ARCTIC OCEAN
218

S0-BMV-187

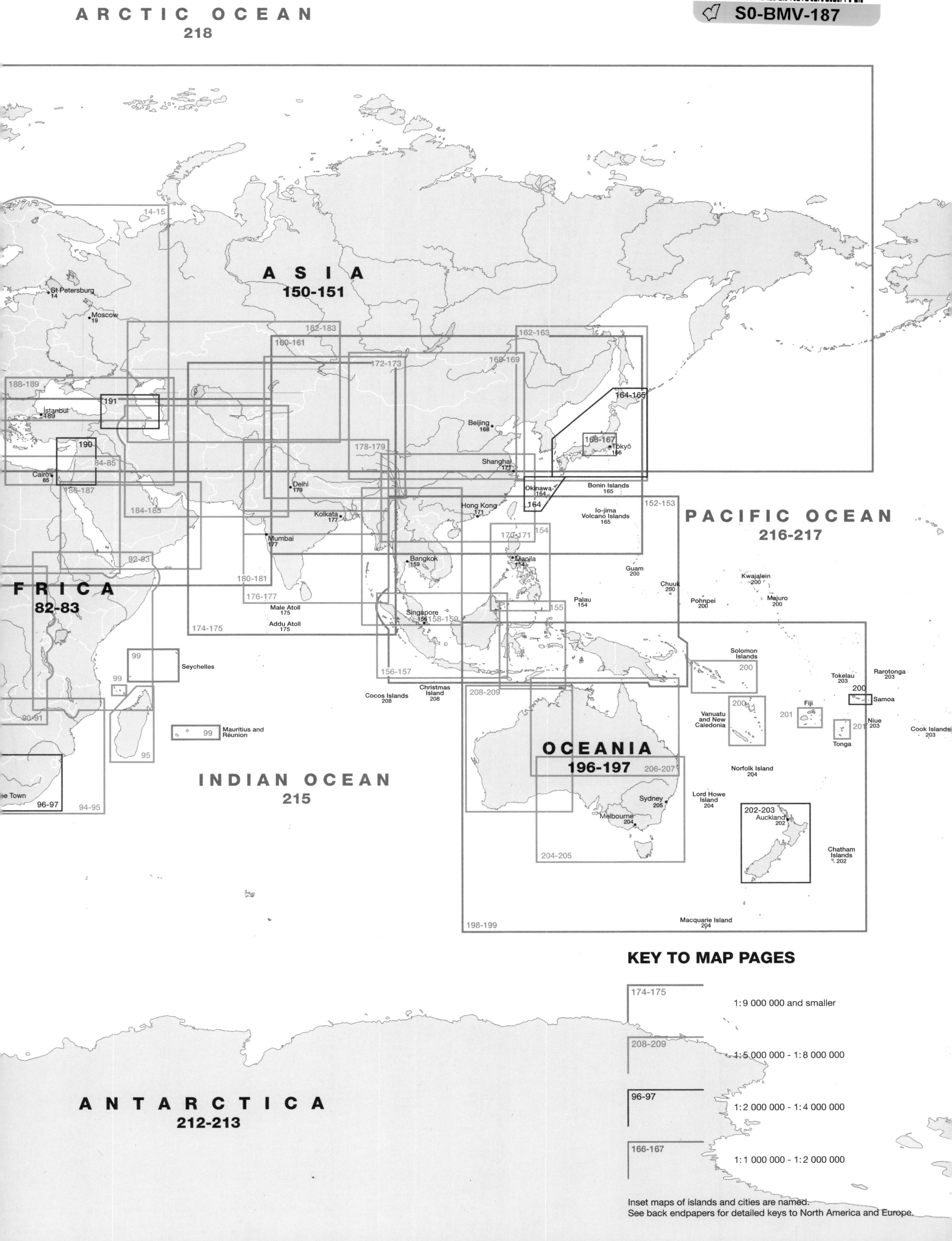

ASIA
150-151

188-189

191

190

84-85

186-187

184-185

92-93

14-15

182-183

180-161

172-173

178-179

168-169

162-163

164-165

166-167

Beijing
168

Shanghai
171

Tōkyō
166

St Petersburg
14

Moscow
19

İstanbul
189

Cairo
85

Delhi
179

Kolkata
177

Mumbai
177

Okinawa
164

164

Hong Kong
171

Bonin Islands
165

Io-jima
Volcano Islands
165

152-153

PACIFIC OCEAN
216-217

AFRICA
82-83

99

99

Seychelles

99

Mauritius and
Réunion

90-91

95

180-181

176-177

Male Atoll
175

Addu Atoll
175

174-175

170-171

154

Bangkok
159

Manila
154

155

Singapore
158-159

156-157

Cocos Islands
208

Christmas
Island
208

Guam
200

Palau
154

Chuuk
200

Kwajalein
200

Pohnpei
200

Majuro
200

Solomon
Islands
200

Vanuatu
and New
Caledonia

200

201

Fiji

Tonga

Tokelau
203

Samoa
200

Niue
203

Rarotonga
203

Cook Islands
203

201

INDIAN OCEAN
215

Cape Town
96-97

94-95

208-209

OCEANIA
196-197

204-205

206-207

Norfolk Island
204

Lord Howe
Island
204

Sydney
205

Melbourne
204

202-203
Auckland
202

Chatham
Islands
202

198-199

Macquarie Island
204

KEY TO MAP PAGES

174-175

1:9 000 000 and smaller

208-209

1:5 000 000 - 1:8 000 000

96-97

1:2 000 000 - 1:4 000 000

ANTARCTICA
212-213

166-167

1:1 000 000 - 1:2 000 000

Inset maps of islands and cities are named.
See back endpapers for detailed keys to North America and Europe.

ENCYCLOPÆDIA

Britannica®

WORLD
ATLAS

ENCYCLOPÆDIA

Britannica®

WORLD

ATLAS

ENCYCLOPÆDIA
Britannica®

CHICAGO LONDON NEW DEHLI PARIS SEOUL SYDNEY TAIPEI TOKYO

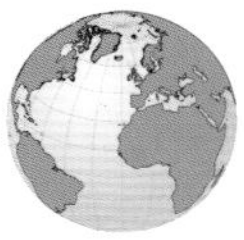

AFRICA

NORTH AMERICA

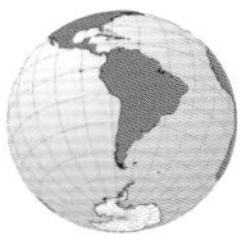

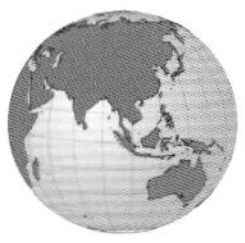

OCEANIA

OCEANS AND POLES

INDEX

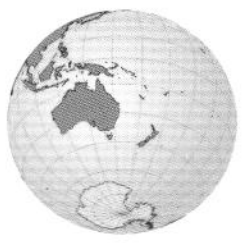

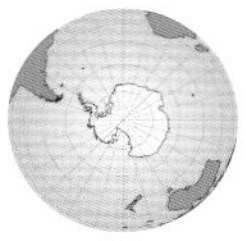

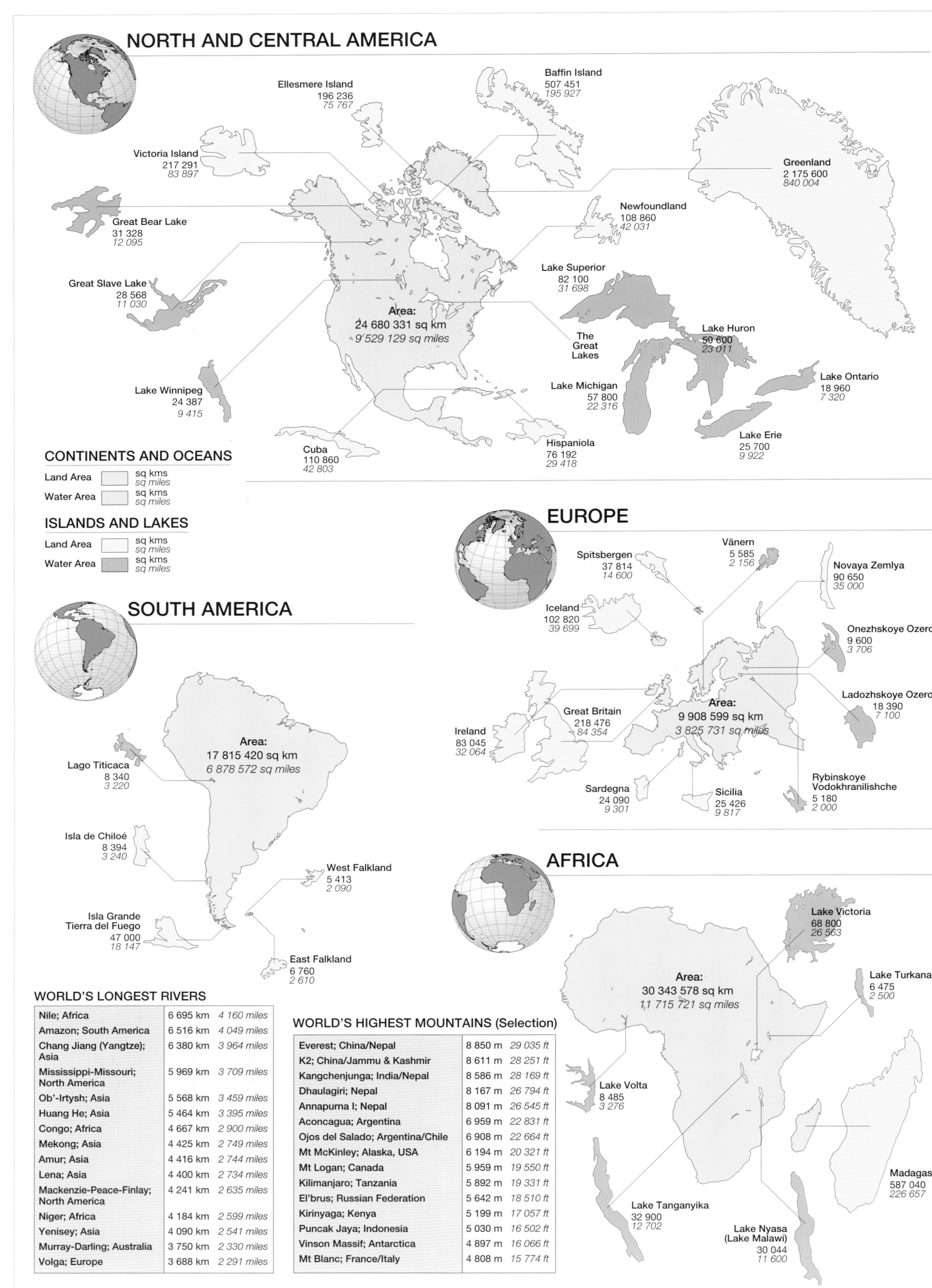

NORTH AND CENTRAL AMERICA

Ellesmere Island
196 236
75 767

Baffin Island
507 451
195 927

Victoria Island
217 291
83 897

Greenland
2 175 600
840 004

Great Bear Lake
31 328
12 095

Newfoundland
108 860
42 031

Great Slave Lake
28 568
11 030

Lake Superior
82 100
31 698

Area:
24 680 331 sq km
9 529 129 sq miles

The
Great
Lakes

Lake Huron
59 600
23 011

Lake Ontario
18 960
7 320

Lake Winnipeg
24 387
9 415

Lake Michigan
57 800
22 316

Lake Erie
25 700
9 922

Cuba
110 860
42 803

Hispaniola
76 192
29 418

CONTINENTS AND OCEANS

Land Area	sq kms *sq miles*
Water Area	sq kms *sq miles*

ISLANDS AND LAKES

Land Area	sq kms *sq miles*
Water Area	sq kms *sq miles*

SOUTH AMERICA

Area:
17 815 420 sq km
6 878 572 sq miles

Lago Titicaca
8 340
3 220

Isla de Chiloé
8 394
3 240

West Falkland
5 413
2 090

Isla Grande
Tierra del Fuego
47 000
18 147

East Falkland
6 760
2 610

EUROPE

Spitsbergen
37 814
14 600

Vänern
5 585
2 156

Novaya Zemlya
90 650
35 000

Iceland
102 820
39 699

Onezhskoye Ozero
9 600
3 706

Area:
9 908 599 sq km
3 825 731 sq miles

Ladozhskoye Ozero
18 390
7 100

Great Britain
218 476
84 354

Ireland
83 045
32 064

Sardegna
24 090
9 301

Sicilia
25 426
9 817

Rybinskoye
Vodokhranilishche
5 180
2 000

AFRICA

Lake Victoria
68 800
26 563

Lake Turkana
6 475
2 500

Area:
30 343 578 sq km
1,1 715 721 sq miles

Lake Volta
8 485
3 276

Madagasc
587 040
226 657

Lake Tanganyika
32 900
12 702

Lake Nyasa
(Lake Malawi)
30 044
11 600

WORLD'S LONGEST RIVERS

Nile; Africa	6 695 km	*4 160 miles*
Amazon; South America	6 516 km	*4 049 miles*
Chang Jiang (Yangtze); Asia	6 380 km	*3 964 miles*
Mississippi-Missouri; North America	5 969 km	*3 709 miles*
Ob'-Irtysh; Asia	5 568 km	*3 459 miles*
Huang He; Asia	5 464 km	*3 395 miles*
Congo; Africa	4 667 km	*2 900 miles*
Mekong; Asia	4 425 km	*2 749 miles*
Amur; Asia	4 416 km	*2 744 miles*
Lena; Asia	4 400 km	*2 734 miles*
Mackenzie-Peace-Finlay; North America	4 241 km	*2 635 miles*
Niger; Africa	4 184 km	*2 599 miles*
Yenisey; Asia	4 090 km	*2 541 miles*
Murray-Darling; Australia	3 750 km	*2 330 miles*
Volga; Europe	3 688 km	*2 291 miles*

WORLD'S HIGHEST MOUNTAINS (Selection)

Everest; China/Nepal	8 850 m	*29 035 ft*
K2; China/Jammu & Kashmir	8 611 m	*28 251 ft*
Kangchenjunga; India/Nepal	8 586 m	*28 169 ft*
Dhaulagiri; Nepal	8 167 m	*26 794 ft*
Annapurna I; Nepal	8 091 m	*26 545 ft*
Aconcagua; Argentina	6 959 m	*22 831 ft*
Ojos del Salado; Argentina/Chile	6 908 m	*22 664 ft*
Mt McKinley; Alaska, USA	6 194 m	*20 321 ft*
Mt Logan; Canada	5 959 m	*19 550 ft*
Kilimanjaro; Tanzania	5 892 m	*19 331 ft*
El'brus; Russian Federation	5 642 m	*18 510 ft*
Kirinyaga; Kenya	5 199 m	*17 057 ft*
Puncak Jaya; Indonesia	5 030 m	*16 502 ft*
Vinson Massif; Antarctica	4 897 m	*16 066 ft*
Mt Blanc; France/Italy	4 808 m	*15 774 ft*

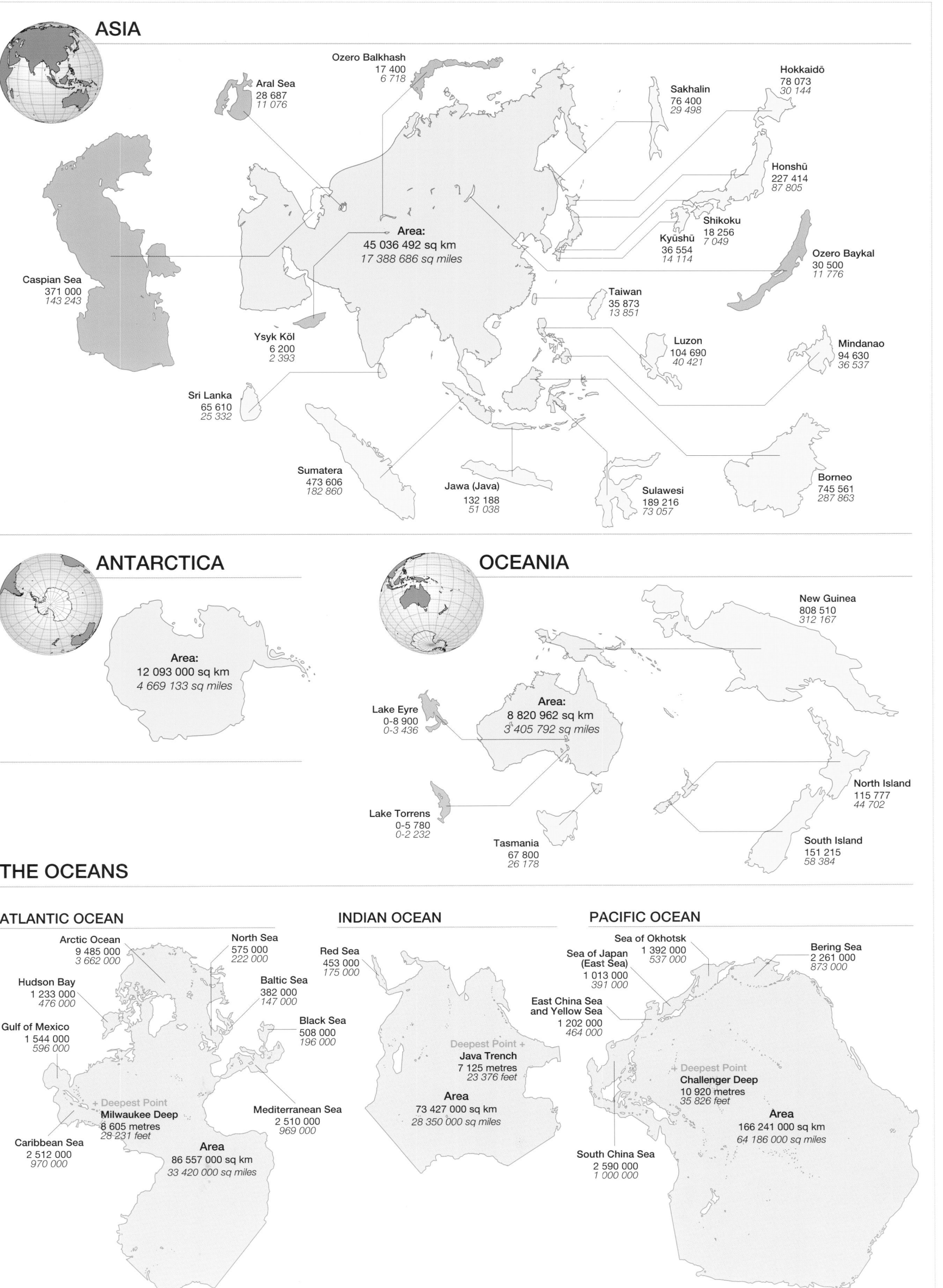

ASIA

Ozero Balkhash
17 400
6 718

Aral Sea
28 687
11 076

Hokkaidō
78 073
30 144

Sakhalin
76 400
29 498

Honshū
227 414
87 805

Shikoku
18 256
7 049

Kyūshū
36 554
14 114

Ozero Baykal
30 500
11 776

Area:
45 036 492 sq km
17 388 686 sq miles

Caspian Sea
371 000
143 243

Taiwan
35 873
13 851

Ysyk Köl
6 200
2 393

Luzon
104 690
40 421

Mindanao
94 630
36 537

Sri Lanka
65 610
25 332

Sumatera
473 606
182 860

Jawa (Java)
132 188
51 038

Sulawesi
189 216
73 057

Borneo
745 561
287 863

ANTARCTICA

Area:
12 093 000 sq km
4 669 133 sq miles

OCEANIA

New Guinea
808 510
312 167

Lake Eyre
0-8 900
0-3 436

Area:
8 820 962 sq km
3 405 792 sq miles

North Island
115 777
44 702

Lake Torrens
0-5 780
0-2 232

Tasmania
67 800
26 178

South Island
151 215
58 384

THE OCEANS

ATLANTIC OCEAN

Arctic Ocean
9 485 000
3 662 000

North Sea
575 000
222 000

Hudson Bay
1 233 000
476 000

Baltic Sea
382 000
147 000

Gulf of Mexico
1 544 000
596 000

Black Sea
508 000
196 000

+ Deepest Point
Milwaukee Deep
8 605 metres
28 231 feet

Mediterranean Sea
2 510 000
969 000

Caribbean Sea
2 512 000
970 000

Area
86 557 000 sq km
33 420 000 sq miles

INDIAN OCEAN

Red Sea
453 000
175 000

Deepest Point +
Java Trench
7 125 metres
23 376 feet

Area
73 427 000 sq km
28 350 000 sq miles

PACIFIC OCEAN

Sea of Okhotsk
1 392 000
537 000

Sea of Japan
(East Sea)
1 013 000
391 000

Bering Sea
2 261 000
873 000

East China Sea
and Yellow Sea
1 202 000
464 000

+ Deepest Point
Challenger Deep
10 920 metres
35 826 feet

Area
166 241 000 sq km
64 186 000 sq miles

South China Sea
2 590 000
1 000 000

THE SOLAR SYSTEM

The origins of the Solar System have been a matter of much debate, but it is now believed that it was created about 4 600 million years ago from of a large collapsing cloud or nebula. The nebula consisted of predominantly hydrogen and helium, and over time the cloud collapsed to form a rotating disk around a dense core. As pressure in the core increased, material was heated enough to allow the nuclear fusion of hydrogen. As the disk cooled, the heavier elements began to condense and agglomerate, and larger bodies grew rapidly by sweeping up much of the remaining smaller material. Nearby volatile disk material was pushed into the outer Solar System, where it condensed and accumulated on the more distant planetary cores. This left the Inner Planets as small rocky bodies and produced the Gas Giants of the outer system. Bombardment of the planets by a decreasing number of small bodies continued for several hundred million years, causing the craters now seen on many of the planets and moons. Outgassing of volatile materials from Earth's interior and perhaps also collisions with icy comets provided our planet with its atmosphere and water. These, along with other factors, created an environment which has enabled life to form and flourish on Earth.

MERCURY

Mercury's long period of rotation, close proximity to the Sun, and minimal atmosphere make its surface an extremely hostile environment with temperatures ranging from 427 to minus 173°C between its day and night side. Mercury is similar to Earth's Moon in size and appearance; its cratered surface was first photographed in detail in the mid-1970s by the Mariner 10 space probe. However, the internal structure differs from the Moon; analysis of its magnetic field suggests the presence of an at least partially molten core of iron, which is believed to occupy 40 per cent of the planet's volume. Mercury has a very eccentric orbit with its orbital distance varying from 46 to 70 million km.

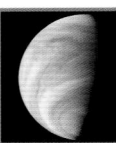

VENUS

Venus' thick atmosphere of carbon dioxide and nitrogen creates not only a huge surface pressure of ninety times that on Earth but also a greenhouse effect producing temperatures in excess of 450°C. Traces of sulphur dioxide and water vapour form clouds of dilute sulphuric acid, making the atmosphere extremely corrosive. The clouds reflect almost all incident visible radiation and prevent direct observation of surface features. In 1990 use of radar imaging enabled the Magellan space probe to see through the cloud. Magellan mapped 98 per cent of the planet during three years to find a surface covered in craters, volcanoes, mountains and solidified lava flows. Venus is the brightest object in the sky after the Sun and Moon and is unusual in that its year is less than its rotation period.

NEPTUNE

URANUS

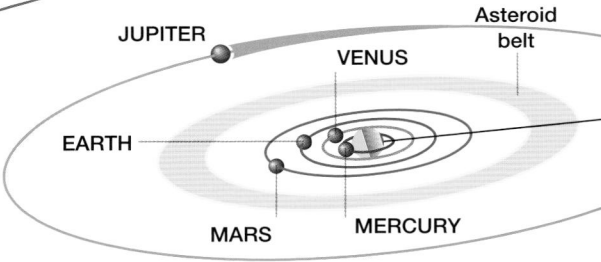

JUPITER   Asteroid belt

VENUS

EARTH

MARS   MERCURY

THE SUN

The Sun is a typical star. It accounts for 99.85 per cent of the total mass contained within the Solar System, ensuring that it provides a dominating gravitational hold on its orbiting planets. The tremendous amount of heat and light produced by the Sun is the result of nuclear fusion reactions which occur in its core. In this process, hydrogen is converted into helium to produce a core temperature of roughly 15 million°C. Intense magnetic fields can induce cooling zones seen as dark sun spots on the Sun's surface. The Sun constantly emits a stream of charged particles which form the solar wind and cause auroral activity which can be seen on Earth.

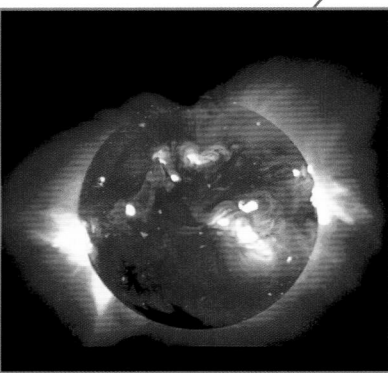

	Sun	Mercury	Venus	Earth	Mars	Jupiter	Saturn	Uranus	Neptune	Pluto
Mass (Earth=1)	332 830	0.055	0.815	1 (6 x 10²⁴ kg)	0.107	317.82	95.161	14.371	17.147	0.002
Volume (Earth=1)	1 306 000	0.05	0.88	1	0.15	1 316	755	52	44	0.01
Density (Water=1)	1.41	5.43	5.24	5.52	3.94	1.33	0.7	1.3	1.76	~2
Equatorial diameter (km)	1 392 000	4 879.4	12 103.6	12 756.3	6 794	142 984	120 536	51 118	49 528	2 390
Polar flattening	0	0	0	0.003	0.007	0.065	0.098	0.023	0.017	0
Surface gravity (Earth=1)	27.5	0.38	0.91	1	0.38	2.53	1.07	0.9	1.14	0.06
Number of satellites > 100 km diameter	-	0	0	1	0	7	13	8	6	1
Total number of satellites	-	0	0	1	2	>60	>30	>25	>10	1
Rotation period (Earth days)	25–36	58.65	-243	23hr 56m 4s	1.03	0.41	0.44	-0.72	0.67	-6.39
Year (Earth days/years)	-	88 days	224.7 days	365.24 days	687 days	11.86 years	29.42 years	83.8 years	163.8 years	248 years
Mean orbital distance (million km)	-	57.9	108.2	149.6	227.9	778.4	1 426.7	2 871.0	4 498.3	5 906.4
Orbital eccentricity	-	0.2056	0.0068	0.0167	0.0934	0.0484	0.0542	0.0472	0.0086	0.2488
Mean orbital velocity (km/s)	-	47.87	35.02	29.79	24.13	13.07	9.67	6.84	5.48	4.75
Inclination of equator to orbit (deg.)	-	0	177.3	23.45	25.19	3.12	26.73	97.86	29.58	119.61
Orbital inclination (w.r.t. ecliptic)	-	7.005	3.395	0.00005	1.851	1.305	2.485	0.77	1.769	17.142
Mean surface temperature (°C)	5 700	167	457	15–20	-90– -5	-108 (at 1 bar level)	-139 (at 1 bar level)	-197 (at 1 bar level)	-200 (at 1 bar level)	-215.2
Atmospheric pressure at surface (bars)	-	10⁻¹⁵	90	1	0.007–0.010	-	-	-	-	8 x 10⁻⁵
Atmospheric composition	H₂ 92.1%	H	CO₂ 96%	N₂ 77%	CO₂ 95.3%	H₂ 90%	H₂ 97%	H₂ 83%	H₂ 85%	N₂
(selected gas components)	He 7.8%	He	N₂ 3%	O₂ 21%	N₂ 2.7%	He 10%	He 3%	He 15%	He 13%	CO
	O₂ 0.061%	Na		Ar 1.6%				CH₄ 2%	CH₄ 2%	CH₄

EARTH

Earth is the largest of the Inner Planets. Created some 4 500 million years ago, the core, rocky mantle and crust are similar in structure to Venus. The Earth's core is composed almost entirely of iron and oxygen compounds which exist in a molten state at temperatures of around 5 000°C. Earth is the only planet with vast quantities of life-sustaining water, with the oceans covering 70.8 per cent of its surface. The action of plate tectonics has created vast mountain ranges and is responsible for much of the planet's volcanic activity. The Moon is Earth's only natural satellite and, with a diameter of over one quarter that of Earth, makes the Earth-Moon system a near double-planet.

MARS

Named after the Roman god of war because of its blood-red appearance, Mars is the outermost of the Inner Planets. The red colour comes from the high concentration of iron oxides on its surface. Mars has impressive surface features, including the highest known peak in the Solar System, Olympus Mons, an inactive volcano reaching a height of 23 km above the surrounding plains, and Valles Marineris, a 2 500 km long canyon four times as deep as the Grand Canyon. Much of the Martian surface is shaped by intense dust storms which often engulf the entire planet. Mars has polar caps composed of water and carbon dioxide ice which partially evaporate during their summers. Spacecraft observations reveal that water flowed on Mars in the ancient past and suggest that large amounts of frozen water exist beneath its surface.

JUPITER

Jupiter is by far the most massive of the planets and is the dominant body in the Solar System after the Sun. It is the innermost of the Gas Giants. The dense upper atmosphere is predominantly hydrogen, with helium, water vapour, and methane. Below this is a layer of liquid hydrogen, then an even deeper layer of metallic hydrogen. Unlike solid bodies, Jupiter's rotation period is somewhat ill-defined, with equatorial regions rotating faster than the polar caps; this, combined with convection currents in lower layers, cause intense magnetic fields and rapidly varying visible surface features. Most notable of these is the Great Red Spot, a giant rotating storm visible since early telescopic observations of Jupiter in the 1600s. Jupiter possesses a narrow ring system made of large numbers of dust- and grit-sized particles.

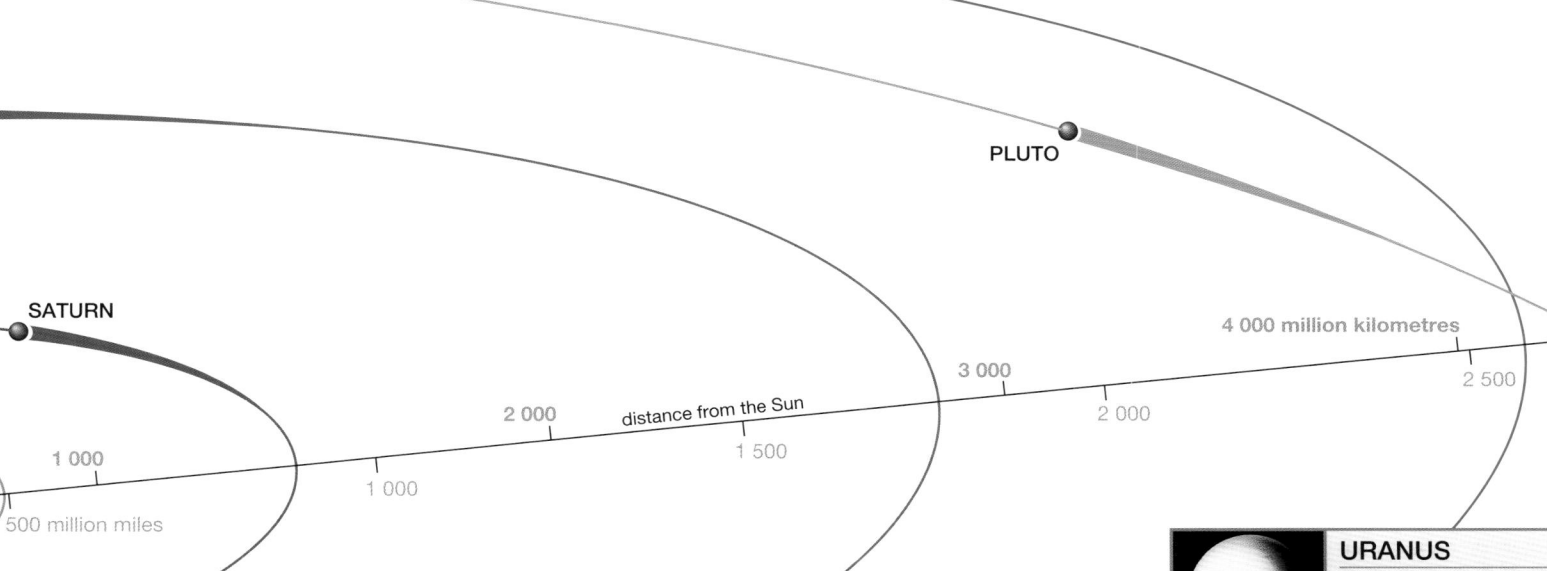

PLUTO

SATURN

4 000 million kilometres

3 000

2 500

2 000

2 000

distance from the Sun

1 500

1 000

1 000

1 000

500 million miles

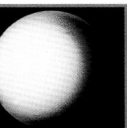

URANUS

Uranus has many surprising features; the most prominent of these is the tilt of its rotation axis by over 90 degrees caused by a series of large collisions in its early history. Like the other Gas Giants, Uranus is predominantly hydrogen and helium with a small proportion of methane and other gases. However, because Uranus is colder than Jupiter and Saturn, the methane forms ice crystals which give Uranus a featureless blue-green colour. The interior is also different from that expected. Instead of having a gaseous atmosphere above liquid and metallic hydrogen layers, Uranus has a super-dense gas and ice interior extending down to its rocky core. Uranus' magnetic field is inclined at 60 degrees to the rotation axis, and is off centre by one third of the planet's radius, which suggests that it is not generated by the core. The system of eleven narrow rings around Uranus is prevented from spreading by the interaction of nearby 'shepherd' moons.

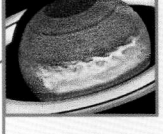

SATURN

Although only slightly smaller that Jupiter, Saturn is a mere one-third of Jupiter's mass, and the least dense of all the planets - less dense than water. The low mass, combined with a fast rotation rate, leads to the planet's significant polar flattening. Saturn's visible surface shows many variable features similar to those on Jupiter, including coloured spots, bands, eddies, and rotating storms. Saturn exhibits a striking ring system, more than twice the diameter of the planet; the rings consist of countless small particles, largely of ice, which vary in size from grains of sand to tens of metres in diameter. Distinct bands and gaps in the rings are partially the result of complex interactions between Saturn and its closer moons.

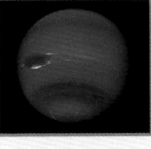

NEPTUNE

Neptune has long been associated with Uranus because of its similar size, composition and appearance, but, unexpectedly, Neptune's atmosphere is more active than that of Uranus. This was shown by Voyager 2 in 1989 with the observation of the Great Dark Spot, Neptune's equivalent to Jupiter's Great Red Spot. Voyager 2 recorded the fastest winds ever seen in the Solar System, 2 000 km per hour, around the Dark Spot. This feature disappeared in 1994, but has been replaced by a similar storm in the northern hemisphere. The planet's deep blue colour is due to the absorption of red light by methane gas in the atmosphere. Like Uranus, Neptune has a magnetic field highly inclined to the planet's axis of rotation and off-centre by more than half of the planet's radius. The cause of this magnetic field is convection currents in conducting fluid layers outside the core. Neptune is encircled by a system of five faint rings.

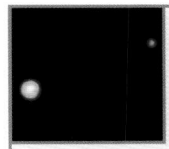

PLUTO

Pluto was discovered in 1930, the third planet (after Uranus and Neptune) to have been found in modern times, as opposed to the five planets observed in the night sky since antiquity. Pluto is by far the smallest planet, only two thirds the diameter of Earth's Moon. Its orbit is highly tilted with respect to the orbits of the other planets and is so eccentric that it occasionally comes inside Neptune's orbit. Its only known moon, Charon, is large relative to the planet it orbits. Rocky materials make up about 70 per cent of Pluto's total mass, with the rest being ice. Pluto's size, large moon, ice-rock composition, and orbital characteristics and, since 1992, the discovery of hundreds of other icy bodies lying beyond Neptune, have called Pluto's status as a planet into question. Astronomers now believe there are thousands of these icy objects - presumed leftovers from the formation of the Gas Giants - many of them perhaps similar in size to Pluto and Charon. These form the Kuiper belt which stretches from Neptune's orbit to about 7 500 million km from the Sun. In this context Pluto (with Charon) can be considered the largest known member of the Kuiper belt.

xii

EARTHQUAKES AND VOLCANOES

The destructive power and terrifying beauty of earthquakes and volcanoes probably capture the imagination more than any other natural phenomena. Earthquakes are associated with the process of plate tectonics – the movement of the separate 'plates' which make up the earth's crust – and most occur along the junctions of these plates. The friction caused by movement of one plate against another causes great stress. When the rocks can no longer bear the pressure, they fracture and enormous energy is released. If the shock waves reach the surface, they are felt as earthquakes. Movement of the surface can cause severe damage to property, which in turn can cause great loss of life.

Volcanic activity is often linked to earthquakes and most occur along subduction zones where two plates collide with one passing underneath the other. Most active volcanoes are in the 'Ring of Fire' around the Pacific plate, or along the southern edge of the Eurasian plate. The forces involved in the collision of plates can cause the surrounding rock to melt to form magma. The heat generated creates upward pressure and the magma is forced through weaknesses in the rock. If the pressure is great enough, material breaks through the surface as a volcano.

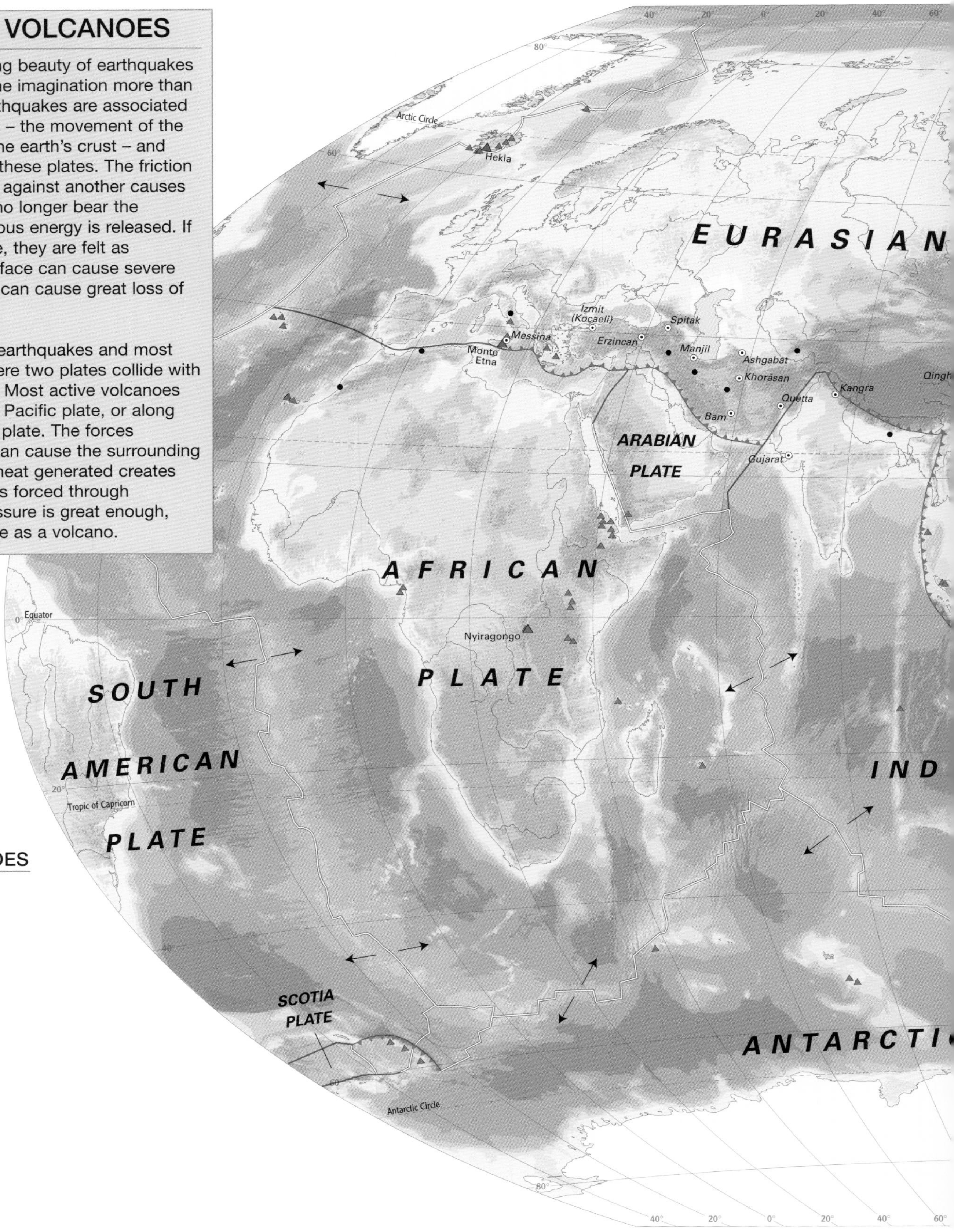

DISTRIBUTION OF MAJOR EARTHQUAKES AND VOLCANOES

Winkel Tripel Projection
Scale 1:86 000 000

SYMBOLS

▲ Major volcanoes
▲ Volcanoes active between 1900 and 2003
• Earthquakes between 1900 and 2003 causing over 10 000 deaths
⊙ Deadliest earthquakes

PLATE BOUNDARIES

— Constructive – mid ocean ridge
⌃⌃⌃ Destructive
— Conservative

DEADLIEST EARTHQUAKES

YEAR	LOCATION	DEATHS
2003	**Bam**, Iran	26 271
2001	**Gujarat**, India	20 000
1999	**İzmit (Kocaeli)**, Turkey	17 000
1990	**Manjil**, Iran	50 000
1988	**Spitak**, Armenia	25 000
1978	**Khorāsān Province**, Iran	20 000
1976	**Hebei Province**, China	255 000
1976	central **Guatemala**	22 778
1974	**Yunnan and Sichuan Provinces**, China	20 000
1970	**Huánuco Province**, Peru	66 794
1948	**Ashgabat**, Turkmenistan	19 800
1939	**Erzincan**, Turkey	32 700
1939	**Chillán**, Chile	28 000
1935	**Quetta**, Pakistan	30 000
1932	**Gansu Province**, China	70 000
1927	**Qinghai Province**, China	200 000
1923	**Tōkyō**, Japan	142 807
1920	**Ningxia Province**, China	200 000
1917	**Bali**, Indonesia	15 000
1908	**Messina**, Italy	110 000
1905	**Kangra**, India	19 000

MAJOR VOLCANIC ERUPTIONS

YEAR	VOLCANO	COUNTRY
2002	**Nyiragongo**	Democratic Republic of Congo
2001	**Monte Etna**	Italy
2000	**Hekla**	Iceland
1997	**Soufrière Hills**	Montserrat
1994	**Rabaul**	Papua New Guinea
1994	**Volcán Llaima**	Chile
1993	**Volcán Galeras**	Colombia
1993	**Mayon**	Philippines
1991	**Unzen-dake**	Japan
1991	**Mt Pinatubo**	Philippines
1985	**Nevado del Ruiz**	Colombia
1983	**Ō-yama**	Japan
1983	**Kilauea**	Hawaii
1982	**Gunung Galunggung**	Indonesia
1982	**El Chichónal**	Mexico
1980	**Mt St Helens**	USA

PLATE TECTONICS

200 MILLION YEARS AGO

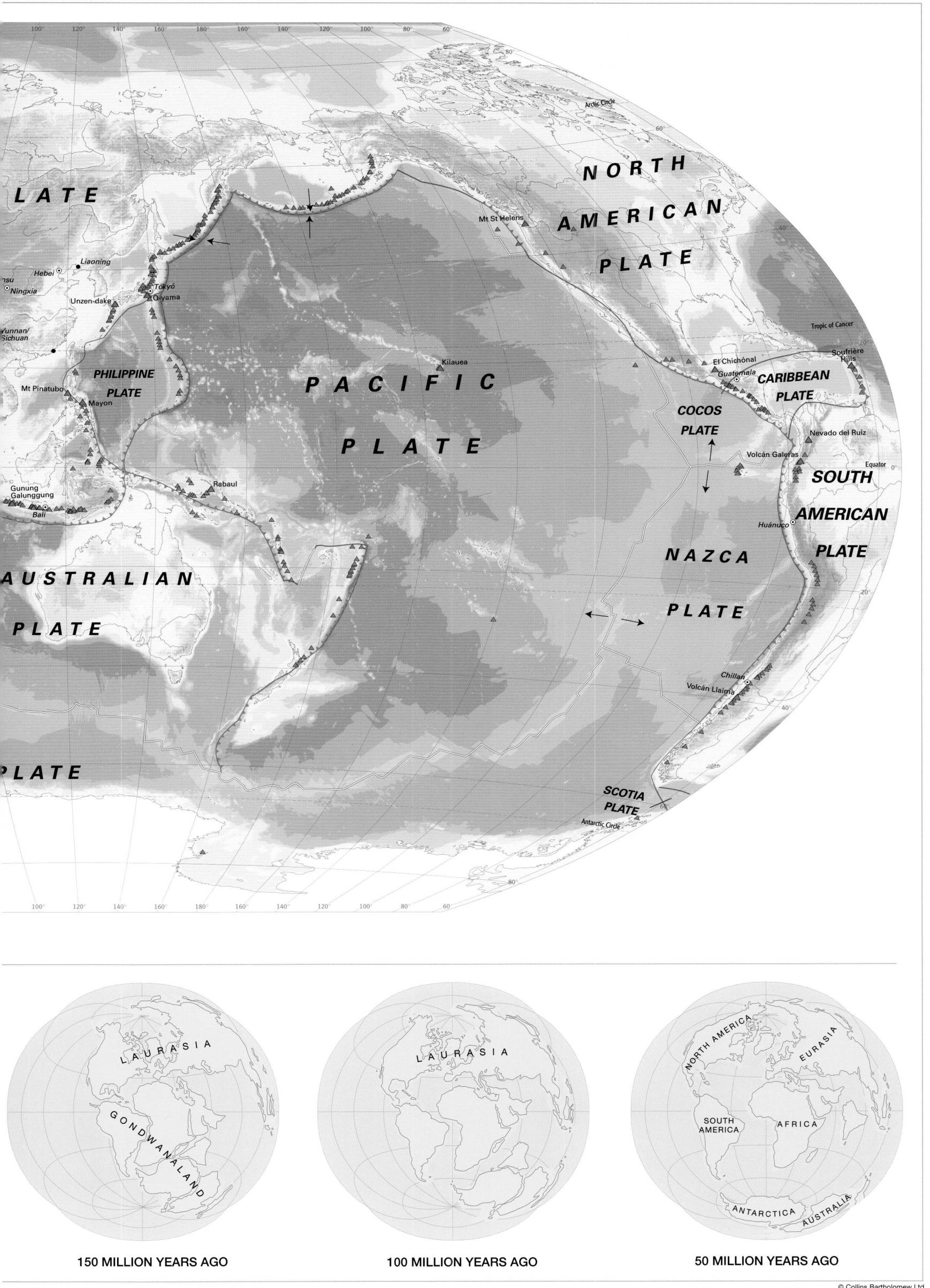

NORTH

AMERICAN

PLATE

Mt St Helens

Arctic Circle

Tropic of Cancer

El Chichónal

Guatemala

CARIBBEAN

PLATE

Soufrière
Hills

COCOS
PLATE

Nevado del Ruiz

Volcán Galeras

SOUTH

Huánuco

AMERICAN

PLATE

NAZCA

PLATE

Equator

Chillán

Volcán Llaima

SCOTIA
PLATE

Antarctic Circle

PACIFIC

PLATE

Kilauea

PHILIPPINE
PLATE

Mt Pinatubo

Mayon

Rabaul

Gunung
Galunggung

Bali

AUSTRALIAN

PLATE

PLATE

Liaoning

Hebei

Ningxia

Tōkyō
Ō-yama

Unzen-dake

Yunnan/
Sichuan

PLATE

LAURASIA

GONDWANALAND

150 MILLION YEARS AGO

LAURASIA

100 MILLION YEARS AGO

NORTH AMERICA

EURASIA

SOUTH
AMERICA

AFRICA

ANTARCTICA

AUSTRALIA

50 MILLION YEARS AGO

THE CLIMATE SYSTEM

The Earth's climate system is a highly complex system involving the atmosphere, hydrosphere (oceans, lakes and rivers), biosphere (the Earth's living resources), cryosphere (particularly sea ice and polar ice caps) and lithosphere (the Earth's crust and upper mantle). This results in a great variety of climate types. The oceans, and the circulation of water throughout them in the form of ocean currents, is critical to the world's climate system. Man's activities are also affecting the system, and the monitoring of human influences upon climate and climate change is now a major issue. Future climate change depends on how quickly and to what extent the concentration of greenhouse gases and aerosols in the atmosphere increases. If we assume that no action is taken to limit future greenhouse gas emissions, then a warming during the 21st century of 0.2 to 0.3°C per decade is likely, with regional variations in changes in both temperature and precipitation.

Tropical storms are perhaps the most powerful and destructive weather systems on Earth. Of the eighty to one hundred which develop annually over the tropical oceans, many make landfall and cause considerable damage to property and loss of life as a result of high winds and heavy rain.

MAJOR CLIMATIC REGIONS AND OCEAN CURRENTS

Robinson Projection
Scale 1: 90 000 000

KEY

1	Ice cap
2	Tundra climate, warmest month below 10°C
3	Sub-arctic, rainy climate with severe cold winters and less than 4 months over 10°C
4	Continental climate, rainy with warmest month below 22°c
5	Continental climate, rainy with warmest month above 20°C
6	Temperate, rainy climate with mild winter, coolest month above 0°C
7	Wet subtropical, coolest month above 0°C, warmest month above 22°C
8	Mediterranean, rainy with mild wet winter, dry summer
9	Semi-arid, dry climate
10	Desert climate
11	Rainy tropical climate, dry season in winter
12	Rainy tropical climate, constantly wet throughout the year

→ Warm current

→ Cold current

→ Seasonal drift during northern winter

∘ Extreme weather location

TEMPERATURE IN THE 2050s

Predicted annual mean temperature change

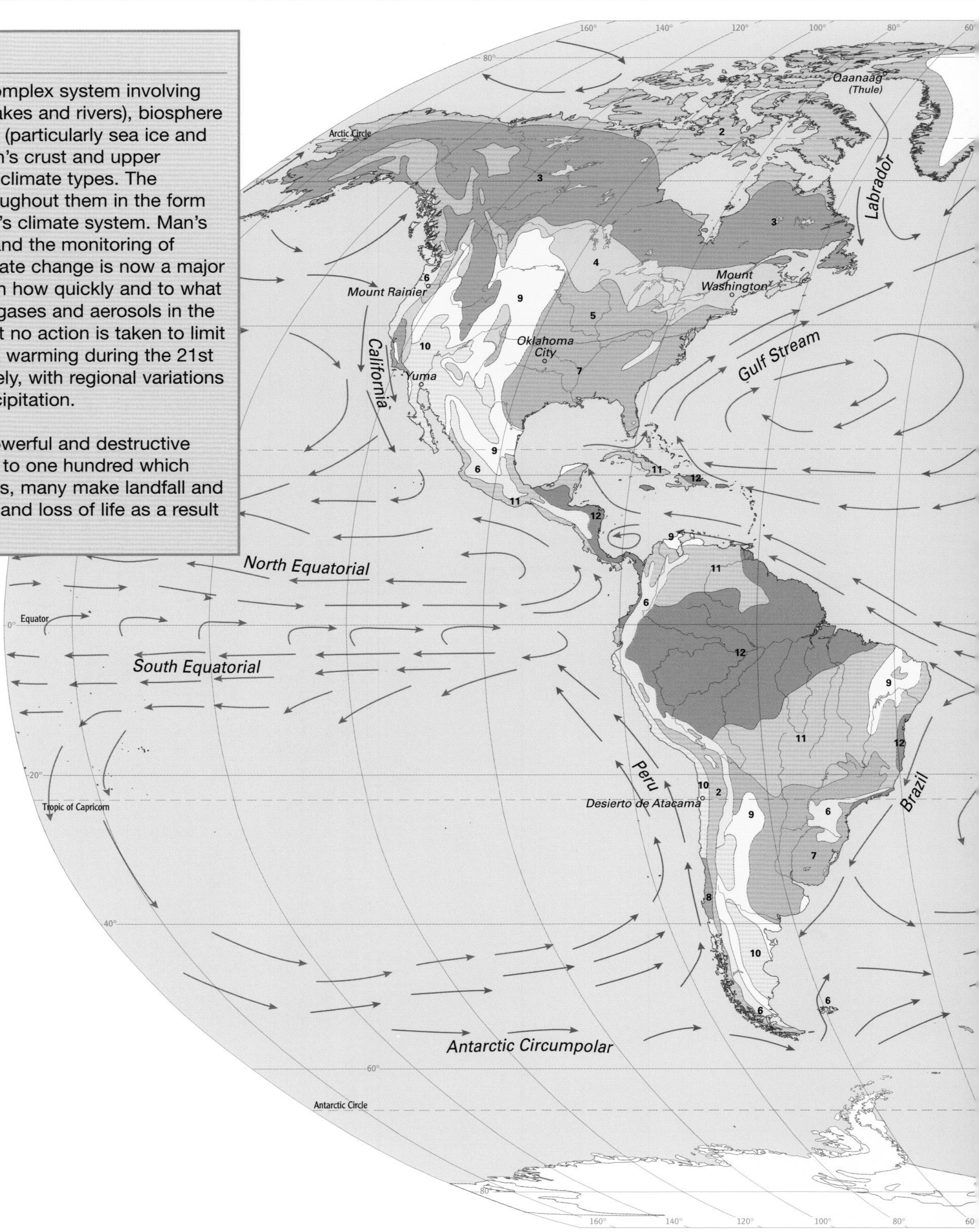

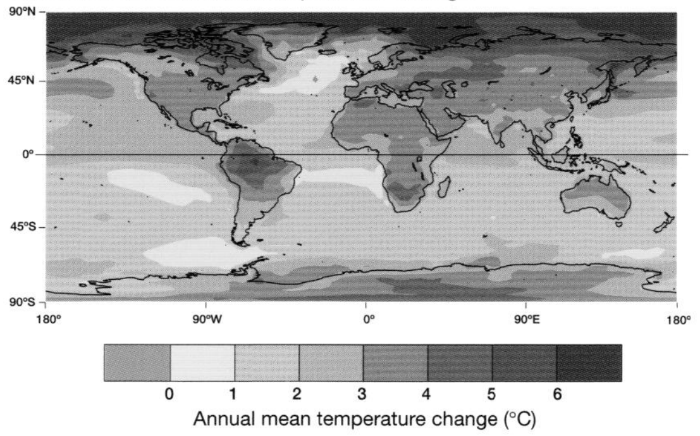

0 1 2 3 4 5 6
Annual mean temperature change (°C)

PRECIPITATION IN THE 2050s

Predicted annual mean precipitation change

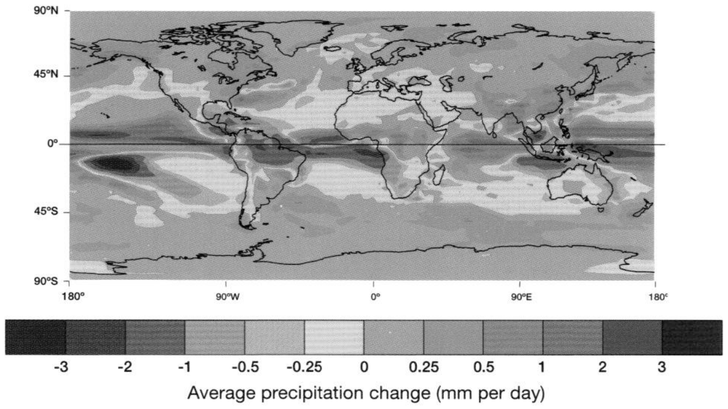

-3 -2 -1 -0.5 -0.25 0 0.25 0.5 1 2 3
Average precipitation change (mm per day)

WORLD WEATHER EXTREMES

Highest shade temperature	57.8°C/136°F Al ʿAzīzīyah, Libya (13th September 1922)
Hottest place — Annual mean	34.4°C/93.9°F Dalol, Ethiopia
Driest place — Annual mean	0.1 mm/0.004 inches Desierto de Atacama, Chile
Most sunshine — Annual mean	90% Yuma, Arizona, USA (over 4 000 hours)
Lowest screen temperature	-89.2°C/-128.6°F Vostok Station, Antarctica (21st July 1983)
Coldest place — Annual mean	-56.6°C/-69.9°F Plateau Station, Antarctica
Wettest place — Annual mean	11 873 mm/467.4 inches Meghalaya, India
Windiest place	322 km per hour/200 miles per hour in gales, Commonwealth Bay, Antarctica
Highest surface windspeed	
High altitude	372 km per hour/231 miles per hour Mount Washington, New Hampshire, USA (12th April 1934)
Low altitude	333 km per hour/207 miles per hour Qaanaaq (Thule), Greenland (8th March 1972)
Tornado	512 km per hour/318 miles per hour Oklahoma City, Oklahoma, USA (3rd May 1999)
Greatest snowfall	31 102 mm/1 224.5 inches Mount Rainier, Washington, USA (19th February 1971 — 18th February 1972)

Qaanaaq (Thule)

Arctic Circle

Labrador

Mount Washington

Mount Rainier

Oklahoma City

Yuma

California

Gulf Stream

North Equatorial

Equator

South Equatorial

Tropic of Capricorn

Peru

Desierto de Atacama

Brazil

Antarctic Circumpolar

Antarctic Circle

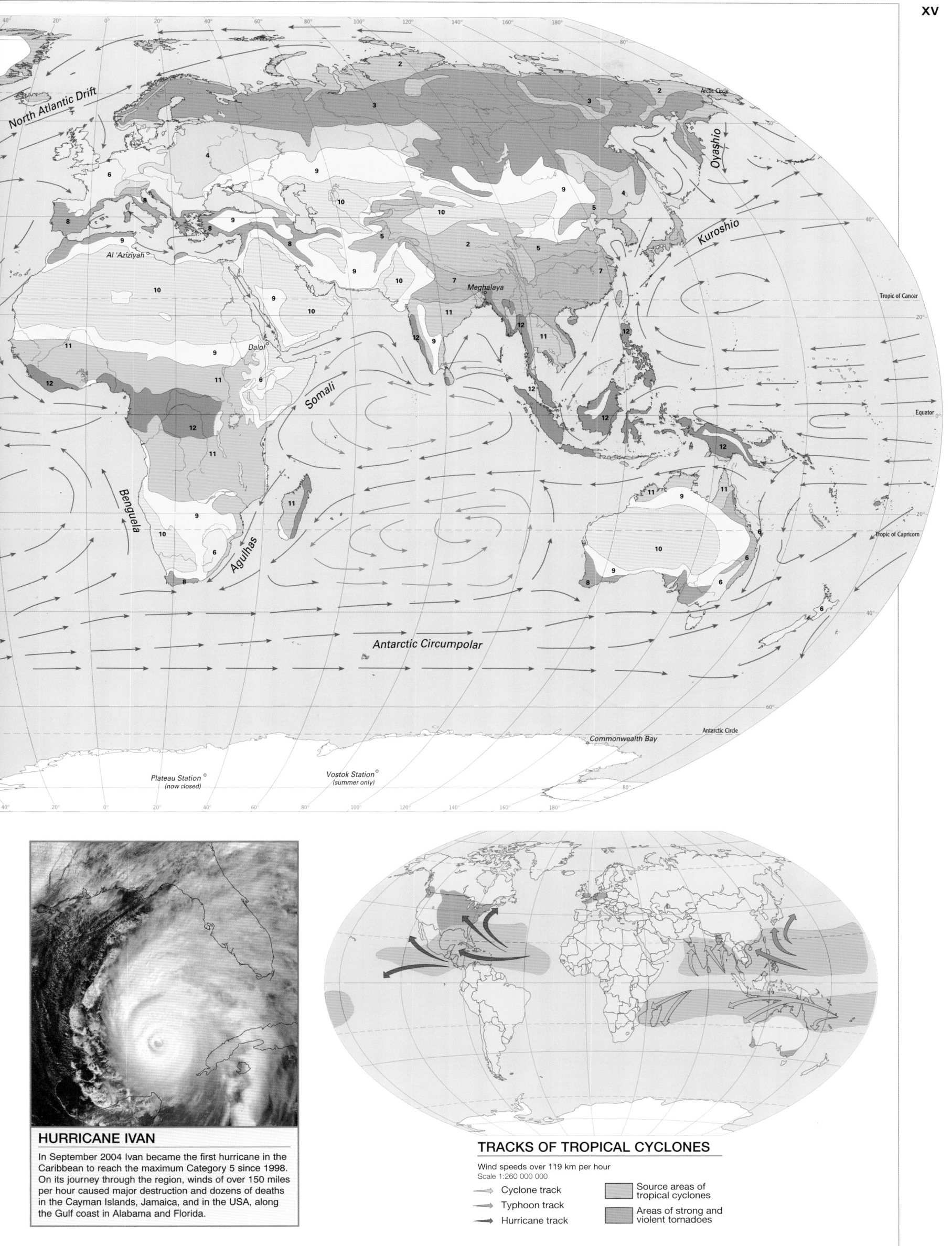

North Atlantic Drift

Arctic Circle

Oyashio

Kuroshio

Al 'Aziziyah

Tropic of Cancer

Meghalaya

Dalol

Equator

Somali

Benguela

Agulhas

Tropic of Capricorn

Antarctic Circumpolar

Antarctic Circle

Commonwealth Bay

Plateau Station
(now closed)

Vostok Station
(summer only)

HURRICANE IVAN

In September 2004 Ivan became the first hurricane in the Caribbean to reach the maximum Category 5 since 1998. On its journey through the region, winds of over 150 miles per hour caused major destruction and dozens of deaths in the Cayman Islands, Jamaica, and in the USA, along the Gulf coast in Alabama and Florida.

TRACKS OF TROPICAL CYCLONES

Wind speeds over 119 km per hour
Scale 1:260 000 000

⇒ Cyclone track
⇒ Typhoon track
⟶ Hurricane track

Source areas of
tropical cyclones

Areas of strong and
violent tornadoes

EUROPE

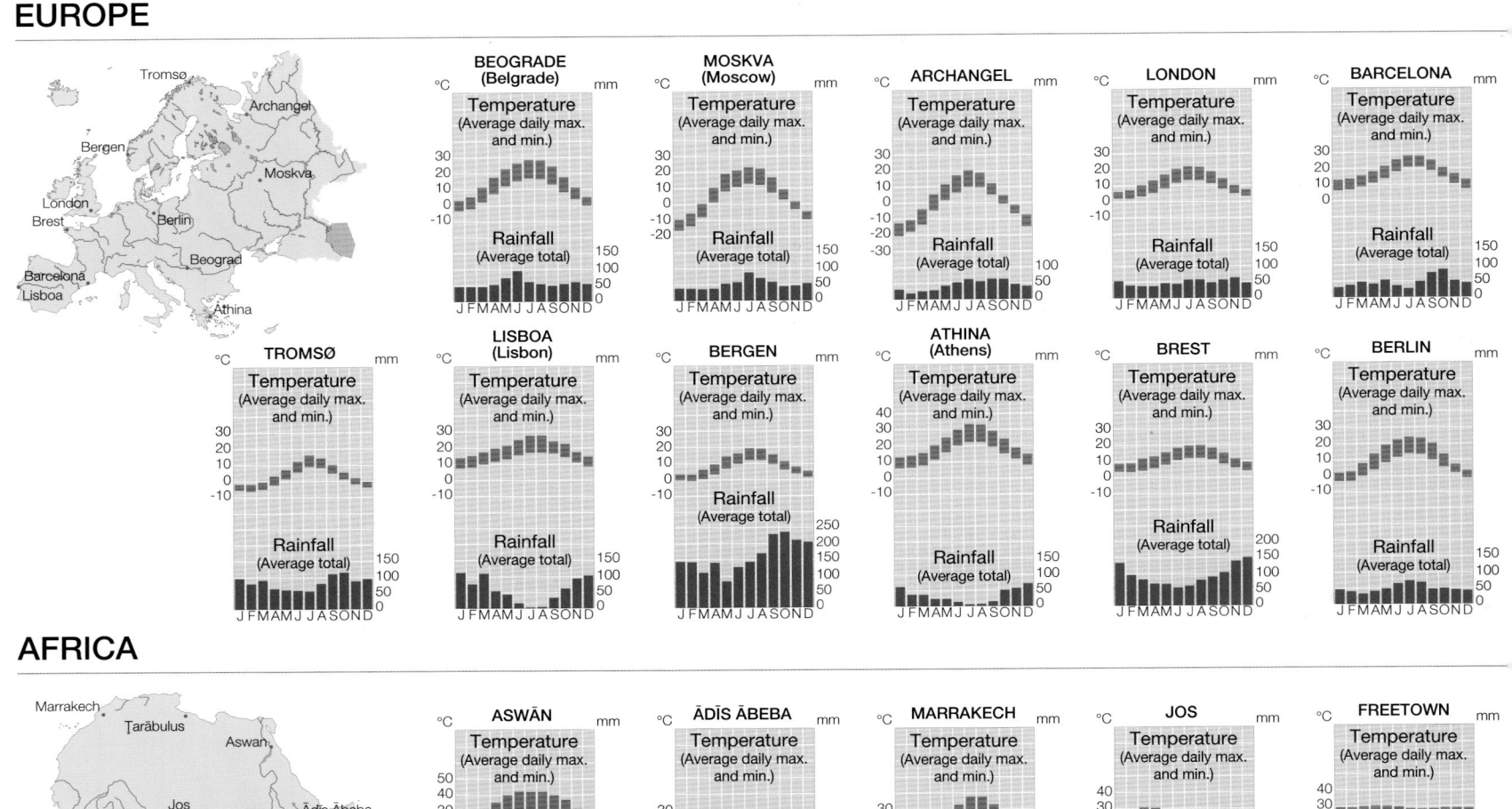
Tromsø
Archangel
Bergen
Moskva
London
Brest
Berlin
Beograd
Barcelona
Lisboa
Athina
BEOGRADE (Belgrade)
MOSKVA (Moscow)
ARCHANGEL
LONDON
BARCELONA
TROMSØ
LISBOA (Lisbon)
BERGEN
ATHINA (Athens)
BREST
BERLIN

AFRICA

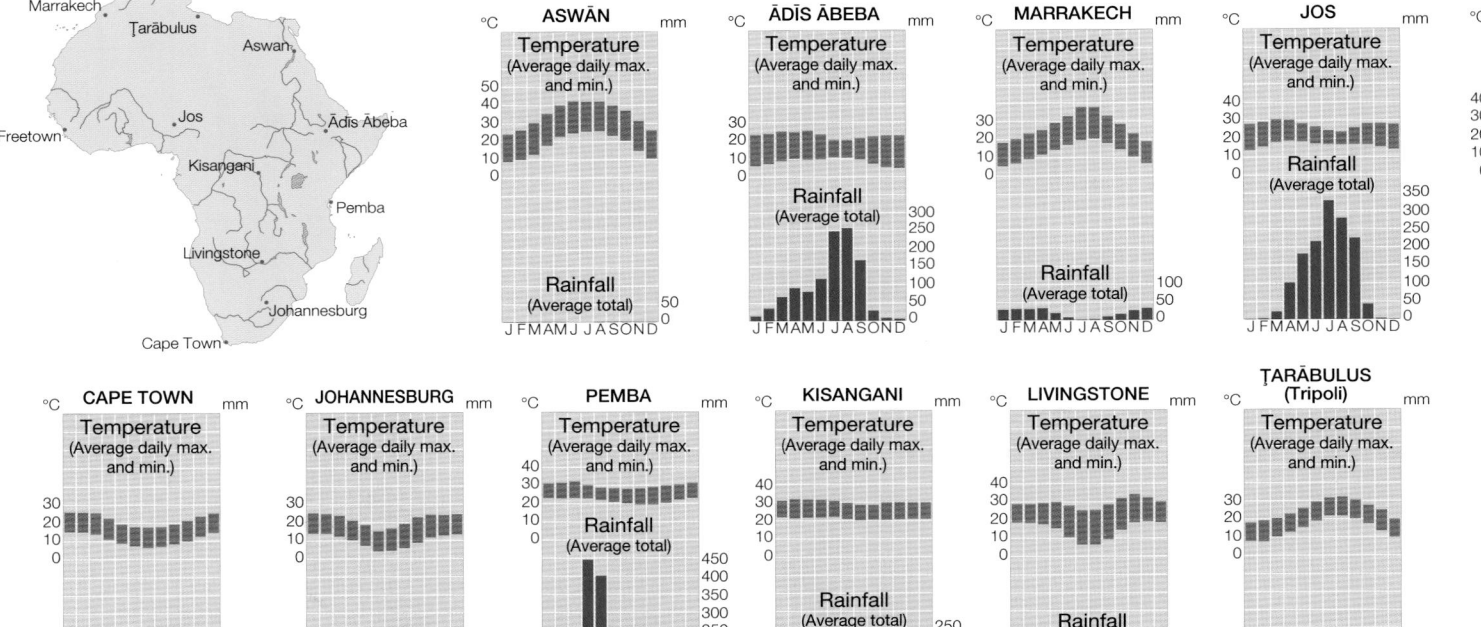
Marrakech
Ţarābulus
Aswan
Freetown
Jos
Ādīs Ābeba
Kisangani
Pemba
Livingstone
Johannesburg
Cape Town
ASWĀN
ĀDĪS ĀBEBA
MARRAKECH
JOS
FREETOWN
CAPE TOWN
JOHANNESBURG
PEMBA
KISANGANI
LIVINGSTONE
ŢARĀBULUS (Tripoli)

NORTH AMERICA

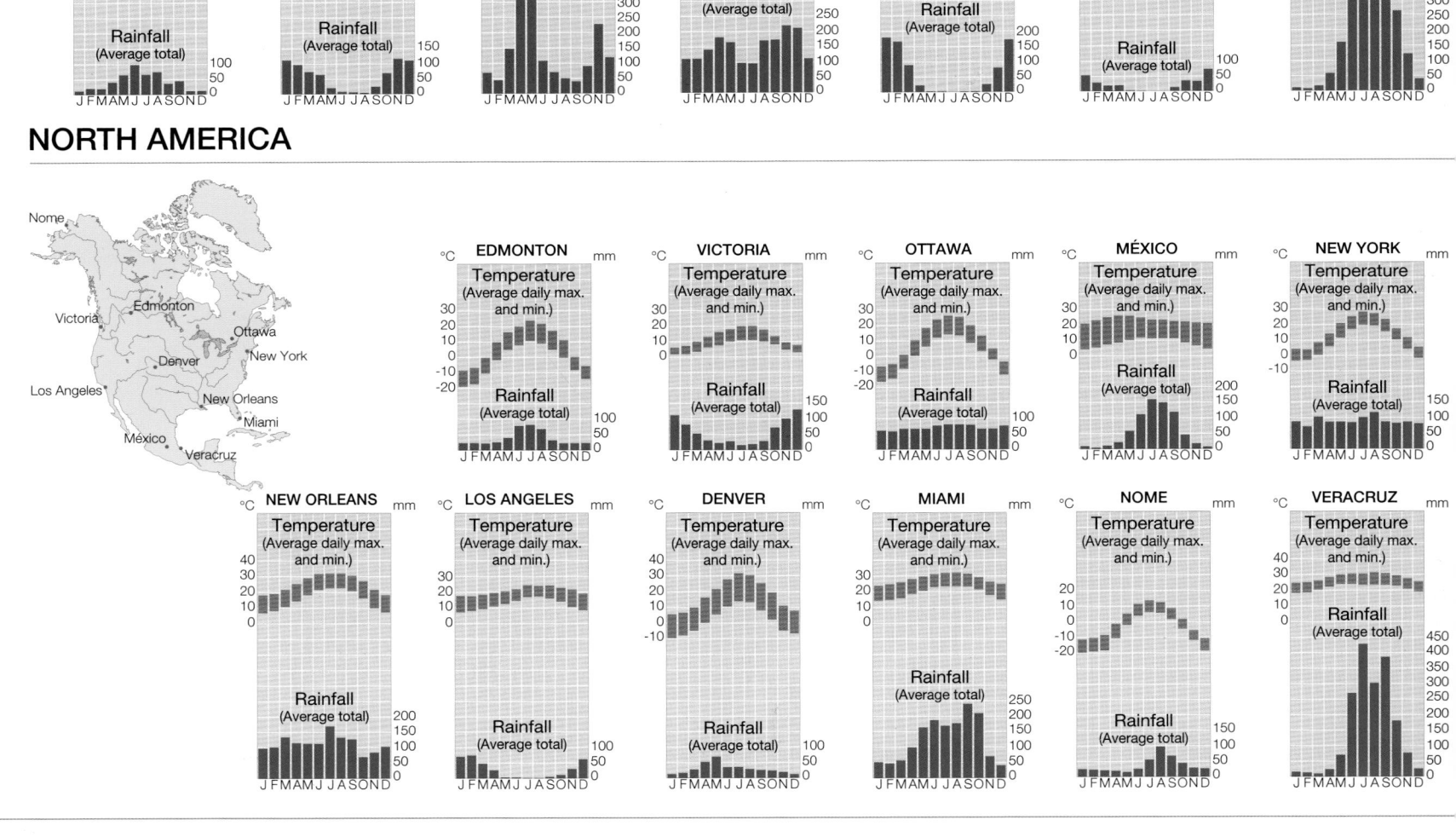
Nome
Edmonton
Victoria
Ottawa
New York
Denver
Los Angeles
New Orleans
Miami
México
Veracruz
EDMONTON
VICTORIA
OTTAWA
MÉXICO
NEW YORK
NEW ORLEANS
LOS ANGELES
DENVER
MIAMI
NOME
VERACRUZ

SOUTH AMERICA

BUENOS AIRES
CÓRDOBA
SARMIENTO
BELÉM
GOIÁS
RIO DE JANEIRO
CARACAS
SANTIAGO
BOGOTÁ
LIMA
PUNTA ARENAS
Temperature (Average daily max. and min.)
Rainfall (Average total)
°C
mm
J F M A M J J A S O N D

Caracas
Bogotá
Belém
Lima
Goiás
Rio de Janeiro
Córdoba
Santiago
Buenos Aires
Sarmiento
Punta Arenas

ASIA

BEIRUT
ULAANBAATAR (Ulan Bator)
KĀBUL
KARACHI
TEHRĀN
TIANJIN
NEW DELHI
TŌKYŌ
SINGAPORE
HONG KONG
Temperature (Average daily max. and min.)
Rainfall (Average total)
°C
mm
J F M A M J J A S O N D

MANILA
Temperature (Average daily max. and min.)
Rainfall (Average total)

Beirut
Tehrān
Kābul
Karachi
New Delhi
Ulaanbaatar
Tianjin
Tōkyō
Hong Kong
Manila
Singapore

OCEANIA

SYDNEY
ALICE SPRINGS
SUVA
WELLINGTON
INVERCARGILL
AUCKLAND
HOBART
PERTH
MACKAY
DARWIN
Temperature (Average daily max. and min.)
Rainfall (Average total)
°C
mm
J F M A M J J A S O N D

PAPEETE
Temperature (Average daily max. and min.)
Rainfall (Average total)

Darwin
Alice Springs
Mackay
Suva
Perth
Sydney
Auckland
Hobart
Wellington
Invercargill
• Papeete
2281 miles (3650 km) east of Suva

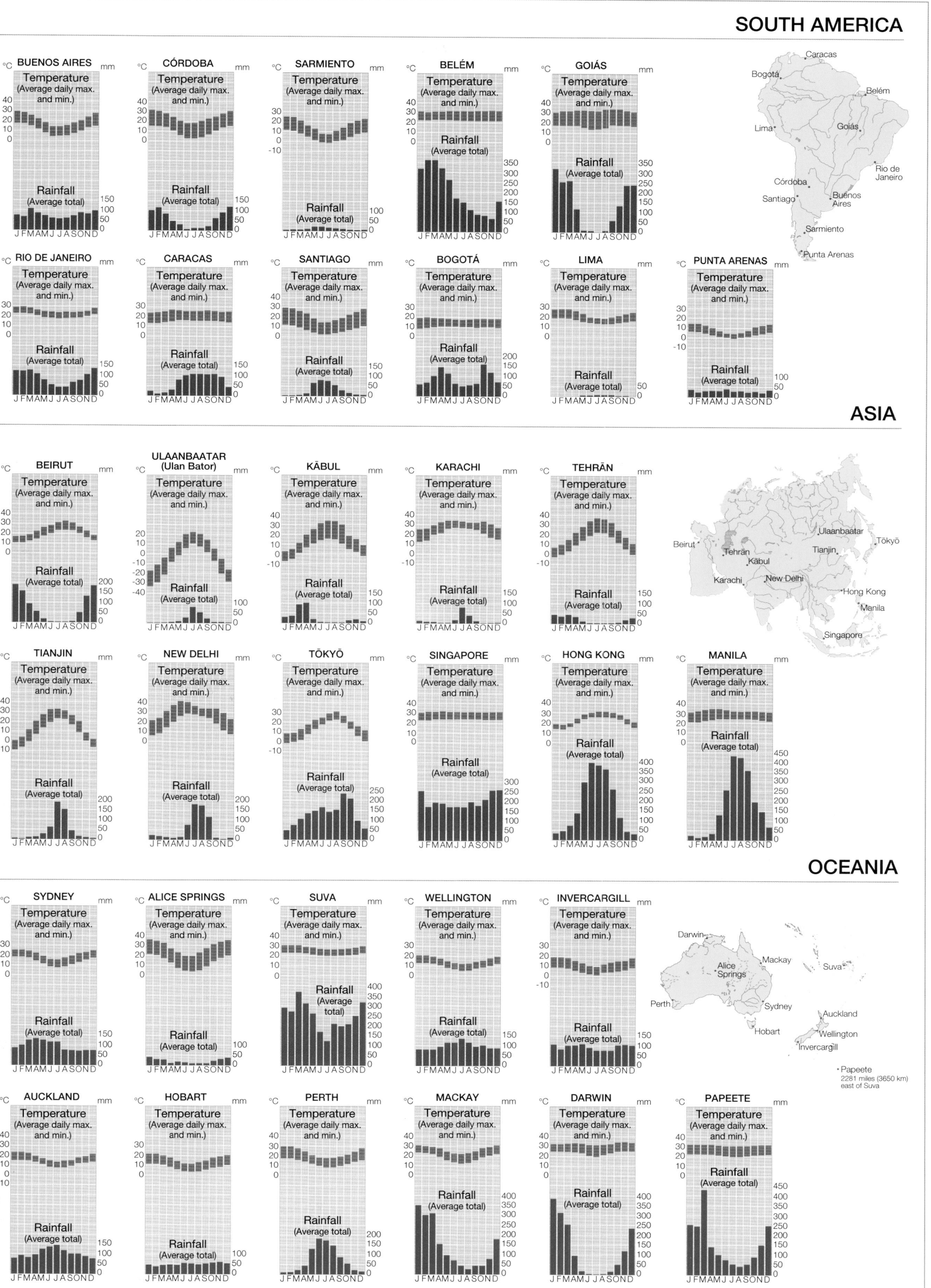

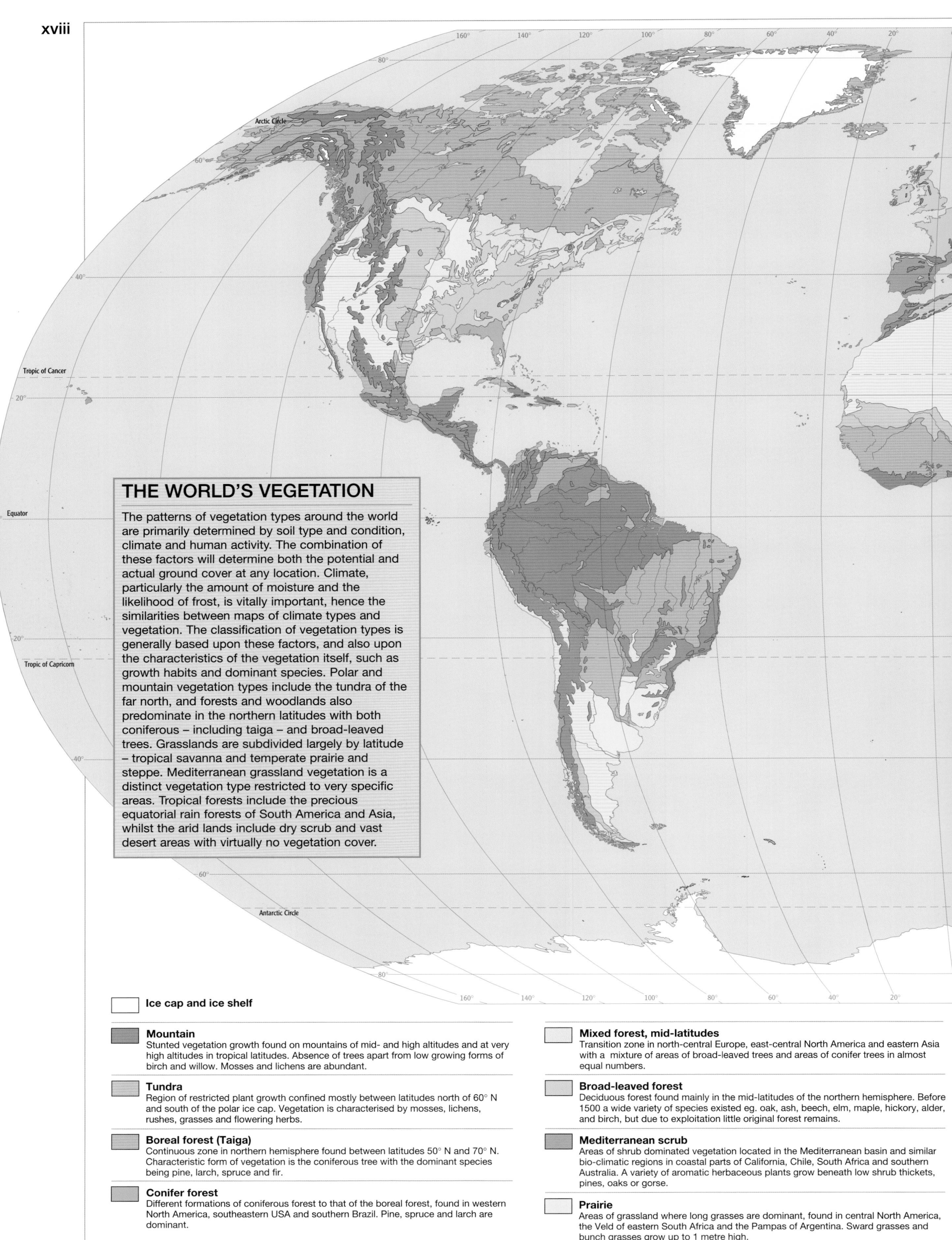

THE WORLD'S VEGETATION

The patterns of vegetation types around the world are primarily determined by soil type and condition, climate and human activity. The combination of these factors will determine both the potential and actual ground cover at any location. Climate, particularly the amount of moisture and the likelihood of frost, is vitally important, hence the similarities between maps of climate types and vegetation. The classification of vegetation types is generally based upon these factors, and also upon the characteristics of the vegetation itself, such as growth habits and dominant species. Polar and mountain vegetation types include the tundra of the far north, and forests and woodlands also predominate in the northern latitudes with both coniferous – including taiga – and broad-leaved trees. Grasslands are subdivided largely by latitude – tropical savanna and temperate prairie and steppe. Mediterranean grassland vegetation is a distinct vegetation type restricted to very specific areas. Tropical forests include the precious equatorial rain forests of South America and Asia, whilst the arid lands include dry scrub and vast desert areas with virtually no vegetation cover.

Ice cap and ice shelf

Mountain
Stunted vegetation growth found on mountains of mid- and high altitudes and at very high altitudes in tropical latitudes. Absence of trees apart from low growing forms of birch and willow. Mosses and lichens are abundant.

Tundra
Region of restricted plant growth confined mostly between latitudes north of 60° N and south of the polar ice cap. Vegetation is characterised by mosses, lichens, rushes, grasses and flowering herbs.

Boreal forest (Taiga)
Continuous zone in northern hemisphere found between latitudes 50° N and 70° N. Characteristic form of vegetation is the coniferous tree with the dominant species being pine, larch, spruce and fir.

Conifer forest
Different formations of coniferous forest to that of the boreal forest, found in western North America, southeastern USA and southern Brazil. Pine, spruce and larch are dominant.

Mixed forest, mid-latitudes
Transition zone in north-central Europe, east-central North America and eastern Asia with a mixture of areas of broad-leaved trees and areas of conifer trees in almost equal numbers.

Broad-leaved forest
Deciduous forest found mainly in the mid-latitudes of the northern hemisphere. Before 1500 a wide variety of species existed eg. oak, ash, beech, elm, maple, hickory, alder, and birch, but due to exploitation little original forest remains.

Mediterranean scrub
Areas of shrub dominated vegetation located in the Mediterranean basin and similar bio-climatic regions in coastal parts of California, Chile, South Africa and southern Australia. A variety of aromatic herbaceous plants grow beneath low shrub thickets, pines, oaks or gorse.

Prairie
Areas of grassland where long grasses are dominant, found in central North America, the Veld of eastern South Africa and the Pampas of Argentina. Sward grasses and bunch grasses grow up to 1 metre high.

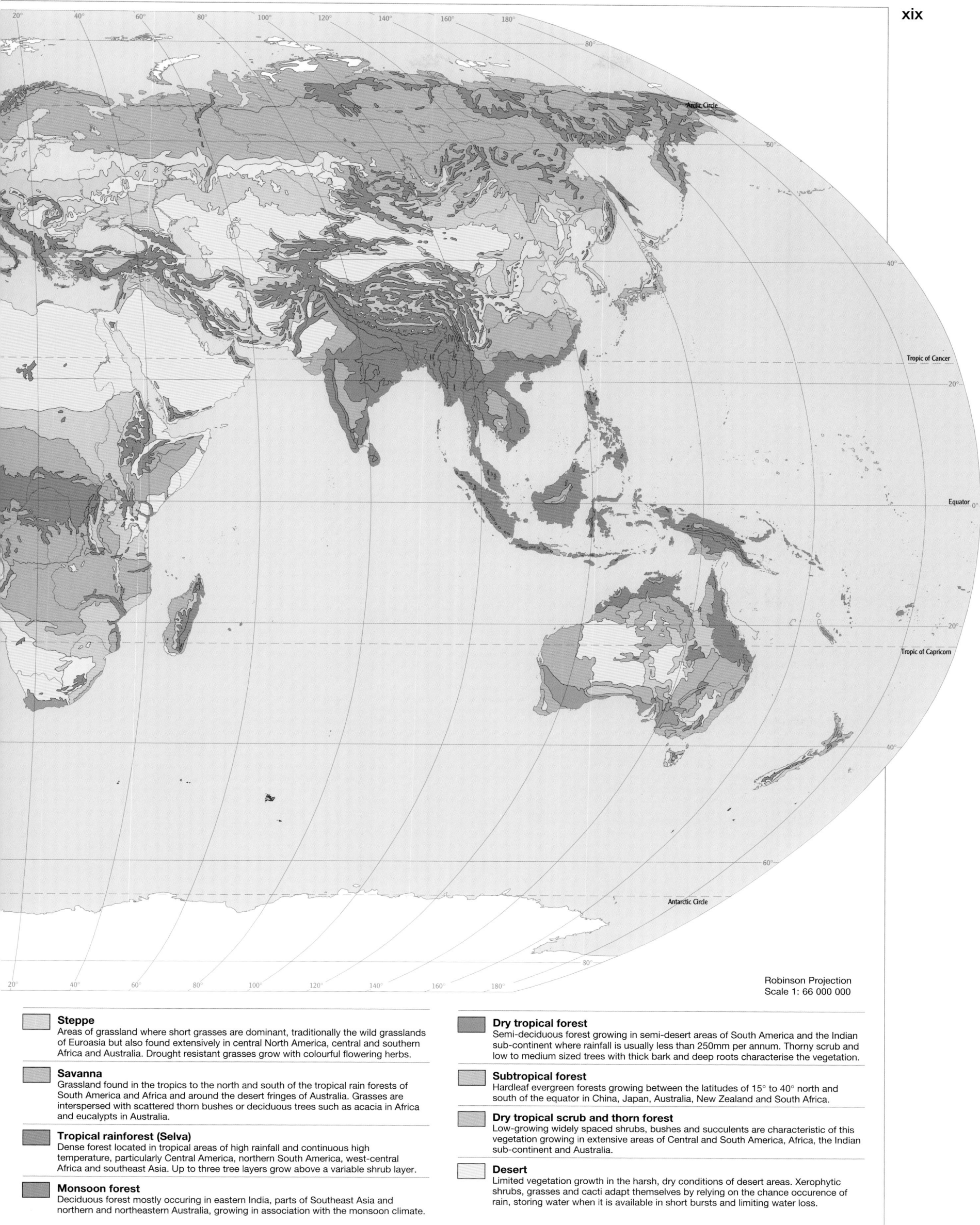

Robinson Projection
Scale 1: 66 000 000

Steppe
Areas of grassland where short grasses are dominant, traditionally the wild grasslands of Euroasia but also found extensively in central North America, central and southern Africa and Australia. Drought resistant grasses grow with colourful flowering herbs.

Savanna
Grassland found in the tropics to the north and south of the tropical rain forests of South America and Africa and around the desert fringes of Australia. Grasses are interspersed with scattered thorn bushes or deciduous trees such as acacia in Africa and eucalypts in Australia.

Tropical rainforest (Selva)
Dense forest located in tropical areas of high rainfall and continuous high temperature, particularly Central America, northern South America, west-central Africa and southeast Asia. Up to three tree layers grow above a variable shrub layer.

Monsoon forest
Deciduous forest mostly occuring in eastern India, parts of Southeast Asia and northern and northeastern Australia, growing in association with the monsoon climate.

Dry tropical forest
Semi-deciduous forest growing in semi-desert areas of South America and the Indian sub-continent where rainfall is usually less than 250mm per annum. Thorny scrub and low to medium sized trees with thick bark and deep roots characterise the vegetation.

Subtropical forest
Hardleaf evergreen forests growing between the latitudes of 15° to 40° north and south of the equator in China, Japan, Australia, New Zealand and South Africa.

Dry tropical scrub and thorn forest
Low-growing widely spaced shrubs, bushes and succulents are characteristic of this vegetation growing in extensive areas of Central and South America, Africa, the Indian sub-continent and Australia.

Desert
Limited vegetation growth in the harsh, dry conditions of desert areas. Xerophytic shrubs, grasses and cacti adapt themselves by relying on the chance occurence of rain, storing water when it is available in short bursts and limiting water loss.

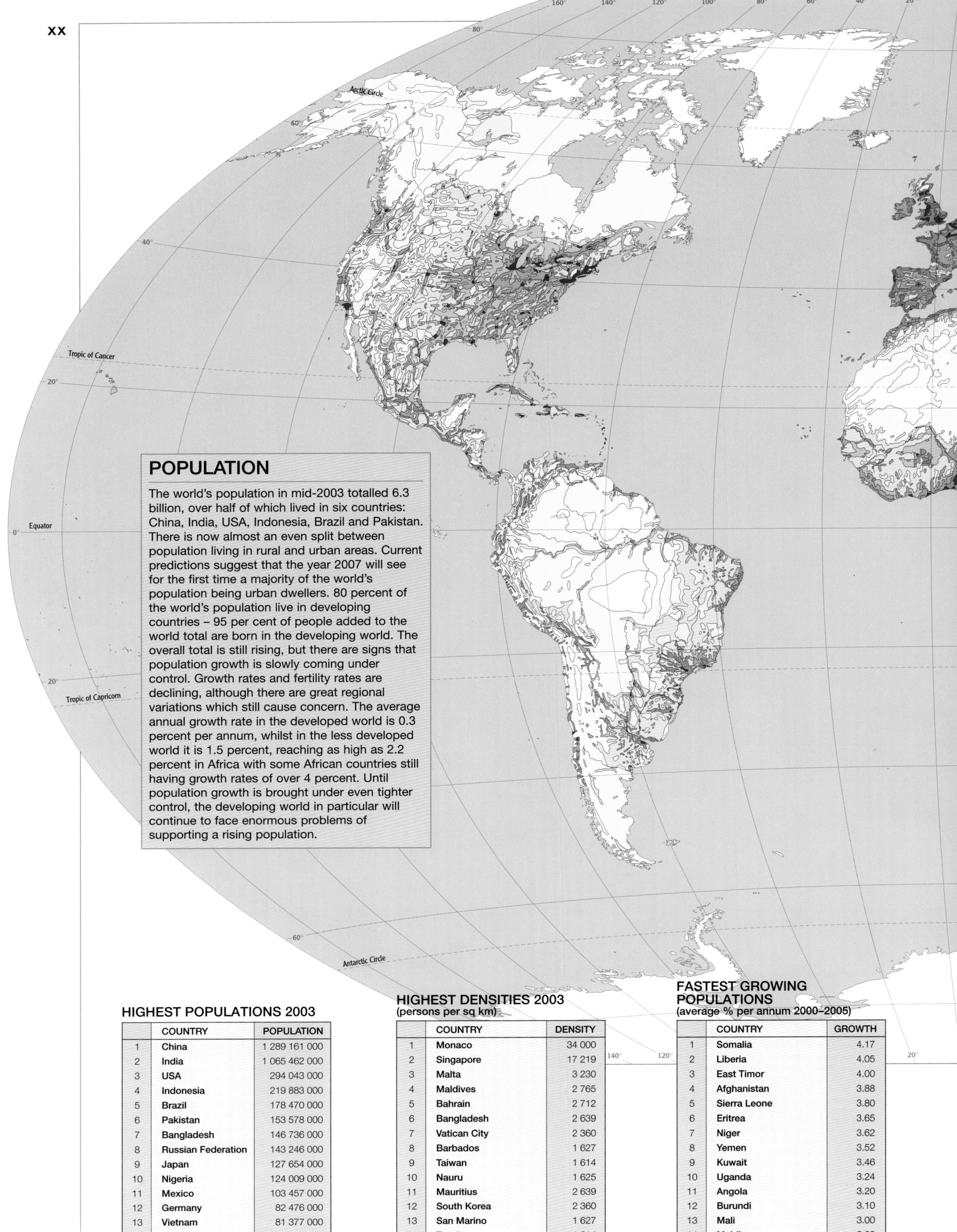

POPULATION

The world's population in mid-2003 totalled 6.3 billion, over half of which lived in six countries: China, India, USA, Indonesia, Brazil and Pakistan. There is now almost an even split between population living in rural and urban areas. Current predictions suggest that the year 2007 will see for the first time a majority of the world's population being urban dwellers. 80 percent of the world's population live in developing countries – 95 per cent of people added to the world total are born in the developing world. The overall total is still rising, but there are signs that population growth is slowly coming under control. Growth rates and fertility rates are declining, although there are great regional variations which still cause concern. The average annual growth rate in the developed world is 0.3 percent per annum, whilst in the less developed world it is 1.5 percent, reaching as high as 2.2 percent in Africa with some African countries still having growth rates of over 4 percent. Until population growth is brought under even tighter control, the developing world in particular will continue to face enormous problems of supporting a rising population.

HIGHEST POPULATIONS 2003

	COUNTRY	POPULATION
1	China	1 289 161 000
2	India	1 065 462 000
3	USA	294 043 000
4	Indonesia	219 883 000
5	Brazil	178 470 000
6	Pakistan	153 578 000
7	Bangladesh	146 736 000
8	Russian Federation	143 246 000
9	Japan	127 654 000
10	Nigeria	124 009 000
11	Mexico	103 457 000
12	Germany	82 476 000
13	Vietnam	81 377 000
14	Philippines	79 999 000
15	Egypt	71 931 000

HIGHEST DENSITIES 2003
(persons per sq km)

	COUNTRY	DENSITY
1	Monaco	34 000
2	Singapore	17 219
3	Malta	3 230
4	Maldives	2 765
5	Bahrain	2 712
6	Bangladesh	2 639
7	Vatican City	2 360
8	Barbados	1 627
9	Taiwan	1 614
10	Nauru	1 625
11	Mauritius	2 639
12	South Korea	2 360
13	San Marino	1 627
14	Tuvalu	1 614
15	Comoros	1 625

FASTEST GROWING POPULATIONS
(average % per annum 2000–2005)

	COUNTRY	GROWTH
1	Somalia	4.17
2	Liberia	4.05
3	East Timor	4.00
4	Afghanistan	3.88
5	Sierra Leone	3.80
6	Eritrea	3.65
7	Niger	3.62
8	Yemen	3.52
9	Kuwait	3.46
10	Uganda	3.24
11	Angola	3.20
12	Burundi	3.10
13	Mali	3.00
14	Maldives	2.98
15	Mauritania	2.98

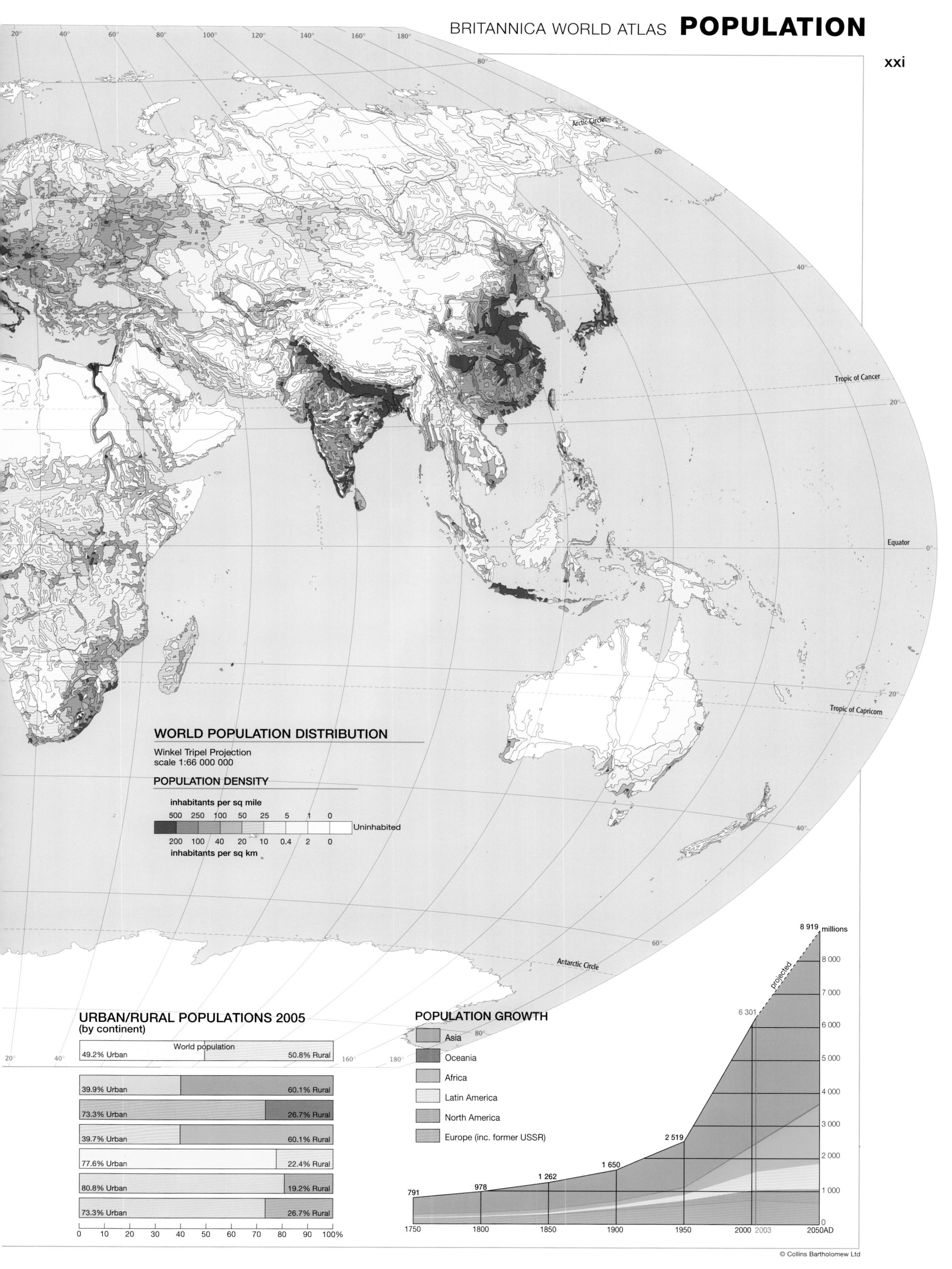

WORLD POPULATION DISTRIBUTION

Winkel Tripel Projection
scale 1:66 000 000

POPULATION DENSITY

inhabitants per sq mile

500	250	100	50	25	5	1	0	
200	100	40	20	10	0.4	2	0	Uninhabited

inhabitants per sq km

URBAN/RURAL POPULATIONS 2005
(by continent)

World population

| 49.2% Urban | 50.8% Rural |

| 39.9% Urban | 60.1% Rural |

| 73.3% Urban | 26.7% Rural |

| 39.7% Urban | 60.1% Rural |

| 77.6% Urban | 22.4% Rural |

| 80.8% Urban | 19.2% Rural |

| 73.3% Urban | 26.7% Rural |

0 10 20 30 40 50 60 70 80 90 100%

POPULATION GROWTH

- Asia
- Oceania
- Africa
- Latin America
- North America
- Europe (inc. former USSR)

8 919 millions

8 000

7 000

6 301

6 000

5 000

4 000

3 000

2 519

2 000

1 650

1 262

1 000

978

791

projected

1750 1800 1850 1900 1950 2000 2003 2050AD

© Collins Bartholomew Ltd

CITIES

World population is urbanizing rapidly but the current level of urbanization – the proportion of the population living in urban conditions – varies greatly across the world, as does its rate of increase. In the hundred years up to 1950 the greatest changes in urban population patterns took place in Europe and North America. Relatively few large cities developed elsewhere and most of these were in coastal locations with good trading connections with the imperial and industrial nations. This legacy is still highly visible on the world map of major cities. The main feature of the past half century has been the massive growth in the numbers of urban dwellers in the less developed regions due to a combination of in-migration and natural increase. This process is still accelerating, posing an even greater logistical challenge during the next few decades than it did in the closing decades of the twentieth century.

There has been a large increase in the number and size of cities. In 1950, New York and Tōkyō were the only urban agglomerations with over 10 million inhabitants. There are expected to be twenty-two such cities by 2015. This increase is principally an Asian phenomenon and today Asia dominates any list of the world's largest cities.

WORLD CITIES

Figures are for the urban agglomeration, defined as the population contained within the contours of a contiguous territory inhabited at urban levels without regard to administrative boundaries. They incorporate the population within the city plus the suburban fringe lying outside of, but adjacent to, the city boundaries.

AFGHANISTAN		**CANADA**		**COTE D'IVOIRE**		**HAITI**	
Kābul	3 288 000	Montréal	3 511 000	Abidjan	3 516 000	Port-au-Prince	2 090 000
ALGERIA		Ottawa	1 120 000	**CUBA**		**HUNGARY**	
Alger	3 260 000	Toronto	5 060 000	La Habana	2 192 000	Budapest	1 670 000
ANGOLA		Vancouver	2 125 000	**CZECH REPUBLIC**		**INDIA**	
Luanda	2 839 000	**CHILE**		Praha	1 164 000	Ahmadabad	5 171 000
ARGENTINA		Santiago	5 623 000	**DEMOCRATIC**		Bangalore	6 532 000
Buenos Aires	13 349 000	**CHINA**		**REPUBLIC OF CONGO**		Calicut	917 000
Córdoba	1 592 000	Anshan	1 459 000	Kinshasa	5 717 000	Chennai	6 915 000
Rosario	1 312 000	Baotou	1 367 000	**DENMARK**		Delhi	15 334 000
ARMENIA		Beijing	10 849 000	København	1 091 000	Hyderabad	6 145 000
Yerevan	1 066 000	Changchun	3 092 000	**DOMINICAN REPUBLIC**		Jaipur	2 796 000
AUSTRALIA		Chengdu	3 478 000	Santo Domingo	1 920 000	Kanpur	3 040 000
Adelaide	1 137 000	Chongqing	4 975 000	**ECUADOR**		Kolkata	14 299 000
Brisbane	1 769 000	Dalian	2 709 000	Guayaquil	2 387 000	Lucknow	2 589 000
Melbourne	3 663 000	Fushun	1 425 000	Quito	1 514 000	Mumbai	18 336 000
Perth	1 484 000	Fuzhou	1 398 000	**EGYPT**		Nagpur	2 359 000
Sydney	4 388 000	Guangzhou	3 881 000	Al Iskandarīyah	3 760 000	Patna	2 066 000
AUSTRIA		Guiyang	2 467 000	Al Qāhirah	11 146 000	Pune	4 485 000
Wien	2 190 000	Hangzhou	1 955 000	**EL SALVADOR**		Surat	3 671 000
AZERBAIJAN		Harbin	2 898 000	San Salvador	1 472 000	**INDONESIA**	
Bakı	1 830 000	Hong Kong	7 182 000	**ETHIOPIA**		Bandung	4 020 000
BANGLADESH		Huai'an	1 297 000	Ādīs Ābeba	2 899 000	Jakarta	13 194 000
Chittagong	4 171 000	Jilin	1 496 000	**FINLAND**		Medan	2 109 000
Dhaka	12 560 000	Jinan	2 654 000	Helsinki	1 103 000	Semarang	816 000
BELARUS		Kunming	1 748 000	**FRANCE**		Surabaya	2 735 000
Minsk	1 709 000	Lanzhou	1 788 000	Lyon	1 408 000	**IRAN**	
BELGIUM		Luoyang	1 594 000	Marseille	1 384 000	Eşfahān	1 547 000
Bruxelles	1 027 000	Nanchang	1 742 000	Paris	9 854 000	Mashhad	2 147 000
BOLIVIA		Nanjing	2 806 000	**GEORGIA**		Tehrān	7 352 000
La Paz	1 533 000	Qiqihar	1 452 000	T'bilisi	1 042 000	**IRAQ**	
BRAZIL		Shanghai	12 665 000	**GERMANY**		Baghdād	5 910 000
Belém	2 097 000	Shenyang	4 916 000	Berlin	3 328 000	**ISRAEL**	
Belo Horizonte	5 304 000	Shijiazhuang	1 733 000	Düsseldorf	3 325 000	Tel Aviv-Yafo	3 025 000
Brasília	3 341 000	Taiyuan	2 516 000	Essen-Dortmund	6 566 000	**ITALY**	
Curitiba	2 871 000	Tangshan	1 773 000	Hamburg	2 686 000	Milano	4 007 000
Fortaleza	3 261 000	Tianjin	9 346 000	Köln	3 084 000	Napoli	2 905 000
Porto Alegre	3 795 000	Wuhan	6 003 000	München	2 318 000	Roma	2 628 000
Recife	3 527 000	Xi'an	3 256 000	Stuttgart	2 705 000	Torino	1 182 000
Rio de Janeiro	11 469 000	Zhengzhou	2 250 000	**GREECE**		**JAPAN**	
São Paulo	18 333 000	Zibo	2 775 000	Athina	3 238 000	Ōsaka	11 286 000
Salvador	3 331 000	**COLOMBIA**		**GUATEMALA**		Hiroshima	1 005 000
BULGARIA		Bogotá	7 594 000	Guatemala	982 000	Kita-Kyūshū	2 815 000
Sofiya	1 045 000	Cali	2 583 000			Kyōto	1 805 000
		Medellín	3 236 000			Nagoya	3 189 000
		CONGO					
		Brazzaville	1 153 000				

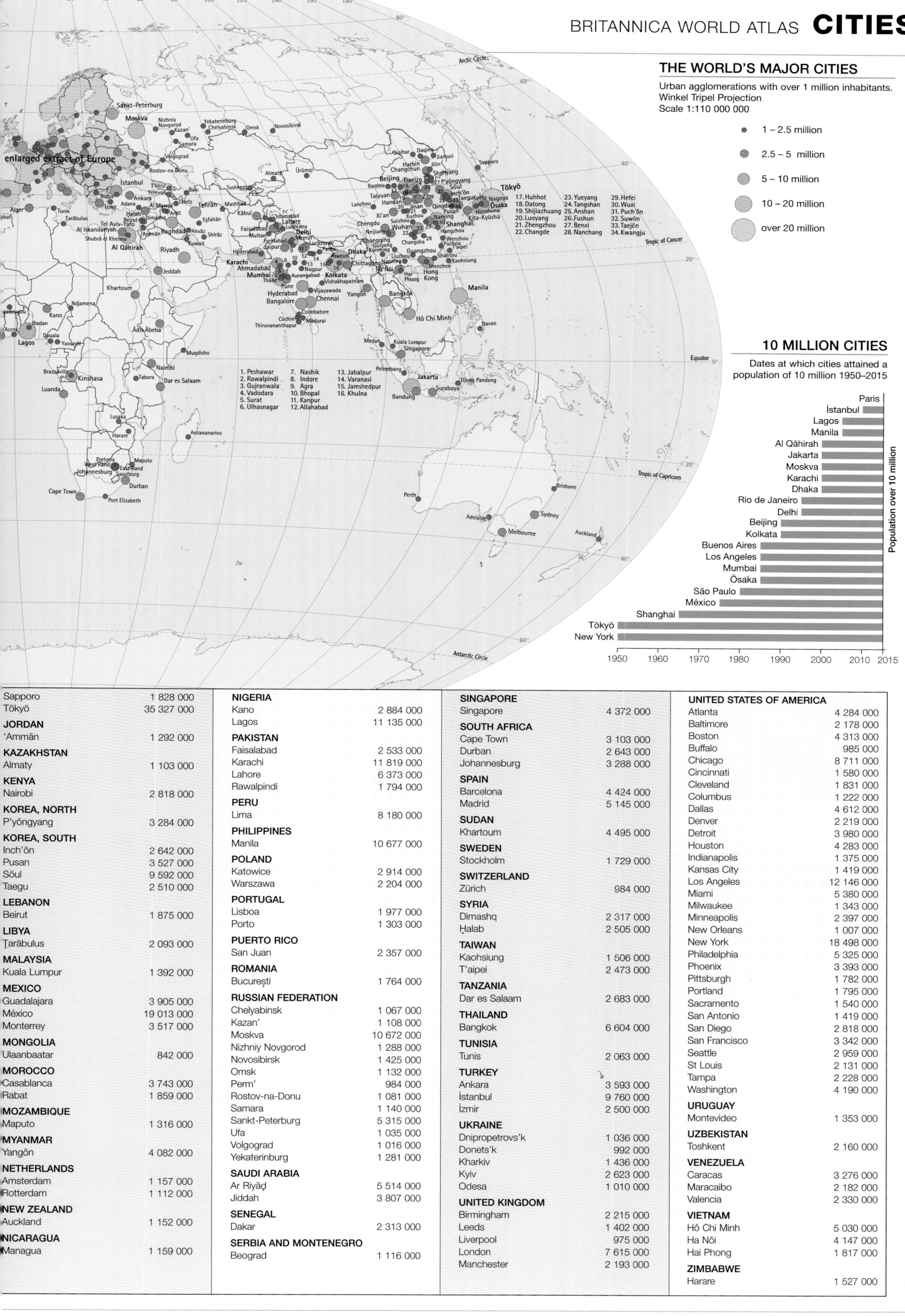

THE WORLD'S MAJOR CITIES

Urban agglomerations with over 1 million inhabitants.
Winkel Tripel Projection
Scale 1:110 000 000

- 1 – 2.5 million
- 2.5 – 5 million
- 5 – 10 million
- 10 – 20 million
- over 20 million

1. Peshawar
2. Rawalpindi
3. Gujranwala
4. Vadodara
5. Surat
6. Ulhasnagar
7. Nashik
8. Indore
9. Agra
10. Bhopal
11. Kanpur
12. Allahabad
13. Jabalpur
14. Varanasi
15. Jamshedpur
16. Khulna

17. Huhhot
18. Datong
19. Shijiazhuang
20. Luoyang
21. Zhengzhou
22. Changde
23. Yueyang
24. Tangshan
25. Anshan
26. Fushun
27. Benxi
28. Nanchang
29. Hefei
30. Wuxi
31. Puch'ŏn
32. Suwŏn
33. Taejŏn
34. Kwangju

10 MILLION CITIES

Dates at which cities attained a
population of 10 million 1950–2015

City	
Paris	
İstanbul	
Lagos	
Manila	
Al Qāhirah	
Jakarta	
Moskva	
Karachi	
Dhaka	
Rio de Janeiro	
Delhi	
Beijing	
Kolkata	
Buenos Aires	
Los Angeles	
Mumbai	
Ōsaka	
São Paulo	
México	
Shanghai	
Tōkyō	
New York	

Population over 10 million

1950 1960 1970 1980 1990 2000 2010 2015

Sapporo	1 828 000
Tōkyō	35 327 000
JORDAN	
'Ammān	1 292 000
KAZAKHSTAN	
Almaty	1 103 000
KENYA	
Nairobi	2 818 000
KOREA, NORTH	
P'yŏngyang	3 284 000
KOREA, SOUTH	
Inch'ŏn	2 642 000
Pusan	3 527 000
Sŏul	9 592 000
Taegu	2 510 000
LEBANON	
Beirut	1 875 000
LIBYA	
Ṭarābulus	2 093 000
MALAYSIA	
Kuala Lumpur	1 392 000
MEXICO	
Guadalajara	3 905 000
México	19 013 000
Monterrey	3 517 000
MONGOLIA	
Ulaanbaatar	842 000
MOROCCO	
Casablanca	3 743 000
Rabat	1 859 000
MOZAMBIQUE	
Maputo	1 316 000
MYANMAR	
Yangôn	4 082 000
NETHERLANDS	
Amsterdam	1 157 000
Rotterdam	1 112 000
NEW ZEALAND	
Auckland	1 152 000
NICARAGUA	
Managua	1 159 000

NIGERIA	
Kano	2 884 000
Lagos	11 135 000
PAKISTAN	
Faisalabad	2 533 000
Karachi	11 819 000
Lahore	6 373 000
Rawalpindi	1 794 000
PERU	
Lima	8 180 000
PHILIPPINES	
Manila	10 677 000
POLAND	
Katowice	2 914 000
Warszawa	2 204 000
PORTUGAL	
Lisboa	1 977 000
Porto	1 303 000
PUERTO RICO	
San Juan	2 357 000
ROMANIA	
Bucureşti	1 764 000
RUSSIAN FEDERATION	
Chelyabinsk	1 067 000
Kazan'	1 108 000
Moskva	10 672 000
Nizhniy Novgorod	1 288 000
Novosibirsk	1 425 000
Omsk	1 132 000
Perm'	984 000
Rostov-na-Donu	1 081 000
Samara	1 140 000
Sankt-Peterburg	5 315 000
Ufa	1 035 000
Volgograd	1 016 000
Yekaterinburg	1 281 000
SAUDI ARABIA	
Ar Riyāḍ	5 514 000
Jiddah	3 807 000
SENEGAL	
Dakar	2 313 000
SERBIA AND MONTENEGRO	
Beograd	1 116 000

SINGAPORE	
Singapore	4 372 000
SOUTH AFRICA	
Cape Town	3 103 000
Durban	2 643 000
Johannesburg	3 288 000
SPAIN	
Barcelona	4 424 000
Madrid	5 145 000
SUDAN	
Khartoum	4 495 000
SWEDEN	
Stockholm	1 729 000
SWITZERLAND	
Zürich	984 000
SYRIA	
Dimashq	2 317 000
Ḥalab	2 505 000
TAIWAN	
Kaohsiung	1 506 000
T'aipei	2 473 000
TANZANIA	
Dar es Salaam	2 683 000
THAILAND	
Bangkok	6 604 000
TUNISIA	
Tunis	2 063 000
TURKEY	
Ankara	3 593 000
İstanbul	9 760 000
İzmir	2 500 000
UKRAINE	
Dnipropetrovs'k	1 036 000
Donets'k	992 000
Kharkiv	1 436 000
Kyiv	2 623 000
Odesa	1 010 000
UNITED KINGDOM	
Birmingham	2 215 000
Leeds	1 402 000
Liverpool	975 000
London	7 615 000
Manchester	2 193 000

UNITED STATES OF AMERICA	
Atlanta	4 284 000
Baltimore	2 178 000
Boston	4 313 000
Buffalo	985 000
Chicago	8 711 000
Cincinnati	1 580 000
Cleveland	1 831 000
Columbus	1 222 000
Dallas	4 612 000
Denver	2 219 000
Detroit	3 980 000
Houston	4 283 000
Indianapolis	1 375 000
Kansas City	1 419 000
Los Angeles	12 146 000
Miami	5 380 000
Milwaukee	1 343 000
Minneapolis	2 397 000
New Orleans	1 007 000
New York	18 498 000
Philadelphia	5 325 000
Phoenix	3 393 000
Pittsburgh	1 782 000
Portland	1 795 000
Sacramento	1 540 000
San Antonio	1 419 000
San Diego	2 818 000
San Francisco	3 342 000
Seattle	2 959 000
St Louis	2 131 000
Tampa	2 228 000
Washington	4 190 000
URUGUAY	
Montevideo	1 353 000
UZBEKISTAN	
Toshkent	2 160 000
VENEZUELA	
Caracas	3 276 000
Maracaibo	2 182 000
Valencia	2 330 000
VIETNAM	
Hô Chi Minh	5 030 000
Ha Nôi	4 147 000
Hai Phong	1 817 000
ZIMBABWE	
Harare	1 527 000

ENERGY

The world's energy resources and their uses are unevenly distributed, with just three countries, the USA, Russian Federation and China, dominating both the production and consumption of energy. Some countries produce much more than they consume, but many of the most advanced industrial economies, such as the USA and Japan, consume more energy than they produce. The USA is the largest single energy consumer, using over a quarter of the world's energy. Proven energy reserves are also unevenly distributed. Nearly two-thirds of oil reserves are concentrated in the Middle East whilst reserves of natural gas are dominated by the Former Soviet Union and the Middle East. Coal reserves are more evenly distributed between the Asia Pacific region, North America and the Former Soviet Union.

Alternatives to traditional energy sources are nuclear power and renewable resources. Asia Pacific and South and Central America have experienced the highest growth in nuclear power over the past decade, led by Japan, which generates two-thirds of its electricity from nuclear sources. The question of sustainability has underpinned the search for new sources of energy which are less detrimental to the environment, hence the emergence of renewable resources such as geothermal, wind, solar, biomass and hydropower. The most successful form of renewable energy has been hydroelectric power, consumption of which has risen significantly since the early 1990s with South and Central America showing the largest rise.

WORLD'S TOP 10 ENERGY PRODUCERS AND CONSUMERS 2001

PRODUCERS		CONSUMERS	
USA	1 804	USA	2 446
Russian Federation	1 131	China	1 000
China	964	Russian Federation	711
Saudi Arabia	513	Japan	552
Canada	459	Germany	362
UK	281	India	322
Iran	265	Canada	315
Norway	258	France	265
Australia	253	UK	247
Mexico	242	Brazil	221
World total	10 166	World total	10 179

Million tonnes of oil equivalent

PROVEN ENERGY RESERVES 2002

REGION	OIL (1000 million barrels)	%	NATURAL GAS (trillion cubic metres)	%	COAL (million tonnes)	%
North America[1]	49.9	4.8	7.15	4.6	257 783	26.2
South and Central America	98.6	9.4	7.08	4.5	21 752	2.2
Europe	19.7	1.9	5.75	3.7	125 395	12.7
Former Soviet Union[2]	77.8	7.4	55.29	35.5	229 975	23.4
Middle East	685.6	65.4	56.06	36.0	1 710	-
Africa	77.4	7.4	11.84	7.6	55 367	5.8
Asia Pacific	38.7	3.7	12.61	8.1	292 471	29.7
World	1 047.7	100	155.78	100	984 453	100

1. Canada, USA and Mexico.
2. Comprises: Russian Federation, Estonia, Latvia, Lithuania, Belarus, Ukraine, Moldova, Georgia, Armenia, Azerbaijan, Kazakhstan, Uzbekistan, Turkmenistan, Tajikistan and Kyrgyzsta

PRIMARY ENERGY CONSUMPTION

Million tonnes of oil equivalent.

Legend:
- World
- North America[1]
- South and Central America
- Europe
- Former Soviet Union[2]
- Middle East
- Africa
- Asia Pacific

1. Canada, USA and Mexico.
2. See footnote for Proven Energy Reserves 2002.

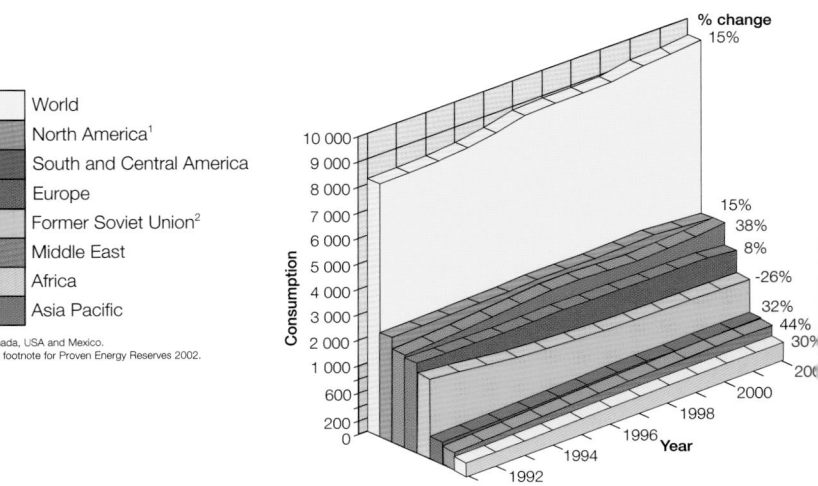

DISTRIBUTION OF RESOURCES

Winkel Tripel Projection
Scale 1:92 000 000

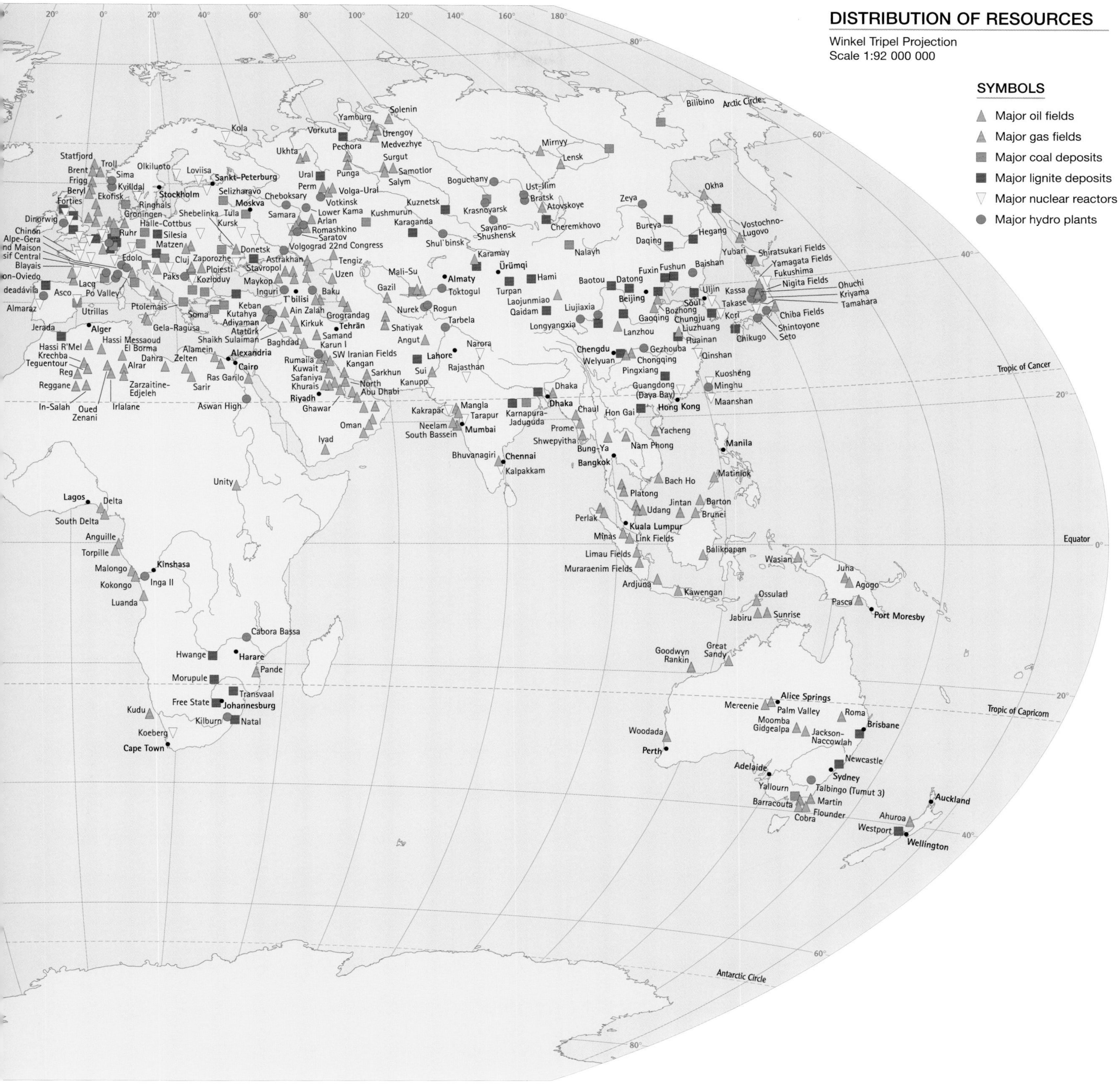

SYMBOLS

▲ Major oil fields
▲ Major gas fields
■ Major coal deposits
■ Major lignite deposits
▽ Major nuclear reactors
● Major hydro plants

NUCLEAR ENERGY CONSUMPTION

Million tonnes of oil equivalent.

% change
22%
17%
19%
39%
12%
57%
24%

Consumption
700
600
500
400
300
200
100
50
30
10
0

Year
1992 1994 1996 1998 2000 2002

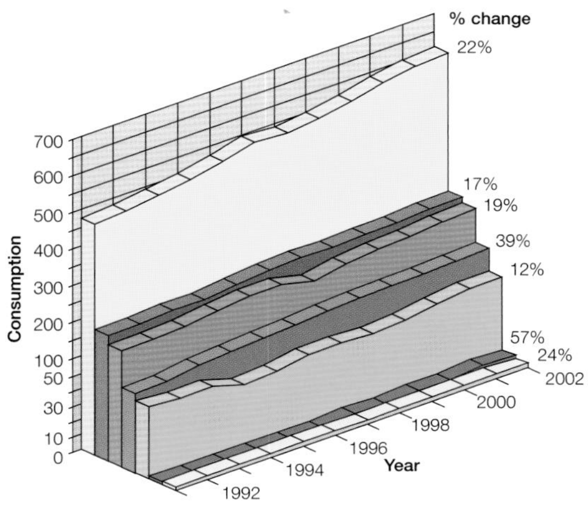

HYDROELECTRICITY CONSUMPTION

Million tonnes of oil equivalent.

% change
16%
6%
5%
34%
38%
-2%
35%
-30%

Consumption
600
500
400
300
200
100
50
30
10

Year
1992 1994 1996 1998 2000 2002

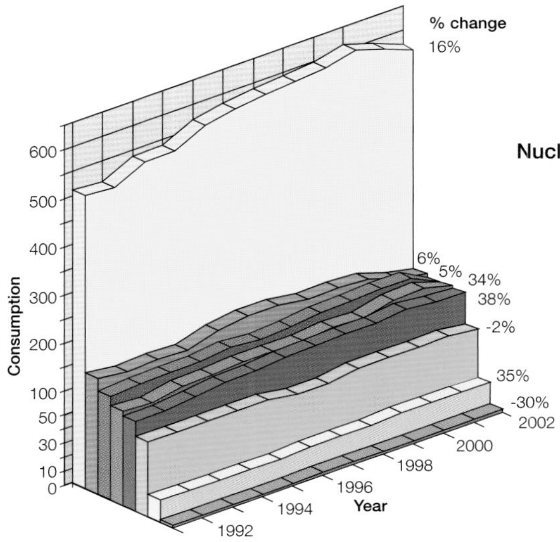

FUEL SHARES IN WORLD TOTAL PRIMARY ENERGY SUPPLY, 2000

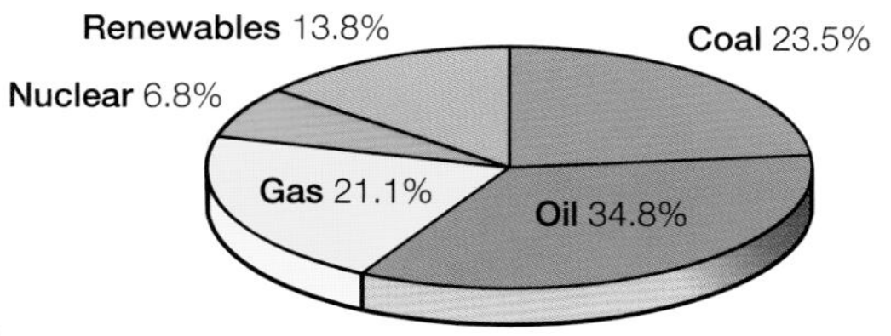

Renewables 13.8%
Nuclear 6.8%
Gas 21.1%
Coal 23.5%
Oil 34.8%

ENCYCLOPÆDIA

Britannica®

WORLD

ATLAS

ATLAS MAPPING

The Encyclopædia Britannica World Atlas includes a variety of styles and scales of mapping which together provide comprehensive coverage of all parts of the world; the map styles and editorial policies followed are introduced here. The area covered by each map is shown on the front and back endpapers.

Each continent is introduced by a satellite image and a politically coloured map, followed by reference maps of sub-continental regions and then more detailed reference mapping of regions and individual countries. Scales for continental maps (see 1) range between 1:15 000 000 and 1:27 000 000 and regional maps (see 2) are in the range 1:11 000 000 to 1:13 000 000. Mapping for most countries is at scales between 1:3 000 000 and 1:7 500 000 (see 3), although selected, more densely populated areas of

Europe, North America and Asia are mapped at larger scales, up to 1:1 000 000 (see 4). Large-scale city plans of a selection of the world's major cities (see 5) are included on the appropriate map pages. A suite of maps covering the world's oceans and poles (see 6) at a variety of scales concludes the main reference map section.

The symbols and place name abbreviations used on the maps are fully explained on pages 4-5 and a glossary of geographical terms is included at the back of the atlas on pages 219-222. The alphanumeric reference system used in the index is based on latitude and longitude, and the number and letter for each graticule square are shown within each map frame, in red. The numbers of adjoining or overlapping pages are shown by arrows in the page frame and accompanying numbers in the margin.

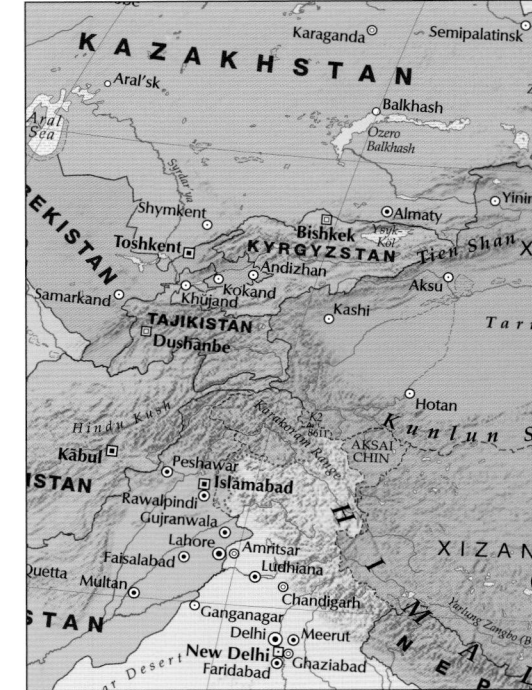

1. CONTINENTAL MAP OF ASIA (extract from pages 150-151)

BOUNDARIES

The status, names and boundaries of nations are shown in this atlas as they are at the time of going to press, as far as can be ascertained. Where an international boundary symbol appears in the sea or ocean it does not necessarily infer a legal maritime boundary, but shows which off-shore islands belong to which country.

Where international boundaries are the subject of dispute it may be that no portrayal of them will meet with the approval of any of the countries involved, but it is not seen as the function of this atlas to try to adjudicate between the rights and wrongs of political issues. The atlas aims to take a neutral viewpoint of all such cases. Although reference mapping at atlas scales is not the ideal medium for indicating territorial claims, every reasonable attempt is made to show where an active territorial dispute exists, and where there is an important difference between 'de facto' (existing in fact, on the ground) and 'de jure' (according to law) boundaries. This is done by the use of a different symbol where international boundaries are disputed, or where the alignment is unconfirmed, to that used for settled international boundaries. Cease-fire lines are also shown by a separate symbol. For clarity, disputed boundaries and areas are annotated where this is considered necessary, but it is impossible to represent all the complexities of territorial disputes on maps at atlas scales.

The latest internal administrative division boundaries are shown on the maps for selected countries where the combination of map scale and the number of divisions permits, with recent changes to local government systems being taken into account as far as possible. Towns which are first-order and second-order administrative centres are also symbolized where scale permits.

2. SOUTHEAST ASIA 1:13 000 000 (extract from pages 152-153)

3. EAST CENTRAL AFRICA 1:7 500 000 (extract from pages 92-93)

PLACE NAMES

NAME-FORM POLICY

The spelling of place names on maps has always been a matter of great complexity, because of the variety of the world's languages and the systems used to write them down. There is no standard way of spelling names or of converting them from one alphabet, or symbol set, to another. Instead, conventional ways of spelling have evolved in each of the world's major languages, and the results often differ significantly from the name as it is spelled in the original language. Familiar examples of English conventional names include Munich (München), Florence (Firenze) and Moscow (from the transliterated form, Moskva).

In this atlas, local name-forms are used where they are in the Roman alphabet. These local forms are those which are recognized by the government of the country concerned, usually as represented by its official mapping agency. This is a basic principle laid down by the United Kingdom government's Permanent Committee on Geographical Names for British Official Use (PCGN).

For languages in non-Roman alphabets or symbol sets,

names need to be 'Romanized' through a process of transliteration (the conversion of characters or symbols from one alphabet into another) or transcription (conversion of names based on pronunciation). Different systems often exist for this process, but PCGN and its United States counterpart, the Board on Geographic Names (BGN), usually follow the same Romanization principles, and the general policy for this atlas is to follow their lead. One notable change in this edition is that PCGN and BGN principles are now followed for Arabic names in Egypt ('Al' style - for example, Al Qahirah for Cairo), where previous editions followed PCGN's former policy of using a local Survey of Egypt system ('El' style – El Qâhira).

Local name-form mapping is the nearest that the cartographer can achieve to an international standard. It is in fact impossible, and perhaps unnecessary, to provide English names for the majority of mapped features, and translating names into English is fraught with linguistic hazards. Consequently, a local name-form map is more internally consistent than a partly anglicized one.

Although local forms in this atlas are given precedence, prominent English-language conventional names and historic names are not neglected. The names of countries, continents, oceans, seas and underwater features in international waters appear in English throughout the atlas, as do those of other international features where such an English form exists. Significant superseded names and other alternative spellings are included in brackets on the maps where space permits, and variants and former names are cross-referenced in the index.

NAME CHANGES

Continuing changes in official languages, in writing systems and in Romanization methods, have to be taken into account by cartographers. In many countries different languages are in use in different regions or side-by-side in the same region, and there is potential for widely varying name-forms even within a single country. A worldwide trend towards national, regional and ethnic self-determination is operating at the same time as pressure towards increased international standardization.

MAP PROJECTIONS

The creation of computer-generated maps presents the opportunity to select projections specifically for the area and scale of each map. As the only way to show the Earth with absolute accuracy is on a globe, all map projections are compromises. Some projections seek to maintain correct area relationships (equal area projections), true distances and bearings from a point (equidistant projections) or correct angles and shapes (conformal projections); others attempt to achieve a balance between these properties. The choice of projections used in this atlas has been made on an individual continental and regional basis. Projections used, and their individual parameters, have been defined to minimize distortion and to reduce scale errors (shown as percentage figures in the accompanying diagrams) as much as possible.

For world maps, the Bartholomew version of the Winkel Tripel Projection is used. This projection combines elements of conformality with that of equal area, and shows, over the world as a whole, relatively true shapes and reasonably equal areas. The Mercator Projection (see 7) has been selected for the regional maps of southeast Asia along the Equator, while in higher latitudes, particularly in Europe and to some extent in North America, the Conic Equidistant Projection (see 8) has been used extensively for regional mapping. The Lambert Azimuthal Equal Area Projection (see 9) has been employed in both South America and Australia.

9. LAMBERT AZIMUTHAL EQUAL AREA PROJECTION

Points are projected onto a plane in contact with the globe at the centre point (25ºS, 135ºE in this illustration). Scale is correct at the centre, and scale errors increase in concentric circles away from it. Areas are true in relation to the corresponding areas on the globe.

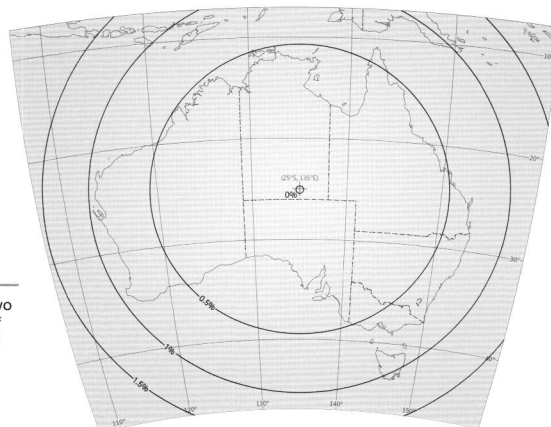

7. MERCATOR PROJECTION

This rectangular or cylindrical projection is constructed on the basis of a cylinder in contact with the globe, in this case around the Equator. Scale is correct along the Equator and distortion increases away from it in both directions.

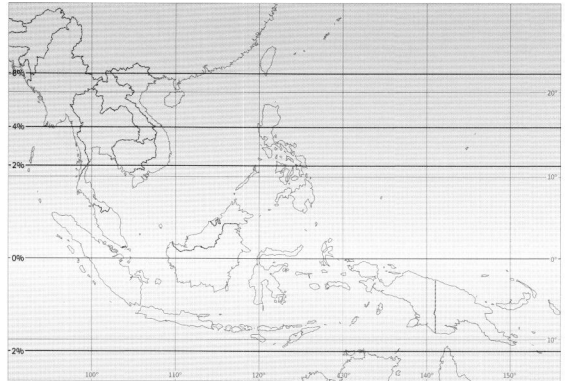

8. CONIC EQUIDISTANT PROJECTION

Constructed on the basis of a cone intersecting the globe along two standard parallels (55ºN and 75ºN in this illustration), along both of which scale is correct. Lines of equal scale error are parallel to the standard lines, with distortion increasing away from each.

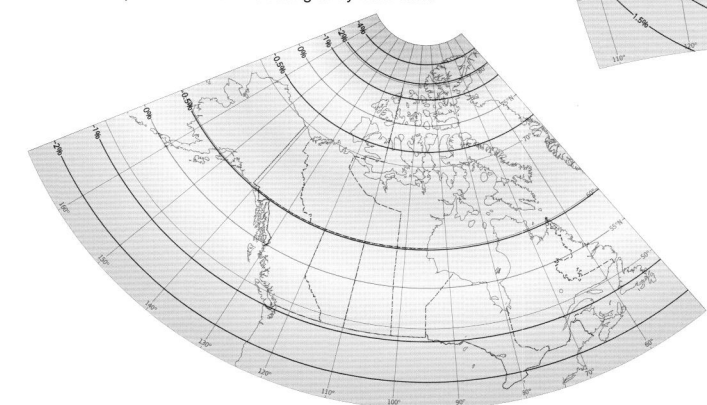

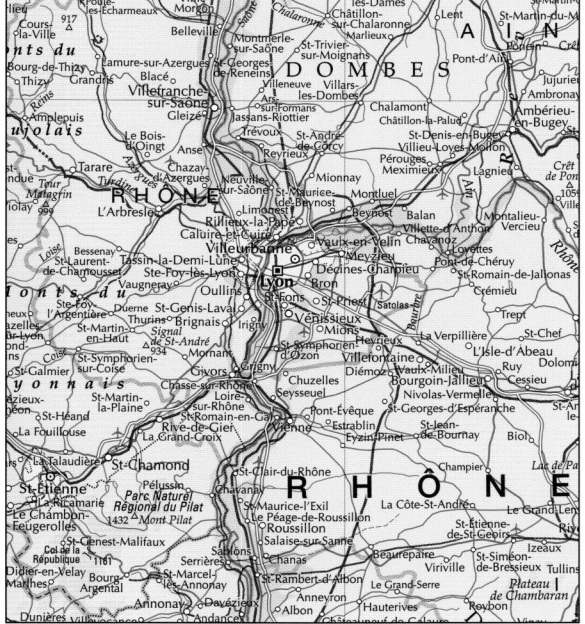

4. SOUTHEAST FRANCE 1:1 200 000 (extract from pages 40-41)

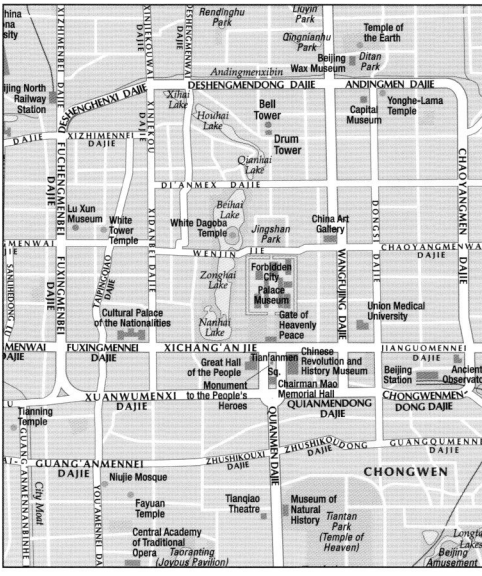

5. BEIJING CITY PLAN (extract from page 168)

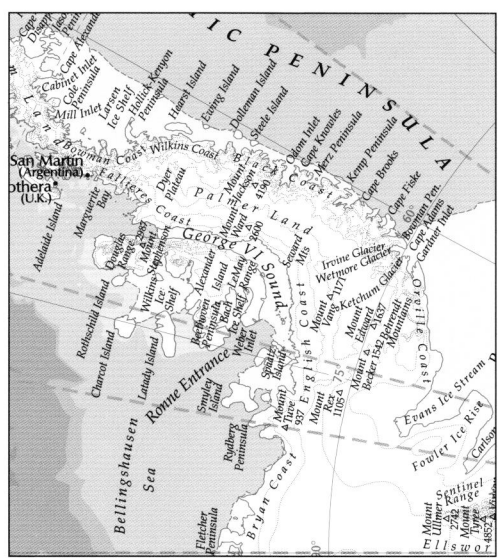

6. ANTARCTICA 1:18 000 000 (extract from pages 212-213)

Place names are, to an extent, a mirror for the changes that continue to transform the political world. Changes of territorial control may have a significant effect on name-forms. Yet even in countries where name-forms could be expected to have long been largely standardized, there are sometimes continuing issues for the cartographer to address. In the UK, for example, there is a trend for more Gaelic and Welsh-language names to be given official recognition. Similarly, there is an increase in the official recognition and use of indigenous name-forms in for instance New Zealand (Maori) and Canada (Inuit and Indian names). Name spelling issues are, in fact, likely to emerge in almost any part of the world.

Reflecting trends across the world, systematic alterations affecting various countries are reflected in this atlas. The dissolution of the former USSR has given rise to the greatest changes in recent years, and this atlas continues the policy established in the previous edition of names being converted from Russian to the main national language in Belarus, Ukraine, Moldova, Armenia, Georgia, Azerbaijan, Kyrgyzstan and Tajikistan. Uzbekistan is the

latest to have been converted in this way, using the new Uzbek Roman alphabet. Russian naturally continues to be used as the main form in the Russian Federation and also continues to be used as the prime language on maps of Kazakhstan. Here, local-language name-forms (derived from Kazakh Cyrillic) are included for main place names where space permits on the maps, with additional alternatives in the index. In Turkmenistan, main Turkmen Cyrillic-derived names are similarly covered, but native sources are starting to apply a finalized Roman alphabet, pointing the way to a future in which Cyrillic names will be dropped entirely. Main examples of new Turkmen forms are included as cross-references in the index.

In Spain, account is taken of the official prominence now given to Catalan, Galician and some Basque spellings, which results in name-forms such as Eivissa for Ibiza and A Coruña for La Coruña. Reflecting these changes, many names are now represented in dual form on official Spanish mapping. Depending on their specific treatment on local mapping, some of these are shown in this atlas as hyphenated (for example Gijón-Xixón or Elche-Elx) while

others include the second forms as alternative names.

Chinese name-forms, which follow the official Pinyin Romanization system, continue to change. Name-forms are in line with the latest official sources, continuing to follow the principle whereby numerous towns which are the centres of administrative units such as the county or 'xian' officially take the name of the county itself. The alternative place name in common local use is shown in brackets on the map. The index also includes numerous cross-references for Chinese name-forms as they were before the introduction of Pinyin – taking account of the main so-called 'Post Office' spellings such as Tientsin (now Tianjin), and more particularly of the long-familiar Wade-Giles Romanization, which gives, for instance, Pei-ching as against the Pinyin form Beijing.

As well as systematic changes in name-forms such as those outlined above, occasionally places are given entirely new names for a variety of reasons. One significant example is the official renaming of Calcutta as Kolkata, following earlier changes by the Indian authorities to Bombay (now Mumbai) and Madras (now Chennai).

REFERENCE MAPS

CITIES AND TOWNS

Population	National Capital	Administrative Capital (Shown for selected countries only) First order	Administrative Capital Second order (Scales larger than 1:9 000 000)	Other City or Town	
over 10 million	TŌKYŌ ◙	Karachi ◙	Los Angeles ◉	New York ◉	
5 million to 10 million	SANTIAGO ◙	Tianjin ◙	Chicago ◉	Hong Kong ◉	
1 million to 5 million	KĀBUL ◙	Sydney ◙	Tangshan ◎	Kaohsiung ◎	
500 000 to 1 million	BANGUI ▣	Trujillo ▣	Agra ◎	Jiddah ◎	
100 000 to 500 000	WELLINGTON ▣	Mansa ▣	Naogaon ◎	Apucarana ◎	
50 000 to 100 000	PORT OF SPAIN ▢	Potenza ▢	Trier ◦	Arecibo ◦	
10 000 to 50 000	MALABO ▢	Chinhoyi ▢	Willimantic ◦	Ceres ◦	
1 000 to 10 000	VALLETTA ▫	Ati ▫	Nepalganj ◦	Abla ◦	
under 1000 (Scales 1:4 000 000 and larger)		Chhukha ▫	Carmel ◦	Lopigna ◦	

Built-up area

MISCELLANEOUS FEATURES

---------- National park   ················ Regional park   ················ Reserve or special land area   ∴ Site of specific interest   ∿∿∿∿∿∿ Wall

BOUNDARIES

▬▬▬	International boundary
⬛⬛⬛⬛	Disputed international boundary or alignment unconfirmed
╱▬▬	Undefined international boundary in the sea. All land within this boundary is part of state or territory named.
▬ ▬ ▬	Administrative boundary, first order internal division. Scales 1:4 000 000 and larger. Shown for selected countries only.
▬▬▬	Administrative boundary, first order internal division. Scales smaller than 1:4 000 000. Shown for selected countries only.
▬▬▬	Administrative boundary, second order internal division. Scales 1:4 000 000 and larger. Shown for selected countries only.
◆▬◆▬◆	Disputed administrative boundary Scales 1:4 000 000 and larger. Shown for selected countries only.
••••••	Ceasefire line or other boundary described on the map

RELIEF

Contour intervals used in layer-colouring for land height and sea depth

Scales 1:4 000 000 and larger

METRES	FEET
6000	19686
5000	16404
4000	13124
3000	9843
2000	6562
1500	4921
1000	3281
500	1640
200	656
100	328
0	0 below sea level
50	164
200	656
2000	6562
4000	13124
6000	19686

Scales smaller than 1:4 000 000

METRES	FEET
6000	19686
5000	16404
4000	13124
3000	9843
2000	6562
1000	3281
500	1640
200	656
0	0 below sea level
200	656
2000	6562
4000	13124
6000	19686

Oceans and Antarctica (Pages 212–218)

METRES	FEET
6000	19686
5000	16404
4000	13124
3000	9843
2000	6562
1000	3281
500	1640
200	656
0	0 below sea level
200	656
2000	6562
3000	9843
4000	13124
5000	16404
6000	19686
7000	22967

1234 △ Summit Height in metres

-123 Spot height Surface height in metres for depressions and areas below sea level.

5678 Ocean deep In metres. Ocean pages only.

LAND AND SEA FEATURES

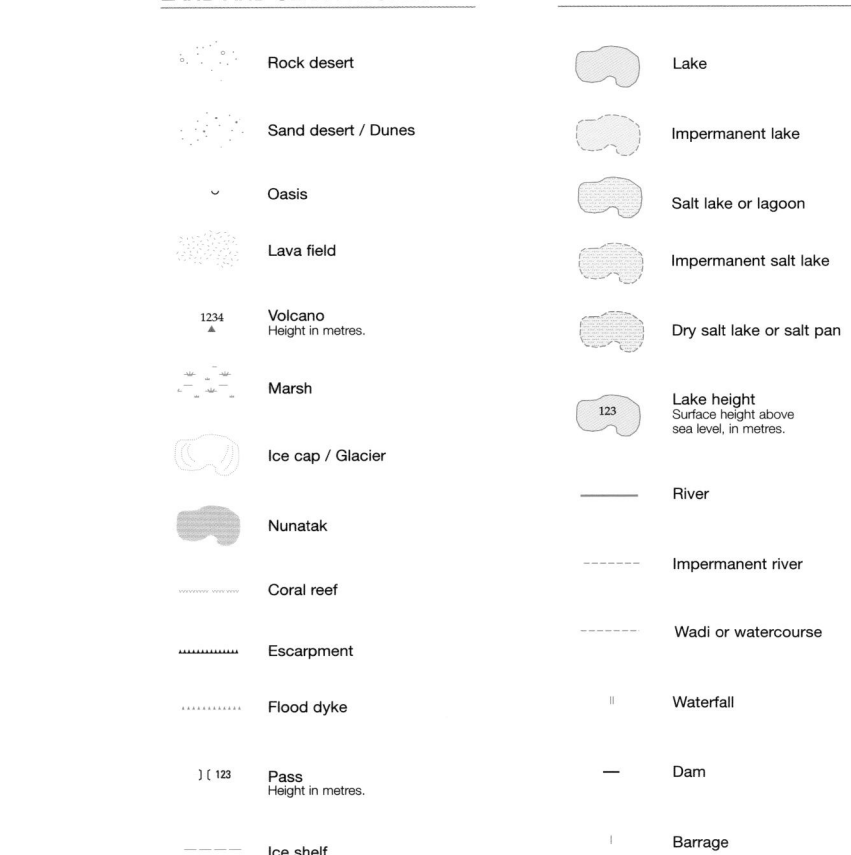

	Rock desert
	Sand desert / Dunes
	Oasis
	Lava field
1234 ▲	Volcano Height in metres.
	Marsh
	Ice cap / Glacier
	Nunatak
	Coral reef
	Escarpment
	Flood dyke
}[123	Pass Height in metres.
	Ice shelf

LAKES AND RIVERS

	Lake
	Impermanent lake
	Salt lake or lagoon
	Impermanent salt lake
	Dry salt lake or salt pan
123	Lake height Surface height above sea level, in metres.
▬▬▬	River
– – –	Impermanent river
- - -	Wadi or watercourse
‖	Waterfall
—	Dam
∣	Barrage

STYLES OF LETTERING

Cities and towns are explained separately

Country	**FRANCE**
Overseas Territory/Dependency	**Guadeloupe**
Disputed Territory	AKSAI CHIN
Administrative name, first order internal division. Shown for selected countries only.	SCOTLAND
Administrative name, second order internal division. Scales 1:4 000 000 and larger. Shown for selected countries only.	MANCHE
Area name	ARTOIS

Physical features

Island	*Gran Canaria*
Lake	*LAKE ERIE*
Mountain	*Mt Blanc*
River	*Thames*
Region	*PAMPAS*

TRANSPORT

══════ under construction	Motorway Scales 1:4 000 000 and larger.	▬▬▬ under construction	Main railway
▬▬▬ under construction	Main road	▬ ▬ ▬ under construction	Secondary railway
▬▬▬ under construction	Secondary road	◆▬◆▬ under construction	Railway tunnel
═┈┈═	Motorway tunnel	··········	Canal
▬┈┈▬	Road tunnel	▬▬▬	Minor canal
– – –	Track	⊕	Main airport
		✈	Regional airport

CITY PLANS

	Built-up area
	Cemetery
	Park
	Place of worship
	General place of interest
	Transport location
	Academic / municipal building

CONTINENTAL MAPS

BOUNDARIES

——	International boundary
-------	Disputed international boundary or alignment unconfirmed
/	Undefined international boundary in the sea. All land within this boundary is part of state or territory named.
••••••••	Ceasefire line
– – – – –	Administrative boundary Shown for selected countries only.

CITIES AND TOWNS

Population	National Capital	Other City or Town
over 10 million	México ▣	Mumbai ◉
5 million to 10 million	London ▣	Belo Horizonte ◉
1 million to 5 million	Kabul ▣	Kaohsiung ◉
500 000 to 1 million	Bangui ▣	Khulna ◉
100 000 to 500 000	Wellington ▣	Iquitos ⊙
50 000 to 100 000	Port of Spain ▢	Naga ○
10 000 to 50 000	Malabo ▢	Ushuaia ○
under 10 000	Valletta ▢	Arviat ○

ABBREVIATIONS

Abbr.	Term	Language	Meaning
A.C.T.	Australian Capital Territory		
Arch.	Archipelago		
	Archipiélago	Spanish	archipelago
B.	Bay		
	Bahia, Baía	Portuguese	bay
	Bahía	Spanish	bay
	Baie	French	bay
Bol.	Bol'shaya, Bol'shoy, Bol'shoye	Russian	big
C.	Cape		
	Cabo	Portuguese, Spanish	cape, headland
	Cap	Catalan, French	cape, headland
Cach.	Cachoeira	Portuguese	waterfall, rapids
Can.	Canal	French, Portuguese, Spanish	canal, channel
Cd	Ciudad	Spanish	city, town
Chan.	Channel		
Co	Cerro	Spanish	hill, mountain, peak
Cord.	Cordillera	Spanish	mountain range
Cr.	Creek		
Cuch.	Cuchilla	Spanish	hills, mountain range
D.	Dağ, Dağı	Turkish	mountain
	Dāgh	Farsi	mountain, mountains
	Dağları	Turkish	mountain range
	Danau	Indonesian, Malay	lake
Div.	Division		
Dr	Doctor		
E.	East, Eastern		
Emb.	Embalse	Spanish	reservoir
Est.	Estero	Spanish	estuary, inlet
	Estrecho	Spanish	strait
Fj.	Fjörður	Icelandic	fjord, inlet
Ft	Fort		
G.	Gebel	Arabic	hill, mountain
	Golfo	Italian, Spanish	gulf, bay
	Gora	Russian	mountain
	Gunung	Indonesian, Malay	hill, mountain
Gd	Grand	French	big
Gde	Grande	French, Italian, Portuguese, Spanish	big
Geb.	Gebergte	Afrikaans, Dutch	mountain range
Gen.	General		
Gl.	Glacier		
Gp	Group		
Gt	Great		
Harb.	Harbour		
Hd	Head		
I.	Island, Isle		
	Ilha	Portuguese	island
	Isla	Spanish	island
Î.	Île	French	island
im.	imeni	Russian	'in the name of'
Ind. Res.	Indian Reservation		
Ing.	Ingeniero	Spanish	engineer
Is	Islands, Isles		
	Islas	Spanish	islands
Îs	Îles	French	islands
J.	Jabal, Jebel	Arabic	mountain, mountains
Kep.	Kepulauan	Indonesian, Malay	archipelago, islands
Khr.	Khrebet	Russian	mountain range
L.	Lake		
	Loch	(Scotland)	lake
	Lough	(Ireland)	lake
	Lac	French	lake
	Lago	Portuguese, Spanish	lake
Lag.	Laguna	Spanish	lagoon
M.	Mys	Russian	cape, point
Mt	Mount		
	Mont	French	hill, mountain
Mt.	Mountain		

Abbr.	Term	Language	Meaning
Mte	Monte	Portuguese, Spanish	hill, mountain
Mts	Mountains		
	Monts	French	hills, mountains
N.	North, Northern		
Nev.	Nevado	Spanish	peak
Nat.	National		
Nat. Park	National Park		
Nat. Res.	Nature Reserve		
Nizh.	Nizhniy, Nizhnyaya	Russian	lower
N.E.	Northeast, Northeastern		
N.H.S.	National Heritage Site		
N.W.	Northwest, Northwestern		
O.	Ostrov	Russian	island
O-va	Ostrova	Russian	islands
Oz.	Ozero	Russian, Ukrainian	lake
P.	Paso	Spanish	pass
	Pulau	Indonesian, Malay	island
Pass.	Passage		
Peg.	Pegunungan	Indonesian, Malay	mountain range
Pen.	Peninsula		
	Península	Spanish	peninsula
Pk	Peak		
	Puncak	Indonesian	mountain, peak
P-ov	Poluostrov	Russian	peninsula
P. P.	Pulau-pulau	Indonesian	islands
Psa	Presa	Spanish	reservoir
Pt	Point		
Pta	Punta	Italian, Spanish	cape, point
Pte	Pointe	French	cape, point
Pto	Porto	Portuguese	harbour, port
	Puerto	Spanish	harbour, port
R.	River		
	Rio	Portuguese	river
	Río	Spanish	river
	Rivière	French	river
	Rūd	Farsi	river
Ra.	Range		
Rec.	Recreation		
Res.	Reservation, Reserve		
Resr	Reservoir		
S.	South, Southern		
	Salar, Salina, Salinas	Spanish	salt pan, salt pans
Sa	Serra	Portuguese	mountain range
	Sierra	Spanish	mountain range
Sd	Sound		
S.E.	Southeast, Southeastern		
Serr.	Serranía	Spanish	mountain range
Sk.	Shuiku	Chinese	reservoir
Sr.	Sredniy, Srednyaya	Russian	middle, central
St	Saint		
	Sankt	German, Russian	saint
	Sint	Dutch	saint
Sta	Santa	Italian, Portuguese, Spanish	saint
Ste	Sainte	French	saint
Sto	Santo	Italian, Portuguese, Spanish	saint
Str.	Strait		
S.W.	Southwest, Southwestern		
Tg	Tanjong, Tanjung	Indonesian, Malay	cape, point
Tk	Teluk, Telukan	Indonesian, Malay	bay, gulf
Tte	Teniente	Spanish	lieutenant
Va	Villa	Spanish	town
Vdkhr.	Vodokhranilishche	Russian	reservoir
Verkh.	Verkhniy, Verkhnyaya	Russian	upper
Vol.	Volcano		
	Volcan	French	volcano
	Volcán	Spanish	volcano
Vozv.	Vozvyshennost'	Russian	hills, upland
W.	West, Western		
	Wadi, Wādi, Wādī	Arabic	watercourse

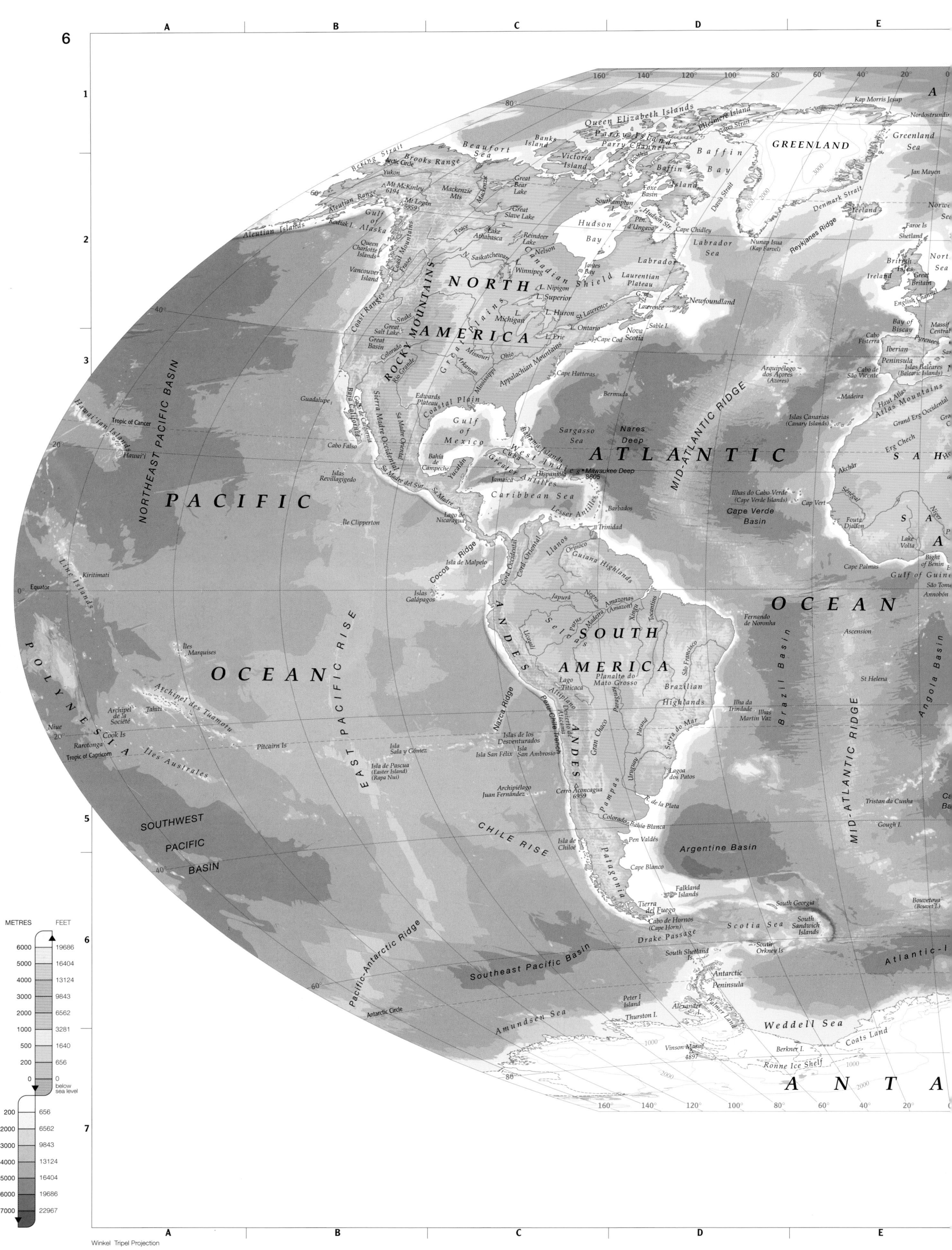

METRES | FEET

6000 | 19686
5000 | 16404
4000 | 13124
3000 | 9843
2000 | 6562
1000 | 3281
500 | 1640
200 | 656
0 | 0
 | below
 | sea level

200 | 656
2000 | 6562
3000 | 9843
4000 | 13124
5000 | 16404
6000 | 19686
7000 | 22967

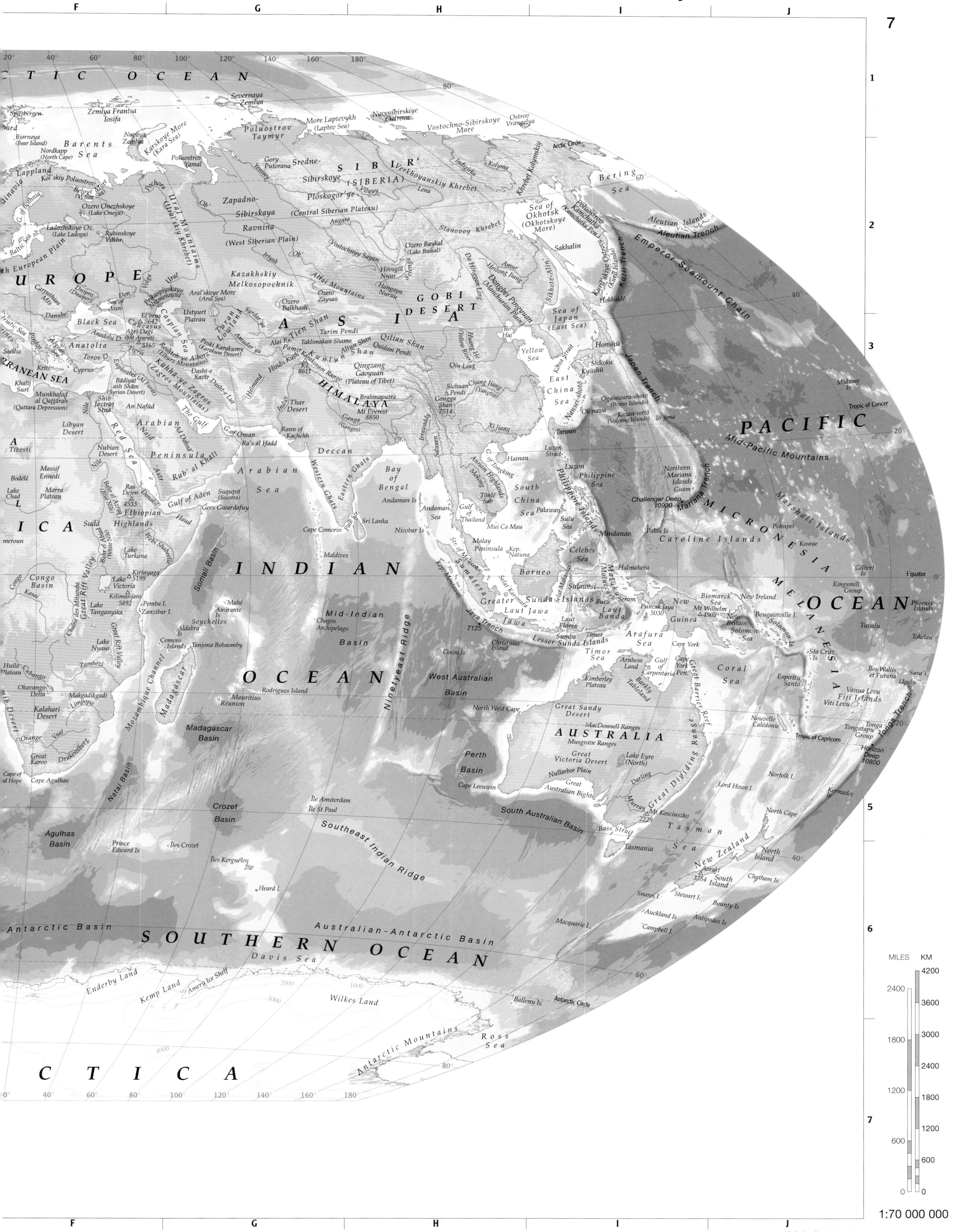

F　G　H　I　J

7

40° 60° 80° 100° 120° 140° 160° 180° 80°

1

CTIC OCEAN

Spitsbergen
Bjørnøya
(Bear Island)
Zemlya Frantsa
Iosifa
Severnaya
Zemlya
More Laptevykh
(Laptev Sea)
Novosibirskiye
Ostrova
Ostrov
Vrangelya
Arctic Circle

Bard
Nordkapp
(North Cape)
Novaya
Zemlya
Karskoye More
(Kara Sea)
Poluostrov
Taymyr
Vostochno-Sibirskoye
More
Bering
Sea

B a r e n t s
S e a
Poluostrov
Yamal
Gory
Putorana
Sredne-
Sibirskoye
S I B I R'
(SIBERIA)
Verkhoyanskiy Khrebet
Indigirka
Kolyma
Khrebet Kolymskiy
60

Lappland
Kol'skiy Poluostrov
Pechora
Yenisey
Ob'
Ploskogor'ye
(Central Siberian Plateau)
Lena
Aleutian Islands
Aleutian Trench

2

Beloye
(White)
Sea
Zapadno-
Sibirskaya
Angara
Stanovoy Khrebet
Sea of
Okhotsk
(Okhotskoye
More)
Sakhalin
Emperor Seamount Chain

Ladozhskoye Oz.
(Lake Ladoga)
Ozero Onezhskoye
(Lake Onega)
Rybinskoye
Vdkhr.
Ural
Mtns.
Ravnina
(West Siberian Plain)
Irtysh
Ob'
Vostochnyy Sayan
Ozero Baykal
(Lake Baikal)
Amur
Sikhote-Alin'
Hokkaidō
40

Baltic Sea
G. of Bothnia
n European Plain
U R A L
E U R O P E
Volga
Kazakhskiy
Melkosopochnik
Altai Mountains
Khangayn Nuruu
Hövsgöl Nuur
A S I A
Songhua
Dongbei Pingyuan
(Manchurian Plain)
Helong Jiang
Kuril Islands
Sea of
Japan
(East Sea)
Honshū
Japan Trench

3

Carpathian
Mts.
Dnipro (Dnieper)
Don
Caspian
Aral'skoye More
(Aral Sea)
Syrdar'ya
Tien Shan
Ozero Zaysan
Ozero
Balkhash
G O B I
D E S E R T
Huang He
(Yellow R.)
Qin Ling
Bo
Hai
Yellow
Sea
Shikoku
Kyūshū
Kōhu Strait
East
China
Sea

Black Sea
El'brus 5642
Caucasus
Agri Dagi (Mt Ararat) 5165
Turan
Lowland
Amudar'ya
Alai Ra.
Tarim Pendi
Taklimakan Shamo
(Takla Makan Desert)
Altun Shan
Qilian Shan
Qaidam Pendi
Chang Jiang (Yangtze)
Ogasawara-shotō
(Bonin Islands)
Midway Is

Danube
Anatolia
Anadolu D.
Ustyurt
Plateau
Peski Karakumy
(Karakum Desert)
Pamir
Kunlun Shan
Qingzang
Gaoyuan
(Plateau of Tibet)
Sichuan
Pendi
Tropic of Cancer

riatic Sea
Toros D.
Kriti
Cyprus
Tigris
Resht-ye Elburz
(Elburz Mountains)
Hindu Kush
Karakoram Range 8611
H I M A L A Y A
Mt Everest 8850
Brahmaputra
(Ganges)
Gongga Shan 7514
Xi Jiang
Kazan-rettō
(Volcano Islands)
Iō-jima

ERRANEAN SEA
Khalij Surt
Euphrates (Al Furat)
Zagros Mountains
Dasht-e Lut
Indus
Thar
Desert
Ganga
(Ganges)
Namsei-shotō
Okinawa
P A C I F I C

Munkhafad al Qattarah
(Qattara Depression)
Badiyat ash Shām
(Syrian Desert)
The Gulf
Rann of
Kachchh
Deccan
G. of Tongking
Hainan
Luzon
Strait
Northern
Mariana
Islands
Guam
Mid-Pacific Mountains

Nile
Shib Jozjrat Sina
An Nafūd
Dasht-e Kavir
G. of Oman
Western Ghats
Eastern Ghats
Bay
of
Bengal
Annam Highlands
South
China
Sea
Luzon
Philippine
Sea
Challenger Deep 10920
Mariana Trench
M I C R O N E S I A
Marshall Islands

Libyan
Desert
Nubian
Desert
Red Sea
Arabian
Najd
Rub' al Khali
G. of Oman
Ra's al Hadd
Arabian
Sea
Suqutrā (Socotra)
Mekong
Tônlé Sab
Palawan
Philippine Islands
Sulu
Sea
Mindanao
Palau Is
Caroline Islands
Pompei
Kosrae
Gilbert Is

A
Tibesti
Bodélé
Massif Ennedi
Lake Chad
Marra Plateau
Ethiopian
Highlands
Ras Dejen 4533
Gees Gwardafuy
Haud
Maldives
Mui Ca Mau
Malay
Peninsula
Kep. Natuna
Celebes
Sea
Halmahera
Equator

I C A
Sudd
Baro
Bahr el Abiad (White Nile)
Bahr el Azraq (Blue Nile)
Lake Turkana
Kirinyaga 5199
Chagos
Archipelago
Str. of Malacca
Sumatera
Borneo
Sulawesi
Maluku
(Moluccas)
Seram
New
Guinea
Bismarck
Sea
Mt Wilhelm 4509
New Ireland
Kingsmill
Group

meroun
Congo
Basin
Kasai
Lake
Victoria
Kilimanjaro 5892
Pemba I.
Zanzibar I.
Seychelles
Aldabra
Comoro Islands
I N D I A N
Mid-Indian
Basin
7125
Java Trench
Greater
Sunda Islands
Jawa
Laut Jawa
Laut
Banda
Puncak Jaya 5030
New
Britain
Solomon
Sea
Bougainville I.
Solomon Is
Tuvalu
Phoenix Islands

Congo
Lualaba
Chaine des Mitumba
Great Rift Valley
Lake
Tanganyika
Mahé
Amirante
Is
Tanjona Bobaomby
O C E A N
Cocos Is
Christmas Island
Lesser Sunda Islands
Sumba
Arafura
Sea
Cape York
Coral
Sea
Espíritu
Santo
Vanua Levu
Viti Levu
Fiji Islands
Îles Wallis et Futuna
Savai'i
Upolu
Tokelau

Huila Plateau
Cubango
Lake Nyasa
Zambezi
Madagascar
Mozambique Channel
Mauritius
Réunion
Rodrigues Island
West Australian
Basin
Timor
Sea
Arnhem
Land
Gulf of
Carpentaria
Cape York Pen.
Barkly Tableland
Great Barrier Reef
Nouvelle
Calédonie
Lord Howe I.

Okavango
Delta
th Desert
Makgadikgadi
Limpopo
Madagascar
Basin
Mauritius
Ninetyeast Ridge
North West Cape
Great Sandy
Desert
MacDonnell Ranges
Kimberley
Plateau
A U S T R A L I A
Musgrave Ranges
Tropic of Capricorn

Orange
Vaal
Great
Karoo
Drakensberg
Crozet
Basin
Ile Amsterdam
Île St Paul
Perth
Basin
Great Victoria
Desert
Great
Australian
Bight
Lake Eyre
(North)
Darling
Murray
Great Dividing Range
Mt Kosciuszko 2226
Norfolk I.
Kermadec

Cape of
d Hope
Cape Agulhas
Agulhas
Basin
Prince Edward Is
Îles Crozet
Natal Basin
Cape Leeuwin
Nullarbor Plain
South Australian Basin
Bass Strait
Tasmania
T a s m a n
S e a
North Cape

5

Îles Kerguélen
Southeast Indian Ridge
New Zealand
Aoraki 3754
South Island
Chatham Is
40

Heard I.
Snares I.
Stewart I.
Bounty Is
Antipodes Is

Antarctic Basin
Australian-Antarctic Basin
Macquarie I.
Campbell I.
Auckland Is

6

S O U T H E R N   O C E A N
Davis Sea
60

Enderby Land
Kemp Land
Amery Ice Shelf
2000
1000
Wilkes Land
Antarctic Circle
Balleny Is
Antarctic Circle

3000
4000
Antarctic Mountains
80
Ross
Sea

C T I C A

40 60 80 100 120 140 160 180

MILES　KM

2400　4200

3600

1800　3000

2400

1200　1800

600　1200

600

0　0

1:70 000 000

8

A B C D E

ARCTIC

Beaufort Sea

Point Hope
Arctic Circle
Bering Strait
Yukon
Inuvik

Greenland
(Denmark)

Victoria Island

Baffin Bay

Jan Mayen
(Norway)

U.S.A.
Anchorage
Gulf of Alaska
Whitehorse

Great Bear Lake

Mackenzie

Baffin Island

ICELAND
Reykjavík

Faroe Islands
(Denmark)

NOR
Shetland Islands
Be

Aleutian Islands

C A N A D A

Great Slave Lake

Hudson Bay

Iqaluit
Nuuk

UNITED KINGDOM

North Sea
DENM
NE

Vancouver
Calgary
Edmonton

Winnipeg
Lake Superior

Newfoundland
St John's
St Pierre and Miquelon
(France)

Edinburgh
Belfast
Dublin
London
Paris

REPUBLIC OF IRELAND
Amsterdam
Gravenhage
Bruxelles
Ber

Portland
Seattle
Boise
Missouri

Ottawa
Montréal
Lake Ontario
Toronto

Lake Huron
Lake Michigan
Milwaukee
Detroit
Cleveland
Boston
New York

PORTUGAL
Lisboa
Madrid
Barcelona
Valencia
M

SPAIN
FRANC
Mars

UNITED STATES
San Francisco
Denver
Chicago
St Louis
Indianapolis
Philadelphia
Washington D.C.

Azores
(Portugal)

Sevilla
Oran
Alg

OF AMERICA
Los Angeles
Colorado
Phoenix
Memphis
Atlanta

Madeira
(Portugal)
Rabat
Casablanca

San Diego
El Paso
Dallas

Bermuda
(U.K.)

Canary Islands (Spain)
Laâyoune
MOROCCO

Guadalupe (Mexico)
San Antonio
Houston
New Orleans
Jacksonville

ALGERI

Tropic of Cancer

Baja California

Gulf of Mexico
Miami

WESTERN SAHARA

Hawai'ian Islands
(U.S.A.)

Monterrey
Nassau
THE BAHAMAS

MAURITANIA
Nouakchott
MALI

Guadalajara
La Habana
CUBA
DOMINICAN REP.

MEXICO

PACIFIC

México
BELIZE
Kingston
HAITI
Santo Domingo
Puerto Rico (U.S.A.)
ANTIGUA

CAPE VERDE
Praia
Dakar
SENEGAL
Banjul
THE GAMBIA

Islas Revillagigedo

Guatemala
GUATEMALA
Belmopan
HONDURAS
Tegucigalpa
San Salvador
JAMAICA
DOMINICA
Guadeloupe (France)
Martinique (France)
ST LUCIA

Bissau
GUINEA-BISSAU
GUINEA
Conakry

Bamako
BURKINA
Ouagadougou
BENIN
Niam
NIG
TOGO
Lor

Île Clipperton
EL SALVADOR
NICARAGUA
Managua
San José
ST VINCENT
GRENADA
BARBADOS
TRINIDAD AND TOBAGO

Yamoussoukro
CÔTE D'IVOIRE
GHANA
Accra

SIERRA LEONE
Freetown
Monrovia
LIBERIA
Abidjan

OCEAN

COSTA RICA
PANAMA
Panamá
Barranquilla
Maracaibo
Caracas

Medellín
VENEZUELA
Georgetown
GUYANA
Paramaribo
SUR.
Cayenne
French Guiana

EQUAT.
G
SÃO TOMÉ AND PRÍNCIPE

Equator
KIRIBATI

Cali
Bogotá
COLOMBIA

Quito
ECUADOR
Guayaquil

Manaus
Amazonas (Amazon)
Belém

Fortaleza
Natal

Fernando de Noronha (Brazil)

Ascension (U.K.)

Îles Marquises

Islas Galápagos (Ecuador)

Trujillo
PERU
Lima

BRAZIL
Teresina
Recife

ATLANTIC

American Samoa

Archipel des Tuamotu

Arequipa
La Paz
BOLIVIA
Sucre
Santa Cruz
Brasília
Goiânia
Salvador
Belo Horizonte

Ilhas Martin Vaz (Brazil)

St Helena (U.K.)

Niue (N.Z.)
Cook Islands (N.Z.)
Tahiti
Archipel de la Société
French Polynesia

Rarotonga
Îles Australes
Pitcairn Is (U.K.)

Isla de Pascua (Easter Island) (Chile)

Isla Sala y Gómez (Chile)

PARAGUAY
San Miguel de Tucumán
Asunción
Paraná
São Paulo
Curitiba
Rio de Janeiro

Trindade (Brazil)

OCEAN

Tropic of Capricorn

Porto Alegre

Tristan da Cunha (U.K.)

Archipélago Juan Fernández (Chile)

Santiago
Córdoba
URUGUAY
Buenos Aires
Montevideo

Gough Island (U.K.)

ARGENTINA
CHILE

Mar del Plata

Falkland Islands (U.K.)

South Georgia and South Sandwich Islands (U.K.)

S

Bo
(No

Punta Arenas
Stanley

Cabo de Hornos

South Shetland Islands (U.K.)

South Orkney Islands (U.K.)

Antarctic Peninsula

Weddell Sea

A.	ANDORRA	LEB.	LEBANON
AL.	ALBANIA	LITH.	LITHUANIA
ARM.	ARMENIA	M.	MACEDONIA
AUST.	AUSTRIA	MOL.	MOLDOVA
AZER.	AZERBAIJAN	NETH.	NETHERLANDS
B.	BURUNDI	R.	RWANDA
BEL.	BELGIUM	R.F.	RUSSIAN FEDERATION
B.H.	BOSNIA-HERZEGOVINA	ROM.	ROMANIA
BULG.	BULGARIA	SL.	SLOVENIA
CR.	CROATIA	SLA.	SLOVAKIA
CZ.R.	CZECH REPUBLIC	S.M.	SERBIA AND MONTENEGRO
EST.	ESTONIA	SUR.	SURINAME
GEOR.	GEORGIA	SW.	SWITZERLAND
HUN.	HUNGARY	TAJIK.	TAJIKISTAN
ISR.	ISRAEL	TURKM.	TURKMENISTAN
JOR.	JORDAN	U.A.E.	UNITED ARAB EMIRATES
L.	LUXEMBOURG	U.S.A.	UNITED STATES OF AMERICA
LAT.	LATVIA	UZBEK.	UZBEKISTAN

ANTA

Winkel Tripel Projection

A B C D E

9

F G H I J

1

OCEAN

Zemlya Frantsa-Iosifa

Severnaya
Zemlya

albard
(orway)

*Barents
Sea*

Novaya
Zemlya

Arctic Circle

noya (-
way)

Murmansk

Yenisey

Lena

Yakutsk

*Bering
Sea*

Aleutian Islands

2

SWEDEN

FINLAND

Stockholm Helsinki

enhavn

EST. Tallinn

Riga LAT.

Berlin LITH.
R.F.

burg Vilnius

Arkhangel'sk

Nizhniy
Novgorod

Perm'

Yekaterinburg

Krasnoyarsk

Novosibirsk

Novokuznetsk

Irkutsk

*Ozero
Baykal*

Komsomol'sk-na-Amure

Khabarovsk

*Sea
of
Okhotsk*

RUSSIAN FEDERATION

Ob'

Sapporo

Moskva

Chelyabinsk

Omsk

BELARUS

y POLAND Minsk
Warszawa

Praha SLA.

Kharkiv

Kazan'

Samara

Astana

Karaganda

Ulaanbaatar

Yichun

Qiqihar

Harbin

Vladivostok

jana
UKRAINE

Budapest HUN. RDM.

CR.

ajevo S.M.

Kyiv

Volgograd

Rostov-
na-Donu

Krasnodar

KAZAKHSTAN

*Aral
Sea*

Bishkek Almaty

Ürümqi

MONGOLIA

Changchun

Shenyang

N. KOREA

Beijing

P'yŏngyang

Sŏul

JAPAN

Sendai

Tōkyō

Beograd

Sofiya

BULG.

ITALY Skopje

Tirane AL.

GREECE

Athína

Izmir

TURKEY

Black Sea

Istanbul

Ankara

GEOR.

ARM.
AZER.

T'bilisi

Baki

Toshkent
UZBEK.

KYRGYZSTAN

TURKM.

TAJIK.

Ashgabat Dushanbe

Lanzhou

Xi'an

CHINA

Huang He

Tianjin

Dalian

Jinan

S. KOREA

Pusan

Fukuoka

Kōbe

Kyōto

Osaka

Nagoya

Yokohama

Kagoshima

*East
China
Sea*

Ogasawara-shotō
(Bonin Islands)
(Japan)

PACIFIC

Midway
Islands
(U.S.A.)

NISIA

Palermo

CYPRUS

Lefkosia

SYRIA

LEB.

Dimashq

Al Mawsil

Mashhad

Kābul

IRAN

Tabriz

Tehrān

Esfahan

Islamabad

AFGHANISTAN

Lahore

Faisalabad

Delhi

Lhasa

Chengdu

Chongqing

Chang Jiang

Wuhan

Nanjing

Shanghai

Fuzhou

T'aipei

TAIWAN

Kaohsiung

*Volcano Islands)
(Japan)*

Kazan-rettō

Tropic of Cancer

Tirane

Jerusalem ISR.
Beirut
JOR.

Baghdad

Amman

IRAQ

Al Başrah

KUWAIT

Al Kuwayt

BAHRAIN

Shīrāz

PAKISTAN

New Delhi

Jaipur

Karachi

NEPAL
Kathmandu

BHUTAN

Lucknow

Patna

Kunming

Nanning

Guangzhou

Macau

Hong
Kong

Zhanjiang

20°

LIBYA

EGYPT

Al Iskandariyah

Al Jizah

Al Qāhirah

SAUDI

Ar Riyāḍ

QATAR

Abū
U.A.E.

Masqaṭ

OMAN

The Gulf

Ahmadābād

Bhopal

INDIA

Mumbai

Pune

Hyderabad

Bhutan

Kolkata
(Calcutta)

BANGLADESH

Dhaka

Khulna

Chittagong

Mandalay

MYANMAR

Hainan

Ha Noi

*South
China
Sea*

Luzon

OCEAN

Northern Mariana
Islands
(U.S.A.)

Jiddah

ARABIA

Makkah

Red Sea

Nile

*Arabian
Sea*

Vijayawada

Chennai

Bangalore

*Andaman
Islands
(India)*

Yangon

LAOS

Viangchan

THAILAND

VIETNAM

Manila

Guam
(U.S.A.)

MARSHALL
ISLANDS

Delap-Uliga-Djarrit

CHAD

SUDAN

Khartoum

Ndjamena

Asmara

ERITREA

Adis
Abeba

ETHIOPIA

Sanʿā

YEMEN

Adan

DJIBOUTI

Djibouti

SOMALIA

Trivandrum

Sri Jayewardenepura Kotte

SRI LANKA

Bangkok

CAMBODIA

Phnum Penh

Hồ Chí Minh

PHILIPPINES

Mindanao

Koror

Palikir

Caroline Islands

FEDERATED STATES

Bairiki
Gilbert
Islands

Equator

CENTRAL
AFRICAN
REPUBLIC

unde

Bangui

ville

DEM. REP.
OF
CONGO

UGANDA

Kampala

Kigali R.

Bujumbura B.

KENYA

Nairobi

Muqdisho

MALDIVES

Male

British
Indian Ocean
Territory

Medan

Kuala Lumpur

MALAYSIA

BRUNEI

Bandar
Seri Begawan

SINGAPORE

Borneo

Sulawesi

PALAU

OF MICRONESIA

Yaren
NAURU

KIRIBATI

Kingsmill
Group

*Phoenix
Islands*

Kinshasa

azzaville

Luanda

TANZANIA

Dodoma

Dar es Salaam

*Lake
Victoria*

Victoria

SEYCHELLES

Putrajaya

Padang

Sumatera

Palembang

Jakarta

Jawa

Surabaya

INDONESIA

Irian
Jaya

New
Guinea

PAPUA

NEW GUINEA

SOLOMON

Honiara

TUVALU

Vaiaku

Tokelau
(N. Z.)

ANGOLA

ZAMBIA

Lusaka

Lilongwe

COMOROS

Moroni

Mayotte
(France)

Cocos Islands
(Australia)

Christmas
Island
(Australia)

Dili

EAST TIMOR

Timor

Port Moresby

ISLANDS

Darwin

*Coral
Sea*

Wallis and
Futuna
Islands
(France)

SAMOA

Apia

ZIMBABWE

MOZAMBIQUE

Harare

Bulawayo

MADAGASCAR

Antananarivo

Port Louis

MAURITIUS

INDIAN

VANUATU

FIJI

Port
Vila

Suva

TONGA

NAMIBIA

dhoek

BOTSWANA

Gaborone

Johannesburg

Pretoria

Maputo

SWAZILAND

Mbabane

Maseru LESOTHO

REPUBLIC OF
SOUTH AFRICA

Cape
Town

Cape Agulhas

Réunion
(France)

OCEAN

AUSTRALIA

Alice
Springs

New
Caledonia
(France)

Nouméa

Norfolk
Island
(Australia)

Kermadec
Islands
(N.Z.)

Tropic of Capricorn

20°

Île Amsterdam
Île St Paul

Perth

Darling

Brisbane

Lord Howe
Island
(Australia)

French Southern and
Antarctic Lands

Prince Edward Island
(South Africa)

Îles Crozet

Adelaide

Murray

Sydney

Canberra

Melbourne

*Tasman
Sea*

Auckland

North
Island

NEW
ZEALAND

Îles Kerguélen

Heard Island
(Australia)

Hobart

Tasmania

Christchurch

*South
Island*

Dunedin

Wellington

Chatham
Islands
(N.Z.)

UTHERN OCEAN

Snares
Islands
(N.Z.)

Bounty
Islands
(N.Z.)

Antipodes
Islands
(N.Z.)

Macquarie
Island
(Australia)

Auckland
Islands
(N.Z.)

Campbell
Island
(N.Z.)

Antarctic Circle

CTICA

*Ross
Sea*

20° 40° 60° 80° 100° 120° 140° 160° 180°

F G H I J

1:70 000 000

MILES KM

2400 4200

3600

1800 3000

2400

1200 1800

1200

600 600

0 0

© Collins Bartholomew Ltd

© Collins Bartholomew Ltd
Data from the 1km AVHRR Global Land dataset project by
ESA,CEOS, IGBP, NASA, NOAA, USGS, IONIA processed
by ESA/ESRIN distributed by Eurimage S.p.A

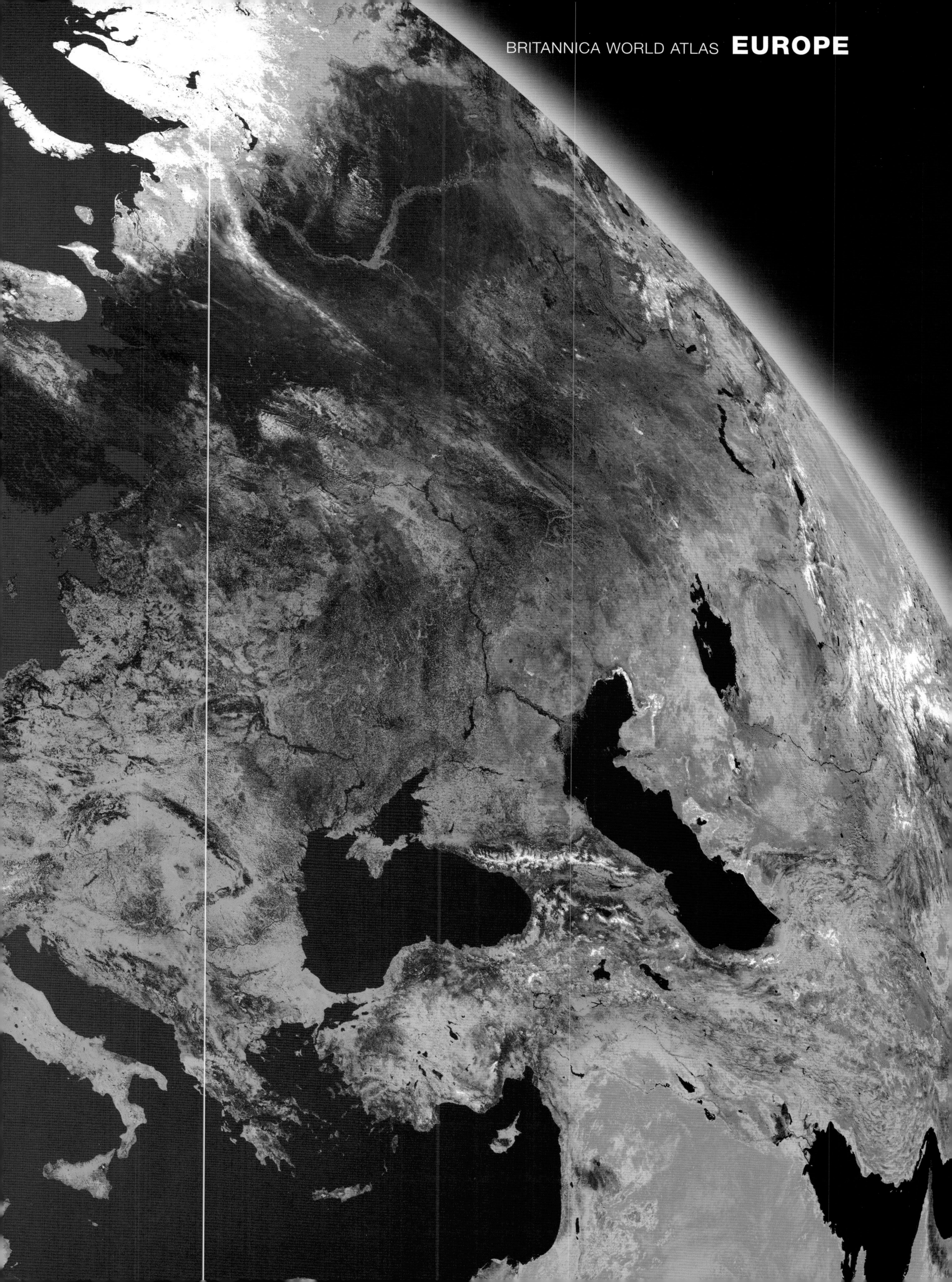

NORTH AMERICA

Baffin Bay

Greenland

Arctic Circle

75°

60°

45°

NORTH SEA

Denmark Strait

Svalbard (Norway)

Longyearbyen

Spitsbergen

Nordaustlandet

Greenland Sea

BARENTS SEA

Bjørnøya (Norway)

Jan Mayen (Norway)

Zemlya Frantsa-Josifa

Nordkapp

ICELAND

Reykjavík

NORWEGIAN

SEA

Trondheim

N
O
R
W
A
Y

S
W
E
D
E
N

Gulf of B

Faroe Islands (Denmark)

Tórshavn

Shetland Islands

Orkney Islands

Bergen

Oslo

Stockh

Vänern

Vätter

Göteborg

SCOTLAND

Glasgow   Edinburgh

Outer Hebrides

DENMARK

Álborg

Skagerrak *Kattegat*

København   Malm

Odense   *Born*

NORTH

SEA

NORTHERN IRELAND

Belfast

UNITED KINGDOM

Manchester   Leeds

Liverpool

Hamburg

Bremen   **Berl**

Dublin

REPUBLIC OF IRELAND

WALES

Birmingham

ENGLAND

Cardiff

NETHERLANDS
Amsterdam

Hannover   Bielefeld

's-Gravenhage

GERMAN

Essen   Leipzig

London

Rotterdam

Düsseldorf   Köln

Bruxelles   Aachen   Bonn

BELGIUM   Frankfurt am Main

Lille

LUXEMBOURG

Luxembourg

Nürnbe

Mannheim

Stuttgart

English Channel

Channel Islands

Paris   Strasbourg   Münche

Brest   Rennes   Orléans

Loire

Dijon

Zürich   **LIECHTEN-STEIN**

Bern   Innsbru

SWITZERLAND

Genève

A
T
L
A
N
T
I
C

O
C
E
A
N

FRANCE

Nantes

Milano

Lyon

Rhône

Torino

Bay of

Biscay

Bordeaux

Genov

MONACO
Nice

A Coruña

Bilbao

Pyrenees

Ebro

Marseille   *Corse*

Andorra la Vella   **ANDORRA**

Toulouse

Coroo

Flores

Arquipélago dos Açores

São Jorge   *Terceira*

Faial

Pico

Azores (Portugal)   *São Miguel*

Ponta Delgada

Santa Maria

Porto

P
O
R
T
U
G
A
L

Salamanca

Madrid

Zaragoza

Barcelona

Islas Baleares

Menorca

Valencia   *Sardegna*

Mallorca

SPAIN

Tajo

Eivissa

Lisboa

Córdoba

Cartagena

M
E
D

Sevilla

Cádiz   Málaga

Gibraltar (U.K.)

Ceuta (Spain)

Melilla (Spain)

A   F

Arquipélago da Madeira

Madeira (Portugal)

Ilha de Porto Santo

Funchal

F
G
H
I
J
1
2
3
4
5
6
7
Karskoye More
Novaya Zemlya
Ostrov Kolguyev
Vorkuta
Ural'skiy Khrebet (Ural Mountains)
Pechora
Ob'
Yenisey
Arctic Circle
Irtysh
Murmansk
Beloye More
Arkhangel'sk
Syktyvkar
Severnaya Dvina
RUSSIAN FEDERATION
ASIA
Altai Mountains
Perm'
Kirov
Izhevsk
Naberezhnyye Chelny
Ufa
Petrozavodsk
Onezhskoye Ozero
Ladozhskoye Ozero
FINLAND
Tampere
Turku
Helsinki
Sankt-Peterburg
Vologda
Rybinskoye Vodokhranilishche
Volga
Yaroslavl'
Nizhniy Novgorod
Kazan'
Ozero Balkhash
Tien Shan
Tallinn
ESTONIA
Lake Peipus
Samara
Orenburg
Ul'yanovsk
RUSSIA
Moskva
LATVIA
Riga
Tula
Penza
Smolensk
Saratov
LITHUANIA
Vitsyebsk
Mahilyow
Vilnius
Minsk
Kaliningrad
RUS. FED.
Gdańsk
Hrodna
BELARUS
Voronezh
Aral Sea
Homyel'
Białystok
Brest
Chernihiv
Sumy
Belgorod
Kharkiv
Don
Volgograd
Volga
Astrakhan'
POLAND
Wisła
Warszawa
Łódź
Kyiv
UKRAINE
Rivne
Dnipropetrovs'k
Rostov-na-Donu
Donets'k
Odra
Wrocław
Katowice
Kraków
L'viv
Dnister (Dniester)
Kirovohrad
Caspian Sea
Hindu Kush
Praha
CZECH REPUBLIC
SLOVAKIA
Košice
Brno
Carpathian Mountains
MOLDOVA
Iași
Chișinău
Mykolayiv
Dnipro (Dnieper)
Sea of Azov
Krasnodar
Stavropol'
Groznyy
Zaliv Kara-Bogaz-Gol
Bratislava
Debrecen
Odesa
Wien
Budapest
Oradea
Simferopol'
Novorossiysk
Caucasus
El'brus
Salzburg
AUSTRIA
HUNGARY
ROMANIA
Brașov
Szeged
Timișoara
Black Sea
SLOVENIA
Zagreb
Ljubljana
Trieste
CROATIA
București
Craiova
Venezia
BOSNIA-HERZEGOVINA
Beograd
SERBIA AND MONTENEGRO
Sarajevo
Niš
Pleven
Varna
Burgas
BULGARIA
Sofiya
SAN MARINO
Split
Podgorica
Edirne
İstanbul
Marmara Denizi
TURKEY
Adriatic Sea
Skopje
MACEDONIA
Tiranë
ALBANIA
Thessaloniki
VATICAN CITY
Roma
ITALY
Bari
Napoli
Larisa
Aegean Sea
GREECE
Nahr Dijlah (Tigris)
Al Furāt (Euphrates)
Kūhhā-ye Zagros (Zagros Mountains)
Tyrrhenian Sea
Cosenza
Ionian Sea
Athina
Dodekanisos
Rodos
Palermo
Messina
Sicilia
Siracusa
Cyprus
The Gulf
Kriti
Valletta
MALTA
MEDITERRANEAN SEA
AFRICA
MILES
KM
0
200
400
600
0
200
400
600
800
1000
1:15 000 000

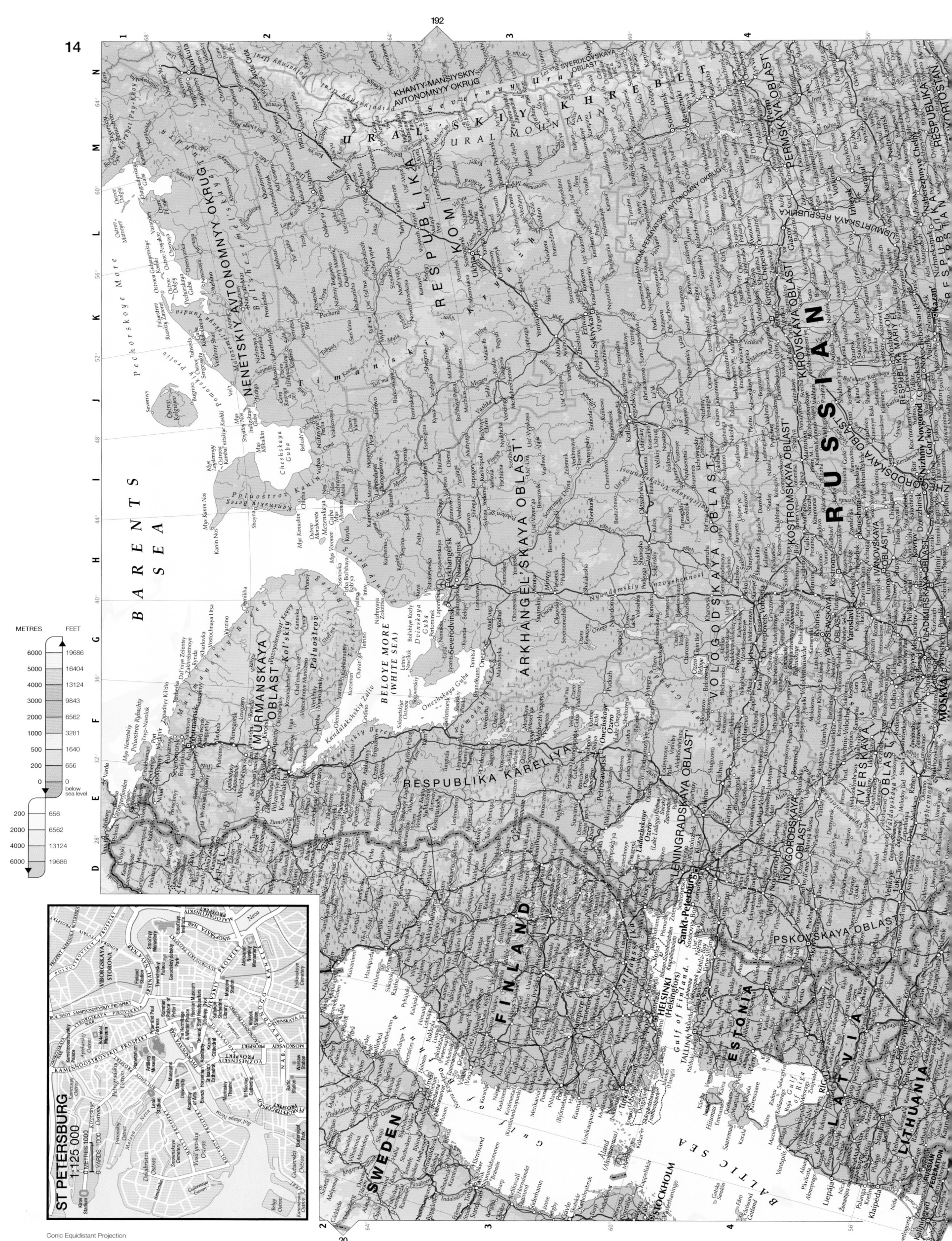
192
20
BARENTS SEA
BELOYE MORE (WHITE SEA)
RUSSIA
FINLAND
SWEDEN
ESTONIA
LATVIA
LITHUANIA
BALTIC SEA
Gulf of Finland
Gulf of Riga
RESPUBLIKA KARELIYA
RESPUBLIKA KOMI
ARKHANGEL'SKAYA OBLAST'
VOLOGODSKAYA OBLAST'
MURMANSKAYA OBLAST'
LENINGRADSKAYA OBLAST'
PSKOVSKAYA OBLAST'
NOVGORODSKAYA OBLAST'
TVERSKAYA OBLAST'
KOSTROMSKAYA OBLAST'
KIROVSKAYA OBLAST'
PERMSKAYA OBLAST'
SVERDLOVSKAYA OBLAST'
NENETSKIY AVTONOMNYY OKRUG
KHANTY-MANSIYSKIY AVTONOMNYY OKRUG
KOMI-PERMYATSKIY AVTONOMNYY OKRUG
URAL'SKIY KHREBET
URAL MOUNTAINS
HELSINKI (Helsingfors)
STOCKHOLM
TALLINN
Sankt-Peterburg
MOSKVA
METRES
FEET
6000
5000
4000
3000
2000
1000
500
200
0
19686
16404
13124
9843
6562
3281
1640
656
below sea level
ST PETERSBURG
1:125 000

Conic Equidistant Projection

15

RUSSIAN FEDERATION

KAZAKHSTAN

ZAPADNY KAZAKHSTAN

ATYRAUSKAYA OBLAST

MANGISTAUSKAYA OBLAST

CASPIAN SEA

TURKMENISTAN

ORENBURGSKAYA OBLAST'

SAMARSKAYA (Kuybyshev) OBLAST'

Samara (Kuybyshev)

ULYANOVSKAYA OBLAST'

Ulyanovsk

SARATOVSKAYA OBLAST'

PENZENSKAYA OBLAST'

RESPUBLIKA MORDOVIYA

TAMBOVSKAYA OBLAST'

VOLGOGRADSKAYA OBLAST'

Volgograd (Stalingrad)

Astrakhan'

ASTRAKHANSKAYA OBLAST'

RESPUBLIKA KALMYKIYA - KHALMG-TANGCH

Chernyye Zemli

RESPUBLIKA DAGESTAN

Makhachkala

Kaspiysk

Derbent

AZERBAIJAN

BAKI

LIPETSKAYA OBLAST'

VORONEZHSKAYA OBLAST'

Voronezh

ROSTOVSKAYA OBLAST'

Rostov-na-Donu

Shakhty

Novocherkassk

STAVROPOL'SKIY KRAY

Stavropol'

KRASNODARSKIY KRAY

Krasnodar

Sochi

KARACHAYEVO-CHERKESSKAYA RESPUBLIKA

KABARDINO-BALKARSKAYA RESPUBLIKA

Nal'chik

RESPUBLIKA SEVERNAYA OSETIYA - ALANIYA

Vladikavkaz

CHECHNYA

Groznyy

GEORGIA

T'BILISI

ARMENIA

TURKEY

Trabzon

BELARUS

MINSK

UKRAINE

KYYIV (KIEV)

Kharkiv

Donets'k

Dnipropetrovs'k

Zaporizhzhya

Mariupol'

Kherson

Mykolayiv

Odesa

Simferopol'

Sevastopol'

MOLDOVA

CHIȘINĂU

ROMANIA

BUCUREȘTI

BULGARIA

POLAND

BLACK SEA

Sea of Azov

Autonomous Republics in Russian Federation numbered on the map:
1. RESPUBLIKA INGUSHETIYA (I8)
2. RESPUBLIKA SEVERNAYA OSETIYA - ALANIYA (I8)

Longitude 40° east of Greenwich

MILES	KM
300	500
	400
200	300
	200
100	100
0	0

1:7 200 000

55

POLAND
BELARUS
UKRAINE
SLOVAKIA
HUNGARY
ROMANIA
MOLDOVA
SERBIA AND MONTENEGRO
BRESTSKAYA VOBLASTS'
MINSKAYA VOBLASTS'
HOMYEL'SKAYA VOBLASTS'
HRODZYENSKAYA VOBLASTS'
MAHILYOWSKAYA VOBLASTS'
PRIPET MARSHES
VOLYNS'KA OBLAST'
RIVNENS'KA OBLAST'
ZHYTOMYRS'KA OBLAST'
KYIVS'KA OBLAST'
L'VIVS'KA OBLAST'
TERNOPILS'KA OBLAST'
KHMEL'NYTS'KA OBLAST'
VINNYTS'KA OBLAST'
IVANO-FRANKIVS'KA OBLAST'
ZAKARPATS'KA OBLAST'
CHERNIVETS'KA OBLAST'
ODES'KA OBLAST'
CHERKAS'KA
KIROVOHRADS'KA
NIZINA MAZOWIECKA
WYŻYNA LUBELSKA
CARPATHIAN MOUNTAINS
CARPAŢII MERIDIONALI
TRANSYLVANIAN ALPS
Warszawa (Warsaw)
Brest
Lublin
Kyiv (Kiev)
L'viv
Chernivtsi
Chişinău (Kishinev)
Odesa
Bucureşti (Bucharest)
Ostriv Zmiyinyy (Ukraine)
METRES
FEET
6000
5000
4000
3000
2000
1500
1000
500
200
100
0
19686
16404
13124
9843
6562
4921
3281
1640
656
328
below sea level
50
200
2000
4000
6000
164
656
6562
13124
19686
18
47
77
Conic Equidistant Projection

RUSSIAN FEDERATION
BRYANSKAYA OBLAST'
ORLOVSKAYA OBLAST'
LIPETSKAYA OBLAST'
TAMBOVSKAYA OBLAST'
KURSKAYA OBLAST'
VORONEZHSKAYA OBLAST'
CHERNIHIVS'KA OBLAST'
SUMS'KA OBLAST'
BELGORODSKAYA OBLAST'
POLTAVS'KA OBLAST'
KHARKIVS'KA OBLAST'
LUHANS'KA OBLAST'
DONETS'KA OBLAST'
DNIPROPETROVS'KA OBLAST'
ZAPORIZ'KA OBLAST'
KHERSONS'KA OBLAST'
ROSTOVSKAYA OBLAST'
KRASNODARSKIY KRAY
RESPUBLIKA KRYM (CRIMEA)
Sea of Azov
BLACK SEA
Kharkiv
Dnipropetrovs'k
Zaporizhzhya
Donets'k
Luhans'k
Poltava
Sumy
Kursk
Belgorod
Voronezh
Mariupol'
Melitopol'
Kherson
Mykolayiv
Simferopol'
Sevastopol'
Kerch
Rostov-na-Donu
Krasnodar
Novorossiysk
MILES
KM
1:3 000 000
© Collins Bartholomew Ltd

GULF OF BOTHNIA
Åland (Ahvenanmaa)
FINLAND
LÄNSI-SUOMI
ETELÄ-SUOMI
HELSINKI (Helsingfors)
SWEDEN
UPPSALA
STOCKHOLM
Gotland (Sweden)
GOTLAND
GULF OF FINLAND
BALTIC SEA
ESTONIA
TALLINN
Hiiumaa
Saaremaa
Lake Peipus
Lake Pskov
GULF OF RIGA
Irbe Strait
LATVIA
RĪGA
PSKOVSKAYA O
LITHUANIA
VILNIUS
RUSSIAN FEDERATION
KALININGRADSKAYA OBLAST'
Gulf of Gdańsk
Courland Lagoon
POLAND
POJEZIERZE MAZURSKIE
NIZINA MAZOWIECKA
WARSZAWA (Warsaw)
BELARUS
MINSKAYA VOBLASTS'
MINSK
VITSYEBSKAYA VOBLASTS'
HRODZYENSKAYA VOBLASTS'
BRESTSKAYA VOBLASTS'
METRES
FEET
6000
19686
5000
16404
4000
13124
3000
9843
2000
6562
1500
4921
1000
3281
500
1640
200
656
100
328
0
0
below sea level
50
164
200
656
2000
6562
4000
13124
6000
19686

Conic Equidistant Projection

ESTONIA, LATVIA, LITHUANIA AND **RUSSIA** Moscow Region

MOSCOW
1:80 000
0 METRES 750
0 YARDS 750

RUSSIAN FEDERATION

LENINGRADSKAYA OBLAST'
VOLOGODSKAYA OBLAST'
NOVGORODSKAYA OBLAST'
TVERSKAYA OBLAST'
YAROSLAVSKAYA OBLAST'
IVANOVSKAYA OBLAST'
MOSKOVSKAYA OBLAST'
VLADIMIRSKAYA OBLAST'
SMOLENSKAYA OBLAST'
KALUZHSKAYA OBLAST'
RYAZANSKAYA OBLAST'
TUL'SKAYA OBLAST'
BRYANSKAYA OBLAST'
ORLOVSKAYA OBLAST'
LIPETSKAYA OBLAST'
MAHILYOWSKAYA VOBLASTS'

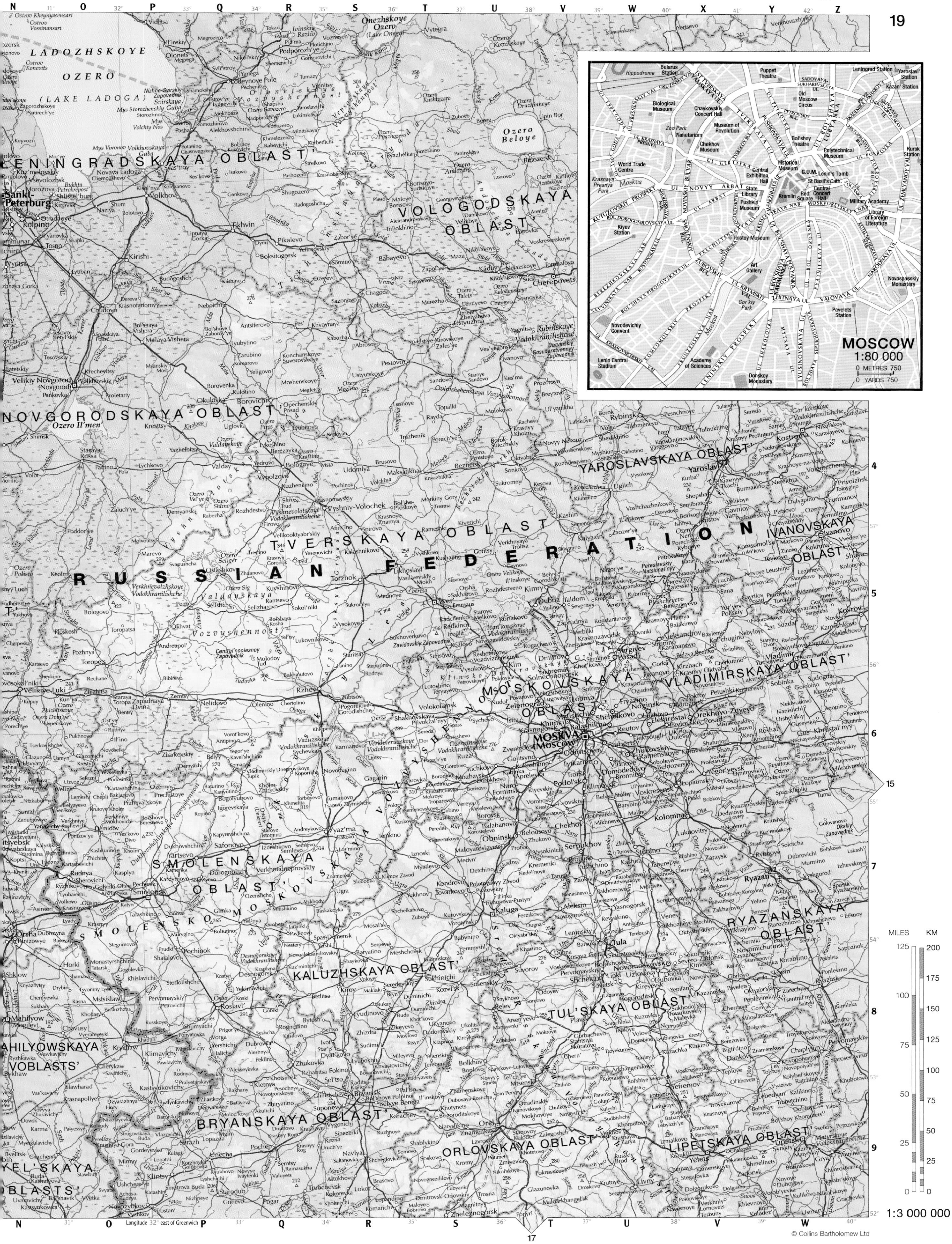

LADOZHSKOYE OZERO (LAKE LADOGA)
Sankt-Peterburg
Moskva (Moscow)

MILES / KM

1:3 000 000

© Collins Bartholomew Ltd

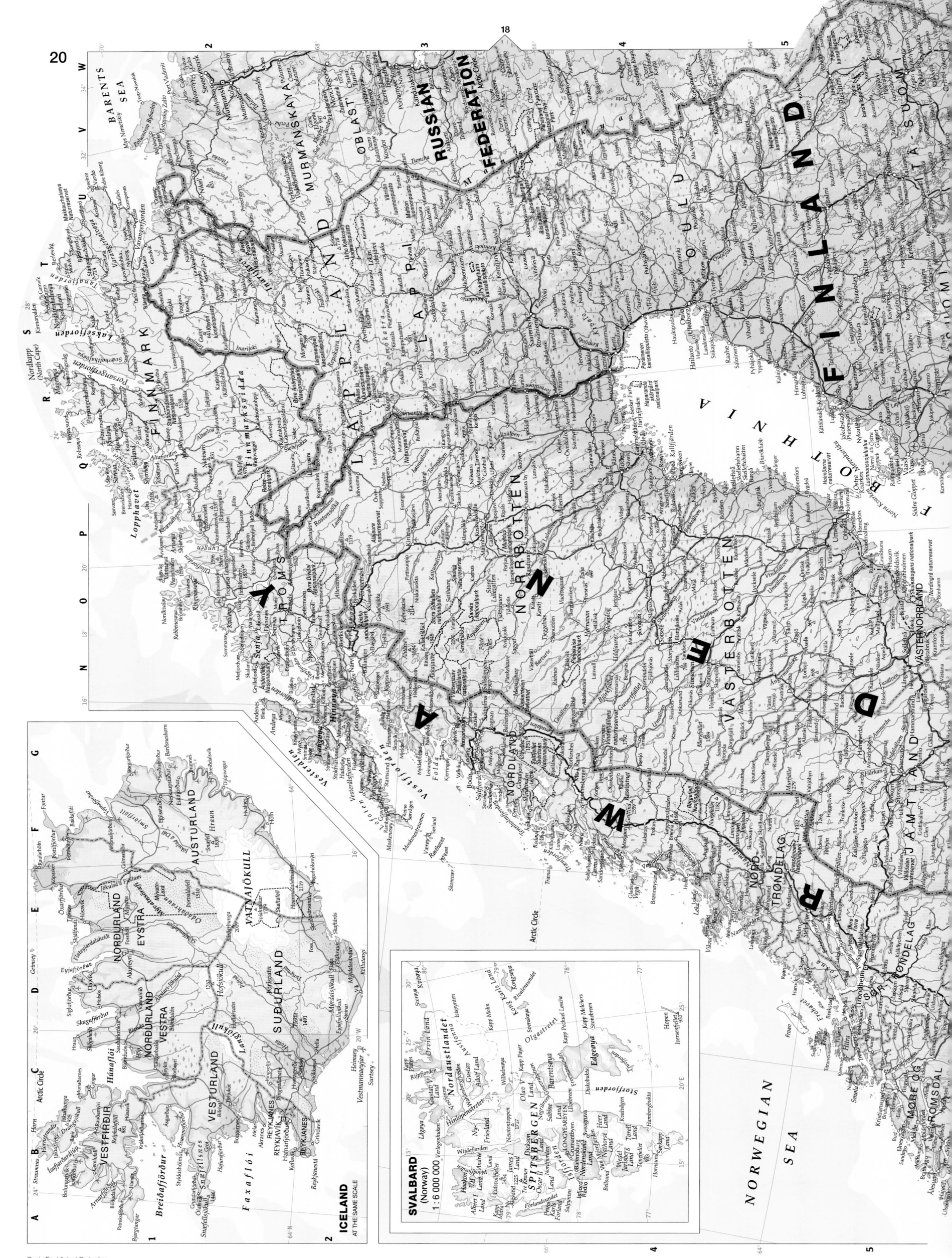

BARENTS SEA

RUSSIAN FEDERATION

FINLAND

FINNMARK

LAPPLAND

LAPPI

OULU

MURMANSKAYA OBLAST

TROMS

NORRBOTTEN

VÄSTERBOTTEN

VÄSTERNORRLAND

NORDLAND

JÄMTLAND

NORD-TRØNDELAG

SØR-TRØNDELAG

MØRE OG ROMSDAL

NORWEGIAN SEA

Arctic Circle

ICELAND
AT THE SAME SCALE

VESTFIRÐIR

VESTURLAND

NORÐURLAND VESTRA

NORÐURLAND EYSTRA

AUSTURLAND

VATNAJÖKULL

SUÐURLAND

Arctic Circle

SVALBARD
(Norway)
1 : 6 000 000

SPITSBERGEN

Nordaustlandet

Edgeøya

Conic Equidistant Projection

ICELAND, NORWAY, SWEDEN AND FINLAND

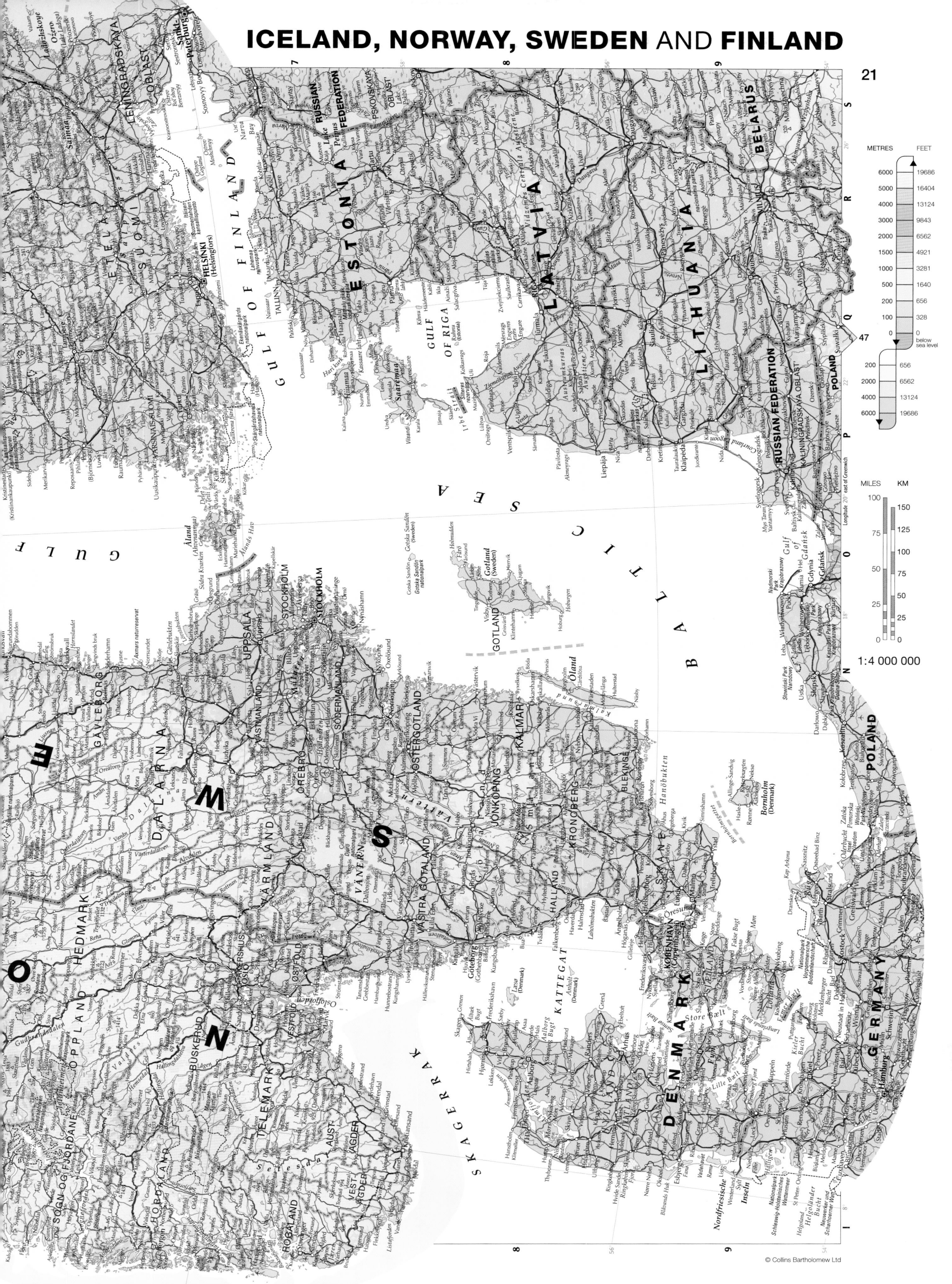
METRES
FEET
6000 19686
5000 16404
4000 13124
3000 9843
2000 6562
1500 4921
1000 3281
500 1640
200 656
100 328
0 0
below sea level
200 656
2000 6562
4000 13124
6000 19686
MILES
KM
1:4 000 000
47
ESTONIA
LATVIA
LITHUANIA
BELARUS
POLAND
GERMANY
DENMARK
RUSSIAN FEDERATION
GULF OF FINLAND
GULF OF RIGA
BALTIC SEA
SKAGERRAK
KATTEGAT
STOCKHOLM
HELSINKI (Helsingfors)
TALLINN
RĪGA
VILNIUS
KØBENHAVN (Copenhagen)
OSLO
Gotland
Öland
Bornholm (Denmark)
Åland (Ahvenanmaa)

20

NORWAY

HORDALAND

BUSKERUD

HEDMARK

AKERSHUS

OSLO

VÅRML...

ØSTFOLD

TELEMARK

VESTFOLD

ROGALAND

AUST-AGDER

VEST-AGDER

Stavanger

Bergen

Kristiansand

SKAGERRAK

SW

VÄST GÖTA

HALLAN

KATTEGAT

Skagen

Grenen

Frederikshavn

Hirtshals

Aalborg

NORDJYLLAND

Aalborg Bugt

Læsø (Denmark)

Anholt (Denmark)

Göteborg Gothenburg

Halmstad

VIBORG

ÅRHUS

Århus

Hessela

Helsingborg

RINGKØBING

Ringkøbing Fjord

JYLLAND

DENMARK

(JUTLAND)

Herning

Randers

Helsingør

FREDERIKSBORG

VEJLE

Vejle

Esbjerg

RIBE

Samsø

KØBENHAVN
COPENHAGEN

Copenhagen

ROSKILDE

Amager

Malmö

Fredericia

Kolding

Odense

FYN

VESTSJÆLLAND

SJÆLLAND
(ZEALAND)

Ringsted

Korsør

SØNDERJYLLAND

Als

STORSTRØM

Møn

Nordfriesische Inseln

Flensburg (Flensborg)

Falster

Loland

Nykøbing

Rødbyhavn

Femer Bælt

Fehmarn

Mecklenburger Bucht

GERMANY

Helgoländer Bucht

Kieler Bucht

Kiel

Rü...

Conic Equidistant Projection

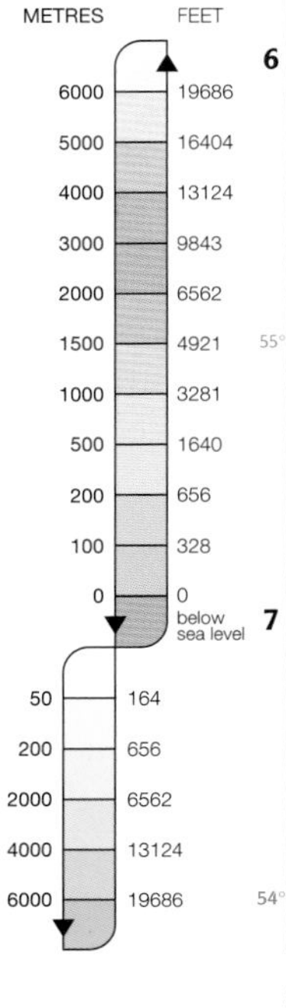

METRES · FEET
6000 · 19686
5000 · 16404
4000 · 13124
3000 · 9843
2000 · 6562
1500 · 4921
1000 · 3281
500 · 1640
200 · 656
100 · 328
0 · 0
below sea level

50 · 164
200 · 656
2000 · 6562
4000 · 13124
6000 · 19686

48

50

1:2 250 000

© Collins Bartholomew Ltd

DALARNA
GÄVLEBORG
UPPSALA
VÄSTMANLAND
STOCKHOLM
ÖREBRO
SÖDERMANLAND
ÖSTERGOTLAND
JÖNKÖPING
KALMAR
KRONOBERG
BLEKINGE
SWEDEN
Åland (Ahvenanmaa)
FINLAND
LÄNSI-SUOMI
Ålands Hav
Södra Kvarken
Skärgårdshavets Nationalpark
ESTONIA
Hiiumaa
Saaremaa
Irbe Strait
LATVIA
LITHUANIA
RUSSIAN FEDERATION
POLAND
GOTLAND
GOTLAND (Sweden)
Gotska Sandön (Sweden)
ÖLAND
BORNHOLM
Bornholm (Denmark)
Bornholmsgattet
Hanöbukten
Kalmarsund
BALTIC SEA
Gulf of Gdańsk
Courland Lagoon
Stockholm
Uppsala
Gävle
Västerås
Örebro
Norrköping
Linköping
Jönköping
Växjö
Kalmar
Karlskrona
Visby
Ventspils
Liepāja
Klaipėda
Kaliningrad
Gdańsk
Gdynia
Elbląg
Koszalin
Słupsk
Rønne
Turku (Åbo)
Mariehamn
Kuressaare
MILES
KM

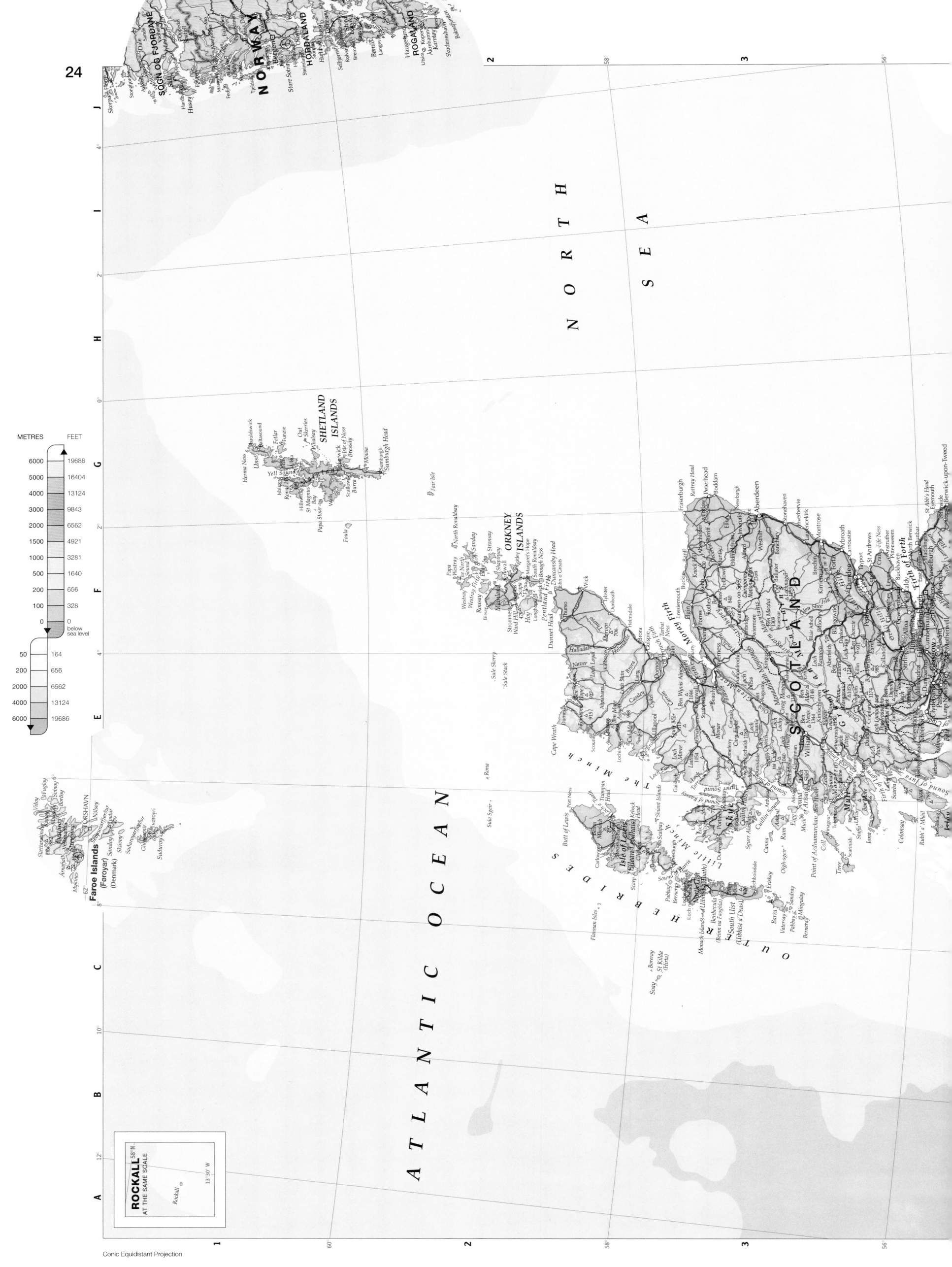

Conic Equidistant Projection

NORWAY
SOGN OG FJORDANE
HORDALAND
ROGALAND
Bergen
NORTH SEA
ATLANTIC OCEAN
SHETLAND ISLANDS
ORKNEY ISLANDS
SCOTLAND
OUTER HEBRIDES
Faroe Islands (Føroyar) (Denmark)
TÓRSHAVN
Aberdeen
Dundee
Glasgow
Inverness
Moray Firth
Firth of Forth
Isle of Lewis
Skye
Mull
Fair Isle
Foula
Sule Skerry
Rona
Sula Sgeir
St Kilda (Hirta)
The Minch
Little Minch
Pentland Firth
Cape Wrath
Butt of Lewis
Sumburgh Head
METRES
FEET
6000 19686
5000 16404
4000 13124
3000 9843
2000 6562
1500 4921
1000 3281
500 1640
200 656
100 328
0 0
below sea level
50 164
200 656
2000 6562
4000 13124
6000 19686
ROCKALL
AT THE SAME SCALE
58° N
13°30' W
Rockall

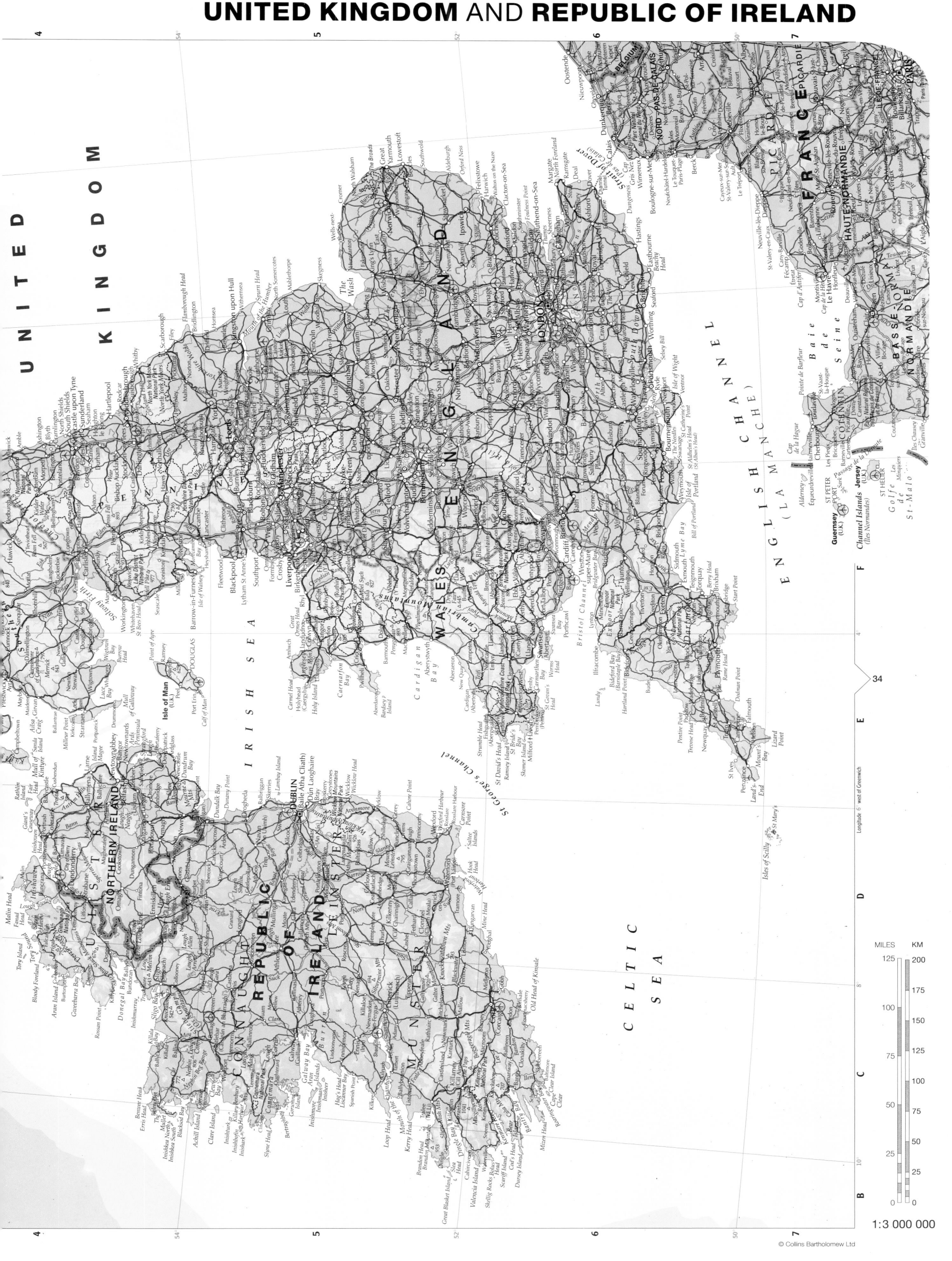

1:3 000 000

MILES   KM

© Collins Bartholomew Ltd

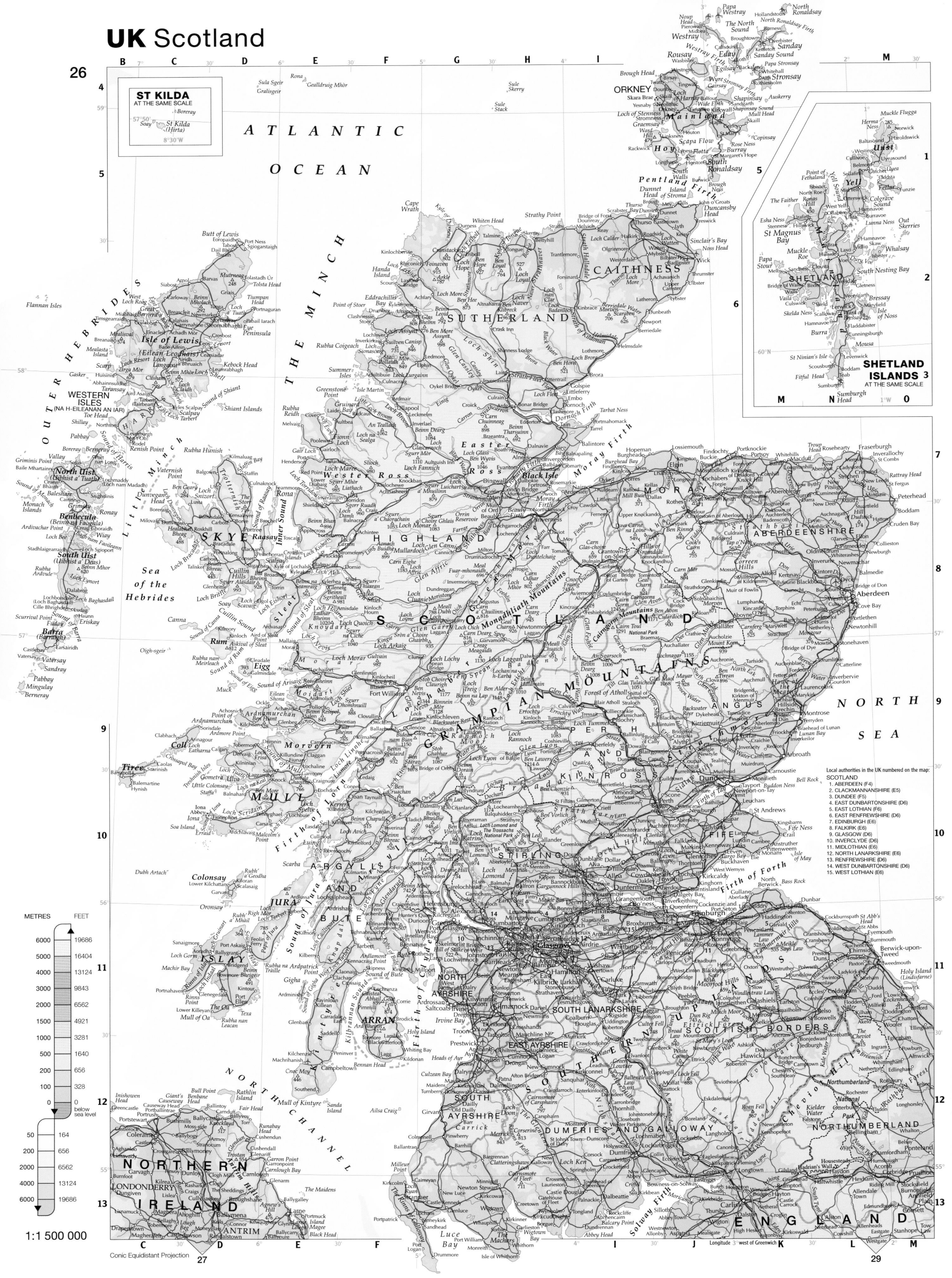

UK Scotland

ATLANTIC

OCEAN

ST KILDA
AT THE SAME SCALE

St Kilda
(Hirta)

THE MINCH

OUTER HEBRIDES

WESTERN
ISLES
(NA H-EILEANAN AN IAR)

Isle of Lewis
(Eilean Leòdhais)

Sea
of the
Hebrides

SKYE

HIGHLAND

SCOTLAND

GRAMPIAN MOUNTAINS

MULL

ARGYLL
AND
BUTE

ISLAY

ARRAN

NORTH
AYRSHIRE

EAST
AYRSHIRE

SOUTH
AYRSHIRE

SOUTH LANARKSHIRE

DUMFRIES AND GALLOWAY

NORTHERN
IRELAND

ENGLAND

NORTH

SEA

ORKNEY

CAITHNESS

SUTHERLAND

Wester Ross

MORAY

ABERDEENSHIRE

PERTH
AND
KINROSS

ANGUS

FIFE

STIRLING

SCOTTISH BORDERS

NORTHUMBERLAND

SHETLAND
ISLANDS
AT THE SAME SCALE

SHETLAND

Local authorities in the UK numbered on the map:
SCOTLAND
1. ABERDEEN (F4)
2. CLACKMANNANSHIRE (E5)
3. DUNDEE (F5)
4. EAST DUNBARTONSHIRE (D6)
5. EAST LOTHIAN (F6)
6. EAST RENFREWSHIRE (D6)
7. EDINBURGH (E6)
8. FALKIRK (E6)
9. GLASGOW (D6)
10. INVERCLYDE (D6)
11. MIDLOTHIAN (E6)
12. NORTH LANARKSHIRE (E6)
13. RENFREWSHIRE (D6)
14. WEST DUNBARTONSHIRE (D6)
15. WEST LOTHIAN (E6)

METRES FEET
6000 19686
5000 16404
4000 13124
3000 9843
2000 6562
1500 4921
1000 3281
500 1640
200 656
100 328
0
below
sea level
50 164
200 656
2000 6562
4000 13124
6000 19686

1:1 500 000

Conic Equidistant Projection

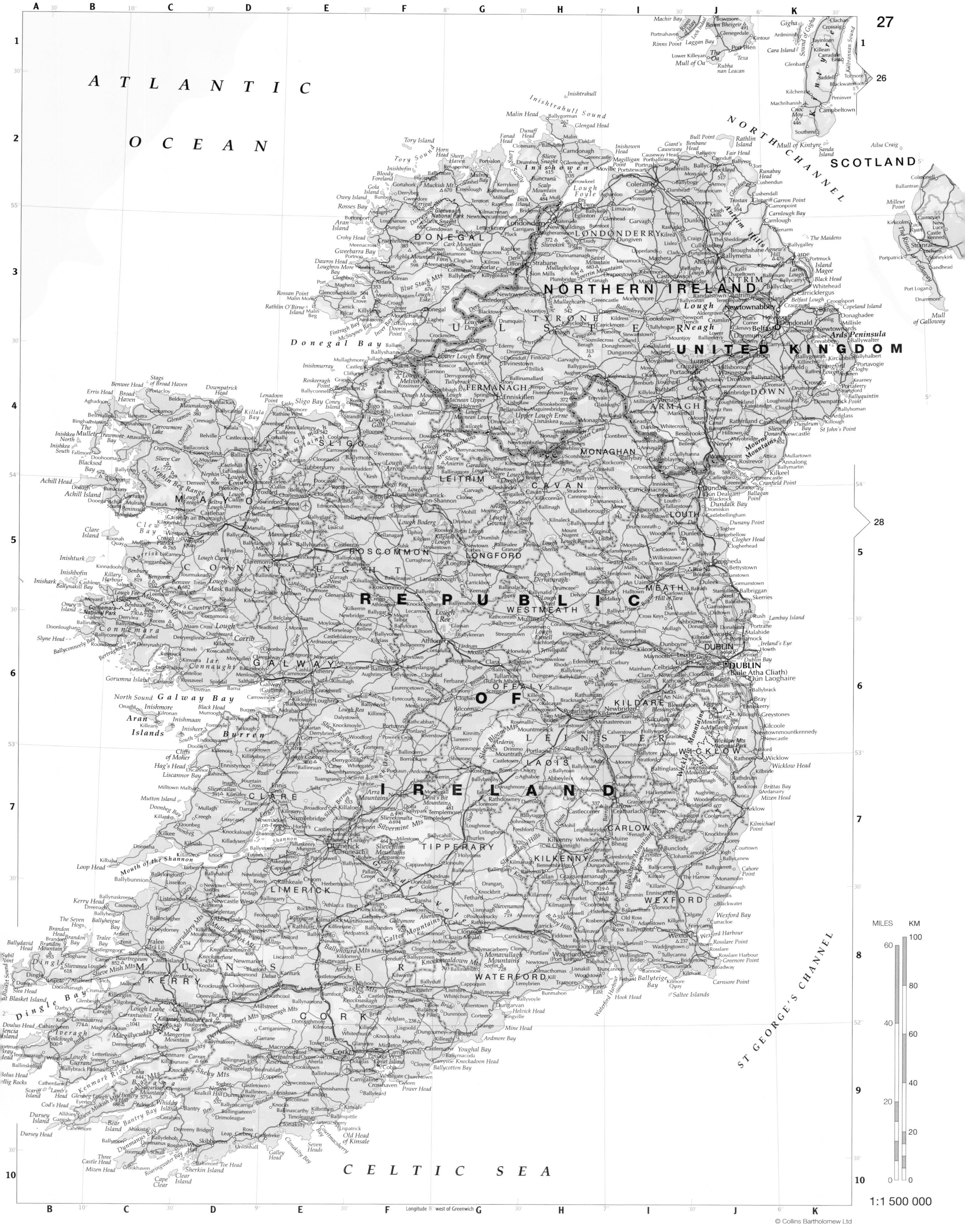

27

ATLANTIC

OCEAN

SCOTLAND

NORTH CHANNEL

NORTHERN IRELAND

DONEGAL

ULSTER

TYRONE

FERMANAGH

LONDONDERRY

ANTRIM

UNITED KINGDOM

ARMAGH

DOWN

MONAGHAN

LEITRIM

CAVAN

LOUTH

SLIGO

MAYO

ROSCOMMON

LONGFORD

MEATH

CONNAUGHT

WESTMEATH

REPUBLIC

OF

GALWAY

OFFALY

DUBLIN

KILDARE

LEINSTER

IRELAND

WICKLOW

CLARE

LAOIS

CARLOW

KILKENNY

LIMERICK

TIPPERARY

WEXFORD

KERRY

MUNSTER

WATERFORD

CORK

Donegal Bay

Galway Bay

Aran Islands

Dingle Bay

CELTIC SEA

ST GEORGE'S CHANNEL

Longitude 8 west of Greenwich

MILES	KM
60	100
	80
40	60
	40
20	
	20
0	0

1:1 500 000

© Collins Bartholomew Ltd

NORTHERN IRELAND
UNITED
REPUBLIC OF IRELAND
ULSTER
LEINSTER
NORTH CHANNEL
IRISH SEA
Isle of Man
(U.K.)
DOUGLAS
DUBLIN
(Baile Átha Cliath)
Belfast
Londonderry
ANTRIM
LONDONDERRY
TYRONE
FERMANAGH
ARMAGH
DOWN
DONEGAL
MONAGHAN
CAVAN
LEITRIM
LONGFORD
WESTMEATH
MEATH
LOUTH
OFFALY
KILDARE
LAOIS
WICKLOW
CARLOW
KILKENNY
WEXFORD
TIPPERARY
Lough Neagh
ARGYLL AND BUTE
ISLAY
JURA
ARRAN
NORTH AYRSHIRE
EAST AYRSHIRE
SOUTH AYRSHIRE
DUMFRIES AND
STIRLING
ISLE OF ANGLESEY
Caernarfon Bay
REP. OF IRELAND
U.K.
METRES
FEET
6000
19686
5000
16404
4000
13124
3000
9843
2000
6562
1500
4921
1000
3281
500
1640
200
656
100
328
0
0
below sea level
50
164
200
656
2000
6562
4000
13124
6000
19686

Conic Equidistant Projection

Local authorities in the UK numbered on the map:

SCOTLAND	ENGLAND
1. CLACKMANNANSHIRE (F1)	15. BLACKPOOL (F4)
2. EAST DUNBARTONSHIRE (E2)	16. DARLINGTON (H3)
3. EAST LOTHIAN (G2)	17. HARTLEPOOL (H3)
4. EAST RENFREWSHIRE (E2)	18. KINGSTON UPON HULL (I4)
5. EDINBURGH (F2)	19. MIDDLESBROUGH (H3)
6. FALKIRK (F2)	20. NORTH EAST LINCOLNSHIRE (I4)
7. GLASGOW (E2)	21. STOCKTON-ON-TEES (H3)
8. INVERCLYDE (E2)	22. STOKE-ON-TRENT (G4)
9. MIDLOTHIAN (F2)	
10. NORTH LANARKSHIRE (F2)	
11. PERTH AND KINROSS (F1)	
12. RENFREWSHIRE (E2)	
13. WEST DUNBARTONSHIRE (E2)	
14. WEST LOTHIAN (F2)	

NORTH SEA

MILES   KM

1:1 200 000

Local authorities in the UK numbered on the map:

ENGLAND
1. BATH AND N.E. SOMERSET (E3)
2. BRACKNELL FOREST (G3)
3. BRIGHTON AND HOVE (G4)
4. BRISTOL (E3)
5. BOURNEMOUTH (F4)
6. GREATER MANCHESTER (E1)
7. LUTON (G3)
8. MILTON KEYNES (G2)
9. NOTTINGHAM (F2)
10. PLYMOUTH (C4)
11. POOLE (F4)
12. PORTSMOUTH (F4)
13. READING (G3)
14. SLOUGH (G3)
15. SOUTHAMPTON (F4)
16. SOUTHEND (H3)
17. STOKE-ON-TRENT (E1)
18. SWINDON (F3)
19. THURROCK (H3)
20. TORBAY (D4)
21. WEST MIDLANDS (F2)
22. WINDSOR AND MAIDENHEAD (G3)
23. WOKINGHAM (G3)

WALES
24. BLAENAU GWENT (D3)
25. BRIDGEND (D3)
26. CAERPHILLY (D3)
27. CARDIFF (D3)
28. MERTHYR TYDFIL (D3)
29. NEWPORT (E3)
30. RHONDDA CYNON TAFF (D3)
31. TORFAEN (D3)

ISLES OF SCILLY
CONTINUATION AT THE SAME SCALE

Isles of Scilly

Conic Equidistant Projection

METRES   FEET
6000   19686
5000   16404
4000   13124
3000   9843
2000   6562
1500   4921
1000   3281
500   1640
200   656
100   328
0   0
          below sea level

50   164
200   656
2000   6562
4000   13124
6000   19686

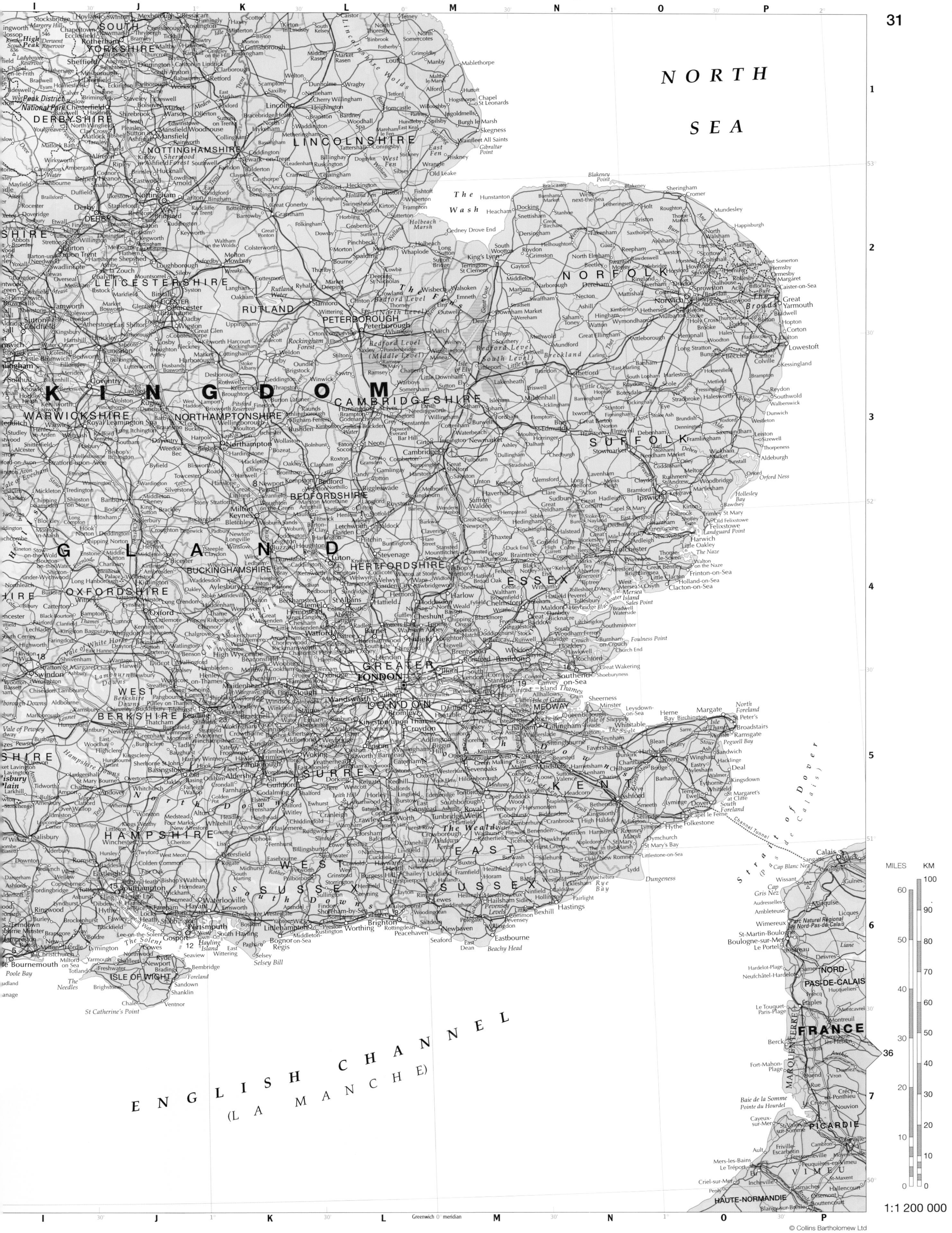

31

NORTH

SEA

SOUTH YORKSHIRE

DERBYSHIRE

LINCOLNSHIRE

The Wash

NOTTINGHAMSHIRE

NORFOLK

The Broads

LEICESTERSHIRE

RUTLAND

The Fens

KINGDOM

CAMBRIDGESHIRE

SUFFOLK

WARWICKSHIRE

NORTHAMPTONSHIRE

Bedford Level

BEDFORDSHIRE

ENGLAND

BUCKINGHAMSHIRE

HERTFORDSHIRE

ESSEX

OXFORDSHIRE

GREATER LONDON

Thames

BERKSHIRE

MEDWAY

KENT

Strait of Dover
(Pas de Calais)

SURREY

HAMPSHIRE

WEST SUSSEX

EAST SUSSEX

The Weald

South Downs

North Downs

ISLE OF WIGHT

Channel Tunnel

Calais

Cap Blanc Nez

NORD-PAS-DE-CALAIS

FRANCE

PICARDIE

HAUTE-NORMANDIE

ENGLISH CHANNEL
(LA MANCHE)

MILES KM
60 100
50 80
40 60
30 40
20 20
10 10
0 0

36

1:1 200 000

Greenwich 0° meridian

© Collins Bartholomew Ltd

CENTRAL LONDON
1:30 000

YARDS   METRES
7000   7000
         6000
6000   5000
5000   4000
4000
3000   3000
2000   2000
1000   1000
         0

1:125 000

© Collins Bartholomew Ltd

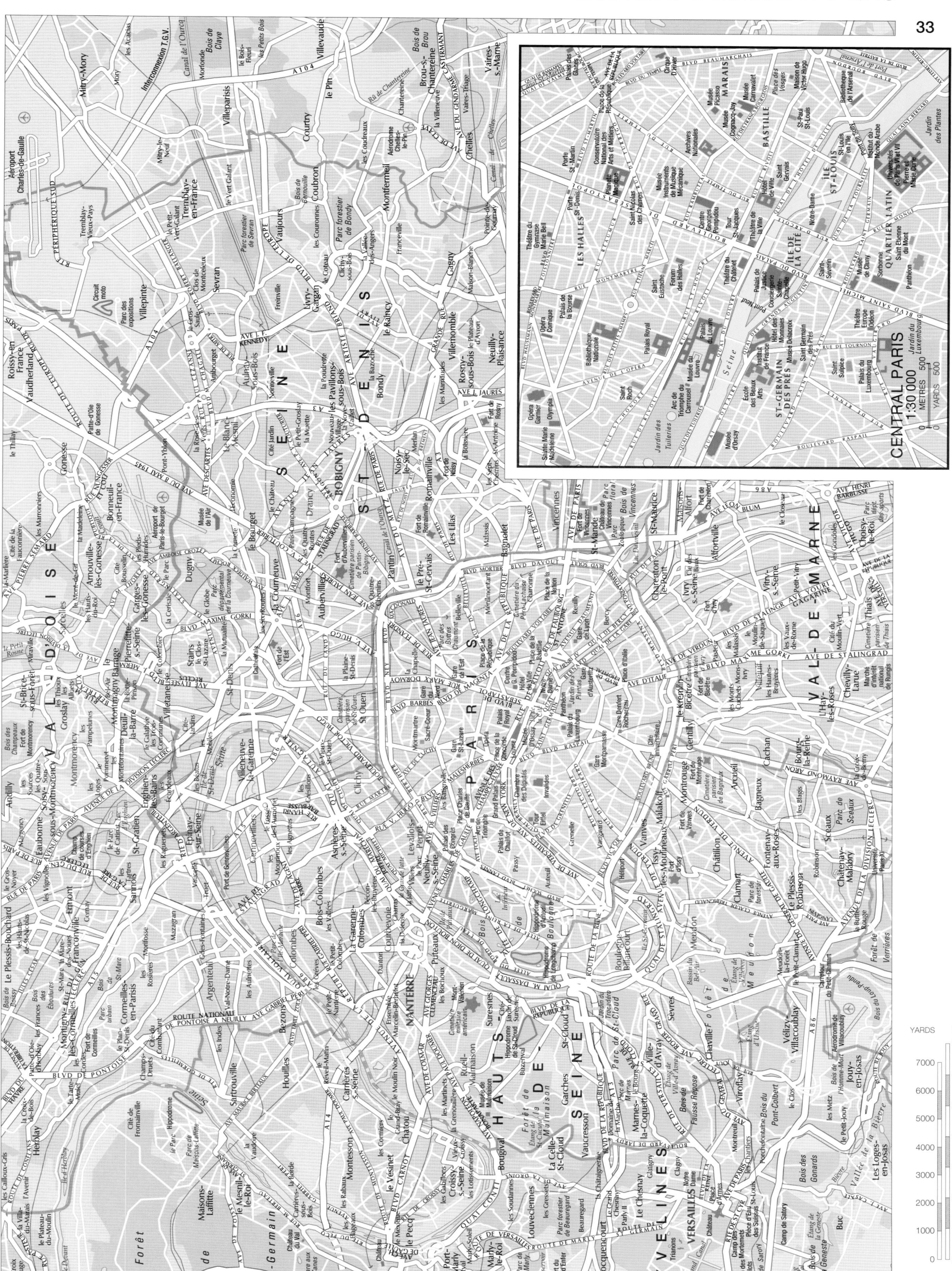

CENTRAL PARIS
1:30 000

METRES 500
YARDS 500

YARDS   METRES
7000
7000   6000
6000
5000   5000
4000
4000   3000
3000
2000   2000
1000
1000
0

1:125 000

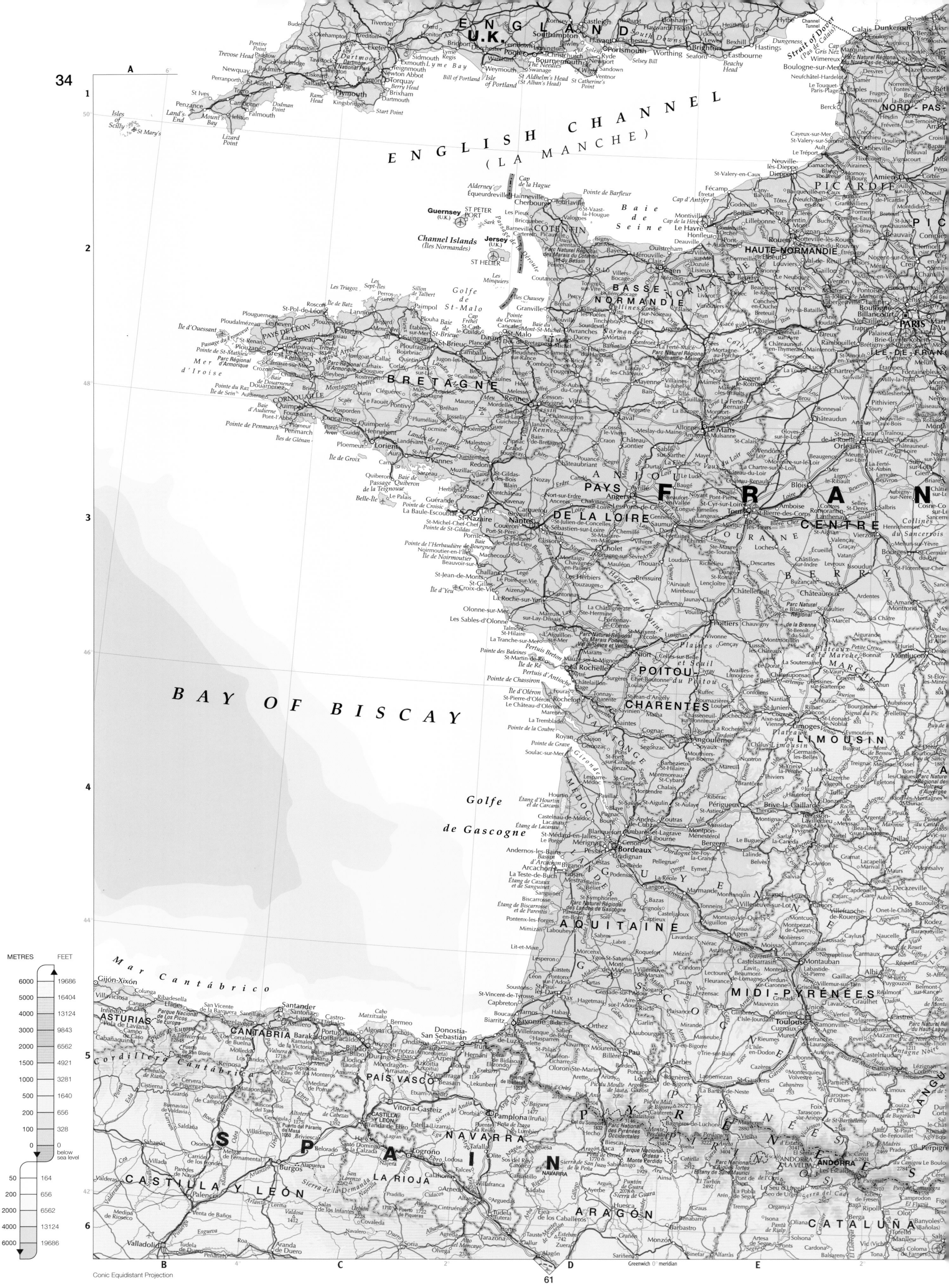
ENGLAND
U.K.
ENGLISH CHANNEL
(LA MANCHE)
Channel Islands
(Îles Normandes)
Guernsey (U.K.)
Jersey (U.K.)
Baie de Seine
Golfe de St-Malo
HAUTE-NORMANDIE
BASSE-NORMANDIE
BRETAGNE
PAYS DE LA LOIRE
CENTRE
FRANCE
POITOU-CHARENTES
LIMOUSIN
AQUITAINE
MIDI-PYRÉNÉES
NORD-PAS-DE-CALAIS
PICARDIE
ÎLE-DE-FRANCE
PARIS
BAY OF BISCAY
Golfe de Gascogne
Mar Cantábrico
Cordillera Cantábrica
ASTURIAS
CANTABRIA
PAÍS VASCO
NAVARRA
LA RIOJA
CASTILLA Y LEÓN
ARAGÓN
CATALUÑA
SPAIN
ANDORRA
PYRENEES
Strait of Dover (Pas de Calais)
METRES
FEET
6000
19686
5000
16404
4000
13124
3000
9843
2000
6562
1500
4921
1000
3281
500
1640
200
656
100
328
0
0
below sea level
50
164
200
656
2000
6562
4000
13124
6000
19686
Conic Equidistant Projection

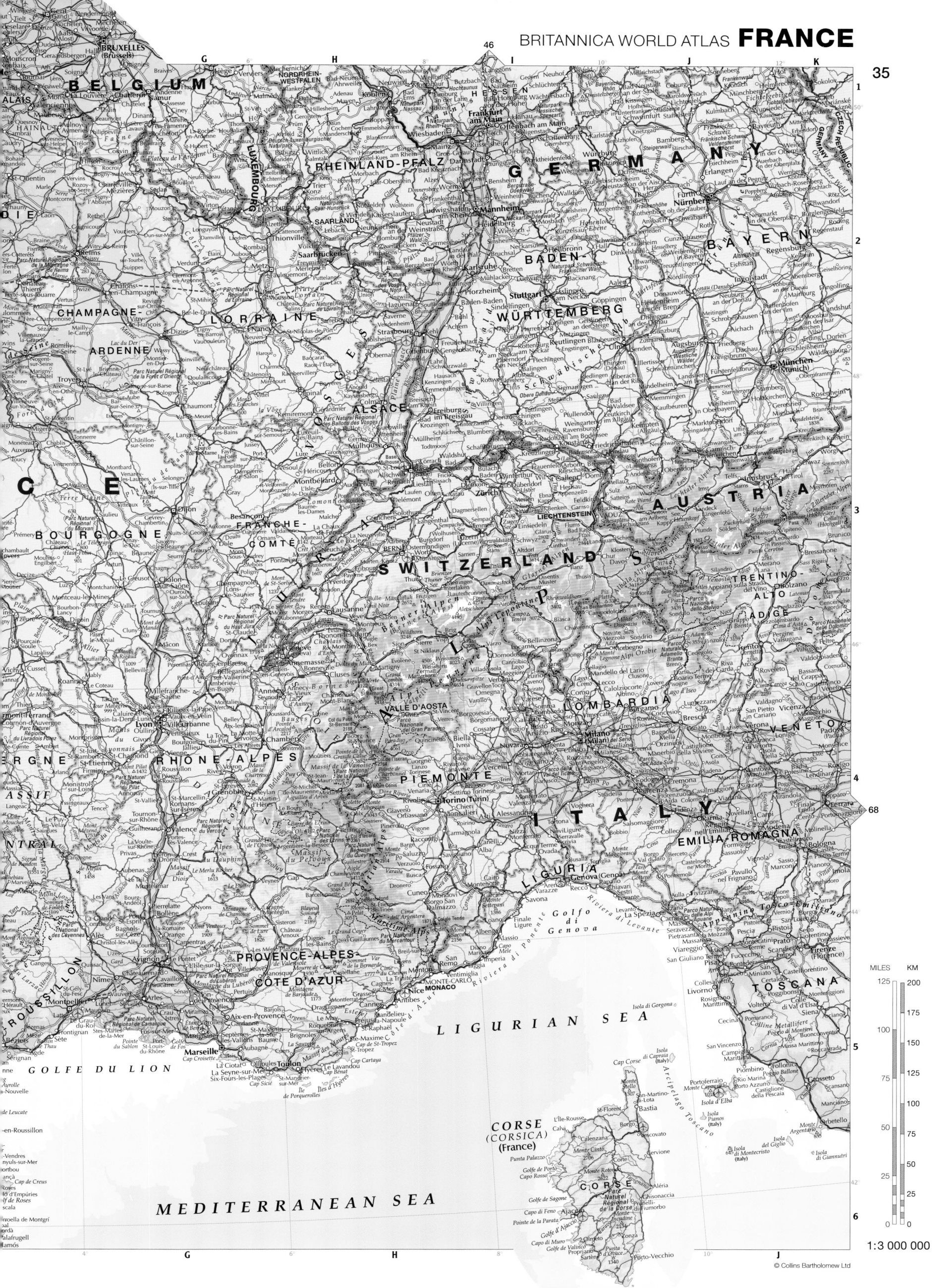

1:3 000 000

© Collins Bartholomew Ltd

BELGIUM
LUXEMBOURG
GERMANY
RHEINLAND-PFALZ
SAARLAND
HESSEN
BADEN-WÜRTTEMBERG
BAYERN
CZECH REPUBLIC
CHAMPAGNE-ARDENNE
LORRAINE
ALSACE
BOURGOGNE
FRANCHE-COMTÉ
RHÔNE-ALPES
PROVENCE-ALPES-CÔTE D'AZUR
SWITZERLAND
LIECHTENSTEIN
AUSTRIA
TRENTINO-ALTO ADIGE
LOMBARDIA
VENETO
VALLE D'AOSTA
PIEMONTE
LIGURIA
EMILIA-ROMAGNA
TOSCANA
ITALY
MONACO
LIGURIAN SEA
MEDITERRANEAN SEA
GOLFE DU LION
Golfo di Genova
CORSE (CORSICA) (France)
Bruxelles (Brussels)
Frankfurt am Main
Mannheim
Stuttgart
München (Munich)
Nürnberg
Strasbourg
Zürich
Bern
Genève
Lyon
Grenoble
Torino (Turin)
Milano (Milan)
Genova (Genoa)
Marseille
Toulon
Nice
Bologna
Firenze (Florence)
Livorno
Ajaccio
Bastia
MILES
KM
G
J
K
2
4
5
6
46
68

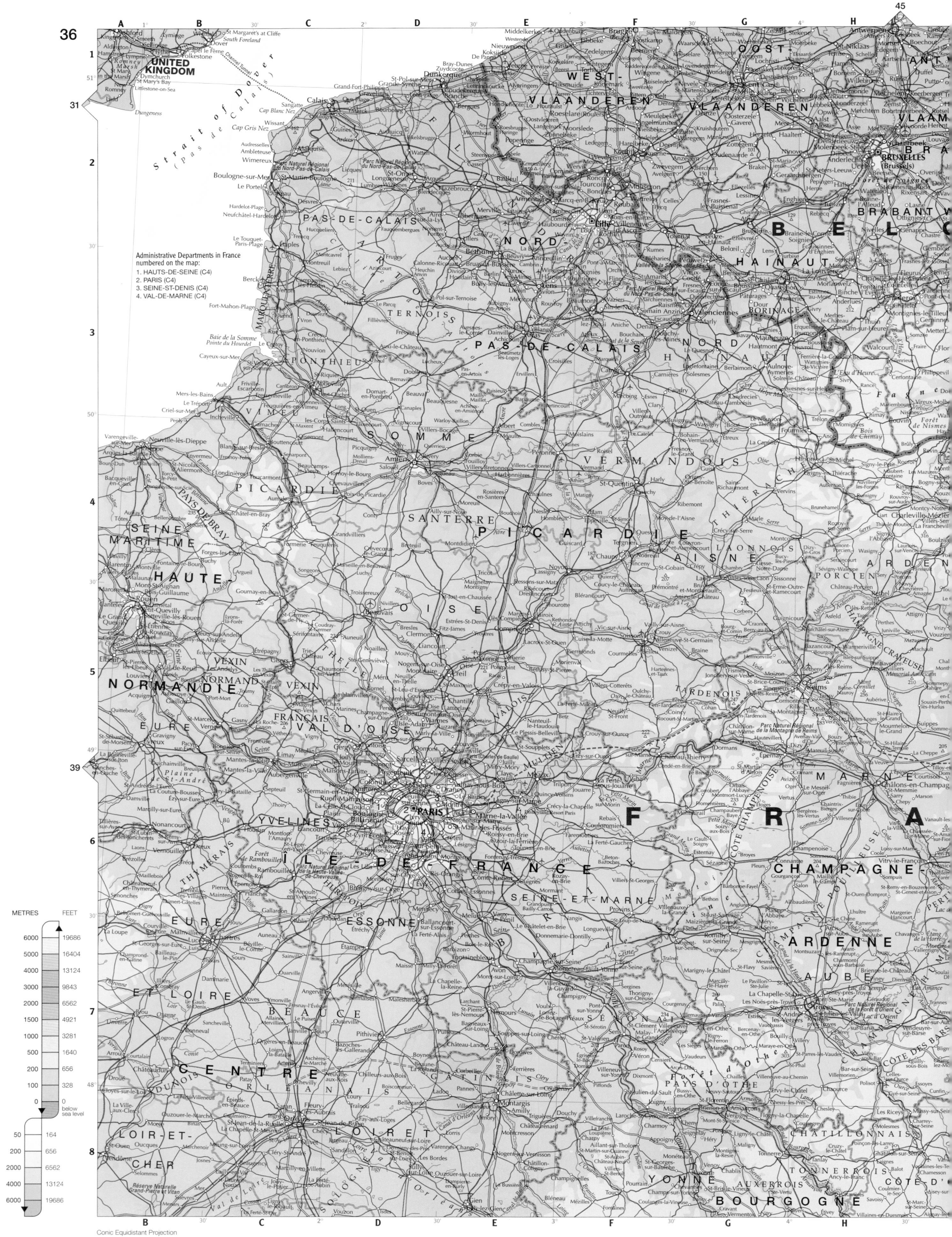

Administrative Departments in France
numbered on the map:
1. HAUTS-DE-SEINE (C4)
2. PARIS (C4)
3. SEINE-ST-DENIS (C4)
4. VAL-DE-MARNE (C4)

METRES | FEET
6000 | 19686
5000 | 16404
4000 | 13124
3000 | 9843
2000 | 6562
1500 | 4921
1000 | 3281
500 | 1640
200 | 656
100 | 328
0 | 0
 | below
 | sea level
50 | 164
200 | 656
2000 | 6562
4000 | 13124
6000 | 19686

Conic Equidistant Projection

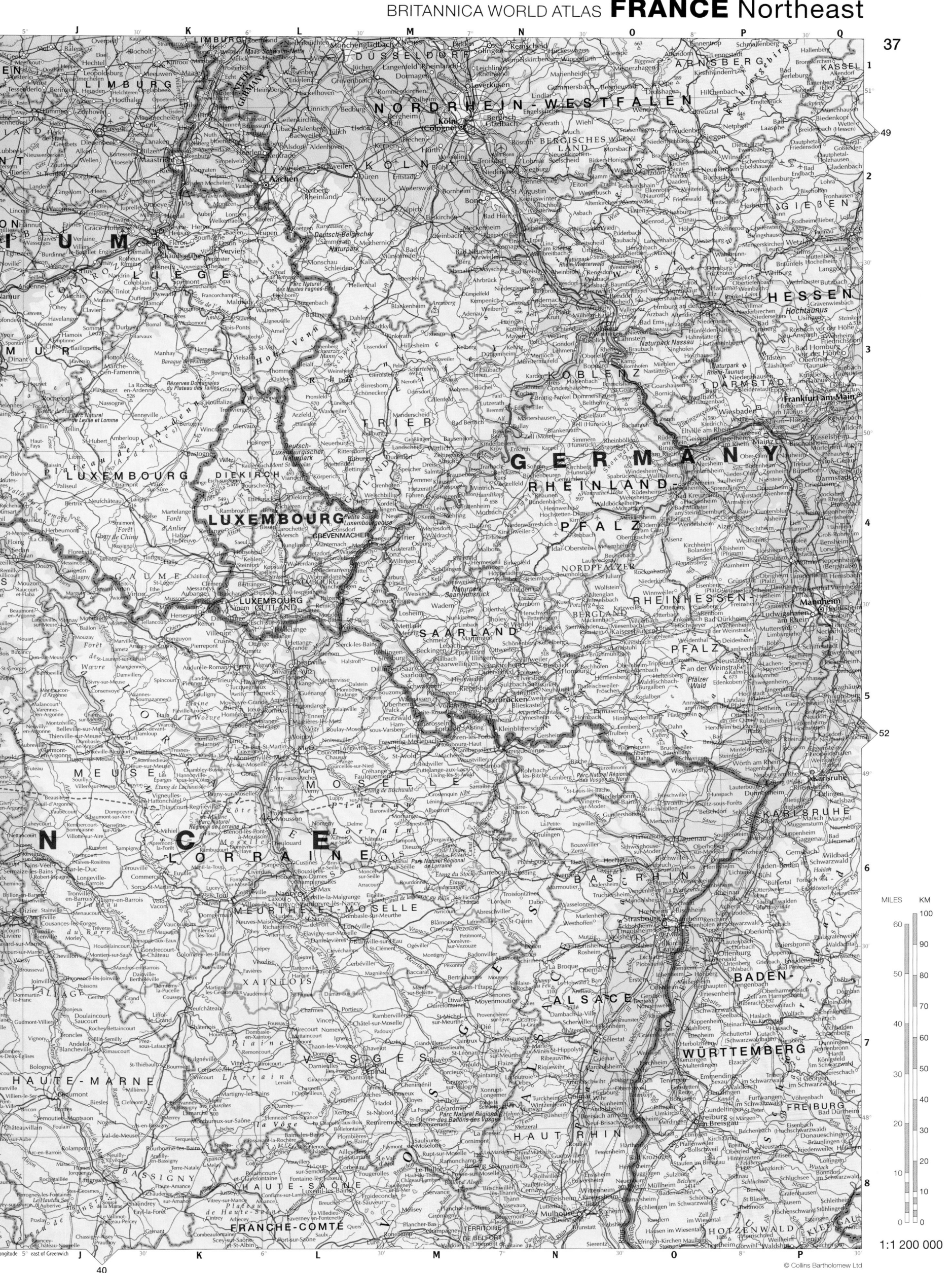

1:1 200 000

© Collins Bartholomew Ltd

NORDRHEIN-WESTFALEN
DÜSSELDORF
KÖLN
ARNSBERG
HESSEN
KOBLENZ
DARMSTADT
TRIER
GERMANY
RHEINLAND-PFALZ
LUXEMBOURG
DIEKIRCH
GREVENMACHER
SAARLAND
RHEINHESSEN-PFALZ
KARLSRUHE
BADEN-WÜRTTEMBERG
FREIBURG
LIEGE
LIMBURG
ALSACE
BAS-RHIN
HAUT-RHIN
LORRAINE
MOSELLE
MEURTHE-ET-MOSELLE
MEUSE
VOSGES
HAUTE-MARNE
HAUTE-SAÔNE
FRANCHE-COMTÉ
TERRITOIRE DE BELFORT
MILES
KM

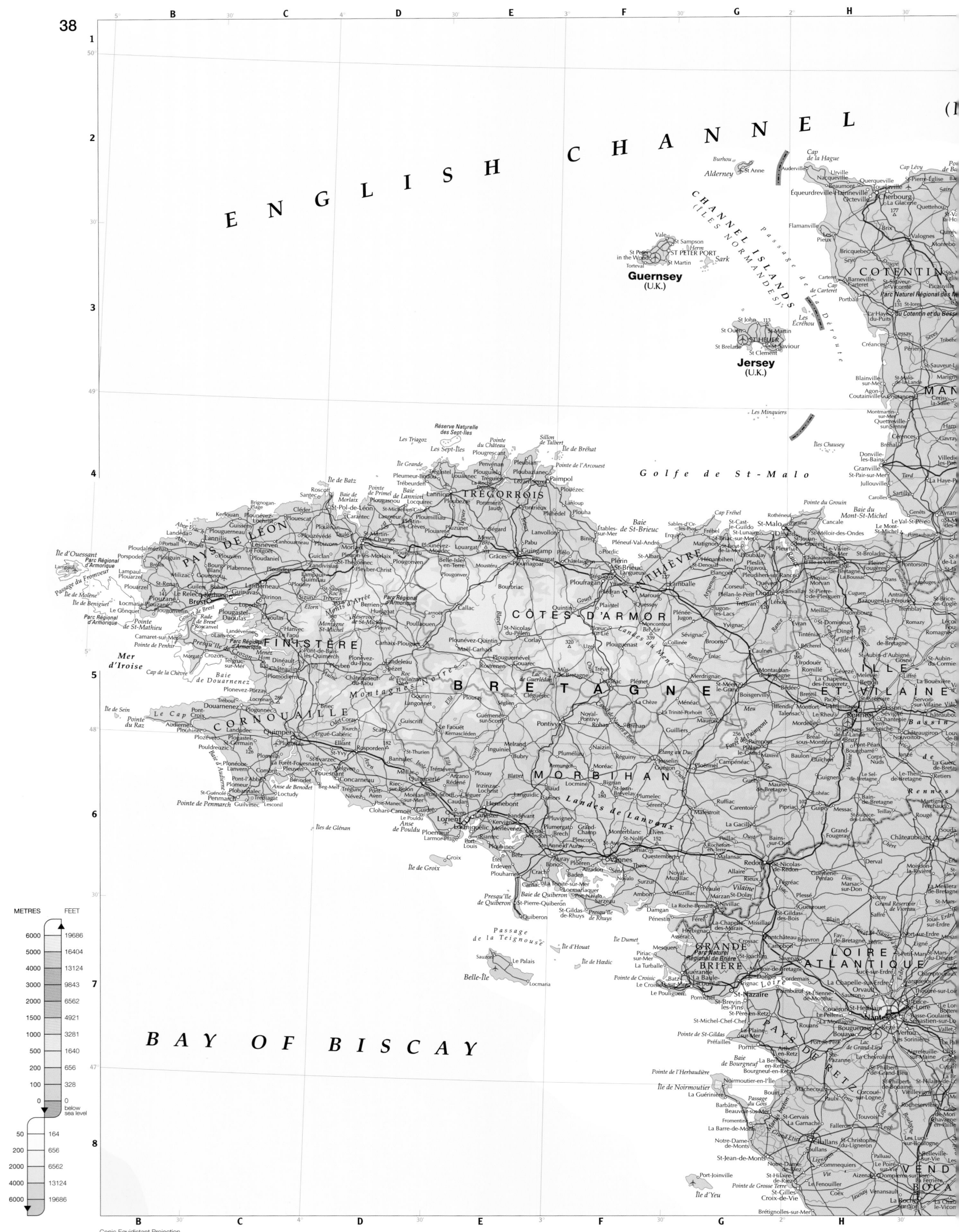
ENGLISH CHANNEL
CHANNEL ISLANDS (ÎLES NORMANDES)
Alderney
Guernsey (U.K.)
Jersey (U.K.)
Sark
Herm
ST PETER PORT
ST HELIER
Passage de la Déroute
Les Écréhou
Les Minquiers
Îles Chausey
Golfe de St-Malo
COTENTIN
Cherbourg
TRÉGORROIS
PAYS DE LÉON
FINISTÈRE
CÔTES-D'ARMOR
PENTHIÈVRE
BRETAGNE
CORNOUAILLE
MORBIHAN
ILLE-ET-VILAINE
LOIRE-ATLANTIQUE
GRANDE BRIÈRE
PAYS DE RETZ
Brest
Quimper
Lorient
Vannes
St-Brieuc
St-Malo
Rennes
Nantes
St-Nazaire
Belle-Île
Île de Groix
Île de Noirmoutier
Île d'Yeu
Île d'Ouessant
Mer d'Iroise
Baie de Douarnenez
Baie de Quiberon
Landes de Lanvaux
Montagnes Noires
Monts d'Arrée
BAY OF BISCAY
METRES
FEET
6000 19686
5000 16404
4000 13124
3000 9843
2000 6562
1500 4921
1000 3281
500 1640
200 656
100 328
0 0
below sea level
50 164
200 656
2000 6562
4000 13124
6000 19686

Conic Equidistant Projection

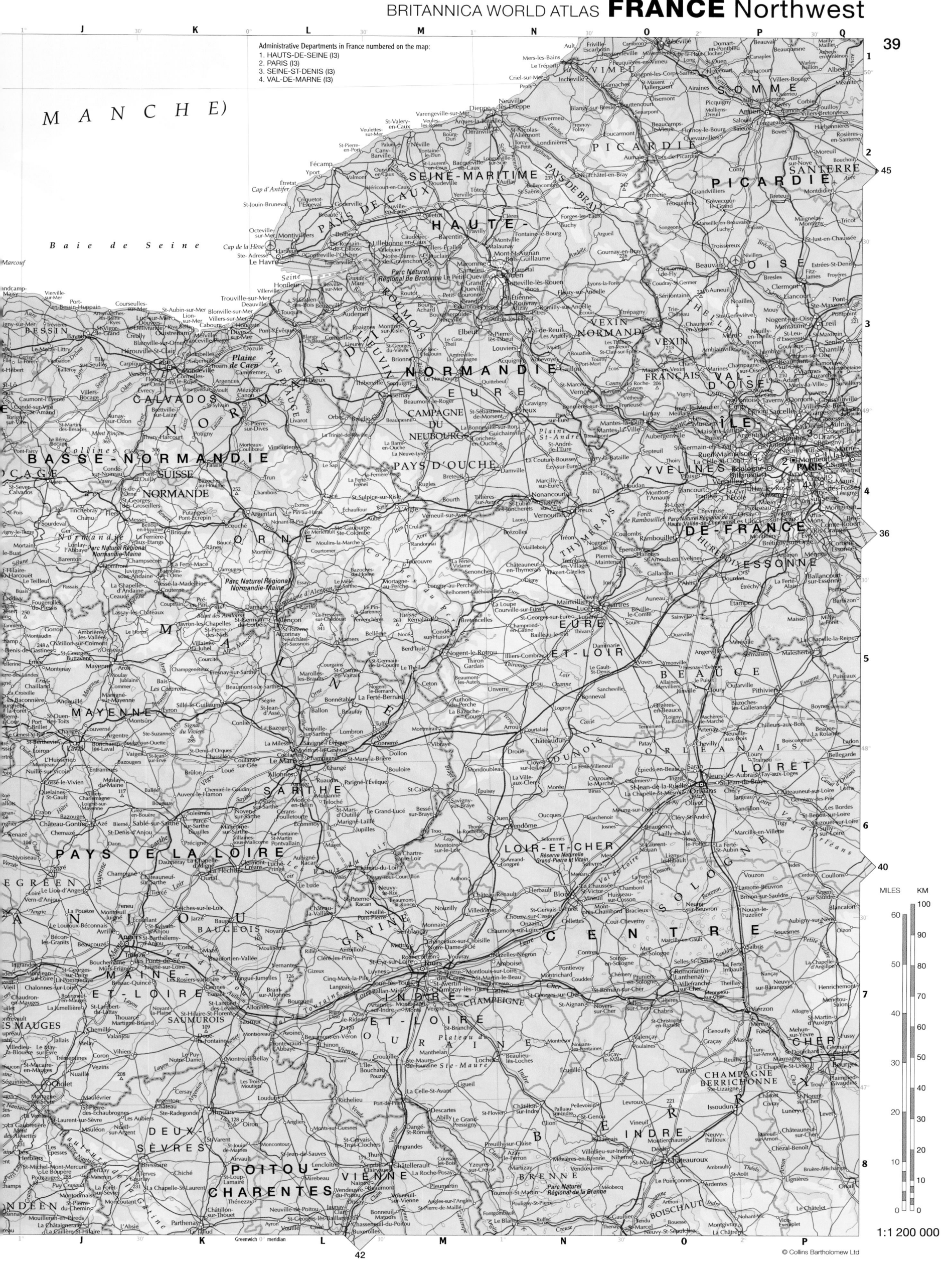

Administrative Departments in France numbered on the map:
1. HAUTS-DE-SEINE (I3)
2. PARIS (I3)
3. SEINE-ST-DENIS (I3)
4. VAL-DE-MARNE (I3)

M A N C H E)

Baie de Seine

SEINE-MARITIME

HAUTE-

PICARDIE

SANTERRE

PICARDIE

VIMEU

SOMME

OISE

VEXIN NORMAND

VEXIN

FRANÇAIS

VAL-D'OISE

ÎLE-DE-FRANCE

PARIS

YVELINES

ESSONNE

NORMANDIE

EURE

CAMPAGNE DU NEUBOURG

PAYS D'OUCHE

BESSIN

CALVADOS

BASSE-NORMANDIE

BOCAGE

SUISSE NORMANDE

ORNE

THYMERAIS

EURE-ET-LOIR

BEAUCE

MAINE

MAYENNE

SARTHE

DUNOIS

ORLÉANAIS

LOIRET

SOLOGNE

PAYS DE LA LOIRE

ANJOU

BAUGEOIS

MAINE-ET-LOIRE

MAUGES

LOIR-ET-CHER

CENTRE

CHAMPEIGNE

INDRE-ET-LOIRE

TOURAINE

CHER

DEUX-SÈVRES

VIENNE

POITOU-CHARENTES

BRENNE

INDRE

CHAMPAGNE BERRICHONNE

BOISCHAUT

MILES   KM
100
60   90
50   80
70
60
40   50
30   40
20   30
20
10   10
0   0

1:1 200 000

© Collins Bartholomew Ltd

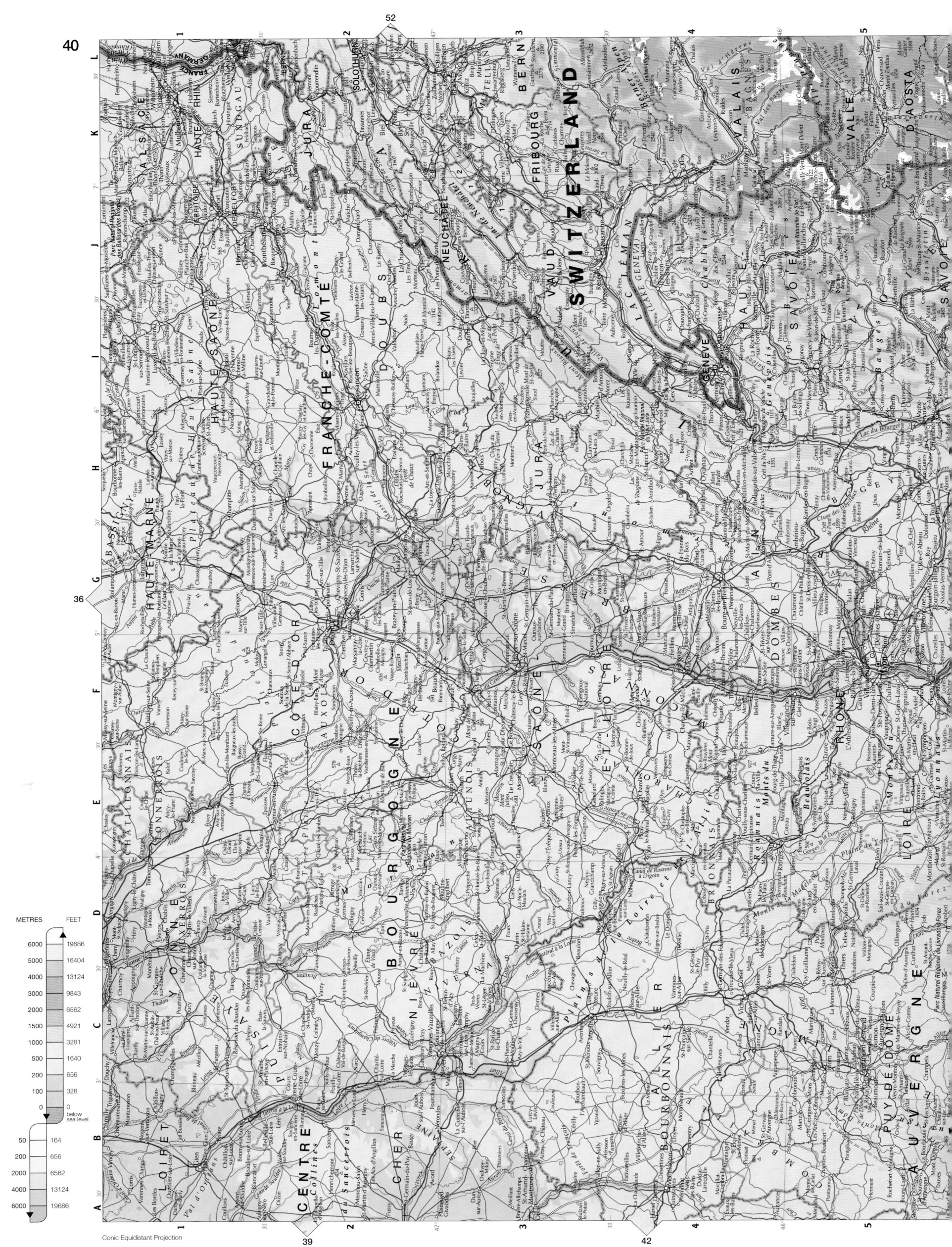

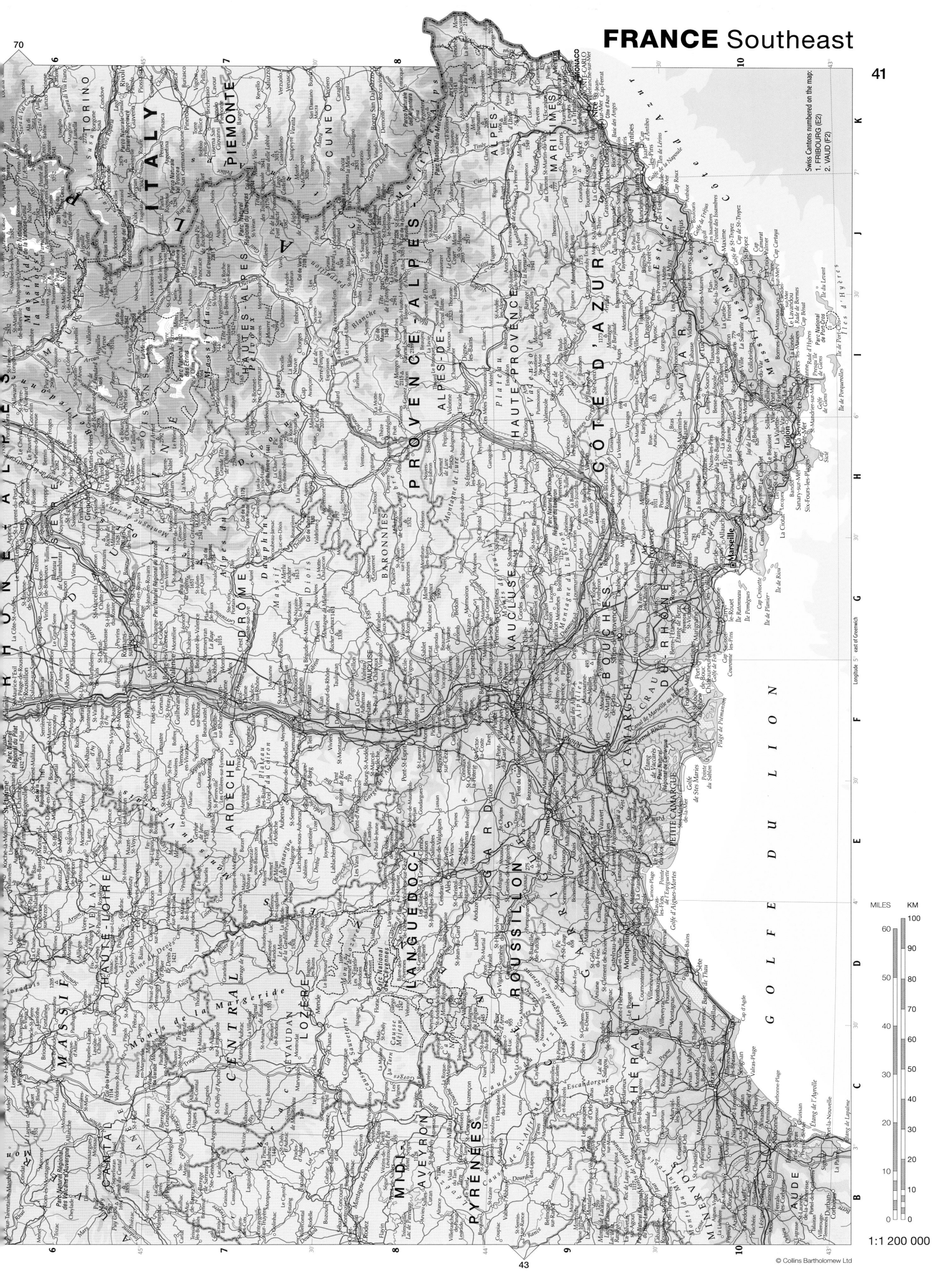

Swiss Cantons numbered on the map:
1. FRIBOURG (E2)
2. VAUD (F2)

1:1 200 000

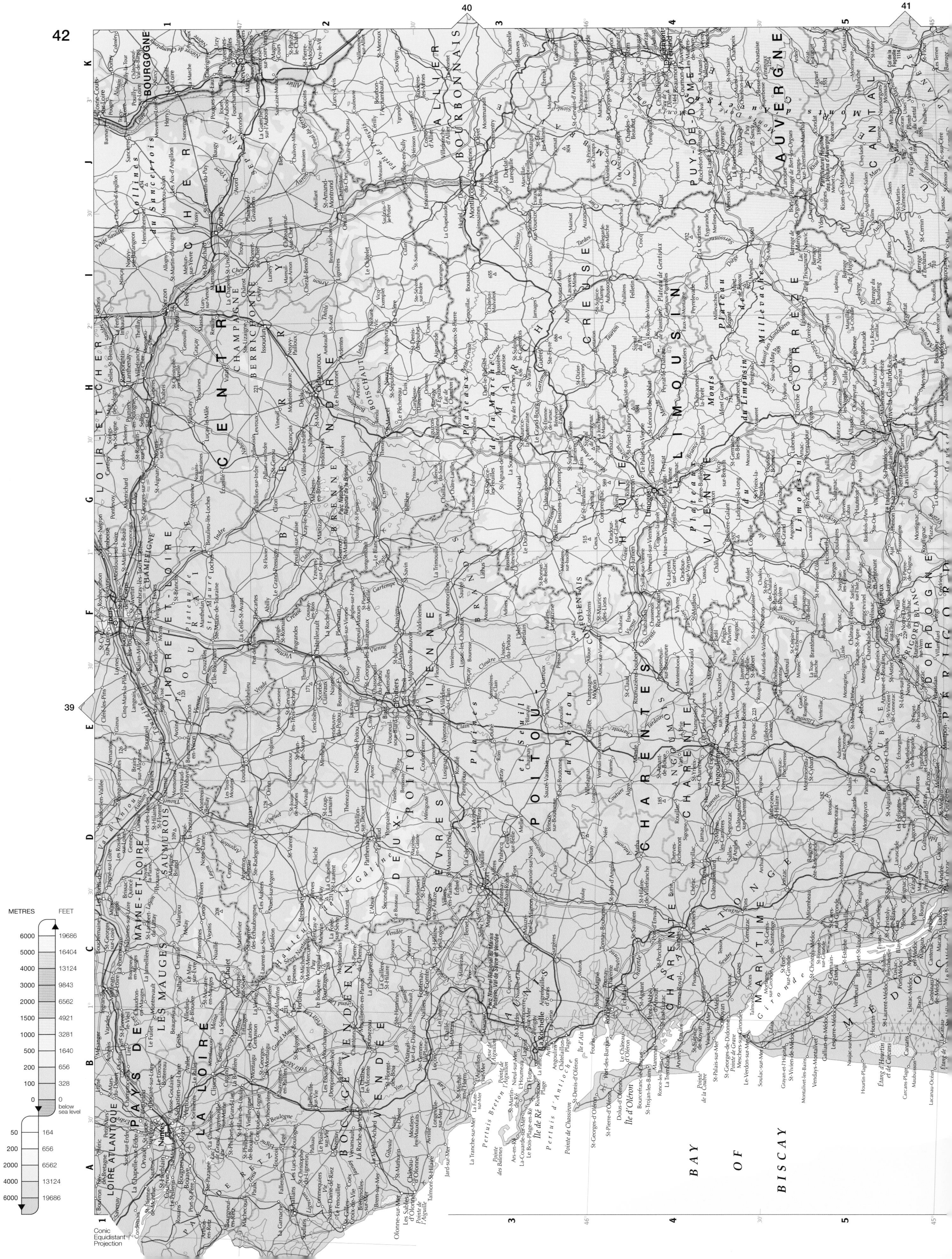

PAYS DE LA LOIRE
CENTRE
LIMOUSIN
POITOU-CHARENTES
AUVERGNE
BOURGOGNE
LOIR-ET-CHER
INDRE-ET-LOIRE
MAINE-ET-LOIRE
LOIRE-ATLANTIQUE
VENDÉE
DEUX-SÈVRES
VIENNE
INDRE
CHER
ALLIER
CREUSE
HAUTE-VIENNE
CHARENTE
CHARENTE-MARITIME
CORRÈZE
CANTAL
PUY-DE-DÔME
DORDOGNE
GIRONDE
BOURBONNAIS
CHAMPAGNE BERRICHONNE
BRENNE
BOISCHAUT
SAUMUROIS
LES MAUGES
BOCAGE VENDÉEN
Plateau de Millevaches
Monts du Limousin
Monts d'Auvergne
Monts du Cantal
Collines du Sancerrois
Gâtine
Plaine et Seuil du Poitou
Île d'Oléron
Île de Ré
Pertuis Breton
Pertuis d'Antioche
BAY OF BISCAY
Nantes
La Rochelle
Poitiers
Limoges
Angoulême
Niort
Tours
Bourges
Châteauroux
Montluçon
Saintes
Cholet
Saumur
Clermont-Ferrand
Tulle
Brive-la-Gaillarde
Périgueux
Royan
Rochefort
Les Sables-d'Olonne
La Roche-sur-Yon
Châtellerault
Vierzon
Nevers
Guéret
Issoudun
Cognac
METRES FEET
6000 19686
5000 16404
4000 13124
3000 9843
2000 6562
1500 4921
1000 3281
500 1640
200 656
100 328
0 0 below sea level
50 164
200 656
2000 6562
4000 13124
6000 19686
Conic Equidistant Projection
39
40
41

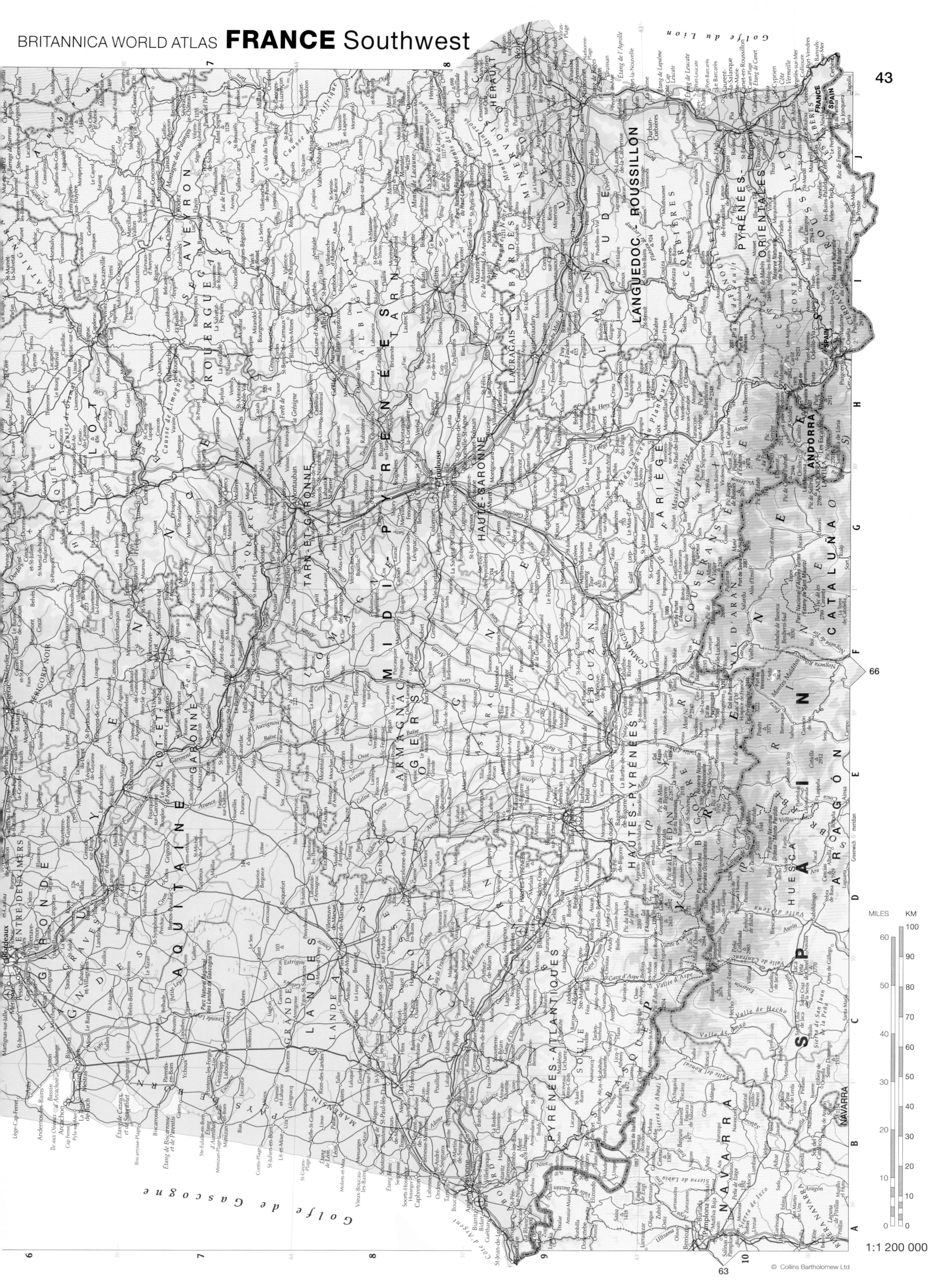

43

1:1 200 000

© Collins Bartholomew Ltd

Golfe du Lion
Golfe de Gascogne
FRANCE
SPAIN
ANDORRA
NAVARRA
AQUITAINE
MIDI-PYRÉNÉES
LANGUEDOC-ROUSSILLON
PYRÉNÉES-ATLANTIQUES
HAUTES-PYRÉNÉES
HAUTE-GARONNE
TARN-ET-GARONNE
PYRÉNÉES-ORIENTALES
Toulouse
Bordeaux
MILES
KM
66
63

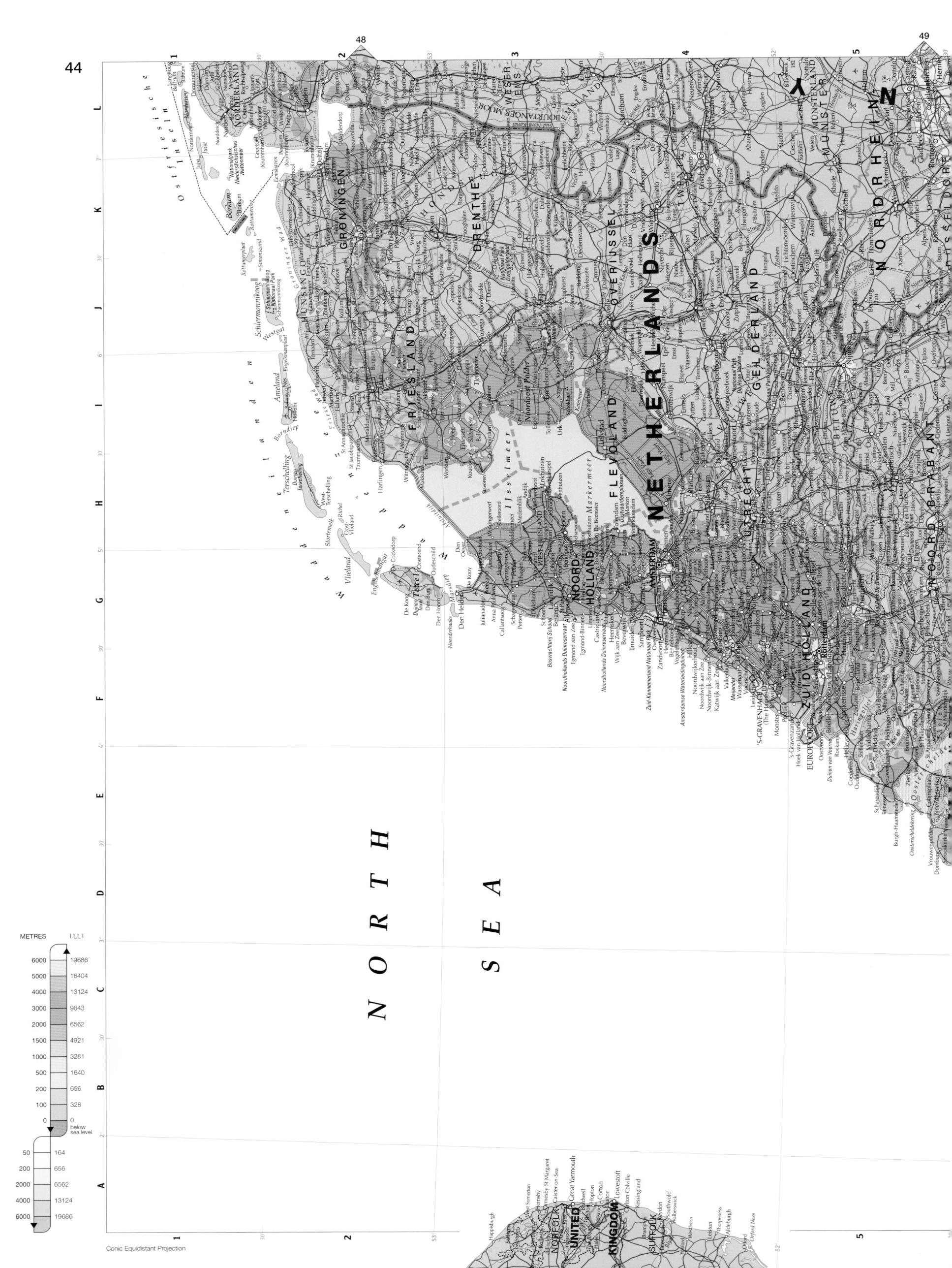
NORTH SEA
NETHERLANDS
GRONINGEN
FRIESLAND
DRENTHE
OVERIJSSEL
FLEVOLAND
GELDERLAND
UTRECHT
NOORD-HOLLAND
ZUID-HOLLAND
NOORD-BRABANT
NORDRHEIN-WESTFALEN
UNITED KINGDOM
NORFOLK
SUFFOLK
AMSTERDAM
Rotterdam
'S-GRAVENHAGE (The Hague)
IJsselmeer
Markermeer
Waddenzee
Ostfriesische Inseln
METRES
FEET
6000
19686
5000
16404
4000
13124
3000
9843
2000
6562
1500
4921
1000
3281
500
1640
200
656
100
328
0
0
below sea level
50
164
200
656
2000
6562
4000
13124
6000
19686

Conic Equidistant Projection

NETHERLANDS, BELGIUM AND LUXEMBOURG

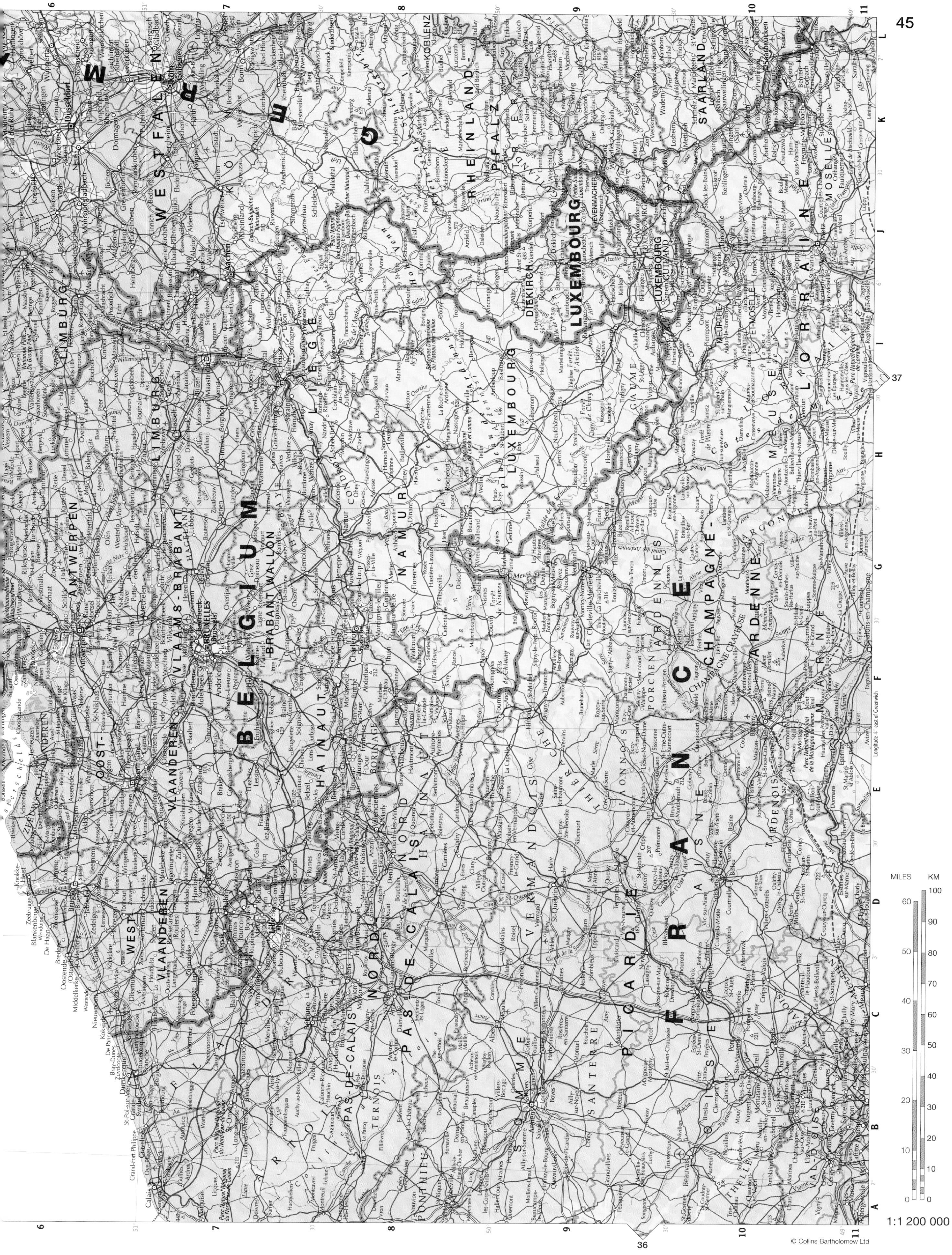

45

1:1 200 000

MILES   KM

DENMARK
NORTH SEA
NETHERLANDS
BELGIUM
LUXEMBOURG
GERMANY
FRANCE
SWITZERLAND
LIECHTENSTEIN
AUSTRIA
ITALY
ALPS
SCHLESWIG-HOLSTEIN
MECKLENBURG-VORPOMMERN
NIEDERSACHSEN
NORDRHEIN-WESTFALEN
SACHSEN-ANHALT
HESSEN
THÜRINGEN
RHEINLAND-PFALZ
SAARLAND
BADEN-WÜRTTEMBERG
BAYERN (BAVARIA)
NORD PAS-DE-CALAIS
PICARDIE
CHAMPAGNE-ARDENNE
LORRAINE
ALSACE
BOURGOGNE
FRANCHE COMTÉ
RHÔNE-ALPES
TRENTINO-ALTO ADIGE
LOMBARDIA
PIEMONTE
VENETO
FRIULI VENEZIA GIULIA
Ostfriesische Inseln
Waddenzee
IJsselmeer
Vosges
Jura
Amsterdam
Rotterdam
'S-GRAVENHAGE (The Hague)
BRUXELLES (Brussel)
Hamburg
Bremen
Hannover
Köln (Cologne)
Düsseldorf
Frankfurt am Main
Stuttgart
München (Munich)
Nürnberg
Zürich
BERN
METRES
FEET
6000 19686
5000 16404
4000 13124
3000 9843
2000 6562
1500 4921
1000 3281
500 1640
200 656
100 328
0 0
below sea level
50 164
200 656
2000 6562
4000 13124
6000 19686

Conic Equidistant Projection

22
35
68

BALTIC SEA

Gulf of Gdańsk

RUSSIAN FEDERATION

LITHUANIA

POLAND

WARSZAWA (Warsaw)

MAZOWIECKA

BELARUS

CZECH REPUBLIC

BOHEMIA

MORAVIA

SLOVAKIA

CARPATHIAN MOUNTAINS

UKRAINE

WIEN (Vienna)

BRATISLAVA

BUDAPEST

HUNGARY

ROMANIA

SLOVENIA

CROATIA

MILES
KM

125 — 200

100 — 175

— 150

75 — 125

— 100

50 — 75

25 — 50

— 25

0 — 0

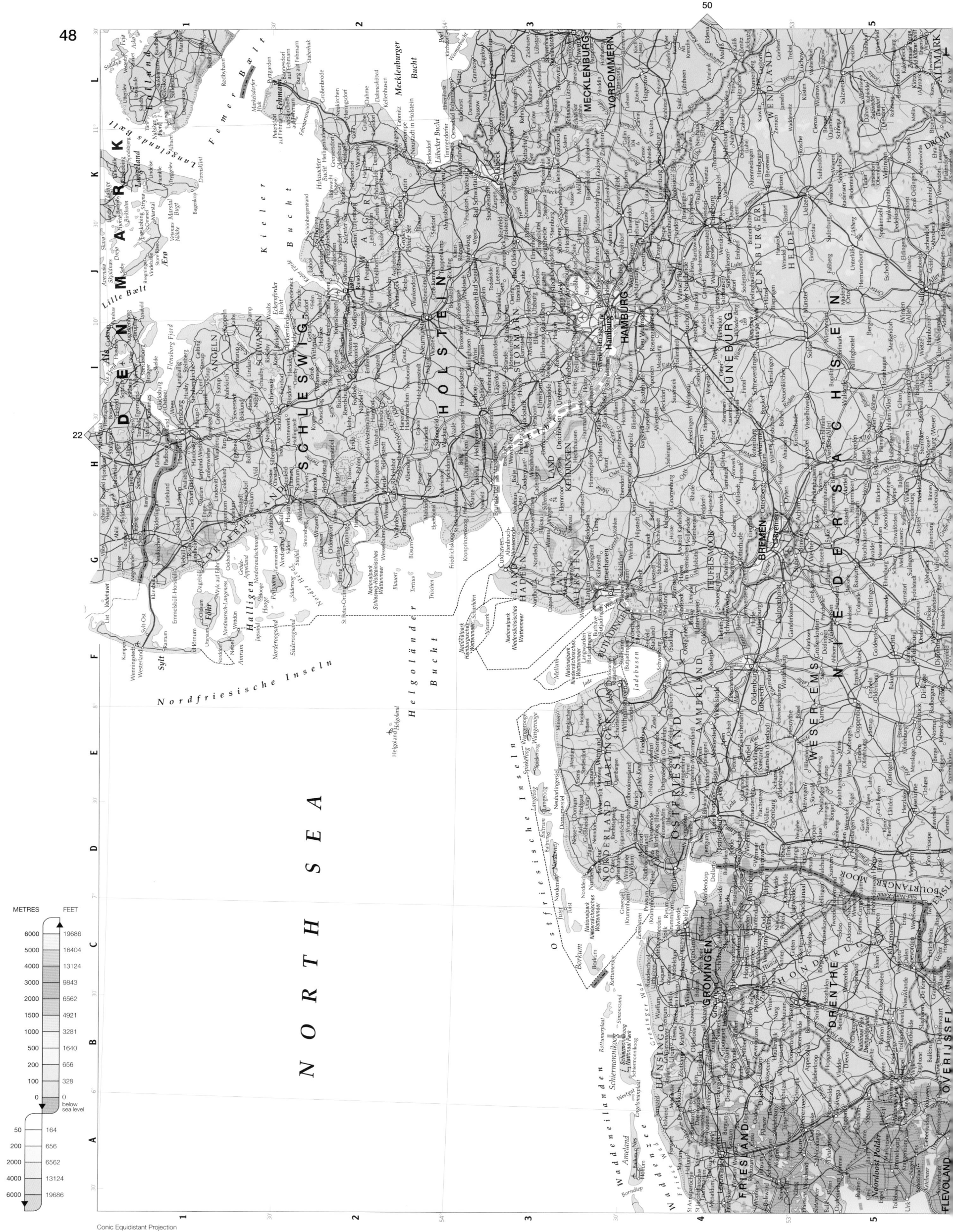

NORTH SEA

Helgoländer Bucht

Nordfriesische Inseln

DEN MARK

SCHLESWIG-HOLSTEIN

NIEDERSACHSEN

HAMBURG

BREMEN

MECKLENBURG-VORPOMMERN

GRONINGEN

DRENTHE

FRIESLAND

OVERIJSSEL

Kieler Bucht

Lübecker Bucht

Mecklenburger Bucht

METRES   FEET
6000   19686
5000   16404
4000   13124
3000   9843
2000   6562
1500   4921
1000   3281
500   1640
200   656
100   328
0   0
          below
          sea level
50   164
200   656
2000   6562
4000   13124
6000   19686

Conic Equidistant Projection

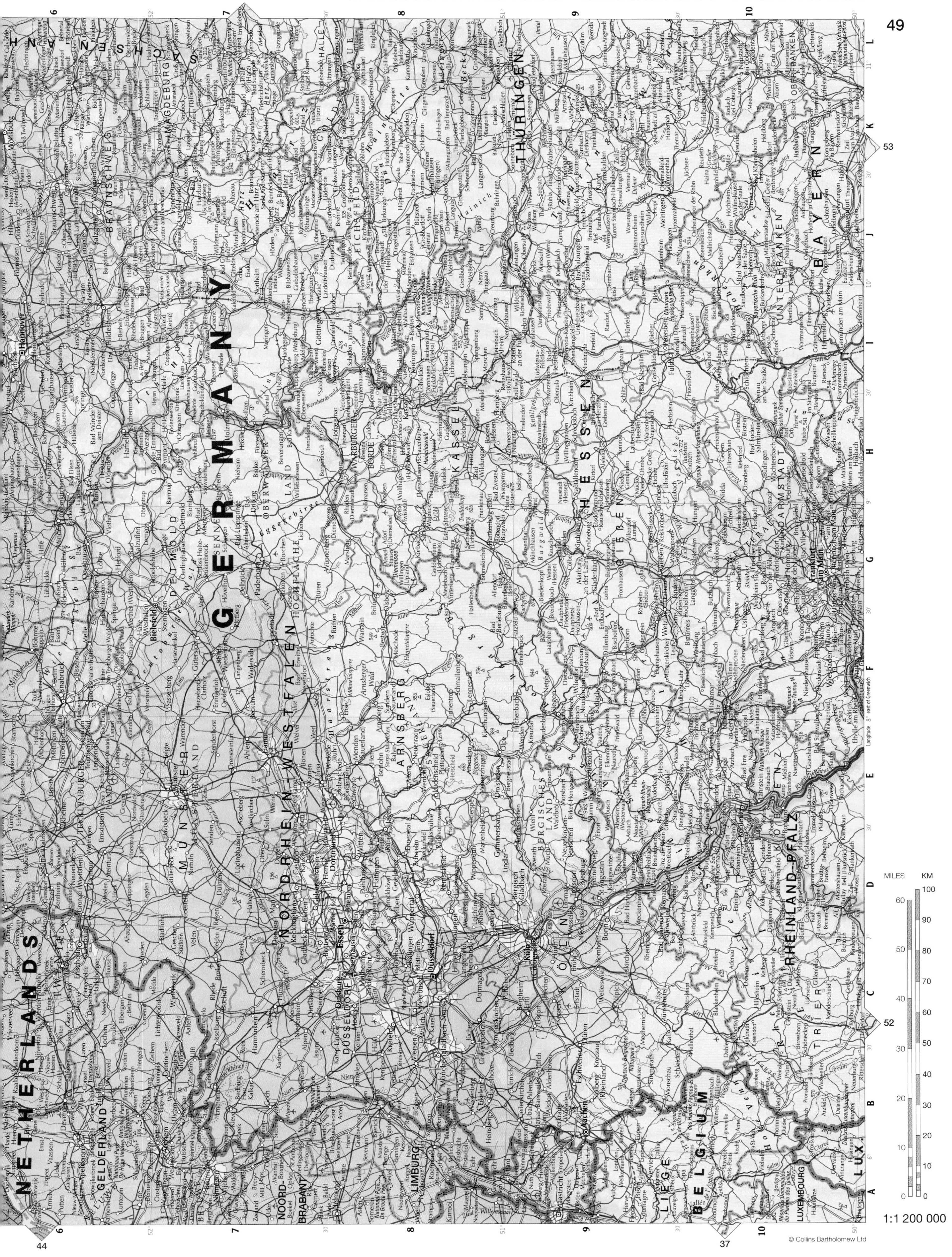

49

53

52

GERMANY

NETHERLANDS

BELGIUM

NIEDERSACHSEN

SACHSEN

MAGDEBURG

BRAUNSCHWEIG

NORDRHEIN-WESTFALEN

HESSEN

THÜRINGEN

BAYERN

RHEINLAND-PFALZ

GELDERLAND

NOORD-BRABANT

LIMBURG

LUXEMBOURG

LIÈGE

Hannover

Bielefeld

Düsseldorf

Essen

Köln

Bonn

Kassel

Frankfurt am Main

TEUTOBURGER WALD

MÜNSTERLAND

SAUERLAND

ARNSBERG

BERGISCHES LAND

EIFEL

TRIER

DARMSTADT

UNTERFRANKEN

OBERFRANKEN

HOHE RHÖN

MILES / KM

1:1 200 000

© Collins Bartholomew Ltd

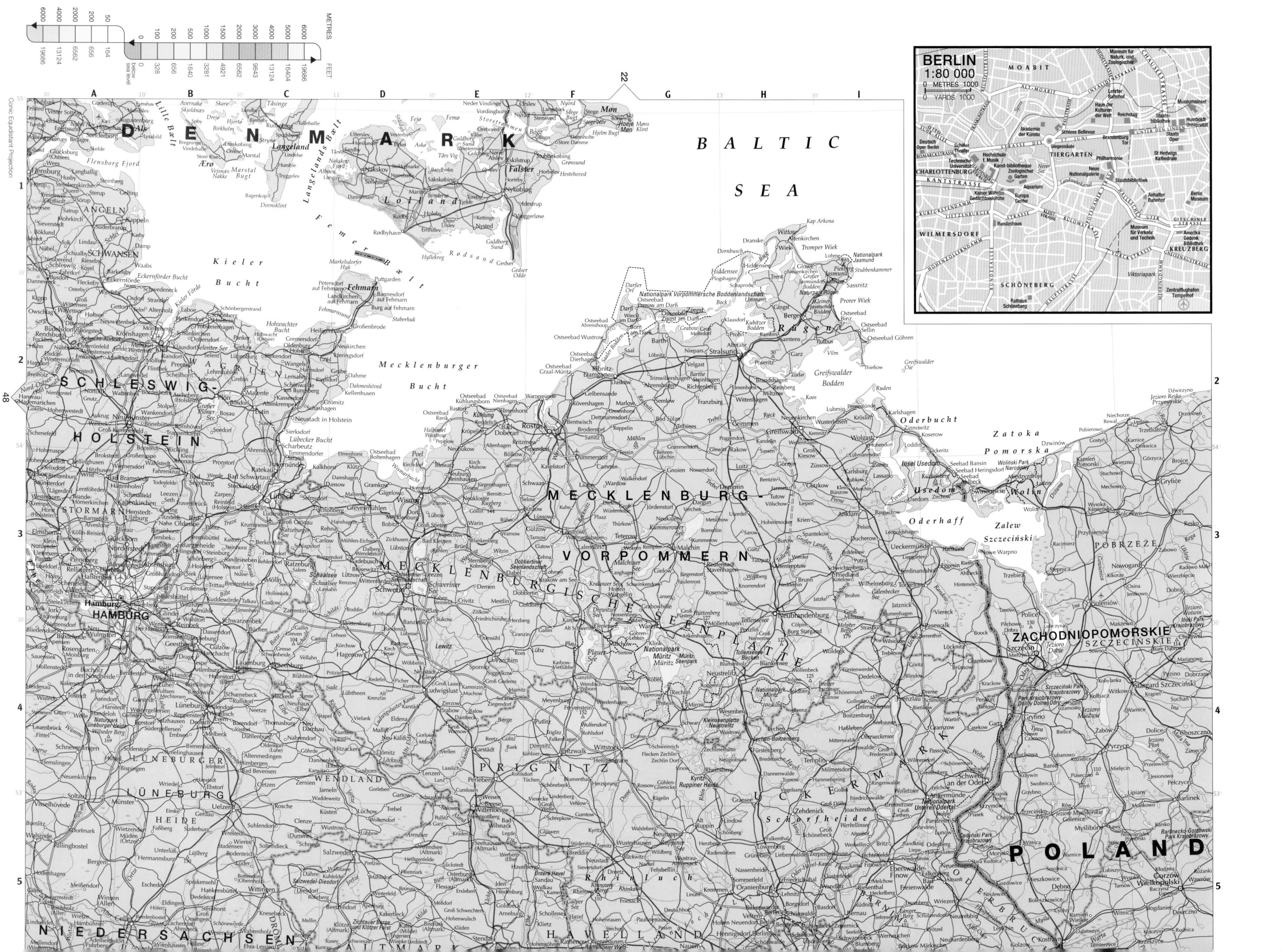

METRES
FEET
below sea level
BERLIN
1:80 000
METRES 1000
YARDS 1000
MOABIT
TIERGARTEN
CHARLOTTENBURG
WILMERSDORF
SCHÖNEBERG
KREUZBERG
Conic Equidistant Projection
DENMARK
BALTIC SEA
SCHLESWIG-HOLSTEIN
MECKLENBURG-VORPOMMERN
MECKLENBURGISCHE SEENPLATTE
NIEDERSACHSEN
ZACHODNIOPOMORSKIE
POLAND
HAMBURG
Kieler Bucht
Mecklenburger Bucht
Fehmarn
Rügen
Lolland
Falster
Møn
Langeland
Ærø
Als
Stralsund
Rostock
Lübeck
Kiel
Schwerin
Wismar
Neubrandenburg
Szczecin
Greifswald
Usedom
Wolin
Oderhaff
Zalew Szczeciński
PRIGNITZ
UCKERMARK
HAVELLAND
ALTMARK
WENDLAND
LÜNEBURGER HEIDE
Lüneburg
Zatoka Pomorska
Oderbucht
Pommersche Bucht

22

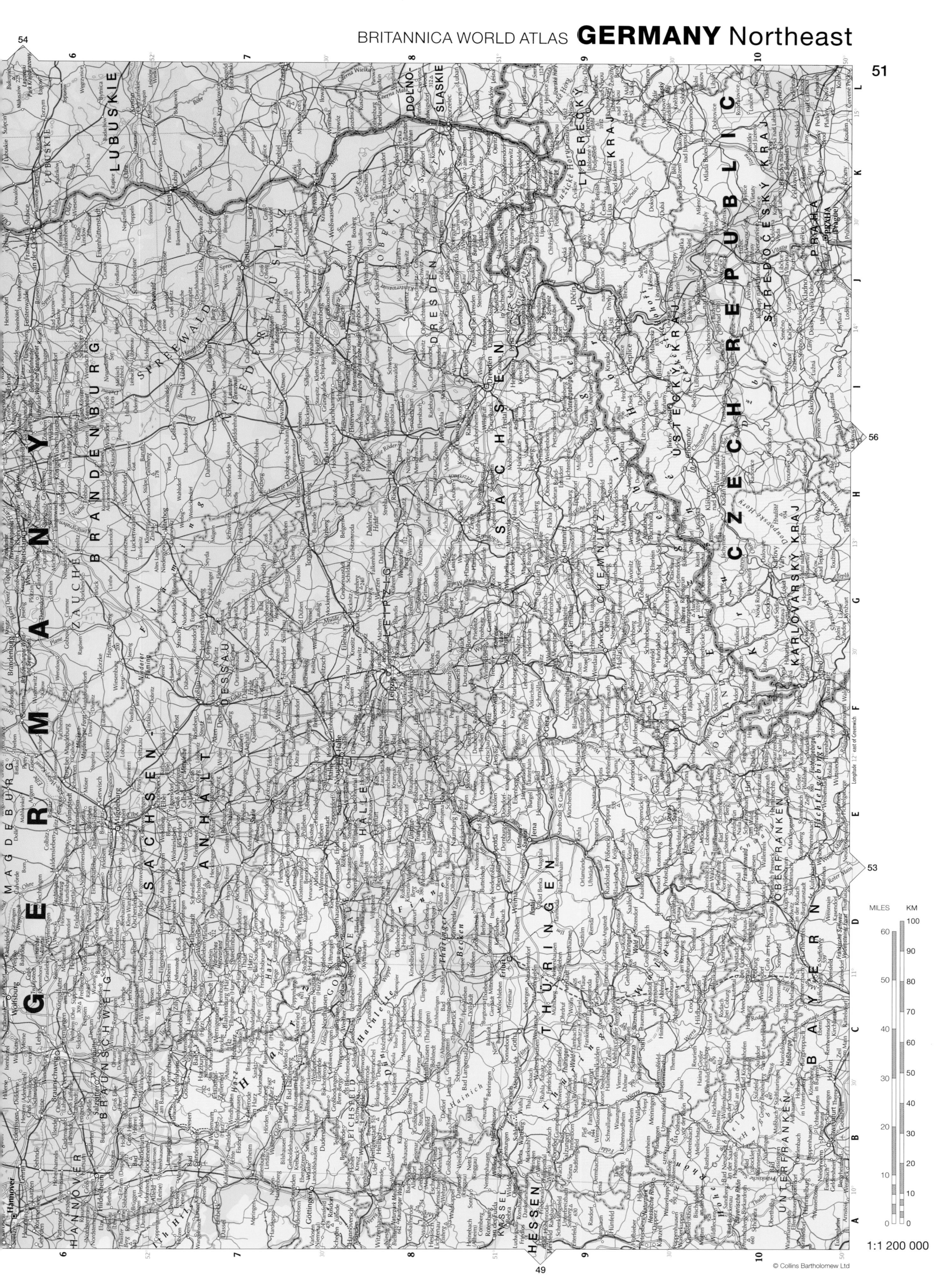

1:1 200 000

© Collins Bartholomew Ltd

54
51
GERMANY
CZECH REPUBLIC
SACHSEN
THÜRINGEN
SACHSEN - ANHALT
BRANDENBURG
MAGDEBURG
DRESDEN
LEIPZIG
CHEMNITZ
HALLE
DESSAU
LEIPZIG
HESSEN
KASSEL
BAYERN
OBERFRANKEN
UNTERFRANKEN
HANNOVER
BRAUNSCHWEIG
LUBUSKIE
DOLNO- ŚLĄSKIE
LIBERECKÝ KRAJ
ÚSTECKÝ KRAJ
KARLOVARSKÝ KRAJ
STŘEDOČESKÝ KRAJ
PRAHA
SPREEWALD
OBERLAUSITZ
NIEDERLAUSITZ
Longitude 12° east of Greenwich
56
53
MILES
KM
60
50
40
30
10
100
90
80
70
60
50
40
30
10
49

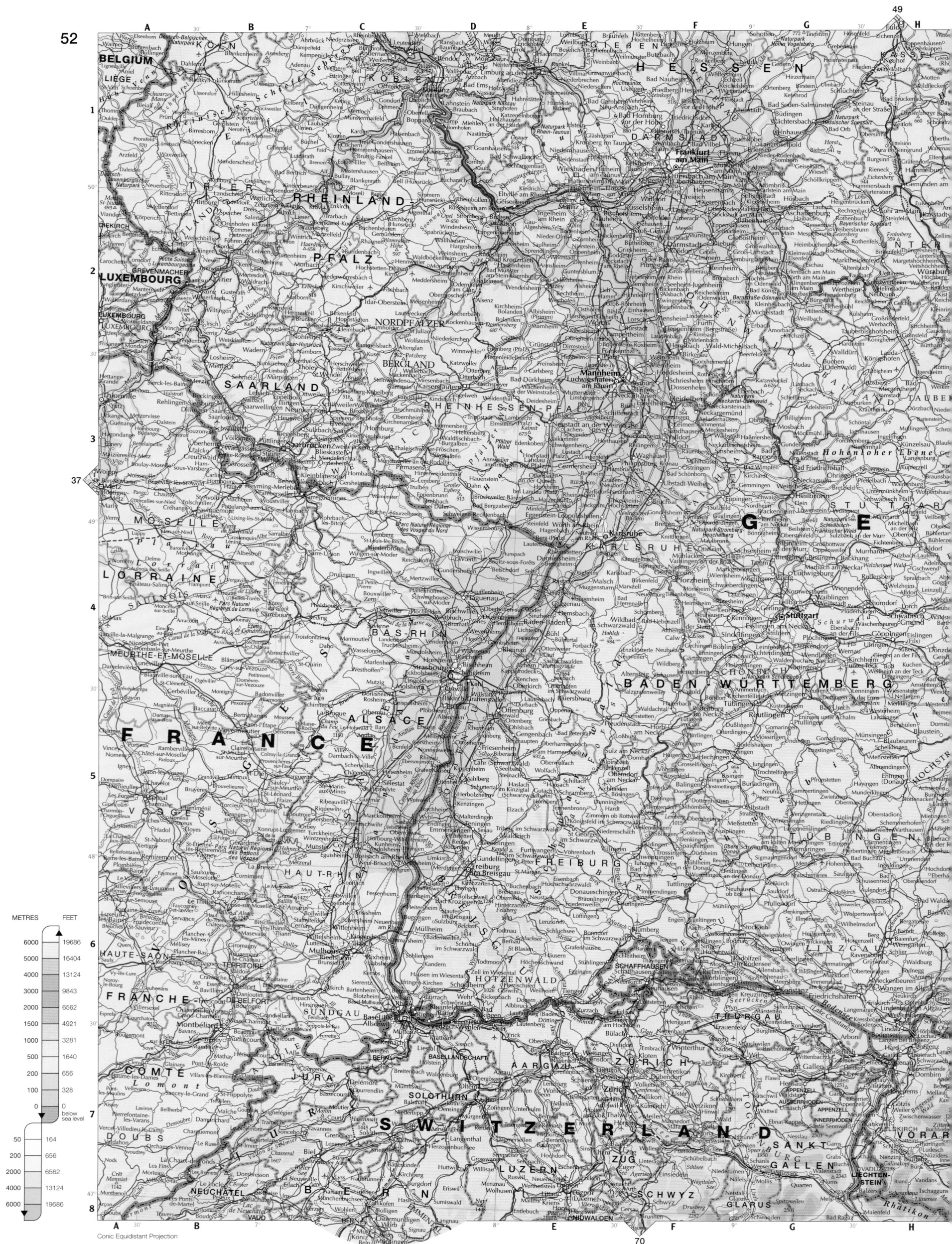
BELGIUM
LUXEMBOURG
FRANCE
SWITZERLAND
HESSEN
RHEINLAND-PFALZ
SAARLAND
BADEN-WÜRTTEMBERG
ALSACE
LORRAINE
MOSELLE
BAS-RHIN
HAUT-RHIN
MEURTHE-ET-MOSELLE
VOSGES
HAUTE-SAÔNE
FRANCHE-COMTÉ
DOUBS
JURA
NEUCHÂTEL
BERN
SOLOTHURN
BASELLANDSCHAFT
AARGAU
ZÜRICH
THURGAU
LUZERN
ZUG
SCHWYZ
GLARUS
APPENZELL
SANKT GALLEN
LIECHTENSTEIN
NORDPFÄLZER BERGLAND
STUTTGART
KARLSRUHE
FREIBURG
TÜBINGEN
KÖLN
KOBLENZ
TRIER
GIESSEN
DARMSTADT
KASSEL
Frankfurt am Main
Mannheim
Ludwigshafen am Rhein
Karlsruhe
Stuttgart
Strasbourg
Mulhouse
Basel
Zürich
Freiburg im Breisgau
Saarbrücken
Luxembourg
Heidelberg
Heilbronn
Mainz
Wiesbaden
Metz
Nancy
Bodensee
A B C D E F G H
1 2 3 4 5 6 7 8
49 37 70
METRES FEET
6000 19686
5000 16404
4000 13124
3000 9843
2000 6562
1500 4921
1000 3281
500 1640
200 656
100 328
0 0
below sea level
50 164
200 656
2000 6562
4000 13124
6000 19686

Conic Equidistant Projection

1:1 200 000

© Collins Bartholomew Ltd

THÜRINGEN
CHEMNITZ
VOGTLAND
ÚSTECKÝ KRAJ
KARLOVARSKÝ KRAJ
STŘEDOČESKÝ KRAJ
CZECH REPUBLIC
PLZEŇSKÝ KRAJ
JIHOČESKÝ KRAJ
OBERFRANKEN
MITTELFRANKEN
OBERPFALZ
GERMANY
BAYERN (BAVARIA)
NIEDERBAYERN
SCHWABEN
OBERBAYERN
OBERÖSTERREICH
AUSTRIA
SALZBURG
TIROL
OSTTIROL
KÄRNTEN
ITALY
Nürnberg
Regensburg
Augsburg
Ingolstadt
München (Munich)
Salzburg
Innsbruck
Plzeň
Fürth
Erlangen
Bamberg
Bayreuth
Landshut
Passau
Rosenheim
Longitude 12° east of Greenwich
51
54
56
58
MILES
KM

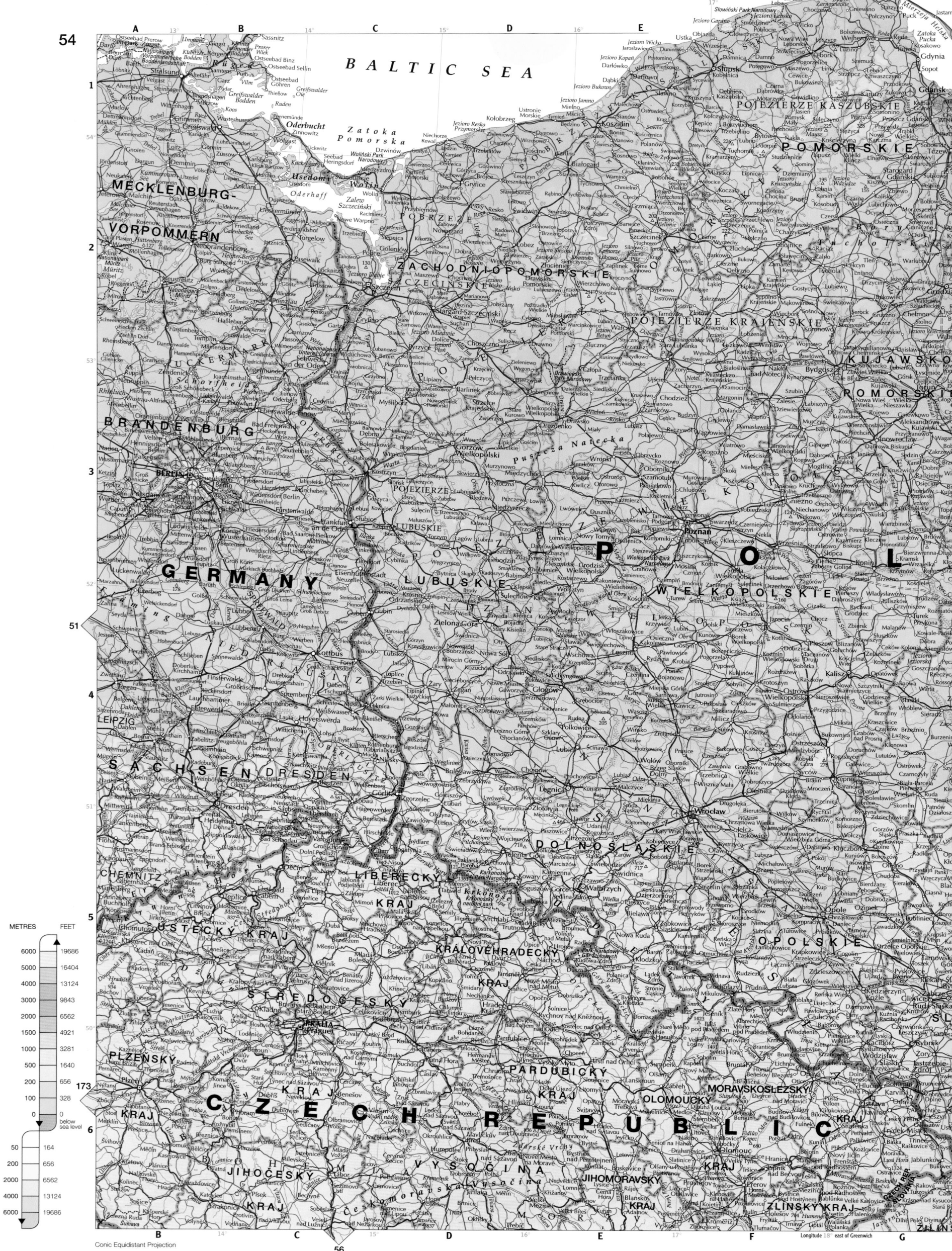
BALTIC SEA
MECKLENBURG-VORPOMMERN
BRANDENBURG
BERLIN
GERMANY
SACHSEN
DRESDEN
LEIPZIG
CHEMNITZ
ZACHODNIOPOMORSKIE
POMORSKIE
KUJAWSKO-POMORSKIE
WIELKOPOLSKIE
LUBUSKIE
DOLNOŚLĄSKIE
OPOLSKIE
POL
Poznań
Wrocław
Szczecin
Gdańsk
Gdynia
Koszalin
Słupsk
Bydgoszcz
Zielona Góra
Gorzów Wielkopolski
Legnica
Opole
Kalisz
Cottbus
Frankfurt an der Oder
Görlitz
LIBERECKÝ KRAJ
ÚSTECKÝ KRAJ
KRÁLOVÉHRADECKÝ KRAJ
STŘEDOČESKÝ KRAJ
PRAHA (Prague)
PLZEŇSKÝ KRAJ
PARDUBICKÝ KRAJ
OLOMOUCKÝ KRAJ
MORAVSKOSLEZSKÝ KRAJ
JIHOČESKÝ KRAJ
VYSOČINA
JIHOMORAVSKÝ KRAJ
ZLÍNSKÝ KRAJ
CZECH REPUBLIC
METRES
FEET
6000 19686
5000 16404
4000 13124
3000 9843
2000 6562
1500 4921
1000 3281
500 1640
200 656
100 328
0 0
below sea level
50 164
200 656
2000 6562
4000 13124
6000 19686
Longitude 18° east of Greenwich

51
173
56

Conic Equidistant Projection

GULF
OF
DAŃSK

RUSSIAN FEDERATION

LITHUANIA

WARMIŃSKO-MAZURSKIE

HRODZYENSKAYA

VOBLASTS'

BELARUS

PODLASKIE

Białystok

BRESTSKAYA

MAZOWIECKIE

WARSZAWA
(Warsaw)

VOBLASTS'

Brest

MAZOWIECKA

ŁÓDZKIE

Łódź

LUBELSKIE

Lublin

WYŻYNA LUBELSKA

WYŻYNA MAŁOPOLSKA

ŚWIĘTOKRZYSKIE

UKRAINE

MAŁOPOLSKIE

Kraków

PODKARPACKIE

CARPATHIAN MOUNTAINS

SLOVAKIA

PREŠOVSKÝ KRAJ

MILES
KM

1:1 800 000

© Collins Bartholomew Ltd

CZECH REPUBLIC
GERMANY
AUSTRIA
SLOVENIA
CROATIA
ITALY
SACHSEN
CHEMNITZ
ÚSTECKÝ KRAJ
LIBERECKÝ KRAJ
DOLNOŚLĄSKIE
KRÁLOVÉHRADECKÝ KRAJ
KARLOVARSKÝ KRAJ
STŘEDOČESKÝ KRAJ
PARDUBICKÝ KRAJ
OLOMOUCKÝ
OBERFRANKEN
PLZEŇSKÝ KRAJ
OBERPFALZ
VYSOČINA
JIHOČESKÝ KRAJ
JIHOMORAVSKÝ KRAJ
BAYERN
NIEDERBAYERN
NIEDERÖSTERREICH
OBERÖSTERREICH
BRATISLAVSKÝ KRAJ
OBERBAYERN
GYŐR-MOSON-SOPRON
TIROL
SALZBURG
STEIERMARK
BURGENLAND
VAS
KÄRNTEN
ZALA
VENETO
FRIULI-VENEZIA GIULIA
PRAHA (Prague)
WIEN (Vienna)
BRATISLAVA
LJUBLJANA
ZAGREB
METRES
FEET
6000
5000
4000
3000
2000
1500
1000
500
200
100
0
19686
16404
13124
9843
6562
4921
3281
1640
656
328
below sea level
50
200
2000
4000
164
656
6562
13124

Conic Equidistant Projection

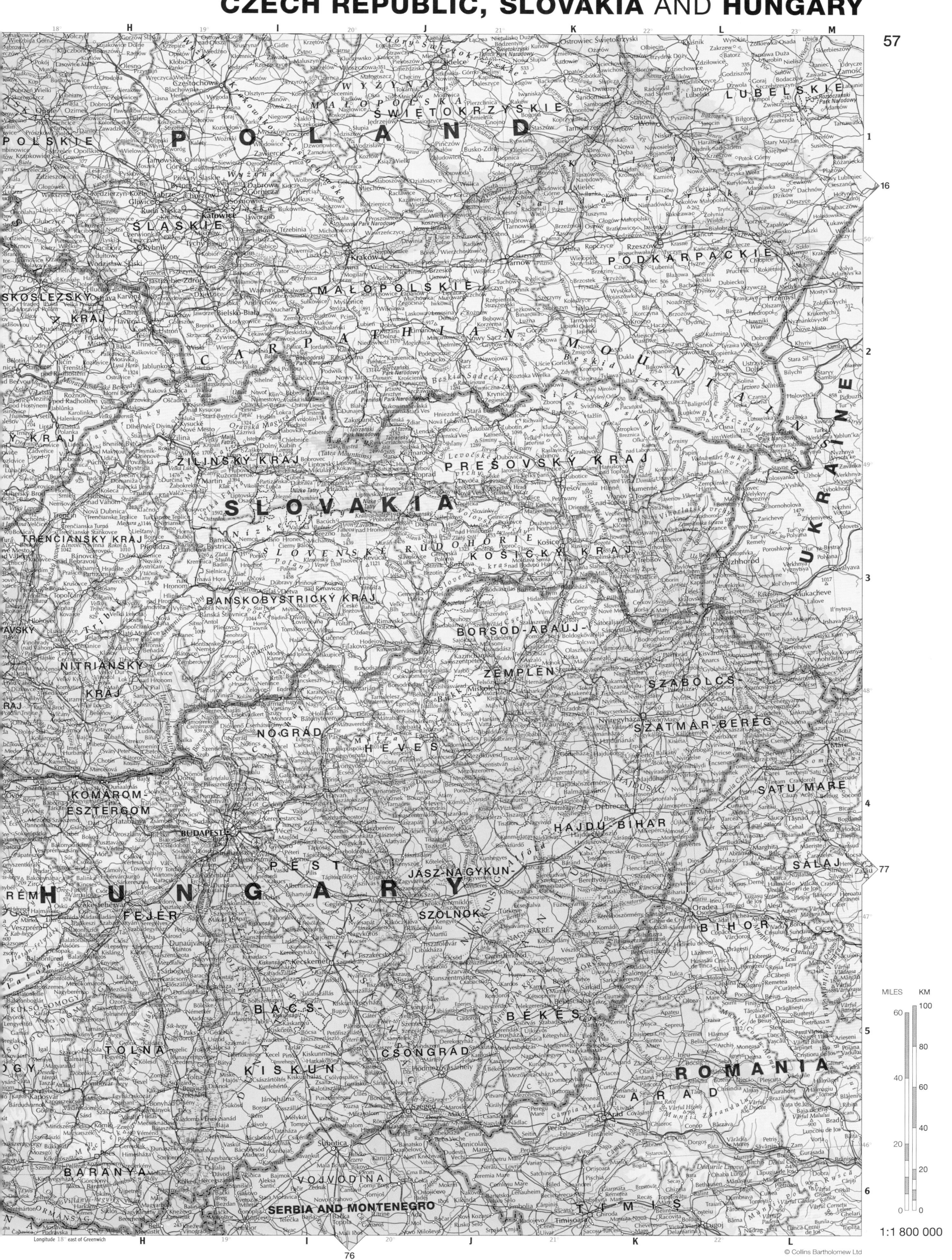

1:1 800 000

© Collins Bartholomew Ltd

CZECH REPUBLIC, SLOVAKIA AND HUNGARY
POLAND
SLOVAKIA
HUNGARY
UKRAINE
ROMANIA
SERBIA AND MONTENEGRO
CARPATHIAN MOUNTAINS
ŚWIĘTOKRZYSKIE
MAŁOPOLSKIE
ŚLĄSKIE
PODKARPACKIE
LUBELSKIE
ŽILINSKÝ KRAJ
PREŠOVSKÝ KRAJ
KOŠICKÝ KRAJ
BANSKOBYSTRICKÝ KRAJ
TRENČIANSKY KRAJ
NITRIANSKY KRAJ
BORSOD-ABAÚJ-ZEMPLÉN
SZABOLCS-SZATMÁR-BEREG
NÓGRÁD
HEVES
KOMÁROM-ESZTERGOM
PEST
JÁSZ-NAGYKUN-SZOLNOK
HAJDÚ-BIHAR
FEJÉR
BÁCS-KISKUN
BÉKÉS
CSONGRÁD
TOLNA
BARANYA
VOJVODINA
SATU MARE
SĂLAJ
BIHOR
ARAD
TIMIŞ
BUDAPEST
Kraków
Debrecen
Uzhhorod
Oradea
Szeged
Arad
Timişoara
Subotica
Katowice
Rzeszów
Tarnów
Košice
Prešov
Miskolc
Nyíregyháza
Kecskemét
Pécs
Longitude 18° east of Greenwich
MILES
KM

GERMANY
AUSTRIA
SWITZERLAND
ITALY
BAYERN
OBERBAYERN
NIEDERBAYERN
OBERPFALZ
MITTELFRANKEN
SCHWABEN
BADEN
WÜRTTEMBERG
STUTTGART
TÜBINGEN
TIROL
OSTTIROL
VORARLBERG
SALZBURG
GRAUBÜNDEN
BOLZANO
TRENTINO
ALTO ADIGE
TRENTO
BELLUNO
VENETO
VICENZA
TREVISO
LOMBARDIA
SONDRIO
BRESCIA
BERGAMO
FRIULI
PORDENONE
VENEZIA GIULIA
München (Munich)
Innsbruck
Salzburg
Augsburg
Regensburg
Ingolstadt
Bolzano
Trento
53
52
70
A B C D E F G
1 2 3 4 5 6 7 8
Longitude 12° east of Greenwich
Conic Equidistant Projection

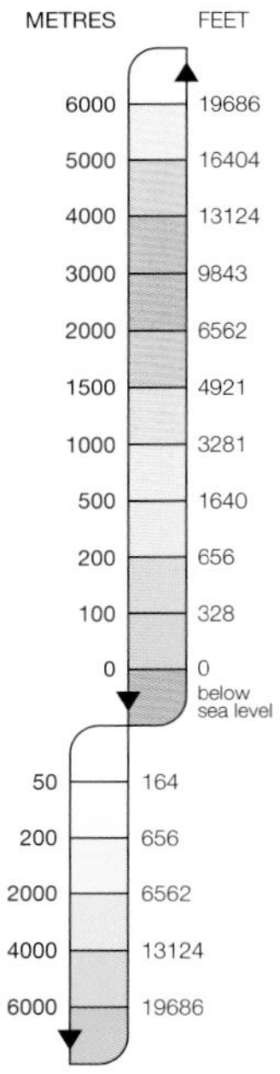
METRES
FEET
6000 19686
5000 16404
4000 13124
3000 9843
2000 6562
1500 4921
1000 3281
500 1640
200 656
100 328
0 0
below sea level
50 164
200 656
2000 6562
4000 13124
6000 19686

CZECH REPUBLIC

JIHOČESKÝ KRAJ

VYSOČINA

JIHOMORAVSKÝ KRAJ

NIEDERÖSTERREICH

WIEN

WIEN
(Vienna)

OBERÖSTERREICH

STEIERMARK

KÄRNTEN

BURGENLAND

HUNGARY

VAS

ZALA

SLOVENIA

CROATIA

ZAGREB

LJUBLJANA

GYÖR-MOSON-SOPRON

AUSTRIA
SLOVAKIA

MILES   KM

1:1 200 000

© Collins Bartholomew Ltd

ATLANTIC OCEAN

Mar Cantábrico

BAYO

GALICIA

CORDILLERA CANTÁBRICA

ASTURIAS

CANTABRIA

CASTILLA Y LEÓ

VIANA DO CASTELO

MINHO

BRAGA

VILA REAL

BRAGANÇA

PORTO

VISEU

BEIRA ALTA

GUARDA

P O R T U G A L

COIMBRA

CASTELO BRANCO

LEIRIA

SANTAREM

EXTREMADURA

E S P A

MADRID

CAS

LA

LISBOA

PORTALEGRE

ÉVORA

SETÚBAL

BEJA

SIERRA MORENA

ANDALUCÍA

ALGARVE

FARO

GOLFO DE CÁDIZ

Costa del Sol

Costa

Strait of Gibralta

MOROCCO

TANGER-TETOUAN

ORIENTAL

METRES	FEET
6000	19686
5000	16404
4000	13124
3000	9843
2000	6562
1500	4921
1000	3281
500	1640
200	656
100	328
0	0
	below sea level
50	164
200	656
2000	6562
4000	13124
6000	19686

Conic Equidistant Projection

Longitude 8° west of Greenwich

34
BISCAY
FRANCE
AQUITAINE
MIDI-PYRÉNÉES
LANGUEDOC
ROUSSILLON
PROVENCE-ALPES-CÔTE-D'AZUR
GOLFE DU LION
PYRÉNÉES
ANDORRA
NAVARRA
LA RIOJA
ARAGÓN
CATALUÑA
VALENCIA
MURCIA
Toulouse
Marseille
Montpellier
Bayonne
Pau
Perpignan
Donostia-San Sebastián
Vitoria-Gasteiz
Pamplona (Iruña)
Logroño
Zaragoza
Lleida
Tarragona
Barcelona
Girona (Gerona)
Teruel
Castelló de la Plana
Valencia
Alicante
Albacete
Murcia
Cartagena
Almería
Costa Brava
Costa Dorada
Costa del Azahar
Costa Blanca
Golfo de Valencia
Illes Columbretes
ILLES BALEARS
ISLAS BALEARES (BALEARIC ISLANDS)
Mallorca (Majorca)
Palma de Mallorca
Menorca (Minorca)
Mahón (Maó)
Eivissa (Ibiza)
Formentera
Cabrera
MEDITERRANEAN SEA
ALGERIA
CANARY ISLANDS
(Spain)
AT THE SAME SCALE
ATLANTIC OCEAN
ISLAS CANARIAS (CANARY ISLANDS)
La Palma
El Hierro
La Gomera
Tenerife
Gran Canaria
Fuerteventura
Lanzarote
Santa Cruz de Tenerife
Las Palmas de Gran Canaria
Puerto del Rosario
Arrecife
MILES
KM
1:3 000 000

Mar Cantábrico
ATLANTIC OCEAN
PORTUGAL
GALICIA
A CORUÑA
LUGO
OURENSE
PONTEVEDRA
ASTURIAS
OVIEDO
LEÓN
ZAMORA
SALAMANCA
CÁCERES
EXTREMADURA
VIANA DO CASTELO
MINHO
BRAGA
VILA REAL
BRAGANÇA
TRÁS-OS-MONTES
PORTO
DOURO
AVEIRO
VISEU
BEIRA ALTA
GUARDA
COIMBRA
CASTELO BRANCO
BEIRA BAIXA
LEIRIA
A Coruña (La Coruña)
Santiago de Compostela
Ferrol
Lugo
Ourense (Orense)
Vigo
Pontevedra
Porto (Oporto)
Braga
Viana do Castelo
Aveiro
Coimbra
Viseu
Guarda
Bragança
Vila Real
Castelo Branco
Leiria
Figueira da Foz
Oviedo
Avilés
Ponferrada
Astorga
Zamora
Salamanca
Ciudad Rodrigo
Plasencia
Cáceres
Cabo Ortegal
Cabo Fisterra (Cape Finisterre)
Cabo Touriñán
Cabo Mondego
Cabo de Peñas
Parque Nacional da Peneda Gerês
Parque Natural da Serra da Estrela
Serra da Estrela
Sierra de Gata
Sierra de la Culebra
Sierra de Gredos
Douro
Tajo (Tagus)
METRES
FEET
6000
5000
4000
3000
2000
1500
1000
500
200
100
0
19686
16404
13124
9843
6562
4921
3281
1640
656
328
below sea level
50
164
A B C D E F G H I
1 2 3 4 5 6 7 8 9

Conic Equidistant Projection

64

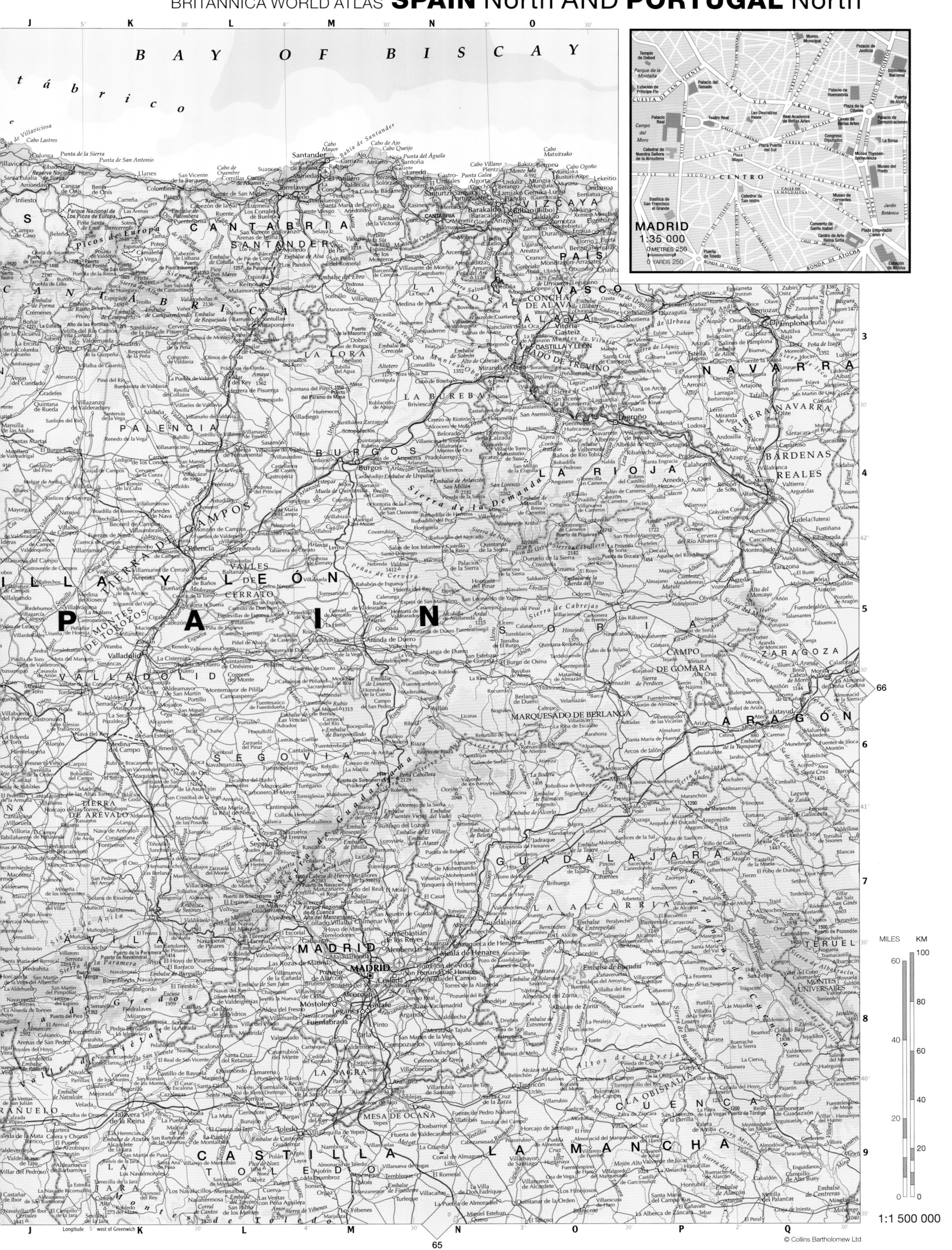

BAY OF BISCAY

MADRID
1:35 000

SPAIN

PORTUGAL

© Collins Bartholomew Ltd

1:1 500 000

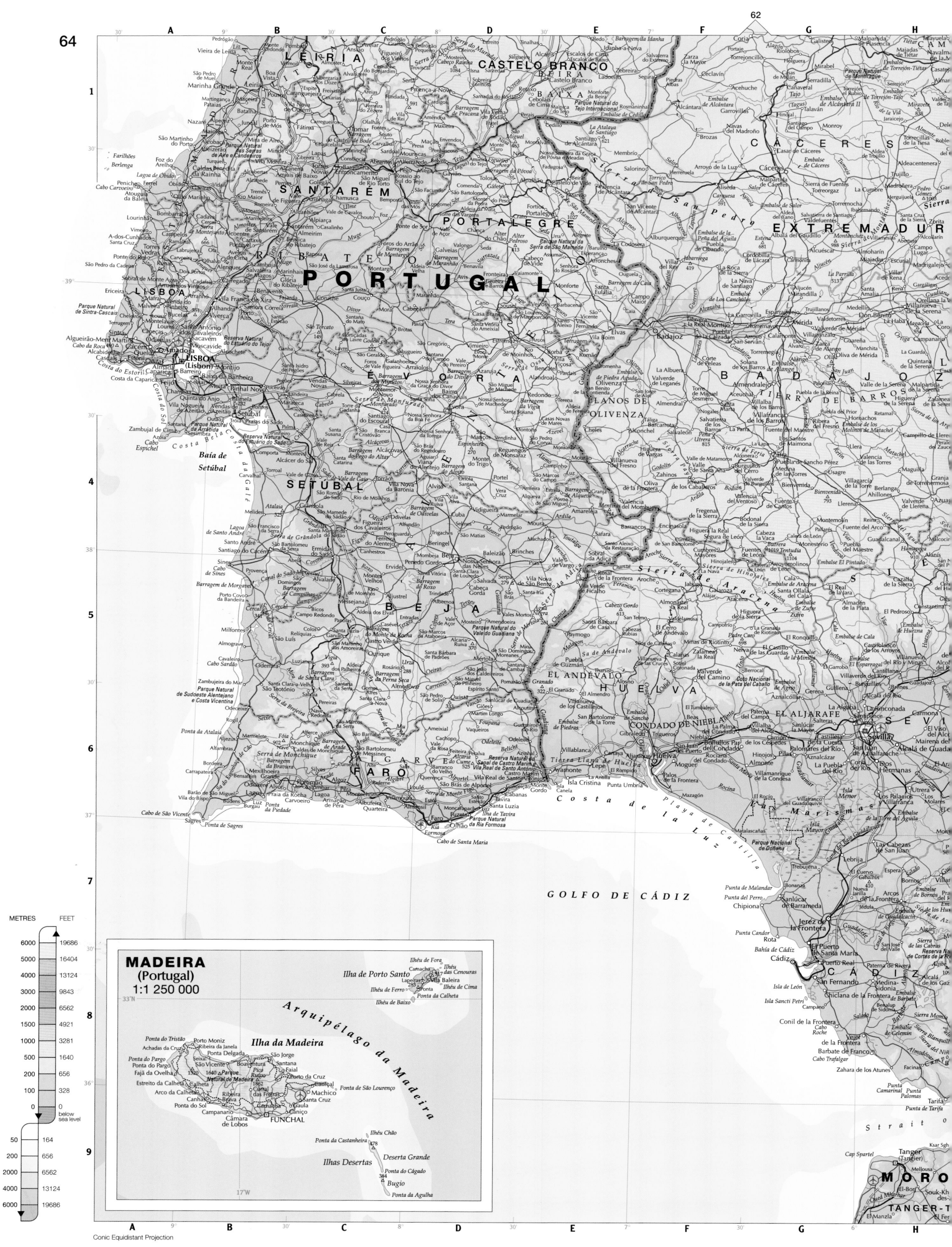
62
A B C D E F G H
1 4 5 6 7 8 9
PORTUGAL
LEIRIA
CASTELO BRANCO
BEIRA BAIXA
SANTARÉM
RIBATEJO
PORTALEGRE
LISBOA
Lisboa (Lisbon)
ÉVORA
ALENTEJO
SETÚBAL
BEJA
ALGARVE
FARO
CÁCERES
EXTREMADURA
BADAJOZ
TIERRA DE BARROS
LLANOS DE OLIVENZA
HUELVA
EL ANDÉVALO
CONDADO DE NIEBLA
EL ALJARAFE
CÁDIZ
Sevilla
Badajoz
Mérida
Cáceres
Huelva
Cádiz
Jerez de la Frontera
Tanger
Sierra de San Pedro
Sierra de Aracena
Baía de Setúbal
Costa do Sol
Costa da Galé
Costa de la Luz
Playa de Castilla
GOLFO DE CÁDIZ
Las Marismas
Parque Nacional de Doñana
Cabo de São Vicente
Cabo de Santa Maria
Strait
MORO
TANGER-T
MADEIRA
(Portugal)
1:1 250 000
Arquipélago da Madeira
Ilha da Madeira
Ilha de Porto Santo
Ilhas Desertas
Deserta Grande
Bugio
FUNCHAL
Machico
Câmara de Lobos
33°N
17°W
METRES FEET
6000 19686
5000 16404
4000 13124
3000 9843
2000 6562
1500 4921
1000 3281
500 1640
200 656
100 328
0 0
below sea level
50 164
200 656
2000 6562
4000 13124
6000 19686

Conic Equidistant Projection

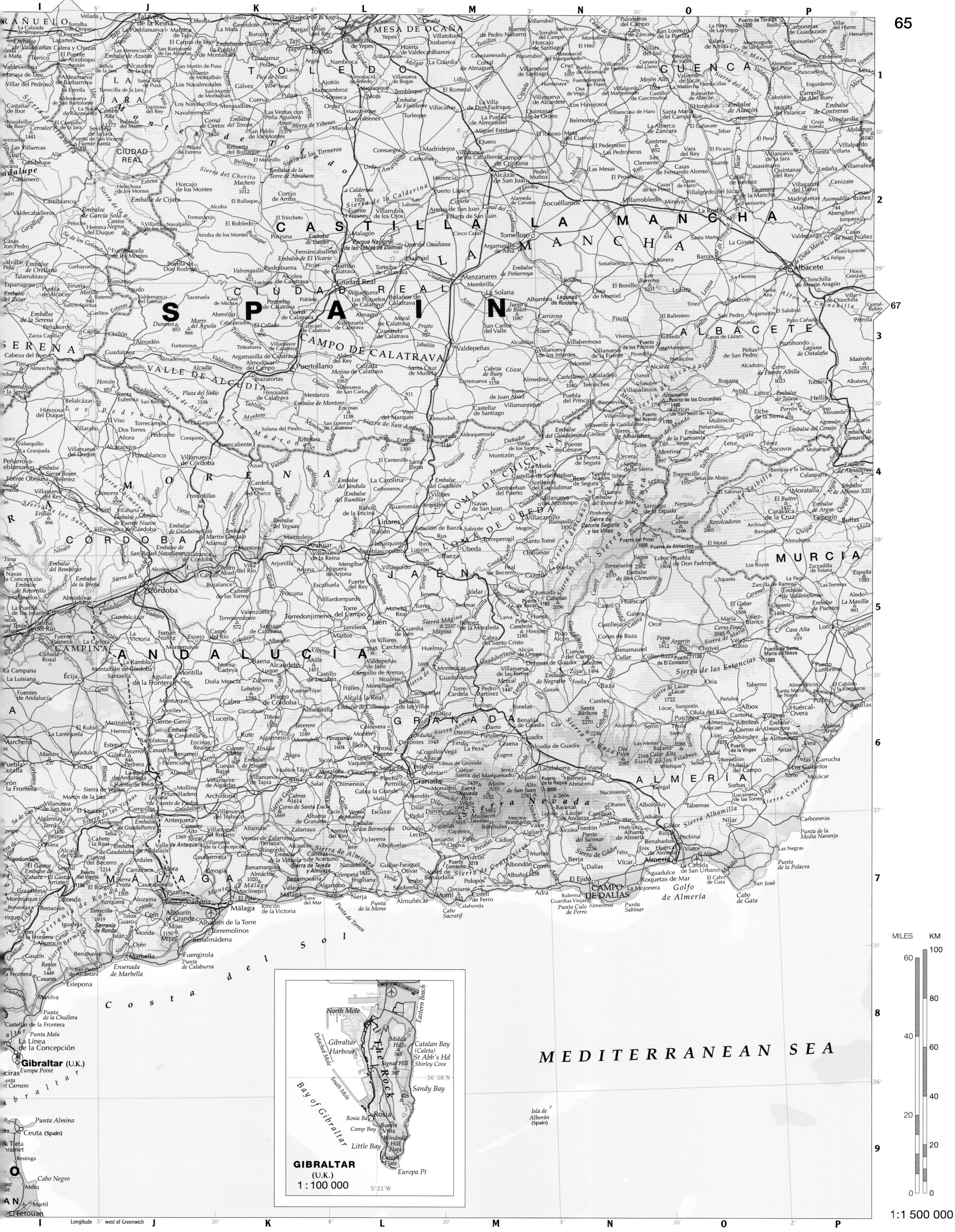
63
67
SPAIN
CASTILLA-LA MANCHA
TOLEDO
CUENCA
CIUDAD REAL
ALBACETE
MURCIA
CÓRDOBA
JAÉN
GRANADA
ALMERÍA
MÁLAGA
ANDALUCÍA
MESA DE OCAÑA
CAMPO DE CALATRAVA
VALLE DE ALCUDIA
Sierra Morena
Sierra Nevada
LOMA DE CHICLANA
LOMA DE ÚBEDA
CAMPO DE DALÍAS
Costa del Sol
MEDITERRANEAN SEA
Golfo de Almería
Gibraltar (U.K.)
Ceuta (Spain)
Isla de Alborán (Spain)
Toledo
Ciudad Real
Albacete
Córdoba
Jaén
Granada
Almería
Málaga
Puertollano
Linares
Úbeda
Valdepeñas
Manzanares
Tomelloso
Alcázar de San Juan
Estepona
Marbella
Fuengirola
Torremolinos
Motril
Nerja
La Línea de la Concepción
Lorca
Hellín
GIBRALTAR
(U.K.)
1 : 100 000
North Mole
Gibraltar Harbour
The Rock
Catalan Bay (Caleta)
Eastern Beach
Sandy Bay
Rosia Bay
Camp Bay
Little Bay
Europa Pt
Bay of Gibraltar
5°21'W
36°08'N
Longitude 5° west of Greenwich
MILES
KM

1:1 500 000

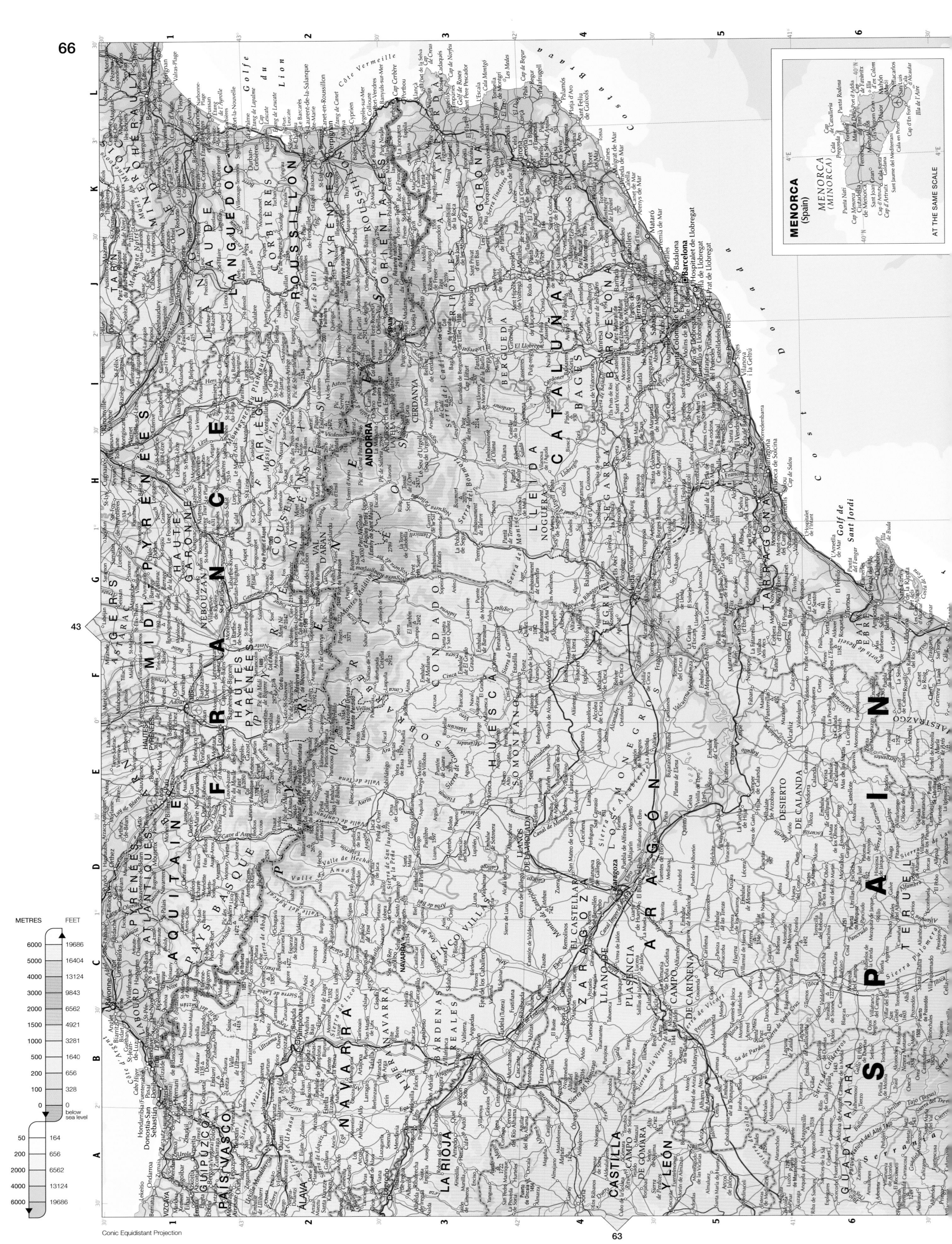

Conic Equidistant Projection

MENORCA
(Spain)

MENORCA
(MINORCA)

AT THE SAME SCALE

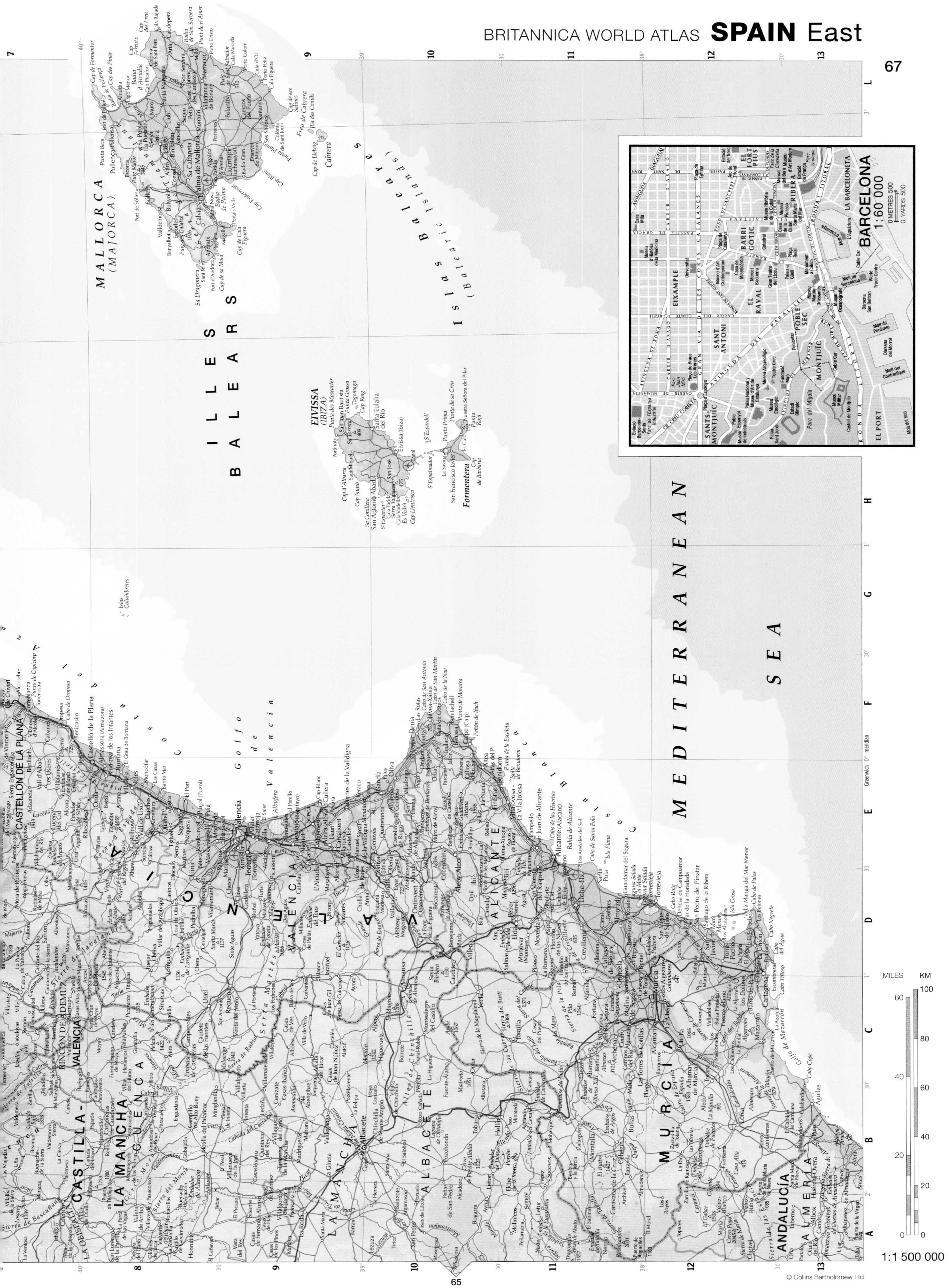
MALLORCA (MAJORCA)
Palma de Mallorca
ILLES BALEARS
Islas Baleares (Balearic Islands)
EIVISSA (IBIZA)
Formentera
Cabrera
MEDITERRANEAN SEA
Golfo de Valencia
Costa Blanca
CASTELLÓN DE LA PLANA
Castelló de la Plana
Valencia
VALENCIA
ALICANTE
Alicante
Benidorm
Elche-Elx
Cartagena
MURCIA
Murcia
ALBACETE
Albacete
CASTILLA-LA MANCHA
CUENCA
LA MANCHA
ANDALUCÍA
ALMERÍA
BARCELONA
1:60 000
EIXAMPLE
BARRI GÒTIC
EL RAVAL
POBLE SEC
SANT ANTONI
MONTJUÏC
EL PORT
LA BARCELONETA
RIBERA
SANTS-MONTJUÏC
MILES
KM
1:1 500 000

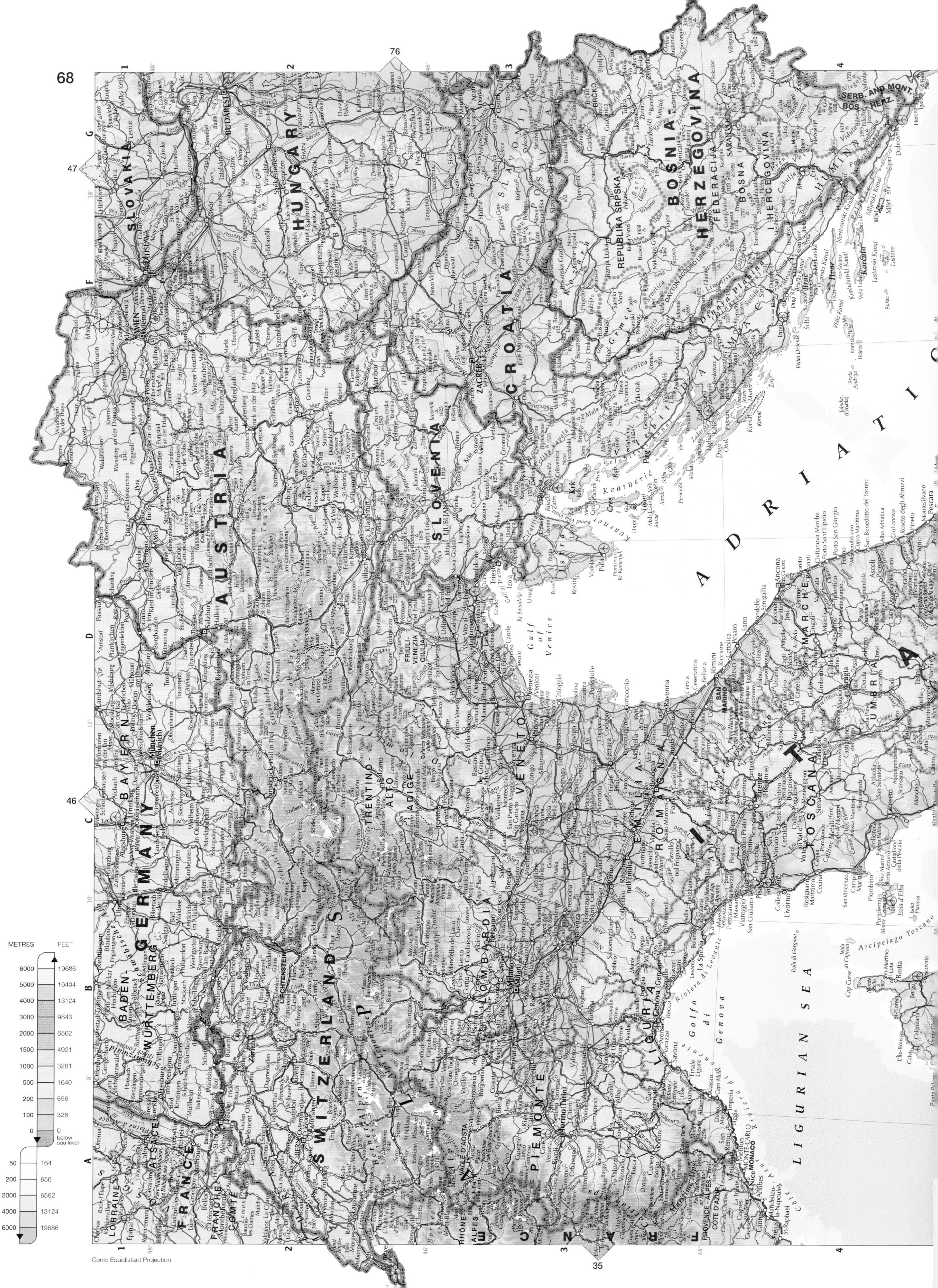

AUSTRIA
GERMANY
BAYERN
BADEN-WÜRTTEMBERG
SWITZERLAND
LIECHTENSTEIN
FRANCE
ALSACE
LORRAINE
FRANCHE-COMTÉ
RHÔNE-ALPES
PROVENCE-ALPES-CÔTE D'AZUR
MONACO
ITALY
VALLE D'AOSTA
PIEMONTE
LOMBARDIA
LIGURIA
TRENTINO-ALTO ADIGE
VENETO
FRIULI-VENEZIA GIULIA
EMILIA-ROMAGNA
TOSCANA
UMBRIA
MARCHE
SAN MARINO
SLOVENIA
CROATIA
HUNGARY
SLOVAKIA
BOSNIA-HERZEGOVINA
REPUBLIKA SRPSKA
FEDERACIJA BOSNA I HERCEGOVINA
SERB. AND MONT.
DAYTON ACCORD LINE 1995
ADRIATIC SEA
Gulf of Venice
Golfo di Genova
LIGURIAN SEA
Arcipelago Toscano
METRES
FEET
6000 19686
5000 16404
4000 13124
3000 9843
2000 6562
1500 4921
1000 3281
500 1640
200 656
100 328
0 0 below sea level
50 164
200 656
2000 6562
4000 13124
6000 19686
Conic Equidistant Projection
76
35

ITALY, SLOVENIA, CROATIA AND BOSNIA-HERZEGOVINA

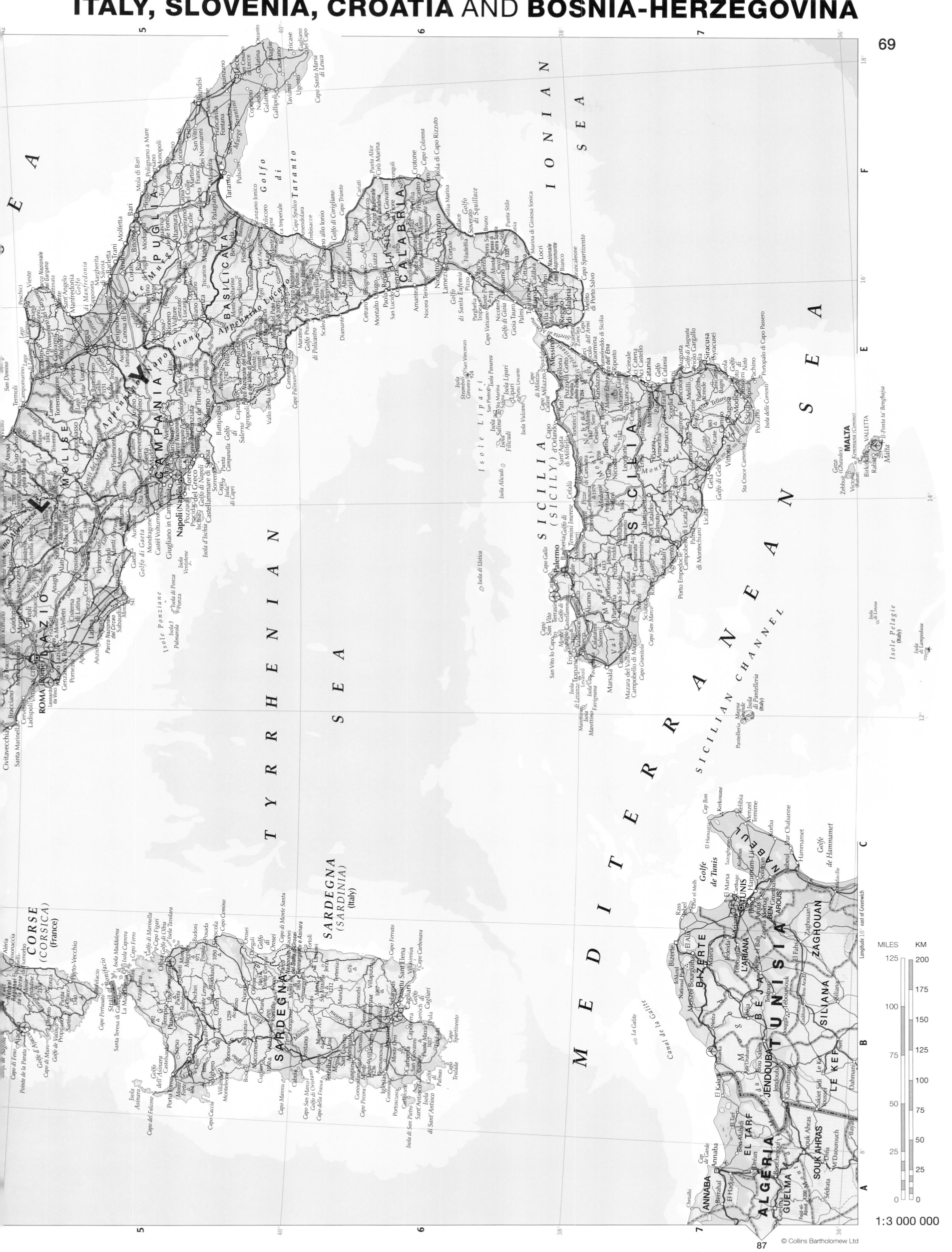
TYRRHENIAN SEA
IONIAN SEA
MEDITERRANEAN SEA
SICILIAN CHANNEL
SICILIA (SICILY)
SARDEGNA (SARDINIA) (Italy)
CORSE (CORSICA) (France)
MALTA
VALLETTA
TUNISIA
ALGERIA
LAZIO
CAMPANIA
BASILICATA
CALABRIA
PUGLIA
MOLISE
ROMA
Napoli (Naples)
Palermo
Catania
Messina
Cagliari
Sassari
Taranto
Bari
TUNIS
Golfo di Taranto
Isole Lipari
Isole Pelagie (Italy)
MILES
KM
1:3 000 000

Swiss Cantons numbered on the map:
1. APPENZELL AUSSERRHODEN (E1)
2. APPENZELL INNERRHODEN (E1)
3. FRIBOURG (B2)
4. VAUD (C2)

METRES FEET
6000 19686
5000 16404
4000 13124
3000 9843
2000 6562
1500 4921
1000 3281
500 1640
200 656
100 328
0 0
below sea level

50 164
200 656
2000 6562
4000 13124
6000 19686

Conic Equidistant Projection

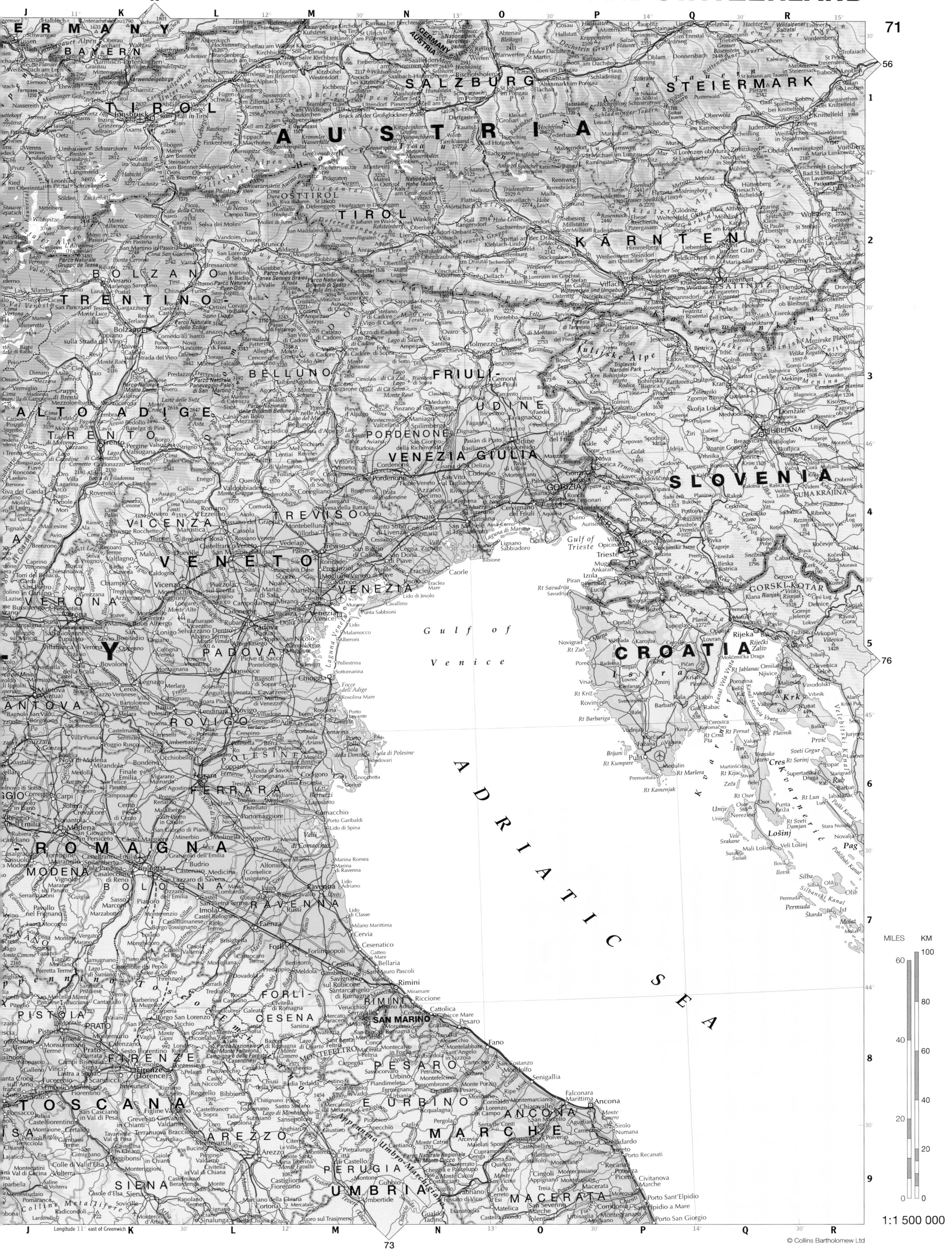
AUSTRIA
SLOVENIA
CROATIA
SALZBURG
STEIERMARK
TIROL
KÄRNTEN
BAYERN
BOLZANO
TRENTINO-
ALTO ADIGE
TRENTO
BELLUNO
FRIULI-
VENEZIA GIULIA
UDINE
PORDENONE
GORIZIA
TREVISO
VICENZA
VENETO
VERONA
PADOVA
VENEZIA
ROVIGO
MANTOVA
FERRARA
ROMAGNA
MODENA
BOLOGNA
RAVENNA
FORLÌ-
CESENA
RIMINI
SAN MARINO
PESARO
E URBINO
ANCONA
MARCHE
MACERATA
PERUGIA
UMBRIA
AREZZO
SIENA
FIRENZE
TOSCANA
PISTOIA
PRATO
Gulf of Venice
Gulf of Trieste
ADRIATIC SEA
Trieste
Ljubljana
Rijeka
Cres
Lošinj
Krk
Pag
MILES
KM
Longitude 11° east of Greenwich

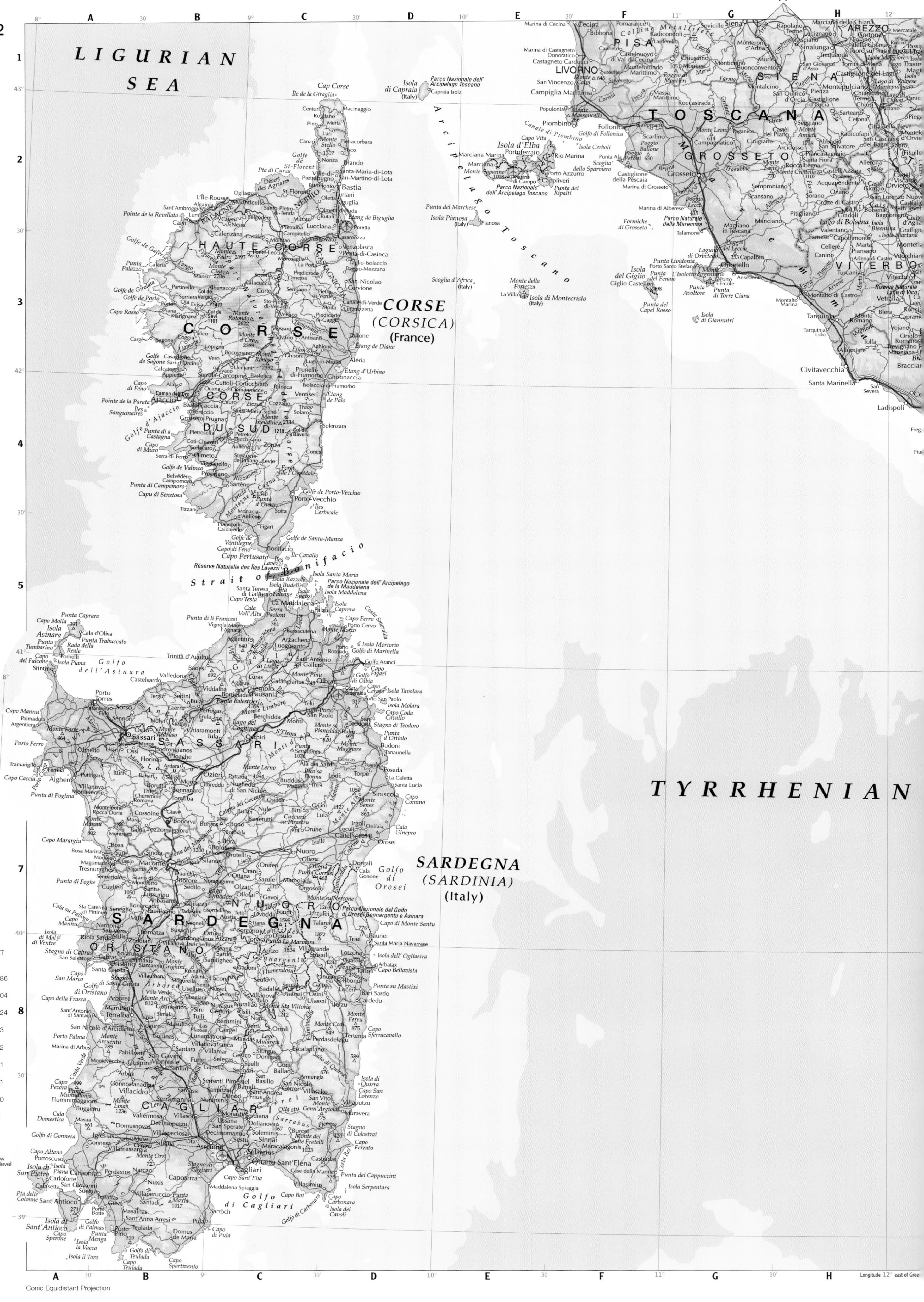
LIGURIAN SEA
TYRRHENIAN
CORSE
(CORSICA)
(France)
SARDEGNA
(SARDINIA)
(Italy)
HAUTE-CORSE
CORSE-DU-SUD
SASSARI
NUORO
ORISTANO
CAGLIARI
TOSCANA
PISA
LIVORNO
SIENA
GROSSETO
VITERBO
AREZZO
Strait of Bonifacio
Arcipelago Toscano
Golfo dell'Asinara
Golfo di Orosei
Golfo di Cagliari
Isola d'Elba
Isola di Capraia
Isola Pianosa
Isola di Montecristo
Isola del Giglio
Isola Asinara
Isola di San Pietro
Isola di Sant'Antioco
Bastia
Ajaccio
Porto-Vecchio
Bonifacio
Sassari
Alghero
Olbia
Nuoro
Oristano
Cagliari
Iglesias
Civitavecchia
Piombino
Cap Corse
Capo Teulada
Capo Carbonara
Conic Equidistant Projection

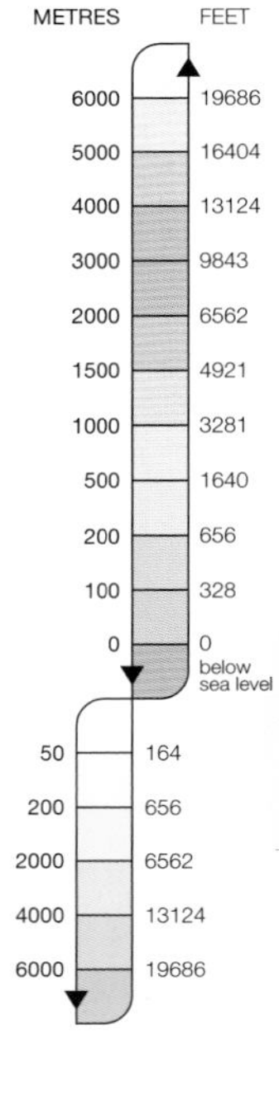
METRES
FEET
6000 19686
5000 16404
4000 13124
3000 9843
2000 6562
1500 4921
1000 3281
500 1640
200 656
100 328
0 0
below sea level
50 164
200 656
2000 6562
4000 13124
6000 19686

ITALY Central

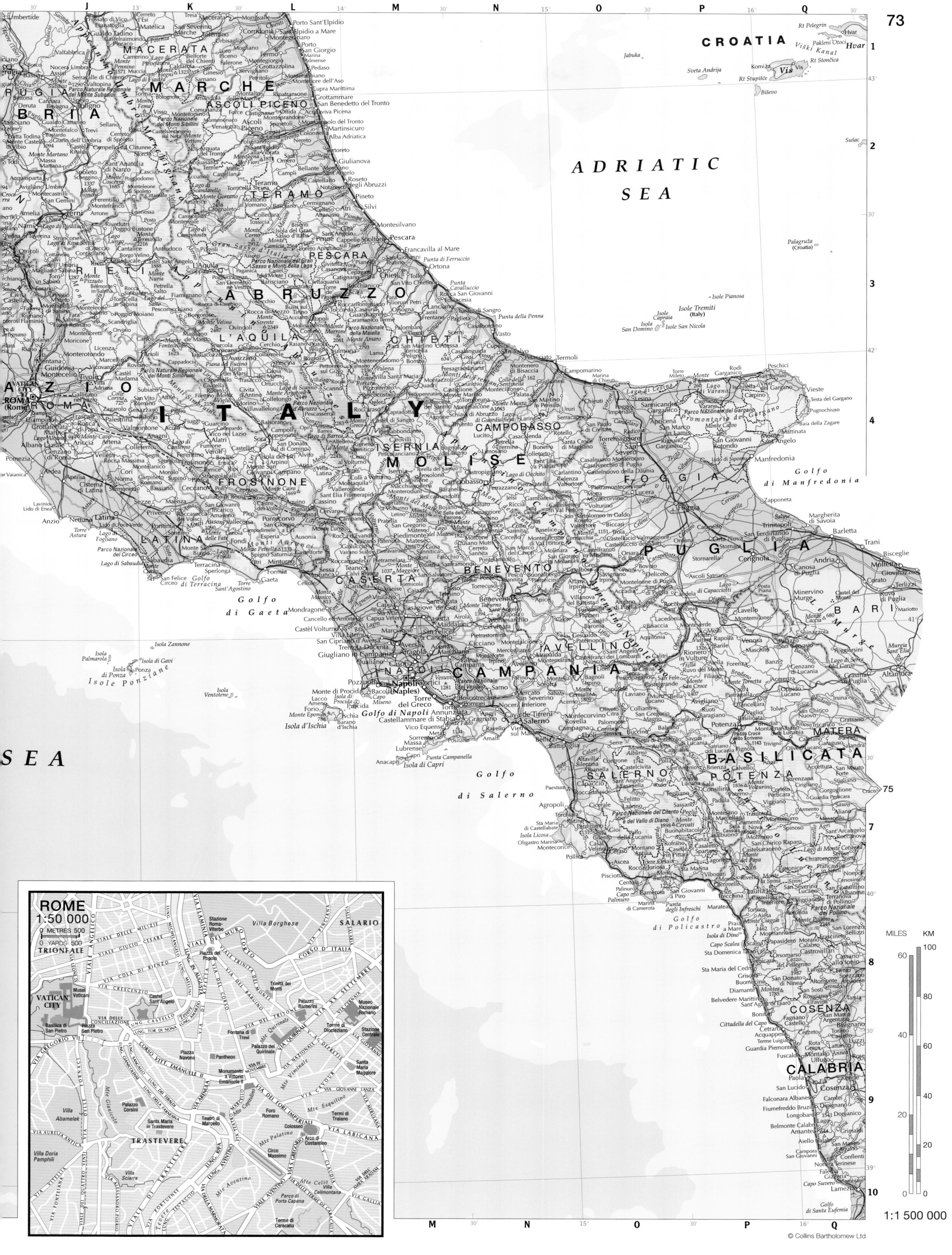

CROATIA

ADRIATIC SEA

SEA

MARCHE
MACERATA
ASCOLI PICENO
TERAMO
ABRUZZO
PESCARA
L'AQUILA
CHIETI
ROMA
ROMA (Rome)
VATICAN CITY
ITALY
MOLISE
ISERNIA
CAMPOBASSO
FROSINONE
LATINA
CASERTA
BENEVENTO
FOGGIA
PUGLIA
AVELLINO
CAMPANIA
NAPOLI (Naples)
BARI
SALERNO
POTENZA
BASILICATA
MATERA
COSENZA
CALABRIA

Golfo di Manfredonia
Golfo di Gaeta
Golfo di Napoli
Golfo di Salerno
Golfo di Policastro
Golfo di Sant'Eufemia

Isole Tremiti (Italy)
Isola di Ponza
Isole Ponziane
Isola d'Ischia
Isola di Capri

Promontorio del Gargano

ROME 1:50 000
0 METRES 500
0 YARDS 500

VATICAN CITY
Basilica di San Pietro
Piazza San Pietro
Castel Sant'Angelo
Villa Borghese
Pantheon
Fontana di Trevi
Palazzo del Quirinale
Terme di Diocleziano
Stazione Centrale
Santa Maria Maggiore
Colosseo
Foro Romano
Circo Massimo
Terme di Caracalla
TRASTEVERE
TRIONFALE
SALARIO

MILES KM

1:1 500 000

© Collins Bartholomew Ltd

A 11° 30' B 12° C 30' D 13° E 30' F 14° G H

TYRRHENIAN SEA

METRES FEET
6000 19686
5000 16404
4000 13124
3000 9843
2000 6562
1500 4921
1000 3281
500 1640
200 656
100 328
0 0
below
sea level
50 164
200 656
2000 6562
4000 13124
6000 19686

Isola Zannone
Isola
Palmarola
Isola di Gavi
Isola di Ponza
Ponza
Isole Ponziane

Isola Ventotene

CASERTA
BENEVENTO
Mondragone
Cancello ed Arnone
Castèl Volturno
San Cipriano d'Aversa
Trentola-Ducenta
Giugliano in Campania
Marano di Napoli
Napoli
Naples
CAMP
Pozzuoli
Monte di Procida
Bacoli
Isola di Procida
Capo
Miseno
Lacco Ameno
Forio
Procida
Monte Epomeo
Torre del Greco
Ischia
Torre
Annunziata
Isola d'Ischia
Barano
d'Ischia
Castellammare di Stabia
Vico Equense
Sorrento
Massa Lubrense
Praiano
Anacapri
Capri
Punta
Campanella
Isola di Capri

Golfo di Napoli
Golfo
di Salerno

Sta Maria di Castel
Isola Licosi
Oligastro M

Isola di Ustica
Ustica

Isole Lipar

Isola Alicudi
Filicudi
Porto
Isola Filicudi

Isola Lipar

Porto L
Isola Vule

Capo San Vito
Punta
Raisi
Isola delle
Femmine
Capo Gallo
Mondello
Golfo
di Castellammare
Golfo
di Palermo
SICILIA
(SICILY)
Capo d'Orlando

San Vito lo Capo
Terrasini
Carini
Montelepre
Palermo
Capo Zafferano
Sant'Agata di Militello
Custonaci
Erice
Valderice
Monreale
Bagheria
Golfo
di Termini Imerese
Cefalù
Sto Stefano
Isola
Marettimo
Isola di Levanzo
Trapani
Castellammare
del Golfo
Balestrate
Belmonte Mezzagno
Termini Imerese di Roccella
Caronia
San Fratello
Marettimo
Levanzo
Misilmeri
Piana degli Albanesi
Trabia
Collesano
Castelbuono
Mistretta
Favignana
Calatafimi
Camporeale
San Cipirello
Bauclna
Isnello
Madonie
Petralia Sottana
Nicosia
Isola
Favignana
Isola
Grande
Vita
San Giuseppe Iato
Marineo
Cesarò
Troina
Marsala
TRAPANI
Salemi
Corleone
Vicari
Montemaggiore
Cerami
Petrosino
Gibellini
Roccamena
Alia
Valledolmo
Sperlinga
Partanna
Monreale
Contessa
Prizzi
Lercara
Cammarata
ENNA
Castelvetrano
Sambuca
Chiusa
Sclafani
Palazzo
Adriano
SICILIA
Mazara del Vallo
Campobello
di Mazara
Menfi
Burgio
Bivona
San
Giovanni
Gemini
Villalba
Enna
Caltanissetta
CATANIA
Sta Caterina
Villarosa
Castelfranco
Villarosa
Sciacca
Ribera
AGRIGENTO
Racalmuto
Aragona
Favara
Naro
Agrigento
CALTANISSETTA
Pietraperzia
Piazza
Armerina
Porto
Empedocle
Canicattì
Campobello
di Licata
Riesi
Mazzarino
Caltagirone
Licata
Gela
Golfo di Gela
Vittoria
RAGUSA
Ragusa

Cap Bon
El Haouaria
Kerkouane
TUNISIA
Kelibia

SICILIAN CHANNEL

SICILIAN CHANNEL

Pantelleria
Isola di Pantelleria
(Italy)
Scauri

A 30' B 12° C D 13° E 30' F 14°

Conic Equidistant Projection

75

ADRIATIC

SEA

Strait of Otranto

PUGLIA

BRINDISI

LECCE

GOLFO

DI

TARANTO

BASILICATA

POTENZA

MATERA

COSENZA

LA SILA

CROTONE

CALABRIA

CATANZARO

Golfo di Santa Eufemia

Golfo di Squillace

IONIAN

SEA

VIBO VALENTIA

Golfo di Gioia

REGGIO DI CALABRIA

Golfo di Catania

Golfo di Augusta

Golfo di Noto

MALTA
1 : 500 000

Gozo
(Ghawdex)

Malta

Kemmuna (Comino)

MILES   KM

60   100

80

40   60

40

20

20

0   0

1 : 1 500 000

Longitude 16° east of Greenwich

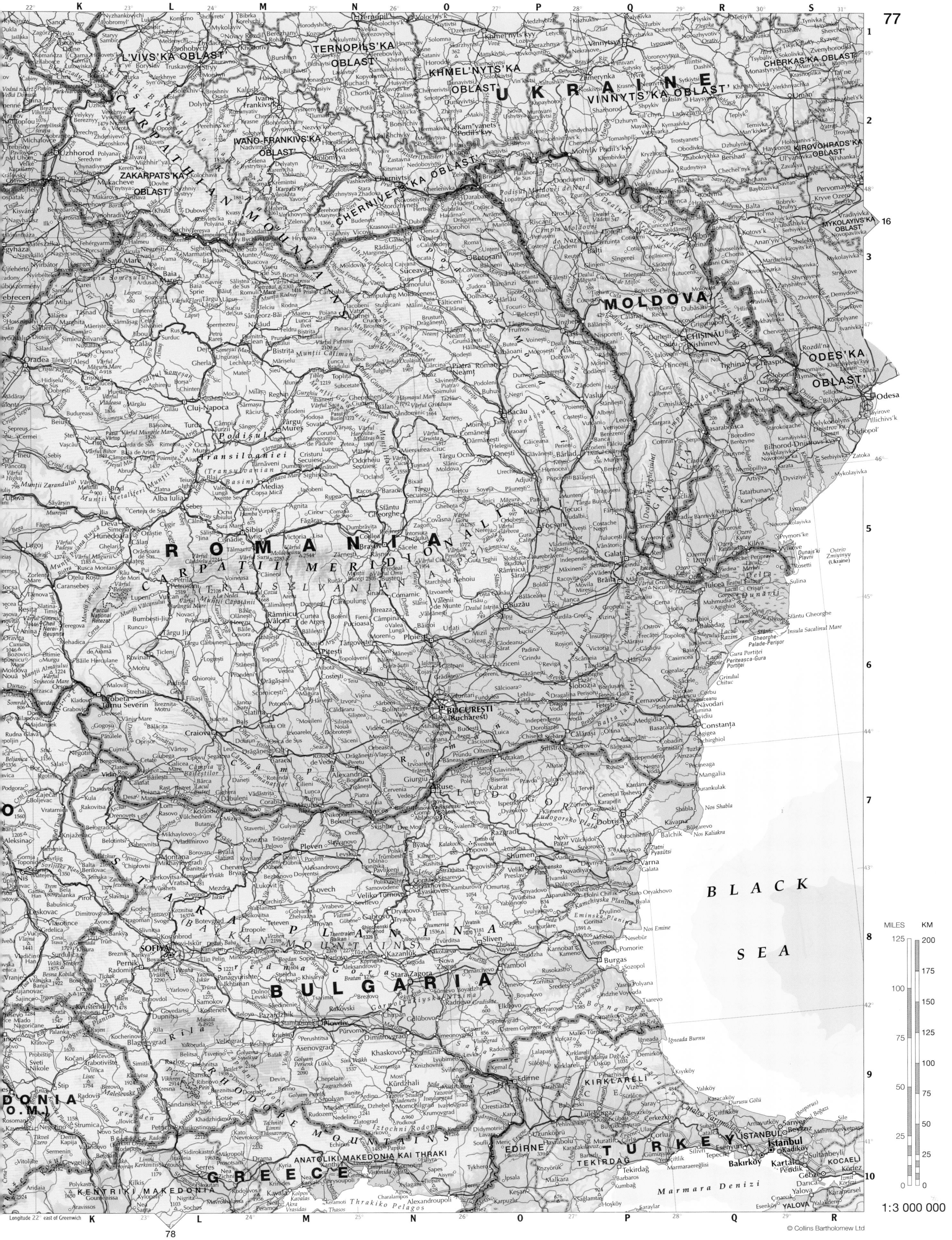

UKRAINE

L'VIVS'KA OBLAST'

TERNOPIL'S'KA OBLAST'

IVANO-FRANKIVS'KA OBLAST'

KHMEL'NYTS'KA OBLAST'

VINNYTS'KA OBLAST'

CHERKAS'KA OBLAST'

KIROVOHRADS'KA OBLAST'

ZAKARPATS'KA OBLAST'

CHERNIVETS'KA OBLAST'

MOLDOVA

CHIŞINĂU (Kishinev)

ODES'KA OBLAST'

Odesa

CARPATHIAN MOUNTAINS

Cluj-Napoca

Podişul Transilvaniei (Transylvanian Basin)

R O M A N I A

CARPAȚII MERIDIONALI (TRANSYLVANIAN ALPS)

Sibiu

Galaţi

Brăila

Ploieşti

Piteşti

BUCUREŞTI Bucuresti

Craiova

Constanţa

Ruse

L U D O G O R I E

Ludogorsko Plato

SOFIYA

B U L G A R I A

STARA PLANINA (BALKAN MOUNTAINS)

Plovdiv

Shumen

Varna

Burgas

RODOPI MOUNTAINS

PIRIN

Blagoevgrad

DONIJA O.M.I.

GREECE

ANATOLIKI MAKEDONIA KAI THRAKI

KENTRIKI MAKEDONIA

KIRKLARELI

TEKIRDAG

EDIRNE

T U R K E Y

İSTANBUL

KOCAELI

Marmara Denizi

Thrakiko Pelagos

B L A C K

S E A

MILES	KM
125	200
100	175
	150
75	125
	100
50	75
25	50
	25
0	0

1:3 000 000

Longitude 22° east of Greenwich

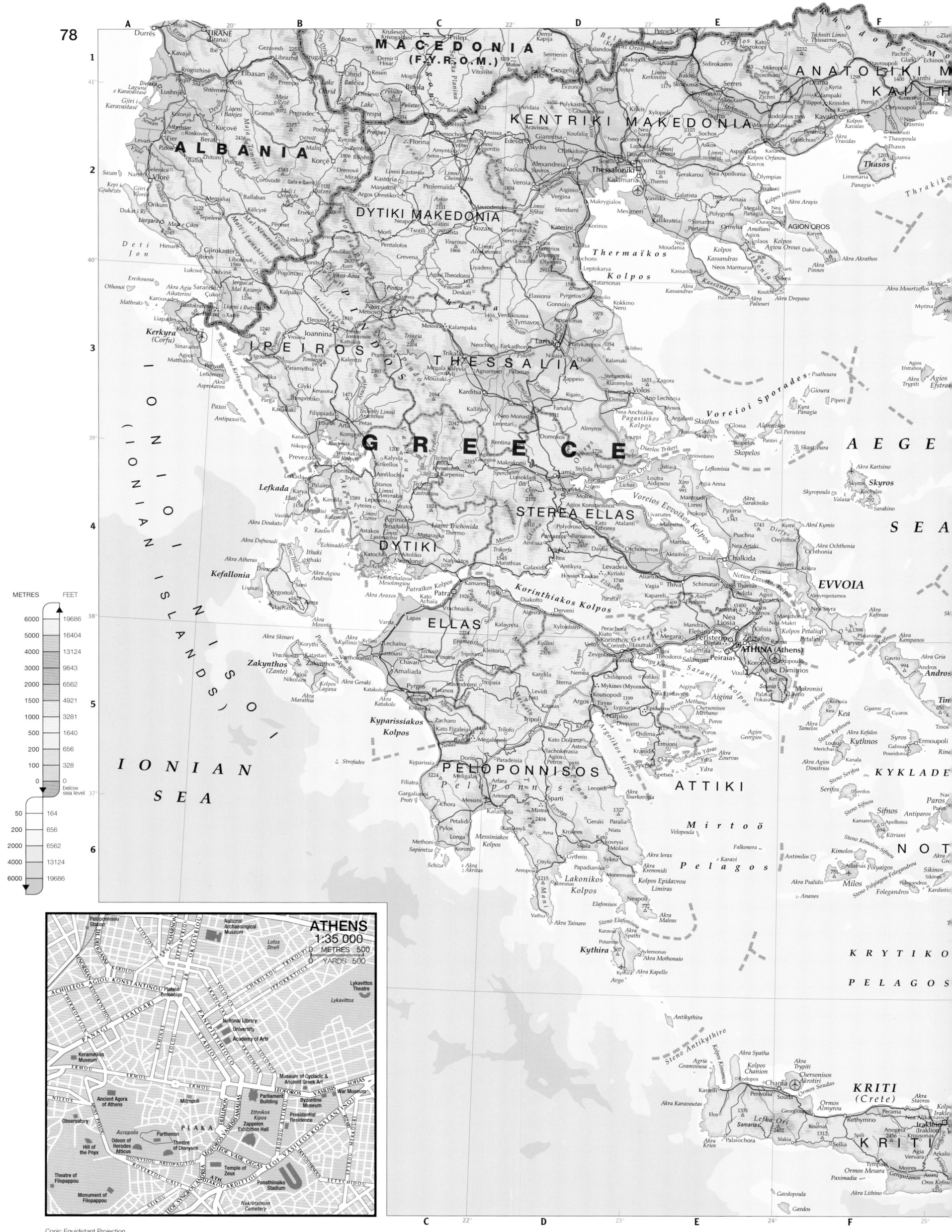

ALBANIA

MACEDONIA
(F.Y.R.O.M.)

KENTRIKI MAKEDONIA

DYTIKI MAKEDONIA

ANATOLIKI M
KAI TH

IPEIROS

THESSALIA

GREECE

STEREA ELLAS

DYTIKI

ELLAS

EVVOIA

AEGE

SEA

PELOPONNISOS

ATTIKI

KYKLADE

NOT

ATHINA (Athens)

KRYTIKO

PELAGOS

Mirtoö

Pelagos

KRITI
(Crete)

KRITI

Voreioi Sporades

IONIAN SEA

Deti Jon

Ionian Islands (NISOI)

METRES   FEET
6000   19686
5000   16404
4000   13124
3000   9843
2000   6562
1500   4921
1000   3281
500   1640
200   656
100   328
0   below
           sea level
50   164
200   656
2000   6562
4000   13124
6000   19686

ATHENS
1:35 000
METRES   500
YARDS   500

National Archaeological Museum

Lykavittos Theatre

Lykavittos

National Library
University
Academy of Arts

Museum of Cycladic & Ancient Greek Art

Kerameikos Museum

Ancient Agora of Athens

Mitropoli

Parliament Building

Byzantine Museum

Presidential Residence

War Museum

Observatory

Acropolis

Parthenon

PLAKA

Ethnikos Kipos

Zappeion Exhibition Hall

Odeon of Herodes Atticus

Theatre of Dionysos

Temple of Zeus

Hill of the Pnyx

Theatre of Filopappou

Monument of Filopappou

Panathinaiko Stadium

Nekrotafeio Cemetery

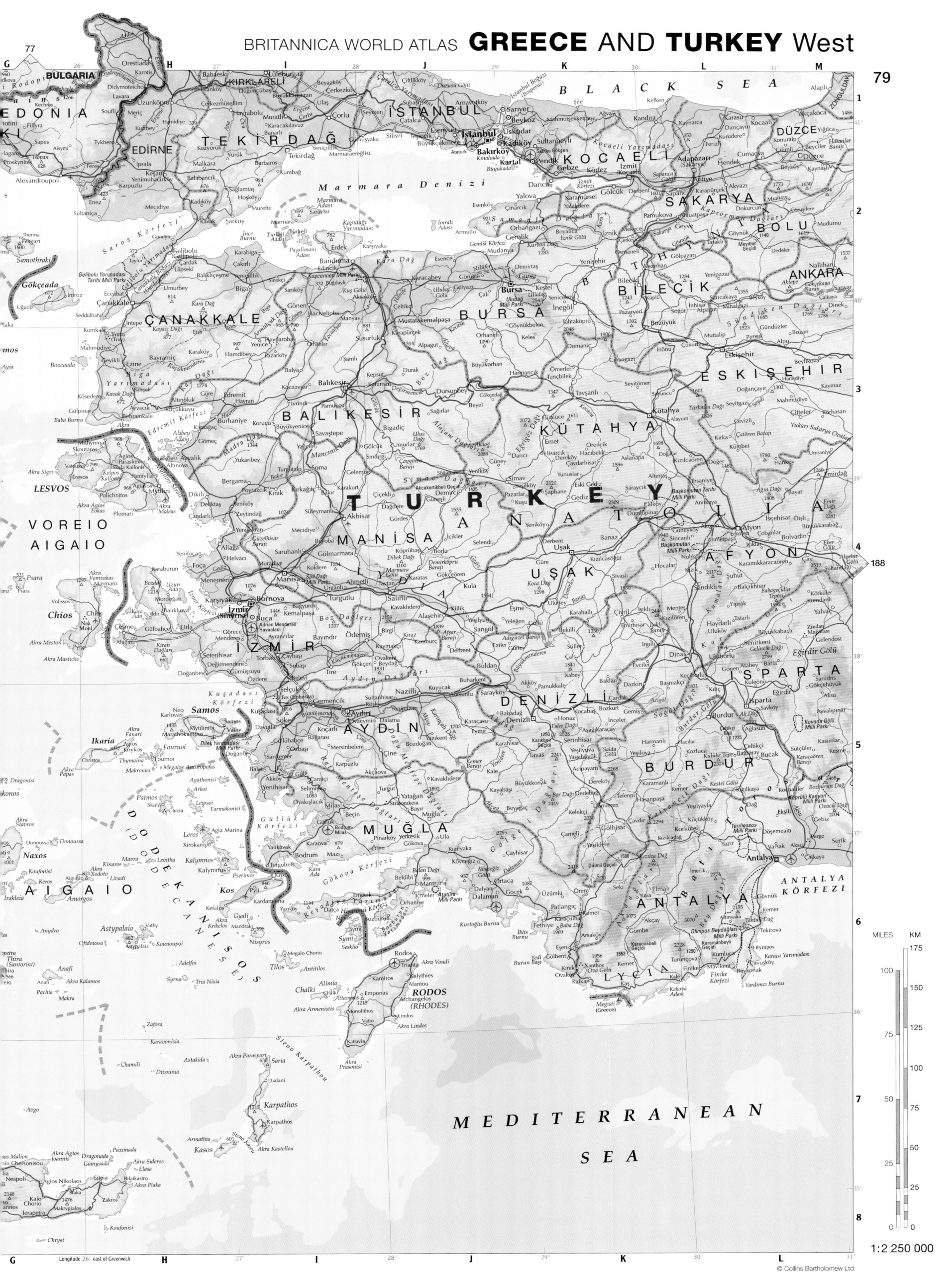

BULGARIA

BLACK SEA

KIRKLARELİ

İSTANBUL

TEKİRDAĞ

EDİRNE

İstanbul

Bakırköy

Kartal

KOCAELİ

DÜZCE

Marmara Denizi

SAKARYA

BOLU

ÇANAKKALE

BURSA

Bursa

ANKARA

BİLECİK

Gökçeada

ESKİŞEHİR

BALIKESİR

KÜTAHYA

LESVOS

TURKEY ANATOLIA

VOREIO
AIGAIO

MANİSA

AFYON

188

Chios

LYDIA

UŞAK

Karşıyaka
İzmir
(Smyrna)
Buca

İZMİR

ISPARTA

Egirdir Gölü

Samos

AYDIN

DENİZLİ

Ikaria

BURDUR

D
O
D
E
K
A
N
I
S
O
S

MUĞLA

Naxos

AIGAIO

Kos

ANTALYA
KÖRFEZİ

Antalya

ANTALYA

RODOS
(RHODES)

LYCIA

MEDITERRANEAN

SEA

Karpathos

Kasos

MILES KM

1:2 250 000

Longitude 26° east of Greenwich

© Collins Bartholomew Ltd

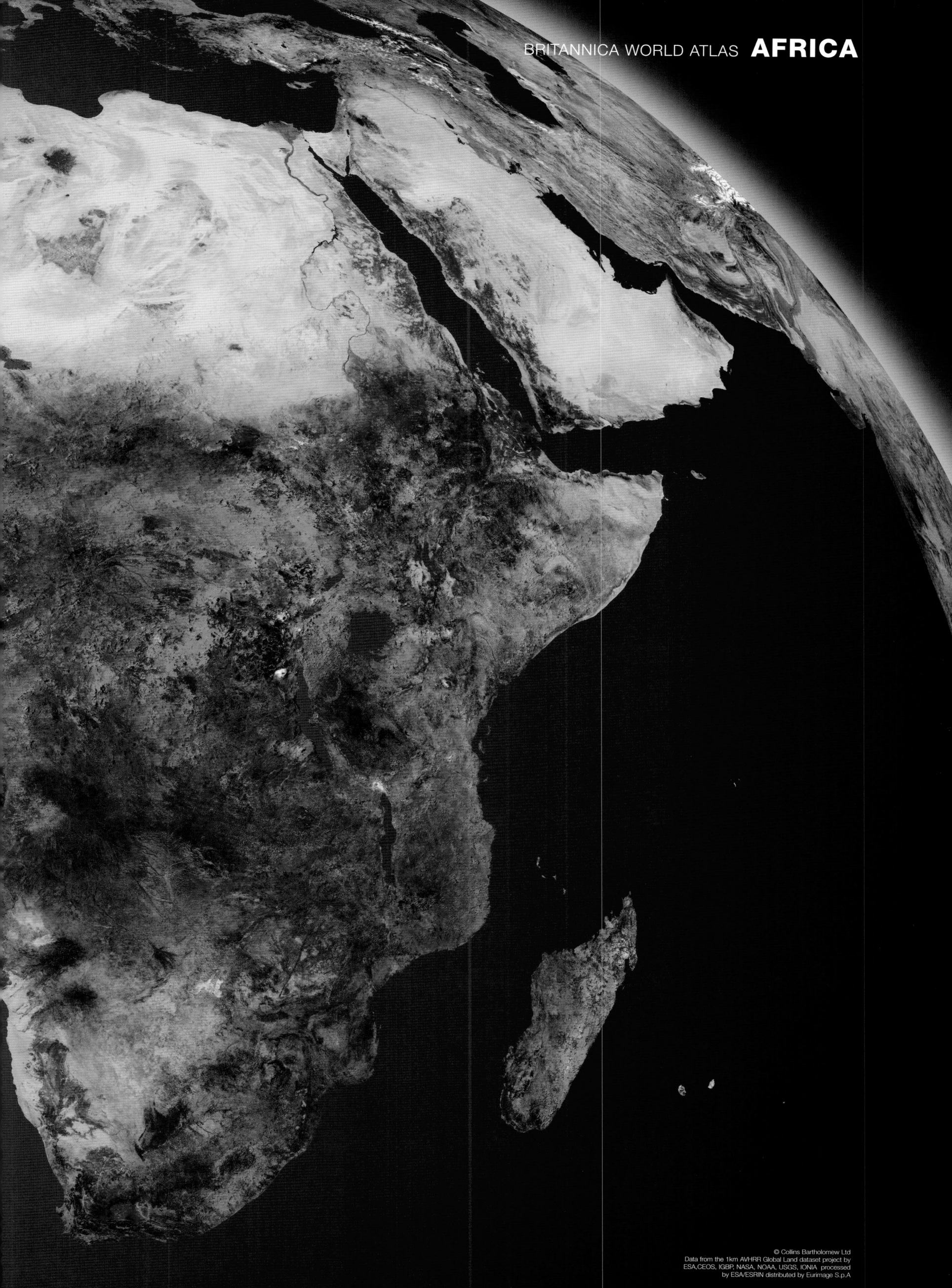

A   B   C   D   E

30°   15°

E U R O P E

Pyrenees

Corse

Sardegna

Tyrrhen Sea

MEDIT

Alger Bejaïa Skikda

Tanger Oran Ech Chélif Annaba **Tunis**

Str. of Gibraltar Sfax

Rabat Fès Sidi Bel Abbès Constantine *Golfe de Ga*

Casablanca Gabes

MOROCCO Beni Laghouat **TUNISIA**

Beni Mellal Béchar Tarâbu

Marrakech

Arquipélago dos Açores

45°

45°

Arquipélago da Madeira

Islas Canarias *Lanzarote* **ALGERIA**

(Spain)

Tenerife **Las Palmas**

de Gran Canaria

Islas *Gran* **Laâyoune** *Hoggar*

Canarias *Canaria* *Mt Tahat*

2918

WESTERN SAHARA **S A H**

Ténéré du Tafassâsset

Nouâdhibou **N I G**

MAURITANIA

Agadez

M A L I

Nouakchott

St Louis Gao

Senegal Zinder

30° **SENEGAL** Kayes Ségou *Niger* Mopti **Niamey**

60° Dakar Sokoto Kano

Tropic of Cancer Kaolack **BURKINA**

CAPE VERDE *Santo Antão* *Boa Vista* Bamako **Ouagadougou**

Santiago **THE GAMBIA** **Banjul** Bobo-Dioulasso Kaduna Gombé

Fogo **Praia** **GUINEA** *Fouta Djallon* *Kainji* *Shiroro* **NIGERIA**

BISSAU *Reservoir* *Reservoir*

Bissau **BENIN** Parakou

GUINEA Kankan **CÔTE** Tamale **Abuja**

Conakry **D'IVOIRE** *Black Volta* **TOGO** Ogbomosho

Freetown **SIERRA** Bouaké **GHANA** **Porto-** Ibadan Onitsha

LEONE *Lac de Kossou* Novo Lagos **CAME**

LIBERIA **Yamoussoukro** Kumasi *Lake Volta* **Lomé** Wari

Monrovia Abidjan **Accra** Port **Malabo** Douala

Cape Coast Harcourt *Bioco* Yaou

Gulf **EQUATORIAL**

of **GUINEA** Bata

SÃO TOMÉ AND PRÍNCIPE Libreville

Príncipe

São Tomé **São Tomé** **GA**

A T L A N T I C

Annobón Port-Gentil

(Equatorial Guinea)

Pointe-Noire

CABIND

(Ango

Equator 0°

O C E A N Ascension

(U.K.)

Namibi

SOUTH

AMERICA

15°

St Helena

(U.K.)

Ilha da Trindade *Ilhas Martin Vaz*

Tropic of Capricorn

30° 45° 30° 15° 0°

A B C D E

Orthographic Projection

F G H I J

Black Sea

Kríti

Ionian
Sea

Misrātah

Khalīj Surt Banghāzī

Al Baydā'

Cyprus

Caspian
Sea

Aral
Sea

A S I A

60°

30° 45°

Mişrātah

MEDITERRANEAN SEA

Al Iskandarīyah Tanța Būr Sa'īd
Shrubā al Khaymah Al Jīzah
Munkhafad **Al Qāhirah**
Libyan al Qaṭṭārah As Suways
Plateau
Al Minyā Khalīj
Plateau as Suways Gulf
Asyūṭ of Aqaba

LIBYA

Al Hulayq
al Kabīr

R A

Tibesti

Emi Koussi
3415

Libyan

Desert

EGYPT

Qinā
Nile
Al Uqṣur

Aswān

Buḥayrat Naşīr

**Nubian
Desert**

Red
Sea

Dasht-e
Kavīr

Kūh-e-ye Zagros

The Gulf

Gulf of Oman

**Arabian
Peninsula**

H I M A L A Y A

Tropic of Cancer

CHAD

Lake Chad

Abéché

uguri **Ndjamena**

Maroua

Sarh

Moundou

aoundéré **CENTRAL**

Bossangoa

Bouar **AFRICAN REPUBLIC**

Bangui

Ubangi

Congo

anceville **CONGO**

Lac
Mai-Ndombe

zaville Bandundu

atadi **Kinshasa**

Kikwit

Kananga

Mbandaka Kisangani

DEMOCRATIC

REPUBLIC OF CONGO

Mbuji-Mayi

Marra
Plateau

Baiyuda
Desert Nile

Omdurman **Khartoum**

El Obeid Wad Medani

SUDAN

Gedaref

Bahir Dar

Wau

Juba

Lake
Albert

Lake
Edward

UGANDA

Kampala

Lake Kivu **RWANDA**

Bukavu **Kigali**

BURUNDI

Bujumbura

Kigoma

Port Sudan

Ras
Dejen
4533

T'ana Hāyk'

ERITREA

Asmara

Mek'elē

ETHIOPIA

Ādīs Ābeba Dirē Dawa

DJIBOUTI

Djibouti

Hargeysa

Gulf of Aden

Suqutrā

**ARABIAN
SEA**

15°

Lake
Turkana

Kisumu **KENYA**

Lake
Victoria Nakuru Kirinyaga
5199

Nairobi

Mwanza

SOMALIA

Webi Shabeelle

Muqdisho

Kismaayo

Maldives

O C E A N

INDIAN

0°

Kalemie

Karnina

Likasi Kasama

Lubumbashi Mansa

Solwezi Chingola

Mongu Ndola

ZAMBIA

Kabwe

Lusaka

Mpika

Lake
Mweru

Lake
Bangweulu

Chaîne des Mitumba

Lake
Tanganyika

TANZANIA

Tanga

Mtera
Reservoir **Dodoma**

Lake Rukwa Iringa

Mbeya

Arusha Kilimanjaro
5892

Mombasa

Pemba Island

Rufiji

Zanzibar
Zanzibar Island

Dar es Salaam

Mafia Island

Ruvuma

SEYCHELLES

Aldabra Islands
(Seychelles)

Victoria Mahé

Coëtivy

Farquhar Islands
(Seychelles)

Chagos
Archipelago

Equator

0°

ANGOLA

ito Huambo

guela

ango

**Barragem
do Gove**

nda

Etosha Pan

Okavango
Delta

NAMIBIA

Windhoek

Desert

Cuando

Cabora

Zambezi

Victoria
Falls Livingstone

Lake
Kariba Tete

ZIMBABWE

Harare Chitungwiza

Gweru Mutare

Bulawayo

BOTSWANA

Makgadikgadi

Francistown

Kalahari
Desert Gaborone

Orange

Lake
Nyasa

MALAWI

Lilongwe

Blantyre

MOZAMBIQUE

Nacala

Nampula

Quelimane

Beira

Limpopo

Inhambane

Xai-Xai

Maputo

Chipata

Pemba

COMOROS

Njazidja **Moroni**

Îles
Glorieuses
(France)

Mayotte
(France)

Tanjona
Bobaomby

Antsiranana

Mozambique Channel

Mahajanga

MADAGASCAR

Toamasina

Antananarivo

Fianarantsoa

Toliara

Bassas da India
(France)

Juan de
Nova
(France)

Île Europa
(France)

Île Tromelin
(France)

Cargados Carajos
Islands
(Mauritius)

Agalega Islands
(Mauritius)

MAURITIUS

Port Louis

St-Denis
Réunion
(France)

Rodrigues Island
(Mauritius)

15°

REPUBLIC OF
SOUTH AFRICA

Great
Karoo

Little
Karoo

Cape Town
Khayelitsha

Cape of
Good Hope Cape Agulhas

Kimberley

Bloemfontein **Maseru**
LESOTHO

East
London

Port
Elizabeth

Durban

Johannesburg
Pretoria
Carletonville Soweto
Mbabane
SWAZILAND

Drakensberg

Tropic of Capricorn

MILES KM

1000
750
500
250

1500
1250
1000
750
500
250
0

1:24 000 000

© Collins Bartholomew Ltd

30° 45° 60° 75° 90°

F G H I J

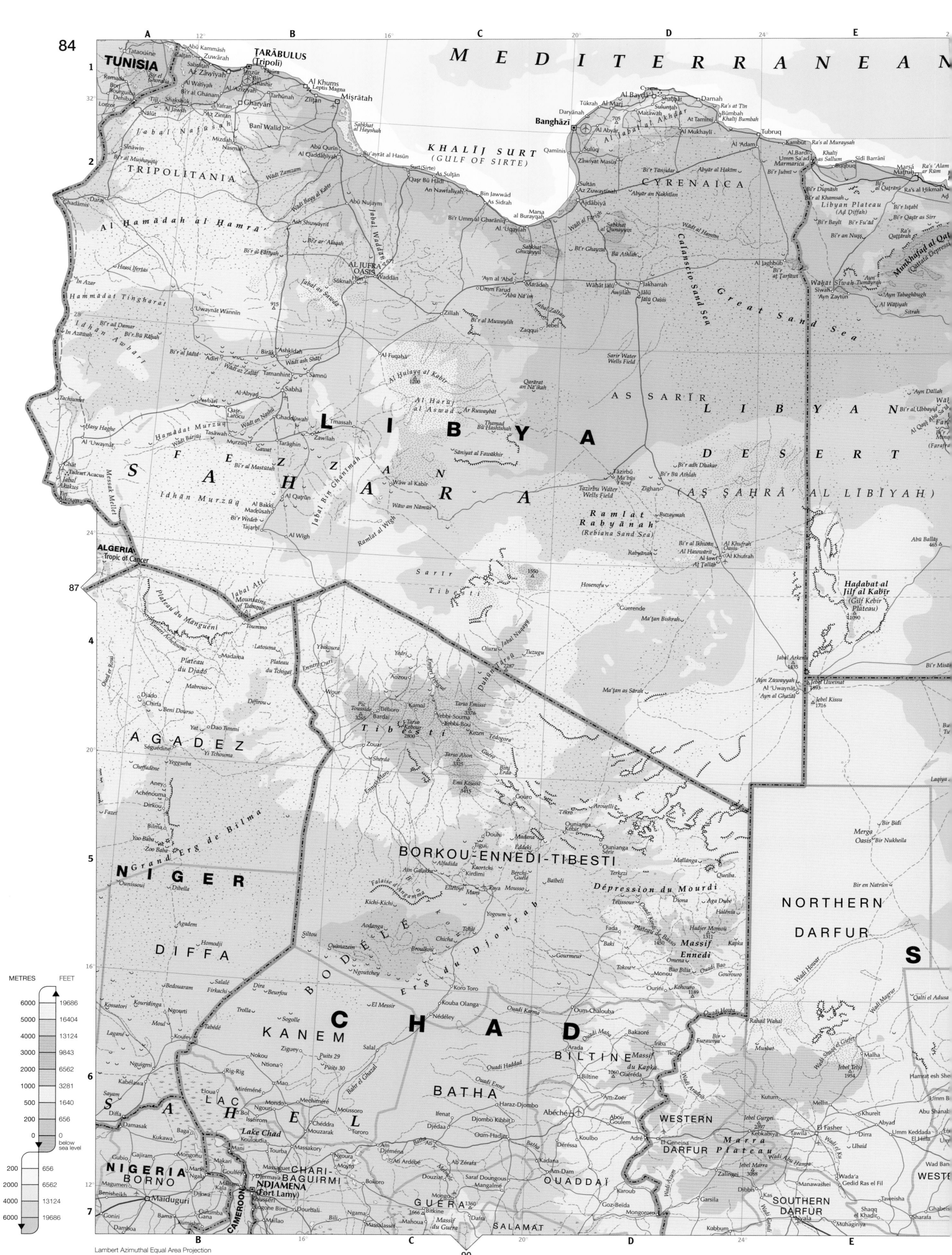

TUNISIA

MEDITERRANEAN

TARĀBULUS
(Tripoli)

Banghāzī

KHALĪJ SURT
(GULF OF SIRTE)

CYRENAICA

TRIPOLITANIA

Al Hamādah al Hamrā'

AL JUFRA
OASIS

Hammādat Tingharat

Idhān Awbāri

Hammādat Murzūq

Idhān Murzūq

L I B Y A

F E Z Z A N

S A H A R A

A S   S A R Ī R

L I B Y A N

D E S E R T

(AṢ ṢAḤRĀ' AL LĪBĪYAH)

Calanscio Sand Sea

Great Sand Sea

Libyan Plateau
(Aḍ Ḍiffah)

Munkhafaḍ al Qaṭ...
(Qattara Depressi...

Sarir Water
Wells Field

Tazirbu Water
Wells Field

Ramlat
Rabyānah
(Rebiana Sand Sea)

Sarir
Tibesti

Hadabat al Jilf al Kabīr
(Gilf Kebir Plateau)

ALGERIA
Tropic of Cancer

Jabal Aïr
Mountains of Tummo

Plateau du Manguéni

Emmer Achécuma

Plateau
du Djado

Plateau
du Tchigaï

Enneri Ouri

Tibesti

Pic
Toussidé
3265

Tarso Emissi
3376

Emi Koussi
3415

BORKOU-ENNEDI-TIBESTI

Dépression du Mourdi

NORTHERN
DARFUR

N I G E R

AGADEZ

DIFFA

Grand Erg de Bilma

B
O
D
É
L
É

Erg du Djourab

C H A D

KANEM

BATHA

BILTINE

Massif
du Kapka

Massif
Ennedi

Plateau de Bianco

WESTERN
DARFUR

Marra
Darfur Plateau

SOUTHERN
DARFUR

SAHEL

LAC

Lake Chad

NIGERIA
BORNO

CHARI-
BAGUIRMI

NDJAMENA
(Fort Lamy)

CAMEROON

GUERA

SALAMAT

OUADDAÏ

S

METRES	FEET
6000	19686
5000	16404
4000	13124
3000	9843
2000	6562
1000	3281
500	1640
200	656
0	0 below sea level
200	656
2000	6562
4000	13124
6000	19686

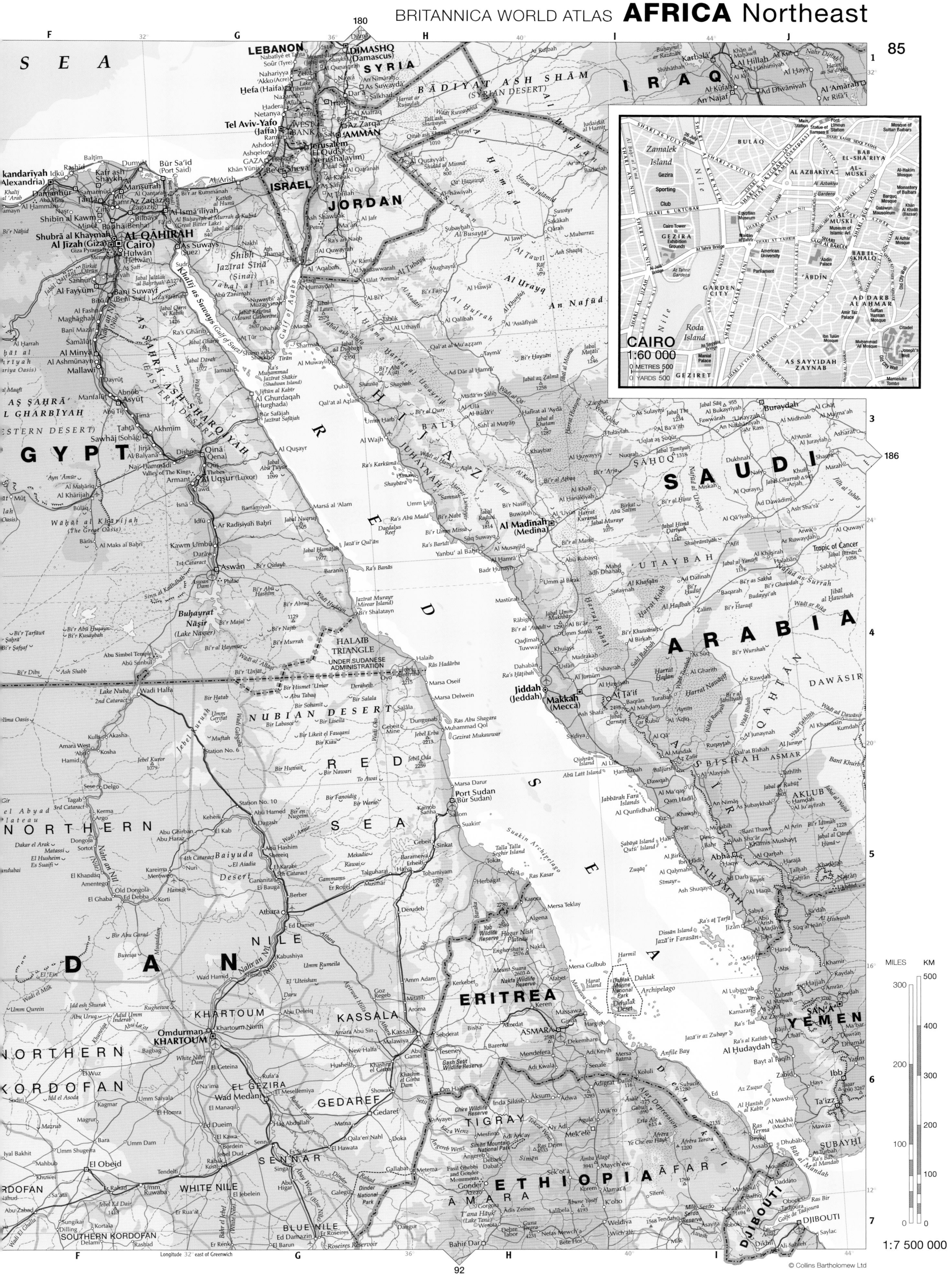
SEA
LEBANON
DIMASHQ (Damascus)
SYRIA
BĀDIYAT ASH SHĀM (SYRIAN DESERT)
IRAQ
Tel Aviv-Yafo (Jaffa)
'AMMĀN
Jerusalem El Quds Yerushalayim
ISRAEL
JORDAN
Būr Sa'īd (Port Said)
Al Iskandarīyah (Alexandria)
AL QĀHIRAH (Cairo)
Al Jīzah (Giza)
As Suways (Suez)
Jazīrat Sīnā' (Sinai)
AL HAMAD
An Nafūd
CAIRO
1:60 000
METRES 500
YARDS 500
Zamalek Island
Gezira
Roda Island
GARDEN CITY
AL AZBAKIYA
BULAQ
ABDIN
AS SAYYIDAH ZAYNAB
GEZIRET
AṢ ṢAḤRĀ' AL GHARBĪYAH
(WESTERN DESERT)
EGYPT
AṢ ṢAḤRĀ' ASH SHARQĪYAH (EASTERN DESERT)
Al Uqşur (Luxor)
Aswān
Buḥayrat Nāşir (Lake Nasser)
RED SEA
HIJAZ
SAUDI ARABIA
Al Madīnah (Medina)
Jiddah (Jeddah)
Makkah (Mecca)
Tropic of Cancer
HALAIB TRIANGLE
UNDER SUDANESE ADMINISTRATION
NUBIAN DESERT
Port Sudan (Būr Sudan)
NORTHERN
SUDAN
NILE
KHARTOUM
Omdurman
KASSALA
ERITREA
ASMARA
Dahlak Archipelago
YEMEN
ṢAN'Ā'
Al Ḥudaydah
GEDAREF
SENNAR
WHITE NILE
BLUE NILE
KORDOFAN
SOUTHERN KORDOFAN
ETHIOPIA
TIGRAY
ĀMARA
ĀFAR
Afar Depression
DJIBOUTI
Gulf of Aden
MILES
KM
1:7 500 000
Longitude 32° east of Greenwich
180
186
92

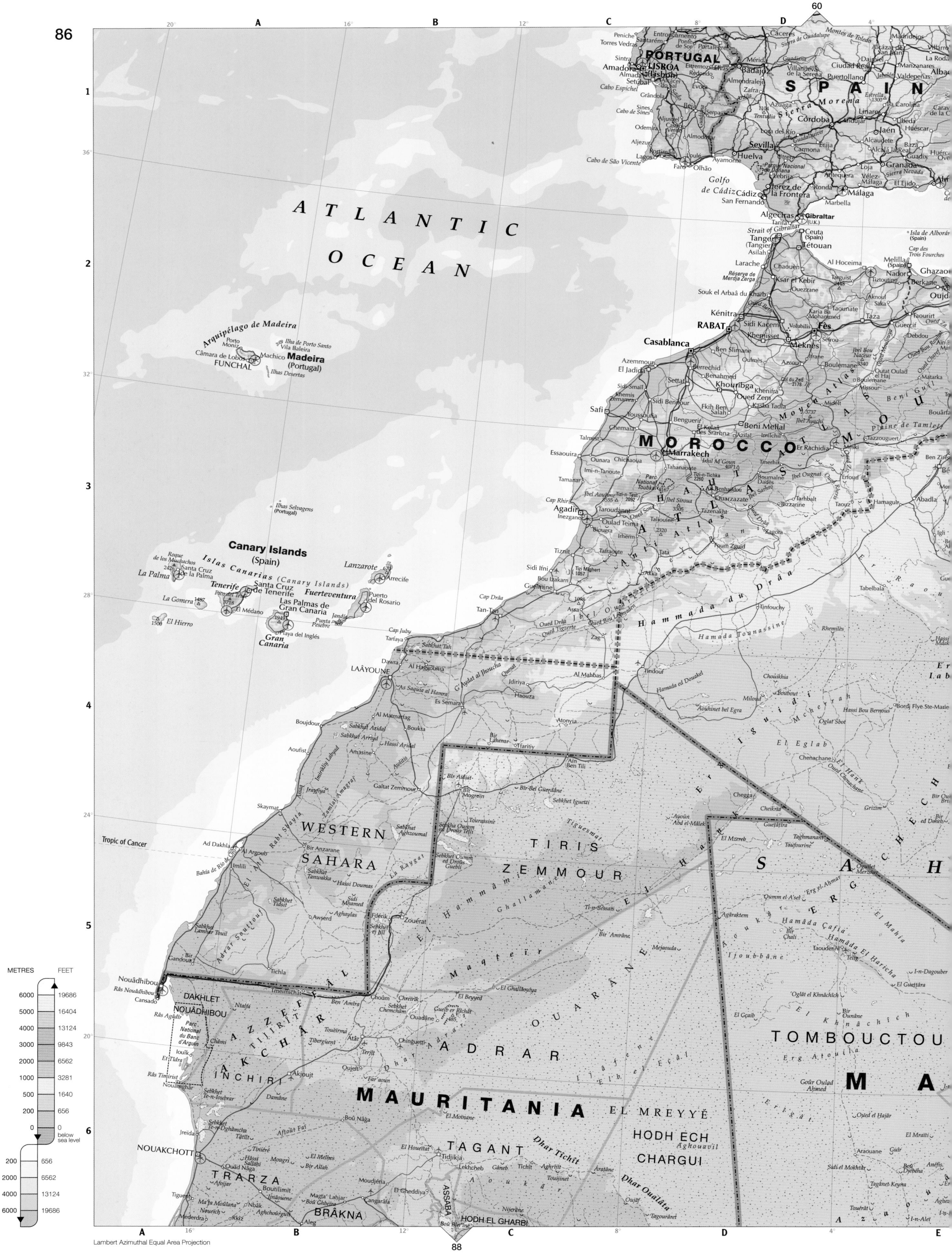

60

A 20° 16° B 12° C 8° D 4°

ATLANTIC

OCEAN

Peniche
Torres Vedras
Entroncamento
Cáceres
Madridejos
Montes de Toledo
Sintra
PORTUGAL
Amadora **LISBOA** (Lisbon)
Almada Setúbal
Estremoz
Badajoz
Mérida
Villanueva de la Serena
Ciudad Real
La Roda
SPAIN
Cabo Espichel
Grândola
Évora
Serpa
Zafra
Almendralejo
Puertollano
Valdepeñas
Cabo de Sines
Sines
Odemira
Beja
Mértola
Aljustrel
Pozoblanco
La Carolina
Linares
Úbeda
Caravaca
de la C
Aljezur
Portimão
Loulé
Ayamonte
Huelva
Sevilla
Carmona
Écija
Córdoba
Jaén
Granada
Huéscar
Guadix
Cabo de São Vicente
Faro
Olhão
Lagos
Antequera
Loja
Sierra Nevada
Vélez-Málaga
El Ejido
Golfo
de Cádiz Cádiz
Jerez de la Frontera
Ronda
Málaga
San Fernando
Algeciras **Gibraltar**
Marbella
Isla de Alborán (Spain)
Strait of Gibraltar
Ceuta (Spain)
Tanger (Tangier)
Tétouan
Cap des Trois Fourches
Tarifa
Asilah
Larache
Al Hoceima
Melilla (Spain)
Ghazao
Chaouèn
Réserve de Mèrdja Zerga
Ksar el Kebir
Souk el Arbaâ du Kharb
Ouezzane
Taourirt
Aknoul
Nador
Berkane
Taza
Oujd
Taouma
Taguist
Tiztoutine
Tizi Ouzli

Casablanca
Azemmour
El Jadida
Sidi Smaïl
Berrechid
Benahmed
Oulmès
Khouribga
Oued Zem
Khémisset
Sidi Kacem
RABAT
Kénitra
Sidi Slimane
Ben Slimane
Settat
Meknes
Fès
Sefrou
Debdou

Safi
Youssoufia
Sidi Bennour
Kasba Tadla
Beni Mellal
El Kelâa des Srarhna
Benguerir
Chemaïa
Talmest
Essaouira
Marrakech
Ounara Chichaoua
Amizmiz
Tahanaoute
Azilal
Imilchil
El Rachidia
Ifni M'Goun
Tassent
Jbel Ayachi
Boumalne Dades
Ouarzazate
Erfoud
MOROCCO
Cap Rhir
Taroudannt
Agadir
Inezgane
Oulad Teima
Biougra
Irherm
Talioune
Tazenakht
Zagora
Tinerhir
Ben Zi
Abadla

Tiznit
Tafraoute
Tata
Akka
Foum Zguid
Sidi Ifni
Bou Izakarn
Guelmine
Tan-Tan
Cap Draa
Oued Drâa
Assa
Zag
Tindouf
Tabelbala
Rhemilès
Er
La b

Tarfaya
Tarfaya
Sabkhat Tah
Al Haggoûnia
Ouest
Idiriya
Haouza
Al Mahbas
Hamada ed Douakel

LAÂYOUNE
Dawra
As Saquia al Hamra
Es Semara
Chouikhia
Benbout
Bordj Flye Ste-Marie
Hassi Bou Bernous

Boujdour
Sabkhat Aridal
Hassi Aridal
Boukta
Atonyia
Aouïnet bel Egra
Oglat Sbot

Aoufist
Bir Lahmar
Tfaritiy
Amasine
Galtat Zemmour
Bir Aidiat
Bir Mogrein
Bir-Bel Guerdâne
Chenachane
Oued Haut
El Eglab

Skaymat
Zamila Lahyal
Bir Amrâne
Cheggab
Cheïkria
Grizim

WESTERN
SAHARA
Ad Dakhla
Bir Anzarane
Sabkhat Aghzoumal
Tourassine
TIRIS
ZEMMOUR
Ayoûn Abd el-Mâlek
Bir ed Dhaba
Bir ed Deheb
Guetfâra

Bir Argoub
Imlili
Sabkhat Tanwakka
Sabkha Oumm Drous Telli
El Mzereb
Taghmananrt

Tropic of Cancer
Bahía de Río de Oro
Hassi Doumas
Sabkhat Oumm ed Drous Guebi
Oumm el A'sel
Erg Chech
S A H A
Ouânet Merzouka

Sidi Tidsil
Fdérik
Sidi Mhamed
Ti-n-Bessaïs
Hamâda Çafia
Hamâda El Hariche

Asward
Aghaylas
Sebkhet el Jill
Zouérat
Taoudenni
I-n-Dagouber
El Guettâra

Nouâdhibou
Râs Nouâdhibou
Cansado
Tichla
Mejaouda
'Ijoubbâne
El Khnâchich

DAKHLET
NOUADHIBOU
Gandour
Bir Gandou
Imeimiuat
Chôum
Chreïk
El Ghallaouiya
El Gaib
El Khnâchich

Râs Agadir
Parc National du Banc d'Arguin
Ntalfa
Ben Amira
Sebkhet Chemchami
Ouâdâne
El Beyyed
OUARÂNE

Ioulk
Chami
Tiberguent
Touêrma
Atâr
Terjit
Bir
'Oglât el Khnâchich
TOMBOUCTOU

Er Ti Timtrist
Nouâmghâr
Râs Timiris
Akjoujt
Ouîni
Oujeft
Faa'roun
Goûr Oulad Ahmed
Erg Atouila
M A
INCHIRI
Damâne

ADRAR

METRES FEET
6000 19686
5000 16404
4000 13124
3000 9843
2000 6562
1000 3281
500 1640
200 656
0 below sea level
200 656
2000 6562
4000 13124
6000 19686

MAURITANIA
El Moinane
EL MREYYÉ
Oued el Hâjar

NOUAKCHOTT
Ireida
Aftoût Faï
El Melhes
Tidjikja
Aghouavil
HODH ECH
CHARGUI
El Mratti
Araouane
Guïr

TRARZA
Ouad Nâga
Boû Nâga
TAGANT
Dhar Tichît
El Gheddiya
Tichît
Aratâne
Sidi el Mokhtar

Tiguent
Afojjar
Mongri
Bir Allah
Moudjéria
Toujinet
Dhar Oualâta
Tenaghet-Keyna

Boutilimit
Magta' Lahjar
Lekhcheb
Ganeb
Aghrijît
ASSABA
Tamourt en Naaj
Diébba

Aleg
Magta' Moûlana
Nbak
BRÂKNA
HODH EL GHARBI
Néma

A 16° B 12° 88 C 8° D 4°

Lambert Azimuthal Equal Area Projection

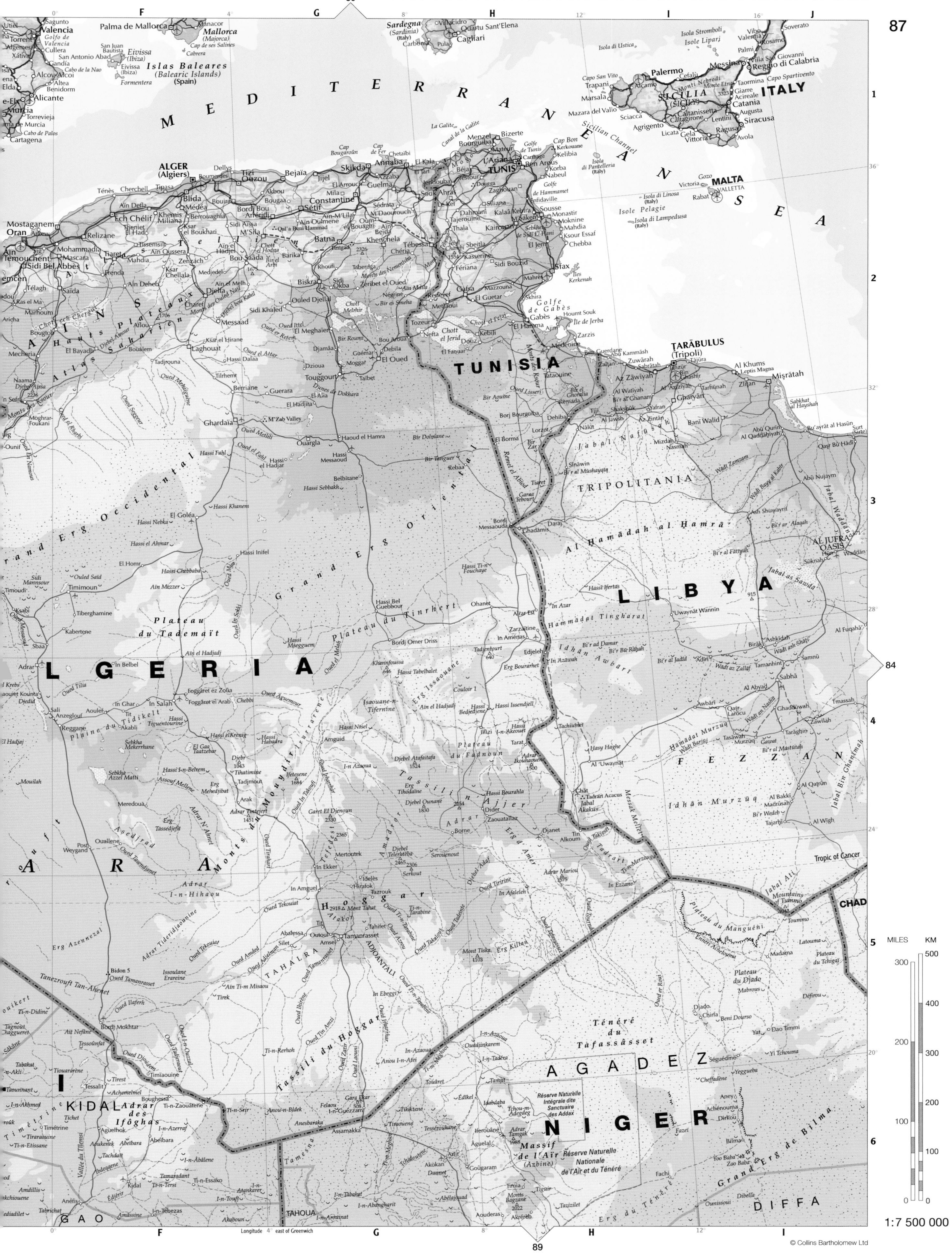
MEDITERRANEAN SEA
ALGERIA
TUNISIA
LIBYA
NIGER
CHAD
ITALY
MALTA
SICILIA (SICILY)
Islas Baleares (Balearic Islands) (Spain)
Sardegna (Sardinia) (Italy)
ALGER (Algiers)
TUNIS
ṬARĀBULUS (Tripoli)
TRIPOLITANIA
FEZZAN
AGADEZ
DIFFA
KIDAL
GAO
TAHOUA
Grand Erg Occidental
Grand Erg Oriental
Plateau du Tademaït
Tassili n'Ajjer
Hoggar
Ténéré du Tafassâsset
Massif de l'Aïr (Azbine)
Tropic of Cancer
MILES
KM
1:7 500 000
Longitude east of Greenwich
© Collins Bartholomew Ltd

86

A 16° B 12° C 8° D 4° E

MAURITANIA

DAKHLET NOUADHIBOU
INCHIRI
AKCHÂR
ADRAR
SAHA
Châmi
Atâr
Tiberguent
Terjit

El Mreyyé

Parc National du Banc d'Arguin
Oujeft
Fai'aoun
Akjoujt

TRARZA
NOUAKCHOTT
Damâne

TAGANT
HODH ECH CHARGUI
TOMBOUCTOU

BRÂKNA

ASSABA
GORGOL
HODH
EL GHARBI

GUIDIMAKA

St-Louis

SENEGAL

DAKAR
Thiès
Rufisque
Mbour
Kaolack

THE GAMBIA
BANJUL

GUINEA-BISSAU
BISSAU

KAYES
KOULIKORO
SÉGOU
SÉGOU
BAMAKO

MOPTI

MALI

SIKASSO

MA

MOYENNE-GUINÉE

GUINÉE-MARITIME

GUINEA
HAUTE-GUINÉE

CONAKRY

BURKINA
OUAGADOUGOU

Bobo-Dioulasso

UPPER WEST

NORTHERN

NORTHERN
SIERRA LEONE
EASTERN
SOUTHERN

GUINÉE-FORESTIÈRE

CÔTE D'IVOIRE

GHANA

BRONG-AHAFO

ASHANTI

FREETOWN
WESTERN AREA

LIBERIA
MONROVIA

Buchanan

YAMOUSSOUKRO

Bouaké

Kumasi

WESTERN

CENTRAL

Abidjan

Cape Palmas

ATLANTIC OCEAN

METRES FEET

METRES	FEET
6000	19686
5000	16404
4000	13124
3000	9843
2000	6562
1000	3281
500	1640
200	656
0	0
	below sea level
200	656
2000	6562
4000	13124
6000	19686

CAPE VERDE
AT THE SAME SCALE

24°W

Santo Antão
Ponta do Sol
Pombas
Porto Novo
Mindelo
São Vicente
Santa Luzia
Branco
Raso
São Nicolau

Sal
Pedra Lume
Santa Maria

Boa Vista
Sal Rei
Fundo das Figueiras
Curral Velho

16°N

Ilhas do Cabo Verde

Santiago
Maio

Fogo
Brava
Vila Nova Sintra
Ilhéus Secos
São Filipe
Porto Rincão
Porto Inglês
PRAIA

Equator

0°

Longitude 4° west of Greenwich

Lambert Azimuthal Equal Area Projection

B 12° C 8° D 4° E

MILES KM

300 — 500

— 400

200 — 300

— 200

100 —

— 100

0 — 0

1:7 500 000

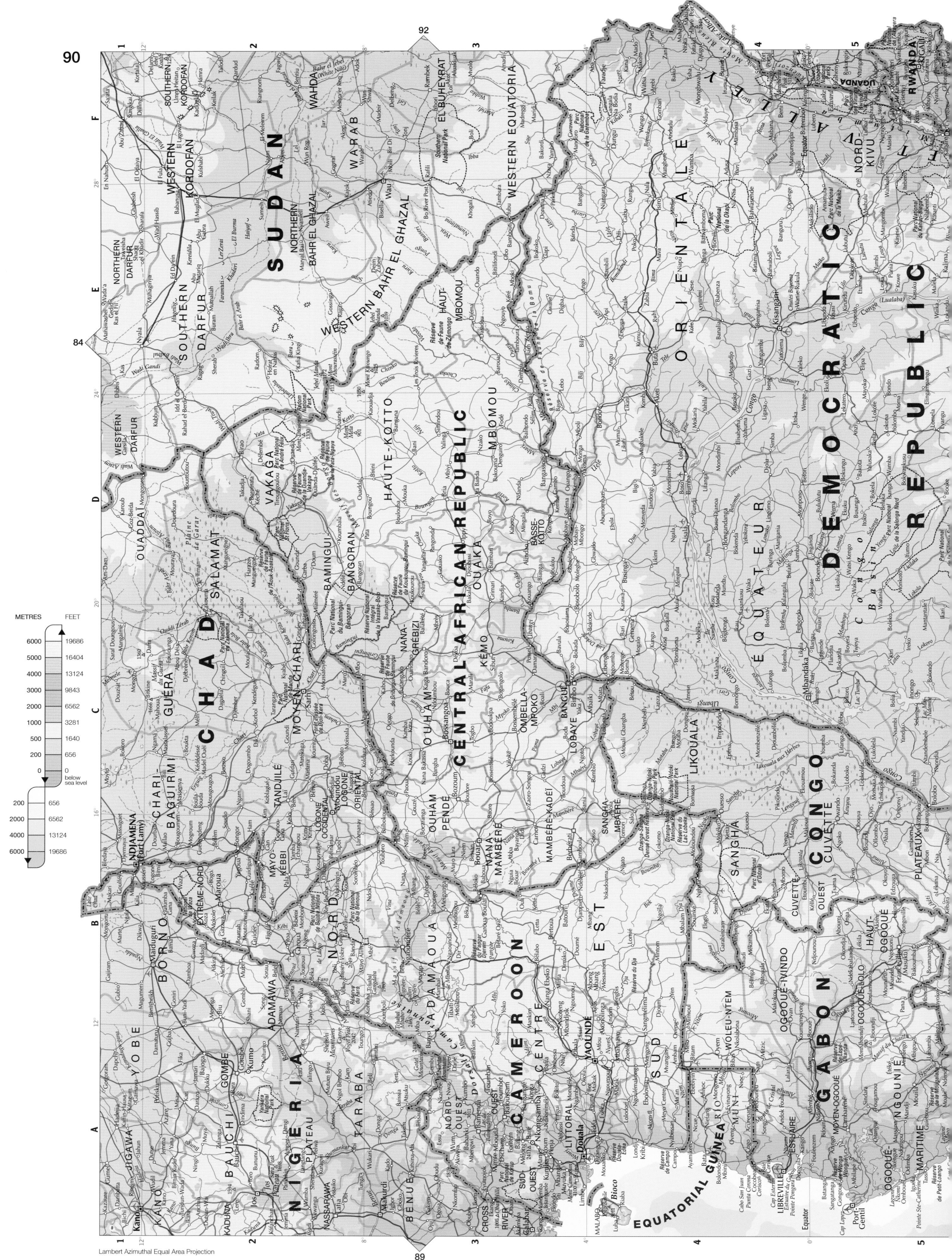
SUDAN
CHAD
CENTRAL AFRICAN REPUBLIC
CAMEROON
NIGERIA
GABON
CONGO
DEMOCRATIC REPUBLIC
EQUATORIAL GUINEA
UGANDA
RWANDA
METRES
FEET
6000
19686
5000
16404
4000
13124
3000
9843
2000
6562
1000
3281
500
1640
200
656
0
0
below sea level
200
656
2000
6562
4000
13124
6000
19686

Lambert Azimuthal Equal Area Projection

ATLANTIC
OCEAN
ANGOLA
ZAMBIA
NAMIBIA
CONGO
BOTSWANA
ZIMBABWE
TANZANIA
MOZAMBIQUE
BURUNDI
KATANGA
LUNDA NORTE
LUNDA SUL
MOXICO
CUANDO CUBANGO
HUILA
CUNENE
NAMIBE
BENGUELA
HUAMBO
BIÉ
MALANJE
UIGE
ZAIRE
BENGO
LUANDA
CABINDA (Angola)
KINSHASA
BRAZZAVILLE
BANDUNDU
BAS-CONGO
KASAÏ-OCCIDENTAL
KASAÏ-ORIENTAL
NORTH-WESTERN
COPPERBELT
CENTRAL
LUSAKA
SOUTHERN
WESTERN
NORTHERN
LUAPULA
Lake Tanganyika
MILES
KM
1:7 500 000

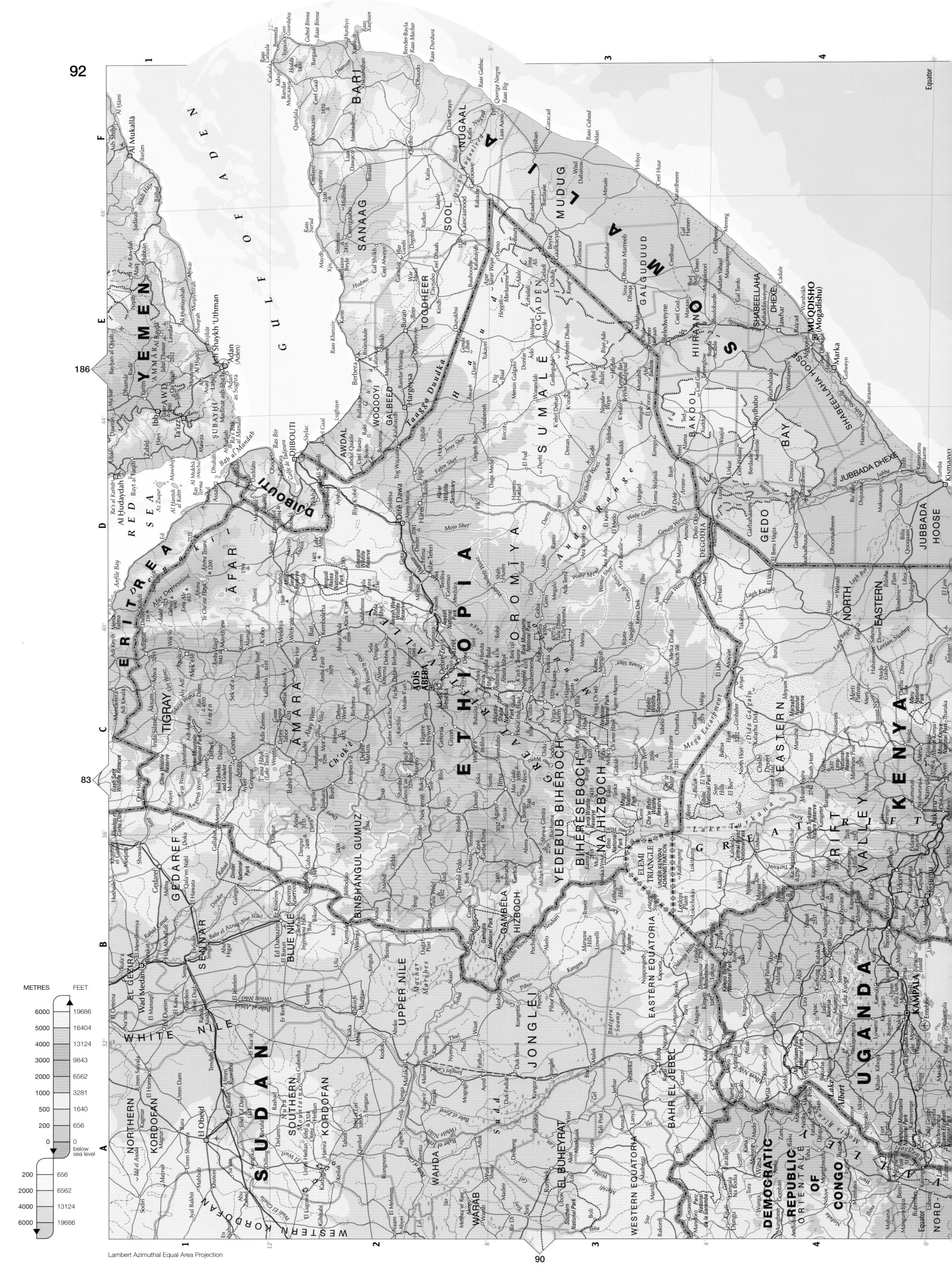
YEMEN
GULF OF ADEN
RED SEA
ERITREA
DJIBOUTI
ETHIOPIA
SOMALIA
SUDAN
KENYA
UGANDA
DEMOCRATIC REPUBLIC OF CONGO
ADIS ABEBA
DJIBOUTI
MUQDISHO (Mogadishu)
KAMPALA
Adan (Aden)
Al Mukallā
Lake Turkana
ELEMI TRIANGLE UNDER KENYAN ADMINISTRATION
186
83
90
METRES
FEET
6000
19686
5000
16404
4000
13124
3000
9843
2000
6562
1000
3281
500
1640
200
656
0
0
below sea level
200
656
2000
6562
4000
13124
6000
19686

Lambert Azimuthal Equal Area Projection

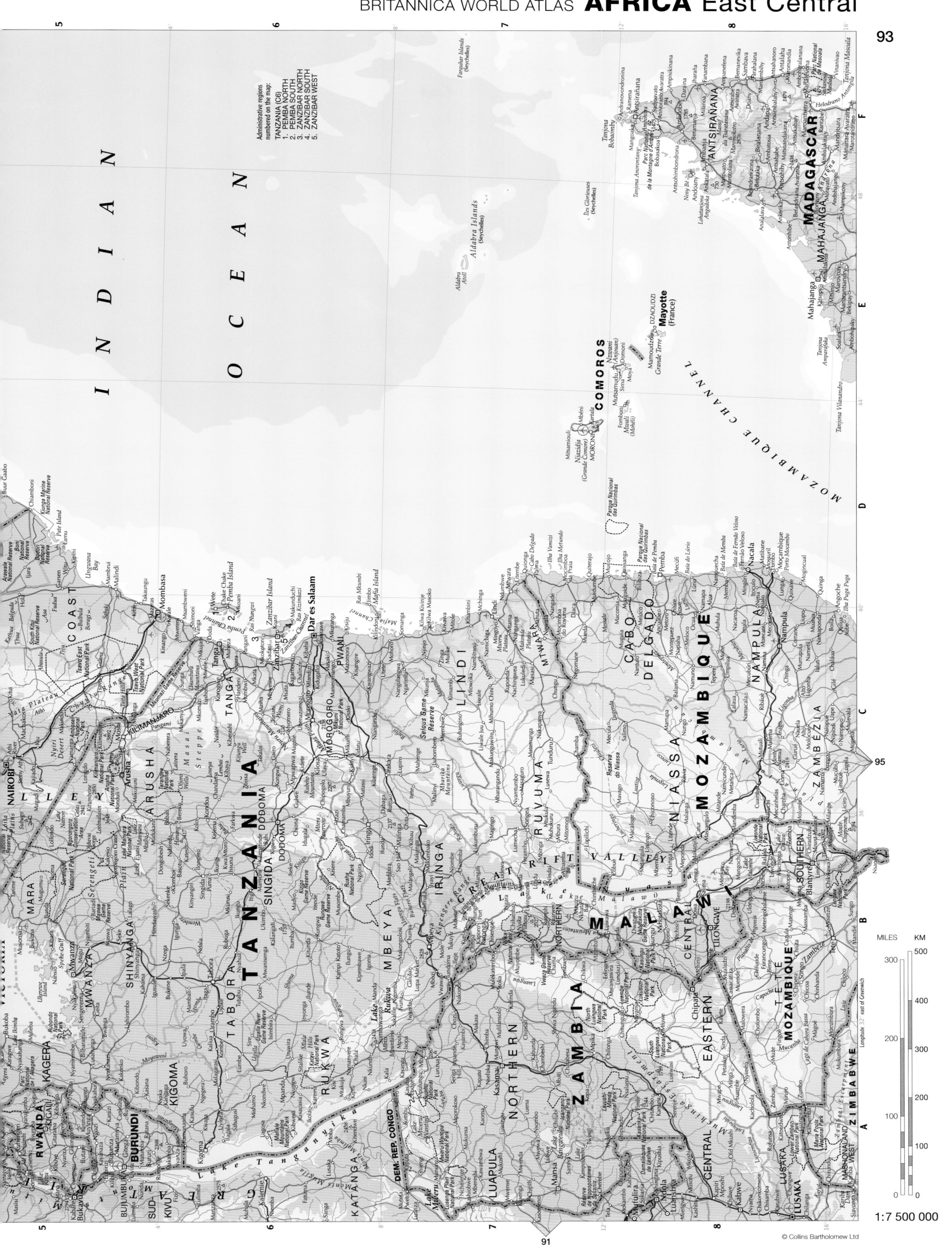

Administrative regions
numbered on the map:
TANZANIA (C6)
1. PEMBA NORTH
2. PEMBA SOUTH
3. ZANZIBAR NORTH
4. ZANZIBAR SOUTH
5. ZANZIBAR WEST

INDIAN OCEAN

MOZAMBIQUE CHANNEL

MADAGASCAR

ANTSIRANANA

MAHAJANGA

Mahajanga

COMOROS

MORONI

Mayotte (France)
DZAOUDZI

Aldabra Islands
(Seychelles)

Farquhar Islands
(Seychelles)

TANZANIA

KENYA

NAIROBI

Mombasa

Dar es Salaam

Zanzibar Island

Pemba Island

Mafia Island

COAST

ARUSHA

KILIMANJARO

TANGA

DODOMA

MOROGORO

PWANI

LINDI

MWARA

RUVUMA

IRINGA

MBEYA

SINGIDA

TABORA

SHINYANGA

MWANZA

KAGERA

KIGOMA

MARA

RWANDA

BURUNDI

BUJUMBURA

DEM. REP. CONGO

KIVU

KATANGA

ZAMBIA

LUSAKA

NORTHERN

LUAPULA

MALAWI

LILONGWE

CENTRAL

SOUTHERN

NORTHERN

Blantyre

Lake
Malawi
(Lake Nyasa)

GREAT RIFT VALLEY

MOZAMBIQUE

NIASSA

CABO DELGADO

NAMPULA

ZAMBÉZIA

TETE

EASTERN

Nacala

Nampula

ZIMBABWE

Lake
Tanganyika

Lake
Rukwa

Lake
Victoria

MILES   KM
300   500

200   400
          300
100   200
          100
0   0

Longitude 32° east of Greenwich

1:7 500 000

© Collins Bartholomew Ltd

95

91

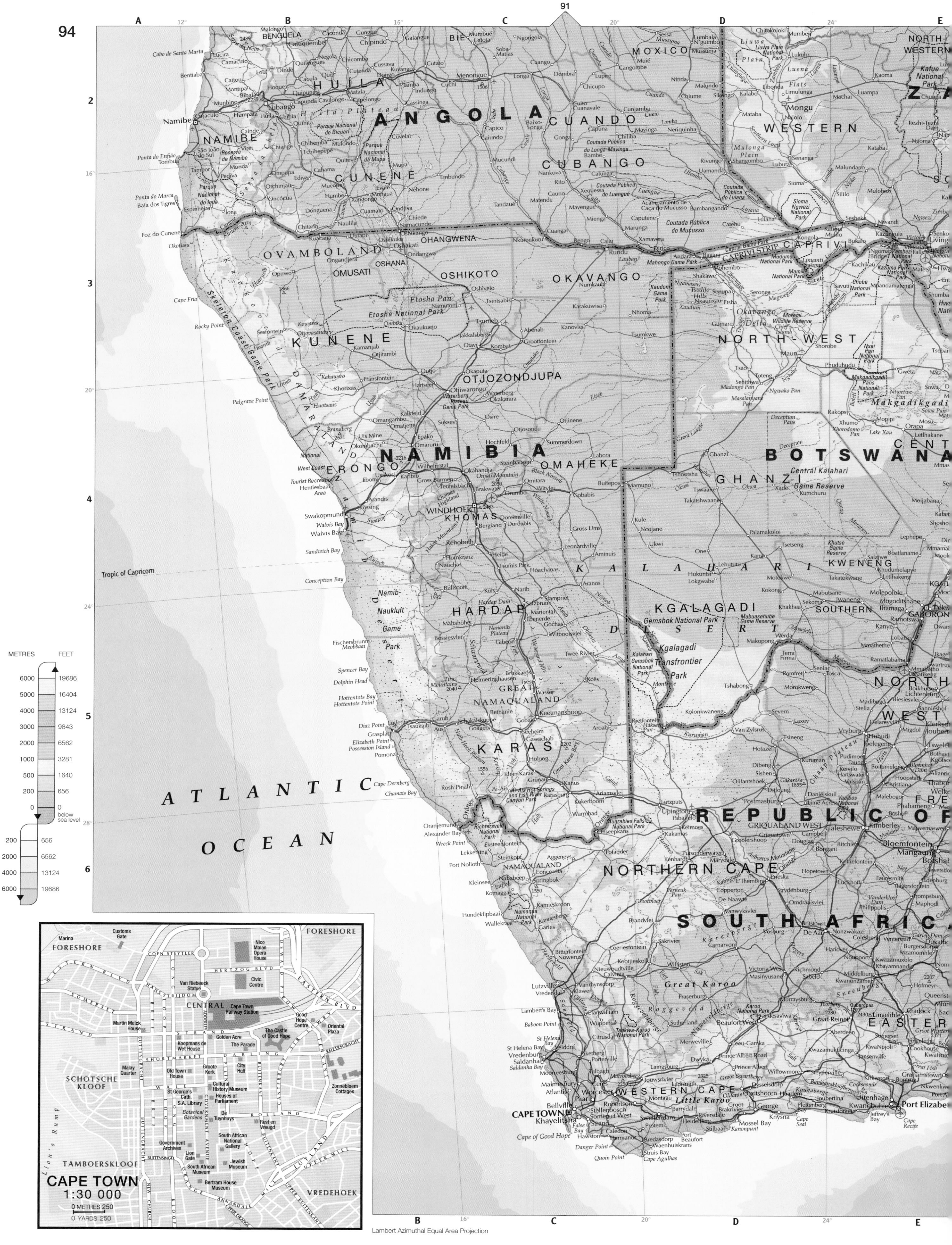
91
A
B
C
D
E
ANGOLA
NAMIBIA
BOTSWANA
REPUBLIC OF SOUTH AFRICA
ATLANTIC OCEAN
Tropic of Capricorn
HUILA
Huila Plateau
NAMIBE
CUNENE
CUANDO CUBANGO
MOXICO
BENGUELA
BIE
WESTERN
NORTH-WESTERN
OVAMBOLAND
OMUSATI
OSHANA
OHANGWENA
OSHIKOTO
OKAVANGO
KUNENE
Etosha Pan
Etosha National Park
Skeleton Coast Game Park
DAMARALAND
OTJOZONDJUPA
ERONGO
OMAHEKE
KHOMAS
WINDHOEK
Swakopmund
Walvis Bay
HARDAP
KALAHARI DESERT
Namib-Naukluft Game Park
Namib Desert
GREAT NAMAQUALAND
KARAS
Keetmanshoop
Lüderitz
Caprivi Strip
CAPRIVI
NORTH-WEST
Okavango Delta
Makgadikgadi
GHANZI
Central Kalahari Game Reserve
KWENENG
KGALAGADI
SOUTHERN
GABORONE
Kgalagadi Transfrontier Park
NORTH WEST
GRIQUALAND WEST
Kimberley
Bloemfontein
NORTHERN CAPE
NAMAQUALAND
SOUTH AFRICA
Great Karoo
WESTERN CAPE
Little Karoo
CAPE TOWN
Cape of Good Hope
Cape Agulhas
Port Elizabeth
EASTERN
Orange
METRES
FEET
6000 19686
5000 16404
4000 13124
3000 9843
2000 6562
1000 3281
500 1640
200 656
0 0
below sea level
200 656
2000 6562
4000 13124
6000 19686
CAPE TOWN
1:30 000
0 METRES 250
0 YARDS 250
FORESHORE
CENTRAL
SCHOTSCHE KLOOF
TAMBOERSKLOOF
VREDEHOEK
Lion's Rump
Lambert Azimuthal Equal Area Projection

MILES   KM

1:7 500 000

MADAGASCAR
AT THE SAME SCALE

© Collins Bartholomew Ltd

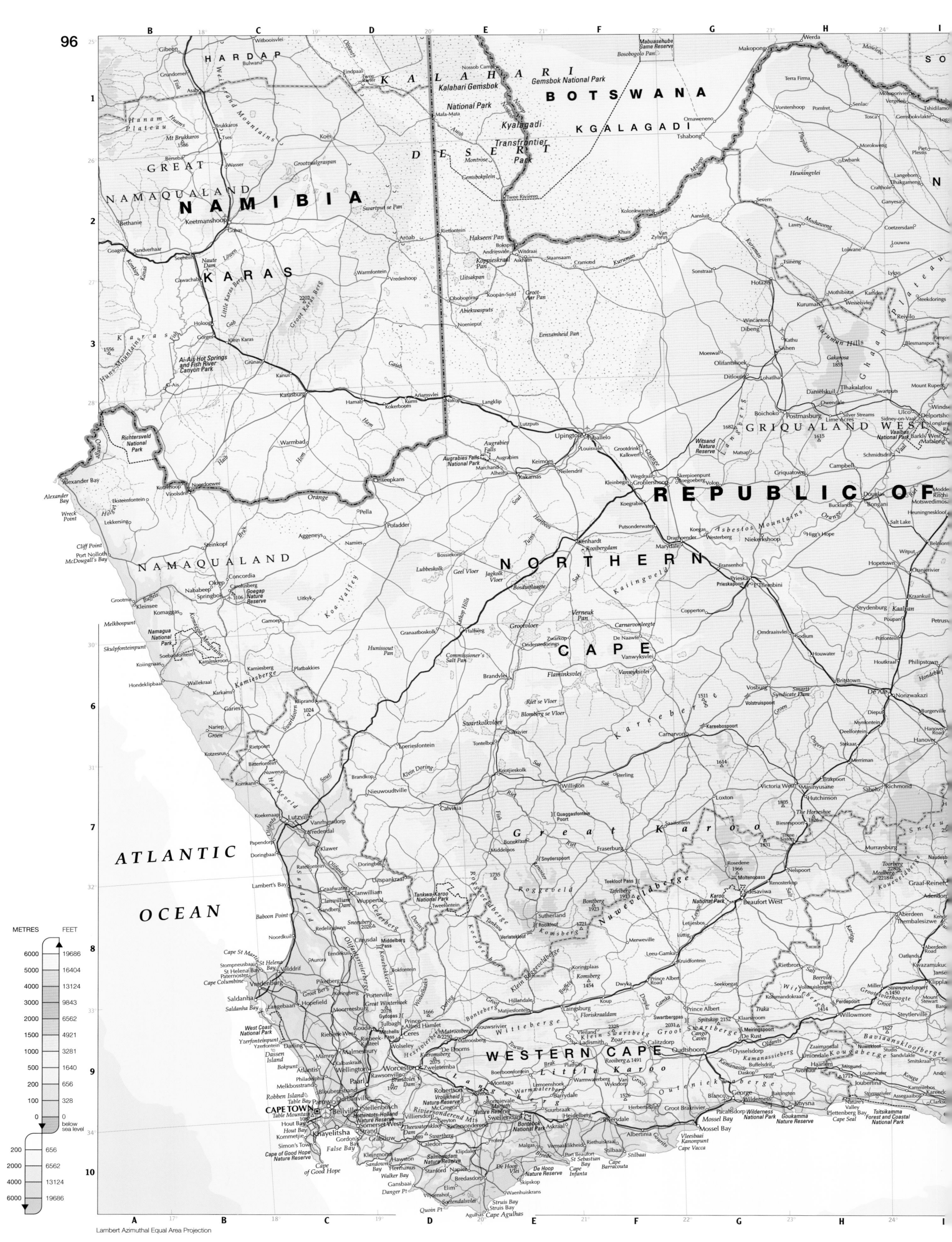
NAMIBIA
BOTSWANA
REPUBLIC OF
HARDAP
KARAS
KGALAGADI
K A L A H A R I
D E S E R T
GREAT NAMAQUALAND
NAMAQUALAND
GRIQUALAND WEST
NORTHERN CAPE
WESTERN CAPE
Great Karoo
Little Karoo
ATLANTIC OCEAN
Kalahari Gemsbok National Park
Gemsbok National Park
Kgalagadi Transfrontier Park
Ai-Ais Hot Springs and Fish River Canyon Park
Richtersveld National Park
Augrabies Falls National Park
Namaqua National Park
Goegap Nature Reserve
Tankwa-Karoo National Park
Karoo National Park
West Coast National Park
Bontebok National Park
Wilderness National Park
Goukamma Nature Reserve
Tsitsikamma Forest and Coastal National Park
Keetmanshoop
Karasburg
Upington
Kuruman
Springbok
Calvinia
Kenhardt
Prieska
De Aar
Beaufort West
Vredenburg
Saldanha
CAPE TOWN
Bellville
Paarl
Stellenbosch
Worcester
Swellendam
Oudtshoorn
George
Mossel Bay
Knysna
Cape of Good Hope
Cape Agulhas
Orange
METRES
FEET
6000
19686
5000
16404
4000
13124
3000
9843
2000
6562
1500
4921
1000
3281
500
1640
200
656
100
328
0
0
below sea level
200
656
2000
6562
4000
13124
6000
19686

Lambert Azimuthal Equal Area Projection

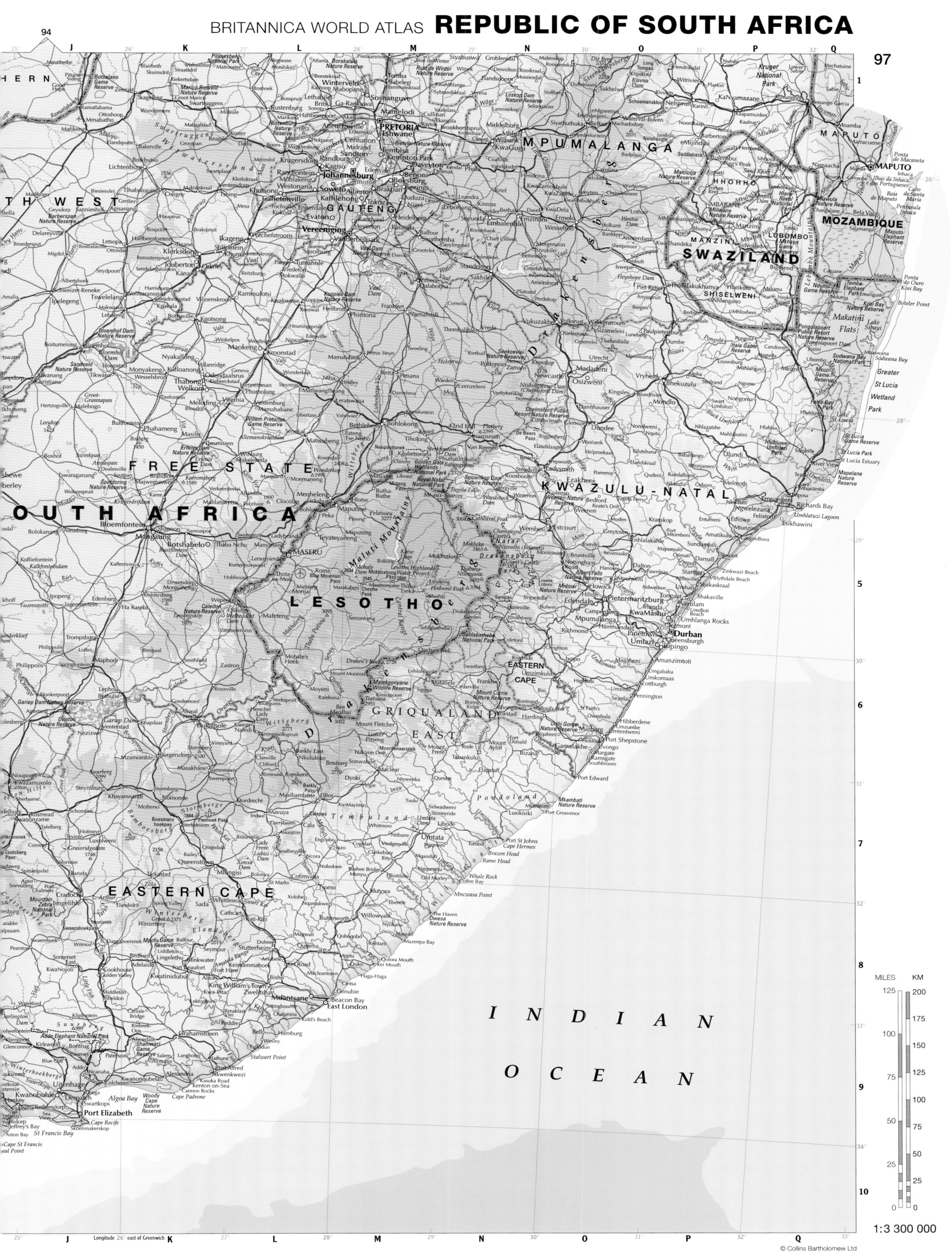
MPUMALANGA
GAUTENG
PRETORIA
Tshwane
Johannesburg
MAPUTO
MOZAMBIQUE
SWAZILAND
FREE STATE
SOUTH AFRICA
KWAZULU-NATAL
LESOTHO
MASERU
Bloemfontein
Durban
Pietermaritzburg
EASTERN CAPE
GRIQUALAND EAST
Port Elizabeth
East London
INDIAN OCEAN
MILES
KM
1:3 300 000

ATLANTIC OCEAN ISLANDS

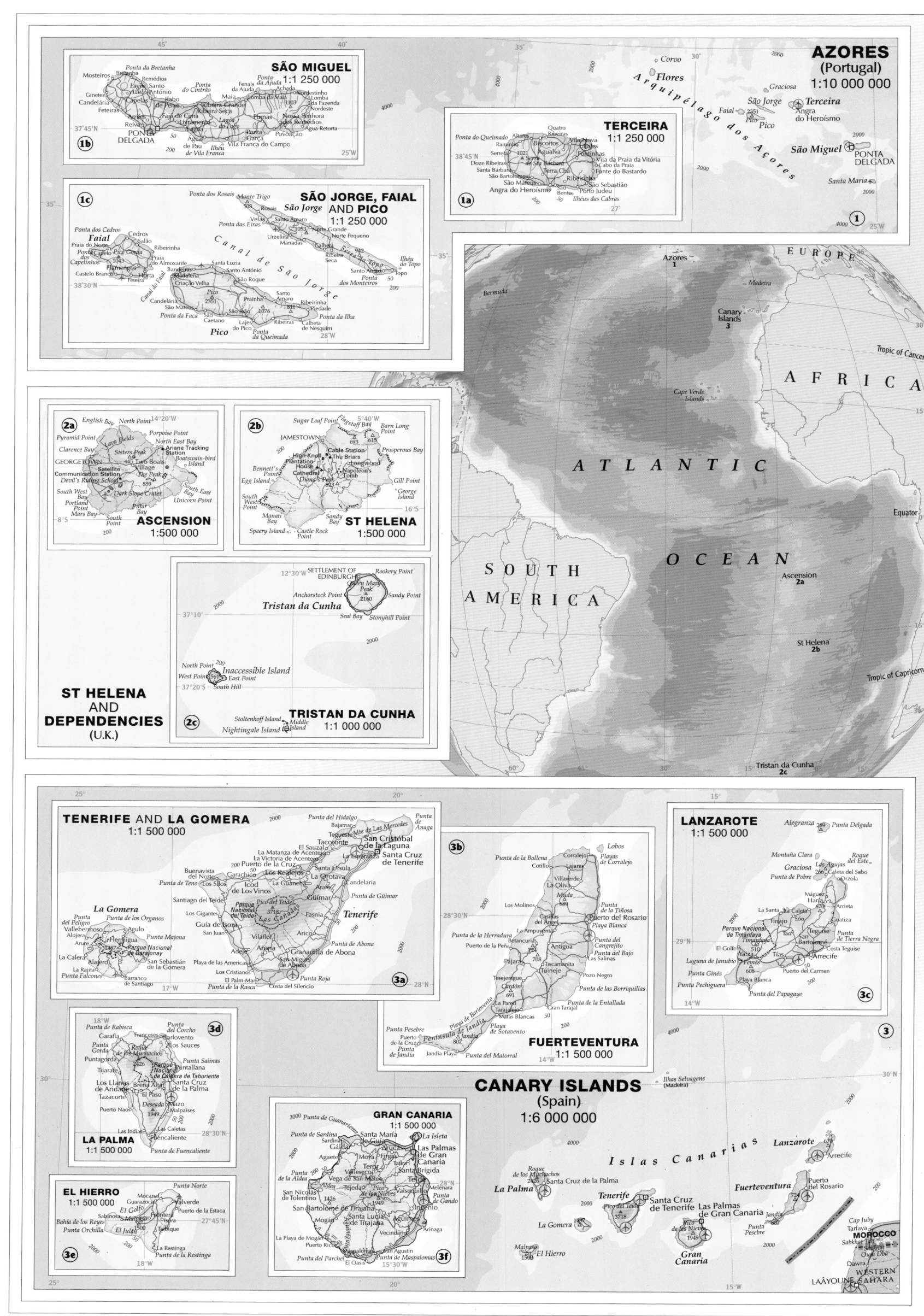
AZORES
(Portugal)
1:10 000 000
Arquipélago dos Açores
Corvo
Flores
Graciosa
São Jorge
Terceira
Angra do Heroísmo
Faial
Pico
São Miguel
PONTA DELGADA
Santa Maria
SÃO MIGUEL
1:1 250 000
TERCEIRA
1:1 250 000
SÃO JORGE, FAIAL AND PICO
1:1 250 000
Canal de São Jorge
EUROPE
AFRICA
ATLANTIC
OCEAN
SOUTH AMERICA
Bermuda
Madeira
Canary Islands
Cape Verde Islands
Tropic of Cancer
Equator
Tropic of Capricorn
Ascension
St Helena
Tristan da Cunha
ASCENSION
1:500 000
GEORGETOWN
ST HELENA
1:500 000
JAMESTOWN
TRISTAN DA CUNHA
1:1 000 000
Tristan da Cunha
Inaccessible Island
Nightingale Island
ST HELENA AND DEPENDENCIES
(U.K.)
TENERIFE AND LA GOMERA
1:1 500 000
Tenerife
La Gomera
Santa Cruz de Tenerife
FUERTEVENTURA
1:1 500 000
LANZAROTE
1:1 500 000
LA PALMA
1:1 500 000
EL HIERRO
1:1 500 000
GRAN CANARIA
1:1 500 000
Las Palmas de Gran Canaria
CANARY ISLANDS
(Spain)
1:6 000 000
Islas Canarias
La Palma
Tenerife
La Gomera
El Hierro
Gran Canaria
Fuerteventura
Lanzarote
Ilhas Selvagens (Madeira)
MOROCCO
WESTERN SAHARA
LAÂYOUNE

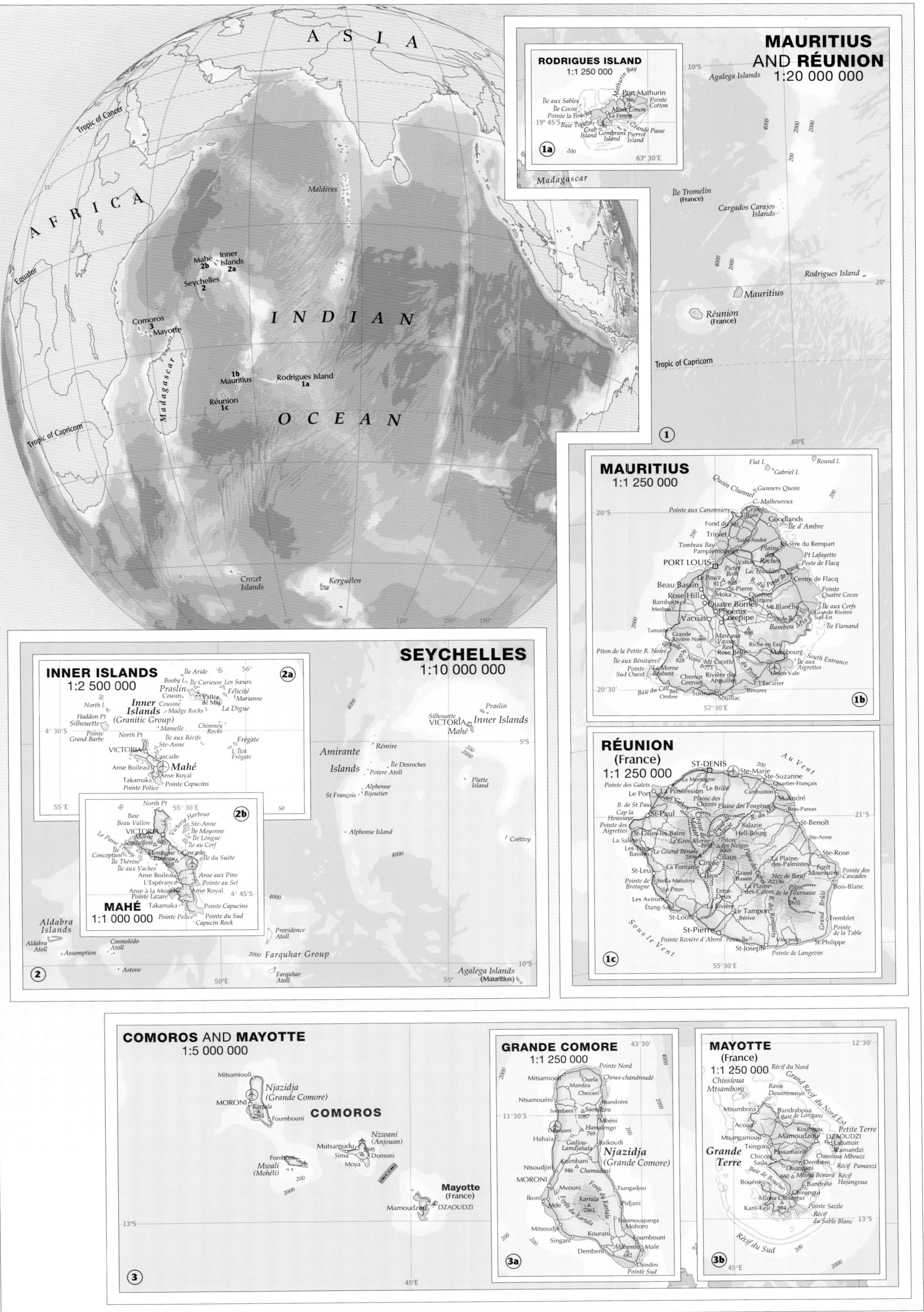

RODRIGUES ISLAND
1:1 250 000

Mathurin Bay

Île aux Sables
Île Cocos
Pointe la Fouche
Baie Topaze

Port Mathurin
Mont Limon
396
La Ferme
Grande Passe
Pierrot Island
Pointe Cotton

Crab Island
Gombrani Island

63° 30'E

19° 45'S

200

1a

Madagascar

MAURITIUS AND RÉUNION
1:20 000 000

Agalega Islands

10°S

Île Tromelin (France)

Cargados Carajos Islands

Rodrigues Island

20°

Mauritius

Réunion (France)

Tropic of Capricorn

60°E

1

MAURITIUS
1:1 250 000

Flat I.
Gabriel I.
Round I.

Quoin Channel
Gunners Quoin
C. Malheureux

20°S

Pointe aux Canonniers
Grande Baie
Goodlands
Île d'Ambre

Fond du Sac
Triolet
Saint André
Rivière du Rempart

Tombeau Bay
Pamplemousses
Plaine
Roche
Pt Lafayette
Poste de Flacq

PORT LOUIS
Piton
811
St-Pierre
Quartier Militaire
Centre de Flacq

Beau Bassin
Moka
Pointe Quatre Cocos

Rose Hill
Quatre Bornes
Phoenix
Curepipe
Île aux Cerfs

Bambou
Vacoas
Grande Rivière
Bambou Mts
Île Flamand

Tamarin
Grande Rivière Noire
Mare aux
Riche en Eau

Piton de la Petite R. Noire
828
Noire
Mt Cocotte
771
Rose Belle
Mahébourg
South Entrance

Pointe Sud Ouest
Le Morne Brabant
Chemin Grenier
Rivière des Anguilles
Île aux Aigrettes
Union Vale

Baie du Cap
Souillac
Surinam
Benares

20° 30'

Ombre

57° 30'E

1b

RÉUNION (France)
1:1 250 000

Au Vent

ST-DENIS
Ste-Marie
Ste-Suzanne
Quartier-Français

Pointe des Galets
La Montagne
Le Brûle
St-André

Le Port
Plaine des Chicots
plaine des Fougères
Bras-Panon

B. de St-Paul
Cap la Houssaye
St-Paul
Salazie
Hell-Bourg

21°S

Pointe des Aigrettes
Le Gros Morne
Piton des Neiges
3069
Ste-Anne

La Saline
Le Grand Bénare
2896
Cirque
Gilaos
La Plaine-des-Palmistes
Ste-Rose

St-Gilles-les-Bains
La Fontaine
Chaos
Nez de Bœuf
Forêt de Mourouvin
Forêt des Cascades

St-Leu
Stella Matutina
Grand
Bassin
2136
Bois-Blanc

Pointe de Bretagne
La Plaine
Piton de la Fournaise
2632

Les Avirons
Deux
Étang-Salé
La Rivière
Le Tampon
Piton de la Table

St-Louis
Bérive
Tremblet

St-Pierre
Sous le Vent
Vincendo
St-Philippe

Pointe Rivière d'Abord
Petite Île
St-Joseph
Pointe de Langevin

55° 30'E

1c

SEYCHELLES
1:10 000 000

Praslin
Inner Islands

5°S

Silhouette
VICTORIA
Mahé

Amirante Islands
Rémire
Île Desroches
Poivre Atoll

Alphonse
St François
Bijoutier
Platte Island

Alphonse Island

Coëtivy

4000

INNER ISLANDS
1:2 500 000

Île Aride
56°

Booby I.
Île Curieuse
Les Sœurs

Praslin
Cousin
Cousine
Vallée
de Mai
Félicité
Marianne

Inner Islands (Granitic Group)
Madge Rocks
La Digue

North I.
Haddon Pt
Silhouette
Île au Recifs
Mamelle
Chimney Rocks

4° 30'S
Pointe Grand Barbe
North Pt
Ste-Anne
Frégate

VICTORIA
L'Îlot Frégate

Cascade

Anse Boileau
Mahé

Takamaka
Anse Royal

Pointe Police
Pointe Capucins

55°E

2a

MAHÉ
1:1 000 000

North Pt
55° 30'E
Baie

Beau Vallon
VICTORIA
Victoria Harbour

Le Passe
Morne Seychellois
Ste-Anne
Île Moyenne

Île
Conception
Montagne
Plateau
Île Longue
Île au Cerf

Île Thérèse
Cascade
Île du Suète

Île aux Vaches

Anse Boileau
Anse aux Pins
L'Espérance
Pointe au Sel

Anse à la Mouche
Anse Royal
4° 45'S

Pointe Lazare

Takamaka
Pointe Capucins

Pointe Police
Pointe du Sud
Capucin Rock

Providence Atoll

Farquhar Group

Aldabra Islands

Aldabra Atoll
Assomption

Cosmolédo Atoll

2000
Astove

Farquhar Atoll

10°S

Agalega Islands (Mauritius)

50°E
55°

2

COMOROS AND MAYOTTE
1:5 000 000

Mitsamiouli
Njazidja (Grande Comore)

MORONI
Karthala
2361
Foumbouni

COMOROS

Nzwani (Anjouan)
Mutsamudu
595
Sima
Domoni
Moya

Fomboni
Mwali
(Mohéli)
200
2000

Mayotte (France)
Mamoudzou
DZAOUDZI

13°S

45°E

3

GRANDE COMORE
1:1 250 000

43° 30'
Pointe Nord

Mitsamiouli
Ouela
Choua-chandroudé
Mandza
Chezani

Ntsaoueni
Ivembeni
Saolézou
1087

11° 30'S
Mbéni
Hamalengo
769

Hahaïa
Itsikoudi

Mamoudzou
Lamfiabou
946
Kombani
Chamdani

Njazidja (Grande Comore)

MORONI
Mvouni
Forêt de Kouni
Tsangadjou

Ikoni
Mde
Forêt de Nioumbadjou
Pidjani

Karthala
2361
Thélmouapanga
Mohoro

Singani
660
682
Foumbouni
Male

Kourani

Dembeni
Ambvamba

Pointe Sud

3a

MAYOTTE (France)
1:1 250 000

12° 30'
Récif du Nord

Chissioua Mtsamboro
Rassi
Douamounyo
Grand Récif du Nord Est

Mtsamboro
Bandraboua
Baie de Longani

Acoua
Koungou
Petite Terre

Mtsangamouji
Mamoudzou
DZAOUDZI
Labattoir

Tsingoni
Passamainti
Pamandzi

Chiconi
Sada
Dembeni
Récif Pamanzi

Ouangani
Chissioua Mbouzi

Grande Terre
Bandrélé
Baie de Bouéni
Mlima Bénara
660
Récif Hajangoua

Bouéni
Chirongui
Mlima Choungui
594
Pointe Sazile

Kani-Kéli
Récif du Sable Blanc

13°S
45°E
Récif du Sud

3b

© Collins Bartholomew Ltd

A B C D E

1

ASIA

ARCTIC

OCEAN

60° Arctic Circle
75° 120°
150° 105°
165° 135° 90°

Chukchi
Sea

Point
Hope

Queen
Is.
Ring

BEAUFORT SEA

Prince
Patrick
Island

Mackenzie
King I.

Melville Island

BERING

Barrow

2

Attu
Island

St. Matthew
Island

St. Lawrence
Island

Bering Strait

Nome
Norton
Sound

Parr

Banks
Island

Viscount Me
Sound

Victoria
Island

SEA

Pribilof
Islands

Nunivak
Island

Brooks Range

Sachs Harbour

McClure Strait

Stefansson
Island

ALASKA

Andreanof Islands

Aleutian Islands

Bristol Bay

Kuskokwim Mts

Mount
McKinley

Mackenzie
Bay

Inuvik

Richardson
Mountains

Amundsen
Gulf

Coronation
Gulf

Vict

Napaktulik
Lake

N

3

Tropic of Cancer

Fox Islands

Alaska Range

Anchorage

Mount
St. Elias

Aleutian Range

Kodiak
Island

**Gulf of
Alaska**

Yukon

Wrangell
Mountains

Ogilvie
Mountains

Great
Bear Lake

Déline

Mackenzie Mountains

**YUKON
TERRITORY**

Whitehorse

Watson
Lake

Fort
Simpson

Yellowknife

Hottah L.

Lac la
Martre

MacKay
Lake

Great Slave
Lake

Trout
Lake

Contwoyto
Lake

Avance

Bathurst
Inlet

NU

MacA

Selwyn

NORTHWEST

TERRITORIES

Juneau

Alexander Archipelago

C

A

Fort
Nelson

Peace

L. Claire

Lake
Athabasca

Uranium City

N

4

Midway
Islands
(U.S.A.)

15°

Queen Charlotte
Islands

Prince Rupert

Queen Charlotte
Sound

COAST

Williston L.

Dawson
Creek

Hecate Strait

Grande
Prairie

**BRITISH
COLUMBIA**

Prince
George

Fraser

MOUNTAINS

Fort
McMurray

ALBERTA

Cree L.

Lesser
Slave Lake

Edmonton

Jasper

Lloydminster

N. Saskatchewan

SASKATCHEWA

Prince
Albert

Lac la
Ro

Sask

5

Kaua'i

O'ahu
Honolulu
Maui

HAWAII

**Hawai'ian Islands
(U.S.A.)**

Hawai'i

Vancouver
Island

Vancouver

Victoria

Kamloops

ROCK

Calgary

Saskatoon

Saskatchewan

Winnipe

Medicine
Hat

Lethbridge

Regin

Seattle

Spokane

WASHINGTON

Olympia

Portland

Salem

Eugene

Columbia

Great Falls

MONTANA

Helena

Bitterroot Mts.

Billings

Bism

N

6

0°
Equator

PACIFIC

OCEAN

Coast Ranges

Cascade Range

Snake

OREGON

IDAHO

Boise

Twin Falls

Great Salt Lake

Salt Lake City

NEVADA

Reno

Sacramento

Carson
City

San Francisco

San Jose

Sierra Nevada

Mount
Whitney

CALIFORNIA

Las Vegas

Los Angeles

Riverside

San Diego

Tijuana

Ensenada

Mexicali

ARIZONA

Phoenix

Tucson

Uinta
Mountains

Great
Basin

UTAH

Colorado
Plateau

UNITED STA

Albuquerque

NEW

MEXICO

El Paso

Rio Grande

Ciudad
Juárez

Bighorn
Mountains

Rapid
City

Casper

WYOMING

Cheyenne

COLORADO

Denver

Colorado
Springs

Santa Fe

Sacramento Mts.

D

N
Pla

Lubbock

Ama

T

7

Line Islands

Guadalupe
(Mexico)

Baja California

Villa Insurgentes

La Paz

Golfo de California

Hermosillo

Chihuahua

Sierra Madre Occidental

MEXI

Durango

Mazatlán

Tepic

Guadalajara

Bolsón
de Mapimí

Los
Mochis

Torreón

Sierra Madre Oriental

Mont

San Lu
Potc

Morel

Islas
Revillagigedo
(Mexico)

Ile Clipperton
(France)

Administrative regions abbreviated on the map:

U.S.A.		CANADA	
CONN.	CONNECTICUT	P.E.I.	PRINCE EDWARD ISLAND
DEL.	DELAWARE		
MD	MARYLAND		
MASS.	MASSACHUSETTS		
N.H.	NEW HAMPSHIRE		
N.J.	NEW JERSEY		
R.I.	RHODE ISLAND		
VER.	VERMONT		
W. VIRG.	WEST VIRGINIA		

165° 15° 150° 0° 135° 120° 105°

A B C D E

EUROPE
AFRICA
ATLANTIC OCEAN
NORTH AMERICA
SOUTH AMERICA
Greenland (Kalaallit Nunaat) (Denmark)
Greenland Sea
Denmark Strait
Iceland
Baffin Bay
Baffin Island
Davis Strait
Labrador Sea
Hudson Strait
HUDSON BAY
Nuuk
Ilulissat
Ammassalik
Nanortalik
Uummannaq
Nuussuaq
Clyde River
Iqaluit
Cape Dorset
Coral Harbour
Repulse Bay
Arviat
Nain
NEWFOUNDLAND AND LABRADOR
QUÉBEC
ONTARIO
MANITOBA
James Bay
Chisasibi
Moosonee
Sept-Îles
Gulf of St Lawrence
Gander
St John's
Cape Race
St Pierre and Miquelon (France)
NEW BRUNSWICK
P.E.I.
NOVA SCOTIA
Charlottetown
Fredericton
Halifax
Sable Island
Cape Sable
Timmins
Rouyn-Noranda
Chicoutimi
Québec
Montréal
Ottawa
North Bay
Sault Sainte Marie
Thunder Bay
International Falls
Lake Superior
Lake Michigan
Lake Huron
Lake Erie
Lake Ontario
Toronto
Duluth
MINNESOTA
Minneapolis
St Paul
WISCONSIN
MICHIGAN
IOWA
ILLINOIS
INDIANA
OHIO
PENNSYLVANIA
NEW YORK
MAINE
Augusta
Montpelier
Concord
Boston
Providence
Hartford
Albany
New York
Philadelphia
Trenton
Dover
Baltimore
Annapolis
Washington
Richmond
Harrisburg
Pittsburgh
Cleveland
Columbus
Detroit
Chicago
Milwaukee
Madison
Lansing
Grand Rapids
Toledo
Fort Wayne
Indianapolis
Springfield
Des Moines
Omaha
Lincoln
Kansas City
Topeka
MISSOURI
Jefferson City
St Louis
Cincinnati
Frankfort
Charleston
W. VIRGINIA
VIRGINIA
KENTUCKY
TENNESSEE
NORTH CAROLINA
SOUTH CAROLINA
Raleigh
Charlotte
Columbia
Cape Hatteras
Nashville
Knoxville
Chattanooga
Memphis
Huntsville
Atlanta
Macon
GEORGIA
Savannah
ARKANSAS
Little Rock
MISSISSIPPI
Jackson
ALABAMA
Montgomery
Tallahassee
Jacksonville
Shreveport
Dallas
Baton Rouge
Mobile
LOUISIANA
New Orleans
Houston
San Antonio
Corpus Christi
Ozark Plateau
Appalachian Mountains
Tulsa
Wichita
FLORIDA
Orlando
Tampa
West Palm Beach
Miami
Cape Canaveral
Bermuda (U.K.)
GULF OF MEXICO
Matamoros
Tampico
Poza Rica
Veracruz
Puebla
Oaxaca
Villahermosa
Mérida
Bahía de Campeche
Yucatán
Yucatan Channel
Straits of Florida
THE BAHAMAS
Nassau
Great Abaco
Turks and Caicos Is (U.K.)
CUBA
La Habana
Santa Clara
Holguín
Cayman Is (U.K.)
JAMAICA
Kingston
Montego Bay
HAITI
Port-au-Prince
DOMINICAN REPUBLIC
Santo Domingo
Puerto Rico (U.S.A.)
San Juan
Hispaniola
Greater Antilles
Lesser Antilles
Leeward Islands
Windward Islands
Virgin Is (U.K.)
Virgin Is (U.S.A.)
Anguilla (U.K.)
ANTIGUA AND BARBUDA
ST KITTS AND NEVIS
Montserrat (U.K.)
Guadeloupe (France)
DOMINICA
Martinique (France)
ST LUCIA
BARBADOS
ST VINCENT AND THE GRENADINES
GRENADA
TRINIDAD AND TOBAGO
Port of Spain
Aruba (Neth.)
Netherlands Antilles
Bonaire
Curaçao
CARIBBEAN SEA
BELIZE
Belmopan
GUATEMALA
Guatemala
San Pedro Sula
HONDURAS
Tegucigalpa
EL SALVADOR
San Salvador
NICARAGUA
Managua
Lago de Nicaragua
COSTA RICA
San José
PANAMA
Panamá
Colón
Golfo de Panamá
Golfo de Tehuantepec
Arquipélago dos Açores
Arquipélago da Madeira
Islas Canarias
Ilhas do Cabo Verde
Tropic of Cancer
Equator
Arctic Circle
F G H I J
1 2 3 4 5 6 7

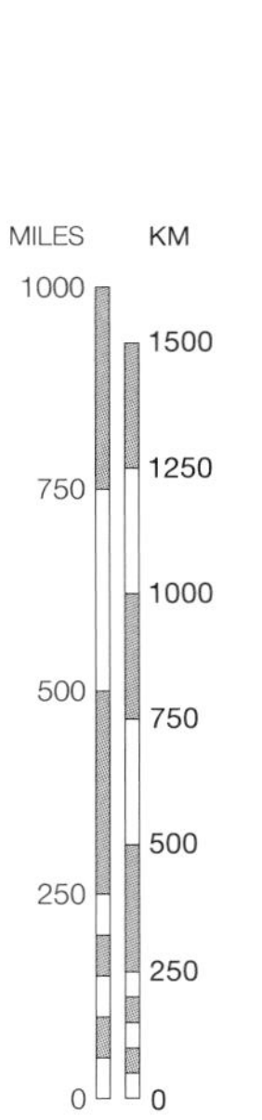
MILES
KM
1000
750
500
250
0
1500
1250
1000
750
500
250
0

1:27 000 000

BERING SEA
ARCTIC OCEAN
BEAUFORT SEA
GULF OF ALASKA
PACIFIC OCEAN
RUSSIAN FEDERATION
U.S.A.
ALASKA
ALEUTIAN ISLANDS
CANADA
YUKON TERRITORY
NORTHWEST TERRITORIES
BRITISH COLUMBIA
ALBERTA
SASKATCHEWAN
WASHINGTON
OREGON
IDAHO
MONTANA
WYOMING
NEVADA
UTAH
CALIFORNIA
NORTH DAKOTA
SOUTH DAKOTA
NEBRASKA
UNITED STATES OF AMERICA
Brooks Range
Philip Smith Mountains
Alaska Range
Kuskokwim Mountains
Mackenzie Mountains
Coast Mountains
Rocky Mountains
Cassiar Mountains
Columbia Mountains
Anchorage
Fairbanks
Juneau
Whitehorse
Yellowknife
Edmonton
Calgary
Vancouver
Victoria
Seattle
Portland
Spokane
Boise
Salt Lake City
Sacramento
San Francisco
San Jose
Regina
Saskatoon
Billings
Lambert Conformal Conic Projection
METRES FEET
6000 19686
5000 16404
4000 13124
3000 9843
2000 6562
1000 3281
500 1640
200 656
0 0 below sea level
200 656
2000 6562
4000 13124
6000 19686

Greenland
(Kalaallit Nunaat)
(Denmark)
GREENLAND SEA
ICELAND
REYKJAVIK
Denmark Strait
BAFFIN BAY
Davis Strait
LABRADOR SEA
HUDSON BAY
James Bay
Hudson Strait
Foxe Basin
Foxe Channel
Ungava Bay
NUNAVUT
NUNAVIK
QUEEN ELIZABETH ISLANDS
Ellesmere Island
Baffin Island
Devon Island
Lancaster Sound
Southampton Island
Lincoln Sea
Nares Strait
Kane Basin
Cumberland Sound
Cumberland Peninsula
Melville Peninsula
Boothia Peninsula
Gulf of Boothia
Prince of Wales Island
Somerset Island
North Magnetic Pole (2004)
North Geomagnetic Pole (2004)
MANITOBA
ONTARIO
QUÉBEC
CANADIAN SHIELD
NEWFOUNDLAND AND LABRADOR
Newfoundland
Labrador
NEW BRUNSWICK
NOVA SCOTIA
PRINCE EDWARD ISLAND
MAINE
VERMONT
NEW HAMPSHIRE
NEW YORK
PENNSYLVANIA
MICHIGAN
WISCONSIN
MINNESOTA
IOWA
Lake Superior
Lake Michigan
Lake Huron
Lake Erie
Lake Winnipeg
Gulf of St Lawrence
Gulf of Maine
Bay of Fundy
Cabot Strait
Île d'Anticosti
St Pierre and Miquelon (France)
Sable Island
ATLANTIC OCEAN
OTTAWA
Montréal
Québec
Toronto
Boston
New York
Philadelphia
Chicago
Detroit
Cleveland
Buffalo
Milwaukee
Minneapolis
Winnipeg
Halifax
St John's
Thunder Bay
NUUK (Godthåb)
Iqaluit (Frobisher Bay)
Longitude 70° west of Greenwich
MILES
KM
600
400
200
0
1000
800
600
400
200
0

1:15 000 000

113

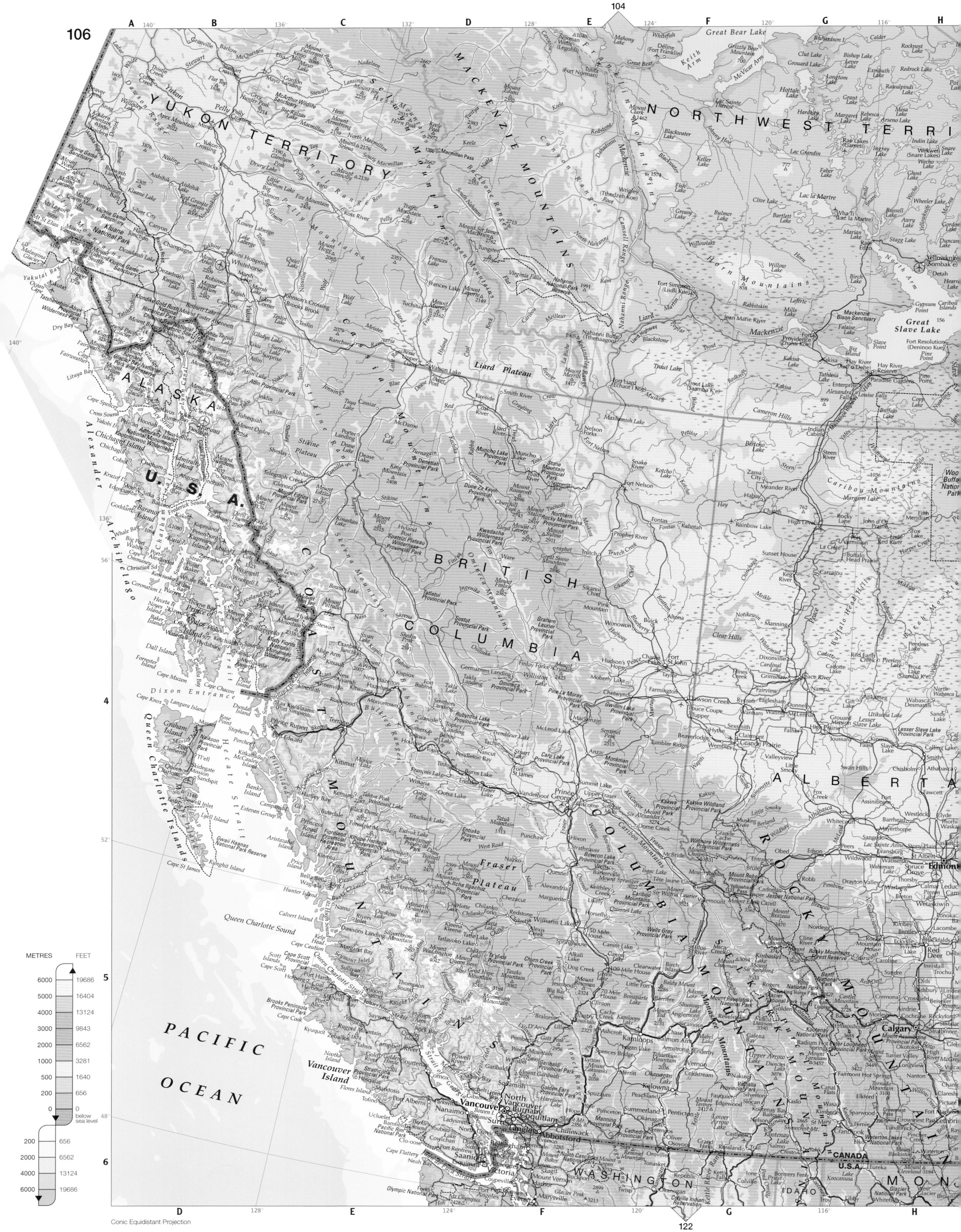

Major regions

YUKON TERRITORY

NORTHWEST TERRITORIES

ALASKA U.S.A.

BRITISH COLUMBIA

ALBERTA

WASHINGTON

IDAHO

MONTANA

PACIFIC OCEAN

CANADA
U.S.A.

Major physical features

MACKENZIE MOUNTAINS

Great Bear Lake

Great Slave Lake

Liard Plateau

COAST MOUNTAINS

ROCKY MOUNTAINS

COLUMBIA MOUNTAINS

SELKIRK MOUNTAINS

PURCELL MOUNTAINS

Fraser Plateau

Queen Charlotte Islands

Vancouver Island

Queen Charlotte Sound

Dixon Entrance

Hecate Strait

Alexander Archipelago

Graham Island

Cassiar Mountains

Skeena Mountains

Omineca Mountains

Cariboo Mountains

Caribou Mountains

Wood Buffalo National Park

Selected settlements

Whitehorse, Vancouver, North Vancouver, Burnaby, Surrey, Coquitlam, Abbotsford, Chilliwack, Victoria, Nanaimo, Prince George, Prince Rupert, Kitimat, Kamloops, Kelowna, Penticton, Fort Nelson, Fort St John, Dawson Creek, Grande Prairie, Calgary, Edmonton, Fort Simpson, Hay River

Scale

METRES	FEET
6000	19686
5000	16404
4000	13124
3000	9843
2000	6562
1000	3281
500	1640
200	656
0	0 below sea level
200	656
2000	6562
4000	13124
6000	19686

Conic Equidistant Projection

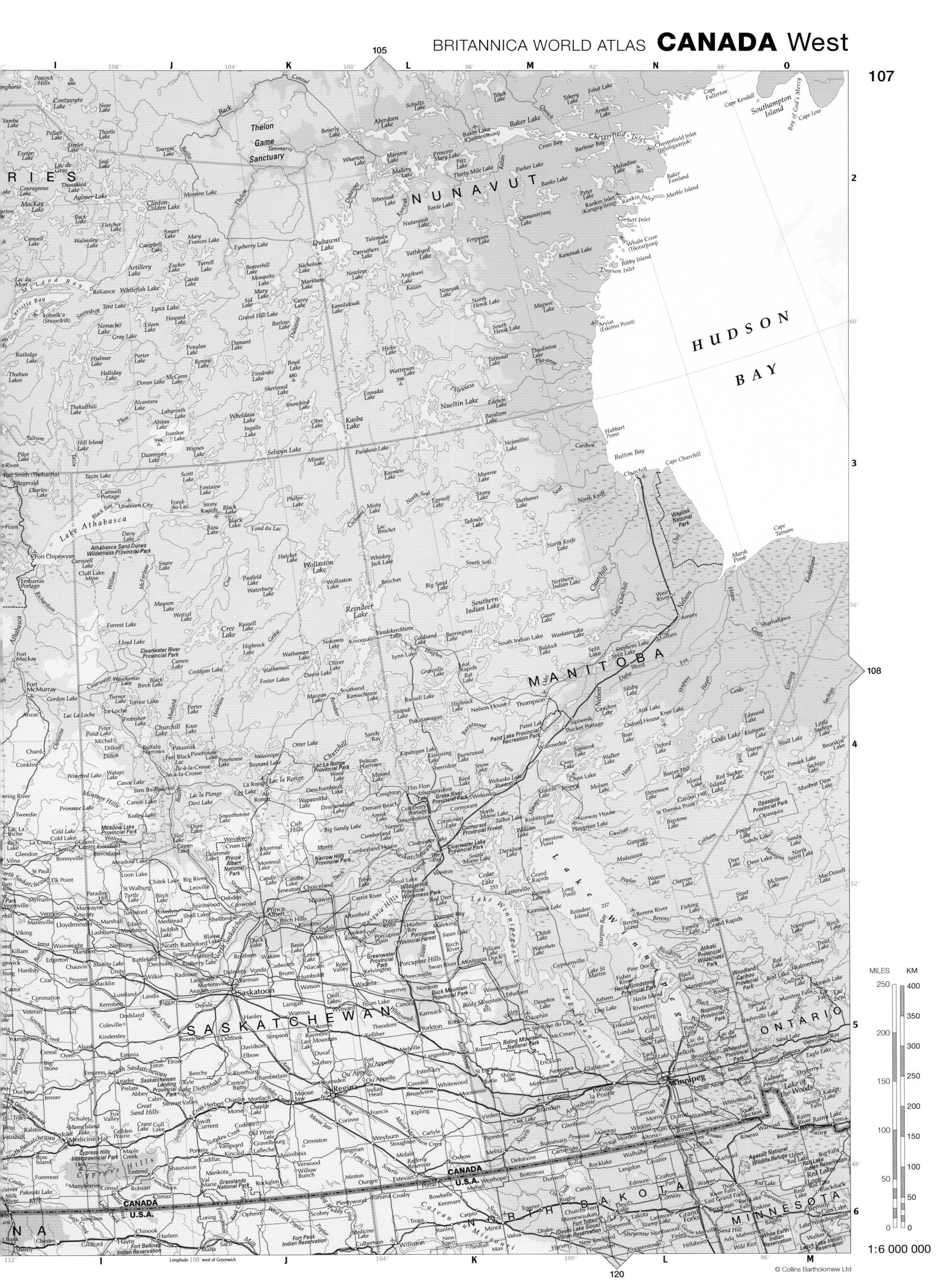

MILES KM

1:6 000 000

© Collins Bartholomew Ltd

NUNAVUT
MANITOBA
SASKATCHEWAN
ONTARIO
NORTH DAKOTA
MINNESOTA
HUDSON BAY
CANADA
U.S.A.
Thelon Game Sanctuary
Lake Athabasca
Reindeer Lake
Southern Indian Lake
Lake Winnipeg
Lake Winnipegosis
Lake Manitoba
Lake of the Woods
Wollaston Lake
Baker Lake
Dubawnt Lake
Nueltin Lake
Churchill
Thompson
Flin Flon
The Pas
Prince Albert
Saskatoon
Regina
Moose Jaw
Brandon
Winnipeg
Swift Current
Medicine Hat
Lloydminster
North Battleford
Yorkton
Dauphin
Grand Forks
Minot
Williston
Fort McMurray
Fort Chipewyan
Uranium City
Arviat (Eskimo Point)
Rankin Inlet (Kangiqcliniq)
Chesterfield Inlet
Southampton Island
Prince Albert National Park
Riding Mountain National Park
Wapusk National Park
Grasslands National Park
Longitude 108° west of Greenwich
105
120
108
250
200
150
100
50
400
350
300
250
200
150
100
50

HUDSON BAY
James Bay
ONTARIO
MANITOBA
MINNESOTA
WISCONSIN
MICHIGAN
NEW YORK
CANADIAN SHIELD
LAKE SUPERIOR
LAKE MICHIGAN
LAKE HURON
LAKE ERIE
LAKE ONTARIO
Georgian Bay
North Channel
CANADA
U.S.A.
OTTAWA
Toronto
Chicago
Milwaukee
Detroit
Cleveland
Buffalo
Rochester
Thunder Bay
Duluth
Sudbury
Hamilton
London
Windsor
Kingston
Albany
Belcher Islands
Akimiski Island
Polar Bear Provincial Park
Algonquin Provincial Park
Lake Nipigon
Lake of the Woods
Lake Nipissing
Lake Abitibi
Adirondack Mountains
METRES
FEET
6000
5000
4000
3000
2000
1000
500
200
0
19686
16404
13124
9843
6562
3281
1640
656
below sea level
Conic Equidistant Projection

120
114

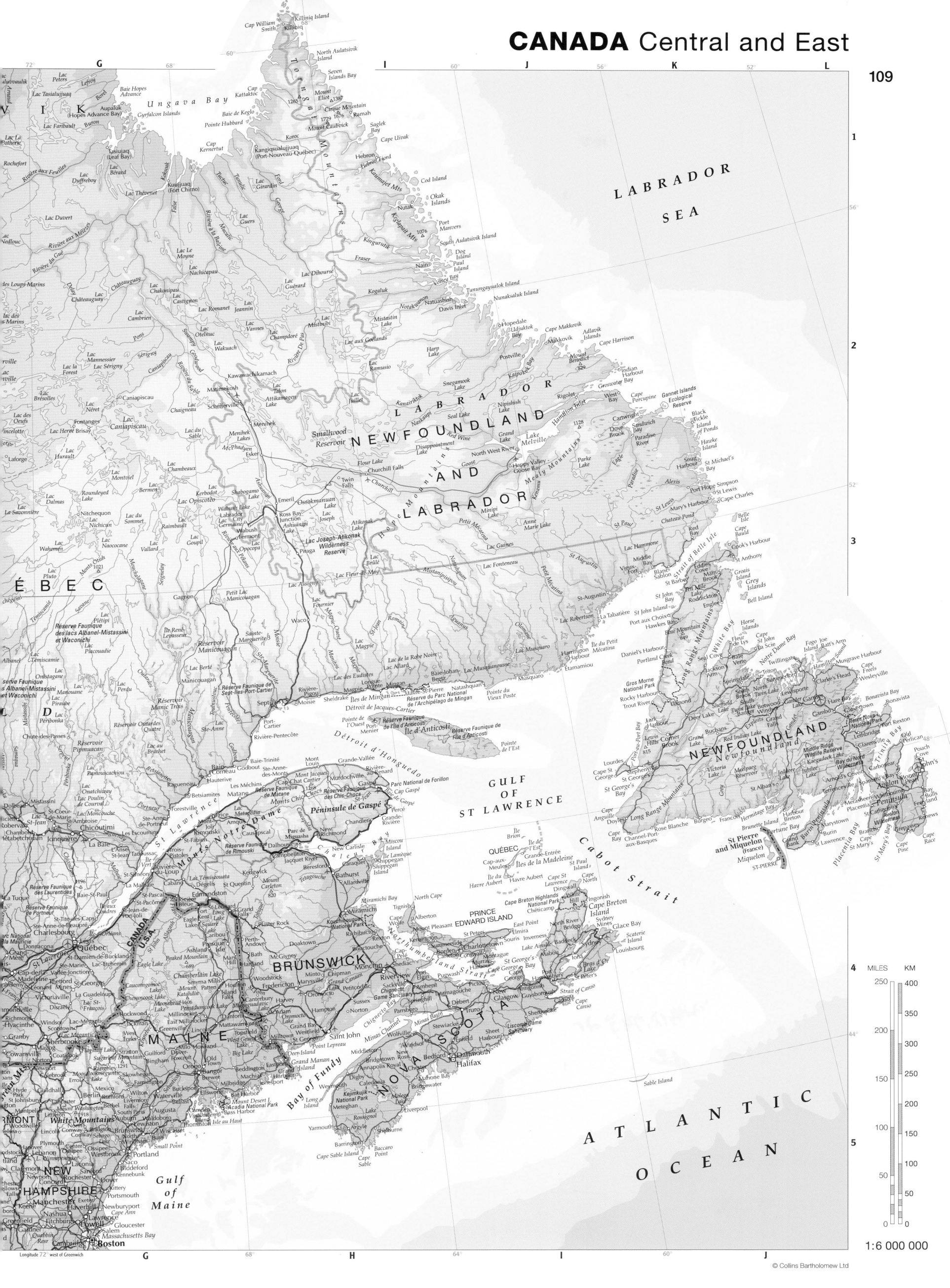

LABRADOR
SEA

Ungava Bay

LABRADOR

NEWFOUNDLAND

AND

LABRADOR

É B E C

NEWFOUNDLAND

GULF
OF
ST LAWRENCE

QUÉBEC

Cabot Strait

St Pierre
and Miquelon
(France)

PRINCE
EDWARD ISLAND

BRUNSWICK

NOVA SCOTIA

MAINE

Bay of Fundy

NEW
HAMPSHIRE

Gulf
of
Maine

ATLANTIC

OCEAN

MILES   KM
250 — 400
        350
200
        300
150 — 250
        200
100
        150
50 — 100
     50
0 — 0

108
METRES
FEET
6000
5000
4000
3000
2000
1500
1000
500
200
100
0
below sea level
19686
16404
13124
9843
6562
4921
3281
1640
656
328
50
164
LAKE SUPERIOR
MINNESOTA
WISCONSIN
MICHIGAN
LAKE MICHIGAN
UNITED STATES OF AMERICA
IOWA
MISSOURI
ILLINOIS
INDIANA
Quetico Provincial Park
Voyageurs National Park
Thunder Bay
Isle Royale
Isle Royale National Park
Apostle Islands
Apostle Islands National Lakeshore
Keweenaw Peninsula
Pictured Rocks National Lakeshore
Sleeping Bear Dunes National Lakeshore
Lake Superior Provincial Park
Duluth
Superior
Minneapolis
St Paul
Rochester
La Crosse
Eau Claire
Wausau
Green Bay
Appleton
Oshkosh
Madison
Milwaukee
Racine
Kenosha
Waukegan
Chicago
Gary
Rockford
Joliet
Peoria
Bloomington
Kankakee
South Bend
Fort Wayne
Kalamazoo
Grand Rapids
Lansing
Muskegon
Marquette
Escanaba
Sault Ste Marie
CHICAGO
1:50 000
METRES 500
YARDS 500
RIVER NORTH
NEAR NORTH
THE LOOP
PRINTERS ROW
Lake Michigan
Monroe Harbor
Chicago Harbor
Burnham Park Harbor
Navy Pier
Sears Tower
Union Station
Northwestern Station
Field Museum of Natural History
John G. Shedd Aquarium
Adler Planetarium
Soldier Field
120
114

Conic Equidistant Projection

Scale 1:3 000 000

MILES / KM

© Collins Bartholomew Ltd

104

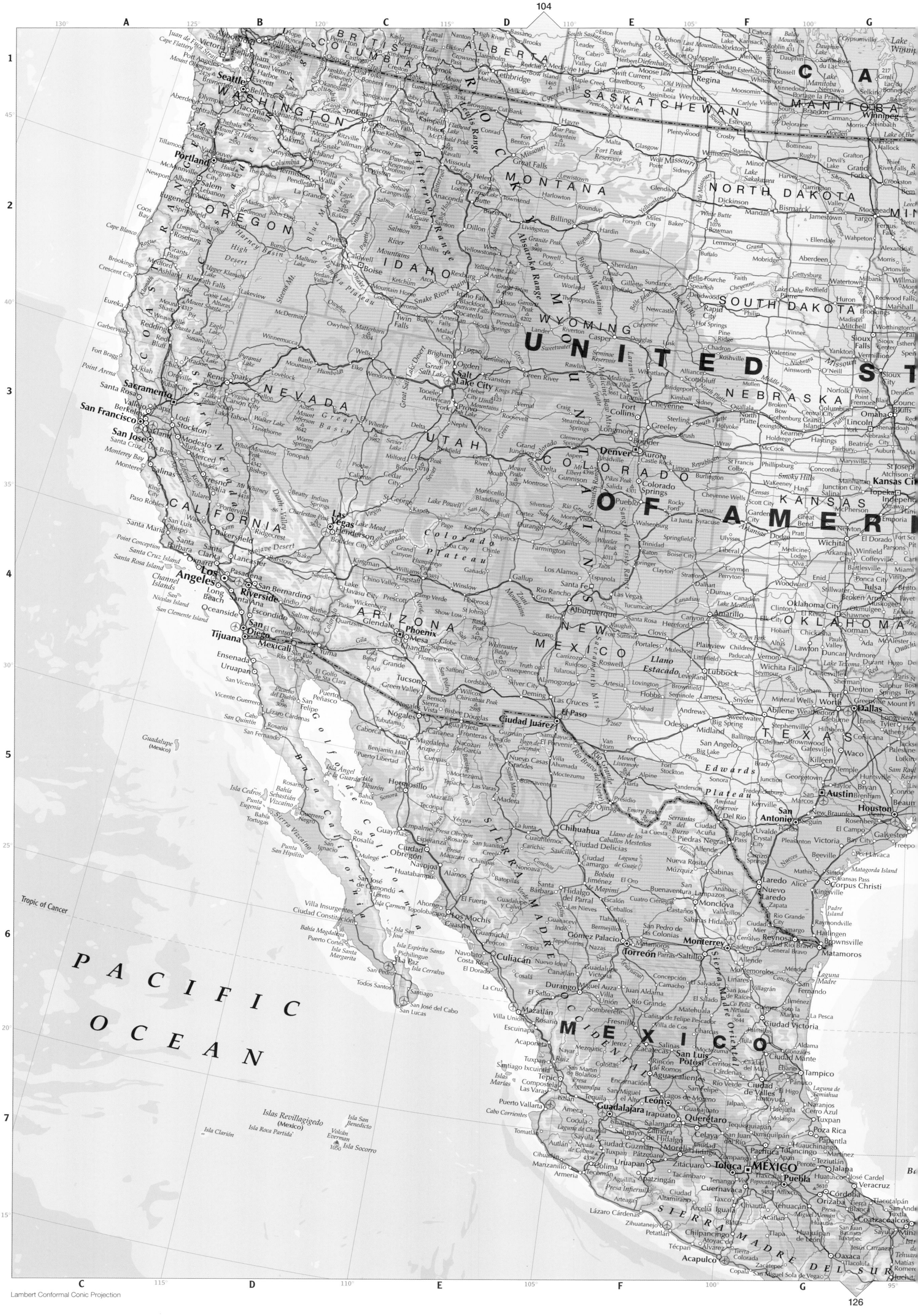

BRITISH COLUMBIA · ALBERTA · SASKATCHEWAN · MANITOBA

CANADA

WASHINGTON · OREGON · IDAHO · MONTANA · NORTH DAKOTA

WYOMING · SOUTH DAKOTA · NEBRASKA

UNITED STATES

NEVADA · UTAH · COLORADO · KANSAS

CALIFORNIA · ARIZONA · NEW MEXICO · OKLAHOMA

OF AMERICA

TEXAS

Colorado Plateau

Sierra Madre Occidental · Sierra Madre Oriental

MEXICO

PACIFIC OCEAN

Tropic of Cancer

Legend (elevation)

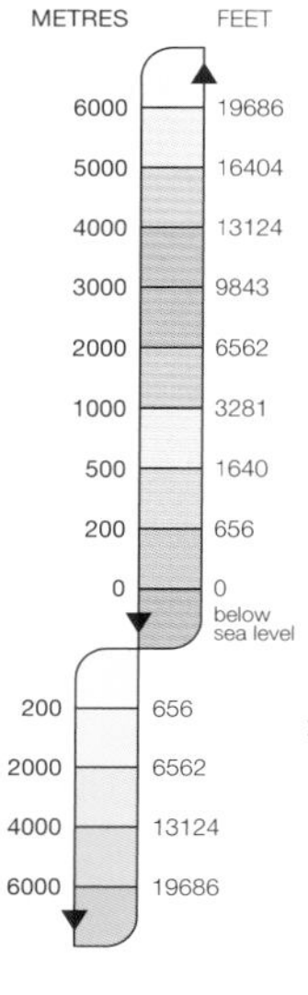

METRES	FEET
6000	19686
5000	16404
4000	13124
3000	9843
2000	6562
1000	3281
500	1640
200	656
0	0 below sea level
200	656
2000	6562
4000	13124
6000	19686

Lambert Conformal Conic Projection

ATLANTIC

OCEAN

GULF OF MEXICO

THE BAHAMAS

WEST INDIES

Tropic of Cancer

CUBA

LA HABANA (Havana)

Cayman Islands (U.K.)

JAMAICA

YUCATÁN

GUATEMALA

BELIZE

CARIBBEAN SEA

Turks and Caicos Islands

HISPANIOLA

HAITI

PORT-AU-PRINCE

SANTO DOMINGO

DOMINICAN REPUBLIC

Puerto Rico (U.S.A.)

131

MILES KM
500 800
700
400 600
500
300 400
200 300
100 200
100
0 0

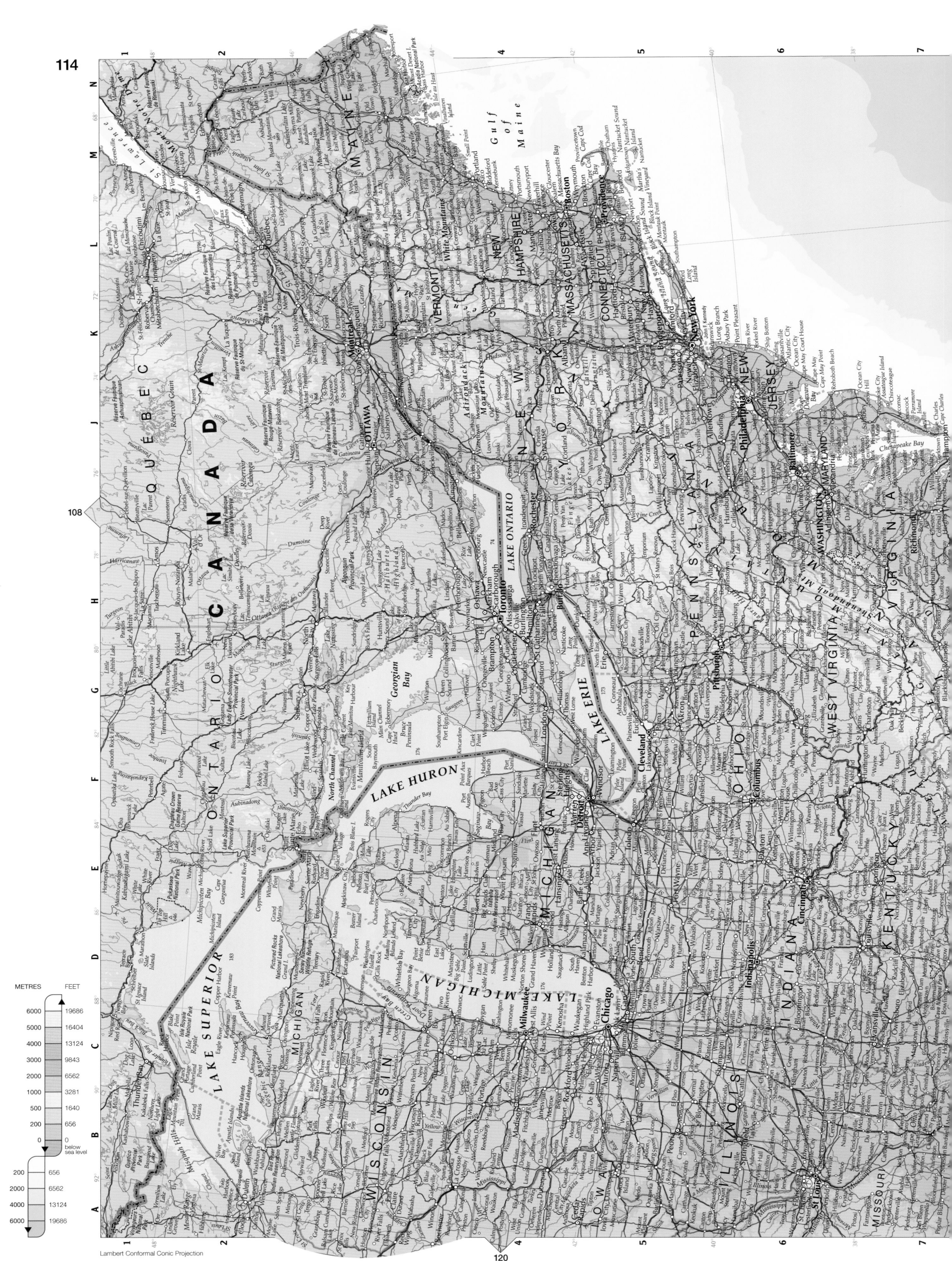
CANADA
ONTARIO
QUÉBEC
MAINE
NEW YORK
PENNSYLVANIA
OHIO
MICHIGAN
INDIANA
ILLINOIS
WISCONSIN
KENTUCKY
WEST VIRGINIA
VIRGINIA
NEW JERSEY
LAKE SUPERIOR
LAKE HURON
LAKE MICHIGAN
LAKE ERIE
LAKE ONTARIO
Georgian Bay
Gulf of Maine
METRES
FEET
below sea level

Lambert Conformal Conic Projection

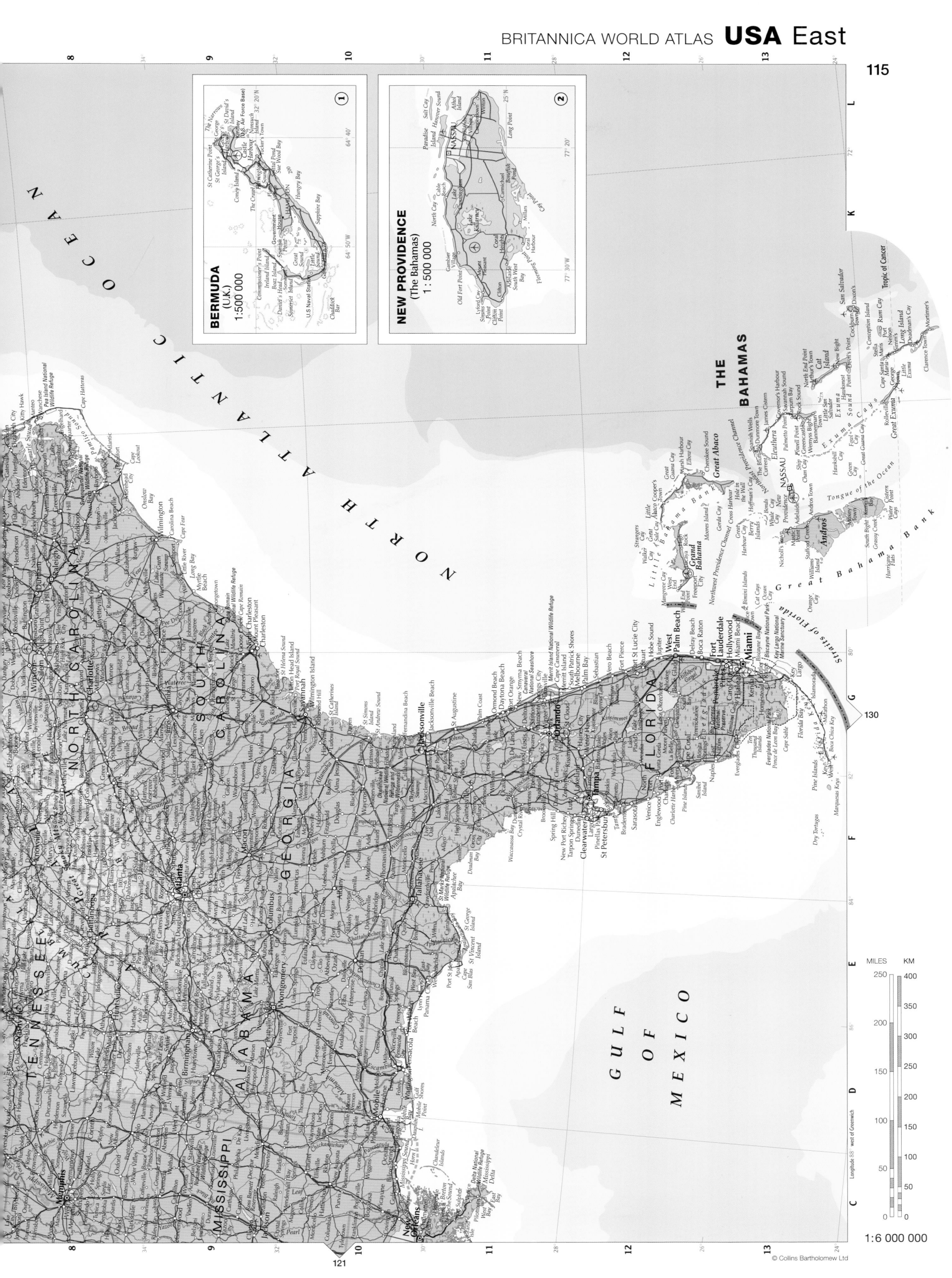

BERMUDA
(U.K.)
1:500 000

NEW PROVIDENCE
(The Bahamas)
1:500 000

NORTH CAROLINA

SOUTH CAROLINA

GEORGIA

ALABAMA

MISSISSIPPI

TENNESSEE

FLORIDA

THE BAHAMAS

NORTH ATLANTIC OCEAN

GULF OF MEXICO

Atlanta

Charlotte

Columbia

Savannah

Jacksonville

Orlando

Tampa

Miami

Fort Lauderdale

Hollywood

West Palm Beach

Montgomery

Birmingham

Mobile

Nashville

Memphis

New Orleans

Tallahassee

NASSAU

Grand Bahama

Great Abaco

Andros

Eleuthera

Freeport

MILES

KM

250 — 400
— 350
200 — 300
— 250
150 — 200
— 150
100 —
— 100
50 —
50 —
0 — 0

1:6 000 000

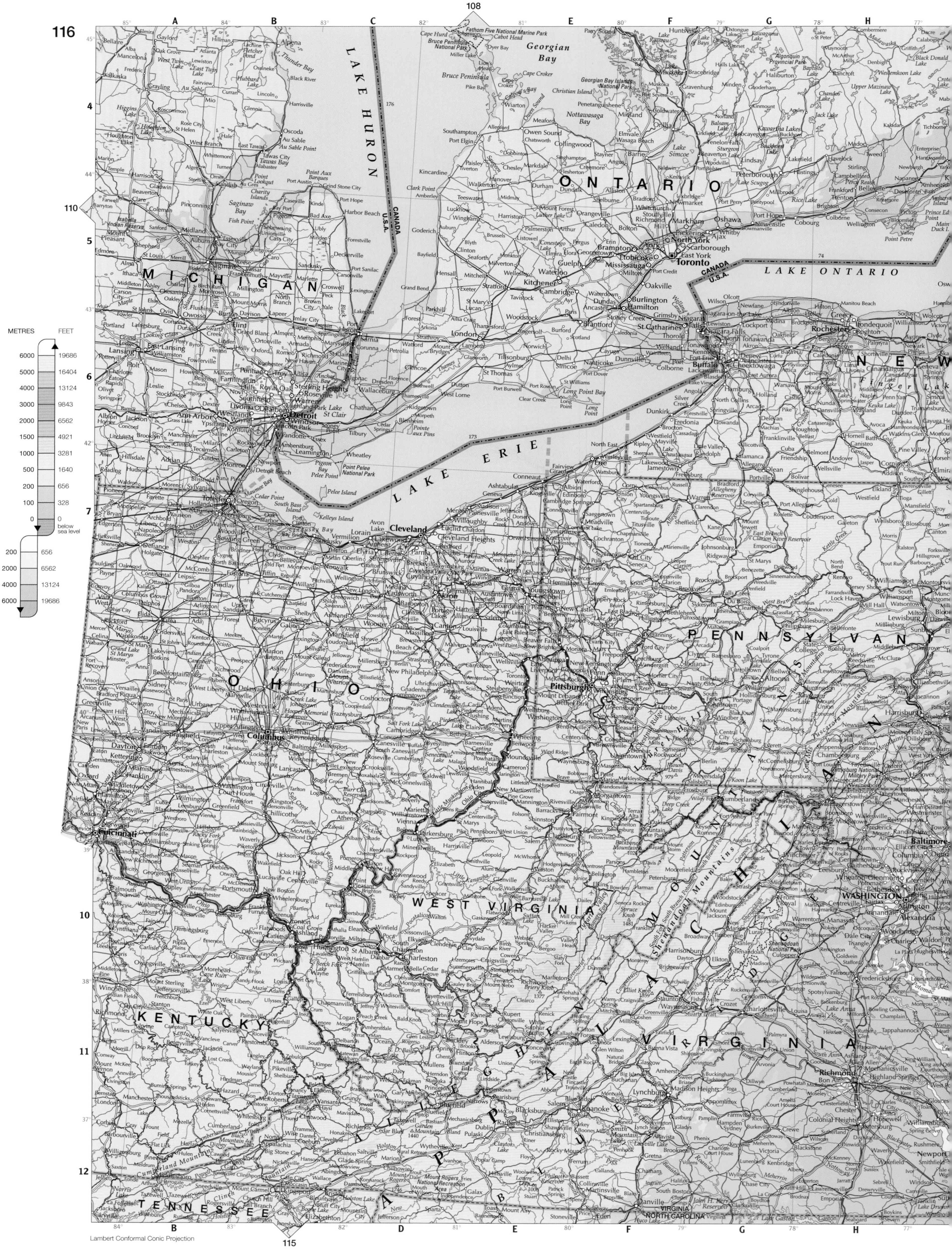

MICHIGAN

ONTARIO

OHIO

PENNSYLVANIA

NEW YORK

WEST VIRGINIA

KENTUCKY

VIRGINIA

TENNESSEE

NORTH CAROLINA

LAKE HURON

Georgian Bay

LAKE ONTARIO

LAKE ERIE

CANADA

U.S.A.

APPALACHIAN MOUNTAINS

ALLEGHENY MOUNTAINS

Toronto

Detroit

Cleveland

Columbus

Cincinnati

Pittsburgh

Buffalo

Rochester

WASHINGTON

Baltimore

Richmond

METRES	FEET
6000	19686
5000	16404
4000	13124
3000	9843
2000	6562
1500	4921
1000	3281
500	1640
200	656
100	328
0	below sea level
200	656
2000	6562
4000	13124
6000	19686

Lambert Conformal Conic Projection

MAINE
CONTINUATION AT THE SAME SCALE

MILES   KM
125   200

100   175
        150
75   125
        100
50   75

25   50
        25

0   0

1:3 000 000

© Collins Bartholomew Ltd

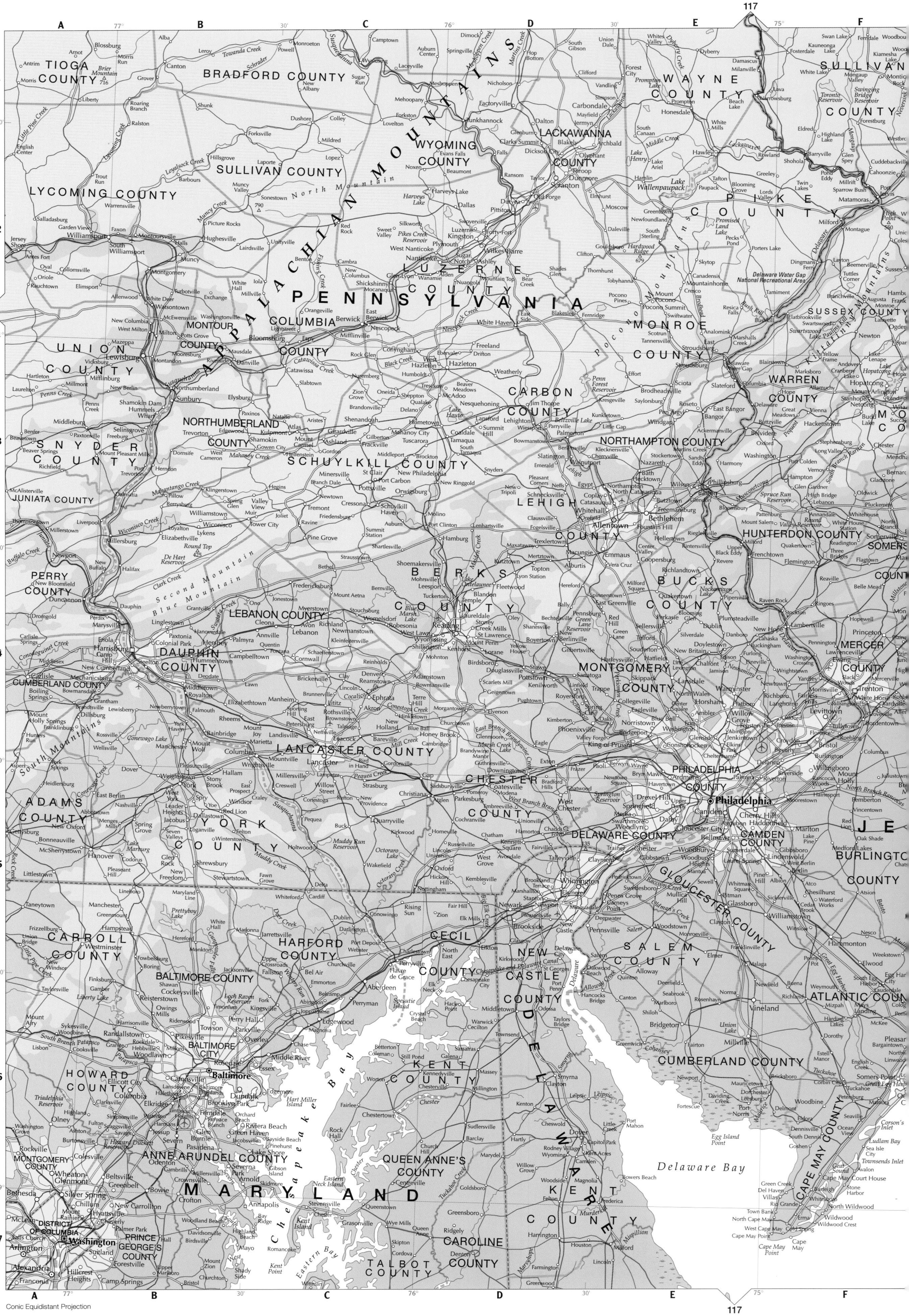
A
B
C
D
E
F
1
2
3
4
5
6
7
117
TIOGA COUNTY
BRADFORD COUNTY
SULLIVAN COUNTY
LYCOMING COUNTY
WYOMING COUNTY
LACKAWANNA COUNTY
WAYNE COUNTY
PIKE COUNTY
APPALACHIAN MOUNTAINS
LUZERNE COUNTY
PENNSYLVANIA
MONTOUR COUNTY
COLUMBIA COUNTY
UNION COUNTY
MONROE COUNTY
CARBON COUNTY
NORTHUMBERLAND COUNTY
SNYDER COUNTY
SCHUYLKILL COUNTY
NORTHAMPTON COUNTY
JUNIATA COUNTY
LEHIGH COUNTY
WARREN COUNTY
HUNTERDON COUNTY
SUSSEX COUNTY
PERRY COUNTY
BERKS COUNTY
BUCKS COUNTY
LEBANON COUNTY
DAUPHIN COUNTY
CUMBERLAND COUNTY
MONTGOMERY COUNTY
MERCER COUNTY
LANCASTER COUNTY
CHESTER COUNTY
PHILADELPHIA COUNTY
Philadelphia
ADAMS COUNTY
YORK COUNTY
DELAWARE COUNTY
CAMDEN COUNTY
BURLINGTON COUNTY
GLOUCESTER COUNTY
CARROLL COUNTY
HARFORD COUNTY
CECIL COUNTY
NEW CASTLE COUNTY
SALEM COUNTY
BALTIMORE COUNTY
BALTIMORE CITY
Baltimore
ATLANTIC COUNTY
CUMBERLAND COUNTY
HOWARD COUNTY
KENT COUNTY
DELAWARE
Chesapeake Bay
Delaware Bay
ANNE ARUNDEL COUNTY
QUEEN ANNE'S COUNTY
CAPE MAY COUNTY
MONTGOMERY COUNTY
MARYLAND
KENT COUNTY
DISTRICT OF COLUMBIA
Washington
PRINCE GEORGE'S COUNTY
CAROLINE COUNTY
TALBOT COUNTY
Conic Equidistant Projection

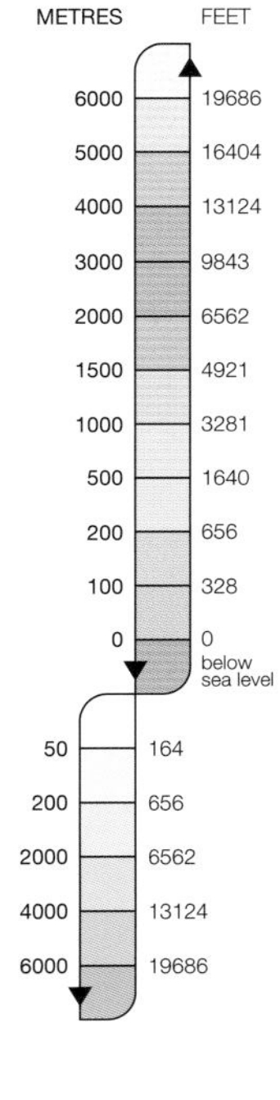
METRES
FEET
6000 19686
5000 16404
4000 13124
3000 9843
2000 6562
1500 4921
1000 3281
500 1640
200 656
100 328
0 0
below sea level
50 164
200 656
2000 6562
4000 13124
6000 19686

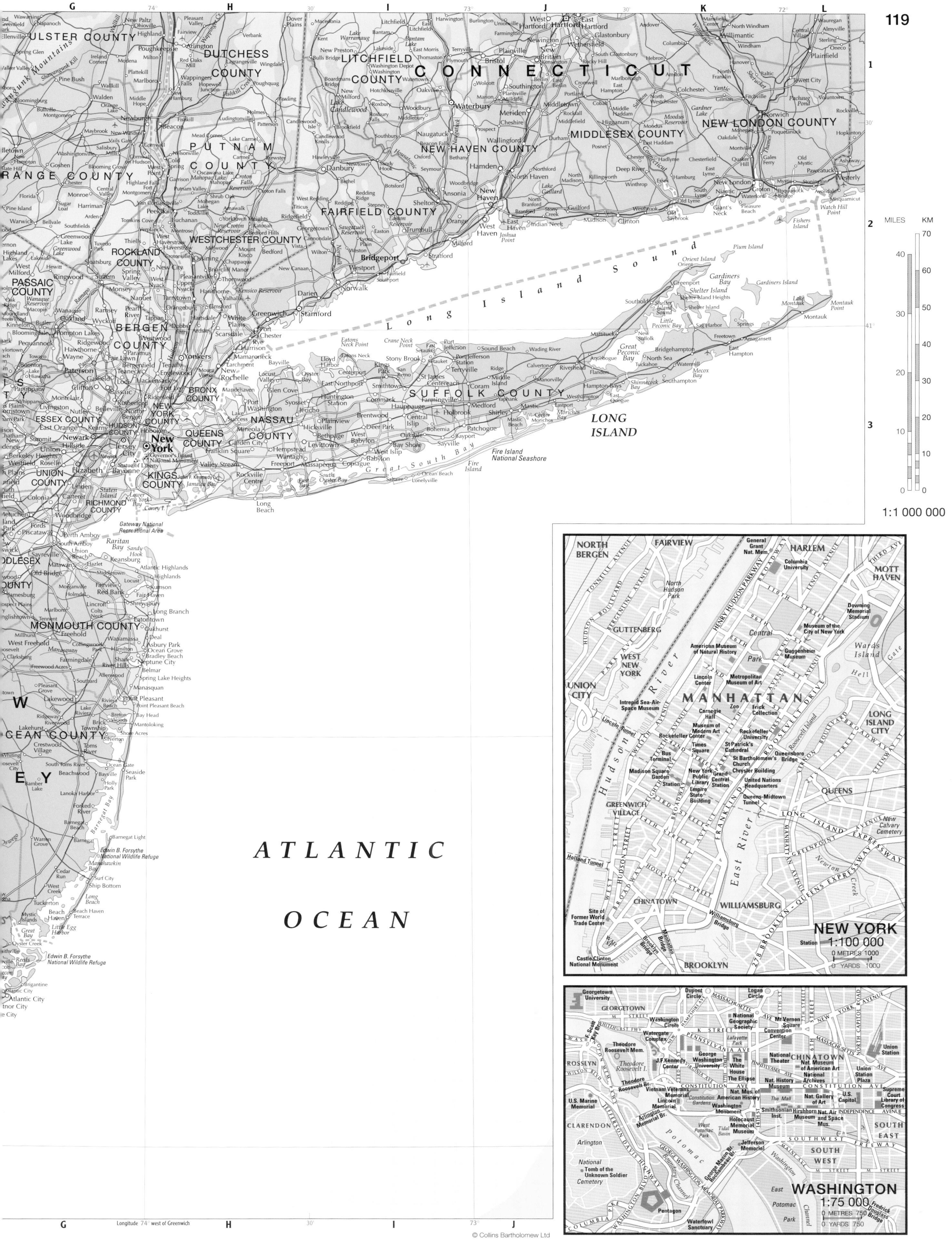

G 74° H 30° I 73° J 30° K 72° L

ULSTER COUNTY
DUTCHESS COUNTY
LITCHFIELD COUNTY
CONNECTICUT
ORANGE COUNTY
PUTNAM COUNTY
NEW HAVEN COUNTY
MIDDLESEX COUNTY
NEW LONDON COUNTY
PASSAIC COUNTY
ROCKLAND COUNTY
WESTCHESTER COUNTY
FAIRFIELD COUNTY
BERGEN COUNTY

Poughkeepsie
Newburgh
Danbury
Waterbury
Meriden
Bridgeport
Stamford
Norwalk
New Haven
New London

Long Island Sound

Gardiners Bay
Gardiners Island
Shelter Island
Greenport
Montauk
Montauk Point

SUFFOLK COUNTY

NEW YORK
New York
BRONX COUNTY
NEW YORK COUNTY
QUEENS COUNTY
NASSAU COUNTY
KINGS COUNTY
RICHMOND COUNTY

HUDSON COUNTY
UNION COUNTY
ESSEX COUNTY
Newark
Elizabeth
Staten Island

LONG ISLAND

Great South Bay
Fire Island National Seashore
Jones Beach
Long Beach
John F. Kennedy International Airport

MIDDLESEX COUNTY
MONMOUTH COUNTY
Freehold
Asbury Park
Long Branch
Red Bank
Sandy Hook
Raritan Bay
Perth Amboy
Gateway National Recreational Area

OCEAN COUNTY
Toms River
Lakewood
Point Pleasant
Seaside Park
Barnegat Bay
Barnegat Light

ATLANTIC

OCEAN

Edwin B. Forsythe National Wildlife Refuge
Long Beach
Beach Haven
Little Egg Harbor
Atlantic City
Brigantine

MILES | KM
1:1 000 000

NEW YORK
1:100 000

NORTH BERGEN | **FAIRVIEW** | **HARLEM** | **MOTT HAVEN**
General Grant Nat. Mem.
Columbia University
North Hudson Park
GUTTENBERG
Museum of the City of New York
WEST NEW YORK
American Museum of Natural History
Guggenheim Museum
UNION CITY
Central Park
MANHATTAN
Metropolitan Museum of Art
Frick Collection
Lincoln Center
Intrepid Sea-Air-Space Museum
Carnegie Hall
Zoo
Museum of Modern Art
Rockefeller University
Rockefeller Center
Queensboro Bridge
LONG ISLAND CITY
Times Square
St Patrick's Cathedral
Chrysler Building
St Bartholomew's Church
Bus Terminal
Lincoln Tunnel
Madison Square Garden
New York Public Library
Grand Central Station
Empire State Building
United Nations Headquarters
Queens-Midtown Tunnel
QUEENS
GREENWICH VILLAGE
New Calvary Cemetery
Holland Tunnel
CHINATOWN
WILLIAMSBURG
Williamsburg Bridge
Site of Former World Trade Center
Manhattan Bridge
Brooklyn Bridge
Castle Clinton National Monument
BROOKLYN
Hudson River
East River
Wards Island
Hell Gate
Roosevelt Island
Randall's Island
Station

0 metres 1000
0 yards 1000

WASHINGTON
1:75 000

Georgetown University
GEORGETOWN
Dupont Circle
Logan Circle
Washington Circle
Watergate Complex
National Geographic Society
National Convention Center
Theodore Roosevelt Mem.
J.F. Kennedy Center
George Washington University
Lafayette Park
National Theater
CHINATOWN
Nat. Museum of American Art
National Archives
Union Station
ROSSLYN
Theodore Roosevelt I.
Theodore Roosevelt Br.
The White House
The Ellipse
Nat. History Museum
Nat. Gallery of Art
Union Station Plaza
U.S. Marine Memorial
Vietnam Veterans Memorial
Constitution Gardens
American History Museum
The Mall
Smithsonian Inst.
Hirshhorn Museum
Nat. Air and Space Mus.
Supreme Court
Library of Congress
U.S. Capitol
Lincoln Memorial
Washington Monument
Holocaust Memorial
CLARENDON
Arlington Memorial Br.
Jefferson Memorial
Tidal Basin
SOUTH EAST
National Tomb of the Unknown Soldier Cemetery
Pentagon
Potomac River
Anacostia River
SOUTH WEST
Waterfowl Sanctuary
Potomac Park

0 metres 750
0 yards 750

Longitude 74° west of Greenwich

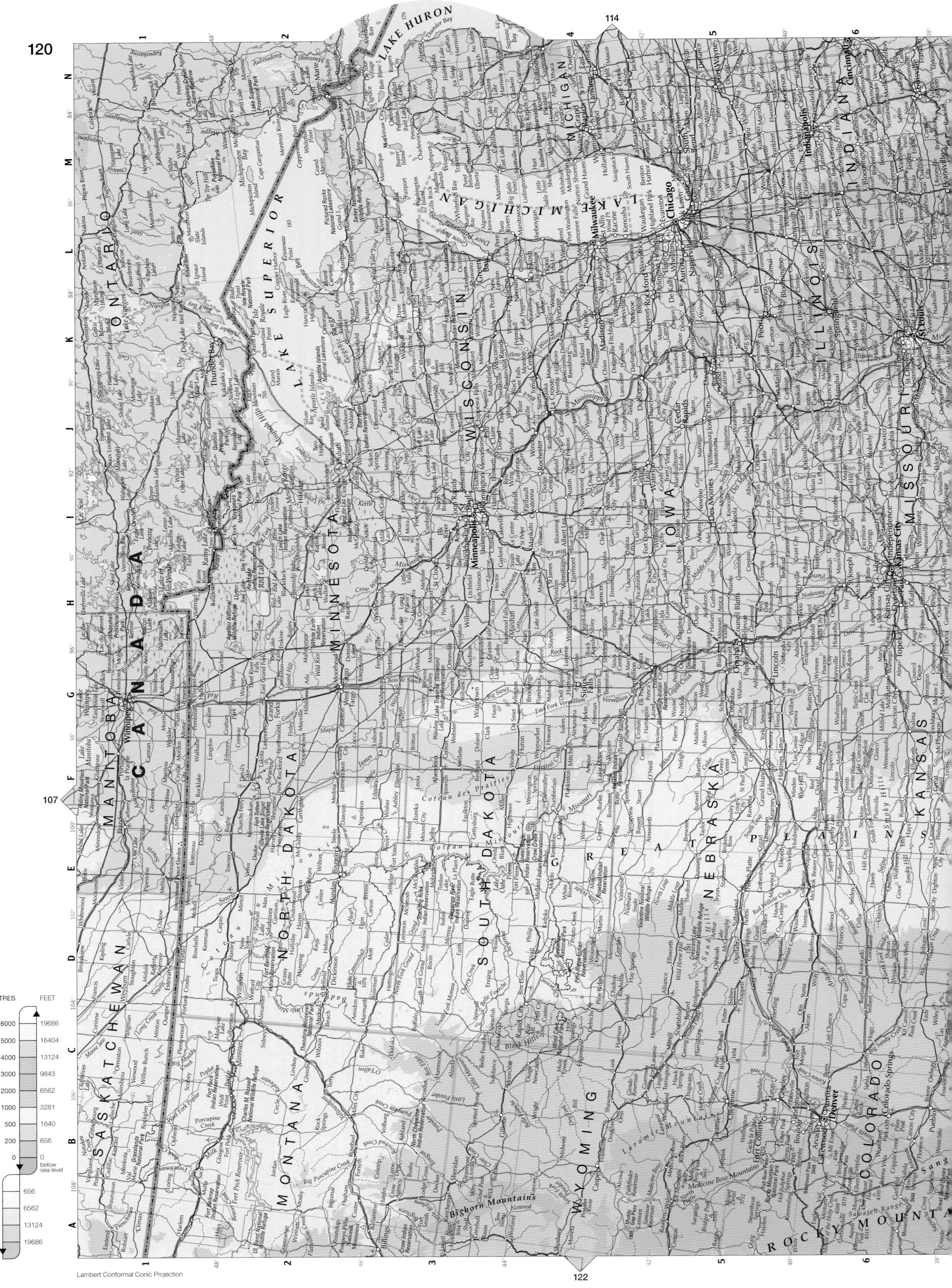
LAKE HURON
LAKE SUPERIOR
LAKE MICHIGAN
ONTARIO
MANITOBA
SASKATCHEWAN
CANADA
MINNESOTA
WISCONSIN
MICHIGAN
ILLINOIS
INDIANA
IOWA
MISSOURI
NORTH DAKOTA
SOUTH DAKOTA
NEBRASKA
KANSAS
MONTANA
WYOMING
COLORADO
GREAT PLAINS
ROCKY MOUNTAINS
Bighorn Mountains
Black Hills
Sand Hills
Thunder Bay
Winnipeg
Duluth
Minneapolis
St Paul
Milwaukee
Chicago
Madison
Green Bay
Des Moines
Omaha
Lincoln
Kansas City
St Louis
Springfield
Indianapolis
Cincinnati
Fort Wayne
Lansing
Fargo
Bismarck
Pierre
Sioux Falls
Rapid City
Denver
Fort Collins
Colorado Springs
Pueblo
Cheyenne
Casper
Billings
Topeka
Peoria
Cedar Rapids
METRES
FEET
6000 19686
5000 16404
4000 13124
3000 9843
2000 6562
1000 3281
500 1640
200 656
0 0 below sea level
200 656
2000 6562
4000 13124
6000 19686
114
107
122

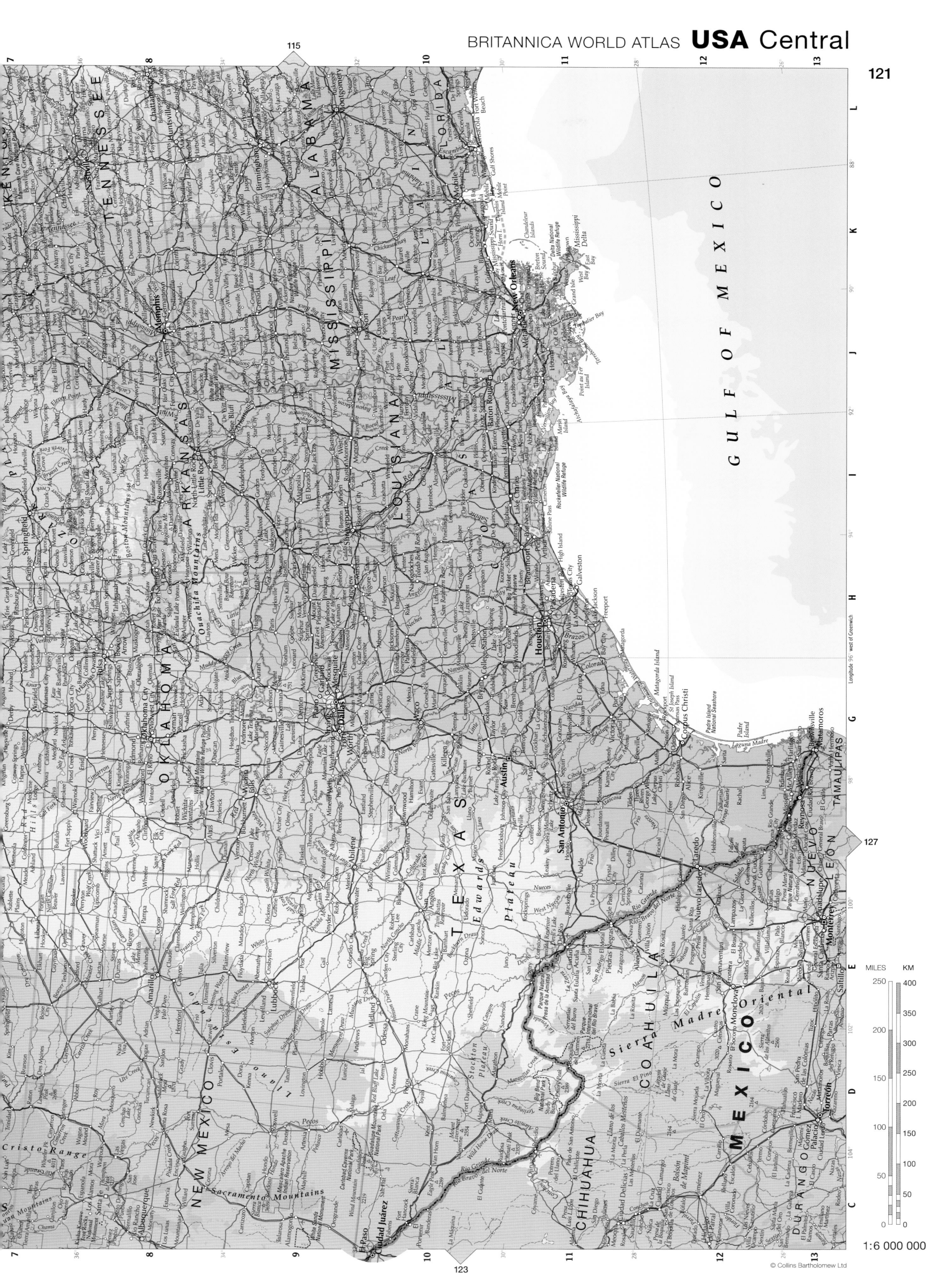

1:6 000 000

© Collins Bartholomew Ltd

GULF OF MEXICO
TEXAS
LOUISIANA
MISSISSIPPI
ALABAMA
ARKANSAS
OKLAHOMA
TENNESSEE
NEW MEXICO
MEXICO
COAHUILA
CHIHUAHUA
NUEVO LEON
TAMAULIPAS
DURANGO
FLORIDA
MILES
KM

120

106

CANADA

SASKATCHEWAN

ALBERTA

BRITISH COLUMBIA

NORTH DAKOTA

SOUTH DAKOTA

NEBRASKA

MONTANA

WYOMING

IDAHO

WASHINGTON

OREGON

ROCKY MOUNTAINS

BITTERROOT RANGE

COLUMBIA MOUNTAINS

COLUMBIA PLATEAU

COAST RANGE

KLAMATH MOUNTAINS

Vancouver Island

Calgary

Saskatoon

Regina

Vancouver

Seattle

Portland

Salem

Eugene

Spokane

Boise

Billings

Salt Lake City

Bighorn Mountains

Absaroka Range

Wind River Range

Lewis Range

Cabinet Mountains

Strait of Georgia

METRES	FEET
6000	19686
5000	16404
4000	13124
3000	9843
2000	6562
1000	3281
500	1640
200	656
0	below sea level
200	656
2000	6562
4000	13124
6000	19686

Lambert Conformal Conic Projection

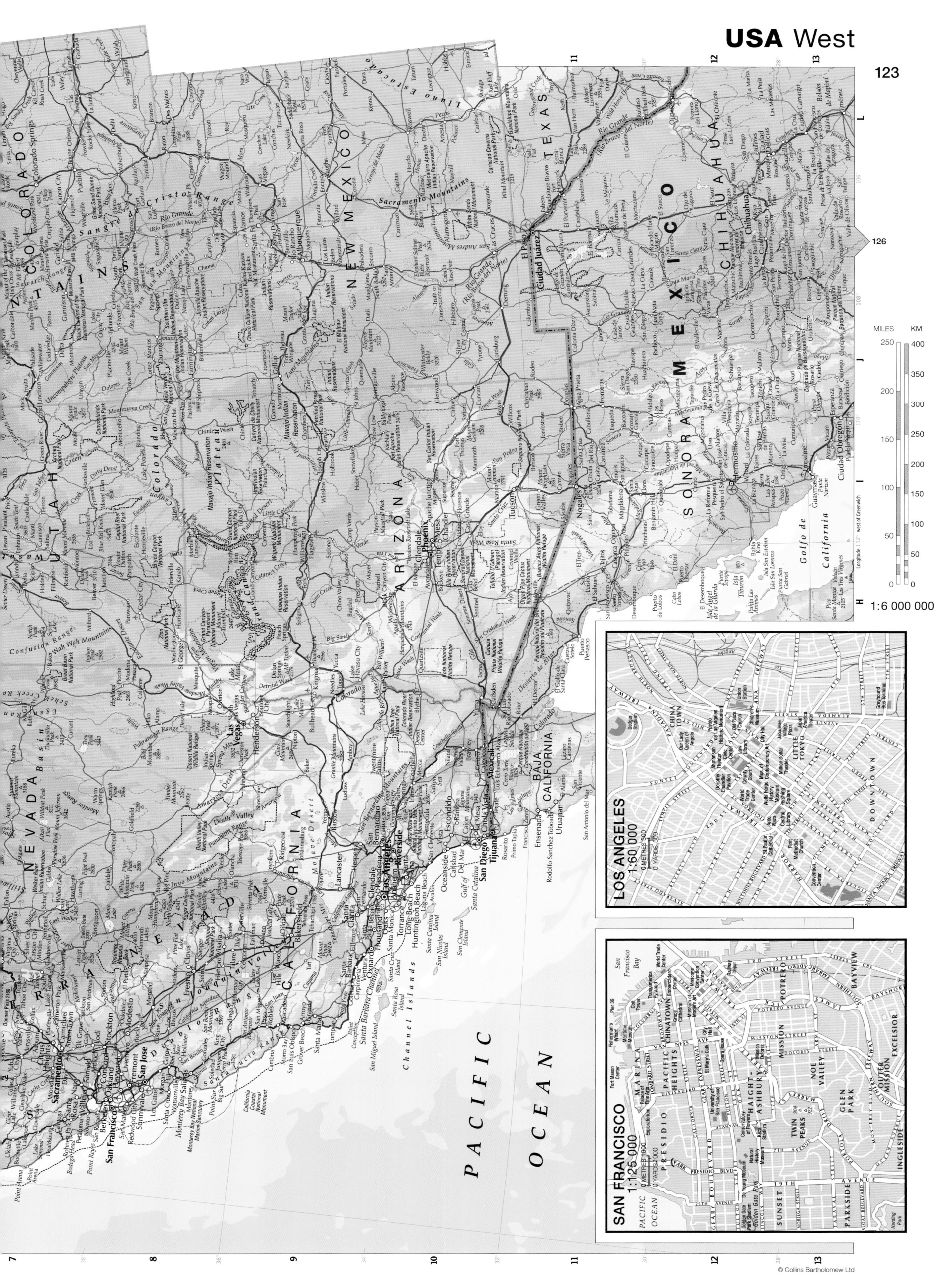

1:6 000 000

MILES   KM
250   400
         350
200   300
         250
150   200
100   150
         100
50   50
         0

LOS ANGELES 1:60 000
0 METRES 500
0 YARDS 500

SAN FRANCISCO 1:125 000
0 METRES 1000
0 YARDS 1000

PACIFIC OCEAN

© Collins Bartholomew Ltd

122

PACIFIC OCEAN
COAST RANGES
SIERRA NEVADA
CALIFORNIA
NEVADA
Sacramento Valley
San Joaquin Valley
San Francisco
Oakland
San Jose
Sacramento
Stockton
Modesto
Fresno
Bakersfield
Los Angeles
San Diego
Tijuana
Reno
Santa Barbara
Lake Tahoe
Mono Lake
Death Valley National Park
Yosemite National Park
Sequoia National Park
Kings Canyon National Park
CHANNEL ISLANDS
Gulf of Santa Catalina
San Pedro Channel
Santa Barbara Channel
METRES
FEET
6000
5000
4000
3000
2000
1500
1000
500
200
100
0
19686
16404
13124
9843
6562
4921
3281
1640
656
328
below sea level
HAWAIIAN ISLANDS
1 : 3 000 000
1 : 1 200 000
Kaua'i
O'ahu
Moloka'i
Lāna'i
Maui
Kaho'olawe
HAWAI'I
HAWAII
HONOLULU COUNTY
Honolulu
Kaua'i Channel
Kaiwi Channel
'Alenuihāhā Channel
Ni'ihau
PACIFIC OCEAN

Lambert Conformal Conic Projection

GREAT BASIN

UTAH

COLORADO

ARIZONA

NEW MEXICO

WASATCH RANGE

Great Salt Lake

Great Salt Lake Desert

Sevier Desert

Escalante Desert

COLORADO PLATEAU

Grand Canyon National Park

Navajo Indian Reservation

Hopi Indian Reservation

Kaiparowits Plateau

Mogollon Plateau

Las Vegas

North Las Vegas

Henderson

Boulder City

Lake Mead

Hoover Dam

Lake Mead National Recreation Area

Kingman

Bullhead City

Lake Havasu City

Needles

Flagstaff

Winslow

Holbrook

Petrified Forest National Park

Prescott

Sedona

Cottonwood

Phoenix

Glendale

Mesa

Tempe

Chandler

Gilbert

Scottsdale

Peoria

Avondale

Buckeye

Sun City

Apache Junction

Globe

San Carlos Indian Reservation

Fort Apache Indian Reservation

Tucson

Saguaro National Park

Green Valley

Nogales

Yuma

Mexicali

MEXICO

BAJA CALIFORNIA

SONORA

Salton Sea

Imperial Valley

El Centro

Brawley

Joshua Tree National Park

Zion National Park

Bryce Canyon National Park

Cedar City

St George

Kanab

Page

Lake Powell

Glen Canyon National Recreation Area

Canyonlands National Park

Arches National Park

Moab

Grand Junction

Provo

Springville

Nephi

Delta

Fillmore

Richfield

Price

Colorado River

Gila River

Little Colorado

Longitude 116° west of Greenwich

MILES 125 100 75 50 25 0

KM 200 175 150 125 100 75 50 25 0

1:3 000 000

© Collins Bartholomew Ltd

123
ARIZONA
NEW MEXICO
UNITED
SONORA
CHIHUAHUA
BAJA CALIFORNIA
BAJA CALIFORNIA SUR
Golfo de California
SIERRA MADRE OCCIDENTAL
SINALOA
DURANGO
COAHUILA
ZACATECAS
NAYARIT
JALISCO
COLIMA
MEXICO
PACIFIC
Tropic of Cancer
Guadalupe
Rocas Alijos
Islas Marías
136
CENTRAL AMERICA
CONTINUATION AT THE SAME SCALE
BELIZE
GUATEMALA
HONDURAS
EL SALVADOR
NICARAGUA
COSTA RICA
PANAMA
COLOMBIA
MOSQUITIA
Gulf of Honduras
CARIBBEAN SEA
PACIFIC OCEAN
TEGUCIGALPA
MANAGUA
SAN JOSÉ
PANAMÁ
Golfo de Panamá
METRES
FEET
6000
19686
5000
16404
4000
13124
3000
9843
2000
6562
1000
3281
500
1640
200
656
0
0
below sea level
200
656
2000
6562
4000
13124
6000
19686

Lambert Conformal Conic Projection

GULF OF MEXICO

STATES OF AMERICA

TEXAS

LOUISIANA

MISSISSIPPI

ALABAMA

FLORIDA

TAMAULIPAS

SAN LUIS POTOSÍ

VERACRUZ

GUANAJUATO

HIDALGO

MÉXICO

MICHOACÁN

GUERRERO

PUEBLA

MORELOS

OAXACA

SIERRA MADRE DEL SUR

CHIAPAS

TABASCO

CAMPECHE

YUCATÁN

QUINTANA ROO

Bahía de Campeche

Golfo de Tehuantepec

GUATEMALA

HONDURAS

EL SALVADOR

BELIZE

PACIFIC OCEAN

Tropic of Cancer

Yucatán Channel

1:6 600 000

© Collins Bartholomew Ltd

MILES

KM

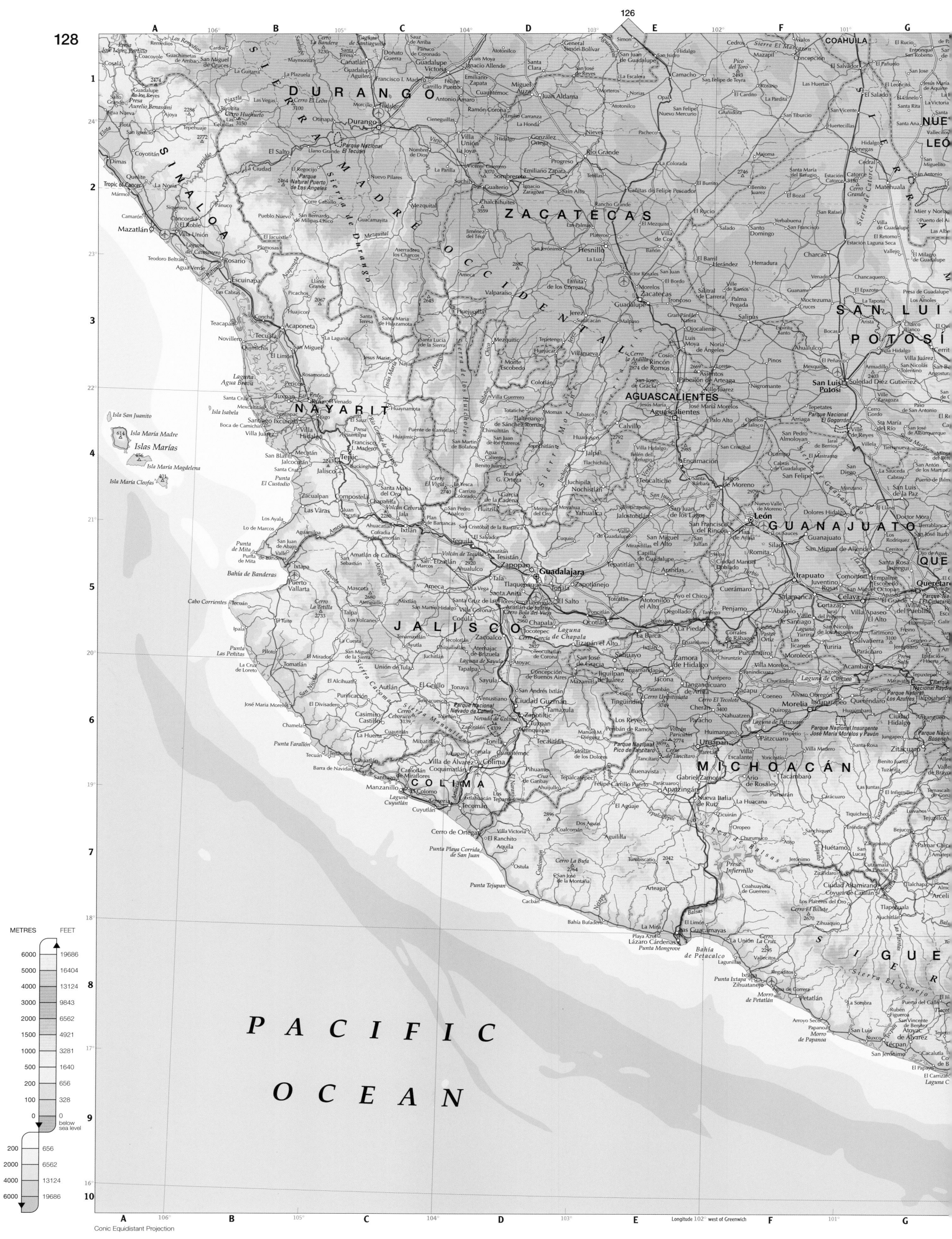

PACIFIC

OCEAN

DURANGO

SINALOA

ZACATECAS

SAN LUIS POTOSÍ

NUE LEÓ

COAHULA

AGUASCALIENTES

NAYARIT

JALISCO

GUANAJUATO

QUE

COLIMA

MICHOACÁN

GUE

Islas Marías

METRES FEET

6000	19686
5000	16404
4000	13124
3000	9843
2000	6562
1500	4921
1000	3281
500	1640
200	656
100	328
0	0
	below sea level
200	656
2000	6562
4000	13124
6000	19686

Conic Equidistant Projection

Longitude 102° west of Greenwich

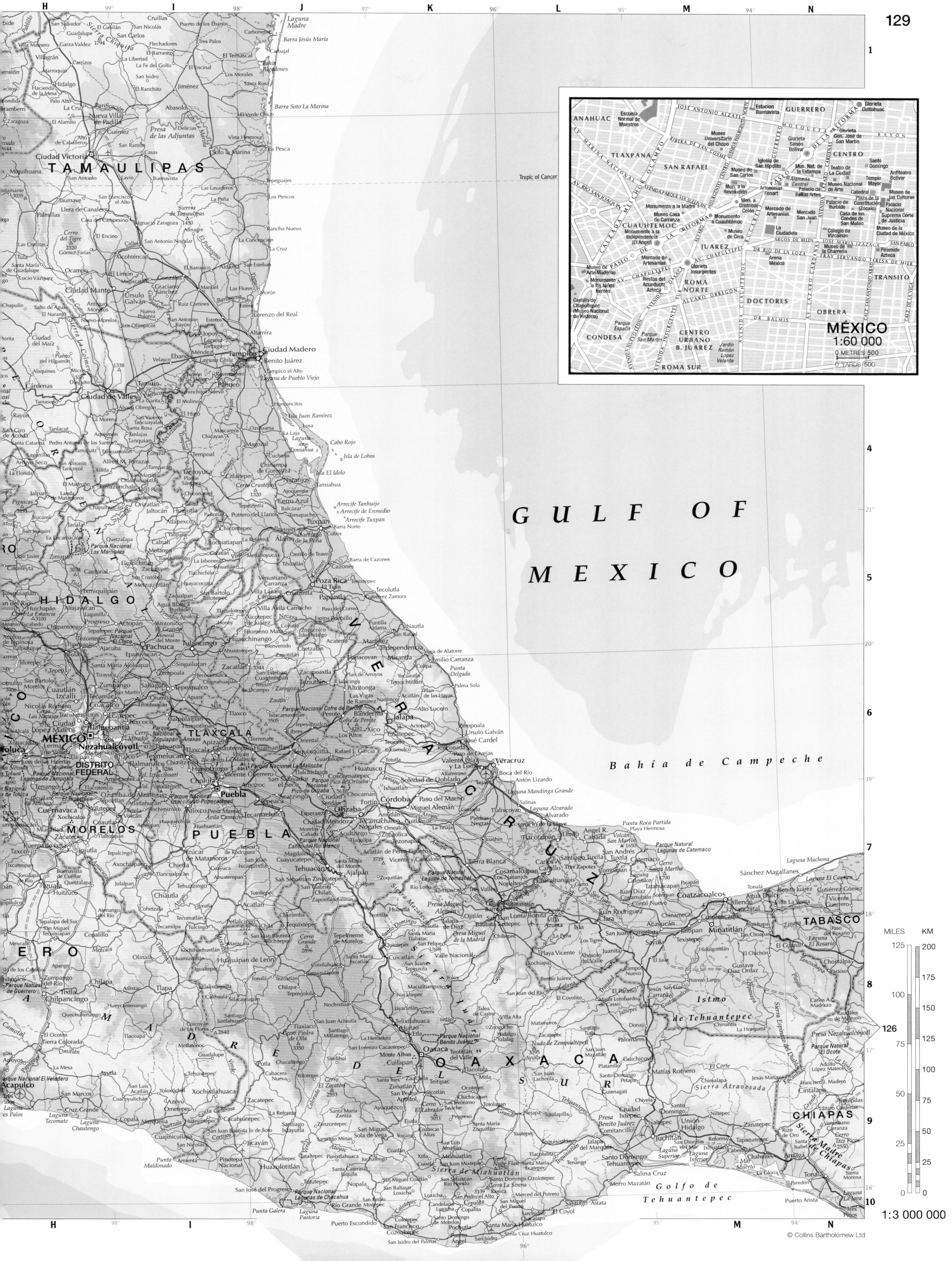

TAMAULIPAS

Tropic of Cancer

HIDALGO

GULF OF

MEXICO

Bahía de Campeche

Punta Roca Partida

VERACRUZ

TLAXCALA

MÉXICO
Nezahualcóyotl
DISTRITO FEDERAL
Puebla
Cuernavaca
MORELOS
PUEBLA

Acapulco

SIERRA MADRE DEL SUR

OAXACA

Oaxaca

TABASCO

Coatzacoacos
Minatitlán

Istmo de Tehuantepec

Golfo de Tehuantepec

CHIAPAS

Sierra Madre de Chiapas

MÉXICO
1:60 000
0 METRES 500
0 YARDS 500

ANAHUAC
TLAXPANA
GUERRERO
CENTRO
SAN RAFAEL
CUAUHTÉMOC
JUÁREZ
ROMA NORTE
DOCTORES
OBRERA
CONDESA
CENTRO URBANO B. JUÁREZ
ROMA SUR
TRANSITO

Museo Nacional de Arte
Palacio de Bellas Artes
Catedral
Plaza de la Constitución (Zócalo)
Monumento a la Independencia (El Ángel)

MILES   KM
125 ——— 200
         175
100 ——— 150
         125
75 ——— 100
         75
50 ———
         50
25 ———
         25
0   ——— 0

1:3 000 000

© Collins Bartholomew Ltd

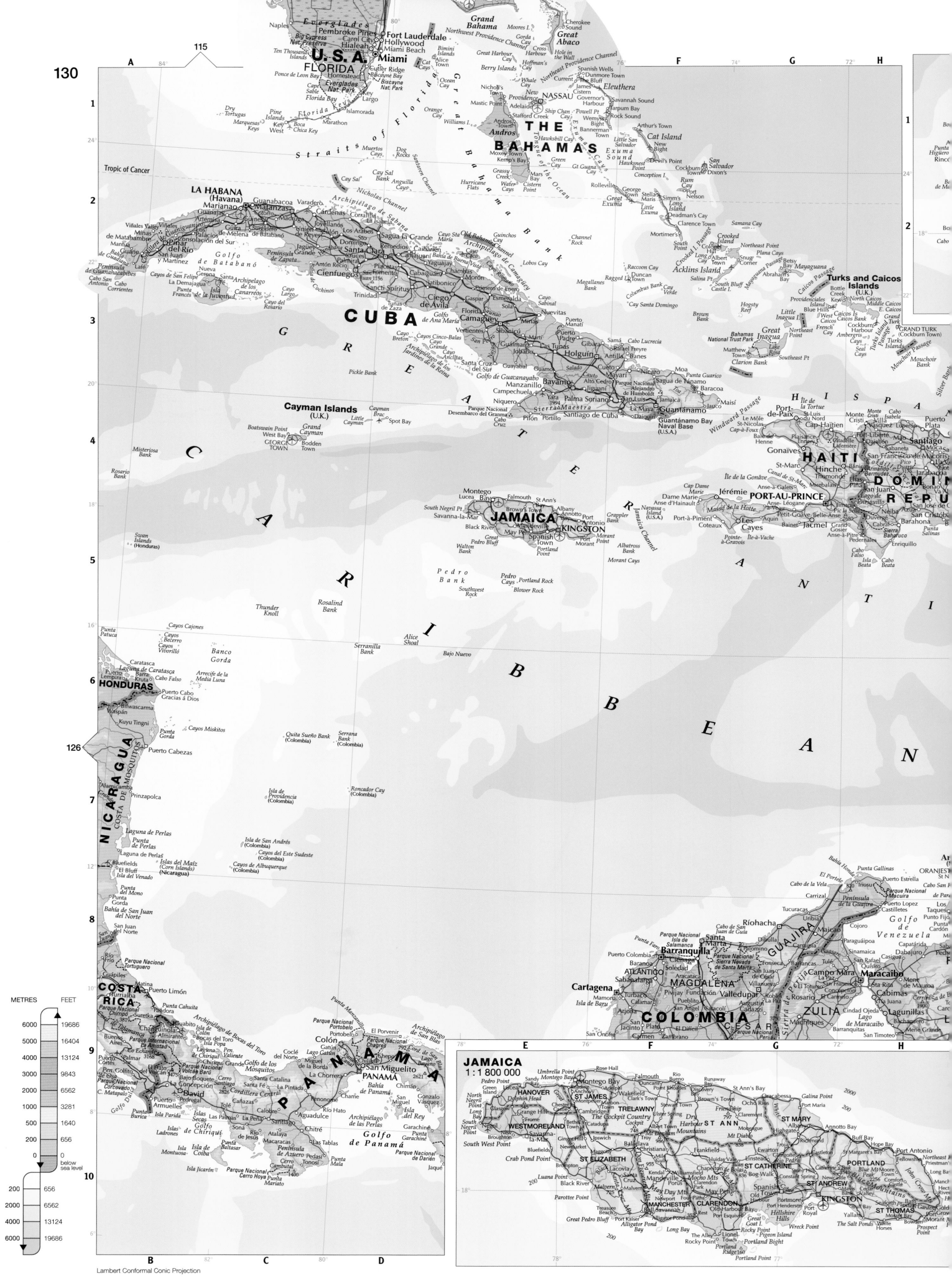
U.S.A.
FLORIDA
Miami
Fort Lauderdale
Hollywood
Hialeah
Miami Beach
Naples
Everglades
Key West
Straits of Florida
Tropic of Cancer
Grand Bahama
Great Abaco
Andros
NASSAU
Eleuthera
Cat Island
THE BAHAMAS
Great Bahama Bank
Acklins Island
Great Inagua
Turks and Caicos Islands (U.K.)
GRAND TURK (Cockburn Town)
LA HABANA (Havana)
Matanzas
Pinar del Río
Santa Clara
Cienfuegos
Sancti Spíritus
Ciego de Ávila
Camagüey
Las Tunas
Holguín
Bayamo
Santiago de Cuba
Guantánamo
Guantánamo Bay Naval Base (U.S.A.)
CUBA
Golfo de Batabanó
Isla de la Juventud
Cayman Islands (U.K.)
Grand Cayman
GEORGE TOWN
Cayman Brac
Little Cayman
Windward Passage
HAITI
PORT-AU-PRINCE
Cap-Haïtien
Gonaïves
Jérémie
Jacmel
Les Cayes
Santiago
JAMAICA
KINGSTON
Montego Bay
Spanish Town
Mandeville
Pedro Bank
CARIBBEAN SEA
GREATER ANTILLES
HONDURAS
NICARAGUA
COSTA DE MOSQUITOS
Puerto Cabezas
Bluefields
COSTA RICA
Puerto Limón
PANAMA
PANAMÁ
Colón
David
Golfo de Panamá
Golfo de los Mosquitos
Golfo de Chiriquí
COLOMBIA
Barranquilla
Cartagena
Santa Marta
Ríohacha
Valledupar
Maracaibo
Lago de Maracaibo
Golfo de Venezuela
GUAJIRA
ZULIA
MAGDALENA
ATLÁNTICO
Isla de San Andrés (Colombia)
Isla de Providencia (Colombia)
Serranilla Bank
Alice Shoal
Bajo Nuevo
Rosalind Bank
Thunder Knoll
Quita Sueño Bank (Colombia)
Serrana Bank (Colombia)
Roncador Cay (Colombia)
115
126
METRES
FEET
6000
19686
5000
16404
4000
13124
3000
9843
2000
6562
1000
3281
500
1640
200
656
0
0
below sea level
200
656
2000
6562
4000
13124
6000
19686
JAMAICA
1 : 1 800 000
HANOVER
ST JAMES
TRELAWNY
ST ANN
ST MARY
WESTMORELAND
ST ELIZABETH
MANCHESTER
CLARENDON
ST CATHERINE
ST ANDREW
PORTLAND
ST THOMAS
KINGSTON
Montego Bay
Negril Point
Black River
Mandeville
May Pen
Spanish Town
Ocho Rios
Port Antonio
Morant Point
Portland Point
Blue Mountains

Lambert Conformal Conic Projection

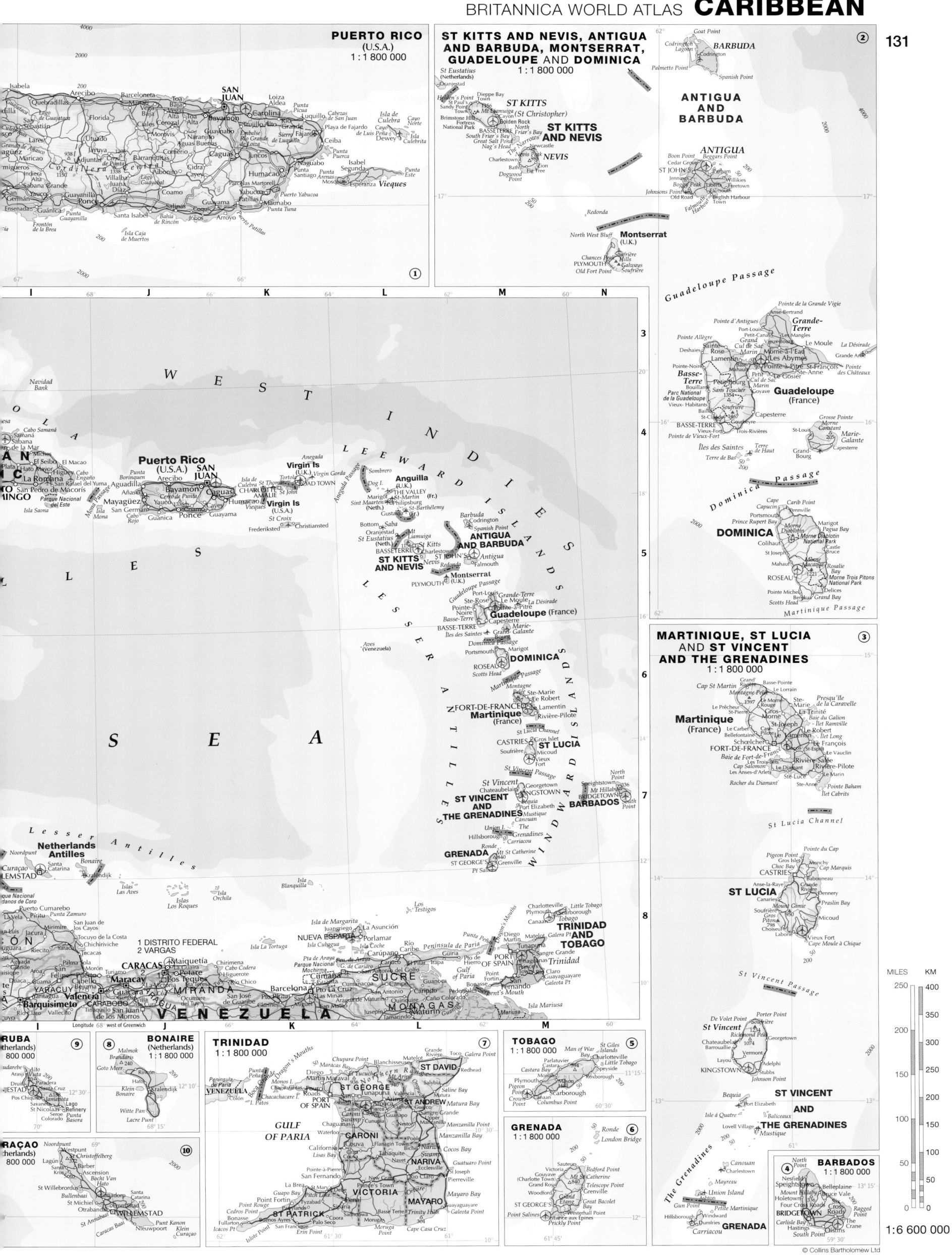

PUERTO RICO
(U.S.A.)
1:1 800 000

ST KITTS AND NEVIS, ANTIGUA
AND BARBUDA, MONTSERRAT,
GUADELOUPE AND DOMINICA
1:1 800 000

MARTINIQUE, ST LUCIA
AND ST VINCENT
AND THE GRENADINES
1:1 800 000

ARUBA
(Netherlands)
1 800 000

BONAIRE
(Netherlands)
1:1 800 000

TRINIDAD
1:1 800 000

TOBAGO
1:1 800 000

GRENADA
1:1 800 000

CURAÇAO
(Netherlands)
800 000

BARBADOS
1:1 800 000

1:6 600 000

© Collins Bartholomew Ltd

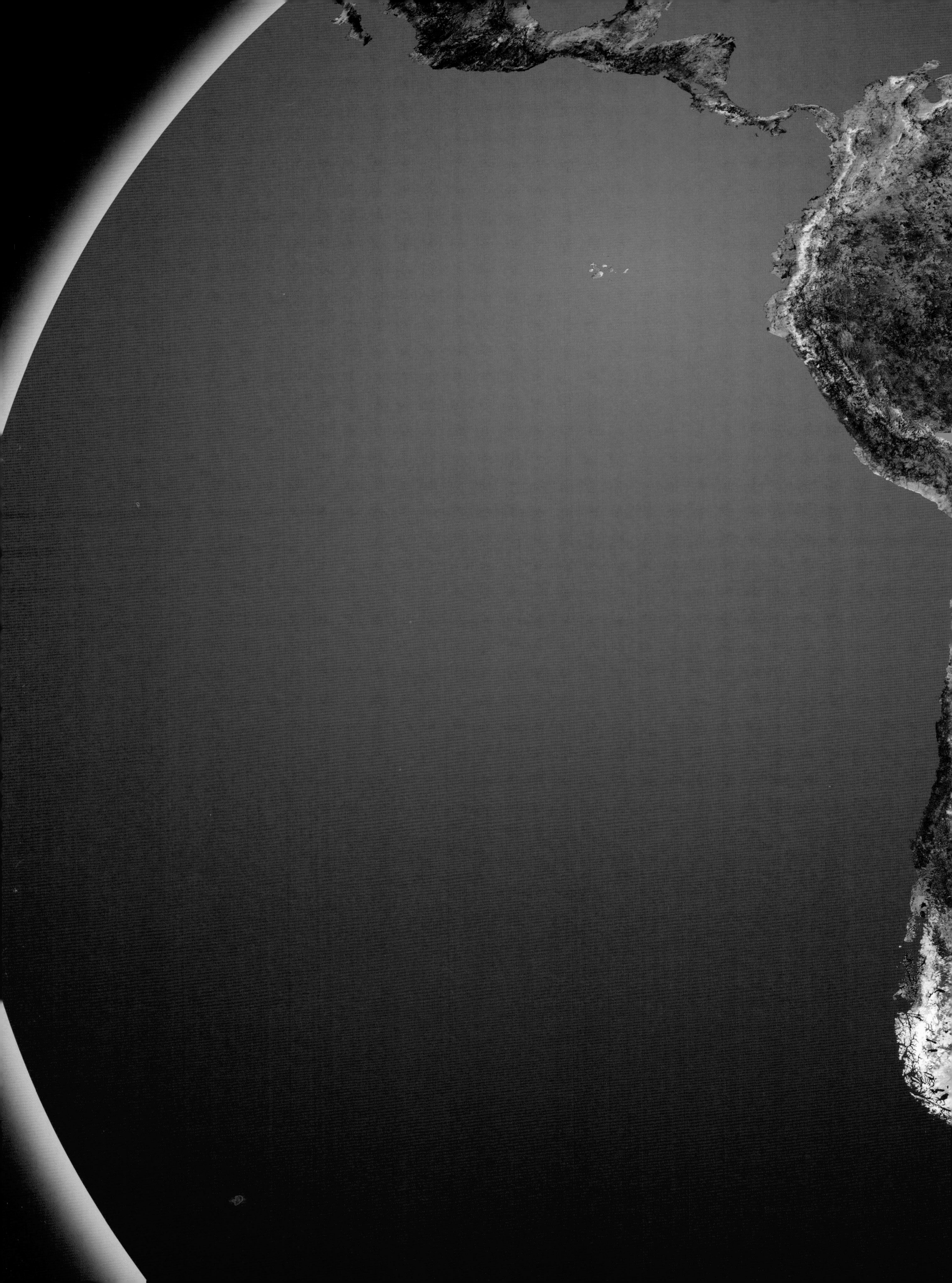

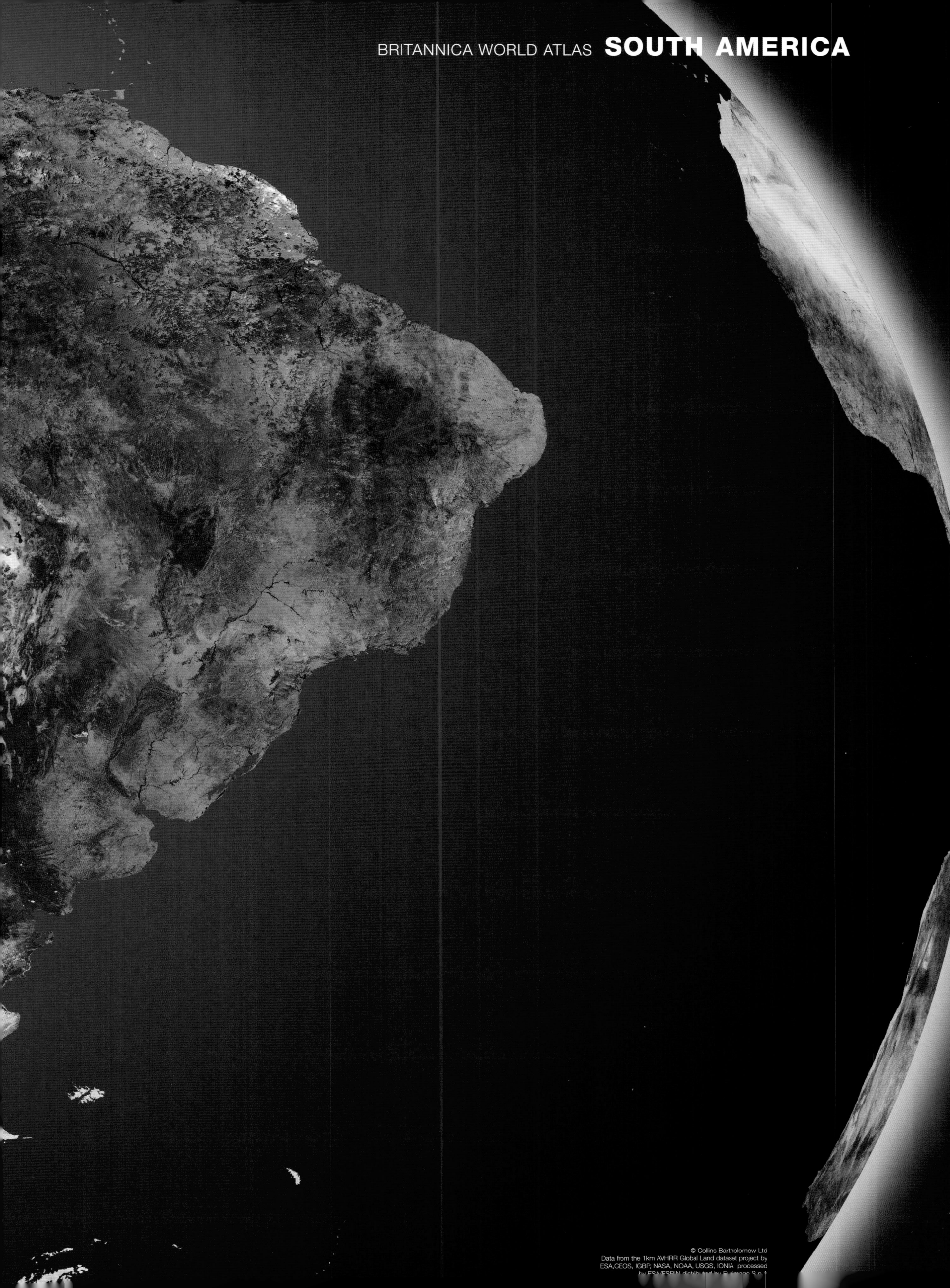

A　　　　　　B　　　　　　C　　　　　　D　　　　　　E

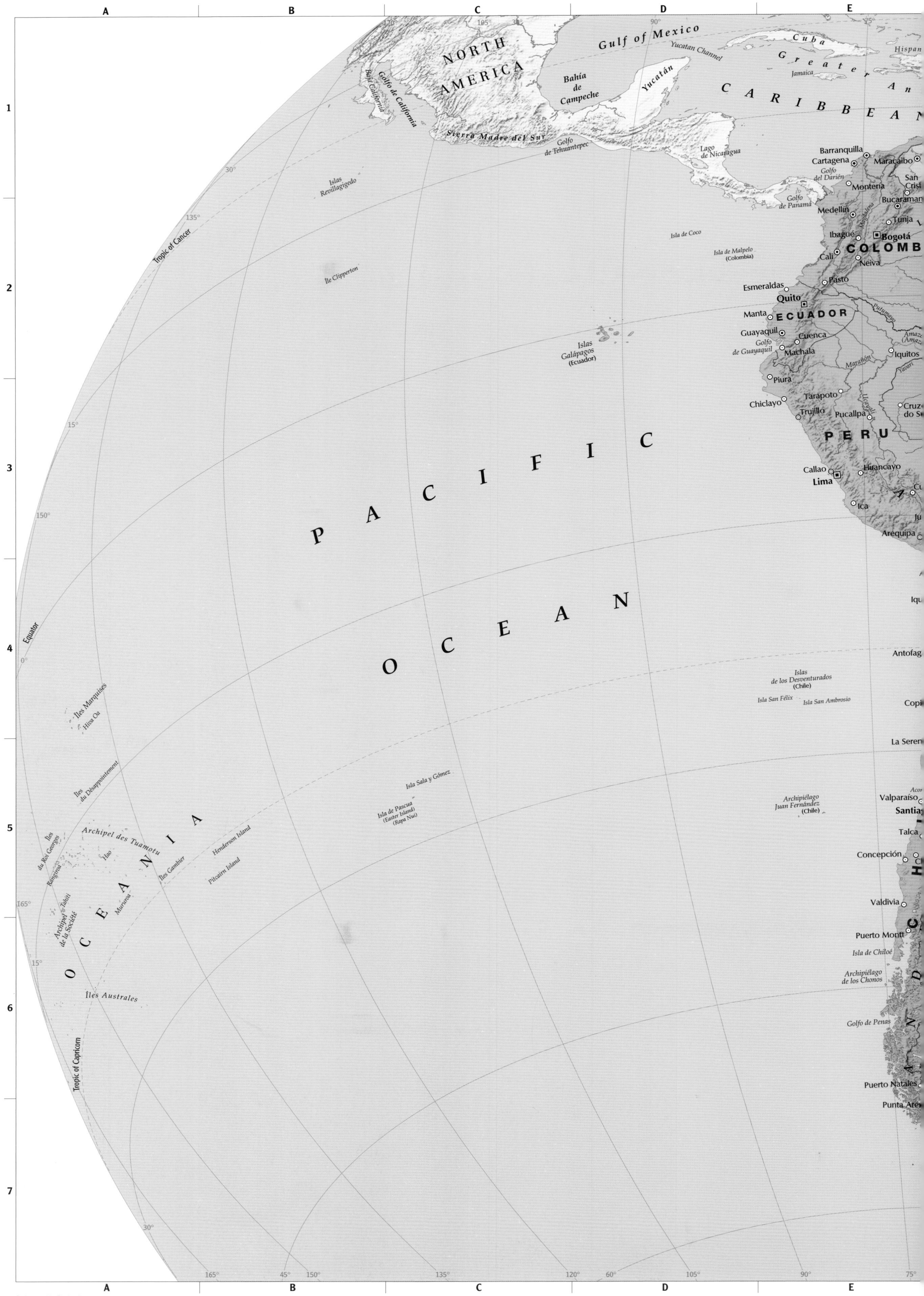

NORTH
AMERICA

Gulf of Mexico

Cuba

Hispan

Greater An

C A R I B B E A N

Yucatan Channel

*Bahía
de
Campeche*

Yucatán

Sierra Madre del Sur

*Golfo
de Tehuantepec*

*Lago
de Nicaragua*

Barranquilla

Cartagena　　Maracaibo

*Golfo
del Darién*

San
Crist

Montería

Bucaraman

Medellín

Tunja

*Islas
Revillagigedo*

Tropic of Cancer

Isla de Coco

Ibagué　　**Bogotá**

*Isla de Malpelo
(Colombia)*

Cali　　**COLOMB**

Neiva

Ile Clipperton

Esmeraldas　　Pasto

Quito

Manta　　**ECUADOR**

Guayaquil　　Cuenca

*Golfo
de Guayaquil*　　Machala

*Amaz
Amaz*

Iquitos

*Islas
Galápagos
(Ecuador)*

Piura

Marañón

Tarapoto

Chiclayo　　Pucallpa

Trujillo

Cruze
do Su

P A C I F I C

P E R U

Callao　　Huancayo

Lima

Ica

Arequipa

O C E A N

Antofag

*Islas
de los Desventurados
(Chile)*

Isla San Félix　　*Isla San Ambrosio*

Copi

La Seren

Iles Marquises

Hiva Oa

Isla Sala y Gómez

*Archipiélago
Juan Fernández
(Chile)*

Valparaíso

*Iles
du Désappointement*

Santia

O　C　E　A　N　I　A

Archipel des Tuamotu

Talca

*Isla de Pascua
(Easter Island)
(Rapa Nui)*

Henderson Island

Concepción

*Iles
du Roi Georges*

Hao

Iles Gambier

Pitcairn Island

Rangiroa

Valdivia

Tahiti

Makatea

Puerto Montt

*Archipel
de la Société*

Isla de Chiloé

*Archipiélago
de los Chonos*

Iles Australes

Golfo de Penas

Tropic of Capricorn

Puerto Natales

Punta Are

A　　　　　　B　　　　　　C　　　　　　D　　　　　　E

Orthographic Projection

F G H I J

Puerto Rico
Virgin Is
Anguilla
Barbuda
St Kitts-Nevis
Montserrat
Antigua
Guadeloupe
Dominica
Lesser Antilles
Martinique
St Lucia
Barbados
St Vincent
and the Grenadines
Grenada
Tobago
Trinidad
Arquipélago
da Madeira
Islas
Canarias
Gran
Canaria

S E A

Caracas
Maracay
quisimeto
Cumaná

Tropic of Cancer

Ciudad Bolívar

Orinoco

VENEZUELA
Guiana Highlands
GUYANA
Georgetown
Paramaribo
Cayenne
SURINAME
French
Guiana

Santo Antão
Ilhas
do Cabo Verde
Boa Vista
Santiago

Puerto
Ayacucho

Boa Vista

Orinoco

Branco

Senegal

Macapá

Mouths of the Amazon

Negro

Manaus

Amazonas (Amazon)

Santarém
Belém
São Luís

Parnaíba

São Pedro e
São Paulo
(Brazil)

Niger

Carauari

Purus
Madeira
Xingu
Iriri
Tapajós

Teresina

Maraba
Tocantins

Fortaleza

Atol
das Rocas

Branco

Porto
Velho

B R A Z I L

Araguaína

Natal

Fernando de Noronha
(Brazil)

A F R I C A

Gulf
of
Guinea

erto Maldonado

Guaporé

Trinidad

Palmas

Araguaia

Floresta

Juàzeiro

João Pessoa
Recife
Maceió
Aracaju

Barragem
de Sobradinho

Equator

La Paz
BOLIVIA

Cochabamba
Santa Cruz

Cuiabá

Brasília
Goiânia

Represa
Serra da Mesa

Salvador

Ilhéus

15

Potosí
Sucre

Campo
Grande

Patos
de Minas

Teófilo
Otôni

Ascension

Tarija

PARAGUAY

Uberaba

Araçatuba
Ribeirão
Preto

Belo
Horizonte

Vitória

A T L A N T I C

San Salvador
de Jujuy

Gran Chaco

Pedro Juan
Caballero

Paraguai

Maringá

Campinas
São Paulo
Santos

Rio
de Janeiro

Ilha da Trindade
(Brazil)

Ilhas
Martim Vaz
(Brazil)

San Miguel
de Tucumán

Formosa

Asunción
Coronel
Oviedo
Encarnación

Paraná

Iguaçu

Curitiba

O C E A N

atamarca

Resistencia

Corrientes
Posadas

Rioja

Salinas
de Ambargasta

Santa Maria

St Helena

Grandes

Laguna
Mar Chiquita

Córdoba

Santa Fé

Concórdia

Paraná

Florianópolis

Porto Alegre

Lagoa
dos Patos

endoza

Rosario

Paysandú

Rio Grande

San Luis

Pampas

Paraná

URUGUAY

Buenos
Aires
La Plata

Montevideo

Rio de la Plata

Tropic of Capricorn

15

el

ARGENTINA

Santa Rosa

Mar del Plata

quén

Negro

Bahía Blanca

Viedma

Golfo San Matías

N I A

Trelew

Comodoro Rivadavia
Golfo de San Jorge

Tristan
da Cunha

Falkland
Islands
(U.K.)

Gallegos

Stanley

Grande
rra del Fuego
shuaia
Isla de los Estados

Cabo de Hornos

Shag
Rocks

South Georgia

750

1250

1000

1000

ke Passage

South Georgia
and
South Sandwich
Islands
(U.K.)

South
Sandwich
Islands

Traversay Islands
Candlemas Island
Saunders Island

500

750

500

South Shetland
Islands

Antarctic Peninsula

South Orkney
Islands

Southern Thule

Bristol Island
Montagu Island

250

250

60°
45°
30°
60°
15°
0°
15°
30°

F G H I J

1:27 000 000

© Collins Bartholomew Ltd

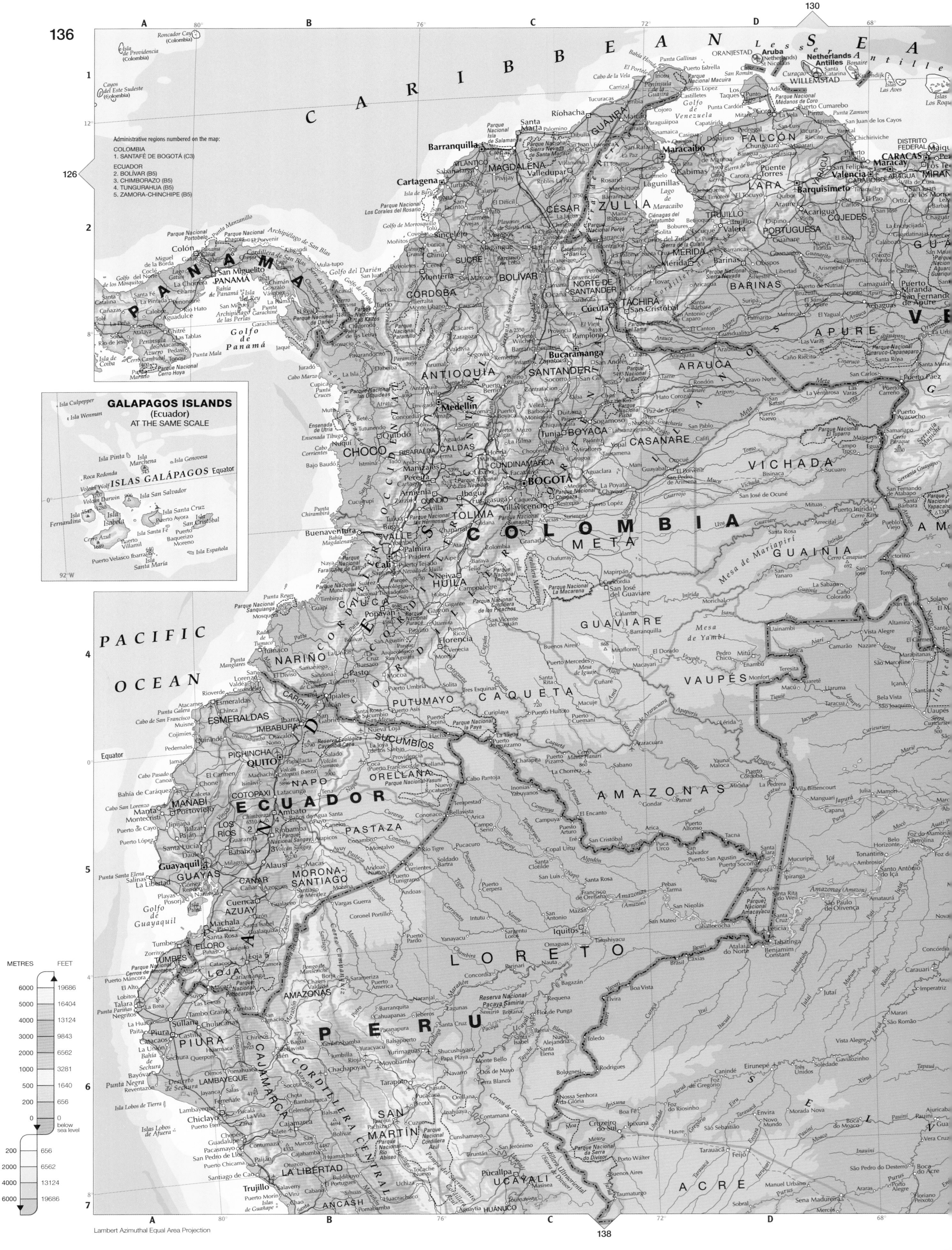
130
126
138
CARIBBEAN SEA
PACIFIC OCEAN
Administrative regions numbered on the map:
COLOMBIA
1. SANTAFÉ DE BOGOTÁ (C3)
ECUADOR
2. BOLÍVAR (B5)
3. CHIMBORAZO (B5)
4. TUNGURAHUA (B5)
5. ZAMORA-CHINCHIPE (B5)
GALAPAGOS ISLANDS
(Ecuador)
AT THE SAME SCALE
ISLAS GALÁPAGOS
Equator
PANAMA
COLOMBIA
ECUADOR
PERU
Golfo de Panamá
Golfo de Guayaquil
Netherlands Antilles
Aruba
Curaçao
Bonaire
ORANJESTAD
WILLEMSTAD
Golfo de Venezuela
Lago de Maracaibo
Barranquilla
Cartagena
Medellín
BOGOTÁ
Cali
Bucaramanga
Cúcuta
QUITO
Guayaquil
Iquitos
Maracaibo
CARACAS
Valencia
Barquisimeto
Maracay
ANTIOQUIA
CHOCÓ
SANTANDER
BOYACÁ
CASANARE
VICHADA
META
GUAINÍA
GUAVIARE
VAUPÉS
CAQUETÁ
PUTUMAYO
AMAZONAS
NARIÑO
CAUCA
HUILA
TOLIMA
VALLE
CÓRDOBA
SUCRE
BOLÍVAR
MAGDALENA
CESAR
GUAJIRA
ARAUCA
ZULIA
FALCÓN
LARA
TRUJILLO
MÉRIDA
BARINAS
TÁCHIRA
APURE
PORTUGUESA
COJEDES
ESMERALDAS
IMBABURA
PICHINCHA
SUCUMBÍOS
NAPO
ORELLANA
PASTAZA
MORONA-SANTIAGO
MANABÍ
GUAYAS
LOS RÍOS
COTOPAXI
CAÑAR
AZUAY
EL ORO
LOJA
TUMBES
PIURA
CAJAMARCA
LAMBAYEQUE
AMAZONAS
SAN MARTÍN
LA LIBERTAD
ANCASH
HUÁNUCO
UCAYALI
LORETO
ACRE
CORDILLERA CENTRAL
METRES
FEET
6000
19686
5000
16404
4000
13124
3000
9843
2000
6562
1000
3281
500
1640
200
656
0
0
below sea level
200
656
2000
6562
4000
13124
6000
19686
A
B
C
D
1
2
3
4
5
6
7
80°
76°
72°
68°
12°
8°
0°
4°
Lambert Azimuthal Equal Area Projection

ATLANTIC

OCEAN

MILES KM

300 — 500
— 400
200 — 300
— 200
100 —
— 100

1:7 500 000

V E N E Z U E L A

BOLÍVAR

GUYANA

GUIANA HIGHLANDS

La Gran Sabana

Pakaraima Mountains

SURINAME

French Guiana

GEORGETOWN

PARAMARIBO

CAYENNE

AMAPÁ

Parque Nacional de Cabo Orange

Cabo Orange

Mouths of the Amazon

Equator

Macapá

Ilha de Marajó

RORAIMA

Boa Vista

A M A Z O N A S

Manaus

Manacapuru

B R A Z I L

PARÁ

RONDÔNIA

MATO GROSSO

136

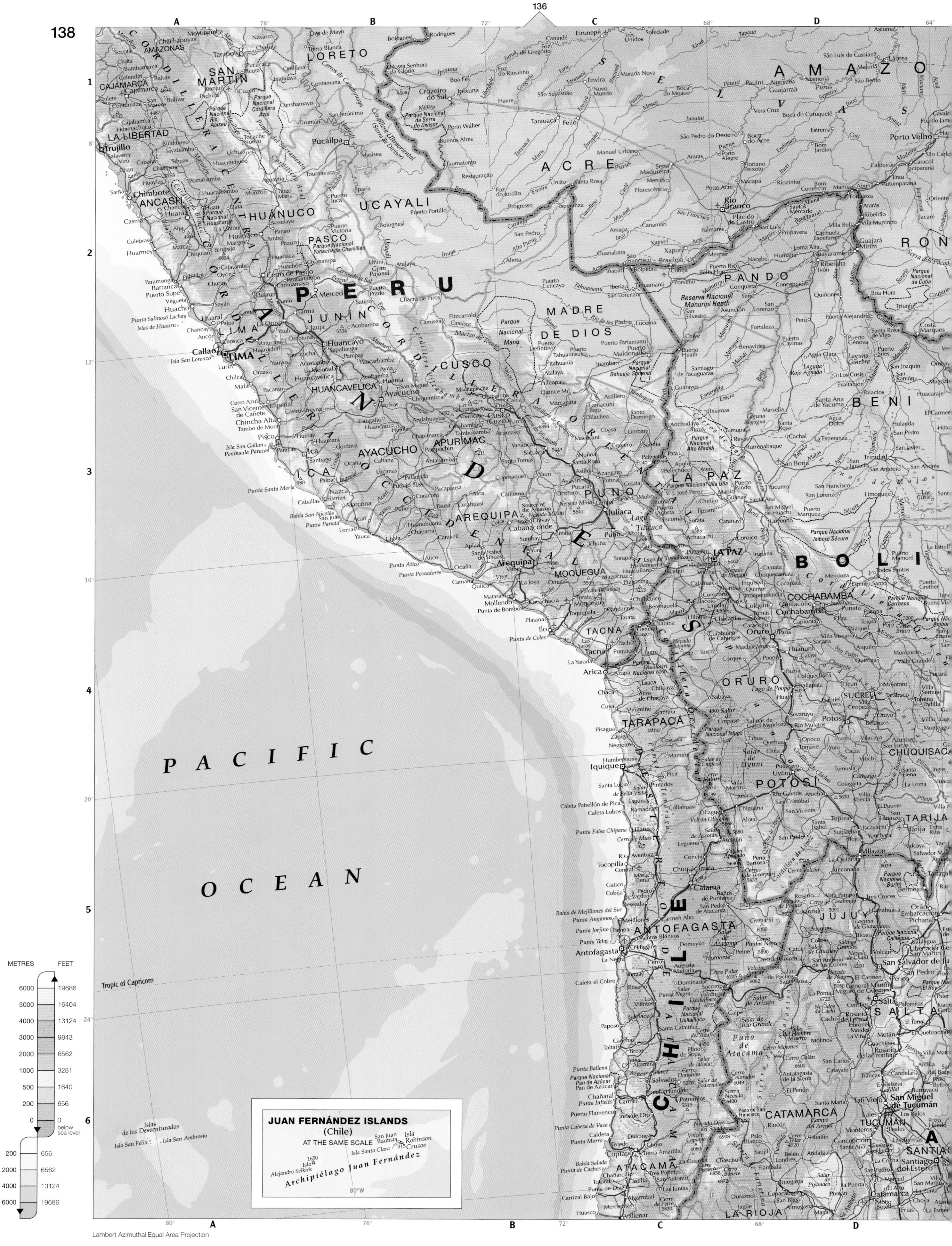

A   76°   B   72°   C   68°   D   64°

PERU

CORDILLERA CENTRAL

CORDILLERA OCCIDENTAL

CORDILLERA ORIENTAL

BOLIVIA

CHILE

AMAZONAS
SAN MARTÍN
LA LIBERTAD
CAJAMARCA
ANCASH
HUÁNUCO
PASCO
LORETO
UCAYALI
ACRE
JUNÍN
LIMA
HUANCAVELICA
AYACUCHO
ICA
APURÍMAC
CUSCO
AREQUIPA
PUNO
MOQUEGUA
TACNA
MADRE DE DIOS
PANDO
BENI
LA PAZ
COCHABAMBA
ORURO
POTOSÍ
CHUQUISACA
TARIJA
TARAPACÁ
ANTOFAGASTA
ATACAMA
JUJUY
SALTA
CATAMARCA
LA RIOJA
TUCUMÁN
SANTIAGO del ESTERO
RON...

Trujillo
Chimbote
Lima
Callao
Ayacucho
Cusco
Arequipa
Juliaca
Puno
La Paz
Cochabamba
Oruro
Sucre
Potosí
Iquique
Antofagasta
Calama
Tarija
Salta
San Salvador de Jujuy
San Miguel de Tucumán
Pucallpa
Río Branco

Lago Titicaca
Lago de Poopó
Salar de Uyuni
Salar de Coipasa
Salar de Atacama

PACIFIC OCEAN

Tropic of Capricorn

Isla San Lorenzo
Islas de Huaura
Islas de los Desventurados
Isla San Félix
Isla San Ambrosio

80°   A   76°   B   72°   C   68°   D

8°, 1, 2, 12°, 3, 16°, 4, 20°, 5, 24°, 6

JUAN FERNÁNDEZ ISLANDS
(Chile)
AT THE SAME SCALE
San Juan Bautista
Isla Robinson Crusoe
Isla Santa Clara
Alejandro Selkirk
Archipiélago Juan Fernández
80°W

METRES / FEET
6000 / 19686
5000 / 16404
4000 / 13124
3000 / 9843
2000 / 6562
1000 / 3281
500 / 1640
200 / 656
0 / 0 below sea level
200 / 656
2000 / 6562
4000 / 13124
6000 / 19686

Lambert Azimuthal Equal Area Projection

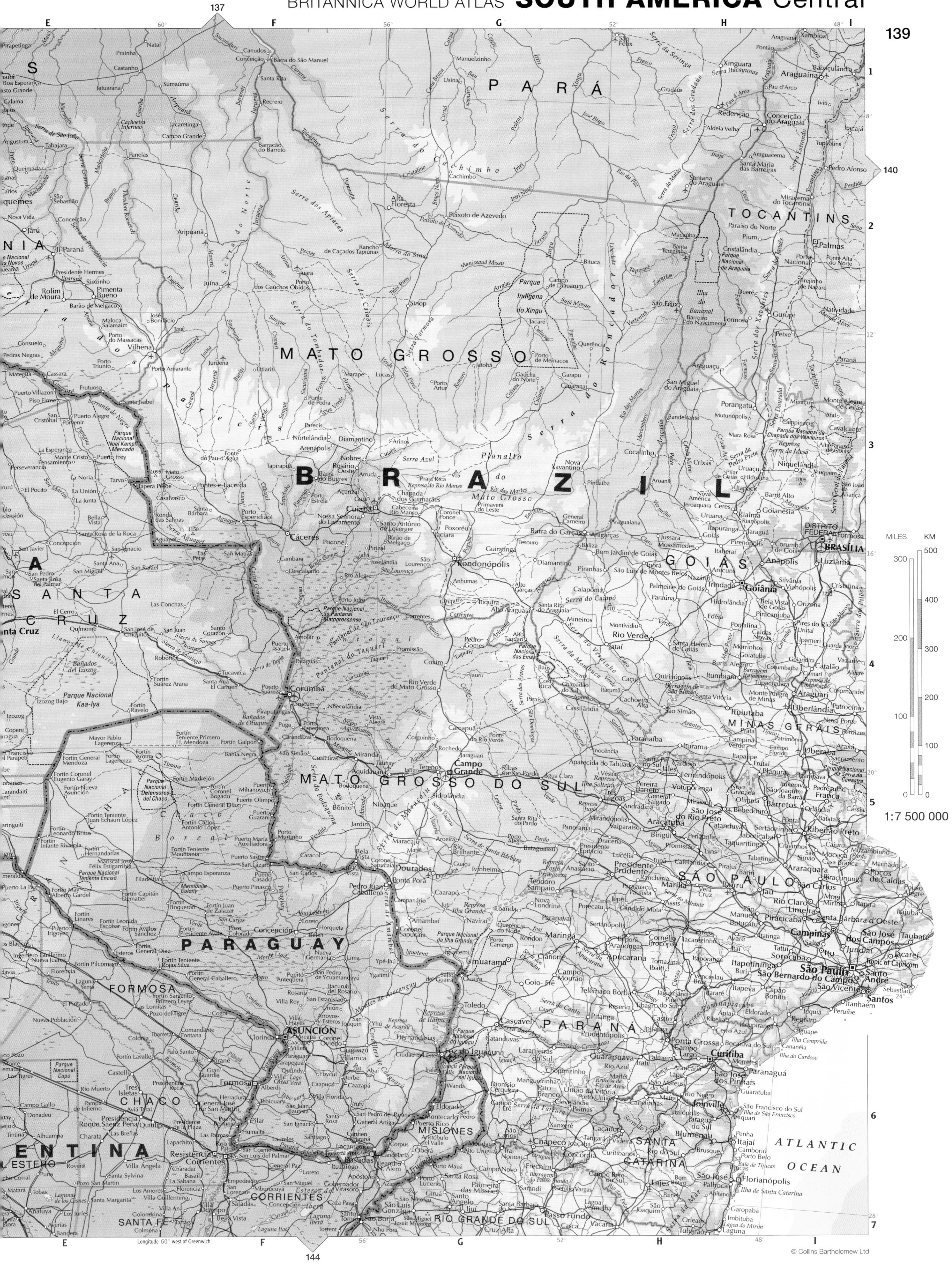
PARÁ
TOCANTINS
MATO GROSSO
BRAZIL
GOIÁS
DISTRITO FEDERAL
BRASÍLIA
MINAS GERAIS
MATO GROSSO DO SUL
SÃO PAULO
PARANÁ
SANTA CATARINA
RIO GRANDE DO SUL
PARAGUAY
ASUNCIÓN
SANTA CRUZ
CHACO
FORMOSA
CORRIENTES
MISIONES
SANTA FE
ARGENTINA
ATLANTIC OCEAN
Cuiabá
Campo Grande
Goiânia
São Paulo
Curitiba
Florianópolis
Santos
Campinas
Corumbá
Tropic of Capricorn
Planalto do Mato Grosso
Pantanal
MILES
KM
1:7 500 000
Longitude 60° west of Greenwich
137
140
144
© Collins Bartholomew Ltd

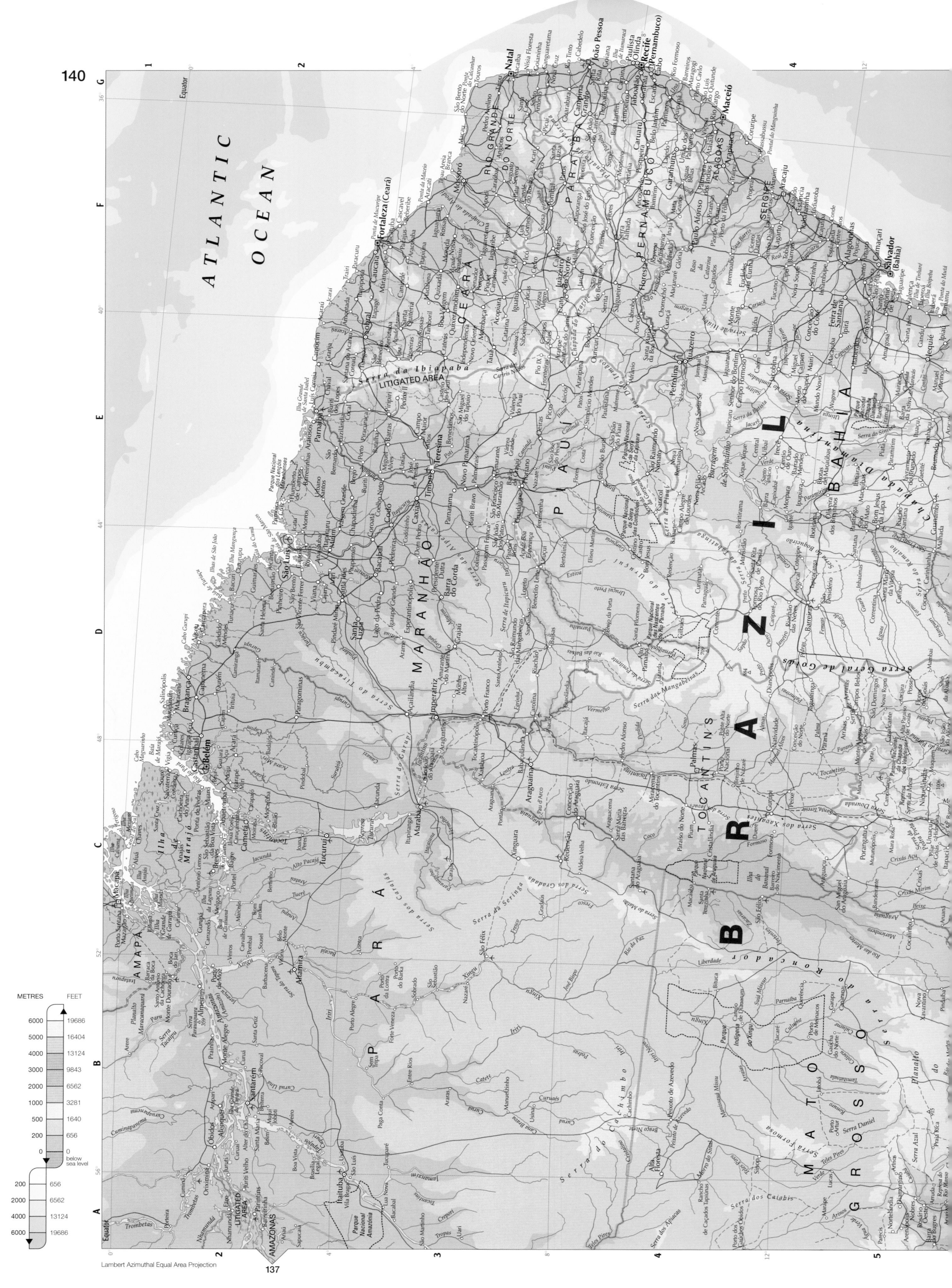

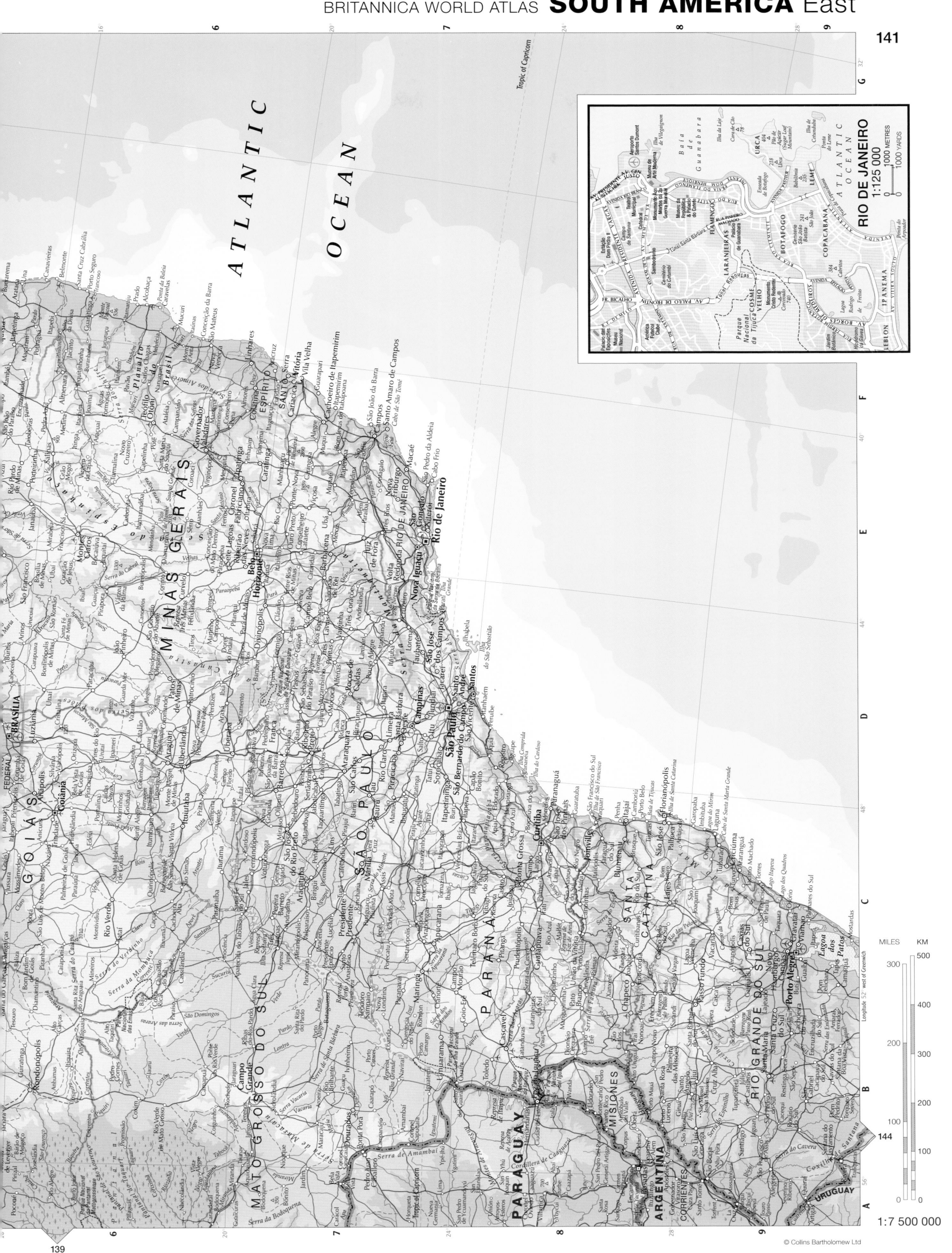

ATLANTIC

OCEAN

RIO DE JANEIRO
1:125 000

1000 METRES
1000 YARDS

Tropic of Capricorn

MINAS GERAIS

ESPÍRITO SANTO

GOIÁS

BRASÍLIA
FEDERAL

Goiânia

MATO GROSSO DO SUL

SÃO PAULO

São Paulo

RIO DE JANEIRO

Rio de Janeiro

PARANÁ

Curitiba

SANTA CATARINA

Florianópolis

RIO GRANDE DO SUL

Porto Alegre

Lagoa dos Patos

PARAGUAY

Tropic of Capricorn

ARGENTINA

CORRIENTES

MISIONES

URUGUAY

MILES   KM

300   500

             400

200   300

             200

100
             100

1:7 500 000

144

© Collins Bartholomew Ltd

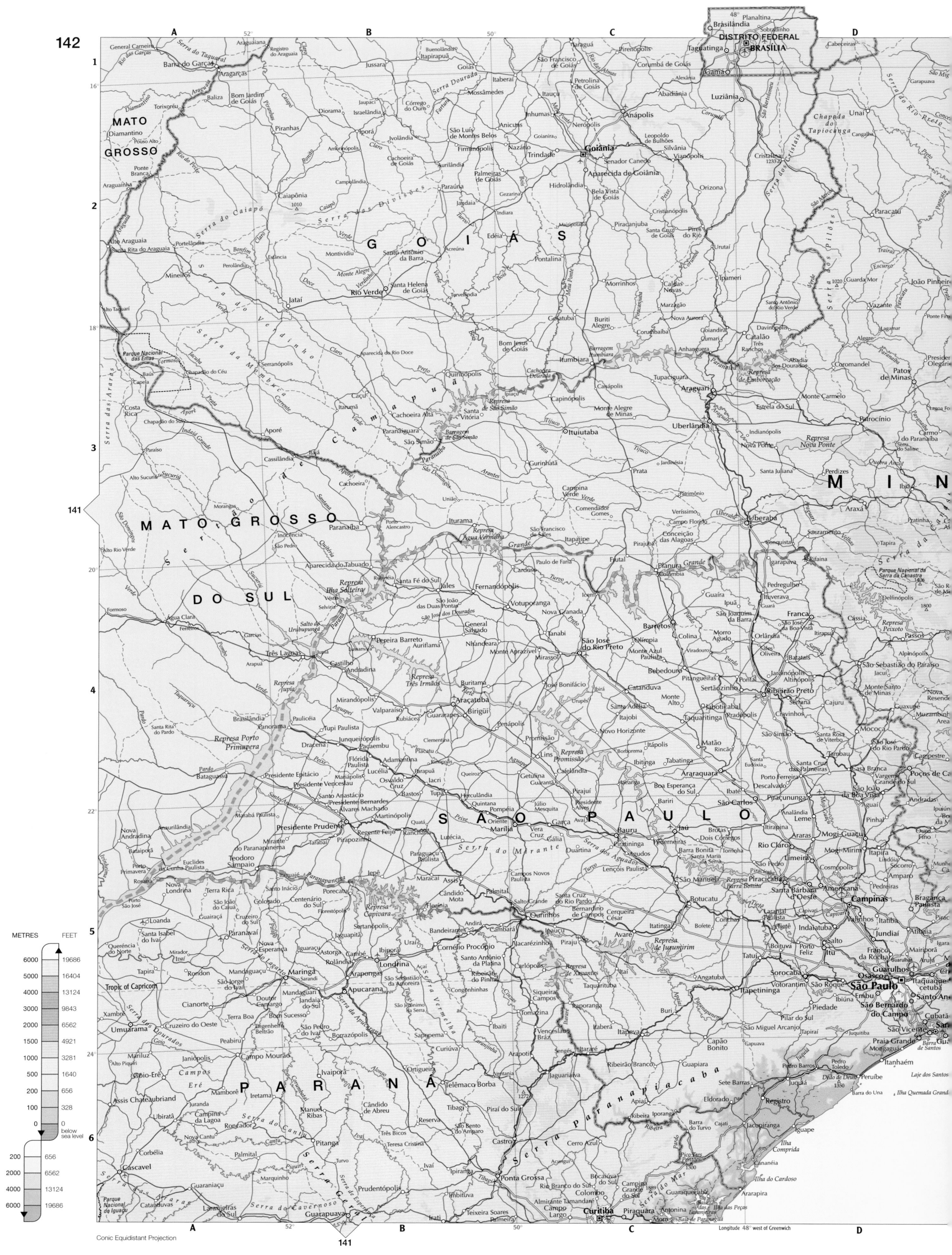

MATO
(Diamantino)

GROSSO

G O I Á S

M A T O   G R O S S O

D O   S U L

S Ã O   P A U L O

M I N

DISTRITO FEDERAL
BRASÍLIA

P A R A N Á

METRES   FEET
6000   19686
5000   16404
4000   13124
3000   9843
2000   6562
1500   4921
1000   3281
500   1640
200   656
100   328
0   0
          below
          sea level

200   656
2000   6562
4000   13124
6000   19686

Tropic of Capricorn

Conic Equidistant Projection

Longitude 48° west of Greenwich

ATLANTIC

OCEAN

MILES KM
125 200

175

100
150

125

75
100

50
75

50
25
25

0 0

1:3 300 000

Tropic of Capricorn

SÃO PAULO
1:125 000
0 METRES 1000
0 YARDS 1000

© Collins Bartholomew Ltd

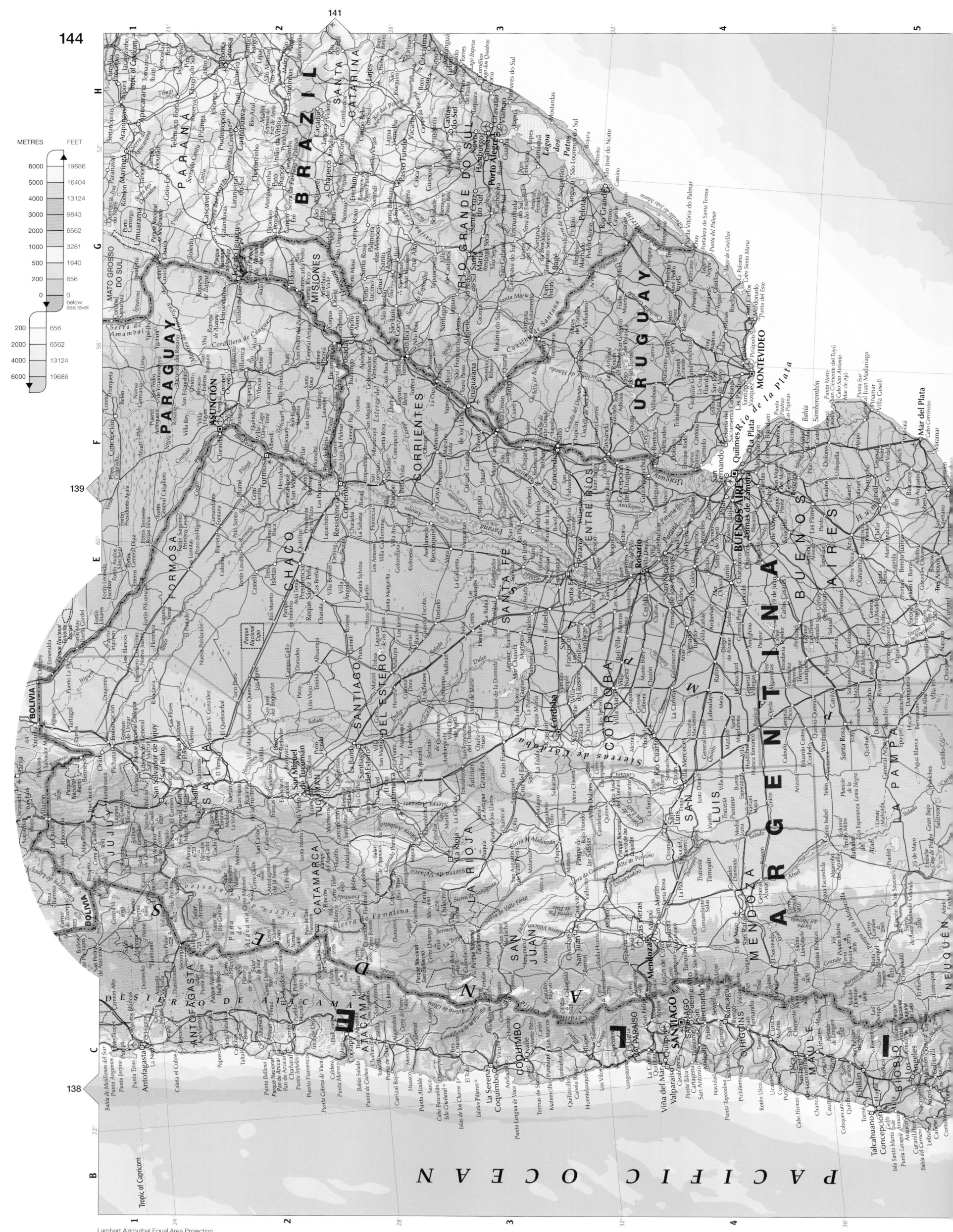

METRES FEET

6000 19686
5000 16404
4000 13124
3000 9843
2000 6562
1000 3281
500 1640
200 656
0 below
sea level

200 656
2000 6562
4000 13124
6000 19686

BRAZIL

PARAGUAY

ASUNCIÓN

BOLIVIA

ARGENTINA

URUGUAY

MONTEVIDEO

BUENOS AIRES

Rosario

Córdoba

SANTIAGO

Mar del Plata

PACIFIC OCEAN

Lambert Azimuthal Equal Area Projection

139

138

141

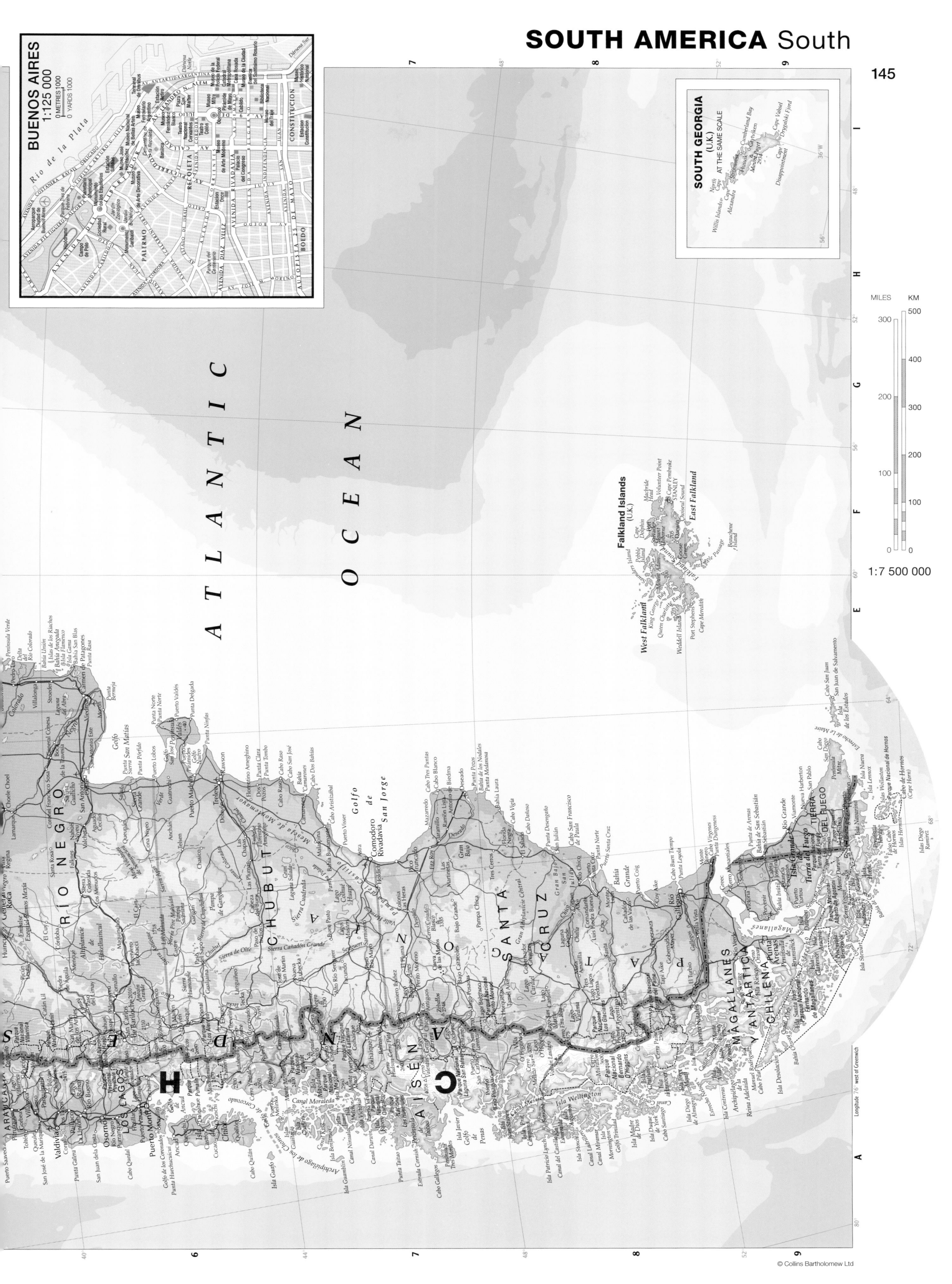

BUENOS AIRES
1:125 000
0 METRES 1000
0 YARDS 1000

SOUTH GEORGIA
(U.K.)
AT THE SAME SCALE

ATLANTIC

OCEAN

Falkland Islands
(U.K.)

West Falkland

East Falkland

MILES   KM
300   500

             400

200   300

             200
100
             100

0   0

1:7 500 000

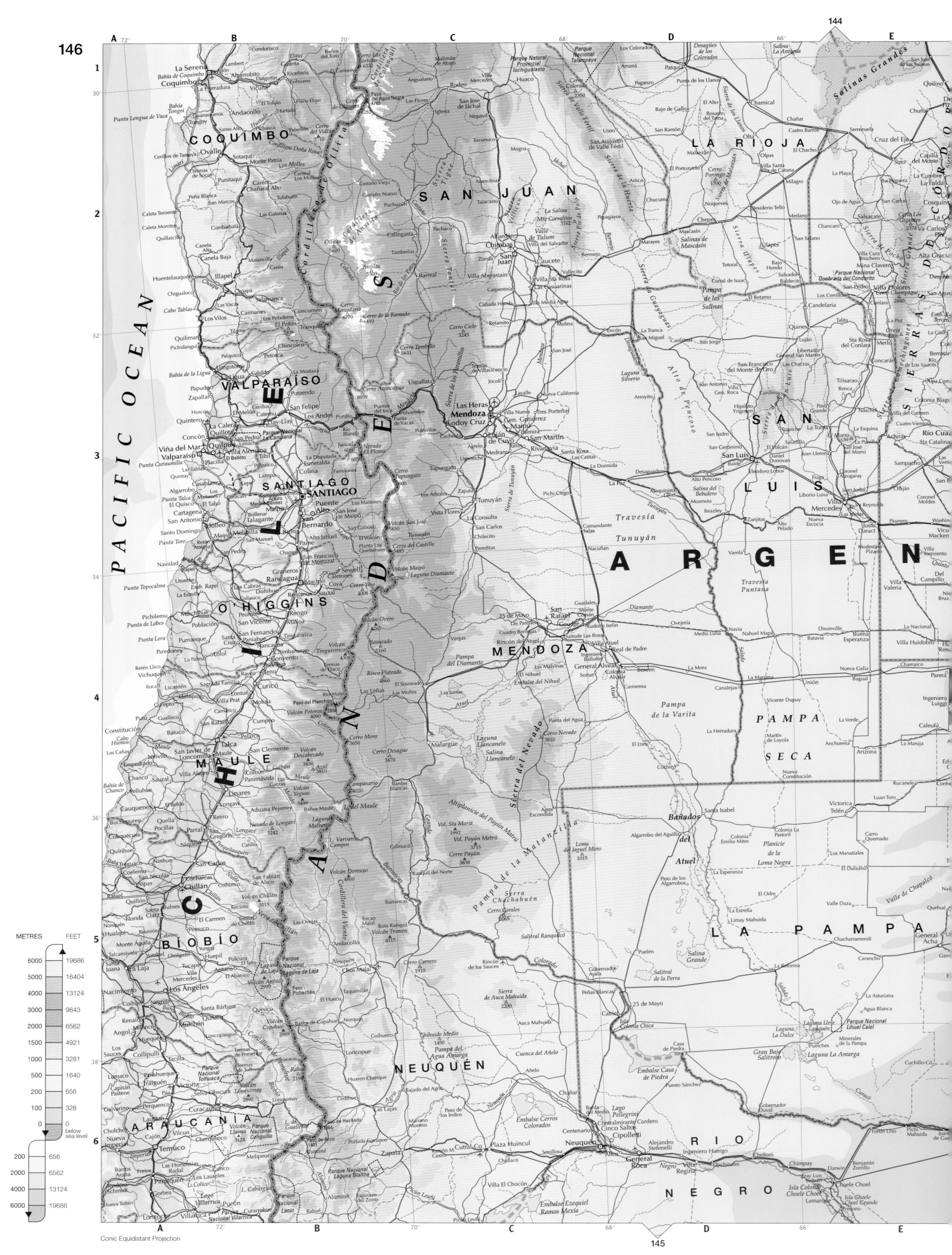

Conic Equidistant Projection

METRES FEET

6000	19686
5000	16404
4000	13124
3000	9843
2000	6562
1500	4921
1000	3281
500	1640
200	656
100	328
0	0 below sea level

200	656
2000	6562
4000	13124
6000	19686

PACIFIC OCEAN

COQUIMBO

VALPARAÍSO

SANTIAGO

O'HIGGINS

MAULE

BÍOBÍO

ARAUCANÍA

SAN JUAN

LA RIOJA

SAN LUIS

MENDOZA

ARGEN

LA PAMPA

NEUQUÉN

RIO NEGRO

Mendoza

Santiago

La Serena

Coquimbo

Valparaíso

Neuquén

PAMPA SECA

CORRIENTES

BRAZIL

ARTIGAS

SALTO

SANTA FÉ

CORDOBA

ENTRE RÍOS

PAYSANDÚ

URUGUAY

TACUAREMBÓ

RÍO NEGRO

DURAZNO

SORIANO

FLORES

FLORIDA

COLONIA

SAN JOSÉ

Rosario

Paraná

Santa Fé

Córdoba

Villa María

Concordia

Salto

Paysandú

Gualeguaychú

Gualeguay

San Nicolás de los Arroyos

Pergamino

Junín

Lincoln

Pilar

Luján

Mercedes

San Fernando

Tigre

BUENOS AIRES

Avellaneda

Lomas de Zamora

Quilmes

Berazategui

La Plata

Moreno

Marcos Paz

MONTEVIDEO

CANELONES

Las Piedras

Colonia del Sacramento

BUENOS AIRES

Azul

Olavarría

Tandil

Coronel Suárez

Tres Arroyos

Bahía Blanca

Punta Alta

Necochea

Mar del Plata

Villa Gesell

Río de la Plata

Bahía Samborombón

Bahía Blanca

ATLANTIC OCEAN

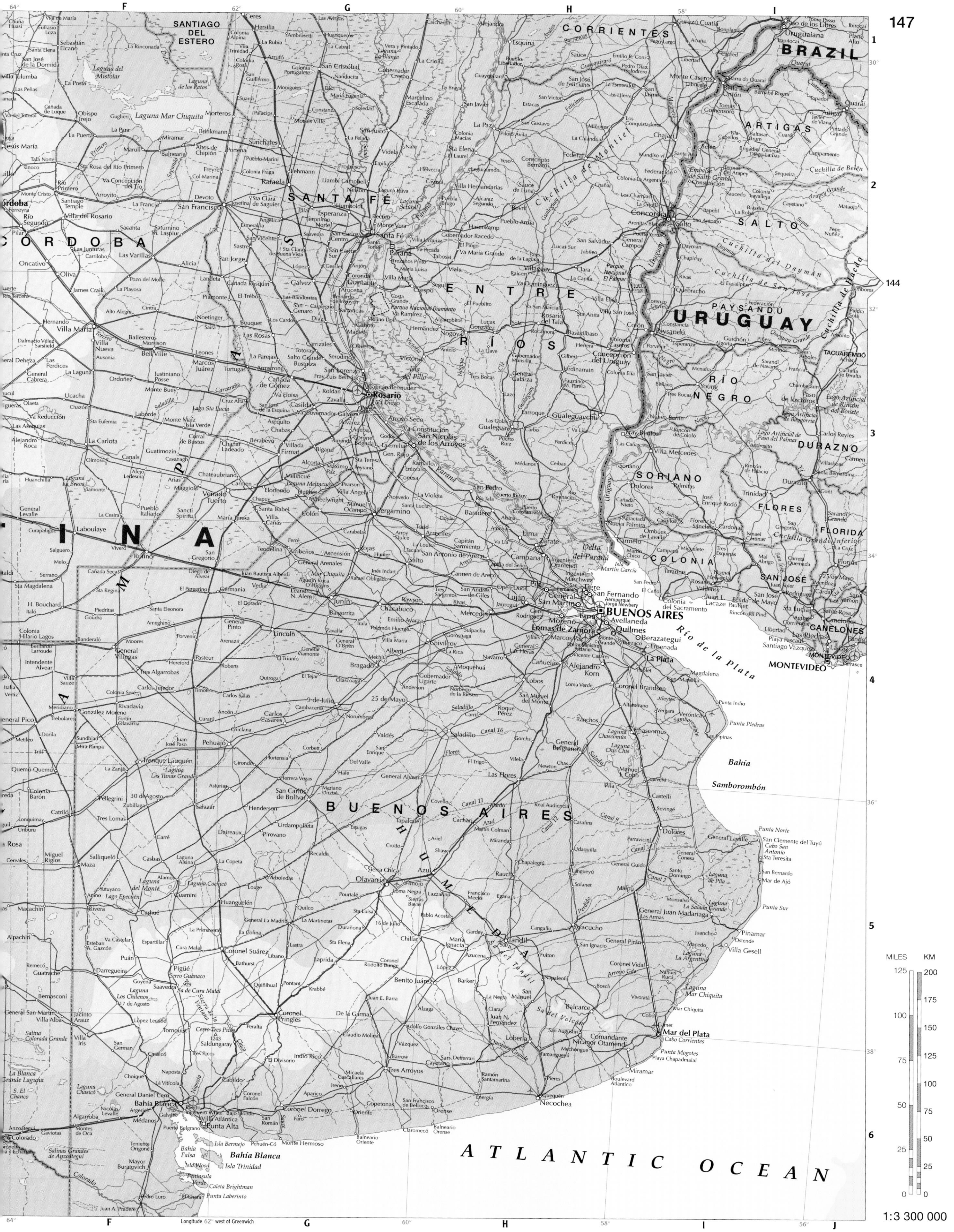

SANTIAGO DEL ESTERO

Longitude 62° west of Greenwich

1:3 300 000

© Collins Bartholomew Ltd

MILES 125 100 75 50 25 0

KM 200 175 150 125 100 75 50 25 0

A B C D E

ARCTI

Karskoye More

Gulf of Bothnia
Beloye More
Arctic Circle

Baltic Sea
EUROPE
RUSSIAN
Noril'sk
Urengoy
Ob'
Obskaya Guba

Ural'skiy Khrebet
(Ural Mountains)

Surgut
Yekaterinburg
Tobol'sk
Chelyabinsk
Omsk
Tomsk
Novosibirsk
Krasnoyars
Ob'
Novokuznetsk

Sea of Azov
Pavlodar
Astana
Barnaul

Carpathian Mountains
Alps

Black Sea
Caucasus
Atyrau
Aktobe
KAZAKHSTAN
Karaganda
Semipalatinsk
Ust'-Kamenogorsk
Ulaangom
45

Bursa
Samsun
GEORGIA
T'bilisi
Kızılırmak
Sivas
Erzurum
ARMENIA AZERBAIJAN
Yerevan
AZ.
Baki
Aral'sk
Balkhash
Ozero
Zaysan
Altay
Altai Mountains
İzmir
Ankara
TURKEY
Konya
Kayseri
Malatya
Gaziantep
Tabriz
Ardabil
Aral Sea
Aktau
Caspian Sea
Zaliv Kara-Bogaz-Gol
Turkmenbashi
Shymkent
UZBEKISTAN
Almaty
Yining
Ürümqi
Tacheng
Ozero Balkhash
Turpan

Antalya
Adana
Lefkosia
CYPRUS
Halab
Al Mawsil
Arbil
Kırkük
Kermānshāh
Qom
Gorgān
Mashhad
Toshkent
Samarkand
KYRGYZSTAN
Bishkek
Andizhan
Kokand
Khujand
Tien Shan
Yeyk-Kol
Aksu
Korla
XINJIANG UYGUR ZIZHIQ
(SINKIANG)
Kashi
Lop Nur

Mediterranean Sea
Beirut
LEBANON
SYRIA
Dimashq
ISRAEL
Tel Aviv-Yafo
Gaza
Amman
Jerusalem
JORDAN
Baghdad
IRAQ
An Najaf
Borūjerd
Eşfahān
Tehrān
Daşht-e Kavir
TURKMENISTAN
Ashgabat
TAJIKISTAN
Dushanbe
Hindu Kush
AFGHANISTAN
Kābul
Herāt
Birjand
Peshawar
Islāmābād
Rawalpindi
Kunlun Shan
Hotan
Tarim Pendi
Qaidam P
Golmud

30
Euphrates
Al Furāt
Birjand
IRAN
Kermān
Zāhedān
Kandahār
PAKISTAN
Quetta
Multan
Gujranwala
Lahore
Faisalābād
Ludhiāna
Amritsar
XIZANG ZIZHIQU
(TIBET)
AKSAI CHIN
Karakoram Range
Lhasa
Xigazê
Nam Co
Siling Co

Ahvāz
Ābādān
Al Başrah
Shīrāz
Bandar-e 'Abbās
Pasni
Karachi
Hyderabad
Thar Desert
Chandigarh
Delhi
Meerut
New Delhi
Ghaziabad
Faridabad
Ganganagar
HIMALAYA
Mount Everest
Kathmandu
NEPAL
Thimphu
BHUTAN
Dibrugarh
Darjiling
Brahmaputra

Al Kuwayt
KUWAIT
An Nafūd
Būshehr
The Gulf
Ad Dammām
BAHRAIN
Al Manāmah
QATAR
Ad Dawḩah
Dubayy
Abū Z̧aby
UNITED ARAB
EMIRATES
Gulf of Oman
Ibrā'
Ṣūr
Masqaţ
Jaipur
Jodhpur
Agra
Gwalior
Lucknow
Kanpur
Gorakhpur
Beawar
Kota
Allahabad
Varanasi
Patna
Ganga (Ganges)
Guwahati
Shillong
Thimphu
BANGLADESH
Dhaka
Chittagong
MY

Al Madīnah
Al Hufūf
Ar Riyāḑ
SAUDI
Jiddah
Makkah
ARABIA
Rub' al Khālī
OMAN
Maqrah
ARABIAN
SEA
Ahmadabad
Vadodara
Surat
Indore
Bhopal
Jabalpur
Nagpur
Ranchi
Jamshedpur
Asansol
Calcutta
(Kolkata)
Khulna
Mouths of the Ganges
Manda

15
Tropic of Cancer
Red Sea
Nile
Libyan Desert
An Nafūd
Şan'ā'
Al Hudaydah
YEMEN
Ta'izz
Al Mukallā
Salālah
Nashik
Thane
Mumbai
Ulhasnagar
Pune
Aurangabad
INDIA
Deccan
Solapur
Hyderabad
Krishna
Vishakhapatnam
Vijayawada
BAY
OF BENGAL
Meikti
Sittwe
Yange
Bassein

Adan
Gulf of Aden
Suquṭrá
(Yemen)
Dharwad
Kurnool
Nellore
Mangalore
Bangalore
Mysore
Chennai
Salem
Andaman
Islands
(India)
Andam
Sea

AFRICA
Calicut
Coimbatore
Cochin
Tiruchirappalli
Madurai
Jaffna
Trincomalee
Nicobar
Islands
(India)

30
Trivandrum
Gulf of
Mannar
Kandy
SRI LANKA
Colombo
Sri Jayewardenepura
Kotte
Banda
Aceh

Lake
Victoria
Equator
Male
MALDIVES
Simeulue

Lake
Nyasa
Mahé
Seychelles
Coëtivy
INDIAN OCEAN

Njazidja
Comoros
Mayotte
Aldabra Islands
(Seychelles)
Farquhar Islands
(Seychelles)
Agalega Islands
(Mauritius)
British
Indian Ocean
Territory
Chagos
Archipelago
Diego Garcia

15

A B C D E

Orthographic Projection

15 30 45 60 75 90

OCEAN

180°

150°

165°

105°

120°

135°

Tiksi

Arctic Circle

Bering Strait

-60°

Khrebet Kolymskiy

Ugol'nye Kopi

SREDNE - SIBIRSKOYE

Verkhoyanskiy Khrebet

Susuman

BERING
SEA

Pribilof
Islands

PLOSKOGOR'YE

Mirnyy

Yakutsk

Aldan

Lena

FEDERATION

Magadan

Poluostrov Kamchatka

45°

1

Bratsk

Ust'- Kut

Bodaybo

Aldan

Stanovoy Khrebet

Tynda

Sea
of Okhotsk

Petropavlovsk-
Kamchatskiy

Aleutian
Islands

Irkutsk

Ozero
Baykal

Chita

Komsomol'sk-
na-Amure

Sakhalin

Aldan

Amur

Heilong Jiang

Blagoveshchensk

Khabarovsk

Yuzhno-
Sakhalinsk

Korsakov

2

Ulan-Ude

Darhan

Hailar

Qiqihar

Daqing

Suihua

Jiamusi

Wakkanai

MONGOLIA

Ulaanbaatar

Jargalant

Da Hinggan Ling

Hulun
Nur

Buir
Nur

Harbin

Vladivostok

Sapporo

Hokkaidō

Hakodate

GOBI

Changchun

Jilin

Sea

Akita

Dalandzadgad

NEI MONGOL ZIZHIQU
(INNER MONGOLIA)

Shenyang

Fushun

NORTH
KOREA

Ch'ŏngjin

of Japan

Niigata

Sendai

Yumen

Jining

Zhangjiakou

Hohhot

Anshan

Benxi

(East Sea)

Wuhai

Baotou

Datong

Beijing

Tangshan

Dalian

P'yŏngyang

Kanazawa

JAPAN

Qinghai Hu

Yinchuan

Shijiazhuang

Tianjin

Bo Hai

Korea
Bay

Puch'ŏn

Sŏul

Suwŏn

Kyōto

Tōkyō

Yokohama

Tian Shan

Taiyuan

Handan

Jinan

Yantai

Inch'ŏn

SOUTH
KOREA

Taejŏn

Kōbe

Osaka

Nagoya

Xining

Lanzhou

Weinan

Zibo

Qingdao

Yellow

Taegu

Pusan

Kita-Kyūshū

Hiroshima

Honshū

Izu-shotō
(Japan)

30°

3

Xi'an

Luoyang

Zhengzhou

Xuzhou

Sea

Mokp'o

Kwangju

Fukuoka

Shikoku

Qinghai Hu

Pingdingshan

Huaian

Nanjing

Changzhou

Shanghai

Nagasaki

Kumamoto

Kyūshū

Chengdu

Nanchong

Suizhou

Hefei

Wuhu

Wuxi

Jiaxing

Kagoshima

CHINA

Neijiang

Chongqing

Changde

Wuhan

Jingdezhen

Hangzhou

Ningbo

East China

Yibin

Zhaotong

Guiyang

Yueyang

Nanchang

Quzhou

Wenzhou

Sea

Ogasawara-shotō
(Japan)

Tropic of Cancer

Panzhihua

Changsha

Hengyang

Fuzhou

Okinawa

PACIFIC

165°

yitkyina

Qujing

Liuzhou

Meizhou

Xiamen

Nansei-shotō
(Japan)

Kazan-rettō
(Japan)

4

Kunming

Nanning

Guangzhou

Shenzhen

Shantou

T'aipei

Taiwan Strait

Macau

Hong Kong

Kaohsiung

T'aitung

TAIWAN

OCEAN

Ha Nôi

Zhanjiang

Batan Islands

Northern
Mariana
Islands

Pagan

Hai Phong

Haikou

Luzon Strait

Gulf
of Tongking

Hainan

Aparri

15°

Chiang
Mai

Louangphrabang

LAOS

VIETNAM

Saipan

Tinian

Rota

Mekong

Huê

Da Nǎng

Paracel Islands

Luzon

PHILIPPINES

Guam

Viangchan

SOUTH

Quezon
City

toulmein

THAILAND

CHINA

Manila

Naga

Yap

Nakhon
Ratchasima

Nha Trang

SEA

Mindoro

Masbate

Samar

5

Bangkok

Tônlé
Sap

Iloilo

Panay

Cebu

Caroline Islands

CAMBODIA

Phnum
Penh

Ho Chi Minh

Spratly Islands

Palawan

Negros

Dipolog

Surigao

Chuuk

Gulf of Thailand

Sihanoukville

Sulu

Mindanao

PALAU

Koror

Mortlock
Islands

Nakhon Si
Thammarat

Sea

Zamboanga

Davao

Kota Bharu

Kota Kinabalu

Sandakan

Sulu
Archipelago

Kepulauan
Talaud

6

George
Town

Ipoh

BRUNEI

SABAH

Sulu
Sea

Kepulauan
Sangir

Equator

0°

MALAYSIA

Bandar Seri
Begawan

Kuala
Lumpur

Putrajaya

Celebes

Manado

Strait of Malacca

Kuching

Sibu

Sri Aman

Sea

Molucca Sea

Halmahera

Singapore

Sumatera

Pontianak

Borneo

Palu

Ketapang

Bismarck Archipelago

Kepulauan
Lingga

Siberut

Padang

Balikpapan

Makassar Strait

Kepulauan
Sula

Jazirah
Doberai

Pegunungan Van Rees

Jayapura

Bismarck
Sea

New Britain

Mentawai

Ketapang

Sulawesi

Buru

Seram

Seram Sea

Puncak Jaya

Central Range

Bougainville
Island

Bangka

Palembang

Banjarmasin

Parepare

NEW

Bengkulu

Enggano

Java Sea

Makassar

Buton

Banda Sea

Kepulauan
Aru

GUINEA

Digul

Solomon
Sea

Bandar
Lampung

Jakarta

Semarang

Surabaya

Bali
Sea

Wetar

Kepulauan
Tanimbar

Gulf
of Papua

7

Bandung

Jawa
(Java)

Madura

Surakarta

Flores Sea

Dili

EAST
TIMOR

Arafura Sea

OCEANIA

Yogyakarta

INDONESIA

Lombok

Sumbawa

Raba

Flores

Sawu
Sea

Sumba

Timor

Cape
York

New Ireland

CORAL
SEA

105°

120°

125°

150°

Melville Island

Kupang

Rote

Torres Strait

York
Peninsula

Mannington Public Library

MILES

KM

1000

1500

750

1250

1000

500

750

250

500

250

0

1 : 24 000 000

F

G

H

I

J

Mercator Projection

CHINA
YUNNAN · **GUIZHOU** · **GUANGXI ZHUANGZU ZIZHIQU** · **GUANGDONG** · **HUNAN** · **JIANGXI** · **FUJIAN** · **HAINAN**

Panzhihua (Dukou) · Kunming (Huangcaoba) · Guiyang · Duyun · Anshun (Xixiu) · Yongzhou · Guilin · Liuzhou · Nanning · Yulin · Guangzhou (Canton) · Shenzhen · Hong Kong · Kowloon · Macau · Shantou · Xiamen (Amoy) · Fuzhou · T'AIPEI · Kaohsiung · Haikou

MYANMAR · **LAOS** · **THAILAND** · **VIETNAM** · **CAMBODIA**

Mandalay · HA NOI · Hai Phong · VIANGCHAN (Vientiane) · Chiang Mai · BANGKOK (Krung Thep) · PHNUM PENH · Huê · Đà Nẵng · Quy Nhon · Nha Trang · Hô Chi Minh (Saigon)

SOUTH CHINA SEA · Paracel Islands (Xisha Qundao) · Spratly Islands · Scarborough Shoal

PHILIPPINES · **LUZON** · MANILA · Quezon City · SULU SEA

MALAYSIA · **SARAWAK** · **SABAH** · **BRUNEI** · BANDAR SERI BEGAWAN · Kota Kinabalu · Kuching · **BORNEO (KALIMANTAN)**

SINGAPORE · KUALA LUMPUR · PUTRAJAYA · George Town · Johor Bahru

SUMATERA · Medan · Padang · Palembang · Bandar Lampung

INDONESIA · JAKARTA · Bandung · Semarang · Surabaya · **JAWA (JAVA)** · Bali · Denpasar

SULAWESI (CELEBES) · Makassar (Ujung Pandang)

CELEBES SEA · **LAUT JAWA (JAVA SEA)** · **INDIAN OCEAN** · **Gulf of Tongking** · **Gulf of Thailand**

METRES / FEET
6000 / 19686 · 5000 / 16404 · 4000 / 13124 · 3000 / 9843 · 2000 / 6562 · 1000 / 3281 · 500 / 1640 · 200 / 656 · 0 / 0 below sea level

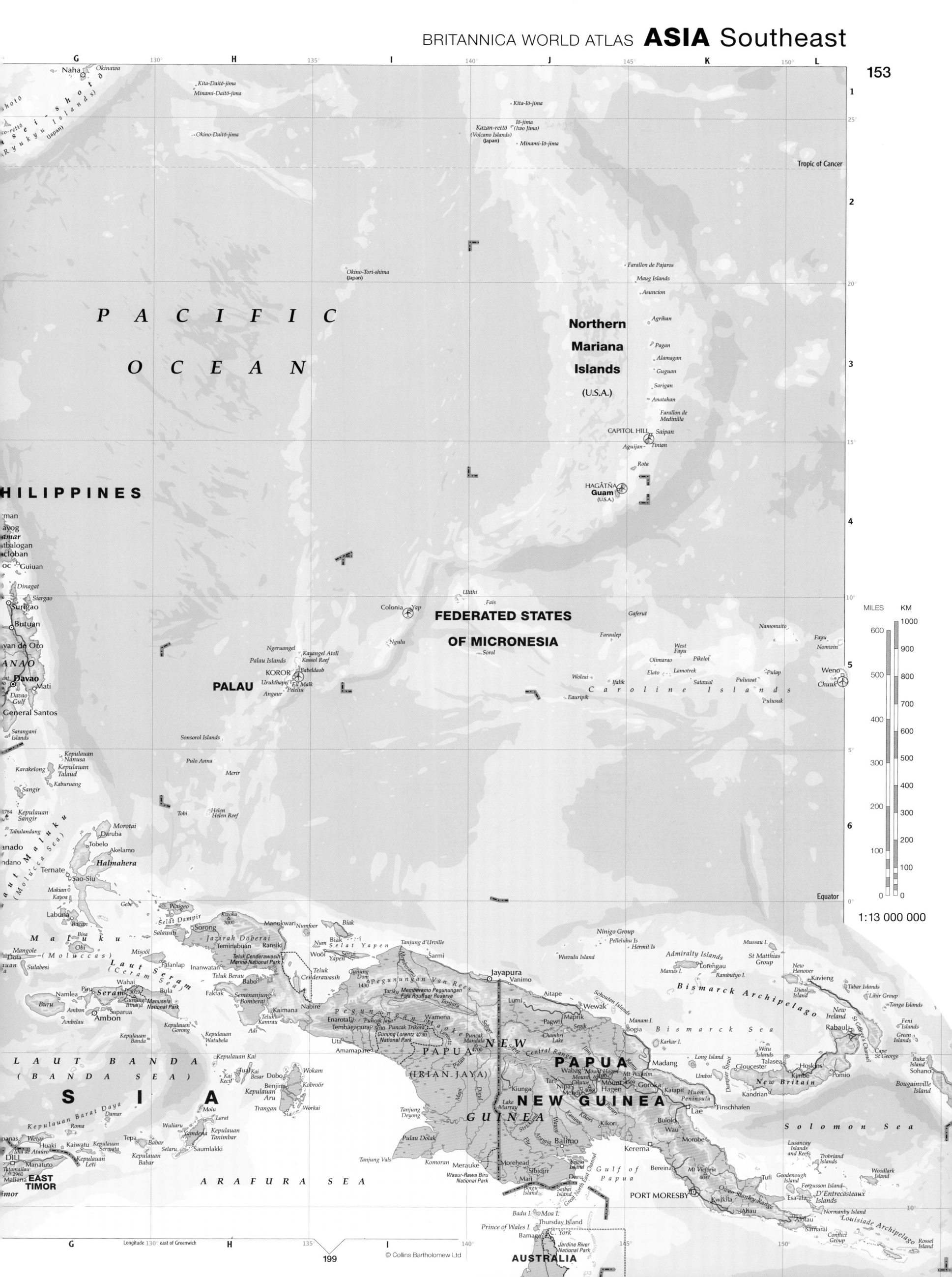

PACIFIC

OCEAN

PHILIPPINES

Northern
Mariana
Islands

(U.S.A.)

CAPITOL HILL · Saipan
Aguijan · Tinian

HAGÅTÑA
Guam
(U.S.A.)

Farallon de Pajaros
Maug Islands
· Asuncion
Agrihan
· Pagan
· Alamagan
· Guguan
Sarigan
· Anatahan
Farallon de
Medinilla

Rota

Naha · Okinawa
Kita-Daitō-jima
Minami-Daitō-jima

Okino-Daitō-jima

Okino-Tori-shima
(Japan)

Kita-Iō-jima
Iō-jima
Kazan-rettō (Iō Jima)
(Volcano Islands)
(Japan)
Minami-Iō-jima

Tropic of Cancer

man
ayog
amar
atbalogan
acloban
oc · Guiuan
· Dinagat
· Siargao
Surigao
Butuan
yan de Oro
ANAO
Davao
· Mati
Davao
Gulf
General Santos
Sarangani
Islands

Ulithi
Fais

Colonia· Yap
Ngulu
· Sorol

FEDERATED STATES

OF MICRONESIA

Gaferut
Faraulep
Olimarao
Elato
Woleai
Ifalik
Eauripik

West
Fayu
Pikelot
Lamotrek
Satawal
Puluwat
Pulusuk

Namonuito
Fayu
Nomwin
Pulap
Weno
Chuuk

Caroline Islands

MILES KM
600 1000
900
500 800
700
400 600
500
300 400
300
200
200
100 100
0 0

Ngeruangel
Palau Islands Kayangel Atoll
Kossol Reef
KOROR· Babeldaob
Urukthapel ·Eil Malk
Angaur Peleliu

PALAU

Sonsorol Islands

Pulo Anna

Merir

Tobi · Helen
Helen Reef

Karakelong
Kepulauan
Nanusa
Kepulauan
Talaud
· Sangir
Kaburuang
4784
Kepulauan
Sangir
Tahulandang
Morotai
Daruba
· Tobelo
Akelamo
ndano
(Molucca Sea)
Ternate
Makian·
Kayoa
Halmahera

Matuku
Mangole
(Moluccas)
Obi
Dofa·
uan
Sulabesi

Equator

1:13 000 000

Waigeo
Kwoka
& 3000
Sorong
Salawati
Selat Dampir
Misōōl
Fafanlap
Inanwatan
Wahai
Kepulauan
Seram
Gorong
Namlea
Piru Gunung
Manusela
Manusela National Park
Buru
Ambon· Saparua
Ambelau

Manokwari Numfoor
Jazirah Doberai
Temirabuan Ransiki
Teluk Cenderawasih
Marine National Park
Teluk Berau Babo
Fakfak
Semenanjung
Bomberai
Kaimana
Teluk
Kamrau
Kepulauan
Adi

Biak
Num Serui
Selat Yapen
Wool Yapen
Teluk Cenderawasih
Nabire

Ninigo Group
Pelleluhu Is
Wuwulu Island
Hermit Is

Admiralty Islands
Mamus I. Lorengau
Rambutyo I.

Mussau I.
St Matthias
Group
New
Hanover
Kavieng
Tabar Islands

Tanjung d'Urville
Sarmi
Gunung
Dom
1430
Tarku
Membramo Pegunungan
Foja Rouffaer Reserve
Tembagapura
Tarijiti

Pegunungan Van Rees
Jayapura
Vanimo
Lumi
Aitape

Schouten Islands
Manam I.
Bogia Karkar I.

Lihir Group

New
Ireland

Feni
Islands
Rabaul
Green
Islands

LAUT

S I A

Bisa
Mangole

Matuku

EAST
TIMOR

Kepulauan
Banda

LAUT BANDA
(B A N D A S E A)

Kepulauan Kai

Dobo Wokam

Tual
Kai
Besar
Kai
Kecil

Kepulauan
Aru

Kobroör

Trangan Workai

SERAM
Seram
3030
Bula

Pegunungan Maoke
Wamena
Puncak Jaya
Gunung Lorentz
National Park
Puncak Trikora
5030
Amamapare
Utu

Wewak
Maprik
Sepik
Chambri
Lake

PAPUA
(IRIAN JAYA)

Puncak
Mandala
4700

NEW

GUINEA

Wabag
Mount Hagen
Mount
Hagen

Pagwi

Angoram

Wuvulu Island

Bismarck Archipelago

Bismarck Sea

Witu
Islands
Long Island
Madang Talasea
Umboi
Gloucester

Central Ran
PAPUA
Goroka
Kaiapit Huon
Peninsula
Finschhafen

Djaul
Tanga Islands

New
Britain
Kimbe
Hoskins Pomio

Bougainville
Island

Solomon Sea

Kepulauan
Barat Daya
Wetar
Roma
Huaki
Kaiwatu
Babar
DILI
Kepulauan
Leti
Kepulauan
Tanimbar
Saumlakki
Kepulauan
Babar
Selaru

Tepa
Damar
Wuliaru
Larat
Sia
Selu
Camdena

Tanjung
Deyong

Pulau Dōlak

Tanjung Vals

Wasur-Rawa Biru
National Park
Merauke

Komoran

Morehead

NEW GUINEA

Balimo

Lake
Murray

Kiunga
Mendi
Mount
Mt Wilhelm

Kikori
Bulolo
Wau

Lae
Morobe

Lusancay
Islands
and Reefs
Trobriand
Islands

Goodenough Island
Fergusson Island

Woodlark
Island

D'Entrecasteaux
Islands

ARAFURA SEA

Mari
Sibidiri
boju
Saibai
Island
Badu I. Moa I.
Prince of Wales I.
Thursday Island
Bamaga Cape
York

Kerema
Bereina

PORT MORESBY

Kwikila

Gulf of
Papua

Daru
Island

Great North East Channel

Great Barrier Reef

Mt Victoria
4037

Owen Stanley Range

Abau

Tufi

Cape
St George
Buka I.
Sohano

Green
Islands

Feni
Islands

Esa-ala

Samarai

Conflict
Group

Rossel Island

Louisiade Archipelago

AUSTRALIA

Jardine River
National Park

Longitude 130° east of Greenwich

PHILIPPINES

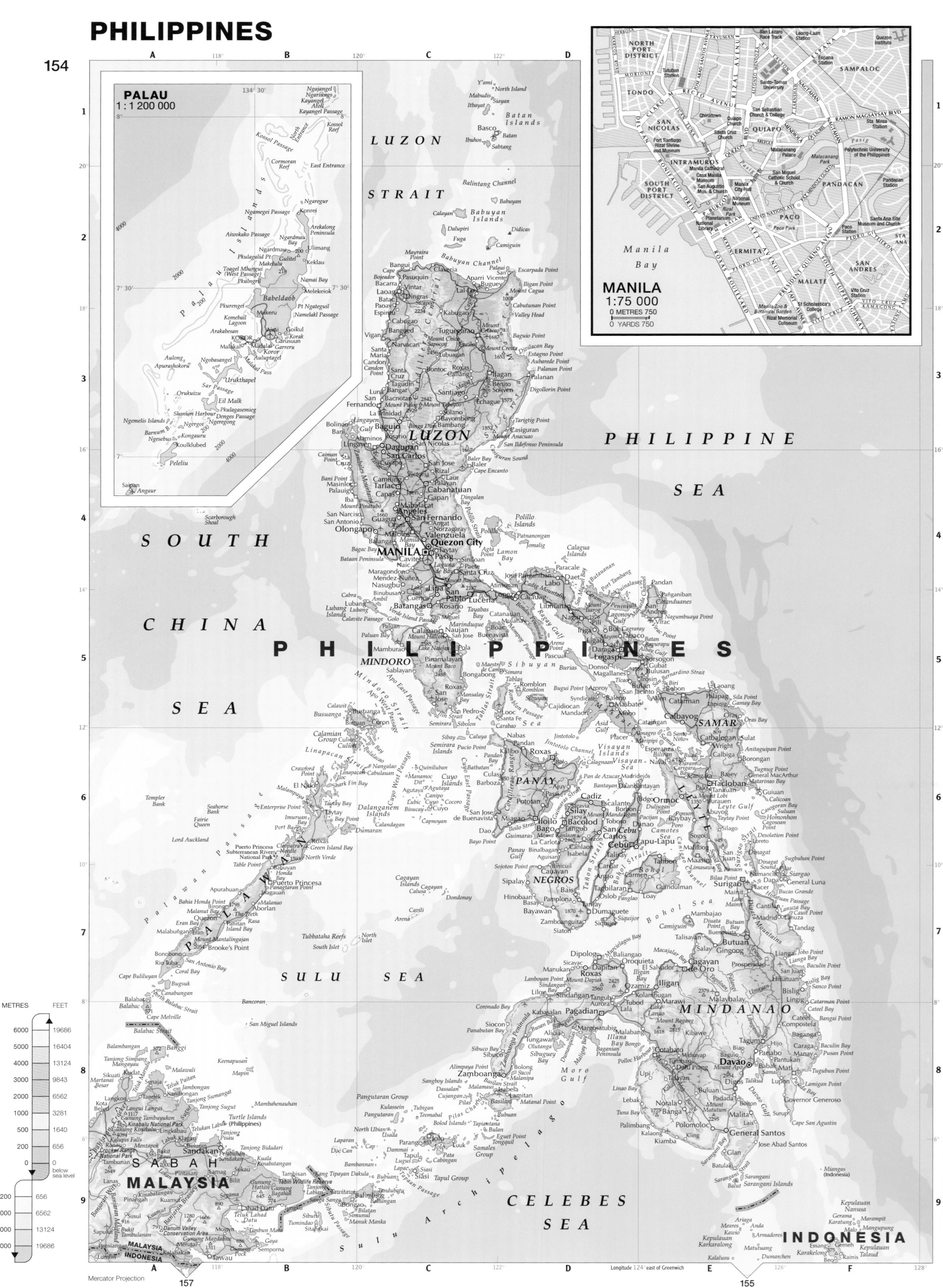
PALAU
1 : 1 200 000
Babeldaob
Koror
Peleliu
Angaur
MANILA
1:75 000
0 METRES 750
0 YARDS 750
NORTH PORT DISTRICT
TONDO
SAN NICOLAS
INTRAMUROS
SOUTH PORT DISTRICT
ERMITA
PACO
MALATE
SAMPALOC
QUIAPO
PANDACAN
SAN ANDRES
Manila Bay
LUZON STRAIT
PHILIPPINE SEA
SOUTH CHINA SEA
SULU SEA
CELEBES SEA
PHILIPPINES
LUZON
MINDORO
PANAY
NEGROS
SAMAR
LEYTE
MINDANAO
PALAWAN
SABAH
MALAYSIA
INDONESIA
MANILA
Quezon City
Baguio
Cebu
Iloilo
Bacolod
Tacloban
Zamboanga
Davao
Cagayan de Oro
General Santos
Puerto Princesa
Sandakan
Sulu Archipelago
Moro Gulf
Bohol Sea
Visayan Sea
Sibuyan Sea
Batan Islands
Babuyan Islands
Polillo Islands
Calamian Group
Cuyo Islands
Mercator Projection
Longitude 124° east of Greenwich
METRES
FEET
6000
5000
4000
3000
2000
1000
500
200
0
19686
16404
13124
9843
6562
3281
1640
656
below sea level
157
155

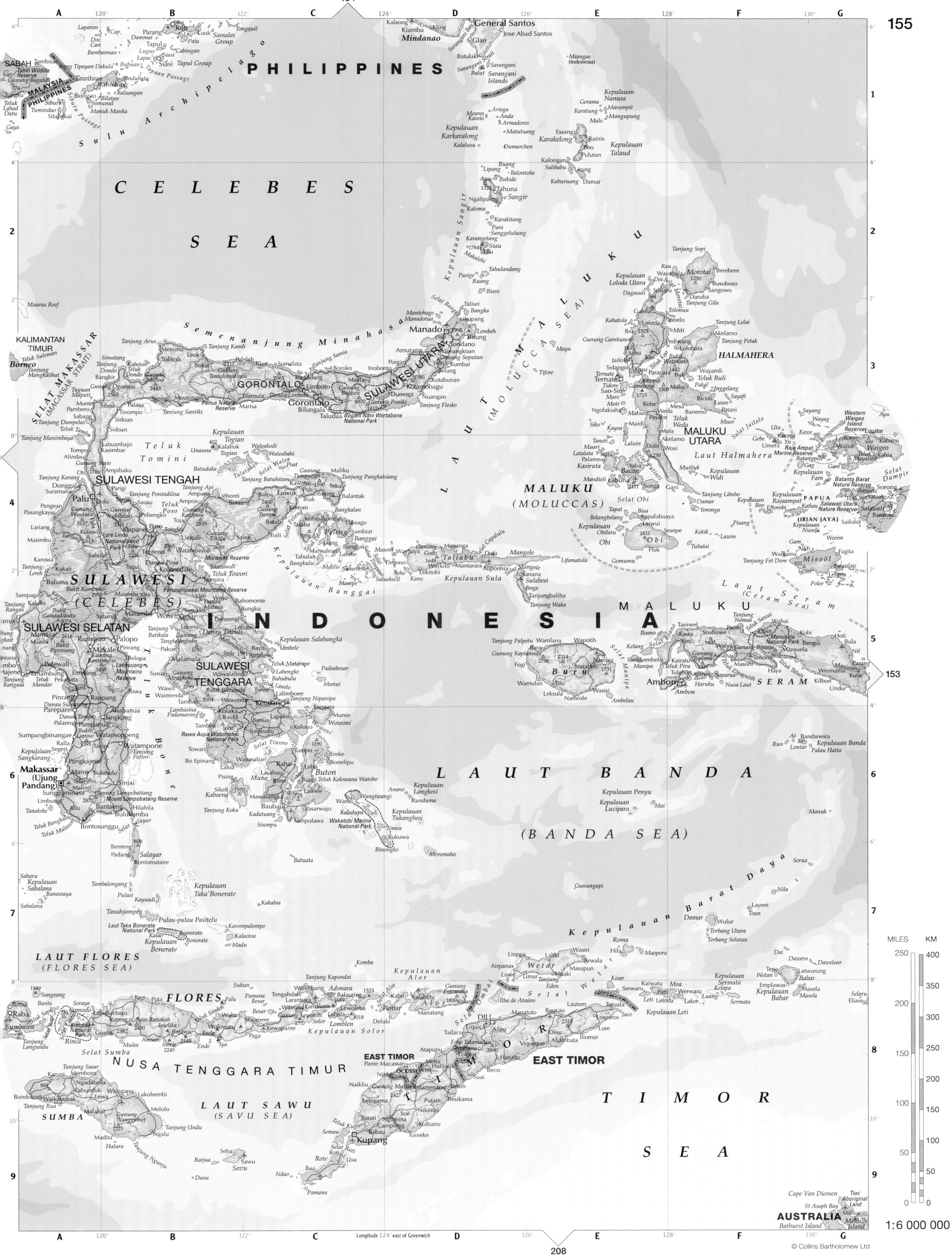
154
PHILIPPINES
Mindanao
General Santos
Sulu Archipelago
CELEBES SEA
MALAYSIA
SABAH
KALIMANTAN TIMUR
Borneo
SELAT MAKASSAR (MACASSAR STRAIT)
Semenanjung Minahasa
Manado
GORONTALO
Gorontalo
SULAWESI UTARA
Teluk Tomini
SULAWESI TENGAH
Palu
SULAWESI (CELEBES)
SULAWESI SELATAN
SULAWESI TENGGARA
INDONESIA
Makassar (Ujung Pandang)
Kendari
Buton
Kepulauan Banggai
Kepulauan Sula
Kepulauan Talaud
Kepulauan Sangir
LAUT MALUKU (MOLUCCA SEA)
MALUKU (MOLUCCAS)
MALUKU UTARA
HALMAHERA
Morotai
Ternate
Obi
Selat Obi
Laut Halmahera
Waigeo
Misoöl
PAPUA (IRIAN JAYA)
Laut Seram (Ceram Sea)
MALUKU
Buru
SERAM
Ambon
153
LAUT BANDA (BANDA SEA)
Kepulauan Banda
Kepulauan Barat Daya
Wetar
Selat Wetar
Alor
Kepulauan Alor
Kepulauan Leti
Kepulauan Babar
Kepulauan Sermata
FLORES
LAUT FLORES (FLORES SEA)
Kepulauan Solor
Selat Sumba
NUSA TENGGARA TIMUR
SUMBA
LAUT SAWU (SAVU SEA)
Sawu
Savu
EAST TIMOR
DILI
TIMOR
Kupang
TIMOR SEA
AUSTRALIA
Salayar
Kepulauan Taka'Bonerate
Sumbawa
Longitude 124° east of Greenwich
208
MILES
KM
1:6 000 000

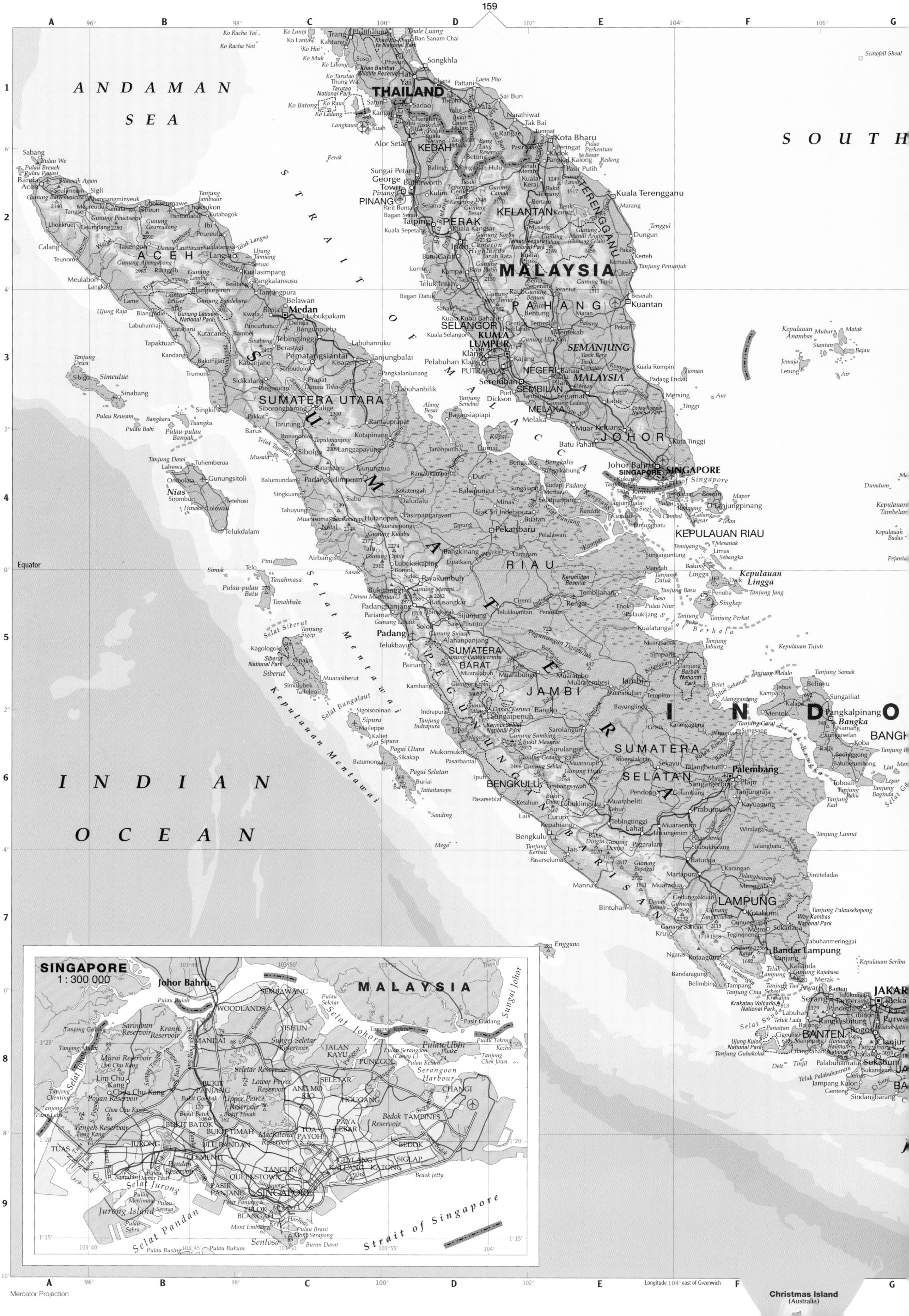

159

ANDAMAN SEA

SOUTH

THAILAND

KEDAH

Ko Racha Yai
Ko Racha Noi
Ko Lanta
Ko Lantai
Ko Hai
Ko Muk
Ko Tarutao National Park
Ko Batong
Ko Rawi
Ko Ladang
Langkawi
Kuah

Trang
Phatthalung
Thale Luang
Khao Ko-Khao Ya Nakonsi Rai
Ban Sanam Chai
Songkhla
Khao Banthat Wildlife Reserve
Hat Yai
Chana
Pattani
Laem Pho
Sai Buri
Sadao
Thepha
Yala
Narathiwat
Tak Bai
Kota Bharu
Peringat
Pulau Perhentian
Redang
Pangkal Kalong

Sabang
Pulau We
Pulau Breueh
Pulau Panasi
Banda Aceh
Seulimeum
Sigli
Lhokseumawe

George Town
PINANG
Butterworth
Kuala Terengganu
Marang
Dungun
Kerteh
Paka
Tanjung Penunjuk

PERAK
KELANTAN
TERENGGANU
Taiping
Kuala Kangsar
Ipoh
Gunung Korbu
Cameron Highlands
Tanah Rata
Taman Negara National Park

ANDAMAN

ACEH
Calang
Teunom
Meulaboh
Lame
Labuhanhaji

Gunung Bateméucica
Gunung Peuetsagu
Gunung Geureudong
Gunung Abongabong
Danau Laut Tawar
Takengon
Kualasimpang
Tanjungpura
Belawan
Medan
Lubukpakam

MALAYSIA
PAHANG
Kuantan
Beserah
Gunung Tapis
Kuala Lumpur

SELANGOR
KUALA LUMPUR
PUTRAJAYA
Port Klang
Klang
Kajang
NEGERI SEMBILAN
Seremban
MELAKA
Melaka
Muar

SUMATERA UTARA
Pematangsiantar
Sidikalang
Prapat
Danau Toba
Balige
Tarutung

JOHOR
Kota Tinggi
Johor Bahru
SINGAPORE

STRAIT OF MALACCA

SUMATERA BARAT
Padang
Bukittinggi
Padangpanjang
Pariaman

Equator

RIAU
Pekanbaru
Dumai
Bengkalis

KEPULAUAN RIAU
Tanjungpinang
Bintan

JAMBI
Jambi
Muarabungo

INDIAN OCEAN

BENGKULU
Bengkulu
Curup

SUMATERA SELATAN
Palembang
Plaju

Bangka
Pangkalpinang

LAMPUNG
Bandar Lampung
Kotabumi

JAKARTA
BANTEN
Serang

SINGAPORE
1 : 300 000

Johor Bahru
MALAYSIA
SEMBAWANG
WOODLANDS
YISHUN
MANDAI
Sungei Seletar Reservoir
JALAN KAYU
PUNGGOL
Kranji Reservoir
Sarimbun Reservoir
Murai Reservoir
Lim Chu Kang
Poyan Reservoir
Tengeh Reservoir
CHOA CHU KANG
BUKIT PANJANG
Upper Peirce Reservoir
Lower Peirce Reservoir
ANG MO KIO
SELETAR
HOUGANG
Serangoon Harbour
CHANGI
TAMPINES
PAYA LEBAR
Bedok Reservoir
BEDOK
SIGLAP
GEYLANG
KALLANG
KATONG
MacRitchie Reservoir
TOA PAYOH
BUKIT TIMAH
BUKIT BATOK
CLEMENTI
ULU PANDAN
QUEENSTOWN
PASIR PANJANG
JURONG
TUAS
TANGLIN
SINGAPORE
Jurong Island
Sentosa
Selat Pandan
Selat Jurong
Strait of Singapore

Pulau Ubin
Pulau Tekong

METRES / FEET

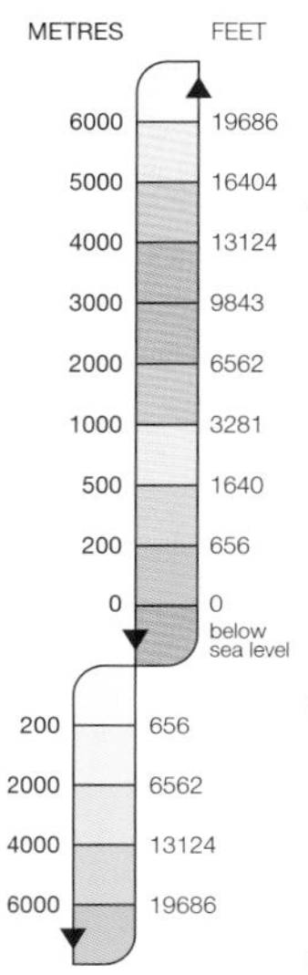

METRES	FEET
6000	19686
5000	16404
4000	13124
3000	9843
2000	6562
1000	3281
500	1640
200	656
0	0 below sea level
200	656
2000	6562
4000	13124
6000	19686

Longitude 104° east of Greenwich

Christmas Island (Australia)

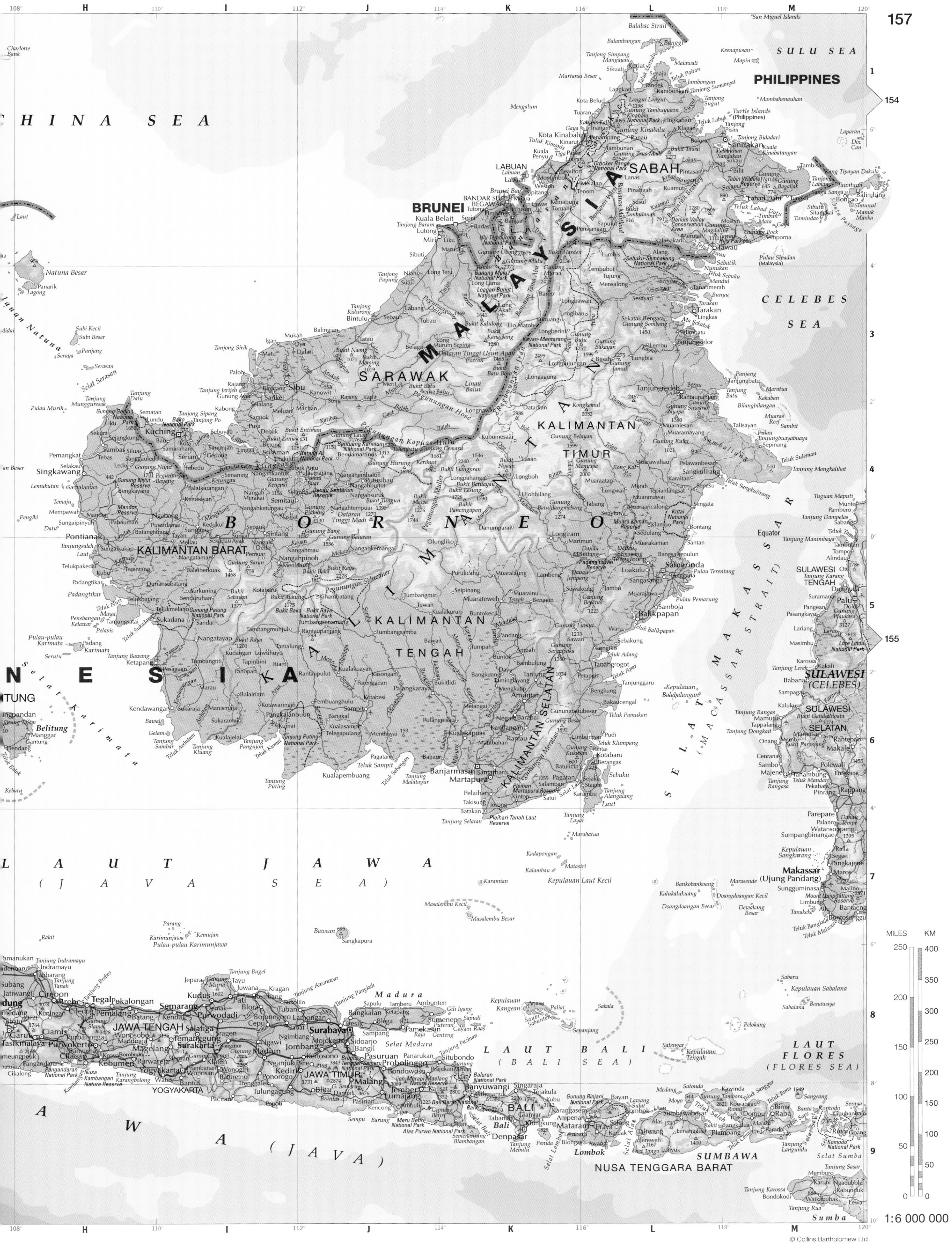

CHINA SEA

SULU SEA

PHILIPPINES

CELEBES SEA

BRUNEI

BANDAR SERI BEGAWAN

SABAH

SARAWAK

MALAYSIA

KALIMANTAN TIMUR

BORNEO

KALIMANTAN BARAT

Kuching

Pontianak

KALIMANTAN TENGAH

KALIMANTAN SELATAN

Banjarmasin
Martapura

Balikpapan

Samarinda

SULAWESI TENGAH

SULAWESI (CELEBES)

SULAWESI SELATAN

Makassar (Ujung Pandang)

SELAT MAKASSAR (MACASSAR STRAIT)

Equator

INDONESIA

Singkawang

Belitung

LAUT JAWA
(J A V A S E A)

Semarang
Surabaya
Surakarta
JAWA TENGAH
JAWA TIMUR
YOGYAKARTA

Bandung

J A W A (J A V A)

Madura

LAUT BALI
(BALI SEA)

BALI
Denpasar
Mataram
Lombok

SUMBAWA
NUSA TENGGARA BARAT

LAUT FLORES
(FLORES SEA)

Sumba

MILES
250
200
150
100
50

KM
400
350
300
250
200
150
100
50
0

1 : 6 000 000

© Collins Bartholomew Ltd

171

METRES | FEET

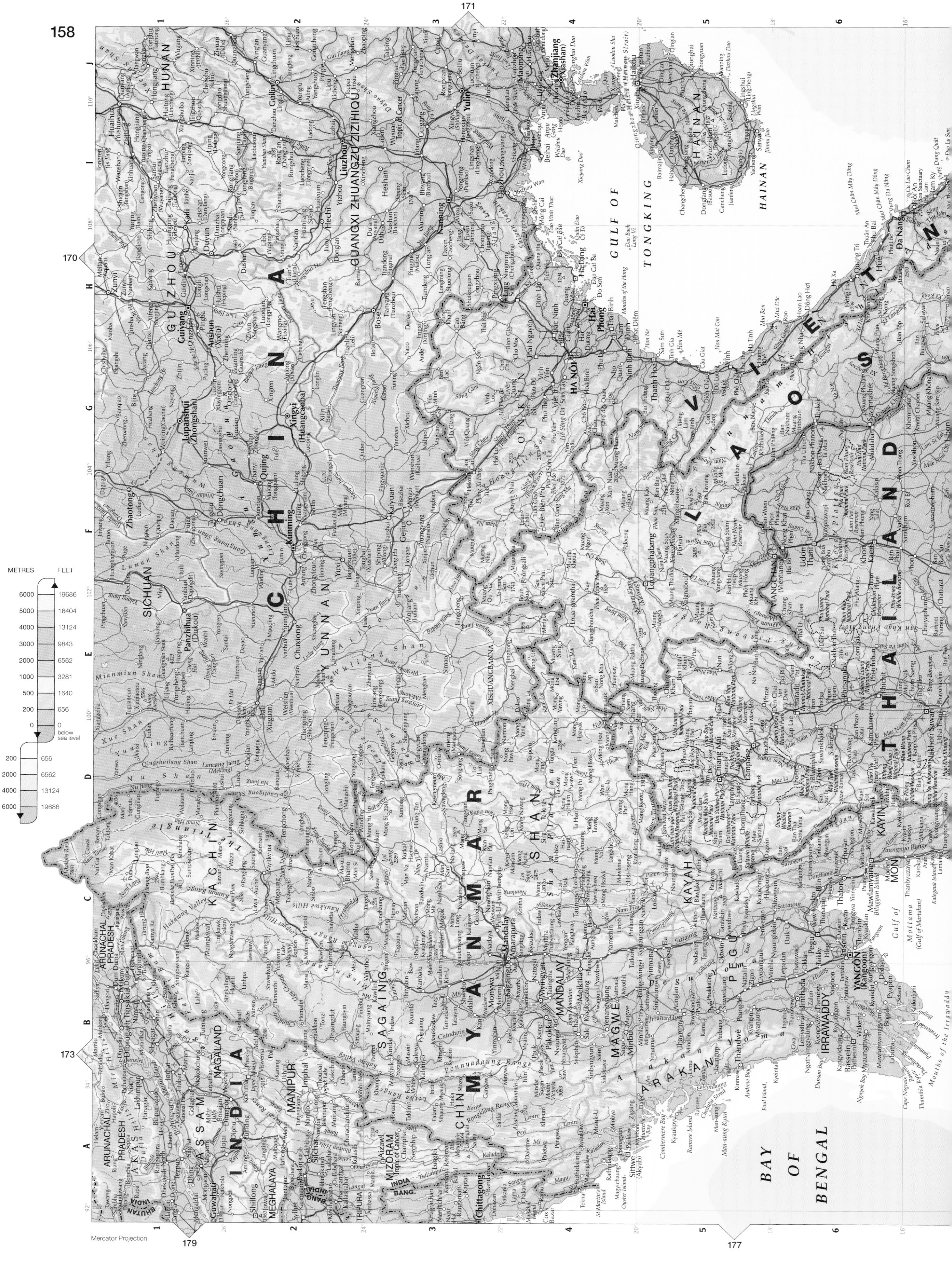

METRES	FEET
6000	19686
5000	16404
4000	13124
3000	9843
2000	6562
1000	3281
500	1640
200	656
0	0 below sea level
200	656
2000	6562
4000	13124
6000	19686

CHINA

INDIA

MYANMAR

THAILAND

LAOS

VIETNAM

HUNAN

GUIZHOU

GUANGXI ZHUANGZU ZIZHIQU

YUNNAN

HAINAN

GULF OF TONGKING

BAY OF BENGAL

SICHUAN

ASSAM

NAGALAND

MANIPUR

MIZORAM

ARUNACHAL PRADESH

MEGHALAYA

TRIPURA

BANGLADESH

BHUTAN

KACHIN

SAGAING

CHIN

MAGWE

RAKHINE (ARAKAN)

PEGU

IRRAWADDY

MON

KAYIN

KAYAH

SHAN

XISHUANGBANNA

Kunming

Guiyang

Liuzhou

Nanning

Haikou

Zhanjiang

HÀ NỘI

Hải Phòng

Da Nang

Huế

Mandalay

Amarapura

Sagaing

Monywa

Nay Pyi Taw

YANGON (Rangon)

Mawlamyaing

Thaton

Pegu

Bassein (Pathein)

Chittagong

Guwahati

Shillong

Imphal

Aizawl

Thandwe

Sittwe (Akyab)

Mercator Projection

MYANMAR, THAILAND, LAOS, CAMBODIA AND VIETNAM

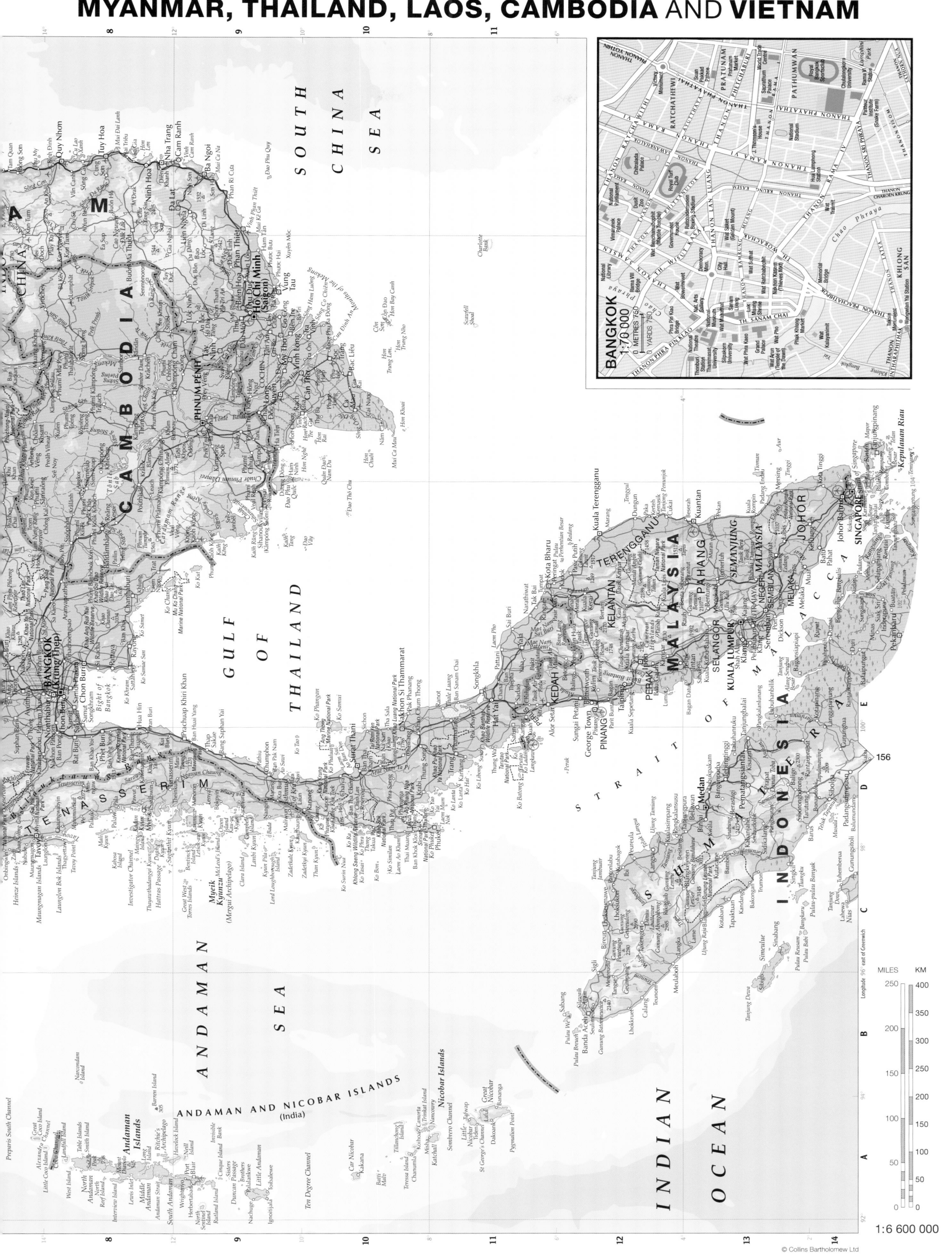

BANGKOK
1:70 000

SOUTH CHINA SEA

CAMBODIA

GULF OF THAILAND

ANDAMAN SEA

ANDAMAN AND NICOBAR ISLANDS
(India)

INDIAN OCEAN

MALAYSIA

KUALA LUMPUR

Singapore

INDONESIA

SUMATRA

STRAIT OF MALACCA

MILES / KM

1:6 600 000

© Collins Bartholomew Ltd

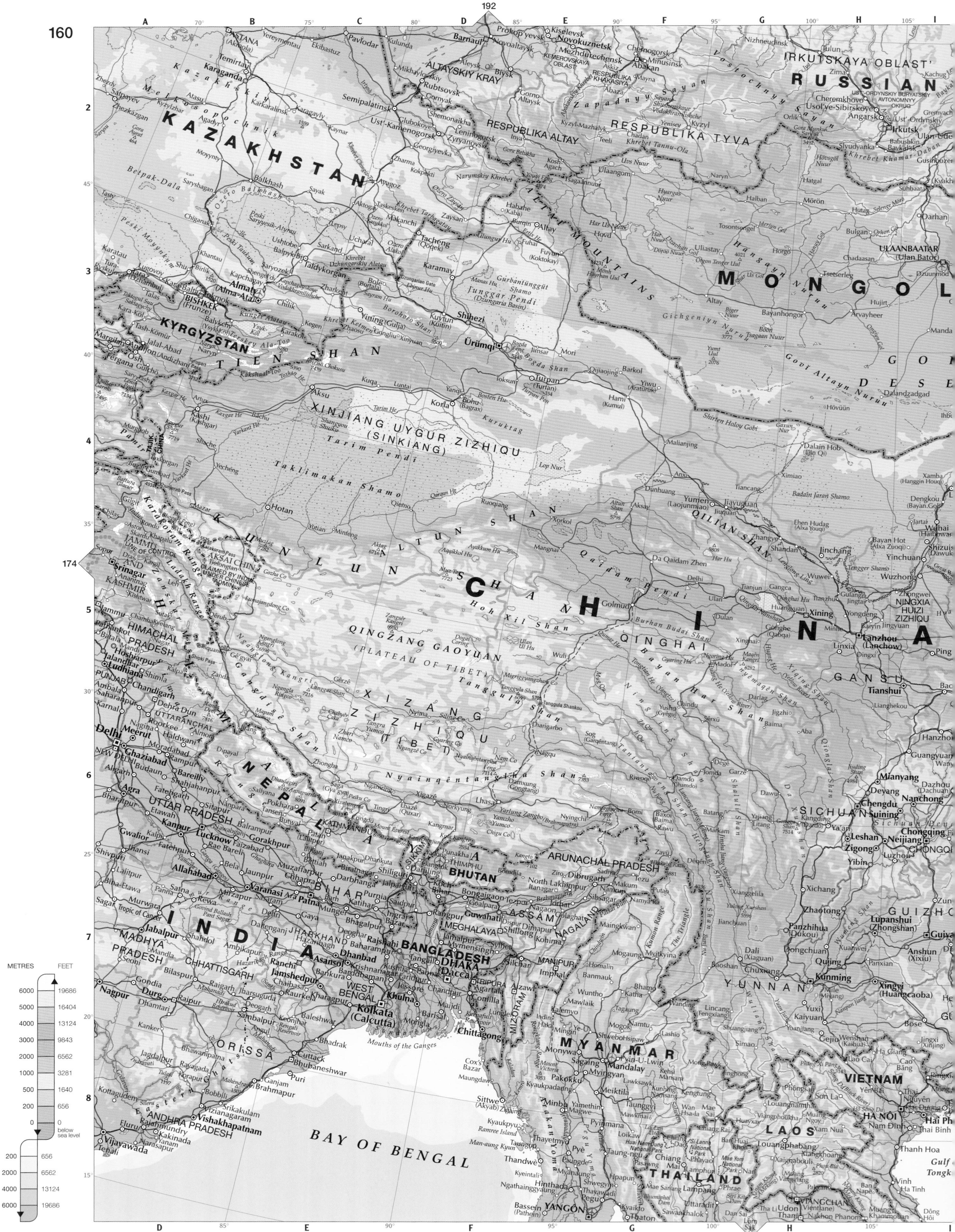

A · B · C · D · E · F · G · H · I

RUSSIAN

IRKUTSKAYA OBLAST'

MONGOLIA

KAZAKHSTAN

Karagandy (Karaganda)
Astana (Akmola)
Balkhash
Almaty
Alma-Ata
BISHKEK (Frunze)

KYRGYZSTAN

RESPUBLIKA ALTAY

RESPUBLIKA TYVA

ALTAY MOUNTAINS

ALTAYSKIY KRAY

Barnaul
Novosibirsk
Novoaltaysk
Novokuznetsk
Semipalatinsk
Ust'-Kamenogorsk

T I E N   S H A N

ULAANBAATAR (Ulan Bator)

G O B I   D E S E R T

XINJIANG UYGUR ZIZHIQU (SINKIANG)

Ürümqi
Turpan (Turfan)
Kashi (Kashgar)
Aksu
Korla
Hotan

Tarim Pendi
Taklimakan Shamo

K U N L U N   S H A N

QILIAN SHAN

ALTUN SHAN

C H I N A

QINGHAI
Xining
Lanzhou (Lanchow)

GANSU

Tianshui

QINGZANG GAOYUAN
(PLATEAU OF TIBET)

XIZANG ZIZHIQU (TIBET)

Lhasa
Xigazê

NINGXIA HUIZU ZIZHIQU

Chengdu
Nanchong
Mianyang
Deyang

SICHUAN

Chongqing
Leshan
Zigong
Neijiang

GUIZHOU

JAMMU AND KASHMIR
Srinagar
LINE OF CONTROL
AKSAI CHIN
Leh
LADAKH

HIMACHAL PRADESH

PUNJAB
Ludhiana
Chandigarh
Jalandhar
Hoshiarpur

Delhi
Meerut
Ghaziabad
NEW DELHI

UTTARANCHAL

UTTAR PRADESH
Agra
Kanpur
Lucknow
Allahabad
Varanasi
Bareilly

NEPAL
KATHMANDU
Pokhara

BHUTAN
THIMPHU

SIKKIM

ARUNACHAL PRADESH

ASSAM
Guwahati
Dispur

MEGHALAYA
Shillong

NAGALAND
Kohima

MANIPUR
Imphal

MIZORAM
Aizawl

TRIPURA
Agartala

I N D I A

MADHYA PRADESH
Jabalpur

CHHATTISGARH
Raipur

JHARKHAND
Ranchi
Jamshedpur
Dhanbad

BIHAR
Patna

WEST BENGAL
Kolkata (Calcutta)
Asansol
Durgapur

BANGLADESH
DHAKA (Dacca)
Khulna
Chittagong

ORISSA
Bhubaneswar
Cuttack
Brahmapur

ANDHRA PRADESH
Vishakhapatnam
Vijayawada
Rajahmundry
Kakinada

Nagpur
Durg

Mouths of the Ganges

MYANMAR
Mandalay
Myingyan
Monywa
Sagaing
Pakokku
Magwe
Pyinmana

Sittwe (Akyab)
Cox's Bazar

THAILAND

LAOS
HA NOI

VIETNAM

YANGON (Pathein)

BAY OF BENGAL

Gulf of Tongking

Tropic of Cancer

Albers Equal Area Conic Projection

METRES	FEET
6000	19686
5000	16404
4000	13124
3000	9843
2000	6562
1000	3281
500	1640
200	656
0	0
below sea level
200	656
2000	6562
4000	13124
6000	19686

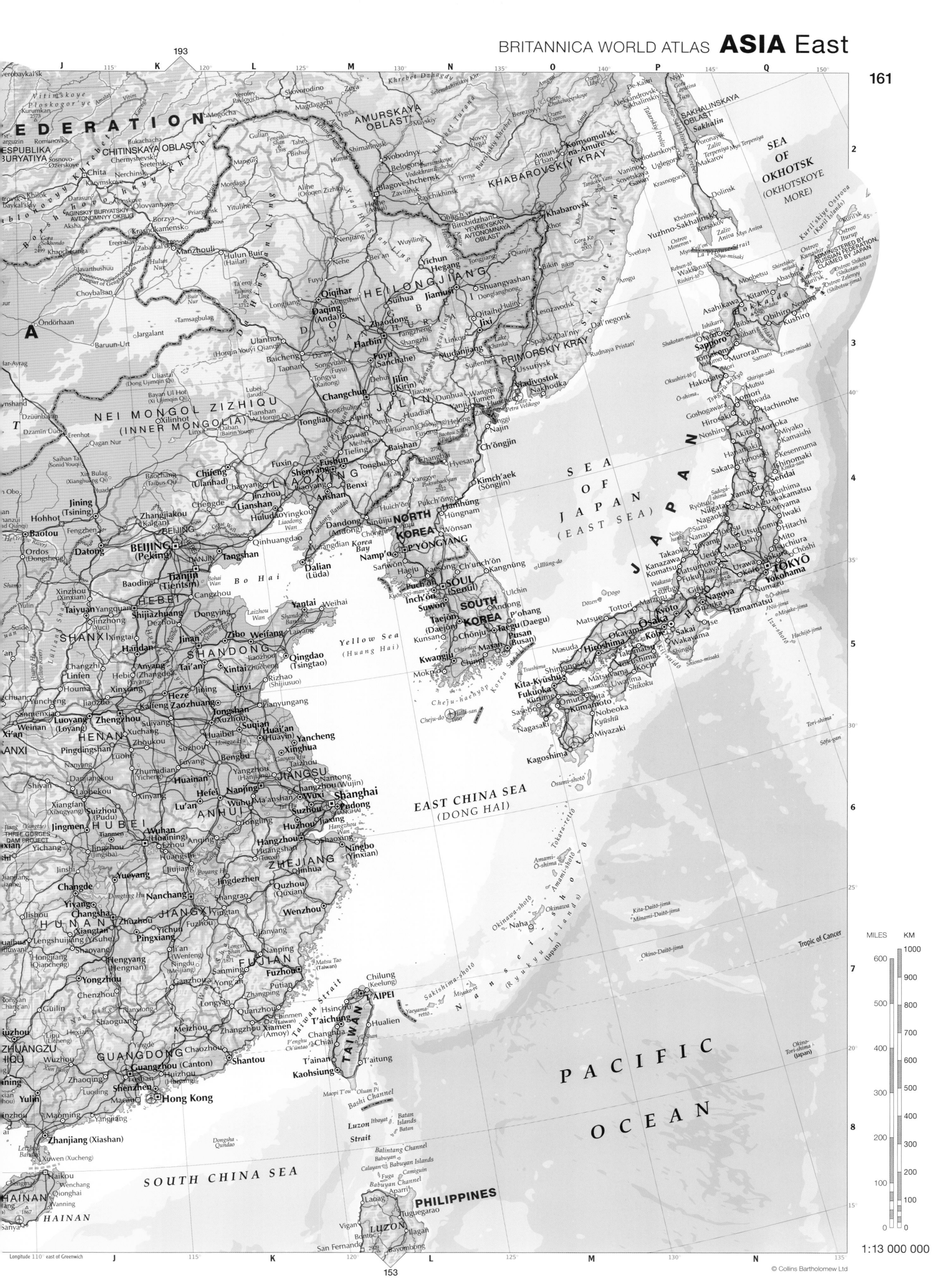

1:13 000 000

© Collins Bartholomew Ltd

SEA OF OKHOTSK (OKHOTSKOYE MORE)
SEA OF JAPAN (EAST SEA)
YELLOW SEA (HUANG HAI)
EAST CHINA SEA (DONG HAI)
SOUTH CHINA SEA
PACIFIC OCEAN
Bo Hai
JAPAN
NORTH KOREA
SOUTH KOREA
TAIWAN
PHILIPPINES
HEILONGJIANG
JILIN
LIAONING
HEBEI
SHANDONG
SHANXI
HENAN
JIANGSU
ANHUI
HUBEI
ZHEJIANG
JIANGXI
HUNAN
FUJIAN
GUANGDONG
HAINAN
NEI MONGOL ZIZHIQU (INNER MONGOLIA)
KHABAROVSKIY KRAY
PRIMORSKIY KRAY
AMURSKAYA OBLAST'
CHITINSKAYA OBLAST'
SAKHALINSKAYA OBLAST'
BEIJING (Peking)
Tianjin (Tientsin)
Shanghai
P'YÖNGYANG
SÖUL (Seoul)
TŌKYŌ
Hong Kong
Vladivostok
Khabarovsk
Harbin
Dalian (Lüda)
Ōsaka
Nagoya
Sapporo
Busan
Taipei
Kaohsiung
Luzon Strait
Taiwan Strait
Tropic of Cancer
MILES
KM
Longitude 110° east of Greenwich

RUSSIAN FEDERATION
CHINA
SAKHALIN
SAKHALINSKAYA OBLAST'
HOKKAIDŌ
KHABAROVSKIY KRAY
AMURSKAYA OBLAST'
YEVREYSKAYA AVTONOMNAYA OBLAST'
PRIMORSKIY KRAY
CHITINSKAYA OBLAST'
HEILONGJIANG
JILIN
NEI MONGOL ZIZHIQU (INNER MONGOLIA)
DONGBEI (MANCHURIA)
Tatarskiy Proliv
La Pérouse Strait
Khabarovsk
Komsomol'sk-na-Amure
Blagoveshchensk
Yuzhno-Sakhalinsk
Vladivostok
Harbin
Qiqihar
Changchun
Jilin
Sapporo

METRES
FEET
6000
19686
5000
16404
4000
13124
3000
9843
2000
6562
1000
3281
500
1640
200
656
0
0
below sea level
200
656
2000
6562
4000
13124
6000
19686

193

Conic Equidistant Projection

169

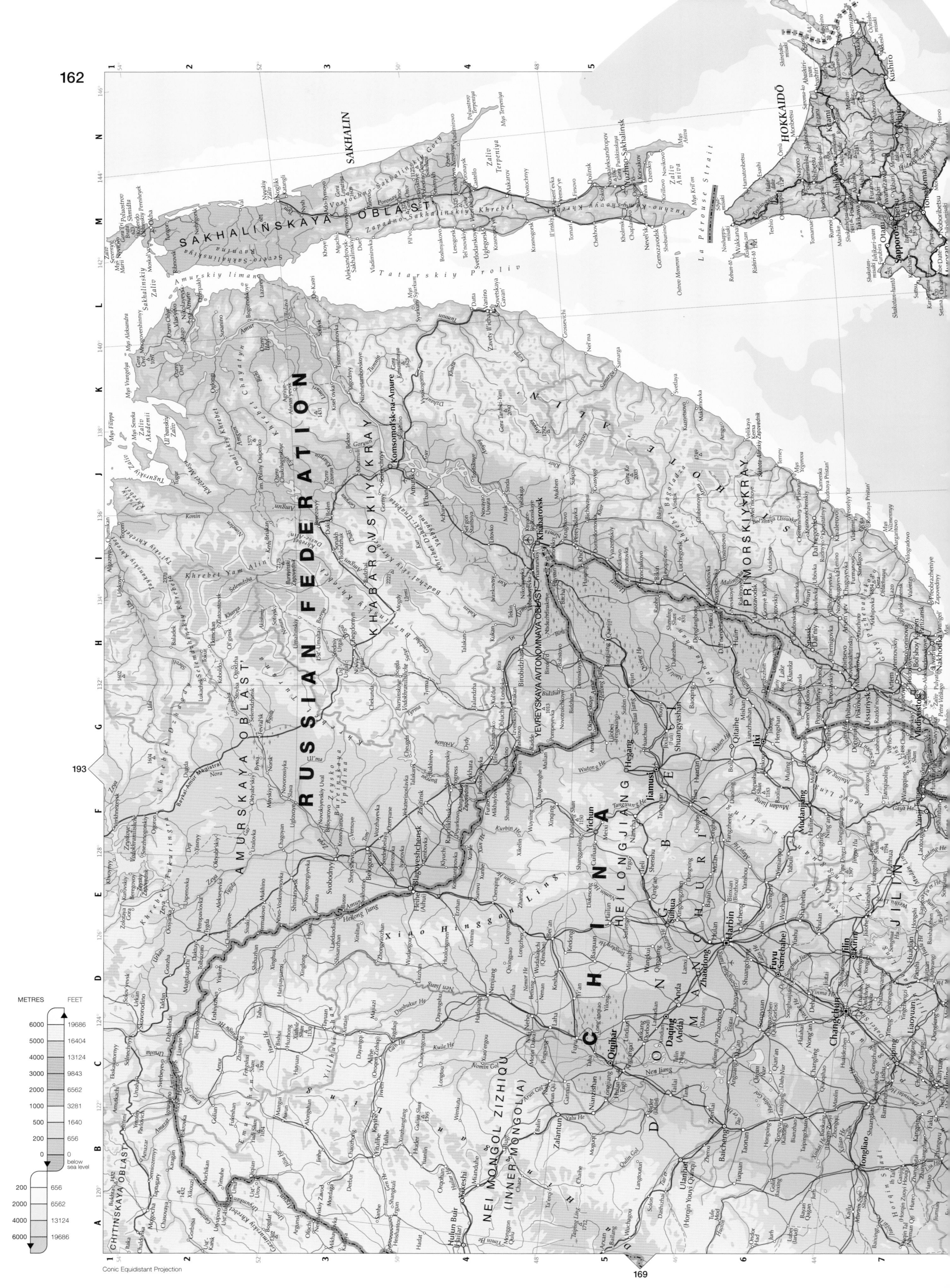

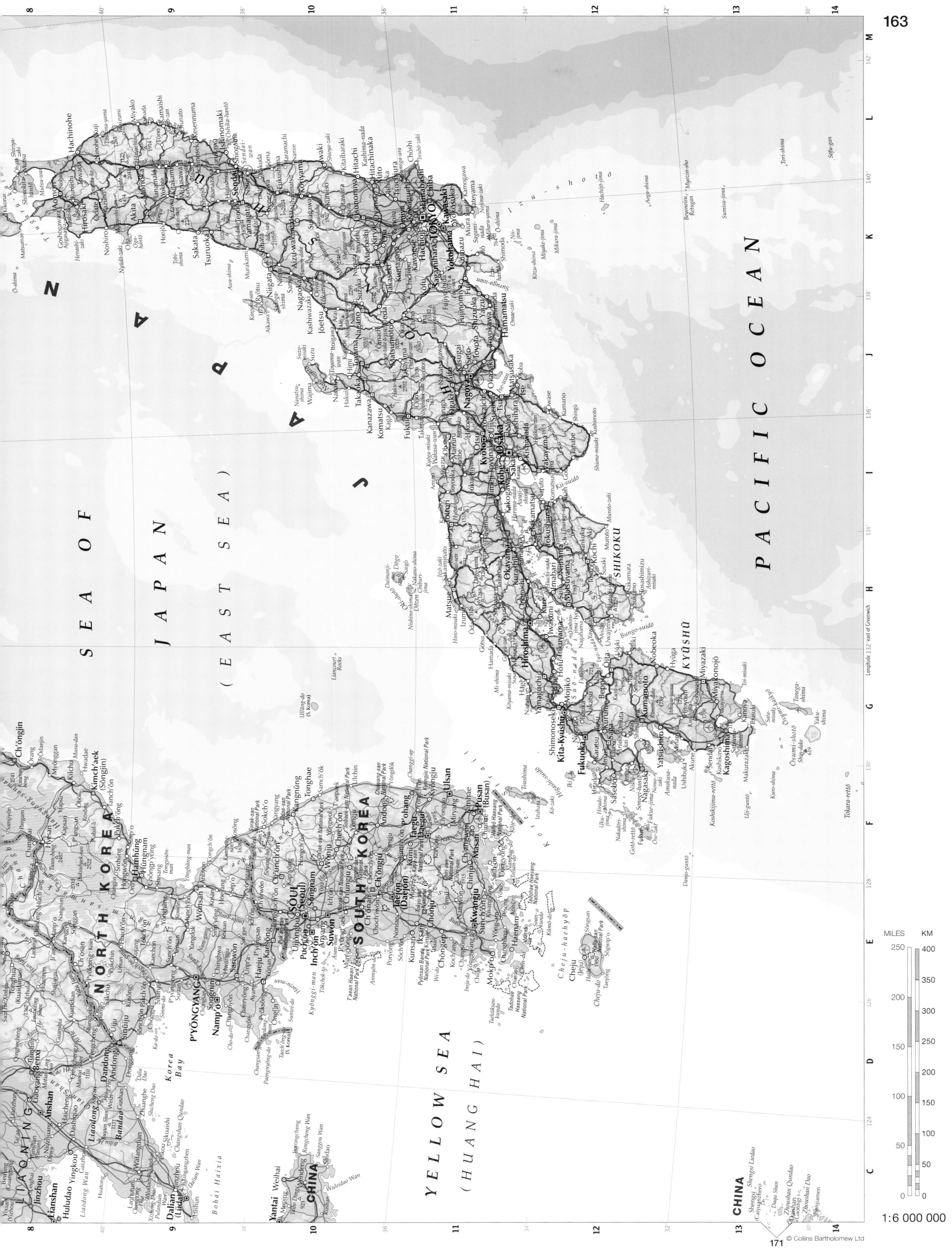

NORTH KOREA

SOUTH KOREA

CHINA

PYŎNGYANG

SŎUL (Seoul)

TOKYO

SEA OF JAPAN (EAST SEA)

PACIFIC OCEAN

YELLOW SEA (HUANG HAI)

Korea Bay

HONSHŪ

SHIKOKU

KYŪSHŪ

Iwo-shotō

Tokara-rettō

Longitude 132° east of Greenwich

MILES   KM
250   400
         350
200   300
         250
150   200
100   150
         100
50   50
0   0

1:6 000 000

© Collins Bartholomew Ltd

171

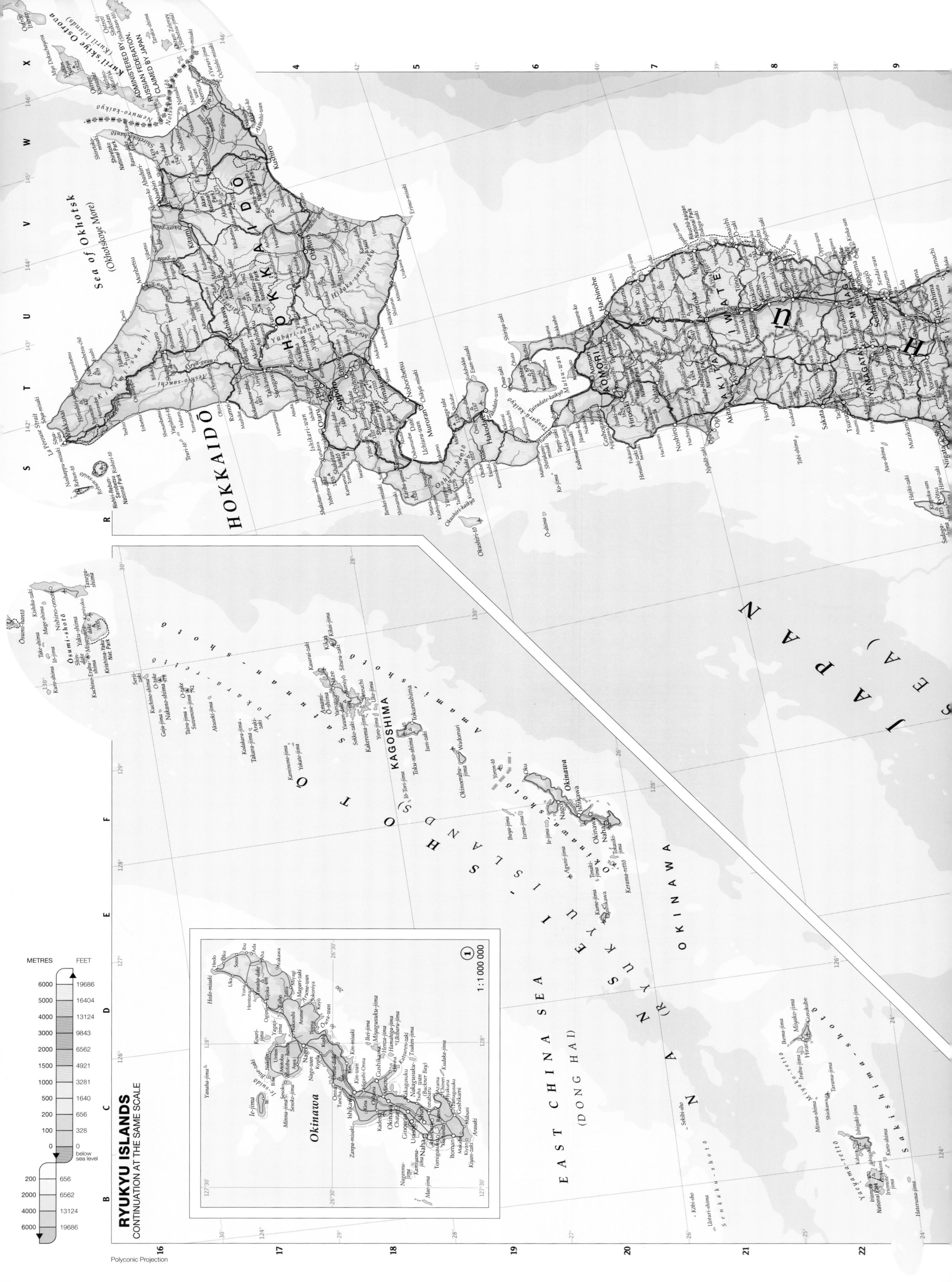

RYUKYU ISLANDS
CONTINUATION AT THE SAME SCALE

Polyconic Projection

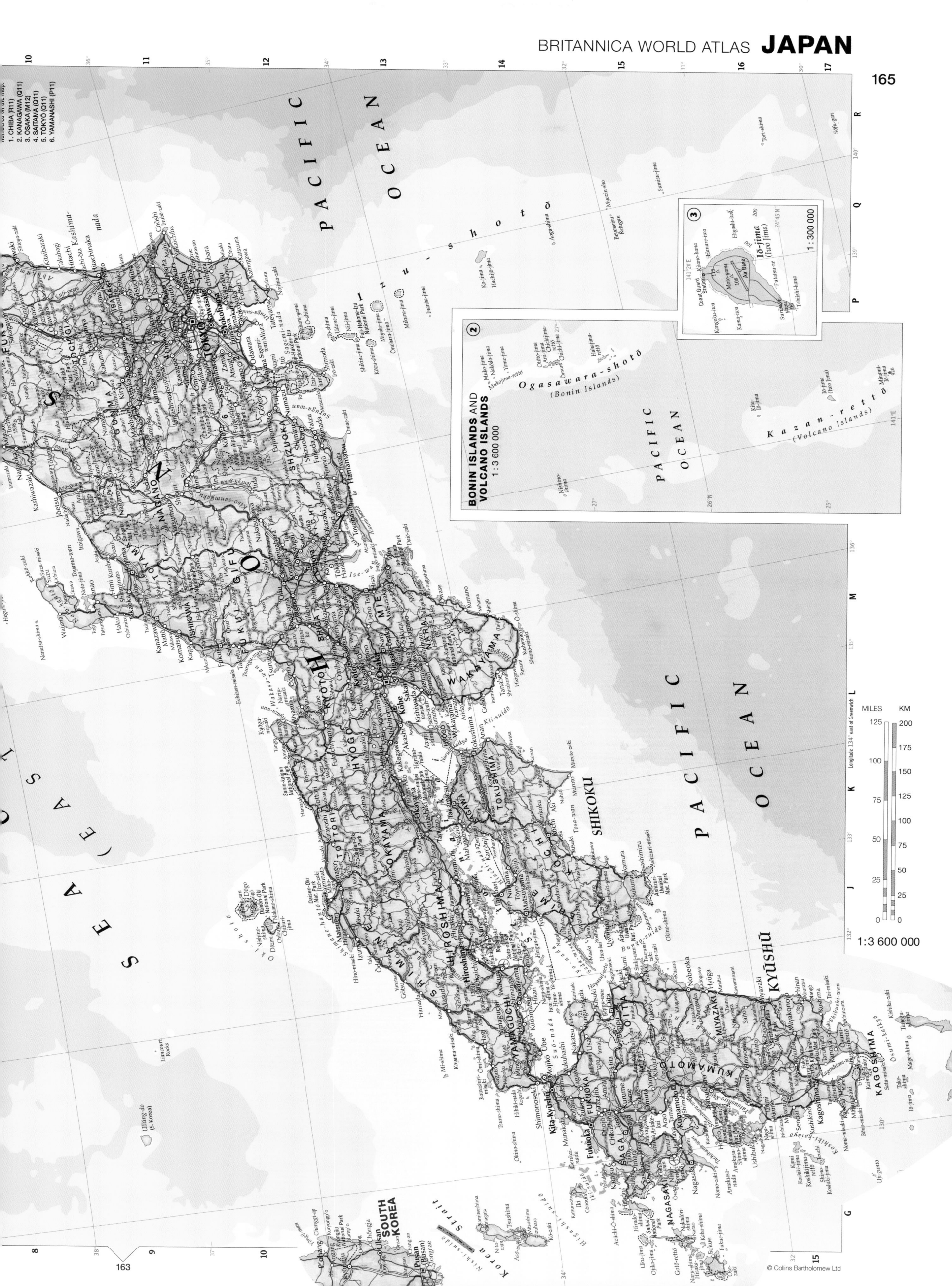

PACIFIC OCEAN

I z u - s h o t ō

③ Iō-jima (Iuo-jima) 1:300 000

② BONIN ISLANDS AND VOLCANO ISLANDS 1:3 600 000

Ogasawara-shotō (Bonin Islands)

Kazan-rettō (Volcano Islands)

PACIFIC OCEAN

SEA OF JAPAN (EAST SEA)

KYŌTO

NAGANO

GIFU

SHIZUOKA

TŌKYŌ

KANAGAWA

MIE

WAKAYAMA

HYŌGO

OKAYAMA

HIROSHIMA

TOTTORI

SHIMANE

YAMAGUCHI

SHIKOKU

TOKUSHIMA

KŌCHI

EHIME

KAGAWA

PACIFIC OCEAN

KYŪSHŪ

FUKUOKA

ŌITA

MIYAZAKI

KUMAMOTO

KAGOSHIMA

NAGASAKI

SAGA

SOUTH KOREA

Korea Strait

MILES / KM
125 / 200
100 / 175
/ 150
75 / 125
/ 100
50 / 75
25 / 50
/ 25
0 / 0

1:3 600 000

Longitude 134 east of Greenwich

1. CHIBA (R11)
2. KANAGAWA (Q11)
3. ŌSAKA (M12)
4. SAITAMA (Q11)
5. TŌKYŌ (Q11)
6. YAMANASHI (P11)

S E A

O F

J A P A N

(EAST SEA)

TŌKYŌ
1:125 000
0 METRES 1000
0 YARDS 1000

TOSHIMA-KU
BUNKYŌ-KU
SHINJUKU-KU
TAITŌ-KU
CHŪŌ-KU
CHIYODA-KU
MINATO KU

Toyama-wan

Noto-hantō
National Park

TOYAMA

ISHIKAWA

Kanazawa

FUKUI

Fukui

Wakasa-wan

Wakasa-wan
Quasi National Park

GIFU

O

KYŌTO

SHIGA

HYŌGO

Kyōto

AICHI

Nagoya

Ōtsu

Biwa-ko Quasi
National Park

METRES   FEET
6000   19686
5000   16404
4000   13124
3000   9843
2000   6562
1500   4921
1000   3281
500   1640
200   656
100   328
0   0
         below
         sea level
50   164
200   656
2000   6562
4000   13124
6000   19686

Kōbe

Ōsaka

OSAKA

Harima-
nada

Akashi-kaikyo

Awaji-
shima

HYŌGO

Wakayama

Ōsaka-wan

MIE

NARA

Ise-shima
National Park

Enshū-nada

P A
C

O

SHIKOKU

TOKUSHIMA

WAKAYAMA

Kii-suido

Conic Equidistant Projection

FUKUSHIMA

NIIGATA

TOCHIGI

GUNMA

Nikkō
National Park

IBARAKI

Kashima-
nada

NAGANO

SAITAMA

Hitachi

Mito

Tsukuba

Chichibu-Tama
National Park

TOKYO

TOKYO

Chiba

Tōkyō-
wan

YAMANASHI

Kawasaki

Yokohama

CHIBA

Bōsō-
hantō

KANAGAWA

Yokosuka

Sagami-wan

Fuji-Hakone-Izu
National Park

SHIZUOKA

Sagami-nada

Izu-
hantō

Ō-shima
Mihara-
yama
764

Fuji-Hakone-Izu
National Park

To-shima

Udone-jima

Nii-jima

Shikine-jima

Kōzu-shima

Miyake-
jima
Ō-yama
813

Ōnohara-jima

P A C I F I C

O C E A N

Mikura-jima

MILES KM

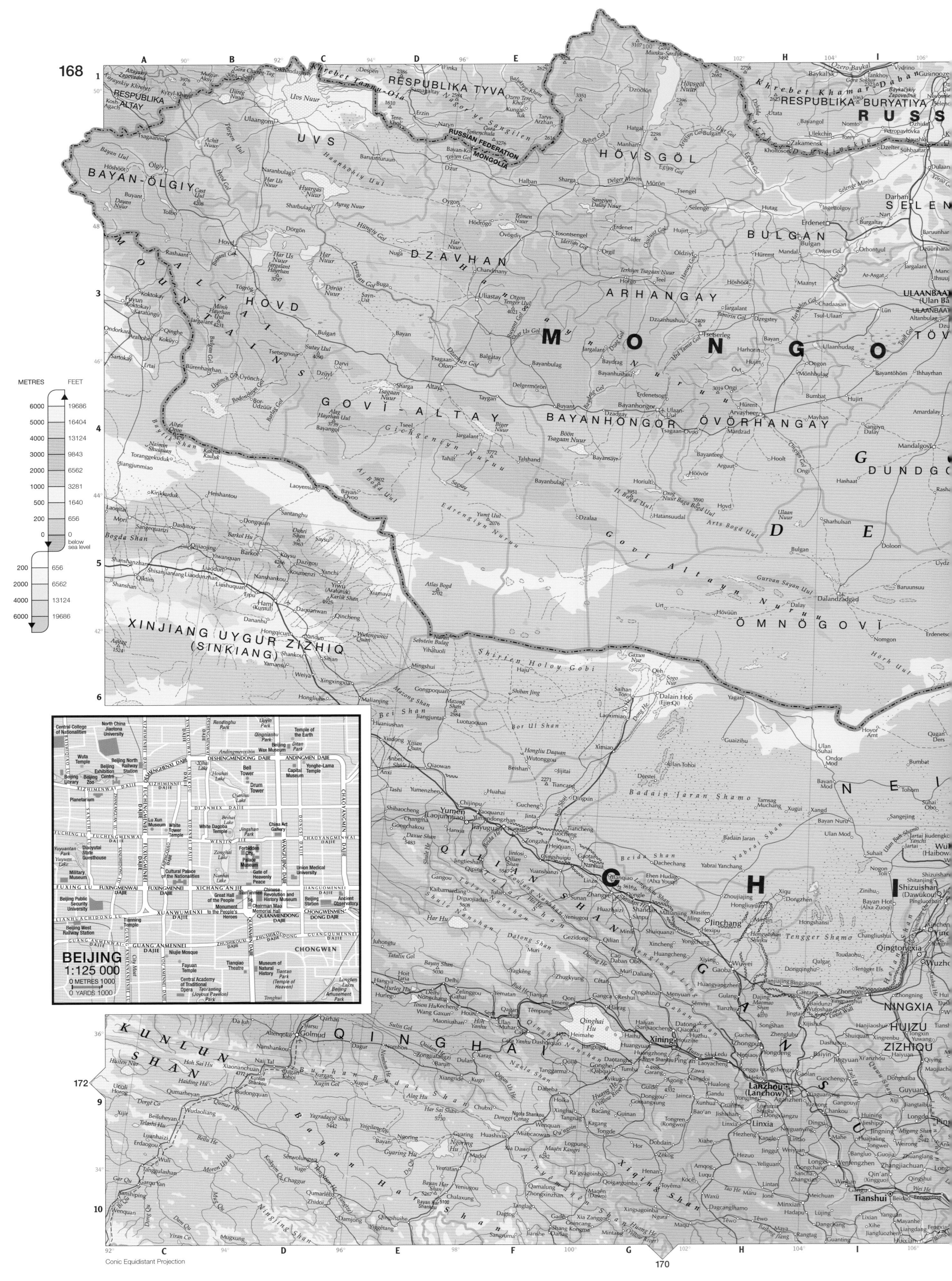

BEIJING
1:125 000

0 METRES 1000

0 YARDS 1000

Conic Equidistant Projection

170

172

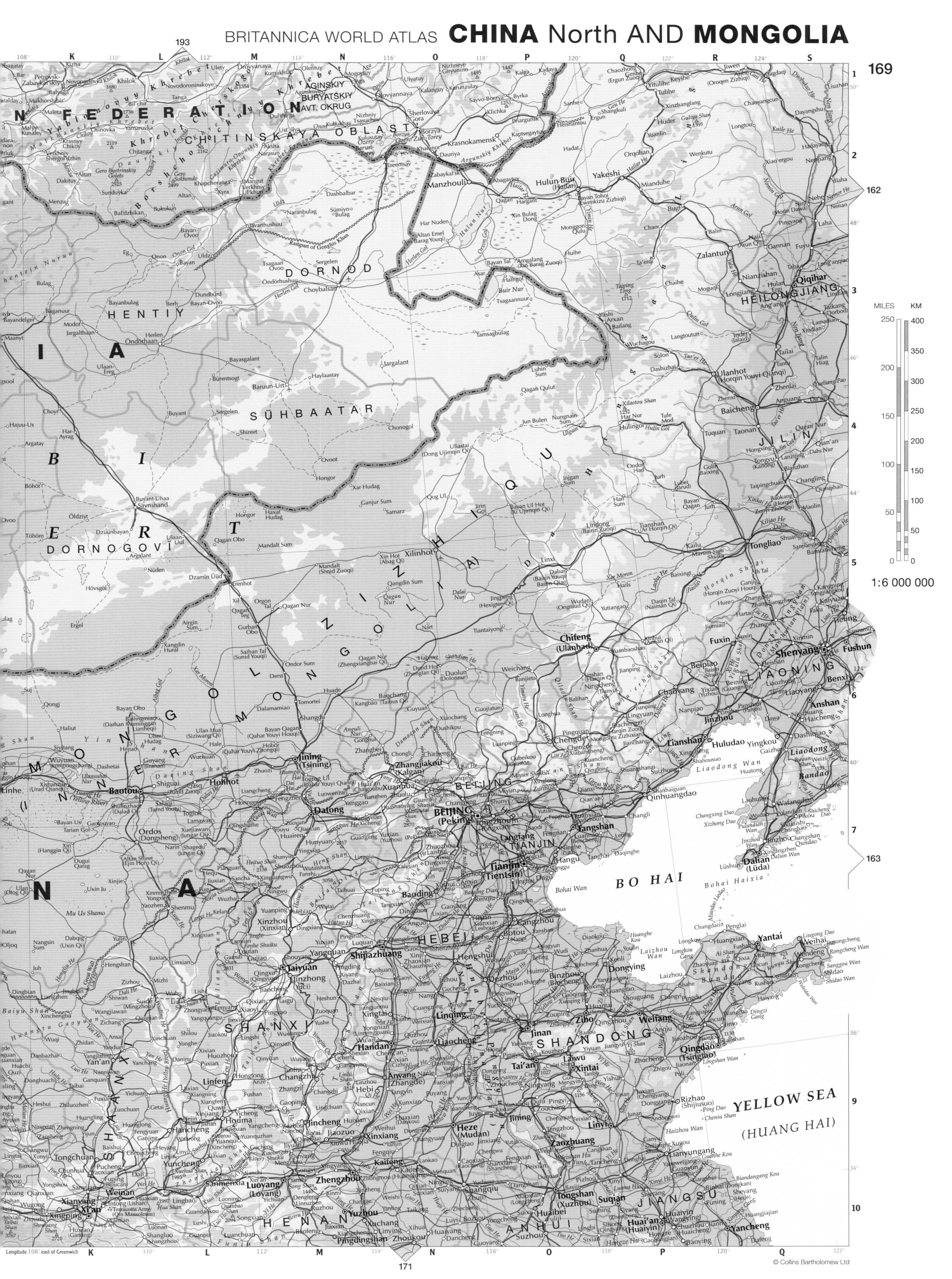

162

MILES KM
250 400
350
200 300
250
150 200
100 150
100
50 50
0 0

1:6 000 000

163

YELLOW SEA

(HUANG HAI)

Longitude 108° east of Greenwich

© Collins Bartholomew Ltd

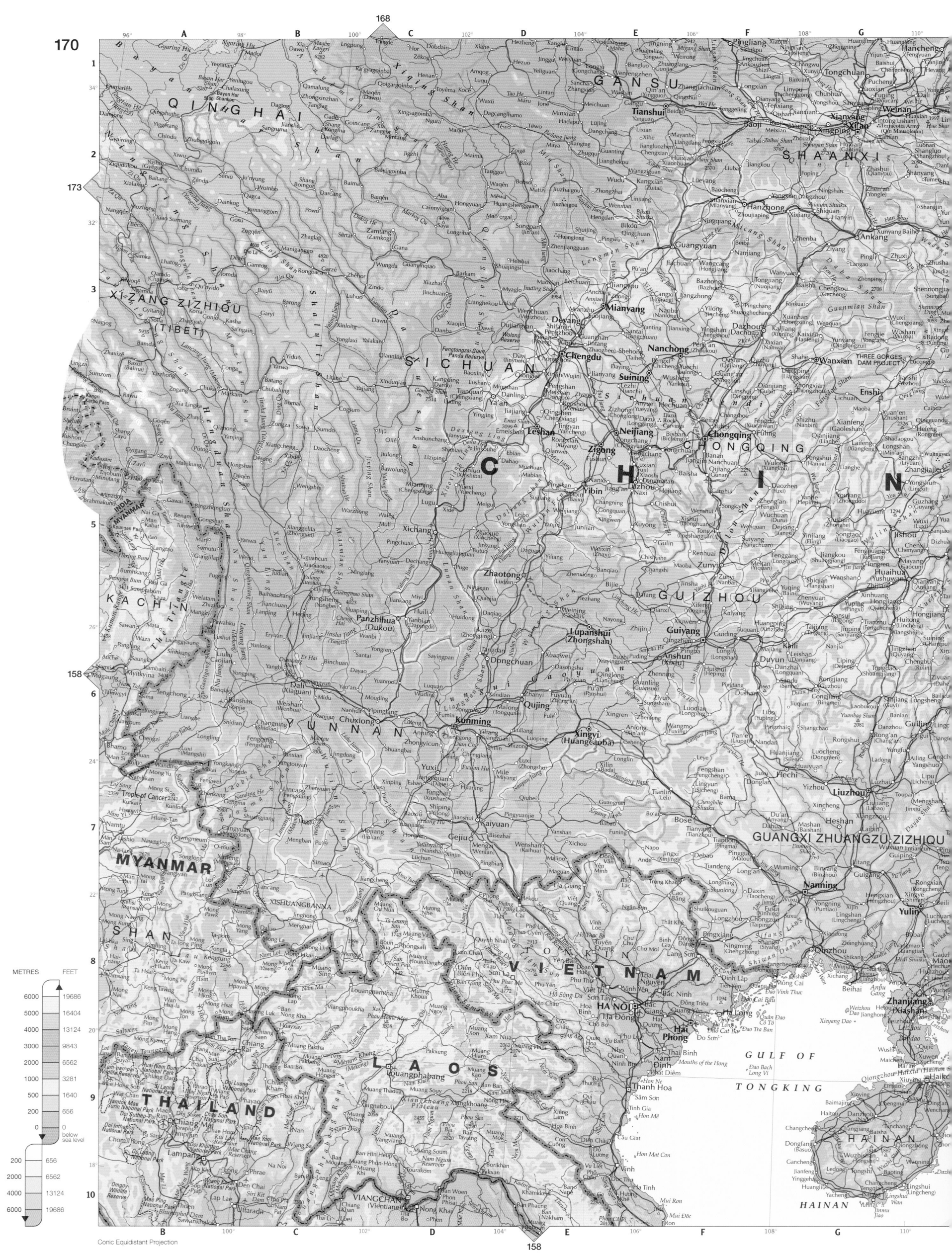
QINGHAI
GANSU
SHAANXI
XIZANG ZIZHIQU (TIBET)
SICHUAN
CHONGQING
CHINA
GUIZHOU
YUNNAN
GUANGXI ZHUANGZU ZIZHIQU
KACHIN
MYANMAR
SHAN
THAILAND
LAOS
VIETNAM
HAINAN
GULF OF TONGKING
Chengdu
Chongqing
Kunming
Guiyang
Nanning
HA NOI
VIANGCHAN (Vientiane)
Tropic of Cancer
METRES
FEET
6000 19686
5000 16404
4000 13124
3000 9843
2000 6562
1000 3281
500 1640
200 656
0 0 below sea level
200 656
2000 6562
4000 13124
6000 19686

Conic Equidistant Projection

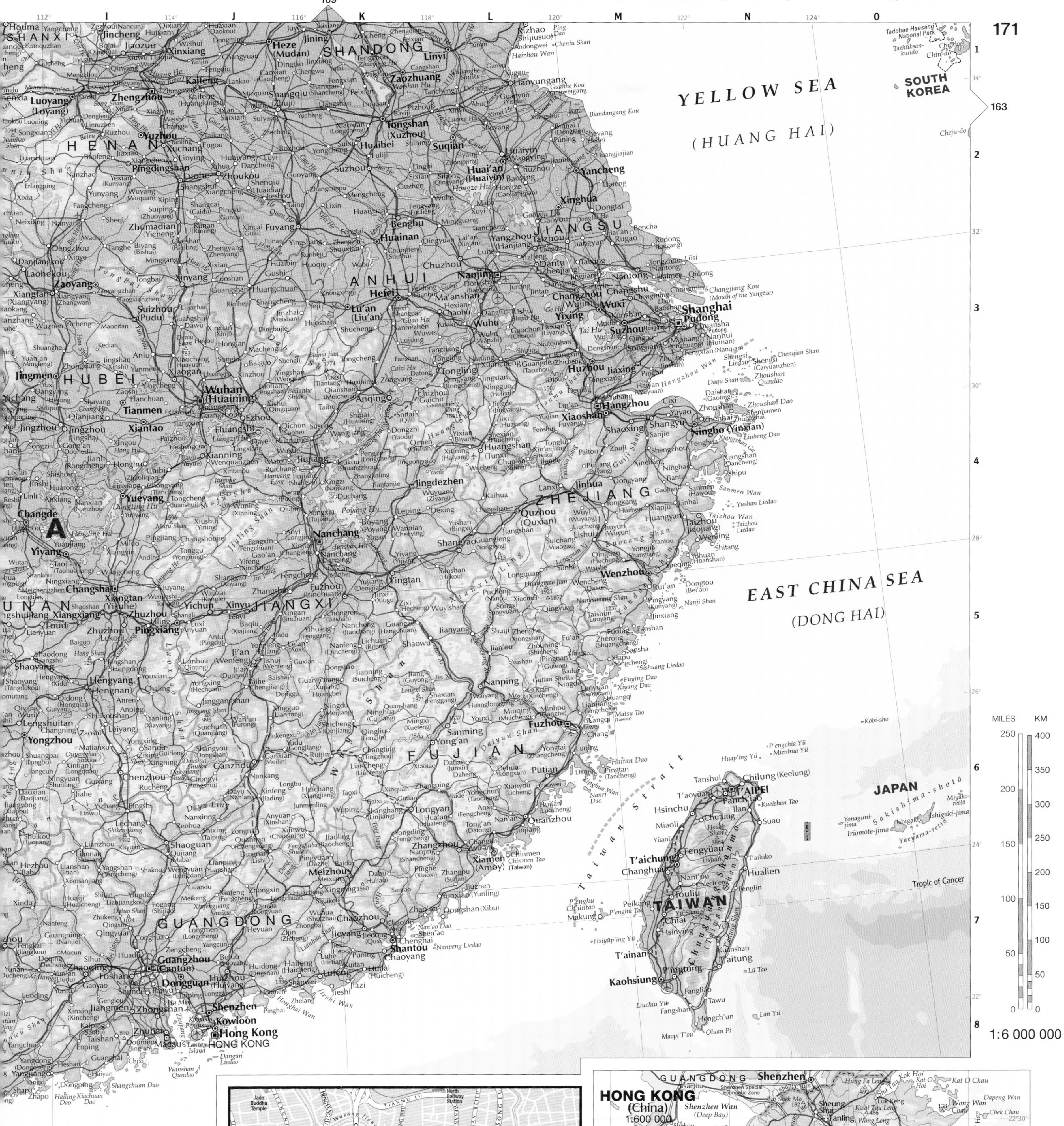
169
163
YELLOW SEA
(HUANG HAI)
EAST CHINA SEA
(DONG HAI)
SOUTH KOREA
JAPAN
SHANDONG
HENAN
JIANGSU
ANHUI
HUBEI
ZHEJIANG
JIANGXI
FUJIAN
GUANGDONG
TAIWAN
Taiwan Strait
Tropic of Cancer
Shanghai
Pudong
Nanjing
Hefei
Wuhan (Huaining)
Hangzhou
Ningbo (Yinxian)
Nanchang
Changsha
Fuzhou
Xiamen (Amoy)
Shantou
Guangzhou (Canton)
Shenzhen
Kowloon
Hong Kong
HONG KONG
Macau
T'AIPEI
Kaohsiung
Zhengzhou
Luoyang (Loyang)
Kaifeng
Xuzhou
Wenzhou
Jingdezhen
MILES
KM
1:6 000 000
Longitude 112° east of Greenwich

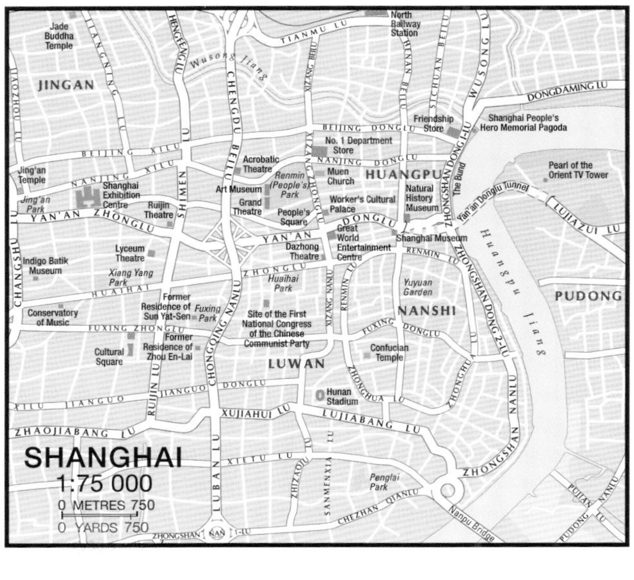
JINGAN
HUANGPU
NANSHI
LUWAN
PUDONG
SHANGHAI
1:75 000
0 METRES 750
0 YARDS 750

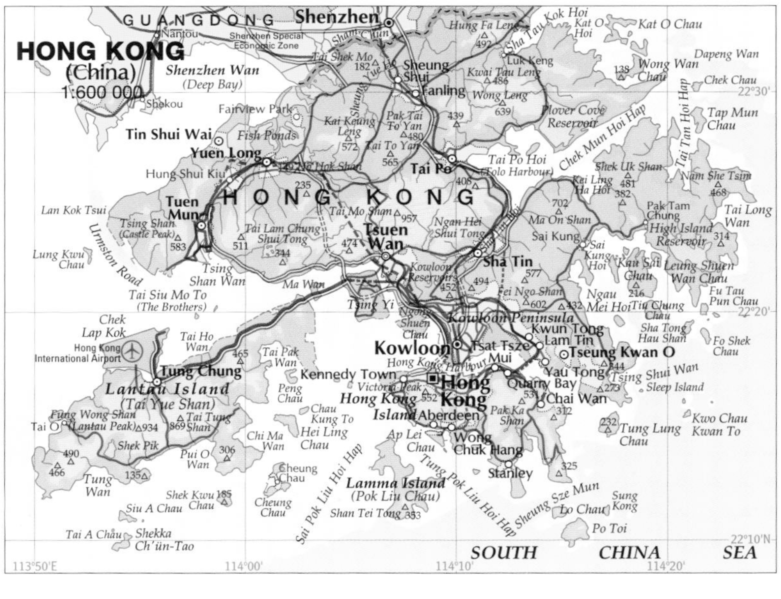
HONG KONG
(China)
1:600 000
GUANGDONG
Shenzhen
HONG KONG
Kowloon
Hong Kong Island
Lantau Island
(Tai Yue Shan)
Tsuen Wan
Sha Tin
Tuen Mun
Yuen Long
Tai Po
SOUTH CHINA SEA

168

183

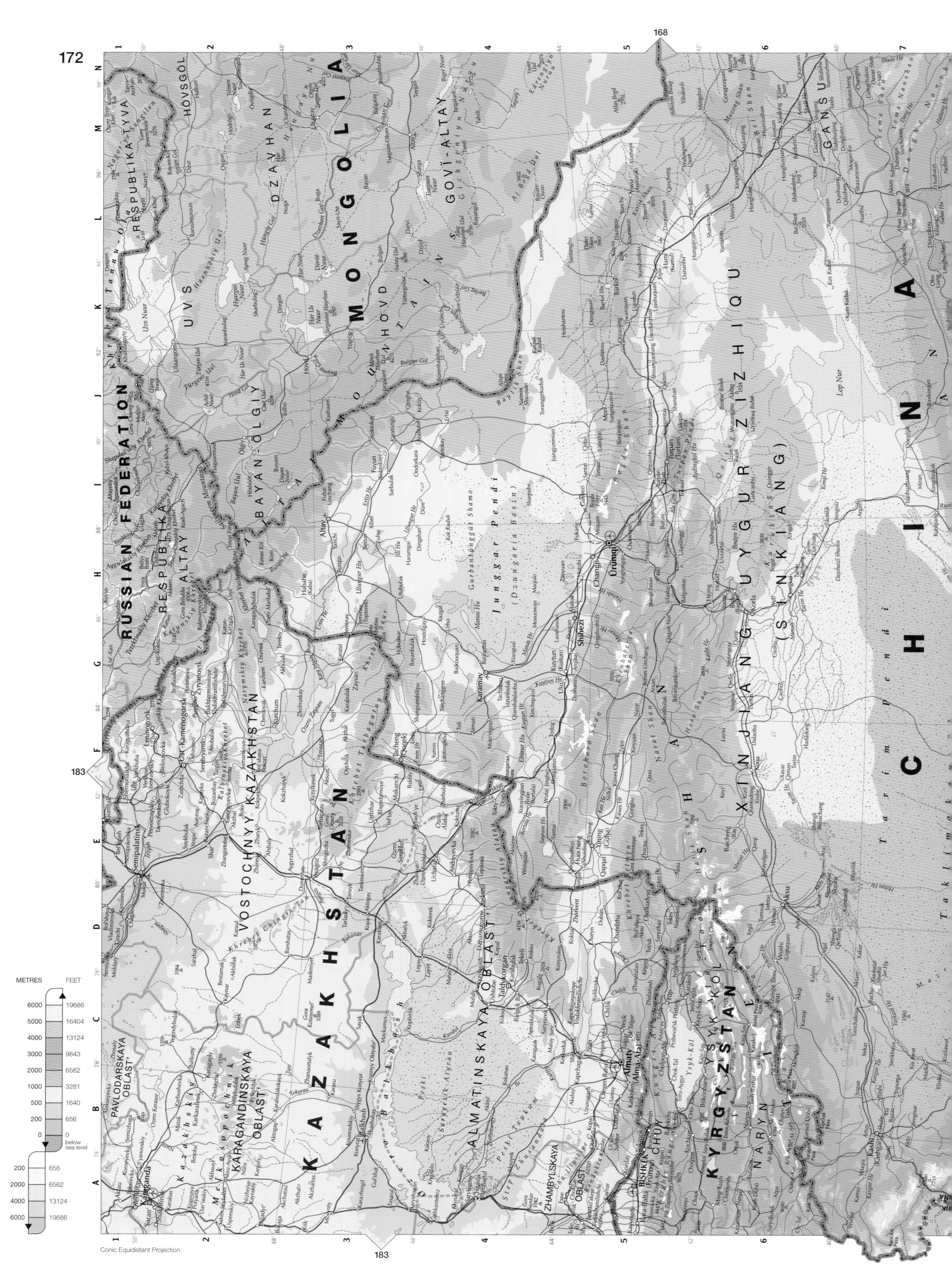

RUSSIAN FEDERATION
RESPUBLIKA TYVA
RESPUBLIKA ALTAY
MONGOLIA
UVS
HÖVSGÖL
DZAVHAN
HOVD
BAYAN-ÖLGIY
GOVĬ-ALTAY
KAZAKHSTAN
VOSTOCHNYY KAZAKHSTAN
PAVLODARSKAYA OBLAST'
KARAGANDINSKAYA OBLAST'
ALMATINSKAYA OBLAST'
ZHAMBYLSKAYA OBLAST'
KYRGYZSTAN
CHUY
NARYN
YSYK-KÖL
XINJIANG UYGUR ZIZHIQU
(SINKIANG)
GANSU
CHINA
Ürümqi
Almaty (Alma-Ata)
Bishkek (Frunze)
Semipalatinsk
Ust'-Kamenogorsk
Karaganda
Balkhash
Taldykorgan
Karamay
Shihezi
Changji
Turpan (Turfan)
Hami (Kumul)
Korla
Aksu
Kashi (Kashgar)
Junggar Pendi
(Dzungaria Basin)
Tarim Pendi
Taklimakan
Lop Nur
METRES
FEET
6000
19686
5000
16404
4000
13124
3000
9843
2000
6562
1000
3281
500
1640
200
656
0
0
below sea level
200
656
2000
6562
4000
13124
6000
19686

Conic Equidistant Projection

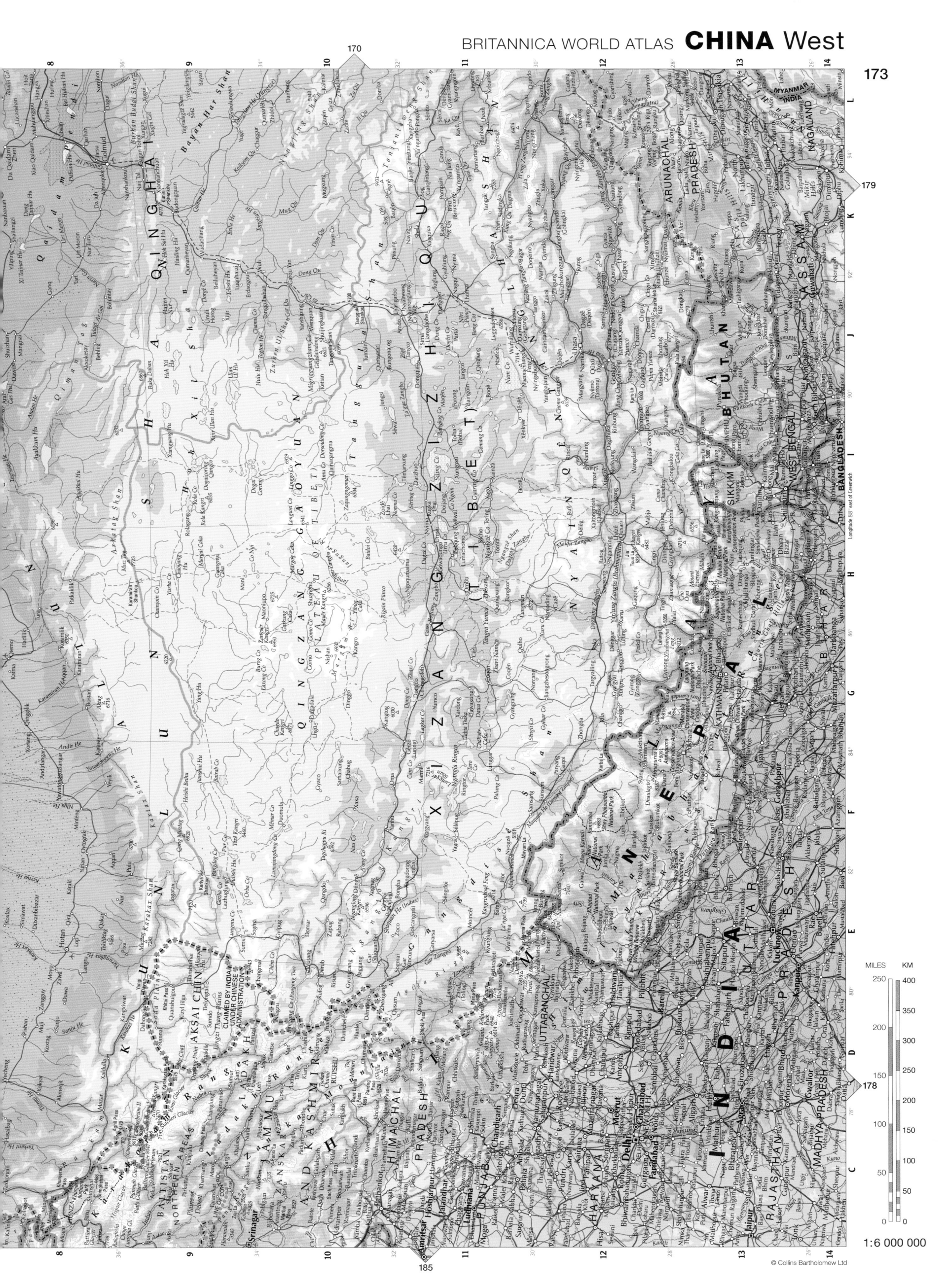

1:6 000 000

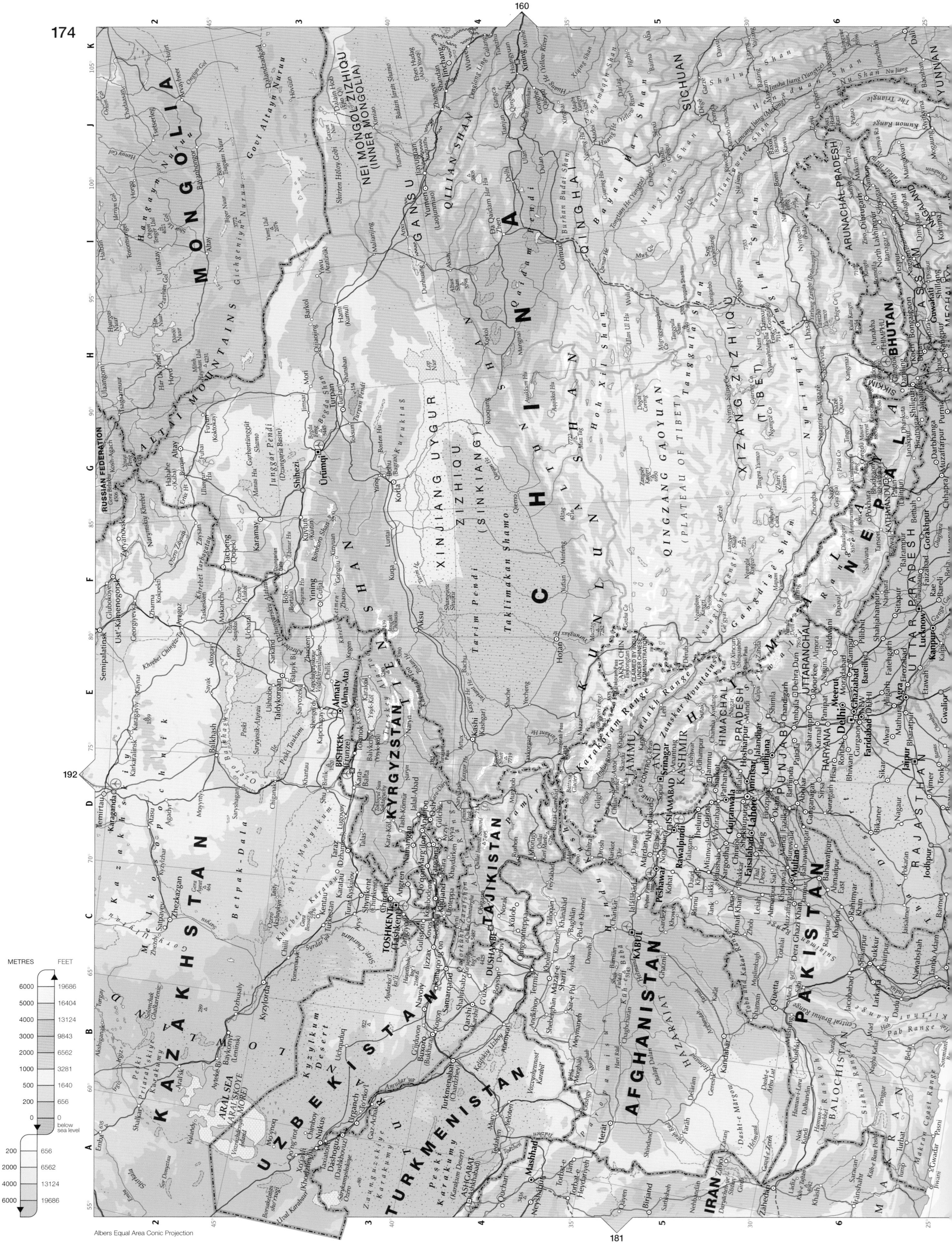
160
181
192
METRES
FEET
6000 19686
5000 16404
4000 13124
3000 9843
2000 6562
1000 3281
500 1640
200 656
0 0
below sea level
200 656
2000 6562
4000 13124
6000 19686
MONGOLIA
KAZAKHSTAN
UZBEKISTAN
TURKMENISTAN
KYRGYZSTAN
TAJIKISTAN
AFGHANISTAN
PAKISTAN
CHINA
NEPAL
BHUTAN
IRAN
RUSSIAN FEDERATION
XINJIANG UYGUR ZIZHIQU (SINKIANG)
XIZANG ZIZHIQU (TIBET)
NEI MONGOL ZIZHIQU (INNER MONGOLIA)
QINGHAI
GANSU
SICHUAN
YUNNAN
ARUNACHAL PRADESH
ASSAM
SIKKIM
UTTAR PRADESH
UTTARANCHAL
HIMACHAL PRADESH
PUNJAB
HARYANA
RAJASTHAN
JAMMU AND KASHMIR
BALOCHISTAN
HAZARAJAT
ARAL SEA
Taklimakan Shamo
Tarim Pendi
QINGZANG GAOYUAN (PLATEAU OF TIBET)
KUNLUN SHAN
ALTUN SHAN
TIEN SHAN
ALTAI MOUNTAINS
Karakoram Range
HIMALAYA
Hindu Kush
Kyzylkum Desert
Karakumy
Betpak-Dala
Ürümqi
Almaty (Alma-Ata)
BISHKEK
TOSHKENT (Tashkent)
DUSHANBE
KABUL
ISLAMABAD
Lahore
DELHI
KATHMANDU
THIMPHU
ASHGABAT
Samarqand
Kashi (Kashgar)
Lhasa
Albers Equal Area Conic Projection

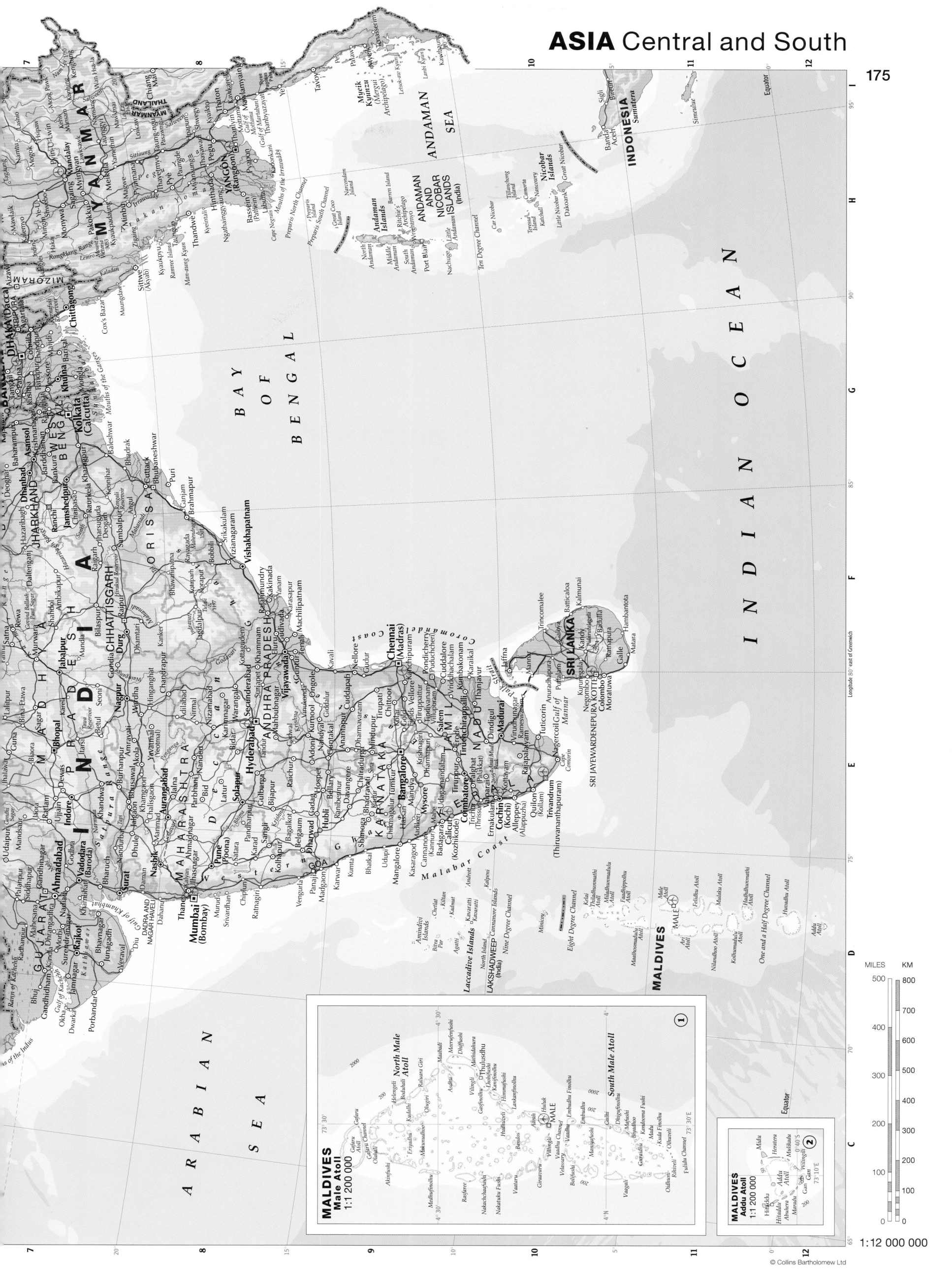

1:12 000 000

MILES   KM

© Collins Bartholomew Ltd

BAY OF BENGAL
INDIAN OCEAN
ARABIAN SEA
ANDAMAN SEA
INDIA
MYANMAR
SRI LANKA
MALDIVES
INDONESIA
ANDAMAN AND NICOBAR ISLANDS (India)
LAKSHADWEEP (India)
Andaman Islands
Nicobar Islands
Laccadive Islands
Ten Degree Channel
Nine Degree Channel
Eight Degree Channel
One and a Half Degree Channel
Equator
Malabar Coast
Coromandel Coast
Gulf of Mannar
Palk Strait
GUJARAT
MAHARASHTRA
KARNATAKA
ANDHRA PRADESH
TAMIL NADU
ORISSA
CHHATTISGARH
JHARKHAND
WEST BENGAL
MADHYA PRADESH
MIZORAM
TRIPURA
Mumbai (Bombay)
Chennai (Madras)
Kolkata (Calcutta)
Bangalore
Hyderabad
YANGON (Rangoon)
DHAKA
Colombo
SRI JAYEWARDENEPURA KOTTE
MALE
Longitude 80° east of Greenwich
MALDIVES Male Atoll 1:1 200 000
North Male Atoll
South Male Atoll
MALDIVES Addu Atoll 1:1 200 000
Addu Atoll

178

A 70° **B** 72° **C** 74° **D** 76° **E** 78° **F** 80° **G** 82°

Tropic of Cancer

GUJARAT

MADHYA PRADESH

Ahmadabad

Bhopal

Jabalpur

CHHATTISG

Indore

Porbandar

Rajkot

Surat

Vadodara
(Baroda)

Nagpur

Durg
Bhilai

Diu

Gulf of Khambhat

Nashik

Aurangabad

MAHARASHTRA

I N D I A

Mumbai
(Bombay)

Navi Mumbai

Thane

Pune
(Poona)

Solapur

D E C C A N

Chandrapur

ARABIAN

SEA

Kolhapur

Bidar

Secunderabad

Hyderabad

Warangal

Khammam

ANDHRA PRADESH

Belgaum

GOA

Dharwad
Hubli

Guntakal

Kurnool

Vijayawada

Guntur

Coromandel Coast

Laccadive

Islands

Davangere

KARNATAKA

Shimoga

Cuddapah

Nellore

LAKSHADWEEP
(India)

Amindivi Islands

Mangalore

Bangalore

Kolar

Chennai
(Madras)

Kanchipuram

Cannanore Islands

Mysore

Salem

Pondicherry
(Puducherry)

Cuddalore

Calicut
(Kozhikode)

TAMIL

Nine Degree Channel

Coimbatore

Tiruchirappalli

NADU

Cochin
(Kochi)

KERALA

Madurai

Alleppey
(Alappuzha)

Palk
Strait

Jaffna

Gulf of
Mannar

Quilon
(Kollam)

Tuticorin

Trivandrum
(Thiruvananthapuram)

Nagercoil

Cape
Comorin

Eight Degree Channel

Minicoy

SRI LANKA

MALDIVES

Colombo

SRI JAYEWARDENEPURA KOTTE

METRES	FEET
6000	19686
5000	16404
4000	13124
3000	9843
2000	6562
1000	3281
500	1640
200	656
0	0
	below
	sea level
200	656
2000	6562
4000	13124
6000	19686

Conic Equidistant Projection

BAY OF BENGAL
INDIAN OCEAN
BANGLADESH
MYANMAR
BIHAR
WEST BENGAL
ORISSA
CHITTAGONG
CHIN
SAGAING
MANDALAY
MAGWE
PEGU
IRRAWADDY
YANGON
Kolkata (Calcutta)
Dhaka
Chittagong
Sittwe (Akyab)
Bhubaneshwar
Cuttack
Vishakhapatnam
Mouths of the Ganges
Mouths of the Irrawaddy
ANDAMAN AND NICOBAR ISLANDS (India)
Andaman Islands
Nicobar Islands
Port Blair
Ten Degree Channel
Administrative divisions in India numbered on the map:
1. DADRA AND NAGAR HAVELI (C2)
2. DAMAN AND DIU (B2, C2)
3. PONDICHERRY (D7, F7, H4)
KOLKATA
1:70 000
0 METRES 750
0 YARDS 750
MUMBAI
1:90 000
0 METRES 1000
0 YARDS 1000
Arabian Sea
Back Bay
Mumbai Harbour
158
MILES KM
1:6 000 000
Longitude 84° east of Greenwich

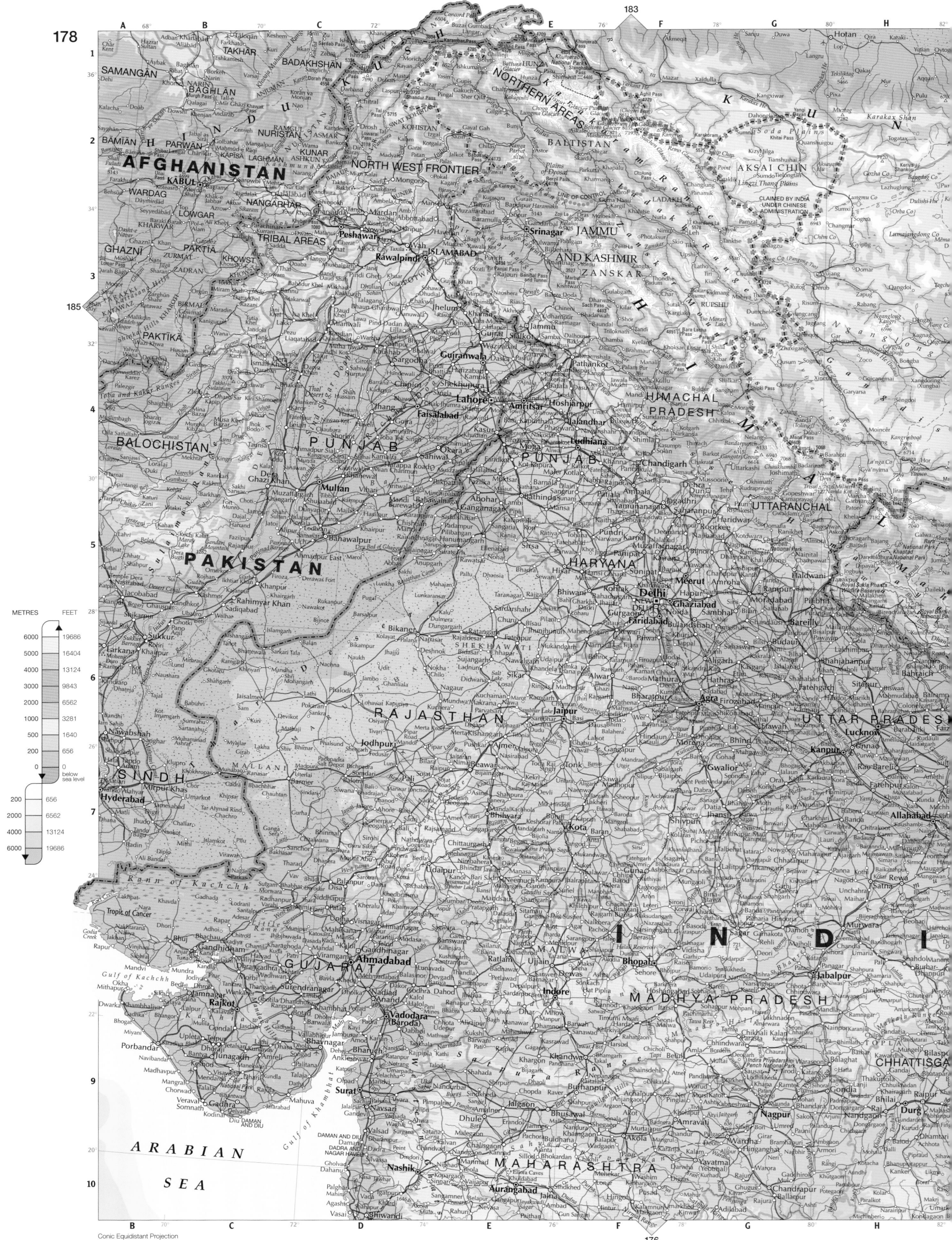

AFGHANISTAN

PAKISTAN

PUNJAB

BALOCHISTAN

SINDH

JAMMU
AND KASHMIR

HIMACHAL
PRADESH

UTTARANCHAL

HARYANA

PUNJAB

RAJASTHAN

UTTAR PRADESH

GUJARAT

MADHYA PRADESH

MAHARASHTRA

CHHATTISGARH

MALWA

ARABIAN

SEA

Gulf of Kachchh

Gulf of Khambhat

Rann of Kachchh

Tropic of Cancer

TRIBAL AREAS

NORTH WEST FRONTIER

NORTHERN AREAS

BALTISTAN

LADAKH

ZANSKAR

ZANSKAR

RUPSHU

AKSAI CHIN

CLAIMED BY INDIA
UNDER CHINESE
ADMINISTRATION

LINE OF CONTROL

KABUL

Islamabad

Rawalpindi

Peshawar

Srinagar

Lahore

Amritsar

Faisalabad

Multan

Ludhiana

Chandigarh

Bahawalpur

Rahimyar Khan

Khanpur

Sukkur

Larkana

Hyderabad

Mirpur Khas

Nawabshah

Bikaner

Jodhpur

Jaipur

Ajmer

Kota

Bhilwara

Udaipur

Delhi

NEW
DELHI

Meerut

Faridabad

Ghaziabad

Gwalior

Agra

Bareilly

Kanpur

Lucknow

Allahabad

Bhopal

Indore

Jabalpur

Nagpur

Ahmadabad

Gandhinagar

Vadodara
Baroda

Rajkot

Bhavnagar

Surat

Navsari

Nashik

Aurangabad

METRES   FEET
6000   19686
5000   16404
4000   13124
3000   9843
2000   6562
1000   3281
500   1640
200   656
0   below
          sea level
200   656
2000   6562
4000   13124
6000   19686

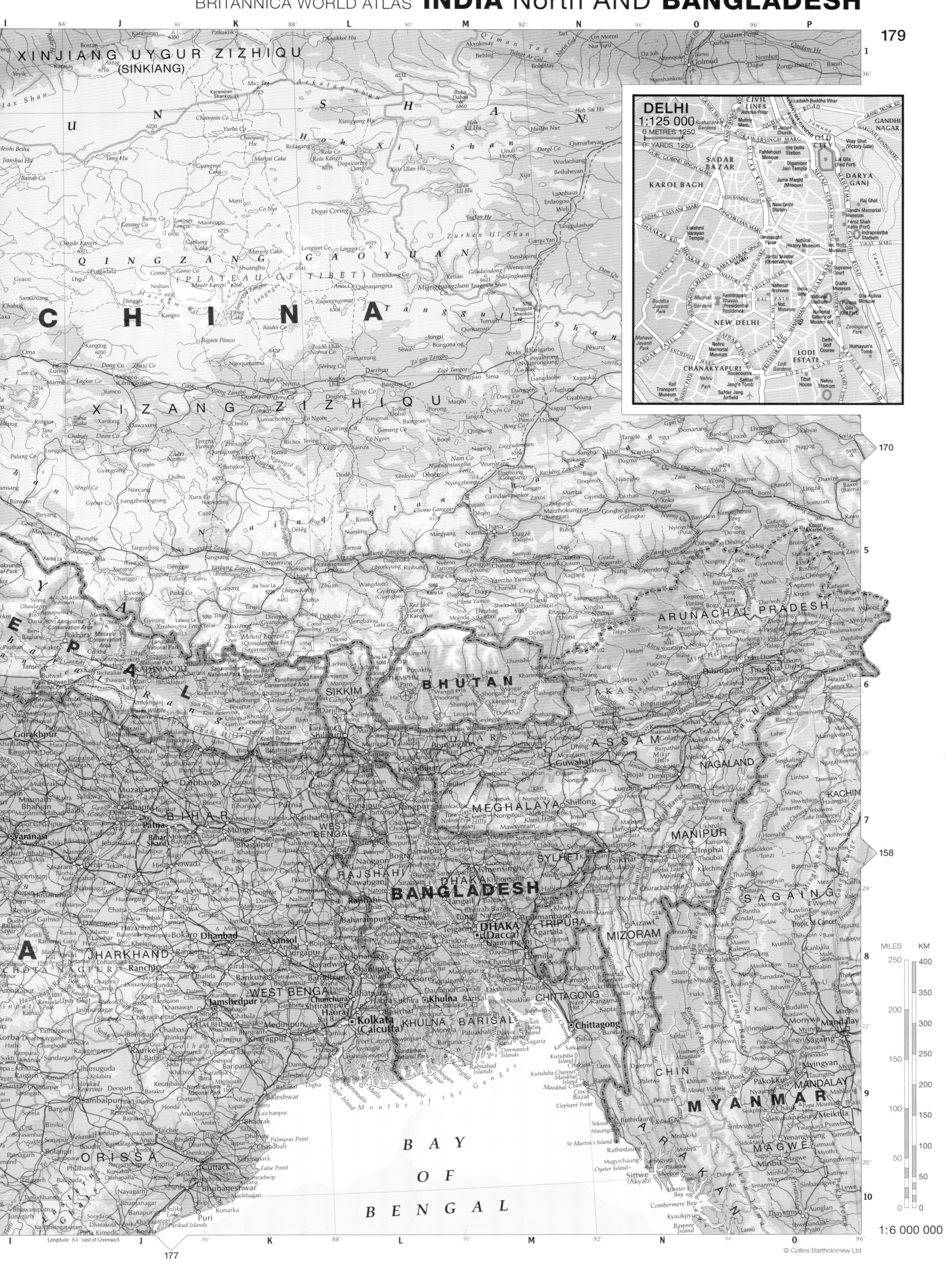
DELHI
1:125 000
0 METRES 1250
0 YARDS 1250
XINJIANG UYGUR ZIZHIQU (SINKIANG)
CHINA
QINGZANG GAOYUAN
PLATEAU OF TIBET
XIZANG ZIZHIQU
NEPAL
BHUTAN
SIKKIM
ARUNACHAL PRADESH
ASSAM
NAGALAND
MEGHALAYA
MANIPUR
MIZORAM
TRIPURA
BIHAR
JHARKHAND
WEST BENGAL
ORISSA
BANGLADESH
DHAKA (Dacca)
Kolkata (Calcutta)
MYANMAR
BAY OF BENGAL
Mouths of the Ganges
MILES
KM
1:6 000 000
Longitude 84° east of Greenwich

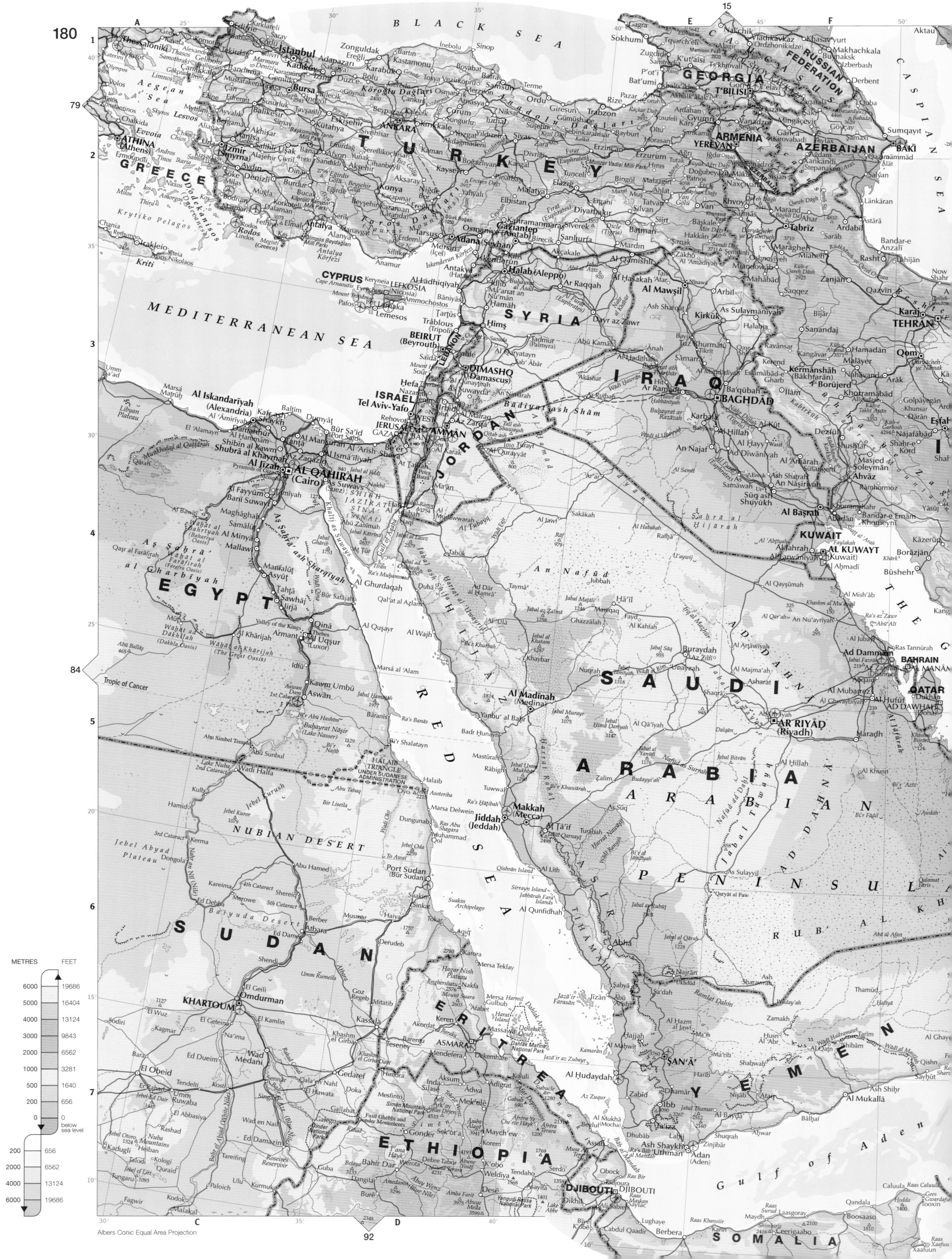
BLACK SEA
CASPIAN SEA
MEDITERRANEAN SEA
RED SEA
Gulf of Aden
TURKEY
GREECE
GEORGIA
ARMENIA
AZERBAIJAN
RUSSIAN FEDERATION
CYPRUS
SYRIA
LEBANON
ISRAEL
JORDAN
IRAQ
KUWAIT
BAHRAIN
QATAR
SAUDI ARABIA
ARABIAN PENINSULA
YEMEN
EGYPT
SUDAN
ERITREA
ETHIOPIA
DJIBOUTI
SOMALIA
HALAIB TRIANGLE UNDER SUDANESE ADMINISTRATION
NUBIAN DESERT
An Nafūd
Rub' al Khālī
Ad Dahnā'
Tropic of Cancer
İstanbul
ANKARA
ATHINA (Athens)
LEFKOSIA (Nicosia)
BEIRUT (Beyrouth)
DIMASHQ (Damascus)
JERUSALEM
AMMAN
Tel Aviv-Yafo
AL QAHIRAH (Cairo)
Al Iskandarīyah (Alexandria)
BAGHDĀD
TEHRAN
T'BILISI
YEREVAN
BAKI
AL KUWAYT (Kuwait)
AR RIYĀḌ (Riyadh)
Makkah (Mecca)
Jiddah (Jeddah)
Al Madīnah (Medina)
ṢAN'Ā'
Adan (Aden)
KHARTOUM
Omdurman
ASMARA
DJIBOUTI
METRES
FEET
6000 19686
5000 16404
4000 13124
3000 9843
2000 6562
1000 3281
500 1640
200 656
0 0 below sea level
200 656
2000 6562
4000 13124
6000 19686
Albers Conic Equal Area Projection

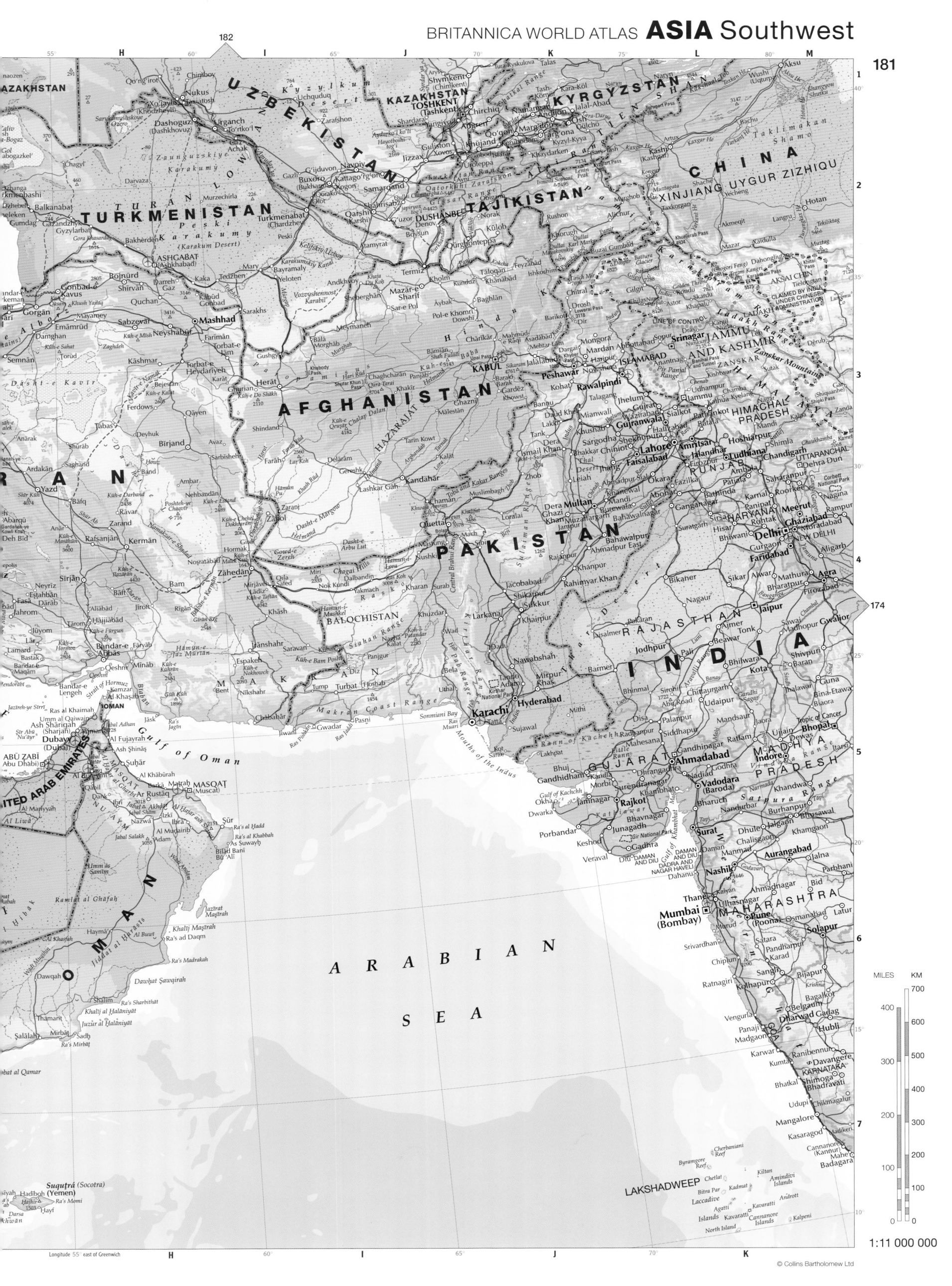

ARABIAN

SEA

1:11 000 000

© Collins Bartholomew Ltd

182
174
J
K
2
3
4
5
6
7
UZBEKISTAN
KAZAKHSTAN
KYRGYZSTAN
TAJIKISTAN
TURKMENISTAN
CHINA
XINJIANG UYGUR ZIZHIQU
AFGHANISTAN
PAKISTAN
INDIA
OMAN
UNITED ARAB EMIRATES
JAMMU AND KASHMIR
HIMACHAL PRADESH
RAJASTHAN
GUJARAT
MADHYA PRADESH
MAHARASHTRA
PUNJAB
HARYANA
UTTARANCHAL
BALOCHISTAN
LAKSHADWEEP
Gulf of Oman
Gulf of Kachchh
Gulf of Khambhat
Mouths of the Indus
LINE OF CONTROL
AKSAI CHIN
CLAIMED BY INDIA UNDER CHINESE ADMINISTRATION
TOSHKENT (Tashkent)
DUSHANBE
KABUL
ISLAMABAD
NEW DELHI
MASQAT (Muscat)
ABŪ ZABĪ (Abu Dhabi)
ASHGABAT (Ashkhabad)
Karachi
Mumbai (Bombay)
Delhi
Lahore
Hyderabad
Ahmadabad
Jaipur
Mashhad
Herat
Kandahar
Quetta
Peshawar
Rawalpindi
Srinagar
Samarqand
Bukhara
Dubayy (Dubai)
Longitude 55° east of Greenwich
MILES KM

182

A 46° B 48° C 50° D 14 52° E 54° F 56° G 58° H 60° I 62° J 64° K

1

52°

2

50°

3

48°

4

METRES FEET
6000 19686
5000 16404
4000 13124
3000 9843
2000 6562
1000 3281
500 1640
200 656
0 below
sea level
200 656
2000 6562
4000 13124
6000 19686

RUSSIAN FEDERATION

RESPUBLIKA BASHKORTOSTAN

SAMARSKAYA OBLAST'

CHELYABINSKAYA OBLAST'

SARATOVSKAYA OBLAST'

ORENBURGSKAYA OBLAST'

KOSTANAYSKAYA OBLAST'

Z A P A D N Y Y

K A Z A K H S T A N

A T Y R A U S K A Y A O B L A S T'

Ryn-
Peski

AKTYUBINSKAYA OBLAST'

K A Z A K

ASTRAKHANSKAYA OBLAST'

Astrakhan

Prikaspiyskaya Nizmennost'
(Caspian Lowland)

Atyrau
(Gur'yev)

KYZYLORDINSKAYA OBLAST'

ARAL SEA
(Aral'skoye More)

C A S P I A N

S E A

RESPUBLIKA
DAGESTAN

Makhachkala

Poluostrov Buzachi

MANGISTAUSKAYA
OBLAST' Plateau

Aktau
(Shevchenko)

Ustyurt Plateau

QORAQALPOG'ISTON-RESPUBLIKASI

(RESPUBLIKA KARAKALPAKISTAN)

K Y Z Y L K U M

D E S E R T

U Z B E K I S T A N

NAVOIY

Zaliv
Kara-Bogaz-
Gol

Vpadina
Assake-Audan

Nukus

DASHOGUZSKAYA

OBLAST'

Dashoguz
(Dashkhovuz)

BUXORO

AZERBAIJAN

BAKI

Turkmenbashi

BALKANSKAYA OBLAST'

Zaunguzskiye
Karakumy

T U R K M E N I S T A N

T u r

BUXORO

Bukhara

LEBAPSKAYA
OBLAST'

Turkmenabat
(Chardzhev)

Administrative divisions in Uzbekistan
numbered on the map:
1. ANDIJON (O7)
2. FARG'ONA (N7)
3. NAMANGAN (N7)

PESKI KARAKUMY
(Karakum Desert)

AKHAL'SKAYA OBLAST'

ASHGABAT
(Ashkhabad)

MARYYSKAYA

OBLAST'

9

36°

MAZANDARAN

GOLESTAN

I R A N

SEMNAN

KHORASAN

D 52° E 54° F 56° G 58° H 60° I 62° J 64° K

184

Conic Equidistant Projection

KAZAKHSTAN, UZBEKISTAN AND KYRGYZSTAN

172

185

MILES KM

1:6 000 000

© Collins Bartholomew Ltd

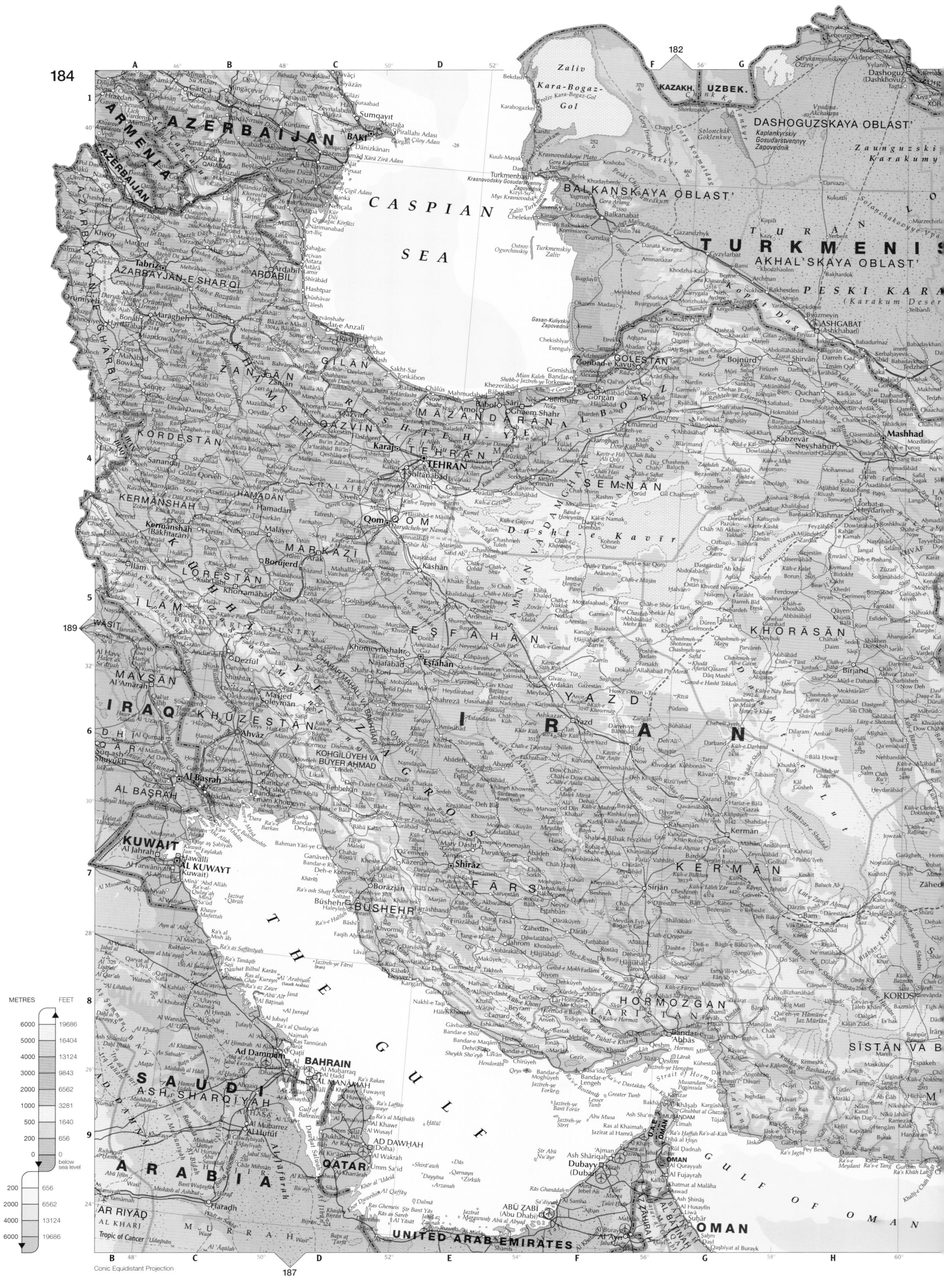

AZERBAIJAN
ARMENIA
AZERBAIJAN
KAZAKH.
UZBEK.
DASHOGUZSKAYA OBLAST'
BALKANSKAYA OBLAST'
TURKMENIS
AKHAL'SKAYA OBLAST'
Zaliv Kara-Bogaz-Gol
CASPIAN SEA
Zaunguzski Karakumy
PESKI KARA (Karakum Deser
ASHGABAT (Ashkhabad)
Dashoguz (Dashkhovuz)
Türkmenbashi
Balkanabat
BAKI
Sumqayit
Tabriz
Ardabil
ÄZARBAYJĀN-E SHARQĪ
ARDABĪL
GĪLĀN
ZANJĀN
QAZVĪN
MĀZANDARĀN
GOLESTĀN
TEHRĀN
SEMNĀN
QOM
MARKAZĪ
HAMADĀN
KORDESTĀN
KERMĀNSHĀH
LORESTĀN
ĪLĀM
KHŪZESTĀN
EŞFAHĀN
YAZD
KHORĀSĀN
CHAHAR MAHAL VA BAKHTĪĀRĪ
KOHGĪLŪYEH VA BŪYER AHMAD
FĀRS
BŪSHEHR
KERMĀN
HORMOZGĀN
SĪSTĀN VA B
IRAN
Dasht-e Kavīr
ZAGROS
Mashhad
Esfahan
Shiraz
Kerman
Yazd
Ahvāz
Bandar-e 'Abbās
IRAQ
WĀSIT
MAYSĀN
AL BAŞRAH
Al Başrah
KUWAIT
AL KUWAYT (Kuwait)
SAUDI ARABIA
ASH SHARQĪYAH
Ad Dammām
AR RIYĀḌ
BAHRAIN
AL MANĀMAH
QATAR
AD DAWḤAH (Doha)
UNITED ARAB EMIRATES
ABŪ ẒABI (Abu Dhabi)
Dubayy (Dubai)
OMAN
THE GULF
GULF OF OMAN
Strait of Hormuz
Tropic of Cancer
METRES FEET
6000 19686
5000 16404
4000 13124
3000 9843
2000 6562
1000 3281
500 1640
200 656
0 0 below sea level
200 656
2000 6562
4000 13124
6000 19686
182
187
189

Conic Equidistant Projection

KAZAKHSTAN

UZBEKISTAN

KYRGYZSTAN

TAJIKISTAN

CHINA

XINJIANG UYGUR ZIZHIQU

TURKMENISTAN

AFGHANISTAN

HERĀT

GHOWR

FARĀH

NĪMRŪZ

HELMAND

KANDAHĀR

BALOCHISTAN

PAKISTAN

PUNJAB

SINDH

INDIA

RAJASTHAN

HARYANA

GUJARĀT

KASHMIR

JAMMU AND KASHMIR

NORTH WEST FRONTIER

TRIBAL AREAS

Kabul
Kābul
Islamabad
Rawalpindi
Peshawar
Lahore
Amritsar
Faisalabad
Multan
Quetta
Karachi
Hyderabad
Dushanbe
Srinagar
Jammu

MILES   KM
250   400
        350
200   300
        250
150   200
100   150
        100
50
        50
0   0

1:6 000 000

© Collins Bartholomew Ltd

190
EGYPT
JORDAN
IRAQ
AL MUTHANNÁ
AL JAWF
AL HUDŪD ASH SHAMĀLĪYAH
TABŪK
JANŪB SĪNĀ'
SHIBH JAZĪRAT SĪNĀ' (SINAI)
An Nafūd
ḤĀ'IL
AL QAṢĪM
AL MADĪNAH
Al Madīnah (Medina)
AR RIYĀḌ (Riyadh)
SAUDI ARABIA
QINĀ
AL BAḤR AL AḤMAR
ASWĀN
Tropic of Cancer
HALAIB TRIANGLE UNDER SUDANESE ADMINISTRATION
NUBIAN DESERT
RED SEA
Port Sudan (Bûr Sudan)
SUDAN
NILE
KASSALA
GEDAREF
SENNAR
BLUE NILE
ERITREA
ASMARA
ETHIOPIA
TIGRAY
ĀFAR
ĀMARA
Jiddah (Jeddah)
Makkah (Mecca)
MAKKAH
At Ṭā'if
AL BĀḤAH
'ASĪR
Abhā
JĪZĀN
NAJRĀN
ṢA'DAH
AL JAWF
YEMEN
ṢAN'Ā'
HAJJAH
AMRĀN
MA'RIB
AL ḤUDAYDAH
DHAMĀR
IBB
TA'IZZ
AḌ ḌĀLI'
LAḤIJ
'ADAN
ABYĀN
SHABWAH
AL BAYḌĀ'
ERITREA
DJIBOUTI
Dahlak Archipelago
Suakin Archipelago
Farasān
85
92
METRES
FEET
6000
19686
5000
16404
4000
13124
3000
9843
2000
6562
1000
3281
500
1640
200
656
0
0
below sea level
200
656
2000
6562
4000
13124
6000
19686

Conic Equidistant Projection

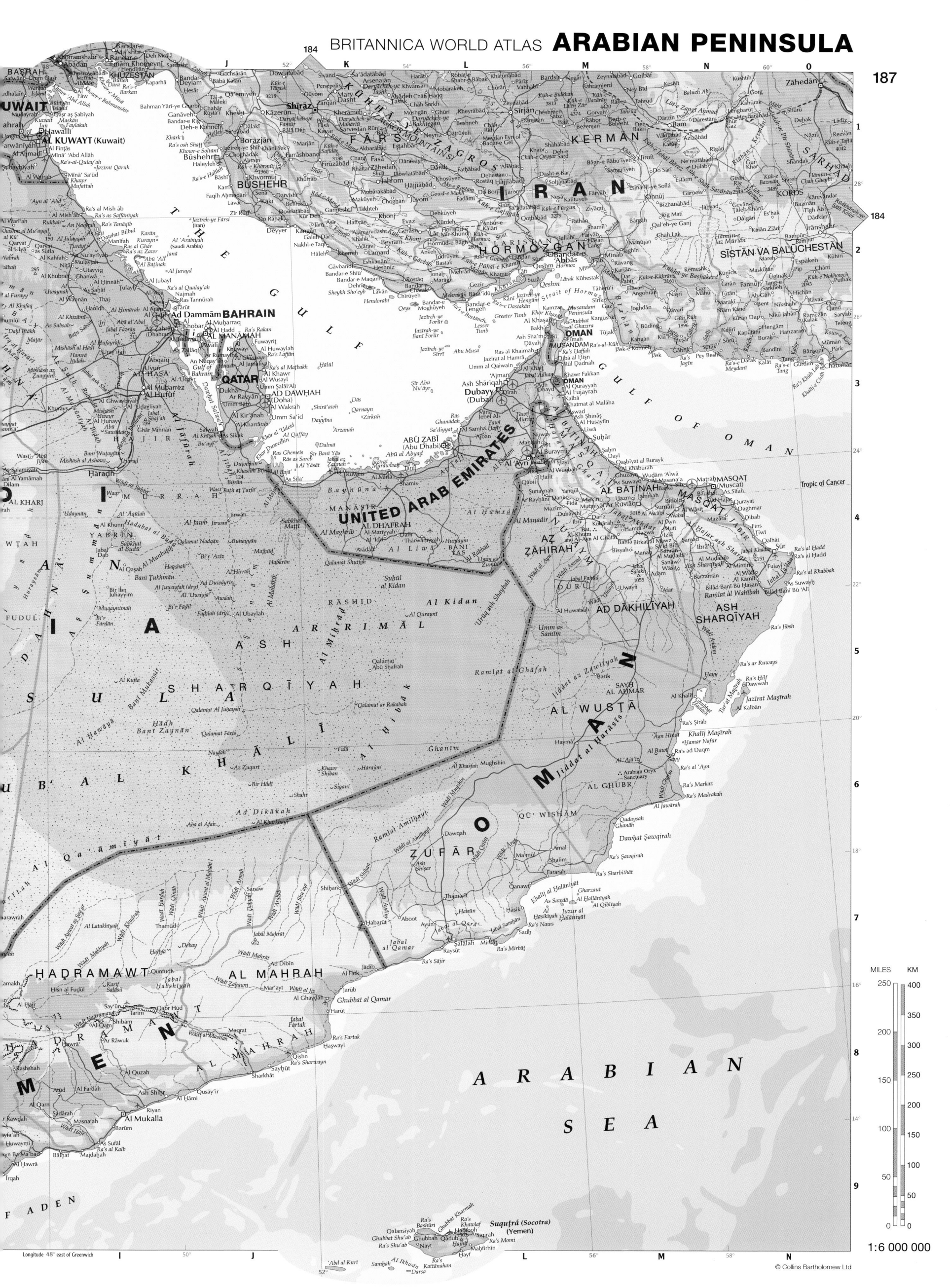

1:6 000 000

© Collins Bartholomew Ltd

184
IRAN
KERMĀN
FĀRS
BŪSHEHR
HORMOZGĀN
SĪSTĀN VA BALŪCHESTĀN
ZAGROS MOUNTAINS
KHUZESTĀN
KUWAIT
AL KUWAYT (Kuwait)
BAHRAIN
AL MANĀMAH
QATAR
AD DAWḨAH (Doha)
THE GULF
UNITED ARAB EMIRATES
ABŪ ẒABĪ (Abu Dhabi)
Dubayy (Dubai)
Ash Shāriqah
OMAN
MUSANDAM
GULF OF OMAN
MASQAṬ (Muscat)
AL BĀṬINAH
AẒ ẒĀHIRAH
AD DĀKHILĪYAH
ASH SHARQĪYAH
AL WUSṬĀ
ẒUFĀR
Ṣalālah
AR RUB' AL KHĀLĪ
ASH SHARQĪYAH
AL MAHRAH
ḨAḌRAMAWT
YEMEN
Al Mukallā
ARABIAN SEA
GULF OF ADEN
Suquṭrá (Socotra) (Yemen)
Strait of Hormuz
Tropic of Cancer
Shīrāz
Bandar-e 'Abbās
Ad Dammām
Al Hufūf
Al 'Ayn
Ṣūr
Jazīrat Maṣīrah
MILES
KM
Longitude 48° east of Greenwich

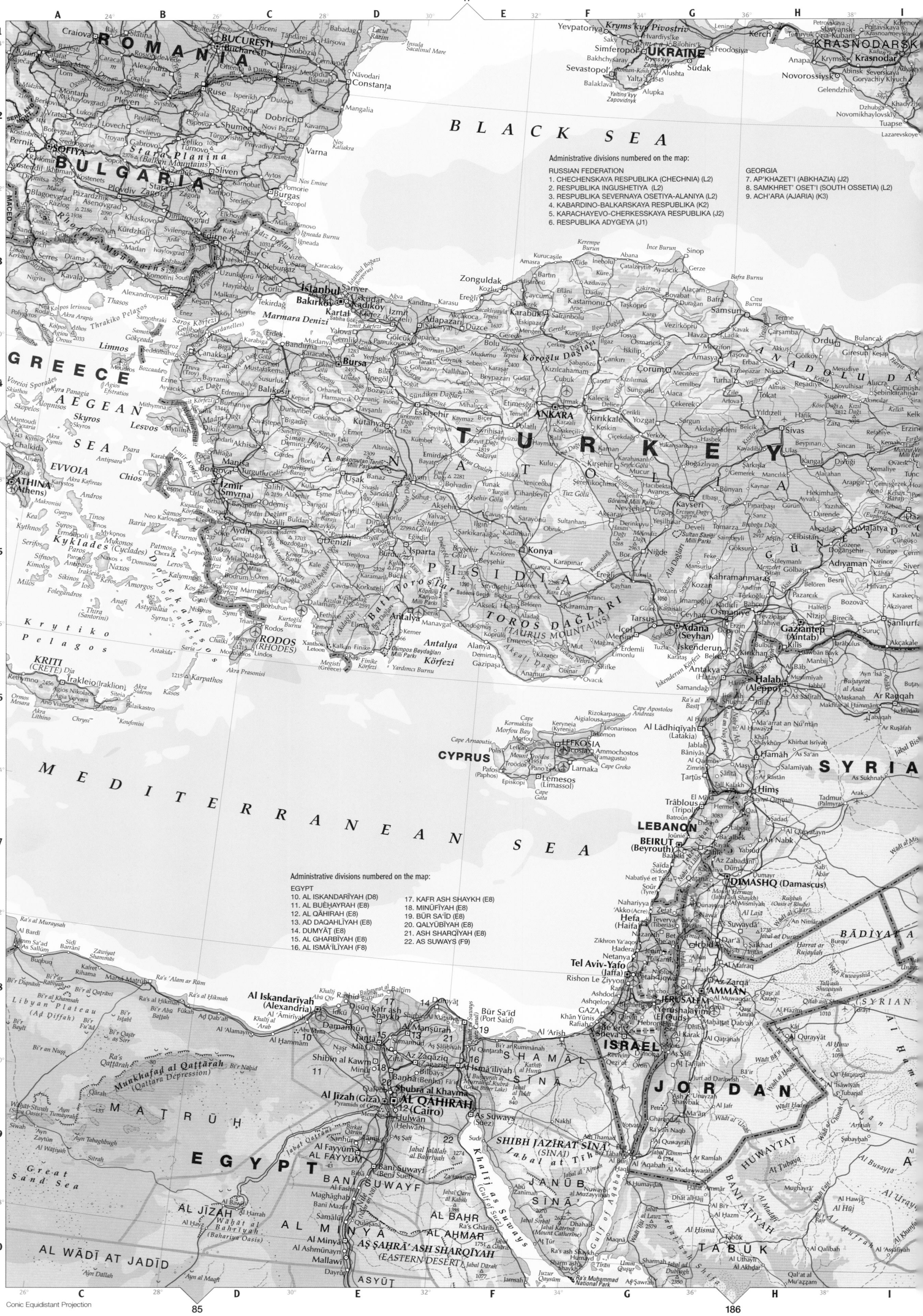
BLACK SEA
Administrative divisions numbered on the map:
RUSSIAN FEDERATION
1. CHECHENSKAYA RESPUBLIKA (CHECHNIA) (L2)
2. RESPUBLIKA INGUSHETIYA (L2)
3. RESPUBLIKA SEVERNAYA OSETIYA-ALANIYA (L2)
4. KABARDINO-BALKARSKAYA RESPUBLIKA (K2)
5. KARACHAYEVO-CHERKESSKAYA RESPUBLIKA (J2)
6. RESPUBLIKA ADYGEYA (J1)
GEORGIA
7. AP'KHAZET'I (ABKHAZIA) (J2)
8. SAMKHRET' OSET'I (SOUTH OSSETIA) (L2)
9. ACH'ARA (AJARIA) (K3)
ROMANIA
BUCUREŞTI (Bucharest)
BULGARIA
SOFIYA
UKRAINE
KRASNODARSK
GREECE
ATHINA (Athens)
AEGEAN SEA
TURKEY
ANKARA
İstanbul
ANADOLU
TOROS DAĞLARI (TAURUS MOUNTAINS)
KRITI (CRETE)
RODOS (RHODES)
CYPRUS
LEFKOSIA (Nicosia)
MEDITERRANEAN SEA
SYRIA
DIMASHQ (Damascus)
LEBANON
BEIRUT (Beyrouth)
ISRAEL
Tel Aviv-Yafo (Jaffa)
JERUSALEM
JORDAN
'AMMĀN
EGYPT
AL QĀHIRAH (Cairo)
Al Iskandarīyah (Alexandria)
Administrative divisions numbered on the map:
EGYPT
10. AL ISKANDARĪYAH (D8)
11. AL BUḤAYRAH (E8)
12. AL QĀHIRAH (E8)
13. AD DAQAHLĪYAH (E8)
14. DUMYĀṬ (E8)
15. AL GHARBĪYAH (E8)
16. AL ISMĀ'ĪLĪYAH (F8)
17. KAFR ASH SHAYKH (E8)
18. MINŪFĪYAH (E8)
19. BŪR SA'ĪD (E8)
20. QALYŪBĪYAH (E8)
21. ASH SHARQĪYAH (E8)
22. AS SUWAYS (F9)
AL WĀDĪ AT JADĪD
Conic Equidistant Projection

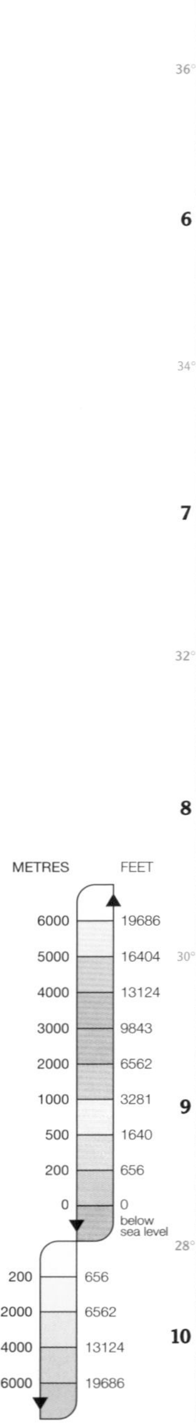
METRES
FEET
6000 19686
5000 16404
4000 13124
3000 9843
2000 6562
1000 3281
500 1640
200 656
0 0
below sea level
200 656
2000 6562
4000 13124
6000 19686

TURKEY, IRAQ, SYRIA AND TRANS-CAUCASIAN REPUBLICS

İSTANBUL
1:60 000

1:6 000 000

© Collins Bartholomew Ltd

MIDDLE EAST

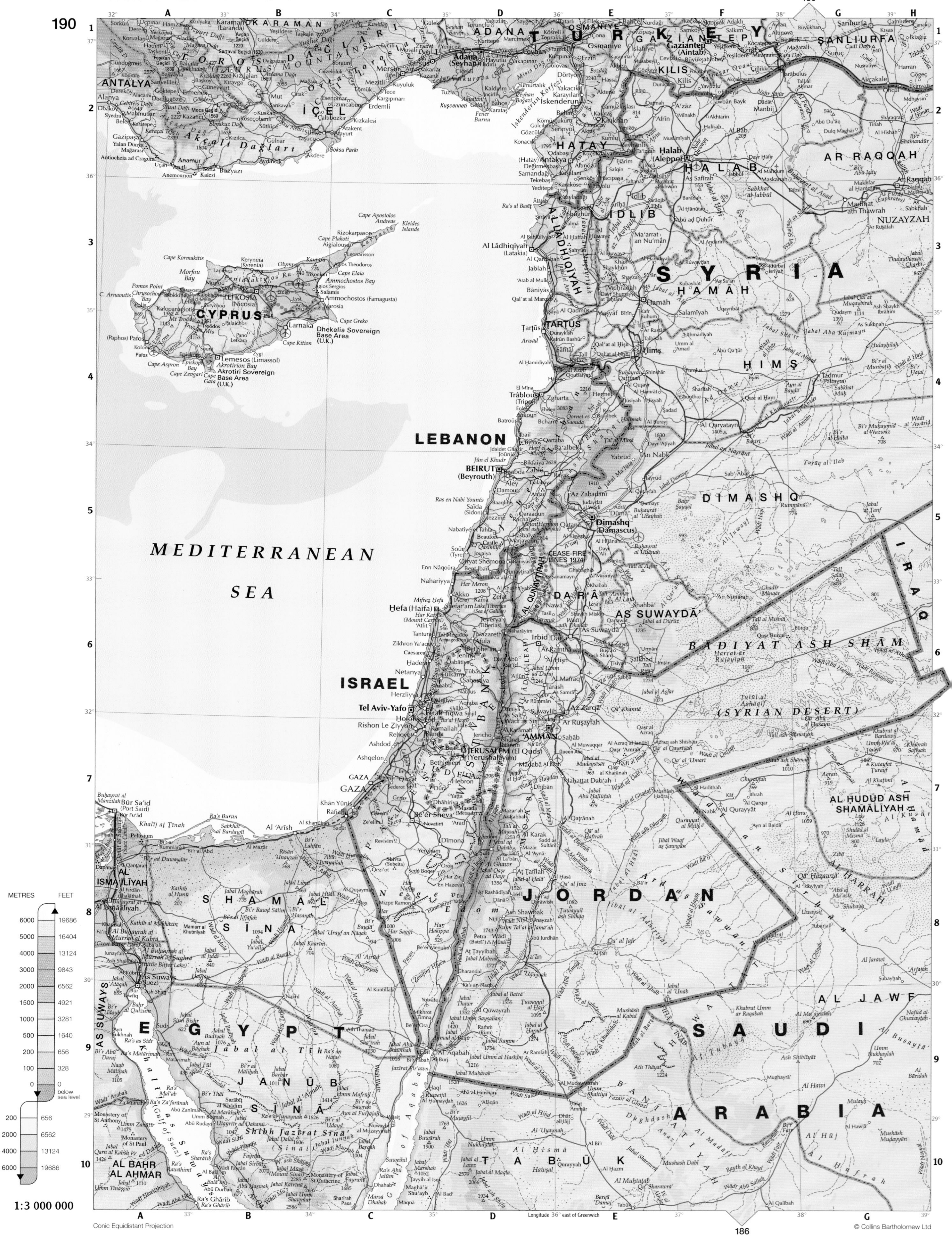

TURKEY
SYRIA
LEBANON
ISRAEL
JORDAN
IRAQ
SAUDI ARABIA
EGYPT
CYPRUS
MEDITERRANEAN SEA
WEST BANK
GAZA
ANTALYA
KARAMAN
İÇEL
ADANA
HATAY
GAZIANTEP
KILIS
ŞANLIURFA
HALAB
IDLIB
AL LĀDHIQĪYAH
HAMĀH
ṬARṬŪS
ḤIMṢ
AR RAQQAH
DIMASHQ
AL QUNAYṬIRAH
DAR'Ā
AS SUWAYDĀ'
AL ḤUDŪD ASH SHAMĀLĪYAH
AL JAWF
TABŪK
SHAMĀL SĪNĀ'
JANŪB SĪNĀ'
AS SUWAYS
AL BAḤR AL AḤMAR
AL ISMĀ'ĪLĪYAH
BĀDIYAT ASH SHĀM
(SYRIAN DESERT)
BEIRUT (Beyrouth)
Dimashq (Damascus)
'AMMĀN
JERUSALEM (El Quds) (Yerushalayim)
Tel Aviv-Yafo
Halab (Aleppo)
LEFKOSIA (Nicosia)
CEASE-FIRE LINES 1974
Dhekelia Sovereign Base Area (U.K.)
Akrotiri Sovereign Base Area (U.K.)
METRES
FEET
6000
5000
4000
3000
2000
1500
1000
500
200
100
0
19686
16404
13124
9843
6562
4921
3281
1640
656
328
below sea level
1:3 000 000
Conic Equidistant Projection
Longitude east of Greenwich
© Collins Bartholomew Ltd
189
186

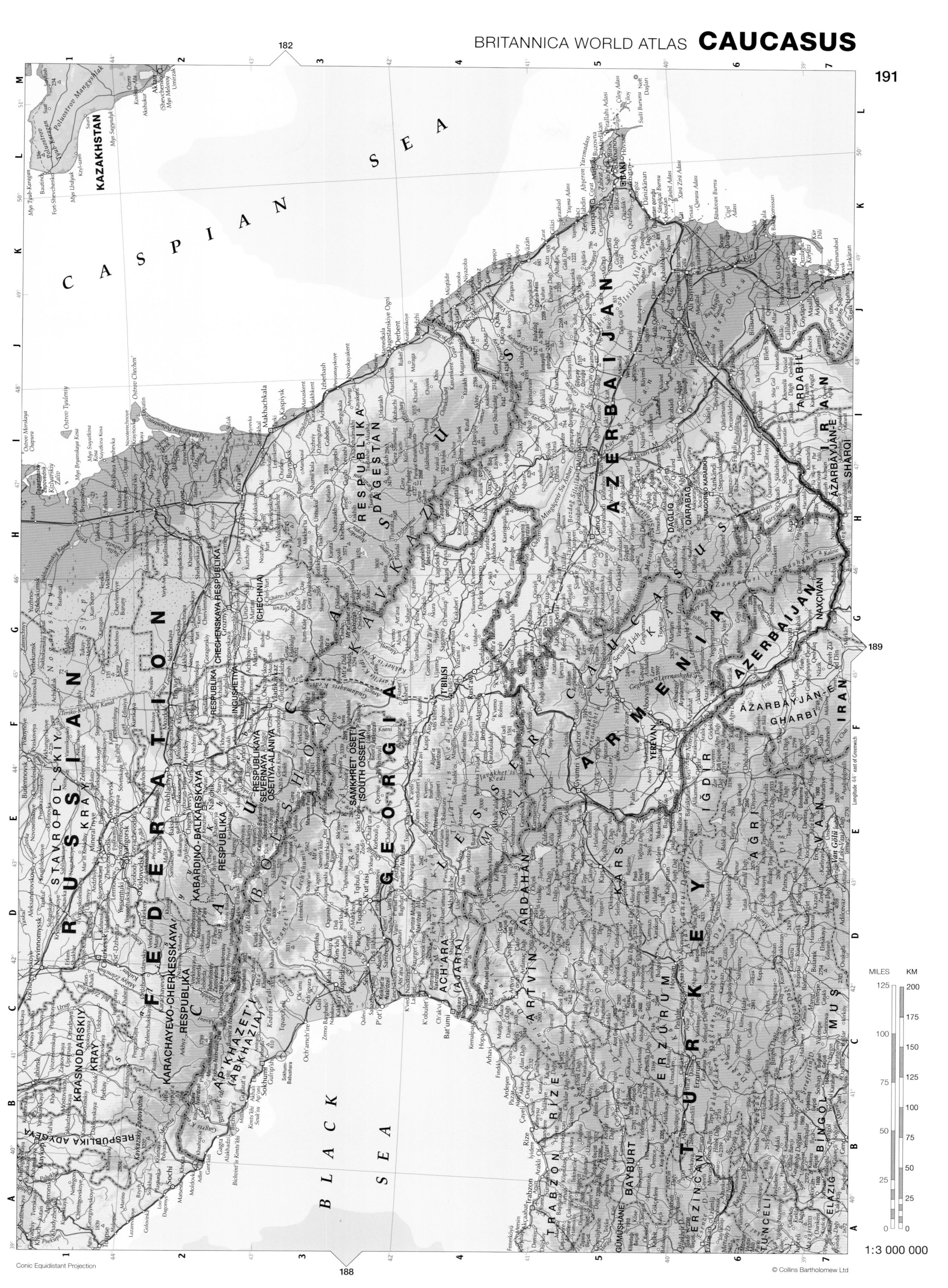

CASPIAN SEA

BLACK SEA

KAZAKHSTAN

RUSSIAN FEDERATION

STAVROPOL'SKIY KRAY

KRASNODARSKIY KRAY

RESPUBLIKA ADYGEA

KARACHAYEVO-CHERKESSKAYA RESPUBLIKA

KABARDINO-BALKARSKAYA RESPUBLIKA

RESPUBLIKA SEVERNAYA OSETIYA-ALANIYA

RESPUBLIKA INGUSHETIYA

CHECHENSKAYA RESPUBLIKA

CHECHNIA

RESPUBLIKA DAGESTAN

GEORGIA

APKHAZET'I (ABKHAZIA)

ACH'ARA (AJARIA)

SAMKHRET OSET'I (SOUTH OSSETIA)

T'BILISI

GREATER CAUCASUS

LESSER CAUCASUS

ARMENIA

YEREVAN

AZERBAIJAN

NAXÇIVAN

DAĞLIQ QARABAĞ NAGORNO KARABAKH

BAKI

SUMQAYIT

TURKEY

TRABZON

RIZE

BAYBURT

GÜMÜŞHANE

ERZURUM

ERZINCAN

ARTVİN

ARDAHAN

KARS

IĞDIR

AĞRI

VAN

MUŞ

BİNGÖL

TUNCELİ

ELAZIĞ

IRAN

ĀZARBĀYJĀN-E SHARQI

ĀZARBĀYJĀN-E GHARBI

ARDABĪL

Derbent

Makhachkala

Kaspiysk

Sochi

Bat'umi

Nevinnomyssk

Conic Equidistant Projection

© Collins Bartholomew Ltd

1:3 000 000

MILES   KM

125   200

100   175
         150
75   125
         100
50   75

25   50
         25

0   0

Longitude 44 east of Greenwich

METRES | FEET
6000 | 19686
5000 | 16404
4000 | 13124
3000 | 9843
2000 | 6562
1000 | 3281
500 | 1640
200 | 656
0 | 0
below sea level
200 | 656
2000 | 6562
4000 | 13124
6000 | 19686

Conic Equidistant Projection

RUSSIAN FEDERATION

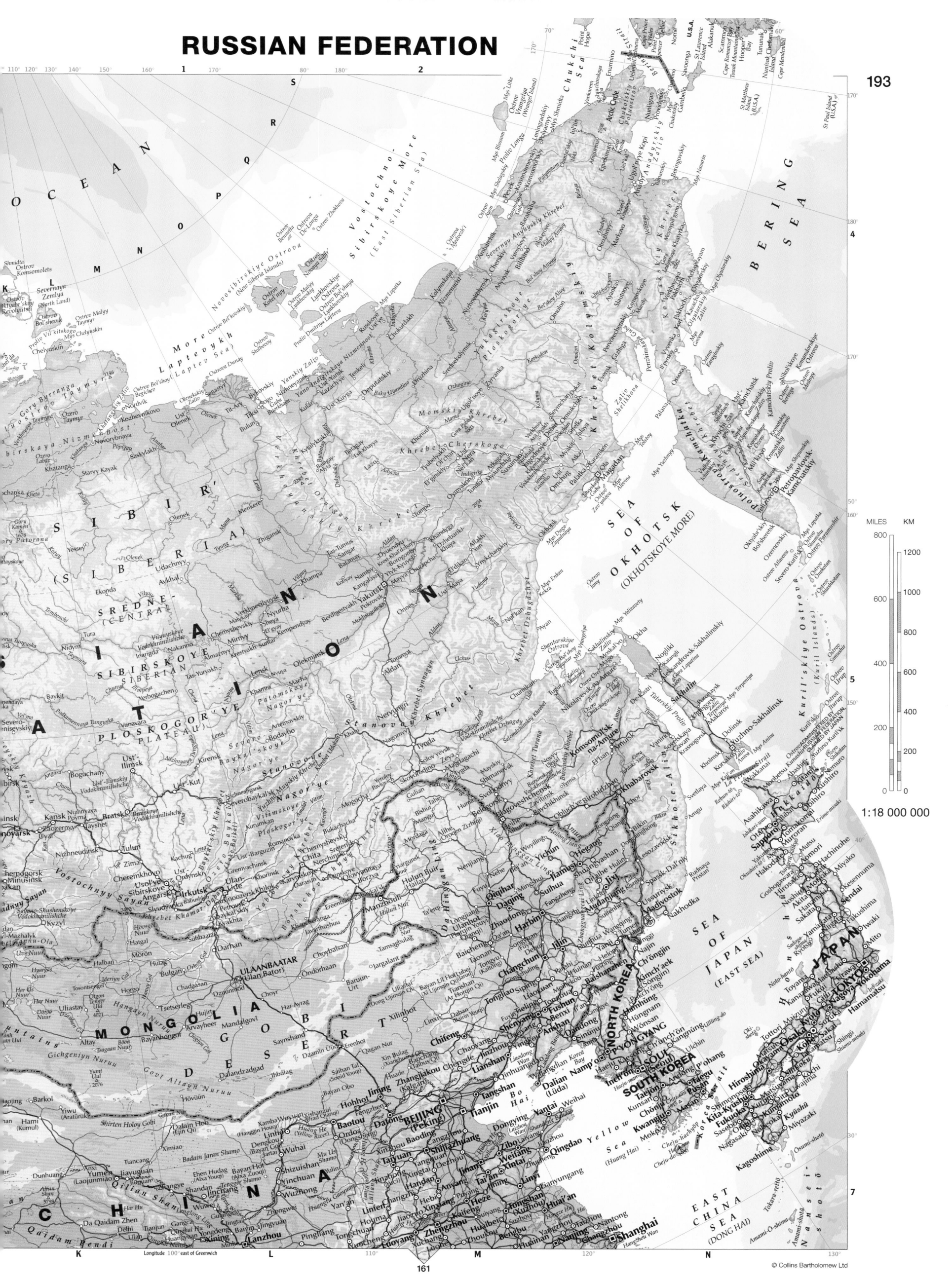
SIBERIA
SIBIR'
SREDNE-SIBIRSKOYE PLOSKOGOR'YE
CENTRAL SIBERIAN PLATEAU
Vostochno-Sibirskoye More
(East Siberian Sea)
More Laptevykh
(Laptev Sea)
SEA OF OKHOTSK
(OKHOTSKOYE MORE)
BERING SEA
SEA OF JAPAN
(EAST SEA)
EAST CHINA SEA
(DONG HAI)
Yellow Sea
(Huang Hai)
Bo Hai
MONGOLIA
GOBI DESERT
CHINA
NORTH KOREA
SOUTH KOREA
JAPAN
U.S.A.
ULAANBAATAR
(Ulan Bator)
BEIJING
(Peking)
P'YONGYANG
SEOUL
TOKYO
Shanghai
Vladivostok
Khabarovsk
Irkutsk
Yakutsk
Magadan
Petropavlovsk-Kamchatskiy
Sakhalin
Kamchatka
Hokkaidō
Kuril'skiye Ostrova
(Kuril Islands)
Novosibirskiye Ostrova
(New Siberian Islands)
Severnaya Zemlya
(North Land)
Ostrov Vrangelya
(Wrangel Island)
Chukotskiy Poluostrov
Khrebet Cherskogo
Verkhoyanskiy Khrebet
Stanovoy Khrebet
Khrebet Kolymskiy
Arctic Circle
Longitude 100° east of Greenwich
MILES
KM
1:18 000 000

A S I A

Sea of Japan
(East Sea)

Hokkaidō

Kuril'skiye Ost

East
China
Sea

Honshū

Kyūshū

Shikoku

Ogasawara-shotō

Kazan-rettō

Nansei-shotō

Chang Jiang

Taiwan Strait

Xun Jiang

Luzon Strait

Luzon

Hainan

Samar

Pagan

Tinian   Saipan   **Northern Mariana
Islands**
Rota   (U.S.A.)

Guam □ **Hagåtña**
(U.S.A.)

Ulithi   Fais
Yap   Faraulep   Pikelot   Hall Island

Ngulu   Sorol   Chuuk

C a r o l i n e   I s l a n d s

Eauripik

FEDERATED STAT

Palau Islands

Mor
Isla

Gulf of
Thailand

Palawan

Sulu
Sea

Panay   Negros

Mindanao

Celebes
Sea

Halmahera

Laut Maluka

Mussau Island

Admiralty Islands   New Hanover

New Ire

Vanimo   ● Wewak

Bismarck
Sea

Rabaul

Bay
of Bengal

90°

South China Sea

Makassar Strait

Borneo

Sulawesi

New
Guinea

Sepik

Madang

Mt Wilhelm
4509   ● Goroka
● Lae

Boug

PAPUA

Solo

Strait of Malacca

Laut
Jawa

Laut Banda

Laut Flores

Arafura Sea

Kerema   **NEW GUINEA**

Wood
Isla

Balimo

Gulf
of Papua

Port
Moresby

D'Entrecastea
Islands

Louisiade Archip

Daru

15°

Sumatera

Timor

Melville
Island

Wessel Islands

Cape Arnhem

Cape
York

Torres   Strait   Cape York

Coral Sea
Islands
Territory

(Australia)

Kepulauan Mentawai

Sumbawa

Flores

Sumba

Bali

Jawa (Java)

Timor Sea

Bathurst Island

Darwin

Arnhem
Land

Gulf
of Carpentaria

Groote
Eylandt

York
Peninsula

Cape

Wellesley
Islands

Cooktown

Gilbert

Mitchell

Great Barrier Reef

Cora
Se

Cor

**Ashmore and Cartier
Islands**
(Australia)

Cape
Londonderry

Cairns

Normanton

Townsville

Christmas Island
(Australia)

I N D I A N

O C E A N

Equator

Cape Lévêque

Broome

Halls
Creek

Wyndham

N O R T H E R N

T E R R I T O R Y

Q U E E N S L A N D

Mackay

Rockhampte
Gladsto

75°

Port
Hedland

Great Sandy
Desert

Mount Liebig
1524

Mount Isa

Cloncurry

Longreach

Gre
Divid
Range

Cocos Islands
(Australia)

Karratha

Lake
Mackay

Alice
Springs

Maryboro

Barrow Island

Newman

Lake
Disappointment

A U S T R A L I A

Charleville

Balonne

Brisba

North West Cape

Paraburdoo

Lake
Amadeus

Copper Creek (Barcoo Creek)

Toowoomba

Gold C

Darling

Grafte

Meekatharra

W E S T E R N
A U S T R A L I A

Great Victoria

S O U T H

Lake Eyre
(North)

Oodnadatta

N E W   S O U T H

Tamwor

Mount
Magnet

Leonora

Desert

A U S T R A L I A

Woomera

Port Augusta

Broken Hill

W A L E S

Newc

Lithgow

Orange

Geraldton

Lake
Moore

Kalgoorlie

Ceduna

Whyalla

Port Pirie

Wagga Wagga

Murray

Albury

Sydney
Wollonge

Great
Australian
Bight

Port Lincoln

Cape Carnot   Adelaide ⊙

A.C.T. ■ Canberra

Esperance

Kangaroo
Island

Bendigo

VICTORIA

Perth ⊙

Fremantle

Bunbury

Albany

Mount Gambier   ⊙ Melbourne
Geelong

Bass Strait   Flinders Island

Cape Leeuwin

King Island

Devonport ● Launceston

TASMANIA

⊙ Hobart

15°

South East
Cape

Tropic of Capricorn

60°   30°   75°   90°   45°   105°   120°   135°   150°

A   B   C   D   E

Orthographic Projection

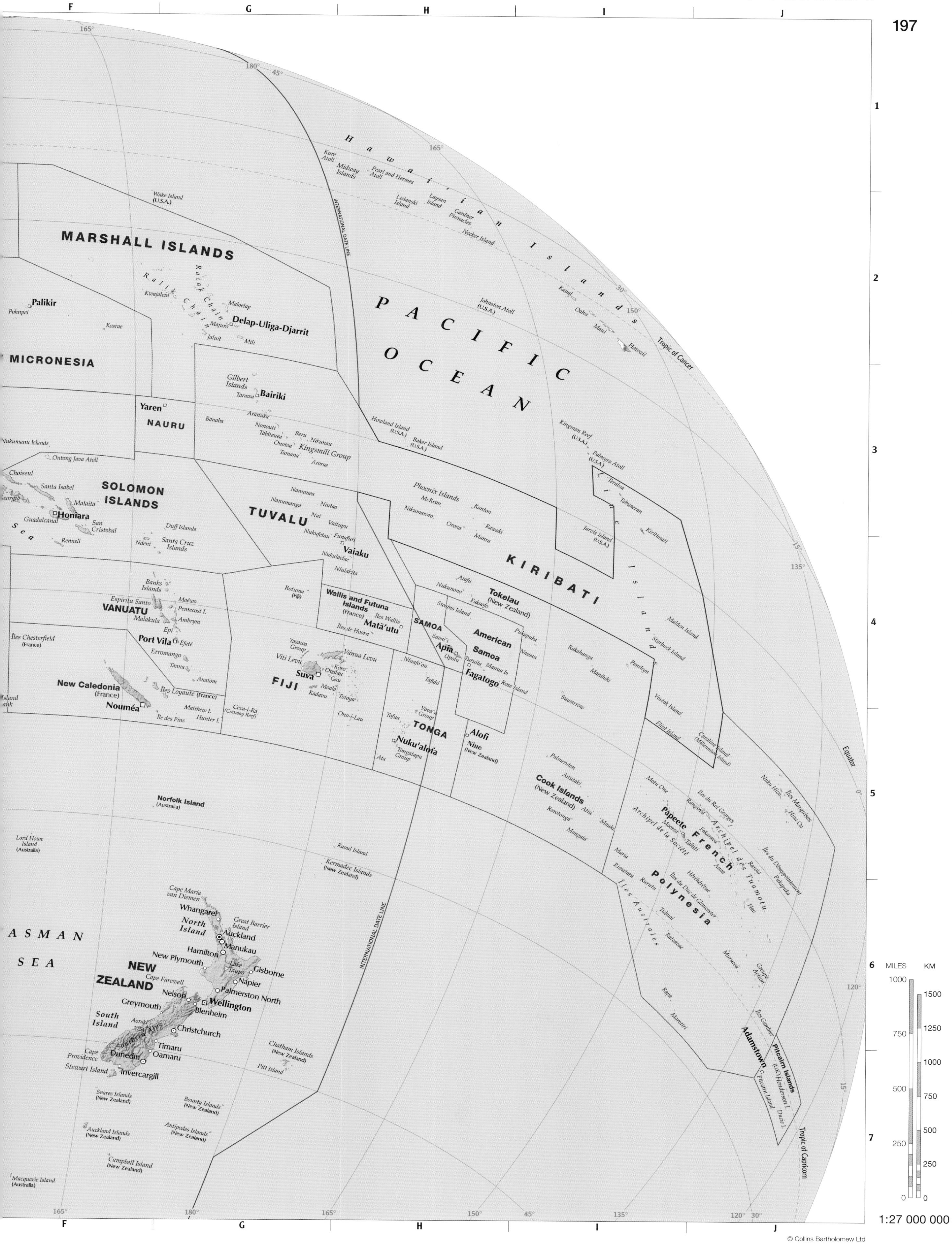

F G H I J

Hawaiian Islands

PACIFIC

OCEAN

Kure Atoll
Midway Islands
Pearl and Hermes Atoll
Lisianski Island
Laysan Island
Gardner Pinnacles
Necker Island
Kauai
Oahu
Maui
Hawaii
Tropic of Cancer

Wake Island (U.S.A.)
Johnston Atoll (U.S.A.)

MARSHALL ISLANDS

Ralik Chain *Ratak Chain*
Kwajalein
Maloelap
Majuro
Jaluit
Mili

Palikir
Pohnpei
Kosrae

MICRONESIA

Delap-Uliga-Djarrit

Gilbert Islands
Tarawa **Bairiki**

Yaren
NAURU
Banaba

Nukumanu Islands
Ontong Java Atoll

Aranuka
Nonouti
Tabiteuea
Beru Nikunau
Onotoa
Tamana
Arorae
Kingsmill Group

Howland Island (U.S.A.)
Baker Island (U.S.A.)

Kingman Reef (U.S.A.)
Palmyra Atoll (U.S.A.)
Teraina
Tabuaeran

SOLOMON ISLANDS
Choiseul
Santa Isabel
Malaita
Georgia
Guadalcanal
Honiara
San Cristobal
Rennell

Duff Islands
Ndeni
Santa Cruz Islands

Nanumea
Nanumanga Niutao
Nui Vaitupu
Nukufetau Funafuti
Vaiaku
Nukulaelae
Niulakita

Phoenix Islands
McKean
Nikumaroro
Orona
Manra
Kanton
Rawaki
Birnie

Jarvis Island (U.S.A.)
Kiritimati

TUVALU

KIRIBATI

Malden Island
Starbuck Island

Sea

Rotuma (Fiji)
Nukunonu
Atafu
Swains Island
Fakaofo
Tokelau (New Zealand)

Banks Islands
Espíritu Santo
VANUATU
Malakula
Maêwo
Pentecost I.
Ambrym
Epi
Efaté
Erromango
Tanna
Anatom

Wallis and Futuna Islands (France)
Îles Wallis
Matā'utu
Îles de Hoorn

SAMOA
Sava'i
Apia
Upolu
American Samoa
Tutuila Manua Is.
Fagatogo
Rose Island

Pukapuka
Nassau
Rakahanga
Manihiki

Penrhyn
Suwarrow

Vostok Island
Caroline Island (Millennium Island)
Flint Island

Îles Chesterfield (France)

Port Vila

Yasawa Group
Viti Levu
Vanua Levu
Koro
Ovalau Gau
Suva
Moala
Kadavu
Totoya

Niuafo'ou
Tafahi
Niuatoputapu

New Caledonia (France)
Îles Loyauté (France)
Nouméa
Île des Pins
Matthew I.
Hunter I.
Ceva-i-Ra (Conway Reef)
Ono-i-Lau

Vava'u Group
Tofua
FIJI
Ata

TONGA
Nuku'alofa
Tongatapu Group

Alofi
Niue (New Zealand)

Cook Islands (New Zealand)
Palmerston
Aitutaki
Atiu
Rarotonga Mauke
Mangaia

Maria
Rimatara
Rurutu
Tubuai

Mota One
Manuae
Maupiti
Bora Bora
Raiatea
Ranairo
Îles du Roi Georges
Îles Marquises
Nuku Hiva
Hiva Oa
Papeete French
Moorea Tahiti
Anaa
Hereheretue
Hao
Îles du Duc de Gloucester
Archipel des Tuamotu
Makatea
Îles Disappointment
Pukapuka
Rangiroa
Fakarava
Archipel de la Société
Îles Australes
Raivavae
Rapa
Marotiri
Polynesia

Norfolk Island (Australia)

Lord Howe Island (Australia)

Raoul Island
Kermadec Islands (New Zealand)

TASMAN SEA

Cape Maria van Diemen
Whangarei
North Island
Great Barrier Island
Auckland
Manukau
Hamilton
New Plymouth
Lake Taupo
Gisborne
Napier
Palmerston North
Cape Farewell
Nelson
Wellington
Greymouth
Blenheim

NEW ZEALAND

South Island
Aoraki
Southern Alps
Christchurch
Timaru
Cape Providence
Dunedin
Oamaru
Stewart Island
Invercargill

Chatham Islands (New Zealand)
Pitt Island

Adamstown
Pitcairn Islands (U.K.)
Henderson I.
Pitcairn Island
Ducie I.
Oeno I.
Îles Gambier

Snares Islands (New Zealand)
Bounty Islands (New Zealand)
Auckland Islands (New Zealand)
Antipodes Islands (New Zealand)
Campbell Island (New Zealand)
Macquarie Island (Australia)

International Date Line

Equator
Tropic of Capricorn

MILES KM
1000 1500
1250
750 1000
750
500 500
250
250
0 0

1:27 000 000

© Collins Bartholomew Ltd

INDONESIA
AUSTRALIA
INDIAN OCEAN
TIMOR SEA
ARAFURA SEA
GULF OF CARPENTARIA
Great Australian Bight
Bass Strait
BORNEO
KALIMANTAN
Sulawesi (Celebes)
LAUT JAWA (JAVA SEA)
JAWA (JAVA)
Laut Flores (Flores Sea)
Laut Banda (Banda Sea)
Laut Sawu (Savu Sea)
MALUKU (MOLUCCAS)
Halmahera
Seram
Timor
EAST TIMOR
DILI
NEW GUINEA
PAPUA NEW GUINEA
Bismarck Archipelago
Torres Strait
Gulf of Papua
PORT MORESBY
Jayapura
Makassar (Ujung Pandang)
Surabaya
Denpasar
Kupang
Ambon
Manado
Balikpapan
Samarinda
Banjarmasin
Ashmore and Cartier Islands (Australia)
WESTERN AUSTRALIA
NORTHERN TERRITORY
SOUTH AUSTRALIA
QUEENSLAND
NEW SOUTH WALES
VICTORIA
TASMANIA
Cape York Peninsula
Arnhem Land
Kimberley
Great Sandy Desert
Gibson Desert
Great Victoria Desert
Tanami Desert
Simpson Desert
Sturt Stony Desert
Barkly Tableland
Nullarbor Plain
Macdonnell Ranges
Musgrave Ranges
Hamersley Range
Lake Eyre (North)
Lake Eyre (South)
Lake Torrens
Lake Gairdner
Lake Frome
Lake Mackay
Lake Amadeus
Lake Disappointment
GREAT DIVIDING RANGE
GREAT BARRIER REEF
Darwin
Katherine
Tennant Creek
Alice Springs
Uluru (Ayers Rock) 867
Mount Isa
Townsville
Cairns
Port Hedland
Broome
Derby
Carnarvon
Geraldton
Perth
Fremantle
Bunbury
Albany
Esperance
Kalgoorlie
Adelaide
Port Augusta
Port Lincoln
Broken Hill
Mildura
Melbourne
Geelong
Hobart
Launceston
Tropic of Capricorn
Equator
METRES FEET
6000 19686
5000 16404
4000 13124
3000 9843
2000 6562
1000 3281
500 1640
200 656
0 0 below sea level
200 656
2000 6562
4000 13124
6000 19686
Longitude 140° east of Greenwich

Lambert Azimuthal Equal Area Projection

Kapingamarangi (Micronesia)

Abaiang Marakei
Tarawa
BAIRIKI Maiana
Kuria Abemama
Aranuka
Nonouti

Equator

Lyra Reef

Kavieng
Tabar Is.
Lihir Group
Tanga Is.
New Ireland
Namatanai
Feni Is.
Green Is.
C. St George
Kilinailau Is.
Buka I.
Sohano
Rabaul
Pomio
Bougainville Island
Buin Korovou
Choiseul

NEA

Nuguria Is.
Takuu Is.
Ontong Java Atoll
Roncador Reef

Nukumanu Is.

Nauru
YAREN

Banaba
(Ocean I.)

Tabiteuea
Onotoa Nikunau
Kingsmill Group
Tamana

Arorae

K I R I B A T I

Howland I.
(U.S.A.)

Baker I.
(U.S.A.)

Kanton
Enderbury
McKean Birnie
Phoenix Islands
Orona Rawaki
Manra

Nikumaroro

SOLOMON
ISLANDS

New Georgia
Santa Isabel
Buala
Vella Lavella
Kolombangara
Ranongga Gizo
New Georgia Islands
Munda
Stewart Islands
Malu'u
Malaita
HONIARA
Guadalcanal Aola
Avuavu
Maramasike

Trobriand Is.
Woodlark I.
Fergusson I.
Normanby I.
D'Entrecasteaux Is.
Louisiade Archipelago
Misima I.
Tagula I.
Conflict Group
Bwagaoia

Yandina
Kirakira
San Cristobal (Makira)
Rennell

Nupani
Lata Ndeni
Duff Islands
Swallow Islands
Santa Cruz Islands

Vanikoro Is.
Tikopia

Utupua

Cherry I.
Mitre I.

Nanumea
Niutao
Nanumanga
Nui
Nukufetau
Vaitupu

TUVALU
Funafuti VAIAKU
Nukulaelae

Niulakita

Rotuma
(Fiji)

Wallis and
Futuna Islands
(France)

MATĀ'UTU
Îles Wallis

Île Futuna Sigave
Îles de Hoorn Île Alofi

Atafu
Nukunono

Tokelau
(New Zealand)
Fakaofo

Swains I.

SAMOA

Mt Silisili Safotu
Falelima Safotu
Savai'i APIA
Poutasi Upolu
Tutuila FAGATOGO

American
Samoa
(U.S.A.)
Manua Maia'na

CORAL
SEA

Coral Sea
Islands
Territory
(Australia)

Marion Reef

Réefs
d'Entrecasteaux
Récif
Grand Passage
Grand Récif de Cook
Récifs de l'Astrolabe

Úreparapara
Mota Lava
Vanua Lava
Banks Islands
Santa Maria I.

Torres Is.

Espíritu Santo
Luganville
Norsup Mt Mérum
Malakula Maéwo
Milip Pentecost I.
Lamen Ambrym
Emaé Shepherd Is.
Úléi

VANUATU

Îles Chesterfield

PORT VILA
Efaté

Cikobia
Vetauua
Great Sea Reef
Yasawa Group
Bligh Water
Labasa Vanua Levu
Nadi (Nandi)
Lautoka
Viti Levu
Sigatoka SUVA
Vatulele
Kadavu (Kandavu)

Somosomo
Taveuni
Rabi
Koro
Koro Sea
Ovalau Levuka
Nairai
Gau
Moala
Totoya
Matuku

Northern
Lau Group
Vanua Balavu
Lakeba
Oneata

Southern
Lau Group

F I J I

Niuafo'ou
Tafahi
Niuatoputapu

Hihifo

Fonualei Tokú
Vava'u Group
Neiafu
Late Vava'u

TONGA

Ha'apai Group
Nomuka
NUKU'ALOFA
Tongatapu Group
Tongatapu 'Eua

ALOFI
Niue
(New Zealand)

Récifs d'Entrecasteaux
Récif de Cook
Grand Récif
Belep
Français
Koumac
Poindimié
Ouvéa Fayaoue
Houaïlou Lifou
Bourail Tadin Maré
Boulouparis
Dumbéa
Nouvelle Calédonie
(New Caledonia)
New Caledonia
(France)
NOUMÉA
Mont-Dore
Yaté
Grand Récif du Sud
Île des Pins

Îles Loyauté

Erromango
Anatom (Aneityum)
Tanna Yasur
Lénakel
Futuna

Matthew I.
Hunter I.

Ceva-i-Ra
(Conway Reef)

Tuvana-i-Ra
Tuvana-i-Colo
Ono-i-Lau
Vatoa

Ata

C O R A L   S E A

Swain
Reefs

Saumarez
Reef

Capricorn Channel
Rockhampton
Gladstone
Bustard Head
Miriam Vale

Cato Island
& Bank

Rockhampton
Gladstone
Bundaberg
Hervey Bay
Maryborough
Fraser Island
Childers
Gympie
Tewantin
Kingaroy
Maroochydore
Nambour
Caboolture
Toowoomba
Oakey
Beenleigh
Brisbane
Gold Coast
Beaudesert
Murwillumbah
Stanthorpe
Casino Lismore
Ballina
Glen Innes
Grafton
Coffs Harbour
Armidale
Macksville
Tamworth
Kempsey
Port Macquarie
Mount Barrington
Taree
Forster
Gloucester
Singleton
Maitland
Newcastle
The Entrance
Gosford
Wollongong
Sydney
JERVIS BAY TERRITORY
Nowra

P A C I F I C   O C E A N

Middleton Reef

Elizabeth Reef

Norfolk Island
(Australia)

Minerva
Reefs

Tropic of Capricorn

Lord Howe I.
(Australia)

T A S M A N   S E A

Three Kings
Islands
Cape Maria van Diemen
North Cape

Awanui
Kaitaia
Kawakawa
Whangarei
Dargaville
Takapuna
Great Barrier I.
Auckland
Manukau
Hamilton
Thames
Whakaari
Te Awamutu
Tauranga
Whakatane
East Cape
Te Kuiti
Rotorua
Taumarunui
Taupo Gisborne
New Plymouth
Mt Taranaki (Mt Egmont)
Wairoa
Hawera Hawke Bay
Wanganui Napier
Feilding Hastings
Palmerston North
Masterton
Richmond Lower Hutt
Westport WELLINGTON
C. Palliser

NORTH ISLAND

Raoul I.
Macauley I.
Curtis I.
Havre Rock
L'Espérance Rock

Kermadec Islands
(New Zealand)

SOUTH ISLAND
Aoraki (Mt Cook)
Greymouth
Hokitika
Cape Farewell
Nelson
Blenheim
Riwaka Tasman Bay
Kaikoura

Rangiora
Christchurch
Banks Peninsula
Ashburton
Timaru
Oamaru
Mt Aspiring
Queenstown
Alexandra
Invercargill
Milton
Balclutha
Port Chalmers
Dunedin
Bluff
Stewart I.

Chatham Islands
(New Zealand)
Chatham I.
Waitangi
Pitt I.

NEW ZEALAND

Cape Providence
South West
Snares Islands
(New Zealand)

Bounty Islands
(New Zealand)

Auckland
Islands
(New Zealand)

Antipodes Islands
(New Zealand)

Campbell I.
(New Zealand)

Macquarie
Island
(Australia)

MILES KM

800
1200
600 1000
800
400 600
400
200
200

1:18 000 000

GUAM
(U.S.A.)
1:1 000 000

SAMOA AND
AMERICAN SAMOA
1:2 500 000

SAMOA

American Samoa
(U.S.A.)

MARSHALL ISLANDS
Majuro
1:1 000 000

MARSHALL ISLANDS
Kwajalein
1:2 000 000

MICRONESIA
Pohnpei
1:1 000 000

MICRONESIA
Chuuk
1:1 500 000

VANUATU AND
NEW CALEDONIA
1:7 500 000

New Caledonia
(Nouvelle Calédonie)
(France)

Îles Loyauté
(Loyalty Islands)
(France)

Nouvelle Calédonie
(New Caledonia)

**PAPUA
NEW GUINEA**

SOLOMON ISLANDS
1:6 000 000

S O L O M O N

I S L A N D S

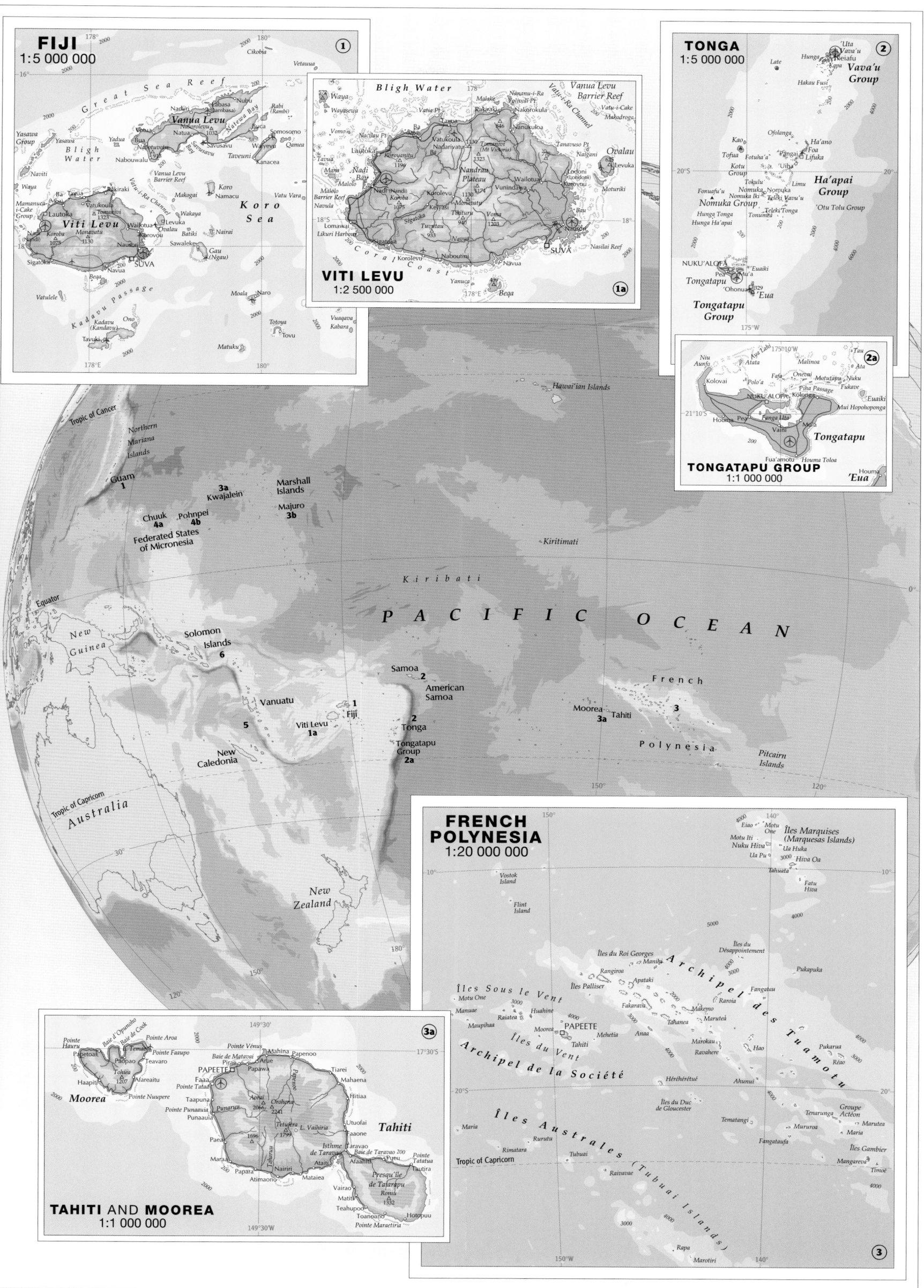

FIJI
1:5 000 000

VITI LEVU
1:2 500 000

TONGA
1:5 000 000

TONGATAPU GROUP
1:1 000 000

FRENCH POLYNESIA
1:20 000 000

TAHITI AND MOOREA
1:1 000 000

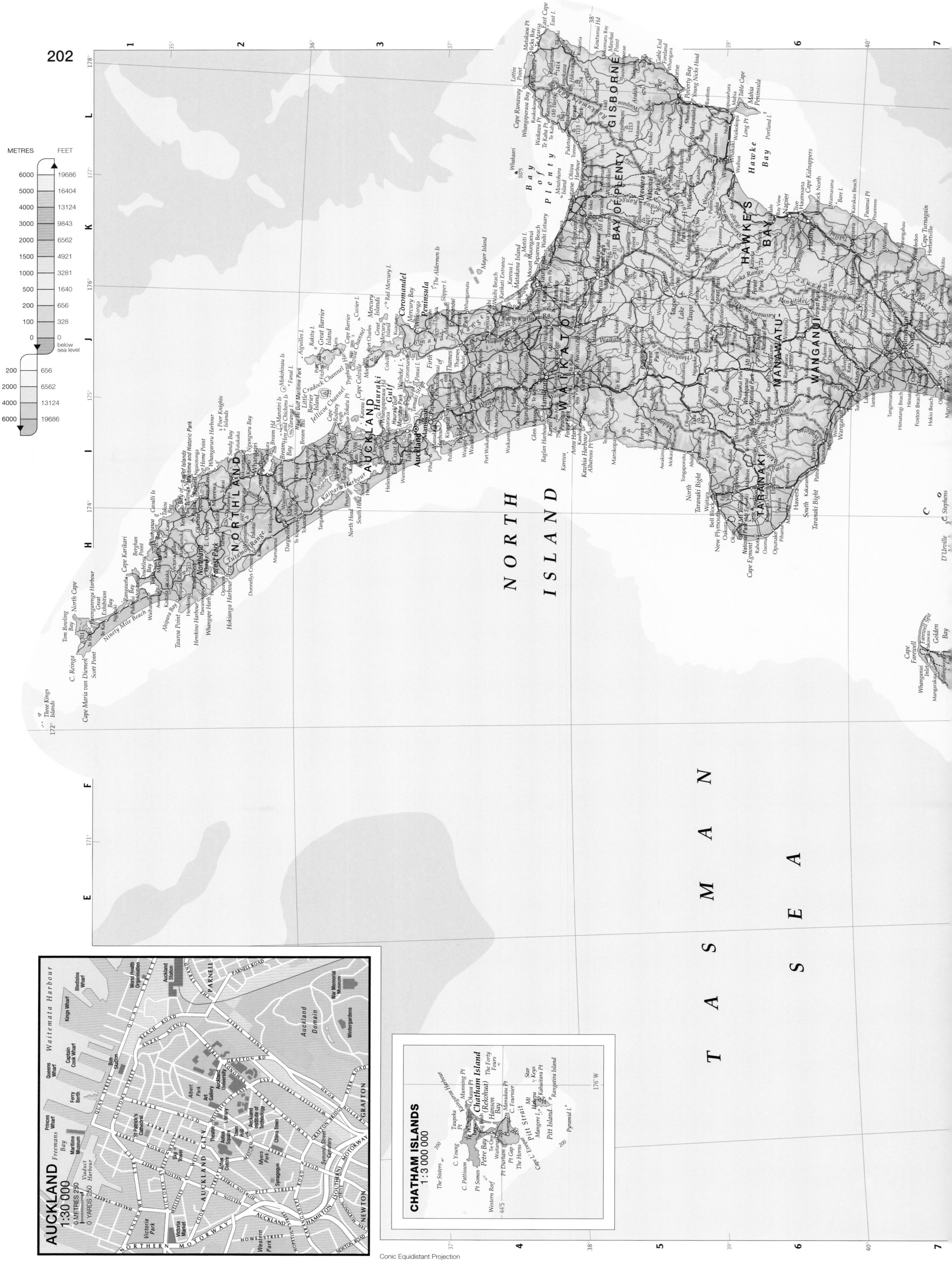
METRES
FEET
6000 19686
5000 16404
4000 13124
3000 9843
2000 6562
1500 4921
1000 3281
500 1640
200 656
100 328
0 0
below sea level
200 656
2000 6562
4000 13124
6000 19686
NORTH ISLAND
TASMAN SEA
NORTHLAND
AUCKLAND
WAIKATO
BAY OF PLENTY
GISBORNE
HAWKE'S BAY
TARANAKI
MANAWATU-WANGANUI
Bay of Plenty
Hawke Bay
Hauraki Gulf
Coromandel Peninsula
Auckland
Hamilton
Tauranga
Rotorua
Napier
Hastings
Gisborne
New Plymouth
Wanganui
Palmerston North
Taupo
Lake Taupo
Whangarei
North Cape
East Cape
Cape Egmont
Cape Reinga
Three Kings Islands
Great Barrier Island
Kaipara Harbour
North Taranaki Bight
South Taranaki Bight
Golden Bay
AUCKLAND
1:30 000
0 METRES 250
0 YARDS 250
Waitemata Harbour
Auckland Domain
Victoria Park
Western Park
CHATHAM ISLANDS
1:3 000 000
Chatham Island (Rekohua)
Pitt Island
Pitt Strait
Conic Equidistant Projection

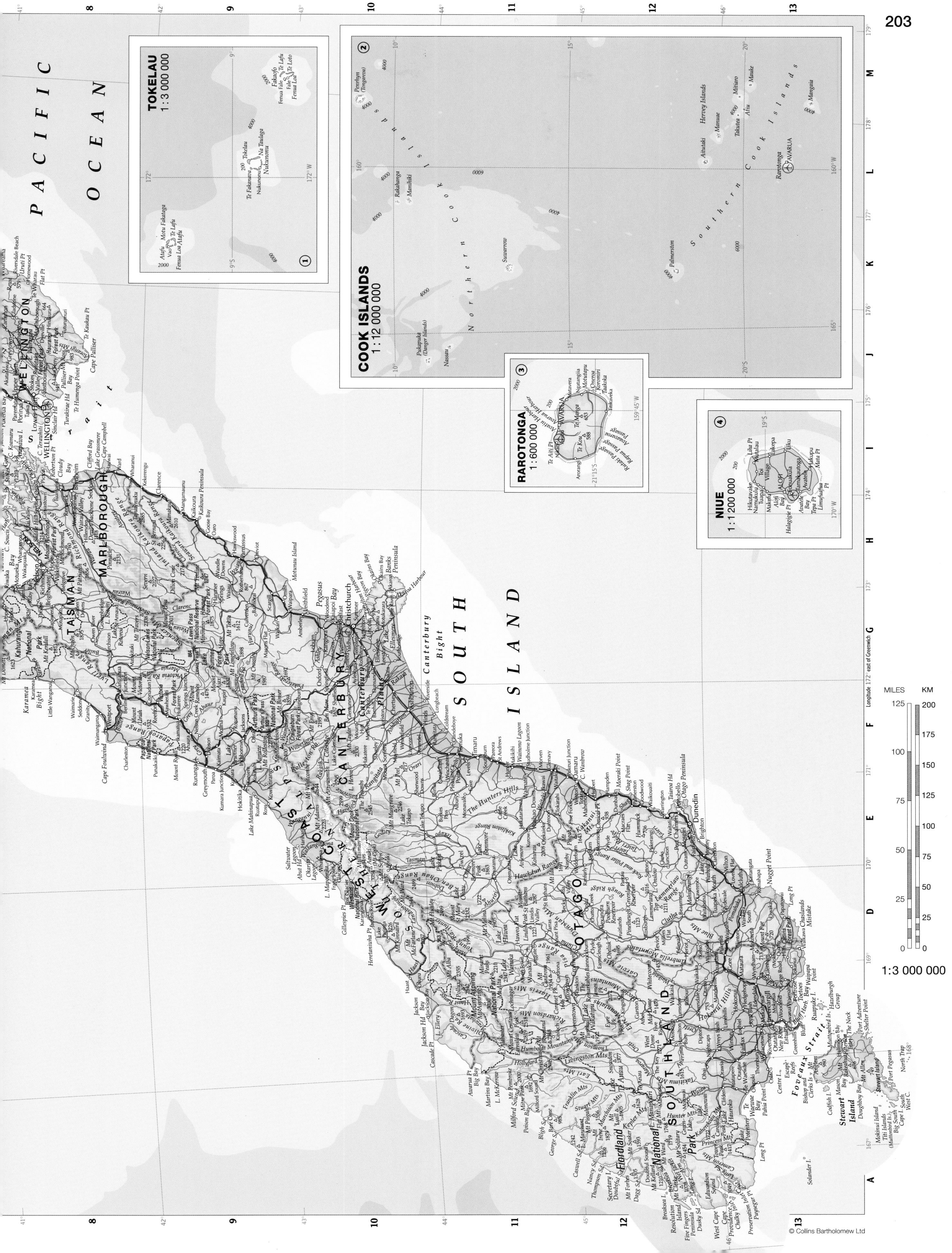

PACIFIC OCEAN

TOKELAU
1 : 3 000 000

Atafu
Motu Fakataga
Te Lafu
Vao
Fenua Loa Atafu

Te Fakanava
Nukunonu
Na Taulaga
Nukunonu

Fakaofo
Fenua Fala
Fale
Te Lulu
Te Loto
Te Lafu

COOK ISLANDS
1 : 12 000 000

Penrhyn
(Tongareva)

Rakahanga
Manihiki

Pukapuka
(Danger Islands)

Nassau

Suwarrow

Palmerston

Northern Cook

Southern Cook Islands

Cook Islands

Nassau

Hervey Islands
Manuae
Aitutaki
Manuae
Takutea
Atiu
Miti'aro
Mauke

Rarotonga
AVARUA
Mangaia

RAROTONGA
1 : 600 000

AVARUA
Matavera
Ngatangiia
Te Manga
653
Motu
Takitaki

North Harbour
Te Aiti Pt
Te Koi
588

Raemaru
Arorangi
Rutaki Passage
Avana
Harbour

NIUE
1 : 1 200 000

Hikutavake
Namukulu
Makefu
Alofi
Bay
ALOFI
Hakupu
Liku
Avatele

Mata Pt
Tepa Pt
Limufuefue
Bay
Halagigie Pt
Tamakautoga

PACIFIC OCEAN

WELLINGTON

Cape Palliser
Palliser Bay

Cook Strait

MARLBOROUGH

TASMAN

National Park

Kahurangi National Park

Cape Farewell

WEST COAST

SOUTH ISLAND

Christchurch

Pegasus Bay

Banks Peninsula

CANTERBURY

Canterbury Bight

Mount Cook National Park

Mount Aspiring National Park

Arthur's Pass National Park

Timaru

Oamaru

Dunedin

OTAGO

SOUTHLAND

Fiordland National Park

Stewart Island

Foveaux Strait

Bluff

Invercargill

Nugget Point

MILES
125
100
75
50
25
0

KM
200
175
150
125
100
75
50
25
0

1 : 3 000 000

Longitude 172° east of Greenwich

© Collins Bartholomew Ltd

SOUTH AUSTRALIA
WESTERN AUSTRALIA
GREAT VICTORIA DESERT
GREAT AUSTRALIAN BIGHT
Nullarbor Plain
Anangu Pitjantjatjara Aboriginal Lands
Warakurna-Wingellina-Irrunytju Aboriginal Reserve
Great Victoria Desert Conservation Park
Great Victoria Desert Nature Reserve
Maralinga-Tjarutja Aboriginal Lands
Woomera Prohibited Area
Nullarbor Regional Reserve
Nullarbor National Park
Musgrave Ranges
Tomkinson Ranges
Simpson Desert Regional Reserve
Sturt Stony Desert
Lake Eyre (North)
Lake Eyre (South)
Lake Torrens
Lake Gairdner
Lake Frome
FLINDERS RANGES
Gawler Ranges
Eyre Peninsula
Spencer Gulf
Gulf St Vincent
Kangaroo Island
Investigator Strait
Adelaide
Port Augusta
Port Pirie
Port Lincoln
Whyalla
Mount Gambier
Ceduna
Coober Pedy
Woomera
206
209
NORFOLK ISLAND ①
1 : 900 000
LORD HOWE ISLAND ②
1 : 900 000
MACQUARIE ISLAND ③
1 : 900 000
METRES
FEET
6000 19686
5000 16404
4000 13124
3000 9843
2000 6562
1000 3281
500 1640
200 656
0 0 below sea level
200 656
2000 6562
4000 13124
6000 19686
MELBOURNE
1:30 000
METRES 250
YARDS 250
Longitude 140° east of Greenwich
Lambert Azimuthal Equal Area Projection

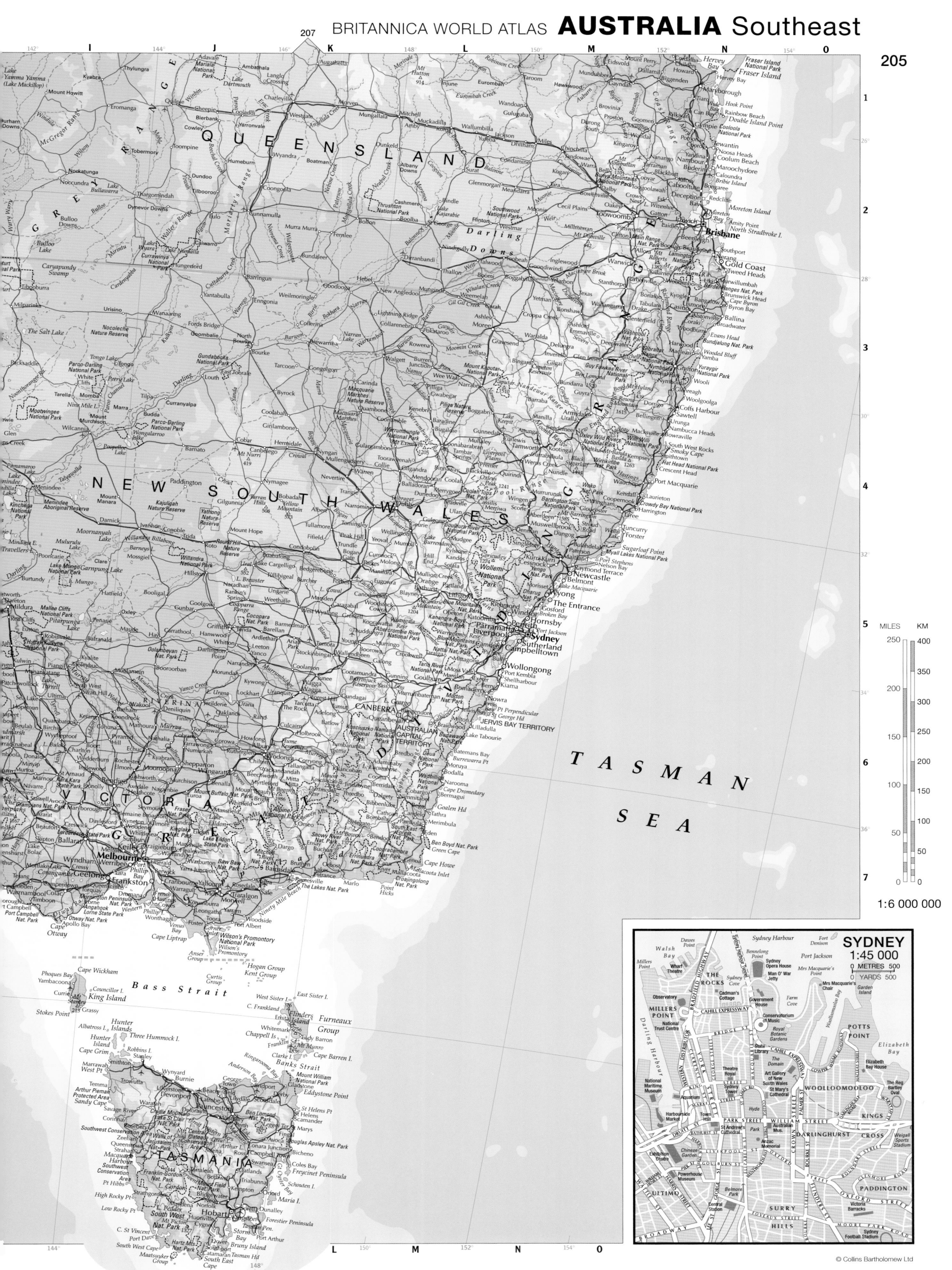

© Collins Bartholomew Ltd

207
QUEENSLAND
NEW SOUTH WALES
VICTORIA
TASMANIA
AUSTRALIAN CAPITAL TERRITORY
JERVIS BAY TERRITORY
TASMAN SEA
Bass Strait
GREY RANGE
GREAT DIVIDING RANGE
Brisbane
Sydney
Canberra
Melbourne
Hobart
Newcastle
Wollongong
Gold Coast
Toowoomba
Geelong
Launceston
Fraser Island
King Island
Furneaux Group
Flinders Island
MILES
KM
1:6 000 000
SYDNEY
1:45 000
METRES 500
YARDS 500
Sydney Harbour
Darling Harbour
THE ROCKS
MILLERS POINT
POTTS POINT
WOOLLOOMOOLOO
KINGS CROSS
DARLINGHURST
PADDINGTON
SURRY HILLS
ULTIMO
Sydney Opera House
Royal Botanic Gardens
Hyde Park
Sydney Tower
Central Station
Sydney Football Stadium

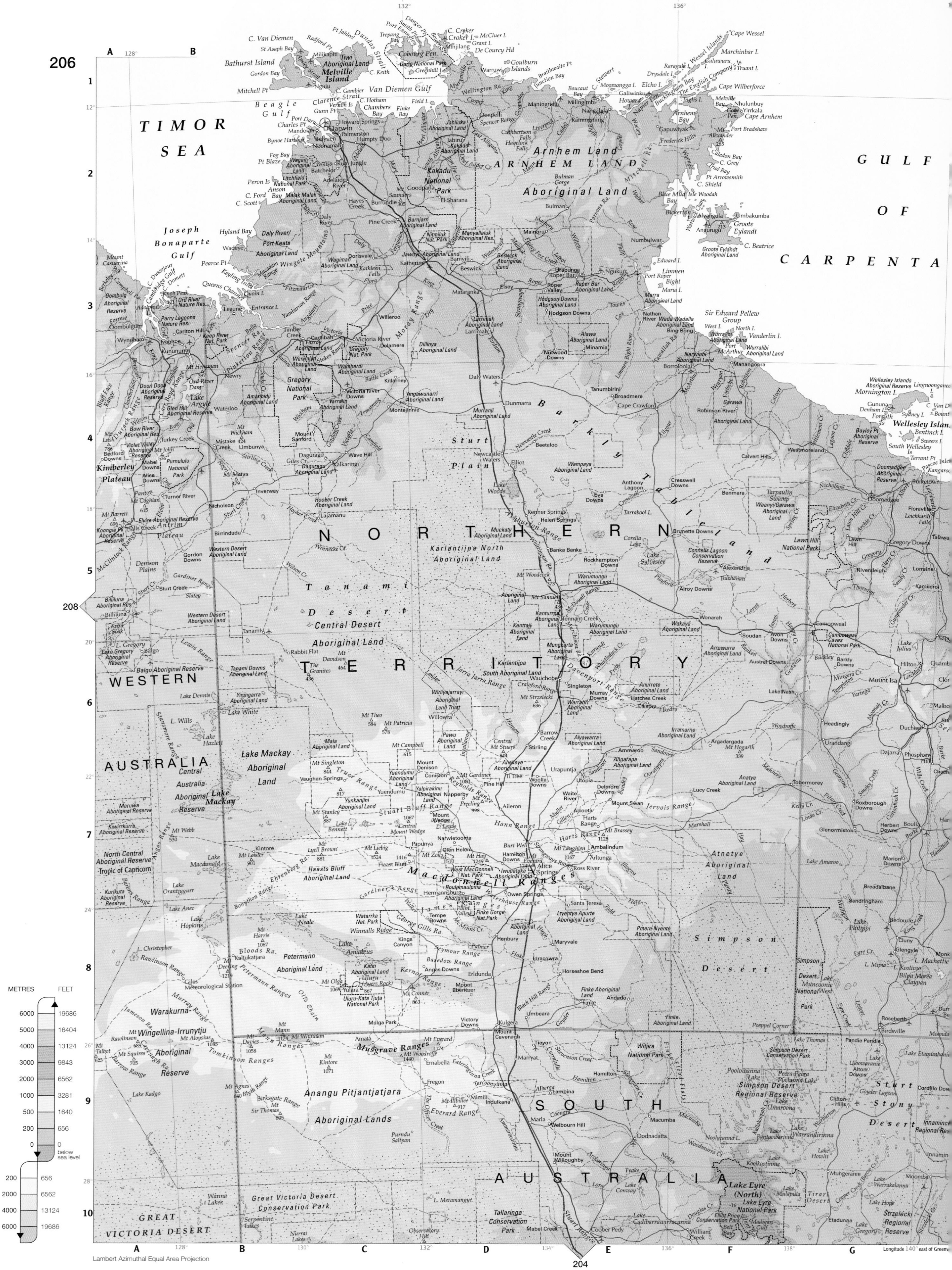

TIMOR
SEA

*Joseph
Bonaparte
Gulf*

GULF
OF
CARPENTARIA

Beagle
Gulf

Van Diemen Gulf

Bathurst Island

Melville
Island

Tiwi
Aboriginal Land

Cobourg Pen.

Arnhem Land
ARNHEM LAND
Aboriginal Land

Kakadu
National
Park

Darwin

Katherine

Daly Waters

Barkly Tableland

Gregory
National
Park

Lake
Argyle

Kimberley
Plateau

NORTHERN

Sturt
Plain

Tanami

Desert

Central Desert
Aboriginal Land

Lake
Woods

Tennant Creek

TERRITORY

WESTERN

AUSTRALIA

Lake Mackay
Aboriginal
Land

Central
Australia
Aboriginal
Reserve

Lake
Mackay

Tanami
Desert

Reynolds Range

Macdonnell Ranges

Alice Springs

Hann Range

Harts Range

Atnetye
Aboriginal
Land

Tropic of Capricorn

Haasts Bluff
Aboriginal Land

Petermann
Aboriginal Land

Musgrave Ranges

Simpson
Desert

Uluru-Kata Tjuta
National Park

Anangu Pitjantjatjara
Aboriginal Lands

Warakurna

Wingellina-Irrunytju
Aboriginal
Reserve

SOUTH

Simpson Desert
Regional Reserve

Sturt
Stony
Desert

Lake Eyre
(North)

Lake Eyre
National Park

AUSTRALIA

GREAT

VICTORIA DESERT

Great Victoria Desert
Conservation Park

Lambert Azimuthal Equal Area Projection

Longitude 140° east of Greenwich

METRES   FEET
6000   19686
5000   16404
4000   13124
3000   9843
2000   6562
1000   3281
500   1640
200   656
0   0
          below
          sea level
200   656
2000   6562
4000   13124
6000   19686

AUSTRALIA Northeast

PAPUA NEW GUINEA

C O R A L   S E A

Coral Sea Islands Territory

CAPE YORK PENINSULA

GREAT DIVIDING RANGE

Q U E E N S L A N D

GREAT BARRIER REEF

Great Barrier Reef Marine Park (Far North Section)

Great Barrier Reef Marine Park (Cairns Section)

Great Barrier Reef Marine Park (Central Section)

Great Barrier Reef Marine Park (Capricorn Section)

Gregory Range

Cairns

Townsville

Rockhampton

Gladstone

Bundaberg

Maryborough

Fraser Island National Park

Brisbane

Tropic of Capricorn

Darling Downs

Carnarvon National Park

Swain Reefs

Willis Group

Herald Cays

Flinders Reefs

1:6 000 000

MILES / KM

250 / 400
350
200 / 300
250
150 / 200
100 / 150
50 / 100
50
0 / 0

© Collins Bartholomew Ltd

205

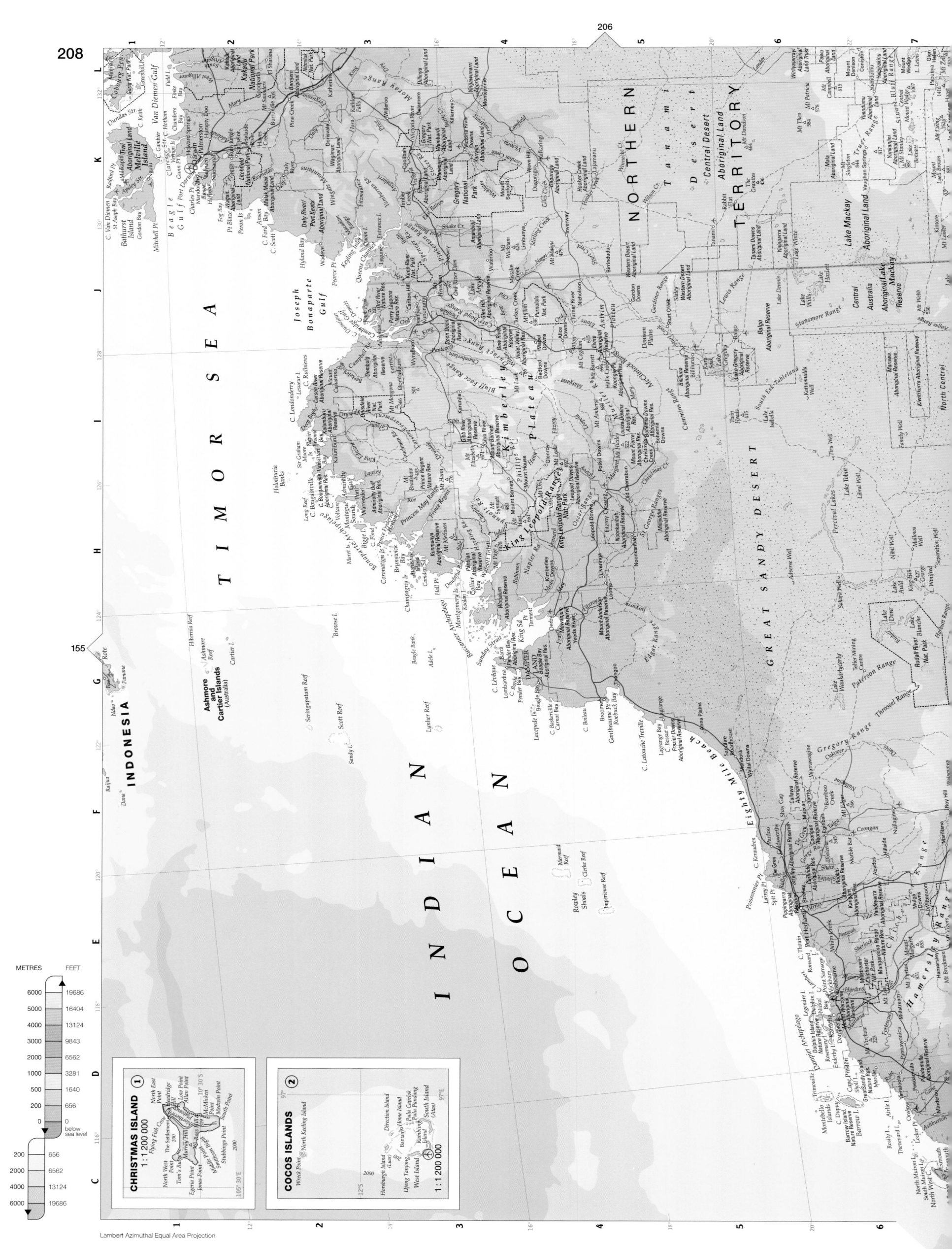

155

METRES | FEET

6000 | 19686
5000 | 16404
4000 | 13124
3000 | 9843
2000 | 6562
1000 | 3281
500 | 1640
200 | 656
0 |
| below
| sea level

200 | 656
2000 | 6562
4000 | 13124
6000 | 19686

CHRISTMAS ISLAND ①
1:1 200 000

COCOS ISLANDS ②
1:1 200 000

Lambert Azimuthal Equal Area Projection

1:6 000 000

© Collins Bartholomew Ltd

WESTERN AUSTRALIA
SOUTH AUSTRALIA
GREAT AUSTRALIAN BIGHT
GIBSON DESERT
GREAT VICTORIA DESERT
Little Sandy Desert
Nullarbor Plain
Great Victoria Desert Nature Reserve
Gibson Desert Nature Reserve
Nullarbor National Park
Nullarbor Regional Reserve
Maralinga-Tjarutja Aboriginal Lands
Anangu Pitjantjatjara Aboriginal Lands
Perth
Fremantle
Mandurah
Bunbury
Geraldton
Kalgoorlie
Esperance
Albany
Carnarvon
Shark Bay
Houtman Abrolhos
Eucla
Tropic of Capricorn
Longitude 120° east of Greenwich
MILES
KM

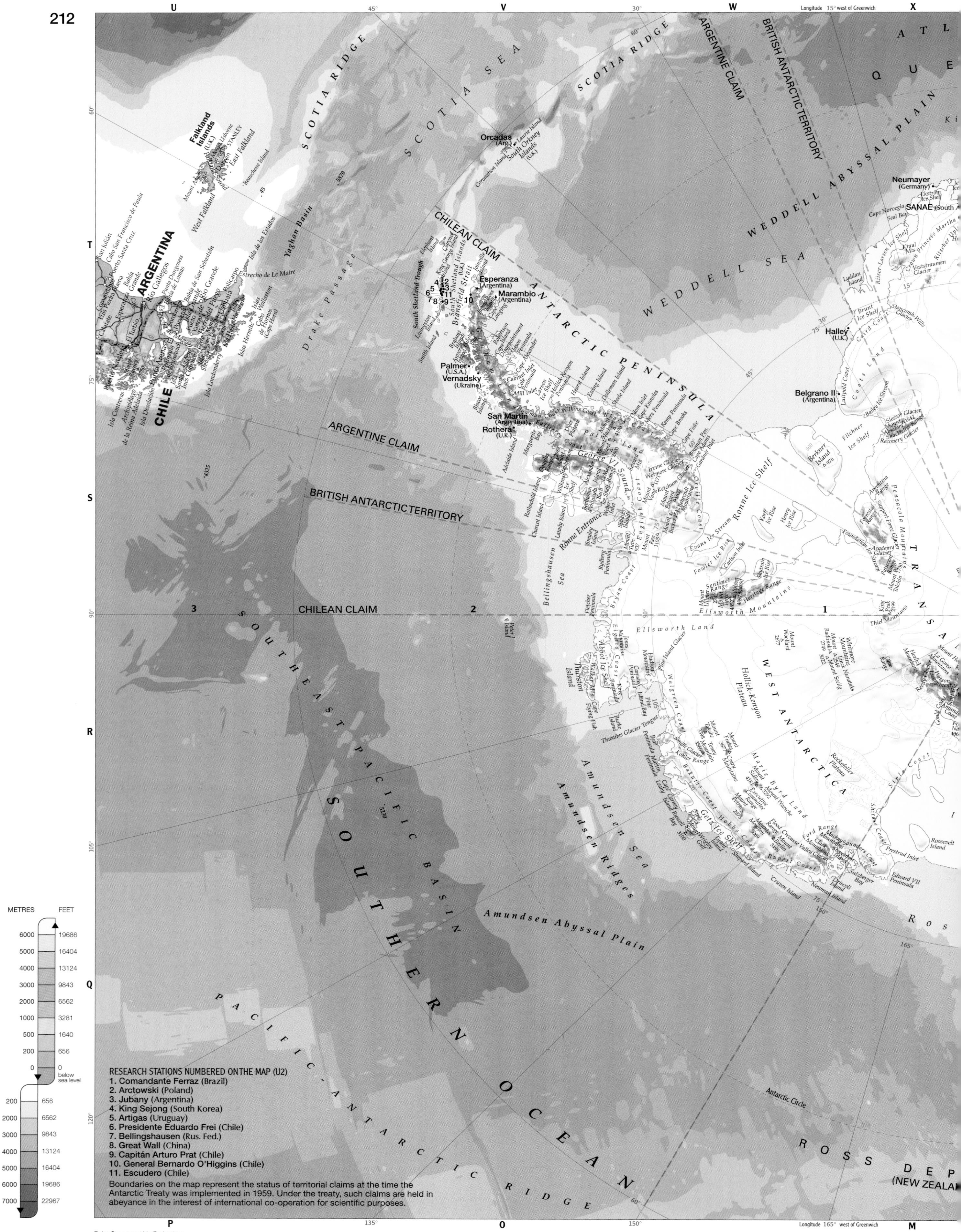

U 45° V 30° W Longitude 15° west of Greenwich X

SCOTIA RIDGE
SCOTIA SEA
SCOTIA RIDGE
ARGENTINE CLAIM
BRITISH ANTARCTIC TERRITORY

WEDDELL ABYSSAL PLAIN

Orcadas (Arg.)
South Orkney Islands (U.K.)

Neumayer (Germany)
SANAE (South Af.)

Falkland Islands (U.K.)
Stanley
East Falkland
West Falkland

ARGENTINA
CHILE

CHILEAN CLAIM

Esperanza (Argentina)
Marambio (Argentina)

WEDDELL SEA

Halley (U.K.)

ANTARCTIC PENINSULA

Drake Passage

South Shetland Islands
Bransfield Strait

Palmer (U.S.A.)
Vernadsky (Ukraine)

Belgrano II (Argentina)

San Martin (Argentina)
Rothera (U.K.)

ARGENTINE CLAIM

George VI Sound

Ronne Ice Shelf

Berkner Island

Filchner Ice Shelf

BRITISH ANTARCTIC TERRITORY

Pensacola Mountains

Bellingshausen Sea

Ronne Entrance

Fowler Ice Rise

90° CHILEAN CLAIM 2

SOUTH EAST PACIFIC BASIN

Sentinel Range
Ellsworth Mountains
Heritage Range

Peter I Island

3

Ellsworth Land

WEST ANTARCTICA

Hollick-Kenyon Plateau

Abbot Ice Shelf
Thurston Island

Amundsen Sea

Marie Byrd Land

Amundsen Ridges

Thwaites Glacier Tongue

Getz Ice Shelf

Amundsen Abyssal Plain

Executive Committee Range

Ford Ranges

Rockefeller Plateau

Roosevelt Island

Eduard VII Peninsula

PACIFIC-ANTARCTIC RIDGE

SOUTHERN OCEAN

Antarctic Circle

ROSS SEA

ROSS DEPENDENCY (NEW ZEALAND)

Polar Stereographic Projection

METRES | FEET
6000 | 19686
5000 | 16404
4000 | 13124
3000 | 9843
2000 | 6562
1000 | 3281
500 | 1640
200 | 656
0 | 0
| below sea level
200 | 656
2000 | 6562
3000 | 9843
4000 | 13124
5000 | 16404
6000 | 19686
7000 | 22967

RESEARCH STATIONS NUMBERED ON THE MAP (U2)
1. Comandante Ferraz (Brazil)
2. Arctowski (Poland)
3. Jubany (Argentina)
4. King Sejong (South Korea)
5. Artigas (Uruguay)
6. Presidente Eduardo Frei (Chile)
7. Bellingshausen (Rus. Fed.)
8. Great Wall (China)
9. Capitán Arturo Prat (Chile)
10. General Bernardo O'Higgins (Chile)
11. Escudero (Chile)

Boundaries on the map represent the status of territorial claims at the time the
Antarctic Treaty was implemented in 1959. Under the treaty, such claims are held in
abeyance in the interest of international co-operation for scientific purposes.

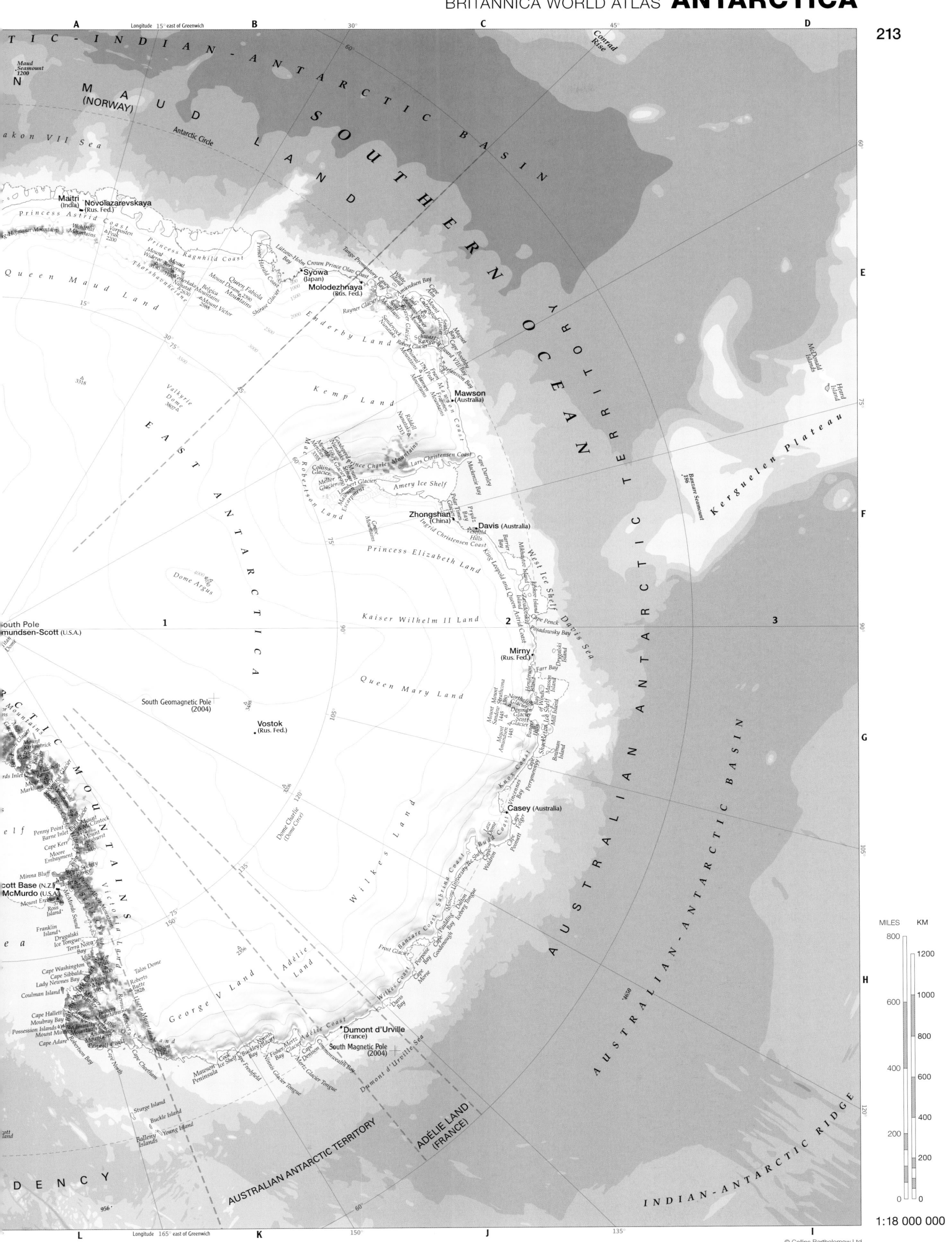

1:18 000 000

© Collins Bartholomew Ltd

F
G
J
K
2
3
Longitude 15° east of Greenwich
Longitude 165° east of Greenwich
SOUTHERN OCEAN
ATLANTIC-INDIAN-ANTARCTIC BASIN
AUSTRALIAN-ANTARCTIC BASIN
INDIAN-ANTARCTIC RIDGE
Kerguelen Plateau
Conrad Rise
McDonald Islands
Heard Island
Banzare Seamount 186
Maud Seamount 1200
MAUD LAND (NORWAY)
Antarctic Circle
Princess Astrid Coast
Princess Ragnhild Coast
Queen Maud Land
Enderby Land
Kemp Land
Mac Robertson Land
Princess Elizabeth Land
Kaiser Wilhelm II Land
Queen Mary Land
Wilkes Land
Adélie Land
George V Land
EAST ANTARCTICA
Valkyrie Dome 3807
Dome Argus
Dome Charlie (Dome Circe)
Talos Dome
AUSTRALIAN ANTARCTIC TERRITORY
ADÉLIE LAND (FRANCE)
Maitri (India)
Novolazarevskaya (Rus. Fed.)
Syowa (Japan)
Molodezhnaya (Rus. Fed.)
Mawson (Australia)
Zhongshan (China)
Davis (Australia)
Mirny (Rus. Fed.)
Casey (Australia)
Dumont d'Urville (France)
Vostok (Rus. Fed.)
South Pole
Amundsen-Scott (U.S.A.)
Scott Base (N.Z.)
McMurdo (U.S.A.)
South Geomagnetic Pole (2004)
South Magnetic Pole (2004)
Amery Ice Shelf
Lambert Glacier
Prince Charles Mountains
Lars Christensen Coast
Mawson Coast
Ingrid Christensen Coast
West Ice Shelf
Shackleton Ice Shelf
Davis Sea
Knox Coast
Budd Coast
Sabrina Coast
Banzare Coast
Wilkes Coast
Adélie Coast
Dumont d'Urville Sea
Mertz Glacier Tongue
Ninnis Glacier Tongue
Mawson Peninsula
Pennell Coast
Cape Adare
Balleny Islands
Sturge Island
Buckle Island
Young Island
Coulman Island
Ross Island
Mount Erebus
McMurdo Sound
Victoria Land
Cape Hallett
Drygalski Ice Tongue
Terra Nova Bay
Roberts Butte 2828
Mount Kirkpatrick
Possession Islands
Moubray Bay
Cape North
Frost Glacier
Cape Darnley
Mackenzie Bay
Amundsen Bay
Cape Poinsett
Vincennes Bay
Bowman Island
Mill Island
Masson Island
Drygalski Island
Cape Penck
Posadowsky Bay
Farr Bay
MILES
KM
600
400
200
1200
1000
600
400
200

ATLANTIC OCEAN

1:48 000 000

Lambert Azimuthal Equal Area Projection

© Collins Bartholomew Ltd

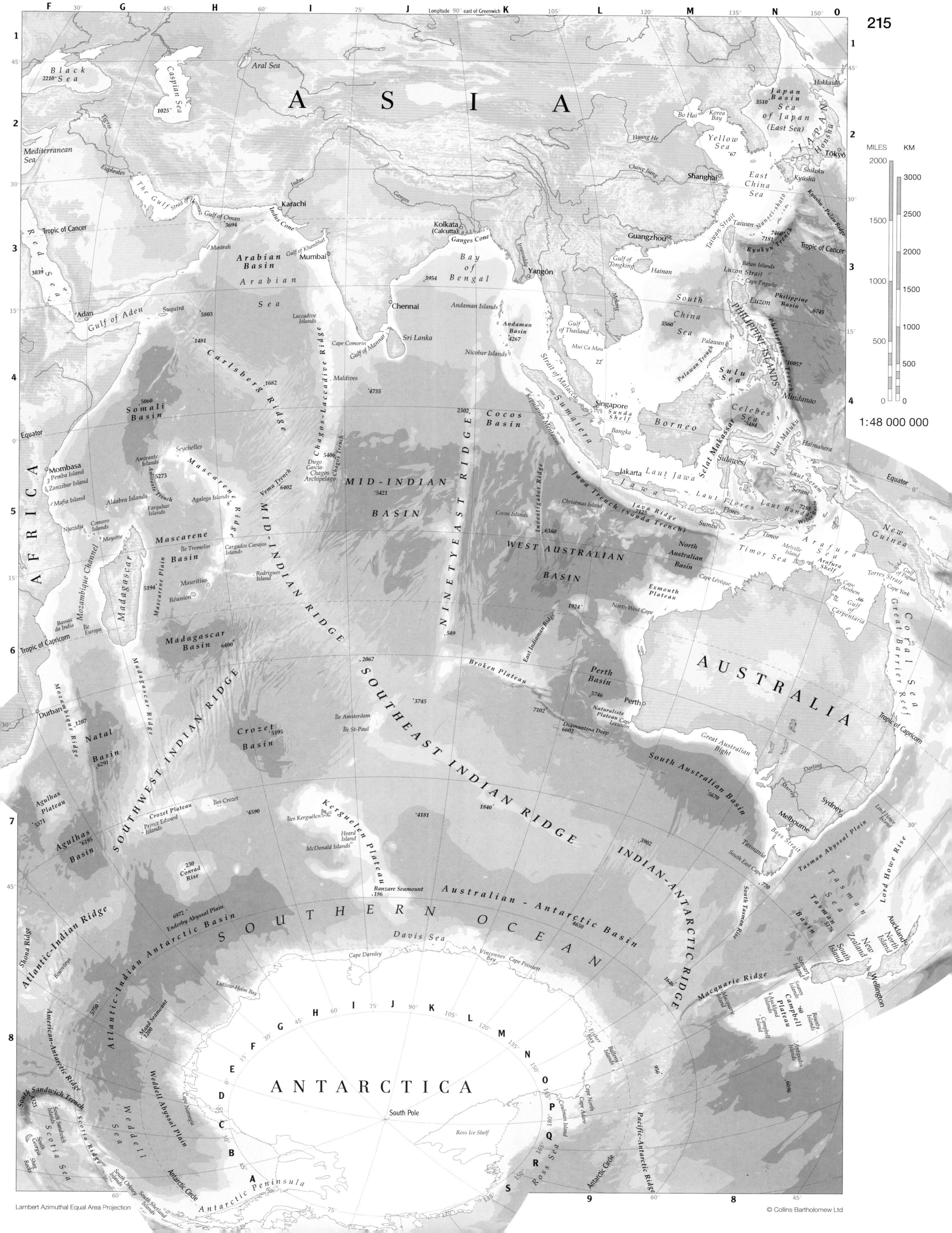

Longitude 90° east of Greenwich

MILES KM
2000 — 3000
1500 — 2500
— 2000
1000 — 1500
— 1000
500 — 500
0 — 0

1:48 000 000

A S I A

Black Sea 2210
Aral Sea
Caspian Sea 1025
Mediterranean Sea
Euphrates
Tigris
Red Sea 3039
Tropic of Cancer

Strait of Hormuz
Gulf of Oman
The Gulf
Karachi
Indus
Indus Cone 3694
Mastrah
Gulf of Aden
Adan
Suqutra 5803

Arabian Basin
Gulf of Khambhat
Mumbai
Arabian Sea
1481
Laccadive Islands
Cape Comorin
Gulf of Mannar
Chennai
Sri Lanka
3954
Maldives 4735

Ganges
Kolkata (Calcutta)
Ganges Cone
Bay of Bengal
Yangon
Andaman Islands
Andaman Basin 4267
Nicobar Islands

Huang He
Chang Jiang
Shanghai
Guangzhou
Gulf of Tongking
Hainan
South China Sea 5560
Gulf of Thailand
Mui Ca Mau 22
Strait of Malacca
Singapore
Sunda Shelf

Bo Hai
Yellow Sea 67
Korea Bay
East China Sea
Taiwan Strait
Ryukyu Trench 7460 7181
Batan Islands
Luzon Strait
Cape Engaño
Luzon
Philippine Basin 6745
PHILIPPINE ISLANDS
10057
Mindanao

Japan Basin Sea of Japan (East Sea) 3510
Hokkaido
Honshu
Tokyo
Shikoku
Kyushu
Tropic of Cancer

Carlsberg Ridge
1682
Somali Basin 5060
Seychelles
Amirante Islands 5273
Adnirante Trench
Aldabra Islands
Farquhar Islands
Agalega Islands
Mascarene Ridge

Chagos-Laccadive Ridge
Vema Trench 5406
Diego Garcia
Chagos Archipelago
Chagos Trench 6402

MID-INDIAN BASIN 5421

NINETYEAST RIDGE
2302
Cocos Basin
Cocos Islands
6360
WEST AUSTRALIAN BASIN

Investigator Ridge
Sumatera
Kepulauan Mentawai
Java Trench (Sunda Trench) 7125
Christmas Island
Java Ridge

Jakarta
Laut Jawa
Jawa
Bangka
Borneo
Selat Makassar
Sulawesi
Laut Banda 7258
Flores
Laut Flores
Sumba
Timor
Arafura Sea
North Australian Basin
Timor Sea

Celebes Sea 5484
Laut Maluku
Halmahera
New Guinea
Equator

AFRICA
Mombasa
Pemba Island
Zanzibar Island
Mafia Island
Njazidja
Comoro Islands
Mayotte

Mascarene Basin
Île Tromelin
Cargados Carajos Islands
Mauritius
Réunion
Rodrigues Island

Madagascar
Mascarene Plain 5194
MID-INDIAN RIDGE

Madagascar Basin 6400
2067
3745

Exmouth Plateau
1924
North West Cape
Cape Léveque
Arafura Shelf
Cape Arnhem
Cape York
Gulf of Carpentaria
Torres Strait
Gulf of Papua
66

AUSTRALIA

Broken Plateau
East Indiaman Ridge
7102
Perth Basin 5746
Perth
Naturaliste Plateau Cape Leeuwin
Diamantina Deep 6602
Great Australian Bight
South Australian Basin 5670
Darling
Murray
Sydney
Melbourne

SOUTHWEST INDIAN RIDGE
SOUTHEAST INDIAN RIDGE
Île Amsterdam
Île St-Paul
Crozet Basin 5195
Îles Crozet
Îles Kerguelen
Heard Island
McDonald Islands
Kerguelen Plateau
4590
4181
1840
3902

INDIAN-ANTARCTIC RIDGE
Tasmania
South East Cape
770
South Tasman Rise
Tasman Abyssal Plain
Bass Strait
Tasman Basin 5596
Lord Howe Rise
Lord Howe Island
New Zealand
North Island
South Island
Wellington
Auckland Islands
Campbell Plateau 90
Campbell Island
Bounty Islands
Antipodes Islands
Snares Islands
Stewart Island
Macquarie Ridge
Macquarie Island
956

Durban
Mozambique Ridge 1207
Natal Basin 6291
Bassas da India
Île Europa
Mozambique Channel
Madagascar Ridge
Crozet Plateau
Prince Edward Islands
230 Conrad Rise
Banzare Seamount 186
Australian-Antarctic Basin 4650

Agulhas Plateau 5371
Agulhas Basin 6195

Atlantic-Indian Ridge
Shona Ridge
Bouvetøya
American-Antarctic Ridge
Atlantic-Indian Antarctic Ridge
6972 Enderby Abyssal Plain
SOUTHERN OCEAN
Davis Sea
Cape Darnley
Vincennes Bay Cape Poinsett
Cape North
Cape Adare
Pacific-Antarctic Ridge
Antarctic Circle
6606

Maud Seamount 1200
5750
South Sandwich Trench 8125
South Sandwich Islands
Scotia Ridge
South Georgia
Shag Rocks
Scotia Sea
South Orkney Islands
South Shetland Islands
Weddell Abyssal Plain
Weddell Sea
Lützow-Holm Bay
Filchner Ice Shelf
Ross Ice Shelf
Ross Sea
Enderby
Coulman Island
Antarctic Circle

ANTARCTICA
Antarctic Peninsula
Cape Norvegia
South Pole

Lambert Azimuthal Equal Area Projection

ASIA

Arctic Circle

Ostrov Vrangelya
Chukchi Sea

Antadyrskiy Zaliv
St Lawrence Island
Nunivak Island
Pribilof Islands

Bering Sea

Kamchatka Basin
Ostrov Beringa
Ostrov Medriny
Aleutian Basin
Bowers

Sea of Okhotsk

Sakhalin

Heilong Jiang

Kuril Basin
Kuril'skiye Ostrova
Kuril Trench

Aleutian Islands
Attu Island
Andreanof Islands
7679
7622

Emperor Seamount Chain

Chinook Trough

Huang He
Rio Hai
Korea Bay
Yellow Sea
Japan Basin
Hokkaido
Japan Trench

Beijing

Qian Tang
Chang Jiang
Shanghai

Honshu
Sea of Japan (East Sea)
JAPAN
Shikoku
Kyushu
Tokyo
6412

NORTHWEST PACIFIC BASIN

Empire of Trough
7900

Tropic of Cancer

Kolkata (Calcutta)

Ganges

Ganges Cone

Bay of Bengal

Yangon
3954

East China Sea
Nansei-shoto

Ramapo Deep
9780
Ogasawara-shoto

MID - PACIFIC MOUNTAINS

Kure Atoll
Midway Islands
Laysan Island
Gardner Pinnacles
Necker Island

Chennai

Andaman Islands

Taiwan
Taiwan Strait
7460
Hainan
Luzon Strait

Ryukyu Trench

Kyushu - Palau Ridge
Kazan-retto
9156

6345

Wake Island
18

Hawaiian

Guangzhou
Gulf of Tongking

Batan Islands
Cape Engaño

South Honshu Ridge

West Mariana Basin

Mariana Ridge

Magellan Seamounts

MICRONESIA

Johnston Atoll

Sri Lanka

Nicobar Islands

Andaman Basin
5560
4267

South China Sea
5484

Philippine Islands
Luzon
Philippine Basin
6745

Palawan Trough
10057

Challenger Deep 10920
8967
8054

Rota
Saipan
Guam
East Mariana Basin
1564

Yap Trench
Palau Islands
Yap

Eauripik Rise
New Guinea Rise

Caroline Islands
Pikelot
Gaferut
Chuuk
Hall Islands
Pohnpei
Mortlock Islands
Kosrae

Enewetak
Bikini
Rongelap
Kwajalein
Ujelang
Wotje
Ailinglaplap

6530

Taongi

Marshall Islands

Central Pacific Basin

6957

Mui Ca Mau

Strait of Malacca

Sumatera

Sulu Sea
Mindanao

Celebes Sea

West Caroline Basin
East Caroline Basin

Kapingamarangi

Nauru
Banaba
Butaritari
Abaiang
Nonouti
Tabiteuea
Onotoa

Melanesian Basin

Gilbert Islands

Howland Island
Baker Island

McKean
Phoenix Islands
Nikumaroro

Kanton
Rawaki
Orona

Singapore

Sunda Shelf

Borneo

Sulawesi

Halmahera

Laut Maluku

New Guinea Rise

Admiralty Islands
7208

Kapingamarangi

MELANESIA

Nanumea

Nikufetau
Funafuti
Vaitupu

Nukulaelae

Atafu
Nukunonu
Fakaofo
Tokelau

POLYNESIA

Equator
2302
Cocos Basin

Bangka

Laut Jawa

Laut Banda
7288

Laut Seram
Seram

Bismarck Sea
New Ireland
New Britain
Bougainville Island
Solomon Islands

Solomon Sea

San Cristobal
8322
Santa Cruz Islands

Rotuma

Iles Wallis
Iles de Hoorn

Savai'i
Upolu
Tutuila

Samoa Basin

Suwarrow

Jakarta
Laut Flores
Flores
Sumba
Jawa

Timor

Arafura Sea

Gulf of Papua
Torres Strait
Cape York

Guadalcanal
D'Entrecasteaux Islands
Louisiade Archipelago
Rennell

Banks Islands

Espiritu Santo
Malakula

13
Swains Island

Pukapuka
Nassau

Mid - Indian Basin

Investigator Ridge

Java Trench
Java Ridge
7125 (Sunda Trench)

Timor Sea

Melville Island

Arafura Shelf

Cape Arnhem
66
Gulf of Carpentaria

Great Barrier Reef

Coral Sea Basin

Ambrym
Efate
Erromango
Tanna
Anatom
7073

Vanua Levu
Viti Levu
Fiji Islands

Iles Loyauté
7633

Hunter Island
New Hebrides Trench

Vava'u Group
Tofua
Tongatapu Group

Tonga Trench

Niue

Horizon Deep 10800

Cocos Islands

Ninetyeast Ridge

6360

North Australian Basin

Cape Lévêque

Nouvelle Calédonie
Ile des Pins

New Caledonia Ridge

South Fiji Basin

Kermadec Islands

10047

Kermadec Trench

Louisville Ridge

WEST AUSTRALIAN BASIN

Exmouth Plateau

North West Cape
1924

AUSTRALIA

Darling

Lord Howe Rise

Lord Howe Island

Norfolk Island Ridge
Norfolk Island

Perth Basin

Perth

Naturaliste Plateau
Cape Leeuwin
5746

Great Australian Bight

Sydney

Murray

Melbourne

Bass Strait
Tasmania

Tasman Abyssal Plain

Tasman Sea

Auckland
North Island

New Zealand
Wellington
South Island

Chatham Rise
Chatham Islands

Bounty Trough
Bounty Islands

Broken Plateau

East Indiaman Ridge

Diamantina Deep
6602

South Australian Basin
5670

South East Cape Basin
770

South East Cape Basin

South Tasman Rise

Stewart Island
Snares Islands

60
Auckland Islands

Campbell Plateau
Campbell Island

Antipodes Islands
6096

SOUTHEAST INDIAN RIDGE

Ile Amsterdam
Ile St-Paul

2067

3902

INDIAN - ANTARCTIC RIDGE

Macquarie Island

Macquarie Ridge

956

SOUTHERN PACIFIC

Tropic of Capricorn

3840

AUSTRALIAN - ANTARCTIC BASIN
4650

1646

Fisher Bay
Balleny Islands
Cape North
Cape Adare

Ross Ice Shelf

ANTARCTICA

Antarctic Circle

Lambert Azimuthal Equal Area Projection

METRES	FEET
6000	19686
5000	16404
4000	13124
3000	9843
2000	6562
1000	3281
500	1640
200	656
0	0 below sea level
200	656
2000	6562
3000	9843
4000	13124
5000	16404
6000	19686
7000	22967

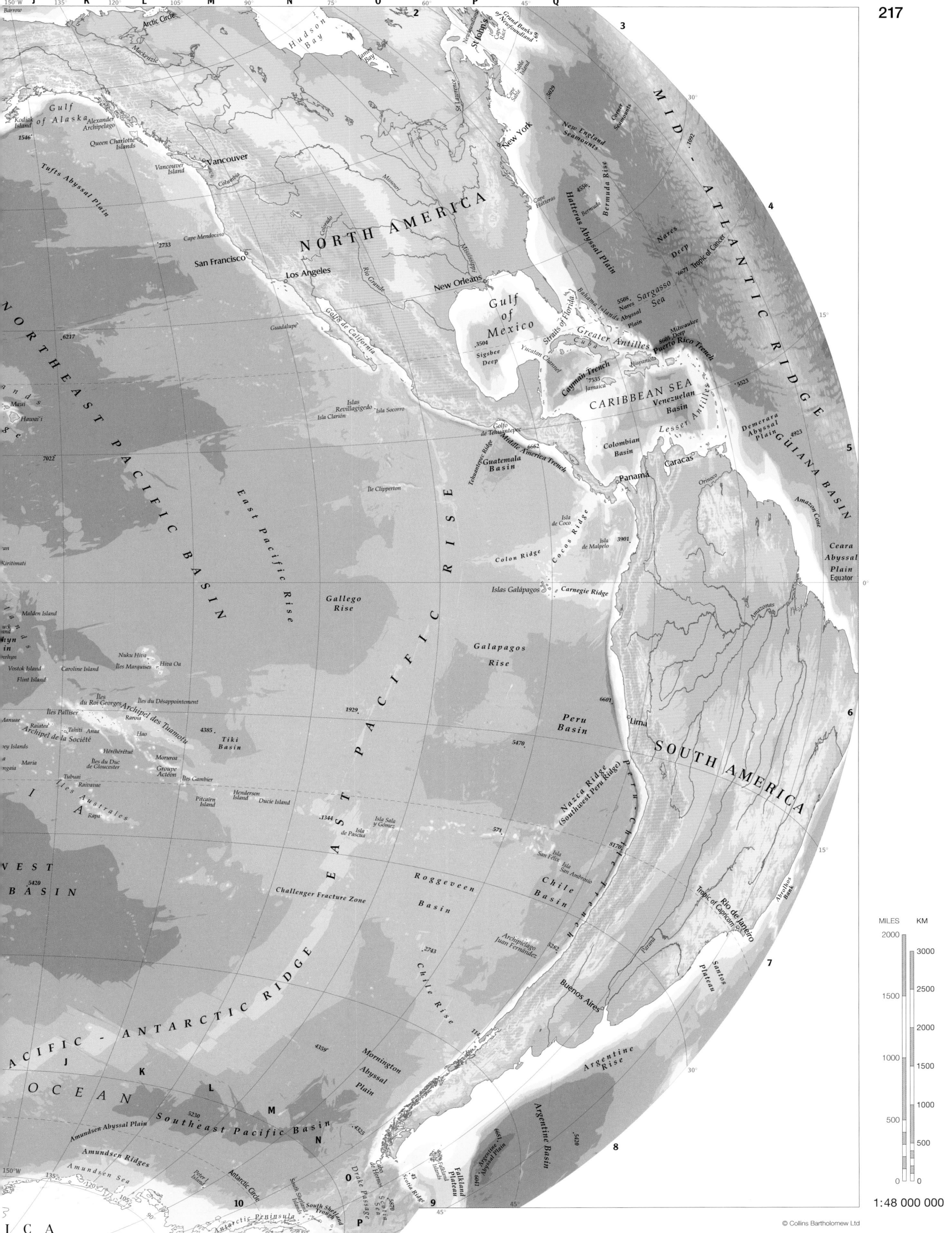
NORTH AMERICA
SOUTH AMERICA
NORTHEAST PACIFIC BASIN
EAST PACIFIC RISE
MID - ATLANTIC RIDGE
PACIFIC - ANTARCTIC RIDGE
OCEAN
Gulf of Alaska
Hudson Bay
James Bay
Gulf of Mexico
CARIBBEAN SEA
Sargasso Sea
Greater Antilles
Lesser Antilles
Puerto Rico Trench
Cayman Trench
Sigsbee Deep
Yucatan Channel
Straits of Florida
Bahama Islands
Cuba
Jamaica
Hispaniola
Venezuelan Basin
Colombian Basin
Guatemala Basin
Middle America Trench
Golfo de Tehuantepec
Tehuantepec Ridge
Golfo de California
Demerara Abyssal Plain
GUIANA BASIN
Amazon Cone
Ceara Abyssal Plain
Equator
Nares Deep
Nares Abyssal Plain
Milwaukee Deep
Tropic of Cancer
Hatteras Abyssal Plain
Bermuda Rise
Bermuda
New England Seamounts
Corner Seamounts
Grand Banks of Newfoundland
Newfoundland
St John's
Cape Race
Sable Island
Cape Sable
New York
Cape Hatteras
St Lawrence
Arctic Circle
Mackenzie
Barrow
Kodiak Island
Alexander Archipelago
Queen Charlotte Islands
Vancouver Island
Vancouver
Columbia
Tufts Abyssal Plain
Missouri
Mississippi
Colorado
Rio Grande
Cape Mendocino
San Francisco
Los Angeles
New Orleans
Guadalupe
Islas Revillagigedo
Isla Socorro
Isla Clarión
Maui
Hawai'i
Kiritimati
Malden Island
Vostok Island
Caroline Island
Flint Island
Île Clipperton
East Pacific Rise
Isla de Coco
Cocos Ridge
Colon Ridge
Isla de Malpelo
Islas Galápagos
Carnegie Ridge
Panamá
Caracas
Orinoco
Amazonas
Gallego Rise
Galapagos Rise
Nuku Hiva
Hiva Oa
Îles Marquises
Îles du Roi Georges
Îles du Désappointement
Îles Palliser
Archipel des Tuamotu
Raroia
Hao
Tahiti
Anaa
Raiatea
Archipel de la Société
Hérēhérétué
Îles du Duc de Gloucester
Moruroa
Groupe Actéon
Îles Gambier
Tubuai
Raivavae
Îles Australes
Rapa
Maria
Pitcairn Island
Henderson Island
Ducie Island
Tiki Basin
Peru Basin
Lima
Nazca Ridge (Southwest Peru Ridge)
Peru - Chile Trench
Isla Sala y Gómez
Isla de Pascua
Isla San Félix
Isla San Ambrosio
Chile Basin
Roggeveen Basin
Challenger Fracture Zone
Archipiélago Juan Fernández
Chile Rise
Tropic of Capricorn
Rio de Janeiro
Abrolhos Bank
Paraná
Santos Plateau
Buenos Aires
Argentine Rise
Argentine Basin
Argentine Abyssal Plain
Falkland Plateau
Falkland Islands
Mornington Abyssal Plain
Southeast Pacific Basin
Amundsen Abyssal Plain
Amundsen Ridges
Amundsen Sea
Peter I Island
Antarctic Circle
Antarctic Peninsula
South Shetland Islands
South Shetland Trough
Drake Passage
Cabo de Hornos
Scotia Ridge
Scotia Sea
MILES KM
1:48 000 000

© Collins Bartholomew Ltd

ARCTIC OCEAN

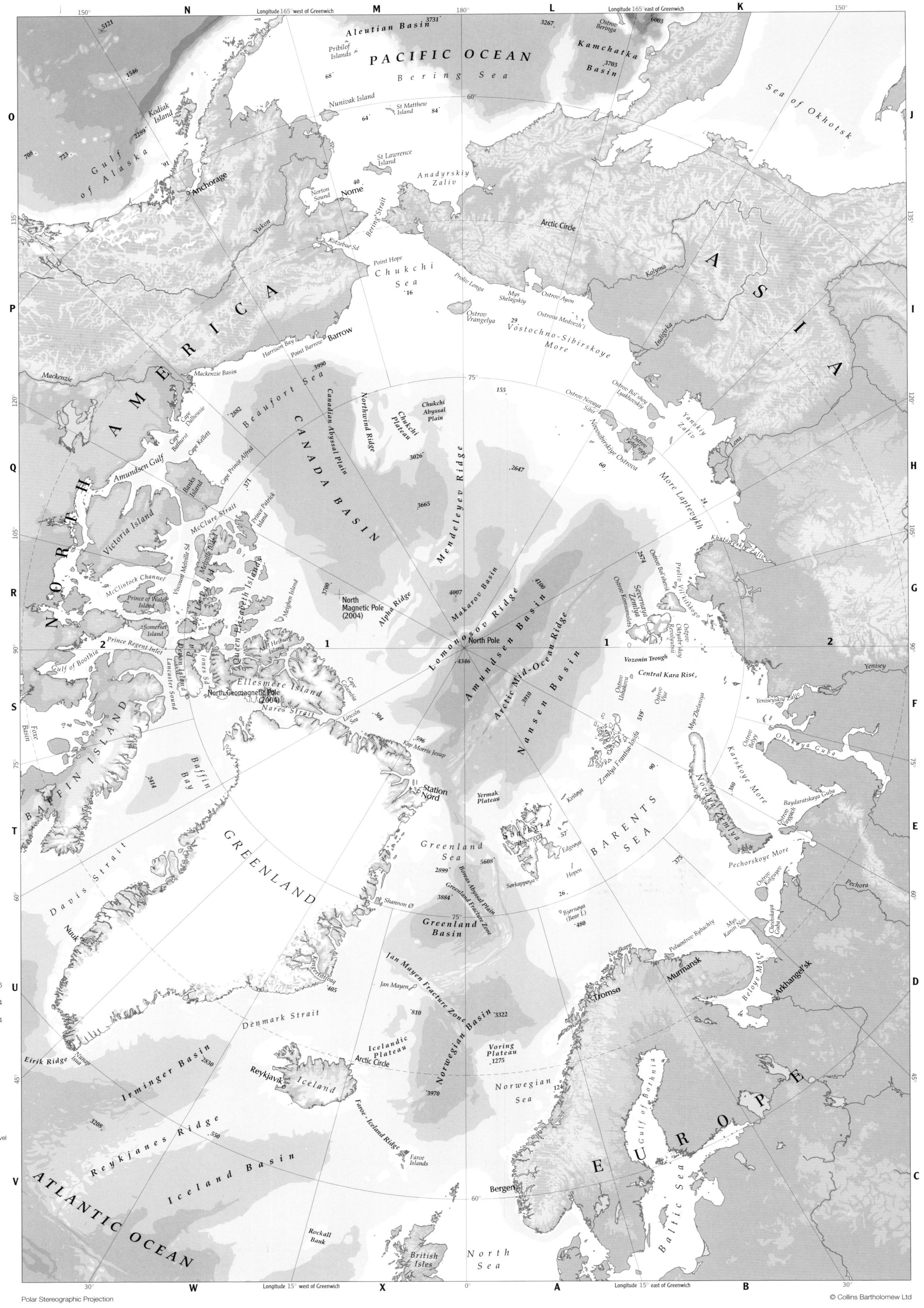

Polar Stereographic Projection

1:24 000 000

MILES KM

METRES FEET

© Collins Bartholomew Ltd

PACIFIC OCEAN

Bering Sea

Aleutian Basin

Kamchatka Basin

Sea of Okhotsk

Pribilof Islands

Nunivak Island

St Matthew Island

St Lawrence Island

Norton Sound

Nome

Anchorage

Kodiak Island

Gulf of Alaska

NORTH AMERICA

ASIA

Arctic Circle

Chukchi Sea

Point Hope

Barrow

Point Barrow

Harrison Bay

Mackenzie

Mackenzie Basin

Beaufort Sea

CANADA BASIN

Canadian Abyssal Plain

Canadian Abyssal Plain

Northwind Ridge

Chukchi Plateau

Chukchi Abyssal Plain

Mendeleyev Ridge

Vostochno-Sibirskoye More

Ostrov Vrangelya

Ostrova Medvezh'i

Mys Shelagskiy

Ostrov Ayon

Kolyma

Indigirka

Yanskiy Zaliv

Lena

More Laptevykh

Khatangskiy Zaliv

Amundsen Gulf

Cape Dalhousie

Cape Bathurst

Cape Kellett

Banks Island

Cape Prince Alfred

Prince Patrick Island

Victoria Island

McClure Strait

Viscount Melville Sd

Melville Island

Mackenzie King Island

Alpha Ridge

North Magnetic Pole (2004)

Makarov Basin

Lomonosov Ridge

North Pole

Amundsen Basin

Arctic Mid-Ocean Ridge

Nansen Basin

Severnaya Zemlya

Ostrov Bol'shevik

Ostrov Oktyabr'skoy Revolyutsii

Ostrov Komsomolets

Proliv Vil'kitskogo

Vozonin Trough

Central Kara Rise

McClintock Channel

Prince of Wales Island

Somerset Island

North Geomagnetic Pole (2004)

Queen Elizabeth Islands

Axel Heiberg Island

Amund Ringnes Island

Ellef Ringnes Island

Meighen Island

Ellesmere Island

Cape Columbia

Lincoln Sea

Nares Strait

Kap Morris Jesup

Station Nord

Prince Regent Inlet

Gulf of Boothia

Lancaster Sound

Jones Sd

Devon Island

Yermak Plateau

Svalbard

Spitsbergen

Edgeøya

Hopen

Sørkappøya

Bjørnøya (Bear I.)

Zemlya Frantsa-Iosifa

Novaya Zemlya

Karskoye More

Ostrov Belyy

Obskaya Guba

Yeniseyskiy Zaliv

Ostrov Vize

Ostrov Ushakova

Baydaratskaya Guba

Yenisey

Ostrov Kolguyev

Pechorskoye More

Pechora

BARENTS SEA

Foxe Basin

Baffin Island

Baffin Bay

BAFFIN ISLAND

Davis Strait

GREENLAND

Greenland Sea

Barents Abyssal Plain

Greenland Fracture Zone

Greenland Basin

Shannon Ø

Nioghalvfjerdsfjorden

Kangerlussuaq

Nuuk

Denmark Strait

Jan Mayen Fracture Zone

Jan Mayen

Norwegian Basin

Vøring Plateau

Norwegian Sea

Nordkapp

Murmansk

Arkhangel'sk

Beloye More

Poluostrov Rybachiy

Mys Kanin Nos

Cheshskaya Guba

Tromsø

Bergen

EUROPE

Eirik Ridge

Irminger Basin

Reykjanes Ridge

Iceland Basin

Reykjavik

Iceland

Icelandic Plateau

Arctic Circle

Faroe-Iceland Ridge

Faroe Islands

Rockall Bank

British Isles

North Sea

ATLANTIC OCEAN

Gulf of Bothnia

Baltic Sea

Bering Strait

Kotzebue Sd

Yukon

Proliv Longa

Ostrov Bol'shoy Lyakhovskiy

Novosibirskiye Ostrova

Anadyrskiy Zaliv

Ostrov Beringa

GLOSSARY

Geographical term	Language	Meaning
A		
-á	Icelandic	river
-å	Danish	river
Āb	Farsi	river
Abajo	Spanish	lower
Abbaye	French	abbey
Abhainn	Gaelic	river
Abyār	Arabic	wells
Açude	Portuguese	reservoir
Adası	Azeri, Turkish	island
Adrar	Berber	hills, mountains
Agia, Agios	Greek	saint
Agioi	Greek	saints
Aiguille	French	peak
Ain, 'Ain, 'Aïn, Aïn, 'Aïn	Arabic	spring, well
Akra	Greek	cape, point
Ala-	Finnish	lower
Allt	Gaelic	river
Alpi	Italian	mountain range
Alpe	Slovene	mountain range
Alpen	German	mountain range
Alpes	French	mountain range
Alt-	German	old
Alta	Italian, Portuguese, Spanish	upper
Altiplanicie	Spanish	high plain
Alto	Italian, Portuguese, Spanish	upper
Alto	Spanish	summit
-älv, -älven	Swedish	river
Ano	Greek	upper
Anou, Ânou	Berber	well
Anse	French	bay
Ao	Thai	bay
Archipel	French	archipelago
Archipiélago	Spanish	archipelago
Arenas	Spanish	sands
Argelanots'	Armenian	reserve
Arkhipelag	Russian	archipelago
Arquipélago	Portuguese	archipelago
Arrecife	Spanish	reef
Arriba	Spanish	upper
Arroio	Portuguese	watercourse
Arroyo	Spanish	watercourse
Augstiene	Latvian	hill region
Aust-	Norwegian	east, eastern
Austur-	Icelandic	east, eastern
Avtonomnaya, Avtonomnyy	Russian	autonomous
Āw	Kurdish	river
'Ayn	Arabic	spring, waterhole, well
B		
Baai, -baai	Afrikaans, Dutch	bay
Bāb	Arabic	strait
Bad	German	spa
Badia	Catalan	bay
Bādiyah	Arabic	desert
Bælt	Danish	strait
Bagh	Gaelic	bay
Bahia	Portuguese	bay
Bahía	Spanish	bay
Bahr, Bahr, Bahr	Arabic	bay, lake, canal, river, watercourse
Bahra, Bahra	Arabic	lagoon, lake
Baía	Portuguese	bay
Baie	French	bay
Baixa, Baixo	Portuguese	lower
Baja	Spanish	lower
Bajja	Maltese	bay
Bajo	Spanish	depression, lower
Bālā	Farsi	upper
Ban	Laotian, Thai	village
Banc	Welsh	hill
Banco	Spanish	shoal
Bandao	Chinese	peninsula
Bandar	Arabic, Farsi, Somali	anchorage, inlet, port, harbour
Bandar	Malay	port, town
Banī	Arabic	desert
Banjaran	Malay	mountain range
Baraj, Barajı	Turkish	dam
Barat	Indonesian, Malay	west, western
Barra	Portuguese, Spanish	sandbank, sandbar, spit
Barrage	French	dam
Barragem	Portuguese	dam, reservoir
Barranco	Spanish	gorge, ravine
Baruun	Mongolian	west, western
Bas, Basse	French	lower
Bassin	French	basin
Bāṭin, Baṭn	Arabic	depression
-beek	Afrikaans, Dutch	river
Beg, Beag	Gaelic, Irish	small
Bei	Chinese	north, northern

Geographical term	Language	Meaning
bei	German	at, near
Beinn	Gaelic	mountain
Belogor'ye	Russian	mountain range
Ben	Gaelic	mountain
Bereg	Russian	coastal area
-berg, -berge	German, Norwegian, Swedish, Afrikaans	mountain, mountains
Besar	Indonesian, Malay	big
Bi'ār	Arabic	wells
Bir, Bi'r, Bīr	Arabic	waterhole, well
Birkat	Arabic	waterhole, well
-bjerg	Danish	hill
Boca	Portuguese, Spanish	mouth
Bodden	German	bay
Boğazı	Turkish	strait, pass
Bois	French	forest, wood
Boloto	Russian	marsh
Bol'shaya, Bol'shiye, Bol'shoy, Bol'shoye	Russian	big
-bong	Korean	mountain
Boquerón	Spanish	pass
Bory	Polish	woods
-botn	Norwegian	valley floor
-botten	Swedish	valley floor
Böyük	Azeri	big
Braţul	Romanian	arm, branch
-bre, -breen	Norwegian	glacier
Bredning	Danish	bay
Breg	Croatian, Serbian	hill
-bron	Afrikaans	spring, well
Brücke	German	bridge
Bucht	German	bay
Bugt	Danish	bay
-bugten	Danish	bay
Bukhta	Russian	bay
Bukit	Indonesian, Malay	hill, mountain
-bukt, -bukta	Norwegian	bay
-bukten	Swedish	bay
Bulag	Mongolian	spring
Bulak	Russian, Uighur	spring
Bum	Burmese	mountain
Burnu, Burun	Turkish	cape, point
Büyük	Turkish	big
Bwlch	Welsh	pass
C		
Cabo	Portuguese, Spanish	cape, point
Cachoeira	Portuguese	waterfall
Caka	Tibetan	salt lake
Cala	Catalan, Italian	bay
Caleta	Spanish	inlet
Câmpia	Romanian	plain
Campo	Italian, Spanish	plain
Cañada, Cañadón	Spanish	ravine, gorge
Canal	French, Portuguese, Spanish	canal, channel
Caño	Spanish	river
Cañon	Spanish	canyon
Caol	Gaelic	hill
Cap	Catalan, French	cape, point
Capo	Italian	cape, point
Carn	Welsh	hill
Castell	Catalan	castle
Causse	French	limestone plateau
Çay, -çay, Çayı, -çayı	Azeri, Turkish	river
Cayo	Spanish	island
Cefn	Welsh	hill, ridge
Cerro	Spanish	hill, mountain, peak
Česká, České, Český	Czech	Czech
Chaco	Spanish	plain
Chāh	Farsi	river
Chaîne	French	mountain range
Cham	Kurdish	river
Chapada	Portuguese	hills, uplands
Château	French	castle, palace
Chau	Chinese	island
Chaung	Burmese	river
Chāy	Kurdish	river
Chhu	Dzongkha (Bhutan)	river
Chiang	Thai	town
Chink	Russian	hill range
Chiyā	Kurdish	mountain, hill range
Chott	Arabic	salt lake
Chuan	Chinese	river
Chuôr Phnum	Cambodian	mountain range
Ci	Indonesian	river
Ciénaga	Spanish	marshy lake
Cima	Italian	peak
Cime	French	peak
Città	Italian	city
Ciudad	Spanish	town, city
Cnoc	Gaelic	hill
Co	Tibetan	lake
Col	French	pass
Collado	Spanish	mountain
Colle	Italian	pass
Colline	French	hill
Cona	Tibetan	lake
Cordillera	Spanish	mountain range

Geographical term	Language	Meaning
Corno	Italian	peak
Coronel	Spanish	colonel
Costa	Catalan, Italian, Portuguese, Spanish	coastal area
Côte	French	coast, hill region, slope
Coutada	Portuguese	reserve
Coxilha	Portuguese	mountain pasture
Cratère	French	crater
Creag	Gaelic	mountain
Cruz	Spanish	cross
Cu Lao	Vietnamese	island
Cuchilla	Spanish	mountain range
Cuenca	Spanish	deep valley, river basin
Cueva	Spanish	cave
Cumbre	Spanish	mountain
-cun	Chinese	village
D		
Da	Chinese	big
Da	Vietnamese	river
Dağ, Dağı	Azeri, Turkish	hill(s), mountain(s)
Dāgh	Farsi	mountain(s)
Dağları	Turkish	mountains
-dake	Japanese	hill, mountain
-dal	Afrikaans, Danish, Swedish	valley
-dal, -dalen	Norwegian	valley
-dalur	Icelandic	valley
-dan	Korean	cape, point
Danau	Indonesian, Malay	lake
Dao	Chinese	island
Đao	Vietnamese	island
Daqq	Farsi	salt flat, salt lake
-dara	Tajik	river
Darreh	Farsi	valley
Dar'ya	Russian	river
Daryācheh	Farsi	lake
Dashan	Chinese	mountain
Dasht	Farsi	desert
Dataran Tinggi	Malay	plateau
Davan	Kazakh	pass
Dawhat	Arabic	bay
Dayr	Arabic	monastery
Dealul	Romanian	hill, mountain
Dealurile	Romanian	hills
Deh	Farsi	village
Deir	Arabic	monastery
Denizi	Turkish	sea
Deresi	Turkish	river
Desierto	Spanish	desert
Détroit	French	channel
-diep	Dutch	channel
Dingzi	Chinese	hill, small mountain
Djebel	Arabic	mountain
-do	Korean	island
Dolna, Dolni	Bulgarian	lower
Dolna, Dolne, Dolny	Polish	lower
Dolní	Czech	lower
Dong	Chinese	east, eastern
-dong	Korean	village
Donja, Donji	Croatian, Serbian	lower
Dorf	German	village
-dorp	Afrikaans, Dutch	village
Druim	Gaelic	hill, mountain
Dund	Mongolian	middle, central
Düzü	Azeri	plain
-dyngja	Icelandic	hill, mountain
Dzüün	Mongolian	east, eastern
E		
Eilean	Gaelic	island
-elv, -elva	Norwegian	river
Embalse	Spanish	reservoir
'Emeq	Hebrew	plain
Ensenada	Spanish	bay
Erg, 'Erg, 'Erg	Arabic	sand dunes
Eski	Turkish	old
Estany	Catalan	pond
Estero	Spanish	estuary, inlet, lagoon
Estrada	Spanish	bay
Estrecho	Spanish	strait
Étang	French	lagoon, lake
-ey, -eyjar	Icelandic	island, islands
-eyri	Icelandic	sandbar
ežeras	Lithuanian	lake
ezers	Latvian	lake
F		
Falaise	French	cliff, escarpment
Farihy	Malagasy	lake
Fayḍat	Arabic	waterhole
-fell	Icelandic	hill, mountain
Fels	German	rock
Feng	Chinese	mountain
Fiume	Italian	river

Geographical term	Language	Meaning
-fjäll, -fjällen, -fjället	Swedish	hill(s), mountain(s)
-fjallgarður	Icelandic	mountains
-fjara	Icelandic	beach
-fjell, -fjellet	Norwegian	mountain
-fjöll	Icelandic	hill(s), mountain(s)
Fjord, -fjord, -fjorden	Danish, Norwegian, Swedish	fjord
-fjörður	Icelandic	fjord
Fliegu	Maltese	channel
-fljót	Icelandic	river
-flói	Icelandic	bay
-fócsatorna	Hungarian	canal
Foel	Welsh	hill
Förde	German	inlet
Forêt	French	forest
Forst	German	forest
-foss	Icelandic	waterfall
-foss, -fossen	Norwegian	rapids, waterfall
Fuente	Spanish	source, well
Fulayj	Arabic	watercourse

G

Geographical term	Language	Meaning
-gan	Japanese	rock
Gang	Dzongkha (Bhutan)	mountain
Gang	Chinese	bay, river
-gang	Korean	river
Gaoyuan	Chinese	plateau
Gardaneh	Farsi	pass
-gat	Dutch	channel
-gata	Japanese	inlet, lagoon, lake
Gau	German	district
Gave	French	torrent
-gawa	Japanese	river
Gebel	Arabic	mountain
Gebergte	Dutch	mountain range
Gebiet	German	district, region
Gebirge	German	mountains
Geodha	Gaelic	inlet
Gezâ'ir	Arabic	islands
Gezirat	Arabic	island
Ghard	Arabic	sand dunes
Ghubba	Arabic	bay
Gjiri	Albanian	bay
Gletscher	German	glacier
Gobernador	Spanish	governor
Gobi	Mongolian	desert
Gol	Mongolian	river
Göl	Azeri	lake
Golets	Russian	mountain
Golf	Catalan	gulf
Golfe	French	bay, gulf
Golfo	Italian, Spanish	bay, gulf
Gölü	Azeri, Turkish	lake
Gora	Bulgarian, Croatian, Russian, Serbian	mountain(s)
Gorges	French	gorge
Górka	Polish	hill
Gornja, Gornje, Gornji	Croatian, Serbian	upper
Gorno-	Russian	mountainous
Gory	Russian	mountains
Góry	Polish	mountains
Gou	Chinese	river
Graben	German	trench
-grad	Bulgarian, Croatian, Russian, Serbian	town
Grand, Grande	French	big
-gród	Polish	town
Groot	Afrikaans, Dutch	big
Gross, Grosse, Grossen, Grosser (also Groß-)	German	big
Grotta	Italian	cave
Grotte	French	cave
Grotte	Italian	caves
Groupe	French	group
Grund	German	ground, valley
Gruppo	Italian	group
Gryada	Russian	mountains
Guan	Chinese	pass
Guba	Russian	bay, gulf
Gubed	Somali	bay
-guntō	Japanese	islands
Gunung	Indonesian, Malay	mountain
Guri	Albanian	peak

H

Geographical term	Language	Meaning
Ḥafar	Arabic	wells
Hafen	German	port, harbour
Haff	German	bay
Hai	Chinese	lake, sea
Haixia	Chinese	channel, strait
-háls	Icelandic	ridge
-halvøya	Norwegian	peninsula
Hamada, Hammada	Arabic	plateau
-hamn	Norwegian, Swedish	port, harbour
-hamrar	Icelandic	cliffs
Hāmūn	Farsi	marsh, salt pan
-hantō	Japanese	peninsula
Har	Hebrew	mountain
Hara	Belorussian	hill
Hardt	German	wooded hills
Ḥarrat, Ḥarrāt	Arabic	lava field
Hassi	Arabic	well
-haug, -haugen	Norwegian	hill
-havn	Danish, Faroese, Norwegian	bay, harbour, port
Hawr	Arabic	lake, impermanent lake, marsh
Hāyk'	Amharic	lake
He	Chinese	river
-hegység	Hungarian	hills, mountains
-hei	Norwegian	heath, moor
-heide	Dutch	heath, marsh
Heide	German	heath, moor
-heiði	Icelandic	heath

Geographical term	Language	Meaning
Helodrano	Malagasy	bay
Higashi-	Japanese	east, eastern
-hisar	Turkish	castle
Ḥiṣn	Arabic	fort
Hka	Burmese	river
-hnjúkur	Icelandic	hill
-ho	Korean	lake
-hø	Norwegian	peak
Hoch	German	high
Hoek	Dutch	cape, point
-höfði	Icelandic	hill, mountain
-höfn	Icelandic	cove
Hög	Swedish	height, high
-högda	Norwegian	height
Höhe	German	height
Hohen-	German	high
Hoi, Hoi Hap	Chinese	bay, channel, harbour, inlet
-høj, -høje	Danish	hill, hills
Hon	Vietnamese	island
Hoog	Dutch	high
Hora, Hory	Czech, Ukrainian	mountain(s)
-horn	Icelandic	cape, point, peak
Horn, -horn	German	mountain, peak
Horná, Horné, Horní, Horný	Czech	upper
Ḥorvot	Hebrew	ruins
-hot	Mongolian	town
-hrad	Czech	town
-hraun	Icelandic	lava field
Hu	Chinese	lake

I

Geographical term	Language	Meaning
Idd	Arabic	well
Île	French	island
Ilha, Ilhéu	Portuguese	island
Illa	Catalan	island
im	German	in
imeni	Russian	in the name of
Inish	Irish	island
Insel, Inseln	German	island, islands
Insula	Romanian	island
Irq, 'Irq	Arabic	hill, sand dune, sand dunes
Isla	Spanish	island
Iso-	Finnish	big
Isola, Isole	Italian	island, islands
Isolte	Catalan	island
Isthme	French	isthmus
Istmo	Spanish	isthmus
-iwa	Japanese	island

J

Geographical term	Language	Meaning
Jabal	Arabic	mountain
järv	Estonian	lake
-järvi	Finnish	lake
Jasiired	Somali	island
Jaun-	Latvian	new
-jaure	Lappish	lake
Jazirah, Jazīreh, Jazīrat	Arabic	island
Jbel, Jebel	Arabic	mountain
Jezero, jezero	Croatian, Serbian, Slovene	lake
Jezioro	Polish	lake
Jiang	Chinese	river
Jiao	Chinese	cape, point
Jibāl	Arabic	mountains
-jima	Japanese	island
Jing	Chinese	well
-jõgi	Estonian	river
-joki	Finnish	river
-jokka	Lappish	river
-jökull, jökullen	Icelandic, Norwegian	glacier, ice cap

K

Geographical term	Language	Meaning
Kaap	Afrikaans	cape, point
-kai	Japanese	bay, channel
-kaigan	Japanese	coastal area
-kaikyō	Japanese	channel, strait
Kali	Indonesian, Malay	river
kalnas, kalnis	Lithuanian	hill
Kalns	Latvian	hill
Kamen'	Russian	rock
Kamm	German	ridge, crest
Kâmpóng	Cambodian	town, village
-kanaal	Dutch	canal
Kanal	German, Russian	canal
Kanał	Polish	canal
Kanalı	Azeri	canal
Kaôh	Cambodian	island
Kap	Danish	cape, point
Kapp	Norwegian	cape, point
Karang	Indonesian, Malay	reef
Kato	Greek	lower
Kavīr	Farsi	salt desert
-kawa	Japanese	river
Kecil	Indonesian, Malay	small
K'edi	Georgian	hills
Kefar	Hebrew	village
Kepi	Albanian	cape, point
Kepulauan	Indonesian	islands
Keski-	Finnish	middle, central
Khabrah, Khabrat	Arabic	impermanent lake
Khalīg, Khalīj	Arabic	bay, gulf
Khao	Thai	peak
Khashm	Arabic	hill
Khawr	Arabic	bay, channel
Khor, Khōr	Arabic	bay
Khowr	Farsi	bay, inlet
Khrebet	Russian	mountain range
Kis-	Hungarian	small
Kita-	Japanese	north, northern
Klein	Afrikaans	small
Klein, Kleine, Kleiner	German	small

K (continued)

Geographical term	Language	Meaning
Klint	Danish	cliff
-kloof	Afrikaans	pass
Knock	Irish	hill
-ko	Japanese	lake
Ko	Thai	island
-kōchi, -kōgen	Japanese	plateau
Koh	Farsi	mountain
Kok	Chinese	cape, point
Köl	Kazakh, Kyrgyz	lake
Kolpos	Greek	gulf
Koog	German	polder (reclaimed land)
-kop	Afrikaans	hill, mountain
Kopf	German	hill
Körfezi	Turkish	bay, gulf
kõrgustik	Estonian	upland
Kosa	Russian, Ukrainian	spit
Kou	Chinese	river mouth
-köy	Turkish	village
Kraj	Croatian, Czech, Polish, Serbian	region
Krajobrazowy	Polish	regional
Kray	Russian	territory
Kryazh	Russian	hills, ridge
Kuala	Malay	river mouth
Küçük	Turkish	small
Kuduk	Uighur	well
Kūh	Farsi	mountain
Kūhhā	Farsi	mountain range
Kul'	Russian	lake
-kūl	Tajik	lake
-küla	Estonian	village
Kum	Russian	sandy desert
-kundo	Korean	islands
Kuppe	German	hill top
kurk	Estonian	channel, strait
K'vemo	Georgian	upper
-kvísl, kvíslar	Icelandic	river, rivers
-kylä	Finnish	village
Kyun	Burmese	island

L

Geographical term	Language	Meaning
La	Tibetan	pass
Lac	French	lake
Lacul	Romanian	lake
Laem	Thai	cape, point
Lago	Italian, Portuguese, Spanish	lake
Lagoa	Portuguese	lagoon
Laguna	Spanish	lagoon, lake
Lagune	French	lagoon
laht	Estonian	bay
-laid	Estonian	island
Lam	Thai	river
Län	Swedish	county
Land	German	province
Lande	French	heath, sandy moor
Las	Polish	wood, forest
Laut	Indonesian, Malay	sea
Lerr	Armenian	mountain
Lerrnashght'a	Armenian	mountains
Lich	Armenian	lake
Liedao	Chinese	islands
Liel-	Latvian	big
Lille	Danish, Norwegian	small
Liman	Russian	bay, lagoon, lake
Limni	Greek	lagoon, lake
Limnothalassa	Greek	inlet, lagoon
Ling	Chinese	mountain range
Liqeni	Albanian	lake
Llano	Spanish	plain, prairie
Llyn	Welsh	lake
Loch, Lochan	Gaelic	lake, small lake
Lohatanjona	Malagasy	cape, point
Loi	Burmese	mountain
looduskaitseala	Estonian	reserve
Luonnonpuisto	Finnish	nature reserve
-luoto	Finnish	rocky island
Lyman	Ukrainian	bay, lake

M

Geographical term	Language	Meaning
Macizo	Spanish	mountain range
Madh	Albanian	big
Madīnat	Arabic	town
Mae, Mae Nam	Thai	river
mägi	Estonian	hill
Măgura	Romanian	hill, mountain
Maḥaṭṭat	Arabic	station
Maja	Albanian	mountain
Mal	Albanian	mountain(s)
Mala	Croatian, Serbian	small
Malá	Czech, Slovak	small
Mali	Albanian	mountain
Mali	Croatian, Serbian, Ukrainian	small
Malo	Croatian, Serbian	small
Maloye	Russian	small
Maly, Malyya	Belorussian	small
-man	Korean	bay
Mar	Spanish	lagoon, lake
Marais	French	marsh, swamp
Mare	Italian	sea
Mare	Romanian	big
marios	Lithuanian	lake
Marsa	Arabic	anchorage, bay, inlet
Marsch	German	fen, marsh
Masabb	Arabic	estuary
Massif	French	mountains, upland
Ma'ṭan	Arabic	well
Mayor	Spanish	higher, larger
Maz-	Latvian	small
Meall	Gaelic	hill, mountain
Meer	Dutch, German	lake
Mega, Megalo-	Greek	big
Men	Chinese	gate

Geographical term	Language	Meaning
Menor	Portuguese, Spanish	smaller, lesser
Mersa	Arabic	anchorage, inlet
Mesa, Meseta	Spanish	tableland
Mesto	Croatian, Serbian	town
Město	Czech	town
Mets	Armenian	big
Mezzo	Italian	middle, central
Miao	Chinese	temple
Miasto	Polish	town
Mic, Mica	Romanian	small
Mikra, Mikri	Greek	small
Mīnā'	Arabic	port, harbour
Minami-	Japanese	south, southern
-mine	Japanese	mountain
-misaki	Japanese	cape, point
Mishāsh	Arabic	well
Mittel-, Mitten-	German	middle, central
Moel	Welsh	hill
Monasterio	Spanish	monastery
Moni	Greek	monastery
Mont	French	hill, mountain
Montagna	Italian	mountain
Montagne	French	mountain
Monte	Italian, Portuguese, Spanish	hill, mountain
Monti	Italian	mountains
Moor	German	marsh, moor, swamp
Moos	German	marsh, moss
More	Russian	sea
Mörön	Mongolian	river
Morro	Portuguese	hill
Morro	Spanish	cape, point
-mose	Danish	marsh, moor
Moyen	French	middle, central
Mt'a	Georgian	mountain
Muang	Laotian, Thai	town
Muara	Indonesian, Malay	estuary
Mui	Vietnamese	cape, point
Mun	Chinese	channel
Munţii	Romanian	mountains
Mynydd	Welsh	mountain
-mýri	Icelandic	marsh
Mys	Russian	cape, point

N

Geographical term	Language	Meaning
na	Croatian, Czech, Russian, Serbian, Slovak, Slovene	on
Nacional	Portuguese, Spanish	national
nacionalinis	Lithuanian	national
nad	Czech, Polish, Slovak	above, over
-nada	Japanese	bay, gulf
Nafūd	Arabic	desert, sand dunes
Nagor'ye	Russian	mountains, plateau
Nagy-	Hungarian	big
Nahr	Arabic	river
Nakhon	Thai	town
Nakrdzali	Georgian	reserve
Nam	Burmese, Laotian	river
Nam	Korean, Vietnamese	south, southern
Nan	Chinese	south, southern
Nanshan	Chinese	mountain range
Narodowy	Polish	national
Nationaal	Dutch	national
Naturreservat	Norwegian, Swedish	nature reserve
Natuurreservaat	Dutch	nature reserve
Naviglio	Italian	canal
Nawa-	Urdu	new
Nazionale	Italian	national
Neder-	Dutch	lower
Nehri	Turkish	river
Nei	Chinese	inner
Nek	Afrikaans	pass
-nes	Icelandic	cape, point
Neu-	German	new
Neuf, Neuve	French	new
Nevado, Nevada	Spanish	snow-covered mountain(s)
Nieder-	German	lower
Nieuw, Nieuwe, Nieuwer	Dutch	new
nina	Estonian	cape, point
Nishi-	Japanese	west, western
Nizhneye, Nizhniy, Nizhniye, Nizhnyaya	Russian	lower
Nizina	Belorussian	lowland
Nízke	Slovak	low
Nizmennost'	Russian	lowland
Nižní	Czech	lower
Nižný	Slovak	lower
Noguera	Catalan	river
Noord	Dutch	north, northern
Nord	French, German	north, northern
Nord-, Nordre	Danish	north, northern
Norður	Icelandic	north, northern
Norra	Swedish	north, northern
Nørre	Danish	north, northern
Norte	Portuguese, Spanish	north, northern
Nos	Bulgarian, Russian	cape, point, spit
Nosy	Malagasy	island
Nou	Romanian	new
Nouveau, Nouvelle	French	new
Nova	Bulgarian, Croatian, Portuguese, Serbian, Slovene, Ukrainian	new
Nová	Czech	new
Novaya	Russian	new
Nové	Czech, Slovak	new
Novi	Bulgarian, Croatian, Serbian, Ukrainian	new
Novo	Portuguese, Slovene	new
Novo-, Novoye	Russian	new
Novy	Belorussian	new
Nový	Czech	new
Novyy, Novyye	Russian, Ukrainian	new
Novyya	Belorussian	new
Nowa, Nowe, Nowy	Polish	new
Nueva, Nuevo	Spanish	new
-numa	Japanese	lake

Geographical term	Language	Meaning
-núpur	Icelandic	hill
Nur	Chinese, Mongolian	lake
Nuruu	Mongolian	mountain range
Nuur	Mongolian	lake
Ny-	Danish, Norwegian, Swedish	new

O

Geographical term	Language	Meaning
-ø	Danish	island
-ö	Swedish	island
oaivi, oaivve	Lappish	hill, mountain
Obanbari	Tajik	reservoir
Ober-	German	upper
Oblast'	Russian, Ukrainian	administrative division
-odde	Danish, Norwegian	cape, point
Oeste	Spanish	west, western
Okrug	Russian	administrative district
-ön	Swedish	island
Öndör-	Mongolian	upper
-oog	German	island
Oost, Ooster	Dutch	east, eastern
-öræfi	Icelandic	lava field
Oriental	Spanish	east, eastern
Ormos	Greek	bay
Oros	Greek	mountain
-ós	Icelandic	river mouth
Ost-	German	east, eastern
Øster-	Danish, Norwegian	east, eastern
Östra-	Swedish	east, eastern
Ostriv	Ukrainian	island
Ostrov, Ostrova	Russian	island, islands
Oud, Oude, Ouden, Ouder	Dutch	old
Oued	Arabic	watercourse
Ovası	Turkish	plain
Over-	Danish, Dutch	upper
Över-, Øvre-	Norwegian, Swedish	upper
-oy	Faroese	island
Ozero	Russian, Ukrainian	lake

P

Geographical term	Language	Meaning
-pää	Finnish	hill
Pampa	Spanish	plain
Pantà	Catalan	reservoir
Pantanal	Portuguese	marsh
Pao	Chinese	small lake
Parbat	Urdu	mountain
Parc	French	park
Parc Naturel	French	nature reserve
Parco	Italian	park
parkas	Lithuanian	park
Parque	Portuguese, Spanish	park
-pas	Afrikaans	pass
Paso	Spanish	pass
Paß	German	pass
Passage	French	channel
Passe	French	channel
Passo	Italian	pass
Pasul	Romanian	pass
Pegunungan	Indonesian, Malay	mountain range
Pelabuhan	Malay	port, harbour
Pen	Welsh	hill
Peña	Spanish	cliff, rock
Pendi	Chinese	basin
Península	Spanish	peninsula
Péninsule	French	peninsula
Penisola	Italian	peninsula
Pereval	Russian	pass
Pervo-, Pervyy	Russian	first
Peski	Russian	desert
Petit, Petite	French	small
Phou	Laotian	mountain
Phu	Thai, Vietnamese	mountain
Phumĭ	Cambodian	town, village
Pic	Catalan, French	peak
Picacho	Spanish	peak
Pico	Spanish	peak
Pik	Russian	peak
Pingyuan	Chinese	plain
Pivostriv	Ukrainian	peninsula
Pizzo	Italian	peak
-plaat	Dutch	flat, sandbank, shoal
Plage	French	beach
Plaine	French	plain
Planalto	Portuguese	plateau
Planina	Bulgarian, Croatian, Serbian	mountain(s)
Platforma	Romanian	plateau
Plato	Bulgarian, Russian	plateau
Playa	Spanish	beach
Plaza	Spanish	market-place, square
Ploskogor'ye	Russian	plateau
Po	Chinese	lake
pod	Czech, Russian, Slovak	under, sub-, near
Podişul	Romanian	plateau
Pointe	French	cape, point
Pojezierze	Polish	area of lakes
Polje	Croatian, Serbian	plain
Poluostrov	Russian	peninsula
Pont	French	bridge
Ponta	Maltese, Portuguese	cape, point
Ponte	Portuguese	bridge
poolsaar	Estonian	peninsula
Porogi	Russian	rapids
Port	Catalan, French, Maltese, Russian	port, harbour
Portella	Italian	pass
Portillo	Spanish	gap, pass
Porto	Italian, Portuguese, Spanish	bay, port, harbour, pass
Pradesh	Hindi	state

Geographical term	Language	Meaning
Praia	Portuguese	beach, shore
Prêk	Cambodian	lake, river
près	French	near, beside
Presa	Spanish	reservoir
Presqu'île	French	peninsula
Pri-	Russian	near, by
Proliv	Russian	channel, strait
Protoka	Russian	channel, watercourse
Pueblo	Spanish	village
Puente	Spanish	bridge
Puerta	Spanish	narrow pass
Puerto	Spanish	pass, port, harbour
Puig	Catalan	hill, mountain
Puk-	Korean	north, northern
Pulau	Indonesian, Malay	island
Pulau-pulau	Indonesian, Malay	islands
Puncak	Indonesian, Malay	hill, mountain, summit
Punta	Italian, Spanish	cape, point
Punta	Italian	hill, mountain
Puntan	Marshallese	cape, point
Puy	French	peak

Q

Geographical term	Language	Meaning
Qā'	Arabic	depression, salt flat, impermanent lake
Qabr	Arabic	tomb
Qafa	Albanian	pass
Qala	Maltese	bay
Qalamat	Arabic	well
Qalti	Arabic	well
Qâret	Arabic	hill
Qatorkŭhi	Tajik	mountain range
Qi	Chinese	banner (administrative division)
Qiao	Chinese	bridge
Qiryat	Hebrew	town
Qolleh	Farsi	mountain
Qoor, Qooriga	Somali	bay
qoruğu	Azeri	reserve
Qu	Tibetan	river
Quan	Chinese	spring, well
Quebrada	Spanish	ravine, river
Qullai	Tajik	mountain
Qundao	Chinese	islands

R

Geographical term	Language	Meaning
Raas	Somali	cape, point
Rade	French	harbour
rags	Latvian	cape, point
Rambla	Catalan	river
Ramla	Maltese	bay, harbour
Ramlat	Arabic	sandy desert
-rani	Icelandic	spur
Ras	Arabic, Maltese	cape, point
Ra's	Arabic, Farsi	cape, point
Râs, Rās	Arabic	cape, point
Ravnina	Russian	plain
Récif	French	reef
Represa	Portuguese, Spanish	reservoir
Reserva	Portuguese, Spanish	reserve
Réserve de Faune, Réserve Faunique	French	wildlife reserve
Réserve Naturelle	French	nature reserve
Reshteh	Farsi	mountain range
Respublika	Russian	republic
-rettō	Japanese	island chain, island group
rezervatas	Lithuanian	reserve
-ri	Korean	village
Ri	Tibetan	mountain
Ría	Spanish	estuary, inlet, river mouth
Ribeirão, Ribeiro	Portuguese	river
Rio	Portuguese	river
Río	Spanish	river
Riserva	Italian	reserve
-rivier	Afrikaans	river
Riviera	Italian	coastal area
Rivière	French	river
Roca	Spanish	rock
Rocher	French	rock
Rt	Croatian, Serbian	cape, point
Rū, Rūbār	Kurdish	river
Rubh', Rubha	Gaelic	cape, point
Rūd, Rūdkhāneh	Farsi	river
Rujm	Arabic	hill

S

Geographical term	Language	Meaning
-saar	Estonian	island
-saari	Finnish	island
Sabkhat, Sabkhet	Arabic	impermanent lake, salt flat, salt marsh
Sadd, Saddat	Arabic	dam
Sagar, Sagara	Hindi	lake
Şaghīr, Şaghīr	Arabic	small
Şaḥrā'	Arabic	desert
-saki	Japanese	cape, point
Salar, Salina	Spanish	salt pan
Salto	Portuguese, Spanish	waterfall
San	Italian, Maltese, Portuguese, Spanish	saint
San	Laotian	mountain
-san	Japanese, Korean	mountain
-sanchi	Japanese	mountain range
-sandur	Icelandic	sandy area
Sankt	German, Russian	saint
-sanmaek	Korean	mountain range
-sanmyaku	Japanese	mountain range
Sant	Catalan	saint
Sant'	Italian	saint

Geographical term	Language	Meaning
Santa	Italian, Portuguese, Spanish	saint
Santo	Italian, Portuguese, Spanish	saint
São	Portuguese	saint
Sar	Kurdish	mountain
Sarīr	Arabic	desert
Satu	Romanian	village
Say	Kyrgyz	river
Schloß	German	castle, mansion
Scoglio	Italian	reef, rock
Sebkha, Sebkhet	Arabic	salt flat, salt marsh
See, -see	German	lake
-şehir	Turkish	town
Selat	Indonesian, Malay	channel, strait
Selatan	Indonesian, Malay	south, southern
-selkä	Finnish	lake, open water, ridge
Selo	Croatian, Russian, Serbian	village
Selva	Portuguese, Spanish	forest
Semenanjung	Indonesian, Malay	peninsula
Seno	Spanish	bay, sound
Serra	Catalan, Portuguese	hills, mountains
Serranía	Spanish	mountain range
-seter	Norwegian	mountain pasture
-seto	Japanese	channel, strait
Severnaya, Severnoye, Severnyy, Severo-	Russian	north, northern
Sfântu	Romanian	saint
Sgeir	Gaelic	island
Sgor, Sgorach, Sgorr, Sgurr	Gaelic	hill
Shahr	Farsi	town
Sha'īb, Sha'īān	Arabic	watercourse
Shamo	Chinese	desert
Shan	Chinese	hill(s), mountain(s)
Shang	Chinese	next to, upper
Shankou	Chinese	pass
Sharm	Arabic	bay
Shatt	Arabic	estuary, river mouth, watercourse
Shën-	Albanian	saint
Shet'	Amharic	watercourse
Shi	Chinese	city
-shima	Japanese	island
-sho	Japanese	island
-shotō	Japanese	islands
Shui	Chinese	river
Shui Tong	Chinese	reservoir
Shuiku	Chinese	reservoir
Sierra	Spanish	mountain range
Silsiläsi	Azeri	hills
-sjø	Norwegian	lake
-sjö, -sjön	Swedish	lake
-sjór	Icelandic	lake
-sker	Icelandic	island
-skog	Norwegian	wood
Slieau	Manx	hill, mountain
Slieve	Irish	hill, mountain
Sloboda	Russian	large village
Sø	Danish, Norwegian	lake
Söder, Södra	Swedish	south, southern
Solonchak	Russian	salt lake
Sommet	French	peak, summit
Sønder-, Søndre	Danish	south, southern
Sông	Vietnamese	river
Sopka	Russian	hill, mountain, volcano
Sør-	Norwegian	south, southern
Sor	Russian	salt pan
sous	French	under
Sovkhoz	Russian	state farm
Spitze	German	peak
Sredna, Sredno	Bulgarian	middle, central
Sredne-, Sredneye, Sredniy, Srednyaya	Russian	middle, central
Sron	Gaelic	hill
Stac	Gaelic	hill, stack
-stad	Afrikaans, Norwegian, Swedish	town
-stadt	German	town
-staður	Icelandic	town
Stagno	Italian	lagoon, lake
Stara, Stari	Croatian, Serbian, Ukrainian	old
Stará, Staré, Starý	Czech	old
Staraya, Stary, Staryya	Belorussian	old
Staraya, Staroye, Staryy, Staryye	Russian	old
Stare, Staro-, Staryy	Ukrainian	old
Stausee	German	reservoir
Steno	Greek	strait
Step'	Russian	plain, steppe
Stob	Gaelic	hill, mountain
Stœng	Cambodian	river
Stór-, Stóra, Stóri	Icelandic	big
Stor, Stora	Swedish	big
Store	Danish	big
Strand	Danish, German	beach
-strand	Norwegian, Swedish	beach
Straße	German	street
Stretta	Italian	strait
-strönd	Icelandic	beach
Sud	French	south, southern
Süd-, Süder-	German	south, southern
Suður-	Icelandic	south, southern
Suid	Afrikaans	south, southern
-suidō	Japanese	channel, strait
Sul	Portuguese	south, southern
sul, sull'	Italian	on
Sund	Swedish	strait, sound
Sungai	Indonesian, Malay	river
-suo	Finnish	marsh, swamp
Superior	Spanish	upper
Sūq	Arabic	market
Sur	Spanish	south, southern
sur	French	on
Suur	Estonian	big
Sveti	Croatian, Serbian	saint
Syðra, Syðri	Icelandic	south, southern
sýsla	Icelandic	county

Geographical term	Language	Meaning
Szent-	Hungarian	saint
-sziget	Hungarian	island

T

Geographical term	Language	Meaning
-tag	Uighur	mountain
-take	Japanese	hill, mountain
Tal	German	valley
Tall	Arabic	hill
Tanjona	Malagasy	cape, point
Tanjong, Tanjung	Indonesian, Malay	cape, point
Tao	Chinese	island
Tassili	Berber	plateau
Tau	Russian	mountain(s)
Taung	Burmese	mountain
Tba	Georgian	lake
Techniti Limni	Greek	reservoir
tekojärvi	Finnish	reservoir
Tell	Arabic	hill, mountain
Teluk, Telukan	Indonesian, Malay	bay, gulf
Tengah	Indonesian, Malay	middle, central
Teniente	Spanish	lieutenant
Tepe, Tepesi	Turkish	hill, mountain
Terara	Amharic	mountain
Terre	French	land
Thale	Thai	lake
Thamad	Arabic	well
Tierra	Spanish	land
Timur	Indonesian, Malay	east, eastern
-tind, -tinden	Norwegian	peak
-tindar	Icelandic	peak
-tindur	Faroese, Icelandic	peak
Tir'at	Arabic	canal, river, watercourse
Tizi	Berber	pass
-tjåkkå	Lappish	mountain
-tjärro	Lappish	mountain
-tó	Hungarian	lake
-tō	Japanese	island
-to	Korean	island
-tōge	Japanese	pass
-tong	Korean	village
Tônlé	Cambodian	lake, river
Too	Kyrgyz	mountain range
-topp, -toppen	Norwegian	peak
T'ou	Chinese	cape, point
Tsentral'nyy	Russian	central
Tso	Tibetan	lake
Tsqalsats'avi	Georgian	reservoir
Tsui	Chinese	cape, point
Túnel	Spanish	tunnel
-tunturi	Finnish	treeless mountain

U

Geographical term	Language	Meaning
Über-	German	upper
-udden	Swedish	cape, point
Ugheltekhili	Georgian	pass
Új-	Hungarian	new
Ujung	Indonesian	cape, point
Unter-, unter	German	below, lower
'Uqlat	Arabic	well
-ura	Japanese	inlet
'Urayq, 'Urūq	Arabic	sand dunes
Ust'-, Ust'ye	Russian	river mouth
Utara	Indonesian, Malay	north, northern
Uttar	Hindi	north, northern
Uul	Mongolian	mountain range
Uval	Russian	hills
'Uyūn	Arabic	springs

V

Geographical term	Language	Meaning
v	Czech	in
-vaara, -vaarat	Finnish	hill(s), mountain(s)
Vaart, -vaart	Dutch	canal
-vaðall	Icelandic	inlet
-våg	Norwegian	bay
-vágur	Faroese	bay
Väike-	Estonian	small
väin	Estonian	bay, channel, strait
Val	French, Portuguese, Spanish	valley
Vale	Portuguese, Romanian	valley
Vall	Catalan, Spanish	valley
Valle	Italian, Spanish	valley
Vallée	French	valley
Valli	Italian	valleys
Vallon	French	small valley
Vârful	Romanian	hill, mountain
-város	Hungarian	town
-varre	Norwegian	mountain
Väster, Västra	Swedish	west, western
-vatn	Icelandic	lake
-vatn, -vatnet	Norwegian	lake
-vatten, -vattnet	Swedish	lake
Vaux	French	valleys
Vechi	Romanian	old
veehoidla	Estonian	lake
-veld	Afrikaans	field
Velha, Velho	Portuguese	old
Velika	Croatian, Slovene, Serbian	big
Velikaya, Velikiy, Velikiye	Russian	big
Velike	Slovene	big
Veliki	Croatian, Serbian	big
Velká, Velké, Velký	Czech	big
Veľká, Veľké, Veľký	Slovak	big
-vellir	Icelandic	plain
Velyka	Ukrainian	big
Verkhne-, Verkhneye, Verkhniy, Verkhnyaya	Russian	upper
-vesi	Finnish	lake, water
Viaduc	French	viaduct
-vidda	Norwegian	plateau

Geographical term	Language	Meaning
Vieja, Viejo	Spanish	old
Vieux	French	old
Vig	Danish	bay
-vík	Icelandic	bay
-vik	Norwegian	bay, inlet
Vila	Portuguese	small town
Ville	French	town
Vinh	Vietnamese	bay
-víz	Hungarian	river
-víztároló	Hungarian	reservoir
-vlei	Afrikaans	lake, salt pan
-vloer	Afrikaans	salt pan
Voblasts'	Belorussian	province
Vodaskhovishcha	Belorussian	reservoir
Vodná nádrž	Slovak	reservoir
Vodní nádrž	Czech	reservoir
Vodokhranilishche	Russian	reservoir
Vodoskhovyshche	Ukrainian	reservoir
-vogur	Icelandic	bay
Volcán	Spanish	volcano
Vostochno-, Vostochnyy	Russian	east, eastern
-võtn	Icelandic	lakes
Vozvyshennost'	Russian	hills, upland
Vozyera	Belorussian	lake
Vpadina	Russian	depression
Vrchovina	Czech	hills, mountain region
Vrŭkh	Bulgarian	hill, mountain
Vulkan	Russian	volcano
Vyalikaya, Vyalikaye, Vyaliki, Vyalikiya	Belorussian	big
Vyerkhnya	Belorussian	upper
Vysokaya, Vysokoye	Russian	upper

W

Geographical term	Language	Meaning
-waard	Dutch	polder (reclaimed land)
Wad	Dutch	sandflat
Wadi, Wâdi, Wādī	Arabic	watercourse
Wai	Chinese	outer
Wald	German	forest
Wan	Chinese	bay
-wan	Japanese	bay
Wand	German	cliff
Wasser	German	water
Wāw	Arabic	well
Webi	Somali	river
Wenz	Amharic	river, watercourse
Wielka, Wielki, Wielkie, Wielko-	Polish	big
-woud	Dutch	wood, forest
Wysoka, Wysoki, Wysokie	Polish	upper
Wyżna	Polish	lowland
Wzvyshsha	Belorussian	upland

X

Geographical term	Language	Meaning
Xé	Vietnamese	river
Xi	Chinese	river, west, western
Xia	Chinese	gorge, lower
Xian	Chinese	county
Xiao	Chinese	small

Y

Geographical term	Language	Meaning
Yam	Hebrew	lake, sea
-yama	Japanese	mountain
Yang	Chinese	channel
Yangi	Russian	new
Yarımadası	Azeri, Turkish	peninsula
Yazovir	Bulgarian	reservoir
Ye	Burmese	island
Yeni	Turkish	new
Yli-	Finnish	upper
Ynys	Welsh	island
Yoma	Burmese	mountain range
You	Chinese	right
Ytra-, Ytri-	Icelandic	outer
Ytre-	Norwegian	outer
Ytter-	Norwegian, Swedish	outer
Yuan	Chinese	spring
Yumco	Tibetan	lake
Yunhe	Chinese	canal
Yuzhno-, Yuzhnyy	Russian	south, southern

Z

Geographical term	Language	Meaning
Za-	Russian	behind, beyond
-zaki	Japanese	cape, point
Zalew	Polish	bay
Zaliv	Russian	bay, gulf, inlet
-zan	Japanese	mountain
Zand	Dutch	sandbank, sandhill
Zangbo	Tibetan	river
Zapadnaya, Zapadno-, Zapadnyy	Russian	west, western
Zapavyednik	Belorussian	reserve
Zapovednik	Russian	reserve
Zapovidnyk	Ukrainian	reserve
Zatoka	Polish, Ukrainian	bay, gulf, lagoon
-zee	Dutch	lake, sea
Zemlya	Russian	land
Zemo	Georgian	upper
Zhen	Chinese	town
Zhong	Chinese	middle, central
Zhou	Chinese	island
Zizhiqu	Chinese	autonomous region
Zuid, Zuider	Dutch	south, southern
Zuo	Chinese	left

INTRODUCTION TO THE INDEX

The index includes names shown on the maps in the Atlas of the World. Each entry includes the country or geographical area in which the feature is located, a page number and an alphanumeric reference. Additional details within the entries are explained below. Abbreviations used in the index are explained in the table below.

REFERENCING

Names are referenced by page number, the first element of each entry, and by a grid reference. The grid reference correlates to the alphanumeric values which appear within each map frame. These reflect the graticule on the map – the letter relates to longitude divisions, the number to latitude divisions.

Names are generally referenced to the largest scale map page on which they appear. For large geographical features, including countries, the reference is to the largest scale map on which the feature appears in its entirety, or on which the majority of it appears.

Rivers are referenced to their lowest downstream point – either their mouth or their confluence with another river. The river name will generally be positioned as close to this point as possible, but may not necessarily be in the same grid square.

ALTERNATIVE NAMES

Alternative names or name forms appear as cross-references and refer the user to the entry for the map form of the name.

For rivers with multiple names – for example those which flow through several countries – all alternative name forms are included within the main index entries, with details of the countries in which each form applies. Different types of name used are: alternative forms or spellings currently in use (alt.); English conventional name forms normally used in English-language contexts (conv.); and long names – full forms of names which are most commonly used in the abbreviated form.

ADMINISTRATIVE QUALIFIERS

Entries within the following countries include the main administrative division in which they occur: Australia, Canada, China, India, U.K., U.S.A. and Yugoslavia. Administrative divisions are also included to differentiate duplicate names – entries of exactly the same name and feature type within the one country – where these division names are shown on the maps. In such cases, duplicate names are alphabetized in the order of the administrative division names.

Additional qualifiers are included for names within selected geographical areas, to indicate more clearly their location. In particular, this has been applied to island nations to indicate the island group, or individual island, on which a feature occurs.

DESCRIPTORS

Entries, other than those for towns and cities, include a descriptor indicating the type of geographical feature. Descriptors are not included where the type of feature is implicit in the name itself, unless there is a town or city of exactly the same name.

INSETS

Entries relating to names appearing on insets are indicated by a small box symbol: □, followed by an inset number if there is more than one inset on the page, or by a grid reference if the inset has its own alphanumeric values.

NAME FORMS AND ALPHABETICAL ORDER

Name forms are as they appear on the maps, with additional alternative forms included as cross-references. Names appear in full in the index, although they may appear in abbreviated form on the maps.

The Icelandic characters Þ and þ are transliterated and alphabetized as 'Th' and 'th'. The German character ß is alphabetized as 'ss'. Names beginning with Mac or Mc are alphabetized exactly as they appear. The terms Saint, Sainte, etc, are abbreviated to St, Ste, etc, but alphabetized as if in the full form.

Name form policies are explained in the Introduction to the Atlas (pp 66-67).

NUMERICAL ENTRIES

Entries beginning with numerals appear at the beginning of the index, in numerical order. Elsewhere, numerals appear before 'a'.

PERMUTED TERMS

Names beginning with generic, geographical terms are permuted – the descriptive term is placed after, and the index alphabetized by, the main part of the name. For example, Lake Superior is indexed as Superior, Lake; Mount Everest as Everest, Mount. This policy is applied to all languages. Permuting has not been applied to names of towns, cities or administrative divisions beginning with such geographical terms. These remain in their full form, for example, Lake Isabella, California, USA.

The definite article is not permuted in any language.

INDEX ABBREVIATIONS

A.C.T.	Australian Capital Territory	est.	estuary	Moz.	Mozambique	rf	reef
admin. dist.	administrative district	Eth.	Ethiopia	MS	Mississippi	RI	Rhode Island
admin. div.	administrative division	Fin.	Finland	MT	Montana	Rus. Fed.	Russian Federation
admin. reg.	administrative region	FL	Florida	mt.	mountain	S.	South
Afgh.	Afghanistan	for.	forest	mts	mountains	S.A.	South Australia
AK	Alaska	Fr. Guiana	French Guiana	mun.	municipality	Sask.	Saskatchewan
AL	Alabama	Fr. Polynesia	French Polynesia	N.	North	SC	South Carolina
Alg.	Algeria	g.	gulf	N.B.	New Brunswick	SD	South Dakota
alt.	alternative name form	GA	Georgia	NC	North Carolina	sea chan.	sea channel
Alta	Alberta	Gd Bahama	Grand Bahama	ND	North Dakota	Serb. and Mont.	Serbia and Montenegro
Andhra Prad.	Andhra Pradesh	Ger.	Germany	NE	Nebraska	Sing.	Singapore
AR	Arkansas	Guat.	Guatemala	Neth.	Netherlands	str.	strait
Arg.	Argentina	hd	headland	Nfld.	Newfoundland	Switz.	Switzerland
Arun. Prad.	Arunachal Pradesh	Heilong.	Heilongjiang	NH	New Hampshire	Tajik.	Tajikistan
Austr.	Australia	HI	Hawaii	Nic.	Nicaragua	Tanz.	Tanzania
aut. comm.	autonomous community	Hima. Prad.	Himachal Pradesh	NJ	New Jersey	Tas.	Tasmania
aut. div.	autonomous division	H.K.	Hong Kong	NM	New Mexico	terr.	territory
aut. prov.	autonomous province	Hond.	Honduras	N.S.	Nova Scotia	Thai.	Thailand
aut. reg.	autonomous region	i.	island	N.S.W.	New South Wales	TN	Tennessee
aut. rep.	autonomous republic	is	islands	N.T.	Northern Territory	Trin. and Tob.	Trinidad and Tobago
AZ	Arizona	IA	Iowa	NV	Nevada	tun.	tunnel
Azer.	Azerbaijan	ID	Idaho	N.W.T.	Northwest Territories	Turkm.	Turkmenistan
b.	bay	IL	Illinois	NY	New York	TX	Texas
Bangl.	Bangladesh	imp. l.	impermanent lake	N.Z.	New Zealand	U.A.E.	United Arab Emirates
B.C.	British Columbia	IN	Indiana	OH	Ohio	U.K.	United Kingdom
B.I.O.T.	British Indian Ocean Territory	Indon.	Indonesia	OK	Oklahoma	Ukr.	Ukraine
Bol.	Bolivia	isth.	isthmus	Ont.	Ontario	Uru.	Uruguay
Bos.-Herz.	Bosnia-Herzegovina	Kazakh.	Kazakhstan	OR	Oregon	U.S.A.	United States of America
Bulg.	Bulgaria	KS	Kansas	PA	Pennsylvania	UT	Utah
c.	cape	KY	Kentucky	Pak.	Pakistan	Uttar Prad.	Uttar Pradesh
CA	California	Kyrg.	Kyrgyzstan	Para.	Paraguay	Uzbek.	Uzbekistan
Can.	Canada	l.	lake	P.E.I.	Prince Edward Island	VA	Virginia
C.A.R.	Central African Republic	LA	Louisiana	pen.	peninsula	val.	valley
CO	Colorado	lag.	lagoon	Phil.	Philippines	Venez.	Venezuela
Col.	Colombia	Lith.	Lithuania	plat.	plateau	Vic.	Victoria
conv.	conventional name form	Lux.	Luxembourg	P.N.G.	Papua New Guinea	vol.	volcano
CT	Connecticut	MA	Massachusetts	Pol.	Poland	vol. crater	volcanic crater
Czech Rep.	Czech Republic	Madag.	Madagascar	Port.	Portugal	VT	Vermont
DC	District of Columbia	Madh. Prad.	Madhya Pradesh	pref.	prefecture	W.	West, Western
DE	Delaware	Mahar.	Maharashtra	prov.	province	W.A.	Western Australia
Dem. Rep. Congo	Democratic Republic of Congo	Man.	Manitoba	Qld	Queensland	WA	Washington
depr.	depression	Maur.	Mauritania	Que.	Québec	WI	Wisconsin
dept	department	MD	Maryland	r.	river	WV	West Virginia
des.	desert	ME	Maine	r. mouth	river mouth	WY	Wyoming
Dom. Rep.	Dominican Republic	Mex.	Mexico	reg.	region	Y.T.	Yukon Territory
E.	East, Eastern	MI	Michigan	Rep.	Republic		
Equat. Guinea	Equatorial Guinea	MN	Minnesota	research stn	research station		
esc.	escarpment	MO	Missouri	resr	reservoir		

1st Cataract to Afmadow

224

1

85 G3 **1st Cataract** *rapids* Egypt
207 J2 **1st Three Mile Opening** *sea chan. Qld* Austr.
85 F4 **2nd Cataract** *rapids* Sudan
207 I2 **2nd Three Mile Opening** *sea chan. Qld* Austr.
85 F5 **3rd Cataract** *rapids* Sudan
85 G5 **4th Cataract** *rapids* Sudan
85 G5 **5th Cataract** *rapids* Sudan
147 G4 **9 de Julio** Arg.
147 G5 **16 de Julio** Arg.
147 F5 **17 de Agosto** Arg.
147 G4 **25 de Mayo** *Buenos Aires* Arg.
146 D5 **25 de Mayo** *La Pampa* Arg.
146 C4 **25 de Mayo** *Mendoza* Arg.
147 I4 **25 de Mayo** Uru.
191 K6 **26 Bakı Komissarı** Azer.
147 F5 **30 de Agosto** Arg.
97 N4 **42nd Hill** S. Africa
106 F5 **70 Mile House** *B.C.* Can.
106 F5 **100 Mile House** *B.C.* Can.
106 F4 **150 Mile House** *B.C.* Can.

A

36 D1 **Aa** *r.* France
49 B7 **Aa** *r.* Ger.
49 E7 **Aa** *r.* Ger.
22 F6 **Aabenraa** Denmark
52 F6 **Aach** Ger.
52 G6 **Aach** *r.* Ger.
49 B9 **Aachen** Ger.
92 E4 **Aadan Yabaal** Somalia
70 F1 **Aadorf** Switz.
23 K6 **Aakirkeby** *Bornholm* Denmark
22 F4 **Aalborg** Denmark
22 G5 **Aalborg Bugt** *b.* Denmark
53 I4 **Aalen** Ger.
22 F5 **Aalestrup** Denmark
Aalesund Norway *see* **Ålesund**
Aaley Lebanon *see* **Aley**
44 G4 **Aalsmeer** Neth.
45 F7 **Aalst** Belgium
45 H6 **Aalst** Neth.
44 K5 **Aalten** Neth.
45 D6 **Aalter** Belgium
20 R5 **Äänekoski** Fin.
96 G2 **Aansluit** S. Africa
Aar *r.* Switz. *see* **Aare**
175 □1 **Aarah** *i. N. Male* Maldives
70 E1 **Aarau** Switz.
70 C1 **Aarberg** Switz.
70 D1 **Aarburg** Switz.
45 D6 **Aardenburg** Neth.
70 E1 **Aare** *r.* Switz.
20 Q3 **Aareavaara** Sweden
70 E1 **Aargau** *canton* Switz.
Aarhus Denmark *see* **Århus**
44 I6 **Aarle** Neth.
Aarlen Belgium *see* **Arlon**
62 D2 **A Armada** Spain
22 F5 **Aars** Denmark
45 G7 **Aarschot** Belgium
45 F6 **Aartselaar** Belgium
22 G6 **Aarup** Denmark
52 D7 **Aarwangen** Switz.
105 M3 **Aasiaat** Greenland
Aath Belgium *see* **Ath**
20 Q3 **Aavasaksa** Fin.
170 C2 **Aba** *Sichuan* China
90 F4 **Aba** Dem. Rep. Congo
57 H4 **Aba** Hungary
89 G5 **Aba** Nigeria
186 G2 **Abā ad Dūd** Saudi Arabia
187 J6 **Abā al Afan** *oasis* Saudi Arabia
190 D9 **Abā al Hinshan** Saudi Arabia
137 G6 **Abacaxis** *r.* Brazil
184 C6 **Ābādān** Iran
184 C6 **Ābādān, Jazīrah** *i.* Iran/Iraq
184 F3 **Abadan Tappeh** Iran
184 E6 **Ābādeh** Iran
184 E7 **Ābādeh Ţashk** Iran
62 G7 **Abadengo** *reg.* Spain
63 L7 **Abades** Spain
142 D3 **Abadia dos Dourados** Brazil
142 C2 **Abadiânia** Brazil
62 F2 **Abadín** Spain
86 E3 **Abadla** Alg.
57 J4 **Abádszalók** Hungary
191 B1 **Abadzekhskaya** Rus. Fed.
143 E3 **Abaeté** Brazil
143 E3 **Abaeté** *r.* Brazil
140 C2 **Abaetetuba** Brazil
169 O2 **Abagaytuy** Rus. Fed.
139 G6 **Abaí** Para.
199 H1 **Abaiang** *atoll* Kiribati
62 D2 **A Baiuca** Spain
89 G4 **Abaji** Nigeria
125 W4 **Abajo Peak** *UT* U.S.A.
89 H5 **Abakaliki** Nigeria
160 F1 **Abakan** Rus. Fed.
160 E1 **Abakanskiy Khrebet** *mts* Rus. Fed.
90 B5 **Abala** Congo
89 F3 **Abala** Niger
89 G3 **Abalak** Niger
87 G5 **Abalessa** Alg.
18 N7 **Abalyanka** *r.* Belarus
188 G3 **Abana** Turkey
63 P7 **Abánades** Spain
138 B3 **Abancay** Peru
90 A5 **Abanga** *r.* Gabon
67 C11 **Abanilla** Spain
71 L5 **Abano Terme** Italy
138 E4 **Abapó** Bol.
67 C11 **Abarán** Spain
184 E6 **Abarkūh, Kavīr-e** *des.* Iran
184 E6 **Abarqū** Iran
62 E3 **A Barrela** Spain
57 J4 **Abasár** Hungary
191 D3 **Abasha** Georgia
164 V2 **Abashiri** Japan
164 V3 **Abashiri-ko** *l.* Japan
164 V2 **Abashiri-wan** *b.* Japan
128 F5 **Abasolo** *Guanajuato* Mex.
129 I1 **Abasolo** *Tamaulipas* Mex.
129 L8 **Abasolo del Valle** Mex.
191 D4 **Abast'umani** Georgia
93 C5 **Abasula** *waterhole* Kenya
153 K9 **Abau** P.N.G.
57 K3 **Abaújszántó** Hungary
18 E4 **Abava** *r.* Latvia
183 O3 **Abay** *Karagandinskaya Oblast'* Kazakh.
Abaya, Lake Eth. *see* **Ābaya Hāyk'**
92 C3 **Ābaya Hāyk'** *l.* Eth.
Abay Bazar Kazakh. *see* **Abay**
85 G6 **Ābay Wenz** *r.* Eth. *alt.* **Azraq, Bahr el (Sudan),** *conv.* **Blue Nile**
160 F1 **Abaza** Rus. Fed.
90 B3 **Abba** C.A.R.
72 H2 **Abbadia San Salvatore** Italy
189 P8 **Abbāsābād** *Fārs* Iran
184 H5 **Abbāsābād** *Khorāsān* Iran
184 G3 **'Abbāsābad** Iran
184 F5 **Abbāsābād Mehr Jān** Iran
72 B7 **Abbasanta** *Sardegna* Italy
Abbatis Villa France *see* Abbeville
110 F3 **Abbaye, Point** *MI* U.S.A.
92 D2 **Abbe, Lake** Djibouti/Eth.
31 N4 **Abberton Reservoir** *England* U.K.
36 C3 **Abbeville** France
115 E10 **Abbeville** *AL* U.S.A.
115 F10 **Abbeville** *GA* U.S.A.
121 I11 **Abbeville** *LA* U.S.A.
115 F8 **Abbeville** *SC* U.S.A.
107 I5 **Abbey** *Sask.* Can.
27 C8 **Abbeydorney** Rep. of Ireland
27 D8 **Abbeyfeale** Rep. of Ireland
26 I13 **Abbey Head** *Scotland* U.K.
27 H7 **Abbeyleix** Rep. of Ireland
29 K4 **Abbey Town** *Cumbria, England* U.K.
70 F5 **Abbiategrasso** Italy
20 O4 **Abborrträsk** Sweden
207 K6 **Abbot, Mount** *Qld* Austr.
207 K5 **Abbot Bay** *Qld* Austr.
212 R2 **Abbot Ice Shelf** Antarctica
31 I2 **Abbots Bromley** *Staffordshire, England* U.K.
30 G6 **Abbotsbury** *Dorset, England* U.K.
106 F5 **Abbotsford** *B.C.* Can.
110 D5 **Abbotsford** *WI* U.S.A.
31 L4 **Abbots Langley** *Hertfordshire, England* U.K.
118 B5 **Abbotstown** *PA* U.S.A.
123 L8 **Abbott** *NM* U.S.A.
116 E11 **Abbott** *VA* U.S.A.
116 E10 **Abbott** *WV* U.S.A.
185 O4 **Abbottabad** Pak.
18 M7 **Abchuha** Belarus
44 G4 **Abcoude** Neth.
57 G4 **Abda** Hungary
189 J5 **'Abd al 'Azīz, Jabal** *hill* Syria
187 K9 **'Abd al Kūrī** *i.* Yemen
189 N9 **'Abd Allah, Khawr** *sea chan.* Iraq/Kuwait
190 G8 **Abd al Ma'asīr** *well* Saudi Arabia
184 B5 **Ābdānān** Iran
14 J5 **Abdi** Rus. Fed.
184 G4 **Abdolabād** Iran
184 G3 **Abdollāhābād** *Khorāsān* Iran
184 E4 **Abdollāhābād** *Semnān* Iran
182 E1 **Abdulino** Rus. Fed.
84 D6 **Abéché** Chad
167 H6 **Abe-gawa** *r.* Japan
89 F2 **Abeïbara** Mali
89 F2 **Abeïbara** *well* Mali
63 O5 **Abejar** Spain
67 D8 **Abejuela** Spain
89 G5 **Abejukolo** Nigeria
64 B4 **Abela** Port.
89 G2 **Abélajouad** *well* Niger
88 E2 **Abelbod** *well* Mali
45 C7 **Abele** Belgium
62 C4 **Abelleiro, Punta** *pt* Spain
Abellinum Italy *see* **Avellino**
203 H7 **Abel Tasman National Park** *South I.* N.Z.
20 K4 **Abelvær** Norway
199 H1 **Abemama** *atoll Gilbert Is* Kiribati
94 C3 **Abenab** Namibia
53 J3 **Abenberg** Ger.
65 P2 **Abengibre** Spain
88 E5 **Abengourou** Côte d'Ivoire
65 K3 **Abenójar** Spain
Åbenrå Denmark *see* **Aabenraa**
53 L4 **Abens** *r.* Ger.
53 L4 **Abensberg** Ger.
89 F5 **Abeokuta** Nigeria
92 B3 **Abera** Eth.
30 D3 **Aberaeron** *Ceredigion, Wales* U.K.
30 F4 **Aberaman** *Rhondda Cynon Taff, Wales* U.K.
30 E4 **Aberavon** *Neath Port Talbot, Wales* U.K.
38 B4 **Aber Benoît** *inlet* France
30 F4 **Abercanaid** *Merthyr Tydfil, Wales* U.K.
30 B4 **Abercastle** *Pembrokeshire, Wales* U.K.
26 K7 **Aberchirder** *Aberdeenshire, Scotland* U.K.
205 L5 **Abercrombie** *r. N.S.W.* Austr.
205 L6 **Abercrombie River National Park** *N.S.W.* Austr.
30 F4 **Abercynon** *Rhondda Cynon Taff, Wales* U.K.
30 F4 **Aberdare** *Rhondda Cynon Taff, Wales* U.K.
92 C5 **Aberdare National Park** Kenya
30 C2 **Aberdaron** *Gwynedd, Wales* U.K.
205 M5 **Aberdeen** *N.S.W.* Austr.
171 □J7 **Aberdeen** *H.K.* China
96 I8 **Aberdeen** S. Africa
26 L8 **Aberdeen** *Aberdeen, Scotland* U.K.
26 L8 **Aberdeen** *admin. div. Scotland* U.K.
118 C6 **Aberdeen** *MD* U.S.A.
121 K9 **Aberdeen** *MS* U.S.A.
116 B10 **Aberdeen** *OH* U.S.A.
120 F3 **Aberdeen** *SD* U.S.A.
122 C3 **Aberdeen** *WA* U.S.A.
Aberdeen Island *H.K.* China *see* **Ap Lei Chau**
107 L1 **Aberdeen Lake** *Nunavut* Can.
96 I8 **Aberdeen Road** S. Africa
26 K8 **Aberdeenshire** *admin. div. Scotland* U.K.
26 J10 **Aberdour** *Fife, Scotland* U.K.
30 D2 **Aberdovey** *Gwynedd, Wales* U.K.
Aberdyfi *Gwynedd, Wales* U.K. *see* **Aberdovey**
26 I9 **Aberfeldy** *Perth and Kinross, Scotland* U.K.
30 D1 **Aberffraw** *Isle of Anglesey, Wales* U.K.
29 O6 **Aberford** *West Yorkshire, England* U.K.
26 H10 **Aberfoyle** *Stirling, Scotland* U.K.
30 F4 **Abergavenny** *Monmouthshire, Wales* U.K.
92 C1 **Ābergelē** Eth.
30 E1 **Abergele** *Conwy, Wales* U.K.
Abergwaun *Pembrokeshire, Wales* U.K. *see* **Fishguard**
30 E3 **Abergwesyn** *Powys, Wales* U.K.
30 E2 **Abergynolwyn** *Gwynedd, Wales* U.K.
Aberhonddu *Powys, Wales* U.K. *see* **Brecon**
30 E4 **Aberkenfig** *Bridgend, Wales* U.K.
26 K10 **Aberlady** *East Lothian, Scotland* U.K.
26 K9 **Aberlemno** *Angus, Scotland* U.K.
26 J8 **Aberlour** *Moray, Scotland* U.K.
Abermaw *Gwynedd, Wales* U.K. *see* **Barmouth**
Abermaw *Wales* U.K. *see* **Barmouth**
121 E9 **Abernathy** *TX* U.S.A.
26 J10 **Abernethy** *Perth and Kinross, Scotland* U.K.
30 C3 **Aberporth** *Ceredigion, Wales* U.K.
30 C2 **Abersoch** *Gwynedd, Wales* U.K.
30 F4 **Abersychan** *Torfaen, Wales* U.K.
56 B1 **Abertamy** Czech Rep.
Aberteifi *Ceredigion, Wales* U.K. *see* **Cardigan**
30 F4 **Abertillery** *Blaenau Gwent, Wales* U.K.
64 H2 **Abertura** Spain
26 I10 **Aberuthven** *Perth and Kinross, Scotland* U.K.
38 B4 **Aber Vrac'h** *inlet* France
30 D3 **Aberystwyth** *Ceredigion, Wales* U.K.
Abeshr Chad *see* **Abéché**
14 M2 **Abez'** Rus. Fed.
58 G6 **Abfaltersbach** Austria
184 H8 **Āb Gāh** Iran
15 I6 **Abganerovo** Rus. Fed.
186 F6 **Abhā** Saudi Arabia
186 E3 **Abhā, Jabal** *hill* Saudi Arabia
26 B7 **Abhainnsuidhe** *Western Isles, Scotland* U.K.
178 H9 **Abhanpur** *Chhattisgarh* India
184 C3 **Abhar** Iran
184 C4 **Abhar Rūd** *r.* Iran
89 G5 **Abia** *state* Nigeria
85 G6 **Abiad, Bahr el** *r.* Sudan/Uganda *alt.* **Jebel, Bahr el,** *conv.* **White Nile**
63 P8 **Abia de la Obispalía** Spain
92 C3 **Ābīata Hāyk'** *l.* Eth.
136 B2 **Abibe, Serranía de** *mts* Col.
88 D5 **Abidjan** Côte d'Ivoire
66 E3 **Abiego** Spain
96 E3 **Abiekwasputs** *salt pan* S. Africa
92 C3 **Abijatta-Shalla National Park** Eth.
167 L4 **Abiko** Japan
48 G1 **Abild** Denmark
120 G6 **Abilene** *KS* U.S.A.
121 F9 **Abilene** *TX* U.S.A.
39 M8 **Abilly** France
31 J4 **Abingdon** *Oxfordshire, England* U.K.
118 C6 **Abingdon** *MD* U.S.A.
116 C12 **Abingdon** *VA* U.S.A.
26 I12 **Abington** *South Lanarkshire, Scotland* U.K.
117 O6 **Abington** *MA* U.S.A.
118 E4 **Abington** *PA* U.S.A.
207 L5 **Abington Reef** *Coral Sea Is Terr.* Austr.
15 G7 **Abinsk** Rus. Fed.
63 N5 **Abión** *r.* Spain
20 O2 **Abisko nationalpark** *nat. park* Sweden
107 J2 **Abitau Lake** *N.W.T.* Can.
108 D3 **Abitibi** *r. Ont.* Can.
108 D3 **Abitibi, Lake** *Ont./Que.* Can.
Abkhazia *aut. rep.* Georgia *see* **Ap'khazet'i**
184 G4 **Ab Khūr** Iran
65 N6 **Abla** Spain
36 C6 **Ablis** France
63 Q5 **Ablitas** Spain
189 L7 **Āb Naft** *r.* Iraq
85 F3 **Abnūb** Egypt
Åbo Fin. *see* **Turku**
66 C2 **Abodi, Sierra de** *mts* Spain
178 E4 **Abohar** *Punjab* India
62 D5 **Aboim das Choças** Port.
88 E5 **Aboisso** Côte d'Ivoire
92 B2 **Aboke** Sudan
89 F5 **Abomey** Benin
98 □3a **Abona, Punta de** *pt Tenerife* Canary Is
40 J4 **Abondance** France
156 B2 **Abongabong, Gunung** *mt.* Indon.
89 I6 **Abong Mbang** Cameroon
57 J4 **Abony** Hungary
88 E5 **Abooso** Ghana
187 K7 **Aboot** Oman
154 B7 **Aborlan** *Palawan* Phil.
166 G3 **Abō-tōge** *pass* Japan
90 C2 **Abou Déia** Chad
84 D6 **Abou Goulem** Chad
90 B5 **Aboumi** Gabon
90 E2 **Abourasséin, Mont** *mt.* C.A.R.
89 G3 **Abouraya** *well* Niger
191 F5 **Abovyan** Armenia
26 K8 **Aboyne** *Aberdeenshire, Scotland* U.K.
187 I3 **Abqaiq** Saudi Arabia
145 B9 **Abra, Canal** *sea chan.* Chile
145 E6 **Abra, Laguna del** *l.* Arg.
186 H8 **Abrād, Wādī** *watercourse* Yemen
62 D6 **Abragão** Port.
130 G2 **Abraham's Bay** *Mayaguana* Bahamas
89 G5 **Abraka** Nigeria
57 L4 **Abram** Romania
29 L6 **Abram** *Greater Manchester, England* U.K.
14 H2 **Abramov, Mys** *pt* Rus. Fed.
17 U2 **Abramovka** Rus. Fed.
110 F5 **Abrams** *WI* U.S.A.
57 L4 **Abrămuţ** Romania
64 C2 **Abrantes** Port.
144 D1 **Abra Pampa** Arg.
191 G6 **Äbraqunis** Azer.
17 Q9 **Abrau Dyurso** Rus. Fed.
62 E7 **Abraveses** Port.
143 F4 **Abre Campo** Brazil
62 F6 **Abreiro** Port.
126 C4 **Abreojos, Punta** *pt* Mex.
66 I4 **Abrera** Spain
37 N6 **Abreschviller** France
40 C4 **Abrest** France
85 F4 **'Abri** Sudan
41 J7 **Abriès** France
143 H3 **Abrolhos, Arquipélago dos** *is* Brazil
214 G7 **Abrolhos Bank** *sea feature* S. Atlantic Ocean
19 S3 **Abrosovo** Rus. Fed.
65 N6 **Abrucena** Spain
77 L4 **Abrud** Romania
18 F3 **Abruka** *i.* Estonia
Abruzzi *admin. reg.* Italy *see* Abruzzo
73 L3 **Abruzzo** *admin. reg.* Italy
73 L4 **Abruzzo, Parco Nazionale d'** *nat. park* Italy
186 F7 **'Abs** Yemen
212 W1 **Absalom, Mount** Antarctica
58 E5 **Absam** Austria
122 I4 **Absaroka Range** *mts WY* U.S.A.
53 J3 **Absberg** Ger.
59 M3 **Absdorf** Austria
119 G6 **Absecon** *NJ* U.S.A.
119 G6 **Absecon Bay** *NJ* U.S.A.
191 K5 **Abşeron Yarımadası** *pen.* Azer.
18 K6 **Absterna, Vozyera** *l.* Belarus
190 F4 **Abtar, Jabal al** *hills* Syria
59 H4 **Abtenau** Austria
52 H4 **Abtsgmünd** Ger.
165 I12 **Abu** Japan
190 F3 **Abū aḑ Ḑuhūr** Syria
187 K3 **Abū al Abyaḑ** *i.* U.A.E.
190 G6 **Abū al Ḩusayn, Qā'** *imp. l.* Jordan
187 I2 **Abū 'Alī** *i.* Saudi Arabia
190 E8 **Abū 'Āmūd, Wādī** *watercourse* Jordan
186 F7 **Abū 'Arīsh** Saudi Arabia
84 E3 **Abū Ballāş** *hill* Egypt
186 G7 **Abū Dā'ir** *des.* Yemen
85 G6 **Abu Deleiq** Sudan
Abu Dhabi U.A.E. *see* Abū Ẓabī
186 D4 **Abū Ḑībā'** *waterhole* Saudi Arabia
190 G2 **Abū Du'ān** Syria
190 B10 **Abū Durbah** Egypt
137 F6 **Abufari** Brazil
90 E2 **Abu Gabra** Sudan
85 H6 **Abu Gamel** Sudan
85 G5 **Abu Ghirban** Sudan
92 A2 **Abu Gubeiha** Sudan
190 B10 **Abū Ḩād, Wādī** *watercourse* Egypt
190 G6 **Abū Ḩafnah, Wādī** *watercourse* Jordan
190 E7 **Abū Ḩallūfah, Jabal** *hill* Jordan
85 G5 **Abu Hamed** Sudan
84 E6 **Abu Hamra, Wadi** *watercourse* Sudan
85 G5 **Abu Haraz** Sudan
85 G5 **Abu Hashim** Sudan
190 B10 **Abū Ḩaşwah, Jabal** *hill* Egypt
175 □2 **Abuhera** *i. Addu Atoll* Maldives
85 G6 **Abu Higar** Sudan
89 G4 **Abuja** Nigeria
190 C10 **Abū Jalūm, Ra's** *pt* Egypt
187 H3 **Abū Jifān** *well* Saudi Arabia
190 D8 **Ābū Jurdhān** Jordan
189 J6 **Abū Kamāl** Syria
84 A1 **Abū Kammāsh** Libya
55 M2 **Abukhava** Belarus
167 L1 **Abukuma-gawa** *r.* Japan
167 M2 **Abukuma-kōchi** *plat.* Japan
85 F6 **Abu La'ot** *watercourse* Sudan
186 E6 **Abū Latt Island** Saudi Arabia
186 C3 **Abū Madd, Ra's** *hd* Saudi Arabia
90 E2 **Abu Matariq** Sudan
188 D8 **Abu Mena** *tourist site* Egypt
90 D4 **Abumombazi** Dem. Rep. Congo
187 L3 **Abu Musa** *i.* The Gulf
Abū Mūsá, Jazīreh-ye *i.* The Gulf *see* **Abu Musa**
138 D2 **Abunã** *r.* Bol.
138 D2 **Abunã** Brazil
136 E5 **Abunai** Brazil
84 C2 **Abū Nā'im** *well* Libya
92 C1 **Ābune Yosēf** *mt.* Eth.
84 B2 **Abū Nujaym** Libya
190 F4 **Abū Qa'ţūr** Syria
188 E8 **Abū Qīr, Khalīj** *b.* Egypt
84 B2 **Abū Qurīn** Libya
186 C2 **Abū Rāqah** *well* Saudi Arabia
190 C9 **Abū Rawthah, Jabal** *mt.* Egypt
166 E4 **Aburazaka-tōge** *pass* Japan
90 F4 **Aburo** *mt.* Dem. Rep. Congo
178 D7 **Abu Road** *Rajasthan* India
186 D4 **Abū Rubayq** Saudi Arabia
190 B10 **Abū Rudays** Egypt
190 G4 **Abū Rujmayn, Jabal** *mts* Syria
190 F10 **Abū Sallah, Wādī** *watercourse* Saudi Arabia
187 I3 **Abū Sawādah** *well* Saudi Arabia
85 H4 **Abu Shagara, Ras** *pt* Sudan
84 E6 **Abu Shanab** Sudan
85 F4 **Abu Simbel Temple** *tourist site* Egypt
189 L8 **Abū Şukhayr** Iraq
85 F4 **Abū Sunbul** Egypt
164 R4 **Abuta** Japan
85 G4 **Abu Tabaq** *well* Sudan
186 C2 **Abū Ţāqah** Saudi Arabia
190 B9 **Abū Ţarfā', Wādī** *watercourse* Egypt
203 E10 **Abut Head** *South I.* N.Z.
85 F3 **Abū Tīj** Egypt
85 G3 **Abū Ţuyūr, Jabal** *mt.* Egypt
85 F6 **Abu Uruq** *well* Sudan
190 C8 **Abū 'Uwayqilah** *well* Egypt
92 C2 **Abuye Meda** *mt.* Eth.
154 E6 **Abuyog** *Leyte* Phil.
85 F6 **Abu Zabad** Sudan
187 L3 **Abū Ẓabī** U.A.E.
184 C6 **Abūzam** Iran
85 G2 **Abū Zanīmah** Egypt
184 D5 **Abū Zeydābād** Iran
92 B2 **Abwong** Sudan
23 M3 **Åby** Sweden
84 E6 **Abyad** Sudan
190 F4 **Abyaḑ, Jabal al** *mts* Syria
186 G9 **Abyān** *governorate* Yemen
84 D2 **Abyār al Hakīm** *well* Libya
84 D2 **Abyār an Nakhīlan** *well* Libya
208 E6 **Abydos** *W.A.* Austr.
90 F2 **Abyei** Sudan
189 O5 **Ābyek** Iran
20 P4 **Åbyn** Sweden
Abyssinia *country* Africa *see* **Ethiopia**
182 H1 **Abzakovo** Rus. Fed.
182 G2 **Abzanovo** Rus. Fed.
84 C6 **Ab Zérafa** Chad
136 C4 **Acacias** Col.
Acacus, Jabal *mts* Libya *see* Akakus, Jabal
Academy Bay Rus. Fed. *see* Akademii, Zaliv
212 T1 **Academy Glacier** Antarctica
117 □Q4 **Acadia National Park** *ME* U.S.A.
142 B5 **Açaí** Brazil
140 D3 **Açailândia** Brazil
140 F4 **Acajutiba** Brazil
127 O11 **Acajutla** El Salvador
127 M9 **Acala** Mex.
128 G5 **Acambaro** Mex.
129 H6 **Acambay** Mex.
91 D9 **Acampamento de Caça do Mucusso** Angola
127 O7 **Acancéh** Mex.
136 B2 **Acandí** Col.
62 D4 **A Cañiza** Spain
128 B3 **Acaponeta** Mex.
128 B3 **Acaponeta** *r.* Mex.
129 H9 **Acapulco** Mex.
Acapulco de Juárez Mex. *see* Acapulco
140 C2 **Acará** Brazil
140 C2 **Acará** *r.* Brazil
137 F6 **Acará, Lago** *l.* Brazil
137 G4 **Acarai Mountains** *hills* Brazil/Guyana
140 C2 **Acará Miri** *r.* Brazil
140 E2 **Acaraú** Brazil
140 E2 **Acaraú** *r.* Brazil
139 G6 **Acaray, Represa de** *resr* Para.
62 C2 **A Carballa** Spain
140 F3 **Acarí** Brazil
143 E1 **Acari** *r.* Brazil
138 B3 **Acarí** Peru
138 B3 **Acarí** *r.* Peru
136 D2 **Acarigua** Venez.
62 D2 **A Carreira** Spain
77 K3 **Acâş** Romania
74 G9 **Acate** *Sicilia* Italy
129 J5 **Acateno** Mex.
129 I7 **Acatlan** *Puebla* Mex.
129 K6 **Acatlán** *Veracruz* Mex.
128 D5 **Acatlán de Juárez** Mex.
129 K7 **Acatlán de Pérez Figueroa** Mex.
129 J7 **Acatzingo** Mex.
144 D2 **Acay, Nevado de** *mt.* Arg.
129 M8 **Acayucán** Mex.
73 O5 **Accadia** Italy
70 B7 **Acceglio** Italy
73 Q7 **Accettura** Italy
Accho Israel *see* **'Akko**
73 L3 **Acciano** Italy
117 J11 **Accomac** *VA* U.S.A.
Accomack *VA* U.S.A. *see* Accomac
43 C10 **Accous** France
88 E5 **Accra** Ghana
29 M6 **Accrington** *Lancashire, England* U.K.
73 K2 **Accumoli** Italy
147 G3 **Aceba** Arg.
62 G8 **Acebo** Spain
64 H2 **Acedera** Spain
63 P3 **Acedo** Spain
144 G3 **Aceguá** Brazil
156 B2 **Aceh** *admin. dist.* Indon.
62 G9 **Acehuche** Spain
62 H8 **Aceituna** Spain
63 Q6 **Acered** Spain
73 P6 **Acerenza** Italy
73 O6 **Acerno** Italy
73 M6 **Acerra** Italy
64 G3 **Aceuchal** Spain
147 G3 **Acevedo** Arg.
58 G3 **Ach** Austria
53 K4 **Ach** *r.* Ger.
53 K6 **Ach** *r.* Ger.
138 C4 **Achacachi** Bol.
98 □1b **Achada** *São Miguel* Azores
64 □ **Achadas da Cruz** Madeira
26 C6 **Achadh Mòr** *Western Isles, Scotland* U.K.
136 D3 **Achaguas** Venez.
178 F9 **Achalpur** *Mahar.* India
176 F4 **Achampet** *Andhra Prad.* India
162 J4 **Achan** Rus. Fed.
62 D4 **A Chan** Spain
176 G4 **Achanta** *Andhra Prad.* India
147 I3 **Achar** Uru.
191 D4 **Ach'ara** *aut. rep.* Georgia
26 E9 **Acharacle** *Highland, Scotland* U.K.
191 C4 **Acharistsqali** *r.* Georgia
26 J6 **Achavanich** *Highland, Scotland* U.K.
193 S3 **Achayvayam** Rus. Fed.
84 A5 **Achegour** *well* Niger
Acheh *admin. dist.* Indon. *see* Aceh
45 H6 **Achel** Belgium
78 C4 **Acheloös** *r.* Greece
87 F5 **Achemelmel** *well* Mali
88 D2 **Achemmîm** *well* Maur.
162 E6 **Acheng** *Heilong.* China
58 E4 **Achenkirch** Austria
89 I2 **Achénouma** Niger
58 E5 **Achensee** *l.* Austria
52 E4 **Achern** Ger.
89 H3 **Achétinamou** *well* Niger
36 E3 **Acheux-en-Amiénois** France
26 G6 **Achfary** *Highland, Scotland* U.K.
178 H9 **Achhota** *Chhattisgarh* India
166 G5 **Achi** Japan
36 E3 **Achicourt** France
191 C3 **Ach'igvara** Georgia
191 F1 **Achikulak** Rus. Fed.
27 B5 **Achill Head** Rep. of Ireland
27 B5 **Achill Island** Rep. of Ireland
27 C5 **Achill Sound** Rep. of Ireland
26 F6 **Achiltibuie** *Highland, Scotland* U.K.
48 H4 **Achim** Ger.
Achin *admin. dist.* Indon. *see* Aceh
193 K4 **Achinsk** Rus. Fed.
26 F8 **Achintee** *Highland, Scotland* U.K.
146 E3 **Achiras** Arg.
183 M6 **Achisay** Kazakh.
191 I3 **Achisu** Rus. Fed.
14 L4 **Achit** Rus. Fed.
168 B2 **Achit Nuur** *l.* Mongolia
191 G2 **Achkhoy-Martan** Rus. Fed.
79 G6 **Achlades, Akra** *pt* Greece
190 B3 **Achna** Cyprus
26 F7 **Achnasheen** *Highland, Scotland* U.K.
19 O9 **Achosa-Rudnya** Belarus
26 D9 **Achosnich** *Highland, Scotland* U.K.
53 N4 **Achslach** Ger.
52 H5 **Achstetten** Ger.
48 H1 **Achtrup** Ger.
15 G7 **Achuyevo** Rus. Fed.
75 I8 **Aci Castello** *Sicilia* Italy
75 I8 **Aci Catena** *Sicilia* Italy
79 K5 **Acıgöl** *l.* Turkey
191 H4 **Acınohur** *depr.* Azer.
79 K5 **Acıpayam** Turkey
75 I8 **Acireale** *Sicilia* Italy
75 I8 **Aci Sant'Antonio** *Sicilia* Italy
121 K9 **Ackerman** *MS* U.S.A.
118 E3 **Ackermanville** *PA* U.S.A.
120 I4 **Ackley** *IA* U.S.A.
130 F2 **Acklins Island** Bahamas
29 O6 **Ackworth Moor Top** *West Yorkshire, England* U.K.
31 P2 **Acle** *Norfolk, England* U.K.
138 B3 **Acobamba** *Huancavelica* Peru
138 B2 **Acobamba** *Junín* Peru
40 C3 **Acolin** *r.* France
138 C3 **Acomayo** *Cusco* Peru
138 A2 **Acomayo** *Huánuco* Peru
29 M4 **Acomb** *Northumberland, England* U.K.
146 B3 **Aconcagua** *r.* Chile
146 B3 **Aconcagua, Cerro** *mt.* Arg.
140 F3 **Acopiara** Brazil
138 C3 **Acora** Peru
98 □1 **Açores, Arquipélago dos** *is* N. Atlantic Ocean
62 D2 **A Coruña** Spain
62 D2 **A Coruña** *prov.* Spain
138 B3 **Acostambo** Peru
99 □3b **Acoua** Mayotte
126 □Q12 **Acoyapa** Nic.
74 H6 **Acquacalda** *Isole Lipari* Italy
71 N8 **Acqualagna** Italy
75 L4 **Acquaniti** *r.* Italy
72 H2 **Acquapendente** Italy
73 P9 **Acquappesa** Italy
75 K6 **Acquaro** Italy
70 F3 **Acquarossa** Switz.
73 K2 **Acquasanta Terme** Italy
73 J2 **Acquasparta** Italy
73 L2 **Acquaviva Picena** Italy
74 H7 **Acquedolci** *Sicilia* Italy
36 B5 **Acquigny** France
70 E6 **Acqui Terme** Italy
117 K6 **Acra** *NY* U.S.A.
Acragas *Sicilia* Italy *see* Agrigento
204 E5 **Acraman, Lake** *salt flat S.A.* Austr.
138 D2 **Acre** *r.* Brazil
138 C2 **Acre** *state* Brazil
Acre Israel *see* **'Akko**
142 B2 **Acreúna** Brazil
75 K5 **Acri** Italy
62 F3 **A Cruz de Incio** Spain
57 H4 **Ács** Hungary
57 I4 **Acsa** Hungary
Actaeon Group *is Arch. des Tuamotu* Fr. Polynesia *see* **Actéon, Groupe**
201 □3 **Actéon, Groupe** *is Arch. des Tuamotu* Fr. Polynesia
129 I7 **Acteopan** Mex.
111 N6 **Acton** *Ont.* Can.
31 N3 **Acton** *Suffolk, England* U.K.
124 N7 **Acton** *CA* U.S.A.
129 I5 **Actopán** Mex.
129 K6 **Actopan** Mex.
138 D1 **Açuã** *r.* Brazil
143 F3 **Açuçena** Brazil
129 H5 **Aculco de Espinosa** Mex.
129 J7 **Acultzingo** Mex.
147 I1 **Acuña** Arg.
142 C6 **Acungui** Brazil
89 H6 **Acurenam** Equat. Guinea
139 F3 **Açurizal** Brazil
73 K4 **Acuto** Italy
89 F5 **Ada** Ghana
76 I5 **Ada** *Vojvodina, Srbija* Serb. and Mont.
120 G2 **Ada** *MN* U.S.A.
116 B8 **Ada** *OH* U.S.A.
121 G8 **Ada** *OK* U.S.A.
92 C3 **Ādaba** Eth.
Adabazar Turkey *see* Adapazarı
200 □1 **Adacao** Guam
87 H5 **Adaf, Djebel** *mts* Alg.
17 Q8 **Adagum** *r.* Rus. Fed.
66 E3 **Adahuesca** Spain
110 D9 **Adair** *IL* U.S.A.
63 K5 **Adaja** *r.* Spain
20 O4 **Adak** Sweden
104 A4 **Adak** *AK* U.S.A.
104 A4 **Adak Island** *AK* U.S.A.
191 B6 **Adaklı** *Bingöl* Turkey
190 F1 **Adaklı** *Gaziantep* Turkey
92 E3 **Adale** *well* Eth.
Adalia Turkey *see* **Antalya**
187 M4 **Adam** Oman
145 F8 **Adam, Mount** *hill* Falkland Is
142 B4 **Adamantina** Brazil
89 I5 **Adamaoua** *prov.* Cameroon
89 I5 **Adamaoua, Massif de l'** *mts* Cameroon
78 F6 **Adamas** *Milos* Greece
89 H4 **Adamawa** *state* Nigeria
77 P6 **Adamclisi** Romania
70 J3 **Adamello** *mt.* Italy
70 I3 **Adamello-Brenta, Parco Naturale** *nature res.* Italy
205 L7 **Adaminaby** *N.S.W.* Austr.
92 C3 **Ādamī Tulu** Eth.
54 E6 **Adamov** Czech Rep.
182 H2 **Adamovka** Rus. Fed.
55 K4 **Adamów** *Lubelskie* Pol.
55 L5 **Adamów** *Lubelskie* Pol.
55 K5 **Adamówka** Pol.
16 G4 **Adampil'** Ukr.
116 C10 **Adams** *KY* U.S.A.
117 L6 **Adams** *MA* U.S.A.
110 B6 **Adams** *MN* U.S.A.
117 I5 **Adams** *NY* U.S.A.
110 E6 **Adams** *WI* U.S.A.
212 T2 **Adams, Cape** Antarctica
203 E10 **Adams, Mount** *South I.* N.Z.
176 F8 **Adam's Bridge** *sea feature* India/Sri Lanka
117 I5 **Adams Center** *NY* U.S.A.
118 A5 **Adams County** *county PA* U.S.A.
106 G5 **Adams Lake** *B.C.* Can.
125 Q3 **Adams McGill Reservoir** *NV* U.S.A.
106 D4 **Adams Mountain** *AK* U.S.A.
Adam's Peak Sri Lanka *see* Sri Pada
124 L2 **Adams Peak** *CA* U.S.A.
27 I8 **Adamstown** Rep. of Ireland
118 C4 **Adamstown** *PA* U.S.A.
65 J4 **Adamuz** Spain
186 G9 **'Adan** Yemen
186 G9 **'Adan** *governorate* Yemen
188 G5 **Adana** Turkey
190 D1 **Adana** *prov.* Turkey
Adana Yemen *see* **'Adan**
186 G9 **'Adan as Sughra** Yemen
77 O3 **Adâncata** Romania
57 H5 **Ádánd** Hungary
63 K7 **Adanero** Spain
157 L5 **Adang, Teluk** *b.* Indon.
89 G5 **Adani** Nigeria
62 F8 **Adão** Port.
79 L2 **Adapazarı** Turkey
186 G9 **Adaran, Jabal** *mt.* Yemen
27 E7 **Adare** Rep. of Ireland
213 L2 **Adare, Cape** Antarctica
186 B5 **Adarmo, Khawr** *watercourse* Sudan
164 R9 **Adatara-san** *vol.* Japan
92 D3 **Ada Terra** Eth.
207 J8 **Adavale** *Qld* Austr.
18 H4 **Ādaži** Latvia
185 M3 **Adban** Afgh.
179 I9 **Adbhar** *Chhattisgarh* India
70 H5 **Adda** *r.* Italy
84 F2 **Aḑ Ḑab'ah** Egypt
Ad Dabbah Sudan *see* Ed Debba
186 E4 **Ad Dafīnah** Saudi Arabia
189 L7 **Ad Daghghārah** Iraq
186 H5 **Ad Dahnā'** *des.* Saudi Arabia
187 M5 **Ad Dākhilīyah** *admin. reg.* Oman
86 B5 **Ad Dakhla** Western Sahara
186 G9 **Aḑ Ḑāli'** Yemen
186 G9 **Aḑ Ḑāli'** *governorate* Yemen
Ad Damir Sudan *see* **Ed Damer**
187 J2 **Ad Dammām** Saudi Arabia
176 F5 **Addanki** *Andhra Prad.* India
70 H4 **Adda Nord, Parco dell'** *park* Italy
188 E8 **Ad Daqahlīyah** *governorate* Egypt
186 C2 **Ad Dār al Ḩamrā'** Saudi Arabia
186 F7 **Ad Darb** Saudi Arabia
70 H5 **Adda Sud, Parco dell'** *park* Italy
176 H4 **Addatigala** *Andhra Prad.* India
186 G3 **Ad Dawādimī** Saudi Arabia
187 J3 **Ad Dawḩah** Qatar
189 K6 **Ad Dawr** Iraq
190 F4 **Ad Daww** *plain* Syria
89 H2 **Addax, Réserve Naturelle Intégrale dite Sanctuaire des** *nature res.* Niger
189 M8 **Ad Dayr** Iraq
31 J3 **Adderbury** *Oxfordshire, England* U.K.
186 H2 **Ad Dibdibah** *plain* Saudi Arabia
187 J7 **Ad Dibīn** Yemen
187 J6 **Ad Dikākah** *des.* Saudi Arabia
187 H4 **Ad Dilam** Saudi Arabia
29 N6 **Addingham** *West Yorkshire, England* U.K.
186 H3 **Ad Dir'īyah** Saudi Arabia
Addis Ababa Eth. *see* Ādīs Ābeba
116 H6 **Addison** *NY* U.S.A.
189 L8 **Ad Dīwānīyah** Iraq
Ad Dīwānīyah *governorate* Iraq *see* **Al Qādisīyah**
31 L5 **Addlestone** *Surrey, England* U.K.
97 J9 **Addo** S. Africa
97 J9 **Addo Elephant National Park** S. Africa
175 □2 **Addu Atoll** Maldives
189 K8 **Ad Duwayd** *well* Saudi Arabia
186 G2 **Ad Duwayḩirah** Saudi Arabia
Ad Duwaym Sudan *see* **Ed Dueim**
187 J4 **Ad Duwayris** *well* Saudi Arabia
98 □3a **Adeje** *Tenerife* Canary Is
115 F10 **Adel** *GA* U.S.A.
120 H5 **Adel** *IA* U.S.A.
204 G6 **Adelaide** *S.A.* Austr.
206 C2 **Adelaide** *r. N.T.* Austr.
130 E1 **Adelaide** *New Prov.* Bahamas
97 K8 **Adelaide** S. Africa
212 T2 **Adelaide Island** Antarctica
206 C2 **Adelaide River** *N.T.* Austr.
70 D3 **Adelboden** Switz.
49 I7 **Adelebsen** Ger.
208 G3 **Adele Island** *W.A.* Austr.
75 L1 **Adelfia** Italy
79 H6 **Adelfoi** *i.* Greece
48 J5 **Adelheidsdorf** Ger.
147 E3 **Adelia María** Arg.
Adélie Coast *reg.* Antarctica *see* **Adélie Land**
213 J2 **Adélie Land** *reg.* Antarctica
52 H4 **Adelmannsfelden** Ger.
205 L6 **Adelong** *N.S.W.* Austr.
209 F10 **Adelong Aboriginal Reserve** *W.A.* Austr.
130 □ **Adelphi** Jamaica
131 □3 **Adelphi** St Vincent
53 K4 **Adelschlag** Ger.
53 J2 **Adelsdorf** Ger.
52 G3 **Adelsheim** Ger.
53 J5 **Adelsried** Ger.
53 K5 **Adelzhausen** Ger.
67 C7 **Ademuz** Spain
Aden Yemen *see* **'Adan**
180 F7 **Aden, Gulf of** Somalia/Yemen
116 E8 **Adena** *OH* U.S.A.
49 C10 **Adenau** Ger.
48 J4 **Adendorf** Ger.
96 I8 **Adendorp** S. Africa
49 I7 **Adenstedt** Ger.
89 G3 **Aderbissinat** Niger
Aderno *Sicilia* Italy *see* **Adrano**
178 C8 **Adesar** *Gujarat* India
92 C2 **Ādēt** Eth.
Adhámas *Milos* Greece *see* Adamas
187 M3 **Adhan, Jabal** *mt.* U.A.E.
186 G8 **Adhanah, Wādī** *watercourse* Yemen
187 L3 **Adh Dhayd** U.A.E.
186 G2 **Adh Dhāyūf** *well* Saudi Arabia
189 J9 **'Adhfā'** *well* Saudi Arabia
185 N5 **Adhi Kot** Pak.
190 E8 **'Ādhirīyāt, Jibāl al** *mts* Jordan
178 C8 **Adhoi** *Gujarat* India
153 H7 **Adi** *i. Papua* Indon.
88 E5 **Adiaké** Côte d'Ivoire
92 C1 **Ādī Ārk'ay** Eth.
64 E4 **Adiça, Serra da** *hills* Port.
136 D2 **Adícora** Venez.
186 D8 **Ādī Da'iro** Eth.
85 F6 **'Adid Umm Inderab** *well* Sudan
71 M5 **Adige** *r.* Italy
Adigey Autonomous Oblast *aut. rep.* Rus. Fed. *see* **Adygeya, Respublika**
92 C1 **Ādīgrat** Eth.
79 K4 **Adıgüzel Barajı** *resr* Turkey
85 H6 **Adi Keyih** Eritrea
85 H6 **Adi Kwala** Eritrea
176 F3 **Adilabad** *Andhra Prad.* India
92 B4 **Adilang** Uganda
189 K4 **Adilcevaz** Turkey
122 D6 **Adin** *CA* U.S.A.
Adîncata Romania *see* Adâncata
45 C6 **Adinkerke** Belgium
84 B3 **Adīrī** Libya
117 K4 **Adirondack Mountains** *NY* U.S.A.
92 C2 **Ādīs Ābeba** Eth.
92 C1 **Ādīs Zemen** Eth.
188 I5 **Adıyaman** Turkey
Adjaria *aut. rep.* Georgia *see* Ach'ara
87 F5 **Adjelman, Oued** *watercourse* Alg.
77 P4 **Adjud** Romania
92 A4 **Adjumani** Uganda
131 □1 **Adjuntas** Puerto Rico
109 J2 **Adlavik Islands** *Nfld and Lab.* Can.
191 A2 **Adler** Rus. Fed.
29 L6 **Adlington** *Lancashire, England* U.K.
70 F1 **Adliswil** Switz.
53 M4 **Adlkofen** Ger.
208 H3 **Admiralty Gulf** *W.A.* Austr.
208 H3 **Admiralty Gulf Aboriginal Reserve** *W.A.* Austr.
105 J2 **Admiralty Inlet** *Nunavut* Can.
105 H3 **Admiralty Island** *Nunavut* Can.
104 E4 **Admiralty Island** *AK* U.S.A.
104 E4 **Admiralty Island National Monument - Kootznoowoo Wilderness** *nat. park AK* U.S.A.
204 □2 **Admiralty Islands** *Lord Howe I.* Austr.
153 K7 **Admiralty Islands** P.N.G.
213 L2 **Admiralty Mountains** Antarctica
59 J4 **Admont** Austria
79 I4 **Adnan Menderes Havaalani** *airport* Turkey
92 E3 **Ādo** Eth.
89 G5 **Ado-Ekiti** Nigeria
166 D5 **Adogawa** Japan
166 D5 **Ado-gawa** *r.* Japan
90 F2 **Adok** Sudan
147 G6 **Adolfo Gonzáles Chaves** Arg.
129 N9 **Adolfo López Mateos** Mex.
20 N3 **Adolfsström** Sweden
208 J3 **Adolphus Island** *W.A.* Austr.
155 C8 **Adonara** *i.* Indon.
176 E5 **Adoni** *Andhra Prad.* India
57 H4 **Adony** Hungary
51 F10 **Adorf** *Sachsen* Ger.
51 G9 **Adorf** *Sachsen* Ger.
49 G8 **Adorf (Diemelsee)** Ger.
64 A2 **A-dos-Cunhados** Port.
162 M3 **Ado-Tymovo** *Sakhalin* Rus. Fed.
62 E6 **Adoufe** Port.
43 A8 **Adour** *r.* France
179 K8 **Adra** *W. Bengal* India
65 M7 **Adra** Spain
65 N7 **Adra** *r.* Spain
190 E5 **'Adrā'** Syria
63 P6 **Adradas** Spain
63 L6 **Adrados** Spain
Adramyttium Turkey *see* **Edremit**
Adramyttium, Gulf of Turkey *see* **Edremit Körfezi**
74 H8 **Adrano** *Sicilia* Italy
87 E4 **Adrar** Alg.
87 G4 **Adrar** *mts* Alg.
86 C5 **Adrar** *admin. reg.* Maur.
87 G5 **Adrar Tedjorart** *well* Alg.
190 B2 **Adras Dağı** *mt.* Turkey
185 J5 **Adraskand** *r.* Afgh.
185 M1 **Adrasmon** Tajik.
84 D6 **Adré** Chad
71 M5 **Adria** Italy
111 J8 **Adrian** *MI* U.S.A.
121 D8 **Adrian** *TX* U.S.A.
Adrianople Turkey *see* **Edirne**
Adrianopolis Turkey *see* **Edirne**
68 D3 **Adriatic Sea** Europe
42 F3 **Adriers** France
27 C9 **Adrigole** Rep. of Ireland
Adua Eth. *see* **Ādwa**
146 B5 **Aduana Pejerrey** Chile
44 J2 **Aduard** Neth.
70 G3 **Adula Gruppe** *mts* Switz.
Adunara *i.* Indon. *see* **Adonara**
176 E8 **Adur** *Kerala* India
90 F4 **Adusa** Dem. Rep. Congo
18 J6 **Adutiškis** Lith.
Aduwa Eth. *see* **Ādwa**
208 G6 **Adverse Well** *W.A.* Austr.
92 C1 **Ādwa** Eth.
29 O6 **Adwick le Street** *South Yorkshire, England* U.K.
88 E5 **Adwufia** Ghana
193 O3 **Adycha** *r.* Rus. Fed.
191 C1 **Adyge-Khabl'** Rus. Fed.
Adygeya *aut. rep.* Rus. Fed. *see* **Adygeya, Respublika**
191 B1 **Adygeya, Respublika** *aut. rep.* Rus. Fed.
15 G7 **Adygeysk** Rus. Fed.
Adygeyskaya Avtonomnaya Oblast' *aut. rep.* Rus. Fed. *see* **Adygeya, Respublika**
15 I7 **Adyk** Rus. Fed.
67 E7 **Adzaneta** Spain
67 E10 **Adzaneta de Albaida** Spain
17 L5 **Adzhamka** Ukr.
Adzharia *aut. rep.* Georgia *see* Ach'ara
184 F3 **Adzhiyan** Turkm.
88 E5 **Adzopé** Côte d'Ivoire
14 M2 **Adz'va** *r.* Rus. Fed.
14 L2 **Adz'vavom** Rus. Fed.
79 F4 **Aegean Sea** Greece/Turkey
Aegeri, Lake of Switz. *see* **Ägerisee**
Aegina *i.* Greece *see* **Aigina**
18 H2 **Aegna** *i.* Estonia
18 I2 **Aegviidu** Estonia
Aegyptus *country* Africa *see* **Egypt**
Aela Jordan *see* **Al 'Aqabah**
Aelana Jordan *see* **Al 'Aqabah**
Aelōnlaplap *atoll* Marshall Is *see* **Ailinglaplap**
Aenus Turkey *see* **Enez**
22 G7 **Ærø** *i.* Denmark
17 N8 **Aeroflots'kyy** Ukr.
30 D3 **Aeron** *r. Wales* U.K.
48 J1 **Ærøskøbing** Denmark
49 H6 **Aerzen** Ger.
62 C3 **A Escusa** Spain
62 C4 **A Esfarrapada** Spain
62 D3 **A Estrada** Spain
78 C2 **Aetos** Greece
21 Q6 **Äetsä** Fin.
201 □3a **Afaahiti** *Tahiti* Fr. Polynesia
85 H5 **Afabet** Eritrea
92 E3 **Afaf Badane** *well* Eth.
189 L5 **Afan** Iran
17 R3 **Afanas'yevka** Rus. Fed.
14 K4 **Afanas'yevo** Rus. Fed.
Afándou *Rodos* Greece *see* Afantou
79 J6 **Afantou** *Rodos* Greece
92 D1 **Āfar** *admin. reg.* Eth.
187 M4 **Afar** Oman
85 I6 **Afar Depression** Eritrea/Eth.
201 □3a **Afareaitu** *Moorea* Fr. Polynesia
92 D2 **Āfdem** Eth.
38 G6 **Aff** *r.* France
88 E5 **Afféri** Côte d'Ivoire
73 K4 **Affile** Italy
53 J5 **Affing** Ger.
70 E1 **Affoltern am Albis** Switz.
26 F8 **Affric, Loch** *l. Scotland* U.K.
Afghānestān *country* Asia *see* Afghanistan
185 K5 **Afghanistan** *country* Asia
92 E4 **Afgooye** Somalia
200 □2 **Afi, Mount** Samoa
200 □2 **Afiamalu** Samoa
186 F4 **'Afīf** Saudi Arabia
62 C5 **Afife** Port.
89 G5 **Afikpo** Nigeria
19 R4 **Afim'ino** Rus. Fed.
17 R9 **Afipskiy** Rus. Fed.
190 D6 **Afiq** Syria
Afiun Karahissar Turkey *see* Afyon
184 D4 **Afjeh** Iran
20 K5 **Åfjord** Norway
45 D6 **Afleidingskanaal van de Leie** *canal* Belgium
59 L4 **Aflenz Kurort** Austria
87 F2 **Aflou** Alg.
92 D4 **Afmadow** Somalia

104 C4 Afognak Island AK U.S.A.
88 B2 Afojjar well Maur.
62 F2 A Fonsagrada Spain
143 E4 Afonso Cláudio Brazil
62 E4 A Forxa Galicia Spain
62 E4 A Forxa Galicia Spain
71 M8 Afra r. Italy
73 M6 Afragola Italy
140 E4 Afrânio Brazil
92 D1 Áfrèra Terara vol. Eth.
92 D1 Áfrèra YeChe'ew Häyk' l. Eth.
82 'Africa continent
190 E2 'Afrin Syria
190 E2 'Afrin, Nahr r. Syria/Turkey
59 I6 Afritz Austria
79 J4 Afşar Baraji resr Turkey
188 H4 Afsluitdijk barrage Neth.
44 H3 Afsluitdijk barrage Neth.
92 E4 Aftar Iran
92 E3 Aftol well Eth.
117 I5 Afton NY U.S.A.
122 I5 Afton WY U.S.A.
26 H12 Afton Bridgend East Ayrshire, Scotland U.K.
88 B2 Aftoûf Faï depr. Maur.
137 I5 Afua Brazil
190 D6 'Afula Israel
79 L4 Afyon Turkey
79 L4 Afyon prov. Turkey
79 L4 Afyonkarahisar Turkey see Afyon
78 E3 Afyssos Greece
51 F9 Aga Japan
169 N1 Aga Rus. Fed.
169 N1 Aga-Buryat Autonomous Okrug admin. div. Rus. Fed. see Aginsky Buryatskiy Avtonomnyy Okrug
89 I2 Agadem well Niger
89 G2 Agadez Niger see Agadez
89 H2 Agadez dept Niger
86 C3 Agadir Morocco
86 A5 Agâdîr, Râs pt Maur.
84 D5 Aga Dubé well Chad
183 O3 Agadyr' Kazakh.
98 □3f Agaete Gran Canaria Canary Is
89 G4 Agaie Nigeria
99 □1 Agalega Islands Mauritius
62 H8 Agallas Spain
126 □Q10 Agalta nat. park Hond.
126 □Q10 Agalta, Sierra de mts Hond.
62 D2 A Gándara Galicia Spain
62 D1 A Gándara de Altea Galicia Spain
168 H9 Aganzhen Gansu China
182 H1 Agapovka Rus. Fed.
178 F8 Agar Madh. Prad. India
191 D4 Agara Georgia
89 G2 Agaié well Niger
86 D5 Agâraktem well Mali
92 C3 Agaro r. Eth.
92 E3 Agar Sarar Weyn well Eth.
57 I5 Agárd Hungary
78 C3 Ágasegyháza Hungary
120 H1 Agassiz B.C. Can.
176 C3 Agassiz Fracture Zone sea feature S. Pacific Ocean
120 H1 Agassiz National Wildlife Refuge nature res. MN U.S.A.
200 □1 Agat Guam
108 D3 Agate Ont. Can.
79 H5 Agathe France see Agde
79 H5 Agathonisi i. Greece
167 I2 Agatsuma Japan
51 J2 Agatsuma-gawa r. Japan
176 O7 Agatti i. India
110 J2 Agawa r. Ont. Can.
Agayani Georgia see Aghaiani
124 N7 Agoura CA U.S.A.
89 F2 Agoza-n-Ehsel well Mali
43 H8 Agout r. France
166 E7 Agoo Rep. of Ireland
119 A1 Agoy Rus. Fed.
178 G6 Agra Uttar Prad. India
147 H3 Agrada Uru.
78 C4 Agrafiotis r. Greece
191 I2 Agrakhanskiy Poluostrov pen. Rus. Fed.
65 P4 Agreda Spain
66 H4 Agramunt Spain
70 G4 Agrate Brianza Italy
92 B3 Agred r. Sudan
191 I4 Agri r. Italy
73 R7 Agri r. Italy
189 K4 Ağrı Turkey
191 H6 Ağrı prov. Turkey
78 E7 Agria Gramvousa i. Greece
72 C2 Agriates, Désert des hills Corse France
191 F6 Ağrı Dağı mt. Turkey
188 I4 Agrigan i. N. Mariana Is see Agrigan
74 E8 Agrigento Sicilia Italy
74 E8 Agrigento prov. Sicilia Italy
74 E8 Agrigentum Sicilia Italy see Agrigento
153 K3 Agrihan r. N. Mariana Is
77 T13 Agrij r. Romania
78 C4 Agrinio Greece
64 G6 Agrio, Embalse de resr Spain
52 F5 Agrochão Port.
191 I4 Agryz Rus. Fed.
191 A4 Ağsu r. Azer. see Ağdaş
206 D7 Ahakeye Aboriginal Land res. N.T. Austr.
53 M4 Aham Ger.
184 B2 Ahar Iran
203 F9 Ahaura South I. N.Z.
203 F9 Ahaura r. South I. N.Z.
49 D6 Ahaus Ger.
48 H4 Ahausen Ger.
27 E9 Ahenny Rep. of Ireland
27 E9 Aherla Rep. of Ireland
27 G8 Aherlow r. Rep. of Ireland
99 □3a Ahibamba hill Njazidja Comoros
62 H8 Ahigal Spain
62 H6 Ahigal de Villarino Spain
43 E7 Ahillo mt. Spain
64 H3 Ahillones Spain
202 K5 Ahimanawa Range mts North I. N.Z.
42 H3 Ahinski, Kanal canal Belarus
163 D8 Ahipara North I. N.Z.
138 A2 Ahipara Bay North I. N.Z.
176 D3 Ahiri Mahar. India
167 J4 Aikawa Kanagawa Japan
166 P8 Aikawa Niigata Japan
115 G9 Aiken SC U.S.A.
170 G6 Ailao Shan mts Yunnan China
178 H7 Ailefroide France
206 D7 Ailette r. France
155 D8 Aileu East Timor
126 □T13 Ailigandi Panama
170 G6 Ailing Guangxi China
191 D3 Ailingalaplap atoll Marshall Is see Ailinglaplap
178 E9 Ailinglaplap atoll Marshall Is
89 Q5 Ailsa Mahar. India
179 C1 Ailsa Nigeria
226 F1 Ailt an Chorráin Rep. of Ireland
178 E3 Ailsa Craig Ont. Can.
126 F12 Ailsa Craig i. Scotland U.K.
41 E9 Aimargues France
168 D4 Aij Bogd Uul mts Mongolia
153 Q6 Ajdābiyā Libya
155 B8 Aimere Flores Indon.
143 Q3 Aimogasta Arg.
164 R6 Aimon r. France
187 H2 Ain Tunisia
143 G2 Aimorés, Serra dos hills Brazil
154 □ Ain dept France
40 L4 Ain France
57 L4 Ajka Hungary
18 L9 Aksu r. Turkey
18 M7 Aktuma Kazakh.

78 E5 Agios Dimitrios Attiki Greece
78 D2 Agios Dimitrios Makedonia Greece
78 F5 Agios Dimitrios, Akra pt Kythnos Greece
78 F3 Agios Efstratios Greece
78 G3 Agios Efstratios i. Greece
79 H3 Agios Fokas, Akra pt Lesvos Greece
78 E5 Agios Georgios Greece
78 E5 Agios Georgios i. Greece
79 G7 Agios Ioannis, Akra pt Kriti Greece
79 H5 Agios Kirykos Ikaria Greece
78 D4 Agios Konstantinos Greece
78 A3 Agios Matthaios Kerkyra Greece
78 E2 Agios Nikolaos Kentriki Makedonia Greece
79 G7 Agios Nikolaos Kriti Greece
78 B5 Agios Nikolaos Zakynthos Greece
79 H3 Agios Paraskevi Lesvos Greece
78 D5 Agios Petros Greece
190 B3 Agios Sergios Cyprus
78 E4 Agios Stefanos Greece
190 C3 Agios Theodoros Cyprus
78 E4 Agios Thomas Greece
62 B4 Agiou Andreou, Akra pt Greece
78 E2 Agiou Orous, Kolpos b. Greece
74 H8 Agira Sicilia Italy
68 G5 Agirwat Hills Sudan
97 J2 Agisanang S. Africa
28 D3 Agivey Northern Ireland U.K.
52 F3 Aglasterhausen Ger.
79 L5 Ağlasun Turkey
71 K8 Agliana Italy
72 C5 Aglientu Sardegna Italy
43 K10 Agly r. France
70 H5 Agnadello Italy
78 C3 Agnanteri Greece
39 I3 Agneaux France
41 J7 Agnel, Col pass France
42 B5 Agnena r. Italy
73 M4 Agnone Italy
166 F2 Agō Japan
89 F4 Ago-Are Nigeria
70 F5 Agogna r. Italy
89 F4 Agogo Ghana
Agoitz Spain see Aoiz
62 D3 Agolada Spain
88 E5 Agona Ghana
42 F5 Agonac France
146 C3 Agon-Coutainville France
168 G8 Agong'echeng China
179 I7 Agori Uttar Prad. India
167 J4 Agose Japan
67 D11 Agost Spain
43 D9 Agout r. France
57 K4 Ágota Spain see Aoiz
89 E5 Agnibilékrou Côte d'Ivoire
77 M5 Agnita Romania
162 K3 Agniye-Afanas'yevsk Rus. Fed.
71 K4 Agno r. Italy
73 N4 Agno Switz.
166 E7 Agoo Japan
89 F4 Agogo Ghana
70 F5 Agogna r. Italy
62 D8 Aguieira, Barragem da resr Port.
153 K4 Aguijan i. N. Mariana Is
41 H7 Águila r. Spain
125 A8 Aguila AZ U.S.A.
63 N2 Aguila, Punta del pt Spain
63 L6 Aguilafuente Spain
63 L3 Aguilar CO U.S.A.
66 D6 Aguilar de Alfambra Spain
63 L3 Aguilar de Campóo Spain
63 L3 Aguilar de Campóo, Embalse de resr Spain
65 J5 Aguilar de la Frontera Spain
63 Q5 Aguilar del Río Alhama Spain
95 P6 Águilas Spain
128 E7 Aguililla Mex.
62 D8 Aguim Port.
98 □3f Agüimes Gran Canaria Canary Is
98 □3f Aguineguín r. Gran Canaria Canary Is
154 D6 Aguisan Negros Phil.
63 N6 Aguisejo r. Spain
92 C1 Agula'i Eth.
64 □ Agulhas, Ponta da pt Madeira
96 E10 Agulhas, Cape S. Africa
214 K9 Agulhas Basin sea feature Southern Ocean
143 E5 Agulhas Negras mt. Brazil
215 F7 Agulhas Plateau sea feature Southern Ocean
214 J8 Agulhas Ridge sea feature S. Atlantic Ocean
66 K3 Agullana Spain
70 D10 Agullent Spain
98 □3a Agulo La Gomera Canary Is
164 □E20 Aguni-jima i. Nansei-shotō Japan
154 C5 Agusan r. Mindanao Phil.
147 G4 Agustín Roca O'Higgins Arg.
154 C6 Agutaya Phil.
154 C6 Agutaya i. Phil.
79 K1 Ağva Turkey
191 H3 Agvali Rus. Fed.
89 G4 Agwarra Nigeria
92 B3 Agwei r. Sudan
191 I4 Ağyazı Turkey
Agyrium Sicilia Italy see Agira
84 Okinawa Japan

98 □1b Agua Retorta São Miguel Azores
136 E2 Aguaro-Guariquito, Parque Nacional nat. park Venez.
66 C5 Aguarón Spain
126 F5 Aguaruto Mex.
201 □3 Ahunui atoll Arch. des Tuamotu Fr. Polynesia
203 E11 Ahuriri r. South I. N.Z.
203 A12 Ahuroa North I. N.Z.
23 K6 Ahus Sweden
184 C6 Ahväz Iran
Ahvenanmaa is Åland Fin. see Åland
63 R5 Ainzón Spain
165 L12 Aioi Gunma Japan
136 C4 Aipe Col.
138 D4 Aiquile Bol.
156 G3 Air r. Indon.
154 □ Airai Palau
137 F5 Airão Brazil
27 O6 Airasca Italy
156 C4 Airbangis Sumatera Indon.
26 C7 Aird of Sleat Highland, Scotland U.K.
26 E8 Aird r. Brazil
169 L5 Aibag Gol r. China
63 R3 Aibar Spain
164 T3 Aibetsu Japan
59 L6 Aibl Austria
131 □1 Aibonito Puerto Rico
53 K5 Aichach Ger.
52 E5 Aichhalden Ger.
166 F6 Aichi pref. Japan
166 F5 Aichi-kōgen Quasi National Park Japan
53 I6 Aichstetten Ger.
178 F7 Aichwara Madh. Prad. India
116 C10 Aid OH U.S.A.
165 L12 Aida Japan
53 O4 Aidenbach Ger.
49 J10 Aidhausen Ger.
184 F2 Aïdin Turkey see Aydın
74 G6 Aidone Sicilia Italy
Aiea HI U.S.A.
124 □D12 Aïea
73 G9 Aiello Calabro Italy
73 P8 Aieta Italy
42 D3 Aiffres France
78 D4 Aigeira Greece
156 D1 Air Muda, Tasik l. Malaysia
73 N5 Airola Italy
157 D7 Airolo Switz.
156 D1 Air Pedu, Tasik l. Malaysia
107 J4 Air Ronge Sask. Can.
26 I10 Airth Falkirk, Scotland U.K.
29 M5 Airton North Yorkshire, England U.K.
42 D2 Airvault France
158 A4 Aisatung Mountain Myanmar
145 B7 Aisén admin. reg. Chile
137 G4 Aishalton Guyana
169 Q8 Ai Shan hill Shandong China
106 B2 Aishihik Y.T. Can.
106 B2 Aishihik Lake Y.T. Can.
40 I5 Aisne dept France
37 E5 Aisne r. France
62 C5 Aïssa, Djebel mt. Alg.
40 I2 Aissey France
79 G1 Aisymi Greece
40 I1 Aisy-sur-Armançon France
20 R3 Aitamännikkö Fin.
67 E10 Aitana mt. Spain
153 J7 Aitape P.N.G.
42 D4 Ait Benhaddou tourist site Morocco
53 N4 Aiterach r. Ger.
53 J5 Aiterhofen Ger.
203 O7 Aitutaki i. Cook Is
77 L4 Aiud Romania
155 E4 Ain dept France
40 L4 Ain France
57 L4 Ajka Hungary

129 I7 Ahuatempan Mex.
129 I5 Ahuazotepec Mex.
128 D6 Ahuijullo Mex.
42 I3 Ahun France
89 F3 Ahunapanu Estonia
203 E11 Ahuriri r. South I. N.Z.
203 A12 Ahuroa North I. N.Z.
23 K6 Åhus Sweden
184 C6 Ahväz Iran
Ahvenanmaa is Åland Fin. see Åland
63 R5 Ainzón Spain
165 L12 Aioi Gunma Japan
136 C4 Aipe Col.
138 D4 Aiquile Bol.
156 G3 Air r. Indon.
154 □ Airai Palau
137 F5 Airão Brazil
156 C4 Airbangis Sumatera Indon.
203 □1 Ai-Ais Namibia
94 C5 Ai-Ais Hot Springs and Fish River Canyon Park nature res. Namibia
137 F6 Aiapuá, Lago l. Brazil
136 D4 Aiari r. Brazil
169 L5 Aibag Gol r. China
164 T3 Aibetsu Japan
59 L6 Aibl Austria
131 □1 Aibonito Puerto Rico
53 K5 Aichach Ger.
52 E5 Aichhalden Ger.
166 F6 Aichi pref. Japan
166 F5 Aichi-kōgen Quasi National Park Japan
53 I6 Aichstetten Ger.
178 F7 Aichwara Madh. Prad. India
116 C10 Aid OH U.S.A.
165 L12 Aida Japan
53 O4 Aidenbach Ger.
49 J10 Aidhausen Ger.
Aïdin Turkey see Aydın
74 G6 Aidone Sicilia Italy
124 □D12 Aiea HI U.S.A.
73 G9 Aiello Calabro Italy
73 P8 Aieta Italy
42 D3 Aiffres France
78 D4 Aigeira Greece
59 L2 Aigen im Ennstal Austria
59 I2 Aigen im Mühlkreis Austria
78 G6 Aigiali Greece
78 E5 Aigina Greece
78 E5 Aigina i. Greece
78 D2 Aiginio Greece
78 D3 Aigio Greece
70 B3 Aigle Switz.
42 I5 Aigle, Barrage de l' dam France
41 J7 Aigle de Chambeyron mt. France
41 I8 Aiglun France
43 E8 Aignan France
36 I8 Aignay-le-Duc France
41 D8 Aigoual, Mont mt. France
42 E4 Aigre France
42 C3 Aigrefeuille-d'Aunis France
41 A4 Aigrefeuille-sur-Maine France
99 □1b Aigrettes, Île aux i. Mauritius
99 □1c Aigrettes, Pointe des pt Réunion
62 D4 Aigua Uru.
40 M4 Aiguebelette France
40 I5 Aiguebelle France
111 P1 Aiguebelle, Parc de Conservation d' nature res. Que. Can.
40 C4 Aigueblanche France
40 C4 Aigueperse France
41 E8 Aigues r. France
41 E9 Aigues-Mortes France
41 D10 Aigues-Mortes, Golfe d' b. France
66 G2 Aigües Tortes i Estany de Sant Maurici, Parc Nacional d' nat. park Spain
41 I6 Aiguilhe France
40 C5 Aiguille, Mont mt. France
40 A3 Aiguille, Pointe de l' pt France
40 K5 Aiguille d'Argentière mt. France/Switz.
40 K5 Aiguille de la Grande Sassière mt. France
41 J6 Aiguille de Péclet mt. France
40 C4 Aiguille de Scolette mt. France/Italy
40 J5 Aiguille du Midi mt. France
41 J7 Aiguilles France
41 I6 Aiguilles d'Arves mts France
40 J5 Aiguilles des Glaciers mts France
202 J3 Aiguilles Island North I. N.Z.
40 I5 Aiguille Verte mt. France
43 E7 Aiguillon France
41 E9 Aiguillon, Anse de l' b. France
42 B3 Aiguillon, Pointe de l' pt France
42 H3 Aigurande France
163 D8 Aiha Peru
138 A2 Aija Peru
167 J4 Aikawa Kanagawa Japan
166 P8 Aikawa Niigata Japan
115 G9 Aiken SC U.S.A.
178 H7 Ailao Shan mts Yunnan China
206 D7 Ailette r. France
155 D8 Aileu East Timor
126 □T13 Ailigandi Panama
170 G6 Ailing Guangxi China
191 D3 Ailinglaplap atoll Marshall Is
89 Q5 Ailsa Mahar. India
179 C1 Ailsa Craig Ont. Can.
26 F12 Ailsa Craig i. Scotland U.K.
41 E9 Aimargues France
168 D4 Aij Bogd Uul mts Mongolia
153 Q6 Aimere Flores Indon.
143 Q3 Aimogasta Arg.
143 G2 Aimorés Brazil
143 G2 Aimorés, Serra dos hills Brazil
40 L4 Ain dept France
40 L4 Ain France
57 L4 Ajka Hungary

53 N6 Ainring Ger.
66 F3 Ainsa Spain
29 K6 Ainsdale Merseyside, England U.K.
87 E2 Aïn Sefra Alg.
109 I4 Ainslie, Lake N.S. Can.
120 F4 Ainsworth NE U.S.A.
Aintab Turkey see Gaziantep
87 F5 Aïn Ti-m Misaou well Alg.
87 F5 Aïntree Merseyside, England U.K.
63 R5 Ainzón Spain
165 L12 Aioi Gunma Japan
136 C4 Aipe Col.
138 D4 Aiquile Bol.
156 G3 Air r. Indon.
154 □ Airai Palau
137 F5 Airão Brazil
27 O6 Airasca Italy
156 C4 Airbangis Sumatera Indon.
26 C7 Aird of Sleat Highland, Scotland U.K.
89 H5 Akamkpa Nigeria
164 V3 Akan Japan
164 U3 Akan-ko l. Japan
164 V3 Akan National Park Japan
89 G3 Akarkar well Niger
78 B4 Akarnanika mts Greece
203 Q10 Akaroa South I. N.Z.
203 D11 Akaroa Harbour South I. N.Z.
203 D11 Akas reg. India
165 K11 Akasaki Japan
85 G8 Akasha Sudan
180 D3 'Akāshāt Iraq
167 H3 Akāshat Iraq
165 A6 Akashi Japan
97 M1 Akasia S. Africa
20 Q3 Äkäsjoensuu Fin.
20 Q3 Äkäsjokisuu Fin.
163 J8 Akatarawa North I. N.Z.
105 K3 Air Force Island Nunavut Can.
169 L5 Airgin Sum Nei Mongol China
157 I6 Airhitam r. Indon.
184 F2 Airidu, Teluk b. Indon.
26 C6 Airidh a'Bhruaich Western Isles, Scotland U.K.
23 S1 Airisto Estfan i. Fin.
207 L6 Airlie Beach Old Austr.
208 C6 Airlie Island W.A. Austr.
156 D1 Air Muda, Tasik l. Malaysia
73 N5 Airola Italy
157 D7 Airolo Switz.
156 D1 Air Pedu, Tasik l. Malaysia
107 J4 Air Ronge Sask. Can.
26 I10 Airth Falkirk, Scotland U.K.
29 M5 Airton North Yorkshire, England U.K.
42 D2 Airvault France
158 A4 Aisatung Mountain Myanmar
145 B7 Aisén admin. reg. Chile
137 G4 Aishalton Guyana
169 Q8 Ai Shan hill Shandong China
106 B2 Aishihik Y.T. Can.
106 B2 Aishihik Lake Y.T. Can.
40 I5 Aisne dept France
37 E5 Aisne r. France
62 C5 Aïssa, Djebel mt. Alg.
40 I2 Aissey France
79 J3 Aisymi Greece
79 M1 Akçakoca Turkey
190 B2 Akçakale Turkey
79 K6 Akçay r. Turkey
79 I5 Akçay r. Turkey
191 C6 Akçaova Turkey
79 K6 Akçay Turkey
191 E5 Akçay Kars Turkey
191 I5 Akçaabat Turkey
191 A4 Akçaabat Turkey
184 H1 Akchakaya, Vpadina depr. Turkm.
82 H7 Ak-Say r. Kyrg.
87 L6 Akchâr reg. Maur.
183 O4 Akchatau Kazakh.
183 N5 Akchi Kazakh. see Akshiy
15 I7 Akchi Volgogradskaya Oblast' Rus. Fed.
17 S6 Akcsuat r. Rus. Fed.
173 D9 Aksai Chin terr. Asia
79 J2 Aksakal Turkey
77 P7 Aksakovo Bulg.
18 K5 Aksakovo Rus. Fed.
188 G4 Aksaray Turkey
192 H3 Aksarka Rus. Fed.
191 C2 Aksay r. Rus. Fed.
172 L7 Aksay Gansu China
182 E7 Aksay Kazakh.
184 H1 Aksay Turkm.
183 P4 Ak-Say r. Kyrg.

87 F4 Akabli Alg.
167 J3 Akabori Japan
89 F2 Akaboun well Mali
162 K1 Akademii, Zaliv b. Rus. Fed.
Akademii Nauk, Khrebet mt. Tajik. see Akademiyai Fanho, Qaтörküni
185 N2 Akademiyai Fanho, Qaтörküni mt. Tajik.
165 P9 Akadomari Japan
182 K5 Akadyr Kazakh.
188 H3 Akaki Turkey
184 F1 Akkyr, Gory hills Turkm.
166 E6 Aklampa Benin
104 E3 Aklavik N.W.T. Can.
178 F7 Aklera Rajasthan India
186 G6 Aklub reg. Saudi Arabia
18 F6 Akmena r. Lith.
18 E5 Akmenė Lith.
18 E5 Akmenrags pt Latvia
173 C8 Akmeqit Xinjiang China
183 N3 Akmeshit Kazakh.
Akmola Kazakh. see Astana
Akmola Oblast admin. div. Kazakh. see Akmolinskaya Oblast'
183 N2 Akmolinskaya Oblast' admin. div. Kazakh.
79 J4 Ak-Moyun Kyrg.
18 I5 Akniste Latvia
86 E2 Aknoul Morocco
165 L12 Akō Japan
92 B3 Akobo Sudan
92 B3 Akobo Wenz r. Eth./Sudan
178 F8 Akodia Madh. Prad. India
89 G2 Akokan Niger
176 D3 Akola Mahar. India
178 F9 Akola Mahar. India
89 H6 Akom II Cameroon
172 C6 Akongkür Xinjiang China
89 I6 Akonolinga Cameroon
90 F2 Akop Sudan
85 H6 Akordat Eritrea
79 L4 Akören Afyon Turkey
188 T5 Akören Konya Turkey
178 F9 Akot well Sudan
90 F3 Akot Sudan
126 G6 Akoupé Côte d'Ivoire
105 L3 Akpatok Island Nunavut Can.
172 D6 Akqi Xinjiang China
114 Akraifnio Greece
20 Akrainess Iceland
78 F2 Akrathos, Akra pt Greece
22 B2 Akrehamn Norway
89 H2 Akrérèb Niger
78 C6 Akritas, Akra pt Greece
120 D5 Akron CO U.S.A.
110 H8 Akron IN U.S.A.
116 G5 Akron NY U.S.A.
116 D7 Akron OH U.S.A.
118 C4 Akron PA U.S.A.
190 A4 Akrotiri Bay Cyprus
Akrotirion Bay Cyprus see Akrotiri Bay
190 B4 Akrotiriou, Kolpos b. Cyprus
190 A4 Akrotiri Sovereign Base Area military base Cyprus
173 D9 Aksai Chin terr. Asia
79 J2 Aksakal Turkey
77 P7 Aksakovo Bulg.
18 K5 Aksakovo Rus. Fed.
188 G4 Aksaray Turkey
192 H3 Aksarka Rus. Fed.
191 C2 Aksay r. Rus. Fed.

183 N6 Akkol' Zhambylskaya Oblast' Kazakh.
79 I5 Akköy Aydın Turkey
79 K5 Akköy Denizli Turkey
44 I2 Akkrum Neth.
183 Q2 Akkum Kazakh.
182 K5 Akkum Kazakh.
188 H3 Akkuş Turkey
184 F1 Akkyr, Gory hills Turkm.
89 G2 Aklampa Benin
104 E3 Aklavik N.W.T. Can.
178 F7 Aklera Rajasthan India
186 G6 Aklub reg. Saudi Arabia
18 F6 Akmena r. Lith.
18 E5 Akmenė Lith.
18 E5 Akmenrags pt Latvia
173 C8 Akmeqit Xinjiang China
183 N3 Akmeshit Kazakh.
Akmola Kazakh. see Astana
Akmola Oblast admin. div. Kazakh. see Akmolinskaya Oblast'
183 N2 Akmolinskaya Oblast' admin. div. Kazakh.
79 J4 Ak-Moyun Kyrg.
18 I5 Akniste Latvia
86 E2 Aknoul Morocco
165 L12 Akō Japan
92 B3 Akobo Sudan
92 B3 Akobo Wenz r. Eth./Sudan
178 F8 Akodia Madh. Prad. India
89 G2 Akokan Niger
176 D3 Akola Mahar. India
178 F9 Akola Mahar. India
89 H6 Akom II Cameroon
172 C6 Akongkür Xinjiang China
89 I6 Akonolinga Cameroon
90 F2 Akop Sudan
85 H6 Akordat Eritrea
79 L4 Akören Afyon Turkey
188 T5 Akören Konya Turkey
178 F9 Akot well Sudan
90 F3 Akot Sudan
126 G6 Akoupé Côte d'Ivoire
105 L3 Akpatok Island Nunavut Can.
172 D6 Akqi Xinjiang China
89 H4 Akrafnio Greece
172 G7 Aktam Xinjiang China
14 K5 Aktanysh Rus. Fed.
182 F5 Aktas Kazakh.
182 E4 Aktas Kazakh.
189 J4 Aktaş Dağı mt. Turkey
191 A4 Aktaş Turkey
183 T4 Aktash Uzbek. see Oqtosh
183 O2 Aktau Karagandinskaya Oblast' Rus. Fed.
183 O2 Aktau Karagandinskaya Oblast' Rus. Fed.
182 D6 Aktau Mangistauskaya Oblast' Kazakh.
190 E2 Aktepe Turkey
190 C2 Aktepe Turkey
173 G8 Aktogay Xinjiang China
172 D6 Aktogay Xinjiang China
182 G5 Aktobe Xinjiang China
182 D5 Aktobe Kazakh.
182 D5 Aktobe Rize Turkey
189 L4 Aktas Dağı mt. Turkey
191 I2 Aktash r. Rus. Fed.
183 O2 Aktau Karagandinskaya Oblast' Rus. Fed.
20 S2 Aktse Sweden see Ak-Tüz
19 U6 Akula Dem. Rep. Congo
19 U6 Akulichi Rus. Fed.
105 K3 Akulivik Que. Can.

85 M3 **'Alīābād** Afgh.
91 H4 **Äliabad** Azer.
84 F3 **'Alīābād** *Golestān* Iran
84 F7 **'Alīābād** *Hormozgan* Iran
84 H5 **'Alīābād** *Khorāsān* Iran
84 I6 **'Alīābād** *Khorāsān* Iran
84 B3 **'Alīābād** *Kordestān* Iran
84 B4 **'Alīābād** *Kordestān* Iran
84 D4 **'Alīābād** *Qom* Iran
84 D4 **Alīābād, Kūh-e** *mt.* Iran
66 D6 **Aliaga** Spain
79 H4 **Aliağa** Turkey
67 C8 **Aliaguilla** Spain
78 D2 **Aliakmonas** *r.* Greece
78 C2 **Aliakmonas, Limni** *l.* Greece
84 B5 **'Alī al Gharbī** Iraq
55 E8 **Aliambata** East Timor
73 Q7 **Aliano** Italy
78 E4 **Aliartos** Greece
76 C3 **Alibag** *Mahar.* India
85 M9 **Ali Bandar** Pak.
91 G5 **Älibäyli** Azer.
91 J6 **Äli Bayramlı** Azer.
79 H3 **Alibey Adası** *i.* Turkey
92 C2 **Ālībo** Eth.
76 I5 **Alibunar** *Vojvodina, Srbija* Serb. and Mont.
91 I5 **Älicançay** *r.* Azer.
67 E11 **Alicante** Spain
67 D10 **Alicante** *prov.* Spain
67 E11 **Alicante, Bahía de** *b.* Spain
07 J7 **Alice** *Qld* Austr.
07 H3 **Alice** *r. Qld* Austr.
07 J8 **Alice** *watercourse Qld* Austr.
97 K8 **Alice** S. Africa
21 F12 **Alice** *TX* U.S.A.
75 M5 **Alice, Punta** *pt* Italy
06 D4 **Alice Arm** *B.C.* Can.
97 K9 **Alicedale** S. Africa
08 I4 **Alice Downs** *W.A.* Austr.
30 D5 **Alice Shoal** *sea feature* Caribbean Sea
06 D7 **Alice Springs** *N.T.* Austr.
30 D1 **Alice Town** Bahamas
21 K9 **Aliceville** *AL* U.S.A.
91 D5 **Aliçeyrek** Turkey
85 O3 **Alichur** Tajik.
85 O3 **Alichur** *r.* Tajik.
85 O3 **Alichuri Janubí, Qatorkŭhi** *mts* Tajik.
47 F2 **Alicia** Arg.
54 D8 **Alicia** *Mindanao* Phil.
07 H6 **Alick Creek** *r. Qld* Austr.
74 G6 **Alicudi, Isola** *i. Isole Lipari* Italy
65 M5 **Alicún de Ortega** Spain
87 K4 **Al 'Idd** U.A.E.
86 F2 **Al 'Idwah** *well* Saudi Arabia
89 G3 **Aliero** Nigeria
73 M5 **Alife** Italy
79 L2 **Alifuatpaşa** Turkey
78 F7 **Aligarh** *Rajasthan* India
78 G6 **Aligarh** *Uttar Prad.* India
84 C5 **Alīgūdarz** Iran
69 R1 **Alihe** *Nei Mongol* China
62 I4 **Alija del Infantado** Spain
Alija de los Melones Spain *see* **Alija del Infantado**
62 F6 **Alijó** Port.
84 D6 **Alījūq, Kūh-e** *mt.* Iran
91 E6 **Alikamerli** Turkey
91 I2 **Alikazgan** *r.* Rus. Fed.
85 M5 **'Alī Kheyl** Afgh.
87 K9 **Al Ikhwān** *is* Yemen
14 I5 **Alikovo** Rus. Fed.
90 C5 **Alima** *r.* Congo
74 G8 **Alimena** *Sicilia* Italy
79 I6 **Alimia** *i.* Greece
62 E4 **A Limia** *reg.* Spain
74 F8 **Aliminusa** *Sicilia* Italy
54 C8 **Alimpaya Point** *Mindanao* Phil.
90 D3 **Alindao** C.A.R.
55 A4 **Alindau** *Sulawesi* Indon.
85 N4 **Alinghar** *r.* Afgh.
22 I4 **Alingsås** Sweden
92 D3 **Alintale** *well* Eth.
79 J3 **Aliova** *r.* Turkey
78 G9 **Alipur** *Mahar.* India
85 N7 **Alipur** Pak.
79 L6 **Alipur Duar** *W. Bengal* India
16 E8 **Aliquippa** *PA* U.S.A.
78 E8 **Alirajpur** *Madh. Prad.* India
92 D2 **Ali Sabieh** Djibouti
88 H8 **Al 'Īsāwīyah** Saudi Arabia
64 F2 **Aliseda** Spain
40 E1 **Alise-Ste-Reine** France
84 A2 **Alī Shah** Iran
85 F2 **Al Iskandarīyah** Egypt
88 D8 **Al Iskandarīyah** *governorate* Egypt
89 L7 **Al Iskandarīyah** Iraq
93 R3 **Aliskerovo** Rus. Fed.
85 G2 **Al Ismā'īlīyah** Egypt
90 A8 **Al Ismā'īlīyah** *governorate* Egypt
91 D5 **Alisofu** Turkey
62 H5 **Aliste** *r.* Spain
20 N3 **Alitåive** *mt.* Sweden
75 I7 **Alì Terme** *Sicilia* Italy
78 F4 **Aliveri** Greece
78 E4 **Aliwal** *Punjab* India
97 K6 **Aliwal North** S. Africa
06 H4 **Alix** *Alta* Can.
16 I8 **Aliyaha** *r.* Ukr.
85 N5 **Alizai** Pak.
36 B5 **Alizay** France
90 E8 **Al Jafr** Jordan
87 J3 **Al Jāfūrah** *des.* Saudi Arabia
84 E2 **Al Jaghbūb** Libya
89 M9 **Al Jahrah** Kuwait
87 J3 **Al Jamalīyah** Qatar
64 E6 **Aljaraque** Spain
90 G8 **Al Jarāwī** *well* Saudi Arabia
86 D3 **Al Jarf** *mts* Saudi Arabia
Al Jauf Saudi Arabia *see* **Al Jawf**
87 M6 **Al Jawārah** *well* Oman
87 J4 **Al Jawb** *reg.* Saudi Arabia
84 D3 **Al Jawf** Libya
88 I9 **Al Jawf** *Al Jawf* Saudi Arabia
86 F6 **Al Jawf** *'Asīr* Saudi Arabia
86 D1 **Al Jawf** *prov.* Saudi Arabia
86 G7 **Al Jawf** *governorate* Yemen
Al Jawlān *hills* Syria *see* **Golan**
84 A1 **Al Jawsh** Libya
Al Jaza'ir Alg. *see* **Alger**
84 F3 **Alj Beyk** Iran
64 B6 **Aljezur** Port.
87 J3 **Al Jībān** *reg.* Saudi Arabia
64 H7 **Aljibe** *mt.* Spain
86 G5 **Al Ji'lān** *hills* Saudi Arabia
86 G2 **Al Jilh** *esc.* Saudi Arabia
86 E2 **Al Jithāmīyah** Saudi Arabia
85 F2 **Al Jīzah** Egypt
88 D9 **Al Jīzah** *governorate* Egypt
90 D7 **Al Jīzah** Jordan
86 F6 **Al Ju'ayfirah** Saudi Arabia
62 C9 **Aljubarrota** Port.
87 I2 **Al Jubayl** Saudi Arabia
87 H3 **Al Jubayl** *hills* Saudi Arabia
86 H3 **Al Jubaylah** Saudi Arabia
86 F2 **Al Jubb** Saudi Arabia
64 G2 **Aljucén** Spain
64 G3 **Aljucén** *r.* Spain
86 E2 **Al Jufayfah** Saudi Arabia
84 B2 **Al Jufra Oasis** Libya
86 G1 **Al Julaydah** *well* Saudi Arabia
87 I2 **Al Julayqah** *well* Saudi Arabia
86 F6 **Al Jumah** Saudi Arabia
86 D5 **Al Jumūm** Saudi Arabia
86 F5 **Al Junaynah** Saudi Arabia
87 J2 **Al Jurayd** *i.* Saudi Arabia
86 G3 **Al Jurayfah** Saudi Arabia
86 F5 **Al Jurayr** *well* Saudi Arabia
86 F3 **Al Jurdhāwīyah** Saudi Arabia
64 C5 **Aljustrel** Port.
90 F5 **Al Juwayf** *depr.* Syria
87 J4 **Al Juwayfah** *well* Saudi Arabia
86 F2 **Al Kahfah** *Al Qaşīm* Saudi Arabia
87 I2 **Al Kahfah** *Ash Sharqīyah* Saudi Arabia
187 N5 **Al Kalbān** Oman
106 F5 **Alkali Lake** *B.C.* Can.
16 J8 **Alkaliya** *r.* Ukr.
89 H3 **Alkamari** Niger
187 N4 **Al Kāmil** Oman
190 D7 **Al Karak** Jordan
190 D7 **Al Karāmah** Jordan
189 L7 **Al Kāẓimīyah** Iraq
45 H7 **Alken** Belgium
187 M4 **Al Khābūrah** Oman
186 F1 **Al Khaḍrā'** *well* Saudi Arabia
187 H2 **Al Khafaq** *well* Saudi Arabia
186 E4 **Al Khafqān** *salt pan* Saudi Arabia
187 M3 **Al Khafṭ** U.A.E.
186 E3 **Al Khalf** Saudi Arabia
187 N5 **Al Khalīf** Oman
189 L7 **Al Khāliş** Iraq
186 G5 **Al Khamāsīn** Saudi Arabia
186 H4 **Al Kharfah** Saudi Arabia
85 F3 **Al Khārijah** Egypt
187 H4 **Al Kharj** *reg.* Saudi Arabia
187 J6 **Al Kharkhayr** *oasis* Saudi Arabia
187 J3 **Al Kharrārah** Qatar
190 B7 **Al Kharrūbah** Egypt
187 M2 **Al Khaşab** Oman
187 L6 **Al Khasfah** *well* Oman
186 F4 **Al Khāşirah** Saudi Arabia
187 L3 **Al Khatam** *reg.* U.A.E.
190 G7 **Al Khaṭīmī** *vol.* Saudi Arabia
186 F9 **Al Khawkhah** Yemen
187 J3 **Al Khawr** Qatar
186 F8 **Al Khawtamah** *i.* Yemen
189 L8 **Al Khiḍr** Iraq
187 J3 **Al Khīşah** *well* Saudi Arabia
187 I2 **Al Khizāmī** *well* Saudi Arabia
187 J2 **Al Khobar** Saudi Arabia
187 I2 **Al Khubrah** Saudi Arabia
186 G3 **Al Khuff** *reg.* Saudi Arabia
84 D3 **Al Khufrah** Libya
84 D3 **Al Khufrah Oasis** Libya
84 B1 **Al Khums** Libya
186 D1 **Al Khunfah** *sand area* Saudi Arabia
187 I4 **Al Khunn** Saudi Arabia
190 D5 **Al Khushnīyah** Syria
187 J2 **Al Khuwayr** Qatar
187 L4 **Al Kidan** *well* Saudi Arabia
189 L7 **Al Kifl** Iraq
187 J3 **Al Kir'ānah** Qatar
190 E5 **Al Kiswah** Syria
44 G3 **Alkmaar** Neth.
59 J3 **Alkoven** Austria
190 A8 **Al Kūbrī** Egypt
189 L7 **Al Kūfah** Iraq
187 I5 **Al Kufla** *well* Saudi Arabia
186 F2 **Al Kuhayfīyah** Saudi Arabia
189 M7 **Al Kumayt** Iraq
190 C9 **Al Kuntillah** Egypt
186 D3 **Al Kurá** *lava field* Saudi Arabia
190 G7 **Al Kusūr** *hills* Saudi Arabia
189 L7 **Al Kūt** Iraq
189 M9 **Al Kuwayt** Kuwait
190 D8 **Al La'bān** Jordan
189 J9 **Al Labbah** *plain* Saudi Arabia
89 F5 **Allada** Benin
190 D3 **Al Lādhiqīyah** Syria
190 D3 **Al Lādhiqīyah** *governorate* Syria
176 F5 **Allagadda** *Andhra Prad.* India
117 □P1 **Allagash** *r. ME* U.S.A.
117 □P2 **Allagash Lake** *ME* U.S.A.
178 H7 **Allahabad** *Uttar Prad.* India
191 D5 **Allahüekber Dağları** *mts* Turkey
191 D5 **Allahüekber Tepe** *mt.* Turkey
72 B8 **Allai** *Sardegna* Italy
36 E4 **Allaines** France
36 C7 **Allaines-Mervilliers** France
38 G6 **Allaire** France
190 E6 **Al Lajā** *lava field* Syria
104 C3 **Allakaket** *AK* U.S.A.
193 O3 **Allakh-Yun'** Rus. Fed.
118 F3 **Allamuchy** *NJ* U.S.A.
41 F7 **Allan** France
41 B6 **Allanche** France
97 L4 **Allandale** S. Africa
208 □1 **Allan Point** Christmas I.
97 K3 **Allanridge** S. Africa
28 J2 **Allanton** *North Lanarkshire, Scotland* U.K.
176 G3 **Allapalli** *Mahar.* India
85 G4 **'Allāqī, Wādī al** *watercourse* Egypt
191 J6 **Allar** Azer.
109 H4 **Allardville** *N.B.* Can.
200 □6 **Allardyce** *Sta Isabel* Solomon Is
62 E4 **Allariz** Spain
37 N7 **Allarmont** France
42 G5 **Allassac** France
187 I7 **Al Latakhīyah** *well* Yemen
41 G10 **Allauch** France
95 F4 **Alldays** S. Africa
70 C1 **Alle** Switz.
110 I7 **Allegan** *MI* U.S.A.
116 G6 **Allegany** *NY* U.S.A.
71 M3 **Alleghe** Italy
116 F8 **Allegheny** *r. PA* U.S.A.
116 C12 **Allegheny Mountains** U.S.A.
116 G7 **Allegheny Reservoir** *PA* U.S.A.
41 D6 **Allègre** France
131 □2 **Allègre, Pointe** *pt* Guadeloupe
41 G9 **Alleins** France
97 L4 **Allemanskraaldam** *resr* S. Africa
41 I6 **Allemond** France
146 D6 **Allen** Arg.
154 E5 **Allen** *Samar* Phil.
28 D7 **Allen** Rep. of Ireland
116 A7 **Allen** *MI* U.S.A.
27 F4 **Allen, Lough** *l.* Rep. of Ireland
203 B14 **Allen, Mount** *hill Stewart I.* N.Z.
115 G9 **Allendale** *SC* U.S.A.
29 M4 **Allendale Town** *Northumberland, England* U.K.
127 I3 **Allende** *Coahuila* Mex.
127 I5 **Allende** *Nuevo León* Mex.
129 M7 **Allende** *Veracruz* Mex.
49 G8 **Allendorf (Eder)** Ger.
49 G9 **Allendorf (Lumda)** Ger.
111 M5 **Allenford** *Ont.* Can.
29 M4 **Allenheads** *Northumberland, England* U.K.
52 G6 **Allensbach** Ger.
116 C9 **Allensville** *OH* U.S.A.
116 H8 **Allensville** *PA* U.S.A.
118 F4 **Allentown** *NJ* U.S.A.
118 D3 **Allentown** *PA* U.S.A.
59 L2 **Allentsteig** Austria
27 I6 **Allenwood** Rep. of Ireland
119 G4 **Allenwood** *NJ* U.S.A.
118 B2 **Allenwood** *PA* U.S.A.
176 E8 **Alleppey** *Kerala* India
66 D7 **Allepuz** Spain
48 H5 **Aller** *r.* Ger.
40 F3 **Allerey-sur-Saône** France
72 H2 **Allerona** Italy
53 K3 **Allersberg** Ger.
53 L5 **Allershausen** Ger.
41 I6 **Allevard** France
41 F7 **Allex** France
53 I6 **Allgäu** *reg.* Ger.
58 B5 **Allgäuer Alpen** *mts* Austria
31 N5 **Allhallows** *Medway, England* U.K.
137 H3 **Allianc** Suriname
120 D4 **Alliance** *NE* U.S.A.
116 D8 **Alliance** *OH* U.S.A.
36 H6 **Allibaudières** France
40 C4 **Allier** *dept* France
40 C3 **Allier** *r.* France
189 K8 **Al Līfīyah** *well* Iraq
207 H4 **Alligator Point** *Qld* Austr.
130 □ **Alligator Pond** Jamaica
130 □ **Alligator Pond Bay** Jamaica
40 E2 **Alligny-en-Morvan** France
187 H2 **Al Lihābah** *well* Saudi Arabia
27 B9 **Allihies** Rep. of Ireland
176 E3 **Allikher** *Karnataka* India
40 I4 **Allinges** France
23 K6 **Allinge-Sandvig** *Bornholm* Denmark
186 H2 **Al Lişāfah** *well* Saudi Arabia
190 D7 **Al Lisān** *pen.* Jordan
120 I4 **Allison** *IA* U.S.A.
75 O4 **Alliste** Italy
111 O5 **Alliston** *Ont.* Can.
186 E5 **Al Līth** Saudi Arabia
187 K4 **Al Liwā'** *oasis* U.A.E.
52 H5 **Allmendingen** Ger.
63 P3 **Allo** Spain
26 I10 **Alloa** *Clackmannanshire, Scotland* U.K.
39 P7 **Allogny** France
29 K4 **Allonby** *Cumbria, England* U.K.
42 E1 **Allonnes** *Pays de la Loire* France
39 L6 **Allonnes** *Pays de la Loire* France
43 D7 **Allons** France
205 N3 **Allora** *Qld* Austr.
41 J8 **Allos** France
41 J8 **Allos, Col d'** *pass* France
42 F3 **Alloue** France
110 F5 **Allouez** *WI* U.S.A.
27 E8 **Allow** *r.* Rep. of Ireland
26 G12 **Alloway** *South Ayrshire, Scotland* U.K.
118 E5 **Alloway** *NJ* U.S.A.
118 D6 **Alloway Creek** *r. NJ* U.S.A.
63 Q3 **Alloz, Embalse de** *resr* Spain
66 D6 **Alloza** Spain
70 D1 **Allschwil** Switz.
51 D8 **Allstedt** Ger.
155 A6 **Allu** *Sulawesi* Indon.
186 F8 **Al Luḥayyah** Yemen
111 Q4 **Allumettes, Île aux** *i. Que.* Can.
72 H3 **Allumiere** Italy
176 G5 **Allur** *Andhra Prad.* India
176 G5 **Alluru Kottapatnam** *Andhra Prad.* India
189 K8 **Al Lussuf** *well* Iraq
40 D2 **Alluy** France
109 G3 **Alma** *Que.* Can.
115 F10 **Alma** *GA* U.S.A.
120 G6 **Alma** *KS* U.S.A.
110 J6 **Alma** *MI* U.S.A.
120 F5 **Alma** *NE* U.S.A.
189 K8 **Al Ma'ānīyah** Iraq
Alma-Ata Kazakh. *see* **Almaty**
Alma-Ata Oblast *admin. div.* Kazakh. *see* **Almatinskaya Oblast'**
66 F4 **Almacelles** Spain
65 K7 **Almáchar** Spain
65 O5 **Almaciles, Puerto de** *pass* Spain
64 A3 **Almada** Port.
186 C1 **Al Madāfi'** *plat.* Saudi Arabia
189 L9 **Al Ma'danīyāt** *well* Iraq
186 F7 **Al Maḍāyā** Saudi Arabia
207 J4 **Almaden** *Qld* Austr.
65 J3 **Almadén** Spain
64 G5 **Almadén de la Plata** Spain
65 J3 **Almadenejos** Spain
65 P4 **Almadenes, Embalse de** *resr* Spain
184 B6 **Al Madīnah** Iraq
186 D3 **Al Madīnah** Saudi Arabia
186 E3 **Al Madīnah** *prov.* Saudi Arabia
190 E6 **Al Mafraq** Jordan
147 E3 **Almafuerte** Arg.
187 K4 **Al Maghrib** *reg.* U.A.E.
129 I2 **Almagre** Mex.
154 E6 **Almagro** *i.* Phil.
65 L3 **Almagro** Spain
67 B13 **Almagro, Sierra de** *hills* Spain
187 J4 **Al Mahākīk** *reg.* Saudi Arabia
85 F3 **Al Maḥāriq** Egypt
186 E5 **Al Maḥāwiyah** Saudi Arabia
86 C4 **Al Mahbas** Western Sahara
186 E5 **Al Mahḍam** Saudi Arabia
190 F2 **Al Mahdum** Syria
186 D2 **Al Maḥiā** *depr.* Saudi Arabia
189 L7 **Al Maḥmūdīyah** Iraq
187 J7 **Al Mahrah** *governorate* Yemen
187 J8 **Al Mahrah** *reg.* Yemen
186 F8 **Al Maḥwīt** Yemen
186 F8 **Al Maḥwīt** *governorate* Yemen
187 J4 **Al Majann** *ridge* Saudi Arabia
63 P5 **Almajano** Spain
186 G3 **Al Majma'ah** Saudi Arabia
77 K6 **Almăjului, Munţii** *mts* Romania
85 F3 **Al Maks al Baḥrī** Egypt
191 H4 **Almalı** Azer.
187 I3 **Al Malsūnīyah** *reg.* Saudi Arabia
63 P6 **Almaluez** Spain
Almalyk Uzbek. *see* **Olmaliq**
187 L4 **Al Manadir** *reg.* Oman
187 J2 **Al Manāmah** Bahrain
186 G4 **Al Manjūr** *well* Saudi Arabia
124 K1 **Almanor, Lake** *CA* U.S.A.
67 C10 **Almansa** Spain
67 C10 **Almansa, Embalse de** *resr* Spain
64 C6 **Almansil** Port.
64 B3 **Almansor** *r.* Port.
85 F2 **Al Manşūrah** Egypt
189 L6 **Al Manşūrīyah** Iraq
63 J3 **Almanza** Spain
63 J8 **Almanzor** *mt.* Spain
65 P6 **Almanzora** *r.* Spain
186 E6 **Al Ma'qaş** Saudi Arabia
189 M8 **Al Ma'qil** Iraq
185 K4 **Almār** Afgh.
63 J7 **Almar** *r.* Spain
62 I9 **Almaraz** Spain
65 I6 **Almargen** Spain
187 K4 **Al Mariyyah** U.A.E.
84 D1 **Al Marj** Libya
190 B9 **Al Markhah** *spring* Egypt
63 P5 **Almarza** Spain
140 D4 **Almas** Brazil
57 L5 **Almaş** Romania
77 L3 **Almaş** *r.* Romania
142 C1 **Almas, Rio das** *r.* Brazil
187 M4 **Al Masana'a** Oman
57 H4 **Almásfüzitő** Hungary
57 G6 **Almás-patak** *r.* Hungary
67 E8 **Almassora** Spain
188 F8 **Al Maṭarīyah** Egypt
183 Q5 **Almatinskaya Oblast'** *admin. div.* Kazakh.
86 B4 **Al Matmarfag** Western Sahara
183 Q6 **Almaty** Kazakh.
Almaty Oblast *admin. div.* Kazakh. *see* **Almatinskaya Oblast'**
Almaty Oblysy *admin. div.* Kazakh. *see* **Almatinskaya Oblast'**
189 K5 **Al Mawşil** Iraq
189 J6 **Al Mayādīn** Syria
63 O6 **Almazán** Spain
190 B7 **Al Mazār** Egypt
193 M3 **Almaznyy** Rus. Fed.
Almazora *Valencia* Spain *see* **Almassora**
190 D7 **Al Mazra'ah** Jordan
63 P5 **Almazul** Spain
53 P4 **Alm Berg** *mt.* Ger.
49 G7 **Alme** *r.* Ger.
67 C11 **Almeces** *mt.* Spain
65 N3 **Almedina** Spain
65 K6 **Almedinilla** Spain
62 G7 **Almeida** Port.
62 H6 **Almeida de Sayago** Spain
137 H5 **Almeirim** Brazil
64 B2 **Almeirim** Port.
44 K4 **Almelo** Neth.
66 G4 **Almenar** Spain
143 G2 **Almenara** Brazil
67 E8 **Almenara** Spain
67 B12 **Almenara** *hill* Spain
67 B12 **Almenara, Sierra de** *hills* Spain
65 O3 **Almenaras** *mt.* Spain
63 P5 **Almenar de Soria** Spain
62 F6 **Almendra** Port.
62 H6 **Almendra** Spain
62 H6 **Almendra, Embalse de** *resr* Spain
64 F3 **Almendral** Spain
64 G3 **Almendralejo** Spain
65 P6 **Almendricos** Spain
44 H4 **Almere** Neth.
65 O7 **Almería** Spain
65 O6 **Almería** *prov.* Spain
65 O7 **Almería, Golfo de** *b.* Spain
65 N7 **Almerimar** Spain
Almetievsk Rus. Fed. *see* **Al'met'yevsk**
15 K5 **Al'met'yevsk** Rus. Fed.
23 K5 **Älmhult** Sweden
186 G3 **Al Midhnab** Saudi Arabia
187 K5 **Al Miḥrāḍ** *reg.* Saudi Arabia
65 L7 **Almijara, Sierra de** *mts* Spain
65 I9 **Almina, Punta** *pt Ceuta* Spain
186 E5 **Al Mindak** Saudi Arabia
187 N4 **Al Mintirib** Oman
85 F2 **Al Minyā** Egypt
188 E9 **Al Minyā** *governorate* Egypt
145 C9 **Almirantazgo, Seno del** *sea chan.* Chile
126 □R13 **Almirante** Panama
142 C6 **Almirante Tamandaré** Brazil
187 K3 **Al Mirfa** U.A.E.
Almirós Greece *see* **Almyros**
187 I1 **Al Mish'āb** Saudi Arabia
190 E5 **Al Mismīyah** Syria
44 G5 **Almkerk** Neth.
64 C5 **Almodôvar** Port.
63 M8 **Almodóvar** *hill* Spain
64 H8 **Almodóvar** *r.* Spain
65 K3 **Almodóvar del Campo** Spain
63 Q9 **Almodóvar del Pinar** Spain
65 I5 **Almodóvar del Río** Spain
62 E7 **Almofala** Port.
65 J7 **Almogía** Spain
64 B5 **Almograve** Port.
63 O8 **Almoguera** Spain
64 G2 **Almoharín** Spain
128 G7 **Almoloya** Mex.
63 R6 **Almonacid de la Sierra** Spain
63 O9 **Almonacid del Marquesado** Spain
63 O8 **Almonacid del Zorita** Spain
63 M9 **Almonacid de Toledo** Spain
64 F5 **Almonaster la Real** Spain
26 J10 **Almond** *r. Scotland* U.K.
26 I10 **Almondbank** *Perth and Kinross, Scotland* U.K.
30 G4 **Almondsbury** *South Gloucestershire, England* U.K.
111 K7 **Almont** *MI* U.S.A.
111 R4 **Almonte** *Ont.* Can.
64 F6 **Almonte** Spain
62 H9 **Almonte** *r.* Spain
178 G5 **Almora** *Uttaranchal* India
67 D11 **Almoradí** Spain
65 I3 **Almorchón** Spain
63 L8 **Almorox** Spain
57 K4 **Álmosd** Hungary
62 D9 **Almoster** Port.
64 B2 **Almoster** *r.* Port.
89 G3 **Al Mota** *well* Niger
89 F2 **Almoustarat** Mali
59 I4 **Almsee** *l.* Austria
49 I6 **Almstedt** Ger.
190 G9 **Al Mu'ayzīlah** *hill* Saudi Arabia
187 I3 **Al Mubarrez** Saudi Arabia
187 N4 **Al Muḍaibī** Oman
187 N4 **Al Muḍairib** Oman
186 D3 **Al Mudarraj** Saudi Arabia
190 E9 **Al Mudawwarah** Jordan
65 P4 **Almudema** Spain
66 D3 **Almudévar** Spain
187 J2 **Al Muḥarraq** Bahrain
190 E10 **Al Muḥtaṭab** *depr.* Saudi Arabia
187 I8 **Al Mukallā** Yemen
186 F9 **Al Mukhā** Yemen
84 D1 **Al Mukhaylī** Libya
186 G4 **Al Mulayḥ** Saudi Arabia
187 I4 **Al Munbaṭiḥ** *des.* Saudi Arabia
186 G6 **Al Mundafan** *pass* Saudi Arabia
65 L7 **Almuñécar** Spain
66 E4 **Almuniente** Spain
59 I4 **Almünster** Austria
189 L7 **Al Muqdādīyah** Iraq
65 M3 **Álmuradiel** Spain
64 D2 **Almuro** *r.* Port.
189 I9 **Al Murūt** *well* Saudi Arabia
188 H3 **Almus** Turkey
186 H1 **Al Musannāh** *ridge* Saudi Arabia
186 D3 **Al Musayjīd** Saudi Arabia
67 E9 **Almussafes** Spain
186 C2 **Al Muṭalla'** Saudi Arabia
189 L8 **Al Muthanná** *governorate* Iraq
190 E7 **Al Muwaqqar** Jordan
186 E4 **Al Muwayh** Saudi Arabia
186 B2 **Al Muwayliḥ** Saudi Arabia
78 F4 **Almyropotamos** Greece
78 D3 **Almyros** Greece
78 F7 **Almyrou, Ormos** *b. Kriti* Greece
119 L1 **Almyville** *CT* U.S.A.
26 H7 **Alness** *Highland, Scotland* U.K.
Alness *r. Scotland* U.K. *see* **Averon**
29 N3 **Alnmouth** *Northumberland, England* U.K.
29 N3 **Alnwick** *Northumberland, England* U.K.
67 C7 **Alobras** Spain
63 O7 **Alocén** Spain
203 □4 **Alofi** Niue
199 I3 **Alofi, Île** *i.* Wallis and Futuna Is
203 □4 **Alofi Bay** Niue
200 □4b **Alohkapw** *Pohnpei* Micronesia
92 B4 **Aloi** Uganda
18 H4 **Aloja** Latvia
98 □3a **Alojera** *La Gomera* Canary Is
18 M5 **Alol'** Rus. Fed.
18 L5 **Alolya** *r.* Rus. Fed.
179 O5 **Along** *Arun. Prad.* India
162 B3 **Alongshan** *Nei Mongol* China
78 E3 **Alonnisos** *i.* Greece
142 B6 **Alonso** *r.* Brazil
155 D8 **Alor** *i.* Indon.
155 D8 **Alor, Kepulauan** *is* Indon.
155 C8 **Alor, Selat** *sea chan.* Indon.
65 J7 **Álora** Spain
156 D1 **Alor Setar** Malaysia
Alor Star Malaysia *see* **Alor Setar**
66 H2 **Alós d'Ensil** Spain
64 E5 **Alosno** Spain
Alost Belgium *see* **Aalst**
178 E8 **Alot** *Madh. Prad.* India
138 D5 **Alota** Bol.
153 L9 **Alotau** P.N.G.
39 J8 **Alouettes, Mont des** *hill* France
63 N7 **Alovera** Spain
40 F2 **Aloxe-Corton** France
209 J9 **Aloysius, Mount** *W.A.* Austr.
65 J7 **Alozaina** Spain
14 E2 **Alozero** Rus. Fed.
66 I3 **Alp** Spain
147 F5 **Alpachiri** Arg.
146 E3 **Alpa Corral** Arg.
79 J3 **Alpagut** *Bursa* Turkey
79 L2 **Alpagut** *Eskişehir* Turkey
64 D2 **Alpalhão** Port.
63 O6 **Alpanseque** Spain
124 M6 **Alpaugh** *CA* U.S.A.
58 E5 **Alpbach** Austria
63 L7 **Alpedrete** Spain
62 F8 **Alpedrinha** Port.
62 C9 **Alpedriz** Port.
49 C7 **Alpen** Ger.
111 K4 **Alpena** *MI* U.S.A.
49 E9 **Alpenrod** Ger.
66 J3 **Alpens** Spain
67 C10 **Alpera** Spain
140 D3 **Alpercatas, Serra das** *hills* Brazil
41 I8 **Alpes-de-Haute-Provence** *dept* France
41 K9 **Alpes-Maritimes** *dept* France
58 D6 **Alpetta, Punta dell'** *mt.* Italy
70 E3 **Alpe Veglia, Parco Naturale** *nature res.* Italy
207 K7 **Alpha** *Qld* Austr.
97 P3 **Alpha** S. Africa
207 K7 **Alpha Creek** *r. Qld* Austr.
218 P1 **Alpha Ridge** *sea feature* Arctic Ocean
44 G6 **Alphen** Neth.
44 G4 **Alphen aan den Rijn** Neth.
99 □2 **Alphonse** *i.* Seychelles
99 □2 **Alphonse Island** Seychelles
70 I7 **Alpi Apuane, Parco Naturale delle** *nature res.* Italy
64 B2 **Alpiarça** Port.
66 G4 **Alpicat** Spain
Alpi Dolomitiche *mts* Italy *see* **Dolomiti**
41 F9 **Alpilles** *hills* France
41 F9 **Alpilles, Canal des** France
125 W8 **Alpine** *AZ* U.S.A.
124 P9 **Alpine** *CA* U.S.A.
111 R7 **Alpine** *NY* U.S.A.
121 D10 **Alpine** *TX* U.S.A.
122 I5 **Alpine** *WY* U.S.A.
205 K7 **Alpine National Park** *Vic.* Austr.
142 D4 **Alpinópolis** Brazil
52 E5 **Alpirsbach** Ger.
70 E2 **Alpnach** Switz.
59 O5 **Alpokalja** *mts* Hungary
71 K5 **Alpone** *r.* Italy
64 D6 **Alportel** *r.* Port.
70 B5 **Alps** *mts* Europe
79 L3 **Alpu** Turkey
67 D8 **Alpuente** Spain
190 B10 **Al Qā'** *val.* Egypt
186 E5 **Al Qā'** *Makkah* Saudi Arabia
186 E6 **Al Qā'** *Makkah* Saudi Arabia
187 H7 **Al Qa'āmīyāt** *reg.* Saudi Arabia
84 B2 **Al Qaddāḥīyah** Libya
189 L8 **Al Qādisīyah** *governorate* Iraq
190 E3 **Al Qadmūs** Syria
187 K3 **Al Qaffāy** *i.* U.A.E.
186 G8 **Al Qafrah** Yemen
85 F2 **Al Qāhirah** Egypt
188 E9 **Al Qāhirah** *governorate* Egypt
186 E6 **Al Qaḥmah** Saudi Arabia
186 F3 **Al Qā'īyah** Saudi Arabia
186 G2 **Al Qā'īyah** *well* Saudi Arabia
186 C1 **Al Qalībah** Saudi Arabia
189 J5 **Al Qāmishlī** Syria
85 G2 **Al Qanṭarah** Egypt
186 H2 **Al Qar'ah** *well* Saudi Arabia
190 E6 **Al Qar'ah** *lava field* Syria
190 E3 **Al Qardāḥah** Syria
85 I5 **Al Qarḥah** Saudi Arabia
187 H8 **Al Qarn** Yemen
190 F7 **Al Qarqar** Saudi Arabia
190 F4 **Al Qaryatayn** Syria
186 G3 **Al Qaşab** *Ar Riyāḍ* Saudi Arabia
187 I4 **Al Qaşab** *Ash Sharqīyah* Saudi Arabia
186 F3 **Al Qaşīm** *prov.* Saudi Arabia
85 F3 **Al Qaşr** Egypt
186 E2 **Al Qaşr** Saudi Arabia
84 E3 **Al Qaşş Abū Sa'īd** *plat.* Egypt
187 J2 **Al Qaṭīf** Saudi Arabia
187 I8 **Al Qaṭn** Yemen
190 E7 **Al Qaṭrānah** Jordan
84 B3 **Al Qaṭrūn** Libya
186 G5 **Al Qawnas** *reg.* Saudi Arabia
186 H1 **Al Qayşūmah** Saudi Arabia
189 K9 **Al Qāyşūmah** *well* Saudi Arabia
187 M7 **Al Qiblīyah** *i.* Oman
67 E10 **Alquería de la Condesa** Spain
64 D4 **Alqueva** Port.
64 E4 **Alqueva, Barragem de** *resr* Port.
66 F3 **Alquézar** Spain
186 E2 **Al Qufayfah** Saudi Arabia
65 M6 **Alquife** Spain
187 I1 **Al-Qulay'ah, Ra's-** *pt* Kuwait
Al Qumur *country* Africa *see* **Comoros**
190 D5 **Al Qunayṭirah** Syria
190 D5 **Al Qunayṭirah** *governorate* Syria
186 E6 **Al Qunfidhah** Saudi Arabia
186 F3 **Al Qurayn** Saudi Arabia
187 K5 **Al Qurayni** *oasis* Saudi Arabia
186 F3 **Al Qurayyah** Saudi Arabia
187 M3 **Al Qurayyah** U.A.E.
188 H8 **Al Qurayyāt** Saudi Arabia
189 M8 **Al Qurnah** Iraq
190 C8 **Al Quşaymah** Egypt
85 G3 **Al Quşayr** Egypt
189 L8 **Al Qusayr** Iraq
190 E4 **Al Quşayr** Syria
190 E5 **Al Quṭayfah** Syria
186 F2 **Al Quwārah** Saudi Arabia
186 G4 **Al Quwayi'** Saudi Arabia
186 G3 **Al Quwayīyah** Saudi Arabia
190 D9 **Al Quwayrah** Jordan
187 I8 **Al Quzah** Yemen
187 L4 **Al Rabbād** *reg.* U.A.E.
41 B8 **Alrance** France
87 H3 **Alrar Est** Alg.
31 O4 **Alresford** *Essex, England* U.K.
31 I2 **Alrewas** *Staffordshire, England* U.K.
206 F5 **Alroy Downs** *N.T.* Austr.
22 F6 **Als** *i.* Denmark
63 M2 **Alsa, Embalse de** *resr* Spain
37 N7 **Alsace** *admin. reg.* France
37 N7 **Alsace** *reg.* France
37 N8 **Alsace, Plaine d'** *val.* France
29 M7 **Alsager** *Cheshire, England* U.K.
184 F9 **Al Samha** U.A.E.
189 K8 **Al Samīt** *well* Iraq
107 I5 **Alsask** *Sask.* Can.
Alsasua Spain *see* **Altsasu**
Alsatia *reg.* France *see* **Alsace**
52 F2 **Alsbach** Ger.
49 B9 **Alsdorf** Ger.
106 B3 **Alsek** *r. AK* U.S.A.
52 D3 **Alsenborn** Ger.
70 H6 **Alseno** Italy
52 D2 **Alsenz** Ger.
49 H9 **Alsfeld** Ger.
48 I1 **Als Fjord** *inlet* Denmark
26 E8 **Alsh, Loch** *sea chan. Scotland* U.K.
52 E2 **Alsheim** Ger.
147 H3 **Alsina** Arg.
162 J1 **Al'skiy Khrebet** *mt.* Rus. Fed.
51 E7 **Alsleben (Saale)** Ger.
57 I4 **Alsónémedi** Hungary
57 G4 **Alsóörs** Hungary
57 J3 **Alsóvadász** Hungary
57 J3 **Alsózsolca** Hungary
23 M5 **Alsterån** *r.* Sweden
23 L5 **Alstermo** Sweden
37 M5 **Alsting** France
29 M4 **Alston** *Cumbria, England* U.K.
205 N3 **Alstonville** *N.S.W.* Austr.
18 E5 **Alsunga** Latvia
18 J4 **Alsviķi** Latvia
20 Q2 **Alta** Norway
23 O2 **Älta** Sweden
203 C11 **Alta, Mount** *South I.* N.Z.
70 H1 **Altach** Austria
71 K2 **Altacroce, Monte** *mt.* Italy
124 N7 **Altadena** *CA* U.S.A.
20 Q2 **Altaelva** *r.* Norway
20 Q1 **Altafjorden** *sea chan.* Norway
139 F2 **Alta Floresta** Brazil
66 H5 **Altafulla** Spain
146 E2 **Alta Gracia** Arg.
126 □Q12 **Alta Gracia** Nic.
172 H2 **Altai Mountains** Asia
147 E4 **Alta Italia** Arg.
115 G10 **Altamaha** *r. GA* U.S.A.
136 E4 **Altamira** *Amazonas* Brazil
137 H5 **Altamira** *Pará* Brazil
144 C2 **Altamira** Chile
136 C4 **Altamira** Col.
126 □Q12 **Altamira** Costa Rica
129 J3 **Altamíra** Mex.
63 L2 **Altamira, Cuevas de** *tourist site* Spain
65 I1 **Altamira, Sierra de** *mts* Spain
147 H4 **Altamirano** Arg.
127 M9 **Altamirano** *Chiapas* Mex.
129 K6 **Altamirano** *Veracruz* Mex.
115 G11 **Altamonte Springs City** *FL* U.S.A.
66 K3 **Alt Empordà** *reg.* Spain
73 R6 **Altamura** Italy
169 K2 **Altan** *Chitinskaya Oblast'* Rus. Fed.
169 L2 **Altan** *Chitinskaya Oblast'* Rus. Fed.
168 J3 **Altanbulag** Mongolia
169 O2 **Altan Emel** *Nei Mongol* China
72 A9 **Altano, Capo** *c. Sardegna* Italy
168 B4 **Altan Ovoo** *mt.* China/Mongolia
169 K7 **Altan Shiret** *Nei Mongol* China
Altan Xiret *Nei Mongol* China *see* **Altan Shiret**
140 D5 **Alta Paraiso de Goiás** Brazil
137 E2 **Altapirire** Venez.
126 D2 **Altar** Mex.
123 I11 **Altar** *r.* Mex.
126 B1 **Altar, Desierto de** *des.* Mex.
70 E7 **Altare** Italy
98 □1a **Altares** *Terceira* Azores
126 F5 **Altata** Mex.
59 I4 **Altaussee** Austria
59 I4 **Altausseer See** *l.* Austria
70 D7 **Alta Valle Pesio, Parco Naturale dell'** *nature res.* Italy
70 D4 **Alta Val Sesia, Parco Naturale** *nature res.* Italy
74 H2 **Altavilla Irpina** Italy
73 O6 **Altavilla Silentina** Italy
116 F11 **Altavista** *VA* U.S.A.
172 I3 **Altay** *Xinjiang* China
168 E3 **Altay** Mongolia
168 A1 **Altay, Respublika** *aut. rep.* Rus. Fed.
Altay Kray *admin. div.* Rus. Fed. *see* **Altayskiy Kray**
183 U2 **Altayskiy** Rus. Fed.
Altayskiy Khrebet *mts* Asia *see* **Altai Mountains**
183 T2 **Altayskiy Kray** *admin. div.* Rus. Fed.
168 A1 **Altayskiy Zapovednik** *nature res.* Rus. Fed.
51 J7 **Altdöbern** Ger.
53 M4 **Altdorf** Ger.
70 F2 **Altdorf** Switz.
53 K3 **Altdorf bei Nürnberg** Ger.
48 I2 **Alt Duvenstedt** Ger.
64 C6 **Alte** Port.
67 E10 **Altea** Spain
50 D4 **Alte Elde** *r.* Ger.
50 H2 **Altefähr** Ger.
53 M4 **Alteglofsheim** Ger.
20 Q1 **Alteidet** Norway
49 E8 **Altena** Ger.
49 C9 **Altenahr** Ger.
49 J7 **Altenau** Ger.
49 G7 **Altenbeken** Ger.
51 I9 **Altenberg** Ger.
49 D6 **Altenberge** Ger.
48 G3 **Altenbruch-Westerende** Ger.
52 G2 **Altenbuch** Ger.
51 F9 **Altenburg** Ger.
49 E10 **Altendiez** Ger.
49 K9 **Altenfeld** Ger.
59 I3 **Altenfelden** Austria
52 C2 **Altenglan** Ger.
49 K8 **Altengottern** Ger.
50 E2 **Altenhagen** Ger.
52 D5 **Altenheim** Ger.
50 I5 **Altenhof** Ger.
48 J2 **Altenholz** Ger.
50 H1 **Altenkirchen** Ger.
49 E9 **Altenkirchen (Westerwald)** Ger.
48 K2 **Altenkrempe** Ger.
53 N5 **Altenmarkt an der Alz** Ger.
59 M3 **Altenmarkt an der Triesting** Austria
59 K4 **Altenmarkt bei Sankt Gallen** Austria
59 H5 **Altenmarkt im Pongau** Austria
48 K4 **Altenmedingen** Ger.
53 J5 **Altenmünster** Ger.
168 D8 **Altenqoke** *Qinghai* China
53 I5 **Altenstadt** *Bayern* Ger.
53 J6 **Altenstadt** *Bayern* Ger.
49 G10 **Altenstadt** *Hessen* Ger.
53 M2 **Altenstadt an der Waldnaab** Ger.
52 F4 **Altensteig** Ger.
50 H3 **Altentreptow** Ger.
51 E7 **Altenweddingen** Ger.
50 J5 **Alte Oder** *r.* Ger.
137 H5 **Alter do Chão** Brazil
64 D2 **Alter do Chão** Port.
64 D2 **Alter Pedroso** *hill* Port.
51 H6 **Altes Lager** Ger.
20 O2 **Altevatnet** *l.* Norway
53 M5 **Altfraunhofen** Ger.
53 K5 **Althegnenberg** Ger.
58 H3 **Altheim** Austria
52 G5 **Altheim** Ger.
53 I4 **Altheim (Alb)** Ger.
52 F4 **Althengstett** Ger.
59 J6 **Althofen** Austria
191 J5 **Altıağaç** Azer.
41 D8 **Altier** France
41 D8 **Altier** *r.* France
191 A6 **Altınbasak** Turkey
191 A5 **Altındere** *park* Turkey
15 F8 **Altınkaya Barajı** *resr* Turkey
189 L6 **Altin Köprü** Iraq
79 H3 **Altınoluk** Turkey
142 D4 **Altinópolis** Brazil
79 H3 **Altınova** *Balıkesir* Turkey
190 F1 **Altınova** *Şanlıurfa* Turkey
190 E2 **Altınözü** Turkey
79 L3 **Altıntaş** Turkey
79 L6 **Altınyaka** Turkey
138 C4 **Altiplano** *plain* Bol.
191 E6 **Altıyol** Turkey
40 K1 **Altkirch** France
51 F9 **Altkirchen** Ger.
50 D4 **Alt Krenzlin** Ger.
50 I5 **Altlandsberg** Ger.
53 L4 **Altmannstein** Ger.
50 D5 **Altmark** *reg.* Ger.
51 G9 **Altmittweida** Ger.
53 L4 **Altmühl** *r.* Ger.
53 K4 **Altmühltal** *park* Ger.
26 G9 **Altnafeadh** *Highland, Scotland* U.K.
26 H6 **Altnaharra** *Highland, Scotland* U.K.
110 I7 **Alto** *MI* U.S.A.
71 L5 **Alto, Monte** *hill* Italy
147 F3 **Alto Alegre** Arg.
142 A2 **Alto Araguaia** Brazil
130 F3 **Alto Cedro** Cuba
91 C7 **Alto Chicapa** Angola
63 P5 **Alto Cruz** *mt.* Spain
127 N10 **Alto Cuchumatanes** *mts* Guat.
129 H2 **Alto de Caballeros** Mex.
63 N3 **Alto de Cabezas** *mt.* Spain
62 F4 **Alto de Covelo** *pass* Spain
63 K3 **Alto de las Portillas** *pass* Spain
63 Q5 **Alto del Moncayo** *mt.* Spain
62 I3 **Alto del Rabizo** *pass* Spain
146 D3 **Alto de Pencoso** *hills* Arg.
65 M6 **Alto de San Juan** *mt.* Spain
62 F4 **Alto do Canizo** *pass* Spain
62 D8 **Alto do Trevim** *mt.* Port.
62 F5 **Alto Douro Wine Region** *reg.* Port.
74 E7 **Altofonte** *Sicilia* Italy
141 B6 **Alto Garças** Brazil
146 B3 **Alto Jahuel** Chile
95 H2 **Alto Ligonha** Moz.
129 K6 **Alto Lucero** Mex.
138 C3 **Alto Madidi, Parque Nacional** *nat. park* Bol.
63 O8 **Altomira, Sierra de** *mts* Spain
95 H2 **Alto Molócuè** Moz.
73 Q8 **Altomonte** Italy
53 K5 **Altomünster** Ger.
31 K5 **Alton** *Hampshire, England* U.K.
31 I2 **Alton** *Staffordshire, England* U.K.
120 J6 **Alton** *IL* U.S.A.
121 J7 **Alton** *MO* U.S.A.
117 □N5 **Alton** *NH* U.S.A.
106 F3 **Altona** *B.C.* Can.
107 L5 **Altona** *Man.* Can.
204 G2 **Alton Downs** *S.A.* Austr.
145 B7 **Alto Nevado** *mt.* Chile
116 G8 **Altoona** *PA* U.S.A.
110 C5 **Altoona** *WI* U.S.A.
137 I5 **Alto Pacajá** *r.* Brazil
140 D4 **Alto Parnaíba** Brazil
71 J8 **Altopascio** Italy
146 D3 **Alto Pelado** Arg.
146 D3 **Alto Pencoso** Arg.
142 A6 **Alto Piquiri** Brazil
138 C2 **Alto Purús** *r.* Peru
62 E5 **Alto Rabagão, Barragem do** *resr* Port.
143 F4 **Alto Rio Doce** Brazil
145 C7 **Alto Río Senguerr** Arg.
142 A3 **Alto Rio Verde** Brazil
66 F4 **Altorricón** Spain
140 E3 **Altos** Brazil
63 O8 **Altos de Cabrejas** *mts* Spain
138 C4 **Altos de Chacaya** Chile
65 P3 **Altos de Chinchilla** *mts* Spain
147 F2 **Altos de Chipión** Arg.
142 A3 **Alto Sucuriú** Brazil
63 P7 **Alto Tajo, Parque Natural del** *nature res.* Spain
142 A2 **Alto Taquarí** Brazil
63 M3 **Altotero** *mt.* Spain
129 J6 **Altotonga** Mex.
53 N5 **Altötting** Ger.
141 B8 **Alto Uruguai** Brazil
131 □9 **Alto Vista** *hill* Aruba
50 J5 **Altranft** Ger.
52 B2 **Altrich** Ger.
29 M7 **Altrincham** *Greater Manchester, England* U.K.
50 G5 **Alt Ruppin** Ger.
63 P3 **Altsasu** Spain
50 F3 **Alt Schwerin** Ger.
52 H6 **Altshausen** Ger.
70 H1 **Altstätten** Switz.
191 E2 **Altud** Rus. Fed.
19 R9 **Altukhovo** Rus. Fed.
191 B6 **Altunkent** Turkey
172 K7 **Altun Shan** *mt. Qinghai* China
173 H8 **Altun Shan** *mts* China
67 E8 **Altura** Spain
122 D6 **Alturas** *CA* U.S.A.
121 F8 **Altus** *OK* U.S.A.
53 I6 **Altusried** Ger.
49 J6 **Alt Wallmoden** Ger.
17 M2 **Altynivka** Ukr.
18 H2 **Alu** Estonia
95 H2 **Alua** Moz.
90 F3 **Aluakluak** Sudan
187 J4 **Al Ubaylah** Saudi Arabia
188 I3 **Alucra** Turkey
187 I3 **Al 'Uḍaylīyah** Saudi Arabia
186 F9 **Al Udayn** Yemen
18 K4 **Alūksne** Latvia
18 K4 **Alūksnes** *l.* Latvia
186 C2 **Al 'Ulā** Saudi Arabia
186 G8 **Al'ulah** *reg.* Yemen
184 C5 **Alūm** Iran
116 E9 **Alum Bridge** *WV* U.S.A.
116 C8 **Alum Creek Lake** *OH* U.S.A.
146 B6 **Aluminé** Arg.
146 B6 **Aluminé** *r.* Arg.
146 B6 **Aluminé, Lago** *l.* Arg.
23 O1 **Alunda** Sweden
77 M4 **Aluniş** Romania
17 N9 **Alupka** Ukr.
84 C2 **Al 'Uqaylah** Libya
Al 'Uqaylah Saudi Arabia *see* **An Nabk**
187 J3 **Al 'Uqayr** Saudi Arabia
Al Uqşur Egypt *see* **El Uqşur**
176 E5 **Alur** *Andhra Prad.* India
188 I9 **Al Urayq** *des.* Saudi Arabia
Alur Setar Malaysia *see* **Alor Setar**
17 N9 **Alushta** Ukr.
63 Q7 **Alustante** Spain
184 A4 **'Ālūt** Iran
186 C1 **Al Uthaylī** Saudi Arabia
200 □1 **Alutom, Mount** *hill* Guam
200 □1 **Alutom Island** Guam
Aluva *Kerala* India *see* **Alwaye**
186 G4 **Al 'Uwayjā'** *well* Saudi Arabia
187 J4 **Al 'Uwayjā'** *well* Saudi Arabia
187 I2 **Al 'Uwaynah** *well* Saudi Arabia
84 E4 **Al 'Uwaynāt** *Al Kufrah* Libya
84 A3 **Al 'Uwaynāt** *Awbārī* Libya
186 C2 **Al 'Uwaynidhiyah** *i.* Saudi Arabia
189 K8 **Al 'Uwayqīlah** Saudi Arabia
186 H3 **Al Uyainah** Saudi Arabia
190 E10 **Al 'Uyaynah** *well* Saudi Arabia
186 D3 **Al 'Uyūn** *Al Madīnah* Saudi Arabia
186 F2 **Al 'Uyūn** *Al Qaşīm* Saudi Arabia
186 F2 **Al 'Uẓaym** Saudi Arabia
189 M8 **Al 'Uzayr** Iraq
62 D8 **Alva** *r.* Port.
26 I10 **Alva** *Clackmannanshire, Scotland* U.K.
121 F7 **Alva** *OK* U.S.A.
62 D9 **Alvaiázere** Port.
64 C5 **Alvalade** Port.
191 I5 **Älvänd** Azer.
184 C4 **Alvand, Kūh-e** *mt.* Iran
70 H2 **Alvaneu** Switz.
62 E6 **Alvão, Parque Natural do** *nature res.* Port.
62 E6 **Alvão, Serra de** *mts* Spain
191 C6 **Alvar** Turkey
129 L7 **Alvarado** Mex.
121 G9 **Alvarado** *TX* U.S.A.
129 L7 **Alvarado, Laguna** *lag.* Mex.
137 E5 **Alvarães** Brazil
62 C5 **Alvarães** Port.
143 G3 **Alvarenga** Brazil
62 D7 **Alvarenga** Port.
62 D8 **Álvares** Port.
142 B5 **Álvares Machado** Brazil
147 G3 **Alvarez** Arg.
62 E9 **Álvaro** Port.
128 F6 **Álvaro Obregón** Mex.
129 I4 **Álvaro Obregón** Mex.
21 M6 **Älvdalen** Sweden
21 J1 **Alvdalen** *val.* Sweden
31 I3 **Alvechurch** *Worcestershire, England* U.K.
62 D2 **Alvedro** *airport* Spain
64 C2 **Alvega** Port.
30 H3 **Alveley** *Shropshire, England* U.K.
62 D9 **Alvelos, Serra de** *mts* Port.
64 A3 **Alverca** Port.
62 F7 **Alverca da Beira** Port.
45 C6 **Alveringem** Belgium
26 J7 **Alves** *Moray, Scotland* U.K.
48 I3 **Alveslohe** Ger.
23 K5 **Alvesta** Sweden
30 G4 **Alveston** *South Gloucestershire, England* U.K.
73 I2 **Alviano** Italy
26 I8 **Alvie** *Highland, Scotland* U.K.
43 H6 **Alvignac** France
22 C1 **Ålvik** Norway
21 N5 **Alvik** Sweden
121 H11 **Alvin** *TX* U.S.A.
110 F4 **Alvin** *WI* U.S.A.
143 F4 **Alvinópolis** Brazil
62 E7 **Alvite** Port.
73 L4 **Alvito** Italy
64 D4 **Alvito** Port.
64 D4 **Alvito, Barragem do** *resr* Port.
23 N1 **Älvkarleby** Sweden
73 P6 **Alvo** *r.* Italy
62 E8 **Alvoco da Serra** Port.
64 B6 **Alvor** Port.

Älvsbyn to Anglesona

228

20 P4 Älvsbyn Sweden
188 C10 Al Wādī at Jadīd governorate Egypt
187 N4 Al Wāfī Oman
189 M9 Al Wafrah Kuwait
186 C2 Al Wajh Saudi Arabia
187 J3 Al Wakrah Qatar
187 I2 Al Wannān Saudi Arabia
186 G1 Al Waqbá well Saudi Arabia
178 F6 Alwar Rajasthan India
187 H2 Al Warī'ah Saudi Arabia
187 N4 Al Wāsiṭ Oman
84 E2 Al Wāṭiyah well Egypt
84 A1 Al Watīyah Libya
176 E7 Alwaye Kerala India
30 E1 Alwen Reservoir Wales U.K.
55 H5 Alwernia Pol.
189 J7 Al Widyān plat. Iraq/Saudi Arabia
84 B3 Al Wīgh Libya
84 C3 Al Wīgh, Ramlat des. Libya
187 M4 Al Wuqbah Oman
187 J3 Al Wusayl Qatar
186 G1 Al Wusayṭ well Saudi Arabia
187 M5 Al Wusṭá admin. reg. Oman
Alxa Youqi Nei Mongol China see Ehen Hudag
Alxa Zuoqi Nei Mongol China see Bayan Hot
186 D4 'Alyā Saudi Arabia
187 H3 Al Yamāmah Saudi Arabia
206 F2 Alyangula N.T. Austr.
187 J3 Al Yāsāt i. U.A.E.
206 E6 Alyawarra Aboriginal Land res. N.T. Austr.
186 F6 Āl Yazīd Saudi Arabia
183 L2 Alyp Kazakh.
26 J9 Alyth Perth and Kinross, Scotland U.K.
18 H7 Alytus Lith.
53 N5 Alz r. Ger.
122 L4 Alzada MT U.S.A.
147 H5 Alzaga Arg.
70 H4 Alzano Lombardo Italy
49 H10 Alzenau in Unterfranken Ger.
45 J9 Alzette r. Lux.
52 E2 Alzey Ger.
67 E9 Alzira Spain
41 C9 Alzon France
43 I9 Alzonne France
97 L8 Amabele S. Africa
136 D5 Amacayacu, Parque Nacional nat. park Col.
129 H8 Amacuzac r. Mex.
21 M6 Åmådalen Sweden
206 C8 Amadeus, Lake salt flat N.T. Austr.
90 F3 Amadi Sudan
105 K3 Amadjuak Lake Nunavut Can.
125 U10 Amado AZ U.S.A.
64 A3 Amadora Port.
87 G4 Amadror plain Alg.
136 C3 Amaga Col.
167 I5 Amaga-dake mt. Japan
119 K3 Amagansett NY U.S.A.
166 B6 Amagasaki Japan
22 I6 Amager i. Denmark
165 H13 Amagi Japan
167 I6 Amagi-san vol. Japan
167 I6 Amagi-tōge pass Japan
167 I6 Amagiyugashima Japan
36 I4 Amagne France
166 D5 Amagoi-dake mt. Japan
155 F5 Amahai Seram Indon.
186 F5 Amā'ir Saudi Arabia
66 C1 Amaiur-Maia Spain
129 I4 Amajac r. Mex.
167 G2 Amakazari-yama mt. Japan
165 H14 Amakusa-Kami-shima i. Japan
165 G14 Amakusa-nada b. Japan
165 H14 Amakusa-Shimo-shima i. Japan
187 L6 Amal Oman
22 I2 Åmål Sweden
89 F3 Amalaoulaou well Mali
176 H4 Amalapuram Andhra Prad. India
161 K1 Amalat r. Rus. Fed.
73 N6 Amalfi Italy
97 J3 Amalia S. Africa
78 C5 Amaliada Greece
178 E9 Amalner Mahar. India
55 L1 Amalvas l. Lith.
153 I7 Amamapare Papua Indon.
139 G5 Amambaí Brazil
139 G5 Amambaí, Serra de hills Brazil/Para.
164 □G18 Amami-Ō-shima i. Nansei-shotō Japan
164 □F20 Amami-shotō is Japan
90 E5 Amamula Dem. Rep. Congo
21 M6 Åmån r. Sweden
146 D2 Amaná Arg.
137 E5 Amanã, Lago l. Brazil
136 E5 Amana, Reserva de Desenvolvimento Sustentável nature res. Brazil
206 B4 Amanbidji Aboriginal Land res. N.T. Austr.
37 L8 Amance France
37 K8 Amance r. France
36 H7 Amance, Lac l. France
40 I2 Amancey France
116 C9 Amanda OH U.S.A.
73 K2 Amandola Italy
182 H3 Amangel'dy Aktyubinskaya Oblast' Kazakh.
182 K2 Amangel'dy Kostanayskaya Oblast' Kazakh.
182 K1 Amankaragay Kazakh.
Amankeldi Aktyubinskaya Oblast' Kazakh. see Amangel'dy
Amankeldi Kostanayskaya Oblast' Kazakh. see Amangel'dy
23 M2 Åmänningen l. Sweden
182 I4 Amanotkel' Kazakh.
Amanqaraghay Kazakh. see Amankaragay
73 Q9 Amantea Italy
95 E3 Amanzamnyama watercourse Zimbabwe
97 O6 Amanzimtoti S. Africa
138 C2 Amapa Brazil
137 I4 Amapá Brazil
137 I4 Amapá state Brazil
129 K7 Amapa r. Mex.
126 □P11 Amapala Hond.
137 I4 Amapari r. Brazil
92 C2 Āmara admin. reg. Eth.
85 G6 Amara Abu Sin Sudan
77 L6 Amaradia r. Romania
141 B9 Amaral Ferrador Brazil
140 E3 Amarante Brazil
62 D6 Amarante Port.
140 D3 Amarante do Maranhão Brazil
158 C4 Amarapura Myanmar
176 F7 Amaravati r. India
85 F4 Amara West Sudan
168 J3 Amardalay Mongolia
62 D5 Amarela, Serra mts Port.
64 E4 Amareleja Port.
62 D5 Amares Port.
140 F5 Amargosa Brazil
123 F8 Amargosa watercourse CA U.S.A.
125 P5 Amargosa Desert NV U.S.A.
124 P5 Amargosa Range mts CA U.S.A.
125 P5 Amargosa Valley NV U.S.A.
65 M2 Amarguillo r. Spain
Amargura Island Tonga see Fonualei
121 E8 Amarillo TX U.S.A.
144 C4 Amarillo, Cerro mt. Arg.
178 H8 Amarkantak Chhattisgarh India
73 M3 Amaro, Monte mt. Italy
75 K6 Amaroni Italy
206 G7 Amaroo, Lake salt flat Qld Austr.
178 H8 Amarpur Madh. Prad. India
179 M8 Amarpur Tripura India
178 G8 Amarwara Madh. Prad. India
110 F3 Amasa MI U.S.A.
166 E1 Ama-saki pt Japan
73 K5 Amaseno Italy
73 K5 Amaseno r. Italy
191 E5 Amasia Armenia
Amasia Turkey see Amasya
86 B4 Amasine Western Sahara
188 F3 Amasra Turkey
89 F2 Amâssine well Mali
188 G3 Amasya Turkey
204 C2 Amata S.A. Austr.
137 G5 Amatari Brazil
136 D5 Amataurá Brazil
127 M9 Amatenango Mex.
128 G7 Amatepec Mex.
97 P5 Amatikulu S. Africa
126 □O10 Amatique, Bahía de b. Guat.
128 D5 Amatitán Mex.
129 K7 Amatlán Mex.
128 C5 Amatlán de Cañas Mex.
75 K6 Amato r. Italy
97 K8 Amatola Range mts S. Africa
73 K2 Amatrice Italy
167 L5 Amatsu-kominato Japan
119 H2 Amawalk NY U.S.A.
45 H7 Amay Belgium
63 L3 Amaya mt. Spain
162 B2 Amazar Rus. Fed.
162 B2 Amazar r. Rus. Fed.
137 I4 Amazon r. S. America alt. Amazonas
137 I4 Amazon, Mouths of the Brazil
138 C3 Amazon, Source of the Peru
137 E6 Amazonas state Brazil
136 D5 Amazonas dept Col.
136 B6 Amazonas dept Peru
137 I4 Amazonas r. S. America conv. Amazon
137 E4 Amazonas state Venez.
214 F5 Amazon Cone sea feature S. Atlantic Ocean
137 G6 Amazónia, Parque Nacional nat. park Brazil
185 O4 Amb Pak.
92 C1 Āmba Ālagē mt. Eth.
176 D3 Ambad Mahar. India
92 C2 Amba Farit mt. Eth.
95 □I4 Ambahikily Madag.
176 E3 Ambajogai Mahar. India
178 F4 Ambala Haryana India
95 □J3 Ambalajanakomby Madag.
95 □J2 Ambalakida Madag.
95 □K2 Ambalakirajy Madag.
176 G9 Ambalangoda Sri Lanka
95 □J4 Ambalatany Madag.
95 □J4 Ambalavao Madag.
206 E7 Ambalindum N.T. Austr.
89 H6 Ambam Cameroon
95 □K2 Ambanja Madag.
184 H6 Ambar Iran
193 R3 Ambarchik Rus. Fed.
42 D6 Ambarès-et-Lagrave France
144 D3 Ambargasta, Salinas de salt pan Arg.
14 F2 Ambarnyy Rus. Fed.
63 J3 Ambasaguas Spain
176 E8 Ambasamudram Tamil Nadu India
179 M8 Ambassa Tripura India
207 J8 Ambathala Qld Austr.
136 B5 Ambato Ecuador
144 D3 Ambato, Sierra mts Arg.
95 □J3 Ambato Boeny Madag.
95 □J4 Ambato Finandrahana Madag.
95 □J4 Ambatolahy Madag.
95 □J3 Ambatolampy Madag.
95 □J3 Ambatomainty Madag.
95 □J3 Ambatomanoina Madag.
95 □K3 Ambatondrazaka Madag.
95 □K2 Ambatosia Madag.
95 □K3 Ambatosoratra Madag.
42 G4 Ambazac France
42 G4 Ambazac, Monts d' hills France
Ambejogai Mahar. India see Ambajogai
185 O4 Ambela Pak.
155 E5 Ambelau i. Maluku Indon.
Ambelón Greece see Ampelonas
Amber Rajasthan India see Amer
53 L3 Amberg Ger.
110 G4 Amberg WI U.S.A.
29 O7 Ambergate Derbyshire, England U.K.
127 P8 Ambergris Cay i. Belize
130 H3 Ambergris Cays is Turks and Caicos Is
40 G5 Ambérieu-en-Bugey France
111 M5 Amberley Ont. Can.
203 G10 Amberley South I. N.Z.
45 I8 Amberloup Belgium
40 D5 Ambert France
42 C5 Ambès France
178 H9 Ambgaon Mahar. India
43 I8 Ambialet France
Ambianum France see Amiens
88 C3 Ambidédi Mali
40 D4 Ambierle France
178 D9 Ambika r. India
179 I8 Ambikapur Chhattisgarh India
154 C5 Ambil i. Phil.
95 □J4 Ambila Madag.
39 L7 Ambillou France
95 □K2 Ambilobe Madag.
106 D3 Ambition, Mount B.C. Can.
36 D5 Amblainville France
29 N3 Amble Northumberland, England U.K.
30 H3 Amblecote West Midlands, England U.K.
104 C3 Ambler AK U.S.A.
118 E4 Ambler PA U.S.A.
29 L5 Ambleside Cumbria, England U.K.
36 C2 Ambleteuse France
45 I8 Amblève r. Belgium
45 I8 Amblève, Vallée de l' val. Belgium
179 K9 Ambo Orissa India
138 A2 Ambo Peru
95 □J5 Amboasary Madag.
95 □K3 Amboasary Gara Madag.
95 □K3 Amboavory Madag.
200 □3a Ambo Channel Kwajalein Marshall Is
95 □K3 Ambodifotatra Madag.
95 □K4 Ambodiharina Madag.
95 □K3 Ambodilazana Madag.
95 □J3 Ambohidratrimo Madag.
95 □K3 Ambohijanahary Madag.
95 □J4 Ambohimahasoa Madag.
95 □I4 Ambohimahavelona Madag.
95 □J3 Ambohipaky Madag.
95 □K2 Ambohitra mt. Madag.
95 □K2 Ambohitralanana Madag.
Amboina Maluku Indon. see Ambon
42 F1 Amboise France
91 B7 Amboiva Angola
38 F6 Ambon France
155 F5 Ambon Maluku Indon.
155 E5 Ambon i. Maluku Indon.
95 □J5 Ambondro Madag.
36 H5 Ambonnay France
138 D4 Amboró, Parque Nacional nat. park Bol.
93 C5 Amboseli National Park Kenya
95 □J4 Ambositra Madag.
95 □J5 Ambovombe Madag.
Ambow i. Fiji see Bau
125 Q7 Amboy CA U.S.A.
110 E8 Amboy IL U.S.A.
39 O8 Ambrault France
Ambre, Cap d' c. Madag. see Bobaomby, Tanjona
99 □1b Ambre, Île d' i. Mauritius
39 J5 Ambrières-les-Vallées France
Ambrim i. Vanuatu see Ambrym
91 B6 Ambriz Angola
91 B6 Ambriz, Coutada do nature res. Angola
191 E3 Ambrolauri Georgia
40 G4 Ambronay France
31 J4 Ambrosden Oxfordshire, England U.K.
147 G2 Ambrosetti Arg.
136 D5 Ambrosio Brazil
200 □5 Ambrym i. Vanuatu
157 J9 Ambulu Jawa Indon.
157 J8 Ambunten Jawa Indon.
176 F6 Ambur Tamil Nadu India
207 L9 Amby Qld Austr.
104 A4 Amchitka Island AK U.S.A.
22 E2 Åmdals Verk Norway
84 D6 Am-Dam Chad
87 F5 Amded, Oued watercourse Alg.
192 H3 Amderma Rus. Fed.
89 E2 Amdillis well Mali
84 C6 Am Djéména Chad
173 J10 Amdo Xizang China
128 G5 Amealco Mex.
128 C5 Ameca Jalisco Mex.
128 D3 Ameca Zacatecas Mex.
128 B5 Ameca r. Mex.
129 I6 Amecameca Mex.
92 C2 Amedamit mt. Eth.
147 F4 Ameghino Arg.
70 H7 Ameglia Italy
59 I2 Ameisberg hill Austria
64 D6 Ameixial Port.
45 J8 Amel Belgium
44 I2 Ameland i. Neth.
73 I2 Amelia Italy
116 H11 Amelia Court House VA U.S.A.
43 J11 Amélie-les-Bains-Palalda France
48 J4 Amelinghausen Ger.
178 H6 Amellu Uttar Prad. India
62 D9 Amêndoa Port.
64 D5 Amendoeira Port.
75 L4 Amendolara Italy
75 J8 Amendolea r. Italy
117 L7 Amenia NY U.S.A.
85 F5 Amentego Sudan
173 B13 Amer Rajasthan India
66 K3 Amer Spain
67 L8 Amer, Punta de n' pt Spain
53 M6 Amerang Ger.
62 E4 A Merca Spain
124 K3 American, North Fork r. CA U.S.A.
142 D5 Americana Brazil
214 H9 American-Antarctic Ridge sea feature S. Atlantic Ocean
122 H5 American Falls ID U.S.A.
122 H5 American Falls Reservoir ID U.S.A.
125 U1 American Fork UT U.S.A.
200 □2 American Samoa terr. S. Pacific Ocean
115 E9 Americus GA U.S.A.
59 K5 Ameringkogel mt. Austria
44 H5 Amerongen Neth.
44 H4 Amersfoort Neth.
97 N3 Amersfoort S. Africa
31 K4 Amersham Buckinghamshire, England U.K.
107 M3 Amery Man. Can.
213 E2 Amery Ice Shelf Antarctica
120 I4 Ames IA U.S.A.
31 I5 Amesbury Wiltshire, England U.K.
117 O6 Amesbury MA U.S.A.
178 D7 Amet Rajasthan India
178 H6 Amethi Uttar Prad. India
66 A1 Amezketa Spain
62 F4 A Mezquita Spain
78 C4 Amfilochia Greece
78 D4 Amfissa Greece
39 M3 Amfreville-la-Campagne France
193 O3 Amga Rus. Fed.
169 P2 Amgalang Nei Mongol China
162 J6 Amgu Rus. Fed.
193 T3 Amguema Rus. Fed.
87 G4 Amguid Alg.
161 O1 Amgun' r. Rus. Fed.
109 H4 Amherst N.S. Can.
117 M6 Amherst MA U.S.A.
116 C7 Amherst OH U.S.A.
116 F11 Amherst VA U.S.A.
208 I5 Amherst, Mount hill W.A. Austr.
111 K7 Amherstburg Ont. Can.
116 D11 Amherstdale WV U.S.A.
111 R5 Amherst Island Ont. Can.
111 R5 Amherstview Ont. Can.
167 L3 Ami Japan
64 B2 Amiais de Baixo Port.
72 H2 Amiata, Monte mt. Italy
Amida Turkey see Diyarbakır
120 D2 Amidon ND U.S.A.
64 D4 Amieira Port.
62 E9 Amieira do Tejo Port.
36 D4 Amiens France
189 J7 'Amīj, Wādī watercourse Iraq
188 H5 Amik Ovası marsh Turkey
187 K6 Amilḥayt, Wādī al r. Oman
36 E8 Amilly France
184 E6 'Amīnābād Iran
Amíndhaion Greece see Amyntaio
Amindivi atoll India see Amini
176 C7 Amindivi Islands Lakshadweep India
176 C7 Amini atoll India
92 D3 Amino Eth.
166 B4 Amino Japan
94 C4 Aminuis Namibia
190 D4 Amioun Lebanon
178 G5 Amipshahr Uttar Prad. India
185 L4 Amīr, Band-e lakes Afgh.
184 D5 Amīrābād Eşfahān Iran
184 B5 Amīrābād Īlām Iran
Amirabad Iran see Fūlād Maïalleh
99 □2 Amirante Islands Seychelles
215 H5 Amirante Trench sea feature Indian Ocean
185 J7 Amir Chah Pak.
107 K4 Amisk Lake Sask. Can.
Amistad, Represa de resr Mex./U.S.A. see Amistad Reservoir
127 I3 Amistad Reservoir Mex./U.S.A.
121 J10 Amite LA U.S.A.
121 J10 Amite Creek r. MS U.S.A.
207 N9 Amity Point Qld Austr.
178 E8 Amjhera Madh. Prad. India
178 G9 Amla Madh. Prad. India
186 F6 Amlaḥ, Jabal al hill Saudi Arabia
89 F5 Amlamé Togo
184 D3 Amlash Iran
179 J6 Amlekhganj Nepal
22 E3 Åmli Norway
104 A4 Amlia Island AK U.S.A.
30 D1 Amlwch Isle of Anglesey, Wales U.K.
85 H5 'Amm Adam Sudan
190 D7 'Ammān Jordan
184 F2 Ammanazar Turkm.
30 E4 Ammanford Carmarthenshire, Wales U.K.
14 E2 Ämmänsaari Fin.
186 G8 'Ammār reg. Yemen
190 E6 'Ammār, Tall hill Syria
20 N4 Ammarnäs Sweden
206 E6 Ammaroo N.T. Austr.
204 D2 Ammaroodinna watercourse S.A. Austr.
105 O3 Ammassalik Greenland
53 K6 Ammer r. Ger.
20 N5 Ammerån r. Sweden
52 F4 Ammerbuch Ger.
58 C5 Ammergauer Alpen mts Austria/Ger.
53 J6 Ammergebirge nature res. Ger.
48 E4 Ammerland reg. Ger.
49 J8 Ammern Ger.
48 J3 Ammersbek Ger.
37 N7 Ammerschwihr France
53 K6 Ammersee l. Ger.
78 C2 Ammochori Greece
190 B3 Ammochostos Cyprus
190 C3 Ammochostos Bay Cyprus
186 F9 Am Nābiyah Yemen
Amne Machin Range mts China see A'nyêmaqên Shan
37 L5 Amnéville France
178 D9 Amod Gujarat India
62 E4 Amoeiro Spain
170 D7 Amo Jiang r. Yunnan China
184 E3 Amol Iran
139 F4 Amolar Brazil
78 E2 Amoliani i. Greece
17 N2 Amon' Rus. Fed.
62 C5 Amonde Port.
49 G9 Amöneburg Ger.
140 F2 Amontada Brazil
63 L9 Amor mt. Spain
52 G2 Amorbach Ger.
144 F3 Amores r. Arg.
79 G6 Amorgos i. Greece
142 B2 Amorinópolis Brazil
121 K8 Amory MS U.S.A.
108 E3 Amos Que. Can.
22 H6 Åmose r. Denmark
22 F2 Åmot Buskerud Norway
22 D2 Åmot Telemark Norway
21 N6 Åmot Sweden
136 A6 Amotape, Cerros de mts Peru
22 I2 Åmotfors Sweden
43 C8 Amou France
87 F2 Amour, Djebel mts Alg.
88 D2 Amourj Maur.
Amoy Fujian China see Xiamen
129 I6 Amozoc Mex.
157 K5 Ampah Kalimantan Indon.
155 B4 Ampana Sulawesi Indon.
95 □K2 Ampanefena Madag.
177 H3 Ampani Orissa India
95 □J5 Ampanihy Madag.
95 □K3 Ampanotoamaizina Madag.
95 □J2 Amparafaka, Tanjona pt Madag.
95 □K3 Amparafaravola Madag.
176 G9 Amparai Sri Lanka
142 D5 Amparo Brazil
95 □K3 Ampasimanolotra Madag.
95 □K3 Ampasimbe Madag.
58 D5 Ampass Austria
78 D3 Ampelonas Greece
157 L9 Ampenan Lombok Indon.
53 L5 Amper r. Ger.
89 H4 Amper Nigeria
214 I3 Ampere Seamount sea feature N. Atlantic Ocean
71 N3 Ampezzo Italy
53 M5 Ampfing Ger.
53 P5 Ampflwang im Hausruckwald Austria
152 D3 Amphitrite Group is Paracel Is
155 B4 Ampibaku Sulawesi Indon.
95 □K2 Ampisikinana Madag.
Ampitsikinana Madag. see Ampisikinana
40 E5 Amplepuis France
155 B4 Ampoa Sulawesi Indon.
31 I5 Amport Hampshire, England U.K.
66 G6 Amposta Spain
31 L3 Ampthill Bedfordshire, England U.K.
63 K5 Ampudia Spain
63 N2 Ampuero Spain
41 I9 Ampus France
168 H9 Amqog Gansu China
109 H3 Amqui Que. Can.
176 F4 Amrabad Andhra Prad. India
186 F3 'Amrah, Jabal hill Saudi Arabia
186 F8 Amrān Yemen
186 F7 Amrān governorate Yemen
Amraoti Mahar. India see Amravati
178 F9 Amravati Mahar. India
178 C9 Amreli Gujarat India
185 M8 Amri Pak.
179 N7 Amring Assam India
70 G1 Amriswil Switz.
178 E4 Amritsar Punjab India
178 G5 Amroha Uttar Prad. India
48 F1 Amrum i. Ger.
87 G5 Amsel Alg.
20 O4 Åmsele Sweden
44 G3 Amstelmeer l. Neth.
44 G4 Amstelveen Neth.
44 G4 Amsterdam Neth.
97 O2 Amsterdam S. Africa
117 K6 Amsterdam NY U.S.A.
116 E8 Amsterdam OH U.S.A.
215 J7 Amsterdam, Île i. Indian Ocean
44 H5 Amsterdam-Rijnkanaal canal Neth.
44 F4 Amsterdamse Waterleidingduinen nature res. Neth.
59 K3 Amstetten Austria
52 H4 Amstetten Ger.
119 K1 Amston CT U.S.A.
90 D2 Am Timan Chad
191 C2 Amtqeli Georgia
52 H6 Amtzell Ger.
136 C4 Amú r. Col.
173 I10 Amu Co l. Xizang China
182 H5 Amudar'ya r. Asia
Amudaryo r. Asia see Amudar'ya
105 I2 Amund Ringnes Island Nunavut Can.
213 G2 Amundsen, Mount Antarctica
217 K10 Amundsen Abyssal Plain sea feature Southern Ocean
218 B1 Amundsen Basin sea feature Arctic Ocean
213 D2 Amundsen Bay Antarctica
212 O1 Amundsen Coast Antarctica
212 N1 Amundsen Glacier Antarctica
104 F2 Amundsen Gulf N.W.T. Can.
217 K10 Amundsen Ridge sea feature Southern Ocean
213 A1 Amundsen-Scott research stn Antarctica
212 Q2 Amundsen Sea Antarctica
157 K6 Amuntai Kalimantan Indon.
162 C2 Amur Heilong. China
162 E3 Amur r. Rus. Fed. alt. Heilong Jiang (China)
162 I4 Amur r. Rus. Fed.
85 G5 'Amur, Wadi watercourse Sudan
155 D3 Amurang Sulawesi Indon.
Amur Oblast admin. div. Rus. Fed. see Amurskaya Oblast'
63 O2 Amurrio Spain
162 J3 Amursk Rus. Fed.
162 F2 Amurskaya Oblast' admin. div. Rus. Fed.
17 N8 Amurs'ke Ukr.
182 H1 Amurskiy Rus. Fed.
162 L2 Amurskiy liman str. Rus. Fed.
162 G5 Amurzet Rus. Fed.
75 K7 Amusa r. Italy
63 L4 Amusco Spain
162 C1 Amutkachi Rus. Fed.
78 C4 Amvrakia, Limni l. Greece
78 B4 Amvrakikos Kolpos b. Greece
17 R6 Amvrosiyivka Ukr.
Amyderya r. Asia see Amudar'ya
78 C2 Amyntaio Greece
110 J1 Amyot Ont. Can.
77 Q7 Amzacea Romania
89 F2 Amzérakad well Mali
84 D6 Am-Zoer Chad
158 B5 An Myanmar
79 I1 Ana r. Turkey
201 □3 Anaa atoll Arch. des Tuamotu Fr. Polynesia
155 B5 Anabanua Sulawesi Indon.
193 M2 Anabar r. Rus. Fed.
205 H6 Ana Branch r. N.S.W. Austr.
190 D6 Anabtā West Bank
124 M7 Anacapa Islands CA U.S.A.
73 M6 Anacapri Italy
137 E2 Anaco Venez.
122 H3 Anaconda MT U.S.A.
122 C2 Anacortes WA U.S.A.
154 C3 Anacuao, Mount Phil.
121 F8 Anadarko OK U.S.A.
62 D8 Anadia Port.
188 H3 Anadolu Dağları mts Turkey
193 S3 Anadyr' Rus. Fed.
193 S3 Anadyr' r. Rus. Fed.
Anadyr, Gulf of Rus. Fed. see Anadyrskiy Zaliv
193 T3 Anadyrskiy Zaliv b. Rus. Fed.
79 G6 Anafi Greece
79 G6 Anafi i. Greece
98 □3a Anaga, Punta de pt Tenerife Canary Is
140 E5 Anagé Brazil
73 K4 Anagni Italy
Anagnia Italy see Anagni
189 J6 'Ānah Iraq
124 O8 Anaheim CA U.S.A.
106 E4 Anahim Lake B.C. Can.
124 □B11 Anahola HI U.S.A.
127 I4 Anáhuac Nuevo León Mex.
129 J3 Anáhuac Veracruz Mex.
121 H11 Anahuac TX U.S.A.
124 □C12 'Anahulu r. HI U.S.A.
176 E7 Anaimalai Hills India
176 E7 Anai Mudi Peak Kerala India
Anaiteum i. Vanuatu see Anatom
137 I5 Anajás Brazil
137 I5 Anajás, Ilha i. Brazil
140 D2 Anajatuba Brazil
95 □I4 Anakao Madag.
177 H4 Anakapalle Andhra Prad. India
207 K7 Anakie Qld Austr.
95 □J2 Analalava Madag.
95 □K3 Analamaitso mts Madag.
142 D5 Analândia Brazil
95 □I4 Analavelona mts Madag.
118 E2 Analomink PA U.S.A.
137 F5 Anamã Brazil
130 D3 Ana María, Golfo de b. Cuba
156 F3 Anambas, Kepulauan is Indon.
89 G5 Anambra state Nigeria
166 E1 Anamizu Japan
120 J4 Anamosa IA U.S.A.
137 G4 Anamu r. Brazil
188 F5 Anamur Turkey
167 G5 Anan Nagano Japan
166 A8 Anan Tokushima Japan
178 D8 Anand Gujarat India
179 K9 Anandapur Orissa India
178 F4 Anandpur Punjab India
179 K8 Anandpur r. W. Bengal India
78 F6 Ananes i. Greece
183 Q6 Anan'ev Kyrg.
204 C2 Anangu Pitjantjatjara Aboriginal Lands res. S.A. Austr.
155 D6 Anano i. Indon.
176 E5 Anantapur Andhra Prad. India
178 E3 Anantnag Jammu and Kashmir
178 G6 Anant Peth Madh. Prad. India
Ananyev Ukr. see Anan'yiv
Anan'yevo Kyrg. see Anan'ev
16 I6 Anan'yiv Ukr.
15 G7 Anapa Rus. Fed.
75 I9 Anapo r. Sicilia Italy
78 G8 Anapodaris r. Kriti Greece
142 C2 Anápolis Brazil
137 I5 Anapú r. Brazil
184 F6 Anār Iran
184 E5 Anārak Iran
184 D4 Anarbar r. Iran
184 G4 Anarbat Iran
57 L3 Anarcs Hungary
185 I5 Anardara Afgh.
213 L2 Anare Mountains Antarctica
204 □3 Anare Station S. Pacific Ocean
27 B8 Anascaul Rep. of Ireland
131 □1 Añasco Puerto Rico
131 □1 Añasco, Río Grande de r. Puerto Rico
20 P4 Ånäset Sweden
17 R6 Anastasiyevka Rus. Fed.
17 Q8 Anastasiyevskaya Rus. Fed.
153 K3 Anatahan i. N. Mariana Is
Anatajan i. N. Mariana Is see Anatahan
79 J4 Anatolia reg. Turkey
78 G1 Anatoliki Makedonia kai Thraki admin. reg. Greece
200 □5 Anatom i. Vanuatu
144 E3 Añatuya Arg.
206 F7 Anatye Aboriginal Land res. N.T. Austr.
137 F4 Anauá r. Brazil
142 A5 Anaurilândia Brazil
137 F5 Anavilhanas, Arquipélago das is Brazil
63 J7 Anaya de Alba Spain
Anaypazari Turkey see Gülnar
190 E10 Anaz mts Saudi Arabia
184 C2 'Anbarān Iran
168 E6 Anbei Gansu China
Anbu Guangdong China see Chao'an
184 C3 Anbūh Iran
184 F8 Anbūr-e Kālārī Iran
163 E9 Anbyon N. Korea
62 C8 Ançã Port.
62 F3 Ancares, Serra dos mts Spain
138 A2 Ancash dept Peru
111 O6 Ancaster Ont. Can.
31 K2 Ancaster Lincolnshire, England U.K.
144 D3 Ancasti, Sierra mts Arg.
41 D7 Ance r. France
41 I7 Ancelle France
38 I7 Ancenis France
37 J6 Ancerville France
145 D6 Anchán Arg.
170 E3 Anchang Sichuan China
89 H4 Anchau Nigeria
143 G4 Anchieta Brazil
138 C3 Anchodaya Bol.
104 D3 Anchorage AK U.S.A.
207 M1 Anchorage Reefs P.N.G.
111 L7 Anchor Bay MI U.S.A.
146 E4 Anchorena Arg.
98 □2c Anchorstock Point Tristan da Cunha S. Atlantic Ocean
130 □ Anchovy Jamaica
Anchuthengu Kerala India see Anjengo
55 L1 Ančia l. Lith.
18 F6 Ančia r. Lith.
63 P3 Ancín Spain
130 D3 Anclitas, Cayo i. Cuba
An Cóbh Rep. of Ireland see Cobh
147 G4 Ancón Arg.
138 A2 Ancón Peru
71 P8 Ancona Italy
71 N9 Ancona prov. Italy
36 D4 Ancre r. France
26 K11 Ancrum Scottish Borders, Scotland U.K.
93 C8 Ancuabe Moz.
95 G3 Ancuaze Moz.
145 B6 Ancud Chile
145 B6 Ancud, Golfo de g. Chile
36 H8 Ancy-le-Franc France
Ancyra Turkey see Ankara
162 D5 Anda Heilong. China
Anda Heilong. China see Daqing
155 D1 Anda i. Indon.
21 I6 Anda Norway
146 B5 Andacollo Arg.
146 B2 Andacollo Chile
206 E8 Andado N.T. Austr.
138 B3 Andahuaylas Peru
95 □K3 Andaingo Gara Madag.
179 K8 Andal W. Bengal India
144 D2 Andalgalá Arg.
71 K3 Andalo Italy
20 I5 Åndalsnes Norway
65 K5 Andalucía aut. comm. Spain
Andalusia aut. comm. Spain see Andalucía
115 D10 Andalusia AL U.S.A.
187 N5 Andām, Wādī r. Oman
159 A9 Andaman and Nicobar Islands union terr. India
175 H9 Andaman and Nicobar Islands union terr. India
215 K4 Andaman Basin sea feature Indian Ocean
177 M6 Andaman Islands Andaman & Nicobar Is India
159 B9 Andaman Sea Indian Ocean
177 M6 Andaman Strait Andaman & Nicobar Is India
204 F4 Andamooka S.A. Austr.
41 F6 Andance France
95 □K2 Andapa Madag.
94 D3 Andara Namibia
185 M4 Andarāb Afgh.
65 N7 Andarax r. Spain
185 N3 Andarob Tajik.
59 P4 Andau Austria
62 I5 Andavías Spain
170 F7 Ande Guangxi China
186 E8 Andeba Ye Midir Zerf Chaf pt Eritrea
53 K6 Andechs Ger.
70 G2 Andeer Switz.
14 K2 Andeg Rus. Fed.
Andegavum France see Angers
70 F1 Andelfingen Switz.
36 B5 Andelle r. France
37 J7 Andelot-Blancheville France
40 H3 Andelot-en-Montagne France
58 A5 Andelsbuch Austria
44 I5 Andelst Neth.
20 N2 Andenes Norway
45 H8 Andenne Belgium
89 F3 Andéramboukane Mali
20 N2 Ånderdalen Nasjonalpark nat. park Norway
45 F7 Anderlecht Belgium
45 F8 Anderlues Belgium
70 F2 Andermatt Switz.
49 D10 Andernach Ger.
43 B6 Andernos-les-Bains France
Anderob Tajik. see Andarob
23 N1 Andersbo Sweden
200 □1 Andersen Airforce Base Guam
147 G4 Anderson Arg.
104 F3 Anderson r. N.W.T. Can.
104 D3 Anderson AK U.S.A.
124 J1 Anderson CA U.S.A.
114 E5 Anderson IN U.S.A.
121 H7 Anderson MO U.S.A.
115 F8 Anderson SC U.S.A.
205 K9 Anderson Bay Tas. Austr.
124 K4 Anderson Reservoir CA U.S.A.
116 B9 Andersonville OH U.S.A.
49 E5 Andervenne Ger.
136 C3 Andes Col.
138 B3 Andes mts S. America
64 E5 Andévalo, Sierra de hills Spain
20 N2 Andfjorden sea chan. Norway
Andhíparos i. Greece see Antiparos
176 C3 Andhra Lake India
176 F4 Andhra Pradesh state India
191 H3 Andi Rus. Fed.
63 Q3 Andía, Sierra de mts Spain
44 H3 Andijk Neth.
183 O7 Andijon Andijon Uzbek.
183 O7 Andijon admin. div. Uzbek.
Andijon Wiloyati admin. div. Uzbek. see Andijon
Andikíra Greece see Antikyra
Andikithira i. Greece see Antikythira
95 □K3 Andilamena Madag.
95 □K3 Andilanatoby Madag.
37 K8 Andilly-en-Bassigny France
184 C5 Andīmeshk Iran
Andímilos i. Greece see Antimilos
171 I4 Anding Hunan China
Andípaxoi i. Greece see Antipaxoi
Andípsara i. Greece see Antipsara
142 B5 Andirá Brazil
173 F8 Andir He r. China
188 H5 Andırın Turkey
173 F8 Andirlangar Xinjiang China
191 H3 Andiyskoye Koysu r. Rus. Fed.
176 E7 Andiyur Tamil Nadu India
Andizhan Uzbek. see Andijon
Andizhan Oblast admin. div. Uzbek. see Andijon
185 K3 Andkhui r. Afgh.
185 K3 Andkhvoy Afgh.
37 N7 Andlau France
37 O6 Andlau r. France
66 A1 Andoain Spain
95 □K2 Andoany Madag.
136 B5 Andoas Peru
136 B5 Andoas Nuevo Ecuador
57 G5 Andocs Hungary
19 U2 Andoga r. Rus. Fed.
19 U2 Andogskaya Gryada hills Rus. Fed.
95 □J5 Andohahela, Réserve d' nature res. Madag.
95 □K2 Andohajango Madag.
90 A4 Andok Foula Gabon
176 F4 Andol Andhra Prad. India
176 E4 Andola Karnataka India
37 N7 Andolsheim France
Andong Liaoning China see Dandong
163 F10 Andong S. Korea
169 P9 Andongwei Shandong China
207 H2 Andoom Qld Austr.
59 I3 Andorf Austria
57 J4 Andornaktálya Hungary
70 E4 Andorno Micca Italy
66 I2 Andorra country Europe
66 E6 Andorra Spain
66 I2 Andorra, Valls d' val. Andorra
66 I2 Andorra la Vella Andorra
Andorra la Vieja Andorra see Andorra la Vella
63 Q4 Andosilla Spain
39 J5 Andouillé France
57 H4 Andovce Slovakia
31 J5 Andover Hampshire, England U.K.
119 K1 Andover CT U.S.A.
117 N6 Andover MA U.S.A.
117 N5 Andover NH U.S.A.
118 F3 Andover NJ U.S.A.
116 H6 Andover NY U.S.A.
116 E7 Andover OH U.S.A.
20 M2 Andøya i. Norway
19 U2 Andozero, Ozero l. Rus. Fed.
41 E6 Andrable r. France
142 D5 Andradas Brazil
125 R9 Andrade CA U.S.A.
142 B4 Andradina Brazil
Andraitx Spain see Andratx
95 □J3 Andramasina Madag.
95 □J3 Andramy Madag.
75 O4 Andrano Italy
95 □J3 Andranomavo Madag.
95 □K3 Andranomena Madag.
95 □I4 Andranopasy Madag.
95 □K2 Andranovondronina Madag.
95 □J4 Andranovory Madag.
67 J8 Andratx Spain
104 A4 Andreanof Islands AK U.S.A.
19 P5 Andreapol' Rus. Fed.
28 I5 Andreas Isle of Man
20 □ Andrée Land reg. Svalbard
90 D2 André Félix, Parc National de nat. park C.A.R.
143 G1 André Fernandes Brazil
143 E4 Andrelândia Brazil
143 E3 Andrequicé Brazil
147 I3 Andresito Uru.
55 H4 Andrespol Pol.
43 E9 Andrest France
107 H4 Andrew Alta Can.
158 B5 Andrew Bay Myanmar
115 H9 Andrews SC U.S.A.
121 D9 Andrews TX U.S.A.
183 S5 Andreyevka Almatinskaya Oblast' Kazakh.
182 D1 Andreyevka Rus. Fed.
Andreyevskoye Rus. Fed. see Dneprovskoye
17 M1 Andreykovichi Rus. Fed.
19 R6 Andreykovo Rus. Fed.
40 E5 Andrézieux-Bouthéon France
73 Q5 Andria Italy
95 □J3 Andriamena Madag.
95 □J3 Andriba Madag.
57 L4 Andrid Romania
96 I9 Andrieskraal S. Africa
96 E2 Andriesvale S. Africa
95 □J4 Andringitra mts Madag.
17 P7 Andrivka Ukr.
16 G3 Andriyevychi Ukr.
17 P6 Andriyivka Dnipropetrovs'ka Oblast' Ukr.
17 Q6 Andriyivka Donets'ka Oblast' Ukr.
17 P4 Andriyivka Kharkivs'ka Oblast' Ukr.
17 M9 Andriyivka Respublika Krym Ukr.
17 M3 Andriyivka Sums'ka Oblast' Ukr.
17 P6 Andriyivka Zaporiz'ka Oblast' Ukr.
95 □J5 Androka Madag.
95 □K2 Androna reg. Madag.
19 W4 Androniki Rus. Fed.
130 D1 Andros i. Bahamas
78 F5 Andros Andros Greece
78 F5 Andros i. Greece
117 P5 Androscoggin r. ME/NH U.S.A.
182 C1 Androsovka Rus. Fed.
130 E1 Andros Town Andros Bahamas
176 C7 Andrott i. India
Andrushevka Ukr. see Andrushivka
16 I3 Andrushivka Ukr.
16 I4 Andrushky Ukr.
55 H6 Andrychów Pol.
55 K3 Andrzejewo Pol.
20 O2 Andselv Norway
20 P1 Andsnes Norway
90 F4 Andudu Dem. Rep. Congo
184 G6 Andūhjerd Iran
65 K4 Andújar Spain
91 C7 Andulo Angola
41 D8 Anduze France
191 E1 Andzhiyevskiy Rus. Fed.
209 J7 Anec, Lake salt flat W.A. Austr.
145 C6 Anecón Grande mt. Arg.
89 F2 Anéfis Mali
88 E2 Anéfis well Mali
131 K4 Anegada i. Virgin Is (U.K.)
145 E6 Anegada, Bahía b. Arg.
131 L4 Anegada Passage Virgin Is (U.K.)
125 T9 Anegam AZ U.S.A.
89 F5 Aného Togo
Aneityum i. Vanuatu see Anatom
200 □3b Aneju i. Majuro Marshall Is
176 E6 Anekal Karnataka India
200 □5 Anelghowhat Vanuatu
146 C6 Añelo Arg.
190 A2 Anemourıon tourist site Turkey
200 □3b Anemwanot i. Majuro Marshall Is
16 I7 Anenii Noi Moldova
87 G6 Anesbaraka well Alg.
36 B6 Anet France
Anetchom, Île i. Vanuatu see Anatom
66 G2 Aneto mt. Spain
Ānewetak atoll Marshall Is see Enewetak
89 I2 Aney Niger
Aneytioum, Île i. Vanuatu see Anatom
85 I6 Anfile Bay Eritrea
58 B8 Anfo Italy
171 J5 Anfu Jiangxi China
176 E7 Angadippuram Kerala India
95 □J2 Angadoka, Lohatanjona hd Madag.
205 I8 Angahook Lorne State Park nature res. Vic. Austr.
206 C3 Angalarri r. N.T. Austr.
84 C5 Angamma, Falaise d' esc. Chad
145 B8 Angamos, Isla i. Chile
138 C5 Angamos, Punta pt Chile
128 G6 Angangueo Mex.
169 R3 Ang'angxi Heilong. China
160 H1 Angara r. Rus. Fed.
89 F4 Angaradébou Benin
206 E7 Angarapa Aboriginal Land res. N.T. Austr.
160 H1 Angarsk Rus. Fed.
206 D8 Angas Downs N.T. Austr.
208 J7 Angas Range hills W.A. Austr.
204 G6 Angaston S.A. Austr.
154 C4 Angat Luzon Phil.
Angatau atoll Arch. des Tuamotu Fr. Polynesia see Fangatau
142 C5 Angatuba Brazil
154 □ Angaur i. Palau
21 M5 Ånge Sweden
62 C7 Angeja Port.
137 F3 Angel, Salto waterfall Venez.
126 C3 Ángel de la Guarda, Isla i. Mex.
154 C4 Angeles Luzon Phil.
Angel Falls Venez. see Angel, Salto
22 I5 Ängelholm Sweden
20 R2 Angeli Fin.
147 G2 Angelica Arg.
121 H10 Angelina r. TX U.S.A.
207 K9 Angellala Creek r. Qld Austr.
48 I1 Angeln reg. Ger.
209 D7 Angelo r. W.A. Austr.
129 L7 Angel R. Cabada Mex.
124 L3 Angels Camp CA U.S.A.
23 J5 Angelstad Sweden
40 E1 Angely France
53 N6 Anger Ger.
92 C1 Āngereb Eth.
92 C1 Āngereb Wenz r. Eth.
20 N5 Ångermanälven r. Sweden
50 J4 Angermünde Ger.
51 E6 Angern Ger.
59 O3 Angern an der March Austria
39 J7 Angers France
36 D7 Angerville France
41 K9 Anges, Baie des b. France
157 L5 Anggana Kalimantan Indon.
71 M8 Anghiari Italy
140 D4 Angical Brazil
140 F3 Angicos Brazil
107 L2 Angikuni Lake Nunavut Can.
124 M6 Angiola CA U.S.A.
78 E2 Angitis r. Greece
159 F8 Angkor tourist site Cambodia
42 C5 Anglade France
42 I5 Anglards-de-Salers France
30 B4 Angle Pembrokeshire, Wales U.K.
203 B13 Anglem, Mount hill Stewart I. N.Z.
106 G5 Anglemont B.C. Can.
43 J8 Anglès France
66 K4 Anglès Spain
30 D1 Anglesey i. Wales U.K.
66 H4 Anglesona Spain

Column 1

136 D3 Arauca dept Col.
136 E3 Arauca r. Venez.
146 A6 Araucanía admin. reg. Chile
141 C8 Araucária Brazil
144 B5 Arauco Chile
144 B5 Arauco, Golfo de b. Chile
41 E6 Araules France
136 E3 Arauquita Col.
136 D2 Araure Venez.
125 V9 Aravaipa Creek watercourse AZ U.S.A.
178 D7 Aravalli Range mts India
18 I2 Aravete Estonia
63 P5 Aravis r. Spain
40 I5 Aravis mts France
40 I5 Aravis, Col des pass France
78 D2 Aravissos Greece
200 □1 Arawa P.N.G.
93 D5 Arawale National Reserve nature res. Kenya
Arawata r. South I. N.Z. see Arawhata
202 L5 Arawhana mt. North I. N.Z.
203 C11 Arawhata r. South I. N.Z.
142 D3 Araxá Brazil
78 C4 Araxos, Akra pt Greece
Araya Spain see Araia
137 E2 Araya, Península de pen. Venez.
131 K8 Arayıt Dağı mt. Turkey
188 E4 Araz r. Azer.
191 J6 Araz r. Azer.
 alt. Arak's (Armenia),
 alt. Aras Nehri (Turkey),
 conv. Aras, hist. Araxes
62 C8 Arazede Port.
66 C4 Arba r. Spain
66 C3 Arba de Biel r. Spain
66 C3 Arba de Luesia r. Spain
 Arballu Iraq see Arbīl
92 C3 Árba Minch Eth.
43 F10 Arbas France
189 L6 Arbat Iraq
72 D8 Arbatax Sardegna Italy
14 J4 Arbazh Rus. Fed.
66 G4 Arbeca Spain
37 K8 Arbecey France
70 G3 Arbedo Switz.
 Arbela Iraq see Arbīl
40 H4 Arbent France
43 D10 Arbéost France
23 J3 Arberg Ger.
59 K2 Arbesbach Austria
63 F7 Arbeteta Spain
71 K9 Arbia r. Italy
189 L5 Arbil Iraq
189 K6 Arbil governorate Iraq
63 P3 Arbizu Spain
23 L2 Arboga Sweden
40 H3 Arbois France
65 O6 Arboleas Spain
147 G5 Arboledas Arg.
136 B2 Arboletes Col.
147 I3 Arbolito Uru.
70 G1 Arbon Switz.
72 B8 Arborea Sardegna Italy
72 B8 Arborea r. Sardegna Italy
107 K4 Arborfield Sask. Can.
107 L5 Arborg Man. Can.
70 E5 Arborio Italy
21 N6 Arbrå Sweden
26 K9 Arbroath Angus, Scotland U.K.
66 K4 Arbúcies Spain
124 J2 Arbu Lut, Dasht-e des. Afgh.
185 J7 Arbus France
43 C9 Arbus Sardegna Italy
72 B8 Arbus Sardegna Italy
17 K6 Arbuzynka Ukr.
41 G9 Arc r. France
41 I5 Arc r. France
43 B6 Arcachon France
43 B6 Arcachon, Bassin d' inlet France
116 G6 Arcade NY U.S.A.
123 I8 Arcadia FL U.S.A.
121 I9 Arcadia LA U.S.A.
110 H5 Arcadia WI U.S.A.
116 G8 Arcadia PA U.S.A.
110 C5 Arcadia WI U.S.A.
40 I5 Arcalod, Pointe d' mt. France
116 A9 Arcanum OH U.S.A.
127 N7 Arcas, Cayos is Mex.
122 B6 Arcata CA U.S.A.
124 O3 Arc Dome mt. NV U.S.A.
73 L4 Arce Italy
128 G7 Arcelia Mex.
44 J6 Arcen Neth.
37 J8 Arc-en-Barrois France
63 N2 Arceniega Spain
42 C4 Arces France
36 G7 Arces-Dilo France
40 H2 Arc-et-Senans France
71 N8 Arcevia Italy
 Archangel Rus. Fed. see Arkhangel'sk
 Archangel Oblast admin. div. Rus. Fed. see Arkhangel'skaya Oblast'
79 J6 Archar r. Bulg.
77 K7 Archar r. Bulg.
118 D2 Archbald PA U.S.A.
116 A7 Archbold OH U.S.A.
67 C11 Archena Spain
207 H2 Archer r. Qld Austr.
207 I2 Archer Bend National Park Qld Austr.
121 F9 Archer City TX U.S.A.
37 M7 Arches France
125 W3 Arches National Park UT U.S.A.
88 E2 Arch Henda well Mali
42 D4 Archiac France
65 K6 Archidona Spain
206 G3 Archie Creek r. Qld Austr.
109 I3 Archipiélago de Mingan, Réserve du Parc National de l' nat. park Que. Can.
57 L5 Archiş Romania
65 P4 Archível Spain
184 G2 Archman Turkm.
72 B8 Arci, Monte hill Italy
72 H2 Arcidosso Italy
72 C5 Arcipelago de la Maddalena, Parco Nazionale dell' nat. park Sardegna Italy
72 G2 Arcipelago Toscano, Parco Nazionale dell' nat. park Italy
36 H6 Arcis-sur-Aube France
184 C2 Árçivan Azer.
204 E3 Arckaringa watercourse S.A. Austr.
40 H2 Arc-lès-Gray France
71 J4 Arco Italy
122 H5 Arco ID U.S.A.
144 B6 Arco, Paso de pass Chile
64 □ Arco da Calheta Madeira
62 E6 Arco de Baúlhe Port.
70 H7 Arcola Italy
116 H10 Arcola VA U.S.A.
40 I3 Arçon France
40 D4 Arconce r. France
63 M4 Arçonnay France
143 E4 Arcos Brazil
58 H3 Arcos Port.
63 M4 Arcos Spain
63 P6 Arcos de Jalón Spain
64 H7 Arcos de la Frontera Spain
67 C8 Arcos de las Salinas Spain
176 F6 Arcos de Valdevez Port.
176 F6 Arcot Tamil Nadu India
38 E4 Arcouest, Pointe de l' pt France
140 F4 Arcoverde Brazil
62 E7 Arcozelo Braga Port.
62 E7 Arcozelo Guarda Port.
62 C6 Arcozelo Porto Port.
62 C6 Arcozelo Viana do Castelo Port.
40 G2 Arc-sur-Tille France
105 J2 Arctic Bay Nunavut Can.
 Arctic Institute Islands is see Arkticheskogo Instituta, Ostrova
218 B1 Arctic Mid-Ocean Ridge sea feature Arctic Ocean
218 Arctic Ocean

Column 2

104 E3 Arctic Red r. N.W.T. Can.
212 N8 Arctowski research stn Antarctica
72 B8 Arcuentu, Monte hill Italy
66 F3 Arcusa Spain
40 D1 Arcy-sur-Cure France
188 C3 Arda r. Bulg.
 alt. Ardas (Greece)
70 I5 Arda r. Italy
184 D2 Ardabīl Iran
184 B2 Ardabīl prov. Iran
59 K3 Ardagger Markt Austria
27 D8 Ardagh Rep. of Ireland
189 K3 Ardahan Turkey
191 D4 Ardahan prov. Turkey
184 D3 Ardak Iran
184 E6 Ardakān Färs Iran
184 D3 Ardakān Yazd Iran
63 N5 Ardal Iran
24 I6 Årdal Norway
63 N5 Ardal mt. Spain
65 J7 Ardales Spain
20 D8 Årdalstangen Norway
21 I6 Årdalstangen Norway
21 J7 Ardanairy Rep. of Ireland
43 B10 Ardanuç Turkey
191 D4 Ardanuç Turkey
72 B6 Ardara Sardegna Italy
27 F3 Ardara Rep. of Ireland
188 C3 Ardas r. Greece
 alt. Arda (Bulgaria)
190 F8 Ard as Sawwān plain Jordan
15 H5 Ardatov Nizhegorodskaya Oblast' Rus. Fed.
15 I5 Ardatov Respublika Mordoviya Rus. Fed.
27 F7 Ardconry Rep. of Ireland
73 J4 Ardea Italy
41 F7 Ardèche dept France
41 F8 Ardèche r. France
41 E8 Ardèche, Gorges de l' France
27 I5 Ardee Rep. of Ireland
26 G10 Arden Argyll and Bute, Scotland U.K.
119 G2 Arden NY U.S.A.
204 F5 Arden, Mount hill S.A. Austr.
45 G9 Ardennes, Plateau de l' Belgium
 Ardennes plat. Belgium see Ardennes, Plateau de l'
36 I4 Ardennes dept France
36 H5 Ardennes r. France
37 I4 Ardennes, Canal des France
42 H2 Ardentes France
26 G10 Ardentinny Argyll and Bute, Scotland U.K.
124 K3 Arden Town CA U.S.A.
27 G6 Arden hill Rep. of Ireland
26 H7 Ardersier Highland, Scotland U.K.
41 C6 Ardes France
191 C4 Ardeşen Turkey
184 E5 Ardestān Iran
70 I2 Ardez Switz.
27 C8 Ardfert Rep. of Ireland
27 D8 Ardfinnan Rep. of Ireland
26 H7 Ardgay Highland, Scotland U.K.
27 K4 Ardglass Northern Ireland U.K.
191 B6 Ardıcın Dağı mt. Turkey
64 E4 Ardila r. Italy
77 N9 Ardino Bulg.
 Ardiwachar Point Scotland U.K.
202 L5 Ardkeen Northern I. N.Z.
27 K4 Ardkeen Northern Ireland U.K.
26 F11 Ardlamont Point Scotland U.K.
31 N4 Ardleigh Essex, England U.K.
205 K6 Ardlethan N.S.W. Austr.
212 V1 Ardley Island Antarctica
26 G10 Ardlui Argyll and Bute, Scotland U.K.
40 I6 Ardlussa Argyll and Bute, Scotland U.K.
214 F9 Argentine Abyssal Plain sea feature S. Atlantic Ocean
26 F7 Ardmair Highland, Scotland U.K.
214 G8 Argentine Basin sea feature S. Atlantic Ocean
26 E11 Ardminish Argyll and Bute, Scotland U.K.
27 E6 Ardmolich Highland, Scotland U.K.
27 C6 Ardmore Rep. of Ireland
121 G8 Ardmore OK U.S.A.
118 E4 Ardmore PA U.S.A.
26 D9 Ardmore Bay Rep. of Ireland
27 E7 Ardmore Point Scotland U.K.
26 D9 Ardnacrusha Rep. of Ireland
147 F6 Argerich Arg.
65 O5 Argerin mt. Spain
77 O6 Argeş r. Romania
63 L9 Argés Spain
77 M6 Argeşel r. Romania
17 L1 Ardon' r. Rus. Fed.
191 F1 Ardon Rus. Fed.
191 F2 Ardon r. Rus. Fed.
70 C3 Ardon Switz.
85 G5 Ardooie Belgium
75 K7 Ardore Italy
26 E11 Ardpatrick Point Scotland U.K.
78 B5 Ardpatrick Point Scotland U.K.
95 P4 Ardres France
110 H8 Ardrishaig Argyll and Bute, Scotland U.K.
204 F6 Ardrossan S.A. Austr.
26 G11 Ardrossan North Ayrshire, Scotland U.K.
38 I5 Ardsalla Rep. of Ireland
28 D7 Ardsalla Rep. of Ireland
147 F6 Ardsley NY U.S.A.
119 H2 Ardsley NY U.S.A.
27 L4 Ards Peninsula Northern Ireland U.K.
77 H3 Ardusat Romania
77 L3 Ardusat Romania
38 G4 Ardvasar Highland, Scotland U.K.
26 A8 Ardvule, Rubha pt Scotland U.K.
20 L5 Åre Sweden
63 O2 Areatza Spain
62 A3 Areado Brazil
40 J5 Arêches France
131 □1 Arecibo Puerto Rico
124 O6 Argus Range mts CA U.S.A.
168 H4 Arguut Mongolia
109 H5 Argyle N.S. Can.
110 C3 Argyle IA U.S.A.
52 H4 Argyle, Lake WA U.S.A.
26 F10 Argyll reg. Scotland U.K.
26 F11 Argyll and Bute admin. div. Scotland U.K.
14 J4 Arhangel Azer.
23 M2 Arhavi Turkey
41 D6 Arlanc France
200 □□ Arhangai prov. Mongolia
63 G3 Arhavi Turkey
22 G5 Århus Denmark
22 G5 Århus county Denmark
114 Bugt b. Denmark
22 G5 Århus-Tirstrup airport Denmark
75 I6 Aria, Monte hill Isole Lipari Italy
176 J6 Ariadnoye Rus. Fed.
155 D1 Ariah l. Indon.
205 K6 Ariah Park N.S.W. Austr.
155 H13 Ariake-ko l. Japan
54 J11 Arialah Namibia
79 I5 Ariamsvlei Namibia
98 □2a Ariana Tracking Station Ascension S. Atlantic Ocean
71 M6 Ariano, Isola d' i. Italy
73 O5 Ariano Irpino Italy
74 D1 Ariano nel Polesine Italy
89 F4 Aribinda Burkina

Column 3

50 D5 Arendsee l. Ger.
212 N8 Arendsee (Altmark) Ger.
43 C7 Arengosse France
30 E2 Arenig Fawr hill Wales U.K.
43 D5 Arenillas Spain
43 C6 Arenillas Ecuador
147 I2 Arenitas Blancas Uru.
67 D7 Arenos, Embalse de resr Spain
65 K4 Arenosillo r. Spain
65 K4 Arenoso r. Spain
49 I8 Arenshausen Ger.
75 K5 Arente r. Italy
66 K4 Arenys de Mar Spain
70 F7 Arenzano Italy
78 D6 Areopoli Greece
62 C5 Areosa Port.
126 F4 Areponapuchi Mex.
138 C4 Arequipa Peru
138 B3 Arequipa dept Peru
147 G3 Arequito Arg.
137 H5 Arere Brazil
92 C3 Árëre Eth.
43 B6 Ares France
62 D2 Ares Spain
18 I3 Aresa r. Belarus
53 K4 Aresga Spain
63 N2 Areso Spain
184 F5 Arestán Iran
43 C9 Arette France
43 A5 Arette-Pierre-St-Martin France
63 J7 Arevalillo Spain
63 K6 Arevalillo r. Spain
63 K6 Arévalo r. Spain
62 E6 Arez Port.
186 D8 Areza Eritrea
 Arezzaf well Mali see Aghezzaf
62 C3 Arezzo Italy
71 H5 Arezzo prov. Italy
43 F7 Arfara Greece
78 B5 Arfons France
63 Q4 Arga r. Spain
206 F6 Argadargada N.T. Austr.
168 I3 Argalant Mongolia
78 E3 Argalasti Greece
65 I4 Argallón Spain
66 C3 Argamasilla de Alba Spain
65 M2 Argamasilla de Calatrava Spain
65 O3 Argamasón Spain
172 I6 Argan Xinjiang China
63 N8 Arganda Spain
62 D8 Arganil Port.
62 G3 Arganza Spain
71 I8 Argañín Italy
26 E9 Arisaig Highland, Scotland U.K.
26 E9 Arisaig, Sound of sea chan. Scotland U.K.
137 G3 Arisans Falls Guyana
190 B7 'Arīsh, Wādī al watercourse Egypt
136 D2 Arismendi Venez.
128 C3 Arista Mex.
108 D3 Aristazabal Island B.C. Can.
178 H9 Aristi Greece
145 D7 Aristizábal, Cabo c. Arg.
144 G2 Aristóbulo del Valle Arg.
185 O6 Aritwala Pak.
72 C8 Aritzo Sardegna Italy
95 □J3 Arivonimamo Madag.
142 G5 Ariya waterhole Kenya
176 F7 Ariyalur Tamil Nadu India
62 E7 Ariza Spain
63 P6 Ariza Spain
43 G10 Arize r. France
43 G10 Arize, Massif de l' mts France
63 O2 Arizgoiti Spain
63 Q3 Arizkia Spain
146 E4 Arizona Arg.
125 U7 Arizona state U.S.A.
126 D2 Arizpe Mex.
17 M7 'Arjah Saudi Arabia
23 J1 Årjäng Sweden
157 K8 Arjasa Jawa Indon.
20 N3 Arjeplog Sweden
79 C2 Ärjo Eth.
136 C2 Arjona Col.
64 G5 Arjona Spain
65 K5 Arjonilla Spain
19 I9 Arju Chhattisgarh India
179 H9 Arjuni Mahar. India
15 H6 Arkadak Rus. Fed.
17 Q4 Arkadivka Ukr.
193 P3 Arkagala Rus. Fed.
26 F9 Arkaig, Loch l. Scotland U.K.
176 E6 Arkalgud Karnataka India
79 J1 Arkalochori Kriti Greece
185 N4 Arkalyk Kazakh.
121 J9 Arkansas r. AR U.S.A.
121 J9 Arkansas state U.S.A.
121 J7 Arkansas City AR U.S.A.
121 G7 Arkansas City KS U.S.A.
183 K7 Arkata r. Bulg.
173 I8 Arkatag Shan mts China
106 C2 Arkell, Mount Y.T. Can.
14 H2 Arkenu, Jabal mt. Libya
28 B6 Arkhavas Rep. of Ireland
15 L5 Arkhangel'sk Rus. Fed.

Column 4

66 C2 Aribe Spain
119 H1 Arlington NY U.S.A.
116 B8 Arlington OH U.S.A.
122 D4 Arlington OR U.S.A.
118 A7 Arlington VA U.S.A.
110 E6 Arlington SD U.S.A.
110 F7 Arlington Heights IL U.S.A.
89 G2 Arlit Niger
45 I9 Arlon Belgium
206 E7 Arltunga N.T. Austr.
70 F4 Arluno Italy
40 I5 Arly r. France
40 I5 Arly r. France
41 D5 Arm r. Sask. Can.
64 C6 Armação de Pêra Port.
116 C6 Armada MI U.S.A.
209 C12 Armadale W.A. Austr.
26 I11 Armadale West Lothian, Scotland U.K.
128 G3 Armadillo Mex.
155 D1 Armadores i. Indon.
 Armageddon tourist site Israel see Tel Megiddo
27 I4 Armagh Northern Ireland U.K.
27 I4 Armagh county Northern Ireland U.K.
43 E8 Armagnac reg. France
187 J7 Armaḥ, Wādī r. Yemen
63 P7 Armallones Spain
191 F6 Armaşı r. Armenia
85 Q3 Armant Egypt
20 Q3 Armasjärvi Sweden
36 G8 Armançon r. France
36 G8 Armance r. France
130 H4 Armando Bermudez nat. park Dom. Rep.
191 F5 Armavir Armenia
15 H7 Armavir Rus. Fed.
183 M2 Armavirskiy Kazakh.
43 B9 Armendáris France
191 F5 Armenia county Asia
136 C3 Armenia Col.
79 I6 Armenistis, Akra pt Rodos Greece
19 X4 Armenī Rus. Fed.
70 E4 Armeno Italy
137 G3 Armenopolis Romania see Gherla
18 G6 Armogia Lith.
131 □1 Aripo, Mount hill Trin. and Tob.
19 I3 Ariporo r. Col.
139 H2 Aripuanã Brazil
137 F6 Aripuanã r. Brazil
139 G2 Ariquemes Brazil
141 B3 Ariranhá r. Brazil
26 E9 Armamar Port.
36 E2 Armance r. France
36 G8 Armançon r. France
108 C3 Aroland Ont. Can.
70 C3 Arolla Switz.
49 H8 Arolsen Ger.
85 H6 Aroma Sudan
124 K5 Aromas CA U.S.A.
39 J5 Aron France
40 C3 Aron r. France
39 J5 Aron r. France
178 F7 Aron Madh. Prad. India
98 □3a Arona Tenerife Canary Is
70 F4 Arona Italy
177 O2 Aroostook r. N.B. Can.
117 O2 Aroostook r. ME U.S.A.
200 □6 Aropa P.N.G.
199 H2 Arorae i. Gilbert Is Kiribati
203 □ Arorangi Rarotonga Cook Is
209 C12 Aroroa i. Gilbert Is Kiribati
189 J7 Arorae
84 C3 Ar Ruwaybat well Libya
186 G2 Ar Ruwaydah Ar Riyāḍ Saudi Arabia
186 G4 Ar Ruwaydah Ar Riyāḍ Saudi Arabia
190 E8 Ar Ruwaydat Syria
206 F6 Arruwurra Aboriginal Land res. N.T. Austr.
37 L5 Arry France
43 A3 Ars Iran
79 K6 Arsaköy Turkey
66 I3 Arsèguel Spain
184 E7 Arsenajân Iran
106 H1 Arseno Lake N.W.T. Can.
A2 A3 Arsen-Ré France
19 T8 Arsen'yevo Rus. Fed.
176 J6 Arsen'yev Rus. Fed.
183 O2 Arshaly Kazakh.
43 L4 Arshaly Kazakh.
18 M7 Arshanskaye Wzvyshsha hills Belarus
73 K2 Arsiè Italy
71 K4 Arsiero Italy
176 E4 Arsikere Karnataka India
191 A5 Arsin Turkey
14 J4 Arsk Rus. Fed.
 Arslanbob Kyrg. see
73 K3 Arsoli Italy
40 F5 Ars-sur-Formans France
185 K7 Ars-sur-Moselle France
200 □□5 Art, Île i. New Caledonia
78 B3 Arta Greece
67 L8 Arta Spain
63 Q3 Artajona Spain
191 A5 Art'ana Georgia
67 E8 Artana Spain
70 E4 Artavaz r. Italy
39 M7 Artannes-sur-Indre France
191 C5 Artashat Armenia
127 I5 Arteaga Coahuila Mex.
128 E7 Arteaga Michoacán Mex.
67 D8 Arteas de Abajo r. Spain
40 H5 Artemare France
130 B2 Artemisa Cuba
78 D5 Artemisia Greece
17 R6 Artemivka Donets'ka Oblast' Ukr.

Column 5

119 H1 Arlington NY U.S.A.
116 B8 Arlington OH U.S.A.
122 D4 Arlington OR U.S.A.
118 A7 Arlington VA U.S.A.
110 E6 Arlington SD U.S.A.
110 F7 Arlington Heights IL U.S.A.
89 G2 Arlit Niger
45 I9 Arlon Belgium
206 E7 Arltunga N.T. Austr.
70 F4 Arluno Italy
40 I5 Arly r. France
41 D5 Arm r. Sask. Can.
64 C6 Armação de Pêra Port.
116 C6 Armada MI U.S.A.
209 C12 Armadale W.A. Austr.
26 I11 Armadale West Lothian, Scotland U.K.
128 G3 Armadillo Mex.
155 D1 Armadores i. Indon.
27 I4 Armagh Northern Ireland U.K.
27 I4 Armagh county Northern Ireland U.K.
43 E8 Armagnac reg. France
187 J7 Armaḥ, Wādī r. Yemen
63 P7 Armallones Spain
191 F6 Armamar Port.
85 Q3 Armant Egypt
20 Q3 Armasjärvi Sweden
36 G8 Armance r. France
130 H4 Armando Bermudez nat. park Dom. Rep.
191 F5 Armavir Armenia
15 H7 Armavir Rus. Fed.
183 M2 Armavirskiy Kazakh.
43 B9 Armendáris France
191 F5 Armenia county Asia
136 C3 Armenia Col.
79 I6 Armenistis, Akra pt Rodos Greece
19 X4 Armenī Rus. Fed.
70 E4 Armeno Italy
137 G3 Armenopolis Romania see Gherla
129 I9 Armenta Mex.
63 J7 Armenteros Spain
36 E2 Armentières France
73 Q7 Armenia Italy
128 D7 Armeria Mex.
128 D7 Armería r. Mex.
136 D3 Armenia Col.
141 B6 Armi, Capo dell' c. Italy
205 M4 Armidale N.S.W. Austr.
65 L6 Armilla Spain
79 J3 Arminda Arg.
119 I9 Armington MT U.S.A.
206 C4 Armit r. N.T. Austr.
106 G5 Armit Lake Nunavut Can.
107 N1 Armit Lake Nunavut Can.
145 D7 Armit Lake Nunavut Can.
37 M6 Armoy Northern Ireland U.K.
52 E2 Armoy Northern Ireland U.K.
43 E3 Armour SD U.S.A.
147 G3 Armstrong Arg.
206 C4 Armstrong r. N.T. Austr.
106 G5 Armstrong B.C. Can.
108 B3 Armstrong Ont. Can.
106 C2 Armstrong, Mount Y.T. Can.
212 W2 Armstrong Mills OH U.S.A.
162 J5 Armu r. Rus. Fed.
63 L6 Armuña Spain
72 C3 Armuña Sardegna Italy
62 I3 Armuña Spain
176 F3 Armur Andhra Prad. India
79 L2 Armutçuk Dağı mts Turkey
79 J2 Armutlu Turkey
 Armutova Turkey see Gömeç
186 D4 Armyans'k Ukr.
 Armyanskaya S.S.R. country Asia see Armenia
22 E7 Arnå r. Denmark
78 D6 Arna Greece
127 N2 Arnac-Pompadour France
184 G2 Arnad Italy
36 □1 Arnafjörður inlet Iceland
109 G1 Arnaud r. Que. Can.
191 C5 Arnauti, Cape Cyprus
176 E6 Arnauti, Cape Cyprus
79 J1 Arnautovka Turkey
185 N4 Arnawai Pak.
43 C9 Arnay-le-Duc France
53 N3 Arnbruck Ger.
79 I9 Arncliffe North Yorkshire, England U.K.
30 H6 Arne Dorset, England U.K.
50 F5 Arneberg Ger.
63 P4 Arnedillo Spain
63 P4 Arnedo Spain
63 M4 Arneguy France
20 P4 Arnemark Sweden
44 H4 Arnemuiden Neth.
22 H1 Årnes Norway
24 □ Årnes Iceland
121 F7 Arnett OK U.S.A.
44 I5 Arnhem Neth.
206 F2 Arnhem, Cape N.T. Austr.
206 E2 Arnhem Land reg. N.T. Austr.
206 D2 Arnhem Land Aboriginal Land res. N.T. Austr.

Column 6

43 E8 Arnage France
187 H7 Armaḥ, Wādī r. Yemen
63 P7 Armallones Spain
191 E5 Arpa r. Armenia/Turkey
183 P7 Arpa Kyrg.
189 B9 Arpaçay Turkey
192 H6 Arpajon-sur-Cère France
43 I6 Arpajon France
36 D6 Arpajon France
185 O1 Arpapirid Uzbek.
200 □5 Arpa r. Pak.
63 Q3 Arpa r. Armenia/Turkey
122 I3 Arpa r. Armenia/Turkey
128 D7 Armeria Mex.
73 K2 Arpino Italy
 Arpinum Italy see Arpino
73 K2 Arpino Italy
176 E6 Arquata del Tronto Italy
191 F5 Arquata Scrivia Italy
43 I10 Arques Languedoc-Roussillon France
36 D2 Arques Nord-Pas-de-Calais France
66 D5 Ariño Spain
139 G3 Arinos Mato Grosso Brazil
143 F2 Arinos Minas Gerais Brazil
40 H4 Arinthod France
128 F6 Ario de Rosáles Mex.
18 G6 Arogala Lith.
191 F5 Arquillos Spain
95 G4 Arquipélago de Bazaruto, Parque Nacional de nat. park Moz.
185 O1 Arquipélago dos Açores aut. reg. N. Atlantic Ocean
78 B3 Arra r. Pak.
63 Q3 Arta, Golfo di b. Greece
187 J3 Ar Rabbah Jordan
191 G3 Art'ana Georgia
70 D7 Ar Rabbah Jordan
 Arrábida, Parque Natural da nature res. Port.
207 H9 Arrabury Qld Austr.
37 M6 Arrach Ger.
43 B9 Arracourt France
85 G3 Ar Radīsīyah Baḥrī Egypt
73 E6 Arradon France
186 G3 Ar Raghbah Saudi Arabia
88 E5 Arrah Côte d'Ivoire
 Arrah Bihar India see Ara
189 K7 Ar Raḥḥālīyah Iraq
186 E5 Ar Rāḥidah Yemen
186 C3 Ar Raḥmān Syria
14 J6 Ar Ramādī Iraq
188 G5 Ar Ramlah Jordan
27 F7 Arra Mountains hills Rep. of Ireland
190 E6 Ar Ramthā Jordan
21 J3 Arran i. Scotland U.K.
37 K5 Arrancy-sur-Crusne France
64 A3 Arranhol Port.
190 H3 Ar Raqqah Syria
190 G2 Ar Raqqah governorate Syria
88 F2 Arraou well Chad
36 D2 Arras France
 Ar Ra's al Abyaḍ pt Saudi Arabia
43 D10 Arras-en-Lavedan France
81 D8 Ar Rashādīyah Jordan
186 F5 Ar Rass Saudi Arabia
190 E4 Ar Rastān Syria
39 L9 Arrats r. France
37 M3 Arraute-Charritte France
189 K3 Ar Rawḍ well Saudi Arabia
186 E2 Ar Rawdah Ḥaḍramawt Saudi Arabia
186 F5 Ar Rawdah Makkah Saudi Arabia
187 H8 Ar Rawḍah Yemen
187 H8 Ar Rawḍah Yemen
187 I4 Ar Rayḥānī Oman
186 G4 Ar Rayn Saudi Arabia
186 H4 Ar Rayyān Qatar
186 F5 Ar Rayyān Al Madīnah Saudi Arabia
186 B4 Ar Rayyān Makkah Saudi Arabia
43 E10 Arreau France
98 □3c Arrecife Lanzarote Canary Is
63 J2 Arrecifes Arg.
62 B4 Arredondo Spain
64 C1 Arrée, Monts d' hills France
36 I7 Arrentières France
21 I4 Arrenjarka Sweden
59 I6 Arriach Austria
129 N9 Arriaga Mex.
128 F4 Arriaga Mex.
63 L6 Arriate Spain
44 I5 Arriba CO U.S.A.
98 □3c Arrieta Lanzarote Canary Is
186 D4 Ar Rifā'ī Iraq
67 G2 Arrifana Aveiro Port.
62 C7 Arrifana Coimbra Port.
62 E7 Arrifana Guarda Port.

Column 7

108 C3 Aroland Ont. Can.
70 C3 Arolla Switz.
49 H8 Arolsen Ger.
85 H6 Aroma Sudan
124 K5 Aromas CA U.S.A.
39 J5 Aron France
40 C3 Aron r. France
39 J5 Aron r. France
178 F7 Aron Madh. Prad. India
98 □3a Arona Tenerife Canary Is
70 F4 Arona Italy
117 O2 Aroostook r. ME U.S.A.
200 □6 Aropa P.N.G.
199 H2 Arorae i. Gilbert Is Kiribati
203 □ Arorangi Rarotonga Cook Is
209 C12 Aroroa i. Gilbert Is Kiribati
189 J7 Arorae
84 C3 Ar Ruwaybat well Libya
186 G2 Ar Ruwaydah Ar Riyāḍ Saudi Arabia
186 G4 Ar Ruwaydah Ar Riyāḍ Saudi Arabia
 Arpa r. Armenia/Turkey
191 E5 Arpa r. Armenia/Turkey
183 P7 Arpa Kyrg.
189 B9 Arpaçay Turkey
192 H6 Arpajon-sur-Cère France
43 I6 Arpajon France
36 D6 Arpajon France
185 O1 Arpapirid Uzbek.
200 □5 Arafa r. Pak.
14 J4 Arslanbob Kyrg. see
207 H9 Arrabury Qld Austr.
37 M6 Arrach Ger.
43 B9 Arracourt France
85 G3 Ar Radīsīyah Baḥrī Egypt
73 E6 Arradon France
186 G3 Ar Raghbah Saudi Arabia
88 E5 Arrah Côte d'Ivoire
189 K7 Ar Raḥḥālīyah Iraq
186 E5 Ar Rāḥidah Yemen
186 C3 Ar Raḥmān Syria
14 J6 Ar Ramādī Iraq
188 G5 Ar Ramlah Jordan
27 F7 Arra Mountains hills Rep. of Ireland
190 E6 Ar Ramthā Jordan
21 J3 Arran i. Scotland U.K.
37 K5 Arrancy-sur-Crusne France
64 A3 Arranhol Port.
190 H3 Ar Raqqah Syria
190 G2 Ar Raqqah governorate Syria
88 F2 Arraou well Chad
36 D2 Arras France
71 L3 Artèn Italy
73 J4 Artena Italy
59 I6 Artenay France
51 I8 Artern (Unstrut) Ger.
66 H4 Artesa de Segre Spain
125 W3 Artesia AZ U.S.A.
123 L10 Artesia NM U.S.A.
70 F1 Arth Switz.
43 I8 Arthès France
43 J2 Arthez-d'Asson France
43 C8 Arthez-de-Béarn France
39 O8 Arthon-en-Retz France
209 C8 Arthur r. W.A. Austr.
111 N6 Arthur Ont. Can.
120 E5 Arthur NE U.S.A.
116 B12 Arthur IL U.S.A.
204 F4 Arthur, Lake salt flat S.A. Austr.
97 J8 Arthur, Lake S. Africa
116 E8 Arthur, Lake PA U.S.A.
205 K9 Arthur Lake Tas. Austr.
205 J9 Arthur Pieman Protected Area Tas. Austr.
207 M7 Arthur r. Qld Austr.
203 F9 Arthur's Pass South I. N.Z.
203 F9 Arthur's Pass South I. N.Z.
130 T1 Arthur's Town Cat I. Bahamas
28 D3 Articlave Northern Ireland U.K.
72 G7 Artieda Spain
22 D1 Artigas research stn Antarctica
212 U2 Artigas research stn Antarctica
147 I2 Artigas Uru.
147 I2 Artigas dept Uru.
43 G9 Artigat France
191 E5 Art'ik Armenia
107 I2 Artillery Lake N.W.T. Can.
94 C5 Artisia Botswana
13 I1 Artjärvi Fin.
48 J1 Artlenburg Ger.
36 O4 Artois reg. France
36 B3 Artois, Collines d' hills France
189 K4 Artova Turkey
191 B5 Artova Turkey
66 □ Artrutx, Cap d' c. Spain

Column 8

128 F8 Arroyo Seco Guerrero Mex.
129 H4 Arroyo Seco Querétaro Mex.
139 F6 Arroyos-y-Esteros Para.
186 D4 Ar Rubaḍ Saudi Arabia
186 C2 Ar Ruba'īyah Saudi Arabia
139 F3 Arruda Brazil
64 A3 Arruda dos Vinhos Port.
147 G2 Arrufó Arg.
187 K2 Ar Ruwayat Saudi Arabia
187 J3 Ar Ruwaythā Bahrain
189 L8 Ar Ruwaythā Iraq
190 J6 Ar Rumman Jordan
186 H1 Ar Ruq'ī well Saudi Arabia
189 J6 Ar Ruṭbah Iraq
84 C3 Ar Ruwaybat well Libya
186 G2 Ar Ruwaydah Ar Riyāḍ Saudi Arabia
186 G4 Ar Ruwaydah Ar Riyāḍ Saudi Arabia
190 E8 Ar Ruwaydat Syria
206 F6 Arruwurra Aboriginal Land res. N.T. Austr.
37 L5 Arry France
43 A3 Ars Iran
79 K6 Arsaköy Turkey
66 I3 Arsèguel Spain
184 E7 Arsenajân Iran
106 H1 Arseno Lake N.W.T. Can.
42 A3 Arsen-Ré France
19 T8 Arsen'yevo Rus. Fed.
176 J6 Arsen'yev Rus. Fed.
183 O2 Arshaly Kazakh.
43 L4 Arshaly Kazakh.
18 M7 Arshanskaye Wzvyshsha hills Belarus
73 K2 Arsiè Italy
71 K4 Arsiero Italy
176 E4 Arsikere Karnataka India
191 A5 Arsin Turkey
14 J4 Arsk Rus. Fed.
73 K3 Arsoli Italy
40 F5 Ars-sur-Formans France
185 K7 Ars-sur-Moselle France
200 □5 Art, Île i. New Caledonia
78 B3 Arta Greece
67 L8 Arta Spain
63 Q3 Artajona Spain
191 A5 Art'ana Georgia
67 E8 Artana Spain
70 E4 Artavaz r. Italy
39 M7 Artannes-sur-Indre France
191 C5 Artashat Armenia
127 I5 Arteaga Coahuila Mex.
128 E7 Arteaga Michoacán Mex.
67 D8 Arteas de Abajo r. Spain
40 H5 Artemare France
130 B2 Artemisa Cuba
78 D5 Artemisia Greece
17 R6 Artemivka Donets'ka Oblast' Ukr.
17 O4 Artemivka Kharkivs'ka Oblast' Ukr.
17 O4 Artemivka Poltavs'ka Oblast' Ukr.
17 R5 Artemivs'k Donets'ka Oblast' Ukr.
17 R5 Artemivs'k Luhans'ka Oblast' Ukr.
193 M4 Artemovskiy Irkutskaya Oblast' Rus. Fed.
162 H7 Artemovskiy Primorskiy Kray Rus. Fed.
71 L3 Artèn Italy
73 J4 Artena Italy
59 I6 Artenay France
51 I8 Artern (Unstrut) Ger.
66 H4 Artesa de Segre Spain
125 W3 Artesia AZ U.S.A.
123 L10 Artesia NM U.S.A.
70 F1 Arth Switz.
43 I8 Arthès France
43 J2 Arthez-d'Asson France
43 C8 Arthez-de-Béarn France
39 O8 Arthon-en-Retz France
209 C8 Arthur r. W.A. Austr.
111 N6 Arthur Ont. Can.
120 E5 Arthur NE U.S.A.
116 B12 Arthur IL U.S.A.
204 F4 Arthur, Lake salt flat S.A. Austr.
97 J8 Arthur, Lake S. Africa
116 E8 Arthur, Lake PA U.S.A.
205 K9 Arthur Lake Tas. Austr.
205 J9 Arthur Pieman Protected Area Tas. Austr.
207 M7 Arthur r. Qld Austr.
203 F9 Arthur's Pass South I. N.Z.
130 T1 Arthur's Town Cat I. Bahamas
28 D3 Articlave Northern Ireland U.K.
72 G7 Artieda Spain
212 U2 Artigas research stn Antarctica
147 I2 Artigas Uru.
147 I2 Artigas dept Uru.
43 G9 Artigat France
191 E5 Art'ik Armenia
107 I2 Artillery Lake N.W.T. Can.
94 C5 Artisia Botswana
13 I1 Artjärvi Fin.
48 J1 Artlenburg Ger.
36 O4 Artois reg. France
36 B3 Artois, Collines d' hills France
189 K4 Artova Turkey
66 □ Artrutx, Cap d' c. Spain
183 K4 Ars Bogd Uul mts Mongolia
183 K4 Artsiz Ukr.
16 I8 Artsvz Ukr.
172 C7 Artux Xinjiang China
191 C4 Artvin Turkey
191 C4 Artvin prov. Turkey
183 N4 Arvs Kazakh.
99 F4 Aru Dem. Rep. Congo
153 I8 Aru, Kepulauan is Indon.
92 A4 Arua Uganda
140 C5 Aruanã Brazil
131 □3a Aruba terr. West Indies
131 □3a Aruba Gran Canaria Canary Is
64 C2 Aruch Armenia
110 C1 Arun r. China
201 □3a Arue Tahiti Fr. Polynesia
200 □□6 Arujá Brazil
 Arulího Guadalcanal Solomon Is
143 F6 Arumã Brazil
 Arumae Okinawa Japan
137 F6 Aru Meadow sh. Okinawa Japan
179 K6 Arun r. Nepal
203 C11 Arunachal Pradesh state India
203 N6 Arundel South I. N.Z.
31 K8 Arundel West Sussex, England U.K.
93 C5 Arusha Tanz.
93 C5 Arusha admin. reg. Tanz.

Arusha to Auchel
231

93 C5 Arusha National Park Tanz.
57 I6 Arut r. Indon.
37 E5 Aruti Brazil
90 D4 Aruwimi r. Dem. Rep. Congo
20 C6 Arvada CO U.S.A.
27 G5 Arvagh Rep. of Ireland
41 I6 Arvan r. France
68 H3 Arvayheer Mongolia
40 I4 Arve r. France
42 B4 Arvert France
43 D6 Arveyres France
78 G9 Arvi Mahar. India
07 M2 Arviat Nunavut Can.
44 L1 Arvida Que. Can.
20 O4 Arvidsjaur Sweden
41 B8 Arvieu France
41 J7 Arvieux France
22 I2 Arvika Sweden
20 P1 Årviksand Norway
24 N6 Arvin CA U.S.A.
75 K5 Arvo, Lago l. Italy
16 G11 Arvonia VA U.S.A.
36 G4 Arwā' Saudi Arabia
90 D4 Arwād i. Syria
55 E7 Arwala Maluku Indon.
59 P3 Arxan Nei Mongol China
72 G5 Arxan Xinjiang China
14 K4 Aryazh Rus. Fed.
33 M1 Arykbalyk Kazakh.
Aryqbayq Kazakh. see Arykbalyk
33 M6 Arys' Kazakh.
33 M6 Arys' r. Kazakh.
33 L5 Arys, Ozero salt l. Kazakh.
72 C5 Arzachena Sardegna Italy
43 D8 Arzacq-Arraziguet France
45 H5 Arzamas Rus. Fed.
72 D8 Arzana Sardegna Italy
37 K3 Arzanah i. U.A.E.
38 E6 Arzano France
49 E10 Arzbach Ger.
51 F10 Arzberg Bayern Ger.
51 H7 Arzberg Sachsen Ger.
43 I9 Arzens France
37 E2 Arzew Alg.
49 B10 Arzfeld Ger.
15 I7 Arzgir Rus. Fed.
71 K4 Arzignano Italy
Arzila Morocco see Asilah
58 C5 Arzl im Pitztal Austria
41 D6 Arzon r. France
62 D3 Arzúa Spain
45 I6 As Belgium
56 B1 Aš Czech Rep.
93 C5 Asa waterhole Kenya
22 I4 Åsa Sweden
22 G4 Asaa Denmark
96 B1 Asab Namibia
67 G6 Asaba Japan
89 G5 Asaba Nigeria
90 G2 Asad, Buḥayrat al resr Syria
85 N4 Asadābād Afgh.
84 C4 Asadābād Hamadān Iran
84 H4 Asadābād Khorāsān Iran
84 E6 Asadābād Yazd Iran
91 H5 Aşağı Ağcakänd Azer.
91 G4 Aşağı Äskipara Azer.
91 G5 Aşağı Ayıblı Azer.
91 E5 Aşağı Dağ mt. Turkey
91 E6 Aşağıdalören Turkey
79 K5 Aşağıkaraçay Turkey
91 C5 Aşağıkatıklı Turkey
91 I4 Aşağı Köynük Azer.
91 E6 Aşağıküpkıran Turkey
91 H5 Aşağı Oratağ Azer.
91 F7 Aşağısağmallı Turkey
91 C6 Aşağısöylemez Turkey
88 D5 Asagny, Parc National d' nat. park Côte d'Ivoire
66 A5 Asago Japan
56 C3 Asahan r. Indon.
66 F5 Asahi Aichi Japan
67 M4 Asahi Chiba Japan
66 D4 Asahi Fukui Japan
66 F3 Asahi Gifu Japan
67 M3 Asahi Ibaraki Japan
67 K5 Asahi Kanagawa Japan
66 E5 Asahi Mie Japan
67 G3 Asahi Nagano Japan
66 G2 Asahi Toyama Japan
64 Q8 Asahi-dake mt. Japan
64 T3 Asahi-dake vol. Japan
65 K12 Asahi-gawa r. Japan
64 T3 Asahikawa Japan
67 J1 Asahi-take mt. Japan
67 K4 Asaka Japan
83 O7 Asaka Uzbek.
67 L1 Asakawa Japan
66 E5 Asake-gawa r. Japan
90 A9 'Asal Egypt
92 D1 Āsalē l. Eth.
84 C3 Asālem Iran
84 E6 'Asalū, Chāh-e well Iran
66 E7 Asamaga-take hill Japan
88 E5 Asamankese Ghana
67 I3 Asama-yama vol. Japan
00 □1 Asan Guam
88 E5 Asankranguaa Ghana
63 E10 Asan-man b. S. Korea
79 K8 Asansol W. Bengal India
88 E5 Asanwenso Ghana
67 K4 Asao Japan
69 O3 Asar Nei Mongol China
67 H3 Asashina Japan
43 C9 Asasp-Arros France
00 □2 Asau Samoa
92 D2 Āsayita Eth.
49 D9 Asbach Ger.
53 J4 Asbach-Bäumenheim Ger.
14 L3 Asbestos Que. Can.
96 G5 Asbestos Mountains S. Africa
92 D2 Āsbe Teferi Eth.
23 L3 Åsbro Sweden
17 K8 Asbury Park NJ U.S.A.
43 A9 Ascain France
Ascalon Israel see Ashqelon
73 O7 Ascea Italy
47 G4 Ascensión Arg.
39 E3 Ascensión Bol.
26 F2 Ascensión Chihuahua Mex.
29 H1 Ascensión Nuevo León Mex.
31 □10 Ascension Curaçao Neth. Antilles
98 □2a Ascension i. S. Atlantic Ocean
53 N3 Ascha Ger.
53 M3 Ascha r. Ger.
59 J3 Aschach an der Donau Austria
52 G2 Aschaffenburg Ger.
58 E5 Aschau im Zillertal Austria
53 M6 Aschau in Chiemgau Ger.
59 K3 Aschbach Markt Austria
49 E7 Ascheberg Ger.
48 J2 Ascheberg (Holstein) Ger.
53 O4 Aschenstein hill Ger.
36 D7 Aschères-le-Marché France
51 D7 Aschersleben Ger.
53 L5 Aschheim Ger.
71 L9 Asciano Italy
75 K5 Ascione, Colle d' pass Italy
72 C3 Asco Corse France
47 E2 Ascochinga Arg.
73 L2 Ascoli Piceno Italy
73 L2 Ascoli Piceno prov. Italy
73 P5 Ascoli Satriano Italy
70 F3 Ascona Switz.
31 K5 Ascot Windsor and Maidenhead, England U.K.
38 C5 Ascotán Chile
38 C5 Ascotán, Salar de salt flat Chile
43 H10 Ascou France
62 C4 As Covas Spain
Asculum Italy see Ascoli Piceno
Asculum Picenum Italy see Ascoli Piceno
17 M5 Ascutney VT U.S.A.
75 □1 Asdhu i. N. Male Maldives
Asdu i. N. Male Maldives see Asdhu
20 M2 Åse Norway
Āseb Eritrea see Assab
23 L4 Åseda Sweden
87 F4 Asedjrad plat. Alg.
182 E1 Asekeyevo Rus. Fed.
92 C3 Āsela Eth.
20 N4 Åsele Sweden
21 L6 Åsen Sweden
92 C3 Āsendabo Eth.
48 H5 Asendorf Niedersachsen Ger.
48 I4 Asendorf Niedersachsen Ger.
77 M8 Asenovgrad Bulg.
22 D3 Åseral Norway
18 J2 Aseri Estonia
62 C3 A Serra de Outes Spain
128 C2 Aserradero los Charcos Mex.
184 G4 Aşfāk Iran
190 E6 Aşfar, Jabal al mt. Jordan
190 E5 Aşfar, Tall al hill Syria
36 H5 Asfeld France
31 K2 Asfordby Leicestershire, England U.K.
20 □C1 Ásgarður Iceland
31 O5 Ash Kent, England U.K.
31 K5 Ash Surrey, England U.K.
14 L5 Asha Rus. Fed.
166 G2 Ashahi-dake mt. Japan
88 E5 Ashanti admin. reg. Ghana
14 L4 Ashap Rus. Fed.
186 G3 Asharat Saudi Arabia
186 F3 Ash 'arīyah Saudi Arabia
119 L2 Ashaway RI U.S.A.
27 J5 Ashbourne Rep. of Ireland
29 N7 Ashbourne Derbyshire, England U.K.
115 F10 Ashburn GA U.S.A.
209 C6 Ashburton watercourse W.A. Austr.
203 F10 Ashburton South I. N.Z.
203 F11 Ashburton r. South I. N.Z.
30 E6 Ashburton Devon, England U.K.
110 H1 Ashburton Bay Ont. Can.
206 D5 Ashburton Range hills N.T. Austr.
31 I4 Ashbury Oxfordshire, England U.K.
31 J2 Ashby de la Zouch Leicestershire, England U.K.
183 L5 Ashchikol', Ozero salt l. Kazakh.
183 N6 Ashchikol', Ozero salt l. Kazakh.
30 H4 Ashchurch Gloucestershire, England U.K.
Ashchysay Kazakh. see Achisay
30 G5 Ashcott Somerset, England U.K.
106 F5 Ashcroft B.C. Can.
190 C7 Ashdod Israel
121 H9 Ashdown AR U.S.A.
31 M5 Ashdown Forest reg. England U.K.
115 H8 Asheboro NC U.S.A.
121 G8 Asher OK U.S.A.
107 L5 Ashern Man. Can.
115 F8 Asheville NC U.S.A.
18 M4 Ashevo Rus. Fed.
108 C2 Asheweig r. Ont. Can.
205 M3 Ashford N.S.W. Austr.
27 J6 Ashford Rep. of Ireland
28 E8 Ashford r. Rep. of Ireland
31 I6 Ashford Hampshire, England U.K.
31 N5 Ashford Kent, England U.K.
31 L5 Ashford Surrey, England U.K.
125 T6 Ash Fork AZ U.S.A.
184 H3 Ashgabat Turkm.
202 J7 Ashhurst North I. N.Z.
164 T3 Ashibetsu Japan
167 I4 Ashigawa Japan
167 J3 Ashikaga Japan
165 H14 Ashikita Japan
31 N2 Ashill Norfolk, England U.K.
29 N3 Ashington Northumberland, England U.K.
167 J5 Ashino-ko l. Japan
167 J2 Ashio Japan
167 J3 Ashio-sanchi mts Japan
110 F6 Ashippun WI U.S.A.
164 S6 Ashiro Japan
167 I4 Ashiwada Japan
166 B6 Ashiya Japan
165 K14 Ashizuri-misaki pt Japan
165 J14 Ashizuri-Uwakai National Park Japan
184 F6 Ashkazar Iran
Ashkelon Israel see Ashqelon
Ashkhabad Turkm. see Ashgabat
Ashkhabadskaya Oblast' admin. div. Turkm. see Akhal'skaya Oblast'
84 B3 Ashkīdah Libya
26 K12 Ashkirk Scottish Borders, Scotland U.K.
110 G9 Ashkum IL U.S.A.
185 N4 Ashkun reg. Afgh.
115 E9 Ashland AL U.S.A.
121 F7 Ashland KS U.S.A.
116 C10 Ashland KY U.S.A.
117 □Q2 Ashland ME U.S.A.
121 K8 Ashland MS U.S.A.
122 K4 Ashland MT U.S.A.
120 G5 Ashland NE U.S.A.
117 N5 Ashland NH U.S.A.
116 C8 Ashland OH U.S.A.
122 C5 Ashland OR U.S.A.
118 C3 Ashland PA U.S.A.
116 H11 Ashland VA U.S.A.
110 D3 Ashland WI U.S.A.
115 D7 Ashland City TN U.S.A.
205 L3 Ashley N.S.W. Austr.
203 G10 Ashley r. South I. N.Z.
31 M3 Ashley Cambridgeshire, England U.K.
110 I8 Ashley IN U.S.A.
110 J6 Ashley MI U.S.A.
120 F2 Ashley ND U.S.A.
116 C8 Ashley OH U.S.A.
118 D2 Ashley PA U.S.A.
208 G2 Ashmore and Cartier Islands terr. Austr.
208 G2 Ashmore Reef Ashmore & Cartier Is Austr.
18 I7 Ashmyanskaye Wzvyshsha hills Belarus
18 I7 Ashmyany Hrodzyenskaya Voblasts' Belarus
18 J7 Ashmyany Hrodzyenskaya Voblasts' Belarus
178 F7 Ashoknagar Madh. Prad. India
164 U3 Ashoro Japan
191 E4 Ashots'k' Armenia
190 C7 Ashqelon Israel
186 F6 Ash Sha'ār Saudi Arabia
189 K8 Ash Shabakah Iraq
85 F4 Ash Shabb well Egypt
189 J5 Ash Shaddādah Syria
186 E5 Ash Shafa Saudi Arabia
190 A8 Ash Shallūfah Egypt
Ash Sham Syria see Dimashq
187 M2 Ash Sha'm U.A.E.
189 L8 Ash Shanāfīyah Iraq
189 J9 Ash Shaqīq well Saudi Arabia
186 G3 Ash Sha'rā' Saudi Arabia
187 H7 Ash Sharawrah Saudi Arabia
187 L3 Ash Shāriqah U.A.E.
189 K6 Ash Sharqāṭ Iraq
188 E8 Ash Sharqīyah governorate Egypt
187 N5 Ash Sharqīyah admin. reg. Oman
187 N4 Ash Sharqīyah reg. Oman
187 J5 Ash Sharqīyah prov. Saudi Arabia
189 M8 Ash Shaṭrah Iraq
190 A9 Ash Shaṭṭ Egypt
190 D8 Ash Shawbak Jordan
186 E1 Ash Shaybānī well Saudi Arabia
190 G3 Ash Shaykh Ibrāhīm Syria
186 G9 Ash Shaykh 'Uthman Yemen
190 F9 Ash Shiblīyāt hill Saudi Arabia
187 I8 Ash Shiḥr Yemen
187 M3 Ash Shināṣ Oman
187 K6 Ash Shiṣar well Oman
186 F2 Ash Shu'āybah Saudi Arabia
186 G1 Ash Shu'bah Saudi Arabia
186 F3 Ash Shubaykīyah Saudi Arabia
187 H2 Ash Shumlūl Saudi Arabia
186 F7 Ash Shuqayq Saudi Arabia
84 B2 Ash Shuwayrif Libya
178 F8 Ashta Madh. Prad. India
176 D4 Ashta Mahar. India
116 E7 Ashtabula OH U.S.A.
191 F5 Ashtarak Armenia
176 D3 Ashti Mahar. India
176 F3 Ashti Mahar. India
178 G9 Ashti Mahar. India
96 E9 Ashton S. Africa
131 □3 Ashton St Vincent
29 L7 Ashton Cheshire, England U.K.
122 I4 Ashton ID U.S.A.
110 E8 Ashton IL U.S.A.
118 A6 Ashton MD U.S.A.
29 M7 Ashton-under-Lyne Greater Manchester, England U.K.
191 I4 Ashty Rus. Fed.
109 H2 Ashuanipi r. Nfld and Lab. Can.
109 H2 Ashuanipi Lake Nfld and Lab. Can.
114 K1 Ashuapmushuan r. Que. Can.
108 F3 Ashuapmushuan, Réserve Faunique nature res. Que. Can.
Ashur Iraq see Ash Sharqāṭ
31 I6 Ashurst Hampshire, England U.K.
31 M5 Ashurst Kent, England U.K.
115 D9 Ashville AL U.S.A.
117 □Q4 Ashville ME U.S.A.
116 G8 Ashville PA U.S.A.
110 D3 Ashwabay, Mount hill WI U.S.A.
110 F5 Ashwaubenon WI U.S.A.
30 G5 Ashwick Somerset, England U.K.
190 E4 'Āṣī r. Lebanon/Syria
190 E2 'Āṣī, Nahr al r. Asia alt. Asi (Turkey), hist. Orontes
150 Asia continent
71 L4 Asiago Italy
154 D5 Asid Gulf Masbate Phil.
128 E3 Asientos Mex.
176 F3 Asifabad Andhra Prad. India
177 I3 Asika Orissa India
21 R6 Asikkala Fin.
86 D2 Asilah Morocco
138 C3 Asillo Peru
78 G7 Asimi Kriti Greece
66 C3 Asín Spain
72 B6 Asinara, Golfo dell' b. Sardegna Italy
72 A5 Asinara, Isola i. Sardegna Italy
178 E7 Asind Rajasthan India
192 J4 Asino Rus. Fed.
19 N7 Asintorf Belarus
18 L8 Asipovichy Belarus
184 E8 Asīr Iran
186 E5 'Asīr prov. Saudi Arabia
186 E5 'Asīr reg. Saudi Arabia
Asisium Italy see Assisi
18 E1 Askainen Fin.
178 E2 Askale Jammu and Kashmir
189 J4 Aşkale Turkey
17 M7 Askaniya Nova Ukr.
17 M7 Askaniya Nova Zapovidnyk nature res. Ukr.
182 H1 Askarovo Rus. Fed.
27 E7 Askeaton Rep. of Ireland
97 L7 Askeaton S. Africa
22 G2 Asker Norway
191 A7 Asker Dağı mt. Turkey
29 O6 Askern South Yorkshire, England U.K.
23 K3 Askersund Sweden
96 E2 Askham S. Africa
27 F4 Askill Rep. of Ireland
22 H2 Askim Norway
14 L4 Askino Rus. Fed.
78 C2 Askio mt. Greece
89 I4 Askira Nigeria
26 D9 Askival hill Scotland U.K.
160 F1 Askiz Rus. Fed.
48 L1 Askø i. Denmark
21 R6 Askola Fin.
23 M2 Äsköping Sweden
78 E2 Askos Greece
178 H5 Askot Uttaranchal India
22 B1 Askøy i. Norway
96 E10 Askraal S. Africa
21 H6 Askvoll Norway
191 H6 Askyaran Azer.
186 G5 Aslam, Wādī watercourse Saudi Arabia
79 K3 Aslanapa Turkey
184 B2 Aşlāndūz Iran
18 M8 Aslik r. Belarus
185 N4 Asmar Afgh.
185 N4 Asmar reg. Afgh.
186 F6 Asmar reg. Saudi Arabia
85 H6 Asmara Eritrea
186 E2 Asmarah, Jabal mts Saudi Arabia
62 D2 As Mariñas reg. Spain
Āsmera Eritrea see Asmara
23 K5 Åsnen l. Sweden
62 D2 As Neves Galicia Spain
62 D4 As Neves Galicia Spain
62 F3 As Nogais Spain
73 L1 Aso r. Italy
167 L4 Asō Japan
137 G4 Asoenangka Brazil
165 I14 Aso-Kuju National Park Japan
70 I5 Asola Italy
71 L4 Asolo Italy
65 P2 Asomadilla hill Spain
179 O5 Asonli Arun. Prad. India
78 D5 Asopos r. Greece
78 E4 Asopos r. Greece
92 B2 Āsosa Eth.
165 I14 Aso-san vol. Japan
85 H4 Asoteriba, Jebel mt. Sudan
122 F3 Asotin WA U.S.A.
57 I5 Ásotthalom Hungary
165 G12 Asō-wan b. Japan
14 L4 Aspa Rus. Fed.
59 H3 Aspach Austria
59 N4 Aspang-Markt Austria
184 C3 Aspar Iran
183 O6 Aspara Kazakh.
59 N2 Asparn an der Zaya Austria
77 P8 Asparukhovo Bulg.
20 M5 Aspås Sweden
29 K4 Aspatria Cumbria, England U.K.
67 D11 Aspe Spain
43 C10 Aspe, Vallée d' val. France
20 N5 Aspeå Sweden
123 K7 Aspen CO U.S.A.
44 H5 Asperen Neth.
22 H2 Asperen l. Norway
52 G4 Asperg Ger.
121 E9 Aspermont TX U.S.A.
118 A5 Aspers PA U.S.A.
43 F9 Aspet France
43 E10 Aspin, Col d' pass France
191 E4 Aspindza Georgia
41 C9 Aspiran France
203 C11 Aspiring, Mount South I. N.Z.
62 E2 As Pontes de García Rodríguez Spain
41 H7 Aspremont France
41 H7 Aspres-sur-Buëch France
43 I6 Asprières France
Aspro, Cape Cyprus see Aspron, Cape
78 B3 Asprokavos, Akra pt Kerkyra Greece
75 J7 Aspromonte, Parco Nazionale dell' nat. park Italy
190 A4 Aspron, Cape Cyprus
Aspropotamos r. Greece see Acheloös
78 G6 Aspros Gremnos, Akra pt Greece
78 E2 Asprovalta Greece
178 E8 Aspur Rajasthan India
107 J4 Asquith Sask. Can.
71 K4 Assa r. Italy
86 C3 Assa Morocco
191 G2 Assa r. Rus. Fed.
190 F3 As Sa'an Syria
85 I6 Assab Eritrea
88 C2 Assaba admin. reg. Maur.
186 E2 As Sab'ān Saudi Arabia
190 H3 As Sabkhah Syria
187 I2 As Sabsab well Saudi Arabia
164 R5 Assabu Japan
190 E5 Aş Şafā lava field Syria
85 F2 Aş Şaff Egypt
190 D7 Aş Şāfī Jordan
190 F2 As Safīrah Syria
186 D3 Aş Şafrā Saudi Arabia
186 F2 Aş Safrā Saudi Arabia
187 I2 Aş Şaḥāf Saudi Arabia
186 F8 Aş Şaḥīf Yemen
85 F3 Aş Şaḥrā' al Gharbīyah des. Egypt
85 G3 Aş Şaḥrā' ash Sharqīyah des. Egypt
89 H4 Assaiko Nigeria
Assake Uzbek. see Asaka
182 G6 Assake-Audan, Vpadina depr. Uzbek.
85 I7 'Assal, Lac l. Djibouti
187 H3 As Salamiyah Saudi Arabia
188 F8 Aş Şāliḥīyah Egypt
189 J6 Aş Şāliḥīyah Syria
188 B8 As Sallūm Egypt
189 L8 As Salmān Iraq
190 D6 As Salṭ Jordan
179 M6 Assam state India
89 G2 Assamakka Niger
189 L8 As Samāwah Iraq
190 E6 As Samrā' Jordan
52 H3 Assamstadt Ger.
187 J5 Aş Şanām reg. Saudi Arabia
190 E5 Aş Şanamayn Syria
86 B4 Assaq watercourse Western Sahara
86 B4 As Saquia al Hamra watercourse Western Sahara
186 G2 As Sarīf well Saudi Arabia
84 D3 As Sarīr reg. Libya
43 D9 Assat France
117 J10 Assateague Island MD U.S.A.
117 J11 Assateague Island National Seashore nature res. VA U.S.A.
186 G4 As Sawādah reg. Saudi Arabia
187 L7 As Sawdā i. Oman
186 D2 Aş Şawrah Al Madīnah Saudi Arabia
186 B2 Aş Şawrah Tabūk Saudi Arabia
186 H4 As Sayḥ Saudi Arabia
186 E5 As Sayl al Kabīr Saudi Arabia
45 F7 Asse Belgium
41 H9 Asse r. France
96 I9 Assegaaibos S. Africa
72 C9 Assemini Sardegna Italy
44 K2 Assen Neth.
44 G4 Assendelft Neth.
45 E6 Assenede Belgium
22 F6 Assens Denmark
38 G7 Assérac France
73 L3 Assergi Italy
45 H8 Assesse Belgium
84 C2 As Sidrah Libya
43 H6 Assier France
187 N4 As Sīfah Oman
109 H2 Assigny, Lac l. Nfld and Lab. Can.
187 J3 As Sikak Saudi Arabia
187 J4 As Sila' U.A.E.
107 J5 Assiniboia Sask. Can.
107 L5 Assiniboine r. Man./Sask. Can.
106 H5 Assiniboine, Mount Alta/B.C. Can.
108 F3 Assinica, Réserve Faunique nature res. Que. Can.
142 B5 Assis Brazil
142 A6 Assis Chateaubriand Brazil
73 J1 Assisi Italy
49 F9 Aßlar Ger.
58 G6 Assling Austria
53 M6 Aßling Ger.
70 G4 Asso Italy
88 □ Assomada Santiago Cape Verde
99 □2 Assomption i. Aldabra Is Seychelles
43 D9 Asson France
74 G8 Assoro Sicilia Italy
87 F4 Assouf Mellene watercourse Alg.
189 M9 Aş Şubayḥīyah Kuwait
186 F6 As Subaykhah Saudi Arabia
187 I8 As Sufāl Yemen
186 G1 Aş Şufayrī well Saudi Arabia
190 G4 As Sukhnah Syria
189 L6 As Sulaymānīyah Iraq
189 L6 As Sulaymānīyah governorate Iraq
186 E2 As Sulaymī Saudi Arabia
186 G5 As Sulayyil Saudi Arabia
187 I3 Aş Şulb reg. Saudi Arabia
84 C2 As Sulṭān Libya
64 E2 Assumar Port.
186 H2 Aş Şummān plat. Saudi Arabia
187 I5 Aş Şummān plat. Saudi Arabia
186 E5 As Sūq Saudi Arabia
189 J6 Aş Şuwar Syria
190 E6 As Suwaydā' Syria
190 E6 As Suwaydā' governorate Syria
187 N4 As Suwayḥ Oman
187 M4 As Suwayq Oman
189 L7 Aş Şuwayrah Iraq
186 E4 As Suwayriqīyah Saudi Arabia
As Suways Egypt see El Suweis
190 A9 As Suways governorate Egypt
186 G8 As Suwwādīyah Yemen
26 F6 Assynt, Loch l. Scotland U.K.
21 K6 Asta r. Norway
71 L3 Asta, Cima d' mt. Italy
43 F7 Astaffort France
79 H7 Astakida i. Greece
78 C4 Astakos Greece
Astalu Island Pak. see Astola Island
183 N2 Astana Kazakh.
184 C3 Astaneh Iran
184 C2 Āstārā Iran
43 E8 Astarac reg. France
43 F9 Astarac, Barrage de l' dam France
22 J1 Åsteby Sweden
59 J3 Asten Austria
45 I6 Asten Neth.
Asterabad Iran see Gorgān
70 E6 Asti Italy
70 E6 Asti prov. Italy
146 D2 Astica Arg.
71 L4 Astico r. Italy
57 L4 Aştileu Romania
138 C3 Astillero Peru
Astin Tag mts China see Altun Shan
Astipálaia i. Greece see Astypalaia
185 J9 Astola Island Pak.
43 H10 Aston r. France
97 I10 Aston Bay S. Africa
31 K4 Aston Clinton Buckinghamshire, England U.K.
178 E2 Astor Jammu and Kashmir
185 P4 Astor r. Pak.
142 B5 Astorga Brazil
62 H4 Astorga Spain
110 D9 Astoria IL U.S.A.
122 C3 Astoria OR U.S.A.
22 I5 Åstorp Sweden
99 □2 Astove i. Aldabra Is Seychelles
145 D7 Astra Arg.
Astrabad Iran see Gorgān
Astrakhan' Kazakh. see Astrakhanka
182 C4 Astrakhan' Rus. Fed.
Astrakhan' Bazar Azer. see Cälilabad
183 M2 Astrakhanka Kazakh.
17 O7 Astrakhanka Ukr.
Astrakhan Oblast admin. div. Rus. Fed. see Astrakhanskaya Oblast'
182 B4 Astrakhanskaya Oblast' admin. div. Rus. Fed.
18 I7 Astravyets Belarus
191 J5 Astraxanka Azer.
Astrida Rwanda see Butare
200 □6 Astrolabe, Cape Malaita Solomon Is
200 □5 Astrolabe, Récifs de l' rf New Caledonia
78 D5 Astros Greece
18 M6 Astrowna Belarus
18 H8 Astryna Belarus
19 O8 Astsyer r. Belarus
63 L4 Astudillo Spain
73 J5 Astura r. Italy
147 F5 Asturias Arg.
62 H1 Asturias airport Spain
62 H2 Asturias aut. comm. Spain
Asturica Augusta Spain see Astorga
31 I3 Astwood Bank Worcestershire, England U.K.
79 H6 Astypalaia Greece
79 H6 Astypalaia i. Greece
183 T3 Asubulak Kazakh.
Asūbulaq Kazakh. see Asubulak
200 □2 Asuisui, Cape Samoa
166 C7 Asuka Japan
166 F5 Asuke Japan
138 D2 Asunción Bol.
123 H11 Asunción r. Mex.
153 K3 Asuncion i. N. Mariana Is
139 F6 Asunción Para.
127 O10 Asunción Mita Guat.
23 O4 Asunden i. Sweden
22 J4 Åsunden l. Sweden
23 L4 Åsunden l. Sweden
72 B8 Asuni Sardegna Italy
166 D3 Asuwa-gawa r. Japan
18 L5 Asvyeya Belarus
18 L5 Asvyeyskaye, Vozyera l. Belarus
92 A4 Aswa r. Uganda
187 M3 Aswad Oman
186 D5 Aswad, Ar Ra's al pt Saudi Arabia
187 L5 Aswad, Wādī watercourse Oman
85 G3 Aswān Egypt
186 A3 Aswān governorate Egypt
85 G3 Aswan Dam Egypt
85 F3 Asyūṭ Egypt
188 E10 Asyūṭ governorate Egypt
57 J3 Aszaló Hungary
201 □2a Ata i. Tonga
136 E3 Atabapo r. Col./Venez.
183 M6 Atabay Kazakh.
79 L5 Atabey Turkey
144 C2 Atacama admin. reg. Chile
144 C2 Atacama, Desierto de des. Chile
138 C5 Atacama, Salar de salt flat Chile
136 B4 Atacames Ecuador
136 C4 Ataco Col.
87 G4 Atafaitafa, Djebel mt. Alg.
203 □1 Atafu atoll Tokelau
203 □1 Atafu i. Tokelau
166 C5 Atago-san hill Japan
167 K5 Atago-yama hill Japan
201 □3a Ataiti Tahiti Fr. Polynesia
183 M7 Atakent Kazakh.
190 C2 Atakent Turkey
191 J5 Atakişili Azer.
87 G5 Atakor mts Alg.
89 F4 Atakora, Chaîne de l' mts Benin
89 F5 Atakpamé Togo
140 G4 Atalaia Brazil
64 B4 Atalaia hill Port.
64 B6 Atalaia, Ponta da pt Port.
136 D6 Atalaia do Norte Brazil
Atalándi Greece see Atalanti
78 E4 Atalanti Greece
126 □S13 Atalaya Panama
138 C3 Atalaya Madre de Dios Peru
138 B2 Atalaya Ucayali Peru
65 P6 Atalaya Arabe hill Spain
143 G3 Ataléia Brazil
198 C2 Atambua Timor Indon.
167 J5 Atami Japan
144 E3 Atamisqui Arg.
105 M3 Atammik Greenland
185 K3 Atamyrat Turkm.
Ataniya Turkey see Adana
57 J4 Átány Hungary
63 M4 Atapuerca tourist site Spain
155 D8 Atapupu Timor Indon.
186 H8 'Ataq Yemen
190 A9 'Atāqah, Jabal hill Egypt
63 K6 Ataquines Spain
86 B5 Atâr Maur.
158 C6 Ataran r. Myanmar
129 H4 Atarjea Mex.
124 L6 Atascadero CA U.S.A.
121 F11 Atascosa watercourse TX U.S.A.
183 N3 Atasu Kazakh.
201 □2a Atata i. Tonga
173 I7 Atatan He r. China
188 D3 Ataturk airport Turkey
79 J6 Atatürk Milli Parkı nat. park Turkey
155 D8 Ataúro, Ilha de i. East Timor
Atáviros mt. Rodos Greece see Attavyros
184 H1 Atayab Turkm.
190 B2 Atayurt Turkey
85 G5 Atbara Sudan
85 G5 Atbara r. Sudan
183 M2 Atbasar Kazakh.
183 P7 At-Bashy Kyrg.
121 J11 Atchafalaya Bay LA U.S.A.
120 H6 Atchison KS U.S.A.
118 F5 Atco NJ U.S.A.
63 Q6 Atea Spain
88 E5 Atebubu Ghana
63 Q6 Ateca Spain
62 E6 Atei Port.
62 F4 A Teixeira Spain
73 M4 Ateleta Italy
73 P6 Atella Italy
73 P6 Atella r. Italy
128 D5 Atemajac de Brizuela Mex.
167 I1 Atema-yama mt. Japan
138 C3 Aten Bol.
73 P7 Atena Lucana Italy
129 H7 Atenango del Río Mex.
128 C4 Atengo r. Mex.
128 C5 Atenguillo Mex.
128 C5 Atenguillo r. Mex.
128 D6 Atenquique Mex.
Ateransk Kazakh. see Atyrau
73 L3 Aterno r. Italy
184 E4 Āteshān Iran
185 I5 Āteshkhāneh, Kūh-e hill Afgh.
73 M3 Atessa Italy
186 G7 'Aṭfayn, Wādī watercourse Yemen
118 D5 Atglen PA U.S.A.
45 E7 Ath Belgium
106 H4 Athabasca Alta Can.
106 I3 Athabasca r. Alta Can.
107 I3 Athabasca, Lake Alta/Sask. Can.
107 I3 Athabasca Sand Dunes Wilderness Provincial Park nature res. Sask. Can.
179 J9 Athagarh Orissa India
116 C10 Athalia OH U.S.A.
107 K4 Athapapuskow Lake Man. Can.
185 O6 Atharan Hazari Pak.
27 I5 Athboy Rep. of Ireland
27 D8 Athea Rep. of Ireland
Athenae Greece see Athina
27 E6 Athenry Rep. of Ireland
111 S5 Athens Ont. Can.
Athens Greece see Athina
115 D8 Athens AL U.S.A.
115 F9 Athens GA U.S.A.
117 L6 Athens NY U.S.A.
116 C9 Athens OH U.S.A.
116 I7 Athens PA U.S.A.
115 E8 Athens TN U.S.A.
121 H9 Athens TX U.S.A.
49 K7 Athenstedt Ger.
78 B4 Atheras, Akra pt Kefallonia Greece
30 D6 Atherington Devon, England U.K.
31 I2 Atherstone Warwickshire, England U.K.
207 J4 Atherton Qld Austr.
29 M6 Atherton Greater Manchester, England U.K.
93 C5 Athi r. Kenya
36 E4 Athies France
36 G4 Athies-sous-Laon France
78 E5 Athina Greece
Athínai Greece see Athina
93 C5 Athi River Kenya
39 K4 Athis-de-l'Orne France
36 D6 Athis-Mons France
27 E8 Athlacca Rep. of Ireland
27 F5 Athleague Rep. of Ireland
27 G6 Athlone Rep. of Ireland
190 G6 Athnā', Wādī al watercourse Jordan
176 D4 Athni Karnataka India
203 C12 Athol South I. N.Z.
117 M6 Athol MA U.S.A.
115 □2 Athol Island New Prov. Bahamas
26 H9 Atholl, Forest of reg. Scotland U.K.
78 F2 Athos mt. Greece
Athos, Mount admin. div. Greece see Agion Oros
85 G2 Ath Thamad Egypt
189 K6 Ath Tharthār, Wādī r. Iraq
190 E9 Ath Thāyat mt. Saudi Arabia
186 G2 Ath Thumāmī well Saudi Arabia
27 I7 Athy Rep. of Ireland
84 C6 Ati Chad
84 B4 Ati, Jabal mts Libya
184 H4 Aṭīābād Iran
92 B4 Atiak Uganda
202 K5 Atiamuri North I. N.Z.
84 C6 Ati Ardébé Chad
142 D5 Atibaia Brazil
138 B4 Atico Peru
138 B4 Atico, Punta pt Peru
90 E3 Atiedo Sudan
63 O6 Atienza Spain
128 F7 Atijo Mex.
107 L5 Atikaki Provincial Wilderness Park park Man. Can.
106 H4 Atikameg Alta Can.
108 D2 Atikameg r. Ont. Can.
107 M4 Atik Lake Man. Can.
108 B3 Atikokan Ont. Can.
109 H2 Atikonak Lake Nfld and Lab. Can.
201 □3a Atimaono Tahiti Fr. Polynesia
154 C4 Atimonan Luzon Phil.
73 L4 Atina Italy
127 O10 Atiquizaya El Salvador
176 F7 Atirampattinam Tamil Nadu India
127 N10 Atitlán Guat.
127 N10 Atitlán, Parque Nacional nat. park Guat.
203 □2 Atiu i. Cook Is
Atjeh admin. dist. Indon. see Aceh
186 H2 'Atk, Wādī al watercourse Saudi Arabia
193 Q3 Atka Rus. Fed.
104 A4 Atka AK U.S.A.
104 A4 Atka Island AK U.S.A.
57 I4 Atkár Hungary
15 I6 Atkarsk Rus. Fed.
121 I8 Atkins AR U.S.A.
155 G4 Atkri Papua Indon.
129 H6 Atlacomulco Mex.
97 L1 Atlanta S. Africa
115 E9 Atlanta GA U.S.A.
110 E9 Atlanta IL U.S.A.
111 J4 Atlanta MI U.S.A.
121 H9 Atlanta TX U.S.A.
188 F4 Atlantı Turkey
120 H5 Atlantic IA U.S.A.
117 □Q4 Atlantic ME U.S.A.
115 I8 Atlantic NC U.S.A.
117 K9 Atlantic City NJ U.S.A.
118 F6 Atlantic County county NJ U.S.A.
119 G4 Atlantic Highlands NJ U.S.A.
213 H3 Atlantic-Indian-Antarctic Basin sea feature S. Atlantic Ocean
215 D8 Atlantic-Indian Ridge sea feature Southern Ocean
136 C2 Atlántico dept Col.
214 Atlantic Ocean
122 J5 Atlantic Peak WY U.S.A.
96 C9 Atlantis S. Africa
129 I4 Atlapexco Mex.
118 C3 Atlas PA U.S.A.
168 E5 Atlas Bogd mt. Mongolia
Atlas Méditerranéen mts Alg. see Atlas Tellien
86 D3 Atlas Mountains Africa
193 Q4 Atlasova, Ostrov i. Kuril'skiye O-va Rus. Fed.
87 F2 Atlas Saharien mts Alg.
87 F2 Atlas Tellien mts Alg.
129 I7 Atlatlahucan Mex.
106 C3 Atlin B.C. Can.
106 C3 Atlin Lake B.C./Y.T. Can.
106 C3 Atlin Provincial Park B.C. Can.
190 C6 'Atlit Israel
129 I7 Atlixco Mex.
129 I8 Atlixtac Mex.
176 F5 Atmakur Andhra Prad. India
176 F5 Atmakur Andhra Prad. India
115 D10 Atmore AL U.S.A.
21 K6 Atna Norway
178 F9 Atner Madh. Prad. India
206 F7 Atnetye Aboriginal Land res. N.T. Austr.
176 E4 Atnur Karnataka India
165 I12 Atō Japan
138 D5 Atocha Bol.
121 G8 Atoka OK U.S.A.
91 B7 Atome Angola
86 C4 Atonyia Western Sahara
200 □6 Atori Malaita Solomon Is
129 I5 Atotonico El Grande Mex.
128 D1 Atotonilco Durango Mex.
128 E1 Atotonilco Zacatecas Mex.
128 E5 Atotonilco el Alto Mex.
158 H6 Atouat mt. Laos
64 A2 Atouguia da Baleia Port.
128 D5 Atoyac Mex.
129 I7 Atoyac r. Mex.
129 J9 Atoyac r. Mex.
129 K6 Atoyac r. Mex.
128 G8 Atoyac de Álvarez Mex.
176 D4 Atpadi Mahar. India
Atqan Xinjiang China see Aqqan
104 C2 Atqasuk AK U.S.A.
179 L7 Atrai r. India
22 I5 Ätran r. Sweden
178 G6 Atranh Uttar Prad. India
136 B2 Atrato r. Col.
129 M9 Atravesada, Sierra mts Mex.
184 G3 Atrek r. Iran/Turkm. alt. Etrek
73 L2 Atri Italy
Atria Italy see Adria
73 N6 Atripalda Italy
Atropatene country Asia see Azerbaijan
191 D3 Ats'ana Georgia
78 G3 Atsiki Limnos Greece
118 F5 Atsion NJ U.S.A.
167 J5 Atsugi Japan
89 H5 Atsuku Nigeria
166 F6 Atsumi Aichi Japan
164 Q8 Atsumi Yamagata Japan
166 F6 Atsumi-hantō pen. Japan
164 S3 Atsuta Japan
187 L3 Aṭ Ṭaff reg. U.A.E.
190 D8 Aṭ Ṭafīlah Jordan
186 E5 Aṭ Ṭā'if Saudi Arabia
57 H5 Attala Hungary
Attalea Turkey see Antalya
Attalia Turkey see Antalya
115 D8 Attalla AL U.S.A.
84 D3 Aṭ Ṭallāb oasis Libya
189 K6 At Ta'mīm governorate Iraq
84 D1 At Tamīmī Libya
28 C8 Attanagh Rep. of Ireland
159 H7 Attapu Laos
87 G2 Attar, Oued el watercourse Alg.
75 □ Attard Malta
27 C4 Attavalley Rep. of Ireland
79 I6 Attavyros mt. Rodos Greece
108 D2 Attawapiskat Ont. Can.
108 D2 Attawapiskat r. Ont. Can.
108 C2 Attawapiskat Lake Ont. Can.
85 H2 Aṭ Ṭawīl mts Saudi Arabia
186 E5 Aṭ Ṭāwlah Saudi Arabia
186 F1 At Taysīyah plat. Saudi Arabia
190 D8 Aṭ Ṭayyibah Jordan
202 H7 Attempt Hill South I. N.Z.
49 E8 Attendorn Ger.
53 L4 Attenkirchen Ger.
97 M1 Atteridgeville S. Africa
59 I4 Attersee Austria
59 I4 Attersee l. Austria
45 I9 Attert Belgium
45 J9 Attert r. Lux.
27 J4 Attica Northern Ireland U.K.
114 D5 Attica IN U.S.A.
116 G6 Attica NY U.S.A.
116 C7 Attica OH U.S.A.
36 F5 Attichy France
73 I2 Attigliano Italy
40 G4 Attignat France
36 I5 Attigny France
109 H2 Attikamagen Lake Nfld and Lab. Can.
78 E5 Attiki admin. reg. Greece
84 D1 At Tīn, Ra's pt Libya
190 A7 Aṭ Ṭīnah Egypt
176 E8 Attingal Kerala India
117 N7 Attleboro MA U.S.A.
31 O2 Attleborough Norfolk, England U.K.
31 O2 Attlebridge Norfolk, England U.K.
59 I3 Attnang Austria
185 O5 Attock City Pak.
Attopeu Laos see Attapu
105 M3 Attu Greenland
188 H9 Aṭ Ṭubayq reg. Saudi Arabia
216 G2 Attu Island AK U.S.A.
186 G2 Aṭ Ṭulayḥī well Saudi Arabia
205 M4 Attunga N.S.W. Austr.
85 G2 Aṭ Ṭūr Egypt
176 E7 Attur Tamil Nadu India
176 F7 Attur Tamil Nadu India
186 F9 At Turbah Ta'izz Yemen
186 G9 At Turbah Ta'izz Yemen
186 E2 Aṭ Ṭuwayyah well Saudi Arabia
27 E6 Attymon Rep. of Ireland
147 H3 Atucha Arg.
187 I8 Atūd Yemen
146 D5 Atuel r. Arg.
42 F5 Atur France
23 L3 Åtvidaberg Sweden
179 L6 Atwari Bangl.
124 L4 Atwater CA U.S.A.
120 E6 Atwood KS U.S.A.
15 I5 Atyashevo Rus. Fed.
182 D4 Atyrau Kazakh.
Atyrau Oblast admin. div. Kazakh. see Atyrauskaya Oblast'
Atyraū Oblysy admin. div. Kazakh. see Atyrauskaya Oblast'
182 D4 Atyrauskaya Oblast' admin. div. Kazakh.
15 H5 Atyur'yevo Rus. Fed.
17 L2 Atyusha Ukr.
72 C8 Atzara Sardegna Italy
59 M3 Atzenbrugg Austria
51 E7 Atzendorf Ger.
58 A5 Au Austria
70 H1 Au Switz.
136 E5 Auati-Paraná r. Brazil
53 I2 Aub Ger.
49 H10 Aubach r. Ger.
41 H10 Aubagne France
41 E9 Aubais France
45 I9 Aubange Belgium
154 D3 Aubarede Point Luzon Phil.
42 H5 Aubazines France
39 M4 Aube France
36 H7 Aube dept France
36 G6 Aube r. France
95 H3 Aúbe Moz.
45 I7 Aubel Belgium
41 E7 Aubenas France
36 H4 Aubenton France
36 C6 Aubergenville France
36 H5 Aubérive France
37 J8 Auberive France
42 E5 Aubeterre-sur-Dronne France
36 F6 Aubetin r. France
36 B5 Aubevoye France
43 F8 Aubiet France
41 G8 Aubignan France
39 L6 Aubigné-Racan France
41 H8 Aubignosc France
36 E3 Aubigny-en-Artois France
39 P7 Aubigny-sur-Nère France
43 I6 Aubin France
108 D4 Aubinadong r. Ont. Can.
43 D10 Aubisque, Col d' pass France
70 A2 Aubonne Switz.
41 E9 Aubord France
37 K5 Auboué France
41 B7 Aubrac mts France
37 J5 Aubreville France
125 T6 Aubrey Cliffs mts AZ U.S.A.
104 F3 Aubry Lake N.W.T. Can.
207 M8 Auburn r. Qld Austr.
111 M6 Auburn Ont. Can.
115 E9 Auburn AL U.S.A.
124 K3 Auburn CA U.S.A.
120 K6 Auburn IL U.S.A.
114 E5 Auburn IN U.S.A.
117 N6 Auburn MA U.S.A.
117 □O4 Auburn ME U.S.A.
111 J6 Auburn MI U.S.A.
120 H5 Auburn NE U.S.A.
116 I6 Auburn NY U.S.A.
118 C3 Auburn PA U.S.A.
122 C3 Auburn WA U.S.A.
118 C1 Auburn Center PA U.S.A.
110 D5 Auburndale WI U.S.A.
207 M8 Auburn Range hills Qld Austr.
42 I4 Aubusson France
36 F3 Auby France
146 C5 Auca Mahuida Arg.
146 C5 Auca Mahuida, Sierra de mt. Arg.
43 G8 Aucamville France
18 F5 Auce Latvia
43 F8 Auch France
26 J9 Auchallater Aberdeenshire, Scotland U.K.
28 G2 Auchbraad Argyll and Bute, Scotland U.K.
158 C2 Auche Myanmar
36 D2 Auchel France

159 G10 Bac Liêu Vietnam
158 H4 Bắc Ninh Vietnam
154 C5 Bacnotan Luzon Phil.
154 C5 Baco, Mount Mindoro Phil.
126 D2 Bacoachi Mex.
123 I12 Bacoachi watercourse Mex.
126 E4 Bacobampo Mex.
73 M6 Bacoli Italy
154 D6 Bacolod Negros Phil.
108 F1 Bacou, Pic de mt. France see Guerreys, Pic de
36 A4 Bacqueville, Lac l. Que. Can.
57 I5 Bacqueville-en-Caux France
57 I5 Bácsalmás Hungary
57 I5 Bácsbokod Hungary
57 I5 Bácsborsód Hungary
57 I5 Bács-Kiskun county Hungary
126 F5 Bactra Afgh. see Balkh
57 I3 Bacubirito Mex.
57 I3 Baculin Slovakia
154 F8 Baculin Bay Mindanao Phil.
154 F7 Baculin Point Mindanao Phil.
29 M6 Bacup Lancashire, England U.K.
140 D2 Bacuri Brazil
54 D3 Baczyna Pol.
120 E3 Bad r. SD U.S.A.
92 C3 Bad mt. Eth.
159 D9 Bada i. Myanmar
56 G5 Bad Abbach Ger.
53 M4 Badagara Kerala India
176 D7 Bad Aibling Ger.
168 H7 Badain Jaran Nei Mongol China
168 G6 (Badain Jaran Shamo des. Nei Mongol China)
137 F5 Badajós Amazonas Brazil
140 D2 Badajós Pará Brazil
137 F5 Badajós, Lago l. Brazil
64 G3 Badajoz Spain
185 N3 Badajoz prov. Spain
Badakhshan prov. Afgh.
Badakhshan aut. rep. Tajik. see Kŭhistoni Badakhshon
66 J5 Badalona Spain
70 D8 Badalucco Italy
63 N2 Bádames Spain
176 D5 Badami Karnataka India
179 K8 Badampaharh Orissa India
189 J8 Badanah Saudi Arabia
26 H6 Badanloch, Loch l. Scotland U.K.
Badaojiang Jilin China see Baishan
63 O4 Badaran Spain
181 G4 Badarinath Uttaranchal India
157 N7 Badarpur Assam India
157 K7 Badas Brunei
178 H3 Badas, Kepulauan is Indon.
178 H7 Badausa Uttar Prad. India
59 I4 Bad Aussee Austria
111 L6 Bad Axe MI U.S.A.
49 D6 Bad Bentheim Ger.
48 E5 Badbergen Ger.
52 D3 Bad Bergzabern Ger.
51 F9 Bad Berka Ger.
49 F8 Bad Berleburg Ger.
51 E10 Bad Berneck im Fichtelgebirge Ger.
49 D10 Bad Bertrich Ger.
48 K4 Bad Bevensen Ger.
53 O5 Bad Bibra Ger.
49 J10 Bad Blankenburg Ger.
59 I6 Bad Bleiberg Austria
49 J10 Bad Bocklet Ger.
51 F10 Bad Brambach Ger.
48 I3 Bad Bramstedt Ger.
49 D10 Bad Breisig Ger.
52 H5 Bad Buchau Ger.
26 F7 Bad Camberg Ger.
Badcaul Highland, Scotland U.K.
109 I4 Baddeck N.S. Can.
49 J6 Baddeckenstedt Ger.
20 Q2 Badderen Norway
185 K7 Baddo r. Pak.
50 E2 Bad Doberan Ger.
51 H7 Bad Driburg Ger.
51 G7 Bad Düben Ger.
51 F8 Bad Dürkheim Ger.
51 F8 Bad Dürrenberg Ger.
51 D7 Bad Dürrheim Ger.
51 D7 Badeborn Ger.
42 G5 Badefols-d'Ans France
89 G3 Badéguichéri Niger
49 H6 Bad Eilsen Ger.
51 F10 Bad Elster Ger.
Bademli Turkey see Aladağ
188 E5 Bademli Geçidi pass Turkey
49 E10 Bad Ems Ger.
59 N3 Baden Austria
38 F6 Baden France
70 E1 Baden Switz.
52 E4 Badenas Spain
52 E4 Baden-Baden Ger.
49 G9 Bad Endbach Ger.
58 M3 Bad Endorf Ger.
49 J7 Badenhausen Ger.
26 L8 Badenoch reg. Scotland U.K.
Badenscoth Aberdeenshire, Scotland U.K.
52 D6 Badenweiler Ger.
52 F5 Baden-Württemberg land Ger.
89 G3 Badér Niger
71 P5 Baderna Croatia
52 D2 Badersleben Ger.
47 B6 Badesi Sardegna Italy
53 M6 Bad Essen Ger.
50 I5 Bad Feilnbach Ger.
49 G5 Bad Freienwalde Ger.
52 G3 Bad Friedrichshall Ger.
53 O5 Bad Füssing Ger.
178 E2 Badgam Jammu and Kashmir
52 L6 Bad Gams Austria
58 H5 Bad Gandersheim Ger.
105 L2 Badgastein Austria
85 J4 Bádgīs prov. Afgh.
59 M6 Bad Gleichenberg Austria
59 I4 Bad Goisern Austria
59 K2 Bad Großpertholz Austria
59 J3 Bad Hall Austria
59 I2 Bad Häring Austria
53 K6 Bad Harzburg Ger.
44 K2 Bad Heilbrunn Ger.
85 J4 Bad Herrenalb Ger.
49 I9 Bad Hersfeld Ger.
49 J4 Badhoevedorp Neth.
58 H5 Bad Hofgastein Austria
49 G10 Bad Homburg vor der Höhe Ger.
49 D9 Bad Honnef Ger.
88 B4 Badi i. Guinea
71 L2 Badia Italy
71 K4 Badia Calavena Italy
67 K9 Badia Gran Spain
71 K5 Badia Polesine Italy
71 M8 Badia Tedalda Italy
71 N6 Bad Iburg Ger.
83 N7 Badi r. Pak.
92 A3 Badigeru Swamp Sudan
57 J3 Badin Col.
55 J5 Badin Slovakia
57 I3 Badinko, Réserve du nature res. Mali
88 C3 Badiraguato Mex.
59 J4 Bad Ischl Austria
85 I4 Badkhyzsky Zapovednik nature res. Turkm.
49 J10 Bad Kissingen Ger.
50 D3 Bad Kleinen Ger.
59 I6 Bad Kleinkirchheim Austria
52 G2 Bad Kohlgrub Ger.
52 G2 Bad König Ger.
51 E8 Bad Königshofen im Grabfeld Ger.
51 E8 Bad Kösen Ger.

59 K3 Bad Kreuzen Austria
52 D2 Bad Kreuznach Ger.
49 F9 Bad Krozingen Ger.
49 F9 Bad Laasphe Ger.
49 F6 Bad Laer Ger.
120 D2 Badlands reg. ND U.S.A.
120 D4 Badlands reg. SD U.S.A.
120 D4 Badlands National Park SD U.S.A.
49 K8 Bad Langensalza Ger.
51 E8 Bad Lauchstädt Ger.
51 E8 Bad Lausick Ger.
49 J7 Bad Lauterberg im Harz Ger.
48 K1 Bad Leonfelden Austria
176 E6 Bad Liebenwerda Ger.
179 L8 Bad Liebenzell Ger.
43 J10 Bad Lippspringe Ger.
66 I4 Bages France
41 B10 Bages reg. Spain
Bages et de Sigean, Étang de lag. France
178 G5 Bageshwar Uttaranchal India
176 E4 Bagevadi Karnataka India
23 L2 Baggå Sweden
122 K6 Baggs WY U.S.A.
30 D5 Baggy Point England U.K.
51 B8 Bagh Madh. Prad. India
185 O5 Bagh i. Indon.
Bagh a'Chaisteil Western Isles, Scotland U.K. see Castlebay
185 K7 Baghak Afgh.
26 B8 Baghasdail, Loch inlet
184 I3 Baghbaghū Iran
189 L7 Baghdad Iraq
189 L7 Baghdad governorate Iraq
191 D3 Baghdat'i Georgia
184 G7 Bāgh-e Bābū'īyeh Iran
184 C6 Bāgh-e Malek Iran
Baghmüller France
Bagherhat Bangl. see Bagerhat
74 F7 Bagheria Sicilia Italy
184 G6 Bāghīn Iran
185 M3 Baghlān Afgh.
185 M4 Baghlān prov. Afgh.
184 B2 Bāghlī Da hill Iran
26 B8 Bagh nam Faoileann b. Scotland U.K.
191 E5 Baghramyan Armenia
185 K5 Baghwāri Pak.
185 L8 Baghwana Pak.
30 F1 Bagillt Flintshire, Wales U.K.
156 G6 Baginda, Tanjung pt Indon.
191 A6 Bagirpaşa Dağ mt. Turkey
191 C7 Bağır Turkey
120 H2 Bagley MN U.S.A.
191 B Baglung Nepal
52 G3 Bad Rappenau Ger.
59 M6 Badr Radkersburg Austria
186 D4 Badr Ḥunayn Saudi Arabia
Badrinath Peaks Uttaranchal India see Chaukhamba
21 J6 Bagn Norway
71 L7 Bagnacavallo Italy
43 I6 Bagnara-sur-Célé France
75 J7 Bagnara Calabra Italy
71 L4 Bagnaria Italy
70 E7 Bagnaria Arsa Italy
36 E7 Bagneaux-sur-Loing France
43 F10 Bagnères-de-Bigorre France
43 F10 Bagnères-de-Luchon France
70 C3 Bagnes reg. Switz.
70 C3 Bagnes, Val des val. Switz.
70 H3 Bagni di Masino Italy
71 J3 Bagni di Rabbi Italy
71 L8 Bagno di Romagna Italy
39 M4 Bagnoles-de-l'Orne France
73 M4 Bagnoli del Trigno Italy
71 L5 Bagnoli di Sopra Italy
73 O6 Bagnoli Irpino Italy
71 J6 Bagnolo in Piano Italy
71 K6 Bagnolo Mella Italy
41 K7 Bagnolo Piemonte Italy
41 K6 Bagnolo San Vito Italy
41 I7 Bagnols-en-Forêt France
41 D7 Bagnols-les-Bains France
41 I7 Bagnols-sur-Cèze France
65 L4 Bailén Spain
77 M5 Baile Olănești Romania
77 L6 Băilești Romania
77 L6 Băilești, Câmpia plain Romania
97 K2 Bailey S. Africa
209 G10 Bailey Range hills W.A. Austr.
116 C12 Baileyton TN U.S.A.
171 J3 Bailiangdeng China
170 H6 Bailicun Guangxi China
27 I5 Bailieborough Rep. of Ireland
169 L6 Bailingmiao Nei Mongol China
137 I4 Bailique Brazil
36 B7 Bailleau-le-Pin France
36 B2 Bailleul France
107 J1 Bailleul r. Nunavut Can.
131 □2 Baillif Guadeloupe
45 H8 Baillonville Belgium
66 D2 Bailo Spain
170 C2 Bailong Jiang r. Gansu/Qinghai China
91 B8 Bailundo Angola
190 Q8 Baima Xizang China see Baxoi
170 C2 Baima Jian mt. Anhui China
170 G9 Baimajing Hainan China
29 Q7 Bain r. England U.K.
184 I2 Baimang Xizang China
164 I4 Bainang Xizang China
29 M5 Bainbridge North Yorkshire, England U.K.
115 E10 Bainbridge GA U.S.A.
110 B9 Bainbridge NY U.S.A.
118 B4 Bainbridge OH U.S.A.
52 H6 Bain-de-Bretagne France
130 D4 Baindt Ger.
178 D4 Bainduru Karnataka India
130 G4 Bainet Haiti
173 J11 Baini r. China
37 I4 Bains-les-Bains France
38 G5 Bains-sur-Oust France

173 K11 Bagar Xizang China
183 T3 Bagar watercourse Kazakh.
79 I5 Bağarası Turkey
41 E8 Bagard France
89 G3 Bagaré well Niger
89 G3 Bagaroua Niger
136 C6 Bagazán Peru
85 F6 Bagbag Sudan
125 S7 Bagdad AZ U.S.A.
Bagdad Georgia see Baghdat'i
57 K6 Bağdadı Georgia see Baghdat'i
40 F4 Bâgé-le-Châtel France
73 Q4 Bagenkop Denmark
179 I8 Bageshwar Uttaranchal India
176 E4 Bagevadi Karnataka India
23 L2 Baggå Sweden
178 G5 Bageshwar Uttaranchal India
155 C5 Baggy Point England U.K.
185 I9 Bagh Madh. Prad. India
19 N7 Bagh i. Indon.
77 O3 Bagh a'Chaisteil see Castlebay
77 Q6 Baghak Afgh.
77 K6 Baghasdail, Loch inlet
89 E9 Baghbaghū Iran
57 L5 Baghdad Iraq
73 Q4 Baghdad governorate Iraq
91 A9 Baghdat'i Georgia
91 B8 Bāgh-e Bābū'īyeh Iran
137 I5 Bāgh-e Malek Iran
72 D6 Baghmüller France
74 D8 Bagheria Sicilia Italy
179 K5 Bāghīn Iran
84 D5 Baghlān Afgh.
90 B3 Baghlān prov. Afgh.
187 L6 Bāghlī Da hill Iran
172 E6 Bagh nam Faoileann b.
77 N5 Baghramyan Armenia
173 H10 Baghwāri Pak.
171 K6 Baghwana Pak.
172 L6 Bagillt Flintshire, Wales U.K.
168 I8 Baginda, Tanjung pt Indon.
109 I3 Bagirpaşa Dağ mt. Turkey
131 □2 Bağır Turkey
59 H4 Bagley MN U.S.A.
53 K3 Bagn Norway
74 F7 Bagnacavallo Italy

85 F3 Bahrīyah, Wāḥāt al oasis Egypt
178 F6 Bahror Rajasthan India
138 C3 Bahuaja-Sonene, Parque Nacional nat. park Peru
155 C5 Bahubulu i. Indon.
185 I9 Bāhushewsk Belarus
19 N7 Bahushewsk Belarus
77 O3 Baia Tulcea Romania
77 Q6 Baia Suceava Romania
77 K6 Baia de Aramă Romania
89 E9 Baía de Henne Haiti
57 L5 Baia de Criș Romania
73 Q4 Baia della Zagare Italy
91 A9 Baía dos Tigres Angola
91 B8 Baia Mare Romania
137 I5 Baião Brazil
72 D6 Baia Sprie Romania
74 D8 Baia i. Sicilia Italy
179 K5 Baïbeli well Chad
84 D5 Bāïbeli well Chad
90 B3 Baïbokoum Chad
169 R4 Baicheng Jilin China
172 E6 Baicheng Xinjiang China
77 N5 Baidoa Somalia see Baydhabo
173 H10 Baidoi Co l. Xizang China
171 K6 Baidu Guangdong China
172 L6 Baidunzi Gansu China
168 I8 Baidunzi Gansu China
109 G3 Baie-Comeau Que. Can.
130 C4 Baie de Henne Haiti
109 I3 Baie-du-Poste Que. Can. see Mistissini
131 □2 Baie-Johan-Beetz Que. Can.
98 □3b Baie-Mahault b. Guadeloupe
80 B1 Baie, Punta del pt Fuerteventura Canary Is
32 E4 Baie Baudó Col.
126 □R13 Bajo Boquete Panama
145 C7 Bajo Caracoles Arg.
146 D2 Bajo de Gallo Arg.
89 H4 Bajoga Nigeria
145 C7 Bajo Grande Arg.
64 H6 Bajo Guadalquivir, Canal del Spain
147 G6 Bajo Hondo Buenos Aires Arg.
146 E2 Bajo Hondo La Rioja Arg.
95 H3 Bajone Moz.
130 D6 Bajo Nuevo sea feature Col.
207 M7 Bajool Qld Austr.
57 H4 Bajot Hungary
63 J6 Bajor r. Spain
179 J3 Bajrakot Orissa India
76 I8 Bajram Curri Albania
57 I6 Bajša Vojvodina, Srbija Serb. and Mont.
56 F5 Baka Slovakia
157 L1 Baka, Bukit mt. Indon.
185 J4 Bālā Morghāb Afgh.
37 I4 Balan Champagne-Ardenne France
40 G5 Balan Rhône-Alpes France
77 N4 Balan Rajasthan India
127 N4 Balan India
178 F9 Balan Mahar. India
179 K8 W. Bengal India
178 F9 Balangir Orissa India
179 J6 Balan Mex.
15 H6 Bălăneşti Moldova
56 G5 Balanga Luzon Phil.
91 C6 Balangala Dem. Rep. Congo

57 L4 Baktalórántháza Hungary
Baku Azer. see Baki
48 F5 Baku Dem. Rep. Congo
156 F4 Bakung i. Indon.
18 H9 Bakuny Belarus
191 E4 Bakuriani Georgia
191 E4 Bakutis Coast Antarctica
212 P2 Baku Azer. see Baki
193 P3 Baky Uyandino r. Rus. Fed.
188 F4 Bala Gwynedd, Wales U.K.
30 E2 Bala, Cerros de mts Bol.
154 A7 Balaban Phil.
154 A8 Balabac i. Phil.
157 L1 Balabac Strait Malaysia/Phil.
184 E5 Balabalagan, Kepulauan atolls Indon.
79 N2 Balabancık Turkey
19 T6 Bălăceanu Romania
200 □5 Balabio, i. New Caledonia
185 J5 Bālā Bolūk Afgh.
17 O6 Bălăceanu Romania
77 P5 Balaci Romania
184 C3 Bālā Deh Iran
184 D3 Baladeh Māzandarān Iran
184 D3 Baladeh Māzandarān Iran
162 H2 Baladek Rus. Fed.
178 F6 Balaghat Madh. Prad. India
178 F6 Balaghat Range hills India
72 B2 Balagne reg. Corse France
184 D5 Balaguer Spain
178 F6 Balahera Rajasthan India
184 H6 Balā Ḩowẕ Iran
157 I5 Balaikuak Kalimantan Indon.
157 I4 Balaikarangan Kalimantan Indon.
156 D4 Balaipungut Sumatera Indon.
157 I6 Balaiiriam Kalimantan Indon.
93 B8 Balaïtous mt. France
93 H4 Balakan Azer.
90 C3 Balaketé C.A.R.
14 H4 Balakhna Rus. Fed.
204 G6 Balakirevo S.A. Austr.
17 M9 Balaklava Ukr.
17 P4 Balakliya Ukr.
182 H2 Balakovo Rus. Fed.
30 E2 Bala Lake Wales U.K.
26 C6 Balallan Western Isles, Scotland U.K.
95 H2 Balama Moz.
157 L1 Balambangan i. Malaysia
185 J4 Bālā Morghāb Afgh.

154 D5 Baleno Masbate Phil.
154 C4 Baler Luzon Phil.
154 C4 Baler Bay Luzon Phil.
65 N7 Balerna Spain
92 C4 Balesa well Kenya
26 B7 Baleshare i. Scotland U.K.
191 K9 Baleshwar Orissa India
21 I6 Balestrand Norway
74 E7 Balestrate Sicilia Italy
89 F3 Baléyara Niger
14 K4 Balezino Rus. Fed.
126 □P10 Balfate Hond.
207 J6 Balfe's Creek Qld Austr.
106 G5 Balfour B.C. Can.
203 C12 Balfour South I. N.Z.
97 K8 Balfour Eastern Cape S. Africa
97 M2 Balfour Mpumalanga S. Africa
26 K4 Balfour Downs W.A. Austr.
26 H10 Balfron Stirling, Scotland U.K.
168 E3 Balgatay Mongolia
48 H5 Balge Ger.
208 I6 Balga W.A. Austr.
208 J6 Balgo Aboriginal Reserve W.A. Austr.
26 D7 Balgown Highland, Scotland U.K.
93 C5 Balguda well Kenya
172 H5 Balguntay Xinjiang China
187 K8 Balḩāf Yemen
92 D1 Bala Djibouti
178 D7 Bali Rajasthan India
178 D7 Bali Rajasthan India
157 K9 Bali i. Indon.
157 K9 Bali prov. Indon.
186 F2 Bali reg. Saudi Arabia
157 K8 Bali, Laut sea Indon.
154 D7 Baliangao Mindanao Phil.
179 K9 Baligol Orissa India
157 K9 Bali Barat National Park Indon.
131 □3 Baliceaux i. St Vincent
179 K8 Balichak W. Bengal India
55 K6 Baligród Pol.
179 I9 Baliguda Orissa India
169 P6 Balihan Nei Mongol China
188 E4 Balıkesir Turkey
79 J3 Balıkhane pt Turkey
189 K4 Balik Gölü l. Turkey
190 H3 Balıklı r. Syria/Turkey
79 I2 Balıklıçeşme Turkey
188 H4 Balıklova Turkey
157 L5 Balikpapan Kalimantan Indon.
157 L5 Balikpapan, Teluk b. Indon.
77 P5 Bălileşti Romania
154 B9 Balimbing Phil.
176 H3 Balimila Reservoir India
153 J8 Balimo P.N.G.
169 R2 Balin Nei Mongol China
156 D2 Baling Malaysia
23 N2 Bälinge Sweden
49 J9 Balingen Ger.
157 J3 Balingian Sarawak Malaysia
157 J3 Balingian r. Malaysia
57 H4 Balinka Hungary
169 N4 Balinqiao Nei Mongol China see Bairin Qiao
57 K6 Baliint Romania
154 C2 Balintang Channel Phil.
26 I7 Balintore Argyll and Bute, Scotland U.K.
90 B3 Balira C.A.R.
169 □3 Balitondo C.A.R.
142 A2 Balíza Brazil
48 H3 Balje Ger.
186 E6 Baljurshi Saudi Arabia
44 I3 Balk Neth.
184 E7 Balkan Turkm.
Balkan Mountains Bulg./Yugo. see Stara Planina
Balkan Oblast admin. div. Turkm. see Balkanskaya Oblast'
184 I1 Balkanabat Turkm.
admin. div. Turkm.
57 K4 Balkány Hungary
183 M1 Balkashino Kazakh.
44 J3 Balk Neth.
185 L3 Balkh Afgh.
185 L3 Balkh prov. Afgh.
183 P4 Balkhash Kazakh.
Balkhash, Lake Kazakh. see Balkhash, Ozero
183 O5 Balkhash, Ozero l. Kazakh.
176 E3 Balki Andhra Prad. India
179 M7 Balkonda Andhra Prad. India
78 I2 Balladam Turkey
28 B5 Ballabeg Isle of Man
26 F9 Ballabio Italy
209 G12 Balladonia W.A. Austr.
205 L4 Balladoran N.S.W. Austr.
57 J1 Ballagan Point Rep. of Ireland
27 E5 Ballaghaderreen Rep. of Ireland
36 D6 Ballancourt-sur-Essonne France
39 M7 Ballan-Miré France
40 J4 Ballantrae South Ayrshire, Scotland U.K.
72 C8 Ballao Sardegna Italy
205 F10 Ballarat Vic. Austr.
209 F10 Ballard, Lake salt flat W.A. Austr.
176 F3 Ballarpur Mahar. India
28 H5 Ballasalla Isle of Man
26 J8 Ballater Aberdeenshire, Scotland U.K.
28 H5 Ballaugh Isle of Man
204 □1 Ball Bay Norfolk I.
88 C3 Ballé Mali
39 K6 Ballée France
144 C2 Ballena, Punta pt Chile
145 C9 Ballenero, Canal sea chan. Chile
213 K6 Balleny Islands Antarctica
39 J7 Ballerup Denmark
22 I6 Ballerup Denmark
179 J8 Ballesteros r. Phil.
28 C8 Ballibay Rep. of Ireland
27 E8 Ballina Mayo Rep. of Ireland
27 F5 Ballina N.S.W. Austr.
27 F5 Ballinadee Rep. of Ireland
27 F5 Ballinagar Rep. of Ireland
27 H5 Ballinagh Rep. of Ireland
27 G4 Ballinakill Rep. of Ireland
27 F4 Ballinalack Rep. of Ireland
27 F5 Ballinalee Rep. of Ireland
27 G4 Ballinamallard Northern Ireland U.K.
27 E5 Ballinamore Rep. of Ireland
27 F6 Ballinascarthy Rep. of Ireland
27 F6 Ballindery Rep. of Ireland
27 F5 Ballinderry r. Northern Ireland U.K.
27 G4 Ballindine Rep. of Ireland
27 E5 Ballindooly Rep. of Ireland
27 E5 Ballineen Rep. of Ireland
27 C8 Ballingarry Tipperary Rep. of Ireland
27 D9 Ballingarry Limerick Rep. of Ireland
27 C6 Ballingeary Rep. of Ireland
121 C6 Ballinger TX U.S.A.
27 G4 Ballinlough Rep. of Ireland
26 K9 Ballinluig Perth and Kinross, Scotland U.K.
27 E5 Ballinrobe Rep. of Ireland
27 B7 Ballinskelligs Rep. of Ireland
27 B7 Ballinskelligs Bay Rep. of Ireland
37 E9 Ballinsdale r. France
27 G4 Ballinspittle Rep. of Ireland
27 E5 Ballintober Rep. of Ireland
27 D4 Ballintoy Northern Ireland U.K.
27 E5 Ballintra Rep. of Ireland
27 E9 Ballinhassig Rep. of Ireland

Ballinlough to Bardaale
234

27 E5 Ballinlough Rep. of Ireland
26 I9 Ballinluig Perth and Kinross, Scotland U.K.
27 D5 Ballinrobe Rep. of Ireland
27 E7 Ballinruan Rep. of Ireland
27 B9 Ballinskelligs Rep. of Ireland
27 E9 Ballinspittle Rep. of Ireland
27 J2 Ballintoy Northern Ireland U.K.
26 J9 Ballintuim Perth and Kinross, Scotland U.K.
27 G7 Ballinure Rep. of Ireland
27 I5 Ballivor Rep. of Ireland
53 I4 Ballmertshofen Ger.
66 F4 Ballobar Spain
26 G11 Balloch West Dunbartonshire, Scotland U.K.
39 L5 Ballon France
28 D8 Ballon Rep. of Ireland
37 M8 Ballon d'Alsace mt. France
37 M8 Ballons des Vosges, Parc Naturel Régional des nature res. France
57 I5 Ballószög Hungary
39 I6 Ballots France
78 A2 Ballsh Albania
204 □2 Ball's Pyramid i. Lord Howe I. Austr.
49 K8 Ballstädt Ger.
117 L5 Ballston Spa NY U.S.A.
44 I2 Ballum Neth.
27 F3 Ballure Rep. of Ireland
118 D4 Bally PA U.S.A.
27 E8 Ballyagran Rep. of Ireland
27 I4 Ballybay Rep. of Ireland
27 G3 Ballybofey Rep. of Ireland
27 J5 Ballyboghil Rep. of Ireland
27 I2 Ballybogy Northern Ireland U.K.
27 J6 Ballybrack Dublin Rep. of Ireland
27 B9 Ballybrack Kerry Rep. of Ireland
27 G7 Ballybrophy Rep. of Ireland
27 C7 Ballybunnion Rep. of Ireland
27 G7 Ballycahill Rep. of Ireland
27 H7 Ballycallan Rep. of Ireland
27 J7 Ballycanew Rep. of Ireland
27 I7 Ballycarney Rep. of Ireland
27 D5 Ballycarra Rep. of Ireland
27 K3 Ballycarry Northern Ireland U.K.
27 D4 Ballycastle Rep. of Ireland
27 J2 Ballycastle Northern Ireland U.K.
27 K3 Ballyclare Northern Ireland U.K.
27 B6 Ballyconneely Rep. of Ireland
27 B6 Ballyconneely Bay Rep. of Ireland
27 G4 Ballyconnell Cavan Rep. of Ireland
27 E4 Ballyconnell Sligo Rep. of Ireland
27 G9 Ballycotton Bay Rep. of Ireland
27 C4 Ballycroy Rep. of Ireland
27 G6 Ballycumber Rep. of Ireland
27 F6 Ballydangan Rep. of Ireland
27 F6 Ballydavid Rep. of Ireland
27 B8 Ballydavid Head Rep. of Ireland
27 D9 Ballydehob Rep. of Ireland
27 D8 Ballydesmond Rep. of Ireland
27 F8 Ballyduff Rep. of Ireland
27 D5 Ballyfarnagh Rep. of Ireland
27 F4 Ballyfarnan Rep. of Ireland
27 F9 Ballyfeard Rep. of Ireland
28 C7 Ballyfin Rep. of Ireland
27 F6 Ballyforan Rep. of Ireland
27 H6 Ballyfore Rep. of Ireland
27 K3 Ballygalley Northern Ireland U.K.
27 F5 Ballygar Rep. of Ireland
27 J7 Ballygarrett Rep. of Ireland
27 H4 Ballygawley Northern Ireland U.K.
27 D5 Ballyglass Mayo Rep. of Ireland
27 E5 Ballyglass Mayo Rep. of Ireland
27 H2 Ballygorman Rep. of Ireland
27 K3 Ballygowan Northern Ireland U.K.
26 D11 Ballygrant Argyll and Bute, Scotland U.K.
27 I8 Ballyhack Rep. of Ireland
27 E8 Ballyhaght Rep. of Ireland
27 D7 Ballyhahill Rep. of Ireland
28 C5 Ballyhaise Rep. of Ireland
27 L4 Ballyhalbert Northern Ireland U.K.
27 E5 Ballyhaunis Rep. of Ireland
27 C8 Ballyheigue Rep. of Ireland
27 C8 Ballyheigue Bay Rep. of Ireland
27 F8 Ballyhooly Rep. of Ireland
27 K4 Ballyhornan Northern Ireland U.K.
27 E8 Ballyhoura Mountains hills Rep. of Ireland
27 H5 Ballyjamesduff Rep. of Ireland
27 G6 Ballykeeran Rep. of Ireland
27 H2 Ballykelly Northern Ireland U.K.
27 H6 Ballykilleen Rep. of Ireland
27 F8 Ballylanders Rep. of Ireland
27 F5 Ballyleague Rep. of Ireland
28 D5 Ballyleny Northern Ireland U.K.
27 H2 Ballyliffen Rep. of Ireland
27 D7 Ballylongford Rep. of Ireland
27 H7 Ballylynan Rep. of Ireland
27 G8 Ballymacarberry Rep. of Ireland
27 C8 Ballymacelligott Rep. of Ireland
27 H7 Ballymack Rep. of Ireland
28 C5 Ballymackilroy Northern Ireland U.K.
27 G8 Ballymacmague Rep. of Ireland
27 G9 Ballymacoda Rep. of Ireland
27 H3 Ballymagorry Northern Ireland U.K.
27 G5 Ballymahon Rep. of Ireland
27 D9 Ballymakeery Rep. of Ireland
27 K4 Ballymartin Northern Ireland U.K.
27 J3 Ballymena Northern Ireland U.K.
27 F5 Ballymoe Rep. of Ireland
27 I2 Ballymoney Northern Ireland U.K.
27 G2 Ballymore Donegal Rep. of Ireland
27 G6 Ballymore Westmeath Rep. of Ireland
27 E4 Ballymote Rep. of Ireland
27 I7 Ballymurphy Rep. of Ireland
27 F5 Ballymurry Rep. of Ireland
27 I8 Ballynabola Rep. of Ireland
27 D9 Ballynacarriga Rep. of Ireland
28 B6 Ballynacarrigy Rep. of Ireland
27 H5 Ballynafid Rep. of Ireland
27 C6 Ballynahinch Rep. of Ireland
27 K4 Ballynahinch Northern Ireland U.K.
27 G6 Ballynahowen Rep. of Ireland
27 B5 Ballynakill Bay Rep. of Ireland
27 E8 Ballynamona Rep. of Ireland
27 C8 Ballynaskreena Rep. of Ireland
27 E7 Ballyneety Rep. of Ireland
28 E7 Ballynockan Rep. of Ireland
27 F8 Ballynoe Rep. of Ireland
27 K3 Ballynure Northern Ireland U.K.
27 F8 Ballyporeen Rep. of Ireland
27 L4 Ballyquintin Point Northern Ireland U.K.
27 H7 Ballyragget Rep. of Ireland
27 H7 Ballyroan Rep. of Ireland
27 I3 Ballyronan Northern Ireland U.K.
27 C9 Ballyroon Rep. of Ireland
27 F3 Ballyshannon Rep. of Ireland
27 E7 Ballysteen Rep. of Ireland
27 I8 Ballyteige Bay Rep. of Ireland
27 I6 Ballytore Rep. of Ireland
27 D6 Ballyvaughan Rep. of Ireland
27 F6 Ballyvoneen Rep. of Ireland
27 J2 Ballyvoy Northern Ireland U.K.
27 G8 Ballyvoyle Rep. of Ireland
27 L3 Ballywalter Northern Ireland U.K.
28 E5 Ballyward Northern Ireland U.K.
27 I8 Ballywilliam Rep. of Ireland
26 E8 Balmacara Highland, Scotland U.K.
145 C7 Balmaceda Aisén Chile
138 C6 Balmaceda Antofagasta Chile
26 G10 Balmaha Stirling, Scotland U.K.
Balmartin Western Isles, Scotland U.K. see Baile Mhartainn
63 N2 Balmaseda Spain
57 K4 Balmazújváros Hungary
70 C5 Balme Italy
26 L8 Balmedie Aberdeenshire, Scotland U.K.
Balmer Rajasthan India see Barmer
107 M5 Balmertown Ont. Can.
70 D3 Balmhorn mt. Switz.
204 H7 Balmoral Vic. Austr.
203 G9 Balmoral South I. N.Z.
121 D10 Balmorhea TX U.S.A.
70 E4 Balmuccia Italy
26 F8 Balnacra Highland, Scotland U.K.
26 D10 Balnahard Argyll and Bute, Scotland U.K.
26 H7 Balnapaling Highland, Scotland U.K.
147 F2 Balnearia Arg.
66 E2 Balneario de Panticosa Huesca Spain
147 H6 Balneario Orense Arg.
147 G6 Balneario Oriente Arg.
155 C4 Baloa Sulawesi Indon.
70 E5 Balocco Italy
185 L7 Balochistan prov. Pak.
181 I4 Balochistan reg. Pak.
178 H9 Balod Chhattisgarh India
179 I8 Baloda Chhattisgarh India
178 I9 Baloda Bazar Chhattisgarh India
56 F4 Balogunyom Hungary
157 G6 Balok, Teluk b. Indon.
91 B8 Balombo Angola
205 L3 Balonne r. Qld Austr.
155 D2 Balontohe i. Indon.
36 H8 Balot France
57 I5 Balotaszállás Hungary
178 D7 Balotra Rajasthan India
191 D6 Balotu Turkey
16 D1 Baloty Belarus
50 E4 Balow Ger.
179 K7 Balpahari Reservoir India
183 R5 Balpyk Bi Kazakh.
Balqash Kazakh. see Balkhash
Balqash Köli l. Kazakh. see Balkhash, Ozero
26 H10 Balquhidder Stirling, Scotland U.K.
178 I6 Balrampur Uttar Prad. India
205 I6 Balranald N.S.W. Austr.
27 J5 Balrath Rep. of Ireland
27 J5 Balrothery Rep. of Ireland
77 M6 Balş Romania
67 C9 Balsa de Ves Spain
111 O3 Balsam Creek Ont. Can.
111 P5 Balsam Lake Ont. Can.
110 B4 Balsam Lake WI U.S.A.
67 C12 Balsa Pintada Spain
136 B6 Balsapuerto Peru
66 I4 Balsareny Spain
140 D3 Balsas Brazil
129 H7 Balsas Mex.
128 E8 Balsas r. Mex.
136 B6 Balsas Peru
140 D3 Balsas, Rio das r. Brazil
19 N9 Bal'shavik Belarus
67 D12 Balsicas Spain
73 L4 Balsorano Italy
23 N2 Bålsta Sweden
70 D1 Balsthal Switz.
26 □O1 Balta i. Scotland U.K.
16 I6 Balta Ukr.
77 K7 Balta Berilovac Srbija Serb. and Mont.
63 L5 Baltanás Spain
62 E5 Baltar Spain
147 I2 Baltasar Brum Uru.
14 J4 Baltasi Rus. Fed.
26 □O1 Baltasound Shetland, Scotland U.K.
182 B1 Baltay Rus. Fed.
16 G6 Bălţi Moldova
119 K1 Baltic CT U.S.A.
23 M6 Baltic Sea g. Europe
85 F2 Balţīm Egypt
27 D10 Baltimore Rep. of Ireland
95 F4 Baltimore S. Africa
118 B6 Baltimore MD U.S.A.
116 C9 Baltimore OH U.S.A.
118 B6 Baltimore City county MD U.S.A.
118 B6 Baltimore County county MD U.S.A.
118 B6 Baltimore Highlands MD U.S.A.
18 K5 Baltinava Latvia
27 I7 Baltinglass Rep. of Ireland
178 E2 Baltistan reg. Jammu and Kashmir
18 C7 Baltiysk Rus. Fed.
55 H1 Baltiyskaya Kosa spit Rus. Fed.
18 I7 Baltoji Vokė Lith.
178 F2 Baltoro Glacier Jammu and Kashmir
55 J4 Bałtów Pol.
48 D3 Baltrum Ger.
48 D3 Baltrum i. Ger.
128 A3 Baluarie r. Mex.
140 E4 Baluarte Brazil
121 G12 Baluarte, Arroyo watercourse TX U.S.A.
184 H7 Baluch Ab well Iran
Baluchistan reg. Pak. see Balochistan
157 J3 Balui r. Malaysia
179 J8 Balumath Jharkhand India
204 F5 Balumbah S.A. Austr.
156 C4 Balumundam Sumatera Indon.
18 J5 Balupe r. Latvia
157 J5 Baluran, Gunung mt. Indon.
157 K8 Baluran National Park Indon.
179 L7 Balurghat W. Bengal India
77 O3 Băluşeni Romania
154 E9 Balut i. Phil.
73 P6 Balvano Italy
20 M3 Balvatnet l. Norway
49 E8 Balve Ger.
18 K4 Balvi Latvia
79 I3 Balya Turkey
169 K1 Balyaga Rus. Fed.
183 Q6 Balykchy Kyrg.
182 D4 Balykshi Kazakh.
168 E1 Balyktyg-Khem r. Rus. Fed.
Balyqshy Kazakh. see Balykshi
75 □ Balzan Malta
136 B5 Balzar Ecuador
52 H7 Balzers Liechtenstein
184 H7 Bam Iran
184 G3 Bām Iran
170 F6 Bama Guangxi China
89 I4 Bama Nigeria
207 I1 Bamaga Qld Austr.
108 B3 Bamaji Lake Ont. Can.
88 D3 Bamako Mali
90 C3 Bamba r. C.A.R.
91 C6 Bamba Dem. Rep. Congo
88 E2 Bamba Mali
90 B5 Bambama Congo
136 B6 Bambamarca Peru
154 C3 Bambang Luzon Phil.
91 D9 Bambangando Angola
154 C9 Bambannan i. Phil.
90 D3 Bambari C.A.R.
91 C9 Bambe Angola
156 B3 Bambel Sumatera Indon.
29 L6 Bamber Bridge Lancashire, England U.K.
53 J2 Bamberg Ger.
115 G9 Bamberg SC U.S.A.
119 G5 Bamber Lake NJ U.S.A.
92 B2 Bambesi Eth.
88 A3 Bambey Senegal
90 E4 Bambili Dem. Rep. Congo
90 C4 Bambio C.A.R.
97 K7 Bamboesberg mts S. Africa
88 E4 Bamboi Ghana
208 F6 Bamboo Creek W.A. Austr.
88 E2 Bambou well Mali
88 C3 Bambouk reg. Mali
99 □1b Bambou Mountains hills Mauritius
99 □1b Bambous Mauritius
90 E3 Bambouti C.A.R.
92 B2 Bambudi Eth.
143 E4 Bambuí Brazil
157 K5 Bambulung Kalimantan Indon.
29 N2 Bamburgh Northumberland, England U.K.
170 A3 Bamda Xizang China
184 C6 Bāmdezh Iran
89 H5 Bamenda Cameroon
89 H5 Bamendjing, Lac de l. Cameroon
106 E5 Bamfield B.C. Can.
184 G2 Bami Turkm.
185 L4 Bāmīān Afgh.
185 L4 Bāmīān prov. Afgh.
169 S5 Bamiancheng Liaoning China
90 D3 Bamingui C.A.R.
90 C2 Bamingui r. C.A.R.
90 D2 Bamingui-Bangoran pref. C.A.R.
90 C2 Bamingui-Bangoran, Parc National du nat. park C.A.R.
185 M4 Bamiyan r. Afgh.
155 G4 Bamkeri Papua Indon.
52 F3 Bammental Ger.
89 H3 Bammo well Niger
159 G8 Bâmnak Cambodia
158 E7 Bamnet Narong Thai.
126 E5 Bamoa Mex.
178 G6 Bamor Madh. Prad. India
178 G8 Bamori Madh. Prad. India
185 J8 Bam Posht reg. Iran
185 J8 Bam Posht, Kūh-e mts Iran
30 F6 Bampton Devon, England U.K.
31 I4 Bampton Oxfordshire, England U.K.
184 I8 Bampūr Iran
184 H8 Bampūr watercourse Iran
184 I5 Bamrūd Iran
Bamy Turkm. see Bami
206 D3 Bamyili N.T. Austr.
88 E3 Ban Burkina
57 G4 Bana Hungary
186 G9 Bana, Wādī watercourse Yemen
199 G2 Banaba i. Kiribati
140 F3 Banabuiu, Açude resr Brazil
146 D5 Bañados del Atuel marsh Arg.
139 E4 Bañados del Izozog swamp Bol.
139 F4 Bañados de Otuquis marsh Bol.
154 C4 Banahao, Mount vol. Luzon Phil.
90 E4 Banalia Dem. Rep. Congo
88 D3 Banamba Mali
126 D3 Banámichi Mex.
170 F4 Banan Chongqing China
207 M8 Banana Qld Austr.
88 B4 Banana Islands Sierra Leone
140 C4 Bananal, Ilha do i. Brazil
177 M9 Bananga Andaman & Nicobar Is India
88 C4 Banankoro Guinea
177 I3 Banapur Orissa India
72 B6 Banari Sardegna Italy
79 I1 Banarlı Turkey
178 F7 Banas r. India
85 G4 Banās, Ra's pt Egypt
41 C8 Banassac France
76 J5 Banatski Karlovac Vojvodina, Srbija Serb. and Mont.
57 J5 Banatsko Aranđelovo Vojvodina, Srbija Serb. and Mont.
57 J6 Banatsko Veliko Selo Vojvodina, Srbija Serb. and Mont.
155 A7 Banawaya i. Indon.
79 K4 Banaz Turkey
79 K4 Banaz r. Turkey
158 F5 Ban Ban Laos
173 L11 Banbar Xizang China
170 C9 Ban Bo Laos
27 J4 Banbridge Northern Ireland U.K.
158 E7 Ban Bua Chum Thai.
158 F7 Ban Bua Yai Thai.
158 H7 Ban Bungxai Laos
31 J3 Banbury Oxfordshire, England U.K.
43 B9 Banca France
77 P4 Banca Romania
158 F4 Ban Cang Vietnam
86 A5 Banc d'Arguin, Parc National du nat. park Maur.
158 F6 Ban Chiang tourist site Thai.
26 L8 Banchory Aberdeenshire, Scotland U.K.
154 B8 Bancoran i. Phil.
108 E4 Bancroft Ont. Can.
Bancroft Zambia see Chililabombwe
184 G5 Band Iran
89 I4 Banda Cameroon
91 A5 Banda Congo
90 E3 Banda Dem. Rep. Congo
178 G7 Banda Madh. Prad. India
178 H7 Banda Uttar Prad. India
155 F6 Banda, Kepulauan is Maluku Indon.
155 G6 Banda, Laut sea Indon.
156 A2 Banda Aceh Sumatera Indon.
205 N4 Banda Banda, Mount N.S.W. Austr.
185 N5 Banda Daud Shah Pak.
156 B3 Bandahara, Gunung mt. Indon.
164 Q9 Bandai-Asahi National Park Japan
22 E2 Bandak l. Norway
88 D5 Bandama r. Côte d'Ivoire
88 D4 Bandama Blanc r. Côte d'Ivoire
184 I6 Bandān Iran
155 F6 Bandaneira Maluku Indon.
184 I6 Bandān Kūh mts Iran
95 G3 Bandar Moz.
Bandar Abbas Iran see Bandar-e 'Abbās
156 F7 Bandaragung Sumatera Indon.
176 G9 Bandarawela Sri Lanka
179 N8 Bandarban Bangl.
184 G8 Bandar-e 'Abbās Iran
184 C3 Bandar-e Anzalī Iran
184 F8 Bandar-e Chārak Iran
184 D6 Bandar-e Deylam Iran
184 C6 Bandar-e Emām Khomeynī Iran
184 F8 Bandar-e Lengeh Iran
184 E8 Bandar-e Maqām Iran
184 C6 Bandar-e Ma'shur Iran
184 F8 Bandar-e Moghūyeh Iran
Bandar-e Pahlavī Iran see Bandar-e Anzalī
184 D7 Bandar-e Rīg Iran
Bandar-e Shāh Iran see Bandar-e Torkeman
Bandar-e Shāhpūr Iran see Bandar-e Emām Khomeynī
184 E8 Bandar-e Shīū' Iran
184 E3 Bandar-e Torkeman Iran
156 F7 Bandar Lampung Sumatera Indon.
92 F2 Bandar Murcaayo Somalia
178 G4 Bandarpunch mt. Uttaranchal India
157 K2 Bandar Seri Begawan Brunei
92 E2 Bandar Wanaag Somalia
Banda Sea Indon. see Banda, Laut
62 E4 Bande Spain
185 L3 Band-e Amīr, Daryā-ye r. Afgh.
143 G1 Bandeira Brazil
140 C5 Bandeirante Brazil
142 B5 Bandeirantes Brazil
98 □1c Bandeiras Pico Azores
143 G4 Bandeiras, Pico de mt. Brazil
50 D4 Bandenitz Ger.
144 E3 Bandera Arg.
121 F11 Bandera TX U.S.A.
147 F4 Banderaló Arg.
126 G2 Banderas Mex.
128 B5 Banderas, Bahía de b. Mex.
129 K6 Banderilla Mex.
184 F4 Band-e Sar Qom Iran
179 J8 Bandgaon Jharkhand India
185 M8 Bandhi Pak.
178 H8 Bandhogarh Madh. Prad. India
48 L1 Bandholm Denmark
178 D7 Bandi r. Rajasthan India
178 E6 Bandi r. Rajasthan India
176 G3 Bandia r. India
88 E3 Bandiagara Mali
88 E3 Bandiagara, Falaise de esc. Mali
185 K7 Band-i-Khan Jahan Pak.
178 F6 Bandikui Rajasthan India
184 H9 Bandīnī Iran
178 E2 Bandipur Jammu and Kashmir
179 J6 Bandipur Nepal
176 E7 Bandipur National Park India
79 I2 Bandırma Turkey
Bandjarmasin Kalimantan Indon. see Banjarmasin
76 H7 Bandjer pass Serb. and Mont.
41 H10 Bandol France
27 E9 Bandon Rep. of Ireland
27 E9 Bandon r. Rep. of Ireland
122 B5 Bandon OR U.S.A.
159 D10 Ban Don, Ao b. Thai.
175 □1 Bandos i. N. Male Maldives
191 K6 Bändovan Burnu pt Azer.
184 C6 Band Qīr Iran
176 C3 Bandra Mahar. India
99 □3b Bandraboua Mayotte
99 □3b Bandrélé Mayotte
95 G3 Bandua Moz.
95 G3 Bandula Moz.
91 C5 Bandundu Dem. Rep. Congo
91 C6 Bandundu prov. Dem. Rep. Congo
157 G8 Bandung Jawa Indon.
209 G10 Bandya W.A. Austr.
77 P6 Băneasa Constanţa Romania
77 O6 Băneasa Giurgiu Romania
184 A4 Bāneh Iran
155 F3 Banemo Halmahera Indon.
178 E7 Banera Rajasthan India
130 F3 Banes Cuba
88 C4 Banfèlè Guinea
106 H5 Banff Alta Can.
26 K7 Banff Aberdeenshire, Scotland U.K.
106 G5 Banff National Park Alta Can.
88 D4 Banfora Burkina
90 B3 Bang C.A.R.
157 J4 Bang, Gunung mt. Indon.
91 B7 Banga Angola
91 D6 Banga Dem. Rep. Congo
154 E8 Banga Mindanao Phil.
154 E8 Banga r. Mindanao Phil.
90 E3 Bangadi Dem. Rep. Congo
154 F8 Bangai Point Mindanao Phil.
207 J7 Bangall Creek watercourse Qld Austr.
176 E6 Bangalore Karnataka India
205 N3 Bangalow N.S.W. Austr.
90 D3 Bangana C.A.R.
176 F5 Banganapalle Andhra Prad. India
178 G6 Banganga r. India
89 H5 Bangangté Cameroon
179 L8 Bangaon W. Bengal India
157 K2 Bangar Brunei
154 C3 Bangar Luzon Phil.
179 L9 Bangara r. Bangl.
176 F6 Bangarapet Karnataka India
90 D3 Bangassou C.A.R.
90 C3 Bangba C.A.R.
173 E9 Bangdag Co salt l. China
158 G6 Bangfai, Xé r. Laos
155 C4 Banggai Sulawesi Indon.
155 C4 Banggai i. Indon.
155 C4 Banggai, Kepulauan is Indon.
152 F7 Banggai, Kepulauan is Indon.
157 L1 Banggi i. Malaysia
84 D1 Banghāzī Libya
158 G6 Banghiang, Xé r. Laos
157 J8 Bangil Jawa Indon.
156 G6 Bangka i. Indon.
155 D3 Bangka i. Indon.
156 F6 Bangka, Selat sea chan. Indon.
155 D2 Bangka, Selat sea chan. Indon.
156 G6 Bangka-Belitung prov. Indon.
157 J6 Bangkal Kalimantan Indon.
155 A6 Bangkala, Teluk b. Indon.
157 J8 Bangkalan Jawa Indon.
155 C4 Bangkalan i. Indon.
156 B3 Bangkaru i. Indon.
156 D4 Bangkinang Sumatera Indon.
155 B3 Bangkir Sulawesi Indon.
156 E6 Bangko Sumatera Indon.
173 I11 Bangkog Co salt l. China
159 E8 Bangkok Thai.
159 E8 Bangkok, Bight of b. Thai.
173 H11 Bangkor Xizang China
157 K6 Bangkuang Kalimantan Indon.
155 C4 Bangkulu i. Indon.
157 M9 Bangkulua Sumbawa Indon.
179 L8 Bangladesh country Asia
156 D1 Bang Lang Reservoir Thai.
168 I9 Bangluo Gansu China
170 B7 Bangma Shan mts Yunnan China
158 E6 Bang Mun Nak Thai.
20 M4 Bångnäs Sweden
159 I9 Ba Ngoi Vietnam
88 D5 Bangolo Côte d'Ivoire
178 G3 Bangong Co salt l. China/Jammu and Kashmir
30 D1 Bangor Gwynedd, Wales U.K.
27 K3 Bangor Northern Ireland U.K.
117 □Q4 Bangor ME U.S.A.
110 H7 Bangor MI U.S.A.
118 E3 Bangor PA U.S.A.
90 D2 Bangoran C.A.R.
179 K8 Bangriposi Orissa India
125 S5 Bangs, Mount AZ U.S.A.
157 L5 Bangsalsepulun Kalimantan Indon.
159 D9 Bang Saphan Yai Thai.
20 K4 Bangsund Norway
90 C5 Bangu Équateur Dem. Rep. Congo
91 D7 Bangu Katanga Dem. Rep. Congo
154 C3 Bangued Luzon Phil.
90 C3 Bangui C.A.R.
154 C2 Bangui Luzon Phil.
90 C4 Bangui-Motaba Congo
93 B8 Bangula Malawi
156 C3 Bangunpurba Sumatera Indon.
90 E4 Banguru Dem. Rep. Congo
91 F7 Bangweulu, Lake Zambia
85 F2 Banhā Egypt
31 O3 Banham Norfolk, England U.K.
95 G4 Banhine, Parque Nacional de nat. park Moz.
158 F5 Ban Hin Heup Laos
158 E5 Ban Huai Khon Thai.
159 D9 Ban Huai Yang Thai.
89 E3 Bani Burkina
90 D3 Bani C.A.R.
130 H4 Baní Dom. Rep.
88 D3 Bani r. Mali
154 B3 Bani Luzon Phil.
86 C3 Bani, Jbel ridge Morocco
90 C3 Bania C.A.R.
188 H9 Bani Atiyah reg. Saudi Arabia
89 F3 Bani-Bangou Niger
130 H4 Bánica Dom. Rep.
54 C2 Banie Pol.
55 K1 Banie Mazurskie Pol.
88 D3 Banifing r. Mali
88 D3 Banifing r. Mali
184 F8 Banī Forūr, Jazīreh-ye i. Iran
178 E3 Banihal Pass and Tunnel Jammu and Kashmir
186 E6 Banī'Īsá Saudi Arabia
186 G6 Banī Khaţmah reg. Saudi Arabia
186 G6 Banī Khurb hills Saudi Arabia
89 F4 Banikoara Benin
186 G6 Banī Ma'āriḍ des. Saudi Arabia
186 F6 Banī Mālik Saudi Arabia
85 F2 Banī Mazār Egypt
187 I5 Banī Mukassir des. Saudi Arabia
154 B4 Bani Point Luzon Phil.
57 L4 Bănişor Romania
116 G12 Banister r. VA U.S.A.
85 F2 Banī Suwayf Egypt
188 D9 Banī Suwayf governorate Egypt
77 N9 Banite Bulg.
186 F6 Banī Thawr Saudi Arabia
77 L7 Banitsa Bulg.
187 I4 Banī Ţukhmān reg. Saudi Arabia
84 B2 Banī Walīd Libya
187 I3 Banī Wuţayfān well Saudi Arabia
190 D5 Bāniyās Al Qunayţirah Syria
190 D3 Bāniyās Ţarţūs Syria
187 L4 Bani Yas reg. U.A.E.
76 H7 Banja Srbija Serb. and Mont.
68 F3 Banja Luka Bos.-Herz.
178 F4 Banjar Hima. Prad. India
157 K6 Banjarbaru Kalimantan Indon.
157 K6 Banjarmasin Kalimantan Indon.
76 I10 Banjes, Liqeni i resr Albania
172 I5 Banjiegou Xinjiang China
169 O6 Banjieta Hebei China
59 I7 Banjšice plat. Slovenia
88 A3 Banjul Gambia
191 K6 Bankä Azer.
179 K7 Banka Bihar India
206 E5 Banka Banka N.T. Austr.
159 G7 Ban Kadian Laos
176 D5 Bankapur Karnataka India
88 E3 Bankass Mali
23 K4 Bankeryd Sweden
26 I9 Bankfoot Perth and Kinross, Scotland U.K.
159 E8 Ban Khai Thai.
159 D8 Ban Khao Yoi Thai.
159 D10 Ban Khok Kloi Thai.
179 J9 Banki Orissa India
89 F3 Bankilaré Niger
89 H5 Bankim Cameroon
97 O2 Bankkop S. Africa
88 C4 Banko, Massif de mt. Guinea
157 L7 Bankobankoang i. Indon.
176 C4 Bankol Mahar. India
88 C4 Bankon Guinea
106 D4 Banks Island B.C. Can.
104 F2 Banks Island N.W.T. Can.
200 □5 Banks Islands Vanuatu
107 M2 Banks Lake Nunavut Can.
122 E3 Banks Lake WA U.S.A.
203 H10 Banks Peninsula South I. N.Z.
205 L9 Banks Strait Tas. Austr.
179 K8 Bankura W. Bengal India
77 K8 Bankya Pernik Bulg.
77 L8 Bankya Sofiya-Grad Bulg.
159 F7 Ban Lamduan Thai.
170 G6 Banlan Guangxi China
158 D7 Ban Le Kathe Thai.
76 J5 Banloc Romania
158 C5 Ban Mae La Luang Thai.
158 D5 Ban Mae Mo Thai.
158 D5 Ban Mae Suya Thai.
158 B2 Banmauk Myanmar
170 C9 Ban Mouang Laos
27 I7 Bann r. Rep. of Ireland
27 I2 Bann r. Northern Ireland U.K.
158 G6 Ban Nakham Laos
38 D6 Bannalec France
158 G5 Ban Napè Laos
159 D10 Ban Na San Thai.
40 B2 Bannay France
130 E1 Bannerman Town Eleuthera Bahamas
116 E12 Bannertown NC U.S.A.
50 D2 Bannesdorf auf Fehmarn Ger.
124 P8 Banning CA U.S.A.
Banningville Dem. Rep. Congo see Bandundu
16 H8 Bannivka Ukr.
203 D12 Bannockburn South I. N.Z.
26 I10 Bannockburn Stirling, Scotland U.K.
158 C6 Ban Noi Myanmar
158 E4 Ban Nong Kha Laos
158 H7 Ban Nongmek Laos
27 I8 Bannow Rep. of Ireland
185 N5 Bannu Pak.
181 K3 Bannu admin. div. Pak.
62 G7 Bañobárez Spain
Bañolas Spain see Banyoles
41 H8 Banon France
128 E2 Bañón Mex.
66 C6 Bañón Spain
136 B5 Baños de Agua Santa Ecuador
146 B5 Baños de Copahue Arg.
65 L4 Baños de la Encina Spain
146 B1 Baños del Toro Chile
62 E4 Baños de Molgas Spain
62 I8 Baños de Montemayor Spain
138 C5 Baños de Puritama Chile
63 O4 Baños de Río Tobía Spain
63 M5 Baños de Valdearados Spain
146 B5 Baños Maule Chile
57 G3 Bánov Czech Rep.
57 H3 Bánov Slovakia
57 H3 Bánovce nad Bebravou Slovakia
68 G3 Banovići Bos.-Herz.
Banow Afgh. see Andarāb
158 E5 Ban Pak-Leng Laos
159 D9 Ban Pak Nam Thai.
158 G6 Ban Phaeng Thai.
158 F6 Ban Phai Thai.
158 D7 Banphot Phisai Thai.
158 D6 Ban Phran Katai Thai.
159 D8 Ban Pong Thai.
168 G7 Banqiao Gansu China
170 B6 Banqiao Yunnan China
170 E5 Banqiao Yunnan China
159 E11 Ban Sanam Chai Thai.
88 B3 Bansang Gambia
159 D9 Ban Sawi Thai.
179 I6 Bansgaon Uttar Prad. India
27 F8 Bansha Rep. of Ireland
179 K7 Bansi Bihar India
178 E7 Bansi Rajasthan India
178 G7 Bansi Uttar Prad. India
179 I6 Bansi Uttar Prad. India
179 L7 Bansihari W. Bengal India
57 I3 Banská Bystrica Slovakia
57 H3 Banská Štiavnica Slovakia
77 L9 Bansko Bulg.
57 I3 Banskobystrický Kraj admin. reg. Slovakia
179 K7 Bansloi r. India
184 I9 Bānsont Iran
31 L5 Banstead Surrey, England U.K.
158 D6 Ban Sut Ta Thai.
176 E3 Banswada Andhra Prad. India
178 E8 Banswara Rajasthan India
44 I3 Bant Neth.
155 A8 Banta i. Indon.
155 A6 Bantaeng Sulawesi Indon.
208 □2 Bantam Cocos Is
Bantam Jawa Indon. see Banten
119 I1 Bantam CT U.S.A.
119 I1 Bantam Lake CT U.S.A.
158 F5 Ban Taviang Laos
154 D6 Bantayan i. Phil.
89 F4 Bantè Benin
27 E8 Banteer Rep. of Ireland
156 G8 Banten Jawa Indon.
156 G8 Banten prov. Indon.
159 D10 Ban Tha Chang Thai.
159 D10 Ban Tha Kham Thai.
30 E7 Bantham Devon, England U.K.
158 C6 Ban Tha Song Yang Thai.
Banthat mts Cambodia see Cardamom Range
158 E7 Ban Tha Tako Thai.
158 D4 Ban Tha Ton Thai.
158 F7 Ban Tha Tum Thai.
159 E11 Ban Thepha Thai.
37 J5 Bantheville France
159 D8 Ban Thung Luang Thai.
158 H6 Ban Tôp Laos
27 D9 Bantry Rep. of Ireland
27 C9 Bantry Bay Rep. of Ireland
157 I8 Bantul Indon.
178 C9 Bantva Gujarat India
176 D6 Bantval Karnataka India
158 D6 Ban Wang Chao Thai.
158 G6 Ban Wang Ta Mua Thai.
30 G5 Banwell North Somerset, England U.K.
158 F5 Ban Woen Laos
158 H7 Ban Xepian Laos
156 B3 Banyak, Pulau-pulau is Indon.
67 K8 Banyalbufar Spain
159 D8 Ban Yang Yong Thai.
17 M2 Banychi Ukr.
67 D10 Banyeres de Mariola Spain
89 H5 Banyo Cameroon
66 K3 Banyoles Spain
156 F6 Banyuasin r. Indon.
43 K11 Banyuls-sur-Mer France
157 H8 Banyumas Jawa Indon.
157 K9 Banyuwangi Jawa Indon.
213 I2 Banzare Coast Antarctica
215 J8 Banzare Seamount sea feature Indian Ocean
Banzart Tunisia see Bizerte
73 Q6 Banzi Italy
50 E3 Banzkow Ger.
84 D5 Bao, Ouadi watercourse Chad
168 H9 Bao'an Qinghai China
84 D5 Bao Bilia well Chad
169 N6 Baochang Nei Mongol China
Baocheng Hainan China see Baoting
170 F2 Baocheng Shaanxi China
169 O7 Baodi Tianjin China
169 N7 Baoding Hebei China
171 I2 Baofeng Henan China
169 J9 Baoji Shaanxi China
169 J9 Baoji Shaanxi China
171 H3 Baokang Hubei China
169 R4 Baokang Nei Mongol China
158 G3 Bao Lac Vietnam
162 F6 Baolin Heilong. China
200 □6 Baolo Sta Isabel Solomon Is
159 H9 Bao Lôc Vietnam
162 H5 Baoqing Heilong. China
90 B3 Baoro C.A.R.
171 M3 Baoshan Shanghai China
170 B6 Baoshan Yunnan China
170 G9 Baoting Hainan China
169 L6 Baotou Nei Mongol China
163 F8 Baotou Shan mt. China/N. Korea
88 C3 Baoulé r. Mali
88 D3 Baoulé r. Mali
170 D3 Baoxing Sichuan China
170 D7 Baoxiu Yunnan China
171 L2 Baoying Jiangsu China
178 D6 Bap Rajasthan India
176 G5 Bapatla Andhra Prad. India
36 E3 Bapaume France
111 P4 Baptiste Lake Ont. Can.
186 F2 Baq'ā' oasis Saudi Arabia
184 E5 Baqam Iran
190 A7 Baqar, Maşrif Baḩr al canal Egypt
186 F4 Baqarah Saudi Arabia
173 K10 Baqên Xizang China
173 L11 Baqên Xizang China
171 J5 Baqiu Jiangxi China
186 E5 Baqrān Saudi Arabia
Baqty Kazakh. see Bakhty
189 L7 Ba'qūbah Iraq
37 I4 Bar r. France
169 J1 Bar Rus. Fed.
76 H8 Bar Crna Gora Serb. and Mont.
16 G4 Bar Ukr.
178 H7 Bara Uttar Prad. India
155 E5 Bara Buru Indon.
89 H4 Bara Nigeria
57 K6 Bara Romania
85 F6 Bara Sudan
90 E2 Bara well Sudan
92 E4 Baraawe Somalia
157 K6 Barabai Kalimantan Indon.
178 H6 Barabanki Uttar Prad. India
19 V7 Barabanovo Rus. Fed.
57 L3 Barabás Hungary
162 G6 Barabash-Levada Rus. Fed.
Barabhas Western Isles, Scotland U.K. see Barvas
179 K8 Barabhum W. Bengal India
192 I4 Barabinsk Rus. Fed.
110 E6 Baraboo WI U.S.A.
110 E6 Baraboo r. WI U.S.A.
88 E3 Baraboulé Burkina
16 J7 Baraboy r. Ukr.
Baracaldo País Vasco Spain see Barakaldo
130 F3 Baracoa Cuba
57 H5 Baracs Hungary
57 H4 Baracska Hungary
190 E5 Baradá, Nahr r. Syria
190 F3 Baradah Syria
147 H3 Baradero Arg.
205 L4 Baradine N.S.W. Austr.
205 L4 Baradine r. N.S.W. Austr.
110 F3 Baraga MI U.S.A.
77 P6 Bărăganului, Câmpia plain Romania
73 P6 Baragiano Italy
92 C4 Baragoi Kenya
136 D2 Baragua Venez.
136 D2 Baragua, Sierra de mts Venez.
130 H4 Barahona Dom. Rep.
63 O6 Barahona Spain
178 G4 Barahoti Uttaranchal India
179 N7 Barail Range mts India
88 E2 Bara Issa r. Mali
63 O8 Barajas de Melo Spain
76 I6 Barajevo Srbija Serb. and Mont.
185 N3 Barak Afgh.
179 N7 Barak r. India
85 H5 Baraka watercourse Eritrea/Sudan
63 O2 Barakaldo Spain
92 B1 Barakat Sudan
185 M5 Barakī Barak Afgh.
97 I8 Barakke S. Africa
179 J9 Barakot Orissa India
19 W7 Barakovo Rus. Fed.
183 L1 Barakpay Kazakh.
207 L8 Baralaba Qld Austr.
178 F3 Bara Lacha Pass Hima. Prad. India
191 E4 Baralet'i Georgia
62 F3 Baralla Spain
107 L3 Baralzon Lake Man. Can.
179 K8 Baram W. Bengal India
157 J2 Baram r. Malaysia
157 J2 Baram, Tanjung pt Malaysia
137 G3 Baramanni Guyana
176 D3 Baramati Mahar. India
207 M8 Barambah r. Qld Austr.
85 H5 Barameiya Sudan
178 E2 Baramulla Jammu and Kashmir
19 N7 Baran' Belarus
178 F7 Baran Rajasthan India
191 I6 Barān Iran
185 M9 Baran r. Pak.
184 I5 Bārān, Kūh-e mts Iran
63 Q3 Barañain Spain
18 J8 Baranavichy Belarus
63 O2 Baranbio Spain
57 K4 Báránd Hungary
73 N4 Baranello Italy
193 R3 Baranikha Rus. Fed.
85 G4 Baranīs Egypt
16 G3 Baranivka Ukr.
182 F4 Barankul Kazakh.
178 H7 Barannda Madh. Prad. India
130 F8 Baranoa Col.
73 L6 Barano d'Ischia Italy
106 C3 Baranof AK U.S.A.
104 E4 Baranof Island AK U.S.A.
Baranovichi Belarus see Baranavichy
182 B1 Baranovka Rus. Fed.
55 K4 Baranów Lubelskie Pol.
54 G4 Baranów Wielkopolskie Pol.
Baranowicze Belarus see Baranavichy
55 J2 Baranowo Pol.
55 J5 Baranów Sandomierska Pol.
18 K6 Barany Belarus
57 H5 Baranya county Hungary
57 H6 Baranyai-dombság hills Hungary
143 F3 Barão de Cocais Brazil
140 E3 Barão de Grajaú Brazil
139 G4 Barão de Melgaço Brazil
139 E2 Barão de Melgaco Brazil
64 B6 Barão de São Miguel Port.
77 N4 Baraolt Romania
88 D3 Baraouéli Mali
Baraqbay Kazakh. see Barakpay
45 I8 Baraque de Fraiture hill Belgium
43 I7 Baraqueville France
139 F1 Bararati r. Brazil
16 H3 Barashi Ukr.
66 F3 Barasona, Embalse de resr Spain
155 D7 Barat Daya, Kepulauan is Maluku Indon.
155 C8 Barati Timor Indon.
17 L7 Barativka Ukr.
204 G5 Baratta S.A. Austr.
137 F4 Barauaná, Serra mts Brazil
178 F5 Baraut Uttar Prad. India
18 L6 Baravukha Belarus
136 C4 Baraya Col.
143 F4 Barbacena Minas Gerais Brazil
137 H5 Barbacena Pará Brazil
64 E3 Barbacena Port.
136 E2 Barbacoas Venez.
62 E4 Barbadás Spain
63 N4 Barbadillo de Herreros Spain
63 N4 Barbadillo del Mercado Spain
63 N4 Barbadillo del Pez Spain
131 □4 Barbados country West Indies
72 C7 Barbagia mts Sardegna Italy
71 Q5 Barban Croatia
190 B9 Barbar, Jabal mt. Egypt
108 C3 Barbara Lake Ont. Can.
71 L5 Barbarano Vicentino Italy
129 J3 Barbarena r. Mex.
67 H10 Barbaria, Cap de c. Spain
71 P5 Barbariga, Rt pt Croatia
79 I2 Barbaros Turkey
43 E7 Barbaste France
66 F3 Barbastro Spain
71 R6 Barbat Croatia
64 H8 Barbate r. Spain
64 H8 Barbate, Embalse de resr Spain
64 H8 Barbate de Franco Spain
38 G8 Barbâtre France
43 F9 Barbazan France
43 E9 Barbazan-Debat France
126 F4 Barbechitos Mex.
18 H5 Bārbele Latvia
41 F9 Barbentane France
131 □10 Barber Curaçao Neth. Antilles
71 K7 Barberino di Mugello Italy
111 N1 Barber's Bay Ont. Can.
97 J2 Barberspan Nature Reserve S. Africa
124 □C12 Barbers Point HI U.S.A.
97 P1 Barberton S. Africa
116 D7 Barberton OH U.S.A.
42 D5 Barbezieux-St-Hilaire France
179 J7 Barbigha Bihar India
179 J8 Barbil Orissa India
36 E7 Barbizon France
29 L5 Barbon Cumbria, England U.K.
36 G6 Barbonne-Fayel France
136 C3 Barbosa Col.
43 D8 Barbotan-les-Thermes France
107 M2 Barbour Bay Nunavut Can.
118 B2 Barbours PA U.S.A.
116 B12 Barbourville KY U.S.A.
154 D6 Barboza Panay Phil.
131 □2 Barbuda i. Antigua and Barbuda
31 J3 Barby Northamptonshire, England U.K.
51 E7 Barby (Elbe) Ger.
77 L7 Bârca Romania
63 O6 Barca Spain
66 F3 Barcabo Spain
62 G6 Barca de Alva Port.
131 □9 Barcadera Aruba
207 J7 Barcaldine Qld Austr.
64 F3 Barcarrota Spain
77 J3 Barcău r. Romania
Barce Libya see Al Marj
62 C5 Barcelinhos Port.
75 I7 Barcellona Pozzo di Gotto Sicilia Italy
66 J5 Barcelona Spain
66 I4 Barcelona prov. Spain
137 E2 Barcelona Venez.
131 □1 Barceloneta Puerto Rico
43 D8 Barcelonne-du-Gers France
41 J8 Barcelonnette France
137 F5 Barcelos Brazil
62 C5 Barcelos Port.
62 G3 Bárcena, Embalse de resr Spain
62 G2 Bárcena del Monasterio Spain
63 L2 Bárcena de Pie de Concha Spain
63 M2 Barcenillas de Cerezos Spain
49 J9 Barchfeld Ger.
55 J1 Barciany Pol.
41 H8 Barcillonnette France
54 F3 Barcin Pol.
54 E1 Barcino Pol.
Barcino Spain see Barcelona
71 N3 Barcis Italy
118 D6 Barclay MD U.S.A.
88 C5 Barclayville Liberia
63 O6 Barcones Spain
207 I8 Barcoo watercourse Qld Austr.
Barcoo Creek watercourse Qld/S.A. Austr. see Cooper Creek
62 E6 Barcos Port.
56 G6 Barcs Hungary
57 G5 Barcsi Ősborókás park Hungary
43 C9 Barcus France
55 I2 Barczewo Pol.
40 E2 Bard, Montagne de hill France
191 I5 Bärdä Azer.
14 K4 Barda Rus. Fed.
92 E3 Bardaale Somalia

Barda del Medio to **Bay Canh, Hon**
235

146 C6 **Barda del Medio** Arg.
84 C4 **Bardai** Chad
20 □E1 **Bárðarbunga** mt. Iceland
146 C4 **Bardas Blancas** Arg.
184 G4 **Bardaskan** Iran
190 G7 **Bardawil, Khabrat al** salt pan Saudi Arabia
190 B7 **Bardawīl, Sabkhat al** lag. Egypt
179 K8 **Barddhaman** W. Bengal India
57 K2 **Bardejov** Slovakia
66 C3 **Bárdena** Spain
63 Q4 **Bárdenas Reales** reg. Spain
51 G6 **Bardenitz** Ger.
Bardera Somalia see **Baardheere**
208 G4 **Bardi** W.A. Austr.
178 I7 **Bardi** Madh. Prad. India
70 H6 **Bardi** Italy
70 E7 **Bardineto** Italy
29 Q7 **Bardney** Lincolnshire, England U.K.
54 E5 **Bardo** Pol.
71 J4 **Bardolino** Italy
70 B5 **Bardonecchia** Italy
43 B9 **Bardos** France
48 J4 **Bardowick** Ger.
29 K5 **Bardsea** Cumbria, England U.K.
30 C2 **Bardsey Island** Wales U.K.
30 C2 **Bardsey Sound** sea chan. Wales U.K.
184 D5 **Bard Shah** Iran
184 G7 **Bardsir** Iran
20 □G1 **Barðsneshorn** pt Iceland
114 E7 **Bardstown** KY U.S.A.
57 G5 **Bardudvarnok** Hungary
Barduli Italy see **Barletta**
121 K7 **Bardwell** KY U.S.A.
89 H5 **Baré** Cameroon
92 D3 **Barē** Eth.
203 B11 **Bare Cone** hill South I. N.Z.
43 E10 **Barèges** France
178 G5 **Bareilly** Uttar Prad. India
202 L6 **Bare Island** North I. N.Z.
178 G8 **Bareli** Madh. Prad. India
205 K6 **Barellan** N.S.W. Austr.
48 G5 **Barenburg** Ger.
48 K4 **Barendorf** Ger.
179 M7 **Barengapara** Meghalaya India
51 K7 **Bärenklau** Ger.
51 H10 **Bärenstein** Sachsen Ger.
51 I9 **Bärenstein** Sachsen Ger.
36 A4 **Barentin** France
39 J4 **Barenton** France
20 □ **Barentsburg** Svalbard
Barents Island Svalbard see **Barentsøya**
20 □ **Barentsøya** i. Svalbard
218 C1 **Barents Sea** Arctic Ocean
85 H6 **Barentu** Eritrea
157 K3 **Bareo** Sarawak Malaysia
118 C4 **Bareville** PA U.S.A.
38 I2 **Barfleur** France
38 I2 **Barfleur, Pointe de** pt France
173 E11 **Barga** Xizang China
70 I7 **Barga** Italy
92 F2 **Bargaal** Somalia
70 G7 **Bargagli** Italy
184 G8 **Bārgāh** Iran
118 F6 **Bargaintown** NJ U.S.A.
207 N8 **Bargara** Qld Austr.
179 I9 **Bargarh** Orissa India
63 L9 **Bargas** Spain
92 C3 **Bargē** Eth.
70 C6 **Barge** Italy
41 J9 **Bargemon** France
70 F1 **Bargen** Switz.
48 H2 **Bargenstedt** Ger.
70 I4 **Barghe** Italy
178 G8 **Bargi** Madh. Prad. India
50 I3 **Bargischow** Ger.
55 K2 **Bargłów Kościelny** Pol.
30 F4 **Bargoed** Caerphilly, Wales U.K.
26 G12 **Bargrennan** Dumfries and Galloway, Scotland U.K.
48 H4 **Bargstedt** Ger.
48 J3 **Bargteheide** Ger.
43 F7 **Barguelonne** r. France
179 M8 **Barguna** Bangl.
176 E7 **Bargur** Tamil Nadu India
191 H6 **Bārgūşad** r. Azer.
90 E3 **Barh** C.A.R.
179 J7 **Barh** Bihar India
179 I7 **Barhaj** Uttar Prad. India
179 I6 **Barhalganj** Uttar Prad. India
205 J6 **Barham** N.S.W. Austr.
31 O5 **Barham** Kent, England U.K.
117 □Q4 **Bar Harbor** ME U.S.A.
179 K7 **Barharwa** Jharkhand India
31 M3 **Bar Hill** Cambridgeshire, England U.K.
90 C4 **Bari** Dem. Rep. Congo
178 F6 **Bari** Rajasthan India
75 L1 **Bari** Italy
73 R6 **Bari** prov. Italy
92 F2 **Bari** admin. reg. Somalia
159 H9 **Ba Ria** Vietnam
93 B5 **Bariadi** Tanz.
186 C3 **Barīdī, Ra's** hd Saudi Arabia
185 O6 **Bari Doab** lowland Pak.
187 M5 **Barik** Oman
87 G2 **Barika** Alg.
185 N4 **Barikot** Afgh.
178 I5 **Barikot** Nepal
73 P6 **Barile** Italy
186 F9 **Barīm** i. Yemen
137 G2 **Barima** r. Guyana
67 C11 **Barinas** Spain
136 D2 **Barinas** Venez.
136 D2 **Barinas** state Venez.
110 B9 **Baring** MO U.S.A.
90 D4 **Baringa** Dem. Rep. Congo
92 C4 **Baringo, Lake** Kenya
179 K9 **Baripada** Orissa India
142 C5 **Bariri** Brazil
85 F3 **Bārīs** Egypt
178 E7 **Bari Sadri** Rajasthan India
191 F3 **Barisakho** Georgia
179 M8 **Barisal** Bangl.
179 M8 **Barisal** admin. div. Bangl.
156 D5 **Barisan, Pegunungan** mts Indon.
72 D8 **Bari Sardo** Sardegna Italy
73 L3 **Barisciano** Italy
157 K6 **Barito** r. Indon.
144 D1 **Baritú, Parque Nacional** nat. park Arg.
Barium Italy see **Bari**
41 E8 **Barjac** France
41 I9 **Barjaude, Montagne de** mt. France
41 I9 **Barjols** France
179 K8 **Barjora** W. Bengal India
84 B3 **Barjūj, Wādī** watercourse Libya
186 C7 **Barka** prov. Eritrea
187 M4 **Barkā** Oman
179 N8 **Barkal** Bangl.
170 D3 **Barkam** Sichuan China
184 C6 **Barkan, Ra's-e** pt Iran
18 J5 **Barkava** Latvia
48 I1 **Barkelsby** Ger.
147 H5 **Barker** Arg.
209 F11 **Barker, Lake** salt flat W.A. Austr.
106 F4 **Barkerville** B.C. Can.
88 B2 **Barkéwol el Abiod** Maur.
185 M7 **Barkhan** Pak.
178 F8 **Barkhera** Madh. Prad. India
179 J7 **Barki Saraiya** Jharkhand India
111 Q4 **Bark Lake** Ont. Can.
114 D7 **Barkley, Lake** KY U.S.A.
106 E5 **Barkley Sound** inlet B.C. Can.
206 G6 **Barkly Downs** Qld Austr.
97 L6 **Barkly East** S. Africa
97 L7 **Barkly Pass** S. Africa
206 E5 **Barkly Tableland** reg. N.T. Austr.
96 I4 **Barkly West** S. Africa
168 C5 **Barkol** Xinjiang China
168 C5 **Barkol Hu** salt l. Xinjiang China
178 G4 **Barkot** Uttaranchal India
54 F2 **Barkowo** Pol.
31 M3 **Barkway** Hertfordshire, England U.K.
79 L4 **Barla** Turkey
77 P4 **Bârlad** Romania
77 P4 **Bârladului, Podişul** plat. Romania
168 C4 **Barlag Gol** watercourse Mongolia
30 H2 **Barlaston** Staffordshire, England U.K.
29 O7 **Barlborough** Derbyshire, England U.K.
30 E5 **Barle** r. England U.K.
51 E6 **Barleben** Ger.
37 J6 **Bar-le-Duc** France
209 E10 **Barlee, Lake** salt flat W.A. Austr.
209 C7 **Barlee Range** hills W.A. Austr.
209 C7 **Barlee Range Nature Reserve** W.A. Austr.
41 I8 **Barles** France
73 Q5 **Barletta** Italy
31 M3 **Barley** Hertfordshire, England U.K.
36 E3 **Barlin** France
50 L5 **Barlinecko-Gorzowski Park Krajobrazowy** Pol.
54 D3 **Barlinek** Pol.
88 B4 **Barlo Point** Sierra Leone
22 D10 **Barlovento** La Palma Canary Is
106 B2 **Barlow** YT Can.
107 K2 **Barlow Lake** N.W.T. Can.
17 L6 **Barmashove** Ukr.
205 K6 **Barmedman** N.S.W. Austr.
178 C7 **Barmer** Rajasthan India
204 H6 **Barmera** S.A. Austr.
189 O8 **Barm Fīrūz, Kūh-e** mt. Iran
30 D2 **Barmouth** Gwynedd, Wales U.K.
30 D2 **Barmouth Bay** Wales U.K.
48 I3 **Barmstedt** Ger.
27 D6 **Barna** Rep. of Ireland
57 L6 **Bârna** Romania
178 E8 **Barnagar** Madh. Prad. India
178 E4 **Barnala** Punjab India
106 B3 **Barnard, Mount** Can./U.S.A.
29 N4 **Barnard Castle** Durham, England U.K.
205 J4 **Barnato** N.S.W. Austr.
27 C4 **Barnatra** Rep. of Ireland
53 M2 **Bärnau** Ger.
160 D1 **Barnaul** Rus. Fed.
59 L5 **Barnbach** Austria
119 G5 **Barnegat** NJ U.S.A.
119 G5 **Barnegat Bay** NJ U.S.A.
119 G5 **Barnegat Beach** NJ U.S.A.
119 G5 **Barnegat Light** NJ U.S.A.
213 K1 **Barne Inlet** Antarctica
204 J7 **Barnes** N.S.W. Austr.
116 G8 **Barnesboro** PA U.S.A.
105 K2 **Barnes Icecap** Nunavut Can.
115 F9 **Barnesville** GA U.S.A.
120 G2 **Barnesville** MN U.S.A.
116 D9 **Barnesville** OH U.S.A.
31 L4 **Barnet** Greater London, England U.K.
117 M4 **Barnet** VT U.S.A.
44 I4 **Barneveld** Neth.
38 H3 **Barneville-Carteret** France
50 G5 **Barnewitz** Ger.
27 E5 **Barneycarroll** Rep. of Ireland
205 J5 **Barneys Lake** imp. l. N.S.W. Austr.
125 U4 **Barney Top** mt. UT U.S.A.
121 E10 **Barnhart** TX U.S.A.
50 H5 **Barnim** reg. Ger.
31 N3 **Barningham** Suffolk, England U.K.
206 D3 **Barnjarn Aboriginal Land** res. N.T. Austr.
98 □2b **Barn Long Point** St Helena
27 J4 **Barnmeen** Northern Ireland U.K.
29 M6 **Barnoldswick** Lancashire, England U.K.
77 P3 **Bârnova, Dealul** hill Romania
54 C3 **Barnówko** Pol.
121 G7 **Barnsdall** OK U.S.A.
29 O6 **Barnsley** South Yorkshire, England U.K.
117 O7 **Barnstable** MA U.S.A.
51 E8 **Barnstädt** Ger.
30 D5 **Barnstaple** Devon, England U.K.
30 D5 **Barnstaple Bay** England U.K.
48 G5 **Barnstorf** Ger.
29 L7 **Barnton** Cheshire, England U.K.
49 H7 **Barntrup** Ger.
154 □ **Barnum Bay** Palau
115 G9 **Barnwell** SC U.S.A.
89 G4 **Baro** Nigeria
Baroda Gujarat India see **Vadodara**
178 F7 **Baroda** Madh. Prad. India
97 J7 **Baroda** S. Africa
96 I9 **Baroe** S. Africa
59 K6 **Bärofen** mt. Austria
185 O3 **Baroghil Pass** Afgh.
178 H7 **Baronda** Madh. Prad. India
70 E4 **Barone, Monte** mt. Italy
170 B3 **Barong** Sichuan China
72 D7 **Baronia** reg. Sardegna Italy
19 P8 **Baron'ki** Belarus
41 G8 **Baronnies** reg. France
209 I8 **Barons Range** hills W.A. Austr.
37 M6 **Baronville** France
200 □6 **Barora Fa** i. Solomon Is
200 □6 **Barora Ite** i. Solomon Is
90 E3 **Barou** C.A.R.
92 B2 **Barou Wenz** r. Eth.
18 K6 **Barowka** Belarus
179 N6 **Barpathar** Assam India
179 M6 **Barpeta** Assam India
Bar Pla Soi Thai. see **Chon Buri**
187 I3 **Barqā ad Dumrān** esc. Saudi Arabia
186 G7 **Barqā al Ashqar** reg. Yemen
190 E10 **Barqā Damaj** well Saudi Arabia
190 C10 **Barqah, Jabal** mt. Egypt
67 C12 **Barqueros** Spain
110 H4 **Barques, Point Aux** MI U.S.A.
111 L5 **Barques, Point Aux** MI U.S.A.
64 C2 **Barquinha** Port.
136 D2 **Barquisimeto** Venez.
37 N7 **Barr** France
26 G12 **Barr** South Ayrshire, Scotland U.K.
140 E4 **Barra** Brazil
26 A9 **Barra** i. Scotland U.K.
26 B8 **Barra, Sound of** sea chan. Scotland U.K.
205 M4 **Barraba** N.S.W. Austr.
142 C5 **Barra Bonita** Brazil
142 C5 **Barra Bonita, Represa** resr Brazil
137 H5 **Barraca da Boca** Brazil
139 F2 **Barracão do Barreto** Brazil
67 D7 **Barracas** Spain
66 C6 **Barrachina** Spain
116 E9 **Barrackville** WV U.S.A.
96 F10 **Barracouta, Cape** S. Africa
140 E5 **Barra da Estiva** Brazil
129 J5 **Barra de Cazones** Mex.
128 C6 **Barra de Navidad** Mex.
142 D6 **Barra de Santos** inlet Brazil
143 G3 **Barra de São Francisco** Brazil
143 G5 **Barra de São João** Brazil
139 F3 **Barra do Bugres** Brazil
140 D3 **Barra do Corda** Brazil
91 B7 **Barra do Cuanza** Angola
143 G3 **Barra do Cuieté** Brazil
142 A1 **Barra do Garças** Brazil
140 E4 **Barrado Mendes** Brazil
143 F5 **Barra do Piraí** Brazil
147 I2 **Barra do Quaraí** Brazil
139 F1 **Barra do São Manuel** Brazil
142 C6 **Barra do Turvo** Brazil
142 D6 **Barra do Una** Brazil
95 G4 **Barra Falsa, Ponta da** pt Moz.
74 G9 **Barrafranca** Sicilia Italy
Barraigh i. Scotland U.K. see **Barra**
126 □R10 **Barra Kruta** Hond.
62 D4 **Barral** Spain
72 C9 **Barrali** Sardegna Italy
143 F4 **Barra Longa** Brazil
143 E5 **Barra Mansa** Brazil
85 G3 **Barrāmīyah** Egypt
43 E8 **Barran** France
185 O6 **Barrana** Pak.
138 A2 **Barranca** Peru
136 C2 **Barranca** Venez.
136 C3 **Barrancabermeja** Col.
126 F4 **Barranca del Cobre, Parque Natural** nature res. Mex.
146 C5 **Barrancas** Neuquén Arg.
147 G3 **Barrancas** Santa Fé Arg.
146 C5 **Barrancas** r. Arg.
147 H2 **Barrancas** r. Arg.
130 G8 **Barrancas** Col.
136 D2 **Barrancas** Barinas Venez.
137 F2 **Barrancas** Monagas Venez.
136 C2 **Barranco de Loba** Col.
98 □3a **Barranco de Santiago** La Gomera Canary Is
64 D6 **Barranco do Velho** Port.
64 F4 **Barrancos** Port.
65 P4 **Barranda** Spain
129 J5 **Barra Norte** Mex.
136 C2 **Barranquilla** Atlántico Col.
136 C4 **Barranquilla** Guaviare Col.
136 B6 **Barranquita** Peru
131 □1 **Barranquitas** Puerto Rico
136 C2 **Barranquitas** Venez.
26 C10 **Barrapoll** Argyll and Bute, Scotland U.K.
140 E3 **Barras** Brazil
111 Q1 **Barraute** Que. Can.
65 O2 **Barrax** Spain
117 M6 **Barre** MA U.S.A.
117 M4 **Barre** VT U.S.A.
73 L4 **Barrea, Lago di** l. Italy
146 C2 **Barreal** Arg.
41 D8 **Barre-des-Cévennes** France
41 I7 **Barre des Ecrins** mt. France
140 D5 **Barreiras** Brazil
137 G5 **Barreirinha** Brazil
140 E2 **Barreirinhas** Brazil
141 B5 **Barreiro** r. Brazil
64 A3 **Barreiro** Port.
140 C4 **Barreiro do Nascimento** Brazil
140 G4 **Barreiros** Brazil
41 I9 **Barrême** France
177 M6 **Barren Island** Andaman & Nicobar Is India
104 C4 **Barren Islands** AK U.S.A.
142 C4 **Barretos** Brazil
124 P9 **Barrett, Lake** CA U.S.A.
208 I5 **Barrett, Mount** hill W.A. Austr.
106 H4 **Barrhead** Alta Can.
26 H11 **Barrhead** East Renfrewshire, Scotland U.K.
203 F10 **Barrhill** South I. N.Z.
26 G12 **Barrhill** South Ayrshire, Scotland U.K.
186 F7 **Barri** i. Saudi Arabia
66 J4 **Barriada Nueva** Spain
108 E4 **Barrie** Ont. Can.
62 C3 **Barrié de la Maza, Encoro de** resr Spain
111 L4 **Barrie Island** Ont. Can.
202 J3 **Barrier, Cape** North I. N.Z.
213 F2 **Barrier Bay** Antarctica
106 F5 **Barrière** B.C. Can.
204 H4 **Barrier Range** hills N.S.W. Austr.
127 O9 **Barrier Reef** Belize
200 □1 **Barrigada** Guam
109 H5 **Barrington** N.S. Can.
96 F9 **Barrington** S. Africa
205 M5 **Barrington, Mount** N.S.W. Austr.
107 K3 **Barrington Lake** Man. Can.
205 M5 **Barrington Tops National Park** N.S.W. Austr.
205 J3 **Barringun** N.S.W. Austr.
67 D12 **Barrio del Peral** Spain
67 E8 **Barrio Mar** Spain
62 I3 **Barrios de Luna, Embalse de** resr Spain
62 E6 **Barrô** Port.
140 C5 **Barro Alto** Brazil
62 E8 **Barroca** Port.
143 F2 **Barrocão** Brazil
62 D4 **Barroças e Taias** Port.
37 J6 **Barrois, Plateau du** France
143 H2 **Barrolândia** Brazil
110 C4 **Barron** WI U.S.A.
110 C4 **Barronett** WI U.S.A.
146 A6 **Barros Arana** Chile
62 C5 **Barroselas** Port.
143 F4 **Barroso** Brazil
127 I4 **Barrotarán** Mex.
131 □3 **Barrouallie** St Vincent
147 G6 **Barrow** Arg.
27 I8 **Barrow** r. Rep. of Ireland
104 C2 **Barrow** AK U.S.A.
104 C2 **Barrow, Point** AK U.S.A.
31 K2 **Barrowby** Lincolnshire, England U.K.
206 D6 **Barrow Creek** N.T. Austr.
29 M6 **Barrowford** Lancashire, England U.K.
29 K5 **Barrow-in-Furness** Cumbria, England U.K.
208 C6 **Barrow Island** W.A. Austr.
208 C6 **Barrow Island Nature Reserve** W.A. Austr.
207 J3 **Barrow Point** Qld Austr.
209 I9 **Barrow Range** hills W.A. Austr.
105 I2 **Barrow Strait** Nunavut Can.
29 Q6 **Barrow upon Humber** North Lincolnshire, England U.K.
209 F9 **Barr Smith Range** hills W.A. Austr.
62 G6 **Barruecopardo** Spain
63 L3 **Barruelo de Santullán** Spain
30 F5 **Barry** Vale of Glamorgan, Wales U.K.
96 E9 **Barrydale** S. Africa
205 K7 **Barry Mountains** Vic. Austr.
108 E4 **Barrys Bay** Ont. Can.
116 A5 **Barryton** MI U.S.A.
202 J5 **Barryville** North I. N.Z.
118 F2 **Barryville** NY U.S.A.
57 L5 **Bârsa** Romania
43 D6 **Barsac** France
182 H5 **Barsakel'mes, Poluostrov** pen. Kazakh.
182 I5 **Barsakel'messkiy Zapovednik** nature res. Kazakh.
88 E3 **Barsalogo** Burkina
178 D5 **Barsalpur** Rajasthan India
77 M3 **Bârsana** Romania
48 J3 **Barsbüttel** Ger.
183 R3 **Barshatas** Kazakh.
Barshi Mahar. India see **Barsi**
176 D3 **Barsi** Mahar. India
49 H6 **Barsinghausen** Ger.
22 F6 **Barsø** i. Denmark
179 K7 **Barsoi** Bihar India
48 E4 **Barßel** Ger.
124 O7 **Barstow** CA U.S.A.
18 E5 **Barstyčiai** Lith.
19 U7 **Barsuki** Rus. Fed.
176 G3 **Barsur** Chhattisgarh India
36 I7 **Bar-sur-Aube** France
36 H7 **Bar-sur-Seine** France
18 E5 **Bārta** Latvia
18 E5 **Bārta** r. Latvia
185 N2 **Bartang** Tajik.
185 N3 **Bartang** r. Tajik.
40 K1 **Bartenheim** France
52 H3 **Bartenstein** Ger.
50 G2 **Barth** Ger.
50 G2 **Barthe** r. Ger.
52 H4 **Bartholomä** Ger.
121 I9 **Bartholomew, Bayou** r. LA U.S.A.
137 G3 **Bartica** Guyana
188 F3 **Bartın** Turkey
207 J4 **Bartle Frere, Mount** Qld Austr.
116 C10 **Bartles** OH U.S.A.
125 V2 **Bartles, Mount** UT U.S.A.
121 G7 **Bartlesville** OK U.S.A.
120 F5 **Bartlett** NE U.S.A.
117 N4 **Bartlett** NH U.S.A.
106 G2 **Bartlett Lake** N.W.T. Can.
125 U8 **Bartlett Reservoir** AZ U.S.A.
202 L5 **Bartletts** North I. N.Z.
55 I2 **Bartniki** Pol.
55 L1 **Bartninkai** Lith.
29 L6 **Barton** Lancashire, England U.K.
117 M4 **Barton** VT U.S.A.
31 L4 **Barton-le-Clay** Bedfordshire, England U.K.
31 I2 **Barton-under-Needwood** Staffordshire, England U.K.
29 Q6 **Barton-upon-Humber** North Lincolnshire, England U.K.
110 E9 **Bartonville** IL U.S.A.
23 Q7 **Bartoszyce** Pol.
115 G12 **Bartow** FL U.S.A.
20 N3 **Barturte** mt. Sweden
18 E5 **Bartuva** r. Lith.
136 C2 **Barú, Isla de** i. Col.
55 H3 **Baruchowo** Pol.
179 L8 **Baruipur** W. Bengal India
64 E2 **Barulho** Port.
187 I8 **Barūm** Yemen
72 C8 **Barumini** Sardegna Italy
156 D3 **Barumun** r. Indon.
168 E8 **Barun** Qinghai China
157 J9 **Barung** i. Indon.
Barunga N.T. Austr. see **Bamyili**
169 N1 **Barun-Torey, Ozero** l. Rus. Fed.
156 C3 **Barus** Sumatera Indon.
51 I6 **Baruth** Brandenburg Ger.
51 K8 **Baruth** Sachsen Ger.
168 J2 **Baruunharaa** Mongolia
168 I5 **Baruunsuu** Mongolia
168 D2 **Baruunturuun** Mongolia
169 M3 **Baruun-Urt** Mongolia
177 I3 **Baruva** Andhra Prad. India
26 C6 **Barvas** Western Isles, Scotland U.K.
45 H8 **Barvaux** Belgium
48 G5 **Barver** Ger.
17 Q5 **Barvinkove** Ukr.
179 J8 **Barwa** Jharkhand India
178 F8 **Barwah** Madh. Prad. India
178 D8 **Barwala** Gujarat India
178 E5 **Barwala** Haryana India
178 F8 **Barwani** Madh. Prad. India
178 G7 **Barwa Sagar** Uttar Prad. India
48 K5 **Barwedel** Ger.
Barwéli Mali see **Baraouéli**
54 E2 **Barwice** Pol.
205 K4 **Barwon** r. N.S.W. Austr.
19 R7 **Baryatino** Rus. Fed.
19 U6 **Barybino** Rus. Fed.
54 E4 **Barycz** r. Pol.
Barygaza Gujarat India see **Bharuch**
18 L7 **Barysaw** Belarus
15 I5 **Barysh** Rus. Fed.
17 K3 **Baryshivka** Ukr.
187 N4 **Barzamān** Oman
62 I2 **Bárzana** Spain
57 L5 **Bârzava** Romania
185 K3 **Basaga** Turkm.
184 F8 **Bāsa'īdū** Iran
144 F2 **Basail** Arg.
159 G9 **Basăk, Tônlé** r. Cambodia
207 J5 **Basalt** r. Qld Austr.
Basalt Island H.K. China see **Fo Shek Chau**
91 E6 **Basanga** Dem. Rep. Congo
90 C4 **Basankusu** Dem. Rep. Congo
179 K6 **Basantpur** Bihar India
176 E3 **Basar** Mahar. India
16 H7 **Basarabeasca** Moldova
77 Q6 **Basarabi** Romania
147 H3 **Basavilbaso** Arg.
154 D7 **Basay** Negros Phil.
191 C5 **Başçakmak** Turkey
77 O5 **Bâsca Mică** r. Romania
66 K3 **Bàscara** Spain
37 K4 **Bascharage** Lux.
30 G2 **Baschurch** Shropshire, England U.K.
73 L2 **Basciano** Italy
154 C1 **Basco** Phil.
204 E5 **Bascombe Well Conservation Park** nature res. S.A. Austr.
63 M3 **Bascondillos del Tozo** Spain
91 B6 **Bas-Congo** prov. Dem. Rep. Congo
43 D8 **Bascons** France
43 E8 **Bascous** France
144 C3 **Bascuñán, Cabo** c. Chile
63 P8 **Bascuñana, Sierra de** mts Spain
48 H4 **Basdahl** Ger.
50 H5 **Basdorf** Ger.
191 A5 **Başdurak** Turkey
45 E7 **Basècles** Belgium
206 D8 **Basedow Range** hills N.T. Austr.
70 D1 **Basel** Switz.
71 K3 **Baselga di Pinè** Italy
73 N5 **Baselice** Italy
70 D1 **Basellandschaft** canton Switz.
40 L1 **Basel-Mulhouse** airport France
41 E6 **Bas-en-Basset** France
73 Q6 **Basentello** r. Italy
73 R7 **Basento** r. Italy
43 F10 **Baserca, Embalse de** resr Spain
77 P3 **Başeu** r. Romania
154 E6 **Basey** Samar Phil.
184 E8 **Bashākerd, Kūhhā-ye** mts Iran
Bashan Jiangxi China see **Chongren**
Bashanta Rus. Fed. see **Gorodovikovsk**
106 H4 **Bashaw** Alta Can.
183 U2 **Bashchelakskiy Khrebet** mts Rus. Fed.
97 M8 **Bashee** r. S. Africa
97 M7 **Bashee Bridge** S. Africa
185 N4 **Bashgul** r. Afgh.
184 D7 **Bāshī** Iran
152 F2 **Bashi Channel** Taiwan
91 E6 **Bashimuke** Dem. Rep. Congo
172 H1 **Bashkaus** r. Rus. Fed.
Bashkiria aut. rep. Rus. Fed. see **Bashkortostan, Respublika**
Bashkirskaya A.S.S.R. aut. rep. Rus. Fed. see **Bashkortostan, Respublika**
182 G1 **Bashkirskiy Zapovednik** nature res. Rus. Fed.
191 F4 **Bashk'oi** Georgia
182 G1 **Bashkortostan, Respublika** aut. rep. Rus. Fed.
15 H5 **Bashmakovo** Rus. Fed.
184 D6 **Bāsht** Iran
17 L6 **Bashtanka** Ukr.
187 K9 **Bashūri, Ra's** pt Suquţrā Yemen
178 F6 **Basi** Rajasthan India
179 J8 **Basia** Jharkhand India
207 M1 **Basilaki Island** P.N.G.
154 C8 **Basilan** i. Phil.
154 D8 **Basilan Strait** Phil.
31 M4 **Basildon** Essex, England U.K.
121 I10 **Basile** LA U.S.A.
89 H6 **Basile, Pico** vol. Equat. Guinea
71 O3 **Basiliano** Italy
73 P6 **Basilicata** admin. reg. Italy
75 I6 **Basiluzzo, Isola** i. Isole Lipari Italy
122 J4 **Basin** WY U.S.A.
23 M1 **Bäsingen** l. Sweden
31 J5 **Basingstoke** Hampshire, England U.K.
107 J4 **Basin Lake** Sask. Can.
189 L6 **Başīra** r. Iraq
184 H6 **Başīrān** Iran
179 L8 **Basirhat** W. Bengal India
190 D3 **Basīţ, Ra's al** pt Syria
17 O2 **Basivka** Ukr.
68 E3 **Baška** Croatia
57 H2 **Baška** Czech Rep.
117 □R3 **Baskahegan Lake** ME U.S.A.
19 R7 **Baskakovka** Rus. Fed.
189 L4 **Başkale** Turkey
108 F4 **Baskatong, Réservoir** resr Que. Can.
208 G4 **Baskerville, Cape** W.A. Austr.
79 L4 **Başkomutan Milli Parkı** nat. park Turkey
79 L4 **Başkomutan Tarıhı Milli Parkı** nat. park Turkey
191 B5 **Başköy** Erzurum Turkey
190 A2 **Başköy** Karaman Turkey
15 I6 **Baskunchak, Ozero** l. Rus. Fed.
191 I4 **Baş Layski** Azer.
Basle Switz. see **Basel**
191 H6 **Başlıbel** Azer.
29 N7 **Baslow** Derbyshire, England U.K.
79 L5 **Başmakçı** Turkey
176 E3 **Basmat** Mahar. India
191 J6 **Baş Muğan Kanalı** canal Azer.
156 E5 **Baso** i. Indon.
178 F8 **Basoda** Madh. Prad. India
70 E3 **Basodino** mt. Italy/Switz.
90 D4 **Basoko** Dem. Rep. Congo
91 D6 **Basongo** Dem. Rep. Congo
Basora, Punt pt Aruba see **Basora, Punta**
131 □9 **Basora, Punta** pt Aruba
93 B6 **Basotu** Tanz.
191 I5 **Baş Qärvänd** Azer.
Basque Country aut. comm. Spain see **País Vasco**
43 F7 **Bas-Quercy** reg. France
Basra Iraq see **Al Başrah**
37 O6 **Bas-Rhin** dept France
72 C5 **Bassacutena** Sardegna Italy
72 C5 **Bassacutena** r. Italy
78 C5 **Bassae** tourist site Greece
107 H5 **Bassano** Alta Can.
71 L4 **Bassano del Grappa** Italy
72 I3 **Bassano Romano** Italy
89 F4 **Bassar** Togo
215 G6 **Bassas da India** rf Indian Ocean
176 C6 **Bassas de Pedro Padua Bank** sea feature India
88 D4 **Bassawa** Côte d'Ivoire
70 C1 **Bassecourt** Switz.
38 I7 **Basse-Goulaine** France
158 B6 **Bassein** Myanmar
158 B6 **Bassein** r. Myanmar
90 D3 **Basse-Kotto** pref. C.A.R.
39 K4 **Basse-Normandie** admin. reg. France
29 K4 **Bassenthwaite Lake** England U.K.
131 □3 **Basse-Pointe** Martinique
Basses-Alpes dept France see **Alpes-de-Haute-Provence**
88 B3 **Basse Santa Su** Gambia
41 H9 **Basses Gorges du Verdon** France
131 □2 **Basse-Terre** Guadeloupe
131 □2 **Basse-Terre** i. Guadeloupe
131 □2 **Basseterre** St Kitts and Nevis
131 □7 **Basse Terre** Trin. and Tob.
120 F4 **Bassett** NE U.S.A.
116 F12 **Bassett** VA U.S.A.
125 V9 **Bassett Peak** AZ U.S.A.
117 □Q4 **Bass Harbor** ME U.S.A.
73 K4 **Bassiano** Italy
43 G10 **Bassiès, Pic Rouge de** mt. France
37 J8 **Bassigny** reg. France
88 D3 **Bassikounou** Maur.
89 F4 **Bassila** Benin
31 L3 **Bassingbourn** Cambridgeshire, England U.K.
29 P7 **Bassingham** Lincolnshire, England U.K.
84 D5 **Basso, Plateau de** Chad
43 E8 **Bassoues** France
26 K10 **Bass Rock** i. Scotland U.K.
205 K8 **Bass Strait** Tas./Vic. Austr.
48 G5 **Bassum** Ger.
108 B3 **Basswood Lake** Ont. Can.
110 C1 **Basswood Lake** MN U.S.A.
40 H5 **Bassy** France
22 I5 **Båstad** Sweden
184 F8 **Bastak** Iran
189 Q5 **Bastam** Iran
184 B3 **Bastānābād** Iran
73 J2 **Bastardo** Italy
72 C3 **Bastelica** Corse France
72 B4 **Bastelicaccia** Corse France
43 C8 **Bastennes** France
49 J10 **Bastheim** Ger.
179 I6 **Basti** Uttar Prad. India
72 C2 **Bastia** Corse France
73 J1 **Bastia** Italy
116 D11 **Bastian** VA U.S.A.
45 I8 **Bastogne** Belgium
50 E2 **Bastorf** Ger.
142 B4 **Bastos** Brazil
121 J9 **Bastrop** LA U.S.A.
121 G10 **Bastrop** TX U.S.A.
20 P4 **Bastuträsk** Sweden
16 F1 **Bastyn'** Belarus
155 E5 **Basu, Tanjung** pt Indon.
185 K9 **Basul** r. Pak.
Basuo Hainan China see **Dongfang**
Basutoland country Africa see **Lesotho**
19 O8 **Basya** r. Belarus
190 A2 **Başyayla** Turkey
Bas-Zaïre prov. Dem. Rep. Congo see **Bas-Congo**
68 F4 **Bat** mt. Croatia
187 M4 **Bat, Al Khutm and Al Ayn** tourist site Oman
89 H6 **Bata** Equat. Guinea
57 H5 **Báta** Hungary
57 L5 **Bata** Romania
154 C4 **Bataan Peninsula** Luzon Phil.
130 B2 **Batabanó, Golfo de** b. Cuba
154 C2 **Batac** Luzon Phil.
126 E4 **Batacosa** Mex.
193 O3 **Batagay** Rus. Fed.
193 O3 **Batagay-Alyta** Rus. Fed.
142 A4 **Bataguassu** Brazil
142 A5 **Bataiporã** Brazil
77 M9 **Batak** Bulg.
157 K7 **Batakan** Kalimantan Indon.
178 E4 **Batala** Punjab India
140 E3 **Batalha** Brazil
62 C9 **Batalha** Port.
156 F4 **Batam** i. Indon.
90 E4 **Batama** Dem. Rep. Congo
193 N3 **Batamay** Rus. Fed.
182 H2 **Batamshinskiy** Kazakh.
Batamshy Kazakh. see **Batamshinskiy**
171 M1 **Batan** Jiangsu China
154 D1 **Batan** i. Phil.
154 E5 **Batan** i. Phil.
170 B3 **Batang** Sichuan China
157 H8 **Batang** Jawa Indon.
90 A5 **Batanga** Gabon
90 C3 **Batangafo** C.A.R.
157 J4 **Batang Ai National Park** Malaysia
154 C5 **Batangas** Luzon Phil.
156 F5 **Batanghari** r. Indon.
155 G4 **Batangpele** i. Papua Indon.
157 I4 **Batangtarang** Kalimantan Indon.
156 C4 **Batangtoru** Sumatera Indon.
154 D1 **Batan Islands** Phil.
155 G4 **Batanta** i. Papua Indon.
57 K5 **Batăr** Romania
57 H5 **Bátaszék** Hungary
142 D4 **Batatais** Brazil
146 E4 **Batavia** Arg.
137 H3 **Batavia** Suriname
110 F8 **Batavia** IL U.S.A.
116 G6 **Batavia** NY U.S.A.
116 A9 **Batavia** OH U.S.A.
19 P8 **Batayeva** Rus. Fed.
15 G7 **Bataysk** Rus. Fed.
154 C6 **Batbatan** i. Phil.
111 J2 **Batchawana** Ont. Can.
111 J3 **Batchawana** r. Ont. Can.
110 J3 **Batchawana Bay** Ont. Can.
108 C4 **Batchawana Mountain** hill Ont. Can.
206 C2 **Batchelor** N.T. Austr.
159 F8 **Bătdâmbâng** Cambodia
66 F5 **Batea** Spain
156 A2 **Bateemeucica, Gunung** mt. Indon.
91 B5 **Batéké, Plateaux** Congo
205 M6 **Batemans Bay** N.S.W. Austr.
20 S1 **Båteng** Norway
65 J3 **Baterno** Spain
204 □1 **Bates, Mount** hill Norfolk I.
115 G9 **Batesburg** SC U.S.A.
209 F9 **Bates Range** hills W.A. Austr.
121 J8 **Batesville** AR U.S.A.
121 K8 **Batesville** MS U.S.A.
19 N3 **Batetskiy** Rus. Fed.
109 H4 **Bath** N.B. Can.
111 R5 **Bath** Ont. Can.
130 □ **Bath** Jamaica
131 □2 **Bath** St Kitts and Nevis
30 H5 **Bath** Bath and North East Somerset, England U.K.
110 D9 **Bath** IL U.S.A.
117 □P5 **Bath** ME U.S.A.
116 H6 **Bath** NY U.S.A.
118 E3 **Bath** PA U.S.A.
84 C6 **Batha** pref. Chad
84 C6 **Batha** watercourse Chad
30 H5 **Bath and North East Somerset** admin. div. England U.K.
30 H5 **Batheaston** Bath and North East Somerset, England U.K.
30 H5 **Bathford** Bath and North East Somerset, England U.K.
26 I11 **Bathgate** West Lothian, Scotland U.K.
178 E4 **Bathinda** Punjab India
44 J4 **Bathmen** Neth.
147 G5 **Bathurst** Arg.
205 L5 **Bathurst** N.S.W. Austr.
109 H4 **Bathurst** N.B. Can.
Bathurst Gambia see **Banjul**
97 K9 **Bathurst** S. Africa
104 F2 **Bathurst, Cape** N.W.T. Can.
207 J3 **Bathurst Bay** Qld Austr.
104 H3 **Bathurst Inlet** Nunavut Can.
104 H3 **Bathurst Inlet** inlet Nunavut Can.
206 C1 **Bathurst Island** N.T. Austr.
105 I2 **Bathurst Island** Nunavut Can.
92 D2 **Bati** Eth.
89 F4 **Batia** Benin
88 E4 **Batié** Burkina
155 B5 **Batikala, Tanjung** pt Indon.
201 □1 **Batiki** i. Fiji
37 K5 **Batilly** France
79 I5 **Batı Menteşe Dağları** mts Turkey
186 H1 **Bāţin, Wādī al** watercourse Asia
57 H6 **Batina** Croatia
140 E4 **Batista, Serra da** hills Brazil
79 L6 **Batı Toroslar** mts Turkey
57 J2 **Batizovce** Slovakia
183 N7 **Batken** Kyrg.
183 N8 **Batken** admin. div. Kyrg.
191 H3 **Batlaich** Rus. Fed.
184 E5 **Bāţlāq-e Gavkhūnī** marsh Iran
29 N6 **Batley** West Yorkshire, England U.K.
205 L6 **Batlow** N.S.W. Austr.
189 J5 **Batman** Turkey
87 G2 **Batna** Alg.
187 J4 **Baţn aţ Ţarfā'** depr. Saudi Arabia
167 L2 **Batō** Japan
76 J6 **Batočina** Srbija Serb. and Mont.
156 □ **Batok, Bukit** Sing.
156 □ **Batok, Bukit** hill Sing.
91 E9 **Batoka** Zambia
159 D11 **Batong, Ko** i. Thai.
121 J10 **Baton Rouge** LA U.S.A.
57 I4 **Bátonyterenye** Hungary
126 F4 **Batopilas** Mex.
57 H4 **Bátorove Kosihy** Slovakia
55 K5 **Batorz** Pol.
178 E3 **Batote** Jammu and Kashmir
90 B4 **Batouala** Gabon
89 I5 **Batouri** Cameroon
57 H3 **Bátovce** Slovakia
186 C3 **Batrā, Jabal** mt. Saudi Arabia
190 D9 **Batrā', Jabal al** mt. Jordan
57 L5 **Bătrâna, Vârful** mt. Romania
159 H9 **Ba Tri** Vietnam
190 D4 **Batroûn** Lebanon
20 T1 **Båtsfjord** Norway
118 F5 **Batsto** r. NJ U.S.A.
Battambang Cambodia see **Bătdâmbâng**
49 G8 **Battenberg (Eder)** Ger.
70 D1 **Bätterkinden** Switz.
178 E4 **Batti** Punjab India
176 G9 **Batticaloa** Sri Lanka
177 M8 **Batti Malv** i. Andaman & Nicobar Is India
73 N6 **Battipaglia** Italy
107 I4 **Battle** r. Alta/Sask. Can.
31 M6 **Battle** East Sussex, England U.K.
206 C3 **Battle Creek** r. N.T. Austr.
107 I5 **Battle Creek** r. Can./U.S.A.
110 I7 **Battle Creek** MI U.S.A.
95 F3 **Battlefields** Zimbabwe
107 I4 **Battleford** Sask. Can.
124 P1 **Battle Mountain** NV U.S.A.
124 O1 **Battle Mountain** mt. NV U.S.A.
57 K5 **Battonya** Hungary
178 E1 **Battura Glacier** Jammu and Kashmir
92 C3 **Batu** mt. Eth.
157 J3 **Batu, Bukit** mt. Malaysia
156 C5 **Batu, Pulau-pulau** is Indon.
157 M3 **Batu, Tanjung** pt Indon.
155 C7 **Batuata** i. Indon.
157 K4 **Batuayau, Bukit** mt. Indon.
156 G6 **Batubetumbang** Indon.
157 K3 **Batu Bora, Bukit** mt. Malaysia
146 B4 **Batuco** Chile
155 B4 **Batudaka** i. Indon.
156 D2 **Batu Gajah** Malaysia
155 C4 **Batuhitam, Tanjung** pt Indon.
155 C4 **Batui** Sulawesi Indon.
154 E9 **Batulaki** Mindanao Phil.
157 L6 **Batulicin** Kalimantan Indon.
157 K4 **Batulilangmebang, Gunung** mt. Indon.
Batum Georgia see **Bat'umi**
191 C4 **Bat'umi** Georgia
156 D6 **Batumonga** Indon.
156 E4 **Batu Pahat** Malaysia
156 D2 **Batu Putih, Gunung** mt. Malaysia
156 F7 **Baturaja** Sumatera Indon.
157 I9 **Baturetno** Jawa Indon.
19 P6 **Baturino** Rus. Fed.
17 L2 **Baturyn** Ukr.
156 D5 **Batusangkar** Sumatera Indon.
57 H5 **Bátya** Hungary
55 M5 **Batyatychi** Ukr.
15 I5 **Batyrevo** Rus. Fed.
38 C4 **Batz, Île de** i. France
38 G7 **Batz-sur-Mer** France
137 H6 **Bau** r. Brazil
201 □1a **Bau** i. Fiji
157 I4 **Bau** Sarawak Malaysia
92 B2 **Bau** Sudan
155 C6 **Baubau** Sulawesi Indon.
155 E8 **Baucau** East Timor
89 H4 **Bauchi** Nigeria
89 H4 **Bauchi** state Nigeria
74 F8 **Baucina** Sicilia Italy
38 E6 **Baud** France
120 H1 **Baudette** MN U.S.A.
136 B3 **Baudo, Serranía de** mts Col.
41 I9 **Bauduen** France
70 F2 **Bauen** Switz.
204 □3 **Bauer Bay** S. Pacific Ocean
92 E3 **Bauet** well Eth.
39 K6 **Baugé** France
39 K6 **Baugeois** reg. France
40 I5 **Bauges** mts France
31 J5 **Baughurst** Hampshire, England U.K.
40 B2 **Baugy** France
207 L8 **Bauhinia** Qld Austr.
Baukau East Timor see **Baucau**
155 B6 **Baula** Sulawesi Indon.
52 G3 **Bauland** reg. Ger.
109 K3 **Bauld, Cape** Nfld and Lab. Can.
38 H6 **Baulon** France
105 J2 **Baumann Fiord** inlet Nunavut Can.
40 I2 **Baume-les-Dames** France
52 C2 **Baumholder** Ger.
49 K11 **Baunach** Ger.
49 K11 **Baunach** r. Ger.
200 □6 **Baunani** Malaita Solomon Is
178 E3 **Baundal** Hima. Prad. India
72 D7 **Baunei** Sardegna Italy
27 C8 **Baurtregaum** hill Rep. of Ireland
142 C5 **Bauru** Brazil
142 A3 **Baús** Brazil
49 C10 **Bausendorf** Ger.
187 N4 **Baushar** Oman
18 H5 **Bauska** Latvia
182 D5 **Bautino** Kazakh.
51 J8 **Bautzen** Ger.
183 N6 **Bauyrzhan Momyshuly** Kazakh.
40 J2 **Bavans** France
Bavaria reg. Ger. see **Bayern**
36 G3 **Bavay** France
176 C4 **Bavda** Mahar. India
44 G5 **Bavel** Neth.
72 C4 **Bavella, Col de** pass France
23 M2 **Båven** l. Sweden
70 F4 **Baveno** Italy
96 H9 **Baviaanskloofberge** mts S. Africa
40 J1 **Bavilliers** France
126 E2 **Bavispe** Mex.
126 E3 **Bavispe** r. Mex.
178 D8 **Bavla** Gujarat India
19 W5 **Bavleny** Rus. Fed.
15 K5 **Bavly** Rus. Fed.
56 D2 **Bavorov** Czech Rep.
90 C3 **Bavula** Dem. Rep. Congo
158 B3 **Baw** Myanmar
178 F5 **Bawal** Haryana India
157 I6 **Bawal** i. Indon.
157 J5 **Bawan** Kalimantan Indon.
157 H5 **Bawang, Tanjung** pt Indon.
205 K7 **Baw Baw National Park** Vic. Austr.
31 O2 **Bawdeswell** Norfolk, England U.K.
31 O3 **Bawdsey** Suffolk, England U.K.
158 C3 **Bawdwin** Myanmar
157 J7 **Bawean** i. Indon.
48 D5 **Bawinkel** Ger.
88 E4 **Bawku** Ghana
158 C5 **Bawlake** Myanmar
28 B5 **Bawnboy** Rep. of Ireland
170 C4 **Bawolung** Sichuan China
29 O7 **Bawtry** South Yorkshire, England U.K.
170 D2 **Baxi** Sichuan China
Baxian Chongqing China see **Banan**
Baxian Hebei China see **Bazhou**
172 J7 **Baxkorgan** Xinjiang China
115 F10 **Baxley** GA U.S.A.
170 A3 **Baxoi** Xizang China
117 □Q2 **Baxter State Park** ME U.S.A.
Bay Xinjiang China see **Baicheng**
92 D4 **Bay** admin. reg. Somalia
154 C4 **Bay, Laguna de** lag. Luzon Phil.
88 E3 **Bay, Réserve de** nature res. Mali
88 E5 **Baya** r. Côte d'Ivoire
69 B8 **Bayad** Alg.
130 E3 **Bayamo** Cuba
131 □1 **Bayamón** Puerto Rico
191 H5 **Bayan** Azer.
162 E5 **Bayan** Heilong. China
168 E9 **Bayan** Qinghai China
157 L9 **Bayan** Lombok Indon.
168 H3 **Bayan** Arhangay Mongolia
168 D3 **Bayan** Govĭ-Altay Mongolia
169 L2 **Bayan** Hentiy Mongolia
185 K4 **Bāyan, Band-e** mts Afgh.
178 F6 **Bayana** Rajasthan India
183 P2 **Bayanaul** Kazakh.
168 F3 **Bayanbulag** Bayanhongor Mongolia
168 F4 **Bayanbulag** Bayanhongor Mongolia
169 K3 **Bayanbulag** Hentiy Mongolia
172 G3 **Bayanbulak** Xinjiang China
172 G5 **Bayanbulak** Xinjiang China
169 K3 **Bayandelger** Mongolia
157 H4 **Bayang, Pegunungan** mts Indon.
90 C4 **Bayanga** C.A.R.
90 B3 **Bayanga-Didi** C.A.R.
Bayan Gol Nei Mongol China see **Dengkou**
168 D4 **Bayangol** Mongolia
168 H1 **Bayangol** Rus. Fed.
170 A1 **Bayan Har Shan** mt. Qinghai China
168 D9 **Bayan Har Shan** mts China
168 E9 **Bayan Har Shankou** pass Qinghai China
168 G3 **Bayanhongor** Mongolia
168 F4 **Bayanhongor** prov. Mongolia
168 I7 **Bayan Hot** Nei Mongol China
168 G3 **Bayanhushuu** Mongolia
168 E2 **Bayan-Kol** Rus. Fed.
168 I6 **Bayan Mod** Nei Mongol China
168 I6 **Bayan Nuru** Nei Mongol China
126 □T13 **Bayano, Lago** l. Panama
169 K6 **Bayan Obo** Nei Mongol China
168 A2 **Bayan-Ölgiy** prov. Mongolia
168 D4 **Bayan-Ovoo** Govĭ-Altay Mongolia
169 L2 **Bayan-Ovoo** Hentiy Mongolia
169 M3 **Bayan-Ovoo** Hentiy Mongolia
169 M6 **Bayan Qagan** Nei Mongol China
169 Q4 **Bayan Qagan** Nei Mongol China
168 F4 **Bayansayr** Mongolia
168 E8 **Bayan Shan** mt. China
172 G5 **Bayansumküre** Xinjiang China
169 O2 **Bayan Tal** Nei Mongol China
168 G4 **Bayanteeg** Mongolia
169 P2 **Bayan Tohoi** Nei Mongol China
168 I3 **Bayantöhöm** Mongolia
169 O4 **Bayan Ul Hot** Nei Mongol China
169 K6 **Bayan Us** Nei Mongol China
168 A2 **Bayan Uul** mts Mongolia
65 N6 **Bayárcal** Spain
120 D5 **Bayard** NE U.S.A.
116 F9 **Bayard** WV U.S.A.
41 I7 **Bayard, Col** pass France
37 J6 **Bayard-sur-Marne** France
63 O3 **Bayas** r. Spain
169 M3 **Bayasgalant** Mongolia
79 L4 **Bayat** Afyon Turkey
Bayat Antalya Turkey see **Akçay**
154 D7 **Bayawan** Negros Phil.
184 F6 **Bayāẓ** Iran
154 E6 **Baybay** Leyte Phil.
115 I8 **Bayboro** NC U.S.A.
116 C7 **Bay Bridge** OH U.S.A.
109 K4 **Bay Bulls** Nfld and Lab. Can.
189 J3 **Bayburt** Turkey
191 B5 **Bayburt** prov. Turkey
16 I5 **Baybuzivka** Ukr.
159 H10 **Bay Canh, Hon** i. Vietnam

Baychunas to Belo Jardim

236

182 E4 **Baychunas** Kazakh.
111 K6 **Bay City** *MI* U.S.A.
121 G11 **Bay City** *TX* U.S.A.
29 K5 **Baycliff** *Cumbria, England* U.K.
186 D3 **Baydā, Jabal al** *hill* Saudi Arabia
192 H3 **Baydaratskaya Guba** Rus. Fed.
92 D4 **Baydhabo** Somalia
168 F3 **Baydrag** Mongolia
168 F4 **Baydrag Gol** *r.* Mongolia
109 K3 **Bay du Nord Wilderness** *nature res. Nfld and Lab.* Can.
Baydzhansay Kazakh. *see* **Bayzhansay**
90 D3 **Baye** Dem. Rep. Congo
36 G6 **Baye** France
184 D3 **Bāyeh** Iran
37 I7 **Bayel** France
89 G5 **Bayelsa** *state* Nigeria
53 O5 **Bayerbach** Ger.
53 M4 **Bayerbach bei Ergoldsbach** Ger.
53 O3 **Bayerisch Eisenstein** Ger.
55 H10 **Bayerische Rhön** *park* Ger.
52 G2 **Bayerischer Spessart** *park* Ger.
53 M3 **Bayerischer Wald** *mts* Ger.
53 N3 **Bayerischer Wald** *nat. park* Ger.
53 N6 **Bayerisch Gmain** Ger.
51 C10 **Bayern** *reg.* Ger.
53 K6 **Bayersoien** Ger.
53 O4 **Bayer Wald, Nationalpark** *nat. park* Ger.
39 J3 **Bayeux** France
19 O7 **Bayeva** Belarus
183 S1 **Bayevo** Rus. Fed.
111 M6 **Bayfield** *Ont.* Can.
110 D3 **Bayfield** *WI* U.S.A.
182 F3 **Bayganin** Kazakh.
183 L5 **Baygekum** Kazakh.
182 J1 **Baygora** Kazakh.
17 S1 **Baygora** *r.* Rus. Fed.
147 I3 **Baygorria, Lago Artificial de** *resr* Uru.
186 G8 **Bayhan al Qişab** Yemen
119 G4 **Bay Head** *NJ* U.S.A.
169 O9 **Bayiji** *Jiangsu* China
191 I5 **Bāyimli** Azer.
79 I4 **Bayındır** Turkey
79 J5 **Bayır** Turkey
173 L12 **Bayizhen** *Xizang* China
189 K6 **Bayjī** Iraq
168 I1 **Baykal, Ozero** *l.* Rus. Fed.
162 F2 **Baykal-Amur Magistral** Rus. Fed.
Baykal Range *mts* Rus. Fed. *see* **Baykal'skiy Khrebet**
168 I1 **Baykal'sk** Rus. Fed.
160 I1 **Baykal'skiy Khrebet** *mts* Rus. Fed.
168 I1 **Baykal'skiy Zapovednik** *nature res.* Rus. Fed.
189 J4 **Baykan** Turkey
182 J5 **Bay-Khozha** Kazakh.
14 L5 **Baykibashevo** Rus. Fed.
193 K3 **Baykit** Rus. Fed.
Baykonur *Gorod Baykonyr* Kazakh. *see* **Baykonyr**
182 L4 **Baykonur** *Karagandinskaya Oblast'* Kazakh.
182 J5 **Baykonyr** *Gorod Baykonyr* Kazakh.
206 G4 **Bayley Point Aboriginal Reserve** *Qld* Austr.
182 H1 **Baymak** Rus. Fed.
115 D10 **Bay Minette** *AL* U.S.A.
187 K4 **Baynūna'h** *reg.* U.A.E.
Bayo Spain *see* **Baio**
202 I2 **Bay of Islands Maritime and Historic Park** *nature res. North I.* N.Z.
202 K4 **Bay of Plenty** *admin. reg. North I.* N.Z.
154 C3 **Bayombong** *Luzon* Phil.
37 L7 **Bayon** France
Bayona *Galicia* Spain *see* **Baiona**
43 B9 **Bayonne** France
119 G3 **Bayonne** *NJ* U.S.A.
154 C6 **Bayo Point** *Panay* Phil.
136 A6 **Bayóvar** Peru
154 B6 **Bay Point** Phil.
111 K6 **Bay Port** *MI* U.S.A.
119 I3 **Bayport** *NY* U.S.A.
Bayqongyr Kazakh. *see* **Baykonyr**
17 N4 **Bayrak** Ukr.
191 E5 **Bayraktutan** Turkey
185 J3 **Bayramaly** Turkm.
79 H3 **Bayramiç** Turkey
53 L2 **Bayreuth** Ger.
118 C7 **Bay Ridge** *MD* U.S.A.
53 M6 **Bayrischzell** Ger.
Bayrūt Lebanon *see* **Beirut**
108 E4 **Bays, Lake of** *Ont.* Can.
121 K10 **Bay St Louis** *MS* U.S.A.
186 F7 **Baysh** *watercourse* Saudi Arabia
Bayshonas Kazakh. *see* **Baychunas**
119 I3 **Bay Shore** *NY* U.S.A.
118 C6 **Bayside Beach** *MD* U.S.A.
121 K10 **Bay Springs** *MS* U.S.A.
30 G2 **Bayston Hill** *Shropshire, England* U.K.
Baysun Uzbek. *see* **Boysun**
183 L8 **Baysuntau, Gory** *mts* Uzbek.
186 F8 **Bayt al Faqīh** Yemen
168 B4 **Baytik Shan** *mts* China
Bayt Lahm West Bank *see* **Bethlehem**
121 H11 **Baytown** *TX* U.S.A.
155 C5 **Bayu** *Sulawesi* Indon.
63 O5 **Bayubas de Abajo** Spain
156 E5 **Bayunglincir** *Sumatera* Indon.
202 K6 **Bay View** *North I.* N.Z.
119 G5 **Bayville** *NJ* U.S.A.
119 H3 **Bayville** *NY* U.S.A.
84 B2 **Bayy al Kabīr, Wādī** *watercourse* Libya
Bayyrqum Kazakh. *see* **Bairkum**
183 M6 **Bayzhansay** Kazakh.
65 N5 **Baza** Spain
65 N5 **Baza** *r.* Spain
65 N6 **Baza, Sierra de** *mts* Spain
56 F5 **Bázakerettye** Hungary
16 F4 **Bazaliya** Ukr.
36 H5 **Bazancourt** France
16 I2 **Bazar** Ukr.
182 D3 **Bazarchulan** Kazakh.
191 I4 **Bazardyuzyu, Gora** *mt.* Azer./Rus. Fed.
184 C3 **Bāzār-e Māsāl** Iran
189 L4 **Bāzargān** Iran
183 M8 **Bazarkhanym, Gora** *mt.* Uzbek.
183 O7 **Bazar-Korgon** Kyrg.
Bazar Kurgan Kyrg. *see* **Bazar-Korgon**
182 B1 **Bazarnyy Karabulak** Rus. Fed.
15 I5 **Bazarnyy Syzgan** Rus. Fed.
Bazarshulan Kazakh. *see* **Bazarchulan**
182 D3 **Bazartobe** Kazakh.
95 G4 **Bazaruto, Ilha do** *i.* Moz.
43 D7 **Bazas** France
17 N6 **Bazavluk** *r.* Ukr.
185 K8 **Bazdar** Pak.
37 I4 **Bazeilles** France
43 E9 **Bazet** France
191 G1 **Bazhigan** Rus. Fed.
170 F3 **Bazhong** *Sichuan* China
169 O7 **Bazhou** *Hebei* China
Bazhou *Sichuan* China *see* **Bazhong**
43 H9 **Baziège** France
43 E9 **Bazillac** France
108 F4 **Bazin** *r. Que.* Can.
88 C4 **Baziwehn** Liberia
184 I8 **Bazmān** Iran
184 I7 **Bazmān, Kūh-e** *mt.* Iran
40 D2 **Bazoches** France
39 K4 **Bazoches-au-Houlme** France
36 D7 **Bazoches-les-Gallerandes** France
39 L4 **Bazoches-sur-Hoëne** France
184 D6 **Bāzoft, Āb-e** *r.* Iran
40 D2 **Bazois** *reg.* France
39 J5 **Bazougers** France
39 J6 **Bazouges** France
38 H5 **Bazouges-la-Pérouse** France
66 C1 **Baztán, Valle del** *val.* France/Spain
190 E4 **Bcharré** Lebanon
Bé, Nossi *i.* Madag. *see* **Bé, Nosy**
95 □K2 **Bé, Nosy** *i.* Madag.
159 H9 **Be, Sông** *r.* Vietnam
120 D2 **Beach** *ND* U.S.A.
111 R4 **Beachburg** *Ont.* Can.
116 D8 **Beach City** *OH* U.S.A.
119 G3 **Beach Glen** *NJ* U.S.A.
119 G5 **Beach Haven** *NJ* U.S.A.
119 G5 **Beach Haven Terrace** *NJ* U.S.A.
118 E1 **Beach Lake** *PA* U.S.A.
204 H7 **Beachport** *S.A.* Austr.
119 G5 **Beachwood** *NJ* U.S.A.
31 M6 **Beachy Head** *England* U.K.
209 D11 **Beacon** *W.A.* Austr.
117 L7 **Beacon** *NY* U.S.A.
97 L8 **Beacon Bay** S. Africa
119 I2 **Beacon Falls** *CT* U.S.A.
205 K9 **Beaconsfield** *Tas.* Austr.
31 K4 **Beaconsfield** *Buckinghamshire, England* U.K.
29 N2 **Beadnell** *Northumberland, England* U.K.
29 N2 **Beadnell Bay** *England* U.K.
28 B3 **Beagh, Lough** *l.* Rep. of Ireland
145 C9 **Beagle, Canal** *sea chan.* Arg.
208 G3 **Beagle Bank** *rf W.A.* Austr.
208 G4 **Beagle Bay** *W.A.* Austr.
208 G4 **Beagle Bay Aboriginal Reserve** *W.A.* Austr.
206 B2 **Beagle Gulf** *N.T.* Austr.
209 C10 **Beagle Island** *W.A.* Austr.
95 □K2 **Bealanana** Madag.
Béal an Átha Rep. of Ireland *see* **Ballina**
Béal Átha na Sluaighe Rep. of Ireland *see* **Ballinasloe**
27 E9 **Bealnablath** Rep. of Ireland
121 E9 **Beals Creek** *r. TX* U.S.A.
30 G6 **Beaminster** *Dorset, England* U.K.
95 □J5 **Beampingaratra** *mts* Madag.
63 Q8 **Beamud** Spain
95 □K2 **Beandrarezona** Madag.
122 H6 **Bear** *r. ID* U.S.A.
27 C9 **Beara** *reg.* Rep. of Ireland
Bearalváhki Norway *see* **Berlevåg**
118 D2 **Bear Creek** *PA* U.S.A.
121 E7 **Bear Creek** *r. KS* U.S.A.
108 C3 **Beardmore** *Ont.* Can.
213 L1 **Beardmore Glacier** Antarctica
120 J5 **Beardstown** *IL* U.S.A.
Bear Island Arctic Ocean *see* **Bjørnøya**
111 N3 **Bear Island** *Ont.* Can.
108 D2 **Bear Island** *i. Nunavut* Can.
27 C9 **Bear Island** Rep. of Ireland
62 D4 **Beariz** Spain
107 L4 **Bear Lake** *Man.* Can.
110 H5 **Bear Lake** *MI* U.S.A.
122 I5 **Bear Lake** *l. ID* U.S.A.
178 G7 **Bearma** *r. Madh. Prad.* India
120 D4 **Bear Mountain** *SD* U.S.A.
43 C9 **Béarn** *reg.* France
Bearnaraigh *i. Western Isles, Scotland* U.K. *see* **Berneray**
122 J2 **Bear Paw Mountain** *MT* U.S.A.
122 J2 **Bearpaw Mountains** *MT* U.S.A.
212 Q2 **Bear Peninsula** Antarctica
26 H11 **Bearsden** *East Dunbartonshire, Scotland* U.K.
107 N4 **Bearskin Lake** *Ont.* Can.
31 N5 **Bearsted** *Kent, England* U.K.
178 E4 **Beas** *r.* India
64 F6 **Beas** Spain
66 A1 **Beasain** Spain
65 M6 **Beas de Granada** Spain
65 N4 **Beas de Segura** Spain
130 H5 **Beata, Cabo** *c.* Dom. Rep.
130 H5 **Beata, Isla** *i.* Dom. Rep.
120 G5 **Beatrice** *NE* U.S.A.
95 F3 **Beatrice** Zimbabwe
206 F3 **Beatrice, Cape** *N.T.* Austr.
26 J12 **Beattock** *Dumfries and Galloway, Scotland* U.K.
106 F3 **Beatton** *r. B.C.* Can.
124 P5 **Beatty** *NV* U.S.A.
108 E3 **Beattyville** *Que.* Can.
116 B11 **Beattyville** *KY* U.S.A.
99 □1b **Beau Bassin** Mauritius
41 F9 **Beaucaire** France
36 C4 **Beaucamps-le-Vieux** France
36 C7 **Beauce** *reg.* France
41 F7 **Beauchastel** France
111 P3 **Beauchêne, Lac** *l. Que.* Can.
145 F9 **Beauchene Island** Falkland Is
40 J2 **Beaucourt** France
39 J7 **Beaucouzé** France
43 E9 **Beaudéan** France
207 N9 **Beaudesert** *Qld* Austr.
39 L5 **Beaufay** France
205 I7 **Beaufort** *Vic.* Austr.
40 G3 **Beaufort** *Franche-Comté* France
40 J5 **Beaufort** *Rhône-Alpes* France
157 K2 **Beaufort** *Sabah* Malaysia
27 C8 **Beaufort** Rep. of Ireland
115 I8 **Beaufort** *NC* U.S.A.
115 G9 **Beaufort** *SC* U.S.A.
190 D5 **Beaufort Castle** *tourist site* Lebanon
42 D1 **Beaufort-en-Vallée** France
40 J5 **Beaufortin** *mts* France
104 F2 **Beaufort Sea** Can./U.S.A.
96 G8 **Beaufort West** S. Africa
36 C8 **Beaugency** France
117 L3 **Beauharnois** *Que.* Can.
41 I8 **Beaujeu** *Provence-Alpes-Côte d'Azur* France
40 F4 **Beaujeu** *Rhône-Alpes* France
40 F4 **Beaujolais, Monts du** *hills* France
41 E9 **Beaulieu** France
39 N7 **Beaulieu-lès-Loches** France
42 H6 **Beaulieu-sur-Dordogne** France
40 B1 **Beaulieu-sur-Loire** France
40 D3 **Beaulon** France
26 H8 **Beauly** *Highland, Scotland* U.K.
26 H8 **Beauly** *r. Scotland* U.K.
26 H8 **Beauly Firth** *est. Scotland* U.K.
43 E8 **Beaumarchés** France
30 D1 **Beaumaris** *Isle of Anglesey, Wales* U.K.
25 E5 **Beaumaris** *tourist site Wales* U.K.
41 G8 **Beaumes-de-Venise** France
39 M3 **Beaumesnil** France
36 E3 **Beaumetz-lès-Loges** France
45 F8 **Beaumont** Belgium
43 F6 **Beaumont** *Aquitaine* France
40 C5 **Beaumont** *Auvergne* France
38 H2 **Beaumont** *Basse-Normandie* France
39 L8 **Beaumont** *Poitou-Charentes* France
203 D12 **Beaumont** *South I.* N.Z.
124 P8 **Beaumont** *CA* U.S.A.
121 K10 **Beaumont** *MS* U.S.A.
118 D2 **Beaumont** *PA* U.S.A.
121 H10 **Beaumont** *TX* U.S.A.
43 F8 **Beaumont-de-Lomagne** France
41 H9 **Beaumont-de-Pertuis** France
37 J4 **Beaumont-en-Argonne** France
39 L7 **Beaumont-en-Véron** France
39 M6 **Beaumont-la-Ronce** France
39 M3 **Beaumont-le-Roger** France
39 M5 **Beaumont-les-Autels** France
41 F7 **Beaumont-lès-Valence** France
36 D5 **Beaumont-sur-Oise** France
39 L5 **Beaumont-sur-Sarthe** France
40 F2 **Beaune** France
36 D7 **Beaune-la-Rolande** France
39 J7 **Beaupréau** France
36 D3 **Beauquesne** France
45 G8 **Beauraing** Belgium
40 K5 **Beauregard, Lago di** *l.* Italy
41 G6 **Beaurepaire** France
40 G3 **Beaurepaire-en-Bresse** France
41 H7 **Beaurières** France
107 L5 **Beauséjour** *Man.* Can.
37 J6 **Beausite** France
41 K9 **Beausoleil** France
200 □5 **Beautemps Beaupré** *atoll Îles Loyauté* New Caledonia
36 F4 **Beautor** France
36 D5 **Beauvais** France
107 J4 **Beauval** *Sask.* Can.
36 D3 **Beauval** France
99 □2b **Beau Vallon, Baie** *b. Mahé* Seychelles
41 J8 **Beauvezer** France
43 F7 **Beauville** France
38 G8 **Beauvoir-sur-Mer** France
42 D3 **Beauvoir-sur-Niort** France
41 E9 **Beauvoisin** France
41 E6 **Beauzac** France
43 G8 **Beauzelle** France
107 J4 **Beaver** *r. Alta/Sask.* Can.
108 C2 **Beaver** *r. Ont.* Can.
106 C2 **Beaver** *r. Y.T.* Can.
106 E3 **Beaver** *r. Y.T.* Can.
121 E7 **Beaver** *OK* U.S.A.
125 T3 **Beaver** *UT* U.S.A.
121 E7 **Beaver** *r. OK* U.S.A.
125 T2 **Beaver** *r. UT* U.S.A.
120 F5 **Beaver City** *NE* U.S.A.
106 A2 **Beaver Creek** *Y.T.* Can.
121 I7 **Beaver Creek** *r. MO* U.S.A.
122 K2 **Beaver Creek** *r. MT* U.S.A.
120 E2 **Beaver Creek** *r. ND* U.S.A.
120 F5 **Beaver Creek** *r. NE* U.S.A.
114 D7 **Beaver Dam** *KY* U.S.A.
110 F6 **Beaver Dam** *WI* U.S.A.
110 F6 **Beaver Dam Lake** *WI* U.S.A.
116 E8 **Beaver Falls** *PA* U.S.A.
213 D2 **Beaver Glacier** Antarctica
122 H4 **Beaverhead** *r. MT* U.S.A.
122 H4 **Beaverhead Mountains** *MT* U.S.A.
107 H4 **Beaverhill Lake** *Alta* Can.
107 M4 **Beaver Hill Lake** *Man.* Can.
107 J2 **Beaverhill Lake** *N.W.T.* Can.
110 I4 **Beaver Island** *MI* U.S.A.
121 I7 **Beaver Lake** *resr AR* U.S.A.
106 G4 **Beaverlodge** *Alta* Can.
118 D3 **Beaver Meadows** *PA* U.S.A.
116 F8 **Beaver Run Reservoir** *PA* U.S.A.
118 A3 **Beaver Springs** *PA* U.S.A.
108 E4 **Beaverton** *Ont.* Can.
110 J6 **Beaverton** *MI* U.S.A.
122 C4 **Beaverton** *OR* U.S.A.
118 A3 **Beavertown** *PA* U.S.A.
178 E6 **Beawar** *Rajasthan* India
146 D3 **Beazley** Arg.
57 J5 **Beba Veche** Romania
146 D3 **Bebedero, Salina del** *salt pan* Arg.
90 C2 **Bébédjia** Chad
142 C4 **Bebedouro** Brazil
140 F3 **Beberibe** Brazil
51 D6 **Bebertal** Ger.
29 K7 **Bebington** *Merseyside, England* U.K.
90 C2 **Béboto** Chad
49 I9 **Bebra** Ger.
170 A3 **Bêca** *Qinghai* China
67 K8 **Beca, Punta** *pt* Spain
40 J5 **Becca du Lac** *mt.* France
31 P3 **Beccles** *Suffolk, England* U.K.
71 K4 **Becco di Filadonna** *mt.* Italy
62 I8 **Becedas** Spain
66 F6 **Beceite** Spain
76 I5 **Bečej** *Vojvodina, Srbija* Serb. and Mont.
62 F3 **Becerreá** Spain
65 J6 **Becerrero** *hill* Spain
63 K4 **Becerril de Campos** Spain
126 □R10 **Becerro, Cayos** *is* Hond.
128 A2 **Béchar** Alg.
104 C4 **Becharof Lake** *AK* U.S.A.
52 D2 **Becherbach** Ger.
38 H5 **Bécherel** France
14 G4 **Bechevinka** Rus. Fed.
53 J4 **Bechhofen** *Bayern* Ger.
52 C3 **Bechhofen** *Rheinland-Pfalz* Ger.
51 J10 **Bechlín** Czech Rep.
118 D4 **Bechtelsville** *PA* U.S.A.
52 E2 **Bechtheim** Ger.
Bechuanaland *country* Africa *see* **Botswana**
56 D2 **Bechyně** Czech Rep.
57 K6 **Becicherecu Mic** Romania
63 J4 **Becilla de Valderaduey** Spain
79 I5 **Beçin** Turkey
48 I4 **Beckdorf** Ger.
48 H6 **Beckedorf** Ger.
49 G5 **Beckeln** Ger.
212 T1 **Becker, Mount** Antarctica
52 B3 **Beckingen** Ger.
29 P7 **Beckingham** *Nottinghamshire, England* U.K.
116 D11 **Beckley** *WV* U.S.A.
57 G3 **Beckov** Slovakia
203 D11 **Becks** *South I.* N.Z.
49 F7 **Beckum** Ger.
125 R2 **Becky Peak** *NV* U.S.A.
77 M3 **Beclean** Romania
155 D8 **Beco** East Timor
39 J7 **Bécon-les-Granits** France
51 I10 **Bečov** Czech Rep.
56 B1 **Bečov nad Teplou** Czech Rep.
56 F5 **Becsehely** Hungary
56 F5 **Becsvölgye** Hungary
57 G2 **Bečva** *r.* Czech Rep.
92 D2 **Beda Häyk'** *l.* Eth.
29 N5 **Bedale** *North Yorkshire, England* U.K.
90 C2 **Bédan** Chad
41 C9 **Bédarieux** France
41 F8 **Bédarrides** France
49 C9 **Bedburg** Ger.
49 B7 **Bedburg-Hau** Ger.
30 F4 **Beddau** *Rhondda Cynon Taff, Wales* U.K.
30 D1 **Beddgelert** *Gwynedd, Wales* U.K.
31 M6 **Beddingham** *East Sussex, England* U.K.
117 □Q4 **Beddington** *ME* U.S.A.
38 H5 **Bédée** France
59 M7 **Bedekovčina** Croatia
Bedel', Pereval *pass* China/Kyrg. *see* **Bedel Pass**
92 C2 **Bedelē** Eth.
172 D6 **Bedel Pass** China/Kyrg.
48 G3 **Bederkesa** Ger.
92 D2 **Bedēsa** Eth.
14 L5 **Bedeyeva Polyana** Rus. Fed.
109 I4 **Bedford** *N.S.* Can.
111 M3 **Bedford** *Que.* Can.
97 K8 **Bedford** *Eastern Cape* S. Africa
97 O4 **Bedford** *KwaZulu-Natal* S. Africa
31 L3 **Bedford** *Bedfordshire, England* U.K.
120 H5 **Bedford** *IA* U.S.A.
114 D6 **Bedford** *IN* U.S.A.
114 E6 **Bedford** *KY* U.S.A.
119 H2 **Bedford** *NY* U.S.A.
116 G8 **Bedford** *PA* U.S.A.
116 F11 **Bedford** *VA* U.S.A.
207 J3 **Bedford, Cape** *Qld* Austr.
208 I4 **Bedford Downs** *W.A.* Austr.
116 D7 **Bedford Heights** *OH* U.S.A.
119 H2 **Bedford Hills** *NY* U.S.A.
31 L3 **Bedford Level (Middle Level)** *lowland England* U.K.
31 L2 **Bedford Level (North Level)** *lowland England* U.K.
31 M3 **Bedford Level (South Level)** *lowland England* U.K.
131 □6 **Bedford Point** Grenada
31 L3 **Bedfordshire** *admin. div. England* U.K.
205 K5 **Bedgerebong** *N.S.W.* Austr.
178 C8 **Bedi** *Gujarat* India
191 F4 **Bediani** Georgia
156 G6 **Bedinggong** Indon.
55 H4 **Będków** Pol.
178 D7 **Bedla** *Rajasthan* India
29 N3 **Bedlington** *Northumberland, England* U.K.
55 H3 **Bedlno** Pol.
65 M5 **Bedmar** Spain
59 M7 **Bednja** Croatia
68 F2 **Bednja** *r.* Croatia
15 H5 **Bednodem'yanovsk** Rus. Fed.
41 G8 **Bédoin** France
156 □ **Bedok** Sing.
156 □ **Bedok, Sungai** *r.* Sing.
156 □ **Bedok Jetty** Sing.
156 □ **Bedok Reservoir** Sing.
71 K3 **Bedollo** Italy
70 H6 **Bedonia** Italy
89 I3 **Bedouaram** *well* Niger
206 G8 **Bedourie** *Qld* Austr.
43 C9 **Bedous** France
125 X3 **Bedrock** *CO* U.S.A.
43 H6 **Béduer** France
44 K2 **Bedum** Neth.
30 F4 **Bedwas** *Caerphilly, Wales* U.K.
31 J3 **Bedworth** *Warwickshire, England* U.K.
55 H5 **Będzin** Pol.
54 D1 **Będzino** Pol.
26 B8 **Bee, Loch** *l. Scotland* U.K.
207 J9 **Beechal Creek** *watercourse Qld* Austr.
110 G8 **Beecher** *IL* U.S.A.
117 N3 **Beecher Falls** *VT* U.S.A.
116 C10 **Beech Fork Lake** *WV* U.S.A.
205 K7 **Beechworth** *Vic.* Austr.
107 J5 **Beechy** *Sask.* Can.
48 J5 **Beedenbostel** Ger.
29 Q6 **Beeford** *East Riding of Yorkshire, England* U.K.
44 I5 **Beek** *Gelderland* Neth.
44 I5 **Beek** *Noord-Brabant* Neth.
44 I4 **Beekbergen** Neth.
209 C10 **Beekeepers Nature Reserve** *W.A.* Austr.
51 G6 **Beelitz** Ger.
118 F2 **Beemerville** *NJ* U.S.A.
51 D6 **Beendorf** Ger.
207 N9 **Beenleigh** *Qld* Austr.
50 H4 **Beenz** Ger.
92 E3 **Beer** Somalia
30 F6 **Beer** *Devon, England* U.K.
52 F2 **Beerfelden** Ger.
209 D10 **Beeringnurding, Mount** *hill W.A.* Austr.
190 D8 **Be'er Menuḥa** Israel
45 D6 **Beernem** Belgium
190 C9 **Be'ér Ora** Israel
44 I5 **Beers** Neth.
45 G6 **Beerse** Belgium
45 F7 **Beersel** Belgium
Beersheba Israel *see* **Be'ér Sheva'**
190 C7 **Be'ér Sheva'** Israel
190 C7 **Be'ér Sheva'** *watercourse* Israel
45 C6 **Beerst** Belgium
44 L2 **Beerta** Neth.
96 H9 **Beervlei Dam** S. Africa
51 E7 **Beesenstedt** Ger.
51 J6 **Beeskow** Ger.
97 L1 **Beestekraal** S. Africa
49 E6 **Beesten** Ger.
31 J2 **Beeston** *Nottinghamshire, England* U.K.
206 D4 **Beetaloo** *N.T.* Austr.
212 T2 **Beethoven Peninsula** Antarctica
31 N2 **Beetley** *Norfolk, England* U.K.
44 J2 **Beetsterzwaag** Neth.
50 D5 **Beetzendorf** Ger.
51 G6 **Beetzsee** *l.* Ger.
121 G11 **Beeville** *TX* U.S.A.
90 D4 **Befale** Dem. Rep. Congo
95 □J4 **Befandriana Atsimo** Madag.
95 □K2 **Befandriana Avaratra** Madag.
95 □J4 **Befasy** Madag.
90 D4 **Befori** Dem. Rep. Congo
95 □J4 **Befotaka** *Fianarantsoa* Madag.
95 □K2 **Befotaka** *Mahajanga* Madag.
27 J3 **Beg, Lough** *l. Northern Ireland* U.K.
205 L7 **Bega** *N.S.W.* Austr.
155 D5 **Bega** *Maluku* Indon.
77 J5 **Bega** *r.* Romania
43 C8 **Bégaar** France
42 C5 **Bégadan** France
179 M8 **Begamganj** Bangl.
38 E4 **Bégard** France
185 M7 **Begari** *r.* Pak.
57 K5 **Begécsivíztároló** *resr* Hungary
131 □2 **Beggars Point** Antigua and Barbuda
Begicheva, Ostrov *i.* Rus. Fed. *see* **Bol'shoy Begichev, Ostrov**
65 L5 **Begíjar** Spain
45 G6 **Begijnendijk** Belgium
43 C6 **Bègles** France
38 D6 **Beg-Meil** France
22 G1 **Begna** *r.* Norway
62 E2 **Begonte** Spain
88 E5 **Begoro** Ghana
Begovat Uzbek. *see* **Bekobod**
178 E7 **Begun** *Rajasthan* India
66 L4 **Begur** Spain
66 L4 **Begur, Cap de** *c.* Spain
179 K7 **Begusarai** *Bihar* India
184 H5 **Behābād** Iran
137 I3 **Behague, Pointe** *pt* Fr. Guiana
95 □J5 **Behara** Madag.
184 D6 **Behbehān** Iran
173 J8 **Beheiqi** *Qinghai* China
48 K3 **Behlendorf** Ger.
106 D4 **Behm Canal** *sea chan. AK* U.S.A.
79 H3 **Behramkale** Turkey
212 T2 **Behrendt Mountains** Antarctica
37 M5 **Behren-lès-Forbach** France
50 C3 **Behren-Lübchin** Ger.
49 K8 **Behringen** Ger.
184 E7 **Behrūsī** Iran
184 E3 **Behshahr** Iran
185 L4 **Behsūd** Afgh.
97 I8 **Behulpsaam** S. Africa
162 E4 **Bei'an** *Heilong.* China
Bei'ao *Zhejiang* China *see* **Dongtou**
170 F2 **Beiba** *Shaanxi* China
170 F4 **Beibei** *Chongqing* China
170 E3 **Beichuan** *Sichuan* China
Beida Libya *see* **Al Bayḍā'**
168 F7 **Beida He** *r. Gansu* China
170 E1 **Beidao** *Gansu* China
168 G7 **Beida Shan** *mts Nei Mongol* China
51 G9 **Beierfeld** Ger.
29 O7 **Beighton** *South Yorkshire, England* U.K.
92 B2 **Beigi** Eth.
70 F7 **Beigua, Monte** *mt.* Italy
170 G8 **Beihai** *Guangxi* China
173 L8 **Bei Hulsan Hu** *salt l. Qinghai* China
171 I7 **Bei Jiang** *r.* China
169 O7 **Beijing** *Beijing* China
169 O6 **Beijing** *mun.* China
44 K3 **Beilen** Neth.
170 H7 **Beiliu** *Guangxi* China
53 K3 **Beilngries** Ger.
51 H7 **Beilrode** Ger.
52 G3 **Beilstein** Ger.
173 K9 **Beilu He** *r. Qinghai* China
168 C9 **Beiluheyan** *Qinghai* China
52 H5 **Beimerstetten** Ger.
90 B2 **Béinamar** Chad
70 D5 **Beinasco** Italy
36 H5 **Beine-Nauroy** France
70 D7 **Beinette** Italy
169 Q6 **Beining** *Liaoning* China
28 F2 **Beinn an Tuirc** *hill Scotland* U.K.
26 E8 **Beinn Bhan** *hill Scotland* U.K.
26 D11 **Beinn Bheigeir** *hill Scotland* U.K.
28 F1 **Beinn Bhreac** *hill Argyll and Bute, Scotland* U.K.
26 F10 **Beinn Bhreac** *hill Argyll and Bute, Scotland* U.K.
26 F11 **Beinn Bhreac** *hill Argyll and Bute, Scotland* U.K.
26 D8 **Beinn Bhreac** *hill Highland, Scotland* U.K.
26 G10 **Beinn Bhuidhe** *hill Scotland* U.K.
26 F10 **Beinn Chapull** *hill Scotland* U.K.
26 G7 **Beinn Dearg** *mt. Highland, Scotland* U.K.
26 I9 **Beinn Dearg** *mt. Perth and Kinross, Scotland* U.K.
26 G9 **Beinn Dorain** *mt. Scotland* U.K.
24 E3 **Beinn Heasgarnich** *mt. Scotland* U.K.
26 G10 **Beinn Ime** *mt. Scotland* U.K.
26 G6 **Beinn Leoid** *hill Scotland* U.K.
26 C6 **Beinn Mholach** *hill Scotland* U.K.
26 F10 **Beinn Mhòr** *hill Scotland* U.K.
26 B8 **Beinn Mhòr** *hill Western Isles, Scotland* U.K.
26 C7 **Beinn Mhòr** *hill Western Isles, Scotland* U.K.
Beinn na Faoghla *i. Scotland* U.K. *see* **Benbecula**
26 G9 **Beinn na Lap** *hill Scotland* U.K.
26 E8 **Beinn na Seamraig** *hill Scotland* U.K.
26 E9 **Beinn Resipol** *hill Scotland* U.K.
26 E8 **Beinn Sgritheall** *hill Scotland* U.K.
26 F9 **Beinn Sgulaird** *hill Scotland* U.K.
26 H7 **Beinn Tharsuinn** *hill Scotland* U.K.
26 H9 **Beinn Udlamain** *mt. Scotland* U.K.
70 E1 **Beinwil** Switz.
170 F6 **Beipan Jiang** *r. Guizhou* China
169 Q6 **Beipiao** *Liaoning* China
95 G3 **Beira** Moz.
64 E2 **Beira** Port.
62 E7 **Beira Alta** *reg.* Port.
62 F9 **Beira Baixa** *reg.* Port.
62 D8 **Beira Litoral** *reg.* Port.
63 Q4 **Beire** Spain
171 J2 **Beiru He** *r.* China
190 D5 **Beirut** Lebanon
106 H5 **Beiseker** *Alta* Can.
168 F6 **Beishan** *Nei Mongol* China
168 D6 **Bei Shan** *mts* China
169 M7 **Beitai Ding** *mts* China
95 F4 **Beitbridge** Zimbabwe
26 G11 **Beith** *North Ayrshire, Scotland* U.K.
190 D7 **Beit Jālā** West Bank
20 K5 **Beitstadfjorden** *sea chan.* Norway
172 H3 **Beitun** *Xinjiang* China
77 K4 **Beiuș** Romania
162 D4 **Beixing** *Heilong.* China
Beizhen *Liaoning* China *see* **Beining**
140 C2 **Beja** Brazil
64 D4 **Beja** Port.
64 C5 **Beja** *admin. dist.* Port.
87 H1 **Béja** Tunisia
87 H1 **Béja** *admin. div.* Tunisia
87 G1 **Bejaïa** Alg.
62 I8 **Béjar** Spain
184 H4 **Bejestān** Iran
185 M7 **Beji** *r.* Pak.
67 D8 **Bejís** Spain
128 G7 **Bejucos** Mex.
131 I8 **Bejuma** Venez.
89 I6 **Bek** *r.* Cameroon
89 I5 **Béka** *Adamaoua* Cameroon
89 I5 **Béka** *Est* Cameroon
89 I4 **Béka** *Nord* Cameroon
Bekabad Uzbek. *see* **Bekobod**
176 D6 **Bekal** *Kerala* India
95 □J3 **Bekapaika** Madag.
156 G8 **Bekasi** *Jawa* Indon.
182 E4 **Bekbike** Kazakh.
184 E1 **Bekdash** Turkm.
91 E7 **Beke** Dem. Rep. Congo
57 K5 **Békés** Hungary
57 K5 **Békés** *county* Hungary
57 K5 **Békéscsaba** Hungary
57 J5 **Békéssámson** Hungary
57 J5 **Békésszentandrás** Hungary
14 G3 **Beketovskaya** Rus. Fed.
17 L7 **Bekhtery** Ukr.
79 K4 **Bekilli** Turkey
95 □J5 **Bekily** Madag.
95 □J3 **Bekipay** Madag.
95 □J5 **Bekitro** Madag.
164 W3 **Bekkai** Japan
181 J1 **Bekobod** Uzbek.
95 □J3 **Bekodoka** Madag.
92 C3 **BeK'ojī** Eth.
95 □J3 **Bekopaka** Madag.
95 □I4 **Bekoropoka-Antongo** Madag.
15 H5 **Bekovo** Rus. Fed.
88 E5 **Bekwai** Ghana
88 E5 **Bekyem** Ghana
179 J7 **Bela** *Bihar* India
178 H7 **Bela** *Uttar Prad.* India
185 L8 **Bela** Pak.
57 H2 **Belá** Slovakia
185 M7 **Belab** *r.* Pak.
95 F5 **Bela-Bela** S. Africa
89 I5 **Bélabo** Cameroon
42 G2 **Bélâbre** France
76 J6 **Bela Crkva** *Vojvodina, Srbija* Serb. and Mont.
57 H3 **Beladice** Slovakia
57 H2 **Belá-Dulice** Slovakia
157 J3 **Belaga** *Sarawak* Malaysia
183 S2 **Bel'agash** Kazakh.
38 F5 **Bel Air** *hill* France
118 C5 **Bel Air** *MD* U.S.A.
90 D5 **Belaka** Dem. Rep. Congo
65 I3 **Belalcázar** Spain
56 B2 **Bělá nad Radbuzou** Czech Rep.
155 D3 **Belang** *Sulawesi* Indon.
155 E4 **Belangbelang** *i. Maluku* Indon.
77 K7 **Bela Palanka** *Srbija* Serb. and Mont.
57 J3 **Bélapátfalva** Hungary
56 D1 **Bělá pod Bezdězem** Czech Rep.
56 G1 **Bělá pod Pradědem** Czech Rep.
176 D3 **Belapur** *Mahar.* India
15 E5 **Belarus** *country* Europe
63 Q3 **Belascoáin** Spain
Belasica *mts* Bulg./Macedonia *see* **Belasitsa**
77 K9 **Belasitsa** *mts* Bulg./Macedonia
91 B6 **Bela Vista** *Bengo* Angola
136 E4 **Bela Vista** *Amazonas* Brazil
139 F5 **Bela Vista** *Mato Grosso do Sul* Brazil
95 G5 **Bela Vista** Moz.
142 C2 **Bela Vista de Goiás** Brazil
156 C3 **Belawan** *Sumatera* Indon.
92 C2 **Belaya** *mt.* Eth.
17 Q3 **Belaya** Rus. Fed.
193 S3 **Belaya** *r.* Rus. Fed.
17 S8 **Belaya** *r.* Rus. Fed.
17 M1 **Belaya Berezka** Rus. Fed.
15 H7 **Belaya Glina** Rus. Fed.
15 H6 **Belaya Kalitva** Rus. Fed.
14 J4 **Belaya Kholunitsa** Rus. Fed.
157 L5 **Belayan** *r.* Indon.
157 K4 **Belayan, Gunung** *mt.* Indon.
19 W5 **Belaya Rechka** Rus. Fed.
Belaya Tserkva Ukr. *see* **Bila Tserkva**
62 D7 **Belazaima do Chão** Port.
89 G3 **Belbédji** Niger
70 F6 **Belbo** *r.* Italy
43 H10 **Belcaire** France
118 C6 **Belcamp** *MD* U.S.A.
43 I7 **Belcastel** France
77 P3 **Belceşti** Romania
55 H4 **Bełchatów** Pol.
52 D6 **Belchen** *mt.* Ger.
116 C11 **Belcher** *KY* U.S.A.
108 E1 **Belcher Islands** *Nunavut* Can.
185 K4 **Belchiragh** Afgh.
66 D5 **Belchite** Spain
56 C2 **Bělčice** Czech Rep.
188 H4 **Belcik** Turkey
27 E6 **Belclare** Rep. of Ireland
111 Q1 **Belcourt** *Que.* Can.
179 L8 **Beldanga** *W. Bengal* India
55 J2 **Bełdany, Jezioro** *l.* Pol.
124 K1 **Belden** *CA* U.S.A.
27 C4 **Belderg** Rep. of Ireland
79 J6 **Beldibi** Turkey
110 I6 **Belding** *MI* U.S.A.
Beleapani *rf* India *see* **Cherbaniani Reef**
182 F1 **Belebey** Rus. Fed.
56 G4 **Beled** Hungary
92 E3 **Beledweyne** Somalia
88 C5 **Belefuanai** Liberia
71 Q6 **Belej** Croatia
184 E2 **Belek** Turkm.
88 D3 **Béléko** Mali
89 I5 **Bélèl** Cameroon
89 I4 **Belel** Nigeria
140 C2 **Belém** Brazil
90 B2 **Bélèm** Chad
144 D2 **Belén** Arg.
139 F5 **Belén** Para.
190 A2 **Belen** *Antalya* Turkey
188 H5 **Belen** *Hatay* Turkey
147 I2 **Belén** Uru.
123 K9 **Belen** *NM* U.S.A.
147 I2 **Belén, Cuchilla de** *hills* Uru.
63 N7 **Beleña, Embalse de** *resr* Spain
128 E4 **Belén del Refugio** Mex.
77 N7 **Belene** Bulg.
17 P3 **Belenikhino** Rus. Fed.
63 J2 **Beleño** Spain
200 □5 **Belep, Îles** *is* New Caledonia
62 E3 **Belesar, Embalse de** *resr* Spain
43 H10 **Bélesta** France
19 T8 **Belev** Rus. Fed.
79 I4 **Belevi** Turkey
56 F5 **Belezna** Hungary
203 G10 **Belfast** *South I.* N.Z.
97 O1 **Belfast** S. Africa
27 K3 **Belfast** *Northern Ireland* U.K.
117 □P4 **Belfast** *ME* U.S.A.
116 G6 **Belfast** *NY* U.S.A.
28 E4 **Belfast International** *airport Northern Ireland* U.K.
27 K3 **Belfast Lough** *inlet Northern Ireland* U.K.
45 J6 **Belfeld** Neth.
120 D2 **Belfield** *ND* U.S.A.
92 B2 **Bēlfodiyo** Eth.
29 N2 **Belford** *Northumberland, England* U.K.
40 J1 **Belfort** France
43 H7 **Belfort-du-Quercy** France
73 K1 **Belforte del Chienti** Italy
176 D5 **Belgaum** *Karnataka* India
41 I10 **Belgentier** France
51 H8 **Belgern** Ger.
51 G8 **Belgershain** Ger.
Belgian Congo *country* Africa *see* **Congo, Democratic Republic of**
Belgicafjella *mts* Antarctica *see* **Belgica Mountains**
213 C2 **Belgica Mountains** Antarctica
België *country* Europe *see* **Belgium**
70 G5 **Belgioioso** Italy
Belgique *country* Europe *see* **Belgium**
45 F7 **Belgium** *country* Europe
72 C2 **Belgodère** *Corse* France
15 G6 **Belgorod** Rus. Fed.
Belgorod-Dnestrovskyy Ukr. *see* **Bilhorod-Dnistrovs'kyy**
Belgorod Oblast *admin. div.* Rus. Fed. *see* **Belgorodskaya Oblast'**
15 G6 **Belgorodskaya Oblast'** *admin. div.* Rus. Fed.
Belgrade *Srbija* Serb. and Mont. *see* **Beograd**
117 □P4 **Belgrade** *ME* U.S.A.
122 I4 **Belgrade** *MT* U.S.A.
212 V1 **Belgrano II** *research stn* Antarctica
203 G8 **Belgrove** *South I.* N.Z.
43 C7 **Belhade** France
87 G3 **Belhirane** Alg.
36 B6 **Belhomert-Guéhouville** France
71 Q5 **Beli** Croatia
88 B4 **Béli** Guinea-Bissau
89 H5 **Beli** Nigeria
66 H4 **Belianes** Spain
59 O7 **Belica** Croatia
74 D8 **Belice** *r. Sicilia* Italy
64 E6 **Beliche** *r.* Port.
74 F8 **Belici** *r. Sicilia* Italy
76 I8 **Beli Drim** *r.* Serb. and Mont.
191 J4 **Belidzhi** Rus. Fed.
77 O7 **Beli Lom** *r.* Bulg.
68 G3 **Beli Manastir** Croatia
156 F7 **Belimbing** *Sumatera* Indon.
159 I14 **Belimbing, Tanjung** *pt* Indon.
43 C7 **Belin-Béliet** France
63 N8 **Belinchón** Spain
90 B4 **Bélinga** Gabon
116 F9 **Belington** *WV* U.S.A.
15 H5 **Belinskiy** Rus. Fed.
77 J5 **Belinț** Romania
156 F5 **Belinyu** Indon.
77 K6 **Beli Timok** *r.* Serb. and Mont.
55 N2 **Belitsa** Belarus
77 L9 **Belitsa** Bulg.
17 O2 **Belitsa** Rus. Fed.
157 H6 **Belitung** *i.* Indon.
57 L5 **Beliu** Romania
91 B6 **Belize** Angola
127 O9 **Belize** Belize
127 O9 **Belize** *country* Central America
137 H3 **Bélizon** Fr. Guiana
77 J6 **Beljanica** *mt.* Serb. and Mont.
193 O2 **Bel'kovskiy, Ostrov** *i. Novosibirskiye O-va* Rus. Fed.
207 M9 **Bell** *Qld* Austr.
205 L5 **Bell** *r. N.S.W.* Austr.
108 E3 **Bell** *r. Que.* Can.
49 D10 **Bell** Ger.
97 L9 **Bell** S. Africa
49 D10 **Bell (Hunsrück)** Ger.
204 D5 **Bell, Point** *S.A.* Austr.
73 P6 **Bella** Italy
106 D4 **Bella Bella** *B.C.* Can.
42 G3 **Bellac** France
40 I5 **Bellacha, Mont** *mt.* France
147 I3 **Bellaco** Uru.
106 E4 **Bella Coola** *B.C.* Can.
106 E4 **Bella Coola** *r. B.C.* Can.
27 C4 **Bellacorick** Rep. of Ireland
138 D2 **Bella Flor** Bol.
27 I3 **Bellaghy** *Northern Ireland* U.K.
70 G4 **Bellagio** Italy
27 E5 **Bellahy** Rep. of Ireland
110 I5 **Bellaire** *MI* U.S.A.
121 H11 **Bellaire** *TX* U.S.A.
27 F5 **Bellanagare** Rep. of Ireland
27 G4 **Bellanaleck** *Northern Ireland* U.K.
27 F3 **Bellanamore** Rep. of Ireland
27 F6 **Bellaneeny** Rep. of Ireland
70 G3 **Bellano** Italy
73 L2 **Bellante** Italy
71 M7 **Bellaria** Italy
176 E5 **Bellary** *Karnataka* India
205 L3 **Bellata** *N.S.W.* Austr.
147 I2 **Bella Unión** Uru.
28 B5 **Bellavally Gap** *pass* Rep. of Ireland
27 D5 **Bellavary** Rep. of Ireland
144 F3 **Bella Vista** *Corrientes* Arg.
145 C8 **Bella Vista** *Santa Cruz* Arg.
139 E3 **Bella Vista** Bol.
139 F5 **Bella Vista** Para.
136 B6 **Bellavista** *Cajamarca* Peru
136 C5 **Bellavista** *Loreto* Peru
72 D8 **Bellavista, Capo** *c. Sardegna* Italy
138 C5 **Bella Vista, Salar de** *salt flat* Chile
202 I6 **Bell Block** *North I.* N.Z.
207 M6 **Bell Cay** *rf Qld* Austr.
66 G4 **Bellcaire d'Urgell** Spain
116 D10 **Belle** *WV* U.S.A.
130 G4 **Belle-Anse** Haiti
51 E7 **Belleben** Ger.
41 H6 **Belledonne** *mts* France
27 F4 **Belleek** *Northern Ireland* U.K.
27 J4 **Belleek** *Northern Ireland* U.K.
37 L7 **Bellefontaine** France
131 □3 **Bellefontaine** Martinique
116 B8 **Bellefontaine** *OH* U.S.A.
116 H8 **Bellefonte** *PA* U.S.A.
120 D3 **Belle Fourche** *SD* U.S.A.
120 D3 **Belle Fourche** *r. SD* U.S.A.
36 D8 **Bellegarde** *Centre* France
41 F9 **Bellegarde** *Languedoc-Roussillon* France
42 I4 **Bellegarde-en-Marche** France
40 H4 **Bellegarde-sur-Valserine** France
115 G12 **Belle Glade** *FL* U.S.A.
38 E7 **Belle-Île** *i.* France
109 K3 **Belle Isle** *i. Nfld and Lab.* Can.
109 J3 **Belle Isle, Strait of** *Nfld and Lab.* Can.
38 E4 **Belle-Isle-en-Terre** France
39 M5 **Bellême** France
118 F4 **Belle Mead** *NJ* U.S.A.
125 U6 **Bellemont** *AZ* U.S.A.
40 C4 **Bellenaves** France
53 I5 **Bellenberg** Ger.
36 B4 **Bellencombre** France
131 □4 **Belleplaine** Barbados
40 C4 **Bellerive-sur-Allier** France
37 M6 **Belles-Forêts** France
108 E4 **Belleterre** *Que.* Can.
36 F5 **Belleu** France
40 J4 **Bellevaux** France
40 G3 **Bellevesvre** France
108 E4 **Belleville** *Ont.* Can.
40 F4 **Belleville** France
120 G6 **Belleville** *KS* U.S.A.
119 G3 **Belleville** *NJ* U.S.A.
40 B1 **Belleville-sur-Loire** France
37 J5 **Belleville-sur-Meuse** France
38 I8 **Belleville-sur-Vie** France
114 B4 **Bellevue** *IA* U.S.A.
110 I7 **Bellevue** *MI* U.S.A.
120 H5 **Bellevue** *NE* U.S.A.
116 C7 **Bellevue** *OH* U.S.A.
122 C3 **Bellevue** *WA* U.S.A.
41 D6 **Bellevue-la-Montagne** France
40 H5 **Belley** France
88 C5 **Belle Yella** Liberia
110 F9 **Bellflower** *IL* U.S.A.
52 E3 **Bellheim** Ger.
40 J2 **Bellherbe** France
40 H4 **Bellignat** France
205 N4 **Bellingen** *N.S.W.* Austr.
29 M3 **Bellingham** *Northumberland, England* U.K.
122 C2 **Bellingham** *WA* U.S.A.
212 U2 **Bellingshausen** *research stn* Antarctica
212 S2 **Bellingshausen Sea** Antarctica
44 L2 **Bellingwolde** Neth.
70 F4 **Bellinzago Novarese** Italy
70 G3 **Bellinzona** Switz.
109 K3 **Bell Island** *Nfld and Lab.* Can
106 D4 **Bell Island Hot Springs** *AK* U.S.A.
73 N6 **Bellizzi** Italy
118 E5 **Bellmawr** *NJ* U.S.A.
136 C3 **Bello** Col.
63 R7 **Bello** Spain
43 C8 **Bellocq** France
200 □6 **Bellona** *i.* Solomon Is
39 K4 **Bellou-en-Houlme** France
117 M5 **Bellows Falls** *VT* U.S.A.
185 M7 **Bellpat** Pak.
66 H4 **Bellpuig** Spain
26 L10 **Bell Rock** *i. Scotland* U.K.
26 H11 **Bellshill** *North Lanarkshire, Scotland* U.K.
20 □ **Bellsund** *inlet* Svalbard
71 M3 **Belluno** Italy
71 M3 **Belluno** *prov.* Italy
176 E6 **Belluru** *Karnataka* India
119 G2 **Bellvale** *NY* U.S.A.
66 I3 **Bellver de Cerdanya** Spain
147 F3 **Bell Ville** Arg.
96 C9 **Bellville** S. Africa
116 C8 **Bellville** *OH* U.S.A.
121 G11 **Bellville** *TX* U.S.A.
116 G8 **Bellwood** *PA* U.S.A.
106 H5 **Belly** *r. Alta* Can.
49 F6 **Belm** Ger.
119 G4 **Belmar** *NJ* U.S.A.
57 K5 **Bélmegyer** Hungary
65 I4 **Bélmez** Spain
65 M5 **Bélmez de la Moraleda** Spain
205 M5 **Belmont** *N.S.W.* Austr.
43 E8 **Belmont** France
96 I5 **Belmont** S. Africa
26 □O1 **Belmont** *Shetland, Scotland* U.K.
117 N5 **Belmont** *NH* U.S.A.
116 G6 **Belmont** *NY* U.S.A.
40 E4 **Belmont-de-la-Loire** France
143 H1 **Belmonte** Brazil
62 F8 **Belmonte** Port.
62 H2 **Belmonte** *Asturias* Spain
63 O9 **Belmonte** *Castilla-La Mancha* Spain
73 Q9 **Belmonte Calabro** Italy
73 M4 **Belmonte del Sannio** Italy
73 J3 **Belmonte in Sabina** Italy
74 E7 **Belmonte Mezzagno** *Sicilia* Italy
41 B9 **Belmont-sur-Rance** France
127 O9 **Belmopan** Belize
207 H5 **Belmore Creek** *r. Qld* Austr.
27 C4 **Belmullet** Rep. of Ireland
95 □J4 **Belo** Madag.
141 E5 **Belo Campo** Brazil
45 E7 **Belœil** Belgium
183 T1 **Beloglazovo** Rus. Fed.
162 F3 **Belogorsk** Rus. Fed.
Belogorsk Ukr. *see* **Bilohirs'k**
17 T3 **Belogor'ye** Rus. Fed.
77 K7 **Belogradchik** Bulg.
95 □J5 **Beloha** Madag.
136 E5 **Belo Horizonte** *Amazonas* Brazil
143 F3 **Belo Horizonte** *Minas Gerais* Brazil
120 F6 **Beloit** *KS* U.S.A.
110 E7 **Beloit** *WI* U.S.A.
140 F4 **Belo Jardim** Brazil

Column 1

205 I6 Beulah *Vic.* Austr.
30 E3 Beulah *Powys, Wales* U.K.
110 H5 Beulah *MI* U.S.A.
120 E2 Beult r. *England* U.K.
31 M5 Beult i. *England* U.K.
44 I5 Beuningen Neth.
49 J8 Beuren Ger.
84 B6 Beurfou *well* Chad
52 F5 Beuron Ger.
37 I7 Beurville France
40 E3 Beuvray, Mont *hill* France
40 D2 Beuvron r. France
39 N7 Beuvron r. France
36 E2 Beuvry France
39 L3 Beuzeville France
73 O2 Bevagna Italy
70 B2 Bevaix Switz.
49 E6 Bever r. Ger.
41 L9 Bévéra r. France
209 D12 Beverley *W.A.* Austr.
29 Q6 Beverley *East Riding of Yorkshire, England* U.K.
117 O6 Beverly *MA* U.S.A.
118 F4 Beverly *NJ* U.S.A.
116 D9 Beverly *OH* U.S.A.
124 N7 Beverly Hills *CA* U.S.A.
107 K1 Beverly Lake *Nunavut* Can.
49 H7 Bevern Ger.
48 G4 Beverstedt Ger.
49 H7 Beverungen Ger.
44 G4 Beverwijk Neth.
36 C7 Béville-le-Comte France
30 H3 Bewdley *Worcestershire, England* U.K.
31 M5 Bewl Water *resr England* U.K.
70 C3 Bex Switz.
52 C3 Bexbach Ger.
31 M6 Bexhill *East Sussex, England* U.K.
79 J5 Beyağaç Turkey
189 M6 Beyǎnli Iran
79 I1 Beyazköy Turkey
43 D6 Beychac-et-Caillau France
79 M2 Beyciler Turkey
79 J4 Beydağ Turkey
79 L6 Bey Dağları *mts* Turkey
191 B7 Beydoğan Turkey
79 J3 Beyel Turkey
51 E6 Beyendorf Ger.
79 L6 Beykonak Turkey
79 M2 Beyköy Turkey
79 L2 Beyköy *Eskişehir* Turkey
79 K1 Beyköy Turkey
88 C4 Beyla Guinea
Beylagan Azer. see Beyläqan
191 I6 Beyläqan Azer.
79 M3 Beylikova Turkey
85 I6 Beylul Eritrea
43 G6 Beynac-et-Cazenac France
158 F5 Beynat France
45 I7 Beyne-Heusay Belgium
182 F5 Beyneu Kazakh.
40 G5 Beynost France
79 I4 Beyobası Turkey
165 Q15 Beyoneisu-retsugan i. Japan
38 E3 Beypazarı Turkey
188 H4 Beypazarı Turkey
176 D7 Beypore *Kerala* India
92 E3 Beyra Somalia
184 E8 Beyram Iran
Beyrouth Lebanon see Beirut
188 E5 Beyşehir Turkey
188 E5 Beyşehir Gölü l. Turkey
17 S8 Beysug Rus. Fed.
17 R7 Beysug r. Rus. Fed.
17 R7 Beysugskiy Liman *lag.* Rus. Fed.
17 R8 Beysuzhek r. Rus. Fed.
162 D2 Beytonovo Rus. Fed.
189 K5 Beytüşşebap Turkey
41 G7 Bez r. France
184 G4 Bezameh Iran
67 C7 Bezas Spain
58 A5 Bezau Austria
14 J4 Bezbozhnik Rus. Fed.
76 G5 Bezdan *Vojvodina, Srbija* Serb. and Mont.
40 G2 Bèze France
191 E2 Bezengi Rus. Fed.
184 G7 Bezenjān Iran
56 G4 Bezenye Hungary
18 M5 Bezhanitskaya Vozvyshennost' *hills* Rus. Fed.
18 M5 Bezhanitsy Rus. Fed.
77 M7 Bezhanovo Bulg.
19 T4 Bezhetsk Rus. Fed.
19 T4 Bezhetskiy Verkh *reg.* Rus. Fed.
191 H3 Bezhta Rus. Fed.
41 C10 Béziers France
55 I1 Bezledy Pol.
Bezmein Turkm. see Byuzmeýin
41 F9 Bezouce France
57 L3 Bežovce Slovakia
178 D7 Bhabhar *Gujarat* India
179 I7 Bhabhua *Bihar* India
178 E8 Bhabra *Madh. Prad.* India
178 C8 Bhachau *Gujarat* India
178 C8 Bhachbhar *Rajasthan* India
178 B9 Bhadar r. India
178 E3 Bhadarwah *Jammu and Kashmir* India
185 P6 Bhadaur *Punjab* India
178 F7 Bhadaura *Madh. Prad.* India
178 G8 Bhadgaon Nepal
179 I7 Bhadohi *Uttar Prad.* India
178 E5 Bhadra *Rajasthan* India
176 G4 Bhadrachalam *Andhra Prad.* India
178 D7 Bhadrajan *Rajasthan* India
179 K9 Bhadrak *Orissa* India
176 D6 Bhadra Reservoir India
176 D6 Bhadravati *Karnataka* India
185 L7 Bhag Pak.
173 C10 Bhag r. Pak.
179 K7 Bhagalpur *Bihar* India
179 K6 Bhagirathi r. India
178 E3 Bhainsa *Andhra Prad.* India
178 F9 Bhainsdehi *Madh. Prad.* India
179 M7 Bhairab Bazar Bangl.
179 I6 Bhairawa Nepal
Bhairawaha Nepal see Bhairawa
181 I4 Bhairi Hol mt. Pak.
185 N6 Bhakkar Pak.
Bhaktapur Nepal see Bhadgaon
Bhaleshear i. *Scotland* U.K. see Baleshare
176 E3 Bhalki India
185 O5 Bhalwal Pak.
178 F9 Bhamgarh *Madh. Prad.* India
158 C2 Bhamo Myanmar
176 G3 Bhamragarh *Mahar.* India
178 G9 Bhandara *Mahar.* India
178 G8 Bhander *Madh. Prad.* India
178 H6 Bhangaha *Uttar Prad.* India
177 I3 Bhanjanagar *Orissa* India
178 G8 Bhanrer Range *hills Madh. Prad.* India
178 H9 Bhanupratappur *Chhattisgarh* India
178 F6 Bharatpur *Rajasthan* India
179 J6 Bharatpur Nepal
179 N6 Bhareli r. India
185 J9 Bharī r. Pak.
178 G6 Bharthana *Uttar Prad.* India
178 D3 Bharuch *Gujarat* India
178 H9 Bharuaghat *Chhattisgarh* India
178 G4 Bhatapara India
179 L8 Bhatiapara Ghat Bangl.
Bhatinda *Punjab* India see Bathinda
176 D3 Bhatkal *Karnataka* India
178 B9 Bhatpara *W. Bengal* India
185 O5 Bhaun Gharibwal Pak.
176 E3 Bhavani *Tamil Nadu* India
176 E7 Bhavani r. India
176 E7 Bhavani Sagar l. India

Column 2

178 D9 Bhavnagar *Gujarat* India
185 O6 Bhawana Pak.
177 H3 Bhawanipatna *Orissa* India
Bhearnaraigh, Eilean i. *Western Isles, Scotland* U.K. see Berneray
Bheemavaram *Andhra Prad.* India see Bhimavaram
97 O3 Bhekuzulu S. Africa
178 H7 Bhelki *Madh. Prad.* India
185 O5 Bhera Pak.
178 H5 Bheri r. Nepal
89 G4 Bhida Nigeria
157 M2 Bhidadari, Tanjung pt Malaysia
176 E4 Bhidar *Karnataka* India
43 A9 Bhidart France
178 E6 Bhidasar *Rajasthan* India
187 N4 Bhiddid Oman
117 O5 Bhiddeford *ME* U.S.A.
31 N5 Bhiddenden *Kent, England* U.K.
44 I4 Bhiddinghuizen Neth.
29 M7 Bhiddulph *Staffordshire, England* U.K.
26 F9 Bhidean nam Bian mt. *Scotland* U.K.
30 D5 Bhideford *Devon, England* U.K.
Bhideford Bay *England* U.K. see Barnstaple Bay
71 M7 Bhidford r. Italy
31 I3 Bhidford-on-Avon *Warwickshire, England* U.K.
20 Q2 Bhidjugadje Norway
184 Q7 Bhidkhan, Kūh-e mt. Iran
184 H4 Bhidokh India
87 F5 Bhidon 5 *tourist site* Alg.
43 C9 Bhidos r. France
43 B8 Bhidouze r. France
57 K3 Bhidovce Slovakia
162 G5 Bhidzhan Rus. Fed.
162 H5 Bhidzhar r. Rus. Fed.
43 B8 Bhie *prov.* Angola
43 H10 Bhieber Ger.
52 E2 Bhiebesheim am Rhein Ger.
55 K2 Bhiebrza r. Pol.
55 K2 Bhiebrzański Park Narodowy *nat. park* Pol.
55 J6 Bhiecz Pol.
52 D3 Bhiedenkopf Ger.
55 I6 Bhiederitz Ger.
66 D3 Bhiel Spain
50 C1 Bhiel Switz.
57 I1 Bhielańsko-Tyniecki Park Krajobrazowy Pol.
55 K3 Bhielany-Żylaki Pol.
55 I3 Bhielawa Pol.
74 F9 Bhiancavilla *Sicilia* Italy
75 K7 Bhianco Italy
71 L5 Bhianco, Canale *canal* Italy
74 E9 Bhianco, Capo c. *Sicilia* Italy
70 D4 Bhianco, Corno mt. Italy
169 Q9 Bhiandangang Kou r. mouth China
70 E5 Bhiandrate Italy
90 D3 Bhianga C.A.R.
88 E5 Bhiankouma Côte d'Ivoire
88 E5 Bhiankouan Côte d'Ivoire
40 I3 Bhians-les-Usiers France
70 E5 Bhiasca Switz.
169 R4 Bhianzhou *Jilin* China
Bhianzhuang *Shandong* China see Cangshan
154 D8 Bhiao *Mindanao* Phil.
178 F8 Bhiaora *Madh. Prad.* India
67 D10 Bhiar Spain
184 F3 Bhiārjmand Iran
155 D2 Bhiaro i. Indon.
43 J9 Bhiarritz France
42 H6 Bhiars-sur-Cère France
186 G3 Bhi'ār Tabrāk *well Saudi Arabia*
43 B7 Bhias *Aquitaine* France
43 F7 Bhias *Aquitaine* France
70 F3 Bhiasca Switz.
147 I2 Bhiassini Uru.
57 H4 Bhiatorbágy Hungary
85 F2 Bhibā Egypt
164 S3 Bhibai Japan
91 B8 Bhibala Angola
90 A4 Bhibas Gabon
205 L7 Bhibbenluke *N.S.W.* Austr.
71 L8 Bhibbiena Italy
71 J9 Bhibbona Italy
107 M2 Bhibby Island *Nunavut* Can.
89 I4 Bhibémi Cameroon
52 E5 Bhiberach Ger.
52 H5 Bhiberach an der Riß Ger.
53 I4 Bhiberbach Ger.
53 J3 Bhibert r. Ger.
88 E5 Bhibiani Ghana
176 G9 Bhibile Sri Lanka
71 O4 Bhibione Italy
19 P5 Bhibirevo Rus. Fed.
179 M7 Bhibiyana r. Bangl.
52 E2 Bhibis Ger.
16 D4 Bhibrka Ukr.
31 I4 Bhibury *Gloucestershire, England* U.K.
18 J5 Bhicanu ezers l. Latvia
143 F4 Bhicas Brazil
57 M4 Bhicaz *Maramureş* Romania
77 O4 Bhicaz *Neamţ* Romania
73 O5 Bhiccari Italy
188 E4 Bhiçer Turkey
31 J4 Bhicester *Oxfordshire, England* U.K.
31 I3 Bhichabberra *Rajasthan* India
131 I7 Bhiche *Trin. and Tob.*
92 C2 Bhicheng Eth.
Bhicheng *Chongqing* China see Bishan
205 L9 Bhichena *Tas.* Austr.
162 I5 Bhichevaya Rus. Fed.
162 K2 Bhichi r. Rus. Fed.
53 K6 Bhichl Ger.
58 C5 Bhichlbach Ger.
176 C5 Bhichliram *Goa* India
191 F5 Bhichvan *Azer.*
169 J1 Bhichura Rus. Fed.
191 G3 Bhichvint'i Georgia
191 B2 Bhichvint'is Konts'khi pt Georgia
52 F2 Bhickenbach Ger.
97 N4 Bhickersdorp S. Africa
208 D3 Bhickerton Island *N.T.* Austr.
30 D7 Bhickleigh *Devon, England* U.K.
30 E6 Bhickleigh *Devon, England* U.K.
31 N4 Bhicknacre *Essex, England* U.K.

Column 3

125 U3 Bicknell *UT* U.S.A.
191 J5 Bico *Azer.*
155 F3 Bicoli *Halmahera* Indon.
67 D9 Bicorp Spain
64 C5 Bicos Port.
57 H4 Bicske Hungary
32 G2 Bicske *Shropshire, England* U.K.
91 B8 Bicuari, Parque Nacional do *nat. park* Angola
176 D3 Bidar *Mahar.* India
89 G4 Bida Nigeria
43 B9 Bidar India
157 M2 Bidadari, Tanjung pt Malaysia
176 E4 Bidar *Karnataka* India
43 A9 Bidart France
178 E6 Bidasar *Rajasthan* India
187 N4 Bidbid Oman
117 O5 Biddeford *ME* U.S.A.
31 N5 Biddenden *Kent, England* U.K.
44 I4 Biddinghuizen Neth.
29 M7 Biddulph *Staffordshire, England* U.K.
26 F9 Bidean nam Bian mt. *Scotland* U.K.
30 D5 Bideford *Devon, England* U.K.
Bideford Bay *England* U.K. see Barnstaple Bay
71 M7 Bidford r. Italy
31 I3 Bidford-on-Avon *Warwickshire, England* U.K.
20 Q2 Bidjugadje Norway
184 Q7 Bidkhan, Kūh-e mt. Iran
184 H4 Bidokh India
87 F5 Bidon 5 *tourist site* Alg.
43 C9 Bidos r. France
43 B8 Bidouze r. France
57 K3 Bidovce Slovakia
162 G5 Bidzhan Rus. Fed.
162 H5 Bidzhar r. Rus. Fed.
43 B8 Bie *prov.* Angola
43 H10 Bieber Ger.
52 E2 Biebesheim am Rhein Ger.
55 K2 Biebrza r. Pol.
55 K2 Biebrzański Park Narodowy *nat. park* Pol.
55 J6 Biecz Pol.
52 D3 Biedenkopf Ger.
55 I6 Biederitz Ger.
66 D3 Biel Spain
50 C1 Biel Switz.
Bieler See l. Switz.
54 C2 Bielawa Pol.
55 J3 Bielawy Pol.
70 E4 Biella Italy
70 E4 Biella *prov.* Italy
43 D9 Bielle France
66 F2 Bielsa Spain
55 H3 Bielsko-Biała Pol.
55 L3 Bielsk Podlaski Pol.
49 I8 Bielstein *hill* Ger.
48 J4 Bienenbüttel Ger.
159 H9 Biên Hoa Vietnam
54 D4 Bieniów Pol.
55 N3 Bienservida Spain
64 G4 Bienvenida Spain
63 P7 Bienvenida *hill* Spain
22 J5 Bienvenüe *mt.* France
137 H4 Bienville, Lac l. *Que.* Can.
91 B8 Bié Plateau Angola
55 H1 Bierawa Pol.
54 G5 Bierawka r. Pol.
207 J9 Bierbank *Qld* Austr.
55 J6 Bierdzany Pol.
51 F7 Biere Ger.
70 A2 Bière Switz.
55 J3 Bierge Spain
39 J6 Bierné France
43 G10 Biert France
55 H5 Bieruń Pol.
54 E3 Bierutów Pol.
54 G3 Bierzwienna-Długa Pol.
54 D2 Bierzwnik Pol.
50 E5 Biese r. Ger.
50 E5 Biesenkier Pol.
54 E1 Biesiekierz Pol.
97 J2 Biesiesvlei S. Africa
37 J7 Biesles France
54 E1 Biesowice Pol.
96 H7 Biesresspoort S. Africa
55 K6 Bieszczadzki Park Narodowy *nat. park* Pol.
52 E4 Bietenfeld Ger.
52 G4 Bietigheim-Bissingen Ger.
50 I4 Bietsche Ger.
70 D3 Bietschhorn mt. Switz.
45 H9 Bièvre Belgium
73 O4 Biferno r. Italy
20 C1 Bifoun Gabon
20 C1 Bifröst Iceland
164 T2 Biga Japan
79 I2 Biga Turkey
79 J3 Biga r. Turkey
79 J3 Bigadiç Turkey
147 G3 Bigand Arg.
73 F7 Biganos France
67 O11 Biganre Spain
73 J9 Biga Yarımadası pen. Turkey
122 I3 Big Baldy Mountain *MT* U.S.A.
106 F5 Big Bar Creek *B.C.* Can.
203 C11 Big Bay *South I.* N.Z.
110 D3 Big Bay *MI* U.S.A.
200 □⁵ Big Bay Vanuatu
110 D4 Big Bay de Noc *MI* U.S.A.
124 P7 Big Bear Lake *CA* U.S.A.
122 I3 Big Belt Mountains *MT* U.S.A.
97 P7 Big Bend Swaziland
121 D11 Big Bend National Park *TX* U.S.A.
121 J9 Big Black r. *MS* U.S.A.
120 G6 Big Blue r. *NE* U.S.A.
30 E7 Bigbury Bay *England* U.K.
30 E7 Bigbury-on-Sea *Devon, England* U.K.
202 □ Big Bush *Chatham I.* S. Pacific Ocean
121 K9 Big Canyon *watercourse TX* U.S.A.
115 G13 Big Cypress National Preserve *nature res. FL* U.S.A.
204 H6 Big Desert Wilderness Park *nature res. Vic.* Austr.
110 E5 Big Eau Pleine Reservoir *WI* U.S.A.
200 □³ᵃ Bigej i. *Kwajalein* Marshall Is
200 □³ᵃ Bigej Channel *Kwajalein* Marshall Is
118 D5 Big Elk Creek r. *MD* U.S.A.
26 L4 Bigga *Highland, Scotland* U.K.
120 I1 Big Falls *MN* U.S.A.
110 A1 Big Fork r. *MN* U.S.A.
107 J4 Biggar *Sask.* Can.
26 I11 Biggar *South Lanarkshire, Scotland* U.K.
200 □³ᵃ Biggarenn i. *Kwajalein* Marshall Is
97 N4 Biggarsberg S. Africa
208 H3 Bigge Island *W.A.* Austr.
31 L4 Biggin *Derbyshire, England* U.K.
31 L4 Biggin Hill *Greater London, England* U.K.
31 K3 Biggleswade *Bedfordshire, England* U.K.
57 I6 Biggs *CA* U.S.A.
122 G2 Biggs *OR* U.S.A.
122 H4 Big Hole r. *MT* U.S.A.
122 G3 Bighorn r. *MT/WY* U.S.A.
122 K4 Bighorn Mountains *WY* U.S.A.
89 J3 Bigi Dem. Rep. Congo
200 □³ᵃ Bigi i. *Kwajalein* Marshall Is
19 W8 Bigo'il Rus. Fed.
191 I5 Bığır Azer.
105 K3 Big Island *Nunavut* Can.
106 G2 Big Island *N.W.T.* Can.
116 F11 Big Island *VA* U.S.A.
106 C2 Big Island *Ont.* Can.
121 E10 Big Lake *TX* U.S.A.
117 O3 Big Lake *l. ME* U.S.A.
122 L2 Big Lost r. *ID* U.S.A.
122 I2 Big Muddy Creek r. *MT* U.S.A.
38 F6 Bignan France
70 F3 Bignasco Switz.
88 A3 Bignona Senegal
91 E6 Bigogo Dem. Rep. Congo
116 F11 Big Otter r. *VA* U.S.A.
124 O2 Big Pine *CA* U.S.A.
124 M7 Big Pine Peak *CA* U.S.A.
122 K3 Big Porcupine Creek r. *MT* U.S.A.
106 C3 Big Port Walter *AK* U.S.A.
110 I6 Big Rapids *MI* U.S.A.
110 E5 Big Rib r. *WI* U.S.A.
107 J4 Big River *Sask.* Can.
110 H5 Big Sable Point *MI* U.S.A.
106 C2 Big Salmon *Y.T.* Can.
106 C2 Big Salmon r. *Y.T.* Can.
107 J4 Big Sand Lake *Man.* Can.
122 I2 Big Sandy *MT* U.S.A.
122 J6 Big Sandy r. *WY* U.S.A.
125 S7 Big Sandy *watercourse AZ* U.S.A.
120 D6 Big Sandy Creek r. *CO* U.S.A.
107 J4 Big Sandy Lake *Sask.* Can.
110 A3 Big Sandy Lake *MN* U.S.A.
120 G3 Big Sioux r. *SD* U.S.A.
124 O3 Big Smoky Valley *NV* U.S.A.
203 B14 Big South Cape Island *Stewart I.* N.Z.
121 E9 Big Spring *TX* U.S.A.
120 E3 Big Springs *NE* U.S.A.
107 I5 Big Stone *MN* U.S.A.
120 G3 Big Stone City *SD* U.S.A.
116 C12 Big Stone Gap *VA* U.S.A.
107 M4 Bigstone Lake *Man.* Can.
121 H10 Big Thicket National Preserve *nature res. TX* U.S.A.
122 J4 Big Timber *MT* U.S.A.
108 B2 Big Trout Lake *Ont.* Can.
108 B2 Big Trout Lake l. *Ont.* Can.
66 C2 Biguglia *Corse* France
72 C2 Biguglia, Étang de *lag. Corse* France
106 H4 Big Valley *Alta* Can.
125 U4 Big Water *UT* U.S.A.
111 O4 Bigwin *Ont.* Can.
68 E3 Bihać Bos.-Herz.
179 J7 Bihar *state* India
57 K4 Biharamulo Tanz.
179 K7 Bihariganj *Bihar* India
57 K4 Biharkeresztes Hungary
179 J7 Biharnagybajom Hungary
179 J7 Bihar Sharif *Bihar* India
57 K5 Biharugrai-halastavak *lakes* Hungary
57 L5 Bihor *county* Romania
77 K4 Bihor, Vârful mt. Romania
164 V3 Bihoro Japan
57 L5 Bihorului, Munţii mts Romania
179 N6 Bihpuriagaon *Assam* India
182 F4 Biikzhal Kazakh.
178 E9 Bijagarh *Madh. Prad.* India
88 A4 Bijagós, Arquipélago dos is Guinea-Bissau
178 E7 Bijainagar *Rajasthan* India
178 F6 Bijaipur *Madh. Prad.* India
178 D6 Bijapur *Karnataka* India
184 B4 Bijār Iran
176 G3 Bijapur *Chhattisgarh* India
178 D7 Bijawar *Madh. Prad.* India
68 F4 Bijeljina Bos.-Herz.
68 E3 Bijelo Polje *Crna Gora* Serb. and Mont.
76 H7 Bijelo Polje *Crna Gora* Serb. and Mont.
178 H8 Bijeraghogarh *Madh. Prad.* India
170 E3 Bijie *Guizhou* China
178 I3 Bijji *Chhattisgarh* India
178 G6 Bijnor *Uttar Prad.* India
185 N7 Bijnot Pak.
67 E8 Bijuela *Rajasthan* India
187 J3 Bijoutier i. Seychelles
187 J3 Bijrān, Khashm *hill*
178 D6 Bikampur *Rajasthan* India
177 H4 Bikaner *Rajasthan* India
179 H6 Bira *Daqing Qarabağ* Azer.
191 L5 Bikaş Azer.
162 I5 Bikin Rus. Fed.
162 I5 Bikin r. Rus. Fed.
189 L7 Bināb Iran
95 F4 Bikita Zimbabwe
92 B2 Bikori Sudan
91 E5 Bikoro Dem. Rep. Congo
170 E2 Bikou *Gansu* China
170 E2 Bikou Shuiku *resr Gansu* China
57 I6 Bikovo *Vojvodina, Srbija* Serb. and Mont.
17 H4 Bila r. Ukr.
91 E5 Bila *r. Dem. Rep. Congo*
154 E7 Bilaa Point *Mindanao* Phil.
191 K5 Bilacari *Azer.*
187 M8 Bilād Banī Bū 'Alī Oman
187 M8 Bilād Banī Bū Ḥasan Oman
186 E5 Bilād Sawāb *reg. Saudi Arabia*
186 C6 Bilād Zahrān *reg. Saudi Arabia*
191 M6 Bila Krynytsya Ukr.
191 B7 Bilaloğlu Turkey
187 M4 Bilangbilangan i. Indon.
178 D6 Bilara *Rajasthan* India
178 I8 Bilaspur *Chhattisgarh* India
183 J7 Bilaspur *Hima. Prad.* India
16 F2 Bila Tserkva Ukr.
191 J6 Bilasuvar *Azer.*
91 D5 Bilati *r. Dem. Rep. Congo*
95 C4 Bilauri Nepal
205 M3 Bilbao Spain
69 O2 Bilbays Egypt
176 M6 Bilbo Spain see Bilbao
178 D7 Bilbor Romania
178 D6 Bilara *Rajasthan* India
178 I8 Bilaspur *Chhattisgarh* India
207 L9 Bildh *Qld* Austr.
91 C6 Bindu Dem. Rep. Congo
31 O5 Birchington *Kent, England* U.K.
205 I6 Birchip *Vic.* Austr.

Column 4

49 E8 Biggesee l. Ger.
31 M5 Biggin Hill *Greater London, England* U.K.
31 L3 Biggleswade *Bedfordshire, England* U.K.
124 K2 Biggs *CA* U.S.A.
122 G2 Biggs *OR* U.S.A.
122 H4 Big Hole r. *MT* U.S.A.
122 G3 Bighorn r. *MT/WY* U.S.A.
122 K4 Bighorn Mountains *WY* U.S.A.
89 J3 Bigi Dem. Rep. Congo
200 □³ᵃ Bigi i. *Kwajalein* Marshall Is
19 W8 Bigo'il Rus. Fed.
191 I5 Bığır Azer.
105 K3 Big Island *Nunavut* Can.
117 O3 Big Lake *l. ME* U.S.A.
122 L2 Big Lost r. *ID* U.S.A.
122 I2 Big Muddy Creek r. *MT* U.S.A.
38 F6 Bignan France
70 F3 Bignasco Switz.
88 A3 Bignona Senegal
91 E6 Bigogo Dem. Rep. Congo
43 D10 Bigorre reg. France
116 F11 Big Otter r. *VA* U.S.A.
124 O2 Big Pine *CA* U.S.A.
124 M7 Big Pine Peak *CA* U.S.A.
122 K3 Big Porcupine Creek r. *MT* U.S.A.
106 C3 Big Port Walter *AK* U.S.A.
110 I6 Big Rapids *MI* U.S.A.
110 E5 Big Rib r. *WI* U.S.A.
107 J4 Big River *Sask.* Can.
110 H5 Big Sable Point *MI* U.S.A.
106 C2 Big Salmon *Y.T.* Can.
106 C2 Big Salmon r. *Y.T.* Can.
107 J4 Big Sand Lake *Man.* Can.
122 I2 Big Sandy *MT* U.S.A.
122 J6 Big Sandy r. *WY* U.S.A.
125 S7 Big Sandy *watercourse AZ* U.S.A.
120 D6 Big Sandy Creek r. *CO* U.S.A.
107 J4 Big Sandy Lake *Sask.* Can.
110 A3 Big Sandy Lake *MN* U.S.A.
120 G3 Big Sioux r. *SD* U.S.A.
124 O3 Big Smoky Valley *NV* U.S.A.
203 B14 Big South Cape Island *Stewart I.* N.Z.
40 C5 Billom France
22 H3 Bille r. Ger.
48 J3 Bille Denmark
49 D7 Bille r. Ger.
31 N4 Billericay *Essex, England* U.K.
40 H4 Billiat France
204 H6 Billiat Conservation Park *nature res. S.A.* Austr.
52 G3 Billigheim Ger.
208 I5 Billiluna *W.A.* Austr.
208 I5 Billiluna Aboriginal Reserve *W.A.* Austr.
214 J2 Billingford *Norfolk, England* U.K.
29 O4 Billingham *Stockton-on-Tees, England* U.K.
29 Q7 Billinghay *Lincolnshire, England* U.K.
122 J4 Billings *MT* U.S.A.
31 L5 Billingshurst *West Sussex, England* U.K.
31 P2 Billockby *Norfolk, England* U.K.
30 G6 Bill of Portland hd *England* U.K.
40 C5 Billom France
22 H3 Billund Denmark
21 J9 Billund *airport* Denmark
125 R7 Bill Williams r. *AZ* U.S.A.
125 T6 Bill Williams Mountain *AZ* U.S.A.
89 I4 Billy France
185 P4 Bilma Niger
92 C2 Bilo Eth.
17 J3 Bilohir"ya Ukr.
17 N3 Bilohorivka Ukr.
17 S4 Biloluts'k Ukr.
17 L3 Bilopillya Ukr.
17 Q3 Biloluts'k Ukr.
57 G2 Bilovice Czech Rep.
17 S4 Bilovods'k Ukr.
121 K10 Biloxi *MS* U.S.A.
17 L7 Bilozerka Ukr.
17 Q5 Bilozers'ke Ukr.
206 G8 Bilpa Morea Claypan *salt flat Qld* Austr.
49 J2 Bilshausen Ger.
16 D4 Bil'shivtsi Ukr.
77 N3 Bilsi *Uttar Prad.* India
17 N3 Bil'ky Ukr.
16 F2 Bilston *Midlothian, Scotland* U.K.
44 H3 Bilthoven Neth.
178 E7 Biltine Chad
178 F6 Biltine *pref.* Chad
184 B4 Bīlūna r. Iran
157 I3 Biluku r. Indon.
95 C3 Bilugyun Island Myanmar
17 O4 Bilukhivka Ukr.
91 C6 Bilwa *Sulawesi* Indon.
126 □R10 Bilwascarma Nic.
16 J7 Bilyayivka Ukr.
55 K6 Bilychi Ukr.
17 J3 Bilyne Ukr.
17 O5 Bily's'ke Ukr.
165 K6 Bily's'ke Ukr.
17 P3 Bilytsya Ukr.
16 I5 Bilzen Belgium
17 R4 Bima r. Indon.
91 D5 Bima *r. Dem. Rep. Congo*
157 M9 Bima, Teluk b. Sumbawa Indon.
91 B7 Bimbe Angola
178 I3 Bimbila Rajasthan India
90 C3 Bimbo C.A.R.
86 C2 Bimbo *Rajasthan* India
89 H4 Bimini Islands Bahamas
177 H4 Bimlipatam *Andhra Prad.* India
179 H6 Bimli *Daqing Qarabağ* Azer.
191 J4 Bina-Etawa *Madh. Prad.* India
170 E2 Binaija, Gunung mt. *Seram* Indon.
154 D6 Binalbagan *Negros* Phil.
184 H3 Binālūd, Kūh-e mts Iran
91 B6 Binanga Dem. Rep. Congo
191 B7 Binar *pass* Iran
155 H3 Binarowo Pol.
157 I3 Binatang *Sarawak* Malaysia
187 K6 Binbee *Qld* Austr.
188 H4 Binboğa Daği mts Turkey
91 C6 Bina Dem. Rep. Congo
14 G3 Bindki *Uttar Prad.* India
184 E3 Binalood Iran
45 F8 Binche Belgium
169 P8 Bincheng *Shandong* China

Column 5

55 K5 Biłgoraj Pol.
93 A5 Bilharamulo Tanz.
16 J7 Bilhaur *Uttar Prad.* India
90 E3 Bili Dem. Rep. Congo
90 D3 Bili r. Dem. Rep. Congo
193 R3 Bilibino Rus. Fed.
93 D8 Bilibiza Moz.
191 B6 Biliçe Turkey
Bilikǒl l. Kazakh. see Biylikol', Ozero
191 B6 Bilil Dem. Rep. Congo
158 C6 Bilin Myanmar
56 C1 Bilina Czech Rep.
73 Q6 Bilioso r. Italy
105 K3 Big Island *Nunavut* Can.
78 B2 Bilişt Albania
92 D4 Bilis Qooqaani Somalia
157 M2 Bilit Sabah Malaysia
169 R7 Biliu He r. China
57 M3 Bilky Ukr.
105 U5 Bill *WY* U.S.A.
212 L5 Bill *WY* U.S.A.
31 L6 Biliran i. Phil.
17 N8 Biliran i. Phil.
16 F4 Bilohorodka Khmel'nyts'ka Oblast' Ukr.
16 J3 Bilohorodka Kyivs'ka Oblast' Ukr.
68 E3 Bilo Gora hills Croatia
69 P4 Bilolichka Ukr.
17 O4 Bilohorivka Ukr.
17 Q4 Bilolichka Ukr.
162 H4 Bira r. Rus. Fed.
162 H4 Bira r. Rus. Fed.
186 C2 Bi'r Abā al 'Ajjāj *well Saudi Arabia*
85 G4 Bir Abu Battah *well* Egypt
188 G4 Bi'r Abū Battah *well* Egypt
190 A9 Bi'r Abū Daraj *well* Egypt
85 F5 Bir Abu Garad *well* Sudan
85 G4 Bi'r Abū Hashīm *well* Egypt
85 G5 Bi'r Abū Jady oasis Syria
84 A3 Bi'r Abū Minqār *well* Egypt
86 C4 Bi'r Abū Mūsá *well* Egypt
189 J4 Bingöl Turkey
188 H5 Binecik Turkey
86 F4 Bir ed Deheb *well* Alg.
87 G2 Bir el Arbi *well* Alg.
91 C6 Bingöl Daği mt. Turkey
170 D4 Binh Dinh Vietnam
159 I8 Binh Dinh Vietnam
158 H4 Binh Gia Vietnam
38 F4 Binic France
154 D7 Binidit *Negros* Phil.
84 C4 Bini Erda *well* Chad
66 D2 Binisale Spain
179 I9 Binika *Orissa* India
67 K8 Binisalem Spain
156 C3 Binjai *Sumatera* Indon.
84 C2 Bin Jawwad Libya
84 E2 Bir Fu'ad *well* Egypt
205 L4 Binnaway *N.S.W.* Austr.
26 G9 Binnein Mòr mt. *Scotland* U.K.
48 H5 Binnen Ger.
155 D7 Binongko i. Indon.
191 D6 Binpur W. Bengal India
203 F10 Binser, Mount South I. N.Z.
92 B2 Binshangul Gumuz admin. reg. Eth.
53 J4 Binswangen Ger.
156 C5 Bintan i. Indon.
156 D2 Bintang, Bukit mts Malaysia
156 C5 Bintuan Phil.
157 I1 Bintulu Sarawak Malaysia
154 C5 Binubusan *Luzon* Phil.
162 E6 Binxian *Heilong.* China
169 K9 Binxian *Shaanxi* China
184 B5 Birjand Iran
169 J3 Binyang *Guangxi* China
191 B7 Bin-Yauri Nigeria
52 D6 Binzen Ger.
169 J5 Binzhou *Guangxi* China see Binyang
169 P8 Binzhou *Heilong.* China see Binxian
187 I4 Bin Jāhayyim
187 I4 Bi'r Ibn Ghunaym *well Saudi Arabia*
186 C3 Bi'r Ibn Hirmās *Saudi Arabia* see Al Bi'r
186 F6 Bi'r Ibn Sarrār *well Saudi Arabia*
186 G6 Bi'r Iḍimah *well Saudi Arabia*
142 B4 Birigüi Brazil
23 E3 Birin Syria
191 G4 Birini *Şäki* Azer.
90 D3 Birini C.A.R.
84 E1 Bi'r Iṣṭabl *well* Egypt
184 H5 Birjand Iran
189 K8 Bi'r Jaydah *well Saudi Arabia*
188 G8 Bi'r Jifn *well* Yemen
84 E2 Bi'r Jubni *well* Libya
186 F5 Bi'r Jugjug *well Saudi Arabia*
186 E3 Bi'r Jurjug *well Saudi Arabia*
186 E3 Birkat Abū Salim *waterhole Saudi Arabia*
189 K8 Birkat al 'Aqabah *well* Iraq
186 F1 Birkat al Ḥamrā *well Saudi Arabia*
187 M4 Birkat al Mawz Oman
189 K9 Birkat Zubālah *waterhole Saudi Arabia*

Column 6

189 J4 Bingöl Turkey
188 H5 Bingöl *prov.* Turkey
191 J4 Bingöl Daği mt. Turkey
191 C6 Bingöl Dağları mts Turkey
170 D4 Binh Dinh Vietnam
159 I8 Binh Dinh Vietnam
38 F4 Binic France
154 D7 Binidit *Negros* Phil.
66 D2 Binisale Spain
179 I9 Binika *Orissa* India
67 K8 Binisalem Spain
156 C3 Binjai *Sumatera* Indon.
84 C2 Bin Jawwad Libya
205 L4 Binnaway *N.S.W.* Austr.
26 G9 Binnein Mòr mt. *Scotland* U.K.
48 H5 Binnen Ger.
155 D7 Binongko i. Indon.
191 D6 Binpur W. Bengal India
203 F10 Binser, Mount South I. N.Z.
92 B2 Binshangul Gumuz admin. reg. Eth.
53 J4 Binswangen Ger.
156 C5 Bintan i. Indon.
156 D2 Bintang, Bukit mts Malaysia
156 C5 Bintuan Phil.
157 I1 Bintulu Sarawak Malaysia
154 C5 Binubusan *Luzon* Phil.
162 E6 Binxian *Heilong.* China
169 K9 Binxian *Shaanxi* China
169 J3 Binyang *Guangxi* China
191 B7 Bin-Yauri Nigeria
52 D6 Binzen Ger.
169 J5 Binzhou *Guangxi* China see Binyang
169 P8 Binzhou *Heilong.* China see Binxian
170 G7 Binyang *Guangxi* China
154 E5 Biri r. Phil.
146 A5 Bíobío *admin. reg.* Chile
146 A5 Bíobío r. Chile
146 A5 Bíobio r. Chile
31 P2 Biobio *r. Equat. Guinea*
68 E2 Biograd na Moru Croatia
76 H8 Biograda Gora *nat. park* Serb. and Mont.
91 G4 Bioko i. Equat. Guinea
84 A7 Bioko
40 C5 Billom France
22 C5 Billum Denmark
21 J9 Billund Denmark
107 I5 Big Stone *MN* U.S.A.
68 F2 Bioska Serb. and Mont.
41 K9 Biot France
66 C3 Biota Spain
86 C3 Biougra Morocco
48 E5 Bippen Ger.
173 K10 Bi Qu r. *Qinghai* China
143 E3 Biquinhas Brazil
84 B3 Bir *Mahar.* India see Bid
89 J4 Bir, Ras *pt* Djibouti
162 H4 Bira Rus. Fed.
162 H4 Bira r. Rus. Fed.
186 C2 Bi'r Abā al 'Ajjāj *well Saudi Arabia*
188 G4 Bi'r Abū Battah *well* Egypt
190 A9 Bi'r Abū Daraj *well* Egypt
85 F5 Bir Abu Garad *well* Sudan
85 G4 Bi'r Abū Garad *well* Sudan
190 G2 Bi'r Abū Jady *oasis* Syria
84 A3 Bi'r Abū Minqār *well* Egypt
84 D3 Bi'r ad Damar *well* Libya
190 A8 Bi'r ad Duwaydār *well* Egypt
84 D3 Bi'r adh Dhakar *well* Libya
84 B6 Bi'r al 'Abd *well* Egypt
190 B7 Bi'r al 'Abd *well* Egypt
190 B8 Bi'r al Amīr *well Saudi Arabia*
85 F3 Bi'r al Aṭbaq *well* Egypt
84 B2 Bi'r al Fāṭīyah *well* Libya
84 A5 Bi'r al Ghanam Libya
84 B1 Bi'r al Ghanam Libya
84 A4 Bi'r al Ḥaymūr *well* Egypt
190 C6 Bi'r al Ḥiswah *well Saudi Arabia*
84 B4 Bi'r al Jadīd *well* Libya
84 A3 Bi'r al Jāhilīyah *well* Egypt
190 C6 Bir al Khamsah *well* Egypt
190 B8 Bi'r al Mālihah *well* Egypt
190 B7 Bi'r al Mashī *well* Egypt
84 B7 Bi'r al Mulūsī *well* Iraq
88 D1 Bi'r al Munbaṭiḥ *well* Syria
84 A1 Bi'r al Mushayqiq *well* Egypt
84 C2 Bi'r al Muwaylih *well* Libya
84 A3 Bi'r al Qaṭrānī *well* Egypt
84 B4 Bi'r al Qurr *well Saudi Arabia*
84 C2 Bi'r al Ubaydq *well* Egypt
84 B3 Bi'r al 'Udayd *well* Egypt
84 A3 Bi'r 'Amrāne *well* Egypt
84 B4 Bi'r al Murrah *well* Egypt
84 E4 Bi'r an Nuṣṣ *well* Egypt
84 B4 Bir Anzarane Western Sahara
87 G2 Bir Aouine *well* Tunisia
84 A4 Bi'r Araf *well Saudi Arabia*
55 F8 Bi'r 'Arjā *well Saudi Arabia*
84 F2 Bi'r ar Rummānah *well* Egypt
84 B2 Bi'r as Sakhā *well* Egypt
84 B3 Birak Libya
49 I4 Birakan Rus. Fed.
190 B7 Bi'r al 'Abd Egypt
85 G4 Bi'r al Ghanam *well Saudi Arabia*
186 F3 Bi'r Basīr *well Saudi Arabia*
186 E4 Bi'r Buwayridah *well Saudi Arabia*
186 B3 Bi'r Buṭaym *well Saudi Arabia*
186 F3 Bi'r Buraym *well Saudi Arabia*
186 F6 Bi'r Ba'dā *well Saudi Arabia*
186 E4 Bi'r Budayr *well Saudi Arabia*
205 K3 Birrie r. *N.S.W.* Austr.
186 D3 Bi'r al Rāḥah *well* Libya
173 K11 Biru *Xizang* China

Column 7

189 J4 Bingöl Turkey
188 H5 Bingöl *prov.* Turkey
191 J4 Bingöl Daği mt. Turkey
191 C6 Bingöl Dağları mts Turkey
159 I8 Binh Dinh Vietnam
158 H4 Binh Gia Vietnam
38 F4 Binic France
154 D7 Binidit *Negros* Phil.
66 D2 Binisale Spain
179 I9 Binika *Orissa* India
67 K8 Binisalem Spain
156 C3 Binjai *Sumatera* Indon.
84 C2 Bin Jawwad Libya
205 L4 Binnaway *N.S.W.* Austr.
26 G9 Binnein Mòr mt. *Scotland* U.K.
48 H5 Binnen Ger.
155 D7 Binongko i. Indon.
191 D6 Binpur W. Bengal India
169 J3 Binyang *Guangxi* China
191 B7 Bin-Yauri Nigeria
52 D6 Binzen Ger.
170 G7 Binyang *Guangxi* China
169 J5 Binzhou *Guangxi* China see Binyang
52 H2 Birkenfeld *Baden-Württemberg* Ger.
52 C3 Birkenfeld *Rheinland-Pfalz* Ger.
53 K6 Birkenfeld *Bayern* Ger.
29 K7 Birkenhead *Merseyside, England* U.K.
49 E9 Birken-Honigsessen Ger.
51 H5 Birkenwerder Berlin Ger.
48 L1 Birket Denmark
59 M3 Birkfeld Austria
48 J1 Birkholm i. Denmark
186 C2 Bi'r Khurbah *well Saudi Arabia*
186 E4 Bi'r Khuwārah *well Saudi Arabia*
84 B3 Birāk Libya
162 G4 Birakan Rus. Fed.
85 A4 Birkat al 'Aqabah
189 L5 Birkim Iraq
186 F4 Bi'r Kiau *well* Sudan
189 L5 Birkirkara Malta
78 E3 Birkim Iraq
204 C2 Birksgate Range *hills S.A.* Austr.
85 G4 Bi'r Kusaybah *well* Egypt
17 N3 Birky Ukr.
85 G4 Bir Labasoi *well* Sudan
185 L6 Birland Hormuz *well* Egypt
90 B7 Bi'r Laḥfān *well* Egypt
84 E4 Bi'r Lahmar Western Sahara
183 O5 Birlik *Zhambylskaya Oblast'* Kazakh.
183 O6 Birlik *Zhambylskaya Oblast'* Kazakh.
186 E4 Bi'r Likeit el Fauqani *well* Sudan
85 G4 Bir Liseila *well* Sudan
85 F4 Bi'r Majal *well* Egypt
185 M5 Birmal *reg.* Afgh.
31 I3 Birmingham *West Midlands, England* U.K.
115 D9 Birmingham *AL* U.S.A.
84 E2 Bi'r Mişāḥ *well* Egypt
84 C4 Bir Mogreïn Maur.
84 B5 Bi'r Muḥaymid al Wazwaz *well* Syria
190 D9 Bi'r Murayr *well* Egypt
84 E2 Bi'r Murrah *well* Egypt
200 □⁵ Birnie i. Kiribati
89 G4 Birnin-Gaouré Niger
89 G3 Birnin Kebbi Nigeria
89 H4 Birnin Konni Niger
89 H3 Birnin Kudu Nigeria
89 F3 Birniwa Nigeria
89 F3 Bir Nukheila *well* Sudan
84 F4 Birofeld Rus. Fed.
43 F6 Birong Palawan Phil.
88 C3 Biro France
84 G4 Bir Ould Brini *well* Egypt
89 K6 Bir Oumarsi *well* Mali
84 C2 Bir Ounâne *well* Mali
84 B5 Bir El Guerdane *well* Maur.
84 C2 Bir Ben Takout *well* Alg.
89 H3 Birnin Kudu Nigeria
84 E4 Bir Qalayb *well* Egypt
190 B7 Bi'r Qayfah *well* Egypt
84 C10 Birresborn Ger.
205 K3 Birrie r. *N.S.W.* Austr.
85 B5 Birrindudu *N.T.* Austr.
187 H3 Birrimbah *N.T.* Austr.
21 L6 Birsay *Orkney, Scotland* U.K.
14 L4 Birsk Rus. Fed.
50 D4 Birsfelden Switz.
31 J2 Birstall *Leicestershire, England* U.K.
49 H10 Birstein Ger.
18 F7 Birštonas Lith.
190 D9 Bi'r Tabah Egypt
85 G4 Bi'r Talhah *well Saudi Arabia*
84 B3 Bi'r Tanguer *well* Egypt
85 F4 Bi'r Tarfāwī *well* Egypt
85 F4 Bi'r Tarfāwī *well* Libya
20 B9 Birtavarre Norway
207 I2 Birthday Mountain *hill Qld* Austr.
187 L5 Bi'r Thāl *well* Saudi Arabia
173 K11 Biru *Xizang* China

Column 8

206 D3 Birdum r. *N.T.* Austr.
188 H5 Birecik Turkey
86 E4 Bir ed Deheb *well* Alg.
87 G2 Bir el Arbi *well* Alg.
87 H4 El el Ghoralia *well* Tunisia
87 E4 Bir El Hadjaj *well* Alg.
93 A5 Birenga Rwanda
84 E5 Bir en Natrūn *well* Sudan
88 G5 Bir en Nugeim *well* Sudan
87 G2 Bir es Smeha *well* Alg.
156 B2 Bireun Sumatera Indon.
187 I4 Bi'r Fāḍil *well Saudi Arabia*
186 C1 Bi'r Fajr *well Saudi Arabia*
85 G5 Bir Faoidig *well* Sudan
187 I4 Bi'r Fardān *well Saudi Arabia*
84 E2 Bir Fu'ad *well* Egypt
84 E4 Bi'r Fuwwah *well* Sudan
86 A5 Bir Gandouz Western Sahara
86 A5 Bir Ghawdah *well Saudi Arabia*
84 D2 Bi'r Ghayzal *well* Libya
79 J4 Birgi Turkey
75 □ Birgu Malta
187 J6 Bi'r Ḥaā oasis *Saudi Arabia*
190 H4 Bi'r Ḥajal *well* Syria
92 C2 Birhan mt. Eth.
186 F4 Bi'r Haraqī *well Saudi Arabia*
190 B8 Bi'r Ḥasanā *well* Egypt
84 G4 Bir Hatab *well* Sudan
186 D2 Bi'r Ḥayzān *well Saudi Arabia*
85 G4 Bir Hismet 'Umar *well* Sudan
84 F4 Bi'r Ḥudūf *well Saudi Arabia*
84 E4 Bir Huwait *well* Sudan
85 G4 Bi'r Ḥuwaymidah *well Saudi Arabia*
84 E3 Bi'ri l. Phil.
186 C3 Bi'r Ibn Ghunayn *well Saudi Arabia*
Bi'r Ibn Hirmās *Saudi Arabia* see Al Bi'r
186 F6 Bi'r Ibn Sarrār *well Saudi Arabia*
186 G6 Bi'r Iḍimah *well Saudi Arabia*
142 B3 Birigüi Brazil
191 G4 Birini *Şäki* Azer.
90 D3 Birini C.A.R.
84 E1 Bi'r Iṣṭabl *well* Egypt
184 H5 Birjand Iran
189 K8 Bi'r Jaydah *well Saudi Arabia*
188 G8 Bi'r Jifn *well* Yemen
84 E2 Bi'r Jubni *well* Libya
186 F5 Bi'r Jugjug *well Saudi Arabia*
186 E3 Birkat Abū Salim *waterhole Saudi Arabia*
189 K8 Birkat al 'Aqabah *well* Iraq
186 F1 Birkat al Ḥamrā *well Saudi Arabia*
187 M4 Birkat al Mawz Oman
189 K9 Birkat Zubālah *waterhole Saudi Arabia*
22 J2 Birkeland Norway
52 F2 Birkenau Ger.
52 H2 Birkenfeld *Baden-Württemberg* Ger.
52 C3 Birkenfeld *Rheinland-Pfalz* Ger.
53 K6 Birkenfeld *Bayern* Ger.
29 K7 Birkenhead *Merseyside, England* U.K.
49 E9 Birken-Honigsessen Ger.
51 H5 Birkenwerder Berlin Ger.
48 L1 Birket Denmark
59 M3 Birkfeld Austria
48 J1 Birkholm i. Denmark
186 E4 Birkat
49 J8 Birkungen Ger.
85 F4 Bi'r Kusaybah *well* Egypt
17 N3 Birky Ukr.
85 G4 Bir Labasoi *well* Sudan
84 E4 Bir Lahmar Western Sahara
183 O5 Birlik *Zhambylskaya Oblast'* Kazakh.
183 O6 Birlik *Zhambylskaya Oblast'* Kazakh.
186 E4 Bi'r Likeit el Fauqani *well* Sudan
85 G4 Bir Liseila *well* Sudan
85 F4 Bi'r Majal *well* Egypt
185 M5 Birmal *reg.* Afgh.
31 I3 Birmingham *West Midlands, England* U.K.
115 D9 Birmingham *AL* U.S.A.
84 E2 Bi'r Mişāḥ *well* Egypt
84 C4 Bir Mogreïn Maur.
84 B5 Bi'r Muḥaymid al Wazwaz *well* Syria
190 D9 Bi'r Murayr *well* Egypt
84 E2 Bi'r Murrah *well* Egypt
200 □⁵ Birnie i. Kiribati
89 G4 Birnin-Gaouré Niger
89 G3 Birnin Kebbi Nigeria
89 H4 Birnin Konni Niger
89 H3 Birnin Kudu Nigeria
89 F3 Birniwa Nigeria
162 H4 Birobidzhan Rus. Fed.
43 E6 Biron France
187 L6 Bi'r Qasb *well* Oman
85 G4 Bi'r Qubaḥ *well Saudi Arabia*
89 K6 Bir Oumarsi *well* Mali
84 G4 Bir Qalayb *well* Egypt
18 H7 Biržai Lith.
84 F2 Bi'r Rawd Sālim *well* Egypt
84 C10 Birresborn Ger.
205 K3 Birrie r. *N.S.W.* Austr.
206 B5 Birrindudu *N.T.* Austr.
187 H3 Birrimbah *N.T.* Austr.
21 L6 Birsay *Orkney, Scotland* U.K.
14 L4 Birsk Rus. Fed.
50 D4 Birsfelden Switz.
31 J2 Birstall *Leicestershire, England* U.K.
49 H10 Birstein Ger.
18 F7 Birštonas Lith.
190 D9 Bi'r Tabah Egypt
85 G4 Bi'r Talhah *well Saudi Arabia*
84 B3 Bi'r Tanguer *well* Egypt
85 F4 Bi'r Tarfāwī *well* Egypt
20 B9 Birtavarre Norway
207 I2 Birthday Mountain *hill Qld* Austr.
187 L5 Bi'r Thāl *well* Saudi Arabia
173 K11 Biru *Xizang* China

Bi'r Udayb to **Bogarra** 239

90 A9 **Bi'r Udayb** *well* Egypt
16 H6 **Biruința** Moldova
84 C2 **Bi'r Umm al Gharānīq** Libya
86 A3 **Bi'r Umm Fawākhīr** *well* Egypt
86 C3 **Bi'r Umm Missā** *well* Saudi Arabia
Biruni Uzbek. *see* **Beruniy**
85 G4 **Bi'r 'Unjāt** *well* Egypt
76 D6 **Birur** *Karnataka* India
86 H4 **Bi'r Usaylīlah** *well* Saudi Arabia
85 G5 **Bir Wario** *well* Sudan
84 B3 **Bi'r Wedeb** *well* Libya
86 F5 **Bi'r Wurshah** *well* Saudi Arabia
17 R3 **Biryuch** Rus. Fed.
91 I2 **Biryuchek** Rus. Fed.
18 H5 **Biržai** Lith.
87 H3 **Bir Zar** *well* Tunisia
75 □ **Birżebbuġa** Malta
59 M6 **Biš** Slovenia
55 E4 **Bisa** *i. Maluku* Indon.
73 O5 **Bisaccia** Italy
74 E8 **Bisacquino** *Sicilia* Italy
66 E5 **Bisai** Japan
78 G5 **Bisalpur** *Uttar Prad.* India
78 E5 **Bisau** *Rajasthan* India
66 D2 **Bisaurín** *mt.* Spain
25 W10 **Bisbee** *AZ* U.S.A.
Biscari *Sicilia* Italy *see* **Acate**
43 B7 **Biscarrosse** France
43 B7 **Biscarrosse et de Parentis, Étang de** *l.* France
43 B7 **Biscarrosse-Plage** France
34 B4 **Biscay, Bay of** *sea* France/Spain
14 I3 **Biscay Abyssal Plain** *sea feature* N. Atlantic Ocean
15 G13 **Biscayne Bay** *FL* U.S.A.
15 G13 **Biscayne National Park** *FL* U.S.A.
73 R5 **Bisceglie** Italy
53 J2 **Bischberg** Ger.
52 G2 **Bischbrunn** Ger.
37 O6 **Bischheim** France
49 F9 **Bischoffen** Ger.
49 J8 **Bischofferode** Ger.
53 L1 **Bischofsgrün** Ger.
52 E2 **Bischofsheim** Ger.
49 J10 **Bischofsheim an der Rhön** Ger.
58 H5 **Bischofshofen** Austria
53 O4 **Bischofsmais** Ger.
51 J8 **Bischofswerda** Ger.
53 N6 **Bischofswiesen** Ger.
70 G1 **Bischofszell** Switz.
37 M6 **Bischwald, Étang de** *l.* France
37 O6 **Bischwiller** France
12 T2 **Biscoe Islands** Antarctica
98 □1a **Biscoitos** *Terceira* Azores
08 D4 **Biscotasi Lake** *Ont.* Can.
08 D4 **Biscotasing** *Ont.* Can.
64 □1 **Bise** *Okinawa* Japan
90 E3 **Bisellia** Sudan
73 L2 **Bisenti** Italy
72 H2 **Bisentina, Isola** *i.* Italy
14 L4 **Biser** Rus. Fed.
14 K4 **Biserovo** Rus. Fed.
14 L4 **Bisert'** *r.* Rus. Fed.
77 O7 **Bisertsi** Bulg.
68 E4 **Biševo** *i.* Croatia
64 □1 **Bise-zaki** *pt Okinawa* Japan
70 D7 **Bisezhai** *Yunnan* China
85 H6 **Bisha** Eritrea
86 F6 **Bīshah** *reg.* Saudi Arabia
86 G5 **Bīshah, Wādī** *watercourse* Saudi Arabia
70 F4 **Bishan** *Chongqing* China
Bishbek Kyrg. *see* **Bishkek**
89 N7 **Bīsheh** Iran
79 P5 **Bishemnagar** *Arun. Prad.* India
83 P6 **Bishkek** Kyrg.
79 K8 **Bishnupur** *W. Bengal* India
97 L8 **Bisho** S. Africa
24 N4 **Bishop** *CA* U.S.A.
03 B13 **Bishop and Clerks Islands** *Stewart I.* N.Z.
29 N4 **Bishop Auckland** *Durham, England* U.K.
26 H11 **Bishopbriggs** *East Dunbartonshire, Scotland* U.K.
06 G1 **Bishop Lake** *N.W.T.* Can.
30 G3 **Bishop's Castle** *Shropshire, England* U.K.
30 H4 **Bishop's Cleeve** *Gloucestershire, England* U.K.
30 F5 **Bishop's Hull** *Somerset, England* U.K.
31 J3 **Bishop's Itchington** *Warwickshire, England* U.K.
30 F5 **Bishop's Lydeard** *Somerset, England* U.K.
31 M4 **Bishop's Stortford** *Hertfordshire, England* U.K.
30 D5 **Bishop's Tawton** *Devon, England* U.K.
30 E6 **Bishopsteignton** *Devon, England* U.K.
31 J6 **Bishop's Waltham** *Hampshire, England* U.K.
26 H11 **Bishopton** *Renfrewshire, Scotland* U.K.
15 G8 **Bishopville** *SC* U.S.A.
88 I6 **Bishrī, Jabal** *hills* Syria
76 H9 **Bishti i Pallës** *pt* Albania
62 C2 **Bishui** *Heilong.* China
Bishui *Henan* China *see* **Biyang**
97 N6 **Bisi** S. Africa
73 Q8 **Bisignano** Italy
36 D3 **Bisinaca** Col.
52 F5 **Bisingen** Ger.
87 G2 **Biskra** Alg.
55 K4 **Biskupice** *Lubelskie* Pol.
54 G4 **Biskupice** *Opolskie* Pol.
57 I3 **Biskupice** Slovakia
55 H2 **Biskupiec** *Warmińsko-Mazurskie* Pol.
55 I2 **Biskupiec** *Warmińsko-Mazurskie* Pol.
30 H4 **Bisley** *Gloucestershire, England* U.K.
54 F7 **Bislig** *Mindanao* Phil.
54 F7 **Bislig Bay** *Mindanao* Phil.
20 E2 **Bismarck** *ND* U.S.A.
53 K7 **Bismarck Archipelago** *is* P.N.G.
98 E2 **Bismarck Range** *mts* P.N.G.
53 K7 **Bismarck Sea** P.N.G.
50 E5 **Bismark (Altmark)** Ger.
89 J5 **Bismil** Turkey
21 J6 **Bismo** Norway
20 D3 **Bison** *SD* U.S.A.
84 B4 **Bīsotūn** Iran
20 N5 **Bispgården** Sweden
48 J4 **Bispingen** Ger.
77 H3 **Bissamcuttak** *Orissa* India
88 B4 **Bissau** Guinea-Bissau
89 H5 **Bissaula** Nigeria
45 J9 **Bissen** Lux.
49 F6 **Bissendorf** Ger.
48 I5 **Bissendorf (Wedemark)** Ger.
07 M5 **Bissett** *Man.* Can.
88 C4 **Bissikrima** Guinea
58 C7 **Bissina, Lago di** *l.* Italy
53 J4 **Bissingen** Ger.
88 B3 **Bissorã** Guinea-Bissau
70 E6 **Bistagno** Italy
06 G3 **Bistcho Lake** *Alta* Can.
76 I9 **Bistra** *mt.* Macedonia
77 K5 **Bistra** *r.* Romania
76 I8 **Bistra** *mt.* Serb. and Mont.
77 L7 **Bistreț** Romania
77 L7 **Bistreț, Lacul** *l.* Romania
59 M7 **Bistrica** *Šmarje pri Jelšah* Slovenia
59 J7 **Bistrica** *Tržič* Slovenia
77 M3 **Bistrița** Romania
77 M3 **Bistrița** *r.* Romania
77 O4 **Bistrița** *r.* Romania
77 M3 **Bistrița Bârgăului** Romania
77 N3 **Bistriței, Munții** *mts* Romania
77 L9 **Bistritsa** *r.* Bulg.
154 C6 **Bisucay** *i.* Phil.
178 H6 **Biswan** *Uttar Prad.* India
187 M4 **Bīsyah** Oman
23 Q7 **Bisztynek** Pol.
175 □1 **Bitadhoo** *i. S. Male* Maldives
Bitadoo *i. S. Male* Maldives *see* **Bitadhoo**
90 A4 **Bitam** Gabon
92 C3 **Bitata** Eth.
52 B2 **Bitburg** Ger.
37 N5 **Bitche** France
75 L1 **Bitetto** Italy
178 H6 **Bithur** *Uttar Prad.* India
79 K2 **Bithynia** *reg.* Turkey
182 D2 **Bitik** Kazakh.
90 E3 **Bitilifondi** C.A.R.
90 C2 **Bitkine** Chad
189 K4 **Bitlis** Turkey
76 J9 **Bitola** Macedonia
Bitolj Macedonia *see* **Bitola**
75 L1 **Bitonto** Italy
186 G4 **Bitrān, Jabal** *hill* Saudi Arabia
176 C7 **Bitra Par** *rf* India
37 N8 **Bitschwiller-lès-Thann** France
125 W2 **Bitter Creek** *r. UT* U.S.A.
122 J6 **Bitter Creek** *r. WY* U.S.A.
51 F7 **Bitterfeld** Ger.
96 C7 **Bitterfontein** S. Africa
122 G3 **Bitterroot** *r. MT* U.S.A.
122 G3 **Bitterroot Range** *mts ID* U.S.A.
124 L5 **Bitterwater** *CA* U.S.A.
72 C7 **Bitti** *Sardegna* Italy
51 E6 **Bittkau** Ger.
30 H5 **Bitton** *South Gloucestershire, England* U.K.
89 E4 **Bittou** Burkina
140 B4 **Bituca** Brazil
155 D3 **Bitung** *Sulawesi* Indon.
97 M7 **Bityi** S. Africa
15 G6 **Bityug** *r.* Rus. Fed.
52 G5 **Bitz** Ger.
89 I4 **Biu** Nigeria
91 D7 **Biula** Angola
63 Q3 **Biurrun** Spain
97 P3 **Bivane** *r.* S. Africa
70 H3 **Bivio** Switz.
77 P3 **Bivolari** Romania
74 E8 **Bivona** *Sicilia* Italy
110 B2 **Biwabik** *MN* U.S.A.
166 C5 **Biwa-ko** *l.* Japan
166 D5 **Biwa-ko Quasi National Park** Japan
Biwmares *Wales* U.K. *see* **Beaumaris**
77 N4 **Bixad** Romania
92 E2 **Bixinduule** Somalia
26 □N2 **Bixter** *Shetland, Scotland* U.K.
183 U1 **Biya** *r.* Rus. Fed.
171 I2 **Biyang** *Henan* China
92 D2 **Bīye K'obē** Eth.
183 N6 **Biylikol', Ozero** *l.* Kazakh.
92 E3 **Biyo Ado** *well* Eth.
183 U1 **Biysk** Rus. Fed.
97 N6 **Bizana** S. Africa
41 B10 **Bizanet** France
43 D9 **Bizanos** France
58 A5 **Bizau** Austria
41 B10 **Bize-Minervois** France
165 L12 **Bizen** Japan
Bizerta Tunisia *see* **Bizerte**
87 H1 **Bizerte** Tunisia
69 B7 **Bizerte** *admin. div.* Tunisia
184 H8 **Bīzhanābād** Iran
20 □A1 **Bjargtangar** *hd* Iceland
20 N2 **Bjarkøy** Norway
23 J5 **Bjärnum** Sweden
23 J6 **Bjärsjölagård** Sweden
20 O5 **Bjästa** Sweden
76 H8 **Bjelasica** *mts* Serb. and Mont.
68 G4 **Bjelašnica** *mts* Bos.-Herz.
68 F3 **Bjelovar** Croatia
20 N2 **Bjerkvik** Norway
48 K1 **Bjerreby** Denmark
22 F5 **Bjerringbro** Denmark
20 M3 **Bjøllånes** Norway
22 G1 **Bjoneroa** Norway
23 K1 **Björbo** Sweden
22 C3 **Bjordal** Norway
20 K5 **Bjørgan** Norway
22 H2 **Bjørkelangen** Norway
20 N3 **Björkfjället** *mts* Sweden
20 O2 **Björkliden** Sweden
23 N1 **Björklinge** Sweden
22 H1 **Bjørknes** *Akershus* Norway
20 T2 **Bjørknes** *Finnmark* Norway
22 H4 **Björkö** Sweden
23 P2 **Björkö** *i.* Sweden
20 O4 **Björksele** Sweden
21 J5 **Bjorli** Norway
20 O5 **Björna** Sweden
22 B1 **Bjørnafjorden** *b.* Norway
22 C2 **Bjørnanuten** *mt.* Norway
22 D1 **Bjornesfjorden** *l.* Norway
20 T2 **Bjørnevatn** Norway
20 O2 **Bjørnfjell** Norway
218 B2 **Bjørnøya** *i.* Arctic Ocean
20 U2 **Bjørnstad** Norway
22 I1 **Bjurberget** Sweden
20 O5 **Bjurholm** Sweden
20 P4 **Bjuröklubb** *pt* Sweden
23 L1 **Bjursås** Sweden
88 D3 **Bla** Mali
26 D8 **Bla Bheinn** *hill Scotland* U.K.
40 F4 **Blacé** France
76 I8 **Blace** *Kosovo, Srbija* Serb. and Mont.
76 J7 **Blace** *Srbija* Serb. and Mont.
54 G5 **Blachownia** Pol.
107 L5 **Black** *r. Man.* Can.
108 D3 **Black** *r. Ont.* Can.
110 H1 **Black** *r. Ont.* Can.
130 □ **Black** *r.* Jamaica
Black Mauritius *see* **Grande Rivière Noire**
113 H3 **Black** *r. AR* U.S.A.
121 J8 **Black** *r. AR* U.S.A.
125 V8 **Black** *r. AZ* U.S.A.
111 L7 **Black** *r. MI* U.S.A.
115 H9 **Black** *r. SC* U.S.A.
110 C5 **Black** *r. WI* U.S.A.
26 L11 **Blackadder Water** *r. Scotland* U.K.
207 J8 **Blackall** *Qld* Austr.
108 B3 **Black Bay** *Ont.* Can.
107 I3 **Black Bay** *Sask.* Can.
108 B2 **Blackbear** *r. Ont.* Can.
110 A2 **Blackberry** *MN* U.S.A.
107 J3 **Black Birch Lake** *Sask.* Can.
204 □1 **Blackbourne, Point** Norfolk I.
31 I4 **Black Bourton** *Oxfordshire, England* U.K.
207 H4 **Blackbull** *Qld* Austr.
28 E7 **Black Bull** Rep. of Ireland
26 L8 **Blackburn** *Aberdeenshire, Scotland* U.K.
29 M6 **Blackburn** *Blackburn with Darwen, England* U.K.
26 I11 **Blackburn** *West Lothian, Scotland* U.K.
29 M6 **Blackburn with Darwen** *admin. div. England* U.K.
207 N9 **Blackbutt** *Qld* Austr.
124 J2 **Black Butte** *mt. CA* U.S.A.
124 J2 **Black Butte Lake** *CA* U.S.A.
125 R6 **Black Canyon** *gorge AZ* U.S.A.
125 T7 **Black Canyon City** *AZ* U.S.A.
123 K7 **Black Canyon of the Gunnison National Park** *CO* U.S.A.
212 T2 **Black Coast** Antarctica
29 K5 **Black Combe** *hill England* U.K.
28 I3 **Blackcraig Hill** *Scotland* U.K.
110 F5 **Black Creek** *WI* U.S.A.
118 C2 **Black Creek** *r. PA* U.S.A.
125 W6 **Black Creek** *watercourse AZ* U.S.A.
106 E4 **Black Dome** *mt. B.C.* Can.
111 R4 **Black Donald Lake** *Ont.* Can.
30 F6 **Black Down Hills** *England* U.K.
207 L7 **Blackdown Tableland National Park** *Qld* Austr.
120 H2 **Blackduck** *MN* U.S.A.
23 M2 **Blacken** *b.* Sweden
106 H4 **Blackfalds** *Alta* Can.
122 H2 **Blackfeet Indian Reservation** *res. MT* U.S.A.
31 J6 **Blackfield** *Hampshire, England* U.K.
122 H5 **Blackfoot** *ID* U.S.A.
122 H3 **Black Foot** *r. MT* U.S.A.
Black Forest *mts* Ger. *see* **Schwarzwald**
122 I5 **Blackfoot Reservoir** *ID* U.S.A.
26 I10 **Blackford** *Perth and Kinross, Scotland* U.K.
27 D6 **Black Head** Rep. of Ireland
30 B7 **Black Head** *England* U.K.
27 K3 **Black Head** *Northern Ireland* U.K.
29 N6 **Black Hill** *England* U.K.
206 D8 **Black Hill Range** *hills N.T.* Austr.
104 H5 **Black Hills** *SD* U.S.A.
122 L4 **Black Hills** *SD* U.S.A.
26 J11 **Blackhope Scar** *hill Scotland* U.K.
107 L5 **Black Island** *Man.* Can.
26 H7 **Black Isle** *pen. Scotland* U.K.
107 J3 **Black Lake** *Sask.* Can.
107 J3 **Black Lake** *l. Sask.* Can.
111 J4 **Black Lake** *MI* U.S.A.
28 B5 **Blacklion** Rep. of Ireland
26 J9 **Blacklunans** *Perth and Kinross, Scotland* U.K.
131 □4 **Blackman's** Barbados
125 W8 **Black Mesa** *mt. AZ* U.S.A.
125 V5 **Black Mesa** *ridge AZ* U.S.A.
30 E5 **Blackmoor Gate** *Devon, England* U.K.
31 M4 **Blackmore** *Essex, England* U.K.
30 E4 **Black Mountain** *hills Wales* U.K.
124 O6 **Black Mountain** *CA* U.S.A.
116 C12 **Black Mountain** *KY* U.S.A.
30 F4 **Black Mountains** *hills Wales* U.K.
125 R6 **Black Mountains** *AZ* U.S.A.
94 C4 **Black Nossob** *watercourse* Namibia
31 N4 **Black Notley** *Essex, England* U.K.
29 K6 **Blackpool** *Blackpool, England* U.K.
205 I7 **Black Range State Park** *nature res. Vic.* Austr.
130 □ **Black River** Jamaica
111 K5 **Black River** *MI* U.S.A.
117 J4 **Black River** *NY* U.S.A.
Black River *r.* Vietnam *see* **Đa, Sông**
110 D5 **Black River Falls** *WI* U.S.A.
27 J5 **Blackrock** Rep. of Ireland
122 E6 **Black Rock Desert** *NV* U.S.A.
116 E11 **Blacksburg** *VA* U.S.A.
15 G8 **Black Sea** Asia/Europe
122 J6 **Blacks Fork** *r. WY* U.S.A.
117 □S3 **Blacks Harbour** *N.B.* Can.
115 F10 **Blackshear** *GA* U.S.A.
27 B4 **Blacksod Bay** Rep. of Ireland
124 M2 **Black Springs** *NV* U.S.A.
27 I7 **Blackstairs Mountains** *hills* Rep. of Ireland
106 F2 **Blackstone** *r. N.W.T.* Can.
116 G11 **Blackstone** *VA* U.S.A.
110 F1 **Black Sturgeon** *r. Ont.* Can.
205 M4 **Black Sugarloaf** *mt. N.S.W.* Austr.
109 K2 **Black Tickle** *Nfld and Lab.* Can.
27 G3 **Blacktown** *Northern Ireland* U.K.
97 P4 **Black Umfolozi** *r.* S. Africa
205 M4 **Blackville** *N.S.W.* Austr.
88 E4 **Black Volta** *r.* Africa *alt.* **Mouhoun**, *alt.* **Volta Noire**
207 L7 **Blackwater** *Qld* Austr.
207 J8 **Blackwater** *watercourse Qld* Austr.
106 E2 **Blackwater** *r. N.W.T.* Can.
27 I3 **Blackwater** *r.* N. Ireland/Rep. of Ireland
27 J8 **Blackwater** Rep. of Ireland
27 I5 **Blackwater** *r.* Rep. of Ireland
27 G8 **Blackwater** *r.* Rep. of Ireland
31 N4 **Blackwater** *r. England* U.K.
26 H6 **Black Water** *r. Highland, Scotland* U.K.
26 H7 **Black Water** *r. Highland, Scotland* U.K.
116 I12 **Blackwater** *r. VA* U.S.A.
121 E9 **Blackwater** *watercourse NM/TX* U.S.A.
26 F12 **Blackwaterfoot** *North Ayrshire, Scotland* U.K.
106 F2 **Blackwater Lake** *N.W.T.* Can.
26 G9 **Blackwater Reservoir** *Scotland* U.K.
28 D5 **Blackwatertown** *Northern Ireland* U.K.
209 C13 **Blackwood** *r. W.A.* Austr.
30 F4 **Blackwood** *Caerphilly, Wales* U.K.
207 K6 **Blackwood National Park** *Qld* Austr.
45 H6 **Bladel** Neth.
207 I7 **Bladensburg National Park** *Qld* Austr.
30 E2 **Blaenau Ffestiniog** *Gwynedd, Wales* U.K.
30 F4 **Blaenau Gwent** *admin. div. Wales* U.K.
30 F4 **Blaenavon** *Torfaen, Wales* U.K.
30 E4 **Blaengarw** *Bridgend, Wales* U.K.
30 E4 **Blaengwrach** *Neath Port Talbot, Wales* U.K.
20 L4 **Blåfjellshatten** *mt.* Norway
30 G5 **Blagdon** *North Somerset, England* U.K.
43 G8 **Blagnac** France
37 J4 **Blagny** France
183 T4 **Blagodarnoye** Kazakh.
15 H7 **Blagodarnyy** Rus. Fed.
183 O2 **Blagodatnoye** Kazakh.
17 N2 **Blagodatnoye** Rus. Fed.
77 L8 **Blagoevgrad** Bulg.
183 L1 **Blagoveshchenka** Kazakh.
183 R1 **Blagoveshchenka** Rus. Fed.
162 E3 **Blagoveshchensk** *Amurskaya Oblast'* Rus. Fed.
14 L5 **Blagoveshchensk** *Respublika Bashkortostan* Rus. Fed.
Blagoveshchenskoye *Severnyy Kazakhstan* Kazakh. *see* **Blagoveshchenka**
59 K7 **Blagovica** Slovenia
17 N7 **Blahodatne** *Khersons'ka Oblast'* Ukr.
17 K6 **Blahodatne** *Mykolayivs'ka Oblast'* Ukr.
17 N6 **Blahovishchenka** *Zaporiz'ka Oblast'* Ukr.
17 P6 **Blahovishchenka** *Zaporiz'ka Oblast'* Ukr.
53 N3 **Blaibach** Ger.
26 F9 **Blaich** *Highland, Scotland* U.K.
53 I6 **Blaichach** Ger.
106 H5 **Blaikiston, Mount** *B.C.* Can.
38 H7 **Blain** France
116 H8 **Blain** *PA* U.S.A.
110 A4 **Blaine** *MN* U.S.A.
122 C2 **Blaine** *WA* U.S.A.
107 J4 **Blaine Lake** *Sask.* Can.
37 L6 **Blainville-sur-l'Eau** France
38 H3 **Blainville-sur-Mer** France
39 K3 **Blainville-sur-Orne** France
120 G5 **Blair** *NE* U.S.A.
110 C5 **Blair** *WI* U.S.A.
207 K7 **Blair Athol** *Qld* Austr.
26 I9 **Blair Atholl** *Perth and Kinross, Scotland* U.K.
97 K1 **Blairbeth** S. Africa
26 J9 **Blairgowrie** *Perth and Kinross, Scotland* U.K.
116 F12 **Blairs** *VA* U.S.A.
124 L2 **Blairsden** *CA* U.S.A.
118 F3 **Blairstown** *NJ* U.S.A.
115 F8 **Blairsville** *GA* U.S.A.
116 F8 **Blairsville** *PA* U.S.A.
37 I6 **Blaise** *r.* France
37 I7 **Blaiserives** France
40 F2 **Blaisy-Bas** France
77 L4 **Blaj** Romania
43 F9 **Blajan** France
57 L5 **Blăjeni** Romania
182 I2 **Blak** Rus. Fed.
115 E10 **Blakely** *GA* U.S.A.
118 D2 **Blakely** *PA* U.S.A.
30 H4 **Blakeney** *Gloucestershire, England* U.K.
31 O2 **Blakeney** *Norfolk, England* U.K.
31 N2 **Blakeney Point** *England* U.K.
110 F1 **Blake Point** *MI* U.S.A.
118 D2 **Blakeslee** *PA* U.S.A.
88 C5 **Blama** Sierra Leone
157 K9 **Blambangan, Semenanjung** *pen.* Indon.
37 M6 **Blâmont** France
43 I8 **Blan** France
67 K9 **Blanc, Cap** *c.* Spain
43 B8 **Blanc, Étang** *l.* France
67 C11 **Blanca** Spain
147 G6 **Blanca, Bahía** *b.* Arg.
138 A2 **Blanca, Cordillera** *mts* Peru
65 J7 **Blanca, Sierra** *mts* Spain
123 L10 **Blanca, Sierra** *mt. NM* U.S.A.
39 Q6 **Blancafort** France
123 L8 **Blanca Peak** *CO* U.S.A.
63 R7 **Blancas** Spain
28 E7 **Blanchardstown** Rep. of Ireland
41 I8 **Blanche** *r.* France
41 I8 **Blanche** *ridge* France
204 E5 **Blanche, Cape** *S.A.* Austr.
204 G3 **Blanche, Lake** *salt flat S.A.* Austr.
208 G7 **Blanche, Lake** *salt flat W.A.* Austr.
200 □6 **Blanche Channel** *New Georgia Is* Solomon Is
116 B9 **Blanchester** *OH* U.S.A.
204 G6 **Blanchetown** *S.A.* Austr.
131 □7 **Blanchisseuse** Trin. and Tob.
36 C2 **Blanc Nez, Cap** *c.* France
144 C3 **Blanco** *r.* Arg.
138 D3 **Blanco** *r.* Bol.
136 C6 **Blanco** *r.* Peru
96 G9 **Blanco** S. Africa
65 I5 **Blanco** *r.* Spain
126 □Q13 **Blanco, Cabo** *c.* Costa Rica
Blanco, Cabo *c.* Spain *see* **Blanc, Cap**
122 B5 **Blanco, Cape** *OR* U.S.A.
109 J3 **Blanc-Sablon** *Que.* Can.
205 K5 **Bland** *r. N.S.W.* Austr.
116 D11 **Bland** *VA* U.S.A.
20 □C1 **Blanda** *r.* Iceland
30 H6 **Blandford Camp** *Dorset, England* U.K.
30 H6 **Blandford Forum** *Dorset, England* U.K.
125 W4 **Blanding** *UT* U.S.A.
110 D9 **Blandinsville** *IL* U.S.A.
118 D4 **Blandon** *PA* U.S.A.
66 K4 **Blanes** Spain
110 I3 **Blaney Park** *MI* U.S.A.
156 □ **Blangah, Telok** *b.* Sing.
156 B3 **Blangkejeren** *Sumatera* Indon.
156 B3 **Blangpidie** *Sumatera* Indon.
39 L3 **Blangy-le-Château** France
36 C4 **Blangy-sur-Bresle** France
56 D2 **Blanice** *r.* Czech Rep.
56 D2 **Blanice** *r.* Czech Rep.
56 D2 **Blaník** *park* Czech Rep.
23 M4 **Blankaholm** Sweden
50 E3 **Blankenberg** Ger.
45 D6 **Blankenberge** Belgium
49 K7 **Blankenburg (Harz)** Ger.
51 H6 **Blankenfelde** Ger.
51 F9 **Blankenhain** *Sachsen* Ger.
51 D9 **Blankenhain** *Thüringen* Ger.
49 C10 **Blankenheim** *Nordrhein-Westfalen* Ger.
51 D7 **Blankenheim** *Sachsen-Anhalt* Ger.
49 D10 **Blankenrath** Ger.
50 H4 **Blankensee** Ger.
51 E10 **Blankenstein** Ger.
43 C6 **Blanquefort** France
137 E2 **Blanquilla, Isla** *i.* Venez.
64 H8 **Blanquilla, Sierra** *mts* Spain
65 N4 **Blanquillo** *mt.* Spain
56 F2 **Blansko** Czech Rep.
93 B8 **Blantyre** Malawi
42 E5 **Blanzac-Porcheresse** France
40 C5 **Blanzat** France
42 E3 **Blanzay** France
40 E3 **Blanzy** France
44 H4 **Blaricum** Neth.
27 E9 **Blarney** Rep. of Ireland
116 G6 **Blasdell** *NY* U.S.A.
43 D6 **Blasimon** France
22 C2 **Blåsjø** *l.* Norway
21 I6 **Blaskavlen** *mt.* Norway
27 A8 **Blasket Sound** *sea chan.* Rep. of Ireland
20 L5 **Blåstöten** *mt.* Sweden
54 G4 **Błaszki** Pol.
56 C2 **Blatná** Czech Rep.
56 G3 **Blatné** Slovakia
45 E7 **Blaton** Belgium
20 N4 **Blattniksele** Sweden
155 C3 **Blau** *Sulawesi* Indon.
52 H5 **Blaubeuren** Ger.
52 H3 **Blaufelden** Ger.
48 G2 **Blauort** *i.* Ger.
52 H5 **Blaustein** Ger.
22 E6 **Blåvands Huk** *pt* Denmark
Blaven *hill Scotland* U.K. *see* **Bla Bheinn**
38 E6 **Blavet** *r.* France
14 B2 **Blåviksjön** Sweden
41 D6 **Blavozy** France
29 N4 **Blaydon** *Tyne and Wear, England* U.K.
42 C5 **Blaye** France
43 I7 **Blaye-les-Mines** France
41 I8 **Blayeul Sommet** *mt.* France
205 L5 **Blayney** *N.S.W.* Austr.
206 C2 **Blaze, Point** *N.T.* Austr.
55 L6 **Blazhiv** Ukr.
16 G2 **Blazhove** Ukr.
55 J4 **Błaziny Górne** Pol.
59 O1 **Blažovice** Czech Rep.
55 K6 **Błażowa** Pol.
65 I4 **Blázquez** Spain
31 O5 **Blean** *Kent, England* U.K.
48 K4 **Bleckede** Ger.
66 E3 **Blecua** Spain
59 J7 **Bled** Slovenia
90 B1 **Bledaya** Chad
55 I4 **Błędów** Pol.
54 G2 **Błędowo** Pol.
54 D3 **Bledzew** Pol.
157 J8 **Blega** *Jawa* Indon.
59 J7 **Blegoš** *mt.* Slovenia
45 D7 **Bléharies** Belgium
49 B10 **Bleialf** Ger.
59 K6 **Bleiburg** Austria
49 K8 **Bleicherode** Ger.
49 F10 **Bleidenstadt** Ger.
20 M2 **Bleik** Norway
58 H4 **Bleikogel** *mt.* Austria
51 E9 **Bleilochtalsperre** *resr* Ger.
44 G4 **Bleiswijk** Neth.
48 K2 **Blekendorf** Ger.
23 K5 **Blekinge** *county* Sweden
29 K4 **Blencathra** *hill England* U.K.
36 D2 **Blendecques** France
48 H5 **Blender** Ger.
36 E8 **Bléneau** France
108 D5 **Blenheim** *Ont.* Can.
203 H8 **Blenheim** *South I.* N.Z.
31 J4 **Blenheim Palace** *tourist site England* U.K.
37 L6 **Blénod-lès-Pont-à-Mousson** France
37 K6 **Blénod-lès-Toul** France
41 H8 **Bléone** *r.* France
72 I3 **Blera** Italy
36 F4 **Blérancourt** France
42 F1 **Bléré** France
45 J6 **Blerick** Neth.
66 D5 **Blesa** Spain
44 G5 **Bleskensgraaf** Neth.
41 C6 **Blesle** France
96 I3 **Blesmanspos** S. Africa
27 I6 **Blessington** Rep. of Ireland
27 I6 **Blessington Lakes** Rep. of Ireland
40 B3 **Blet** France
31 K3 **Bletchley** *Milton Keynes, England* U.K.
22 F2 **Bletoppen** *mt.* Norway
40 G3 **Bletterans** France
111 P3 **Bleu, Lac** *l. Que.* Can.
90 F4 **Bleus, Monts** *mts* Dem. Rep. Congo
31 J4 **Blewbury** *Oxfordshire, England* U.K.
48 G3 **Blexen (Nordenham)** Ger.
57 J3 **Blh** *r.* Slovakia
87 F1 **Blida** Alg.
48 I4 **Bliedersdorf** Ger.
52 C3 **Blies** *r.* Ger.
52 C3 **Blieskastel** Ger.
203 B11 **Bligh Sound** *inlet South I.* N.Z.
201 □1a **Bligh Water** *b.* Fiji
36 I7 **Bligny** France
40 F2 **Bligny-sur-Ouche** France
44 L2 **Blijham** Neth.
62 I2 **Blimea** Spain
59 K3 **Blindenmarkt** Austria
50 I4 **Blindow** Ger.
108 D4 **Blind River** *Ont.* Can.
97 K8 **Blinkwater** S. Africa
204 G4 **Blinman** *S.A.* Austr.
70 E3 **Blinnenhorn** *mt.* Italy/Switz.
122 G5 **Bliss** *ID* U.S.A.
111 K8 **Blissfield** *MI* U.S.A.
116 D8 **Blissfield** *OH* U.S.A.
31 K3 **Blisworth** *Northamptonshire, England* U.K.
157 J9 **Blitar** *Jawa* Indon.
54 G4 **Blizanów** Pol.
53 N3 **Blížejov** Czech Rep.
56 E3 **Blížkovice** Czech Rep.
55 J6 **Blizne** Pol.
Bliznetsy Ukr. *see* **Blyznyuky**
Bliznyuki Ukr. *see* **Blyznyuky**
55 I4 **Bliżyn** Pol.
117 N7 **Block Island** *RI* U.S.A.
117 N7 **Block Island** *i. RI* U.S.A.
117 N7 **Block Island Sound** *sea chan. RI* U.S.A.
31 I3 **Blockley** *Gloucestershire, England* U.K.
97 O3 **Bloedrivier** S. Africa
97 K5 **Bloemfontein** S. Africa
97 J3 **Bloemhof** S. Africa
97 J3 **Bloemhof Dam** S. Africa
97 J3 **Bloemhof Dam Nature Reserve** S. Africa
39 N6 **Blois** France
44 I3 **Blokzijl** Neth.
49 H7 **Blomberg** Ger.
96 E6 **Blomberg se Vloer** *salt pan* S. Africa
22 A1 **Blomøy** *i.* Norway
20 □D1 **Blöndulón** *l.* Iceland
20 □C1 **Blönduós** Iceland
157 L9 **Blongas** *Lombok* Indon.
55 H3 **Błonie** *Łódzkie* Pol.
55 I3 **Błonie** *Mazowieckie* Pol.
51 G7 **Blönsdorf** Ger.
39 L3 **Blonville-sur-Mer** France
206 B8 **Bloods Range** *mts N.T.* Austr.
117 I10 **Bloodsworth Island** *MD* U.S.A.
107 L5 **Bloodvein** *r. Man.* Can.
27 F2 **Bloody Foreland** *pt* Rep. of Ireland
110 C4 **Bloomer** *WI* U.S.A.
111 Q6 **Bloomfield** *Ont.* Can.
120 I5 **Bloomfield** *IA* U.S.A.
114 D6 **Bloomfield** *IN* U.S.A.
121 K7 **Bloomfield** *MO* U.S.A.
123 K8 **Bloomfield** *NM* U.S.A.
207 J3 **Bloomfield River** *Qld* Austr.
119 G1 **Bloomingburg** *NY* U.S.A.
119 G2 **Bloomingdale** *NJ* U.S.A.
118 E4 **Blooming Glen** *PA* U.S.A.
119 G2 **Blooming Grove** *NY* U.S.A.
118 E2 **Blooming Grove** *PA* U.S.A.
110 A6 **Blooming Prairie** *MN* U.S.A.
110 F9 **Bloomington** *IL* U.S.A.
114 D6 **Bloomington** *IN* U.S.A.
110 A5 **Bloomington** *MN* U.S.A.
111 R8 **Bloomsburg** *PA* U.S.A.
207 L6 **Bloomsbury** *Qld* Austr.
118 E3 **Bloomsbury** *NJ* U.S.A.
157 I8 **Blora** *Jawa* Indon.
111 Q8 **Blossburg** *PA* U.S.A.
105 P3 **Blosseville Kyst** *coastal area* Greenland
193 S2 **Blossom, Mys** *pt* Rus. Fed.
40 K1 **Blotzheim** France
95 F4 **Blouberg Nature Reserve** S. Africa
96 C9 **Bloubergstrand** S. Africa
97 K4 **Bloudrif** S. Africa
115 E10 **Blountstown** *FL* U.S.A.
116 C12 **Blountville** *TN* U.S.A.
43 E9 **Blousson-Sérian** France
56 C2 **Blovice** Czech Rep.
50 E3 **Blowatz** Ger.
130 E5 **Blower Rock** *i.* Jamaica
31 J3 **Bloxham** *Oxfordshire, England* U.K.
29 N6 **Blubberhouses** *North Yorkshire, England* U.K.
58 A5 **Bludenz** Austria
58 A5 **Bludesch** Austria
106 D3 **Blue** *r. B.C.* Can.
121 H9 **Blue** *r. OK* U.S.A.
125 W8 **Blue** *watercourse AZ* U.S.A.
28 B7 **Blue Ball** Rep. of Ireland
118 C4 **Blue Ball** *PA* U.S.A.
118 E4 **Blue Bell** *PA* U.S.A.
125 U3 **Blue Bell Knoll** *mt. UT* U.S.A.
106 F3 **Blueberry** *r. B.C.* Can.
97 J9 **Blue Cliff** S. Africa
Blue Creek *r.* Mex. *see* **Azul**
115 G12 **Blue Cypress Lake** *FL* U.S.A.
125 Q5 **Blue Diamond** *NV* U.S.A.
120 H4 **Blue Earth** *MN* U.S.A.
120 H3 **Blue Earth** *r. MN* U.S.A.
116 D11 **Bluefield** *VA* U.S.A.
116 D11 **Bluefield** *WV* U.S.A.
130 □ **Bluefields** Jamaica
126 □R11 **Bluefields** Nic.
27 D8 **Blueford** Rep. of Ireland
97 L6 **Bluegums** S. Africa
117 □Q4 **Blue Hill** *ME* U.S.A.
120 F5 **Blue Hill** *NE* U.S.A.
130 G3 **Blue Hills** Turks and Caicos Is
116 G8 **Blue Knob** *hill PA* U.S.A.
91 E8 **Blue Lagoon National Park** Zambia
118 C4 **Blue Marsh Lake** *PA* U.S.A.
109 J3 **Blue Mountain** *hill Nfld and Lab.* Can.
179 N8 **Blue Mountain** *Mizoram* India
118 B4 **Blue Mountain** *ridge PA* U.S.A.
117 K5 **Blue Mountain Lake** *NY* U.S.A.
97 L5 **Blue Mountain Pass** Lesotho
130 □ **Blue Mountain Peak** Jamaica
205 L5 **Blue Mountains** *N.S.W.* Austr.
130 □ **Blue Mountains** Jamaica
203 D13 **Blue Mountains** *South I.* N.Z.
122 E4 **Blue Mountains** *OR* U.S.A.
205 M5 **Blue Mountains National Park** *N.S.W.* Austr.
206 F2 **Blue Mud Bay** *N.T.* Austr.
92 B2 **Blue Nile** *r.* Eth. *alt.* **Ābay Wenz (Ethiopia)**, *alt.* **Azraq, Bahr el (Sudan)**
92 B2 **Blue Nile** *state* Sudan
104 G3 **Bluenose Lake** *Nunavut* Can.
120 G6 **Blue Rapids** *KS* U.S.A.
115 E8 **Blue Ridge** *GA* U.S.A.
116 F11 **Blue Ridge** *VA* U.S.A.
116 E12 **Blue Ridge** *mts VA* U.S.A.
106 G4 **Blue River** *B.C.* Can.
27 F3 **Blue Stack Mountains** *hills* Rep. of Ireland
116 E11 **Bluestone Lake** *WV* U.S.A.
207 L7 **Bluff** *Qld* Austr.
203 C13 **Bluff** *South I.* N.Z.
125 W4 **Bluff** *UT* U.S.A.
116 C12 **Bluff City** *TN* U.S.A.
125 U1 **Bluffdale** *UT* U.S.A.
208 I4 **Bluff Face Range** *hills W.A.* Austr.
203 C13 **Bluff Harbour** *South I.* N.Z.
209 E13 **Bluff Knoll** *mt. W.A.* Austr.
209 C9 **Bluff Point** *W.A.* Austr.
114 E5 **Bluffton** *IN* U.S.A.
116 B8 **Bluffton** *OH* U.S.A.
59 N5 **Blumau in Steiermark** Austria
52 F6 **Blumberg** *Baden-Württemberg* Ger.
50 I5 **Blumberg** *Brandenburg* Ger.
141 C8 **Blumenau** Brazil
50 I3 **Blumenhagen** Ger.
50 H4 **Blumenholz** Ger.
50 F4 **Blumenthal** Ger.
70 D3 **Blümlisalp** *mt.* Switz.
120 E3 **Blunt** *SD* U.S.A.
106 F5 **Blustry Mountain** *B.C.* Can.
122 D5 **Bly** *OR* U.S.A.
17 K2 **Blystova** Ukr.
206 E2 **Blyth** *r. N.T.* Austr.
111 M6 **Blyth** *Ont.* Can.
29 N3 **Blyth** *Northumberland, England* U.K.
29 O7 **Blyth** *Nottinghamshire, England* U.K.
31 P3 **Blyth** *r. England* U.K.
26 J11 **Blyth Bridge** *Scottish Borders, Scotland* U.K.
97 P5 **Blythdale Beach** S. Africa
125 R8 **Blythe** *CA* U.S.A.
121 K8 **Blytheville** *AR* U.S.A.
209 J9 **Blyth Range** *hills W.A.* Austr.
29 P7 **Blyton** *Lincolnshire, England* U.K.
17 P5 **Blyznyuky** Ukr.
22 F2 **Bø** Norway
88 C5 **Bo** Sierra Leone
154 C5 **Boac** Phil.
126 □Q11 **Boaco** Nic.
62 H7 **Boada** Spain
66 K3 **Boadella, Pantà de** *resr* Spain
63 M8 **Boadilla del Monte** Spain
63 K4 **Boadilla de Rioseco** Spain
139 E1 **Boa Esperança** *Amazonas* Brazil
143 E4 **Boa Esperança** *Minas Gerais* Brazil
137 F4 **Boa Esperança** *Roraima* Brazil
140 E3 **Boa Esperança, Açude** *resr* Brazil
142 C4 **Boa Esperança do Sul** Brazil
138 B1 **Boa Fé** Brazil
138 D2 **Boa Hora** Brazil
169 M9 **Bo'ai** *Henan* China
170 F7 **Bo'ai** *Yunnan* China
28 B4 **Boa Island** *Northern Ireland* U.K.
62 G2 **Boal** Spain
62 D5 **Boalhosa** Port.
90 C3 **Boali** C.A.R.
116 H8 **Boalsburg** *PA* U.S.A.
97 Q2 **Boane** Moz.
155 E5 **Boano** *i. Maluku* Indon.
155 E5 **Boano, Selat** *sea chan. Maluku* Indon.
140 E5 **Boa Nova** Brazil
71 L5 **Boara Pisani** Italy
116 E7 **Boardman** *OH* U.S.A.
119 I1 **Boardmans Bridge** *CT* U.S.A.
26 H7 **Boath** *Highland, Scotland* U.K.
94 E4 **Boatlaname** Botswana
207 K9 **Boatman** *Qld* Austr.
26 I8 **Boat of Garten** *Highland, Scotland* U.K.
98 □2a **Boatswain-bird Island** *Ascension* S. Atlantic Ocean
130 C4 **Boatswain Point** Cayman Is
64 □ **Boaventura** Madeira
140 F3 **Boa Viagem** Brazil
136 C6 **Boa Vista** *Amazonas* Brazil
137 E5 **Boa Vista** *Amazonas* Brazil
137 H5 **Boa Vista** *Pará* Brazil
137 F4 **Boa Vista** *Roraima* Brazil
88 □ **Boa Vista** *i.* Cape Verde
62 C9 **Boa Vista** Port.
115 □1 **Boaz Island** Bermuda
205 K5 **Bobadah** *N.S.W.* Austr.
65 J6 **Bobadilla** *Andalucía* Spain
63 O4 **Bobadilla** *La Rioja* Spain
63 J6 **Bobadilla del Campo** Spain
170 H7 **Bobai** *Guangxi* China
95 □K1 **Bobaomby, Tanjona** *c.* Madag.
95 □K2 **Bobasakoa** Madag.
51 F7 **Bobbau** Ger.
177 H3 **Bobbili** *Andhra Prad.* India
70 G6 **Bobbio** Italy
70 C6 **Bobbio Pellice** Italy
111 P5 **Bobcaygeon** *Ont.* Can.
52 E2 **Bobenheim-Roxheim** Ger.
16 F2 **Bober** *r.* Ukr.
16 B4 **Boberka** Ukr.
62 G2 **Bobia** *mt.* Spain
54 E2 **Bobięcińskie Wielkie, Jezioro** *l.* Pol.
36 D6 **Bobigny** France
53 K6 **Böbing** Ger.
53 J5 **Bobingen** Ger.
50 D3 **Bobitz** Ger.
19 W6 **Bobkovo** Rus. Fed.
52 G4 **Böblingen** Ger.
55 M4 **Bobly** Ukr.
88 D4 **Bobo-Dioulasso** Burkina
54 E2 **Bobolice** Pol.
154 E5 **Bobon** *Samar* Phil.
95 F4 **Bobonong** Botswana
62 D4 **Boborás** Spain
57 L4 **Bobota** Romania
Bobotov Kuk *mt.* Serb. and Mont. *see* **Durmitor**
77 L8 **Bobovdol** Bulg.
57 L3 **Bobove** Ukr.
55 I6 **Bobowa** Pol.
54 G2 **Bobowo** Pol.
183 N7 **Boboyob, Gora** *mt.* Uzbek.
18 M7 **Bobr** Belarus
18 L7 **Bobr** *r.* Belarus
54 D3 **Bóbr** *r.* Pol.
53 O3 **Böbrach** Ger.
Bobrinets Ukr. *see* **Bobrynets'**
15 H6 **Bobrov** Rus. Fed.
57 I2 **Bobrov** Slovakia
57 I2 **Bobrovec** Slovakia
Bobrovitsa Ukr. *see* **Bobrovytsya**
17 Q2 **Bobrovo-Dvorskoye** Rus. Fed.
17 K3 **Bobrovytsya** Ukr.
51 L7 **Bobrowice** Pol.
54 D3 **Bobrówko** Pol.
54 G3 **Bobrowniki** *Kujawsko-Pomorskie* Pol.
55 L2 **Bobrowniki** *Podlaskie* Pol.
55 H2 **Bobrowo** Pol.
Bobruysk Belarus *see* **Babruysk**
18 J9 **Bobryk** *r.* Belarus
16 J6 **Bobryk-Druhyy** Ukr.
17 L5 **Bobrynets'** Ukr.
17 P2 **Bobryshevo** Rus. Fed.
111 R5 **Bobs Lake** *Ont.* Can.
170 D2 **Bobso** *Sichuan* China
116 F9 **Bobtown** *PA* U.S.A.
92 B2 **Bobuk** Sudan
136 D2 **Bobures** Venez.
95 □J4 **Boby** *mt.* Madag.
59 M7 **Boč** *hill* Slovenia
62 H7 **Bocacara** Spain
115 G13 **Boca Chica Key** *i. FL* U.S.A.
128 B4 **Boca de Camichin** Mex.
63 K3 **Boca de Huérgano** Spain
145 D6 **Boca de la Travesía** Arg.
137 E2 **Boca del Pao** Venez.
129 K6 **Boca del Río** Mex.
137 F2 **Boca de Macareo** Venez.
137 F2 **Boca de Uracoa** Venez.
138 D2 **Boca do Acre** Brazil
137 F6 **Boca do Capanã** Brazil
138 D2 **Boca do Curuquetê** Brazil
137 I5 **Boca do Jari** Brazil
138 C1 **Boca do Moaco** Brazil
39 I4 **Bocage** *reg.* France
39 I8 **Bocage Vendéen** *reg.* France
131 □7 **Boca Grande** *r. mouth* Trin. and Tob./Venez.
143 E5 **Bocaina de Minas** Brazil
67 D10 **Bocairent** Spain
143 F2 **Bocaiúva** Brazil
142 C6 **Bocaiúva do Sul** Brazil
137 E4 **Boca Mavaca** Venez.
88 D5 **Bocanda** Côte d'Ivoire
57 J6 **Bočar** *Vojvodina, Srbija* Serb. and Mont.
90 B3 **Bocaranga** C.A.R.
115 G12 **Boca Raton** *FL* U.S.A.
128 F3 **Bocas** Mex.
126 □R13 **Bocas del Toro** Panama
126 □R13 **Bocas del Toro, Archipiélago de** *is* Panama
75 L5 **Bocchigliero** Italy
63 M6 **Boceguillas** Spain
56 F5 **Bocfölde** Hungary
137 F3 **Bochinche** Venez.
55 I6 **Bochnia** Pol.
45 I6 **Bocholt** Belgium
49 C7 **Bocholt** Ger.
56 C1 **Bochov** Czech Rep.
49 D8 **Bochum** Ger.
95 F4 **Bochum** S. Africa
50 G2 **Bock** *i.* Ger.
49 J6 **Bockenem** Ger.
53 L5 **Bockhorn** *Bayern* Ger.
48 F4 **Bockhorn** *Niedersachsen* Ger.
48 E4 **Bockhorst** Ger.
55 L3 **Boćki** Pol.
72 C3 **Bocognano** *Corse* France
91 B8 **Bocoio** Angola
57 J4 **Boconád** Hungary
126 F4 **Bocoyna** Mex.
45 G8 **Bocq** *r.* Belgium
57 J3 **Bőcs** Hungary
57 I5 **Bócsa** Hungary
77 J5 **Bocșa** *Caraș-Severin* Romania
57 L4 **Bocșa** *Sălaj* Romania
57 K5 **Bocsig** Romania
54 C3 **Boczów** Pol.
90 C3 **Boda** C.A.R.
21 M6 **Boda** Sweden
23 N4 **Böda** *Öland* Sweden
55 L5 **Bodaczów** Pol.
23 K4 **Bodafors** Sweden
23 L5 **Boda glasbruk** Sweden
57 H4 **Bodajk** Hungary
205 M7 **Bodalla** *N.S.W.* Austr.
209 E11 **Bodallin** *W.A.* Austr.
193 M4 **Bodaybo** Rus. Fed.
26 M8 **Boddam** *Aberdeenshire, Scotland* U.K.
26 □N3 **Boddam** *Shetland, Scotland* U.K.
130 C4 **Bodden Town** Cayman Is
50 D3 **Boddin** Ger.
209 D12 **Boddington** *W.A.* Austr.
51 E7 **Bode** *r.* Ger.
124 I3 **Bodega Head** *CA* U.S.A.
44 G4 **Bodegraven** Neth.
52 F5 **Bodelshausen** Ger.
30 F1 **Bodelwyddan** *Denbighshire, Wales* U.K.
20 P4 **Boden** Sweden
49 I7 **Bodenfelde** Ger.
30 G3 **Bodenham** *Herefordshire, England* U.K.
52 E2 **Bodenheim** Ger.
53 M5 **Bodenkirchen** Ger.
53 O3 **Bodenmais** Ger.
52 G6 **Bodensee** *l.* Ger./Switz.
48 K5 **Bodenteich** Ger.
49 I7 **Bodenwerder** Ger.
59 K4 **Bodenwies** *mt.* Austria
53 M3 **Bodenwöhr** Ger.
27 G5 **Boderg, Lough** *l.* Rep. of Ireland
89 G4 **Bode-Sadu** Nigeria
77 O3 **Bodești** Romania
124 N6 **Bodfish** *CA* U.S.A.
176 E3 **Bodhan** *Andhra Prad.* India
179 J7 **Bodh Gaya** *Bihar* India
31 J3 **Bodicote** *Oxfordshire, England* U.K.
124 M3 **Bodie** *CA* U.S.A.
176 E7 **Bodinayakkanur** *Tamil Nadu* India
64 F4 **Bodión** *r.* Spain
52 G6 **Bodman** Ger.
30 C7 **Bodmin** *Cornwall, England* U.K.
30 C6 **Bodmin Moor** *moorland England* U.K.
52 H6 **Bodnegg** Ger.
20 M3 **Bodø** Norway
140 F3 **Bodocó** Brazil
52 H6 **Bodolz** Ger.
64 F4 **Bodonal de la Sierra** Spain
168 C4 **Bodonchiyn Gol** *watercourse* Mongolia
139 F4 **Bodoquena** *Mato Grosso do Sul* Brazil
139 F5 **Bodoquena** *Mato Grosso do Sul* Brazil
139 F5 **Bodoquena, Serra da** *hills* Brazil
90 C3 **Bodoukpa** C.A.R.
57 K3 **Bodrog** *r.* Hungary
57 K3 **Bodroghalom** Hungary
79 I5 **Bodrum** Turkey
188 C5 **Bodrum-Milas** *airport* Turkey
20 M5 **Bodsjö** Sweden
20 P3 **Bodträskfors** Sweden
175 □1 **Boduhali** *i. N. Male* Maldives
57 J3 **Bódva** *r.* Hungary
57 J3 **Bodva** *r.* Slovakia
57 J3 **Bódvaszilas** Hungary
55 I3 **Bodzanów** Pol.
55 I5 **Bodzentyn** Pol.
43 F7 **Boé** France
88 B4 **Boé** Guinea-Bissau
45 F6 **Boechout** Belgium
63 K5 **Boecillo** Spain
63 L4 **Boedo** *r.* Spain
40 I4 **Boëge** France
96 G4 **Boegoeberg** S. Africa
44 I5 **Boekel** Neth.
45 E6 **Boekhoute** Belgium
40 E5 **Boën** France
90 D5 **Boende** Dem. Rep. Congo
155 B6 **Bo Epinang** *Sulawesi* Indon.
96 E9 **Boerboonfontein** S. Africa
121 F11 **Boerne** *TX* U.S.A.
97 K9 **Boesmans** *r.* S. Africa
97 K7 **Boesmans hoekpas** *pass* S. Africa
121 J10 **Boeuf** *r. LA* U.S.A.
62 H3 **Boeza** Spain
62 G3 **Boeza** *r.* Spain
142 C5 **Bofete** Brazil
88 B4 **Boffa** Guinea
41 F7 **Boffres** France
49 H7 **Boffzen** Ger.
27 G5 **Bofin Lough** *l.* Rep. of Ireland
22 F2 **Bøfjell** *hill* Norway
20 T1 **Boftsa** Norway
179 O5 **Boga** *Arun. Prad.* India
57 J4 **Bogács** Hungary
62 G7 **Bogajo** Spain
158 B6 **Bogale** Myanmar
158 B7 **Bogale** *r.* Myanmar
121 K10 **Bogalusa** *LA* U.S.A.
205 K3 **Bogan** *r. N.S.W.* Austr.
89 E3 **Bogandé** Burkina
205 K5 **Bogan Gate** *N.S.W.* Austr.
90 C3 **Bogangolo** C.A.R.
155 C3 **Bogani Nani Wartabone National Park** Indon.
207 K7 **Bogantungan** *Qld* Austr.
65 O3 **Bogarra** Spain

Bosagha Kazakh. see Bosaga
Bosaginskiy Kazakh. see Bosaga
72 A7 Bosa Marina Sardegna Italy
77 O3 Bosanci Romania
68 F3 Bosanska Dubica Bos.-Herz.
68 F3 Bosanska Gradiška Bos.-Herz.
68 F3 Bosanska Kostajnica Bos.-Herz.
68 G3 Bosanska Krupa Bos.-Herz.
68 G3 Bosanski Brod Bos.-Herz.
68 G3 Bosanski Novi Bos.-Herz.
68 G3 Bosanski Petrovac Bos.-Herz.
68 G3 Bosanski Šamac Bos.-Herz.
68 G3 Bosansko Grahovo Bos.-Herz.
57 H3 Bošany Slovakia
56 G4 Bósárkány Hungary
48 J2 Bosau Ger.
97 K4 Bosberg mt. S. Africa
30 H3 Bosbury Herefordshire, England U.K.
30 C6 Boscastle Cornwall, England U.K.
117 N5 Boscawen NH U.S.A.
147 H5 Bosch Alg.
73 I1 Bosco Italy
110 D6 Boscobel WI U.S.A.
70 E4 Bosco Chiesanuova Italy
70 E5 Bosco della Partecipiano e Lucedio, Parco Naturale nature res. Italy
70 F6 Bosco Marengo Italy
73 M6 Boscotrecase Italy
48 J2 Bösdorf Ger.
170 F7 Bosduiflaagte salt pan S. Africa
48 E4 Bösel Ger.
128 G6 Bosencheve, Parque Nacional nat. park Mex.
31 K6 Bosham West Sussex, England U.K.
Boshchakul' Kazakh. see Boshakol'
162 M4 Boshnyakovo Sakhalin Rus. Fed.
97 I4 Boshoek S. Africa
97 J4 Boshof S. Africa
184 G5 Boshrüyeh Iran
77 K8 Bosilegrad Srbija Serb. and Mont.
Bosilegrad Srbija Serb. and Mont. see Bosilegrad
52 F5 Bösingen Ger.
182 I1 Boskol' Kazakh.
56 F2 Boskovice Czech Rep.
117 H3 Boslanti Suriname
68 G3 Bosna r. Bos.-Herz.
77 P8 Bosna hills Bulg.
Bosna i Hercegovina country Europe see Bosnia-Herzegovina
Bosnia and Herzegovina, Federation of aut. div. Bos.-Herz. see Federacija Bosna i Hercegovina
68 F3 Bosnia-Herzegovina country Europe
90 C4 Boso Dem. Rep. Congo
96 C1 Bosobogolo Pan salt pan Botswana
90 C3 Bosobolo Dem. Rep. Congo
167 L5 Bōsō-hantō pen. Japan
90 D3 Boosama Dem. Rep. Congo
Boosot Spain see Bòssost
59 O1 Bosovýce Czech Rep.
97 K2 Bospoort S. Africa
Bosporus str. Turkey see Istanbul Boğazı
Bossaanga C.A.R. see Basaga
21 M6 Bossbod Sweden
90 C3 Bossembélé C.A.R.
Bossemptélé C.A.R. see Bossentélé
90 C3 Bossentélé C.A.R.
42 E6 Bossier City LA U.S.A.
96 E5 Bossiekom Namibia
88 D4 Bossora Burkina
66 G2 Bossost Spain
97 L1 Bosspruit S. Africa
208 F5 Bossut, Cape W.A. Austr.
173 G8 Bostan Xinjiang China
184 B6 Bostān Iran
185 L6 Bostan Pak.
182 C3 Bostandyk Kazakh.
184 H5 Bostāneh, Ra's-e pt Iran
172 H6 Bostan Hu i. China
27 E6 Boston Rep. of Ireland
31 L2 Boston Lincolnshire, England U.K.
117 N6 Boston MA U.S.A.
204 E6 Boston Bay S.A. Austr.
111 O1 Boston Creek Ont. Can.
121 H8 Boston Mountains AR U.S.A.
29 O6 Boston Spa West Yorkshire, England U.K.
68 G3 Bosut r. Croatia
44 G3 Boswachterij Schoorl nature res. Neth.
116 H9 Boswell IN U.S.A.
116 F8 Boswell PA U.S.A.
178 C6 Botad Gujarat India
17 M8 Botanichne Ukr.
88 C5 Botë Liberia
20 N5 Botë Sweden
97 J2 Boteler Point S. Africa
88 C5 Boteta Liberia
76 N3 Botevi Romania
31 O3 Botesdale Suffolk, England U.K.
94 E4 Boteti r. Botswana
15 D8 Botev mt. Bulg.
77 L8 Botevgrad Bulg.
97 K3 Bothaville S. Africa
88 A5 Bothel Ger.
29 K4 Bothel Cumbria, England U.K.
22 C3 Bothell WA U.S.A.
30 G6 Bothenhampton Dorset, England U.K.
21 O6 Bothnia, Gulf of Fin./Sweden
205 K10 Bothwell Tas. Austr.
11 M7 Bothwell Ont. Can.
62 E5 Boticas Port.
94 E4 Boteli r. Botswana
58 E3 Botev mt. Bos.-Herz.
59 M8 Botinec Stupnički Croatia
17 O7 Botiyevo Ukr.
57 L4 Botiz Romania
16 H2 Botkins OH U.S.A.
15 H2 Botkul', Ozero i. Kazakh./Rus. Fed.
91 H3 Bot Makak Cameroon
89 H6 Bot Md U.S.A.
66 C4 Botorrita Spain
77 O3 Botoșani Romania
169 C7 Botou Hebei China
175 L6 Botricello Italy
88 C5 Botro Côte d'Ivoire
97 I1 Botsalano Game Reserve nature res. S. Africa
19 I2 Botsford CT U.S.A.
97 K5 Botshabelo S. Africa
20 P4 Botsmark Sweden
22 D2 Botsvati i. Norway
94 D3 Botswana country Africa
75 K5 Botte Donato, Monte mt. Italy
48 E5 Bottendorf (Burgwald) Ger.
48 H5 Bottendorf (Obernholz) Ger.
31 K2 Bottesford Leicestershire, England U.K.
29 P6 Bottesford North Lincolnshire, England U.K.
72 C7 Bottidda Sardegna Italy
33 I1 Bottineau ND U.S.A.
30 D3 Bottle Creek Turks and Caicos Is

Brest to Buffalo Lake
242

38 C5 Brest France
38 C5 Brest, Rade de inlet France
59 L8 Brestanica Slovenia
59 M6 Bresternica Slovenia
Brest-Litovsk Belarus see Brest
Brest Oblast admin. div. Belarus see Brestskaya Voblasts'
77 J7 Brestovac Srbija Serb. and Mont.
57 K6 Brestovăț Romania
Brestskaya Oblast' admin. div. Belarus see Brestskaya Voblasts'
18 I9 Brestskaya Voblasts' admin. div. Belarus
41 F5 Bretagne admin. reg. France
99 □1c Bretagne, Pointe de pt Réunion
43 E8 Bretagne-d'Armagnac France
136 C6 Bretana Peru
22 G2 Bretangen b. Norway
98 □1b Bretanha São Miguel Azores
98 □1b Bretanha, Ponta da pt São Miguel Azores
77 O4 Brețcu Romania
38 H5 Breteil France
43 H6 Bretenoux France
39 M4 Breteuil Haute-Normandie France
36 D4 Breteuil Picardie France
38 H8 Brétignolles-sur-Mer France
36 D6 Brétigny-sur-Orge France
51 J8 Bretnig Ger.
62 I5 Bretocino Spain
106 H4 Breton Alta Can.
130 D3 Breton, Cayo i. Cuba
39 M5 Bretoncelles France
121 K11 Breton Sound b. LA U.S.A.
119 G4 Breton Woods NJ U.S.A.
52 F3 Bretten Ger.
30 G1 Bretton Flintshire, Wales U.K.
39 K3 Brettville-sur-Laize France
52 D2 Bretzenheim Ger.
52 G3 Bretzfeld Ger.
138 B2 Breu r. Brazil/Peru
52 G2 Breuberg-Neustadt Ger.
37 L8 Breuches France
37 L8 Breuchin r. France
156 A2 Breueh, Pulau i. Indon.
44 I5 Breugel Neth.
70 D4 Breuil-Cervinia Italy
42 C4 Breuil-Magné France
36 B6 Breuilpont France
44 H4 Breukelen Neth.
49 H8 Breuna Ger.
37 K7 Breuvannes-en-Bassigny France
115 F8 Brevard NC U.S.A.
137 I5 Breves Brazil
22 F2 Brevik Norway
22 I2 Breviken Sweden
40 J4 Brévon r. France
49 H7 Brevörde Ger.
205 K3 Brewarrina N.S.W. Austr.
117 □Q4 Brewer ME U.S.A.
88 C5 Brewerville Liberia
30 H2 Brewood Staffordshire, England U.K.
120 F5 Brewster NE U.S.A.
119 H2 Brewster NY U.S.A.
116 D8 Brewster OH U.S.A.
122 E2 Brewster WA U.S.A.
205 J5 Brewster, Lake imp. l. N.S.W. Austr.
115 D10 Brewton AL U.S.A.
97 N2 Breyten S. Africa
19 U3 Breytovo Rus. Fed.
57 I2 Breza Slovakia
59 L7 Breze Slovenia
56 F3 Březí Czech Rep.
68 E3 Brežice Slovenia
59 N7 Breznica Croatia
57 K2 Breznica Slovakia
56 C2 Březnice Czech Rep.
77 K8 Breznik Bulg.
77 L6 Breznița-Motru Romania
77 L9 Breznitsa Bulg.
51 H10 Březno Czech Rep.
57 I3 Brezno Slovakia
36 B6 Brézolles France
57 G2 Březová Czech Rep.
57 G3 Brezová pod Bradlom Slovakia
57 L3 Brezovec Slovakia
59 N7 Brezovica Slovenia
77 N8 Brezovo Bulg.
68 F3 Brezovo Polje plain Croatia
90 D3 Bria C.A.R.
162 I2 Briakan Rus. Fed.
42 G4 Briance r. France
41 J7 Briançon France
125 T4 Brian Head mt. UT U.S.A.
30 E3 Brianne, Llyn resr Wales U.K.
119 H2 Briarcliff Manor NY U.S.A.
40 B1 Briare France
36 E8 Briare, Canal de France
43 H8 Briatexte France
75 K6 Briatico Italy
207 N9 Bribie Island Qld Austr.
41 K7 Bric Bouchet mt. France/Italy
16 G5 Briceni Moldova
41 J7 Bric Froid mt. France/Italy
Brichany Moldova see Briceni
70 C6 Bricherasio Italy
27 E5 Brickeens Rep. of Ireland
118 C4 Brickerville PA U.S.A.
118 F6 Bricksboro NJ U.S.A.
119 G4 Brick Township NJ U.S.A.
37 I7 Bricon France
38 H3 Bricquebec France
27 G8 Bride r. Rep. of Ireland
41 J6 Brides-les-Bains France
31 O5 Bridge Kent, England U.K.
119 K3 Bridgehampton NY U.S.A.
27 I7 Bridgeland Rep. of Ireland
110 H8 Bridgeman MI U.S.A.
27 H2 Bridgend Rep. of Ireland
26 K9 Bridgend Angus, Scotland U.K.
26 D11 Bridgend Argyll and Bute, Scotland U.K.
30 E4 Bridgend Bridgend, Wales U.K.
26 J8 Bridgend Moray, Scotland U.K.
30 E4 Bridgend admin. div. Wales U.K.
26 I10 Bridge of Allan Stirling, Scotland U.K.
26 H9 Bridge of Balgie Perth and Kinross, Scotland U.K.
26 J9 Bridge of Cally Perth and Kinross, Scotland U.K.
26 J9 Bridge of Craigisla Angus, Scotland U.K.
26 L8 Bridge of Don Aberdeen, Scotland U.K.
26 K9 Bridge of Dun Angus, Scotland U.K.
26 K9 Bridge of Dye Aberdeenshire, Scotland U.K.
26 J10 Bridge of Earn Perth and Kinross, Scotland U.K.
26 I5 Bridge of Forss Highland, Scotland U.K.
26 G9 Bridge of Orchy Argyll and Bute, Scotland U.K.
26 □M2 Bridge of Walls Shetland, Scotland U.K.
26 G11 Bridge of Weir Renfrewshire, Scotland U.K.
115 E8 Bridgeport AL U.S.A.
124 M3 Bridgeport CA U.S.A.
119 G3 Bridgeport CT U.S.A.
111 K6 Bridgeport MI U.S.A.
120 D5 Bridgeport NE U.S.A.
118 E4 Bridgeport PA U.S.A.
121 G9 Bridgeport TX U.S.A.
124 M3 Bridgeport Reservoir CA U.S.A.
122 J4 Bridger MT U.S.A.
122 K6 Bridger Peak WY U.S.A.
118 E6 Bridgeton NJ U.S.A.
209 D12 Bridgetown W.A. Austr.
131 □4 Bridgetown Barbados
109 H4 Bridgetown N.S. Can.
27 I8 Bridgetown Rep. of Ireland
117 J10 Bridgeville DE U.S.A.
205 K10 Bridgewater Tas. Austr.
109 H4 Bridgewater N.S. Can.
117 O7 Bridgewater MA U.S.A.
117 □R2 Bridgewater ME U.S.A.
117 J6 Bridgewater NY U.S.A.
116 G10 Bridgewater VA U.S.A.
204 H8 Bridgewater, Cape Vic. Austr.
30 H2 Bridgnorth Shropshire, England U.K.
117 □O4 Bridgton ME U.S.A.
30 F5 Bridgwater Somerset, England U.K.
30 F5 Bridgwater Bay England U.K.
56 G2 Břidličná Czech Rep.
29 Q5 Bridlington East Riding of Yorkshire, England U.K.
29 Q5 Bridlington Bay England U.K.
205 K9 Bridport Tas. Austr.
30 G6 Bridport Dorset, England U.K.
42 E4 Brie France
36 E7 Brie reg. France
38 D5 Briec France
36 E6 Brie-Comte-Robert France
49 D10 Briedel Ger.
Brieg Pol. see Brzeg
44 F5 Brielle Neth.
36 I7 Brienne-le-Château France
40 E4 Briennon France
36 G7 Brienon-sur-Armançon France
70 E2 Brienz Switz.
73 P7 Brienza Italy
70 E2 Brienzer Rothorn mt. Switz.
70 D2 Brienzer See l. Switz.
38 G7 Brière, Parc Naturel Régional de nature res. France
118 A1 Brier Mountain hill PA U.S.A.
116 E10 Briery Knob mt. WV U.S.A.
51 J6 Briescht Ger.
50 G5 Brieselang Ger.
51 J6 Briesen Ger.
51 I8 Brieske Ger.
51 K6 Brieskow-Finkenheerd Ger.
51 K7 Briesnig Ger.
48 J4 Brietlingen Ger.
37 I5 Brieulles-sur-Bar France
63 O4 Brieva de Cameros Spain
37 K5 Briey France
70 D3 Brig Switz.
52 F6 Brigach r. Ger.
147 I2 Brigadier General Diego Lamas Uru.
119 G6 Brigantine NJ U.S.A.
29 Q6 Brigg North Lincolnshire, England U.K.
122 L6 Briggsdale CO U.S.A.
110 E6 Briggsville WI U.S.A.
29 K4 Brigham Cumbria, England U.K.
122 H6 Brigham City UT U.S.A.
29 N6 Brighouse West Yorkshire, England U.K.
31 J6 Brighstone Isle of Wight, England U.K.
205 K7 Bright Vic. Austr.
31 O4 Brightlingsea Essex, England U.K.
147 F6 Brightman, Caleta inlet Arg.
111 Q5 Brighton Ont. Can.
203 E12 Brighton South I. N.Z.
31 L6 Brighton Brighton and Hove, England U.K.
122 L7 Brighton CO U.S.A.
111 K7 Brighton MI U.S.A.
116 H5 Brighton NY U.S.A.
116 C10 Brighton WV U.S.A.
31 L6 Brighton and Hove admin. div. England U.K.
207 H7 Brighton Downs Qld Austr.
203 D12 Brightwater South I. N.Z.
40 F5 Brignais France
43 F8 Brignemont France
38 C4 Brignogan-Plage France
41 I10 Brignoles France
26 H10 Brig o'Turk Stirling, Scotland U.K.
31 K3 Brigstock Northamptonshire, England U.K.
63 O7 Brihuega Spain
71 P6 Brijuni nat. park Croatia
88 A3 Brikama Gambia
110 F5 Brillion WI U.S.A.
37 J6 Brillon-en-Barrois France
49 G8 Brilon Ger.
29 O7 Brimington Derbyshire, England U.K.
110 J3 Brimley MI U.S.A.
20 □G1 Brimnes Iceland
110 C2 Brimson MN U.S.A.
131 □2 Brimstone Hill Fortress National Park St Kitts and Nevis
64 D4 Brinches Port.
62 H6 Brincones Spain
75 N2 Brindisi Italy
75 N2 Brindisi prov. Italy
73 P6 Brindisi Montagna Italy
204 D4 Bring, Lake salt flat S.A. Austr.
68 E3 Brinje Croatia
121 J8 Brinkley AR U.S.A.
147 F2 Brinkmann Arg.
48 E4 Brinkum Niedersachsen Ger.
48 G4 Brinkum Niedersachsen Ger.
204 G5 Brinkworth S.A. Austr.
40 C2 Brinon-sur-Beuvron France
39 P6 Brinon-sur-Sauldre France
29 O7 Brinsley Nottinghamshire, England U.K.
37 L6 Brin-sur-Seille France
29 O7 Brinsworth South Yorkshire, England U.K.
41 C7 Brion France
109 I4 Brion, Île i. Que. Can.
63 O3 Briones Spain
40 E4 Brionnais reg. France
39 M3 Brionne France
41 C6 Brioude France
42 D3 Brioux-sur-Boutonne France
39 K4 Briouze France
109 G2 Brisay Que. Can.
207 N9 Brisbane Qld Austr.
71 L7 Brisighella Italy
39 K7 Brissac-Quincé France
117 □R2 Bristol N.B. Can.
30 G5 Bristol Bristol, England U.K.
30 G5 Bristol admin. div. England U.K.
117 M7 Bristol CT U.S.A.
115 E10 Bristol FL U.S.A.
118 B7 Bristol MD U.S.A.
117 N5 Bristol NH U.S.A.
118 F4 Bristol PA U.S.A.
117 N7 Bristol RI U.S.A.
116 C12 Bristol TN U.S.A.
117 L4 Bristol VT U.S.A.
104 B4 Bristol Bay AK U.S.A.
30 D5 Bristol Channel est. England U.K.
135 G7 Bristol Island S. Sandwich Is
125 Q7 Bristol Lake CA U.S.A.
125 P7 Bristol Mountains CA U.S.A.
31 O2 Briston Norfolk, England U.K.
121 G8 Bristow OK U.S.A.
30 G5 Brit r. England U.K.
62 D5 Britelo Port.
212 S2 British Antarctic Territory Antarctica
106 F5 British Columbia prov. Can.
105 J1 British Empire Range mts Nunavut Can.
British Guiana country S. America see Guyana
150 C7 British Indian Ocean Territory terr. Indian Ocean
214 J6 British Isles N. Atlantic Ocean
59 J7 Britof Slovenia
97 L1 Brits S. Africa
96 H6 Britstown S. Africa
27 J6 Brittas Rep. of Ireland
27 J7 Brittas Bay Rep. of Ireland
26 D8 Brittle, Loch b. Scotland U.K.
120 G3 Britton SD U.S.A.
50 I5 Britz Ger.
42 H5 Brive-la-Gaillarde France
41 D6 Brives-Charensac France
63 N3 Briviesca Spain
38 H2 Brix France
58 F5 Brixen im Thale Austria
30 E7 Brixham Torbay, England U.K.
Brixia Italy see Brescia
58 E5 Brixlegg Austria
31 K3 Brixworth Northamptonshire, England U.K.
71 P4 Brkini reg. Slovenia
Brlik Kazakh. see Birlik
51 K9 Brniště Czech Rep.
56 F2 Brno Czech Rep.
23 N2 Bro Sweden
Broach Gujarat India see Bharuch
115 G8 Broad r. SC U.S.A.
117 K5 Broadalbin NY U.S.A.
209 F11 Broad Arrow W.A. Austr.
108 E3 Broadback r. Que. Can.
30 F6 Broadclyst Devon, England U.K.
205 J7 Broadford Vic. Austr.
27 E7 Broadford Clare Rep. of Ireland
27 E8 Broadford Limerick Rep. of Ireland
26 E8 Broadford Highland, Scotland U.K.
27 C4 Broad Haven b. Rep. of Ireland
30 B4 Broad Haven Pembrokeshire, Wales U.K.
30 H3 Broadheath Worcestershire, England U.K.
26 J12 Broad Law hill Scotland U.K.
30 H6 Broadmayne Dorset, England U.K.
206 E4 Broadmere N.T. Austr.
31 N6 Broad Oak East Sussex, England U.K.
185 Q4 Broad Peak China/Jammu and Kashmir
207 L7 Broad Sound sea chan. Qld Austr.
207 M7 Broad Sound Channel Qld Austr.
207 L7 Broadsound Range hills Qld Austr.
31 O5 Broadstairs Kent, England U.K.
122 L4 Broadus MT U.S.A.
107 K5 Broadview Sask. Can.
205 N3 Broadwater N.S.W. Austr.
120 D5 Broadwater NE U.S.A.
27 J8 Broadway Rep. of Ireland
31 I3 Broadway Worcestershire, England U.K.
116 G10 Broadway VA U.S.A.
30 H6 Broadwey Dorset, England U.K.
30 G6 Broadwindsor Dorset, England U.K.
202 H2 Broadwood North I. N.Z.
48 I1 Broager Denmark
23 K5 Broby Sweden
70 C2 Broc Switz.
43 C7 Brocas France
18 F5 Brocēni Latvia
26 D8 Brochel Highland, Scotland U.K.
107 K3 Brochet Man. Can.
107 K3 Brochet, Lac l. Man. Can.
29 L6 Brock r. England U.K.
48 I4 Brockel Ger.
48 J5 Bröckel Ger.
49 K7 Brocken mt. Ger.
31 I6 Brockenhurst Hampshire, England U.K.
105 G2 Brock Island N.W.T. Can.
208 D7 Brockman, Mount W.A. Austr.
116 H5 Brockport NY U.S.A.
116 G7 Brockport PA U.S.A.
117 N6 Brockton MA U.S.A.
118 C3 Brockton PA U.S.A.
49 F6 Brockum Ger.
108 F4 Brockville Ont. Can.
117 □R3 Brockway N.B. Can.
116 G7 Brockway PA U.S.A.
30 H4 Brockworth Gloucestershire, England U.K.
116 F6 Brocton NY U.S.A.
54 E2 Broczyno Pol.
78 C2 Brod Macedonia
76 J9 Brod Macedonia
56 G2 Brodek u Přerova Czech Rep.
Broderick Falls Kenya see Webuye
50 F2 Broderstorf Ger.
16 H4 Brodets'ke Ukr.
105 J2 Brodeur Peninsula Nunavut Can.
110 E7 Brodhead WI U.S.A.
118 E3 Brodhead r. PA U.S.A.
118 E3 Brodheadsville PA U.S.A.
26 F11 Brodick North Ayrshire, Scotland U.K.
116 G12 Brodnax VA U.S.A.
55 H2 Brodnica Kujawsko-Pomorskie Pol.
54 E3 Brodnica Wielkopolskie Pol.
47 I2 Brodnicki Park Krajobrazowy Pol.
56 G3 Brodské Slovakia
54 C4 Brody Lubuskie Pol.
54 D3 Brody Lubuskie Pol.
16 E3 Brody Ukr.
97 J2 Broedersput S. Africa
44 J6 Broekhuizenvorst Neth.
97 J6 Broekpoort r. S. Africa
39 M3 Broglie France
49 D10 Brohl Ger.
50 I3 Brohm Ger.
40 G2 Broin France
54 G3 Brójce Pol.
54 D2 Brojce Pol.
55 J3 Brok Pol.
55 J3 Brok r. Pol.
48 H3 Brokdorf Ger.
22 E1 Brokefjell mt. Norway
209 D13 Broke Inlet W.A. Austr.
121 H7 Broken Arrow OK U.S.A.
205 M5 Broken Bay N.S.W. Austr.
120 F5 Broken Bow NE U.S.A.
121 I8 Broken Bow OK U.S.A.
121 H8 Broken Bow Reservoir OK U.S.A.
116 H10 Brokenburg VA U.S.A.
107 L5 Brokenhead r. Man. Can.
204 H4 Broken Hill N.S.W. Austr.
Broken Hill Zambia see Kabwe
215 K7 Broken Plateau sea feature Indian Ocean
137 H3 Brokopondo Suriname
48 I3 Brokstedt Ger.
74 H7 Brolo Sicilia Italy
53 J3 Brombachsee l. Ger.
Bromberg Pol. see Bydgoszcz
48 K5 Brome Ger.
30 G3 Bromfield Shropshire, England U.K.
31 K3 Bromham Bedfordshire, England U.K.
30 H5 Bromham Wiltshire, England U.K.
31 L5 Bromley Greater London, England U.K.
22 F1 Bromma Norway
41 B7 Brommat France
23 J3 Brommö i. Sweden
20 O1 Bromnes Norway
157 J8 Bromo-Tengger-Semeru National Park Indon.
130 □ Brompton Jamaica
29 O5 Brompton North Yorkshire, England U.K.
29 N5 Brompton on Swale North Yorkshire, England U.K.
23 M5 Brömsebro Sweden
30 H3 Bromsgrove Worcestershire, England U.K.
49 G8 Bromskirchen Ger.
30 G3 Bromyard Herefordshire, England U.K.
40 F5 Bron France
30 E2 Bronaber Gwynedd, Wales U.K.
63 Q7 Bronchales Spain
22 F4 Brønderslev Denmark
88 E5 Brong-Ahafo admin. reg. Ghana
70 G5 Broni Italy
51 K7 Bronice Pol.
97 M1 Bronkhorstspruit S. Africa
19 V6 Bronnitsy Rus. Fed.
20 L4 Brønnøysund Norway
115 F11 Bronson FL U.S.A.
110 I8 Bronson MI U.S.A.
74 H8 Bronte Sicilia Italy
119 H3 Bronx County county NY U.S.A.
16 G3 Bronyts'ka Huta Ukr.
70 H4 Bronzone, Monte mt. Italy
31 O2 Brooke Norfolk, England U.K.
116 H10 Brooke VA U.S.A.
27 H4 Brookeborough Northern Ireland U.K.
154 A7 Brooke's Point Palawan Phil.
119 I1 Brookfield CT U.S.A.
120 I6 Brookfield MO U.S.A.
110 F6 Brookfield WI U.S.A.
121 J10 Brookhaven MS U.S.A.
122 B5 Brookings OR U.S.A.
120 G3 Brookings SD U.S.A.
118 D5 Brookland Terrace DE U.S.A.
117 N6 Brookline MA U.S.A.
110 D9 Brooklyn IL U.S.A.
111 J7 Brooklyn MI U.S.A.
118 B6 Brooklyn Park MD U.S.A.
110 A4 Brooklyn Park MN U.S.A.
116 G11 Brookneal VA U.S.A.
110 A4 Brook Park MN U.S.A.
107 I5 Brooks Alta Can.
117 □P4 Brooks ME U.S.A.
116 E11 Brooks WV U.S.A.
212 T2 Brooks, Cape Antarctica
106 C2 Brooks Brook Y.T. Can.
118 D5 Brookside DE U.S.A.
106 E5 Brooks Peninsula Provincial Park park B.C. Can.
104 D3 Brooks Range mts AK U.S.A.
110 H9 Brookston IN U.S.A.
110 B3 Brookston MN U.S.A.
115 F11 Brooksville FL U.S.A.
116 A10 Brooksville KY U.S.A.
209 D12 Brookton W.A. Austr.
117 □R3 Brookton ME U.S.A.
114 E6 Brookville IN U.S.A.
116 F7 Brookville PA U.S.A.
26 F7 Broom, Loch inlet Scotland U.K.
208 G4 Broome W.A. Austr.
209 D12 Broomehill W.A. Austr.
27 I4 Broomfield Rep. of Ireland
31 M4 Broomfield Essex, England U.K.
38 G5 Broons France
41 B8 Broquiès France
26 I6 Brora Highland, Scotland U.K.
26 I6 Brora r. Scotland U.K.
26 I6 Brora, Loch l. Scotland U.K.
23 K6 Brösarp Sweden
30 H2 Broseley Shropshire, England U.K.
16 D5 Broshniv Osada Ukr.
27 D8 Brosna Rep. of Ireland
27 G6 Brosna r. Rep. of Ireland
42 D5 Brossac France
20 N2 Brøstadbotn Norway
77 N3 Broșteni Romania
116 F12 Brosville VA U.S.A.
142 C5 Brotas Brazil
64 C3 Brotas Port.
140 E5 Brotas de Macaúbas Brazil
177 M7 Brothers is Andaman & Nicobar Is India
122 D5 Brothers OR U.S.A.
204 □3 Brothers Point S. Pacific Ocean
66 E2 Broto Spain
39 M3 Brotonne, Parc Naturel Régional de nature res. France
37 J7 Brottes France
29 P4 Brotton Redcar and Cleveland, England U.K.
36 B7 Brou France
29 M4 Brough Cumbria, England U.K.
29 P6 Brough East Riding of Yorkshire, England U.K.
26 J5 Brough Highland, Scotland U.K.
28 B7 Broughal Rep. of Ireland
26 J4 Brough Head Scotland U.K.
26 K5 Brough Ness pt Scotland U.K.
27 J3 Broughshane Northern Ireland U.K.
30 G1 Broughton Flintshire, Wales U.K.
31 K3 Broughton Northamptonshire, England U.K.
29 P6 Broughton North Lincolnshire, England U.K.
26 J11 Broughton Scottish Borders, Scotland U.K.
31 J2 Broughton Astley Leicestershire, England U.K.
29 K5 Broughton in Furness Cumbria, England U.K.
26 K4 Broughtown Orkney, Scotland U.K.
84 C5 Broulkou well Chad
56 F1 Broumov Czech Rep.
37 I7 Brousseval France
37 M7 Brouvelieures France
44 E5 Brouwershaven Neth.
16 J3 Brovary Ukr.
207 M9 Brovinia Qld Austr.
22 F4 Brovst Denmark
120 H2 Browerville MN U.S.A.
209 E11 Brown, Lake salt flat W.A. Austr.
204 G5 Brown, Mount hill S.A. Austr.
204 D5 Brown, Point S.A. Austr.
130 F3 Brown Bank sea feature Bahamas
111 L6 Brown City MI U.S.A.
207 I4 Brown Creek r. Qld Austr.
110 G6 Brown Deer WI U.S.A.
29 M7 Brown Edge Staffordshire, England U.K.
209 H8 Browne Range hills W.A. Austr.
121 D9 Brownfield TX U.S.A.
31 I2 Brownhills West Midlands, England U.K.
122 H2 Browning MT U.S.A.
124 O6 Brown Mountain CA U.S.A.
110 D6 Brownsdale MN U.S.A.
118 F5 Browns Mills NJ U.S.A.
130 □ Brown's Town Jamaica
114 D6 Brownstown IN U.S.A.
118 C4 Brownstown PA U.S.A.
120 G3 Browns Valley MN U.S.A.
114 D7 Brownsville KY U.S.A.
116 F8 Brownsville PA U.S.A.
121 K8 Brownsville TN U.S.A.
121 G13 Brownsville TX U.S.A.
137 H3 Brownsweg Suriname
117 □P3 Brownville ME U.S.A.
117 □P3 Brownville Junction ME U.S.A.
121 F10 Brownwood TX U.S.A.
127 J2 Brownwood, Lake TX U.S.A.
208 G3 Browse Island W.A. Austr.
26 J11 Broxburn West Lothian, Scotland U.K.
70 C2 Broye r. Switz.
36 G6 Broyes France
51 J10 Brozany Czech Rep.
62 G9 Brozas Spain
18 M9 Brozha Belarus
70 I4 Brozzo Italy
56 E2 Brtnice Czech Rep.
26 I9 Bruar Water r. Scotland U.K.
36 E3 Bruay-la-Bussière France
Bruce Barbados see Bruce Vale
121 K9 Bruce MS U.S.A.
110 C4 Bruce WI U.S.A.
208 E7 Bruce, Mount W.A. Austr.
110 E3 Bruce Crossing MI U.S.A.
111 M5 Bruce Peninsula Ont. Can.
108 D4 Bruce Peninsula pen. Ont. Can.
111 M4 Bruce Peninsula National Park Ont. Can.
209 E11 Bruce Rock W.A. Austr.
131 □4 Bruce Vale Barbados
37 O6 Bruche r. France
48 H5 Bruchhausen-Vilsen Ger.
49 G10 Bruchköbel Ger.
52 C3 Bruchmühlbach Ger.
52 F3 Bruchsal Ger.
52 D3 Bruchweiler-Bärenbach Ger.
51 G6 Brück Ger.
58 G5 Bruck an der Großglocknerstraße Austria
59 O3 Bruck an der Leitha Austria
59 L5 Bruck an der Mur Austria
53 L4 Bruckberg Ger.
52 C2 Brücken Ger.
52 C3 Brücken (Pfalz) Ger.
53 M3 Bruck in der Oberpfalz Ger.
59 K6 Brückl Austria
53 L6 Bruckmühl Ger.
75 I9 Brucoli Sicilia Italy
55 H3 Brudzeń Duży Pol.
47 I2 Brudzeński Park Krajobrazowy Pol.
54 G3 Brudzew Pol.
30 G5 Brue r. England U.K.
41 H9 Brue-Auriac France
53 I1 Brüel Ger.
39 P8 Bruère-Allichamps France
45 F7 Brugelette Belgium
Bruges Belgium see Brugge
70 E1 Brugg Switz.
45 D6 Brugge Belgium
49 I6 Brüggen Niedersachsen Ger.
48 B8 Brüggen Nordrhein-Westfalen Ger.
70 H7 Brugnato Italy
71 N4 Brugnera Italy
43 G8 Bruguières France
20 I5 Bruhagen Norway
52 F3 Brühl Baden-Württemberg Ger.
49 C9 Brühl Nordrhein-Westfalen Ger.
116 B10 Bruin KY U.S.A.
116 F7 Bruin PA U.S.A.
44 F5 Bruinisse Neth.
125 V2 Bruin Point mt. UT U.S.A.
179 P5 Bruint Arun. Prad. India
94 C5 Brukkaros Namibia
96 B1 Brukkaros, Mount Namibia
106 G4 Brûlé Alta Can.
110 D3 Brule WI U.S.A.
109 I3 Brûlé, Lac l. Que. Can.
39 K6 Brûlon France
45 G9 Brûly Belgium
143 E4 Brumadinho Brazil
140 E5 Brumado Brazil
37 O6 Brumath France
207 M1 Brumer Islands P.N.G.
44 J4 Brummen Neth.
57 H2 Brumov-Bylnice Czech Rep.
57 H2 Brumovice Czech Rep.
21 K6 Brumunddal Norway
72 F2 Bruna r. Italy
27 J5 Brú Na Bóinne tourist site Rep. of Ireland
50 D5 Brunau Ger.
31 O2 Brundall Norfolk, England U.K.
31 O3 Brundish Suffolk, England U.K.
Brundisium Italy see Brindisi
122 G5 Bruneau ID U.S.A.
122 G5 Bruneau r. ID U.S.A.
122 G5 Bruneau, East Fork r. ID/NV U.S.A.
122 G5 Bruneau, West Fork r. ID/NV U.S.A.
36 H4 Brunehamel France
157 K2 Brunei country Asia
Brunei Brunei see Bandar Seri Begawan
157 K2 Brunei Bay Malaysia
63 M8 Brunete Spain
206 E5 Brunette Downs N.T. Austr.
109 K4 Brunette Island Nfld and Lab. Can.
20 M5 Brunflo Sweden
71 L2 Brunico Italy
43 H7 Bruniquel France
59 L6 Brunn Austria
Brünn Czech Rep. see Brno
50 H3 Brunn Ger.
23 N2 Brunna Sweden
59 N3 Brunn am Gebirge Austria
70 F1 Brunnen Switz.
203 F9 Brunner, Lake South I. N.Z.
118 C4 Brunnerville PA U.S.A.
107 J4 Bruno Sask. Can.
110 B3 Bruno MN U.S.A.
48 H3 Brunsbüttel Ger.
45 I7 Brunssum Neth.
37 N8 Brunstatt France
Brunswick Ger. see Braunschweig
115 G10 Brunswick GA U.S.A.
116 H9 Brunswick MD U.S.A.
117 □P5 Brunswick ME U.S.A.
120 I6 Brunswick MO U.S.A.
116 D7 Brunswick OH U.S.A.
145 C9 Brunswick, Peninsula de pen. Chile
208 H3 Brunswick Bay W.A. Austr.
205 N3 Brunswick Head N.S.W. Austr.
209 C12 Brunswick Junction W.A. Austr.
108 D3 Brunswick Lake Ont. Can.
56 G2 Bruntál Czech Rep.
212 W2 Brunt Ice Shelf Antarctica
97 O5 Bruntville S. Africa
205 K10 Bruny Island Tas. Austr.
76 J7 Brus Srbija Serb. and Mont.
Brusa Turkey see Bursa
58 D7 Brusago Italy
22 B3 Brusand Norway
18 J5 Brusenets Rus. Fed.
50 D3 Brüsewitz Ger.
120 D5 Brush CO U.S.A.
117 K4 Brushton NY U.S.A.
70 I3 Brusio Switz.
57 I3 Brusno Slovakia
19 S4 Brusovo Rus. Fed.
141 C8 Brusque Brazil
41 B9 Brusque France
Brussel Belgium see Bruxelles
Brussels Belgium see Bruxelles
111 M6 Brussels Ont. Can.
50 J4 Brüssow Ger.
57 L4 Brusturi Romania
77 O3 Brusturi-Drăgănești Romania
54 F2 Brusy Pol.
16 I3 Brusyliv Ukr.
205 K7 Bruthen Vic. Austr.
30 H5 Bruton Somerset, England U.K.
49 D10 Bruttig-Fankel Ger.
45 F7 Bruxelles Belgium
37 M7 Bruyères France
36 G4 Bruyères-et-Montbérault France
38 H5 Bruz France
136 D2 Bruzual Venez.
75 K7 Bruzzano, Capo c. Italy
57 H2 Brvniště Slovakia
55 I3 Brwinów Pol.
120 M5 Bryan OH U.S.A.
121 G10 Bryan TX U.S.A.
204 G5 Bryan, Mount hill S.A. Austr.
212 S2 Bryan Coast Antarctica
17 R5 Bryanka Ukr.
19 R8 Bryansk Rus. Fed.
191 I1 Bryanskaya Kosa, Mys pt Rus. Fed.
19 Q8 Bryanskaya Oblast' admin. div. Rus. Fed.
Bryansk Oblast admin. div. Rus. Fed. see Bryanskaya Oblast'
191 H1 Bryanskoye Rus. Fed.
121 I8 Bryant AR U.S.A.
110 E4 Bryant WI U.S.A.
121 I7 Bryant Creek r. MO U.S.A.
117 □O4 Bryant Pond ME U.S.A.
125 T4 Bryce Canyon National Park UT U.S.A.
125 W8 Bryce Mountain AZ U.S.A.
30 □ Bryher i. England U.K.
17 M7 Brylivka Ukr.
30 G1 Brymbo Wrexham, Wales U.K.
19 S8 Bryn' Rus. Fed.
30 E4 Brynamman Carmarthenshire, Wales U.K.
22 B3 Bryne Norway
30 F1 Brynford Flintshire, Wales U.K.
55 H5 Brynica r. Pol.
15 G7 Bryn'kovskaya Rus. Fed.
30 F4 Brynmawr Blaenau Gwent, Wales U.K.
118 E4 Bryn Mawr PA U.S.A.
111 Q3 Bryson, Lac l. Que. Can.
115 F8 Bryson City NC U.S.A.
15 G7 Bryukhovetskaya Rus. Fed.
16 C4 Bryukhovychi Ukr.
76 I5 Brzava r. Serb. and Mont.
54 F5 Brzeg Pol.
54 E4 Brzeg Dolny Pol.
54 G3 Brześć Kujawski Pol.
Brześć nad Bugiem Belarus see Brest
55 I6 Brzesko Pol.
55 H6 Brzeszcze Pol.
54 G3 Brzezie Kujawsko-Pomorskie Pol.
54 E2 Brzezie Pomorskie Pol.
55 H4 Brzeziny Łódzkie Pol.
55 J6 Brzeziny Podkarpackie Pol.
54 G4 Brzeziny Wielkopolskie Pol.
55 H6 Brzeźnica Małopolskie Pol.
55 J5 Brzeźnica Podkarpackie Pol.
54 G4 Brzeźnio Pol.
55 L4 Brzeźno Lubelskie Pol.
54 G3 Brzeźno Wielkopolskie Pol.
54 D2 Brzeźno Zachodniopomorskie Pol.
55 J6 Brzostek Pol.
57 J3 Brzotín Slovakia
55 J4 Brzóza Pol.
55 K6 Brzozów Pol.
55 K2 Brzozówka r. Pol.
55 H2 Brzuze Pol.
55 K5 Brzyska Wola Pol.
36 C6 Bû France
186 G7 Bū well Yemen
91 B6 Bua Angola
201 □1 Bua Vanua Levu Fiji
22 I4 Bua Sweden
92 D4 Bu'aale Somalia
154 E6 Buad i. Phil.
39 J4 Buais France
200 □6 Buala Sta Isabel Solomon Is
Buandougou Côte d'Ivoire see Bouandougou
155 D2 Buang i. Indon.
62 C8 Buarcos Port.
156 D4 Buatan Sumatera Indon.
84 D2 Bū Athlah well Libya
187 J3 Bu'ayj well Saudi Arabia
84 B2 Bu'ayrāt al Hasūn Libya
88 B4 Buba Guinea-Bissau
66 E2 Búbal, Embalse de resr Spain
93 A5 Bubanza Burundi
53 K2 Bubenreuth Ger.
95 F4 Bubi r. Zimbabwe
189 N9 Būbīyān Island Kuwait
38 E6 Bubry France
154 C8 Bubuan i. Phil.
154 C9 Bubuan i. Phil.
29 P6 Bubwith East Riding of Yorkshire, England U.K.
201 □1 Buca Vanua Levu Fiji
79 I4 Buca Turkey
79 L5 Bucak Turkey
57 G3 Bučany Slovakia
191 I4 Bucaq Azer.
136 C3 Bucaramanga Col.
129 H4 Bucareli Mex.
154 E7 Bucas Grande i. Phil.
208 G4 Buccaneer Archipelago is W.A. Austr.
74 H9 Buccheri Sicilia Italy
73 M3 Bucchianico Italy
71 K7 Bucciana, Monte mt. Italy
70 G5 Buccinasco Italy
73 O6 Buccino Italy
77 O3 Bucecea Romania
77 N5 Bucegi, Munții mts Romania
64 A3 Bucelas Port.
40 H2 Bucey-lès-Gy France
53 I5 Buch Ger.
16 E4 Buchach Ukr.
53 M5 Buch am Erlbach Ger.
205 L7 Buchan Vic. Austr.
206 F5 Buchanan watercourse N.T. Austr.
88 C5 Buchanan Liberia
115 E9 Buchanan GA U.S.A.
110 H8 Buchanan MI U.S.A.
119 H2 Buchanan NY U.S.A.
116 F11 Buchanan VA U.S.A.
207 J6 Buchanan, Lake salt flat Qld Austr.
209 G8 Buchanan, Lake salt flat W.A. Austr.
121 F10 Buchanan, Lake TX U.S.A.
105 K2 Buchan Gulf Nunavut Can.
109 J3 Buchans Nfld and Lab. Can.
Bucharest Romania see București
53 M5 Buchbach Ger.
58 A5 Buchboden Austria
49 D10 Büchel Ger.
48 K4 Büchen Ger.
52 G2 Buchen (Odenwald) Ger.
52 E6 Buchenbach Ger.
53 K3 Büchenbach Ger.
53 I6 Buchenberg Ger.
52 C2 Büchenbeuren Ger.
50 F4 Buchholz Ger.
48 I5 Buchholz (Aller) Ger.
49 D9 Buchholz (Westerwald) Ger.
59 J3 Buchkirchen Austria
53 P4 Büchlberg Ger.
53 J5 Buchloe Ger.
56 G2 Buchlovice Czech Rep.
26 H10 Buchlyvie Stirling, Scotland U.K.
48 I4 Bucholz in der Nordheide Ger.
124 L6 Buchon, Point CA U.S.A.
70 G1 Buchs Switz.
146 A5 Buchupureo Chile
36 B4 Buchy France
77 N4 Bucin, Pasul pass Romania
71 L9 Bucine Italy
118 C5 Buck PA U.S.A.
121 E10 Buckburn Draw watercourse TX U.S.A.
31 L3 Buckden Cambridgeshire, England U.K.
29 M5 Buckden North Yorkshire, England U.K.
49 H6 Bückeburg Ger.
48 H5 Bücken Ger.
125 T8 Buckeye AZ U.S.A.
30 E7 Buckfastleigh Devon, England U.K.
116 E10 Buckhannon WV U.S.A.
116 F9 Buckhannon r. WV U.S.A.
26 J10 Buckhaven Fife, Scotland U.K.
111 P5 Buckhorn Ont. Can.
111 P5 Buckhorn Lake Ont. Can.
26 K7 Buckie Moray, Scotland U.K.
111 S4 Buckingham Que. Can.
128 C4 Buckingham Mex.
31 K3 Buckingham Buckinghamshire, England U.K.
118 E4 Buckingham PA U.S.A.
116 G11 Buckingham VA U.S.A.
206 E2 Buckingham Bay N.T. Austr.
31 K4 Buckinghamshire admin. div. England U.K.
104 B3 Buckland AK U.S.A.
96 H5 Bucklands S. Africa
207 L8 Buckland Tableland reg. Qld Austr.
204 F5 Buckleboo S.A. Austr.
31 J5 Bucklebury West Berkshire, England U.K.
213 K2 Buckle Island Antarctica
204 □3 Buckles Bay S. Pacific Ocean
206 F6 Buckley watercourse Qld Austr.
30 F1 Buckley Flintshire, Wales U.K.
110 F9 Buckley IL U.S.A.
213 J2 Buckley Bay Antarctica
59 M4 Bucklige Welt reg. Austria
121 F7 Bucklin KS U.S.A.
50 J5 Buckow Märkische Schweiz Ger.
26 L8 Bucksburn Aberdeen, Scotland U.K.
118 E4 Bucks County county PA U.S.A.
125 S7 Buckskin Mountains AZ U.S.A.
124 K2 Bucks Mountain CA U.S.A.
117 □Q4 Bucksport ME U.S.A.
50 F5 Bückwitz Ger.
56 G2 Bučovice Czech Rep.
91 B6 Buco-Zau Angola
57 K4 Bucsa Hungary
77 N6 Bucșani Romania
77 O6 București Romania
36 G4 Bucy-lès-Pierrepont France
116 C8 Bucyrus OH U.S.A.
55 H4 Buczek Pol.
20 I5 Bud Norway
19 R8 Buda Rus. Fed.
66 G6 Buda, Illa de i. Spain
51 L6 Budachów Pol.
57 H4 Budai park Hungary
19 N9 Buda-Kashalyova Belarus
57 H4 Budakeszi Hungary
158 B3 Budalin Myanmar
57 H4 Budaörs Hungary
57 I4 Budapest Hungary
178 G5 Budaun Uttar Prad. India
205 M6 Budawang National Park N.S.W. Austr.
186 F4 Budayyi'ah well Saudi Arabia
92 E3 Bud Bud Somalia
209 C10 Budd, Mount hill W.A. Austr.
205 J4 Budda N.S.W. Austr.
213 H2 Budd Coast Antarctica
51 D6 Büddenstedt Ger.
92 D3 Buddi Eth.
118 F3 Budd Lake NJ U.S.A.
26 K10 Buddon Ness pt Scotland U.K.
72 C6 Buddusò Sardegna Italy
30 C6 Bude Cornwall, England U.K.
121 J10 Bude MS U.S.A.
30 C6 Bude Bay England U.K.
45 I6 Budel Neth.
72 C5 Budelli, Isola i. Sardegna Italy
48 I2 Büdelsdorf Ger.
16 E5 Budenets' Ukr.
49 F10 Budenheim Ger.
191 F1 Budennovsk Rus. Fed.
64 B6 Budens Port.
207 N9 Buderim Qld Austr.
77 O6 Budești Romania
185 M9 Budhapur Pak.
185 P7 Budhlada Punjab India
63 O7 Budia Spain
57 I3 Budiná Slovakia
184 G8 Būdīng Iran
49 H10 Büdingen Ger.
59 N7 Budinšćina Croatia
57 G2 Budišov nad Budišovkou Czech Rep.
190 B9 Budīyah, Jabal hills Egypt
190 B9 Budīyah, Jabal mt. Egypt
90 C4 Budjala Dem. Rep. Congo
54 F5 Budkowiczanka r. Pol.
30 F6 Budleigh Salterton Devon, England U.K.
19 P2 Budogoshch' Rus. Fed.
71 N3 Budoia Italy
168 C9 Budongquan Qinghai China
72 D6 Budoni Sardegna Italy
71 L6 Budrio Italy
55 J1 Budry Pol.
187 I4 Budū', Sabkhat al salt pan Saudi Arabia
77 K4 Budureasa Romania
57 L4 Buduslău Romania
76 G8 Budva Crna Gora Serb. and Mont.
55 K1 Būdviečiai Lith.
Budweis Czech Rep. see České Budějovice
51 J10 Budyně nad Ohří Czech Rep.
18 M6 Budzilava Belarus
55 H4 Budziszewice Pol.
55 H6 Budzów Pol.
54 E3 Budzyń Pol.
89 H5 Buea Cameroon
41 H8 Buëch r. France
124 L7 Buellton CA U.S.A.
66 C6 Bueña Spain
118 F5 Buena NJ U.S.A.
63 P9 Buenache de Alarcón Spain
63 P8 Buenache de la Sierra Spain
146 E4 Buena Esperanza Arg.
136 B4 Buenaventura Col.
126 F3 Buenaventura Mex.
63 K8 Buenaventura Spain
138 E4 Buena Vista Bol.
65 □ Buena Vista Gibraltar
128 E6 Buenavista Michoacán Mex.
129 I2 Buenavista Tamaulipas Mex.
154 E7 Buenavista Mindanao Phil.
154 C5 Buenavista Phil.
123 K7 Buena Vista CO U.S.A.
115 E9 Buena Vista GA U.S.A.
116 F11 Buena Vista VA U.S.A.
130 D2 Buena Vista, Bahía de b. Cuba
129 H7 Buenavista de Cuéllar Mex.
98 □3a Buenavista del Norte Tenerife Canary Is
63 K3 Buenavista de Valdavia Spain
63 O8 Buendía Spain
63 O8 Buendia, Embalse de resr Spain
91 B6 Buenga r. Angola
91 B6 Buengas Angola
142 B1 Buenolândia Brazil
143 E2 Buenópolis Brazil
147 H4 Buenos Aires Arg.
147 G5 Buenos Aires prov. Arg.
138 B2 Buenos Aires Brazil
136 D5 Buenos Aires Amazonas Col.
136 C4 Buenos Aires Guaviare Col.
126 □R13 Buenos Aires Costa Rica
145 B7 Buenos Aires, Lago l. Arg./Chile
125 U10 Buenos Aires National Wildlife Refuge nature res. AZ U.S.A.
131 □7 Buenos Ayres Trin. and Tob.
145 C7 Buen Pasto Arg.
145 C8 Buen Tiempo, Cabo c. Arg.
141 F5 Buerarema Brazil
136 B4 Buesaco Col.
40 J4 Buet, Le Mont mt. France
62 C4 Bueu Spain
65 M3 Buey, Cabeza de mt. Spain
67 C11 Buey, Sierra del mts Spain
126 G4 Búfalo Mex.
106 H2 Buffalo r. Alta/N.W.T. Can.
120 I3 Buffalo MN U.S.A.
121 I7 Buffalo MO U.S.A.
116 G6 Buffalo NY U.S.A.
116 D9 Buffalo OH U.S.A.
121 F7 Buffalo OK U.S.A.
120 D3 Buffalo SD U.S.A.
121 G10 Buffalo TX U.S.A.
110 C5 Buffalo WI U.S.A.
122 K4 Buffalo WY U.S.A.
121 I7 Buffalo r. AR U.S.A.
115 D8 Buffalo r. TN U.S.A.
110 C5 Buffalo r. WI U.S.A.
118 A4 Buffalo Creek r. PA U.S.A.
106 G3 Buffalo Head Hills Y.T. Can.
106 G3 Buffalo Head Prairie Alta Can.
122 G4 Buffalo Hump mt. ID U.S.A.
106 H2 Buffalo Lake N.W.T. Can.

Buffalo Narrows to Bystrzyckie, Góry
243

107 I4 Buffalo Narrows Sask. Can.
95 F4 Buffalo Range Zimbabwe
124 O1 Buffalo Valley NV U.S.A.
130 □ Buff Bay Jamaica
97 O4 Buffels r. KwaZulu-Natal S. Africa
96 E9 Buffels r. Western Cape S. Africa
96 B5 Buffels watercourse S. Africa
96 G9 Buffelsdrif S. Africa
95 E4 Buffels Drift S. Africa
40 F4 Buffières France
49 K8 Bufleben Ger.
115 E8 Buford GA U.S.A.
77 N6 Buftea Romania
50 H1 Bug pen. Ger.
55 L4 Bug r. Pol.
136 B4 Buga Col.
168 D3 Buga Mongolia
89 G4 Buga Nigeria
57 I5 Bugac Hungary
92 B5 Bugala Island Uganda
205 L4 Bugaldie N.S.W. Austr.
89 G5 Bugana Nigeria
169 J2 Bugant Mongolia
43 I10 Bugarach, Pic de mt. France
31 J3 Bugbrooke Northamptonshire, England U.K.
92 E3 Bugda Acable Somalia
79 I2 Buğdaylı Turkey
184 F2 Bugdayli Turkm.
42 H4 Bugeat France
157 I8 Bugel, Tanjung pt Indon.
40 H5 Bugey reg. France
45 F6 Buggenhout Belgium
72 A9 Buggerru Sardegna Italy
52 D6 Buggingen Ger.
75 □ Buġibba Malta
64 □ Bugio i. Madeira
191 C7 Buğlan Geçidi pass Turkey
73 L3 Bugnara Italy
43 C9 Bugnein France
68 F3 Bugojno Bos.-Herz.
20 T2 Bugøyfjord Norway
14 J1 Bugrino Rus. Fed.
154 A7 Bugsuk i. Phil.
169 Q2 Bugt Nei Mongol China
154 C2 Buguey Luzon Phil.
154 D5 Bugui Point Masbate Phil.
15 K5 Bugul'ma Rus. Fed.
182 I4 Bugun' Kazakh.
182 E1 Buguruslan Rus. Fed.
57 I4 Bugyi Hungary
179 N6 Buha Arun. Prad. India
184 F6 Būhābād Iran
79 J5 Buharkent Turkey
95 F3 Buhera Zimbabwe
168 F8 Buh He r. China
154 D5 Buhi Luzon Phil.
52 E4 Bühl Ger.
122 G5 Buhl ID U.S.A.
110 B2 Buhl MN U.S.A.
52 E4 Bühlertal Ger.
52 H3 Bühlertann Ger.
52 H3 Bühlerzell Ger.
49 K7 Bühne Ger.
93 A6 Buhoro Tanz.
93 B7 Buhoro Flats plain Tanz.
16 F3 Buhryn Ukr.
189 K5 Bühtan r. Turkey
93 B6 Buhu r. Tanz.
77 O4 Buhuşi Romania
71 O3 Buia Italy
106 F3 Buick B.C. Can.
26 E10 Buie, Loch b. Scotland U.K.
30 F3 Builth Wells Powys, Wales U.K.
146 B3 Buin Chile
184 D4 Bū'īn Iran
200 □6 Buin P.N.G.
88 E4 Bui National Park Ghana
15 J5 Buinsk Rus. Fed.
184 B4 Bu'in Soflā Iran
184 D4 Bu'in Zahrā Iran
169 O3 Buir Nur l. Mongolia
41 G8 Buis-les-Baronnies France
44 J2 Buitenpost Neth.
94 C4 Buitepos Namibia
63 M7 Buitrago del Lozoya Spain
18 I7 Būivydžiai Lith.
65 K5 Bujalance Spain
77 J8 Bujanovac Srbija Serb. and Mont.
66 E5 Bujaraloz Spain
71 P5 Buje Croatia
77 N7 Bujoru Romania
93 A5 Bujumbura Burundi
59 O5 Bük Hungary
54 E3 Buk Pol.
161 K1 Bukachacha Rus. Fed.
55 M6 Bukachivtsi Ukr.
173 J8 Buka Daban mt. Qinghai/Xinjiang China
153 L8 Buka Island P.N.G.
94 E3 Bukalo Namibia
91 E7 Bukama Dem. Rep. Congo
19 R8 Bukan' Rus. Fed.
184 E6 Būkand Iran
183 S1 Bukanskoye Rus. Fed.
90 F5 Bukavu Dem. Rep. Congo
91 C6 Bukedi Dem. Rep. Congo
93 B6 Bukene Tanz.
91 E7 Bukeya Dem. Rep. Congo
Bukhara Buxoro Uzbek. see Buxoro
Bukhara Oblast admin. div. Uzbek. see Buxoro
18 M6 Bukhava Belarus
Bukhoro Uzbek. see Buxoro
Bukhoro Wiloyati admin. div. Uzbek. see Buxoro
162 B1 Bukhta Rus. Fed.
183 U3 Bukhtarminskoye Vodokhranilishche resr Kazakh.
155 D2 Bukide i. Indon.
93 B5 Bukima Tanz.
157 J5 Bukit Baka - Bukit Raya National Park Indon.
157 J6 Bukitlidi Kalimantan Indon.
156 □ Bukit Timah Sing.
156 □ Bukit Timah hill Sing.
156 D5 Bukittinggi Sumatera Indon.
57 J3 Bükk mts Hungary
57 J4 Bükkábrány Hungary
57 J4 Bükkalja hills Hungary
176 E5 Bukkapatnam Andhra Prad. India
57 J3 Bükki nat. park Hungary
57 G5 Bükkösd Hungary
57 J4 Bükkzsérc Hungary
51 F7 Buko Ger.
93 A5 Bukoba Tanz.
18 H6 Bukonys Lith.
57 H2 Bukovec Czech Rep.
59 J8 Bukovje Slovenia
57 L2 Bukovské vrchy hills Slovakia
55 K5 Bukowa r. Pol.
54 F3 Bukowe Pol.
54 F4 Bukowice Pol.
54 G2 Bukowiec Kujawsko-Pomorskie Pol.
54 D3 Bukowiec Lubuskie Pol.
51 L6 Bukowiec hill Pol.
54 F1 Bukowina Pol.
55 I6 Bukowina Tatrzańska Pol.
54 G4 Bukownica Pol.
55 H5 Bukowno Pol.
54 F2 Bukowo Pol.
23 M7 Bukowo, Jezioro lag. Pol.
55 K6 Bukowsko Pol.
Bükreş Romania see Bucureşti
156 F5 Buku, Tanjung pt Indon.
169 L2 Bukukun Rus. Fed.
156 □ Bukum, Pulau i. Sing.
16 J4 Buky Ukr.
184 E6 Būl, Kūh-e mt. Iran
88 B3 Bula Guinea-Bissau
155 G5 Bula Seram Indon.
91 B7 Bula Atumba Angola
70 F1 Bülach Switz.
169 K2 Bulag Mongolia
169 J2 Bulagtay Mongolia
205 N5 Bulahdelah N.S.W. Austr.
154 C6 Bulalacao i. Phil.
156 E4 Bulan i. Indon.
154 D5 Bulan Luzon Phil.
154 C8 Bulan i. Phil.
188 I3 Bulancak Turkey
178 F5 Bulandshahr Uttar Prad. India
189 K4 Bulanık Turkey
182 F1 Bulanovo Rus. Fed.
85 F3 Būlāq Egypt
162 L3 Bulava Rus. Fed.
155 C3 Bulawa, Gunung mt. Indon.
95 F4 Bulawayo Zimbabwe
183 N1 Bulayevo Kazakh.
188 H5 Bulbul Syria
90 E2 Bulbul, Wadi watercourse Sudan
93 C5 Bulbula waterhole Kenya
79 J4 Buldan Turkey
178 F9 Buldhana Mahar. India
138 A2 Buldibuyo Peru
104 A4 Buldir Island AK U.S.A.
178 F4 Buldur Hima. Prad. India
182 E2 Buldurta Kazakh.
Buldyrty Kazakh. see Buldurta
185 J8 Buleda reg. Pak.
92 E3 Bulei well Eth.
97 P1 Bulembu Swaziland
88 E4 Bulenga Ghana
31 I5 Bulford Wiltshire, England U.K.
168 H2 Bulgan Bulgan Mongolia
Bulgan Hovd Mongolia see Bürenhayrhan
168 C3 Bulgan Hovd Mongolia
168 G1 Bulgan Hövsgöl Mongolia
168 H4 Bulgan Ömnögovĭ Mongolia
168 H2 Bulgan prov. Mongolia
168 B3 Bulgan Gol r. Mongolia
Bulgar Rus. Fed. see Bolgar
77 Q7 Bŭlgarevo Bulg.
77 N8 Bulgaria country Europe
Bŭlgariya country Europe see Bulgaria
186 E3 Bulghah Saudi Arabia
73 O7 Bulgheria, Monte mt. Italy
37 K7 Bulgnéville France
191 D5 Bulgurlu Turkey
17 M9 Bulhanak r. Ukr.
155 F3 Buli Halmahera Indon.
155 F3 Buli, Teluk b. Halmahera Indon.
154 A7 Buliluyan, Cape Palawan Phil.
92 A4 Bulisa Uganda
48 G3 Bülkau Ger.
31 J3 Bulkington Warwickshire, England U.K.
106 D4 Bulkley Ranges mts B.C. Can.
55 I3 Bulkowo Pol.
65 K3 Bullaque r. Spain
65 P4 Bullas Spain
207 I9 Bullawarra, Lake salt flat Qld Austr.
92 E2 Bullaxaar Somalia
49 D10 Bullay Ger.
130 □ Bull Bay Jamaica
70 C2 Bulle Switz.
205 H4 Bullea, Lake salt flat N.S.W. Austr.
131 □10 Bullenbaai b. Curaçao Neth. Antilles
203 F8 Buller r. South I. N.Z.
207 I4 Bulleringa National Park Qld Austr.
209 E11 Bullfinch W.A. Austr.
125 R6 Bullhead City AZ U.S.A.
205 M6 Bulli N.S.W. Austr.
45 J8 Büllingen Belgium
125 P7 Bullion Mountains CA U.S.A.
20 P4 Bullmark Sweden
206 B3 Bullo r. N.T. Austr.
63 P7 Bullones r. Spain
205 I3 Bulloo watercourse Qld Austr.
205 I3 Bulloo Downs Qld Austr.
205 I3 Bulloo Lake salt flat Qld Austr.
27 J2 Bull Point Northern Ireland U.K.
202 J7 Bulls North I. N.Z.
130 □ Bull Savannah Jamaica
119 I1 Bulls Bridge CT U.S.A.
121 I7 Bull Shoals Lake AR U.S.A.
94 C5 Büllsport Namibia
119 G1 Bullville NY U.S.A.
36 E3 Bully-les-Mines France
206 E2 Bulman N.T. Austr.
206 E2 Bulman Gorge N.T. Austr.
106 F2 Bulmer Lake N.W.T. Can.
31 N3 Bulmer Tye Essex, England U.K.
146 A5 Bulnes Chile
156 □ Buloh, Pulau i. Sing.
205 I7 Buloke, Lake dry lake Vic. Austr.
153 K8 Bulolo P.N.G.
76 I9 Bulqizë Albania
72 C7 Bultei Sardegna Italy
97 K4 Bultfontein S. Africa
157 L3 Bulu, Gunung mt. Indon.
154 E8 Buluan Mindanao Phil.
155 B6 Bulubulu Sulawesi Indon.
92 C3 Buluk well Kenya
155 B6 Bulukumba Sulawesi Indon.
90 D5 Bulukutu Dem. Rep. Congo
193 N2 Bulun Rus. Fed.
185 P2 Bulungkol Xinjiang China
91 C6 Bulungu Bandundu Dem. Rep. Congo
91 D6 Bulungu Kasaï-Occidental Dem. Rep. Congo
183 L8 Bulung'ur Uzbek.
154 E5 Bulusan Luzon Phil.
96 C1 Bulwana Namibia
97 N5 Bulwer S. Africa
57 L5 Bulz Romania
72 B6 Bulzi Sardegna Italy
200 □6 Buma Malaita Solomon Is
91 C6 Bumba Bandundu Dem. Rep. Congo
90 D4 Bumba Équateur Dem. Rep. Congo
84 D1 Būmbah Libya
84 D1 Bumbah, Khalīj b. Libya
168 I6 Bumbat Nei Mongol China
168 I3 Bumbat Mongolia
77 L5 Bumbeşti-Jiu Romania
88 C4 Bumbuna Sierra Leone
158 C1 Bumhkang Myanmar
158 C1 Bumpha Bum mt. Myanmar
91 C5 Buna Dem. Rep. Congo
92 C4 Buna Kenya
27 C5 Bunacurry Rep. of Ireland
187 J4 Bunayyān well Saudi Arabia
93 A5 Bunazi Tanz.
27 F2 Bunbeg Rep. of Ireland
209 C12 Bunbury W.A. Austr.
29 L7 Bunbury Cheshire, England U.K.
27 I7 Bunclody Rep. of Ireland
27 H2 Buncrana Rep. of Ireland
93 B5 Bunda Tanz.
207 N8 Bundaberg Qld Austr.
205 K3 Bundaleer Qld Austr.
205 M4 Bundarra N.S.W. Austr.
48 D4 Bunde Ger.
49 G6 Bünde Ger.
52 C2 Bundenbach Ger.
48 D4 Bunderhee Ger.
206 E6 Bundey watercourse N.T. Austr.
178 E7 Bundi Rajasthan India
92 A4 Bundibugyo Uganda
205 N3 Bundjalung National Park N.S.W. Austr.
27 F4 Bundoran Rep. of Ireland
179 J8 Bundu Jharkhand India
92 A3 Bunduqiya Sudan
76 H9 Bunë r. Albania/Yugo.
184 C6 Būneh i. Iran
187 I1 Būneh Dara b. Iran
185 O4 Buner reg. Pak.
89 H3 Bunga r. Nigeria
166 C5 Bunga-dake mt. Japan
156 C6 Bungalaut, Selat sea chan. Indon.
31 O3 Bungay Suffolk, England U.K.
158 E7 Bung Boraphet l. Thai.
205 L6 Bungendore N.S.W. Austr.
213 G2 Bunger Hills Antarctica
155 C6 Bungi Sulawesi Indon.
207 L9 Bungil Creek r. Qld Austr.
155 B5 Bungku Sulawesi Indon.
91 B6 Bungo Angola
92 B4 Bungoma Kenya
173 J10 Bungona'og Xizang China
165 J13 Bungo-suidō sea chan. Japan
165 I13 Bungo-takada Japan
90 F4 Bunia Dem. Rep. Congo
63 M4 Buniel Spain
57 L6 Bunila Romania
209 G11 Buningonia well W.A. Austr.
89 I4 Buni-Yadi Nigeria
178 E2 Bunji Jammu and Kashmir
121 J7 Bunker MO U.S.A.
207 N7 Bunker Group atolls Qld Austr.
91 E7 Bunkeya Dem. Rep. Congo
121 I10 Bunkie LA U.S.A.
21 L6 Bunkris Sweden
27 H8 Bunmahon Rep. of Ireland
27 C4 Bunnahowen Rep. of Ireland
27 E4 Bunnanadden Rep. of Ireland
115 G11 Bunnell FL U.S.A.
44 H4 Bunnik Neth.
27 D4 Bunnyconnellan Rep. of Ireland
202 J7 Bunnythorpe North I. N.Z.
67 D9 Buñol Spain
44 H4 Bunschoten-Spakenburg Neth.
173 F11 Bünsum Xizang China
89 G3 Bunsuru watercourse Nigeria
57 L5 Bunteşti Romania
209 D10 Buntine W.A. Austr.
31 L4 Buntingford Hertfordshire, England U.K.
157 K5 Buntok Kalimantan Indon.
157 K5 Buntokecil Kalimantan Indon.
63 R5 Buñuel Spain
89 H4 Bununu Nigeria
207 M9 Bunya Mountains National Park Qld Austr.
188 G4 Bünyan Turkey
67 K8 Bunyola Spain
157 L3 Bunyu i. Indon.
89 G3 Bunza Nigeria
68 F3 Buoač Bos.-Herz.
73 P7 Buonabitacolo Italy
73 N5 Buonalbergo Italy
72 G1 Buonconvento Italy
159 I8 Buôn Hô Vietnam
159 I8 Buôn Ma Thuôt Vietnam
73 P8 Buonvicino Italy
193 O2 Buorkhaya, Guba b. Rus. Fed.
173 H12 Bup r. China
186 F2 Buqay'ā Saudi Arabia
Buqayq Saudi Arabia see Abqaiq
84 E2 Buqbuq Egypt
Buqtyrma Bögeni resr Kazakh. see Bukhtarminskoye Vodokhranilishche
93 C5 Bura Kenya
92 F2 Buraan Somalia
184 H9 Burak Iran
209 D11 Burakin W.A. Austr.
90 E2 Buram Sudan
183 U3 Buran Kazakh.
156 □ Buran Darat rf Sing.
178 H4 Burang Xizang China
143 G2 Buranhaém Brazil
143 H2 Buranhaém r. Brazil
182 F2 Burannoye Rus. Fed.
71 N8 Burano r. Italy
190 E5 Burāq Syria
154 E6 Burauen Leyte Phil.
185 O4 Burawai Pak.
178 E9 Buray r. India
186 F2 Buraydah Saudi Arabia
14 K5 Burayevo Rus. Fed.
49 F9 Burbach Ger.
31 I5 Burbage Wiltshire, England U.K.
66 C5 Burbáguena Spain
124 N7 Burbank CA U.S.A.
72 C9 Burcei Sardegna Italy
17 O6 Burchak Ukr.
110 D1 Burchell Lake Ont. Can.
205 K5 Burcher N.S.W. Austr.
92 E2 Burco Somalia
44 I2 Burdaard Neth.
185 K2 Burdalyk Turkm.
207 K5 Burdekin r. Qld Austr.
207 K6 Burdekin Falls Qld Austr.
40 H4 Burdet, Mont mt. France
Burdigala France see Bordeaux
45 H7 Burdinne Belgium
79 L5 Burdur Turkey
79 L5 Burdur prov. Turkey
79 L5 Burdur Gölü l. Turkey
Burdwan W. Bengal India see Barddhaman
92 C2 Burē Āmara Eth.
92 B2 Burē Oromīya Eth.
31 P2 Bure r. England U.K.
41 H7 Bure, Pic de mt. France
20 P4 Bureå Sweden
162 H3 Bureinskiy Khrebet mts Rus. Fed.
85 F5 Bureiqa well Sudan
63 L3 Burejo r. Spain
62 F1 Burela, Cabo c. Spain
49 G7 Büren Ger.
44 H5 Buren Neth.
70 C1 Büren an der Aare Switz.
168 B3 Bürenhayrhan Mongolia
169 L3 Bürentsogt Mongolia
146 A5 Bureo r. Chile
31 N4 Bures Suffolk, England U.K.
162 F4 Bureya r. Rus. Fed.
Bureya Range mts Rus. Fed. see Bureinskiy Khrebet
162 I3 Bureyinski Zapovednik nature res. Rus. Fed.
111 N6 Burford Ont. Can.
31 I4 Burford Oxfordshire, England U.K.
190 A7 Būr Fu'ād Egypt
43 E9 Burg France
51 J7 Burg Ger.
48 H3 Burg (Dithmarschen) Ger.
168 I2 Burgaltay Mongolia
62 I5 Burganes de Valverde Spain
77 P8 Burgas Bulg.
59 N5 Burgau Austria
53 I5 Burgau Ger.
64 B6 Burgau Port.
50 D2 Burg auf Fehmarn Ger.
115 I8 Burgaw NC U.S.A.
51 E6 Burg bei Magdeburg Ger.
53 I6 Burgberg im Allgäu Ger.
53 I3 Burgbernheim Ger.
49 D10 Burgbrohl Ger.
49 J6 Burgdorf Niedersachsen Ger.
49 J6 Burgdorf Niedersachsen Ger.
70 D1 Burgdorf Switz.
53 J2 Burgebrach Ger.
51 E9 Bürgel Ger.
59 N5 Burgenland land Austria
109 J4 Burgeo Nfld and Lab. Can.
97 K6 Burgersdorp S. Africa
95 F5 Burgersfort S. Africa
96 I6 Burgerville S. Africa
209 F11 Burges, Mount hill W.A. Austr.
117 I11 Burgess VA U.S.A.
31 L6 Burgess Hill West Sussex, England U.K.
84 E4 Burget Tuyur waterhole Sudan
53 J2 Burghaslach Ger.
49 I9 Burghaun Ger.
53 N5 Burghausen Ger.
29 K4 Burgh by Sands Cumbria, England U.K.
31 J5 Burghclere Hampshire, England U.K.
26 J7 Burghead Moray, Scotland U.K.
26 I7 Burghead Bay Scotland U.K.
53 K4 Burgheim Ger.
31 J5 Burghfield Common West Berkshire, England U.K.
44 E5 Burgh-Haamstede Neth.
30 G3 Burghill Herefordshire, England U.K.
29 R7 Burgh le Marsh Lincolnshire, England U.K.
74 E8 Burgio Sicilia Italy
74 H9 Burgio, Serra di hill Sicilia Italy
58 H3 Burgkirchen Austria
53 N5 Burgkirchen an der Alz Ger.
51 D10 Burgkunstadt Ger.
70 G1 Bürglen Thurgau Switz.
70 F2 Bürglen Uri Switz.
53 M3 Burglengenfeld Ger.
53 J3 Burgoberbach Ger.
63 K8 Burgohondo Spain
63 M6 Burgomillodo, Embalse de resr Spain
72 B7 Burgos Sardegna Italy
127 J5 Burgos Mex.
63 M4 Burgos Spain
63 M4 Burgos prov. Spain
49 K10 Burgpreppach Ger.
52 H5 Burgrieden Ger.
53 K3 Burgsalach Ger.
49 I10 Burgsinn Ger.
52 G2 Bürgstadt Ger.
51 G9 Burgstädt Ger.
50 H4 Burg Stargand Ger.
23 O4 Burgsvik Gotland Sweden
53 K3 Burgthann Ger.
49 K8 Burgtonna Ger.
66 C2 Burgui Spain
63 K8 Burguillo, Embalse de resr Spain
64 H5 Burguillos Spain
64 F4 Burguillos del Cerro Spain
44 J2 Burgum Neth.
49 G9 Burgwald for. Ger.
53 J2 Burgwindheim Ger.
179 K9 Burhabalanga r. India
168 D9 Burhan Budai Shan mts China
79 H3 Burhaniye Turkey
178 F9 Burhanpur Madh. Prad. India
179 M8 Burhanuddin Bangl.
178 H8 Burhar-Dhanpuri Madh. Prad. India
48 F3 Burhave (Butjadingen) Ger.
179 K7 Burhi Gandak r. India
38 G2 Burhou i. Channel Is
142 C5 Buri Brazil
156 D6 Buriai Indon.
154 D5 Burias i. Phil.
70 C6 Buriasco Italy
Buriat-Mongol Republic aut. rep. Rus. Fed. see Buryatiya, Respublika
182 H2 Buribay Rus. Fed.
126 □R13 Burica, Punta pt Costa Rica
42 D4 Burie France
179 I6 Buri Gandak r. Nepal
109 K4 Burin Nfld and Lab. Can.
109 K4 Burin Peninsula Nfld and Lab. Can.
158 F7 Buriram Thai.
142 B4 Buritama Brazil
140 E2 Buriti Brazil
139 F3 Buriti r. Brazil
142 C3 Buriti Alegre Brazil
140 E3 Buriti Bravo Brazil
140 E2 Buriti dos Lopes Brazil
140 E4 Buritirama Brazil
141 D5 Buritis Brazil
143 E2 Buritizeiro Brazil
185 L6 Burj Pak.
67 E8 Burjassot Spain
172 I5 Burjay Xinjiang China
57 L6 Burjuc Romania
53 I3 Burk Ger.
183 Q7 Burkan-Suu r. Kyrg.
49 I10 Burkardroth Ger.
121 F8 Burkburnett TX U.S.A.
206 G7 Burke watercourse Qld Austr.
120 F4 Burke SD U.S.A.
106 E5 Burke Channel B.C. Can.
212 Q2 Burke Island Antarctica
203 E11 Burkes Pass South I. N.Z.
114 E7 Burkesville KY U.S.A.
206 G4 Burketown Qld Austr.
116 G11 Burkeville VA U.S.A.
193 P3 Burkhala Rus. Fed.
88 E4 Burkina country Africa
Burkina Faso country Africa see Burkina
108 E4 Burk's Falls Ont. Can.
183 Q3 Burkutty Kazakh.
183 R1 Burla Rus. Fed.
183 R1 Burla r. Rus. Fed.
63 Q3 Burlada Spain
52 G5 Burladingen Ger.
43 I8 Burlats France
207 I6 Burleigh Qld Austr.
118 F6 Burleigh NJ U.S.A.
31 I6 Burley Hampshire, England U.K.
122 H5 Burley ID U.S.A.
30 G3 Burley Gate Herefordshire, England U.K.
29 N6 Burley in Wharfedale West Yorkshire, England U.K.
182 I1 Burli Kazakh.
182 E2 Burlin Kazakh.
124 J4 Burlingame CA U.S.A.
108 E5 Burlington Ont. Can.
120 D6 Burlington CO U.S.A.
119 J1 Burlington CT U.S.A.
114 B5 Burlington IA U.S.A.
110 H9 Burlington IN U.S.A.
120 H6 Burlington KS U.S.A.
120 M6 Burlington KY U.S.A.
115 H7 Burlington NC U.S.A.
118 F4 Burlington NJ U.S.A.
117 L4 Burlington VT U.S.A.
122 C2 Burlington WA U.S.A.
110 F7 Burlington WI U.S.A.
118 F5 Burlington County county NJ U.S.A.
182 G1 Burly Rus. Fed.
Burma country Asia see Myanmar
14 J4 Burmakino Kirovskaya Oblast' Rus. Fed.
19 X4 Burmakino Yaroslavskaya Oblast' Rus. Fed.
14 M3 Burmantovo Rus. Fed.
19 X8 Burminka Rus. Fed.
58 G4 Bürmoos Austria
106 F5 Burnaby B.C. Can.
28 C8 Burnchurch Rep. of Ireland
26 K4 Burness Orkney, Scotland U.K.
121 F10 Burnet TX U.S.A.
207 N8 Burnett r. Qld Austr.
207 N8 Burnett Heads Qld Austr.
122 D6 Burney CA U.S.A.
145 B9 Burney, Monte vol. Chile
27 E8 Burnfoot Rep. of Ireland
27 I3 Burnfoot Northern Ireland U.K.
203 G10 Burnham South I. N.Z.
31 K4 Burnham Buckinghamshire, England U.K.
117 □P4 Burnham ME U.S.A.
116 H8 Burnham PA U.S.A.
31 N2 Burnham Market Norfolk, England U.K.
31 N4 Burnham-on-Crouch Essex, England U.K.
30 G5 Burnham-on-Sea Somerset, England U.K.
28 H2 Burnhouse North Ayrshire, Scotland U.K.
205 J9 Burnie Tas. Austr.
116 B11 Burning Springs KY U.S.A.
29 Q5 Burniston North Yorkshire, England U.K.
29 M6 Burnley Lancashire, England U.K.
26 L11 Burnmouth Scottish Borders, Scotland U.K.
29 N4 Burnopfield Durham, England U.K.
Burnoye Kazakh. see Bauyrzhan Momyshuly
122 E5 Burns OR U.S.A.
104 H3 Burnside r. Nunavut Can.
209 G8 Burnside, Lake salt flat W.A. Austr.
122 F5 Burns Junction OR U.S.A.
106 E4 Burns Lake B.C. Can.
110 A5 Burnsville MN U.S.A.
116 E10 Burnsville WV U.S.A.
116 E10 Burnsville Lake WV U.S.A.
122 F4 Burnt r. OR U.S.A.
26 J10 Burntisland Fife, Scotland U.K.
Burnt Lake Que. Can. see Brûlé, Lac
204 □1 Burnt Pine Norfolk I.
107 L4 Burntwood r. Man. Can.
31 I2 Burntwood Green Staffordshire, England U.K.
107 K4 Burntwood Lake Man. Can.
173 G9 Burog Co l. Xizang China
109 G1 Buron r. Que. Can.
191 F3 Buron Rus. Fed.
63 J2 Burón Spain
70 E5 Buronzo Italy
43 D9 Buros France
50 H3 Burow Ger.
172 H3 Burqin Xinjiang China
172 H3 Burqin He r. China
190 G6 Burqu' Jordan
204 G5 Burra S.A. Austr.
26 □N2 Burra i. Scotland U.K.
26 □N1 Burravoe Shetland, Scotland U.K.
26 K5 Burray i. Scotland U.K.
76 I9 Burrel Albania
124 M5 Burrel CA U.S.A.
26 J9 Burrelton Perth and Kinross, Scotland U.K.
27 D6 Burren Rep. of Ireland
27 D5 Burren Rep. of Ireland
27 D6 Burren reg. Rep. of Ireland
28 E5 Burren Northern Ireland U.K.
205 L5 Burrendong, Lake resr N.S.W. Austr.
205 L4 Burren Junction N.S.W. Austr.
205 M6 Burrewarra Point N.S.W. Austr.
67 E8 Burriana Spain
205 L6 Burrinjuck Reservoir N.S.W. Austr.
127 H3 Burro, Serranías del mts Mex.
110 C6 Burr Oak IA U.S.A.
116 C9 Burr Oak Reservoir OH U.S.A.
125 S7 Burro Creek watercourse AZ U.S.A.
28 I4 Burrow Head Scotland U.K.
206 C2 Burrundie N.T. Austr.
144 D2 Burruyacú Arg.
30 D4 Burry Inlet Wales U.K.
30 D4 Burry Port Carmarthenshire, Wales U.K.
58 A5 Bürs Austria
79 K2 Bursa Turkey
79 J2 Bursa prov. Turkey
85 G3 Būr Safājah Egypt
85 G2 Būr Sa'īd Egypt
188 F8 Būr Sa'īd governorate Egypt
29 L6 Burscough Lancashire, England U.K.
29 L6 Burscough Bridge Lancashire, England U.K.
49 I7 Bursfelde Ger.
16 D4 Burshtyn Ukr.
162 G3 Bursinskoye Vodokhranilishche resr Rus. Fed.
52 E2 Bürstadt Ger.
31 L5 Burstow Surrey, England U.K.
204 H5 Burta N.S.W. Austr.
190 A9 Būr Tawfīq Egypt
53 I5 Burtenbach Ger.
110 J4 Burt Lake MI U.S.A.
18 I4 Burtnieku ezers l. Latvia
31 I6 Burton Dorset, England U.K.
111 K7 Burton MI U.S.A.
108 E2 Burton, Lac l. Que. Can.
30 G6 Burton Bradstock Dorset, England U.K.
29 L5 Burton-in-Kendal Cumbria, England U.K.
31 K3 Burton Latimer Northamptonshire, England U.K.
29 O5 Burton Leonard North Yorkshire, England U.K.
27 F3 Burtonport Rep. of Ireland
118 B6 Burtonsville MD U.S.A.
29 P6 Burton upon Stather North Lincolnshire, England U.K.
31 I2 Burton upon Trent Staffordshire, England U.K.
20 P4 Burträsk Sweden
117 □S2 Burtts Corner N.B. Can.
205 I5 Burtundy N.S.W. Austr.
206 D7 Burt Well N.T. Austr.
155 E5 Buru i. Maluku Indon.
183 O5 Burubaytal Kazakh.
63 L9 Burujón Spain
190 B8 Burūk, Wādī al watercourse Egypt
17 N8 Burul'cha r. Ukr.
188 E8 Burullus, Buḩayrat al lag. Egypt
Burullus, Lake lag. Egypt see Burullus, Buḩayrat al
Burultokay Xinjiang China see Fuhai
190 B7 Burūn, Ra's pt Egypt
93 A5 Burundi country Africa
93 A5 Bururi Burundi
89 G5 Burutu Nigeria
30 G3 Burwarton Shropshire, England U.K.
31 M6 Burwash East Sussex, England U.K.
106 B2 Burwash Landing Y.T. Can.
31 M3 Burwell Cambridgeshire, England U.K.
120 F5 Burwell NE U.S.A.
26 K5 Burwick Orkney, Scotland U.K.
29 M6 Bury Greater Manchester, England U.K.
Buryatia aut. rep. Rus. Fed. see Buryatiya, Respublika
168 H1 Buryatiya, Respublika aut. rep. Rus. Fed.
Buryatskaya Mongolskaya A.S.S.R. aut. rep. Rus. Fed. see Buryatiya, Respublika
Būrylbaytal Kazakh. see Burubaytal
17 M2 Buryn' Ukr.
182 D5 Burynshyk Kazakh.
31 N3 Bury St Edmunds Suffolk, England U.K.
147 H4 Burzaco Arg.
54 G4 Burzenin Pol.
41 E7 Burzet France
178 E2 Burzil Pass Jammu and Kashmir
72 B7 Busachi Sardegna Italy
70 F6 Busalla Italy
186 F8 Būs'ān Yemen
70 I7 Busana Italy
154 D8 Busan Bay Mindanao Phil.
90 D5 Busanga Dem. Rep. Congo
122 K4 Busby MT U.S.A.
70 C6 Busca Italy
59 N2 Buschberg hill Austria
50 G5 Buschow Ger.
48 I2 Busdorf Ger.
Buseire Syria see Al Buşayrah
74 D7 Buseto Palizzolo Sicilia Italy
28 D3 Bush r. Northern Ireland U.K.
16 H5 Busha Ukr.
16 F3 Bushcha Ukr.
184 D7 Būshehr Iran
184 D7 Būshehr prov. Iran
92 A5 Bushenyi Uganda
31 L4 Bushey Hertfordshire, England U.K.
Bushire Iran see Būshehr
118 E2 Bushkill PA U.S.A.
118 F2 Bush Kill r. PA U.S.A.
27 I2 Bushmills Northern Ireland U.K.
115 F11 Bushnell FL U.S.A.
110 D9 Bushnell IL U.S.A.
76 I9 Bushtricë Albania
92 B4 Busia Kenya
36 F3 Busigny France
57 I3 Bušince Slovakia
156 □ Busing, Pulau i. Sing.
90 D4 Businga Dem. Rep. Congo
90 C5 Busira r. Dem. Rep. Congo
22 J1 Busjön l. Sweden
16 D4 Bus'k Ukr.
22 E1 Buskerud county Norway
55 I5 Busko-Zdrój Pol.
Buskul' Kazakh. see Boskol'
54 E2 Buślary Pol.
155 F2 Busobuso Maluku Indon.
190 E6 Buşrá ash Shām Syria
37 M8 Bussang France
162 E3 Busse Rus. Fed.
209 C12 Busselton W.A. Austr.
73 P7 Bussento r. Italy
90 F3 Busseri watercourse Sudan
70 I5 Busseto Italy
42 F4 Bussière-Badil France
42 H3 Bussière-Dunoise France
42 G4 Bussière-Galant France
42 F3 Bussière-Poitevine France
70 B2 Bussigny Switz.
73 L3 Bussi sul Tirino Italy
51 D9 Büßleben Ger.
71 J5 Bussolengo Italy
70 C5 Bussoleno Italy
44 H4 Bussum Neth.
36 G7 Bussy-en-Othe France
40 F1 Bussy-le-Grand France
127 I4 Bustamante Nuevo León Mex.
129 H2 Bustamante Tamaulipas Mex.
Bustandyk Kazakh. see Bostandyk
199 F4 Bustard Head Qld Austr.
77 N5 Buşteni Romania
126 F3 Bustillos, Lago l. Mex.
147 G3 Bustinza Arg.
62 H1 Busto, Cabo c. Spain
70 F4 Busto Arsizio Italy
63 O2 Busturi-Axpe Spain
154 B5 Busuanga Phil.
154 B5 Busuanga i. Phil.
90 D4 Busu-Djanoa Dem. Rep. Congo
48 G2 Büsum Ger.
90 C4 Busu Modanda Dem. Rep. Congo
71 O3 But r. Italy
90 E4 Buta Dem. Rep. Congo
92 C2 Butajīra Eth.
185 J7 Butak Pak.
77 L7 Butan Bulg.
146 C5 Buta Ranquil Arg.
93 A5 Butare Rwanda
216 G6 Butaritari atoll Kiribati
154 D4 Butauanan pt Luzon Phil.
26 F11 Bute i. Scotland U.K.
26 F11 Bute, Sound of sea chan. Scotland U.K.
77 O3 Butea Romania
106 D4 Butedale B.C. Can.
106 E5 Bute Inlet B.C. Can.
90 F4 Butembo Dem. Rep. Congo
57 L5 Buteni Romania
74 G9 Butera Sicilia Italy
45 J8 Bütgenbach Belgium
97 M4 Butha-Buthe Lesotho
158 A4 Buthidaung Myanmar
40 K5 Buthier di Valpelline r. Italy
141 C9 Butiá Brazil
92 A4 Butiaba Uganda
48 F3 Butjadingen reg. Ger.
121 K9 Butler AL U.S.A.
115 E9 Butler GA U.S.A.
110 J8 Butler IN U.S.A.
116 A10 Butler KY U.S.A.
120 H6 Butler MO U.S.A.
119 G2 Butler NJ U.S.A.
116 F8 Butler PA U.S.A.
27 H4 Butlers Bridge Rep. of Ireland
155 C6 Buton i. Indon.
155 C6 Buton, Selat sea chan. Indon.
16 I6 Butor Moldova
17 P3 Butovo Rus. Fed.
50 F4 Bütow Ger.
64 G4 Butrera mt. Spain
55 M1 Butrimonys Alytus Lith.
18 I7 Butrimonys Vilnius Lith.
78 B3 Butrint tourist site Albania
78 B3 Butrintit, Liqeni i l. Albania
55 I2 Butryny Pol.
70 G1 Bütschwil Switz.
55 M4 Butsyn Ukr.
121 K9 Buttahatchee r. MS U.S.A.
176 G9 Buttala Sri Lanka
122 H3 Butte MT U.S.A.
120 F4 Butte NE U.S.A.
52 F2 Büttelborn Ger.
51 D8 Buttelstedt Ger.
53 K2 Buttenheim Ger.
53 J4 Buttenwiesen Ger.
29 K4 Buttermere Cumbria, England U.K.
110 D3 Butternut WI U.S.A.
29 Q5 Butterwick North Yorkshire, England U.K.
156 D2 Butterworth Malaysia
97 M8 Butterworth S. Africa
124 L2 Buttes, Sierra mt. CA U.S.A.
27 E8 Buttevant Rep. of Ireland
52 H2 Bütthard Ger.
26 D5 Butt of Lewis hd Scotland U.K.
107 M3 Button Bay Man. Can.
105 L3 Button Islands Nunavut Can.
124 M6 Buttonwillow CA U.S.A.
51 D8 Buttstädt Ger.
49 J8 Büttstedt Ger.
209 F12 Butty Head W.A. Austr.
118 E3 Buttzville NJ U.S.A.
154 E7 Butuan Mindanao Phil.
154 E7 Butuan Bay Mindanao Phil.
16 I6 Butuceni Moldova
170 D5 Butuo Sichuan China
15 H6 Buturlinovka Rus. Fed.
179 I6 Butwal Nepal
49 G10 Butzbach Ger.
50 E3 Bützow Ger.
118 E3 Butztown PA U.S.A.
92 E2 Buuhoodle Somalia
92 E4 Buulobarde Somalia
Buurakan r. Kyrg. see Burkan-Suu
93 D5 Buur Gaabo Somalia
92 E4 Buurhabaka Somalia
44 K4 Buurse Neth.
20 M2 Buvåg Norway
92 B4 Buvuma Island Uganda
190 C10 Buwārah, Jabal mt. Saudi Arabia
186 D3 Buwāṭah Saudi Arabia
179 J7 Buxar Bihar India
39 L8 Buxerolles France
53 K4 Buxheim Ger.
40 B4 Buxières-les-Mines France
182 K8 Buxoro Uzbek.
182 J7 Buxoro admin. div. Uzbek.
31 M6 Buxted East Sussex, England U.K.
48 I4 Buxtehude Ger.
29 N7 Buxton Derbyshire, England U.K.
40 F3 Buxy France
14 H4 Buy Rus. Fed.
14 K4 Buy r. Rus. Fed.
168 F3 Buyant Bayanhongor Mongolia
168 A2 Buyant Bayan-Ölgiy Mongolia
169 L3 Buyant Hentiy Mongolia
168 B2 Buyant Gol r. Mongolia
168 E3 Buyant Gol r. Mongolia
169 J4 Buyant-Ovoo Mongolia
169 L4 Buyant-Uhaa Mongolia
110 B1 Buyck MN U.S.A.
191 I3 Buynaksk Rus. Fed.
16 H2 Buynavichy Belarus
88 D5 Buyo Côte d'Ivoire
88 D5 Buyo, Lac de l. Côte d'Ivoire
170 C8 Buyuan Jiang r. Yunnan China
79 K2 Büyükada i. Turkey
189 L4 Büyük Ağrı Dağı mt. Turkey
191 E5 Büyükçatak Turkey
79 J1 Büyükçekmece Turkey
191 B6 Büyükgeçit Turkey
190 G1 Büyükhan Turkey
79 L4 Büyükkabaca Turkey
79 M4 Büyükkarabağ Turkey
79 I1 Büyükkarıştıran Turkey
79 K5 Büyükkonak Turkey
79 I5 Büyükmenderes r. Turkey
79 J3 Büyükorhan Turkey
190 F2 Büyükşahinbey Turkey
79 I3 Büyükyenice Turkey
169 R6 Buyun Shan mt. Liaoning China
182 D5 Buzachi, Poluostrov pen. Kazakh.
185 P3 Buzai Gumbad Afgh.
42 G2 Buzançais France
37 I5 Buzancy France
77 O5 Buzău Romania
77 O5 Buzău r. Romania
77 P5 Buzău r. Romania
84 D3 Buzaymah oasis Libya
15 K5 Buzdyak Rus. Fed.
71 P5 Buzet Croatia
43 E7 Buzet-sur-Baïse France
43 H8 Buzet-sur-Tarn France
19 X6 Buzha r. Rus. Fed.
95 G3 Búzi Moz.
95 G3 Búzi r. Moz.
77 J5 Buziaş Romania
57 K3 Buzica Slovakia
143 G5 Búzios, Cabo dos c. Brazil
143 E5 Búzios, Ilha dos i. Brazil
Büzmeyin Turkm. see Byuzmeyin
191 L5 Buzovna Azer.
183 L2 Buzuluk Kazakh.
182 E1 Buzuluk Rus. Fed.
15 H6 Buzuluk r. Rus. Fed.
43 D9 Buzy France
117 O7 Buzzards Bay MA U.S.A.
153 L9 Bwagaoia P.N.G.
93 A5 Bwanga Tanz.
Bwcle Flintshire, Wales U.K. see Buckley
Bwcle Wales U.K. see Buckley
90 F5 Bwindi National Park Uganda
176 D5 Byadgi Karnataka India
18 L7 Byahoml' Belarus
77 N7 Byala Ruse Bulg.
77 P8 Byala Varna Bulg.
79 H1 Byala Reka r. Bulg.
77 L7 Byala Slatina Bulg.
18 M8 Byalynichy Belarus
19 P8 Byalynkavichy Belarus
Byam Martin atoll Arch. des Tuamotu Fr. Polynesia see Ahunui
105 H2 Byam Martin Island Nunavut Can.
18 I8 Byarezina r. Belarus
18 N9 Byarezina r. Belarus
18 L7 Byarezinski Biyasfyerny Zapavyednik nature res. Belarus
18 H9 Byaroza Belarus
18 I8 Byarozawka Belarus
55 M3 Byarozna Belarus
190 D4 Byblos tourist site Lebanon
55 K4 Bychawa Pol.
54 G5 Bycina Pol.
54 G4 Byczyna Pol.
54 F2 Bydgoski, Kanał canal Pol.
54 G2 Bydgoszcz Pol.
18 I9 Byelaazyorsk Belarus
16 F2 Byelavusha Belarus
18 G9 Byelavyezhskaya Pushcha park Belarus
55 L3 Byelavyezhski Belarus
55 M2 Byelaye, Vozyera l. Belarus
17 P8 Byelins'ke Ukr.
19 N9 Byelitsk Belarus
18 K6 Byel'ki Belarus
Byelorussia country Europe see Belarus
55 N1 Byenyakoni Belarus
18 L8 Byerazino Minskaya Voblasts' Belarus
18 L7 Byerazino Vitsyebskaya Voblasts' Belarus
18 K9 Byeraznyaki Belarus
122 L7 Byers CO U.S.A.
18 H8 Byershty Belarus
18 M6 Byeshankovichy Belarus
116 D9 Byesville OH U.S.A.
19 O9 Byesyedz' r. Belarus
207 M7 Byfield Qld Austr.
31 J3 Byfield Northamptonshire, England U.K.
207 M7 Byfield National Park Qld Austr.
31 L5 Byfleet Surrey, England U.K.
20 P4 Bygdeå Sweden
20 P4 Bygdsiljum Sweden
22 D3 Bygland Norway
22 D3 Byglandsfjord Norway
22 D3 Byglandsfjorden l. Norway
51 J7 Byhleguhre Ger.
17 P5 Byk r. Ukr.
19 N8 Bykhaw Belarus
Bykhov Belarus see Bykhaw
16 G3 Bykivka Ukr.
22 D2 Bykle Norway
17 P3 Bykovka Rus. Fed.
17 Q2 Bykovo Kurskaya Oblast' Rus. Fed.
15 I6 Bykovo Volgogradskaya Oblast' Rus. Fed.
193 N2 Bykovskiy Rus. Fed.
125 V8 Bylas AZ U.S.A.
30 E1 Bylchau Conwy, Wales U.K.
48 H1 Bylderup-Bov Denmark
183 P3 Bylkyldak Kazakh.
105 K2 Bylot Island Nunavut Can.
191 D2 Bylym Rus. Fed.
111 N4 Byng Inlet Ont. Can.
207 H4 Bynoe r. Qld Austr.
206 C2 Bynoe Harbour N.T. Austr.
176 B7 Byramgore Reef India
213 K1 Byrd Glacier Antarctica
169 P1 Byrka Rus. Fed.
22 C3 Byrkjedal Norway
21 I6 Byrkjelo Norway
17 L3 Byrlivka Ukr.
205 K4 Byrock N.S.W. Austr.
110 E7 Byron IL U.S.A.
117 □O4 Byron ME U.S.A.
116 B6 Byron MI U.S.A.
205 N3 Byron, Cape N.S.W. Austr.
205 N3 Byron Bay N.S.W. Austr.
193 K2 Byrranga, Gory mts Rus. Fed.
17 M1 Byryne Ukr.
16 I3 Byshiv Ukr.
56 D1 Byšice Czech Rep.
20 P4 Byske Sweden
20 P4 Byskeälven r. Sweden
162 G2 Byssa Rus. Fed.
162 G2 Byssa r. Rus. Fed.
55 H6 Bystra Pol.
57 I2 Bystrá mt. Slovakia
56 F2 Bystré Czech Rep.
57 K2 Bystré Slovakia
18 L4 Bystretsovo Rus. Fed.
57 H3 Bystričany Slovakia
57 H2 Bystřice Moravskoslezský kraj Czech Rep.
56 D2 Bystřice Středočeský kraj Czech Rep.
56 E1 Bystřice r. Czech Rep.
56 F2 Bystřice nad Pernštejnem Czech Rep.
57 G2 Bystřice pod Hostýnem Czech Rep.
169 L2 Bystrinskiy Golets, Gora mt. Rus. Fed.
16 D5 Bystrytsya Ukr.
16 C4 Bystrytsya r. Ukr.
183 U1 Bystryy Istok Rus. Fed.
14 K5 Bystryy Tanyp r. Rus. Fed.
54 F5 Bystrzyca Pol.
54 E4 Bystrzyca r. Pol.
55 K4 Bystrzyca r. Pol.
54 E5 Bystrzyca Kłodzka Pol.
56 F1 Bystrzyckie, Góry mts Czech Rep./Pol.

193 O3 Bytantay r. Rus. Fed.
57 H2 Bytča Slovakia
54 D3 Bytnica Pol.
54 G5 Bytom Pol.
54 D4 Bytom Odrzański Pol.
19 R8 Bytosh' Rus. Fed.
23 N7 Bytów Pol.
93 A5 Byumba Rwanda
184 F2 Byurgyutli Turkm.
184 H2 Byuzmeyin Turkm.
16 J2 Byval'ki Belarus
23 N4 Byxelkrok Öland Sweden
56 G3 Bzenec Czech Rep.
191 B2 Bzip'i r. Georgia
191 B2 Bzip'is K'edi hills Georgia
55 I3 Bzura r. Pol.
191 A2 Bzych Rus. Fed.

C

158 G5 Ca, Sông r. Vietnam
139 F6 Caacupé Para.
139 F6 Caaguazú Para.
139 G6 Caaguazú, Cordillera de hills Para.
91 B8 Caála Angola
137 F5 Caapiranga Brazil
139 F6 Caapucú Para.
141 B7 Caarapó Brazil
143 E2 Caatinga Brazil
139 F6 Caazapá Para.
92 F3 Cabaad, Raas pt Somalia
139 F3 Cabaçal r. Brazil
129 J9 Cabacera Nueva Mex.
66 G5 Cabacés Spain
130 D2 Cabaiguán Cuba
43 D10 Cabaliros, Pic de mt. France
138 B3 Caballas Peru
65 M6 Caballo mt. Spain
136 D5 Caballococha Peru
123 K10 Caballo Reservoir NM U.S.A.
138 A2 Cabana Ancash Peru
138 B3 Cabana Ayacucho Peru
43 E9 Cabanac France
43 C6 Cabanac-et-Villagrains France
138 C3 Cabanaconde Peru
62 D5 Cabana Maior Port.
62 I2 Cabañaquinta Spain
64 D6 Cabanas Port.
65 N5 Cabañas mt. Spain
62 I9 Cabañas del Castillo Spain
62 E8 Cabanas de Viriato Port.
62 G3 Cabañas Raras Spain
154 C4 Cabanatuan Luzon Phil.
30 E3 Caban Coch Reservoir Wales U.K.
43 G9 Cabanères hill France
67 F7 Cabanes Spain
41 F9 Cabannes France
109 G4 Cabano Que. Can.
68 E3 Čabar Croatia
43 I9 Cabardès reg. France
41 I10 Cabasse France
92 D2 Cabdul Qaadir Somalia
62 E4 Cabe r. Spain
64 D5 Cabeça Gorda Port.
64 C3 Cabeção Port.
139 G3 Cabeceira Rio Manso Brazil
142 D1 Cabeceiras Brazil
62 E5 Cabeceiras de Basto Port.
64 D2 Cabeço de Vide Port.
62 E9 Cabeço Rainha mt. Port.
140 G3 Cabedelo Brazil
43 J10 Cabestany France
57 L5 Căbești Romania
129 M9 Cabestrada Mex.
62 H6 Cabeza de Framontanos Spain
145 C6 Cabeza del Buey Arg.
65 I3 Cabeza del Buey Spain
62 G6 Cabeza del Caballo Spain
144 C2 Cabeza de Vaca, Punta pt Chile
64 G4 Cabeza la Vaca Spain
63 N9 Cabezamesada Spain
125 S9 Cabeza Prieta National Wildlife Refuge nature res. AZ U.S.A.
65 K3 Cabezarados Spain
139 E4 Cabezas Bol.
63 J7 Cabezas del Villar Spain
131 □1 Cabezas de San Juan pt Puerto Rico
64 E5 Cabezas Rubias Spain
63 Q6 Cabezo de Morés mt. Spain
67 C11 Cabezo de Torres Spain
64 E5 Cabezo Gordo hill Spain
63 K5 Cabezón Spain
63 O4 Cabezón de Cameros Spain
63 L2 Cabezón de la Sal Spain
63 K2 Cabezón de Liébana Spain
62 I8 Cabezuela del Valle Spain
Cabicorp, Punta pt Spain see Capicorp, Punta de
147 G6 Cabildo Arg.
146 B3 Cabildo Chile
136 D2 Cabimas Venez.
91 B6 Cabinda Angola
91 B6 Cabinda prov. Angola
212 T2 Cabinet Inlet Antarctica
122 G2 Cabinet Mountains MT U.S.A.
154 C9 Cabingan i. Phil.
57 K2 Čabiny Slovakia
Cabistra Turkey see Ereğli
110 C3 Cable WI U.S.A.
115 □2 Cable Beach New Prov. Bahamas
140 G4 Cabo Brazil
145 D7 Cabo Blanco Arg.
98 □1a Cabo da Praia Terceira Azores
95 H2 Cabo Delgado prov. Moz.
143 F5 Cabo Frio Brazil
143 G5 Cabo Frio, Ilha do i. Brazil
63 P6 Cabolafuente Spain
108 E4 Cabonga, Réservoir resr Que. Can.
121 I7 Cabool MO U.S.A.
207 N9 Caboolture Qld Austr.
137 I4 Cabo Orange, Parque Nacional de nat. park Brazil
136 C5 Cabo Pantoja Peru
Cabora Bassa, Lake resr Moz. see Cahora Bassa, Lago de
145 D7 Cabo Raso Arg.
126 C2 Caborca Mex.
111 M4 Cabot Head Ont. Can.
109 I4 Cabot Strait Nfld and Lab./N.S. Can.
39 K3 Cabourg France
Cabo Verde country N. Atlantic Ocean see Cape Verde
88 □ Cabo Verde, Ilhas do is N. Atlantic Ocean
154 C5 Cabra i. Phil.
65 K6 Cabra Spain
65 J5 Cabra r. Spain
62 C5 Cabração Port.
66 H5 Cabra del Camp Spain
65 M5 Cabra del Santo Cristo Spain
67 D7 Cabra de Mora Spain
130 H4 Cabral Dom. Rep.
143 E2 Cabral, Serra do mts Brazil
72 B8 Cabras Sardegna Italy
128 G4 Cabras Mex.
65 K6 Cabras mt. Spain
89 G6 Cabras, Ilha das i. São Tomé and Príncipe
98 □1a Cabras, Ilhéus das is Azores
72 A8 Cabras, Stagno di l. Sardegna Italy
128 F4 Cabras de Guadalupe Mex.
191 I6 Cäbrayıl Azer.
41 H7 Cabre, Col de pass France
147 I1 Cabred Arg.
62 D5 Cabreira, Serra da mts Port.
63 O5 Cabrejas, Sierra de mts Spain
63 O5 Cabrejas del Pinar Spain
64 C3 Cabrela Port.
64 B3 Cabrela r. Port.
130 I4 Cabrera Dom. Rep.
67 K9 Cabrera i. Spain
65 K4 Cabrera r. Spain
65 O6 Cabrera, Sierra mts Spain
43 H6 Cabrerets France
146 A5 Cabrero Chile
107 I5 Cabri Sask. Can.
63 R10 Cabriel r. Spain
41 H9 Cabrières-d'Aigues France
62 E8 Cabril Port.
62 H3 Cabrillanes Spain
62 H7 Cabrillas Spain
63 P7 Cabrillas r. Spain
66 E6 Cabrillas, Puerto de pass Spain
131 □3 Cabrits, Îlet i. Martinique
140 F4 Cabrobó Brazil
136 E3 Cabruta Venez.
154 C3 Cabugao Luzon Phil.
154 C6 Cabulauan i. Phil.
68 F4 Čabulja mt. Bos.-Herz.
126 E2 Cabullona Mex.
57 G6 Cabuna Croatia
146 B6 Caburgua, Lago l. Chile
154 D2 Cabutunan Point Luzon Phil.
62 G3 Cacabelos Spain
141 C8 Caçador Brazil
129 I9 Cacahuatepec Mex.
76 I7 Čačak Srbija Serb. and Mont.
128 G8 Cacalutla Mex.
137 H3 Cacao Fr. Guiana
143 E5 Cacapava Brazil
141 B9 Caçapava do Sul Brazil
116 G9 Cacapon r. WV U.S.A.
62 H5 Caçarelhos Port.
136 C3 Cácares Col.
128 D7 Cacbán Mex.
74 F8 Caccamo Sicilia Italy
72 A6 Caccia, Capo c. Sardegna Italy
73 Q5 Caccia, Monte hill Italy
75 L5 Caccuri Italy
64 A3 Cacém Port.
141 B9 Cacequi Brazil
139 F4 Cáceres Brazil
64 G2 Cáceres Spain
62 H9 Cáceres prov. Spain
64 G2 Cáceres, Embalse de resr Spain
138 D3 Cachal Bol.
147 H5 Cachari Arg.
121 K7 Cache r. IL U.S.A.
88 A3 Cacheau r. Guinea-Bissau
106 F5 Cache Creek B.C. Can.
124 K3 Cache Creek r. CA U.S.A.
122 L6 Cache la Poudre r. CO U.S.A.
122 H5 Cache Peak ID U.S.A.
88 A3 Cacheu Guinea-Bissau
146 C3 Cacheuta Arg.
144 D2 Cachi Arg.
144 D2 Cachi, Nevados de mts Arg.
140 B4 Cachimbo Brazil
140 B4 Cachimbo, Serra do hills Brazil
91 D7 Cachimo Angola
144 C2 Cachina r. Chile
91 C8 Cachingues Angola
136 C3 Cáchira Col.
140 F5 Cachoeira Bahia Brazil
142 B3 Cachoeira Mato Grosso do Sul Brazil
142 B3 Cachoeira Alta Brazil
142 B2 Cachoeira de Goiás Brazil
140 C2 Cachoeira do Arari Brazil
143 E3 Cachoeira dos Macacos Brazil
141 B9 Cachoeira do Sul Brazil
143 E5 Cachoeira Paulista Brazil
143 F5 Cachoeiras de Macacu Brazil
143 G4 Cachoeiro de Itapemirim Brazil
64 D6 Cachopo Port.
144 C2 Cachos, Punta de pt Chile
57 G3 Čachtice Slovakia
138 D2 Cachuela Esperanza Bol.
62 C7 Cacia Port.
65 L6 Cacín Spain
65 K6 Cacín r. Spain
88 B4 Cacine Guinea-Bissau
137 I4 Caciporé, Cabo c. Brazil
91 C7 Cacolo Angola
128 B5 Cacoma, Sierra mts Mex.
91 B8 Caconda Angola
91 B6 Cacongo Angola
121 D7 Cactus TX U.S.A.
124 O4 Cactus Range mts NV U.S.A.
142 B3 Caçu Brazil
91 B7 Cacuaco Angola
91 B8 Cacula Angola
91 C7 Caculama Angola
140 E5 Caculé Brazil
143 H2 Cacumba, Ilha i. Brazil
91 B7 Cacuso Angola
64 A2 Cadafais Port.
30 E2 Cadair Idris hills Wales U.K.
92 E4 Cadale Somalia
43 H8 Cadalen France
63 L8 Cadalso de los Vidrios Spain
28 B7 Cadamstown Rep. of Ireland
66 L3 Cadaqués Spain
64 A2 Cadaval Port.
57 G6 Čađavica Croatia
57 H2 Čadca Slovakia
92 D2 Caddabassa I. Eth.
31 L4 Caddington Bedfordshire, England U.K.
121 I9 Caddo Lake TX U.S.A.
71 J6 Cadelbosco di Sopra Italy
206 E2 Cadell r. N.T. Austr.
207 H7 Cadell Creek watercourse Qld Austr.
70 F3 Cadenazzo Switz.
48 H3 Cadenberge Ger.
41 G9 Cadenet France
70 H6 Cadeo Italy
127 I5 Cadereyta Nuevo León Mex.
129 H5 Cadereyta Querétaro Mex.
Cader Idris hills Wales U.K. see Cadair Idris
41 F8 Caderousse France
66 I3 Cadí, Serra del mts Spain
66 I3 Cadí, Túnel de tun. Spain
65 M7 Cádiar Spain
204 E3 Cadibarrawirracanna, Lake salt flat S.A. Austr.
154 D4 Cadig Mountains Luzon Phil.
111 P1 Cadillac Que. Can.
107 J5 Cadillac Sask. Can.
43 D6 Cadillac France
110 I5 Cadillac MI U.S.A.
144 D2 Cadillal, Embalse el resr Arg.
191 D4 Çadır Dağı mt. Turkey
191 B6 Çadırkaya Turkey
154 D6 Cadiz Negros Phil.
64 G7 Cádiz Spain
64 H8 Cádiz prov. Spain
125 Q7 Cadiz CA U.S.A.
114 D7 Cadiz KY U.S.A.
116 E8 Cadiz OH U.S.A.
64 G7 Cádiz, Bahía de b. Spain
64 E7 Cádiz, Golfo de g. Spain
125 Q7 Cadiz Lake CA U.S.A.
53 J3 Cadolzburg Ger.
106 G4 Cadomin Alta Can.
71 L5 Cadoneghe Italy
71 M3 Cadore reg. Italy
110 C5 Cadott WI U.S.A.
106 G3 Cadotte r. Alta Can.
106 G3 Cadotte Lake Alta Can.
43 G8 Cadours France
209 D11 Cadoux W.A. Austr.
140 E4 Caém Brazil
39 K3 Caen France
39 K3 Caen, Plaine de plain France
30 F5 Caerau Cardiff, Wales U.K.
Caerdydd Cardiff, Wales U.K. see Cardiff
Caere Italy see Cerveteri
Caerffili Caerphilly, Wales U.K. see Caerphilly
Caerfyrddin Carmarthenshire, Wales U.K. see Carmarthen
30 F1 Caergwrle Flintshire, Wales U.K.
30 E1 Caerhun Conwy, Wales U.K.
30 G4 Caerleon Newport, Wales U.K.
30 D1 Caernarfon Gwynedd, Wales U.K.
30 C1 Caernarfon Bay Wales U.K.
30 D1 Caernarfon Castle tourist site Wales U.K.
Caernarvon Gwynedd, Wales U.K. see Caernarfon
30 F4 Caerphilly Caerphilly, Wales U.K.
30 F4 Caerphilly admin. div. Wales U.K.
30 F2 Caersws Powys, Wales U.K.
30 G4 Caerwent Monmouthshire, Wales U.K.
Caesarea Alg. see Cherchell
190 C6 Caesarea tourist site Israel
Caesarea Philippi Syria see Bāniyās
Caesaromagus Essex, England U.K. see Chelmsford
143 F3 Caeté Brazil
138 C2 Caeté r. Brazil
140 E5 Caetité Brazil
70 D5 Cafasse Italy
144 D2 Cafayate Arg.
142 C4 Cafelândia Brazil
Caffa Ukr. see Feodosiya
136 D3 Cafifi Col.
99 □1c Cafres, Plaine des hills Réunion
137 G4 Cafuini r. Brazil
64 □ Cágado, Ponta do pt Madeira
154 C7 Cagayan i. Phil.
154 C2 Cagayan r. Luzon Phil.
154 E7 Cagayan de Oro Mindanao Phil.
154 C7 Cagayan Islands Phil.
73 P6 Caggiano Italy
71 N8 Cagli Italy
72 C9 Cagliari Sardegna Italy
72 C9 Cagliari prov. Sardegna Italy
72 C9 Cagliari, Golfo di b. Sardegna Italy
72 B9 Cagliari, Stagno di l. Sardegna Italy
72 B4 Cagna, Montagne de mts Corse France
43 I8 Cagnac-les-Mines France
73 P4 Cagnano Varano Italy
41 K9 Cagnes-sur-Mer France
154 E6 Cagosoan Point Phil.
154 D2 Cagua, Mount vol. Phil.
136 C5 Caguán r. Col.
131 □1 Caguas Puerto Rico
27 C9 Caha hill Rep. of Ireland
115 D9 Cahaba r. AL U.S.A.
91 B9 Cahama Angola
27 C9 Caha Mountains hills Rep. of Ireland
27 E7 Caher Rep. of Ireland
27 B9 Cahermore Rep. of Ireland
Cahersiveen Rep. of Ireland see Cahirciveen
27 G8 Cahir Rep. of Ireland
27 B9 Cahirciveen Rep. of Ireland
118 F2 Cahoonzie NY U.S.A.
95 F2 Cahora Bassa, Lago de resr Moz.
27 J7 Cahore Point Rep. of Ireland
43 G7 Cahors France
136 B6 Cahuapanas Peru
126 □R13 Cahuita, Punta pt Costa Rica
16 H8 Cahul Moldova
43 H8 Cahuzac-sur-Vère France
95 G3 Caia Moz.
64 E3 Caia Port.
64 E3 Caia r. Port.
64 E2 Caia, Barragem do resr Port.
139 F3 Caiabis, Serra dos hills Brazil
91 D7 Caianda Angola
142 B1 Caiapó r. Brazil
142 A2 Caiapó, Serra do mts Brazil
142 B2 Caiapônia Brazil
91 D7 Caiaza Angola
73 M5 Caiazzo Italy
130 D2 Caibarién Cuba
158 H4 Cai Bâu, Đao i. Vietnam
159 H9 Cai Be Vietnam
137 E3 Caicara Venez.
140 F3 Caicó Brazil
130 H3 Caicos Bank sea feature Turks and Caicos Is
130 H3 Caicos Islands Turks and Caicos Is
130 G3 Caicos Passage Bahamas/Turks and Caicos Is
171 J3 Caidian Hubei China
91 D7 Caifuche Angola
209 H12 Caiguna W.A. Austr.
170 H3 Caihua Hubei China
138 C3 Cailloma Peru
128 A3 Caimanero, Laguna del lag. Mex.
146 B2 Caimanes Chile
154 B4 Caiman Point Luzon Phil.
91 B8 Caimbambo Angola
63 Q7 Caimodorro mt. Spain
16 H6 Căinar r. Moldova
91 B8 Cainde Angola
77 M5 Câineni Romania
125 U3 Caineville UT U.S.A.
170 D2 Cainnyigoin Sichuan China
159 G10 Cai Nước Vietnam
62 C2 Caión Spain
144 C2 Caipe Arg.
41 F8 Cairanne France
212 W1 Caird Coast Antarctica
Cairinis Scotland U.K. see Carinish
26 F10 Cairnbaan Argyll and Bute, Scotland U.K.
26 G10 Cairndow Argyll and Bute, Scotland U.K.
26 I10 Cairneyhill Fife, Scotland U.K.
26 I8 Cairn Gorm mt. Scotland U.K.
26 I8 Cairngorm Mountains Scotland U.K.
26 I8 Cairngorms National Park Scotland U.K.
26 F13 Cairnryan Dumfries and Galloway, Scotland U.K.
207 J4 Cairns Qld Austr.
26 H12 Cairnsmore of Carsphairn hill Scotland U.K.
26 H13 Cairnsmore of Fleet hill Scotland U.K.
26 I8 Cairn Toul mt. Scotland U.K.
Cairo Egypt see Al Qāhirah
115 E10 Cairo GA U.S.A.
121 K7 Cairo IL U.S.A.
73 L4 Cairo, Monte mt. Italy
70 E7 Cairo Montenotte Italy
Caisleán an Bharraigh Rep. of Ireland see Castlebar
41 E9 Caissargues France
26 F11 Caisteal Abhail hill Scotland U.K.
31 P2 Caister-on-Sea Norfolk, England U.K.
29 Q7 Caistor Lincolnshire, England U.K.
26 J6 Caithness reg. Scotland U.K.
91 B8 Caitou Angola
91 C8 Caiundo Angola
205 J3 Caiwarro Qld Austr.
171 K6 Caixi Fujian China
138 D5 Caiza Bol.
171 K3 Caizi Hu l. China
138 A1 Cajabamba Peru
131 □1 Caja de Muertos, Isla i. Puerto Rico
138 A1 Cajamarca Peru
136 B6 Cajamarca dept Peru
140 D2 Cajapió Brazil
43 H7 Cajarc France
140 D2 Cajari Brazil
138 A2 Cajatambo Peru
142 C6 Cajati Brazil
140 F3 Cajàzeiras Brazil
76 H7 Čajetina Srbija Serb. and Mont.
154 D5 Cajidiocan Phil.
57 H3 Čajkov Slovakia
68 G4 Čajniče Bos.-Herz.
146 A6 Cajón Chile
126 □R9 Cajones, Cayos is Hond.
129 L8 Cajonos r. Mex.
138 D4 Cajuata Bol.
142 D4 Cajuru Brazil
77 N3 Cajvana Romania
168 F8 Caka Qinghai China
57 H3 Čakajovce Slovakia
168 F8 Caka Yanhu l. Qinghai China
191 A7 Çakırkaş Turkey
79 I2 Çakırlı Turkey
191 E5 Çakmak Turkey
191 D6 Çakmak Dağı mts Turkey
68 F2 Čakovec Croatia
79 K4 Çal Denizli Turkey
Çal Hakkâri Turkey see Çukurca
97 L7 Cala S. Africa
64 G5 Cala Spain
64 G5 Cala r. Spain
64 G5 Cala, Embalse de resr Spain
89 H5 Calabar Nigeria
67 B13 Calabardina Spain
111 R4 Calabogie Ont. Can.
136 E2 Calabozo Venez.
73 Q9 Calabria admin. reg. Italy
75 L5 Calabria, Parco Nazionale della nat. park Italy
65 J7 Calaburra, Punta de pt Spain
66 F5 Calaceite Spain
138 C4 Calacoto Bol.
72 C3 Calacuccia Corse France
66 □ Cala d'Alcaufar Spain
72 A5 Cala d'Oliva Sardegna Italy
67 L9 Cala d'Or Spain
66 □ Cala en Porter Spain
66 I4 Calaf Spain
77 K7 Calafat Romania
145 B8 Calafate Arg.
66 I5 Calafell Spain
67 L9 Cala Figuera Spain
67 K9 Cala Figuera, Cap de c. Spain
77 O3 Calafindeşti Romania
73 P5 Calaggio r. Italy
154 D6 Calagnaan i. Phil.
72 D7 Cala Gonone Sardegna Italy
126 D4 Calagua Mex.
154 D4 Calagua Islands Phil.
Calagurris Spain see Calahorra
65 M7 Calahonda Spain
63 Q4 Calahorra Spain
91 C9 Calai Angola
36 C2 Calais France
117 □R3 Calais ME U.S.A.
127 O8 Calakmus tourist site Mex.
144 D2 Calalasteo, Sierra de mts Arg.
200 □3b Calalin i. Majuro Marshall Is
200 □3b Calalin Channel Majuro Marshall Is
71 M3 Calalzo di Cadore Italy
139 E2 Calama Brazil
138 C5 Calama Chile
70 E6 Calamandrana Italy
136 C2 Calamar Bolívar Col.
136 C4 Calamar Guaviare Col.
138 C4 Calamarca Bol.
154 B6 Calamian Group is Phil.
67 L8 Cala Millor Spain
66 C6 Calamocha Spain
64 G3 Calamonte Spain
67 L9 Cala Murada Spain
77 L5 Călan Romania
Calanais Scotland U.K. see Callanish
Calanais Western Isles, Scotland U.K. see Callanish
137 E5 Calanaque Brazil
64 F5 Calañas Spain
70 G3 Calancasca r. Switz.
66 E6 Calanda Spain
66 E5 Calanda, Desierto de reg. Spain
66 E6 Calanda, Embalse de resr Spain
154 C6 Calandagan i. Phil.
91 C7 Calandula Angola
156 A2 Calang Sumatera Indon.
72 C6 Calangianus Sardegna Italy
75 J7 Calanna Italy
84 D2 Calanscio Sand Sea des. Libya
154 C5 Calapan Mindoro Phil.
97 L7 Calapas pass S. Africa
67 L8 Cala Rajada Spain
65 N6 Calar Alta mt. Spain
16 H6 Călăraşi Moldova
77 P6 Călăraşi Romania
65 N4 Calar del Mundo mts Spain
66 □ Cala Santa Galdana Spain
74 G8 Calascibetta Sicilia Italy
72 A9 Calasetta Sardegna Italy
65 P4 Calasparra Spain
74 D8 Calatafimi Sicilia Italy
63 O5 Calatañazor Spain
67 H10 Cala Tarida Spain
63 Q6 Calatayud Spain
63 R5 Calatorao Spain
65 K3 Calatrava, Campo de reg. Spain
51 I7 Calau Ger.
154 D5 Calauag Luzon Phil.
51 I7 Calau-Altdöbern-Reddern park Ger.
74 H7 Calavà, Capo c. Sicilia Italy
67 H10 Cala Vadella Spain
65 I4 Calaveruela hill Spain
154 C5 Calavite Passage Phil.
154 B5 Calawit i. Phil.
154 C2 Calayan i. Phil.
154 E5 Calbayog Samar Phil.
51 E7 Calbe (Saale) Ger.
49 K6 Calberlah Ger.
154 E6 Calbiga Samar Phil.
138 C3 Calca Peru
140 G3 Calcanhar, Ponta do pt Brazil
127 M3 Calcasieu r. LA U.S.A.
121 I11 Calcasieu Lake LA U.S.A.
72 B3 Calcatoggio Corse France
136 A5 Calceta Ecuador
147 G1 Calchaqui Arg.
70 J8 Calci Italy
73 Q6 Calciano Italy
70 I5 Calcinato Italy
70 H4 Calcio Italy
137 I4 Calçoene Brazil
Calcutta W. Bengal India see Kolkata
77 M6 Căldăraru Romania
58 D7 Caldaro, Lago di l. Italy
73 K1 Caldarola Italy
71 K3 Caldaro sulla Strada del Vino Italy
136 C3 Caldas dept Col.
64 A2 Caldas da Rainha Port.
Caldas de Mombuy Cataluña Spain see Caldes de Montbui
64 B6 Caldas de Monchique Port.
62 C3 Caldas de Reis Spain
62 D6 Caldas de Vizela Port.
142 C2 Caldas Novas Brazil
29 K4 Caldbeck Cumbria, England U.K.
66 D3 Caldearenas Spain
31 K2 Caldecott Rutland, England U.K.
138 D2 Caldeirão Brazil
64 C6 Caldeirão, Serra de mts Port.
62 D5 Caldelas Port.
62 D6 Caldelas Taipas Port.
49 H8 Calden Ger.
106 G1 Calder r. N.W.T. Can.
26 I5 Calder, Loch l. Scotland U.K.
144 C2 Caldera Chile
98 □3d Caldera de Taburiente, Parque Nacional de nat. park La Palma Canary Is
26 I11 Caldercruix North Lanarkshire, Scotland U.K.
63 Q7 Caldereros, Sierra de mts Spain
127 O8 Calderitas Mex.
207 K8 Caldervale Qld Austr.
66 J4 Caldes de Montbui Spain
66 K4 Caldes d'Estrac Spain
29 L4 Caldew r. England U.K.
30 C4 Caldey Island Wales U.K.
30 G4 Caldicot Monmouthshire, Wales U.K.
191 E6 Çaldıran Van Turkey
189 K4 Çaldıran Van Turkey
71 L4 Caldogno Italy
71 K3 Caldonazzo Italy
71 K3 Caldonazzo, Lago di l. Italy
29 N4 Caldwell North Yorkshire, England U.K.
122 F5 Caldwell ID U.S.A.
121 G7 Caldwell KS U.S.A.
116 D9 Caldwell OH U.S.A.
121 G10 Caldwell TX U.S.A.
111 O6 Caledon Ont. Can.
97 K6 Caledon r. Lesotho/S. Africa
96 D10 Caledon S. Africa
28 D5 Caledon Northern Ireland U.K.
206 F2 Caledon Bay N.T. Austr.
109 H4 Caledonia N.S. Can.
111 O6 Caledonia Ont. Can.
110 I7 Caledonia MI U.S.A.
110 C6 Caledonia MN U.S.A.
116 H6 Caledonia NY U.S.A.
97 K5 Caledon Nature Reserve S. Africa
66 K4 Calella Spain
207 L6 Calen Qld Austr.
62 C6 Calendário Port.
72 B2 Calenzana Corse France
71 K8 Calenzano Italy
115 D9 Calera AL U.S.A.
64 G4 Calera de León Spain
63 J9 Calera y Chozas Spain
63 N5 Caleruega Spain
Caleta b. Gibraltar see Catalan Bay
98 □3c Caleta del Sebo Canary Is
138 C6 Caleta el Cobre Chile
145 C9 Caleta Josefina Chile
138 C5 Caleta Lobos Chile
146 B2 Caleta Morritos Chile
138 C5 Caleta Pabellón de Pica Chile
146 B2 Caleta Teniente Chile
146 B4 Caletones Chile
146 E4 Caleufú Arg.
125 Q9 Calexico CA U.S.A.
28 H5 Calf of Man i. Isle of Man
26 K4 Calfsound Orkney, Scotland U.K.
106 H5 Calgary Alta Can.
26 D9 Calgary Argyll and Bute, Scotland U.K.
98 □1c Calheta São Jorge Azores
64 □ Calheta Madeira
64 □ Calheta, Ponta da pt Madeira
98 □1c Calheta de Nesquim Pico Azores
115 E8 Calhoun GA U.S.A.
114 D7 Calhoun KY U.S.A.
136 B4 Cali Col.
79 J2 Çalı Turkey
154 E6 Calicoan i. Phil.
176 D7 Calicut Kerala India
125 R4 Caliente NV U.S.A.
131 □7 California Trin. and Tob.
120 I6 California MO U.S.A.
124 L4 California state U.S.A.
126 C2 California, Golfo de g. Mex.
124 K4 California Aqueduct canal CA U.S.A.
124 N8 California Coastal National Monument nat. park CA U.S.A.
66 F7 Cálig Spain
43 E7 Calignac France
129 I8 Calihualá Mex.
191 J6 Cälilabad Azer.
144 D1 Calilegua Arg.
138 D5 Calilegua, Parque Nacional nat. park Arg.
77 M5 Călimăneşti Romania
77 M3 Călimani, Munţii mts Romania
75 O3 Calimera Italy
146 C2 Calingasta Arg.
Calininsc Moldova see Cupcina
129 J7 Calipan Mex.
125 Q8 Calipatria CA U.S.A.
124 J3 Calistoga CA U.S.A.
73 O6 Calitri Italy
96 F9 Calitzdorp S. Africa
70 E7 Calizzano Italy
79 L6 Çalkaya Antalya Turkey
79 M2 Çalkaya Eskişehir Turkey
127 N7 Calkiní Mex.
79 L4 Çalköy Turkey
204 H3 Callabonna, Lake salt flat S.A. Austr.
204 H3 Callabonna Creek watercourse S.A. Austr.
38 E5 Callac France
116 E11 Callaghan VA U.S.A.
124 P2 Callaghan, Mount NV U.S.A.
115 G10 Callahan FL U.S.A.
27 H7 Callan Rep. of Ireland
28 D5 Callan r. Northern Ireland U.K.
108 E4 Callander Ont. Can.
26 H10 Callander Stirling, Scotland U.K.
116 F12 Callands VA U.S.A.
154 C3 Callang Luzon Phil.
26 C6 Callanish Western Isles, Scotland U.K.
44 G3 Callantsoog Neth.
138 A3 Callao Peru
125 S2 Callao UT U.S.A.
41 J9 Callas France
208 F6 Callawa Aboriginal Reserve W.A. Austr.
43 D7 Callen France
129 I2 Calles Mex.
62 I2 Callezuela Spain
41 J9 Callian France
70 E5 Calliano Italy
117 J7 Callicoon NY U.S.A.
207 M8 Callide Qld Austr.
106 H4 Calling Lake Alta Can.
106 H4 Calling Lake l. Alta Can.
30 D6 Callington Cornwall, England U.K.
207 M8 Calliope Qld Austr.
Callipolis Turkey see Gelibolu
67 E10 Callosa d'En Sarrià Spain
67 D11 Callosa de Segura Spain
111 N3 Callum Ont. Can.
209 C8 Callyharra Springs W.A. Austr.
106 H4 Calmar Alta Can.
110 C6 Calmar IA U.S.A.
77 N7 Călmăţui r. Romania
43 H9 Calmont Midi-Pyrénées France
43 J7 Calmont Midi-Pyrénées France
146 C5 Calmucó Arg.
129 I5 Calnali Mex.
30 H5 Calne Wiltshire, England U.K.
77 L5 Câlnic Romania
77 N6 Câlniştea r. Romania
126 □S13 Calobre Panama
70 G4 Calolziocorte Italy
63 Q8 Calomarde Spain
91 D7 Calonda Angola
66 L4 Calonge Spain
43 E7 Calonges France
36 D3 Calonne-Ricouart France
115 G12 Caloosahatchee r. FL U.S.A.
73 N5 Calore Italy
73 M5 Calore r. Italy
73 O6 Calore r. Italy
127 O7 Calotmul Mex.
207 N9 Caloundra Qld Austr.
57 G4 Čalovec Slovakia
Calp Spain see Calpe
67 F10 Calpe Spain
111 M5 Calpoy's Bay Ont. Can.
129 H5 Calpulalpan Mex.
129 I6 Calpulálpan Mex.
108 C3 Calstock Ont. Can.
74 E8 Caltabellotta Sicilia Italy
74 H9 Caltagirone Sicilia Italy
74 H9 Caltagirone r. Sicilia Italy
74 G9 Caltanissetta Sicilia Italy
74 F8 Caltanissetta prov. Sicilia Italy
74 F8 Caltavuturo Sicilia Italy
190 B2 Çaltıbozkır Turkey
70 F4 Caltignaga Italy
63 O6 Caltojar Spain
27 F6 Caltraghlea Rep. of Ireland
91 C7 Caluanga Angola
91 C7 Calucinga Angola
40 F5 Caluire-et-Cuire France
91 B7 Calulo Angola
110 F2 Calumet MI U.S.A.
110 A2 Calumet MN U.S.A.
91 D8 Calunda Angola
91 C9 Calunga Angola
91 B8 Caluquembe Angola
154 C7 Calusa i. Phil.
70 D5 Caluso Italy
92 F2 Caluula Somalia
92 F2 Caluula, Raas pt Somalia
154 C6 Caluya i. Phil.
39 K3 Calvados dept France
62 C8 Calvão Port.
62 I7 Calvarrasa de Abajo Spain
62 I7 Calvarrasa de Arriba Spain
73 P7 Calvello Italy
29 N7 Calver Derbyshire, England U.K.
27 I6 Calverstown Rep. of Ireland
206 F4 Calvert r. N.T. Austr.
206 F4 Calvert Hills N.T. Austr.
106 D5 Calvert Island B.C. Can.
119 J3 Calverton NY U.S.A.
209 G7 Calvert Range hills W.A. Austr.
72 B2 Calvi Corse France
72 F1 Calvi, Monte hill Italy
67 K8 Calvià Spain
73 J3 Calvi dell'Umbria Italy
43 H7 Calvignac France
128 E4 Calvillo Mex.
26 I9 Calvine Perth and Kinross, Scotland U.K.
43 I6 Calvinet France
96 D7 Calvinia S. Africa
73 M5 Calvi Risorta Italy
41 E9 Calvisson France
62 I8 Calvitero mt. Spain
74 G10 Calvo, Monte hill Italy
73 P4 Calvo, Monte mt. Italy
51 D6 Calvörde Ger.
62 E5 Calvos Spain
52 F4 Calw Ger.
65 L3 Calzada de Calatrava Spain
62 I6 Calzada de Valdunciel Spain
62 G8 Calzadilla Spain
31 M3 Cam r. England U.K.
91 B7 Camabatela Angola
140 F5 Camaçari Brazil
64 □ Camacha Madeira
64 □ Camacha Madeira
124 L3 Camache Reservoir CA U.S.A.
108 E4 Camachigama r. Que. Can.
111 R2 Camachigama, Lac l. Que. Can.
128 E1 Camacho Mex.
91 B8 Camacuio Angola
91 C8 Camacupa Angola
136 E2 Camaguán Venez.
130 E3 Camagüey Cuba
130 D2 Camagüey, Archipiélago de is Cuba
156 D2 Camah, Gunung mt. Malaysia
70 I8 Camaiore Italy
137 G6 Camaiú r. Brazil
130 D2 Camajuaní Cuba
Çamalan Turkey see Gülek
71 L8 Camaldoli Italy
63 K2 Camaleño Spain
140 F5 Camamu Brazil
138 B4 Camana Peru
138 B4 Camaná r. Peru
66 C6 Camañas Spain
91 D7 Camanongue Angola
141 B6 Camapuã Brazil
141 C9 Camaquã Brazil
141 C9 Camaquã r. Brazil
77 K3 Camăr Romania
137 F5 Camará Brazil
64 □ Câmara de Lobos Madeira
136 D4 Camarão Brazil
139 F3 Camararé r. Brazil
66 G4 Camarasa Spain
41 J10 Camarat, Cap c. France
63 L8 Camarena Spain
67 C7 Camarena r. Spain
67 C7 Camarena de la Sierra Spain
41 B9 Camarès France
41 F8 Camaret-sur-Aigues France
38 B5 Camaret-sur-Mer France
138 D5 Camargo Bol.
127 J4 Camargo Mex.
127 J4 Camargo, Parque Natural nature res. Mex.
41 F9 Camargue reg. France
41 F10 Camargue, Parc Naturel Régional de nature res. France
146 B4 Camarico Chile
65 P4 Camarillas, Embalse de resr Spain
124 M7 Camarillo CA U.S.A.
64 H8 Camarinal, Punta pt Spain
62 B2 Camariñas Spain
62 B2 Camariñas, Ría de inlet Spain
128 A2 Camarón Mex.
126 □Q10 Camarón, Cabo c. Hond.
145 D7 Camarones Arg.
129 H1 Camarones Mex.
145 D7 Camarones, Bahía b. Arg.
27 I8 Camaross Rep. of Ireland
62 H4 Camarzana de Tera Spain
64 G6 Camas Spain
122 C4 Camas WA U.S.A.
122 G5 Camas r. ID U.S.A.
122 H5 Camas Creek r. ID U.S.A.
26 F9 Camasnacroise Highland, Scotland U.K.
74 F9 Camastra Sicilia Italy
159 G10 Ca Mau Vietnam
91 C7 Camaxilo Angola
147 G4 Cambaceres Arg.
62 C3 Cambados Spain
139 F4 Cambara Brazil
142 B5 Cambará Brazil
Cambay Gujarat India see Khambhat
142 B5 Cambé Brazil
31 K5 Camberley Surrey, England U.K.
43 D6 Cambes France
159 G8 Cambodia country Asia
43 B9 Cambo-les-Bains France
43 I8 Cambon France
91 B8 Cambonda, Serra mts Angola
141 C8 Camboriú Brazil
30 B7 Camborne Cornwall, England U.K.
118 C2 Cambra PA U.S.A.
204 G6 Cambrai S.A. Austr.
36 F3 Cambrai France
62 D2 Cambre Spain
39 L3 Cambremer France
62 E6 Cambres Port.
96 I9 Cambria S. Africa
124 K6 Cambria CA U.S.A.
30 E2 Cambrian Mountains hills Wales U.K.
108 D5 Cambridge Ont. Can.
130 □ Cambridge Jamaica
202 J4 Cambridge North I. N.Z.
31 M3 Cambridge Cambridgeshire, England U.K.
120 J5 Cambridge IL U.S.A.
117 N6 Cambridge MA U.S.A.
117 I10 Cambridge MD U.S.A.
110 A4 Cambridge MN U.S.A.
117 L5 Cambridge NY U.S.A.
116 D8 Cambridge OH U.S.A.
118 D4 Cambridge PA U.S.A.
117 M4 Cambridge VT U.S.A.
110 E6 Cambridge WI U.S.A.
105 H3 Cambridge Bay Nunavut Can.
208 J3 Cambridge Gulf W.A. Austr.
31 M3 Cambridgeshire admin. div. England U.K.
116 E7 Cambridge Springs PA U.S.A.
109 G1 Cambrien, Lac l. Que. Can.
66 H5 Cambrils Spain
36 E2 Cambrin France
36 C3 Cambron France
50 E3 Cambs Ger.
142 D5 Cambuí Brazil
91 D6 Cambulo Angola
91 C7 Cambundi-Catembo Angola
143 E4 Cambuquira Brazil
51 E8 Camburg Ger.
99 □1c Cambuston Réunion
136 A3 Cambutal, Cerro mt. Panama
173 F10 Cam Co l. Xizang China
205 M6 Camden N.S.W. Austr.
115 D9 Camden AL U.S.A.
121 I9 Camden AR U.S.A.
118 D6 Camden DE U.S.A.
117 □P4 Camden ME U.S.A.
115 I7 Camden NC U.S.A.
118 E5 Camden NJ U.S.A.
117 J5 Camden NY U.S.A.
116 A9 Camden OH U.S.A.
115 G8 Camden SC U.S.A.
121 K7 Camden TN U.S.A.
104 D2 Camden Bay AK U.S.A.
118 E5 Camden County county NJ U.S.A.
208 H3 Camden Sound sea chan. W.A. Austr.
120 I6 Camdenton MO U.S.A.
91 D7 Cameia Angola
91 D7 Cameia, Parque Nacional da nat. park Angola
30 C6 Camelford Cornwall, England U.K.
79 K5 Çameli Turkey
16 H5 Camenca Moldova
71 P8 Camerano Italy
73 K1 Camerino Italy
Camerinum Italy see Camerino
66 G6 Camerles Spain
125 U6 Cameron AZ U.S.A.
121 I11 Cameron LA U.S.A.
120 H6 Cameron MO U.S.A.
121 G10 Cameron TX U.S.A.
110 C4 Cameron WI U.S.A.
116 E9 Cameron WV U.S.A.
156 D2 Cameron Highlands mts Malaysia
106 G3 Cameron Hills Y.T. Can.
105 H2 Cameron Island Nunavut Can.
203 A13 Cameron Mountains South I. N.Z.
124 L3 Cameron Park CA U.S.A.
89 I5 Cameroon country Africa
73 O7 Camerota Italy
Caméroun country Africa see Cameroon
89 H5 Cameroun, Mont vol. Cameroon
29 K4 Camerton Cumbria, England U.K.
147 I5 Camet Arg.
137 E6 Cametá Amazonas Brazil
137 I5 Cametá Pará Brazil
206 C4 Camfield r. N.T. Austr.
191 D4 Çam Geçidi pass Turkey
79 I5 Çamiçi Turkey
73 L3 Camicia, Monte mt. Italy
79 I5 Çamiçi Gölü l. Turkey
154 C2 Camiguin i. Phil.
154 E7 Camiguin i. Phil.
190 D2 Camili Turkey
154 C4 Camiling Luzon Phil.
115 E10 Camilla GA U.S.A.
48 K4 Camin Ger.
138 C4 Camiña Chile
62 C5 Caminha Port.
62 H8 Caminomorisco Spain
66 C6 Caminreal Spain
140 D2 Camiranga Brazil
138 E5 Camiri Bol.
138 B2 Camisea Peru
138 B2 Camisea r. Peru
91 D7 Camissombo Angola
191 C5 Çamlıca Turkey
190 H1 Çamlıdere Turkey
191 C4 Çamlıhemşin Turkey
191 D5 Çamlıkale Turkey
191 C5 Çamlıkaya Turkey
191 B5 Çamlıkoz Turkey
209 E12 Camm, Lake salt flat W.A. Austr.
74 F8 Cammarata Sicilia Italy
74 F8 Cammarata, Monte mt. Sicilia Italy
51 G6 Cammer Ger.
50 F3 Cammin Ger.
140 E2 Camocim Brazil
27 J7 Camolin Rep. of Ireland
36 D4 Camon France
70 I4 Camonica, Val val. Italy
206 G5 Camooweal Qld Austr.
206 G6 Camooweal Caves National Park Qld Austr.
137 H4 Camopi Brazil
65 J7 Camorro Alto mt. Spain
38 F6 Camors France
177 M8 Camorta i. Andaman & Nicobar Is India
154 E6 Camotes Sea g. Phil.
128 C6 Camotlán de Miraflores Mex.
27 H3 Camowen r. Northern Ireland U.K.
27 C8 Camp Rep. of Ireland
73 O6 Campagna Italy
41 C8 Campagnac France
72 G2 Campagnatico Italy
43 C8 Campagne Aquitaine France
43 F6 Campagne Aquitaine France
36 C3 Campagne-lès-Hesdin France
126 □P10 Campamento Hond.
147 I2 Campamento Uru.
147 H4 Campana Arg.
75 L5 Campana Italy
126 H4 Campana Mex.
147 I4 Campana Uru.
145 B8 Campana, Isla i. Chile
146 B4 Campanario mt. Arg./Chile
139 G5 Campanário Mato Grosso do Sul Brazil
143 G3 Campanário Minas Gerais Brazil
64 □ Campanario Madeira
64 H3 Campanario Spain
73 M6 Campanella, Punta pt Italy
143 E4 Campanha Brazil
73 N5 Campania admin. reg. Italy
106 D4 Campania Island B.C. Can.
64 G8 Campano Spain
136 B6 Campanquiz, Cerro hills Peru
63 K3 Camparredondo, Embalse de resr Spain
207 K6 Campaspe r. Qld Austr.
63 L6 Campaspero Spain
65 □ Camp Bay Gibraltar
96 H4 Campbell S. Africa
124 K4 Campbell CA U.S.A.
116 E7 Campbell OH U.S.A.
203 I8 Campbell, Cape South I. N.Z.
206 C6 Campbell, Mount hill N.T. Austr.
108 E4 Campbellford Ont. Can.
116 B8 Campbell Hill OH U.S.A.
159 D9 Campbell Island Myanmar
199 G6 Campbell Island N.Z.
107 J2 Campbell Lake N.W.T. Can.
216 G9 Campbell Plateau sea feature S. Pacific Ocean
208 I3 Campbell Range hills W.A. Austr.
106 E5 Campbell River B.C. Can.
111 R4 Campbells Bay Que. Can.
110 F6 Campbellsport WI U.S.A.
116 A9 Campbellstown OH U.S.A.
114 E7 Campbellsville KY U.S.A.
109 H4 Campbellton N.B. Can.
205 M6 Campbelltown N.S.W. Austr.
205 K9 Campbell Town Tas. Austr.
118 B4 Campbelltown PA U.S.A.

Catastrophe, Cape to Challenger Deep
247

94 E6 Catastrophe, Cape S.A. Austr.
91 B8 Catata Nova Angola
86 C2 Catatumbo Bari nat. park Col.
48 D4 Catavi Bol.
10 D4 Catawba WI U.S.A.
15 G8 Catawba r. SC U.S.A.
11 R9 Catawissa PA U.S.A.
18 C3 Catawissa Creek r. PA U.S.A.
58 H4 Cat Ba, Đao i. Vietnam
54 E6 Catbalogan Samar Phil.
40 D1 Cat Cays is Bahamas
54 F8 Cateel Mindanao Phil.
54 F8 Cateel Bay Mindanao Phil.
91 D9 Catehu Angola
29 L7 Catemaco Mex.
29 L7 Catemaco, Laguna l. Mex.
97 Q2 Catembe Moz.
46 B3 Catemu Chile
72 C7 Catena del Goceano mts Sardegna Italy
72 B7 Catena del Marghine mts Sardegna Italy
74 H8 Catenanuova Sicilia Italy
91 B8 Catengue Angola
31 L5 Caterham Surrey, England U.K.
72 B2 Cateri Corse France
91 B7 Catete Angola
47 H6 Catete r. Brazil
95 L7 Cathcart N.S.W. Austr.
97 L8 Cathcart S. Africa
25 P8 Cathedral City CA U.S.A.
97 N4 Cathedral Peak Lesotho
96 F5 Cathedral Provincial Park B.C. Can.
27 B9 Catherdaniel Rep. of Ireland
15 D9 Catherine AL U.S.A.
Catherine, Mount Egypt see Kātrīnā, Jabal
25 T3 Catherine, Mount UT U.S.A.
30 □ Catherine's Peak hill Jamaica
24 L4 Catheys Valley CA U.S.A.
22 C3 Cathlamet WA U.S.A.
66 F7 Catí Spain
73 L3 Catignano Italy
46 B5 Catillo Chile
88 B4 Catió Guinea-Bissau
47 F3 Catisimiña Venez.
30 F1 Cat Island Bahamas
62 E7 Cativelos Port.
91 C6 Çatkale Turkey
98 B3 Cat Lake Ont. Can.
16 C10 Catlettsburg KY U.S.A.
03 D13 Catlins Forest Park nature res. South I. N.Z.
27 P7 Catoche, Cabo c. Mex.
62 C3 Catoira Spain
39 F4 Cato Island and Bank rf Coral Sea Is Terr. Austr.
30 F3 Catolé do Rocha Brazil
91 C7 Catolo Angola
29 L5 Caton Lancashire, England U.K.
75 J7 Catona r. Italy
18 B6 Catonsville MD U.S.A.
28 G2 Catorce Mex.
28 G2 Catorce, Sierra de mts Mex.
79 L3 Çatören Barajı resr Turkey
91 C8 Catota Angola
62 H3 Catoute mt. Spain
67 D11 Catral Spain
71 N9 Catria, Monte mt. Italy
46 D5 Catriel Arg.
47 F5 Catriló Arg.
47 F4 Catrimani Brazil
47 F4 Catrimani r. Brazil
26 H11 Catrine East Ayrshire, Scotland U.K.
30 H3 Catshill Worcestershire, England U.K.
17 L6 Catskill NY U.S.A.
17 K6 Catskill Mountains NY U.S.A.
87 L5 Cattenom France
49 K9 Catterfeld Ger.
29 N5 Catterick North Yorkshire, England U.K.
29 N5 Catterick Garrison North Yorkshire, England U.K.
26 L9 Catterline Aberdeenshire, Scotland U.K.
03 E11 Cattle Creek South I. N.Z.
71 N8 Cattolica Italy
74 E9 Cattolica Eraclea Sicilia Italy
44 D1 Catúa Arg.
95 G5 Catuane Moz.
95 G2 Catur Moz.
43 G6 Catus France
74 F8 Catuso, Monte mt. Italy
67 L4 Căuaş Romania
40 C2 Cauaxi r. Brazil
54 D7 Cauayan Negros Phil.
09 I1 Caubvick, Mount Nfld and Lab. Can.
36 B4 Cauca dept Col.
36 C2 Cauca r. Col.
40 F2 Caucaia Brazil
36 C3 Caucasia Col.
91 B2 Caucasus mts Asia/Europe
46 C2 Caucete Arg.
44 D1 Cauchari, Salar de salt flat Arg.
47 L4 Cauchon Lake Man. Can.
17 □P2 Caucomgomoc Lake ME U.S.A.
38 E6 Caudan France
42 F6 Caudau r. France
39 M2 Caudebec-en-Caux France
43 F7 Caudecoste France
57 D10 Caudete Spain
57 C8 Caudete de las Fuentes Spain
57 D8 Caudiel Spain
43 I10 Caudiès de-Fenouillèdes France
36 F3 Caudry France
58 G5 Câu Giat Vietnam
54 F7 Cauit Point Mindanao Phil.
43 G9 Caujac France
38 G5 Caulnes France
75 K7 Caulonia Italy
43 G7 Caumont Midi-Pyrénées France
43 G9 Caumont Midi-Pyrénées France
39 J3 Caumont-l'Éventé France
41 F9 Caumont-sur-Durance France
30 D2 Caunao r. Cuba
43 J9 Caunes-Minervois France
91 C7 Caungula Angola
91 C9 Cauno Angola
46 A4 Cauquenes Chile
37 E3 Caura r. Venez.
37 F5 Caurés r. Brazil
72 B4 Cauro Corse France
09 H3 Causapscal Que. Can.
46 I7 Căuşeni Moldova
27 C8 Causeway Rep. of Ireland
27 I2 Causeway Head Northern Ireland U.K.
43 H7 Caussade France
38 D3 Cautário r. Brazil
43 D10 Cauterets France
06 E5 Caution, Cape B.C. Can.
30 E3 Cauto r. Cuba
91 J5 Cavad Azer.
73 N6 Cava de'Tirreni Italy
62 C5 Cávado r. Port.
70 E5 Cavaglià Italy
41 G9 Cavaillon France
41 J10 Cavalaire-sur-Mer France
40 D5 Cavalcante Goiás Brazil
38 E2 Cavalcante Rondônia Brazil
54 B5 Cavaleiro Port.
71 K3 Cavalese Italy
20 G1 Cavalier ND U.S.A.
56 □ Cavalleria, Cap de c. Spain
70 D6 Cavallermaggiore Italy
02 H1 Cavalli Islands North I. N.Z.
71 N5 Cavallino Italy
72 C5 Cavallo, Île i. Corse France
73 N3 Cavalluccio, Punta pt Italy
38 D5 Cavally r. Côte d'Ivoire
70 G5 Cava Manara Italy
27 H5 Cavan Rep. of Ireland
27 H5 Cavan county Rep. of Ireland
47 F3 Cavanagh Arg.
70 G3 Cavargna Italy
71 M5 Cavarzere Italy
71 O3 Cavazzo Carnico Italy
79 K3 Çavdarhisar Turkey
79 K5 Çavdır Turkey
203 E11 Cave South I. N.Z.
121 J7 Cave City AR U.S.A.
114 E7 Cave City KY U.S.A.
125 U8 Cave Creek AZ U.S.A.
71 P3 Cave del Predil Italy
71 J3 Cavedine, Lago di l. Italy
143 F2 Caveira Brazil
41 E9 Caveirac France
209 J9 Cavenagh Range W.A. Austr.
205 I7 Cavendish Vic. Austr.
141 B9 Cavera, Serra do hills Brazil
142 A6 Cavernoso, Serra do mts Brazil
30 H2 Caverswall Staffordshire, England U.K.
116 B10 Cave Run Lake KY U.S.A.
62 E5 Cavês Port.
71 K6 Cavezzo Italy
137 I4 Caviana, Ilha i. Brazil
42 D5 Cavignac France
154 C7 Cavili rf Phil.
154 C4 Cavite Luzon Phil.
71 Q5 Čavle Croatia
77 L3 Cavnic Romania
73 J4 Cavo, Monte hill Italy
72 D9 Cavoli, Isola dei i. Sardegna Italy
75 L3 Cavone r. Italy
91 C8 Cavongo Angola
70 C6 Cavour Italy
110 F4 Cavour WI U.S.A.
70 E5 Cavour, Canale canal Italy
71 J6 Cavriago Italy
71 K8 Cavriglia Italy
188 E4 Çavuşçu Turkey
79 M2 Çavuşdere Turkey
79 L6 Çavuşköy Turkey
26 I7 Cawdor Highland, Scotland U.K.
205 H5 Cawndilla Lake imp. l. N.S.W. Austr.
29 O6 Cawood North Yorkshire, England U.K.
116 B12 Cawood KY U.S.A.
31 O2 Cawston Norfolk, England U.K.
143 E4 Caxambu Brazil
62 C9 Caxarias Port.
136 D6 Caxias Amazonas Brazil
140 E3 Caxias Maranhão Brazil
141 C9 Caxias do Sul Brazil
91 B7 Caxito Angola
137 I5 Caxiuana, Baía de l. Brazil
79 M4 Çay Turkey
136 B5 Cayambe-Coca, Parque Nacional nat. park Ecuador
191 D5 Çayarası Turkey
147 G2 Cayastá Arg.
79 I4 Çaybaşı İzmir Turkey
Çaybaşı Rize Turkey see Çayeli
115 G9 Cayce SC U.S.A.
188 F3 Çaycuma Turkey
189 J3 Çayeli Turkey
137 H3 Cayenne Fr. Guiana
147 I2 Cayetano Uru.
36 C3 Cayeux-sur-Mer France
131 □1 Cayey Puerto Rico
131 □1 Cayey, Sierra de hills Puerto Rico
79 J3 Çaygören Barajı resr Turkey
188 G5 Çayhan Turkey
79 J6 Çayhisar Turkey
188 E3 Çayırhan Turkey
191 B6 Çayırlı Turkey
191 B5 Çaykara Turkey
191 H6 Çaylaqqala Azer.
43 H7 Caylus France
130 D4 Cayman Brac i. Cayman Is
130 C4 Cayman Islands terr. West Indies
214 D4 Cayman Trench sea feature Caribbean Sea
92 E2 Caynabo Somalia
30 G3 Caynham Shropshire, England U.K.
131 □2 Cayon St Kitts and Nevis
115 □2 Cay Point New Prov. Bahamas
191 G5 Çay Räsullu Azer.
41 D7 Cayres France
130 C2 Cay Sal i. Bahamas
130 C2 Cay Sal Bank sea feature Bahamas
130 F3 Cay Santa Domingo i. Bahamas
29 P7 Caythorpe Lincolnshire, England U.K.
29 Q5 Cayton North Yorkshire, England U.K.
124 L6 Cayucos CA U.S.A.
111 O7 Cayuga Ont. Can.
116 I6 Cayuga Heights NY U.S.A.
116 I6 Cayuga Lake NY U.S.A.
130 F2 Cay Verde i. Bahamas
91 D7 Cazage Angola
Cazaje Angola see Cazage
63 K8 Cazalegas Spain
64 H5 Cazalla de la Sierra Spain
43 G6 Cazals Midi-Pyrénées France
43 H7 Cazals Midi-Pyrénées France
77 P6 Căzăneşti Romania
144 F3 Caza Pava Arg.
43 D8 Cazaubon France
43 B7 Cazaux et de Sanguinet, Étang de l. France
173 H11 Cazê Xizang China
117 J6 Cazenovia NY U.S.A.
43 G9 Cazères France
43 G7 Cazes-Mondenard France
43 I9 Cazilhac France
68 F3 Čazma Croatia
91 D7 Cazombo Angola
129 J5 Cazones Mex.
129 J5 Cazones r. Mex.
65 N5 Cazorla Spain
65 M5 Cazorla, Sierra de mts Spain
43 G6 Cazoulès France
71 N3 Cà Zul, Lago di l. Italy
95 G2 Cazula Moz.
63 K4 Cea Castilla y León Spain
62 E4 Cea Galicia Spain
63 I4 Cea r. Spain
Ceadâr-Lunga Moldova see Ciadîr-Lunga
Ceanannus Mór Rep. of Ireland see Kells
26 B7 Ceann a' Bhàigh Western Isles, Scotland U.K.
63 O2 Ceanuri-Elexondo Spain
Ceará Brazil see Fortaleza
140 F3 Ceará state Brazil
214 G6 Ceara Abyssal Plain sea feature S. Atlantic Ocean
26 C6 Cearsiadar Western Isles, Scotland U.K.
77 Q5 Ceatalchioi Romania
Ceatharlach Rep. of Ireland see Carlow
39 J5 Ceaucé France
41 D6 Céaux-d'Allègre France
126 G4 Ceballos Mex.
62 G1 Cebes, Cabo c. Spain
190 A2 Cebireis Dağı mt. Turkey
62 E9 Cebolais de Cima Port.
63 K9 Cebolla Spain
144 D3 Cebollar Arg.
63 O4 Cebollera, Sierra mts Spain
128 C6 Ceboruco, Cerro mt. Mex.
128 C4 Ceboruco, Volcán vol. Mex.
57 I3 Čebovce Slovakia
63 L8 Cebreros Spain
154 D6 Cebu Cebu Phil.
154 D6 Cebu i. Phil.
73 K4 Ceccano Italy
57 H5 Cece Hungary
58 E7 Cece, Cima di mt. Italy
62 D2 Cecebre, Encoro de resr Spain
57 K3 Čečejovce Slovakia
56 E2 Čechtice Czech Rep.
57 H3 Čechynce Slovakia
110 F5 Cecil WI U.S.A.
118 D5 Cecil County county MD U.S.A.
207 M9 Cecil Plains Qld Austr.
209 F8 Cecil Rhodes, Mount hill W.A. Austr.
118 D6 Cecilton MD U.S.A.
71 J9 Cecina Italy
71 I9 Cecina r. Italy
75 K5 Cecita, Lago di l. Italy
62 G9 Ceclavín Spain
62 F6 Cedães Port.
110 J6 Cedar r. MI U.S.A.
120 E2 Cedar r. ND U.S.A.
120 G5 Cedar r. NE U.S.A.
116 D11 Cedar Bluff VA U.S.A.
118 F5 Cedar Brook NJ U.S.A.
125 S4 Cedar City UT U.S.A.
121 G9 Cedar Creek Reservoir TX U.S.A.
123 K7 Cedaredge CO U.S.A.
120 I4 Cedar Falls IA U.S.A.
131 □2 Cedar Grove Antigua and Barbuda
124 N5 Cedar Grove CA U.S.A.
110 G6 Cedar Grove WI U.S.A.
116 D10 Cedar Grove WV U.S.A.
117 J11 Cedar Island VA U.S.A.
107 K4 Cedar Lake Man. Can.
111 P3 Cedar Lake Ont. Can.
116 B7 Cedar Point OH U.S.A.
114 B5 Cedar Rapids IA U.S.A.
125 U5 Cedar Ridge AZ U.S.A.
110 G4 Cedar River MI U.S.A.
119 G5 Cedar Run NJ U.S.A.
111 L7 Cedar Springs Ont. Can.
110 I6 Cedar Springs MI U.S.A.
115 E8 Cedartown GA U.S.A.
130 □ Cedar Valley Jamaica
97 N6 Cedarville S. Africa
110 E7 Cedarville IL U.S.A.
111 J4 Cedarville MI U.S.A.
116 B9 Cedarville OH U.S.A.
70 I3 Cedegolo Italy
62 D1 Cedeira Spain
62 C2 Cedeira hill Spain
62 D1 Cedeira, Ría de inlet Spain
63 L9 Cedena r. Spain
126 □P11 Cedeño Hond.
96 C8 Cederberg mts S. Africa
62 F9 Cedillo Spain
62 F9 Cedillo, Embalse de resr Port./Spain
63 M8 Cedillo del Condado Spain
127 P7 Cedral Quintana Roo Mex.
128 G2 Cedral San Luis Potosí Mex.
66 D7 Cedrillas Spain
72 D7 Cedrino r. Sardegna Italy
140 F3 Cedro Brazil
98 □1c Cedros Faial Azores
126 □P10 Cedros Hond.
126 E4 Cedros Sonora Mex.
128 F1 Cedros Zacatecas Mex.
126 B3 Cedros, Isla i. Mex.
98 □1c Cedros, Ponta dos pt Faial Azores
131 □7 Cedros Point Trin. and Tob.
54 G1 Cedry Wielkie Pol.
204 D5 Ceduna S.A. Austr.
54 C3 Cedynia Pol.
50 J5 Cedyński Park Krajobrazowy Pol.
62 B3 Cee Spain
92 E2 Ceel Afweyn Somalia
92 F2 Ceelayo Somalia
92 D2 Ceel Baxay Somalia
92 E3 Ceelbuur Somalia
92 E2 Ceel Dhaab Somalia
92 E4 Ceeldheere Somalia
92 D2 Ceel Gaal Awdal Somalia
92 F2 Ceel Gaal Bari Somalia
92 E3 Ceel Garas well Somalia
92 E3 Ceel God Somalia
92 F3 Ceel Huur Somalia
92 D4 Ceel Walaaq well Somalia
92 E2 Ceerigaabo Somalia
57 K5 Cefa Romania
74 G7 Cefalù Sicilia Italy
30 F2 Cefn-mawr Wrexham, Wales U.K.
63 K5 Cega r. Spain
71 N4 Ceggia Italy
57 I4 Cegléd Hungary
57 I4 Ceglédbercel Hungary
75 N2 Ceglie Messapica Italy
55 J3 Cegłów Pol.
173 K10 Cêgnê Xizang China
76 I9 Čegrane Macedonia
57 L4 Cehal Romania
65 P4 Cehegín Spain
170 E6 Ceheng Guizhou China
76 G7 Čehotina r. Serb. and Mont.
77 L3 Cehu Silvaniei Romania
131 □1 Ceiba Puerto Rico
147 H3 Ceibas Arg.
57 L5 Ceica Romania
41 C9 Ceilhes-et-Rocozels France
63 J4 Ceinos de Campos Spain
37 L6 Ceintrey France
62 D8 Ceira Port.
62 D8 Ceira r. Port.
56 F3 Čejč Czech Rep.
57 K3 Čejkov Slovakia
59 O2 Čejkovice Czech Rep.
54 G2 Cekcyn Pol.
188 G3 Çekerek Turkey
54 G4 Ceków-Kolonia Pol.
66 C7 Celadas Spain
56 D1 Čelákovice Czech Rep.
73 L3 Celano Italy
62 E4 Celanova Spain
127 O10 Celaque, Parque Nacional nat. park Hond.
128 G5 Celaya Mex.
27 I6 Celbridge Rep. of Ireland
43 H7 Célé r. France
Celebes i. Indon. see Sulawesi
155 B2 Celebes Sea Indon./Phil.
191 E7 Çelebibağı Turkey
62 D5 Celeiros Port.
64 H8 Celemin, Embalse de resr Spain
136 B6 Celendín Peru
73 N4 Celenza Valfortore Italy
127 N7 Celestún Mex.
75 K5 Celico Italy
191 D6 Çelikli Turkey
120 M5 Celina OH U.S.A.
115 E7 Celina TN U.S.A.
68 E2 Celje Slovenia
66 C7 Cella Spain
56 G4 Celldömölk Hungary
48 J5 Celle Ger.
72 H3 Cellere Italy
45 D7 Celles Belgium
43 H10 Celles France
42 D3 Celles-sur-Belle France
40 D5 Celles-sur-Durolle France
36 H7 Celles-sur-Ource France
39 N6 Cellettes France
71 N3 Cellina r. Italy
73 L2 Cellino Attanasio Italy
75 N3 Cellino San Marco Italy
73 L5 Cellole Italy
73 P4 Celone r. Italy
62 F7 Celorico da Beira Port.
62 E6 Celorico de Basto Port.
66 K3 Celrà Spain
25 D6 Celtic Sea Rep. of Ireland/U.K.
214 I2 Celtic Shelf sea feature N. Atlantic Ocean
79 L5 Çeltikçi Burdur Turkey
79 J2 Çeltikçi Bursa Turkey
79 L5 Çeltikçi Beli pass Turkey
30 E2 Celyn, Llyn l. Wales U.K.
191 D6 Cem r. Turkey
157 K4 Cemaru, Gunung mt. Indon.
71 K3 Cembra Italy
188 G3 Cemilbey Turkey
188 I4 Çemişgezek Turkey
30 E2 Cemmaes Powys, Wales U.K.
157 M9 Cempi, Teluk b. Sumbawa Indon.
59 K7 Čemšeniška planina mt. Slovenia
43 G6 Cénac-et-St-Julien France
76 I4 Cenad Romania
65 P4 Cenajo, Embalse del resr Spain
71 L3 Cencenighe Agordino Italy
153 I7 Cenderawasih, Teluk b. Papua Indon.
41 E8 Cendras France
42 F6 Cendrieux France
76 I5 Cenei Romania
71 K5 Ceneselli Italy
70 E7 Cengio Italy
63 O4 Cenicero Spain
63 L8 Ceniclentos Spain
41 J6 Cenis, Col du Mont pass France
65 P2 Cenizate Spain
191 A6 Cennetpınar Turkey
70 I6 Ceno r. Italy
43 C6 Cenon France
64 □ Cenouras, Ilhéu das i. Madeira
155 A5 Cenrana Sulawesi Indon.
76 I5 Čenta Vojvodina, Srbija Serb. and Mont.
70 D6 Centallo Italy
203 C11 Centaur Peak South I. N.Z.
Centellas Spain see Centelles
66 J4 Centelles Spain
146 C6 Centenario Arg.
142 B5 Centenário do Sul Brazil
95 F3 Centenary Zimbabwe
125 T8 Centennial Wash watercourse AZ U.S.A.
120 E2 Center ND U.S.A.
120 G4 Center NE U.S.A.
121 H10 Center TX U.S.A.
116 C8 Centerburg OH U.S.A.
119 I3 Centereach NY U.S.A.
115 E8 Center Hill Lake resr TN U.S.A.
119 J3 Center Moriches NY U.S.A.
117 □N5 Center Ossipee NH U.S.A.
115 D9 Center Point AL U.S.A.
119 I3 Centerport NY U.S.A.
118 E4 Center Square PA U.S.A.
118 E3 Center Valley PA U.S.A.
120 I5 Centerville IA U.S.A.
121 J7 Centerville MO U.S.A.
116 C10 Centerville OH U.S.A.
116 F7 Centerville PA U.S.A.
116 F8 Centerville PA U.S.A.
115 D8 Centerville TN U.S.A.
121 H10 Centerville TX U.S.A.
116 E9 Centerville WV U.S.A.
71 K6 Cento Italy
73 O7 Centola Italy
137 G3 Centraal Suriname Natuurreservaat nature res. Suriname
Centrafricaine, République country Africa see Central African Republic
94 E4 Central admin. dist. Botswana
140 E4 Central Brazil
138 C5 Central Chile
88 E5 Central admin. reg. Ghana
92 C5 Central prov. Kenya
93 B8 Central admin. reg. Malawi
123 J10 Central NM U.S.A.
91 F8 Central prov. Zambia
138 D4 Central, Cordillera mts Bol.
136 B4 Central, Cordillera mts Col.
130 H4 Central, Cordillera mts Dom. Rep.
126 □S13 Central, Cordillera mts Panama
138 A2 Central, Cordillera mts Peru
154 C3 Central, Cordillera mts Luzon Phil.
131 □1 Central, Cordillera mts Puerto Rico
Central African Empire country Africa see Central African Republic
90 D3 Central African Republic country Africa
208 J6 Central Australia Aboriginal Reserve W.A. Austr.
185 L7 Central Brahui Range mts Pak.
107 J5 Central Butte Sask. Can.
120 J4 Central City IA U.S.A.
120 F5 Central City NE U.S.A.
116 G8 Central City PA U.S.A.
143 G3 Central de Minas Brazil
206 C6 Central Desert Aboriginal Land res. N.T. Austr.
117 N7 Central Falls RI U.S.A.
120 K6 Centralia IL U.S.A.
122 C3 Centralia WA U.S.A.
92 C4 Central Island National Park nat. park Kenya
119 I3 Central Islip NY U.S.A.
94 D4 Central Kalahari Game Reserve nature res. Botswana
146 B2 Central Los Molles Chile
185 K8 Central Makran Range mts Pak.
206 D6 Central Mount Stuart hill N.T. Austr.
206 C7 Central Mount Wedge N.T. Austr.
19 P5 Central'noolesnoy Zapovednik nature res. Rus. Fed.
216 G5 Central Pacific Basin sea feature Pacific Ocean
205 K9 Central Plateau Conservation Area nature res. Tas. Austr.
97 M5 Central Range mts Lesotho
153 J7 Central Range mts P.N.G.
Central Siberian Plateau Rus. Fed. see Sredne-Sibirskoye Ploskogor'ye
117 I5 Central Square NY U.S.A.
119 G2 Central Valley NY U.S.A.
119 L1 Central Village CT U.S.A.
89 H5 Centre prov. Cameroon
42 H1 Centre admin. reg. France
115 E8 Centre AL U.S.A.
40 E3 Centre, Canal du France
99 □1b Centre de Flacq Mauritius
203 B13 Centre Island South I. N.Z.
115 D9 Centreville AL U.S.A.
118 C6 Centreville MD U.S.A.
110 I8 Centreville MI U.S.A.
116 H10 Centreville VA U.S.A.
72 C2 Centuri Corse France
97 M1 Centurion S. Africa
74 H8 Centuripe Sicilia Italy
115 D10 Century FL U.S.A.
171 H7 Cenxi Guangxi China
43 G6 Céou r. France
73 M3 Cepagatti Italy
Cephaloedium Sicilia Italy see Cefalù
Cephalonia i. Greece see Kefallonia
68 G3 Čepin Croatia
18 H8 Čepkelių nature res. Lith.
62 E7 Cepões Port.
59 I7 Čepovan Slovenia
36 E7 Cepoy France
74 H1 Ceppaloni Italy
73 L4 Ceprano Italy
157 I8 Cepu Jawa Indon.
76 H6 Cer hills Serb. and Mont.
74 H8 Cerami Sicilia Italy
74 G8 Cerami r. Sicilia Italy
Ceram i. Maluku Indon. see Seram
Ceram Sea Indon. see Seram, Laut
70 F5 Cerano Italy
55 K3 Ceranów Pol.
39 L6 Cérans-Foulletourte France
75 J7 Cerasi Italy
73 O7 Ceraso Italy
72 D6 Ceraso, Capo c. Sardegna Italy
57 L6 Cerbăl Romania
125 R6 Cerbat Mountains AZ U.S.A.
43 K11 Cerbère France
66 L3 Cerbère, Cap c. France/Spain
72 C4 Cerbicale, Îles is Corse France
72 F2 Cerboli, Isola i. Italy
64 B2 Cercal Lisboa Port.
64 B5 Cercal Setúbal Port.
64 B5 Cercal hill Port.
64 B5 Cercal, Serra do mts Port.
56 D2 Čerčany Czech Rep.
63 L7 Cercedilla Spain
73 N5 Cercemaggiore Italy
73 L3 Cerchio Italy
56 B2 Čerchov mt. Czech Rep.
40 D3 Cercy-la-Tour France
74 F8 Cerda Sicilia Italy
43 I11 Cerdagne reg. France
Cerdaña reg. France see Cerdagne
66 I3 Cerdanya reg. Spain
66 J5 Cerdanyola del Vallès Spain
62 D3 Cerdedo Spain
62 E8 Cerdeira Port.
39 P6 Cerdon France
43 H6 Cère r. France
71 K5 Cerea Italy
107 I5 Cereal Alta Can.
147 F5 Cereales Arg.
63 N3 Cereceda, Embalse de resr Spain
57 I3 Cered Hungary
30 E3 Ceredigion admin. div. Wales U.K.
71 L5 Ceregnano Italy
54 F3 Cerekwica Pol.
38 I4 Cérences France
75 L5 Cerenzia Italy
147 G1 Ceres Arg.
140 C5 Ceres Brazil
70 C5 Ceres Italy
96 D9 Ceres S. Africa
124 L4 Ceres CA U.S.A.
41 K6 Ceresole, Lago di l. Italy
70 C5 Ceresole Reale Italy
71 L5 Ceresone r. Italy
41 H9 Céreste France
43 J11 Céret France
136 C2 Cereté Col.
63 M6 Cerezo de Abajo Spain
63 M6 Cerezo de Arriba Spain
63 N3 Cerezo de Ríotirón Spain
99 □2b Cerf, Île au i. Inner Islands Seychelles
111 S3 Cerf, Lac du l. Que. Can.
45 F8 Cerfontaine Belgium
99 □1b Cerfs, Îles aux is Mauritius
57 K2 Čergov mts Slovakia
36 D5 Cergy France
51 L10 Cerhenice Czech Rep.
173 G11 Cêri Xizang China
70 E7 Ceriale Italy
70 D8 Ceriana Italy
73 P5 Cerignola Italy
188 F4 Çerikli Turkey
146 B3 Cerillos Chile
146 B2 Cerillos de Tamaya Chile
40 B3 Cérilly France
Cêringgolêb Xizang China see Dongco
36 F7 Cerisiers France
39 J3 Cerisy-la-Forêt France
38 I3 Cerisy-la-Salle France
39 J8 Cerizay France
71 R4 Cerk mt. Slovenia
188 F3 Çerkeş Turkey
79 K2 Çerkeşli Turkey
79 J1 Çerkezköy Turkey
79 I1 Çerkezmüsellim Turkey
59 M8 Cerklje Brežice Slovenia
59 J7 Cerklje Kranj Slovenia
68 E3 Cerknica Slovenia
59 J8 Cerkniško jezero l. Slovenia
59 I7 Cerkno Slovenia
54 D1 Cerkwica Pol.
191 D5 Çerme Turkey
77 J4 Cermei Romania
73 L2 Cermignano Italy
188 I4 Çermik Turkey
77 Q5 Cerna Romania
77 K5 Cerna r. Romania
77 K6 Cerna r. Romania
77 M6 Cerna r. Romania
62 D9 Cernache do Bonjardim Port.
62 H5 Cernadilla, Embalse de resr Spain
56 F2 Černá Hora Czech Rep.
56 C3 Černá Hora mt. Czech Rep.
77 O5 Cernat Romania
Cernăuţi Ukr. see Chernivtsi
77 Q6 Cernavodă Romania
37 N8 Cernay France
36 I5 Cernay-en-Dormois France
56 C1 Černčice Czech Rep.
63 M3 Cernégula Spain
59 N6 Černelavci Slovenia
70 B1 Cernier Switz.
57 H3 Černík Slovakia
57 L2 Černiny hill Slovakia
70 G4 Cernobbio Italy
56 D2 Černošice Czech Rep.
56 B2 Černošín Czech Rep.
56 D2 Černovice Czech Rep.
43 H7 Cérou r. France
71 Q5 Cerovica Croatia
71 Q5 Cerovlje Croatia
57 I3 Cerovo Slovakia
142 C5 Cerqueira César Brazil
62 G7 Cerralbo Spain
127 J4 Cerralvo Mex.
126 E5 Cerralvo, Isla i. Mex.
63 K5 Cerrato, Valles de reg. Spain
70 I7 Cerreto, Passo del pass Italy
71 N9 Cerreto d'Esi Italy
73 J2 Cerreto di Spoleto Italy
73 N5 Cerreto Sannita Italy
30 E1 Cerrigydrudion Conwy, Wales U.K.
76 H9 Cërrik Albania
144 D2 Cerrillos Arg.
128 G5 Cerritos Guanajuato Mex.
128 G3 Cerritos San Luis Potosí Mex.
73 M4 Cerro al Volturno Italy
142 C6 Cerro Azul Brazil
129 J4 Cerro Azul Mex.
138 A3 Cerro Azul Peru
144 C2 Cerro Bonete mt. Arg.
64 H5 Cerro del Hiero Spain
128 D7 Cerro de Ortega Mex.
138 A2 Cerro de Pasco Peru
128 G4 Cerro Gordo Mex.
126 □S14 Cerro Hoya, Parque Nacional nat. park Panama
145 C9 Cerro Manantiales Chile
65 M7 Cerrón mt. Spain
136 D2 Cerrón, Cerro mt. Venez.
138 C5 Cerro Negro Chile
126 F4 Cerro Prieto Mex.
146 C6 Cerros Colorados, Embalse resr Arg.
136 A5 Cerros de Amotape, Parque Nacional nat. park Peru
39 K7 Cersay France
73 Q7 Cersosimo Italy
71 K8 Certaldo Italy
77 K5 Certeju de Sus Romania
57 K2 Čertižne Slovakia
70 G5 Certosa di Pavia Italy
70 D7 Certosa di Pesio Italy
62 E6 Cerva Port.
62 C5 Cervães Port.
63 J9 Cervales mt. Spain
209 C11 Cervantes W.A. Austr.
145 B8 Cervantes, Cerro mt. Arg.
73 L5 Cervaro Italy
73 P4 Cervaro r. Italy
73 O7 Cervati, Monte mt. Italy
63 K4 Cervatos de la Cueza Spain
56 F1 Červená Voda Czech Rep.
51 L10 Červené Pečky Czech Rep.
77 N7 Cervenia Romania
56 G2 Červenka Czech Rep.
66 H4 Cervera Spain
66 F6 Cervera r. Spain
63 Q6 Cervera de la Cañada Spain
63 P9 Cervera del Llano Spain
63 K8 Cervera de los Montes Spain
63 Q4 Cervera del Río Alhama Spain
63 L3 Cervera de Pisuerga Spain
72 I4 Cerveteri Italy
71 M7 Cervia Italy
73 O6 Cervialto, Monte mt. Italy
71 O4 Cervignano del Friuli Italy
71 K2 Cervina, Punta mt. Italy
73 N5 Cervinara Italy
56 E2 Červiná Řečice Czech Rep.
72 C3 Cervione Corse France
70 E8 Cervo Italy
70 E5 Cervo r. Italy
62 F1 Cervo Spain
40 D2 Cervon France
73 Q9 Cerzeto Italy
71 O8 Cesano r. Italy
136 C2 César dept Col.
136 C2 César r. Col.
74 H8 Cesarò Sicilia Italy
58 F8 Cesen, Monte mt. Italy
71 M7 Cesena Italy
71 M7 Cesenatico Italy
70 D7 Cesio Italy
18 I4 Cēsis Latvia
56 D1 Česká Kamenice Czech Rep.
56 D1 Česká Lípa Czech Rep.
Česká Republika country Europe see Czech Republic
56 F1 Česká Skalice Czech Rep.
57 I3 České Brezovo Slovakia
56 D3 České Budějovice Czech Rep.
56 C1 České Středohoří hills Czech Rep.
59 K2 České Velenice Austria
56 D2 Českomoravská Vysočina hills Czech Rep.
56 D1 Český Brod Czech Rep.
51 K9 Český Dub Czech Rep.
56 D3 Český Krumlov Czech Rep.
56 B2 Český Les mts Czech Rep./Ger.
56 E1 Český Ráj park Czech Rep.
59 L1 Český Rudolec Czech Rep.
57 H2 Český Těšín Czech Rep.
68 F3 Česma r. Croatia
79 H4 Çeşme Turkey
62 I7 Cespedosa Spain
71 N4 Cessalto Italy
41 B10 Cesse r. France
41 C10 Cessenon-sur-Orb France
40 G5 Cessieu France
205 M5 Cessnock N.S.W. Austr.
38 H5 Cesson-Sévigné France
43 C6 Cestas France
88 C5 Cestos r. Liberia
62 D2 Cesuras Spain
18 J5 Cesvaine Latvia
154 D3 Cetaceo, Mount Phil.
168 G8 Cêtar Qinghai China
57 L4 Cetariu Romania
77 L6 Cetate Romania
Cetatea Albă Ukr. see Bilhorod-Dnistrovs'kyy
68 F4 Cetina r. Croatia
63 Q6 Cetina Spain
76 G8 Cetinje Crna Gora Serb. and Mont.
70 I3 Ceto Italy
39 M5 Ceton France
72 H2 Cetona Italy
73 P8 Cetraro Italy
43 C10 Cette-Eygun France
200 □1 Cetti Bay Guam
41 H7 Céüse France
41 H7 Céüse, Montagne de mt. France
60 D5 Ceuta N. Africa
67 C11 Ceutí Spain
70 E7 Ceva Italy
199 H4 Ceva-i-Ra rf Fiji
71 J3 Cevedale, Monte mt. Italy
41 C9 Cévennes mts France
41 D8 Cévennes, Parc National des nat. park France
63 L5 Cevico de la Torre Spain
63 L5 Cevico Navero Spain
40 I5 Cevins France
70 F3 Cevio Switz.
191 C5 Cevizli Erzurum Turkey
79 L3 Cevizli Eskişehir Turkey
190 F2 Cevizli Gaziantep Turkey
54 F1 Cewice Pol.
55 K5 Cewków Pol.
188 G5 Ceyhan Turkey
190 D2 Ceyhan r. Turkey
190 D2 Ceyhan Boğazı r. mouth Turkey
189 J5 Ceylanpınar Turkey
191 K5 Çeyldağ Azer.
Ceylon country Asia see Sri Lanka
191 K5 Ceyranbatan Azer.
41 H10 Ceyreste France
40 G4 Ceyzériat France
42 D5 Cézac France
41 F8 Cèze r. France
62 E5 Chã Port.
184 I3 Chaacha Turkm.
44 G6 Chaam Neth.
184 I9 Chābahār Iran
42 F4 Chabanais France
147 G3 Chabas Arg.
41 H8 Chabestan France
41 G7 Chabeuil France
55 H4 Chabielice Pol.
40 J4 Chablais mts France
127 N9 Chablé Mex.
36 G8 Chablis France
42 F4 Chabrac France
41 H8 Chabre ridge France
40 D5 Chabreloche France
39 O7 Chabris France
173 L13 Chabua Assam India
173 F10 Chabug Xizang China
173 G11 Chabyêr Caka salt l. China
138 C4 Chaca Chile
147 G4 Chacabuco Arg.
131 □7 Chacachacare Island Trin. and Tob.
129 L7 Chacaltianguis Mex.
129 J8 Chacaltongo Mex.
138 C4 Chacarilla Bol.
136 B6 Chachapoyas Peru
146 E5 Chacharramendi Arg.
178 F7 Chachaura-Binaganj Madh. Prad. India
Chäche Turkm. see Chaacha
19 N9 Chachersk Belarus
18 M8 Chachevichy Belarus
159 E8 Chachoengsao Thai.
185 N9 Chachro Pak.
62 G6 Chacim Port.
144 E2 Chaco prov. Arg.
139 F5 Chaco Boreal reg. Para.
123 K8 Chaco Culture National Historical Park nat. park NM U.S.A.
106 C4 Chacon, Cape AK U.S.A.
137 G6 Chacorão, Cachoeira da waterfall Brazil
138 B2 Chacra de Piros Peru
84 C6 Chad country Africa
84 B6 Chad, Lake Africa
168 H3 Chadaasan Mongolia
160 F1 Chadan Rus. Fed.
115 □1 Chaddock Bar rf Bermuda
118 D5 Chadds Ford PA U.S.A.
95 G2 Chadiza Zambia
41 D6 Chadrac France
120 D4 Chadron NE U.S.A.
Chadyr-Lunga Moldova see Ciadîr-Lunga
158 D5 Chae Hom Thai.
183 P7 Chaek Kyrg.
163 D9 Chaeryŏng N. Korea
158 D5 Chae Son National Park Thai.
61 E5 Chafarinas, Islas is N. Africa
89 G4 Chafe Nigeria
121 K7 Chaffee MO U.S.A.
145 B7 Chaffers, Isla i. Chile
110 B3 Chaffey WI U.S.A.
136 C4 Chafurray Col.
185 K7 Chagai Pak.
185 J7 Chagai Hills Afgh./Pak.
176 F5 Chagalamarri Andhra Prad. India
182 K5 Chagan Kyzylordinskaya Oblast' Kazakh.
183 R2 Chagan Vostochnyy Kazakhstan Kazakh.
172 I1 Chaganuzun Rus. Fed.
173 G9 Chagdo Kangri mt. China
30 E6 Chagford Devon, England U.K.
173 L9 Chaggur Qinghai China
184 D6 Chaghā Khūr mt. Iran
185 K4 Chaghcharān Afgh.
183 M1 Chaglinka r. Kazakh.
40 F3 Chagny France
19 S2 Chagoda Rus. Fed.
19 S2 Chagoda r. Rus. Fed.
19 T3 Chagodoshcha r. Rus. Fed.
215 I5 Chagos Archipelago is B.I.O.T.
215 I5 Chagos-Laccadive Ridge sea feature Indian Ocean
215 I5 Chagos Trench sea feature Indian Ocean
162 F2 Chagoyan Rus. Fed.
182 C1 Chagra r. Rus. Fed.
126 □T13 Chagres, Parque Nacional nat. park Panama
131 □7 Chaguanas Trin. and Tob.
131 □7 Chaguaramas Trin. and Tob.
136 E2 Chaguaramas Venez.
184 F1 Chagyl Turkm.
184 E1 Chagyllyshor, Vpadina depr. Turkm.
16 I8 Chaha r. Ukr.
185 J6 Chahah Burjal Afgh.
184 H5 Chāhak Iran
184 H5 Chāh Ākhvor Iran
184 E6 Chah 'Ali Iran
184 G4 Chāh 'Ali Akbar Iran
185 N4 Chaharbagh Afgh.
184 D5 Chahār Maḩāll va Bakhtīārī prov. Iran
184 D7 Chahār Rūstā'ī Iran
184 B3 Chahār Ţāq Iran
184 F4 Chah Baba well Iran
184 E5 Chāh Badam Iran
184 I9 Chāh Bahār, Khalīj-e b. Iran
184 I3 Chahchaheh Turkm.
185 M3 Chāh-e Āb Afgh.
184 H5 Chāh-e Bābā well Iran
184 F6 Chāh-e Bāgh well Iran
184 E6 Chāh-e Dow Chāhī Iran
184 E5 Chāh-e Gonbad well Iran
184 G4 Chāh-e Kavīr well Iran
184 F4 Chāh-e Khorāsān well Iran
184 G5 Chāh-e Khoshāb Iran
184 E5 Chāh-e Malek well Iran
184 F6 Chāh-e Malek Mīrzā well Iran
184 E5 Chāh-e Mirzā well Iran
184 F4 Chāh-e Mūjān well Iran
184 F5 Chāh-e Nūklok Iran
184 E5 Chāh-e Nūklok well Iran
184 F4 Chāh-e Pansu well Iran
184 F7 Chāh-e Qeyşar well Iran
184 E4 Chāh-e Qobād well Iran
184 F7 Chāh-e Rāh Iran
184 H6 Chāh-e Raḩmān well Iran
185 I5 Chah-e Rig Afgh.
184 F5 Chāh-e Shūr Iran
184 E4 Chāh-e Shūr well Iran
184 E6 Chāh-e Ţāqestān well Iran
184 H5 Chāh-e Tūnī well Iran
184 I7 Chah Gheybī, Hāmūn-e salt pan Iran
184 F4 Chāh Haji Abdulla well Iran
184 F7 Chāh Ḩaqq Iran
184 E6 Chāh Kūh Iran
184 G8 Chāh Lak Iran
184 E5 Chāh Pās well Iran
184 H6 Chāh Ru'ī well Iran
185 J7 Chah Sandan Pak.
184 E4 Chah Shirin Iran
184 E7 Chāh Sorkh Iran
129 M9 Chahuites Mex.
179 J8 Chaibasa Jharkhand India
109 H2 Chaigneau, Lac l. Que. Can.
162 B5 Chaihe Nei Mongol China
162 C7 Chai He r. China
185 M9 Chailar Pak.
31 L6 Chailey East Sussex, England U.K.
42 G3 Chaillac France
39 J5 Chailland France
42 B3 Chaillé-les-Marais France
36 G7 Chailley France
90 A5 Chaillu, Massif du mts Gabon
158 E7 Chainat Thai.
41 D6 Chaîne du Devès mts France
173 H9 Chainjoin Co l. Xizang China
36 H6 Chaintrix-Bierges France
158 D5 Chai Prakan Thai.
159 E8 Chai Si r. Thai.
145 B6 Chaitén Chile
171 □J7 Chai Wan H.K. China
172 H5 Chaiwopu Xinjiang China
159 D10 Chaiya Thai.
158 E7 Chaiyaphum Thai.
146 E3 Chaján Arg.
147 I2 Chajarí Arg.
179 K7 Chakai Bihar India
185 O4 Chakai Pak.
185 P5 Chak Amru Pak.
185 M7 Chakar r. Pak.
95 F3 Chakari Zimbabwe
179 N9 Chakaria Bangl.
185 O4 Chakdarra Pak.
93 C6 Chake Chake Tanz.
185 J6 Chakhānsūr Afgh.
179 I7 Chakia Uttar Prad. India
185 O6 Chak Jhumra Pak.
185 L8 Chakku Pak.
109 G1 Chakonipau, Lac l. Que. Can.
179 J8 Chakradharpur Jharkhand India
179 K8 Chakulia Jharkhand India
191 C4 Ch'ak'vi Georgia
185 O5 Chakwal Pak.
138 B3 Chala Peru
93 A6 Chala Tanz.
93 A7 Chalabesa Zambia
43 I10 Chalabre France
40 H3 Chalain, Lac de l. France
42 E5 Chalais France
70 D3 Chalais Switz.
40 G4 Chalamont France
185 K5 Chalap Dalan mts Afgh.
40 F4 Chalaronne r. France
126 □O10 Chalatenango El Salvador
95 H3 Chaláua Moz.
168 E9 Chalaxung Qinghai China
92 C4 Chalbi Desert Kenya
128 D2 Chalchihuites Mex.
129 I6 Chalco Mex.
162 A2 Chaldonka Rus. Fed.
31 J6 Chale Isle of Wight, England U.K.
42 F4 Chaleix France
41 F7 Chalencon France
173 K7 Chalengkou Qinghai China
36 E7 Châlette-sur-Loing France
109 H3 Chaleur Bay inlet N.B./Que. Can.
Chaleurs, Baie de inlet N.B./Que. Can. see Chaleur Bay
118 E4 Chalfont PA U.S.A.
31 K4 Chalfont St Peter Buckinghamshire, England U.K.
30 H4 Chalford Gloucestershire, England U.K.
179 I8 Chalgali Chhattisgarh India
31 J4 Chalgrove Oxfordshire, England U.K.
145 C8 Chalía r. Arg.
55 H3 Chalin Pol.
37 J8 Chalindrey France
171 I5 Chaling Hunan China
93 C6 Chalinze Tanz.
178 E9 Chalisgaon Mahar. India
176 E7 Chalisseri Kerala India
40 B3 Chalivoy-Milon France
79 I6 Chalki Notio Aigaio Greece
78 D3 Chalki Thessalia Greece
79 I6 Chalki i. Greece
78 E4 Chalkida Greece
78 D2 Chalkidona Greece
183 R6 Chalkudysu Kazakh.
203 A13 Chalky Inlet South I. N.Z.
146 C6 Challacó Arg.
176 E5 Challakere Karnataka India
38 H8 Challans France
138 D4 Challapata Bol.
216 E5 Challenger Deep sea feature N. Pacific Ocean

Challenger Fracture Zone to Cherán
248

217 L8 Challenger Fracture Zone sea feature S. Pacific Ocean
36 I5 Challerange France
40 H5 Challes-les-Eaux France
122 G4 Challis ID U.S.A.
121 K11 Chalmette LA U.S.A.
14 G2 Chal'mny-Varre Rus. Fed.
40 D3 Chalmoux France
40 E3 Chaloire r. France
42 C1 Chalonnes-sur-Loire France
36 H6 Châlons-en-Champagne France
Châlons-sur-Marne France see Châlons-en-Champagne
40 F3 Chalon-sur-Saône France
43 C8 Chalosse reg. France
191 E3 Chalovani Georgia
178 E1 Chalt Jammu and Kashmir
17 S6 Chaltyr' Rus. Fed.
162 D7 Chaluhe Jilin China
97 L9 Chalumna S. Africa
42 F4 Châlus France
184 D3 Chālūs Iran
184 D3 Chālūs, Rūd-e r. Iran
53 N3 Cham Ger.
70 E1 Cham Switz.
184 D5 Cham, Kūh-e hill Iran
123 K8 Chama NM U.S.A.
123 K8 Chama r. NM U.S.A.
93 B7 Chama Zambia
99 □3a Chamadani hill Njazidja Comoros
146 E4 Chamaico Arg.
94 B5 Chamais Bay Namibia
40 C5 Chamalières France
41 G7 Chamaloc France
93 B6 Chamamba Tanz.
185 L6 Chaman Pak.
184 G3 Chaman Bid Iran
159 E8 Chamao, Khao mt. Thai.
53 N3 Chamb r. Ger.
178 F3 Chamba Hima. Prad. India
95 H2 Chamba Moz.
93 C7 Chamba Tanz.
178 G6 Chambal r. India
191 G5 Chambarak Armenia
41 G6 Chambaran, Plateau de France
130 D2 Chambas Cuba
109 G2 Chambeaux, Lac l. Que. Can.
42 H4 Chamberet France
40 H4 Chambéria France
208 I4 Chamberlain r. W.A. Austr.
107 J5 Chamberlain Sask. Can.
147 I3 Chamberlain Uru.
120 F4 Chamberlain SD U.S.A.
117 □P2 Chamberlain Lake ME U.S.A.
125 W6 Chambers AZ U.S.A.
206 C2 Chambers Bay N.T. Austr.
116 H9 Chambersburg PA U.S.A.
110 G4 Chambers Island WI U.S.A.
40 H5 Chambéry France
93 A7 Chambeshi Zambia
87 H2 Chambi, Jebel mt. Tunisia
136 C6 Chambira r. Peru
37 K5 Chambley-Bussières France
36 D5 Chambly France
39 L4 Chambois France
40 F2 Chambolle-Musigny France
42 H3 Chambon, Lac de l. France
40 B5 Chambon-sur-Lac France
42 I3 Chambon-sur-Voueize France
109 F3 Chambord Que. Can.
39 O6 Chambord France
185 K8 Chambor Kalat Pak.
42 H5 Chamboulive France
39 M7 Chambray-lès-Tours France
153 J7 Chambri Lake P.N.G.
36 G4 Chambry France
189 L6 Chamchamāl Iraq
179 M5 Chamda Xizang China
126 □T13 Chame Panama
41 H6 Chamechaude mt. France
184 C5 Cham-e Ḩannā Iran
128 B6 Chamela Mex.
53 N3 Chamerau Ger.
36 I8 Chamesson France
95 G3 Chametengo Moz.
42 H5 Chameyrat France
86 B5 Châmi well Maur.
146 D2 Chamical Arg.
79 H7 Chamili i. Greece
191 B1 Chamlykskaya Rus. Fed.
92 C3 Ch'amo Häyk' l. Eth.
70 D4 Chamois Italy
Chamoli Uttaranchal India see Gopeshwar
40 J5 Chamonix-Mont-Blanc France
Chamouchouane r. Que. Can. see Ashuapmushuan
41 H8 Chamouse, Montagne de mt. France
40 I5 Chamoux-sur-Gelon France
146 B3 Champa Chile
179 I8 Champa Chhattisgarh India
42 I5 Champagnac France
42 F5 Champagnac-de-Belair France
41 D6 Champagnac-le-Vieux France
106 B2 Champagne Y.T. Can.
39 L5 Champagné France
36 H6 Champagne-Ardenne admin. reg. France
39 O7 Champagne Berrichonne reg. France
97 N5 Champagne Castle mt. S. Africa
36 H5 Champagne Crayeuse reg. France
40 H5 Champagne-en-Valromey France
36 H7 Champagne Humide reg. France
42 E4 Champagne-Mouton France
36 G7 Champagne Pouilleuse reg. France
36 D5 Champagne-sur-Oise France
36 E7 Champagne-sur-Seine France
37 M8 Champagney France
40 H3 Champagnole France
208 H3 Champagny Islands W.A. Austr.
114 C5 Champaign IL U.S.A.
29 J2 Champany Falkirk, Scotland U.K.
146 E2 Champaqui, Cerro mt. Arg.
138 A2 Champara mt. Peru
159 G7 Champasak Laos
36 G6 Champaubert France
178 H5 Champawat Uttaranchal India
42 F5 Champcevinel France
42 D3 Champdeniers-St-Denis France
40 E1 Champ-d'Oiseau France
109 H2 Champdoré, Lac l. Que. Can.
37 N7 Champ du Feu mt. France
39 M7 Champeigne reg. France
40 C5 Champeix France
70 B3 Champéry Switz.
70 C3 Champex Switz.
40 F3 Champforgeuil France
39 K5 Champgenéteux France
179 N8 Champhai Mizoram India
41 G6 Champier France
39 J6 Champigné France
36 F8 Champignelles France
37 L6 Champigneulles France
36 I7 Champignol-lez-Mondeville France
36 F7 Champigny France
106 H5 Champion Alta Can.
110 G3 Champion MI U.S.A.
117 L4 Champlain NY U.S.A.
116 I10 Champlain VA U.S.A.
108 F4 Champlain, Lake Can./U.S.A.
117 L5 Champlain Canal NY U.S.A.
40 C2 Champlemy France
40 H1 Champlitte France
111 Q1 Champneuf Que. Can.
42 E4 Champniers France
41 I7 Champoléon France
40 D5 Champoly France
127 N8 Champotón Mex.
36 B7 Champrond-en-Gâtine France
39 J4 Champsecret France
41 B6 Champs-sur-Tarentaine-Marchal France
36 G8 Champs-sur-Yonne France
41 H6 Champ-sur-Drac France
41 I8 Champtercier France
38 I7 Champtoceaux France
40 G2 Champvans France
176 F7 Chamrajnagar Karnataka India
41 H6 Chamrousse France
184 D6 Cham Siyāh Iran
173 J9 Chamu Co l. Qinghai China
64 C2 Chamusca Port.
Chamyndy Naryn Kyrg. see Chemyndy
15 I5 Chamzinka Rus. Fed.
159 E11 Chana Thai.
41 C8 Chanac France
Chanak Turkey see Çanakkale
127 M9 Chanal Mex.
147 H2 Chañar Entre Ríos Arg.
146 E2 Chañar La Rioja Arg.
146 C6 Chañar Neuquén Arg.
144 C2 Chañaral Chile
144 C3 Chañaral, Isla i. Chile
146 B2 Chañaral Alto Chile
184 H3 Chanārān Iran
144 C2 Chañarcillo Chile
147 F3 Chañar Ladeado Arg.
137 F3 Chanaro, Cerro mt. Venez.
41 F6 Chanas France
64 D2 Chança Port.
Chança r. Port./Spain see Chanza
146 E2 Chancani Arg.
128 G3 Chancaquero Mex.
138 A2 Chancay Peru
40 F1 Chanceaux France
39 M7 Chanceaux-sur-Choisille France
42 F5 Chancelade France
62 C9 Chancelaria Port.
131 □2 Chances Peak vol. Montserrat
127 O8 Chanchén Mex.
146 A4 Chanco Chile
146 A4 Chanco, Bahía de b. Chile
138 A2 Chancos Peru
Chanda Mahar. India see Chandrapur
104 D3 Chandalar r. AK U.S.A.
93 C6 Chandama Tanz.
178 H5 Chandan Chauki Uttar Prad. India
179 I9 Chandarpur Chhattisgarh India
178 F5 Chandausi Uttar Prad. India
179 K9 Chandbali Orissa India
179 O7 Chandel Manipur India
121 K11 Chandeleur Islands LA U.S.A.
178 G7 Chanderi Madh. Prad. India
178 H9 Chandia Madh. Prad. India
178 F4 Chandigarh Chandigarh India
178 F4 Chandigarh union terr. India
179 K8 Chandil Jharkhand India
109 H3 Chandler Que. Can.
125 U8 Chandler AZ U.S.A.
121 G8 Chandler OK U.S.A.
138 C2 Chandless r. Brazil
168 E2 Chandmany Mongolia
111 Q5 Chandos Lake Ont. Can.
179 M8 Chandpur Bangl.
178 G5 Chandpur Uttar Prad. India
176 F6 Chandragiri Andhra Prad. India
176 F3 Chandrapur Mahar. India
62 F4 Chandrexa de Queixa, Embalse de resr Spain
178 G9 Chandur Mahar. India
178 E9 Chandvad Mahar. India
184 F2 Chandyr r. Turkm.
63 L6 Chañe Spain
184 I8 Chānf Iran
159 F8 Chang, Ko i. Thai.
97 Q2 Changalane Moz.
169 K9 Chang'an Shaanxi China
165 G11 Chang-an S. Korea
95 G5 Changane r. Moz.
95 G3 Changara Moz.
163 F8 Changbai Jilin China
163 E8 Changbai Shan mts China/N. Korea
Chang Cheng research stn Antarctica see Great Wall
170 G9 Changcheng Hainan China
170 G9 Changcheng Hainan China
Changchow Jiangsu China see Changzhou
162 D7 Changchun Jilin China
162 D8 Changdao Shandong China
171 H4 Changde Hunan China
39 J5 Changé Pays de la Loire France
39 L6 Changé Pays de la Loire France
171 K2 Changfeng Anhui China
169 M9 Changge Henan China
163 F10 Changgi-ap pt S. Korea
173 G12 Changgo Xizang China
171 I3 Chang Hu l. China
171 M6 Changhua Taiwan
170 G9 Changhua Jiang r. China
165 G13 Changhŭng S. Korea
156 □ Changi Sing.
156 □ Changi Airport airport Sing.
172 H5 Changji Xinjiang China
170 G9 Changjiang Hainan China
161 L5 Chang Jiang r. China
alt. Jinsha Jiang,
alt. Tongtian He,
conv. Yangtze,
long Yangtze Kiang
171 M3 Changjiang Kou r. mouth China
163 E8 Changjin N. Korea
163 E8 Changjin-gang r. N. Korea
173 L13 Changlang Arun. Prad. India
171 L6 Changle Fujian China
169 P7 Changli Hebei China
169 R4 Changling Jilin China
168 I7 Changliushui Nei Mongol China
156 D1 Changlun Malaysia
178 F2 Changlung Jammu and Kashmir
168 E7 Changma Gansu China
173 E9 Changmar Xizang China
171 I5 Changning Hunan China
170 E4 Changning Sichuan China
170 B6 Changning Yunnan China
163 D9 Changnyŏn N. Korea
Ch'ang-pai Shan mts China/N. Korea see Changbai Shan
169 O6 Changping Beijing China
163 D9 Changsan-got pt N. Korea
171 I4 Changsha Hunan China
171 L4 Changshan Zhejiang China
169 R7 Changshan Qundao is China
170 E5 Changshi Guizhou China
170 F4 Changshou Chongqing China
171 I4 Changshoujie Hunan China
171 M3 Changshu Jiangsu China
163 E11 Changsŏng S. Korea
171 K6 Changtai Fujian China
Changteh Hunan China see Changde
171 K6 Changting Fujian China
162 F6 Changting Heilong. China
162 D7 Changtu Liaoning China
126 □R13 Changuinola Panama
173 K7 Changweiliang Qinghai China
163 F11 Ch'angwŏn S. Korea
169 J9 Changwu Shaanxi China
171 L3 Changxing Zhejiang China
169 Q7 Changxing Dao i. China
40 E4 Changy France
171 H3 Changyang Hubei China
169 P8 Changyi Shandong China
163 D9 Changyŏn N. Korea
169 N9 Changyuan Henan China
169 M8 Changzhi Shanxi China
169 M9 Changzhi Shanxi China
171 L3 Changzhou Jiangsu China
144 D2 Chañi, Nevado de mt. Arg.
78 F7 Chania Kriti Greece
42 C4 Chaniers France
78 E7 Chanion, Kolpos b. Kriti Greece
168 I9 Chankou Gansu China
158 I6 Chân Mây Đông, Mui pt Vietnam
176 D5 Channagiri Karnataka India
176 E6 Channapatna Karnataka India
38 F3 Channel Islands English Chan.
124 M8 Channel Islands CA U.S.A.
124 M7 Channel Islands National Park CA U.S.A.
109 J4 Channel-Port-aux-Basques Nfld and Lab. Can.
130 E2 Channel Rock i. Bahamas
25 H6 Channel Tunnel France/U.K.
110 F3 Channing MI U.S.A.
121 D8 Channing TX U.S.A.
178 D7 Chanod Rajasthan India
62 E3 Chantada Spain
193 S3 Chantal'skiy mt. Rus. Fed.
40 C4 Chantelle France
38 H5 Chantepie France
159 F8 Chanthaburi Thai.
36 D5 Chantilly France
42 B2 Chantonnay France
37 L7 Chantraine France
40 D2 Chantrans France
39 J4 Chanu France
177 M8 Chanumla Andaman & Nicobar Is India
121 H7 Chanute KS U.S.A.
185 O5 Chanuwala Pak.
192 I4 Chany, Ozero salt l. Rus. Fed.
64 D5 Chanza r. Port./Spain
138 A2 Chao Peru
62 E2 Chao Spain
64 □ Chão, Ilhéu i. Madeira
171 K7 Chao'an Guangdong China
169 O7 Chaobai Xinhe r. China
171 K3 Chaohu Anhui China
171 K3 Chao Hu l. China
159 E8 Chao Phraya r. Thai.
169 Q2 Chaor Nei Mongol China
86 D2 Chaouèn Morocco
60 D5 Chaouèn prov. Morocco
40 G2 Chaource France
171 K7 Chaoyang Guangdong China
169 Q6 Chaoyang Liaoning China
169 S2 Chaoyangcun Nei Mongol China
173 H9 Chaoyang Hu l. Xizang China
169 Q1 Chaozhong Nei Mongol China
171 K7 Chaozhou Guangdong China
140 E5 Chapada Diamantina, Parque Nacional nat. park Brazil
139 G3 Chapada dos Guimarães Brazil
140 D5 Chapada dos Veadeiros, Parque Nacional da nat. park Brazil
142 A3 Chapadão do Céu Brazil
141 B6 Chapadão do Sul Brazil
140 E2 Chapadinha Brazil
108 F3 Chapais Que. Can.
185 K3 Chapak Guzar Afgh.
128 D5 Chapala Mex.
128 D5 Chapala, Laguna de l. Mex.
146 E5 Chapalcó, Valle de val. Arg.
147 H5 Chapaleofú Arg.
128 C4 Chapalilla Mex.
129 H5 Chapantongo Mex.
138 D3 Chapare r. Bol.
41 H6 Chapareillan France
138 B3 Chaparra Peru
136 C4 Chaparral Col.
182 D2 Chapayev Kazakh.
17 O4 Chapayeve Ukr.
17 L4 Chapayevka Ukr.
182 C1 Chapayevsk Rus. Fed.
183 O1 Chapayevskoye Kazakh.
40 B5 Chapdes-Beaufort France
141 B8 Chapecó Brazil
141 B8 Chapecó r. Brazil
29 N7 Chapel-en-le-Frith Derbyshire, England U.K.
29 M4 Chapelfell Top hill England U.K.
115 H8 Chapel Hill NC U.S.A.
45 F8 Chapelle-lez-Herlaimont Belgium
29 R7 Chapel St Leonards Lincolnshire, England U.K.
130 □ Chapelton Jamaica
27 J3 Chapeltown Northern Ireland U.K.
29 O7 Chapeltown South Yorkshire, England U.K.
147 I2 Chapicuy Uru.
138 B3 Chapimarca Peru
63 L8 Chapinería Spain
162 M5 Chaplanovo Rus. Fed.
108 D4 Chapleau Ont. Can.
108 D3 Chapleau Crown Game Reserve nature res. Ont. Can.
107 J5 Chaplin Sask. Can.
Chaplinka Ukr. see Chaplynka
107 J5 Chaplin Lake l. Sask. Can.
193 T3 Chaplino Rus. Fed.
17 M2 Chapliyivka Ukr.
19 W8 Chaplygin Rus. Fed.
17 P5 Chaplyne Ukr.
17 M7 Chaplynka Ukr.
17 M7 Chaplyns'kyy Kanal canal Ukr.
17 Q2 Chaplyzhnoye Rus. Fed.
106 G5 Chapman, Mount B.C. Can.
116 F7 Chapmanville PA U.S.A.
116 C11 Chapmanville WV U.S.A.
119 H2 Chappaqua NY U.S.A.
120 D5 Chappell NE U.S.A.
205 K9 Chappell Islands Tas. Austr.
Chapra Bihar India see Chhapra
185 K4 Chapri Pass Afgh.
129 I4 Chapulhuacán Mex.
147 G3 Chapuy Arg.
178 F3 Char Jammu and Kashmir
144 F2 Charadai Arg.
139 E4 Charagua Bol.
138 C4 Charaña Bol.
136 C5 Charapita Col.
144 E2 Charata Arg.
126 E4 Charay Mex.
40 E3 Charbonnat France
41 K6 Charbonnel, Pointe de mt. France
128 F2 Charcas Mex.
40 H2 Charcenne France
40 H4 Charchilla France
128 G3 Charco Blanco Mex.
212 S2 Charcot Island Antarctica
107 I4 Chard Alta Can.
30 G6 Chard Somerset, England U.K.
183 L7 Chardara, Step' plain Kazakh.
183 M7 Chardarinskoye Vodokhranilishche resr Kazakh./Uzbek.
184 B5 Chardāvol Iran
184 F3 Chardeh Iran
116 D7 Chardon OH U.S.A.
30 G6 Chardstock Devon, England U.K.
Chardzhev Lebapskaya Oblast' Turkm. see Turkmenabat
87 F2 Charef Alg.
86 E2 Charef, Oued watercourse Morocco
42 E4 Charente dept France
42 C4 Charente r. France
42 C4 Charente-Maritime dept France
40 B3 Charenton-du-Cher France
39 M3 Charentonne r. France
191 F5 Ch'arents'avan Armenia
30 F4 Charfield South Gloucestershire, England U.K.
184 E7 Charg Iran
40 H2 Chargey-lès-Gray France
90 B1 Chari r. Cameroon/Chad
184 G6 Chārī Iran
90 C2 Chari-Baguirmi pref. Chad
185 M4 Chārīkār Afgh.
179 K6 Charikot Nepal
31 N5 Charing Kent, England U.K.
120 I5 Chariton IA U.S.A.
120 I6 Chariton r. IA U.S.A.
111 K5 Charity Island MI U.S.A.
17 M6 Charivne Ukr.
189 O8 Charkas Iran
14 K2 Charkayuvom Rus. Fed.
185 L3 Chār Kent Afgh.
178 G7 Charkhari Uttar Prad. India
178 F5 Charkhi Dadri Haryana India
31 J4 Charlbury Oxfordshire, England U.K.
97 N2 Charl Cilliers S. Africa
27 I4 Charlemont Northern Ireland U.K.
45 F8 Charleroi Belgium
117 J11 Charles, Cape VA U.S.A.
109 G4 Charlesbourg Que. Can.
120 I4 Charles City IA U.S.A.
116 H11 Charles City VA U.S.A.
107 I3 Charles Lake Alta Can.
122 K3 Charles M. Russell National Wildlife Refuge nature res. MT U.S.A.
206 C2 Charles Point N.T. Austr.
203 F8 Charleston South I. N.Z.
121 H8 Charleston AR U.S.A.
120 I5 Charleston IA U.S.A.
120 K6 Charleston IL U.S.A.
121 K7 Charleston MO U.S.A.
121 J8 Charleston MS U.S.A.
115 H9 Charleston SC U.S.A.
116 D10 Charleston WV U.S.A.
125 Q5 Charleston Peak NV U.S.A.
27 E5 Charlestown Rep. of Ireland
97 N3 Charlestown S. Africa
131 □2 Charlestown St Kitts and Nevis
131 □3 Charlestown St Vincent
118 D5 Charlestown MD U.S.A.
117 M5 Charlestown NH U.S.A.
117 N7 Charlestown RI U.S.A.
116 H9 Charles Town WV U.S.A.
Charlestown of Aberlour Moray, Scotland U.K. see Aberlour
207 K9 Charleville Qld Austr.
36 I4 Charleville-Mézières France
110 I4 Charlevoix MI U.S.A.
106 F3 Charlie Lake B.C. Can.
40 E4 Charlieu France
110 J7 Charlotte MI U.S.A.
115 G8 Charlotte NC U.S.A.
131 □ Charlotte Amalie Virgin Is (U.S.A.)
157 G1 Charlotte Bank sea feature S. China Sea
116 G11 Charlotte Court House VA U.S.A.
115 F12 Charlotte Harbor b. FL U.S.A.
106 E4 Charlotte Lake B.C. Can.
22 I2 Charlottenberg Sweden
116 G10 Charlottesville VA U.S.A.
109 I4 Charlottetown P.E.I. Can.
Charlotte Town Grenada see Gouyave
131 □5 Charlotteville Trin. and Tob.
205 I7 Charlton Vic. Austr.
31 J5 Charlton Hampshire, England U.K.
30 H4 Charlton Wiltshire, England U.K.
108 E2 Charlton Island Nunavut Can.
30 H4 Charlton Kings Gloucestershire, England U.K.
31 L5 Charlwood Surrey, England U.K.
36 F6 Charly France
42 E4 Charmé France
37 L7 Charmes France
41 F6 Charmes-sur-Rhône France
70 C2 Charmey Switz.
30 H6 Charminster Dorset, England U.K.
37 L7 Charmois-l'Orgueilleux France
36 H7 Charmont-sous-Barbuise France
30 G6 Charmouth Dorset, England U.K.
36 F8 Charmoy France
40 F4 Charnay-lès-Mâcon France
64 A3 Charneca Port.
19 N7 Charnitsa r. Belarus
208 H4 Charnley r. W.A. Austr.
36 F8 Charny France
55 M4 Charnyany Belarus
37 J5 Charny-sur-Meuse France
40 E4 Charolles France
40 E4 Charollais reg. France
18 K6 Charomkhava Belarus
39 P8 Chârost France
14 G3 Charozero Rus. Fed.
40 J2 Charquemont France
70 C3 Charrat Switz.
36 I8 Charrey-sur-Seine France
40 D3 Charrin France
107 M4 Charron Lake Man. Can.
42 E3 Charroux France
36 C5 Chars France
185 N4 Charsadda Pak.
185 K3 Charshanga Turkm.
18 L6 Charstsvyatskaye, Vozyera l. Belarus
55 H5 Charsznica Pol.
116 B10 Charters KY U.S.A.
207 K6 Charters Towers Qld Austr.
31 O5 Chartham Kent, England U.K.
36 B7 Chartres France
70 C4 Charvensod Italy
40 I4 Charvonnex France
183 R6 Charyn Kazakh.
183 R6 Charyn r. Kazakh.
183 T1 Charysh r. Rus. Fed.
183 T2 Charyshskoye Rus. Fed.
54 F2 Charzykowskie, Jezioro l. Pol.
54 F2 Charzykowy Pol.
54 D1 Charzyno Pol.
147 H4 Chas Arg.
179 K8 Chas Jharkhand India
62 D7 Chãs mt. Port.
144 C2 Chaschuil Arg.
147 H4 Chascomús Arg.
147 H4 Chascomús, Laguna l. Arg.
106 G5 Chase B.C. Can.
118 C6 Chase MD U.S.A.
110 I6 Chase MI U.S.A.
116 G12 Chase City VA U.S.A.
185 I3 Chashkent Turkm.
184 F4 Chashmeh Baluch Iran
184 G4 Chashmeh Nūrī Iran
184 E4 Chashmeh Tuleh Iran
184 G5 Chashmeh-ye Ab-e Garm spring Iran
184 H5 Chashmeh-ye Garm Ab spring Iran
184 G5 Chashmeh-ye Magu well Iran
184 G5 Chashmeh-ye Mūkīk spring Iran
184 E4 Chashmeh-ye Palasi Iran
184 G5 Chashmeh-ye Safīd spring Iran
184 F5 Chashmeh-ye Shotoran well Iran
18 M7 Chashniki Belarus
189 P6 Chāsht Khvāran Iran
78 C3 Chasia reg. Greece
147 F6 Chasicó Arg.
145 D6 Chasico Arg.
147 F6 Chasicó, Laguna l. Arg.
17 Q5 Chasiv Yar Ukr.
120 I3 Chaska MN U.S.A.
203 D13 Chaslands Mistake c. South I. N.Z.
163 E8 Chasŏng N. Korea
162 A2 Chasovaya Rus. Fed.
14 H2 Chasovenskaya Arkhangel'skaya Oblast' Rus. Fed.
19 Q1 Chasovenskaya Leningradskaya Oblast' Rus. Fed.
39 L8 Chasseneuil-du-Poitou France
42 E4 Chasseneuil-sur-Bonnieure France
42 F4 Chassenon France
41 D7 Chasseradès France
70 C1 Chasseral mt. Switz.
40 F5 Chasse-sur-Rhône France
41 E8 Chassezac r. France
37 J8 Chassigny-Aisey France
39 K5 Chassillé France
42 B3 Chassiron, Pointe de pt France
184 F5 Chastab, Kūh-e mts Iran
42 I5 Chastang, Barrage du dam France
45 G7 Chastre Belgium
14 K4 Chastyye Rus. Fed.
136 B6 Chasuta Peru
184 F3 Chāt Iran
40 H5 Chat, Mont du mt. France
43 I6 Châtaigneraie reg. France
110 E9 Chatauqua Lake IL U.S.A.
38 E4 Chateau, Pointe du pt France
41 H8 Château-Arnoux France
131 □4 Chateaubelair St Vincent
42 D4 Châteaubernard France
38 I5 Châteaubourg France
147 G3 Chateaubriand Arg.
38 I6 Châteaubriant France
40 D1 Château-Chinon France
70 C3 Château-d'Oex Switz.
42 A2 Château-d'Olonne France
39 L6 Château-du-Loir France
36 B7 Châteaudun France
40 C5 Châteaugay France
117 K4 Chateaugay NY U.S.A.
38 H5 Châteaugiron France
39 J6 Château-Gontier France
117 L3 Châteauguay Que. Can.
109 G1 Châteauguay r. Que. Can.
109 G1 Châteauguay, Lac l. Que. Can.
36 E7 Château-Landon France
39 L6 Château-la-Vallière France
39 I5 Château-l'Évêque France
38 C5 Châteaulin France
41 F9 Châteauneuf-de-Gadagne France
41 F6 Châteauneuf-de-Galaure France
41 D7 Châteauneuf-de-Randon France
38 H4 Châteauneuf-d'Ille-et-Vilaine France
38 D5 Châteauneuf-du-Faou France
41 F8 Châteauneuf-du-Pape France
41 F8 Châteauneuf-du-Rhône France
36 B6 Châteauneuf-en-Thymerais France
42 H4 Châteauneuf-la-Forêt France
40 B4 Châteauneuf-les-Bains France
41 G10 Châteauneuf-les-Martigues France
42 D4 Châteauneuf-sur-Charente France
39 P8 Châteauneuf-sur-Cher France
36 D8 Châteauneuf-sur-Loire France
39 K6 Châteauneuf-sur-Sarthe France
40 C2 Châteauneuf-Val-de-Bargis France
109 J2 Chateau Pond l. Nfld and Lab. Can.
42 G3 Châteauponsac France
36 H4 Château-Porcien France
41 I8 Châteauredon France
36 E8 Châteaurenard Centre France
41 F9 Châteaurenard Provence-Alpes-Côte d'Azur France
40 G3 Châteaurenaud France
39 M6 Château-Renault France
42 H2 Châteauroux Centre France
41 J7 Châteauroux Provence-Alpes-Côte d'Azur France
37 M6 Château-Salins France
36 F5 Château-Thierry France
37 I7 Châteauvillain France
131 □2 Châteaux, Pointe des pt Guadeloupe
106 G3 Chateh Alta Can.
40 J4 Châtel France
42 B3 Châtelaillon-Plage France
38 F4 Châtelaudren France
40 D1 Châtel-Censoir France
40 D5 Châteldon France
45 G8 Châtelet Belgium
42 D1 Châtelet-Gérard France
40 C5 Châtelguyon France
42 F2 Châtellerault France
40 D4 Châtel-Montagne France
40 D4 Châtelperron France
70 B2 Châtel-St-Denis Switz.
37 L7 Châtel-sur-Moselle France
42 I3 Châtelus-Malvaleix France
37 N7 Châtenois Alsace France
37 K7 Châtenois Lorraine France
40 J1 Châtenois-les-Forges France
40 E3 Châtenoy-le-Royal France
116 C8 Chatfield OH U.S.A.
108 D5 Chatham Ont. Can.
31 N5 Chatham Medway, England U.K.
106 C3 Chatham AK U.S.A.
117 P7 Chatham MA U.S.A.
118 F5 Chatham NJ U.S.A.
117 L6 Chatham NY U.S.A.
118 D5 Chatham PA U.S.A.
116 F12 Chatham VA U.S.A.
145 B8 Chatham, Isla i. Chile
202 □ Chatham Island Chatham Is S. Pacific Ocean
202 □ Chatham Islands S. Pacific Ocean
216 H8 Chatham Rise sea feature S. Pacific Ocean
106 D4 Chatham Sound sea chan. B.C. Can.
106 C3 Chatham Strait AK U.S.A.
45 I9 Châtillon Belgium
70 D4 Châtillon Italy
36 E8 Châtillon-Coligny France
40 D2 Châtillon-en-Bazois France
41 G7 Châtillon-en-Diois France
40 H4 Châtillon-en-Michaille France
40 G5 Châtillon-la-Palud France
36 I8 Châtillonnais reg. France
40 F4 Châtillon-sur-Chalaronne France
39 J5 Châtillon-sur-Colmont France
42 G2 Châtillon-sur-Indre France
40 B1 Châtillon-sur-Loire France
36 G5 Châtillon-sur-Marne France
36 I8 Châtillon-sur-Seine France
39 K8 Châtillon-sur-Thouet France
183 N7 Chatkal r. Kyrg.
183 N7 Chatkal Range mts Kyrg.
121 K10 Chatom AL U.S.A.
179 J7 Chatra Jharkhand India
179 K6 Chatra Nepal
178 E6 Chatsu Rajasthan India
206 H6 Chatsworth Qld Austr.
111 N5 Chatsworth Ont. Can.
115 E8 Chatsworth GA U.S.A.
110 F9 Chatsworth IL U.S.A.
118 F5 Chatsworth NJ U.S.A.
95 F3 Chatsworth Zimbabwe
Chattagam Bangl. see Chittagong
115 E10 Chattahoochee FL U.S.A.
115 E10 Chattahoochee r. GA U.S.A.
115 E8 Chattanooga TN U.S.A.
41 G6 Chatte France
31 M3 Chatteris Cambridgeshire, England U.K.
Chattisgarh state India see Chhattisgarh
203 D12 Chatto Creek South I. N.Z.
29 N2 Chatton Northumberland, England U.K.
158 E7 Chatturat Thai.
41 G7 Chatuzange-le-Goubet France
118 D5 Chatwood PA U.S.A.
Chatyrkël', Ozero l. Kyrg. see Chatyr-Köl
183 P7 Chatyr-Köl l. Kyrg.
183 Q7 Chatyr-Tash Kyrg.
185 N6 Chaubara Pak.
65 L6 Chauchina Spain
17 O8 Chauda, Mys pt Ukr.
37 K8 Chaudenay France
41 C7 Chaudes-Aigues France
41 D7 Chaudeyrac France
45 I7 Chaudfontaine Belgium
159 G9 Châu Đốc Vietnam
39 J7 Chaudron-en-Mauges France
40 E4 Chauffailles France
41 I7 Chauffayer France
178 C7 Chauhtan Rajasthan India
158 B4 Chauk Myanmar
178 H6 Chauka r. India
178 G4 Chaukhamba mts Uttaranchal India
171 □J7 Chau Kung To i. H.K. China
176 C3 Chaul Mahar. India
36 E4 Chaulnes France
40 D2 Chaumeçon, Barrage de dam France
40 G3 Chaumergy France
37 J7 Chaumont France
36 C5 Chaumont-en-Vexin France
36 H4 Chaumont-Porcien France
37 J6 Chaumont-sur-Aire France
39 N7 Chaumont-sur-Loire France
42 E3 Chaunay France
116 C9 Chauncey OH U.S.A.
159 D8 Chaungwabyin Myanmar
193 R3 Chaunskaya Guba b. Rus. Fed.
36 F4 Chauny France
158 I7 Châu Ô Vietnam
Chau Phu Vietnam see Châu Đốc
178 G8 Chaurai Madh. Prad. India
42 D3 Chauray France
38 H4 Chausey, Îles is France
40 G3 Chaussin France
166 G5 Chausu-yama mt. Japan
Chausy Belarus see Chavusy
116 F6 Chautauqua, Lake NY U.S.A.
129 H9 Chautengo, Laguna l. Mex.
185 L6 Chauter Pak.
183 O7 Chauvay Kyrg.
42 F2 Chauvigny France
107 I4 Chauvin Alta Can.
40 H2 Chaux, Forêt de for. France
38 I8 Chavagnes-en-Paillers France
176 G8 Chavakachcheri Sri Lanka
140 E2 Chaval Brazil
41 F6 Chavanay France
14 G2 Chavan'ga Rus. Fed.
36 I6 Chavanges France
41 D6 Chavaniac-Lafayette France
40 G5 Chavanoz France
184 B5 Chavār Iran
78 C5 Chavari Greece
37 L7 Chavelot France
137 I5 Chaves Brazil
62 F5 Chaves Port.
136 B6 Chaves Valdivia Peru
108 F1 Chavigny, Lac l. Que. Can.
136 C3 Chaviva Col.
91 D8 Chavuma Zambia
19 N8 Chavusy Belarus
185 L7 Chawal r. Pak.
159 D10 Chawang Thai.
158 G4 Chay, Sông r. Vietnam
138 D4 Chayanta r. Bol.
162 J2 Chayatyn, Khrebet ridge Rus. Fed.
Chayek Kyrg. see Chaek
19 U3 Chayevo Rus. Fed.
Ch'ayk'end Armenia see Dprabak
14 K4 Chaykovskiy Rus. Fed.
40 F5 Chazay-d'Azergues France
42 E4 Chazelles France
40 E5 Chazelles-sur-Lyon France
14 K3 Chazhegovo Rus. Fed.
147 F3 Chazón Arg.
129 J7 Chazumba Mex.
117 L4 Chazy NY U.S.A.
29 M7 Cheadle Greater Manchester, England U.K.
31 I2 Cheadle Staffordshire, England U.K.
116 F9 Cheat r. WV U.S.A.
56 B1 Cheb Czech Rep.
110 G8 Chebanse IL U.S.A.
87 H2 Chebba Tunisia
87 F4 Chebbi salt l. Alg.
14 I4 Cheboksarskoye Vodokhranilishche resr Rus. Fed.
14 I4 Cheboksary Rus. Fed.
110 J4 Cheboygan MI U.S.A.
63 Q7 Checa Spain
16 I5 Chechel'nyk Ukr.
191 I2 Chechen', Ostrov i. Rus. Fed.
171 M7 Ch'ech'eng Taiwan
191 G2 Chechenskaya Respublika aut. rep. Rus. Fed.
97 M5 Cheche Pass Lesotho
Chechnia aut. rep. Rus. Fed. see Chechenskaya Respublika
Chechnya aut. rep. Rus. Fed. see Chechenskaya Respublika
163 F10 Chech'ŏn S. Korea
16 D5 Chechva r. Ukr.
55 I5 Chęciny Pol.
121 H8 Checotah OK U.S.A.
36 D8 Chécy France
169 Q8 Chedao Shandong China
31 N3 Chedburgh Suffolk, England U.K.
30 G5 Cheddar Somerset, England U.K.
29 M7 Cheddleton Staffordshire, England U.K.
84 C6 Chéddra Chad
Cheduba Island Myanmar see Man-aung Kyun
158 A5 Cheduba Strait Myanmar
37 I6 Chée r. France
27 I8 Cheekpoint Rep. of Ireland
116 G6 Cheektowaga NY U.S.A.
108 D3 Cheepash r. Ont. Can.
207 J9 Cheepie Qld Austr.
213 K2 Cheetham, Cape Antarctica
42 D3 Chef-Boutonne France
89 I2 Cheffadène well Niger
104 B3 Chefornak AK U.S.A.
162 H3 Chegdomyn Rus. Fed.
Chegem 1 Rus. Fed. see Chegem Pervyy
191 E2 Chegem r. Rus. Fed.
191 E2 Chegem Pervyy Rus. Fed.
86 D4 Chegga Maur.
88 C2 Cheggué watercourse Maur.
88 D2 Chegguet Ti-n-Kerkâz des. Maur.
95 F3 Chegutu Zimbabwe
122 C3 Chehalis WA U.S.A.
122 C3 Chehalis r. WA U.S.A.
184 G3 Chehar Burj Iran
184 G5 Chehardeh Iran
189 M7 Chehariz tourist site Iraq
184 B4 Chehel Chashmeh, Kūh-e hill Iran
184 I6 Chehel Dokhtarān, Kūh-e mt. Iran
184 G6 Chehell'āyeh Iran
86 D4 Cheikria well Alg.
77 J5 Cheil Nerei-Beușnița nat. park Romania
78 C2 Cheimaditis, Limni l. Greece
41 J9 Cheiron, Cime du mt. France
163 E12 Cheju S. Korea
163 E12 Cheju-do i. S. Korea
163 E12 Cheju-haehyŏp sea chan. S. Korea
19 T7 Chekalin Rus. Fed.
14 K5 Chekan Rus. Fed.
171 □J7 Chek Chau i. H.K. China
19 U6 Chekhov Moskovskaya Oblas[t'] Rus. Fed.
162 L5 Chekhov Sakhalin Rus. Fed.
Chekichler Turkm. see Chekishlyar
184 E3 Chekishlyar Turkm.
156 □ Chek Jawa, Tanjong pt Sing[.]
171 □I7 Chek Lap Kok reg. H.K. Chi[na]
171 □J7 Chek Mun Hoi Hap sea chan[.] H.K. China
14 H4 Chekshino Rus. Fed.
162 H3 Chekunda Rus. Fed.
91 B9 Chela, Serra da mts Angola
43 F9 Chélan France
122 D3 Chelan WA U.S.A.
122 D2 Chelan, Lake WA U.S.A.
17 R7 Chelbas r. Rus. Fed.
17 S8 Chelbasskaya Rus. Fed.
64 A3 Cheleiros Port.
64 A3 Cheleiros r. Port.
184 E2 Cheleken Turkm.
64 E3 Cheles Spain
146 D6 Chelforó Arg.
95 G4 Cheline Moz.
182 D2 Chelkar Zapadnyy Kazakhsta[n] Kazakh.
67 D9 Chella Spain
55 L4 Chełm Pol.
55 H5 Chełmek Pol.
31 N4 Chelmer r. England U.K.
55 I6 Chełmiec Pol.
54 G2 Chełmno Kujawsko-Pomorski[e] Pol.
54 G3 Chełmno Wielkopolskie Pol.
31 M4 Chelmsford Essex, England U.K.
117 N6 Chelmsford MA U.S.A.
97 N3 Chelmsford Public Resort Nature Reserve S. Africa
16 C2 Chełmski Park Krajobrazow[y] Pol.
56 F1 Chełmy, Park Krajobrazowy Pol.
54 G2 Chełmża Pol.
111 J7 Chelsea MI U.S.A.
117 M5 Chelsea VT U.S.A.
202 J7 Cheltenham North I. N.Z.
30 H4 Cheltenham Gloucestershire, England U.K.
118 E4 Cheltenham PA U.S.A.
67 D8 Chelva Spain
192 H4 Chelyabinsk Rus. Fed.
182 I1 Chelyabinskaya Oblast' admin. div. Rus. Fed.
Chelyabinsk Oblast admin. div. Rus. Fed. see Chelyabinskaya Oblast'
17 P8 Chelyadinove Ukr.
116 D10 Chelyan WV U.S.A.
193 L2 Chelyuskin Rus. Fed.
193 L2 Chelyuskin, Mys c. Rus. Fed.
86 C2 Chemaïa Morocco
127 P7 Chemax Mex.
39 J6 Chemazé France
95 G3 Chemba Moz.
91 F7 Chembe Zambia
86 B5 Chemchâm, Sebkhet salt flat Maur.
173 D9 Chêm Co l. China
185 J4 Chemenibit Turkm.
16 F4 Chemerivtsi Ukr.
39 N7 Chémery France
55 M6 Chemeryntsi Ukr.
37 I4 Chémery-sur-Bar France
42 C1 Chemillé France
40 G3 Chemin France
99 □1b Chemin Grenier Mauritius
37 I6 Cheminon France
39 K6 Chemiré-le-Gaudin France
Chemmis Egypt see Akhmīm
51 G9 Chemnitz Ger.
51 G9 Chemnitz admin. reg. Ger.
117 □P2 Chemquasabamticook Lake ME U.S.A.
122 D5 Chemult OR U.S.A.
111 R8 Chemung r. NY U.S.A.
183 P7 Chemyndy Naryn Kyrg.
178 C5 Chenab r. India/Pak.
86 D4 Chenachane Alg.
86 E4 Chenachane, Oued watercourse Alg.
117 J6 Chenango r. NY U.S.A.
117 J6 Chenango Bridge NY U.S.A.
40 F4 Chénas France
92 C3 Ch'ench'a Eth.
156 D2 Chenderoh, Tasik resr Malaysia
Chendir r. Turkm. see Chand[yr]
40 H2 Chenecey-Buillon France
42 I3 Chénérailles France
121 G7 Cheney Reservoir KS U.S.A.
176 G6 Chengalpattu Tamil Nadu India
176 F6 Chengam Tamil Nadu India
169 N8 Cheng'an Hebei China
170 F6 Chengbihe Shuiku resr Chin[a]
170 H5 Chengbu Hunan China
169 K9 Chengcheng Shaanxi China
169 O6 Chengde Hebei China
169 P6 Chengde Hebei China
170 E3 Chengdu Sichuan China
183 M7 Chengel'dy Kazakh.
179 P5 Chengele Arun. Prad. India
170 D6 Chenggong Yunnan China
171 K7 Chenghai Guangdong China
170 C5 Cheng Hai l. China
170 D6 Chengjiang Yunnan China
170 G3 Chengkou Chongqing China
170 H9 Chengmai Hainan China
169 O9 Chengqian Shandong China
Chengqiao Shanghai China see Chongming
Chengtu Sichuan China see Chengdu
169 N9 Chengwu Shandong China
170 E2 Chengxian Gansu China
Chengxian Guizhou China see Fuquan
170 A6 Chengzi Yunnan China
37 M7 Cheniménil France
169 P9 Cheniu Shan i. China
176 G9 Chenkaladi Sri Lanka
176 G6 Chennai Tamil Nadu India
110 F9 Chenoa IL U.S.A.
39 N7 Chenonceaux France
40 G2 Chenôve France
171 N3 Chenqian Shan i. China
162 E4 Chenqing Heilong. China
Chenqingqiao Heilong. China see Chenqing
Chenstokhov Pol. see Częstochowa
169 J2 Chentejn Nuruu mts Mongolia
156 □ Chenting, Tanjong pt Sing.
170 H5 Chenxi Hunan China
36 G8 Cheny France
Chenyang Hunan China see Chenxi
171 I6 Chenzhou Hunan China
169 N7 Chenzhuang Hebei China
Cheom Ksan Cambodia see Chŏâm Khsant
77 M9 Chepelare Bulg.
136 B6 Chepén Peru
146 D2 Chepes Arg.
17 P4 Chepil' Ukr.
19 O6 Chepli Rus. Fed.
126 □T13 Chepo Panama
30 G4 Chepstow Monmouthshire, Wales U.K.
14 J4 Cheptsa r. Rus. Fed.
36 H6 Chepy France
184 B5 Cheqād Kabūd Iran
110 D3 Chequamegon Bay WI U.S.A.
39 P7 Cher dept France
42 E1 Cher r. France
67 D8 Chera Spain
42 D4 Chérac France
75 M3 Cheradi, Isole is Italy
40 H5 Chéran r. France
128 F6 Cherán Mex.

Cherangany Hills to **Chop**
249

92 B4 **Cherangany Hills** Kenya
70 D6 **Cherasco** Italy
35 N5 **Cherat** Pak.
43 C9 **Chéraute** France
15 H8 **Cheraw** SC U.S.A.
76 B6 **Cherbaniani Reef** India
38 H2 **Cherbourg** France
37 F1 **Cherchell** Alg.
15 J5 **Cherdakly** Rus. Fed.
13 T3 **Cherdoyak** Kazakh.
14 L3 **Cherdyn'** Rus. Fed.
38 H6 **Chère** r. France
Chereapani rf India see **Byramgore Reef**
57 L4 **Cherechiu** Romania
91 F2 **Cherek** r. Rus. Fed.
18 L4 **Cherekha** r. Rus. Fed.
15 G6 **Cheremisinovo** Rus. Fed.
50 H1 **Cheremkhovo** Rus. Fed.
33 T1 **Cheremnoye** Rus. Fed.
52 I6 **Cheremshany** Rus. Fed.
14 J4 **Cheremukhovka** Rus. Fed.
72 B6 **Cheremule** Sardegna Italy
92 J4 **Cherepanovo** Rus. Fed.
Cherepkovo Moldova see Ciripcău
19 U2 **Cherepovets** Rus. Fed.
14 I3 **Cherevkovo** Rus. Fed.
37 E2 **Chergui, Chott ech** imp. l. Alg.
37 G2 **Chéria** Alg.
76 F4 **Cherial** Andhra Prad. India
70 H4 **Cherio** r. Italy
31 J5 **Cheriton** Hampshire, England U.K.
17 J11 **Cheriton** VA U.S.A.
76 C7 **Cheriyam** atoll India
16 K4 **Cherkas'ka Oblast'** admin. div. Ukr.
17 O5 **Cherkas'ke** Dnipropetrovs'ka Oblast' Ukr.
17 Q5 **Cherkas'ke** Donets'ka Oblast' Ukr.
Cherkasskaya Oblast' admin. div. Ukr. see **Cherkas'ka Oblast'**
Cherkassy Ukr. see **Cherkasy**
17 L4 **Cherkasy** Ukr.
Cherkasy Oblast admin. div. Ukr. see **Cherkas'ka Oblast'**
91 D1 **Cherkessk** Rus. Fed.
19 W5 **Cherkutino** Rus. Fed.
76 G3 **Cherla** Andhra Prad. India
33 P1 **Cherlak** Rus. Fed.
16 F5 **Cherlenivka** Ukr.
91 F2 **Chermen** Rus. Fed.
91 D8 **Chermenze** Angola
14 L4 **Chermoz** Rus. Fed.
19 T8 **Chern'** Rus. Fed.
19 T8 **Chern'** r. Rus. Fed.
33 M6 **Chernak** Kazakh.
19 V9 **Chernava** Lipetskaya Oblast' Rus. Fed.
19 W8 **Chernava** Ryazanskaya Oblast' Rus. Fed.
14 L1 **Chernaya** Rus. Fed.
14 L1 **Chernaya** r. Rus. Fed.
18 K3 **Chernaya** r. Rus. Fed.
17 T3 **Chernaya Kalitva** r. Rus. Fed.
14 J4 **Chernaya Kholunitsa** Rus. Fed.
17 M2 **Chernecha Sloboda** Ukr.
17 O4 **Cherneshchyna** Ukr.
19 V7 **Chernevo** Moskovskaya Oblast' Rus. Fed.
18 L3 **Chernevo** Pskovskaya Oblast' Rus. Fed.
Chernigov Ukr. see **Chernihiv**
52 H6 **Chernigovka** Rus. Fed.
Chernigov Oblast admin. div. Ukr. see **Chernihivs'ka Oblast'**
91 A1 **Chernigovskaya** Rus. Fed.
Chernigovskaya Oblast' admin. div. Ukr. see Chernihivs'ka Oblast'
91 A1 **Chernigovskoye** Rus. Fed.
17 K2 **Chernihiv** Ukr.
Chernihiv Oblast admin. div. Ukr. see **Chernihivs'ka Oblast'**
17 L2 **Chernihivs'ka Oblast'** admin. div. Ukr.
77 N7 **Cherni Lom** r. Bulg.
17 P6 **Cherninivka** Ukr.
55 M6 **Cherniv** Ukr.
16 F5 **Chernivets'ka Oblast'** admin. div. Ukr.
Chernivetskaya Oblast' admin. div. Ukr. see Chernivets'ka Oblast'
77 L8 **Cherni Vrŭkh** mt. Bulg.
16 E5 **Chernivtsi** Chernivets'ka Oblast' Ukr.
16 H5 **Chernivtsi** Vinnyts'ka Oblast' Ukr.
Chernivtsi Oblast admin. div. Ukr. see **Chernivets'ka Oblast'**
16 D5 **Cherniyiv** Ukr.
Chernobyl' Ukr. see Chornobyl'
50 F1 **Chernogorsk** Rus. Fed.
91 E1 **Chernolesskoye** Rus. Fed.
92 J3 **Chernoostrovskoye** Rus. Fed.
14 K3 **Chernorechenskiy** Rus. Fed.
91 G2 **Chernorech'ye** Rus. Fed.
33 Q1 **Chernoretskoye** Kazakh.
19 P1 **Chernoushevo** Rus. Fed.
14 I4 **Chernovskoye** Rus. Fed.
Chernovtsy Ukr. see Chernivtsi
Chernovtsy Oblast admin. div. Ukr. see Chernivets'ka Oblast'
Chernoye More sea Asia/Europe see **Black Sea**
14 L4 **Chernushka** Rus. Fed.
16 H3 **Chernyakhiv** Ukr.
18 E7 **Chernyakhovsk** Rus. Fed.
15 G6 **Chernyanka** Rus. Fed.
52 D2 **Chernyayeve** Rus. Fed.
91 I2 **Chernyayevskiy** Rus. Fed.
19 N7 **Chernyewka** Belarus
32 H5 **Chernysheva, Zaliv** b. Kazakh.
51 K1 **Chernyshevsk** Rus. Fed.
93 M3 **Chernyshevskiy** Rus. Fed.
15 H6 **Chernyshkovskiy** Rus. Fed.
17 M8 **Chernyshove** Ukr.
15 I7 **Chernyye Zemli** reg. Rus. Fed.
Chernyy Irtysh r. China/Kazakh. see **Ertix He**
32 F2 **Chernyy Otrog** Rus. Fed.
14 F3 **Chernyy Porog** Rus. Fed.
15 I6 **Chernyy Yar** Rus. Fed.
20 H4 **Cherokee** IA U.S.A.
21 F7 **Cherokee** OK U.S.A.
15 F7 **Cherokee Lake** TN U.S.A.
21 H7 **Cherokees, Lake o' the** OK U.S.A.
30 E1 **Cherokee Sound** Gt Abaco Bahamas
36 F7 **Chéroy** France
19 N5 **Cherpessa** Rus. Fed.
46 A6 **Cherquenco** Chile
79 M7 **Cherrapunji** Meghalaya India
29 Q6 **Cherry Burton** East Riding of Yorkshire, England U.K.
20 E3 **Cherry Creek** r. SD U.S.A.
25 R1 **Cherry Creek Mountains** NV U.S.A.
17 □R4 **Cherryfield** ME U.S.A.
18 E5 **Cherry Hill** NJ U.S.A.
99 G3 **Cherry Island** Solomon Is
24 M3 **Cherry Lake** CA U.S.A.
11 Q6 **Cherry Valley** Ont. Can.
18 D3 **Cherryville** PA U.S.A.
29 Q7 **Cherry Willingham** Lincolnshire, England U.K.
18 L4 **Cherskaya** Rus. Fed.
93 R3 **Cherskiy** Rus. Fed.
Cherskiy Range mts Rus. Fed. see Cherskogo, Khrebet
69 L1 **Cherskogo, Khrebet** mts Rus. Fed.
193 P3 **Cherskogo, Khrebet** mts Rus. Fed.
78 D1 **Cherso** Greece
70 C6 **Chersogno, Monte** mt. Italy
78 F7 **Chersonisos Akrotiri** pen. Kriti Greece
78 E5 **Chersonisos Methano** pen. Greece
66 F6 **Chert** Spain
Chertkov Ukr. see **Chortkiv**
15 H6 **Chertkovo** Rus. Fed.
19 Q5 **Chertolino** Rus. Fed.
203 F10 **Chertsey** South I. N.Z.
31 K5 **Chertsey** Surrey, England U.K.
19 X6 **Cherusti** Rus. Fed.
42 G5 **Cherveix-Cubas** France
77 M7 **Cherven Bryag** Bulg.
42 D4 **Cherves-Richemont** France
191 G2 **Chervlennaya** Rus. Fed.
191 G1 **Chervlennyye Buruny** Rus. Fed.
17 M5 **Chervona Kam''yanka** Ukr.
17 N2 **Chervone** Sums'ka Oblast' Ukr.
16 H4 **Chervone** Zhytomyrs'ka Oblast' Ukr.
17 Q6 **Chervone Pole** Ukr.
17 K3 **Chervoni Partyzany** Ukr.
16 H3 **Chervonoarmiys'k** Zhytomyrs'ka Oblast' Ukr.
17 N7 **Chervonoarmiys'ke** Ukr.
Chervonograd Ukr. see Chervonohrad
16 D3 **Chervonohrad** Ukr.
17 N6 **Chervonohryhorivka** Ukr.
17 Q4 **Chervonooskil's'ke Vodoskhovyshche** resr Ukr.
Chervonopartizansk Ukr. see Chervonopartyzans'k
17 S5 **Chervonopartyzans'k** Ukr.
17 M3 **Chervonozavods'ke** Ukr.
16 J6 **Chervonoznam''yanka** Ukr.
17 P4 **Chervonyy Donets'** Ukr.
17 M7 **Chervonyy Mayak** Ukr.
18 L8 **Chervyen'** Belarus
31 J4 **Cherwell** r. England U.K.
19 O8 **Cherykaw** Belarus
111 J6 **Chesaning** MI U.S.A.
117 I12 **Chesapeake** VA U.S.A.
118 D5 **Chesapeake and Delaware Canal** DE U.S.A.
118 C7 **Chesapeake Bay** MD/VA U.S.A.
116 I10 **Chesapeake Beach** MD U.S.A.
118 D5 **Chesapeake City** MD U.S.A.
31 K4 **Chesham** Buckinghamshire, England U.K.
29 M7 **Cheshire** admin. div. England U.K.
119 J2 **Cheshire** CT U.S.A.
117 L6 **Cheshire** MA U.S.A.
29 L7 **Cheshire Plain** England U.K.
184 G7 **Cheshmeh Sabz** Iran
185 I2 **Cheshme Vtoroy** Turkm.
191 G3 **Chesho** Georgia
14 I2 **Cheshskaya Guba** b. Rus. Fed.
185 P3 **Cheshtebe** Tajik.
185 J4 **Chesht-e Sharīf** Afgh.
31 L4 **Cheshunt** Hertfordshire, England U.K.
30 G6 **Chesil Beach** England U.K.
118 F5 **Chesilhurst** NJ U.S.A.
111 M5 **Chesley** Ont. Can.
36 H8 **Chesley** France
182 I1 **Chesma** Rus. Fed.
36 G7 **Chessy-les-Prés** France
67 D9 **Cheste** Spain
109 H4 **Chester** N.S. Can.
29 L7 **Chester** Cheshire, England U.K.
124 K1 **Chester** CA U.S.A.
119 K2 **Chester** CT U.S.A.
120 K7 **Chester** IL U.S.A.
118 C7 **Chester** MD U.S.A.
122 I2 **Chester** MT U.S.A.
118 F3 **Chester** NJ U.S.A.
119 G2 **Chester** NY U.S.A.
116 D9 **Chester** OH U.S.A.
118 E5 **Chester** PA U.S.A.
115 G8 **Chester** SC U.S.A.
116 H11 **Chester** VA U.S.A.
118 C7 **Chester** r. MD U.S.A.
130 □ **Chester Castle** Jamaica
118 D4 **Chester County** county PA U.S.A.
29 O7 **Chesterfield** Derbyshire, England U.K.
119 K2 **Chesterfield** CT U.S.A.
120 J6 **Chesterfield** MO U.S.A.
115 G8 **Chesterfield** SC U.S.A.
116 H11 **Chesterfield** VA U.S.A.
199 F3 **Chesterfield, Îles** is New Caledonia
107 N2 **Chesterfield Inlet** Nunavut Can.
107 M2 **Chesterfield Inlet** inlet Nunavut Can.
29 N4 **Chester-le-Street** Durham, England U.K.
26 K12 **Chesters** Scottish Borders, Scotland U.K.
118 C6 **Chestertown** MD U.S.A.
117 L5 **Chestertown** NY U.S.A.
117 J3 **Chesterville** Ont. Can.
118 D6 **Chesterville** MD U.S.A.
116 F8 **Chestnut Ridge** PA U.S.A.
117 □P2 **Chesuncook Lake** ME U.S.A.
118 D6 **Cheswold** DE U.S.A.
87 G1 **Chetaïbi** Alg.
110 C4 **Chetek** WI U.S.A.
109 I4 **Chéticamp** N.S. Can.
176 C7 **Chetlat** i. India
121 H7 **Chetopa** KS U.S.A.
127 O8 **Chetumal** Mex.
203 I7 **Chetwode Islands** South I. N.Z.
106 F4 **Chetwynd** B.C. Can.
162 G3 **Cheugda** Rus. Fed.
171 □J7 **Cheung Chau** H.K. China
41 I8 **Cheval Blanc, Sommet du** mt. France
42 D5 **Chevanceaux** France
36 G8 **Chevannes** France
125 V7 **Chevelon Creek** r. AZ U.S.A.
57 K6 **Chevereșu Mare** Romania
118 B7 **Cheverly** MD U.S.A.
40 G2 **Chevigny-St-Sauveur** France
37 J6 **Chevillon** France
36 C7 **Chevilly** France
203 H9 **Cheviot** South I. N.Z.
116 A9 **Cheviot** OH U.S.A.
29 L3 **Cheviot Hills** England U.K.
207 I8 **Cheviot Range** hills Qld Austr.
108 F2 **Chevreulx** r. Que. Can.
36 D6 **Chevreuse** France
92 C3 **Che'w Bahir** salt l. Eth.
92 C3 **Che'w Bahir Wildlife Reserve** nature res. Eth.
122 F2 **Chewelah** WA U.S.A.
30 G5 **Chew Magna** Bath and North East Somerset, England U.K.
30 G5 **Chew Valley Lake** resr England U.K.
121 F8 **Cheyenne** OK U.S.A.
122 L6 **Cheyenne** WY U.S.A.
120 E3 **Cheyenne** r. SD U.S.A.
120 E3 **Cheyenne River Indian Reservation** res. SD U.S.A.
120 D6 **Cheyenne Wells** CO U.S.A.
41 B6 **Cheylade** France
209 E13 **Cheyne Bay** W.A. Austr.
176 G6 **Cheyur** Tamil Nadu India
176 F6 **Cheyyar** r. India
106 E4 **Chezacut** B.C. Can.
39 P8 **Chezal-Benoît** France
99 □3a **Chezani** Njazidja Comoros
43 D10 **Chèze** France
178 F7 **Chhabra** Rajasthan India
159 F9 **Chhâk Sihanoukville** b. Cambodia
178 E6 **Chhapar** Rajasthan India
179 J7 **Chhapra** Bihar India
178 F6 **Chhata** Uttar Prad. India
179 M7 **Chhatak** Bangl.
179 J7 **Chhatarpur** Jharkhand India
178 G7 **Chhatarpur** Madh. Prad. India
185 M7 **Chhatr** Pak.
177 I3 **Chhatrapur** Orissa India
178 H9 **Chhattisgarh** state India
159 F9 **Chhay Arêng, Stœng** r. Cambodia
178 G6 **Chhibramau** Uttar Prad. India
178 G8 **Chhindwara** Madh. Prad. India
178 F7 **Chhipa Barod** Rajasthan India
178 G4 **Chhitkul** Hima. Prad. India
159 G8 **Chhlong, Prêk** r. Cambodia
178 G8 **Chhota Chhindwara** Madh. Prad. India
178 E8 **Chhota Udepur** Gujarat India
178 H9 **Chhuikhadan** Chhattisgarh India
179 L6 **Chhukha** Bhutan
158 G7 **Chi, Mae Nam** r. Thai.
143 F4 **Chiador** Brazil
171 M7 **Chiai** Taiwan
163 F10 **Ch'iak-san National Park** S. Korea
93 D5 **Chiamboni** Kenya
71 K4 **Chiampo** Italy
71 K5 **Chiampo** r. Italy
72 H1 **Chianciano Terme** Italy
158 D5 **Chiang Dao** Thai.
91 B8 **Chiange** Angola
158 E5 **Chiang Kham** Thai.
158 E6 **Chiang Khan** Thai.
158 D5 **Chiang Mai** Thai.
158 D5 **Chiang Rai** Thai.
158 E4 **Chiang Saen** Thai.
72 I2 **Chiani** r. Italy
71 J8 **Chianni** Italy
127 M9 **Chiapa** Mex.
129 N9 **Chiapas** state Mex.
127 M9 **Chiapilla** Mex.
74 H9 **Chiaramonte Gulfi** Sicilia Italy
72 B6 **Chiaramonti** Sardegna Italy
71 O8 **Chiaravalle** Italy
75 K6 **Chiaravalle Centrale** Italy
70 H4 **Chiari** Italy
73 Q7 **Chiaromonte** Italy
71 O3 **Chiarso** r. Italy
71 M9 **Chiascio** r. Italy
70 G4 **Chiasso** Italy
191 E3 **Chiat'ura** Georgia
129 I6 **Chiautempan** Mex.
129 I7 **Chiautla** Mex.
129 I6 **Chiautzingo** Mex.
70 G7 **Chiavari** Italy
70 H5 **Chiavenna** r. Italy
70 G3 **Chiavenno** Italy
167 L4 **Chiba** Japan
167 L5 **Chiba** pref. Japan
95 G4 **Chibabava** Moz.
164 □1 **Chibana** Okinawa Japan
91 B8 **Chibemba** Angola
171 I4 **Chibi** Hubei China
Chibi Zimbabwe see **Chivi**
91 B8 **Chibia** Angola
172 H1 **Chibit** Rus. Fed.
95 G4 **Chiboma** Moz.
108 F3 **Chibougamau** Que. Can.
108 F3 **Chibougamau** r. Que. Can.
108 F3 **Chibougamau, Lac** l. Que. Can.
165 K10 **Chibu** Japan
165 K11 **Chiburi-jima** i. Japan
166 G3 **Chibu-Sangaku National Park** Japan
95 G5 **Chibuto** Moz.
91 F8 **Chibwe** Zambia
146 E2 **Chica, Sierra** mts Arg.
110 G8 **Chicago** IL U.S.A.
110 G8 **Chicago Heights** IL U.S.A.
110 G8 **Chicago O'Hare** airport IL U.S.A.
91 C8 **Chicala** Bié Angola
91 C7 **Chicala** Moxico Angola
95 G3 **Chicamba** Moz.
91 D6 **Chicapa** r. Angola
129 I4 **Chicayan** Mex.
129 I3 **Chicayán** r. Mex.
109 H3 **Chic-Chocs, Monts** mts Que. Can.
109 H3 **Chic-Chocs, Réserve Faunique des** nature res. Que. Can.
77 M5 **Chicera Hamba** hill Romania
84 C5 **Chicha** well Chad
106 B3 **Chichagof** AK U.S.A.
104 E4 **Chichagof Island** AK U.S.A.
185 K8 **Chichak** r. Pak.
86 C3 **Chichaoua** Morocco
138 D5 **Chichas, Cordillera de** mts Bol.
39 K8 **Chiché** France
169 N6 **Chicheng** Hebei China
127 O7 **Chichén Itzá** tourist site Mex.
31 K6 **Chichester** West Sussex, England U.K.
208 E7 **Chichester Range** mts W.A. Austr.
178 H9 **Chichgarh** Mahar. India
167 J4 **Chichibu** Japan
167 J3 **Chichibu-gawa** r. Japan
167 I4 **Chichibu-Tama National Park** Japan
129 K9 **Chichicapan** Mex.
129 H8 **Chichihualco** Mex.
165 □2 **Chichi-jima** i. Ogasawara-shotō Japan
165 □2 **Chichijima-rettō** is Ogasawara-shotō Japan
146 D6 **Chichinales** Arg.
136 D2 **Chichiriviche** Venez.
178 F9 **Chicholi** Madh. Prad. India
116 I11 **Chickahominy** r. VA U.S.A.
115 E8 **Chickamauga Lake** TN U.S.A.
121 K10 **Chickasawhay** r. MS U.S.A.
121 G8 **Chickasha** OK U.S.A.
30 G6 **Chickerell** Dorset, England U.K.
147 G4 **Chiclana** Arg.
64 G8 **Chiclana de la Frontera** Spain
136 B6 **Chiclayo** Peru
147 G6 **Chico** r. Arg.
145 C6 **Chico** r. Arg.
145 C8 **Chico** r. Arg.
145 D7 **Chico** r. Arg.
128 D3 **Chico** r. Mex.
124 K2 **Chico** CA U.S.A.
95 G2 **Chicoa** Moz.
Chicobea i. Fiji see **Cikobia**
111 P1 **Chicobi, Lac** l. Que. Can.
91 B8 **Chicomba** Angola
95 G5 **Chicomo** Moz.
127 M10 **Chicomucelo** Mex.
129 I4 **Chiconamel** Mex.
99 □3b **Chiconi** Mayotte
93 B8 **Chiconono** Moz.
129 I4 **Chicontepec** Mex.
117 M6 **Chicopee** MA U.S.A.
154 C3 **Chico Sapocoy, Mount** Luzon Phil.
99 □1c **Chicots, Plaine des** hills Réunion
109 G3 **Chicoutimi** Que. Can.
109 G3 **Chicoutimi** r. Que. Can.
95 F4 **Chicualacuala** Moz.
91 B8 **Chicuma** Angola
91 C8 **Chicupo** Angola
176 F7 **Chidambaram** Tamil Nadu India
31 K5 **Chiddingfold** Surrey, England U.K.
95 G5 **Chidenguele** Moz.
105 L3 **Chidley, Cape** Nfld and Lab./Nunavut Can.
163 E11 **Chido** S. Korea
91 C9 **Chiede** Angola
115 F11 **Chiefland** FL U.S.A.
94 D3 **Chief's Island** Botswana
53 M6 **Chiemgauer Alpen** mts Ger.
53 N6 **Chieming** Ger.
53 M6 **Chiemsee** l. Ger.
71 L2 **Chienes** Italy
91 F7 **Chiengi** Zambia
Chiengmai Thai. see Chiang Mai
71 P9 **Chienti** r. Italy
159 D10 **Chieo Lan Reservoir** Thai.
70 D5 **Chieri** Italy
37 J4 **Chiers** r. France
70 H3 **Chiesa in Valmalenco** Italy
57 L4 **Chieșd** Romania
71 I5 **Chiese** r. Italy
73 M3 **Chieti** Italy
73 M3 **Chieti** prov. Italy
73 O4 **Chieuti** Italy
31 J5 **Chieveley** West Berkshire, England U.K.
45 E7 **Chièvres** Belgium
169 P5 **Chifeng** Nei Mongol China
143 G2 **Chifre, Serra do** mts Brazil
95 G2 **Chifunde** Moz.
183 O5 **Chiganak** Kazakh.
167 J5 **Chigasaki** Japan
Chigil, Ostrov i. Azer. see Çigil Adası
104 C4 **Chiginagak Volcano, Mount** AK U.S.A.
17 T2 **Chigla** r. Rus. Fed.
129 I6 **Chignahuapán** Mex.
109 H4 **Chignecto Bay** N.B./N.S. Can.
109 H4 **Chignecto Game Sanctuary** nature res. N.S. Can.
104 C4 **Chignik** AK U.S.A.
40 I5 **Chignin** France
136 B3 **Chigorodó** Col.
173 J12 **Chigu** Xizang China
146 B2 **Chigualoco** Chile
138 D5 **Chiguana** Bol.
95 G4 **Chigubo** Moz.
173 J12 **Chigu Co** l. China
31 M4 **Chigwell** Essex, England U.K.
126 F3 **Chihuahua** Mex.
126 F3 **Chihuahua** state Mex.
146 C6 **Chihuido Medio** mt. Arg.
183 L5 **Chiili** Kazakh.
168 E6 **Chijinpu** Gansu China
191 G4 **Chikaani** Georgia
178 F9 **Chikalda** Mahar. India
170 H8 **Chikan** Guangdong China
121 G7 **Chikaskia** r. KS U.S.A.
176 E6 **Chik Ballapur** Karnataka India
18 M4 **Chikhachevo** Rus. Fed.
178 G8 **Chikhali Kalan Parasia** Madh. Prad. India
178 F9 **Chikhli** Mahar. India
Chikishlyar Turkm. see Chekishlyar
176 D6 **Chikmagalur** Karnataka India
176 D4 **Chikodi** Karnataka India
176 D4 **Chikodi Road** Karnataka India
191 E2 **Chikola** Rus. Fed.
91 F8 **Chikonkomene** Zambia
168 J1 **Chikoy** Rus. Fed.
169 J1 **Chikoy** r. Rus. Fed.
165 H13 **Chikugo** Japan
167 I1 **Chikuma-gawa** r. Japan
167 K6 **Chikura** Japan
165 H13 **Chikushino** Japan
93 B7 **Chikwa** Zambia
93 B8 **Chikwawa** Malawi
164 S4 **Chikyū-misaki** pt Japan
91 B8 **Chila** Angola
129 J8 **Chila** Mex.
129 I3 **Chila, Laguna** l. Mex.
91 F8 **Chilanga** Zambia
106 F4 **Chilanko** r. B.C. Can.
106 E4 **Chilanko Forks** B.C. Can.
129 H8 **Chilapa** Guerrero Mex.
129 J8 **Chilapa** Oaxaca Mex.
178 E2 **Chilas** Jammu and Kashmir
176 F9 **Chilaw** Sri Lanka
138 A3 **Chilca** Peru
138 C4 **Chilcaya** Chile
67 E8 **Chilches** Spain
30 G5 **Chilcompton** Somerset, England U.K.
106 F5 **Chilcotin** r. B.C. Can.
207 M4 **Chilcott Island** Coral Sea Is Terr. Austr.
207 N8 **Childers** Qld Austr.
121 E8 **Childress** TX U.S.A.
31 J4 **Childrey** Oxfordshire, England U.K.
145 B7 **Chile** country S. America
217 N8 **Chile Basin** sea feature S. Pacific Ocean
145 C7 **Chile Chico** Chile
144 D3 **Chilecito** La Rioja Arg.
146 C3 **Chilecito** Mendoza Arg.
91 B8 **Chilengue, Serra do** mts Angola
217 N8 **Chile Rise** sea feature S. Pacific Ocean
138 A1 **Chilete** Peru
15 I7 **Chilgir** Rus. Fed.
31 N5 **Chilham** Kent, England U.K.
116 D12 **Chilhowie** VA U.S.A.
77 R5 **Chilia Veche** Romania
91 D8 **Chiliba** Angola
136 B2 **Chilibre** Panama
183 R6 **Chilik** Kazakh.
183 R6 **Chilik** r. Kazakh.
177 I3 **Chilika Lake** India
91 E8 **Chililabombwe** Zambia
Chilimanzi Zimbabwe see Chirumanzu
78 D5 **Chiliomodi** Greece
106 C3 **Chilkat** r. Can./U.S.A.
106 F4 **Chilko** r. B.C. Can.
106 E5 **Chilko Lake** B.C. Can.
104 E4 **Chilkoot Trail National Historic Site** nat. park AK U.S.A.
207 J4 **Chillagoe** Qld Austr.
146 A5 **Chillán** Chile
146 A5 **Chillán** r. Chile
146 B5 **Chillán, Nevado** mts Chile
146 B5 **Chillán, Volcán** vol. Chile
147 H5 **Chillar** Arg.
36 D7 **Chilleurs-aux-Bois** France
110 E9 **Chillicothe** IL U.S.A.
120 I6 **Chillicothe** MO U.S.A.
116 C9 **Chillicothe** OH U.S.A.
138 C4 **Chilliculco** Peru
178 E1 **Chillinji** Jammu and Kashmir
106 F5 **Chilliwack** B.C. Can.
65 J3 **Chillón** Spain
65 M4 **Chilluévar** Spain
118 B7 **Chillum** MD U.S.A.
184 F1 **Chil'mamedkum, Peski** des. Turkm.
179 L7 **Chilmari** Bangl.
178 D6 **Chilo** Rajasthan India
145 B6 **Chiloé, Isla de** i. Chile
Chiloé, Isla Grande de i. Chile see **Chiloé, Isla de**
63 N7 **Chiloeches** Spain
91 D8 **Chilombo** Angola
93 A8 **Chilonga** Zambia
122 D5 **Chiloquin** OR U.S.A.
129 H8 **Chilpancingo** Mex.
178 H8 **Chilpi** Chhattisgarh India
116 B6 **Chilson** MI U.S.A.
129 K8 **Chiltepec** Mex.
205 K7 **Chiltern** Vic. Austr.
31 K4 **Chiltern Hills** England U.K.
110 F5 **Chilton** WI U.S.A.
91 D7 **Chiluage** Angola
91 F7 **Chilubi** Zambia
93 B7 **Chilumba** Malawi
171 M6 **Chilung** Taiwan
93 B8 **Chilwa, Lake** Malawi
93 B7 **Chimala** Tanz.
129 M9 **Chimalapa** Mex.
127 N10 **Chimaltenango** Guat.
128 D4 **Chimaltitán** Mex.
126 □T13 **Chimán** Panama
95 G3 **Chimanimani** Zimbabwe
171 □J7 **Chi Ma Wan** H.K. China
45 F8 **Chimay** Belgium
45 F8 **Chimay, Bois de** for. Belgium
93 A7 **Chimba** Zambia
146 B4 **Chimbarongo** Chile
146 C2 **Chimbas** Arg.
Chimbay Uzbek. see **Chimboy**
136 B5 **Chimborazo** mt. Ecuador
138 A2 **Chimbote** Peru
182 H6 **Chimboy** Uzbek.
65 L6 **Chimeneas** Spain
185 P6 **Chimian** Pak.
136 C2 **Chimichaguá** Col.
Chimishliya Moldova see Cimișlia
Chimkent Kazakh. see **Shymkent**
99 □2a **Chimney Rocks** is Inner Islands Seychelles
95 G3 **Chimoio** Moz.
65 J4 **Chimorra** hill Spain
65 J4 **Chimorra, Sierra** mts Spain
146 D6 **Chimpay** Arg.
185 M2 **Chimtargha, Qullai** mt. Tajik.
Chimtorga, Gora mt. Tajik. see **Chimtargha, Qullai**
183 N7 **Chimyon** Uzbek.
158 A4 **Chin** state Myanmar
160 E4 **China** country Asia
127 J5 **China** Mex.
126 G5 **Chinacates** Mex.
127 N9 **Chinajá** Guat.
124 O6 **China Lake** CA U.S.A.
117 □P4 **China Lake** ME U.S.A.
129 M7 **Chinameca** Mex.
129 J4 **Chinampa de Gorostiza** Mex.
70 C6 **Chinanale** Italy
126 □P11 **Chinandega** Nic.
129 M8 **Chinantla** Mex.
124 N9 **China Point** CA U.S.A.
123 L12 **Chinati Peak** TX U.S.A.
Chinaz Uzbek. see **Chinoz**
136 B4 **Chinca** Ecuador
138 A3 **Chincha Alta** Peru
106 G3 **Chinchaga** r. Alta Can.
207 M9 **Chinchilla** Qld Austr.
65 P3 **Chinchilla de Monte Aragón** Spain
176 E4 **Chincholi** Karnataka India
63 N8 **Chinchón** Spain
127 P8 **Chinchorro, Banco** sea feature Mex.
146 B3 **Chincolco** Chile
117 J11 **Chincoteague** VA U.S.A.
117 J11 **Chincoteague Bay** MD/VA U.S.A.
95 H3 **Chinde** Moz.
99 □3a **Chindini** Njazidja Comoros
163 E11 **Chindo** S. Korea
163 E11 **Chin-do** i. S. Korea
40 H5 **Chindrieux** France
170 A2 **Chindu** Qinghai China
158 B4 **Chindwin** r. Myanmar
164 □1 **Chinen** Okinawa Japan
178 E3 **Chineni** Jammu and Kashmir
95 H2 **Chinga** Moz.
136 C3 **Chingaza, Parque Nacional** nat. park Col.
31 L4 **Chingford** Greater London, England U.K.
163 D9 **Chinghwa** N. Korea
182 F2 **Chingirlau** Kazakh.
183 R3 **Chingiz-Tau, Khrebet** mts Kazakh.
Chingleput Tamil Nadu India see **Chengalpattu**
91 E8 **Chingola** Zambia
91 C8 **Chinguanja** Angola
91 C8 **Chinguar** Angola
86 B5 **Chinguețți** Maur.
90 C2 **Chinguil** Chad
163 F11 **Chinhae** S. Korea
95 G2 **Chinhanda** Moz.
95 F3 **Chinhoyi** Zimbabwe
138 C3 **Chiñijo** Bol.
185 O6 **Chiniot** Pak.
126 E4 **Chinipas** Mex.
159 G8 **Chinit, Stœng** r. Cambodia
163 F11 **Chinju** S. Korea
90 D3 **Chinko** r. C.A.R.
125 W5 **Chinle** AZ U.S.A.
125 W5 **Chinle Valley** AZ U.S.A.
125 W5 **Chinle Wash** watercourse AZ U.S.A.
171 L6 **Chinmen** Taiwan
171 L6 **Chinmen Tao** i. Taiwan
176 G5 **Chinna Ganjam** Andhra Prad. India
176 E8 **Chinnamanur** Tamil Nadu India
176 F7 **Chinna Salem** Tamil Nadu India
31 K4 **Chinnor** Oxfordshire, England U.K.
176 F3 **Chinnur** Andhra Prad. India
167 H4 **Chino** Japan
124 O7 **Chino** CA U.S.A.
125 T7 **Chino Creek** watercourse AZ U.S.A.
209 E12 **Chinocup, Lake** salt flat W.A. Austr.
209 E12 **Chinocup Nature Reserve** W.A. Austr.
42 E1 **Chinon** France
122 J2 **Chinook** MT U.S.A.
216 H3 **Chinook Trough** sea feature N. Pacific Ocean
125 T7 **Chino Valley** AZ U.S.A.
183 M7 **Chinoz** Uzbek.
93 B7 **Chinsali** Zambia
176 G3 **Chintalnar** Chhattisgarh India
176 F6 **Chintamani** Karnataka India
77 L4 **Chinteni** Romania
93 B7 **Chintheche** Malawi
129 I3 **Chintón de las Flores** Mex.
136 C2 **Chinú** Col.
45 H9 **Chiny** Belgium
45 H9 **Chiny, Forêt de** for. Belgium
91 D8 **Chinyama Litapi** Zambia
14 K3 **Chin'yavoryk** Rus. Fed.
95 G3 **Chioco** Moz.
71 M5 **Chioggia** Italy
70 B5 **Chiomonte** Italy
93 B6 **Chiona** Tanz.
79 H4 **Chios** Chios Greece
79 G4 **Chios** i. Greece
79 H4 **Chios Strait** Greece
127 N10 **Chipam** Guat.
95 G3 **Chipanga** Moz.
93 B8 **Chipata** Zambia
173 C9 **Chip Chap** r. China/India
145 C6 **Chipchihua, Sierra de** mts Arg.
95 G2 **Chipera** Moz.
91 C8 **Chipeta** Angola
159 H9 **Chiphu** Cambodia
91 F7 **Chipili** Zambia
91 B8 **Chipindo** Angola
169 O8 **Chiping** Shandong China
Chipinga Zimbabwe see Chipinge
95 G4 **Chipinge** Zimbabwe
64 G7 **Chipiona** Spain
115 E10 **Chipley** FL U.S.A.
176 C4 **Chiplun** Mahar. India
109 H4 **Chipman** N.B. Can.
93 C6 **Chipogolo** Tanz.
91 C8 **Chipoia** Angola
30 H5 **Chippenham** Wiltshire, England U.K.
95 G3 **Chipperone, Monte** mt. Moz.
120 H3 **Chippewa** r. MN U.S.A.
110 B5 **Chippewa** r. WI U.S.A.
110 C4 **Chippewa, Lake** WI U.S.A.
110 C5 **Chippewa Falls** WI U.S.A.
31 I3 **Chipping Campden** Gloucestershire, England U.K.
31 I4 **Chipping Norton** Oxfordshire, England U.K.
31 M4 **Chipping Ongar** Essex, England U.K.
30 H4 **Chipping Sodbury** South Gloucestershire, England U.K.
70 D3 **Chippis** Switz.
66 E5 **Chiprana** Spain
77 K7 **Chiprovtsi** Bulg.
91 F8 **Chipundu** Central Zambia
91 F8 **Chipundu** Luapula Zambia
Chipuriro Zimbabwe see **Guruve**
177 H3 **Chipurupalle** Andhra Prad. India
177 H4 **Chipurupalle** Andhra Prad. India
117 □R3 **Chiputneticook Lakes** Can./U.S.A.
138 A2 **Chiquian** Peru
127 O9 **Chiquibul National Park** Belize
127 P7 **Chiquilá** Mex.
128 D5 **Chiquilistlán** Mex.
127 O10 **Chiquimula** Guat.
136 C3 **Chiquinquira** Col.
138 B3 **Chiquintirca** Peru
147 G4 **Chiquita, Mar** l. Arg.
129 H1 **Chiquita, Sierra** mts Mex.
128 F7 **Chiquito** r. Mex.
139 E4 **Chiquitos, Llanos de** plain Bol.
15 H6 **Chir** r. Rus. Fed.
41 C7 **Chirac** France
176 G5 **Chirada** Andhra Prad. India
93 B8 **Chiradzulu** Malawi
191 I4 **Chirag** Rus. Fed.
191 J4 **Chirakhchay** r. Rus. Fed.
176 D7 **Chirakkal** Kerala India
176 G5 **Chirala** Andhra Prad. India
95 G3 **Chiramba** Moz.
136 B3 **Chirambirá, Punta** pt Col.
185 K4 **Chiras** Afgh.
173 B12 **Chirawa** Rajasthan India
30 F2 **Chirbury** Shropshire, England U.K.
183 M7 **Chirchiq** Uzbek.
183 M7 **Chirchiq** r. Uzbek.
95 F4 **Chiredzi** Zimbabwe
92 C1 **Chire Wildlife Reserve** Eth.
84 B4 **Chirfa** Niger
136 E2 **Chirgua** r. Venez.
125 W9 **Chiricahua National Monument** nat. park AZ U.S.A.
125 W10 **Chiricahua Peak** AZ U.S.A.
136 C2 **Chiriguaná** Col.
104 C4 **Chirikof Island** AK U.S.A.
131 J8 **Chirimena** Venez.
136 B6 **Chirinos** Peru
126 □R13 **Chiriquí, Golfo de** b. Panama
126 □R13 **Chiriquí, Laguna de** b. Panama
130 C9 **Chiriquí, Punta** pt Panama
126 □R13 **Chiriquí Grande** Panama
163 E11 **Chiri-san** mt. S. Korea
163 E11 **Chiri-san National Park** S. Korea
65 O5 **Chirivel** Spain
191 G2 **Chiri-Yurt** Rus. Fed.
30 F2 **Chirk** Wrexham, Wales U.K.
26 L11 **Chirnside** Scottish Borders, Scotland U.K.
99 □3b **Chirongui** Mayotte
185 L2 **Chiroqchi** Uzbek.
40 F4 **Chiroubles** France
200 □6 **Chirovanga** Choiseul Solomon Is
77 N8 **Chirpan** Bulg.
126 □R13 **Chirripó, Parque Nacional** nat. park Costa Rica
95 F3 **Chirumanzu** Zimbabwe
95 F3 **Chirundu** Zimbabwe
128 F5 **Chiruntzio** Mex.
184 E8 **Chīrūyeh** Iran
166 F5 **Chiryū** Japan
91 F8 **Chisamba** Zambia
91 E8 **Chisasa** Zambia
108 E2 **Chisasibi** Que. Can.
147 I4 **Chis Chis, Laguna** l. Arg.
127 N10 **Chisec** Guat.
91 E9 **Chisekesi** Zambia
31 I4 **Chiseldon** Swindon, England U.K.
77 O6 **Chiselet** Romania
93 B7 **Chisenga** Malawi
15 K5 **Chishmy** Rus. Fed.
106 H4 **Chisholm** Alta Can.
117 □O4 **Chisholm** ME U.S.A.
110 B2 **Chisholm** MN U.S.A.
185 O7 **Chishtian Mandi** Pak.
170 E4 **Chishui** Guizhou China
170 E5 **Chishuihe** Sichuan China
170 E4 **Chishui He** r. China
Chisimaio Somalia see Kismaayo
16 H6 **Chișinău** Moldova
57 L5 **Chisindia** Romania
77 J4 **Chișineu-Criș** Romania
57 L4 **Chișlaz** Romania
70 D6 **Chisola** r. Italy
70 C6 **Chisone** r. Italy
99 □3b **Chissioua Mbouzi** i. Mayotte
99 □3b **Chissioua Mtsamboro** i. Mayotte
14 J5 **Chistopol'** Rus. Fed.
183 L1 **Chistopol'ye** Kazakh.
183 N1 **Chistyakovskoye** Kazakh.
55 K1 **Chistye-Prudy** Rus. Fed.
138 D5 **Chita** Bol.
136 C3 **Chita** Col.
166 E6 **Chita** Japan
161 J1 **Chita** Rus. Fed.
93 B7 **Chita** Tanz.
184 D6 **Chitab** Iran
91 B9 **Chitado** Angola
166 E6 **Chita-hantō** pen. Japan
Chitaldrug Karnataka India see Chitradurga
178 C7 **Chitalwana** Rajasthan India
93 A8 **Chitambo** Zambia
169 L1 **Chitanga** Rus. Fed.
Chita Oblast admin. div. Rus. Fed. see **Chitinskaya Oblast'**
91 D6 **Chitato** Angola
166 E6 **Chita-wan** b. Japan
14 J3 **Chitayevo** Rus. Fed.
107 J4 **Chitek Lake** Sask. Can.
107 L4 **Chitek Lake** l. Man. Can.
91 C8 **Chitembo** Angola
71 L8 **Chitignano** Italy
162 A3 **Chitinskaya Oblast'** admin. div. Rus. Fed.
93 B7 **Chitipa** Malawi
Chitkul Hima. Prad. India see Chhitkul
95 G4 **Chitobe** Moz.
91 D8 **Chitokoloki** Zambia
91 E9 **Chitongo** Zambia
Chitor Rajasthan India see Chittaurgarh
164 S4 **Chitose** Japan
176 E5 **Chitradurga** Karnataka India
178 H7 **Chitrakoot** Uttar Prad. India
185 N4 **Chitral** Pak.
185 N4 **Chitral** r. Pak.
176 F5 **Chitravati** r. India
126 □S14 **Chitré** Panama
178 C8 **Chitrod** Gujarat India
179 M8 **Chittagong** Bangl.
179 M8 **Chittagong** admin. div. Bangl.
179 K8 **Chittaranjan** W. Bengal India
178 E7 **Chittaurgarh** Rajasthan India
176 F6 **Chittoor** Andhra Prad. India
Chittorgarh Rajasthan India see **Chittaurgarh**
176 E7 **Chittur** Kerala India
93 B8 **Chitungulu** Zambia
95 F3 **Chitungwiza** Zimbabwe
93 C7 **Chiulezi** r. Moz.
91 D8 **Chiume** Angola
95 H2 **Chiúre Novo** Moz.
70 H3 **Chiuro** Italy
71 L2 **Chiusa** Italy
70 D7 **Chiusa di Pesio** Italy
71 O3 **Chiusaforte** Italy
74 E8 **Chiusa Sclafani** Sicilia Italy
70 D8 **Chiusavecchia** Italy
72 G1 **Chiusdino** Italy
70 D5 **Chiusella** r. Italy
72 H1 **Chiusi** Italy
72 H1 **Chiusi, Lago di** l. Italy
71 L8 **Chiusi della Verna** Italy
95 G2 **Chiúta** Moz.
67 D9 **Chiva** Spain
70 D5 **Chivasso** Italy
126 D4 **Chívato, Punta** pt Mex.
138 C3 **Chivay** Peru
138 C3 **Chive** Bol.
91 C8 **Chiveio** Angola
129 M9 **Chivela** Mex.
95 F3 **Chivhu** Zimbabwe
95 F4 **Chivi** Zimbabwe
147 G4 **Chivilcoy** Arg.
171 I8 **Chixi** Guangdong China
Chiyirchik, Pereval pass Kyrg. see **Chyyyrchyk Ashuusu**
167 J3 **Chiyoda** Gunma Japan
167 L3 **Chiyoda** Ibaraki Japan
167 K3 **Chiyogawa** Japan
95 E3 **Chizarira Hills** Zimbabwe
95 E3 **Chizarira National Park** Zimbabwe
42 D3 **Chizé** France
14 I2 **Chizha** Rus. Fed.
182 C2 **Chizha Vtoraya** Kazakh.
171 K3 **Chizhou** Anhui China
165 L11 **Chizu** Japan
17 N6 **Chkalove** Ukr.
183 N1 **Chkalovo** Kazakh.
14 H4 **Chkalovsk** Rus. Fed.
17 P4 **Chkalovs'ke** Ukr.
162 H6 **Chkalovskoye** Rus. Fed.
191 D3 **Ch'khari** Georgia
57 G2 **Chlebičov** Czech Rep.
57 I2 **Chlebnice** Slovakia
54 C3 **Chlebowo** Pol.
Chlef Alg. see **Ech Chélif**
55 I4 **Chlewiska** Pol.
57 K3 **Chlmec** r. Slovakia
55 K6 **Chłopice** Pol.
125 R6 **Chloride** AZ U.S.A.
54 E3 **Chludowo** Pol.
53 O2 **Chlumčany** Czech Rep.
56 C1 **Chlumec** Czech Rep.
56 E1 **Chlumec nad Cidlinou** Czech Rep.
56 D3 **Chlum u Třeboně** Czech Rep.
162 L2 **Chlya, Ozero** l. Rus. Fed.
57 H2 **Chmeľová** hill Slovakia
55 I5 **Chmielnik** Pol.
54 E2 **Chmielno** Pol.
55 K4 **Chmiel Pierwszy** Pol.
156 □ **Choa Chu Kang** Sing.
156 □ **Choa Chu Kang** hill Sing.
159 G7 **Chŏâm Khsant** Cambodia
146 B2 **Choapa** Chile
146 B2 **Choapa** r. Chile
94 E3 **Chobe** admin. dist. Botswana
94 E3 **Chobe National Park** Botswana
54 E4 **Chobienia** Pol.
54 D3 **Chobienice** Pol.
158 G4 **Chô Bo** Vietnam
129 J6 **Chocamán** Mex.
131 □3 **Choc Bay** St Lucia
56 F1 **Choceň** Czech Rep.
55 H3 **Choceń** Pol.
163 E10 **Choch'iwŏn** S. Korea
57 G3 **Chocholná-Velčice** Slovakia
158 G4 **Chơ Chu** Vietnam
54 D4 **Chocianów** Pol.
54 D2 **Chociwel** Pol.
136 B3 **Choco** dept Col.
125 Q8 **Chocolate Mountains** AZ/CA U.S.A.
136 C3 **Chocontá** Col.
115 D10 **Choctawhatchee** r. FL U.S.A.
54 F4 **Chocz** Pol.
54 F1 **Choczewo** Pol.
176 G4 **Chodavaram** Andhra Prad. India
55 H3 **Chodecz** Pol.
55 K4 **Chodel** Pol.
55 J4 **Chodelka** r. Pol.
163 D9 **Cho-do** i. N. Korea
56 B1 **Chodov** Czech Rep.
56 B2 **Chodová Planá** Czech Rep.
55 K3 **Chodów** Mazowieckie Pol.
55 H3 **Chodów** Wielkopolskie Pol.
172 I1 **Chodro** Rus. Fed.
54 E3 **Chodzież** Pol.
146 E6 **Choele Choel** Arg.
146 E6 **Choele Choel Grande, Isla** i. Arg.
95 F2 **Chofombo** Moz.
167 K4 **Chōfu** Japan
184 D7 **Choghādak** Iran
184 E7 **Choghān** Iran
178 E2 **Chogo Lungma Glacier** Jammu and Kashmir
Chogori Feng mt. China/Jammu and Kashmir see **K2**
15 I7 **Chograyskoye Vodokhranilishche** resr Rus. Fed.
107 J4 **Choiceland** Sask. Can.
147 F6 **Choique** Arg.
200 □6 **Choiseul** i. Solomon Is
131 □3 **Choiseul** St Lucia
145 F8 **Choiseul Sound** sea chan. Falkland Is
40 I5 **Choisy** France
126 E4 **Choix** Mex.
54 C3 **Chojna** Pol.
54 F2 **Chojnice** Pol.
54 D4 **Chojnów** Pol.
16 A1 **Chojnowski Park Krajobrazowy** Pol.
164 R7 **Chōkai-san** vol. Japan
92 C2 **Ch'ok'ē** mts Eth.
191 D3 **Ch'okhatauri** Georgia
183 P6 **Chokpar** Kazakh.
183 Q6 **Chok-Tal** Kyrg.
Chokue Moz. see **Chókwé**
193 P2 **Chokurdakh** Rus. Fed.
95 G5 **Chókwé** Moz.
170 B3 **Cho La** pass Sichuan China
124 L6 **Cholame** CA U.S.A.
124 L6 **Cholame Creek** r. CA U.S.A.
170 B2 **Chola Shan** mts Sichuan China
146 A6 **Cholchol** Chile
42 C1 **Cholet** France
146 A5 **Cholguán** Chile
126 □P10 **Choloma** Hond.
183 P6 **Cholpon** Kyrg.
183 Q6 **Cholpon-Ata** Kyrg.
31 J4 **Cholsey** Oxfordshire, England U.K.
129 I6 **Cholula** Mex.
126 □P11 **Choluteca** Hond.
91 E9 **Choma** Zambia
163 F10 **Chŏmch'ŏn** S. Korea
41 D6 **Chomelix** France
41 F7 **Chomérac** France
173 I12 **Chomo Ganggar** mt. Xizang China
158 G4 **Chơ Moi** Vietnam
179 L6 **Chomo Lhari** mt. Bhutan
158 D5 **Chom Thong** Thai.
178 E6 **Chomun** Rajasthan India
56 C1 **Chomutov** Czech Rep.
56 C1 **Chomutovka** r. Czech Rep.
193 L3 **Chona** r. Rus. Fed.
167 L5 **Chōnan** Japan
163 E10 **Ch'ŏnan** S. Korea
159 E8 **Chon Buri** Thai.
145 B6 **Chonchi** Chile
136 A5 **Chone** Ecuador
163 D9 **Ch'ŏngch'ŏn-gang** r. N. Korea
163 F11 **Ch'ongdo** S. Korea
165 G11 **Chŏngja** S. Korea
163 F8 **Ch'ŏngjin** N. Korea
163 D9 **Chŏngju** N. Korea
163 E10 **Ch'ŏngju** S. Korea
159 F8 **Chŏng Kal** Cambodia
169 N6 **Chongli** Hebei China
171 M3 **Chongming** Shanghai China
171 M3 **Chongming Dao** i. China
91 B8 **Chongoroi** Angola
163 E9 **Chŏngp'yŏng** N. Korea
170 F4 **Chongqing** Chongqing China
Chongqing Sichuan China see Chongzhou
170 F3 **Chongqing** mun. China
171 J5 **Chongren** Jiangxi China
163 E11 **Chŏngŭp** S. Korea
91 F8 **Chongwe** Zambia
171 J4 **Chongyang** Hubei China
171 L5 **Chongyang Xi** r. China
171 J6 **Chongyi** Jiangxi China
170 D3 **Chongzhou** Sichuan China
170 F7 **Chongzuo** Guangxi China
17 N7 **Chonhar, Pivostriv** pen. Ukr.
163 E11 **Chŏnju** S. Korea
169 N4 **Chonogol** Mongolia
129 N8 **Chontalpa** Mex.
159 H9 **Chơn Thanh** Vietnam
179 K5 **Cho Oyu** mt. China/Nepal
37 I3 **Chooz** France
16 B5 **Chop** Ukr.

Chopan to Clowne
250

179 I7 Chopan Uttar Prad. India
178 E9 Chopda Mahar. India
141 B8 Chopimzinho Brazil
16 H3 Chopovychi Ukr.
117 I10 Choptank r. MD U.S.A.
184 C6 Choqāy Zanbil tourist site Iran
138 D4 Choquecamata Bol.
185 M9 Chor Pak.
78 C5 Chora Greece
188 C5 Chora tourist site Greece
79 H5 Chorá tourist site Greece
41 I7 Chorges France
65 K2 Chorito, Sierra del mts Spain
29 L6 Chorley Lancashire, England U.K.
31 K4 Chorleywood Hertfordshire, England U.K.
16 I6 Chorna Ukr.
17 M9 Chorna r. Ukr.
16 D5 Chorna Tysa Ukr.
16 E1 Chornaye, Vozyera l. Belarus
55 M5 Chorniyiv Ukr.
17 L4 Chornobay Ukr.
16 J2 Chornobyl' Ukr.
57 L3 Chornoholova Ukr.
17 J7 Chornomors'ke Odes'ka Oblast' Ukr.
15 F7 Chornomors'ke Respublika Krym Ukr.
17 K7 Chornomors'kyy Zapovidnyk nature res. Ukr.
16 I4 Chornorudka Ukr.
17 L3 Chornukhy Ukr.
17 J5 Chornyy Tashlyk r. Ukr.
191 C4 Chorokhi r. Georgia/Turkey
55 K2 Choroszcz Pol.
207 I7 Chorregon Qld Austr.
140 F4 Chorrochó Brazil
16 E4 Chortkiv Ukr.
185 L3 Chorvoq Uzbek.
183 M7 Chorvoq suv ombori resr Kazakh./Uzbek.
178 C9 Chorwad Gujarat India
163 E9 Ch'ŏrwŏn S. Korea
55 I2 Chorzele Pol.
54 G5 Chorzów Pol.
163 D8 Ch'osan N. Korea
167 M4 Chōshi Japan
145 B5 Choshuenco, Volcán vol. Chile
138 A2 Chosica Peru
146 B5 Chos Malal Arg.
146 D3 Chosmes Arg.
54 D2 Choszczno Pol.
136 B6 Chota Peru
179 I8 Chota Nagpur reg. Chhattisgarh India
57 K2 Chotča Slovakia
122 H3 Choteau MT U.S.A.
56 E2 Chotěboř Czech Rep.
53 O2 Chotěšov Czech Rep.
185 N7 Choti Pak.
178 C8 Chotila Gujarat India
57 H4 Chotín Slovakia
99 □3a Choua-chandroudé i. Comoros
86 D4 Chouikhia well Alg.
36 H5 Chouilly France
86 B5 Choûm Maur.
64 C2 Chouto Port.
39 N6 Chouzy-sur-Cisse France
124 L4 Chowchilla CA U.S.A.
176 D7 Chowghat Kerala India
204 H5 Chowilla Regional Reserve nature res. S.A. Austr.
106 G4 Chown, Mount Alta Can.
144 D3 Choya Arg.
183 V2 Choya Rus. Fed.
169 N3 Choybalsan Mongolia
40 H2 Choye France
169 K3 Choyr Mongolia
62 I3 Chozas de Abajo Spain
93 B7 Chozi Zambia
56 E2 Chrast Czech Rep.
56 C2 Chrást Czech Rep.
56 D1 Chrastava Czech Rep.
86 B5 Chreïrîk well Maur.
51 J9 Chřibská Czech Rep.
56 G2 Chřiby hills Czech Rep.
120 L6 Chrisman IL U.S.A.
97 O2 Chrissiesmeer S. Africa
203 G10 Christchurch South I. N.Z.
31 I6 Christchurch Dorset, England U.K.
105 L2 Christian, Cape Nunavut Can.
130 □ Christiana Jamaica
97 J3 Christiana S. Africa
118 D5 Christiana PA U.S.A.
111 N5 Christian Island Ont. Can.
116 E11 Christiansburg VA U.S.A.
22 F6 Christiansfeld Denmark
Christianshåb Greenland see Qasigiannguit
23 L6 Christiansø i. Denmark
106 C4 Christian Sound sea chan. AK U.S.A.
131 K5 Christiansted Virgin Is (U.S.A.)
110 D5 Christie WI U.S.A.
107 I2 Christie Bay N.W.T. Can.
107 I3 Christina r. Alta Can.
203 C11 Christina, Mount South I. N.Z.
29 L7 Christleton Cheshire, England U.K.
208 H5 Christmas Creek W.A. Austr.
208 H5 Christmas Creek r. W.A. Austr.
208 □1 Christmas Island terr. Indian Ocean
Christmas Island atoll Kiribati see Kiritimati
29 N2 Christon Bank Northumberland, England U.K.
209 I8 Christopher, Lake salt flat W.A. Austr.
79 H5 Christos Ikaria Greece
56 E2 Chrudim Czech Rep.
55 H3 Chruślin Pol.
79 G8 Chrysi i. Greece
190 A3 Chrysochou Bay Cyprus
Chrysochous, Kolpos b. Cyprus see Chrysochou Bay
78 F2 Chrysoupoli Greece
28 I2 Chryston North Lanarkshire, Scotland U.K.
55 H5 Chrzanów Pol.
54 F4 Chrząstowa Wielka Pol.
54 G5 Chrząstowice Pol.
54 E3 Chrzypsko Wielkie Pol.
183 L5 Chu r. Kazakh.
179 L8 Chuadanga Bangl.
171 M3 Chuansha Shanghai China
170 B4 Chubalung Sichuan China
17 P6 Chubarivka Ukr.
19 T6 Chubarovo Rus. Fed.
Chubartau Kazakh. see Barshatas
122 H5 Chubbuck ID U.S.A.
17 R7 Chuburka r. Rus. Fed.
145 C6 Chubut prov. Arg.
145 D6 Chubut r. Arg.
168 F9 Chubxi Qinghai China
128 F6 Chucándiro Mex.
57 H2 Chuchelná Czech Rep.
15 H5 Chuchkovo Rus. Fed.
125 Q8 Chuckwalla Mountains CA U.S.A.
147 E3 Chucul Arg.
146 D2 Chucuma Arg.
126 □U13 Chucunaque r. Panama
30 E6 Chudleigh Devon, England U.K.
16 H3 Chudniv Ukr.
54 G5 Chudoba Pol.
19 O2 Chudovo Rus. Fed.
18 J9 Chudzin Belarus
104 D3 Chugach Mountains AK U.S.A.
165 J12 Chūgoku-sanchi mts Japan
Chuguyev Ukr. see Chuhuyiv
162 H6 Chuguyevka Rus. Fed.
122 L6 Chugwater WY U.S.A.
17 P4 Chuhuyiv Ukr.
183 P5 Chu-Iliyskiye Gory mts Kazakh.
170 B4 Chuka Xizang China
Chukai Malaysia see Cukai
162 J2 Chukchagirskoye, Ozero l. Rus. Fed.
Chukchi Peninsula Rus. Fed. see Chukotskiy Poluostrov
218 M1 Chukchi Plateau sea feature Arctic Ocean
104 A3 Chukchi Sea Rus. Fed./U.S.A.
14 H4 Chukhloma Rus. Fed.
193 T3 Chukotskiy, Mys c. Rus. Fed.
193 T3 Chukotskiy Poluostrov pen. Rus. Fed.
17 L7 Chulakivka Ukr.
158 E6 Chulaphon Reservoir Thai.
14 I2 Chulasa Rus. Fed.
124 O9 Chula Vista CA U.S.A.
67 D8 Chulilla Spain
19 T8 Chulkovo Rus. Fed.
30 E6 Chulmleigh Devon, England U.K.
138 C6 Chulo Chile
136 A6 Chulucanas Peru
185 Q4 Chulung Pass Pak.
168 G2 Chuluut Gol r. Mongolia
192 J4 Chulym Rus. Fed.
172 H1 Chulyshman r. Rus. Fed.
14 M2 Chum Rus. Fed.
138 C3 Chuma Bol.
17 N6 Chumaky Ukr.
178 G3 Chumar Jammu and Kashmir
92 C3 Chumba Eth.
144 D3 Chumbicha Arg.
170 A2 Chumda Qinghai China
183 U3 Chumek Kazakh.
77 N8 Chumerna mt. Bulg.
162 I1 Chumikan Rus. Fed.
191 G4 Ch'umlaqi Georgia
158 F6 Chum Phae Thai.
159 D9 Chumphon Thai.
158 E7 Chum Saeng Thai.
146 E2 Chuña Arg.
193 K4 Chuna r. Rus. Fed.
147 E1 Chuña Huasi Arg.
171 L4 Chun'an Zhejiang China
20 V3 Chuna-Tundra plain Rus. Fed.
163 E10 Ch'unch'ŏn S. Korea
179 L8 Chunchura W. Bengal India
183 R6 Chundzha Kazakh.
91 E8 Chunga Zambia
Chung-hua Jen-min Kung-ho-kuo country Asia see China
163 E10 Ch'ungju S. Korea
Chungking Chongqing China see Chongqing
163 D9 Chŭngsan N. Korea
93 C7 Chungu Tanz.
171 M7 Chungyang Shanmo mts Taiwan
162 G7 Chunhua Jilin China
170 G1 Chunhua Shaanxi China
127 O8 Chunhuhux Mex.
Chunxi Jiangsu China see Gaochun
193 K3 Chunya r. Rus. Fed.
93 B7 Chunya Tanz.
Chuosijia Sichuan China see Guanyinqiao
14 F2 Chupa Rus. Fed.
17 N3 Chupakhivka Ukr.
131 □7 Chupara Point Trin. and Tob.
184 B3 Chūplū Iran
16 J4 Chupyra Ukr.
138 C5 Chuquicamata Chile
138 D5 Chuquisaca dept Bol.
Chuqung Qinghai China see Chindu
70 H2 Chur Switz.
179 N7 Churachandpur Manipur India
14 K4 Churaki Rus. Fed.
184 F7 Chūrān Iran
193 O3 Churapcha Rus. Fed.
14 K5 Churayevo Rus. Fed.
31 M3 Church End Essex, England U.K.
28 B4 Church Hill Rep. of Ireland
118 D6 Church Hill MD U.S.A.
116 C12 Church Hill TN U.S.A.
107 M3 Churchill Man. Can.
107 M3 Churchill r. Man. Can.
109 I2 Churchill r. Nfld and Lab. Can.
107 M3 Churchill, Cape Man. Can.
109 I2 Churchill Falls Nfld and Lab. Can.
107 I4 Churchill Lake Sask. Can.
213 K1 Churchill Mountains Antarctica
106 E3 Churchill Peak B.C. Can.
108 E1 Churchill Sound sea chan. Nunavut Can.
29 M7 Church Lawton Cheshire, England U.K.
120 F1 Churchs Ferry ND U.S.A.
30 G2 Church Stretton Shropshire, England U.K.
118 B7 Churchton MD U.S.A.
27 E8 Churchtown Cork Rep. of Ireland
27 F9 Churchtown Cork Rep. of Ireland
118 D4 Churchtown PA U.S.A.
118 C5 Churchville MD U.S.A.
116 F10 Churchville VA U.S.A.
168 B1 Chureg-Tag, Gora mt. Rus. Fed.
179 J6 Churia Ghati Hills Nepal
19 N6 Churilovo Rus. Fed.
138 A2 Churin Peru
191 H3 Churkey Rus. Fed.
191 H3 Churkeyskoye Vodokhranilishche resr Rus. Fed.
106 F5 Churn Creek Provincial Park B.C. Can.
14 I4 Churov Rus. Fed.
17 L1 Churovichi Rus. Fed.
178 E5 Churu Rajasthan India
Churubay Nura Kazakh. see Abay
110 I8 Churubusco IN U.S.A.
136 D2 Churuguara Venez.
164 U4 Chūrui Japan
185 K1 Churuk Uzbek.
128 F7 Churumuco Mex.
70 H2 Churwalden Switz.
17 N7 Churyuk, Ostriv i. Ukr.
159 I8 Chu Sê Vietnam
178 G3 Chushul Jammu and Kashmir
125 W5 Chuska Mountains NM U.S.A.
14 L4 Chusovaya r. Rus. Fed.
14 L4 Chusovoy Rus. Fed.
14 L3 Chusovskoye Rus. Fed.
183 N7 Chust Uzbek.
109 G3 Chute-des-Passes Que. Can.
111 R3 Chute-Rouge Que. Can.
179 N6 Chutia Assam India
17 O4 Chutove Ukr.
171 M6 Chutung Taiwan
200 □4a Chuuk is Micronesia
14 L3 Chuval Rus. Fed.
Chuvashia aut. rep. Rus. Fed. see Chuvashskaya Respublika
Chuvashskaya A.S.S.R. aut. rep. Rus. Fed. see Chuvashskaya Respublika
15 I5 Chuvashskaya Respublika aut. rep. Rus. Fed.
191 I4 Chuvek Rus. Fed.
163 F10 Chuwang-san National Park S. Korea
170 C6 Chuxiong Yunnan China
183 P6 Chüy admin. div. Kyrg.
144 G4 Chuy Uru.
159 I8 Chư Yang Sin mt. Vietnam
Chuyskaya Oblast' admin. div. Kyrg. see Chüy
40 F5 Chuzelles France
167 J2 Chūzenji-ko l. Japan
171 L2 Chuzhou Anhui China
171 L2 Chuzhou Jiangsu China
166 D5 Chūzu Japan
56 D3 Chvalšiny Czech Rep.
189 L6 Chwārtā Iraq
54 G1 Chwaszczyno Pol.
54 G6 Chybie Pol.
16 K6 Chychykliya r. Ukr.
18 M8 Chyhirynskaye Vodaskhovishcha resr Belarus
17 L4 Chyhyryn Ukr.
Chymyshliya Moldova see Cimişlia
16 B5 Chynadiyeve Ukr.
51 J10 Chyňava Czech Rep.
55 J4 Chynów Pol.
55 M2 Chyrvonae Syalo Belarus
18 L9 Chyrvonaya Slabada Belarus
16 G1 Chyrvonaye, Vozyera l. Belarus
17 N9 Chysten'ke Ukr.
17 P8 Chystopillya Ukr.
93 C5 Chyulu Range mts Kenya
183 O7 Chyyyrchyk Ashuusu pass Kyrg.
55 M6 Chyzhykiv Ukr.
76 J5 Ciacova Romania
Ciadâr-Lunga Moldova see Ciadîr-Lunga
16 H7 Ciadîr-Lunga Moldova
43 F9 Ciadoux France
73 P8 Ciagola, Monte mt. Italy
131 □1 Ciales Puerto Rico
72 C4 Ciamannacce Corse France
157 H8 Ciamis Jawa Indon.
73 J4 Ciampino Italy
73 J4 Ciampino airport Italy
74 E8 Cianciana Sicilia Italy
156 G8 Cianjur Jawa Indon.
142 A5 Cianorte Brazil
41 K9 Cians r. France
54 G5 Ciasna Pol.
54 F3 Ciążeń Pol.
156 G8 Cibadak Jawa Indon.
57 J5 Cibakháza Hungary
157 H8 Cibatu Jawa Indon.
125 V7 Cibecue AZ U.S.A.
156 G8 Cibinong Jawa Indon.
93 A5 Cibitoke Burundi
121 G11 Cibolo Creek r. TX U.S.A.
64 C3 Ciborro Port.
156 G8 Ci Buni r. Indon.
126 D2 Cibuta Mex.
126 D2 Cibuta, Sierra mt. Mex.
70 G7 Cicagna Italy
68 D3 Ćićarija mts Croatia
73 N6 Cicciano Italy
188 G4 Çiçekdağı Turkey
190 D2 Çiçekli İçel Turkey
79 J3 Çiçekli Manisa Turkey
73 O7 Cicerale Italy
110 G8 Cicero IL U.S.A.
140 F4 Cícero Dantas Brazil
76 J7 Ćićevac Srbija Serb. and Mont.
54 E4 Cicha Woda r. Pol.
55 L3 Cicibór Duży Pol.
57 G4 Čičov Slovakia
63 Q4 Cidacos r. Spain
156 G8 Cidaun Jawa Indon.
188 F3 Cide Turkey
56 E1 Cidlina r. Czech Rep.
63 O5 Cidones Spain
131 □1 Cidra Puerto Rico
55 I3 Ciechanów Pol.
55 K3 Ciechanowiec Pol.
54 G3 Ciechocinek Pol.
130 D3 Ciego de Ávila Cuba
55 I4 Cielądz Pol.
146 C3 Cielo, Cerro mt. Arg.
156 G8 Ciemas Jawa Indon.
63 M8 Ciempozuelos Spain
136 C2 Ciénaga Col.
136 D2 Ciénagas del Catatumbo nat. park Venez.
127 I5 Ciénega Mex.
128 C1 Cieneguillas Mex.
130 C2 Cienfuegos Cuba
54 F3 Cienin Zaborny Pol.
55 J4 Ciepielów Pol.
54 E5 Ciepłowody Pol.
43 F10 Cier-de-Luchon France
57 G3 Čierna Voda Slovakia
57 K3 Čierna voda r. Slovakia
57 H3 Čierne Kľačany Slovakia
57 I3 Čierny Balog Slovakia
43 F10 Cierp-Gaud France
54 F2 Cierznie Pol.
62 C4 Cíes, Illas is Spain
55 L5 Cieszanów Pol.
54 F4 Cieszków Pol.
54 G6 Cieszyn Śląskie Pol.
54 F4 Cieszyn Wielkopolskie Pol.
43 E9 Cieutat France
42 G4 Cieux France
67 C11 Cieza Spain
55 I6 Ciężkowice Pol.
190 F2 Çiflikköy Turkey
79 M3 Çifteler Turkey
191 C6 Çiftlikköy Erzurum Turkey
79 J1 Çiftlikköy İstanbul Turkey
63 O7 Cifuentes Spain
63 K5 Cigales Spain
57 K3 Cigánd Hungary
191 C6 Çiğdemli Turkey
156 F8 Cigeulis Jawa Indon.
191 K6 Çigil Adası i. Azer.
70 E5 Cigliano Italy
63 M10 Cigüela r. Spain
188 F4 Cihanbeyli Turkey
79 K3 Cihangazi Turkey
128 C6 Cihuatlán Mex.
65 J2 Cijara, Embalse de resr Spain
57 J6 Čik r. Serb. and Mont.
Cikai Yunnan China see Gongshan
157 H8 Cikalong Jawa Indon.
78 A2 Çikes, Maja e mt. Albania
201 □1 Cikobia i. Fiji
68 F4 Čikola r. Croatia
157 H8 Cilacap Jawa Indon.
156 G8 Cilangkahan Jawa Indon.
99 □1c Cilaos Réunion
99 □1c Cilaos, Cirque de vol. crater Réunion
189 K3 Çıldır Turkey
189 K3 Çıldır Gölü l. Turkey
190 F2 Çıldıroba Turkey
157 H8 Ciledug Jawa Indon.
73 O7 Cilento e del Vallo di Diano, Parco Nazionale del nat. park Italy
191 A5 Çilhorozdağı Geçidi pass Turkey
171 H4 Cili Hunan China
190 B2 Cilicia reg. Turkey
Cilician Gates pass Turkey see Gülek Boğazı
77 M7 Cilieni Romania
79 M2 Çilimli Turkey
63 Q7 Cillas Spain
26 B8 Cille Bhrighde Western Isles, Scotland U.K.
62 G8 Cilleros Spain
191 F6 Çilli Geçidi pass Turkey
189 L5 Cilo Dağı mt. Turkey
191 L5 Çiloy Azer.
191 L5 Çiloy Adası i. Azer.
30 E4 Cilybebyll Neath Port Talbot, Wales U.K.
30 E3 Cilycwm Carmarthenshire, Wales U.K.
125 Q6 Cima CA U.S.A.
64 □ Cima, Ilhéu de i. Madeira
156 G8 Cimahi Jawa Indon.
62 I3 Cimanes del Tejar Spain
121 E7 Cimarron KS U.S.A.
123 L8 Cimarron NM U.S.A.
121 G7 Cimarron r. OK U.S.A.
123 L8 Cimarron Creek r. CO U.S.A.
63 Q6 Cimballa Spain
74 F8 Ciminna Sicilia Italy
72 I3 Cimino, Monte mt. Italy
16 H7 Cimişlia Moldova
71 M3 Cimolais Italy
71 J7 Cimone, Monte mt. Italy
Cîmpeni Romania see Câmpeni
Cîmpia Turzii Romania see Câmpia Turzii
Cîmpina Romania see Câmpina
Cîmpulung Romania see Câmpulung
Cîmpulung la Tisa Romania see Câmpulung la Tisa
Cîmpulung Moldovenesc Romania see Câmpulung Moldovenesc
156 F7 Cina, Tanjung c. Indon.
189 J5 Çınar Turkey
79 K2 Çınarcık Turkey
136 E3 Cinaruco r. Venez.
136 E3 Cinaruco-Capanaparo, Parque Nacional nat. park Venez.
66 F3 Cinca r. Spain
66 F5 Cinca r. Spain
68 F4 Cincar mt. Bos.-Herz.
120 M6 Cincinnati OH U.S.A.
117 J6 Cincinnatus NY U.S.A.
130 D3 Cinco-Balas, Cayos is Cuba
65 M2 Cinco Casas Spain
146 C6 Cinco Saltos Arg.
66 C3 Cinco Villas reg. Spain
66 E6 Cinctorres Spain
77 M5 Cincu Romania
130 H8 Cindad Ojeda Venez.
30 H4 Cinderford Gloucestershire, England U.K.
79 J5 Çine Turkey
79 I5 Çine r. Turkey
62 I3 Ciñera Spain
45 H8 Ciney Belgium
62 D6 Cinfães Port.
71 O9 Cingoli Italy
72 G2 Cinigiano Italy
70 G4 Cinisello Balsamo Italy
74 E7 Cinisi Sicilia Italy
57 I3 Cinobaňa Slovakia
39 L7 Cinq-Mars-la-Pile France
75 K7 Cinquefrondi Italy
177 M7 Cinque Island Andaman & Nicobar Is India
70 H7 Cinque Terre reg. Italy
129 N9 Cintalapa Mex.
43 H9 Cintegabelle France
72 B3 Cinto, Monte mt. France
147 F3 Cintra Arg.
98 □1b Cintrão, Ponta do pt São Miguel Azores
37 K8 Cintrey France
63 Q4 Cintruénigo Spain
97 M8 Cintsa S. Africa
142 B5 Cinzas r. Brazil
77 O6 Ciolpani Romania
57 L6 Ciordan, Dealul hill Romania
68 F4 Čiovo i. Croatia
157 H8 Cipatuja Jawa Indon.
140 F4 Cipó Brazil
143 E3 Cipo r. Brazil
146 D6 Cipolletti Arg.
143 F4 Cipotânea Brazil
191 H5 Çıraqdärä Azer.
67 E7 Cirat Spain
156 G8 Cirata, Waduk resr Jawa Indon.
62 I3 Cirbanal mt. Spain
73 N5 Circello Italy
73 K5 Circeo, Monte hill Italy
73 J5 Circeo, Parco Nazionale del nat. park Italy
104 D3 Circle AK U.S.A.
122 L3 Circle MT U.S.A.
116 C9 Circleville OH U.S.A.
125 T3 Circleville UT U.S.A.
157 H8 Cirebon Jawa Indon.
31 I4 Cirencester Gloucestershire, England U.K.
Cirene tourist site Libya see Cyrene
156 D5 Cirenti Sumatera Indon.
37 I7 Cirey-sur-Blaise France
37 M6 Cirey-sur-Vezouze France
63 Q5 Ciria Spain
70 D5 Ciriè Italy
73 Q7 Cirigliano Italy
16 H5 Ciripcău Moldova
18 J5 Cirišs l. Latvia
75 □ Cirkewwa, Il-Ponta tac- pt Malta
75 M5 Cirò Italy
57 K3 Cirocha r. Slovakia
75 M5 Cirò Marina Italy
43 D6 Ciron r. France
109 I1 Cirque Mountain Nfld and Lab. Can.
Cirta Alg. see Constantine
63 M9 Ciruelos Spain
40 E3 Ciry-le-Noble France
70 H7 Cisa, Passo della pass Italy
70 E7 Cisano sul Neva Italy
125 W3 Cisco UT U.S.A.
58 E7 Cismòn r. Italy
55 K6 Cisna Pol.
77 M5 Cisnădie Romania
63 K4 Cisneros Spain
71 M4 Cisòn di Valmarino Italy
57 J1 Cisowsko-Orłowiński Park Krajobrazowy Pol.
39 L8 Cissé France
73 J4 Cisterna di Latina Italy
75 M2 Cisternino Italy
130 E2 Cistern Point Andros Bahamas
63 J3 Cistierna Spain
130 G4 Citadelle Laferrière tourist site Haiti
71 M9 Citerna Italy
129 J4 Citlaltepec Mex.
68 F4 Čitluk Bos.-Herz.
43 J9 Citou France
121 K10 Citronelle AL U.S.A.
96 D8 Citrusdal S. Africa
124 K3 Citrus Heights CA U.S.A.
71 L4 Cittadella Italy
73 P8 Cittadella del Capo c. Italy
72 I2 Città della Pieve Italy
71 M9 Città di Castello Italy
70 D5 Città di Torino airport Italy
73 J3 Cittaducale Italy
75 K7 Cittanova Italy
73 K2 Cittareale Italy
73 M2 Città Sant'Angelo Italy
70 F4 Cittiglio Italy
27 H2 City of Derry airport Northern Ireland U.K.
77 N5 Ciucaş, Vârful mt. Romania
77 K4 Ciucea Romania
127 I3 Ciudad Acuña Mex.
128 G7 Ciudad Altamirano Mex.
137 F2 Ciudad Bolívar Venez.
126 G4 Ciudad Camargo Mex.
126 D5 Ciudad Constitución Mex.
127 N10 Ciudad Cuauhtémoc Mex.
127 N8 Ciudad del Carmen Mex.
139 G6 Ciudad del Este Para.
126 G3 Ciudad Delicias Mex.
129 H3 Ciudad del Maíz Mex.
129 H4 Ciudad de Valles Mex.
137 F2 Ciudad Guayana Venez.
128 D6 Ciudad Guzmán Mex.
128 G6 Ciudad Hidalgo Mex.
129 L9 Ciudad Ixtepec Mex.
126 F2 Ciudad Juárez Mex.
126 H5 Ciudad Lerdo Mex.
129 H6 Ciudad López Mateos Mex.
129 J3 Ciudad Madero Mex.
129 I3 Ciudad Mante Mex.
128 F5 Ciudad Manuel Doblado Mex.
129 J7 Ciudad Mendoza Mex.
127 J4 Ciudad Mier Mex.
126 E4 Ciudad Obregón Mex.
137 F3 Ciudad Piar Venez.
65 L3 Ciudad Real Spain
65 M3 Ciudad Real prov. Spain
127 J5 Ciudad Río Bravo Mex.
62 G7 Ciudad Rodrigo Spain
129 J7 Ciudad Serdán Mex.
127 M10 Ciudad Tecún Uman Guat.
129 H2 Ciudad Victoria Mex.
77 J5 Ciudanoviţa Romania
57 L4 Ciuhoi Romania
16 G6 Ciuhur r. Moldova
16 H6 Ciulucal de Mijloc r. Moldova
77 N4 Ciumani Romania
57 K5 Ciumeghiu Romania
66 □ Ciutadella de Menorca Spain
188 H3 Cıva Burnu pt Turkey
42 F3 Civaux France
71 M3 Civetta, Monte mt. Italy
71 O3 Cividale del Friuli Italy
73 Q8 Civita Italy
73 I3 Civita Castellana Italy
73 K4 Civita d'Antino Italy
71 P9 Civitanova Marche Italy
73 L3 Civitaquana Italy
72 H3 Civitavecchia Italy
72 H2 Civitella, Monte mt. Italy
73 L3 Civitella Casanova Italy
72 I2 Civitella d'Agliano Italy
71 L7 Civitella di Romagna Italy
71 L9 Civitella in Val di Chiana Italy
73 K4 Civitella Roveto Italy
39 P8 Civray Centre France
42 E3 Civray Poitou-Charentes France
79 K4 Çivril Turkey
72 C9 Cixerri r. Sardegna Italy
171 M3 Cixi Zhejiang China
169 N8 Cixian Hebei China
169 O9 Ciyao Shandong China
57 L4 Cizer Romania
Cizhou Hebei China see Cixian
51 J10 Čížkovice Czech Rep.
189 K5 Cizre Turkey
56 C2 Čkyně Czech Rep.
26 C9 Clabhach Argyll and Bute, Scotland U.K.
26 E11 Clachan Argyll and Bute, Scotland U.K.
26 D8 Clachan Highland, Scotland U.K.
122 C4 Clackamas r. OR U.S.A.
26 I10 Clackmannanshire admin. div. Scotland U.K.
31 O4 Clacton-on-Sea Essex, England U.K.
26 F10 Cladich Argyll and Bute, Scotland U.K.
28 B4 Clady Northern Ireland U.K.
27 I3 Clady Northern Ireland U.K.
30 E3 Claerwen Reservoir Wales U.K.
26 E9 Claggan Highland, Scotland U.K.
26 C7 Claidh, Loch inlet Scotland U.K.
42 F2 Clain r. France
43 E7 Clairac France
107 H3 Claire, Lake Alta Can.
122 C6 Clair Engle Lake resr CA U.S.A.
106 G4 Clairmont Alta Can.
36 E5 Clairoix France
43 I7 Clairvaux-d'Aveyron France
40 H3 Clairvaux-les-Lacs France
42 F2 Claise r. France
41 H6 Claix France
40 D2 Clamecy France
110 D3 Clam Lake WI U.S.A.
28 C4 Clanabogan Northern Ireland U.K.
124 O2 Clan Alpine Mountains NV U.S.A.
203 F11 Clandeboye South I. N.Z.
27 I6 Clane Rep. of Ireland
31 I4 Clanfield Oxfordshire, England U.K.
41 K8 Clans France
115 D9 Clanton AL U.S.A.
97 L7 Clanville S. Africa
96 C8 Clanwilliam S. Africa
96 C8 Clanwilliam Dam S. Africa
26 F11 Claonaig Argyll and Bute, Scotland U.K.
31 L3 Clapham Bedfordshire, England U.K.
29 M5 Clapham North Yorkshire, England U.K.
26 H6 Clar, Loch nan l. Scotland U.K.
147 H2 Clara Arg.
207 H5 Clara r. Qld Austr.
27 G6 Clara Rep. of Ireland
145 D6 Clara, Punta pt Arg.
159 C9 Clara Island Myanmar
207 H5 Claraville Qld Austr.
147 H5 Claraz Arg.
29 P7 Clarborough Nottinghamshire, England U.K.
205 I5 Clare N.S.W. Austr.
204 G5 Clare S.A. Austr.
27 E7 Clare county Rep. of Ireland
27 D6 Clare r. Rep. of Ireland
31 N3 Clare Suffolk, England U.K.
110 J6 Clare MI U.S.A.
27 E7 Clarecastle Rep. of Ireland
27 G6 Clareen Rep. of Ireland
27 E6 Claregalway Rep. of Ireland
27 B5 Clare Island Rep. of Ireland
130 □ Claremont Jamaica
117 M5 Claremont NH U.S.A.
207 I2 Claremont Isles Qld Austr.
121 H7 Claremore OK U.S.A.
27 E5 Claremorris Rep. of Ireland
205 N3 Clarence r. N.S.W. Austr.
203 H9 Clarence South I. N.Z.
203 H9 Clarence r. South I. N.Z.
145 C9 Clarence, Isla i. Chile
98 □2a Clarence Bay Ascension S. Atlantic Ocean
212 U2 Clarence Island Antarctica
206 C1 Clarence Strait N.T. Austr.
106 C3 Clarence Strait AK U.S.A.
130 F2 Clarence Town Long I. Bahamas
130 □ Clarendon parish Jamaica
203 E13 Clarendon South I. N.Z.
121 J8 Clarendon AR U.S.A.
116 F7 Clarendon PA U.S.A.
121 E8 Clarendon TX U.S.A.
130 □ Clarendon Park Jamaica
97 M4 Clarens S. Africa
109 K3 Clarenville Nfld and Lab. Can.
106 H5 Claresholm Alta Can.
41 D9 Claret Languedoc-Roussillon France
41 H8 Claret Provence-Alpes-Côte d'Azur France
67 E9 Clariano r. Spain
207 H4 Clarina Creek r. Qld Austr.
120 H5 Clarinda IA U.S.A.
131 K9 Clarines Venez.
116 E9 Clarington OH U.S.A.
120 I4 Clarion IA U.S.A.
116 F7 Clarion PA U.S.A.
116 F7 Clarion r. PA U.S.A.
112 D7 Clarión, Isla i. Mex.
130 G3 Clarion Bank sea feature Bahamas
202 J3 Claris North I. N.Z.
120 G3 Clark SD U.S.A.
106 F1 Clark, Mount N.W.T. Can.
118 B4 Clark Creek r. PA U.S.A.
125 T7 Clarkdale AZ U.S.A.
207 J5 Clarke r. Qld Austr.
97 M7 Clarkebury S. Africa
205 L9 Clarke Island Tas. Austr.
207 K6 Clarke Range mts Qld Austr.
207 J5 Clarke River Qld Austr.
207 H4 Clarkes Creek r. Qld Austr.
109 K3 Clarke's Head Nfld and Lab. Can.
115 F8 Clarkesville GA U.S.A.
122 F2 Clark Fork r. ID U.S.A.
122 F2 Clark Fork r. MT U.S.A.
115 F9 Clark Hill Reservoir GA/SC U.S.A.
125 Q6 Clark Mountain CA U.S.A.
212 O1 Clark Mountains Antarctica
108 D4 Clark Point Ont. Can.
119 G4 Clarksburg NJ U.S.A.
116 E9 Clarksburg WV U.S.A.
121 J8 Clarksdale MS U.S.A.
122 J4 Clark's Fork Yellowstone r. MT U.S.A.
203 E12 Clarks Junction South I. N.Z.
96 I10 Clarkson S. Africa
118 D1 Clarks Summit PA U.S.A.
122 F3 Clarkston WA U.S.A.
130 □ Clark's Town Jamaica
121 I8 Clarksville AR U.S.A.
118 B6 Clarksville MD U.S.A.
115 D7 Clarksville TN U.S.A.
121 H9 Clarksville TX U.S.A.
116 G12 Clarksville VA U.S.A.
142 B1 Claro r. Brazil
142 B3 Claro r. Brazil
70 G3 Claro Switz.
147 G6 Claromecó Arg.
36 F3 Clary France
26 H7 Clashmore Highland, Scotland U.K.
26 F6 Clashnessie Highland, Scotland U.K.
122 C3 Clatskanie OR U.S.A.
26 H12 Clatteringshaws Loch l. Scotland U.K.
121 E8 Claude TX U.S.A.
143 E4 Cláudio Brazil
147 G6 Claudio Molina Arg.
27 H3 Claudy Northern Ireland U.K.
51 H9 Clausnitz Ger.
118 D3 Claussville PA U.S.A.
49 J7 Clausthal-Zellerfeld Ger.
71 N3 Claut Italy
71 N3 Clauzetto Italy
154 C2 Claveria Luzon Phil.
31 M4 Clavering Essex, England U.K.
105 P2 Clavering Ø i. Greenland
30 H2 Claverley Shropshire, England U.K.
45 H8 Clavier Belgium
115 G9 Claxton GA U.S.A.
118 C4 Clay PA U.S.A.
116 D10 Clay WV U.S.A.
117 L4 Clayburg NY U.S.A.
120 G6 Clay Center KS U.S.A.
120 F5 Clay Center NE U.S.A.
116 B11 Clay City KY U.S.A.
29 O7 Clay Cross Derbyshire, England U.K.
31 O3 Claydon Suffolk, England U.K.
36 E6 Claye-Souilly France
28 I5 Clay Head Isle of Man
125 S4 Clayhole Wash watercourse AZ U.S.A.
118 E5 Claymont DE U.S.A.
29 P7 Claypole Lincolnshire, England U.K.
125 V8 Claypool AZ U.S.A.
125 V7 Clay Springs AZ U.S.A.
31 L6 Clayton West Sussex, England U.K.
115 E10 Clayton AL U.S.A.
118 D6 Clayton DE U.S.A.
115 F8 Clayton GA U.S.A.
118 E5 Clayton NJ U.S.A.
121 D7 Clayton NM U.S.A.
117 I4 Clayton NY U.S.A.
121 H8 Clayton OK U.S.A.
117 □P2 Clayton Lake ME U.S.A.
29 M6 Clayton-le-Moors Lancashire, England U.K.
116 E11 Claytor Lake VA U.S.A.
147 H3 Clé r. Arg.
26 D9 Cleadale Highland, Scotland U.K.
29 O4 Cleadon Tyne and Wear, England U.K.
27 C9 Cleady Rep. of Ireland
27 C10 Clear, Cape Rep. of Ireland
116 E10 Clearco WV U.S.A.
111 N7 Clear Creek Ont. Can.
125 U2 Clear Creek UT U.S.A.
125 V7 Clear Creek r. AZ U.S.A.
122 K4 Clear Creek r. WY U.S.A.
116 G7 Clearfield PA U.S.A.
122 H6 Clearfield UT U.S.A.
121 F9 Clear Fork Brazos r. TX U.S.A.
106 G3 Clear Hills Y.T. Can.
27 D10 Clear Island Rep. of Ireland
120 I4 Clear Lake IA U.S.A.
120 G3 Clear Lake SD U.S.A.
110 B4 Clear Lake WI U.S.A.
124 J2 Clear Lake l. CA U.S.A.
125 T2 Clear Lake l. UT U.S.A.
124 J2 Clearlake Oaks CA U.S.A.
122 D6 Clear Lake Reservoir CA U.S.A.
122 K4 Clearmont WY U.S.A.
116 H9 Clear Spring MD U.S.A.
106 G5 Clearwater B.C. Can.
106 H4 Clearwater r. Alta Can.
107 I3 Clearwater r. Alta/Sask. Can.
115 F12 Clearwater FL U.S.A.
122 F3 Clearwater r. ID U.S.A.
120 G2 Clearwater r. MN U.S.A.
107 K4 Clearwater Lake Man. Can.
110 E4 Clearwater Lake WI U.S.A.
107 K4 Clearwater Lake Provincial Park Man. Can.
122 G4 Clearwater Mountains ID U.S.A.
107 I3 Clearwater River Provincial Park Sask. Can.
29 J4 Cleator Moor Cumbria, England U.K.
121 G9 Cleburne TX U.S.A.
39 K4 Clécy France
38 C4 Cléder France
30 G3 Cleehill Shropshire, England U.K.
122 D3 Cle Elum WA U.S.A.
29 Q6 Cleethorpes North East Lincolnshire, England U.K.
37 K7 Clefmont France
38 E6 Cléguer France
38 E5 Cléguérec France
30 G3 Clehonger Herefordshire, England U.K.
77 N6 Clejani Romania
41 H7 Clelles France
45 I9 Clémency Lux.
137 H4 Clément Fr. Guiana
156 □ Clementi Sing.
142 B4 Clementina Brazil
115 F8 Clemson SC U.S.A.
116 D10 Clendenin WV U.S.A.
116 D8 Clendening Lake OH U.S.A.
48 K5 Clenze Ger.
30 H3 Cleobury Mortimer Shropshire, England U.K.
36 B5 Cléon France
118 C4 Cleona PA U.S.A.
41 F7 Cléon-d'Andran France
154 B6 Cleopatra Needle mt. Palawan Phil.
39 L7 Cléré-les-Pins France
36 B4 Clères France
36 H7 Clérey France
Clerf Lux. see Clervaux
111 P1 Cléricy Que. Can.
41 F6 Clérieux France
203 A12 Clerke, Mount South I. N.Z.
208 E4 Clerke Reef W.A. Austr.
40 F4 Clermain France
207 K7 Clermont Qld Austr.
43 G9 Clermont Midi-Pyrénées France
36 D5 Clermont Picardie France
97 O5 Clermont S. Africa
115 G11 Clermont FL U.S.A.
39 K6 Clermont-Créans France
42 F6 Clermont-de-Beauregard France
37 J5 Clermont-en-Argonne France
40 C5 Clermont-Ferrand France
41 C9 Clermont-l'Hérault France
40 J2 Clerval France
45 J8 Clervaux Lux.
45 J9 Clervé r. Lux.
36 E7 Cléry r. France
36 C8 Cléry-St-André France
71 K3 Cles Italy
204 F5 Cleve S.A. Austr.
30 G5 Clevedon North Somerset, England U.K.
115 F8 Cleveland GA U.S.A.
121 J9 Cleveland MS U.S.A.
116 D7 Cleveland OH U.S.A.
115 E8 Cleveland TN U.S.A.
121 H10 Cleveland TX U.S.A.
125 V2 Cleveland UT U.S.A.
116 C12 Cleveland VA U.S.A.
110 G6 Cleveland WI U.S.A.
207 K5 Cleveland, Cape Qld Austr.
122 H2 Cleveland, Mount MT U.S.A.
207 K5 Cleveland Bay Qld Austr.
116 D7 Cleveland Heights OH U.S.A.
29 O5 Cleveland Hills England U.K.
141 B8 Clevelândia Brazil
106 C4 Cleveland Peninsula AK U.S.A.
29 K6 Cleveleys Lancashire, England U.K.
27 C5 Clew Bay Rep. of Ireland
97 N1 Clewer S. Africa
115 G12 Clewiston FL U.S.A.
203 B13 Clifden South I. N.Z.
27 B6 Clifden Rep. of Ireland
206 G4 Cliffdale r. Qld Austr.
31 M5 Cliffe Medway, England U.K.
31 M5 Cliffe Woods Medway, England U.K.
27 F4 Cliffoney Rep. of Ireland
97 L7 Clifford S. Africa
118 D1 Clifford PA U.S.A.
203 I8 Clifford Bay South I. N.Z.
96 A5 Cliff Point S. Africa
116 E10 Clifftop WV U.S.A.
207 M9 Clifton Qld Austr.
115 □2 Clifton New Prov. Bahamas
31 L3 Clifton Bedfordshire, England U.K.
125 W8 Clifton AZ U.S.A.
110 G9 Clifton IL U.S.A.
120 G6 Clifton KS U.S.A.
119 G3 Clifton NJ U.S.A.
118 D2 Clifton PA U.S.A.
207 J4 Clifton Beach Qld Austr.
116 F11 Clifton Forge VA U.S.A.
204 G2 Clifton Hills S.A. Austr.
117 L6 Clifton Park NY U.S.A.
115 □2 Clifton Point New Prov. Bahamas
107 I5 Climax Sask. Can.
110 I7 Climax MI U.S.A.
116 B12 Clinch r. TN U.S.A.
116 C11 Clinchco VA U.S.A.
116 C12 Clinch Mountain mts TN/VA U.S.A.
116 C12 Clinchport VA U.S.A.
106 G4 Cline River Alta Can.
45 F6 Clinge Neth.
49 K8 Clingen Ger.
106 F5 Clinton B.C. Can.
108 D5 Clinton Ont. Can.
203 D13 Clinton South I. N.Z.
121 I8 Clinton AR U.S.A.
119 J2 Clinton CT U.S.A.
114 B5 Clinton IA U.S.A.
120 K5 Clinton IL U.S.A.
121 K7 Clinton KY U.S.A.
121 J10 Clinton LA U.S.A.
117 □P4 Clinton ME U.S.A.
111 K7 Clinton MI U.S.A.
120 I6 Clinton MO U.S.A.
121 J9 Clinton MS U.S.A.
115 H8 Clinton NC U.S.A.
117 J5 Clinton NY U.S.A.
116 D8 Clinton OH U.S.A.
121 F8 Clinton OK U.S.A.
115 E7 Clinton TN U.S.A.
107 J1 Clinton-Colden Lake N.W.T. Can.
110 F5 Clintonville WI U.S.A.
116 E11 Clintonville WV U.S.A.
116 C11 Clintwood VA U.S.A.
115 E10 Clio AL U.S.A.
111 K6 Clio MI U.S.A.
39 N8 Clion France
102 E7 Clipperton, Île terr. N. Pacific Ocean
26 C7 Clisham hill Scotland U.K.
38 I7 Clisson France
29 M6 Clitheroe Lancashire, England U.K.
202 K6 Clive North I. N.Z.
106 G2 Clive Lake N.W.T. Can.
138 D4 Cliza Bol.
209 B7 Cloates, Point W.A. Austr.
97 L4 Clocolan S. Africa
27 H7 Clogh Kilkenny Rep. of Ireland
27 J7 Clogh Wexford Rep. of Ireland
27 J3 Clogh Northern Ireland U.K.
27 G3 Cloghan Donegal Rep. of Ireland
27 G6 Cloghan Offaly Rep. of Ireland
28 C6 Cloghan Westmeath Rep. of Ireland
27 B8 Cloghane Rep. of Ireland
27 E3 Cloghboy Rep. of Ireland
27 G8 Clogheen Rep. of Ireland
27 D5 Clogher Rep. of Ireland
27 H4 Clogher Northern Ireland U.K.
27 J5 Clogherhead Rep. of Ireland
27 J5 Clogher Head Rep. of Ireland
27 J2 Clogh Mills Northern Ireland U.K.
27 L4 Cloghy Northern Ireland U.K.
27 I7 Clohamon Rep. of Ireland
38 D6 Clohars-Carnoët France
207 H6 Clonagh Qld Austr.
27 E9 Clonakilty Rep. of Ireland
27 E9 Clonakilty Bay Rep. of Ireland
27 H6 Clonare Rep. of Ireland
28 B7 Clonaslee Rep. of Ireland
206 H6 Cloncurry Qld Austr.
207 H5 Cloncurry r. Qld Austr.
27 J6 Clondalkin Rep. of Ireland
27 H8 Clonea Rep. of Ireland
27 J6 Clonee Rep. of Ireland
27 G8 Cloneen Rep. of Ireland
27 I7 Clonegal Rep. of Ireland
27 H4 Clones Rep. of Ireland
27 H2 Clonmany Rep. of Ireland
27 G8 Clonmel Rep. of Ireland
27 H5 Clonmellon Rep. of Ireland
27 I7 Clonmore Carlow Rep. of Ireland
27 G7 Clonmore Tipperary Rep. of Ireland
27 G6 Clonony Rep. of Ireland
27 G7 Clonoulty Rep. of Ireland
27 I8 Clonroche Rep. of Ireland
27 J6 Clontarf Rep. of Ireland
27 I4 Clontibret Rep. of Ireland
27 H6 Clonygowan Rep. of Ireland
27 E4 Cloonacool Rep. of Ireland
27 D8 Cloonbannin Rep. of Ireland
27 D6 Cloonboo Rep. of Ireland
27 G5 Cloone Rep. of Ireland
28 B6 Clooneagh Rep. of Ireland
27 E5 Cloonfad Roscommon Rep. of Ireland
27 F6 Cloonfad Roscommon Rep. of Ireland
27 D5 Cloonkeen Rep. of Ireland
27 E5 Cloontia Rep. of Ireland
106 E5 Clo-oose B.C. Can.
48 F5 Cloppenburg Ger.
110 B3 Cloquet MN U.S.A.
110 B2 Cloquet r. MN U.S.A.
144 F2 Clorinda Arg.
26 I12 Closeburn Dumfries and Galloway, Scotland U.K.
110 E1 Cloud Bay Ont. Can.
104 H5 Cloud Peak WY U.S.A.
122 K4 Cloud Peak WY U.S.A.
203 I8 Cloudy Bay South I. N.Z.
42 E3 Clouère r. France
27 K4 Clough Northern Ireland U.K.
29 Q5 Cloughton North Yorkshire, England U.K.
26 □N2 Clousta Shetland, Scotland U.K.
108 F3 Clova Que. Can.
26 J9 Clova Angus, Scotland U.K.
30 D5 Clovelly Devon, England U.K.
26 K11 Clovenfords Scottish Borders, Scotland U.K.
125 T1 Clover UT U.S.A.
124 I3 Cloverdale CA U.S.A.
124 M5 Clovis CA U.S.A.
121 D8 Clovis NM U.S.A.
26 F9 Clovullin Highland, Scotland U.K.
29 O7 Clowne Derbyshire, England U.K.

Cloyes-sur-le-Loir to **Conquista** 251

36 B8 **Cloyes-sur-le-Loir** France
11 Q5 **Cloyne** Ont. Can.
27 F9 **Cloyne** Rep. of Ireland
Cluain Meala Rep. of Ireland see **Clonmel**
26 F8 **Cluanie, Loch** l. Scotland U.K.
07 I3 **Cluff Lake Mine** Sask. Can.
42 H2 **Cluis** France
77 L4 **Cluj-Napoca** Romania
41 I8 **Clumanc** France
30 F3 **Clun** Shropshire, England U.K.
30 G3 **Clun** r. England U.K.
26 G9 **Clunes** Highland, Scotland U.K.
06 G8 **Cluny** Qld Austr.
40 F4 **Cluny** France
40 G5 **Cluse des Hôpitaux** gorge France
40 J4 **Cluses** France
Clusium Italy see **Chiusi**
70 H4 **Clusone** Italy
16 G12 **Cluster Springs** VA U.S.A.
03 D13 **Clutha** r. South I. N.Z.
06 G1 **Clut Lake** N.W.T. Can.
09 I8 **Clutterbuck Hills** W.A. Austr.
30 G5 **Clutton** Bath and North East Somerset, England U.K.
30 F1 **Clwydian Range** hills Wales U.K.
30 E4 **Clydach** Swansea, Wales U.K.
30 F4 **Clydach Vale** Rhondda Cynon Taff, Wales U.K.
06 H4 **Clyde** Alta Can.
03 D12 **Clyde** South I. N.Z.
26 H11 **Clyde** r. Scotland U.K.
16 I5 **Clyde** NY U.S.A.
16 C7 **Clyde** OH U.S.A.
26 G12 **Clyde, Firth of** est. Scotland U.K.
26 H11 **Clydebank** West Dunbartonshire, Scotland U.K.
05 L2 **Clyde River** Nunavut Can.
26 I11 **Clydesdale** val. Scotland U.K.
03 D13 **Clydevale** South I. N.Z.
10 F6 **Clyman** WI U.S.A.
16 F8 **Clymer** PA U.S.A.
30 C4 **Clynderwen** Carmarthenshire, Wales U.K.
30 F3 **Clyro** Powys, Wales U.K.
30 E3 **Clywedog Reservoir, Llyn** Wales U.K.
55 J5 **Ćmielów** Pol.
26 I8 **Cnoc Fraing** hill Scotland U.K.
26 E12 **Cnoc Moy** hill Scotland U.K.
62 F6 **Côa** r. Port.
29 H6 **Coacalco** Mex.
25 P8 **Coachella** CA U.S.A.
25 P8 **Coachella Canal** CA U.S.A.
27 E9 **Coachford** Rep. of Ireland
28 A1 **Coacoyole** Mex.
29 I9 **Coacoyulichán** Mex.
27 I3 **Coagh** Northern Ireland U.K.
28 F7 **Coahuayutla de Guerrero** Mex.
26 H4 **Coahuila** state Mex.
06 E3 **Coal** r. Y.T. Can.
26 I11 **Coalburn** South Lanarkshire, Scotland U.K.
10 F8 **Coal City** IL U.S.A.
28 D7 **Coalcomán** Mex.
28 D7 **Coalcomán** r. Mex.
07 H5 **Coaldale** Alta Can.
24 O3 **Coaldale** NV U.S.A.
18 D3 **Coaldale** PA U.S.A.
21 G8 **Coalgate** OK U.S.A.
16 C10 **Coal Grove** OH U.S.A.
06 E5 **Coal Harbour** B.C. Can.
24 L5 **Coalinga** CA U.S.A.
03 A13 **Coal Island** South I. N.Z.
27 I3 **Coalisland** Northern Ireland U.K.
16 G8 **Coalport** PA U.S.A.
06 E3 **Coal River** B.C. Can.
25 Q4 **Coal Valley** NV U.S.A.
97 N2 **Coalville** S. Africa
31 J2 **Coalville** Leicestershire, England U.K.
22 I6 **Coalville** UT U.S.A.
31 □1 **Coamo** Puerto Rico
62 G1 **Coaña** Spain
37 F6 **Coari** Brazil
37 F6 **Coari** r. Brazil
37 F6 **Coari, Lago** l. Brazil
43 D9 **Coarraze** France
24 M4 **Coarsegold** CA U.S.A.
38 C3 **Coasa** Peru
93 D5 **Coast** prov. Kenya
77 O2 **Coasta Ibăneştilor** ridge Romania
21 H10 **Coastal Plain** U.S.A.
06 E4 **Coast Mountains** B.C. Can.
07 M8 **Coast Range** hills Qld Austr.
24 I1 **Coast Ranges** mts CA U.S.A.
26 H11 **Coatbridge** North Lanarkshire, Scotland U.K.
29 K9 **Coatecas Altas** Mex.
29 K6 **Coatepec** Mex.
29 H7 **Coatepec Harinas** Mex.
27 N10 **Coatepeque** Guat.
18 D5 **Coatesville** PA U.S.A.
09 G4 **Coaticook** Que. Can.
29 K9 **Coatlán** Mex.
05 J3 **Coats Island** Nunavut Can.
12 V1 **Coats Land** reg. Antarctica
29 M7 **Coatzacoalcos** Mex.
29 M7 **Coatzacoalcos** r. Mex.
29 J5 **Coatzintla** Mex.
77 Q6 **Cobadin** Romania
11 O2 **Cobalt** Ont. Can.
19 J1 **Cobalt** CT U.S.A.
27 N10 **Cobán** Guat.
91 G4 **Çobandağ** hill Azer./Georgia
79 L4 **Çobanlar** Turkey
91 B6 **Çobantaş Geçidi** pass Turkey
05 J4 **Cobar** N.S.W. Austr.
05 L7 **Cobargo** N.S.W. Austr.
09 I8 **Cobb, Lake** salt flat W.A. Austr.
05 I8 **Cobden** Vic. Austr.
11 R4 **Cobden** Ont. Can.
63 M8 **Cobeja** Spain
63 P7 **Cobeta** Spain
27 F9 **Cobh** Rep. of Ireland
07 M4 **Cobham** r. Man./Ont. Can.
31 L5 **Cobham** Surrey, England U.K.
38 C2 **Cobija** Bol.
38 C5 **Cobija** Chile
Coblenz Ger. see **Koblenz**
17 K6 **Cobleskill** NY U.S.A.
28 D7 **Coblinstown** Rep. of Ireland
47 I5 **Cobo** Arg.
06 C3 **Cobol** AK U.S.A.
29 J5 **Cobos** Mex.
08 E5 **Cobourg** Ont. Can.
06 D1 **Cobourg Peninsula** N.T. Austr.
46 A5 **Cobquecura** Chile
09 D8 **Cobra** W.A. Austr.
05 J6 **Cobram** Vic. Austr.
38 D5 **Cobres** Arg.
64 D5 **Cobres** r. Port.
93 B8 **Cóbuè** Moz.
49 K10 **Coburg** Ger.
05 K2 **Coburg Island** Nunavut Can.
36 B5 **Coca** Orellana Ecuador
63 K6 **Coca** Spain
38 C4 **Cocachacra** Peru
40 E2 **Cocal** Brazil
18 C4 **Cocalico Creek** r. PA U.S.A.
40 C5 **Cocalinho** Brazil
38 D4 **Cocapata** Bol.
73 P7 **Coccovello, Monte** mt. Italy
67 E10 **Cocentaina** Spain
38 D4 **Cochabamba** Bol.
38 D4 **Cochabamba** dept Bol.
45 B6 **Cochamó** Chile
46 A5 **Cocharcas** Chile
37 F2 **Coche, Isla** i. Venez.
49 D10 **Cochem** Ger.
46 D4 **Cochicó** Arg.
47 F5 **Cochicó, Laguna** l. Arg.
76 E8 **Cochin** Kerala India
59 G9 **Cochin** reg. Vietnam
30 C2 **Cochinos, Bahía de** b. Cuba
25 W9 **Cochise** AZ U.S.A.
25 W9 **Cochise Head** mt. AZ U.S.A.
15 F9 **Cochran** GA U.S.A.
06 H5 **Cochrane** Alta Can.
08 D3 **Cochrane** Ont. Can.
107 K3 **Cochrane** r. Sask. Can.
145 B7 **Cochrane** Chile
145 B7 **Cochrane, Lago** l. Arg./Chile
116 E7 **Cochranton** PA U.S.A.
118 D5 **Cochranville** PA U.S.A.
51 D7 **Cochstedt** Ger.
57 L5 **Cociuba Mare** Romania
204 E6 **Cockaleechie** S.A. Austr.
26 J8 **Cock Bridge** Aberdeenshire, Scotland U.K.
204 H5 **Cockburn** S.A. Austr.
130 H3 **Cockburn Harbour** Turks and Caicos Is
108 D4 **Cockburn Island** Ont. Can.
26 L11 **Cockburnspath** Scottish Borders, Scotland U.K.
130 F1 **Cockburn Town** San Salvador Bahamas
Cockburn Town Turks and Caicos Is see **Grand Turk**
29 N2 **Cockenheugh** hill England U.K.
26 K11 **Cockenzie and Port Seton** East Lothian, Scotland U.K.
29 J4 **Cocker** r. England U.K.
29 L6 **Cockerham** Lancashire, England U.K.
29 K4 **Cockermouth** Cumbria, England U.K.
30 E4 **Cockett** Swansea, Wales U.K.
118 B6 **Cockeysville** MD U.S.A.
209 I12 **Cocklebiddy** W.A. Austr.
130 □ **Cockpit** hill Jamaica
97 I9 **Cockscomb** mt. S. Africa
126 □S13 **Coclé del Norte** Panama
140 C4 **Coco** r. Brazil
126 □R10 **Coco** r. Hond./Nic.
130 D2 **Coco, Cayo** i. Cuba
217 N5 **Coco, Isla de** i. N. Pacific Ocean
Cocoa Island Rodrigues I. Mauritius see **Cocos, Île**
90 A4 **Cocobeach** Gabon
177 M6 **Coco Channel** India
126 F3 **Cocomórachic** Mex.
125 S6 **Coconino Plateau** AZ U.S.A.
205 K6 **Cocopara National Park** N.S.W. Austr.
205 K5 **Cocoparra Range** hills N.S.W. Austr.
136 C3 **Cocorná** Col.
154 C6 **Cocoro** i. Phil.
140 D5 **Cocos** Brazil
99 □1a **Cocos, Île** i. Rodrigues I. Mauritius
215 K4 **Cocos Basin** sea feature Indian Ocean
131 □7 **Cocos Bay** Trin. and Tob.
200 □1 **Cocos Island** Guam
208 □2 **Cocos Islands** terr. Indian Ocean
217 N5 **Cocos Ridge** sea feature N. Pacific Ocean
99 □1b **Cocotte, Mont** hill Mauritius
128 D5 **Cocula** Mex.
43 E7 **Cocumont** France
117 O7 **Cod, Cape** MA U.S.A.
72 D6 **Coda Cavallo, Capo** c. Sardegna Italy
77 P4 **Codăeşti** Romania
137 F5 **Codajás** Brazil
29 O5 **Cod Beck** r. England U.K.
31 O3 **Coddenham** Suffolk, England U.K.
29 P7 **Coddington** Nottinghamshire, England U.K.
137 E2 **Codera, Cabo** c. Venez.
107 J5 **Coderre** Sask. Can.
71 M5 **Codevigo** Italy
203 B13 **Codfish Island** Stewart I. N.Z.
72 D8 **Codi, Monte** hill Italy
31 L4 **Codicote** Hertfordshire, England U.K.
71 M6 **Codigoro** Italy
146 B6 **Codihue** Arg.
109 I1 **Cod Island** Nfld and Lab. Can.
77 N5 **Codlea** Romania
29 O7 **Codnor** Derbyshire, England U.K.
140 E3 **Codó** Brazil
70 H5 **Codogno** Italy
67 H10 **Codol** airport Spain
118 B5 **Codorus** PA U.S.A.
63 R6 **Codos** Spain
140 D3 **Codózinho** Brazil
131 □2 **Codrington** Antigua and Barbuda
213 D2 **Codrington, Mount** Antarctica
131 □2 **Codrington Lagoon** Antigua and Barbuda
71 N4 **Codroipo** Italy
72 B6 **Codrongianos** Sardegna Italy
16 H7 **Codru** Moldova
57 L5 **Codru-Moma, Munții** mts Romania
30 H2 **Codsall** Staffordshire, England U.K.
27 B9 **Cod's Head** Rep. of Ireland
122 J4 **Cody** WY U.S.A.
116 C12 **Coeburn** VA U.S.A.
97 J9 **Coega** S. Africa
146 A5 **Coelemu** Chile
140 E3 **Coelho Neto** Brazil
207 I2 **Coen** Qld Austr.
207 I2 **Coen** r. Qld Austr.
128 F6 **Coeneo** Mex.
97 J9 **Coerney** S. Africa
137 G4 **Coeroeni** r. Suriname
49 D7 **Coesfeld** Ger.
99 □2 **Coëtivy** i. Seychelles
97 I8 **Coetzeesberg** mts S. Africa
96 I2 **Coetzersdam** S. Africa
122 F3 **Coeur d'Alene** ID U.S.A.
122 F3 **Coeur d'Alene** r. ID U.S.A.
122 F3 **Coeur d'Alene Indian Reservation** res. ID U.S.A.
122 F3 **Coeur d'Alene Lake** ID U.S.A.
44 K3 **Coevorden** Neth.
38 H8 **Coëx** France
97 N7 **Coffee Bay** S. Africa
106 B2 **Coffee Creek** Y.T. Can.
121 K9 **Coffeeville** MS U.S.A.
121 H7 **Coffeyville** KS U.S.A.
204 E6 **Coffin Bay** S.A. Austr.
204 E6 **Coffin Bay** b. S.A. Austr.
204 E6 **Coffin Bay National Park** S.A. Austr.
204 E6 **Coffin Bay Peninsula** S.A. Austr.
205 N4 **Coffs Harbour** N.S.W. Austr.
97 L8 **Cofimvaba** S. Africa
126 □O10 **Cofradía** Hond.
128 C5 **Cofradia de Camotlán** Mex.
129 J6 **Cofre de Perote** mt. Mex.
129 J6 **Cofre de Perote, Parque Nacional** nat. park Mex.
67 C9 **Cofrentes** Spain
Cogâlniceni Moldova see **Cogîlniceni**
77 Q6 **Cogealac** Romania
63 L5 **Cogeces del Monte** Spain
31 N4 **Coggeshall** Essex, England U.K.
72 B3 **Coggia** Corse France
70 E4 **Coggiola** Italy
72 B6 **Coghinas** r. Italy
72 C6 **Coghinas, Lago del** l. Sardegna Italy
97 M7 **Coghlan** S. Africa
208 I5 **Coghlan, Mount** hill W.A. Austr.
66 G3 **Cogigar** r. Spain
16 H6 **Cogîlniceni** Moldova
42 D4 **Cognac** France
42 G4 **Cognac-la-Forêt** France
70 C4 **Cogne** Italy
40 H5 **Cognin** France
89 H6 **Cogo** Equat. Guinea
144 F2 **Cogoi** Arg.
70 F7 **Cogoleto** Italy
41 J10 **Cogolin** France
63 M4 **Cogollos** Spain
63 L4 **Cogollos** r. Spain
65 L6 **Cogollos Vega** Spain
63 N7 **Cogolludo** Spain
170 C4 **Cogsum** Sichuan China
62 F7 **Cogula** Port.
95 G5 **Coguno** Moz.
118 E6 **Cohansey** r. NJ U.S.A.
129 I7 **Cohetzala** Mex.
63 L2 **Cohilla, Embalse de** resr Spain
20 R2 **Čohkarášša** mt. Norway
116 H6 **Cohocton** r. NY U.S.A.
117 L6 **Cohoes** NY U.S.A.
205 J6 **Cohuna** Vic. Austr.
126 □S14 **Coiba, Isla de** i. Panama
129 I8 **Coicoyán de las Flores** Mex.
212 T3 **Coig** r. Arg.
26 F6 **Coigeach, Rubha** pt Scotland U.K.
145 B7 **Coihaique** Chile
145 C7 **Coihaique Alto** Chile
146 A5 **Coihüe** Chile
146 B5 **Coihueco** Arg.
146 B5 **Coihueco** Chile
176 E7 **Coimbatore** Tamil Nadu India
62 D8 **Coimbra** Port.
62 D8 **Coimbra** admin. dist. Port.
65 J7 **Coín** Spain
36 F5 **Coincy** France
138 C4 **Coipasa, Salar de** salt flat Bol.
Coire Switz. see **Chur**
41 F7 **Coiron, Plateau du** France
40 E5 **Coise** r. France
129 J8 **Coixtlahuaca** Mex.
62 E8 **Coja** Port.
77 N6 **Cojasca** Romania
138 C3 **Cojata** Peru
136 D2 **Cojedes** state Venez.
136 A4 **Cojimíes** Ecuador
136 D2 **Cojoro** Venez.
145 C7 **Cojudo Blanco, Cerro** mt. Arg.
57 J6 **Čoka** Vojvodina, Srbija Serb. and Mont.
122 I5 **Cokeville** WY U.S.A.
205 I8 **Colac** Vic. Austr.
203 B13 **Colac** South I. N.Z.
146 C1 **Colangüil, Cordillera de** mts Arg.
190 H2 **Colap** watercourse Turkey
140 C2 **Colares** Brazil
143 G3 **Colatina** Brazil
129 I5 **Colatlán** Mex.
43 F7 **Colayrac-St-Cirq** France
49 G9 **Cölbe** Ger.
Colbert Alg. see **Aïn Oulmene**
51 E6 **Colbitz** Ger.
71 N8 **Colbordola** Italy
111 Q6 **Colborne** Ont. Can.
146 B4 **Colbún** Chile
146 B4 **Colbún, Lago** l. Chile
120 E6 **Colby** KS U.S.A.
110 D5 **Colby** WI U.S.A.
138 B3 **Colca** r. Peru
77 O6 **Colceag** Romania
97 J9 **Colchester** S. Africa
31 N4 **Colchester** Essex, England U.K.
119 K1 **Colchester** CT U.S.A.
110 D9 **Colchester** IL U.S.A.
104 B4 **Cold Bay** AK U.S.A.
31 J6 **Colden Common** Hampshire, England U.K.
26 L11 **Coldingham** Scottish Borders, Scotland U.K.
51 G8 **Colditz** Ger.
51 G8 **Colditzer Forst** park Ger.
107 I4 **Cold Lake** Alta Can.
107 I4 **Cold Lake** l. Alta/Sask. Can.
118 F7 **Cold Spring** NJ U.S.A.
119 H2 **Cold Spring** NY U.S.A.
121 H10 **Coldspring** TX U.S.A.
124 O2 **Cold Springs** NV U.S.A.
106 G5 **Coldstream** B.C. Can.
203 F11 **Coldstream** South I. N.Z.
26 L11 **Coldstream** Scottish Borders, Scotland U.K.
111 O5 **Coldwater** Ont. Can.
121 F7 **Coldwater** KS U.S.A.
110 J8 **Coldwater** MI U.S.A.
121 J8 **Coldwater** r. MS U.S.A.
121 E7 **Coldwater Creek** r. OK U.S.A.
110 H1 **Coldwell** Ont. Can.
117 N4 **Colebrook** NH U.S.A.
97 N5 **Coleford** S. Africa
30 G4 **Coleford** Gloucestershire, England U.K.
30 H5 **Coleford** Somerset, England U.K.
207 H3 **Coleman** r. Qld Austr.
118 C6 **Coleman** MD U.S.A.
110 J6 **Coleman** MI U.S.A.
121 F10 **Coleman** TX U.S.A.
110 F4 **Coleman** WI U.S.A.
97 N4 **Colenso** S. Africa
77 N6 **Colentina** r. Romania
212 T2 **Cole Peninsula** Antarctica
204 H7 **Coleraine** Vic. Austr.
27 I2 **Coleraine** Northern Ireland U.K.
110 A2 **Coleraine** MN U.S.A.
203 F10 **Coleridge, Lake** South I. N.Z.
30 H5 **Colerne** Wiltshire, England U.K.
176 F7 **Coleroon** r. India
138 C4 **Coles, Punta de** pt Peru
205 L10 **Coles Bay** Tas. Austr.
97 J6 **Colesberg** S. Africa
31 I2 **Coleshill** Warwickshire, England U.K.
118 A6 **Colesville** MD U.S.A.
118 F2 **Colesville** NJ U.S.A.
107 I5 **Coleville** Sask. Can.
124 M3 **Coleville** CA U.S.A.
124 L2 **Colfax** CA U.S.A.
110 F9 **Colfax** IL U.S.A.
121 I10 **Colfax** LA U.S.A.
122 F3 **Colfax** WA U.S.A.
110 C5 **Colfax** WI U.S.A.
179 K7 **Colgong** Bihar India
26 □O1 **Colgrave Sound** str. Scotland U.K.
145 C7 **Colhué Huapí, Lago** l. Arg.
146 B4 **Coliauco** Chile
77 M6 **Colibaşi** Romania
70 G3 **Colico** Italy
146 B6 **Colico, Lago** l. Chile
40 G4 **Coligny** France
97 K2 **Coligny** S. Africa
131 □2 **Colihaut** Dominica
44 E5 **Colijnsplaat** Neth.
128 D6 **Colima** Mex.
128 D6 **Colima** state Mex.
128 D6 **Colima, Nevado de** vol. Mex.
142 C4 **Colina** Brazil
146 B3 **Colina** Chile
140 D3 **Colinas** Brazil
63 N2 **Colindres** Spain
26 F11 **Colintraive** Argyll and Bute, Scotland U.K.
129 K6 **Colipa** Mex.
140 B5 **Coliseu** r. Brazil
26 C9 **Coll** i. Scotland U.K.
63 Q8 **Collado Bajo** mt. Spain
63 M6 **Collado Hermoso** Spain
63 M7 **Collado Villalba** Spain
70 I7 **Collagna** Italy
138 C5 **Collahuasi** Chile
58 F6 **Collalto** mt. Austria/Italy
62 I2 **Collanzo** Spain
205 L3 **Collarenebri** N.S.W. Austr.
73 L3 **Collarmele** Italy
73 I2 **Collazzone** Italy
66 J3 **Coll de Merolla** pass Spain
70 I6 **Collecchio** Italy
73 L2 **Colledara** Italy
71 K9 **Colle di Val d'Elsa** Italy
95 F4 **Colleen Dawn** Zimbabwe
73 K4 **Colleferro** Italy
115 E9 **College Park** GA U.S.A.
121 G10 **College Station** TX U.S.A.
118 E4 **Collegeville** PA U.S.A.
70 D5 **Collegno** Italy
71 K2 **Colle Isarco** Italy
73 L4 **Collelongo** Italy
73 K4 **Collepardo** Italy
75 O3 **Collepasso** Italy
205 K3 **Collerina** N.S.W. Austr.
70 I8 **Collesalvetti** Italy
73 N5 **Colle Sannita** Italy
74 F8 **Collesano** Sicilia Italy
73 N4 **Colletorto** Italy
118 C1 **Colley** PA U.S.A.
73 O6 **Colliano** Italy
73 M4 **Colli a Volturno** Italy
205 L4 **Collie** N.S.W. Austr.
209 D12 **Collie** W.A. Austr.
208 H4 **Collier Bay** W.A. Austr.
209 E8 **Collier Range** hills W.A. Austr.
209 E8 **Collier Range National Park** W.A. Austr.
121 K8 **Collierville** TN U.S.A.
26 M8 **Collieston** Aberdeenshire, Scotland U.K.
30 C6 **Colliford Reservoir** England U.K.
26 I12 **Collin** Dumfries and Galloway, Scotland U.K.
72 B8 **Collinas** Sardegna Italy
38 F5 **Collinée** France
29 P7 **Collingham** Nottinghamshire, England U.K.
48 E4 **Collinghorst (Rhauderfehn)** Ger.
108 D4 **Collingwood** Ont. Can.
202 G7 **Collingwood** South I. N.Z.
119 G4 **Collingwood Park** NJ U.S.A.
121 K10 **Collins** MS U.S.A.
213 E2 **Collins Glacier** Antarctica
124 K2 **Collins Lake** CA U.S.A.
105 H2 **Collinson Peninsula** Nunavut Can.
207 K6 **Collinsville** Qld Austr.
115 E8 **Collinsville** AL U.S.A.
121 H7 **Collinsville** OK U.S.A.
116 F12 **Collinsville** VA U.S.A.
58 B8 **Collio** Italy
43 K10 **Collioure** France
146 A5 **Collipulli** Chile
51 H8 **Collmberg** hill Ger.
41 I10 **Collobrières** France
70 B3 **Collombey** Switz.
118 A2 **Collomsville** PA U.S.A.
27 J5 **Collon** Rep. of Ireland
40 H4 **Collonges** France
42 H5 **Collonges-la-Rouge** France
27 F4 **Collooney** Rep. of Ireland
37 N7 **Colmar** France
147 F2 **Col Marina** Arg.
41 J8 **Colmars** France
53 I3 **Colmberg** Ger.
62 E8 **Colmeal** Port.
144 E3 **Colmena** Arg.
65 K7 **Colmenar** Spain
62 I8 **Colmenar de Montemayor** Spain
63 N8 **Colmenar de Oreja** Spain
63 M7 **Colmenar Viejo** Spain
40 C2 **Colméry** France
26 G12 **Colmonell** South Ayrshire, Scotland U.K.
31 I4 **Coln** r. England U.K.
26 J8 **Colnabaichin** Aberdeenshire, Scotland U.K.
31 K5 **Colnbrook** Windsor and Maidenhead, England U.K.
29 M6 **Colne** Lancashire, England U.K.
31 N4 **Colne** r. England U.K.
31 L4 **Colney Heath** Hertfordshire, England U.K.
48 F5 **Colnrade** Ger.
205 M5 **Colo** r. N.S.W. Austr.
75 K3 **Colobraro** Italy
71 K5 **Cologna Veneta** Italy
43 F8 **Cologne** France
Cologne Ger. see **Köln**
118 F6 **Cologne** NJ U.S.A.
66 □ **Colom, Illa d'en** i. Spain
110 H7 **Coloma** MI U.S.A.
110 E5 **Coloma** WI U.S.A.
Colomb-Béchar Alg. see **Béchar**
39 K3 **Colombelles** France
36 D6 **Colombes** France
37 K6 **Colombey-les-Belles** France
37 I7 **Colombey-les Deux-Églises** France
142 C4 **Colômbia** Brazil
136 C4 **Colombia** Col.
127 J4 **Colombia** Mex.
136 C4 **Colombia** country S. America
214 D5 **Colombian Basin** sea feature S. Atlantic Ocean
70 B2 **Colombier** Switz.
40 I5 **Colombier, Mont** mt. France
43 I7 **Colombiès** France
142 C6 **Colombo** Brazil
176 F9 **Colombo** Sri Lanka
111 O1 **Colombourg** Que. Can.
63 K2 **Colombres** Spain
65 L6 **Colomera** Spain
65 L6 **Colomera** r. Spain
65 L6 **Colomera, Embalse de** resr Spain
66 K3 **Colomers** Spain
43 G8 **Colomiers** France
147 G3 **Colón** Buenos Aires Arg.
147 H3 **Colón** Entre Ríos Arg.
130 C2 **Colón** Cuba
128 G5 **Colón** Mex.
126 □T13 **Colón** Panama
110 I8 **Colon** MI U.S.A.
131 □7 **Colón** Venez.
Colón, Archipiélago de is Pacific Ocean see **Galápagos, Islas**
126 □R13 **Colón, Isla de** i. Panama
204 D4 **Colona** S.A. Austr.
178 H6 **Colonelganj** Uttar Prad. India
130 F2 **Colonel Hill** Bahamas
126 A2 **Colonet, Cabo** c. Mex.
144 E2 **Colonia** Arg.
153 I5 **Colonia** Yap Micronesia
147 I4 **Colonia** dept Uru.
119 G3 **Colonia** NJ U.S.A.
147 F2 **Colonia Alpina** Arg.
146 D4 **Colonia Alvear** Arg.
147 F5 **Colonia Barón** Arg.
146 E3 **Colonia Biagorria** Arg.
147 H3 **Colonia Caseros** Arg.
146 D5 **Colonia Chica, Isla** i. Arg.
146 E6 **Colonia Choele Choel, Isla** i. Arg.
147 I4 **Colonia del Sacramento** Uru.
67 L9 **Colònia de Sant Jordi** Spain
67 L8 **Colònia de Sant Pere** Spain
126 E2 **Colonia Díaz** Mex.
144 E3 **Colonia Dora** Arg.
147 H3 **Colonia Elía** Arg.
146 D5 **Colonia Emilio Mitre** Arg.
147 G2 **Colonia Fraga** Arg.
147 F4 **Colonia Hilario Lagos** Arg.
Colonia Julia Fenestris Italy see **Fano**
147 H2 **Colonia La Argentina** Arg.
146 D5 **Colonia La Pastoril** Arg.
145 C7 **Colonia Las Heras** Arg.
147 I2 **Colonia Lavalleja** Uru.
116 H11 **Colonial Heights** VA U.S.A.
118 B4 **Colonial Park** PA U.S.A.
147 H2 **Colonia Macías** Arg.
147 G2 **Colonia Portugalete** Arg.
125 T10 **Colonia Reforma** Mex.
147 G2 **Colonia Rosa** Arg.
147 F4 **Colonia Seré** Arg.
144 F4 **Colonia Suiza** Uru.
75 M5 **Colonna, Capo** c. Italy
72 A9 **Colonne, Punta delle** pt Sardegna Italy
73 L2 **Colonnella** Italy
217 M5 **Colon Ridge** sea feature Pacific Ocean
26 D10 **Colonsay** i. Scotland U.K.
147 F6 **Colorada Grande, Salina** salt l. Arg.
146 C2 **Colorado** r. Arg.
146 F6 **Colorado** r. Arg.
144 D3 **Colorado** r. Arg.
142 B5 **Colorado** Brazil
146 B4 **Colorado** r. Chile
129 J9 **Colorado** r. Mex.
126 B2 **Colorado** r. Mex./U.S.A.
121 G11 **Colorado** r. TX U.S.A.
125 X2 **Colorado** state U.S.A.
146 D2 **Colorado, Cerro** mt. Arg.
145 E5 **Colorado, Delta del Río** Arg.
125 S5 **Colorado City** AZ U.S.A.
121 E9 **Colorado City** TX U.S.A.
125 P8 **Colorado Desert** CA U.S.A.
125 X2 **Colorado National Monument** nat. park CO U.S.A.
125 W4 **Colorado Plateau** CO U.S.A.
125 R7 **Colorado River Aqueduct** canal CA U.S.A.
125 R8 **Colorado River Indian Reservation** res. AZ/CA U.S.A.
144 C2 **Colorados, Cerro** mt. Arg.
123 L7 **Colorado Springs** CO U.S.A.
70 I6 **Colorno** Italy
64 C5 **Colos** Port.
72 D9 **Colostrai, Stagno di** lag. Sardegna Italy
41 H9 **Colostre** r. France
129 K10 **Colotepec** Mex.
129 J10 **Colotepec** r. Mex.
128 D3 **Colotlán** Mex.
50 H3 **Cölpin** Ger.
138 D4 **Colquechaca** Bol.
26 J11 **Colquhar** Scottish Borders, Scotland U.K.
138 D4 **Colquiri** Bol.
115 E10 **Colquitt** GA U.S.A.
191 K4 **Çölquşçu** Azer.
37 N7 **Colroy-la-Grande** France
116 C11 **Colson** KY U.S.A.
31 K2 **Colsterworth** Lincolnshire, England U.K.
122 K4 **Colstrip** MT U.S.A.
31 O2 **Coltishall** Norfolk, England U.K.
124 O7 **Colton** CA U.S.A.
117 K4 **Colton** NY U.S.A.
125 U2 **Colton** UT U.S.A.
119 G4 **Colts Neck** NJ U.S.A.
67 C12 **Columbares** hill Spain
119 K1 **Columbia** CT U.S.A.
114 E7 **Columbia** KY U.S.A.
121 I9 **Columbia** LA U.S.A.
118 B6 **Columbia** MD U.S.A.
120 I6 **Columbia** MO U.S.A.
121 K10 **Columbia** MS U.S.A.
115 I8 **Columbia** NC U.S.A.
118 E3 **Columbia** NJ U.S.A.
118 B4 **Columbia** PA U.S.A.
115 G9 **Columbia** SC U.S.A.
115 D8 **Columbia** TN U.S.A.
122 C3 **Columbia** r. WA U.S.A.
105 K1 **Columbia, Cape** Nunavut Can.
118 A7 **Columbia, District of** admin. dist. U.S.A.
106 G4 **Columbia, Mount** Alta/B.C. Can.
126 B3 **Columbia, Sierra** mts Mex.
114 E5 **Columbia City** IN U.S.A.
118 C2 **Columbia County** county PA U.S.A.
117 □R4 **Columbia Falls** ME U.S.A.
122 G2 **Columbia Falls** MT U.S.A.
106 F4 **Columbia Mountains** B.C. Can.
115 D9 **Columbiana** AL U.S.A.
116 E8 **Columbiana** OH U.S.A.
122 E3 **Columbia Plateau** U.S.A.
96 B8 **Columbine, Cape** S. Africa
67 G8 **Columbretes, Islas** is Spain
115 E9 **Columbus** GA U.S.A.
114 E6 **Columbus** IN U.S.A.
121 H7 **Columbus** KS U.S.A.
121 K9 **Columbus** MS U.S.A.
122 J4 **Columbus** MT U.S.A.
115 F8 **Columbus** NC U.S.A.
120 G5 **Columbus** NE U.S.A.
118 F4 **Columbus** NJ U.S.A.
123 K11 **Columbus** NM U.S.A.
116 B9 **Columbus** OH U.S.A.
116 F7 **Columbus** PA U.S.A.
121 G11 **Columbus** TX U.S.A.
110 E6 **Columbus** WI U.S.A.
130 F3 **Columbus Bank** sea feature Bahamas
116 A8 **Columbus Grove** OH U.S.A.
131 □5 **Columbus Point** Trin. and Tob.
124 N3 **Columbus Salt Marsh** NV U.S.A.
143 F3 **Coluna** Brazil
63 J2 **Colunga** Spain
124 J2 **Colusa** CA U.S.A.
202 J3 **Colville** North I. N.Z.
122 F2 **Colville** WA U.S.A.
104 C2 **Colville** r. AK U.S.A.
202 J3 **Colville, Cape** North I. N.Z.
209 I10 **Colville, Lake** salt flat W.A. Austr.
202 J3 **Colville Channel** North I. N.Z.
122 E2 **Colville Indian Reservation** res. WA U.S.A.
104 F3 **Colville Lake** N.W.T. Can.
31 I2 **Colwich** Staffordshire, England U.K.
30 E1 **Colwyn Bay** Conwy, Wales U.K.
42 G5 **Coly** France
30 F6 **Colyton** Devon, England U.K.
71 M6 **Comacchio** Italy
71 M6 **Comacchio, Valli di** lag. Italy
65 M7 **Comacho, Puerto** pass Spain
173 J12 **Comai** Xizang China
128 D6 **Comala** Mex.
127 M8 **Comalcalco** Mex.
129 I4 **Comales** r. Mex.
145 C6 **Comallo** Arg.
77 O6 **Comana** Romania
77 N5 **Comana de Sus** Romania
121 F10 **Comanche** TX U.S.A.
212 U2 **Comandante Ferraz** research stn Antarctica
144 F2 **Comandante Fontana** Arg.
145 C8 **Comandante Luis Piedra Buena** Arg.
147 I6 **Comandante Nicanor Otamendi** Arg.
146 C3 **Comandante Salas** Arg.
77 O4 **Comăneşti** Romania
66 H2 **Coma Pedrosa, Pic de** mt. Andorra
77 N5 **Comarnic** Romania
126 □P10 **Comayagua** Hond.
115 G9 **Combahee** r. SC U.S.A.
146 B2 **Combarbalá** Chile
37 K8 **Combeaufontaine** France
40 I5 **Combe de Savoie** val. France
30 D5 **Combe Martin** Devon, England U.K.
27 K3 **Comber** Northern Ireland U.K.
111 Q4 **Combermere** Ont. Can.
158 A5 **Combermere Bay** Myanmar
31 M3 **Comberton** Cambridgeshire, England U.K.
30 G6 **Combe St Nicholas** Somerset, England U.K.
45 I8 **Comblain-au-Pont** Belgium
40 F2 **Comblanchien** France
36 E3 **Combles** France
40 J5 **Combloux** France
156 E4 **Combol** i. Indon.
70 I3 **Combolo, Monte** mt. Italy/Switz.
38 H5 **Combourg** France
40 A4 **Combraille** reg. France
38 C6 **Combrit** France
40 C5 **Combronde** France
146 E3 **Comechingones, Sierra de** mts Arg.
71 N2 **Comeglians** Italy
71 N2 **Comèlico Superiore** Italy
108 F3 **Comencho, Lac** l. Que. Can.
64 D2 **Comenda** Port.
142 C3 **Comendador Gomes** Brazil
143 G2 **Comercinho** Brazil
131 □1 **Comerio** Puerto Rico
71 M8 **Comero, Monte** mt. Italy
207 L7 **Comet** Qld Austr.
207 L7 **Comet** r. Qld Austr.
121 F10 **Comfort** TX U.S.A.
116 D10 **Comfort** WV U.S.A.
130 □ **Comfort Castle** Jamaica
179 M8 **Comilla** Bangl.
63 L2 **Comillas** Spain
45 C7 **Comines** Belgium
Comino i. Malta see **Kemmuna**
72 D6 **Comino, Capo** c. Sardegna Italy
74 H10 **Comiso** Sicilia Italy
129 L9 **Comitancillo** Mex.
127 M9 **Comitán de Domínguez** Mex.
74 F9 **Comitini** Sicilia Italy
57 J6 **Comloşu Mare** Romania
119 I3 **Commack** NY U.S.A.
111 O4 **Commanda** Ont. Can.
27 G3 **Commeen** Rep. of Ireland
40 G3 **Commenailles** France
43 C7 **Commensacq** France
40 B4 **Commentry** France
38 H8 **Commequiers** France
39 J5 **Commer** France
37 K6 **Commercy** France
43 F10 **Comminges** reg. France
115 □1 **Commissioner's Point** Bermuda
96 D6 **Commissioner's Salt Pan** S. Africa
105 J3 **Committee Bay** Nunavut Can.
97 O3 **Commondale** S. Africa
213 J2 **Commonwealth Bay** Antarctica
70 G4 **Como** Italy
70 G4 **Como** prov. Italy
70 G4 **Como, Lago di** l. Italy
Como, Lake Italy see **Como, Lago di**
129 L7 **Comoapan** Mex.
173 I12 **Como Chamling** l. China
146 B3 **Comodoro Arturo Merino Benitez** airport Chile
145 D7 **Comodoro Rivadavia** Arg.
128 G5 **Comonfort** Mex.
Comores country Africa see **Comoros**
176 E8 **Comorin, Cape** India
99 □3 **Comoros** country Africa
106 E5 **Comox** B.C. Can.
65 L7 **Cómpeta** Spain
70 H6 **Compiano** Italy
36 E5 **Compiègne** France
43 I7 **Compolibat** France
64 B4 **Comporta** Port.
128 C4 **Compostela** Mex.
154 F8 **Compostela** Mindanao Phil.
42 G4 **Compreignac** France
142 D6 **Comprida, Ilha** i. Brazil
41 J9 **Comps-sur-Artuby** France
124 N8 **Compton** CA U.S.A.
110 E8 **Compton** IL U.S.A.
63 K3 **Compuerto, Embalse de** resr Spain
16 H7 **Comrat** Moldova
26 I10 **Comrie** Perth and Kinross, Scotland U.K.
121 E11 **Comstock** TX U.S.A.
73 K2 **Comunanza** Italy
74 G9 **Comunelli** r. Sicilia Italy
158 G5 **Con, Sông** r. Vietnam
159 I8 **Con, Sông** r. Vietnam
173 J13 **Cona** Xizang China
71 M5 **Cona** Italy
190 E1 **Çona** Turkey
88 B4 **Conakry** Guinea
136 B5 **Conambo** Ecuador
136 B5 **Conambo** r. Ecuador
145 D6 **Cona Niyeo** Arg.
205 K9 **Conara Junction** Tas. Austr.
144 C3 **Conay** Chile
72 C4 **Conca** Corse France
71 N8 **Conca** r. Italy
146 E3 **Concarán** Arg.
38 D6 **Concarneau** France
72 D6 **Concas** Sardegna Italy
137 F5 **Conceição** Amazonas Brazil
139 F1 **Conceição** Mato Grosso Brazil
140 F3 **Conceição** Paraíba Brazil
139 E2 **Conceição** Rondônia Brazil
137 F4 **Conceição** Roraima Brazil
142 E2 **Conceição** r. Brazil
64 D6 **Conceição** Port.
143 H3 **Conceição da Barra** Brazil
142 C3 **Conceição das Alagoas** Brazil
143 G5 **Conceição de Macabu** Brazil
140 C4 **Conceição do Araguaia** Brazil
140 F4 **Conceição do Coité** Brazil
143 F3 **Conceição do Mato Dentro** Brazil
137 G4 **Conceição do Maú** Brazil
140 D5 **Conceição do Norte** Brazil
143 E4 **Conceição do Rio Verde** Brazil
144 F3 **Concepción** Corrientes Arg.
144 D2 **Concepción** Tucumán Arg.
138 D2 **Concepción** Beni Bol.
139 E4 **Concepción** Santa Cruz Bol.
144 B5 **Concepción** Chile
128 F1 **Concepción** Mex.
126 C2 **Concepción** r. Mex.
139 F5 **Concepción** Para.
136 D2 **Concepción** Venez.
145 B8 **Concepción, Canal** sea chan. Chile
126 D4 **Concepción, Punta** pt Mex.
128 D6 **Concepción de Buenos Aires** Mex.
147 H3 **Concepción del Uruguay** Arg.
99 □2b **Conception, Île** i. Inner Islands Seychelles
124 L7 **Conception, Point** CA U.S.A.
94 B4 **Conception Bay** Namibia
130 F2 **Conception Island** Bahamas
70 I4 **Concesio** Italy
95 F3 **Concession** Zimbabwe
128 B3 **Concha** Mex.
63 N2 **Concha** Spain
63 O3 **Concha de Álava** reg. Spain
142 C5 **Conchas** Brazil
123 L9 **Conchas** NM U.S.A.
62 E5 **Conchas, Embalse das** resr Spain
123 L9 **Conchas Lake** NM U.S.A.
36 A6 **Conches-en-Ouche** France
138 C5 **Conchi** Chile
126 G4 **Concho** Mex.
125 W7 **Concho** AZ U.S.A.
121 F10 **Concho** r. TX U.S.A.
127 K5 **Conchos** r. Nuevo León/Tamaulipas Mex.
126 G3 **Conchos** r. Mex.
146 B3 **Concón** Chile
124 J4 **Concord** CA U.S.A.
110 J7 **Concord** MI U.S.A.
115 G8 **Concord** NC U.S.A.
117 N5 **Concord** NH U.S.A.
116 H8 **Concord** PA U.S.A.
116 G11 **Concord** VA U.S.A.
117 N4 **Concord** VT U.S.A.
147 I2 **Concordia** Arg.
136 E6 **Concórdia** Amazonas Brazil
141 B8 **Concórdia** Santa Catarina Brazil
136 C3 **Concordia** Antioquia Col.
136 C4 **Concordia** Meta Col.
128 A2 **Concordiá** Mex.
136 C6 **Concordia** Peru
96 B5 **Concordia** S. Africa
120 G6 **Concordia** KS U.S.A.
71 N4 **Concordia Sagittaria** Italy
185 O3 **Concord Peak** Afgh.
43 G6 **Concorès** France
43 H7 **Concots** France
146 B2 **Concumén** Chile
158 G5 **Con Cuông** Vietnam
91 B7 **Conda** Angola
66 F3 **Condado** reg. Spain
64 G6 **Condado de Niebla** reg. Spain
63 O3 **Condado de Treviño** reg. Spain
207 M9 **Condamine** Qld Austr.
207 L9 **Condamine** r. Qld Austr.
159 H10 **Côn Đao** Vietnam
41 B6 **Condat** France
42 G4 **Condat-sur-Vienne** France
140 F4 **Conde** Brazil
36 G5 **Condé-en-Brie** France
126 □P11 **Condega** Nic.
140 C2 **Condeixa** Brazil
62 D8 **Condeixa-a-Nova** Port.
39 M5 **Condé-sur-Huisne** France
36 G3 **Condé-sur-l'Escaut** France
39 J4 **Condé-sur-Noireau** France
39 I3 **Condé-sur-Vire** France
141 E5 **Condeúba** Brazil
71 J4 **Condino** Italy
205 K5 **Condobolin** N.S.W. Austr.
95 G3 **Condoe** Moz.
75 J7 **Condofuri** Italy
43 E8 **Condom** France
122 D4 **Condon** OR U.S.A.
136 B6 **Condor, Cordillera del** mts Ecuador/Peru
146 B1 **Condoriaco** Chile
70 C5 **Condove** Italy
30 G2 **Condover** Shropshire, England U.K.
45 G8 **Condroz** reg. Belgium
115 D10 **Conecuh** r. AL U.S.A.
71 M4 **Conegliano** Italy
126 H4 **Conejos** Mex.
123 K8 **Conejos** CO U.S.A.
123 L8 **Conejos** r. CO/NM U.S.A.
111 O9 **Conemaugh** r. PA U.S.A.
71 P8 **Conero, Monte** hill Italy
147 G3 **Conesa** Arg.
118 C5 **Conestoga** PA U.S.A.
118 C4 **Conestoga Creek** r. PA U.S.A.
111 N6 **Conestogo Lake** Ont. Can.
116 H6 **Conesus Lake** NY U.S.A.
116 D8 **Conesville** OH U.S.A.
118 B4 **Conewago Creek** r. PA U.S.A.
118 B4 **Conewago Lake** PA U.S.A.
37 L8 **Coney** r. France
115 □1 **Coney Island** Bermuda
27 E4 **Coney Island** Rep. of Ireland
119 H3 **Coney Island** NY U.S.A.
37 K5 **Conflans-en-Jarnisy** France
37 L8 **Conflans-sur-Lanterne** France
43 I10 **Conflent** reg. France
73 Q9 **Conflenti** Italy
153 L9 **Conflict Group** is P.N.G.
116 F9 **Confluence** PA U.S.A.
42 F3 **Confolens** France
42 F4 **Confolentais** reg. France
125 S3 **Confusion Range** mts UT U.S.A.
139 F6 **Confuso** r. Para.
27 D5 **Cong** Rep. of Ireland
170 B3 **Conga** Xizang China
30 D6 **Congdon's Shop** Cornwall, England U.K.
173 H12 **Congdü** Xizang China
171 I7 **Conghua** Guangdong China
170 G6 **Congjiang** Guizhou China
29 M7 **Congleton** Cheshire, England U.K.
90 B5 **Congo** country Africa
91 B6 **Congo** r. Congo/Dem. Rep. Congo
Congo (Brazzaville) country Africa see **Congo**
Congo (Kinshasa) country Africa see **Congo, Democratic Republic of**
90 D5 **Congo, Democratic Republic of** country Africa
Congo, Republic of country Africa see **Congo**
90 D5 **Congo Basin** Dem. Rep. Congo
214 J6 **Congo Cone** sea feature S. Atlantic Ocean
Congo Free State country Africa see **Congo, Democratic Republic of**
143 F4 **Congonhas** Brazil
142 B5 **Congonhinhas** Brazil
62 H3 **Congosto** Spain
63 K3 **Congosto de Valdavia** Spain
30 G5 **Congresbury** North Somerset, England U.K.
125 T7 **Congress** AZ U.S.A.
39 I6 **Congrier** France
146 B6 **Conguillo, Parque Nacional** nat. park Chile
146 E5 **Conhelo** Arg.
127 O8 **Conhuas** Mex.
203 E12 **Conical Peak** hill South I. N.Z.
145 C6 **Cónico, Cerro** mt. Arg.
36 B7 **Conie** r. France
64 G8 **Conil de la Frontera** Spain
67 K9 **Conills, Illa des** i. Spain
29 Q7 **Coningsby** Lincolnshire, England U.K.
29 O7 **Conisbrough** South Yorkshire, England U.K.
206 D7 **Coniston** N.T. Austr.
108 D4 **Coniston** Ont. Can.
29 K5 **Coniston** Cumbria, England U.K.
29 K5 **Coniston Water** l. England U.K.
207 J5 **Conjuboy** Qld Austr.
65 M7 **Conjuros** hill Spain
127 O7 **Conkal** Mex.
107 I4 **Conklin** Alta Can.
91 A5 **Conkouati, Réserve de Faune** nature res. Congo
146 E3 **Conlara** Arg.
146 E3 **Conlara** r. Arg.
39 K5 **Conlie** France
40 H3 **Conliège** France
27 K3 **Conlig** Northern Ireland U.K.
108 E2 **Conn** r. Que. Can.
27 D4 **Conn, Lough** l. Rep. of Ireland
Connacht reg. Rep. of Ireland see **Connaught**
30 F1 **Connah's Quay** Flintshire, Wales U.K.
36 G6 **Connantre** France
111 N1 **Connaught** Ont. Can.
27 D5 **Connaught** reg. Rep. of Ireland
41 F8 **Connaux** France
116 E7 **Conneaut** OH U.S.A.
116 E7 **Conneaut Lake** PA U.S.A.
116 E7 **Conneautville** PA U.S.A.
119 K2 **Connecticut** r. CT U.S.A.
117 M7 **Connecticut** state U.S.A.
26 F10 **Connel** Argyll and Bute, Scotland U.K.
206 F5 **Connells Lagoon Conservation Reserve** nature res. N.T. Austr.
116 F8 **Connellsville** PA U.S.A.
207 I8 **Connemara** Qld Austr.
27 C6 **Connemara** reg. Rep. of Ireland
27 C5 **Connemara National Park** Rep. of Ireland
206 C8 **Conner, Mount** hill N.T. Austr.
39 L5 **Connerré** France
114 E6 **Connersville** IN U.S.A.
27 D7 **Connolly** Rep. of Ireland
106 C2 **Connolly, Mount** Y.T. Can.
26 D13 **Connor** Northern Ireland U.K.
207 L6 **Connors Range** hills Qld Austr.
205 J5 **Conoble** N.S.W. Austr.
118 B4 **Conodoguinet Creek** r. PA U.S.A.
136 C5 **Cononaco** Ecuador
136 C5 **Cononaco** r. Ecuador
26 H7 **Conon Bridge** Highland, Scotland U.K.
57 K5 **Conop** Romania
57 I6 **Čonoplja** Vojvodina, Srbija Serb. and Mont.
110 E3 **Conover** WI U.S.A.
50 H4 **Conow** Ger.
118 C5 **Conowingo** MD U.S.A.
43 I6 **Conques** France
43 I9 **Conques-sur-Orbiel** France
138 D2 **Conquista** Bol.

Conquista to Cozia, Vârful

252

142 D3 Conquista Brazil
65 J4 Conquista Spain
122 I2 Conrad MT U.S.A.
214 L9 Conrad Rise sea feature Southern Ocean
121 H10 Conroe TX U.S.A.
121 H10 Conroe, Lake TX U.S.A.
71 L6 Consandolo Italy
142 H2 Conscripto Bernardi Arg.
45 J9 Consdorf Lux.
111 Q5 Consecon Ont. Can.
127 O8 Consejo Belize
143 F4 Conselheiro Lafaiete Brazil
143 G3 Conselheiro Pena Brazil
71 L6 Conselice Italy
67 K8 Consell Spain
37 J5 Consenvoye France
29 N4 Consett Durham, England U.K.
118 E4 Conshohocken PA U.S.A.
130 B2 Consolación del Sur Cuba
159 H10 Côn Son, Đao i. Vietnam
107 I4 Consort Alta Can.
Constance Ger. see Konstanz
Constance, Lake Ger./Switz. see Bodensee
64 C2 Constância Port.
147 H3 Constancia Uru.
137 F6 Constância dos Baetas Brazil
77 Q6 Constanța Romania
66 H5 Constantí Spain
62 H5 Constantim Bragança Port.
62 E6 Constantim Vila Real Port.
64 H5 Constantina Spain
87 G1 Constantine Alg.
30 B7 Constantine Cornwall, England U.K.
110 I8 Constantine MI U.S.A.
104 C4 Constantine, Cape AK U.S.A.
130 □ Constant Spring Jamaica
147 G2 Constanza Arg.
63 K7 Constanzana Spain
146 A4 Constitución Chile
147 I2 Constitución Uru.
126 B1 Constitución de 1857, Parque Nacional nat. park Mex.
65 L2 Consuegra Spain
207 L8 Consuelo Qld Austr.
139 E3 Consuelo Brazil
107 I5 Consul Sask. Can.
107 K1 Consul r. Nunavut Can.
122 G6 Contact NV U.S.A.
143 F4 Contagalo Brazil
143 E3 Contagem Brazil
138 B1 Contamana Peru
71 M5 Contarina Italy
140 F5 Contas r. Brazil
72 A7 Conte, Porto b. Sardegna Italy
97 I4 Content S. Africa
74 E8 Contessa Entellina Sicilia Italy
70 C3 Conthey Switz.
73 J3 Contigliano Italy
26 G7 Contin Highland, Scotland U.K.
116 A7 Continental OH U.S.A.
37 B7 Contis-Plage France
117 N5 Contoocook r. NH U.S.A.
127 P7 Contoy, Isla i. Mex.
146 C6 Contralmirante Cordero Arg.
74 G8 Contrasto, Colle del pass Italy
136 C3 Contratacion Col.
65 M7 Contraviesa, Sierra de mts Spain
63 Q9 Contreras, Embalse de resr Spain
145 B8 Contreras, Isla i. Chile
42 G1 Contres France
37 K7 Contrexéville France
143 E3 Contria Brazil
73 O6 Controne Italy
144 B5 Contulmo Chile
138 A1 Contumazá Peru
73 O6 Contursi Terme Italy
107 I1 Contwoyto Lake N.W.T./Nunavut Can.
36 D4 Conty France
136 C2 Convención Col.
121 J10 Convent LA U.S.A.
146 B4 Convento Viejo Chile
75 M2 Conversano Italy
116 A8 Convoy OH U.S.A.
97 J7 Conway S. Africa
Conway Conwy, Wales U.K. see Conwy
121 I8 Conway AR U.S.A.
116 A11 Conway KY U.S.A.
120 G1 Conway ND U.S.A.
117 □N5 Conway NH U.S.A.
119 H5 Conway SC U.S.A.
207 L6 Conway, Cape Qld Austr.
204 E3 Conway, Lake salt flat S.A. Austr.
207 L6 Conway National Park Qld Austr.
Conway Reef Fiji see Ceva-i-Ra
121 G7 Conway Springs KS U.S.A.
30 E1 Conwy Conwy, Wales U.K.
30 E1 Conwy admin. div. Wales U.K.
30 E1 Conwy r. Wales U.K.
30 D1 Conwy Bay Wales U.K.
118 C3 Conyngham PA U.S.A.
73 O6 Conza, Lago di l. Italy
204 E3 Coober Pedy S.A. Austr.
Cooch Behar W. Bengal India see Koch Bihar
207 L9 Coogoon r. Qld Austr.
204 C4 Cook S.A. Austr.
110 B2 Cook MN U.S.A.
145 C9 Cook, Bahía de b. Chile
201 □3a Cook, Baie de b. Moorea Fr. Polynesia
106 E5 Cook, Cape B.C. Can.
106 B2 Cook, Mount Can./U.S.A.
Cook, Mount South I. N.Z. see Aoraki
123 K10 Cookes Peak NM U.S.A.
115 E7 Cookeville TN U.S.A.
31 K4 Cookham Windsor and Maidenhead, England U.K.
97 J8 Cookhouse S. Africa
213 K2 Cook Ice Shelf Antarctica
104 C3 Cook Inlet sea chan. AK U.S.A.
203 □2 Cook Islands S. Pacific Ocean
30 H3 Cookley Worcestershire, England U.K.
Cook's Bay Moorea Fr. Polynesia see Cook, Baie de
117 K6 Cooksburg NY U.S.A.
26 J8 Cook's Cairn hill Scotland U.K.
109 K3 Cook's Harbour Nfld and Lab. Can.
207 J3 Cooks Passage Qld Austr.
27 I3 Cookstown Northern Ireland U.K.
203 I7 Cook Strait South I. N.Z.
118 A6 Cooksville MD U.S.A.
207 J3 Cooktown Qld Austr.
27 F4 Coola Rep. of Ireland
205 K4 Coolabah N.S.W. Austr.
207 J9 Cooladdi Qld Austr.
205 L4 Coolah N.S.W. Austr.
205 M4 Coolah Tops National Park N.S.W. Austr.
205 K6 Coolamon N.S.W. Austr.
27 E4 Coolaney Rep. of Ireland
36 H6 Coole France
36 H6 Coole r. France
28 C6 Coole Rep. of Ireland
209 F11 Coolgardie W.A. Austr.
27 H7 Coolgrange Rep. of Ireland
27 J7 Coolgreany Rep. of Ireland
206 C3 Coolibah N.T. Austr.
125 U9 Coolidge AZ U.S.A.
209 C10 Coolimba W.A. Austr.
27 J6 Coolock Rep. of Ireland
207 N9 Cooloola National Park Qld Austr.
27 H8 Coolroebeg Rep. of Ireland
207 N9 Coolum Beach Qld Austr.
205 L7 Cooma N.S.W. Austr.
27 B9 Coomacarrea hill Rep. of Ireland
204 H5 Coombah N.S.W. Austr.
30 C6 Coombe Cornwall, England U.K.
31 I5 Coombe Bissett Wiltshire, England U.K.
205 L4 Coonabarabran N.S.W. Austr.
204 G6 Coonalpyn S.A. Austr.
205 L4 Coonamble N.S.W. Austr.
209 G11 Coonana W.A. Austr.
209 G11 Coonana Aboriginal Reserve W.A. Austr.
204 H7 Coonawarra S.A. Austr.
204 E4 Coondambo S.A. Austr.
208 E6 Coongan r. W.A. Austr.
208 E6 Coongan Aboriginal Reserve W.A. Austr.
207 J9 Coongoola Qld Austr.
204 E2 Coongra watercourse S.A. Austr.
110 A4 Coon Rapids MN U.S.A.
206 D2 Cooper r. N.T. Austr.
121 H9 Cooper TX U.S.A.
204 F3 Cooper Creek watercourse Qld/S.A. Austr.
116 C8 Cooperdale OH U.S.A.
205 N4 Coopernook N.S.W. Austr.
118 E3 Coopersburg PA U.S.A.
117 □P4 Coopers Mills ME U.S.A.
115 I12 Cooper's Town Bahamas
120 F2 Cooperstown ND U.S.A.
117 K6 Cooperstown NY U.S.A.
205 L7 Coopracambra National Park Vic. Austr.
131 □7 Coora Trin. and Tob.
204 D4 Coorabie S.A. Austr.
209 D8 Coor-de-Wandy hill W.A. Austr.
204 G7 Coorong National Park S.A. Austr.
209 D10 Coorow W.A. Austr.
207 N9 Cooroy Qld Austr.
115 D9 Coosa r. AL U.S.A.
122 B5 Coos Bay OR U.S.A.
122 B5 Coos Bay b. OR U.S.A.
205 L6 Cootamundra N.S.W. Austr.
27 H4 Cootehill Rep. of Ireland
176 G6 Cooum r. India
207 M9 Cooyar Qld Austr.
144 D3 Copacabana Arg.
57 L5 Copăcel Romania
146 B5 Copahue, Volcán vol. Chile
127 M9 Copainalá Mex.
129 I9 Copala Mex.
129 H7 Copalillo Mex.
129 K10 Copalita Mex.
129 K10 Copalita r. Mex.
136 C5 Copal Urcu Peru
126 □O10 Copán tourist site Hond.
75 L6 Copanello Italy
120 D6 Cope CO U.S.A.
67 C13 Cope, Cabo c. Spain
27 L3 Copeland Island Northern Ireland U.K.
110 I5 Copemish MI U.S.A.
Copenhagen Denmark see København
139 E4 Copere Bol.
75 O3 Copertino Italy
147 G6 Copetonas Arg.
205 M3 Copeton Reservoir N.S.W. Austr.
158 G6 Cô Pi, Phou mt. Laos/Vietnam
119 I3 Copiague NY U.S.A.
144 C2 Copiapó Chile
144 C2 Copiapo, Volcán vol. Chile
26 K5 Copinsay i. Scotland U.K.
118 E3 Coplay PA U.S.A.
204 G4 Copley S.A. Austr.
29 N4 Copley Durham, England U.K.
29 O6 Copmanthorpe York, England U.K.
139 E6 Copo, Parque Nacional nat. park Arg.
66 I4 Copons Spain
138 C3 Coporaque Peru
70 G5 Coppa r. Italy
71 L6 Copparo Italy
27 E9 Coppeen Rep. of Ireland
137 G3 Coppename r. Suriname
49 I6 Coppenbrügge Ger.
49 I7 Coppengrave Ger.
91 E8 Copperbelt prov. Zambia
108 D4 Copper Cliff Ont. Can.
207 I4 Copperfield r. Qld Austr.
110 G2 Copper Harbor MI U.S.A.
Coppermine Nunavut Can. see Kugluktuk
104 G3 Coppermine r. Nunavut Can.
108 C4 Coppermine Point Ont. Can.
95 F3 Copper Queen Zimbabwe
96 G5 Copperton S. Africa
125 T1 Copperton UT U.S.A.
106 H2 Copp Lake N.W.T. Can.
30 E6 Copplestone Devon, England U.K.
77 M4 Copşa Mică Romania
31 L5 Copthorne Surrey, England U.K.
31 I6 Copythorne Hampshire, England U.K.
173 G11 Coqên Xizang China
173 G11 Coqên Xizang China
131 □1 Coqui Puerto Rico
122 B5 Coquille OR U.S.A.
128 D6 Coquimatlán Mex.
146 B1 Coquimbo Chile
146 B2 Coquimbo admin. reg. Chile
146 B1 Coquimbo, Bahía de b. Chile
106 F5 Coquitlam B.C. Can.
77 M7 Corabia Romania
143 E2 Coração de Jesus Brazil
75 L6 Corace r. Italy
Coracesium Turkey see Alanya
138 B3 Coracora Peru
176 C6 Cora Dive sea feature India
205 N3 Coraki N.S.W. Austr.
209 B7 Coral Bay W.A. Austr.
154 A7 Coral Bay Palawan Phil.
201 □1a Coral Coast Fiji
146 C5 Corales, Cerro mt. Arg.
115 □2 Coral Harbour New Prov. Bahamas
105 J3 Coral Harbour Nunavut Can.
115 □2 Coral Heights New Prov. Bahamas
200 □5 Coral Sea S. Pacific Ocean
216 F6 Coral Sea Basin S. Pacific Ocean
199 F3 Coral Sea Islands Territory terr. Austr.
27 H6 Coralstown Rep. of Ireland
119 I3 Coram NY U.S.A.
205 I8 Corangamite, Lake Vic. Austr.
144 D1 Coranzuli Arg.
116 E8 Coraopolis PA U.S.A.
191 K5 Corat Azer.
73 Q5 Corato Italy
38 D5 Coray France
66 D7 Corbalán Spain
27 D4 Corbally Rep. of Ireland
72 I2 Corbara, Lago di l. Italy
36 D6 Corbeil-Essonnes France
36 E7 Corbeilles France
142 A6 Corbélia Brazil
40 H5 Corbelin France
37 L8 Corbenay France
36 G5 Corbeny France
66 F5 Corbera d'Ebre Spain
147 G4 Corbett Arg.
107 M2 Corbett Inlet Nunavut Can.
178 G5 Corbett National Park India
36 E4 Corbie France
43 I10 Corbières reg. France
70 C2 Corbières Switz.
40 D2 Corbigny France
116 A12 Corbin KY U.S.A.
118 F6 Corbin City NJ U.S.A.
66 G4 Corbins Spain
71 M5 Corbola Italy
65 H5 Corbones r. Spain
29 M4 Corbridge Northumberland, England U.K.
77 Q6 Corbu Romania
31 K3 Corby Northamptonshire, England U.K.
66 L4 Corçà Spain
Corcaigh Rep. of Ireland see Cork
40 G2 Corcelles-lès-Cîteaux France
73 I3 Corchiano Italy
98 □3d Corcho, Punta del pt La Palma Canary Is
73 I1 Corciano Italy
37 M7 Corcieux France
65 M2 Córcoles r. Spain
124 M5 Corcoran CA U.S.A.
38 H8 Corcoué-sur-Logne France
145 C6 Corcovado Arg.
145 B6 Corcovado, Golfo de sea chan. Chile
126 □R13 Corcovado, Parque Nacional nat. park Costa Rica
62 B3 Corcubión Spain
62 B3 Corcubión, Ría de b. Spain
27 D8 Cordal Rep. of Ireland
207 N8 Cordalba Qld Austr.
143 F5 Cordeiro Brazil
115 F10 Cordele GA U.S.A.
124 J3 Cordelia CA U.S.A.
121 F8 Cordell OK U.S.A.
38 H7 Cordemais France
71 N4 Cordenòns Italy
43 H7 Cordes France
71 M3 Cordevole r. Italy
71 M4 Cordignano Italy
138 B1 Cordillera Azul, Parque Nacional nat. park Peru
136 C4 Cordillera de los Picachos, Parque Nacional nat. park Col.
154 D6 Cordilleras Range mts Panay Phil.
204 H2 Cordillo Downs S.A. Austr.
62 C8 Cordinhã Port.
143 E3 Cordisburgo Brazil
147 E2 Córdoba Córdoba Arg.
145 C6 Córdoba Río Negro Arg.
147 F3 Córdoba prov. Arg.
136 C2 Córdoba dept Col.
126 H4 Córdoba Durango Mex.
129 K7 Córdoba Veracruz Mex.
65 J5 Córdoba Spain
65 J4 Córdoba prov. Spain
65 J5 Córdoba, Sierra de hills Spain
146 E3 Córdoba, Sierras de mts Arg.
65 J6 Cordobilla, Embalse de resr Spain
64 G2 Cordobilla de Lácara Spain
138 B3 Cordova Peru
Cordova Spain see Córdoba
104 D3 Cordova AK U.S.A.
118 D7 Cordova MD U.S.A.
106 C4 Cordova Bay AK U.S.A.
63 O4 Cordovín Spain
Corduba Spain see Córdoba
63 Q7 Corduente Spain
140 E2 Coreaú Brazil
71 J7 Coreglia Antelminelli Italy
207 H5 Corella r. Qld Austr.
63 Q4 Corella Spain
206 E5 Corella Lake salt flat N.T. Austr.
62 I5 Coreses Spain
30 H6 Corfe Castle Dorset, England U.K.
30 H6 Corfe Mullen Dorset, England U.K.
207 I6 Corfield Qld Austr.
73 L3 Corfinio Italy
Corfu i. Ionioi Nisoi Greece see Kerkyra
116 G6 Corfu NY U.S.A.
62 E6 Corgo r. Port.
141 B6 Corguinho Brazil
73 J4 Cori Italy
62 G9 Coria Spain
64 G6 Coria del Río Spain
71 N8 Coriano Italy
140 D5 Coribe Brazil
205 M5 Coricudgy mt. N.S.W. Austr.
75 L4 Corigliano, Golfo di b. Italy
75 L4 Corigliano Calabro Italy
71 O8 Corinaldo Italy
207 M4 Coringa Islands Coral Sea Is Terr. Austr.
Corinium Gloucestershire, England U.K. see Cirencester
205 J9 Corinna Tas. Austr.
107 J5 Corinne Sask. Can.
Corinth Peloponnisos Greece see Korinthos
121 K8 Corinth MS U.S.A.
117 L5 Corinth NY U.S.A.
143 E3 Corinto Brazil
126 □P11 Corinto Nic.
65 I7 Coripe Spain
89 H6 Corisco i. Equat. Guinea
139 F4 Corixa Grande r. Bol./Brazil
139 F4 Corixinha r. Brazil
27 F9 Cork Rep. of Ireland
27 E8 Cork county Rep. of Ireland
38 E5 Corlay France
28 B6 Corlea Rep. of Ireland
27 D4 Corlee Rep. of Ireland
74 E8 Corleone Sicilia Italy
73 Q7 Corleto Perticara Italy
79 I1 Çorlu Turkey
79 I1 Çorlu r. Turkey
40 F3 Cormatin France
62 B2 Corme e Laxe, Ría de b. Spain
39 L3 Cormeilles France
39 K3 Cormelles-le-Royal France
62 C2 Corme Porto Spain
42 C4 Corme-Royal France
36 G5 Cormicy France
71 O4 Cormons Italy
137 H4 Cormontibo Fr. Guiana
36 H5 Cormontreuil France
71 O4 Cormor r. Italy
154 □ Cormoran Reef Palau
107 K4 Cormorant Man. Can.
107 K4 Cormorant Lake Man. Can.
107 K4 Cormorant Provincial Forest nature res. Man. Can.
73 O5 Cornacchia, Monte mt. Italy
27 G6 Cornafulla Rep. of Ireland
63 P4 Cornago Spain
27 D5 Cornamona Rep. of Ireland
70 G4 Cornaredo Italy
41 F7 Cornas France
48 F5 Cornau Ger.
49 I8 Cornberg Ger.
39 K7 Corné France
71 K3 Cornedo all'Isarco Italy
43 J10 Corneilla-del-Vercol France
97 M3 Cornelia S. Africa
142 B5 Cornélio Procópio Brazil
144 H3 Cornélios Brazil
137 G3 Corneliskondre Suriname
110 C4 Cornell WI U.S.A.
66 J5 Cornellà de Llobregat Spain
66 K3 Cornellà de Terri Spain
62 H2 Cornellana Spain
109 J3 Corner Brook Nfld and Lab. Can.
205 K8 Corner Inlet b. Vic. Austr.
65 P5 Corneros r. Spain
214 F3 Corner Seamounts sea feature N. Atlantic Ocean
16 H6 Corneşti Moldova
71 K4 Cornetto mt. Italy
116 B11 Cornettsville KY U.S.A.
57 L6 Cornetu, Vârful hill Romania
26 K7 Cornhill Aberdeenshire, Scotland U.K.
29 M2 Cornhill-on-Tweed Northumberland, England U.K.
29 M6 Cornholme West Yorkshire, England U.K.
77 O3 Corni Romania
72 F2 Cornia r. Italy
70 I7 Corniglio Italy
36 H5 Cornillet, Mont hill France
37 M8 Cornimont France
121 J7 Corning AR U.S.A.
124 J2 Corning CA U.S.A.
120 H5 Corning IA U.S.A.
116 H6 Corning NY U.S.A.
116 C9 Corning OH U.S.A.
207 J7 Cornish watercourse Qld Austr.
145 B7 Cornish, Estrada b. Chile
Corn Islands is Nic. see Maíz, Islas del
73 J2 Corno r. Italy
73 L3 Corno, Monte mt. Italy
70 I3 Corno di Campo mt. Italy/Switz.
38 C5 Cornouaille reg. France
110 C3 Cornucopia WI U.S.A.
71 M4 Cornuda Italy
63 N3 Cornudilla Spain
41 C9 Cornus France
108 F4 Cornwall Ont. Can.
109 I4 Cornwall P.E.I. Can.
130 □ Cornwall reg. Jamaica
30 C6 Cornwall admin. div. England U.K.
119 G2 Cornwall NY U.S.A.
118 C4 Cornwall PA U.S.A.
30 □ Cornwall, Cape England U.K.
105 I2 Cornwallis Island Nunavut Can.
105 I2 Cornwall Island Nunavut Can.
119 G2 Cornwall on Hudson NY U.S.A.
204 F6 Corny Point S.A. Austr.
136 D2 Coro Venez.
62 F5 Coroa, Serra da mts Port.
143 F3 Coroaci Brazil
140 D3 Coroatá Brazil
138 C4 Corocoro Bol.
137 F2 Corocoro, Isla i. Venez.
27 D7 Corofin Rep. of Ireland
202 J3 Coroglen North I. N.Z.
138 D4 Coroico Bol.
142 D3 Coromandel Brazil
202 J3 Coromandel North I. N.Z.
176 G7 Coromandel Coast India
202 J4 Coromandel Forest Park nature res. North I. N.Z.
202 J3 Coromandel Peninsula North I. N.Z.
202 J3 Coromandel Range hills North I. N.Z.
39 J7 Coron France
154 C5 Coron Phil.
64 C4 Corona r. Port.
63 R3 Corona mt. Spain
124 O8 Corona CA U.S.A.
123 L9 Corona NM U.S.A.
89 H6 Corona, Punta pt Equat. Guinea
62 C6 Coronado Port.
124 O9 Coronado CA U.S.A.
126 □R13 Coronado, Bahiá de b. Costa Rica
154 D8 Coronado Bay Mindanao Phil.
107 I4 Coronation Alta Can.
104 G3 Coronation Gulf Nunavut Can.
212 U2 Coronation Island S. Orkney Is Atlantic Ocean
106 C4 Coronation Island AK U.S.A.
208 H3 Coronation Islands W.A. Austr.
154 C6 Coron Bay Phil.
147 G2 Coronda Arg.
146 E3 Coronel Alzogaray Arg.
147 G3 Coronel Bogada Arg.
147 H4 Coronel Brandsen Arg.
147 G6 Coronel Dorrego Arg.
143 F3 Coronel Fabriciano Brazil
147 G6 Coronel Falcón Arg.
145 D6 Coronel Francisco Sosa Arg.
147 E6 Coronel Juliá y Echarrán Arg.
146 E3 Coronel Moldes Córdoba Arg.
144 D2 Coronel Moldes Salta Arg.
143 F2 Coronel Murta Brazil
139 F6 Coronel Oviedo Para.
139 G3 Coronel Ponce Brazil
136 B5 Coronel Portillo Peru
147 G5 Coronel Pringles Arg.
147 G5 Coronel Rodolfo Bunge Arg.
139 G5 Coronel Sapucaia Mato Grosso do Sul Brazil
139 G5 Coronel Sapucaia Mato Grosso do Sul Brazil
147 G5 Coronel Suárez Arg.
147 I5 Coronel Vidal Arg.
128 G5 Coroneo Mex.
203 C11 Coronet Peak South I. N.Z.
78 B2 Çorovodë Albania
205 K6 Corowa N.S.W. Austr.
127 O8 Corozal Belize
129 I4 Corozal Mex.
131 □1 Corozal Puerto Rico
137 F2 Corozal Venez.
136 E2 Corozo Pando Venez.
145 C8 Corpen Aike Arg.
41 H7 Corps France
38 H6 Corps-Nuds France
144 G2 Corpus Arg.
121 G12 Corpus Christi TX U.S.A.
121 G11 Corpus Christi, Lake TX U.S.A.
138 D4 Corque Bol.
145 B5 Corral Chile
62 I7 Corral mt. Spain
63 N9 Corral de Almaguer Spain
147 F3 Corral de Bustos Arg.
65 K3 Corral de Calatrava Spain
63 L9 Corral de Cantos mt. Spain
146 D2 Corral de Isaac Arg.
98 □3b Corralejo Fuerteventura Canary Is
121 C13 Corrales Mex.
62 I6 Corrales Spain
128 F5 Corrales de Rábago Mex.
130 C2 Corralilla Cuba
124 K5 Corralitos CA U.S.A.
146 D2 Corralitos, Monte mt. Arg.
129 L7 Corral Nuevo Mex.
65 Q3 Corral-Rubio Spain
209 C8 Corrandibby Range hills W.A. Austr.
95 H2 Corrane Moz.
72 C7 Corrasi, Punta mt. Sardegna Italy
27 C5 Corraun Peninsula Rep. of Ireland
37 L8 Corre France
128 C2 Corre Caballo Mex.
26 K8 Correen Hills Scotland U.K.
71 J6 Correggio Italy
142 B2 Córrego do Ouro Brazil
143 F3 Córrego Novo Brazil
140 D4 Corrente Brazil
142 B3 Corrente r. Brazil
140 E5 Corrente r. Brazil
143 F3 Corrente Grande r. Brazil
141 B6 Correntes Brazil
139 G4 Correntes r. Brazil
69 E7 Correnti, Isola delle i. Sicilia Italy
140 D5 Correntina Brazil
Correntina r. Brazil see Éguas
42 H5 Corrèze France
42 H5 Corrèze dept France
42 G5 Corrèze r. France
27 D6 Corrib, Lough l. Rep. of Ireland
71 P9 Corridonia Italy
26 F11 Corrie North Ayrshire, Scotland U.K.
144 F2 Corrientes Arg.
147 H1 Corrientes prov. Arg.
144 F3 Corrientes r. Arg.
136 C5 Corrientes r. Peru
147 I6 Corrientes, Cabo c. Arg.
136 B3 Corrientes, Cabo c. Col.
130 A3 Corrientes, Cabo c. Cuba
128 B5 Corrientes, Cabo c. Mex.
121 H10 Corrigan TX U.S.A.
209 D12 Corrigin W.A. Austr.
31 M4 Corringham Thurrock, England U.K.
30 E2 Corris Gwynedd, Wales U.K.
137 G3 Corriverton Guyana
36 G6 Corrobert France
62 B3 Corrubedo, Cabo c. Spain
116 F7 Corry PA U.S.A.
205 K7 Corryong Vic. Austr.
70 D7 Corsaglia r. Italy
75 O4 Corsano Italy
72 C3 Corse admin. reg. France
72 A3 Corse i. France
72 C1 Corse, Cap c. Corse France
72 B4 Corse-du-Sud dept Corse France
26 H12 Corserine hill Scotland U.K.
38 G5 Corseul France
30 H5 Corsham Wiltshire, England U.K.
Corsica i. France see Corse
121 G9 Corsicana TX U.S.A.
70 G5 Corsico Italy
90 A4 Corsico, Baie de b. Gabon
26 I12 Corsock Dumfries and Galloway, Scotland U.K.
118 F6 Corson's Inlet NJ U.S.A.
75 K6 Cortale Italy
128 G5 Cortazar Mex.
72 C3 Corte Corse France
64 F3 Corte de Peleas Spain
62 D4 Cortegada Spain
64 F5 Cortegana Spain
70 E6 Cortemilia Italy
70 I3 Corteno Golgi Italy
70 G5 Corteolona Italy
63 R5 Cortes Spain
Cortes, Sea of g. Mex. see California, Golfo de
66 D6 Cortes de Aragón Spain
65 N5 Cortes de Baza Spain
65 I7 Cortes de la Frontera Spain
64 H7 Cortes de la Frontera, Reserva Nacional de nature res. Spain
67 D9 Cortes de Pallás Spain
123 J8 Cortez CO U.S.A.
125 P1 Cortez Mountains NV U.S.A.
64 C3 Cortiçadas de Lavre Port.
66 G5 Cortiella r. Spain
65 K2 Cortijo de Arriba Spain
129 I9 Cortijos r. Mex.
65 N4 Cortijos Nuevos Spain
71 M2 Cortina d'Ampezzo Italy
117 I6 Cortland NY U.S.A.
116 E7 Cortland OH U.S.A.
58 E8 Corto, Lago del l. Italy
31 P2 Corton Suffolk, England U.K.
71 L9 Cortona Italy
88 B4 Corubal r. Guinea-Bissau
64 B3 Coruche Port.
Çoruh Turkey see Artvin
191 C4 Çoruh r. Turkey
189 J3 Çoruh r. Turkey
62 G3 Corullón Spain
188 G3 Çorum Turkey
139 F4 Corumbá Brazil
142 C3 Corumbá r. Brazil
142 C1 Corumbá de Goiás Brazil
142 C3 Corumbaíba Brazil
142 B5 Corumbataí r. Brazil
143 H2 Corumbaú, Ponta pt Brazil
62 D2 Coruña, Ría da b. Spain
77 N4 Corund Romania
57 L4 Corund r. Romania
116 C6 Corunna Ont. Can.
Corunna Spain see A Coruña
111 J7 Corunna MI U.S.A.
140 F4 Coruripe Brazil
122 C4 Corvallis OR U.S.A.
71 L2 Corvara in Badia Italy
30 G3 Corve Dale val. England U.K.
67 C12 Corvera Spain
73 J4 Corvia, Colle hill Italy
98 □1 Corvo i. Azores
30 F2 Corwen Denbighshire, Wales U.K.
120 I5 Corydon IA U.S.A.
114 D6 Corydon IN U.S.A.
31 N4 Coryton Thurrock, England U.K.
116 G7 Coryville PA U.S.A.
Cos i. Greece see Kos
66 C6 Cosa Spain
128 A1 Cosalá Mex.
129 L7 Cosamaloapan Mex.
191 A5 Coşandere Turkey
31 J2 Cosby Leicestershire, England U.K.
138 C4 Coscaya Chile
73 J2 Coscerno, Monte mt. Italy
75 L4 Coscile r. Italy
129 J6 Coscomatepec Mex.
63 P6 Coscurita Spain
Cosentia Italy see Cosenza
73 Q9 Cosenza Italy
73 Q9 Cosenza prov. Italy
77 O6 Coşereni Romania
75 L4 Coserie r. Italy
26 I9 Coshieville Perth and Kinross, Scotland U.K.
116 D8 Coshocton OH U.S.A.
128 E3 Cosío Mex.
70 D7 Cosio di Arroscia Italy
63 M8 Coslada Spain
99 □2 Cosmolédo Atoll Aldabra Is Seychelles
209 G10 Cosmo Newbery Aboriginal Reserve W.A. Austr.
142 D5 Cosmópolis Brazil
40 B2 Cosne-Cours-sur-Loire France
40 B4 Cosne-d'Allier France
129 M8 Cosoleacaque Mex.
75 J7 Cosoleto Italy
146 E2 Cosquín Arg.
70 E4 Cossato Italy
51 I8 Cossebaude Ger.
39 J6 Cossé-le-Vivien France
72 B7 Cossoine Sardegna Italy
36 B8 Cosson r. France
70 B2 Cossonay Switz.
140 E3 Costa Brazil
64 A4 Costa Bela coastal area Port.
67 E11 Costa Blanca coastal area Spain
66 L5 Costa Brava coastal area Spain
71 N9 Costacciaro Italy
77 P5 Costache Negri Romania
64 A3 Costa da Caparica Port.
64 B4 Costa da Galé coastal area Port.
66 G6 Costa de Fora coastal area Spain
64 E6 Costa de la Luz coastal area Spain
67 E8 Costa del Azahar coastal area Spain
98 □3a Costa del Silencio Tenerife Canary Is
65 I8 Costa del Sol coastal area Spain
126 □R11 Costa de Mosquitos coastal area Nic.
66 J5 Costa Dorada coastal area Spain
64 A3 Costa do Sol coastal area Port.
147 G3 Costa Grande Arg.
138 D3 Costa Marques Brazil
72 D9 Costa Rei coastal area Sardegna Italy
142 A3 Costa Rica Brazil
130 A8 Costa Rica country Central America
126 F5 Costa Rica Mex.
72 D5 Costa Smeralda coastal area Sardegna Italy
98 □3c Costa Teguise Lanzarote Canary Is
72 A9 Costa Verde coastal area Sardegna Italy
62 G1 Costa Verde coastal area Spain
70 I4 Costa Volpino Italy
57 K6 Costeiu Romania
27 C6 Costelloe Rep. of Ireland
Costermansville Dem. Rep. Congo see Bukavu
31 O2 Costessey Norfolk, England U.K.
16 G6 Costeşti Moldova
77 M6 Costeşti Argeş Romania
77 P4 Costeşti Vaslui Romania
117 □Q3 Costigan ME U.S.A.
107 J3 Costigan Lake Sask. Can.
70 E6 Costigliole d'Asti Italy
70 C6 Costigliole Saluzzo Italy
66 C5 Cosuenda Spain
77 L6 Coşuştea r. Romania
51 I8 Coswig Sachsen Ger.
51 E7 Coswig Sachsen-Anhalt Ger.
138 B3 Cotabambas Peru
154 E8 Cotabato Mindanao Phil.
138 D4 Cotacajes r. Bol.
138 D5 Cotagaita Bol.
138 B3 Cotahuasi Peru
143 G3 Cotaxé r. Brazil
129 K7 Cotaxtla Mex.
106 D3 Cote, Mount AK U.S.A.
120 F3 Coteau des Prairies slope SD U.S.A.
120 D1 Coteau du Missouri slope ND U.S.A.
120 E3 Coteau du Missouri slope SD U.S.A.
117 K3 Coteau Station Que. Can.
130 F4 Coteaux Haiti
36 G6 Côte Champenoise reg. France
43 A9 Côte d'Argent coastal area France
41 K9 Côte d'Azur airport France
41 K9 Côte d'Azur coastal area France
36 H7 Côte des Bars reg. France
88 D5 Côte d'Ivoire country Africa
36 I8 Côte-d'Or dept France
40 F3 Côte d'Or reg. France
Côte Française de Somalis country Africa see Djibouti
140 D4 Cotegipe Brazil
38 I3 Cotentin pen. France
38 F5 Côtes-d'Armor dept France
37 I4 Côtes de Meuse ridge France
37 K6 Côtes de Moselle hills France
Côtes-du-Nord dept France see Côtes-d'Armor
43 K10 Côte Vermeille coastal area France
30 D4 Cothi r. Wales U.K.
138 D2 Coti r. Brazil
72 B4 Coti-Chiavari Corse France
66 F2 Cotiella mt. Spain
41 I9 Cotignac France
71 L7 Cotignola Italy
128 E6 Cotija Mex.
98 □3b Cotillo Fuerteventura Canary Is
137 F4 Cotingo r. Brazil
16 H6 Cotiujeni Moldova
16 H6 Cotiujenii Mici Moldova
77 M6 Cotmeana r. Romania
Coton, Pointe pt Rodrigues I. Mauritius see Cotton, Pointe
64 G5 Coto Nacional de la Pata del Caballo nature res. Spain
89 F5 Cotonou Benin
136 B5 Cotopaxi prov. Ecuador
136 B5 Cotopaxi, Volcán vol. Ecuador
130 B2 Cotorro Cuba
75 L5 Cotronei Italy
30 H4 Cotswold Hills England U.K.
122 C5 Cottage Grove OR U.S.A.
73 J3 Cottanello Italy
51 J7 Cottbus Ger.
176 G6 Cotteliar r. India
31 M3 Cottenham Cambridgeshire, England U.K.
31 K2 Cottesmore Rutland, England U.K.
41 J8 Cottian Alps mts France/Italy
137 H4 Cottica Suriname
Cottiennes, Alpes mts France/Italy see Cottian Alps
29 Q6 Cottingham East Riding of Yorkshire, England U.K.
31 K2 Cottingham Northamptonshire, England U.K.
110 B2 Cotton MN U.S.A.
99 □1a Cotton, Pointe pt Rodrigues I. Mauritius
206 G7 Cottonbush Creek watercourse Qld Austr.
125 T7 Cottonwood AZ U.S.A.
124 J1 Cottonwood CA U.S.A.
122 F3 Cottonwood ID U.S.A.
120 G6 Cottonwood r. KS U.S.A.
120 H3 Cottonwood r. MN U.S.A.
121 D10 Cottonwood Creek watercourse TX U.S.A.
120 G6 Cottonwood Falls KS U.S.A.
125 V7 Cottonwood Wash watercourse AZ U.S.A.
130 H4 Cotuí Dom. Rep.
121 F11 Cotulla TX U.S.A.
77 O2 Coţuşca Romania
41 D6 Coubon France
40 F3 Couches France
208 I3 Couchman Range hills W.A. Austr.
64 C3 Couço Port.
41 D7 Coucouron France
36 F4 Coucy-le-Château-Auffrique France
39 N7 Couddes France
36 D1 Coudekerque-Branche France
116 G7 Coudersport PA U.S.A.
109 G4 Coudres, Île aux i. Que. Can.
204 F7 Couedic, Cape du S.A. Austr.
38 H7 Couëron France
38 H4 Couesnon r. France
43 G10 Couflens France
43 H8 Coufouleux France
42 E3 Couhé France
43 I10 Couiza France
39 L5 Coulaines France
36 G8 Coulanges-la-Vineuse France
40 C2 Coulanges-lès-Nevers France
40 D1 Coulanges-sur-Yonne France
39 L5 Coulans-sur-Gée France
42 F5 Coulaures France
122 E3 Coulee City WA U.S.A.
122 E3 Coulee Dam WA U.S.A.
40 B3 Couleuvre France
39 P6 Coullons France
213 L2 Coulman Island Antarctica
36 H8 Coulmier-le-Sec France
36 C8 Coulmiers France
36 C2 Coulogne France
36 G5 Coulognes-Cohan France
87 H4 Couloir 1 well Alg.
42 E3 Coulombiers France
36 C6 Coulombs France
36 F6 Coulommiers France
41 F9 Coulon r. France
108 E4 Coulonge r. Que. Can.
42 C3 Coulonges-sur-l'Autize France
42 F5 Coulounieix-Chamiers France
26 G10 Coulport Argyll and Bute, Scotland U.K.
124 L4 Coulterville CA U.S.A.
122 F4 Council ID U.S.A.
120 H5 Council Bluffs IA U.S.A.
120 G6 Council Grove KS U.S.A.
205 J8 Councillor Island Tas. Austr.
31 J2 Countesthorpe Leicestershire, England U.K.
26 J9 Coupar Angus Perth and Kinross, Scotland U.K.
122 C2 Coupeville WA U.S.A.
41 B9 Coupiac France
39 K5 Couptrain France
62 C5 Coura Port.
107 I1 Courageous Lake N.W.T. Can.
137 G3 Courantyne r. Guyana
45 F8 Courcelles Belgium
117 □O3 Courcelles Que. Can.
37 L5 Courcelles-Chaussy France
37 L5 Courcelles-sur-Nied France
40 J1 Courchaton France
41 J6 Courchevel France
39 N6 Cour-Cheverny France
39 K5 Courcité France
42 C3 Courçon France
36 H5 Courcy France
62 F4 Courel, Serra do mts Spain
39 L5 Courgains France
36 G7 Courgenay France
70 C1 Courgenay Switz.
18 E6 Courland Lagoon b. Lith./Rus. Fed.
40 G3 Courlaoux France
39 J8 Courlay France
36 F7 Courlon-sur-Yonne France
70 B4 Courmayeur Italy
36 F5 Courmelles France
40 C5 Cournon-d'Auvergne France
41 D9 Cournonterral France
41 G10 Couronne, Cap c. France
40 D5 Courpière France
70 C1 Courrendlin Switz.
43 E8 Courrensan France
36 E3 Courrières France
40 B2 Cours France
42 F5 Coursac France
41 C10 Coursan France
41 K9 Coursegoules France
39 K3 Courseulles-sur-Mer France
40 E4 Cours-la-Ville France
40 C1 Courson-les-Carrières France
70 C1 Court Switz.
36 B7 Courtalain France
70 C1 Courtelary Switz.
40 K1 Courtelevant France
106 E5 Courtenay B.C. Can.
36 F7 Courtenay France
41 F8 Courthézon France
36 I6 Courtisols France
116 H12 Courtland VA U.S.A.
27 E9 Courtmacsherry Rep. of Ireland
27 E9 Courtmacsherry Bay Rep. of Ireland
39 L4 Courtomer France
27 J7 Courtown Rep. of Ireland
45 G7 Court-St-Etienne Belgium
36 B7 Courville-sur-Eure France
40 G3 Cousance France
37 J6 Cousances-les-Forges France
43 F10 Couserans reg. France
121 I9 Coushatta LA U.S.A.
40 D1 Cousin r. France
99 □2a Cousin i. Inner Islands Seychelles
99 □2a Cousine i. Inner Islands Seychelles
62 C4 Couso, Punta de pt Spain
42 G4 Coussac-Bonneval France
39 M8 Coussay-les-Bois France
36 H8 Coussegrey France
37 K7 Coussey France
41 G9 Coustellet France
43 J11 Coustouges France
38 I3 Coutances France
39 K4 Couterne France
143 F3 Couto de Magalhães de Minas Brazil
42 D5 Coutras France
107 I5 Coutts Alta Can.
42 E4 Couture r. France
131 □7 Couva Trin. and Tob.
70 B2 Couvet Switz.
45 G8 Couvin Belgium
36 G4 Couvron-et-Aumencourt France
43 F6 Couze r. France
43 F6 Couze-et-St-Front France
42 G4 Couzeix France
62 I8 Covacha del Losar mt. Spain
62 E3 Cova da Serpe, Sierra da mts Spain
63 O5 Covaleda Spain
63 N4 Covarrubias Spain
57 K5 Covăsinț Romania
77 O5 Covasna Romania
26 E7 Cove Highland, Scotland U.K.
26 L8 Cove Bay Aberdeen, Scotland U.K.
125 T3 Cove Fort UT U.S.A.
111 M4 Cove Island Ont. Can.
147 H5 Covello Arg.
124 I2 Covelo CA U.S.A.
116 G9 Cove Mountains PA U.S.A.
136 C2 Coveñas Col.
138 D3 Covendo Bol.
31 I3 Coventry West Midlands, England U.K.
29 N5 Cover r. England U.K.
30 B7 Coverack Cornwall, England U.K.
125 T9 Covered Wells AZ U.S.A.
116 G11 Covesville VA U.S.A.
62 F8 Covilhã Port.
115 F9 Covington GA U.S.A.
114 D5 Covington IN U.S.A.
116 A9 Covington KY U.S.A.
121 J10 Covington LA U.S.A.
110 F3 Covington MI U.S.A.
116 A8 Covington OH U.S.A.
121 K8 Covington TN U.S.A.
116 E11 Covington VA U.S.A.
111 K2 Cow r. Ont. Can.
205 K5 Cowal, Lake dry lake N.S.W. Austr.
116 B10 Cowan KY U.S.A.
209 F11 Cowan, Lake salt flat W.A. Austr.
109 F4 Cowansville Que. Can.
31 L2 Cowbit Lincolnshire, England U.K.
30 F5 Cowbridge Vale of Glamorgan, Wales U.K.
209 D11 Cowcowing Lakes salt flat W.A. Austr.
26 J10 Cowdenbeath Fife, Scotland U.K.
204 F5 Cowell S.A. Austr.
116 E10 Cowen WV U.S.A.
205 J8 Cowes Vic. Austr.
31 J6 Cowes Isle of Wight, England U.K.
31 L6 Cowfold West Sussex, England U.K.
29 M4 Cow Green Reservoir England U.K.
26 I10 Cowie Stirling, Scotland U.K.
207 J9 Cowley Qld Austr.
29 M6 Cowling North Yorkshire, England U.K.
122 C3 Cowlitz r. WA U.S.A.
116 F11 Cowpasture r. VA U.S.A.
205 L5 Cowra N.S.W. Austr.
29 M4 Cowshill Durham, England U.K.
206 E3 Cox r. N.T. Austr.
43 G8 Cox France
31 M5 Coxheath Kent, England U.K.
29 N4 Coxhoe Durham, England U.K.
144 G3 Coxilha de Santana hills Brazil/Uru.
141 B9 Coxilha Grande hills Brazil
141 B6 Coxim Brazil
141 B6 Coxim r. Brazil
117 L6 Coxsackie NY U.S.A.
179 M9 Cox's Bazar Bangl.
29 O5 Coxwold North Yorkshire, England U.K.
146 B4 Coya Chile
88 B4 Coyah Guinea
145 C8 Coy Aike Arg.
121 C11 Coyame Mex.
121 D10 Coyanosa Creek watercourse TX U.S.A.
30 E4 Coychurch Bridgend, Wales U.K.
26 H12 Coylton South Ayrshire, Scotland U.K.
26 I8 Coylumbridge Highland, Scotland U.K.
123 H11 Coyote r. Mex.
126 D5 Coyote, Punta pt Mex.
124 P6 Coyote Lake CA U.S.A.
125 R9 Coyote Peak hill AZ U.S.A.
124 N5 Coyote Peak CA U.S.A.
128 G5 Coyotillos Mex.
128 A2 Coyotitán Mex.
128 G9 Coyuca, Laguna l. Mex.
128 G8 Coyuca de Benitez Mex.
128 G7 Coyuca de Catalán Mex.
129 J5 Coyutla Mex.
120 F5 Cozad NE U.S.A.
65 M3 Cózar Spain
42 C4 Cozes France
77 M5 Cozia, Vârful mt. Romania

Cozie, Alpi mts France/Italy see Cottian Alps
127 P7 Cozumel Mex.
127 P7 Cozumel, Isla de i. Mex.
72 C4 Cozzano Corse France
73 Q8 Cozzo del Pellegrino mt. Italy
68 E2 Craanford Rep. of Ireland
207 I1 Crab Island Qld Austr.
99 □1a Crab Island Rodrigues I. Mauritius
130 □ Crab Pond Point Jamaica
38 E6 Crach France
73 Q7 Craco Italy
207 M8 Cracow Qld Austr.
205 K9 Cradle Mountain Lake St Clair National Park Tas. Austr.
30 H3 Cradley Herefordshire, England U.K.
Cracow Pol. see Kraków
204 G4 Cradock S.A. Austr.
97 J8 Cradock S. Africa
202 J3 Cradock Channel North I. N.Z.
70 J4 Craffaro r. Italy
96 I2 Crafthole S. Africa
26 K9 Craichie Angus, Scotland U.K.
57 L4 Craidorolt Romania
57 L4 Craig Highland, Scotland U.K.
106 C4 Craig AK U.S.A.
122 K6 Craig CO U.S.A.
27 K3 Craigavad Northern Ireland U.K.
27 J4 Craigavon Northern Ireland U.K.
26 H12 Craigdarroch East Ayrshire, Scotland U.K.
26 F11 Craigdhive Argyll and Bute, Scotland U.K.
205 J7 Craigieburn Vic. Austr.
203 F10 Craigieburn South I. N.Z.
203 F10 Craigieburn Forest Park nature res. South I. N.Z.
26 E10 Craignure Argyll and Bute, Scotland U.K.
27 J3 Craigs Northern Ireland U.K.
116 F10 Craigsville VA U.S.A.
116 E10 Craigsville WV U.S.A.
26 K10 Craig Fife, Scotland U.K.
53 I3 Crailsheim Ger.
77 L6 Craiova Romania
118 B5 Craley PA U.S.A.
36 G6 Cramant France
29 N3 Cramlington Northumberland, England U.K.
43 H9 Cramond S. Africa
28 C3 Crampagna France
29 M7 Cranage Cheshire, England U.K.
27 J4 Cranagh Northern Ireland U.K.
106 D4 Cranberry Junction B.C. Can.
118 F3 Cranberry Lake NJ U.S.A.
117 K4 Cranberry Lake I. NY U.S.A.
107 K4 Cranberry Portage Man. Can.
30 H6 Cranborne Chase for. England U.K.
205 J8 Cranbourne Vic. Austr.
209 D13 Cranbrook W.A. Austr.
106 H5 Cranbrook B.C. Can.
31 N5 Cranbrook Kent, England U.K.
119 F4 Cranbury NJ U.S.A.
119 I4 Crandon WI U.S.A.
122 E5 Crane OR U.S.A.
121 D10 Crane TX U.S.A.
107 I5 Crane Lake Sask. Can.
111 I3 Crane Lake MN U.S.A.
119 I3 Crane Neck Point NY U.S.A.
31 K3 Cranfield Bedfordshire, England U.K.
27 J4 Cranfield Point Northern Ireland U.K.
28 B3 Cranford Rep. of Ireland
39 F5 Cran-Gevrier France
31 L5 Cranleigh Surrey, England U.K.
43 I6 Cransac France
26 L11 Cranshaws Scottish Borders, Scotland U.K.
70 C3 Crans-sur-Sierre Switz.
26 G6 Cranstackie hill Scotland U.K.
116 B10 Cranston KY U.S.A.
117 N7 Cranston RI U.S.A.
31 K2 Cranwell Lincolnshire, England U.K.
140 D3 Craolândia Brazil
39 J6 Craon France
36 G5 Craonne France
77 Q5 Crapina, Lacul l. Romania
41 H6 Craponne-sur-Arzon France
212 M1 Crary Ice Rise Antarctica
212 P1 Crary Mountains Antarctica
26 G6 Crask Inn Highland, Scotland U.K.
77 K3 Crasna Romania
77 K3 Crasna r. Romania
16 I7 Crasnoe Moldova
122 C5 Crater Lake National Park OR U.S.A.
122 H5 Craters of the Moon National Monument nat. park ID U.S.A.
140 D3 Crateús Brazil
26 J8 Crathie Aberdeenshire, Scotland U.K.
73 Q8 Crati r. Italy
140 F3 Crato Brazil
64 D2 Crato Port.
41 F9 Crau reg. France
27 E6 Craughwell Rep. of Ireland
70 E4 Cravagliana Italy
40 J1 Cravanche France
36 G8 Cravant France
139 F3 Cravari r. Brazil
31 K3 Craven Arms Shropshire, England U.K.
142 D4 Cravinhos Brazil
138 D3 Cravo Norte Col.
120 D4 Crawford NE U.S.A.
122 F2 Crawford Bay B.C. Can.
26 I12 Crawfordjohn South Lanarkshire, Scotland U.K.
154 B6 Crawford Point Palawan Phil.
206 D6 Crawford Range hills N.T. Austr.
203 F9 Crawford Range mts South I. N.Z.
114 D5 Crawfordsville IN U.S.A.
115 E10 Crawfordville FL U.S.A.
115 F9 Crawfordville GA U.S.A.
49 K9 Crawinkel Ger.
31 L5 Crawley West Sussex, England U.K.
122 I3 Crazy Mountains MT U.S.A.
26 E9 Creag Ghoraidh Scotland U.K. see Creagorry
26 G9 Creag Meagaidh mt. Scotland U.K.
26 B8 Creagorry Western Isles, Scotland U.K.
38 H3 Créances France
40 F2 Créancey France
107 J4 Crean Lake Sask. Can.
62 D4 Crecente Spain
36 G4 Crèches-sur-Saône France
36 E5 Crécy-en-Ponthieu France
36 G4 Crécy-la-Chapelle France
36 G3 Crécy-sur-Serre France
30 E6 Credenhill Herefordshire, England U.K.
30 E7 Crediton Devon, England U.K.
107 J3 Cree r. Sask. Can.
30 F5 Creech St Michael Somerset, England U.K.
123 K8 Creede CO U.S.A.
26 F7 Creegh Rep. of Ireland
27 D7 Creeslough Rep. of Ireland
111 N5 Creemore Ont. Can.
26 H13 Creetown Dumfries and Galloway, Scotland U.K.
27 D4 Creevagh Rep. of Ireland
27 I5 Creggan Northern Ireland U.K.
27 C5 Creggan Rep. of Ireland
27 F5 Creggs Rep. of Ireland

53 I3 Creglingen Ger.
28 H5 Cregneash Isle of Man
37 M5 Créhange France
107 K4 Creighton Sask. Can.
97 N6 Creighton S. Africa
36 D5 Creil France
44 I3 Creil Neth.
41 C8 Creissels France
70 H5 Crema Italy
40 D5 Cremeaux France
63 J3 Crémenes Spain
40 G5 Crémieu France
49 K6 Cremlingen Ger.
70 I5 Cremona Italy
70 I5 Cremona prov. Italy
43 D6 Créon France
137 G6 Crépori r. Brazil
36 D5 Crépy France
36 E5 Crépy-en-Valois France
49 K10 Crera, Loch inlet Scotland U.K.
68 E3 Cres i. Croatia
68 E3 Cres Croatia
122 D5 Crescent OR U.S.A.
122 B6 Crescent City CA U.S.A.
115 G11 Crescent City FL U.S.A.
152 D3 Crescent Group is Paracel Is
205 N4 Crescent Head N.S.W. Austr.
125 W3 Crescent Junction UT U.S.A.
120 D5 Crescent Lake National Wildlife Refuge nature res. NE U.S.A.
124 P1 Crescent Peak NV U.S.A.
124 P1 Crescent Valley NV U.S.A.
110 B6 Cresco IA U.S.A.
118 E2 Cresco PA U.S.A.
70 G5 Crespano d'Adda tourist site Italy
71 L6 Crespino Italy
147 G3 Crespo Arg.
63 K7 Crespos Spain
42 H5 Cressensac France
52 C7 Cressier Switz.
118 C3 Cressona PA U.S.A.
206 E5 Cresswell watercourse N.T. Austr.
206 E4 Cresswell Downs N.T. Austr.
205 I8 Cressy Vic. Austr.
41 G7 Crest France
154 D3 Cresta, Mount Phil.
116 C8 Crestline OH U.S.A.
106 G5 Creston B.C. Can.
120 H5 Creston IA U.S.A.
115 D10 Crestview FL U.S.A.
40 J5 Crest-Voland France
29 O7 Crestwood Village NJ U.S.A.
26 H7 Creswell Derbyshire, England U.K.
118 C5 Creswell PA U.S.A.
205 I7 Creswick Vic. Austr.
71 N2 Creta Forata, Monte mt. Italy
66 F6 Crete i. Greece
40 H4 Crêt de la Neige mt. France
40 H4 Crêt de Pont mt. France
40 H4 Crêt des Eculaz mt. France
40 H4 Crêt du Nu mt. France
66 F6 Crete i. Greece see Kriti
120 G5 Crete NE U.S.A.
36 D6 Créteil France
39 J3 Crêt Monniot mt. France
41 C6 Creully France
66 L3 Creus, Cap de c. Spain
42 I3 Creuse dept France
42 F1 Creuse r. France
53 L2 Creußen France
53 L2 Creußen r. Ger.
49 J8 Creuzburg Ger.
43 F6 Creuzier-le-Vieux France
71 K6 Crevacore Italy
42 H3 Crevant France
212 O1 Crevasse Valley Glacier Antarctica
37 L6 Crévéchamps France
36 D4 Crèvecœur-le-Grand France
67 D11 Crevillent France
67 D11 Crevillente, Sierra de mts Spain
29 M7 Crewe Cheshire, England U.K.
116 C11 Crewe VA U.S.A.
30 D6 Crewkerne Somerset, England U.K.
29 K7 Criccieth Gwynedd, Wales U.K.
141 C9 Criciúma Brazil
31 I4 Crickhowell Powys, Wales U.K.
31 K4 Cricklade Wiltshire, England U.K.
16 H6 Cricova Moldova
77 O6 Cricovu Sărat r. Romania
118 A6 Cridersville OH U.S.A.
26 I10 Crieff Perth and Kinross, Scotland U.K.
36 B3 Criel-sur-Mer France
29 N6 Crigglestone West Yorkshire, England U.K.
68 E3 Crikvenica Croatia
106 B3 Crillon, Mount AK U.S.A.
28 D5 Crilly Northern Ireland U.K.
Crimea aut. rep. Ukr. see Krym, Respublika
26 M7 Crimond Aberdeenshire, Scotland U.K.
31 O2 Cringleford Norfolk, England U.K.
51 I7 Crinan Argyll and Bute, Scotland U.K.
123 L7 Cripple Creek CO U.S.A.
31 N6 Cripp's Corner East Sussex, England U.K.
39 L2 Criquetot-l'Esneval France
77 R5 Crişan Romania
117 J11 Crisfield MD U.S.A.
78 M2 Crispiano Italy
70 C6 Crissolo Italy
142 D2 Cristais, Serra dos mts Brazil
90 A4 Cristal, Monts de mts Equat. Guinea/Gabon
140 C4 Cristalândia Brazil
142 D2 Cristalina Brazil
139 G2 Cristalina r. Brazil
71 M2 Cristallo mt. Italy
142 C2 Cristalópolis Brazil
143 E5 Cristina Brazil
140 D4 Cristino Castro Brazil
57 L5 Cristior de Jos Romania
62 I8 Cristóbal Panama
77 M4 Cristolţu Colombo airport Italy
77 N4 Cristuru Secuiesc Romania
77 J4 Crişul Alb r. Romania
77 J4 Crişul Negru r. Romania
77 M4 Crişul Repede r. Romania
77 J4 Crişurilor, Câmpia plain Romania
29 P4 Criterion mt. Peru

71 Q6 Crna Pta, Rt pt Croatia
77 K8 Crna Trava Srbija Serb. and Mont.
76 I9 Crni Drim r. Macedonia
71 R5 Crni Lug Croatia
77 K7 Crni Timok r. Serb. and Mont.
68 E2 Crni vrh mt. Slovenia
68 E3 Crnomelj Slovenia
77 K8 Crnook mt. Serb. and Mont.
27 F3 Croagh Rep. of Ireland
27 F3 Croagheheen hill Rep. of Ireland
27 C5 Croagh Patrick hill Rep. of Ireland
205 L7 Croajingolong National Park Vic. Austr.
68 E3 Croatia country Europe
75 L6 Crocchio r. Italy
75 K7 Crocco, Monte mt. Italy
71 K3 Croce, Monte mt. Italy
73 P6 Croce dello Scrivano, Passo pass Italy
73 I2 Croce di Serra, Monte hill Italy
49 K10 Crock Ger.
157 K2 Crocker, Banjaran mts Malaysia
157 L2 Crocker Range National Park Malaysia
26 I12 Crockettord Dumfries and Galloway, Scotland U.K.
121 H10 Crockett TX U.S.A.
27 G3 Crockmore Rep. of Ireland
42 I4 Crocq France
71 M2 Croda dei Toni mt. Italy
71 M2 Croda Rossa mt. Italy
70 E3 Crodo Italy
30 E4 Croeserw Neath Port Talbot, Wales U.K.
30 B4 Croesgoch Pembrokeshire, Wales U.K.
29 O6 Crofton West Yorkshire, England U.K.
118 B6 Crofton MD U.S.A.
120 G4 Crofton NE U.S.A.
30 D4 Crofty Swansea, Wales U.K.
27 F5 Croghan Rep. of Ireland
117 J5 Croghan NY U.S.A.
29 L4 Croglin Cumbria, England U.K.
73 K2 Crognaleto Italy
27 F3 Crohy Head Rep. of Ireland
27 E3 Croick Highland, Scotland U.K.
41 I6 Croisette, Cap c. France
38 E7 Croisic, Pointe de pt France
36 E3 Croisilles France
203 H8 Croisilles Harbour South I. N.Z.
70 C5 Croix-Rousse mt. Italy
206 D1 Croker, Cape N.T. Austr.
111 N5 Croker, Lake Ont. Can.
206 D1 Croker Island N.T. Austr.
27 C8 Cromane Rep. of Ireland
26 H7 Cromarty Highland, Scotland U.K.
26 H7 Cromarty Firth est. Scotland U.K.
26 I8 Cromdale, Hills of Scotland U.K.
31 N2 Cromer Norfolk, England U.K.
30 H4 Cromhall South Gloucestershire, England U.K.
203 D12 Cromwell South I. N.Z.
119 J1 Cromwell CT U.S.A.
110 B3 Cromwell MN U.S.A.
203 F9 Cronadun South I. N.Z.
40 D3 Cronat France
41 C6 Cronce r. France
31 K5 Crondall Hampshire, England U.K.
29 N4 Crook Durham, England U.K.
122 D4 Crooked r. OR U.S.A.
110 C1 Crooked Island Bahamas
110 C1 Crooked Island Passage Bahamas
107 K4 Crooked Lake Can./U.S.A.
110 C1 Crooked River Sask. Can.
27 C10 Crookhaven Rep. of Ireland
120 G2 Crookston MN U.S.A.
27 E9 Crookstown Rep. of Ireland
116 C9 Crooksville OH U.S.A.
205 L6 Crookwell N.S.W. Austr.
75 L6 Cropalati Italy
75 L4 Cropani Italy
207 I3 Croppa Creek N.S.W. Austr.
203 F9 Crosbie r. Qld Austr.
26 D6 Crosbost Western Isles, Scotland U.K.
29 K7 Crosby Merseyside, England U.K.
29 P6 Crosby North Lincolnshire, England U.K.
120 I2 Crosby MN U.S.A.
120 D1 Crosby ND U.S.A.
29 L4 Crosby Ravensworth Cumbria, England U.K.
121 B9 Crosbyton TX U.S.A.
75 L4 Crosia Italy
89 H5 Cross r. Nigeria
38 G7 Crossac France
28 C6 Crossaig Argyll and Bute, Scotland U.K.
28 C6 Crossakeel Rep. of Ireland
110 C3 Crossapol Bay Scotland U.K.
27 I5 Cross Bay Nunavut Can.
107 M2 Cross Bay Nunavut Can.
110 A2 Crosscanonby Cumbria, England U.K.
27 J10 Crossdoney Rep. of Ireland
121 I9 Crossett AR U.S.A.
29 M4 Cross Fell hill England U.K.
106 H5 Crossfield Alta Can.
26 I11 Crossford South Lanarkshire, Scotland U.K.
27 K4 Crossgar Northern Ireland U.K.
27 I2 Crossgare Northern Ireland U.K.
30 F3 Crossgates Powys, Wales U.K.
26 H11 Crosshands East Ayrshire, Scotland U.K.
130 E1 Cross Harbour b. Gt Abaco Bahamas
26 G12 Crosshill South Ayrshire, Scotland U.K.
28 H2 Crosshouse East Ayrshire, Scotland U.K.
30 D3 Cross Inn Ceredigion, Wales U.K.
27 I5 Crosskeys Rep. of Ireland
27 I5 Cross Keys Rep. of Ireland
107 L4 Cross Lake Man. Can.
107 L4 Cross Lake l. Man. Can.
116 I5 Cross Lake NY U.S.A.
203 G9 Cross Lake, Mount South I. N.Z.
27 K4 Crossmaglen Northern Ireland U.K.
125 R7 Crossman Peak AZ U.S.A.
26 I13 Crossmichael Dumfries and Galloway, Scotland U.K.
89 H5 Cross River state Nigeria
115 E8 Crossville TN U.S.A.
118 C2 Crosswicks NJ U.S.A.
71 J6 Crostolo r. Italy
29 P7 Croston Lancashire, England U.K.
111 L6 Croswell MI U.S.A.
110 C4 Croton Italy see Crotone
75 L5 Crotone Italy
75 L5 Crotone prov. Italy
119 H2 Croton Falls NY U.S.A.
119 H2 Croton Falls Reservoir NY U.S.A.
119 H2 Crotonville NY U.S.A.
41 I7 Crots France
51 G10 Crottendorf Ger.
147 G5 Crotto Arg.
31 N4 Crouch r. England U.K.
31 K4 Croughton Northamptonshire, England U.K.
42 E2 Croutelle France

36 F5 Crouy France
36 F5 Crouy-sur-Ourcq France
39 L7 Crouzilles France
27 E3 Crove Rep. of Ireland
122 K4 Crow r. B.C. Can.
122 K4 Crow Agency MT U.S.A.
205 K4 Crowal watercourse N.S.W. Austr.
31 M5 Crowborough East Sussex, England U.K.
122 L6 Crow Creek r. CO U.S.A.
120 D7 Crow Creek r. CO U.S.A.
120 D6 Crow Creek Indian Reservation res. SD U.S.A.
205 N4 Crowdy Bay National Park N.S.W. Austr.
121 F8 Crowell TX U.S.A.
30 G4 Crow Hill Herefordshire, England U.K.
147 I2 Crow Indian Reservation res. MT U.S.A.
205 J5 Crowl watercourse N.S.W. Austr.
31 L2 Crowland Lincolnshire, England U.K.
29 P6 Crowle North Lincolnshire, England U.K.
121 I10 Crowley LA U.S.A.
124 N4 Crowley, Lake CA U.S.A.
26 E8 Crowlin Islands Scotland U.K.
131 □5 Crown Point Trin. and Tob.
114 D5 Crown Point IN U.S.A.
123 J9 Crownpoint NM U.S.A.
117 L5 Crown Point NY U.S.A.
213 C2 Crown Prince Olav Coast Antarctica
212 W1 Crown Princess Martha Coast Antarctica
130 C3 Crownsville MD U.S.A.
207 N9 Crows Nest Qld Austr.
106 H5 Crowsnest Pass Alta Can.
106 H5 Crowsnest Pass pass Alta/B.C. Can.
31 K5 Crowthorne Bracknell Forest, England U.K.
120 H2 Crow Wing r. MN U.S.A.
26 H7 Croy Highland, Scotland U.K.
207 I5 Croydon Qld Austr.
31 L5 Croydon Greater London, England U.K.
118 F4 Croydon PA U.S.A.
42 H3 Crozant France
116 G10 Crozet VA U.S.A.
215 H6 Crozet, Îles is Indian Ocean
99 □1 Crozet Basin sea feature Indian Ocean
215 G7 Crozet Plateau sea feature Indian Ocean
127 N10 Crozier Channel N.W.T. Can.
104 F2 Crozier, Cape Antarctica
38 C5 Crozon France
38 B5 Crozon, Presqu'île de pen. France
41 F7 Cruas France
77 N3 Crucea Romania
138 C2 Crucero Peru
130 C2 Cruces Cuba
136 B3 Cruces, Punta pt Col.
75 L5 Crucoli Italy
26 M8 Cruden Bay Aberdeenshire, Scotland U.K.
129 I1 Cruillas Mex.
26 C6 Cruilivig Western Isles, Scotland U.K.
116 C11 Crum WV U.S.A.
30 E7 Crumlin Caerphilly, Wales U.K.
27 J3 Crumlin Northern Ireland U.K.
29 K4 Crummock Water l. England U.K.
40 E7 Cruseilles France
27 E7 Crusheen Rep. of Ireland
37 K5 Crusnes France
37 K5 Crusnes r. France
129 J4 Crustepec, Cerro mt. Mex.
129 □9 Cruz, Cabo c. Cuba
147 G3 Cruz Alta Arg.
141 A9 Cruz Alta Brazil
128 D6 Cruz de Garibay Mex.
146 E2 Cruz del Eje Arg.
142 A5 Cruzeiro Brazil
142 A5 Cruzeiro do Oeste Brazil
138 B1 Cruzeiro do Sul Acre Brazil
142 A4 Cruzeiro do Sul Paraná Brazil
212 O2 Cruz Island Antarctica
129 H9 Cruz Grande Mex.
41 B10 Cruzy France
36 H8 Cruzy-le-Châtel France
77 I2 Crvenka Vojvodina, Srbija Serb. and Mont.
209 D9 Cue W.A. Austr.
91 C8 Cuebe r. Angola
91 B6 Cueio r. Angola
91 B6 Cuemba Angola
138 B5 Cuenca Ecuador
154 B4 Cuenca Luzon Phil.
63 P8 Cuenca Spain
63 P9 Cuenca prov. Spain
63 P7 Cuenca, Serranía de mts Spain
126 H5 Cuencamé Mex.
129 H7 Cuernavaca Mex.
121 G11 Cuero TX U.S.A.
41 I10 Cuers France
63 P7 Cuerva Spain
63 O6 Cuervo r. Spain
130 C2 Cueto Cuba
129 J5 Cuetzalan Mex.
145 C7 Cueva de las Manos cave Arg.
65 K6 Cuevas Altas hill Spain
65 K6 Cuevas Bajas Spain
65 P6 Cuevas de Almanzora Spain
65 P6 Cuevas de Almanzora, Embalse resr Spain
65 I7 Cuevas del Becerro hill Spain
65 N5 Cuevas del Campo Spain
63 M4 Cuevas de San Clemente Spain
66 F7 Cuevas de Vinromá Spain
63 K4 Cuevas Labradas Spain
63 K4 Cuézar r. Spain
31 M4 Cuffley Hertfordshire, England U.K.
77 H10 Cugir Romania
77 I10 Cugir r. Romania
72 B7 Cuglieri Sardegna Italy
40 C6 Cugnaux France

143 G3 Cuité r. Brazil
129 K7 Cuitláhuac Mex.
91 D9 Cuito r. Angola
91 C8 Cuito Cuanavale Angola
129 K7 Cuitzeo Mex.
128 D6 Cuitzeo, Laguna de l. Mex.
128 D6 Cuixtla Mex.
156 E2 Cukai Malaysia
78 B3 Çukë Albania
191 E6 Çukurca Turkey
189 J5 Çukurkuyu Turkey
191 A5 Çukurören Turkey
191 A6 Çukurhisar Turkey
190 D2 Çukurova plat. Turkey
16 H6 Cula r. Moldova
169 O8 Culai Shan mt. Shandong China
42 I2 Culan France
159 I8 Cu Lao Cham i. Vietnam
159 I8 Cu Lao Xanh i. Vietnam
16 H6 Culciu Romania
27 H2 Culdaff Rep. of Ireland
26 L8 Culdrain Aberdeenshire, Scotland U.K.
66 I5 Culebra, Isla de i. Puerto Rico
138 A2 Culebras Peru
131 □1 Culebrinas r. Puerto Rico
44 H5 Culemborg Neth.
191 G7 Cuffa Azer.
126 F5 Culiacán Mex.
154 D6 Culion Phil.
154 D6 Culion i. Phil.
28 B5 Culkey Northern Ireland U.K.
67 E7 Culla Spain
28 C8 Cullahill Rep. of Ireland
65 N5 Cúllar Spain
65 N5 Cúllar-Baza Spain
27 I4 Cullaville Northern Ireland U.K.
27 D4 Culleens Rep. of Ireland
26 K7 Cullen Moray, Scotland U.K.
65 I9 Cullen r. Spain
207 I1 Cullen Point Qld Austr.
67 E9 Cullera Spain
26 H7 Cullicudden Highland, Scotland U.K.
27 D5 Cullin, Lough l. Rep. of Ireland
115 D8 Cullman AL U.S.A.
70 B3 Cully Switz.
27 J3 Cullybackey Northern Ireland U.K.
27 I4 Cullyhanna Northern Ireland U.K.
26 F6 Cul Mòr hill Scotland U.K.
27 H2 Culmore Northern Ireland U.K.
30 F6 Culmstock Devon, England U.K.
26 F7 Culnacraig Highland, Scotland U.K.
26 D7 Culnaknock Highland, Scotland U.K.
65 N7 Culo de Perro, Punta pt Spain
40 H5 Culoz France
116 H10 Culpeper VA U.S.A.
136 □ Culpepper, Isla i. Islas Galápagos Ecuador
26 H7 Culrain Highland, Scotland U.K.
26 M2 Culswick Shetland, Scotland U.K.
190 H2 Cülük watercourse Turkey
26 L8 Culter Fell hill Scotland U.K.
26 L8 Cults Aberdeen, Scotland U.K.
140 D2 Culuene r. Brazil
110 H6 Culver IN U.S.A.
209 H12 Culver, Point W.A. Austr.
203 G8 Culverden South I. N.Z.
136 B5 Cumaná Venez.
136 D2 Cumaná Venez.
136 C3 Cumanacoa Venez.
191 H4 Cumayeri Turkey
136 C2 Cumbal, Nevado de vol. Col.
116 C12 Cumberland KY U.S.A.
130 A3 Cumberland MD U.S.A.
116 D9 Cumberland VA U.S.A.
111 K6 Cumberland WI U.S.A.
110 B12 Cumberland r. KY/TN U.S.A.
125 R1 Cumberland, Lake Sask. Can.
116 B12 Cumberland, Lake KY U.S.A.
118 A4 Cumberland County county PA U.S.A.
107 K4 Cumberland House Sask. Can.
115 □ Cumberland Island GA U.S.A.
207 L4 Cumberland Islands Qld Austr.
75 O3 Cumberland Lake Sask. Can.
115 E8 Cumberland Mountains KY/TN U.S.A.
105 L3 Cumberland Peninsula Nunavut Can.
115 E8 Cumberland Plateau KY/TN U.S.A.
105 L3 Cumberland Sound sea chan. Nunavut Can.
26 I11 Cumbernauld North Lanarkshire, Scotland U.K.
65 K9 Cumbre Alta mt. Spain
126 F3 Cumbres de Majalca, Parque Nacional nat. park Mex.
127 I5 Cumbres de Monterrey, Parque Nacional nat. park Mex.
64 F4 Cumbres de San Bartolomé Spain
64 F4 Cumbres Mayores Spain
29 L4 Cumbria admin. div. England U.K.
29 L4 Cumbrian Mountains England U.K.
64 C6 Cumeada Port.
137 G4 Cuminá r. Brazil
137 G4 Cuminapanema r. Brazil
26 L7 Cuminestown Aberdeenshire, Scotland U.K.
115 □ Cummings GA U.S.A.
204 E4 Cummins S.A. Austr.
208 I5 Cummins Range hills W.A. Austr.
205 L5 Cumnock N.S.W. Austr.
26 H12 Cumnock East Ayrshire, Scotland U.K.
31 J4 Cumnor Oxfordshire, England U.K.
126 C3 Cumpas Mex.
190 D2 Çumra Turkey
137 F4 Cumuruxatiba Brazil
91 C7 Cuna r. Angola

137 I4 Cunani Brazil
136 C4 Cuñaré Col.
39 K7 Cunault France
209 G11 Cundeelee Aboriginal Reserve W.A. Austr.
209 D11 Cunderdin W.A. Austr.
136 C3 Cundinamarca dept Col.
97 N4 Cundycleugh S. Africa
43 E6 Cuneges France
127 N10 Cuen Guat.
91 B9 Cunene r. Angola
91 B9 Cunene r. Angola/Namibia alt. Kunene
70 D7 Cuneo Italy
70 D7 Cuneo prov. Italy
51 K8 Cunewalde Ger.
36 I7 Cunfin France
204 E5 Cungena S.A. Austr.
159 I8 Cung Sơn Vietnam
188 I4 Çüngüş Turkey
143 E5 Cunha Brazil
62 F7 Cunha Port.
91 C8 Cunhinga Angola
16 H6 Cunicea Moldova
66 I5 Cunit Spain
91 D8 Cunjamba Angola
40 D5 Cunlhat France
205 J3 Cunnamulla Qld Austr.
115 □2 Cunningham, Lake New Prov. Bahamas
26 □N2 Cunningsburgh Shetland, Scotland U.K.
138 B1 Cunshamayo Peru
62 C3 Cuntis Spain
77 J6 Cunupia Trin. and Tob.
70 D5 Cuorgnè Italy
26 J10 Cupar Fife, Scotland U.K.
137 H5 Cupari r. Brazil
57 L4 Cupari, Dealul hill Romania
16 G5 Cupcina Moldova
73 N3 Cupello Italy
136 B3 Cupica Col.
73 L1 Cupra Marittima Italy
71 O9 Cupramontana Italy
76 J7 Cuprija Serb. and Mont.
43 H8 Cupula, Pico mt. Mex.
128 D5 Cuq-Toulza France
128 D5 Cuquío Mex.
137 F6 Curaçá Brazil
137 F6 Curaçá r. Brazil
131 □10 Curaçao i. Neth. Antilles
146 B6 Curacautín Chile
146 B3 Curacaví Chile
91 B8 Curaculo Angola
138 C4 Curahuara de Carangas Bol.
147 F5 Cura Malal Arg.
146 B6 Curanilahue Chile
138 C2 Curanja r. Peru
146 A5 Curarrehue Chile
137 F3 Curatabaca Venez.
57 L1 Curăţele Romania
144 F3 Curaumilla, Punta pt Chile
136 D5 Curaray r. Ecuador
40 D1 Cure r. France
70 E4 Cureggio Italy
99 □1b Curepipe Mauritius
146 A4 Curepto Chile
137 F3 Curiapo Venez.
136 C5 Curicó Chile
136 E5 Curicuriari, Serra hill Brazil
137 I4 Curieuriari r. Brazil
99 □2a Curieuse, Île i. Inner Islands Seychelles
140 D4 Curimatá Brazil
142 C6 Curitiba Brazil
142 A5 Curitibanos Brazil
142 B6 Curiúva Brazil
205 L3 Curlewis N.S.W. Austr.
204 C4 Curnamona S.A. Austr.
91 A8 Curoca r. Angola
71 J2 Curon Venosta Italy
137 F2 Curral Velho Cape Verde
111 K5 Curran MI U.S.A.
27 G3 Curragh Rep. of Ireland
27 J8 Curragh West Rep. of Ireland
27 F5 Curragh West Rep. of Ireland
27 D7 Curraglass Rep. of Ireland
143 G3 Curral de Dentro Brazil
143 I2 Curralinho Brazil
204 E2 Curralulla watercourse S.A. Austr.
137 F2 Curral Velho Cape Verde
111 K9 Curran MI U.S.A.
26 L7 Currane, Lough l. Rep. of Ireland
125 R1 Currant NV U.S.A.
205 J4 Curranyalpa N.S.W. Austr.
205 J3 Currás Spain
205 J3 Curranvinna National Park Qld Austr.
130 D1 Current Eleuthera Bahamas
121 J7 Current r. MO U.S.A.
205 I8 Currie Tas. Austr.
125 R1 Currie NV U.S.A.
115 I7 Currituck NC U.S.A.
26 F7 Curry Rivel Somerset, England U.K.
75 M5 Cursi Italy
77 M5 Curtea de Argeş Romania
77 J4 Curtici Romania
209 G11 Curtin W.A. Austr.
207 N4 Curtis Group is Tas. Austr.
207 M8 Curtis Island Qld Austr.
199 I5 Curtis Island N.Z.
57 L4 Curtuişeni Romania
137 F4 Curuá r. Brazil
137 G4 Curuá, Ilha i. Brazil
140 B3 Curuaés r. Brazil
140 C3 Curuaí Brazil
137 H5 Curuapanema r. Brazil
140 C3 Curuá Una r. Brazil
140 B3 Curumu Brazil
137 F4 Curupira, Serra mts Brazil/Venez.
139 E3 Cururú Bol.
137 G5 Cururupu Brazil
137 F4 Cururú, Cerro mt. Venez.
143 H1 Curuzú Cuatiá Arg.
143 E3 Curvelo Brazil
107 J4 Curwood, Mount MI U.S.A.
72 C2 Cusa, Punta de pt Corse France
73 N5 Cusano Mutri Italy
73 J4 Cusco Peru
138 C3 Cusco dept Peru
27 J2 Cushendall Northern Ireland U.K.
27 J2 Cushendun Northern Ireland U.K.
28 C7 Cushina Rep. of Ireland
121 G7 Cushing OK U.S.A.
72 C2 Cusna, Monte mt. Italy
72 C2 Cussac France
42 C5 Cussac-Fort-Médoc France
40 D7 Cussac-sur-Loire France
94 B2 Cussava Angola

Column 1

40 C4 **Cusset** France
115 E9 **Cusseta** GA U.S.A.
40 E2 **Cussy-les-Forges** France
120 K3 **Custer** MT U.S.A.
120 D4 **Custer** SD U.S.A.
37 L6 **Custines** France
74 D7 **Custonaci** Sicilia Italy
91 C8 **Cutato** Angola
122 H2 **Cut Bank** MT U.S.A.
122 H7 **Cut Bank Creek** r. MT U.S.A.
94 B2 **Cutenda** Angola
115 E10 **Cuthbert** GA U.S.A.
206 D2 **Cuthbertson Falls** N.T. Austr.
71 J7 **Cutigliano** Italy
124 M5 **Cutler** CA U.S.A.
117 □H4 **Cutler** ME U.S.A.
115 G13 **Cutler Ridge** FL U.S.A.
74 H8 **Cuto** r. Sicilia Italy
121 J11 **Cut Off** LA U.S.A.
27 E6 **Cutra, Lough** l. Rep. of Ireland
146 C6 **Cutral-Co** Arg.
75 L5 **Cutro** Italy
75 O3 **Cutrofiano** Italy
205 O3 **Cuttaburra Creek** r. Qld Austr.
179 J9 **Cuttack** Orissa India
72 B4 **Cuttoli-Corticchiato** Corse France
128 G7 **Cutzamala** r. Mex.
128 G7 **Cutzamala de Pinzón** Mex.
91 B8 **Cuvelai** Angola
90 B5 **Cuvette** admin. reg. Congo
90 B5 **Cuvette Ouest** admin. reg. Congo
209 B8 **Cuvier, Cape** W.A. Austr.
202 J3 **Cuvier Island** North I. N.Z.
41 R1 **Cuvillier, Lac** l. Que. Can.
43 I9 **Cuxac-d'Aude** France
41 E10 **Cuxac-d'Aude** France
191 J6 **Çuxanlı** Azer.
48 G3 **Cuxhaven** Ger.
191 J5 **Çuxuryud** Azer.
138 C4 **Cuya** Chile
116 D7 **Cuyahoga Falls** OH U.S.A.
116 D7 **Cuyahoga Valley National Park** OH U.S.A.
124 M7 **Cuyama** CA U.S.A.
124 L7 **Cuyama** r. CA U.S.A.
154 C4 **Cuyapo** Luzon Phil.
154 C6 **Cuyo** Phil.
154 C6 **Cuyo** i. Phil.
154 C6 **Cuyo East Passage** Phil.
154 C6 **Cuyo Islands** Phil.
154 C6 **Cuyo West Passage** Phil.
137 G3 **Cuyuni** r. Guyana
128 C7 **Cuyutlán** Mex.
128 C7 **Cuyutlán, Laguna** lag. Mex.
42 H6 **Cuzance** France
Cuzco Cusco Peru see **Cusco**
138 A1 **Cuzco** San Martín Peru
65 J4 **Cuzna** r. Spain
43 F6 **Cuzorn** France
51 K9 **Cvikov** Czech Rep.
30 F4 **Cwm** Blaenau Gwent, Wales U.K.
30 E4 **Cwmafan** Neath Port Talbot, Wales U.K.
30 F3 **Cwmbach** Powys, Wales U.K.
30 F4 **Cwmbrân** Torfaen, Wales U.K.
30 E4 **Cwmllynfell** Neath Port Talbot, Wales U.K.
93 A5 **Cyangugu** Rwanda
54 C3 **Cybinka** Pol.
54 D2 **Cychowo** Pol.
50 K5 **Cybowy** Pol.
Cyclades is Greece see **Kyklades**
55 L4 **Cycow** Pol.
Cydonia Kriti Greece see **Chania**
205 K10 **Cygnet** Tas. Austr.
116 B7 **Cygnet** OH U.S.A.
30 E3 **Cynghordy** Carmarthenshire, Wales U.K.
30 D4 **Cynin** r. Wales U.K.
116 A10 **Cynthiana** KY U.S.A.
30 D4 **Cynwyl Elfed** Carmarthenshire, Wales U.K.
107 I5 **Cypress Hills** Sask. Can.
107 I5 **Cypress Hills Interprovincial Park** B.C. Can.
190 B3 **Cyprus** country Asia
84 D1 **Cyrenaica** reg. Libya
84 D1 **Cyrene** tourist site Libya
36 F2 **Cysoing** France
30 D4 **Cywyn** r. Wales U.K.
54 E3 **Czacz** Pol.
54 G4 **Czajków** Pol.
54 E2 **Czaplinek** Pol.
107 I4 **Czar** Alta Can.
55 J3 **Czarna** Podkarpackie Pol.
55 K5 **Czarna** Podkarpackie Pol.
55 H4 **Czarna** r. Pol.
55 J5 **Czarna** r. Pol.
55 J5 **Czarna** r. Pol.
55 L2 **Czarna Białostocka** Pol.
54 F1 **Czarna Dąbrówka** Pol.
55 K6 **Czarna Górna** Pol.
55 L2 **Czarna Hańcza** r. Pol.
55 I5 **Czarna Nida** r. Pol.
54 G3 **Czarna Struga** r. Pol.
54 G2 **Czarna Woda** Pol.
55 H5 **Czarnca** Pol.
54 E2 **Czarnia** Pol.
55 J2 **Czarnia** Pol.
54 E3 **Czarnków** Pol.
50 K5 **Czarne** Pol.
54 G4 **Czarnożyły** Pol.
55 H6 **Czarny Dunajec** Pol.
57 I2 **Czarny Dunajec** r. Pol.
54 G4 **Czastary** Pol.
55 I2 **Czchów** Pol.
55 I6 **Czechowice-Dziedzice** Pol.
56 E2 **Czech Republic** country Europe
54 E2 **Czechy** Pol.
55 J4 **Czekarzewice** Pol.
55 K4 **Czemierniki** Pol.
55 L5 **Czempiń** Pol.
54 F4 **Czeremcha** Pol.
54 D4 **Czerna Mała** r. Pol.
54 D4 **Czerna Wielka** r. Pol.
54 E3 **Czernica** r. Pol.
54 E3 **Czernica** r. Pol.
55 I2 **Czernice Borowe** Pol.
54 F3 **Czerniejewo** Pol.
55 I4 **Czerniewice** Pol.
54 G3 **Czernikowo** Pol.
54 E4 **Czernina** Pol.
Czernowitz Ukr. see **Chernivtsi**
54 F2 **Czersk** Pol.
55 J4 **Czerwień** Pol.
55 J3 **Czerwin** Pol.
55 I3 **Czerwińsk nad Wisłą** Pol.
54 G5 **Czerwionka-Leszczyny** Pol.
54 E3 **Czerwonak** Pol.
55 L8 **Czerwona Woda** Pol.
55 J3 **Czerwonka Włościańska** Pol.
54 H4 **Częstków** Pol.
55 H5 **Częstochowa** Pol.
54 F4 **Czeszów** Pol.
54 E2 **Człopa** Pol.
54 F2 **Człuchów** Pol.
51 K8 **Czorneboh** hill Ger.
55 I6 **Czorsztyn, Jezioro** resr Pol.
55 I3 **Czosnów** Pol.
55 I6 **Czudec** Pol.
55 L3 **Czyże** Pol.
55 K3 **Czyżew-Osada** Pol.

D

158 G4 **Đạ, Sông** r. Vietnam
49 E9 **Daaden** Ger.
169 S4 **Da'an** Jilin China
154 D6 **Daanbantayan** Phil.
44 K4 **Daarle** Neth.
173 D11 **Daba** Xizang China
190 D7 **Daba, àbbal aq** mt. Jordan
93 D7 **Dabaga** Tanz.

Column 2

136 D2 **Dabajuro** Venez.
88 D4 **Dabakala** Côte d'Ivoire
169 P5 **Daban** Nei Mongol China
168 G8 **Daban Shan** mts China
170 D4 **Daban** Sichuan China
57 I4 **Dabas** Hungary
170 G2 **Daba Shan** mts China
92 C1 **Dabat** Eth.
Dabba Sichuan China see **Daocheng**
136 B3 **Dabeiba** Col.
158 C6 **Dabein** Myanmar
50 E3 **Dabel** Ger.
176 C4 **Dabhoi** Gujarat India
178 D8 **Dabhol** Mahar. India
190 E7 **Dab'l, Wādī aq** watercourse Jordan
54 D3 **Dąbie** Lubuskie Pol.
54 C2 **Dąbie** Wielkopolskie Pol.
54 C2 **Dąbie, Jezioro** l. Pol.
168 D7 **Dabiegai** Gansu China
171 J3 **Dabie Shan** mts China
23 M7 **Dabki** Pol.
190 E9 **Dabl, Wādī** watercourse Saudi Arabia
178 C6 **Daboh** Madh. Prad. India
88 C4 **Dabola** Guinea
88 D5 **Dabou** Côte d'Ivoire
169 K7 **Dabqig** Nei Mongol China
178 C7 **Dabra** Madh. Prad. India
18 J9 **Dabraslawka** Belarus
55 M3 **Dabravolya** Belarus
54 G3 **Dąbroszyn** Lubuskie Pol.
54 G3 **Dąbroszyn** Wielkopolskie Pol.
54 F3 **Dąbroszyn** Kujawsko-Pomorskie Pol.
54 F5 **Dąbrowa** Opolskie Pol.
54 F5 **Dąbrowa** Opolskie Pol.
55 L2 **Dąbrowa Białostocka** Pol.
54 G3 **Dąbrowa Biskupia** Pol.
55 H5 **Dąbrowa Chełmińska** Pol.
55 H5 **Dąbrowa Górnicza** Pol.
55 I5 **Dąbrowa Tarnowska** Pol.
55 H3 **Dąbrowice** Pol.
54 D3 **Dąbrówka Wielkopolska** Pol.
55 I2 **Dąbrówno** Pol.
168 D8 **Dabsan** Qinghai China
173 L8 **Dabsan Hu** salt l. Qinghai China
171 K6 **Dabu** Guangdong China
55 M3 **Dabuchyn** Belarus
77 M7 **Dabuleni** Romania
Dacca Bangl. see **Dhaka**
53 K5 **Dachau** Ger.
168 G7 **Dachang** Nei Mongol China
169 P6 **Dachengzi** Liaoning China
176 F4 **Dachepalle** Andhra Prad. India
55 L5 **Dachnów** Pol.
49 J8 **Dachrieden** Ger.
53 J2 **Dachsbach** Ger.
59 I4 **Dachstein Gruppe** mts Austria
Dachuan Sichuan China see **Dazhou**
53 K6 **Dačice** Czech Rep.
41 H4 **Dacre** Ont. Can.
29 L4 **Dacre** Cumbria, England U.K.
57 H4 **Dad** Hungary
55 I2 **Dadaj, Jezioro** l. Pol.
200 □6 **Dadale** Sta Isabel Solomon Is
137 G4 **Dadanawa** Guyana
191 C6 **Dadaş** Turkey
190 F2 **Dādāt** Syria
188 F3 **Dadáy** Turkey
92 D1 **Daddato** Djibouti
115 F11 **Dade City** FL U.S.A.
115 E9 **Dadeville** AL U.S.A.
185 L7 **Dadhar** Pak.
184 I8 **Dadkan** Iran
Dadong Liaoning China see **Donggang**
43 H8 **Dadou** r. France
178 D9 **Dadra** Dadra India
Dadra Mahar. India see **Achalpur**
Dadra and Nagar Haveli union terr. India
178 D9 **Dadri** Madh. Prad. India
Dadu r. Sichuan China see **Dadu He**
185 K5 **Dadu** Pak.
170 D3 **Dadu** Sichuan China
186 C3 **Daedalus Reef** Saudi Arabia
Daegu S. Korea see **Daegu**
165 K11 **Dai-sen** vol. Japan
Daejeon S. Korea see **Taejŏn**
164 T3 **Daisetsu-zan National Park** Japan
171 J3 **Daishan** Zhejiang China
166 C6 **Daitō** Osaka Japan
167 H6 **Daitō** Shizuoka Japan
171 L6 **Daiya-gawa** r. Japan
130 H4 **Dajabón** Dom. Rep.
185 N7 **Dajal** Pak.
166 E5 **Dajan** Japan
206 G6 **Dajarra** Qld Austr.
170 C3 **Dajin Chuan** r. Sichuan China
28 G11 **Dajing** Gansu China
168 D8 **Da Juh** Qinghai China
88 A3 **Dakar** Senegal
85 F5 **Dakar el Arak** well Sudan
190 A10 **Dakhal, Wādī ad** watercourse Egypt
85 F3 **Dākhilah, Wāḥāt al** oasis Egypt
179 M8 **Dakhin Shahbazpur Island** Bangl.
Dakhla Oasis Egypt see **Ad Dakhla**
Dakhilah, Wāḥāt ad Egypt see **Dākhilah, Wāḥāt al**
Dakhlet Nouâdhibou admin. reg. Maur.
191 J3 **Dakhovskaya** Rus. Fed.
89 G4 **Dakingari** Nigeria
169 K2 **Dakituy** Rus. Fed.
159 I8 **Đăk Lăk, Cao Nguyên** plat. Vietnam
177 M7 **Dakoank** Andaman & Nicobar Is India
18 L2 **Dakol'ka** r. Belarus
178 D8 **Dakor** Gujarat India
89 G3 **Dakoro** Niger
120 D4 **Dakota City** IA U.S.A.
120 G4 **Dakota City** NE U.S.A.
76 I8 **Đakovica** Kosovo, Srbija Serb. and Mont.
68 G3 **Đakovo** Croatia
162 G2 **Dakp-Rung** N. Korea
91 D7 **Dala** Angola
209 □D1 **Dala** Vojvodina, Srbija Serb. and Mont.
200 □6 **Dala** Malaita Solomon Is
154 C2 **Dalupiri** i. Phil.
79 J6 **Dala** Turkey
79 J6 **Dalaman** Turkey
124 J6 **Dalaoyaa** Belarus
206 C3 **Daly River/Port Keats Aboriginal Land** res.

Column 3

186 D5 **Dahabān** Saudi Arabia
106 E2 **Dahadinni** r. N.W.T. Can.
Dahalach, Isole is Eritrea see **Dahlak Archipelago**
Dahana des. Saudi Arabia see **Ad Dahnā'**
82 I3 **Dahana** Qinghai China
176 C3 **Dahana** Qinghai China
168 F9 **Dahaban** India
169 L6 **Dahei He** r. China
162 F5 **Daheiding Shan** mt. China
187 M2 **Dahin, Ḥarrat ad** lava field Saudi Arabia
21 H6 **Da Hinggan Ling** mts China
176 D4 **Dahivadi** Mahar. India
49 B10 **Dahlak Archipelago** is Eritrea
49 B10 **Dahlak Marine National Park** Eritrea
44 K3 **Dahl al Furayy** well Saudi Arabia
97 M2 **Dahl Ifākh** well Saudi Arabia
158 A5 **Dahlem** Ger.
158 A5 **Dahlen** Ger.
116 E10 **Dahlenburg** Ger.
118 D2 **Dahlener Heide** reg. Ger.
21 M6 **Dahlenwarsleben** Ger.
44 J3 **Dahlet Qorrot** b. Gozo Malta
189 H1 **Dahl Iftākh** well Saudi Arabia
209 D9 **Dahlonega** GA U.S.A.
205 L7 **Dahlwitz-Hoppegarten** Ger.
209 C8 **Dahmani** Tunisia
26 J10 **Dahme** Brandenburg Ger.
119 H2 **Dahme** Schleswig-Holstein Ger.
109 H3 **Dahme** r. Ger.
178 F3 **Dahmeshöved** hd Ger.
104 F2 **Dähre** Ger.
169 L8 **Dahod** Gujarat India
96 H4 **Dahomey** country Africa see **Benin**
184 E4 **Dahongliutan** Aksai Chin
184 E4 **Dahra** Senegal see **Dara**
43 E7 **Dähre** Ger.
91 B6 **Dahua** Guangxi China
37 N7 **Dahûk** Iraq
89 F4 **Dahûk** governorate Iraq
89 H3 **Dahyah** N. Yemen
50 E4 **Dai** i. Maluku Indon.
89 I4 **Daibosatsu-rei** mt. Japan
59 I1 **Daicheng** Hebei China
130 L4 **Daigo** Japan
14 G4 **Dai Hai** l. China
50 C6 **Dai Island** Solomon Is
94 B2 **Daik** Indon.
91 N7 **Daik-anvik** Sweden
89 H4 **Daik** r. Myanmar
50 E4 **Đai Lanh, Mui** pt Vietnam
91 D5 **Dailekh** Nepal
54 F1 **Dailey** WV U.S.A.
178 G8 **Dailly** South Ayrshire, Scotland U.K.
88 E4 **Daim** Iran
145 C6 **Daimanji-san** hill Japan
68 G3 **Daimiel** Spain
26 J11 **Daimon** Japan
179 K7 **Daimon-tōge** pass Japan
207 N8 **Daimugen-zan** mt. Japan
26 J7 **Daimava** Lith.
122 C4 **Daingean** Rep. of Ireland
118 D2 **Daingerfield** TX U.S.A.
121 G9 **Dainichiga-take** vol. Japan
118 B5 **Dainichi-gawa** r. Japan
50 H5 **Dainichi-zan** mt. Japan
178 H9 **Daiping** Sichuan China
104 E4 **Daintree** Qld Austr.
92 D1 **Daintree National Park** Qld Austr.
89 F3 **Daiō** Japan
187 K3 **Daiō-zaki** pt Japan
40 J2 **Daiquirí** Cuba
26 G12 **Dairen** Liaoning China see **Dalian**
26 K10 **Dairsie** Fife, Scotland U.K.
119 F1 **Dairyland** NY U.S.A.
179 K8 **Dairyland** WI U.S.A.
70 H4 **Daisen-Oki National Park** Japan
165 K11 **Dai-sen** vol. Japan

Column 4

207 K6 **Dalbeg** Qld Austr.
50 D1 **Dalbo-Wendelstorf** Ger.
110 A4 **Dalbo** MN U.S.A.
21 J1 **Dalbosjön** l. Sweden
207 M9 **Dalby** Qld Austr.
28 H5 **Dalby** Isle of Man
22 J6 **Dalby** Sweden
145 B6 **Dalcahue** Chile
22 B1 **Dale** Hordaland Norway
21 H6 **Dale** Sogn og Fjordane Norway
21 H6 **Dale** Pembrokeshire, Wales U.K.
116 H10 **Dale City** VA U.S.A.
118 C1 **Dale Hollow Lake** TN U.S.A.
49 B10 **Daleiden** Ger.
17 M8 **Daleke** Ukr.
44 K3 **Dalen** Neth.
Dalešice, Vodní nádrž resr Czech Rep.
97 M2 **Daleside** S. Africa
158 A5 **Dalet** Myanmar
158 A5 **Daletme** Myanmar
116 E10 **Daleville** AL U.S.A.
118 D2 **Daleville** PA U.S.A.
21 M6 **Dalfors** Sweden
44 J3 **Dalfsen** Neth.
189 H1 **Dalgān** Iran
209 D9 **Dalgaranger, Mount** hill W.A. Austr.
205 L7 **Dalgety** N.S.W. Austr.
209 C8 **Dalgety** r. N.S.W. Austr.
26 J10 **Dalgety Bay** Fife, Scotland U.K.
119 H2 **Dalhart** TX U.S.A.
109 H3 **Dalhousie** N.B. Can.
178 F3 **Dalhousie** Hima. Prad. India
104 F2 **Dalhousie, Cape** N.W.T. Can.
181 J5 **Dali** Shaanxi China
170 C6 **Dali** Yunnan China
170 D4 **Dali** China
181 I3 **Dali** Cyprus
39 L5 **Daliburgh** Western Isles, Scotland U.K. see **Dalabrog**
169 N8 **Daliang** China
191 L8 **Dali He** r. China
55 H4 **Dālī He** r. China
191 H5 **Dālīlār** Azer.
191 H5 **Dälimämmädli** Azer.
169 R5 **Daling** Nei Mongol China
169 O6 **Daling He** r. China
163 E8 **Dalizi** Jilin China
68 G3 **Dalj** Croatia
26 J11 **Dalkeith** Midlothian, Scotland U.K.
179 K7 **Dalkola** W. Bengal India
207 N8 **Dallarnil** Qld Austr.
26 J7 **Dallas** Moray, Scotland U.K.
122 C4 **Dallas** OR U.S.A.
118 D2 **Dallas** PA U.S.A.
121 G9 **Dallas** TX U.S.A.
118 B5 **Dallas City** IL U.S.A.
50 H5 **Dallgow** Ger.
178 H9 **Dalli** Chhattisgarh India
104 E4 **Dall Island** AK U.S.A.
92 D1 **Dallol** Eth.
89 F3 **Dallol Bosso** watercourse Mali/Niger
187 K3 **Dalmā** i. U.A.E.
40 J2 **Dalmacio Vélez Sarsfield** Arg.
147 F3 **Dalmally** Argyll and Bute, Scotland U.K.
26 G10 **Dalmatia** PA U.S.A.
118 D2 **Dalmatia** reg. Croatia
121 D5 **Dalmatia** reg. Croatia
118 D2 **Dalmeny** Sask. Can.
179 K8 **Dalmi** Jharkhand India
70 H4 **Dalmine** Italy
115 H7 **Dalnevalnoye** Rus. Fed.
88 D5 **Dan, Monts des** hills Côte d'Ivoire
155 B9 **Dana** i. Indon.
190 D8 **Dānā** Jordan
179 I5 **Dana** Nepal
124 M4 **Dana, Mount** CA U.S.A.
191 H4 **Danaçı** Azer.
65 M4 **Dan'ádò** r. ...
88 C5 **Danané** Côte d'Ivoire
207 M1 **Dalolola Group** is P.N.G.
170 F5 **Dalou** Shan mts China
55 G10 **Dalovice** Czech Rep.
186 G3 **Dalqān** well Saudi Arabia
26 G11 **Dalry** North Ayrshire, Scotland U.K.

Column 5

94 C4 **Damaraland** reg. Namibia
117 □P4 **Damariscotta Lake** ME U.S.A.
156 □ **Damar Laut, Pulau** i. Sing.
89 I3 **Damas** Syria see **Dimashq**
37 L7 **Damas-aux-Bois** France
116 H9 **Damascus** MD U.S.A.
116 D12 **Damascus** PA U.S.A.
118 E1 **Damascus** VA U.S.A.
89 H4 **Damaturu** Nigeria
184 E4 **Dāmāvand** Iran
184 E4 **Dāmāvand, Qolleh-ye** mt. Iran
43 E7 **Damazan** France
91 B6 **Damba** Angola
37 N7 **Damba** Ger.
89 F4 **Dambai** Ghana
89 H3 **Dambatta** Nigeria
50 E4 **Dambeck** Ger.
89 I4 **Damboa** Nigeria
59 O1 **Dâmbovița** r. Romania
77 M6 **Dâmbovița** r. Romania
176 G9 **Dambulla** Sri Lanka
179 N7 **Damchara** Assam India
182 K2 **Damdy** Kazakh.
37 I6 **Dame Marie** Haiti
130 F4 **Dame Marie, Cap** c. Haiti
31 I6 **Damerham** Hampshire, England U.K.
43 H8 **Damerstown** Rep. of Ireland
49 J9 **Damery** France
36 G5 **Damgan** France
184 F3 **Damghan** Iran
26 E7 **Damh, Loch** l. Scotland U.K.
27 I2 **Damhead** Northern Ireland U.K.
43 H8 **Damietta** Egypt see **Dumyāṭ**
39 L5 **Damigny** France
169 N8 **Daming** Hebei China
170 D4 **Daming Shan** mt. Guangxi China
191 J5 **Dämirçi** Azer.
170 D6 **Dämiyā** Jordan
170 A2 **Damjong** Qinghai China
154 C9 **Damlacik** mt. Turkey
Dammam Saudi Arabia see **Ad Dammām**
191 L6 **Dämirçi** Azer.
45 D6 **Damme** Belgium
48 F5 **Damme** Ger.
178 G8 **Damoh** Madh. Prad. India
88 E4 **Damongo** Ghana
190 D5 **Damour** Lebanon
48 I1 **Damp** Ger.
156 E3 **Dampar, Tasik** l. Malaysia
48 G2 **Dampelas, Tanjung** pt Indon.
208 D6 **Dampier** W.A. Austr.
208 D6 **Dampier Archipelago** is W.A. Austr.
208 G4 **Dampier Land** reg. W.A. Austr.
40 E2 **Dampierre** France
40 E8 **Dampierre-en-Burly** France
40 I1 **Dampierre-sur-Linotte** France
40 H1 **Dampierre-sur-Salon** France
153 K8 **Dampier Strait** P.N.G.
155 G4 **Dampit** Java Indon.
40 J2 **Damprichard** France
173 K10 **Dam Qu** r. Qinghai China
159 G9 **Dâmrei, Chuŏr Phnum** mts Cambodia
179 O5 **Damroh** Arun. Prad. India
51 G6 **Damsdorf** Ger.
50 D3 **Damshagen** Ger.
50 F1 **Damsholte** Denmark
58 A5 **Damüls** Austria
70 B1 **Damvant** Switz.
36 B6 **Damville** France
26 H12 **Damvillers** France
35 H2 **Damwoude** Neth.
Damxoi Xizang China see **Comai**
76 C4 **Dao** Panay Phil.
62 D6 **Dão** r. Port.
170 C4 **Daocheng** Sichuan China
170 C4 **Daojiang** Hunan China see **Daoxian**
39 J6 **Daon** France
168 G8 **Daotanghe** Qinghai China
89 I1 **Dar Timmi** Niger
36 B4 **Daoud** Alg. see **Aïn Beïda**
88 E3 **Daoudi** well Maur.
88 D5 **Daoukro** Côte d'Ivoire
170 F4 **Daoxian** Hunan China
170 E5 **Daozhen** Guizhou China
184 E7 **Dapaong** Togo
89 H5 **Dapchi** Nigeria
171 □J7 **Dapeng Wan** b. H.K. China
179 P6 **Daphabum** mt. Arun. Prad. India
190 A8 **Daphnae** tourist site Egypt
115 D10 **Daphne** AL U.S.A.

Column 6

92 B2 **Dangur** mt. Eth.
92 B2 **Dangur** mts Eth.
171 H3 **Dangyang** Hubei China
54 G5 **Dani** Pol.
120 I5 **Daniel** WY U.S.A.
140 E5 **Daniel, Serra** hills Brazil
116 I7 **Daniel Donovan** Arg.
109 J3 **Daniel's Harbour** Nfld and Lab. Can.
96 H4 **Daniel's Head** Bermuda
117 N7 **Danielson** CT U.S.A.
97 M3 **Danielsrus** S. Africa
115 F8 **Danielsville** GA U.S.A.
19 U2 **Danilovka** Rus. Fed.
14 H4 **Danilov** Rus. Fed.
76 H8 **Danilovgrad** Crna Gora Serb. and Mont.
183 N1 **Danilovka** Kazakh.
15 I6 **Danilovka** Rus. Fed.
14 G4 **Danilovskaya Vozvyshennost'** hills Rus. Fed.
169 L8 **Daning** Shanxi China
173 H3 **Dänizkänarı** Azer.
171 H2 **Danjiangkou** Hubei China
171 H2 **Danjiangkou Shuiku** resr China
163 F12 **Danjo-guntō** is Japan
40 J1 **Danjoutin** France
187 M4 **Dank** Oman
186 E9 **Dankalia** prov. Eritrea
51 D7 **Dankerode** Ger.
184 D7 **Dankhar** Hima. Prad. India
14 H5 **Dankov** Rus. Fed.
183 Q7 **Dankova, Pik** mt. Kyrg.
156 □P10 **Dankó** Hungary
170 D3 **Danling** Sichuan China
105 P1 **Danmark Fjord** inlet Greenland
49 K6 **Danndorf** Ger.
20 H4 **Dannemarie** Denmark
40 K1 **Dannemarie** France
37 L4 **Dannenberg** Ger.
50 H4 **Dannenberg (Elbe)** Ger.
50 H4 **Dannenwalde** Ger.
89 G2 **Dannet** well Niger
202 K7 **Dannevirke** North I. N.Z.
48 I2 **Dannewerk** Ger.
97 O4 **Dannhauser** S. Africa
88 E4 **Dano** Burkina
145 D8 **Dañoso, Cabo** c. Arg.
158 E6 **Dan Sai** Thai.
116 H6 **Dansville** NY U.S.A.
116 I6 **Danta** Gujarat India
179 K9 **Dantan** W. Bengal India
116 C12 **Dante** VA U.S.A.
77 G5 **Dante** r. Europe
alt. **Donau** (Aust./Germany),
alt. **Duna** (Hungary),
alt. **Dunaj** (Slovakia),
alt. **Dunărea** (Romania)
Danube Delta Romania see **Dunării, Delta**
158 B6 **Danubyu** Myanmar
157 K4 **Danumparai** Kalimantan Indon.
157 L2 **Danum Valley Conservation Area** nature res. Malaysia
121 I8 **Danville** AR U.S.A.
114 C5 **Danville** IL U.S.A.
114 E7 **Danville** KY U.S.A.
111 R9 **Danville** OH U.S.A.
111 F12 **Danville** VA U.S.A.
117 M4 **Danville** VT U.S.A.
171 L3 **Danyang** Jiangsu China
170 D5 **Danzhai** Guizhou China
170 F5 **Danzhou** Guangxi China
170 G9 **Danzhou** Hainan China
77 O4 **Danzig** Pol. see **Gdańsk**
Danzig, Gulf of Pol./Rus. Fed. see **Gdańsk, Gulf of**
154 C6 **Dao** Panay Phil.
62 D6 **Dão** r. Port.
170 C4 **Daocheng** Sichuan China
170 C4 **Daojiang** Hunan China see **Daoxian**
39 J6 **Daon** France
168 G8 **Daotanghe** Qinghai China

Column 7

92 B2 **Dangur** mt. Eth.
171 H3 **Dangyang** Hubei China
170 B2 **Darcang** Sichuan China
69 O7 **D'Arci** Italy
54 G5 **Dani** Pol.
106 F5 **Dar Chaoui** Morocco
68 G3 **Darda** Croatia
121 I8 **Dardanelle** AR U.S.A.
124 M3 **Dardanelle** CA U.S.A.
121 I8 **Dardanelle, Lake** AR U.S.A.
115 □1 **Dardanelles** str. Turkey see **Çanakkale Boğazı**
96 H4 **Dardanelle** Bermuda
117 N7 **Dardesheim** Ger.
49 K7 **Dardha** Albania
71 J3 **Darë** Italy
170 H2 **Dar el Beida** Morocco see **Casablanca**
188 H4 **Darende** Turkey
93 C6 **Dar es Salaam** Tanz.
184 F7 **Dārestān** Kermān Iran
184 H7 **Dārestān** Kermān Iran
203 G10 **Dareton** N.S.W. Austr.
70 I4 **Darfield** South I. N.Z.
185 N4 **Darfo Boario Terme** Italy
181 I5 **Darga** Pak.
184 I2 **Dargan-Ata** Turkm.
202 H2 **Dargaville** North I. N.Z.
55 J1 **Dargin, Jezioro** l. Pol.
89 F3 **Dargo** Vic. Austr.
50 G3 **Dargun** Ger.
168 I2 **Darhan** Mongolia
79 N6 **Darhan Muminggan Lianheqi** Nei Mongol China see **Bailingmiao**
79 L3 **Darıca** Turkey
79 L1 **Darıçayırı** Turkey
119 I2 **Darien** CT U.S.A.
115 G10 **Darien** GA U.S.A.
136 B2 **Darién, Golfo del** g. Col.
126 □U14 **Darién, Parque Nacional de** nat. park Panama
126 □T13 **Darién, Serranía del** mts Panama/Col.
185 K8 **Daripa** Pak.
191 A7 **Darkent** Turkey
183 O3 **Dar'inskiy** Kazakh.
182 D2 **Dar'inskoye** Kazakh.
126 □P11 **Dario** Nic.
79 K5 **Darıveren** Turkey
183 Q3 **Dar'inskiy** Kazakh. see **Dar'inskiy**
187 M4 **Dariz** Oman
W. Bengal India see **Darjeeling**
179 L6 **Darjiling** W. Bengal India
209 D12 **Darkan** W.A. Austr.
184 C6 **Darkë Peak** S.A. Austr.
184 C6 **Darkhazineh** Iran
27 I4 **Darkhovin** Iran
98 □2a **Dark Slope Crater** Ascension S. Atlantic Ocean
207 J3 **Darling** r. N.S.W. Austr.
49 K7 **Darlingerode** Ger.
105 K2 **Darling Peninsula** Nunavut Can.
209 C13 **Darling Range** hills W.A. Austr.
29 N4 **Darlington** Darlington, England U.K.
29 N4 **Darlington** admin. div. England U.K.
115 E5 **Darlington** MD U.S.A.
115 E5 **Darlington** SC U.S.A.
110 D7 **Darlington** WI U.S.A.
97 J9 **Darlington Dam** resr S. Africa
205 K6 **Darlington Point** N.S.W. Austr.
209 K9 **Darlot, Lake** salt flat W.A. Austr.
23 M7 **Dartowo** Pol.
77 G4 **Dārmāneşti** Romania
173 E11 **Darma Pass** China/India
176 F7 **Darmaraopet** Andhra Prad. India

Column 8

27 B8 **Darby's Bridge** Rep. of Ireland
170 B2 **Darcang** Sichuan China
69 O7 **D'Arcy** B.C. Can.
68 G3 **Darda** Croatia
121 I8 **Dardanelle** AR U.S.A.
124 M3 **Dardanelle** CA U.S.A.
121 I8 **Dardanelle, Lake** AR U.S.A.
49 K7 **Dardha** Albania
71 J3 **Darè** Italy
188 H4 **Darende** Turkey
93 C6 **Dar es Salaam** Tanz.
184 F7 **Dārestān** Kermān Iran
184 H7 **Dārestān** Kermān Iran
203 G10 **Dareton** N.S.W. Austr.
70 I4 **Darfield** South I. N.Z.
185 N4 **Darfo Boario Terme** Italy
181 I5 **Darga** Pak.
184 I2 **Dargan-Ata** Turkm.
202 H2 **Dargaville** North I. N.Z.
55 J1 **Dargin, Jezioro** l. Pol.
89 F3 **Dargol** Niger
50 G3 **Dargun** Ger.
168 I2 **Darhan** Mongolia
79 L3 **Darıca** Turkey
79 L1 **Darıçayırı** Turkey
119 I2 **Darien** CT U.S.A.
115 G10 **Darien** GA U.S.A.
136 B2 **Darién, Golfo del** g. Col.
126 □U14 **Darién, Parque Nacional de** nat. park Panama
126 □T13 **Darién, Serranía del** mts Panama/Col.
185 K8 **Daripa** Pak.
191 A7 **Darkent** Turkey
183 O3 **Dar'inskiy** Kazakh.
182 D2 **Dar'inskoye** Kazakh.
126 □P11 **Dario** Nic.
79 K5 **Darıveren** Turkey
79 N6 **Darjeeling** W. Bengal India
209 D12 **Darkan** W.A. Austr.
204 D6 **Darke Peak** S.A. Austr.
184 C6 **Darkhazineh** Iran
27 I4 **Darkhovin** Iran
98 □2a **Dark Slope Crater** Ascension S. Atlantic Ocean
207 J3 **Darling** r. N.S.W. Austr.
49 K7 **Darlingerode** Ger.
105 K2 **Darling Peninsula** Nunavut Can.
209 C13 **Darling Range** hills W.A. Austr.
29 N4 **Darlington** Darlington, England U.K.
29 N4 **Darlington** admin. div. England U.K.
115 E5 **Darlington** MD U.S.A.
115 E5 **Darlington** SC U.S.A.
110 D7 **Darlington** WI U.S.A.
97 J9 **Darlington Dam** resr S. Africa
205 K6 **Darlington Point** N.S.W. Austr.
209 K9 **Darlot, Lake** salt flat W.A. Austr.
23 M7 **Darłowo** Pol.
77 G4 **Dărmăneşti** Romania
173 E11 **Darma Pass** China/India
176 F7 **Darmaraopet** Andhra Prad. India
188 H4 **Darmcık** Iran
53 I4 **Darmstadt** Ger.
53 I4 **Darmstadt** admin. reg. Ger.
178 D1 **Darna** r. India
84 D1 **Darnah** Libya
97 P5 **Darnall** S. Africa
37 L7 **Darney** France
66 K3 **Darnick** N.S.W. Austr.
37 L7 **Darnieulles** France
66 K3 **Darnius** Spain
213 C2 **Darnley, Cape** Antarctica
63 N6 **Darnley Bay** N.W.T. Can.
89 F7 **Daroca** Spain
14 H4 **Darovskoy** Rus. Fed.
14 I4 **Dar Pahn** Iran
207 I7 **Darr** watercourse Qld Austr.
26 F6 **Darra** Aberdeenshire, Scotland U.K.
147 F5 **Darragh** r. Rep. of Ireland
89 F7 **Darragueira** Arg.
184 D7 **Darreh Bīd** Iran
185 J7 **Darreh Gaz** Iran
184 H3 **Darreh Gozarı** r. Iran see **Gīzeh Rūd**
184 F5 **Darreh-ye Bāghī** Iran
184 B5 **Darreh-ye Shahr** Iran
185 M4 **Darreh-ye Shekārī** r. Afgh.
109 H4 **Darrow** LA U.S.A.
30 E7 **Darshi** Devon, England U.K.
204 H7 **Dartmoor** Vic. Austr.
30 E7 **Dartmoor** hills England U.K.
30 E7 **Dartmoor National Park** England U.K.
109 I4 **Dartmouth** N.S. Can.
30 E7 **Dartmouth** Devon, England U.K.
207 J9 **Dartmouth, Lake** salt flat Qld Austr.
205 K7 **Dartmouth Reservoir** Vic. Austr.
29 N6 **Darton** South Yorkshire, England U.K.
31 O3 **Dartford** Kent, England U.K.
30 E7 **Dartington** Devon, England U.K.
153 P1 **Daru** P.N.G.
88 C5 **Daru** Sierra Leone
85 G5 **Daru** waterhole Sudan
66 A5 **Daruba** Maluku Indon.
146 E6 **Daruga-mine** mt. Japan
184 G7 **Daruvar** Croatia
19 U3 **Darvishi** Iran
185 N2 **Darvoz, Qatorkūhi** mts Tajik.
29 M6 **Darwen** Blackburn with Darwen, England U.K.
95 F3 **Darwendale** Zimbabwe
146 E6 **Darwha** Mahar. India
206 C1 **Darwin** Arg.
145 C9 **Darwin** Falkland Is
145 C9 **Darwin** N.T. Austr.
145 C9 **Darwin, Canal** sea chan. Chile
145 C9 **Darwin, Monte** mt. Chile

Column 1

36 □ Darwin, Volcán vol. Islas Galápagos Ecuador
125 R6 Darwin, Volcán vol. Islas Galápagos Ecuador
109 I2 Darwin Island Islas Galápagos Ecuador see Culpepper, Isla
85 N6 Darya Khan Pak.
82 K5 Dar'yalyktakyr, Ravnina plain Kazakh.
84 D1 Daryānah Libya
Dar''yoi Amu r. Asia see Amudar'ya
73 I10 Darzhuo Xizang China
74 H7 Dārzīn Iran
87 K3 Dās i. U.A.E.
78 C8 Dasada Gujarat India
69 N7 Dasha He r. China
79 J9 Dashapalla Orissa India
55 M6 Dashava Ukr.
69 N2 Dashballar Mongolia
69 K6 Dashetai Nei Mongol China
Dashoguz Turkm. see Dashoguz
69 R6 Dashiqiao Liaoning China
68 B5 Dashitou Xinjiang China
16 I4 Dashiv Ukr.
69 Q3 Dashizhai Nei Mongol China
19 N8 Dashkawka Belarus
Dashkesan Azer. see Daşkäsän
Dashkhovuz Dashoguzskaya Oblast' Turkm. see Dashoguz
Dashkhovuz Oblast admin. div. Turkm. see Dashoguzskaya Oblast'
84 H1 Dashoguz Dashoguzskaya Oblast' Turkm.
84 H1 Dashoguzskaya Oblast' admin. div. Turkm.
85 J8 Dasht Iran
85 I9 Dasht r. Pak.
84 G7 Dashtak Iran
186 E6 Dashtak Iran
Dashtak Qal'ehsi Iran see Dashtak
84 G7 Dasht-e Bar Iran
84 E7 Dasht-e Palang r. Iran
85 I9 Dashtiari Iran
83 M7 Dashtobod Uzbek.
68 J8 Dashuikeng Ningxia China
68 F8 Dashuiqiao Qinghai China
68 I8 Dashuitou Gansu China
58 E1 Dašice Czech Rep.
53 K5 Dasing Ger.
85 P5 Daska Pak.
91 H5 Daşkäsän Azer.
96 G9 Daskop S. Africa
50 G2 Daskow Ger.
70 E5 Dasongshu Yunnan China
85 O3 Dasqat mt. Pak.
89 F5 Dassa Benin
49 I7 Dassel Ger.
54 C8 Dassalan i. Phil.
48 J4 Dassendorf Ger.
96 C3 Dassen Island S. Africa
48 K5 Dassow Ger.
85 I8 Dastakan, Ra's-e pt Iran
91 H6 Dastakert Armenia
84 G4 Dastgardān Iran
84 H5 Dastgerd Iran
62 G7 Da Suifen He r. China
78 E4 Dasuya Punjab India
97 M2 Dasville S. Africa
57 K4 Daszyna Pol.
25 S9 Datadian Kalimantan Indon.
79 I6 Datça Turkey
64 R4 Date Japan
25 S7 Date Creek watercourse AZ U.S.A.
25 S9 Dateland AZ U.S.A.
78 D3 Datha Gujarat India
78 D7 Datia Madh. Prad. India
71 K6 Datian Fujian China
71 H7 Datian Ding mt. Guangdong China
78 J8 Datil NM U.S.A.
71 K3 Datong Anhui China
62 D6 Datong Heilong. China
68 G8 Datong Qinghai China
69 M6 Datong Shanxi China
69 H8 Datong He r. China
68 F8 Datong Shan mts China
82 L4 Datta Rus. Fed.
85 M5 Datta Khel Pak.
76 F2 Dattapur Mahar. India
49 D7 Datteln Ger.
49 J8 Datterode (Ringgau) Ger.
57 H4 Datu, Tanjung c. Indon./Malaysia
25 S9 Datuk, Tanjung pt Indon.
54 E8 Datu Piang Mindanao Phil.
79 M8 Daudkandi Bangl.
85 N5 Daud Khel Pak.
79 J7 Daudnagar Bihar India
18 I5 Daudzeva Latvia
18 I6 Daugai Lith.
18 H4 Daugava r. Latvia alt. Zakhodnyaya Dzvina, alt. Zapadnaya Dvina, conv. Western Dvina
18 J6 Daugavpils Latvia
49 I7 Daugyvenė r. Lith.
85 L3 Daulatabad Afgh.
85 L3 Daulatpur Bangl.
86 D4 Daule Ecuador
43 G9 Daumazan-sur-Arize France
39 K6 Daumeray France
49 C10 Daun Ger.
76 D3 Daund Mahar. India
84 D8 Daung Kyun i. Myanmar
58 J3 Daungyu r. Myanmar
41 H9 Dauphin France
18 B4 Dauphin PA U.S.A.
18 B4 Dauphin County county PA U.S.A.
41 G6 Dauphiné reg. France
41 G6 Dauphiné, Alpes du mts France
21 K10 Dauphin Island AL U.S.A.
07 L5 Dauphin Lake Man. Can.
85 H3 Daura Nigeria
69 O2 Daurie Creek r. W.A. Austr.
82 G2 Dauriya Rus. Fed.
19 L2 Daurskiy Khrebet mts Rus. Fed.
78 F6 Dausa Rajasthan India
59 N7 Dāu Tiëng, Hô resr Vietnam
49 J9 Dautphetal-Friedensdorf Ger.
49 G9 Dautphetal-Holzhausen Ger.
26 I8 Dava Moray, Scotland U.K.
91 J4 Dāvāçi Azer.
76 D5 Davangere Karnataka India
54 E8 Davao Mindanao Phil.
54 E8 Davao Gulf Mindanao Phil.
84 D4 Dāvarān Iran
84 H8 Dāvar Hormozgan Iran
85 J8 Dāvar Panāh Iran
74 F2 Davarzan Iran
14 N3 Davel S. Africa
22 E3 Davenport IA U.S.A.
17 K6 Davenport NY U.S.A.
22 E3 Davenport WA U.S.A.
06 E6 Davenport Downs Qld Austr.
206 E6 Davenport Range hills N.T. Austr.
31 I3 Daventry Northamptonshire, England U.K.
97 M2 Daveyton S. Africa
41 F6 Davézieux France
26 CR13 David Panama
20 G5 David City NE U.S.A.
06 C10 Davidson Sask. Can.
06 E2 Davidson, Mount N.T. Austr.
23 L4 Davidson Lake Man. Can.
25 R8 Davidsonville MD U.S.A.
04 L4 Davie FL U.S.A.
11 K7 Davie CA U.S.A.
04 B2 Davies, Mount W.A. Austr.
04 D2 Davies, Mount W.A. Austr.
46 H3 Davies, Mount Antarctica
86 E3 Dávila Peru
16 D4 Davis research stn Antarctica
05 I9 Davis S.A. Austr.
24 B1 Davis CA U.S.A.
16 K9 Davis WV U.S.A.
04 D3 Davis r. W.A. Austr.
13 I2 Davis Bay Antarctica

Column 2

125 R6 Davis Dam AZ U.S.A.
125 R6 Davis Dam dam AZ U.S.A.
109 I2 Davis Inlet Nfld and Lab. Can.
111 K6 Davison MI U.S.A.
213 G2 Davis Sea Antarctica
105 M3 Davis Strait Can./Greenland
15 K5 Davlekanovo Rus. Fed.
78 D4 Davlia Greece
57 H5 Dávod Hungary
75 K6 Davoli Italy
70 H2 Davos Switz.
191 J6 Dāvūd Qeshlāqī Iran
79 I5 Davutlar Turkey
116 D11 Davy WV U.S.A.
191 G2 Davyd-Haradok Belarus
16 G1 Davydivka Ukr.
55 M6 Davydiv Ukr.
17 O7 Davydivka Ukr.
17 S2 Davydivka Rus. Fed.
19 V4 Davydovo Rus. Fed.
107 I3 Davy Lake Sask. Can.
169 R6 Dawa Liaoning China
173 G11 Dawa Co l. Xizang China
186 G5 Dawásir, Wādī ad watercourse Saudi Arabia
92 D3 Dawa Wenz r. Eth.
173 G11 Dawaxung Xizang China
170 D3 Dawê Sichuan China
44 H4 De Bilt Neth.
193 Q3 Dawêloor i. Maluku Indon.
155 G7 Dawen He r. China
155 G7 Dawera i. Maluku Indon.
187 I2 Dawhat Bilbul b. Saudi Arabia
18 K7 Dawhinava Belarus
30 F6 Dawlish Devon, England U.K.
16 I2 Dawley Shropshire, England U.K.
158 C6 Dawna Taungdan mts Myanmar/Thai.
187 L6 Dawqah Oman
186 E6 Dawqah Saudi Arabia
86 B4 Dawra Western Sahara
88 B4 Dawran Yemen
27 E3 Dawros Head r. Rep. of Ireland
207 L7 Dawson r. Qld Austr.
104 E3 Dawson Y.T. Can.
115 E10 Dawson GA U.S.A.
120 F2 Dawson ND U.S.A.
145 C9 Dawson, Isla i. Chile
145 G5 Dawson, Mount B.C. Can.
92 G2 Dawson Bay Man. Can.
106 F4 Dawson Creek B.C. Can.
107 M2 Dawson Inlet Nunavut Can.
106 A2 Dawson Range mts Y.T. Can.
106 E5 Dawsons Landing B.C. Can.
54 D2 Dębsko Pol.
115 E8 Dawsonville GA U.S.A.
170 C3 Dawu Hubei China
171 J3 Dawu Shan hill Hubei China
173 J8 Dawusi Qinghai China
187 N5 Dax France
Daxian Sichuan China see Dazhou
170 F3 Daxian Sichuan China
170 D4 Daxiang Ling mts Sichuan China
92 C2 Daxin Guangxi China
176 E3 Daxue Shan mt. China
108 E4 Da Xueshan mts Sichuan China
191 G3 Dayang Rus. Fed.
187 M3 Dāyah U.A.E.
173 K13 Dayang r. India
169 R7 Dayang He r. China
162 D3 Dayangshu Nei Mongol China
169 S2 Dayangshu Nei Mongol China
168 A2 Dayan Nuur l. Mongolia
170 C6 Dayao Yunnan China
170 H7 Dayao Shan mts China
170 A6 Dayican Sichuan China
171 J3 Dayi Hubei China
170 D3 Dayi Sichuan China
122 K4 Dayiguang Myanmar
40 C3 Decize France
111 L6 Deckerville MI U.S.A.
75 K5 De Cocksdorp Neth.
191 G3 Daykhokh, Gora mt. Rus. Fed.
206 D1 De Courcy Head N.T. Austr.
57 H5 Decs Hungary
91 O7 Dayman r. Uru.
31 J4 Dayman, Cuchilla del hills Uru.
79 K5 Dayrabad Uttar Prad. India
188 J5 Dayr Abū Sa'īd Jordan
191 E6 Dayr 'Alī Syria
88 I4 Dayr az Zawr Syria
189 J6 Dayr az Zawr Syria
92 D2 Dayr Ḥāfir Syria
57 J3 Dayr Shumayyil at Taḥtānī Syria
85 J7 Dayrūt Egypt
107 H4 Daysland Alta Can.
110 A4 Dayton MN U.S.A.
116 A9 Dayton OH U.S.A.
115 E8 Dayton TN U.S.A.
121 H8 Dayton TX U.S.A.
122 E3 Dayton WA U.S.A.
115 G12 Daytona Beach FL U.S.A.
171 J6 Dayu Jiangxi China
157 K6 Dayu Kalimantan Indon.
171 I6 Dayu Ling mts China
171 L2 Da Yunhe canal China
169 O9 Da Yunhe canal China
171 L2 Da Yunhe canal China
169 O7 Da Yunhe canal China
122 E4 Dayville OR U.S.A.
187 K3 Dayyina i. U.A.E.
165 Q3 Dazaifu Japan
184 A3 Dazgir Iran
169 M8 Dazhai Shanxi China
170 H9 Dazhipo Hainan China
70 F3 Dazhou Sichuan China
170 F3 Dazhou Dao i. China
158 E4 Dazu Sichuan China
168 G5 Dazigou Xinjiang China
79 K5 Dazkırı Turkey
70 C3 Dazu Chongqing China
122 O4 Dazu Rock Carvings tourist site Chongqing China
96 I6 De Aar S. Africa
27 E7 Dead r. MI U.S.A.
117 O3 Dead r. ME U.S.A.
110 C3 Dead r. MI U.S.A.
115 F11 Deadman Bay FL U.S.A.
130 F2 Deadman's Cay Long I. Bahamas
209 J8 Dead Mountains i. NV U.S.A.
104 H4 Dead Island NB. Can.
103 I2 Dead Island W.A. Austr.
107 M4 Deadman Lake Nfld and Lab. Can.
107 M4 Deer Lake l. Ont. Can.
107 M4 Deer Lake l. Ont. Can.
76 B2 Deerlijk Belgium
122 J4 Deer Lodge MT U.S.A.
119 J3 Deer Park WA U.S.A.
122 F3 Deer Park WA U.S.A.
190 D2 Dead River Storage Dam resr MI U.S.A.
35 J4 Dead Sea salt l. Asia
14 O5 Deadwood SD U.S.A.
206 D2 Deaf Adder Creek r. N.T. Austr.
209 J11 Deakin W.A. Austr.
31 O5 Deal Kent, England U.K.
97 J4 Dealesville S. Africa
106 E4 Dean r. B.C. Can.
171 J4 De'an Jiangxi China
30 C4 Dean, Forest of England U.K.
122 G6 Dean Channel B.C. Can.
146 E2 Deán Funes Arg.
44 D3 Dean Water r. Scotland U.K.
116 E7 Dean r. MI U.S.A.
118 D5 Dearborn MI U.S.A.
29 O4 Dearham Cumbria, England U.K.
29 O7 Dease r. England U.K.
106 I2 Deary ID U.S.A.
106 D3 Dease Arm b. N.W.T. Can.
106 D3 Dease Lake B.C. Can.
88 E2 Défale de Tosaye gorge Mali
103 H4 Dease Plateau B.C. Can.
115 D10 Dease Strait Nunavut Can.
124 O5 Death Valley depr. CA U.S.A.

Column 3

125 P5 Death Valley Junction CA U.S.A.
124 O5 Death Valley National Park CA U.S.A.
39 L3 Deauville France
122 J4 Deaver WY U.S.A.
191 I4 Deavgay, Gora mt. Rus. Fed.
179 L8 Debagram W. Bengal India
157 I4 Debak Sarawak Malaysia
17 R5 Debal'tseve Ukr.
Debal'tsovo Ukr. see Debal'tseve
170 F7 Debao Guangxi China
76 I9 Debar Macedonia
92 C1 Debark Eth.
187 J7 Debay well Yemen
107 J4 Debden Sask. Can.
191 D5 Debe Trin. and Tob.
97 N4 De Beers Pass S. Africa
31 O3 Debenham Suffolk, England U.K.
109 I4 Debert N.S. Can.
14 K4 Debesy Rus. Fed.
191 G4 Debet r. Armenia
55 J5 Dębica Pol.
44 G5 De Biesbosch, Nationaal Park nat. park Neth.
87 G2 Debila Alg.
44 H4 De Bilt Neth.
193 Q3 Debin Rus. Fed.
55 J4 Dębin Pol.
54 I1 Dębki Kaszubska Pol.
55 I6 Dębno Małopolskie Pol.
54 C3 Dębno Zachodniopomorskie Pol.
88 D3 Dêbo, Lac l. Mali
209 E11 Deborah East, Lake salt flat W.A. Austr.
209 E11 Deborah West, Lake salt flat W.A. Austr.
55 I4 Dęborzeczka Pol.
55 H4 Dębowa Kłoda Pol.
55 H2 Dębowa Łąka Pol.
207 N1 Deboyne Islands P.N.G.
92 C2 Debre Birhan Eth.
54 K4 Debrecen Hungary
92 C2 Debre Markos Eth.
92 C2 Debre Sina Eth.
76 I9 Debreste Macedonia
92 G2 Debre Tabor Eth.
92 C2 Debre Werk' Eth.
92 C2 Debre Zeyit Eth.
54 D2 Dębrzno Pol.
Decan Kosovo, Srbija Serb. and Mont. see Dečani
76 I8 Dečani Kosovo, Srbija Serb. and Mont.
115 I8 Decatur AL U.S.A.
115 E9 Decatur GA U.S.A.
114 C6 Decatur IL U.S.A.
115 I6 Decatur IN U.S.A.
110 I7 Decatur MI U.S.A.
121 K9 Decatur MS U.S.A.
115 E8 Decatur TN U.S.A.
121 E9 Decatur TX U.S.A.
115 E8 Decaturville TN U.S.A.
41 F4 Decazeville France
76 C5 Deccan plat. India
108 E4 Decelles, Lac resr Que. Can.
94 E4 Deception watercourse Botswana
207 N9 Deception Bay Qld Austr.
94 D4 Deception Pans salt pan Botswana
170 D5 Dechang Sichuan China
Decheng Guangdong China see Deqing
57 G3 Dechtice Slovakia
72 B9 Decimomannu Sardegna Italy
72 B9 Decimoputzu Sardegna Italy
56 D1 Děčín Czech Rep.
40 F5 Décines-Charpieu France
40 C3 Decize France
122 K4 Decker MT U.S.A.
111 L6 Deckerville MI U.S.A.
75 G5 De Cocksdorp Neth.
75 K5 Decorah IA U.S.A.
206 D1 De Courcy Head N.T. Austr.
57 H5 Decs Hungary
Dédéagach Greece see Alexandroupoli
31 J4 Deddington Oxfordshire, England U.K.
79 K6 Dedegöl Dağları mts Turkey
79 L2 Dedegöl Turkey
79 K6 Dededagöl Turkey
188 E5 Dededagöl Turkey
49 K6 Dedeleben Ger.
79 L2 Dedeler Turkey
191 E6 Dedeli Turkey
48 K5 Dedelow Ger.
79 L7 Dedelstorf Ger.
188 E4 Dedemli Turkey
44 J3 Dedemsvaart Neth.
92 D2 Deder Eth.
57 J3 Dédestapolcsány Hungary
31 M4 Dedham Essex, England U.K.
19 W6 Dedino r. Rus. Fed.
142 D6 Dedo de Deus mt. Brazil
96 D9 De Doorns S. Africa
191 H4 Dedop'listsqaro Georgia
88 D3 Dédougou Burkina
18 M4 Dedovichi Rus. Fed.
182 F7 Dedoplis Rus. Fed.
93 B8 Dedza Malawi
95 G2 Dedza Mountain Malawi
27 J5 Dee r. Rep. of Ireland
30 F1 Dee est. Wales U.K.
30 E3 Dee r. England/Wales U.K.
26 L8 Dee r. Scotland U.K.
178 F6 Deeg Rajasthan India
27 O4 Deel r. Rep. of Ireland
27 I6 Deel r. Rep. of Ireland
27 E5 Deel r. Rep. of Ireland
27 E6 Deele r. Rep. of Ireland
90 F2 Deep r. NC U.S.A.
115 G11 Deep r. NC U.S.A.
124 M6 Deep Lake salt l. UT U.S.A.
118 C3 Deep r. NJ U.S.A.
125 T3 Deep Creek r. MD U.S.A.
124 L2 Deep Creek Lake MD U.S.A.
206 C3 Deep Creek Range mts UT U.S.A.
29 L7 Deeping St Nicholas Lincolnshire, England U.K.
185 J5 Deep Bight inlet W.A. Austr.
116 F9 Deep Creek Lake MD U.S.A.
125 S2 Deep Creek Range mts UT U.S.A.
L2 Deeping St Nicholas
185 M5 Deep Afgh.
97 J2 Deepdale W.A. Austr.
104 A7 Deepdale N.S.W. Austr.
110 E6 Deep River Ont. Can.
205 M4 Deep River CT U.S.A.
118 E5 Deepwater N.S.W. Austr.
119 M4 Deep Water Bay H.K. China
150 F4 Deer r. MI U.S.A.
118 C3 Deer Creek r. MD U.S.A.
118 J10 Deer Creek r. MD U.S.A.
116 B9 Deer Creek Reservoir UT U.S.A.
118 C3 Deerfield NJ U.S.A.
116 D7 Deerfield OH U.S.A.
118 E3 Deerfield r. NY U.S.A.
92 D3 Deeri Somalia
209 J8 Deering, Mount W.A. Austr.
104 H4 Deer Island NB. Can.
104 H4 Deer Island NB. Can.
117 O3 Deer Isle ME U.S.A.
118 E5 Deer Lake Nfld and Lab. Can.
118 J7 Deerlijk Belgium
29 L8 Deerlodge Ont. U.S.A.
122 H2 Deer Lodge MT U.S.A.
118 A4 Deersville OH U.S.A.
26 I8 Deer Park WA U.S.A.
122 F3 Deer Park WA U.S.A.
16 J3 Deerpark Rep. of Ireland
110 B4 Deer River MN U.S.A.
16 J3 Deersbrook Rep. of Ireland
44 F5 Deest Neth.
122 I3 Deer Park WA U.S.A.
121 O6 Defeng Guizhou China see Liping
21 P6 Defiance OH U.S.A.
43 G6 Dégagnac France

Column 4

142 D4 Delfinópolis Brazil
44 F4 Delft Neth.
176 F6 Delft Island Sri Lanka
44 K2 Delfzijl Neth.
129 K6 Delgada, Punta pt Mex.
93 D7 Delgado, Cabo c. Moz.
168 F3 Delgermörön r. Mongolia
168 G2 Delger Mörön r. Mongolia
85 F4 Delgo Sudan
118 F6 Del Haven NJ U.S.A.
44 H4 Del Dolder Neth.
44 F6 Del Dungen Neth.
44 I5 Den Dungen Neth.
44 L4 Denekamp Neth.
76 J8 Đeneral Janković Kosovo, Srbija Serb. and Mont.
14 L3 Denezhkin Kamen', Gora mt. Rus. Fed.
89 H3 Denge Nigeria
89 G3 Denge Nigeria
154 □ Dengas Passage Palau
169 M9 Dengfeng Henan China
173 G12 Dênggên Xizang China
89 H4 Dengî Nigeria
169 J6 Dengkou Nei Mongol China
173 L11 Dêngqên Xizang China
171 J7 Dengta Guangdong China
43 D9 Denguin France
90 D3 Denguiro C.A.R.
171 J7 Dengzhou Henan China
Dengzhou Shandong China see Penglai
173 K8 Dêngqên Xizang China
177 I2 Dengzhou Henan China
43 D9 Denguin France
90 D3 Denguiro C.A.R.
209 B8 Denham W.A. Austr.
208 J3 Denham r. W.A. Austr.
44 K4 Den Ham Neth.
31 L4 Denham Buckinghamshire, England U.K.
130 □ Denham, Mount hill Jamaica
206 G4 Denham Range mts Qld Austr.
209 B8 Denham Sound sea chan. W.A. Austr.
44 G3 Den Helder Neth.
107 I4 Denholm Sask. Can.
26 K12 Denholm Scottish Borders, Scotland U.K.
29 N6 Denholme West Yorkshire, England U.K.
44 I4 Den Hoorn Neth.
67 F10 Denia Spain
204 D5 Denial Bay S.A. Austr.
204 D5 Denial Bay b. S.A. Austr.
205 J6 Deniliquin N.S.W. Austr.
179 P6 Denio Arun. Prad. India
122 E6 Denio NV U.S.A.
17 K1 Deniskovichi Rus. Fed.
120 H4 Denison IA U.S.A.
121 G9 Denison TX U.S.A.
208 J5 Denison Plains W.A. Austr.
182 I1 Denisovka Kazakh.
79 K5 Denizli prov. Turkey
41 J8 Denjuan, Sommet de mt. France
Denkendorf Baden-Württemberg Ger.
Denkendorf Bayern Ger.
Denklingen Baden-Württemberg Ger.
Denkingen Baden-Württemberg Ger.
49 K6 Denman N.S.W. Austr.
205 M5 Denman N.S.W. Austr.
213 G2 Denman Glacier Antarctica
209 D13 Denmark W.A. Austr.
22 G5 Denmark WI U.S.A.
110 G5 Denmark country Europe
Denmark Fjord inlet Greenland see Danmark Fjord
105 P3 Denmark Strait Greenland/Iceland
31 J6 Dennead Hampshire, England U.K.
44 L4 Dennekamp Neth.
131 □7 Dennery St Lucia
44 E6 Denneville Ger.
97 N1 Denniston S. Africa
31 O3 Dennington Suffolk, England U.K.
208 J6 Dennis, Lake salt flat W.A. Austr.
116 D6 Dennison OH U.S.A.
116 C10 Dennisville NJ U.S.A.
26 I10 Denny Falkirk, Scotland U.K.
44 J5 Den Oever Neth.
183 L8 Denov Uzbek.
169 M5 Denman Nei Mongol China
168 G6 Denstei Nei Mongol China
173 D10 Dêrsum Ger.
92 D2 Dêntang Xizang China
96 G9 De Rust S. Africa
73 I2 Dent Blanche mt. Switz.
26 D9 Dent de Rez hill France
45 D7 Dentergem Belgium
53 J3 Dentlein am Forst Ger.
29 M7 Denton Greater Manchester, England U.K.
29 N4 Denton Norfolk, England U.K.
118 D5 Denton MD U.S.A.
121 G8 Denton TX U.S.A.
209 C13 D'Entrecasteaux, Point W.A. Austr.
199 G3 D'Entrecasteaux, Récifs rf New Caledonia
153 L8 D'Entrecasteaux Islands P.N.G.
209 D13 D'Entrecasteaux National Park W.A. Austr.
70 B3 Dents du Midi mt. Switz.
31 M4 Denver Norfolk, England U.K.
123 L5 Denver CO U.S.A.
118 C4 Denver PA U.S.A.
70 G3 Denzlingen Ger.

Column 5

158 E6 Den Chai Thai.
157 G6 Dendang Indon.
88 D2 Dendâra Maur.
45 F7 Denderleeuw Belgium
45 F6 Dendermonde Belgium
44 H4 Den Dolder Neth.
45 I8 Dendre r. Belgium
44 I5 Den Dungen Neth.
44 L4 Denekamp Neth.
48 J3 Delisle Sask. Can.
156 C3 Delitua Sumatera Indon.
51 F7 Delitzsch Ger.
58 H6 Dellach Austria
59 I7 Dellach im Drautal Austria
40 K1 Delle France
49 I7 Delligsen Ger.
70 I5 Dello Italy
120 G4 Dell Rapids SD U.S.A.
87 F1 Dellys Alg.
124 O9 Del Mar CA U.S.A.
117 J10 Delmar DE U.S.A.
45 M5 Delmas S. Africa
37 L6 Delme France
48 G4 Delmenhorst Ger.
18 F6 Delmont NJ U.S.A.
206 E7 Delmore Downs N.T. Austr.
68 E3 Delnice Croatia
123 K8 Del Norte CO U.S.A.
193 Q2 De-Longa, Ostrova is Rus. Fed.
De Long Islands is Rus. Fed. see De-Longa, Ostrova
104 B3 De Long Mountains AK U.S.A.
205 K9 Deloraine Tas. Austr.
107 K5 Deloraine Man. Can.
29 M6 Delph Greater Manchester, England U.K.
78 D4 Delphi tourist site Greece
115 I5 Delphi IN U.S.A.
114 A7 Delphos OH U.S.A.
116 A8 Delphos OH U.S.A.
41 J8 Delphos OH U.S.A.
96 I4 Delportshoop S. Africa
115 G12 Delray Beach FL U.S.A.
121 C11 Del Rio Mex.
121 D7 Del Rio TX U.S.A.
21 N6 Delsbo Sweden
89 G5 Delta state Nigeria
123 J7 Delta CO U.S.A.
116 A7 Delta OH U.S.A.
118 C5 Delta PA U.S.A.
137 T2 Delta Amacuro state Venez.
207 H4 Delta Downs Qld Austr.
88 A3 Delta du Saloum, Parc National du nat. park Senegal
104 D3 Delta Junction AK U.S.A.
121 K11 Delta National Wildlife Refuge nature res. LA U.S.A.
117 J5 Delta Reservoir NY U.S.A.
66 G6 Deltebre Spain
115 G11 Deltona FL U.S.A.
205 M3 Delungra N.S.W. Austr.
44 L4 De Lutte Neth.
147 G4 Del Valle Arg.
27 H5 Delvin Rep. of Ireland
78 B3 Delvinë Albania
16 I5 Delyatyn Ukr.
182 F1 Dema r. Rus. Fed.
89 G4 Demak Jawa Indon.
162 L3 Demanda, Sierra de la mts Spain
85 H6 Demas-aux-Eaux France
Demavend mt. Iran see Damāvand, Qolleh-ye
91 D5 Demba Dem. Rep. Congo
18 H6 Demba Chio Angola
92 C2 Dembeni Njazidja Comoros
99 □3a Dembeni Mayotte
92 C2 Dembî Eth.
92 C2 Dembî Dolo Eth.
57 K3 Dekonta Hungary
44 K3 De Krim Neth.
30 C6 Delabole Cornwall, England U.K.
147 G5 De la Garma Arg.
155 D8 Delaki Indon.
124 N4 Delamar Lake NV U.S.A.
206 C3 Delamere N.T. Austr.
29 L7 Delamere Cheshire, England U.K.
90 F2 Delami Sudan
156 C2 Delano CA U.S.A.
115 G11 Delano CA U.S.A.
124 M6 Delano Peak UT U.S.A.
118 C3 Delano PA U.S.A.
79 J3 Delanta Iran
191 E6 Delaram Afgh.
104 A4 Delarof Islands AK U.S.A.
110 E9 Delaronde Lake Sask. Can.
118 E6 Delaware r. U.S.A.
116 B9 Delaware OH U.S.A.
118 D5 Delaware NJ U.S.A.
118 E6 Delaware OH U.S.A.
118 E5 Delaware r. KS U.S.A.
116 C10 Delaware state U.S.A.
118 E5 Delaware, East Branch r. NY U.S.A.
118 J7 Delaware, West Branch r. NY U.S.A.
118 E6 Delaware Bay DE/NJ U.S.A.
118 D5 Delaware City DE U.S.A.
118 E5 Delaware County county PA U.S.A.
118 D5 Delaware Water Gap PA U.S.A.
118 C3 Delaware Water Gap National Recreational Area park NJ/PA U.S.A.
109 G1 Delay r. Que. Can.
116 C11 De Land FL U.S.A.
124 M6 Delano UT U.S.A.
137 G3 Delbarton WV U.S.A.
49 I8 Delbrück Ger.
107 H4 Delburne Alta Can.
146 E4 Del Campillo Arg.
146 D4 Del Carmen Arg.
175 C9 Delčevo Macedonia
Delcommune, Lac l. Dem. Rep. Congo see Nzilo, Lac
44 F5 Den Bommel Neth.

Column 6 / 7

44 G2 Den Bosch Neth. see 's-Hertogenbosch
29 N6 Denby Dale West Yorkshire, England U.K.
36 I6 Der, Lac du l. France
92 C2 Dera Eth.
178 F4 Dera Hima. Prad. India
185 M7 Dera Bugti Pak.
185 N6 Dera Ghazi Khan Pak.
85 G4 Dera el Sudan
185 N6 Dera Ismail Khan Pak.
185 N6 Derajat reg. Pak.
213 C2 Derawar, Mount Antarctica
185 N7 Derawar Fort Pak.
16 F3 Derazhne Ukr.
16 E5 Derazhnya Ukr.
17 O5 Derazhnya Ukr.
191 J3 Derbent Rus. Fed.
79 L2 Derbent Kocaeli Turkey
79 K4 Derbent Manisa Turkey
79 K4 Derbent Uşak Turkey
Derbent Nei Mongol China see Darband
162 B3 Derbent Nei Mongol China
205 K9 Derby Tas. Austr.
208 G4 Derby W.A. Austr.
97 L1 Derby S. Africa
31 J2 Derby Derby, England U.K.
31 J2 Derby admin. div. England U.K.
121 G7 Derby KS U.S.A.
117 M3 Derby Line VT U.S.A.
29 N7 Derbyshire admin. div. England U.K.
191 C5 Derebaşı Turkey
57 K4 Derecske Hungary
31 N2 Dereham Norfolk, England U.K.
190 A1 Dereiçi Turkey
57 J5 Derekegyháza Hungary
190 A2 Dereköy Antalya Turkey
79 K5 Dereköy Denizli Turkey
79 K3 Dereköy Kütahya Turkey
49 K7 Derenburg Ger.
84 D6 Deréssa Chad
19 P2 Dereva Rus. Fed.
17 O5 Derezuvate Ukr.
27 D9 Derg, r. Rep. of Ireland/U.K.
27 E5 Derg, Lough l. Rep. of Ireland
27 F3 Derg, Lough l. Rep. of Ireland
182 C2 Dergachi Rus. Fed.
Dergachi Ukr. see Derhachi
204 H7 Dergholm State Park nature res. Vic. Austr.
17 P3 Derhachi Ukr.
178 G7 Deri Uttar Prad. India
121 I10 De Ridder LA U.S.A.
44 G3 De Rijp Neth.
189 J5 Derik Turkey
191 B6 Derinçay Turkey
191 D6 Derinkuyu Turkey
188 G4 Deriyivka Ukr.
92 D4 Derkali well Kenya
15 T5 Derkul r. Rus. Fed./Ukr.
49 J9 Derra Ger.
93 B6 Dermbach Ger.
182 J5 Dermenshe Kazakh.
Derna Libya see Darnah
57 L4 Derna Romania
94 B5 Dernberg, Cape Namibia
191 F5 Dernekpazarı Turkey
16 E3 Derno Ukr.
170 A4 Dêrong Sichuan China
182 C9 Derov r. Turkey
27 H5 Derrabeg Rep. of Ireland
95 H3 Derre Moz.
27 J4 Derreen Rep. of Ireland
27 D9 Derreenaragh Rep. of Ireland
27 D9 Derreeny Bridge Rep. of Ireland
27 I7 Derry Rep. of Ireland
Derry Northern Ireland U.K. see Londonderry
27 I7 Derry Rep. of Ireland
117 N6 Derry NH U.S.A.
27 NH U.S.A. Derry NH U.S.A.
27 G3 Derrybeg Rep. of Ireland
27 D9 Derryerglinna Northern Ireland U.K.
27 F3 Derrygonnelly Northern Ireland U.K.
27 F7 Derrygoolin Rep. of Ireland
28 D9 Derrylin Northern Ireland U.K.
27 D9 Derrynacreeve Rep. of Ireland
27 D9 Derrynasaggart Mountains hills Rep. of Ireland
27 C7 Derrynane Northern Ireland U.K.
28 E5 Derryrush Rep. of Ireland
28 E5 Derrytrasna Northern Ireland U.K.
27 F3 Derryveagh Mountains hills Rep. of Ireland
57 L3 Dersca Romania
31 M2 Dersingham Norfolk, England U.K.
169 M5 Derst Nei Mongol China
168 G6 Derstei Nei Mongol China
173 D10 Dêrtang Xizang China
63 H3 Derudeb Sudan
96 G9 De Rust S. Africa
73 I2 Deruta Italy
26 D9 Dervaig Argyll and Bute, Scotland U.K.
40 E3 Derval France
78 A3 Derveni Greece
74 D6 Dervock Bos.-Herz.
70 G3 Dervio Italy
205 K10 Derwent r. Tas. Austr.
31 J2 Derwent r. Derbyshire, England U.K.
29 N4 Derwent r. N.E. England U.K.
29 N5 Derwent r. N. Yorkshire, England U.K.
29 N7 Derbyshire, England U.K.
29 N4 Derwent Reservoir Durham/Northumberland, England U.K.
29 N7 Derwent Reservoir Derbyshire, England U.K.
29 K4 Derwent Water l. England U.K.
Derweze Turkm. see Darvaza
17 O1 Deryugino Rus. Fed.
19 R5 Derža r. Rus. Fed.
182 J2 Derzhavinsk Kazakh.
77 L7 Desa Romania
146 B4 Descabezado, Volcán vol. Chile
139 F4 Descalvado Mato Grosso Brazil
142 E3 Descalvado São Paulo Brazil
62 G2 Descargamaría Spain
84 C4 Deschambault Lake Sask. Can.
107 K4 Deschambault Lake l. Sask. Can.
122 C3 Deschutes r. OR U.S.A.
143 H2 Descoberto Brazil
92 C1 Desē Eth.
144 C8 Deseado Arg.
144 C7 Deseado r. Arg.
201 □3 Désappointement, Îles du is Arch. des Tuamotu Fr. Polynesia
138 C5 Descabezado, Volcán vol. La Palma Canary I.
146 A4 Deseada Chile
145 D2 Deseado r. Arg.
57 G5 Deseda-tározó l. Hungary

Doa to Drâa, Oued
257

95 G3 Doa Moz.
185 L4 Doāb Afgh.
185 N5 Doaba Pak.
185 L4 Do Āb-e Mīkh-e Zarrīn Afgh.
27 J3 Doagh Northern Ireland U.K.
28 C3 Doagh Isle pen. Rep. of Ireland
109 H4 Doaktown N.B. Can.
157 L7 Doangdoangan Besar i. Indon.
157 L7 Doangdoangan Kecil i. Indon.
158 G4 Doan Hung Vietnam
95 □K2 Doany Madag.
43 C8 Doazit France
90 C2 Doba Chad
57 L4 Doba Romania
18 N9 Dobasna r. Belarus
50 F3 Dobbertin Ger.
50 F3 Dobbertiner Seenlandschaft park Ger.
71 M2 Dobbiaco Italy
111 M5 Dobbinton Ont. Can.
119 H2 Dobbs Ferry NY U.S.A.
55 I6 Dobczyce Pol.
168 G9 Dobdain Qinghai China
18 G5 Dobele Latvia
51 H8 Döbeln Ger.
153 H7 Doberai, Jazirah pen. Papua Indon.
Doberai Peninsula Papua Indon. see Doberai, Jazirah
51 I7 Doberlug-Kirchhain Ger.
51 K7 Döbern Ger.
59 L2 Dobersberg Austria
48 J2 Dobersdorf Ger.
51 J8 Dobershau Ger.
54 D3 Dobiegniew Pol.
55 J4 Dobieszyn Pol.
59 L6 Dobl Austria
147 E5 Doblas Arg.
153 H8 Dobo Maluku Indon.
68 G3 Doboj Bos.-Herz.
184 F7 Do Borjī Iran
59 M8 Dobova Slovenia
57 K5 Doboz Hungary
55 I6 Dobra Małopolskie Pol.
54 G4 Dobra Wielkopolskie Pol.
54 C2 Dobra Zachodniopomorskie Pol.
54 D2 Dobra Zachodniopomorskie Pol.
57 L6 Dobra Romania
51 E10 Döbraberg hill Ger.
57 I3 Dobrá Niva Slovakia
56 C2 Dobřany Czech Rep.
59 L2 Dobra Stausee resr Austria
59 K2 Dobrá Voda Czech Rep.
54 G3 Dobre Kujawsko-Pomorskie Pol.
55 J3 Dobre Mazowieckie Pol.
17 L6 Dobre Ukr.
23 Q8 Dobre Miasto Pol.
77 K4 Dobrești Romania
77 P7 Dobrich Bulg.
15 H5 Dobrinka Rus. Fed.
56 D2 Dobříš Czech Rep.
51 F6 Dobritz Ger.
53 P2 Dobřív Czech Rep.
59 L7 Dobrna Slovenia
59 K8 Dobrnič Slovenia
63 M3 Dobro Spain
54 G5 Dobrodzień Pol.
57 H5 Döbrököz Hungary
54 E5 Dobromierz Pol.
16 B4 Dobromyl' Ukr.
55 H4 Dobroń Pol.
57 L3 Dobron' Ukr.
56 E2 Dobronín Czech Rep.
17 Q5 Dobropillya Ukr.
Dobropol'ye Ukr. see Dobropillya
55 L5 Dobrosyn Ukr.
54 F4 Dobroszyce Pol.
77 M6 Dobrotești Romania
55 M5 Dobrotvir Ukr.
77 P4 Dobrovăț Romania
51 K10 Dobrovice Czech Rep.
17 P5 Dobrovillya Ukr.
59 N6 Dobrovnik Slovenia
18 F7 Dobrovol'sk Rus. Fed.
55 I5 Dobrowoda Pol.
19 W9 Dobroye Rus. Fed.
18 K3 Dobruchi Rus. Fed.
77 P7 Dobrudzhansko Plato plat. Bulg.
77 M6 Dobrun Romania
17 K1 Dobrush Belarus
17 M8 Dobrushyne Ukr.
56 F1 Dobruška Czech Rep.
14 L4 Dobryanka Rus. Fed.
17 K1 Dobryanka Ukr.
19 U6 Dobrynikha Rus. Fed.
55 I3 Dobrzankowo Pol.
54 D2 Dobrzany Pol.
54 F5 Dobrzeń Wielki Pol.
54 F4 Dobrzyca Pol.
54 E2 Dobrzyca r. Pol.
55 H3 Dobrzyków Pol.
55 H3 Dobrzyń nad Wisłą Pol.
57 J3 Dobšiná Slovakia
55 J1 Dobskie, Jezioro l. Pol.
203 F9 Dobson South I. N.Z.
203 D11 Dobson r. South I. N.Z.
115 G7 Dobson NC U.S.A.
30 C7 Dobwalls Cornwall, England U.K.
173 I12 Dobzha Xizang China
57 J5 Dóc Hungary
154 B9 Doc Can rf Phil.
142 B3 Doce r. Brazil
143 H3 Doce r. Brazil
26 H10 Dochart r. Scotland U.K.
26 H8 Dochgarroch Highland, Scotland U.K.
185 M6 Do China Qala Afgh.
31 N2 Docking Norfolk, England U.K.
49 C10 Dockweiler Ger.
128 G2 Doctor Arroyo Mex.
126 F3 Doctor Belisario Domínguez Mex.
121 F13 Doctor Coss Mex.
209 H10 Doctor Hicks Range hills W.A. Austr.
128 G4 Doctor Mora Mex.
93 C6 Doda Tanz.
185 M7 Dodapur Pak.
176 E6 Dod Ballapur Karnataka India
31 M4 Doddinghurst Essex, England U.K.
29 M2 Doddington Northumberland, England U.K.
173 I11 Dodê Xizang China
Dodecanese is Greece see Dodekanisos
79 I7 Dodekanisos is Greece
44 I5 Dodewaard Neth.
110 B5 Dodge Center MN U.S.A.
121 E7 Dodge City KS U.S.A.
110 D7 Dodgeville WI U.S.A.
71 K4 Dodici, Cima mt. Italy
30 C7 Dodman Point England U.K.
92 C3 Dodola Eth.
93 B6 Dodoma Tanz.
93 B6 Dodoma admin. reg. Tanz.
93 D5 Dodori National Reserve nature res. Kenya
107 I5 Dodsland Sask. Can.
116 B9 Dodsonville OH U.S.A.
44 J4 Doesburg Neth.
44 J5 Doetinchem Neth.
55 D4 Dofa Maluku Indon.
77 N5 Doftana r. Romania
108 B3 Dog r. Ont. Can.
173 I9 Dogai Coring salt l. China
173 I9 Dogaicoring Qangco salt l. China
79 L3 Doğalar Turkey
79 I5 Doğanbey Aydın Turkey
79 H4 Doğanbey İzmir Turkey
79 L3 Doğançayır Turkey
88 H4 Doğanşehir Turkey
91 D6 Doğansu Turkey
106 F5 Dog Creek B.C. Can.
29 Q7 Dogdyke Lincolnshire, England U.K.
173 J11 Dogên Co l. China
167 J2 Dōgen-ko l. Japan
79 L3 Döğer Turkey
52 E6 Dogern Ger.
184 I4 Doghārūn Iran
131 L4 Dog Island Anguilla
109 I1 Dog Island Nfld and Lab. Can.
107 L5 Dog Lake Man. Can.
108 B3 Dog Lake Ont. Can.
108 C3 Dog Lake Ont. Can.
70 D6 Dogliani Italy
77 J5 Dognecea Romania
165 K10 Dōgo i. Japan
88 D4 Dogo Mali
92 E2 Dogoble well Somalia
89 G3 Dogondoutchi Niger
90 C2 Dogoumbo Chad
165 K11 Dōgo-yama mt. Japan
130 D1 Dog Rocks is Bahamas
189 L4 Doğubeyazıt Turkey
191 B5 Doğu Karadenız Dağları mts Turkey
79 J5 Doğu Menteşe Dağları mts Turkey
131 □2 Dogwood Point St Kitts and Nevis
173 H12 Dogxung Zangbo r. Xizang China
Doha Qatar see Ad Dawḥah
Dohad Gujarat India see Dahod
179 N8 Dohazari Bangl.
51 E10 Döhlau Ger.
51 I9 Dohna Ger.
97 L8 Dohne S. Africa
48 E5 Dohren Ger.
173 F13 Dohrighat Uttar Prad. India
199 I4 Doi i. Fiji
155 E2 Doi i. Maluku Indon.
158 D5 Doi Inthanon National Park Thai.
173 I11 Doijang Xizang China
158 D5 Doi Khuntan National Park Thai.
158 D5 Doi Luang National Park Thai.
Doïranis, Limni l. Greece/Macedonia see Dojran, Lake
62 G2 Doiras, Embalse de resr Spain
158 D5 Doi Saket Thai.
179 J8 Doisanagar Jharkhand India
45 G8 Doische Belgium
142 C5 Dois Córregos Brazil
140 E4 Dois Irmãos, Serra dos hills Brazil
64 A2 Dois Portos Port.
158 D5 Doi Suthep-Pui National Park Thai.
56 G3 Dojč Slovakia
77 K9 Dojran, Lake Greece/Macedonia
Dojransko Ezero l. Greece/Macedonia see Dojran, Lake
85 G6 Doka Sudan
184 F5 Dokali Iran
87 G2 Dokhara, Dunes de des. Alg.
21 K6 Dokka Norway
20 P3 Dokkas Sweden
44 I2 Dokkum Neth.
44 I2 Dokkumer Ee r. Neth.
88 C4 Doko Guinea
170 C3 Dokog He r. Sichuan China
78 E5 Dokos i. Greece
185 M8 Dokri Pak.
18 K7 Dokshytsy Belarus
56 D1 Doksy Liberecký kraj Czech Rep.
51 J10 Doksy Středočeský kraj Czech Rep.
164 X2 Dokuchayeva, Mys c. Kuril'skiye O-va Rus. Fed.
17 Q6 Dokuchayevs'k Ukr.
191 C5 Dokumacılar Turkey
79 L2 Dokurcun Turkey
153 I8 Dolak, Pulau i. Papua Indon.
120 F3 Doland SD U.S.A.
30 F2 Dolanog Powys, Wales U.K.
125 R6 Dolan Springs AZ U.S.A.
145 D6 Dolavón Arg.
109 F3 Dolbeau Que. Can.
30 D2 Dolbenmaen Gwynedd, Wales U.K.
70 D8 Dolceacqua Italy
38 H4 Dol-de-Bretagne France
40 G2 Dole France
71 R4 Dolenja Vas Slovenia
59 L8 Dolenjske Toplice Slovenia
40 K5 Dolent, Mont mt. France/Italy
30 F3 Dolfor Powys, Wales U.K.
30 E1 Dolgarrog Conwy, Wales U.K.
17 Q7 Dolgaya, Kosa spit Rus. Fed.
30 E2 Dolgellau Gwynedd, Wales U.K.
50 H4 Dolgen Ger.
117 K5 Dolgeville NY U.S.A.
14 K1 Dolgiy, Ostrov i. Rus. Fed.
14 L1 Dolgiy, Ostrov i. Rus. Fed.
17 O2 Dolgiye Budy Rus. Fed.
55 I1 Dolgorukovo Kaliningradskaya Oblast' Rus. Fed.
19 V9 Dolgorukovo Lipetskaya Oblast' Rus. Fed.
19 W8 Dolgoye Lipetskaya Oblast' Rus. Fed.
15 G5 Dolgoye Orlovskaya Oblast' Rus. Fed.
19 V9 Dolgusha Rus. Fed.
77 O3 Dolhasca Romania
55 M5 Dołhobyczów Pol.
72 C9 Dolianova Sardegna Italy
54 D2 Dolice Pol.
Dolina Ukr. see Dolyna
23 N7 Dolina Słupi, Park Krajobrazowy Pol.
57 I1 Dolinki Krakowskie, Park Krajobrazowy Pol.
191 E1 Dolinovka Rus. Fed.
162 M5 Dolinsk Sakhalin Rus. Fed.
47 G3 Doliny Bobru, Park Krajobrazowy Pol.
50 J4 Doliny Dolnej Odry, Park Krajobrazowy Pol.
Dolisie Congo see Loubomo
155 E4 Dolit Halmahera Indon.
77 J7 Doljevac Srbija Serb. and Mont.
27 F7 Dolla Rep. of Ireland
26 I10 Dollar Clackmannanshire, Scotland U.K.
48 D4 Dollart Ger.
51 E6 Dolle Ger.
212 T2 Dolleman Island Antarctica
37 N8 Doller r. France
48 I3 Dollern Ger.
51 F8 Döllnitz Ger.
53 K4 Dollnstein Ger.
39 M5 Dollon France
49 K8 Döllstädt Ger.
49 J9 Dolmar hill Ger.
183 M1 Dolmatovo Kazakh.
77 N7 Dolna Lipnitska Bulg.
57 I3 Dolná Strehová Slovakia
57 H3 Dolné Vestenice Slovakia
57 H2 Dolní Benešov Czech Rep.
51 J10 Dolní Beřkovice Czech Rep.
59 P2 Dolní Bojanovice Czech Rep.
56 E1 Dolní Bousov Czech Rep.
59 K1 Dolní Bukovsko Czech Rep.
77 P8 Dolni Chiflik Bulg.
77 M7 Dolni Dŭbnik Bulg.
59 O2 Dolní Dunajovice Czech Rep.
56 D3 Dolní Dvořiště Czech Rep.
56 F2 Dolní Kounice Czech Rep.
57 G3 Dolní Němčí Czech Rep.
56 D1 Dolní Podluží Czech Rep.
51 J9 Dolní Poustevna Czech Rep.
56 F2 Dolní Újezd Czech Rep.
56 B1 Dolní Šandov Czech Rep.
77 L8 Dolno Kamartsi Bulg.
77 M8 Dolno Levski Bulg.
54 E4 Dolnośląskie prov. Pol.
57 I2 Dolný Kubín Slovakia
57 H3 Dolný Pial Slovakia
57 G4 Dolný štál Slovakia
155 A4 Dolo Sulawesi Indon.
71 M5 Dolo Italy
70 J7 Dolo r. Italy
200 □4b Dolohmwar hill Pohnpei Micronesia
40 H5 Dolomieu France
Dolomites mts Italy see Dolomiti
71 L4 Dolomiti mts Italy
71 L3 Dolomiti Bellunesi, Parco Nazionale delle nat. park Italy
71 M2 Dolomiti di Sesto, Parco Naturale nature res. Italy
Dolon, Pereval pass Kyrg. see Dolon Ashuusu
183 P7 Dolon Ashuusu pass Kyrg.
Dolonnur Nei Mongol China see Duolun
92 D3 Dolo Odo Eth.
168 I4 Doloon Mongolia
147 I5 Dolores Arg.
127 O9 Dolores Guat.
126 D5 Dolores Mex.
67 D11 Dolores Spain
147 H3 Dolores Uru.
125 W3 Dolores r. CO U.S.A.
128 G4 Dolores Hidalgo Mex.
76 I6 Dolovo Vojvodina, Srbija Serb. and Mont.
145 F8 Dolphin, Cape Falkland Is
104 G3 Dolphin and Union Strait Nunavut Can.
130 □ Dolphin Head hill Jamaica
94 B5 Dolphin Head Namibia
208 D6 Dolphin Island W.A. Austr.
208 D6 Dolphin Island Nature Reserve W.A. Austr.
29 K2 Dolphinton South Lanarkshire, Scotland U.K.
58 G6 Dölsach Austria
54 F4 Dolsk Pol.
55 M4 Dol's'k Ukr.
55 K3 Dołubowo Pol.
158 G5 Đô Lương Vietnam
42 B4 Dolus-d'Oléron France
16 C5 Dolyna Ukr.
17 L5 Dolyns'ka Ukr.
17 Q7 Dolzhanskaya Rus. Fed.
17 O2 Dolzhenkovo Rus. Fed.
18 M3 Dolzhitsy Rus. Fed.
153 I7 Dom, Gunung mt. Papua Indon.
57 J3 Domaháza Hungary
178 G5 Domaila Uttaranchal India
79 K3 Domaniç Turkey
55 K3 Domanice Pol.
73 Q9 Domanico Italy
55 H3 Domaniewice Łódzkie Pol.
55 I4 Domaniewice Mazowieckie Pol.
57 H2 Domaniža Slovakia
179 L6 Domar Bangl.
173 E10 Domar Xizang China
55 J6 Domaradz Pol.
173 L11 Domartang Xizang China
36 D3 Domart-en-Ponthieu France
59 O7 Domašinec Croatia
57 J5 Domaszek Hungary
54 E5 Domaszków Pol.
54 F4 Domaszowice Pol.
70 G2 Domat Ems Switz.
36 F7 Domats France
56 B2 Domažlice Czech Rep.
173 L10 Domba Qinghai China
184 B5 Dom Bākh Iran
182 H2 Dombarovskiy Rus. Fed.
21 J5 Dombås Norway
37 J5 Dombasle-en-Argonne France
37 K7 Dombasle-en-Xaintois France
37 L6 Dombasle-sur-Meurthe France
191 C2 Dombay Rus. Fed.
95 G3 Dombe Moz.
91 B8 Dombe Grande Angola
57 K5 Dombegyház Hungary
40 F4 Dombes reg. France
91 D6 Dombi Dem. Rep. Congo
57 H5 Dombóvár Hungary
91 C8 Dombra Angola
57 K3 Dombrád Hungary
Dombrau Pol. see Dąbrowa Górnicza
70 B1 Dombresson Switz.
Dombrovitsa Ukr. see Dubrovytsya
Dombrowa Pol. see Dąbrowa Górnicza
44 E5 Domburg Neth.
143 F3 Dom Cavati Brazil
40 B5 Dôme, Monts mts France
213 F1 Dome Argus ice feature Antarctica
213 H2 Dome Charlie ice feature Antarctica
Dome Circe ice feature Antarctica see Dome Charlie
106 F4 Dome Creek B.C. Can.
58 F7 Domegge di Cadore Italy
18 G7 Domeikava Lith.
41 H6 Domène France
40 B4 Domérat France
125 R8 Dome Rock Mountains AZ U.S.A.
51 D6 Domersleben Ger.
72 A9 Domestica, Cala b. Sardegna Italy
208 J3 Domett, Cape W.A. Austr.
203 G8 Domett, Mount South I. N.Z.
37 K6 Domèvre-en-Haye France
37 M6 Domèvre-sur-Vezouze France
138 C5 Domeyko Antofagasta Chile
144 C3 Domeyko Atacama Chile
43 C9 Domezaine-Berraute France
141 B9 Dom Feliciano Brazil
39 J4 Domfront France
37 K6 Domgermain France
138 C6 Dominador Chile
143 G4 Domingos Martins Brazil
62 E8 Dominguiso Port.
131 □2 Dominica country West Indies
126 □R13 Dominical Costa Rica
Dominicana, República country West Indies see Dominican Republic
130 H4 Dominican Republic country West Indies
131 □2 Dominica Passage Dominica/Guadeloupe
105 K3 Dominion, Cape Nunavut Can.
91 D6 Domiongo Dem. Rep. Congo
50 D4 Dömitz Ger.
143 F3 Dom Joaquim Brazil
179 M6 Domkhar Bhutan
37 I7 Dommartin-le-Franc France
36 I6 Dommartin-Varimont France
43 G6 Domme France
44 H5 Dommel r. Neth.
49 D10 Dommershausen Ger.
51 G7 Dommitzsch Ger.
77 M5 Domnești Argeș Romania
77 N6 Domnești București Romania
50 E5 Dömnitz r. Ger.
55 I1 Domnovo Rus. Fed.
92 E3 Domo Eth.
19 U6 Domodedovo Rus. Fed.
70 E3 Domodossola Italy
78 D3 Domokos Greece
99 □3 Domoni Nzwani Comoros
36 D5 Domont France
57 H4 Dömös Hungary
19 Q1 Domozhirovo Rus. Fed.
37 L7 Dompaire France
37 J6 Dompcevrin France
141 B9 Dom Pedrito Brazil
140 D3 Dom Pedro Brazil
40 E4 Dompierre-les-Ormes France
40 D3 Dompierre-sur-Besbre France
42 B3 Dompierre-sur-Mer France
38 I8 Dompierre-sur-Yon France
157 M9 Dompu Sumbawa Indon.
37 K7 Domrémy-la-Pucelle France
57 I4 Dömsöd Hungary
50 E4 Domsühl Ger.
72 B10 Domus de Maria Sardegna Italy
72 B9 Domusnovas Sardegna Italy
146 B5 Domuyo, Volcán vol. Arg.
17 O7 Domuzla r. Ukr.
205 M3 Domville, Mount hill Qld Austr.
68 E2 Domžale Slovenia
207 L5 Don r. Qld Austr.
38 H6 Don r. France
176 E4 Don r. India
126 E4 Don Mex.
19 L8 Don r. Rus. Fed.
26 L8 Don r. Scotland U.K.
158 G7 Don, Xé r. Laos
27 J6 Donabate Rep. of Ireland
71 M5 Donada Italy
144 E2 Donadeu Arg.
27 H4 Donagh Northern Ireland U.K.
27 K3 Donaghadee Northern Ireland U.K.
27 J4 Donaghcloney Northern Ireland U.K.
27 G7 Donaghmore Laois Rep. of Ireland
27 J6 Donaghmore Meath Rep. of Ireland
27 I3 Donaghmore Northern Ireland U.K.
129 L8 Donaji Mex.
205 I7 Donald Vic. Austr.
121 J10 Donaldsonville LA U.S.A.
144 C2 Donalnes, Cerro mt. Chile
115 E10 Donalsonville GA U.S.A.
64 G3 Don Álvaro Spain
65 P2 Doña María Cristina, Canal de Spain
65 K5 Doña Mencía Spain
64 G7 Doñana, Parque Nacional de nat. park Spain
27 I6 Donard Rep. of Ireland
146 B2 Doña Rosa, Cordillera mts Chile
128 C1 Donato Guerra Mex.
58 E2 Donau r. Austria/Ger.
alt. Duna (Hungary),
alt. Dunaj (Slovakia),
alt. Dunărea (Romania),
alt. Dunav (Serb. and Mont.),
conv. Danube
59 O3 Donau-Auen, Nationalpark nat. park Austria
52 E6 Donaueschingen Ger.
53 K4 Donaumoos reg. Ger.
53 I4 Donauried reg. Ger.
53 M3 Donaustauf Ger.
53 J4 Donauwörth Ger.
64 H3 Don Benito Spain
184 D5 Donbī Iran
29 O6 Doncaster South Yorkshire, England U.K.
37 I4 Donchery France
91 B7 Dondo Angola
95 G3 Dondo Moz.
155 B3 Dondo, Tanjung pt Indon.
155 B3 Dondo, Teluk b. Indon.
154 C7 Dondonay i. Phil.
176 G10 Dondra Head Sri Lanka
16 G5 Dondușeni Moldova
Dondyushany Moldova see Dondușeni
63 P3 Done Bikendi Harana Spain
27 F3 Donegal Rep. of Ireland
27 F3 Donegal county Rep. of Ireland
27 F3 Donegal Bay Rep. of Ireland
Dönenbay Kazakh. see Dunenbay
17 S5 Donetsk Rus. Fed.
17 Q6 Donets'k Ukr.
17 Q5 Donets'ka Oblast' admin. div. Ukr.
Donetskaya Oblast' admin. div. Ukr. see Donets'ka Oblast'
17 P2 Donetskaya Seymitsa r. Rus. Fed.
Donetsko-Amrovsiyevka Ukr. see Amvrosiyivka
Donetsk Oblast admin. div. Ukr. see Donets'ka Oblast'
17 R5 Donets'kyy Ukr.
17 Q5 Donets'kyy Kryazh hills Rus. Fed./Ukr.
66 B1 Doneztebe Spain
92 E3 Donfar Eth.
130 □ Don Figuerero Mountains hills Jamaica
21 J6 Dønfoss Norway
89 H4 Donga r. Cameroon/Nigeria
89 H5 Donga Nigeria
171 H5 Dong'an Hunan China
209 C10 Dongara W.A. Austr.
178 H9 Dongargaon Chhattisgarh India
178 H9 Dongargarh Chhattisgarh India
172 L6 Dongbatu Gansu China
161 M2 Dongbei reg. Heilong. China
169 Q5 Dongbei Pingyuan plain China
170 D5 Dongchuan Yunnan China
173 G10 Dongco Xizang China
173 G10 Dong Co l. Xizang China
170 F8 Đông Đăng Vietnam
169 O8 Dong'e Shandong China
44 G5 Dongen Neth.
38 G7 Donges France
170 G9 Dongfang Hainan China
162 H5 Dongfanghong Heilong. China
162 D7 Dongfeng Jilin China
155 A4 Donggala Sulawesi Indon.
163 D9 Donggang Liaoning China
169 P9 Donggang Shandong China
168 F9 Donggi Conag l. Qinghai China
Donggou Liaoning China see Donggang
168 G9 Donggou Qinghai China
171 J5 Donggu Jiangxi China
171 I7 Dongguan Guangdong China
158 H6 Đông Ha Vietnam
169 P9 Donghai Jiangsu China
Dong Hai sea N. Pacific Ocean see East China Sea
168 I8 Donghaiba Ningxia China
170 H8 Donghai Dao i. China
170 F3 Dong He r. China
168 G5 Dong He watercourse China
158 H6 Đông Hơi Vietnam
169 K8 Donghuachi Gansu China
171 I7 Dong Jiang r. China
152 D1 Dongjiang Shuiku resr Hunan China
162 F6 Dongjingcheng Heilong. China
155 A5 Dongkait, Tanjung pt Indon.
173 J12 Dongkar Xizang China
170 H5 Dongkou Hunan China
170 F6 Donglan Guangxi China
168 G7 Dongle Gansu China
169 R5 Dongliao He r. China
172 I7 Donglük Xinjiang China
169 N9 Dongming Shandong China
162 G6 Dongning Heilong. China
91 B8 Dongo Angola
91 C6 Dongo Dem. Rep. Congo
70 G3 Dongo Italy
93 B6 Dongobesh Tanz.
85 F5 Dongola Sudan
92 B3 Dongotona Mountains Sudan
90 C4 Dongou Congo
158 E7 Dong Phraya Yen esc. Thai.
171 I8 Dongping Guangdong China
Dongping Hunan China see Anhua
169 O8 Dongping Hu l. China
173 J11 Dongqiao Xizang China
168 I8 Dongqinghu Nei Mongol China
173 K10 Dong Qu r. Qinghai China
168 C5 Dongquan Xinjiang China
171 K7 Dongshan Fujian China
170 H8 Dongshan Guangdong China
171 L3 Dongshan Jiangsu China
171 M3 Dongshan Jiangsu China
171 J5 Dongshao Jiangxi China
152 E2 Dongsha Qundao is China
171 M2 Dongtai Jiangsu China
171 M2 Dongtai He r. China
173 L8 Dong Taijnar Hu l. Qinghai China
171 I4 Dongting Hu l. China
171 M5 Dongtou Zhejiang China
158 H4 Đông Triều Vietnam
91 B9 Donguena Angola
90 A4 Donguila Gabon
170 E7 Đông Văn Vietnam
168 H9 Dongxiangzu Gansu China
170 F8 Dongxing Guangxi China
162 E5 Dongxing Heilong. China
171 M4 Dongyang Zhejiang China
169 P8 Dongying Shandong China
171 J7 Dongyuan Guangdong China
168 H7 Dongzhen Gansu China
171 K3 Dongzhi Anhui China
146 B4 Doñihue Chile
31 L2 Donington Lincolnshire, England U.K.
121 J7 Doniphan MO U.S.A.
76 J8 Donja Dubnica Kosovo, Srbija Serb. and Mont.
59 O7 Donja Dubrava Croatia
59 N7 Donja Konjšćina Croatia
59 M8 Donja Stubica Croatia
59 N7 Donja Višnjica Croatia
59 N8 Donja Zelina Croatia
106 A2 Donjek r. Y.T. Can.
37 J7 Donjeux France
68 G3 Donji Miholjac Croatia
77 K6 Donji Milanovac Srbija Serb. and Mont.
68 F3 Donji Vakuf Bos.-Herz.
68 E3 Donji Zemunik Croatia
44 J2 Donkerbroek Neth.
97 J6 Donkerpoort S. Africa
179 M9 Donmanick Islands Bangl.
20 L3 Dønna i. Norway
109 G4 Donnacona Que. Can.
74 H10 Donnalucata Sicilia Italy
70 D4 Donnas Italy
106 G4 Donnelly Alta Can.
202 H2 Donnellys Crossing North I. N.Z.
36 F7 Donnemarie-Dontilly France
124 L2 Donner Pass CA U.S.A.
59 J5 Donnersbach Austria
52 D2 Donnersberg hill Ger.
53 I2 Donnersdorf Ger.
30 H2 Donnington Telford and Wrekin, England U.K.
209 C12 Donnybrook W.A. Austr.
27 F7 Donohill Rep. of Ireland
37 N6 Donon mt. France
72 C9 Donori Sardegna Italy
66 B1 Donostia - San Sebastián Spain
27 E9 Donoughmore Rep. of Ireland
79 G5 Donoussa Greece
79 G5 Donoussa i. Greece
110 G9 Donovan IL U.S.A.
17 Q6 Dons'ke Ukr.
17 T6 Donskoy Rostovskaya Oblast' Rus. Fed.
19 V8 Donskoy Tul'skaya Oblast' Rus. Fed.
19 V9 Donskoye Lipetskaya Oblast' Rus. Fed.
15 H7 Donskoye Stavropol'skiy Kray Rus. Fed.
17 S3 Donskoye Belogor'ye hills Rus. Fed.
154 D5 Donsol Luzon Phil.
158 C6 Donthami r. Myanmar
17 L8 Donuzlav, Ozero l. Ukr.
38 H4 Donville-les-Bains France
43 F7 Donzac France
52 H4 Donzdorf Ger.
71 M6 Donzella, Isola della i. Italy
42 H5 Donzenac France
41 F8 Donzère France
40 C2 Donzy France
27 B5 Dooagh Rep. of Ireland
27 E4 Doocastle Rep. of Ireland
27 B5 Dooega Rep. of Ireland
27 C5 Dooghbeg Rep. of Ireland
27 B4 Doogort Rep. of Ireland
27 C4 Doohooma Rep. of Ireland
28 C4 Dooish Northern Ireland U.K.
208 E6 Dooleena hill W.A. Austr.
27 D6 Doolin Rep. of Ireland
206 G4 Doomadgee Qld Austr.
206 G4 Doomadgee Aboriginal Reserve Qld Austr.
27 F7 Doon Rep. of Ireland
26 G12 Doon r. Scotland U.K.
26 H12 Doon, Loch l. Scotland U.K.
27 C7 Doonaha Rep. of Ireland
27 C7 Doonbeg Rep. of Ireland
27 C7 Doonbeg r. Rep. of Ireland
27 C7 Doonbeg Bay Rep. of Ireland
208 J4 Doon Doon Aboriginal Reserve W.A. Austr.
27 B6 Doonloughan Rep. of Ireland
27 B8 Doonmanagh Rep. of Ireland
27 F3 Doorin Point Rep. of Ireland
44 H4 Doorn Neth.
44 I4 Doornspijk Neth.
110 G5 Door Peninsula WI U.S.A.
92 F2 Dooxo Nugaaleed val. Somalia
54 E3 Dopiewo Pol.
173 K11 Doqêmo Xizang China
173 J12 Doqoi Xizang China
170 A1 Do Qu r. Qinghai China
185 I6 Dor watercourse Afgh.
19 S6 Dor Rus. Fed.
121 D9 Dora NM U.S.A.
208 G7 Dora, Lake salt flat W.A. Austr.
70 E5 Dora Baltea r. Italy
40 J5 Dora di Ferret r. Italy
40 K5 Dora di Veny r. Italy
126 G4 Dorado Mex.
184 D8 Do Rāhak Iran
185 N3 Dorah Pass Pak.
179 J8 Doranda Jharkhand India
107 I2 Doran Lake N.W.T. Can.
70 D5 Dora Riparia r. Italy
139 E5 D'Orbigny Bol.
Dorbiljin Xinjiang China see Emin
76 J8 Đorče Petrov Macedonia
30 H6 Dorchester Dorset, England U.K.
118 F6 Dorchester NJ U.S.A.
94 C4 Dordabis Namibia
36 E7 Dordives France
42 F5 Dordogne dept France
40 B5 Dordogne r. France
31 I2 Dordon Warwickshire, England U.K.
44 G5 Dordrecht Neth.
97 L7 Dordrecht S. Africa
40 C4 Dore r. France
40 B6 Dore, Monts mts France
94 C4 Doreenville Namibia
107 J4 Doré Lake Sask. Can.
107 J4 Doré Lake l. Sask. Can.
41 D6 Dore-l'Église France
58 A5 Doren Austria
49 H6 Dörentrup Ger.
26 H8 Dores Highland, Scotland U.K.
143 F3 Dores de Guanhães Brazil
143 E3 Dores do Indaiá Brazil
88 E3 Dorey Mali
53 M5 Dorfen Ger.
58 H5 Dorfgastein Austria
48 I5 Dorfmark Ger.
50 D3 Dorf Mecklenburg Ger.
72 D7 Dorgali Sardegna Italy
168 C9 Dorgê Co l. Qinghai China
168 C2 Dörgön Mongolia
57 K5 Dorgoș Romania
185 K6 Dori r. Afgh.
89 E3 Dori Burkina
147 F4 Dorila Arg.
96 C7 Doring r. S. Africa
96 D8 Doring r. S. Africa
96 C7 Doringbaai S. Africa
96 D7 Doringbos S. Africa
78 C5 Dorio Greece
206 C3 Dorisvale N.T. Austr.
31 L5 Dorking Surrey, England U.K.
37 N6 Dorlisheim France
88 E5 Dormaa-Ahenkro Ghana
49 C8 Dormagen Ger.
57 J4 Dormánd Hungary
36 G5 Dormans France
70 F4 Dormelletto Italy
52 F5 Dormettingen Ger.
162 I5 Dormidontovka Rus. Fed.
176 G4 Dornakal Andhra Prad. India
59 M7 Dornava Slovenia
49 H8 Dörnberg (Habichtswald) Ger.
58 A5 Dornbirn Austria
51 E8 Dornburg (Saale) Ger.
49 F9 Dornburg-Frickhofen Ger.
48 H3 Dornbusch Ger.
50 H1 Dornbusch pen. Ger.
49 J9 Dorndorf Ger.
51 E8 Dorndorf-Steudnitz Ger.
62 E5 Dornelas Port.
40 C3 Dornes France
49 I8 Dörnhagen (Fuldabrück) Ger.
52 F5 Dornhan Ger.
26 E8 Dornie Highland, Scotland U.K.
51 F6 Dörnitz Ger.
70 F5 Dorno Italy
26 H7 Dornoch Highland, Scotland U.K.
26 H7 Dornoch Firth est. Scotland U.K.
169 N2 Dornod prov. Mongolia
169 K4 Dornogovĭ prov. Mongolia
118 B3 Dornsife PA U.S.A.
52 H5 Dornstadt Ger.
52 E5 Dornstetten Ger.
48 D3 Dornum Ger.
48 D3 Dornumersiel Ger.
88 E2 Doro Mali
77 O6 Dorobanțu Romania
19 U8 Dorobino Rus. Fed.
57 H4 Dorog Hungary
57 I4 Dorogháza Hungary
19 Q7 Dorogobuzh Rus. Fed.
14 I2 Dorogorskoye Rus. Fed.
77 O3 Dorohoi Romania
55 L4 Dorohusk Pol.
19 T6 Dorokhovo Rus. Fed.
184 H5 Dorokhsh Iran
57 L4 Dorolț Romania
168 C3 Döröö Nuur salt l. Mongolia
17 K6 Doroshivka Ukr.
16 E3 Dorosyni Ukr.
20 N4 Dorotea Sweden
118 F6 Dorothy NJ U.S.A.
95 F3 Dorowa Zimbabwe
48 D5 Dörpen Ger.
209 B8 Dorre Island W.A. Austr.
205 N4 Dorrigo N.S.W. Austr.
122 D6 Dorris CA U.S.A.
89 H5 Dorsale Camerounaise slope Cameroon/Nigeria
111 P4 Dorset Ont. Can.
30 H6 Dorset admin. div. England U.K.
116 E7 Dorset OH U.S.A.
30 F6 Dorset and East Devon Coast tourist site U.K.
173 I10 Dorsoidong Co l. Xizang China
49 K6 Dorstadt Ger.
49 C7 Dorsten Ger.
40 H4 Dortan France
49 D7 Dortmund Ger.
49 E7 Dortmund-Ems-Kanal canal Ger.
116 C11 Dorton KY U.S.A.
188 H5 Dörtyol Turkey
54 G4 Doruchów Pol.
191 D6 Dorukdibi Turkey
48 G3 Dorum Ger.
90 E3 Doruma Dem. Rep. Congo
184 G4 Dorūneh Iran
184 G4 Dorūneh, Kūh-e mts Iran
48 H5 Dörverden Ger.
Dorylaeum Turkey see Eskişehir
52 H3 Dörzbach Ger.
128 E7 Dos Aguas Mex.
67 D9 Dos Aguas Spain
184 G7 Do Sārī Iran
145 D7 Dos Bahías, Cabo c. Arg.
63 N9 Dosbarrios Spain
125 W9 Dos Cabezas Mountain AZ U.S.A.
136 C6 Dos de Mayo Peru
79 L5 Döşemealtı Turkey
185 I4 Do Shākh, Kūh-e mt. Afgh.
64 H6 Dos Hermanas Spain
167 J4 Dōshi Japan
179 O6 Dosing Arun. Prad. India
127 O9 Dos Lagunos Guat.
158 H4 Đo Sơn Vietnam
124 L5 Dos Palos CA U.S.A.
77 M9 Dospat Bulg.
77 M9 Dospat r. Bulg.
65 N6 Dos Picos mt. Spain
145 D6 Dos Pozos Arg.
50 F5 Dosse r. Ger.
52 F3 Dossenheim Ger.
90 C2 Dosséo, Bahr r. Chad
89 F3 Dosso Niger
89 F3 Dosso dept Niger
89 F3 Dosso, Réserve Partielle de nature res. Niger
70 E3 Dossola, Val val. Italy
182 E4 Dossor Kazakh.
183 M7 Do'stlik Uzbek.
65 J4 Dos Torres Spain
183 T5 Dostyk Kazakh.
Dostyq Kazakh. see Dostyk
115 E10 Dothan AL U.S.A.
48 F5 Dötlingen Ger.
52 F5 Dotternhausen Ger.
70 E1 Döttingen Switz.
36 F3 Douai France
88 C4 Douako Guinea
89 H5 Douala Cameroon
89 H6 Douala-Edéa, Réserve nature res. Cameroon
38 C5 Douarnenez France
38 C5 Douarnenez, Baie de b. France
42 E5 Double reg. France
207 N8 Double Island Point Qld Austr.
121 E9 Double Mountain Fork r. TX U.S.A.
124 N6 Double Peak CA U.S.A.
207 K4 Double Point Qld Austr.
115 D8 Double Springs AL U.S.A.
56 E2 Doubrava r. Czech Rep.
40 I3 Doubs France
40 I2 Doubs dept France
40 G3 Doubs r. France/Switz.
208 H3 Doubtful Bay W.A. Austr.
209 E13 Doubtful Island Bay W.A. Austr.
203 B12 Doubtful Sound South I. N.Z.
203 A12 Doubtful Sound inlet South I. N.Z.
202 H1 Doubtless Bay North I. N.Z.
Doucan Shaanxi China see Fuping
36 F8 Douchy France
36 F3 Douchy-les-Mines France
40 H3 Doucier France
39 M2 Doudeville France
42 D1 Doué-la-Fontaine France
88 E3 Douentza Mali
88 E3 Douentza, Réserve de nature res. Mali
28 G2 Dougarie North Ayrshire, Scotland U.K.
87 H1 Dougga tourist site Tunisia
203 B14 Doughboy Bay Stewart I. N.Z.
27 F4 Dough Mountain hill Rep. of Ireland
25 E4 Douglas Isle of Man
202 I6 Douglas North I. N.Z.
27 F9 Douglas Rep. of Ireland
96 H5 Douglas S. Africa
26 I11 Douglas South Lanarkshire, Scotland U.K.
106 C3 Douglas AK U.S.A.
125 W10 Douglas AZ U.S.A.
115 F10 Douglas GA U.S.A.
122 L5 Douglas WY U.S.A.
205 L9 Douglas Apsley National Park Tas. Austr.
28 C4 Douglas Bridge Northern Ireland U.K.
106 D4 Douglas Channel B.C. Can.
204 F3 Douglas Creek watercourse S.A. Austr.
125 X1 Douglas Creek r. CO U.S.A.
212 T2 Douglas Range mts Antarctica
118 D4 Douglassville PA U.S.A.
26 K9 Douglastown Angus, Scotland U.K.
115 E9 Douglasville GA U.S.A.
89 H3 Dougoulé well Niger
84 C5 Douhi Chad
Douhudi Hubei China see Gong'an
78 B4 Doukato, Akra pt Lefkada Greece
37 J7 Doulaincourt-Saucourt France
36 D3 Doullens France
27 B9 Doulus Head Rep. of Ireland
90 D2 Doum C.A.R.
89 F4 Doumè Benin
89 I5 Doumé Cameroon
89 I5 Doumé r. Cameroon
171 I7 Doumen Guangdong China
88 E3 Douna Mali
26 J4 Dounby Orkney, Scotland U.K.
26 H10 Doune Stirling, Scotland U.K.
26 G10 Doune Hill Scotland U.K.
89 F4 Dounkassa Benin
26 I5 Dounreay Highland, Scotland U.K.
56 C1 Doupovské Hory mts Czech Rep.
45 E8 Dour Belgium
142 C3 Dourada, Cachoeira waterfall Brazil
142 B2 Dourada, Serra hills Brazil
140 C5 Dourada, Serra mts Brazil
141 B7 Dourados Brazil
141 B7 Dourados r. Brazil
142 A5 Dourados, Serra dos hills Brazil
90 B2 Dourbali Chad
41 C8 Dourbie r. France
41 C8 Dourbies France
36 D6 Dourdan France
41 A7 Dourdou r. France
41 B9 Dourdou r. France
90 D2 Dourdoura Chad
43 I9 Dourgne France
36 C3 Douriez France
62 C6 Douro r. Port.
alt. Duero (Spain)
62 D6 Douro reg. Port.
62 G6 Douro Internacional, Parque Natural do nature res. Port.
Doushi Hubei China see Gong'an
171 J6 Doushui Shuiku resr China
40 I5 Doussard France
142 A5 Doutor Camargo Brazil
40 I4 Douvaine France
38 I3 Douve r. France
39 K3 Douvres-la-Délivrande France
41 F6 Doux r. France
87 H2 Douz Tunisia
43 D8 Douze r. France
84 C6 Douziat Chad
42 E5 Douzillac France
37 J4 Douzy France
71 L7 Dovadola Italy
16 H3 Dovbysh Ukr.
31 I2 Dove r. Derbyshire/Staffordshire, England U.K.
29 P5 Dove r. North Yorkshire, England U.K.
31 O3 Dove r. Suffolk, England U.K.
109 J2 Dove Brook Nfld and Lab. Can.
105 P2 Dove Bugt b. Greenland
125 X4 Dove Creek CO U.S.A.
205 K10 Dover Tas. Austr.
31 O5 Dover Kent, England U.K.
118 D6 Dover DE U.S.A.
117 □O5 Dover NH U.S.A.
118 F3 Dover NJ U.S.A.
116 D8 Dover OH U.S.A.
118 B5 Dover PA U.S.A.
115 D7 Dover TN U.S.A.
209 H12 Dover, Point W.A. Austr.
25 H6 Dover, Strait of France/U.K.
117 □P3 Dover-Foxcroft ME U.S.A.
31 I2 Doveridge Derbyshire, England U.K.
119 H1 Dover Plains NY U.S.A.
Dovey r. Wales U.K. see Dyfi
184 C6 Doveyrīch, Rūd-e r. Iran/Iraq
16 C5 Dovhe Ukr.
16 E3 Dovhoshyyi Ukr.
55 L1 Dovinė r. Lith.
22 G7 Dovnsklint cliff Denmark
21 J5 Dovrefjell mts Norway
21 J5 Dovrefjell Nasjonalpark nat. park Norway
17 O3 Dovzhyk Ukr.
93 B8 Dowa Malawi
110 H8 Dowagiac MI U.S.A.
26 I9 Dowally Perth and Kinross, Scotland U.K.
184 F6 Dow Chāhī Iran
184 H3 Dowgha'ī Iran
156 B4 Dowi, Tanjung pt Indon.
184 F3 Dow Kūh mt. Iran
185 J5 Dowlatābād Afgh.
185 K3 Dowlatābād Afgh.
184 E7 Dowlatābād Būshehr Iran
184 D7 Dowlatābād Fārs Iran
184 F7 Dowlatābād Fārs Iran
184 G3 Dowlatābād Khorāsān Iran
184 H4 Dowlatābād Khorāsān Iran
185 I3 Dowlatābād Khorāsān Iran
185 K4 Dowl at Yār Afgh.
27 K4 Down county Northern Ireland U.K.
124 N8 Downey CA U.S.A.
31 M2 Downham Market Norfolk, England U.K.
124 L2 Downieville CA U.S.A.
110 B9 Downing MO U.S.A.
118 D4 Downingtown PA U.S.A.
27 K4 Downpatrick Northern Ireland U.K.
27 D4 Downpatrick Head Rep. of Ireland
120 F6 Downs KS U.S.A.
117 K6 Downsville NY U.S.A.
110 C5 Downsville WI U.S.A.
31 I6 Downton Wiltshire, England U.K.
106 E4 Downton, Mount B.C. Can.
27 F4 Dowra Rep. of Ireland
184 C5 Dow Rūd Iran
184 B4 Dow Sar Iran
31 L2 Dowsby Lincolnshire, England U.K.
185 M4 Dowshī Afgh.
19 N8 Dowsk Belarus
19 N6 Dowzha Belarus
173 L12 Doxong Xizang China
40 B4 Doyet France
147 H3 Doyle Arg.
124 L1 Doyle CA U.S.A.
109 J4 Doyles Nfld and Lab. Can.
118 E4 Doylestown PA U.S.A.
77 M7 Doyrentsi Bulg.
184 G8 Dozdān r. Iran
165 J10 Dōzen is Japan
98 □1a Doze Ribeiras Terceira Azores
108 E4 Dozois, Réservoir resr Que. Can.
39 K3 Dozulé France
191 G5 Dprabak Armenia
86 C3 Drâa, Cap c. Morocco
86 C3 Drâa, Oued watercourse Morocco

Drabiv to Dusmenys

258

17 L4 Drabiv Ukr.
17 K4 Drabivka Ukr.
41 H6 Drac r. France
142 B4 Dracena Brazil
77 J9 Dračevo Macedonia
51 J7 Drachhausen Ger.
18 L8 Drachkava Belarus
53 O3 Drachselsried Ger.
44 J2 Drachten Neth.
54 G2 Dragacz Pol.
77 P6 Dragalina Romania
57 L5 Dragan r. Romania
20 M4 Dragan l. Sweden
57 L5 Drăgănești Romania
77 M6 Drăgănești-Olt Romania
77 N6 Drăgănești-Vlașca Romania
77 M6 Drăgășani Romania
48 J4 Drage Ger.
57 L5 Drăgești Romania
96 G5 Draghoender S. Africa
77 K8 Dragoman Bulg.
79 H7 Dragonada i. Greece
144 E1 Dragones Arg.
73 M5 Dragoni Italy
79 G5 Dragonisi i. Greece
209 E12 Dragon Rocks Nature Reserve W.A. Austr.
131 □7 Dragon's Mouths str. Trin. and Tob./Venez.
125 V9 Dragoon AZ U.S.A.
22 I6 Dragør Denmark
77 P6 Dragoș Vodă Romania
21 Q6 Dragsfjärd Fin.
41 I9 Draguignan France
77 O2 Drăgușeni Botoșani Romania
77 P5 Drăgușeni Galați Romania
56 G2 Drahanovice Czech Rep.
16 E1 Drahichyn Belarus
51 I7 Drahnsdorf Ger.
205 N3 Drake N.S.W. Austr.
120 E2 Drake ND U.S.A.
48 H5 Drakenburg Ger.
97 M5 Drakensberg mts Lesotho/S. Africa
95 F5 Drakensberg mts S. Africa
97 N5 Drakensberg Garden S. Africa
97 M6 Draken's Rock mt. S. Africa
214 E9 Drake Passage S. Atlantic Ocean
124 I4 Drakes Bay CA U.S.A.
191 G5 Drakhtik Armenia
16 I8 Drakulya r. Ukr.
78 F1 Drama Greece
22 G2 Drammen Norway
36 D6 Drancy France
159 H8 Drang, Prêk r. Cambodia
20 □B1 Drangajökull ice cap Iceland
27 G7 Drangan Rep. of Ireland
22 F2 Drangedal Norway
178 M6 Drangme Chhu r. Bhutan
48 G3 Drangstedt Ger.
77 R6 Dranov, Lacul l. Romania
40 J4 Dranse r. France
50 G4 Dranse Ger.
49 I8 Dransfeld Ger.
50 H1 Dranske Ger.
125 U1 Draper UT U.S.A.
106 B3 Draper, Mount AK U.S.A.
27 I3 Draperstown Northern Ireland U.K.
178 E2 Dras Jammu and Kashmir
185 O3 Drasan Pak.
59 O2 Drasenhofen Austria
59 N4 Draßmarkt Austria
58 J6 Drau r. Austria
alt. Drava (Croatia),
alt. Dráva (Hungary)
68 G3 Drava r. Croatia
alt. Drau (Austria),
alt. Dráva (Hungary)
68 G3 Dráva r. Hungary
alt. Drau (Austria),
alt. Drava (Croatia)
57 G6 Drávafok Hungary
68 E2 Dravinja r. Slovenia
68 E2 Dravograd Slovenia
54 D3 Drawa r. Pol.
54 D2 Drawieński Park Narodowy nat. park Pol.
54 D2 Drawno Pol.
47 H2 Drawski Park Krajobrazowy Pol.
54 E3 Drawsko Pol.
54 E2 Drawsko, Jezioro l. Pol.
54 D2 Drawsko Pomorskie Pol.
31 O2 Drayton Norfolk, England U.K.
31 J4 Drayton Oxfordshire, England U.K.
106 H4 Drayton Valley Alta Can.
55 J2 Drążdżewo Pol.
59 M6 Dražen Vrh Slovenia
59 J7 Dražgoše Slovenia
185 N6 Drazinda Pak.
69 A7 Dréa Alg.
69 A7 Dréan Alg.
48 F5 Drebber Ger.
51 J7 Drebkau Ger.
40 E3 Drée r. France
27 C8 Dreenagh Rep. of Ireland
50 F5 Dreetz Ger.
30 D4 Drefach Carmarthenshire, Wales U.K.
57 I3 Drégelypalánk Hungary
26 G11 Dreghorn North Ayrshire, Scotland U.K.
49 G10 Dreieich Ger.
58 F5 Dreiherrnspitze mt. Austria
51 D6 Dreileben Ger.
52 B2 Dreis Ger.
52 D5 Dreisam r. Ger.
53 P4 Dreisesselberg mt. Ger.
49 I10 Dreistelzberge hill Ger.
48 J1 Drejø i. Denmark
55 K4 Drelów Pol.
48 H1 Drelsdorf Ger.
29 L1 Drem East Lothian, Scotland U.K.
71 P3 Drenchia Italy
68 G3 Drenovci Croatia
78 B2 Drenovë Albania
77 K7 Drenovets Bulg.
50 I4 Drense Ger.
49 E7 Drensteinfurt Ger.
44 K3 Drenthe prov. Neth.
44 J3 Drentse Hoofdvaart canal Neth.
48 G5 Drentwede Ger.
78 D5 Drepano Greece
78 E3 Drepano, Akra pt Greece
111 L7 Dresden Ont. Can.
51 I8 Dresden Ger.
51 J8 Dresden admin. reg. Ger.
121 K7 Dresden TN U.S.A.
14 K1 Dresvyanka Rus. Fed.
18 M6 Dretun' Belarus
54 E1 Dretyń Pol.
44 H5 Dreumel Neth.
36 B6 Dreux France
57 G2 Dřevnice r. Czech Rep.
21 L6 Drevsjø Norway
51 F6 Drewitz Ger.
50 F3 Drewitzer See l. Ger.
54 G1 Drewnica Pol.
116 H12 Drewryville VA U.S.A.
118 E5 Drexel Hill PA U.S.A.
54 D3 Drezdenko Pol.
18 K5 Dricēni Latvia
18 K6 Dridža l. Latvia
44 H4 Driebergen Neth.
63 N8 Driebes Spain
49 F9 Driedorf Ger.
57 K3 Drienov Slovakia
44 J2 Driesum Neth.
29 Q5 Driffield East Riding of Yorkshire, England U.K.
31 I4 Driffield Gloucestershire, England U.K.
118 D3 Drifton PA U.S.A.
116 G7 Driftwood PA U.S.A.
122 I5 Driggs ID U.S.A.
207 M9 Drillham Qld Austr.
17 K2 Drimaylivka Ukr.
27 G6 Drimmo Rep. of Ireland
26 E9 Drimnin Highland, Scotland U.K.
27 D9 Drimoleague Rep. of Ireland
76 H8 Drin r. Albania
68 G3 Drina r. Bos.-Herz./Yugo.
77 K6 Drincea r. Romania
76 I8 Drini i Zi r. Albania
76 H9 Drinit, Gjiri i b. Albania
78 B2 Drino r. Albania
116 B11 Drip Rock KY U.S.A.
27 E9 Dripsey Rep. of Ireland
212 O1 Driscoll Island Antarctica
59 J1 Dříteň Czech Rep.
20 J5 Driva Norway
56 F3 Drnholec Czech Rep.
68 F4 Drniš Croatia
59 O7 Drnje Croatia
71 J4 Dro Italy
22 G2 Drøbak Norway
77 K6 Drobeta - Turnu Severin Romania
41 E8 Drobie r. France
55 H3 Drobin Pol.
17 Q4 Drobysheve Ukr.
57 L5 Drocea, Vârful hill Romania
16 G5 Drochia Moldova
48 H3 Drochtersen Ger.
44 J2 Drogeham Neth.
27 J5 Drogheda Rep. of Ireland
Drogichin Belarus see Drahichyn
Drogobych Ukr. see Drohobych
55 K3 Drohiczyn Pol.
16 C4 Drohobych Ukr.
Droichead Átha Rep. of Ireland see Drogheda
Droichead Nua Rep. of Ireland see Newbridge
30 H3 Droitwich Spa Worcestershire, England U.K.
Drokiya Moldova see Drochia
179 M6 Drokung Arun. Prad. India
49 E8 Drolshagen Ger.
27 F4 Dromahair Rep. of Ireland
205 J8 Dromana Vic. Austr.
27 J4 Dromara Northern Ireland U.K.
41 G7 Drôme dept France
41 F7 Drôme r. France
39 J3 Drôme r. France
205 M7 Dromedary, Cape N.S.W. Austr.
118 A4 Dromgold PA U.S.A.
27 J5 Dromiskin Rep. of Ireland
48 K5 Drömling reg. Ger.
27 G5 Dromod Rep. of Ireland
27 H3 Dromore Northern Ireland U.K.
27 J4 Dromore Northern Ireland U.K.
27 E4 Dromore West Rep. of Ireland
70 C7 Dronero Italy
29 O7 Dronfield Derbyshire, England U.K.
26 H12 Drongan East Ayrshire, Scotland U.K.
45 E6 Drongen Belgium
42 D5 Dronne r. France
105 N3 Dronning Ingrid Land reg. Greenland
105 P2 Dronning Louise Land reg. Greenland
44 I3 Dronten Neth.
44 G3 Droogmakerij De Beemster tourist site Neth.
43 D6 Dropt r. France
59 M2 Drosendorf Austria
185 N4 Drosh Pak.
78 E4 Drosia Greece
59 O2 Drösing Austria
19 U9 Droskovo Rus. Fed.
36 B7 Droué France
169 M1 Drovyanaya Rus. Fed.
108 C3 Drowning r. Ont. Can.
51 F8 Droyßig Ger.
16 G2 Drozdyn' Ukr.
185 N6 Drug Pak.
30 F2 Druid Denbighshire, Wales U.K.
131 □9 Druif Aruba
28 F2 Druimdrishaig Argyll and Bute, Scotland U.K.
18 J6 Drūkšių ežeras l. Belarus/Lith.
Druk-Yul country Asia see Bhutan
37 N6 Drulingen France
27 E7 Drumandoora Rep. of Ireland
27 H5 Drumanespick Rep. of Ireland
27 K4 Drumaness Northern Ireland U.K.
26 F6 Drumbeg Highland, Scotland U.K.
27 J4 Drumbilla Rep. of Ireland
27 G4 Drumcard Northern Ireland U.K.
28 I2 Drumclog South Lanarkshire, Scotland U.K.
27 J6 Drumcondra Rep. of Ireland
27 I5 Drumconrath Rep. of Ireland
27 H5 Drumcree Rep. of Ireland
27 G4 Drumduff Northern Ireland U.K.
40 H5 Drumettaz-Clarafond France
27 H2 Drumfree Rep. of Ireland
27 F5 Drumharlow, Lough l. Rep. of Ireland
107 H5 Drumheller Alta Can.
27 F4 Drumkeeran Rep. of Ireland
28 B5 Drumlea Rep. of Ireland
27 G5 Drumlish Rep. of Ireland
26 L9 Drumlithie Aberdeenshire, Scotland U.K.
27 I8 Drummin Rep. of Ireland
122 H3 Drummond MT U.S.A.
110 C3 Drummond WI U.S.A.
116 I12 Drummond, Lake VA U.S.A.
111 K4 Drummond Island MI U.S.A.
207 K8 Drummond Range hills Qld Austr.
109 F4 Drummondville Que. Can.
26 G13 Drummore Dumfries and Galloway, Scotland U.K.
27 G3 Drumnacross Rep. of Ireland
26 H8 Drumnadrochit Highland, Scotland U.K.
28 C4 Drumnakilly Northern Ireland U.K.
27 H3 Drumquin Northern Ireland U.K.
28 B7 Drumraney Rep. of Ireland
27 F4 Drumshanbo Rep. of Ireland
28 B6 Drumsna Rep. of Ireland
44 H5 Drunen Neth.
28 C5 Drung Rep. of Ireland
106 C2 Drury Lake Y.T. Can.
70 F1 Drusberg mt. Switz.
37 O6 Drusenheim France
Druskieniki Lith. see Druskininkai
18 H8 Druskininkai Lith.
18 I4 Drusti Latvia
44 I5 Druten Neth.
18 N8 Druts' r. Belarus
18 K6 Druya Belarus
40 C1 Druyes-les-Belles-Fontaines France
55 H4 Drużbice Pol.
Druzhba Kazakh. see Dostyk
55 J1 Druzhba Rus. Fed.
17 L3 Druzhba Chernihivs'ka Oblast' Ukr.
17 M1 Druzhba Sums'ka Oblast' Ukr.
17 N7 Druzhbivka Ukr.
193 P3 Druzhina Rus. Fed.
19 U1 Druzhinnoye, Ozero l. Rus. Fed.
17 Q5 Druzhkivka Ukr.
Druzhkovka Donets'ka Oblast' Ukr. see Druzhkivka
19 N2 Druzhnaya Gorka Rus. Fed.
16 E1 Druzhylavichy Belarus
55 H1 Druzno, Jezioro l. Pol.
57 K3 Družstevná pri Hornáde Slovakia
55 J4 Drwalew Pol.
55 G2 Drwęca r. Pol.
55 H2 Drwęckie, Jezioro l. Pol.
55 I5 Drwinia Pol.
206 D3 Dry r. N.T. Austr.
77 N8 Dryanovo Bulg.
17 S1 Dryazgi Rus. Fed.
18 L3 Dryazhno Rus. Fed.
106 B3 Dry Bay AK U.S.A.
107 M5 Dryberry Lake Ont. Can.
19 O7 Drybin Belarus
30 G4 Drybrook Gloucestershire, England U.K.
121 E7 Dry Cimarron r. KS U.S.A.
108 A3 Dryden Ont. Can.
117 I6 Dryden NY U.S.A.
116 C12 Dryden VA U.S.A.
122 L5 Dry Fork r. WY U.S.A.
145 □ Drygalski Fjord inlet S. Georgia
213 L1 Drygalski Ice Tongue Antarctica
213 G2 Drygalski Island Antarctica
55 K2 Drygały Pol.
30 E3 Drygarn Fawr hill Wales U.K.
130 □ Dry Harbour Mountains hills Jamaica
97 I3 Dry Harts r. S. Africa
125 R5 Dry Lake NV U.S.A.
124 O2 Dry Lake l. NV U.S.A.
26 H10 Drymen Stirling, Scotland U.K.
18 K6 Drysa r. Belarus
208 I3 Drysdale r. W.A. Austr.
206 E1 Drysdale Island N.T. Austr.
208 I3 Drysdale River National Park W.A. Austr.
Drysyvaty Vozyera l. Belarus/Lith. see Drūkšių ežeras
115 F13 Dry Tortugas is FL U.S.A.
54 G3 Drzewce Pol.
54 E2 Drzewiany Pol.
55 I4 Drzewica Pol.
54 E2 Drzonowo Zachodniopomorskie Pol.
50 L2 Drzonowo Zachodniopomorskie Pol.
54 G2 Drzycim Pol.
89 H5 Dschang Cameroon
90 D4 Dua r. Dem. Rep. Congo
184 C4 Dūāb r. Iran
131 I8 Duaca Venez.
72 B7 Dualchi Sardegna Italy
170 G7 Du'an Guangxi China
99 □3b Duangani Mayotte
207 L7 Duaringa Qld Austr.
179 M6 Duars reg. Assam India
130 H4 Duarte, Pico mt. Dom. Rep.
142 C5 Duartina Brazil
62 H6 Duas Igrejas Port.
88 E5 Duayaw-Nkwanta Ghana
56 D1 Dubá Czech Rep.
186 B2 Ḍubā Saudi Arabia
Dubai U.A.E. see Dubayy
Dubai U.A.E. see Dubayy
124 I1 Dubakella Mountain CA U.S.A.
16 I6 Dubăsari Moldova
16 I6 Dubău Moldova
107 L2 Dubawnt r. Nunavut Can.
107 K2 Dubawnt Lake N.W.T./Nunavut Can.
187 M4 Dubayshī Oman
187 L3 Dubayy U.A.E.
186 B2 Dubbagh, Jabal ad mt. Saudi Arabia
205 L5 Dubbo N.S.W. Austr.
88 D5 Dube r. Liberia
16 D2 Dubechne Ukr.
55 L4 Dubeczno Pol.
51 I7 Duben Ger.
51 F7 Düben Ger.
70 F1 Dübendorf Switz.
51 G7 Dübener Heide park Ger.
51 F7 Dübener Heide reg. Ger.
55 K1 Dubeninki Pol.
15 I5 Dubenki Rus. Fed.
182 G2 Dubenskiy Rus. Fed.
Dubesar' Moldova see Dubăsari
26 C10 Dubh Artach i. Scotland U.K.
51 I9 Dubí Czech Rep.
18 H7 Dubičiai Lith.
55 K6 Dubiecko Pol.
55 L4 Dubienka Pol.
76 H8 Dubinës, Maja e mt. Albania
18 I6 Dubingiai Lith.
70 G3 Dubino Italy
16 F5 Dubivka Ukr.
17 K4 Dubiyivka Ukr.
191 H2 Dubki Rus. Fed.
17 N9 Dubky Ukr.
126 F2 Dublán Mex.
110 G1 Dublin Ont. Can.
27 J6 Dublin Rep. of Ireland
27 J6 Dublin county Rep. of Ireland
115 F9 Dublin GA U.S.A.
118 C5 Dublin MD U.S.A.
118 E4 Dublin PA U.S.A.
116 E11 Dublin VA U.S.A.
27 J6 Dublin Bay Rep. of Ireland
56 D2 Dublovice Czech Rep.
16 C4 Dublyany L'vivs'ka Oblast' Ukr.
16 D4 Dublyany L'vivs'ka Oblast' Ukr.
55 M2 Dubna Belarus
18 J5 Dubna r. Latvia
19 U5 Dubna Moskovskaya Oblast' Rus. Fed.
19 T7 Dubna Tul'skaya Oblast' Rus. Fed.
56 G3 Dubňany Czech Rep.
56 D3 Dubné Czech Rep.
57 H3 Dubnica nad Váhom Slovakia
16 E3 Dubno Ukr.
122 H4 Dubois ID U.S.A.
116 G7 Du Bois PA U.S.A.
122 J5 Dubois WY U.S.A.
Dubossary Moldova see Dubăsari
19 T8 Dubovaya Roshcha Rus. Fed.
16 C5 Dubove Ukr.
57 J2 Dubovica Slovakia
17 O5 Dubovi Hryady Ukr.
19 V8 Dubovka Tul'skaya Oblast' Rus. Fed.
15 I6 Dubovka Volgogradskaya Oblast' Rus. Fed.
Dubovo Moldova see Dubău
19 X6 Dubovoye, Ozero l. Rus. Fed.
15 H7 Dubovskoye Rus. Fed.
17 M2 Dubov''yazivka Ukr.
191 J5 Dübrar Dağı mt. Azer.
191 J5 Dübrar Pass Azer.
59 O8 Dubrava Croatia
57 I2 Dúbrava Slovakia
59 M8 Dubravica Croatia
57 I3 Dúbravy Slovakia
88 B4 Dubréka Guinea
Dubris Kent, England U.K. see Dover
16 G3 Dubrivka Ukr.
19 W7 Dubrovichi Rus. Fed.
19 Q8 Dubrovka Bryanskaya Oblast' Rus. Fed.
18 L5 Dubrovka Pskovskaya Oblast' Rus. Fed.
18 M4 Dubrovka Pskovskaya Oblast' Rus. Fed.
68 G4 Dubrovnik Croatia
183 M1 Dubrovnoye Kazakh.
55 L6 Dubrovytsya L'vivs'ka Oblast' Ukr.
16 F2 Dubrovytsya Rivnens'ka Oblast' Ukr.
19 N7 Dubrowna Belarus
183 S6 Dubun Kazakh.
114 B4 Dubuque IA U.S.A.
16 J5 Dubynove Ukr.
18 G6 Dubysa r. Lith.
38 G6 Duc, Étang au l. France
159 H9 Đưc Bôn Vietnam
201 □3 Duc de Gloucester, Îles du is Arch. des Tuamotu Fr. Polynesia
38 I4 Ducey France
171 K4 Duchang Jiangxi China
207 N1 Duchateau Entrance sea chan. P.N.G.
50 I3 Ducherow Ger.
125 V1 Duchesne UT U.S.A.
125 W1 Duchesne r. UT U.S.A.
206 G6 Duchess Qld Austr.
107 I5 Duchess Alta Can.
51 I9 Duchov Czech Rep.
207 I2 Ducie r. Qld Austr.
217 K7 Ducie Island Pitcairn Is
115 D7 Duck r. TN U.S.A.
107 K4 Duck Bay Man. Can.
208 D7 Duck Creek r. W.A. Austr.
31 M4 Duck End Essex, England U.K.
107 J4 Duck Lake Sask. Can.
106 K5 Duck Mountain Provincial Park Man. Can.
122 F6 Duck Valley Indian Reservation res. ID/NV U.S.A.
125 Q3 Duckwater NV U.S.A.
125 Q3 Duckwater Peak NV U.S.A.
39 M3 Duclair France
159 H9 Đưc Linh Vietnam
131 □3 Ducos Martinique
159 I7 Đưc Phô Vietnam
158 G5 Duc Tho Vietnam
136 C4 Duda r. Col.
57 G4 Dudar Hungary
17 M6 Dudchany Ukr.
29 M2 Duddo Northumberland, England U.K.
29 K5 Duddon r. England U.K.
45 J10 Dudelange Lux.
49 C11 Dudeldorf Ger.
49 J7 Duderstadt Ger.
76 I4 Dudeștii Vechi Romania
179 I7 Dudhi Uttar Prad. India
179 M7 Dudhnai Assam India
178 H5 Dudhwa Uttar Prad. India
57 H3 Dudince Slovakia
70 C2 Düdingen Switz.
192 J3 Dudinka Rus. Fed.
30 H2 Dudley West Midlands, England U.K.
125 V9 Dudleyville AZ U.S.A.
176 E3 Dudna r. India
19 S8 Dudorovskiy Rus. Fed.
178 E6 Dudu Rajasthan India
92 E3 Dudub Eth.
97 M2 Duduza S. Africa
68 F2 Dudváh r. Slovakia
26 L8 Dudwick, Hill of Scotland U.K.
162 M3 Due Sakhalin Rus. Fed.
88 D5 Duékoué Côte d'Ivoire
156 E6 Duen, Bukit vol. Indon.
63 K5 Dueñas Spain
23 L7 Dueodde pt Bornholm Denmark
140 C4 Dueré Brazil
62 I4 Duerna r. Spain
40 F5 Duerne France
62 G6 Duero r. Spain
alt. Douro (Portugal)
71 L4 Dueville Italy
111 P1 Dufault, Lac l. Que. Can.
45 G6 Duffel Belgium
108 E1 Dufferin, Cape Que. Can.
122 E6 Duffer Peak NV U.S.A.
31 J2 Duffield Derbyshire, England U.K.
116 C12 Duffield VA U.S.A.
200 □6 Duff Islands Santa Cruz Is Solomon Is
109 G1 Duffreboy, Lac l. Que. Can.
26 J8 Dufftown Moray, Scotland U.K.
70 D4 Dufourspitze mt. Italy/Switz.
107 L5 Dufrost Man. Can.
206 H5 Dugald r. Qld Austr.
68 E3 Duga Resa Croatia
193 P4 Duga-Zapadnaya, Mys c. Rus. Fed.
162 F2 Dugda Rus. Fed.
190 E9 Dughdash mts Saudi Arabia
Dughoba Uzbek. see Dugob
68 E3 Dugi Otok i. Croatia
68 F4 Dugi Rat Croatia
19 T7 Dugna Rus. Fed.
37 J5 Dugny-sur-Meuse France
183 L8 Dugob Uzbek.
68 F4 Dugopolje Croatia
68 F3 Dugo Selo Croatia
169 K7 Dugui Qarag Nei Mongol China
79 I1 Düğüncübaşı Turkey
125 T1 Dugway UT U.S.A.
170 H2 Du He r. China
43 D8 Duhort-Bachen France
84 C4 Duhūn Tārsū mts Chad/Libya
137 E4 Duida-Marahuaca, Parque Nacional nat. park Venez.
207 H2 Duifken Point Qld Austr.
44 H2 Duinen Terschelling nature res. Neth.
44 G2 Duinen Texel nature res. Neth.
44 F5 Duinen van Voorne nature res. Neth.
49 I6 Duingen Ger.
71 P4 Duino Italy
184 D5 Duir Iran
49 C8 Duisburg Ger.
136 C3 Duitama Col.
44 J5 Duiven Neth.
95 F4 Duiwelskloof S. Africa
170 D3 Dujiangyan Sichuan China
92 D4 Dujuuma Somalia
189 L6 Dukān Dam Iraq
193 Q3 Dukat Rus. Fed.
77 K8 Dukat mt. Serb. and Mont.
97 K6 Dukathole S. Africa
78 A2 Dukat i Ri Albania
106 D4 Duke Island AK U.S.A.
Duke of Gloucester Islands Arch. des Tuamotu Fr. Polynesia see Duc de Gloucester, Îles du
Duke of York atoll Tokelau see Atafu
92 A3 Duk Fadiat Sudan
92 A3 Duk Faiwil Sudan
187 J3 Dukhān Qatar
186 F3 Dukhnah Saudi Arabia
182 C1 Dukhovnitskoye Rus. Fed.
19 P6 Dukhovshchina Rus. Fed.
19 O6 Dukhovshehinskaya Vozvyshennost' hills Rus. Fed.
185 M6 Duki Pak.
162 I3 Duki Rus. Fed.
162 I3 Duki r. Rus. Fed.
89 H4 Dukku Nigeria
55 J6 Dukla Pol.
18 J6 Dūkštas Lith.
94 E4 Dukwe Botswana
168 J2 Dulaanhaan Mongolia
184 H7 Dūlab Iran
121 J11 Dulac LA U.S.A.
168 F8 Dulan Qinghai China
Dulawan Mindanao Phil. see Datu Piang
147 F2 Dulce r. Arg.
63 O7 Dulce r. Spain
123 K8 Dulce NM U.S.A.
126 □R13 Dulce, Golfo b. Costa Rica
126 □Q10 Dulce Nombre de Culmí Hond.
144 C2 Dulcinea Chile
169 M1 Dul'durga Rus. Fed.
27 J5 Duleek Rep. of Ireland
193 O3 Dulgalakh r. Rus. Fed.
77 P7 Dŭlgopol Bulg.
207 I1 Dulhunty r. Qld Austr.
18 K6 Dulina Belarus
173 E9 Dulishi Hu salt l. China
157 J3 Dulit, Pegunungan mts Malaysia
170 G6 Duliu Jiang r. China
154 E6 Duljugan Point Leyte Phil.
179 N7 Dullabchara Assam India
31 M3 Dullingham Cambridgeshire, England U.K.
97 O1 Dullstroom S. Africa
49 D7 Dülmen Ger.
178 D5 Dulmera Rajasthan India
26 I8 Dulnain r. Scotland U.K.
26 I8 Dulnain Bridge Highland, Scotland U.K.
18 L4 Dulovka Rus. Fed.
77 P7 Dulovo Bulg.
190 G2 Dulq Maghār Syria
110 B3 Duluth MN U.S.A.
120 I2 Duluth/Superior airport MN U.S.A.
30 E5 Dulverton Somerset, England U.K.
19 X4 Dulyapino Rus. Fed.
190 E5 Dūmā Syria
154 D7 Dumaguete Negros Phil.
156 D4 Dumai Sumatera Indon.
191 A5 Dumanlı Turkey
191 E5 Dumanlı Dağı mt. Turkey
191 B6 Dumanlı Tepe mt. Turkey
154 D8 Dumanquilas Bay Mindanao Phil.
154 C6 Dumaran i. Phil.
155 D1 Dumarchen i. Indon.
205 M3 Dumaresq r. N.S.W. Austr.
121 J9 Dumas AR U.S.A.
121 E8 Dumas TX U.S.A.
190 E5 Ḍumayr Syria
190 E5 Ḍumayr, Jabal mts Syria
Dumbakh Iran see Dom Bākh
26 G11 Dumbarton West Dunbartonshire, Scotland U.K.
97 O3 Dumbe S. Africa
200 □5 Dumbéa New Caledonia
57 I3 Ďumbier mt. Slovakia
209 D12 Dumbleyung W.A. Austr.
209 D12 Dumbleyung, Lake salt flat W.A. Austr.
89 H5 Dumbo Cameroon
57 L6 Dumbrava Romania
77 M4 Dumbrăveni Sibiu Romania
77 P5 Dumbrăveni Vrancea Romania
77 N5 Dumbrăvița Brașov Romania
57 K6 Dumbrăvița Timiș Romania
62 B2 Dumbría Spain
178 G3 Dumchele Jammu and Kashmir
156 G4 Dumdum i. Indon.
179 O6 Dum Duma Assam India
77 P4 Dumești Romania
38 F7 Dumet, Île i. France
131 □3 Dumfries Grenada
26 I12 Dumfries Dumfries and Galloway, Scotland U.K.
26 I12 Dumfries and Galloway admin. div. Scotland U.K.
19 S8 Duminichi Kaluzhskaya Oblast' Rus. Fed.
19 S8 Duminichi Kaluzhskaya Oblast' Rus. Fed.
77 M3 Dumitra Romania
179 K7 Dumka Jharkhand India
191 C5 Dumlu Turkey
191 C5 Dumlu Dağı mt. Turkey
190 A2 Dumluğöze Turkey
79 K4 Dumlupınar Turkey
176 G4 Dummagudem Andhra Prad. India
48 F5 Dümmer l. Ger.
49 F5 Dümmer, Naturpark nature res. Ger.
50 F3 Dummerstorf Ger.
155 D3 Dumoga Sulawesi Indon.
108 E4 Dumoine r. Que. Can.
111 Q3 Dumoine, Lac l. Que. Can.
111 R3 Dumont, Lac l. Que. Can.
213 J2 Dumont d'Urville research stn Antarctica
213 I2 Dumont d'Urville Sea Antarctica
49 C10 Dümpelfeld Ger.
179 J7 Dumraon Bihar India
186 F7 Dumsuk i. Saudi Arabia
85 F2 Dumyāṭ Egypt
188 E8 Dumyāṭ governorate Egypt
43 H9 Dun France
49 J8 Dün ridge Ger.
68 G3 Duna r. Hungary
alt. Donau (Aust./Germany),
alt. Dunaj (Slovakia),
alt. Dunărea (Romania),
alt. Dunav (Serb. and Mont.),
conv. Danube
57 H4 Dunaalmás Hungary
Dünaburg Latvia see Daugavpils
57 H5 Dunaegyháza Hungary
57 H5 Dunafalva Hungary
27 G2 Dunaff Head Rep. of Ireland
57 H5 Dunaföldvár Hungary
57 I4 Dunaharaszti Hungary
68 F2 Dunaj r. Slovakia
alt. Donau (Aust./Germany),
alt. Duna (Hungary),
alt. Dunărea (Romania),
alt. Dunav (Serb. and Mont.),
conv. Danube
55 I5 Dunajec r. Pol.
56 G3 Dunajská Lužná Slovakia
57 G4 Dunajská Streda Slovakia
16 I8 Dunajs'ki Plavni nature res. Ukr.
57 I4 Dunakeszi Hungary
56 G4 Dunakiliti Hungary
205 K10 Dunalley Tas. Austr.
Dunanbay Kazakh. see Dunenbay
27 J5 Dunany Point Rep. of Ireland
57 I5 Dunapataj Hungary
77 Q5 Dunărea r. Romania
alt. Donau (Aust./Germany),
alt. Duna (Hungary),
alt. Dunaj (Slovakia),
alt. Dunav (Serb. and Mont.),
conv. Danube
77 R5 Dunării, Delta Romania
57 G4 Dunaszeg Hungary
57 H5 Dunaszekcső Hungary
57 H5 Dunaszentgyörgy Hungary
56 G4 Dunasziget Hungary
57 I5 Dunatetétlen Hungary
57 I5 Duna-Tisza Köze reg. Hungary
57 H5 Dunaújváros Hungary
77 F2 Dunav r. Serb. and Mont.
alt. Donau (Aust./Germany),
alt. Duna (Hungary),
alt. Dunaj (Slovakia),
alt. Dunărea (Romania),
conv. Danube
57 I4 Dunavarsány Hungary
57 H5 Dunavecse Hungary
77 K7 Dunavtsi Bulg.
193 N2 Dunay, Ostrova is Rus. Fed.
16 F4 Dunayivtsi Khmel'nyts'ka Oblast' Ukr.
16 F5 Dunayivtsi Khmel'nyts'ka Oblast' Ukr.
203 E12 Dunback South I. N.Z.
207 I4 Dunbar Qld Austr.
26 K10 Dunbar East Lothian, Scotland U.K.
116 F9 Dunbar PA U.S.A.
110 F4 Dunbar WI U.S.A.
116 D10 Dunbar WV U.S.A.
26 J6 Dunbeath Highland, Scotland U.K.
26 I10 Dunblane Stirling, Scotland U.K.
27 J6 Dunboyne Rep. of Ireland
106 F5 Duncan B.C. Can.
125 W9 Duncan AZ U.S.A.
121 G8 Duncan OK U.S.A.
108 D2 Duncan, Cape Nunavut Can.
108 E2 Duncan, Lac l. Que. Can.
106 G5 Duncan Lake B.C. Can.
106 H2 Duncan Lake N.W.T. Can.
27 I8 Duncannon Rep. of Ireland
111 Q9 Duncannon PA U.S.A.
27 D8 Duncannon Bridge Rep. of Ireland
177 M7 Duncan Passage Andaman & Nicobar Is India
130 □ Duncans Jamaica
26 J5 Duncansby Head Scotland U.K.
130 F2 Duncan Town Bahamas
31 J3 Dunchurch Warwickshire, England U.K.
27 I8 Duncormick Rep. of Ireland
18 F4 Dundaga Latvia
26 E10 Dun da Ghaoithe hill Scotland U.K.
111 N5 Dundalk Ont. Can.
27 J4 Dundalk Rep. of Ireland
118 B6 Dundalk MD U.S.A.
27 J5 Dundalk Bay Rep. of Ireland
108 E5 Dundas Ont. Can.
Dundas Greenland see Uummannaq
209 F12 Dundas, Lake salt flat W.A. Austr.
106 D4 Dundas Island B.C. Can.
209 G12 Dundas Nature Reserve W.A. Austr.
104 G2 Dundas Peninsula N.W.T. Can.
206 C1 Dundas Strait N.T. Austr.
169 L3 Dundbürd Mongolia
Dún Dealgan Rep. of Ireland see Dundalk
97 O4 Dundee S. Africa
26 K10 Dundee Dundee, Scotland U.K.
26 K10 Dundee admin. div. Scotland U.K.
111 K8 Dundee MI U.S.A.
116 I6 Dundee NY U.S.A.
168 I4 Dundgovĭ prov. Mongolia
169 O5 Dund Hot Nei Mongol China
27 K3 Dundonald Northern Ireland U.K.
26 G11 Dundonald South Ayrshire, Scotland U.K.
207 J9 Dundoo Qld Austr.
26 G8 Dundreggan Highland, Scotland U.K.
26 I13 Dundrennan Dumfries and Galloway, Scotland U.K.
27 J6 Dundrum Dublin Rep. of Ireland
27 F7 Dundrum Tipperary Rep. of Ireland
27 K4 Dundrum Northern Ireland U.K.
27 K4 Dundrum Bay Northern Ireland U.K.
178 I6 Dundwa Range mts India/Nepal
108 F1 Dune, Lac l. Que. Can.
26 I11 Duneaton Water r. Scotland U.K.
26 L8 Dunecht Aberdeenshire, Scotland U.K.
203 E12 Dunedin South I. N.Z.
115 F11 Dunedin FL U.S.A.
205 L5 Dunedoo N.S.W. Austr.
183 S3 Dunenbay Kazakh.
43 F7 Dunes France
106 E3 Dune Za Keyih Provincial Park B.C. Can.
28 B3 Dunfanaghy Rep. of Ireland
26 J10 Dunfermline Fife, Scotland U.K.
27 I3 Dungannon Northern Ireland U.K.
Dún Garbhán Rep. of Ireland see Dungarvan
178 E5 Dungargarh Rajasthan India
178 D8 Dungarpur Rajasthan India
27 H7 Dungarvan Kilkenny Rep. of Ireland
27 G8 Dungarvan Waterford Rep. of Ireland
53 N4 Dungau reg. Ger.
173 J11 Dung Co l. Xizang China
31 N6 Dungeness hd England U.K.
145 C9 Dungeness, Punta pt Arg.
49 D10 Düngenheim Ger.
27 I3 Dungiven Northern Ireland U.K.
27 F3 Dungloe Rep. of Ireland
205 M5 Dungog N.S.W. Austr.
27 F9 Dungourney Rep. of Ireland
158 I7 Dung Quất, Vung b. Vietnam
90 F4 Dungu Dem. Rep. Congo
156 E2 Dungun Malaysia
85 H4 Dungunab Sudan
29 Q7 Dunholme Lincolnshire, England U.K.
162 F7 Dunhua Jilin China
172 L6 Dunhuang Gansu China
41 E6 Dunières France
54 E1 Duninowo Pol.
207 L9 Dunkeld Qld Austr.
205 I7 Dunkeld Vic. Austr.
26 I9 Dunkeld Perth and Kinross, Scotland U.K.
27 E6 Dunkellin r. Rep. of Ireland
59 L3 Dunkelsteiner Wald for. Austria
36 D1 Dunkerque France
27 G7 Dunkerrin Rep. of Ireland
30 E5 Dunkery Hill England U.K.
27 F3 Dunkineely Rep. of Ireland
Dunkirk France see Dunkerque
31 N5 Dunkirk Kent, England U.K.
116 F6 Dunkirk NY U.S.A.
116 B8 Dunkirk OH U.S.A.
207 K4 Dunk Island Qld Austr.
88 E5 Dunkwa Ghana
27 J6 Dún Laoghaire Rep. of Ireland
120 H5 Dunlap IA U.S.A.
110 I8 Dunlap IN U.S.A.
115 E8 Dunlap TN U.S.A.
27 I6 Dunlavin Rep. of Ireland
27 J5 Dunleer Rep. of Ireland
42 H3 Dun-le-Palestel France
40 E2 Dun-les-Places France
28 A3 Dunlewy Rep. of Ireland
26 G11 Dunlop East Ayrshire, Scotland U.K.
27 J2 Dunloy Northern Ireland U.K.
25 D4 Dunluce tourist site Northern Ireland U.K.
27 C9 Dunmanus Rep. of Ireland
27 C10 Dunmanus Bay Rep. of Ireland
27 D9 Dunmanway Rep. of Ireland
206 D4 Dunmarra N.T. Austr.
27 G8 Dunmoon Rep. of Ireland
27 E5 Dunmore Rep. of Ireland
118 D2 Dunmore PA U.S.A.
116 F10 Dunmore WV U.S.A.
27 I8 Dunmore East Rep. of Ireland
130 E1 Dunmore Town Eleuthera Bahamas
27 K3 Dunmurry Northern Ireland U.K.
115 H8 Dunn NC U.S.A.
27 H3 Dunnamanagh Northern Ireland U.K.
115 F11 Dunnellon FL U.S.A.
26 J5 Dunnet Highland, Scotland U.K.
26 J5 Dunnet Bay Scotland U.K.
26 J5 Dunnet Head Scotland U.K.
124 K3 Dunnigan CA U.S.A.
26 I10 Dunning Perth and Kinross, Scotland U.K.
120 E5 Dunning NE U.S.A.
52 F5 Dunningen Ger.
29 P6 Dunnington York, England U.K.
209 E12 Dunn Rock Nature Reserve W.A. Austr.
209 E8 Dunns Range hills W.A. Austr.
111 O7 Dunnville Ont. Can.
36 B8 Dunois reg. France
205 I7 Dunolly Vic. Austr.
26 G11 Dunoon Argyll and Bute, Scotland U.K.
27 B8 Dunquin Rep. of Ireland
26 J11 Dun Rig hill Scotland U.K.
26 L11 Duns Scottish Borders, Scotland U.K.
203 G10 Dunsandel South I. N.Z.
209 C12 Dunsborough W.A. Austr.
26 I12 Dunscore Dumfries and Galloway, Scotland U.K.
120 E1 Dunseith ND U.S.A.
48 G5 Dünsen Ger.
27 I5 Dunshaughlin Rep. of Ireland
122 C6 Dunsmuir CA U.S.A.
31 K4 Dunstable Bedfordshire, England U.K.
203 D12 Dunstan Mountains South I. N.Z.
30 F5 Dunster Somerset, England U.K.
40 B3 Dun-sur-Auron France
37 J5 Dun-sur-Meuse France
26 H8 Duntelchaig, Loch l. Scotland U.K.
203 E11 Duntroon South I. N.Z.
48 E3 Dunum Ger.
28 H3 Dunure South Ayrshire, Scotland U.K.
30 D4 Dunvant Swansea, Wales U.K.
26 C8 Dunvegan Highland, Scotland U.K.
26 C7 Dunvegan, Loch b. Scotland U.K.
26 C7 Dunvegan Head Scotland U.
107 J2 Dunvegan Lake N.W.T. Can.
31 P3 Dunwich Suffolk, England U.
185 N7 Dunyapur Pak.
169 S2 Duobukur He r. China
169 O5 Duolun Nei Mongol China
173 F9 Duomula Xizang China
159 G9 Dương Đông Vietnam
176 F5 Dupadu Andhra Prad. India
171 H6 Dupang Ling mts China
111 O1 Duparquet Que. Can.
111 O1 Duparquet, Lac l. Que. Can.
Duperré Alg. see Aïn Defla
59 K7 Duplica Slovenia
77 L8 Dupnitsa Bulg.
120 E3 Dupree SD U.S.A.
208 C6 Dupuy, Cape W.A. Austr.
186 F7 Duqaylah i. Saudi Arabia
Duque de Bragança Angola see Calandula
143 F5 Duque de Caxias Brazil
145 B8 Duque de York, Isla i. Chile
110 B3 Duquette MN U.S.A.
114 C6 Du Quoin IL U.S.A.
92 C2 Dura r. Eth.
190 D7 Dūrā West Bank
71 M2 Dura, Cima mt. Italy
53 I6 Durach Ger.
198 C3 Durack r. W.A. Austr.
208 I4 Durack Range hills W.A. Aust
Dura Europos Syria see Aş Şāliḩīyah
188 G3 Durağan Turkey
178 F8 Duraha Madh. Prad. India
79 J3 Durak Turkey
63 O3 Durana Spain
43 E7 Durance France
41 F9 Durance r. France
111 K7 Durand MI U.S.A.
110 C5 Durand WI U.S.A.
200 □5 Durand, Récif rf New Caledonia
65 J3 Duranes hill Spain
125 Q9 Durango Baja California Mex.
128 C1 Durango Durango Mex.
128 C1 Durango state Mex.
63 O2 Durango Spain
123 K8 Durango CO U.S.A.
128 B2 Durango, Sierra de mts Mex
185 L6 Durani reg. Afgh.
77 Q7 Durankulak Bulg.
71 M3 Duranno, Monte mt. Italy
147 G5 Durañona Arg.
121 K9 Durant MS U.S.A.
121 G8 Durant OK U.S.A.
43 E6 Duras France
63 L5 Duratón r. Spain
43 G6 Duravel France
190 E4 Duraykīsh Syria
144 C3 Durazno Arg.
147 I3 Durazno Uru.
147 I3 Durazno dept Uru.
Durazzo Albania see Durrës
52 E4 Durbach Ger.
43 G9 Durban France
97 P5 Durban S. Africa
41 B11 Durban-Corbières France
96 C9 Durbanville S. Africa
52 F5 Dürbheim Ger.
116 F10 Durbin WV U.S.A.
37 L7 Durbion r. France
185 K7 Durbun Pak.
45 H8 Durbuy Belgium
65 L7 Dúrcal Spain
65 M7 Dúrcal r. Spain
57 H2 Ďurčiná Slovakia
40 B4 Durdat-Larequille France
39 M2 Durdent r. France
68 F2 Đurđevac Croatia
92 F2 Durdura, Raas pt Somalia
172 I3 Düre Xinjiang China
49 B9 Düren Ger.
184 G5 Duren Iran
184 G5 Duren, Kūh-e mt. Iran
41 D9 Durfort France
178 H9 Durg Chhattisgarh India
179 M7 Durgapur Bangl.
179 K8 Durgapur W. Bengal India
111 N5 Durham Ont. Can.
29 N4 Durham Durham, England U.
29 M4 Durham admin. div. England U.K.
124 K2 Durham CA U.S.A.
119 J2 Durham CT U.S.A.
115 H8 Durham NC U.S.A.
117 □O5 Durham NH U.S.A.
202 □ Durham, Point Chatham Is S. Pacific Ocean
117 □S2 Durham Bridge N.B. Can.
207 H9 Durham Downs Qld Austr.
92 D3 Durhi well Eth.
156 D4 Duri Sumatera Indon.
157 H5 Duriansebatang Kalimantan Indon.
26 I12 Durisdeer Dumfries and Galloway, Scotland U.K.
16 H6 Durlești Moldova
59 M7 Durmanec Croatia
36 G1 Durme r. Belgium
52 H5 Dürmentingen Ger.
52 E4 Durmersheim Ger.
76 H7 Durmitor mt. Serb. and Mont
76 G7 Durmitor nat. park Serb. and Mont.
26 G5 Durness Highland, Scotland U.K.
26 G5 Durness, Kyle of inlet Scotland U.K.
59 O3 Dürnkrut Austria
207 M9 Durong South Qld Austr.
Durovernum Kent, England U.K. see Canterbury
76 H9 Durrës Albania
206 H8 Durrie Qld Austr.
53 I5 Dürrlauingen Ger.
51 J8 Dürröhrsdorf-Dittersbach Ger.
27 H7 Durrow Rep. of Ireland
53 I3 Dürrwangen Ger.
27 B9 Dursey Head Rep. of Ireland
27 B9 Dursey Island Rep. of Irelanc
30 H4 Dursley Gloucestershire, England U.K.
79 J3 Dursunbey Turkey
39 K6 Durtal France
90 F4 Duru r. Dem. Rep. Congo
187 M4 Duru reg. Oman
190 F2 Duruca Turkey
63 O5 Duruelo de la Sierra Spain
184 I5 Dūruḩ Iran
92 E2 Durukhsi Somalia
79 J1 Durusu Gölü l. Turkey
190 E6 Durūz, Jabal ad mt. Syria
153 I7 D'Urville, Tanjung pt Papua Indon.
202 H7 D'Urville Island South I. N.Z.
118 D2 Duryea PA U.S.A.
26 □N2 Dury Voe inlet Scotland U.K.
185 K4 Durzab Afgh.
18 I6 Dusetos Lith.
185 K7 Dushai Pak.
184 H3 Dushak Turkm.
170 F6 Dushan Guizhou China
185 M2 Dushanbe Tajik.
172 G4 Dushanzi Xinjiang China
17 L1 Dushatino Rus. Fed.
191 F3 Dushet'i Georgia
169 N6 Dushikou Hebei China
111 R8 Dushore PA U.S.A.
18 G7 Dusia l. Lith.
203 A12 Dusky Sound inlet South I. N.Z
55 M1 Dusmenys Lith.

Eilerts de Haan, Natuurreservaat to Embarcación

260

137 G4 Eilerts de Haan, Natuurreservaat nature res. Suriname
137 G4 Eilerts de Haan Gebergte mts Suriname
154 □ Eil Malk i. Palau
51 D6 Eilsleben Ger.
49 I6 Eime Ger.
49 I7 Eimen Ger.
48 J5 Eimke Ger.
22 G1 Eina Norway
26 C6 Einacleit Western Isles, Scotland U.K.
207 J5 Einasleigh Qld Austr.
207 I4 Einasleigh r. Qld Austr.
22 G1 Einavatnet l. Norway
49 I7 Einbeck Ger.
45 H6 Eindhoven Neth.
96 D1 Eindpaal Namibia
51 E7 Eine r. Ger.
52 F2 Einhausen Ger.
26 G7 Einig r. Scotland U.K.
158 B6 Einme Myanmar
51 G9 Einsiedel Ger.
70 F1 Einsiedeln Switz.
37 L6 Einville-au-Jard France
190 D8 Ein Yahav Israel
98 □1c Eiras, Ponta das pt São Jorge Azores
214 G2 Eirik Ridge sea feature N. Atlantic Ocean
Eiriosgaigh i. Scotland U.K. see Eriskay
136 D6 Eiru r. Brazil
136 D6 Eirunepé Brazil
49 I8 Eisberg hill Ger.
45 J9 Eisch r. Lux.
45 I7 Eisden Belgium
49 J7 Eisdorf Ger.
94 D3 Eiseb watercourse Namibia
53 M5 Eiselfing Ger.
49 J9 Eisenach Ger.
52 E6 Eisenbach (Hochschwarzwald) Ger.
51 E9 Eisenberg Ger.
52 E2 Eisenberg (Pfalz) Ger.
59 K4 Eisenerz Austria
59 J4 Eisenerzer Alpen mts Austria
Eisenhower, Mount Alta Can. see Castle Mountain
59 I6 Eisenhut mt. Austria
51 K6 Eisenhüttenstadt Ger.
59 K7 Eisenkappel Austria
59 O4 Eisenstadt Austria
59 K4 Eisenwurzen reg. Austria
49 K10 Eisfeld Ger.
26 E8 Eishort, Loch inlet Scotland U.K.
18 H7 Eišiškės Lith.
24 J1 Eislandet Norway
51 E7 Eisleben Lutherstadt Ger.
52 H4 Eislingen (Fils) Ger.
202 J4 Eistow North I. N.Z.
Eitape P.N.G. see Aitape
53 K4 Eitensheim Ger.
49 I9 Eiterfeld Ger.
49 D9 Eitorf Ger.
46 E1 Eitzum (Despetal) Ger.
21 H6 Eivinvik Norway
67 H10 Eivissa Spain
67 I9 Eivissa i. Spain
62 F4 Eixe, Serra do mts Spain
62 C7 Eixo Port.
62 D6 Eja Port.
66 C3 Ejea de los Caballeros Spain
95 □J5 Ejeda Madag.
Ejin Horo Qi Nei Mongol China see Altan Shiret
Ejin Qi Nei Mongol China see Dalain Hob
86 B5 Ej Jill, Sebkhet salt flat Maur.
Ejmiadzin Armenia see Ejmiatsin
191 F5 Ejmiatsin Armenia
66 D6 Ejulve Spain
88 E5 Ejura Ghana
129 K9 Ejutla Mex.
122 L4 Ekalaka MT U.S.A.
89 H5 Ekang Nigeria
97 M1 Ekangala S. Africa
90 B4 Ékata Gabon
165 J13 Ekawasaki Japan
21 Q7 Ekenäs Fin.
23 J3 Ekenäs Sweden
21 Q7 Ekenäskärgårds nationalpark nat. park Fin.
45 F6 Ekeren Belgium
23 N2 Ekerö Sweden
89 G5 Eket Nigeria
202 J7 Eketahuna North I. N.Z.
Ekhinos Greece see Echinos
Ekhmīm Egypt see Akhmīm
183 P2 Ekibastuz Kazakh.
162 H2 Ekimchan Rus. Fed.
190 H2 Ekinyazı Turkey
89 G5 Ekiti state Nigeria
23 M4 Eknö i. Sweden
90 E5 Ekoli Dem. Rep. Congo
23 N2 Ekoln l. Sweden
193 L3 Ekonda Rus. Fed.
89 H5 Ekondo Titi Cameroon
20 V3 Ekostrovskaya Imandra, Ozero l. Rus. Fed.
90 C4 Ekouamou Congo
89 G5 Ekpoma Nigeria
45 E6 Eksaarde Belgium
45 H6 Eksel Belgium
Eksere Turkey see Gündoğmuş
22 J1 Ekshärad Sweden
79 L5 Ekşili Turkey
23 K4 Eksjö Sweden
162 C1 Ekskavatornyy Rus. Fed.
96 B4 Eksteenfontein S. Africa
212 X2 Ekström Ice Shelf Antarctica
20 O4 Ekträsk Sweden
90 D5 Ekuku Dem. Rep. Congo
108 D2 Ekwan r. Ont. Can.
108 D2 Ekwan Point Ont. Can.
158 C5 Ela Myanmar
El Aaiún Western Sahara see Laâyoune
146 B5 El Abanico Chile
85 F6 El Abbasiya Sudan
78 D6 Elafonisos i. Greece
78 D6 Elafonisou, Steno sea chan. Greece
88 D2 El Aghlâf well Maur.
128 E7 El Aguaje Mex.
190 C3 Elaia, Cape Cyprus
85 G5 El Aiadia well Sudan
78 F2 Elaiochori Greece
86 A5 El 'Aïouej well Maur.
El 'Alamein Egypt see Al 'Alamayn
129 H2 El Alamito Mex.
126 A2 El Alamo Mex.
128 C6 El Alcihuatl Mex.
67 D12 El Algar Spain
62 I1 El Alia Alg.
69 B7 El Alia Tunisia
64 G6 El Aljarafe reg. Spain
65 E5 El Almendro Spain
65 O7 El Alquián Spain
144 D3 El Alto Catamarca Arg.
146 D2 El Alto La Rioja Arg.
136 A6 El Alto Peru
36 C6 Élancourt France
64 E5 El Andévalo reg. Spain
97 O1 Elands r. S. Africa
97 J5 Elands r. S. Africa
97 K8 Elandsberg mt. S. Africa
97 N1 Elandsdoorn S. Africa
97 J8 Elandsdrif S. Africa
97 O4 Elandskraal S. Africa
97 N4 Elandslaagte S. Africa
97 K1 Elandsputte S. Africa
30 E3 Elan Village Powys, Wales U.K.
Elar Armenia see Abovyan
64 H6 El Arahal Spain
126 C3 El Arco Mex.
63 J8 El Arenal Castilla y León Spain
87 E2 El Aricha Alg.
207 K4 El Arish Qld Austr.
87 G1 El Arrouch Alg.
79 H7 Elasa i. Greece
El Asnam Alg. see Ech Chélif
78 D3 Elassona Greece
63 K3 El Astillero Spain
190 C9 Elat Israel
63 N7 El Atazar, Embalse de resr Spain
86 B5 El 'Aṭf reg. Western Sahara
78 B4 Elati mt. Lefkada Greece
153 K5 Elato atoll Micronesia
188 I4 Elazığ Turkey
191 A7 Elazığ prov. Turkey
115 D10 Elba AL U.S.A.
72 E2 Elba, Isola d' i. Italy
65 O3 El Ballestero Spain
162 J3 El'ban Rus. Fed.
136 C2 El Banco Col.
88 D2 El Bânoûn well Maur.
62 I8 El Barco de Ávila Spain
63 K8 El Barraco Spain
129 I1 El Barranco Tamaulipas Mex.
129 I3 El Barranco Tamaulipas Mex.
126 F2 El Barreal salt l. Mex.
128 E2 El Barril Mex.
92 B2 El Barun Sudan
76 I9 Elbasan Albania
188 G4 Elbaşı Turkey
85 G5 El Bauga Sudan
136 D2 El Baúl Venez.
87 F2 El Bayadh Alg.
48 H3 Elbe r. Ger.
alt. Labe (Czech Rep.)
122 C3 Elbe WA U.S.A.
51 E6 Elbe-Havel-Kanal canal Ger.
62 C3 'Elb el Fçâl des. Maur.
146 B3 El Belloto airport Chile
48 K3 Elbe-Lübeck-Kanal canal Ger.
190 E4 El Béqaa val. Lebanon
49 D6 Elbergen Ger.
88 C2 El Berié well Maur.
63 M7 El Berrueco Spain
123 K7 Elbert, Mount CO U.S.A.
110 H5 Elberta MI U.S.A.
125 U2 Elberta UT U.S.A.
115 F8 Elberton GA U.S.A.
92 D4 El Beru Hagia Somalia
92 C4 El Bes well Kenya
36 B5 Elbeuf France
190 F2 Elbeyli Turkey
88 C2 El Beyyeş well Maur.
86 C5 El Beyyeş well Maur.
62 F4 El Bierzo reg. Spain
58 B5 Elbigenalp Austria
128 F7 El Billete, Cerro mt. Mex.
Elbing Pol. see Elbląg
49 K7 Elbingerode (Harz) Ger.
188 H4 Elbistan Turkey
64 I9 El-Biutz Morocco
23 P7 Elbląg Pol.
55 H1 Elbląski, Kanał canal Pol.
126 □R11 El Bluff Nic.
62 G8 El Bodón Spain
146 A4 El Boldo Chile
145 C6 El Bolsón Arg.
65 N3 El Bonillo Spain
128 E3 El Bordo Mex.
64 H9 El-Borj Morocco
87 H3 El Borma Tunisia
65 I7 El Bosque Spain
El Boulaïda Alg. see Blida
107 J5 Elbow Sask. Can.
115 I12 Elbow Cay i. Bahamas
120 G2 Elbow Lake MN U.S.A.
128 F2 El Bozal Mex.
127 I4 El Brasil Mex.
191 D2 El'brus Rus. Fed.
191 D2 El'brus mt. Rus. Fed.
191 D2 El'brusskiy Rus. Fed.
51 J9 Elbsandstein Gebirge hills Ger.
90 F3 El Buheyrat state Sudan
65 P4 El Buitre mt. Spain
65 K2 El Bullaque Spain
44 I4 Elburg Neth.
65 J7 El Burgo Spain
63 O3 Elburgo Spain
63 D4 El Burgo de Ebro Spain
63 N5 El Burgo de Osma Spain
63 J4 El Burgo Ranero Spain
90 E2 El Burma well Sudan
128 E2 El Burrito Mex.
Elburz Mountains Iran see Alborz, Reshteh-ye
63 Q5 El Buste Spain
17 S7 El'buzd r. Rus. Fed.
62 H7 El Cabaco Spain
65 P6 El Cabildo y la Campana Spain
65 O7 El Cabo de Gata Spain
145 C6 El Cain Arg.
124 P9 El Cajon CA U.S.A.
126 □P10 El Cajón, Represa dam Hond.
137 F3 El Callao Venez.
El Caló Spain see Es Caló
129 G8 El Camotal, Sierra mts Mex.
63 J9 El Campillo de la Jara Spain
El Campo Spain see Campo Lugar
121 G11 El Campo TX U.S.A.
63 J7 El Campo de Peñaranda Spain
63 P9 El Cañavate Spain
128 G1 El Canelo Mex.
147 I4 El Caño Uru.
136 D3 El Canton Venez.
121 E12 El Capulín r. Mex.
128 F1 El Cardito Mex.
136 D2 El Carmelo Venez.
144 D2 El Carmen Jujuy Arg.
146 C1 El Carmen San Juan Arg.
138 E3 El Carmen Beni Bol.
139 F4 El Carmen Santa Cruz Bol.
146 B5 El Carmen Chile
136 B5 El Carmen Ecuador
136 E4 El Carmen Venez.
129 N7 El Carmen, Laguna l. Mex.
67 D9 El Caroche mt. Spain
65 K5 El Carpio Spain
63 L9 El Carpio de Tajo Spain
128 G9 El Carrizal Mex.
63 N7 El Casar Spain
63 L8 El Casar de Escalona Spain
126 G5 El Casco Mex.
67 D7 El Castellar Spain
66 C4 El Castellar reg. Spain
64 G5 El Castillo de las Guardas Spain
127 M10 El Cebú, Cerro mt. Mex.
65 L4 El Centenillo Spain
125 Q9 El Centro CA U.S.A.
139 E4 El Cerro Bol.
64 F5 El Cerro de Andévalo Spain
62 E4 El Chacho Arg.
147 F6 El Chanco, Salina salt pan Arg.
137 E2 El Chaparro Venez.
129 H3 El Chapulín Mex.
147 F6 El Chara Arg.
67 D11 Elche, Embalse de resr Spain
65 O4 Elche de la Sierra Spain
67 D11 Elche-Elx Spain
129 M8 El Chichón Mex.
127 M9 El Chichónal vol. Mex.
129 I5 El Chico, Parque Nacional nat. park Mex.
126 G3 El Chilicote Mex.
53 I5 Elchingen Ger.
110 E4 Elcho WI U.S.A.
206 E1 Elcho Island N.T. Austr.
63 O3 Elciego Spain
128 G5 El Cimatario, Parque Nacional nat. park Mex.
El Coca Ecuador see Coca
136 C3 El Cocuy, Parque Nacional nat. park Col.
65 K3 El Collado hill Spain
128 C6 El Colomo Mex.
128 G8 El Conejo, Sierra mts Mex.
66 J5 El Congost r. Spain
65 O5 El Contador, Puerto de pass Spain
64 H6 El Coronil Spain
129 M8 El Corte r. Mex.
129 L10 El Coyol Mex.
129 L8 El Coyolito Mex.
62 H7 El Cubo de Don Sancho Spain
62 I6 El Cubo de Tierra del Vino Spain
64 G7 El Cuervo Spain
128 B4 El Custodio, Punta pt Mex.
145 C5 El Cuy Arg.
127 P7 El Cuyo Mex.
67 D11 Elda Spain
67 D10 Elda, Embalse de resr Spain
92 B4 Eldama Ravine Kenya
66 L3 El Daró r. Spain
126 C3 El Dátil Mex.
92 D3 El Debb well Eth.
111 O3 Eldee Ont. Can.
50 D4 Eldena Ger.
110 E8 Eldena IL U.S.A.
204 □3 Elder, Mount hill S. Pacific Ocean
110 E5 Elderon WI U.S.A.
123 H12 El Desemboque Mex.
20 □D2 Eldhraun lava field Iceland
126 H3 El Diamante Mex.
136 C2 El Difícil Col.
193 O3 El'dikan Rus. Fed.
48 J5 Eldingen Ger.
128 G8 El Divisadero Mex.
136 B4 El Diviso Col.
147 G6 El Divisorio Arg.
El Djezair Alg. see Alger
126 B2 El Doctor Mex.
120 I6 Eldon MO U.S.A.
120 I4 Eldora IA U.S.A.
118 F6 Eldora NJ U.S.A.
147 G4 El Dorado Arg.
144 G2 Eldorado Arg.
142 C6 Eldorado Brazil
136 D4 El Dorado Col.
126 F5 El Dorado Mex.
121 I9 El Dorado AR U.S.A.
121 G7 El Dorado KS U.S.A.
121 E10 Eldorado TX U.S.A.
137 F3 El Dorado Venez.
125 R6 Eldorado Mountains NV U.S.A.
92 B4 Eldoret Kenya
118 F1 Eldred NY U.S.A.
146 E5 El Durazno Arg.
Elea, Cape Cyprus see Elaia, Cape
116 D10 Eleanor WV U.S.A.
122 I4 Electric Peak MT U.S.A.
78 E4 Elefsina Greece
86 D4 El Eglab plat. Alg.
85 F5 El 'Ein well Sudan
18 G3 Eleja Latvia
65 N7 El Ejido Spain
57 K5 Elek Hungary
183 V2 Elekmonar Rus. Fed.
18 H7 Elektrėnai Lith.
19 V6 Elektrogorsk Rus. Fed.
19 V6 Elektrostal' Rus. Fed.
19 V6 Elektrougli Rus. Fed.
89 G5 Elele Nigeria
92 B3 Elemi Triangle terr. Africa
77 N8 Elena Bulg.
66 E5 Elena, Planas de plain Spain
136 C5 El Encanto Col.
125 P9 El Encinal Baja California Mex.
129 I3 El Encinal Tamaulipas Mex.
129 H2 El Encino Mex.
49 K7 Elend Ger.
146 D3 Eleodoro Lobos Arg.
78 B3 Eleousa Greece
128 G3 El Epazote Mex.
176 C3 Elephanta Caves tourist site Mahar. India
123 K10 Elephant Butte Reservoir NM U.S.A.
212 U2 Elephant Island Antarctica
176 G8 Elephant Pass Sri Lanka
179 N9 Elephant Point Bangl.
91 E6 Éléphants de Kaniama, Réserve des nature res. Dem. Rep. Congo
91 F7 Éléphants de Sakania, Réserve Partielle aux nature res. Dem. Rep. Congo
63 L7 El Escorial Spain
77 L9 Eleshnitsa Bulg.
189 K4 Eleşkirt Turkey
64 G5 El Esparragal, Embalse resr Spain
63 L7 El Espinar Spain
127 O10 El Estor Guat.
67 D12 El Estrecho Spain
147 I2 El Eucaliptus Uru.
130 E1 Eleuthera i. Bahamas
121 C5 Eleva WI U.S.A.
121 J7 Eleven Point r. MO U.S.A.
69 B7 El Fahs Tunisia
El Faiyûm Egypt see Al Fayyūm
87 H2 El Faouar Tunisia
84 E6 El Fasher Sudan
60 D5 El Fendek Morocco
El Ferrol Spain see Ferrol
El Ferrol del Caudillo Spain see Ferrol
49 I10 Elfershausen Ger.
66 L3 El Fluvià r. Spain
66 H5 El Francolí r. Spain
88 B2 El Freïoua well Maur.
63 K3 El Fresno Spain
125 W10 Elfrida AZ U.S.A.
92 D3 El Fud Eth.
126 E4 El Fuerte Mex.
90 F2 El Fula Sudan
21 K5 Elgå Norway
87 F4 El Gaa Taatzebar basin Alg.
65 O5 El Gabar mt. Spain
66 H5 El Gaià r. Spain
92 C4 El Gal waterhole Kenya
128 G5 El Gallo Mex.
65 Q5 El Garrobo Spain
65 I7 El Gastor Spain
129 I1 El Gavilán Mex.
86 D5 El Gçaib well Mali
180 C6 El Geili Sudan
84 D6 El Geneina Sudan
49 H8 Elgershausen (Schauenburg) Ger.
63 P2 Elgeta Spain
85 G6 El Geteina Sudan
85 G6 El Gezira state Sudan
88 E3 El Ghaba Sudan
85 F5 El Ghaba Sudan
90 E2 El Ghalla, Wadi watercourse Sudan
86 C5 El Ghallâouïya well Maur.
88 C2 El Gheddiya Maur.
22 H2 Elgheia hill Norway
El Ghor plain Jordan/West Bank see Al Ghawr
26 J7 Elgin Moray, Scotland U.K.
110 F7 Elgin IL U.S.A.
120 E2 Elgin ND U.S.A.
125 R4 Elgin NV U.S.A.
122 F4 Elgin OR U.S.A.
121 G10 Elgin TX U.S.A.
207 K7 Elgin Down Qld Austr.
193 P3 El'ginskiy Rus. Fed.
85 F5 El Gir well Sudan
El Gîza Egypt see Al Jīzah
128 G4 El Gogorrón, Parque Nacional nat. park Mex.
63 P2 Elgoibar Spain
26 D8 Elgol Highland, Scotland U.K.
87 G3 El Goléa Alg.
98 □3c El Golfo Lanzarote Canary Is
98 □3e El Golfo b. El Hierro Canary Is
126 B2 El Golfo de Santa Clara Mex.
92 B4 Elgon, Mount Uganda
20 U2 Elgoras, Gora hill Rus. Fed.
21 K5 Elgpiggen mt. Norway
66 F3 El Grado Spain
66 F3 El Grado, Embalse de resr Spain
64 E5 El Granado Spain
67 E8 El Grau de Borriana Spain
128 C6 El Grullo Jalisco Mex.
127 J5 El Grullo Tamaulipas Mex.
129 N8 El Guanal Mex.
126 G2 El Guante Mex.
87 H2 El Guetar Tunisia
86 E5 El Guettâra well Mali
193 M3 El'gyay Rus. Fed.
69 A7 El Hadjar Alg.
87 G2 El Hadjira Alg.
87 H2 El Hamma Tunisia
86 C5 El Ḥammâmi reg. Maur.
86 D4 El Hank reg. Alg.
86 C5 El Ḥank esc. Mali/Maur.
69 C7 El Haouaria Tunisia
186 B9 El Hasira Sudan
126 □R13 El Hato del Volcán Panama
85 G6 El Hawata Sudan
El Hazim Jordan see Al Hazīm
98 □3e El Hierro i. Canary Is
129 I4 El Higo Mex.
84 E6 El Hilla Sudan
63 O9 El Hito Spain
87 F3 El Homr Alg.
85 F6 El Homra Sudan
88 C2 El Houeïtat well Maur.
63 L7 El Hoyo de Pinares Spain
146 B5 El Huecu Arg.
85 F5 El Husheim well Sudan
89 H2 Eli well Niger
155 G8 Eliase Maluku Indon.
91 D7 Elias Garcia Angola
130 H4 Elías Piña Dom. Rep.
73 L2 Elice Italy
Elichpur Mahar. India see Achalpur
116 A8 Elida OH U.S.A.
129 J4 El Ídolo, Isla i. Mex.
26 K10 Elie Fife, Scotland U.K.
176 C7 Elikalpeni Bank sea feature India
78 D4 Elikonas mts Greece
90 E5 Elila Dem. Rep. Congo
91 E5 Elila r. Dem. Rep. Congo
96 D10 Elim S. Africa
104 B3 Elim AK U.S.A.
18 J1 Elimäki Fin.
Elimberrum France see Auch
118 A2 Elimsport PA U.S.A.
128 G6 El Infiernillo Mex.
31 J6 Eling Hampshire, England U.K.
90 E5 Elingampangu Dem. Rep. Congo
77 L8 Elin Pelin Bulg.
191 F2 Elin-Yurt Rus. Fed.
73 P4 Elio, Monte d' hill Italy
109 I1 Eliot, Mount Nfld and Lab. Can.
90 E5 Elipa Dem. Rep. Congo
90 D4 Elisabetha Dem. Rep. Congo
Élisabethville Dem. Rep. Congo see Lubumbashi
140 E4 Eliseu Martins Brazil
El Iskandarîya Egypt see Al Iskandarīyah
15 I7 Elista Rus. Fed.
58 H4 Elixhausen Austria
172 C7 Elixku Xinjiang China
117 K8 Elizabeth NJ U.S.A.
116 D9 Elizabeth WV U.S.A.
208 I4 Elizabeth, Mount hill W.A. Austr.
117 □S1 Elizabeth, Mount hill N.B. Can.
115 I7 Elizabeth City NC U.S.A.
206 G5 Elizabeth Creek r. Qld Austr.
117 O7 Elizabeth Islands MA U.S.A.
94 B5 Elizabeth Point Namibia
199 F4 Elizabeth Reef Austr.
116 C12 Elizabethton TN U.S.A.
121 K7 Elizabethtown IL U.S.A.
114 E7 Elizabethtown KY U.S.A.
115 H8 Elizabethtown NC U.S.A.
117 L4 Elizabethtown NY U.S.A.
118 B4 Elizabethtown PA U.S.A.
111 R9 Elizabethville PA U.S.A.
66 B1 Elizalde Spain
66 B1 Elizondo Spain
128 B2 El Jacuixtle Mex.
86 C2 El Jadida Morocco
126 G4 El Jaralito Mex.
62 G8 Eljas Spain
129 H5 El Jazmín Mex.
85 G6 El Jebelein Sudan
87 H2 El Jem Tunisia
126 □P11 El Jicaro Nic.
128 G3 El Jilguero Mex.
129 M8 El Juile Mex.
98 □3e El Julán slope El Hierro Canary Is
106 H5 Elk r. B.C. Can.
55 K2 Ełk Pol.
55 K2 Ełk r. Pol.
118 D6 Elk r. MD U.S.A.
115 D8 Elk r. TN U.S.A.
85 G5 El Kab Sudan
120 J4 Elkader IA U.S.A.
87 H1 El Kala Alg.
180 C6 El Kamlin Sudan
85 G5 El Karabi Sudan
18 I4 Elkas kalns hill Latvia
116 B11 Elkatawa KY U.S.A.
85 G6 El Kawa Sudan
121 F8 Elk City OK U.S.A.
124 J2 Elk Creek CA U.S.A.
206 E6 Elkedra N.T. Austr.
206 F6 Elkedra watercourse N.T. Austr.
86 D2 El Kelaâ des Srarhna Morocco
49 E9 Elkenroth Ger.
92 D3 El Kerê Eth.
106 H5 Elkford B.C. Can.
124 K3 Elk Grove CA U.S.A.
85 F5 El Khandaq Sudan
El Khârga Egypt see Al Khārijah
114 E5 Elkhart IN U.S.A.
121 E7 Elkhart KS U.S.A.
El Khartûm Sudan see Khartoum
El Khenachich esc. Mali see El Khnâchîch
86 D5 El Khnâchîch esc. Mali
110 F7 Elkhorn WI U.S.A.
120 G5 Elkhorn r. NE U.S.A.
116 C11 Elkhorn City KY U.S.A.
191 F2 El'khotovo Rus. Fed.
77 O8 Elkhovo Bulg.
Elki Turkey see Beytüşşebap
115 G7 Elkin NC U.S.A.
116 F10 Elkins WV U.S.A.
118 E4 Elkins Park PA U.S.A.
107 H4 Elk Island National Park Alta Can.
108 D4 Elk Lake Ont. Can.
110 I5 Elk Lake MI U.S.A.
118 D5 Elkland PA U.S.A.
118 D5 Elk Mills MD U.S.A.
122 K6 Elk Mountain WY U.S.A.
118 D5 Elk Neck MD U.S.A.
106 H5 Elko B.C. Can.
122 G6 Elko NV U.S.A.
92 E3 El K'oran Eth.
107 I4 Elk Point Alta Can.
120 G4 Elk Point SD U.S.A.
118 B6 Elkridge MD U.S.A.
110 A4 Elk River MN U.S.A.
El Ksaib Ounane well Mali see El Gçaib
125 X1 Elk Springs CO U.S.A.
116 C11 Elkton KY U.S.A.
118 D5 Elkton MD U.S.A.
116 G10 Elkton VA U.S.A.
116 D10 Elkview WV U.S.A.
129 K9 El Labrador, Cerro mt. Mex.
90 F2 El Lagowa Sudan
23 O1 Ellan Sweden
191 H4 Ellançyu Dağı hill Azer.
Ellas country Europe see Greece
147 G2 El Laurel Arg.
209 C8 Ellavalla W.A. Austr.
115 E9 Ellaville GA U.S.A.
58 D5 Ellbögen Austria
38 D6 Ellé r. France
51 F10 Ellefeld Ger.
105 H2 Ellef Ringnes Island Nunavut Can.
92 C4 El Lēh Eth.
92 D5 El Lein well Kenya
188 E4 Ellek Turkey
209 D13 Elleker W.A. Austr.
84 C5 Elléloyé well Chad
125 V3 Ellen, Mount UT U.S.A.
178 E5 Ellenabad Haryana India
53 I3 Ellenberg Ger.
116 D9 Ellenboro WV U.S.A.
117 K4 Ellenburg Depot NY U.S.A.
117 J10 Ellendale DE U.S.A.
120 F2 Ellendale ND U.S.A.
122 D3 Ellensburg WA U.S.A.
119 G1 Ellenville NY U.S.A.
128 B1 El León, Cerro mt. Mex.
128 G1 El Leoncito Mex.
200 □3a Eller i. Kwajalein Marshall Is
48 I3 Ellerau Ger.
48 I3 Ellerbek Ger.
48 I3 Ellerhoop Ger.
203 C11 Ellery, Lake South I. N.Z.
203 E11 Ellesmere South I. N.Z.
30 G2 Ellesmere Shropshire, England U.K.
203 G10 Ellesmere, Lake South I. N.Z.
105 J2 Ellesmere Island Nunavut Can.
29 L7 Ellesmere Port Cheshire, England U.K.
45 E7 Ellezelles Belgium
38 D6 Elliant France
105 H3 Ellice r. Nunavut Can.
Ellice Island atoll Tuvalu see Funafuti
Ellice Islands country S. Pacific Ocean see Tuvalu
118 B6 Ellicott City MD U.S.A.
116 G6 Ellicottville NY U.S.A.
115 E8 Ellijay GA U.S.A.
128 F7 El Limón Guerrero Mex.
128 B3 El Limón Nayarit Mex.
129 I3 El Limón Tamaulipas Mex.
53 J3 Ellingen Ger.
29 N2 Ellingham Northumberland, England U.K.
29 N3 Ellington Northumberland, England U.K.
206 D4 Elliot N.T. Austr.
97 L7 Elliot S. Africa
207 K5 Elliot, Mount Qld Austr.
97 M7 Elliotdale S. Africa
116 F10 Elliot Knob mt. VA U.S.A.
108 D4 Elliot Lake Ont. Can.
204 F3 Elliot Price Conservation Park nature res. S.A. Austr.
204 □3 Elliott Reef S. Pacific Ocean
122 G4 Ellis ID U.S.A.
120 F6 Ellis KS U.S.A.
204 E5 Elliston S.A. Austr.
116 E11 Elliston VA U.S.A.
121 K10 Ellisville MS U.S.A.
128 G4 El Llano Mex.
62 F2 El Llano Spain
66 I4 El Llobregat r. Spain
58 F4 Ellmau Austria
26 L8 Ellon Aberdeenshire, Scotland U.K.
178 E9 Ellora Caves tourist site Mahar. India
146 D4 El Loro Arg.
22 H3 Ellös Sweden
62 I8 El Losar del Barco Spain
29 P6 Elloughton East Riding of Yorkshire, England U.K.
49 K7 Ellrich Ger.
147 G2 Ellsa Arg.
120 F6 Ellsworth KS U.S.A.
117 □Q4 Ellsworth ME U.S.A.
120 E4 Ellsworth NE U.S.A.
110 B5 Ellsworth WI U.S.A.
212 R1 Ellsworth Land reg. Antarctica
212 S1 Ellsworth Mountains Antarctica
53 I4 Ellwangen (Jagst) Ger.
116 E8 Ellwood City PA U.S.A.
48 F4 Ellwürden Ger.
48 H3 Elm Ger.
70 G2 Elm Switz.
31 M2 Elm Cambridgeshire, England U.K.
55 I1 Ełma r. Pol.
131 I4 El Macao Dom. Rep.
129 H4 El Madroño Mex.
El Maestral reg. Spain see El Maestrazgo
66 E7 El Maestrazgo reg. Spain
86 E5 El Mahia reg. Mali
145 C6 El Maitén Arg.
191 D6 Elmakaya Turkey
190 B2 Elmakuz Dağı mt. Turkey
79 K6 Elmalı Turkey
123 K9 El Malpais National Monument nat. park NM U.S.A.
85 G6 El Manaqil Sudan
136 E4 El Mango Venez.
El Manşûra Egypt see Al Manṣūrah
137 F3 El Manteco Venez.
60 D5 El Manzla Morocco
69 C7 El Marsa Tunisia
128 F1 El Mascarón, Sierra mts Mex.
66 G5 El Masroig Spain
128 F4 El Mastranto Mex.
88 C2 El Mechoual well Maur.
98 □3a El Médano Tenerife Canary Is
126 D5 El Médano Mex.
92 D3 El Medo Eth.
87 G2 El Meghaïer Alg.
90 F2 El Melemm Sudan
88 B2 El Melẓes well Maur.
146 B3 El Melón Chile
58 C5 Elmen Austria
50 D3 Elmenhorst Mecklenburg-Vorpommern Ger.
50 F2 Elmenhorst Mecklenburg-Vorpommern Ger.
50 H2 Elmenhorst Mecklenburg-Vorpommern Ger.
48 J3 Elmenhorst Schleswig-Holstein Ger.
48 K3 Elmenhorst Schleswig-Holstein Ger.
118 E5 Elmer NJ U.S.A.
85 G6 El Mesellemiya Sudan
84 C6 El Messir well Chad
126 E4 El Mezquite Mex.
118 D4 Elmhurst PA U.S.A.
137 F3 El Miamo Venez.
128 G2 El Milagro de Guadalupe Mex.
88 E5 Elmina Ghana
190 D4 El Mina Lebanon
111 N6 Elmira Ont. Can.
109 I4 Elmira P.E.I. Can.
110 J4 Elmira MI U.S.A.
111 R7 Elmira NY U.S.A.
128 C5 El Mirador Mex.
129 J4 El Mirador, Cerro mt. Mex.
125 T8 El Mirage AZ U.S.A.
88 C2 El Moïnane well Maur.
63 M7 El Molar Spain
65 K2 El Molinillo Spain
126 D3 El Molino Mex.
129 I4 El Moral Mex.
65 O5 El Moral Spain
205 J7 Elmore Vic. Austr.
116 B7 Elmore OH U.S.A.
66 H5 El Morell Spain
146 E3 El Morro mt. Arg.
88 C3 El Mraïfig well Maur.
88 D2 El Mreïti well Maur.
88 D2 El Mreyyé reg. Maur.
119 H2 Elmsford NY U.S.A.
48 I3 Elmshorn Ger.
52 D3 Elmstein Ger.
31 N3 Elmswell Suffolk, England U.K.
90 E2 El Muglad Sudan
63 O9 El Mugrón mt. Spain
111 O5 Elmvale Ont. Can.
110 E9 Elmwood IL U.S.A.
110 B5 Elmwood WI U.S.A.
86 D4 El Mzereb well Mali
129 H3 El Naranjo Mex.
128 D7 El Naranjo r. Mex.
20 I5 Elnesvågen Norway
154 B6 El Nido Palawan Phil.
146 C4 El Nihuel Arg.
98 □3f El Oasis Gran Canaria Canary Is
125 Q9 El Oasis Mex.
85 F6 El Obeid Sudan
129 N9 El Ocote, Parque Natural nature res. Mex.
129 H8 El Ocotito Mex.
85 F6 El Odaiya Sudan
146 D5 El Odre Arg.
90 B4 Elogo Congo
111 N6 Elora Ont. Can.
38 C5 Elorn r. France
136 B5 El Oro prov. Ecuador
126 H4 El Oro Coahuila Mex.
128 G6 El Oro México Mex.
63 O2 Elorrio Spain
147 G3 Elortondo Arg.
63 Q3 Elorz Spain
78 E7 Elos Kriti Greece
63 K7 El Oso Spain
57 H5 Előszállás Hungary
128 A2 Elota Mex.
128 A2 Elota r. Mex.
87 G2 El Oued Alg.
129 I5 Eloxochitlán Mex.
125 U9 Eloy AZ U.S.A.
37 M7 Éloyes France
137 F3 El Palmar Venez.
147 H2 El Palmar, Parque Nacional nat. park Arg.
126 G5 El Palmito Mex.
98 □3a El Palm-Mar Tenerife Canary Is
65 K7 El Palo Spain
128 G1 El Pañuelo Mex.
137 F2 El Pao Bolívar Venez.
136 D2 El Pao Cojedes Venez.
128 G8 El Papayo Mex.
155 F5 Elpaputih, Teluk b. Seram Indon.
126 □P11 El Paraíso Hond.
129 L8 El Paraíso Mex.
98 □3d El Paso La Palma Canary Is
110 F9 El Paso IL U.S.A.
El Paso KS U.S.A. see Derby
123 K11 El Paso TX U.S.A.
62 G8 El Payo Spain
65 N2 El Pedernoso Spain
129 I3 El Pedregoso r. Mex.
65 H5 El Pedroso Spain
63 J6 El Pedroso de la Armuña Spain
128 G3 El Peñasco Mex.
144 D2 El Peñón Arg.
146 B3 El Peñón mt. Chile
63 Q9 El Peral Spain
62 I6 El Perdigón Spain
147 F4 El Peregrino Arg.
66 G6 El Perelló Cataluña Spain
67 E9 El Perelló Valencia Spain
48 H2 Elpersbüttel Ger.
27 F5 Elphin Rep. of Ireland
26 F5 Elphin Highland, Scotland U.K.
65 O2 El Picazo Spain
137 F2 El Pilar Venez.
129 I4 El Pinal Mex.
66 G5 El Pinell de Bray Spain
62 I6 El Piñero Spain
147 H2 El Pingo Arg.
126 H3 El Pino, Sierra mts Mex.
144 E2 El Pintado Arg.
64 H4 El Pintado, Embalse resr Spain
66 H5 El pla de Santa Maria Spain
146 B3 El Plomo, Nevado mt. Chile
145 C7 El Pluma Arg.
66 D6 El Pobo Spain
63 Q7 El Pobo de Dueñas Spain
139 E3 El Pocito Bol.
67 E8 El Port Spain
124 M4 El Portal CA U.S.A.
66 L3 El Port de la Selva Spain
136 C1 El Portete b. Col.
146 D2 El Portozuelo Arg.
136 B7 El Portugues Peru
136 D3 El Porvenir Col.
124 P9 El Porvenir Mex.
126 G2 El Porvenir Mex.
126 □T13 El Porvenir Panama
129 H4 El Potosí, Parque Nacional nat. park Mex.
66 J5 El Prat de Llobregat Spain
El Progreso Guat. see Guastatoya
126 □P10 El Progreso Hond.
65 N2 El Provencio Spain
147 H3 El Pueblito Arg.
138 D5 El Puente Bol.
126 □P11 El Puente Nic.
63 N2 El Puente Spain
63 J9 El Puente de Arzobispo Spain
64 G7 El Puerto de Santa María Spain
El Qâhira Egypt see Al Qāhirah
190 D5 El Qasimiye r. Lebanon
El Quds Israel/West Bank see Jerusalem
144 D2 El Quebrachal Arg.
128 G3 El Quelital Mex.
146 B2 Elqui r. Chile
146 B3 El Quisco Chile
128 D7 El Ranchito Michoacán Mex.
129 I1 El Ranchito Tamaulipas Mex.
63 O4 El Rasillo Spain
126 □U13 El Real Panama
64 G5 El Real de la Jara Spain
63 K8 El Real de San Vicente Spain
63 P7 El Recuenco Spain
128 G4 El Refugio Mex.
128 B2 El Regocijo Mex.
121 G8 El Reno OK U.S.A.
146 D3 El Retamo Arg.
128 D2 El Retorno Mex.
144 D2 El Rey, Parque Nacional nat. park Arg.
124 M7 El Rio CA U.S.A.
128 A2 El Roble Mex.
65 K2 El Robledo Spain
64 G6 El Rocío Spain
63 N9 El Romeral Spain
64 E4 El Rompido Spain
64 G5 El Ronquillo Spain
129 N8 El Rosario, Laguna l. Mex.
107 I5 Elrose Sask. Can.
110 D6 Elroy WI U.S.A.
63 O5 El Royo Spain
65 J6 El Rubio Spain
128 G1 El Rucio Nuevo León Mex.
128 E2 El Rucio Zacatecas Mex.
106 C2 Elsa Y.T. Can.
74 H9 Elsa r. Sicilia Italy
71 J8 Elsa r. Italy
127 J4 El Sabinal, Parque Nacional nat. park Mex.
66 C3 El Sabinar Aragón Spain
65 O4 El Sabinar Murcia Spain
126 C2 El Sahuaro Mex.
145 D8 El Salado Arg.
128 G1 El Salado Mex.
67 B9 El Saler Spain
65 P3 El Salobral Spain
128 B2 El Salto Durango Mex.
128 D5 El Salto Jalisco Mex.
127 O11 El Salvador country Central America
144 C2 El Salvador Chile
128 D5 El Salvador Jalisco Mex.
128 G1 El Salvador Zacatecas Mex.
154 F7 El Salvador Mindanao Phil.
136 D3 El Samán de Apure Venez.
66 G4 Els Arcs Spain
111 L1 Elsas Ont. Can.
Elsass reg. France see Alsace
65 I6 El Saucejo Spain
62 G8 El Saugo Spain
126 F3 El Sauz Chihuahua Mex.
128 C4 El Sauz Nayarit Mex.
98 □3a El Sauzal Tenerife Canary Is
124 P10 El Sauzal Mex.
52 G2 Elsava r. Ger.
58 H4 Elsbethen Austria
29 M3 Elsdon Northumberland, England U.K.
48 H4 Elsdorf Niedersachsen Ger.
49 C9 Elsdorf Nordrhein-Westfalen Ger.
48 I2 Elsdorf-Westermühlen Ger.
49 G6 Else r. Ger.
131 I4 El Seibo Dom. Rep.
45 J8 Elsenborn Belgium
53 L4 Elsendorf Ger.
52 G2 Elsenfeld Ger.
52 F3 Elsenz r. Ger.
66 I2 El Serrat Andorra
206 D3 Elsey N.T. Austr.
48 J6 Elsfleth Ger.
206 D2 El Sharana N.T. Austr.
110 J6 Elsie MI U.S.A.
124 O8 Elsinore CA U.S.A.
125 T3 Elsinore UT U.S.A.
124 O8 Elsinore Lake CA U.S.A.
45 I7 Elsloo Neth.
118 D5 Elsmere DE U.S.A.
20 P2 Elsnes Norway
51 G7 Elsnig Ger.
51 F7 Elsnigk Ger.
126 H4 El Socorro Mex.
66 G5 El Solerás Spain
146 C4 El Sosneado Arg.
44 I4 Elspeet Neth.
66 I4 Els Prats de Rei Spain
44 I5 Elst Gelderland Neth.
44 H5 Elst Utrecht Neth.
31 K5 Elstead Surrey, England U.K.
51 G7 Elster Ger.
51 F9 Elsterberg Ger.
51 I8 Elsterniederung und Westliche Oberlausitzer Heide park Ger.
51 I8 Elsterwerda Ger.
31 L4 Elstree Hertfordshire, England U.K.
126 F3 El Sueco Mex.
85 G2 El Suweis Egypt
146 B3 El Tabo Chile
129 J5 El Tajín tourist site Mex.
136 C3 El Tama, Parque Nacional nat. park Venez.
87 H1 El Tarf Alg.
69 B7 El Tarf prov. Alg.
128 F6 El Tecolote, Cerro mt. Mex.
128 C2 El Tecuán, Parque Nacional nat. park Mex.
147 G4 El Tejar Arg.
62 H4 El Teleno mt. Spain
129 I1 El Temascal Mex.
59 N5 Eltendorf Austria
129 H6 El Tepozteco, Parque Nacional nat. park Mex.
66 L3 El Ter r. Spain
51 G9 Elterlein Ger.
202 I6 Eltham North I. N.Z.
63 L8 El Tiemblo Spain
137 E2 El Tigre Venez.
127 N9 El Tigre, Parque Nacional nat. park Guat.
53 J2 Eltmann Ger.
63 O9 El Toboso Spain
136 D2 El Tocuyo Venez.
144 C3 El Tofo Coquimbo Chile
146 B2 El Tololo Chile
27 F8 Elton Rep. of Ireland
182 B3 El'ton Rus. Fed.
31 L2 Elton Cambridgeshire, England U.K.
29 L7 Elton Cheshire, England U.K.
182 B3 El'ton, Ozero l. Rus. Fed.
122 E3 Eltopia WA U.S.A.
62 I8 El Torno Spain
146 B5 El Toro Biobío Chile
136 C2 El Totumo Venez.
147 G3 El Trébol Arg.
129 H9 El Treinta Mex.
126 F4 El Tren Mex.
147 H4 El Trigo Arg.
65 K2 El Trincheto Spain
147 G4 El Triunfo Arg.
126 D6 El Triunfo Mex.
131 □7 El Tucuche hill Trin. and Tob.
128 B5 El Tuito Mex.
64 F6 El Tumbalejo Spain
144 D2 El Tunal Arg.
136 D3 El Tuparro, Parque Nacional nat. park Col.
145 B8 El Turbio Chile
66 G3 El Turbón mt. Spain
49 F10 Eltville am Rhein Ger.
88 E5 Elubo Ghana
85 G3 El Uqşur Egypt
176 G4 Eluru Andhra Prad. India
85 G5 El 'Uteishan well Sudan
18 J3 Elva Estonia
126 E3 El Vallecillo Mex.
26 I12 Elvanfoot South Lanarkshire, Scotland U.K.
64 E3 Elvas Port.
20 Q2 Elvebakken Norway
20 N2 Elvegard Norway
129 H9 El Velador, Parque Nacional nat. park Mex.
38 F6 Elven France
128 C4 El Venado Mex.
66 I5 El Vendrell Spain
129 J1 El Verde Chico Mex.
67 F10 El Verger Spain
118 D4 Elverson PA U.S.A.
21 K6 Elverum Norway
65 L2 El Vicario, Embalse de resr Spain
136 C3 El Viejo mt. Col.
126 □P11 El Viejo Nic.
128 C4 El Viejo, Cerro mt. Mex.
63 M7 El Villar, Embalse de resr Spain
29 P6 Elvington York, England U.K.
136 D5 Elvira Brazil
208 J4 Elvire r. W.A. Austr.
208 I5 Elvire Aboriginal Reserve W.A. Austr.
65 J4 El Viso Spain
64 H6 El Viso del Alcor Spain
20 U2 Elvnes Norway
70 E5 Elvo r. Italy
146 D3 El Volcán Arg.
146 B3 El Volcán Chile
92 D4 El Wak Kenya
110 F8 Elwood IL U.S.A.
114 E5 Elwood IN U.S.A.
120 F5 Elwood NE U.S.A.
118 F5 Elwood NJ U.S.A.
92 A2 El Wurl watercourse Sudan
85 F6 El Wuz Sudan
49 K8 Elxleben Ger.
31 M3 Ely Cambridgeshire, England U.K.
30 F5 Ely Cardiff, Wales U.K.
110 C2 Ely MN U.S.A.
125 R2 Ely NV U.S.A.
31 M3 Ely, Isle of reg. England U.K.
136 D3 El Yagual Venez.
92 C3 El Yibo well Kenya
116 C7 Elyria OH U.S.A.
119 R9 Elysburg PA U.S.A.
49 F10 Elz Ger.
52 D5 Elz r. Ger.
129 J9 El Zacatón, Cerro mt. Mex.
52 E5 Elzach Ger.
126 G5 El Zape Mex.
49 I6 Elze Ger.
49 I6 Elze (Wedemark) Ger.
200 □5 Émaé i. Vanuatu
40 H2 Émagny France
18 H3 Emajõgi r. Estonia
184 F3 Emām Qolī Iran
185 F3 Emāmrūd Iran
185 M3 Emām Ṣaḥēb Afgh.
184 H3 Emām Taqī Iran
23 M4 Emån r. Sweden
97 Q2 Emangusi S. Africa
200 □5 Émao i. Vanuatu
E. Martínez Mex. see Emiliano Martínez
142 A3 Emas, Parque Nacional das nat. park Brazil
183 T4 Emazar Kazakh.
183 H3 Emba Kazakh.
182 E4 Emba r. Kazakh.
97 N2 Embalenhle S. Africa
144 D1 Embarcación Arg.

Embarras Portage to Essonne
261

07 I3 Embarras Portage Alta Can.
0 B2 Embarrass MN U.S.A.
Embetsu Japan see Enbetsu
Embi Kazakh. see Emba
56 □ Embiah, Mount hill Sing.
53 Q7 Embid Spain
53 Q6 Embid de Ariza Spain
Embira r. Brazil see Envira
29 N2 Embleton Northumberland, England U.K.
26 I7 Embo Highland, Scotland U.K.
Émbonas Rodos Greece see Emponas
90 C4 Embondo Dem. Rep. Congo
42 D3 Emborcação, Represa de resr Brazil
Emborion Greece see Emporeio
52 F7 Embrach Switz.
18 D5 Embreeville PA U.S.A.
17 J3 Embrun Ont. Can.
41 I7 Embrun France
48 J4 Embsen Ger.
42 D5 Embu Brazil
92 C5 Embu Kenya
75 □1 Embudhu i. S. Male Maldives
75 □1 Embudhu Finolhu i. S. Male Maldives
91 C9 Embundo Angola
48 D4 Emden Ger.
79 I6 Emecik Turkey
Emei Sichuan China see Emeishan
70 D4 Emeishan Sichuan China
70 D4 Emei Shan mt. Sichuan China
83 S4 Emel' r. Kazakh.
07 L7 Emerald Qld Austr.
05 J7 Emerald Vic. Austr.
18 D3 Emerald PA U.S.A.
05 G2 Emerald Isle i. N.W.T. Can.
09 H2 Emeril Nfld and Lab. Can.
38 D3 Emero r. Bol.
07 L5 Emerson Man. Can.
16 B10 Emerson KY U.S.A.
25 U3 Emery UT U.S.A.
79 K3 Emet Turkey
97 O1 eMgwenya S. Africa
24 M3 Emigrant Basin Wilderness nature res. CA U.S.A.
24 L2 Emigrant Gap CA U.S.A.
22 F6 Emigrant Pass NV U.S.A.
25 Q4 Emigrant Valley NV U.S.A.
97 P1 eMijindini S. Africa
84 C5 Emi Koussi mt. Chad
06 G2 Emile r. N.W.T. Can.
47 G2 Emilia Arg.
26 G5 Emiliano Martínez Mex.
27 N9 Emiliano Zapata Chiapas Mex.
28 D1 Emiliano Zapata Durango Mex.
28 D2 Emiliano Zapata Zacatecas Mex.
70 K7 Emilia-Romagna admin. reg. Italy
47 G4 Emilio Ayarza Arg.
29 K6 Emilio Carranza Veracruz Mex.
28 D1 Emilio Carranza Zacatecas Mex.
47 H2 Emilio R. Coni Arg.
70 C4 Emilius, Monte mt. Italy
72 F3 Emin Xinjiang China
77 P8 Emine, Nos pt Bulg.
21 J7 Eminence MO U.S.A.
72 F3 Emin He r. China
77 P8 Eminska Planina hills Bulg.
79 M3 Emirdağ Turkey
79 M4 Emir Dağı mt. Turkey
79 K4 Emirhisar Turkey
05 K9 Emita Tas. Austr.
48 I2 Emkendorf Ger.
16 F7 Emlenton PA U.S.A.
48 C5 Emlichheim Ger.
27 F8 Emly Rep. of Ireland
23 L5 Emmaboda Sweden
31 □10 Emmastad Curaçao Neth. Antilles
18 F3 Emmaste Estonia
19 T5 Emmaus Rus. Fed.
18 E3 Emmaus PA U.S.A.
05 M3 Emmaville N.S.W. Austr.
70 D1 Emme r. Switz.
44 I3 Emmeloord Neth.
48 G1 Emmelsbüll-Horsbüll Ger.
49 E10 Emmelshausen Ger.
44 K3 Emmen Neth.
52 E7 Emmen Switz.
52 D5 Emmendingen Ger.
70 D1 Emmental reg. Switz.
49 H6 Emmer r. Ger.
44 L3 Emmer-Compascuum Neth.
44 K3 Emmer-Erfscheidenveen Neth.
49 B7 Emmerich Ger.
53 K5 Emmering Ger.
53 N5 Emmerting Ger.
07 J8 Emmet Qld Austr.
20 H4 Emmetsburg IA U.S.A.
22 F5 Emmett ID U.S.A.
16 C6 Emmett MI U.S.A.
76 E5 Emmiganuru Andhra Prad. India
16 H9 Emmitsburg MD U.S.A.
18 C6 Emmorton MD U.S.A.
31 M2 Emneth Norfolk, England U.K.
07 M5 Emo Ont. Can.
57 J4 Emőd Hungary
21 H9 Emory TX U.S.A.
21 D11 Emory Peak TX U.S.A.
88 B4 Empada Guinea-Bissau
26 D4 Empalme Mex.
28 G5 Empalme Escobedo Mex.
61 E4 Empanadas mt. Spain
97 P4 Empangeni S. Africa
44 F2 Empedrado Arg.
46 A4 Empedrado Chile
44 H5 Empel Neth.
16 G2 Emperor Seamount Chain sea feature N. Pacific Ocean
16 G2 Emperor Trough sea feature N. Pacific Ocean
38 C5 Empexa, Salar de salt flat Bol.
52 F5 Empfingen Ger.
10 H5 Empire MI U.S.A.
55 F8 Emplawas Maluku Indon.
71 J8 Empoli Italy
79 I6 Emponas Rodos Greece
79 G6 Emporeio Greece
20 G6 Emporia KS U.S.A.
16 H12 Emporia VA U.S.A.
16 G7 Emporium PA U.S.A.
07 I5 Empress Alta Can.
95 F3 Empress Mine Zimbabwe
45 H8 Emptinne Belgium
Empty Quarter des. Saudi Arabia see Rub' al Khālī
41 F6 Empurany France
84 H4 'Emrānī Iran
48 D4 Ems r. Ger.
49 D6 Emsbüren Ger.
11 O4 Emsdale Ont. Can.
49 E6 Emsdetten Ger.
48 E4 Ems-Jade-Kanal canal Ger.
53 J2 Emskirchen Ger.
48 D5 Emsland reg. Ger.
44 I4 Emst Neth.
48 F5 Emstek Ger.
31 K6 Emsworth Hampshire, England U.K.
97 O1 Emthonjeni S. Africa
48 G5 Emtinghausen Ger.
07 H4 Emu Creek r. Qld Austr.
18 J3 Emumägi hill Estonia
07 M7 Emu Park Qld Austr.
62 D2 Emur He r. China
62 C2 Emur Shan mts China
27 I4 Emyvale Rep. of Ireland
97 N2 Emzinoni S. Africa
66 F5 Ena Japan
20 L5 Enafors Sweden
36 D4 Enambú Col.
37 F3 Enamuna Brazil
21 N6 Enånger Sweden
53 I7 Enarotali Papua Indon.
66 G5 Ena-san mt. Japan
83 Q3 Enbek Kazakh.
164 S2 Enbetsu Japan
66 F6 Encanadé mt. Spain
141 B9 Encantadas, Serra das hills Brazil
129 N9 Encantado r. Mex.
154 C4 Encanto, Cape Luzon Phil.
128 E4 Encarnación Mex.
139 G6 Encarnación Para.
42 I5 Enchanet, Barrage d' dam France
88 E5 Enchi Ghana
65 P2 Encina r. Spain
66 C5 Encinacorba Spain
121 F11 Encinal TX U.S.A.
65 L3 Encinas mt. Spain
63 J7 Encinas de Abajo Spain
64 F4 Encinasola Spain
65 K6 Encinas Reales Spain
62 G4 Encinedo Spain
124 O8 Encinitas CA U.S.A.
123 L9 Encino NM U.S.A.
63 P4 Enciso Spain
146 D3 Encón Arg.
136 C2 Encontrados Venez.
204 G6 Encounter Bay S.A. Austr.
141 E5 Encruzilhada Brazil
141 B9 Encruzilhada do Sul Brazil
57 K3 Encs Hungary
57 L4 Encsencs Hungary
106 E4 Endako B.C. Can.
156 E3 Endau r. Malaysia
152 B6 Endau-Rompin National Park Malaysia
155 B8 Ende Flores Indon.
155 B8 Ende i. Indon.
207 H1 Endeavour Strait Qld Austr.
22 G6 Endelave i. Denmark
199 I2 Enderbury i. Kiribati
106 G5 Enderby B.C. Can.
31 J2 Enderby Leicestershire, England U.K.
214 L9 Enderby Abyssal Plain sea feature Southern Ocean
208 D6 Enderby Island W.A. Austr.
213 D2 Enderby Land reg. Antarctica
67 K9 Enderrocat, Cap c. Spain
104 C3 Endicott Mountains AK U.S.A.
138 D2 Endimari r. Brazil
70 H4 Endine, Lago di l. Italy
52 D5 Endingen Ger.
18 J3 Endla riiklik looduskaitseala nature res. Estonia
89 I6 Endom Cameroon
57 I3 Endrefalva Hungary
62 I7 Endrinal Spain
43 H10 Endron, Pique d' mt. France
111 R7 Endwell NY U.S.A.
18 I4 Endzele Latvia
138 B2 Ene r. Peru
209 C10 Eneabba W.A. Austr.
22 H2 Enebakk Norway
71 L4 Enego Italy
17 R9 Enem Rus. Fed.
137 G3 Enemutu Brazil
182 H2 Energetik Rus. Fed.
147 H6 Energía Arg.
Energodar Ukr. see Enerhodar
17 N6 Enerhodar Ukr.
56 G4 Enese Hungary
216 G6 Enewetak atoll Marshall Is
79 H2 Enez Turkey
190 D4 Enfe Lebanon
62 C3 Enfesta Spain
91 A8 Enfião, Ponta do pt Angola
87 H1 Enfidaville Tunisia
109 I4 Enfield N.S. Can.
31 L4 Enfield Greater London, England U.K.
115 I7 Enfield NC U.S.A.
110 I3 Engadine MI U.S.A.
20 J5 Engan Norway
131 I4 Engaño, Cabo c. Dom. Rep.
215 M3 Engaño, Cape Luzon Phil.
164 U2 Engaru Japan
97 L7 Engcobo S. Africa
49 D6 Engden Ger.
190 D7 En Gedi Israel
70 E2 Engelberg Switz.
115 J8 Engelhard NC U.S.A.
59 O3 Engelhartstetten Austria
59 I2 Engelhartszell Austria
48 G5 Engeln Ger.
182 B2 Engel's Rus. Fed.
53 N5 Engelsberg Ger.
44 G2 Engelschmangat sea chan. Neth.
51 F8 Engelsdorf Ger.
49 D9 Engelskirchen Ger.
44 J2 Engelsmanplaat i. Neth.
52 F6 Engen Ger.
142 A5 Engenheiro Beltrão Brazil
143 F2 Engenheiro Navarro Brazil
204 E3 Engenina watercourse S.A. Austr.
49 G6 Enger Ger.
21 K6 Engerdal Norway
50 D5 Engersen Ger.
48 G1 Enge-Sande Ger.
156 E7 Enggano i. Indon.
85 H5 Enghershatu mt. Eritrea
45 F7 Enghien Belgium
106 C3 Engineer B.C. Can.
45 H7 Engis Belgium
157 I4 Engkilili Sarawak Malaysia
29 O8 England admin. div. U.K.
124 K2 Englebright Reservoir CA U.S.A.
109 K3 Englee Nfld and Lab. Can.
36 G3 Englefontaine France
108 E4 Englehart Ont. Can.
115 F12 Englewood FL U.S.A.
119 H3 Englewood NJ U.S.A.
116 A9 Englewood OH U.S.A.
107 M5 English r. Ont. Can.
114 D6 English IN U.S.A.
98 □2a English Bay Ascension S. Atlantic Ocean
English Bazar W. Bengal India see Ingraj Bazar
118 A2 English Center PA U.S.A.
25 G7 English Channel France/U.K.
212 S2 English Coast Antarctica
118 F6 English Creek NJ U.S.A.
131 □2 English Harbour Town Antigua and Barbuda
119 G4 Englishtown NJ U.S.A.
43 G10 Engomer France
14 F2 Engozero Rus. Fed.
52 G5 Engstingen Ger.
67 D10 Enguera Spain
67 D10 Enguera, Serra de mts Spain
63 Q9 Enguidanos Spain
18 G4 Engure Latvia
18 G4 Engures ezers l. Latvia
191 C3 Enguri r. Georgia
190 D8 'En Hazeva Israel
97 O5 Enhlalakahle S. Africa
121 G7 Enid OK U.S.A.
200 □3b Enigu i. Majuro Marshall Is
52 G5 Eningen unter Achalm Ger.
78 D3 Enipefs r. Greece
164 S4 Eniwa Japan
Eniwetok atoll Marshall Is see Enewetak
65 N7 Enix Spain
193 P4 Enkan, Mys pt Rus. Fed.
Enkeldoorn Zimbabwe see Chivhu
37 O5 Enkenbach Ger.
44 H3 Enkhuizen Neth.
52 C2 Enkirch Ger.
18 D1 Enklinge Åland Fin.
23 N2 Enköping Sweden
129 J4 Enmedio, Arrecife de rf Mex.
74 G8 Enna Sicilia Italy
74 H8 Enna prov. Sicilia Italy
70 H4 Enna r. Italy
107 K2 Ennadai Lake Nunavut Can.
85 F6 En Nahud Sudan
87 E3 En Namous, Oued watercourse Alg.
89 H3 E-n-Nassamé well Niger
84 C6 Enné, Ouadi watercourse Chad
84 D5 Ennedi, Massif mts Chad
27 H6 Ennell, Lough l. Rep. of Ireland
49 D8 Ennepetal Ger.
97 L2 Ennerdale S. Africa
29 K4 Ennerdale Water l. England U.K.
84 B4 Enneri Achelouma watercourse Niger
84 C5 Enneri Maro watercourse Chad
84 B4 Enneri Ouri watercourse Chad
84 C4 Enneri Yebigué watercourse Chad
37 L5 Ennery France
130 G4 Ennery Haiti
40 C5 Ennezat France
205 J3 Enngonia N.S.W. Austr.
49 F7 Ennigerloh Ger.
185 P5 Enninabad Pak.
120 D3 Enning SD U.S.A.
27 E7 Ennis Rep. of Ireland
122 I4 Ennis MT U.S.A.
121 G9 Ennis TX U.S.A.
27 I7 Enniscorthy Rep. of Ireland
27 E9 Enniskean Rep. of Ireland
27 J6 Enniskerry Rep. of Ireland
27 G4 Enniskillen Northern Ireland U.K.
27 D7 Ennistymon Rep. of Ireland
200 □3a Enniwetak i. Kwajalein Marshall Is
190 D5 Enn Nâqoûra Lebanon
59 J3 Enns Austria
59 K3 Enns r. Austria
59 J4 Ennstaler Alpen mts Austria
200 □3a Ennubuj i. Kwajalein Marshall Is
200 □3a Ennumennet i. Kwajalein Marshall Is
176 G6 Ennur Tamil Nadu India
200 □3a Ennylabagan i. Kwajalein Marshall Is
20 U5 Eno Fin.
125 S4 Enoch UT U.S.A.
156 E5 Enok Sumatera Indon.
118 B4 Enola PA U.S.A.
20 T5 Enonkoski Fin.
20 Q2 Enontekiö Fin.
115 G8 Enoree r. SC U.S.A.
117 M4 Enosburg Falls VT U.S.A.
171 I7 Enping Guangdong China
155 A5 Enrekang Sulawesi Indon.
154 C3 Enrile Luzon Phil.
130 H5 Enriquillo Dom. Rep.
130 H4 Enriquillo, Lago de l. Dom. Rep.
44 I3 Ens Neth.
205 K7 Ensay Vic. Austr.
44 K4 Enschede Neth.
53 L3 Ensdorf Ger.
49 F8 Ense Ger.
147 I4 Ensenada Arg.
126 A2 Ensenada Baja California Mex.
126 E6 Ensenada Baja California Sur Mex.
131 □1 Ensenada Puerto Rico
136 B3 Ensenada de Utria nat. park Col.
52 C3 Ensheim Ger.
170 G3 Enshi Hubei China
166 G7 Enshū-nada g. Japan
37 N8 Ensisheim France
115 D10 Ensley FL U.S.A.
31 J4 Enstone Oxfordshire, England U.K.
41 G10 Ensuès-la-Redonne France
92 B4 Entebbe Uganda
44 K4 Enter Neth.
26 I12 Enterkinfoot Dumfries and Galloway, Scotland U.K.
106 G2 Enterprise N.W.T. Can.
111 R5 Enterprise Ont. Can.
115 E10 Enterprise AL U.S.A.
122 F4 Enterprise OR U.S.A.
125 S4 Enterprise UT U.S.A.
154 B6 Enterprise Point Palawan Phil.
106 E4 Entiako Provincial Park B.C. Can.
157 J4 Entimau, Bukit hill Malaysia
70 E2 Entlebuch Switz.
70 C7 Entracque Italy
64 C5 Entradas Port.
41 F8 Entraigues-sur-la-Sorgue France
40 C2 Entrains-sur-Nohain France
39 J6 Entrammes France
106 G4 Entrance Alta Can.
206 B3 Entrance Island N.T. Austr.
41 J8 Entraunes France
41 B7 Entraygues-sur-Truyère France
200 □5 Entrecasteaux, Récifs d' rf New Caledonia
99 □1c Entre-Deux Réunion
43 D6 Entre-deux-Mers reg. France
63 O7 Entrepeñas, Embalse de resr Spain
147 H3 Entre Ríos prov. Arg.
138 D5 Entre Ríos Bol.
140 F4 Entre Rios Bahia Brazil
137 H6 Entre Rios Pará Brazil
143 E4 Entre Rios de Minas Brazil
41 J9 Entrevaux France
64 C2 Entroncamento Port.
128 G1 Entronque San Roberto Mex.
94 E3 Entuba Zimbabwe
97 P4 Entumeni S. Africa
89 G5 Enugu Nigeria
89 G5 Enugu state Nigeria
193 T3 Enurmino Rus. Fed.
66 I2 Envalira, Port d' pass Andorra
62 E9 Envendos Port.
36 B4 Envermeu France
136 C3 Envigado Col.
138 C1 Envira Brazil
138 C1 Envira r. Brazil
91 E5 Enyamba Dem. Rep. Congo
57 H5 Enying Hungary
203 F10 Enys, Mount South I. N.Z.
52 G3 Enz r. Ger.
70 J6 Enza r. Italy
167 I4 Enzan Japan
59 O3 Enzersdorf an der Fischa Austria
52 E4 Enzklösterle Ger.
200 □5 Eo atoll Îles Loyauté New Caledonia
62 F2 Eo r. Spain
62 F1 Eo, Ría del inlet Spain
116 C11 Eolia KY U.S.A.
Eooa i. Tonga see 'Eua
26 D5 Eoropaidh Western Isles, Scotland U.K.
39 L3 Épaignes France
94 C4 Epako Namibia
70 B2 Epalignes Switz.
129 I5 Epazoyucan Mex.
44 I4 Epe Neth.
89 F5 Epe Nigeria
147 F5 Epecuén, Lago l. Arg.
90 C4 Epéna Congo
57 J5 Eperjes Hungary
36 G5 Épernay France
36 C6 Épernon France
52 F5 Epfendorf Ger.
Ephesus tourist site Turkey see Efes
125 U2 Ephraim UT U.S.A.
118 C4 Ephrata PA U.S.A.
122 E3 Ephrata WA U.S.A.
200 □5 Epi i. Vanuatu
Epidamnus Albania see Durrës
78 E5 Epidavros tourist site Greece
78 E6 Epidavrou Limiras, Kolpos b. Greece
36 C8 Épieds-en-Beauce France
41 I6 Épierre France
61 F2 Épila Spain
40 F3 Épinac France
37 L7 Épinal France
137 G3 Epira Guyana
Epirus admin. reg. Greece see Ipeiros
40 D2 Epiry France
190 A4 Episkopi Cyprus
190 A4 Episkopi Bay Cyprus
Episkopis, Kolpos b. Cyprus see Episkopi Bay
128 G5 Epitacio Huerta Mex.
40 E1 Époisses France
73 L6 Epomeo, Monte vol. Italy
52 B3 Eppelborn Ger.
52 F3 Eppelheim Ger.
52 D3 Eppenbrunn Ger.
51 H9 Eppendorf Ger.
52 F2 Eppertshausen Ger.
36 F4 Eppeville France
31 M4 Epping Essex, England U.K.
117 □N5 Epping NH U.S.A.
52 F3 Eppingen Ger.
207 K7 Epping Forest National Park Qld Austr.
53 J5 Eppishausen Ger.
49 F10 Eppstein Ger.
30 F3 Eppynt, Mynydd hills Wales U.K.
31 L5 Epsom Surrey, England U.K.
36 C5 Epte r. France
39 M6 Épuisay France
146 E5 Epu-pel Arg.
145 C6 Epuyén Arg.
29 P6 Epworth North Lincolnshire, England U.K.
184 E6 Eqlīd Iran
90 D4 Équateur prov. Dem. Rep. Congo
89 H6 Equatorial Guinea country Africa
137 F3 Equeipa Venez.
38 H2 Équeurdreville-Hainneville France
71 J8 Era r. Italy
207 J9 Erac Creek watercourse Qld Austr.
71 N4 Eraclea Italy
71 N4 Eraclea Mare Italy
88 E2 Erakchiouene well Mali
66 B1 Erakurri mt. Spain
178 G8 Eran Madh. Prad. India
154 A7 Eran Palawan Phil.
154 A7 Eran Bay Palawan Phil.
63 O2 Erandio Spain
178 E9 Erandol Mahar. India
97 M1 Erasmia S. Africa
159 D7 Erawan National Park Thai.
70 G4 Erba Italy
85 H4 Erba, Jebel mt. Sudan
188 H3 Erbaa Turkey
52 H5 Erbach Baden-Württemberg Ger.
52 G2 Erbach Hessen Ger.
53 M2 Erbendorf Ger.
52 C2 Erbeskopf hill Ger.
70 F5 Erbognone r. Italy
38 I6 Erbray France
190 B3 Ercan airport Cyprus
43 G10 Ercé France
189 K4 Erçek Turkey
146 A6 Ercilla Chile
189 K4 Erciş Turkey
188 G4 Erciyes Dağı mt. Turkey
57 H4 Ercsi Hungary
57 H4 Érd Hungary
Erdaobaihe Jilin China see Baihe
168 C9 Erdaogou Qinghai China
162 E7 Erdao Jiang r. China
51 E8 Erdeborn Ger.
79 I2 Erdek Turkey
188 G5 Erdemli Turkey
168 F2 Erdenet Hövsgöl Mongolia
168 I2 Erdenet Orhon Mongolia
168 G3 Erdenetsogt Bayanhongor Mongolia
168 J5 Erdenetsogt Ömnögovĭ Mongolia
38 E6 Erdeven France
53 L5 Erding Ger.
53 L5 Erdinger Moos marsh Ger.
51 H9 Erdmannsdorf Ger.
15 I7 Erdniyevskiy Rus. Fed.
63 P3 Erdoñana Spain
38 H7 Erdre r. France
53 K5 Erdweg Ger.
136 C5 Eré Peru
142 A6 Eré, Campos hills Brazil
38 G5 Éréac France
137 E3 Erebato r. Venez.
213 L1 Erebus, Mount vol. Antarctica
189 L8 Erech tourist site Iraq
141 B8 Erechim Brazil
169 N2 Ereentsav Mongolia
188 G5 Ereğli Konya Turkey
188 E3 Ereğli Zonguldak Turkey
Erego Moz. see Errego
74 G8 Erei, Monti mts Sicilia Italy
78 A3 Ereikoussa i. Greece
155 C6 Ereke Sulawesi Indon.
128 G7 Eréndira Mex.
172 G5 Erenhaberga Shan mts China
169 M5 Erenhot Nei Mongol China
76 I8 Erenik r. Serb. and Mont.
191 D7 Erentepe Turkey
184 G5 Eresk Iran
63 K6 Eresma r. Spain
79 G3 Eresos Lesvos Greece
78 E4 Eretria Greece
Erevan Armenia see Yerevan
147 G3 Erézcano Arg.
48 H2 Erfde Ger.
97 K4 Erfenis Dam resr S. Africa
97 K4 Erfenis Dam Nature Reserve S. Africa
86 D3 Erfoud Morocco
49 C9 Erftstadt Ger.
51 D9 Erfurt Ger.
189 I4 Ergani Turkey
86 D5 Erg Atouila des. Mali
87 E5 Erg Azennezal des. Alg.
87 H4 Erg Bourarhet des. Alg.
86 D5 'Erg Chech des. Alg./Mali
87 H4 Erg d' Amer des. Alg.
84 C6 Erg du Djourab des. Chad
89 H2 Erg du Ténéré des. Niger
169 K5 Ergel Mongolia
86 D5 'Erg el AŞmar des. Mali
87 E4 Erg el Krebs des. Alg.
18 I4 Ērģeme Latvia
79 H2 Ergene r. Turkey
53 I2 Ergersheim Ger.
86 E4 Erg labès des. Alg.
86 D4 Erg Iguidi des. Alg./Maur.
87 E5 'Erg I-n-Sâkâne des. Mali
87 G4 Erg Issaouane des. Alg.
87 H5 Erg Kilian des. Alg.
18 I5 Ērgļi Latvia
87 F4 Erg Mehedjibat des. Alg.
53 M4 Ergolding Ger.
53 M4 Ergoldsbach Ger.
87 F4 Erg Tassedjefit des. Alg.
87 G4 Erg Tihodaïne des. Alg.
162 F5 Ergu Heilong. China
38 C5 Ergué-Gabéric France
90 B2 Erguig r. Chad
169 Q1 Ergun Nei Mongol China
Ergun He r. China/Rus. Fed. see Argun'
Ergun Youqi Nei Mongol China see Ergun
170 C6 Er Hai l. China
53 N5 Erharting Ger.
85 H5 Erheib Sudan
163 D8 Erhulai Liaoning China
62 I4 Eria r. Spain
26 G6 Eriboll Highland, Scotland U.K.
26 G6 Eriboll, Loch inlet Scotland U.K.
44 K3 Erica Neth.
74 D7 Erice Sicilia Italy
63 Q3 Erice Spain
64 A3 Ericeira Port.
26 J9 Ericht r. Scotland U.K.
26 H9 Ericht, Loch l. Scotland U.K.
107 L5 Erickson Man. Can.
121 H7 Erie KS U.S.A.
116 E6 Erie PA U.S.A.
111 N7 Erie, Lake Can./U.S.A.
Erieddu i. N. Male Maldives see Eriyadhu
88 D2 'Erîgât des. Mali
192 D2 Erik Eriksenstretet sea chan. Svalbard
Erikoússa i. Greece see Ereikoussa
107 L5 Eriksdale Man. Can.
23 L5 Eriksmåla Sweden
65 I4 Erillas hill Spain
Erímanthos Óros mts Greece see Erymanthos
164 U4 Erimo Japan
164 U5 Erimo-misaki c. Japan
111 N6 Erin Ont. Can.
115 D7 Erin TN U.S.A.
53 O5 Ering Ger.
23 L5 Eringsboda Sweden
131 □7 Erin Point Trin. and Tob.
26 B8 Eriskay i. Scotland U.K.
52 H6 Eriskirch Ger.
26 C6 Erisort, Loch inlet Scotland U.K.
31 N3 Eriswell Suffolk, England U.K.
70 D1 Eriswil Switz.
Erithraí Greece see Erythres
Erithropótamos r. Greece see Erydropotamos
85 H6 Eritrea country Africa
175 □1 Eriyadhu i. N. Male Maldives
Eriyadu i. N. Male Maldives see Eriyadhu
183 O8 Erkech-Tam Kyrg.
49 B8 Erkelenz Ger.
36 D2 Erkelsbrugge France
23 O2 Erken l. Sweden
191 C1 Erken-Shakhar Rus. Fed.
53 I5 Erkheim Ger.
79 L4 Erkmen Turkey
51 I6 Erkner Ger.
186 C6 Erkowit Sudan
58 F4 Erl Austria
66 D3 Erla Spain
70 C1 Erlach Switz.
53 K2 Erlangen Ger.
171 H2 Erlangping Henan China
53 P4 Erlau r. Ger.
59 L3 Erlauf Austria
59 L3 Erlauf r. Austria
59 L4 Erlaufsee l. Austria
51 F10 Erlbach Ger.
206 D8 Erldunda N.T. Austr.
52 G2 Erlenbach am Main Ger.
49 G10 Erlensee Ger.
70 E7 Erli Italy
209 F9 Erlistoun watercourse W.A. Austr.
162 F7 Erlong Shan mt. China
118 F7 Erma NJ U.S.A.
Ermak Kazakh. see Aksu
169 M2 Ermana, Khrebet mts Rus. Fed.
44 I4 Ermelo Neth.
62 E6 Ermelo Port.
97 N2 Ermelo S. Africa
188 F5 Ermenek Turkey
190 B2 Ermenek r. Turkey
62 C6 Ermesinde Port.
64 C4 Ermidas do Sado Port.
84 E6 Ermil Sudan
78 E5 Ermioni Greece
128 D3 Ermita de los Correas Mex.
36 D6 Ermont France
78 F5 Ermoupoli Syros Greece
52 G4 Erms r. Ger.
51 D7 Ermsleben Ger.
63 O2 Ermua Spain
204 D2 Ernabella S.A. Austr.
176 E8 Ernakulam Kerala India
49 F9 Erndtebrück Ger.
27 F4 Erne r. Rep. of Ireland/U.K.
39 J5 Ernée France
39 J5 Ernée r. France
209 G9 Ernest Giles Range hills W.A. Austr.
106 C4 Ernest Sound sea chan. AK U.S.A.
59 N2 Ernstbrunn Austria
52 A2 Ernz Noire r. Lux.
176 E7 Erode Tamil Nadu India
200 □3b Eroj i. Majuro Marshall Is
53 I5 Erolzheim Ger.
207 I9 Eromanga Qld Austr.
94 B4 Erongo admin. reg. Namibia
88 E2 'Eroûg well Mali
44 I5 Erp Neth.
57 K4 Érpatak Hungary
49 D9 Erpel Ger.
191 H3 Erpeli Rus. Fed.
168 C5 Erpu Xinjiang China
45 F8 Erquelinnes Belgium
38 G4 Erquy France
209 C9 Errabiddy Hills W.A. Austr.
86 D3 Er Rachidia Morocco
85 F6 Er Rahad Sudan
26 D10 Erraid i. Scotland U.K.
176 E5 Erramala Hills India
86 E3 Er Raoui des. Alg.
66 C1 Erratzu Spain
95 H3 Errego Moz.
92 B2 Er Renk Sudan
Errenteria Spain see Rentería
66 A1 Errezil Spain
27 F2 Errigal hill Rep. of Ireland
27 G7 Errill Rep. of Ireland
50 E1 Errindlev Denmark
205 L7 Errinundra National Park Vic. Austr.
27 B4 Erris Head Rep. of Ireland
70 E6 Erro r. Italy
66 C2 Erro r. Spain
26 H9 Errochty, Loch l. Scotland U.K.
26 I9 Errochty Water r. Scotland U.K.
85 G5 Er Rogel Sudan
26 H8 Errogie Highland, Scotland U.K.
117 □N4 Errol NH U.S.A.
200 □5 Erromango i. Vanuatu
Erronan i. Vanuatu see Futuna
92 B2 Er Roseires Sudan
85 G6 Er Rua'at Sudan
57 H5 Érsekcsanád Hungary
78 B2 Ersekë Albania
57 I3 Érsekvadkert Hungary
49 J8 Ershausen Ger.
162 D2 Ershiyizhan Heilong. China
120 G2 Erskine MN U.S.A.
37 O7 Erstein France
70 F2 Erstfeld Switz.
92 D1 Erta Ale vol. Eth.
168 B3 Ertai Xinjiang China
15 H6 Ertil' Rus. Fed.
52 G5 Ertingen Ger.
172 G2 Ertix He r. China/Kazakh.
71 M3 Erto Italy
200 □3a Eru i. Kwajalein Marshall Is
204 G4 Erudina S.A. Austr.
89 G4 Erufu Nigeria
189 K5 Eruh Turkey
72 B6 Erula Sardegna Italy
18 I2 Eru laht b. Estonia
89 F5 Eruwa Nigeria
144 G4 Erval Brazil
143 F4 Ervália Brazil
39 K6 Erve r. France
62 F6 Ervedosa do Douro Port.
64 C5 Ervidel Port.
36 E3 Ervillers France
62 F5 Ervões Port.
36 G7 Ervy-le-Châtel France
115 F7 Erwin TN U.S.A.
49 F7 Erwitte Ger.
50 E5 Erxleben Sachsen-Anhalt Ger.
51 D6 Erxleben Sachsen-Anhalt Ger.
79 H1 Erydropotamos r. Greece
78 C5 Erymanthos mts Greece
78 C5 Erymanthos r. Greece
78 E4 Erythres Greece
170 B5 Eryuan Yunnan China
76 H9 Erzen r. Albania
Erzerum Turkey see Erzurum
51 H9 Erzgebirge mts Czech Rep./Ger.
162 E4 Erzhan Heilong. China
52 F2 Erzhausen Ger.
168 D1 Erzin Rus. Fed.
188 H5 Erzin Turkey
188 I4 Erzincan Turkey
191 A6 Erzincan prov. Turkey
189 J4 Erzurum Turkey
191 C5 Erzurum prov. Turkey
18 F6 Eržvilkas Lith.
153 L8 Esa-ala P.N.G.
71 N9 Esanatoglia Italy
164 S5 Esan-misaki pt Japan
75 M5 Esaro r. Italy
73 Q8 Esaro r. Italy
164 R5 Esashi Hokkaidō Japan
164 T2 Esashi Hokkaidō Japan
164 S7 Esashi Iwate Japan
22 E6 Esbjerg Denmark
22 E6 Esbjerg airport Denmark
36 E6 Esbly France
Esbo Fin. see Espoo
140 G4 Escada Brazil
62 E3 Escairón Spain
154 D6 Escalante Negros Phil.
63 N2 Escalante Spain
125 U4 Escalante UT U.S.A.
125 V4 Escalante r. UT U.S.A.
125 S4 Escalante Desert UT U.S.A.
72 C8 Escalaplano Sardegna Italy
66 G3 Escales, Embassament d' resr Spain
62 G7 Escalhão Port.
43 B9 Escaliers, Pic des mt. France
66 H2 Escaló Spain
67 I10 Es Caló Spain
126 G4 Escalón Mex.
124 L4 Escalon CA U.S.A.
63 L8 Escalona Spain
63 L6 Escalona del Prado Spain
62 F9 Escalos de Baixo Port.
62 F9 Escalos de Cima Port.
63 O6 Escalote r. Spain
115 D10 Escambia r. FL U.S.A.
63 O7 Escamilla Spain
110 G4 Escanaba MI U.S.A.
67 D7 Escandón, Puerto de pass Spain
41 C9 Escandorgue ridge France
65 K5 Escañuela Spain
203 B13 Escape Reefs South I. N.Z.
127 N8 Escárcega Mex.
63 N8 Escariche Spain
62 F8 Escarigo Port.
66 C2 Escároz Spain
154 D2 Escarpada Point Luzon Phil.
43 G8 Escatalens France
66 E5 Escatrón Spain
36 F3 Escaudain France
45 D7 Escaut r. Belgium
44 H5 Esch Neth.
53 I6 Eschach r. Ger.
37 O7 Eschau France
52 G2 Eschau Ger.
49 G10 Eschborn Ger.
48 C5 Esche Ger.
48 J4 Escheburg Ger.
48 J5 Eschede Ger.
70 E1 Eschenbach Switz.
53 L2 Eschenbach in der Oberpfalz Ger.
49 F9 Eschenburg-Eibelshausen Ger.
49 I8 Eschenstruth (Helsa) Ger.
49 I7 Eschershausen Ger.
58 D6 Eschio r. Italy
53 N3 Eschlkam Ger.
70 D2 Escholzmatt Switz.
45 I10 Esch-sur-Alzette Lux.
45 I9 Esch-sur-Sûre Lux.
49 J8 Eschwege Ger.
49 B9 Eschweiler Ger.
131 I4 Escocesa, Bahía b. Dom. Rep.
138 C3 Escoma Bol.
67 D12 Escombreras Spain
121 E11 Escondido r. Mex.
126 □R11 Escondido r. Nic.
124 O8 Escondido CA U.S.A.
67 K8 Escorca Spain
66 D6 Escorihuela Spain
43 B9 Escos France
43 I10 Escouloubre France
43 B7 Escource France
43 B7 Escource r. France
41 J9 Escragnolles France
66 D6 Escucha Spain
212 W2 Escudero research stn Antarctica
125 W8 Escudilla mt. AZ U.S.A.
128 B3 Escuinapa Mex.
127 N10 Escuintla Guat.
127 M10 Escuintla Mex.
136 D2 Escuque Venez.
64 H2 Escurial Spain
66 D5 Escuriza r. Spain
40 C4 Escurolles France
142 D2 Escurso r. Brazil
63 K8 Escusa mt. Spain
65 L6 Escúzar Spain
89 H6 Eséka Cameroon
193 O3 Ese-Khayya Rus. Fed.
79 K6 Eşen Turkey
79 K6 Eşen r. Turkey
79 J2 Esence Turkey
191 A6 Esence Dağları mts Turkey
191 F6 Eşengöl Dağı mt. Iran/Turkey
184 E3 Esenguly Turkm.
79 J2 Esenköy Turkey
190 C2 Esenpınar Turkey
48 E3 Esens Ger.
191 B5 Esenyurt Erzurum Turkey
79 J1 Esenyurt İstanbul Turkey
66 F3 Ésera r. Spain
184 D5 Eşfahān Iran
184 E5 Eşfahān prov. Iran
185 J8 Esfandak Iran
184 E6 Esfandāran Iran
184 G3 Esfarayen, Reshteh-ye mts Iran
184 H5 Esfīdeh Iran
62 E4 Esgos Spain
63 K5 Esgueva r. Spain
63 L5 Esguevillas de Esgueva Spain
184 H8 Es'hak Iran
170 D6 Eshan Yunnan China
26 □M2 Esha Ness hd Scotland U.K.
31 L5 Esher Surrey, England U.K.
191 B2 Eshera Georgia
91 E6 Eshimba Dem. Rep. Congo
185 M3 Eshkamesh Afgh.
184 E8 Eshkanān Iran
97 P4 Eshowe S. Africa
184 D4 Eshtehārd Iran
95 F4 Esigodini Zimbabwe
97 Q4 Esikhawini S. Africa
71 O8 Esino r. Italy
191 B5 Esirçölü Tepe mt. Turkey
97 O3 eSizameleni S. Africa
207 N9 Esk Qld Austr.
205 K9 Esk r. Tas. Austr.
29 K5 Esk r. Cumbria, England U.K.
29 K4 Esk r. England/Scotland U.K.
26 J11 Esk r. Midlothian/Scottish Borders, Scotland U.K.
202 K6 Eskdale North I. N.Z.
26 J12 Eskdale val. Scotland U.K.
26 J12 Eskdalemuir Dumfries and Galloway, Scotland U.K.
27 F3 Eske, Lough l. Rep. of Ireland
109 H2 Esker Nfld and Lab. Can.
17 P4 Eskhar Ukr.
20 □F1 Eskifjörður Iceland
79 K3 Eski Gediz Turkey
50 E1 Eskilstrup Denmark
23 M2 Eskilstuna Sweden
104 E3 Eskimo Lakes N.W.T. Can.
Eskimo Point Nunavut Can. see Arviat
189 K5 Eski Mosul Iraq
183 O7 Eski-Nookat Kyrg.
188 F3 Eskipazar Turkey
79 L3 Eskişehir Turkey
79 M3 Eskişehir prov. Turkey
63 H6 Esla r. Spain
184 B4 Eslāmābād-e Gharb Iran
184 H4 Eslām Qal'eh Iran
53 N2 Eslarn Ger.
63 R3 Eslava Spain
79 K5 Esler Dağı mt. Turkey
49 F8 Eslohe (Sauerland) Ger.
22 J6 Eslöv Sweden
184 G7 Esmā'īlī-ye Soflá Iran
79 J4 Eşme Turkey
191 D5 Eşmeçayır Turkey
191 D6 Esmer Turkey
147 G2 Esmeralda Arg.
146 B3 Esmeralda Chile
130 D3 Esmeralda Cuba
145 B8 Esmeralda, Isla i. Chile
143 E3 Esmeraldas Brazil
136 B4 Esmeraldas Ecuador
136 B4 Esmeraldas prov. Ecuador
138 D3 Esmeraldo r. Bol.
66 □ Es Migjorn Gran Spain
116 G11 Esmont VA U.S.A.
62 C7 Esmoriz Port.
108 C3 Esnagami Lake Ont. Can.
110 J1 Esnagi Lake Ont. Can.
36 F3 Esnes France
45 I7 Esneux Belgium
67 D8 Espada, Serra d' mts Spain
67 E8 Espadàn mt. Spain
62 H4 Espadañedo Spain
184 I8 Espakeh Iran
41 B7 Espalion France
41 D6 Espaly-St-Marcel France
111 M3 Espanola Ont. Can.
123 K8 Espanola NM U.S.A.
136 □ Española, Isla i. Islas Galápagos Ecuador
64 G3 Esparragalejo Spain
65 I3 Esparragosa Spain
66 I4 Esparreguera Spain
41 H9 Esparron France
126 □P10 Esparta Hond.
147 F5 Espartillar Arg.
124 J3 Esparto CA U.S.A.
66 C2 Esparza de Salazar Spain
183 P6 Espe Kazakh.
62 G7 Espeja Spain
63 N5 Espeja de San Marcelino Spain
65 J5 Espejo Spain
63 N5 Espejón Spain
44 I3 Espel Neth.
43 B9 Espelette France
49 G6 Espelkamp Ger.
49 H8 Espenau Ger.
64 H7 Espera Spain
64 E2 Esperança Port.
142 B6 Esperança, Serra de mts Brazil
209 F12 Esperance W.A. Austr.
209 F13 Esperance Bay W.A. Austr.
140 D3 Esperantinópolis Brazil
212 U2 Esperanza research stn Antarctica
145 C8 Esperanza Santa Cruz Arg.
147 G2 Esperanza Santa Fé Arg.
129 J7 Esperanza Puebla Mex.
126 E4 Esperanza Sonora Mex.
138 C2 Esperanza Peru
154 E6 Esperanza Masbate Phil.
131 □1 Esperanza Puerto Rico
147 I3 Esperanza Uru.
43 I10 Espéraza France
73 L5 Esperia Italy
43 I10 Espezel France
64 A4 Espichel, Cabo c. Port.
65 J4 Espiel Spain
141 C8 Espigão, Serra do mts Brazil
147 G5 Espigas Arg.
63 K3 Espigüete mt. Spain
41 E9 Espiguette, Pointe de l' pt France
129 J5 Espina Mex.
63 K2 Espinama Spain
41 I8 Espinasses France
127 I4 Espinazo Mex.
129 M8 Espinazo del Diablo, Sierra mts Mex.
146 B6 Espinazo del Zorro Arg.
143 F2 Espinhaço, Serra do mts Brazil
64 B6 Espinhaço de Cão, Serra do mts Port.
62 D8 Espinhal Port.
91 B9 Espinheira Angola
64 D4 Espinheira hill Port.
62 C6 Espinho Port.
141 B9 Espinilho, Serra do hills Brazil
63 L2 Espinilla Spain
137 E2 Espino Venez.
141 E5 Espinosa Brazil
63 M5 Espinosa de Cerrato Spain
63 N7 Espinosa de Henares Spain
63 M2 Espinosa de los Monteros Spain
63 K9 Espinoso del Rey Spain
41 B9 Espinouse, Monts de l' mts France
43 J10 Espira-de-l'Agly France
143 G3 Espírito Santo state Brazil
64 D5 Espírito Santo Port.
154 C3 Espiritu Luzon Phil.
138 D4 Espiritu Santo Bol.
128 F3 Espíritu Santo Mex.
200 □5 Espíritu Santo i. Vanuatu
127 P8 Espíritu Santo, Bahía del b. Mex.
126 D5 Espíritu Santo, Isla i. Mex.
127 O7 Espita Mex.
62 C9 Espite Port.
140 F4 Esplanada Brazil
63 P7 Esplegares Spain
66 J5 Esplugues de Llobregat Spain
66 F4 Esplús Spain
66 L3 Espolla Spain
41 C10 Espondeilham France
66 K3 Esponellà Spain
21 R6 Espoo Fin.
67 K8 Esporles Spain
62 C5 Esposende Port.
66 H2 Espot Spain
40 I1 Esprels France
65 P5 Espuña mt. Spain
67 B12 Espuña, Sierra de mts Spain
95 G4 Espungabera Moz.
118 C2 Espy PA U.S.A.
126 E2 Esqueda Mex.
145 C6 Esquel Arg.
106 F5 Esquimalt B.C. Can.
147 H2 Esquina Arg.
127 O10 Esquipulas Guat.
63 M8 Esquivias Spain
20 P3 Esrange Sweden
22 I5 Esrum Sø l. Denmark
92 A1 Es Samalat Sudan
155 E1 Essang Sulawesi Indon.
86 C3 Essaouira Morocco
39 L4 Essay France
89 H5 Essé Cameroon
48 I5 Essel Ger.
86 C4 Es Semara Western Sahara
45 F6 Essen Belgium
49 D8 Essen Ger.
48 E5 Essen (Oldenburg) Ger.
53 M4 Essenbach Ger.
209 F8 Essendon, Mount hill W.A. Austr.
40 J1 Essert France
111 L7 Essex Ont. Can.
31 N4 Essex admin. div. England U.K.
125 Q7 Essex CA U.S.A.
119 K2 Essex CT U.S.A.
117 O6 Essex MA U.S.A.
118 C6 Essex MD U.S.A.
117 L4 Essex NY U.S.A.
119 G3 Essex County county NJ U.S.A.
117 L4 Essex Junction VT U.S.A.
Essexvale Zimbabwe see Esigodini
111 K6 Essexville MI U.S.A.
53 I4 Essingen Ger.
30 H2 Essington Staffordshire, England U.K.
52 G4 Esslingen am Neckar Ger.
193 Q4 Esso Rus. Fed.
36 F5 Essômes-sur-Marne France
36 D6 Essonne dept France

Essonne to Farson

262

36 D6 Essonne r. France
36 I7 Essoyes France
89 H5 Essu Cameroon
18 J2 Essu Estonia
85 F5 Es Suaifi well Sudan
85 G6 Es Suki Sudan
89 I5 Est prov. Cameroon
37 L7 Est, Canal de l' France
109 I4 Est, Île de l' i. Que. Can.
117 □P1 Est, Lac de l' l. Que. Can.
109 I3 Est, Pointe de l' pt Que. Can.
62 E1 Estaca de Bares, Punta de pt Spain
147 H2 Estacas Arg.
128 G2 Estación Catorce Mex.
125 R9 Estación Coahuila Mex.
65 L4 Estación de Baeza Spain
128 G2 Estación Laguna Seca Mex.
66 F3 Estadilla Spain
43 J10 Estagel France
154 D3 Estagno Point Luzon Phil.
184 F7 Eşţahbān Iran
41 B7 Estaing France
111 N3 Estaire Ont. Can.
36 E2 Estaires France
142 B2 Estância Goiás Brazil
140 F4 Estância Sergipe Brazil
123 K9 Estancia NM U.S.A.
145 C9 Estancia Camerón Chile
145 C9 Estancia Carmen Arg.
184 I6 Estand, Kūh-e mt. Iran
43 D8 Estang France
67 K9 Estanyol de Mitjorn Spain
184 H7 Estārm Iran
62 C7 Estarreja Port.
66 D2 Estarrón r. Spain
66 H2 Estats, Pic d' mt. France/Spain
70 B2 Estavayer-le-Lac Switz.
97 N5 Estcourt S. Africa
48 I3 Este r. Ger.
71 L5 Este Italy
131 I4 Este, Parque Nacional del nat. park Dom. Rep.
131 □1 Este, Punta pt Puerto Rico
66 D4 Esteban hill Spain
147 F5 Esteban A. Gazcón Arg.
144 D1 Esteban de Urizar Arg.
50 D5 Estedt Ger.
62 C6 Estela Port.
126 □P11 Estelí Nic.
63 P3 Estella Spain
118 F6 Estell Manor NJ U.S.A.
64 G2 Estena hill Spain
65 J2 Estena r. Spain
53 I2 Estenfeld Ger.
65 J6 Estepa Spain
63 M4 Estepar Spain
65 I8 Estepona Spain
65 J3 Esteras r. Spain
63 P6 Esteras de Medinaceli Spain
66 D6 Estercuel Spain
41 J9 Esterel reg. France
43 B9 Estérençuby France
53 K6 Estergebirge mts Ger.
107 K5 Esterhazy Sask. Can.
90 A4 Esterias, Cap c. Gabon
36 G6 Esternay France
59 I2 Esternberg Austria
129 J3 Estero Mex.
124 K6 Estero Bay CA U.S.A.
70 C8 Esteron r. Italy
129 I3 Esteros Mex.
139 E5 Esteros Para.
66 H2 Esterri d'Aneu Spain
48 E5 Esterwegen Ger.
122 L6 Estes Park CO U.S.A.
136 A1 Este Sudeste, Cayos del is Col.
107 K5 Estevan Sask. Can.
106 D4 Estevan Group is B.C. Can.
120 H4 Estherville IA U.S.A.
41 E6 Estiavreilles France
115 G9 Estill SC U.S.A.
43 F7 Estillac France
45 F8 Estinnes-au-Mont Belgium
36 G7 Estissac France
143 D5 Estiva Brazil
140 D3 Estiva r. Brazil
40 B4 Estivareilles France
67 E8 Estivella Spain
64 D6 Estói Port.
64 C6 Estômbar Port.
107 I5 Eston Sask. Can.
29 O4 Eston Redcar and Cleveland, England U.K.
18 I3 Estonia country Europe
Estonskaya S.S.R. country Europe see Estonia
48 H3 Estorf Niedersachsen Ger.
48 H5 Estorf Niedersachsen Ger.
64 A3 Estoril Port.
64 A3 Estoril, Costa do coastal area Port.
41 I9 Estoublon France
40 F5 Estrablin France
36 E5 Estrées-St-Denis France
144 H3 Estreito Brazil
62 E9 Estreito Port.
64 □ Estreito da Calheta Madeira
64 E4 Estrela Port.
62 E8 Estrela, Serra da mts Port.
143 E3 Estrela do Indaiá Brazil
142 D3 Estrela do Sul Brazil
65 L4 Estrella mt. Spain
126 B2 Estrella, Punta pt Mex.
125 T8 Estrella, Sierra mts AZ U.S.A.
200 □6 Estrella Bay Sta Isabel Solomon Is
138 D2 Estrema Brazil
62 B10 Estremadura reg. Port.
63 N8 Estremera Spain
63 N8 Estremera, Canal de Spain
63 O8 Estremera, Embalse de resr Spain
64 D3 Estremoz Port.
63 O6 Estriégala Spain
43 C8 Estrigon r. France
140 C4 Estrondo, Serra hills Brazil
90 A4 Estuaire prov. Gabon
64 B4 Estuário do Sado, Reserva Natural do nature res. Port.
64 B3 Estuário do Tejo, Reserva Natural do nature res. Port.
184 C4 Estūh Iran
Esu Cameroon see Essu
90 D4 Esumba, Île i. Dem. Rep. Congo
67 H10 Es Vedrà i. Spain
39 M7 Esvres France
57 K4 Esztár Hungary
57 H4 Esztergom Hungary
38 F4 Étables-sur-Mer France
204 G3 Etadunna S.A. Austr.
42 F4 Étagnac France
178 G6 Etah Uttar Prad. India
37 K5 Étain France
40 C1 Étais-la-Sauvin France
40 F1 Étalante France
45 I9 Étalle Belgium
109 J3 Étamamiou Que. Can.
36 D7 Étampes France
204 G2 Etamunbanie, Lake salt flat S.A. Austr.
99 □1c Étang-Salé Réunion
40 E3 Étang-sur-Arroux France
36 C2 Étaples France
42 B4 Étaules France
42 C5 Étauliers France
178 F7 Etawah Rajasthan India
178 G6 Etawah Uttar Prad. India
200 □3a Etcharai i. Kwajalein Marshall Is
126 E4 Etchojoa Mex.
90 A5 Étéké Gabon
38 E6 Étel France
21 S6 Etelä-Suomi prov. Fin.
41 I6 Étendard, Pic de l' mt. France
40 I2 Éternoz France
97 O2 eThandakukhanya S. Africa
45 I9 Ethe Belgium
209 E8 Ethel watercourse W.A. Austr.
107 K5 Ethelbert Man. Can.
208 F7 Ethel Creek W.A. Austr.
207 I3 Ethel Creek r. Qld Austr.
96 G5 E'Thembini S. Africa
207 I4 Etheridge r. Qld Austr.
92 C3 Ethiopia country Africa
79 H3 Etili Turkey
188 F4 Etimesğut Turkey
40 H3 Étival France
37 M7 Étival-Clairefontaine France
26 F10 Etive, Loch inlet Scotland U.K.
36 H8 Étivey France
129 K8 Etla Mex.
21 K6 Etna r. Norway
75 I8 Etna, Monte vol. Sicilia Italy
Etna, Mount vol. Sicilia Italy see Etna, Monte
74 H8 Etna, Parco dell' park Italy
22 B2 Etne Norway
111 O6 Etobicoke Ont. Can.
36 G6 Étoges France
41 G10 Étoile, Chaîne de l' hills France
41 F7 Étoile-sur-Rhône France
90 D4 Etoka Dem. Rep. Congo
104 E4 Etolin Island AK U.S.A.
207 L6 Eton Qld Austr.
31 K5 Eton Windsor and Maidenhead, England U.K.
94 B3 Etosha National Park Namibia
94 C3 Etosha Pan salt pan Namibia
90 B4 Etoumbi Congo
119 F4 Etra NJ U.S.A.
36 D7 Étréchy France
184 F3 Etrek Turkm.
36 C5 Étrépagny France
39 L2 Étretat France
36 G4 Étreux France
77 M8 Etropole Bulg.
70 C4 Etroubles Italy
43 C10 Etsaut France
94 D3 Etsha Botswana
45 J9 Ettelbruck Lux.
200 □4a Etten i. Chuuk Micronesia
52 D5 Ettenheim Ger.
44 G5 Etten-Leur Neth.
26 H8 Etteridge Highland, Scotland U.K.
51 D8 Ettersburg Ger.
88 A2 Et Tîdra i. Maur.
31 I3 Ettington Warwickshire, England U.K.
52 E4 Ettlingen Ger.
26 J12 Ettrick Scottish Borders, Scotland U.K.
29 L2 Ettrickbridge Scottish Borders, Scotland U.K.
26 J11 Ettrick Forest reg. Scotland U.K.
26 K11 Ettrick Water r. Scotland U.K.
49 D10 Ettringen Ger.
176 E8 Ettumanur Kerala India
90 E5 Etumba Dem. Rep. Congo
40 H2 Étuz France
31 I2 Etwall Derbyshire, England U.K.
66 B1 Etxalar Spain
Etxarri Spain see Echarri
63 P3 Etxarri-Aranatz Spain
128 C5 Etzatlán Mex.
107 I5 Etzicom Coulee r. Alta Can.
36 B3 Eu France
201 □2a 'Eua i. Tonga
205 K5 Euabalong N.S.W. Austr.
201 □2a 'Euaiki i. Tonga
Eubarca, Cabo c. Spain see Albarca, Cap d'
52 H2 Eubigheim Ger.
Euboea i. Greece see Evvoia
209 J11 Eucla W.A. Austr.
116 D7 Euclid OH U.S.A.
140 F4 Euclides da Cunha Brazil
142 A5 Euclides da Cunha Paulista Brazil
205 L7 Eucumbene, Lake N.S.W. Austr.
109 H3 Eudistes, Lac des l. Que. Can.
121 J9 Eudora AR U.S.A.
204 G6 Eudunda S.A. Austr.
'Eueiki i. Tonga see 'Euaiki
49 J10 Euerbach Ger.
49 J10 Euerdorf Ger.
115 E10 Eufaula AL U.S.A.
121 H8 Eufaula OK U.S.A.
121 H8 Eufaula Lake resr OK U.S.A.
147 F1 Eufrasio Loza Arg.
58 H4 Eugendorf Austria
122 C4 Eugene OR U.S.A.
139 F2 Eugênia r. Brazil
126 B4 Eugenia, Punta pt Mex.
43 D8 Eugénie-les-Bains France
43 A10 Eugi, Embalse de resr Spain
205 L5 Eugowra N.S.W. Austr.
63 P3 Eulate Spain
205 J3 Eulo Qld Austr.
62 E2 Eume r. Spain
62 E2 Eume, Encoro do resr Spain
143 H2 Eunápolis Brazil
207 L6 Eungella Qld Austr.
207 L6 Eungella National Park Qld Austr.
121 I10 Eunice LA U.S.A.
121 D9 Eunice NM U.S.A.
45 J7 Eupen Belgium
51 G7 Euper Ger.
180 D2 Euphrates r. Asia alt. Al Furāt (Iraq/Syria), alt. Fırat (Turkey)
121 K9 Eupora MS U.S.A.
21 Q6 Eura Fin.
21 P6 Eurajoki Fin.
53 K5 Eurasburg Bayern Ger.
53 K6 Eurasburg Bayern Ger.
59 K3 Euratsfeld Austria
36 B5 Eure dept France
36 B5 Eure r. France
36 B7 Eure-et-Loir dept France
122 B6 Eureka CA U.S.A.
121 G7 Eureka KS U.S.A.
122 G2 Eureka MT U.S.A.
125 Q2 Eureka NV U.S.A.
116 C10 Eureka OH U.S.A.
120 F3 Eureka SD U.S.A.
125 T2 Eureka UT U.S.A.
105 J2 Eureka Sound sea chan. Nunavut Can.
121 I7 Eureka Springs AR U.S.A.
124 O4 Eureka Valley CA U.S.A.
204 H4 Eurinilla watercourse S.A. Austr.
205 H4 Euriowie N.S.W. Austr.
205 J7 Euroa Vic. Austr.
207 L8 Eurombah Qld Austr.
207 L8 Eurombah Creek r. Qld Austr.
83 H6 Europa, Île i. Indian Ocean
63 J2 Europa, Picos de mts Spain
Europa, Punta de pt Gibraltar see Europa Point
65 □ Europa Flats Gibraltar
65 □ Europa Point Gibraltar
12 Europe continent
44 F5 Europoort reg. Neth.
37 J6 Eurville-Bienville France
49 C9 Euskirchen Ger.
49 I10 Eußenheim Ger.
115 G11 Eustis FL U.S.A.
205 I6 Euston N.S.W. Austr.
115 D9 Eutaw AL U.S.A.
48 K2 Eutin Ger.
52 F5 Eutingen im Gäu Ger.
106 E4 Eutsuk Lake B.C. Can.
51 G7 Eutzsch Ger.
37 K6 Euville France
206 E4 Eva Downs N.T. Austr.
91 B9 Evale Angola
70 D4 Evançon r. Italy
97 N2 Evander S. Africa
108 E3 Evans, Lac l. Que. Can.
120 C6 Evans, Mount CO U.S.A.
106 H4 Evansburg Alta Can.
116 E8 Evans City PA U.S.A.
118 C2 Evans Falls PA U.S.A.
205 N3 Evans Head N.S.W. Austr.
212 S1 Evans Ice Stream Antarctica
105 J3 Evans Strait Nunavut Can.
110 G7 Evanston IL U.S.A.
122 I6 Evanston WY U.S.A.
108 D4 Evansville Ont. Can.
114 D7 Evansville IN U.S.A.
110 E7 Evansville WI U.S.A.
122 K5 Evansville WY U.S.A.
121 F10 Evant TX U.S.A.
26 H7 Evanton Highland, Scotland U.K.
110 I6 Evart MI U.S.A.
97 L2 Evaton S. Africa
40 A4 Évaux-les-Bains France
184 F8 Evaz Iran
191 F6 Evci Turkey
79 K4 Evciler Turkey
190 C1 Evcili Turkey
110 B2 Eveleth MN U.S.A.
121 J7 Evening Shade AR U.S.A.
31 J4 Evenlode r. England U.K.
193 Q3 Evensk Rus. Fed.
20 N2 Evenskjær Norway
204 E4 Everard, Lake salt flat S.A. Austr.
206 D7 Everard, Mount N.T. Austr.
204 D2 Everard, Mount S.A. Austr.
204 D2 Everard Range hills S.A. Austr.
30 G5 Evercreech Somerset, England U.K.
44 H5 Everdingen Neth.
Everek Turkey see Develi
179 K6 Everest, Mount China/Nepal
117 □R1 Everett N.B. Can.
116 G8 Everett PA U.S.A.
122 C3 Everett WA U.S.A.
45 E6 Evergem Belgium
115 G12 Everglades swamp FL U.S.A.
115 G13 Everglades City FL U.S.A.
115 G13 Everglades National Park FL U.S.A.
115 D10 Evergreen AL U.S.A.
112 D7 Everman, Volcán vol. Mex.
122 C2 Everson WA U.S.A.
137 G3 Everton Guyana
21 L6 Evertsberg Sweden
207 I7 Evesham Qld Austr.
31 I3 Evesham Worcestershire, England U.K.
31 I3 Evesham, Vale of val. England U.K.
49 K6 Evessen Ger.
40 J4 Évian-les-Bains France
20 Q5 Evijärvi Fin.
89 H6 Evinayong Equat. Guinea
116 F11 Evington VA U.S.A.
78 C4 Evinos r. Greece
72 B3 Evisa Corse France
22 D3 Evje Norway
70 D3 Evolène Switz.
64 D3 Évora Port.
64 D3 Évora admin. dist. Port.
64 D3 Évora-Monte Port.
162 J3 Evoron, Ozero l. Rus. Fed.
78 D2 Evosmo Greece
184 A2 Evowghlī Iran
38 H5 Évran France
39 I7 Èvre r. France
39 J3 Évrecy France
36 B5 Évreux France
39 K5 Évron France
79 H2 Evros r. Greece/Turkey alt. Meriç (Turkey), alt. Maritsa (Bulgaria)
78 D6 Evrotas r. Greece
36 D6 Évry France
190 A3 Evrychou Cyprus
Evrykhou Cyprus see Evrychou
162 J3 Evur r. Rus. Fed.
78 F4 Evvoia i. Greece
78 D1 Evzonoi Greece
124 □C12 'Ewa HI U.S.A.
124 □D12 'Ewa Beach HI U.S.A.
207 J5 Ewan Qld Austr.
130 □ Ewarton Jamaica
92 D4 Ewaso Ngiro r. Kenya
96 H2 Ewbank S. Africa
26 E7 Ewe, Loch b. Scotland U.K.
31 L5 Ewell Surrey, England U.K.
110 E3 Ewen MI U.S.A.
Ewenkizu Zizhiqi Nei Mongol China see Bayan Tohoi
31 L5 Ewhurst Surrey, England U.K.
118 F4 Ewing NJ U.S.A.
212 T2 Ewing Island Antarctica
172 H5 Ewirgol Xinjiang China
90 B5 Ewo Congo
138 D3 Exaltación Bol.
78 D5 Examilia Greece
97 L4 Excelsior S. Africa
124 M3 Excelsior Mountain CA U.S.A.
124 N3 Excelsior Mountains NV U.S.A.
120 H6 Excelsior Springs MO U.S.A.
118 B2 Exchange PA U.S.A.
42 G5 Excideuil France
30 F6 Exe r. England U.K.
30 E5 Exebridge Somerset, England U.K.
212 P1 Executive Committee Range mts Antarctica
110 C4 Exeland WI U.S.A.
205 M6 Exeter N.S.W. Austr.
111 M6 Exeter Ont. Can.
30 E6 Exeter Devon, England U.K.
124 M5 Exeter CA U.S.A.
117 □O6 Exeter NH U.S.A.
107 I1 Exeter Lake N.W.T. Can.
41 J6 Exilles Italy
44 K3 Exloo Neth.
39 L4 Exmes France
30 F6 Exminster Devon, England U.K.
30 E5 Exmoor hills England U.K.
30 E5 Exmoor National Park England U.K.
117 J11 Exmore VA U.S.A.
208 C6 Exmouth W.A. Austr.
30 F6 Exmouth Devon, England U.K.
205 L4 Exmouth, Mount N.S.W. Austr.
208 C7 Exmouth Gulf W.A. Austr.
106 H1 Exmouth Lake N.W.T. Can.
215 L6 Exmouth Plateau sea feature Indian Ocean
207 L8 Expedition National Park Qld Austr.
207 L8 Expedition Range mts Qld Austr.
109 K3 Exploits r. Nfld and Lab. Can.
106 H5 Exshaw Alta Can.
118 D4 Exton PA U.S.A.
129 H4 Extoraz r. Mex.
62 N10 Extremadura aut. comm. Spain
89 I4 Extrême-Nord prov. Cameroon
62 D5 Extremo Port.
130 E1 Exuma Cays is Bahamas
130 F1 Exuma Sound sea chan. Bahamas
15 G7 Eya r. Rus. Fed.
29 N7 Eyam Derbyshire, England U.K.
90 D5 Eyangu Dem. Rep. Congo
93 B5 Eyasi, Lake salt l. Tanz.
41 H6 Eybens France
42 H5 Eyburie France
43 G10 Eycheil France
22 E3 Eydehavn Norway
48 G5 Eydelstedt Ger.
31 L2 Eye Peterborough, England U.K.
31 O3 Eye Suffolk, England U.K.
107 J2 Eyeberry Lake N.W.T. Can.
14 M2 Eyelenoborsk Rus. Fed.
26 L11 Eyemouth Scottish Borders, Scotland U.K.
26 D6 Eye Peninsula Scotland U.K.
27 C9 Eyeries Rep. of Ireland
41 G8 Eygues r. France
41 H8 Eyguians France
41 G9 Eyguières France
42 I4 Eygurande France
42 E5 Eygurande-et-Gardedeuil France
20 □D2 Eyjafjallajökull ice cap Iceland
20 □D1 Eyjafjörður inlet Iceland
92 F3 Eyl Somalia
Eylau Rus. Fed. see Bagrationovsk
43 E6 Eymet France
79 J5 Eymir Turkey
42 H4 Eymoutiers France
184 B5 'Eyn Gazān Iran
26 B8 Eynort, Loch inlet Scotland U.K.
31 M5 Eynsford Kent, England U.K.
31 J4 Eynsham Oxfordshire, England U.K.
41 F9 Eyragues France
42 C5 Eyrans France
43 B6 Eyre r. France
204 F3 Eyre (North), Lake salt flat S.A. Austr.
27 F6 Eyrecourt Rep. of Ireland
206 G9 Eyre Creek watercourse Qld Austr.
42 H5 Eyrein France
203 C12 Eyre Mountains South I. N.Z.
203 C12 Eyre Peak South I. N.Z.
204 E5 Eyre Peninsula S.A. Austr.
41 F7 Eyrieux r. France
43 C6 Eysines France
48 H5 Eystrup Ger.
192 A3 Eysturoy i. Faroe Is
24 D1 Eysturoy i. Faroe Is
31 O5 Eythorne Kent, England U.K.
93 C5 Eyuku waterhole Kenya
89 H5 Eyumojok Cameroon
184 E4 Eyvānakī Iran
40 F6 Eyzin-Pinet France
97 O4 Ezakheni S. Africa
97 N2 eZamokuhle S. Africa
63 O4 Ezcaray Spain
41 K9 Èze France
116 B11 Ezel KY U.S.A.
97 M3 Ezenzeleni S. Africa
146 C6 Ezequiel Ramos Mexía, Embalse resr Arg.
18 K5 Ezernieki Latvia
18 K5 Ežezers l. Latvia
171 J3 Ezhou Hubei China
14 J3 Ezhva Rus. Fed.
79 J4 Eziler Turkey
79 H3 Ezine Turkey
188 H3 Ezinepazar Turkey
66 B1 Ezkurra Spain
190 A4 Ezousa r. Cyprus
189 M8 Ezra's Tomb tourist site Iraq
36 B6 Ézy-sur-Eure France

F

201 □3a Faaa Tahiti Fr. Polynesia
22 G6 Faaborg Denmark
176 C10 Faadhippolhu Atoll Maldives
175 D10 Faadhippolhu Atoll Maldives
92 D4 Faafxadhuun Somalia
59 I6 Faaker See l. Austria
201 □3a Faaone Tahiti Fr. Polynesia
Faarava atoll Arch. des Tuamotu Fr. Polynesia see Fakarava
201 □3a Faaupo, Pointe pt Moorea Fr. Polynesia
66 F5 Fabara Spain
43 G9 Fabas France
123 K11 Fabens TX U.S.A.
156 □ Faber, Mount hill Sing.
106 G2 Faber Lake N.W.T. Can.
62 G3 Fabero Spain
57 L4 Fábiánháza Hungary
55 H3 Fabianki Pol.
57 J5 Fábiánsebestyén Hungary
57 I3 Fabova hoľa mt. Slovakia
41 D9 Fabrègues France
71 N9 Fabriano Italy
73 I3 Fabrica di Roma Italy
65 O3 Fábricas de San Juan de Alcaraz Spain
75 K7 Fabrizia Italy
72 I2 Fabro Italy
98 □1c Faca, Ponta da pt Pico Azores
136 C3 Facatativá Col.
91 D6 Facauma Angola
62 C5 Facha Port.
89 H2 Fachi Niger
64 H8 Facinas Spain
207 M7 Facing Island Qld Austr.
200 □1 Facpi Point Guam
118 D1 Factoryville PA U.S.A.
145 C7 Facundo Arg.
84 D5 Fada Chad
64 E2 Fadagosa Port.
184 F7 Fadāmī Iran
89 F3 Fada-N'Gourma Burkina
57 H5 Fadd Hungary
189 J6 Fadghāmī Syria
187 J4 Faḑīlah well Saudi Arabia
186 G9 Faḑli reg. Yemen
87 H4 Fadnoun, Plateau du Alg.
88 C4 Fadugu Sierra Leone
71 O3 Faedis Italy
71 L7 Faenza Italy
Færoerne terr. N. Atlantic Ocean see Faroe Islands
Faeroes terr. N. Atlantic Ocean see Faroe Islands
Faesulae Italy see Fiesole
72 G2 Faete, Monte hill Italy
90 C3 Fafa r. C.A.R.
201 □2a Fafa i. Tonga
155 G5 Fafanlap Papua Indon.
62 D6 Fafe Port.
92 E3 Fafen Shet' watercourse Eth.
92 D5 Fafi waterhole Kenya
89 F3 Faga watercourse Burkina
71 O3 Fagagna Italy
200 □2 Fagaloa Bay Samoa
200 □2 Fagamalo Samoa
77 M5 Făgăraş Romania
Fagatau atoll Arch. des Tuamotu Fr. Polynesia see Fangatau
200 □2 Fagatogo American Samoa
20 J5 Fagerhaug Norway
21 J6 Fagernes Norway
23 L2 Fagersta Sweden
77 K5 Făget Romania
155 G4 Fagita Papua Indon.
145 C9 Fagnano, Lago l. Arg./Chile
73 Q8 Fagnano Castello Italy
45 F8 Fagne reg. Belgium
36 H6 Fagnières France
89 G2 Fagochia well Niger
88 D2 Faguibine, Lac l. Mali
20 □E2 Fagurhólsmýri Iceland
92 A2 Fagwir Jonglei Sudan
90 F2 Fagwir Wahda Sudan
28 C3 Fahan Rep. of Ireland
87 G3 Fahl, Oued el watercourse Alg.
184 D6 Fahlīān, Rūdkhāneh-ye watercourse Iran
184 F6 Fahraj Iran
48 I1 Fahrdorf Ger.
48 J3 Fahrenkrug Ger.
53 L5 Fahrenzhausen Ger.
51 H6 Fahrland Ger.
187 M4 Fahūd, Jabal hill Oman
98 □1c Faial i. Azores
64 □ Faial Madeira
98 □1c Faial, Canal do sea chan. Azores
73 M5 Faicchio Italy
200 □4a Faichuk is Chuuk Micronesia
85 G2 Fā'id Egypt
49 D10 Faid Ger.
70 F3 Faido Switz.
62 G5 Failde Port.
111 R1 Faillon, Lac l. Que. Can.
45 H7 Faimes Belgium
40 E1 Fain-lès-Montbard France
37 J6 Fains-Véel France
104 D3 Fairbanks AK U.S.A.
116 A9 Fairborn OH U.S.A.
120 G5 Fairbury NE U.S.A.
110 D5 Fairchild WI U.S.A.
203 C13 Fairfax South I. N.Z.
116 H10 Fairfax VA U.S.A.
117 L4 Fairfax VT U.S.A.
203 E12 Fairfield South I. N.Z.
124 J3 Fairfield CA U.S.A.
119 I2 Fairfield CT U.S.A.
120 J5 Fairfield IA U.S.A.
122 G5 Fairfield ID U.S.A.
120 K6 Fairfield IL U.S.A.
116 A9 Fairfield OH U.S.A.
121 G10 Fairfield TX U.S.A.
125 T1 Fairfield UT U.S.A.
116 F11 Fairfield VA U.S.A.
119 I2 Fairfield County county CT U.S.A.
31 I4 Fairford Gloucestershire, England U.K.
111 K6 Fairgrove MI U.S.A.
117 O7 Fairhaven MA U.S.A.
119 G4 Fair Haven NJ U.S.A.
117 L5 Fair Haven VT U.S.A.
27 J2 Fair Head Northern Ireland U.K.
118 D5 Fair Hill MD U.S.A.
154 A6 Fairie Queen sea feature Phil.
26 □M3 Fair Isle i. Scotland U.K.
119 G3 Fair Lawn NJ U.S.A.
118 C6 Fairlee MD U.S.A.
117 M5 Fairlee VT U.S.A.
118 F4 Fairless Hills PA U.S.A.
203 E11 Fairlie South I. N.Z.
26 G11 Fairlie North Ayrshire, Scotland U.K.
207 J3 Fairlight Qld Austr.
31 N6 Fairlight East Sussex, England U.K.
120 H4 Fairmont MN U.S.A.
116 E9 Fairmont WV U.S.A.
106 H5 Fairmont Hot Springs B.C. Can.
31 J6 Fair Oak Hampshire, England U.K.
121 J8 Fair Oaks AR U.S.A.
110 H7 Fair Plain MI U.S.A.
123 L7 Fairplay CO U.S.A.
110 H4 Fairport MI U.S.A.
118 E6 Fairton NJ U.S.A.
207 J3 Fairview Qld Austr.
106 G3 Fairview Alta Can.
110 D9 Fairview IL U.S.A.
116 B10 Fairview KY U.S.A.
111 J5 Fairview MI U.S.A.
119 G4 Fairview NJ U.S.A.
119 H1 Fairview NY U.S.A.
121 F7 Fairview OK U.S.A.
116 E6 Fairview PA U.S.A.
125 U2 Fairview UT U.S.A.
110 D6 Fairview WI U.S.A.
171 □J7 Fairview Park H.K. China
118 D5 Fairville PA U.S.A.
106 B3 Fairweather, Cape AK U.S.A.
106 B3 Fairweather, Mount Can./U.S.A.
28 C4 Fairy Water r. Northern Ireland U.K.
153 J5 Fais i. Micronesia
185 O6 Faisalabad Pak.
36 I4 Faissault France
120 D3 Faith SD U.S.A.
73 M6 Faito, Monte mt. Italy
Faizabad Badakhshān Afgh. see Feyzābād
185 K3 Faizabad Fāryāb Afgh.
178 I6 Faizabad Uttar Prad. India
64 □ Fajã da Ovelha Madeira
98 □1b Fajã de Cima São Miguel Azores
62 E8 Fajão Port.
64 B3 Fajarda Port.
131 □1 Fajardo Puerto Rico
188 I9 Fajr, Wādī watercourse Saudi Arabia
55 K4 Fajsławice Pol.
57 H5 Fajsz Hungary
203 □1 Fakaofo atoll Tokelau
Fakaofu atoll Tokelau see Fakaofo
201 □3 Fakarava atoll Arch. des Tuamotu Fr. Polynesia
14 K4 Fakel Rus. Fed.
31 N2 Fakenham Norfolk, England U.K.
20 M5 Fåker Sweden
182 C3 Fakeyevo Kazakh.
153 H7 Fakfak Papua Indon.
184 E6 Fakhrabad Iran
179 M6 Fakiragram Assam India
77 P8 Fakiyska Reka r. Bulg.
22 I6 Fakse Denmark
22 I6 Fakse Bugt b. Denmark
169 R5 Faku Liaoning China
30 C7 Fal r. England U.K.
88 C4 Falaba Sierra Leone
62 E2 Faladoira, Serra da mts Spain
89 F3 Falagountou Burkina
39 K4 Falaise France
106 G2 Falaise Lake N.W.T. Can.
179 L6 Falakata W. Bengal India
158 A3 Falam Myanmar
184 D5 Falavarjan Iran
71 L3 Falcade Italy
27 F2 Falcarragh Rep. of Ireland
63 Q4 Falces Spain
77 Q4 Fălciu Romania
37 M5 Falck France
71 L8 Falco, Monte mt. Italy
62 B3 Falcoeira, Punta c. Spain
136 D2 Falcón state Venez.
74 G9 Falconara Sicilia Italy
73 Q9 Falconara Albanese Italy
71 O8 Falconara Marittima Italy
75 I7 Falcone Sicilia Italy
72 A6 Falcone, Capo del c. Sardegna Italy
72 C5 Falcone, Punta pt Sardegna Italy
98 □3a Falcones, Punta pt La Gomera Canary Is
107 M5 Falcon Lake Man. Can.
127 J4 Falcon Lake Mex./U.S.A.
146 E2 Falda del Carmen Arg.
203 □1 Fale Tokelau
200 □2 Falealupo Samoa
200 □2 Falefa Samoa
200 □2 Falelatai Samoa
200 □2 Falelima Samoa
88 B3 Falémé r. Mali/Senegal
14 J4 Falenki Rus. Fed.
73 I3 Faleria Italy
Falerii Italy see Civita Castellana
73 Q9 Falerna Italy
73 K1 Falerone Italy
Faleshty Moldova see Făleşti
16 G6 Făleşti Moldova
200 □2 Fale'ula Samoa
121 F12 Falfurrias TX U.S.A.
106 G4 Falher Alta Can.
186 D7 Falkat watercourse Eritrea
49 J8 Falken Ger.
53 M2 Falkenberg Bayern Ger.
53 N5 Falkenberg Bayern Ger.
50 I5 Falkenberg Brandenburg Ger.
51 H7 Falkenberg Brandenburg Ger.
22 I5 Falkenberg Sweden
50 F4 Falkenhagen Ger.
51 G8 Falkenhain Ger.
50 H5 Falkensee Ger.
53 M3 Falkenstein Bayern Ger.
51 F10 Falkenstein Sachsen Ger.
50 H5 Falkenthal Ger.
26 I11 Falkirk Falkirk, Scotland U.K.
26 I11 Falkirk admin. div. Scotland U.K.
26 J10 Falkland Fife, Scotland U.K.
214 F9 Falkland Escarpment sea feature S. Atlantic Ocean
145 F8 Falkland Islands terr. S. Atlantic Ocean
214 F9 Falkland Plateau sea feature S. Atlantic Ocean
145 E9 Falkland Sound sea chan. Falkland Is
145 D6 Falkner Arg.
78 E6 Falkonera i. Greece
22 J3 Falköping Sweden
55 I4 Fałków Pol.
121 H7 Fall r. KS U.S.A.
116 C12 Fall Branch TN U.S.A.
124 O8 Fallbrook CA U.S.A.
110 C5 Fall Creek WI U.S.A.
70 C4 Fallère, Monte mt. Italy
38 H8 Falleron France
20 P4 Fällfors Sweden
212 T2 Fallieres Coast Antarctica
26 I10 Fallin Stirling, Scotland U.K.
48 I5 Fallingbostel Ger.
27 B4 Fallmore Rep. of Ireland
97 L9 Fallodon S. Africa
124 N2 Fallon NV U.S.A.
117 N7 Fall River MA U.S.A.
122 L6 Fall River Pass CO U.S.A.
118 D2 Falls PA U.S.A.
118 A7 Falls Church VA U.S.A.
120 H5 Falls City NE U.S.A.
116 G7 Falls Creek PA U.S.A.
118 F4 Fallsington PA U.S.A.
118 C5 Fallston MD U.S.A.
70 F3 Falmenta Italy
131 □2 Falmouth Antigua and Barbuda
130 □ Falmouth Jamaica
30 B7 Falmouth Cornwall, England U.K.
116 A10 Falmouth KY U.S.A.
117 O7 Falmouth MA U.S.A.
117 □O5 Falmouth ME U.S.A.
118 B4 Falmouth PA U.S.A.
116 H10 Falmouth VA U.S.A.
30 B7 Falmouth Bay England U.K.
131 □2 Falmouth Harbour Antigua and Barbuda
88 D3 Falo Mali
88 D3 Falou Mali
147 F6 Falsa, Bahía b. Arg.
138 C5 Falsa Chipana, Punta pt Chile
109 G1 False r. Que. Can.
96 C10 False Bay S. Africa
97 Q3 False Bay Park S. Africa
104 B4 False Pass AK U.S.A.
179 K9 False Point India
66 G5 Falset Spain
130 H5 Falso, Cabo c. Dom. Rep.
126 □R10 Falso, Cabo c. Hond.
145 C9 Falso Cabo de Hornos c. Chile
22 H7 Falster i. Denmark
29 M3 Falstone Northumberland, England U.K.
77 O3 Fălticeni Romania
23 L1 Falun Sweden
71 M2 Falzarego, Passo di pass Italy
155 G4 Fam, Kepulauan is Papua Indon.
Famagusta Cyprus see Ammochostos
Famagusta Bay Cyprus see Ammochostos Bay
62 F8 Famalicão Port.
144 D3 Famatina Arg.
144 C3 Famatina, Sierra de mts Arg.
49 J9 Fambach Ger.
37 L5 Fameck France
184 C4 Famenin Iran
45 G8 Famenne val. Belgium
209 G8 Fame Range hills W.A. Austr.
107 M5 Family Lake Man. Can.
208 I7 Family Well W.A. Austr.
184 D7 Fāmūr, Daryācheh-ye l. Iran
88 D3 Fana Mali
27 G2 Fanad Head Rep. of Ireland
200 □4a Fanaik i. Chuuk Micronesia
202 J2 Fanal Island North I. N.Z.
95 □K2 Fanambana Madag.
200 □4a Fanan i. Chuuk Micronesia
200 □4a Fananenei, Mochun sea chan. Chuuk Micronesia
95 □K3 Fanandrana Madag.
71 J7 Fanano Italy
200 □4a Fanapanges i. Chuuk Micronesia
79 H5 Fanari, Akra pt Ikaria Greece
171 L3 Fanchang Anhui China
95 □J4 Fandriana Madag.
27 J5 Fane r. Rep. of Ireland
71 M2 Fanes Sennes Braies, Parco Naturale nature res. Italy
200 □4a Fanew, Mochun sea chan. Chuuk Micronesia
158 D5 Fang Thai.
92 A2 Fangak Sudan
66 G6 Fangar, Punta del pt Spain
201 □3 Fangatau atoll Arch. des Tuamotu Fr. Polynesia
201 □3 Fangataufa atoll Arch. des Tuamotu Fr. Polynesia
201 □2a Fanga Uta inlet Tongatapu Tonga
Fangcheng Guangxi China see Fangchenggang
171 I2 Fangcheng Henan China
170 G8 Fangchenggang Guangxi China
170 G3 Fangdou Shan mts China
171 M7 Fangliao Taiwan
72 B3 Fango r. Corse France
23 M3 Fångö i. Sweden
171 M7 Fangshan Taiwan
170 H2 Fangxian Hubei China
162 F6 Fangzheng Heilong. China
76 H9 Fani i Vogël r. Albania
18 K8 Fanipal' Belarus
43 I9 Fanjeaux France
170 G3 Fankuai Sichuan China
Fankuaidian Sichuan China see Fankuai
171 □J7 Fanling H.K. China
66 E2 Fanlo Spain
26 F7 Fannich, Loch l. Scotland U.K.
Fanning Island atoll Kiribati see Tabuaeran
20 J5 Fannrem Norway
184 H8 Fannūj Iran
22 E6 Fanø i. Denmark
71 O8 Fano Italy
22 E6 Fanø Bugt b. Denmark
200 □4a Fanos i. Chuuk Micronesia
Fanoualie i. Tonga see Fonualei
171 K3 Fanshan Anhui China
171 M5 Fanshan Zhejiang China
169 M7 Fanshi Shanxi China
57 K5 Fântâna Rece hill Romania
57 K5 Fântânele Romania
Fanum Fortunae Italy see Fano
169 N9 Fanxian Shandong China
62 C5 Fão Port.
184 D7 Faqīh Aḩmadān Iran
Farab Turkm. see Farap
88 C3 Faraba Mali
Farab-Pristan' Turkm. see Dzheykhun
90 F4 Faradje Dem. Rep. Congo
95 □J4 Farafangana Madag.
88 B3 Farafenni Gambia
73 M3 Fara Filiorum Petri Italy
84 F3 Farāfirah, Wāḩāt al oasis Egypt
Farafra Oasis Egypt see Farāfirah, Wāḩāt al
184 E6 Farāgheh Iran
185 J5 Farāh Afgh.
185 I5 Farāh prov. Afgh.
95 □K2 Farahalana Madag.
185 I6 Farah Rūd watercourse Afgh.
73 J3 Fara in Sabina Italy
185 M4 Farakhulm Afgh.
128 B6 Farallón, Punta pt Mex.
153 K3 Farallon de Medinilla i. N. Mariana Is
153 J2 Farallon de Pajaros vol. N. Mariana Is
136 B4 Farallones de Cali, Parque Nacional nat. park Col.
124 I4 Farallon National Wildlife Refuge nature res. CA U.S.A.
62 I5 Faramontanos de Tábara Spain
90 E2 Faramuti I. Sudan
88 C4 Faranah Guinea
185 P4 Faranshat Jammu and Kashmir
77 O4 Faraoani Romania
88 B2 Far'aoun well Maur.
185 J2 Farap Turkm.
187 L7 Fararah Oman
186 E7 Farasān Saudi Arabia
186 E7 Farasān, Jazā'ir is Saudi Arabia
73 M3 Fara San Martino Italy
66 C3 Farasdues Spain
95 □J3 Faratsiho Madag.
153 J5 Faraulep atoll Micronesia
77 M3 Farcău, Vârful mt. Romania
53 K6 Farchant Ger.
45 G8 Farciennes Belgium
57 L6 Fârdea Romania
65 N5 Fardes r. Spain
27 G6 Fardrum Rep. of Ireland
37 M5 Farébersviller France
31 J6 Fareham Hampshire, England U.K.
36 F6 Faremoutiers France
202 G7 Farewell, Cape South I. N.Z.
202 G7 Farewell Spit South I. N.Z.
73 J3 Farfa r. Italy
22 I3 Färgelanda Sweden
Farghona Uzbek. see Farg'ona
Farghona Wiloyati admin. div. Uzbek. see Farg'ona
115 F10 Fargo GA U.S.A.
120 G2 Fargo ND U.S.A.
183 N7 Farg'ona Uzbek.
183 N7 Farg'ona admin. div. Uzbek.
43 D6 Fargues-St-Hilaire France
43 E7 Fargues-sur-Ourbise France
48 H1 Fårhus Denmark
120 I3 Faribault MN U.S.A.
109 G1 Faribault, Lac l. Que. Can.
178 F5 Faridabad Haryana India
178 E4 Faridkot Punjab India
179 L8 Faridpur Bangl.
178 G5 Faridpur Uttar Prad. India
84 C2 Fārigh, Wādī al watercourse Libya
21 M6 Färila Sweden
62 A10 Farilhões i. Port.
88 B3 Farim Guinea-Bissau
184 H4 Farīmān Iran
31 I4 Faringdon Oxfordshire, England U.K.
29 L6 Farington Lancashire, England U.K.
140 D3 Farinha r. Brazil
70 H6 Farini Italy
62 H6 Fariza de Sayago Spain
23 M5 Färjestaden Öland Sweden
78 D3 Farkadhon Greece
Farkhar Afgh. see Farkhato
185 M3 Farkhato Afgh.
185 M3 Farkhor Tajik.
93 B6 Farkwa Tanz.
207 L6 Farleigh Qld Austr.
31 J5 Farleigh Wallop Hampshire, England U.K.
66 D4 Farlete Spain
72 G1 Farma r. Italy
184 C4 Farmahin Iran
79 I5 Farmakonisi i. Greece
30 H5 Farmborough Bath and North East Somerset, England U.K.
110 F9 Farmer City IL U.S.A.
108 D1 Farmer Island Nunavut Can.
121 I9 Farmerville LA U.S.A.
119 G4 Farmingdale NJ U.S.A.
106 F4 Farmington B.C. Can.
119 J1 Farmington CT U.S.A.
118 D7 Farmington DE U.S.A.
110 D9 Farmington IL U.S.A.
117 □O4 Farmington ME U.S.A.
121 J7 Farmington MO U.S.A.
117 □N5 Farmington NH U.S.A.
123 J8 Farmington NM U.S.A.
122 I6 Farmington UT U.S.A.
116 B6 Farmington Hills MI U.S.A.
119 I3 Farmingville NY U.S.A.
57 I4 Farmos Hungary
106 E4 Far Mountain B.C. Can.
116 G11 Farmville VA U.S.A.
57 H3 Farná Slovakia
31 K5 Farnborough Hampshire, England U.K.
29 L7 Farndon Cheshire, England U.K.
29 P7 Farndon Nottinghamshire, England U.K.
23 M1 Färnebofjärden l. Sweden
23 M1 Färnebofjärdens nationalpark nat. park Sweden
29 N2 Farne Islands England U.K.
72 H2 Farnese Italy
117 M3 Farnham Que. Can.
31 K5 Farnham Surrey, England U.K.
116 I11 Farnham VA U.S.A.
209 I8 Farnham, Lake salt flat W.A. Austr.
106 G5 Farnham, Mount B.C. Can.
31 K4 Farnham Royal Buckinghamshire, England U.K.
51 E8 Farnstädt Ger.
29 M6 Farnworth Greater Manchester, England U.K.
147 G6 Faro Arg.
137 G5 Faro Brazil
89 I4 Faro r. Cameroon
106 C2 Faro Y.T. Can.
64 D6 Faro Port.
64 C6 Faro admin. dist. Port.
62 E3 Faro mt. Spain
23 P4 Fårö Gotland Sweden
23 P4 Fårö i. Sweden
130 F8 Faro, Punta pt Col.
89 I4 Faro, Réserve du nature res. Cameroon
62 E4 Faro, Serra do mts Spain
24 D1 Faroe Islands terr. N. Atlantic Ocean
70 C4 Faroma, Monte mt. Italy
23 P4 Fårösund Gotland Sweden
99 □2 Farquhar Atoll Seychelles
99 □2 Farquhar Group is Seychelles
209 G9 Farquharson Tableland hills W.A. Austr.
26 H8 Farr Highland, Scotland U.K.
71 M3 Farra d'Alpago Italy
116 H7 Farrandsville PA U.S.A.
27 C8 Farranfore Rep. of Ireland
26 G8 Farrar r. Scotland U.K.
207 H8 Farrars Creek watercourse Qld Austr.
186 F6 Farrāsh, Jabal al hill Saudi Arabia
184 E7 Farrāshband Iran
213 G2 Farr Bay Antarctica
111 S4 Farrellton Que. Can.
146 B3 Farrelones Chile
184 H5 Farrokhī Iran
Farruch, Cabo c. Spain see Ferrutx, Cap
Farrukhabad Uttar Prad. India see Fatehgarh
184 E7 Fārs prov. Iran
191 B1 Fars r. Rus. Fed.
184 F5 Farsakh Iran
78 D3 Farsala Greece
78 D3 Farsaliotis r. Greece
185 J5 Fārsī Afgh.
184 D8 Fārsī, Jazīreh-ye i. Būshehr Iran
189 O9 Fārsī, Jazīreh-ye i. Būshehr Iran
22 F5 Farsø Denmark
122 J5 Farson WY U.S.A.

Column 1

22 C3 Farsund Norway
87 J8 Fartak, Jabal mts Yemen
87 K8 Fartak, Ra's c. Yemen
77 P5 Fărțănești Romania
42 B2 Fartura r. Brazil
81 B8 Fartura, Serra da mts Brazil
84 J3 Fārūj Iran
64 G3 Farūmād Iran
22 F5 Fårvang Denmark
10 J6 Farwell MI U.S.A.
21 D8 Farwell TX U.S.A.
85 K3 Fāryāb prov. Afgh.
84 H3 Fāryāb Hormozgan Iran
84 G7 Fāryāb Kermān Iran
18 L6 Farynava Belarus
84 E7 Fasā Iran
84 E7 Fasano Italy
21 K5 Fåset Norway
90 A2 Faşikan Geçidi pass Turkey
22 C1 Fasil Ghebbi and Gonder Monuments tourist site Eth.
98 □3a Fasnia Tenerife Canary Is
43 J8 Fassberg Ger.
85 I9 Fāsteh, Ra's-e pt Iran
16 I3 Fastiv Ukr.
Fastov Ukr. see Fastiv
90 F4 Fataki Dem. Rep. Congo
73 K5 Fate, Monte delle mt. Italy
78 E5 Fatehabad Haryana India
78 F7 Fatehgarh Madh. Prad. India
78 G6 Fatehgarh Uttar Prad. India
78 F4 Fatehgarh Sahib Punjab India
78 E6 Fatehnagar Rajasthan India
78 E6 Fatehnagar Rajasthan India
78 H7 Fatehpur Pak.
78 G6 Fatehpur Uttar Prad. India
62 F8 Fatela Port.
97 L4 Fateng Tse Ntsho S. Africa
15 I5 Fatevyevka Rus. Fed.
17 N1 Fateyevka Rus. Fed.
17 O1 Fatezh Rus. Fed.
84 F7 Fatḩābād Iran
84 A3 Fathai Sudan
11 M4 Fathom Five National Marine Park Ont. Can.
88 A3 Fatick Senegal
62 C9 Fátima Port.
Fatoilep atoll Micronesia see Faraulep
1 □4 Fatu Hiva i. Fr. Polynesia
91 F6 Fatuma Dem. Rep. Congo
91 C6 Fatundu Dem. Rep. Congo
86 □2a Fatutaka Malaita Solomon Is
37 M8 Faucogney-et-la-Mer France
41 C9 Faugères France
27 H2 Faughan r. Northern Ireland U.K.
70 J8 Fauglia Italy
43 E7 Fauguerolles France
52 G2 Faulbach Ger.
26 I11 Fauldhouse West Lothian, Scotland U.K.
50 G3 Faulkton SD U.S.A.
20 F3 Faulquemont France
37 M5 Faulquemont France
36 D2 Fauquembergues France
00 G5 Fauquier B.C. Can.
67 E8 Faura Spain
99 B8 Faure Island W.A. Austr.
97 J5 Fauresmith S. Africa
86 □ Fauro i. Solomon Is
00 M3 Fauske Norway
06 H4 Faust Alta Can.
44 J6 Fauville-en-Caux France
39 M2 Fauville-en-Caux France
42 E6 Faux France
70 G7 Favale di Malvaro Italy
71 M9 Favalto, Monte mt. Italy
74 F9 Favara Sicilia Italy
67 E9 Favara Spain
66 □ Favàritx, Cap de c. Spain
40 D5 Faverges France
37 L8 Faverney France
31 N5 Faversham Kent, England U.K.
37 K7 Favières France
74 C8 Favignana Sicilia Italy
74 C8 Favignana, Isola i. Sicilia Italy
06 H4 Fawcett Alta Can.
14 J6 Fawley Hampshire, England U.K.
08 B2 Fawn r. Ont. Can.
18 C5 Fawn Grove PA U.S.A.
96 S3 Fawnleas S. Africa
86 F2 Fawwārah Saudi Arabia
20 □B1 Faxaflói b. Iceland
20 N5 Faxälven r. Sweden
57 J5 Faxon PA U.S.A.
88 C3 Faya Chad
00 □5 Fayaoué Îles Loyauté New Caledonia
06 D8 Fay-aux-Loges France
43 H6 Faycelles France
86 F2 Fayd Saudi Arabia
38 H7 Fay-de-Bretagne France
42 E7 Fayence France
15 D9 Fayette AL U.S.A.
56 I4 Fayette MO U.S.A.
0 H5 Fayette MS U.S.A.
21 J10 Fayette MS U.S.A.
17 H5 Fayette OH U.S.A.
21 H7 Fayetteville AR U.S.A.
15 E9 Fayetteville GA U.S.A.
15 H8 Fayetteville NC U.S.A.
17 I5 Fayetteville NY U.S.A.
15 H8 Fayetteville PA U.S.A.
15 D7 Fayetteville TN U.S.A.
16 D10 Fayetteville WV U.S.A.
86 F2 Fayfā Saudi Arabia
37 K8 Fayl-Billot France
37 K8 Fayl-la-Forêt France
86 F5 Faylakah i. Kuwait
90 E5 Faymont France
66 F5 Fayón Spain
84 B10 Fayrān well Egypt
84 B10 Fayrān, Wādī watercourse Egypt
90 C10 Fayrawz, Jabal mt. Egypt
41 G3 Fay-sur-Lignon France
53 L5 Fayū i. Micronesia
90 E3 Fazair al Ghrazi watercourse Saudi Arabia
71 P6 Fažana Croatia
89 F4 Fazao Malfakassa, Parc National de nat. park Togo
89 H2 Fazel well Niger
31 I2 Fazeley Staffordshire, England U.K.
78 E4 Fazilka Punjab India
85 N7 Fazilpur Pak.
87 J2 Fazrān, Jabal hill Saudi Arabia
86 B5 Fderîk Maur.
26 B5 Feale r. Rep. of Ireland
15 I9 Fear, Cape NC U.S.A.
26 B5 Fear, Cape NC U.S.A.
43 C9 Féas France
18 D5 Feasterville PA U.S.A.
14 E3 Feather r. CA U.S.A.
24 K2 Feather, North Fork r. CA U.S.A.
03 J8 Featherston North I. N.Z.
30 H7 Featherstone West Yorkshire, England U.K.
95 F3 Featherstone Zimbabwe
39 L1 Fécamp France
72 C7 Feccia r. Italy
19 H1 Fecht r. France
68 G3 Federacija Bosna i Hercegovina aut. div. Bos.-Herz.
47 I2 Federación Arg.
47 I2 Federación Uru.
47 I2 Federal Arg.
69 G4 Federal Capital Territory admin. div. Nigeria

Column 2

Federal District admin. dist. Brazil see Distrito Federal
Federal District admin. dist. Mex. see Distrito Federal
Federal District admin. dist. Venez. see Distrito Federal
117 J10 Federalsburg MD U.S.A.
52 H5 Federsee l. Ger.
24 J1 Fedje Norway
17 O7 Fedorivka Ukr.
Fedorov Kazakh. see Fedorovka
191 A4 Fedorovka
70 C5 Fedorovka Kostanayskaya Oblast' Kazakh.
57 M6 Fedorovka
183 J1 Fedorovka Pavlodarskaya Oblast' Kazakh.
182 D2 Fedorovka Zapadnyy Kazakhstan Kazakh.
182 F1 Fedorovka Respublika Bashkortostan Rus. Fed.
17 R6 Fedorovka Rostovskaya Oblast' Rus. Fed.
182 C1 Fedorovka Samarskaya Oblast' Rus. Fed.
15 I6 Fedorovka Saratovskaya Oblast' Rus. Fed.
17 R8 Fedorovskaya Rus. Fed.
19 W5 Fedorovskoye Rus. Fed.
17 O7 Fedotova Kosa spit Ukr.
19 X6 Fedotovo Rus. Fed.
178 D6 Fedusar Rajasthan India
27 C5 Fee, Lough l. Rep. of Ireland
27 C5 Feeagh, Lough l. Rep. of Ireland
169 P7 Feenix r. Scotland U.K.
169 O6 Feeny Northern Ireland U.K.
170 B6 Feengong Yunnan China
169 P9 Fegguia Henan China
169 P7 Fégreac France
57 K5 Fehérgyarmat Hungary
57 J5 Fehér-Körös r. Hungary
171 J6 Fehér-tó l. Hungary
162 C2 Fehér-tó l. Hungary
57 J5 Fehér-tó l. Hungary
171 K2 Fehér-to l. Hungary
171 K2 Fehérvárcsurgó Hungary
107 N1 Fehmarn Belt str. Denmark/Ger.
50 D2 Fehmarn Belt str. Denmark/Ger. see Femer Bælt
48 K2 Fehmarn i. Ger.
50 G5 Fehrbellin Ger.
59 N6 Fehring Austria
143 G4 Feia, Lagoa lag. Brazil
Feicheng Shandong China see Feixian
171 K3 Feidong Anhui China
36 G3 Feignies France
138 C2 Feijó Port.
52 D2 Feilbingert Ger.
171 K3 Feilding North I. N.Z.
51 E10 Feilitzsch Ger.
49 J5 Feillens France
171 □J7 Feio r. Brazil see Aguapeí
140 F5 Feira de Santana Brazil
62 E2 Feira do Monte Spain
40 I5 Feissons-sur-Isère France
59 K6 Feistritz im Rosental Austria
64 D6 Feistritz ob Bleiburg Austria
171 K3 Feiteira Port.
169 O9 Feixian Shandong China
169 N9 Feixiang Hebei China
87 H2 Fejd-el-Abiod pass Alg.
22 H7 Fejér county Hungary
171 □J7 Feje l. Denmark
53 M3 Feke Turkey
111 K7 Fekete-Körös r. Hungary
203 □1 Fekeetani Spain
87 G6 Felanx well Alg.
50 J4 Felchow Ger.
26 H11 Felda r. East Ayrshire, Scotland U.K.
53 K6 Feldafing Ger.
59 M6 Feldbach Austria
59 K6 Feldberg Ger.
50 H4 Feldberg mt. Ger.
48 I2 Felde Ger.
57 J4 Feldebrő Hungary
58 A5 Feldkirch Austria
52 H7 Feldkirch admin. reg. Austria
17 O8 Feldkirchen bei Graz Austria
59 L5 Feldkirchen in Kärnten Austria
53 L6 Feldkirchen-Westerham Ger.
77 M3 Feldru Romania
62 G6 Felgar Port.
57 J5 Felgyő Hungary
147 H2 Felicidad r. Arg.
99 □2a Félicité i. Inner Islands Seychelles
116 A10 Felicity OH U.S.A.
175 D11 Felidhu Atoll Maldives
175 □1 Felidhu Channel Maldives
30 F3 Felindre Powys, Wales U.K.
41 D6 Félines France
70 I6 Felino Italy
128 C1 Felipe Carrillo Puerto Durango Mex.
128 E6 Felipe Carrillo Puerto Michoacán Mex.
127 O8 Felipe C. Puerto Mex.
73 O7 Felitto Italy
31 O2 Félix Spain
183 O7 Felixdorf Austria
143 E3 Felixlândia Brazil
31 O4 Felixstowe Suffolk, England U.K.
97 F6 Felixton S. Africa
52 B2 Felizzano Italy
30 E5 Fell Ger.
111 N6 Fell, Loch hill Scotland U.K.
27 E7 Fella r. Rep. of Ireland
52 B2 Fellbach Ger.
206 C3 Felletin France
42 I4 Felletin France
29 N4 Felling Tyne and Wear, England U.K.
79 L2 Fellowship Jamaica
116 C10 Fellowship WV U.S.A.
77 J3 Felnac Romania
49 H8 Felsberg Ger.
74 H9 Felsina Italy see Bologna
59 J6 Felsődobsza Hungary
57 J5 Felsőlajos Hungary
88 B3 Felsőnyék Hungary
57 J5 Felsőzentmárton Hungary
57 J4 Felsőtárkány Hungary
59 O6 Felső-Válicka r. Hungary
57 J3 Felsőzsolca Hungary
22 G4 Felsted Denmark
31 N4 Felsted Essex, England U.K.
29 P5 Felton Northumberland, England U.K.
118 D6 Felton DE U.S.A.
118 B5 Felton PA U.S.A.
71 L3 Feltre Italy
31 N3 Feltwell Norfolk, England U.K.
31 L1 Fema, Monte mt. Italy
81 F3 Femea r. Brazil
81 F3 Kemer Bælt str. Denmark/Ger.
23 K5 Femlingen i. Sweden
75 L5 Femme i. Inner Islands
74 H8 Femminamorta, Monte mt. Italy
145 B9 Femminamorta, Portella pass Italy
22 H7 Femø i. Denmark
142 G4 Femø i. Denmark
21 K5 Femsjøen l. Norway
21 L5 Femunden l. Norway
21 L5 Femundsmarka nat. park Norway
65 I5 Fenagh Carlow Rep. of Ireland
28 D5 Fenagh Leitrim Rep. of Ireland
95 I2 Fenaio, Punta del pt Italy
95 I2 Fenais da Ajuda São Miguel Azores

Column 3

95 □J5 Fenambosy, Lohatanjona pt Madag.
200 □1 Fena Valley Reservoir Guam
40 G2 Fénay France
43 H9 Fendeille France
62 D2 Fene Spain
111 P5 Fenelon Falls Ont. Can.
200 □1a Fenepji i. Chuuk Micronesia
190 D2 Fener Burnu hd Turkey
Fénérive Madag. see Fenoarivo Atsinanana
191 A4 Fenerköyü Turkey
70 C5 Fenestrelle Italy
37 N6 Fénétrange France
205 K3 Feneu France
124 M2 Fenevychi Ukr.
58 C5 Fengari mt. Samothraki Greece
118 D2 Fengcheng Fujian China see Anxi
12 I7 Fengcheng Guangxi China see Fengshan
75 K6 Feneglio Valdarno Italy
41 B10 Ferazepore Punjab India see Firozpur
75 K3 Ferrals-les-Corbières France
71 K6 Ferrara Italy
71 L6 Ferrara prov. Italy
71 M6 Ferrarese r. Italy
72 D9 Ferrato, Capo c. Sardegna Italy
73 N4 Ferrazzano Italy
147 G4 Ferré Arg.
62 F1 Ferreira Spain
64 C4 Ferreira do Alentejo Port.
62 D9 Ferreira do Zêzere Port.
137 I4 Ferreira-Gomes Brazil
142 A4 Ferreiros Brazil
62 C4 Ferrel Port.
64 A2 Ferrenafe Peru
116 C10 Ferrellsburg WV U.S.A.
136 B6 Ferreñafe Peru
62 H5 Ferreras de Abajo Spain
62 H5 Ferreras de Arriba Spain
66 □ Ferreries Spain
65 L5 Ferreruela de Huerva Spain
63 L5 Ferreruela de Tábara Spain
40 K1 Ferrette France
147 E2 Ferreyra Arg.
121 J10 Ferriday LA U.S.A.
70 H6 Ferriere Italy
75 J5 Ferrière-la-Grande France
45 I8 Ferrières Belgium
36 E7 Ferrières France
41 C6 Ferrières-St-Mary France
43 H10 Ferrières-sur-Ariège France
76 C5 Ferro, r. Sicilia Italy
64 □ Ferro r. Italy
72 A6 Ferro, Capo c. Sardegna Italy
62 D2 Ferrol Spain
62 D2 Ferrol, Ría de inlet Spain
143 F3 Ferros Brazil
72 D8 Ferru, Monte hill Sardegna Italy
73 M3 Ferruccio, Punta di pt Italy
116 E12 Ferrum VA U.S.A.
67 L8 Ferrutx, Cap c. Spain
27 I8 Ferrycarrig Rep. of Ireland
26 I9 Ferryden Angus, Scotland U.K.
29 N4 Ferryhill Durham, England U.K.
109 K4 Ferryland Nfld and Lab. Can.
52 A2 Ferschweiler Ger.
182 H1 Fershampenuaz Rus. Fed.
72 A6 Fertilia Sardegna Italy
59 O4 Fertőd Hungary
56 F4 Fertőrákos Hungary
59 O4 Fertőszentmiklós Hungary
59 O4 Fertőszéplak Hungary
56 F4 Fertő-tavi nat. park Hungary
62 C3 Fervença Port.
62 C3 Fervenza, Encoro da resr Spain
44 I2 Ferwert Neth.
19 T7 Ferzikovo Rus. Fed.
86 D2 Fès Morocco
91 C6 Feshi Dem. Rep. Congo
26 I8 Feshiebridge Highland, Scotland U.K.
120 F2 Fessenden ND U.S.A.
37 O8 Fessenheim France
36 G4 Festieux France
41 H7 Festre, Col du pass France
155 F4 Fet, Dom, Tanjung pt Papua Indon.
88 B3 Fété Bowé Senegal
98 □1c Feteira Faial Azores
98 □1b Feteira São Miguel Azores
77 P6 Feteşti Romania
77 P6 Feteşti-Gară Romania
26 □N1 Fethaland, Point of Scotland U.K.
27 G8 Fethard Tipperary Rep. of Ireland
27 H8 Fethard Wexford Rep. of Ireland
79 K6 Fethiye Muğla Turkey
182 E6 Fetisovo Kazakh.
26 □O1 Fetlar i. Scotland U.K.
74 B8 Feto, Capo c. Sicilia Italy
26 K9 Fettercairn Aberdeenshire, Scotland U.K.
31 I2 Fettorce r. Scotland U.K.
26 I7 Feucht Ger.
53 K6 Feuchtwangen Ger.
26 I7 Feuilles, Rivière aux r. Que. Can.
26 C4 Feuquières France
36 C3 Feuquières-en-Vimeu France
45 I7 Feurs France
182 G2 Feyzābād Afgh.
185 M5 Feytiat France
184 F6 Feyzābād Afgh.
184 H4 Feyzābād Kermān Iran
184 F3 Feyzābād Khorāsān Iran
85 L3 Fez Morocco see Fès
83 G2 Fezzan reg. Libya
30 E2 Ffestiniog Chwatr.gion, Wales U.K.
43 H8 Fiac France
144 D2 Fiamala Arg.
74 H4 Fiamala Arg.
73 K3 Fiamignano Italy
74 C4 Fian Ghana
95 □J4 Fianarantsoa Madag.
95 □J4 Fianarantsoa prov. Madag.
90 B2 Fianga Chad
70 D5 Fiano Italy
71 H4 Fiano Romano Italy
71 J4 Fiastra r. Italy
71 J4 Fiastra, Lago di l. Italy
71 J4 Fiavè Italy
70 G6 Ficalho mt. Port.
71 K6 Ficarazzi Sicilia Italy
71 K6 Ficarolo Italy
71 L6 Fiché Eth.
53 L2 Fichtelberg Ger.
51 I10 Fichtelberg hills Ger.
111 Q4 Fichtelgebirge park Ger.
62 H6 Fichtelnaab r. Ger.
62 H6 Ficksburg S. Africa
97 I5 Ficulle Italy
74 G9 Ficuzza r. Sicilia Italy
74 D6 Fidå oasis Saudi Arabia
187 K6 Fida'i Oman
27 I6 Fiddown Rep. of Ireland
62 A4 Fidenza Italy
106 C2 Fidjeland Norway
52 G6 Fié, r. Guinea
58 E6 Fiè allo Sciliar Italy
58 E6 Fieni Romania
95 J4 Fenn Núñez Spain
142 D2 Fernão Dias Brazil
95 J2 Fernão Veloso Moz.
106 G5 Fernão Veloso, Baía de b. Moz.
118 B6 Ferndale MD U.S.A.
208 D2 Ferndale NY U.S.A.
18 J5 Ferndale NY U.S.A.

Column 4

122 C2 Ferndale WA U.S.A.
59 I6 Ferndorf Austria
31 I6 Ferndown Dorset, England U.K.
26 I8 Ferness Highland, Scotland U.K.
40 I4 Ferney-Voltaire France
202 K6 Fernhill North I. N.Z.
30 H3 Fernhill Heath Worcestershire, England U.K.
31 K5 Fernhurst West Sussex, England U.K.
106 H5 Fernie B.C. Can.
59 M6 Fernitz Austria
205 K3 Fernlea Qld Austr.
124 M2 Fernley NV U.S.A.
58 C5 Fernpass pass Austria
118 D2 Fernridge PA U.S.A.
27 I7 Ferns Rep. of Ireland
75 K6 Feroleto Antico Italy
131 □2 Fig Tree St Kitts and Nevis
64 C4 Figueira r. Port.
62 C8 Figueira da Foz Port.
62 G7 Figueira de Castelo Rodrigo Port.
64 C4 Figueira dos Cavaleiros Port.
26 J4 Figueira e Barros Port.
62 F1 Figueiró r. Port.
62 F7 Figueiró da Granja Port.
62 D9 Figueiró dos Vinhos Port.
66 K3 Figueras Spain see Figueres
62 H5 Figueruela de Arriba Spain
87 E2 Figuig Morocco
89 I4 Figuil Cameroon
190 E9 Fiha al 'Inab reg. Saudi Arabia
95 □J3 Fihaonana Madag.
201 □1 Fiji country S. Pacific Ocean
216 Q7 Fiji Islands S. Pacific Ocean
75 M5 Fijnaart Neth.
92 D2 Fik' Eth.
89 H4 Fika Nigeria
95 F4 Filabusi Zimbabwe
126 □Q12 Filadelfia Costa Rica
75 K6 Filadelfia Para.
203 B12 Filadelfia Italy
65 C4 Filakovo Slovakia
88 D4 Filamana Mali
18 L4 Filatova-Gora Rus. Fed.
70 H7 Filattiera Italy
212 V1 Filchner Ice Shelf Antarctica
29 N5 Filettino Italy
30 N7 Filey North Yorkshire, England U.K.
29 O5 Filey Bay England U.K.
71 K4 Filiași Romania
83 B3 Filiates Greece
78 C5 Filiatra Greece
143 F3 Filicudi, Isola i. Isole Lipari Italy
74 H6 Filicudi Porto Isole Lipari Italy
89 F3 Filingué Niger
79 G2 Filiouri r. Greece
15 F6 Filipów Pol.
72 D6 Filippa, Mys hd Rus. Fed.
71 K7 Filippiada Greece
111 K1 Filippoi tourist site Greece
106 E3 Filipstad Sweden
120 G4 Firesteel Creek r. SD U.S.A.
98 □3 Firgas Gran Canaria Canary Is
137 E3 Firira Greece
189 I3 Firk, Sha'ib watercourse Iraq
18 L4 Firkachi well Niger
55 L4 Firlej Pol.
147 G3 Firmat Arg.
43 I6 Firmi France
142 B2 Firminópolis Brazil
41 E6 Firminy France
73 O8 Firmo Italy
Firmum Italy see Fermo
Firmum Picenum Italy see Fermo
53 I4 Firngrund reg. Ger.
185 N7 Firovo Rus. Fed.
184 E3 Firozabad Uttar Prad. India
185 K4 Firozkoh reg. Afgh.
178 E6 Firozpur Haryana India
178 D6 Firozpur Punjab India
48 E4 Firrel Ger.
162 N5 Firsovo Rus. Fed.
117 □N3 First Connecticut Lake NH U.S.A.
26 □N2 Firth Shetland, Scotland U.K.
184 E7 Fīrūzābād Iran
184 G3 Fīrūzeh Iran
184 H3 Firyuza Turkm.
66 B2 Fiscal Spain
53 J5 Fischach Ger.
53 I6 Fischbach Ger.
59 M6 Fischbach bei Dahn Ger.
59 L5 Fischbacher Alpen mts Austria
50 F5 Fischbeck Ger.
51 H6 Fischen im Allgäu Ger.
94 B5 Fischersbrunn Namibia
96 E6 Fish r. S. Africa
191 O4 Fishbourne Durham, England U.K.
116 D7 Findlay OH U.S.A.
204 C4 Findon S.A. Austr.
213 J2 Fine Bay Antarctica
213 C2 Fine Glacier Antarctica
107 L5 Fine River Man. Can.
26 J4 Fine NY U.S.A.
117 J4 Fine NY U.S.A.
31 K3 Finedon Northamptonshire, England U.K.
67 L3 Finese, Monte hill Italy
66 J3 Finestres, Serra mts Spain
205 L9 Fingal Tas. Austr.
107 M4 Finger Lake Ont. Can.
116 I6 Finger Lakes NY U.S.A.
178 J9 Fingeshwar Chhattisgarh India
95 F2 Fingoè Moz.
79 L6 Finike Turkey
79 L6 Finike Körfezi b. Turkey
38 B2 Finistère dept France
212 T2 Finister Point Antarctica
Finisterre, Cabo c. Spain see Fisterra, Cabo
62 B3 Finisterre, Cape c. Spain see Fisterra, Cabo
95 □J4 Fianarantsoa Embaïse de resr Spain

Column 5

77 N5 Fieni Romania
78 A2 Ferndort Austria
40 H5 Fier r. France
58 E7 Fiera di Primiero Italy
72 B6 Fierzes, Liqeni i resr Albania
71 K8 Fiesch Switz.
26 K10 Fiesole Italy
110 I5 Fife admin. div. Scotland U.K.
26 K10 Fife Ness pt Scotland U.K.
205 K5 Fifield N.S.W. Austr.
110 D4 Fifield WI U.S.A.
106 H3 Fifth Meridian Alta Can.
61 F5 Figalo, Cap c. Alg.
41 I9 Figanières France
72 C5 Figari r. Corse France
72 D6 Figari, Capo c. Sardegna Italy
43 I6 Figeac France
71 K8 Figline Valdarno Italy
131 □2 Fig Tree St Kitts and Nevis
153 H8 Finschhafen P.N.G.
53 L5 Finsing Ger.
23 O8 Finspång Sweden
10 F2 Finsteraarhorn mt. Switz.
51 I7 Finsterwalde Ger.
26 J4 Finstown Orkney, Scotland U.K.
22 Q4 Finström Åland Fin.
48 I4 Fintel Ger.
57 K2 Fintice Slovakia
Fintînele Romania see Fântânele
77 H4 Fintona Northern Ireland U.K.
27 F3 Fintown Rep. of Ireland
27 E3 Fintragh Bay Rep. of Ireland
26 J9 Fintry Stirling, Scotland U.K.
207 H7 Finucane Range hills Qld Austr.
70 H6 Fiora r. Italy
71 J6 Fiorano Modense Italy
203 B12 Fiordland National Park South I. N.Z.
106 D4 Fiordland Provincial Recreation Area park B.C. Can.
70 H6 Fiorenzuola d'Arda Italy
73 L2 Fiori, Montagna dei mt. Italy
186 G1 Fir reg. Saudi Arabia
180 D2 Fırat r. Turkey alt. Al Furāt (Iraq/Syria), conv. Euphrates
191 A6 Fırat Nehri r. Turkey
95 □J3 Firavahana Madag.
190 O9 Fir'awn, Jazirat i. Egypt
124 C2 Firebaugh CA U.S.A.
107 J2 Firedrake Lake N.W.T. Can.
119 I3 Fire Island N.Y. Can.
119 I3 Fire Island National Seashore nature res. NY U.S.A.
71 K8 Firenze Italy
71 K8 Firenze prov. Italy
71 K7 Firenzuola Italy
54 U1 Fire River Ont. Can.
106 E3 Fireside B.C. Can.
120 G4 Firesteel Creek r. SD U.S.A.
40 I4 Finner Rep. of Ireland
49 E8 Finnentrop Ger.
23 K3 Finnerödja Sweden
207 J3 Finnigan, Mount Qld Austr.
31 O3 Finningham Suffolk, England U.K.
29 P7 Finningley South Yorkshire, England U.K.
206 C2 Finniss r. N.T. Austr.
204 E5 Finniss, Cape S.A. Austr.
204 F3 Finniss Springs Aboriginal Land res. S.A. Austr.
20 R1 Finnmark county Norway
20 Q2 Finnmarksvidda reg. Norway
23 N1 Finnsjön Florarna naturreservat nature res. Sweden
22 I1 Finnskoga Norway
20 N2 Finnsnes Norway
70 O5 Finnowfurt Ger.
50 I5 Finnowkanal canal Ger.
187 N4 Fins Oman
153 K6 Finschhafen P.N.G.
53 L5 Finsing Ger.

Column 6

27 H5 Finnea Rep. of Ireland
49 E8 Finnentrop Ger.
23 K3 Finnerödja Sweden
207 J3 Finnigan, Mount Qld Austr.
31 O3 Finningham Suffolk, England U.K.
29 P7 Finningley South Yorkshire, England U.K.
206 C2 Finniss r. N.T. Austr.
204 E5 Finniss, Cape S.A. Austr.
204 F3 Finniss Springs Aboriginal Land res. S.A. Austr.
20 R1 Finnmark county Norway
20 Q2 Finnmarksvidda reg. Norway
23 N1 Finnsjön Florarna naturreservat nature res. Sweden
22 I1 Finnskoga Norway
20 N2 Finnsnes Norway
70 O5 Finnowfurt Ger.
50 I5 Finnowkanal canal Ger.
187 N4 Fins Oman
153 K6 Finschhafen P.N.G.
53 L5 Finsing Ger.
23 O8 Finspång Sweden
10 F2 Finsteraarhorn mt. Switz.
51 I7 Finsterwalde Ger.
26 J4 Finstown Orkney, Scotland U.K.
22 Q4 Finström Åland Fin.
48 I4 Fintel Ger.
57 K2 Fintice Slovakia
77 H4 Fintona Northern Ireland U.K.
27 F3 Fintown Rep. of Ireland
27 E3 Fintragh Bay Rep. of Ireland
26 J9 Fintry Stirling, Scotland U.K.
207 H7 Finucane Range hills Qld Austr.
72 H3 Fiora r. Italy
71 J6 Fiorano Modense Italy
106 D4 Fiordland Provincial Recreation Area park B.C. Can.
70 H6 Fiorenzuola d'Arda Italy
186 G1 Fir reg. Saudi Arabia
180 D2 Fırat r. Turkey
191 A6 Fırat Nehri r. Turkey
95 □J3 Firavahana Madag.
190 O9 Fir'awn, Jazirat i. Egypt
124 C2 Firebaugh CA U.S.A.
107 J2 Firedrake Lake N.W.T. Can.
119 I3 Fire Island N.Y. U.S.A.
119 I3 Fire Island National Seashore nature res. NY U.S.A.
71 K8 Firenze Italy
71 K8 Firenze prov. Italy
71 K7 Firenzuola Italy
54 U1 Fire River Ont. Can.
106 E3 Fireside B.C. Can.
120 G4 Firesteel Creek r. SD U.S.A.
98 □3 Firgas Gran Canaria Canary Is
204 B5 Fisher S.A. Austr.
213 J2 Fisher Bay Antarctica
213 C2 Fisher Glacier Antarctica
107 L5 Fisher River Man. Can.
119 L2 Fishers Island NY U.S.A.
105 L2 Fisher Strait Nunavut Can.
116 G10 Fishersville VA U.S.A.
30 C4 Fishguard Pembrokeshire, Wales U.K.
117 J10 Fishing Creek MD U.S.A.
117 J10 Fishing Creek PA U.S.A.
107 M4 Fishing Lake Man. Can.
125 M2 Fish Lake UT U.S.A.
111 K6 Fish Point MI U.S.A.
31 M2 Fishtoft Lincolnshire, England U.K.
58 K2 Fiskárdo Greece
31 M2 Fiske Norway
212 L2 Fiske, Cape Antarctica
36 G5 Fismes France
62 B3 Fisterra, Cabo c. Spain
62 B3 Fisterra, Cabo c. Spain
45 I7 Fléron France

Column 7

27 H5 Finnea Rep. of Ireland
73 K4 Fiuggi Italy
71 J7 Fiumalbo Italy
73 O5 Fiumarella r. Italy
73 Q9 Fiumefreddo Bruzio Italy
75 I8 Fiumefreddo di Sicilia Sicilia Italy
75 M5 Fiume Nicà, Punta pt Italy
71 N4 Fiume Veneto Italy
72 I4 Fiumicino Italy
72 C4 Fium'Orbo r. Corse France
26 E9 Fiunary Highland, Scotland U.K.
203 A12 Five Fingers Peninsula South I. N.Z.
203 C12 Five Forks South I. N.Z.
27 H4 Fivemiletown Northern Ireland U.K.
124 L5 Five Points CA U.S.A.
203 C12 Five Rivers South I. N.Z.
70 I7 Fivizzano Italy
41 D6 Fix-St-Geneys France
91 F6 Fizi Dem. Rep. Congo
Fizuli Azer. see Füzuli
20 N4 Fjärdhundra reg. Sweden
23 O2 Fjärdlångs naturreservat nature res. Sweden
50 E1 Fjelie Denmark
22 B1 Fjell Norway
20 N2 Fjellbu Norway
22 F4 Fjerritslev Denmark
86 D2 Fkih Ben Salah Morocco
22 F1 Flå Norway
59 H5 Flachau Austria
53 J3 Flachslanden Ger.
48 D4 Flachsmeer Ger.
26 □N2 Fladdabister Shetland, Scotland U.K.
16 E3 Fladså r. Denmark
49 J9 Fladungen Ger.
20 □2 Flaga Iceland
43 I6 Flagnac France
97 N7 Flagstaff S. Africa
125 U6 Flagstaff AZ U.S.A.
98 □5b Flagstaff Bay St Helena
103 O5 Flagstaff Lake ME U.S.A.
118 F3 Flagtown NJ U.S.A.
108 E1 Flaherty Island Nunavut Can.
40 J4 Flaine France
20 P3 Flakaberg Sweden
21 I6 Flåm Norway
45 I7 Flamand, Île i. Mauritius
38 H2 Flamanville France
77 O3 Flămânzi Romania
110 C4 Flambeau r. WI U.S.A.
29 Q5 Flamborough East Riding of Yorkshire, England U.K.
29 Q5 Flamborough Head England U.K.
52 I3 Flamenco, Isla i. Arg.
98 □1e Flamengos Faial Azores
66 G3 Flamicell r. Spain
51 F6 Fläming hills Ger.
122 L8 Flaming Gorge Reservoir WY U.S.A.
96 F6 Flaminkvlei salt pan S. Africa
107 M4 Flanagan r. Ont. Can.
131 □7 Flanagin Town Trin. and Tob.
45 C7 Flanders reg. Europe
119 J3 Flanders NY U.S.A.
36 D2 Flandre reg. France
90 G5 Flandreau SD U.S.A.
116 C11 Flannagan Lake VA U.S.A.
26 A6 Flannan Isles Scotland U.K.
20 M4 Flåren l. Sweden
41 I10 Flåsjön l. Sweden
20 N5 Flassans-sur-Issole France
42 E7 Flat r. N.W.T. Can.
111 K6 Flat r. MI U.S.A.
118 F2 Flatbrookville NJ U.S.A.
20 □E1 Flateyjardalsheiði reg. Iceland
104 G5 Flathead r. MT U.S.A.
122 G3 Flathead Indian Reservation res. MT U.S.A.
122 G3 Flathead Lake MT U.S.A.
31 H4 Flat Holm i. Wales U.K.
122 H4 Flatiron mt. ID U.S.A.
99 □1b Flat Island Mauritius
163 N6 Flat Island S. China Sea
116 B12 Flat Lick KY U.S.A.
203 B12 Flat Mountain South I. N.Z.
203 J8 Flat Point North I. N.Z.
58 H6 Flattach Austria
207 J3 Flattery, Cape Qld Austr.
122 B2 Flattery, Cape WA U.S.A.
106 B2 Flatnitz Austria
37 M1 Flat Top mt. Y.T. Can.
115 □ Flatts Village Bermuda
122 K3 Flatwillow Creek r. MT U.S.A.
116 C10 Flatwoods KY U.S.A.
116 E10 Flatwoods WV U.S.A.
52 E5 Flaurling Austria
22 C2 Flåvatnet l. Norway
43 I7 Flavignac France
40 F1 Flavigny-sur-Ozerain France
41 B8 Flavin France
70 G1 Flawil Switz.
59 J9 Flaxenpass pass Austria
41 B9 Flaxesc France
129 I1 Flechadores Mex.
51 D6 Flechtingen Ger.
53 J5 Flechtorf Ger. (park Ger.)
48 J2 Flecken Zechlin Ger.
50 J4 Fleckeby Ger.
31 J2 Fleckney Leicestershire, England U.K.
115 □ Fleeming Point New Prov. Bahamas
50 E2 Fleesensee l. Ger.
31 K5 Fleet Hampshire, England U.K.
31 K5 Fleet r. Scotland U.K.
119 L2 Fleet, Loch b. Scotland U.K.
205 N7 Fleetwood Qld Austr.
118 B10 Fleetwood Lancashire, England U.K.
22 C3 Flekkefjord Norway
22 C3 Flekkerøy i. Norway
45 H7 Flémalle Belgium
118 B10 Flemingsburg KY U.S.A.
118 F3 Flemington NJ U.S.A.
N. Atlantic Ocean
31 N4 Flempton Suffolk, England U.K.
71 I1 Fleurbaix Cornwall, England U.K.
23 M2 Flen Sweden

Column 8

73 K4 Fiuggi Italy
71 J7 Fiumalbo Italy
73 O5 Fiumarella r. Italy
73 Q9 Fiumefreddo Bruzio Italy
75 I8 Fiumefreddo di Sicilia Sicilia Italy
75 M5 Fiume Nicà, Punta pt Italy
71 N4 Fiume Veneto Italy
72 I4 Fiumicino Italy
72 C4 Fium'Orbo r. Corse France
26 E9 Fiunary Highland, Scotland U.K.
203 A12 Five Fingers Peninsula South I. N.Z.
203 C12 Five Forks South I. N.Z.
27 H4 Fivemiletown Northern Ireland U.K.
124 L5 Five Points CA U.S.A.
203 C12 Five Rivers South I. N.Z.
70 I7 Fivizzano Italy
41 D6 Fix-St-Geneys France
91 F6 Fizi Dem. Rep. Congo
20 N4 Fjärdhundra reg. Sweden
23 O2 Fjärdlångs naturreservat nature res. Sweden
50 E1 Fjelie Denmark
22 B1 Fjell Norway
20 N2 Fjellbu Norway
22 F4 Fjerritslev Denmark
86 D2 Fkih Ben Salah Morocco
22 F1 Flå Norway
59 H5 Flachau Austria
53 J3 Flachslanden Ger.
48 D4 Flachsmeer Ger.
26 □N2 Fladdabister Shetland, Scotland U.K.
16 E3 Fladså r. Denmark
49 J9 Fladungen Ger.
20 □2 Flaga Iceland
43 I6 Flagnac France
97 N7 Flagstaff S. Africa
125 U6 Flagstaff AZ U.S.A.
98 □5b Flagstaff Bay St Helena
103 O5 Flagstaff Lake ME U.S.A.
118 F3 Flagtown NJ U.S.A.
108 E1 Flaherty Island Nunavut Can.
40 J4 Flaine France
20 P3 Flakaberg Sweden
21 I6 Flåm Norway
45 I7 Flamand, Île i. Mauritius
38 H2 Flamanville France
77 O3 Flămânzi Romania
110 C4 Flambeau r. WI U.S.A.
29 Q5 Flamborough East Riding of Yorkshire, England U.K.
29 Q5 Flamborough Head England U.K.
52 I3 Flamenco, Isla i. Arg.
98 □1e Flamengos Faial Azores
66 G3 Flamicell r. Spain
51 F6 Fläming hills Ger.
122 L8 Flaming Gorge Reservoir WY U.S.A.
96 F6 Flaminkvlei salt pan S. Africa
107 M4 Flanagan r. Ont. Can.
131 □7 Flanagin Town Trin. and Tob.
45 C7 Flanders reg. Europe
119 J3 Flanders NY U.S.A.
36 D2 Flandre reg. France
90 G5 Flandreau SD U.S.A.
116 C11 Flannagan Lake VA U.S.A.
26 A6 Flannan Isles Scotland U.K.
20 M4 Flåren l. Sweden
41 I10 Flåsjön l. Sweden
20 N5 Flassans-sur-Issole France
42 E7 Flat r. N.W.T. Can.
111 K6 Flat r. MI U.S.A.
118 F2 Flatbrookville NJ U.S.A.
20 □E1 Flateyjardalsheiði reg. Iceland
104 G5 Flathead r. MT U.S.A.
122 G3 Flathead Indian Reservation res. MT U.S.A.
122 G3 Flathead Lake MT U.S.A.
31 H4 Flat Holm i. Wales U.K.
122 H4 Flatiron mt. ID U.S.A.
99 □1b Flat Island Mauritius
163 N6 Flat Island S. China Sea
116 B12 Flat Lick KY U.S.A.
203 B12 Flat Mountain South I. N.Z.
203 J8 Flat Point North I. N.Z.
58 H6 Flattach Austria
207 J3 Flattery, Cape Qld Austr.
122 B2 Flattery, Cape WA U.S.A.
106 B2 Flatnitz Austria
37 M1 Flat Top mt. Y.T. Can.
115 □ Flatts Village Bermuda
122 K3 Flatwillow Creek r. MT U.S.A.
116 C10 Flatwoods KY U.S.A.
116 E10 Flatwoods WV U.S.A.
52 E5 Flaurling Austria
22 C2 Flåvatnet l. Norway
43 I7 Flavignac France
40 F1 Flavigny-sur-Ozerain France
41 B8 Flavin France
70 G1 Flawil Switz.
59 J9 Flaxenpass pass Austria
41 B9 Flaxesc France
129 I1 Flechadores Mex.
51 D6 Flechtingen Ger.
115 □3a Fleckney Höhenzug park Ger.
48 J2 Flecken Zechlin Ger.
50 J4 Fleckeby Ger.
31 J2 Fleckney Leicestershire, England U.K.
115 □ Fleeming Point New Prov. Bahamas
50 E2 Fleesensee l. Ger.
31 K5 Fleet Hampshire, England U.K.
31 K5 Fleet r. Scotland U.K.
119 L2 Fleet, Loch b. Scotland U.K.
205 N7 Fleetwood Qld Austr.
118 B10 Fleetwood Lancashire, England U.K.
22 C3 Flekkefjord Norway
22 C3 Flekkerøy i. Norway
45 H7 Flémalle Belgium
118 B10 Flemingsburg KY U.S.A.
118 F3 Flemington NJ U.S.A.
31 N4 Flempton Suffolk, England U.K.
71 I1 Fleurbaix Cornwall, England U.K.
23 M2 Flen Sweden
22 D4 Flensburg Ger.
22 D4 Flensburger Förde inlet Denmark/Ger.
22 D4 Flensburg Fjord inlet Denmark/Ger.
45 I7 Fléron France
39 N8 Flers France
39 N8 Flers France
40 H3 Fléville-Lixières France
44 I2 Flevoland prov. Neth.
31 I2 Fleckbury Cornwall, England U.K.
31 M5 Flimwell East Sussex, England U.K.
70 G2 Flims Switz.

207 H4 **Flinders** r. Qld Austr.
209 C13 **Flinders Bay** W.A. Austr.
204 F6 **Flinders Chase National Park** S.A. Austr.
207 J3 **Flinders Group** is Qld Austr.
207 J3 **Flinders Group National Park** Qld Austr.
204 E5 **Flinders Island** S.A. Austr.
205 L8 **Flinders Island** Tas. Austr.
207 L5 **Flinders Passage** Qld Austr.
204 F5 **Flinders Ranges** mts S.A. Austr.
204 G4 **Flinders Ranges National Park** S.A. Austr.
207 L4 **Flinders Reefs** Coral Sea Is Terr. Austr.
36 I1 **Flines-lez-Raches** France
107 K4 **Flin Flon** Man. Can.
30 F1 **Flint** Flintshire, Wales U.K.
111 K6 **Flint** MI U.S.A.
115 E10 **Flint** r. GA U.S.A.
111 K6 **Flint** r. MI U.S.A.
48 J2 **Flint** Ger.
217 I6 **Flint Island** Kiribati
207 L9 **Flinton** Qld Austr.
30 F1 **Flintshire** admin. div. Wales U.K.
116 G9 **Flintstone** MD U.S.A.
37 K6 **Flirey** France
58 B5 **Flirsch** Austria
22 I1 **Flisa** Norway
21 L6 **Flisa** r. Norway
22 D2 **Fliseggi** mt. Norway
31 L3 **Flitwick** Bedfordshire, England U.K.
66 G5 **Flix** Spain
66 G5 **Flix, Pantà de** resr Spain
36 D4 **Flixecourt** France
36 I4 **Flize** France
22 I4 **Floda** Sweden
29 M2 **Flodden** Northumberland, England U.K.
36 G8 **Flogny-la-Chapelle** France
51 H9 **Flöha** Ger.
51 H9 **Flöha** r. Ger.
37 I4 **Floing** France
43 D6 **Floirac** France
212 P1 **Flood Range** mts Antarctica
110 B3 **Floodwood** MN U.S.A.
29 L5 **Flookburgh** Cumbria, England U.K.
206 C3 **Flora** r. N.T. Austr.
110 H9 **Flora** IN U.S.A.
41 D8 **Florac** France
115 D10 **Florala** AL U.S.A.
37 L5 **Florange** France
207 K4 **Flora Reef** Coral Sea Is Terr. Austr.
206 G5 **Floraville** Qld Austr.
136 C6 **Flor de Punga** Peru
45 G8 **Floreffe** Belgium
111 L7 **Florence** Ont. Can.
 Florence Italy see Firenze
115 D8 **Florence** AL U.S.A.
125 U8 **Florence** AZ U.S.A.
123 L7 **Florence** CO U.S.A.
120 G6 **Florence** KS U.S.A.
118 F4 **Florence** KY U.S.A.
122 B5 **Florence** OR U.S.A.
115 H8 **Florence** SC U.S.A.
110 F4 **Florence** WI U.S.A.
125 U8 **Florence Junction** AZ U.S.A.
117 □R2 **Florenceville** N.B. Can.
144 F3 **Florencia** Formosa Arg.
144 F3 **Florencia** Santa Fé Arg.
136 C4 **Florencia** Col.
147 I3 **Florencio Sánchez** Uru.
45 G8 **Florennes** Belgium
41 C10 **Florensac** France
 Florentia Italy see Firenze
145 D6 **Florentino Ameghino** Arg.
145 D6 **Florentino Ameghino, Embalse** resr Arg.
45 H9 **Florenville** Belgium
147 H4 **Flores** r. Arg.
98 □1 **Flores** i. Azores
140 F3 **Flores** Pernambuco Brazil
140 E3 **Flores** Piauí Brazil
127 O9 **Flores** Guat.
58 B8 **Flores** i. Indon.
147 I3 **Flores** dept Uru.
155 A7 **Flores, Laut** sea Indon.
138 C2 **Florescência** Brazil
63 J7 **Flores de Ávila** Spain
140 D5 **Flores de Goiás** Brazil
 Floreshty Moldova see Floreşti
106 E5 **Flores Island** B.C. Can.
 Flores Sea Indon. see Flores, Laut
140 F4 **Floresta** Brazil
74 H8 **Floresta** Sicilia Italy
91 F7 **Floreşti** Moldova
142 B5 **Florestópolis** Brazil
121 F11 **Floresville** TX U.S.A.
119 G3 **Florham Park** NJ U.S.A.
140 E3 **Floriano** Brazil
138 D2 **Floriano Peixoto** Brazil
142 C4 **Florianópolis** Brazil
138 E4 **Florida** Bol.
146 A5 **Florida** Chile
130 D3 **Florida** Cuba
131 □1 **Florida** Puerto Rico
147 I4 **Florida** Uru.
147 I4 **Florida** dept Uru.
119 G2 **Florida** NY U.S.A.
115 F10 **Florida** state U.S.A.
115 G14 **Florida, Straits of** Bahamas/U.S.A.
115 G13 **Florida Bay** FL U.S.A.
62 I6 **Florida de Liébana** Spain
200 □1 **Florida Islands** Solomon Is
115 G13 **Florida Keys** is FL U.S.A.
145 D8 **Florida Negra** Arg.
142 B4 **Flórida Paulista** Brazil
75 I9 **Floridia** Sicilia Italy
121 C12 **Florida** r. U.S.A.
124 K3 **Florina** Greece
78 C2 **Florina** Greece
72 B6 **Florinas** Sardegna Italy
142 B5 **Florínea** Brazil
96 F9 **Floriskraaldam** I. S. Africa
120 J6 **Florissant** MO U.S.A.
26 J6 **Florø** Norway
49 H10 **Flörsbach** Ger.
49 F10 **Flörsheim am Main** Ger.
52 E2 **Flörsheim-Dalsheim** Ger.
49 G10 **Florstadt** Ger.
53 M2 **Floß** Ger.
53 M2 **Flossenbürg** Ger.
26 J5 **Flotta** i. Scotland U.K.
43 I9 **Floure** France
109 H2 **Flour Lake** Nfld and Lab. Can.
110 B6 **Floyd** IA U.S.A.
116 E12 **Floyd** VA U.S.A.
125 T6 **Floyd, Mount** AZ U.S.A.
121 E9 **Floydada** TX U.S.A.
58 H6 **Flüela Pass** Switz./Austria
70 H2 **Flüelapass** pass Switz.
70 F2 **Flüelen** Switz.
44 I3 **Fluessen** l. Neth.
27 □2 **Fluggufossen** waterfall Iceland
155 E4 **Fluk** Maluku Indon.
106 E4 **Flühorn** r. Sardegna Italy
73 O5 **Flumeri** Italy
72 D7 **Flumendosa** r. Sardegna Italy
72 C8 **Flumineddu** r. Sardegna Italy
72 B9 **Fluminimaggiore** Sardegna Italy
70 G1 **Fluns** Switz.
116 B10 **Flushing** MI U.S.A.
116 E3 **Flushing** OH U.S.A.
72 B7 **Flussio** Sardegna Italy
153 J8 **Fly** r. P.N.G.
213 R2 **Flying Fish, Cape** Antarctica
208 □1 **Flying Fish Cove** Christmas I.
206 E3 **Flying Fox Creek** r. N.T. Austr.
201 □2 **Foa** i. Tonga
107 K5 **Foam Lake** Sask. Can.
70 K4 **Fobello** Italy
64 □ **Foça** Bos.-Herz.
79 H4 **Foça** Turkey

45 H8 **Focant** Belgium
71 M5 **Focce dell'Adige** r. mouth Italy
26 J7 **Fochabers** Moray, Scotland U.K.
125 T2 **Fool Creek Reservoir** UT U.S.A.
97 L2 **Fochville** S. Africa
48 I2 **Fockbek** Ger.
77 P5 **Focşani** Romania
77 P5 **Focuri** Romania
90 D3 **Fodé** C.A.R.
88 □ **Fodékaria** Guinea
39 P7 **Foëcy** France
206 F3 **Foelsche** r. N.T. Austr.
171 I7 **Fogang** Guangdong China
206 C2 **Fog Bay** N.T. Austr.
118 D3 **Fogelsville** PA U.S.A.
87 F4 **Foggáret el Arab** Alg.
87 F4 **Foggáret ez Zoûa** Alg.
73 P5 **Foggia** Italy
73 P5 **Foggia** prov. Italy
72 A7 **Foghe, Punta di** pt Sardegna Italy
155 E5 **Fogi** Buru Indon.
71 N8 **Foglia** r. Italy
73 J5 **Fogliano, Lago di** lag. Italy
21 P6 **Föglö** Åland Fin.
88 □ **Fogo** i. Cape Verde
109 K3 **Fogo Island** Nfld and Lab. Can.
183 M6 **Fogovelo** Kazakh.
59 K5 **Fohnsdorf** Austria
48 G1 **Föhr** i. Ger.
51 F6 **Föhrde** Ger.
52 B2 **Föhren** Ger.
64 B6 **Fóia** hill Port.
71 L9 **Foiano della Chiana** Italy
57 L4 **Foieni** Romania
29 B9 **Foilclough** hill Rep. of Ireland
28 C6 **Foinaven** hill Scotland U.K.
43 H10 **Foix** France
43 G10 **Foix** reg. France
66 I5 **Foix** r. Spain
14 K4 **Foki** Rus. Fed.
19 R8 **Fokino** Rus. Fed.
89 G4 **Fokku** Nigeria
64 □ **Foktő** Hungary
22 D1 **Folarskarnuten** mt. Norway
22 D1 **Folda** sea chan. Norway
202 J6 **Földe** i. Tonga
51 E7 **Förderstedt** Ger.
31 M3 **Foldham** Cambridgeshire, England U.K.
110 G4 **Ford** r. MI U.S.A.
206 B2 **Ford, Cape** N.T. Austr.
124 M6 **Ford City** CA U.S.A.
116 F8 **Ford City** PA U.S.A.
22 B2 **Førde** Hordaland Norway
21 H6 **Førde** Sogn og Fjordane Norway
107 L2 **Forde Lake** Nunavut Can.
202 J6 **Fordell** N.T. I. N.Z.
51 I7 **Förderstedt** Ger.
31 M3 **Fordham** Cambridgeshire, England U.K.
29 M2 **Ford** Northumberland, England U.K.
31 J6 **Fordingbridge** Hampshire, England U.K.
72 B8 **Fordongianus** Sardegna Italy
26 I9 **Fordoun** Aberdeenshire, Scotland U.K.
212 O1 **Ford Range** mts Antarctica
25 I3 **Fords** NJ U.S.A.
205 J3 **Fords Bridge** N.S.W. Austr.
27 I5 **Fordstown** Rep. of Ireland
26 K7 **Fordyce** Aberdeenshire, Scotland U.K.
121 I9 **Fordyce** AR U.S.A.
88 B4 **Forécariah** Guinea
105 O3 **Forel, Mont** mt. Greenland
31 I6 **Foreland** hill England U.K.
30 E5 **Foreland Point** England U.K.
121 H9 **Foreman** AR U.S.A.
107 I5 **Foremost** Alta Can.
73 P6 **Forenza** Italy
106 E4 **Foresight Mountain** B.C. Can.
108 D5 **Forest** Ont. Can.
121 K9 **Forest** MS U.S.A.
116 B8 **Forest** OH U.S.A.
116 F11 **Forest** VA U.S.A.
107 H4 **Forestburg** Alta Can.
118 E1 **Forestburg** NY U.S.A.
118 F1 **Forest City** PA U.S.A.
207 H5 **Forest Creek** r. Qld Austr.
205 K6 **Forest Hill** N.S.W. Austr.
207 J8 **Forest Hill** Qld Austr.
124 L2 **Foresthill** CA U.S.A.
205 L10 **Forestier Peninsula** Tas. Austr.
110 C5 **Forest Junction** WI U.S.A.
110 B4 **Forest Lake** MN U.S.A.
125 V7 **Forest Lakes** AZ U.S.A.
115 E9 **Forest Park** GA U.S.A.
124 K2 **Forest Ranch** CA U.S.A.
31 M5 **Forest Row** East Sussex, England U.K.
109 G3 **Forestville** Que. Can.
124 J3 **Forestville** CA U.S.A.
118 B7 **Forestville** MD U.S.A.
111 L6 **Forestville** MI U.S.A.
116 F6 **Forestville** NY U.S.A.
22 B2 **Føreswick** Norway
88 E4 **Forêt des Deux Balé** nat. park Burkina Faso
89 F5 **Forêt de la** Togo
40 D5 **Forez, Monts du** mts France
40 D5 **Forez, Plaine du** plain France
26 K9 **Forfar** Angus, Scotland U.K.
121 E7 **Forgan** OK U.S.A.
36 C4 **Forges-les-Eaux** France
39 I7 **Forgensee** l. Ger.
26 J7 **Forgie** Moray, Scotland U.K.
40 C4 **Fon Going** ridge Guinea
109 H3 **Forillon, Parc National de** nat. park Que. Can.
73 N6 **Forino** Italy
73 I9 **Forío** Italy
51 D10 **Föritz** Ger.
62 C5 **Forjães** Port.
118 C6 **Fork** MD U.S.A.
121 K8 **Forked Deer** r. TN U.S.A.
117 K9 **Forked River** NJ U.S.A.
27 J4 **Forkhill** Northern Ireland U.K.
122 B3 **Forks** WA U.S.A.
118 D3 **Forks** PA U.S.A.
119 K7 **Fork Union** VA U.S.A.
20 □ **Forlandsundet** str. Svalbard
71 M7 **Forlì** Italy
71 M8 **Forli-Cesena** prov. Italy
71 M7 **Forlimpopoli** Italy
120 D2 **Forman** ND U.S.A.
73 O4 **Formazza** Italy
29 K6 **Formby** Merseyside, England U.K.
67 H10 **Formentera** i. Spain
67 I8 **Formentor, Cap de** c. Spain
36 C4 **Former Yugoslav Republic of Macedonia** country Europe see Macedonia
73 L5 **Formia** Italy
67 D7 **Formiche Alto** Spain
72 F2 **Formiche di Grosseto** is Italy
73 M5 **Formícola** Italy
142 B3 **Formiga** Brazil
71 J6 **Formigine** Italy
71 L6 **Formigueres** France
140 B2 **Formosa** prov. Arg.
144 F2 **Formosa** prov. Arg.
141 F5 **Formosa, Ria** lag. Port.
140 A3 **Formosa, Serra** hills Brazil
140 D6 **Formosa do Rio Preto** Brazil
62 C8 **Formoselha** Port.
142 A4 **Formoso** Mato Grosso do Sul Brazil
140 D5 **Formoso** Minas Gerais Brazil
140 C5 **Formoso** Tocantins Brazil
140 C3 **Formoso** r. Brazil
140 D5 **Formoso** r. Brazil
27 D6 **Formoyle** Rep. of Ireland
22 G5 **Fornæs** r. Denmark
66 D1 **Fornells** Spain
66 □ **Fornelli** Sardegna Italy
66 K4 **Fornells de la Selva** Spain
64 C2 **Fornes** Spain
71 N3 **Forni di Sopra** Italy
71 N3 **Forni di Sotto** Italy
70 C5 **Forno Alpi Graie** Italy
71 N3 **Forno di Zoldo** Italy
95 F6 **Fornos** Moz.
71 L6 **Fornovo di Taro** Italy
71 J6 **Foro** r. Italy
71 M3 **Forolshogna** mt. Norway
20 K5 **Foroyar** terr. N. Atlantic Ocean see Faroe Islands
22 G2 **Fors** Sweden
64 C3 **Foros de Vale Figueira** Port.

71 L3 **Fonzaso** Italy
 Foochow Fujian China see Fuzhou
 Fool Creek Reservoir UT U.S.A.
111 O4 **Fool's Moy** Ont. Can.
170 G2 **Foping** Shaanxi China
70 H3 **Foppolo** Italy
64 □ **Fora, Ilhéu de** i. Madeira
73 J3 **Forano** Italy
184 F4 **Forat** Iran
67 D9 **Forata, Embalse de** resr Spain
 Foraulep atoll Micronesia see Faraulep
37 M5 **Forbach** France
52 E4 **Forbach** Ger.
205 L5 **Forbes** N.S.W. Austr.
120 G6 **Forbes, Mount** Alta Can.
203 A12 **Forbes, Mount** South I. N.Z.
179 K6 **Forbesganj** Bihar India
97 P2 **Forbes Reef** Swaziland
41 I10 **Forcalcuieret** France
66 E6 **Forcall** Spain
41 H9 **Forcalquier** France
62 D3 **Forcarei** Spain
 Forcary Spain see Forcarei
73 K2 **Force** Italy
52 D5 **Forchheim** Baden-Württemberg Ger.
53 K2 **Forchheim** Bayern Ger.
52 H3 **Forchtenberg** Ger.
59 N4 **Forchtenstein** Austria
109 H1 **Ford** r. Que. Can.
26 F10 **Ford** Argyll and Bute, Scotland U.K.
29 M2 **Ford** Northumberland, England U.K.
110 G4 **Ford** r. MI U.S.A.
206 B2 **Ford, Cape** N.T. Austr.
124 M6 **Ford City** CA U.S.A.
116 F8 **Ford City** PA U.S.A.
22 B2 **Førde** Hordaland Norway
21 H6 **Førde** Sogn og Fjordane Norway
107 L2 **Forde Lake** Nunavut Can.
202 J6 **Fordell** N.T. I. N.Z.
51 I7 **Förderstedt** Ger.
31 M3 **Fordham** Cambridgeshire, England U.K.
 Fordsheet ...
57 I5 **Forrayar** terr. N. Atlantic Ocean see Faroe Islands
209 J11 **Forres** Moray, Scotland U.K.
208 J3 **Forrest** r. W.A. Austr.
110 F9 **Forrest** IL U.S.A.
212 U1 **Forrestal Range** mts Antarctica
121 J8 **Forrest City** AR U.S.A.
106 C4 **Forrester Island** AK U.S.A.
107 I3 **Forrest Lake** Sask. Can.
207 I5 **Forrest Lakes** salt flat W.A. Austr.
110 E7 **Forreston** IL U.S.A.
57 K3 **Forró** Hungary
42 D3 **Fors** France
22 C3 **Forsand** Norway
207 I5 **Forsayth** Qld Austr.
22 C2 **Forsbakken** Norway
30 H2 **Forsbrook** Staffordshire, England U.K.
22 J2 **Forshaga** Sweden
26 I6 **Forsinard** Highland, Scotland U.K.
62 D3 **Forsnäs** Sweden
21 Q6 **Forssa** Fin.
52 F3 **Forst** Baden-Württemberg Ger.
51 K7 **Forst** Brandenburg Ger.
205 N5 **Forster** N.S.W. Austr.
53 L5 **Forsth** Ger.
53 L5 **Forstinning** Ger.
115 F9 **Forsyth** GA U.S.A.
121 I7 **Forsyth** MO U.S.A.
122 K3 **Forsyth** MT U.S.A.
111 R1 **Forsythe** Que. Can.
203 I7 **Forsyth Island** South I. N.Z.
206 G4 **Forsyth Islands** Qld Austr.
207 I7 **Forsyth Range** hills Qld Austr.
185 O7 **Fort Abbas** Pak.
108 D2 **Fort Albany** Ont. Can.
138 D2 **Fortaleza** Pando Bol.
138 D3 **Fortaleza** Pando Bol.
140 F2 **Fortaleza** Brazil
62 C4 **Fortaleza de Santa Teresa** Uru.
66 D6 **Fortanete** Spain
125 V8 **Fort Apache Indian Reservation** res. AZ U.S.A.
116 G9 **Fort Ashby** WV U.S.A.
106 H4 **Fort Assiniboine** Alta Can.
107 H4 **Fort Atkinson** WI U.S.A.
26 G8 **Fort Augustus** Highland, Scotland U.K.
58 C2 **Fort Babine** B.C. Can.
97 K8 **Fort Beaufort** S. Africa
122 J2 **Fort Belknap Indian Reservation** res. MT U.S.A.
122 J3 **Fort Benton** MT U.S.A.
120 D2 **Fort Berthold Indian Reservation** res. ND U.S.A.
107 J4 **Fort Black** Sask. Can.
67 C11 **Fort Brabant** N.W.T. Can. see Tuktoyaktuk
124 I2 **Fort Bragg** CA U.S.A.
 Fort Charlet Alg. see Djanet
 Fort Chimo Que. Can. see Kuujjuaq
107 I3 **Fort Chipewyan** Alta Can.
122 L6 **Fort Collins** CO U.S.A.
110 D8 **Fort Constantine** Qld Austr.
114 E5 **Fort-Coulonge** Que. Can.
117 K4 **Fort Covington** NY U.S.A.
121 D10 **Fort Davis** TX U.S.A.
131 □3 **Fort-de-France** Martinique
131 □3 **Fort-de-France, Baie de** b. Martinique
 Fort de Kock Sumatera Indon. see Bukittinggi
115 D9 **Fort Deposit** AL U.S.A.
120 H4 **Fort Dodge** IA U.S.A.
97 N6 **Fort Donald** S. Africa
125 W1 **Fort Duchesne** UT U.S.A.
72 A6 **Forte, Monte** hill Italy
117 K4 **Fort Edward** NY U.S.A.
91 C6 **Forte Nordeste** Angola
111 P7 **Fort Erie** Ont. Can.
208 D6 **Fortescue** r. W.A. Austr.
118 E6 **Fortescue** NJ U.S.A.
137 H6 **Forte Veneza** Brazil
71 L2 **Fortezza** Italy
71 L2 **Fortezza, Monte della** hill Italy
117 □R2 **Fort Fairfield** ME U.S.A.
 Fort Flatters Alg. see Bordj Omer Driss
110 A1 **Fort Frances** Ont. Can.
 Fort Franklin N.W.T. Can. see Déline
115 E10 **Fort Gaines** GA U.S.A.
123 L8 **Fort Garland** CO U.S.A.
116 C10 **Fort Gay** WV U.S.A.
 Fort Gibson Lake OK U.S.A.
104 F3 **Fort Good Hope** N.W.T. Can.
 Fort Gouraud Maur. see Fdérik
26 I11 **Forth** South Lanarkshire, Scotland U.K.
24 F3 **Forth** r. Scotland U.K.
26 J10 **Forth, Firth of** est. Scotland U.K.
122 H5 **Fort Hall Indian Reservation** res. ID U.S.A.
123 L11 **Fort Hancock** TX U.S.A.
97 K8 **Fort Hare** S. Africa
125 K3 **Fortification Range** mts NV U.S.A.
139 K7 **Fortín** Mex.
139 E5 **Fortín Aroma** Para.
139 E5 **Fortín Ávalos Sánchez** Para.
139 E5 **Fortín Boquerón** Para.
139 E5 **Fortín Capitán Demattei** Para.
139 E5 **Fortín Carlos Antonio López** Para.
139 E5 **Fortín Coronel Bogado** Para.
139 E5 **Fortín Coronel Eugenio Garay** Para.
139 F4 **Fortín Galpón** Para.
139 F4 **Fortín General Caballero** Para.
139 E5 **Fortín General Díaz** Para.
139 E5 **Fortín General Díaz** Para.
139 E5 **Fortín General Mendoza** Para.
139 E5 **Fortín Hernandarias** Para.
139 E5 **Fortín Infante Rivarola** Para.
139 E5 **Fortín Juan de Zalazar** Para.
139 E5 **Fortín Lagerenza** Para.
144 E2 **Fortín Lavalle** Arg.
139 E5 **Fortín Leonardo Britos** Para.
139 E5 **Fortín Leonida Escobar** Para.
139 F5 **Fortín Linares** Para.
139 E5 **Fortín Madrejón** Para.
139 F5 **Fortín May Alberto Gardel** Para.
139 F4 **Fortín Nueva Asunción** Para.
144 F1 **Fortín Olavarría** Arg.
139 F5 **Fortín Pilcomayo** Arg.
139 E5 **Fortín Presidente Ayala** Para.
139 E4 **Fortín Ravelo** Bol.
144 F2 **Fortín Sargento Primero Leyes** Arg.
139 E5 **Fortín Suárez Arana** Bol.
139 E5 **Fortín Teniente Juan Echauri López** Para.
139 F5 **Fortín Teniente Montania** Para.
139 E4 **Fortín Teniente Primero H. Mendoza** Para.
139 E4 **Fortín Teniente Rojas Silva** Para.
139 E5 **Fortín Uno** Arg.
117 □Q1 **Fort Kent** ME U.S.A.
117 □3 **Fort Klamath** OR U.S.A.
64 D5 **Fort Lamy** Chad see Ndjamena
122 L5 **Fort Laramie** WY U.S.A.
115 G12 **Fort Lauderdale** FL U.S.A.
124 O7 **Fort Lee** NJ U.S.A.
119 H3 **Fort Lee** VA U.S.A.
107 I3 **Fort Liard** N.W.T. Can.
131 J5 **Fort-Liberté** Haiti
97 M4 **Fort Louden** S. Africa
31 J5 **Fort Mackay** Alta Can.

106 H5 **Fort Macleod** Alta Can.
110 C9 **Fort Madison** IA U.S.A.
36 C3 **Fort-Mahon-Plage** France
110 C9 **Fort McCoy** WI U.S.A.
107 I3 **Fort McMurray** Alta Can.
104 E3 **Fort McPherson** N.W.T. Can.
119 H2 **Fort Montgomery** NY U.S.A.
120 D5 **Fort Morgan** CO U.S.A.
97 O5 **Fort Mtombeni** S. Africa
185 N7 **Fort Munro** Pak.
115 G12 **Fort Myers** FL U.S.A.
106 F2 **Fort Nelson** B.C. Can.
106 F3 **Fort Nelson** r. B.C. Can.
 Fort Norman N.W.T. Can. see Tulita
117 I7 **Fort Orange** NY U.S.A. see Albany
73 O4 **Fort Payne** AL U.S.A.
122 K3 **Fort Peck** MT U.S.A.
122 L2 **Fort Peck Indian Reservation** res. MT U.S.A.
122 K3 **Fort Peck Reservoir** MT U.S.A.
115 G12 **Fort Pierce** FL U.S.A.
122 C3 **Fort Pierre** SD U.S.A.
121 J8 **Fort Portal** Uganda
106 G2 **Fort Providence** N.W.T. Can.
107 K5 **Fort Qu'Appelle** Sask. Can.
 Fort Randall AK U.S.A. see Cold Bay
116 A8 **Fort Recovery** OH U.S.A.
106 H2 **Fort Resolution** N.W.T. Can.
95 F3 **Fort Rixon** Zimbabwe
203 C13 **Fortrose** South I. N.Z.
26 H7 **Fort Rupert** Que. Can. see Waskaganish
106 E4 **Fort St James** B.C. Can.
106 G3 **Fort St John** B.C. Can.
107 M3 **Fort Saskatchewan** Alta Can.
121 H7 **Fort Scott** KS U.S.A.
108 C1 **Fort Severn** Ont. Can.
182 D5 **Fort-Shevchenko** Kazakh.
92 B2 **Fort Simpson** N.W.T. Can.
107 H2 **Fort Smith** N.W.T. Can.
121 H8 **Fort Smith** AR U.S.A.
121 C10 **Fort Stockton** TX U.S.A.
117 I7 **Fort Sumner** NM U.S.A.
125 W8 **Fort Supply** OK U.S.A.
121 F7 **Fort Supply** OK U.S.A.
53 L5 **Fort Thomas** AZ U.S.A.
120 F2 **Fort Totten (Devils Lake Sioux) Indian Reservation** res. ND U.S.A.
189 N5 **Fort Trinquet** Maur. see Bir Mogreïn
122 K6 **Fortuna** Spain
202 J7 **Fortuna** CA U.S.A.
122 C1 **Fortuna** ND U.S.A.
107 I5 **Fortune Bay** Nfld and Lab. Can.
30 H6 **Fortuneswell** Dorset, England U.K.
115 F9 **Fort Valley** GA U.S.A.
106 G3 **Fort Vermilion** Alta Can.
95 F3 **Fort Victoria** Zimbabwe see Masvingo
27 D7 **Fort Walton** FL U.S.A. see Fort Walton Beach
115 D10 **Fort Walton Beach** FL U.S.A.
114 E5 **Fort Washington** PA U.S.A.
114 E5 **Fort Wayne** IN U.S.A.
137 G3 **Fort Wellington** Guyana
158 A3 **Fort White** Myanmar
26 F9 **Fort William** Highland, Scotland U.K.
123 J9 **Fort Wingate** NM U.S.A.
121 F9 **Fort Worth** TX U.S.A.
120 E2 **Fort Yates** ND U.S.A.
118 D2 **Fort Yerba** PA U.S.A.
138 C1 **Foz do Riosinho** Brazil
207 J5 **Fort Yukon** AK U.S.A.
113 J1 **Fort Yukon** AK U.S.A.
62 H7 **Foudre de la Sierra** Spain
66 F4 **Fraga** Spain
75 M3 **Fragagnano** Italy
59 J3 **Fraham** Austria
144 C4 **Frailes** Arg.

36 H3 **Fourmies** France
104 B4 **Four Mountains, Islands of** the AK U.S.A.
36 C3 **Fort-Mahon-Plage** France
41 C7 **Fournels** France
202 □ **Fournier, Cape** Chatham Is S. Pacific Ocean
130 □ **Fournier, Lac** l. Que. Can.
78 C5 **Fournoi** Greece
79 H5 **Fournoi** Greece
31 N6 **Four Oaks** East Sussex, England U.K.
114 D5 **Four Paths** Jamaica
116 H5 **Four Roads** Trin. and Tob.
209 F12 **Fourteen Mile Point** MI U.S.A.
88 B4 **Fouta Djallon** reg. Guinea
203 B13 **Foveaux Strait** South I. N.Z.
118 B5 **Fowbelsburgh** PA U.S.A.
115 I13 **Fowl Cay** i. Bahamas
124 M5 **Fowler** CA U.S.A.
123 L7 **Fowler** CO U.S.A.
114 D5 **Fowler** IN U.S.A.
212 S1 **Fowler Ice Rise** Antarctica
204 D5 **Fowlers Bay** S.A. Austr.
204 D5 **Fowlers Bay** b. S.A. Austr.
110 H9 **Fowlerville** MI U.S.A.
189 N5 **Fowman** Iran
30 G3 **Fownhope** Herefordshire, England U.K.
106 E4 **Fox** r. B.C. Can.
107 M3 **Fox** r. Man. Can.
110 E6 **Fox** r. IL U.S.A.
110 E6 **Fox** r. WI U.S.A.
207 K7 **Fox Creek** r. Qld Austr.
106 G4 **Fox Creek** Alta Can.
28 H5 **Foxdale** Isle of Man.
105 K3 **Foxe Basin** g. Nunavut Can.
105 J3 **Foxe Channel** Nunavut Can.
22 H2 **Foxen** l. Sweden
105 K3 **Foxe Peninsula** Nunavut Can.
27 D5 **Foxford** Rep. of Ireland
203 E10 **Fox Glacier** South I. N.Z.
104 B4 **Fox Islands** AK U.S.A.
106 H3 **Fox Lake** Alta Can.
110 F7 **Fox Lake** IL U.S.A.
106 C2 **Fox Mountain** Y.T. Can.
122 K6 **Foxpark** WY U.S.A.
202 J7 **Foxton** North I. N.Z.
107 I5 **Fox Valley** Sask. Can.
26 H8 **Foyers** Highland, Scotland U.K.
28 B6 **Foygh** Rep. of Ireland
27 H3 **Foyle, Lough** b.
27 E7 **Foyle** r. Rep. of Ireland/U.K.
27 D7 **Foynes** Rep. of Ireland/U.K.
62 C2 **Foz** Spain
62 C2 **Foz** Port.
90 C7 **Foz de Areia, Represa de** resr Brazil
136 D6 **Foz de Gregório** Brazil
64 A2 **Foz do Arelho** Port.
142 A5 **Foz do Copeá** Brazil
91 C8 **Foz do Cunene** Angola
141 B8 **Foz do Iguaçu** Brazil
138 E2 **Foz do Jamari** Brazil
138 C2 **Foz do Jordão** Brazil
138 C2 **Foz do Jutaí** Brazil
138 C1 **Foz do Mamoriá** Brazil
138 C1 **Foz do Riosinho** Brazil
62 E9 **Foz Giraldo** Port.
70 D7 **Fozzano** Corse France
118 F1 **Frackville** PA U.S.A.
66 F4 **Fraga** Spain
67 I1 **Frackville** PA U.S.A.
51 I8 **Fráncis** Ger.
50 E2 **Franzburg** Ger.
203 E10 **Franz Josef Glacier** South I. N.Z.
 Franz Josef Land is Rus. Fed. see Zemlya Frantsa-Iosifa
72 A8 **Frasca, Capo della** c. Sardegna Italy
74 H9 **Frasca, Monte** hill Italy
73 J3 **Frascati** Italy
73 Q8 **Frascineto** Italy
73 Q8 **Frascinetello** Italy
71 J7 **Fraserburgh** Aberdeenshire, Scotland U.K.
96 L7 **Fraserburg** S. Africa
108 D3 **Fraserdale** Ont. Can.
207 N8 **Fraser Island** Qld Austr.
207 N8 **Fraser Island National Park** Qld Austr.
106 E4 **Fraser Lake** B.C. Can.
205 J7 **Fraser National Park** Vic. Austr.
106 E4 **Fraser Plateau** B.C. Can.
209 G12 **Fraser Range** hills W.A. Austr.
202 G5 **Frasertown** North I. N.Z.
40 I3 **Frasne** France
40 I3 **Frasne, Étang de** lag. France
45 F7 **Frasnes-lez-Buissenal** Belgium
45 F7 **Frasnes-lez-Gosselies** Belgium
71 J7 **Frassinoro** Italy
58 A5 **Frastanz** Austria
62 F9 **Fratel** Port.
74 H7 **Fratello** r. Sicilia Italy
77 M7 **Frăteşti** Romania
71 L5 **Fratta** r. Italy
71 L5 **Fratta Polesine** Italy
73 J2 **Fratta Todina** Italy
73 O1 **Fraubrunnen** Switz.
73 O4 **Frauenau** Ger.
59 H4 **Frauenfeld** Austria
50 E3 **Frauenkirchen** Austria
59 L6 **Frauental an der Laßnitz** Austria
49 K9 **Frauenwald** Ger.
53 J4 **Fraunberg** Ger.
74 G4 **Fray Bentos** Uru.
147 I3 **Fray Luis Beltrán** Santa Fé Arg.
147 G3 **Fray Luis Beltrán** Santa Fé Arg.
147 G4 **Fray Marcos** Uru.
 Frayssinet-le-Gélat France
73 O4 **Frazee** MN U.S.A.
118 B4 **Frazer** PA U.S.A.
208 F5 **Frazier Downs Aboriginal Reserve** W.A. Austr.
124 N7 **Frazier Park** CA U.S.A.
52 G3 **Freamunde** Port.
77 O7 **Frecăţei** Romania
72 G6 **Freca** Port.
73 Q5 **Freccheo** Ger.
69 C9 **Frechen** Ger.
63 K3 **Frechilla** Spain
29 K6 **Freckleton** Lancashire, England U.K.
49 I7 **Freden (Leine)** Ger.
50 E3 **Fredenbeck** Ger.
110 J5 **Frederic** WI U.S.A.
110 D5 **Frederic** WI U.S.A.
110 J5 **Frederica** DE U.S.A.
22 F5 **Fredericia** Denmark
116 F11 **Frederick** MD U.S.A.
121 E8 **Frederick** OK U.S.A.
121 E8 **Frederick** SD U.S.A.
 Frederick E. Hyde Fjord inlet Greenland
207 K6 **Frederick Hills** N.T. Austr.
108 B7 **Frederick House Lake** Ont. Can.
206 F5 **Fredericksburg** IA U.S.A.
110 B7 **Fredericksburg** IA U.S.A.

53 I3 **Frankenhöhe** park Ger.
59 K9 **Frankenmarkt** Austria
111 K6 **Frankenmuth** MI U.S.A.
52 E2 **Frankenthal (Pfalz)** Ger.
51 E10 **Frankenthal** park Ger.
130 □ **Frankfield** Jamaica
111 Q5 **Frankford** Ont. Can.
97 M3 **Frankfort** S. Africa
114 C5 **Frankfort** IN U.S.A.
114 H5 **Frankfort** KY U.S.A.
110 H5 **Frankfort** MI U.S.A.
116 B9 **Frankfort** OH U.S.A.
 Frankfurt am Main Ger.
49 G10 **Frankfurt am Main** Ger.
51 K6 **Frankfurt an der Oder** Ger.
125 Q1 **Frankin Lake** NV U.S.A.
53 J4 **Fränkische Alb** hills Ger.
53 K3 **Fränkische Rezat** r. Ger.
49 J10 **Fränkische Saale** r. Ger.
53 K2 **Fränkische Schweiz** reg. Ge
53 I3 **Fränkische Schweiz-Veldensteiner Forst** park Ger.
209 D13 **Frankland** r. W.A. Austr.
205 K8 **Frankland, Cape** Tas. Austr.
30 H3 **Frankley** Worcestershire, England U.K.
97 N6 **Franklin** S. Africa
115 E10 **Franklin** AZ U.S.A.
115 E9 **Franklin** GA U.S.A.
114 D6 **Franklin** IN U.S.A.
118 F5 **Franklin** KY U.S.A.
121 J11 **Franklin** LA U.S.A.
118 F5 **Franklin** MA U.S.A.
117 N4 **Franklin** NH U.S.A.
118 F8 **Franklin** NC U.S.A.
120 F5 **Franklin** NE U.S.A.
117 N5 **Franklin** NJ U.S.A.
121 I3 **Franklin** TX U.S.A.
116 I12 **Franklin** VA U.S.A.
116 D6 **Franklin** WV U.S.A.
121 J11 **Franklin** LA U.S.A.
104 F3 **Franklin Bay** N.W.T. Can.
122 E3 **Franklin D. Roosevelt Lake** WA U.S.A.
110 F7 **Franklin Furnace** OH U.S.A.
205 J10 **Franklin-Gordon National Park** Tas. Austr.
110 E8 **Franklin Grove** IL U.S.A.
204 F5 **Franklin Harbor** b. S.A. Austr.
213 L1 **Franklin Island** Antarctica
106 F2 **Franklin Mountains** N.W.T. Can.
203 B11 **Franklin Mountains** South I. N.Z.
118 F4 **Franklin Park** NJ U.S.A.
205 K9 **Franklin Sound** sea chan. Tas. Austr.
119 H3 **Franklin Square** NY U.S.A.
105 I2 **Franklin Strait** Nunavut Can.
121 J10 **Franklinton** LA U.S.A.
116 C6 **Franklinville** NY U.S.A.
55 I1 **Frankowo** Pol.
52 C4 **Frankrike** Sweden
205 J8 **Frankston** Vic. Austr.
203 C12 **Frankton** South I. N.Z.
40 I2 **Franois** France
96 G4 **Fransenhof** S. Africa
94 E3 **Fransfontein** Namibia
21 N5 **Franske Øer** is Greenland
21 N5 **Fränsta** Sweden
56 B1 **Františkovy Lázně** Czech Rep.
72 C3 **Franz** Ont. Can.
50 E2 **Franzburg** Ger.
203 E10 **Franz Josef Glacier** South I. N.Z.
 Franz Josef Strauss airport Ger.

118 C4	Fredericksburg PA U.S.A.
121 F10	Fredericksburg TX U.S.A.
116 H10	Fredericksburg VA U.S.A.
106 C3	Frederick Sound sea chan. AK U.S.A.
121 J7	Fredericktown MO U.S.A.
116 C8	Fredericktown OH U.S.A.
109 H4	Fredericton N.B. Can.
117 □S3	Fredericton Junction N.B. Can.
22 I6	Frederiksborg county Denmark
	Frederikshåb Greenland see Paamiut
22 G4	Frederikshavn Denmark
22 I6	Frederikssund Denmark
131 K5	Fredericksted Virgin Is (U.S.A.)
22 I6	Frederiksværk Denmark
50 I5	Fredonia AZ U.S.A.
125 T5	Fredonia AZ U.S.A.
121 H7	Fredonia KS U.S.A.
116 E7	Fredonia PA U.S.A.
110 G6	Fredonia WI U.S.A.
20 O4	Fredrika Sweden
23 K1	Fredriksberg Sweden
22 G2	Fredrikstad Norway
55 K6	Fredropol Pol.
117 K8	Freeburg PA U.S.A.
117 K8	Freehold NJ U.S.A.
110 H4	Freeland PA U.S.A.
204 G6	Freeling S.A. Austr.
206 D7	Freeling, Mount N.T. Austr.
204 G4	Freeling Heights hill S.A. Austr.
124 M3	Freel Peak CA U.S.A.
109 K3	Freels, Cape Nfld and Lab. Can.
52 G4	Freeman SD U.S.A.
110 H9	Freeman, Lake IN U.S.A.
118 E3	Freemansburg PA U.S.A.
20 □	Freemansundet sea chan. Svalbard
115 D10	Freeport FL U.S.A.
110 F7	Freeport IL U.S.A.
117 □O5	Freeport ME U.S.A.
119 H3	Freeport NY U.S.A.
116 F8	Freeport PA U.S.A.
121 F11	Freeport TX U.S.A.
115 H12	Freeport City Gd Bahama Bahamas
121 F12	Freer TX U.S.A.
110 H5	Freesoil MI U.S.A.
97 K4	Free State prov. S. Africa
131 □2	Freetown Antigua and Barbuda
88 B4	Freetown Sierra Leone
115 I5	Freetown PA U.S.A.
119 G4	Freewood Acres NJ U.S.A.
99 □2a	Frégate, L'Îlot i. Inner Islands Seychelles
99 □2a	Frégate i. Inner Islands Seychelles
64 F4	Fregenal de la Sierra Spain
72 I4	Freihung Italy
66 G6	Freginals Spain
204 D2	Freijung S.A. Austr.
53 L2	Freihung Ger.
143 G2	Frei Gonzaga Brazil
53 L2	Freiburg Ger.
143 G3	Frei Inocêncio Brazil
65 N5	Freila Spain
53 N6	Freilassing Ger.
52 I2	Freinsheim Ger.
146 A6	Freirina Chile
53 L5	Freisen Ger.
41 J17	Freissinières France
59 K2	Freistadt Austria
37 L5	Freistroff France
51 I9	Freital Ger.
62 F7	Freixeda Port.
62 D9	Freixianda Port.
62 F6	Freixiosa Port.
62 C5	Freixo Port.
62 G6	Freixo de Espada à Cinta Port.
43 I8	Fréjairolles France
41 J10	Fréjus France
41 J10	Fréjus, Golfe de b. France
41 J6	Fréjus Tunnel France/Italy
22 B1	Frekhaug Norway
49 K6	Frelsdorf Ger.
209 C12	Fremantle W.A. Austr.
49 H6	Fremdingen Ger.
30 D5	Fremington Devon, England U.K.
124 K4	Fremont CA U.S.A.
110 E8	Fremont IN U.S.A.
110 I6	Fremont MI U.S.A.
120 G5	Fremont NE U.S.A.
116 B7	Fremont OH U.S.A.
116 F5	Fremont PA U.S.A.
125 V3	Fremont r. UT U.S.A.
118 B11	Frenchburg KY U.S.A.
130 Q3	French Cay i. Turks and Caicos Is
	French Congo country Africa see Congo
116 F7	French Creek r. PA U.S.A.
137 H4	French Guiana terr. S. America see Guiana
	French Guinea country Africa see Guinea
205 J8	French Island Vic. Austr.
122 K2	Frenchman r. MT U.S.A.
117 □O4	Frenchman Bay ME U.S.A.
120 E5	Frenchman Creek r. NE U.S.A.
124 L2	Frenchman Lake CA U.S.A.
125 Q5	Frenchman Lake NV U.S.A.
203 H7	French Pass South I. N.Z.
201 □3	French Polynesia terr. S. Pacific Ocean
9 G6	French Southern and Antarctic Lands terr. Indian Ocean
	French Somaliland country Africa see Djibouti
	French Territory of the Afars and Issas country Africa see Djibouti
18 I3	Frenchtown NJ U.S.A.
17 □Q1	Frenchville ME U.S.A.
87 F2	Frenda Alg.
36 C5	Freneuse France
53 J2	Frenštát pod Radhoštěm Czech Rep.
31 K5	Frensham Surrey, England U.K.
57 H2	Frenštát pod Radhoštěm Czech Rep.
73 M4	Frentani, Monti dei mts Italy
97 N4	Frere S. Africa
59 I6	Fresach Austria
73 I6	Fresagrandinaria Italy
37 I6	Fresco r. Brazil
88 D5	Fresco, Côte d'Ivoire
37 H2	Freshfield, Cape Antarctica
30 C7	Freshwater Isle of Wight, England U.K.
30 C4	Freshwater East Pembrokeshire, Wales U.K.
36 C7	Fresnay-l'Évêque France
39 L5	Fresnay-sur-Sarthe France
43 L5	Fresnedas r. Spain
40 H1	Fresne-St-Mamès France
37 K5	Fresnes-en-Woëvre France
37 K8	Fresnes-sur-Escaut France
36 E2	Fresnillo Mex.
124 M5	Fresno CA U.S.A.

124 L5	Fresno r. CA U.S.A.
62 I7	Fresno r. CA U.S.A.
62 I5	Fresno Alhándiga Spain
62 I6	Fresno de la Ribera Spain
63 J6	Fresno de Sayago Spain
36 B4	Fresno el Viejo Spain
36 F4	Fresnoy-Folny France
39 I6	Fresnoy-le-Grand France
37 M8	Fresse-sur-Moselle France
31 O3	Fressenneville France
21 I6	Fressingfield Suffolk, England U.K.
26 J5	Freswick Highland, Scotland U.K.
40 H2	Fretigney-et-Velloreille France
67 L8	Freu, Cap des c. Spain
67 K9	Freu de Cabrera sea chan. Spain
52 G2	Freudenberg Baden-Württemberg Ger.
53 L3	Freudenberg Bayern Ger.
49 E9	Freudenberg Nordrhein-Westfalen Ger.
52 B2	Freudenstadt Ger.
52 E5	Freudenstadt Ger.
36 D3	Frévent France
39 G4	Frévent France
78 A4	Fria Guinea
128 E4	Fria, Cape Namibia
124 M5	Fria, Sierra mts Mex.
124 M6	Friant CA U.S.A.
144 D3	Friant-Kern Canal CA U.S.A.
63 N3	Frias Arg.
63 N3	Frias Spain
70 C2	Fribourg Switz.
70 C2	Fribourg canton Switz.
70 E1	Frick Switz.
52 G6	Frickingen Ger.
122 C2	Friday Harbor WA U.S.A.
29 P5	Fridaythorpe East Riding of Yorkshire, England U.K.
52 F5	Friedberg an der Donau Ger.
53 N6	Fridolfing Ger.
212 M1	Fridtjof Nansen, Mount Antarctica
49 J6	Frieda (Meinhard) Ger.
59 L3	Friedberg Austria
53 J5	Friedberg (Hessen) Ger.
49 G10	Friedberg (Hessen) Ger.
51 E7	Friedberg (Saale) Ger.
53 M2	Friedenfels Ger.
116 G3	Friedens PA U.S.A.
118 C3	Friedensburg PA U.S.A.
53 E6	Friedenweiler Ger.
51 I6	Friederdorf (Brandenburg Ger.
51 F7	Friedersdorf Sachsen-Anhalt Ger.
49 I9	Friedewald Hessen Ger.
49 E9	Friedewald Rheinland-Pfalz Ger.
49 I8	Friedland Brandenburg Ger.
49 K9	Friedland Mecklenburg-Vorpommern Ger.
51 D7	Friedland Niedersachsen Ger.
49 G10	Friedrichsdorf Ger.
52 H6	Friedrichshafen Ger.
51 K7	Friedrichshain Ger.
51 D6	Friedrichskanal canal Ger.
49 J2	Friedrichskoog Ger.
50 E3	Friedrichsruhe Ger.
48 H2	Friedrichstadt Ger.
50 H5	Friedrichsthal Ger.
50 I4	Friedrichswalde Ger.
49 H9	Frielendorf Ger.
49 J6	Friemar Ger.
120 C5	Friend NE U.S.A.
130 □	Friendship Jamaica
171 K6	Friendship NY U.S.A.
171 M5	Fuding Fujian China
93 C5	Fuuga waterhole Kenya
187 H4	Fuji, Mount Japan
59 J6	Friesach Austria
50 G5	Friesack Ger.
49 E9	Friesenhagen Ger.
52 D5	Friesenheim Ger.
53 J6	Friesenried Ger.
44 I2	Friese Wad tidal flat Neth.
44 I2	Friesland prov. Neth.
48 E4	Friesoythe Ger.
	Frigate Island Inner Islands Seychelles see Frégate
21 N6	Frigesund Sweden
65 L7	Frigiliana Spain
71 J7	Frignano reg. Italy
36 I6	Frignicourt France
31 K5	Frimley Surrey, England U.K.
200 □6	Frindsbury Reef Solomon Is
31 O4	Frinton-on-Sea Essex, England U.K.
121 F11	Frio r. TX U.S.A.
121 F11	Frio r. TX U.S.A.
63 I9	Frio watercourse NM/TX U.S.A.
62 E2	Friol Spain
62 D9	Frisa, Loch l. Scotland U.K.
65 J2	Frisange Lux.
123 K7	Frisco CO U.S.A.
125 S3	Frisco Mountain UT U.S.A.
29 R7	Friskney Lincolnshire, England U.K.
117 L6	Frissell, Mount hill CT U.S.A.
30 D6	Frithelstock Stone Devon, England U.K.
21 L4	Fritsla Sweden
58 E5	Fritzens Austria
49 H8	Fritzlar Ger.
71 O3	Friuli - Venezia Giulia admin. reg. Italy
36 C3	Friville-Escarbotin France
29 N4	Frizington Cumbria, England U.K.
118 A5	Frizzellburg MD U.S.A.
20 J4	Froan nature res. Norway
20 J5	Froan park Norway
	Frobisher Bay Nunavut Can. see Iqaluit
105 L3	Frobisher Bay b. Nunavut Can.
107 I3	Frobisher Lake Sask. Can.
22 G6	Frøbjerg Bavnehøj hill Denmark
58 B7	Frodolfo r. Italy
29 L7	Frodsham Cheshire, England U.K.
37 O6	Frœschwiller France
36 H6	Froges France
20 J5	Frohavet b. Norway
51 E8	Frohburg Ger.
52 H2	Frohnberg hill Ger.
59 L5	Frohnleiten Austria
36 C6	Froideconche France
65 L6	Froissy France
14 K3	Frolovo Rus. Fed.
23 P7	Frombork Pol.
204 F3	Frome watercourse S.A. Austr.
130 □	Frome Jamaica
30 H5	Frome Somerset, England U.K.
30 H6	Frome r. England U.K.
204 G4	Frome, Lake salt flat S.A. Austr.
204 G4	Frome Downs S.A. Austr.
37 I3	Fromelennes France
36 G6	Fromentières France
38 C5	Fromentine France
63 L4	Frómista Spain
38 A5	Fromveur, Passage du str. France

37 J7	Froncles France
49 E8	Fröndenberg Ger.
49 O9	Fronhausen Ger.
43 D6	Fronsac Aquitaine France
43 F10	Fronsac Midi-Pyrénées France
64 D2	Fronteira Brazil
140 E3	Fronteiras Brazil
40 G3	Frontenard France
42 C3	Frontenay-Rohan-Rohan France
53 N4	Frontenhausen Ger.
127 I4	Frontera Coahuila Mex.
127 I4	Frontera Coahuila Mex.
126 E2	Frontera Tabasco Mex.
127 M8	Frontera, Punta pt Mex.
126 E2	Fronteras Mex.
43 I10	Frontignan France
43 G8	Fronton France
131 □1	Frontón de la Brea pt Puerto Rico
116 G10	Front Royal VA U.S.A.
51 D7	Frose Ger.
73 K4	Frosinone Italy
73 K4	Frosinone prov. Italy
73 M4	Frosolone Italy
20 K5	Frosta Norway
116 G9	Frostburg MD U.S.A.
213 I2	Frost Glacier Antarctica
37 L6	Frouard France
62 D1	Frouxeira, Punta da pt Spain
23 L2	Frövi Sweden
20 J5	Frøya i. Norway
36 E5	Froyeres France
36 D2	Fruges France
66 F3	Fruita CO U.S.A.
51 D7	Fruitland MD U.S.A.
125 V1	Fruitland UT U.S.A.
203 D12	Fruitlands South I. N.Z.
110 H6	Fruitport MI U.S.A.
125 X2	Fruitvale CO U.S.A.
19 W7	Frutkovaya Rus. Fed.
63 L6	Frumales Spain
183 N7	Frunze Batken Kyrg.
	Frunze Bishkek Kyrg. see Bishkek
17 N7	Frunze Khersons'ka Oblast' Ukr.
17 N7	Frunze Khersons'ka Oblast' Ukr.
17 N9	Frunzens'ke Ukr.
	Frunzenskoye Kyrg. see Bishkek
16 I6	Frunzivka Ukr.
76 H5	Fruška Gora hills Serb. and Mont.
76 H5	Fruška Gora nat. park Serb. and Mont.
142 C4	Frutal Brazil
70 D2	Frutigen Switz.
139 E3	Frutuoso Brazil
19 V5	Fryanovo Rus. Fed.
19 V6	Fryazino Rus. Fed.
57 H2	Frýdek-Mistek Czech Rep.
56 E1	Frýdlant Czech Rep.
117 □O4	Fryeburg ME U.S.A.
31 M4	Fryerning Essex, England U.K.
55 I2	Frygnowo Pol.
56 D3	Frymburk Czech Rep.
57 G2	Fryšták Czech Rep.
55 J6	Frysztak Pol.
201 □2a	Fua'amotu Tongatapu Tonga
171 L5	Fu'an Fujian China
26 F9	Fuar Bheinn hill Scotland U.K.
70 E6	Fubine Italy
71 J8	Fucecchio Italy
	Fucheng Anhui China see Fengyang
	Fucheng Shaanxi China see Fuxian
53 M2	Fuchsmühl Ger.
50 J4	Fuchstal Ger.
165 K12	Fuchū Hiroshima Japan
167 J4	Fuchū Japan
166 F2	Fuchū Toyama Japan
171 H6	Fuchuan Guangxi China
171 M3	Fuchun Jiang r. China
73 K2	Fucino r. Italy
164 S6	Fudai Japan
26 B8	Fuday i. Scotland U.K.
171 K6	Fude Fujian China
171 M5	Fuding Fujian China
93 C5	Fuuga waterhole Kenya
187 H4	Fuʼud Saudi Arabia
98 □3d	Fuencaliente La Palma Canary Is
65 H5	Fuencaliente Spain
98 □3d	Fuencaliente, Punta de pt La Palma Canary Is
63 R5	Fuenfría Spain
63 M8	Fuengirola Spain
63 O9	Fuenlabrada Spain
63 O7	Fuenlabrada de los Montes Spain
63 O4	Fuenmayor Spain
63 O8	Fuensalida Spain
65 O2	Fuensanta Castilla-La Mancha Spain
65 P5	Fuensanta Murcia Spain
63 C10	Fuente-Álamo Spain
67 C12	Fuente Álamo Spain
65 P3	Fuente Albilla, Cerro de mt. Spain
63 N5	Fuentearmegil Spain
65 O5	Fuentecambrón Spain
63 N5	Fuentecén Spain
64 G4	Fuente de Cantos Spain
64 G4	Fuente del Arco Spain
64 G3	Fuente del Maestre Spain
65 P3	Fuente de Pedro Naharro Spain
63 N4	Fuente de Piedra Spain
65 J6	Fuente de Piedra, Laguna de l. Spain
63 O4	Fuente el Fresno Spain
63 K6	Fuente el Sol Spain
62 G8	Fuenteguinaldo Spain
63 M5	Fuentelapeña Spain
63 O6	Fuentelcésped Spain
63 O6	Fuentelespino de Haro Spain
63 R9	Fuentelespino de Moya Spain
65 O5	Fuentelmonge Spain
63 L4	Fuente Obejuna Spain
64 G4	Fuente Palmera Spain
170 F5	Fuquan Guizhou China
23 L5	Fur Sweden
62 C7	Furadouro Port.
95 G2	Furancungo Moz.
71 L2	Furano Japan
63 I7	Fuenterrebollo Spain
62 I7	Fuenterroble de Salvatierra Spain
63 N3	Furci Italy
69 E7	Furci Siculo Sicilia Italy
164 W3	Füren-gawa r. Japan
164 W3	Füren-ko l. Japan
22 I6	Furese l. Denmark
184 D8	Fürgun, Küh-e mt. Iran
72 C2	Furiani Corse France
65 J6	Furkapass pass Switz.
118 E5	Furlong PA U.S.A.
19 V4	Furmanov Rus. Fed.
121 J2	Furmanov Rus. Fed.
26 F10	Furnace Argyll and Bute, Scotland U.K.
118 B6	Furnace Branch MD U.S.A.
184 H9	Furnas Port.
143 D1	Furnas, Represa resr Brazil
205 L9	Furneaux Group is Tas. Austr.
190 F4	Furqlus Syria
48 E3	Fürstenau Ger.
53 K2	Fürstenberg Brandenburg Ger.
49 H7	Fürstenberg Niedersachsen Ger.
92 D1	Fürstenberg (Lichtenfels) Ger.
92 D1	Gabuli vol. Eth.
55 K5	Gać Pol.
39 L4	Gacé France
55 J5	Gacko Bos.-Herz.
58 E6	Fürstenfeld Austria
53 K5	Fürstenfeldbruck Ger.
51 K5	Fürstenwalde Ger.
50 I4	Fürstenwerder Ger.
58 G8	Fürstenzell Ger.
57 K4	Furta Hungary
72 B8	Furtei Sardegna Italy
52 E5	Furtwangen im Schwarzwald Ger.
164 S3	Furubira Japan
21 M6	Furudal Sweden
167 M1	Furukawa Gifu Japan
166 F3	Furukawa Gifu Japan
164 R8	Furukawa Miyagi Japan
105 J3	Fury and Hecla Strait Nunavut Can.
136 C3	Fusagasugá Col.
73 Q9	Fuscaldo Italy
58 H4	Fuschlsee l. Austria
170 Q9	Fushan Hainan China
169 Q8	Fushan Shandong China
169 L9	Fushan Shanxi China
76 H9	Fushë-Krujë Albania
166 C6	Fushimi Japan
169 R6	Fushun Liaoning China
170 E4	Fushun Sichuan China
200 □2	Fusi Samoa
71 L7	Fusignano Italy
59 I6	Fusine in Valromana Italy
166 E5	Fuso Italy
162 E7	Fusong Jilin China
49 J4	Füßberg Austria
53 J6	Füssen Ger.
39 P7	Fussy France
63 R4	Fustiñana Spain
170 F7	Fusui Guangxi China
167 H4	Futaba Japan
166 F3	Futagawa Japan
165 I13	Futago-san vol. Japan
145 C6	Futaleufú Chile
166 E6	Futami Japan
165 □3	Futaoi-jima i. Japan
171 □J7	Fu Tau Pun Chau i. H.K. China
37 J5	Futeau France
76 H5	Futog Vojvodina, Srbija Serb. and Mont.
167 J5	Futtsu Japan
167 K5	Futtsu-misaki pt Japan
200 □5	Futuna i. Vanuatu
199 I3	Futuna i. Wallis and Futuna Is
	Futuna Islands Wallis and Futuna Is see Hoorn, Îles de
171 K5	Futun Xi r. China
41 H10	Fuveau France
187 I4	Fuwayrit Qatar
169 K9	Fuxian Shaanxi China
170 D6	Fuxian Hu l. China
170 E6	Fuyuan Yunnan China
169 Q5	Fuxin Xinjiang China
169 Q5	Fuxin Liaoning China
169 Q5	Fuxin Liaoning China
	Fuxinzhen Liaoning China see Fuxin
164 Q8	Fuya Japan
171 J2	Fuyang Anhui China
	Fuyang Guangxi China see Fuchuan
171 J7	Fuyang Zhejiang China
169 O7	Fuyang He r. China
170 D2	Fuyang Dao i. China
169 S3	Fuyu Heilong. China
162 B3	Fuyu Jilin China
170 E4	Fuyuan Heilong. China
160 I2	Fuyun Xinjiang China
57 K4	Füzesabony Hungary
57 K4	Füzesgyarmat Hungary
58 I6	Fusi i. Austria
121 E9	Fuzhou Fujian China
171 K5	Fuzhou Jiangxi China
71 R5	Fužine Croatia
191 I6	Füzuli Azer.
31 M4	Fyfield Essex, England U.K.
29 L6	Fylde lowland England U.K.
22 G6	Fyn i. Denmark
26 G10	Fyne, r. Scotland U.K.
26 F11	Fyne, Loch inlet Scotland U.K.
48 I1	Fynshav Denmark
32 E2	Fyns Hoved pt Denmark
22 F2	Fyresdal Norway
22 F1	Fyresvatn l. Norway
23 N2	Fyrisån r. Sweden
26 L8	Fyvie Aberdeenshire, Scotland U.K.
131 □7	Fyzabad Trin. and Tob.

G

175 □1	Gaafaru i. N. Male Maldives
175 □1	Gaafaru Atoll N. Male Maldives
175 □1	Gaafaru Channel Maldives
69 B7	Gaâfour Tunisia
59 K5	Gaal Austria
92 E3	Gaalkacyo Somalia
157 J4	Gaat r. Malaysia
96 B3	Gab watercourse Namibia
93 E3	Gabadadd wi Eth.
92 E3	Gabangab wall Eth.
43 E8	Gabarret France
43 G8	Gabas r. France
92 F2	Gabbac, Raas pt Somalia
59 L3	Gabbauco Slovakia
124 N3	Gabbs Valley Range mts NV U.S.A.
57 G4	Gabčíkovo Slovakia
91 B7	Gabela Angola
59 K5	Gaberl pass Austria
88 E4	Gaberones Botswana see Gaborone
106 C3	Gaberts AK U.S.A.
170 B8	Gabesville Tunisia
87 H2	Gabès Tunisia
87 H2	Gabès, Golfe de g. Tunisia
85 G4	Gäbrä, Wadi watercourse Sudan
91 C6	Gabia Dem. Rep. Congo
92 E3	Gabia la Grande Spain
41 C9	Gabian France
71 N8	Gabiano Italy
55 H3	Gabin Pol.
129 K7	Gabino Barreda Mex.
202 M5	Gable End Foreland hd North I. N.Z.
55 L1	Gabija Co l. China
53 J5	Gablingen Ger.
59 N3	Gablitz Austria
43 E9	Galan France
90 A5	Galana, Cerro mt. Arg.
93 C5	Galana r. Kenya
184 F3	Galand Iran
79 N7	Galanduf France
77 J2	Galanca Brazil
91 B8	Galangue Angola
94 F5	Galaroza Spain
93 C5	Galas r. Kenya
26 K11	Galashiels Scottish Borders, Scotland U.K.
94 C4	Galata Bulg.
92 D1	Galena Co.
20 Q2	Gälaniittu Norway
182 K8	Galata Uzbek.
136 □	Galana, Islas is Pacific Ocean
141 J7	Galápagos Islands is Pacific Ocean
217 M6	Galapagos Rise sea feature Pacific Ocean
136 □	Galapagos Rise sea feature Pacific Ocean
95 C5	Gaba Tula Kenya
77 N8	Gălbinaşi Romania
184 F3	Galandî Iran
77 N3	Gălăneşti Romania
91 C8	Gabo Nigeria
77 P7	Gălăţui Romania

59 M3	Furth bei Göttweig Austria
53 N3	Furth im Wald Ger.
52 E5	Furtwangen im Schwarzwald Ger.
164 R3	Furubira Japan
21 M6	Furudal Sweden
167 M1	Furukawa Gifu Japan
166 F3	Furukawa Gifu Japan
164 R8	Furukawa Miyagi Japan
105 J3	Fury and Hecla Strait Nunavut Can.
136 C3	Fusagasugá Col.
73 Q9	Fuscaldo Italy
58 H4	Fuschlsee l. Austria
170 Q9	Fushan Hainan China
169 Q8	Fushan Shandong China
169 L9	Fushan Shanxi China
76 H9	Fushë-Krujë Albania
166 C6	Fushimi Japan
169 R6	Fushun Liaoning China
170 E4	Fushun Sichuan China
200 □2	Fusi Samoa
71 L7	Fusignano Italy
59 I6	Fusine in Valromana Italy
166 E5	Fuso Italy
162 E7	Fusong Jilin China
49 J4	Füßberg Austria
53 J6	Füssen Ger.
39 P7	Fussy France
63 R4	Fustiñana Spain
170 F7	Fusui Guangxi China
167 H4	Futaba Japan
166 F3	Futagawa Japan
165 I13	Futago-san vol. Japan
145 C6	Futaleufú Chile
166 E6	Futami Japan
165 □3	Futaoi-jima i. Japan
171 □J7	Fu Tau Pun Chau i. H.K. China
37 J5	Futeau France
76 H5	Futog Vojvodina, Srbija Serb. and Mont.
167 J5	Futtsu Japan
167 K5	Futtsu-misaki pt Japan
200 □5	Futuna i. Vanuatu
199 I3	Futuna i. Wallis and Futuna Is
171 K5	Futun Xi r. China
41 H10	Fuveau France
187 I4	Fuwayrit Qatar
169 K9	Fuxian Shaanxi China
170 D6	Fuxian Hu l. China
170 E6	Fuyuan Yunnan China
169 Q5	Fuxin Xinjiang China
169 Q5	Fuxin Liaoning China
169 Q5	Fuxin Liaoning China
164 Q8	Fuya Japan
171 J2	Fuyang Anhui China
171 J7	Fuyang Zhejiang China
169 O7	Fuyang He r. China
170 D2	Fuyang Dao i. China
169 S3	Fuyu Heilong. China
162 B3	Fuyu Jilin China
170 E4	Fuyuan Heilong. China
160 I2	Fuyun Xinjiang China
57 K4	Füzesabony Hungary
57 K4	Füzesgyarmat Hungary
121 E9	Fuzhou Fujian China
171 K5	Fuzhou Jiangxi China
71 R5	Fužine Croatia
191 I6	Füzuli Azer.
31 M4	Fyfield Essex, England U.K.
29 L6	Fylde lowland England U.K.
22 G6	Fyn i. Denmark
26 G10	Fyne, r. Scotland U.K.
26 F11	Fyne, Loch inlet Scotland U.K.
48 I1	Fynshav Denmark
32 E2	Fyns Hoved pt Denmark
22 F2	Fyresdal Norway
22 F1	Fyresvatn l. Norway
23 N2	Fyrisån r. Sweden
26 L8	Fyvie Aberdeenshire, Scotland U.K.
131 □7	Fyzabad Trin. and Tob.

170 B2	Gadê Qinghai China
50 D3	Gadebusch Ger.
49 J6	Gadenstedt (Lahstedt) Ger.
71 L2	Gader r. Italy
178 C8	Gadhada Gujarat India
178 C9	Gadhada Gujarat India
185 L9	Gadhap Pak.
178 B8	Gadhka Gujarat India
178 C8	Gadhra Gujarat India
191 K5	Gädi Dağı mt. Azer.
99 □3a	Gäähe Comoros
	Njazidja Comoros
70 E2	Gadmen Switz.
72 C8	Gadoni Sardegna Italy
65 O7	Gádor Spain
65 N7	Gádor, Sierra de mts Spain
57 J5	Gádoros Hungary
185 L8	Gadra Balochistan Pak.
185 N9	Gadra Sindh Pak.
115 D8	Gadsden AL U.S.A.
125 R9	Gadsden AZ U.S.A.
200 □2	Gadwal Andhra Prad. India
71 L7	Gadžin Han Srbija Serb. and Mont.
64 A2	Gaeiras Port.
105 P2	Gael Hamke Bugt b. Greenland
30 F4	Gaer Powys, Wales U.K.
77 N6	Gäeşti Romania
73 L5	Gaeta Italy
73 L5	Gaeta, Golfo di g. Italy
167 H4	Gaeun Japan
73 L5	Gaffney SC U.S.A.
87 H2	Gafsa Tunisia
155 F4	Gag i. Papua Indon.
78 B2	Gagal Chad
179 L9	Gagan Madh. Prad. India
19 S6	Gagarin Rus. Fed.
183 M7	Gagarin Uzbek.
77 Q5	Găgăuzia rep. Moldova
50 D3	Gägelow Ger.
89 G3	Gagere watercourse Nigeria
52 E4	Gaggenau Ger.
68 F5	Gaggi Sicilia Italy
71 J7	Gaggio Montano Italy
70 E4	Gaglianico Italy
73 L5	Gagliano Castelferrato Sicilia Italy
75 O4	Gagliano del Capo Italy
41 E8	Gagnières France
88 D5	Gagnoa Côte d'Ivoire
109 G3	Gagnon Que. Can.
191 B2	Gagra Georgia
168 E8	Gagyi Qinghai China
94 C6	Gaiab watercourse Namibia
179 L7	Gaibandha Bangl.
77 P4	Găiceana Romania
58 I6	Gail r. Austria
121 E9	Gail TX U.S.A.
52 H4	Gaildorf Ger.
52 F6	Gailingen Ger.
43 H8	Gaillac France
41 B8	Gaillac-d'Aveyron France
119 J2	Gaillard, Lake CT U.S.A.
	Gaillimh Rep. of Ireland see Galway
36 C6	Gaillon France
41 E9	Gaillan-en-Médoc France
70 F5	Gaïnonlid Italy
73 J4	Gaïenne France
50 I4	Gaïnonel ga Lazio Italy
48 K3	Gaïllau Mecklenburg-Vorpommern Ger.
120 I6	Gallatin MO U.S.A.
115 D7	Gallatin TN U.S.A.
122 J4	Gallatin r. MT U.S.A.
66 D4	Galle Sri Lanka
66 N6	Gállego r. Spain
217 L6	Gallego Rise sea feature Pacific Ocean
145 C7	Gallegos r. Arg.
146 B7	Gallegos, Cabo c. Chile
63 J7	Gallegos de Argañán Spain
63 J7	Gallegos de Solmirón Spain
73 J4	Galleno Italy
73 I3	Gallese Italy
27 E9	Galley Head Rep. of Ireland
	Gallia country Europe see France
42 C5	Gallian-en-Médoc France
70 F5	Galliate Italy
73 J4	Gallicano nel Lazio Italy
50 I4	Gallin Mecklenburg-Vorpommern Ger.
48 K3	Gallin Mecklenburg-Vorpommern Ger.
136 D1	Gallinas, Punta pt Col.
71 L4	Gallio Italy
75 O3	Gallipoli Italy
	Gallipoli Turkey see Gelibolu
116 C10	Gallipolis OH U.S.A.
66 C6	Gallipuén, Embalse de resr Spain
20 P3	Gällivare Sweden
59 K6	Gallizien Austria
59 J3	Gallneukirchen Austria
63 R7	Gallo r. Spain
80 M5	Gallo Sweden
74 E7	Gallo, Capo c. Sicilia Italy
70 I2	Gallo, Lago di l. Italy
63 Q7	Gallocanta, Laguna de l. Spain
73 L5	Galluccio Italy
116 C10	Gallup KY U.S.A.
123 J9	Gallup NM U.S.A.
63 R5	Gallur Spain
72 B6	Galt;a reg. Sardegna Italy
89 G4	Galma watercourse Nigeria
73 J4	Galmé Italy
27 G8	Galmoy Rep. of Ireland
205 L6	Galong N.S.W. Austr.
176 G3	Galoya Sri Lanka
176 G9	Gal Oya National Park Sri Lanka
27 G6	Galros Rep. of Ireland
92 E4	Gal Shiilch Somalia
55 L1	Galstas r. Lith.
26 H11	Galston East Ayrshire, Scotland U.K.
124 K3	Galt CA U.S.A.
92 F4	Gal Tardo Somalia
23 M4	Galtås Sweden
58 C6	Galtür Austria
27 F7	Galtwhen mts Rep. of Ireland
27 E8	Galtymore hill Rep. of Ireland
184 H4	Galūgāh-e Āsīyeh Iran
184 C3	Galub Tanz.
146 C3	Galvarino Chile
66 C6	Galve Spain
63 C6	Galve de Sorbe Spain
72 B6	Galvéias Port.
110 F9	Galva IL U.S.A.
121 H11	Galva TX U.S.A.
121 H11	Galveston IN U.S.A.
121 H11	Galveston TX U.S.A.
147 G3	Gálvez Arg.
178 H4	Galwa Nepal
27 D6	Galway Rep. of Ireland
27 D6	Galway county Rep. of Ireland
27 C6	Galway Bay Rep. of Ireland
131 □7	Galways Soufrière vol.
155 F4	Gam i. Papua Indon.

Gam to Gentioux, Plateau de

266

155 G4 Gam i. Papua Indon.
158 G4 Gâm, Sông r. Vietnam
142 C2 Gamá Brazil
145 E6 Gama, Isla i. Arg.
36 C4 Gamaches France
166 F6 Gamagōri Japan
97 O6 Gamalakhe S. Africa
155 E3 Gamalama vol. Maluku Indon.
43 C8 Gamarde-les-Bains France
136 C2 Gamarra Col.
57 G5 Gamás Hungary
89 H3 Gamawa Nigeria
146 E5 Gamay Arg.
154 E5 Gamay Bay Samar Phil.
91 C7 Gamba Angola
Gamba Xizang China see Gongbalou
90 A5 Gamba Gabon
88 E4 Gambaga Ghana
70 I5 Gambara Italy
75 J7 Gambarie Italy
71 J8 Gambassi Terme Italy
73 N4 Gambatesa Italy
92 B2 Gambēla Eth.
92 B3 Gambēla Hizboch admin. reg. Eth.
92 B3 Gambēla National Park Eth.
104 A3 Gambell AK U.S.A.
118 B6 Gamber MD U.S.A.
71 M7 Gambettola Italy
Gambia country Africa see The Gambia
88 A3 Gambia r. Gambia
88 B3 Gambie r. Senegal
206 C1 Gambier, Cape N.T. Austr.
201 □3 Gambier, Îles is Arch. des Tuamotu Fr. Polynesia
204 F6 Gambier Islands S.A. Austr.
Gambier Islands Arch. des Tuamotu Fr. Polynesia see Gambier, Îles
115 □2 Gambier Village New Prov. Bahamas
109 K3 Gambo Nfld and Lab. Can.
90 D3 Gambo C.A.R.
70 F5 Gambolò Italy
90 B5 Gamboma Congo
207 I4 Gamboola Qld Austr.
90 B3 Gamboula C.A.R.
118 B6 Gambrills MD U.S.A.
37 O6 Gambsheim France
59 L4 Gaming Austria
191 H5 Gamış Dağı mt. Azer.
96 F9 Gamka r. S. Africa
155 E3 Gamkunoro, Gunung vol. Halmahera Indon.
23 M4 Gamleby Sweden
31 L3 Gamlingay Cambridgeshire, England U.K.
59 M6 Gamlitz Austria
85 G5 Gammams well Sudan
53 L4 Gammelsdorf Ger.
20 Q4 Gammelstaden Sweden
52 G5 Gammertingen Ger.
204 G4 Gammon Ranges National Park S.A. Austr.
166 D5 Gamō Japan
96 C5 Gamoep S. Africa
62 I2 Gamonal mt. Spain
162 G7 Gamova, Mys pt Rus. Fed.
176 G9 Gampaha Sri Lanka
176 G9 Gampola Sri Lanka
70 G1 Gams Switz.
185 I7 Gamshadzai Kūh mts Iran
170 B3 Gamtog Xizang China
97 J9 Gamtoos r. S. Africa
92 C3 Gamud mt. Eth.
20 T1 Gamvik Norway
43 D9 Gan France
175 □2 Gan Addu Atoll Maldives
175 □2 Gan i. Addu Atoll Maldives
170 C2 Gana Sichuan China
125 W6 Ganado AZ U.S.A.
41 H8 Ganagobie France
85 G5 Gananita Sudan
108 E4 Gananoque Ont. Can.
184 D7 Ganāveh Iran
191 H5 Gäncä Azer.
191 H5 Gäncäçay r. Azer.
172 I6 Gancaohu Xinjiang China
170 G9 Gancheng Hainan China
Gand Belgium see Gent
91 B8 Ganda Angola
173 L11 Ganda Xizang China
155 A5 Gandadiwata, Bukit mt. Indon.
178 H9 Gandai Chhattisgarh India
91 D6 Gandajika Dem. Rep. Congo
179 I6 Gandak Barrage dam Nepal
185 I5 Gandalak Afgh.
178 E2 Gandarbal Jammu and Kashmir
62 D6 Gandarela Port.
185 M7 Gandari Mountain Pak.
185 I5 Gandarra Afgh.
185 L7 Gandava Pak.
70 H4 Gandellino Italy
109 K3 Gander Nfld and Lab. Can.
105 M5 Gander r. Nfld and Lab. Can.
48 G4 Ganderkesee Ger.
109 K3 Gander Lake Nfld and Lab. Can.
66 F5 Gandesa Spain
178 D9 Gandevi Gujarat India
178 C8 Gandhidham Gujarat India
178 D8 Gandhinagar Gujarat India
178 E7 Gandhi Sagar resr India
90 E2 Gandi, Wadi watercourse Sudan
67 E10 Gandía Spain
70 H4 Gandino Italy
98 □3f Gando, Punta de pt Gran Canaria Canary Is
184 D6 Gandomān Iran
191 J4 Gändov Azer.
62 C4 Gandra Viana do Castelo Port.
62 D5 Gandra Viana do Castelo Port.
140 F5 Gandu Brazil
168 H9 Gandu Qinghai China
20 T1 Gandvik Norway
Gandzha Azer. see Gäncä
88 C2 Gâneb well Maur.
62 C4 Ganfei Port.
181 L4 Ganga r. Bangl./India alt. Padma (Bangladesh), conv. Ganges
89 G4 Ganga Nigeria
176 G9 Ganga r. Sri Lanka
Ganga Cone sea feature Indian Ocean see Ganges Cone
176 E3 Gangakher Mahar. India
90 F4 Gangala Na Bodia Dem. Rep. Congo
145 C6 Gangán Arg.
145 C6 Gangán, Pampa de plain Arg.
178 D5 Ganganagar Rajasthan India
176 D3 Gangapur Mahar. India
178 E7 Gangapur Rajasthan India
178 F6 Gangapur Rajasthan India
89 H3 Gangara Niger
179 L9 Ganga Sagar W. Bengal India
178 C7 Ganga Sera Rajasthan India
176 D5 Gangavali r. India
158 B3 Gangaw Myanmar
176 E5 Gangawati Karnataka India
158 C3 Gangaw Range mts Myanmar
168 G8 Gangca Qinghai China
178 E8 Gangdhar Rajasthan India
173 F11 Gangdisê Shan mts Xizang China
181 L4 Ganges r. Bangl./India alt. Ganga, alt. Padma (Bangladesh)
41 D9 Ganges France
179 L9 Ganges, Mouths of the Bangl./India
215 J3 Ganges Cone sea feature Indian Ocean
74 G8 Gangi Sicilia Italy
74 G8 Gangi r. Sicilia Italy
53 N5 Gangkofen Ger.
88 C5 Ganglota Liberia
168 E7 Gangou Qinghai China
168 I9 Gangouyi Gansu China
Gangra Turkey see Çankırı
178 E7 Gangrar Rajasthan India
179 L6 Gangtok Sikkim India
168 I9 Gangu Gansu China
169 N8 Gangziyao Hebei China
169 S2 Gan He r. China
172 I4 Ganhezi Xinjiang China
155 F4 Gani Halmahera Indon.
88 C4 Ganiakali Guinea
177 I3 Ganjam Orissa India
184 D6 Ganjgūn Iran
171 K4 Gan Jiang r. China
169 R5 Ganjig Nei Mongol China
169 L9 Ganjing Shaanxi China
169 N4 Ganjur Sum Nei Mongol China
19 Q2 Gankovo Rus. Fed.
170 D4 Ganluo Sichuan China
169 R3 Gannan Heilong. China
40 C4 Gannat France
109 J2 Gannet Islands Ecological Reserve Nfld and Lab. Can.
122 J5 Gannett Peak WY U.S.A.
16 F3 Gannopil' Ukr.
120 F3 Gannvalley SD U.S.A.
173 K8 Ganq Qinghai China
169 K8 Ganquan Shaanxi China
96 D10 Gansbaai S. Africa
49 D10 Gänsehals hill Ger.
59 O3 Gänserndorf Austria
45 F7 Ganshoren Belgium
170 F4 Ganshui Chongqing China
168 E6 Gansu prov. China
92 D4 Gantamaa Somalia
168 I8 Gantang Nei Mongol China
179 I9 Gantapara Orissa India
208 G4 Gantheaume Point W.A. Austr.
191 B2 Gant'iadi Ap'khazet'i Georgia
191 F4 Gant'iadi Georgia
70 C2 Gantrisch mt. Switz.
157 H6 Gantung Indon.
171 J6 Ganxian Jiangxi China
178 F8 Ganyal r. Madh. Prad. India
89 I4 Ganye Nigeria
96 I2 Ganyesa S. Africa
169 P9 Ganyu Jiangsu China
182 C4 Ganyushkino Kazakh.
171 J6 Ganzhou Jiangxi China
92 A3 Ganzi Sudan
50 F4 Ganzlin Ger.
89 E2 Gao Mali
89 F2 Gao admin. reg. Mali
171 J4 Gao'an Jiangxi China
168 H8 Gaoba Gansu China
169 N7 Gaocheng Hebei China
171 L3 Gaochun Jiangsu China
171 M4 Gaojian Zhejiang China
168 H8 Gaolan Gansu China
170 B6 Gaoligong Shan mts China
169 K9 Gaoling Shaanxi China
169 P8 Gaomi Shandong China
171 H5 Gaomutang Hunan China
169 M9 Gaoping Shanxi China
169 O8 Gaoqing Shandong China
168 F7 Gaotai Gansu China
169 O8 Gaotang Shandong China
Gaoting Zhejiang China see Daishan
169 K7 Gaotouyao Nei Mongol China
88 E4 Gaoua Burkina
88 B4 Gaoual Guinea
Gaoxian Sichuan China see Wenjiang
169 N7 Gaoyang Hebei China
171 I7 Gaoyao Guangdong China
169 N8 Gaoyi Hebei China
171 L2 Gaoyou Jiangsu China
171 L2 Gaoyou Hu l. China
170 H8 Gaozhou Guangdong China
41 I7 Gap France
118 C5 Gap PA U.S.A.
154 C4 Gapan Luzon Phil.
41 I10 Gapeau r. France
90 E3 Gapi Dem. Rep. Congo
206 E2 Gapuwiyak N.T. Austr.
173 F12 Gaqoi Xizang China
179 K5 Gaqung Xizang China
160 D5 Gar Xizang China
185 J8 Gar Pak.
162 F2 Gar' r. Rus. Fed.
57 I5 Gara Hungary
27 F5 Gara, Lough l. Rep. of Ireland
87 H3 Garaa Tebourt well Tunisia
67 C8 Garaballa Spain
185 K2 Garabekevyul Turkm.
90 B4 Garabinzam Congo
41 C7 Garabit, Viaduc de France
92 F3 Garacad Somalia
98 □3a Garachico Tenerife Canary Is
126 □T13 Garachiné Panama
126 □T13 Garachiné, Punta pt Panama
92 E2 Garadag Somalia
28 D7 Garadice Rep. of Ireland
27 G4 Garadice Lough l. Rep. of Ireland
87 G6 Gara Ekar hill Alg.
98 □3d Garafía La Palma Canary Is
184 I6 Garāgheh Iran
136 C3 Garagoa Col.
73 Q6 Garaguso Italy
205 L3 Garah N.S.W. Austr.
185 O4 Garai Pak.
98 □3a Garajonay, Parque Nacional de nat. park La Gomera Canary Is
88 D4 Garalo Mali
90 F4 Garamba r. Dem. Rep. Congo
168 G8 Garang Qinghai China
140 F4 Garanhuns Brazil
97 L1 Ga-Rankuwa S. Africa
140 B5 Garapu Brazil
142 D2 Garapuava Brazil
90 D2 Garar, Plaine de plain Chad
178 G7 Garautha Uttar Prad. India
41 G8 Garaux, Rocher mt. France
206 F4 Garawa Aboriginal Land res. N.T. Austr.
90 D2 Garba C.A.R.
92 D4 Garbahaarrey Somalia
55 J4 Garbatka-Letnisko Pol.
92 C4 Garba Tula Kenya
65 J2 Garbayuela Spain
124 I1 Garberville CA U.S.A.
184 D5 Garbosh, Kūh-e mt. Iran
77 O5 Gârbova, Vârful hill Romania
55 K4 Garbów Pol.
49 I6 Garbsen Ger.
178 H4 Garbyang Uttaranchal India
142 C5 Garça Brazil
142 A1 Garças, Rio das r. Brazil
77 P4 Gârceni Romania
53 N5 Garching an der Alz Ger.
53 L5 Garching bei München Ger.
40 C2 Garchizy France
66 G5 Garcia Spain
128 D5 García, Cerro mt. Mex.
128 D4 Garcia de la Cadena Mex.
142 A4 Garcias Brazil
65 I2 Garcia Sola, Embalse de resr Spain
64 H2 Garciaz Spain
63 J7 Garcihernández Spain
63 L7 Garcillán Spain
77 O4 Gârcina Romania
63 O8 Garcinarro Spain
41 E8 Gard dept France
41 F9 Gard r. France
71 J4 Garda Italy
71 J5 Garda, Lago di l. Italy
191 G4 Gardabani Georgia
77 K4 Gârda de Sus Romania
41 G10 Gardanne France
69 A7 Garde, Cap de c. Alg.
54 G2 Gardeja Pol.
107 J2 Garde Lake N.W.T. Can.
50 D5 Gardelegen Ger.
71 L2 Gardena r. Italy
120 E7 Garden City KS U.S.A.
119 H3 Garden City NY U.S.A.
121 E10 Garden City TX U.S.A.
110 H4 Garden Corners MI U.S.A.
124 O8 Garden Grove CA U.S.A.
107 M4 Garden Hill Man. Can.
209 C12 Garden Island W.A. Austr.
110 I4 Garden Island MI U.S.A.
116 D11 Garden Mountain VA U.S.A.
118 A2 Garden View PA U.S.A.
44 I4 Garderen Neth.
22 G1 Gardermoen airport Norway
147 H5 Gardey Arg.
185 M5 Gardēz Afgh.
117 □P4 Gardiner ME U.S.A.
122 I4 Gardiner MT U.S.A.
206 D7 Gardiner, Mount N.T. Austr.
206 B5 Gardiner Range hills N.T. Austr.
119 K2 Gardiners Bay NY U.S.A.
119 K2 Gardiners Island NY U.S.A.
206 D7 Gardiner's Range mts N.T. Austr.
48 G2 Garding Ger.
Gardner atoll Micronesia see Faraulep
110 F8 Gardner IL U.S.A.
117 N6 Gardner MA U.S.A.
212 T1 Gardner Inlet Antarctica
119 K1 Gardner Lake CT U.S.A.
117 □R4 Gardner Lake ME U.S.A.
197 H2 Gardner Pinnacles is HI U.S.A.
124 M3 Gardnerville NV U.S.A.
23 N7 Gardno, Jezioro lag. Pol.
41 E8 Gardon d'Alès r. France
41 D8 Gardon de St-Jean r. France
71 J4 Gardone Riviera Italy
70 I4 Gardone Val Trompia Italy
43 E6 Gardonne France
57 H4 Gárdony Hungary
43 H9 Gardouch France
20 N4 Gardsjönås Sweden
23 M5 Gärdslösa Öland Sweden
43 C7 Garein France
28 H1 Gare Loch inlet Scotland U.K.
26 G10 Garelochhead Argyll and Bute, Scotland U.K.
68 F3 Garešnica Croatia
70 E7 Garessio Italy
200 □5 Garet, Mount vol. Vanuatu
87 G4 Garet El Djenoun mt. Alg.
137 H3 Gare Tigre Fr. Guiana
123 K7 Garfield CO U.S.A.
119 G3 Garfield NJ U.S.A.
29 O6 Garforth West Yorkshire, England U.K.
73 Q8 Garga r. Italy
78 C5 Gargalianoi Greece
64 H2 Gargáligas Spain
65 H2 Gargáligas r. Spain
66 D6 Gargallo Spain
42 H4 Gargan, Mont hill France
73 P4 Gargano, Parco Nazionale del nat. park Italy
62 I8 Garganta la Olla Spain
108 C4 Gargantua, Cape Ont. Can.
189 N8 Gargar Iran
41 G9 Gargas France
71 K2 Gargazzone Italy
58 A6 Gargellen Austria
36 D6 Garges-lès-Gonesse France
42 H2 Gargilesse-Dampierre France
71 J4 Gargnano Italy
41 D8 Gargo mt. France
29 M6 Gargrave North Yorkshire, England U.K.
26 H10 Gargunnock Hills Scotland U.K.
Gargunsa Xizang China see Gar
18 E6 Gargždai Lith.
178 G8 Garhakota Madh. Prad. India
179 K8 Garhbeta W. Bengal India
178 G8 Garhi Madh. Prad. India
178 E8 Garhi Rajasthan India
185 N7 Garhi Ikhtiar Khan Pak.
185 L7 Garhi Khairo Pak.
178 G7 Garhi Malehra Madh. Prad. India
178 G5 Garhmuktesar Uttar Prad. India
178 F4 Garhshankar Punjab India
179 I7 Garhwa Jharkhand India
73 L5 Gari r. Italy
141 C9 Garibaldi Brazil
106 F5 Garibaldi B.C. Can.
106 F5 Garibaldi, Mount B.C. Can.
106 F5 Garibaldi Provincial Park B.C. Can.
97 J6 Gariep Dam resr S. Africa
97 J6 Gariep Dam Nature Reserve S. Africa
96 B6 Garies S. Africa
73 L5 Garigliano r. Italy
63 Q3 Garínoain Spain
92 C5 Garissa Kenya
18 H4 Garkalne Latvia
173 H10 Garkung Caka l. Xizang China
Gârla Mare r. Moldova see Gîrla Mare
121 G9 Garland TX U.S.A.
70 F5 Garlasco Italy
59 K4 Garlenz Austria
18 G7 Garliava Lith.
77 Q6 Gârliciu Romania
26 H13 Garlieston Dumfries and Galloway, Scotland U.K.
43 D8 Garlin France
65 I3 Garlitos Spain
27 I5 Garlowcross Rep. of Ireland
48 J4 Garlstorf Ger.
Garm Tajik. see Gharm
185 K5 Garmab Afgh.
184 G4 Garmab Iran
184 C6 Garmdasht Iran
184 F5 Garmeh Eşfahān Iran
184 G3 Garmeh Khorāsān Iran
184 C2 Garmī Iran
53 K7 Garmisch-Partenkirchen Ger.
26 E10 Garmony Argyll and Bute, Scotland U.K.
184 E7 Garmosht Iran
184 E4 Garmsar Iran
185 J6 Garmsel reg. Afgh.
185 J6 Garmushki Afgh.
120 I4 Garner IA U.S.A.
116 C11 Garner KY U.S.A.
120 H6 Garnett KS U.S.A.
27 B9 Garnish Rep. of Ireland
184 H7 Gārnow Iran
205 I5 Garnpung Lake imp. l. N.S.W. Austr.
179 M7 Garo Hills Meghalaya India
66 G2 Garona r. Spain
43 C6 Garonne r. France
43 E7 Garonne, Canal latéral à la France
41 E9 Garons France
92 F2 Garoowe Somalia
141 C9 Garopaba Brazil
178 E7 Garoth Madh. Prad. India
88 E2 Garou, Lac l. Mali
89 I4 Garoua Cameroon
89 I5 Garoua Boulai Cameroon
23 K2 Garphyttan Sweden
23 K2 Garphyttans nationalpark nat. park Sweden
173 K10 Gar Qu r. Qinghai China
173 K10 Garqu Yan Qinghai China
62 I3 Garrafe de Torio Spain
43 B10 Garralda Spain
27 D9 Garrane Rep. of Ireland
63 P5 Garray Spain
147 F5 Garré Arg.
48 F5 Garrel Ger.
154 □ Garreru i. Palau
110 I8 Garrett IN U.S.A.
41 D9 Garrigues reg. France
27 F4 Garrison Northern Ireland U.K.
116 B10 Garrison KY U.S.A.
120 I2 Garrison MN U.S.A.
120 E2 Garrison ND U.S.A.
119 H2 Garrison NY U.S.A.
27 J5 Garristown Rep. of Ireland
191 E4 Garrnarrich Armenia
129 L7 Garro Mex.
27 K2 Garronpoint Northern Ireland U.K.
27 K2 Garron Point Northern Ireland U.K.
62 G9 Garrovillas Spain
65 P6 Garrucha Spain
185 K7 Garruk Pak.
26 G8 Garry r. Scotland U.K.
26 G8 Garry, Loch l. Highland, Scotland U.K.
184 G2 Garrygala Turkm.
105 H3 Garry Lake Nunavut Can.
26 C6 Garrynahine Western Isles, Scotland U.K.
97 L7 Garryowen S. Africa
27 F9 Garryvoe Rep. of Ireland
53 M5 Gars am Inn Ger.
59 M2 Gars am Kamp Austria
29 M5 Garsdale Head Cumbria, England U.K.
93 D5 Garsen Kenya
84 D6 Garsila Sudan
23 K6 Gärsnäs Sweden
29 L6 Garstang Lancashire, England U.K.
48 J4 Garstedt Ger.
59 J3 Garsten Austria
203 C12 Garston South I. N.Z.
42 F2 Gartempe r. France
30 E3 Garth Powys, Wales U.K.
30 F2 Garthmyl Powys, Wales U.K.
26 G10 Gartocharn West Dunbartonshire, Scotland U.K.
Gartok Xizang China see Garyarsa
50 D4 Gartow Ger.
52 F4 Gärtringen Ger.
50 J4 Gartz Ger.
94 C5 Garub Namibia
154 □ Garusuun Palau
157 G8 Garut Jawa Indon.
27 G5 Garvagh Rep. of Ireland
27 I3 Garvagh Northern Ireland U.K.
27 H4 Garvaghy Northern Ireland U.K.
26 K11 Garvald East Lothian, Scotland U.K.
26 H8 Garvamore Highland, Scotland U.K.
64 C5 Garvão Port.
26 D10 Garvard Argyll and Bute, Scotland U.K.
26 G7 Garve Highland, Scotland U.K.
203 C12 Garvie Mountains South I. N.Z.
55 J4 Garwolin Pol.
173 E10 Gar Xincun Xizang China
114 D5 Gary IN U.S.A.
116 D11 Gary WV U.S.A.
173 E11 Garyarsa Xizang China
170 B3 Garyi Sichuan China
165 J12 Garyū-zan mt. Japan
50 H2 Garz Ger.
144 E3 Garza Arg.
173 D10 Gar Zangbo r. China
129 H1 Garza Valdez Mex.
170 B3 Garzê Sichuan China
136 C4 Garzón Col.
Gasan-Kuli Turkm. see Esenguly
184 E3 Gasan-Kuliyskiy Zapovednik nature res. Turkm.
54 F3 Gąsawa Pol.
58 B6 Gaschurn Austria
51 F8 Gaschwitz Ger.
43 C8 Gascogne reg. France
34 C5 Gascogne, Golfe de g. France/Spain
120 J6 Gasconade r. MO U.S.A.
Gascony reg. France see Gascogne
Gascony, Gulf of France/Spain see Gascogne, Golfe de
209 C8 Gascoyne r. W.A. Austr.
209 D8 Gascoyne, Mount hill W.A. Austr.
209 C8 Gascoyne Junction W.A. Austr.
63 O8 Gascueña Spain
Gascuña, Golfo de g. France/Spain see Gascogne, Golfe de
173 H11 Gase Xizang China
175 □1 Gasfinolhu i. N. Male Maldives
186 C8 Gash and Setit prov. Eritrea
178 F2 Gasherbrum I mt. Jammu and Kashmir
185 Q4 Gasherbrum II mt. China/Jammu and Kashmir
85 H6 Gash Setit Wildlife Reserve nature res. Eritrea
185 I8 Gasht Iran
173 J7 Gas Hu salt l. China
89 H3 Gashua Nigeria
26 B7 Gasker i. Scotland U.K.
55 K2 Gąski Pol.
36 C5 Gasny France
55 I3 Gąsocin Pol.
130 D3 Gaspar Cuba
156 G6 Gaspar, Selat sea chan. Indon.
109 H3 Gaspé Que. Can.
109 H3 Gaspé, Baie de b. Que. Can.
109 H3 Gaspé, Cap c. Que. Can.
109 H3 Gaspé, Péninsule de pen. Que. Can.
75 L6 Gasperina Italy
59 I3 Gaspoltshofen Austria
88 E3 Gassan Burkina
164 R8 Gassan vol. Japan
88 B3 Gassane Senegal
116 E10 Gassaway WV U.S.A.
44 K3 Gasselte Neth.
44 K3 Gasselternijveen Neth.
65 L2 Gasset, Embalse de resr Spain
41 J10 Gassin France
89 H4 Gassol Nigeria
125 Q5 Gass Peak NV U.S.A.
58 H5 Gasteiner Tal val. Austria
162 M4 Gastello Sakhalin Rus. Fed.
59 L2 Gastern Austria
43 B7 Gastes France
116 H12 Gaston NC U.S.A.
116 H12 Gaston, Lake NC U.S.A.
115 G8 Gastonia NC U.S.A.
78 C5 Gastouni Greece
145 C6 Gastre Arg.
62 G8 Gata Spain
65 O7 Gata, Cabo de c. Spain
190 B4 Gata, Cape Cyprus
62 G8 Gata, Sierra de mts Spain
67 F10 Gata de Gorgos Spain
106 E3 Gataga r. B.C. Can.
76 J5 Gătaia Romania
Gatas, Akra c. Cyprus see Gata, Cape
19 N2 Gatchina Rus. Fed.
116 C12 Gate City VA U.S.A.
26 H13 Gatehouse of Fleet Dumfries and Galloway, Scotland U.K.
57 I5 Gátér Hungary
51 D7 Gatersleben Ger.
29 N4 Gateshead Tyne and Wear, England U.K.
105 H2 Gateshead Island Nunavut Can.
104 C3 Gates of the Arctic National Park and Preserve AK U.S.A.
115 I7 Gatesville NC U.S.A.
121 G10 Gatesville TX U.S.A.
125 X3 Gateway CO U.S.A.
119 G4 Gateway National Recreational Area park NJ U.S.A.
138 C5 Gatico Chile
36 E7 Gâtinais reg. France
39 L7 Gâtine reg. France
108 F4 Gatineau Que. Can.
108 F4 Gatineau r. Que. Can.
65 J4 Gato r. Spain
67 D8 Gátova Spain
59 O3 Gattendorf Austria
71 M7 Gatteo a Mare Italy
41 K9 Gattières France
70 E4 Gattinara Italy
207 N9 Gatton Qld Austr.
136 B2 Gatún Panama
126 □S13 Gatún, Lago l. Panama
184 C5 Gatvand Iran
31 L5 Gatwick airport England U.K.
201 □1 Gau i. Fiji
52 E2 Gau-Algesheim Ger.
140 B5 Gaúcha do Norte Brazil
36 F4 Gauchy France
65 I7 Gaucín Spain
65 J7 Gaudalteba, Embalse de resr Spain
107 L3 Gauer Lake Man. Can.
Gauhati Assam India see Guwahati
18 H4 Gauja r. Latvia
18 I7 Gauja r. Lith.
18 I4 Gaujas nacionālais parks nat. park Latvia
52 H2 Gaukönigshofen Ger.
Gaul country Europe see France
64 □ Gaula Madeira
20 K5 Gaula r. Norway
116 D10 Gauley Bridge WV U.S.A.
45 I9 Gaume reg. Belgium
52 E2 Gau-Odernheim Ger.
21 I6 Gaupne Norway
Gaurdak Turkm. see Govurdak
176 E6 Gauribidanur Karnataka India
179 M8 Gaurnadi Bangl.
22 E2 Gausta mt. Norway
97 M2 Gauteng prov. S. Africa
53 K5 Gauting Ger.
66 E4 Gautizalema r. Spain
185 K4 Gauzan Afgh.
66 J5 Gavà Spain
189 P9 Gāvakān Iran
70 I4 Gavardo Italy
184 H3 Gavāreshg Iran
43 D10 Gavarnie France
43 D10 Gavarnie, Cirque de corrie France/Spain
191 G5 Gavarr Armenia
185 I9 Gavāter Iran
57 K3 Gávavencsellő Hungary
184 E8 Gāvbandī Iran
184 E8 Gāvbūs, Kūh-e mts Iran
78 F8 Gavdopoula i. Greece
78 F8 Gavdos i. Greece
43 B8 Gave r. France
62 D4 Gave Port.
43 D9 Gave d'Arrens r. France
43 C9 Gave d'Aspe r. France
43 B8 Gave d'Oloron r. France
43 C9 Gave d'Ossau r. France
184 B4 Gāveh Rūd r. Iran
45 E7 Gavere Belgium
70 F6 Gavi Italy
73 K6 Gavi, Isola di i. Italy
141 E5 Gavião r. Brazil
64 D2 Gavião Port.
136 D6 Gaviãozinho Brazil
184 B4 Gavīleh Iran
147 F6 Gaviotas Arg.
70 F4 Gavirate Italy
184 E5 Gav Khūnī Iran
23 N1 Gävle Sweden
23 M1 Gävleborg county Sweden
23 N1 Gävlebukten b. Sweden
72 C7 Gavoi Sardegna Italy
72 F2 Gavorrano Italy
38 I4 Gavray France
15 H5 Gavrilovka Vtoraya Rus. Fed.
19 X5 Gavrilov Posad Rus. Fed.
19 W4 Gavrilov-Yam Rus. Fed.
78 F5 Gavrio Andros Greece
94 C5 Gawachab Namibia
158 C1 Gawai Myanmar
179 J7 Gawan Jharkhand India
84 B3 Gawat well Libya
59 O3 Gaweinstal Austria
178 F9 Gawilgarh Hills India
204 G6 Gawler S.A. Austr.
204 E5 Gawler Ranges hills S.A. Austr.
55 K1 Gawliki Wielkie Pol.
54 D4 Gaworzyce Pol.
29 M7 Gawsworth Cheshire, England U.K.
29 M5 Gawthrop Cumbria, England U.K.
89 G4 Gawu Nigeria
Gäwür watercourse Turkm. see Gyaur
168 G5 Gaxun Nur salt l. Nei Mongol China
182 H2 Gay Rus. Fed.
110 F2 Gay MI U.S.A.
179 J7 Gaya Bihar India
157 L1 Gaya i. Malaysia
157 M2 Gaya i. Malaysia
89 F4 Gaya Niger
Gayá r. Spain see El Gaià
162 F7 Gaya He r. China
178 D2 Gayal Gah Jammu and Kashmir
157 K8 Gayam Jawa Indon.
92 A5 Gayaza Uganda
28 C7 Gaybrook Rep. of Ireland
86 C4 G'Aydat al Jhoucha ridge Western Sahara
17 Q9 Gayduk Rus. Fed.
89 F3 Gayéri Burkina
110 J4 Gaylord MI U.S.A.
120 H3 Gaylord MN U.S.A.
207 M8 Gayndah Qld Austr.
19 T4 Gaynovo Rus. Fed.
14 K3 Gayny Rus. Fed.
31 N2 Gayton Norfolk, England U.K.
14 G4 Gayutino Rus. Fed.
184 D5 Gaz Eşfahān Iran
184 G8 Gaz Hormozgan Iran
190 C7 Gaza terr. Asia
190 C7 Gaza Gaza
95 G4 Gaza prov. Moz.
185 I1 Gaz-Achak Turkm.
184 G6 Gazak Iran
183 M7 G'azalkent Uzbek.
185 L7 Gazan Pak.
184 F2 Gazandzhyk Turkm.
89 I4 Gazawa Cameroon
184 F5 Gazestān Iran
90 E4 Gazi Dem. Rep. Congo
188 H5 Gaziantep Turkey
190 F2 Gaziantep prov. Turkey
184 I5 Gazīk Iran
191 E5 Gaziler Turkey
Gazimağusa Cyprus see Ammochostos
162 B2 Gazimur r. Rus. Fed.
169 L2 Gazimuro-Ononskiy Khrebet mts Rus. Fed.
162 A3 Gazimurskiy Khrebet mts Rus. Fed.
188 F5 Gazipaşa Turkey
76 I8 Gazivode Jezero l. Serb. and Mont.
182 J7 Gazli Uzbek.
184 H8 Gaz Māhū Iran
184 E3 Gaznāsarā Iran
Gazojak Turkm. see Gaz-Achak
63 Q3 Gazolaz Spain
71 J5 Gazoldo degli Ippoliti Italy
71 K5 Gazzo Veronese Italy
71 J5 Gazzuolo Italy
88 D5 Gbaaka Liberia
90 D3 Gbadolite Dem. Rep. Congo
88 B5 Gbangbatok Sierra Leone
88 C5 Gbarnga Liberia
88 C5 Gbatala Liberia
57 H4 Gbelce Slovakia
56 G3 Gbely Slovakia
89 F4 Gbérouboué Benin
89 H5 Gboko Nigeria
90 D4 Gbwado Dem. Rep. Congo
23 O7 Gdańsk Pol.
55 H1 Gdańsk, Gulf of Pol./Rus. Fed.
Gdańska, Zatoka g. Pol./Rus. Fed. see Gdańsk, Gulf of
Gdingen Pol. see Gdynia
18 K3 Gdov Rus. Fed.
55 I6 Gdów Pol.
23 O7 Gdynia Pol.
20 Q2 Geaidnovuohppi Norway
26 H8 Geal Charn hill Highland, Scotland U.K.
26 J8 Geal Charn hill Highland, Scotland U.K.
26 E4 Gealldruig Mhòr i. Scotland U.K.
43 I11 Géant, Pic du mt. France
200 □3a Gea Passage Kwajalein Marshall Is
122 D5 Gearhart Mountain OR U.S.A.
Gearraidh na h-Aibhne Scotland U.K. see Garrynahine
28 C7 Geashill Rep. of Ireland
118 F6 Geat Sound b. NJ U.S.A.
43 D8 Geaune France
155 F3 Gebe i. Maluku Indon.
85 H5 Gebeit Sudan
85 H4 Gebeit Mine Sudan
49 K8 Gebesee Ger.
49 E9 Gebhardshain Ger.
54 E3 Gębice Pol.
79 L5 Gebiz Turkey
92 C2 Gebre Guracha Eth.
79 K2 Gebze Turkey
92 B3 Gech'a Eth.
Gecheng Chongqing China see Chengkou
52 F4 Gechingen Ger.
191 C6 Geçit Turkey
156 D6 Gedang, Gunung mt. Indon.
18 H7 Gedanonių kalnas hill Lith.
85 G6 Gedaref Sudan
85 G6 Gedaref state Sudan
31 K3 Geddington Northamptonshire, England U.K.
57 H5 Géderlak Hungary
49 H10 Gedern Ger.
84 E6 Gedid Ras el Fil Sudan
45 G9 Gedinne Belgium
79 K4 Gediz Turkey
79 H4 Gediz r. Turkey
92 E3 Gedlegubē Eth.
31 M2 Gedney Drove End Lincolnshire, England U.K.
92 C2 Gēdo Eth.
92 D4 Gedo admin. reg. Somalia
157 I4 Gedong Sarawak Malaysia
156 □ Gedong, Tanjong pt Sing.
43 E10 Gèdre France
22 H7 Gedser Denmark
22 H7 Gedser Odde c. Denmark
22 F5 Gedsted Denmark
156 F7 Gedungpakuan Sumatera Indon.
Gedzheti Georgia see Gejet'i
45 H6 Geel Belgium
205 J8 Geelong Vic. Austr.
209 B10 Geelvink Channel W.A. Austr.
96 E5 Geel Vloer salt pan S. Africa
45 I7 Geer r. Belgium
44 G5 Geertruidenberg Neth.
48 D5 Geeste Ger.
48 G3 Geeste r. Ger.
44 K4 Geesteren Neth.
50 E5 Geestgottberg Ger.
48 J4 Geesthacht Ger.
45 H7 Geetbets Belgium
51 E10 Gefell Ger.
92 C2 Gefersa Eth.
44 H5 Geffen Neth.
51 E10 Gefrees Ger.
18 E6 Gėgė r. Lith.
57 K3 Gégény Hungary
191 F5 Geghadir Armenia
191 F5 Geghama Lerrnashght'a mts Armenia
191 G5 Geghamasar Armenia
18 H7 Gegužinė Lith.
173 E10 Gê'gyai Xizang China
200 □3a Gehh i. Kwajalein Marshall Is
48 F5 Gehrde Ger.
49 I6 Gehrden Ger.
51 D9 Gehren Ger.
171 L3 Ge Hu l. China
89 H3 Geidam Nigeria
52 G2 Geiersberg hill Ger.
53 N3 Geiersthal Ger.
118 D4 Geigertown PA U.S.A.
107 K3 Geikie r. Sask. Can.
108 B3 Geikie Island Ont. Can.
207 I2 Geikie Range hills Qld Austr.
49 B9 Geilenkirchen Ger.
22 E1 Geilo Norway
166 D6 Geinō Japan
21 I5 Geiranger Norway
49 I9 Geisa Ger.
49 H10 Geiselbach Ger.
53 M4 Geiselhöring Ger.
53 I2 Geiselwind Ger.
53 L4 Geisenfeld Ger.
53 M5 Geisenhausen Ger.
52 D2 Geisenheim Ger.
51 I9 Geising Ger.
52 F6 Geisingen Ger.
49 J8 Geisleden Ger.
52 F5 Geislingen Ger.
52 H4 Geislingen an der Steige Ger.
49 J8 Geismar Ger.
37 O6 Geispolsheim France
58 F5 Geißstein mt. Austria
59 L5 Geistthal Austria
93 B5 Geita Tanz.
51 G8 Geithain Ger.
20 L4 Geittind mt. Norway
191 D3 Gejet'i Georgia
170 D7 Gejiu Yunnan China
184 G2 Gekdepe Turkm.
92 A3 Gel r. Sudan
90 F2 Gel watercourse Sudan
74 G9 Gela Sicilia Italy
74 G9 Gela r. Sicilia Italy
74 G9 Gela, Golfo di g. Sicilia Italy
173 J10 Gêladaindong mt. Qinghai China
92 E3 Geladī Eth.
93 C5 Gelai vol. Tanz.
157 I6 Gelam i. Indon.
41 K8 Gélas, Cime du mt. France/Italy
50 F2 Gelbensande Ger.
53 I2 Gelchsheim Ger.
44 J4 Gelderland prov. Neth.
44 H5 Geldermalsen Neth.
49 B7 Geldern Ger.
49 J10 Geldersheim Ger.
45 I6 Geldrop Neth.
45 I7 Geleen Neth.
79 I3 Gelembe Turkey
92 D2 Gelemso Eth.
51 G9 Gelenau Ger.
79 M4 Gelendost Turkey
15 G7 Gelendzhik Rus. Fed.
92 B2 Gelhak Sudan
79 H2 Gelibolu Turkey
79 H2 Gelibolu Yarımadası pen. Turkey
79 H2 Gelibolu Yarımadası Tarihi Milli Parkı nat. park Turkey
79 L4 Gelincik Dağı mt. Turkey
92 E3 Gelinsoor Somalia
43 E7 Gelise r. France
56 F5 Gellénháza Hungary
30 F4 Gelligaer Caerphilly, Wales U.K.
200 □3a Gellinam i. Kwajalein Marshall Is
184 G5 Gelmord Iran
49 H10 Gelnhausen Ger.
57 J3 Gelnica Slovakia
43 D9 Gelos France
43 C8 Geloux r. France
22 E6 Gels r. Denmark
66 E5 Gelsa Spain
56 F5 Gelse Hungary
49 D7 Gelsenkirchen Ger.
53 K5 Geltendorf Ger.
70 C3 Gelten-Iffigen nature res. Switz.
48 I1 Gelting Ger.
51 G6 Geltow Ger.
156 F6 Gelumbang Sumatera Indon.
156 E3 Gemas Malaysia
45 G7 Gembloux Belgium
89 H5 Gembu Nigeria
40 G2 Gemeaux France
90 C4 Gemena Dem. Rep. Congo
57 H5 Gemenci park Hungary
41 H10 Gémenos France
188 H4 Gemerek Turkey
57 J3 Gemerská Hôrka Slovakia
57 J3 Gemerská Poloma Slovakia
44 I5 Gemert Neth.
79 K5 Gemiş Turkey
79 K2 Gemlik Turkey
79 J2 Gemlik Körfezi b. Turkey
20 □B1 Gemlufall Iceland
52 F3 Gemmingen Ger.
71 O3 Gemona del Friuli Italy
42 C4 Gémozac France
94 D5 Gemsbok National Park Botswana
96 E2 Gemsbokplein well S. Africa
96 I1 Gemsbokvlakte S. Africa
52 C2 Gemünden Ger.
49 G9 Gemünden (Wohra) Ger.
49 I10 Gemünden am Main Ger.
65 I8 Genal r. Spain
92 D3 Genalē Wenz r. Eth.
45 F7 Genappe Belgium
65 N4 Génave Spain
73 J4 Genazzano Italy
191 B7 Genç Turkey
42 E3 Gençay France
56 F4 Gencsapáti Hungary
186 C9 Gendoa r. Eth.
173 C14 Gendoli Rajasthan India
40 H2 Gendrey France
44 J5 Gendringen Neth.
44 I5 Gendt Neth.
40 E3 Génelard France
44 J3 Genemuiden Neth.
146 E5 General Acha Arg.
147 G5 General Alvear Buenos Aires Arg.
146 D4 General Alvear Mendoza Arg.
147 G4 General Arenales Arg.
139 F6 General Artigas Para.
147 H4 General Belgrano Arg.
General Belgrano II research stn Antarctica see Belgrano II
212 U2 General Bernardo O'Higgins research stn Antarctica
127 J5 General Bravo Mex.
147 F3 General Cabrera Arg.
147 H2 General Campos Arg.
142 A1 General Carneiro Brazil
145 B7 General Carrera, Lago l. Arg./Chile
147 I5 General Conesa Buenos Aires Arg.
145 D6 General Conesa Río Negro Arg.
147 F6 General Daniel Cerri Arg.
147 F3 General Deheza Arg.
47 H2 Generał Dezyderego Chłapowskiego, Park Krajobrazowy imieniu Pol.
127 I5 General Escobeda Mex.
147 H3 General Galarza Arg.
147 I5 General Guido Arg.
146 C3 General Gutiérrez Arg.
67 C8 Generalísimo, Embalse del resr Spain
144 F2 General José de San Martín Arg.
147 I5 General Juan Madariaga Arg.
138 C4 General Lagos Chile
147 G5 General La Madrid Arg.
147 H4 General Las Heras Arg.
147 I5 General Lavalle Arg.
147 F4 General Levalle Arg.
154 F7 General Luna Phil.
154 E6 General MacArthur Samar Phil.
General Machado Angola see Camacupa
147 I4 General Mansilla Arg.
144 D2 General Martín Miguel de Güemes Arg.
147 G4 General O'Brien Arg.
144 F2 General Paz Arg.
147 F4 General Pico Arg.
147 G4 General Pinto Arg.
147 I5 General Pirán Arg.
146 D6 General Roca Arg.
147 H4 General Rodriguez Arg.
147 G3 General Rojo Arg.
139 E4 General Saavedra Bol.
142 B4 General Salgado Brazil
147 H4 General San Martín Buenos Aires Arg.
147 F5 General San Martín La Pampa Arg.
154 E8 General Santos Mindanao Phil.
128 D1 General Simón Bolívar Mex.
127 J5 General Terán Mex.
77 Q7 General Toshevo Bulg.
126 F3 General Trías Mex.
147 G4 General Viamonte Arg.
147 F4 General Villegas Arg.
116 H7 Genesee PA U.S.A.
116 H5 Genesee r. NY U.S.A.
116 H6 Geneseo NY U.S.A.
62 H2 Genestoso Spain
92 C2 Genet Eth.
38 I4 Genêts France
97 L3 Geneva S. Africa
Geneva Switz. see Genève
115 E10 Geneva AL U.S.A.
110 F8 Geneva IL U.S.A.
120 G5 Geneva NE U.S.A.
116 H6 Geneva NY U.S.A.
116 E7 Geneva OH U.S.A.
Geneva, Lake France/Switz. see Léman, Lac
110 F7 Geneva, Lake WI U.S.A.
70 A3 Genève Switz.
40 I4 Genève canton Switz.
63 P3 Genevilla Spain
40 I4 Genevois mts France
Genf Switz. see Genève
71 N9 Genga Italy
Gengda Sichuan China see Gana
52 E5 Gengenbach Ger.
171 I7 Genglou Guangdong China
170 B7 Gengma Yunnan China
Gengqing Sichuan China see Dêgê
91 D5 Gengwa Dem. Rep. Congo
Gengxuan Yunnan China see Gengma
169 P1 Gen He r. China
92 B3 Geni r. Sudan
55 L1 Geniai Lith.
65 I5 Genil r. Spain
78 F1 Genisea Greece
43 D6 Génissac France
40 H4 Génissiat, Barrage de dam France
178 D8 Genji Rajasthan India
45 I7 Genk Belgium
165 H13 Genkai-nada b. Japan
40 G2 Genlis France
72 C8 Gennargentu, Monti del mts Sardegna Italy
72 C9 Genn'Argiolas, Monte hill Italy
44 I5 Gennep Neth.
42 D1 Gennes France
205 L7 Genoa Vic. Austr.
Genoa Italy see Genova
110 F7 Genoa IL U.S.A.
41 D8 Génolhac France
72 C8 Genoni Sardegna Italy
42 H3 Genouillac France
42 E3 Genouillé France
39 O7 Genouilly France
70 F7 Genova Italy
70 G7 Genova prov. Italy
70 F7 Genova, Golfo di g. Italy
67 E10 Genovés Spain
136 □ Genovesa, Isla i. Islas Galápagos Ecuador
43 E6 Gensac France
45 E6 Gent Belgium
156 G8 Genteng Jawa Indon.
157 J8 Genteng i. Indon.
51 F6 Genthin Ger.
156 D3 Genting Highlands Malaysia
140 E4 Gentio do Ouro Brazil
42 I4 Gentioux, Plateau de France

Gentioux-Pigerolles to Glubokiy
267

42 H4 Gentioux-Pigerolles France
Genua Italy see Genova
73 Q6 Genzano di Lucania Italy
73 J4 Genzano di Roma Italy
77 L4 Geoagiu r. Romania
26 D10 Geodha, Rubh' a' pt Scotland U.K.
09 C12 Geographe Bay W.A. Austr.
09 B8 Geographe Channel W.A. Austr.
05 P2 Geographical Society Ø i. Greenland
Geok-Tepe Turkm. see Gekdepe
08 D6 George r. W.A. Austr.
09 H1 George r. Que. Can.
96 G9 George S. Africa
09 I4 George, Cape N.S. Can.
05 L6 George, Lake N.S.W. Austr.
04 G7 George, Lake S.A. Austr.
08 G7 George, Lake salt flat W.A. Austr.
92 A4 George, Lake Uganda
15 G11 George, Lake FL U.S.A.
17 L5 George, Lake NY U.S.A.
06 C7 George Gills Range mts N.T. Austr.
30 D5 Georgeham Devon, England U.K.
98 □2b George Island St Helena
53 M2 Georgenberg Ger.
53 K3 Georgensgmünd Ger.
17 M5 Georges Mills NH U.S.A.
03 B11 George Sound inlet South I. N.Z.
07 I5 Georgetown Qld Austr.
05 K9 George Town Tas. Austr.
30 F2 George Town Gt Exuma Bahamas
08 E5 Georgetown Ont. Can.
30 C4 George Town Cayman Is
88 B3 Georgetown Gambia
37 G3 Georgetown Guyana
56 D2 George Town Malaysia
98 □2a Georgetown Ascension S. Atlantic Ocean
31 □3 Georgetown St Vincent
19 I2 Georgetown CT U.S.A.
17 J10 Georgetown DE U.S.A.
15 E10 Georgetown GA U.S.A.
14 E6 Georgetown KY U.S.A.
16 B10 Georgetown OH U.S.A.
15 H9 Georgetown SC U.S.A.
21 G10 Georgetown TX U.S.A.
12 T2 George VI Sound sea chan. Antarctica
13 K2 George V Land reg. Antarctica
21 F11 George West TX U.S.A.
91 E4 Georgia country Asia
15 F9 Georgia state U.S.A.
06 E5 Georgia, Strait of B.C. Can.
15 D10 Georgiana AL U.S.A.
08 D4 Georgian Bay Ont. Can.
11 O5 Georgian Bay Islands National Park Ont. Can.
06 G8 Georgina watercourse Qld Austr.
78 F7 Georgioupoli Kriti Greece
Georgi Traykov Bulg. see Dolni Chiflik
82 G2 Georgiyevka Aktyubinskaya Oblast' Kazakh.
83 S3 Georgiyevka Vostochnyy Kazakhstan Kazakh.
91 E1 Georgiyevsk Rus. Fed.
14 I4 Georgiyevskoye Kostromskaya Oblast' Rus. Fed.
91 A1 Georgiyevskoye Krasnodarskiy Kray Rus. Fed.
19 T2 Georgiyevskoye Vologodskaya Oblast' Rus. Fed.
48 D5 Georgsdorf Ger.
48 D4 Georgsheil Ger.
49 F6 Georgsmarienhütte Ger.
58 C6 Gepatsch, Stausee resr Austria
43 D9 Ger Aquitaine France
39 J4 Ger Basse-Normandie France
66 I3 Ger Spain
51 F9 Gera Ger.
45 E7 Geraardsbergen Belgium
49 K9 Geraberg Ger.
52 H3 Gerabronn Ger.
75 K7 Gerace Italy
75 K7 Gerace r. Italy
74 G8 Geraci Siculo Sicilia Italy
27 C9 Gerahies Rep. of Ireland
78 E2 Gerakarou Greece
78 D6 Geraki Greece
78 B5 Geraki, Akra pt Zakynthos Greece
42 B6 Geral, Serra mts Brazil
40 D4 Geral de Goiás, Serra hills Brazil
03 F11 Geraldine South I. N.Z.
40 D5 Geral do Paraná, Serra hills Brazil
09 C10 Geraldton W.A. Austr.
55 E1 Gerama i. Indon.
78 E5 Geraneia mts Greece
90 C7 Gerar watercourse Israel
37 M7 Gérardmer France
59 M2 Geras Austria
59 N3 Gerasdorf bei Wien Austria
84 F8 Gerāsh Iran
36 H7 Géraudot France
92 B2 Gerba Dima Eth.
24 J1 Gerber CA U.S.A.
37 M7 Gerbéviller France
41 E7 Gerbier de Jonc mt. France
51 E7 Gerbstedt Ger.
56 G4 Gérce Hungary
52 H2 Gerchsheim Ger.
89 J5 Gercüş Turkey
48 J5 Gerdau Ger.
97 K2 Gerdau S. Africa
57 H4 Gerecsei park Hungary
88 F3 Gerede Turkey
88 F3 Gerede r. Turkey
64 G5 Gerena Spain
57 J5 Gerendás Hungary
62 D5 Gerês, Serra do mts Port.
57 H5 Geresdlak Hungary
85 K6 Gereshk Afgh.
58 G3 Geretsberg Austria
53 K6 Geretsried Ger.
65 N6 Gérgal Spain
91 I3 Gergebil' Rus. Fed.
72 C8 Gergei Sardegna Italy
57 K3 Gergely-hegy hill Hungary
40 F3 Gergy France
53 J2 Gerhardshofen Ger.
56 D2 Gerik Malaysia
84 H5 Gerīmenj Iran
63 L9 Gerindote Spain
20 D5 Gering NE U.S.A.
51 G8 Geringswalde Ger.
57 J4 Gerje r. Hungary
57 H5 Gerjen Hungary
22 E6 Gerlach NV U.S.A.
57 J2 Gerlachovský štít mt. Slovakia
52 G4 Gerlingen Ger.
58 F5 Gerlos Austria
58 F5 Gerlospass pass Austria
09 H2 Germaine, Lac l. Que. Can.
47 F4 Germania Arg.
Germania country Europe see Germany
05 Q2 Germania Land reg. Greenland
06 E4 Germansen Landing B.C. Can.
16 H9 Germantown MD U.S.A.
16 A9 Germantown OH U.S.A.
21 K8 Germantown TN U.S.A.
10 F6 Germantown WI U.S.A.
46 E3 Germany country Europe
53 J6 Germaringen Ger.
37 J7 Germay France
79 I5 Germencik Turkey
53 K5 Germering Ger.
52 E3 Germersheim Ger.
36 D8 Germigny-des-Prés France
97 M2 Germiston S. Africa
63 O2 Gernika-Lumo Spain
51 D7 Gernrode Sachsen-Anhalt Ger.
49 J8 Gernrode Thüringen Ger.
52 E4 Gernsbach Ger.
52 E2 Gernsheim Ger.
166 F4 Gero Japan
70 H3 Gerola Alta Italy
51 E10 Geroldsgrün Ger.
53 K5 Gerolsbach Ger.
49 C10 Gerolstein Ger.
53 I2 Gerolzhofen Ger.
Gerona Spain see Girona
78 F7 Geropotamos r. Kriti Greece
71 R4 Gerovo Croatia
45 G8 Gerpinnes Belgium
72 C9 Gerrei reg. Sardegna Italy
Gerri Spain see Guerri de la Sal
43 E8 Gers dept France
43 F7 Gers r. France
70 F2 Gersau Switz.
49 I10 Gersfeld (Rhön) Ger.
52 C3 Gersheim Ger.
176 D5 Gersoppa Karnataka India
48 E5 Gersten Ger.
53 I4 Gerstetten Ger.
37 O7 Gerstheim France
53 J5 Gersthofen Ger.
49 J9 Gerstungen Ger.
50 I4 Gerswalde Ger.
41 G7 Gervanne r. France
51 E6 Gerwisch Ger.
Géryville Alg. see El Bayadh
40 C5 Gerzat France
173 G10 Gêrzê Xizang China
188 G3 Gerze Turkey
53 M4 Gerzen Ger.
49 D7 Gescher Ger.
59 N5 Geschriebenstein hill Austria
49 K9 Geschwenda Ger.
49 G7 Geseke Ger.
72 C8 Gesico Sardegna Italy
Gesoriacum France see Boulogne-sur-Mer
37 I4 Gespunsart France
53 J5 Gessertshausen Ger.
147 G2 Gessler Arg.
70 D7 Gesso r. Italy
67 D8 Gestalgar Spain
39 I7 Gesté France
72 C8 Gesturi Sardegna Italy
73 O5 Gesualdo Italy
45 H8 Gesves Belgium
57 K5 Geszt Hungary
57 K4 Geszteréd Hungary
21 O6 Geta Åland Fin.
63 M8 Getafe Spain
169 L9 Getai Shaanxi China
184 E4 Getcheh, Kūh-e hills Iran
45 H7 Gete r. Belgium
77 L6 Getic, Podişul plat. Romania
38 I7 Gétigné France
191 G5 Getik r. Armenia
48 I2 Gettorf Ger.
118 A5 Gettysburg PA U.S.A.
120 F3 Gettysburg SD U.S.A.
116 H9 Gettysburg National Military Park nat. park PA U.S.A.
170 F6 Getu He r. China
142 C4 Getulina Brazil
141 B8 Getúlio Vargas Brazil
212 P2 Getz Ice Shelf Antarctica
45 I7 Geul r. Neth.
156 B3 Geumapang r. Indon.
156 B2 Geumpang Sumatera Indon.
156 B2 Geureudong, Gunung vol. Indon.
205 L5 Geurie N.S.W. Austr.
184 H8 Gevān-e Ţāleb Khānī Iran
189 K4 Gevaş Turkey
41 C7 Gévaudan reg. France
49 D8 Gevelsberg Ger.
38 H5 Gévezé France
77 K9 Gevgelija Macedonia
64 E2 Gévora r. Spain
176 D3 Gevrai Mahar. India
40 F2 Gevrey-Chambertin France
92 D2 Gewanē Wildlife Reserve nature res. Eth.
40 I4 Gex France
190 A2 Geydik Dağları mts Turkey
51 G9 Geyer Ger.
79 H3 Geyikli Turkey
156 □ Geylang Sing.
156 □ Geylang r. Sing.
179 M6 Geylegphug Bhutan
97 J2 Geysdorp S. Africa
124 J3 Geyserville CA U.S.A.
79 L2 Geyve Turkey
142 C2 Gezarina Brazil
78 B1 Gezavesh Albania
168 G7 Gezidong Qinghai China
184 F8 Gezīr Iran
59 L2 Gföhl Austria
75 □ Ġgantija Temples Gozo Malta
96 H3 Ghaap Plateau S. Africa
190 E5 Ghabāghib Syria
84 E6 Ghabeish Sudan
189 K7 Ghadaf, Wādī al watercourse Iraq
190 E7 Ghadaf, Wādī al watercourse Jordan
185 N4 Ghadai Pak.
Ghadamés Libya see Ghadāmis
84 A2 Ghadāmis Libya
84 B3 Ghaddūwah Libya
184 E3 Ghaem Shahr Iran
185 O7 Ghaggar, Dry Bed of watercourse Pak.
179 J7 Ghaghara r. India
200 □6 Ghaghe i. Solomon Is
179 J8 Ghaghra Jharkhand India
75 □ Għaġin, Xrobb l- pt Malta
185 L8 Ghaibi Dero Pak.
75 □ Għajnsielem Gozo Malta
75 □ Għajn Tuffieħa, Ir-Ramla ta' b. Malta
185 I6 Ghalend Iran
182 J3 Ghalkarteniz, Solonchak salt marsh Kazakh.
Ghallaorol Uzbek. see G'allaorol
75 □ Għallis, Ġebel ta' l- is Malta
88 E4 Ghana country Africa
187 L3 Ghanādah, Rās pt U.A.E.
187 M6 Ghānah well Oman
187 K6 Ghanīm well Saudi Arabia
178 D6 Ghanliala Rajasthan India
178 C8 Ghantila Gujarat India
178 C9 Ghantwar Gujarat India
187 I2 Ghanwā Saudi Arabia
94 D4 Ghanzi Botswana
94 D4 Ghanzi admin. dist. Botswana
187 I2 Ghār, Ras al pt Saudi Arabia
186 F5 Gharāmīl, Jabal al hill Saudi Arabia
190 D8 Gharandal Jordan
190 A9 Gharandal, Wādī watercourse Egypt
75 □ Għarb Gozo Malta
87 F2 Ghardaïa Alg.
69 B7 Ghardimaou Tunisia
69 C7 Ghar el Melh Tunisia
185 K4 Gharghrab Afgh.
179 I8 Gharghoda Chhattisgarh India
75 □ Għargħur Malta
85 G2 Ghārib, Jabal mt. Egypt
190 B10 Ghārib, Ra's pt Egypt
185 N2 Gharm Tajik.
187 M6 Gharm, Wādī r. Oman
187 I3 Ghār Mihnān Saudi Arabia
185 L9 Gharo Pak.
184 C4 Gharq Ābād Iran
84 B1 Gharyān Libya
188 H7 Gharz, Wādī al watercourse Syria
187 M7 Gharzaut i. Oman
84 A3 Ghāt Libya
178 H6 Ghatampur Uttar Prad. India
200 □6 Ghatere Sta Isabel Solomon Is
179 J9 Ghatgan Orissa India
178 E8 Ghatol Rajasthan India
179 K8 Ghatsila Jharkhand India
185 M7 Ghauspur Pak.
Ghawdex i. Malta see Gozo
186 G8 Ghaymān Yemen
84 C6 Ghazal, Bahr el watercourse Chad
90 F2 Ghazal, Bahr el r. Sudan
Ghazalkent Uzbek. see G'azalkent
86 E2 Ghazaouet Alg.
178 F5 Ghaziabad Uttar Prad. India
179 I7 Ghazipur Uttar Prad. India
187 M2 Ghazira, Ghubbat al inlet Oman
185 L6 Ghazluna Pak.
Ghazna Afgh. see Ghaznī
185 M5 Ghaznī Afgh.
185 L5 Ghaznī prov. Afgh.
185 L5 Ghazni r. Afgh.
185 L5 Ghazoor Afgh.
186 E2 Ghazzālah Saudi Arabia
184 G5 Ghebar Gumbad Iran
70 I5 Ghedi Italy
77 K5 Ghelari Romania
77 O5 Ghelința Romania
187 J3 Ghemeis, Ras pt U.A.E.
Gengda Sichuan China see Gana
Ghent Belgium see Gent
116 D11 Ghent WV U.S.A.
77 P6 Gheorghe Lazăr Romania
77 N4 Gheorgheni Romania
176 D4 Gherdi Mahar. India
77 L3 Gherla Romania
70 F4 Ghiffa Italy
Ghijduwon Uzbek. see G'ijduvon
72 B7 Ghilarza Sardegna Italy
185 L6 Ghilzai reg. Afgh.
188 I8 Ghīnah, Wādī al watercourse Saudi Arabia
57 K5 Ghioroc Romania
77 L6 Ghioroiu Romania
57 K6 Ghiroda Romania
45 E7 Ghislenghien Belgium
72 C3 Ghisonaccia Corse France
72 C3 Ghisoni Corse France
185 L5 Ghizao Afgh.
178 D1 Ghizar Jammu and Kashmir
57 K6 Ghizela Romania
185 L9 Ghizri Creek inlet Pak.
200 □6 Ghizunabeana Islands Solomon Is
176 C3 Ghod Mahar. India
176 D3 Ghod r. India
178 D9 Gholvad Mahar. India
185 L9 Ghorabari Pak.
179 L7 Ghoraghat Bangl.
185 K5 Ghorak Afgh.
185 M4 Ghorband r. Afgh.
106 H2 Ghost Lake N.W.T. Can.
178 C6 Ghotaru Rajasthan India
185 M8 Ghotki Pak.
185 K4 Ghowr prov. Afgh.
187 K9 Ghubbah Suquṭrā Yemen
Ghudamis Libya see Ghadāmis
185 O2 Ghŭdara Tajik.
179 K7 Ghugri r. India
176 F3 Ghugus Mahar. India
Ghukasyan Armenia see Ashots'k'
185 M9 Ghulam Mohammed Barrage Pak.
190 F4 Ghunthur Syria
190 F7 Ghurayfah hill Saudi Arabia
184 F7 Ghūrī Iran
185 I4 Ghurian Afgh.
186 G3 Ghurrab, Jabal hill Saudi Arabia
186 F4 Ghurūb, Jabal hill Saudi Arabia
178 H8 Ghutipari Madh. Prad. India
187 M4 Ghuzayn Oman
84 C2 Ghuzayyil, Sabkhat salt marsh Libya
Ghuzor Uzbek. see G'uzor
36 E1 Ghyvelde France
15 H7 Giaginskaya Rus. Fed.
190 B3 Gialias r. Cyprus
159 H8 Gia Nghia Vietnam
158 H6 Gianh, Sông r. Vietnam
78 D2 Giannitsa Greece
72 G3 Giannutri, Isola di i. Italy
73 J2 Giano dell'Umbria Italy
97 N5 Giant's Castle mt. S. Africa
27 I2 Giant's Causeway lava field Northern Ireland U.K.
119 K2 Giant's Neck CT U.S.A.
157 K9 Gianyar Bali Indon.
79 H7 Gianysada i. Greece
159 G10 Gia Rai Vietnam
75 I8 Giardini-Naxos Sicilia Italy
76 J5 Giarmata Romania
74 H9 Giarratana Sicilia Italy
75 I8 Giarre Sicilia Italy
42 I4 Giat France
72 B7 Giave Sardegna Italy
70 C5 Giaveno Italy
70 D4 Giavino, Monte mt. Italy
72 B9 Giba Sardegna Italy
64 H7 Gibalbín hill Spain
130 E3 Gibara Cuba
64 H5 Gibarrayo hill Spain
208 I3 Gibb r. W.A. Austr.
120 F5 Gibbon NE U.S.A.
122 H4 Gibbonsville ID U.S.A.
208 I4 Gibb River W.A. Austr.
208 I4 Gibb River Aboriginal Reserve W.A. Austr.
118 F5 Gibbsboro NJ U.S.A.
115 □1 Gibb's Hill Bermuda
118 E5 Gibbstown NJ U.S.A.
74 D8 Gibellina Nuova Sicilia Italy
94 C5 Gibeon Namibia
39 K3 Giberville France
20 O2 Gibostad Norway
42 A2 Giboule r. France
64 F6 Gibraleón Spain
65 I8 Gibraltar Europe
65 □ Gibraltar, Bay of Gibraltar/Spain
64 H8 Gibraltar, Campo de reg. Spain
86 D2 Gibraltar, Strait of Morocco/Spain
65 □ Gibraltar Harbour Gibraltar
29 R7 Gibraltar Point England U.K.
205 N3 Gibraltar Range National Park N.S.W. Austr.
209 F12 Gibson W.A. Austr.
115 F9 Gibson GA U.S.A.
110 F9 Gibson City IL U.S.A.
209 G8 Gibson Desert W.A. Austr.
209 H8 Gibson Desert Nature Reserve W.A. Austr.
118 C6 Gibson Island MD U.S.A.
106 F5 Gibsons B.C. Can.
55 L1 Giby Pol.
191 K5 Gicäki Dağı mt. Azer.
168 D4 Gichgeniyn Nuruu mts Mongolia
92 B2 Gīdamī Eth.
185 L7 Gidar Pak.
14 K4 Gidayevo Rus. Fed.
92 B2 Gidda Eth.
176 F5 Giddalur Andhra Prad. India
121 G10 Giddings TX U.S.A.
20 O5 Gideälven r. Sweden
55 H5 Gidle Pol.
92 C3 Gīdolē Eth.
52 H2 Giebelstadt Ger.
49 J7 Gieboldehausen Ger.
55 H4 Gieczno Pol.
48 K2 Giekau Ger.
47 K3 Giełczew r. Pol.
55 I4 Gielniów Pol.
50 G3 Gielow Ger.
36 E8 Gien France
53 I4 Giengen an der Brenz Ger.
41 I10 Giens, Golfe de b. France
41 I10 Giens, Presqu'île de pen. France
41 H6 Gières France
45 G6 Gierle Belgium
51 E7 Giersleben Ger.
49 K8 Gierstädt Ger.
55 I2 Gierzwałd Pol.
49 I7 Gieselwerder (Oberweser) Ger.
49 G9 Gießen Ger.
49 G9 Gießen admin. reg. Ger.
44 K2 Gieten Neth.
55 I2 Gietrzwałd Pol.
39 O7 Gièvres France
184 G3 Gīfan Iran
29 L2 Gifford East Lothian, Scotland U.K.
43 I7 Giffou r. France
40 I4 Giffre r. France
49 K6 Gifhorn Ger.
106 H4 Gift Lake Alta Can.
166 E5 Gifu Japan
166 E4 Gifu pref. Japan
15 H7 Gigant Rus. Fed.
126 D4 Giganta, Cerro mt. Mex.
136 C4 Gigante Col.
65 P5 Gigante mt. Spain
41 D9 Gigean France
26 E11 Gigha i. Scotland U.K.
26 E11 Gigha, Sound of sea chan. Scotland U.K.
77 L7 Ghighera Romania
72 F3 Giglio, Isola del i. Italy
72 F3 Giglio Castello Italy
41 D9 Gignac Languedoc-Roussillon France
41 H9 Gignac Provence-Alpes-Côte d'Azur France
70 C4 Gignod Italy
41 G8 Gigondas France
182 K7 G'ijduvon Uzbek.
62 I1 Gijón-Xixón Spain
43 I8 Gijou r. France
93 A5 Gikongoro Rwanda
125 R9 Gila r. AZ U.S.A.
155 F2 Gila, Tanjung pt Maluku Indon.
125 T9 Gila Bend AZ U.S.A.
125 S8 Gila Bend Mountains AZ U.S.A.
125 R9 Gila Mountains AZ U.S.A.
184 C3 Gīlān prov. Iran
184 A4 Gīlān-e Gharb Iran
125 U8 Gila River Indian Reservation res. AZ U.S.A.
77 L4 Gilău Romania
191 K5 Giläzi Azer.
29 P6 Gilberdyke East Riding of Yorkshire, England U.K.
147 H3 Gilbert Arg.
207 H4 Gilbert r. Qld Austr.
125 U8 Gilbert AZ U.S.A.
110 B2 Gilbert MN U.S.A.
116 D11 Gilbert WV U.S.A.
Gilbert Islands country Pacific Ocean see Kiribati
118 C3 Gilberton PA U.S.A.
207 I5 Gilbert Range mts Qld Austr.
216 G6 Gilbert Ridge sea feature Pacific Ocean
207 I5 Gilbert River Qld Austr.
118 D4 Gilbertsville PA U.S.A.
116 B7 Gilboa OH U.S.A.
140 D4 Gilbués Brazil
184 G4 Gil Chashmeh Iran
53 K5 Gilching Ger.
122 I2 Gildford MT U.S.A.
95 H3 Gilé Moz.
65 J6 Gilena Spain
209 E10 Giles, Lake salt flat W.A. Austr.
206 C4 Giles Creek r. N.T. Austr.
209 J8 Giles Meteorological Station W.A. Austr.
206 D6 Giles Range mts N.T. Austr.
41 K9 Gilette France
27 J4 Gilford Northern Ireland U.K.
205 M3 Gilgai N.S.W. Austr.
205 L4 Gilgandra N.S.W. Austr.
191 K4 Gilgilçay Azer.
205 L3 Gil Gil Creek r. N.S.W. Austr.
178 E2 Gilgit Jammu and Kashmir
178 E2 Gilgit r. Jammu and Kashmir
205 K5 Gilgunnia N.S.W. Austr.
157 K8 Gili Iyang i. Indon.
157 K9 Gilimanuk Bali Indon.
Gılındire Turkey see Aydıncık
106 D4 Gil Island B.C. Can.
27 F4 Gill, Lough l. Rep. of Ireland
107 M3 Gillam Man. Can.
29 P5 Gillamoor North Yorkshire, England U.K.
22 I5 Gilleleje Denmark
206 E7 Gillen watercourse N.T. Austr.
209 H9 Gillen, Lake salt flat W.A. Austr.
49 C10 Gillenfeld Ger.
204 F5 Gilles, Lake salt flat S.A. Austr.
203 D10 Gillespies Point South I. N.Z.
116 I7 Gillett PA U.S.A.
110 F5 Gillett WI U.S.A.
122 L4 Gillette WY U.S.A.
20 M5 Gillhov Sweden
207 H6 Gilliat Qld Austr.
207 H6 Gilliat r. Qld Austr.
30 H5 Gillingham Dorset, England U.K.
31 N5 Gillingham Medway, England U.K.
29 N5 Gilling West North Yorkshire, England U.K.
98 □2b Gill Point St Helena
26 J5 Gills Highland, Scotland U.K.
110 G4 Gills Rock WI U.S.A.
40 I5 Gilly-sur-Isère France
40 D3 Gilly-sur-Loire France
119 K1 Gilman CT U.S.A.
110 G9 Gilman IL U.S.A.
110 D4 Gilman WI U.S.A.
121 H9 Gilmer TX U.S.A.
26 I10 Gilmerton Perth and Kinross, Scotland U.K.
105 K4 Gilmour Island Nunavut Can.
77 L6 Gilort r. Romania
124 K4 Gilroy CA U.S.A.
49 H9 Gilserberg Ger.
29 L4 Gilsland Northumberland, England U.K.
26 K11 Gilston Scottish Borders, Scotland U.K.
48 I5 Gilten Ger.
153 J8 Giluwe, Mount P.N.G.
30 F4 Gilwern Monmouthshire, Wales U.K.
44 G5 Gilze Neth.
92 B2 Gīmbī Eth.
131 □3 Gimie, Mount vol. St Lucia
75 L6 Gimigliano Italy
107 L5 Gimli Man. Can.
23 O1 Gimo Sweden
43 G8 Gimone r. France
43 F8 Gimont France
40 C3 Gimouille France
41 H9 Ginasservis France
85 H6 Ginda Eritrea
207 L7 Gindie Qld Austr.
138 D3 Ginebra, Laguna l. Bol.
72 D7 Ginepro, Cala b. Sardegna Italy
98 □3c Ginés, Punta pt Lanzarote Canary Is
41 B10 Ginestas France
98 □1b Ginetes São Miguel Azores
20 □ Ginevrabotnen str. Svalbard
176 G9 Gin Ganga r. Sri Lanka
176 F6 Gingee Tamil Nadu India
45 H7 Gingelom Belgium
52 H4 Gingen an der Fils Ger.
130 □ Ginger Hill Jamaica
207 M8 Gin Gin Qld Austr.
209 C11 Gingin W.A. Austr.
97 P5 Gingindlovu S. Africa
154 E7 Gingoog Mindanao Phil.
50 H2 Gingst Ger.
92 D3 Gīnīr Eth.
18 G6 Ginkūnai Lith.
43 I10 Ginoles France
75 L2 Ginosa Italy
75 I6 Ginostra Isole Lipari Italy
164 □1 Ginowan Okinawa Japan
176 G9 Gintota Sri Lanka
64 D6 Giões Port.
78 G7 Giofyros r. Kriti Greece
73 O7 Gioi Italy
75 J6 Gioia, Golfo di b. Italy
73 L4 Gioia dei Marsi Italy
75 L2 Gioia del Colle Italy
73 M5 Gioia Sannitica Italy
75 J7 Gioia Tauro Italy
75 K7 Gioiosa Ionica Italy
74 H7 Gioiosa Marea Sicilia Italy
Gióna Óros mts Greece see Gkiona
70 F3 Giornico Switz.
78 F3 Gioura i. Greece
73 L3 Giovenco r. Italy
71 J3 Gioveretto mt. Italy
58 C7 Gioveretto, Lago di l. Italy
71 K8 Giovi, Monte hill Italy
73 R5 Giovinazzo Italy
108 F2 Gipouloux r. Que. Can.
205 J8 Gippsland reg. Vic. Austr.
175 □1 Giraavaru i. N. Male Maldives
178 C6 Girab Rajasthan India
57 K2 Giraltovce Slovakia
184 H8 Gīrān Iran
37 L7 Girancourt France
184 H7 Gīrān Rīg mt. Iran
178 G9 Girar Mahar. India
121 H7 Girard KS U.S.A.
116 E7 Girard OH U.S.A.
116 E6 Girard PA U.S.A.
109 H1 Girardin, Lac l. Que. Can.
118 C3 Girardville PA U.S.A.
72 D8 Girasole Sardegna Italy
Giravaru i. N. Male Maldives see Giraavaru
184 G4 Girdab Iran
185 M6 Girdao Pak.
185 K8 Girdar Dhor r. Pak.
185 I6 Girdi Iran
89 I4 Girei Nigeria
188 I3 Giresun Turkey
Girgenti Sicilia Italy see Agrigento
90 C4 Giri r. Dem. Rep. Congo
92 C4 Giribabor well Kenya
179 K7 Giridih Jharkhand India
75 K6 Girifalco Italy
205 K4 Girilambone N.S.W. Austr.
57 K4 Girişu de Criş Romania
16 G6 Gîrla Mare r. Moldova
178 E9 Girna r. India
178 C9 Gir National Park India
57 K6 Giroc Romania
49 E10 Girod Ger.
72 A3 Girolata, Golfe de b. Corse France
37 M8 Giromagny France
136 B5 Girón Ecuador
66 K4 Girona Spain
66 K3 Girona prov. Spain
43 D6 Gironde dept France
42 C4 Gironde est. France
43 D6 Gironde-sur-Dropt France
147 G4 Girondo Arg.
66 I3 Gironella Spain
185 O5 Girot Pak.
43 G8 Girou r. France
43 H8 Giroussens France
31 M3 Girton Cambridgeshire, England U.K.
141 B9 Giruá Brazil
26 G12 Girvan South Ayrshire, Scotland U.K.
14 F3 Girvas Rus. Fed.
178 H7 Girwan Uttar Prad. India
202 M5 Gisborne North I. N.Z.
202 M5 Gisborne admin. reg. North I. N.Z.
29 M6 Gisburn Lancashire, England U.K.
106 F4 Giscome B.C. Can.
93 A5 Gisenyi Rwanda
22 J4 Gislaved Sweden
36 C5 Gisors France
185 L2 Gissar Range mts Tajik./Uzbek.
Gissarskiy Khrebet mts Tajik./Uzbek. see Gissar Range
73 N3 Gissi Italy
45 C6 Gistel Belgium
62 H3 Gistredo, Sierra de mts Spain
70 E2 Giswil Switz.
93 A5 Gitarama Rwanda
93 A5 Gitega Burundi
49 J7 Gittelde Ger.
77 L6 Giubega Romania
70 G3 Giubiasco Switz.
71 J4 Giudicarie, Valli val. Italy
73 M6 Giugliano in Campania Italy
73 K4 Giuliano di Roma Italy
73 L2 Giulianova Italy
70 I7 Giuncugnano Italy
77 N4 Giurgeului, Munţii mts Romania
77 N7 Giurgiu Romania
184 G3 Givar Iran
22 F6 Give Denmark
36 C5 Giverny France
37 I3 Givet France
40 F5 Givors France
45 F8 Givry Belgium
40 F3 Givry France
37 I6 Givry-en-Argonne France
95 F4 Giyani S. Africa
92 C2 Giyon Eth.
Giza Al Jīzah Egypt see Al Jīzah
54 F3 Giżałki Pol.
184 B4 Gīzeh Rūd r. Iran
191 F2 Gizel' Rus. Fed.
39 L7 Gizeux France
193 R3 Gizhiga Rus. Fed.
73 L3 Gizio r. Italy
200 □6 Gizo New Georgia Is Solomon Is
200 □6 Gizo i. New Georgia Is Solomon Is
55 J1 Giżycko Pol.
73 Q10 Gizzeria Italy
76 I8 Gjalicë e Lumës, Mal mt. Albania
21 I6 Gjerde Norway
22 F3 Gjerstad Norway
78 B2 Gjirokastër Albania
105 I3 Gjoa Haven Nunavut Can.
20 □C1 Gjögur Iceland
20 J5 Gjøra Norway
21 K6 Gjøvik Norway
78 A2 Gjuhëzës, Kepi i pt Albania
78 D4 Gkiona mts Greece
109 J4 Glace Bay N.S. Can.
70 D4 Glacier, Monte mt. Italy
106 C3 Glacier Bay AK U.S.A.
104 E4 Glacier Bay National Park and Preserve AK U.S.A.
106 G5 Glacier National Park B.C. Can.
122 H2 Glacier National Park MT U.S.A.
122 D2 Glacier Peak vol. WA U.S.A.
49 C7 Gladbeck Ger.
49 G9 Gladenbach Ger.
116 D12 Glade Spring VA U.S.A.
20 K4 Gladstad Norway
207 M7 Gladstone Qld Austr.
204 G5 Gladstone S.A. Austr.
205 L9 Gladstone Tas. Austr.
107 L5 Gladstone Man. Can.
203 J8 Gladstone North I. N.Z.
110 G4 Gladstone MI U.S.A.
118 F3 Gladstone NJ U.S.A.
116 G11 Gladstone VA U.S.A.
110 J6 Gladwin MI U.S.A.
116 F11 Gladys VA U.S.A.
106 C3 Gladys Lake B.C. Can.
78 F1 Glafki Greece
40 J2 Glainans France
26 J9 Glamis Angus, Scotland U.K.
125 Q9 Glamis CA U.S.A.
68 F3 Glamoč Bos.-Herz.
59 J6 Glan r. Austria
52 D2 Glan r. Ger.
154 E9 Glan Mindanao Phil.
23 L3 Glan l. Sweden
30 E4 Glanaman Carmarthenshire, Wales U.K.
27 C8 Glanaruddery Mountains hills Rep. of Ireland
41 H7 Glandage France
42 G5 Glandon France
41 I6 Glandon r. France
49 F6 Glandorf Ger.
42 F4 Glane r. France
49 E6 Glane r. Ger.
59 J6 Glanegg Austria
44 K4 Glanerbrug Neth.
27 F9 Glanmire Rep. of Ireland
111 M7 Glanworth Ont. Can.
70 E2 Glarner Alpen mts Switz.
52 F8 Glärnisch mts Switz.
27 J3 Glarryford Northern Ireland U.K.
70 G1 Glarus Switz.
70 G2 Glarus canton Switz.
26 G6 Glas Bheinn hill Scotland U.K.
30 F3 Glasbury Powys, Wales U.K.
26 G7 Glascarnoch, Loch l. Scotland U.K.
120 G6 Glasco KS U.S.A.
22 I2 Glasfjorden l. Sweden
110 E9 Glasford IL U.S.A.
130 □ Glasgow Jamaica
26 H11 Glasgow Glasgow, Scotland U.K.
26 H11 Glasgow admin. div. Scotland U.K.
118 D5 Glasgow DE U.S.A.
114 E7 Glasgow KY U.S.A.
122 K2 Glasgow MT U.S.A.
116 F11 Glasgow VA U.S.A.
51 I9 Glashütte Ger.
53 K2 Glashütten Ger.
49 F10 Gläshütten Ger.
22 I2 Glaskogens naturreservat nature res. Norway
27 I4 Glaslough Rep. of Ireland
107 I4 Glaslyn Sask. Can.
26 J9 Glas Maol mt. Scotland U.K.
26 G7 Glass, Loch l. Scotland U.K.
27 G6 Glassan Rep. of Ireland
118 E5 Glassboro NJ U.S.A.
28 I2 Glassford South Lanarkshire, Scotland U.K.
124 N4 Glass Mountain CA U.S.A.
29 K4 Glasson Cumbria, England U.K.
106 C3 Glass Peninsula AK U.S.A.
30 G5 Glastonbury Somerset, England U.K.
119 J1 Glastonbury CT U.S.A.
26 I9 Glas Tulaichean mt. Scotland U.K.
70 E1 Glatt r. Switz.
51 H8 Glaubitz Ger.
51 G9 Glauchau Ger.
77 N6 Glavacioc r. Romania
77 O8 Glavan Bulg.
77 P4 Glăvăneşti Romania
77 O7 Glavinitsa Bulg.
76 J8 Glavnik Kosovo, Srbija Serb. and Mont.
191 I2 Glavnyy Kut Rus. Fed.
19 O6 Glazomichi Rus. Fed.
89 F5 Glazoué Benin
14 K4 Glazov Rus. Fed.
19 T9 Glazunovka Rus. Fed.
19 N6 Glazunovo Rus. Fed.
110 E4 Gleason WI U.S.A.
106 H5 Gleichen Alta Can.
51 E8 Gleina Ger.
59 K5 Gleinalpe mt. Austria
59 M5 Gleisdorf Austria
Gleiwitz Pol. see Gliwice
40 F5 Gleizé France
31 N3 Glemsford Suffolk, England U.K.
20 L5 Glen Sweden
117 □N4 Glen NH U.S.A.
28 F2 Glenacardoch Point Scotland U.K.
26 F8 Glen Affric val. Scotland U.K.
111 N3 Glen Afton Ont. Can.
202 J4 Glen Afton North I. N.Z.
116 H11 Glen Allen VA U.S.A.
27 E5 Glenamaddy Rep. of Ireland
27 C4 Glenamoy Rep. of Ireland
27 C4 Glenamoy r. Rep. of Ireland
38 D6 Glénan, Îles de is France
110 I5 Glen Arbor MI U.S.A.
27 J2 Glenariff Northern Ireland U.K.
27 K3 Glenarm Northern Ireland U.K.
26 H10 Glen Artney val. Scotland U.K.
26 I8 Glen Avon val. Scotland U.K.
203 F11 Glenavy South I. N.Z.
27 J3 Glenavy Northern Ireland U.K.
26 E11 Glenbarr Argyll and Bute, Scotland U.K.
26 E9 Glenbeg Highland, Scotland U.K.
27 C9 Glenbeg Lough l. Rep. of Ireland
27 C8 Glenbeigh Rep. of Ireland
107 L5 Glenboro Man. Can.
26 J12 Glenbreck Scottish Borders, Scotland U.K.
26 D8 Glenbrittle Highland, Scotland U.K.
118 D1 Glenburn PA U.S.A.
118 B6 Glen Burnie MD U.S.A.
26 F8 Glen Cannich val. Scotland U.K.
125 U4 Glen Canyon gorge UT U.S.A.
125 U5 Glen Canyon Dam AZ U.S.A.
125 V4 Glen Canyon National Recreation Area park UT U.S.A.
26 I12 Glencaple Dumfries and Galloway, Scotland U.K.
26 J10 Glencarse Perth and Kinross, Scotland U.K.
26 G6 Glen Cassley val. Scotland U.K.
26 J9 Glen Clova val. Scotland U.K.
108 D5 Glencoe Ont. Can.
97 O4 Glencoe S. Africa
26 F9 Glencoe Highland, Scotland U.K.
26 F9 Glen Coe val. Scotland U.K.
120 H3 Glencoe MN U.S.A.
27 E3 Glencolumbkille Rep. of Ireland
97 J9 Glenconnor S. Africa
119 H3 Glen Cove NY U.S.A.
27 J6 Glencullen Rep. of Ireland
111 J3 Glendale Ont. Can.
125 T8 Glendale AZ U.S.A.
124 N7 Glendale CA U.S.A.
125 T4 Glendale UT U.S.A.
116 G8 Glendale Lake PA U.S.A.
204 E4 Glendambo S.A. Austr.
26 F10 Glendaruel val. Scotland U.K.
26 I8 Glen Dee val. Scotland U.K.
207 L6 Glenden Qld Austr.
122 L3 Glendive MT U.S.A.
107 I4 Glendon Alta Can.
118 E3 Glendon PA U.S.A.
122 L5 Glendo Reservoir WY U.S.A.
27 G3 Glendowan Rep. of Ireland
27 F8 Glenduff Rep. of Ireland
27 J2 Glendun r. Northern Ireland U.K.
26 I10 Gleneagles Perth and Kinross, Scotland U.K.
28 E8 Glenealy Rep. of Ireland
26 D11 Glenegedale Argyll and Bute, Scotland U.K.
204 H8 Glenelg r. Vic. Austr.
26 E8 Glenelg Highland, Scotland U.K.
26 J10 Glenfarg Perth and Kinross, Scotland U.K.
27 G4 Glenfarne Rep. of Ireland
26 I8 Glen Feshie val. Scotland U.K.
31 J2 Glenfield Leicester, England U.K.
117 J5 Glenfield NY U.S.A.
26 F9 Glenfinnan Highland, Scotland U.K.
27 H2 Glengad Head Rep. of Ireland
118 F3 Glen Gardner NJ U.S.A.
27 C9 Glengarriff Rep. of Ireland
26 F8 Glen Garry val. Highland, Scotland U.K.
26 H9 Glen Garry val. Perth and Kinross, Scotland U.K.
209 E9 Glengarry Range hills W.A. Austr.
28 B5 Glengavlen Rep. of Ireland
130 □ Glengoffe Jamaica
206 G8 Glengyle Qld Austr.
203 C13 Glenham South I. N.Z.
27 H2 Glenhead Northern Ireland U.K.
206 D7 Glen Helen N.T. Austr.
208 J4 Glen Hill Aboriginal Reserve W.A. Austr.
205 M3 Glen Innes N.S.W. Austr.
26 K8 Glenkindie Aberdeenshire, Scotland U.K.
26 G13 Glenluce Dumfries and Galloway, Scotland U.K.
26 H9 Glen Lyon val. Scotland U.K.
118 C2 Glen Lyon PA U.S.A.
106 C2 Glenlyon Peak Y.T. Can.
202 I4 Glen Massey North I. N.Z.
118 D4 Glenmoore PA U.S.A.
26 G8 Glen More val. Scotland U.K.
207 L9 Glenmorgan Qld Austr.
26 J9 Glen Muick val. Scotland U.K.
202 I4 Glen Murray North I. N.Z.
124 J2 Glenn CA U.S.A.
125 V10 Glenn, Mount AZ U.S.A.
27 C5 Glennagevlagh Rep. of Ireland
104 D3 Glennallen AK U.S.A.
26 F9 Glen Nevis val. Scotland U.K.
111 K5 Glennie MI U.S.A.
116 I11 Glenns VA U.S.A.
122 G5 Glenns Ferry ID U.S.A.
28 F4 Glenoe Northern Ireland U.K.
106 D3 Glenora B.C. Can.
207 H4 Glenore Qld Austr.
206 G7 Glenormiston Qld Austr.
209 F10 Glenorn Aboriginal Reserve W.A. Austr.
26 G6 Glen Oykel val. Scotland U.K.
205 N4 Glenreagh N.S.W. Austr.
117 K3 Glen Robertson Ont. Can.
118 B5 Glen Rock PA U.S.A.
116 D11 Glen Rogers WV U.S.A.
121 G9 Glen Rose TX U.S.A.
26 J10 Glenrothes Fife, Scotland U.K.
208 I4 Glenroy W.A. Austr.
117 L5 Glens Falls NY U.S.A.
28 D4 Glenshane Pass Northern Ireland U.K.
26 J9 Glen Shee val. Scotland U.K.
26 F8 Glen Shiel val. Scotland U.K.
118 E4 Glenside PA U.S.A.
26 G9 Glen Spean val. Scotland U.K.
118 F2 Glen Spey PA U.S.A.
27 F3 Glenties Rep. of Ireland
27 H2 Glentogher Rep. of Ireland
26 H8 Glen Tromie val. Scotland U.K.
203 F10 Glentunnel South I. N.Z.
27 G2 Glenveagh National Park Rep. of Ireland
116 E10 Glenville WV U.S.A.
28 H5 Glen Vine Isle of Man
110 E1 Glenwater Ont. Can.
116 F11 Glen Wilton VA U.S.A.
121 I8 Glenwood AR U.S.A.
124 □F14 Glenwood HI U.S.A.
120 H5 Glenwood IA U.S.A.
120 H3 Glenwood MN U.S.A.
119 G2 Glenwood NJ U.S.A.
123 J10 Glenwood NM U.S.A.
125 U3 Glenwood UT U.S.A.
116 C10 Glenwood WV U.S.A.
110 B4 Glenwood City WI U.S.A.
123 K7 Glenwood Springs CO U.S.A.
40 J2 Glère France
51 F8 Glesien Ger.
26 □N2 Gletness Shetland, Scotland U.K.
70 E2 Gletsch Switz.
Glevum Gloucestershire, England U.K. see Gloucester
50 G2 Glewitz Ger.
110 D3 Glidden WI U.S.A.
51 J6 Glienicke Ger.
Glikí Greece see Glyki
27 D7 Glin Rep. of Ireland
68 F3 Glina r. Bos.-Herz./Croatia
68 F3 Glina Croatia
48 J3 Glinde Ger.
51 G6 Glindow Ger.
19 R8 Glinishchevo Rus. Fed.
16 G6 Glinjeni Moldova
19 P7 Glinka Rus. Fed.
55 I3 Glinojeck Pol.
31 L2 Glinton Peterborough, England U.K.
21 J6 Glittertinden mt. Norway
54 G5 Gliwice Pol.
54 G5 Gliwicki, Kanał canal Pol.
59 K6 Globasnitz Austria
125 V8 Globe AZ U.S.A.
57 L6 Glodea, Vârful hill Romania
77 O6 Glodeanu-Sărat Romania
16 G6 Glodeni Moldova
77 M4 Glodeni Romania
59 J6 Glödnitz Austria
54 E2 Głodowa Pol.
Glodyany Moldova see Glodeni
Glogau Pol. see Głogów
59 M4 Gloggnitz Austria
70 G2 Glogn r. Switz.
76 I8 Glogovac Kosovo, Srbija Serb. and Mont.
54 E4 Głogów Pol.
54 F5 Głogówek Pol.
55 J5 Głogów Małopolski Pol.
54 G2 Głogowo Pol.
20 L3 Glomfjord Norway
20 O4 Glommersträsk Sweden
53 L6 Glonn Ger.
53 L5 Glonn r. Ger.
58 C6 Glorenza Italy
140 F4 Glória Brazil
64 B2 Glória do Ribatejo Port.
99 □2 Glorieuses, Îles is Indian Ocean
Glorioso Islands Indian Ocean see Glorieuses, Îles
39 M4 Glos-la-Ferrière France
78 E3 Glossa Greece
29 N7 Glossop Derbyshire, England U.K.
51 E7 Glöthe Ger.
15 I5 Glotovka Rus. Fed.
205 M4 Gloucester N.S.W. Austr.
153 K8 Gloucester New Britain P.N.G.
30 H4 Gloucester Gloucestershire, England U.K.
117 O6 Gloucester MA U.S.A.
116 I11 Gloucester VA U.S.A.
30 H4 Gloucester, Vale of val. England U.K.
118 E5 Gloucester City NJ U.S.A.
118 E5 Gloucester County county NJ U.S.A.
207 L6 Gloucester Island Qld Austr.
116 I11 Gloucester Point VA U.S.A.
30 H4 Gloucestershire admin. div. England U.K.
27 F9 Glounthaune Rep. of Ireland
127 P9 Glover Reef Belize
117 K5 Gloversville NY U.S.A.
109 K3 Glovertown Nfld and Lab. Can.
55 J4 Głowaczów Pol.
54 F1 Główczyce Pol.
50 H1 Glowe Ger.
50 F5 Glöwen Ger.
55 H4 Głowno Pol.
54 F5 Głubczyce Pol.
162 I5 Glubinnoye Rus. Fed.
17 T5 Glubokaya r. Rus. Fed.
15 H6 Glubokiy Rostovskaya Oblast' Rus. Fed.

15 H7 Glubokiy Rostovskaya Oblast' Rus. Fed.
183 T2 Glubokoye Kazakh.
18 M1 Glubokoye, Ozero i. Rus. Fed.
54 F5 Głuchołazy Pol.
55 I4 Głuchów Pol.
48 I1 Glücksburg (Ostsee) Ger.
48 H3 Glückstadt Ger.
24 D1 Gluggarnir hill Faroe Is
41 F7 Gluiras France
156 A2 Glumpangminyeuk Sumatera Indon.
29 N6 Glusburn North Yorkshire, England U.K.
17 N2 Glushkovo Rus. Fed.
54 E5 Głuszyca Pol.
54 G3 Głuszyńskie, Jezioro i. Pol.
30 D1 Glyder Fawr hill Wales U.K.
78 B3 Glyki Greece
30 F2 Glyn Ceiriog Wrexham, Wales U.K.
30 E4 Glyncorrwg Neath Port Talbot, Wales U.K.
Glynebwy Wales U.K. see Ebbw Vale
22 E5 Glyngøre Denmark
73 K5 Glynn Northern Ireland U.K.
30 E4 Glynneath Neath Port Talbot, Wales U.K.
Glyn-Nedd Wales U.K. see Glynneath
182 B2 Gmelinka Rus. Fed.
59 I6 Gmünd Kärnten Austria
59 K2 Gmünd Niederösterreich Austria
53 L6 Gmund am Tegernsee Ger.
59 I4 Gmunden Austria
116 D8 Gnadenhutten OH U.S.A.
21 N5 Gnarp Sweden
48 H4 Gnarrenburg Ger.
59 M6 Gnas Austria
27 D8 Gneevgullia Rep. of Ireland
51 G8 Gneisenaustadt Schildau Ger.
75 □ Gnejna, Il-Bajja tal- b. Malta
59 I6 Gnesau Austria
Gnesen Pol. see Gniezno
23 N2 Gnesta Sweden
22 H5 Gniben pt Denmark
59 M6 Gniebing Austria
59 I4 Gniew Pol.
54 G1 Gniewino Pol.
54 G3 Gniewkowo Pol.
55 I5 Gnieździska Pol.
54 F3 Gniezno Pol.
23 O4 Gnisvärd Gotland Sweden
76 J8 Gnjilane Kosovo, Srbija Serb. and Mont.
71 M6 Gnocchetta Italy
50 G3 Gnoien Ger.
54 F5 Gnojna Pol.
55 I6 Gnojnik Pol.
55 I5 Gnojno Pol.
30 H2 Gnosall Staffordshire, England U.K.
53 J3 Gnotzheim Ger.
209 D12 Gnowangerup W.A. Austr.
209 D10 Gnows Nest Range hills W.A. Austr.
48 I2 Gnutz Ger.
176 C5 Goa Goa India
176 D5 Goa state India
94 C5 Goageb Namibia
205 M7 Goalen Head N.S.W. Austr.
179 M6 Goalpara Assam India
155 A8 Goang Flores Indon.
88 E5 Goas Ghana
26 F11 Goat Fell hill Scotland U.K.
131 □2 Goat Point Antigua and Barbuda
92 D3 Goba Eth.
94 C4 Gobabis Namibia
Gobannium Monmouthshire, Wales U.K. see Abergavenny
94 C5 Gobas Namibia
146 C5 Gobernador Ayala Arg.
147 G2 Gobernador Crespo Arg.
146 D6 Gobernador Duval Arg.
145 C8 Gobernador Gregores Arg.
147 H3 Gobernador Mansilla Arg.
145 C8 Gobernador Mayer Arg.
147 G2 Gobernador Racedo Arg.
147 G4 Gobernador Ugarte Arg.
144 F3 Gobernador Virasoro Arg.
168 J4 Gobi Desert China/Mongolia
19 Q8 Gobles Rus. Fed.
59 I3 Göblberg hill Austria
166 B8 Gobō Japan
30 F2 Gobowen Shropshire, England U.K.
79 J6 Göcek Ger.
49 B7 Goch Ger.
94 C5 Gochas Namibia
49 J10 Gochsheim Ger.
159 H9 Go Công Vietnam
59 O6 Göcsej hills Hungary
57 I4 Göd Hungary
51 J8 Göda Ger.
179 L7 Godagari Bangl.
22 F2 Godal Norway
31 K5 Godalming Surrey, England U.K.
176 G4 Godavari r. India
176 H4 Godavari, Cape India
176 H4 Godavari, Mouths of the India
116 H3 Godbout Que. Can.
109 H3 Godbout r. Que. Can.
179 K7 Godda Jharkhand India
106 C3 Goddard AK U.S.A.
124 N4 Goddard, Mount CA U.S.A.
52 F2 Goddelau Ger.
49 G8 Goddelsheim (Lichtenfels) Ger.
92 D3 Godē Eth.
64 C3 Godel hill Port.
77 L7 Godech Bulg.
118 F2 Godeffroy NY U.S.A.
58 F8 Godega di Sant'Urbano Italy
191 F6 Gödek Turkey
67 D9 Godelleta Spain
108 D5 Goderich Ont. Can.
39 L2 Goderville France
178 D8 Godhra Gujarat India
178 B8 Godia Creek b. Gujarat India
52 G6 Godiasco Italy
62 E6 Godinne Belgium
92 E3 Godinlabe Somalia
55 H1 Godkowo Pol.
203 E10 Godley r. South i. N.Z.
31 L3 Godmanchester Cambridgeshire, England U.K.
166 E5 Godo Japan
155 D4 Godo, Gunung mt. Indon.
64 C4 Godolin r. Port./Spain
57 I4 Gödöllő Hungary
59 J8 Godovič Slovenia
147 G3 Godoy Arg.
146 C3 Godoy Cruz Arg.
38 G4 Godre Hungary
107 M3 Gods r. Man. Can.
107 M4 Gods Lake Man. Can.
107 O2 God's Mercy, Bay of Nunavut Can.
31 L5 Godstone Surrey, England U.K.
Godthåb Greenland see Nuuk
20 O2 Goduchowka mt. Sweden
Godwin-Austen, Mount China/Jammu and Kashmir see K2
54 G4 Godziesze Wielkie Pol.
55 K5 Godziszów Pol.
97 K6 Goedemoed S. Africa
44 E5 Goedereede Neth.
96 C5 Goegap Nature Reserve S. Africa
108 E3 Goéland, Lac au i. Que. Can.
109 I2 Goélands, Lac aux i. Que. Can.
44 E5 Goes Neth.
113 I5 Goetzville MI U.S.A.
117 N5 Goffstown NH U.S.A.
59 L2 Göfritz an der Wild Austria
108 D4 Gogama Ont. Can.
165 O12 Gō-gawa r. Japan
110 E3 Gogebic, Lake MI U.S.A.
110 E3 Gogebic Range hills MI U.S.A.
190 H2 Göğer Turkey
52 H4 Göggingen Ger.

191 G6 Gogi Lerr mt. Armenia/Azer.
18 J1 Gogland, Ostrov i. Rus. Fed.
95 G4 Gogoi Moz.
19 O7 Gogolevka Rus. Fed.
54 G5 Gogolin Pol.
77 K6 Gogoşu Romania
89 F4 Gogounou Benin
90 F2 Gogra Jharkhand India see Ghaghra
Gogra r. India see Ghaghara
178 D7 Gogunda Rajasthan India
178 G6 Gohad Madh. Prad. India
178 F5 Gohana Haryana India
178 F2 Gohargani Madh. Prad. India
48 K2 Göhl Ger.
51 F7 Gohrau Ger.
48 K4 Göhrde Ger.
50 G4 Göhren-Lebbin Ger.
140 G3 Goiana Brazil
142 C3 Goiandira Brazil
141 C5 Goianésia Brazil
142 C2 Goiânia Brazil
142 C3 Goianira Brazil
142 B1 Goiás Brazil
142 B2 Goiás state Brazil
142 A6 Goiatuba Brazil
173 E10 Goicangmai Xizang China
184 □ Goikul Palau
26 G10 Goil, Loch inlet Scotland U.K.
170 C2 Goincang Qinghai China
22 J5 Göinge reg. Sweden
142 A6 Goio r. Brazil
142 A6 Goio-Erê Brazil
91 E6 Goi-Pula Dem. Rep. Congo
44 H5 Goirle Neth.
62 D8 Góis Port.
38 G8 Gois, Passage du France
71 J5 Goito Italy
66 C7 Goizueta Spain
79 M2 Gojeb Wenz r. Eth.
164 R7 Gojōme Japan
79 I4 Gökçeada i. Turkey
191 B6 Gökçedere Turkey
79 K5 Gökçedağ Turkey
79 J3 Gökova Muğla Turkey
79 I6 Gökçekaya Baraji resr Turkey
188 H4 Gökçen Turkey
188 G5 Gökçeören Turkey
190 B2 Gökçeşeyh Turkey
Gökdepe Turkm. see Gekdepe
190 A2 Gökdere Turkey
48 J2 Gokels Ger.
188 G3 Gökırmak r. Turkey
184 G1 Goklenkuy, Solonchak salt l. Turkm.
191 C6 Gökoğlan Turkey
79 J5 Gökova Muğla Turkey
79 I6 Gökova Körfezi b. Turkey
185 J9 Gokprosh Hills Pak.
191 C6 Göksu r. Turkey
188 H5 Göksun Turkey
191 B5 Göksu Nehri r. Turkey
50 J5 Göksu Parkı Turkey
51 G6 Göktepe Turkey
90 F5 Gokwe Zimbabwe
93 A5 Gol Norway
52 G5 Gola Croatia
178 F2 Gola Jharkhand India
173 I11 Gola Uttar Prad. India
168 Q9 Gołab Pol.
166 C7 Golac Slovenia
63 P5 Golada Spain see Agolada
63 P5 Golaghat Assam India
52 G5 Gola Island Rep. of Ireland
17 T7 Golak mt. Slovenia
156 □ Golakganj Assam India
90 F4 Golan hills Syria
89 H4 Gołańcz Pol.
89 H4 Golbāf Iran
93 A6 Golbahār Afgh.
79 K6 Gölbaşı Turkey
93 A6 Gölbent Turkey
89 I4 Golbey France
191 G4 Golconda Andhra Prad. India
88 E4 Golconda i. U.S.A.
99 □1a Golconda NV U.S.A.
206 F5 Gölcük Balıkesir Turkey
Gölcük Turkey see Etili
79 I3 Gölcük r. Turkey
64 C5 Gölcük Kocaeli Turkey
64 C5 Gołcza Pol.
26 D10 Gołczewo Pol.
129 H2 Gold PA U.S.A.
129 J5 Goldach Switz.
136 A5 Gołdap Pol.
184 E3 Gołdapa r. Pol.
51 E6 Goldbach Ger.
173 G10 Gold Beach OR U.S.A.
173 G10 Goldbeck Ger.
19 R1 Goldberg Ger.
70 E3 Gold Cliff Newport, Wales U.K.
155 E4 Gold Coast Africa see Ghana
205 N3 Gold Coast Qld Austr.
88 E5 Gold Coast Ghana
184 D3 Goldeck mt. Austria
78 E8 Goldegg Austria
62 F8 Goldelund Ger.
41 H6 Golden B.C. Can.
178 I6 Golden Rep. of Ireland
178 D7 Golden Bay South i. N.Z.
92 E2 Goldendale WA U.S.A.
136 C5 Golden Ears Provincial Park B.C. Can.
50 H4 Goldene Aue reg. Ger.
62 D6 Golden Gate Highlands National Park S. Africa
62 D6 Golden Gate National Recreation Area park CA U.S.A.
130 □ Golden Grove Jamaica
106 E5 Golden Hinde mt. B.C. Can.
108 E4 Golden Lake Ont. Can.
121 J11 Golden Meadow LA U.S.A.
31 K5 Golden Pot Hampshire, England U.K.
107 I5 Golden Prairie Sask. Can.
131 □2 Golden Rock airport St Kitts and Nevis
48 F5 Goldenstedt Ger.
181 L2 Golden Throne mt. Jammu and Kashmir India
37 K6 Golden Vale lowland Rep. of Ireland
37 M6 Golden Vale lowland Rep. of Ireland
43 E8 Golden Valley S. Africa
79 I2 Golden Valley U.K.
79 L5 Golden Valley Zimbabwe
79 I2 Goldfield NV U.S.A.
41 I10 Goldkronach Ger.
39 I2 Goldopiwo, Jezioro i. Pol.
91 C8 Gold River B.C. Can.
172 I3 Gold Sand Lake Man. Can.
173 K12 Goldsboro MD U.S.A.
168 K7 Goldsboro MD U.S.A.
170 H6 Goldstone Lake CA U.S.A.
172 E2 Goldsworthy W.A. Austr.
170 A2 Goldthwaite TX U.S.A.
Goldvila Azer.
168 G8 Goldvein VA U.S.A.
169 N6 Göle Turkey
172 I3 Golenice Pol.
89 I4 Goleniów Pol.
205 K4 Golestān Afgh.
Golestān prov. Iran
168 I6 Goleta CA U.S.A.
170 E4 Golfito Costa Rica
169 O4 Golfo Aranci Sardegna Italy
170 C2 Golfo di Orosei Gennargentu e Asinara, Parco Nazionale del nat. park Sardegna Italy
170 D3 Gölgeli Dağları mts Turkey

79 K5 Gölhisar Turkey
71 N5 Goli i. Croatia
71 R6 Goli i. Croatia
121 G11 Goliad TX U.S.A.
76 I7 Golija nat. park Serb. and Mont.
54 G3 Golina Pol.
169 Q4 Golin Baixing Nei Mongol China
41 B7 Golinhac France
19 U6 Golitsyno Rus. Fed.
188 H3 Gölköy Turkey
52 I2 Gollach r. Ger.
59 N3 Göllersdorf Austria
52 E2 Göllheim Ger.
50 I4 Gollin Ger.
50 E3 Göllin Ger.
58 H4 Golling an der Salzach Austria
51 D8 Göllingen Ger.
50 I4 Gollmitz Ger.
51 G6 Gölm Ger.
79 I4 Gölmarmara Turkey
49 I7 Golmbach Ger.
51 H6 Golmberg hill Ger.
58 E2 Golmes Spain
168 D8 Golmud Qinghai China
168 D8 Golmud He r. China
59 J7 Golnik Slovenia
72 D2 Golo r. Corse France
154 C5 Golo i. Phil.
19 K6 Golobino Rus. Fed.
146 C2 Golondrina Arg.
90 C2 Golongosso C.A.R.
19 X7 Golovanovo Rus. Fed.
190 D2 Gölovası Turkey
17 O3 Golovchino Rus. Fed.
191 A2 Golovinka Rus. Fed.
162 N7 Golovino Kuril'skiye O-va Rus. Fed.
184 D5 Golpayegān Iran
79 L2 Gölpazarı Turkey
62 I6 Golpejas Spain
59 O4 Göls Austria
59 M3 Gölsen r. Austria
26 I7 Golspie Highland, Scotland U.K.
51 I7 Golßen Ger.
59 K7 Golte mts Slovenia
51 F9 Göltzsch r. Ger.
55 H2 Golub-Dobrzyń Pol.
17 Q8 Golubivka Rus. Fed.
183 P7 Golubovka Kazakh.
54 F4 Goluchów Pol.
19 U8 Golun' Rus. Fed.
95 F3 Golungo Alto Angola
184 I5 Gol Vardeh Iran
92 E4 Golweyn Somalia
79 I3 Gölyaka Turkey
77 M8 Golyama Syutkya mt. Bulg.
77 M8 Golyama Zhelyazna Bulg.
77 M9 Golyam Perelik mt. Bulg.
77 M9 Golyam Persenk mt. Bulg.
79 I3 Gölyanı Turkey
191 D7 Gölyazı Turkey
19 O7 Golynki Rus. Fed.
191 B5 Gölyürt Geçidi pass Turkey
50 J5 Golzow Brandenburg Ger.
51 G6 Golzow Brandenburg Ger.
90 F5 Goma Dem. Rep. Congo
93 A5 Goma Uganda
52 G5 Gomadingen Ger.
178 F2 Goma Hanu Jammu and Kashmir India
173 I11 Gomang Co salt l. China
168 Q9 Gomang Qinghai China
166 C7 Gomanodan-zan mt. Japan
63 P5 Gómara Spain
63 P5 Gómara, Campo de reg. Spain
52 G5 Gomaringen Ger.
17 T7 Gomati r. India
156 □ Gombak, Bukit hill Sing.
90 F4 Gombari Dem. Rep. Congo
89 H4 Gombe Nigeria
89 H4 Gombe state Nigeria
93 A6 Gombe r. Tanz.
79 K6 Gömbe Turkey
93 A6 Gombe Stream National Park Tanz.
89 I4 Gombi Nigeria
191 G4 Gömbori Georgia
88 E4 Gomboussougou Burkina
99 □1a Gombrani Island Rodrigues i. Mauritius
Gombroon Iran see Bandar-e 'Abbās
79 I3 Gömeç Turkey
64 C5 Gomecello Spain
Gomel' Belarus see Homyel'
26 D10 Gometra i. Scotland U.K.
129 H2 Gómez Farías Mex.
129 J5 Gómez Palacio Mex.
136 A5 Gómez Rendón Ecuador
184 E3 Gomīshān Iran
51 E6 Gommern Ger.
173 G10 Gomo Xizang China
173 G10 Gomo Co salt l. China
19 R1 Gomorovichi Rus. Fed.
70 E3 Goms reg. Switz.
155 E4 Gomumu i. Maluku Indon.
130 G4 Gonaïves Haiti
95 F4 Gonarezhou National Park Zimbabwe
184 D3 Gonbad-e Kavus Iran
62 F8 Gônc Hungary
41 I6 Gonçalo Port.
178 I6 Goncelin France
178 D7 Gonda Uttar Prad. India
92 D2 Gondal Gujarat India
90 C2 Gonda Libah well Eth.
178 H9 Gonda Col.
62 C6 Gondelsheim Ger.
62 D6 Gondar Braga Port.
62 D6 Gondar Porto Port.
52 F3 Gondelsheim Ger.
48 H5 Gandern Ger.
91 E6 Gonderme Geçidi pass Turkey
49 D10 Gondershausen Ger.
90 C2 Gondey Chad
178 H9 Gondia Mahar. India
62 C6 Gondomar Port.
62 D6 Gondomar Spain
49 D10 Gondorf Ger.
62 D5 Gondorf Port.
37 K6 Gondrecourt-le-Château France
37 K6 Gondreville France
37 M6 Gondrexange, Étang de i. France
43 E8 Gondrin France
79 I2 Gönen Balıkesir Turkey
79 L5 Gönen Isparta Turkey
79 I2 Gönen r. Turkey
41 I10 Gonette France
39 I2 Gonfreville-l'Orcher France
91 C8 Gong Angola
172 I3 Gong'an Hubei China
173 K12 Gonggar Xizang China
168 K7 Gongchakou Gansu China
170 H6 Gongcheng Guangxi China
172 E2 Gonggar Xizang China
170 A2 Gongga Shan mt. Sichuan China
168 G8 Gonghe Qinghai China
169 N6 Gonghui Hebei China
172 I3 Gongliu Xinjiang China
89 I4 Gongola r. Nigeria
205 K4 Gongolgon N.S.W. Austr.
191 G4 Gongora Azer.
168 I6 Gongpoquan Gansu China
170 E4 Gongquan Sichuan China
170 C2 Gongwang Shan mts Yunnan China
170 D3 Gongxian Henan China see Gongyi
27 I7 Gongxian Henan China see Gongyi
169 M9 Gongyi Henan China

162 D7 Gongzhuling Jilin China
72 C8 Goni Sardegna Italy
147 I3 Goñi Uru.
55 K2 Goniądz Pol.
89 I4 Goniri Nigeria
170 B3 Gonjo Xizang China
Gonjo Xizang China see Kasha
72 A9 Gonnesa Sardegna Italy
72 A9 Gonnosfanàdiga Sardegna Italy
78 D3 Gonnoi Greece
72 F9 Gonnosnò Sardegna Italy
72 B8 Gonnesa Sardegna Italy
164 S6 Gonohe Japan
165 G13 Gōnoura Japan
40 I2 Gonsans France
97 M8 Gonubie S. Africa
57 G4 Gönyü Hungary
71 J6 Gonzaga Italy
129 I3 Gonzaga Mex.
124 K5 Gonzales CA U.S.A.
121 G11 Gonzales TX U.S.A.
147 F4 González Moreno Arg.
128 D2 González Ortega Mex.
162 D2 Gonzha Rus. Fed.
116 H11 Goochland VA U.S.A.
116 F11 Goode VA U.S.A.
213 I2 Goodenough, Cape Antarctica
184 D7 Goodenough Island P.N.G.
111 P5 Goodenow Ont. Can.
110 I4 Good Harbor Bay MI U.S.A.
110 I4 Good Hart MI U.S.A.
97 J1 Good Hope Botswana
110 D9 Good Hope IL U.S.A.
96 C10 Good Hope, Cape of S. Africa
106 E5 Good Hope Mountain B.C. Can.
122 G5 Gooding ID U.S.A.
120 E6 Goodland KS U.S.A.
99 □1b Goodlands Mauritius
110 F4 Goodman WI U.S.A.
205 K3 Goodooga N.S.W. Austr.
206 D2 Goodparla N.T. Austr.
110 D4 Goodrich WI U.S.A.
107 I4 Goodsoil Sask. Can.
213 E2 Goodspeed Nunataks nunataks Antarctica
30 C3 Goodwick Pembrokeshire, Wales U.K.
109 G2 Goodwood r. Que. Can.
203 E12 Goodwood South i. N.Z.
29 P6 Goole East Riding of Yorkshire, England U.K.
205 J6 Goolgowi N.S.W. Austr.
204 G6 Goolwa S.A. Austr.
205 K3 Goomadeer r. N.T. Austr.
209 I11 Goomalling W.A. Austr.
205 J3 Goombalie N.S.W. Austr.
207 N9 Goomeri Qld Austr.
95 G3 Goonda Moz.
205 M3 Goondiwindi Qld Austr.
209 F10 Goongarrie, Lake salt flat W.A. Austr.
209 F10 Goongarrie National Park W.A. Austr.
30 B7 Goonhavern Cornwall, England U.K.
207 K6 Goonyella Qld Austr.
44 K4 Goor Neth.
209 D11 Goorly, Lake salt flat W.A. Austr.
109 I2 Goose r. Nfld and Lab. Can.
120 G2 Goose r. ND U.S.A.
203 H9 Goose Bay South i. N.Z.
115 G9 Goose Creek SC U.S.A.
209 I11 Goose Creek r. ID/NV U.S.A.
125 F8 Goose Green Falkland Is
122 D6 Goose Lake CA U.S.A.
124 M6 Goose Lake Canal r. CA U.S.A.
176 E5 Gooty Andhra Prad. India
177 J3 Gop Orissa India
179 L8 Gopalganj Bangl.
179 J6 Gopalganj Bihar India
177 I3 Gopalpur Orissa India
63 O3 Gopegi Spain
178 G4 Gopeshwar Uttaranchal India
176 E7 Gopichettipalayam Tamil Nadu India
18 I7 Gopïganj Uttar Prad. India
54 G3 Gopło, Jezioro i. Pol.
52 H3 Göppingen Ger.
170 A4 Goqên Xizang China
65 N6 Gor Spain
54 C4 Góra Dolnośląskie Pol.
55 H3 Góra Mazowieckie Pol.
65 M6 Gorafe Spain
191 G2 Goragorskiy Rus. Fed.
55 K5 Goraj Pol.
65 I3 Góra Kalwaria Pol.
176 I4 Gorakhpur Uttar Prad. India
191 H5 Goranboy Azer.
55 J4 Góra Puławska Pol.
57 H1 Góra Świętej Anny, Park Krajobrazowy Pol.
54 G2 Gorawino Pol.
88 B3 Goražde Bos.-Herz.
19 U8 Gorbachevo Rus. Fed.
146 A6 Gorbea Chile
18 H4 Gorbeako Atxak mt. Spain
57 I7 Gorbitsa Hungary
162 E1 Gorbitsa Rus. Fed.
14 H4 Görcha Rus. Fed.
55 I6 Gorczański Park Narodowy nat. park Pol.
130 H4 Gorda, Banco sea feature Hond.
98 □3d Gorda, Punta pt La Palma Canary Is
126 □R10 Gorda, Punta pt Nic.
124 H1 Gorda, Punta pt Mex.
65 K6 Gorda, Sierra mts Spain
130 C1 Gorda Cay i. Bahamas
63 N7 Gordaliza del Pino Spain
155 C3 Gorda Point pt AK U.S.A.
89 G3 Gordatza Nigeria
57 I7 Gordeyevka Rus. Fed.
79 J4 Gördes Turkey
191 G7 Gordeyevka Rus. Fed.
19 O9 Gordeyevka Rus. Fed.
70 F3 Gordola Switz.
209 D13 Gordon r. W.A. Austr.
26 K11 Gordon Scottish Borders, Scotland U.K.
120 D4 Gordon NE U.S.A.
118 C3 Gordon PA U.S.A.
110 C3 Gordon WI U.S.A.
145 C10 Gordon, Isla i. Chile
70 G3 Gordola Italy
206 C3 Gordon Lake N.W.T. Can.
107 I3 Gordon Lake Alta Can.
116 G10 Gordonsville VA U.S.A.
118 C4 Gordonville PA U.S.A.
90 C2 Goré Chad
203 C13 Gore South i. N.Z.
116 G9 Gore VA U.S.A.
111 L4 Gore Bay Ont. Can.
27 G5 Gorebridge Midlothian, Scotland U.K.
79 I4 Görece Turkey
27 I5 Goresbridge Rep. of Ireland
27 I5 Gorey Rep. of Ireland

27 J7 Gorey Rep. of Ireland
184 H7 Gorg Iran
184 F3 Gorgān Iran
184 E3 Gorgān, Khalīj-e b. Iran
184 E3 Gorgān, Rūd-e r. Iran
208 E6 Gorge Range hills W.A. Austr.
207 J5 Gorge Range mts Qld Austr.
203 C13 Gorge Road South i. N.Z.
95 G3 Gorgês Namibia
56 G5 Görgeteg Hungary
73 Q7 Gorgoglione Italy
88 B2 Gorgol admin. reg. Maur.
70 H9 Gorgona, Isola di i. Italy
70 G4 Gorgonzola Italy
92 C1 Gorgora Eth.
89 H3 Gorgoram Nigeria
67 F10 Gorgos r. Spain
77 R5 Gorgova, Lacul i. Romania
191 C6 Görgü Turkey
117 N6 Gorham NH U.S.A.
191 F4 Gori Georgia
76 H8 Gorica Crna Gora Serb. and Mont.
59 O7 Goričan Croatia
59 N6 Gorišnica Slovenia
44 G5 Gorinchem Neth.
31 J4 Goring Oxfordshire, England U.K.
71 M6 Gorino Italy
191 H6 Goris Armenia
53 J6 Görisried Ger.
77 P8 Goritsa Bulg.
19 T4 Goritsy Rus. Fed.
50 I4 Göritz Ger.
71 P4 Gorizia Italy
71 P4 Gorizia prov. Italy
59 L8 Gorjanci mts Slovenia
19 V5 Gor'ka Rus. Fed.
191 F1 Gor'kaya Balka r. Rus. Fed.
79 L8 Gorkhā Nepal
14 I4 Gor'kiy Rus. Fed. see Nizhniy Novgorod
19 N4 Gor'kovskoye Vodokhranilishche resr Rus. Fed.
183 S1 Gor'koye, Ozero salt l. Rus. Fed.
183 S1 Gor'koye, Ozero salt l. Rus. Fed.
50 D4 Gorleben Ger.
22 H6 Gørlev Denmark
55 J6 Gorlice Pol.
50 D4 Gorlosen Ger.
19 W8 Gorlovo Rus. Fed.
51 J8 Görlsdorf Ger.
26 D11 Gorm, Loch l. Scotland U.K.
27 J5 Gormanstown Rep. of Ireland
63 O5 Gormaz Spain
178 G6 Gorna Madh. Prad. India
50 H3 Gorna Dzhumaya Bulg. see Blagoevgrad
74 I7 Gornalunga r. Sicilia Italy
77 N7 Gorna Oryakhovitsa Bulg.
51 H9 Gornau Ger.
68 E2 Gornja Dubnik Bulg.
77 J7 Gornja Radgona Slovenia
71 R5 Gornja Toponica Srbija Serb. and Mont.
59 M7 Gornje Jelenje Croatia
57 J6 Gornje Vratno Croatia
59 K7 Gornji Breg Vojvodina, Srbija Serb. and Mont.
54 F2 Gornji Grad Slovenia
77 J7 Gornji Matejevac Srbija Serb. and Mont.
76 I6 Gornji Milanovac Srbija Serb. and Mont.
59 N8 Gornji Tkalec Croatia
64 F4 Gornji Vakuf Bos.-Herz.
55 I5 Gôrno Pol.
77 N7 Gorno Ablanovo Bulg.
183 U2 Gorno-Altaysk Rus. Fed.
Gorno-Altayskaya Avtonomnaya Oblast' aut. rep. Rus. Fed. see Altay, Respublika
192 H3 Gornopravdinsk Rus. Fed.
77 N8 Gornotrakiyska Nizina lowland Bulg.
14 L4 Gornozavodsk Permskaya Rus. Fed.
162 L5 Gornozavodsk Sakhalin Rus. Fed.
172 I3 Gornyak Altayskiy Kray Rus. Fed.
19 W8 Gornyak Ryazanskaya Oblast' Rus. Fed.
162 H6 Gornye Kyuchi Rus. Fed.
162 J3 Gornyy Khabarovskiy Kray Rus. Fed.
17 T6 Gornyy Rostovskaya Oblast' Rus. Fed.
182 C2 Gornyy Saratovskaya Oblast' Rus. Fed.
Gornyy Altay aut. rep. Rus. Fed. see Altay, Respublika
15 I6 Gornyy Balykley Rus. Fed.
92 I3 Goro Eth.
14 H4 Gorodets Rus. Fed.
92 C2 Goro'ah'an Eth.
131 □8 Goro Meer Bonaire
Goto Meer Bonaire see Goro Meer
92 D7 Goroda, Mys pt Rus. Fed.
53 N4 Gorodets Rus. Fed.
53 N4 Gorodishche Rus. Fed.
49 I7 Göttingen Ger.
52 F6 Göttmadingen Ger.
19 Q4 Gorokhovets Rus. Fed.
95 G3 Gorongosa Moz.
95 G3 Gorongosa Moz.
95 G3 Gorongosa, Parque Nacional de nat. park Moz.
155 C3 Gorontalo Sulawesi Indon.
155 C3 Gorontalo prov. Indon.
89 G3 Goronyo Nigeria
57 H4 Gór Opawskich, Park Krajobrazowy Pol.
96 D9 Goroubi watercourse Niger
89 F3 Gorouol r. Burkina/Niger
89 G3 Gorowo Iławeckie Pol.
44 J2 Gorredijk Neth.
70 G6 Gorreto Italy
39 I5 Gorron France
49 K8 Gorsleben Ger.
30 D4 Gorseinon Swansea, Wales U.K.
54 G4 Gorsów r. Croatia
71 Q5 Gorski Kotar reg. Croatia
214 I8 Gorski Sieverodonetsk Rus. Fed.

191 E1 Goryachevodskiy Rus. Fed.
191 J1 Goryachiy Klyuch Rus. Fed.
162 J3 Goryun r. Rus. Fed.
185 J5 Gorzanak Afgh.
73 K2 Gorzano, Monte mt. Italy
37 L5 Görze France
51 F6 Görzke Ger.
55 H4 Gorzkowice Pol.
55 L5 Gorzków-Osada Pol.
54 E2 Górzna Pol.
47 I2 Górzno Pol.
55 H2 Gorzów Śląski Pol.
54 C3 Gorzów Wielkopolski Pol.
54 C3 Górzyca Lubuskie Pol.
54 C3 Górzyca Zachodniopomorskie Pol.
55 J5 Gorzyce Podkarpackie Pol.
55 K5 Gorzyce Podkarpackie Pol.
54 G6 Gorzyce Śląskie Pol.
54 C4 Górzyn Pol.
71 L3 Gosaldo Italy
59 I4 Gosau Austria
31 L2 Gosberton Lincolnshire, England U.K.
54 D3 Gościm Pol.
54 D1 Gościno Pol.
54 G2 Gościszów Pol.
59 M6 Gosdorf Austria
54 G6 Goseck Ger.
51 E8 Goseck Ger.
56 F5 Gősfai Hegy hill Hungary
31 N4 Gosfield Essex, England U.K.
205 M5 Gosford N.S.W. Austr.
29 K5 Gosforth Cumbria, England U.K.
29 N3 Gosforth Tyne and Wear, England U.K.
185 K8 Goshanak Pak.
52 F5 Gosheim Ger.
114 C5 Goshen IN U.S.A.
117 M5 Goshen NH U.S.A.
118 F6 Goshen NJ U.S.A.
117 K7 Goshen NY U.S.A.
116 F11 Goshen VA U.S.A.
166 A7 Goshiki Japan
164 F6 Goshogawara Japan
49 J7 Goslar Ger.
55 H3 Goślice Pol.
38 I5 Gosné France
68 E3 Gospić Croatia
31 K6 Gosport Hampshire, England U.K.
88 A3 Gossas Senegal
51 I7 Gossau Sankt Gallen Switz.
52 F7 Gossau Zürich Switz.
206 E5 Gosse watercourse N.T. Austr.
59 M6 Gössendorf Austria
88 E3 Gossi Mali
92 G2 Gossinga Sudan
59 N3 Gössl Austria
51 F9 Gößnitz Ger.
53 K2 Gößweinstein Ger.
51 E8 Gößweinstein Ger.
17 P3 Gostishchevo Rus. Fed.
59 N7 Gostivar Macedonia
59 K4 Gostling an der Ybbs Austria
54 F2 Gostynin Pol.
54 C1 Gostyń Wielkopolskie Pol.
54 C1 Gostyń Zachodniopomorskie Pol.
55 H3 Gostynin Pol.
47 I2 Gostyń Pol.
54 G4 Goszczanów Pol.
55 I4 Goszczyn Pol.
92 D3 Gota Eth.
22 I4 Göta älv r. Sweden
23 O8 Göta kanal canal Sweden
22 I4 Götaland reg. Sweden
22 I4 Göteborg Sweden
22 I4 Göteborg-Landvetter airport Sweden
89 I3 Gotel Mountains Cameroon/Nigeria
167 I6 Gotenba Shizuoka Japan see Gotenba
22 J3 Götene Sweden
59 N6 Gotenhafen Pol. see Gdynia
71 R4 Goteska Gora mts Slovenia
49 K9 Gotha Ger.
31 J2 Gotham Nottinghamshire, England U.K.
23 O4 Gothem Gotland Sweden
23 O4 Gothemán r. Gotland Sweden
23 O4 Göteborg Sweden
120 E5 Gothenburg NE U.S.A.
89 F3 Gothèye Niger
23 O4 Gotland county Sweden
23 O4 Gotland i. Gotland Sweden
131 □8 Goto Meer Bonaire
165 F14 Gotō-rettō is Japan
77 M8 Gotse Delchev Bulg.
165 J12 Gōtsu Japan
70 H7 Gottero, Monte mt. Italy
53 N4 Gottesgab Czech Rep.
52 G3 Gottfrieding Ger.
49 I7 Göttingen Ger.
52 F6 Gottmadingen Ger.
59 L2 Göttweig Austria
106 E4 Gott Peak B.C. Can.
75 □ Gozo i. Malta

90 C2 Goundi Chad
90 B2 Gounou-Gan Chad
90 B2 Gounou-Gaya Chad
109 G2 Goupil, Lac i. Que. Can.
88 B3 Gouraye Maur.
43 B8 Gourbera France
131 □2 Gourbeyre Guadeloupe
88 E3 Gourcy Burkina
41 J9 Gourdan, Montagne de mt. France
43 F9 Gourdan-Polignan France
43 G6 Gourdon Midi-Pyrénées France
41 J9 Gourdon Provence-Alpes-Côte d'Azur France
26 L9 Gourdon Aberdeenshire, Scotland U.K.
89 H3 Gouré Niger
43 D10 Gourette France
36 H6 Gourgançon France
38 D5 Gourin France
179 M7 Gouripur Bangl.
96 F10 Gourits r. S. Africa
110 J1 Gourlay Lake Ont. Can.
88 E2 Gourma-Rharous Mali
88 C2 Goûrmél well Maur.
36 D5 Gournay-en-Bray France
84 C5 Gouro Chad
86 D5 Goûr Oulad Aḥmed reg. Mali
84 D5 Gorouror well Chad
36 D5 Goussainville France
42 E5 Gout-Rossignol France
44 D5 Goutum Neth.
143 F3 Gouvêa Brazil
62 E8 Gouveia Port.
117 J4 Gouverneur NY U.S.A.
36 D5 Gouvieux France
54 G9 Gouvy Belgium
131 □6 Gouyave Grenada
90 C3 Gouzé C.A.R.
42 I3 Gouzon France
120 D6 Gove KS U.S.A.
91 B8 Gove, Barragem do resr Angola
77 L8 Govedartsi Bulg.
193 H4 Gove, Mys Rus. Fed.
206 F2 Gove Peninsula N.T. Austr.
143 G3 Governador Valadares Brazil
154 F8 Governor Generoso Mindanao Phil.
130 E1 Governor's Harbour Eleuthera Bahamas
119 G3 Governor's Island National Monument nat. park NY U.S.A.
168 F4 Govi-Altay prov. Mongolia
168 F4 Govi Altayn Nuruu mts Mongolia
179 I7 Govind Ballash Pant Sagar resr India
178 H7 Govindgarh Madh. Prad. India
185 L3 Govurdak Turkm.
185 M6 Gowal Pak.
76 G4 Gowanda NY U.S.A.
207 J8 Gowan Range hills Qld Austr.
173 H11 Gowaqungo Xizang China
185 K7 Gowārān Afgh.
55 I4 Gowarczów Pol.
184 F6 Gowd-e Aḥmar Iran
184 I6 Gowd-e Mokh i. Iran
203 B3 Gowenbridge South i. N.Z.
118 B3 Gowen City PA U.S.A.
30 D4 Gower pen. Wales U.K.
204 □2 Gower, Mount hill Lord Howe i. Austr.
111 N2 Gowganda Ont. Can.
111 N2 Gowganda Lake Ont. Can.
54 F1 Gowidlino Pol.
54 G3 Gowienica r. Pol.
185 M5 Gowmal Kalay Afgh.
27 H7 Gowna, Lough i. Rep. of Ireland
55 J3 Gowrie Pol.
27 H7 Gowran Rep. of Ireland
Gowurdak Turkm. see Govurdak
29 L7 Gowy r. England U.K.
29 O6 Goxhill North Lincolnshire, England U.K.
144 F3 Goya Arg.
131 □2 Goyave Guadeloupe
191 H5 Göyçay r. Azer.
191 H5 Göyçay Azer.
191 H5 Göyçay Qoruğu nature res. Azer.
206 E2 Goyder r. N.T. Austr.
206 E8 Goyder watercourse N.T. Austr.
204 C2 Goyder Lagoon salt flat S.A. Austr.
147 F5 Goyena Arg.
191 H5 Göygöl Azer.
89 F3 Göygöl Azer.
23 O4 Goyllē Azer.
191 J5 Göylär Çöl Azer.
79 L6 Göynük Antalya Turkey
79 M3 Göynük Bilecik Turkey
79 L3 Göynük Bolu Turkey
79 L2 Göynük r. Turkey
191 K5 Göynükbelen Turkey
164 S7 Goyō-zan mt. Japan
185 J4 Goz Beida Afgh.
84 D6 Goz-Beïda Chad
190 D2 Gözcüler Turkey
54 C3 Gozdowice Pol.
54 C3 Gozdnica Pol.
167 J2 Gozen-yama Japan
173 E9 Gozha Co salt l. China
190 E2 Gözkaya Turkey
75 □ Gozo i. Malta

96 E6 Graaff-Reinet S. Africa
97 N3 Graafwater S. Africa
59 O3 Gramatneusiedl Austria
58 H5 Gräfelfing Ger.
59 L2 Graben Ger.
52 G3 Grabenstätt Ger.
53 K6 Grabenstätt Ger.
53 J4 Grabfeld plain Ger.
88 D5 Grabo Côte d'Ivoire
53 M3 Grabow Mecklenburg-Vorpommern Ger.
50 E4 Grabow Sachsen-Anhalt Ger.
55 L3 Grabów Pol.
55 I4 Grabów nad Pilicą Pol.
54 F4 Grabów nad Prosną Pol.
55 K4 Grabowiec Pol.
54 F4 Grabowno Wielkie Pol.
54 F2 Grabowo Podlaskie Pol.
55 H4 Grabowo Warmińsko-Mazurskie Pol.
50 E4 Grabs Switz.
71 O6 Gračac Croatia
68 G3 Gračanica Bos.-Herz.
71 K7 Gračac Croatia
68 G3 Gračanica Jezero i. Serb. and Mont.
42 H1 Graçay France
45 H7 Grâce-Hollogne Belgium
207 M7 Gracemere Qld Austr.
38 E4 Grâces France
209 E12 Grace, Lake salt flat W.A. Austr.
108 H4 Gracefield Que. Can.
182 C1 Grachevka Orenburgskaya Oblast' Rus. Fed.

Grachi to Grimari
269

183 R2 Grachi Kazakh.
129 I3 Graciano Sánchez Mex.
126 □O10 Gracias Hond.
98 □1c Graciosa i. Azores
98 □3c Graciosa i. Canary Is
59 N6 Grad Slovenia
68 G3 Gradačac Bos.-Herz.
71 N8 Gradara Italy
140 C3 Gradaús Brazil
140 C4 Gradaús, Serra dos hills Brazil
59 N8 Gradec Croatia
63 J3 Gradefes Spain
77 O8 Gradets Bulg.
43 C6 Gradignan France
77 O8 Gradishte hill Bulg.
Gradiška Bos.-Herz. see Bosanska Gradiška
68 G3 Gradište Croatia
77 O6 Grădiștea Romania
71 O4 Grado Italy
62 H2 Grado Spain
58 H8 Grado, Laguna di lag. Italy
72 H2 Gradoli Italy
121 D8 Grady NM U.S.A.
26 J5 Graemsay i. Scotland U.K.
65 M6 Graena Spain
53 K5 Gräfelfing Ger.
53 K2 Gräfenberg Ger.
49 I10 Gräfendorf Ger.
59 M5 Grafendorf bei Hartberg Austria
51 F7 Gräfenhainichen Ger.
52 E6 Grafenhausen Ger.
49 K9 Gräfenroda Ger.
59 J6 Grafenstein Austria
51 D9 Gräfenthal Ger.
49 K8 Gräfentonna Ger.
53 L2 Grafenwöhr Ger.
59 M3 Grafenworth Austria
72 I2 Graffignano Italy
31 L3 Grafham Water resr England U.K.
49 K6 Grafhorst Ger.
51 D9 Gräfinau-Angstedt Ger.
53 L5 Grafing bei München Ger.
22 F1 Gråfjell mt. Norway
53 N4 Grafling Ger.
53 K5 Grafrath Ger.
20 L5 Gräftåvallen Sweden
205 N3 Grafton N.S.W. Austr.
120 G1 Grafton ND U.S.A.
116 C7 Grafton OH U.S.A.
110 G6 Grafton WI U.S.A.
116 E9 Grafton WV U.S.A.
207 J4 Grafton, Cape Qld Austr.
125 R3 Grafton, Mount NV U.S.A.
207 K4 Grafton Passage Qld Austr.
22 F1 Grågalten hill Norway
73 N6 Gragnano Italy
115 H7 Graham NC U.S.A.
121 F9 Graham TX U.S.A.
125 W9 Graham, Mount AZ U.S.A.
Graham Bell Island Zemlya Frantsa-Iosifa Rus. Fed. see Greem-Bell, Ostrov
106 C4 Graham Island B.C. Can.
105 I2 Graham Island Nunavut Can.
117 □Q4 Graham Lake ME U.S.A.
212 T2 Graham Land reg. Antarctica
106 F3 Graham Laurier Provincial Park park B.C. Can.
105 K2 Graham Moore, Cape Nunavut Can.
97 K9 Grahamstown S. Africa
Grahovo Bos.-Herz. see Bosansko Grahovo
59 I7 Grahovo Slovenia
28 D8 Graigue Rep. of Ireland
27 I7 Graiguenamanagh Rep. of Ireland
31 N5 Grain Medway, England U.K.
31 N5 Grain, Isle of pen. England U.K.
53 K7 Grainau Ger.
53 P4 Grainet Ger.
41 B7 Graissac France
41 C9 Graissessac France
63 Q9 Graja de Iniesta Spain
157 K9 Grajagan Jawa Indon.
63 J4 Grajal de Campos Spain
140 D3 Grajaú Brazil
140 D2 Grajaú r. Brazil
55 K2 Grajewo Pol.
14 J4 Grakhovo Rus. Fed.
26 D4 Gralisgeir i. Scotland U.K.
59 M6 Gralla Austria
22 F6 Gram Denmark
77 K8 Gramada mt. Serb. and Mont.
59 J3 Gramastettan Austria
43 H6 Gramat France
43 H6 Gramat, Causse de hills France
77 P8 Gramatikovo Bulg.
59 N3 Gramatneusiedl Austria
41 H9 Grambois France
50 J4 Grambow Ger.
50 D3 Gramkow Ger.
50 G2 Grammendorf Ger.
74 H9 Grammichele Sicilia Italy
Grammont Belgium see Geraardsbergen
70 D8 Grammont, Mont mt. Italy
78 B2 Grammos mt. Greece
16 G8 Grampian PA U.S.A.
26 G9 Grampian Mountains Scotland U.K.
205 I7 Grampians, The mts Vic. Austr.
205 I7 Grampians National Park Vic. Austr.
30 C7 Grampound Cornwall, England U.K.
44 K3 Gramsbergen Neth.
76 I10 Gramsh Albania
50 J4 Gramzow Ger.
Gran Hungary see Esztergom
70 D6 Grana r. Italy
70 F5 Grana r. Italy
96 D6 Granaatboskolk S. Africa
27 J6 Granabeg Rep. of Ireland
136 C4 Granada Col.
126 □Q12 Granada Nic.
65 L6 Granada Spain
65 M6 Granada prov. Spain
20 D6 Granada CO U.S.A.
98 □3a Granadilla de Abona Tenerife Canary Is
64 E5 Granado hill Spain
145 C8 Gran Altiplanicie Central plain Arg.
27 H5 Granard Rep. of Ireland
71 K6 Granarolo dell'Emilia Italy
58 G5 Granatspitze mt. Austria
65 L3 Granátula de Calatrava Spain
145 D7 Gran Bajo depr. Arg.
146 D6 Gran Bajo Salitroso salt flat Arg.
45 C8 Gran Bajo San Julián val. Arg.
70 B5 Gran Bosco di Salbertrand, Parco Naturale del nature res. Italy
21 G9 Granbury TX U.S.A.
09 F4 Granby Que. Can.
22 K6 Granby CO U.S.A.
98 □3f Gran Canaria i. Canary Is
37 J8 Grancey-le-Château-Nouvelle France
39 E6 Gran Chaco reg. Arg./Para.
31 □7 Gran Couva Trin. and Tob.
37 J7 Grand France
14 D4 Grand r. MO U.S.A.
20 E3 Grand r. SD U.S.A.
20 D3 Grand, North Fork r. SD U.S.A.
20 D3 Grand, South Fork r. SD U.S.A.
41 H7 Grand Armet mt. France
62 G2 Grandas Spain
30 D1 Grand Bahama i. Bahamas
37 N8 Grand Ballon mt. France
09 K4 Grand Bank Nfld and Lab. Can.
214 F3 Grand Banks of Newfoundland sea feature N. Atlantic Ocean
88 E5 Grand-Bassam Côte d'Ivoire
99 □1c Grand Bassin Réunion
131 □2 Grand Bay Dominica
121 K10 Grand Bay AL U.S.A.
109 H4 Grand Bay - Westfield N.B. Can.
108 D5 Grand Bend Ont. Can.
41 J8 Grand Bérard mt. France
88 D5 Grand-Bérébi Côte d'Ivoire
116 B6 Grand Blanc MI U.S.A.
131 □2 Grand-Bourg Guadeloupe
99 □1c Grand Brûlé coastal area Réunion
39 I3 Grandcamp-Maisy France
Grand Canal China see Da Yunhe
27 H6 Grand Canal Rep. of Ireland
Grand Canary i. Canary Is see Gran Canaria
125 T5 Grand Canyon AZ U.S.A.
125 T5 Grand Canyon gorge AZ U.S.A.
125 T5 Grand Canyon National Park AZ U.S.A.
125 S5 Grand Canyon-Parashant National Monument nat. park AZ U.S.A.
130 C4 Grand Cayman i. Cayman Is
107 I4 Grand Centre Alta Can.
88 C5 Grand Cess Liberia
38 F6 Grand-Champ France
40 J1 Grand-Charmont France
40 H5 Grand Colombier mt. France
70 C4 Grand Combin mt. Switz.
122 E3 Grand Coulee WA U.S.A.
36 B5 Grand-Couronne France
131 □2 Grand Cul de Sac Marin b. Guadeloupe
110 E8 Grand Detour IL U.S.A.
146 C5 Grande r. Arg.
139 E4 Grande r. Bol.
138 E4 Grande r. Bol.
142 B3 Grande r. Brazil
140 E4 Grande r. Brazil
74 E8 Grande r. Sicilia Italy
128 E6 Grande r. Jalisco/Michoacán Mex.
129 K8 Grande r. Mex.
129 L9 Grande r. Mex.
129 N9 Grande r. Mex.
126 □R11 Grande r. Nic.
138 B3 Grande r. Peru
67 D9 Grande r. Spain
65 J7 Grande r. Spain
65 L4 Grande r. Spain
145 C8 Grande, Bahía b. Arg.
130 D3 Grande, Cayo i. Cuba
128 G2 Grande, Cerro mt. Mex.
129 J8 Grande, Cerro mt. Mex.
136 C2 Grande, Ciénaga lag. Col.
38 D4 Grande, Île i. France
143 E5 Grande, Ilha i. Brazil
74 C8 Grande, Isola i. Sicilia Italy
41 K6 Grande, Lago l. Italy
74 D8 Grande, Montagna hill Italy
146 D5 Grande, Salina salt flat Arg.
139 E2 Grande, Serra hills Brazil
137 F4 Grande, Serra mt. Brazil
146 E2 Grande, Sierra mts Arg.
131 □2 Grande Anse Guadeloupe
99 □1b Grande Baie Mauritius
99 □2a Grande Barbe, Pointe pt Inner Islands Seychelles
71 M6 Grande Bonifica Ferrarese i. Italy
38 G7 Grande Brière reg. France
106 G4 Grande Cache Alta Can.
Grande Comore i. Comoros see Njazidja
137 F5 Grande de Manacapuru, Lago l. Brazil
109 I4 Grande-Entrée Que. Can.
43 C7 Grande Lande reg. France
43 C7 Grande Leyre r. France
39 M3 Grande Mare l. France
99 □1a Grande Passe Rodrigues I. Mauritius
106 G4 Grande Prairie Alta Can.
89 I2 Grand Erg de Bilma des. Niger
87 E3 Grand Erg Occidental des. Alg.
87 G3 Grand Erg Oriental des. Alg.
109 H3 Grande-Rivière Que. Can.
131 □3 Grande Rivière St Lucia
131 □7 Grande Rivière Trin. and Tob.
99 □1b Grande Rivière Noire Mauritius
99 □1b Grande Rivière Noire r. Mauritius
99 □1b Grande Rivière South East r. Mauritius
99 □1b Grande Rivière Sud-Est Mauritius
99 □1b Grande Rivière Sud-Est r. Mauritius
70 C4 Grande Rochère mt. Italy
122 F3 Grande Ronde r. OR U.S.A.
146 E2 Grandes, Salinas salt marsh Arg.
144 D1 Grandes, Salinas salt marsh Arg.
40 A2 Grande Sauldre r. France
126 C2 Gran Desierto del Pinacate, Parque Natural del nature res. Mex.
40 K5 Grandes Jorasses mts France/Italy
41 I6 Grandes Rousses mts France
36 D1 Grande-Synthe France
131 □6 Grand Étang l. Grenada
131 □2 Grande-Terre i. Guadeloupe
99 □3b Grande Terre i. Mayotte
41 H7 Grande Tête de l'Obiou mt. France
38 G8 Grand Etier r. France
70 D4 Grande Tournalin mt. Italy
43 I6 Grande-Vabre France
109 H3 Grande-Vallée Que. Can.
70 C4 Grand Eyvia r. Italy
109 H4 Grand Falls N.B. Can.
109 K3 Grand Falls Nfld and Lab. Can.
106 G5 Grand Forks B.C. Can.
120 G2 Grand Forks ND U.S.A.
36 D1 Grand-Fort-Philippe France
38 H6 Grand-Fougeray France
43 D10 Grand Gabizos mt. France
117 K6 Grand Gorge NY U.S.A.
130 H4 Grand Gosier Haiti
109 H4 Grand Harbour N.B. Can.
110 H6 Grand Haven MI U.S.A.
106 G1 Grandin, Lac l. N.W.T. Can.
120 F5 Grand Island NE U.S.A.
110 H3 Grand Island i. MI U.S.A.
121 J11 Grand Isle LA U.S.A.
117 □Q1 Grand Isle ME U.S.A.
125 X2 Grand Junction CO U.S.A.
110 H7 Grand Junction MI U.S.A.
88 D5 Grand-Lahou Côte d'Ivoire
109 H4 Grand Lake N.B. Can.
109 I2 Grand Lake Nfld and Lab. Can.
109 J3 Grand Lake Nfld and Lab. Can.
121 I11 Grand Lake LA U.S.A.
121 J11 Grand Lake LA U.S.A.
111 K4 Grand Lake MI U.S.A.
117 □Q2 Grand Lake Matagamon ME U.S.A.
116 A8 Grand Lake St Marys OH U.S.A.
117 □Q2 Grand Lake Seboeis ME U.S.A.
39 I8 Grand Lay r. France
110 J7 Grand Ledge MI U.S.A.
38 H7 Grand-Lieu, Lac de l. France
39 I8 Grand Maine r. France
109 H4 Grand Manan Island N.B. Can.
110 I3 Grand Marais MI U.S.A.
110 D2 Grand Marais MN U.S.A.
110 E6 Grand Marsh WI U.S.A.
109 F4 Grand-Mère Que. Can.
36 E6 Grand Morin r. France
64 B4 Grândola Port.
64 C4 Grândola r. Port.
64 B4 Grândola, Serra de mts Port.
106 B3 Grand Pacific Glacier B.C. Can.
200 □5 Grand Passage New Caledonia
41 H6 Grand Pic de Belledonne mt. France
36 B8 Grand-Pierre et Vitan, Réserve Naturelle nature res. France
110 E2 Grand Portage MN U.S.A.
37 I5 Grandpré France
36 E6 Grandpuits-Bailly-Carrois France
107 L4 Grand Rapids Man. Can.
110 I7 Grand Rapids MI U.S.A.
110 A2 Grand Rapids MN U.S.A.
200 □5 Grand Récif de Cook rf New Caledonia
99 □3b Grand Récif du Nord Est rf Mayotte
200 □5 Grand Récif du Sud rf New Caledonia
38 I6 Grand Réservoir de Vioreau resr France
41 F10 Grand Rhône r. France
41 D7 Grandrieu France
40 E4 Grandris France
131 □3 Grand' Rivière Martinique
41 J6 Grand Roc Noir mt. France
131 □6 Grand Roy Grenada
Grand St Bernard, Col du pass Italy/Switz. see Great St Bernard Pass
137 H3 Grand-Santi Fr. Guiana
70 B2 Grandson Switz.
122 I5 Grand Teton mt. WY U.S.A.
122 I5 Grand Teton National Park WY U.S.A.
110 I5 Grand Traverse Bay MI U.S.A.
130 H3 Grand Turk Turks and Caicos Is
130 H3 Grand Turk i. Turks and Caicos Is
41 C7 Grandval, Barrage de dam France
97 P2 Grand Valley Swaziland
40 I1 Grandvelle-et-le-Perrenot France
110 C3 Grand View WI U.S.A.
40 J1 Grandvillars France
110 I7 Grandville MI U.S.A.
37 M7 Grandvillers France
36 C4 Grandvilliers France
125 R5 Grand Wash watercourse AZ U.S.A.
125 R6 Grand Wash Cliffs mts AZ U.S.A.
110 A4 Grandy MN U.S.A.
41 F7 Grane France
66 E4 Grañén Spain
146 B4 Graneros Chile
27 E7 Graney, Lough l. Rep. of Ireland
23 M2 Granfjärden b. Sweden
27 J5 Grange Louth Rep. of Ireland
27 E4 Grange Sligo Rep. of Ireland
27 G9 Grange Waterford Rep. of Ireland
40 J4 Grange, Mont de mt. France
27 J5 Grangebellow Rep. of Ireland
27 I7 Grangeford Rep. of Ireland
130 □ Grange Hill Jamaica
26 I10 Grangemouth Falkirk, Scotland U.K.
41 E6 Grangent, Barrage de dam France
29 L5 Grange-over-Sands Cumbria, England U.K.
122 J6 Granger WY U.S.A.
23 L1 Grängesberg Sweden
37 M7 Granges-sur-Vologne France
30 F5 Grangetown Cardiff, Wales U.K.
122 F4 Grangeville ID U.S.A.
144 F2 Gran Guardia Arg.
20 P3 Granhult Sweden
40 H6 Granier, Col du pass France
41 H6 Granier, Mont mt. France
106 E4 Granisle B.C. Can.
118 B6 Granite MD U.S.A.
120 J6 Granite City IL U.S.A.
120 H3 Granite Falls MN U.S.A.
124 O1 Granite Mountain NV U.S.A.
125 Q7 Granite Mountains CA U.S.A.
125 Q8 Granite Mountains CA U.S.A.
122 J4 Granite Peak MT U.S.A.
125 S1 Granite Peak UT U.S.A.
110 G3 Granite Point MI U.S.A.
183 O6 Granitogorsk Kazakh.
74 D8 Granitola, Capo c. Sicilia Italy
74 D8 Granitola-Torretta Sicilia Italy
203 F8 Granity South I. N.Z.
140 E2 Granja Brazil
64 E4 Granja Port.
62 I5 Granja de Moreruela Spain
64 H4 Granja de Torrehermosa Spain
62 C8 Granja do Ulmeiro Port.
145 D7 Gran Laguna Salada l. Arg.
123 K12 Gran Morelos Mex.
22 I3 Grann l. Sweden
23 K3 Gränna Sweden
66 J4 Granollers Spain
54 E3 Granowo Pol.
138 B2 Gran Pajonal plain Peru
128 E3 Gran Pánfilo Natera Mex.
70 C4 Gran Paradiso mt. Italy
70 C4 Gran Paradiso, Parco Nazionale del nat. park Italy
58 E6 Gran Pilastro mt. Austria/Italy
Gran San Bernardo, Colle del pass Italy/Switz. see Great St Bernard Pass
73 K2 Gran Sasso d'Italia mts Italy
73 L3 Gran Sasso e Monti della Laga, Parco Nazionale del nat. park Italy
51 F8 Granschütz Ger.
50 H4 Gransee Ger.
28 E5 Gransha Northern Ireland U.K.
23 M3 Gransö i. Sweden
120 E5 Grant NE U.S.A.
124 N3 Grant, Mount NV U.S.A.
124 O2 Grant, Mount NV U.S.A.
98 □3b Gran Tarajal Fuerteventura Canary Is
120 H5 Grant City MO U.S.A.
31 K2 Grantham Lincolnshire, England U.K.
118 B4 Grantham PA U.S.A.
212 P2 Grant Island Antarctica
206 D1 Grant Island N.T. Austr.
106 G1 Grant Lake N.W.T. Can.
110 D5 Granton WI U.S.A.
26 I8 Grantown-on-Spey Highland, Scotland U.K.
110 G8 Grant Park IL U.S.A.
125 Q3 Grant Range mts NV U.S.A.
123 K9 Grants NM U.S.A.
110 B4 Grantsburg WI U.S.A.
26 L11 Grantshouse Scottish Borders, Scotland U.K.
122 C5 Grants Pass OR U.S.A.
116 D10 Grantsville WV U.S.A.
118 B4 Grantville PA U.S.A.
106 B2 Granville Y.T. Can.
38 H4 Granville France
125 W8 Granville AZ U.S.A.
110 E8 Granville IL U.S.A.
117 L5 Granville NY U.S.A.
116 C8 Granville OH U.S.A.
107 K3 Granville Lake Man. Can.
22 C1 Granvin Norway
50 E3 Granzin Ger.
143 F2 Grão Mogol Brazil
124 O5 Grapevine Mountains NV U.S.A.
71 L4 Grappa, Monte mt. Italy
130 F4 Grappler Bank sea feature Caribbean Sea
107 I1 Gras, Lac de l. N.W.T. Can.
20 T1 Grasbakken Norway
48 G4 Grasberg Ger.
95 F5 Graskop S. Africa
51 D6 Grasleben Ger.
22 I1 Gräsmarken Sweden
29 K5 Grasmere Cumbria, England U.K.
23 O1 Gräsö i. Sweden
118 C7 Grasonville MD U.S.A.
94 B5 Grasplatz Namibia
107 L3 Grass r. Man. Can.
117 K4 Grass r. NY U.S.A.
73 Q6 Grassano Italy
53 M6 Grassau Ger.
41 J9 Grasse France
116 G7 Grassflat PA U.S.A.
29 N5 Grassington North Yorkshire, England U.K.
111 J7 Grass Lake MI U.S.A.
107 J5 Grasslands National Park Sask. Can.
203 I8 Grassmere, Lake South I. N.Z.
209 F12 Grass Patch W.A. Austr.
122 J3 Grassrange MT U.S.A.
97 J7 Grassridgedam l. S. Africa
107 K4 Grass River Provincial Park Man. Can.
124 K2 Grass Valley CA U.S.A.
205 J9 Grassy Tas. Austr.
120 D2 Grassy Butte ND U.S.A.
130 E2 Grassy Creek r. Andros Bahamas
48 I1 Gråsten Denmark
22 I3 Grästorp Sweden
66 G5 Gratallops Spain
20 N2 Gratangsbotn Norway
43 G9 Gratens France
43 G8 Gratentour France
110 D7 Gratiot WI U.S.A.
59 L5 Gratkorn Austria
20 O4 Gråträsk Sweden
74 F8 Gratteri Sicilia Italy
59 L5 Gratwein Austria
70 H2 Graubünden canton Switz.
Graudenz Pol. see Grudziądz
49 E10 Grauer Kopf hill Ger.
43 H8 Graulhet France
51 I8 Graupa Ger.
66 F3 Graus Spain
63 Q4 Grávalos Spain
140 G4 Gravata Brazil
141 C9 Gravatai Brazil
20 L2 Gravdal Norway
44 I5 Grave Neth.
42 B4 Grave, Pointe de pt France
70 G3 Gravedona Italy
107 J5 Gravelbourg Sask. Can.
107 K2 Gravel Hill Lake N.W.T. Can.
36 D2 Gravelines France
70 E4 Gravellona Toce Italy
37 L5 Gravelotte France
108 E4 Gravenhurst Ont. Can.
49 F10 Grävenwiesbach Ger.
122 G3 Grave Peak ID U.S.A.
18 K5 Grāveri Latvia
43 C6 Graves reg. France
205 M3 Gravesend N.S.W. Austr.
31 M5 Gravesend Kent, England U.K.
121 H7 Gravette AR U.S.A.
36 B5 Gravigny France
73 R6 Gravina r. Italy
75 L3 Gravina di Matera r. Italy
73 Q6 Gravina in Puglia Italy
106 D4 Gravina Island AK U.S.A.
130 G4 Gravois, Pointe-à- pt Haiti
72 B4 Gravona r. Corse France
110 I5 Grawn MI U.S.A.
40 H2 Gray France
115 F9 Gray GA U.S.A.
116 A12 Gray KY U.S.A.
117 □O5 Gray ME U.S.A.
116 C12 Gray TN U.S.A.
42 B5 Grayan-et-l'Hôpital France
122 C5 Grayback Mountain OR U.S.A.
107 I2 Gray Lake N.W.T. Can.
106 E3 Grayling r. B.C. Can.
110 J5 Grayling MI U.S.A.
29 L5 Grayrigg Cumbria, England U.K.
31 M5 Grays Thurrock, England U.K.
122 B3 Grays Harbor inlet WA U.S.A.
31 K5 Grayshott Hampshire, England U.K.
122 I5 Grays Lake ID U.S.A.
116 C10 Grayson KY U.S.A.
114 D6 Grayville IL U.S.A.
17 O3 Grayvoron Rus. Fed.
59 L5 Graz Austria
41 E6 Grazac France
65 I7 Grazalema Spain
55 H2 Grążawy Pol.
74 G1 Grazzanise Italy
77 K8 Grdelica Srbija Serb. and Mont.
66 C7 Grea de Albarracín Spain
43 H6 Gréalou France
106 F2 Greasy Lake N.W.T. Can.
130 □ Great r. Jamaica
130 E1 Great Abaco i. Bahamas
Great Ararat mt. Turkey see Büyük Ağrı Dağı
198 C5 Great Australian Bight g. Austr.
29 O5 Great Ayton North Yorkshire, England U.K.
131 □6 Great Bacolet Bay Grenada
31 N4 Great Baddow Essex, England U.K.
130 D1 Great Bahama Bank sea feature Bahamas
202 J3 Great Barrier Island North I. N.Z.
207 J1 Great Barrier Reef Qld Austr.
207 K4 Great Barrier Reef Marine Park (Cairns Section) Qld Austr.
207 M6 Great Barrier Reef Marine Park (Capricorn Section) Qld Austr.
207 L5 Great Barrier Reef Marine Park (Central Section) Qld Austr.
207 J2 Great Barrier Reef Marine Park (Far North Section) Qld Austr.
117 L6 Great Barrington MA U.S.A.
31 N3 Great Barton Suffolk, England U.K.
207 J5 Great Basalt Wall National Park Qld Austr.
125 P2 Great Basin NV U.S.A.
125 R3 Great Basin National Park NV U.S.A.
119 G6 Great Bay NJ U.S.A.
106 E1 Great Bear r. N.W.T. Can.
106 G1 Great Bear Lake N.W.T. Can.
Great Belt sea chan. Denmark see Store Bælt
120 F6 Great Bend KS U.S.A.
117 J7 Great Bend PA U.S.A.
31 O4 Great Bentley Essex, England U.K.
26 C6 Great Bernera i. Scotland U.K.
31 N2 Great Bircham Norfolk, England U.K.
Great Bitter Lake Egypt see Murrah al Kubrá, Al Buḩayrah al
27 A8 Great Blasket Island Rep. of Ireland
29 O5 Great Broughton North Yorkshire, England U.K.
29 K4 Great Clifton Cumbria, England U.K.
159 A7 Great Coco Island Cocos Is
31 N3 Great Cornard Suffolk, England U.K.
28 H2 Great Cumbrae i. Scotland U.K.
117 I12 Great Dismal Swamp National Wildlife Refuge nature res. VA U.S.A.
198 E5 Great Dividing Range mts Austr.
29 K4 Great Dodd hill England U.K.
111 L4 Great Duck Island Ont. Can.
31 M4 Great Dunmow Essex, England U.K.
Great Eastern Erg des. Alg. see Grand Erg Oriental
29 L6 Great Eccleston Lancashire, England U.K.
118 F6 Great Egg Harbor r. NJ U.S.A.
118 F6 Great Egg Harbor Inlet NJ U.S.A.
31 N2 Great Ellingham Norfolk, England U.K.
130 C3 Greater Antilles is Caribbean Sea
Greater Khingan Mountains China see Da Hinggan Ling
31 L4 Greater London admin. div. England U.K.
29 M6 Greater Manchester admin. div. England U.K.
97 Q3 Greater St Lucia Wetland Park nature res. S. Africa
187 L2 Greater Tunb i. The Gulf
202 H1 Great Exhibition Bay North I. N.Z.
130 F2 Great Exuma i. Bahamas
122 I3 Great Falls MT U.S.A.
97 L9 Great Fish r. S. Africa
95 E7 Great Fish Point S. Africa
202 J7 Greatford North I. N.Z.
179 J7 Great Gandak r. India
31 J2 Great Glen Leicestershire, England U.K.
130 □ Great Goat Island Jamaica
31 K2 Great Gonerby Lincolnshire, England U.K.
31 L3 Great Gransden Cambridgeshire, England U.K.
130 E1 Great Guana Cay i. Bahamas
115 I12 Great Guana Cay i. Bahamas
31 K5 Greatham Hampshire, England U.K.
29 O4 Greatham Hartlepool, England U.K.
130 E1 Great Harbour Cay i. Bahamas
29 M6 Great Harwood Lancashire, England U.K.
31 I2 Great Haywood Staffordshire, England U.K.
31 N4 Great Horkesley Essex, England U.K.
130 G3 Great Inagua i. Bahamas
27 F9 Great Island Rep. of Ireland
96 H8 Great Karoo plat. S. Africa
97 M8 Great Kei r. S. Africa
207 M7 Great Keppel Island Qld Austr.
205 K9 Great Lake Tas. Austr.
95 F4 Great Limpopo Transfrontier Park nat. park Africa
31 K3 Great Linford Milton Keynes, England U.K.
30 H3 Great Malvern Worcestershire, England U.K.
29 K6 Great Marton Blackpool, England U.K.
118 F3 Great Meadows NJ U.S.A.
202 J3 Great Mercury Island North I. N.Z.
214 H4 Great Meteor Tablemount sea feature N. Atlantic Ocean
116 A9 Great Miami r. OH U.S.A.
31 K4 Great Missenden Buckinghamshire, England U.K.
94 C5 Great Namaqualand reg. Namibia
177 N9 Great Nicobar i. Andaman & Nicobar Is India
153 J8 Great North East Channel Austr./P.N.G.
30 E1 Great Ormes Head Wales U.K.
31 M2 Great Ouse r. England U.K.
205 L10 Great Oyster Bay Tas. Austr.
207 K5 Great Palm Islands Qld Austr.
119 K3 Great Peconic Bay NY U.S.A.
130 □ Great Pedro Bluff pt Jamaica
105 K3 Great Plain of the Koukdjuak Nunavut Can.
120 E4 Great Plains NE U.S.A.
117 O7 Great Point MA U.S.A.
31 K2 Great Ponton Lincolnshire, England U.K.
30 F3 Great Rhos hill Wales U.K.
92 B5 Great Rift Valley Africa
93 C6 Great Ruaha r. Tanz.
117 K5 Great Sacandaga Lake NY U.S.A.
40 K5 Great St Bernard Pass Italy/Switz.
115 H12 Great Sale Cay i. Bahamas
29 L4 Great Salkeld Cumbria, England U.K.
122 H6 Great Salt Lake UT U.S.A.
125 S1 Great Salt Lake Desert UT U.S.A.
131 □2 Great Salt Pond l. St Kitts and Nevis
31 M4 Great Sampford Essex, England U.K.
120 B6 Great Sand Dunes National Park CO U.S.A.
107 I5 Great Sand Hills Sask. Can.
84 E2 Great Sand Sea des. Egypt/Libya
208 G6 Great Sandy Desert W.A. Austr.
Great Sandy Island Qld Austr. see Fraser Island
208 C6 Great Sandy Island Nature Reserve W.A. Austr.
201 □1 Great Sea Reef Fiji
31 M3 Great Shelford Cambridgeshire, England U.K.
106 H2 Great Slave Lake N.W.T. Can.
115 E8 Great Smoky Mountains NC/TN U.S.A.
115 F8 Great Smoky Mountains National Park NC/TN U.S.A.
106 E3 Great Snow Mountain B.C. Can.
115 □1 Great Sound b. Bermuda
119 I3 Great South Bay NY U.S.A.
31 O5 Great Stour r. England U.K.
28 E7 Great Sugar Loaf hill Rep. of Ireland
30 D6 Great Torrington Devon, England U.K.
209 J10 Great Victoria Desert W.A. Austr.
204 B3 Great Victoria Desert Conservation Park nature res. S.A. Austr.
209 J10 Great Victoria Desert Nature Reserve W.A. Austr.
31 N4 Great Wakering Essex, England U.K.
212 U2 Great Wall research stn Antarctica
169 P6 Great Wall tourist site China
31 M4 Great Waltham Essex, England U.K.
117 □R4 Great Wass Island ME U.S.A.
Great Western Erg des. Alg. see Grand Erg Occidental
205 K9 Great Western Tiers mts Tas. Austr.
159 C9 Great West Torres Islands Myanmar
29 N5 Great Whernside hill England U.K.
96 D9 Great Winterhoek mt. S. Africa
30 H2 Great Wyrley Staffordshire, England U.K.
31 P2 Great Yarmouth Norfolk, England U.K.
31 N3 Great Yeldham Essex, England U.K.
95 F4 Great Zimbabwe National Monument tourist site Zimbabwe
22 H3 Grebbestad Sweden
49 H9 Grebenau Ger.
49 J8 Grebendorf (Meinhard) Ger.
49 H10 Grebenhain Ger.
191 H2 Grebenskaya Rus. Fed.
Grebenski Rus. Fed. see Grebenskaya
49 H8 Grebenstein Ger.
48 J2 Grebin Ger.
55 J3 Grębków Pol.
19 W7 Grebnevo Rus. Fed.
54 E4 Grębocice Pol.
54 G2 Grębocin Pol.
55 J5 Grębów Pol.
73 J3 Greccio Italy
73 O5 Greci Italy
77 Q5 Greci, Vârful hill Romania
Greco, Cape Cyprus see Greko, Cape
69 D5 Greco, Monte mt. Italy
53 K3 Greding Ger.
62 I8 Gredos, Sierra de mts Spain
145 C9 Greec Chile
78 C3 Greece country Europe
116 H5 Greece NY U.S.A.
122 L6 Greeley CO U.S.A.
118 F2 Greeley PA U.S.A.
120 F5 Greely Center NE U.S.A.
105 J1 Greely Fiord inlet Nunavut Can.
192 H1 Greem-Bell, Ostrov i. Zemlya Frantsa-Iosifa Rus. Fed.
113 M1 Green r. N.B. Can.
114 D7 Green r. KY U.S.A.
120 D2 Green r. ND U.S.A.
125 W3 Green r. WY U.S.A.
110 F5 Green Bay WI U.S.A.
110 G4 Green Bay b. WI U.S.A.
118 B6 Greenbelt MD U.S.A.
116 E11 Greenbrier r. WV U.S.A.
209 D12 Greenbushes W.A. Austr.
205 M7 Green Cape N.S.W. Austr.
115 I13 Greencastle Bahamas
27 I2 Greencastle Rep. of Ireland
27 H3 Greencastle Northern Ireland U.K.
27 J4 Greencastle Northern Ireland U.K.
114 D6 Greencastle IN U.S.A.
116 H9 Greencastle PA U.S.A.
130 E1 Green Cay i. Bahamas
115 G11 Green Cove Springs FL U.S.A.
118 F6 Green Creek NJ U.S.A.
49 I7 Greene Ger.
110 B7 Greene IA U.S.A.
117 □O4 Greene ME U.S.A.
117 J6 Greene NY U.S.A.
115 F7 Greeneville TN U.S.A.
124 K5 Greenfield CA U.S.A.
120 H5 Greenfield IA U.S.A.
114 E6 Greenfield IN U.S.A.
117 M6 Greenfield MA U.S.A.
121 I7 Greenfield MO U.S.A.
116 B9 Greenfield OH U.S.A.
110 F7 Greenfield WI U.S.A.
119 G1 Greenfield Park NY U.S.A.
28 J2 Greengairs North Lanarkshire, Scotland U.K.
31 J5 Greenham West Berkshire, England U.K.
118 B6 Green Haven MD U.S.A.
209 C11 Green Head W.A. Austr.
209 C11 Green Head hd W.A. Austr.
29 L4 Greenhead Northumberland, England U.K.
206 D1 Greenhill Island N.T. Austr.
203 C13 Greenhills South I. N.Z.
130 □ Green Island Jamaica
27 K3 Greenisland Northern Ireland U.K.
154 B6 Green Island Bay Palawan Phil.
153 L7 Green Islands P.N.G.
107 J4 Green Lake Sask. Can.
106 F5 Green Lake l. B.C. Can.
203 B12 Green Lake South I. N.Z.
110 F6 Green Lake WI U.S.A.
105 N2 Greenland terr. N. America
110 E3 Greenland MI U.S.A.
218 X2 Greenland Basin sea feature Arctic Ocean
203 D12 Greenland Reservoir South I. N.Z.
102 G1 Greenland Sea Greenland/Svalbard
118 E4 Green Lane PA U.S.A.
118 D4 Green Lane Reservoir PA U.S.A.
26 L11 Greenlaw Scottish Borders, Scotland U.K.
26 I10 Greenloaning Perth and Kinross, Scotland U.K.
26 I12 Green Lowther hill Scotland U.K.
204 E6 Greenly Island S.A. Austr.
118 B5 Greenmount MD U.S.A.
117 M4 Green Mountains VT U.S.A.
26 G11 Greenock Inverclyde, Scotland U.K.
29 K5 Greenodd Cumbria, England U.K.
27 J4 Greenore Rep. of Ireland
27 J8 Greenore Point Rep. of Ireland
209 C10 Greenough W.A. Austr.
209 C10 Greenough r. W.A. Austr.
204 □3 Green Point S. Pacific Ocean
119 G2 Green Pond NJ U.S.A.
117 M7 Greenport NY U.S.A.
125 V3 Green River UT U.S.A.
122 J6 Green River WY U.S.A.
115 D9 Greensboro AL U.S.A.
115 F9 Greensboro GA U.S.A.
118 D7 Greensboro MD U.S.A.
115 H7 Greensboro NC U.S.A.
114 E6 Greensburg IN U.S.A.
121 F7 Greensburg KS U.S.A.
114 E7 Greensburg KY U.S.A.
121 J10 Greensburg LA U.S.A.
116 F8 Greensburg PA U.S.A.
125 W7 Greens Peak NM U.S.A.
26 E7 Greenstone Point Scotland U.K.
115 H8 Green Swamp NC U.S.A.
110 I9 Greentown IN U.S.A.
118 E2 Greentown PA U.S.A.
120 K6 Greenup IL U.S.A.
116 C10 Greenup KY U.S.A.
207 J5 Greenvale Qld Austr.
117 K3 Green Valley Ont. Can.
125 V10 Green Valley AZ U.S.A.
106 D4 Greenville B.C. Can.
88 C5 Greenville Liberia
115 D10 Greenville AL U.S.A.
124 L1 Greenville CA U.S.A.
115 F10 Greenville FL U.S.A.
115 E9 Greenville GA U.S.A.
120 K6 Greenville IL U.S.A.
114 D7 Greenville KY U.S.A.
117 □P3 Greenville ME U.S.A.
110 I6 Greenville MI U.S.A.
121 J7 Greenville MO U.S.A.
121 J9 Greenville MS U.S.A.
115 I8 Greenville NC U.S.A.
117 N6 Greenville NH U.S.A.
120 M5 Greenville OH U.S.A.
116 E7 Greenville PA U.S.A.
115 F8 Greenville SC U.S.A.
121 G9 Greenville TX U.S.A.
116 F10 Greenville VA U.S.A.
110 D1 Greenwater Lake Ont. Can.
107 K4 Greenwater Provincial Park Sask. Can.
30 C4 Greenway Pembrokeshire, Wales U.K.
31 L5 Greenwich Greater London, England U.K.
119 H2 Greenwich CT U.S.A.
118 E6 Greenwich NJ U.S.A.
117 L5 Greenwich NY U.S.A.
116 C7 Greenwich OH U.S.A.
121 H8 Greenwood AR U.S.A.
118 D7 Greenwood DE U.S.A.
114 D6 Greenwood IN U.S.A.
121 J9 Greenwood MS U.S.A.
115 F8 Greenwood SC U.S.A.
110 D5 Greenwood WI U.S.A.
119 G2 Greenwood Lake NY U.S.A.
119 G2 Greenwood Lake l. NJ U.S.A.
115 F8 Greer SC U.S.A.
121 I8 Greers Ferry Lake AR U.S.A.
28 D8 Greese r. Rep. of Ireland
48 D3 Greetsiel (Krummhörn) Ger.
136 D6 Gregório r. Brazil
206 G5 Gregory r. Qld Austr.
111 J7 Gregory MI U.S.A.
120 F4 Gregory SD U.S.A.
204 G3 Gregory, Lake salt flat S.A. Austr.
208 I6 Gregory, Lake salt flat W.A. Austr.
209 E8 Gregory, Lake salt flat W.A. Austr.
206 G5 Gregory Downs Qld Austr.
206 C4 Gregory National Park N.T. Austr.
207 I5 Gregory Range hills Qld Austr.
208 F6 Gregory Range hills W.A. Austr.
58 H6 Greifenburg Austria
51 H8 Greifendorf Ger.
70 F1 Greifensee l. Switz.
49 F9 Greifenstein Ger.
50 I4 Greiffenberg Ger.
50 H2 Greifswald Ger.
50 I2 Greifswalder Bodden b. Ger.
50 I2 Greifswalder Oie i. Ger.
59 K3 Grein Austria
51 F9 Greiz Ger.
190 C4 Greko, Cape Cyprus
48 K2 Gremersdorf Ger.
14 G1 Gremikha Rus. Fed.
19 V7 Gremyachev Rus. Fed.
14 L4 Gremyachinsk Permskaya Oblast' Rus. Fed.
160 I1 Gremyachinsk Respublika Buryatiya Rus. Fed.
17 S2 Gremyach'ye Rus. Fed.
22 G5 Grenå Denmark
121 K9 Grenada MS U.S.A.
131 □6 Grenada country West Indies
121 K9 Grenada Lake resr MS U.S.A.
43 G8 Grenade France
43 D8 Grenade-sur-l'Adour France
37 K8 Grenant France
70 C1 Grenchen Switz.
22 G4 Grenen spit Denmark
205 L5 Grenfell N.S.W. Austr.
107 K5 Grenfell Sask. Can.
41 H6 Grenoble France
20 U2 Grense-Jakobselv Norway
131 □6 Grenville Grenada
207 I1 Grenville, Cape Qld Austr.
52 D6 Grenzach-Wyhlen Ger.
41 H9 Gréoux-les-Bains France
50 F2 Gresenhorst Ger.
185 K8 Greshag Pak.
185 L8 Greshak Pak.
122 C4 Gresham OR U.S.A.
157 J8 Gresik Jawa Indon.
26 D6 Gress Western Isles, Scotland U.K.
20 L4 Gressåmoen Nasjonalpark nat. park Norway
70 C4 Gressan Italy
41 H6 Gresse r. France
48 K4 Gresse Ger.
41 H7 Gresse-en-Vercors France
70 D4 Gressoney-la-Trinite Italy
59 L4 Gresten Austria
40 H5 Grésy-sur-Aix France
40 I5 Grésy-sur-Isère France
29 L5 Greta r. England U.K.
72 G2 Gretano r. Italy
26 J13 Gretna Dumfries and Galloway, Scotland U.K.
121 J11 Gretna LA U.S.A.
116 F12 Gretna VA U.S.A.
53 I2 Grettstadt Ger.
49 K8 Greußen Ger.
37 K7 Greux France
71 K8 Greve r. Italy
71 K8 Greve in Chianti Italy
44 E5 Grevelingen sea chan. Neth.
48 K4 Greven Mecklenburg-Vorpommern Ger.
49 E6 Greven Nordrhein-Westfalen Ger.
78 C2 Grevena Greece
45 I6 Grevenbicht Neth.
49 C8 Grevenbroich Ger.
45 J9 Grevenmacher Lux.
45 J9 Grevenmacher admin. dist. Lux.
50 D3 Grevesmühlen Ger.
109 J4 Grey r. Nfld and Lab. Can.
203 F9 Grey r. South I. N.Z.
206 F2 Grey, Cape N.T. Austr.
27 K3 Greyabbey Northern Ireland U.K.
122 J4 Greybull WY U.S.A.
122 J4 Greybull r. WY U.S.A.
106 C2 Grey Hunter Peak Y.T. Can.
109 K3 Grey Islands Nfld and Lab. Can.
97 M2 Greylingstad S. Africa
117 L6 Greylock, Mount MA U.S.A.
203 F9 Greymouth South I. N.Z.
28 F4 Grey Point Northern Ireland U.K.
205 I3 Grey Range hills Qld Austr.
209 C8 Grey's Plains W.A. Austr.
29 L4 Greystoke Cumbria, England U.K.
95 F4 Greystone Zimbabwe
27 J6 Greystones Rep. of Ireland
96 D10 Greyton S. Africa
203 J8 Greytown North I. N.Z.
97 O5 Greytown S. Africa
45 G7 Grez-Doiceau Belgium
39 J6 Grez-en-Bouère France
71 K4 Grezzana Italy
59 I7 Grgar Slovenia
78 F5 Gria, Akra pt Andros Greece
Griais Scotland U.K. see Gress
15 H6 Gribanovskiy Rus. Fed.
90 C2 Gribingui r. C.A.R.
90 C3 Gribingui-Bamingui, Réserve de Faune du nature res. C.A.R.
14 F2 Gridino Rus. Fed.
124 K2 Gridley CA U.S.A.
110 F9 Gridley IL U.S.A.
51 E6 Grieben Ger.
63 Q8 Griegos Spain
37 O6 Gries France
58 D5 Gries am Brenner Austria
52 E5 Griesbach Ger.
53 O5 Griesbach im Rottal Ger.
52 F2 Griesheim Ger.
59 I3 Grieskirchen Austria
51 K7 Grießen Ger.
53 M6 Griesstätt Ger.
59 K6 Griffen Austria
115 E9 Griffin GA U.S.A.
205 K6 Griffith N.S.W. Austr.
111 Q4 Griffith Ont. Can.
104 F2 Griffiths Point N.W.T. Can.
116 D10 Griffithsville WV U.S.A.
Grigan i. N. Mariana Is see Agrihan
72 B8 Grighini, Monte hill Italy
Grigioni canton Switz. see Graubünden
18 I7 Grigiškės Lith.
70 G4 Grigna mt. Italy
70 I4 Grigna r. Italy
41 F8 Grignan France
71 L3 Grigno Italy
71 L3 Grigno r. Italy
43 D7 Grignols France
40 F5 Grigny France
16 I6 Grigoriopol Moldova
63 K4 Grijota Spain
44 J2 Grijpskerk Neth.
Grik Malaysia see Gerik
41 F8 Grillon France
205 J9 Grim, Cape Tas. Austr.
73 Q9 Grimaldi Italy
90 D3 Grimari C.A.R.

Grimaud to Gulumba Gana

270

41 J10 Grimaud France
26 A7 Griminis Point Scotland U.K.
51 G8 Grimma Ger.
50 H2 Grimmen Ger.
59 I4 Grimming mt. Austria
50 I5 Grimnitzsee l. Ger.
29 R7 Grimoldby Lincolnshire, England U.K.
26 B8 Grimsay i. Scotland U.K.
111 O6 Grimsby Ont. Can.
29 Q6 Grimsby North East Lincolnshire, England U.K.
70 E2 Grimsel nature res. Switz.
20 □E1 Grímsey i. Iceland
106 G3 Grimshaw Alta Can.
20 □E1 Grímsstaðir Iceland
22 E3 Grimstad Norway
31 N2 Grimston Norfolk, England U.K.
22 B2 Grindafjord Norway
21 J6 Grindaheim Norway
20 □B2 Grindavík Iceland
70 E2 Grindelwald Switz.
22 E6 Grindsted Denmark
111 L5 Grind Stone City MI U.S.A.
77 O6 Grindu Ialomița Romania
77 Q5 Grindu Tulcea Romania
77 Q6 Grindul Chituc spit Romania
77 O4 Grindușu, Vârful mt. Romania
19 Q9 Grinevo Rus. Fed.
29 P7 Gringley on the Hill Nottinghamshire, England U.K.
120 I5 Grinnell IA U.S.A.
105 I2 Grinnell Peninsula Nunavut Can.
63 M8 Griñón Spain
58 C5 Grins Austria
77 N3 Grințieș Romania
68 E2 Grintovec mt. Slovenia
58 D5 Grinzens Austria
63 R5 Grío r. Spain
Griomasaigh i. Scotland U.K. see Grimsay
97 N6 Griqualand East reg. S. Africa
96 H4 Griqualand West reg. S. Africa
96 H4 Griquatown S. Africa
Grischun canton Switz. see Graubünden
105 J2 Grise Fiord Nunavut Can.
66 C4 Grisén Spain
71 L5 Grisignano di Zocco Italy
156 E6 Grisik Sumatera Indon.
36 C2 Gris Nez, Cap c. France
73 P8 Grisolia Italy
43 G8 Grisolles France
Grisons canton Switz. see Graubünden
23 O1 Grisslehamn Sweden
26 K5 Gritley Orkney, Scotland U.K.
17 R8 Grivenskaya Rus. Fed.
29 K5 Grizebeck Cumbria, England U.K.
86 E4 Grizim well Alg.
106 F1 Grizzly Bear Mountain hill N.W.T. Can.
68 F3 Grmeč mts Bos.-Herz.
109 K3 Groais Island Nfld and Lab. Can.
45 G6 Grobbendonk Belgium
53 K5 Gröbenzell Ger.
51 F8 Gröbers Ger.
18 E5 Grobiņa Latvia
97 N1 Groblersdal S. Africa
96 G4 Groblershoop S. Africa
59 I5 Gröbming Austria
51 E7 Gröbzig Ger.
76 I6 Grocka Srbija Serb. and Mont.
48 G1 Gröde-Appelland i. Ger.
55 K4 Gródek Lubelskie Pol.
55 L2 Gródek Podlaskie Pol.
51 I8 Gröden Ger.
58 H4 Grödig Austria
51 H8 Gröditz Ger.
55 I2 Gródki Pol.
54 F5 Grodków Pol.
Grodno Belarus see Hrodna
55 H2 Grodziczno Pol.
54 G3 Grodziec Pol.
55 K3 Grodzisk Pol.
55 I3 Grodzisk Mazowiecki Pol.
54 E3 Grodzisk Wielkopolski Pol.
96 H6 Groen watercourse Northern Cape S. Africa
96 B6 Groen watercourse S. Africa
44 K4 Groenlo Neth.
97 O3 Groenvlei S. Africa
121 G10 Groesbeck TX U.S.A.
44 I5 Groesbeek Neth.
20 □B1 Gröf Iceland
207 J4 Groganville Qld Austr.
49 H6 Grohnde (Emmerthal) Ger.
57 L6 Grohot, Vârful hill Romania
51 F8 Groitzsch Ger.
38 E6 Groix France
38 E6 Groix, Île de i. France
55 I4 Grójec Pol.
55 I2 Grom Pol.
54 D4 Gromadka Pol.
69 C7 Grombalia Tunisia
48 K2 Grömitz Ger.
55 I6 Gromnik Pol.
70 H4 Gromo Italy
48 G1 Grønå r. Denmark
49 I6 Gronau (Leine) Ger.
49 D6 Gronau (Westfalen) Ger.
73 Q8 Grondo r. Italy
53 I6 Grönenbach Ger.
20 L4 Grong Norway
51 D7 Gröningen Ger.
44 K2 Groningen Neth.
44 K2 Groningen prov. Neth.
137 H3 Groningen Suriname
44 J2 Groninger Wad tidal flat Neth.
Grønland terr. N. America see Greenland
55 H1 Gronowo Pol.
23 L4 Grönskåra Sweden
50 F1 Grønsund sea chan. Denmark
121 E8 Groom TX U.S.A.
125 Q4 Groom Lake NV U.S.A.
27 K3 Groomsport Northern Ireland U.K.
96 I9 Groot r. Eastern Cape S. Africa
96 D8 Groot r. Western Cape S. Africa
96 F9 Groot r. Western Cape S. Africa
96 E3 Groot-Aar Pan salt pan S. Africa
96 C8 Groot Berg r. S. Africa
97 J7 Groot Brak r. S. Africa
96 G10 Groot Brakrivier S. Africa
97 N2 Grootdraaidam dam S. Africa
96 F4 Grootdrink S. Africa
44 H3 Grootebroek Neth.
206 F2 Groote Eylandt i. N.T. Austr.
206 F3 Groote Eylandt Aboriginal Land res. N.T. Austr.
44 J2 Grootegast Neth.
94 C3 Grootfontein Namibia
97 J4 Groot-Grannapan salt pan S. Africa
94 C5 Groot Karas Berg plat. Namibia
94 D4 Groot Laagte watercourse Botswana/Namibia
95 F4 Groot Letaba r. S. Africa
97 K1 Groot Marico S. Africa
96 B5 Grootmis S. Africa
97 K1 Grootpan S. Africa
96 H9 Grootrivierhoogte mts S. Africa
96 F9 Groot Swartberge mts S. Africa
96 C2 Grootvaalgraspan salt pan Namibia
97 M2 Grootvlei S. Africa
96 E5 Grootvloer salt pan S. Africa
97 K8 Groot Winterberg mt. S. Africa
97 I9 Groot-Winterhoekberge mts S. Africa
70 F5 Gropello Cairoli Italy
77 P5 Gropeni Romania
67 D12 Grosa, Isla i. Spain
41 I9 Gros Bessillon hill France
40 F2 Grosbois-en-Montagne France
41 K6 Groscavallo Italy
70 I3 Grosio Italy
131 □3 Gros Islet St Lucia
131 □3 Gros-Morne Martinique
109 J3 Gros Morne National Park Nfld and Lab. Can.
40 F3 Grosne r. France
58 B7 Grosotto Italy
131 □3 Gros Piton mt. St Lucia
67 I9 Grossa, Punta pt Spain
53 J5 Großaitingen Ger.
49 I8 Großalmerode Ger.
51 E6 Groß Ammensleben Ger.
58 H5 Großarl Austria
94 C4 Gross Barmen Namibia
49 J8 Großbartloff Ger.
51 H6 Großbeeren Ger.
48 D5 Groß Berßen Ger.
52 F2 Groß-Bieberau Ger.
49 J8 Großbodungen Ger.
51 G8 Großbothen Ger.
52 G4 Großbottwar Ger.
51 D9 Großbreitenbach Ger.
49 I6 Großburgwedel (Burgwedel) Ger.
49 J8 Großburschla Ger.
50 I5 Groß Dölln Ger.
51 J8 Großdubrau Ger.
49 H5 Große Aue r. Ger.
52 F4 Große Enz r. Ger.
53 N4 Große Laaber r. Ger.
52 H5 Große Lauter r. Ger.
49 J6 Groß Elbe (Elbe) Ger.
52 F5 Grosselfingen Ger.
48 I3 Großenaspe Ger.
50 D2 Großenbrode Ger.
49 G9 Großen-Buseck Ger.
49 K8 Großenehrich Ger.
59 O3 Groß Engersdorf Austria
49 K8 Großengottern Ger.
51 I8 Großenhain Ger.
48 F5 Großenkneten Ger.
49 I9 Großenlüder Ger.
48 J3 Großensee Ger.
51 F9 Großenstein Ger.
48 H1 Großenwiehe Ger.
59 O3 Groß-Enzersdorf Austria
131 □2 Grosse Pointe Guadeloupe
53 O3 Großer Arber mt. Ger.
49 K9 Großer Beerberg hill Ger.
59 J5 Grosser Bösenstein mt. Austria
49 J10 Großer Breitenberg hill Ger.
59 K4 Grosser Buchstein mt. Austria
52 D3 Großer Eyberg hill Ger.
49 K10 Großer Gleichberg hill Ger.
50 H1 Großer Jasmunder Bodden b. Ger.
51 F10 Großer Kornberg hill Ger.
50 H3 Großer Landgraben r. Ger.
58 E5 Grosser Löffler mt. Austria
51 I6 Großer Müggelsee l. Ger.
51 H8 Große Röder r. Ger.
56 C2 Großer Osser mt. Czech Rep./Ger.
48 J2 Großer Plöner See l. Ger.
59 J4 Grosser Priel mt. Austria
53 O4 Großer Rachel mt. Ger.
51 I6 Großer Selchower See l. Ger.
59 I6 Grosser Speikkofel mt. Austria
59 K6 Grosser Speikkogel mt. Austria
51 E10 Großer Waldstein hill Ger.
48 D4 Großes Meer l. Ger.
58 G5 Großes Wiesbachhorn mt. Austria
38 H8 Grosse Terre, Pointe de pt France
72 G2 Grosseto Italy
72 G2 Grosseto prov. Italy
72 B4 Grosseto-Prugna Corse France
162 K5 Grossevichi Rus. Fed.
53 M4 Große Vils r. Ger.
50 I4 Groß Fredenwalde Ger.
49 K8 Großfurra Ger.
50 E5 Groß Garz Ger.
52 E2 Groß-Gerau Ger.
59 K2 Groß-Gerungs Austria
49 I6 Groß Giesen Ger.
51 H6 Groß Glienicke Ger.
58 G5 Großglockner mt. Austria
53 N6 Großgmain Ger.
50 E4 Groß Godems Ger.
59 L2 Großgöttfritz Austria
48 K3 Groß Grönau Ger.
53 J3 Großhabersdorf Ger.
48 J3 Großhansdorf Ger.
59 N2 Großharras Austria
49 J6 Groß Heere (Heere) Ger.
51 K9 Großhennersdorf Ger.
51 E8 Großheringen Ger.
48 D5 Groß-Hesepe Ger.
52 G2 Großheubach Ger.
48 G5 Groß Ippener Ger.
53 M6 Großkarolinenfeld Ger.
51 E8 Großkayna Ger.
50 H2 Groß Kiesow Ger.
59 L6 Großklein Austria
51 F8 Großkorbetha Ger.
51 I6 Groß Köris Ger.
51 J8 Großkoschen Ger.
51 G6 Groß Kreutz Ger.
59 O2 Großkrut Austria
48 J2 Groß Kummerfeld Ger.
50 E4 Groß Laasch Ger.
49 J6 Groß Lafferde (Lahstedt) Ger.
53 I2 Großlangheim Ger.
51 F8 Großlehna Ger.
51 J6 Groß Leine Ger.
51 J6 Groß Leuthen Ger.
51 K6 Groß Lindow Ger.
49 C10 Großlittgen Ger.
49 K8 Großlohra Ger.
51 I8 Großmehlen Ger.
53 L4 Großmehring Ger.
50 I3 Groß Miltzow Ger.
50 G2 Groß Mohrdorf Ger.
51 D8 Großmonra Ger.
51 E7 Groß Mühlingen Ger.
51 I8 Großnaundorf Ger.
51 G7 Groß Naundorf Ger.
50 H4 Groß Nemerow Ger.
48 J5 Groß Oesingen Ger.
51 H9 Großolbersdorf Ger.
51 D7 Großörner Ger.
51 J7 Groß Oßnig Ger.
52 G2 Großostheim Ger.
59 N5 Großpetersdorf Austria
50 G3 Groß Plasten Ger.
51 D7 Groß Quenstedt Ger.
59 K4 Großraming Austria
51 J7 Großräschen Ger.
52 H2 Großrinderfeld Ger.
52 E2 Groß-Rohrheim Ger.
51 J8 Großröhrsdorf Ger.
51 E7 Groß Rosenburg Ger.
52 B3 Großrosseln Ger.
51 D8 Großrudestedt Ger.
59 N3 Großrußbach Austria
59 L6 Groß Sankt Florian Austria
51 J8 Groß Särchen Ger.
51 K7 Groß Schacksdorf Ger.
51 H9 Großschirma Ger.
59 K2 Großschönau Austria
51 K9 Großschönau Ger.
50 I5 Groß Schönebeck Ger.
50 E5 Groß Schwechten Ger.
51 K8 Großschweidnitz Ger.
49 J6 Groß Schwülper (Schwülper) Ger.
59 L2 Groß-Siegharts Austria
48 I1 Großsolt Ger.
48 D5 Groß Stavern Ger.
51 G8 Großsteinberg Ger.
50 D3 Groß Stieten Ger.
51 G7 Großtreben Ger.
49 K6 Groß Twülpstedt Ger.
94 C4 Gross Ums Namibia
52 F2 Groß-Umstadt Ger.
58 F5 Großvenediger mt. Austria
52 G2 Großwallstadt Ger.
70 E1 Grosswangen Switz.
50 E4 Groß Warnow Ger.
49 K8 Großwechsungen Ger.
59 M3 Großweikersdorf Austria
50 F4 Groß Welle Ger.
48 I2 Groß Wittensee Ger.
50 F3 Groß Wokern Ger.
50 F5 Großwudicke Ger.
50 G3 Groß Wüstenfelde Ger.
50 I5 Groß Ziethen Ger.
52 F2 Groß-Zimmern Ger.
37 M6 Grostenquin France
68 E3 Grosuplje Slovenia
213 L1 Grosvenor Mountains Antarctica
122 I5 Gros Ventre Range mts WY U.S.A.
109 J2 Groswater Bay Nfld and Lab. Can.
45 F6 Grote Nete r. Belgium
119 K2 Groton CT U.S.A.
117 I6 Groton NY U.S.A.
120 F3 Groton SD U.S.A.
73 J4 Grottaferrata Italy
75 M2 Grottaglie Italy
73 L2 Grottammare Italy
73 L1 Grottazzolina Italy
74 F9 Grotte Sicilia Italy
72 H2 Grotte di Castro Italy
75 K7 Grotteria Italy
116 G10 Grottoes VA U.S.A.
75 K2 Grottole Italy
44 I2 Grou Neth.
106 G1 Grouard Lake N.W.T. Can.
106 G4 Grouard Mission Alta Can.
38 H4 Grouin, Pointe du pt France
88 E5 Groumania Côte d'Ivoire
108 D3 Groundhog r. Ont. Can.
121 H7 Grove OK U.S.A.
116 B9 Grove City OH U.S.A.
116 E7 Grove City PA U.S.A.
115 D10 Grove Hill AL U.S.A.
21 L5 Grövelsjön Sweden
213 F2 Grove Mountains Antarctica
118 B1 Grover PA U.S.A.
124 L6 Grover Beach CA U.S.A.
117 N4 Groveton NH U.S.A.
121 H10 Groveton TX U.S.A.
118 F4 Groveville NJ U.S.A.
20 N2 Grovfjord Norway
125 S9 Growler Mountains AZ U.S.A.
77 P7 Grozd'ovo Bulg.
191 G2 Groznyy Rus. Fed.
51 D10 Grub am Forst Ger.
22 C3 Grubbåfjellet mt. Norway
45 J6 Grubbenvorst Neth.
50 D2 Grube Ger.
68 F3 Grubišno Polje Croatia
54 G2 Gruczno Pol.
55 I2 Grudusk Pol.
54 G2 Grudziądz Pol.
70 F6 Grue r. Italy
37 L7 Gruey-lès-Surance France
70 D5 Grugliasco Italy
26 E7 Gruinard Bay Scotland U.K.
26 D11 Gruinart, Loch inlet Scotland U.K.
41 C10 Gruissan France
62 H2 Grullos Spain
20 □ Grumantbyen Svalbard
77 O3 Grumăzești Romania
51 I8 Grumbach Ger.
73 P7 Grumento Nova Italy
75 L1 Grumo Appula Italy
22 J2 Grums Sweden
51 G9 Grüna Ger.
59 M3 Grünau Niederösterreich Austria
59 I4 Grünau Oberösterreich Austria
94 C5 Grünau Namibia
51 I6 Grünau-Grünheider Wald und Seengebiet park Ger.
59 M4 Grünbach am Schneeberg Austria
49 G9 Grünberg Ger.
59 J4 Grünburg Austria
21 L5 Grundagssätern Sweden
20 □B1 Grundarfjörður Iceland
21 L6 Grundforsen Sweden
59 I4 Grundlsee l. Austria
59 I4 Grundlsee nature res. Austria
96 B1 Grundorner Namibia
20 O5 Grundsuna Sweden
116 C11 Grundy VA U.S.A.
120 I4 Grundy Center IA U.S.A.
50 H5 Grüneberg Ger.
48 I3 Grünendeich Ger.
51 I8 Grünewald Ger.
51 I7 Grünewalde Ger.
51 I6 Grünheide Ger.
128 F1 Gruñidora Mex.
52 H6 Grünkraut Ger.
51 J6 Grunow Ger.
52 H2 Grünsfeld Ger.
52 E2 Grünstadt Ger.
71 K2 Gruppo de Tessa, Parco Naturale nature res. Italy
40 D3 Grury France
54 G2 Gruta Pol.
26 □N3 Grutness Shetland, Scotland U.K.
121 E7 Gruver TX U.S.A.
70 C2 Gruyères Switz.
18 G5 Gruzdžiai Lith.
Gruzinskaya S.S.R. country Asia see Georgia
19 W9 Gryazi Rus. Fed.
19 W7 Gryaznoye Rus. Fed.
14 H4 Gryazovets Rus. Fed.
55 I6 Grybów Pol.
23 M1 Grycken l. Sweden
54 D2 Gryfice Pol.
54 C2 Gryfino Pol.
54 D4 Gryfów Śląski Pol.
54 F3 Grylewo Pol.
20 N2 Gryllefjord Norway
22 B2 Grytenuten hill Norway
23 N1 Gryttjom Sweden
145 □ Grytviken S. Georgia
55 I2 Gryźliny Pol.
54 E3 Grzebienisko Pol.
54 G3 Grzegorzew Pol.
54 E2 Grzmiąca Pol.
54 C2 Grzybno Pol.
54 G3 Grzymiszew Pol.
54 G2 Grzywna Pol.
58 D5 Gschnitz Austria
59 I4 Gschwandt Austria
52 H4 Gschwend Ger.
70 C3 Gstaad Switz.
53 M6 Gstadt am Chiemsee Ger.
70 C3 Gsteig Switz.
179 J8 Gua Jharkhand India
71 L5 Guà r. Italy
126 □R13 Guabito Panama
128 C2 Guacamayita Mex.
130 E3 Guacanayabo, Golfo de b. Cuba
131 J8 Guacara Venez.
136 D3 Guacharía r. Col.
128 A1 Guachimetas de Arriba Mex.
144 D2 Guachipas Arg.
141 B7 Guaçu Brazil
143 G4 Guaçuí Brazil
65 M5 Guadahortuna Spain
65 N5 Guadahortuna r. Spain
64 G6 Guadaira r. Spain
64 H6 Guadairilla r. Spain
64 F3 Guadajira r. Spain
64 H5 Guadajoz Spain
65 J5 Guadajoz r. Spain
128 D5 Guadalajara Mex.
63 N7 Guadalajara Spain
63 P7 Guadalajara prov. Spain
67 C7 Guadalaviar r. Spain
64 I5 Guadalbacar r. Spain
65 L5 Guadalbullón r. Spain
64 H7 Guadalcacín, Embalse de resr Spain
200 □6 Guadalcanal i. Solomon Is
64 H4 Guadalcanal Spain
65 J5 Guadalcázar Spain
64 H3 Guadalefra r. Spain
65 L4 Guadalén r. Spain
65 M4 Guadalén, Embalse del resr Spain
65 N5 Guadalentín r. Spain
65 Q5 Guadalentín r. Spain
146 D4 Guadales Arg.
67 E10 Guadalest, Embalse de resr Spain
64 G7 Guadalete r. Spain
65 K7 Guadalhorce r. Spain
65 J7 Guadalhorce, Embalse de resr Spain
65 L5 Guadalimar r. Spain
65 I5 Guadalmazán r. Spain
65 J4 Guadalmellato, Embalse de resr Spain
65 N4 Guadalmena r. Spain
65 N4 Guadalmena, Embalse del resr Spain
65 J3 Guadalmez Spain
65 J3 Guadalmez r. Spain
66 E5 Guadalope r. Spain
65 G7 Guadalquivir r. Spain
140 E3 Guadalupe Brazil
127 I5 Guadalupe Nuevo León Mex.
129 J6 Guadalupe Puebla Mex.
129 H1 Guadalupe Tamaulipas Mex.
128 E3 Guadalupe Zacatecas Mex.
129 I9 Guadalupe Mex.
126 A3 Guadalupe i. Mex.
125 P9 Guadalupe watercourse Mex.
136 B6 Guadalupe Peru
65 I2 Guadalupe Spain
125 U8 Guadalupe AZ U.S.A.
124 L7 Guadalupe CA U.S.A.
121 G11 Guadalupe r. TX U.S.A.
121 G11 Guadalupe r. TX U.S.A.
64 H2 Guadalupe, Sierra de mts Spain
128 C1 Guadalupe Aguilera Mex.
123 K11 Guadalupe Bravos Mex.
128 A1 Guadalupe de los Reyes Mex.
123 L11 Guadalupe Mountains National Park TX U.S.A.
121 C10 Guadalupe Peak TX U.S.A.
125 Q9 Guadalupe Victoria Baja California Mex.
128 C1 Guadalupe Victoria Durango Mex.
126 F4 Guadalupe y Calvo Mex.
65 I5 Guadalvacarejo r. Spain
63 O8 Guadamajud r. Spain
65 I3 Guadamatilla r. Spain
64 H3 Guadamez r. Spain
63 L9 Guadamur Spain
63 L7 Guadarrama Spain
63 L9 Guadarrama r. Spain
136 D2 Guadarrama Venez.
63 L7 Guadarrama, Puerto de pass Spain
63 L7 Guadarrama, Sierra de mts Spain
63 Q9 Guadazaón r. Spain
131 □2 Guadeloupe terr. West Indies
131 □ Guadeloupe, Parc National de la nat. park Guadeloupe
131 □2 Guadeloupe Passage Caribbean Sea
64 G7 Guadiamar r. Spain
65 E6 Guadiana r. Port./Spain
130 A2 Guadiana, Bahía de b. Cuba
65 M2 Guadiana, Canal del Spain
65 M5 Guadiana Menor r. Spain
65 I8 Guadiaro r. Spain
65 I5 Guadiato r. Spain
63 P8 Guadiela r. Spain
63 J8 Guadiervas r. Spain
65 M6 Guadix Spain
145 B6 Guafo, Isla i. Chile
154 C4 Guagua Luzon Phil.
141 C9 Guaíba Brazil
131 □7 Guaico Trin. and Tob.
143 E2 Guaiçuí Brazil
139 F5 Guaicuras Brazil
136 B4 Guaillabamba r. Ecuador
130 E3 Guáimaro Cuba
137 F3 Guaina Venez.
136 D4 Guainia dept Col.
136 E4 Guainía r. Col./Venez.
137 F3 Guaiquinima, Cerro mt. Venez.
141 B8 Guaíra Brazil
142 C4 Guaíra Brazil
142 A5 Guairaçá Brazil
145 B6 Guaitecas, Islas is Chile
168 H6 Guaizihu Nei Mongol China
140 C2 Guajará Açu Brazil
138 D2 Guajará Mirim Brazil
137 F6 Guajaratuba Brazil
63 L9 Guajaraz r. Spain
65 L7 Guájar-Faraguit Spain
138 D1 Guajarraã Brazil
131 □1 Guajataca r. Puerto Rico
131 □1 Guajataca, Lago de l. Puerto Rico
126 H3 Guaje, Laguna de l. Mex.
126 H4 Guaje, Llano de plain Mex.
136 C2 Guajira dept Col.
136 B5 Gualaceo Ecuador
124 I3 Gualala CA U.S.A.
127 O10 Gualán Guat.
136 B5 Gualaquiza Ecuador
73 J2 Gualdo Cattaneo Italy
71 N9 Gualdo Tadino Italy
147 H3 Gualeguay Arg.
147 H3 Gualeguay r. Arg.
147 H3 Gualeguaychu Arg.
145 D6 Gualicho, Salina salt flat Arg.
145 C6 Gualjaina Arg.
138 C4 Guallatiri vol. Chile
146 B4 Gualleco Chile
146 B6 Gualletue, Lago de l. Chile
128 D2 Gualterio Mex.
71 J6 Gualtieri Italy
153 J4 Guam terr. N. Pacific Ocean
131 I8 Guama Venez.
145 B7 Guamblin, Isla i. Chile
147 F5 Guamini Arg.
130 E3 Guamo Cuba
137 E3 Guampí, Sierra de mts Venez.
126 E5 Guamúchil Mex.
156 D2 Gua Musang Malaysia
169 O7 Gu'an Hebei China
130 B2 Guanabacoa Cuba
138 C2 Guanabara Brazil
143 F5 Guanabara, Baía de b. Brazil
126 □Q12 Guanacaste, Cordillera de mts Costa Rica
126 □Q12 Guanacaste, Parque Nacional nat. park Costa Rica
126 G5 Guanacevi Mex.
147 F5 Guanaco, Cerro hill Arg.
130 A2 Guanahacabibes, Península de pen. Cuba
126 □Q9 Guanaja Hond.
130 B2 Guanajay Cuba
128 F4 Guanajuato Mex.
128 G4 Guanajuato state Mex.
128 F4 Guanajuato, Sierra de mts Mex.
140 E5 Guanambi Brazil
128 F3 Guaname Mex.
136 B7 Guañape, Islas de is Peru
131 □7 Guanapo Trin. and Tob.
146 B2 Guanaqueros Chile
136 D2 Guanare Venez.
136 E2 Guanare Viejo r. Venez.
136 D2 Guanarito Venez.
136 D2 Guanarito r. Venez.
98 □3f Guanarteme, Punta de pt Gran Canaria Canary Is
138 D3 Guanay Bol.
144 C3 Guandacol Arg.
169 L9 Guandaokou Henan China
169 L8 Guandi Shan mt. Shanxi China
143 G3 Guandu r. Brazil
171 I6 Guandu Guangdong China
130 A2 Guane Cuba
170 F3 Guang'an Sichuan China
171 K5 Guangchang Jiangxi China
171 L3 Guangde Anhui China
171 J7 Guangdong prov. China
171 L4 Guangfeng Jiangxi China
171 I8 Guanghai Guangdong China
170 E3 Guanghan Sichuan China
169 N7 Guangling Shanxi China
170 C5 Guangmao Shan mt. Yunnan China
171 L3 Guangming Ding mt. Anhui China
170 E6 Guangnan Yunnan China
171 I7 Guangning Guangdong China
Guangning Liaoning China see Beining
169 P8 Guangrao Shandong China
171 J3 Guangshan Henan China
171 I3 Guangshui Hubei China
Guangxi aut. reg. China see Guangxi Zhuangzu Zizhiqu
170 G7 Guangxi Zhuangzu Zizhiqu aut. reg. China
170 E2 Guangyuan Sichuan China
171 K5 Guangze Fujian China
171 I7 Guangzhou Guangdong China
169 N8 Guangzong Hebei China
143 F3 Guanhães Brazil
143 F3 Guanhães r. Brazil
169 P9 Guan He r. China
169 P9 Guanhe Kou r. mouth China
131 □1 Guánica Puerto Rico
130 A2 Guaniguanico, Cordillera de mts Cuba
137 F2 Guanipa r. Venez.
170 E6 Guanling Guizhou China
170 G3 Guanmian Shan mts China
137 F2 Guanoca Venez.
170 H2 Guanpo Henan China
163 D8 Guanshui Liaoning China
Guansuo Guizhou China see Guanling
146 B1 Guanta Chile
137 E2 Guanta Venez.
130 F3 Guantánamo Cuba
130 F4 Guantánamo Bay Naval Base military base Cuba
169 N8 Guantao Hebei China
170 E2 Guanting Gansu China
168 H9 Guanting Qinghai China
169 N6 Guanting Shuiku resr China
Guanxian Sichuan China see Dujiangyan
171 H6 Guanyang Guangxi China
170 C3 Guanyinqiao Sichuan China
169 P9 Guanyun Jiangsu China
Guapay r. Bol. see Grande
143 E4 Guapé Brazil
136 B4 Guapí Col.
142 C6 Guapiara Brazil
126 □R12 Guápiles Costa Rica
131 □7 Guapo Bay Trin. and Tob.
138 D3 Guaporé r. Bol./Brazil
141 C9 Guaporé Brazil
138 C4 Guaqui Bol.
142 D4 Guará Brazil
140 D5 Guará r. Brazil
66 E3 Guara, Sierra de mts Spain
140 G3 Guarabira Brazil
143 F4 Guaraciaba Brazil
136 B5 Guaranda Ecuador
143 F4 Guarani Brazil
142 A6 Guaraniaçu Brazil
142 C4 Guarantã Brazil
143 G4 Guarapari Brazil
142 B6 Guarapuava Brazil
142 C6 Guaraqueçaba Brazil
142 B4 Guararapes Brazil
143 H2 Guaratinga Brazil
143 E5 Guaratinguetá Brazil
141 C8 Guaratuba Brazil
138 C3 Guarayos Bol.
98 □3e Guarazoca El Hierro Canary Is
73 K4 Guarcino Italy
62 F7 Guarda Port.
62 F7 Guarda admin. dist. Port.
Guardafui, Cape Somalia see Gwardafuy, Gees
65 N5 Guardal r. Spain
67 D11 Guardamar del Segura Spain
142 D2 Guarda Mor Brazil
136 E2 Guardatinajas Venez.
75 K6 Guardavalle Italy
144 E3 Guardia Escolta Arg.
73 M3 Guardiagrele Italy
73 N4 Guardialfiera, Lago di l. Italy
125 Q9 Guardianes de la Patria Mex.
73 Q7 Guardia Perticara Italy
73 Q9 Guardia Piemontese Italy
73 N5 Guardia Sanframondi Italy
65 N7 Guardias Viejas Spain
66 I3 Guardiola de Berguedà Spain
63 K3 Guardo Spain
62 H6 Guardramiro Spain
62 E9 Guardunha, Serra de mts Port.
64 G3 Guareña Spain
63 J6 Guareña r. Spain
66 E3 Guarga r. Spain
139 E1 Guariba r. Brazil
136 E2 Guárico state Venez.
130 F3 Guarico, Punta pt Cuba
65 J7 Guaro Spain
65 L4 Guarrizas r. Spain
136 D3 Guarrojo r. Col.
65 L4 Guarromán Spain
142 D5 Guarujá Brazil
142 D5 Guarulhos Brazil
142 D5 Guarulhos airport Brazil
130 H8 Guasare r. Venez.
126 E5 Guasave Mex.
136 D3 Guasdualito Venez.
72 C8 Guasila Sardegna Italy
137 F3 Guasipati Venez.
71 J6 Guastalla Italy
El Progreso Guat. see Guastatoya
127 O10 Guastatoya Guat.
179 L9 Guasuba r. India
127 N10 Guatemala country Central America
127 N10 Guatemala Guat.
217 M5 Guatemala Basin sea feature Pacific Ocean
Guatemala City Guat. see Guatemala
147 F3 Guatimozin Arg.
98 □3c Guatiza Lanzarote Canary Is
147 F5 Guatrache Arg.
145 D6 Guatrochi Arg.
131 □7 Guatuaro Point Trin. and Tob.
136 D4 Guaviare dept Col.
136 E3 Guaviare r. Col.
142 D4 Guaxupé Brazil
136 D3 Guayabal Col.
130 E3 Guayabal Cuba
131 □1 Guayabal, Lago l. Puerto Rico
146 D2 Guayaguas, Sierra da mts Arg.
131 □7 Guayaguayare Trin. and Tob.
129 J3 Guayalejo r. Mex.
131 □1 Guayama Puerto Rico
131 □1 Guayanilla Puerto Rico
131 □1 Guayanilla, Punta pt Puerto Rico
136 E3 Guayapo, Serranía mts Venez.
136 B5 Guayaquil Ecuador
136 A5 Guayaquil, Golfo de g. Ecuador
138 D2 Guayaramerín Bol.
136 A5 Guayas prov. Ecuador
144 D1 Guayatayoc, Laguna de imp. l. Arg.
126 D4 Guaymas Mex.
131 □1 Guaynabo Puerto Rico
147 H2 Guayquirard Arg.
147 H2 Guayquiraró r. Arg.
127 N10 Guazacapán Guat.
168 D6 Guazhou Gansu China
92 B2 Guba Eth.
182 H6 Gubadag Turkm.
14 L4 Gubakha Rus. Fed.
92 E2 Guban plain Somalia
154 E5 Gubat Luzon Phil.
28 B5 Gubaveeny Rep. of Ireland
176 E6 Gubbi Karnataka India
71 N9 Gubbio Italy
191 I3 Gubden Rus. Fed.
14 L3 Gubdor Rus. Fed.
92 F2 Gubed Binna b. Somalia
169 O6 Gubeikou Beijing China
51 K7 Guben Ger.
77 N8 Gŭbene Bulg.
55 J1 Guber r. Pol.
54 C4 Gubin Pol.
19 S6 Gubino Rus. Fed.
89 I3 Gubio Nigeria
15 G6 Gubkin Rus. Fed.
168 H8 Gucheng Gansu China
168 F6 Gucheng Gansu China
169 N8 Gucheng Hebei China
171 H2 Gucheng Hubei China
169 L9 Gucheng Shanxi China
176 E7 Gudalur Tamil Nadu India
191 F3 Gudamaqris K'edi hills Georgia
66 D7 Gudar Spain
67 D7 Gudar, Sierra de mts Spain
Gudara Tajik. see Ghŭdara
177 H3 Gudari Orissa India
191 B2 Gudaut'a Georgia
21 J6 Gudbrandsdalen val. Norway
185 M7 Guddu Barrage Pak.
22 G5 Gudenå r. Denmark
49 H8 Gudensberg Ger.
191 H2 Gudermes Rus. Fed.
48 I1 Guderup Denmark
23 K6 Gudhjem Bornholm Denmark
89 H4 Gudi Nigeria
176 G4 Gudivada Andhra Prad. India
176 F6 Gudiyattam Tamil Nadu India
75 □ Gudja Malta
22 G6 Gudme Denmark
37 J7 Gudmont-Villiers France
162 F7 Gudong He r. China
48 K3 Gudow Ger.
185 J8 Gudri r. Pak.
188 F3 Güdül Turkey
176 F5 Gudur Andhra Prad. India
176 F5 Gudur Andhra Prad. India
21 I6 Gudvangen Norway
162 H4 Gudzhal r. Rus. Fed.
18 G6 Gudžiūnai Lith.
109 G1 Gué, Rivière du r. Que. Can.
37 N8 Guebwiller France
Guecho Spain see Algorta
88 C4 Guéckédou Guinea
38 F6 Guégon France
111 Q1 Guéguen, Lac l. Que. Can.
65 M6 Güéjar-Sierra Spain
86 C5 Guelb er Rîchât hill Maur.
90 B2 Guélengdeng Chad
87 G1 Guelma Alg.
69 A7 Guelma prov. Alg.
86 C3 Guelmine Morocco
108 D5 Guelph Ont. Can.
87 E5 Guem waterhole Mali
87 G2 Guémar Alg.
37 N7 Guémar France
38 H6 Guémené-Penfao France
38 E5 Guémené-sur-Scorff France
129 H2 Guémez Mex.
37 L5 Guénange France
88 C2 Guendour well Maur.
89 F4 Guéné Benin
63 N2 Güeñes Spain
38 H6 Guenrouet France
88 B3 Guènt Paté Senegal
38 G6 Guer France
90 C2 Guéra pref. Chad
90 C2 Guéra, Massif du mts Chad
38 G7 Guérande France
87 G2 Guerara Alg.
109 H1 Guérard, Lac l. Que. Can.
86 E2 Guercif Morocco
84 C5 Guéré watercourse Chad
84 D6 Guéréda Chad
84 D4 Guerende Libya
42 H3 Guéret France
40 C2 Guérigny France
89 F4 Guérin-Kouka Togo
38 E5 Guerlédan, Lac de l. France
124 J3 Guerneville CA U.S.A.
Guernica Spain see Gernika-Lumo
38 F3 Guernsey terr. Channel Is
122 L5 Guernsey WY U.S.A.
88 C2 Guérou Maur.
64 E6 Guerreiros do Rio Port.
147 I4 Guerrero Arg.
121 E11 Guerrero Coahuila Mex.
127 J4 Guerrero Tamaulipas Mex.
128 G8 Guerrero state Mex.
64 F3 Guerrero r. Spain
129 H8 Guerrero, Parque Natural de nature res. Mex.
126 B4 Guerrero Negro Mex.
43 E10 Guerreys, Pic de mt. France
66 H3 Guerri de la Sal Spain
109 H1 Guers, Lac l. Que. Can.
86 E3 Guerzim Alg.
66 C2 Güesa Spain
86 D4 Guețâțîra well Mali
43 A9 Guéthary France
40 E3 Gueugnon France
88 D5 Guéyo Côte d'Ivoire
191 F5 Gugark' Armenia
92 C3 Gugē mt. Eth.
200 □3a Gugegwe i. Kwajalein Marshall Is
185 O6 Gugera Pak.
184 E4 Gūgerd, Kūh-e mts Iran
30 □ Gugh i. England U.K.
147 F2 Guglieri Arg.
52 F3 Güglingen Ger.
73 N4 Guglionesi Italy
92 C2 Gugu mts Eth.
153 K3 Guguan i. N. Mariana Is
156 F8 Guhakolak, Tanjung pt Indon.
171 K3 Guhe Anhui China
184 H8 Gūh Kūh mt. Iran
50 G4 Gühlen-Glienicke Ger.
139 F3 Guia Brazil
62 C9 Guia Port.
98 □3a Guía de Isora Tenerife Canary Is
62 G4 Guiana mt. Spain
214 F5 Guiana Basin sea feature N. Atlantic Ocean
135 F2 Guiana Highlands reg. Guyana/Venez.
136 E3 Guiana Highlands mts S. America
88 D5 Guibéroua Côte d'Ivoire
36 B6 Guichainville France
38 H6 Guichen France
204 G7 Guichen Bay S.A. Austr.
Guichi Anhui China see Chizhou
129 L8 Guichicovi Mex.
147 I3 Guichón Uru.
38 D4 Guiclan France
89 G3 Guidan-Roumji Niger
90 C2 Guidari Chad
168 G9 Guide Qinghai China
38 E6 Guidel France
29 N3 Guide Post Northumberland, England U.K.
89 I4 Guider Cameroon
89 H3 Guidiguir Niger
89 I4 Guidiguis Cameroon
88 B3 Guidimaka admin. reg. Maur.
170 F5 Guiding Guizhou China
71 J5 Guidizzolo Italy
171 I6 Guidong Hunan China
73 J4 Guidonia-Montecelio Italy
143 F4 Guidoval Brazil
129 L9 Guienagati Mex.
88 B2 Guier, Lac de l. Senegal
40 H5 Guiers r. France
90 A5 Guietsou Gabon
170 G7 Guigang Guangxi China
71 J7 Guiglia Italy
88 D5 Guiglo Côte d'Ivoire
38 H6 Guignen France
36 E6 Guignes France
36 G5 Guignicourt France
131 J8 Güigüe Venez.
95 G5 Guija Moz.
170 H7 Gui Jiang r. China
171 M4 Guiji Shan mts China
62 H8 Guijo de Coria Spain
62 H8 Guijo de Galisteo Spain
62 H8 Guijo de Granadilla Spain
62 I7 Guijuelo Spain
41 J7 Guil r. France
31 K5 Guildford Surrey, England U.K.
117 N4 Guildhall VT U.S.A.
26 J10 Guildtown Perth and Kinross, Scotland U.K.
38 B5 Guilers France
119 J2 Guilford CT U.S.A.
117 □P3 Guilford ME U.S.A.
41 F7 Guilherand France
Guilherme Capelo Angola see Cacongo
62 D5 Guilhofrei Port.
170 H6 Guilin Guangxi China
105 K4 Guillaume-Delisle, Lac l. Que. Can.
41 J8 Guillaumes France
64 G5 Guillena Spain
41 J7 Guillestre France
38 G5 Guilliers France
40 E1 Guillon France
43 C6 Guillos France
38 C6 Guilvinec France
98 □3a Güímar Tenerife Canary Is
98 □3a Güimar, Punta de pt Tenerife Canary Is
140 D2 Guimarães Brazil
62 D6 Guimarães Port.
154 D6 Guimaras i. Phil.
154 D6 Guimaras Strait Phil.
169 O9 Guimeng Ding mt. Shandong China
89 F4 Guinagourou Benin
168 G9 Guinan Qinghai China
130 D2 Guinchos Cay i. Cuba
154 E7 Guindulman Bohol Phil.
88 C4 Guinea country Africa
89 G6 Guinea, Gulf of Africa
214 I5 Guinea Basin sea feature N. Atlantic Ocean
88 B4 Guinea-Bissau country Africa
Guinea-Conakry country Africa see Guinea
Guinea Ecuatorial country Africa see Equatorial Guinea
Guiné-Bissau country Africa see Guinea-Bissau
Guinée country Africa see Guinea
88 C4 Guinée-Forestière admin. reg. Guinea
88 B4 Guinée-Maritime admin. reg. Guinea
130 B2 Güines Cuba
36 C2 Guînes France
109 I2 Guines, Lac l. Nfld and Lab. Can.
38 E4 Guingamp France
88 B3 Guinguinéo Senegal
126 □Q13 Guiones, Punta pt Costa Rica
38 C5 Guipavas France
170 H7 Guiping Guangxi China
38 H6 Guipry France
66 A1 Guipúzcoa prov. Spain
88 E2 Guîr well Mali
130 B2 Güira de Melena Cuba
141 B6 Guiratinga Brazil
137 F2 Güiria Venez.
137 I3 Guisanbourg Fr. Guiana
63 J8 Guisando Spain
41 J7 Guisane r. France
29 O4 Guisborough Redcar and Cleveland, England U.K.
36 F4 Guiscard France
38 D5 Guiscriff France
36 G4 Guise France
29 N6 Guiseley West Yorkshire, England U.K.
89 F2 Guissefa well Mali
38 C4 Guissény France
66 H4 Guissona Spain
31 N2 Guist Norfolk, England U.K.
62 E2 Guitiriz Spain
42 D5 Guîtres France
88 D5 Guitri Côte d'Ivoire
154 E6 Guiuan Samar Phil.
20 S2 Guivi hill Fin.
Guixi Chongqing China see Dianjiang
170 F5 Guiyang Guizhou China
171 I5 Guiyang Hunan China
171 I6 Guiyang Hunan China
170 F5 Guizhou prov. China
171 H7 Guizi Guangdong China
43 B6 Gujan-Mestras France
178 D8 Gujarat state India
191 E4 Gujaret'i Georgia
185 O5 Gujar Khan Pak.
89 H4 Gujba Nigeria
Gujerat state India see Gujarat
169 M8 Gujiao Shanxi China
185 P5 Gujranwala Pak.
185 P5 Gujrat Pak.
Gukasyan Armenia see Ashots'k'
15 G6 Gukovo Rus. Fed.
184 A3 Gūk Tappeh Iran
178 F3 Gulabgarh Jammu and Kashmir
191 H6 Gülablı Azer.
168 H8 Gulang Gansu China
205 L4 Gulargambone N.S.W. Austr.
79 H4 Gülbahçe Turkey
183 M7 Gulbahor Uzbek.
176 E4 Gulbarga Karnataka India
156 □ Gul Basin dock Sing.
18 J4 Gulbene Latvia
Gul'cha Kyrg. see Gülchö
183 O7 Gülchö Kyrg.
190 D2 Gülcihan Turkey
191 C4 Gül dağı mt. Turkey
50 E1 Guldborg Denmark
50 E1 Guldborg Sund str. Denmark
190 B1 Güldere Turkey
191 A6 Güleç Turkey
188 G5 Gülek Turkey
180 C2 Gülek Boğazı pass Turkey
Gulf of Chihli China see Bo Hai
121 K10 Gulfport MS U.S.A.
115 D10 Gulf Shores AL U.S.A.
205 L5 Gulgong N.S.W. Austr.
175 □1 Gulhi i. S. Male Maldives
162 C2 Gulian Heilong. China
170 E5 Gulin Sichuan China
185 L6 Gulistan Pak.
Gulistan Uzbek. see Guliston
183 M7 Guliston Uzbek.
154 □ Gulitel hill Palau
50 E4 Gülitz Ger.
169 R2 Guliya Shan mt. Nei Mongol China
185 M6 Gul Kach Pak.
15 H7 Gul'kevichi Rus. Fed.
108 B3 Gull r. Ont. Can.
28 D4 Gulladuff Northern Ireland U.K.
26 K10 Gullane East Lothian, Scotland U.K.
21 I6 Gullbrå Norway
110 I4 Gull Island MI U.S.A.
21 Q7 Gullkrona fjärd b. Fin.
107 I5 Gull Lake Sask. Can.
22 H3 Gullmarn inlet Sweden
107 M5 Gullrock Lake Ont. Can.
23 K3 Gullspång Sweden
191 D6 Güllü Erzurum Turkey
79 K4 Güllü Uşak Turkey
79 I5 Güllübahçe Turkey
191 H4 Güllük Azer.
79 I5 Güllük Turkey
79 I5 Güllük Körfezi b. Turkey
188 F5 Gülnar Turkey
45 I7 Gulpen Neth.
50 F5 Gülper See l. Ger.
79 H3 Gülpınar Turkey
185 I4 Gulran Afgh.
191 C3 Gulrip'shi Georgia
188 G4 Gülşehir Turkey
183 P4 Gul'shat Kazakh.
50 H3 Gültz Ger.
92 B4 Gulu Uganda
77 N8 Gŭlŭbovo Bulg.
207 M9 Guluguba Qld Austr.
89 I4 Gulumba Gana Nigeria

Column 1

106 F1 Guluwuru Island N.T. Austr.
26 F9 Gulvain hill Scotland U.K.
93 C6 Gulwe Tanz.
77 M7 Gulyantsi Bulg.
14 K1 Gulyayevskiye Koshki, Ostrova is Rus. Fed.
50 F3 Gülzow Mecklenburg-Vorpommern Ger.
48 J4 Gülzow Schleswig-Holstein Ger.
85 N6 Gumal r. Pak.
94 D3 Gumare Botswana
85 M6 Gumbaz Pak.
Gusev see Gumbinnen Rus. Fed. see Gusev
92 A3 Gumdi mt. Sudan
84 F2 Gumdag Turkm.
89 H3 Gumel Nigeria
63 M5 Gumiel de Hizán Spain
63 M5 Gumiel de Mercado Spain
91 C2 Gumist'is Nakrdzali nature res. Georgia
79 J8 Gumia Jharkhand India
Gumma Japan see Gunma
Gumma pref. Japan see Gunma
49 E8 Gummersbach Ger.
50 F5 Gumpang r. Indon.
49 J9 Gumpelstadt Ger.
89 H5 Gumsi Nigeria
50 F5 Gumtow Ger.
88 I3 Gümüşhane Turkey
91 A5 Gümüşhane prov. Turkey
79 I4 Gümüşsuyu Turkey
78 F7 Guna Madh. Prad. India
57 I6 Gunaroš Vojvodina, Srbija Serb. and Mont.
92 C2 Guna Terara mt. Eth.
105 J6 Gunbar N.S.W. Austr.
Gund r. Tajik. see Gunt
105 J4 Gundabooka National Park N.S.W. Austr.
103 L6 Gundagai N.S.W. Austr.
78 H9 Gundardehi Chhattisgarh India
52 D5 Gundelfingen Ger.
53 I4 Gundelfingen an der Donau Ger.
52 S3 Gundelsheim Baden-Württemberg Ger.
53 J2 Gundelsheim Bayern Ger.
76 E6 Gunderi Karnataka India
37 O6 Gundershoffen France
90 C4 Gundji Dem. Rep. Congo
76 G5 Gundlakamma r. India
76 E7 Gundlupet Karnataka India
88 F5 Gündoğmuş Turkey
Gundorovka Rus. Fed. see Donetsk
79 L3 Gündüzler Turkey
91 D6 Gündüzü Turkey
79 L5 Güneşli Turkey
79 K4 Güney Kütahya Turkey
79 J3 Güney Turkey
79 J2 Güneydoğu Toroslar plat. Turkey
79 L4 Güneyköy Turkey
79 H2 Güneyli Turkey
91 B5 Güneysu Turkey
79 N2 Güneyyurt Turkey
58 D1 Gunglilap Myanmar
90 B4 Gungu Dem. Rep. Congo
91 B8 Gungue Angola
63 M3 Gunib Rus. Fed.
07 L4 Gunisao r. Man. Can.
07 L4 Gunisao Lake Man. Can.
88 A3 Gunja Croatia
68 D3 Gunjur Gambia
79 K3 Günlüce Turkey
73 I2 Gunma Japan
67 I2 Gunma pref. Japan
20 N4 Gunnarn Sweden
20 P3 Gunnarsbyn Sweden
07 J4 Gunnaur Qld Austr.
05 P3 Gunnbjørn Fjeld nunatak Greenland
55 M4 Gunnedah N.S.W. Austr.
99 □1b Gunners Quoin Mauritius
29 P6 Gunness North Lincolnshire, England U.K.
25 L6 Gunning N.S.W. Austr.
30 D6 Gunnislake Cornwall, England U.K.
23 K7 Gunnison CO U.S.A.
25 U2 Gunnison UT U.S.A.
23 J7 Gunnison r. CO U.S.A.
25 U2 Gunnison Reservoir UT U.S.A.
06 C2 Gunn Point N.T. Austr.
Gunung Ayer Sarawak Malaysia see Gunung Ayer
31 □3 Gun Point Grenada
06 G5 Gunpowder Creek r. Qld Austr.
18 C6 Gunpowder Falls r. MD U.S.A.
76 E3 Gun Sangari Mahar. India
89 J1 Gunskirchen Austria
58 C2 Guntakal Andhra Prad. India
78 E5 Guntersberge Ger.
18 K7 Güntersberge Ger.
21 E9 Guntersblum Ger.
52 H2 Güntersdorf Austria
52 H2 Güntersleben Ger.
15 J9 Guntersville AL U.S.A.
62 E3 Guntin de Pallares Spain
53 K7 Guntramsdorf Austria
76 D4 Guntur Andhra Prad. India
06 D4 Gununa Qld Austr.
55 E7 Gunungapi i. Maluku Indon.
57 I3 Gunung Ayer Sarawak Malaysia
57 L6 Gunungbatubesar Kalimantan Indon.
57 N4 Gunung Gading National Park Malaysia
56 C2 Gunung Gede Pangrango National Park Indon.
56 B3 Gunung Halimun National Park Indon.
56 B3 Gunung Leuser National Park Indon.
53 I7 Gunung Lorentz National Park Papua Indon.
57 K2 Gunung Mulu National Park Malaysia
57 H4 Gunung Niyut Reserve nature res. Indon.
57 I5 Gunung Palung National Park Indon.
57 L7 Gunung Rinjani National Park Lombok Indon.
56 B4 Gunungsitoli Sumatera Indon.
56 F7 Gunungsugih Sumatera Indon.
56 C6 Gunungtua Sumatera Indon.
77 N5 Gunupur Orissa India
78 E6 Gunzenhausen Ger.
68 J3 Guochengyi Gansu China
Guo He r. China see Guo He r. China
68 I3 Guojia Gansu China
69 O6 Guojiaba Hubei China
71 K2 Guoyang Anhui China
Guozhen Shaanxi China see Baoji
78 D1 Gupis Jammu and Kashmir
62 J3 Gur r. Rus. Fed.
77 O5 Guradu r. S. Male Maldives see Guraidhu
16 H7 Gura Galbenei Moldova
77 O5 Gurahonț Romania
77 L4 Gura Humorului Romania
75 □1 Guraidhu i. S. Male Maldives
78 C1 Gurais Jammu and Kashmir
78 Q6 Gura Portiței sea chan. Romania
57 J Gurara r. Nigeria
55 E7 Gurasada Romania
57 N6 Gura Suții Romania
77 O5 Gura Teghii Romania

Column 2

90 E4 Gurba r. Dem. Rep. Congo
169 M5 Gurban Obo Nei Mongol China
172 H4 Gurbantünggüt Shamo des. China
126 F2 Gürbulak Turkey
126 F2 Gürbüzler Turkey
183 L8 G'uzor Uzbek.
184 I9 Gurdim Iran
121 I9 Gurdon AR U.S.A.
Gurdzhaani Georgia see Gurjaani
22 F2 Gurvar Norway
162 J5 Gvasyugi Rus. Fed.
17 T3 Gvazda Rus. Fed.
158 B6 Gwa Myanmar
205 L4 Gwabegar N.S.W. Austr.
89 G4 Gwada Nigeria
89 G3 Gwadabawa Nigeria
185 J9 Gwadar Pak.
185 J9 Gwadar Pak.
106 D4 Gwaii Haanas National Park Reserve B.C. Can.
178 G4 Gwai River Zimbabwe
178 E7 Gwalior Uttaranchal India
178 E7 Gwalior Madh. Prad. India
178 G6 Gwalior Madh. Prad. India
195 F4 Gwanda Zimbabwe
90 E3 Gwane Dem. Rep. Congo
92 F7 Gwardafuy, Gees c. Somalia
89 G4 Gwarzo Nigeria
185 K7 Gwash Pak.
185 I9 Gwatar Bay Pak.
30 E4 Gwaun-Cae-Gurwen Neath Port Talbot, Wales U.K.
90 F3 Gwawele Dem. Rep. Congo
95 E3 Gwayi Zimbabwe
95 E3 Gwayi r. Zimbabwe
54 E2 Gwda r. Pol.
54 E2 Gwda Wielka Pol.
158 B2 Gweedaukon Myanmar
27 F3 Gweebarra Bay Rep. of Ireland
27 D2 Gweedore Rep. of Ireland
195 F3 Gwelo Zimbabwe see Gweru
95 F3 Gweru Zimbabwe
94 E4 Gweta Botswana
106 F4 Gwillim Lake Provincial Park B.C. Can.
110 G3 Gwinn MI U.S.A.
120 G2 Gwinner ND U.S.A.
30 B6 Gwithian Cornwall, England U.K.
89 I4 Gwoza Nigeria
205 L3 Gwydir r. N.S.W. Austr.
30 D1 Gwynedd admin. div. Wales U.K.
30 E1 Gwytherin Conwy, Wales U.K.
40 H2 Gy France
173 K11 Gyablung Xizang China
173 K12 Gyaca Xizang China
173 F10 Gyaco Xizang China
173 L11 Gyai Qu r. Xizang China
57 I4 Gyaigé Qinghai China
79 I6 Gyali i. Greece
173 E10 Gyamug Xizang China
Gyandzha Azer. see Gäncä
173 H9 Gyangnyi Caka salt l. China
173 G11 Gyangrang Xizang China
Gyangzê Xizang China see Gyangzê
173 I12 Gyangzê Xizang China
173 E11 Gya'nyima Xizang China
178 G8 Gyaspur Madh. Prad. India
168 E9 Gyaring Qinghai China
173 I11 Gyaring Co l. China
173 E9 Gyaring Hu l. Qinghai China
179 O5 Gyarishing Arun. Prad. India
56 G4 Gyaros i. Greece
78 F5 Gyaros i. Greece
184 F2 Gyaur watercourse Turkm.
192 I2 Gydanskiy Poluostrov pen. Rus. Fed.
56 G5 Gydopas pass S. Africa
56 G5 Gyékényes Hungary
173 K12 Gyêgu Xizang China
57 H4 Gyermely Hungary
173 G11 Gyêsar Co l. China
36 H7 Gyé-sur-Seine France
48 H4 Gyhum Ger.
170 A4 Gyigang Xizang China
173 H10 Gyimda Xizang China
173 E9 Gyipug Xizang China
173 G12 Gyirong Xizang China
173 G12 Gyirong Xizang China
170 A3 Gyitang Xizang China
Gyixong Qinghai China see Gonggar
173 L10 Gyiza Qinghai China
22 H6 Gylденleveshøj hill Denmark
27 F9 Gyleen Rep. of Ireland
20 O3 Gylen Sweden
207 N9 Gympie Qld Austr.
158 B5 Gyobingauk Myanmar
167 J3 Gyoda Japan
57 J5 Gyomaendrőd Hungary
57 I4 Gyömöre Hungary
57 I4 Gyömrő Hungary
56 E4 Gyöngyös Hungary
57 I4 Gyöngyös r. Romania
57 I4 Gyöngyöshalász Hungary
57 I4 Gyöngyöspata Hungary
57 H4 GyömHungary
57 G4 Györ Hungary
56 G4 Győr-Moson-Sopron county Hungary
57 G4 Györgytag Hungary
57 L4 Görtelek Hungary
57 G4 Györújbarát Hungary
57 G4 Györújfalu Hungary
106 H2 Gypsum Point N.W.T. Can.
107 L5 Gyrfalcon Islands Que. Can.
109 C1 Gyrfalcon Islands Que. Can.
78 D6 Gytheio Greece
44 I2 Gytsjerk Neth.
57 K5 Gyula Hungary
57 L5 Gyulafehérvár Romania see Alba Iulia
57 L3 Gyulaháza Hungary
57 K5 Gyulavári Hungary
191 J4 Gyumri Armenia
191 E5 Gyunyuz Turkm.
173 D10 Gyurkovo Bulg.
77 O9 Gyuygör Bair hill Turkey
184 C2 Gyzylarbat Turkm.
19 R6 Gzhatsk Rus. Fed.
75 □ Gżira Malta
55 I3 Gzy Pol.

Column 3 (H)

191 C6 Güzelkent Turkey
170 C2 Güzeloluk Turkey
171 K2 Guzhang Hunan China
127 L7 Güzeloluk Turkey
126 F2 Guzmán Mex.
126 F2 Guzmán, Lago de l. Mex.
183 L8 G'uzor Uzbek.
18 E7 Gvardeysk Rus. Fed.
Gvardeyskoye Rus. Fed. see Elin-Yurt
22 F7 Gvarv Norway
162 J5 Gvasyugi Rus. Fed.
17 T3 Gvazda Rus. Fed.
53 K6 Gvozd Bos.-Herz.
172 H2 Gvozd Xijiang China see La Habana
176 G3 Habana Cuba see La Habana
187 J4 Habarón well Saudi Arabia
53 N1 Habartov Czech Rep.
187 K7 Habarüt Oman
43 C8 Habas France
92 C4 Habaswein Kenya
106 G3 Habay Alta Can.
45 I9 Habay-la-Neuve Belgium
186 H8 Habbān Yemen
185 M3 Habbānīyah, Hawr al l. Iraq
185 L9 Hab Chauki Pak.
186 E6 Habbah ash Shaykh, Harrat lava field Saudi Arabia
58 D5 Habicht mt. Austria
49 H8 Habichtswald park Ger.
179 M7 Habiganj Bangl.
165 N5 Habirao Nei Mongol China
190 D7 Habis, Wādī al r. Jordan
23 K4 Habo Sweden
164 S2 Haboro Japan
53 J2 Habovka Slovakia
179 L8 Habra r. India
56 E2 Habry Czech Rep.
37 N8 Habsheim France
187 J7 Habshīyah, Jabal mts Yemen
136 C5 Hacha Col.
146 B6 Hachado, Paso de pass Arg./Chile
49 H3 Hachel-Siek Ger.
20 L5 Häggenås Sweden
122 H3 Haggin, Mount MT U.S.A.
20 L5 Häggsjövik Sweden
20 M5 Hagi Japan
167 H3 Hachibuse-yama mt. Japan
166 E5 Hachikai r. Japan
166 E4 Hachiman r. Japan
167 L5 Hachiman-misaki c. Japan
167 L4 Hachimantai Japan
166 G3 Hachimori-yama mt. Japan
164 S6 Hachinohe Japan
164 Q6 Hachiryū Japan
191 H6 Hacıalılı Azer.
76 K3 Hacıbekir Turkey
79 K3 Hacıbektaş Turkey
126 H11 Hacienda de la Mesa Mex.
191 E6 Hacıhalit Turkey
79 L5 Hacılar Turkey
63 N5 Hacinas Spain
190 E2 Hacıpaşa Turkey
191 J6 Hacıqabul Gölü l. Azer.
191 J6 Hacıqährämanlı Azer.
79 I2 Hacıvelioba Turkey
191 K5 Hacı Zeynalabdin Azer.
204 G4 Hack, Mount S.A. Austr.
116 C5 Hackberry AZ U.S.A.
52 G2 Hackenheim Ger.
52 D2 Hackensack NJ U.S.A.
116 E10 Hacker Valley WV U.S.A.
27 I7 Hacketstown Rep. of Ireland
118 F3 Hackettstown NJ U.S.A.
31 K3 Hackleton Northamptonshire, England U.K.
31 O5 Hacklinge Kent, England U.K.
29 P5 Hackness North Yorkshire, England U.K.
118 D6 Hack Point MD U.S.A.
91 B7 Haco Angola
95 C4 Hacufera Moz.
187 I4 Hadabat al Budū plain Saudi Arabia
172 F6 Hadagalli Karnataka India
176 D5 Hadagalli Karnataka India
49 F10 Hadamar Ger.
185 L6 Hada Mountains Afgh.
191 H8 Hadan, Harrat lava field Saudi Arabia
167 J5 Hadano Japan
166 E9 Hadapu Gansu China
186 E6 Hadārah i. Saudi Arabia
169 P2 Hadat Nei Mongol China
169 S2 Hadayang Nei Mongol China
187 M3 Hadd, Ra's al pt Oman
84 C6 Haddad, Ouadi watercourse Chad
31 K4 Haddenham Buckinghamshire, England U.K.
26 K11 Haddington East Lothian, Scotland U.K.
31 P2 Haddiscoe Norfolk, England U.K.
118 E5 Haddonfield NJ U.S.A.
99 □3a Haddon Point Inner Islands Seychelles
89 H3 Hadejia Nigeria
89 I3 Hadejia watercourse Nigeria
22 G1 Hadeland reg. Norway
190 D7 Hadera Israel
22 E5 Haderslev Denmark
176 E3 Hadgaon Mahar. India
186 E4 Hādhah Saudi Arabia
181 I5 Hadīb Bani Zaynān pen. Saudi Arabia
175 D11 Hadhdhunmathi Atoll Maldives
Hadhramaut reg. Yemen see Hadramawt
190 K8 Hādī, Jabal al mts Jordan
187 K9 Hadībū Suqutrā Yemen
173 H8 Hadilik Xinjiang China
81 D9 Hadım Turkey
84 D5 Hadjer Momou mt. Chad
31 N3 Hadleigh Suffolk, England U.K.
30 H2 Hadley Telford and Wrekin, England U.K.
105 H2 Hadley Bay Nunavut Can.
119 K2 Hadlyme CT U.S.A.
106 B2 Hadlock, Junction Y.T. Can.
37 I7 Hadol France
170 E8 Ha Đông Vietnam
188 H8 Hadraj, Wādī watercourse Saudi Arabia
187 I7 Hadramawt governorate Yemen
187 H8 Hadramawt reg. Yemen
187 I7 Hadramawt, Wādī watercourse Yemen
59 N2 Hadres Austria
29 M3 Hadrian's Wall tourist site U.K.
191 I6 Hadrut Azer.
20 M2 Hadseløya i. Norway
218 H3 Haabneeme Estonia
22 G5 Hadsten Denmark
22 G5 Hadsund Denmark
17 N3 Hadyach Ukr.
59 N3 Haedo, Cuchilla de hills Uru.
22 □ Haeju N. Korea
45 I6 Haelen Neth.
20 □ Haakon VII Land reg. Svalbard
44 K4 Haaksbergen Neth.
45 F7 Haaltert Belgium
186 G4 Ha'ena HI U.S.A.
163 E11 Haenam S. Korea
85 H4 Haafeng S. Korea
169 P2 Hadet Nei Mongol China
187 M3 'Afar al 'Atk well Saudi Arabia
31 K3 Haapai Group is Tonga
187 M3 Ra's at Pt Oman
50 J3 Haffküste park Ger.
19 R6 Haaga r. Ger.
190 D7 Hafira, Wādī al salt pan Jordan
186 D2 Hafira, Qā' al salt pan Jordan

Column 4

44 G4 Haarlem Neth.
96 H1 Haarlem S. Africa
49 E7 Haarstrang ridge Ger.
203 D10 Haast South l. N.Z.
203 D10 Haast r. South l. N.Z.
206 C7 Haast Bluff N.T. Austr.
203 C11 Haast Range mts South l. N.Z.
44 G5 Haastrecht Neth.
206 C7 Haasts Bluff Aboriginal Land res. N.T. Austr.
92 D4 Haaway Somalia
185 L9 Hab r. Pak.
53 K6 Habah Pak.
172 H2 Habahe Xinjiang China
178 Habana Cuba see La Habana
176 G3 Habanaki-zaki pt Japan
187 M8 Haga-Naga S. Africa
59 O8 Hagagi Croatia
111 N3 Hagar Ont. Can.
176 E5 Hagari r. India
85 H5 Hagar Nish Plateau Eritrea
200 □1 Hagåtña Guam
186 F7 Hagbyån r. Sweden
51 G6 Hageland reg. Belgium
51 G6 Hagelberg hill Ger.
23 H4 Hagfors Sweden
23 J1 Hagen i. Sweden
20 M5 Häggenås Sweden
122 H3 Haggin, Mount MT U.S.A.
20 L5 Häggsjövik Sweden
20 M5 Hagi Japan
49 D8 Hagen Ger.
49 E6 Hagen am Teutoburger Wald Ger.
52 E3 Hagenbach Ger.
49 H6 Hagenburg Ger.
58 H5 Hagengebirge mts Austria
48 G4 Hagen im Bremischen Ger.
50 D4 Hagenow Ger.
106 E4 Hagensborg B.C. Can.
51 K8 Hagenwerder Ger.
92 C2 Hägere Hiywet Eth.
92 C3 Hägere Selam Eth.
116 C11 Hagerhill KY U.S.A.
116 H9 Hagerstown MD U.S.A.
43 C8 Hagetmau France
23 J1 Hagfors Sweden
23 J1 Hagfors Sweden
20 M5 Häggenås Sweden
189 L6 Häggerås Sweden
20 P3 Hakkas Sweden
122 W1 Hag's Head Rep. of Ireland
37 I6 Hagondange France
191 E6 Hague NY U.S.A.
37 O□a Haguenau France
165 □2 Hahajima-rettō is Ogasawara-shotō Japan
49 J7 Hahnbach Ger.
53 L2 Hahnenklee-Bockswiese Ger.
52 F2 Hahnheim Ger.
156 C1 Hahnstätten Ger.
93 C5 Hai, Ko i. Thai.
156 C1 Hai, Ko i. Thai.
170 H8 Hai'an Guangdong China
171 M2 Hai'an Jiangsu China
94 C6 Haib watercourse Namibia
52 C2 Haibach Bayern Ger.
53 N3 Haibach Bayern Ger.
209 Nara Japan
167 H6 Haibara Shizuoka Japan
169 R6 Haicheng Liaoning China
170 C3 Haicheng Ningxia China see Haiyuan
178 M7 Haidargarh Uttar Prad. India
53 M2 Haidenaab r. Ger.
59 J3 Haidershofen Austria
168 C9 Haiding Hu salt l. Qinghai China
58 H4 Haidmühle Ger.
171 J7 Haifa Israel see Hefa
172 F6 Haifeng Guangdong China
171 J7 Haifeng Guangdong China
171 J7 Haifeng Guangdong China see Haifeng
Haifeng Ningxia China see Haiyuan
178 H6 Haiganj Assam India
53 M2 Haigerloch Ger.
91 G7 Haihe He r. China
167 G8 Haiha Gansu China
168 G7 Haihu Qinghai China see Leizhou
165 L6 Haiji Japan
170 H9 Haikakou Hainan China
186 B2 Hā'īl Saudi Arabia
186 B2 Hā'īl prov. Saudi Arabia
186 B2 Hā'īl, Wādī watercourse Saudi Arabia
179 N7 Hailakandi Assam India
Hailar Nei Mongol China see Hulun Buir
169 O2 Hailar He r. China
122 G5 Hailey ID U.S.A.
108 E3 Haileybury Ont. Can.
171 H8 Hailing Dao i. Guangdong China
Hailong Jilin China see Meihekou
169 Q3 Hailong Heilong. China
31 M6 Hailsham East Sussex, England U.K.
162 E5 Hailun Heilong. China
20 R4 Hailuoto i. Fin.
171 M3 Haimen Jiangsu China
53 L5 Haimhausen Ger.
164 □A22 Haimi Nansei-shotō Japan
53 N5 Haiming Ger.
84 D5 Hai'nan I. Chad
49 K10 Haina (Kloster) Ger.
170 H9 Hainan i. China
161 I8 Hainan prov. China
158 C4 Hai-nang Myanmar
45 F8 Hainaut prov. Belgium
59 O3 Hainburg an der Donau Austria
88 B2 Haindi Liberia
104 E4 Haines AK U.S.A.
115 G13 Haines City FL U.S.A.
106 B2 Haines Junction Y.T. Can.
118 F5 Hainesport NJ U.S.A.
106 B2 Haines Road Can./U.S.A.
124 J4 Half Moon Bay CA U.S.A.
204 □3 Halfmoon Bay Stewart I. N.Z.

Column 5

186 H3 Hafirat Nasah Saudi Arabia
187 L4 Hafit Oman
187 L3 Hafit, Jabal mt. U.A.E.
185 O5 Hafizabad Pak.
179 N7 Haflong Assam India
20 □C1 Hafnarfjörður Iceland
59 L3 Hafnerbach Austria
185 L7 Haft Gel Iran
184 D4 Haftoni Azer.
184 E8 Haftvän Iran
20 □B1 Hafursfjörður b. Iceland
85 G6 Hag Abdullah Sudan
167 I6 Hagachi-zaki pt Japan
187 M8 Haga-Naga S. Africa
59 O8 Hagagi Croatia
111 N3 Hagar Ont. Can.
176 E5 Hagari r. India
85 H5 Hagar Nish Plateau Eritrea
200 □1 Hagåtña Guam
23 K4 Häågby Sweden
186 F7 Hagbyån r. Sweden
51 G6 Hageland reg. Belgium
51 G6 Hagelberg hill Ger.
23 H4 Hagfors Sweden
23 J1 Hagen i. Sweden
20 M5 Häggenås Sweden
122 H3 Haggin, Mount MT U.S.A.
20 L5 Häggsjövik Sweden
20 M5 Hagi Japan
185 M9 Hala Pak.
190 D8 Halā', Jabal al mt. Jordan
190 F2 Halab governorate Syria
186 G4 Halabān Saudi Arabia
189 L6 Halabja Iraq
127 N7 Halachó Mex.
203 □4 Halagigie Point Niue
162 D6 Halahai Jilin China
16 G5 Halahora de Sus Moldova
85 H4 Halaib Sudan
188 H8 Halaib Triangle terr. Egypt/Sudan
158 □7 Ha Lam Vietnam
187 M7 Halānīyah, Juzur al is Oman
187 L7 Halānīyah, Khalīj al b. Oman
59 J3 Haslach Austria
188 H3 Halat 'Ammār Saudi Arabia
77 I3 Hălăucești Romania
23 K3 Halavеden hills Sweden
124 □E12 Hālawa HI U.S.A.
190 E4 Halba Lebanon
168 I2 Halban Mongolia
53 J6 Halbe Ger.
59 M6 Halberstadt Austria
30 F6 Halberton Devon, England U.K.
53 J6 Halblech Ger.
208 H3 Half Point W.A. Austr.
118 B2 Halbs PA U.S.A.
23 L2 Hallsberg Sweden
208 I5 Halls Creek W.A. Austr.
111 P4 Halls Lake Ont. Can.
53 J2 Hallstadt Ger.
59 I4 Hallstatt Austria
23 O1 Hallstavik Sweden
117 J7 Hallstead PA U.S.A.
27 I5 Halltown Rep. of Ireland
45 D7 Halluin Belgium
44 I2 Halluin Neth.
20 N3 Hällnäs Sweden
20 M5 Hällnäs Sweden
70 E1 Hallviler See l. Switz.
30 C6 Hallworthy Cornwall, England U.K.
105 L3 Hall Peninsula Nunavut Can.
14 H3 Hall Point W.A. Austr.
118 B2 Halls PA U.S.A.
23 L2 Hallsberg Sweden
59 I4 Hallstatt Austria

Column 6

57 K4 Hajdúnánás Hungary
57 K4 Hajdúböszörmény Hungary
57 K4 Hajdúdorog Hungary
57 K4 Hajdúhadház Hungary
57 K4 Hajdúsámson Hungary
57 K4 Hajdúszoboszló Hungary
57 K4 Hajdúszovát Hungary
187 L9 Hajhir mt. Suqutrā Yemen
164 P8 Hajiki-zaki pt Japan
185 L7 Hajīābād Iran
179 J7 Hajipur Bihar India
187 I3 Hajir reg. Saudi Arabia
186 F8 Hajjah Yemen
184 D4 Hājjīābād-e Māsileh Iran
184 E7 Hājjīābād Fārs Iran
184 E7 Hājjīābād Golestān Iran
184 F7 Hājjīābād Hormozgan Iran
184 F7 Hajjiābād-e Zarrīn Iran
57 H4 Hajmáskér Hungary
55 L3 Hajnówka Pol.
179 M6 Haju Assam India
57 I5 Hajós Hungary
186 E3 Hājrah Saudi Arabia
168 F5 Hajuu-Us Mongolia
158 A3 Haka Myanmar
124 □F14 Hakalau HI U.S.A.
191 H6 Hākāri r. Azer.
165 Q9 Hakase-yama mt. Japan
203 E10 Hakatere South l. N.Z.
201 □2 Hakatea b. Vanua Fatu rf Vava'u Gp Tonga
22 H4 Hakefjord sea chan. Sweden
145 C6 Hakelhuincul, Altiplanicie de plat. Arg.
202 □ Hakepa, Mount Chatham Is S. Pacific Ocean
190 F2 Hakha Myanmar
189 K5 Hakkâri Turkey
20 P3 Hakkas Sweden
164 P6 Hakkōda-san mt. Japan
167 H6 Hakkō-san I. Japan
164 T2 Hako-dake mt. Japan
164 R4 Hakodate Japan
167 J5 Hakone Japan
167 J5 Hakone-tōge pass Japan
94 C4 Hakos Mountains Namibia
96 E2 Hakseen Pan salt pan S. Africa
37 L5 Hagondange France
27 D7 Hag's Head Rep. of Ireland
117 L5 Hague NY U.S.A.
37 O□a Haguenau France
203 □1 Hakupu Niue
166 E3 Hakusan Japan
166 E3 Hakū-san vol. Japan
166 E3 Haku-san National Park Japan
167 H6 Hakui Japan
185 M9 Hala Pak.
190 D8 Halā', Jabal al mt. Jordan
190 F2 Halab governorate Syria
186 G4 Halabān Saudi Arabia
189 L6 Halabja Iraq
127 N7 Halachó Mex.
203 □4 Halagigie Point Niue
162 D6 Halahai Jilin China
16 G5 Halahora de Sus Moldova
85 H4 Halaib Sudan
188 H8 Halaib Triangle terr. Egypt/Sudan
158 □7 Ha Lam Vietnam
187 M7 Halānīyah, Juzur al is Oman
187 L7 Halānīyah, Khalīj al b. Oman
59 J3 Haslach Austria
188 H3 Halat 'Ammār Saudi Arabia
77 I3 Hălăucești Romania
23 K3 Halaveden hills Sweden
124 □E12 Hālawa HI U.S.A.
190 E4 Halba Lebanon
168 I2 Halban Mongolia
53 J6 Halbe Ger.
59 M6 Halberstadt Austria
30 F6 Halberton Devon, England U.K.
53 J6 Halblech Ger.
208 H3 Half Point W.A. Austr.
118 B2 Halbs PA U.S.A.

Column 7

190 F2 Halisah Syria
169 K6 Haliut Nei Mongol China
187 I7 Halīyā well Yemen
176 D5 Haliyal Karnataka India
26 J5 Halkirk Highland, Scotland U.K.
30 F1 Halkyn Flintshire, Wales U.K.
Hall atoll Gilbert Is Kiribati see Maiana
23 O4 Hall Gotland Sweden
28 H2 Hall East Renfrewshire, Scotland U.K.
118 B7 Hall MD U.S.A.
20 N5 Hälla Sweden
24 E7 Halladale r. Scotland U.K.
118 B4 Hallam PA U.S.A.
22 I4 Halland county Sweden
31 M6 Halland East Sussex, England U.K.
22 I5 Hallandsås hills Sweden
22 I5 Hallandsåsen hills Sweden
163 E12 Halla-san mt. S. Korea
163 E12 Halla-san National Park S. Korea
105 J3 Hall Beach Nunavut Can.
53 L5 Hallbergmoos Ger.
45 G6 Halle Antwerpen Belgium
45 E5 Halle Vlaams-Brabant Belgium
49 I7 Halle Ger.
51 E8 Halle admin. reg. Ger.
51 E8 Halle (Saale) Ger.
49 F6 Halle (Westfalen) Ger.
23 K2 Hälleforsnäs Sweden
59 I3 Hallein Austria
20 M5 Hällen Sweden
23 N1 Hällen Sweden
49 G8 Hallenberg Ger.
36 C4 Hallencourt France
51 E8 Halle-Neustadt Ger.
53 J2 Hallerndorf Ger.
53 L5 Hallertau reg. Ger.
213 L2 Hallett, Cape Antarctica
121 G11 Hallettsville TX U.S.A.
22 H3 Hälleviksstrand Sweden
212 W1 Halley research stn Antarctica
212 X2 Halley, Mount Antarctica
23 O4 Hall-Hangvars naturreservat nature res. Gotland Sweden
120 D2 Halliday ND U.S.A.
107 I2 Halliday Lake N.W.T. Can.
48 G1 Halligen is Ger.
21 G6 Hallingby Norway
22 E1 Hallingdal val. Norway
22 F2 Hallingdalselva r. Norway
23 M4 Hallingeberg Sweden
58 E5 Hall in Tirol Austria
216 F5 Hall Islands Micronesia
18 I3 Halliste r. Estonia
20 O4 Hällnäs Sweden
120 G1 Hallock MN U.S.A.
30 H3 Hallow Worcestershire, England U.K.
105 L3 Hall Peninsula Nunavut Can.
208 H3 Hall Point W.A. Austr.
118 B2 Halls PA U.S.A.
23 L2 Hallsberg Sweden
208 I5 Halls Creek W.A. Austr.
111 P4 Halls Lake Ont. Can.
53 J2 Hallstadt Ger.
59 I4 Hallstatt Austria
23 O1 Hallstavik Sweden
117 J7 Hallstead PA U.S.A.
27 I5 Halltown Rep. of Ireland
45 D7 Halluin Belgium
44 I2 Halluin Neth.
20 N3 Hällnäs Sweden
20 M5 Hällnäs Sweden
70 E1 Hallviler See l. Switz.
30 C6 Hallworthy Cornwall, England U.K.
105 L3 Hall Peninsula Nunavut Can.
163 F11 Hallyŏ Haesang National Park S. Korea
77 L4 Hălmagel Romania
22 I5 Halmahera i. Maluku Indon.
155 F4 Halmahera, Laut sea Maluku Indon.
Halmahera Sea Maluku Indon. see Halmahera, Laut
22 I5 Halmstad Sweden
77 L4 Hălmeu Romania
22 I5 Halne Fin.
22 D1 Halnefjorden l. Norway
22 I6 Ha Long Vietnam
170 F8 Ha Long, Vinh b. Vietnam
55 M3 Halowichyy Belarus
24 I5 Haloze reg. Slovenia
22 G5 Hals Denmark
75 □ Hal Saflieni Hypogeum tourist site Malta
51 H9 Halsbrücke Ger.
22 I6 Halsenbach Ger.
Halsingborg Sweden see Helsingborg
31 N4 Halstead Essex, England U.K.
48 I3 Halstenbek Ger.
37 I5 Halstroff France
20 L5 Hallöra Fin.
49 I7 Halver Ger.
73 M4 Halvmåneøya i. Svalbard
30 E7 Halwell Devon, England U.K.
30 E7 Halwill Devon, England U.K.
22 J5 Halych Ukr.
16 D4 Halytsya Ukr.
52 E3 Halze Czech Rep.
186 C2 Ham Chad
96 D4 Ham watercourse Namibia
26 □1a Ham Shetland, Scotland U.K.
36 D4 Ham Namibia
165 J12 Hamada Japan
86 C5 Hamada Çafia pta. Mali
86 C4 Hamada El Haricha des. Mali
86 C2 Hamadān Iran
184 C3 Hamadān prov. Iran
86 D4 Hamada Murzuq plat. Libya
86 C4 Hamada Tounassine des. Alg.
165 K12 Hamada-jima i. Okinawa Japan
166 □F17 Hamada-jima i. Okinawa Japan
166 E7 Hamagawa Japan
164 S3 Hamamas Japan
166 G5 Hamamatsu Japan
Hamamatsu-ko l. Japan
18 □A6 Hamanaka Japan
166 E7 Hamana-ko l. Japan
164 P3 Hamanosa Japan
166 E7 Hamana Spain
167 M5 Hamaoka Japan
187 M6 Hamar Iceland
21 K6 Hamar Norway
190 E2 Hamārūh well Oman
184 B7 Hamamatsu Japan
187 M6 Hamar, Wādī al watercourse Saudi Arabia
191 M9 Hamar Nafūr r. Oman
186 E3 Hamarøy Norway
20 M2 Hamarøy Norway
186 D8 Hamasaka Japan
186 D8 Hamasien prov. Eritrea

Ḥamāṭah, Jabal to Havelländisches Luch

272

85 G3 **Ḥamāṭah, Jabal** *mt.* Egypt
164 T1 **Hamatonbetsu** Japan
37 N5 **Hambach** France
176 G9 **Hambantota** Sri Lanka
20 □ **Hambergbukta** *b.* Svalbard
48 K3 **Hamberge** Ger.
48 G4 **Hambergen** Ger.
204 E5 **Hambidge Conservation Park** *nature res. S.A.* Austr.
31 K4 **Hambleden** *Buckinghamshire, England* U.K.
31 J6 **Hamble-le-Rice** *Hampshire, England* U.K.
29 L6 **Hambleton** *Lancashire, England* U.K.
116 F9 **Hambleton** *WV* U.S.A.
29 O5 **Hambleton Hills** *England* U.K.
52 F3 **Hambrücken** Ger.
48 I5 **Hambühren** Ger.
48 I3 **Hamburg** Ger.
48 I3 **Hamburg** *land* Ger.
97 L9 **Hamburg** S. Africa
121 J9 **Hamburg** *AR* U.S.A.
119 K2 **Hamburg** *CT* U.S.A.
120 H5 **Hamburg** *IA* U.S.A.
118 F2 **Hamburg** *NJ* U.S.A.
116 G6 **Hamburg** *NY* U.S.A.
118 D3 **Hamburg** *PA* U.S.A.
48 F3 **Hamburgisches Wattenmeer, Nationalpark** *nat. park* Ger.
22 H3 **Hamburgsund** Sweden
38 I4 **Hambye** France
186 C3 **Ḥamḍ, Wādī al** *watercourse* Saudi Arabia
186 F6 **Ḥamḍah** Saudi Arabia
89 F3 **Hamdallay** Niger
186 E6 **Ḥamdānah** Saudi Arabia
117 M7 **Hamden** *CT* U.S.A.
79 I3 **Hamdibey** Turkey
190 D1 **Hamdili** Turkey
48 I2 **Hamdorf** Ger.
21 Q6 **Hämeenkangas** *moorland* Fin.
18 I1 **Hämeenkoski** *Etelä-Suomi* Fin.
Hämeenkoski *Länsi-Suomi* Fin. *see* **Koski**
21 Q6 **Hämeenkyrö** Fin.
21 R6 **Hämeenlinna** Fin.
48 H5 **Hämelhausen** Ger.
209 C9 **Hamelin** *W.A.* Austr.
209 C13 **Hamelin, Cape** *W.A.* Austr.
209 C9 **Hamelin Pool** *b. W.A.* Austr.
49 H6 **Hameln** Ger.
92 D3 **Hamero Hadad** Eth.
51 D6 **Hamersleben** Ger.
208 D7 **Hamersley** *W.A.* Austr.
209 E11 **Hamersley Lakes** *salt flat W.A.* Austr.
208 D7 **Hamersley Range** *mts W.A.* Austr.
50 E5 **Hämerten** Ger.
163 F8 **Hamgyŏng-sanmaek** *mts* N. Korea
163 E9 **Hamhŭng** N. Korea
168 C5 **Hami** *Xinjiang* China
59 M8 **Hamica** Croatia
184 C6 **Ḥamīd** Iran
85 F4 **Hamid** Sudan
79 H1 **Hamidiye** Turkey
79 L3 **Hamıdiye** Turkey
206 H7 **Hamilton** *Qld* Austr.
206 E9 **Hamilton** *S.A.* Austr.
206 G7 **Hamilton** *watercourse Qld* Austr.
204 E2 **Hamilton** *watercourse S.A.* Austr.
115 □1 **Hamilton** Bermuda
108 E5 **Hamilton** *Ont.* Can.
202 J4 **Hamilton** *North I.* N.Z.
26 H11 **Hamilton** *South Lanarkshire, Scotland* U.K.
115 D8 **Hamilton** *AL* U.S.A.
115 E9 **Hamilton** *GA* U.S.A.
110 C9 **Hamilton** *IL* U.S.A.
122 G3 **Hamilton** *MT* U.S.A.
119 G4 **Hamilton** *NJ* U.S.A.
117 J6 **Hamilton** *NY* U.S.A.
116 A9 **Hamilton** *OH* U.S.A.
121 F10 **Hamilton** *TX* U.S.A.
204 □3 **Hamilton, Mount** *hill* S. Pacific Ocean
124 K4 **Hamilton, Mount** *CA* U.S.A.
125 Q2 **Hamilton, Mount** *NV* U.S.A.
203 C12 **Hamilton Burn** *South I.* N.Z.
124 J2 **Hamilton City** *CA* U.S.A.
206 D7 **Hamilton Downs** *N.T.* Austr.
109 J2 **Hamilton Inlet** *Nfld and Lab.* Can.
117 K5 **Hamilton Mountain** *hill NY* U.S.A.
28 D5 **Hamilton's Bawn** *Northern Ireland* U.K.
109 K3 **Hamilton Sound** *sea chan. Nfld and Lab.* Can.
84 D2 **Hamīm, Wādī al** *watercourse* Libya
21 S6 **Hamina** Fin.
189 J8 **Ḥamīr, Wādī al** *watercourse* Saudi Arabia
178 F4 **Hamirpur** *Hima. Prad.* India
178 H7 **Hamirpur** *Uttar Prad.* India
Hamitabat Turkey *see* **Isparta**
22 C1 **Hamlagrovatnet** *l.* Norway
115 H8 **Hamlet** *NC* U.S.A.
204 G6 **Hamley Bridge** *S.A.* Austr.
118 E2 **Hamlin** *PA* U.S.A.
121 E9 **Hamlin** *TX* U.S.A.
116 C10 **Hamlin** *WV* U.S.A.
110 H5 **Hamlin Lake** *MI* U.S.A.
49 E7 **Hamm** *Nordrhein-Westfalen* Ger.
52 E2 **Hamm** *Rheinland-Pfalz* Ger.
49 E9 **Hamm (Sieg)** Ger.
86 C3 **Hammada du Drâa** *plat.* Alg.
84 A2 **Hammādat Tingharat** *des.* Libya
48 H3 **Hammah** Ger.
189 K5 **Ḥammām al 'Alīl** Iraq
61 F5 **Hammam Boughrara** Alg.
69 C7 **Hammamet** Tunisia
87 H1 **Hammamet, Golfe de** *g.* Tunisia
69 C7 **Hammam-Lif** Tunisia
97 M1 **Hammanskraal** S. Africa
189 M8 **Ḥammār, Hawr al** *imp. l.* Iraq
21 O6 **Hammarland** *Åland* Fin.
97 O5 **Hammarsdale** S. Africa
23 K6 **Hammarsjön** *l.* Sweden
20 N5 **Hammarstrand** Sweden
45 F6 **Hamme** Belgium
22 F5 **Hammel** Denmark
49 I10 **Hammelburg** Ger.
50 H4 **Hammelspring** Ger.
45 G7 **Hamme-Mille** Belgium
51 F10 **Hammerbrücke** Ger.
20 M5 **Hammerdal** Sweden
20 Q1 **Hammerfest** Norway
31 I2 **Hammerwich** *Staffordshire, England* U.K.
49 C7 **Hamminkeln** Ger.
204 G5 **Hammond** *S.A.* Austr.
114 D5 **Hammond** *IN* U.S.A.
121 J10 **Hammond** *LA* U.S.A.
122 L4 **Hammond** *MT* U.S.A.
111 J4 **Hammond Bay** *MI* U.S.A.
116 H6 **Hammondsport** *NY* U.S.A.
109 J3 **Hammone, Lac** *l. Que.* Can.
118 F5 **Hammonton** *NJ* U.S.A.
26 □N1 **Hamnavoe** *Shetland, Scotland* U.K.
26 □N2 **Hamnavoe** *Shetland, Scotland* U.K.
26 □N2 **Hamnavoe** *Shetland, Scotland* U.K.
159 G9 **Ham Ninh** Vietnam
45 I8 **Hamoir** Belgium
45 H8 **Hamois** Belgium
45 I6 **Hamont** Belgium
118 D5 **Hamorton** *PA* U.S.A.
203 E12 **Hampden** *South I.* N.Z.
117 □Q4 **Hampden Highlands** *ME* U.S.A.
116 G11 **Hampden Sydney** *VA* U.S.A.
176 E5 **Hampi** *Karnataka* India
20 P3 **Håmpjåkk** Sweden
37 M6 **Hampont** France
31 I6 **Hampreston** *Dorset, England* U.K.
31 J5 **Hampshire** *admin. div. England* U.K.
31 I5 **Hampshire Downs** *hills England* U.K.
118 B5 **Hampstead** *MD* U.S.A.
109 H4 **Hampton** *N.B.* Can.
121 I9 **Hampton** *AR* U.S.A.
120 I4 **Hampton** *IA* U.S.A.
117 □O6 **Hampton** *NH* U.S.A.
118 F3 **Hampton** *NJ* U.S.A.
115 G9 **Hampton** *SC* U.S.A.
117 I11 **Hampton** *VA* U.S.A.
119 J3 **Hampton Bays** *NY* U.S.A.
209 I12 **Hampton Tableland** *reg. W.A.* Austr.
187 M4 **Hamrā** Oman
90 F2 **Hamra** Sudan
Hamra, Vâdii *watercourse* Syria/Turkey *see* **Ḥimār, Wādī al**
187 I3 **Ḥamrā Jūdah** *plat.* Saudi Arabia
84 E6 **Hamrat esh Sheikh** Sudan
189 L6 **Ḥamrīn, Jabal** *hills* Iraq
75 □ **Ħamrun** Malta
122 J6 **Hams Fork** *r. WY* U.S.A.
191 A5 **Hamsiköy** Turkey
37 M5 **Ham-sous-Varsberg** France
31 N5 **Hamstreet** *Kent, England* U.K.
45 F8 **Ham-sur-Heure** Belgium
159 H9 **Ham Tân** Vietnam
178 F3 **Hamta Pass** *Hima. Prad.* India
184 H8 **Hāmūn-e Jaz Mūrīān** *salt marsh* Iran
185 I6 **Hāmūn Helmand** *salt flat* Afgh./Iran
185 I6 **Hāmūn Pu** *marsh* Afgh.
189 K4 **Hamur** Turkey
167 J4 **Hamura** Japan
183 N7 **Hamza** Uzbek.
190 A1 **Hamzalar** Turkey
45 H8 **Han, Grotte de** *cave* Belgium
56 G2 **Haná** *r.* Czech Rep.
124 □E13 **Hāna** *HI* U.S.A.
130 C2 **Hanábana** *r.* Cuba
94 D4 **Hanahai** *watercourse* Botswana/Namibia
186 C3 **Ḥanak** Saudi Arabia
191 D4 **Hanak** Turkey
124 □B11 **Hanalei** *HI* U.S.A.
124 □E13 **Hanamaioa, Cape** *HI* U.S.A.
164 S7 **Hanamaki** Japan
124 □B12 **Hanamā'ulu** *HI* U.S.A.
167 L4 **Hanamigawa** Japan
96 B1 **Hanam Plateau** Namibia
93 B6 **Hanang** *mt.* Tanz.
124 □B12 **Hanapēpē** *HI* U.S.A.
165 □3 **Hanare-iwa** *i.* Japan
49 G10 **Hanau** Ger.
124 □D12 **Hanauma Bay** *HI* U.S.A.
167 L2 **Hanawa** Japan
Hâncești Moldova *see* **Hîncești**
18 I8 **Hanchary** Belarus
169 L9 **Hancheng** *Shaanxi* China
36 C6 **Hanches** France
171 I3 **Hanchuan** *Hubei* China
116 G9 **Hancock** *MD* U.S.A.
110 F2 **Hancock** *MI* U.S.A.
117 J7 **Hancock** *NY* U.S.A.
118 E5 **Hancocks Bridge** *NJ* U.S.A.
166 E6 **Handa** Japan
26 F6 **Handa Island** *Scotland* U.K.
169 N8 **Handan** *Hebei* China
48 I4 **Handeloh** Ger.
93 C6 **Handeni** Tanz.
48 H1 **Handewitt** Ger.
57 H3 **Handlová** Slovakia
48 J4 **Handorf** Ger.
48 E5 **Handrup** Ger.
204 □3 **Handspike Point** S. Pacific Ocean
167 K4 **Haneda** *airport* Japan
HaNegev *des.* Israel *see* **Negev**
190 D8 **Haneqarot** *watercourse* Israel
48 H2 **Hanerau-Hademarschen** Ger.
Hanfeng *Chongqing* China *see* **Kaixian**
124 M5 **Hanford** *CA* U.S.A.
122 E3 **Hanford Reach National Monument** *nat. park WA* U.S.A.
176 D5 **Hangal** *Karnataka* India
158 C7 **Hangan** Myanmar
163 E10 **Han-gang** *r.* S. Korea
168 E2 **Hangayn Nuruu** *mts* Mongolia
Hangchow *Zhejiang* China *see* **Hangzhou**
51 I6 **Hangelsberg** Ger.
Hangö Fin. *see* **Hanko**
18 G2 **Hangö östra fjärd** *b.* Fin.
18 F2 **Hangö västra fjärd** *b.* Fin.
169 O7 **Hangu** *Tianjin* China
185 N5 **Hangu** Pak.
168 E8 **Hangya** *Qinghai* China
171 M3 **Hangzhou** *Zhejiang* China
171 M3 **Hangzhou Wan** *b.* China
30 G5 **Hanham** *South Gloucestershire, England* U.K.
189 J4 **Hani** Turkey
187 I2 **Ḥanīdh** Saudi Arabia
79 J2 **Hanife** *r.* Turkey
57 K3 **Haniska** Slovakia
Hanji *Gansu* China *see* **Linxia**
171 K7 **Han Jiang** *r.* China
168 I8 **Hanjiaoshui** *Ningxia* China
162 D2 **Hanjiayuanzi** *Heilong.* China
185 I8 **Hanjīrak** Iran
20 S5 **Hankasalmi** Fin.
48 K5 **Hankensbüttel** Ger.
97 I9 **Hankey** S. Africa
21 Q7 **Hanko** Fin.
79 L3 **Hanköy** Turkey
125 V3 **Hanksville** *UT* U.S.A.
178 G3 **Hanle** Jammu and Kashmir
107 J5 **Hanley** *Sask.* Can.
30 H3 **Hanley Castle** *Worcestershire, England* U.K.
203 G9 **Hanmer Forest Park** *nature res. South I.* N.Z.
203 G9 **Hanmer Springs** *South I.* N.Z.
207 J3 **Hann** *r. Qld* Austr.
208 I4 **Hann** *r. W.A.* Austr.
208 H3 **Hann, Mount** *hill W.A.* Austr.
107 I5 **Hanna** *Alta* Can.
55 L4 **Hanna** Pol.
125 W8 **Hannagan Meadow** *AZ* U.S.A.
108 D3 **Hannah Bay** *Ont.* Can.
120 J6 **Hannibal** *MO* U.S.A.
116 I5 **Hannibal** *NY* U.S.A.
116 E9 **Hannibal** *OH* U.S.A.
85 G5 **Hannik** *well* Sudan
17 M5 **Hannivka** Ukr.
167 J4 **Hannō** Japan
37 K5 **Hannonville-sous-les-Côtes** France
49 I6 **Hannover** Ger.
49 H5 **Hannover** *admin. reg.* Ger.
49 I8 **Hannoversch Münden** Ger.
206 D7 **Hann Range** *mts N.T.* Austr.
45 H7 **Hannut** Belgium
23 K5 **Hanö** *i.* Sweden
23 K6 **Hanöbukten** *b.* Sweden
Hanoi Vietnam *see* **Ha Nôi**
158 G4 **Ha Nôi** Vietnam
166 A8 **Hanoura** Japan
108 D4 **Hanover** *Ont.* Can.
Hanover Ger. *see* **Hannover**
130 □ **Hanover** *parish* Jamaica
96 I7 **Hanover** S. Africa
119 K1 **Hanover** *CT* U.S.A.
117 M5 **Hanover** *NH* U.S.A.
116 C8 **Hanover** *OH* U.S.A.
118 B5 **Hanover** *PA* U.S.A.
116 H11 **Hanover** *VA* U.S.A.
145 B8 **Hanover, Isla** *i.* Chile
118 B4 **Hanoverdale** *PA* U.S.A.
96 I6 **Hanover Road** S. Africa
115 □2 **Hanover Sound** *sea chan. New Prov.* Bahamas
56 G4 **Hanság** *hill* Hungary
56 G4 **Hansagi** *park* Hungary
45 E6 **Hansbeke** Belgium
213 D2 **Hansen Mountains** Antarctica
50 D3 **Hanshagen** Ger.
171 H4 **Hanshou** *Hunan* China
171 J3 **Han Shui** *r.* China
178 F5 **Hansi** *Haryana* India
31 K3 **Hanslope** *Milton Keynes, England* U.K.
20 O2 **Hansnes** Norway
206 D6 **Hanson** *watercourse N.T.* Austr.
204 F4 **Hanson, Lake** *salt flat S.A.* Austr.
202 □ **Hanson Bay** *Chatham Is* S. Pacific Ocean
116 C12 **Hansonville** *VA* U.S.A.
48 J4 **Hanstedt** *Niedersachsen* Ger.
48 J4 **Hanstedt** *Niedersachsen* Ger.
22 E4 **Hanstholm** Denmark
169 P4 **Han Sum** *Nei Mongol* China
37 L6 **Han-sur-Nied** France
Hantengri Feng *mt.* Kazakh./Kyrg. *see* **Khan-Tengri, Pik**
57 H5 **Hantos** Hungary
18 J9 **Hantsavichy** Belarus
178 I7 **Hanumana** *Madh. Prad.* India
178 E5 **Hanumangarh** *Rajasthan* India
187 L7 **Hanūn** *well* Oman
57 K2 **Hanušovce nad Topľou** Slovakia
56 F1 **Hanušovice** Czech Rep.
168 H2 **Hanuy Gol** *r.* Mongolia
38 C5 **Hanvec** France
30 G2 **Hanwood** *Shropshire, England* U.K.
205 K6 **Hanwwod** *N.S.W.* Austr.
168 E7 **Hanxia** *Gansu* China
170 G2 **Hanyin** *Shaanxi* China
167 K3 **Hanyū** Japan
170 D4 **Hanyuan** *Sichuan* China
184 I9 **Hanzaram** Iran
170 F2 **Hanzhong** *Shaanxi* China
201 □3 **Hao** *atoll Arch. des Tuamotu* Fr. Polynesia
Haomen *Qinghai* China *see* **Menyuan**
179 L8 **Haora** *W. Bengal* India
87 G2 **Haoud el Hamra** Alg.
65 I9 **Haouz, Jebel el** *hill* Morocco
86 C4 **Haouza** Western Sahara
20 R4 **Haparanda** Sweden
20 Q4 **Haparanda skärgård nationalpark** *nat. park* Sweden
45 H6 **Hapert** Neth.
179 N6 **Hapoli** *Arun. Prad.* India
53 K3 **Happburg** Ger.
31 P2 **Happisburgh** *Norfolk, England* U.K.
206 F6 **Happy Creek** *watercourse N.T.* Austr.
125 U7 **Happy Jack** *AZ* U.S.A.
109 I2 **Happy Valley - Goose Bay** *Nfld and Lab.* Can.
44 I5 **Haps** Neth.
163 F8 **Hapsu** N. Korea
178 F5 **Hapur** *Uttar Prad.* India
188 G9 **Ḥaql** Saudi Arabia
187 J4 **Haqshah** *well* Saudi Arabia
85 I5 **Ḥaqw** Saudi Arabia
167 H4 **Hara** Japan
92 D2 **Hara Alol** *mt.* Djibouti
187 I3 **Ḥaraḍ** *well* Saudi Arabia
186 F7 **Ḥaraḍ** Yemen
190 D9 **Ḥarad, Jabal al** *mt.* Jordan
187 I3 **Ḥaraḍh** Saudi Arabia
18 J7 **Haradok** *Minskaya Voblasts'* Belarus
18 M6 **Haradok** *Vitsyebskaya Voblasts'* Belarus
18 M6 **Haradotskaye Wzvyshsha** *hills* Belarus
20 P3 **Harads** Sweden
18 J8 **Haradzishcha** *Brestskaya Voblasts'* Belarus
18 M8 **Haradzishcha** *Mahilyowskaya Voblasts'* Belarus
55 M3 **Haradzyets** Belarus
18 J8 **Haradzyeya** Belarus
179 I6 **Haraiya** *Uttar Prad.* India
186 F7 **Ḥarajā** Saudi Arabia
164 R9 **Haramachi** Japan
172 H3 **Haramgai** *Xinjiang* China
178 E2 **Haramukh** *mt.* Jammu and Kashmir
Haran Turkey *see* **Harran**
18 M6 **Harany** Belarus
185 O6 **Harappa Road** Pak.
95 F3 **Harare** Zimbabwe
97 J5 **Ha Rasebi** S. Africa
187 L6 **Ḥarāsīs, Jiddat al** *des.* Oman
55 K5 **Harasiuki** Pol.
184 F6 **Harāt** Iran
85 H5 **Harat Island** Eritrea
187 K6 **Haraym** *well* Saudi Arabia
169 K4 **Har-Ayrag** Mongolia
84 C6 **Haraz-Djombo** Chad
90 D2 **Haraze-Mangueigne** Chad
18 M6 **Harbacheva** Belarus
49 I7 **Harbarnsen** Ger.
88 C5 **Harbel** Liberia
162 E6 **Harbin** *Heilong.* China
51 D6 **Harbke** Ger.
51 D6 **Harbke-Allertal** *park* Ger.
31 O5 **Harbledown** *Kent, England* U.K.
185 L7 **Harboi Hills** Pak.
36 E4 **Harbonnières** France
111 L6 **Harbor Beach** *MI* U.S.A.
110 J4 **Harbor Springs** *MI* U.S.A.
26 D6 **Harbost** *Western Isles, Scotland* U.K.
109 K4 **Harbour Breton** *Nfld and Lab.* Can.
53 J4 **Harburg (Schwaben)** Ger.
31 J3 **Harbury** *Warwickshire, England* U.K.
208 G7 **Harbutt Range** *hills W.A.* Austr.
178 H8 **Harchoka** *Chhattisgarh* India
125 S8 **Harcuvar Mountains** *AZ* U.S.A.
58 A5 **Hard** Austria
178 F8 **Harda** *Madh. Prad.* India
187 I7 **Ḥarḍah, Wādī** *r.* Yemen
22 C1 **Hardanger** *reg.* Norway
22 B2 **Hardangerfjorden** *sea chan.* Norway
22 D1 **Hardangervidda Nasjonalpark** *nat. park* Norway
184 D5 **Hardank** Iran
94 C5 **Hardap** *admin. reg.* Namibia
94 C5 **Hardap Dam** Namibia
21 H6 **Hardbakke** Norway
115 G9 **Hardeeville** *SC* U.S.A.
59 M2 **Hardegg** Austria
49 I7 **Hardegsen** Ger.
36 C2 **Hardelot-Plage** France
157 K2 **Harden, Bukit** *mt.* Indon.
44 K3 **Hardenberg** Neth.
44 I4 **Harderwijk** Neth.
96 C7 **Hardeveld** *mts* S. Africa
209 D7 **Hardey** *r. W.A.* Austr.
52 G2 **Hardheim** Ger.
120 J6 **Hardin** *IL* U.S.A.
122 K4 **Hardin** *MT* U.S.A.
208 D6 **Harding** *r. W.A.* Austr.
97 N6 **Harding** S. Africa
118 F6 **Harding Lakes** *NJ* U.S.A.
208 H4 **Harding Range** *hills W.A.* Austr.
209 D9 **Harding Range** *hills W.A.* Austr.
31 K3 **Hardingstone** *Northamptonshire, England* U.K.
44 G5 **Hardinxveld-Giessendam** Neth.
107 I4 **Hardisty** *Alta* Can.
106 G1 **Hardisty Lake** *N.W.T.* Can.
178 H6 **Hardoi** *Uttar Prad.* India
52 E5 **Hardt** Ger.
Hardwar *Uttaranchal* India *see* **Haridwar**
115 F9 **Hardwick** *GA* U.S.A.
117 M4 **Hardwick** *VT* U.S.A.
204 F6 **Hardwicke Bay** *S.A.* Austr.
118 E2 **Hardwood Ridge** *PA* U.S.A.
121 J7 **Hardy** *AR* U.S.A.
145 C9 **Hardy, Península** *pen.* Chile
109 K3 **Hare Bay** *Nfld and Lab.* Can.
31 L4 **Harefield** *Greater London, England* U.K.
22 I2 **Harefjorden** *l.* Sweden
29 J2 **Hare Hill** *Scotland* U.K.
20 I5 **Hareid** Norway
45 D7 **Harelbeke** Belgium
44 K2 **Haren** Neth.
48 D5 **Haren (Ems)** Ger.
92 D2 **Hārer** Eth.
92 D2 **Hārer Wildlife Sanctuary** *nature res.* Eth.
31 M4 **Hare Street** *Hertfordshire, England* U.K.
92 C2 **Hareto** Eth.
29 N6 **Harewood** *West Yorkshire, England* U.K.
190 D5 **Harf el Mreffi** *mt.* Lebanon
39 L2 **Harfleur** France
118 C5 **Harford County** *county MD* U.S.A.
169 P2 **Hargant** *Nei Mongol* China
Hargeisa Somalia *see* **Hargeysa**
92 D3 **Hargele** Eth.
52 D2 **Hargesheim** Ger.
92 E2 **Hargeysa** Somalia
77 N4 **Harghita, Munții** *mts* Romania
77 N4 **Harghita-Mădăraș, Vârful** *mt.* Romania
85 H6 **Hargigo** Eritrea
45 H8 **Hargimont** Belgium
37 I3 **Hargnies** France
189 J4 **Harhal Dağları** *mts* Turkey
169 J7 **Harhatan** *Nei Mongol* China
168 H3 **Harhorin** Mongolia
168 E7 **Har Hu** *l. Qinghai* China
98 □3c **Haría** *Lanzarote* Canary Is
186 G8 **Harīb** Yemen
178 G5 **Haridwar** *Uttaranchal* India
190 C8 **Ḥarif, Har** *mt.* Israel
176 D5 **Harihar** *Karnataka* India
203 E10 **Harihari** *South I.* N.Z.
176 D6 **Hariharpur** *Karnataka* India
178 C8 **Harij** *Gujarat* India
18 F2 **Hari kurk** *sea chan.* Estonia
190 E2 **Ḥārim** Syria
166 A6 **Harima** Japan
166 A6 **Harima-nada** *b.* Japan
179 L9 **Haringhat** *r.* Bangl.
44 F5 **Haringvliet** *est.* Neth.
20 S5 **Harinkaa** Fin.
166 G2 **Harinoki-dake** *mt.* Japan
176 E8 **Haripad** *Kerala* India
185 O5 **Haripur** Pak.
190 E6 **Ḥarīr, Wādī adh** *r.* Syria
185 I3 **Hari Rūd** *r.* Afgh./Iran
186 F6 **Ḥarjab, Wādī** *watercourse* Saudi Arabia
21 M6 **Härjåsjön** Sweden
21 Q6 **Harjavalta** Fin.
21 L5 **Härjedalen** *reg.* Sweden
20 Q4 **Harjufjärden** *b.* Sweden
56 F4 **Harka** Hungary
57 I5 **Harkakötöny** Hungary
20 M5 **Hårkan** *r.* Sweden
57 H6 **Harkány** Hungary
120 H5 **Harlan** *IA* U.S.A.
116 B12 **Harlan** *KY* U.S.A.
120 F5 **Harlan County Lake** *NE* U.S.A.
77 O3 **Hârlău** Romania
30 D2 **Harlech** *Gwynedd, Wales* U.K.
122 J2 **Harlem** *MT* U.S.A.
31 O3 **Harleston** *Norfolk, England* U.K.
118 E4 **Harleysville** *PA* U.S.A.
44 H2 **Harlingen** Neth.
121 G12 **Harlingen** *TX* U.S.A.
48 E3 **Harlinger Land** *reg.* Ger.
31 L4 **Harlington** *Bedfordshire, England* U.K.
31 M4 **Harlow** *Essex, England* U.K.
122 J3 **Harlowton** *MT* U.S.A.
36 F4 **Harly** France
116 F10 **Harman** *WV* U.S.A.
79 K3 **Harmancık** Turkey
79 K5 **Harmanlı** Turkey
59 N3 **Harmannsdorf** Austria
118 B6 **Harmans** *MD* U.S.A.
44 G4 **Harmelen** Neth.
85 I5 **Harmil** *i.* Eritrea
117 □P4 **Harmony** *ME* U.S.A.
110 B6 **Harmony** *MN* U.S.A.
118 E3 **Harmony** *NJ* U.S.A.
48 K2 **Harmsdorf** *Schleswig-Holstein* Ger.
48 K3 **Harmsdorf** *Schleswig-Holstein* Ger.
176 E6 **Harnahalli** *Karnataka* India
176 C4 **Harnai** *Mahar.* India
185 L6 **Harnai** Pak.
36 E3 **Harnes** France
122 E5 **Harney Basin** *OR* U.S.A.
122 E5 **Harney Lake** *OR* U.S.A.
20 N5 **Härnösand** Sweden
169 O2 **Har Nuden** *Nei Mongol* China
168 C2 **Har Nuur** *l.* Mongolia
168 E2 **Har Nuur** *l.* Mongolia
63 O3 **Haro** Spain
16 I1 **Harochychy** Belarus
116 C11 **Harold** *KY* U.S.A.
26 □O1 **Haroldswick** *Shetland, Scotland* U.K.
37 L7 **Haroué** France
176 D5 **Harpanahalli** *Karnataka* India
31 L4 **Harpenden** *Hertfordshire, England* U.K.
88 D5 **Harper** Liberia
121 F7 **Harper** *KS* U.S.A.
106 H3 **Harper Creek** *r. Alta* Can.
124 O6 **Harper Lake** *CA* U.S.A.
116 H9 **Harpers Ferry** *WV* U.S.A.
109 I2 **Harp Lake** *Nfld and Lab.* Can.
31 K3 **Harpole** *Northamptonshire, England* U.K.
48 G5 **Harpstedt** Ger.
Harqin Qi *Nei Mongol* China *see* **Jinshan**
125 S8 **Harquahala Mountains** *AZ* U.S.A.
178 G8 **Harrai** *Madh. Prad.* India
190 H2 **Harran** Turkey
185 N7 **Harrand** Pak.
186 E4 **Ḥarrāt Kishb** *lava field* Saudi Arabia
26 J4 **Harray, Loch of** *l. Scotland* U.K.
108 E3 **Harricanaw** *r. Ont./Que.* Can.
26 I10 **Harrietfield** *Perth and Kinross, Scotland* U.K.
31 N5 **Harrietsham** *Kent, England* U.K.
119 G2 **Harriman** *NY* U.S.A.
117 M6 **Harriman Reservoir** *VT* U.S.A.
205 N4 **Harrington** *N.S.W.* Austr.
118 D7 **Harrington** *DE* U.S.A.
117 □R4 **Harrington** *ME* U.S.A.
109 J3 **Harrington Harbour** *Que.* Can.
115 □1 **Harrington Sound** *inlet* Bermuda
26 C7 **Harris** *reg. Scotland* U.K.
204 E4 **Harris, Lake** *salt flat S.A.* Austr.
206 B8 **Harris, Mount** *N.T.* Austr.
26 B7 **Harris, Sound of** *sea chan. Scotland* U.K.
97 K3 **Harrisburg** S. Africa
121 J8 **Harrisburg** *AR* U.S.A.
121 K7 **Harrisburg** *IL* U.S.A.
120 D5 **Harrisburg** *NE* U.S.A.
116 B9 **Harrisburg** *OH* U.S.A.
111 R9 **Harrisburg** *PA* U.S.A.
48 H1 **Harrislee** Ger.
209 D12 **Harrismith** *W.A.* Austr.
97 N4 **Harrismith** S. Africa
203 C11 **Harris Mountains** *South I.* N.Z.
121 I7 **Harrison** *AR* U.S.A.
110 J5 **Harrison** *MI* U.S.A.
120 D4 **Harrison** *NE* U.S.A.
119 H3 **Harrison** *NY* U.S.A.
109 J2 **Harrison, Cape** *Nfld and Lab.* Can.
104 C2 **Harrison Bay** *AK* U.S.A.
121 J10 **Harrisonburg** *LA* U.S.A.
116 G10 **Harrisonburg** *VA* U.S.A.
106 F5 **Harrison Lake** *B.C.* Can.
118 B6 **Harrisonville** *MD* U.S.A.
120 H6 **Harrisonville** *MO* U.S.A.
111 N6 **Harriston** *Ont.* Can.
111 K5 **Harrisville** *MI* U.S.A.
117 J4 **Harrisville** *NY* U.S.A.
116 D9 **Harrisville** *WV* U.S.A.
Harrodsville *North I.* N.Z. *see* **Otorohanga**
29 N6 **Harrogate** *North Yorkshire, England* U.K.
116 B12 **Harrogate** *TN* U.S.A.
111 R5 **Harrowsmith** *Ont.* Can.
120 I6 **Harry S. Truman Reservoir** *MO* U.S.A.
21 M6 **Harsa** Sweden
168 E9 **Har Sai Shan** *mt. Qinghai* China
57 J4 **Harsány** Hungary
48 I4 **Harsefeld** Ger.
77 M6 **Hârsești** Romania
49 F7 **Harsewinkel** Ger.
184 B4 **Harsīn** Iran
188 I3 **Harşit** *r.* Turkey
51 D7 **Harsleben** Ger.
77 P6 **Hârșova** Romania
20 O3 **Harsprånget** Sweden
20 N2 **Harstad** Norway
31 M3 **Harston** *Cambridgeshire, England* U.K.
178 F8 **Harsud** *Madh. Prad.* India
49 I6 **Harsum** Ger.
20 K4 **Harsvik** Norway
104 E3 **Hart** *r. Y.T.* Can.
110 H6 **Hart** *MI* U.S.A.
204 F4 **Hart, Lake** *salt flat S.A.* Austr.
208 H4 **Hart, Mount** *hill W.A.* Austr.
57 I5 **Harta** Hungary
169 R5 **Hartao** *Liaoning* China
96 E4 **Hartbees** *watercourse* S. Africa
97 K2 **Hartbeesfontein** S. Africa
97 L1 **Hartbeespoort** S. Africa
59 M5 **Hartberg** Austria
22 D1 **Harteigan** *mt.* Norway
48 J3 **Hartenholm** Ger.
36 F5 **Hartennes-et-Taux** France
51 G9 **Hartenstein** Ger.
29 L5 **Harter Fell** *hill England* U.K.
31 M5 **Hartfield** *East Sussex, England* U.K.
88 C5 **Hartford** Liberia
117 M7 **Hartford** *CT* U.S.A.
114 D7 **Hartford** *KY* U.S.A.
110 H7 **Hartford** *MI* U.S.A.
120 G4 **Hartford** *SD* U.S.A.
110 F6 **Hartford** *WI* U.S.A.
114 E5 **Hartford City** *IN* U.S.A.
51 G8 **Hartha** Ger.
52 E3 **Harthausen** Ger.
52 D6 **Hartheim** Ger.
29 J2 **Harthill** *North Lanarkshire, Scotland* U.K.
77 M5 **Hârtibaciu** *r.* Romania
58 E5 **Hart im Zillertal** Austria
120 G4 **Hartington** *NE* U.S.A.
59 I3 **Hartkirchen** Austria
109 H4 **Hartland** *N.B.* Can.
30 D6 **Hartland** *Devon, England* U.K.
117 □P4 **Hartland** *ME* U.S.A.
30 C5 **Hartland Point** *England* U.K.
30 H3 **Hartlebury** *Worcestershire, England* U.K.
29 O4 **Hartlepool** *Hartlepool, England* U.K.
29 O4 **Hartlepool** *admin. div. England* U.K.
118 A3 **Hartleton** *PA* U.S.A.
31 M5 **Hartley** *Kent, England* U.K.
121 D8 **Hartley** *TX* U.S.A.
106 D4 **Hartley Bay** *B.C.* Can.
31 K5 **Hartley Wintney** *Hampshire, England* U.K.
118 D6 **Hartly** *DE* U.S.A.
53 O3 **Hartmanice** Czech Rep.
51 E9 **Hartmannsdorf** Ger.
118 C6 **Hart Miller Island** *MD* U.S.A.
122 E5 **Hart Mountain National Wildlife Refuge** *nature res. OR* U.S.A.
21 S6 **Hartola** Fin.
96 I4 **Harts** *r.* S. Africa
119 H2 **Hartsdale** *NY* U.S.A.
94 C4 **Hartseer** Namibia
115 D8 **Hartselle** *AL* U.S.A.
53 I4 **Härtsfeld** *hills* Ger.
31 I2 **Hartshill** *Warwickshire, England* U.K.
31 I2 **Hartshorne** *Derbyshire, England* U.K.
121 H8 **Hartshorne** *OK* U.S.A.
23 N3 **Hartsö naturreservat** *nature res.* Sweden
206 E7 **Harts Range** *N.T.* Austr.
206 E7 **Harts Range** *mts N.T.* Austr.
115 G8 **Hartsville** *SC* U.S.A.
115 D7 **Hartsville** *TN* U.S.A.
97 I3 **Hartswater** S. Africa
121 I7 **Hartville** *MO* U.S.A.
116 D8 **Hartville** *OH* U.S.A.
31 K3 **Hartwell** *Northamptonshire, England* U.K.
115 F8 **Hartwell** *GA* U.S.A.
115 F8 **Hartwell Reservoir** *GA/SC* U.S.A.
205 K10 **Hartz Mountains National Park** *Tas.* Austr.
166 D3 **Harue** Japan
155 F5 **Haruku** *i. Maluku* Indon.
167 I3 **Haruna** Japan
167 G5 **Haruno** Japan
176 F6 **Harur** *Tamil Nadu* India
168 C3 **Har Us Nuur** *l.* Mongolia
168 C2 **Har Us Nuur** *salt l.* Mongolia
185 I6 **Harut** *watercourse* Afgh.
187 K7 **Harūt** Yemen
185 I6 **Harut Rud** Afgh.
168 I2 **Haruuhin Gol** *r.* Mongolia
184 G6 **Harūz-e Bālā** Iran
110 F7 **Harvard** *IL* U.S.A.
123 K7 **Harvard, Mount** *CO* U.S.A.
209 C12 **Harvey** *W.A.* Austr.
109 H4 **Harvey** *N.B.* Can.
110 G3 **Harvey** *MI* U.S.A.
120 E2 **Harvey** *ND* U.S.A.
118 C2 **Harveys Lake** *PA* U.S.A.
118 C2 **Harveys Lake** *l. PA* U.S.A.
31 I3 **Harvington** *Worcestershire, England* U.K.
31 J4 **Harwell** *Oxfordshire, England* U.K.
31 O4 **Harwich** *Essex, England* U.K.
117 O7 **Harwich Port** *MA* U.S.A.
119 I1 **Harwington** *CT* U.S.A.
205 N3 **Harwood** *N.S.W.* Austr.
29 O7 **Harworth** *Nottinghamshire, England* U.K.
178 F5 **Haryana** *state* India
16 G1 **Haryn'** *r.* Belarus
Haryn' *r.* Ukr. *see* **Horyn'**
49 J7 **Harz** *hills* Ger.
49 K7 **Harz** *nat. park* Ger.
51 D7 **Harz** *park* Ger.
51 D7 **Harzgerode** Ger.
190 D8 **Har Ẕin** Israel
190 D8 **Ḥaşāh, Wādī al** *watercourse* Jordan
190 F8 **Ḥaşāh, Wādī al** *watercourse* Jordan/Saudi Arabia
173 C8 **Hasalbag** *Xinjiang* China
184 E5 **Ḥasanābād** Iran
190 B8 **Ḥasanah, Wādī** *watercourse* Egypt
191 B5 **Hasan Dağı** *mt.* Turkey
188 G4 **Hasan Dağı** *mts* Turkey
189 J5 **Hasankeyf** Turkey
185 J5 **Hasan Kūleh** Afgh.
184 G8 **Ḥasan Langī** Iran
176 F3 **Hasanparti** *Andhra Prad.* India
79 K5 **Hasanpaşa** Turkey
184 B3 **Ḥasan Sālārān** Iran
176 E7 **Hasanur** *Tamil Nadu* India
191 B6 **Hasbağlar** Turkey
190 D5 **Hasbaïya** Lebanon
188 G7 **Hasbani** *r.* Lebanon
188 G4 **Hasbek** Turkey
49 E6 **Hasbergen** Ger.
26 □O1 **Hascosay** *i. Scotland* U.K.
178 I9 **Hasdo** *r. Madh. Prad.* India
49 D5 **Hase** *r.* Ger.
167 H4 **Hase** Japan
48 I3 **Haseldorf** Ger.
48 D5 **Haselünne** Ger.
147 H2 **Hasenkamp** Arg.
49 J9 **Hasenkopf** *hill* Ger.
70 C1 **Hasenmatt** *mt.* Switz.
168 I4 **Hashaat** Mongolia
190 C6 **HaSharon** *plain* Israel
166 E5 **Hashima** Japan
166 C7 **Hashimoto** Japan
187 N5 **Ḥashīsh, Ghubbat** *b.* Oman
184 D4 **Hashtgerd** Iran
184 C3 **Hashtpar** *Gīlān* Iran
184 B3 **Hashtrud** Iran
187 L7 **Ḥāsik** Oman
185 O7 **Hasilpur** Pak.
121 F9 **Haskell** *TX* U.S.A.
191 D4 **Hasköy** Turkey
59 J2 **Haslach an der Mühl** Austria
52 E5 **Haslach im Kinzigtal** Ger.
29 O7 **Hasland** *Derbyshire, England* U.K.
23 K6 **Hasle** *Bornholm* Denmark
70 D1 **Hasle** Switz.
31 K5 **Haslemere** *Surrey, England* U.K.
22 H6 **Haslev** Denmark
29 M6 **Haslingden** *Lancashire, England* U.K.
48 I3 **Hasloh** Ger.
57 L5 **Hășmaș** Romania
77 N4 **Hășmașul Mare** *mt.* Romania
43 B9 **Hasparren** France
17 N9 **Haspra** Ukr.
191 I6 **Ḥasratān** Iran
191 D6 **Hasretpınar** Turkey
190 F2 **Ḥaşş, Jabal al** *hills* Syria
190 E2 **Hassa** Turkey
176 E6 **Hassan** *Karnataka* India
125 T8 **Hassayampa** *watercourse AZ* U.S.A.
49 J10 **Haßberge** *hills* Ger.
49 K10 **Haßberge** *park* Ger.
48 H5 **Haßbergen** Ger.
86 C6 **Hâsseï Mbârek** *well* Maur.
48 H5 **Hassel (Weser)** Ger.
204 □3 **Hasselborough Bay** S. Pacific Ocean
49 K7 **Hasselfelde** Ger.
23 M4 **Hasselö** *i.* Sweden
45 H7 **Hasselt** Belgium
44 J3 **Hasselt** Neth.
49 K10 **Haßfurt** Ger.
86 B4 **Hassi Aridal** *well* Western Sahara
87 H4 **Hassi Bedjedjene** *well* Alg.
87 G3 **Hassi Bel Guebbour** Alg.
86 E4 **Hassi Bou Bernous** *well* Alg.
87 H4 **Hassi Bourahla** *well* Alg.
87 F3 **Hassi Chebbaba** *well* Alg.
87 F2 **Hassi Dalaa** Alg.
86 B5 **Hassi Doumas** *well* Western Sahara
87 F3 **Hassi el Ahmar** *well* Alg.
87 G3 **Hassi el Hadjar** Alg.
87 F4 **Hassi el Krenig** *well* Alg.
87 F3 **Hassi Fahl** *well* Alg.
88 D2 **Ḥâssi Fouini** *well* Maur.
87 G4 **Hassi Habadra** *well* Alg.
84 A2 **Hassi Ifertas** *well* Libya
87 H4 **Hassi I-n-Akeouet** *well* Alg.
87 F4 **Hassi I-n-Belrem** *well* Alg.
87 F3 **Hassi Inifel** Alg.
87 H4 **Hassi Issendjell** *well* Alg.
88 E2 **Hâssi Karkabane** *well* Mali
87 F3 **Hassi Khanem** *well* Alg.
86 E3 **Hassi Mdakene** *well* Alg.
87 G3 **Hassi Messaoud** Alg.
87 G3 **Hassi Msegguem** *well* Alg.
87 F3 **Hassi Nebka** *well* Alg.
87 G4 **Hassi Ntsel** *well* Alg.
88 B2 **Hâssï SalläŞi** *well* Maur.
87 G3 **Hassi Sebbakh** *well* Alg.
87 G4 **Hassi Tabelbalet** *well* Alg.
87 F4 **Hassi Tiguentourine** *well* Alg.
87 H3 **Hassi Ti-n Fouchaye** *well* Alg.
88 D2 **Hâssi Touîl** *well* Maur.
50 I4 **Haßleben** *Brandenburg* Ger.
51 D8 **Haßleben** *Thüringen* Ger.
23 J5 **Hässleholm** Sweden
52 E3 **Haßloch** Ger.
52 G3 **Haßmersheim** Ger.
23 N1 **Hästbo** Sweden
49 H6 **Haste** Ger.
45 G8 **Hastière-Lavaux** Belgium
205 J8 **Hastings** *Vic.* Austr.
205 N4 **Hastings** *r. N.S.W.* Austr.
131 □4 **Hastings** Barbados
111 Q5 **Hastings** *Ont.* Can.
202 K6 **Hastings** *North I.* N.Z.
31 N6 **Hastings** *East Sussex, England* U.K.
110 I7 **Hastings** *MI* U.S.A.
110 B5 **Hastings** *MN* U.S.A.
120 F5 **Hastings** *NE* U.S.A.
167 K4 **Hasuda** Japan
167 L4 **Hasunuma** Japan
20 Q1 **Hasvik** Norway
187 K8 **Ḥaşwayl** Yemen
84 A3 **Ḥasy Haghe** *well* Libya
57 H2 **Hat'** Czech Rep.
57 L3 **Hat'** Ukr.
179 I6 **Hata** *Uttar Prad.* India
167 G3 **Hata** Japan
168 G4 **Hatansuudal** Mongolia
166 D5 **Hatashō** Japan
Hatay Turkey *see* **Antakya**
190 E2 **Hatay** *prov.* Turkey
118 E4 **Hatboro** *PA* U.S.A.
125 T4 **Hatch** *UT* U.S.A.
206 E6 **Hatches Creek** *N.T.* Austr.
107 K3 **Hatchet Lake** *Sask.* Can.
121 K8 **Hatchie** *r. TN* U.S.A.
77 K5 **Hațeg** Romania
202 K5 **Hatepe** *North I.* N.Z.
164 □A22 **Hateruma-jima** *i. Nansei-shotō* Japan
205 I5 **Hatfield** *N.S.W.* Austr.
31 L4 **Hatfield** *Hertfordshire, England* U.K.
29 P6 **Hatfield** *South Yorkshire, England* U.K.
118 E4 **Hatfield** *PA* U.S.A.
31 M4 **Hatfield Broad Oak** *Essex, England* U.K.
31 N4 **Hatfield Peverel** *Essex, England* U.K.
168 G1 **Hatgal** Mongolia
179 I8 **Hath** *Chhattisgarh* India
205 N4 **Hat Head National Park** *N.S.W.* Austr.
30 D6 **Hatherleigh** *Devon, England* U.K.
31 J2 **Hathern** *Leicestershire, England* U.K.
29 N7 **Hathersage** *Derbyshire, England* U.K.
178 G6 **Hathras** *Uttar Prad.* India
179 M8 **Hatia** Bangl.
179 K6 **Hatia** Nepal
186 D5 **Ḥāṭibah, Ra's** *pt* Saudi Arabia
159 G9 **Ha Tiên** Vietnam
158 G5 **Ha Tinh** Vietnam
131 □8 **Hato** *Bonaire* Neth. Antilles
131 □10 **Hato, Bocht van** *b. Curaçao* Neth. Antilles
136 D3 **Hato Corozal** Col.
Hato Hud East Timor *see* **Hatudo**
137 F3 **Hato la Vergareña** Venez.
131 I4 **Hato Mayor** Dom. Rep.
167 L1 **Hatori-ko** *l.* Japan
178 F8 **Hat Piplia** *Madh. Prad.* India
165 J12 **Hatsukaichi** Japan
167 J5 **Hatsu-shima** *i.* Japan
178 G7 **Hatta** *Madh. Prad.* India
178 H9 **Hatta** *Madh. Prad.* India
205 I6 **Hattah** *Vic.* Austr.
44 J4 **Hattem** Neth.
53 K5 **Hattenhofen** Ger.
115 J8 **Hatteras, Cape** *NC* U.S.A.
214 E4 **Hatteras Abyssal Plain** *sea feature* S. Atlantic Ocean
49 F10 **Hattersheim am Main** Ger.
49 E9 **Hattert** Ger.
20 L4 **Hattfjelldal** Norway
177 H3 **Hatti** *r.* India
121 K10 **Hattiesburg** *MS* U.S.A.
58 D5 **Hatting** Austria
49 D8 **Hattingen** Ger.
26 M8 **Hatton** *Aberdeenshire, Scotland* U.K.
31 I2 **Hatton** *Derbyshire, England* U.K.
157 M2 **Hatton, Gunung** *hill* Malaysia
49 J7 **Hattorf am Harz** Ger.
166 D6 **Hattori-gawa** *r.* Japan
159 C8 **Hattras Passage** Myanmar
48 H1 **Hattstedt** Ger.
21 R6 **Hattula** Fin.
20 U5 **Hattuvaara** Fin.
155 D8 **Hatudo** East Timor
57 I4 **Hatvan** Hungary
159 E11 **Hat Yai** Thai.
52 E3 **Hatzenbühl** Ger.
59 N6 **Hatzendorf** Austria
49 G9 **Hatzfeld (Eder)** Ger.
159 H10 **Hâu, Sông** *r.* Vietnam
36 E2 **Haubourdin** France
92 E2 **Haud** *reg.* Eth.
52 D3 **Hauenstein** Ger.
22 D1 **Haugastøl** Norway
22 C3 **Hauge** Norway
22 B2 **Haugesund** Norway
30 H2 **Haughton** *Staffordshire, England* U.K.
59 N2 **Haugsdorf** Austria
21 R6 **Hauho** Fin.
200 □6 **Hauhui** *Malaita* Solomon Is
202 J5 **Hauhungaroa** *mt. North I.* N.Z.
202 J5 **Hauhungaroa Range** *mts North I.* N.Z.
22 D2 **Haukeligrend** Norway
20 R4 **Haukipudas** Fin.
20 T5 **Haukivesi** *l.* Fin.
21 S5 **Haukivuori** Fin.
44 J2 **Haulerwijk** Neth.
107 J4 **Haultain** *r. Sask.* Can.
202 K6 **Haumoana** *North I.* N.Z.
144 E2 **Haumonia** Arg.
158 C2 **Haungpa** Myanmar
26 B8 **Haunn** *Western Isles, Scotland* U.K.
119 I3 **Hauppauge** *NY* U.S.A.
50 J5 **Hauptgraben** *r.* Ger.
53 K4 **Hauptkanal** *canal* Ger.
97 K2 **Hauptrus** S. Africa
51 I7 **Hauptspree** *r.* Ger.
200 □6 **Hauraha** *San Cristobal* Solomon Is
202 J3 **Hauraki Gulf** *North I.* N.Z.
202 I3 **Hauraki Gulf Maritime Park** *nature res. North I.* N.Z.
203 J8 **Haurangi Forest Park** *nature res. North I.* N.Z.
203 B13 **Hauroko, Lake** *South I.* N.Z.
201 □3a **Hauru, Pointe** *pt Moorea* Fr. Polynesia
59 I5 **Haus** Austria
52 E5 **Hausach** Ger.
51 G8 **Hausdorf** Ger.
53 K2 **Hausen** *Bayern* Ger.
53 M4 **Hausen** *Bayern* Ger.
53 I2 **Hausen bei Würzburg** Ger.
52 D6 **Hausen im Wiesental** Ger.
52 E6 **Häusern** Ger.
53 L6 **Hausham** Ger.
18 H1 **Hausjärvi** Fin.
59 N3 **Hausleiten** Austria
59 M6 **Hausmannstätten** Austria
59 H3 **Hausruck** *mts* Austria
70 G2 **Hausstock** *mt.* Switz.
117 □Q4 **Haut, Isle au** *i. ME* U.S.A.
20 T3 **Hautajärvi** Fin.
86 C3 **Haut Atlas** *mts* Morocco
Haut-Congo *prov.* Dem. Rep. Congo *see* **Orientale**
37 M8 **Haut-du-Them-Château-Lambert** France
37 K8 **Haute-Amance** France
72 C3 **Haute-Corse** *dept Corse* France
40 G4 **Hautecourt-Romanèche** France
42 G5 **Hautefort** France
43 G9 **Haute-Garonne** *dept* France
88 C4 **Haute-Guinée** *admin. reg.* Guinea
90 D3 **Haute-Kotto** *pref.* C.A.R.
41 D6 **Haute-Loire** *dept* France
40 J5 **Hauteluce** France
37 J7 **Haute-Marne** *dept* France
36 B5 **Haute-Normandie** *admin. reg.* France
109 G3 **Hauterive** *Que.* Can.
41 G6 **Hauterives** France
41 I7 **Hautes-Alpes** *dept* France
37 L8 **Haute-Saône** *dept* France
37 K8 **Haute-Saône, Plateau de** France
40 I4 **Haute-Savoie** *dept* France
36 G6 **Haute Seine, Canal de la** France
45 J8 **Hautes Fagnes** *moorland* Belgium
45 J7 **Hautes Fagnes-Eifel, Parc Naturel des** *nature res.* Belgium
43 E9 **Hautes-Pyrénées** *dept* France
42 C2 **Hauteurs de la Gâtine** *reg.* France
42 G4 **Haute-Vienne** *dept* France
40 H5 **Hauteville-Lompnes** France
36 G5 **Hautevillers** France
45 H8 **Haut-Fays** Belgium
40 E3 **Haut-Folin** *hill* France
40 H4 **Haut Jura, Parc Naturel Régional du** *nature res.* France
41 B9 **Haut-Languedoc, Parc Naturel Régional du** *nature res.* France
90 E3 **Haut-Mbomou** *pref.* C.A.R.
36 G3 **Hautmont** France
118 D3 **Hauto, Lake** *PA* U.S.A.
90 B5 **Haut-Ogooué** *prov.* Gabon
43 G6 **Haut-Quercy** *reg.* France
37 N8 **Haut-Rhin** *dept* France
39 P4 **Hauts-de-Seine** *dept* France
87 E2 **Hauts Plateaux** Alg.
Haut-Zaïre *prov.* Dem. Rep. Congo *see* **Orientale**
124 □D12 **Hau'ula** *HI* U.S.A.
Hauvo Fin. *see* **Nagu**
203 I8 **Hauwai** *South I.* N.Z.
43 C9 **Haux** France
53 P4 **Hauzenberg** Ger.
Havana Cuba *see* **La Habana**
110 D9 **Havana** *IL* U.S.A.
31 K6 **Havant** *Hampshire, England* U.K.
77 O2 **Havârna** Romania
125 R7 **Havasu, Lake** *AZ/CA* U.S.A.
20 R1 **Hávdna** Norway
51 E5 **Havel** *r.* Ger.
45 H8 **Havelange** Belgium
50 F5 **Havelberg** Ger.
185 O6 **Haveli** Pak.
185 O4 **Havelian** Pak.
50 F5 **Havelland** *reg.* Ger.
50 F5 **Havelländisches Luch** *marsh* Ger.

Column 1

11 Q5 Havelock Ont. Can.
03 H8 Havelock South I. N.Z.
03 E10 Havelock r. South I. N.Z.
18 I8 Havelock NC U.S.A.
75 Q8 Havelock Falls N.T. Can.
77 M7 Havelock Island Andaman & Nicobar Is India
02 K6 Havelock North North I. N.Z.
44 J3 Havelte Neth.
21 G7 Haven KS U.S.A.
22 I5 Haverdal Sweden
30 C4 Haverfordwest Pembrokeshire, Wales U.K.
31 M3 Haverhill Suffolk, England U.K.
17 N6 Haverhill MA U.S.A.
76 D5 Haveri Karnataka India
49 J6 Haverlah Ger.
21 M5 Haverö Sweden
45 H8 Haversin Belgium
19 H2 Haverstraw NY U.S.A.
18 E5 Havertown PA U.S.A.
57 H2 Havířov Czech Rep.
46 E2 Havlíčkův Brod Czech Rep.
20 R1 Havøysund Norway
57 J2 Havran mt. Slovakia
79 I3 Havran Turkey
79 H3 Havran r. Turkey
45 F8 Havré Belgium
22 J2 Havre MT U.S.A.
09 I4 Havre Aubert Que. Can.
09 I4 Havre Aubert, Île du i. Que. Can.
18 C5 Havre de Grace MD U.S.A.
09 I5 Havre Rock i. N.Z.
17 P5 Havre-St-Pierre Que. Can.
17 P5 Havrylivka Dnipropetrovs'ka Oblast' Ukr.
17 P5 Havrylivka Kharkivs'ka Oblast' Ukr.
16 F5 Havrylivtsi Ukr.
77 O9 Havsa Turkey
90 D2 Havstensfjord inlet Sweden
90 D2 Havutlu Turkey
88 Q3 Havza Turkey
24 ☐F13 Hawai'i i. HI U.S.A.
24 ☐F14 Hawaii state U.S.A.
16 H4 Hawaiian Islands N. Pacific Ocean
16 H4 Hawaiian Ridge sea feature N. Pacific Ocean
24 ☐F14 Hawai'i Volcanoes National Park HI U.S.A.
89 N9 Hawalli Kuwait
30 F1 Hawar i. The Gulf see Huwār
30 F1 Hawarden Flintshire, Wales U.K.
90 A10 Hawashiyah, Wādī watercourse Egypt
03 D11 Hawea, Lake South I. N.Z.
03 D11 Hawea Flat South I. N.Z.
02 I6 Hawera North I. N.Z.
29 N5 Hawes North Yorkshire, England U.K.
14 D7 Hawesville KY U.S.A.
29 L4 Haweswater Reservoir England U.K.
24 ☐F13 Hāwī HI U.S.A.
26 K12 Hawick Scottish Borders, Scotland U.K.
89 M8 Hawkdun Range mts South I. N.Z.
03 D11 Hawke Bay North I. N.Z.
09 K2 Hawke Island Nfld and Lab. Can.
04 G4 Hawker S.A. Austr.
04 G4 Hawkers Gate N.S.W. Austr.
09 J3 Hawkes Bay Nfld and Lab. Can.
02 K6 Hawke's Bay admin. reg. North I. N.Z.
11 N5 Hawkesbury Ont. Can.
206 G6 Hawkesbury South Gloucestershire, England U.K.
110 C4 Hawkeye IA U.S.A.
15 N5 Hawkhurst Kent, England U.K.
06 C3 Hawk Inlet AK U.S.A.
08 S4 Hawkins Peak UT U.S.A.
10 J1 Hawk Junction Ont. Can.
15 E8 Haw Knob mt. NC/TN U.S.A.
30 F1 Hawksbill Cay i. Bahamas
17 ☐R3 Hawkshaw N.B. Can.
29 L5 Hawkshead Cumbria, England U.K.
30 F1 Hawksnest Point Bahamas
22 L6 Hawk Springs WY U.S.A.
03 H9 Hawkswood South I. N.Z.
31 M4 Hawkwell Essex, England U.K.
07 M8 Hawkwood Qld Austr.
31 K5 Hawley Hampshire, England U.K.
18 E2 Hawley PA U.S.A.
19 D2 Hawleyville CT U.S.A.
29 O5 Hawnby North Yorkshire, England U.K.
38 D4 Hawng Luk Myanmar
29 N6 Haworth West Yorkshire, England U.K.
87 I8 Hawrā' Yemen
89 K7 Hawrān, Wādī watercourse Iraq
90 D10 Hawsa hills Saudi Arabia
86 G4 Hawsah, Jibāl al mts Saudi Arabia
15 B8 Hawston S. Africa
19 G3 Hawthorne NJ U.S.A.
24 N3 Hawthorne NV U.S.A.
19 H2 Hawthorne NY U.S.A.
58 D9 Hawzen Eth.
69 M4 Haxat Hudag Nei Mongol China
29 O5 Haxby York, England U.K.
29 P7 Haxey North Lincolnshire, England U.K.
05 J6 Hay r. N.S.W. Austr.
06 F8 Hay watercourse N.T. Austr.
06 H2 Hay r. Can.
10 C5 Hay r. WI U.S.A.
05 F5 Haya Seram Indon.
67 H5 Hayachine-san mt. Japan
66 D3 Hayakawa Japan
67 H5 Haya-kawa r. Japan
54 S4 Hayakita Japan
57 K5 Hayama Japan
57 L5 Hayange France
55 I13 Hayasui-seto sea chan. Japan
17 P6 Haychur r. Ukr.
10 B5 Hay Creek MN U.S.A.
34 A3 Haydarābād Iran
91 L2 Haydarli Turkey
79 L4 Haydaroba Turkey
25 V8 Hayden AZ U.S.A.
25 K2 Hayden CO U.S.A.
22 F3 Hayden ID U.S.A.
29 M4 Haydock Merseyside, England U.K.
31 I4 Haydon Bridge Northumberland, England U.K.
25 C2 Haydon Vic. Austr.
07 M3 Hayes r. Man. Can.
20 E5 Hayes Center NE U.S.A.
05 M2 Hayes Halvø pen. Greenland
15 F8 Hayesville NC U.S.A.
25 M2 Hayes Creek N.T. Austr.
29 N7 Hayfield Derbyshire, England U.K.
10 B6 Hayfield MN U.S.A.
25 G8 Hayfield Reservoir CA U.S.A.
37 M3 Hāyil Oman
25 U2 Hayl, Wādī al r. Syria
30 H4 Hayl, Wādī watercourse Syria

Column 2

30 B7 Hayle Cornwall, England U.K.
31 K6 Hayling Island England U.K.
187 M6 Haymā' Oman
44 H5 Haymana Turkey
207 L6 Haymarket Qld Austr.
116 H10 Haymarket VA U.S.A.
18 L7 Hayna r. Belarus
121 I9 Haynesville LA U.S.A.
115 D9 Hayneville AL U.S.A.
30 F3 Hay-on-Wye Powys, Wales U.K.
23 N1 Hayotboshi Toghi mt. Uzbek. see Hayotboshi tog'i
23 N1 Hayotboshi tog'i mt. Uzbek.
122 F4 Hayrabolu Turkey
191 B5 Hayrat Turkey
106 H2 Hay River N.W.T. Can.
106 H2 Hay River Reserve N.W.T. Can.
120 F6 Hays KS U.S.A.
122 J2 Hays MT U.S.A.
186 F9 Hays Yemen
84 B2 Hayshah, Sabkhat al salt pan Libya
116 C11 Haysi VA U.S.A.
212 N1 Hays Mountains Antarctica
120 D4 Hay Springs NE U.S.A.
121 G7 Haysville KS U.S.A.
16 I5 Haysyn Ukr.
190 D3 Hayṭān, Jabal hill Egypt
29 L4 Hayton Cumbria, England U.K.
29 P6 Hayton East Riding of Yorkshire, England U.K.
179 P5 Hayutang Arun. Prad. India
16 I5 Hayvoron Ukr.
24 J4 Hayward CA U.S.A.
110 C3 Hayward WI U.S.A.
31 L6 Haywards Heath West Sussex, England U.K.
187 N5 Hayy well Oman
185 K5 Hazarajat reg. Afgh.
116 B11 Hazard KY U.S.A.
179 J8 Hazaribagh Jharkhand India
179 I8 Hazaribagh Range mts Bihar India
184 H3 Hazār Masjed, Kūh-e mts Iran
36 E2 Hazebrouck France
203 C13 Hazelburgh Group is South I. N.Z.
29 M7 Hazel Grove Greater Manchester, England U.K.
110 E4 Hazelhurst WI U.S.A.
106 E4 Hazelton B.C. Can.
120 E2 Hazen ND U.S.A.
105 K1 Hazen, Lake Nunavut Can.
105 G2 Hazen Strait N.W.T./Nunavut Can.
185 L3 Hazhdanahr reg. Afgh.
115 F10 Hazlehurst GA U.S.A.
121 J10 Hazlehurst MS U.S.A.
31 K4 Hazlemere Buckinghamshire, England U.K.
119 G4 Hazlet NJ U.S.A.
118 D3 Hazleton PA U.S.A.
208 J6 Hazlett, Lake salt flat W.A. Austr.
57 K2 Hažlín Slovakia
56 B1 Hazlov Czech Rep.
187 M4 Hazm Oman
182 I7 Hazorasp Uzbek.
191 J4 Hāzrā Azer.
185 M4 Hazrat Sultan Afgh.
70 H1 Hazro Turkey
189 M3 Hazro Pak.
166 E6 Hazū Japan
147 F4 H. Bouchard Arg.
16 J2 Hdzyen' Belarus
31 M2 Heacham Norfolk, England U.K.
31 N5 Headcorn Kent, England U.K.
27 D6 Headford Rep. of Ireland
206 G6 Headingly Qld Austr.
31 K5 Headley Hampshire, England U.K.
204 C4 Head of Bight b. S.A. Austr.
208 ☐1 Heads Christmas I.
26 G12 Heads of Ayr Scotland U.K.
110 E4 Headwaters Junction WI U.S.A.
26 C8 Healabhal Bheag hill Scotland U.K.
124 J3 Healdsburg CA U.S.A.
121 G8 Healdton OK U.S.A.
205 J7 Healesville Vic. Austr.
29 Q6 Healing North East Lincolnshire, England U.K.
116 F11 Healing Springs VA U.S.A.
29 O7 Heanor Derbyshire, England U.K.
30 D5 Heanton Punchardon Devon, England U.K.
215 I8 Heard Island Indian Ocean
20 R1 Heargerášša hill Norway
121 G10 Hearne TX U.S.A.
106 H2 Hearne Lake N.W.T. Can.
108 D3 Hearst Ont. Can.
212 T2 Heart Island Antarctica
120 E2 Heart r. ND U.S.A.
138 C3 Heath r. Bol./Peru
29 O7 Heath Derbyshire, England U.K.
205 J7 Heathcote Vic. Austr.
31 M6 Heathfield East Sussex, England U.K.
31 L5 Heathrow airport England U.K.
116 I11 Heathsville VA U.S.A.
121 H8 Hebbronville TX U.S.A.
116 F8 Hebbville MD U.S.A.
29 M6 Hebden Bridge West Yorkshire, England U.K.
169 K7 Hebei prov. China
205 K3 Hebel Qld Austr.
125 V3 Heber AZ U.S.A.
125 Q9 Heber CA U.S.A.
125 U1 Heber City UT U.S.A.
128 C2 Heber Springs AR U.S.A.
53 I5 Hebertsfelden Ger.
49 I8 Hebertshausen Ger.
169 N7 Hebi Henan China
169 M7 Hebian Shanxi China
22 B2 Hebnes Norway
26 C9 Hebrides, Sea of the Scotland U.K.
109 I1 Hebron Nfld and Lab. Can.
119 K1 Hebron CT U.S.A.
110 G8 Hebron IN U.S.A.
117 J10 Hebron MD U.S.A.
120 D2 Hebron ND U.S.A.
120 G3 Hebron NE U.S.A.
190 D7 Hebron West Bank
109 I1 Hebron Fiord inlet Nfld and Lab. Can.
23 M2 Heby Sweden
106 D4 Hecate Strait B.C. Can.
145 E8 Hecelchakán Mex.
161 C6 Hechi Guangxi China
66 D2 Hecho Spain
66 D2 Hecho, Valle de val. Spain
45 H6 Hechtel Belgium
48 H3 Hechthausen Ger.
170 E4 Hechuan Chongqing China
170 H8 Hechun Guangdong China
50 I5 Heckelberg Ger.
31 L2 Heckington Lincolnshire, England U.K.
49 I5 Hecklingen Ger.
169 O7 Hecun Hebei China
172 H5 Hede Xinjiang China
22 F3 Hedberg Sweden
22 G2 Heddalsvatnet l. Norway
49 I2 Heddesheim Ger.

Column 3

38 H5 Hédé France
21 L5 Hede Sweden
22 H3 Hedekas Sweden
44 H5 Hedel Neth.
45 H6 Hedehterren Belgium
23 L1 Hedemora Sweden
20 Q3 Hedenäset Sweden
22 F6 Hedensted Denmark
49 K6 Hedeper Ger.
51 E7 Hedersleben Ger.
23 N1 Hédervár Hungary
23 M1 Hedesunda Sweden
23 M1 Hedesundafjärden l. Sweden
122 F4 He Devil Mountain ID U.S.A.
31 J6 Hedge End Hampshire, England U.K.
203 C13 Hedgehope South I. N.Z.
127 I5 Hedionda Grande Mex.
170 H8 Hedi Shuiku resr China
23 I2 Hednesford Staffordshire, England U.K.
164 ☐1 Hedo Okinawa Japan
164 ☐1 Hedo-misaki c. Okinawa Japan
29 Q6 Hedon East Riding of Yorkshire, England U.K.
48 D5 Heede Ger.
44 I3 Heeg Neth.
49 D6 Heek Ger.
45 I6 Heel Neth.
44 G3 Heemsen Ger.
44 G4 Heemskerk Neth.
44 G4 Heemstede Neth.
45 G8 Heer Belgium
44 J4 Heerde Neth.
44 I3 Heerenveen Neth.
44 H3 Heerhugowaard Neth.
20 ☐1 Heer Land reg. Svalbard
45 I7 Heerlen Neth.
45 H7 Heers Belgium
44 I5 Heesch Neth.
48 H4 Heeslingen Ger.
45 H6 Heeswijk Neth.
49 H6 Heeten Neth.
45 I6 Heeze Neth.
190 C6 Hefa Israel
190 D6 Hefa, Mifraz b. Israel
171 K3 Hefei Anhui China
170 F6 Hefeng Hubei China
115 E9 Heflin AL U.S.A.
162 G5 Hegang Heilong. China
52 F6 Hegau reg. Ger.
176 E6 Heggadadevankote Karnataka India
21 J6 Heggenes Norway
118 B3 Hegins PA U.S.A.
65 O9 Hegura-jima i. Japan
56 G4 Hegyeshalom Hungary
59 O4 Hegykő Hungary
49 H7 Hehlen Ger.
158 C4 Heho Myanmar
92 A2 Heiban Sudan
Heidan r. Jordan see Ḥaydān, Wādī al
51 D7 Heidberg hill Ger.
48 H2 Heide Ger.
94 C4 Heide Namibia
53 K3 Heideck Ger.
97 M2 Heidelberg Gauteng S. Africa
96 E5 Heidelberg Western Cape S. Africa
52 F5 Heidelberg Ger.
49 C7 Heiden Ger.
51 D8 Heiden Switz.
48 I4 Heiden Niedersachsen Ger.
48 I4 Heidenau Sachsen Ger.
53 I4 Heidenheim an der Brenz Ger.
59 L2 Heidenreichstein Austria
118 A5 Heidlersburg PA U.S.A.
164 S7 Hei-gawa r. Japan
49 H10 Heigenbrücken Ger.
29 N4 Heighington Darlington, England U.K.
29 P7 Heighington Lincolnshire, England U.K.
165 J13 Heigun-jima i. Japan
162 E3 Heihe Heilong. China
168 G7 He He r. Qinghai China
97 L3 Heikendorf Ger.
97 I3 Heilbron S. Africa
52 G3 Heilbronn Ger.
59 M5 Heilbrunn Austria
Heiligenbeil Rus. Fed. see Mamonovo
52 G6 Heiligenberg Ger.
50 D5 Heiligenfelde Ger.
50 F4 Heiligengrabe Ger.
49 H6 Heiligenhafen Ger.
49 C8 Heiligenhaus Ger.
59 M6 Heiligenkreuz am Waasen Austria
59 N6 Heiligenkreuz im Lafnitztal Austria
49 J8 Heiligenstadt Heilbad Ger.
53 K2 Heiligenstadt in Oberfranken Ger.
48 H3 Heiligenstedten Ger.
171 ☐J7 Hei Ling Chau i. H.K. China
169 R3 Heilongjiang prov. China
162 I4 Heilong Jiang r. China alt. Amur (Rus. Fed.)
44 G3 Heiloo Neth.
53 J3 Heilsbronn Ger.
31 I6 Heiltz-le-Maurupt France
Heilungkiang prov. China see Heilongjiang
41 E8 Heimaey i. Iceland
124 P8 Heimahe Qinghai China
48 H2 Heimbach Ger.
49 K7 Heimburg Ger.
49 K7 Heimenkirch Ger.
52 F4 Heimertingen Ger.
59 I4 Heimiswil Switz.
48 H3 Heinade Ger.
21 J6 Heinävesi Fin.
51 K7 Heinersbrück Ger.
51 J6 Heinersdorf Ger.
53 L2 Heinersreuth Ger.
49 K6 Heiningen Ger.
44 J4 Heinkenszand Neth.
31 M3 Heinsberg Essex, England U.K.
119 H3 Heinsberg Ger.
121 G10 Heinze Islands Myanmar
159 C7 Heinz Bay Myanmar
52 F2 Heinzenhausen Ger.
48 H3 Heist Belgium
169 M7 Heituo Shan mt. Shanxi China
38 H4 Heiwa Japan
202 I2 Hejaz reg. Saudi Arabia see Hijaz
169 O7 Hejian Hebei China
63 H9 Hejiang Sichuan China
171 H1 He Jiang r. China
169 L8 Hejiao Nei Mongol China
169 N9 Hejin Shanxi China
172 H5 Hejing Xinjiang China
57 J4 Hejnice Czech Rep.
173 F9 Heishi Beihu l. Xizang China
47 D9 Heishui Sichuan China
29 O6 Hekistan West Yorkshire, England U.K.
48 I3 Heist op. Belgium
45 G6 Heist-op-den-Berg Belgium
30 B7 Heist Cornwall, England U.K.
168 H8 Heituo Gansu China
171 J1 Heitou Shan mt. Shanxi China
166 E5 Heiwa Japan
23 O7 Hel Pol.

Column 4

20 L5 Helagsfjället mt. Sweden
179 N6 Helam Arun. Prad. India
168 I8 Helan Shan mts China
45 H6 Helchteren Belgium
49 K10 Heldburg Ger.
131 ☐7 Helden's Point St Kitts and Nevis
53 M5 Heldenstein Ger.
51 D8 Heldrungen Ger.
65 I3 Helechosa de los Montes Spain
77 O4 Helegiu Romania
179 N6 Helen Assam India
153 H6 Helen atoll Palau
124 P4 Helen, Mount NV U.S.A.
121 J8 Helena AR U.S.A.
122 H3 Helena MT U.S.A.
116 B7 Helena OH U.S.A.
175 ☐1 Helengeli i. N. Male Maldives
153 H6 Helen Reef Palau
28 F4 Helen's Bay Northern Ireland U.K.
26 G10 Helensburgh Argyll and Bute, Scotland U.K.
206 D5 Helen Springs N.T. Austr.
202 I3 Helensville North I. N.Z.
190 C7 Helez Israel
59 J2 Helfenberg Austria
118 C3 Helfenstein PA U.S.A.
23 K5 Helgasjön l. Sweden
22 G5 Helgatun Norway
48 E2 Helgoland i. Ger.
48 F2 Helgoländer Bucht g. Ger.
20 N5 Helgum Sweden
31 N2 Helhoughton Norfolk, England U.K.
48 E2 Heligoland i. Ger. see Helgoland
48 E2 Heligoland Bight g. Ger. see Helgoländer Bucht
20 C6 Hella Iceland
99 ☐1c Hell-Bourg Réunion
184 D7 Helleh r. Iran
20 N3 Hellemobotn Norway
44 J4 Hellendoorn Neth.
44 H4 Hellenthal Ger.
118 B3 Hellertown PA U.S.A.
Hellespont str. Turkey see Çanakkale Boğazı
44 F5 Hellevoetsluis Neth.
207 J8 Hellhole Gorge National Park Qld Austr.
124 L2 Hell Hole Reservoir CA U.S.A.
29 M5 Hellifield North Yorkshire, England U.K.
20 P2 Helligskogen Norway
65 P3 Hellín Spain
31 M6 Hellingly East Sussex, England U.K.
122 F4 Hells Canyon gorge ID/OR U.S.A.
130 ☐ Hellshire Hills Jamaica
18 D2 Hellsö Åland Fin.
48 H4 Hellwege Ger.
24 C8 Helm CA U.S.A.
185 J6 Helmand prov. Afgh.
185 I6 Helmand r. Afgh.
51 E10 Helmbrechts Ger.
51 D8 Helme r. Ger.
94 C5 Helmeringhausen Namibia
26 I6 Helmsdale Highland, Scotland U.K.
26 I6 Helmsdale r. Scotland U.K.
29 O5 Helmsley North Yorkshire, England U.K.
207 I3 Helmsley Aboriginal Holding res. Qld Austr.
52 H2 Helmstadt Ger.
51 D6 Helmstedt Ger.
95 ☐K2 Helodrano Antongila b. Madag.
162 F7 Helong Jilin China
36 E3 Helpe Majeure r. France
125 V2 Helper UT U.S.A.
97 O4 Helpmekaar S. Africa
31 L2 Helpringham Lincolnshire, England U.K.
49 J6 Helpsen Ger.
50 I4 Helpter Berge hills Ger.
29 L7 Helsby Cheshire, England U.K.
48 H3 Helse Ger.
22 I5 Helsingborg Sweden
22 I5 Helsinge Denmark
Helsingfors Fin. see Helsinki
22 I5 Helsingør Denmark
21 R6 Helsinki Fin.
30 B7 Helston Cornwall, England U.K.
18 G3 Helterma Estonia
52 D3 Heltersberg Ger.
79 I4 Helvacı Turkey
147 G2 Helvécia Arg.
142 C7 Helvécia Brazil
206 D5 Helvellyn hill England U.K.
29 K4 Helvellyn hill England U.K.
Helvetia country Europe see Switzerland
Helvetinjärven kansallispuisto nat. park Fin.
27 G8 Helvick Head Rep. of Ireland
44 H5 Helvoirt Neth.
36 F2 Hem France
53 I1 Hemau Ger.
31 L4 Hemel Hempstead Hertfordshire, England U.K.
49 E8 Hemer Ger.
124 P8 Hemet CA U.S.A.
120 D4 Hemingford NE U.S.A.
207 L4 Hemingford Grey Cambridgeshire, England U.K.
128 E2 Hemingway SC U.S.A.
202 I5 Hemiksem Belgium
175 ☐2 Hemmendorf Ger.
41 C10 Hemmingstedt Ger.
85 H4 Hemmoor Ger.
121 I10 Hemphill TX U.S.A.
41 F6 Hempnall Norfolk, England U.K.
48 I5 Hempstead Essex, England U.K.
119 H3 Hempstead NY U.S.A.
121 G10 Hempstead TX U.S.A.
52 F2 Hemsbach Ger.
48 H4 Hemsbünde Ger.
203 E12 Hemsby Norfolk, England U.K.
177 M7 Hemsedal Norway
177 M7 Hemsedal val. Norway
52 G2 Hemsloh Ger.
29 Q6 Hemsworth West Yorkshire, England U.K.
96 F10 Hemyock Devon, England U.K.
27 K7 Henan Qinghai China
209 H8 Henan prov. China
22 H3 Henán Sweden
202 I2 Hen and Chickens Islands North I. N.Z.
52 G5 Henares r. Spain
63 H9 Henarejos Spain
63 H9 Henares r. Spain
38 D2 Hénansal France
48 I5 Hendaye France
79 L2 Hendek Turkey
114 B7 Henderson Arg.
114 B7 Henderson KY U.S.A.
119 I2 Henderson NC U.S.A.
124 O2 Henderson NV U.S.A.
119 H2 Henderson NY U.S.A.
115 G5 Henderson TN U.S.A.
121 H5 Henderson TX U.S.A.

Column 5

213 G2 Henderson Island Antarctica
217 K7 Henderson Island Pitcairn Is
115 F8 Hendersonville NC U.S.A.
115 D7 Hendersonville TN U.S.A.
184 C6 Hendījān Iran
31 L4 Hendon Greater London, England U.K.
184 E8 Hendorābī i. Iran
44 G5 Hendrik-Ido-Ambacht Neth.
97 O1 Hendriksdal S. Africa
97 N2 Hendrina S. Africa
Henegouwen prov. Belgium see Hainaut
31 L6 Henfield West Sussex, England U.K.
184 H9 Hengām Iran
184 F8 Hengām, Jazīreh-ye i. Iran
170 C2 Hengch'un Taiwan
170 E2 Hengdian Gansu China
171 I5 Hengdong Hunan China
170 B4 Hengduan Shan mts Xizang China
44 K4 Hengelo Gelderland Neth.
44 K4 Hengelo Overijssel Neth.
44 K4 Hengevelde Neth.
70 F1 Henggart Switz.
Hengnan Hunan China see Hengyang
162 G6 Hengshan Heilong. China
171 I5 Hengshan Hunan China
169 K8 Hengshan Shaanxi China
171 I5 Heng Shan mt. Hunan China
169 N8 Hengshan Hebei China
170 G7 Hengshan Guangxi China
171 I5 Hengyang Hunan China
171 I5 Hengyang Hunan China
171 I5 Hengzhou Guangxi China see Hengxian
17 N7 Henichesk Ukr.
17 N7 Heniches'ke, Ozero l. Ukr.
36 E3 Hénin-Beaumont France
Hénin-Liétard France see Hénin-Beaumont
203 E12 Henley-in-Arden Warwickshire, England U.K.
31 I3 Henley-on-Thames Oxfordshire, England U.K.
117 J10 Henlopen, Cape DE U.S.A.
31 L3 Henlow Bedfordshire, England U.K.
164 ☐1 Henna Okinawa Japan
59 H4 Hennan Switz.
38 E6 Hennebont France
49 D9 Hennef (Sieg) Ger.
97 L3 Henneman S. Africa
16 I5 Hennenman S. Africa
127 I4 Hennetalsperre resr Ger.
53 O2 Hennezel France
51 H6 Hennickendorf Brandenburg Ger.
51 I5 Hennickendorf Brandenburg Ger.
50 H5 Hennigsdorf Berlin Ger.
117 N5 Henniker NH U.S.A.
48 H2 Hennstedt Ger.
52 C2 Hennweiler Ger.
42 J1 Henrichemont France
121 F9 Henrietta TX U.S.A.
108 D2 Henrietta Maria, Cape Ont. Can.
98 ☐3a Henri Pitts, Cape Guadalcanal
125 U4 Henrieville UT U.S.A.
209 C7 Henry r. W.A. Austr.
110 E8 Henry IL U.S.A.
117 I12 Henry, Cape NC U.S.A.
118 E2 Henry, Lake PA U.S.A.
121 H8 Henryetta OK U.S.A.
212 H2 Henry Ice Rise Antarctica
105 L3 Henry Kater, Cape Nunavut Can.
190 D3 Hermon, Mount Lebanon/Syria
54 F5 Henrykowo Pol.
55 I1 Henrykowo Pol.
125 V3 Henry Mountains UT U.S.A.
125 S3 Henrys Fork r. ID U.S.A.
111 M6 Hensall Ont. Can.
124 P8 Henshaw, Lake CA U.S.A.
200 ☐1a Henslow, Cape Guadalcanal Solomon Is
208 J4 Hensman, Mount hill W.A. Austr.
48 I3 Hensted-Ulzburg Ger.
30 H6 Henstridge Somerset, England U.K.
94 B4 Hentiesbaai Namibia
169 L3 Hentiy prov. Mongolia
164 ☐1 Hentona Okinawa Japan
158 C4 Hentona Myanmar
164 ☐1 Henza-jima i. Okinawa Japan
Heping Guizhou China see Huishui
Hepo Guangdong China see Jiexi
45 M6 Heppen Belgium
52 F7 Heppenheim (Bergstraße) Ger.
122 E4 Heppner OR U.S.A.
48 H4 Hepstedt Ger.
Heptanesus is Greece see Ionioi Nisoi
170 G8 Hepu Guangxi China
168 H8 Heqiaoyi Gansu China
170 C5 Heqing Yunnan China
169 L7 Hequ Shanxi China
Heraklion Kriti Greece see Irakleio
207 L4 Herald Cays atolls Coral Sea Is Terr. Austr.
128 E2 Hernández Arg.
202 I5 Herangi hill North I. N.Z.
185 I5 Herāt Afgh.
185 I5 Herāt prov. Afgh.
175 ☐2 Heratera i. Addu Atoll Maldives
41 D9 Hérault dept France
41 C10 Hérault r. France
85 H4 Herbagat Sudan
41 F6 Herbasse r. France
39 M6 Herbaudière, Pointe de l' pt France
207 M7 Herbert watercourse N.T. Austr.
206 D7 Herbert Downs Qld Austr.
206 D7 Herberton Qld Austr.
128 F2 Herbeumont Belgium
202 I5 Herbignac France
185 J4 Herbitzheim France
185 J4 Herbrechtingen Ger.
175 ☐2 Herbsleben Ger.
41 F9 Herbstein Ger.
85 H5 Herby Pol.
41 F6 Hercegfalva Hungary see Mezőfalva
39 M6 Hercegszántó Hungary
39 N6 Herdecke Ger.
142 D2 Herðubreið vol. Iceland
212 I2 Hercules Dome ice feature Antarctica

Column 6

45 I7 Herve Belgium
109 G2 Hervé, Lac l. Que. Can.
207 N8 Hervey Bay Qld Austr.
207 N8 Hervey Bay b. Qld Austr.
203 ☐ Hervey Island Cook Is see Manuae
44 H5 Herwijnen Neth.
52 E3 Herxheim bei Landau (Pfalz) Ger.
36 G8 Héry France
51 H7 Herzberg Brandenburg Ger.
50 E3 Herzberg Mecklenburg-Vorpommern Ger.
49 J7 Herzberg Brandenburg Ger.
49 J7 Herzberg am Harz Ger.
45 E7 Herzebrock-Clarholz Ger.
51 I6 Herzeele France
48 E5 Herzfelde Ger.
49 J6 Herzhorn Ger.
48 E5 Herzlake Ger.
190 C6 Herzliyya Israel
53 J2 Herzogenaurach Ger.
70 D1 Herzogenbuchsee Switz.
59 M3 Herzogenburg Austria
50 F4 Herzsprung Ger.
184 D7 Heşār Iran
184 H9 Heşār Iran
184 C4 Heşar Iran
45 G6 Hesbaye reg. Belgium
36 D3 Hesbaye reg. Belgium
36 E4 Hesdin France
190 D6 Heşdin France
53 J2 Heshan Guangxi China
70 D1 Heshan Guangxi China
171 J3 Heshengqiao Hubei China
184 E8 Heshniz Iran
169 K9 Heshui Gansu China
169 M8 Heshun Shanxi China
124 O7 Hespérange Lux.
124 O7 Hesperia CA U.S.A.
106 E5 Hesquiat B.C. Can.
106 C2 Hess r. Y.T. Can.
53 J2 Heßdorf Ger.
Hesse land Ger. see Hessen
110 J3 Hessel MI U.S.A.
53 J3 Hesselberg hill Ger.
22 H5 Hesselø i. Denmark
22 H5 Hessle nature res. Denmark
49 K6 Hessen Ger.
49 H9 Hessen land Ger.
53 M2 Hessenreuther und Mantler Wald park Ger.
52 E2 Heßheim Ger.
49 I9 Hessische Rhön, Naturpark nature res. Ger.
49 H10 Hessischer Spessart, Naturpark nature res. Ger.
49 I8 Hessisch Lichtenau Ger.
49 I6 Hessisch Oldendorf Ger.
106 C2 Hess Mountains Y.T. Can.
50 F1 Hestehoved hd Denmark
49 J6 Hestern (Adenbüttel) Ger.
20 J5 Hestkjølen mt. Norway
29 K7 Hestvika Norway
158 G4 Het r. Laos
124 J4 Hetch Hetchy Aqueduct canal CA U.S.A.
44 I5 Heteren Neth.
57 G5 Hetes Hungary
56 F5 Hetés hills Hungary
31 O2 Hethersett Norfolk, England U.K.
Hetian Guangdong China see Luhe
170 G8 Hetou Guangdong China
37 L5 Hettange-Grande France
49 I8 Hettenleidelheim Ger.
53 L4 Hettenshausen Ger.
52 G5 Hettingen Ger.
120 D2 Hettinger ND U.S.A.
29 M5 Hetton North Yorkshire, England U.K.
29 O4 Hetton-le-Hole Tyne and Wear, England U.K.
51 E7 Hettstedt Ger.
52 B2 Hetzerath Ger.
52 H4 Heubach Ger.
49 D7 Heubach r. Ger.
52 G2 Heuberg ridge Ger.
49 J9 Heuchelheim Ger.
36 D3 Heuchin France
49 K7 Heudeber Ger.
44 H5 Heukelum Neth.
96 I5 Heuningneskloof S. Africa
97 L3 Heuningspruit S. Africa
96 H2 Heuningvlei salt pan S. Africa
44 H5 Heusden Neth.
45 H6 Heusden Neth.
49 G10 Heusenstamm Ger.
52 I4 Heustreu Ger.
49 J10 Heuthen Ger.
117 J4 Heuvelton NY U.S.A.
56 G5 Héves Hungary
56 G5 Heves county Hungary
57 I4 Hévíz Hungary
56 F5 Hévízgyörk Hungary
56 F5 Hevlín Czech Rep.
119 G2 Hewett, West Bank sea feature North U.S.A.
116 H11 Hewitt NJ U.S.A.
58 H6 Hexham Northumberland, England U.K.
29 M4 Hexham Northumberland, England U.K.
171 L3 Hexi Anhui China
171 L3 Hexi Gansu China
96 I9 Hexrivierberg mts S. Africa
31 M5 Hextable Kent, England U.K.
49 J6 Heyang Hebei China
Nanhe
171 I3 Heyang Shaanxi China
31 M4 Heybridge Essex, England U.K.
184 H7 Heydarabad Iran
184 H7 Heydarābād Sīstān va Baluchestan Iran
65 J3 Heydon S. Africa
66 C5 Heyen Ger.
96 I7 Heygali well Eth.
49 I6 Heyen Ger.
29 L5 Heysham Lancashire, England U.K.
97 O2 Heywood Dam S. Africa
45 I6 Heythuysen Neth.
110 F9 Heyuan Guangdong China
204 D3 Heywood Vic. Austr.
29 M6 Heywood Greater Manchester, England U.K.
170 E5 Hezhang Guizhou China
170 G5 Hezhou Guangxi China
169 L9 Hezuo Gansu China
168 I9 Hezuo Gansu China
115 G13 Hialeah FL U.S.A.
120 H6 Hiawatha KS U.S.A.
186 F9 Hibābīya reg. Saudi Arabia
96 A3 Hibberdene S. Africa
110 B2 Hibbing MN U.S.A.
205 I7 Hibbs, Point Tas. Austr.
208 G2 Hibernia Reef Ashmore & Cartier Is Austr.
165 H12 Hibiki-nada b. Japan
15 ☐1 Hibiki-nada b. Japan
76 E5 Hichan China [?]
121 K5 Hickman KY U.S.A.
118 D5 Hickory NC U.S.A.
205 D6 Hickory, Point Vic. Austr.
202 M4 Hicks Bay North I. N.Z.
205 I5 Hicks Cays is Belize
111 O2 Hicks Lake Nunavut Can.
119 H3 Hicksville NY U.S.A.
116 A7 Hicksville OH U.S.A.
121 F9 Hico TX U.S.A.

166 F5 Hida-gawa r. Japan
164 T4 Hidaka Hokkaidō Japan
166 A5 Hidaka Hyōgo Japan
167 J4 Hidaka Saitama Japan
166 B8 Hidaka Wakayama Japan
164 T4 Hidaka-sammyaku mts Japan
166 F4 Hida-Kiso-gawa Quasi National Park Japan
166 E8 Hida-kōchi plat. Japan
127 J4 Hidalgo Coahuila Mex.
128 C1 Hidalgo Durango Mex.
128 G2 Hidalgo San Luis Potosí Mex.
129 H1 Hidalgo Tamaulipas Mex.
128 D2 Hidalgo Zacatecas Mex.
128 E1 Hidalgo Zacatecas Mex.
129 H5 Hidalgo state Mex.
98 □3a Hidalgo, Punta del pt Tenerife Canary Is
126 G4 Hidalgo del Parral Mex.
129 M8 Hidalgotitlán Mex.
129 K8 Hidalgo Yalalag Mex.
57 H5 Hidas Hungary
166 G3 Hida-sanmyaku mts Japan
57 K3 Hidasnémeti Hungary
49 G6 Hiddenhausen Ger.
50 H1 Hiddensee Ger.
50 H1 Hiddensee i. Ger.
207 K5 Hidden Valley Qld Austr.
190 D2 Hidrli Turkey
77 K4 Hidişelu de Sus Romania
72 C3 Hidra i. Norway
142 C2 Hidrolândia Brazil
140 C5 Hidrolina Brazil
59 K4 Hieflau Austria
63 O6 Hiendelaencina Spain
200 □5 Hienghène New Caledonia
39 J6 Hière r. France
Hierosolyma Israel/West Bank see Jerusalem
63 M7 Hierro, Cabeza de mt. Spain
42 D4 Hiersac France
20 T3 Hietaniemi Fin.
167 L1 Hieva Fin.
165 J12 Higashi-Hiroshima Japan
165 □3 Higashi-iwa i. Japan
167 J6 Higashiizu Japan
167 J3 Higashi-matsuyama Japan
167 J4 Higashimurayama Japan
164 R8 Higashine Japan
166 □1 Higashi-Onna Okinawa Japan
166 C6 Higashi-ōsaka Japan
166 F4 Higashi-shirakawa Japan
165 G13 Higashi-suidō sea chan. Japan
166 E6 Higashiura Aichi Japan
166 A6 Higashiura Hyōgo Japan
166 G2 Higashi-yama mt. Japan
66 B1 Higer, Cabo c. Spain
119 J2 Higganum CT U.S.A.
121 E7 Higgins TX U.S.A.
117 K5 Higgins Bay NY U.S.A.
110 J5 Higgins Lake MI U.S.A.
96 J4 Hige's Hope S. Africa
31 M5 Higham Kent, England U.K.
31 K3 Higham Ferrers Northamptonshire, England U.K.
30 D6 Highampton Devon, England U.K.
High Atlas mts Morocco see Haut Atlas
29 L5 High Bentham North Yorkshire, England U.K.
26 H11 High Blantyre South Lanarkshire, Scotland U.K.
30 G5 Highbridge Somerset, England U.K.
118 F3 High Bridge NJ U.S.A.
31 J5 Highclere Hampshire, England U.K.
122 D5 High Desert OR U.S.A.
Higher Bentham England U.K. see High Bentham
29 N4 High Etherley Durham, England U.K.
110 F4 High Falls Reservoir WI U.S.A.
97 O6 Highflats S. Africa
31 N4 High Garrett Essex, England U.K.
130 □ Highgate Jamaica
31 N5 High Halden Kent, England U.K.
29 P5 High Hawsker North Yorkshire, England U.K.
29 L4 High Hesket Cumbria, England U.K.
77 J4 Highiş, Vârful hill Romania
98 □ High Island H.K. China see Leung Shuen Wan Chau
121 H11 High Island TX U.S.A.
110 I4 High Island MI U.S.A.
171 □J7 High Island Reservoir H.K. China
98 □2b High Knoll hill St Helena
26 D7 Highland admin. div. Scotland U.K.
124 C1 Highland CA U.S.A.
118 B6 Highland MD U.S.A.
110 C2 Highland MN U.S.A.
119 H1 Highland NY U.S.A.
110 D6 Highland WI U.S.A.
118 C7 Highland Beach MD U.S.A.
119 H2 Highland Falls NY U.S.A.
118 F1 Highland Lake NY U.S.A.
119 G2 Highland Lakes NJ U.S.A.
115 K10 Highland Park IL U.S.A.
116 B6 Highland Park MI U.S.A.
119 G4 Highland Park NJ U.S.A.
124 M3 Highland Peak CA U.S.A.
125 R4 Highland Peak NV U.S.A.
116 H11 Highland Springs VA U.S.A.
29 M7 High Legh Cheshire, England U.K.
106 G3 High Level Alta Can.
179 K9 High Level Canal India
33 □ Highley Shropshire, England U.K.
125 Q9 Highline Canal CA U.S.A.
29 K4 High Lorton Cumbria, England U.K.
120 F3 Highmore SD U.S.A.
30 H4 Highnam Gloucestershire, England U.K.
29 N7 High Peak hills England U.K.
115 H8 High Point NC U.S.A.
118 F2 High Point NJ U.S.A.
106 G4 High Prairie Alta Can.
106 H5 High River Alta Can.
115 H12 High Rock G4 Bahama Bahamas
107 K4 Highrock Lake Man. Can.
107 J3 Highrock Lake Sask. Can.
115 G8 High Rock Lake resr NC U.S.A.
205 J10 High Rocky Point Tas. Austr.
29 M5 High Seat hill England U.K.
115 F11 High Springs FL U.S.A.
119 F4 Hightstown NJ U.S.A.
31 I4 Highworth Swindon, England U.K.
31 K4 High Wycombe Buckinghamshire, England U.K.
92 E3 Higlale well Eth.
126 F5 Higos de Abuya Mex.
65 L5 Higuera de Arjona Spain
64 H3 Higuera de la Serena Spain
64 F4 Higuera de la Sierra Spain
64 F4 Higuera de Vargas Spain
65 J4 Higuera de Zaragoza Mex.
64 E4 Higuera la Real Spain
131 □1 Higüero, Punta pt Puerto Rico
131 J8 Higuerote Venez.
67 C10 Higueruela Spain
67 D8 Higüey Dom. Rep.
131 I4 Higuey Dom. Rep.
167 K5 Hiji-gawa r. Japan
199 I3 Hihifo Tonga
20 T3 Hihnavaara Fin.
18 H1 Hiidenvesi l. Fin.
92 E3 Hiiraan admin. reg. Somalia

18 F3 Hiiumaa i. Estonia
190 E5 Hījānah, Buḥayrat al imp. l. Syria
66 E5 Hijar Spain
156 E6 Hijau, Gunung mt. Indon.
186 C2 Hijaz reg. Saudi Arabia
167 H5 Hijiri-dake mt. Japan
154 E8 Hijo Mindanao Phil.
63 O2 Hijuela r. Spain
167 I3 Hikabo-yama mt. Japan
166 I5 Hikami Japan
167 H3 Hikawa Japan
167 M4 Hiketa Japan
165 L12 Hiketa Japan
165 I13 Hikigawa Japan
166 B8 Hiki-gawa r. Japan
166 D5 Hikone Japan
165 H13 Hiko-san mt. Japan
202 I2 Hikurangi North I. N.Z.
202 M4 Hikurangi mt. North I. N.Z.
203 □4 Hikutavake Niue
191 J4 Hil Azer.
155 F7 Hila Maluku Indon.
155 B6 Hilahila Sulawesi Indon.
190 B8 Ḥilāl, Jabal hill Egypt
138 C5 Hilaricos Chile
213 K1 Hilary Coast Antarctica
49 F9 Hilbersdorf Ger.
125 S4 Hildale UT U.S.A.
49 K10 Hildburghausen Ger.
116 E8 Hilferd OH U.S.A.
127 O9 Hill Bank Belize
120 F6 Hill City KS U.S.A.
117 L5 Hill City SD U.S.A.
125 W2 Hill Creek r. UT U.S.A.
118 B7 Hillcrest Heights MD U.S.A.
49 G6 Hille Ger.
44 G4 Hillegom Neth.
205 L5 Hillerød Denmark
22 I6 Hillered Denmark
203 H8 Hillersden South I. N.Z.
49 J6 Hillerse Ger.
49 C10 Hillesheim Ger.
207 J5 Hillgrove Qld Austr.
107 I2 Hill Island Lake N.W.T. Can.
111 K4 Hillman MI U.S.A.
209 D11 Hillman, Lake salt flat W.A. Austr.
120 K6 Hillsboro IL U.S.A.
120 J6 Hillsboro MO U.S.A.
120 G2 Hillsboro ND U.S.A.
117 N5 Hillsboro NH U.S.A.
123 K10 Hillsboro NM U.S.A.
122 C4 Hillsboro OH U.S.A.
121 G9 Hillsboro TX U.S.A.
110 D6 Hillsboro WI U.S.A.
115 G12 Hillsboro Canal FL U.S.A.
131 □3 Hillsborough Grenada
27 J4 Hillsborough Northern Ireland U.K.
207 L6 Hillsborough, Cape Qld Austr.
49 J10 Hillscheid Ger.
110 J8 Hillsdale MI U.S.A.
118 F3 Hillsdale NJ U.S.A.
111 R8 Hillsgrove PA U.S.A.
206 E6 Hillside W.A. Austr.
26 □N2 Hillside Shetland, Scotland U.K.
119 G3 Hillside NJ U.S.A.
108 C3 Hillsport Ont. Can.
205 J5 Hillston N.S.W. Austr.
116 E12 Hillsville VA U.S.A.
26 □N2 Hillswick Shetland, Scotland U.K.
27 J4 Hilltown Northern Ireland U.K.
124 □F14 Hilo HI U.S.A.
35 N3 Hilperton Wiltshire, England U.K.
53 K3 Hilpoltstein Ger.
29 K5 Hilpsford Point England U.K.
37 O7 Hilsenheim France
49 F6 Hilter am Teutoburger Wald Ger.
206 D8 Hilton Qld Austr.
97 O5 Hilton S. Africa
31 I2 Hilton Derbyshire, England U.K.
116 H5 Hilton NY U.S.A.
111 K3 Hilton Beach Ont. Can.
115 G9 Hilton Head Island SC U.S.A.
53 K2 Hiltpoltstein Ger.
188 I5 Hilvan Turkey
44 H6 Hilvarenbeek Neth.
44 H5 Hilversum Neth.
52 F6 Hilzingen Ger.
186 G6 Ḥimá well Saudi Arabia
178 F4 Himachal Pradesh state India
186 E3 Ḥimá Dariyah, Jabal mt. Saudi Arabia
166 F6 Himaga-shima i. Japan
178 F3 Himalaya mts Asia
18 Q4 Himanka Fin.
190 H2 Ḥimār, Wādī al watercourse Syria/Turkey
78 A2 Himarë Albania
202 J7 Himatangi North I. N.Z.
202 J7 Himatangi Beach North I. N.Z.
178 D8 Himatnagar Gujarat India
59 N3 Himberg Austria
48 K4 Himbergen Ger.
186 D8 Himbirti Eritrea
167 G11 Hime-gawa r. Japan
165 L12 Himeji Japan
164 S7 Himekami-dake mt. Japan
74 H5 Himesháza Hungary
165 I13 Hime-shima i. Japan
97 N5 Himeville S. Africa
164 P8 Hime-zaki pt Japan
166 E2 Himi Japan
175 □1 Himmafushi i. N. Male Maldives
59 J6 Himmelberg Austria
22 F5 Himmelbjerget hill Denmark
□ Himmelpforten Ger.
186 C8 Himora Eth.
190 E4 Ḥimş Syria
190 G3 Ḥimş governorate Syria
165 H14 Hinagu Japan
154 □ Hinako i. Indon.
203 J8 Hinakura North I. N.Z.
154 D2 Hinatuan Mindanao Phil.
154 D2 Hinatuan Passage Phil.
121 I8 Hinckley Leicestershire, England U.K.
110 A2 Hinckley MN U.S.A.
117 O4 Hinckley ME U.S.A.
110 B3 Hinckley MN U.S.A.
125 T2 Hinckley UT U.S.A.
117 I6 Hinckley Reservoir NY U.S.A.
190 D9 Hind, Wādī al watercourse Saudi Arabia
91 B6 Hinda Congo
173 C12 Hindan r. India
178 F6 Hindaun Rajasthan India
50 I6 Hindenberg Ger.
29 P2 Hinderwell North Yorkshire, England U.K.

31 K5 Hindhead Surrey, England U.K.
29 L6 Hindley Greater Manchester, England U.K.
116 C11 Hindman KY U.S.A.
205 H7 Hindmarsh, Lake dry lake Vic. Austr.
179 J9 Hindola Orissa India
178 E7 Hindoli Rajasthan India
30 H5 Hindon Wiltshire, England U.K.
178 G8 Hindoria Madh. Prad. India
23 K4 Hindsen i. Sweden
22 G6 Hindsholm pen. Denmark
185 L4 Hindu Kush mts Afgh./Pak.
176 E6 Hindupur Andhra Prad. India
106 G3 Hines Creek Alta Can.
115 G10 Hinesville GA U.S.A.
178 G9 Hinganghat Mahar. India
31 N2 Hingham Norfolk, England U.K.
185 K9 Hingol Pak.
185 K9 Hingol r. Pak.
176 E3 Hingoli Mahar. India
189 L4 Hınıs Turkey
207 N7 Hinkley Cay rf Qld Austr.
118 C4 Hinks Conservation Park nature res. S.A. Austr.
204 F5 Hinks Conservation Park nature res. S.A. Austr.
20 M2 Hinnøya i. Norway
166 D5 Hino Shiga Japan
167 H3 Hino Tōkyō Japan
165 K11 Hino Tottori Japan
154 D7 Hinobaan Negros Phil.
167 J1 Hinoemata Japan
166 D3 Hino-gawa r. Japan
166 D5 Hino-gawa r. Japan
63 H9 Hinojal Spain
64 F4 Hinojales Spain
64 F5 Hinojales, Sierra de hills Spain
65 N5 Hinojares Spain
65 K3 Hinojosas de Calatrava Spain
63 O5 Hinojedo mt. Spain
147 G5 Hinojo Arg.
64 G6 Hinojos Spain
63 Q6 Hinojosa Spain
62 G7 Hinojosa de Duero Spain
66 D6 Hinojosa de Jarque Spain
65 I3 Hinojosa del Duque Spain
60 D2 Hinojosa de San Vicente Spain
165 I14 Hinokage Japan
166 B8 Hino-misaki pt Japan
165 J11 Hino-misaki pt Japan
117 M6 Hinsdale NH U.S.A.
23 M1 Hinsen i. Sweden
48 D4 Hinte Ger.
58 E4 Hinteres Sonnenwendjoch mt. Austria
51 J9 Hinterhermsdorf Ger.
49 K9 Hinternah Ger.
72 G2 Hinterrhein r. Switz.
57 H3 Hinterrhein r. Switz.
57 K3 Hinterschmiding Ger.
56 E2 Hintersee Austria
77 P3 Hlipiceni Romania
71 Q4 Hlinné Slovakia
56 E2 Hinterstoder Austria
53 O4 Hinterweidenthal Ger.
158 B6 Hinthada Myanmar
104 C4 Hinton Alta Can.
121 F8 Hinton OK U.S.A.
116 E11 Hinton WV U.S.A.
202 J4 Hinuera North I. N.Z.
167 M3 Hi-numa l. Japan
70 F1 Hinwil Switz.
43 C8 Hinx France
127 I5 Hipólito Mex.
146 D3 Hipólito Yrigoyen Arg.
58 E5 Hippach Austria
44 G3 Hippolytushoef Neth.
91 E6 Hippopotames, Réserve de nature res. Dem. Rep. Congo
91 E5 Hippopotames, Réserve de Faune des nature res. Dem. Rep. Congo
91 E5 Hippopotames de Sakania, Réserve de nature res. Dem. Rep. Congo
48 G4 Hipstedt Ger.
189 L4 Hirabit Dağ mt. Turkey
165 G13 Hirado Japan
165 G13 Hirado-shima i. Japan
30 E1 Hiraethog, Mynydd hills U.K.
87 G5 Hirafok Alg.
167 J1 Hiraga-take mt. Japan
166 C6 Hirakata Japan
179 J9 Hirakud Reservoir India
93 C5 Hiraman watercourse Kenya
212 P1 Hiram r. Japan
167 M1 Hirata Fukushima Japan
166 E5 Hirata Gifu Japan
165 J11 Hirata Shimane Japan
167 K6 Hiratsuka Japan
89 F5 Hiraya Japan
158 G4 Hirekerur Karnataka India
158 G5 Hirhi-Watta Côte d'Ivoire
158 F3 Hiriyur Karnataka India
Hîrlău Romania see Hârlău
94 E3 Hîrna Eth.
17 Q5 Hirnyk Donets'ka Oblast' Ukr.
55 M5 Hirnyk L'viv'ka Oblast' Ukr.
17 N7 Hirogami Japan
166 B7 Hirokawa Japan
167 M1 Hirono Japan
167 M4 Hiroo Japan
164 R6 Hirosaki Japan
165 K11 Hirose Japan
165 J12 Hiroshima Japan
115 G13 Hiroshima airport Japan
165 J12 Hiroshima pref. Japan
164 S8 Hirota-wan b. Japan
79 J7 Hirrlingen Ger.
53 K2 Hirschaid Ger.
53 L2 Hirschau Ger.
51 E10 Hirschberg Ger.
53 L6 Hirschberg mt. Ger.
Hirschberg Pol. see Jelenia Góra
53 N4 Hirschenstein mt. Ger.
51 I8 Hirschfeld Ger.
51 K9 Hirschfelde Ger.
79 K4 Hirschfelden Ger.
52 F3 Hirschhorn (Neckar) Ger.
22 F3 Hirsholmene nature res. Denmark
40 K1 Hirsingue France
17 O7 Hirs'k Ukr.
17 H5 Hirs'ke Ukr.
16 J5 Hirs'kyy Tikych r. Ukr.
36 H4 Hirson France
63 N7 Hîrşova Romania see Hârşova
Hirta i. Western Isles, Scotland U.K. see St Kilda
59 J6 Hirtenberg Austria
22 F3 Hirtshals Denmark
167 J5 Hiruga-take mt. Japan
49 K7 Hirschbach Ger.
30 E4 Hirwaun Rhondda Cynon Taff, Wales U.K.
49 H10 Hirzenhain Ger.
159 H9 Hirzmann Ger.
165 □2 Hisai-jima i. Japan
165 F14 Hisai Japan
189 N5 Hisar Iran
178 E3 Hisar Haryana India
79 K3 Hisarcık Turkey
78 F3 Hisarönü Turkey
188 D3 Hisarönü körfezi b. Turkey
189 L8 Ḩisb, Sha'īb watercourse Iraq
187 H7 Ḩisn al Fuqūl Yemen
185 M2 Hisor Tajik.
130 L8 Hisoak qo'riqxonasi Uzbek.
130 G3 Hispaniola i. Caribbean Sea
178 E1 Hispur Glacier Jammu and Kashmir
Hisar Haryana India see Hisar
179 J7 Hisua Bihar India
190 F4 Ḩişyah Syria
17 H4 Hisya Syria
71 I4 Hit Iraq
63 N7 Hita Spain

167 M2 Hitachi Japan
167 M3 Hitachi Japan
167 M2 Hitachi-ōta Japan
175 □2 Hitaddu Addu Atoll Maldives
175 □2 Hitaddu i. Addu Atoll Maldives
31 L4 Hitchin Hertfordshire, England U.K.
201 □3a Hitiaa Tahiti Fr. Polynesia
165 H14 Hitoyoshi Japan
29 M6 Hitra i. Norway
31 L4 Hitzacker Ger.
58 A5 Hittisau Austria
50 D4 Hitzacker Ger.
59 L5 Hitzendorf Austria
49 I5 Hitzhofen Ger.
70 E1 Hitzkirch Switz.
200 □5 Hiu i. Vanuatu
167 J2 Hiuchiga-take vol. Japan
165 K12 Hiwasa Japan
163 □3 Hiva Oa i. Fr. Polynesia
201 □3 Hiva Oa i. Fr. Polynesia
189 N4 Hixon B.C. Can.
110 C5 Hixton WI U.S.A.
55 L5 Hiyche Ukr.
190 D8 Hiyon watercourse Israel
166 C5 Hiyoshi Kyōto Japan
166 G4 Hiyoshi Nagano Japan
30 G2 Hiyoshi Japan
167 L7 Hiji-gawa r. Japan
202 H2 Hokianga Harbour North I. N.Z.
167 L7 Hōki-gawa r. Japan
202 J7 Hioki Japan
203 E9 Hokitika South I. N.Z.
162 M7 Hokkaidō i. Japan
164 T3 Hokkaidō pref. Japan
64 H3 Hökensås Sweden
23 J4 Hökensås naturreservat nature res. Sweden
203 C13 Hokonui Hills South I. N.Z.
167 M3 Hokota Japan
166 A6 Hokudan Japan
166 E4 Hokunō Japan
167 H1 Hokura-gawa r. Japan
166 E5 Hokusei Japan
22 E1 Hol Buskerud Norway
20 N2 Hol Hedmark Norway
93 C5 Hola Kenya
169 E9 Hoeyang N. Korea
51 E10 Hof Bayern Ger.
49 E9 Hof Rheinland-Pfalz Ger.
59 O4 Hof am Leithaberge Austria
58 H4 Hof bei Salzburg Austria
49 I9 Hofbieber Ger.
55 O5 Hofbieber Ger.
22 H6 Hofböke Denmark
97 O2 Hoibak S. Africa
31 M2 Holbeach England U.K.

89 F5 Hohoe Ghana
171 □J7 Ho Hok Shan H.K. China
165 H12 Hōhoku Japan
17 N3 Hoholeve Ukr.
17 K3 Hoholiv Ukr.
17 N7 Hoholivka Ukr.
168 C9 Hoh Sai Hu l. Qinghai China
48 K2 Hohwacht (Ostsee) Ger.
48 K2 Hohwachter Bucht b. Ger.
173 J9 Hoh Xil Hu salt l. Qinghai China
173 I9 Hoh Xil Shan mts China
168 F8 Hoh Yanhu salt l. Qinghai China
158 I7 Hôi An Vietnam
168 F9 Hoika Qinghai China
92 A4 Hoima Uganda
48 J3 Hoisdorf Ger.
120 F6 Hoisington KS U.S.A.
168 E8 Hoit Taria Qinghai China
56 E3 Hojagala Turkm. see Khodzha-Kala
179 N7 Hojai Assam India
57 I3 Hojambaz Turkm.
165 J13 Höjby Denmark
N. Myanmar
23 J4 Hökensås hills Sweden
22 E6 Hökerum Sweden
70 D1 Hölstein Switz.
125 U3 Holbrook AZ U.S.A.
205 I6 Holbrook N.S.W. Austr.
208 K6 Holbrook Suffolk, England U.K.
125 V7 Holbrook AZ U.S.A.
119 I3 Holbrook NY U.S.A.
120 D5 Holcombe WI U.S.A.
110 C4 Holcombe Flowage resr WI U.S.A.
107 H4 Holden Alta Can.
26 I12 Holden Lancashire, England U.K.
125 T2 Holden UT U.S.A.
121 G8 Holdenville OK U.S.A.
29 Q6 Holderness pen. England U.K.
49 E10 Holzappel Ger.
49 I7 Holzbach r. Ger.
49 I7 Holzen Ger.
52 G4 Holzgerlingen Ger.
49 E10 Holzhausen an der Haide Ger.
53 I5 Holzheim Bayern Ger.
53 J4 Holzheim Bayern Ger.
49 G10 Holzheim Hessen Ger.
49 G6 Holzkirchen Ger.
50 H5 Holzminden Ger.

14 C3 Holmön i. Sweden
20 P5 Holmsund Sweden
21 N6 Holmsveden Sweden
23 P3 Holmudden pt Gotland Sweden
16 E2 Holoby Ukr.
16 D2 Holohory Ukr.
77 K4 Holod Romania
16 C2 Holod r. Romania
55 L5 Holodowska Pol.
16 C2 Holohory hills Ukr.
16 E3 Holon Israel
190 C6 Holon Israel
94 C5 Holong Namibia
208 H2 Holothuria Banks rf W.A. Austr.
53 P2 Holoubkov Czech Rep.
17 N9 Holovanivs'k Ukr.
48 J3 Holovanivs'k Ukr.
16 D2 Hoĺovets'ko Ukr.
17 L4 Holovkivka Ukr.
16 H3 Holovyne Ukr.
207 H3 Holroyd r. Qld Austr.
209 G9 Holroyd Bluff hills W.A. Austr.
93 I3 Holsljunga Sweden
97 H3 Holste S. Africa
48 G4 Holste Ger.
22 E5 Holstebro Denmark
22 E6 Holsted Denmark
70 D1 Hölstein Switz.
115 H4 Holstein IA U.S.A.
116 B12 Holston r. TN U.S.A.
116 D12 Holston Lake TN U.S.A.
30 D6 Holsworthy Devon, England U.K.
31 O2 Holt Norfolk, England U.K.
30 H1 Holt Wiltshire, England U.K.
30 F1 Holt Wrexham, Wales U.K.
110 J7 Holt MI U.S.A.
44 J4 Holten Neth.
48 E3 Holtgast Ger.
48 E4 Holthusen Ger.
120 H6 Holton KS U.S.A.
110 H6 Holton MI U.S.A.
48 E4 Holtrop (Großefehn) Ger.
48 I2 Holtsee Ger.
125 Q9 Holtville CA U.S.A.
124 C5 Holualoa HI U.S.A.
17 O5 Holubivka Ukr.
44 J1 Holwerd Neth.
44 K2 Holwierde Neth.
27 G7 Holycross Rep. of Ireland
104 C3 Holy Cross AK U.S.A.
123 K7 Holy Cross, Mount of the CO U.S.A.
30 C1 Holyhead Isle of Anglesey, Wales U.K.
30 C1 Holyhead Bay Wales U.K.
16 D2 Holy Island England U.K.
26 F11 Holy Island Scotland U.K.
30 C1 Holy Island Wales U.K.
120 D5 Holyoke CO U.S.A.
117 M6 Holyoke MA U.S.A.
30 F1 Holywell Flintshire, Wales U.K.
27 K7 Holywood Northern Ireland U.K.
26 I12 Holywood Dumfries and Galloway, Scotland U.K.
27 K3 Holywood Northern Ireland U.K.
49 E10 Holzappel Ger.
59 K4 Holzgau Austria
49 I7 Holzdorf Ger.
52 G4 Holzgerlingen Ger.
49 E10 Holzhausen an der Haide Ger.
53 I5 Holzheim Bayern Ger.
53 J4 Holzheim Bayern Ger.
49 G10 Holzheim Hessen Ger.
49 G6 Holzkirchen Ger.
50 H5 Holzminden Ger.
49 K8 Holzthaleben Ger.
49 H7 Holzwickede Ger.
94 C5 Hom watercourse Namibia
92 B5 Homā Iran
92 B5 Homa Bay Kenya
158 C4 Homalin Myanmar
106 E5 Homathko r. B.C. Can.
51 G8 Homberg (Efze) Ger.
49 E6 Homberg (Ohm) Ger.
Homberg Japan see Honbetsu
36 E4 Hombleux France
54 M3 Hombori Mali
37 M3 Homburg-Budange France
37 M5 Hombourg-Haut France
144 D2 Homero Muerto, Salar del salt flat Arg.
49 E10 Homburg Ger.
66 G3 Homen, Cabo de pt Spain
14 L3 Home Bay Nunavut Can.
36 C3 Homécourt France
207 K5 Home Hill Qld Austr.
208 □2 Home Island Cocos Is
62 D2 Home Point North I. N.Z.
49 J9 Homberg Ger.
115 F10 Homerville GA U.S.A.
207 J6 Homestead Qld Austr.
115 G13 Homestead FL U.S.A.
120 L4 Hometown PA U.S.A.
20 K5 Hommelvik Norway
72 D2 Hommersåk Norway
176 F4 Honnabad Karnataka India
77 P4 Honcoava Romania
89 J2 Homodji well Niger
126 F6 Homoine Moz.
57 G5 Homokmégy Hungary
57 G5 Homokszentgyörgy Hungary
57 L3 Homorod r. Romania
21 R6 Homs Libya see Al Khums
17 H4 Homs Syria see Ḩimş
17 K1 Homyel' Belarus
17 K1 Homyel' Oblast admin. div. Belarus see Homyel'skaya Voblasts'
19 M9 Homyel'skaya Voblasts' admin. div. Belarus
116 D11 Honaker VA U.S.A.
188 D5 Honan prov. China see Henan
176 □F14 Honavalli Karnataka India
176 E4 Honavar Karnataka India
79 L5 Honaz Turkey
79 N5 Honaz Dağı mt. Turkey
164 S6 Honbetsu Japan
201 D10 Honbetsu Japan
93 C6 Hondeklipbaai S. Africa
17 N6 Hondo r. Moz.
128 G6 Hondo Col.
95 H2 Hondeblaf r. S. Africa
127 H6 Hondo Mex.
130 □ Hondo r. Belize/Mex.
123 L7 Hondo NM U.S.A.
121 F11 Hondo TX U.S.A.
165 H11 Hondo r. NM U.S.A.
123 L9 Hondo r. NM U.S.A.
165 □1 Hondón de las Nieves Spain
67 D11 Hondón de los Frailes Spain
66 F2 Hondschoote France
44 K2 Hondsrug reg. Neth.

Honduras to Huitzuco
275

30 A6 Honduras country Central America
26 □P9 Honduras, Gulf of Belize/Hond.
70 D4 Hône Italy
22 G1 Honefoss Norway
16 H6 Honeoye Falls NY U.S.A.
18 E1 Honesdale PA U.S.A.
29 I5 Honey Mex.
18 D4 Honey Brook PA U.S.A.
24 L1 Honey Lake CA U.S.A.
13 J3 Honfleur France
58 H4 Hông, Mouths of the Vietnam
58 H4 Hông, Sông r. Vietnam
71 J3 Hong'an Hubei China
68 H8 Hongchengzi Gansu China
63 E10 Hongch'ŏn S. Korea
69 J8 Hongde Gansu China
72 J7 Honggouzi Qinghai China
68 H8 Honggu Gansu China
71 J7 Honghai Wan b. China
70 D7 Honghe Yunnan China
71 J2 Hong He r. China
71 I4 Honghu Hubei China
71 I4 Hong Hu l. China
Hongjialou Shandong China see Licheng
70 G5 Hongjiang Hunan China
70 G5 Hongjiang Hunan China
71 □J7 Hong Kong H.K. China
71 J7 Hong Kong special admin. reg. China
71 □J7 Hong Kong Harbour sea chan. H.K. China
71 □J7 Hong Kong Island H.K. China
68 F6 Hongliu Daquan well Nei Mongol China
68 D6 Hongliuhe Gansu China
69 K7 Hongliu He r. China
72 J7 Hongliuquan Qinghai China
68 H7 Hongliuyuan Gansu China
72 L6 Hongliuyuan Gansu China
59 G9 Hông Ngư Vietnam
69 M4 Hongor Nei Mongol China
69 M4 Hongor Mongolia
71 M3 Hongqiao airport China
68 C5 Hongqicun Xinjiang China
70 B4 Hongshan Yunnan China
68 I7 Hongshansi Nei Mongol China
62 E7 Hongshi Jilin China
70 H7 Hongshui He r. China
69 L8 Hongtong Shanxi China
66 C8 Hongū Japan
09 H3 Honguedo, Détroit d' sea chan. Que. Can.
63 E8 Hongwŏn N. Korea
69 R4 Hongxing Jilin China
68 H7 Hongyashan Shuiku resr Gansu China
70 D2 Hongyuan Sichuan China
71 L2 Hongze Jiangsu China
71 L2 Hongze Hu l. China
00 □6 Honiara Guadalcanal Solomon Is
30 F6 Honiton Devon, England U.K.
67 R7 Honjō Akita Japan
67 R3 Honjo Japan
67 J3 Honjō Saitama Japan
21 Q6 Honkajoki Fin.
67 H5 Honkawane Japan
59 G10 Hon Khoai i. Vietnam
29 N6 Honley West Yorkshire, England U.K.
59 I8 Hon Lon i. Vietnam
58 G5 Hon Mê i. Vietnam
76 D5 Honnali Karnataka India
58 G5 Hon Ne i. Vietnam
20 R1 Honningsvåg Norway
24 □F13 Honoka'a HI U.S.A.
24 □E13 Honokahua HI U.S.A.
02 L4 Honokawa mt. North I. N.Z.
24 □D12 Honolulu HI U.S.A.
24 □ Honolulu County county HI U.S.A.
24 □F14 Honomū HI U.S.A.
10 H5 Honor MI U.S.A.
54 G3 Honoratka Pol.
24 □C12 Honouliuli HI U.S.A.
54 B3 Hönow Ger.
59 G10 Hon Rai i. Vietnam
63 P9 Honrubia Spain
63 M6 Honrubia de la Cuesta Spain
65 K11 Honshū i. Japan
63 P9 Hontacillas Spain
63 L6 Hontalbilla Spain
63 O9 Hontanaya Spain
43 D8 Hontanx France
57 H3 Hontianske Nemce Slovakia
63 M4 Hontoria de la Cantera Spain
63 N5 Hontoria del Pinar Spain
63 M5 Hontoria de Valdearados Spain
59 G10 Hon Tre i. Vietnam
59 H10 Hon Trung Lon i. Vietnam
59 H10 Hon Trung Nho i. Vietnam
24 □F14 Honu'apo HI U.S.A.
76 D4 Honwad Karnataka India
31 N5 Hoo Medway, England U.K.
22 D4 Hood, Mount vol. OR U.S.A.
26 C3 Hood Bay AK U.S.A.
09 E13 Hood Point W.A. Austr.
22 D4 Hood River OR U.S.A.
44 G4 Hoofddorp Neth.
48 G1 Hooge Ger.
48 G1 Hooge i. Ger.
44 F6 Hoogerheide Neth.
44 J3 Hoogersmilde Neth.
44 J3 Hoogeveen Neth.
44 K2 Hoogezand-Sappemeer Neth.
44 G5 Hooge Zwaluwe Neth.
44 K3 Hooghalen Neth.
Hooghly r. mouth India see Hugli
44 H3 Hoogkarspel Neth.
44 J5 Hoog-Keppel Neth.
44 J2 Hoogkerk Neth.
44 H4 Hoogland Neth.
45 G6 Hoogstede Ger.
45 G6 Hoogstraten Belgium
44 F5 Hoogvliet Neth.
29 P6 Hook East Riding of Yorkshire, England U.K.
31 K5 Hook Hampshire, England U.K.
21 E7 Hooker OK U.S.A.
06 C5 Hooker Creek watercourse N.T. Austr.
06 C4 Hooker Creek Aboriginal Land res. N.T. Austr.
27 I8 Hook Head Rep. of Ireland
31 J4 Hook Norton Oxfordshire, England U.K.
Hook of Holland Neth. see Hoek van Holland
07 N8 Hook Point Qld Austr.
07 L5 Hook Reef Qld Austr.
48 F3 Hooksiel Ger.
24 □D12 Ho'olehua HI U.S.A.
68 H4 Hoolt Mongolia
04 E4 Hoonah AK U.S.A.
22 C6 Hoopa Valley Indian Reservation res. CA U.S.A.
04 B3 Hooper Bay AK U.S.A.
17 I10 Hooper Island MD U.S.A.
10 G9 Hoopeston IL U.S.A.
97 J3 Hoopstad S. Africa
22 J6 Höör Sweden
44 H3 Hoorn Neth.
99 I3 Hoorn, Îles de is Wallis and Futuna Is
44 G5 Hoornaar Neth.
67 H4 Hōō-san mt. Japan
17 L6 Hoosick NY U.S.A.
25 R5 Hoover Dam AZ/NV U.S.A.
16 C8 Hoover Memorial Reservoir OH U.S.A.
68 G4 Höövör Mongolia
20 □C1 Hóp lag. Iceland
89 J3 Hopa Turkey
16 F3 Hopatcong NJ U.S.A.
18 F3 Hopatcong, Lake NJ U.S.A.
18 D1 Hop Bottom PA U.S.A.
06 F5 Hope B.C. Can.
03 H8 Hope South I. N.Z.
03 G9 Hope r. South I. N.Z.
30 F1 Hope Flintshire, Wales U.K.
21 I9 Hope AR U.S.A.
118 F3 Hope NJ U.S.A.
204 G3 Hope, Lake salt flat S.A. Austr.
209 F12 Hope, Lake salt flat W.A. Austr.
26 G6 Hope, Loch l. Scotland U.K.
104 B3 Hope, Point AK U.S.A.
130 □ Hope Bay Jamaica
109 I2 Hopedale Nfld and Lab. Can.
121 K11 Hopedale LA U.S.A.
96 C9 Hopefield S. Africa
Hopei prov. China see Hebei
127 O8 Hopelchén Mex.
26 J7 Hopeman Moray, Scotland U.K.
109 I2 Hope Mountains Nfld and Lab. Can.
20 □ Hopen i. Svalbard
Hopes Advance Bay Que. Can. see Aupaluk
109 G1 Hopes Advance, Baie b. Que. Can.
105 L3 Hopes Advance, Cap c. Que. Can.
205 I6 Hopetoun Vic. Austr.
209 F12 Hopetoun W.A. Austr.
96 I5 Hopetown S. Africa
207 J3 Hope Vale Qld Austr.
207 J3 Hope Vale Aboriginal Reserve Qld Austr.
117 N7 Hope Valley RI U.S.A.
118 F4 Hopewell NJ U.S.A.
116 H11 Hopewell VA U.S.A.
108 E1 Hopewell Islands Nunavut Can.
119 H1 Hopewell Junction NY U.S.A.
58 F5 Hopfgarten im Brixental Austria
58 G6 Hopfgarten in Defereggen Austria
125 V6 Hopi Indian Reservation res. AZ U.S.A.
158 C2 Hopin Myanmar
205 I8 Hopkins r. Vic. Austr.
209 J8 Hopkins, Lake salt flat W.A. Austr.
114 D7 Hopkinsville KY U.S.A.
119 L2 Hopkinton RI U.S.A.
124 I3 Hopland CA U.S.A.
158 C4 Hopong Myanmar
52 C2 Hoppstädten Ger.
20 S1 Hopseidet Norway
49 E6 Hopsten Ger.
31 P2 Hopton Norfolk, England U.K.
31 N3 Hopton Suffolk, England U.K.
30 G3 Hoptonheath Shropshire, England U.K.
91 B8 Hoque Angola
122 C3 Hoquiam WA U.S.A.
168 G9 Hor Qinghai China
173 E11 Hor Xizang China
16 J3 Hora Ukr.
92 D2 Hora Califo Eth.
191 I6 Horadiz Azer.
166 E4 Horado Japan
166 G6 Hōrai Japan
166 G6 Hōraiji-san hill Japan
31 M6 Horam East Sussex, England U.K.
189 K3 Horasan Turkey
56 C2 Horažďovice Czech Rep.
52 F5 Horb am Neckar Ger.
50 F1 Horbelev Denmark
31 L2 Horbling Lincolnshire, England U.K.
37 N7 Horbourg-Wihr France
58 A4 Hörbranz Austria
23 J6 Hörby Sweden
63 J5 Horcajo de las Torres Spain
63 K2 Horcajo de los Montes Spain
63 O9 Horcajo de Santiago Spain
63 J7 Horcajo Medianero Spain
126 G3 Horcasitas Mex.
63 N7 Horche Spain
146 B3 Horcón Chile
63 J3 Horcón hill Spain
129 J4 Horconcitos Mex.
144 D2 Horcones r. Arg.
22 E6 Horda Norway
22 C1 Hordaland county Norway
49 J7 Hörden Ger.
31 I6 Hordle Hampshire, England U.K.
30 D3 Horeb Ceredigion, Wales U.K.
202 H2 Horeke North I. N.Z.
77 L5 Horezu Romania
53 J5 Horgau Ger.
70 F1 Horgen Switz.
52 H6 Horgenzell Ger.
168 F2 Horgo Mongolia
76 H4 Horgoš Vojvodina, Srbija Serb. and Mont.
16 C5 Horhany mts Ukr.
168 I5 Hörh Uul mts Mongolia
77 Q5 Horia Romania
56 E1 Hořice Czech Rep.
110 F6 Horicon WI U.S.A.
167 G3 Horigane Japan
169 L6 Horinger Nei Mongol China
167 I1 Horinouchi Japan
59 O4 Horitschon Austria
168 G4 Horiult Mongolia
216 H7 Horizon Deep sea feature S. Pacific Ocean
59 J7 Horjul Slovenia
51 K8 Horka Ger.
19 N7 Horki Belarus
31 L5 Horley Surrey, England U.K.
212 O1 Horlick Mountains Antarctica
51 I7 Hörlitz Ger.
17 R5 Horlivka Ukr.
184 I7 Hormak Iran
131 □ Hormigueros Puerto Rico
63 O4 Hormilla Spain
184 G8 Hormoz i. Iran
184 F8 Hormoz, Kūh-e mt. Iran
184 G8 Hormozgan prov. Iran
184 F8 Hormūd-e Bāgh Iran
184 F8 Hormūd-e Mīr Khūnd Iran
184 G8 Hormuz, Strait of Iran/Oman
59 M2 Horn Austria
104 G2 Horn r. N.W.T. Can.
20 □B1 Horn c. Iceland
Horn, Cape Chile see Hornos, Cabo de
64 G3 Hornachos Spain
65 I5 Hornachuelos Spain
47 J4 Hornád r. Hungary/Slovakia
Hornád r. Hungary/Slovakia see Hernád
57 I2 Horna Orava park Slovakia
56 G3 Horná Potôň Slovakia
57 H3 Horná Štubňa Slovakia
20 N3 Hornavan l. Sweden
52 C3 Hornbach Ger.
49 G7 Horn-Bad Meinberg Ger.
121 I10 Hornbeck LA U.S.A.
52 E5 Hornberg Ger.
22 J3 Hornborgasjöns naturreservat nature res. Sweden
16 C6 Hornbrook CA U.S.A.
49 K6 Hornburg Ger.
29 L5 Hornby Lancashire, England U.K.
29 O7 Horncastle Lincolnshire, England U.K.
23 M1 Horndal Sweden
31 J6 Horndean Hampshire, England U.K.
Horne, Îles de is Wallis and Futuna Is see Hoorn, Îles de
48 I3 Horneburg Ger.
20 O5 Hörnefors Sweden
116 H6 Hornell NY U.S.A.
108 C3 Hornepayne Ont. Can.
119 F4 Hornerstown NJ U.S.A.
57 G3 Horné Saliby Slovakia
57 H2 Horné Srnie Slovakia
27 F2 Horn Head Rep. of Ireland
57 H2 Horní Bečva Czech Rep.
57 G2 Horní Benešov Czech Rep.
51 J10 Horní Beřkovice Czech Rep.
56 C2 Horní Bříza Czech Rep.
56 E2 Horní Cerekev Czech Rep.
56 C1 Horní Jiřetín Czech Rep.
126 E4 Hornillos Mex.
56 G2 Horní Moštěnice Czech Rep.
21 I6 Hornindal Norway
31 O2 Horning Norfolk, England U.K.
56 D3 Horní Planá Czech Rep.
51 J10 Horní Počaply Czech Rep.
52 E4 Hornisgrinde mt. Ger.
207 I1 Horn Island Qld Austr.
121 K10 Horn Island MS U.S.A.
56 B1 Horní Slavkov Czech Rep.
56 D3 Horní Stropnice Czech Rep.
94 C4 Hornkranz Namibia
53 N2 Horn Mountains N.W.T. Can.
65 N4 Hornos Spain
145 D9 Hornos, Cabo de c. Chile
145 D9 Hornos, Parque Nacional de nat. park Chile
17 K1 Hornostayivka Chernihivs'ka Oblast' Ukr.
17 M6 Hornostayivka Khersons'ka Oblast' Ukr.
17 P8 Hornostayivka Respublika Krym Ukr.
51 K7 Hornow Ger.
36 C4 Hornoy-le-Bourg France
106 D2 Horn Peak Y.T. Can.
205 M5 Hornsby N.S.W. Austr.
29 Q6 Hornsea East Riding of Yorkshire, England U.K.
21 N6 Hornslandet pen. Sweden
22 G5 Hornslet Denmark
50 E3 Hornstorf Ger.
20 □B1 Hornstrandir reg. Iceland
20 □ Hornsund inlet Svalbard
48 F1 Hörnum Ger.
57 I3 Horný Tisovník Slovakia
57 L4 Horoatu Crasnei Romania
16 E5 Horodenka Ukr.
16 F2 Horodets' Ukr.
55 M5 Horodło Pol.
17 K2 Horodnya Ukr.
16 G3 Horodnytsya Ukr.
16 F4 Horodok Khmel'nyts'ka Oblast' Ukr.
16 C4 Horodok L'vivs'ka Oblast' Ukr.
17 K4 Horodyshche Cherkas'ka Oblast' Ukr.
17 K2 Horodyshche Chernihivs'ka Oblast' Ukr.
17 S4 Horodyshche Luhans'ka Oblast' Ukr.
16 E4 Horodyshche Ternopils'ka Oblast' Ukr.
164 T2 Horokanai Japan
16 D3 Horokhiv Ukr.
17 Q4 Horokhuvatka Ukr.
51 J10 Horoměřice Czech Rep.
57 L3 Horonda Ukr.
164 S4 Horonobe Japan
172 F5 Horo Shan mts China
164 T4 Horoshiri-dake mt. Japan
164 T1 Horoshiri-yama hill Japan
56 C2 Hořovice Czech Rep.
169 Q5 Horqin Shadi reg. China
139 F5 Horqueta Para.
30 D6 Horrabridge Devon, England U.K.
50 E1 Horreby Denmark
22 I4 Horred Sweden
31 N3 Horringer Suffolk, England U.K.
209 C10 Horrocks W.A. Austr.
173 J11 Horru Xizang China
208 □2 Horsburgh Island Cocos Is
59 J3 Hörsching Austria
122 L6 Horse Creek r. WY U.S.A.
106 F4 Horsefly B.C. Can.
111 R7 Horseheads NY U.S.A.
29 N5 Horsehouse North Yorkshire, England U.K.
109 K3 Horse Islands Nfld and Lab. Can.
49 J8 Hörsel r. Ger.
27 E6 Horseleap Galway Rep. of Ireland
27 G6 Horseleap Westmeath Rep. of Ireland
22 F6 Horsens Denmark
206 E8 Horseshoe Bend N.T. Austr.
122 F5 Horseshoe Bend ID U.S.A.
125 U7 Horseshoe Reservoir AZ U.S.A.
214 H3 Horseshoe Seamounts sea feature N. Atlantic Ocean
31 O2 Horsford Norfolk, England U.K.
29 N6 Horsforth West Yorkshire, England U.K.
205 I7 Horsham Vic. Austr.
31 L5 Horsham West Sussex, England U.K.
118 E4 Horsham PA U.S.A.
16 H3 Horshchyk Ukr.
51 D6 Horsingen Ger.
48 L1 Horslunde Denmark
31 M5 Horsmonden Kent, England U.K.
56 B2 Horšovský Týn Czech Rep.
49 H10 Horst hill Ger.
45 J6 Horst Neth.
48 I3 Horst (Holstein) Ger.
31 O2 Horstead Norfolk, England U.K.
48 H4 Horstedt Ger.
49 E6 Hörstel Ger.
49 D6 Horstmar Ger.
79 J5 Horsunlu Turkey
57 I4 Hort Hungary
98 □1c Horta Faial Azores
22 G2 Horten Norway
147 G4 Hortensia Arg.
63 O6 Hortezuela Spain
63 N4 Hortigüela Spain
57 K4 Hortobágy Hungary
57 K4 Hortobágy-Berettyó canal Hungary
57 K4 Hortobágyi nat. park Hungary
104 F3 Horton r. N.W.T. Can.
31 I6 Horton Heath Hampshire, England U.K.
29 M5 Horton in Ribblesdale North Yorkshire, England U.K.
48 I1 Hørup Denmark
19 N9 Horval' Belarus
70 E1 Horw Switz.
29 L6 Horwich Greater Manchester, England U.K.
108 D3 Horwood Lake Ont. Can.
19 O8 Hory Belarus
16 F2 Horyn' r. Ukr.
55 L5 Horyniec-Zdrój Pol.
55 L6 Horyszów Pol.
166 C6 Hōryūji tourist site Japan
92 C3 Hosa'ina Eth.
52 D3 Hösbach Ger.
176 E6 Hosdurga Karnataka India
157 J3 Hose, Pegunungan mts Malaysia
51 J8 Hosena Ger.
49 H9 Hosenfeld Ger.
84 D4 Hosenofu well Libya
184 B4 Hoseynābād Iran
184 F4 Hoseyniān, Band-e mts Iran
184 C6 Hoseynīyeh Iran
185 J8 Hoshab Pak.
178 F8 Hoshangabad Madh. Prad. India
16 F3 Hoshcha Ukr.
178 E4 Hoshiarpur Punjab India
168 H2 Hōshōōt Arhangay Mongolia
168 A2 Hōshōōt Bayan-Ölgiy Mongolia
45 J8 Hosingen Lux.
153 L8 Hoskins New Britain P.N.G.
79 I2 Hoşköy Turkey
166 G6 Hosoe Japan
176 E5 Hospet Karnataka India
43 F10 Hospice de France France
Hospitalet Cataluña Spain see L'Hospitalet de l'Infant
Hospitalet Cataluña Spain see L'Hospitalet de Llobregat
20 T4 Hossa Fin.
43 B8 Hossegor France
89 I4 Hosséré Vokre mt. Cameroon
78 D4 Hossios Luckas tourist site Greece
52 G4 Hoßkirch Ger.
57 K4 Hosszúpályi Hungary
56 G4 Hosszúpereszteg Hungary
66 K4 Hostalríc Spain
Hostalrich Spain see Hostalríc
145 C9 Hoste, Isla i. Chile
43 C7 Hostens France
56 F3 Hostěradice Czech Rep.
57 H3 Hostie Slovakia
56 E1 Hostinné Czech Rep.
56 D1 Hostivice Czech Rep.
51 J10 Hoštka Czech Rep.
56 C1 Hostomice Czech Rep.
53 N2 Hostouň Czech Rep.
48 H1 Hostrupskov Denmark
176 E6 Hosur Tamil Nadu India
20 M5 Hotagen r. Sweden
Hotahudo East Timor see Hatudo
167 G3 Hotaka Japan
166 G3 Hotaka-dake mt. Japan
167 J2 Hotaka-yama mt. Japan
173 E8 Hotan Xinjiang China
172 E6 Hotan He watercourse China
96 G3 Hotazel S. Africa
119 I1 Hotchkissville CT U.S.A.
125 P3 Hot Creek r. NV U.S.A.
125 P3 Hot Creek Range mts NV U.S.A.
51 D6 Hötensleben Ger.
209 D12 Hotham r. W.A. Austr.
206 C2 Hotham, Cape N.T. Austr.
155 G5 Hoti Seram Indon.
20 N4 Hoting Sweden
59 M7 Hotinja vas Slovenia
201 □3a Hotopuu Tahiti Fr. Polynesia
121 I8 Hot Springs AR U.S.A.
120 D4 Hot Springs SD U.S.A.
122 K6 Hot Sulphur Springs CO U.S.A.
106 G1 Hottah Lake N.W.T. Can.
94 B5 Hottentots Bay Namibia
96 C9 Hottentots-Holland Nature Reserve S. Africa
94 B5 Hottentots Point Namibia
45 H8 Hotton Belgium
52 E6 Hotzenwald reg. Ger.
200 □5 Houaïlu New Caledonia
38 F7 Houat, Île d' i. France
36 E3 Houdain France
36 C6 Houdan France
37 J6 Houdelaincourt France
37 K7 Houécourt France
43 E7 Houeillès France
43 E9 Houeydets France
45 I8 Houffalize Belgium
156 □ Hougang Sing.
207 K5 Houghton r. Qld Austr.
29 L4 Houghton Cumbria, England U.K.
110 F2 Houghton MI U.S.A.
116 G6 Houghton NY U.S.A.
110 J5 Houghton Lake MI U.S.A.
110 J5 Houghton Lake l. MI U.S.A.
29 O4 Houghton le Spring Tyne and Wear, England U.K.
31 K4 Houghton Regis Bedfordshire, England U.K.
158 F4 Houie Moc, Phou mt. Laos
37 M6 Houillères de la Sarve, Canal des France
39 K3 Houlgate France
117 □R2 Houlton ME U.S.A.
169 L9 Houma Shanxi China
201 □2a Houma Tongatapu Tonga
201 □2a Houma Tonga
121 J11 Houma LA U.S.A.
201 □2a Houma Toloa pt Tongatapu Tonga
171 J7 Houmen Guangdong China
87 H2 Houmt Souk Tunisia
88 E4 Houndé Burkina
26 K11 Houndslow Scottish Borders, Scotland U.K.
36 E2 Houplines France
36 C3 Hourdel, Pointe du pt France
168 F8 Houri Qinghai China
26 E8 Hourn, Loch inlet Scotland U.K.
42 B5 Hourtin France
42 B5 Hourtin et de Carcans, Étang d' l. France
42 B5 Hourtin-Plage France
117 L6 Housatonic MA U.S.A.
119 I2 Housatonic r. CT U.S.A.
125 S2 House Range mts UT U.S.A.
29 M3 Housesteads tourist site England U.K.
106 E4 Houston B.C. Can.
118 E7 Houston DE U.S.A.
110 C6 Houston MN U.S.A.
121 J7 Houston MO U.S.A.
121 K9 Houston MS U.S.A.
121 H11 Houston TX U.S.A.
96 C10 Hout Bay S. Africa
96 C10 Hout Bay b. S. Africa
44 H4 Houten Neth.
45 H6 Houthalen Belgium
45 C7 Houthulst Belgium
96 I6 Houtkraal S. Africa
209 B10 Houtman Abrolhos is W.A. Austr.
26 J5 Houton Orkney, Scotland U.K.
21 P6 Houtskär Fin.
96 H6 Houwater S. Africa
172 H5 Houxia Xinjiang China
45 H8 Houyet Belgium
168 G8 Houzihe Qinghai China
22 G6 Hov Denmark
22 G1 Hov Norway
23 K3 Hova Sweden
168 B3 Hovd Hovd Mongolia
168 H4 Hovd Övörhangay Mongolia
168 C3 Hovd prov. Mongolia
22 E3 Hovdefjell hill Norway
22 D2 Hovden park Norway
168 C2 Hovd Gol r. Mongolia
31 L6 Hove Brighton and Hove, England U.K.
49 G7 Hövelhof Ger.
16 D5 Hoverla, Hora mt. Ukr.
31 O2 Hoveton Norfolk, England U.K.
184 C6 Hoveyzeh Iran
23 L1 Hovfjället naturreservat nature res. Sweden
29 P5 Hovingham North Yorkshire, England U.K.
110 E2 Hovland MN U.S.A.
23 L5 Hovmantorp Sweden
191 L5 Hövsan Azer.
169 K5 Hövsgöl Mongolia
168 G1 Hövsgöl prov. Mongolia
168 G1 Hövsgöl Nuur l. Mongolia
17 M4 Hovtva Ukr.
17 M4 Hovtva r. Ukr.
168 H5 Hövüün Mongolia
84 D6 Howa, Ouadi watercourse Chad/Sudan
186 E8 Howakil Bay Eritrea
186 E8 Howakil Island Eritrea
84 E5 Howar, Wadi watercourse Sudan
207 N8 Howard Qld Austr.
121 G7 Howard KS U.S.A.
120 G3 Howard SD U.S.A.
110 F5 Howard WI U.S.A.
110 I6 Howard City MI U.S.A.
118 B6 Howard County county MD U.S.A.
29 O5 Howardian Hills England U.K.
206 E2 Howard Island N.T. Austr.
107 J2 Howard Lake N.W.T. Can.
206 C2 Howard Springs N.T. Austr.
29 P6 Howden East Riding of Yorkshire, England U.K.
110 I8 Howe IN U.S.A.
205 L7 Howe, Cape Vic. Austr.
212 O1 Howe, Mount Antarctica
111 K7 Howell MI U.S.A.
26 K9 Howe of the Mearns reg. Scotland U.K.
120 D3 Howes SD U.S.A.
117 L3 Howick Que. Can.
97 O5 Howick S. Africa
204 G2 Howitt, Lake salt flat S.A. Austr.
117 □Q3 Howland ME U.S.A.
199 I1 Howland Island N. Pacific Ocean
205 K6 Howlong N.S.W. Austr.
Howrah W. Bengal India see Haora
27 J6 Howth Rep. of Ireland
184 H5 Ḥowz well Iran
184 F5 Ḥowz-e Gīvar Iran
184 G5 Ḥowz-e Khān well Iran
184 G6 Ḥowz-e Panj Iran
184 F5 Ḥowz-e Panj waterhole Iran
184 F5 Howz i-Mian i-Tak Iran
158 H6 Hô Xa Vietnam
120 E6 Hoxie KS U.S.A.
49 H7 Höxter Ger.
172 H3 Hoxtolgay Xinjiang China
172 H5 Hoxud Xinjiang China
26 J5 Hoy i. Scotland U.K.
48 H5 Hoya Ger.
167 K4 Hōya Japan
65 P3 Hoya Gonzalo Spain
21 I6 Høyanger Norway
51 J8 Hoyerswerda Ger.
29 K7 Hoylake Merseyside, England U.K.
29 O7 Hoyland South Yorkshire, England U.K.
20 L4 Høylandet Norway
111 M1 Hoyle Ont. Can.
51 D7 Hoym Ger.
63 M7 Hoyo de Manzanares Spain
168 I6 Hoyor Amt Nei Mongol China
62 G8 Hoyos Spain
63 J8 Hoyos del Espino Spain
20 T5 Höytiäinen l. Fin.
188 I4 Hozat Turkey
65 I8 Hozgarganta r. Spain
18 G8 Hozha Belarus
166 C5 Hozu-gawa r. Japan
166 E5 Hozumi Japan
158 C6 Hpa-an Myanmar
158 C5 Hpapun Myanmar
16 I5 Hrabove Ukr.
17 Q3 Hrachivka Ukr.
53 O2 Hracholusky, Vodní nádrž resr Czech Rep.
56 E1 Hradec Králové Czech Rep.
57 G2 Hradec nad Moravicí Czech Rep.
56 F2 Hradec nad Svitavou Czech Rep.
53 P2 Hrádek Czech Rep.
56 D1 Hrádek nad Nisou Czech Rep.
56 C2 Hradešice Czech Rep.
56 C1 Hradiště hill Czech Rep.
57 H3 Hradište Slovakia
17 M4 Hradyz'k Ukr.
18 L8 Hradzyanka Belarus
55 L2 Hrandzichy Belarus
56 B1 Hranice Karlovarský kraj Czech Rep.
57 G2 Hranice Olomoucký kraj Czech Rep.
17 Q6 Hranitne Donets'ka Oblast' Ukr.
16 I3 Hranitne Zhytomyrs'ka Oblast' Ukr.
57 J3 Hranovnica Slovakia
68 G4 Hrasnica Bos.-Herz.
59 L7 Hrastnik Slovenia
20 □C1 Hraun Iceland
20 □F1 Hraun slope Iceland
18 I7 Hrawzhyshki Belarus
191 F5 Hrazdan Armenia
51 J9 Hrazený hill Czech Rep.
17 L3 Hrebinka Ukr.
16 J4 Hrebinky Ukr.
71 R5 Hreljin Croatia
17 M1 Hrem''yach Ukr.
17 L6 Hreyhove Ukr.
57 J3 Hrhov Slovakia
55 L6 Hrimne Ukr.
57 I3 Hriňová Slovakia
16 H5 Hristovaia Moldova
51 I9 Hrob Czech Rep.
57 I3 Hrochoť Slovakia
56 E2 Hrochův Týnec Czech Rep.
18 G8 Hrodna Belarus
Hrodna Oblast admin. div. Belarus see Hrodzyenskaya Voblasts'
55 L2 Hrodnyendskaye Wzvyshsha hills Belarus
18 I8 Hrodzyenskaya Voblasts' admin. div. Belarus
17 N7 Hromivka Ukr.
53 O2 Hromnice Czech Rep.
57 H4 Hron r. Slovakia
57 I3 Hronec Slovakia
56 F1 Hronov Czech Rep.
57 H3 Hronský Beňadik Slovakia
56 F2 Hrotovice Czech Rep.
51 G10 Hroznětín Czech Rep.
55 L5 Hrubieszów Pol.
55 M4 Hrudky Ukr.
17 N3 Hrun' Ukr.
17 N3 Hrun' r. Ukr.
17 P4 Hrushuvakha Ukr.
59 J8 Hrušica mts Slovenia
56 F3 Hrušky Czech Rep.
57 I3 Hrusov Slovakia
56 F3 Hrušovany nad Jevišovkou Czech Rep.
59 O1 Hrušovany u Brna Czech Rep.
57 I2 Hruštín Slovakia
55 K3 Hruszniew Pol.
68 F3 Hrvatska Kostajnica Croatia
17 L2 Hryhorivka Chernihivs'ka Oblast' Ukr.
17 P5 Hryhorivka Dnipropetrovs'ka Oblast' Ukr.
17 M7 Hryhorivka Khersons'ka Oblast' Ukr.
16 F4 Hrymayliv Ukr.
16 D6 Hrynyava Ukr.
16 H4 Hryshkivtsi Ukr.
17 M8 Hryshyne Ukr.
16 G4 Hrytsiv Ukr.
158 C3 Hsenwi Myanmar
Hsiang Chang i. H.K. China see Hong Kong Island
Hsiang Kang H.K. China see Hong Kong
158 C4 Hsi-hseng Myanmar
158 D4 Hsin, Nam r. Myanmar
171 M6 Hsinchu Taiwan
171 M7 Hsinying Taiwan
158 C3 Hsipaw Myanmar
Hsi-sha Ch'un-tao is S. China Sea see Paracel Islands
171 L7 Hsiyüp'ing Yü i. Taiwan
171 M6 Hsüeh Shan mt. Taiwan
171 K6 Hua'an Fujian China
94 B4 Huab watercourse Namibia
169 N8 Huabei Pingyuan plain China
138 A2 Huacaibamba Peru
138 E3 Huacaraje Bol.
138 E5 Huacaya Bol.
171 J6 Huacheng Guangdong China
138 E3 Huachi Bol.
169 K8 Huachi Gansu China
126 E2 Huachinera Mex.
138 A2 Huacho Peru
138 B2 Huachón Peru
162 G5 Huachuan Heilong. China
125 V10 Huachuca City AZ U.S.A.
146 C2 Huaco Arg.
138 A2 Huacrachuco Peru
138 C4 Huacullani Peru
169 M6 Huade Nei Mongol China
162 E7 Huadian Jilin China
171 I7 Huadu Guangdong China
Huafeng Fujian China see Hua'an
168 E6 Huahai Gansu China
172 L7 Huahaizi Qinghai China
159 D8 Hua Hin Thai.
201 □3 Huahine i. Arch. de la Société Fr. Polynesia
169 N6 Huai'an Hebei China
171 L2 Huai'an Jiangsu China
171 K2 Huaibei Anhui China
171 J2 Huaibin Henan China
Huaicheng Guangdong China see Huaiji
162 D7 Huaidezhen Jilin China
158 G6 Huai Had National Park Thai.
171 L2 Huai He r. China
170 G5 Huaihua Hunan China
171 I7 Huaiji Guangdong China
158 D7 Huai Kha Khaeng Wildlife Reserve nature res. Thai.
169 N6 Huailai Hebei China
158 F6 Huai Luang r. Thai.
158 D5 Huai Nam Dung National Park Thai.
171 K2 Huainan Anhui China
171 K3 Huaining Anhui China
169 M7 Huairen Shanxi China
169 O6 Huairou Beijing China
159 G7 Huai Samran r. Thai.
171 J2 Huaiyang Henan China
171 L2 Huaiyin Jiangsu China
Huaiyin Jiangsu China see Huai'an
171 K2 Huaiyuan Anhui China
170 G6 Huaiyuan Guangxi China
168 I9 Huajialing Gansu China
128 B3 Huajicori Mex.
128 C4 Huajimic Mex.
129 J8 Huajuápan de León Mex.
128 G6 Huajúmbaro Mex.
155 E7 Huaki Maluku Indon.
127 J5 Hualahuises Mex.
125 S6 Hualapai Indian Reservation res. AZ U.S.A.
125 S6 Hualapai Peak AZ U.S.A.
144 D2 Hualfín Arg.
171 M6 Hualien Taiwan
138 B3 Hualla Peru
136 C6 Huallaga r. Peru
168 H8 Hualong Qinghai China
146 A5 Hualqui Chile
138 A1 Huamachuco Peru
138 B3 Huamani Peru
129 J6 Huamantla Mex.
91 B8 Huambo Angola
91 B8 Huambo prov. Angola
96 B1 Huams watercourse Namibia
129 I8 Huamuxtitlán Mex.
162 G5 Huanan Heilong. China
136 B6 Huancabamba r. Peru
145 C6 Huancache, Sierra mts Arg.
138 B3 Huancapi Peru
138 B3 Huancavelica Peru
138 B3 Huancavelica dept Peru
138 B3 Huancayo Peru
Huancheng Gansu China see Huanxian
147 F3 Huanchilla Arg.
171 J5 Huangbei Jiangxi China
168 G8 Huangcheng Gansu China
171 J2 Huangchuan Henan China
171 J3 Huanggang Hubei China
Huang Hai sea N. Pacific Ocean see Yellow Sea
169 P8 Huang He r. China
169 P8 Huanghe Kou r. mouth China
169 O7 Huanghua Hebei China
171 M2 Huangjiajian Jiangsu China
170 D5 Huanglianguan Sichuan China
169 K9 Huangling Shaanxi China
170 G9 Huangliu Hainan China
169 K9 Huanglong Shaanxi China
171 L5 Huanglonggang Fujian China
Huanglongsi Henan China see Kaifeng
171 L5 Huangmao Jian mt. Zhejiang China
171 J3 Huangmei Hubei China
162 E7 Huangnihe Jilin China
171 J3 Huangpi Hubei China
170 F5 Huangping Guizhou China
170 H8 Huangpo Guangdong China
171 L5 Huangqi Fujian China
169 M6 Huangqi Hai l. China
171 L4 Huangshan Anhui China
171 K3 Huang Shan mts Anhui China
170 D2 Huangshengguan Sichuan China
171 J3 Huangshi Hubei China
168 H8 Huang Shui r. China
169 J8 Huangtu Gaoyuan plat. China
147 G5 Huanguelén Arg.
169 Q8 Huangxian Shandong China
171 M4 Huangyan Zhejiang China
168 H8 Huangyangzhen Gansu China
168 G8 Huangyuan Qinghai China
168 G8 Huangzhong Qinghai China
Huangzhou Hubei China see Huanggang
170 D6 Huaning Yunnan China
168 D6 Huaniushan Gansu China
170 G6 Huanjiang Guangxi China
169 J8 Huan Jiang r. China
129 I9 Huanjintepec Mex.
147 G2 Huanqueros Arg.
163 D8 Huanren Liaoning China
138 B3 Huanta Peru
169 P8 Huantai Shandong China
138 A2 Huánuco Peru
138 A2 Huánuco dept Peru
138 B3 Huanuhuanu Peru
138 D4 Huanuni Bol.
128 E4 Huanusco Mex.
169 J8 Huanxian Gansu China
170 C5 Huaping Yunnan China
171 N6 Huap'ing Yü i. Taiwan
129 I7 Huaquechula Mex.
138 D4 Huar Bol.
138 A2 Huaral Peru
138 A2 Huaráz Peru
146 B6 Huaren Chenque Arg.
138 A2 Huari Peru
138 A2 Huariaca Peru
136 B6 Huarmaca Peru
138 A2 Huarmey Peru
138 A3 Huarochiri Peru
138 A2 Huaron Peru
171 I4 Huarong Hunan China
Huarte-Araquil Spain see Uharte-Arakil
136 B5 Huasaga r. Peru
138 A2 Huascarán, Parque Nacional nat. park Peru
144 C3 Huasco Chile
169 L9 Hua Shan mt. Shaanxi China
169 N6 Huashaoying Hebei China
168 F9 Huashixia Qinghai China
Huashugou Gansu China see Jingtieshan
126 E4 Huatabampo Mex.
169 Q6 Huatong Liaoning China
129 K6 Huatusco Mex.
129 I5 Huauchinango Mex.
138 A2 Huauru, Islas de is Peru
129 K7 Huautla Mex.
Huaxian Guangdong China see Huadu
169 N9 Huaxian Henan China
169 K9 Huaxian Shaanxi China
129 I5 Huayacocotla Mex.
Huayang Anhui China see Jixi
138 A2 Huaylas Peru
128 C4 Huaynamota Mex.
170 G4 Huayuan Hunan China
158 E4 Huayxay Laos
168 G7 Huazhaizi Gansu China
170 H8 Huazhou Guangdong China
129 J9 Huazolotitlán Mex.
106 B2 Hubbard, Mount Can./U.S.A.
109 H1 Hubbard, Pointe pt Que. Can.
111 K5 Hubbard Lake MI U.S.A.
107 M3 Hubbart Point Man. Can.
171 I3 Hubei prov. China
176 D5 Hubli Karnataka India
57 I2 Hubová Slovakia
55 M5 Hubyn Ukr.
17 O5 Hubynykha Ukr.
147 E5 Hucal Arg.
163 E8 Huch'ang N. Korea
49 B8 Hückelhoven Ger.
49 D8 Hückeswagen Ger.
29 O7 Hucknall Nottinghamshire, England U.K.
36 C2 Hucqueliers France
55 L5 Huczwa r. Pol.
85 G4 Ḥuḍayn, Wādī watercourse Egypt
186 D2 Ḥuḍb Ḥumar mts Saudi Arabia
29 N6 Huddersfield West Yorkshire, England U.K.
49 F5 Hude Ger.
48 F4 Hude (Oldenburg) Ger.
169 Q2 Huder Nei Mongol China
77 O2 Hudeşti Romania
175 □1 Hudhuveli i. N. Male Maldives
21 N6 Hudiksvall Sweden
117 N6 Hudson MA U.S.A.
117 I10 Hudson MD U.S.A.
117 □Q3 Hudson ME U.S.A.
111 J8 Hudson MI U.S.A.
117 N6 Hudson NH U.S.A.
117 L6 Hudson NY U.S.A.
110 B5 Hudson WI U.S.A.
117 L8 Hudson r. NY U.S.A.
Hudson, Baie d' sea Can. see Hudson Bay
145 B7 Hudson, Cerro vol. Chile
Hudson, Détroit d' str. Nunavut/Que. Can. see Hudson Strait
121 H7 Hudson, Lake OK U.S.A.
107 K4 Hudson Bay Sask. Can.
105 J4 Hudson Bay sea Can.
119 G3 Hudson County county NJ U.S.A.
117 L5 Hudson Falls NY U.S.A.
Hudson Island Tuvalu see Nanumanga
105 P2 Hudson Land reg. Greenland
212 R2 Hudson Mountains Antarctica
106 F3 Hudson's Hope B.C. Can.
105 K3 Hudson Strait Nunavut/Que. Can.
158 H6 Huê Vietnam
62 H7 Huebra r. Spain
63 R5 Huecha r. Spain
145 B6 Huechucuicui, Punta pt Chile
65 N7 Huécija Spain
77 L4 Huedin Romania
127 M10 Huehuetán Mex.
127 N10 Huehuetenango Guat.
129 I7 Huehuetlán Mex.
128 B1 Huehueto, Cerro mt. Mex.
129 I6 Huejotzingo Mex.
128 D3 Huejúcar Mex.
128 D3 Huejuqilla Mex.
129 I4 Huejutla Mex.
65 M6 Huélago Spain
38 D5 Huelgoat France
65 M5 Huelma Spain
64 F6 Huelva Spain
64 F5 Huelva prov. Spain
64 G6 Huelva r. Spain
63 O8 Huelves Spain
65 N6 Huéneja Spain
146 B2 Huentelauquén Chile
126 D3 Huépac Mex.
146 B5 Huepil Chile
146 A5 Huequén Chile
65 O7 Huércal de Almería Spain
65 P6 Huércal-Overa Spain
63 O4 Huércanos Spain
123 L7 Huerfano r. CO U.S.A.
63 Q8 Huérguina Spain
63 M3 Huérmeces Spain
63 N5 Huerta del Rey Spain
63 M9 Huerta de Valdecarábanos Spain
63 P7 Huertahernando Spain
128 F1 Huertecillas Mex.
66 E4 Huerto Spain
66 D4 Huerva r. Spain
65 M5 Huesa Spain
66 D5 Huesa del Común Spain
66 E3 Huesca Spain
66 E3 Huesca prov. Spain
65 N5 Huéscar Spain
128 G7 Huétamo Mex.
63 O8 Huete Spain
65 K6 Huétor-Tájar Spain
146 A6 Hueva Toltén Chile
129 H8 Hueycantenango Mex.
129 I6 Hueyotlipan Mex.
115 D9 Hueytown AL U.S.A.
64 H5 Huezna r. Spain
64 H5 Huezna, Embalse de resr Spain
52 E6 Hüfingen Ger.
22 B1 Huftarøy i. Norway
90 E2 Hugeilig I. Sudan
29 P6 Huggate East Riding of Yorkshire, England U.K.
206 E8 Hugh watercourse N.T. Austr.
207 J6 Hughenden Qld Austr.
147 G3 Hughes Arg.
204 B4 Hughes S.A. Austr.
107 K3 Hughes r. Man. Can.
212 T2 Hughes Bay Antarctica
116 I10 Hughesville MD U.S.A.
111 R8 Hughesville PA U.S.A.
124 L4 Hughson CA U.S.A.
30 □ Hugh Town Isles of Scilly, England U.K.
53 K6 Huglfing Ger.
179 K9 Hugli r. mouth India
120 D6 Hugo CO U.S.A.
121 H8 Hugo OK U.S.A.
121 E7 Hugoton KS U.S.A.
57 I3 Hugyag Hungary
Huhehot Nei Mongol China see Hohhot
Huhhot Nei Mongol China see Hohhot
137 E3 Huhucunya Venez.
97 I2 Huhudi S. Africa
20 U5 Huhus Fin.
171 L6 Hui'an Fujian China
168 J8 Hui'anpu Ningxia China
202 K5 Huiarau Range mts North I. N.Z.
94 C5 Huib-Hoch Plateau Namibia
171 J6 Huichang Jiangxi China
129 H5 Huichapán Mex.
Huicheng Guangdong China see Huilai
163 E8 Huich'ŏn N. Korea
171 J7 Huidong Guangdong China
170 D5 Huidong Sichuan China
162 E7 Huifa He r. China
169 P2 Huihe Nei Mongol China
45 F6 Huijbergen Neth.
171 J2 Huiji He r. China
91 B8 Huíla Angola
91 B8 Huíla prov. Angola
136 C4 Huila dept Col.
136 C4 Huila, Nevado de vol. Col.
171 K7 Huilai Guangdong China
91 B8 Huíla Plateau Angola
170 D5 Huili Sichuan China
128 F6 Huimangaro Mex.
127 M9 Huimanguillo Mex.
128 G5 Huimilpan Mex.
169 O8 Huimin Shandong China
138 C4 Huiñaimarca, Lago de l. Bol./Peru
162 E7 Huinan Jilin China
Huinan Shanghai China see Nanhui
146 E4 Huinca Renancó Arg.
168 I9 Huining Gansu China
168 J7 Huinong Ningxia China
53 J4 Huisheim Ger.
30 G5 Huish Episcopi Somerset, England U.K.
Huishi Gansu China see Huining
170 F5 Huishui Guizhou China
26 B7 Huisinis Western Isles, Scotland U.K.
39 L5 Huisne r. France
39 N6 Huisseau-sur-Cosson France
44 I5 Huissen Neth.
168 B9 Huiten Nur l. China
170 G5 Huitong Hunan China
21 Q6 Huittinen Fin.
127 M9 Huitupan Mex.
128 D4 Huitzila Mex.
129 K8 Huitzo Mex.
129 H7 Huitzuco Mex.

Column 1

170 F2 Huixian Gansu China
169 M9 Huixian Henan China
127 M10 Huixtla Mex.
175 D5 Huize Yunnan China
44 H4 Huizen Neth.
171 J7 Huizhou Guangdong China
168 G2 Hujirt Arhangay Mongolia
168 H3 Hujirt Övörhangay Mongolia
168 I3 Hujirt Töv Mongolia
186 E3 Hujr Saudi Arabia
202 J7 Hukanui North I. N.Z.
203 F9 Hukanui South I. N.Z.
158 C1 Hukawng Valley Myanmar
171 K4 Hukou Jiangxi China
94 D4 Hukuntsi Botswana
162 E6 Hulan Heilong. China
169 R3 Hulan Ergi Heilong. China
162 E6 Hulan He r. Heilong. China
186 E2 Hulayfah Saudi Arabia
190 G4 Hulayhilah well Syria
110 I3 Hulbert MI U.S.A.
110 I3 Hulbert Lake MI U.S.A.
116 B12 Hulen KY U.S.A.
184 B5 Hulilan Iran
162 H6 Hulin Heilong. China
56 G2 Hulín Czech Rep.
169 Q4 Hulingol Nei Mongol China
169 S4 Hulin He r. China
108 F4 Hull Que. Can.
 Hull Kingston upon Hull, England U.K. see Kingston upon Hull
117 O6 Hull MA U.S.A.
30 H4 Hullavington Wiltshire, England U.K.
31 N4 Hullbridge Essex, England U.K.
49 G6 Hüllhorst Ger.
 Hull Island Phoenix Is Kiribati see Orona
18 G3 Hullo Estonia
45 I7 Hulsberg Neth.
49 H6 Hülsede Ger.
45 G6 Hulshout Belgium
45 F6 Hulst Neth.
23 M5 Hulterstad Öland Sweden
23 L4 Hultsfred Sweden
169 Q6 Huludao Liaoning China
169 K9 Hulu He r. China
173 J9 Hulu Hu salt l. China
175 □1 Huluk i. N. Male Maldives
 Hulumeedhoo i. Addu Atoll Maldives see Midu
169 P2 Hulun Buir Nei Mongol China
169 O2 Hulun Nur l. China
85 F2 Hulwan Egypt
 Hulwan Egypt see Ḩulwān
17 P6 Hulyaypole Ukr.
162 E3 Huma Heilong. China
131 □1 Humacao Puerto Rico
162 E3 Huma He r. Heilong. China
144 D1 Humahuaca Arg.
138 D2 Humaitá Brazil
139 E1 Humaitá Brazil
139 F6 Humaitá Para.
63 N7 Humanes de Mohernando Spain
97 I10 Humansdorp S. Africa
138 B3 Humay Peru
187 L4 Humaym well U.A.E.
186 G3 Humayyān, Jabal hill Saudi Arabia
91 B9 Humbe Angola
169 M8 Humbe, Serra do mts Angola
29 R6 Humber, Mouth of the England U.K.
29 Q6 Humberside International airport England U.K.
29 Q6 Humberston North East Lincolnshire, England U.K.
138 C5 Humberstone Chile
140 E2 Humberto de Campos Brazil
29 L2 Humbie East Lothian, Scotland U.K.
48 K1 Humble Denmark
147 G2 Humboldt Arg.
107 J4 Humboldt Sask. Can.
125 T7 Humboldt AZ U.S.A.
120 H5 Humboldt NE U.S.A.
124 N1 Humboldt NV U.S.A.
118 C3 Humboldt PA U.S.A.
121 K8 Humboldt TN U.S.A.
124 N1 Humboldt NV U.S.A.
200 □5 Humboldt, Mont mt. New Caledonia
122 B6 Humboldt Bay CA U.S.A.
124 N1 Humboldt Lake NV U.S.A.
203 C11 Humboldt Mountains South I. N.Z.
124 N1 Humboldt Range mts NV U.S.A.
124 O2 Humbolt Salt Marsh NV U.S.A.
207 J9 Humeburn Qld Austr.
147 G5 Humedà plain Arg.
71 Q3 Hu Men sea chan. China
57 G2 Humenec hill Czech Rep.
57 K3 Humenné Slovakia
205 K6 Hume Reservoir N.S.W. Austr.
37 J6 Humes-Jorquenay France
61 J6 Humilladero Spain
68 F3 Humina reg. Bos.-Herz.
68 F3 Humka, Gora hill Croatia
23 M4 Hummeln l. Sweden
44 J4 Hummelo Neth.
118 B4 Hummelstown PA U.S.A.
125 U6 Humphreys Peak AZ U.S.A.
56 E2 Humpolec Czech Rep.
21 Q6 Humppila Fin.
206 C2 Humpty Doo N.T. Austr.
29 M3 Humshaugh Northumberland, England U.K.
84 B2 Hūn Libya
20 □C1 Húnaflói b. Iceland
171 H5 Hunan prov. China
162 C1 Hunchun Jilin China
162 G7 Hunchun He r. China
56 H2 Huncovce Slovakia
51 F7 Hundeluft Ger.
53 N4 Hunderdorf Ger.
22 H6 Hundested Denmark
185 D6 Hundewali Pak.
51 D6 Hundisburg Ger.
30 C4 Hundleton Pembrokeshire, Wales U.K.
21 J6 Hundorp Norway
116 E9 Hundred WV U.S.A.
51 G9 Hundshübel Ger.
53 J5 Hundsheim Denmark
111 □ Hundstein mt. Austria
77 K5 Hunedoara Romania
49 I9 Hünfeld Ger.
49 F10 Hünfelden-Kirberg Ger.
201 M4 Hunga i. Vava'u Gp Tonga
79 H4 Hunga Ha'apai i. Tonga
201 □2 Hunga Tonga i. Tonga
49 G10 Hungen Ger.
53 J4 Hungerberg hill Ger.
205 J3 Hungerford Qld Austr.
31 I5 Hungerford West Berkshire, England U.K.
171 □J7 Hung Fa Leng hill H.K. China
168 C2 Hüngiy Gol r. Mongolia
163 F9 Hüngnam N. Korea
115 □1 Hungry Bay Bermuda
27 C6 Hungry Hill Rep. of Ireland
122 H2 Hungry Horse Reservoir MT U.S.A.
171 □J7 Hung Shui Kiu H.K. China
91 C8 Hungu Angola
176 H4 Hungund Karnataka India
158 H4 Hung Yên Vietnam
169 R6 Hun He r. China

Column 2

26 D7 Hunish, Rubha pt Scotland U.K.
96 D6 Hunissout Pan salt pan S. Africa
163 D8 Hun Jiang r. China
29 Q5 Hunmanby North Yorkshire, England U.K.
22 H3 Hunnebostrand Sweden
45 I6 Hunsel Neth.
44 J2 Hunsingo reg. Neth.
96 B3 Huns Mountains Namibia
37 O6 Hunspach France
31 M2 Hunstanton Norfolk, England U.K.
176 E6 Hunsur Karnataka India
111 M1 Hunta Ont. Can.
49 F4 Hunte r. Ger.
147 G4 Hunter r. Arg.
205 M5 Hunter r. N.S.W. Austr.
203 F11 Hunter r. South I. N.Z.
203 D11 Hunter r. South I. N.Z.
204 □1 Hunter, Point c. Norfolk I.
118 F3 Hunterdon County county NJ U.S.A.
179 J7 Hunterganj Jharkhand India
205 J9 Hunter Island Tas. Austr.
106 D5 Hunter Island B.C. Can.
199 H4 Hunter Island S. Pacific Ocean
205 J9 Hunter Islands Tas. Austr.
203 B12 Hunter Mountains South I. N.Z.
158 A5 Hunter's Bay Myanmar
26 G11 Hunter's Quay Argyll and Bute, Scotland U.K.
118 A4 Hunters Run PA U.S.A.
117 K3 Huntingdon Que. Can.
31 L3 Huntingdon Cambridgeshire, England U.K.
116 H8 Huntingdon TN U.S.A.
121 H7 Huntingdon TN U.S.A.
118 E5 Huntington IN U.S.A.
122 F4 Huntington OR U.S.A.
125 V2 Huntington UT U.S.A.
116 C10 Huntington WV U.S.A.
124 N8 Huntington Beach CA U.S.A.
125 □1 Huntington Creek r. NV U.S.A.
119 I3 Huntington Station NY U.S.A.
58 H5 Huntsen Ger.
202 J4 Huntly North I. N.Z.
26 G11 Huntly Aberdeenshire, Scotland U.K.
122 K4 Hunt Mountain WY U.S.A.
204 F3 Hunt Peninsula S.A. Austr.
108 E4 Huntsville Ont. Can.
115 D8 Huntsville AL U.S.A.
121 I7 Huntsville AR U.S.A.
120 I6 Huntsville MO U.S.A.
121 H10 Huntsville TX U.S.A.
85 G2 Hunūd, Kathib al des. Egypt
190 A8 Hunūd, Kathib al hill Egypt
127 O7 Hunucmá Mex.
57 J5 Hunyani Hungary
 Hunyani r. Moz./Zimbabwe see Manyame
169 M7 Huyuan Shanxi China
178 E1 Hunza Jammu and Kashmir
178 E1 Hunza r. Pak.
185 P4 Hunza r. Pak.
44 K2 Hunze r. Neth.
169 M9 Huocheng Xinjiang China
 Huoer Xizang China see Hor
169 M9 Huojia Henan China
162 D4 Huolongmen Heilong. China
 Huolu Hebei China see Luquan
200 □5 Huon i. New Caledonia
158 G5 Huong Khê Vietnam
153 K8 Huon Peninsula P.N.G.
205 K10 Huonville Tas. Austr.
171 K2 Huoqiu Anhui China
171 K3 Huoshan Anhui China
 Huoshao Tao i. Taiwan see Lü Tao
94 B4 Huoshaowo waterhole Namibia
171 H4 Huoxian Shanxi China
169 L8 Huozhou Shanxi China
17 N4 Hupalivka Ukr.
 Hupeh prov. China see Hubei
49 J8 Hüpstedt Ger.
109 G2 Hurault, Lac l. Que. Can.
190 B8 Ḩuraydīn, Wādī watercourse Egypt
186 H3 Ḩuraymilā' Saudi Arabia
187 H4 Ḩurayslān reg. Saudi Arabia
57 H4 Hurbanovo Slovakia
108 D4 Hurd, Cape Ont. Can.
22 H1 Hurdalssjøen l. Norway
92 F2 Hurdiyo Somalia
204 □3 Hurd Point S. Pacific Ocean
169 O5 Hure Nei Mongol China
168 H3 Hüremt Mongolia
168 H3 Hüremt Mongolia
36 C6 Hure Qi Nei Mongol China
92 C4 Huri mt. Kenya
40 A4 Huri France
17 M5 Hurivka Ukr.
110 F1 Hurkett Ont. Can.
168 E8 Hurleg Qinghai China
168 E8 Hurleg Hu l. Qinghai China
27 E7 Hurler's Cross Rep. of Ireland
117 K7 Hurley NY U.S.A.
110 I3 Hurley WI U.S.A.
110 J10 Hurlock MD U.S.A.
209 E12 Hurlstone, Lake salt flat W.A. Austr.
185 K7 Hurmagai Pak.
124 L5 Huron CA U.S.A.
116 C7 Huron OH U.S.A.
120 F3 Huron SD U.S.A.
111 L5 Huron, Lake Can./U.S.A.
110 I4 Huron Bay MI U.S.A.
110 J3 Huron Beach MI U.S.A.
110 D1 Huronian Ont. Can.
110 G3 Huron Mountains hills MI U.S.A.
125 S4 Hurricane UT U.S.A.
130 D2 Hurricane Flats sea feature Bahamas
31 J5 Hursley Hampshire, England U.K.
31 J5 Hurstbourne Tarrant Hampshire, England U.K.
31 M5 Hurst Green East Sussex, England U.K.
31 L6 Hurstpierpoint West Sussex, England U.K.
146 B2 Hurtado Chile
146 B2 Hurtado r. Chile
48 F5 Hurup Denmark
49 C9 Hürth Ger.
115 E9 Hurtsboro AL U.S.A.
157 J4 Hurung, Gunung mt. Indon.
203 H9 Hurunui r. South I. N.Z.
48 I1 Hürup Ger.
29 N5 Hurworth-on-Tees Darlington, England U.K.
29 N5 Husain Nika Pak.
57 K6 Husasău de Tinca Romania
20 □E1 Húsavík Vestfirðir Iceland
180 □U1 Húsavík reg. Iceland
48 I1 Husby Ger.
21 M3 Husby Sweden
77 M4 Huşi Romania
85 G6 Husheib Sudan
26 E6 Husinec Czech Rep.
85 G6 Huşi Sudan
23 K4 Huskvarna Sweden
104 C3 Huslia AK U.S.A.

Column 3

187 H7 Husn Āl 'Abr Yemen
22 B2 Husnes Norway
2 J1 Husøy i. Norway
179 J7 Hussainabad Jharkhand India
56 F3 Hustopeče Czech Rep.
48 H5 Husum Niedersachsen Ger.
48 H2 Husum Schleswig-Holstein Ger.
20 O5 Husum Sweden
145 □ Husvik S. Georgia
16 F4 Husyatyn Ukr.
17 Q4 Husynka Ukr.
55 K3 Huszlew Pol.
55 I4 Huta Pol.
168 H7 Hutag Mongolia
184 G6 Hūtak Iran
156 C4 Hutanopan Sumatera Indon.
179 J8 Hutar Jharkhand India
186 E2 Hutaym, Ḩarrat lava field Saudi Arabia
96 H7 Hutchinson S. Africa
120 G6 Hutchinson KS U.S.A.
120 H3 Hutchinson MN U.S.A.
125 U7 Hutch Mountain AZ U.S.A.
186 F7 Hūth Yemen
158 D6 Huti Myanmar
162 H6 Hutou Heilong. China
205 I6 Huttah Kulkyne National Park N.S.W. Austr.
58 H5 Hüttau Austria
59 K6 Hüttenberg Austria
50 G3 Hüttenberg Ger.
49 G9 Hüttenberg-Hochheim Ger.
44 A1 Hüttenbusch Ger.
50 G4 Hütten Ger.
53 I4 Hüttlingen Ger.
29 R7 Huttoft Lincolnshire, England U.K.
30 O5 Hutton North Somerset, England U.K.
207 L8 Hutton, Mount hill Qld Austr.
29 Q6 Hutton Cranswick East Riding of Yorkshire, England U.K.
209 G8 Hutton Range hills W.A. Austr.
29 O4 Hutton Rudby North Yorkshire, England U.K.
58 H5 Hüttschlag Austria
70 D1 Huttwil Switz.
172 J4 Hutubi Xinjiang China
172 H4 Hutuo He r. China
169 O7 Hutuo He r. China
17 O3 Huty Ukr.
48 J4 Hützel Ger.
175 D11 Huvadhu Atoll Maldives
185 I8 Hūvār Iran
48 E5 Hüven Ger.
187 J3 Huwār i. The Gulf
186 G5 Huwaynat des. Saudi Arabia
188 H9 Huwayrat reg. Saudi Arabia
55 K6 Huwniki Pol.
171 J5 Huxi Jiangxi China
169 K9 Huxian Shaanxi China
208 I5 Huxley, Mount hill W.A. Austr.
203 D11 Huxley, Mount South I. N.Z.
45 H7 Huy Belgium
16 H3 Huyba r. Ukr.
29 L7 Huyton Merseyside, England U.K.
162 C3 Huyuan Heilong. China
16 H3 Huya r. Ukr.
171 M4 Huzhen Zhejiang China
162 C3 Huzhong Heilong. China
171 M3 Huzhou Zhejiang China
168 G8 Huzhu Qinghai China
176 F4 Huzurnagar Andhra Prad. India
20 □F1 Hvalnes Iceland
20 □1 Hvalfjörður inlet Iceland
20 □E1 Hvannadalshnúkur vol. Iceland
68 F4 Hvar Croatia
68 F4 Hvar i. Croatia
17 O5 Hvardiys'ke Dnipropetrovs'ka Oblast' Ukr.
17 N8 Hvardiys'ke Respublika Krym Ukr.
68 F4 Hvarski Kanal sea chan. Croatia
20 □C1 Hveragerði Iceland
22 E5 Hvide Sande Denmark
20 □D1 Hvítárvatn l. Iceland
22 F7 Hvittingfoss Norway
17 M2 Hvizdivtsi Ukr.
94 E3 Hwange Zimbabwe
94 E3 Hwange National Park Zimbabwe
 Hwang Ho r. China see Huang He
163 D9 Hwangju N. Korea
95 F3 Hwedza Zimbabwe
137 M4 Hwlffordd Pembrokeshire, Wales U.K. see Haverfordwest
166 C5 Hyakuri-take hill Japan
117 O7 Hyannis MA U.S.A.
120 E4 Hyannis NE U.S.A.
168 C2 Hyargas Nuur salt l. Mongolia
118 B7 Hyattsville MD U.S.A.
106 F12 Hydaburg AK U.S.A.
106 C4 Hyder AK U.S.A.
29 M7 Hyde Greater Manchester, England U.K.
209 E12 Hyden W.A. Austr.
116 B11 Hyden KY U.S.A.
117 M4 Hyde Park VT U.S.A.
106 D4 Hyder AK U.S.A.
125 K7 Hyder AZ U.S.A.
176 F3 Hyderabad Andhra Prad. India
185 M9 Hyderabad Pak.
41 I10 Hyères France
41 I11 Hyères, Îles d' is France
41 I10 Hyères, Rade d' b. France
19 K8 Hyermanichy Belarus
163 F8 Hyesan N. Korea
205 K8 Hyland, Mount N.S.W. Austr.
206 B2 Hyland Bay N.T. Austr.
106 D3 Hyland Post B.C. Can.
31 J5 Hylke l. Denmark
49 I8 Hylestad Norway
22 J4 Hyltebruk Sweden
138 D4 Hymont France
116 G9 Hyndman PA U.S.A.
122 H4 Hyndman Peak ID U.S.A.
26 C10 Hynish Argyll and Bute, Scotland U.K.
165 L11 Hyōgo pref. Japan
164 S8 Hyōno-sen mt. Japan
 Hyrra Banda C.A.R. see Ira Banda
77 H4 Hyrynsalmi Fin.
122 K3 Hysham MT U.S.A.
31 L6 Hythe Hampshire, England U.K.
31 N5 Hythe Kent, England U.K.
165 H4 Hyūga Japan
55 K6 Hyźne Pol.

Column 4

142 C4 Iacanga Brazil
140 D5 Iaciara Brazil
138 C2 Iaco r. Brazil
77 M4 Iacobeni Sibiu Romania
77 N3 Iacobeni Suceava Romania
142 C4 Iacri Brazil
142 C4 Iaçu Brazil
116 D11 Iaeger WV U.S.A.
121 H2 Iago TX U.S.A.
77 N3 Ialomiţa r. Romania
77 M4 Ialomiţa r. Romania
77 P6 Ialomiţei, Balta marsh Romania
16 H7 Ialoveni Moldova
77 P5 Ianca Romania
77 M6 Iancu Jianu Romania
191 D3 İanţı Georgia
143 F3 Iapu Brazil
77 L4 Iara r. Romania
137 F4 Iarauarune, Serra mts Brazil
27 D6 Iar Connaught reg. Rep. of Ireland
16 H7 Iargara Moldova
77 P3 Iaşi Romania
78 G1 Iasmos Greece
154 B4 Iba Luzon Phil.
89 F5 Ibadan Nigeria
89 G6 Ibagué Col.
91 D6 Ibanda Kasaï-Occidental Dem. Rep. Congo
91 D6 Ibanga Sud-Kivu Dem. Rep. Congo
125 S1 Ibapah UT U.S.A.
17 L7 Ibar r. Serb. and Mont.
165 K12 Ibara Japan
167 L3 Ibaraki Ibaraki Japan
166 C6 Ibaraki Ōsaka Japan
167 L3 Ibaraki pref. Japan
138 C2 Ibarra Ecuador
104 C3 Ibärstad AK U.S.A.
90 C2 Ibáyúwana Sudan
85 F2 Ibdā Egypt
186 G8 Ibb Yemen
186 G8 Ibb governorate Yemen
90 F3 Ibba watercourse Sudan
49 E6 Ibbenbüren Ger.
89 F3 Ibdeqqene watercourse Mali
63 R3 Ibdes Spain
78 E6 Ibë Albania
63 M4 Ibeas de Juarros Spain
144 F3 Iberá, Esteros del marsh Arg.
144 F3 Iberá, Laguna l. Arg.
64 D1 Iberia Loreto Peru
138 C4 Ibéria Madre de Dios Peru
143 F4 Ibertioga Brazil
117 L3 Iberville, Lac d' l. Que. Can.
109 F2 Iberville, Lac d' l. Que. Can.
20 N2 Ibestad Norway
89 G4 Ibeto Nigeria
158 B2 Ibh Sumatera Indon.
89 H4 Ibi Nigeria
67 D10 Ibi Spain
142 D3 Ibiá Brazil
143 E2 Ibiai Brazil
142 E4 Ibiapaba, Serra da hills Brazil
141 F5 Ibicaraí Brazil
141 F3 Ibicuí Brazil
141 A9 Ibicuí r. Brazil
141 E8 Ibicuy Arg.
141 E8 Ibigawa Japan
166 D4 Ibigawa Japan
91 D7 Ibina watercourse Dem. Rep. Congo
142 B5 Ibiporã Brazil
143 G2 Ibiraçu Brazil
143 G3 Ibiranhém Brazil
143 G2 Ibiraçu Brazil
140 E5 Ibitiara Brazil
142 C4 Ibitinga Brazil
142 D5 Ibitira Brazil
142 D5 Ibiúna Brazil
142 A6 Ibiza Illes Balears Spain see Eivissa
 Ibiza i. Spain see Eivissa
74 N9 Iblei, Monti mts Sicilia Italy
79 J6 Iblis Burnu pt Turkey
186 G2 Ibn Buşayyiş well Saudi Arabia
53 K6 Ibn Hani' Syria
186 E6 Ibn Hādī Saudi Arabia
43 D9 Ibos France
90 A5 Iboundji Gabon
90 A5 Iboundji, Mont hill Gabon
187 N4 Ibrā' Oman
90 E2 Ibra, Wadi watercourse Sudan
15 I5 Ibresi Rus. Fed.
187 M4 Ibrī Oman
31 J2 Ibstock Leicestershire, England U.K.
155 S3 Ibu Halmahera Indon.
164 □1 Ibu Okinawa Japan
79 J6 Ibuhos i. Phil.
166 D5 Ibuki Japan
166 D5 Ibuki-sanchi mts Japan
166 D4 Ibuki-yama mt. Japan
135 H15 Içá r. Brazil
153 I2 Içá Peru
92 B4 Içana Brazil
92 B4 Içana r. Brazil
142 D3 Icaraí Brazil
138 □ Icaria i. Greece see Ikaria
140 E2 Icatu Brazil
176 E5 Iccberg Canyon gorge NV U.S.A.
89 H4 Içel Turkey see Mersin
190 D2 İçel prov. Turkey
105 Q3 Iceland country Europe
214 I1 Iceland Basin sea feature N. Atlantic Ocean
214 I1 Icelandic Plateau sea feature N. Atlantic Ocean
142 C4 Icem Brazil
179 J7 Ichalkaranji Mahar. India
176 D4 Ichalkaranji Mahar. India
53 I5 Ichenhausen Ger.
165 C6 Ichenheim Ger.
167 L3 Ichihara Japan
167 L3 Ichikai Japan
167 K4 Ichikawa Chiba Japan
165 K4 Ichikawa Hyōgo Japan
167 K4 Ichi-kawa r. Japan
165 K11 Ichikawadaimon Japan
166 D4 Ichinomiya Aichi Japan
167 K4 Ichinomiya Aichi Japan
167 L5 Ichinomiya Chiba Japan
167 H3 Ichinomiya Yamanashi Japan
164 S8 Ichinoseki Japan
193 Q4 Ichinskiy, Vulkan vol. Rus. Fed.
166 D6 Ichishi Japan
69 B7 Ichkeul National Park Tunisia
17 L3 Ichnya Ukr.
188 F2 Ich'ŏn N. Korea
45 D6 Ichtegem Belgium
138 C4 Ichuña Peru
177 M7 Icó Brazil
79 J4 Içökler Turkey
14 G1 Icod de los Vinos Tenerife Canary Is
106 C3 Icy Bay AK U.S.A.
106 C3 Icy Strait AK U.S.A.
121 J8 Idabel OK U.S.A.
89 G5 Idah Nigeria
120 H5 Idaho state U.S.A.
122 G5 Idaho City ID U.S.A.

Column 5

122 H5 Idaho Falls ID U.S.A.
207 J8 Idalia National Park Qld Austr.
 Idalion Cyprus see Dali
122 C4 Idanha OR U.S.A.
62 F9 Idanha, Barragem da resr Port.
62 F9 Idanha-a-Nova Port.
178 D8 Idar Gujarat India
52 C2 Idar-Oberstein Ger.
52 C2 Idarwald for. Ger.
203 D12 Ida Valley South I. N.Z.
89 H3 Iday well Niger
92 F3 Iddah Somalia
75 □ Id-Dawwara, Ras pt Malta
85 F6 Idd al Asoda well Sudan
90 E2 Idd el Chanam Sudan
85 E5 Idd esh Shurak well Sudan
166 C6 Idé Japan
22 H2 Idefjorden inlet Norway/Sweden
87 G5 Idelès Alg.
50 E5 Iden Ger.
168 F2 Ideriyn Gol r. Mongolia
85 G3 Idfu Egypt
85 G3 Idfū Egypt
84 B3 Idhān Murzūq des. Libya
84 B3 Idhān Awbārī des. Libya
66 A1 Idiazabal Spain
71 L6 Idice r. Italy
92 D3 Ididole Eth.
91 C6 Idiofa Dem. Rep. Congo
104 C3 Iditarod AK U.S.A.
20 O2 Idivuoma Sweden
85 F2 Idkū Egypt
29 P7 Idle r. England U.K.
190 D3 Idlib Syria
190 E3 Idlib governorate Syria
43 B9 Idmiston Wiltshire, England U.K.
52 D5 Idocin Spain
53 L4 Idoš Albania
79 L3 Idoš Vojvodina, Srbija
57 J6 Idoš Vojvodina, Srbija
206 D8 Idracowra N.T. Austr.
70 I4 Idro Italy
70 I4 Idro, Lago d' l. Italy
43 D9 Idron-Ousse-Sendets France
70 I4 Idro Italy
70 I4 Idstein Ger.
18 I1 Idstein Ger.
167 H2 Iiyama Japan
166 D7 Iinan Japan
164 □1 Iisaka Fin.
20 S5 Iisalmi Fin.
18 I1 Iitti Fin.
167 H2 Iiyama Japan
165 H13 Iizuka Japan
86 C6 Ijâfene des. Maur.
89 G5 Ijebu-Ode Nigeria
89 G5 Ijebu-Ode Nigeria
191 A9 Ijevan Armenia
44 H3 IJlst Neth.
44 G2 IJmuiden Neth.
86 C5 Ijoubâne des. Mali
44 I3 IJssel r. Neth.
44 H3 IJsselmeer l. Neth.
44 H3 IJsselmuiden Neth.
44 I3 IJsselstein Neth.
44 I4 Iju r. Brazil
139 G6 Ijuí Brazil
139 G6 Ijuí r. Brazil
45 C7 IJzer r. Belgium
45 C7 Yser (France)
21 Q6 Ikaalinen Fin.
97 I2 Ikageleng S. Africa
97 L2 Ikageng S. Africa
95 □J3 Ikahavo hill Madag.
95 □J4 Ikalamavony Madag.
203 F9 Ikamatua South I. N.Z.
91 D5 Ikanda-Nord Dem. Rep. Congo
89 H4 Ikara Nigeria
89 H4 Ikara Nigeria
79 L5 Ikaria i. Greece
22 E5 Ikast Denmark
167 H2 Ikawa Japan
203 E11 Ikawai South I. N.Z.
202 K5 Ikawhenua Range mts North I. N.Z.
166 C5 Ikeda Gifu Japan
166 C5 Ikeda Hokkaidō Japan
167 G3 Ikeda Nagano Japan
165 C8 Ikeda Ōsaka Japan
165 K13 Ikeda Tokushima Japan
91 D6 Ikela Dem. Rep. Congo
89 H4 Ikem Nigeria
90 C5 Ikelemba r. Dem. Rep. Congo
90 B5 Ikengo Dem. Rep. Congo
90 A5 Ikéngué Gabon
89 G5 Ikerre Nigeria see Ikere
89 G5 Ikerre Nigeria see Ikere
56 F4 Ikervár Hungary
91 H5 Ikhtiman Bulg.
77 L8 Ikhtiman Bulg.
97 L3 Ikhutseng S. Africa
165 G13 Iki i. Japan
79 L3 Ikiztepe Turkey
165 G13 Iki-suidō sea chan. Japan
93 B6 Ikizu Tanz.
19 Q4 Ikkala Fin.
14 G1 Ikla Estonia
18 H3 Ikla Estonia
106 C5 Ikolik, Cape AK U.S.A.
89 H5 Ikom Nigeria
95 □J4 Ikongo Madag.
95 □3a Ikonju Njazidja Comoros
191 A9 Ikorta Georgia
89 G5 Ikot Ekpene Nigeria
15 H7 Ikouhaouene, Adrar mt. Alg.
95 □J4 Ikrény Hungary
95 □J4 Ikungi Tanz.
93 B6 Ikungu Tanz.
93 B6 Ikuno Japan
165 B6 Ikusaka Japan
206 D4 Ila Nigeria
89 G5 Ilagan Luzon Phil.
154 C2 Ilagan Luzon Phil.
21 T6 Ilaka Atsinanana Madag.
95 □J5 Ilaka Atsinanana Madag.
179 K9 Ilam Nepal
177 I5 Ilam Nepal
184 B3 Ilām Iran
184 C3 Ilām prov. Iran
79 M4 Ilan Taiwan
171 □I7 Ilan Taiwan
19 Q6 Ilanskiy Rus. Fed.
70 G2 Ilanz Switz.
55 H2 Iława Pol.
107 K4 Iława Rus. Fed.
14 K4 Iława Rus. Fed.
89 G5 Ilawe-Ekiti Nigeria
186 E6 Il-Bajda, Ras pt Gozo Malta
140 D2 Ilbono Brazil
168 F4 Il Bogd Uul mts Mongolia
30 □ Ilchester Somerset, England U.K.
79 H4 Ildır Turkey
183 Q5 Ildun r. China/Kazakh.

Column 6

66 I4 Igualada Spain
65 I7 Igualeja Spain
129 I8 Igualtepec Mex.
142 D6 Iguape Brazil
143 E4 Iguaraçu Brazil
143 E4 Iguarapé Brazil
143 E4 Iguatama Brazil
141 B7 Iguatemi Brazil
141 B7 Iguatemi r. Brazil
140 F3 Iguatu Brazil
 Iguaçu, Cataratas do waterfall Arg./Brazil see Iguaçu Falls
89 B7 Iguéla Gabon
62 H3 Igueña Spain
40 E4 Iguerande France
86 C4 Iguetti, Sebkhet salt flat Maur.
93 B6 Igugunu Tanz.
89 G5 Igugbazawa Nigeria
95 F3 Igusi Zimbabwe
93 B5 Igusule Tanz.
95 □K2 Iharaña Madag.
89 G5 Ihiala Nigeria
87 G5 Ihirene, Oued watercourse Alg.
57 J2 Ihľany Slovakia
48 E4 Ihlowerhörn (Ihlow) Ger.
16 H2 Ihnatpil' Ukr.
43 B9 Iholdy France
48 D4 Ihrhove Ger.
52 D5 Ihringen Ger.
53 L4 Ihrlerstein Ger.
79 L3 Ihsaniye Turkey
168 J2 Ihsuuj Mongolia
169 R5 Ih Tal Nei Mongol China
164 D4 Iida Japan
164 □1 Iheya-jima i. Nansei-shotō Japan
168 I3 Ihhayrhan Mongolia
176 C9 Ihavandhippolhu Atoll Maldives
95 J5 Ihbulag Mongolia
56 G5 Iharosberény Hungary
167 G4 Iijima Japan
20 R4 Iisaku Fin.
166 D7 Iinan Japan
167 H2 Iiyama Japan
165 H13 Iizuka Japan
86 C6 Ijâfene des. Maur.
89 G5 Ihiala Nigeria
88 B2 Ijoubâne des. Mali
86 C5 Ijoubâne des. Mali
44 H3 IJssel r. Neth.
44 H3 IJsselmeer l. Neth.
44 I3 IJsselstein Neth.
14 J2 Ijui r. Brazil
100 2 Ijui Brazil
21 Q6 Ikaalinen Fin.
97 I2 Ikageleng S. Africa
97 L2 Ikageng S. Africa
95 □J3 Ikahavo hill Madag.
95 □J4 Ikalamavony Madag.
203 F9 Ikamatua South I. N.Z.
91 D5 Ikanda-Nord Dem. Rep. Congo
89 H4 Ikara Nigeria
79 L5 Ikaria i. Greece
22 E5 Ikast Denmark
167 H2 Ikawa Japan
203 E11 Ikawai South I. N.Z.
202 K5 Ikawhenua Range mts North I. N.Z.
166 C5 Ikeda Gifu Japan
166 C5 Ikeda Hokkaidō Japan
167 G3 Ikeda Nagano Japan
165 C8 Ikeda Ōsaka Japan
165 K13 Ikeda Tokushima Japan
91 D6 Ikela Dem. Rep. Congo
89 H4 Ikem Nigeria
90 C5 Ikelemba r. Dem. Rep. Congo
90 B5 Ikengo Dem. Rep. Congo
90 A5 Ikéngué Gabon
89 G5 Ikerre Nigeria see Ikere
56 F4 Ikervár Hungary
77 L8 Ikhtiman Bulg.
97 L3 Ikhutseng S. Africa
165 G13 Iki i. Japan
79 L3 Ikiztepe Turkey
165 G13 Iki-suidō sea chan. Japan
93 B6 Ikizu Tanz.
19 Q4 Ikkala Fin.
14 G1 Ikla Estonia
18 H3 Ikla Estonia
106 C5 Ikolik, Cape AK U.S.A.
89 H5 Ikom Nigeria
95 □J4 Ikongo Madag.
95 □3a Ikonju Njazidja Comoros
191 A9 Ikorta Georgia
89 G5 Ikot Ekpene Nigeria
87 H4 Ikouhaouene, Adrar mt. Alg.
56 F4 Ikrény Hungary
93 B6 Ikungi Tanz.
93 B6 Ikungu Tanz.
165 H12 Ikuno Japan
165 B6 Ikusaka Japan
166 B4 Ikuta Japan
89 G5 Ila Nigeria
154 C2 Ilagan Luzon Phil.
95 □J5 Ilaka Atsinanana Madag.
179 K9 Ilam Nepal
184 B3 Ilām Iran
184 C3 Ilām prov. Iran
171 □I7 Ilan Taiwan
55 H2 Iława Pol.
14 K4 Iława Rus. Fed.
89 G5 Ilawe-Ekiti Nigeria
186 E6 Il-Bajda, Ras pt Gozo Malta
140 D2 Ilbono Brazil
168 F4 Il Bogd Uul mts Mongolia
30 □ Ilchester Somerset, England U.K.
79 H4 Ildır Turkey

Column 7

122 H5 Idaho Falls ID U.S.A.
207 J8 Idalia National Park Qld Austr.
129 I8 Igualtepec Mex.
142 D6 Iguape Brazil
143 E4 Iguaraçu Brazil
143 E4 Iguarapé Brazil
143 E4 Iguatama Brazil
141 B7 Iguatemi Brazil
141 B7 Iguatemi r. Brazil
140 F3 Iguatu Brazil
144 G2 Iguazú, Parque Nacional del nat. park Arg.
90 A5 Iguéla Gabon
62 H3 Igueña Spain
40 E4 Iguerande France
86 C4 Iguetti, Sebkhet salt flat Maur.
93 B6 Igugunu Tanz.
89 G5 Igugbazawa Nigeria
95 F3 Igusi Zimbabwe
93 B5 Igusule Tanz.
95 □K2 Iharaña Madag.
56 G5 Iharosberény Hungary
176 C9 Ihavandhippolhu Atoll Maldives
95 J5 Ihbulag Mongolia
164 □E19 Iheya-jima i. Nansei-shotō Japan
168 I3 Ihhayrhan Mongolia
89 G5 Ihiala Nigeria
87 G5 Ihirene, Oued watercourse Alg.
57 J2 Ihľany Slovakia
48 E4 Ihlowerhörn (Ihlow) Ger.
16 H2 Ihnatpil' Ukr.
43 B9 Iholdy France
48 D4 Ihrhove Ger.
52 D5 Ihringen Ger.
53 L4 Ihrlerstein Ger.
79 L3 Ihsaniye Turkey
168 J2 Ihsuuj Mongolia
169 R5 Ih Tal Nei Mongol China
68 G4 Iijaš Bos.-Herz.
105 P2 Ilimananngip Nunaa i. Greenland
193 L3 Il'inka Kazakh.
182 G3 Il'inka Kazakh.
180 D1 Il'inka Respublika Altay Rus. Fed.
168 D1 Il'inka Respublika Tyva Rus. Fed.
14 O4 Il'inskiy Permskaya Oblast' Rus. Fed.
19 P1 Il'inskiy Respublika Kareliya Rus. Fed.
162 M5 Il'inskiy Sakhalin Rus. Fed.
14 I3 Il'insko-Podomskoye Rus. Fed.
17 S7 Il'inskoye Krasnodarskiy Kray Rus. Fed.
19 S8 Il'inskoye Orlovskaya Oblast' Rus. Fed.
19 U5 Il'inskoye Tverskaya Oblast' Rus. Fed.
19 V4 Il'inskoye Yaroslavskaya Oblast' Rus. Fed.
15 C5 Il'inskoye-Khovanskoye Rus. Fed.
154 C5 Ilin Strait Phil.
155 E8 Iliomar East Timor
117 J3 Ilion NY U.S.A.
124 D12 'Ilio Point HI U.S.A.
68 E3 Ilirska Bistrica Slovenia
191 H4 Ilisu qoruğu nature res. Azer.
17 Y7 Iliysk Kazakh. see Kapchagay
51 K3 Ilk Hungary
176 E5 Ilkal Karnataka India
31 J2 Ilkeston Derbyshire, England U.K.
29 N6 Ilkley West Yorkshire, England U.K.
51 H3 Il-Kartun Malta
37 O6 Ill r. France
154 D3 Illana Bay Mindanao Phil.
146 B3 Illapel Chile
65 M7 Illar Spain
71 K5 Illasi Italy
43 J10 Illats France
204 D2 Illbillee, Mount S.A. Austr.
38 H5 Ille-et-Vilaine dept France
64 H2 Ille-sur-Têt France
89 G5 Illéla Niger
154 C3 Illéla Niger
63 M8 Illescas Spain
89 G5 Illescas Spain
64 H2 Illes Balears aut. comm. Spain
37 O6 Illiers-Combray France
45 D4 Illkirch-Graffenstaden Ger.
16 I4 Illintsi Ukr.
51 K3 Illmensee Ger.
53 K2 Illmitz Austria
71 K5 Illertissen Italy
51 G9 Illschwang Ger.
37 N8 Illzach France
52 G5 Ilm r. Ger.
21 U2 Ilmajoki Fin.
75 □ Il-Minkba pt Malta
52 G5 Ilmenau Ger.
17 O5 Ilmenskoye Rus. Fed.
58 E8 Il Montello hill Italy
16 C5 Il'nytsya Ukr.
10 Peru
53 C4 Ilobu Brazil
89 G5 Ilobu Nigeria
20 U5 Ilomantsi Fin.
17 L4 Ilovay-Dmitriyevskoye Rus. Fed.
89 G5 Ilorin Nigeria
68 F3 Ilova r. Croatia

Column 8

107 J4 Île-à-la-Crosse Sask. Can.
107 J4 Île-à-la-Crosse, Lac l. Sask. Can.
130 G4 Île-à-Vache i. Haiti
91 D6 Ilebo Dem. Rep. Congo
109 I3 Île d'Anticosti, Réserve Faunique de l' nature res. Que. Can.
36 C6 Île-de-France admin. reg. France
93 B7 Ileje Tanz.
182 E2 Ilek Kazakh.
182 E2 Ilek r. Rus. Fed.
27 D9 Ilen r. Rep. of Ireland
 Ilerda prov. Spain see Lleida
92 C3 Ileret Kenya
89 F4 Ilesa Nigeria
89 F4 Ilesha Nigeria
89 G5 Ilesha Ibariba Nigeria
14 J5 Ilet r. Rus. Fed.
14 I3 Ileza Rus. Fed.
49 K7 Ilfeld Ger.
107 M3 Ilford Man. Can.
31 M4 Ilford Greater London, England U.K.
207 J7 Ilfracombe Qld Austr.
30 D5 Ilfracombe Devon, England U.K.
188 F3 Ilgaz Turkey
188 F3 Ilgaz Dağları mts Turkey
55 M1 Ilgis l. Lith.
75 □ Il-Griebeg, Ras pt Malta
98 □1c Ilha, Ponta da pt Pico Azores
143 E5 Ilhabela Brazil
137 E5 Ilha Grande Brazil
143 E5 Ilha Grande, Baía da b. Brazil
141 B7 Ilha Grande, Parque Nacional da nat. park Brazil
141 B7 Ilha Grande, Represa resr Brazil
75 □ Il-Ħamrija, Ras pt Malta
142 B4 Ilha Solteira, Represa resr Brazil
62 C7 Ílhavo Port.
141 F5 Ilhéus Brazil
77 M5 Ili r. China/Kazakh. see Ile
16 K3 Ilia Romania
104 C4 Iliamna Lake AK U.S.A.
188 I4 İliç Turkey
191 B6 Ilıca Bingöl Turkey
191 C6 Ilıca Erzurum Turkey
191 C1 Ilıch Rus. Fed.
92 F3 Ilig, Raas pt Somalia
154 E7 Iligan Mindanao Phil.
154 E7 Iligan Bay Mindanao Phil.
183 R5 Ili He r. China/Kazakh. see Ile
77 K5 Ilia Romania
104 C4 Iliamna Lake AK U.S.A.
188 I4 İliç Turkey
92 F3 Ilig, Raas pt Somalia
154 E7 Iligan Mindanao Phil.
68 G4 Ilijaš Bos.-Herz.
105 P2 Ilimananngip Nunaa i. Greenland
193 L3 Il'inka Kazakh.
182 G3 Il'inka Kazakh.
162 M5 Il'inskiy Sakhalin Rus. Fed.
14 I3 Il'insko-Podomskoye Rus. Fed.
17 S7 Il'inskoye Krasnodarskiy Kray Rus. Fed.
19 S8 Il'inskoye Orlovskaya Oblast' Rus. Fed.
19 U5 Il'inskoye Tverskaya Oblast' Rus. Fed.
19 V4 Il'inskoye Yaroslavskaya Oblast' Rus. Fed.
154 C5 Ilin Strait Phil.
117 J3 Ilion NY U.S.A.
68 E3 Ilirska Bistrica Slovenia
191 H4 Ilisu qoruğu nature res. Azer.
51 K3 Ilk Hungary
176 E5 Ilkal Karnataka India
31 J2 Ilkeston Derbyshire, England U.K.
29 N6 Ilkley West Yorkshire, England U.K.
75 □ Il-Kartun pt Malta
37 O6 Ill r. France
154 D3 Illana Bay Mindanao Phil.
146 B3 Illapel Chile
65 M7 Illar Spain
71 K5 Illasi Italy
43 J10 Illats France
204 D2 Illbillee, Mount S.A. Austr.
38 H5 Ille-et-Vilaine dept France
64 H2 Ille-sur-Têt France
89 G5 Illéla Niger
63 M8 Illescas Spain
64 H2 Illes Balears aut. comm. Spain
37 O6 Illiers-Combray France
16 I4 Illintsi Ukr.
51 K3 Illmensee Ger.
53 K2 Illmitz Austria
51 G9 Illschwang Ger.
37 N8 Illzach France
52 G5 Ilm r. Ger.
75 □ Il-Minkba pt Malta
52 G5 Ilmenau Ger.
17 O5 Ilmenskoye Rus. Fed.
58 E8 Il Montello hill Italy
16 C5 Il'nytsya Ukr.
53 C4 Ilobu Nigeria
89 G5 Ilobu Nigeria
186 D6 Iloca Panay Phil.
20 U5 Ilomantsi Fin.
17 L4 Ilovay-Dmitriyevskoye Rus. Fed.
89 G5 Ilorin Nigeria
68 F3 Ilova r. Croatia

15 I6	Ilovatka Rus. Fed.
17 R6	Ilovays'k Ukr.
77 K9	Ilovica Macedonia
71 R7	Ilovik Croatia
68 E3	Ilovik i. Croatia
17 R3	Ilovka Rus. Fed.
15 H6	Ilovlya Rus. Fed.
15 H6	Ilovlya r. Rus. Fed.
54 D4	Iłowa Pol.
55 I2	Iłowo Osada Pol.
44 Q4	Ilpendam Neth.
93 R3	Il'pyrskiy Rus. Fed.
	Il'pyrskoye Rus. Fed. see
75 □	Il'pyrskiy
21 N6	Il-Qala, Ras pt Gozo Malta
49 K6	Ilsbo Sweden
45 I6	Ilse r. Ger.
49 K7	Ilsede Ger.
52 H3	Ilsenburg (Harz) Ger.
52 H3	Ilsfeld Ger.
41 I6	Ilshofen Ger.
30 E6	Ilsington Devon, England U.K.
17 P3	Il'skiy Rus. Fed.
18 J6	Ilūkste Latvia
40 M3	Iluilissat Greenland
93 B6	Ilunde Tanz.
93 B6	Ilunde Tanz.
75 □	Il-Wahx, Ras pt Malta
18 K7	Il'ya Belarus
14 L3	Ilych r. Rus. Fed.
55 K1	Iłyushino Rus. Fed.
53 O4	Ilz Austria
53 O4	Ilz r. Ger.
55 J4	Iłża Pol.
55 J4	Iłżanka r. Pol.
65 J12	Imabari Japan
65 J12	Imabetsu Japan
67 G5	Imabū r. Brazil
64 R4	Imadate Japan
64 R4	Imagane Japan
67 K2	Imaichi Japan
66 H3	Imajō Japan
89 L3	Imam al Hamzah Iraq
85 J3	Imam-baba Turkm.
80 E4	Imamoğlu Turkey
62 H6	Iman r. Rus. Fed.
14 F2	Imandra Rus. Fed.
63 M1	Imantau, Ozero l. Kazakh.
65 G13	Imari Japan
88 E3	Imasgo Burkina
	Imassogo Burkina see Imasgo
38 C3	Imataca, Serranía de mts Venez.
21 T6	Imatra Fin.
18 I3	Imavere Estonia
66 D5	Imazu Japan
36 B4	Imbabura prov. Ecuador
37 F3	Imbaimadai Guyana
	Imba-numa l. Japan see
41 C9	Imbituba Brazil
42 B6	Imbituva Brazil
57 L6	Imecik Turkey
57 H4	Imef Slovakia
84 F2	imeni 26 Bakinskikh Komissarov Turkm.
14 H4	imeni Babushkina Rus. Fed.
85 J3	imeni C. A. Niyazova Turkm.
	imeni Chapayeva Turkm. see
	imeni G. I. Petrovskogo Ukr.
93 P3	see Horodyshche
19 X5	imeni Gor'kogo Rus. Fed.
17 O2	imeni Karla Libknekhta Rus. Fed.
84 I3	imeni Kerbabayeva Turkm.
	imeni Khamzy Khakimkzade Uzbek. see Hamza
	imeni Kirova Kazakh. see Kopbirlik
	imeni Kirova Donets'ka Oblast' Ukr. see Kirovs'k
	imeni Kirova Donets'ka Oblast' Ukr. see Kirove
85 J3	imeni Kuybysheva Turkm.
14 I4	imeni M. I. Kalinina Rus. Fed.
62 I2	imeni Poliny Osipenko Rus. Fed.
19 T3	imeni Zhelyabova Rus. Fed.
17 O5	imeni Lenina, Ozero l. Ukr.
71 L3	Imèr Italy
74 S8	Imera r. Sicilia Italy
41 B5	Imeri, Serra mts Brazil
90 C4	Imese Dem. Rep. Congo
92 D3	Imī Eth.
86 D2	Imilchil Morocco
86 C3	Imi-n-Tanoute Morocco
86 B4	Imirikliy Labyad reg. Western Sahara
	Imis̆li Azer. see İmişli
91 J6	İmişli Azer.
78 D1	imit Jammu and Kashmir
63 E11	Imja-do i. S. Korea
63 E10	Imjin-gang r. N. Korea/S. Korea
11 K6	Imlay City MI U.S.A.
86 B5	Imlili Western Sahara
49 J9	Immelborn Ger.
23 K5	Immeln l. Sweden
52 F6	Immendingen Ger.
52 H3	Immenhausen Ger.
52 L2	Immenreuth Ger.
52 G6	Immenstaad am Bodensee Ger.
53 I6	Immenstadt im Allgäu Ger.
29 Q6	Immingham North East Lincolnshire, England U.K.
15 G12	Immokalee FL U.S.A.
89 G5	Imo state Nigeria
71 L7	Imola Italy
68 F4	Imotski Croatia
97 N5	Impendle S. Africa
41 H4	Imperatriz Amazonas Brazil
38 E6	Imperatriz Maranhão Brazil
40 D3	Imperia Italy
70 D2	Imperial prov. Italy
46 A6	Imperial r. Chile
24 E5	Imperial Peru
25 Q9	Imperial CA U.S.A.
20 E5	Imperial NE U.S.A.
24 O9	Imperial Beach CA U.S.A.
25 Q9	Imperial Dam AZ/CA U.S.A.
25 Q9	Imperial Valley plain CA U.S.A.
01 E4	Imperieuse Reef W.A. Austr.
90 C4	Impfondo Congo
79 N7	Imphal Manipur India
40 C3	Imphy France
31 M3	Impington Cambridgeshire, England U.K.
71 K8	Impruneta Italy
13 J2	Imralı Adası i. Turkey
86 G9	Imrän Yemen
32 J2	Imrehegy Hungary
59 G2	İmroz Gökeada Turkey
83 E11	Imsil S. Korea
55 E6	Imten Syria
90 E6	Imtan Syria
34 B6	Imuris Mex.
54 B6	Imuruan Bay Palawan Phil.
93 J3	Imyanin Belarus
92 E1	Imzouren Morocco
60 D7	In r. Rus. Fed.
67 K1	Ina Fukushima Japan
67 L4	Ina Ibaraki Japan
67 H4	Ina Nagano Japan
54 C2	Ina r. Pol.
88 D3	I-n-Abalene well Mali
88 D2	I-n-Abangharit well Niger
66 E5	Inabe Japan
66 C5	Inabu Japan
98 □2c	Inaccessible Island Tristan da Cunha S. Atlantic Ocean
66 D5	Inae Japan
87 H5	I-n-Atelelh well Alg.
67 D7	Inagawa Japan
66 D6	Ina-gawa r. Japan
67 L4	Inage Japan
67 D7	Inagi Japan
67 K4	Inagi Rep. of Ireland

95 H2	Inago Moz.
138 B1	Inahuaya Peru
140 F4	Inajá Brazil
139 H2	Inaja r. Brazil
139 H2	Inaja, Serra do hills Brazil
88 E2	I-n-Akhmed well Mali
87 E5	I-n-Akli well Mali
200 □5	Inakona Guadalcanal Solomon Is.
	Inalahan Guam see Inarajan
89 F2	I-n-Alakam well Mali
88 E2	I-n-Alchi well Mali
89 F2	I-n-Alchig well Mali
88 E2	I-n-'Amar well Maur.
88 C2	Inamba-jima i. Japan see
	Inanba-jima
204 D2	Inambari Peru
91 C8	Inambari r. Peru
	Inambari Angola
	Indur Andhra Prad. India see
	Nizamabad
18 G8	Indura Belarus
176 F4	Indurti Andhra Prad. India
178 G3	Indus r. China/Pak.
	Indus, Mouths of the Pak.
	Indus Cone sea feature Indian Ocean
97 L7	Indwe S. Africa
97 L8	Indwe r. S. Africa
77 P8	Indzhe Voyvoda Bulg.
66 B4	Ine Japan
87 G5	I-n Ebeggi well Alg.
188 F3	Inebolu Turkey
86 E5	I-n-Échaï well Mali
79 K2	İnegöl Turkey
87 G4	In Ekker Alg.
155 B8	Inerie vol. Flores Indon.
147 G4	Ines Indart Arg.
77 J4	Ineu Arad Romania
57 L4	Ineu Bihor Romania
116 C11	Inez KY U.S.A.
86 C3	Inezgane Morocco
87 H5	In Ezzane well Alg.
96 E10	Infanta, Cape S. Africa
136 C3	Infantas Col.
129 M9	Infernillo, Laguna lag. Mex.
139 E2	Infernao, Cachoeira waterfall Brazil
144 C2	Infielés, Punta pt Chile
128 F7	Infiernillo, Presa resr Mex.
63 J2	Infiesto Spain
73 O8	Infreschi, Punta degli pt Italy
158 E4	Inga r. Norway
91 B6	Inga Dem. Rep. Congo
21 R6	Ingå Fin.
144 C2	Inca de Oro Chile
188 G2	Ince Burnu pt Turkey
89 G2	Ince Burun pt Turkey
206 D6	Ingallanna watercourse N.T. Austr.
124 L2	Ingalls, Mount CA U.S.A.
107 J2	Ingalls Lake N.W.T. Can.
90 D5	Ingbando Dem. Rep. Congo
31 M4	Ingatestone Essex, England U.K.
52 H3	Ingelfingen Ger.
52 E2	Ingelheim am Rhein Ger.
45 D7	Ingelmunster Belgium
23 K5	Ingelstad Sweden
90 C5	Ingende Dem. Rep. Congo
146 D4	Ingeniero Balloffet Arg.
144 E1	Ingeniero Guillermo Nueva Juárez Arg.
146 D6	Ingeniero Huergo Arg.
145 D6	Ingeniero Jacobacci Arg.
91 B5	Ingeniero Luiggi Arg.
136 C5	Ingeniero Luisi Arg.
79 L3	Ingeniero Maschwitz Arg.
106 E3	Ingeniero Otamendi Arg.
134 D1	Ingenika r. B.C. Can.
88 E2	I-n-Ghāchef well Mali
87 F5	I-n-Ouzzal, Oued watercourse Alg.
168 H2	Ingettolgoy Mongolia
	Ingezi Dem. Rep. Congo see Ngezi
57 H3	Inggelang i. Maluku Indon.
207 K5	Ingham Qld Austr.
133 A8	In Ghar Alg.
182 L8	Ingichka Uzbek.
63 O3	Ingiers r. Spain
29 M5	Ingleborough hill England U.K.
105 K2	Inglefield Land reg. Greenland
29 N4	Ingleton Durham, England U.K.
29 M5	Ingleton North Yorkshire, England U.K.
29 L6	Inglewhite Lancashire, England U.K.
205 M3	Inglewood Qld Austr.
205 I7	Inglewood Vic. Austr.
203 D6	Inglewood North I. N.Z.
124 N8	Inglewood CA U.S.A.
29 L4	Inglewood Forest England U.K.
105 J2	Ingolf Fjord inlet Greenland
53 K3	Ingolstadt Ger.
23 O4	Ingolstadt S.A. Austr.
204 F2	Ingomar MT U.S.A.
109 I4	Ingonish N.S. Can.
179 L7	Ingraj Bazar W. Bengal India
26 M12	Ingram Northumberland, England U.K.
116 F12	Ingram VA U.S.A.
110 D4	Ingram WI U.S.A.
39 J7	Ingrandes Pays de la Loire France
38 M8	Ingrandes Poitou-Charentes France
147 F4	Ingray Lake N.W.T. Can.
89 E8	Ingre Bol.
70 D2	Ingre France
110 A3	Ingrid Christensen Coast Antarctica
120 E1	I-n-Guezzam Alg.
39 F3	I-n-Guita well Mali
	Ingul r. Ukr. see Inhul
186 D8	Ingul'ets Ukr.
88 E3	Ini-Tillit Mali
26 F10	Intorsura Buzăului Romania
89 F2	I-n-Touft well Mali
121 H11	Intracoastal Waterway canal TX U.S.A.
70 G4	Introbio Italy
14 H2	Intsy Rus. Fed.
95 E3	Intundhla Zimbabwe
136 C5	Intutu Peru
167 M4	Inubō-zaki pt Japan
155 H3	Inukai Japan
108 L1	Inukjuak Que. Can.
103 H3	Inútil, Bahía b. Chile
104 J6	Inuvik N.W.T. Can.
138 B2	Inuya r. Peru
29 N7	Inuyama Japan
14 L4	In'va r. Rus. Fed.
207 N9	Inver Qld Austr.
31 O3	Inver Rep. of Ireland
26 E9	Inverallochy Aberdeenshire, Scotland U.K.
142 C4	Inverarary Argyll and Bute, Scotland U.K.
156 D6	Inveraray Angus, Scotland U.K.
75 □	Inverarity Angus, Scotland U.K.
26 K9	Inverarnan Argyll and Bute, Scotland U.K.
26 G10	Inverbervie Aberdeenshire, Scotland U.K.
105 L3	Inverbervie Aberdeenshire, Scotland U.K.
173 L7	Inver Bay Rep. of Ireland
25 N7	Inverbervie Aberdeenshire, Scotland U.K.
90 C5	Invercargill South I. N.Z.
24 C22	Invercargill South I. N.Z.
26 G11	Inverclyde admin. div. Scotland U.K.
205 M3	Inverell N.S.W. Austr.
26 D7	Inverey Aberdeenshire, Scotland U.K.

17 O8	Indol r. Ukr.
19 U1	Indomanka r. Rus. Fed.
152 D7	Indonesia country Asia
178 E8	Indore Madh. Prad. India
156 E5	Indragiri r. Indon.
157 H8	Indramayu Jawa Indon.
157 H8	Indramayu, Tanjung pt Indon.
156 D6	Indrapura Sumatera Indon.
	Indrapura, Gunung vol. Indon. see Kerinci, Gunung
	Indrapura, Tanjung pt Indon.
156 D6	Indrapura, Tanjung pt Indon.
177 G3	Indre Kiberg Norway
39 G6	Indre dept France
42 E1	Indre r. France
39 M7	Indre-et-Loire dept France
20 U1	Indre Samlen b. Norway
22 C1	Indre Samlen b. Norway
56 G5	Inke Hungary
88 D2	I-n-Kerchef well Mali
17 M9	Inkerman Qld Austr.
106 C3	Inklin B.C. Can.
106 C3	Inklin r. B.C. Can.
185 I3	Inkylap Turkm.
203 H9	Inland Kaikoura Range mts South I. N.Z.
	Inland Sea Japan see Seto-naikai
117 K5	Inlet NY U.S.A.
88 E2	I-n-Milach well Mali
53 I8	Inn r. Europe
105 L2	Innaanganeq c. Greenland
165 □13	Innai Japan
204 H2	Innamincka S.A. Austr.
204 H2	Innamincka Regional Reserve nature res. S.A. Austr.
20 M3	Inndyr Norway
26 G11	Innellan Argyll and Bute, Scotland U.K.
58 A5	Innerbraz Austria
99 □2a	Inner Islands Seychelles
26 J11	Innerleithen Scottish Borders, Scotland U.K.
	Inner Mongolia aut. reg. China see Nei Mongol Zizhiqu
53 O4	Innernzell Ger.
58 F6	Innervillgraten Austria
204 F6	Innes National Park S.A. Austr.
20 M3	Innhavet Norway
75 □	I-n-Niexfa, Ras pt Malta
53 K5	Inning am Ammersee Ger.
207 K4	Innisfail Qld Austr.
181 L8	Innisfail Alta Can.
27 E9	Innishannon Rep. of Ireland
27 J4	Inniskeen Rep. of Ireland
162 F4	Innoketnyevka Rus. Fed.
165 K12	Innoshima Japan
58 D5	Innsbruck Austria
78 B3	Innsbruck Austria
71 K1	Innsbruck airport Austria
108 L1	Innuksuak r. Que. Can.
59 H3	Inny r. Rep. of Ireland
27 E9	Inny r. Rep. of Ireland
155 C13	Inobonto Sulawesi Indon.
142 B3	Inocência r. Brazil
166 E2	Inokuchi Japan
90 C5	Inongo Dem. Rep. Congo
91 B5	Inoni Congo
136 C5	Inonas Peru
79 L3	İnönü Turkey
136 D1	Inosu Col.
88 E2	I-n-Ouchef well Mali
87 F5	I-n-Ouzzal, Oued watercourse Alg.
57 H3	Inovec mt. Slovakia
55 I4	Inowłódz Pol.
54 G3	Inowrocław Pol.
191 E1	Inozemtsevo Rus. Fed.
78 A3	Inönü Nisoi is Greece
167 L2	Iono Japan
193 P4	Iony, Ostrov i. Rus. Fed.
	Iordan Uzbek. see Yordon
191 H4	Iori r. Georgia
78 G6	Ios Greece
79 G6	Ios i. Greece
164 □F19	Iō-shima i. Japan see Iō-jima
164 □F19	Iō-Tori-jima i. Nansei-shotō Japan
88 A2	Iouîk Maur.
120 J5	Iowa r. IA U.S.A.
120 I4	Iowa state U.S.A.
120 J5	Iowa City IA U.S.A.
120 J4	Iowa Falls IA U.S.A.
191 H5	Iō-zan hill Japan
18 E7	Ipa r. Belarus
128 B5	Ipala Mex.
93 B6	Ipala Tanz.
122 C7	Ipameri Brazil
143 G3	Ipanema r. Brazil
140 F4	Ipanema r. Brazil
138 B2	Iparía Peru
143 F3	Ipatinga Brazil
15 H7	Ipatovo Rus. Fed.
145 C5	Ipaucu Brazil
110 D9	Ipava IL U.S.A.
78 B3	Ipeiros admin. reg. Greece
191 E6	İpek Geçidi pass Turkey
57 H4	Ipel' r. Slovakia
57 I3	Ipel' r. Slovakia
97 J3	Ipelegeng S. Africa
57 H4	Ipelská pahorkatina mts Slovakia
53 I2	Iphofen Ger.
142 B3	Ipiaçu Brazil
136 B4	Ipiales Col.
140 F5	Ipiaú Brazil
39 F3	Ipirá Brazil
136 D5	Ipiranga Amazonas Brazil
142 C2	Ipiranga Amazonas Brazil
142 B6	Ipiranga Paraná Brazil
	Ípiros admin. reg. Greece see Ipeiros
200 □1a	Ipis i. Chuuk Micronesia
138 B1	Ipixuna r. Brazil
136 E5	Ipixuna r. Brazil
139 E5	Ipixuna r. Brazil
156 D2	Ipoh Malaysia
140 C2	Ipole Tanz.
57 H4	Ipoly r. Hungary/Slovakia
143 F2	Ipoponga Brazil
142 B2	Iporá Brazil
74 G10	Iport r. Sicilia Italy
110 J3	Ippesheim Ger.
52 E7	Ipplepen Devon, England U.K.
90 D3	Ippy C.A.R.
79 G2	Ipsala Turkey
167 I6	Ipsheim Ger.
142 E1	Ipstones Staffordshire, England U.K.
16 □	Ipswich Qld Austr.
130 □	Ipswich Jamaica
31 O3	Ipswich Suffolk, England U.K.
187 H2	Ipswich SD U.S.A.

27 B4	Inishkea North i. Rep. of Ireland
27 B4	Inishkea South i. Rep. of Ireland
27 C6	Inishmaan i. Rep. of Ireland
27 C6	Inishmore i. Rep. of Ireland
27 H4	Inishmurray i. Rep. of Ireland
27 H2	Inishowen pen.
	Rep. of Ireland
27 H2	Inishowen Head Rep. of Ireland
27 H2	Inishtrahull i. Rep. of Ireland
27 H2	Inishtrahull Sound sea chan. Rep. of Ireland
27 B5	Inishturk i. Rep. of Ireland
169 P4	Injgan Sum Nei Mongol China
92 C2	Injibara Eth.
207 L8	Injune Qld Austr.
182 K5	Inkardar'ya Kazakh.
31 I3	Inkberrow Worcestershire, England U.K.
27 E6	Inishmaan i. Rep. of Ireland
27 C6	Inishmore i. Rep. of Ireland
26 G8	Invergarry Highland, Scotland U.K.
26 H7	Invergordon Highland, Scotland U.K.
26 F10	Inverinan Argyll and Bute, Scotland U.K.
26 K9	Inverkeilor Angus, Scotland U.K.
26 J10	Inverkeithing Fife, Scotland U.K.
26 F6	Inverkirkaig Highland, Scotland U.K.
26 F7	Inverlael Highland, Scotland U.K.
207 H5	Inverleigh Qld Austr.
107 K5	Invermay Sask. Can.
26 G8	Invermoriston Highland, Scotland U.K.
109 I4	Inverness N.S. Can.
26 H8	Inverness Highland, Scotland U.K.
124 J3	Inverness CA U.S.A.
115 F11	Inverness FL U.S.A.
26 F10	Invernoaden Argyll and Bute, Scotland U.K.
26 G10	Inveruglas Stirling, Scotland U.K.
26 G1	Inverurie Aberdeenshire, Scotland U.K.
206 B4	Inverway N.T. Austr.
159 C8	Investigator Channel Myanmar
204 E5	Investigator Group is S.A. Austr.
215 K5	Investigator Ridge sea feature Indian Ocean
204 F6	Investigator Strait S.A. Austr.
177 M7	Invisible Bank sea feature Andaman & Nicobar Is India
116 H8	Inwood WV U.S.A.
97 M7	Inxu r. S. Africa
172 H1	Inya Rus. Fed.
	Inyanga Zimbabwe see Nyanga
95 G3	Inyanga Mountains Zimbabwe
	Inyanga National Park Zimbabwe see Nyanga National Park
95 G3	Inyangani mt. Zimbabwe
	Inyati Zimbabwe see Nyathi
	Inyazura Zimbabwe see Nyazura
124 O4	Inyokern CA U.S.A.
124 N4	Inyo Mountains CA U.S.A.
93 B6	Inyonga Tanz.
15 I5	Inza Rus. Fed.
167 I4	Inzai Japan
53 N6	Inzell Ger.
182 G1	Inzer Rus. Fed.
14 L5	Inzer r. Rus. Fed.
15 H5	Inzhavino Rus. Fed.
58 D5	Inzing Austria
78 B3	Ioannina Greece
78 B3	Ioannina, Limni l. Greece
71 O3	Iöf di Montasio mt. Italy
165 □2	Iō-jima i. Kazan-rettō Japan
87 G5	Iö-jima i. Nansei-shotō Japan
14 G2	Iokanga r. Rus. Fed.
121 H7	Iola KS U.S.A.
118 B2	Iola PA U.S.A.
110 E5	Iola WI U.S.A.
91 B9	Iona Angola
109 I4	Iona N.S. Can.
26 D10	Iona i. Scotland U.K.
	Iona, Parque Nacional do nat. park Angola
26 D10	Iona, Sound of sea chan. Scotland U.K.
26 D10	Iona Abbey tourist site Scotland U.K.
124 O3	Ione NV U.S.A.
122 F2	Ione OR U.S.A.
77 M6	Ioneşti Romania
110 I7	Ionia MI U.S.A.
	Ionian Islands Greece see Ionioi Nisoi
78 A3	Ionian Sea Greece/Italy
78 A3	Ionioi Nisoi is Greece
167 L2	Iono Japan
193 P4	Iony, Ostrov i. Rus. Fed.

26 G8	Invergarry Highland, Scotland U.K.
185 J8	Īrafshān reg. Iran
166 F6	Irago-misaki pt Japan
166 E6	Irago-suidō str. Japan
141 B8	Irai Brazil
207 M1	Irai Island P.N.G.
78 E1	Iraï Brazil
79 G6	Iraklaia i. Greece
78 G7	Irakleio Kriti Greece
78 G7	Irakleiou, Kolpos b. Kriti Greece
	Iráklia i. Greece see Irakleia
	Iraklion Kriti Greece see Irakleio
147 G4	Irala Arg.
139 G6	Irala Para.
140 E5	Iramaia Brazil
184 F6	Iran country Asia
157 K4	Iran, Pegunungan mts Indon.
191 I6	Irānābad Iran
176 G8	Iranamadu Tank resr Sri Lanka
36 G8	Irancy France
184 B3	Īrānshāh Iran
184 F6	Īrānshahr Iran
137 F2	Irapa Venez.
128 F5	Irapuato Mex.
189 K7	Iraq country Asia
87 G4	Irarrarene reg. Alg.
117 M4	Irasville VT U.S.A.
137 H5	Iratapuru r. Brazil
141 B3	Irati Brazil
63 K1	Irati r. Spain
57 K5	Iratoşa Romania
14 K2	Irayel' Rus. Fed.
126 □R13	Irazú, Volcán vol. Costa Rica
18 F4	Irbe r. Latvia
	Irbe šaurums sea chan. Estonia/Latvia see Irbe Strait
18 E4	Irbe Strait Estonia/Latvia
	Irbe vāin sea chan. Estonia/Latvia see Irbe Strait
190 D6	Irbid Jordan
192 H4	Irbit Rus. Fed.
31 K3	Irchester Northamptonshire, England U.K.
59 J4	Irdning Austria
17 K4	Irdyn' Ukr.
90 C5	Irebu Dem. Rep. Congo
140 E4	Irecê Brazil
57 H5	Iregszemcse Hungary
63 R3	Irati r. Spain
90 C5	Ireko Dem. Rep. Congo
27 G5	Ireland, Republic of country Europe
119 G1	Ireland Corners NY U.S.A.
115 □1	Ireland Island Bermuda
27 J6	Ireland's Eye i. Rep. of Ireland
14 L4	Iren' r. Rus. Fed.
147 G4	Irene Arg.
203 B12	Irene, Mount South I. N.Z.
137 G4	Irene r. Guyana/Venez.
142 A6	Iretama Brazil
191 F1	Irgakly Rus. Fed.
191 H4	Irganch'ai Georgia
79 K4	Irgilli Turkey
182 I3	Irgiz Kazakh.
182 J3	Irgiz r. Kazakh.
72 D7	Irgoli Sardegna Italy
87 G3	Irharrhar, Oued watercourse Illizi/Tamanrasset Alg.
20 □B1	İsafjarðardjúp est. Iceland
20 □B1	İsafjörður Iceland
178 F7	Isagarh Madh. Prad. India
165 H13	Isahaya Japan
185 K8	Isai Kalat Pak.
90 C5	Isaka Dem. Rep. Congo
185 N5	Isa Khel Pak.
14 J2	Isakogorka Rus. Fed.
19 Q1	Isakovo Leningradskaya Oblast' Rus. Fed.
19 R6	Isakovo Smolenskaya Oblast' Rus. Fed.
72 D7	Isalle r. Italy
77 L6	Isalniţa Romania
95 □K2	Isalo, Massif de l' mts Madag.
95 □J4	Isalo, Parc National de l' nat. park Madag.
136 D4	Isana r. Col.
90 C5	Isanga Dem. Rep. Congo
93 A7	Isangano National Park Zambia
89 G3	Isanlu Nigeria
87 G4	Isaouane-n-Tifernine des. Alg.
94 N3	Isar r. Ger.
154 D5	Isarog, Mount Phil.
57 I4	Isaszeg Hungary
167 I4	Isawa Japan
36 D2	Isbergues France
26 □N1	Isbister Shetland, Scotland U.K.
26 □O2	Isbister Shetland, Scotland U.K.
63 K6	Íscar Spain
138 D5	Iscayachi Bol.
57 K7	Ischenhausen Ger.
57 I4	Ischgl Austria
73 L6	Ischia, Isola d' i. Italy
73 L6	Ischia Italy
186 C2	Ischitella Italy
208 H4	Isdell r. W.A. Austr.
164 C2	Ise Japan
167 J6	Isehara Japan
93 B6	Iseke Tanz.
58 G6	Isel r. Austria
53 N5	Isen r. Ger.
53 M2	Isen Ger.
97 J2	Is-en-Bassigny France
14 J2	Isenbyevo Rus. Fed.
49 G6	Isenbüttel Ger.
90 C5	Isengi Dem. Rep. Congo
164 □F19	Isen-zaki hd Nansei-shotō Japan
70 H4	Iseo Italy
70 H4	Iseo, Lago d' l. Italy
41 N6	Iseran, Col de l' pass France
36 J4	Isère dept France
42 H3	Isère r. France
41 F7	Isère, Pointe pt Fr. Guiana
49 E8	Iserlohn Ger.
49 I6	Isernhagen Ger.
73 M4	Isernia Italy
73 M4	Isernia prov. Italy
167 J3	Isesaki Japan
66 E6	Ise-shima National Park Japan
166 E6	Ise-wan b. Japan
89 E5	Iseyin Nigeria
183 J8	Isfana Tajik.
20 □	Isfjord Radio Svalbard
191 H5	Isherim, Gora mt. Rus. Fed.
184 C5	Isfahan Iran
164 G3	Ishevskoye Rus. Fed.
164 S7	Ishidoriya Japan
166 B22	Ishigaki-jima i. Nansei-shotō Japan
167 K3	Ishige Japan
166 □	Ishigaki-jima i. Nansei-shotō Japan
167 K3	Ishige Japan
164 G3	Ishikari-gawa r. Japan
164 □1	Ishikari-wan b. Japan
167 H3	Ishikawa Japan
164 C2	Ishikawa Okinawa Japan
66 D2	Ishikawa pref. Japan
192 H4	Ishim Rus. Fed.
172 H1	Ishim r. Kazakh./Rus. Fed.
182 H1	Ishim r. Kazakh./Rus. Fed.
165 N5	Ishinomaki Japan
165 N5	Ishinomaki-wan b. Japan
164 S8	Ishioka Japan
185 N2	Ishkoshim Tajik.

26 F19	İron, Parque Nacional do nat. park Angola
88 E2	I-n-Sokki, Oued watercourse Alg.
90 D3	Insein Myanmar
37 M6	Insein Myanmar
87 F3	Insee Ger.
18 E7	İnsrabuga well Mali
77 M7	Insch Aberdeenshire, Scotland U.K.
115 □1	Insko Pol.
54 D2	Iński Park Krajobrazowy Pol.
37 M6	Insming France
54 C3	Insko, Jezioro l. Pol.
209 B8	Inscription, Cape W.A. Austr.
158 C6	Insein Myanmar
50 J3	Insel Usedom park Ger.
50 M4	Iński Park Krajobrazowy Pol.
54 D2	Ińsko Pol.
52 G2	Institut Azer.
18 E7	Insrar r. Azer.
128 G6	Insurgente José María Morelos y Pavón, Parque Nacional nat. park Mex.
95 E3	Insuza r. Zimbabwe
14 M2	Inta Rus. Fed.
186 B8	Int-n-Tilit Mali
88 E3	Int-n-Tilit Mali
77 O1	International Falls MN U.S.A.
110 A1	International Peace Garden tourist site Can./U.S.A.
87 F2	Intecouo Fr. Guiana
185 I8	Īrafshān Iran

Ishkuman to Jamtara
278

178 D1 Ishkuman Jammu and Kashmir
19 W4 Ishnya Rus. Fed.
110 G3 Ishpeming MI U.S.A.
Ishtikhon Uzbek. see Ishtixon
183 L8 Ishtixon Uzbek.
185 N3 Ishtragh Afgh.
179 L7 Ishurdi Bangl.
138 D3 Isiboro r. Bol.
138 D4 Isiboro Sécure, Parque Nacional nat. park Bol.
39 I4 Isigny-le-Buat France
39 I3 Isigny-sur-Mer France
79 L4 Işıklar Turkey
79 K4 Işıklı Turkey
79 K4 Işıklı Barajı resr Turkey
72 C8 Isili Sardegna Italy
192 I4 Isil'kul' Rus. Fed.
93 B6 Isimbira Tanz.
136 B5 Isinliví Ecuador
92 C4 Isiolo Kenya
97 O5 Isipingo S. Africa
90 E4 Isiro Dem. Rep. Congo
207 J8 Isisford Qld Austr.
20 □ Isispynten pt Svalbard
59 J8 Iška r. Slovenia
185 L3 Iskabad Canal Afgh.
185 N3 Iskan Afgh.
14 K2 Iskateley Rus. Fed.
188 H5 İskenderun Turkey
188 G5 İskenderun Körfezi b. Turkey
188 G3 İskilip Turkey
182 E4 Iskine Kazakh.
182 E4 Iskininskiy Kazakh.
192 J4 Iskitim Rus. Fed.
19 W7 Iskra Rus. Fed.
17 M5 Iskrivka Kirovohrads'ka Oblast' Ukr.
17 O4 Iskrivka Poltavs'ka Oblast' Ukr.
77 M7 Iskŭr r. Bulg.
77 L8 Iskŭr, Yazovir resr Bulg.
92 F2 Iskushuban Somalia
106 D3 Iskut r. B.C. Can.
129 L7 Isla Mex.
26 J9 Isla r. Angus/Perth and Kinross, Scotland U.K.
147 I2 Isla Cabellos Uru.
64 E6 Isla Canela Spain
64 E6 Isla Cristina Spain
136 C2 Isla de Salamanca, Parque Nacional nat. park Col.
207 L8 Isla Gorge National Park Qld Austr.
188 H5 İslahiye Turkey
191 B5 İslâhiye Turkey
185 O5 Islamabad Pak.
145 B7 Isla Magdalena, Parque Nacional nat. park Chile
64 G6 Isla Mayor marsh Spain
64 G6 Isla Menor marsh Spain
185 N8 Islamgarh Pak.
185 N9 Islamkot Pak.
115 G13 Islamorada FL U.S.A.
179 J7 Islampur Bihar India
106 F2 Island r. N.W.T. Can.
Ísland country Europe see Iceland
154 B7 Island Bay Palawan Phil.
117 □Q2 Island Falls ME U.S.A.
204 F4 Island Lagoon salt flat S.A. Austr.
107 M4 Island Lake Man. Can.
107 M4 Island Lake l. Man. Can.
110 B2 Island Lake MN U.S.A.
27 K3 Island Magee pen. Northern Ireland U.K.
122 I4 Island Park ID U.S.A.
117 N4 Island Pond VT U.S.A.
202 I2 Islands, Bay of North I. N.Z.
62 C4 Islas Atlánticas de Galicia, Parque Nacional de las nature res. Spain
126 □Q9 Islas de Bahá, Parque Nacional nat. park Hond.
147 F3 Isla Verde Arg.
26 D11 Islay i. Scotland U.K.
26 D11 Islay, Sound of sea chan. Scotland U.K.
77 M7 Islaz Romania
42 G4 Isle France
42 D6 Isle r. France
31 M3 Isleham Cambridgeshire, England U.K.
30 D1 Isle of Anglesey admin. div. Wales U.K.
28 H5 Isle of Man i. Irish Sea
26 H13 Isle of Whithorn Dumfries and Galloway, Scotland U.K.
31 J6 Isle of Wight admin. div. England U.K.
116 I12 Isle of Wight VA U.S.A.
110 F2 Isle Royale National Park MI U.S.A.
36 H5 Isles-sur-Suippe France
146 B1 Islón Chile
131 □7 Islote Point Trin. and Tob.
138 C4 Isluga, Parque Nacional nat. park Chile
147 I3 Ismael Cortinas Uru.
Ismail Ukr. see Izmayil
Ismâ`ilîya Egypt see Al Ismā'īlīyah
Ismailly Azer. see İsmayıllı
53 L5 Ismaning Ger.
191 J5 İsmayıllı Azer.
191 J5 İsmayıllı qoruğu nature res. Azer.
185 N2 Ismoili Somoní, Qullai mt. Tajik.
85 G3 Isnā Egypt
62 E9 Isna Port.
74 G8 Isnello Sicilia Italy
53 I6 Isny im Allgäu Ger.
95 □J4 Isoanala Madag.
166 E7 Isobe Japan
167 K5 Isogo Japan
21 P5 Isojoki Fin.
93 B7 Isoka Zambia
20 S3 Isokylä Fin.
20 Q5 Isokyrö Fin.
41 K8 Isola France
41 K8 Isola 2000 France
72 C3 Isolaccio-di-Fiumorbo Corse France
73 L2 Isola del Gran Sasso d'Italia Italy
71 K5 Isola della Scala Italy
74 E7 Isola delle Femmine Sicilia Italy
73 L4 Isola del Liri Italy
75 M6 Isola di Capo Rizzuto Italy
38 D6 Isole r. France
70 F6 Isole del Cantone Italy
66 H3 Isona Spain
71 P4 Isonzo r. Italy
93 A7 Isopa Tanz.
98 □3e Isora El Hierro Canary Is
95 □J4 Isorana Madag.
70 I5 Isorella Italy
20 S4 Iso-Syöte hill Fin.
41 D8 Ispagnac France
79 L5 Isparta Turkey
79 L5 Isparta prov. Turkey
77 O7 Isperikh Bulg.
74 H10 Ispica Sicilia Italy
74 H10 Ispica r. Sicilia Italy
185 J8 Ispikan Pak.
189 J3 İspir Turkey
Ispisar Tajik. see Khŭjand
185 L7 Isplinji Pak.
43 B9 Ispoure France
70 F4 Ispra Italy
191 C1 Ispravnaya Rus. Fed.
52 F4 Ispringen Ger.
190 C6 Israel country Asia
142 B2 Israelândia Brazil
209 G12 Israelite Bay W.A. Austr.
Isrā'īl country Asia see Israel
15 I5 Issa Rus. Fed.
18 L5 Issa r. Rus. Fed.
41 J10 Issambres, Pointe des pt France
89 H5 Issanguele Cameroon
137 G3 Issano Guyana
41 E7 Issarlès France
84 B6 Isséirom Chad
49 B7 Isselburg Ger.
37 N8 Issenheim France
166 F6 Isshiki Japan
88 D5 Issia Côte d'Ivoire
43 F6 Issigeac France
70 D4 Issime Italy
155 C3 Issimu Sulawesi Indon.
189 L8 Issin tourist site Iraq
65 P4 Isso Spain
70 D4 Issogne Italy
40 C5 Issoire France
41 I10 Issole r. France
89 F2 Issouanka well Mali
42 H2 Issoudun France
87 F5 Issoulane Erareine slope Alg.
49 B7 Issum Ger.
93 B6 Issuna Tanz.
40 G1 Is-sur-Tille France
Issyk-Kul' Kyrg. see Balykchy
Issyk-Kul', Ozero salt l. Kyrg. see Ysyk-Köl
40 D3 Issy-l'Évêque France
71 R7 Ist Croatia
71 R7 Ist i. Croatia
19 T8 Ista r. Rus. Fed.
186 D3 Iṣṭabl 'Antar Saudi Arabia
189 K6 Iṣṭablāt tourist site Iraq
185 M5 Īstādeh-ye Moqor, Āb-e l. Afgh.
57 J3 Istállós-kő hill Hungary
65 J7 Istán Spain
79 J1 İstanbul Turkey
79 J1 İstanbul prov. Turkey
79 K1 İstanbul Boğazı str. Turkey
31 M5 Istead Rise Kent, England U.K.
54 G6 Istebna Pol.
57 I2 Istebné Slovakia
56 F5 Isten dombja hill Hungary
184 C5 Īstgāh-e Eznā Iran
144 F3 Isthilart Arg.
78 E4 Istiaia Greece
185 P3 Istik r. Tajik.
191 G6 İstisu Azer.
136 B3 Istmina Col.
17 R2 Istobnoye Rus. Fed.
76 I8 Istok Kosovo, Srbija Serb. and Mont.
115 G12 Istokpoga, Lake FL U.S.A.
68 D3 Istra pen. Croatia
19 T6 Istra Rus. Fed.
41 F9 Istres France
Istria pen. Croatia see Istra
77 Q6 Istria Romania
77 O5 Istrița, Dealul hill Romania
43 B9 Isturits France
19 X7 Ist'ya r. Rus. Fed.
66 E3 Isuela r. Aragón Spain
63 R5 Isuela r. Spain
43 B11 Isuerre Spain
167 L5 Isumi Japan
167 L5 Isumi-gawa r. Japan
179 L8 Iswaripur Bangl.
97 O2 Iswepe S. Africa
182 G1 Isyangulovo Rus. Fed.
140 F4 Itabaianinha Brazil
143 G4 Itabapoana Brazil
143 G4 Itabapoana r. Brazil
142 C5 Itaberá Brazil
140 E5 Itaberaba Brazil
142 C2 Itaberaí Brazil
143 F3 Itabira Brazil
143 F4 Itabirito Brazil
137 F6 Itaboca Brazil
143 F5 Itaboraí Brazil
141 F5 Itabuna Brazil
140 C3 Itacaiuna r. Brazil
140 D4 Itacajá Brazil
143 F2 Itacambira Brazil
141 D5 Itacarambi Brazil
140 F5 Itacaré Brazil
139 H1 Itacayunas, Serra hills Brazil
137 G5 Itacoatiara Brazil
136 D6 Itacuaí r. Brazil
139 F6 Itacurubí del Rosario Para.
166 E4 Itadori Japan
140 E5 Itaetê Brazil
93 B6 Itaga Tanz.
Itagmatana Iran see Hamadān
143 H2 Itagmirim Brazil
143 G3 Itaguaçu Brazil
143 F5 Itaguaí Brazil
142 B5 Itaguajé Brazil
143 E4 Itaguara Brazil
138 C3 Itahuania Peru
142 C5 Itaí Brazil
140 E3 Itaim r. Brazil
141 C8 Itaiópolis Brazil
141 B8 Itaipu, Represa de resr Brazil
21 S6 Itäisen Suomenlahden kansallispuisto nat. park Fin.
137 G6 Itaituba Brazil
142 B3 Itajá Brazil
141 C8 Itajaí Brazil
142 C4 Itajobi Brazil
143 E5 Itajubá Brazil
141 F5 Itajuípe Brazil
162 A2 Itaka Rus. Fed.
179 J8 Itaki Jharkhand India
167 M4 Itako Japan
167 K3 Itakura Gunma Japan
167 H1 Itakura Niigata Japan
97 P3 Itala Game Reserve nature res. S. Africa
Italia country Europe see Italy
147 F4 Italó Arg.
68 E5 Italy country Europe
140 G3 Itamaracá, Ilha de i. Brazil
143 H2 Itamaraju Brazil
143 F2 Itamarandiba Brazil
140 D2 Itamataré Brazil
143 G3 Itambacuri Brazil
143 G3 Itambacuri r. Brazil
141 E5 Itambé Brazil
143 F3 Itambé, Pico de mt. Brazil
166 B6 Itami Japan
166 B6 Itami airport Japan
95 □I5 Itampolo Madag.
174 H6 Itanagar Arun. Prad. India
140 D5 Itanguari r. Brazil
142 D6 Itanhaém Brazil
143 E5 Itanhandu Brazil
137 F6 Itanhauã r. Brazil
143 G2 Itanhém Brazil
143 H2 Itanhém r. Brazil
143 G3 Itanhomi Brazil
137 H4 Itany r. Fr. Guiana/Suriname
143 G2 Itaobím Brazil
143 F4 Itaocara Brazil
140 C5 Itapaci Brazil
140 F2 Itapagé Brazil
142 C3 Itapajipe Brazil
137 F6 Itaparaná r. Brazil
140 F4 Itaparica, Represa de resr Brazil
143 H1 Itapebi Brazil
147 I2 Itapebí Uru.
143 E4 Itapecerica Brazil
143 G4 Itapemirim Brazil
143 G4 Itaperuna Brazil
141 E5 Itapetinga Brazil
142 C5 Itapetininga Brazil
142 C5 Itapeva Brazil
141 C9 Itapeva, Lago l. Brazil
137 G5 Itapi r. Brazil
140 E4 Itapicuru Brazil
140 F4 Itapicuru r. Brazil
140 D3 Itapicuru, Serra de hills Brazil
140 D2 Itapicuru Mirim Brazil
140 F4 Itapicuru Mirim r. Brazil
137 F6 Itapinima Brazil
140 F2 Itapipoca Brazil
142 D5 Itapira Brazil
137 G5 Itapiranga Brazil
142 B1 Itapirapuã Brazil
147 I1 Itapitocai Brazil
140 F3 Itapiúna Brazil
142 C4 Itápolis Brazil
140 F3 Itaporanga Paraíba Brazil
142 C5 Itaporanga São Paulo Brazil
141 C9 Itapuã Brazil
141 C5 Itapuranga Brazil
142 D5 Itaquaquecetuba Brazil
141 A9 Itaqui Brazil
143 G3 Itarana Brazil
143 G1 Itarantim Brazil
142 C6 Itararé Brazil
142 C5 Itararé r. Brazil
178 F8 Itarsi Madh. Prad. India
142 B3 Itarumã Brazil
20 T5 Itä-Suomi prov. Fin.
146 A5 Itata r. Chile
139 F7 Itati, Laguna l. Arg.
142 D5 Itatiba Brazil
142 C5 Itatinga Brazil
137 F6 Itatuba Brazil
137 I5 Itatupã Brazil
142 C2 Itauçu Brazil
140 E3 Itaueira r. Brazil
137 E5 Itaúna Amazonas Brazil
143 E4 Itaúna Minas Gerais Brazil
143 H3 Itaúnas Brazil
143 H3 Itaúnas r. Brazil
154 C1 Itbayat i. Phil.
106 E4 Itcha Ilgachuz Provincial Park park B.C. Can.
106 H1 Itchen Lake N.W.T. Can.
138 C4 Ite Peru
78 D4 Itea Greece
90 F5 Itebero Dem. Rep. Congo
183 N1 Itemgen, Ozero l. Kazakh.
93 B6 Itende Tanz.
63 L4 Itero de la Vega Spain
93 C7 Itete Tanz.
42 E3 Iteuil France
91 E8 Itezhi-Tezhi Dam Zambia
Ithaca Greece see Ithaki
Ithaca i. Greece see Ithaki
110 J6 Ithaca MI U.S.A.
116 I6 Ithaca NY U.S.A.
78 B4 Ithaki Greece
78 B4 Ithaki i. Greece
78 B4 Ithakis, Steno sea chan. Greece
49 H6 Ith Hils ridge Ger.
190 F7 Ithrah Saudi Arabia
93 B6 Itigi Tanz.
165 I14 Itihusa-yama mt. Japan
105 M3 Itilleq Greenland
90 D4 Itimbiri r. Dem. Rep. Congo
143 G2 Itinga Brazil
141 B6 Itiquira Brazil
139 F4 Itiquira r. Brazil
142 D5 Itirapina Brazil
142 D4 Itirapuã Brazil
140 F4 Itiúba Brazil
140 F4 Itiúba, Serra de hills Brazil
144 E1 Itiyura r. Arg.
179 J7 Itkhari Jharkhand India
182 E3 Itmurinkol', Ozero l. Kazakh.
167 J6 Itō Japan
95 I2 Itoculo Moz.
167 G1 Itoigawa Japan
90 D5 Itoko Dem. Rep. Congo
164 □1 Itoman Okinawa Japan
36 B5 Iton r. France
95 □J4 Itongafeno mt. Madag.
Iton-Qälla Rus. Fed. see Itum-Kale
166 E5 Itonuki Japan
65 L7 Itrabo Spain
73 L5 Itri Italy
99 □3a Itsandzéni Njazidja Comoros
99 □3a Itsikoudi Njazidja Comoros
165 H14 Itsuki Japan
165 J12 Itsukushima i. Japan
87 G2 Ittel, Oued watercourse Alg.
72 B6 Ittireddu Sardegna Italy
72 B6 Ittiri Sardegna Italy
105 P2 Ittoqqortoormiit Greenland
45 F7 Ittre Belgium
142 D5 Itu Brazil
89 G5 Itu Nigeria
152 D4 Itu Abu Island S. China Sea
140 E5 Ituaçu Brazil
140 F5 Ituberá Brazil
138 C1 Itucumã r. Brazil
62 G8 Ituero de Azaba Spain
136 D6 Ituí r. Brazil
142 C3 Ituiutaba Brazil
91 E5 Itula Dem. Rep. Congo
93 B6 Itumba Tanz.
142 C3 Itumbiara Brazil
142 C3 Itumbiara, Barragem resr Brazil
191 G3 Itum-Kale Rus. Fed.
93 B7 Itungi Port Malawi
137 G3 Ituni Guyana
140 C3 Itupiranga Brazil
142 B3 Iturama Brazil
139 F6 Iturbe Para.
127 O8 Iturbide Campeche Mex.
129 H1 Iturbide Nuevo León Mex.
90 E4 Ituri r. Dem. Rep. Congo
161 Q3 Iturup, Ostrov i. Kuril'skiye O-va Rus. Fed.
143 E4 Itutinga Brazil
142 D4 Ituverava Brazil
138 D1 Ituxi r. Brazil
144 F2 Ituzaingo Arg.
49 K11 Itz r. Ger.
48 I3 Itzehoe Ger.
48 J3 Itzstedt Ger.
136 D4 Iuaretê Brazil
74 H8 Iudica, Monte hill Sicilia Italy
121 K8 Iuka MS U.S.A.
193 T3 Iul'tin Rus. Fed.
95 H2 Iuluti Moz.
143 G4 Iúna Brazil
136 D4 Iutica Brazil
142 B6 Ivaí Brazil
142 A5 Ivaí r. Brazil
142 B6 Ivaiporã Brazil
95 □J4 Ivakoany mt. Madag.
20 S2 Ivalo Fin.
20 S2 Ivalojoki r. Fin.
56 F4 Iván Hungary
55 L6 Ivana Franka Ukr.
16 E1 Ivanava Belarus
56 F2 Ivančice Czech Rep.
68 F2 Ivanec Croatia
18 L2 Ivangorod Rus. Fed.
205 J5 Ivanhoe N.S.W. Austr.
208 J3 Ivanhoe W.A. Austr.
108 D3 Ivanhoe r. Ont. Can.
124 M5 Ivanhoe CA U.S.A.
120 G3 Ivanhoe MN U.S.A.
116 E12 Ivanhoe VA U.S.A.
107 J2 Ivanhoe Lake N.W.T. Can.
111 L1 Ivanhoe Lake Ont. Can.
68 F3 Ivanić-Grad Croatia
17 O2 Ivanino Rus. Fed.
19 X6 Ivanishchi Rus. Fed.
17 Q3 Ivanivka Kharkivs'ka Oblast' Ukr.
17 L7 Ivanivka Khersons'ka Oblast' Ukr.
17 N7 Ivanivka Khersons'ka Oblast' Ukr.
17 K4 Ivanivka Kyivs'ka Oblast' Ukr.
17 R5 Ivanivka Luhans'ka Oblast' Ukr.
16 J7 Ivanivka Odes'ka Oblast' Ukr.
17 M8 Ivanivka Respublika Krym Ukr.
57 L3 Ivanivka Zakarpats'ka Oblast' Ukr.
16 G5 Ivanivtsi Ukr.
76 I7 Ivanjica Srbija Serb. and Mont.
56 G3 Ivanka pri Dunaji Slovakia
16 I3 Ivankiv Ukr.
68 G3 Ivankovo Croatia
19 U7 Ivan'kovo Rus. Fed.
19 X5 Ivan'kovskiy Rus. Fed.
19 T5 Ivan'kovskoye Vodokhranilishche resr Rus. Fed.
162 I4 Ivankovtsy Rus. Fed.
16 D5 Ivano-Frankivs'k Ukr.
16 D5 Ivano-Frankivs'ka Oblast' admin. div. Ukr.
Ivano-Frankivs'k Oblast admin. div. Ukr. see Ivano-Frankivs'ka Oblast'
16 C4 Ivano-Frankove Ukr.
Ivano-Frankovsk Ukr. see Ivano-Frankivs'k
Ivano-Frankovskaya Oblast' admin. div. Ukr. see Ivano-Frankivs'ka Oblast'
Ivano-Frankovsk Oblast admin. div. Ukr. see Ivano-Frankivs'ka Oblast'
16 H4 Ivanopil' Ukr.
17 O3 Ivano-Shyychyne Ukr.
Ivanovka Kazakh. see Kokzhayyk
162 E3 Ivanovka Amurskaya Oblast' Rus. Fed.
182 E1 Ivanovka Orenburgskaya Oblast' Rus. Fed.
Ivanovo Belarus see Ivanava
77 N7 Ivanovo tourist site Bulg.
19 X5 Ivanovo Ivanovskaya Oblast' Rus. Fed.
19 N5 Ivanovo Pskovskaya Oblast' Rus. Fed.
19 U3 Ivanovo Tverskaya Oblast' Rus. Fed.
Ivanovo Oblast admin. div. Rus. Fed. see Ivanovskaya Oblast'
17 R8 Ivanovskaya Rus. Fed.
19 Y4 Ivanovskaya Oblast' admin. div. Rus. Fed.
183 T2 Ivanovskiy Khrebet mts Kazakh.
17 N2 Ivanovskoye Kurskaya Oblast' Rus. Fed.
19 T8 Ivanovskoye Orlovskaya Oblast' Rus. Fed.
19 W5 Ivanovskoye Yaroslavskaya Oblast' Rus. Fed.
125 Q6 Ivanpah Lake CA U.S.A.
68 E2 Ivanšćica mts Croatia
59 O8 Ivanska Croatia
77 P7 Ivanski Bulg.
182 C1 Ivanteyevka Rus. Fed.
Ivantsevichi Belarus see Ivatsevichy
16 D3 Ivanychi Ukr.
17 L3 Ivanytsya Ukr.
95 □J4 Ivato Madag.
18 I9 Ivatsevichy Belarus
77 O9 Ivaylovgrad Bulg.
77 N9 Ivaylovgrad, Yazovir resr Bulg.
14 M3 Ivdel' Rus. Fed.
99 □3a Ivembeni Njazidja Comoros
31 K4 Iver Buckinghamshire, England U.K.
27 C9 Iveragh reg. Rep. of Ireland
20 □ Iversenfjellet hill Svalbard
77 P5 Ivești Galați Romania
77 P4 Ivești Vaslui Romania
90 B5 Ivindo r. Gabon
31 K4 Ivinghoe Buckinghamshire, England U.K.
141 B7 Ivinheima Brazil
142 A5 Ivinheima r. Brazil
19 R1 Ivinskiy Razliv resr Rus. Fed.
139 H1 Iviti Brazil
105 N3 Ivittuut Greenland
17 P2 Ivnya Rus. Fed.
95 □J4 Ivohibe Madag.
142 B2 Ivolândia Brazil
138 D2 Ivón Bol.
116 I12 Ivor VA U.S.A.
Ivory Coast country Africa see Côte d'Ivoire
23 K5 Ivösjön l. Sweden
19 R8 Ivot Rus. Fed.
17 M2 Ivot Ukr.
17 M2 Ivotka r. Ukr.
70 D5 Ivrea Italy
79 I3 İvrindi Turkey
191 F3 Ivris Ugheltekhili pass Georgia
191 G4 Ivris Zegani plat. Georgia
36 B6 Ivry-la-Bataille France
36 D6 Ivry-sur-Seine France
Ivugivik Que. Can. see Ivujivik
105 K3 Ivujivik Que. Can.
93 B7 Ivuna Tanz.
104 E3 Ivvavik National Park Y.T. Can.
18 J8 Ivyanyets Belarus
30 E7 Ivybridge Devon, England U.K.
116 D10 Ivydale WV U.S.A.
166 B7 Iwade Japan
31 N5 Iwade Kent, England U.K.
167 K3 Iwafune Japan
167 K3 Iwai Japan
165 I13 Iwai-shima i. Japan
164 S7 Iwaizumi Japan
167 M1 Iwaki Japan
164 R6 Iwaki-san vol. Japan
165 J12 Iwakuni Japan
166 E5 Iwakura Japan
167 L3 Iwama Japan
165 J13 Iwamatsu Japan
164 S3 Iwamizawa Japan
166 F5 Iwamura Japan
167 H3 Iwamurada Japan
157 K4 Iwan r. Indon.
164 R4 Iwanai Japan
93 B7 Iwanda Tanz.
55 J5 Iwaniska Pol.
164 R8 Iwanuma Japan
164 Q6 Iwasaki Japan
167 L3 Iwase Japan
166 F2 Iwasehama Japan
167 I2 Iwasuge-yama vol. Japan
167 G6 Iwata Japan
166 B4 Iwataki Japan
164 S7 Iwate Japan
164 S7 Iwate pref. Japan
164 R7 Iwate-san vol. Japan
167 K4 Iwatsuki Japan
55 I6 Iwkowa Pol.
89 G5 Iwo Nigeria
206 D7 Iwupataka Aboriginal Land res. N.T. Austr.
18 I8 Iwye Belarus
129 L9 Ixaltepec Mex.
129 I7 Ixcamilpa Mex.
129 H7 Ixcateopan Mex.
129 M9 Ixhuatán Mex.
129 I5 Ixhuatlán Veracruz Mex.
129 K6 Ixhuatlán Veracruz Mex.
138 C3 Ixiamas Bol.
129 H5 Ixmiquilpán Mex.
97 O6 Ixopo S. Africa
129 J6 Ixtacamaxtitlán Mex.
127 M9 Ixtacomitán Mex.
128 F8 Ixtapa Guerrero Mex.
128 B5 Ixtapa Jalisco Mex.
128 F8 Ixtapa, Punta pt Mex.
129 H7 Ixtapan de la Sal Mex.
129 H6 Ixtlahuaca Mex.
128 D6 Ixtlahuacán Mex.
128 E5 Ixtlán Michoacán Mex.
128 C4 Ixtlán Nayarit Mex.
129 K8 Ixtlán Oaxaca Mex.
31 N3 Ixworth Suffolk, England U.K.
155 B8 Iya i. Indon.
160 G1 Iya r. Rus. Fed.
85 F6 Iyal Bakhit Sudan
93 B7 Iyayi Tanz.
191 B4 İyidere Turkey
165 J13 Iyo Japan
165 K13 Iyomishima Japan
165 J13 Iyo-nada b. Japan
77 L3 Iza r. Romania
57 H4 Iža Slovakia
126 □O10 Izabal Guat.
127 O10 Izabal, Lago de l. Guat.
63 N2 Izalde r. Spain
127 O7 Izamal Mex.
127 M10 Izapa tourist site Mex.
164 S4 Izari-dake mt. Japan
63 O3 Izarra Spain
93 B6 Izazi Tanz.
14 H2 Izba Bol'shaya Bab'ya Rus. Fed.
77 M5 Izbășești hill Romania
191 I3 Izberbash Rus. Fed.
55 L5 Izbica Pol.
54 G3 Izbica Kujawska Pol.
63 Q3 Izco, Sierra de mts Spain
19 Q6 Izdeshkovo Rus. Fed.
41 G6 Izeaux France
62 G5 Izeda Port.
45 D7 Izegem Belgium
184 C6 Īzeh Iran
164 □E20 Izena-jima i. Nansei-shotō Japan
40 H4 Izernore France
41 G6 Izeron France
89 H2 Izgagane well Niger
185 O4 Izgal Pak.
14 K4 Izhevsk Rus. Fed.
19 X7 Izhevskoye Rus. Fed.
14 K2 Izhma Respublika Komi Rus. Fed.
14 K2 Izhma r. Rus. Fed.
187 M4 Izkī Oman
Izmail Ukr. see Izmayil
19 U9 Izmalkovo Rus. Fed.
16 H8 Izmayil Ukr.
Izmeny, Proliv sea chan. Japan/Rus. Fed. see Notsuke-suidō
79 I4 İzmir Turkey
79 I4 İzmir prov. Turkey
79 H4 İzmir Körfezi g. Turkey
79 K2 İzmit Turkey
79 K2 İzmit Körfezi b. Turkey
60 E5 Izmorene Morocco
65 K6 Iznájar Spain
65 K6 Iznajar, Embalse de resr Spain
65 L6 Iznalloz Spain
79 K2 İznik Turkey
79 K2 İznik Gölü l. Turkey
19 S7 Iznoski Rus. Fed.
17 O2 Iznoskovo Rus. Fed.
41 J7 Izoard, Col d' pass France
Izobil'noye Rus. Fed. see Izobil'nyy
15 H7 Izobil'nyy Rus. Fed.
68 D3 Izola Slovenia
19 T5 Izoplit Rus. Fed.
139 E4 Izozog Bol.
139 E4 Izozog Bajo Bol.
190 E6 Izra' Syria
57 I5 Izsák Hungary
129 I6 Iztaccihuatl, Volcán vol. Mex.
129 I6 Iztaccihuatl-Popocatépetl, Parque Nacional nat. park Mex.
77 N9 Iztochni Rodopi mts Bulg.
129 I7 Izúcar de Matamoros Mex.
167 I6 Izu-hantō pen. Japan
165 G12 Izuhara Japan
166 E4 Izumi Fukui Japan
167 M2 Izumi Fukushima Japan
165 H14 Izumi Kagoshima Japan
167 J5 Izumi Kanagawa Japan
164 R8 Izumi Miyagi Japan
166 B7 Izumi Ōsaka Japan
166 B6 Izumiōtsu Japan
166 B7 Izumisano Japan
167 L1 Izumizaki Japan
165 J11 Izumo Japan
165 P9 Izumozaki Japan
167 I5 Izunagaoka Japan
216 E3 Izu-Ogasawara Trench sea feature N. Pacific Ocean
166 A5 Izushi Japan
167 J7 Izu-shotō is Japan
192 J2 Izvestiy Tsentral'nogo Ispolnitel'nogo Komiteta, Ostrova Rus. Fed.
162 G4 Izvestkovyy Rus. Fed.
77 N6 Izvoarele Giurgiu Romania
77 M6 Izvoarele Olt Romania
77 O5 Izvoarele Prahova Romania
77 N6 Izvoru Romania
16 F3 Izyaslav Ukr.
14 L2 Iz''yayu Rus. Fed.
182 H5 Izyndy Kazakh.
17 Q4 Izyum Ukr.

J

21 S6 Jaala Fin.
18 K2 Jaama Estonia
186 G9 Ja'ar Yemen
20 R3 Jaatila Fin.
184 G4 Jaba watercourse Iran
63 P8 Jabaga Spain
71 R6 Jabalanac Croatia
185 M4 Jabal as Sirāj Afgh.
65 N5 Jabalcón mt. Spain
187 I4 Jabal Dab Saudi Arabia
65 K3 Jabalón r. Spain
67 C7 Jabaloyas Spain
178 G8 Jabalpur Madh. Prad. India
65 L4 Jabalquinto Spain
64 F2 Jabarriega hill Spain
186 E6 Jabbārah Fara Islands Saudi Arabia
45 D6 Jabbeke Belgium
190 F2 Jabbūl Syria
190 F3 Jabbūl, Sabkhat al salt flat Syria
50 G3 Jabel Ger.
206 D2 Jabiluka Aboriginal Land res. N.T. Austr.
187 N4 Jabir reg. Oman
206 D2 Jabiru N.T. Austr.
190 D3 Jablah Syria
71 Q5 Jablanac, Rt pt Croatia
68 F4 Jablanica Bos.-Herz.
77 J7 Jablanica r. Serb. and Mont.
55 L4 Jabłoń Pol.
56 E1 Jablonec nad Nisou Czech Rep.
56 G3 Jablonica Slovakia
55 H6 Jabłonka Pol.
55 K3 Jabłonka Kościelna Pol.
55 I3 Jabłonna Pol.
55 K3 Jabłonna Lacka Pol.
55 K4 Jabłonna Pierwsza Pol.
56 D1 Jablonné v Podještědí Czech Rep.
55 H2 Jabłonowo Pomorskie Pol.
57 G2 Jablůnka Czech Rep.
57 H2 Jablunkov Czech Rep.
140 G4 Jaboatão Pernambuco Brazil
140 G4 Jaboatão Brazil
142 C4 Jaboticabal Brazil
143 F3 Jaboticatubas Brazil
41 F7 Jabron r. France
64 F5 Jabugo Spain
68 E4 Jabuka i. Croatia
76 I6 Jabuka Vojvodina, Srbija Serb. and Mont.
156 F5 Jabung, Tanjung pt Indon.
137 E6 Jaburu Brazil
137 G6 Jabuti Brazil
66 D2 Jaca Spain
129 H4 Jacala Mex.
127 N10 Jacaltenango Guat.
140 B5 Jacaré Mato Grosso Brazil
138 D2 Jacaré Rondônia Brazil
140 E4 Jacaré r. Brazil
137 F6 Jacaré r. Brazil
137 G6 Jacareacanga Brazil
143 D5 Jacareí Brazil
139 F2 Jacaretinga Brazil
142 C5 Jacarézinho Brazil
143 F4 Jaceaba Brazil
146 D2 Jáchal r. Arg.
53 L6 Jachen r. Ger.
53 K6 Jachenau Ger.
56 B1 Jáchymov Czech Rep.
141 B5 Jaciara Brazil
143 G2 Jacinto Brazil
147 F6 Jacinto Arauz Arg.
141 C9 Jacinto Machado Brazil
138 D2 Jaciparaná Brazil
138 D2 Jaciparaná r. Brazil
207 J3 Jack r. Qld Austr.
110 H1 Jackfish Ont. Can.
107 I4 Jackfish Lake Sask. Can.
111 P5 Jack Lake Ont. Can.
121 I9 Jack Lee, Lake resr AR U.S.A.
117 □O3 Jackman ME U.S.A.
116 A12 Jacksboro TN U.S.A.
121 F9 Jacksboro TX U.S.A.
207 L9 Jackson Qld Austr.
115 D10 Jackson AL U.S.A.
124 L3 Jackson CA U.S.A.
115 F9 Jackson GA U.S.A.
116 B11 Jackson KY U.S.A.
110 J7 Jackson MI U.S.A.
120 H4 Jackson MN U.S.A.
121 K7 Jackson MO U.S.A.
121 J9 Jackson MS U.S.A.
115 I7 Jackson NC U.S.A.
116 C9 Jackson OH U.S.A.
121 K8 Jackson TN U.S.A.
110 F6 Jackson WI U.S.A.
122 I5 Jackson WY U.S.A.
203 I7 Jackson, Cape South I. N.Z.
212 T2 Jackson, Mount Antarctica
203 C10 Jackson Bay South I. N.Z.
203 C10 Jackson Bay b. South I. N.Z.
203 C10 Jackson Head South I. N.Z.
122 I5 Jackson Lake WY U.S.A.
110 G5 Jacksonport WI U.S.A.
203 F9 Jacksons South I. N.Z.
109 J3 Jackson's Arm Nfld and Lab. Can.
115 E9 Jacksonville AL U.S.A.
121 I8 Jacksonville AR U.S.A.
115 G10 Jacksonville FL U.S.A.
120 J6 Jacksonville IL U.S.A.
118 B5 Jacksonville MD U.S.A.
115 I8 Jacksonville NC U.S.A.
116 C9 Jacksonville OH U.S.A.
121 H10 Jacksonville TX U.S.A.
115 G10 Jacksonville Beach FL U.S.A.
130 G4 Jacmel Haiti
155 E8 Jaco i. East Timor
185 M7 Jacobabad Pak.
140 E4 Jacobina Brazil
125 T5 Jacob Lake AZ U.S.A.
97 I5 Jacobsdal S. Africa
110 A2 Jacobson MN U.S.A.
203 D10 Jacobs River South I. N.Z.
118 B6 Jacobsville MD U.S.A.
118 B5 Jacobus PA U.S.A.
128 E6 Jacona Mex.
109 H3 Jacques-Cartier, Détroit de sea chan. Que. Can.
109 H3 Jacques Cartier, Mont mt. Que. Can.
Jacques Cartier Passage Que. Can. see Jacques-Cartier, Détroit de
109 H4 Jacquet River N.B. Can.
142 A3 Jacuba r. Brazil
142 D4 Jacuí Brazil
141 C9 Jacuí r. Brazil
140 F5 Jacuípe r. Brazil
136 D4 Jacumã r. Brazil
140 C3 Jacunda Brazil
137 I5 Jacundá r. Brazil
143 G3 Jacupemba Brazil
142 D6 Jacupiranga Brazil
136 D2 Jacura Venez.
68 G3 Jadar r. Bos.-Herz.
76 H6 Jadar r. Serb. and Mont.
176 F4 Jadcherla Andhra Prad. India
176 H4 Jaddangi Andhra Prad. India
185 J9 Jaddi, Ras pt Pak.
48 F4 Jade r. Ger.
48 F3 Jade sea chan. Ger.
48 F4 Jadebusen b. Ger.
186 E6 Jadhdhānah Saudi Arabia
187 K7 Jādib Yemen
105 N3 J. A. D. Jensen Nunatakker nunataks Greenland
Jadotville Dem. Rep. Congo see Likasi
68 E3 Jadova r. Croatia
68 F3 Jadovnik mt. Bos.-Herz.
55 J3 Jadów Pol.
63 O7 Jadraque Spain
136 B6 Jaén Peru
154 C4 Jaen Luzon Phil.
65 L5 Jaén Spain
65 M4 Jaén prov. Spain
22 B3 Jæren reg. Norway
178 C9 Jafarabad Gujarat India
184 C2 Ja'farābād Ardabīl Iran
184 H3 Ja'farābād Khorāsān Iran
184 C4 Ja'farābād Qazvīn Iran
184 G5 Ja'fārn Iran
Jaffa Israel see Tel Aviv-Yafo
204 G7 Jaffa, Cape S.A. Austr.
176 F8 Jaffna Sri Lanka
117 M6 Jaffrey NH U.S.A.
190 E8 Jafr, Qa' al imp. l. Jordan
178 F4 Jagadhri Haryana India
18 I2 Jägala r. Estonia
176 E5 Jagalur Karnataka India
179 K9 Jagatsinghpur Orissa India
185 M4 Jagdalak Afgh.
176 H3 Jagdalpur Chhattisgarh India
169 S1 Jagdaqi Nei Mongol China
173 E13 Jagdishpur Uttar Prad. India
179 J7 Jagdispur Bihar India
59 M6 Jagerberg Austria
97 J5 Jagersfontein S. Africa
173 D10 Jaggang Xizang China
176 G4 Jaggayyapeta Andhra Prad. India
184 G8 Jaghīn Iran
184 H9 Jagīn watercourse Iran
184 H9 Jagīn, Ra's pt Iran
96 E5 Jagkolk Vloer salt pan S. Africa
76 J7 Jagodina Srbija Serb. and Mont.
55 J2 Jagodne, Jezioro l. Pol.
54 D4 Jagodzin Pol.
Jagsamka Sichuan China see Luding
52 G3 Jagst r. Ger.
52 G3 Jagsthausen Ger.
53 I3 Jagstzell Ger.
176 F3 Jagtial Andhra Prad. India
142 B5 Jaguapitã Brazil
144 G4 Jaguarão r. Brazil/Uru.
144 G4 Jaguarão Uru.
140 E4 Jaguarari Brazil
140 F3 Jaguaretama Brazil
141 B9 Jaguari Brazil
142 C6 Jaguariaíva Brazil
140 F3 Jaguaribe Brazil
140 F5 Jaguaripe Brazil
140 F3 Jaguaruana Brazil
144 C3 Jagüe Arg.
130 C2 Jagüey Grande Cuba
Jahanabad Bihar India see Jehanabad
184 C3 Jahān Dāgh mt. Iran
190 E9 Jahdānīyah, Wādī al watercourse Jordan
206 C1 Jahleel, Point N.T. Austr.
189 L9 Jahmah well Iraq
51 H8 Jahna r. Ger.
51 J5 Jahnsfelde Ger.
184 E7 Jahrom Iran
89 H3 Jahun Nigeria
184 H8 Jāhyad Iran
140 E3 Jaicós Brazil
176 C4 Jaigarh Mahar. India
155 E3 Jailolo Halmahera Indon.
155 F4 Jailolo, Selat sea chan. Maluku Indon.
Jailolo Gilolo i. Maluku Indon. see Halmahera
138 C4 Jaiña Chile
168 H9 Jainca Qinghai China
179 I6 Jainpur Uttar Prad. India
179 N7 Jaintiapur Bangl.
178 E6 Jaipur Rajasthan India
178 H6 Jais Uttar Prad. India
178 C6 Jaisalmer Rajasthan India
178 E7 Jaisamand Lake India
178 H8 Jaisinghnagar Madh. Prad. India
178 E6 Jaitaran Rajasthan India
178 G9 Jaitgarh hill Mahar. India
178 G7 Jaitpur Uttar Prad. India
178 I5 Jajarkot Nepal
68 F3 Jajce Bos.-Herz.
Jajnagar state India see Orissa
179 K9 Jajpur Orissa India
56 F4 Ják Hungary
57 I5 Jakabszállás Hungary
179 M6 Jakar Bhutan
156 G8 Jakarta Jawa Indon.
106 C2 Jakes Corner Y.T. Can.
178 B8 Jakhan Gujarat India
84 D2 Jakharrah Libya
185 L6 Jakin mt. Afgh.
94 C3 Jakkalsberg Namibia
185 I8 Jakkī Kowr Iran
20 N3 Jäkkvik Sweden
178 E5 Jakliat Haryana India
Jako i. East Timor see Jaco
Jakobshavn Greenland see Ilulissat
20 Q5 Jakobstad Fin.
59 M8 Jakovlje Croatia
89 G5 Jakpa Nigeria
55 I3 Jaktorów Pol.
57 J2 Jakubany Slovakia
56 F3 Jakubov Slovakia
76 J9 Jakupica mts Macedonia
121 D9 Jal NM U.S.A.
128 C4 Jala Mex.
129 J6 Jalacingo Mex.
Jalaid Nei Mongol China see Inder
186 G3 Jalājil Saudi Arabia
185 N4 Jalālābād Afgh.
178 E4 Jalalabad Punjab India
178 F5 Jalalabad Uttar Prad. India
178 G6 Jalalabad Uttar Prad. India
183 O7 Jalal-Abad Kyrg.
183 O7 Jalal-Abad admin. div. Kyrg.
Jalal-Abad Oblast admin. div. Kyrg. see Jalal-Abad
85 F2 Jalālah al Baḥrīyah, Jabal plat. Egypt
178 D9 Jalalpur Gujarat India
179 I6 Jalalpur Uttar Prad. India
85 H2 Jalāmid, Ḥazm al ridge Saudi Arabia
187 N4 Ja'lān, Jabal mts Oman
67 C9 Jalance Spain
178 E4 Jalandhar Punjab India
156 □ Jalan Kayu Sing.
127 O10 Jalapa Guat.
127 M9 Jalapa Mex.
129 K6 Jalapa Mex.
126 □P11 Jalapa Nic.
129 K7 Jalapa de Díaz Mex.
129 L9 Jalapa del Marqués Mex.
185 P5 Jalapur Pak.
185 N7 Jalapur Pirwala Pak.
20 Q5 Jalasjärvi Fin.
178 G6 Jalaun Uttar Prad. India
189 L6 Jalawlā' Iraq
206 E3 Jalboi r. N.T. Austr.
128 B4 Jalcocotán Mex.
129 K6 Jalcomulco Mex.
185 L6 Jaldak Afgh.
179 L7 Jaldhaka r. Bangl.
176 E4 Jaldrug Karnataka India
142 B4 Jales Brazil
178 G6 Jalesar Uttar Prad. India
179 K9 Jaleshwar Orissa India
Jaleshwar Nepal see Jaleswar
179 J6 Jaleswar Nepal
178 E9 Jalgaon Mahar. India
45 I7 Jalhay Belgium
189 M8 Jalībah Iraq
40 D4 Jaligny-sur-Besbre France
89 H4 Jalingo Nigeria
128 C4 Jalisco Mex.
128 C6 Jalisco state Mex.
185 O4 Jalkot Pak.
184 G8 Jallābī Iran
39 J7 Jallais France
176 D3 Jalna Mahar. India
185 J8 Jālo Iran
200 □3b Jaloklab i. Majuro Marshall Is
67 E10 Jalón Spain
63 R5 Jalón r. Spain
63 P4 Jalón de Cameros Spain
178 D7 Jalore Rajasthan India
128 E4 Jalostotitlán Mex.
76 H6 Jalovik Srbija Serb. and Mont.
55 L2 Jałówka Pol.
128 F5 Jalpa Guanajuato Mex.
128 D4 Jalpa Zacatecas Mex.
179 L6 Jalpaiguri W. Bengal India
129 H4 Jalpan Mex.
185 M4 Jalrez Afgh.
129 M8 Jaltepec r. Mex.
129 M8 Jaltipan Mex.
129 I4 Jaltocán Mex.
84 D2 Jālū Libya
Jalūlā Iraq see Jalawlā'
84 D2 Jālū Oasis Libya
184 E8 Jam Iran
184 I4 Jām r. Iran
184 I4 Jām reg. Iran
136 A5 Jama Ecuador
92 D4 Jamaame Somalia
130 F3 Jamaica Cuba
130 □ Jamaica country West Indies
119 H3 Jamaica Bay NY U.S.A.
130 F4 Jamaica Channel Haiti/Jamaica
18 F3 Jämaja Estonia
185 L9 Jama Jamot Pak.
179 L7 Jamalpur Bangl.
179 K7 Jamalpur Bihar India
131 □9 Jamanota hill Aruba
137 G6 Jamanxim r. Brazil
129 K6 Jamapa r. Mex.
138 E2 Jamari Brazil
89 H4 Jamari Nigeria
172 F4 Jamati Xinjiang China
91 C8 Jamba Angola
156 E5 Jambi Sumatera Indon.
156 E5 Jambi prov. Indon.
97 O1 Jambila S. Africa
207 M8 Jambin Qld Austr.
178 D6 Jambo Rajasthan India
156 B2 Jamboaye r. Indon.
157 L1 Jambongan i. Malaysia
157 L5 Jambu Kalimantan Indon.
156 B2 Jambuair, Tanjung pt Indon.
178 D8 Jambusar Gujarat India
176 F3 Jamekunte Andhra Prad. India
50 D4 Jameln Ger.
206 F6 James watercourse N.T. Austr.
121 I7 James r. MO U.S.A.
120 G4 James r. ND/SD U.S.A.
116 I11 James r. VA U.S.A.
145 B7 James, Isla i. Chile
185 M9 Jamesabad Pak.
108 D2 James Bay Can.
119 G4 Jamesburg NJ U.S.A.
130 E1 James Cistern Eleuthera Bahamas
147 F3 James Craik Arg.
20 □ James I Land reg. Svalbard
105 P2 Jameson Land reg. Greenland
209 I8 Jameson Range W.A. Austr.
203 C12 James Peak South I. N.Z.
206 D8 James Ranges mts N.T. Austr.
212 U2 James Ross Island Antarctica
105 I3 James Ross Strait Nunavut Can.
204 G5 Jamestown S.A. Austr.
27 H6 Jamestown Rep. of Ireland
97 K7 Jamestown S. Africa
98 □2b Jamestown St Helena
124 L4 Jamestown CA U.S.A.
114 E7 Jamestown KY U.S.A.
120 F2 Jamestown ND U.S.A.
116 F6 Jamestown NY U.S.A.
116 B9 Jamestown OH U.S.A.
116 E7 Jamestown PA U.S.A.
115 E7 Jamestown TN U.S.A.
37 J5 Jametz France
55 H2 Jamielnik Pol.
21 Q6 Jämijärvi Fin.
65 L5 Jamilena Spain
129 J9 Jamiltepec Mex.
118 E4 Jamison PA U.S.A.
23 L5 Jämjö Sweden
176 D4 Jamkhandi Karnataka India
176 D3 Jamkhed Mahar. India
187 M4 Jammah Oman
176 F5 Jammalamadugu Andhra Prad. India
22 F4 Jammerbugten b. Denmark
178 E3 Jammu Jammu and Kashmir
178 F2 Jammu and Kashmir terr. Asia
178 C8 Jamnagar Gujarat India
178 E9 Jamner Mahar. India
178 G7 Jamni r. India
23 M7 Jamno, Jezioro lag. Pol.
45 H9 Jamoigne Belgium
156 G8 Jampang Kulon Jawa Indon.
185 N7 Jampur Pak.
21 R6 Jämsä Fin.
85 G3 Jamsah Egypt
21 R6 Jämsänkoski Fin.
179 K8 Jamshedpur Jharkhand India
172 E6 Jamtai Xinjiang China
179 K8 Jamtara Jharkhand India

169 H5 Jamtari Nigeria
120 L5 Jämtland county Sweden
79 K7 Jamui Bihar India
57 L3 Jamuk, Gunung mt. Indon.
76 J5 Jamu Mare Romania
79 L8 Jamuna r. Bangl.
79 N6 Jamuna r. India
62 I4 Jamuz r. Spain
87 J2 Janaale Somalia
92 E4 Janāb, Wādī al watercourse Jordan
90 E7 Jordan
121 R6 Janakkala Fin.
78 H8 Janakpur Chhattisgarh India
79 J6 Janakpur Nepal
143 F1 Janaúba Brazil
37 I4 Janaucú, Ilha i. Brazil
57 L3 Jand Pak.
85 O5 Jand Pak.
142 B2 Jandaia Brazil
144 F4 Jandaia do Sul Brazil
84 F4 Jandaq Iran
91 G4 Jandari Georgia
53 P4 Jandelsbrunn Ger.
98 □3b Jandía hill Fuerteventura Canary Is
98 □3b Jandía, Peninsula de pen. Fuerteventura Canary Is
98 □3b Jandía, Punta de pt Fuerteventura Canary Is
85 P6 Jandiala Punjab India
98 □3b Jandía Playa Fuerteventura Canary Is
36 D5 Jandiatuba r. Brazil
85 N5 Jandola Pak.
90 D4 Jandongi Dem. Rep. Congo
77 M9 Jandowae Qld Austr.
85 K4 Jándula r. Spain
55 L4 Jándula, Embalse del resr Spain
55 M5 Jandulilla r. Spain
40 D5 Janeiro r. Brazil
37 L6 Janesville CA U.S.A.
24 L1 Janesville WI U.S.A.
10 E7 Janesville WI U.S.A.
20 M4 Jang, Tanjung pt Indon.
21 N6 Jangal Iran
179 I6 Jangamo Moz.
39 K6 Jangaon Andhra Prad. India
178 C8 Jangco Xizang China
36 D5 Jangi Hima. Prad. India
85 N5 Jangipur W. Bengal India
90 D4 Jangngai Ri mts Xizang China
87 I5 Jangngai Zangbo r. Xizang China
54 D4 Jango Brazil
65 J3 Jangy-Bazar Kyrg.
55 L4 Jangy-Jol Kyrg.
89 F5 Jāni Beyglī Iran
55 J5 Jänickendorf Ger.
55 K5 Jani Khel Pak.
184 G9 Janiópolis Brazil
184 G9 Janja Bos.-Herz.
182 G6 Janja r. Bos.-Herz.
55 J6 Janjevo Kosovo, Srbija Serb. and Mont.
55 J6 Jänkälä Fin.
97 I3 Jan Kempdorp S. Africa
51 L4 Jankmajtis Hungary
76 I7 Jankov Kamen mt. Serb. and Mont.
65 I7 Janków Pol.
54 F3 Jankowo Dolne Pol.
12 C2 Jan Mayen i. Arctic Ocean
11 M7 Jannah Iraq
84 D4 Jannatābād Iran
115 D9 Jañona mt. Spain
121 I7 Janos Mex.
115 F10 Jánoshalma Hungary
115 E8 Jánosháza Hungary
116 D6 Jánossomorja Hungary
116 B9 Janovice nad Úhlavou Czech Rep.
115 E8 Janów Podlaskie Pol.
121 I10 Janów Śląskie Pol.
106 G4 Janowiec Pol.
84 C2 Janowiec Kościelny Pol.
76 J5 Janowiec Wielkopolski Pol.
92 A2 Janów Lubelski Pol.
23 O7 Janowo Pol.
68 E3 Janów Podlaski Pol.
54 E2 Jans Bay Sask. Can.
54 H4 Jänschwalde Ger.
55 I4 Jansenville S. Africa
54 G6 Jânua Coeli Brazil
55 K2 Janúaria Brazil
57 I3 Janūbī, Al Fulayj al watercourse Saudi Arabia
57 I4 Janubio, Laguna de l. Lanzarote Canary Is
57 I4 Janūb Sīnā' governorate Egypt
57 J4 Janville France
57 J4 Janwada Karnataka India
57 J4 Janzar mt. Pak.
57 J4 Janzé France
57 J5 Janzūr Libya
57 J4 Jaora Madh. Prad. India
57 J5 Japan country Asia
63 O2 Japan, Sea of N. Pacific Ocean
142 B2 Japan Basin sea feature Sea of Japan
137 G5 Japan Trench sea feature N. Pacific Ocean
65 L7 Jap'aridze Georgia
178 G3 Japsand i. Ger.
176 D4 Japurá r. Brazil
185 M9 Jati Pak.
157 H8 Jatibarang Jawa Indon.
157 H8 Jatinegara Hungary
130 D3 Jati Pak.
156 C5 Jatiluhur, Waduk resr Jawa Indon.
157 H8 Jatiwangi Jawa Indon.
74 F7 Jato r. Sicilia Italy
140 B5 Jatobá Brazil
130 B5 Jatoi Pak.
185 K6 Jat Poti Afgh.
21 N6 Jättendal Sweden
139 E1 Jatuarana Brazil
50 I3 Jatzke Ger.
142 C5 Jaú Brazil
137 F3 Jaú r. Brazil
43 I10 Jaú, Col de pass France
137 I6 Jaú, Parque Nacional do nat. park Brazil
137 F5 Jauaperí r. Brazil
89 G3 Jaua Sarisariñama, Parque Nacional nat. park Venez.
43 E3 Jauco Cuba
138 B2 Jauja Peru
66 D5 Jaujin Spain
129 H2 Jaumave Mex.
40 K3 Jaun Switz.
63 I4 Jauna r. Latvia
18 H4 Jaunanna Latvia
54 E2 Jaunay-Clan France
18 I5 Jaunjelgava Latvia
18 I5 Jaunkalsnava Latvia
18 I5 Jaunlutriņi Latvia
18 G5 Jaunmārupe Latvia
115 I8 Jaunpiebalga Latvia
119 I7 Jaunpils Latvia
59 K6 Jaunpur Uttar Prad. India
142 B2 Jaur r. France
41 J9 Jaur r. France
147 H4 Jauru r. Brazil
116 C8 Jáva i. Indon.
141 H4 Jávea-Xábia Spain
139 F2 Javerzac France
41 J8 Java i. Indon. see Jawa
176 F6 Javadi Hills India
140 C4 Javaés, Serra dos Brazil

37 M7 Jarmen Ger.
23 K1 Jarménil France
23 N2 Järna Dalarna Sweden
42 D4 Järna Stockholm Sweden
42 I3 Jarnac France
23 L3 Järnlunden l. Sweden
22 I2 Järnsjön l. Sweden
37 K5 Jarny France
55 K5 Jarocin Podkarpackie Pol.
54 F4 Jarocin Wielkopolskie Pol.
56 E1 Jaroměř Czech Rep.
56 E2 Jaroměřice nad Rokytnou Czech Rep.
56 F3 Jaroslavice Czech Rep.
55 K5 Jarosław Pol.
54 E1 Jarosławiec Pol.
56 E2 Jarošov nad Nežárkou Czech Rep.
57 K2 Jarovnice Slovakia
20 L5 Järpen Sweden
48 H1 Jarplund-Weding Ger.
183 L9 Jarqo'rgo'n Uzbek.
Jarqo'rgo'n Uzbek. see
184 C6 Jarrāhī watercourse Iran
206 D6 Jarra Jarra Range hills N.T. Austr.
116 H12 Jarratt VA U.S.A.
118 C5 Jarrettsville MD U.S.A.
29 O4 Jarrow Tyne and Wear, England U.K.
168 I7 Jartai Nei Mongol China
168 I7 Jartai Yanchi salt l. Nei Mongol China
178 F9 Jaru Brazil
187 K7 Jarud Yemen
Jarud Nei Mongol China see Lubei
76 I7 Jarut mt. Serb. and Mont.
18 H3 Järvakandi Estonia
21 R6 Järvenpää Fin.
37 L6 Jarville-la-Malgrange France
197 I4 Jarvis Island terr. N. Pacific Ocean
20 M4 Järvsand Sweden
21 N6 Järvsö Sweden
179 I6 Jarwa Uttar Prad. India
39 K6 Jarzé France
178 C8 Jasdan Gujarat India
51 I3 Jas de Laure hill France
57 J3 Jasenie Slovakia
57 K3 Jasenov Slovakia
179 J8 Jashpurnagar Chhattisgarh India
54 D4 Jasień Lubuskie Pol.
54 C3 Jasień Pomorskie Pol.
136 B6 Jasienica Pol.
55 J4 Jasienica Pol.
89 F5 Jasikan Ghana
55 J6 Jasiołka r. Pol.
55 K5 Jasionka Pol.
55 L2 Jasionówka Pol.
184 G9 Jāsk Iran
184 G9 Jāsk-e Kohneh Iran
182 G6 Jasliq Uzbek.
55 J6 Jasliska Pol.
55 J6 Jasło Pol.
57 J3 Jaslovské Bohunice Slovakia
190 E5 Jaśliūnai Lith.
18 I7 Jasmund pen. Ger.
50 I1 Jasmund, Nationalpark nature res. Ger.
50 I1 Jason Peninsula Antarctica
212 T2 Jasov Slovakia
57 H4 Jasová Slovakia
106 G4 Jasper Alta Can.
115 D9 Jasper AL U.S.A.
121 I7 Jasper AR U.S.A.
115 F10 Jasper FL U.S.A.
115 E8 Jasper GA U.S.A.
116 A9 Jasper IN U.S.A.
116 D6 Jasper NY U.S.A.
116 B9 Jasper OH U.S.A.
115 E8 Jasper TN U.S.A.
121 I10 Jasper TX U.S.A.
106 G4 Jasper National Park Alta Can.
84 C2 Jassan Iraq
76 J5 Jasseron-Riottier France
40 G4 Jasseron France
Jassy Romania see Iași
23 O7 Jastarnia Pol.
54 C2 Jastrebarsko Croatia
54 E2 Jastrowie Pol.
55 I4 Jastrząb Pol.
54 G6 Jastrzębia Góra Pol.
55 K2 Jastrzębie-Zdrój Pol.
57 I4 Jaświły Pol.
57 J4 Jászapáti Hungary
57 J4 Jászberény Hungary
57 I4 Jászboldogháza Hungary
57 I4 Jászfényszaru Hungary
57 J4 Jászkarajenő Hungary
57 I4 Jászkisér Hungary
57 J4 Jászladány Hungary
57 J4 Jász-Nagykun-Szolnok
57 I4 Jászszentandrás Hungary
57 I5 Jászszentlászló Hungary
57 I4 Jásztelek Hungary
63 O2 Jata, Monte hill Spain
142 B2 Jatai Brazil
137 G5 Jatapu r. Brazil
65 L7 Jatar Spain
178 G3 Jatara Madh. Prad. India

185 K4 Javand Afgh.
136 D6 Javari r. Brazil/Peru alt. Yavari
215 L5 Java Ridge sea feature Indian Ocean
169 M2 Javarthushu Mongolia
Java Sea Indon. see
215 K5 Java Trench sea feature Indian Ocean
67 F10 Jávea-Xábia Spain
50 E5 Jávenitz Ger.
65 K6 Javerero mt. Spain
42 F4 Javerlhac-et-la-Chapelle-St-Robert France
66 C2 Javier Chile
145 B7 Javier, Isla i. Chile
147 I2 Javier de Viana Uru.
76 I7 Javor mts Serb. and Mont.
56 E2 Javořice hill Czech Rep.
57 I3 Javorie mt. Slovakia
76 H7 Javorje mt. Serb. and Mont.
56 G1 Javorník Czech Rep.
57 H2 Javorník mt. Slovenia
59 J8 Javorník mts Slovakia
57 H2 Javorníky mts Slovakia
20 P4 Jävre Sweden
39 K5 Javron-les-Chapelles France
157 G9 Jawa i. Indon.
157 I7 Jawa, Laut sea Indon. see
156 B4 Jawa Barat prov. Indon.
57 C7 Jawad Madh. Prad. India
57 C7 Jawai r. India
174 F4 Jawala Mukhi Hima. Prad. India
178 F9 Jawar Madh. Prad. India
157 H8 Jawa Tengah prov. Indon.
155 F4 Jawa Timur prov. Indon.
190 F2 Jawbān Bayk Syria
186 G8 Jawf, Wādī al watercourse Yemen
176 C3 Jawhar Mahar. India
92 E4 Jawhar Somalia
55 K6 Jawornik Polski Pol.
55 J4 Jawor Solecki Pol.
54 G6 Jaworze Pol.
55 H6 Jaworzyna mt. Pol.
54 E5 Jaworzyna Śląska Pol.
206 D3 Jawoyn Aboriginal Land res. N.T. Austr.
121 H7 Jay OK U.S.A.
153 I7 Jaya, Puncak mt. Papua Indon.
129 K8 Jayacatlán Mex.
176 C3 Jayakwadi Sagar l. India
136 B6 Jayanca Peru
179 L6 Jayanti W. Bengal India
153 J7 Jayapura Papua Indon.
190 D7 Jayb, Wādī al watercourse Israel/Jordan
65 L7 Jayena Spain
184 C6 Jäyezān Iran
190 C8 Jayfi, Wādī al watercourse Egypt
121 H7 Jay Peak U.S.A.
84 C6 Jayrūd Syria
76 J5 Jaysan Kazakh.
92 A2 Jayton TX U.S.A.
131 □1 Jayuya Puerto Rico
42 E3 Jazeneuil France
55 K2 Jaziewo Pol.
187 L3 Jazīrat al Hamrā U.A.E.
184 D7 Jazīreh-ye Shīf Iran
55 J3 Jażúin Iran
190 D4 Jbaïl Lebanon
209 E12 J. C. Murphey Lake IN U.S.A.
185 M9 Jdaidet Ghazir Lebanon
48 J3 Jdiriya Western Sahara
125 Q6 Jean NV U.S.A.
121 J11 Jeanerette LA U.S.A.
106 F2 Jean Marie River N.W.T. Can.
109 H1 Jeannin, Lac l. Que. Can.
184 G7 Jebāl Bārez, Kūh-e mts Iran
89 G4 Jebba Nigeria
84 C2 Jebel Libya
76 J5 Jebel Romania
92 A2 Jebel, Bahr el r. Sudan/Uganda alt. Abiad, Bahr el, conv. White Nile
85 F5 Jebel Abyad Plateau Sudan
Jebel Ali U.A.E. see Mina Jebel Ali
85 G6 Jebel Dud Sudan
136 B6 Jeberos Peru
60 D5 Jebha Morocco
185 K8 Jebri Pak.
37 N7 Jebsheim France
156 F5 Jebus Indon.
26 K12 Jedburgh Scottish Borders, Scotland U.K.
Jeddah Makkah Saudi Arabia see Jiddah
109 K3 Jeddore Lake Nfld and Lab. Can.
69 B7 Jedeida Tunisia
55 K4 Jedlanka Pol.
55 J6 Jedlicze Pol.
54 E5 Jedlina-Zdrój Pol.
55 J4 Jedlińsk Pol.
55 I4 Jedlnia-Letnisko Pol.
64 H7 Jédula Spain
55 J4 Jedwabne Pol.
55 L2 Jedwabno Pol.
52 F3 Jeetze r. Ger.
115 F8 Jefferson GA U.S.A.
120 H4 Jefferson IA U.S.A.
116 D12 Jefferson NC U.S.A.
116 E7 Jefferson OH U.S.A.
121 H9 Jefferson TX U.S.A.
110 F6 Jefferson WI U.S.A.
122 I4 Jefferson r. MT U.S.A.
124 P3 Jefferson, Mount vol. NV U.S.A.
122 D4 Jefferson, Mount vol. OR U.S.A.
120 I6 Jefferson City MO U.S.A.
115 F8 Jefferson GA U.S.A.
116 H10 Jeffersonton VA U.S.A.
115 F9 Jeffersonville GA U.S.A.
116 B11 Jeffersonville IN U.S.A.
116 B9 Jeffersonville OH U.S.A.
116 D11 Jeffrey WV U.S.A.
97 I10 Jeffrey's Bay S. Africa
89 G3 Jega Nigeria
43 E8 Jegun France
179 J7 Jehanabad Bihar India
52 G3 Jehsing Denmark
115 J5 Jékabpils Latvia
183 R6 Jeki-Ögüz Kyrg.
53 I5 Jelbart Ice Shelf Antarctica
54 F4 Jelcz-Laskowice Pol.
92 D2 Jeldêsa Eth.
53 I5 Jelenec Slovakia
48 I2 Jeleniewo Pol.
54 D5 Jelenia Góra Pol.
55 K1 Jeleniewo Pol.
116 A7 Jeleniowski Park Krajobrazowy Pol.
55 J5 Jeleśnia Pol.
55 H6 Jelgava Latvia
173 Q5 Jelep La pass China/India
156 B6 Jelešnia Pol.
55 G3 Jelka Slovakia
116 A12 Jellico TN U.S.A.
108 C3 Jellicoe Ont. Can.
202 I3 Jellinge Denmark
22 F6 Jelling Denmark
116 C8 Jelloway OH U.S.A.
48 K4 Jelmstorf Ger.
185 O3 Jelondi Kühistoni Badakhshon Tajik.
57 J7 Jelovica mt. Slovenia
184 B5 Jelow Gir Iran
51 H4 Jelšava Slovenia
23 Q8 Jelsi Italy
54 G4 Jelšine Slovakia
73 N3 Jemaja i. Indon.
156 F3 Jemaja i. Indon.
157 G2 Jember Jawa Indon.
49 K6 Jembke Ger.
45 G8 Jemeppe Belgium
190 D5 Jemez Lebanon
178 E8 Jemez Pueblo NM U.S.A.

48 D4 Jemgum Ger.
54 G5 Jemielnica Pol.
54 E4 Jemielno Pol.
172 G3 Jeminay Xinjiang China
183 U4 Jeminay Kazakh.
89 H4 Jemma Bauchi Nigeria
89 H4 Jemma Kaduna Nigeria
56 E2 Jemnice Czech Rep.
51 E9 Jena LA U.S.A.
51 E9 Jena Ger.
58 E5 Jenbach Austria
93 B8 Jenda Malawi
69 B7 Jendouba Tunisia
69 B7 Jendouba admin. div. Tunisia
51 J10 Jénč Czech Rep.
53 J6 Jengen Ger.
172 E5 Jengish Chokusu mt. China/Kyrg.
54 D2 Jenikowo Pol.
190 D6 Jenin West Bank
137 F6 Jenipapo Brazil
116 D11 Jenkinjones WV U.S.A.
116 C11 Jenkins KY U.S.A.
118 E4 Jenkins NJ U.S.A.
173 H12 Jênlung Xizang China
107 I5 Jenner Alta Can.
59 N6 Jennersdorf Austria
129 □2 Jennings r. B.C. Can.
121 I10 Jennings LA U.S.A.
107 L4 Jenpeg Man. Can.
125 W1 Jensen UT U.S.A.
157 I8 Jepara Jawa Indon.
205 I7 Jeparit Vic. Austr.
140 G5 Jequié Brazil
143 E2 Jequitaí Brazil
143 E2 Jequitaí r. Brazil
143 G2 Jequitinhonha Brazil
143 H1 Jequitinhonha r. Brazil
156 E3 Jerantut Malaysia
69 D7 Jerba, Île de i. Tunisia
92 A3 Jerbar Sudan
51 D6 Jerchel Ger.
128 G5 Jerécuaro Mex.
189 O9 Jereh Iran
130 F4 Jérémie Haiti
139 E1 Jeremoabo Brazil
92 D3 Jerer Shet' watercourse Eth.
157 L9 Jerewoh Sumbawa Indon.
128 D3 Jerez Mex.
64 G7 Jerez de la Frontera Spain
65 M6 Jerez del Marquesado Spain
64 F4 Jerez de los Caballeros Spain
20 O4 Jerfojaur Sweden
20 R2 Jergol Norway
78 B3 Jergucat Albania
67 D8 Jérica Spain
207 K7 Jericho Qld U.S.A.
119 H3 Jericho N.Y. U.S.A.
190 D7 Jericho West Bank
51 F5 Jerichow Ger.
87 H2 Jerid, Chott el salt l. Tunisia
157 I3 Jerijeh, Tanjung pt Malaysia
205 J6 Jerilderie N.S.W. Austr.
54 E4 Jerka Pol.
91 G6 Jermuk Armenia
118 D1 Jermyn PA U.S.A.
139 H3 Jeroaquara Brazil
125 T7 Jerome AZ U.S.A.
122 G5 Jerome ID U.S.A.
116 D6 Jerome PA U.S.A.
128 F7 Jerónimo Mex.
147 G2 Jerónimo Norte Arg.
209 E12 Jerramungup W.A. Austr.
185 M9 Jerruck Pak.
48 J3 Jersbek Ger.
38 D3 Jersey terr. Channel Is
38 D3 Jersey i. Channel Is
119 I3 Jersey City NJ U.S.A.
110 E5 Jersey Shore PA U.S.A.
120 J6 Jerseyville IL U.S.A.
62 I8 Jerte Spain
62 H9 Jerte r. Spain
140 E3 Jerumenha Brazil
190 D7 Jerusalem Israel/West Bank
202 J4 Jerusalem North I. N.Z.
205 M6 Jervis Bay Jervis Bay Austr.
205 M6 Jervis Bay b. Jervis Bay Austr.
205 M6 Jervis Bay Territory admin. div. Austr.
106 C6 Jervis Inlet B.C. Can.
206 E7 Jervois Range hills N.T. Austr.
49 K6 Jerxheim Ger.
58 C5 Jerzens Austria
72 D8 Jerzu Sardegna Italy
54 F4 Jerzwałd Pol.
85 G3 Jiftūn al Kabīr i. Egypt
209 F7 Jigalong Aboriginal Reserve W.A. Austr.
89 H3 Jigawa state Nigeria
209 F11 Jiggalong W.A. Austr.
125 Q1 Jiggs NV U.S.A.
130 E3 Jiguani Cuba
172 G2 Jigzhi Qinghai China
59 I5 Jihlava Czech Rep.
56 E3 Jihlava r. Czech Rep.
54 G4 Jihlava Czech Rep.
56 E3 Jihlava hill Czech Rep.
172 H4 Jihlava Czech Rep.
56 E2 Jihomoravský kraj admin. reg. Czech Rep.

56 F2 Jihomoravský kraj admin. reg. Czech Rep.
179 F5 Jhajjar Haryana India
178 D6 Jhajju Rajasthan India
185 L7 Jhal Pak.
87 G1 Jhalakati Bangl.
77 Q2 Jijia r. Romania
92 D2 Jijiga Eth.
184 D4 Jijrud Iran
168 F6 Jijitai Gansu China
67 G10 Jijona-Xixona Spain
170 C4 Jijū Sichuan China
190 D6 Jil'ād reg. Jordan
77 O6 Jilava Romania
209 E11 Jilantai Nei Mongol China
56 E1 Jílemnice Czech Rep.
56 D1 Jílové Czech Rep.
56 D2 Jílové u Prahy Czech Rep.
92 C3 Jima Eth.
92 E3 Jima Ali well Eth.
130 H4 Jima Ali well Eth.
93 A8 Jimbo Tanz.
76 I5 Jimbolia Romania
65 M5 Jimena Spain
65 I8 Jimena de la Frontera Spain
126 G4 Jiménez Chihuahua Mex.
129 I1 Jiménez Coahuila Mex.
128 D2 Jiménez Tamaulipas Mex.
168 F8 Jiménez del Téul Mex.
89 I4 Jimeta Nigeria
153 J7 Jimi r. P.N.G.
206 D2 Jim Jim Creek r. N.T. Austr.
166 E5 Jimo Shandong China
56 F2 Jimramov Czech Rep.
172 I5 Jimsar Xinjiang China
118 D3 Jim Thorpe PA U.S.A.
169 O8 Jinan Shandong China
171 L2 Jince Czech Rep.
168 H7 Jincheng Gansu China
169 M9 Jincheng Shanxi China
168 F7 Jincheng Sichuan China see Leibo
169 P9 Jinchengjiang Guangxi China see Hechi
171 H6 Jinchuan Gansu China
170 D4 Jinchuan Sichuan China see Jinchuan
170 D3 Jind Haryana India
178 F5 Jindabyne N.S.W. Austr.
205 L7 Jinding Guizhou China
57 G1 Jindřichův Hradec Czech Rep.
56 E2 Jindřichův Hradec Czech Rep.
168 F7 Jinfosi Gansu China
171 J7 Jingan Jiangxi China see Jinghe
171 L2 Jingbian Shaanxi China
168 I9 Jingchuan Gansu China
171 L3 Jingde Anhui China
171 K4 Jingdezhen Jiangxi China
170 C6 Jingdong Yunnan China
171 J5 Jinggangshan Jiangxi China
162 F7 Jinggangshan Jiangxi China
171 M2 Jingjiang Jiangsu China
171 M3 Jingjing Jiangsu China
171 H6 Jingkou Hunan China
168 H9 Jingle Shanxi China
170 C7 Jinglong Gansu China
170 D3 Jingmen Hubei China
171 H5 Jingning Gansu China
169 M7 Jingpeng Nei Mongol China
169 Q5 Jingpo Heilong. China
162 F7 Jingpo Hu l. China
178 B2 Jingsha Hubei China see Jingzhou
171 H3 Jingshan Hubei China
168 H8 Jingtai Gansu China
168 E7 Jingtieshan Gansu China
170 E4 Jingxi Guangxi China
170 E4 Jingxian Anhui China
170 E4 Jingxian Hunan China see Jingzhou
169 M8 Jingyang Shaanxi China
169 O6 Jingyu Jilin China
169 Q6 Jingyuan Gansu China
169 R5 Jingyuan Ningxia China
170 C7 Jingzhi Shandong China
170 D6 Jingzhou Hubei China
169 M6 Jingzhou Hunan China
168 H9 Jinhe Nei Mongol China
169 R8 Jinhe Yunnan China see Jinping
171 K3 Jinhua Zhejiang China
168 H3 Jining Nei Mongol China
169 M6 Jining Shandong China
92 B4 Jinja Uganda
162 E7 Jinjiang Fujian China
170 B5 Jinjiang Yunnan China
170 H5 Jin Jiang r. China
170 H4 Jin Jiang r. China
167 H1 Jinka Eth.
37 L5 Jinkou Hubei China
62 D2 Jinmen pt China
128 C3 Jinmu Jiao pt China
130 D6 Jinning Yunnan China
121 H5 Jinniu Hubei China see Jinning
55 I6 Jinping Guizhou China
174 J6 Jinping Yunnan China
174 J6 Jinping Yunnan China
52 B4 Jinping Shan mts Sichuan China
171 K3 Jinsen S. Korea section Inch'ŏn
174 J6 Jinsha Guizhou China
174 J6 Jinsha Jiang r. China alt. Chang Jiang, alt. Tongtian He, conv. Yangtze, conv. Yangtze Kiang
169 P6 Jinshan Nei Mongol China
171 K7 Jinshan Shanghai China see Lufeng
168 I9 Jinshi Hunan China
171 H4 Jinshi Wan b. China
171 J3 Jintan Jiangsu China
171 L3 Jintang Sichuan China
154 C4 Jintianzhen Guangdong China
58 H8 Jintotolo i. Phil.
58 H8 Jintotolo Channel Phil.
186 H7 Jintur Mahar. India
176 F4 Jinxi Jiangxi China
171 L5 Jinxi Liaoning China see Lianshan
171 J3 Jin Xi r. China
171 L5 Jinxian Jiangxi China
169 Q7 Jinxian Liaoning China see Jinzhou
170 C6 Jinxiang Shandong China
170 C6 Jinxiu Guangxi China
170 E4 Jinyang Sichuan China
170 C6 Jinyang Yunnan China
171 J3 Jinyun Zhejiang China
170 C6 Jinzhai Anhui China

169 M8 Jinzhong Shanxi China
169 Q6 Jinzhou Liaoning China
169 Q7 Jinzhou Liaoning China
169 Q7 Jinzhou Wan b. China
166 F2 Jinzū-gawa r. Japan
139 E2 Ji-Paraná Brazil
139 E2 Jiparaná r. Brazil
136 A5 Jipijapa Ecuador
173 N11 Ji Qu r. Qinghai China
126 □11 Jiquilisco El Salvador
128 E6 Jiquilpan de Juárez Mex.
129 N9 Jiquipilas Mex.
143 H2 Jiquitaia Brazil
140 B9 Jirā', Wādī watercourse Egypt
190 G7 Jirānīyāt, Shi'bān al watercourse Saudi Arabia
138 D2 Jirau Brazil
185 N2 Jirgatol Tajik.
179 N7 Jiri r. India
91 O4 Jirin Gol Nei Mongol China
85 F3 Jirja Egypt
56 C1 Jirkov Czech Rep.
44 I2 Jirnsum Neth.
51 K10 Jirny Czech Rep.
184 G7 Jiroft Iran
187 J4 Jirwan Saudi Arabia
187 J4 Jirwan well Saudi Arabia
169 L9 Jishan Shanxi China
168 H9 Jishishan Gansu China
170 G4 Jishou Hunan China
190 E3 Jisr ash Shughūr Syria
56 D2 Jistebnice Czech Rep.
128 F6 Jitian Guangdong China see Lianshan
127 M9 Jitotol Mex.
156 D1 Jitra Malaysia
77 L7 Jiu r. Romania
77 K7 Jiuchenggong Shaanxi China
168 J7 Jiudengkou Nei Mongol China
170 D3 Jiuding Shan mt. Sichuan China
171 J4 Jiugong Shan mt. Hubei China
171 J4 Jiujiang Jiangxi China
171 K4 Jiujiang Jiangxi China
171 J4 Jiulian Yunnan China see Mojiang
171 J4 Jiuling Shan mts China
170 C4 Jiulong Sichuan China
169 Q5 Jiumiao Liaoning China
170 G6 Jiuquan Gansu China see Jiuquan
168 F7 Jiuquan Gansu China
169 R8 Jiurongcheng Shandong China
162 D6 Jiuxi Jilin China
169 L7 Jiuxian Shanxi China
170 F6 Jiuxu Guangxi China
170 E2 Jiuzhaigou Sichuan China
171 K6 Jiuzhen Fujian China
185 I9 Jiwani Pak.
169 M8 Jiwen Nei Mongol China
171 L3 Jixi Anhui China
162 G6 Jixi Heilong. China
169 Q7 Jixian Hebei China see Jizhou
162 E3 Jixian Heilong. China
171 J3 Jixian Shanxi China
169 M9 Jiyuan Henan China
187 K7 Jīzān Saudi Arabia
187 K7 Jīzān prov. Saudi Arabia
56 D1 Jizera r. Czech Rep.
56 E1 Jizerské Hory mts Czech Rep.
56 E1 Jizerské Hory park Czech Rep.
169 N8 Jizhou Hebei China
186 D3 Jizl watercourse Saudi Arabia
167 J2 Jizō-dake mt. Japan
165 K11 Jizō-zaki pt Japan
Jizzakh Uzbek. see Jizzax
183 L7 Jizzax Uzbek.
183 L7 Jizzax admin. div. Uzbek.
141 C8 Joaçaba Brazil
50 I5 Joachimsthal Ger.
129 K7 Joachín Mex.
142 B3 Joaíma Brazil
88 A3 Joal-Fadiout Senegal
137 I5 Joana Peres Brazil
62 D6 Joane Port.
143 F3 João Monlevade Brazil
140 G3 João Pessoa Brazil
142 A1 João Pinheiro Brazil
143 G2 Joaquim Felício Brazil
144 D2 Joaquín V. González Arg.
40 D5 Job France
130 E3 Jobabo Cuba
167 M2 Jōban Japan
185 H4 Jobat Madh. Prad. India
51 H4 Jobbágyi Hungary
154 F7 Jobo Point Mindanao Phil.
131 □1 Jobos Puerto Rico
124 N2 Job Peak NV U.S.A.
58 E5 Jochberg Austria
20 Q3 Jockfall Sweden
52 E3 Jockgrim Ger.
146 C3 Jocoli Arg.
127 M9 Jocotán Guat.
129 H6 Jocotepec Mex.
126 □11 Jocotitlán, Volcán vol. Mex.
129 J8 Jocotitlán Mex.
65 M5 Jódar Spain
130 D6 Jodar Spain
178 C6 Jodhpur Rajasthan India
178 C8 Jodiya Gujarat India
45 F7 Jodoigne Belgium
109 K3 Joe Batt's Arm Nfld and Lab. Can.
20 T5 Joensuu Fin.
20 M4 Joesjö Sweden
125 U2 Joe's Valley Reservoir UT U.S.A.
167 H1 Jōetsu Japan
37 L5 Jœuf France
129 H6 Jofane Moz.
106 H5 Joffre, Mount Alta/B.C. Can.
166 F2 Jōganji-gawa r. Japan
167 K5 Jōga-shima i. Japan
179 K6 Jogbani Bihar India
185 K3 Jogbura Nepal
18 J2 Jõgeva Estonia
184 G2 Joghatāy, Kūh-ye hill Iran
185 G3 Joghdān Iran
179 M6 Jogighopa Assam India
178 F5 Jogindarnagar Hima. Prad. India
18 J2 Jõgeva Estonia
107 J2 Johan Peninsula
179 K6 Johilla r. Madh. Prad. India
208 I4 John, Mount W.A. Austr.
130 □ Jamaica
John Crow Mountains hills
122 E4 John Day OR U.S.A.
122 E4 John Day r. OR U.S.A.
122 E4 John Day, Middle Fork r. OR U.S.A.
122 E4 John Day, South Fork r. OR U.S.A.
106 H3 John d'Or Prairie Alta Can.
117 L8 John F. Kennedy airport U.S.A.
116 G12 John H. Kerr Reservoir VA U.S.A.
106 D3 John Jay, Mount Can./U.S.A.
106 F1 John o'Groats Highland, Scotland U.K.
121 E7 Johnson KS U.S.A.
117 M4 Johnson VT U.S.A.
111 H9 Johnson City NY U.S.A.
115 F7 Johnson City TN U.S.A.

121 F10 **Johnson City** TX U.S.A.
124 N6 **Johnsondale** CA U.S.A.
121 E10 **Johnson Draw** watercourse TX U.S.A.
131 □3 **Johnson Point** St Vincent
106 C2 **Johnson's Crossing** Y.T. Can.
131 □2 **Johnsons Point** Antigua and Barbuda
115 H9 **Johnsonville** SC U.S.A.
30 C4 **Johnston** Pembrokeshire, Wales U.K.
115 G9 **Johnston** SC U.S.A.
209 F12 **Johnston, Lake** salt flat W.A. Austr.
Johnston and Sand Islands atoll N. Pacific Ocean see **Johnston Atoll**
197 H2 **Johnston Atoll** N. Pacific Ocean
26 G11 **Johnstone** Renfrewshire, Scotland U.K.
26 J12 **Johnstonebridge** Dumfries and Galloway, Scotland U.K.
Johnstone Lake Sask. Can. see **Old Wives Lake**
106 E5 **Johnstone Strait** B.C. Can.
209 E10 **Johnston Range** hills W.A. Austr.
27 G7 **Johnstown** Rep. of Ireland
117 K5 **Johnstown** NY U.S.A.
116 C8 **Johnstown** OH U.S.A.
116 G8 **Johnstown** PA U.S.A.
27 I6 **Johnstown Bridge** Rep. of Ireland
167 L3 **Jōhoku** Japan
156 E4 **Johor** state Malaysia
156 □ **Johor, Selat** str. Malaysia/Sing.
156 □ **Johor, Sungai** Malaysia
156 □ **Johor Bahru** Malaysia
51 H9 **Jöhstadt** Ger.
18 K2 **Jõhvi** Estonia
36 F8 **Joigny** France
141 C8 **Joinville** Brazil
37 J7 **Joinville** France
212 U2 **Joinville Island** Antarctica
129 H7 **Jojutla** Mex.
18 H1 **Jokela** Fin.
105 P2 **Jøkelbugten** b. Greenland
21 Q6 **Jokioinen** Fin.
20 Q5 **Jokiperä** Fin.
20 O3 **Jokkmokk** Sweden
20 □B1 **Jökulbunga** hill Iceland
20 □B1 **Jökulfirðir** inlet Iceland
20 □F1 **Jökulsá á Dál** r. Iceland
20 □E1 **Jökulsá á Fjöllum** r. Iceland
129 I7 **Jolalpan** Mex.
71 L6 **Jolanda di Savoia** Italy
176 F6 **Jolarpettai** Tamil Nadu India
189 L4 **Jolfa** Iran
110 F8 **Joliet** IL U.S.A.
118 C3 **Joliet** PA U.S.A.
108 E3 **Joliet, Lac** l. Que. Can.
108 F4 **Joliette** Que. Can.
107 H1 **Jolly Lake** N.W.T. Can.
154 C8 **Jolo** Phil.
154 C9 **Jolo** i. Phil.
40 J5 **Joly, Mont** mt. France
18 C1 **Jomala** Åland Fin.
154 D4 **Jomalig** i. Phil.
207 M1 **Jomard Entrance** sea chan. P.N.G.
157 J8 **Jombang** Jawa Indon.
170 B3 **Jomda** Xizang China
22 F3 **Jomfruland** i. Norway
167 J3 **Jōmine-san** mt. Japan
21 K6 **Jømna** Norway
179 I5 **Jomsom** Nepal
70 F1 **Jona** Switz.
184 F8 **Jonāḥ** Iran
116 C11 **Jonancy** KY U.S.A.
127 O9 **Jonathan Point** Belize
18 H6 **Jonava** Lith.
36 G5 **Jonchery-sur-Vesle** France
40 F3 **Joncy** France
22 C1 **Jondal** Norway
182 K8 **Jondor** Uzbek.
168 H9 **Jonê** Gansu China
166 G3 **Jōnen-dake** mt. Japan
121 J8 **Jonesboro** AR U.S.A.
121 K7 **Jonesboro** IL U.S.A.
110 I9 **Jonesboro** IN U.S.A.
121 I9 **Jonesboro** LA U.S.A.
117 □R4 **Jonesboro** ME U.S.A.
116 C12 **Jonesboro** TN U.S.A.
28 E5 **Jonesborough** Northern Ireland U.K.
116 F8 **Jones Mills** PA U.S.A.
212 R2 **Jones Mountains** Antarctica
208 □1 **Jones Point** Christmas I.
117 □R4 **Jonesport** ME U.S.A.
105 J2 **Jones Sound** sea chan. Nunavut Can.
118 C4 **Jonestown** PA U.S.A.
121 J10 **Jonesville** LA U.S.A.
116 B12 **Jonesville** VA U.S.A.
182 J7 **Jongeldi** Uzbek.
92 A3 **Jonglei** Sudan
92 B3 **Jonglei** state Sudan
92 A3 **Jonglei Canal** Sudan
55 I3 **Joniec** Pol.
18 H5 **Joniškėlis** Lith.
18 G5 **Joniškis** Lith.
179 I9 **Jonk** r. India
23 K4 **Jönköping** Sweden
23 K4 **Jönköping** county Sweden
55 I2 **Jonkowo** Pol.
109 G3 **Jonquière** Que. Can.
41 F8 **Jonquières** France
127 M8 **Jonuta** Mex.
42 D5 **Jonzac** France
92 F2 **Joog-Joogto, Raas** pt Somalia
121 H7 **Joplin** MO U.S.A.
129 I3 **Jopoy** Mex.
118 C6 **Joppatowne** MD U.S.A.
75 J6 **Joppolo** Italy
178 F6 **Jora** Madh. Prad. India
66 D6 **Jorcas** Spain
190 E7 **Jordan** country Asia
190 D7 **Jordan** r. Asia
122 K3 **Jordan** MT U.S.A.
116 I5 **Jordan** NY U.S.A.
122 F5 **Jordan** r. OR U.S.A.
125 T1 **Jordan** r. UT U.S.A.
207 J7 **Jordan Creek** watercourse Qld Austr.
143 G1 **Jordânia** Brazil
41 A7 **Jordanne** r. France
55 H6 **Jordanów** Pol.
54 E5 **Jordanów Śląski** Pol.
122 F5 **Jordan Valley** OR U.S.A.
50 G3 **Jördenstorf** Ger.
21 L6 **Jordet** Norway
22 G6 **Jordløse** Denmark
145 B8 **Jorge Montt, Isla** i. Chile
179 O6 **Jorhat** Assam India
172 D7 **Jor Hu** l. China
191 F4 **Jorjiashvili** Georgia
138 C5 **Jorjino, Punta** pt Chile
48 I3 **Jork** Ger.
22 H4 **Jörlanda** Sweden
185 N3 **Jorm** Afgh.
20 M4 **Jormvattnet** Sweden
20 P4 **Jörn** Sweden
21 S5 **Joroinen** Fin.
157 K6 **Jorong** Kalimantan Indon.
22 C2 **Jørpeland** Norway
65 P2 **Jorquera** Spain
89 H4 **Jos** Nigeria
154 E9 **Jose Abad Santos** Mindanao Phil.
140 B4 **José Bispo** r. Brazil
139 E3 **José Bonifácio** Rondônia Brazil
142 C4 **José Bonifácio** São Paulo Brazil
129 K6 **José Cardel** Mex.
140 E3 **José de Freitas** Brazil
145 C7 **José de San Martin** Arg.
147 I3 **José Enrique Rodó** Uru.
147 F2 **Josefina** Arg.
51 L9 **Josefův Důl** Czech Rep.
139 F4 **Joselândia** Brazil
128 A1 **José López Portillo, Presa** resr Mex.
128 E3 **José Maria Morelos** Mex.
154 D4 **Jose Pañganiban** Luzon Phil.
144 G4 **José Pedro Varela** Uru.
109 H2 **Joseph, Lac** l. Nfld and Lab. Can.
208 J3 **Joseph Bonaparte Gulf** W.A. Austr.
125 V7 **Joseph City** AZ U.S.A.
65 I5 **José Torán, Embalse de** resr Spain
178 G4 **Joshimath** Uttaranchal India
167 H2 **Jōshinetsu-kōgen National Park** Japan
179 K9 **Joshipur** Orissa India
119 J2 **Joshua Point** CT U.S.A.
125 P7 **Joshua Tree** CA U.S.A.
125 Q8 **Joshua Tree National Park** CA U.S.A.
36 C8 **Josnes** France
89 H4 **Jos Plateau** Nigeria
38 F6 **Josselin** France
51 F9 **Jößnitz** Ger.
20 K4 **Jossund** Norway
21 I6 **Jostedalsbreen** glacier Norway
21 I6 **Jostedalsbreen Nasjonalpark** nat. park Norway
18 G6 **Josvainiai** Lith.
21 J6 **Jotunheimen** mts Norway
21 J6 **Jotunheimen Nasjonalpark** nat. park Norway
62 F6 **Jou** Port.
190 D5 **Jouaiya** Lebanon
39 J5 **Jouanne** r. France
36 F6 **Jouarre** France
96 H9 **Joubertina** S. Africa
97 K2 **Jouberton** S. Africa
42 F1 **Joué-lès-Tours** France
38 I6 **Joué-sur-Erdre** France
40 B2 **Jouet-sur-l'Aubois** France
40 I3 **Jougne** France
20 S4 **Joukokylä** Fin.
190 D5 **Joûnié** Lebanon
41 H9 **Jouques** France
121 F11 **Jourdanton** TX U.S.A.
44 I3 **Joure** Neth.
42 F6 **Journiac** France
106 H4 **Joussard** Alta Can.
21 S6 **Joutsa** Fin.
21 T6 **Joutseno** Fin.
20 S3 **Joutsijärvi** Fin.
40 I3 **Joux, Lac de** l. Switz.
70 A2 **Joux, Vallée de** val. Switz.
40 D1 **Joux-la-Ville** France
36 C6 **Jouy** France
37 L5 **Jouy-aux-Arches** France
36 D5 **Jouy-le-Moutier** France
36 C8 **Jouy-le-Potier** France
36 G5 **Jouy-lès-Reims** France
130 C2 **Jovellanos** Cuba
179 N7 **Jowai** Meghalaya India
184 D3 **Jowr Deh** Iran
184 I6 **Jowzak** Iran
184 C4 **Jowzān** Iran
185 K3 **Jowzjān** prov. Afgh.
106 C2 **Joy, Mount** Y.T. Can.
127 O11 **Joya de Cerén** tourist site El Salvador
27 C5 **Joyce's Country** reg. Rep. of Ireland
41 E8 **Joyeuse** France
166 C6 **Jōyō** Japan
179 L7 **Joypurhat** Bangl.
40 C5 **Joze** France
55 J4 **Józefów** Lubelskie Pol.
55 L5 **Józefów** Lubelskie Pol.
55 J3 **Józefów** Mazowieckie Pol.
97 Q3 **Jozini** S. Africa
86 B4 **Jrayfiya** well Western Sahara
88 A2 **Jreïda** Maur.
136 E5 **Juami** r. Brazil
131 □1 **Juana Díaz** Puerto Rico
128 D1 **Juan Aldama** Mex.
147 F6 **Juan A. Pradere** Arg.
147 G4 **Juan Bautista Alberdi** Arg.
169 N9 **Juancheng** Shandong China
147 I5 **Juancho** Arg.
130 □ **Juan de Bolas** hill Jamaica
106 E5 **Juan de Fuca Strait** Can./U.S.A.
146 E6 **Juan de Garay** Arg.
95 □I3 **Juan de Nova** i. Indian Ocean
129 L7 **Juan Díaz Covarrubias** Mex.
147 G5 **Juan E. Barra** Arg.
128 C4 **Juan Escutia** Mex.
138 □ **Juan Fernández, Archipiélago** is S. Pacific Ocean
Juan Fernández Islands S. Pacific Ocean see Juan Fernández, Archipiélago
137 F2 **Juangriego** Venez.
129 L8 **Juanita** Mex.
146 E3 **Juan Jorba** Arg.
147 H2 **Juan Jorge** Arg.
147 F4 **Juan José Paso** Arg.
138 A1 **Juanjuí** Peru
20 T5 **Juankoski** Fin.
41 K9 **Juan-les-Pins** France
147 I4 **Juan L. Lacaze** Uru.
146 E3 **Juan Llerena** Arg.
126 E2 **Juan Mata Ortíz** Mex.
147 H6 **Juan N. Fernández** Arg.
129 J4 **Juan Ramírez, Isla** i. Mex.
129 L7 **Juan Rodriguez Clara** Mex.
147 I4 **Juan Soler** Uru.
145 B7 **Juan Stuven, Isla** i. Chile
89 F5 **Juapon** Ghana
139 F2 **Juara** Brazil
127 I4 **Juaréz** Mex.
129 K8 **Juárez, Sierra** mts Mex.
126 A1 **Juárez, Sierra de** mts Mex.
143 E5 **Juatinga, Ponta da** pt Brazil
140 E4 **Juàzeiro** Brazil
140 F3 **Juàzeiro do Norte** Brazil
88 C5 **Juazohn** Liberia
Juba r. Somalia see **Jubba**
92 A3 **Juba** Sudan
186 A2 **Jūbāl, Jazīrat** i. Egypt
186 G8 **Juban** Yemen
212 U2 **Jubany** research stn Antarctica
92 D5 **Jubba** r. Somalia
92 D4 **Jubbada Dhexe** admin. reg. Somalia
92 D4 **Jubbada Hoose** admin. reg. Somalia
186 E1 **Jubbah** Saudi Arabia
Jubbulpore Madh. Prad. India see **Jabalpur**
48 H1 **Jübek** Ger.
209 I10 **Jubilee Lake** salt flat W.A. Austr.
109 K3 **Jubilee Lake** Nfld and Lab. Can.
147 H2 **Jubileo** Arg.
179 K6 **Jubing** Nepal
39 K5 **Jublains** France
86 B4 **Juby, Cap** c. Morocco
63 P8 **Júcar** r. Spain
67 E9 **Jucar-Turia, Canal** r. Spain
140 F3 **Jucas** Brazil
129 J9 **Juchatengo** Mex.
49 B8 **Jüchen** Ger.
128 D4 **Juchipila** Mex.
128 D4 **Juchipila** r. Mex.
129 L9 **Juchitán** Mex.
128 C5 **Juchitlán** Mex.
55 L2 **Juchnowiec Kościelne** Pol.
54 E2 **Juchowo** Pol.
49 K10 **Jüchsen** Ger.
143 H2 **Jucuruçu** Brazil
143 H2 **Jucuruçu** r. Brazil
22 B2 **Judaberg** Norway
190 C7 **Judaea** reg. Israel
189 J8 **Judaidat al Hamir** Iraq
188 I6 **Judaydah** Syria
190 E5 **Judaydat al Wādī** Syria
189 J8 **Judayyidat 'Ar'ar** well Iraq
51 D10 **Judenbach** Ger.
59 K5 **Judenburg** Austria
63 P6 **Judes** mt. Spain
170 B5 **Judian** Yunnan China
67 C11 **Judio, Embalse del** resr Spain
122 J3 **Judith** r. MT U.S.A.
122 J3 **Judith Gap** MT U.S.A.
65 M3 **Juego de Bolos** mt. Spain
22 G6 **Juelsminde** Denmark
143 H2 **Juerana** Brazil
63 Q7 **Juez** mt. Spain
137 F5 **Jufari** r. Brazil
38 G5 **Jugon-les-Lacs** France
169 K8 **Juh** Nei Mongol China
186 F7 **Juḥā** Saudi Arabia
186 D3 **Juhaynah** reg. Saudi Arabia
49 I8 **Jühnde** Ger.
168 E8 **Juhongtu** Qinghai China
58 E4 **Juifen** mt. Austria
126 □Q11 **Juigalpa** Nic.
39 K7 **Juigné-sur-Loire** France
42 G5 **Juillac** France
43 E9 **Juillan** France
109 I2 **Juillet, Lac** l. Que. Can.
36 E5 **Juilly** France
139 F2 **Juína** Brazil
139 F3 **Juina** r. Brazil
36 D6 **Juine** r. France
48 C3 **Juist** Ger.
48 D3 **Juist** i. Ger.
143 F4 **Juiz de Fora** Brazil
156 D5 **Jujuhan** r. Indon.
40 G4 **Jujurieux** France
144 D1 **Jujuy** prov. Arg.
20 P3 **Jukkasjärvi** Sweden
167 I3 **Jukkoku-tōge** pass Japan
138 D5 **Julaca** Bol.
59 I2 **Julbach** Austria
53 N5 **Julbach** Ger.
120 D5 **Julesburg** CO U.S.A.
138 C4 **Juli** Peru
136 E5 **Julia** Brazil
138 C3 **Juliaca** Peru
207 H6 **Julia Creek** Qld Austr.
207 H6 **Julia Creek** r. Qld Austr.
124 P8 **Julian** CA U.S.A.
108 E2 **Julian, Lac** l. Que. Can.
44 G3 **Julianadorp** Neth.
131 □10 **Julianadorp** Curaçao Neth. Antilles
45 I6 **Juliana Kanaal** canal Neth.
Julian Alps mts Slovenia see **Julijske Alpe**
Julianatop mt. Papua Indon. see **Mandala, Puncak**
137 G4 **Juliana Top** mt. Suriname
Julianehåb Greenland see **Qaqortoq**
27 J5 **Julianstown** Rep. of Ireland
49 B9 **Jülich** Ger.
40 E3 **Julien, Mont** hill France
40 F4 **Juliénas** France
68 D2 **Julijske Alpe** mts Slovenia
126 G3 **Julimes** Mex.
141 B9 **Júlio de Castilhos** Brazil
142 C5 **Júlio Mesquita** Brazil
206 G6 **Julius, Lake** Qld Austr.
118 F4 **Juliustown** NJ U.S.A.
38 H4 **Jullouville** France
Jullundur Punjab India see Jalandhar
128 D6 **Juluapan** Mex.
137 E6 **Juma** r. Brazil
183 L8 **Juma** Uzbek.
169 N7 **Juma He** r. China
170 B2 **Jumanggoin** Sichuan China
92 D5 **Jumba** Somalia
136 B6 **Jumbilla** Peru
41 C6 **Jumeaux** France
42 G5 **Jumilhac-le-Grand** France
67 C11 **Jumilla** Spain
178 I5 **Jumla** Nepal
48 E4 **Jümme** r. Ger.
110 C4 **Jump** r. WI U.S.A.
18 H5 **Jumprava** Latvia
178 C9 **Junagadh** Gujarat India
177 H3 **Junagarh** Orissa India
169 P9 **Junan** Shandong China
190 A8 **Junayfah** Egypt
190 B9 **Junaynah, Ra's al** mt. Egypt
184 H5 **Junbuk** Iran
169 P4 **Jun Bulen** Nei Mongol China
146 B3 **Juncal** mt. Chile
62 C9 **Juncal** Port.
131 □1 **Juncos** Puerto Rico
66 G5 **Juncosa** Spain
121 F10 **Junction** TX U.S.A.
125 T3 **Junction** UT U.S.A.
206 D1 **Junction Bay** N.T. Austr.
120 G6 **Junction City** KS U.S.A.
122 C4 **Junction City** OR U.S.A.
207 I8 **Jundah** Qld Austr.
142 D5 **Jundiaí** Brazil
104 E4 **Juneau** AK U.S.A.
106 C3 **Juneau Icefield** B.C. Can.
66 G4 **Juneda** Spain
205 K6 **Junee** N.S.W. Austr.
190 D5 **Jûn el Khudr** b. Lebanon
128 G6 **Jungapeo** Mex.
70 D2 **Jungfrau** mt. Switz.
172 H4 **Junggar Pendi** basin China
52 G5 **Jungingen** Ger.
45 J9 **Junglinster** Lux.
185 L9 **Jungshahi** Pak.
173 J10 **Jungsi** Xizang China
92 B2 **Junguls** Sudan
111 Q9 **Juniata** r. PA U.S.A.
118 A3 **Juniata County** county PA U.S.A.
76 I8 **Junik** Kosovo, Srbija Serb. and Mont.
147 G4 **Junín** Arg.
146 C3 **Junin** Arg.
138 A2 **Junín** Peru
138 B2 **Junín** dept Peru
116 F10 **Junior** WV U.S.A.
117 □R2 **Juniper** N.B. Can.
125 S6 **Juniper Mountains** AZ U.S.A.
124 K5 **Junipero Serro Peak** CA U.S.A.
36 H5 **Juniville** France
49 C10 **Jünkerath** Ger.
20 M3 **Junkerdalen Balvatnet** nature res. Norway
170 E4 **Junlian** Sichuan China
171 J6 **Junmenling** Jiangxi China
190 C10 **Junnah, Jabal** mts Egypt
176 C3 **Junnar** Mahar. India
121 E10 **Juno** TX U.S.A.
20 Q3 **Junosuando** Sweden
142 B4 **Junqueirópolis** Brazil
20 N5 **Junsele** Sweden
171 K4 **Junshan Hu** l. China
122 E5 **Juntura** OR U.S.A.
20 T4 **Juntusranta** Fin.
170 B2 **Ju'nyung** Sichuan China
Ju'nyunggoin Sichuan China see **Ju'nyung**
167 M2 **Jūō** Japan
18 E6 **Juodkrantė** Lith.
18 I7 **Juodšiliai** Lith.
18 I5 **Juodupė** Lith.
20 Q3 **Juoksengi** Sweden
18 H6 **Juosta** r. Lith.
18 H6 **Juostinikai** Lith.
18 I7 **Juozapinės kalnas** hill Lith.
184 G6 **Jūpār** Iran
143 G3 **Juparanã, Lagoa** l. Brazil
142 B4 **Jupiá** Brazil
142 B4 **Jupía, Represa** resr Brazil
39 L6 **Jupilles** France
115 G12 **Jupiter** FL U.S.A.
45 I7 **Juprelle** Belgium
142 D6 **Juquiá** Brazil
142 D6 **Juquiá** r. Brazil
142 D5 **Juquitiba** Brazil
90 F2 **Jur** r. Sudan
40 H3 **Jura** dept France
40 G5 **Jura** mts France/Switz.
18 F6 **Jūra** r. Lith.
70 C1 **Jura** canton Switz.
26 E10 **Jura** i. Scotland U.K.
26 E11 **Jura, Sound of** sea chan. Scotland U.K.
136 B3 **Juradó** Col.
143 F2 **Juramento** Brazil
43 D9 **Jurançon** France
142 A6 **Juranda** Brazil
18 F6 **Jurbarkas** Lith.
45 E7 **Jurbise** Belgium
140 E4 **Juremal** Brazil
190 D8 **Jurf ad Darāwīsh** Jordan
50 E3 **Jürgenshagen** Ger.
50 G3 **Jürgenstorf** Ger.
208 G5 **Jurgurra** r. W.A. Austr.
169 Q4 **Jurh** Nei Mongol China
169 Q4 **Jurh** Nei Mongol China
18 H2 **Jüri** Estonia
209 C11 **Jurien** W.A. Austr.
209 C11 **Jurien Bay** W.A. Austr.
42 D4 **Jurignac** France
77 Q6 **Jurilovca** Romania
137 G5 **Juriti Velho** Brazil
71 R6 **Jurjevo** Croatia
59 L7 **Jurklošter** Slovenia
18 G5 **Jūrmala** Latvia
21 P7 **Jurmo** Fin.
20 S4 **Jurmu** Fin.
64 E3 **Juromenha** Port.
171 L3 **Jurong** Jiangsu China
156 □ **Jurong** Sing.
156 □ **Jurong, Sungai** r. Sing.
156 □ **Jurong Island** reg. Sing.
137 E5 **Juruá** Brazil
136 E5 **Juruá** r. Brazil
139 F3 **Juruena** Brazil
139 F1 **Juruena** r. Brazil
142 C5 **Jurumirim, Represa de** resr Brazil
139 G2 **Juruna** r. Brazil
138 C1 **Jurupari** r. Brazil
137 G5 **Juruti** Brazil
20 P5 **Jurva** Fin.
164 R5 **Jūsan-ko** l. Japan
137 F2 **Jusepín** Venez.
166 E5 **Jūshiyama** Japan
184 G3 **Jūshqān** Iran
190 E4 **Jūsīyah** Syria
42 I6 **Jussac** France
142 B1 **Jussara** Brazil
18 G2 **Jussarö** i. Fin.
37 K8 **Jussey** France
116 D11 **Justice** WV U.S.A.
147 F3 **Justiniano Posse** Arg.
146 E3 **Justo Daract** Arg.
57 G5 **Juta** Hungary
136 D6 **Jutaí** Brazil
136 E5 **Jutaí** r. Brazil
51 H7 **Jüterbog** Ger.
141 B7 **Juti** Brazil
127 O10 **Jutiapa** Guat.
126 □P10 **Jutiapa** Hond.
126 □P10 **Juticalpa** Hond.
Jutland pen. Denmark see **Jylland**
54 F4 **Jutrosin** Pol.
20 T5 **Juuka** Fin.
21 R6 **Juupajoki** Fin.
18 J1 **Juurikorpi** Fin.
21 S6 **Juva** Fin.
128 G5 **Juventino Rosas** Mex.
39 I5 **Juvigné** France
39 I4 **Juvigny-le-Tertre** France
39 J4 **Juvigny-sous-Andaine** France
185 I6 **Juwain** Afgh.
157 I8 **Juwana** Jawa Indon.
169 P9 **Juxian** Shandong China
169 O9 **Juye** Shandong China
184 H4 **Jūymand** Iran
184 E7 **Jūyom** Iran
37 I7 **Juzennecourt** France
43 F10 **Juzet-d'Izaut** France
94 E5 **Jwaneng** Botswana
22 H6 **Jyderup** Denmark
22 F5 **Jylland** pen. Denmark
183 R6 **Jyrgalang** Kyrg.
21 R5 **Jyväskylä** Fin.

K

178 F2 **K2** mt. China/Jammu and Kashmir
89 G4 **Ka** r. Nigeria
124 □D12 **Ka'a'awa** HI U.S.A.
92 B4 **Kaabong** Uganda
139 E4 **Kaa-Iya, Parque Nacional** nat. park Bol.
Kaakhka Turkm. see **Kaka**
124 □C12 **Ka'ala** mt. HI U.S.A.
200 □5 **Kaala-Gomen** New Caledonia
96 I5 **Kaalpan** salt pan S. Africa
97 P1 **Kaalrug** S. Africa
20 S2 **Kaamanen** Fin.
18 K4 **Kääpa** Estonia
97 P1 **Kaapamuiden** S. Africa
21 Q6 **Kaarina** Fin.
50 D4 **Kaarßen** Ger.
49 C8 **Kaarst** Ger.
88 C3 **Kaarta** reg. Mali
44 H5 **Kaatsheuvel** Neth.
20 T5 **Kaavi** Fin.
Kaba Xinjiang China see **Habahe**
183 V4 **Kaba** r. China/Kazakh.
57 K4 **Kaba** Hungary
155 B6 **Kabaena** i. Indon.
185 J2 **Kabakly** Turkm.
191 D5 **Kabak Tepe** mt. Turkey
88 C4 **Kabala** Sierra Leone
93 A5 **Kabale** Uganda
Kabalega Falls National Park Uganda see **Murchison Falls National Park**
91 E6 **Kabalo** Dem. Rep. Congo
91 E6 **Kabambare** Dem. Rep. Congo
183 L1 **Kaban'** Kazakh.
183 L1 **Kabanbay** Severnyy Kazakhstan Kazakh.
91 C6 **Kabanga** Dem. Rep. Congo
93 A5 **Kabanga** Tanz.
91 D7 **Kabangu** Dem. Rep. Congo
156 C3 **Kabanjahe** Sumatera Indon.
182 D1 **Kabanovka** Rus. Fed.
Kabanye Ukr. see **Krasnorichens'ke**
201 □1 **Kabara** i. Fiji
155 G4 **Kabarai** Papua Indon.
17 Q9 **Kabardinka** Rus. Fed.
Kabardino-Balkarskaya A.S.S.R. aut. rep. Rus. Fed. see **Kabardino-Balkarskaya Respublika**
191 E2 **Kabardino-Balkarskaya Respublika** aut. rep. Rus. Fed.
191 E2 **Kabardino-Balkarskiy Zapovednik** nature res. Rus. Fed.
90 F5 **Kabare** Dem. Rep. Congo
Kabarega National Park Uganda see **Murchison Falls National Park**
154 D8 **Kabasalan** Mindanao Phil.
167 L3 **Kaba-san** hill Japan
165 G14 **Kaba-shima** i. Japan
158 C5 **Kabaung** r. Myanmar
158 B3 **Kabaw Valley** Myanmar
191 B6 **Kabayel** Turkey
89 G5 **Kabba** Nigeria
176 E6 **Kabbani** r. India
20 P3 **Kåbdalis** Sweden
89 I3 **Kabélawa** Niger
110 J1 **Kabenung Lake** Ont. Can.
18 I2 **Kaberneeme** Estonia
87 F3 **Kabertene** Alg.
155 B3 **Kabetan** i. Indon.
110 B1 **Kabetogama Lake** MN U.S.A.
91 E6 **Kabeya** Dem. Rep. Congo
57 G4 **Kab-hegy** hill Hungary
108 C3 **Kabinakagami** r. Ont. Can.
108 C3 **Kabinakagami Lake** Ont. Can.
91 E6 **Kabinda** Dem. Rep. Congo
155 D8 **Kabir** Indon.
190 D3 **Kabīr** r. Syria
164 □B22 **Kabira** Nansei-shotō Japan
184 B5 **Kabīrkūh** mts Iran
191 I6 **Kābirli** Azer.
185 N6 **Kabirwala** Pak.
18 H3 **Kabli** Estonia
178 G9 **Kabneshwar** Mahar. India
90 C3 **Kabo** C.A.R.
Kabodiyon Tajik. see **Kabutiyon**
91 E8 **Kabompo** Zambia
91 D8 **Kabompo** r. Zambia
91 E7 **Kabondo-Dianda** Dem. Rep. Congo
157 I4 **Kabong** Sarawak Malaysia
91 E6 **Kabongo** Dem. Rep. Congo
159 C8 **Kabosa Island** Myanmar
90 D3 **Kabou** C.A.R.
89 F4 **Kabou** Togo
19 S3 **Kabozha** Rus. Fed.
88 A3 **Kabrousse** Senegal
186 F3 **Kabshah, Jabal** hills Saudi Arabia
184 I5 **Kabūdeh** Iran
184 H3 **Kabūd Gonbad** Iran
184 C4 **Kabūd Rāhang** Iran
154 C3 **Kabugao** Luzon Phil.
185 M4 **Kābul** Afgh.
185 M4 **Kābul** prov. Afgh.
185 O5 **Kābul** r. Afgh.
91 F8 **Kabunda** Dem. Rep. Congo
93 A7 **Kabunda** Zambia
155 A8 **Kabunduk** Sumba Indon.
167 J3 **Kabura-gawa** r. Japan
155 E2 **Kaburuang** i. Indon.
85 G5 **Kabushiya** Sudan
184 G6 **Kabūtar Khān** Iran
185 M3 **Kabutiyon** Tajik.
91 F8 **Kabwe** Zambia
182 J3 **Kabyrga** r. Kazakh.
76 J8 **Kačanik** Kosovo, Srbija Serb. and Mont.
155 F4 **Kacepi** Maluku Indon.
17 M9 **Kacha** r. Ukr.
185 K8 **Kacha Daman** Pak.
92 B4 **Kachagalau** mt. Kenya
185 I7 **Kacha Kuh** mts Iran/Pak.
15 I6 **Kachalinskaya** Rus. Fed.
185 K9 **Kachari, Ras** pt Pak.
178 B8 **Kachchh, Gulf of** Gujarat India
185 L6 **Kachh** Pak.
178 E7 **Kachhola** Rajasthan India
179 I7 **Kachhwa** Uttar Prad. India
89 G4 **Kachia** Nigeria
94 E3 **Kachikau** Botswana
158 C1 **Kachin** state Myanmar
183 Q1 **Kachiry** Kazakh.
92 C2 **Kachīsī** Eth.
93 A8 **Kacholola** Zambia
160 I1 **Kachug** Rus. Fed.
92 B4 **Kachung** Uganda
51 I10 **Kačice** Czech Rep.
189 J3 **Kaçkar Dağı** mt. Turkey
191 E6 **Kaçmaz** Turkey
47 H3 **Kaczawa** r. Pol.
54 E2 **Kaczory** Pol.
166 B7 **Kada** Japan
158 C6 **Kadaingti** Myanmar
176 E8 **Kadaiyanallur** Tamil Nadu India
92 B4 **Kadam** mt. Uganda
56 C1 **Kadaň** Czech Rep.
84 D6 **Kadana** Chad
185 K6 **Kadanai** r. Afgh./Pak.
159 D8 **Kadan Kyun** i. Myanmar
157 K7 **Kadapongan** i. Indon.
57 G5 **Kadarkút** Hungary
155 C6 **Kadatuang** i. Indon.
178 G6 **Kadaura** Uttar Prad. India
201 □1 **Kadavu** i. Fiji
201 □1a **Kadavu Passage** Fiji
169 P1 **Kadaya** Rus. Fed.
176 F3 **Kaddam** l. India
88 E5 **Kade** Ghana
164 □1 **Kadena** Okinawa Japan
209 I9 **Kadgo, Lake** salt flat W.A. Austr.
85 F4 **Kadhdhāb, Sinn al** esc. Egypt
178 D8 **Kadi** Gujarat India
88 D4 **Kadiana** Mali
176 E8 **Kadiapattanam** Tamil Nadu India
Kadijica mt. Bulg. see **Kadiytsa**
79 H2 **Kadıköy** Çanakkale Turkey
79 K2 **Kadıköy** İstanbul Turkey
204 F5 **Kadina** S.A. Austr.
158 F5 **Kading** r. Laos
188 F4 **Kadınhanı** Turkey
88 D4 **Kadiolo** Mali
88 C4 **Kadiondola, Mont** mt. Guinea
176 F5 **Kadiri** Andhra Prad. India
188 H5 **Kadirli** Turkey
185 O6 **Kadirpur** Pak.
77 K9 **Kadiytsa** mt. Bulg.
89 F5 **Kadjebi** Ghana
176 C7 **Kadmat** atoll India
14 H4 **Kadnikov** Rus. Fed.
89 H5 **Kado** Nigeria
163 D9 **Ka-do** i. N. Korea
165 I14 **Kadogawa** Japan
156 E2 **Kadok** Malaysia
120 E4 **Kadoka** SD U.S.A.
15 H5 **Kadom** Rus. Fed.
95 F3 **Kadoma** Zimbabwe
158 B7 **Kadonkani** Myanmar
18 J2 **Kadrina** Estonia
90 F2 **Kadugli** Sudan
89 G4 **Kaduna** Nigeria
89 G4 **Kaduna** r. Nigeria
89 G4 **Kaduna** state Nigeria
176 E6 **Kadur** Karnataka India
170 A4 **Kadusam** mt. China/India
19 U2 **Kaduy** Rus. Fed.
14 H4 **Kadyy** Rus. Fed.
Kadzharan Armenia see **K'ajaran**
14 K2 **Kadzherom** Rus. Fed.
Kadzhi-Say Kyrg. see **Kajy-Say**
55 J2 **Kadzidło** Pol.
163 D9 **Kaechon** N. Korea
88 B2 **Kaédi** Maur.
109 K3 **Kaegudeck Lake** Nfld and Lab. Can.
89 I4 **Kaélé** Cameroon
124 □E13 **Ka'elekū** HI U.S.A.
124 □C12 **Ka'ena Point** HI U.S.A.
159 D8 **Kaeng Krachan National Park** Thai.
202 H2 **Kaeo** North I. N.Z.
48 I1 **Kær** Denmark
163 E10 **Kaesŏng** N. Korea
188 H8 **Kāf** Saudi Arabia
91 D7 **Kafakumba** Dem. Rep. Congo
Kafan Armenia see **Kapan**
89 H4 **Kafanchan** Nigeria
97 K5 **Kafferrivier** S. Africa
89 H3 **Kaffin-Hausa** Nigeria
97 J5 **Kaffir** r. S. Africa
88 B3 **Kaffrine** Senegal
90 E2 **Kafia Kingi** Sudan
155 F4 **Kafiau** i. Papua Indon.
78 F4 **Kafireas, Akra** pt Greece
78 F5 **Kafireos, Steno** sea chan. Greece
185 N4 **Kafiristan** reg. Pak.
Kafirnigan Tajik. see **Kofarnihon**
88 D4 **Kafolo** Côte d'Ivoire
85 F2 **Kafr ash Shaykh** Egypt
188 E8 **Kafr ash Shaykh** governorate Egypt
190 E3 **Kafr Buhum** Syria
84 E2 **Kafret Rihama** Egypt
190 E4 **Kafrūn Bashūr** Syria
92 B4 **Kafu** r. Uganda
91 F8 **Kafue** Zambia
91 F8 **Kafue** r. Zambia
91 E8 **Kafue Flats** marsh Zambia
91 E8 **Kafue National Park** Zambia
166 D3 **Kaga** Japan
182 G1 **Kaga** Rus. Fed.
90 C3 **Kaga Bandoro** C.A.R.
17 S6 **Kagal'nik** Rus. Fed.
17 S6 **Kagal'nik** r. Rus. Fed.
15 H7 **Kagal'nitskaya** Rus. Fed.
167 L1 **Kagamiishi** Japan
185 O4 **Kagan** Pak.
Kagan Uzbek. see **Kogon**
168 G9 **Kagang** Qinghai China
Kaganovichabad Tajik. see **Kolkhozobod**
Kagarlyk Ukr. see **Kaharlyk**
165 L12 **Kagawa** pref. Japan
111 L4 **Kagawong** Ont. Can.
20 P4 **Kåge** Sweden
93 A5 **Kagera** admin. reg. Tanz.
Kagera, Parc National de la Rwanda see **Akagera, Parc National de l'**
97 L2 **Kagiso** S. Africa
189 K3 **Kağızman** Turkey
85 F6 **Kagmar** Sudan
156 C5 **Kagologolo** Indon.
90 C2 **Kagopal** Chad
167 I5 **Kagosaka-tōge** pass Japan
165 H15 **Kagoshima** Japan
164 □H15 **Kagoshima** pref. Japan
165 H15 **Kagoshima-wan** b. Japan
184 G3 **Kāhak** Iran
184 C3 **Kahak** Qazvīn Iran
184 D4 **Kahak** Qom Iran
124 □E13 **Kahakuloa** HI U.S.A.
124 □B11 **Kahala Point** HI U.S.A.
124 □D12 **Kahalu'u** HI U.S.A.
93 B5 **Kahama** Tanz.
185 M7 **Kahan** Pak.
124 □D12 **Kahana** HI U.S.A.
16 J4 **Kaharlyk** Ukr.
155 E3 **Kahatola** i. Maluku Indon.
94 B4 **Kahawero** waterhole Namibia
157 K6 **Kahayan** r. Indon.
91 C6 **Kahemba** Dem. Rep. Congo
124 □C12 **Kahe Point** HI U.S.A.
203 B12 **Kaherekoau Mountains** South I. N.Z.
49 G10 **Kahl** r. Ger.
51 E9 **Kahla** Ger.
49 H10 **Kahl am Main** Ger.
106 F3 **Kahntah** B.C. Can.
Kahnu Iran see **Kahnūj**
184 G8 **Kahnūj** Kermān Iran
184 H6 **Kahnūj** Kermān Iran
88 C5 **Kahnwia** Liberia
202 H2 **Kahoe** North I. N.Z.
120 J5 **Kahoka** MO U.S.A.
166 E2 **Kahoku-gata** l. Japan
124 □E13 **Kaho'olawe** i. HI U.S.A.
192 D3 **Kahperusvaarat** mts Fin.
185 I8 **Kahrād** Iran
188 H5 **Kahramanmaraş** Turkey
185 N7 **Kahror** Pak.
188 I5 **Kâhta** Turkey
124 □F13 **Kahuā** HI U.S.A.
184 G4 **Kahugish** well Iran
202 □ **Kahuitara Point** Chatham Is S. Pacific Ocean
124 □D12 **Kahuku** HI U.S.A.
124 □C12 **Kahuku Point** HI U.S.A.
16 H8 **Kahul, Ozero** l. Ukr.
Kahulaui i. HI U.S.A. see **Kaho'olawe**
124 □E13 **Kahului** HI U.S.A.
184 H7 **Kahūrak** Iran
203 G8 **Kahurangi National Park** South I. N.Z.
202 G7 **Kahurangi Point** South I. N.Z.
185 O5 **Kahuta** Pak.
90 E5 **Kahuzi-Biega, Parc National du** nat. park Dem. Rep. Congo
153 H8 **Kai, Kepulauan** is Indon.
92 A3 **Kaia** r. Sudan
202 H2 **Kaiaka** North I. N.Z.
89 F4 **Kaiama** Nigeria
153 K8 **Kaiapit** P.N.G.
203 G10 **Kaiapoi** South I. N.Z.
125 T5 **Kaibab** AZ U.S.A.
125 T5 **Kaibab Plateau** AZ U.S.A.
168 E7 **Kaibamardang** Qinghai China
166 B5 **Kaibara** Japan
153 H8 **Kai Besar** i. Indon.
125 U5 **Kaibito Plateau** AZ U.S.A.
200 □6 **Kaichui, Mount** Guadalcanal Solomon Is
166 G4 **Kaida** Japan
172 H6 **Kaidu He** r. China
137 G3 **Kaieteur Falls** Guyana
169 N9 **Kaifeng** Henan China
169 N9 **Kaifeng** Henan China
202 H2 **Kaihu** North I. N.Z.
171 L4 **Kaihua** Zhejiang China
96 F5 **Kaiingveld** reg. S. Africa
170 F3 **Kaijiang** Sichuan China
153 H8 **Kai Kecil** i. Indon.
171 □J7 **Kai Keung Leng** H.K. China
202 H2 **Kaikohe** North I. N.Z.
203 H9 **Kaikoura** South I. N.Z.
203 H9 **Kaikoura Peninsula** South I. N.Z.
88 C4 **Kailahun** Sierra Leone
178 H5 **Kailali** Nepal
Kailas mt. Xizang China see **Kangrinboqê Feng**
179 N7 **Kailashahar** Tripura India
Kailas Range mts Xizang China see **Gangdisê Shan**
170 F5 **Kaili** Guizhou China
92 B3 **Kailongong** waterhole Kenya
169 Q5 **Kailu** Nei Mongol China
124 □D12 **Kailua** HI U.S.A.
124 □F14 **Kailua-Kona** HI U.S.A.
202 J4 **Kaimai** North I. N.Z.
202 J4 **Kaimai-Mamaku Forest Park** nature res. North I. N.Z.
202 J4 **Kaimai Range** hills North I. N.Z.
153 H7 **Kaimana** Papua Indon.
202 K5 **Kaimanawa Forest Park** nature res. North I. N.Z.
202 J6 **Kaimanawa Mountains** North I. N.Z.
170 A2 **Kaimar** Qinghai China
203 F9 **Kaimata** South I. N.Z.
178 G6 **Kaimganj** Uttar Prad. India
165 H15 **Kaimon-dake** hill Japan
178 H7 **Kaimur Range** hills India
18 F3 **Käina** Estonia
165 L13 **Kainan** Tokushima Japan
166 B7 **Kainan** Wakayama Japan
Kainda Kyrg. see **Kayyngdy**
Kaindy Kyrg. see **Kayyngdy**
158 B4 **Kaing** Myanmar
202 K5 **Kaingaroa Forest** North I. N.Z.
202 □ **Kaingaroa Harbour** b. Chatham Is S. Pacific Ocean
89 F3 **Kaingiwa** Nigeria
89 G4 **Kainji Lake National Park** Nigeria
89 G4 **Kainji Lake National Park** Nigeria
89 G4 **Kainji Reservoir** Nigeria
179 J9 **Kaintaragarh** Orissa India
20 Q3 **Kainulasjärvi** Sweden
202 I3 **Kaipara Flats** North I. N.Z.
202 I3 **Kaipara Harbour** North I. N.Z.
125 U4 **Kaiparowits Plateau** UT U.S.A.
171 I7 **Kaiping** Guangdong China
109 J2 **Kaipokok Bay** Nfld and Lab. Can.
Kaira Gujarat India see **Kheda**
202 K6 **Kairakau Beach** North I. N.Z.
20 S3 **Kairala** Fin.
178 F5 **Kairana** Uttar Prad. India
155 F5 **Kairatu** Seram Indon.
87 H2 **Kairouan** Tunisia
20 O2 **Kaisepakte** Sweden
58 F4 **Kaisergebirge** mts Austria
58 F4 **Kaisergebirge** nature res. Austria
52 D3 **Kaiserslautern** Ger.
213 F2 **Kaiser Wilhelm II Land** reg. Antarctica
162 F7 **Kaishantun** Jilin China
53 J4 **Kaisheim** Ger.
18 H7 **Kaišiadorys** Lith.
156 G6 **Kait, Tanjung** pt Indon.
165 J12 **Kaita** Japan
202 H2 **Kaitaia** North I. N.Z.
203 D13 **Kaitangata** South I. N.Z.
202 L5 **Kaitawa** North I. N.Z.
178 F8 **Kaitha** Madh. Prad. India
178 F5 **Kaithal** Haryana India
20 P3 **Kaitum** Sweden
20 P3 **Kaitumälven** r. Sweden
155 E8 **Kaiwatu** Maluku Indon.
124 □D13 **Kaiwi Channel** HI U.S.A.
170 G3 **Kaixian** Chongqing China
170 F5 **Kaiyang** Guizhou China
169 S5 **Kaiyuan** Liaoning China
170 D7 **Kaiyuan** Yunnan China
Kaiyun Hunan China see **Hengshan**
166 E5 **Kaizu** Japan
166 B7 **Kaizuka** Japan
20 S4 **Kajaani** Fin.
206 H6 **Kajabbi** Qld Austr.
185 K5 **Kajaki** Afgh.
156 D3 **Kajang** Malaysia
185 N7 **Kajanpur** Pak.
207 L9 **Kajarabie, Lake** resr Qld Austr.
191 H6 **K'ajaran** Armenia
57 H5 **Kajdacs** Hungary
185 I8 **Kajdar** Iran
93 C5 **Kajiado** Kenya
167 H4 **Kajikazawa** Japan
165 H15 **Kajiki** Japan
90 E2 **Kajok** Sudan
92 A4 **Kajo Kaji** Sudan
56 D3 **Kájov** Czech Rep.
185 K5 **Kajrān** Afgh.
184 B3 **Kaju** Iran
205 J5 **Kajuligah Nature Reserve** N.S.W. Austr.
89 G4 **Kajuru** Nigeria
183 Q6 **Kajy-Say** Kyrg.
183 L1 **Kak, Ozero** salt l. Kazakh.
92 B2 **Kaka** Sudan
184 H3 **Kaka** Turkm.
157 M3 **Kakaban** i. Indon.
108 B3 **Kakabeka Falls** Ont. Can.
191 G4 **Kakabet'i** Georgia
155 C7 **Kakabia** i. Indon.
206 D2 **Kakadu Aboriginal Land** res. N.T. Austr.
206 D2 **Kakadu National Park** N.T. Austr.
107 M5 **Kakagi Lake** Ont. Can.
154 E8 **Kakal** r. Mindanao Phil.
155 A4 **Kakali** Sulawesi Indon.
96 E4 **Kakamas** S. Africa
92 B4 **Kakamega** Kenya
166 E5 **Kakamigahara** Japan
91 A6 **Kakamoéka** Congo
177 M8 **Kakana** Andaman & Nicobar Is India
68 G3 **Kakanj** Bos.-Herz.
203 E12 **Kakanui Mountains** South I. N.Z.
185 L8 **Kakar** Pak.
89 H3 **Kakarahil** well Niger
202 I6 **Kakaramea** North I. N.Z.
202 J5 **Kakaramea** vol. North I. N.Z.
57 H5 **Kakasd** Hungary
88 C5 **Kakata** Liberia
202 J6 **Kakatahi** North I. N.Z.
179 O7 **Kakching** Manipur India
165 J12 **Kake** Japan
106 C3 **Kake** AK U.S.A.
167 H6 **Kakegawa** Japan
91 D6 **Kakenge** Dem. Rep. Congo
48 I4 **Kakenstorf** Ger.
50 D5 **Kakerbeck** Ger.
164 □G18 **Kakeroma-jima** i. Nansei-shotō Japan
93 B5 **Kakesio** Tanz.
191 C3 **Kakhat'i** Georgia
191 G3 **Kakhet'is K'edi** hills Georgia
191 H3 **Kakhib** Rus. Fed.
17 M7 **Kakhovka** Ukr.
17 M7 **Kakhovs'ke Vodoskhovyshche** resr Ukr.
184 H4 **Kakht** Iran
184 D7 **Kākī** Iran
176 H4 **Kakinada** Andhra Prad. India
76 H8 **Kakinjës, Maja e** mt. Albania
106 G2 **Kakisa** N.W.T. Can.
106 G2 **Kakisa** r. N.W.T. Can.
106 G2 **Kakisa Lake** N.W.T. Can.
18 E5 **Kāķišķe** Latvia
167 H1 **Kakizaki** Japan
91 C6 **Kakobola** Dem. Rep. Congo
166 A6 **Kakogawa** Japan
166 A6 **Kako-gawa** r. Japan
55 K4 **Kąkolewnica Wschodnia** Pol.
54 E4 **Kąkolewo** Pol.
93 A5 **Kakonko** Tanz.
168 B4 **Kakpak Kuduk** well Xinjiang China
88 E4 **Kakpin** Côte d'Ivoire
178 G6 **Kakrala** Uttar Prad. India
88 B4 **Kakrima** r. Guinea
181 L1 **Kakshaal-Too** mts China/Kyrg.
104 D2 **Kaktovik** AK U.S.A.
57 I4 **Kakucs** Hungary
164 R9 **Kakuda** Japan
92 B4 **Kakuma** Kenya
184 D6 **Kakun** Iran
157 J3 **Kakus** r. Malaysia
106 G4 **Kakwa** r. Alta Can.
106 F4 **Kakwa Provincial Park** park B.C. Can.
106 G4 **Kakwa Wildland Provincial Park** Alta Can.
68 E3 **Kal** hill Croatia
57 J4 **Kál** Hungary
89 I3 **Kala** Nigeria
185 N6 **Kala** Pak.
93 A7 **Kala** Tanz.
87 H2 **Kalaâ Kebira** Tunisia
185 N5 **Kalabagh** Pak.
155 D8 **Kalabahi** Indon.
Kalabáka Greece see **Kalampaka**
157 L2 **Kalabakan** Sabah Malaysia
Kalabákion Greece see **Kalampaki**
92 E2 **Kalabaydh** Togdheer Somalia
92 D2 **Kalabaydh** Woqooyi Galbeed Somalia
176 F4 **Kalabgur** Andhra Prad. India
204 H4 **Kalabity** S.A. Austr.
91 D8 **Kalabo** Zambia
15 H6 **Kalach** Rus. Fed.
185 L4 **Kalacha** Afgh.
92 C4 **Kalacha Dida** Kenya
15 H6 **Kalach-na-Donu** Rus. Fed.
158 A4 **Kaladan** r. India/Myanmar
108 E4 **Kaladar** Ont. Can.
176 D4 **Kaladgi** Karnataka India
155 B5 **Kalaena** r. Indon.
158 C3 **Kalagwe** Myanmar
94 D4 **Kalahari Desert** Africa
96 E1 **Kalahari Gemsbok National Park** S. Africa
124 □B12 **Kalaheo** HI U.S.A.
185 J4 **Kala-I-Mor** Turkm.
179 J6 **Kalaiya** Nepal
20 Q4 **Kalajoki** Fin.
20 Q4 **Kalajoki** r. Fin.
20 S1 **Kalak** Norway
77 O7 **Kalakoch** hill Bulg.
89 F4 **Kalalé** Benin
155 B4 **Kalaliok** Sulawesi Indon.
155 D1 **Kalalusu** i. Indon.
178 G9 **Kalam** Mahar. India
185 O4 **Kalam** Pak.
Kalámai Greece see **Kalamata**
78 D3 **Kalamaki** Greece
94 E4 **Kalamare** Botswana
78 D2 **Kalamaria** Greece
78 D5 **Kalamata** Greece
110 I7 **Kalamazoo** MI U.S.A.
110 H7 **Kalamazoo** r. MI U.S.A.
157 K7 **Kalambau** i. Indon.
176 E3 **Kalamnuri** Mahar. India
78 B4 **Kalamos** i. Greece
79 G6 **Kalamos, Akra** pt Greece
78 C3 **Kalampaka** Greece
78 F1 **Kalampaki** Greece
17 M8 **Kalamyts'ka Zatoka** b. Ukr.
18 F3 **Kalana** Estonia
88 C4 **Kalana** Mali
173 C12 **Kalanaur** Haryana India
178 E4 **Kalanaur** Punjab India
17 M7 **Kalanchak** Ukr.
185 J7 **Kalandi** Pak.
92 B5 **Kalangala** Uganda
93 B6 **Kalangali** Tanz.
169 O1 **Kalanguy** Rus. Fed.
209 D11 **Kalannie** W.A. Austr.
178 E5 **Kalanwali** Haryana India
184 H8 **Kālān Zīād** Iran
155 B7 **Kalao** i. Indon.

Kalaoa to Karagan 281

124 □F14 Kalaoa HI U.S.A.
154 E8 Kalaong Mindanao Phil.
155 B7 Kalaotoa i. Indon.
176 F8 Kala Oya r. Sri Lanka
156 F5 Kalapa Indon.
124 □G14 Kalapana HI U.S.A.
184 I9 Kalar watercourse Iran
189 L6 Kalār Iraq
19 S4 Kalashnikovo Rus. Fed.
158 F6 Kalasin Thai.
185 L5 Kalāt Afgh.
Kalāt Khorāsān Iran see Kabūd Gonbad
184 H9 Kalāt Sīstān va Balūchestān Iran
185 K9 Kalat Balochistan Pak.
185 L7 Kalat Balochistan Pak.
184 H4 Kalat, Kūh-e mt. Iran
185 I5 Kalata Barangak Afgh.
184 F3 Kalāteh-ye Molla Iran
124 □E12 Kalaupapa HI U.S.A.
15 I7 Kalaus r. Rus. Fed.
178 C8 Kalavad Gujarat India
78 D4 Kalavryta Greece
54 D3 Kaława Pol.
187 I8 Kalb, Ra's al c. Yemen
187 M3 Kalbā U.A.E.
191 H5 Kälbäcär Azer.
209 C9 Kalbarri W.A. Austr.
209 C9 Kalbarri National Park W.A. Austr.
96 C9 Kalbaskraal S. Africa
50 D5 Kalbe (Milde) Ger.
183 T3 Kalbinskiy Khrebet mts Kazakh.
184 H4 Kalbū Iran
59 J8 Kalce Slovenia
53 K2 Kalchreuth Ger.
17 Q6 Kal'chyk Ukr.
17 Q6 Kal'chyk r. Ukr.
56 G4 Káld Hungary
190 D2 Kaldırım Turkey
182 E3 Kaldygayty r. Kazakh.
79 K6 Kale Antalya Turkey
79 J5 Kale Denizli Turkey
191 A5 Kale Gümüşhane Turkey
191 A4 Kale r. Turkey
188 F3 Kalecik Turkey
155 C6 Kaledupa i. Indon.
49 J7 Kalefeld Ger.
158 C7 Kalegauk Island Myanmar
184 C3 Kaleh Sarai Iran
158 B5 Kaleindaung inlet Myanmar
92 B4 Kalekol Kenya
91 E6 Kalema Dem. Rep. Congo
91 F6 Kalemie Dem. Rep. Congo
158 B3 Kalemyo Myanmar
184 F4 Kāl-e Namak Iran
182 D3 Kalenoye Kazakh.
78 B3 Kalentzi Greece
68 G3 Kalesija Bos.-Herz.
54 G5 Kalety Pol.
20 U4 Kalevala Rus. Fed.
158 B3 Kalewa Myanmar
26 L11 Kale Water r. Scotland U.K.
184 B2 Kaleybar Iran
169 P1 Kalga Rus. Fed.
209 D13 Kalgan r. W.A. Austr.
176 D5 Kalghatgi Karnataka India
209 F11 Kalgoorlie W.A. Austr.
89 H3 Kalguéri Niger
184 H6 Kāl Güsheh Iran
68 E3 Kali Croatia
178 H5 Kali r. India/Nepal
77 Q7 Kaliakra, Nos pt Bulg.
156 F7 Kalianda Sumatera Indon.
154 D6 Kalibo Panay Phil.
116 A8 Kalida OH U.S.A.
156 C6 Kaliet Indon.
185 M3 Kalifgan Afgh.
179 J6 Kali Gandaki r. Nepal
176 F5 Kaligiri Andhra Prad. India
Kalikata W. Bengal India see Kolkata
19 W9 Kalikino Rus. Fed.
90 E5 Kalima Dem. Rep. Congo
157 I6 Kalimantan reg. Indon.
157 I4 Kalimantan Barat prov. Indon.
157 K6 Kalimantan Selatan prov. Indon.
157 J5 Kalimantan Tengah prov. Indon.
157 L3 Kalimantan Timur prov. Indon.
57 G5 Kali-medence park Hungary
Kálimnos i. Greece see Kalymnos
179 L6 Kalimpang W. Bengal India
176 D5 Kalinadi r. India
178 H6 Kali Nadi r. India
93 B7 Kalinda Zambia
177 I3 Kalingapatnam Andhra Prad. India
Kalinin Rus. Fed. see Tver'
Kalininabad Tajik. see Kalininobod
17 M8 Kalinine Ukr.
18 D7 Kaliningrad Rus. Fed.
Kaliningrad Oblast admin. div. Rus. Fed. see Kaliningradskaya Oblast'
18 E7 Kaliningradskaya Oblast' admin. div. Rus. Fed.
18 C7 Kaliningradskiy Zaliv b. Rus. Fed.
191 G4 Kalininkänd Azer.
55 K1 Kalinino Kaliningradskaya Oblast' Rus. Fed.
14 H4 Kalinino Kostromskaya Oblast' Rus. Fed.
17 S8 Kalinino Krasnodarskiy Kray Rus. Fed.
183 O1 Kalinino Omskaya Oblast' Rus. Fed.
14 L4 Kalinino Permskaya Oblast' Rus. Fed.
185 M3 Kalininobod Tajik.
15 I6 Kalininsk Rus. Fed.
15 G7 Kalininskaya Rus. Fed.
17 L6 Kalinins'ke Ukr.
178 E8 Kalinjara Rajasthan India
16 I1 Kalinkavichy Belarus
Kalinkovichi Belarus see Kalinkavichy
191 J6 Kalinovka Azer.
182 F3 Kalinovka Kazakh.
17 N2 Kalinovka Rus. Fed.
Kalinovka Ukr. see Kalynivka
91 G2 Kalinovskaya Rus. Fed.
91 H2 Kalinovskiy Rus. Fed.
54 G4 Kalinowa Pol.
55 K2 Kalinowo Pol.
92 B4 Kaliro Uganda
92 F2 Kalis Somalia
157 J9 Kalisat Jawa Indon.
Kalisch Pol. see Kalisz
176 E1 Kali Sindh r. India
54 G2 Kaliska Pol.
122 G2 Kalispell MT U.S.A.
56 D3 Kaliště hill Czech Rep.
54 G4 Kalisz Pol.
54 D2 Kalisz Pomorski Pol.
184 G7 Kalituyeh Iran
15 H6 Kalitva r. Rus. Fed.
93 A6 Kaliua Tanz.
178 H7 Kaliujar Uttar Prad. India
20 Q4 Kalix Sweden
20 Q4 Kalixälven r. Sweden
178 F4 Kalka Haryana India
17 Q6 Kalka r. Ukr.
59 J4 Kalkalpen, Nationalpark nat. park Austria
79 K6 Kalkan Turkey
191 B5 Kalkandere Turkey
49 B7 Kalkar Ger.
206 C4 Kalkaringi N.T. Austr.
110 I5 Kalkaska MI U.S.A.
94 C4 Kalkfeld Namibia
97 J5 Kalkfonteindam dam S. Africa
97 J5 Kalkfontein Dam Nature Reserve S. Africa
50 D3 Kalkhorst Ger.
176 G9 Kalkudah Sri Lanka
137 G3 Kalkuni Guyana
96 F4 Kalkwerf S. Africa
49 C9 Kall Ger.
176 F7 Kallakkurichchi Tamil Nadu India
204 F2 Kallakoopah Creek watercourse S.A. Austr.
20 N3 Kallaktjåkkå mt. Sweden
176 E3 Kallam Mahar. India
22 J3 Kållandsö i. Sweden
156 □ Kallang Sing.
156 □ Kallang r. Sing.
18 K3 Kallaste Estonia
20 S5 Kallavesi l. Fin.
20 L5 Kållberget Sweden
20 Q4 Kallfjärden b. Sweden
59 I3 Kallham Austria
78 D4 Kallidromo mts Greece
78 C3 Kallifoni Greece
23 L5 Kallinge Sweden
76 H9 Kallmet i Madh Albania
53 L3 Kallmünz Ger.
78 G5 Kalloni Tinos Greece
79 H3 Kallonis, Kolpos b. Lesvos Greece
57 K4 Kállósemjén Hungary
20 L5 Kallsjön l. Sweden
176 E4 Kallur Karnataka India
182 K4 Kalmakkyrgan watercourse Kazakh.
57 K4 Kálmánháza Hungary
183 T1 Kalmanka Rus. Fed.
23 M5 Kalmar Sweden
23 M4 Kalmar county Sweden
23 M4 Kalmarsund sea chan. Sweden
52 E3 Kalmit hill Ger.
17 Q6 Kal'mius r. Ukr.
45 F6 Kalmthout Belgium
45 F6 Kalmthoutse Heide Natuurreservaat nature res. Belgium
184 G3 Kalmūkh Qal'eh Iran
176 G9 Kalmunai Sri Lanka
Kalmykia aut. rep. Rus. Fed. see Kalmykiya - Khalm'g-Tangch, Respublika
15 I7 Kalmykiya - Khalm'g-Tangch, Respublika aut. rep. Rus. Fed.
Kalmytskaya Avtonomnaya Oblast' aut. rep. Rus. Fed. see Kalmykiya - Khalm'g-Tangch, Respublika
179 I8 Kalnai Chhattisgarh India
57 H3 Kalná nad Hronom Slovakia
18 G5 Kalnciems Latvia
179 M7 Kalni r. Bangl.
68 F2 Kalnik mts Croatia
79 G7 Kalo Chorio Kriti Greece
57 H5 Kalocsa Hungary
16 F2 Kalodnaye Belarus
124 □D13 Kalohi Channel HI U.S.A.
190 A3 Kalokhorio Cyprus
91 E6 Kaloko Dem. Rep. Congo
178 D8 Kalol Gujarat India
178 D8 Kalol Gujarat India
155 D2 Kaloma i. Indon.
91 E9 Kalomo Zambia
158 C3 Kalon Myanmar
106 E4 Kalone Peak B.C. Can.
155 E1 Kalongan Sulawesi Indon.
190 A4 Kalopanagiotis Cyprus
200 □6 Kalourat, Mount Malaita Solomon Is
184 B2 Kalow r. Iran
57 H5 Káloz Hungary
20 U3 Kalozhnoye, Ozero l. Rus. Fed.
178 G4 Kalpa Hima. Prad. India
78 B3 Kalpakio Greece
176 C7 Kalpeni atoll India
176 E7 Kalpetta Kerala India
178 G6 Kalpi Uttar Prad. India
172 D6 Kalpin Xinjiang China
176 F8 Kalpitiya Sri Lanka
Kalquduq Uzbek. see Ko'lquduq
189 M6 Kal Safīd Iran
58 G5 Kals am Großglockner Austria
59 L6 Kalsdorf bei Graz Austria
184 G3 Kāl-Shūr, Rūd-e r. Iran
178 F4 Kalsi Uttaranchal India
104 C3 Kaltag AK U.S.A.
18 I6 Kaltanėnai Lith.
14 K5 Kaltasy Rus. Fed.
70 G1 Kaltbrunn Switz.
58 E5 Kaltenbach Austria
48 I3 Kaltenkirchen Ger.
49 J9 Kaltennordheim Ger.
49 J9 Kaltensundheim Ger.
49 J9 Kaltenwestheim Ger.
18 F6 Kaltinėnai Lith.
206 B8 Kaltukatjara N.T. Austr.
89 H4 Kaltungo Nigeria
178 D5 Kalu Rajasthan India
176 C3 Kalu r. India
124 □E12 Kalua'aha HI U.S.A.
76 I6 Kaluđerica Srbija Serb. and Mont.
19 T7 Kaluga Rus. Fed.
Kaluga Oblast admin. div. Rus. Fed. see Kaluzhskaya Oblast'
17 L6 Kaluha Ukr.
157 L7 Kalukalukuang i. Indon.
155 A5 Kaluku Sulawesi Indon.
157 K3 Kalulong, Bukit mt. Malaysia
91 F8 Kalulushi Zambia
208 I3 Kalumburu W.A. Austr.
208 I3 Kalumburu Aboriginal Reserve W.A. Austr.
22 H6 Kalundborg Denmark
91 E7 Kalundwe Dem. Rep. Congo
157 L1 Kalupis Falls Malaysia
185 N5 Kalur Kot Pak.
16 D4 Kalush Ukr.
55 J3 Kałuszyn Pol.
176 F9 Kalutara Sri Lanka
19 S7 Kaluzhskaya Oblast' admin. div. Rus. Fed.
21 H6 Kalvåg Norway
178 E9 Kalvan Mahar. India
18 G7 Kalvarija Lith.
18 I7 Kalveliai Lith.
14 C? Kälviä Fin.
21 S6 Kalvitsa Fin.
21 R6 Kalvola Fin.
55 I2 Kalwa, Jezioro l. Pol.
176 F4 Kalwakurti Andhra Prad. India
59 K5 Kalwang Austria
55 H6 Kalwaria Zebrzydowska Pol.
14 L3 Kal'ya Rus. Fed.
176 C? Kalyan Mahar. India
176 E5 Kalyandurg Andhra Prad. India
176 E4 Kalyani Karnataka India
177 H3 Kalyansingapuram Orissa India
19 U4 Kalyazin Rus. Fed.
16 E2 Kalyena Belarus
79 H6 Kalymnos Greece
79 H5 Kalymnos i. Greece
16 J3 Kalynivka Kyivs'ka Oblast' Ukr.
17 O8 Kalynivka Respublika Krym Ukr.
16 H4 Kalynivka Vinnyts'ka Oblast' Ukr.
19 N6 Kalyshki Belarus
17 K3 Kalyta Ukr.
79 J6 Kalythies Rodos Greece
78 C4 Kalyvia Greece
89 H4 Kam Nigeria
91 E5 Kama Dem. Rep. Congo
158 B5 Kama Myanmar
14 K4 Kama Rus. Fed.
14 K4 Kama r. Rus. Fed.
167 K4 Kamagaya Japan
164 S7 Kamaishi Japan
165 □3 Kama-iwa i. Japan
167 K5 Kamakura Japan
137 G3 Kamakusa Guyana
88 B4 Kamakwie Sierra Leone
84 C4 Kamal Chad
176 F5 Kamalapuram Andhra Prad. India
185 O6 Kamalia Pak.
124 □E12 Kamalō HI U.S.A.
158 C6 Kamamaung Myanmar
178 F6 Kaman Rajasthan India
188 F4 Kaman Turkey
167 I4 Kamanashi-gawa r. Japan
167 H4 Kamanashi-yama mt. Japan
96 G9 Kamanassie r. S. Africa
96 G9 Kamanassieberg mts S. Africa
111 Q4 Kamaniskeg Lake Ont. Can.
94 B3 Kamanjab Namibia
200 □6 Kamaosi Sta Isabel Solomon Is
186 F8 Kamaran Yemen
186 F8 Kamarān i. Yemen
137 F3 Kamarang Guyana
Kamaran Island Yemen see Kamarān
185 L4 Kamard reg. Afgh.
18 H5 Kamarde Latvia
176 F3 Kamareddi Andhra Prad. India
78 C4 Kamares Dytiki Ellas Greece
78 F6 Kamares Sifnos Greece
137 G3 Kamaria Falls Guyana
191 G4 Kämärli Azer.
16 J2 Kamaryn Belarus
Kamashi Uzbek. see Qamashi
178 H7 Kamasin Uttar Prad. India
95 E3 Kamativi Zimbabwe
89 F4 Kamba Nigeria
158 D2 Kambaiti Myanmar
90 C3 Kamba Kota C.A.R.
209 F11 Kambalda W.A. Austr.
14 I1 Kambal'nitskiye Koshki, Ostrova is Rus. Fed.
176 E8 Kambam Tamil Nadu India
156 D5 Kambang Sumatera Indon.
157 H9 Kambangan i. Indon.
91 C6 Kamba-Poko Dem. Rep. Congo
Kambara i. Fiji see Kabara
Kambara Japan see Kanbara
172 E6 Kambardi Xinjiang China
14 K4 Kambarka Rus. Fed.
88 B4 Kambia Sierra Leone
208 □2 Kambling Island Cocos Is
Kambo-san mt. N. Korea see Kwanmo-bong
91 E7 Kambove Dem. Rep. Congo
155 B5 Kambuno, Bukit mt. Indon.
77 O7 Kamburovo Bulg.
84 E2 Kambūt Libya
193 R4 Kamchatka r. Rus. Fed.
193 Q4 Kamchatka, Poluostrov pen. Rus. Fed.
216 G2 Kamchatka Basin sea feature Bering Sea
Kamchatka Peninsula Rus. Fed. see Kamchatka, Poluostrov
193 R4 Kamchatskiy Proliv str. Rus. Fed.
193 R4 Kamchatskiy Zaliv b. Rus. Fed.
77 P7 Kamchiya r. Bulg.
77 P8 Kamchiyska Planina hills Bulg.
96 H3 Kamden S. Africa
185 N4 Kamdesh Afgh.
182 C1 Kamelik r. Rus. Fed.
77 N7 Kamen Bulg.
49 E7 Kamen Ger.
193 K3 Kamen', Gory mts Rus. Fed.
91 E6 Kamende Dem. Rep. Congo
56 D3 Kamenec mt. Czech Rep.
Kamenets-Podol'skiy Ukr. see Kam''yanets'-Podil's'kyy
77 K7 Kamenica Srbija Serb. and Mont.
57 J2 Kamenica Slovakia
56 E2 Kamenice nad Lipou Czech Rep.
51 J9 Kamenický Šenov Czech Rep.
57 H4 Kameničná Slovakia
57 H4 Kamenín Slovakia
188 A3 Kamenitsa mt. Bulg.
77 M7 Kamenitsa r. Bulg.
57 H6 Kamenjak hill Croatia
68 D3 Kamenjak, Rt pt Croatia
182 D2 Kamenka Kazakh.
14 I2 Kamenka Arkhangel'skaya Oblast' Rus. Fed.
19 S7 Kamenka Kaluzhskaya Oblast' Rus. Fed.
18 M1 Kamenka Leningradskaya Oblast' Rus. Fed.
15 I5 Kamenka Penzenskaya Oblast' Rus. Fed.
162 J6 Kamenka Primorskiy Kray Rus. Fed.
19 P6 Kamenka Smolenskaya Oblast' Rus. Fed.
15 G6 Kamenka Voronezhskaya Oblast' Rus. Fed.
Kamenka Ukr. see Kam''yanka
Kamenka-Bugskaya Ukr. see Kam''yanka-Buz'ka
Kamenka-Shevchenkovskaya Ukr. see Kam''yanka
Kamen'-Kashirskiy Ukr. see Kamin'-Kashyrs'kyy
Kamenka-Strumilovskaya Ukr. see Kam''yanka-Buz'ka
19 U5 Kamenki Rus. Fed.
192 J4 Kamen'-na-Obi Rus. Fed.
14 G4 Kamenniki Rus. Fed.
18 M1 Kamennogorsk Rus. Fed.
191 B1 Kamennomostskiy Rus. Fed.
20 U4 Kamennoye, Ozero l. Rus. Fed.
56 D2 Kamenný Přívoz Czech Rep.
56 D3 Kamenný Újezd Czech Rep.
77 P8 Kameno Bulg.
17 T6 Kamenolomni Rus. Fed.
162 H6 Kamen'-Rybolov Rus. Fed.
15 I6 Kamenskiy Rus. Fed.
193 R3 Kamenskoye Koryakskiy Avtonomnyy Okrug Rus. Fed.
19 V9 Kamenskoye Lipetskaya Oblast' Rus. Fed.
15 H6 Kamensk-Shakhtinskiy Rus. Fed.
192 H4 Kamensk-Ural'skiy Rus. Fed.
51 J8 Kamenz Ger.
166 C5 Kameoka Japan
92 B4 Kameramaido Uganda
50 F5 Kamern Ger.
26 F11 Kames Argyll and Bute, Scotland U.K.
19 X5 Kameshkovo Rus. Fed.
173 D11 Kamet mt. Xizang China
166 D6 Kameyama Japan
76 H9 Kamëz Albania
166 A5 Kami Hyōgo Japan
167 G5 Kami Nagano Japan
165 G12 Kamiagata Japan
122 F3 Kamiah ID U.S.A.
166 F2 Kamichi Japan
55 L4 Kamień Lubelskie Pol.
55 K5 Kamień Podkarpackie Pol.
55 I6 Kamienica Pol.
54 E3 Kamieniec Pol.
54 E5 Kamieniec Ząbkowicki Pol.
54 F2 Kamień Krajeński Pol.
55 J4 Kamienna r. Pol.
54 E5 Kamienna Gora Pol.
54 F5 Kamiennik Pol.
54 C2 Kamień Pomorski Pol.
55 H4 Kamieńsk Pol.
50 K5 Kamień Wielkie Pol.
96 C6 Kamiesberg S. Africa
96 C6 Kamiesberge mts S. Africa
96 B6 Kamieskroon S. Africa
167 K4 Kamifukuoka Japan
164 T3 Kamifurano Japan
166 D5 Kami-ishizu Japan
91 D6 Kamiji Dem. Rep. Congo
166 E6 Kami-jima i. Japan
164 T3 Kamikawa Hokkaidō Japan
167 J3 Kamikawa Saitama Japan
167 K2 Kamikawachi Japan
166 C7 Kamikitayama Japan
165 G15 Kami-Koshiki-jima i. Japan
167 I4 Kamikuishiki Japan
206 H5 Kamileroi Qld Austr.
107 K2 Kamilukuak Lake Nunavut Can.
91 E7 Kamina Dem. Rep. Congo
91 E7 Kamina Base Dem. Rep. Congo
166 C5 Kaminaka Japan
107 M2 Kaminak Lake Nunavut Can.
16 D2 Kamin'-Kashyrs'kyy Ukr.
166 F4 Kaminoho Japan
167 K3 Kaminokawa Japan
164 R5 Kaminokuni Japan
164 □G18 Kaminone-jima i. Nansei-shotō Japan
164 R8 Kaminoyama Japan
68 E2 Kaminške in Savinjske Alpe mts Slovenia
19 Y4 Kaminskiy Rus. Fed.
166 F3 Kamioka Japan
55 I3 Kamion Mazowieckie Pol.
55 I4 Kamion Mazowieckie Pol.
55 K4 Kamionka Pol.
79 I6 Kamiros Rodos Greece
166 D3 Kamishihi Japan
164 U3 Kamishihoro Japan
167 M4 Kamisu Japan
166 E3 Kami-taira Japan
166 F3 Kami-takara Japan
165 G12 Kamitsushima Japan
91 F5 Kamituga Dem. Rep. Congo
166 F5 Kami-yahagi Japan
164 □H16 Kamiyaku Japan
167 H3 Kamiyamada Japan
164 U2 Kamiyūbetsu Japan
179 O7 Kamjong Manipur India
183 N5 Kamkaly Kazakh.
179 K6 Kamla r. India
179 N6 Kamla r. India
183 U2 Kamlak Rus. Fed.
106 F5 Kamloops B.C. Can.
106 F5 Kamloops Lake B.C. Can.
53 I5 Kammel r. Ger.
96 I9 Kammiebos S. Africa
53 I5 Kammlach Ger.
Kammuri-jima i. Japan see Kanmuri-jima
Kammuri-yama mt. Japan see Kanmuri-yama
68 E2 Kamnik Slovenia
59 I7 Kamno Slovenia
Kamo Armenia see Gavarr
166 C6 Kamo Kyōto Japan
167 I6 Kamo Yamanashi Japan
202 I2 Kamo North I. N.Z.
85 H5 Kamob Sanha Sudan
166 A8 Kamoda-misaki pt Japan
164 R3 Kamoenai Japan
167 L5 Kamogawa Japan
165 L12 Kamojima Japan
185 P6 Kamoke Pak.
91 E6 Kamola Dem. Rep. Congo
93 A6 Kamonanira Tanz.
59 M3 Kamp r. Austria
49 E10 Kamp Ger.
156 F5 Kampa Indon.
92 B4 Kampala Uganda
78 F4 Kampanos, Akra pt Andros Greece
156 E4 Kampar r. Indon.
156 D2 Kampar Malaysia
179 I8 Kampara Chhattisgarh India
18 F4 Kamparkalns hill Latvia
156 D4 Kamparkiri r. Indon.
48 F1 Kampen Ger.
44 I3 Kampen Neth.
91 E5 Kampene Dem. Rep. Congo
52 F4 Kämpfelbach Ger.
158 D6 Kamphaeng Phet Thai.
93 B6 Kampi Katoto Tanz.
55 I3 Kampinos Pol.
55 I3 Kampinoski Park Narodowy nat. park Pol.
176 E5 Kampli Karnataka India
49 C8 Kamp-Lintfort Ger.
165 G11 Kamp'o S. Korea
91 F7 Kampolombo, Lake Zambia
159 G9 Kâmpóng Cham Cambodia
159 G8 Kâmpóng Chhnăng Cambodia
159 G8 Kâmpóng Khleăng Cambodia
159 G9 Kâmpóng Spœ Cambodia
159 G8 Kâmpóng Thum Cambodia
159 G9 Kâmpóng Trâbêk Cambodia
159 G9 Kâmpóng Tranch Cambodia
159 G9 Kâmpôt Cambodia
88 E4 Kampti Burkina
Kampuchea country Asia see Cambodia
153 H7 Kamrau, Teluk b. Papua Indon.
107 K5 Kamsack Sask. Can.
88 B4 Kamsar Guinea
51 D9 Kamsdorf Ger.
14 K3 Kamskiy Rus. Fed.
15 J5 Kamskoye Ust'ye Rus. Fed.
14 L4 Kamskoye Vodokhranilishche resr Rus. Fed.
92 D4 Kamsuuma Somalia
178 H9 Kamtha Mahar. India
107 K3 Kamuchawie Lake Man./Sask. Can.
164 T4 Kamui-dake mt. Japan
92 B4 Kamuli Uganda
91 E6 Kamungu Dem. Rep. Congo
57 J5 Kamut Hungary
92 A4 Kamwenge Uganda
16 G2 Kam''yane Rivnens'ka Oblast' Ukr.
17 N3 Kam''yane Sums'ka Oblast' Ukr.
16 F5 Kam''yanets'-Podil's'kyy Ukr.
17 L4 Kam''yanka Cherkas'ka Oblast' Ukr.
17 Q4 Kam''yanka Kharkivs'ka Oblast' Ukr.
17 L5 Kam''yanka r. Ukr.
16 D3 Kam''yanka-Buz'ka Ukr.
17 N6 Kam''yanka-Dniprovs'ka Ukr.
16 I8 Kam''yans'ke Odes'ka Oblast' Ukr.
17 O6 Kam''yans'ke Zaporiz'ka Oblast' Ukr.
18 G9 Kamyanyets Belarus
18 G9 Kamyanyuki Belarus
184 B4 Kāmyārān Iran
18 L6 Kamyen' Belarus
18 H8 Kamyenka Belarus
15 G7 Kamyshevatskaya Rus. Fed.
15 I6 Kamyshin Rus. Fed.
15 K5 Kamyshla Rus. Fed.
182 I4 Kamyshlybash Kazakh.
Kamyshnaya r. Rus. Fed./Ukr. see Komyshna
182 C3 Kamysh-Samarskiye Ozera lakes Kazakh.
Kamyslybas Kazakh. see Kamyshlybash
182 I4 Kamyslybas, Ozero l. Kazakh.
182 I2 Kamysty Kazakh.
182 C4 Kamyzyak Rus. Fed.
187 M2 Kamzar Oman
193 K4 Kan r. Rus. Fed.
92 A2 Kan Sudan
90 F4 Kana Dem. Rep. Congo
95 E3 Kana r. Zimbabwe
108 E2 Kanaaupscow r. Que. Can.
125 T4 Kanab UT U.S.A.
125 T5 Kanab Creek r. AZ U.S.A.
201 □1 Kanacea Taveuni Fiji
167 G5 Kanae Japan
104 A4 Kanaga Island AK U.S.A.
167 J5 Kanagawa pref. Japan
164 R6 Kanagi Japan
137 F3 Kanaima Falls Guyana
109 J2 Kanairiktok r. Nfld and Lab. Can.
185 L7 Kanak Pak.
176 E6 Kanakapura Karnataka India
59 I7 Kanal Slovenia
78 F5 Kanala Kythnos Greece
78 B3 Kanali Greece
78 B3 Kanallaki Greece
189 L7 Kan'ān Iraq
20 M4 Kanan Sweden
97 K2 Kanana S. Africa
91 D6 Kananga Dem. Rep. Congo
205 M5 Kanangra-Boyd National Park N.S.W. Austr.
Kanarak Orissa India see Konarka
125 S4 Kanarraville UT U.S.A.
96 B3 Kanas watercourse Namibia
167 L2 Kanasagō Japan
14 I5 Kanash Rus. Fed.
172 H2 Kanas Köl l. China
Kanathea Taveuni Fiji see Kanacea
14 K3 Kanava Rus. Fed.
157 K3 Kanawang, Bukit mt. Malaysia
116 C10 Kanawha r. WV U.S.A.
167 H6 Kanaya Shizuoka Japan
166 B7 Kanaya Wakayama Japan
166 F4 Kanayama Japan
183 S3 Kanayka Kazakh.
166 E2 Kanazawa Ishikawa Japan
167 K5 Kanazawa Kanagawa Japan
166 D3 Kanazu Japan
158 B3 Kanbalu Myanmar
167 I5 Kanbara Japan
159 D8 Kanchanaburi Thai.
Kanchanjanga mt. India/Nepal see Kangchenjunga
179 L6 Kanchenjunga Conservation Area nature res. Nepal
176 F6 Kanchipuram Tamil Nadu India
55 K6 Kańczuga Pol.
185 L6 Kand mt. Pak.
185 L7 Kanda Pak.
185 K6 Kandahār Afgh.
185 K6 Kandahār prov. Afgh.
176 E3 Kandahar Mahar. India
20 V3 Kandalaksha Rus. Fed.
14 F2 Kandalakshskiy Zaliv g. Rus. Fed.
91 C6 Kandale Dem. Rep. Congo
156 B3 Kandang Sumatera Indon.
157 K6 Kandangan Kalimantan Indon.
18 F4 Kandava Latvia
Kandavu i. Fiji see Kadavu
Kandavu Passage Fiji see Kadavu Passage
89 F4 Kandé Togo
52 E3 Kandel Ger.
52 E5 Kandel mt. Ger.
50 H2 Kandelin Ger.
70 D2 Kander r. Switz.
52 D6 Kandern Ger.
70 D3 Kandersteg Switz.
185 M7 Kandhkot Pak.
185 N4 Kandhura Pak.
89 F4 Kandi Benin
185 L7 Kandi Pak.
155 B3 Kandi, Tanjung pt Indon.
185 M8 Kandiaro Pak.
78 B4 Kandila Dytiki Ellas Greece
78 D5 Kandila Peloponnisos Greece
89 H3 Kandil Bouzou well Niger
191 E6 Kandil Dağı mt. Turkey
191 B6 Kandilli Turkey
79 L1 Kandıra Turkey
90 D3 Kandja C.A.R.
178 C8 Kandla Gujarat India
175 □1 Kandooma Fushi i. S. Male Maldives
205 L5 Kandos N.S.W. Austr.
177 J1 Kandra Jharkhand India
95 □J3 Kandreho Madag.
179 I8 Kandri Chhattisgarh India
153 K8 Kandrian New Britain P.N.G.
176 F5 Kandukur Andhra Prad. India
176 G9 Kandy Sri Lanka
182 G3 Kandyagash Kazakh.
116 G7 Kane PA U.S.A.
105 L2 Kane Bassin b. Greenland
184 E8 Kaneh watercourse Iran
84 B6 Kanem pref. Chad
124 □D12 Kāne'ohe HI U.S.A.
124 □D12 Kāne'ohe Bay HI U.S.A.
178 E7 Kanera Rajasthan India
185 L7 Kaneti Pak.
Kanev Ukr. see Kaniv
14 G2 Kanevka Rus. Fed.
15 G7 Kanevskaya Rus. Fed.
166 F5 Kaneyama Gifu Japan
165 R8 Kaneyama Yamagata Japan
71 P5 Kanfanar Croatia
88 B4 Kanfarande Guinea
185 I6 Kang Afgh.
94 D4 Kang Botswana
179 L9 Kanga r. Bangl.
105 M3 Kangaamiut Greenland
105 K2 Kangaarsussuaq c. Greenland
105 M3 Kangaatsiaq Greenland
88 C4 Kangaba Mali
188 H4 Kangal Turkey
193 N3 Kangalassy Rus. Fed.
184 E8 Kangān Būshehr Iran
184 G9 Kangān Hormozgan Iran
208 E6 Kangan Aboriginal Reserve W.A. Austr.
156 D1 Kangar Malaysia
88 C4 Kangaré Mali
204 F6 Kangaroo Island S.A. Austr.
206 G4 Kangaroo Point Qld Austr.
137 G3 Kangaruma Guyana
21 R6 Kangasala Fin.
20 T5 Kangaslampi Fin.
21 S6 Kangasniemi Fin.
184 B4 Kangāvar Iran
176 E7 Kangayam Tamil Nadu India
169 N6 Kangbao Hebei China
179 L6 Kangchenjunga mt. India/Nepal
170 C3 Kangding Sichuan China
157 K8 Kangean, Kepulauan is Indon.
105 L3 Kangeeak Point Nunavut Can.
92 B3 Kangen r. Sudan
105 N3 Kangeq c. Greenland
105 M3 Kangerluarsoruseq Greenland
105 M3 Kangerlussuaq Greenland
105 M2 Kangerlussuaq inlet Greenland
105 M3 Kangerlussuaq inlet Greenland
105 O3 Kangerlussuaq inlet Greenland
105 N3 Kangerlussuatsiaq inlet Greenland
105 M2 Kangersuatsiaq Greenland
105 P2 Kangertittivaq sea chan. Greenland
105 O3 Kangertittivatsiaq inlet Greenland
92 C4 Kangetet Kenya
163 E8 Kanggye N. Korea
105 P2 Kangikajik c. Greenland
105 N3 Kangilinnguit Greenland
109 H1 Kangiqsualujjuaq Que. Can.
105 K3 Kangiqsujuaq Que. Can.
105 K3 Kangirsuk Que. Can.
159 D10 Kang Krung National Park Thai.
168 H9 Kangle Gansu China
173 I12 Kangmar Xizang China
163 F10 Kangnŭng S. Korea
90 A4 Kango Gabon
165 □3 Kangoku-iwa i. Japan
20 Q3 Kangos Sweden
169 R5 Kangping Liaoning China
178 F3 Kangra Hima. Prad. India
179 P5 Kangri Karpo Pass China/India
173 E11 Kangrinboqê Feng mt. Xizang China
173 G10 Kangro Xizang China
154 C9 Kang Tipayan Dakula i. Phil.
173 K13 Kangto mt. China/India
173 G10 Kangtog Xizang China
170 E2 Kangxian Gansu China
173 D8 Kangxiwar Xinjiang China
158 B6 Kangyidaung Myanmar
178 G9 Kanhan r. India
179 I7 Kanhar r. Jharkhand India
176 E3 Kanhargaon Mahar. India
23 O2 Kanholmsfjärden b. Sweden
88 D4 Kani Côte d'Ivoire
184 F8 Kānī Iran
166 F5 Kani Japan
158 B3 Kani Myanmar
91 E6 Kaniama Dem. Rep. Congo
Kanibadam Tajik. see Konibodom
157 L1 Kanibongan Sabah Malaysia
166 E5 Kanie Japan
203 F9 Kaniere South I. N.Z.
203 F9 Kaniere, Lake South I. N.Z.
88 A3 Kanifing Gambia
175 □1 Kanifinolhu i. N. Male Maldives
176 F5 Kanigiri Andhra Prad. India
185 M5 Kaniguram Pak.
99 □3b Kani-Kéli Mayotte
14 I2 Kanin, Poluostrov pen. Rus. Fed.
14 H1 Kanin Nos Rus. Fed.
14 H1 Kanin Nos, Mys c. Rus. Fed.
14 H2 Kaninskiy Bereg coastal area Rus. Fed.
189 L5 Kānī Ŗash Iraq
58 A5 Kanisfluh mt. Austria
164 R5 Kanita Japan
17 K4 Kaniv Ukr.
204 H7 Kaniva Vic. Austr.
17 K3 Kanivs'ke Vodoskhovyshche resr Ukr.
178 G8 Kaniwara Madh. Prad. India
179 I5 Kanjiroba mt. Nepal
76 I4 Kanjiža Vojvodina, Srbija Serb. and Mont.
21 Q6 Kankaanpää Fin.
110 G8 Kankakee IL U.S.A.
110 F8 Kankakee r. IL U.S.A.
88 C4 Kankan Guinea
88 C4 Kankan, Réserve Naturelle de nature res. Guinea
178 H9 Kanker Chhattisgarh India
176 G8 Kankesanturai Sri Lanka
89 G3 Kankiya Nigeria
88 C3 Kankossa Maur.
154 D6 Kanlaon, Mount vol. Phil.
159 D9 Kanmaw Kyun i. Myanmar
166 B4 Kanmuri-jima i. Japan
166 D4 Kanmuri-yama mt. Japan
165 J12 Kanmuri-yama mt. Japan
178 E9 Kannad Mahar. India
167 J3 Kanna-gawa r. Japan
167 I5 Kannami Japan
115 G8 Kannapolis NC U.S.A.
178 G6 Kannauj Uttar Prad. India
51 D8 Kannawurf Ger.
176 E8 Kanniyakumari Tamil Nadu India
178 F8 Kannod Madh. Prad. India
20 R5 Kannonkoski Fin.
166 F1 Kannon-zaki pt Japan
20 Q5 Kannus Fin.
18 K1 Kannuskoski Fin.
155 D5 Kano i. Indon.
89 H3 Kano Nigeria
89 H4 Kano r. Nigeria
89 H4 Kano state Nigeria
167 I5 Kano-gawa r. Japan
131 □10 Kanon, Punt pt Curaçao Neth. Antilles
93 A8 Kanona Zambia
183 R2 Kanonerka Kazakh.
165 K12 Kan'onji Japan
96 F10 Kanonpunt pt S. Africa
178 E7 Kanor Rajasthan India
120 D6 Kanorado KS U.S.A.
125 T3 Kanosh UT U.S.A.
94 C3 Kanovlei Namibia
157 J3 Kanowit Sarawak Malaysia
165 H15 Kanoya Japan
178 H6 Kanpur Uttar Prad. India
185 M7 Kanpur Pak.
167 I3 Kanra Japan
185 L8 Kanrach reg. Pak.
166 B7 Kansai airport Japan
91 E8 Kansanshi Zambia
120 H6 Kansas r. KS U.S.A.
120 F6 Kansas state U.S.A.
120 H6 Kansas City KS U.S.A.
120 H6 Kansas City MO U.S.A.
91 E7 Kansenia Dem. Rep. Congo
193 K4 Kansk Rus. Fed.
172 B7 Kansu Xinjiang China
92 B3 Kanta mt. Eth.
21 S5 Kantala Fin.
159 D11 Kantang Thai.
190 B3 Kantara hill Cyprus
159 G7 Kantaralak Thai.
191 C6 Kantarkaya Turkey
191 B5 Kantarlı Turkey
63 O3 Kantauri Mendilerroa mts Spain
Kantavu i. Fiji see Kadavu
89 F3 Kantchari Burkina
15 G6 Kantemirovka Rus. Fed.
44 K2 Kantens Neth.
178 G5 Kanth Uttar Prad. India
179 K9 Kanthi W. Bengal India
179 J6 Kanti Bihar India
179 J9 Kantilo Orissa India
104 C3 Kantishna r. AK U.S.A.
173 B12 Kantli r. India
167 K4 Kantō-heiya plain Japan
199 I2 Kanton atoll Phoenix Is Kiribati
Kan-Too, Pik mt. Kazakh./Kyrg. see Khan-Tengri, Pik
167 H4 Kanto-sanchi mts Japan
206 D5 Kanttaji Aboriginal Land res. N.T. Austr.
158 C5 Kantulong Myanmar
27 E8 Kanturk Rep. of Ireland
206 E5 Kanturrpa Aboriginal Land res. N.T. Austr.
184 F5 Kanūgar Iran
137 G4 Kanuku Mountains Guyana
167 K2 Kanuma Japan
93 A5 Kanungu Uganda
176 E5 Kanur Andhra Prad. India
94 C5 Kanus Namibia
153 J8 Kanuwe r. P.N.G.
Kanyakubja Uttar Prad. India see Kannauj
97 P1 KaNyamazane S. Africa
94 E5 Kanye Botswana
95 F2 Kanyemba Zimbabwe
19 Q6 Kanyutino Rus. Fed.
166 A5 Kanzaki Japan
155 E3 Kao Halmahera Indon.
89 G3 Kao Niger
201 □2 Kao i. Tonga
155 E3 Kao, Teluk b. Halmahera Indon.
171 M7 Kaohsiung Taiwan
159 F9 Kaôh Tang i. Cambodia
94 B3 Kaokoveld plat. Namibia
88 A3 Kaolack Senegal
200 □6 Kaolo Sta Isabel Solomon Is
91 F7 Kaoma Northern Zambia
91 E8 Kaoma Western Zambia
84 C5 Kaortchi well Chad
90 D3 Kaouadja C.A.R.
201 □2 Kapa i. Vava'u Gp Tonga
124 □B11 Kapa'a HI U.S.A.
124 □F13 Kapa'au HI U.S.A.
183 R5 Kapal Kazakh.
155 E4 Kapalabuaya Maluku Indon.
76 H8 Kapa Moračka mt. Serb. and Mont.
191 H6 Kapan Armenia
91 D7 Kapanga Dem. Rep. Congo
91 F6 Kapangolo Dem. Rep. Congo
78 E4 Kapareli Greece
184 C6 Kaparhā Iran
16 H1 Kapatkyevichy Belarus
93 A7 Kapatu Zambia
183 Q6 Kapchagay Kazakh.
183 Q6 Kapchagayskoye Vodokhranilishche resr Kazakh.
92 B4 Kapchorwa Uganda
18 G8 Kapčiamiestis Lith.
Kap Dan Greenland see Kulusuk
44 E6 Kapelle Neth.
45 F6 Kapellen Belgium
78 E6 Kapello, Akra pt Kythira Greece
23 P2 Kapellskär Sweden
Kapelskär Sweden see Kapellskär
92 B4 Kapenguria Kenya
59 L5 Kapfenberg Austria
59 M6 Kapfenstein Austria
79 I2 Kapıdağı Yarımadası pen. Turkey
179 M6 Kapili r. India
199 F1 Kapingamarangi atoll Micronesia
216 F5 Kapingamarangi Rise sea feature N. Pacific Ocean
79 L2 Kapıorman Dağları mts Turkey
185 M6 Kapip Pak.
91 F8 Kapiri Mposhi Zambia
185 M4 Kāpīsā prov. Afgh.
105 M3 Kapisillit Greenland
108 D2 Kapiskau r. Ont. Can.
111 M2 Kapiskong Lake Ont. Can.
157 J3 Kapit Sarawak Malaysia
17 K5 Kapitanivka Ukr.
203 I7 Kapiti Island North I. N.Z.
137 H4 Kapiting Brazil
84 D5 Kapka well Chad
84 D6 Kapka, Massif du mts Chad
155 E5 Kaplamada, Gunung mt. Buru Indon.
184 F1 Kaplankyr, Chink esc. Turkm./Uzbek.
184 G1 Kaplankyrskiy Gosudarstvennyy Zapovednik nature res. Turkm.
56 D3 Kaplice Czech Rep.
159 D10 Kapoe Thai.
92 B3 Kapoeta Sudan
57 J4 Kápolna Hungary
155 C8 Kapondai, Tanjung pt Flores Indon.
202 I6 Kaponga North I. N.Z.
93 B7 Kaporo Malawi
76 G4 Kapos r. Romania
57 G5 Kaposfő Hungary
57 H5 Kaposszekcső Hungary
57 G5 Kaposvár Hungary
185 J9 Kappar Pak.
52 C2 Kappel Ger.
59 J6 Kappel am Krappfeld Austria
52 D5 Kappel-Grafenhausen Ger.
48 I1 Kappeln Ger.
52 E4 Kappelrodeck Ger.
58 B5 Kappl Austria
178 F7 Kapran Rajasthan India
58 G5 Kaprun Austria
92 B4 Kapsabet Kenya
185 J8 Kap Salt Swamp Pak.
163 F8 Kapsan N. Korea
78 D5 Kapsas Greece
19 Q2 Kapsha r. Rus. Fed.
Kapsukas Lith. see Marijampolė
179 N8 Kaptai Bangl.
169 P2 Kaptsegaytuy Rus. Fed.
16 H1 Kaptsevichy Belarus
55 L2 Kaptsyowka Belarus
157 H5 Kapuas r. Indon.
157 K6 Kapuas r. Indon.
157 J4 Kapuas Hulu, Pegunungan mts Indon./Malaysia
204 G6 Kapunda S.A. Austr.
178 D6 Kapuriya Rajasthan India
178 E4 Kapurthala Punjab India
57 K2 Kapušany Slovakia
108 D3 Kapuskasing Ont. Can.
108 D3 Kapuskasing r. Ont. Can.
15 I6 Kapustin Yar Rus. Fed.
17 K3 Kapustyntsi Kyivs'ka Oblast' Ukr.
17 N3 Kapustyntsi Sums'ka Oblast' Ukr.
91 F7 Kaputa Zambia
184 H9 Kapūtānī Iran
205 M4 Kaputar mt. N.S.W. Austr.
92 B4 Kaputir Kenya
56 G4 Kapuvár Hungary
18 K8 Kapyl' Belarus
163 E10 Kap'yŏng S. Korea
19 P6 Kapyrevshchina Rus. Fed.
173 L11 Ka Qu r. Xizang China
178 H7 Kara Uttar Prad. India
14 N1 Kara r. Rus. Fed.
89 F4 Kara Togo
189 J4 Kara r. Turkey
79 K2 Kara r. Turkey
79 H4 Kara Ada i. Turkey
79 I6 Kara Ada i. Turkey
79 H3 Karaağaç Turkey
188 F4 Karaali Turkey
172 A7 Kara Art Pass Xinjiang China
Karaaul Kazakh. see Karaul
183 O6 Kara-Balta Kyrg.
182 J1 Karabalyk Kazakh.
19 V5 Karabanovo Rus. Fed.
183 O3 Karabas Kazakh.
182 E3 Karabau Kazakh.
182 F6 Karabaur, Uval hills Uzbek.
191 C7 Karabey Turkey
79 I2 Karabiga Turkey
185 J3 Karabil', Vozvyshennost' hills Turkm.
191 B6 Karaboğa Dağları mts Turkey
Kara-Bogaz-Gol Turkm. see Karabogazkel'
184 E1 Kara-Bogaz-Gol, Proliv sea chan. Turkm.
184 E1 Kara-Bogaz-Gol, Zaliv b. Turkm.
184 E1 Karabogazkel' Turkm.
191 I3 Karabudakhkent Rus. Fed.
188 F3 Karabük Turkey
183 R5 Karabulak Almatinskaya Oblast' Kazakh.
183 U4 Karabulak Vostochnyy Kazakhstan Kazakh.
191 F2 Karabulak Rus. Fed.
183 P3 Karabulakskaya Kazakh.
79 J4 Karaburç Turkey
79 H4 Karaburun Turkey
182 I3 Karabutak Kazakh.
79 J2 Karacabey Turkey
188 F5 Karacadağ mts Turkey
79 I1 Karacakılavuz Turkey
188 D3 Karacaköy Turkey
189 I5 Karacalı Dağ mt. Turkey
190 A2 Karaçal Tepe mt. Turkey
79 L5 Karacaören Barajı resr Turkey
79 J5 Karacasu Turkey
79 L6 Karaca Yarımadası pen. Turkey
Karachay-Cherkess Republic aut. rep. Rus. Fed. see Karachayevo-Cherkesskaya Respublika
Karachayevo-Cherkesskaya A.S.S.R. aut. rep. Rus. Fed. see Karachayevo-Cherkesskaya Respublika
191 C2 Karachayevo-Cherkesskaya Respublika aut. rep. Rus. Fed.
191 C2 Karachayevsk Rus. Fed.
19 R8 Karachev Rus. Fed.
185 L9 Karachi Pak.
17 M6 Karachunivs'ke Vodoskhovyshche resr Ukr.
189 K4 Karaçoban Turkey
79 K6 Karaçulha Turkey
Karacurun Turkey see Hilvan
57 G5 Karád Hungary
176 D4 Karad Mahar. India
190 G2 Kara Dağ hill Turkey
79 H2 Kara Dağ hill Turkey
79 J2 Kara Dağ hills Turkey
188 F5 Kara Dağ mt. Turkey
183 O7 Kara-Darya r. Kyrg.
88 E4 Karaga Ghana
162 B2 Karagan Rus. Fed.

Karaganda to Kaynar

282

183 O3 **Karaganda** Kazakh.
183 O3 **Karagandinskaya Oblast'** *admin. div.* Kazakh.
191 G1 **Karagas** Rus. Fed.
183 Q5 **Karagash** Kazakh.
182 D2 **Karagay** Kazakh.
14 K4 **Karagay** Rus. Fed.
183 P3 **Karagayly** Kazakh.
183 U3 **Karagaylybulak** Kazakh.
184 E2 **Karage** Turkm.
184 F2 **Karagez** Turkm.
193 R4 **Karaginskiy, Ostrov** *i.* Rus. Fed.
182 D6 **Karagiye, Vpadina** *depr.* Kazakh.
179 K7 **Karagola** *Bihar* India
191 B6 **Karagöl Dağları** *mts* Turkey
183 T2 **Karaguzhikha** Kazakh.
93 A5 **Karagwe** Tanz.
77 P9 **Karahalil** Turkey
79 K4 **Karahallı** Turkey
188 G4 **Karahasanlı** Turkey
79 J5 **Karahisar** Turkey
14 L5 **Karaidel'** Rus. Fed.
176 F7 **Karaikal** *Pondicherry* India
176 F7 **Karaikkudi** *Tamil Nadu* India
183 U4 **Kara Irtysh** *r.* Kazakh.
188 G5 **Karaisalı** Turkey
157 L4 **Karaitan** *Kalimantan* Indon.
184 D4 **Karaj** Iran
Karakalli Turkey *see* **Özalp**
Karakalpakistan, Respublika *aut. rep.* Uzbek. *see* **Qoraqalpog'iston Respublikasi**
Karakalpakskaya Respublika *aut. rep.* Uzbek. *see* **Qoraqalpog'iston Respublikasi**
191 C5 **Karakamış** Turkey
205 I7 **Kara Kara State Park** *nature res. Vic.* Austr.
Karakax *Xinjiang* China *see* **Moyu**
173 E7 **Karakax He** *r.* China
173 E9 **Karakax Shan** *mts Xinjiang* China
191 C5 **Karakaya** Turkey
191 D6 **Karakaya** *r.* Turkey
191 C6 **Karakaya Tepe** *mt.* Turkey
188 I5 **Karakeçi** Turkey
188 F4 **Karakeçili** Turkey
155 E1 **Karakelong** *i.* Indon.
173 E8 **Karaki** *Xinjiang* China
155 D2 **Karakitang** *i.* Indon.
Karaklis Armenia *see* **Vanadzor**
189 J4 **Karakoçan** Turkey
183 N1 **Karakoga** Kazakh.
Karakoin *salt l.* Kazakh. *see* **Karakoyyn, Ozero**
182 E3 **Karakol'** Kazakh.
183 O7 **Kara-Köl** Kyrg.
183 Q7 **Karakol** *Ysyk-Köl* Kyrg.
183 R6 **Karakol** *Ysyk-Köl* Kyrg.
Karakolka Kyrg. *see* **Karakol**
Karaköprü Turkey *see* **Karaçoban**
178 F2 **Karakoram Pass** China/Jammu and Kashmir
185 P3 **Karakoram Range** *mts* Asia
92 C2 **Kara K'orē** Eth.
88 B3 **Karakoro** *r.* Mali/Maur.
190 D2 **Karaköse** *Hatay* Turkey
79 H3 **Karaköy** Turkey
191 I3 **Karakoysu** *r.* Rus. Fed.
191 F6 **Karakoyunlu** Turkey
183 M4 **Karakoyyn, Ozero** *salt l.* Kazakh.
Karakubbud Ukr. *see* **Komsomol's'ke**
Kara-Kuga Kazakh. *see* **Karakoga**
Kara Kul' Kyrg. *see* **Kara-Köl**
Kara-Kul'dzha Kyrg. *see* **Kara-Kulja**
14 K4 **Karakulino** Rus. Fed.
183 O7 **Kara-Kulja** Kyrg.
182 J1 **Karakul'skoye** Rus. Fed.
183 R4 **Karakum** Kazakh.
182 E5 **Karakum, Peski** *des.* Kazakh.
Karakum Desert Kazakh. *see* **Karakum, Peski**
Karakum Desert Turkm. *see* **Karakumy, Peski**
185 I3 **Karakumskiy Kanal** *canal* Turkm.
184 I2 **Karakumy, Peski** *des.* Turkm.
189 K3 **Karakurt** *Kars* Turkey
79 I3 **Karakurt** *Manisa* Turkey
79 L4 **Karakuş Dağı** *ridge* Turkey
94 C3 **Karakuwisa** Namibia
90 B1 **Karal** Chad
18 E3 **Karala** Estonia
209 E8 **Karalundi** *W.A.* Austr.
155 A5 **Karama** *r.* Indon.
Karamagay *Xinjiang* China *see* **Haramgai**
79 J3 **Karaman** *Balıkesir* Turkey
188 F5 **Karaman** *Karaman* Turkey
190 B1 **Karaman** *prov.* Turkey
79 L6 **Karamanbeyli Geçidi** *pass* Turkey
79 K5 **Karamanlı** Turkey
172 G4 **Karamay** *Xinjiang* China
185 O3 **Karambar Pass** Afgh./Pak.
157 L6 **Karambu** *Kalimantan* Indon.
203 G8 **Karamea** *South I.* N.Z.
203 G8 **Karamea** *r. South I.* N.Z.
203 F8 **Karamea Bight** *b. South I.* N.Z.
182 K2 **Karamendy** Kazakh.
185 K3 **Karamet-Niyaz** Turkm.
157 K7 **Karamian** *i.* Indon.
79 L4 **Karamıkkaracaören** Turkey
173 G8 **Karamiran** *Xinjiang* China
173 G8 **Karamiran He** *r.* China
173 H8 **Karamiran Shankou** *pass Xinjiang* China
193 Q3 **Karamken** Rus. Fed.
79 K2 **Karamürsel** Turkey
55 K1 **Karamyshevo** *Kaliningradskaya Oblast'* Rus. Fed.
18 L4 **Karamyshevo** *Pskovskaya Oblast'* Rus. Fed.
185 N3 **Karan** *r.* Afgh.
Karan *state* Myanmar *see* **Kayin**
187 I2 **Karān** *i.* Saudi Arabia
137 G4 **Karanambo** Guyana
57 I3 **Karancsalja** Hungary
57 I3 **Karancskeszi** Hungary
57 I3 **Karancsság** Hungary
88 A3 **Karang** Senegal
155 A4 **Karang, Tanjung** *pt* Indon.
156 F6 **Karangagung** *Sumatera* Indon.
156 F7 **Karangan** *Sumatera* Indon.
203 D10 **Karangarua** *South I.* N.Z.
157 K9 **Karangasem** *Bali* Indon.
157 H9 **Karangbolong, Tanjung** *pt* Indon.
155 D2 **Karangetang** *vol.* Indon.
90 B4 **Karangoua** *r.* Congo
178 F9 **Karanja** *Mahar.* India
176 E3 **Karanja** *r.* India
178 H8 **Karanjia** *Madh. Prad.* India
179 J9 **Karanjia** *Orissa* India
178 D5 **Karanpura** *Rajasthan* India
183 Q1 **Karaoba** Kazakh.
79 I5 **Karaova** Turkey
79 K6 **Karaovabeli Geçidi** *pass* Turkey
183 P5 **Karaoy** *Almatinskaya Oblast'* Kazakh.
183 P5 **Karaoy** *Almatinskaya Oblast'* Kazakh.
77 P7 **Karapelit** Bulg.
190 E2 **Karapınar** *Gaziantep* Turkey
188 F5 **Karapınar** *Konya* Turkey
79 J3 **Karapürçek** *Balıkesir* Turkey
79 L2 **Karapürçek** *Sakarya* Turkey
172 C6 **Karaqi** *Xinjiang* China
94 C5 **Karas** *admin. reg.* Namibia
96 B3 **Karas** *mts* Namibia
191 A6 **Karasakal Dağları** *mts* Turkey
188 E3 **Karaşar** Turkey
173 F8 **Karasay** *Xinjiang* China
183 Q7 **Kara-Say** Kyrg.
94 C6 **Karasburg** Namibia
Kara Sea Rus. Fed. *see* **Karskoye More**
19 W5 **Karash** Rus. Fed.
183 P2 **Karashoky** Kazakh.
68 G3 **Karašica** *r.* Croatia
57 H6 **Karasica** *r.* Hungary/Romania
17 N8 **Karasivka** *r.* Ukr.
Kárášjohka *Finnmark* Norway *see* **Karasjok**
20 R2 **Kárášjohka** *r.* Norway
20 R2 **Karasjok** *Finnmark* Norway
Karasjokka *r.* Norway *see* **Kárášjohka**
183 P2 **Karasor** Kazakh.
183 M1 **Karasor, Ozero** *l.* Kazakh.
183 P2 **Karasor, Ozero** *salt l.* Kazakh.
183 P3 **Karasor, Ozero** *salt l.* Kazakh.
Kara Strait Rus. Fed. *see* **Karskiye Vorota, Proliv**
166 E6 **Karasu** Japan
183 P4 **Karasu** *Karagandinskaya Oblast'* Kazakh.
182 J2 **Karasu** *Kostanayskaya Oblast'* Kazakh.
182 K1 **Karasu** *Kostanayskaya Oblast'* Kazakh.
183 P1 **Karasu** *r.* Kazakh.
190 E2 **Karasu** *r.* Syria/Turkey
Karasu *Bitlis* Turkey *see* **Hizan**
79 L1 **Karasu** *Sakarya* Turkey
189 K4 **Karasu** *r.* Turkey
167 J3 **Karasu-gawa** *r.* Japan
183 R1 **Karasuk** Rus. Fed.
16 H8 **Karasulak** *r.* Ukr.
183 O7 **Kara-Suu** Kyrg.
167 L2 **Karasuyama** Japan
16 E2 **Karasyn** Ukr.
184 I4 **Karāt** Iran
191 H3 **Karata** Rus. Fed.
183 U4 **Karatal** Kazakh.
188 G5 **Karataş** *Adana* Turkey
190 E2 **Karataş** *Hatay* Turkey
79 J4 **Karatas** Turkey
183 N6 **Karatau** Kazakh.
183 L5 **Karatau, Khrebet** *mts* Kazakh.
14 M1 **Karatayka** Rus. Fed.
190 A2 **Karatepe** Turkey
159 D9 **Karathuri** Myanmar
176 F8 **Karativu** *i.* Sri Lanka
20 O3 **Karatj** *l.* Sweden
182 E3 **Karatobe** Kazakh.
182 H4 **Karatobe, Mys** *pt* Kazakh.
182 H3 **Karatogay** Kazakh.
183 Q4 **Karatol** *r.* Kazakh.
182 J1 **Karatomarskoye Vodokhranilishche** *resr* Kazakh.
182 E4 **Karaton** Kazakh.
20 O3 **Karats** Sweden
165 G13 **Karatsu** Japan
155 E1 **Karatung** *i.* Indon.
168 A3 **Karatüngü** *Xinjiang* China
182 H4 **Karatup, Poluostrov** *pen.* Kazakh.
182 K2 **Kara-Turgay** *r.* Kazakh.
183 R3 **Karaul** Kazakh.
178 F6 **Karauli** *Rajasthan* India
189 K3 **Karaurgan** Turkey
Karavan Kyrg. *see* **Kerben**
78 D6 **Karavas** *Kythira* Greece
76 H10 **Karavastasë, Gjiri i** *b.* Albania
76 H10 **Karavastasë, Laguna e** *lag.* Albania
16 J1 **Karavatsichy** Belarus
19 Y4 **Karavayevo** Rus. Fed.
78 E6 **Karavi** *i.* Greece
79 H7 **Karavonisia** *i.* Greece
190 A3 **Karavostasi** Cyprus
78 E7 **Karavoutas, Akra** *pt Kriti* Greece
90 D4 **Karawa** Dem. Rep. Congo
156 G8 **Karawang** *Jawa* Indon.
59 J6 **Karawanken** *mts* Austria
Karaxahar *r.* China *see* **Kaidu He**
191 D6 **Karayazı** Turkey
190 E2 **Karayılan** Turkey
172 E6 **Karayulgan** *Xinjiang* China
183 N3 **Karazhal** Kazakh.
182 D5 **Karazhanbas** Kazakh.
183 O4 **Karazhingil** Kazakh.
189 L7 **Karbalā'** Iraq
189 K7 **Karbalā'** *governorate* Iraq
49 G10 **Karben** Ger.
50 F4 **Karbow-Vietlübbe** Ger.
183 P3 **Karbushevka** Kazakh.
48 I1 **Karby** Ger.
57 J4 **Karcag** Hungary
57 K3 **Karcsa** Hungary
55 J3 **Karczew** Pol.
55 K4 **Karczmiska** Pol.
77 Q7 **Kardam** Bulg.
79 I6 **Kardamaina** *Kos* Greece
78 D6 **Kardamyli** Greece
59 K1 **Kardašova Řečice** Czech Rep.
49 D10 **Karden** Ger.
Kardhaámaina *Kos* Greece *see* **Kardamaina**
Kardhítsa Greece *see* **Karditsa**
78 G6 **Kardiotissa** *i.* Greece
20 Q3 **Kardis** Sweden
78 C3 **Karditsa** Greece
18 F3 **Kärdla** Estonia
57 J5 **Kardos** Hungary
59 O4 **Kardos-ér** *r.* Hungary
57 J5 **Kardoskút** Hungary
19 P7 **Kardymovo** Rus. Fed.
191 F2 **Kardzhin** Rus. Fed.
97 K4 **Karee** S. Africa
96 F6 **Kareeberge** *mts* S. Africa
96 G6 **Kareebospoort** *pass* S. Africa
96 I9 **Kareedouw** S. Africa
60 D5 **Kareha, Jebel** *mt.* Morocco
85 F5 **Kareima** Sudan
191 E4 **K'areli** Georgia
178 G8 **Kareli** *Madh. Prad.* India
Karelia *aut. rep.* Rus. Fed. *see* **Kareliya, Respublika**
18 J8 **Karelichy** Belarus
14 F3 **Kareliya, Respublika** *aut. rep.* Rus. Fed.
Karel'skaya A.S.S.R. *aut. rep.* Rus. Fed. *see* **Kareliya, Respublika**
14 F2 **Karel'skiy Bereg** *coastal area* Rus. Fed.
93 A6 **Karema** *Rukwa* Tanz.
Karen *state* Myanmar *see* **Kayin**
161 K1 **Karenga** *r.* Rus. Fed.
178 G7 **Karera** *Madh. Prad.* India
20 Q2 **Karesuando** Sweden
184 I8 **Kārevāndar** Iran
202 I4 **Karewa** *i. North I.* N.Z.
202 K4 **Karewa Island** *North I.* N.Z.
185 I5 **Karez Dasht** Afgh.
182 F2 **Kargala** Rus. Fed.
191 H2 **Kargalinskaya** Rus. Fed.
Kargalinski Rus. Fed. *see* **Kargalinskaya**
182 G2 **Kargalinskoye** Kazakh.
183 P3 **Kargaly** Kazakh.
189 J4 **Kargapazarı Dağları** *mts* Turkey
188 G3 **Kargı** Turkey
178 F3 **Kargiakh** Jammu and Kashmir
178 F2 **Kargil** Jammu and Kashmir
190 C2 **Kargıpınarı** Turkey
14 G3 **Kargopol'** Rus. Fed.
54 D3 **Kargowa** Pol.
184 G8 **Kargūshkī** Iran
178 G6 **Karhal** *Uttar Prad.* India
23 N1 **Karholmsbruk** Sweden
89 H4 **Kari** Nigeria
86 D2 **Karia Ba Mohammed** Morocco
184 G8 **Karīān** Iran
17 U1 **Karian** Rus. Fed.
78 E2 **Kariani** Greece
61 E5 **Kariat-Arkmane** Morocco
95 F3 **Kariba** Zimbabwe
91 E9 **Kariba, Lake** *resr* Zambia/Zimbabwe
91 F9 **Kariba Dam** Zambia/Zimbabwe
164 Q4 **Kariba-yama** *vol.* Japan
94 B4 **Karibib** Namibia
96 H9 **Kariega** *r.* S. Africa
187 I7 **Karīf Salāsil** *well* Yemen
20 R2 **Karigasniemi** Fin.
18 J1 **Karijärvi** *l.* Fin.
209 E7 **Karijini National Park** *W.A.* Austr.
202 H1 **Karikari, Cape** *North I.* N.Z.
184 F5 **Karīmābād** Iran
157 H5 **Karimata** *i.* Indon.
157 H5 **Karimata, Pulau-pulau** *is* Indon.
157 H5 **Karimata, Selat** *str.* Indon.
179 N7 **Karimganj** *Assam* India
184 D4 **Karim Khanch** Iran
176 F3 **Karimnagar** *Andhra Prad.* India
156 E4 **Karimun Besar** *i.* Indon.
157 I7 **Karimunjawa** *i.* Indon.
157 I7 **Karimunjawa, Pulau-pulau** *is* Indon.
92 E2 **Karin** Somalia
21 Q6 **Karinainen** Fin.
79 J5 **Karınçalı Dağı** *mts* Turkey
21 L5 **Käringsjön** Sweden
97 P1 **Karino** S. Africa
202 I4 **Karioi** *hill North I.* N.Z.
21 Q6 **Karis** Fin.
93 A5 **Karisimbi, Mont** *vol.* Rwanda
Káristos Greece *see* **Karystos**
184 G5 **Karit** Iran
78 D2 **Karitsa** Greece
166 E6 **Kariya** Japan
95 E3 **Kariyangwe** Zimbabwe
Karjaa Fin. *see* **Karis**
18 G1 **Karjalohja** Fin.
178 D8 **Karjan** *Gujarat* India
176 D3 **Karjat** *Mahar.* India
179 K8 **Karkai** *r. Jharkhand* India
176 D6 **Karkal** *Karnataka* India
176 D4 **Karkamb** *Mahar.* India
96 B6 **Karkams** S. Africa
183 P3 **Karkaralinsk** Kazakh.
154 E9 **Karkaralong, Kepulauan** *is* Indon.
153 K7 **Karkar Island** P.N.G.
184 D5 **Karkas, Kūh-e** *mts* Iran
185 L8 **Karkh** Pak.
184 B6 **Karkheh, Rūdkhāneh-ye** *r.* Iran
17 L8 **Karkinits'ka Zatoka** *g.* Ukr.
21 R6 **Karkkila** Fin.
21 R6 **Kärkölä** Fin.
Karkonoski Park Narodowy *nat. park* Czech Rep./Pol. *see* **Krkonošský narodní park**
54 D5 **Karkonoski Park Narodowy** *nat. park* Pol.
18 I3 **Karksi-Nuia** Estonia
186 C3 **Karkūmā, Ra's** *hd* Saudi Arabia
185 N5 **Karlachi** Pak.
206 D5 **Karlantijpa North Aboriginal Land** *res. N.T.* Austr.
206 D6 **Karlantijpa South Aboriginal Land** *res. N.T.* Austr.
18 D2 **Karlby** *Åland* Fin.
191 C5 **Karlı** Turkey
179 I8 **Karlidi** *Chhattisgarh* India
168 D5 **Karlik Shan** *mts Xinjiang* China
54 D1 **Karlino** Pol.
189 J4 **Karlıova** Turkey
17 O4 **Karlivka** Ukr.
191 E6 **Karlıyayla** Turkey
185 O3 **Karl Marks, Qullai** *mt.* Tajik.
Karl-Marx-Stadt Ger. *see* **Chemnitz**
68 E3 **Karlovac** Croatia
56 B1 **Karlovarský kraj** *admin. reg.* Czech Rep.
56 G1 **Karlovice** Czech Rep.
Karlovka Ukr. *see* **Karlivka**
77 M8 **Karlovo** Bulg.
56 B1 **Karlovy Vary** Czech Rep.
52 F4 **Karlsbad** Ger.
21 M6 **Karlsberg** Sweden
23 K3 **Karlsborg** Sweden
50 I3 **Karlsburg** Ger.
52 F3 **Karlsdorf-Neuthard** Ger.
53 K5 **Karlsfeld** Ger.
50 I2 **Karlshagen** Ger.
23 K5 **Karlshamn** Sweden
48 H4 **Karlshöfen** Ger.
53 K4 **Karlshuld** Ger.
23 K2 **Karlskoga** Sweden
53 K4 **Karlskron** Ger.
23 L5 **Karlskrona** Sweden
23 N4 **Karlsöarna** *i.* Sweden
52 E3 **Karlsruhe** Ger.
52 F4 **Karlsruhe** *admin. reg.* Ger.
22 J2 **Karlstad** Sweden
120 G1 **Karlstad** *MN* U.S.A.
52 H2 **Karlstadt** Ger.
49 H10 **Karlstein am Main** Ger.
59 L2 **Karlstein an der Thaya** Austria
59 M3 **Karlstetten** Austria
104 C4 **Karluk** *AK* U.S.A.
20 □ **Karl XII Øyane** *i.* Svalbard
185 L3 **Karlyuk** Turkm.
19 N8 **Karma** Belarus
89 F3 **Karma** Niger
84 C6 **Karma, Ouadi** *watercourse* Chad
191 F3 **Karmadon** Rus. Fed.
176 D3 **Karmala** *Mahar.* India
19 R6 **Karmanovo** Rus. Fed.
20 O3 **Karmas** Sweden
190 D6 **Karmel, Har** *hill* Israel
22 B2 **Karmøy** *i.* Norway
185 O7 **Karmpur** Pak.
179 N8 **Karnafuli Reservoir** Bangl.
178 F5 **Karnal** *Haryana* India
178 H5 **Karnali** *r.* Nepal
16 J7 **Karnaliyivka** Ukr.
179 M8 **Karnaphuli** *r.* Bangl.
178 G4 **Karnaprayag** *Uttaranchal* India
176 D5 **Karnataka** *state* India
17 N5 **Karnaukhivka** Ukr.
121 G11 **Karnes City** *TX* U.S.A.
54 D1 **Karnice** Pol.
55 I3 **Karniewo** Pol.
58 G6 **Karnische Alpen** *mts* Austria
77 O8 **Karnobat** Bulg.
59 I6 **Kärnten** *land* Austria
185 K8 **Karodi** Pak.
95 F3 **Karoi** Zimbabwe
71 P5 **Karojba** Croatia
158 C7 **Karokpi** Myanmar
173 J12 **Karo La** *pass Xizang* China
57 H2 **Karolinka** Czech Rep.
155 B7 **Karompalompo** *i.* Indon.
179 O7 **Karong** *Manipur* India
93 B7 **Karonga** Malawi
209 G11 **Karonie** *W.A.* Austr.
183 Q7 **Karool-Döbö** Kyrg.
Karool-Tëbë Kyrg. *see* **Karool-Döbö**
96 G8 **Karoo National Park** S. Africa
204 G6 **Karoonda** *S.A.* Austr.
185 N6 **Karor** Pak.
85 H5 **Karora** Eritrea
Káros *i.* Greece *see* **Keros**
155 A4 **Karossa** *Sulawesi* Indon.
157 M9 **Karossa, Tanjung** *pt Sumba* Indon.
79 H1 **Karotis** Greece
88 E2 **Karouassa** *well* Mali
84 D6 **Karoub** Chad
78 A3 **Karousades** *Kerkyra* Greece
50 F3 **Karow** *Mecklenburg-Vorpommern* Ger.
51 F6 **Karow** *Sachsen-Anhalt* Ger.
54 D5 **Karpacz** Pol.
190 C3 **Karpasia** *pen.* Cyprus
Karpas Peninsula Cyprus *see* **Karpasia**
79 I7 **Karpathos** *Karpathos* Greece
79 I7 **Karpathos** *i.* Greece
79 I6 **Karpathou, Steno** *sea chan.* Greece
16 D5 **Karpats'kiy** *nat. park* Ukr.
78 C4 **Karpenisi** Greece
14 M4 **Karpinsk** Rus. Fed.
14 I2 **Karpogory** Rus. Fed.
17 L1 **Karpovychi** Ukr.
79 I5 **Karpuzlu** *Aydın* Turkey
79 H2 **Karpuzlu** *Edirne* Turkey
16 J3 **Karpylivka** *Chernihivs'ka Oblast'* Ukr.
17 M3 **Karpylivka** *Chernihivs'ka Oblast'* Ukr.
16 G2 **Karpylivka** *Rivnens'ka Oblast'* Ukr.
208 D6 **Karratha** *W.A.* Austr.
Karrats Fjord *inlet* Greenland *see* **Nuugaatsiaap Imaa**
50 E4 **Karrenzin** Ger.
184 D7 **Karrī** Iran
97 L6 **Karringmelkspruit** S. Africa
Karroo *plat.* S. Africa *see* **Great Karoo**
209 E10 **Karroun Hill Nature Reserve** *W.A.* Austr.
185 J4 **Karrukh** Afgh.
Karrychirla Turkm. *see* **imeni Kerbabayeva**
189 K3 **Kars** Turkey
191 E5 **Kars** *prov.* Turkey
191 E5 **Kars** *r.* Turkey
183 L4 **Karsakpay** Kazakh.
20 R5 **Kärsämäki** Fin.
18 K5 **Kārsava** Latvia
51 E8 **Karsdorf** Ger.
184 E1 **Karshi** Turkm.
Karshi Uzbek. *see* **Qarshi**
191 C4 **Karşıköy** Turkey
54 F2 **Karsin** Pol.
79 J2 **Karşıyaka** *Balıkesir* Turkey
79 I4 **Karşıyaka** *İzmir* Turkey
179 L6 **Karsiyang** *W. Bengal* India
192 G3 **Karskiye Vorota, Proliv** *str.* Rus. Fed.
50 L5 **Karsko** Pol.
192 I2 **Karskoye More** *sea* Rus. Fed.
50 E4 **Karstädt** *Brandenburg* Ger.
50 D4 **Karstädt** *Mecklenburg-Vorpommern* Ger.
14 D3 **Karstula** Fin.
15 I5 **Karsun** Rus. Fed.
57 I4 **Kartal** Hungary
79 K2 **Kartal** Turkey
99 □3a **Kartala** *vol. Njazidja* Comoros
99 □3a **Kartala, Forêt du** *for. Njazidja* Comoros
182 I1 **Kartaly** Rus. Fed.
178 E4 **Kartarpur** *Punjab* India
19 O6 **Kartashevichi** Rus. Fed.
19 O6 **Kartavshchina** Rus. Fed.
14 K2 **Kartayel'** Rus. Fed.
18 E6 **Kartena** Lith.
116 G7 **Karthaus** *PA* U.S.A.
58 G6 **Kartitsch** Austria
58 G6 **Kartitscher Sattel** *pass* Austria
191 F3 **K'art'lis K'edi** *hills* Georgia
Kartsa Rus. Fed. *see* **Oktyabr'skoye**
19 N5 **Kartsevo** Rus. Fed.
78 F4 **Kartsino, Akra** *pt Skyros* Greece
20 S5 **Karttula** Fin.
137 G3 **Kartuni** Guyana
23 O7 **Kartuzy** Pol.
91 F8 **Karubwe** Zambia
167 I3 **Karuizawa** Japan
184 H7 **Karūk** Iran
164 S6 **Karumai** Japan
207 H4 **Karumba** *Qld* Austr.
184 D6 **Karun, Kūh-e** *hill* Iran
184 C6 **Kārūn, Rūd-e** *r.* Iran
176 E8 **Karunagapalli** *Kerala* India
20 Q3 **Karungi** Sweden
92 B5 **Karungu** Kenya
155 A8 **Karuni** *Sumba* Indon.
208 I4 **Karunjie** *W.A.* Austr.
22 F5 **Karup** Denmark
22 F5 **Karup** *r.* Denmark
176 F7 **Karur** *Tamil Nadu* India
93 A5 **Karuzi** Burundi
176 F6 **Karvetnagar** *Andhra Prad.* India
21 Q5 **Karvia** Fin.
57 H2 **Karviná** Czech Rep.
16 H3 **Karvynivka** Ukr.
176 D5 **Karwar** *Karnataka* India
58 D5 **Karwendelgebirge** *mts* Austria
58 D5 **Karwendelgebirge** *nature res.* Austria
178 H7 **Karwi** *Uttar Prad.* India
55 J2 **Karwica** Pol.
50 D4 **Karwitz** Ger.
78 B4 **Karya** *Lefkada* Greece
78 F2 **Karyes** Greece
161 J1 **Karymskoye** Rus. Fed.
182 E6 **Karynzharyk, Peski** *des.* Kazakh.
78 F4 **Karystos** Greece
17 N2 **Karyzh** Rus. Fed.
84 E6 **Kas** Sudan
79 K6 **Kaş** Turkey
176 C3 **Kasa** *Mahar.* India
93 A7 **Kasaba Lodge** Zambia
108 B2 **Kasabonika** *Ont.* Can.
108 B2 **Kasabonika Lake** *Ont.* Can.
93 A6 **Kasacasia** Tanz.
166 G3 **Kasaga-dake** *mt.* Japan
166 C6 **Kasagi** Japan
166 F4 **Kasagi-yama** *mt.* Japan
166 F5 **Kasahara** Japan
91 C5 **Kasaï** *r.* Dem. Rep. Congo
166 A6 **Kasai** Japan
91 D6 **Kasaï, Plateau du** Dem. Rep. Congo
91 D6 **Kasaï-Occidental** *prov.* Dem. Rep. Congo
91 E6 **Kasaï-Oriental** *prov.* Dem. Rep. Congo
91 D7 **Kasaji** Dem. Rep. Congo
167 J3 **Kasakake** Japan
167 L3 **Kasama** Japan
93 A7 **Kasama** Zambia
166 E5 **Kasamatsu** Japan
Kasan Uzbek. *see* **Koson**
93 A5 **Kasana** Tanz.
94 E3 **Kasane** Botswana
93 A7 **Kasanga** Tanz.
91 B6 **Kasangulu** Dem. Rep. Congo
91 F8 **Kasanka National Park** Zambia
166 D3 **Kasano-misaki** *pt* Japan
Kasansay Uzbek. *see* **Kosonsoy**
91 C6 **Kasanza** Dem. Rep. Congo
85 H5 **Kasar, Ras** *pt* Sudan
176 D6 **Kasaragod** *Kerala* India
164 □G18 **Kasarai-zaki** *hd Nansei-shotō* Japan
18 G3 **Kasari** *r.* Estonia
18 L6 **Kasary** Belarus
162 G4 **Kasatkino** Rus. Fed.
166 D6 **Kasatori-yama** *hill* Japan
107 K2 **Kasba Lake** Can.
86 D2 **Kasba Tadla** Morocco
22 E5 **Kås Bredning** *b.* Denmark
165 H15 **Kaseda** Japan
56 C2 **Kasejovice** Czech Rep.
91 E8 **Kasempa** Zambia
51 D10 **Kasendorf** Ger.
91 D7 **Kasenga** *Katanga* Dem. Rep. Congo
91 F7 **Kasenga** *Katanga* Dem. Rep. Congo
90 F4 **Kasenye** Dem. Rep. Congo
90 E5 **Kasese** Dem. Rep. Congo
92 A4 **Kasese** Uganda
Kasevo Rus. Fed. *see* **Neftekamsk**
178 G6 **Kasganj** *Uttar Prad.* India
170 B3 **Kasha** *Xizang* China
92 D5 **Kasha** *waterhole* Kenya
108 B3 **Kashabowie** *Ont.* Can.
123 K9 **Kasha-Katuwe Tent Rocks National Monument** *nat. park NM* U.S.A.
184 D5 **Kāshān** Iran
15 H6 **Kashary** Rus. Fed.
108 D2 **Kashechewan** *Ont.* Can.
Kashgar *Xinjiang* China *see* **Kashi**
172 C7 **Kashi** *Xinjiang* China
166 C6 **Kashiba** Japan
166 C7 **Kashihara** Japan
167 M4 **Kashima** *Ibaraki* Japan
166 E2 **Kashima** *Ishikawa* Japan
165 H13 **Kashima** *Saga* Japan
167 M3 **Kashima-nada** *b.* Japan
166 G2 **Kashimayaria-dake** *mt.* Japan
166 F4 **Kashimo** Japan
19 U4 **Kashin** Rus. Fed.
19 U4 **Kashinka** *r.* Rus. Fed.
91 F7 **Kashiobwe** Dem. Rep. Congo
178 G5 **Kashipur** *Uttaranchal* India
19 V7 **Kashira** Rus. Fed.
19 V7 **Kashirka** *r.* Rus. Fed.
17 S2 **Kashirskoye** Rus. Fed.
91 F8 **Kashitu** Zambia
167 K4 **Kashiwa** Japan
166 C6 **Kashiwara** Japan
165 P9 **Kashiwazaki** Japan
Kashkadar'ya *r.* Uzbek. *see* **Qashqadaryo**
Kashkadarya Oblast *admin. div.* Uzbek. *see* **Qashqadaryo**
183 O5 **Kashkanteniz** Kazakh.
14 G2 **Kashkarantsy** Rus. Fed.
Kashken-Teniz Kazakh. *see* **Kashkanteniz**
191 E2 **Kashkhatau** Rus. Fed.
184 F6 **Kashku'iyeh** Iran
19 O6 **Kashkurino** Rus. Fed.
17 P6 **Kashlahach** *r.* Ukr.
184 H4 **Kāshmar** Iran
Kashmir *terr.* Asia *see* **Jammu and Kashmir**
178 E2 **Kashmir, Vale of** *reg.* India
185 M7 **Kashmor** Pak.
185 N4 **Kashmund** *reg.* Afgh.
17 M9 **Kashtany** Ukr.
91 E6 **Kashyukulu** Dem. Rep. Congo
179 I6 **Kasia** *Uttar Prad.* India
185 N4 **Kasigar** Afgh.
19 Q8 **Kasilovo** Rus. Fed.
155 A4 **Kasimbar** *Sulawesi* Indon.
79 M5 **Kasımlar** Turkey
15 H5 **Kasimov** Rus. Fed.
59 N8 **Ka...ina** Croatia
90 F4 **Kasingi** Dem. Rep. Congo
155 E4 **Kasiruta** *i. Maluku* Indon.
57 I5 **Kaskantyú** Hungary
120 K7 **Kaskaskia** *r. IL* U.S.A.
107 N3 **Kaskattama** *r. Man.* Can.
183 Q6 **Kaskelen** Kazakh.
21 P5 **Kaskinen** Fin.
Kas Klong *i.* Cambodia *see* **Kŏng, Kaôh**
Kaskö Fin. *see* **Kaskinen**
106 G5 **Kaslo** *B.C.* Can.
107 K3 **Kasmere Lake** *Man.* Can.
19 R6 **Kasnya** *r.* Rus. Fed.
91 F7 **Kasomeno** Dem. Rep. Congo
157 J5 **Kasongan** *Kalimantan* Indon.
91 E6 **Kasongo** Dem. Rep. Congo
91 C6 **Kasongo-Lunda** Dem. Rep. Congo
91 C6 **Kasongo Lunda Falls** Angola/Dem. Rep. Congo
91 E6 **Kasonguele** Dem. Rep. Congo
79 H7 **Kasos** *i.* Greece
79 I7 **Kasou, Steno** *sea chan.* Greece
56 C2 **Kašperské Hory** Czech Rep.
191 F4 **Kaspi** Georgia
191 I3 **Kaspiysk** Rus. Fed.
Kaspiyskiy Rus. Fed. *see* **Lagan'**
19 O7 **Kasplya** Rus. Fed.
19 N6 **Kasplya** *r.* Rus. Fed.
178 E8 **Kasrawad** *Madh. Prad.* India
191 H4 **Kasristsqali** Georgia
Kassa Slovakia *see* **Košice**
18 F3 **Kassaare laht** *b.* Estonia
85 H6 **Kassala** Sudan
85 G6 **Kassala** *state* Sudan
78 E2 **Kassandra** *pen.* Greece
78 E3 **Kassandras, Akra** *pt* Greece
78 E2 **Kassandras, Kolpos** *b.* Greece
78 E2 **Kassandreia** Greece
48 K2 **Kasseedorf** Ger.
49 I8 **Kassel** Ger.
49 H8 **Kassel** *admin. reg.* Ger.
87 H2 **Kasserine** Tunisia
110 B5 **Kasson** *MN* U.S.A.
89 H3 **Kassouloua** *well* Niger
185 I9 **Kastag** Pak.
188 F3 **Kastamonu** Turkey
49 D10 **Kastellaun** Ger.
78 E7 **Kastelli** *Kriti* Greece
79 G7 **Kastelli** *Kriti* Greece
Kastéllion *Kriti* Greece *see* **Kastelli**
Kastellorizon *i.* Greece *see* **Megisti**
79 I7 **Kastellou, Akra** *pt Karpathos* Greece
45 G6 **Kasterlee** Belgium
53 L3 **Kastl** *Bayern* Ger.
53 N5 **Kastl** *Bayern* Ger.
48 K3 **Kastorf** Ger.
78 C2 **Kastoria** Greece
78 C2 **Kastorias, Limni** *l.* Greece
15 G6 **Kastornoye** Rus. Fed.
78 B4 **Kastos** *i.* Greece
78 C4 **Kastrakiou, Techniti Limni** *resr* Greece
18 K3 **Kastre** Estonia
19 P8 **Kastsyukovichy** Belarus
19 N9 **Kastsyukowka** Belarus
166 E5 **Kasuga** *Gifu* Japan
166 B5 **Kasuga** *Hyōgo* Japan
166 E5 **Kasugai** Japan
167 K4 **Kasukabe** Japan
97 K9 **Kasuka Road** S. Africa
167 J3 **Kasukawa** Japan
90 E5 **Kasuku** Dem. Rep. Congo
93 A6 **Kasulu** Tanz.
163 I11 **Kasumi** Japan
167 L3 **Kasumigaura** Japan
167 L3 **Kasumiga-ura** *l.* Japan
191 J4 **Kasumkent** Rus. Fed.
93 B8 **Kasungu** Malawi
93 B8 **Kasungu National Park** Malawi
185 P6 **Kasur** Pak.
57 J5 **Kaszaper** Hungary
54 E4 **Kaszczor** Pol.
54 G1 **Kaszubskie, Pojezierze** *reg.* Pol.
23 O7 **Kaszubski Park Krajobrazowy** Pol.
91 E9 **Kataba** Zambia
89 H3 **Katagum** Nigeria
117 □Q3 **Katahdin, Mount** *ME* U.S.A.
178 G2 **Kataklik** Jammu and Kashmir
91 E5 **Katako-Kombe** Dem. Rep. Congo
78 C5 **Katakolo** Greece
78 C5 **Katakolo, Akra** *pt* Greece
92 B4 **Katakwi** Uganda
89 I3 **Katalui** Chad
90 F5 **Katana** Dem. Rep. Congo
91 D6 **Katanda** Dem. Rep. Congo
91 E7 **Katanga** *prov.* Dem. Rep. Congo
178 G8 **Katangi** *Madh. Prad.* India
178 G9 **Katangi** *Madh. Prad.* India
162 M3 **Katangli** *Sakhalin* Rus. Fed.
209 D12 **Katanning** *W.A.* Austr.
166 C6 **Katano** Japan
90 E5 **Katanti** Dem. Rep. Congo
184 D3 **Kata Pusht** Iran
19 P9 **Katashin** Rus. Fed.
167 J2 **Katashina** Japan
167 J2 **Katashina-gawa** *r.* Japan
78 B5 **Katastari** *Zakynthos* Greece
166 C5 **Katata** Japan
93 A6 **Katavi National Park** Tanz.
185 M5 **Katawaz** Afgh.
185 L5 **Katawaz** *reg.* Afgh.
177 M9 **Katchall** *i. Andaman & Nicobar Is* India
89 F4 **Katchamba** Togo
91 C8 **Katchiungo** Angola
91 E6 **Katea** Dem. Rep. Congo
91 D6 **Katende** Dem. Rep. Congo
78 D2 **Katerini** Greece
16 J5 **Katerynopil'** Ukr.
27 J4 **Katesbridge** *Northern Ireland* U.K.
93 B6 **Katesh** Tanz.
104 E4 **Kate's Needle** *mt.* Can./U.S.A.
93 B8 **Katete** Zambia
191 H4 **Katex** Azer.
179 I8 **Katghora** *Chhattisgarh* India
158 C2 **Katha** Myanmar
206 D3 **Katherine** *N.T.* Austr.
206 C3 **Katherine** *r. N.T.* Austr.
207 I7 **Katherine Creek** *watercourse Qld* Austr.
Katherine Gorge National Park *N.T.* Austr. *see* **Nitmiluk National Park**
178 E9 **Kathi** *Mahar.* India
178 C8 **Kathiawar** *pen. Gujarat* India
186 F8 **Kathīb, Ra's al** *pt* Yemen
176 G8 **Kathiraveli** Sri Lanka
206 C3 **Kathleen Falls** *N.T.* Austr.
97 M2 **Kathlehong** S. Africa
51 J7 **Kathlow** Ger.
179 J6 **Kathmandu** Nepal
96 H3 **Kathu** S. Africa
178 E3 **Kathua** Jammu and Kashmir
93 C5 **Kathua** *watercourse* Kenya
88 C3 **Kati** Mali
157 J3 **Katibas** *r.* Malaysia
57 K4 **Kati-ér** *r.* Hungary
179 K7 **Katihar** *Bihar* India
202 J4 **Katikati** *North I.* N.Z.
97 L8 **Kati-Kati** S. Africa
202 J4 **Katikati Entrance** *sea chan. North I.* N.Z.
94 E3 **Katima Mulilo** Namibia
107 L4 **Katimik Lake** *Man.* Can.
19 W8 **Katino** Rus. Fed.
88 D4 **Katiola** Côte d'Ivoire
206 C8 **Katiti Aboriginal Land** *res. N.T.* Austr.
96 E6 **Katkop Hills** S. Africa
16 H8 **Katlabukh, Ozero** *l.* Ukr.
49 J7 **Katlenburg-Lindau** Ger.
57 G3 **Kátlovce** Slovakia
173 G7 **Katma** *Xinjiang* China
104 C4 **Katmai National Park and Preserve** *AK* U.S.A.
Katmandu Nepal *see* **Kathmandu**
78 C4 **Kato Achaïa** Greece
171 □J7 **Kat O Chau** *i. H.K.* China
78 C4 **Katochi** Greece
78 D5 **Kato Doliana** Greece
78 C5 **Kato Figaleia** Greece
78 D6 **Kato Glykovrysi** Greece
171 □J7 **Kat O Hoi** *b. H.K.* China
178 G9 **Katol** *Mahar.* India
20 Q5 **Kåtölandet** *i.* Fin.
91 D6 **Katombe** Dem. Rep. Congo
79 G6 **Katomeri, Akra** *pt Naxos* Greece
91 E6 **Katompi** Dem. Rep. Congo
119 H2 **Katonah** *NY* U.S.A.
91 F8 **Katondwe** Zambia
78 E1 **Kato Nevrokopi** Greece
156 □ **Katong** Sing.
92 A4 **Katonga** *r.* Uganda
183 U3 **Katon-Karagay** Kazakh.
Katonqaraghay Kazakh. *see* **Katon-Karagay**
205 M5 **Katoomba** *N.S.W.* Austr.
155 B4 **Katoposa, Gunung** *mt.* Indon.
178 D8 **Katosan** *Gujarat* India
78 D4 **Kato Tithorea** Greece
56 C2 **Katovice** Czech Rep.
55 H5 **Katowice** Pol.
179 L8 **Katoya** *W. Bengal* India
178 D9 **Katpur** *Gujarat* India
79 K5 **Katrancık Dağı** *mts* Turkey
85 G2 **Kātrīnā, Jabal** *mt.* Egypt
26 G10 **Katrine, Loch** *l. Scotland* U.K.
23 M3 **Katrineholm** Sweden
59 I5 **Katschberghöhe** *pass* Austria
59 J3 **Katsdorf** Austria
97 M5 **Katse Dam** Lesotho
95 □J2 **Katsepy** Madag.
78 B3 **Katsikas** Greece
89 G3 **Katsina** Nigeria
89 G4 **Katsina** *state* Nigeria
89 H5 **Katsina-Ala** Nigeria
165 G13 **Katsumoto** Japan
167 I4 **Katsunuma** Japan
167 J4 **Katsura-gawa** *r.* Japan
166 C7 **Katsuragi** Japan
166 B7 **Katsuragi-san** *hill* Japan
164 □1 **Katsuren-zaki** *c. Okinawa* Japan
167 L5 **Katsuura** Japan
166 E3 **Katsuyama** *Fukui* Japan
165 K11 **Katsuyama** *Okayama* Japan
109 H1 **Kattaktoc, Cap** *c. Que.* Can.
208 I6 **Kattamudda Well** *W.A.* Austr.
187 K9 **Kattānahan, Ra's** *pt Suquṭrā* Yemen
183 L8 **Kattaqo'rg'on** Uzbek.
Kattaqŭrghon Uzbek. *see* **Kattaqo'rg'on**
185 L5 **Kattasang Hills** Afgh.
79 I7 **Kattavia** *Rodos* Greece
22 H5 **Kattegat** *str.* Denmark/Sweden
20 O4 **Kattisavan** Sweden
Kattowitz Pol. *see* **Katowice**
176 F7 **Kattuputtur** *Tamil Nadu* India
91 E6 **Katumba** Dem. Rep. Congo
93 B7 **Katumbi** Malawi
172 G1 **Katun'** *r.* Rus. Fed.
14 I4 **Katunino** Rus. Fed.
172 G1 **Katunskiy Khrebet** *mts* Rus. Fed.
185 M7 **Katuri** Pak.
Katwa *W. Bengal* India *see* **Katoya**
44 F4 **Katwijk aan Zee** Neth.
55 J2 **Kąty** Pol.
57 I5 **Katymár** Hungary
19 O7 **Katyn'** Rus. Fed.
54 E4 **Kąty Wrocławskie** Pol.
53 M3 **Katzbach** *r.* Ger.
59 N4 **Katzelsdorf** Austria
52 G3 **Katzenbuckel** *hill* Ger.
49 E10 **Katzenelnbogen** Ger.
51 D9 **Katzhütte** Ger.
52 D2 **Katzweiler** Ger.
124 □B11 **Kaua'i** *i. HI* U.S.A.
124 □B12 **Kaua'i Channel** *HI* U.S.A.
49 E10 **Kaub** Ger.
94 D3 **Kaudom Game Park** *nature res.* Namibia
53 J6 **Kaufbeuren** Ger.
53 J5 **Kaufering** Ger.
121 G9 **Kaufman** *TX* U.S.A.
49 I8 **Kaufungen** Ger.
21 Q5 **Kauhajoki** Fin.
21 Q5 **Kauhanevan-Pohjankankaan kansallispuisto** *nat. park* Fin.
20 Q5 **Kauhava** Fin.
110 F5 **Kaukauna** *WI* U.S.A.
158 C2 **Kaukkwè Hills** Myanmar
20 R3 **Kaukonen** Fin.
18 K2 **Kauksi** Estonia
124 □B12 **Kaulakahi Channel** *HI* U.S.A.
45 I6 **Kaulille** Belgium
20 Q3 **Kaulinranta** Fin.
51 D9 **Kaulsdorf** Ger.
202 J7 **Kaumai** *North I.* N.Z.
109 I1 **Kaumajet Mountains** *Nfld and Lab.* Can.
124 □B12 **Kaumakani** *HI* U.S.A.
124 □E13 **Kaumalapau** *HI* U.S.A.
124 □D12 **Kaunakakai** *HI* U.S.A.
18 G7 **Kaunas** Lith.
18 K5 **Kaunata** Latvia
182 E6 **Kaundy, Vpadina** *depr.* Kazakh.
118 F1 **Kauneonga Lake** *NY* U.S.A.
58 C6 **Kaunertal** *val.* Austria
179 L7 **Kaunia** Bangl.
20 Q3 **Kaunisvaara** Sweden
18 H7 **Kauno marios** *l.* Lith.
203 F9 **Kaupiri** *South I.* N.Z.
55 K1 **Kaupiškiai** Lith.
124 □E13 **Kaupō** *HI* U.S.A.
89 G3 **Kaura-Namoda** Nigeria
171 □J7 **Kau Sai Chau** *i. H.K.* China
20 Q5 **Kaustinen** Fin.
45 J9 **Kautenbach** Lux.
20 Q2 **Kautokeino** Norway
59 L2 **Kautzen** Austria
159 D9 **Kau-ye Kyun** *i.* Myanmar
193 R3 **Kavacha** Rus. Fed.
77 K9 **Kavadarci** Macedonia
76 H9 **Kavajë** Albania
79 H2 **Kavak** *Çanakkale* Turkey
188 H3 **Kavak** *Samsun* Turkey
79 H3 **Kavak Dağı** *hill* Turkey
79 J4 **Kavaklıdere** *Manisa* Turkey
79 J5 **Kavaklıdere** *Muğla* Turkey
78 F2 **Kavala** Greece
78 F2 **Kavalas, Kolpos** *b.* Greece
162 I6 **Kavalerovo** Rus. Fed.
176 G5 **Kavali** *Andhra Prad.* India
176 F8 **Kavalpatnam** *Tamil Nadu* India
19 N6 **Kavalyova** Belarus
137 F3 **Kavanayen** Venez.
184 E7 **Kavār** Iran
176 C7 **Kavaratti** *Lakshadweep* India
176 C7 **Kavaratti** *atoll* India
77 Q7 **Kavarna** Bulg.
18 H6 **Kavarskas** Lith.
19 Q6 **Kavel'shchino** Rus. Fed.
50 F3 **Kavelstorf** Ger.
88 B4 **Kavendou, Mont** *mt.* Guinea
176 F7 **Kaveri** *r.* India
176 F6 **Kaveripatnam** *Tamil Nadu* India
178 D8 **Kavi** *Gujarat* India
153 L7 **Kavieng** *New Ireland* P.N.G.
184 D4 **Kavīr** Iran
184 F4 **Kavīr, Dasht-e** *des.* Iran
184 G4 **Kavīr Kūshk** *well* Iran
191 D1 **Kavkazskiy** Rus. Fed.
191 B2 **Kavkazskiy Zapovednik** *nature res.* Rus. Fed.
55 L6 **Kavs'ke** Ukr.
137 H3 **Kaw** Fr. Guiana
155 F5 **Kawa** *Seram* Indon.
164 R7 **Kawabe** *Akita* Japan
166 F5 **Kawabe** *Gifu* Japan
166 B8 **Kawabe** *Wakayama* Japan
167 L4 **Kawachi** *Ibaraki* Japan
166 E3 **Kawachi** *Ishikawa* Japan
167 K2 **Kawachi** *Tochigi* Japan
166 E1 **Kawachi-dake** *hill* Japan
166 C7 **Kawachi-nagano** Japan
108 E4 **Kawagama Lake** *Ont.* Can.
166 E6 **Kawage** Japan
167 J4 **Kawagoe** Japan
167 I1 **Kawaguchi** *Niigata* Japan
167 K4 **Kawaguchi** *Saitama* Japan
167 I4 **Kawaguchiko** Japan
167 I4 **Kawaguchi-ko** *l.* Japan
165 L11 **Kawahara** Japan
166 F3 **Kawai** *Gifu* Japan
164 S7 **Kawai** *Iwate* Japan
124 □F13 **Kawaihae** *HI* U.S.A.
124 □A12 **Kawaihoa Point** *HI* U.S.A.
124 □B11 **Kawaikini** *mt. HI* U.S.A.
124 □C12 **Kawailoa Beach** *HI* U.S.A.
165 J12 **Kawajiri** Japan
167 I4 **Kawakami** *Nagano* Japan
166 C7 **Kawakami** *Nara* Japan
202 I2 **Kawakawa** *North I.* N.Z.
166 E3 **Kawakita** Japan
164 R9 **Kawamata** Japan
91 F7 **Kawambwa** Zambia
165 I14 **Kawaminami** Japan
167 J3 **Kawamoto** Japan
91 E8 **Kawana** Zambia
167 H2 **Kawanakajima** Japan
167 J6 **Kawana-zaki** *pt* Japan
167 H6 **Kawane** Japan
155 D3 **Kawangkoan** *Sulawesi* Indon.
166 C5 **Kawanishi** *Hyōgo* Japan
167 I1 **Kawanishi** *Niigata* Japan
164 R9 **Kawanishi** *Yamagata* Japan
167 J3 **Kawarazawa-gawa** *r.* Japan
178 H8 **Kawardha** *Chhattisgarh* India
108 E4 **Kawartha Lakes** *Ont.* Can.
91 F7 **Kawasa** Dem. Rep. Congo
167 K4 **Kawasaki** Japan
166 E5 **Kawashima** Japan
165 I12 **Kawashiri-misaki** *pt* Japan
155 C4 **Kawato** *Sulawesi* Indon.
164 R5 **Kawauchi** Japan
166 G4 **Kawaue** Japan
202 I3 **Kawau Island** *North I.* N.Z.
165 H14 **Kawaura** Japan
109 H2 **Kawawachikamach** *Que.* Can.
167 I6 **Kawazu** Japan
158 C7 **Kawdut** Myanmar
155 G3 **Kawe** *i. Papua* Indon.
124 N5 **Kaweah, Lake** *CA* U.S.A.
202 K6 **Kaweka** *mt. North I.* N.Z.
202 K6 **Kaweka Forest Park** *nature res. North I.* N.Z.
202 K6 **Kaweka Range** *mts North I.* N.Z.
124 □C12 **Kawela Bay** *HI* U.S.A.
110 C1 **Kawene** *Ont.* Can.
202 K5 **Kawerau** *North I.* N.Z.
202 I5 **Kawhia** *North I.* N.Z.
202 I5 **Kawhia Harbour** *North I.* N.Z.
125 P4 **Kawich Peak** *NV* U.S.A.
125 P4 **Kawich Range** *mts NV* U.S.A.
107 L4 **Kawinaw Lake** *Man.* Can.
157 M9 **Kawinda** *Sumbawa* Indon.
155 D1 **Kawio** *i.* Indon.
186 F8 **Kawkabān** Yemen
158 D6 **Kawkareik** Myanmar
121 G7 **Kaw Lake** *OK* U.S.A.
158 B3 **Kawlin** Myanmar
158 C5 **Kawludo** Myanmar
159 D8 **Kawmapyin** Myanmar
85 G3 **Kawm Umbū** Egypt
158 D3 **Kawngmeum** Myanmar
159 D9 **Kawthaung** Myanmar
Kawthoolei *state* Myanmar *see* **Kayin**
Kawthule *state* Myanmar *see* **Kayin**
Kaxgar *Xinjiang* China *see* **Kashi**
172 C7 **Kaxgar He** *r.* China
172 E5 **Kax He** *r.* China
173 F8 **Kaxtax Shan** *mts* China
14 K4 **Kay** Rus. Fed.
88 E3 **Kaya** Burkina
191 D5 **Kayaaltı** Turkey
79 J5 **Kayabaşı** Turkey
79 H3 **Kayacı Dağı** *hill* Turkey
188 H4 **Kayadibi** Turkey
167 I4 **Kayaga-take** *mt.* Japan
158 C5 **Kayah** *state* Myanmar
191 I3 **Kayakent** Rus. Fed.
93 A7 **Kayambi** Zambia
157 I5 **Kayan** *r.* Indon.
157 L3 **Kayan** *r.* Indon.
158 C6 **Kayan** Myanmar
93 A5 **Kayanaza** Burundi
154 □ **Kayangel Atoll** Palau
154 □ **Kayangel Passage** Palau
176 E8 **Kayankulam** *Kerala* India
157 K3 **Kayan-Mentarang National Park** Indon.
176 F3 **Kayar** *Mahar.* India
155 E3 **Kayasa** *Halmahera* Indon.
191 G1 **Kayasula** Rus. Fed.
Kaybagar, Ozero *l.* Kazakh. *see* **Koybagar, Ozero**
122 K5 **Kaycee** *WY* U.S.A.
91 D7 **Kayembe-Mukulu** Dem. Rep. Congo
125 V5 **Kayenta** *AZ* U.S.A.
91 B6 **Kayes** Congo
88 C3 **Kayes** Mali
88 C3 **Kayes** *admin. reg.* Mali
182 K2 **Kayga** Kazakh.
Kaygy Kazakh. *see* **Kayga**
88 C4 **Kayima** Sierra Leone
158 C5 **Kayin** *state* Myanmar
45 J10 **Kayl** Lux.
79 J4 **Kaymakçı** Turkey
183 P1 **Kaymanachikha** Kazakh.
79 M3 **Kaymaz** Turkey
51 F9 **Kayna** Ger.
191 B6 **Kaynakdüzü** Turkey
183 Q3 **Kaynar** Kazakh.
183 P6 **Kaynar** *Zhambylskaya Oblast'* Kazakh.

Kaynar to Kharwar
283

188 H4 Kaynar Turkey
79 L1 Kaynarca Turkey
77 P9 Kaynarlı r. Turkey
79 M2 Kaynaşlı Turkey
166 B4 Kayo Japan
164 □1 Kayō Okinawa Japan
155 E3 Kayoa i. Maluku Indon.
Kayrakkumskoye Vodokhranilishche resr Tajik. see Obanbori Qayroqqum
182 B3 Kaysatskoye Rus. Fed.
188 G4 Kayseri Turkey
37 N7 Kaysersberg France
155 B7 Kayuadi i. Indon.
156 F6 Kayuagung Sumatera Indon.
92 B4 Kayunga Uganda
91 E5 Kayuyu Dem. Rep. Congo
192 J3 Kayyerkan Rus. Fed.
183 O6 Kayyngdy Kyrg.
19 V8 Kazachka Rus. Fed.
193 O2 Kazach'ye Rus. Fed.
Kazakhdar'ya Uzbek. see Qozoqdaryo
Kazakhskaya S.S.R. country Asia see Kazakhstan
183 N2 Kazakhskiy Melkosopochnik plain Kazakh.
182 E6 Kazakhskiy Zaliv b. Kazakh.
182 T3 Kazakhstan country Asia
19 V9 Kazaki Rus. Fed.
Kazakstan country Asia see Kazakhstan
182 J5 Kazalinsk Kazakh.
107 M2 Kazan r. Nunavut Can.
14 J5 Kazan' Rus. Fed.
191 D6 Kazan Turkey
183 S3 Kazanchunkur Kazakh.
188 F5 Kazancı Turkey
78 B3 Kazanje, Mal mt. Albania
14 J5 Kazanka r. Rus. Fed.
17 L6 Kazanka Ukr.
Kazanketken Uzbek. see Qozonketkan
190 C2 Kazanlı Turkey
77 N8 Kazanlŭk Bulg.
19 V8 Kazanovka Rus. Fed.
55 J4 Kazanów Pol.
165 □2 Kazan-rettō is N. Pacific Ocean
15 H6 Kazanskaya Rus. Fed.
17 O8 Kazantip, Mys pt Ukr.
17 O8 Kazantips'ka Zatoka b. Ukr.
Kazatin Ukr. see Kozyatyn
182 H3 Kazatskiy Kazakh.
89 H3 Kazaure Nigeria
92 C1 Kaza Wenz r. Eth.
191 F3 Kazbek mt. Georgia/Rus. Fed.
79 H3 Kaz Dağı mts Turkey
184 D7 Kāzerūn Iran
183 N1 Kazgorodok Kazakh.
14 J3 Kazhim Rus. Fed.
185 J8 Kazhmak r. Pak.
17 N7 Kazhovs'kyy Mahistral'nyy Kanal canal Ukr.
79 K5 Kazıkbeli Geçidi pass Turkey
16 B2 Kazimierski Park Krajobrazowy Pol.
55 I5 Kazimierza Wielka Pol.
54 G3 Kazimierz Biskupi Pol.
55 J4 Kazimierz Dolne Pol.
57 J3 Kazincbarcika Hungary
17 Q3 Kazinka Belgorodskaya Oblast' Rus. Fed.
19 W9 Kazinka Lipetskaya Oblast' Rus. Fed.
19 W8 Kazinka Ryazanskaya Oblast' Rus. Fed.
17 T3 Kazinka Voronezhskaya Oblast' Rus. Fed.
179 N6 Kaziranga National Park India
18 I8 Kazlowshchyna Hrodzyenskaya Voblasts' Belarus
18 L6 Kazlowshchyna Vitsyebskaya Voblasts' Belarus
18 G7 Kazlų Rūda Lith.
54 E3 Kaźmierz Pol.
56 C2 Kaznějov Czech Rep.
167 K3 Kazo Japan
182 C3 Kaztalovka Kazakh.
94 E3 Kazuma Pan National Park Zimbabwe
91 D6 Kazumba Dem. Rep. Congo
91 E9 Kazungula Zambia
164 R6 Kazuno Japan
167 L5 Kazusa Japan
184 G2 Kazy Turkm.
18 M6 Kazyany Belarus
183 M7 Kazygurt Kazakh.
192 H3 Kazym r. Rus. Fed.
192 H3 Kazymskiy Mys Rus. Fed.
76 H8 Kçirë Albania
54 F3 Kcynia Pol.
56 C2 Kdyně Czech Rep.
78 F5 Kea Kea Greece
78 F5 Kea i. Greece
124 □F14 Kea'au HI U.S.A.
200 □6 Kea'auloa Reef Solomon Is
27 I4 Keady Northern Ireland U.K.
124 □E14 Keahole Point HI U.S.A.
26 D10 Keal, Loch na b. Scotland U.K.
124 □D13 Kealaikahiki Channel HI U.S.A.
124 □F14 Kealakekua HI U.S.A.
124 □F14 Kealakekua Bay HI U.S.A.
124 □F14 Keālia HI U.S.A.
27 D9 Kealkill Rep. of Ireland
125 V6 Keams Canyon AZ U.S.A.
119 G4 Keansburg NJ U.S.A.
27 L4 Kearney Northern Ireland U.K.
120 F5 Kearney NE U.S.A.
116 H9 Kearneysville WV U.S.A.
125 V8 Kearny AZ U.S.A.
119 G3 Kearny NJ U.S.A.
78 F5 Keas, Steno sea chan. Greece
97 O4 Keate's Drift S. Africa
124 □F14 Keauhou HI U.S.A.
124 □E13 Keawakapu HI U.S.A.
188 I4 Keban Turkey
188 I4 Keban Barajı resr Turkey
90 B5 Kébara Congo
157 H6 Kebatu i. Indon.
89 F3 Kebbi state Nigeria
88 A3 Kébémèr Senegal
89 I4 Kébi r. Cameroon
88 D4 Kébi Côte d'Ivoire
87 H2 Kebili Tunisia
190 D4 Kebīr, Nahr al r. Lebanon/Syria
84 E6 Kebkabiya Sudan
20 O3 Kebnekaise mt. Sweden
26 D6 Kebock Head Scotland U.K.
92 E3 K'ebrī Dehar Eth.
157 H8 Kebumen Jawa Indon.
156 E6 Kebur Sumatera Indon.
57 I5 Kecel Hungary
185 J8 Kech reg. Pak.
92 C3 K'ech'a Terara mt. Eth.
90 D2 Kéché C.A.R.
168 E8 Kecheng Qinghai China
106 E3 Kechika r. B.C. Can.
185 M7 Kechi Kalat Pak.
79 G1 Kechros Greece
79 L5 Keçiborlu Turkey
57 I5 Kecskemét Hungary
156 D1 Kedah state Malaysia
18 G6 Kėdainiai Lith.
Kedairu Passage Fiji see Kadavu Passage
173 D11 Kedarnath Peak Uttaranchal India
90 C2 Kédédéssé Chad
109 H4 Kedgwick N.B. Can.
171 I3 Kedian Hubei China
31 M3 Kedington Suffolk, England U.K.
157 J8 Kediri Jawa Indon.
162 E5 Kedong Heilong. China
88 B3 Kédougou Senegal
157 I4 Kedukul Kalimantan Indon.
14 K2 Kedva r. Rus. Fed.
54 G5 Kędzierzyn-Koźle Pol.
29 Q6 Keelby Lincolnshire, England U.K.
106 E1 Keele r. Y.T. Can.
29 M7 Keele Staffordshire, England U.K.
106 D2 Keele Peak Y.T. Can.
124 O5 Keeler CA U.S.A.
107 I4 Keeley Lake Sask. Can.
Keelung Taiwan see Chilung
26 K9 Keen, Mount hill Scotland U.K.
27 G5 Keenagh Rep. of Ireland
154 B8 Keenapusan i. Phil.
124 N6 Keene CA U.S.A.
117 M6 Keene NH U.S.A.
116 D8 Keene OH U.S.A.
206 B3 Keep r. N.T. Austr.
205 M4 Keepit, Lake resr N.S.W. Austr.
206 B3 Keep River National Park N.T. Austr.
45 G7 Keerbergen Belgium
97 K4 Keeromsberg mt. Free State S. Africa
96 D9 Keeromsberg mt. Western Cape S. Africa
207 H2 Keer-weer, Cape Qld Austr.
94 C5 Keetmanshoop Namibia
107 M5 Keewatin Ont. Can.
110 A2 Keewatin MN U.S.A.
Kefallinía i. Greece see Kefallonia
78 B4 Kefallonia i. Greece
79 H6 Kefalos Kos Greece
78 F5 Kefalos, Akra pt Kythnos Greece
155 D8 Kefamenanu Timor Indon.
49 H10 Kefenrod Ger.
59 K3 Kefermarkt Austria
89 G4 Keffi Nigeria
79 L1 Kefken Turkey
20 □B1 Keflavík Iceland
159 I9 Kê Ga, Mui pt Vietnam
176 G9 Kegalla Sri Lanka
Kegayli Uzbek. see Kegeyli
183 R6 Kegen Kazakh.
183 P6 Kegeti Kyrg.
182 H6 Kegeyli Uzbek.
109 H1 Keglo, Baie de b. Que. Can.
106 G3 Keg River Alta Can.
15 I7 Kegul'ta Rus. Fed.
18 H5 Ķegums Latvia
31 J2 Kegworth Leicestershire, England U.K.
85 G5 Keheili Sudan
184 E5 Kehi Iran
52 D4 Kehl Ger.
45 J9 Kehlen Lux.
88 C2 Kehoula well Maur.
18 I2 Kehra Estonia
49 D10 Kehrig Ger.
158 C4 Kehsi Mansam Myanmar
18 H3 Kehtna Estonia
17 O4 Kehychivka Ukr.
29 N6 Keighley West Yorkshire, England U.K.
166 C5 Keihoku Japan
18 H2 Keila Estonia
18 H2 Keila r. Estonia
90 F2 Keilak Sudan
92 B2 Keili Sudan
171 □J7 Kei Ling Ha Hoi b. H.K. China
205 J7 Keilor Vic. Austr.
96 E4 Keimoes S. Africa
97 M8 Kei Mouth S. Africa
97 L8 Kei Road S. Africa
97 L9 Keiskama r. S. Africa
97 L8 Keiskammahoek S. Africa
26 J5 Keiss Highland, Scotland U.K.
89 G3 Keïta Niger
90 C2 Kéita, Bahr r. Chad
20 S5 Keitele Fin.
20 S5 Keitele l. Fin.
204 H7 Keith S.A. Austr.
26 K7 Keith Moray, Scotland U.K.
206 C1 Keith, Cape N.T. Austr.
106 F1 Keith Arm b. N.W.T. Can.
106 F4 Keithley Creek B.C. Can.
201 □1a Keiyasi Viti Levu Fiji
109 H4 Kejimkujik National Park N.S. Can.
166 G2 Kekachi-yama mt. Japan
124 □B12 Kekaha HI U.S.A.
Këk-Art Kyrg. see Kök-Art
18 H5 Ķekava Latvia
Këkaygyr Kyrg. see Kök-Aygyr
57 L3 Kékcse Hungary
203 H9 Kekerengu South I. N.Z.
57 J4 Kékes mt. Hungary
155 F4 Kekik i. Maluku Indon.
176 G8 Kekirawa Sri Lanka
154 □ Keklau Palau
79 K6 Kekova Adası i. Turkey
193 P4 Kekra Rus. Fed.
178 E7 Kekri Rajasthan India
Këk-Tash Kyrg. see Kök-Tash
92 E3 K'elafo Eth.
176 C9 Kelai i. Maldives
169 L7 Kelan Shanxi China
155 E5 Kelang i. Maluku Indon.
Kelang Malaysia see Klang
156 E1 Kelantan r. Malaysia
156 D2 Kelantan state Malaysia
155 F8 Kelapa i. Maluku Indon.
155 A6 Kelara r. Indon.
184 D3 Kelārdasht Iran
157 H5 Kelawar i. Indon.
49 C10 Kelberg Ger.
51 D8 Kelbra (Kyffhäuser) Ger.
57 G2 Kelč Czech Rep.
78 B2 Këlcyrë Albania
191 E4 Kel Dağı mt. Turkey
92 B4 Kele Uganda
57 I5 Kelebia Hungary
79 K5 Kelekçi Turkey
93 B6 Kelema Dodoma Tanz.
79 K3 Keles Turkey
183 M7 Keles Uzbek.
57 K4 Keleti-főcsatorna canal Hungary
57 H5 Kelet-Mecsek park Hungary
53 L4 Kelheim Ger.
87 H1 Kelibia Tunisia
185 L3 Kelif Turkm.
185 J2 Kelifskiy Uzboy marsh Turkm.
184 H9 Kelīrī Iran
49 F10 Kelkheim (Taunus) Ger.
188 I3 Kelkit Turkey
188 H3 Kelkit r. Turkey
52 B2 Kell Ger.
203 A12 Kellard, Mount South I. N.Z.
26 J7 Kellas Moray, Scotland U.K.
18 J2 Kellavere hill Estonia
90 B5 Kéllé Congo
50 D2 Kellenhusen Ger.
209 D11 Kellerberrin W.A. Austr.
106 F2 Keller Lake N.W.T. Can.
183 M1 Kellerovka Kazakh.
104 F2 Kellett, Cape N.W.T. Can.
116 C7 Kelleys Island OH U.S.A.
107 K5 Kelliher Sask. Can.
48 I3 Kellinghusen Ger.
53 I5 Kellmünz an der Iller Ger.
122 F3 Kellogg ID U.S.A.
20 T3 Kelloselkä Fin.
27 B9 Kells Kerry Rep. of Ireland
27 H7 Kells Kilkenny Rep. of Ireland
27 I5 Kells Meath Rep. of Ireland
27 J3 Kells Northern Ireland U.K.
27 J3 Kells r. Northern Ireland U.K.
206 G7 Kelly Creek watercourse Qld Austr.
209 F8 Kelly Range hills W.A. Austr.
27 F6 Kellysgrove Rep. of Ireland
18 F6 Kelmė Lith.
16 F5 Kel'mentsi Ukr.
45 J7 Kelmis Belgium
90 B2 Kelo Chad
200 □6 Keloma i. Solomon Is
106 G5 Kelowna B.C. Can.
106 E5 Kelp Head B.C. Can.
29 L7 Kelsall Cheshire, England U.K.
110 B2 Kelsey MN U.S.A.
124 J3 Kelseyville CA U.S.A.
203 D12 Kelso South I. N.Z.
26 L11 Kelso Scottish Borders, Scotland U.K.
125 Q6 Kelso CA U.S.A.
122 C3 Kelso WA U.S.A.
49 G10 Kelsterbach Ger.
60 D5 Kelti, Jebel mt. Morocco
26 J10 Kelty Fife, Scotland U.K.
156 E4 Keluang Malaysia
20 S3 Kelujärvi Fin.
31 N4 Kelvedon Essex, England U.K.
31 M4 Kelvedon Hatch Essex, England U.K.
107 K4 Kelvington Sask. Can.
108 B3 Kelvin Island Ont. Can.
185 O9 Kelwara Rajasthan India
14 F2 Kem' Rus. Fed.
14 F2 Kem' r. Rus. Fed.
19 U1 Kema r. Rus. Fed.
157 K2 Kemabung Sabah Malaysia
Ke Macina Mali see Massina
188 I4 Kemah Turkey
77 O9 Kemal Turkey
188 I4 Kemaliye Turkey
191 C4 Kemalpaşa Artvin Turkey
79 I4 Kemalpaşa İzmir Turkey
200 □6 Kemalu i. Solomon Is
106 E4 Kemano B.C. Can.
156 E2 Kemasik Malaysia
58 D5 Kematen in Tirol Austria
90 D3 Kemba C.A.R.
157 I4 Kembayan Kalimantan Indon.
90 D3 Kembé C.A.R.
51 G7 Kemberg Ger.
118 D5 Kemblesville PA U.S.A.
92 C2 Kembolcha Eth.
37 N8 Kembs France
56 G4 Kemeneshát hills Hungary
56 G4 Kemenesmagasi Hungary
56 G4 Kemenessömjén Hungary
79 K6 Kemer Antalya Turkey
79 L6 Kemer Antalya Turkey
79 L5 Kemer Burdur Turkey
79 K6 Kemer Muğla Turkey
79 J5 Kemer Barajı resr Turkey
192 J4 Kemerovo Rus. Fed.
Kemerovo Oblast admin. div. Rus. Fed. see Kemerovskaya Oblast'
160 E1 Kemerovskaya Oblast' admin. div. Rus. Fed.
57 H6 Kémes Hungary
59 N5 Kemeten Austria
20 R4 Kemi Fin.
20 T3 Kemihaara Fin.
20 S3 Kemijärvi Fin.
20 S3 Kemijärvi l. Fin.
20 R4 Kemijoki r. Fin.
183 P6 Kemin Kyrg.
20 R4 Keminmaa Fin.
Kemiö Fin. see Kimito
184 E3 Kemir Turkm.
15 I5 Kemlya Rus. Fed.
45 C7 Kemmel Belgium
45 C7 Kemmelberg hill Belgium
122 I6 Kemmerer WY U.S.A.
53 J2 Kemmern Ger.
75 □ Kemmuna i. Malta
75 □ Kemmunett i. Malta
53 L2 Kemnath Ger.
26 L8 Kemnay Aberdeenshire, Scotland U.K.
50 I2 Kemnitz Mecklenburg-Vorpommern Ger.
51 K8 Kemnitz Sachsen Ger.
90 C3 Kémo pref. C.A.R.
121 F9 Kemp, Lake TX U.S.A.
14 M2 Kempazh r. Rus. Fed.
20 R4 Kempele Fin.
49 B8 Kempen Ger.
193 M3 Kempendyay Rus. Fed.
49 D10 Kempenich Ger.
45 H6 Kempisch Kanaal canal Belgium
213 D2 Kemp Land reg. Antarctica
212 U2 Kemp Peninsula Antarctica
130 E1 Kemp's Bay Andros Bahamas
205 N4 Kempsey N.S.W. Austr.
30 H3 Kempsey Worcestershire, England U.K.
31 L3 Kempston Bedfordshire, England U.K.
108 F4 Kempt, Lac l. Que. Can.
53 I6 Kempten (Allgäu) Ger.
205 K10 Kempton Tas. Austr.
97 M2 Kempton Park S. Africa
111 S4 Kemptville Ont. Can.
31 M5 Kemsing Kent, England U.K.
157 I7 Kemujan i. Indon.
178 H7 Ken r. India
26 H13 Ken, Loch l. Scotland U.K.
111 O2 Kenabeek Ont. Can.
104 C3 Kenai AK U.S.A.
104 C4 Kenai Fiords National Park AK U.S.A.
104 C4 Kenai Mountains AK U.S.A.
156 F7 Kenam, Tanjung pt Indon.
109 J2 Kenamu r. Nfld and Lab. Can.
92 B3 Kenamuke Swamp Sudan
115 I8 Kenansville NC U.S.A.
184 I4 Kenar-e Kapeh Afgh.
104 H4 Kenaston Sask. Can.
116 G12 Kenbridge VA U.S.A.
157 J9 Kencong Jawa Indon.
178 I8 Kenda Chhattisgarh India
157 I8 Kendal Jawa Indon.
130 □ Kendal Jamaica
97 M2 Kendal S. Africa
29 L5 Kendal Cumbria, England U.K.
205 N4 Kendall N.S.W. Austr.
207 H3 Kendall r. Qld Austr.
115 G13 Kendall FL U.S.A.
107 O2 Kendall, Cape Nunavut Can.
203 G8 Kendall, Mount South I. N.Z.
114 E5 Kendallville IN U.S.A.
155 C5 Kendari Sulawesi Indon.
157 I6 Kendawangan Kalimantan Indon.
157 I6 Kendawangan r. Indon.
90 C2 Kendégué Chad
57 J4 Kenderes Hungary
Kendhrikí Makedhonía admin. reg. Greece see Kentriki Makedonia
57 K3 Kendice Slovakia
179 K9 Kendrapara Orissa India
96 I8 Kendrew S. Africa
122 F3 Kendrick ID U.S.A.
125 U6 Kendrick Peak AZ U.S.A.
179 L7 Kendua Bangl.
183 P6 Kendyktas mts Kazakh.
182 E6 Kendyrli-Kayasanskoye, Plato plat. Kazakh.
182 F6 Kendyrlisor, Solonchak salt l. Kazakh.
205 L4 Kenebri N.S.W. Austr.
121 G11 Kenedy TX U.S.A.
97 N6 Keneka r. S. Africa
88 C5 Kenema Sierra Leone
157 I4 Kenepai, Gunung mt. Indon.
184 H1 Keneurgench Turkm.
57 K3 Kenézlő Hungary
30 E4 Kenfig Bridgend, Wales U.K.
91 C6 Kenge Dem. Rep. Congo
91 E7 Kengere Dem. Rep. Congo
158 D4 Keng Hkam Myanmar
20 Q3 Kengis Sweden
179 M6 Kengkhar Bhutan
158 E4 Keng Lap Myanmar
158 D4 Keng Lon Myanmar
158 D4 Keng Tawng Myanmar
158 D4 Kengtung Myanmar
91 B5 Kengué Congo
57 J4 Kengyet Hungary
Kengzharyq Kazakh. see Kenzharyk
96 F5 Kenhardt S. Africa
118 D4 Kenhorst PA U.S.A.
88 C3 Kéniéba Mali
88 C3 Kéniébaoulé, Réserve de nature res. Mali
31 I3 Kenilworth Warwickshire, England U.K.
118 D4 Kenilworth PA U.S.A.
86 D2 Kénitra Morocco
191 G3 Kenkhi Rus. Fed.
169 P8 Kenli Shandong China
27 C9 Kenmare Rep. of Ireland
120 E1 Kenmare ND U.S.A.
27 B9 Kenmare River inlet Rep. of Ireland
95 F3 Kenmaur Zimbabwe
26 I9 Kenmore Perth and Kinross, Scotland U.K.
116 G6 Kenmore NY U.S.A.
52 B2 Kenn Ger.
121 D9 Kenna NM U.S.A.
26 F11 Kennacraig Argyll and Bute, Scotland U.K.
120 F4 Kennebec SD U.S.A.
117 □P4 Kennebec r. ME U.S.A.
117 □O5 Kennebunk ME U.S.A.
117 □O5 Kennebunkport ME U.S.A.
207 J5 Kennedy Qld Austr.
207 J3 Kennedy r. Qld Austr.
Kennedy, Cape FL U.S.A. see Canaveral, Cape
209 C8 Kennedy Range hills W.A. Austr.
209 C8 Kennedy Range National Park W.A. Austr.
171 □J7 Kennedy Town H.K. China
118 D6 Kennedyville MD U.S.A.
121 J11 Kenner LA U.S.A.
31 K5 Kennet r. England U.K.
26 K8 Kennethmont Aberdeenshire, Scotland U.K.
209 D7 Kenneth Range hills W.A. Austr.
121 J7 Kennett MO U.S.A.
118 D5 Kennett Square PA U.S.A.
122 E3 Kennewick WA U.S.A.
31 J4 Kennington Oxfordshire, England U.K.
26 J10 Kennoway Fife, Scotland U.K.
108 C3 Kenogami r. Ont. Can.
111 N1 Kenogami Lake Ont. Can.
111 M1 Kenogamissi Lake Ont. Can.
106 C2 Keno Hill Y.T. Can.
107 M5 Kenora Ont. Can.
110 G7 Kenosha WI U.S.A.
116 C10 Kenova WV U.S.A.
14 G3 Kenozero, Ozero l. Rus. Fed.
26 D8 Kensaleyre Highland, Scotland U.K.
119 H2 Kensico Reservoir NY U.S.A.
109 I4 Kensington P.E.I. Can.
119 J1 Kensington CT U.S.A.
31 L4 Kensworth Bedfordshire, England U.K.
31 N5 Kent admin. div. England U.K.
29 L5 Kent r. England U.K.
119 I1 Kent CT U.S.A.
116 D7 Kent OH U.S.A.
123 L11 Kent TX U.S.A.
116 D12 Kent VA U.S.A.
122 C3 Kent WA U.S.A.
31 M5 Kent, Vale of val. England U.K.
118 D6 Kent Acres DE U.S.A.
97 M8 Kentani S. Africa
183 M6 Kentau Kazakh.
118 D6 Kent County county DE U.S.A.
118 C6 Kent County county MD U.S.A.
205 K8 Kent Group is Tas. Austr.
118 C7 Kent Island MD U.S.A.
114 D5 Kentland IN U.S.A.
30 F6 Kenton Devon, England U.K.
118 D6 Kenton DE U.S.A.
110 F3 Kenton MI U.S.A.
116 B8 Kenton OH U.S.A.
97 K9 Kenton-on-Sea S. Africa
104 H3 Kent Peninsula Nunavut Can.
118 C7 Kent Point MD U.S.A.
78 E2 Kentriki Makedonia admin. reg. Greece
116 B11 Kentucky r. KY U.S.A.
116 A11 Kentucky state U.S.A.
121 K7 Kentucky Lake KY U.S.A.
121 J10 Kentwood LA U.S.A.
110 I7 Kentwood MI U.S.A.
Kenxa Rus. Fed. see Kenkhi
92 C4 Kenya country Africa
Kenya, Mount Kenya see Kirinyaga
56 G4 Kenyeri Hungary
156 E2 Kenyir, Tasik resr Malaysia
110 B5 Kenyon MN U.S.A.
191 G2 Ken'yurt Rus. Fed.
167 K5 Ken-zaki pt Japan
183 N3 Kenzharyk Kazakh.
191 E2 Kenzhe Rus. Fed.
52 D5 Kenzingen Ger.
124 □E13 Kēōkea HI U.S.A.
110 C9 Keokuk IA U.S.A.
178 F6 Keoladeo National Park India
124 □D12 Keolu Hills HI U.S.A.
179 J9 Keonjhar Orissa India
120 J5 Keosauqua IA U.S.A.
26 D6 Keose Western Isles, Scotland U.K.
115 F8 Keowee, Lake resr SC U.S.A.
156 E6 Kepahiang Sumatera Indon.
23 M7 Kępice Pol.
200 □4b Kepidau en Pohnahtik sea chan. Pohnpei Micronesia
14 H2 Kepina Rus. Fed.
14 H2 Kepina r. Rus. Fed.
203 B12 Kepler Mountains South I. N.Z.
54 F4 Kępno Pol.
207 M7 Keppel Bay Qld Austr.
156 □ Keppel Harbour sea chan. Sing.
79 J3 Kepsut Turkey
176 D7 Kerala state India
164 □E20 Kerama-rettō is Nansei-shotō Japan
78 F2 Keramoti Greece
205 I6 Kerang Vic. Austr.
78 B3 Kerasona Greece
78 E5 Keratea Greece
208 E5 Keraudren, Cape W.A. Austr.
21 R6 Kerava Fin.
156 E6 Kerbau, Tanjung pt Indon.
Kerbela Iraq see Karbalā'
183 N7 Kerben Kyrg.
162 J2 Kerbi r. Rus. Fed.
109 H2 Kerbodot, Lac l. Que. Can.
75 □ Kercem Gozo Malta
17 P8 Kerch Ukr.
14 K3 Kerchem'ya Rus. Fed.
Kerchens'ka Protoka str. Rus. Fed./Ukr. see Kerch Strait
Kerchenskiy Proliv str. Rus. Fed./Ukr. see Kerch Strait
17 O8 Kerchens'kyy Pivostriv pen. Ukr.
14 L4 Kerchevskiy Rus. Fed.
Kerch Peninsula Ukr. see Kerchens'kyy Pivostriv
17 P8 Kerch Strait Rus. Fed./Ukr.
90 E3 Kéré C.A.R.
92 C3 Kere Eth.
57 J4 Kerecsend Hungary
189 P9 Kereft Iran
90 E2 Kereidila l. Sudan
57 I5 Kerekegyháza Hungary
153 K8 Kerema P.N.G.
106 G5 Keremeos B.C. Can.
188 F2 Kerempe Burun pt Turkey
85 H6 Keren Eritrea
184 B4 Kerend Iran
202 J4 Kerepehi North I. N.Z.
57 I4 Kerepestarcsa Hungary
19 O2 Kerest' r. Rus. Fed.
16 C5 Kerets'ky Ukr.
88 A3 Kerewan Gambia
183 M2 Kerey watercourse Kazakh.
183 M2 Kerey, Ozero salt l. Kazakh.
184 G2 Kergeli Turkm.
215 I8 Kerguélen, Îles is Indian Ocean
Kerguelen Islands Indian Ocean see Kerguélen, Îles
215 I8 Kerguelen Plateau sea feature Indian Ocean
92 B5 Kericho Kenya
157 J4 Kerihun mt. Indon.
202 H2 Kerikeri North I. N.Z.
21 T6 Kerimäki Fin.
156 D6 Kerinci, Danau l. Indon.
156 D5 Kerinci, Gunung vol. Indon.
156 D6 Kerinci Seblat National Park Indon.
Kerintji vol. Indon. see Kerinci, Gunung
92 C4 Kerio watercourse Kenya
173 F7 Keriya He watercourse China
173 E9 Keriya Shankou pass Xinjiang China
76 E4 Kerka r. Romania
44 H5 Kerkdriel Neth.
85 H5 Kerkebet Eritrea
49 B8 Kerken Ger.
87 H2 Kerkenah, Îles is Tunisia
185 K3 Kerkichi Turkm.
78 E1 Kerkinitis, Limni l. Greece
Kérkira i. Greece see Kerkyra
87 H1 Kerkouane tourist site Tunisia
45 J7 Kerkrade Neth.
44 H5 Kerkwijk Neth.
78 A3 Kerkyra Kerkyra Greece
78 A3 Kerkyra i. Greece
38 C4 Kerlouan France
85 F5 Kerma Sudan
199 I5 Kermadec Islands S. Pacific Ocean
216 H8 Kermadec Trench sea feature S. Pacific Ocean
184 G6 Kermān Iran
184 G7 Kermān prov. Iran
124 L5 Kerman CA U.S.A.
184 H7 Kermān, Bīābān-e des. Iran
184 B4 Kermānshāh Iran
184 B4 Kermānshāh prov. Iran
184 F6 Kermānshāhān Iran
Kermānshāhān prov. Iran see Kermānshāh
Kermine Uzbek. see Navoiy
121 D10 Kermit TX U.S.A.
124 M6 Kern r. CA U.S.A.
124 N6 Kern, South Fork r. CA U.S.A.
38 E5 Kernascléden France
109 H1 Kernertut, Cap c. Que. Can.
59 M4 Kernhof Austria
206 D8 Kernot Range hills N.T. Austr.
70 E2 Kerns Switz.
124 N6 Kernville CA U.S.A.
79 G6 Keros i. Greece
14 K3 Keros Rus. Fed.
89 F4 Kérou Benin
88 C4 Kérouané Guinea
49 C9 Kerpen Ger.
213 K1 Kerr, Cape Antarctica
26 E10 Kerrera i. Scotland U.K.
107 I5 Kerrobert Sask. Can.
121 F10 Kerrville TX U.S.A.
27 D8 Kerry county Rep. of Ireland
27 C8 Kerry Head Rep. of Ireland
27 G2 Kerrykeel Rep. of Ireland
92 C3 Kersa Dek Eth.
115 G8 Kershaw SC U.S.A.
29 L3 Kershopefoot Cumbria, England U.K.
51 D8 Kerspleben Ger.
23 M1 Kerstinbo Sweden
60 E5 Kert, Oued r. Morocco
156 E2 Kerteh Malaysia
22 G6 Kerteminde Denmark
57 K4 Kertészsziget Hungary
157 J8 Kertosono Jawa Indon.
157 L9 Keruak Lombok Indon.
Kerulen r. China see Herlen Gol
156 E5 Kerumutan Reserve nature res. Indon.
176 D4 Kerur Karnataka India
19 W6 Kerva Rus. Fed.
38 E6 Kervignac France
190 B3 Keryneia Cyprus
87 E3 Kerzaz Alg.
70 C2 Kerzers Switz.
14 I4 Kerzhenets r. Rus. Fed.
108 E3 Kesagami r. Ont. Can.
108 D3 Kesagami Lake Ont. Can.
21 T6 Kesälahti Fin.
79 H2 Keşan Turkey
188 I3 Keşap Turkey
77 N7 Kesarevo Bulg.
179 J6 Kesariya Bihar India
91 C5 Kese Dem. Rep. Congo
164 S8 Kesennuma Japan
31 O3 Kesgrave Suffolk, England U.K.
27 F4 Kesh Rep. of Ireland
27 G3 Kesh Northern Ireland U.K.
162 D4 Keshan Heilong. China
191 E3 K'eshelt'a Georgia
185 N3 Keshem Afgh.
110 F5 Keshena WI U.S.A.
185 L3 Keshendeh-ye Bala Afgh.
184 H7 Keshīt Iran
178 C9 Keshod Gujarat India
178 F7 Keshorai Patan Rajasthan India
189 N7 Keshvar Iran
188 F4 Keskin Turkey
14 F3 Keskozero Rus. Fed.
19 U3 Kes'ma Rus. Fed.
79 M5 Kesme Turkey
19 U4 Kesova Gora Rus. Fed.
54 F2 Kęsowo Pol.
45 G6 Kessel Belgium
53 J4 Kessel r. Ger.
45 J6 Kessel Neth.
31 P3 Kessingland Suffolk, England U.K.
79 K2 Kestel Bursa Turkey
79 L5 Kestel Gölü l. Turkey
97 M4 Kestell S. Africa
20 U4 Kesten'ga Rus. Fed.
20 S4 Kestilä Fin.
111 O5 Keswick Ont. Can.
29 K4 Keswick Cumbria, England U.K.
56 G5 Keszthely Hungary
56 G5 Keszthelyihegység park Hungary
192 J4 Ket' r. Rus. Fed.
89 F5 Keta Ghana
156 D6 Ketahun Sumatera Indon.
156 □ Ketam, Pulau i. Sing.
157 J8 Ketapang Jawa Indon.
157 I5 Ketapang Kalimantan Indon.
104 E4 Ketchikan AK U.S.A.
122 G5 Ketchum ID U.S.A.
212 T2 Ketchum Glacier Antarctica
57 K5 Kétegyháza Hungary
89 E5 Kete Krachi Ghana
44 I3 Ketelmeer l. Neth.
56 G5 Kéthely Hungary
173 J10 Ketian Qinghai China
185 L9 Keti Bandar Pak.
183 S6 Ketmen', Khrebet mts China/Kazakh.
89 F5 Kétou Benin
17 L6 Ketrysanivka Ukr.
23 R7 Kętrzyn Pol.
57 J5 Kétsoprony Hungary
90 B4 Ketta Congo
89 I5 Ketté Cameroon
48 E5 Kettenkamp Ger.
31 K3 Kettering Northamptonshire, England U.K.
116 A9 Kettering OH U.S.A.
53 I5 Kettershausen Ger.
50 E1 Kettinge Denmark
106 G5 Kettle r. B.C. Can.
110 B4 Kettle r. MN U.S.A.
116 H7 Kettle Creek r. PA U.S.A.
122 E2 Kettle Falls WA U.S.A.
124 M5 Kettleman City CA U.S.A.
110 B3 Kettle River MN U.S.A.
122 E2 Kettle River Range mts WA U.S.A.
26 K4 Kettletoft Orkney, Scotland U.K.
29 M5 Kettlewell North Yorkshire, England U.K.
157 I4 Ketungau r. Indon.
55 H6 Kęty Pol.
51 H8 Ketzerbach r. Ger.
51 G6 Ketzin Ger.
116 H6 Keuka NY U.S.A.
116 H6 Keuka Lake NY U.S.A.
49 K8 Keula Ger.
Keumgang, Mount N. Korea see Kumgang-san
Keumsang, Mount N. Korea see Kumgang-san
88 A2 Keur Massène Maur.
21 R5 Keurusselkä l. Fin.
21 R5 Keuruu Fin.
59 J6 Keutschach am See Austria
59 J6 Keutscharcher See l. Austria
49 B7 Kevelaer Ger.
57 K5 Kevermes Hungary
20 S2 Kevo Fin.
20 S2 Kevon luonnonpuisto nature res. Fin.
130 G3 Kew Turks and Caicos Is
110 E8 Kewanee IL U.S.A.
155 C8 Kewapante Flores Indon.
110 F6 Kewaskum WI U.S.A.
110 G5 Kewaunee WI U.S.A.
110 F3 Keweenaw Bay MI U.S.A.
110 F3 Keweenaw Bay b. MI U.S.A.
110 F2 Keweenaw Peninsula MI U.S.A.
110 G2 Keweenaw Point MI U.S.A.
30 G5 Kewstoke North Somerset, England U.K.
27 F4 Key, Lough l. Rep. of Ireland
92 B3 Keyala Sudan
120 F4 Keya Paha r. NE U.S.A.
108 D4 Key Harbour Ont. Can.
172 F5 Keyi Xinjiang China
169 R1 Keyihe Nei Mongol China
29 Q6 Keyingham East Riding of Yorkshire, England U.K.
115 G13 Key Largo FL U.S.A.
115 G13 Key Largo National Marine Sanctuary nature res. FL U.S.A.
206 B3 Keyling Inlet N.T. Austr.
Keymir Turkm. see Kemir
30 G5 Keynsham Bath and North East Somerset, England U.K.
116 G9 Keyser WV U.S.A.
116 F9 Keysers Ridge MD U.S.A.
121 G7 Keystone Lake OK U.S.A.
111 O9 Keystone Lake PA U.S.A.
125 U10 Keystone Peak AZ U.S.A.
116 G11 Keysville VA U.S.A.
120 I6 Keytesville MO U.S.A.
184 C4 Keytū Iran
14 G2 Keyvy, Vozvyshennost' hills Rus. Fed.
115 G13 Key West FL U.S.A.
31 J2 Keyworth Nottinghamshire, England U.K.
14 K4 Kez Rus. Fed.
117 □O5 Kezar Falls ME U.S.A.
95 F4 Kezi Zimbabwe
57 J2 Kežmarok Slovakia
97 K3 Kgakala S. Africa
94 D5 Kgalagadi admin. dist. Botswana
96 F1 Kgalagadi Transfrontier Park nat. park Botswana/S. Africa
94 E5 Kgatleng admin. dist. Botswana
97 K3 Kgotsong S. Africa
97 M4 Kgubetswana S. Africa
190 E5 Khabab Syria
184 F6 Khabar Iran
14 K2 Khabarikha Rus. Fed.
162 I4 Khabarovsk Rus. Fed.
162 I3 Khabarovskiy Kray admin. div. Rus. Fed.
Khabarovsk Kray admin. div. Rus. Fed. see Khabarovskiy Kray
183 R1 Khabary Rus. Fed.
186 G7 Khabb, Wādī watercourse Yemen
187 N4 Khabbah, Ra's al pt Oman
191 C1 Khabez Rus. Fed.
185 J4 Khabody Pass Afgh.
55 M3 Khabovichy Belarus
184 G7 Khabr Iran
186 E4 Khabrā al'Arn salt pan Saudi Arabia
190 H7 Khabrah Sāfiyah hill Saudi Arabia
180 E2 Khābūr, Nahr al r. Syria
178 E8 Khachrod Madh. Prad. India
187 N4 Khadar, Jabal mt. Oman
186 F7 Khaḑārah Saudi Arabia
90 E2 Khadari watercourse Sudan
186 F1 Khadd, Wādī al watercourse Saudi Arabia
189 N8 Khādeyn Iran
19 O8 Khadun' Belarus
191 A1 Khadyzhensk Rus. Fed.
191 I3 Khadzhalmakhi Rus. Fed.
77 L9 Khadzhidimovo Bulg.
16 J7 Khadzhybeys'kyy Lyman l. Ukr.
55 M2 Khadziloni Belarus
186 H3 Khafs Banbān well Saudi Arabia
187 H4 Khafs Daghrah Saudi Arabia
184 E7 Khāftar Iran
178 H7 Khaga Uttar Prad. India
179 K7 Khagaria Bihar India
179 J7 Khagaul Bihar India
179 M8 Khagrachari Bangl.
Khagrachchari Bangl. see Khagrachari
178 H9 Khairagarh Chhattisgarh India
173 C13 Khairagarh Uttar Prad. India
185 N7 Khairgarh Pak.
178 H5 Khairigarh Uttar Prad. India
185 O7 Khairpur Pak.
185 M8 Khairpur Pak.
178 D8 Khairwara Rajasthan India
191 D3 Khaishi Georgia
184 D6 Khāīz, Kūh-e mt. Iran
185 K3 Khaja du Koh hill Afgh.
185 M5 Khajuri Kach Pak.
160 F1 Khakasiya, Respublika aut. rep. Rus. Fed.
Khakassia aut. rep. Rus. Fed. see Khakasiya, Respublika
Khakasskaya A.S.S.R. aut. rep. Rus. Fed. see Khakasiya, Respublika
185 M4 Khāk-e Jabbar Afgh.
191 G3 Khakhalgi, Gora mt. Rus. Fed.
94 D5 Khakhea Botswana
185 K5 Khakīr Afgh.
185 K6 Khak-rēz Afgh.
185 K6 Khakriz reg. Afgh.
185 K2 Khalach Turkm.
191 I3 Khalagork r. Rus. Fed.
184 D4 Khalajestan reg. Iran
191 H4 Khalakhurkats, Pereval pass Rus. Fed.
18 M6 Khalamyer"ye Belarus
191 E3 Khalatsa, Mt'a Georgia/Rus. Fed.
178 F2 Khalatse Jammu and Kashmir
184 E5 Khalidabad Iran
185 L6 Khalifat mt. Pak.
179 I6 Khalilabad Uttar Prad. India
184 H4 Khalilabad Iran
184 E8 Khalīlī Iran
182 H2 Khalilovo Rus. Fed.
185 J1 Khalkabad Turkm.
184 C3 Khalkhāl Iran
191 G3 Khal-Kiloy Rus. Fed.
177 I3 Khallikot Orissa India
14 N2 Khal'mer-Yu Rus. Fed.
18 L7 Khalopyenichy Belarus
179 J6 Khalte Nepal
Khalturin Rus. Fed. see Orlov
191 H2 Khamamatyurt Rus. Fed.
168 H1 Khamar-Daban, Khrebet mts Rus. Fed.
178 H8 Khamaria Madh. Prad. India
178 B8 Khambhaliya Gujarat India
178 D8 Khambhat Gujarat India
176 B3 Khambhat, Gulf of India
178 F9 Khamgaon Mahar. India
184 F8 Khamīr Iran
186 F7 Khamir Yemen
95 F4 Khami Ruins National Monument tourist site Zimbabwe
186 F6 Khamis Mushayṭ Saudi Arabia
182 D4 Khamit Yergaliyev Kazakh.
158 G5 Khamkkeut Laos
186 H2 Khamma well Saudi Arabia
176 G4 Khammam Andhra Prad. India
193 N3 Khampa Rus. Fed.
158 B3 Khampat Myanmar
193 M3 Khamra Rus. Fed.
190 A8 Khamsah Egypt
184 C4 Khamseh reg. Iran
191 B1 Khamyshki Rus. Fed.
Khamza Uzbek. see Hamza
185 M5 Khan Afgh.
158 F5 Khan, Nam r. Laos
185 M3 Khānābād Afgh.
189 K7 Khān al Baghdādī Iraq
189 L7 Khān al Maḩāwīl Iraq
189 L7 Khān al Mashāhidah Iraq
189 L7 Khān al Muşallá Iraq
176 D5 Khanapur Karnataka India
176 D4 Khanapur Mahar. India
184 A3 Khānaqāh Iran
189 L8 Khān ar Raḩbah Iraq
189 L4 Khanasur Pass Iran/Turkey
184 F3 Khān Bāgh Iran
184 A3 Khānch Iran
205 L7 Khancoban N.S.W. Austr.
168 C1 Khandagayty Rus. Fed.
176 D4 Khandala Mahar. India
178 E6 Khandela Rajasthan India
185 O3 Khandud Afgh.
178 F9 Khandwa Madh. Prad. India
193 O3 Khandyga Rus. Fed.
184 E6 Khāneh Khowreh Iran
185 N6 Khanewal Pak.
185 N7 Khangarh Pak.
193 N4 Khani Rus. Fed.
178 G7 Khaniadhana Madh. Prad. India
19 T7 Khanino Rus. Fed.
184 E7 Khānī Yek Iran
189 L7 Khān Jadwal Iraq
162 H6 Khanka, Lake China/Rus. Fed.
Khanka, Ozero l. China/Rus. Fed. see Khanka, Lake
178 F4 Khanna Punjab India
190 E6 Khannā, Qā' salt pan Jordan
87 G4 Khannfoussa hill Alg.
14 M2 Khanovey Rus. Fed.
185 N7 Khanpur Pak.
Khān Ruḩābah Iraq see Khān ar Raḩbah
190 E3 Khān Shaykhūn Syria
92 E2 Khansiir, Raas pt Somalia
191 A1 Khanskaya Rus. Fed.
17 R7 Khanskoye, Ozero salt l. Rus. Fed.
183 O5 Khantau Kazakh.
193 K3 Khantayskoye, Ozero l. Rus. Fed.
192 J3 Khantayskoye Vodokhranilishche resr Rus. Fed.
183 S6 Khan-Tengri, Pik mt. Kazakh./Kyrg.
192 H3 Khanty-Mansiysk Rus. Fed.
14 M3 Khanty-Mansiyskiy Avtonomnyy Okrug admin. div. Rus. Fed.
Khanty-Mansy Autonomous Okrug admin. div. Rus. Fed. see Khanty-Mansiyskiy Avtonomnyy Okrug
190 C7 Khān Yūnis Gaza
159 E8 Khao Ang Rua Nai Wildlife Reserve nature res. Thai.
159 D11 Khao Banthat Wildlife Reserve nature res. Thai.
159 D10 Khao Chum Thong Thai.
159 D7 Khaoen Si Nakarin National Park Thai.
159 D7 Khao Laem National Park Thai.
158 D7 Khao Laem Reservoir Thai.
159 D10 Khao Luang National Park Thai.
159 D11 Khao Pu-Khao Ya National Park Thai.
159 F8 Khao Soi Dao Wildlife Reserve nature res. Thai.
159 D10 Khao Sok National Park Thai.
159 E7 Khao Yai National Park Thai.
178 G9 Khapa Mahar. India
178 F2 Khapalu Jammu and Kashmir
169 M2 Khapcheranga Rus. Fed.
178 H5 Khaptad National Park Nepal
182 B4 Kharabali Rus. Fed.
191 E3 Kharagauli Georgia
179 K7 Kharagdiha Jharkhand India
178 C8 Kharaghoda Gujarat India
179 K7 Kharagpur Bihar India
179 K8 Kharagpur W. Bengal India
184 G3 Kharakī Iran
184 H8 Khārān r. Iran
185 K7 Kharan Pak.
169 O2 Kharanor Rus. Fed.
55 M3 Kharava Belarus
176 D3 Kharda Mahar. India
176 C3 Khardi Mahar. India
178 F2 Khardung La pass Jammu and Kashmir
185 I4 Kharez Ilias Afgh.
189 M8 Kharfiyah Iraq
162 H2 Kharga r. Rus. Fed.
Kharga Oasis Egypt see Khārijah, Wāḩāt al
178 G7 Khargapur Madh. Prad. India
Khārg Island Iran see Khārk
184 D7 Khārg Islands Iran
178 E9 Khargon Madh. Prad. India
178 E7 Khari r. Rajasthan India
185 O9 Khari r. Rajasthan India
185 O5 Kharian Pak.
179 I9 Khariar Orissa India
85 F3 Khārijah, Wāḩāt al oasis Egypt
190 B8 Kharīm, Jabal hill Egypt
191 E3 Kharist'vala Georgia
184 D7 Khārk i. Iran
178 H9 Kharkhara r. India
178 F5 Kharkhauda Haryana India
Kharkiv r. Rus. Fed./Ukr. see Khar'kov
17 P4 Kharkiv Ukr.
Kharkiv Oblast admin. div. Ukr. see Kharkivs'ka Oblast'
17 P4 Kharkivs'ka Oblast' admin. div. Ukr.
17 P3 Khar'kov r. Rus. Fed./Ukr.
Khar'kov Ukr. see Kharkiv
Kharkov Oblast admin. div. Ukr. see Kharkivs'ka Oblast'
Khar'kovskaya Oblast' admin. div. Ukr. see Kharkivs'ka Oblast'
184 E6 Khār Kūh mt. Iran
14 G1 Kharlovka Rus. Fed.
14 E3 Kharlu Rus. Fed.
187 K9 Kharmah, Ghubbat b. Suquṭrā Yemen
178 F2 Kharmang Jammu and Kashmir
77 N9 Kharmanli Bulg.
178 H9 Kharora Chhattisgarh India
185 M5 Kharoti reg. Afgh.
14 H4 Kharovsk Rus. Fed.
162 J3 Kharpin r. Rus. Fed.
184 D4 Khar Rūd r. Iran
179 J8 Kharsawan Jharkhand India
179 I8 Kharsia Chhattisgarh India
179 M6 Kharteng Arun. Prad. India
85 G6 Khartoum Sudan
85 G6 Khartoum state Sudan
85 G6 Khartoum North Sudan
17 R5 Khartsyz'k Ukr.
Kharuf, Ra's mt. Israel see Ḩarif, Har
14 L2 Kharutoyuvom Rus. Fed.
185 M5 Kharwar reg. Afgh.

Column 1

91 B6 Kintata Dem. Rep. Congo
31 J5 Kintbury West Berkshire, England U.K.
118 E3 Kintersville PA U.S.A.
88 C4 Kintinian Guinea
155 C4 Kintom Sulawesi Indon.
157 K6 Kintap Kalimantan Indon.
206 B7 Kintore N.T. Austr.
26 L8 Kintore Aberdeenshire, Scotland U.K.
204 C2 Kintore, Mount S.A. Austr.
208 J7 Kintore Range hills N.T. Austr.
26 D11 Kintour Argyll and Bute, Scotland U.K.
191 D4 Kintrishis Nakrdzali nature res. Georgia
26 E11 Kintyre pen. Scotland U.K.
158 B3 Kin-U Myanmar
167 L4 Kinu-gawa r. Japan
167 J2 Kinunuma-yama mt. Japan
108 D2 Kinusheo r. Ont. Can.
106 H4 Kinuso Alta Can.
27 E6 Kinvara Rep. of Ireland
27 C6 Kinvarra Rep. of Ireland
30 H3 Kinver Staffordshire, England U.K.
164 □1 Kin-wan i. Okinawa Japan
176 F3 Kinwat Mahar. India
93 B6 Kinyangiri Tanz.
92 B4 Kinyeti mt. Sudan
182 G3 Kinzhaly Kazakh.
52 D4 Kinzig r. Ger.
49 G10 Kinzig r. Ger.
93 B6 Kiomboi Tanz.
191 E3 Kion-Khokh, Gora mt. Rus. Fed.
111 P3 Kiosk Ont. Can.
123 L7 Kiowa CO U.S.A.
121 F7 Kiowa KS U.S.A.
122 L6 Kiowa Creek r. CO U.S.A.
107 K4 Kipahigan Lake Man./Sask. Can.
124 □E13 Kipahulu HI U.S.A.
Kiparissia Greece see Kyparissia
108 E4 Kipawa, Lac l. Que. Can.
172 C6 Kipchak Pass Xinjiang China
14 G4 Kipelovo Rus. Fed.
93 B6 Kipembawe Tanz.
18 M2 Kipen' Rus. Fed.
93 B7 Kipengere Range mts Tanz.
53 K4 Kipfenberg Ger.
93 A6 Kipili Tanz.
93 C6 Kipini Kenya
107 K5 Kipling Sask. Can.
Kipling Station Sask. Can. see Kipling
29 O6 Kippax West Yorkshire, England U.K.
70 D3 Kippel Switz.
26 H10 Kippen Stirling, Scotland U.K.
52 D5 Kippenheim Ger.
27 J6 Kippure hill Rep. of Ireland
183 T1 Kiprino Rus. Fed.
14 I4 Kipshenga Rus. Fed.
17 K2 Kipti' Ukr.
117 J11 Kiptopeke VA U.S.A.
91 E7 Kipushi Dem. Rep. Congo
91 F8 Kipushia Dem. Rep. Congo
166 F6 Kira Japan
191 B6 Kiraçtepe Turkey
179 I7 Kirakat Uttar Prad. India
200 □8 Kirakira San Cristobal Solomon Is
20 T2 Kiráľ Hungary
57 G5 Kiráľ Hungary
57 G5 Királyegyháza Hungary
79 H4 Királyhegyes Hungary
79 H4 Kiran Dağları hills Turkey
176 G3 Kiranchud Chhattisgarh India
88 C3 Kirané Mali
95 □J3 Kiranomena Madag.
190 B2 Kirawa Turkey
18 M8 Kirawsk Belarus
79 J4 Kiraz Turkey
18 G3 Kirbla Estonia
95 □JJ Kirbyville TX U.S.A.
53 N6 Kirchaschöring Ger.
52 F3 Kirchardt Ger.
58 H4 Kirchbach Austria
59 M6 Kirchbach in Steiermark Austria
53 O4 Kirchberg Bayern Ger.
53 O4 Kirchberg Bayern Ger.
51 V9 Kirchberg Sachsen Ger.
70 D1 Kirchberg Bern Switz.
70 G1 Kirchberg St Gallen Switz.
52 C2 Kirchberg (Hunsrück) Ger.
59 M3 Kirchberg am Wagram Austria
59 L2 Kirchberg am Walde Austria
59 L2 Kirchberg am Wechsel Austria
53 I5 Kirchberg an der Iller Ger.
52 H3 Kirchberg an der Jagst Ger.
59 L3 Kirchberg an der Pielach Austria
59 M6 Kirchberg an der Raab Austria
58 F5 Kirchberg in Tirol Austria
58 F4 Kirchbichl Austria
59 J4 Kirchbrak Ger.
50 D3 Kirchdorf Mecklenburg-Vorpommern Ger.
48 G5 Kirchdorf Niedersachsen Ger.
53 N5 Kirchdorf am Inn Ger.
53 L5 Kirchdorf an der Amper Ger.
59 J4 Kirchdorf an der Krems Austria
53 O4 Kirchdorf im Wald Ger.
58 H5 Kirchdorf in Tirol Austria
53 K2 Kirchehrenbach Ger.
49 E9 Kirchen (Sieg) Ger.
51 E10 Kirchenlamitz Ger.
53 L2 Kirchenpingarten Ger.
53 K2 Kirchensittenbach Ger.
52 G4 Kirchentellinsfurt Ger.
53 L2 Kirchenthumbach Ger.
49 G9 Kirchhain Ger.
49 K8 Kirchheilingen Ger.
53 H2 Kirchheim Bayern Ger.
49 I9 Kirchheim Hessen Ger.
52 G3 Kirchheim am Neckar Ger.
53 L5 Kirchheim bei München Ger.
52 G2 Kirchheim-Bolanden Ger.
58 G1 Kirchheim in Schwaben Ger.
52 G4 Kirchheim unter Teck Ger.
49 F8 Kirchhundem Ger.
50 D4 Kirch Jesar Ger.
49 K10 Kirchlauter Ger.
48 H5 Kirchlinteln Ger.
48 H1 Kirch Mulsow Ger.
49 I6 Kirchosten (Emmerthal) Ger.
53 N4 Kirchroth Ger.
59 N4 Kirchschlag in der Buckligen Welt Austria
48 G5 Kirchseelte Ger.
48 H4 Kirchtimke Ger.
48 H4 Kirchwalsede Ger.
48 H4 Kirchweidach Ger.
49 J5 Kirchwistedt Ger.
52 D6 Kirchzarten Ger.
27 K4 Kircubbin Northern Ireland U.K.
91 E5 Kirdami Turkey
84 C5 Kirdimi Chad
91 C5 Kireçli Geçidi pass Turkey
Kirehesjävri Fin. see Kirakkajärvi
93 L4 Kirensk Rus. Fed.
17 K2 Kirey watercourse Kazakh.
Kirey Kazakh. see Kerey
Kirey, Ozero salt l. Kazakh. see Kerey, Ozero
19 U8 Kireyevsk Rus. Fed.
19 S8 Kireykovo Rus. Fed.
Kirghizia country Asia see Kyrgyzstan
63 O6 Kirghiz Range mts Asia
62 F1 Kirgiz-Miyaki Rus. Fed.
Kirgizskaya S.S.R. country Asia see Kyrgyzstan
Kirgizskiy Khrebet mts Asia see Kirghiz Range

Column 2

90 C5 Kirgizstan country Asia see Kyrgyzstan
90 C5 Kiri Dem. Rep. Congo
Kiria Greece see Kyria
199 J2 Kiribati country Pacific Ocean
92 E2 Kiridh Somalia
167 H3 Kiriga-mine mt. Japan
189 J3 Kirikhan Turkey
188 H5 Kirikkale Turkey
202 I2 Kirikopuni North I. N.Z.
19 V2 Kirillov Rus. Fed.
162 M5 Kirillovo Sakhalin Rus. Fed.
18 M1 Kirillovskoye Rus. Fed.
176 G9 Kirinda Sri Lanka
92 C5 Kirinyaga mt. Kenya
185 N6 Kiri Shamozai Pak.
19 P2 Kirishi Rus. Fed.
164 □H15 Kirishima-Yaku National Park Japan
165 H15 Kirishima-yama vol. Japan
217 I5 Kiritimati atoll Kiribati
79 L3 Kirka Turkey
79 I3 Kirkağaç Turkey
26 I13 Kirkbean Dumfries and Galloway, Scotland U.K.
29 K4 Kirkbride Cumbria, England U.K.
184 B3 Kirk Bulāg Dāgi mt. Iran
29 N6 Kirkburton West Yorkshire, England U.K.
29 L7 Kirkby Merseyside, England U.K.
29 O7 Kirkby in Ashfield Nottinghamshire, England U.K.
29 L5 Kirkby Lonsdale Cumbria, England U.K.
29 N5 Kirkby Malzeard North Yorkshire, England U.K.
29 P5 Kirkbymoorside North Yorkshire, England U.K.
29 M5 Kirkby Stephen Cumbria, England U.K.
29 N5 Kirkby Thore Cumbria, England U.K.
26 J10 Kirkcaldy Fife, Scotland U.K.
26 F13 Kirkcolm Dumfries and Galloway, Scotland U.K.
26 I12 Kirkconnel Dumfries and Galloway, Scotland U.K.
26 G13 Kirkcowan Dumfries and Galloway, Scotland U.K.
26 H13 Kirkcudbright Dumfries and Galloway, Scotland U.K.
28 I4 Kirkcudbright Bay Scotland U.K.
52 C3 Kirkel-Neuhäusel Ger.
22 I1 Kirkenær Norway
20 U2 Kirkenes Norway
111 P5 Kirkfield Ont. Can.
29 L6 Kirkham Lancashire, England U.K.
26 I13 Kirkinner Dumfries and Galloway, Scotland U.K.
26 H11 Kirkintilloch East Dunbartonshire, Scotland U.K.
21 R6 Kirkkonummi Fin.
125 T7 Kirkland AZ U.S.A.
110 F7 Kirkland IL U.S.A.
108 D3 Kirkland Lake Ont. Can.
191 A6 Kırklar Dağı mt. Turkey
191 B5 Kırklar Dağı mt. Turkey
188 C3 Kırklareli Turkey
79 I1 Kırklareli prov. Turkey
79 P9 Kırklareli Barajı resr Turkey
29 O5 Kirklevington Stockton-on-Tees, England U.K.
26 J11 Kirkliston Edinburgh, Scotland U.K.
203 E11 Kirkliston Range mts South I. N.Z.
28 H5 Kirk Michael Isle of Man
26 I9 Kirkmichael Perth and Kinross, Scotland U.K.
26 G12 Kirkmichael South Ayrshire, Scotland U.K.
26 I11 Kirkmuirhill South Lanarkshire, Scotland U.K.
18 K1 Kirkonmaanselkä b. Fin.
75 □ Kirkop Malta
29 L4 Kirkoswald Cumbria, England U.K.
26 G12 Kirkoswald South Ayrshire, Scotland U.K.
77 N9 Kirkovo Bulg.
191 C7 Kirköy Turkey
213 L1 Kirkpatrick, Mount Antarctica
26 I12 Kirkpatrick-Fleming Dumfries and Galloway, Scotland U.K.
29 O6 Kirk Sandall South Yorkshire, England U.K.
120 I5 Kirksville MO U.S.A.
28 F1 Kirkton Argyll and Bute, Scotland U.K.
26 L8 Kirkton of Durris Aberdeenshire, Scotland U.K.
26 K9 Kirkton of Menmuir Angus, Scotland U.K.
26 L8 Kirktown of Auchterless Aberdeenshire, Scotland U.K.
26 K7 Kirktown of Deskford Moray, Scotland U.K.
186 L6 Kirkūk Iraq
26 K5 Kirkwall Orkney, Scotland U.K.
97 J9 Kirkwood DE U.S.A.
118 D5 Kirkwood DE U.S.A.
118 C5 Kirkwood DE U.S.A.
29 M2 Kirk Yetholm Scottish Borders, Scotland U.K.
Kirman Iran see Kermān
71 T Kırmır r. Turkey
191 A6 Kırmızıköprü Turkey
52 C2 Kirn Ger.
Kirobasi Turkey see Mağara
19 R7 Kirov Kaluzhskaya Oblast' Rus. Fed.
14 J4 Kirov Kirovskaya Oblast' Rus. Fed.
Kirovabad Azer. see Gäncä
Kirovabad Tajik. see Panj
Kirovakan Armenia see Vanadzor
17 M5 Kirove Donets'ka Oblast' Ukr.
17 O6 Kirove Zaporiz'ka Oblast' Ukr.
182 E2 Kirovo Kazakh.
Kirovo Donets'ka Oblast' Ukr. see Kirovohrad
Kirov Oblast admin. div. Rus. Fed. see Kirovskaya Oblast'
14 J4 Kirovo-Chepetsk Rus. Fed.
Kirovo-Chepetsk Rus. Fed. see Kirovo-Chepetsk
Kirovograd Ukr. see Kirovohrad
Kirovogradskaya Oblast' admin. div. Ukr. see Kirovohrad Oblast
17 L5 Kirovohrad Ukr.
Kirovohrad Oblast admin. div. Ukr. see Kirovohrads'ka Oblast'
16 L5 Kirovohrads'ka Oblast' admin. div. Ukr.
191 J7 Kirovsk Azer.
19 N2 Kirovsk Leningradskaya Oblast' Rus. Fed.
14 J11 Kirovsk Murmanskaya Oblast' Rus. Fed.
Kirovsk Ukr. see Kirovohrad
17 Q4 Kirovs'ke Donets'ka Oblast' Ukr.
17 T7 Kirovs'ke Luhans'ka Oblast' Ukr.
Kirovskaya Oblast' admin. div. Rus. Fed.
17 N5 Kirovs'ke Dnipropetrovs'ka Oblast' Ukr.

Column 3

17 R5 Kirovs'ke Donets'ka Oblast' Ukr.
17 M8 Kirovs'ke Respublika Krym Ukr.
17 O8 Kirovs'ke Respublika Krym Ukr.
182 C5 Kirovskiy Astrakhanskaya Oblast' Rus. Fed.
17 P2 Kirovskiy Kurskaya Oblast' Rus. Fed.
162 H6 Kirovskiy Primorskiy Kray Rus. Fed.
Kirovskoye Kyrg. see Kyzyl-Adyr
Kirovskoye Dnipropetrovs'ka Oblast' Ukr. see Kirovs'ke
Kirovskoye Donets'ka Oblast' Ukr. see Kirovs'ke
Kirovskoye Respublika Krym Ukr. see Kirovs'ke
17 R8 Kirpili r. Rus. Fed.
184 G2 Kirpili Turkm.
17 S8 Kirpil'skaya Rus. Fed.
17 R8 Kirpil'skiy Liman marsh Rus. Fed.
26 J9 Kirriemuir Angus, Scotland U.K.
14 K4 Kirs Rus. Fed.
15 H5 Kirsanov Rus. Fed.
182 E2 Kirsanovo Kazakh.
52 C2 Kirschweiler Ger.
188 G4 Kirşehir Turkey
55 L1 Kirsna r. Lith.
185 I5 Kirtachi Niger
185 L9 Kirthar National Park Pak.
185 L8 Kirthar Range mts Pak.
31 J4 Kirtlington Oxfordshire, England U.K.
31 L2 Kirton Lincolnshire, England U.K.
31 J3 Kirton Suffolk, England U.K.
29 P7 Kirton in Lindsey North Lincolnshire, England U.K.
49 H9 Kirtorf Ger.
191 D3 Kirts'khi Georgia
20 P3 Kiruna Sweden
93 A5 Kirundo Burundi
90 E5 Kirundu Dem. Rep. Congo
212 X2 Kirwan Escarpment Antarctica
15 I5 Kirya Rus. Fed.
167 J3 Kiryū Japan
19 V5 Kirzhach Rus. Fed.
164 O7 Kisakata Japan
93 C6 Kisaki Tanz.
90 C4 Kisangani Dem. Rep. Congo
93 C6 Kisangire Tanz.
91 C6 Kisantete Dem. Rep. Congo
57 L3 Kisar Hungary
155 E8 Kisar i. Maluku Indon.
156 C3 Kisaran Sumatera Indon.
93 C6 Kisarawe Tanz.
167 K5 Kisarazu Japan
190 G1 Kisas Turkey
56 C2 Kis-Balaton park Hungary
166 D7 Kisbér Hungary
160 E1 Kiselëvsk Rus. Fed.
68 G4 Kiseljak Bos.-Herz.
19 P1 Kisel'nya Rus. Fed.
162 K3 Kisel'ovka Rus. Fed.
57 J3 Kiser Hungary
179 K6 Kishanganj Bihar India
178 C6 Kishangarh Madh. Prad. India
178 D6 Kishangarh Rajasthan India
178 E6 Kishangarh Rajasthan India
178 D2 Kishen Ganga r. India/Pak.
89 F4 Kishi Nigeria
166 B7 Kishi-gawa r. Japan
166 B7 Kishi-gawa r. Japan
183 N1 Kishi-Karoy, Ozero salt l. Kazakh.
164 □116 Kishika-zaki pt Japan
Kishinev Moldova see Chişinău
26 I11 Kishorn, Loch inlet Scotland U.K.
183 O1 Kishkenekol' Kazakh.
179 M7 Kishoreganj Bangl.
26 E8 Kishorn, Loch inlet Scotland U.K.
178 E3 Kishtwar Jammu and Kashmir
93 A6 Kisi Tanz.
93 H2 Kisielice Pol.
55 K2 Kisielnica Pol.
93 A3 Kisigo r. Tanz.
93 C6 Kisiju Tanz.
191 E5 Kısır Dağı mt. Turkey
104 A4 Kiska Island AK U.S.A.
107 L4 Kiskittogisu Lake Man. Can.
107 L4 Kiskitto Lake Man. Can.
21 Q6 Kisko Fin.
57 J4 Kiskörei-Víztároló resr Hungary
57 I5 Kiskőrös Hungary
57 I4 Kiskunfélegyháza Hungary
57 I5 Kiskunhalas Hungary
57 I4 Kiskunlacháza Hungary
57 I5 Kiskunmajsa Hungary
57 I5 Kiskunság reg. Hungary
57 I5 Kiskunság nat. park Hungary
57 I5 Kislang Hungary
57 K4 Kisléta Hungary
191 D2 Kislovodsk Rus. Fed.
183 L2 Kislyakovskaya Rus. Fed.
92 E5 Kismaayo Somalia
57 K4 Kismarja Hungary
92 E5 Kismayu Somalia see Kismaayo
166 D4 Kiso Japan
166 D5 Kisofukushima Japan
166 E5 Kiso-gawa r. Japan
166 D5 Kiso-gawa r. Japan
93 A5 Kisoro Uganda
166 D5 Kisosaki Japan
166 D5 Kiso-sanmyaku mts Japan
93 B6 Kisosi Burundi
91 F5 Kisovec Slovenia
106 E4 Kispiox B.C. Can.
106 E4 Kispiox r. B.C. Can.
78 E7 Kissamos, Kolpos b. Kriti Greece
Kisserainig Island Myanmar see Kanmaw Kyun
88 C4 Kissidougou Guinea
115 G11 Kissimmee FL U.S.A.
115 G12 Kissimmee r. FL U.S.A.
115 G12 Kissimmee, Lake FL U.S.A.
52 H5 Kissing Ger.
115 G11 Kissing Lake Man. Can.
52 H6 Kißlegg Ger.
84 E4 Kissu, Jebel mt. Sudan
57 I5 Kisszállás Hungary
68 E4 Kistanje Croatia
52 H2 Kistel Ger.
57 K3 Kistelek Hungary
107 M4 Kistigan Lake Man. Can.
Kistna r. India see Krishna
189 J5 Kistrang Turkey
191 A1 Kistrich Turkey
79 O5 Kisújszállás Hungary
191 H2 Kisüri'yurt Turkey
57 K3 Kisvárda Hungary
92 B3 Kiswah Kenya
57 H5 Kiszkowo Pol.
57 J4 Kiszombor Hungary
57 I3 Kit r. Hungary
191 F2 Kıt' Georgia
78 B3 Kita Hungary
166 C5 Kita Kyōto Japan
161 N6 Kita-Daitō-jima i. Japan
166 E5 Kitagawa Japan

Column 4

165 I14 Kitagawa Japan
164 Q4 Kitahiyama Japan
167 M2 Kitaibaraki Japan
165 □² Kita-Iō-jima vol. Kazan-rettō Japan
166 A7 Kitajima Japan
164 S7 Kitakami Japan
164 S7 Kitakami-gawa r. Japan
164 Q9 Kitakata Fukushima Japan
165 H13 Kitakata Miyazaki Japan
165 H13 Kita-Kyūshū Japan
92 B4 Kitale Kenya
164 U3 Kitami Japan
167 H3 Kitami-sanchi mts Japan
164 T2 Kitamoto Japan
165 □3 Kitanda Dem. Rep. Congo
166 □1 Kitano-hana c. Iō-jima Japan
167 M3 Kitachibana Japan
165 I14 Kitaura Ibaraki Japan
167 M4 Kita-ura l. Japan
165 K8 Kitayama Japan
166 C8 Kitayama Japan
166 B4 Kitayama-gawa r. Japan
120 D6 Kit Carson CO U.S.A.
105 D5 Kitchener Ont. Can.
108 E3 Kitchigama r. Que. Can.
91 E6 Kiteba Dem. Rep. Congo
20 U5 Kitee Fin.
92 D5 Kitendwe Dem. Rep. Congo
92 B4 Kithira i. Greece see Kythira
Kithnos i. Greece see Kythnos
Kithnou, Stenón sea chan. Greece see Kythnou, Steno
Kiti, Cape Cyprus see Kition, Akra
106 D4 Kitimat B.C. Can.
20 S3 Kitinen r. Fin.
190 B4 Kition, Akra c. Cyprus see Kitiou, Akra
Kitiou, Akra c. Cyprus see Kition, Cape
106 D4 Kitkatla B.C. Can.
106 E4 Kitlope Heritage Conservancy Provincial Park B.C. Can.
183 I4 Kitob Uzbek.
19 Y5 Kitovo Rus. Fed.
78 F6 Kitriani i. Greece
23 V2 Kitsa Rus. Fed.
106 D4 Kitsault B.C. Can.
183 K2 Kitsoty Alta Can.
20 N5 Kitsman' Ukr.
59 J7 Kitsee Austria
212 J2 Kittatinny Mountains hills NJ U.S.A.
117 □O5 Kittery ME U.S.A.
22 H4 Kittilä Fin.
Kittittyoa-yama hill Japan
59 P3 Kittsee Austria
53 I2 Kitzbühel Austria
51 G8 Kitzeck im Sausal Austria
58 G5 Kitzsteinhorn mt. Austria
50 I3 Kitzingen Ger.
131 □¹ Kiubo, Chutes de waterfall Dem. Rep. Congo
131 □¹⁰ Kitui Kenya
96 D7 Kitumbeine vol. Tanz.
51 H7 Kitumbini Tanz.
59 H6 Kitunda Tanz.
54 E2 Kitwanga B.C. Can.
118 E3 Kitwe Zambia
106 B2 Kitzbühel Austria
106 A2 Kitzbüheler Alpen mts Austria
106 B2 Kitzbüheler Horn mt. Austria
106 B2 Kitzeck im Sausal Austria
53 I2 Kiucze Pol.
20 S3 Kiukainen Fin.
190 B4 Kiuruvesi Fin.

Column 5

173 D9 Kizyl Jilga Aksai Chin
164 R2 Kizyl-Su Turkm.
22 F5 Kjellerup Denmark
21 K6 Kjerringøy Norway
20 M3 Kjerringøy Norway
20 S1 Kjøllefjord Norway
96 G9 Kjøpsvik Norway
44 F5 Klaarstroom S. Africa
56 C2 Klaaswaal Neth.
53 J1 Klabava r. Czech Rep.
92 B4 Kláden Slovakia
68 G3 Kláden Ger.
80 E5 Kládanj Bos.-Herz.
56 D1 Kladno Czech Rep.
77 K6 Kladovo Srbija Serb. and Mont.
Kladruby Czech Rep.
157 L2 Klagan Sabah Malaysia
59 J6 Klagenfurt Austria
71 Q2 Klagenfurt airport Austria
125 W6 Klagetoh AZ U.S.A.
18 E6 Klaipēda Lith.
55 I6 Klaj Pol.
57 H3 Kļak mt. Slovakia
57 I2 Kļak mt. Slovakia
Klaksvig Faroe Is see Klaksvik
22 J5 Klaksvik Faroe Is
122 B6 Klamath CA U.S.A.
122 B6 Klamath r. CA U.S.A.
122 C6 Klamath Falls OR U.S.A.
122 C6 Klamath Mountains CA U.S.A.
23 N2 Klämmingen l. Sweden
71 Q5 Klana Croatia
156 D3 Klang Malaysia
54 E1 Klanino Pol.
59 M7 Klanjec Croatia
48 G1 Klanxbüll Ger.
106 D3 Klappan r. B.C. Can.
22 J2 Klarälven r. Sweden
20 N5 Klärke Sweden
59 H6 Klasdowa Lubuskie Pol.
54 G3 Kłodawa Wielkopolskie Pol.
54 E5 Kłodzko Pol.
22 H1 Kløfta Norway
55 H5 Kłomnice Pol.
106 C3 Klondike Gold Rush National Historical Park nat. park AK U.S.A.
51 H6 Klonowa Pol.
18 H2 Klooga Estonia
44 F6 Kloosterhaar Neth.
57 J3 Kloptani mt. Norway
76 I9 Klos Albania
59 N8 Klötar Ivanić Croatia
56 C6 Kloštar Podravski Croatia
58 B5 Klosterfelde Ger.
53 J5 Klosterhäseler Ger.
51 D7 Klosterlechfeld Ger.
59 N3 Klosterneuburg Austria
70 H2 Klosters Switz.
51 J8 Klosterwasser r. Ger.
52 F7 Kloster Zinna Ger.
53 O3 Kloten Switz.
49 D10 Klotten Ger.
58 D5 Klötze (Altmark) Ger.
106 B2 Kluane r. Y.T. Can.
106 A2 Kluane Game Sanctuary nature res. Y.T. Can.
106 B2 Kluane National Park Y.T. Can.
156 D5 Kluang Malaysia see Keluang
157 I6 Kluang, Tanjung pt Indon.
55 H5 Kluczbork Pol.
55 H5 Kluczewsko Pol.
55 I4 Kluki Pol.
55 K3 Klukowo Pol.
157 E4 Klukwan AK U.S.A.
191 C4 Klukpmarg, Tepük b. Indon.
44 G5 Klundert Neth.
157 K9 Klungkung Bali Indon.
185 M9 Klupro Pak.
48 D5 Kluse Ger.
52 K2 Kłusy Pol.
50 D3 Klütz Ger.
49 L6 Klwów Pol.
18 L6 Klyastsitsy Belarus
15 L5 Klyavlino r. Belarus
18 J8 Klyaz'ma r. Rus. Fed.
162 I3 Klyetsk Belarus
17 O4 Klymivka Ukr.
167 H1 Klyshky Ukr.
17 M2 Klyshky Ukr.
93 R1 Klyuchevskaya, Sopka vol. Rus. Fed.
Klyuchi Altayskiy Kray Rus. Fed.
162 E4 Klyuchi Amurskaya Oblast' Rus. Fed.
193 R4 Klyuchi Kamchatskaya Oblast' Rus. Fed.
200 □6 k'obulet'i Georgia
22 J3 Knaben Norway
97 K6 Knapdale S. Africa
203 C13 Knapdale South I. N.Z.
26 E11 Knapdale reg. Scotland U.K.
110 D5 Knapp Mound hill WI U.S.A.
29 O5 Knaresborough North Yorkshire, England U.K.
54 F1 Knäsänsk Sweden
23 K1 Knästen hill Sweden
31 L4 Knebworth Hertfordshire, England U.K.
107 M4 Knee Lake Man. Can.
107 J4 Knee Lake Sask. Can.
54 G3 Knesebeck Ger.
71 Q4 Kneža Slovenia
71 Q4 Knežak Slovenia
59 N7 Kneževi Vinogradi Croatia
59 H6 Kneževo Croatia
56 F2 Knežmost Czech Rep.
77 K9 Knič Srbija Serb. and Mont.
120 E2 Knife r. ND U.S.A.
110 C3 Knife River MN U.S.A.
30 H3 Knighton Powys, Wales U.K.
31 J4 Knight Inlet B.C. Can.
191 D6 Knik Knightley Landing Chin
59 P6 Knin Croatia
23 N5 Knislinge Sweden
52 E6 Knittelfeld Austria
52 F3 Knittlingen Ger.
56 D3 Knížeci stolec mt. Czech Rep.
77 K7 Knjaževac Srbija Serb. and Mont.
209 C10 Knobby Head W.A. Austr.
208 J3 Knob Peak hill W.A. Austr.
27 D7 Knock Clare Rep. of Ireland
26 E10 Knock Argyll and Bute, Scotland U.K.
27 D8 Knockacuppen hill Rep. of Ireland
27 E7 Knockadoon Head Rep. of Ireland
27 E4 Knockalongy hill Rep. of Ireland
27 G9 Knockalough Rep. of Ireland
28 E5 Knockananny Rep. of Ireland
27 D8 Knockandhu Moray, Scotland U.K.

Column 6

57 I2 Klin Slovakia
76 I8 Klina Kosovo, Srbija Serb. and Mont.
106 C5 Klinaklini r. B.C. Can.
154 E9 Kling Mindanao Phil.
51 I9 Klingelbach Ger.
52 G2 Klingenberg am Main Ger.
51 F10 Klingenthal Ger.
118 B3 Klingerstown PA U.S.A.
157 I4 Klingkang, Banjaran mts Indon./Malaysia
50 G4 Klink Ger.
56 C1 Klinovec mt. Czech Rep.
19 T5 Klinsko-Dmitrovskaya Gryada ridge Rus. Fed.
23 O4 Klintehamn Gotland Sweden
182 C2 Klintsovka Rus. Fed.
19 P9 Klintsy Rus. Fed.
97 N3 Klip r. S. Africa
90 D10 Klipdale S. Africa
48 H1 Klipfontein S. Africa
22 J5 Klipiev Denmark
96 C6 Klippan Sweden
97 O1 Klipskool S. Africa
68 F4 Klis Croatia
19 V7 Klishino Moskovskaya Oblast' Rus. Fed.
122 B3 Klisura Srbija Serb. and Mont.
77 K8 Klisura Srbija Serb. and Mont.
22 E4 Klitmøller Denmark
51 K8 Klixbüll Ger.
48 G1 Klixbüll Ger.
52 I6 Ključ Bos.-Herz.
68 F3 Klobouky Czech Rep.
54 G5 Kłobuck Pol.
59 H6 Kłóbia Pol.
55 J4 Kłoczew Pol.
54 G5 Klodawa Lubuskie Pol.
54 E5 Kłodawa Wielkopolskie Pol.
22 H1 Kłodzko Pol.
55 H5 Kłomnice Pol.
106 C3 Klondike Gold Rush National Historical Park nat. park AK U.S.A.
18 H2 Klooga Estonia
44 F6 Kloosterhaar Neth.
57 J3 Kloptani mt. Norway
76 I9 Klos Albania
59 N8 Klötar Ivanić Croatia
56 C6 Kloštar Podravski Croatia
58 B5 Klosterfelde Ger.
53 J5 Klosterhäseler Ger.
51 D7 Klosterlechfeld Ger.
59 N3 Klosterneuburg Austria
70 H2 Klosters Switz.
51 J8 Klosterwasser r. Ger.
52 F7 Kloster Zinna Ger.
53 O3 Kloten Switz.
49 D10 Klotten Ger.
58 D5 Klötze (Altmark) Ger.
106 B2 Kluane r. Y.T. Can.
106 A2 Kluane Game Sanctuary nature res. Y.T. Can.
106 B2 Kluane National Park Y.T. Can.
156 D5 Kluang Malaysia see Keluang
157 I6 Kluang, Tanjung pt Indon.
55 H5 Kluczbork Pol.
55 H5 Kluczewsko Pol.
55 I4 Kluki Pol.
55 K3 Klukowo Pol.
157 E4 Klukwan AK U.S.A.
191 C4 Klukpmarg, Tepük b. Indon.
44 G5 Klundert Neth.
157 K9 Klungkung Bali Indon.
185 M9 Klupro Pak.
48 D5 Kluse Ger.
52 K2 Kłusy Pol.
50 D3 Klütz Ger.
49 L6 Klwów Pol.
18 L6 Klyastsitsy Belarus
15 L5 Klyavlino r. Belarus
18 J8 Klyaz'ma r. Rus. Fed.
162 I3 Klyetsk Belarus
17 O4 Klymivka Ukr.
167 H1 Klyshky Ukr.
17 M2 Klyshky Ukr.
93 R1 Klyuchevskaya, Sopka vol. Rus. Fed.
Klyuchi Altayskiy Kray Rus. Fed.
162 E4 Klyuchi Amurskaya Oblast' Rus. Fed.
193 R4 Klyuchi Kamchatskaya Oblast' Rus. Fed.
200 □6 k'obulet'i Georgia
22 J3 Knaben Norway
97 K6 Knapdale S. Africa
203 C13 Knapdale South I. N.Z.
26 E11 Knapdale reg. Scotland U.K.
110 D5 Knapp Mound hill WI U.S.A.
29 O5 Knaresborough North Yorkshire, England U.K.
54 F1 Knäsänsk Sweden
23 K1 Knästen hill Sweden
31 L4 Knebworth Hertfordshire, England U.K.
107 M4 Knee Lake Man. Can.
107 J4 Knee Lake Sask. Can.
54 G3 Knesebeck Ger.
71 Q4 Kneža Slovenia
71 Q4 Knežak Slovenia
59 N7 Kneževi Vinogradi Croatia
59 H6 Kneževo Croatia
56 F2 Knežmost Czech Rep.
77 K9 Knič Srbija Serb. and Mont.
120 E2 Knife r. ND U.S.A.
110 C3 Knife River MN U.S.A.
30 H3 Knighton Powys, Wales U.K.
31 J4 Knight Inlet B.C. Can.
59 P6 Knin Croatia
23 N5 Knislinge Sweden
52 E6 Knittelfeld Austria
52 F3 Knittlingen Ger.
56 D3 Knížecí stolec mt. Czech Rep.
77 K7 Knjaževac Srbija Serb. and Mont.
209 C10 Knobby Head W.A. Austr.
208 J3 Knob Peak hill W.A. Austr.
27 D7 Knock Clare Rep. of Ireland
26 E10 Knock Argyll and Bute, Scotland U.K.
27 D8 Knockacuppen hill Rep. of Ireland
27 E7 Knockadoon Head Rep. of Ireland
27 E4 Knockalongy hill Rep. of Ireland
27 G9 Knockalough Rep. of Ireland
28 E5 Knockananny Rep. of Ireland
27 D8 Knockandhu Moray, Scotland U.K.

Column 7

27 D8 Knockanefune hill Rep. of Ireland
26 G7 Knockban Highland, Scotland U.K.
27 J7 Knockbrandon Rep. of Ireland
27 J7 Knockbridge Rep. of Ireland
27 G7 Knockbrit Rep. of Ireland
27 F5 Knockcroghery Rep. of Ireland
26 K7 Knock Hill Scotland U.K.
27 J2 Knock International airport Rep. of Ireland
19 T5 Knocklayd hill Northern Ireland U.K.
27 F8 Knocklong Rep. of Ireland
27 F8 Knockmealdown Mountains hills Rep. of Ireland
27 D4 Knockmore Rep. of Ireland
27 F6 Knockmoyle Rep. of Ireland
28 E3 Knocknaboul Rep. of Ireland
27 F8 Knocknacarry Northern Ireland U.K.
27 F8 Knocknagree Rep. of Ireland
27 F8 Knocknaskagh hill Rep. of Ireland
27 F9 Knockraha Rep. of Ireland
27 E9 Knocks Rep. of Ireland
45 D6 Knokke-Heist Belgium
50 H3 Knorrendorf Ger.
78 G7 Knosos tourist site Greece
Knossós tourist site Greece see Knosos
29 O6 Knottingley West Yorkshire, England U.K.
31 I3 Knowle West Midlands, England U.K.
212 T2 Knowles, Cape Antarctica
117 □Q2 Knowles Corner ME U.S.A.
117 M3 Knowlton Que. Can.
114 D5 Knox IN U.S.A.
116 F7 Knox PA U.S.A.
106 C4 Knox, Cape B.C. Can.
110 B9 Knox City MO U.S.A.
213 G2 Knox Coast Antarctica
115 F9 Knoxville GA U.S.A.
120 I5 Knoxville IA U.S.A.
115 F8 Knoxville TN U.S.A.
26 E8 Knoydart mts Scotland U.K.
30 F3 Knucklas Powys, Wales U.K.
105 L2 Knud Rasmussen Land reg. Greenland
49 H9 Knüllgebirge hills Ger.
49 H8 Knüllwald-Remsfeld Ger.
54 G5 Knurów Pol.
29 M7 Knutsford Cheshire, England U.K.
14 I5 Knyaginino Rus. Fed.
18 K7 Knyahinin Belarus
162 I4 Knyaze-Bolkonskaye Rus. Fed.
17 M6 Knyaze-Hryhorivka Ukr.
18 L5 Knyazevo Rus. Fed.
55 M5 Knyazhe Ukr.
19 T4 Knyazhikha Rus. Fed.
19 U3 Knyazhiy Pogost Rus. Fed.
55 K2 Knyazhpy Belarus
96 H10 Knysna S. Africa
55 K2 Knyszyn Pol.
162 J5 Ko, Gora mt. Rus. Fed.
90 F2 Koabli, Jebel mt. Sudan
203 I8 Koamaru, Cape South I. N.Z.
93 C6 Koani Tanz.
Koartac Que. Can. see Quaqtaq
96 D5 Koa Valley watercourse S. Africa
156 G6 Koba Indon.
191 A4 Kobadian Belarus
165 H15 Kobarid Slovenia
20 T2 Kobbfoss Norway
155 E3 Kobe Halmahera Indon.
166 C8 Kōbe Japan
17 N4 Kobelyaky Ukr.
22 I6 Kobenhavn Denmark
22 I6 København mun. Denmark
58 K5 Kobenni Maur.
58 K5 Kobeřice Czech Rep.
96 D5 Kobern-Koblenz Ger.
Kobi Indon.
55 H4 Kobiele Wielkie Pol.
54 G5 Kobierzyce Pol.
164 □A21 Kōbi-sho i. Nansei-shotō Japan
90 C2 Koblentz Ger.
49 E10 Koblenz Ger.
49 D10 Koblenz admin. div. Ger.
17 K7 Kobleve Ukr.
92 C1 K'obo Eth.
179 O6 Kobo Assam India
92 A4 Koboko Uganda
162 H2 Kobold Rus. Fed.
20 R4 Kobozha r. Rus. Fed.
14 F4 Kobra r. Rus. Fed.
53 H8 Kobrino Rus. Fed.
28 F7 Kobroör i. Indon.
162 H3 Kobrynevskoye Rus. Fed.
58 K5 Kobryn Belarus see Kobryn
50 C5 Kobrów i. Skyros Greece
54 K4 Kobryn Pol.
53 K6 Kobuchi-zawa Japan
53 K6 Kobuk Valley National Park AK U.S.A.
191 C4 K'obulet'i Georgia
167 I4 Kobushiga-take mt. Japan
191 N3 Koburo Japan

Column 8

27 D8 Knockanefune hill Rep. of Ireland
26 G7 Knockban Highland, Scotland U.K.
27 J7 Knockbrandon Rep. of Ireland
27 J7 Knockbridge Rep. of Ireland
27 G7 Knockbrit Rep. of Ireland
27 F5 Knockcroghery Rep. of Ireland
26 K7 Knock Hill Scotland U.K.
27 J2 Knock International airport Rep. of Ireland
19 T5 Knocklayd hill Northern Ireland U.K.
27 F8 Knocklong Rep. of Ireland
27 F8 Knockmealdown Mountains hills Rep. of Ireland
27 D4 Knockmore Rep. of Ireland
27 F6 Knockmoyle Rep. of Ireland
28 E3 Knocknaboul Rep. of Ireland
27 F8 Knocknacarry Northern Ireland U.K.
27 F8 Knocknagree Rep. of Ireland
27 F8 Knocknaskagh hill Rep. of Ireland
27 F9 Knockraha Rep. of Ireland
27 E9 Knocks Rep. of Ireland
45 D6 Knokke-Heist Belgium
50 H3 Knorrendorf Ger.
78 G7 Knosos tourist site Greece
Knossós tourist site Greece see Knosos
29 O6 Knottingley West Yorkshire, England U.K.
31 I3 Knowle West Midlands, England U.K.
212 T2 Knowles, Cape Antarctica
117 □Q2 Knowles Corner ME U.S.A.
117 M3 Knowlton Que. Can.
114 D5 Knox IN U.S.A.
116 F7 Knox PA U.S.A.
106 C4 Knox, Cape B.C. Can.
110 B9 Knox City MO U.S.A.
213 G2 Knox Coast Antarctica
115 F9 Knoxville GA U.S.A.
120 I5 Knoxville IA U.S.A.
115 F8 Knoxville TN U.S.A.
26 E8 Knoydart mts Scotland U.K.
30 F3 Knucklas Powys, Wales U.K.
105 L2 Knud Rasmussen Land reg. Greenland
49 H9 Knüllgebirge hills Ger.
49 H8 Knüllwald-Remsfeld Ger.
54 G5 Knurów Pol.
29 M7 Knutsford Cheshire, England U.K.
14 I5 Knyaginino Rus. Fed.
18 K7 Knyahinin Belarus
162 I4 Knyaze-Bolkonskaye Rus. Fed.
17 M6 Knyaze-Hryhorivka Ukr.
18 L5 Knyazevo Rus. Fed.
55 M5 Knyazhe Ukr.
19 T4 Knyazhikha Rus. Fed.
19 U3 Knyazhiy Pogost Rus. Fed.
55 K2 Knyazhpy Belarus
96 H10 Knysna S. Africa
55 K2 Knyszyn Pol.
162 J5 Ko, Gora mt. Rus. Fed.
90 F2 Koabli, Jebel mt. Sudan
203 I8 Koamaru, Cape South I. N.Z.
93 C6 Koani Tanz.
Koartac Que. Can. see Quaqtaq
96 D5 Koa Valley watercourse S. Africa
156 G6 Koba Indon.
191 A4 Kobadian Belarus
165 H15 Kobarid Slovenia
20 T2 Kobbfoss Norway
155 E3 Kobe Halmahera Indon.
166 C8 Kōbe Japan
17 N4 Kobelyaky Ukr.
22 I6 København Denmark
22 I6 København mun. Denmark
58 K5 Kobenni Maur.
58 K5 Kobeřice Czech Rep.
96 D5 Kobern-Koblenz Ger.
17 N4 Kobi Indon.
55 H4 Kobiele Wielkie Pol.
54 G5 Kobierzyce Pol.
164 □A21 Kōbi-sho i. Nansei-shotō Japan
90 C2 Koblentz Ger.
49 E10 Koblenz Ger.
49 D10 Koblenz admin. div. Ger.
17 K7 Kobleve Ukr.
92 C1 K'obo Eth.
179 O6 Kobo Assam India
92 A4 Koboko Uganda
162 H2 Kobold Rus. Fed.
20 R4 Kobozha r. Rus. Fed.
14 F4 Kobra r. Rus. Fed.
53 H8 Kobrino Rus. Fed.
28 F7 Kobroör i. Indon.
162 H3 Kobrynevskoye Rus. Fed.
Kobrin Belarus see Kobryn
50 C5 Kobrów i. Skyros Greece
54 K4 Kobryn Pol.
53 K6 Kobuchi-zawa Japan
53 K6 Kobuk Valley National Park AK U.S.A.
191 C4 K'obulet'i Georgia
167 I4 Kobushiga-take mt. Japan
191 N3 Koburo Japan
190 F1 Köçke Turkey

Koshmanivka to **Ksar el Hinare**

287

17 N4 **Koshmanivka** Ukr.
184 F1 **Koshoba** Turkm.
167 H2 **Kōshoku** Japan
Koshtëbë Kyrg. *see* **Kosh-Döbö**
178 F6 **Kosi** *Uttar Prad.* India
178 G5 **Kosi** *r.* India
97 Q2 **Kosi Bay** S. Africa
97 Q3 **Kosi Bay Nature Reserve** S. Africa
57 K3 **Košice** Slovakia
57 K3 **Košický Kraj** *admin. reg.* Slovakia
176 E5 **Kosigi** *Andhra Prad.* India
179 K6 **Kosi Reservoir** Nepal
182 G2 **Kos-Istek** Kazakh.
16 E5 **Kosiv** Ukr.
17 M5 **Kosivka** Ukr.
76 H7 **Kosjerić** *Srbija* Serb. and Mont.
79 J5 **Köşk** Turkey
21 Q6 **Koski** *Länsi-Suomi* Fin.
19 Q7 **Koski** Rus. Fed.
183 L3 **Koskol'** Kazakh.
57 K2 **Koškovce** Slovakia
19 Q1 **Kos'kovo** Rus. Fed.
183 Q5 **Koskuduk** Kazakh.
20 P3 **Koskullskulle** Sweden
14 J3 **Koslan** Rus. Fed.
Köslin Pol. *see* **Koszalin**
14 J2 **Kosma** *r.* Rus. Fed.
51 K10 **Kosmonosy** Czech Rep.
19 X4 **Kosmynino** Rus. Fed.
68 G3 **Košnica** *r.* Croatia
54 F2 **Kosobudy** Pol.
182 K8 **Koson** Uzbek.
163 F8 **Kosŏng** *Hamgyŏng-namdo* N. Korea
163 F9 **Kosŏng** *Kangwŏn-do* N. Korea
183 N7 **Kosonsoy** Uzbek.
17 P1 **Kosorzha** Rus. Fed.
Kosova *prov.* Serb. and Mont. *see* **Kosovo**
76 I8 **Kosovo** *prov.* Serb. and Mont.
Kosovo-Metohija *prov.* Serb. and Mont. *see* **Kosovo**
76 J8 **Kosovo Polje** *Kosovo, Srbija* Serb. and Mont.
76 I8 **Kosovo Polje** *plain* Serb. and Mont.
77 J8 **Kosovska Kamenica** *Kosovo, Srbija* Serb. and Mont.
76 I8 **Kosovska Mitrovica** *Kosovo, Srbija* Serb. and Mont.
55 K3 **Kosów Lacki** Pol.
216 F5 **Kosrae** *atoll* Micronesia
173 C8 **Kosrap** *Xinjiang* China
190 D1 **Kösreli** Turkey
88 D3 **Kossa** *well* Maur.
89 I3 **Kossatori** *well* Niger
51 H8 **Koßdorf** Ger.
53 L2 **Kösseine** *hill* Ger.
58 F4 **Kössen** Austria
53 O5 **Kößlar** *r.* Ger.
154 □ **Kossol Passage** Palau
154 □ **Kossol Reef** Palau
88 D5 **Kossou, Lac de** *l.* Côte d'Ivoire
Kosta-Khetagurovo Rus. Fed. *see* **Nazran'**
182 J1 **Kostanay** Kazakh.
182 J1 **Kostanayskaya Oblast'** *admin. div.* Kazakh.
59 L8 **Kostanjevica** *Krško* Slovenia
59 I8 **Kostanjevica** *Nova Gorica* Slovenia
71 R4 **Kostel** Slovenia
56 D2 **Kostelec nad Černými Lesy** Czech Rep.
51 K10 **Kostelec nad Labem** Czech Rep.
56 F1 **Kostelec nad Orlicí** Czech Rep.
77 L8 **Kostenets** Bulg.
97 K1 **Koster** S. Africa
19 W6 **Kosterevo** Rus. Fed.
22 H3 **Kosteroarna naturreservat** *nature res.* Sweden
85 G6 **Kosti** Sudan
59 O2 **Kostice** Czech Rep.
77 L8 **Kostinbrod** Bulg.
192 J3 **Kostino** Rus. Fed.
17 L1 **Kostobobriv** Ukr.
76 J6 **Kostolac** *Srbija* Serb. and Mont.
54 E4 **Kostomłoty** Pol.
20 U4 **Kostomuksha** Rus. Fed.
20 U4 **Kostomukshskiy Zapovednik** *nature res.* Rus. Fed.
16 F3 **Kostopil'** Ukr.
Kostopol' Ukr. *see* **Kostopil'**
19 X4 **Kostroma** Rus. Fed.
14 H4 **Kostroma** *r.* Rus. Fed.
Kostroma Oblast *admin. div.* Rus. Fed. *see* **Kostromskaya Oblast'**
14 H4 **Kostromskaya Oblast'** *admin. div.* Rus. Fed.
54 C3 **Kostrzyn** *Lubuskie* Pol.
54 F3 **Kostrzyn** *Wielkopolskie* Pol.
55 K3 **Kostrzyń** *r.* Pol.
17 Q5 **Kostyantynivka** *Donets'ka Oblast'* Ukr.
17 O4 **Kostyantynivka** *Kharkivs'ka Oblast'* Ukr.
17 M7 **Kostyantynivka** *Khersons'ka Oblast'* Ukr.
17 O7 **Kostyantynivka** *Zaporiz'ka Oblast'* Ukr.
19 Q7 **Kostyri** Rus. Fed.
Kostyukovichi Belarus *see* **Kastsyukovichy**
18 M4 **Kostyzhitsy** Rus. Fed.
89 F4 **Kosubosu** Nigeria
167 I4 **Kosuge** Japan
166 F2 **Kosugi** Japan
57 L3 **Kosyny** Ukr.
14 L2 **Kos'yu** Rus. Fed.
14 L2 **Kos'yu** *r.* Rus. Fed.
14 L2 **Kos'yuvom** Rus. Fed.
23 M7 **Koszalin** Pol.
54 G5 **Koszęcin** Pol.
56 F4 **Kőszeg** Hungary
56 F4 **Kőszegi** *park* Hungary
59 N5 **Kőszegi-hegység** *hill* Hungary
55 I5 **Koszyce** Pol.
176 G5 **Kota** *Andhra Prad.* India
178 I8 **Kota** *Chhattisgarh* India
178 E7 **Kota** *Rajasthan* India
166 F6 **Kōta** Japan
156 F7 **Kotaagung** *Sumatera* Indon.
Kota Baharu Malaysia *see* **Kota Bharu**
157 I5 **Kotabaru** *Kalimantan* Indon.
157 L6 **Kotabaru** *Kalimantan* Indon.
156 B3 **Kotabaru** *Sumatera* Indon.
157 L1 **Kota Belud** *Sabah* Malaysia
157 J6 **Kotabesi** *Kalimantan* Indon.
156 E1 **Kota Bharu** Malaysia
156 F7 **Kotabumi** *Sumatera* Indon.
155 D3 **Kotabunan** *Sulawesi* Indon.
185 N6 **Kot Addu** Pak.
157 L2 **Kota Kinabalu** *Sabah* Malaysia
20 T3 **Kotala** Fin.
155 D3 **Kotamobagu** *Sulawesi* Indon.
106 E2 **Kotaneelee Range** *mts* *N.W.T./Y.T.* Can.
183 Q4 **Kotanemel', Gora** *mt.* Kazakh.
176 H3 **Kotaparh** *Orissa* India
156 D4 **Kotapinang** *Sumatera* Indon.
178 H7 **Kotar** *Madh. Prad.* India
178 E7 **Kotari** *r.* India
157 I4 **Kota Samarahan** *Sarawak* Malaysia
156 D4 **Kotatengah** *Sumatera* Indon.
156 E4 **Kota Tinggi** Malaysia
157 I6 **Kotawaringin** *Kalimantan* Indon.
179 L8 **Kotchandpur** Bangl.
106 F3 **Kotcho** *r.* *B.C.* Can.
106 F3 **Kotcho Lake** *B.C.* Can.
185 M8 **Kot Diji** Pak.
178 G5 **Kotdwara** *Uttaranchal* India
178 B2 **Koteasro** Afgh.
57 K5 **Kötegyán** Hungary
77 O8 **Kotel** Bulg.
57 J4 **Kőtelek** Hungary
14 J4 **Kotel'nich** Rus. Fed.
15 H7 **Kotel'nikovo** Rus. Fed.
193 O2 **Kotel'nyy, Ostrov** *i.* *Novosibirskiye O-va* Rus. Fed.
50 I3 **Kotelow** Ger.
17 N3 **Kotel'va** Ukr.
202 L6 **Kotemaori** *North I.* N.Z.
185 O4 **Kotgala** Pak.
177 H3 **Kotgar** *Orissa* India
178 F4 **Kotgarh** *Hima. Prad.* India
Kothagudem *Andhra Prad.* India *see* **Kottagudem**
51 E7 **Köthen (Anhalt)** Ger.
178 H7 **Kothi** *Madh. Prad.* India
88 B3 **Kotiari Naoude** Senegal
92 B4 **Kotido** Uganda
162 I5 **Kotikovo** Rus. Fed.
185 M8 **Kot Imamgarh** Pak.
21 S6 **Kotka** Fin.
178 E4 **Kot Kapura** *Punjab* India
14 J2 **Kotkino** Rus. Fed.
54 E4 **Kotla** Pol.
14 I3 **Kotlas** Rus. Fed.
185 O5 **Kotli** Pak.
104 B3 **Kotlik** *AK* U.S.A.
54 F4 **Kotlin** Pol.
55 J5 **Kotlina Sandomierska** *basin* Pol.
19 R3 **Kotlovan** Rus. Fed.
20 □D2 **Kötlutangi** *pt* Iceland
18 L2 **Kotly** Rus. Fed.
166 D5 **Kotō** Japan
89 G4 **Koton-Karifi** Nigeria
164 R6 **Kotooka** Japan
76 G8 **Kotor** *Crna Gora* Serb. and Mont.
59 O7 **Kotoriba** Croatia
89 G3 **Kotorkoshi** Nigeria
19 W4 **Kotorosl'** *r.* Rus. Fed.
68 G3 **Kotorsko** Bos.-Herz.
68 F3 **Kotor Varoš** Bos.-Herz.
88 E4 **Kotouba** Côte d'Ivoire
17 N4 **Kotovka** Ukr.
15 I6 **Kotovo** Rus. Fed.
Kotovsk Moldova *see* **Hîncești**
15 H5 **Kotovsk** Rus. Fed.
16 I6 **Kotovs'k** Ukr.
178 F6 **Kot Putli** *Rajasthan* India
18 H8 **Kotra** *r.* Belarus
178 D7 **Kotra** *Rajasthan* India
185 L7 **Kotra** Pak.
176 G3 **Kotri** *r.* India
185 M9 **Kotri** Pak.
185 L9 **Kotri Allahrakhio Shah** Pak.
78 D6 **Kotronas** Greece
182 H3 **Kotrtas** Kazakh.
185 L10 **Kot Sarae** Pak.
58 H6 **Kötschach** Austria
176 G4 **Kottagudem** *Andhra Prad.* India
176 E8 **Kottayam** *Kerala* India
176 D7 **Kottayam** *Pondicherry* India
49 D10 **Kottenheim** Ger.
59 L3 **Kottes** Austria
59 J6 **Köttmannsdorf** Austria
90 D3 **Kotto** *r.* C.A.R.
176 E5 **Kotturu** *Karnataka* India
201 □2 **Kotu Group** *is* Tonga
55 K3 **Kotuń** Pol.
184 E2 **Koturdepe** Turkm.
193 L2 **Kotuy** *r.* Rus. Fed.
179 I8 **Kotwar Peak** *Chhattisgarh* India
53 I5 **Kötz** Ger.
104 B3 **Kotzebue** *AK* U.S.A.
104 B3 **Kotzebue Sound** *sea chan.* *AK* U.S.A.
96 B4 **Kotzehoop** S. Africa
96 B6 **Kotzesrus** S. Africa
53 N3 **Kötzting** Ger.
90 D3 **Kouango** C.A.R.
84 C6 **Kouba Olanga** Chad
88 C4 **Koubia** Guinea
109 H4 **Kouchibouguac National Park** *N.B.* Can.
46 A3 **Koudekerke** Neth.
88 E3 **Koudougou** Burkina
44 H3 **Koudum** Neth.
96 D8 **Kouebokkeveld** *mts* S. Africa
88 E4 **Kouéré** Burkina
96 H8 **Koueveldberge** *mts* S. Africa
78 D2 **Koufalia** Greece
89 I3 **Koufey** Niger
79 H8 **Koufonisi** *i.* *Kriti* Greece
79 G6 **Koufonisi** *i.* Greece
78 E3 **Koufos** Greece
96 I9 **Kouga** *r.* S. Africa
96 H9 **Kougaberge** *mts* S. Africa
90 B3 **Koui** C.A.R.
88 D5 **Kouibli** Côte d'Ivoire
91 A6 **Kouilou** *admin. reg.* Congo
88 D4 **Kouka** Burkina
90 C3 **Kouki** C.A.R.
90 D3 **Koukourou** C.A.R.
90 C3 **Koukourou** *r.* C.A.R.
90 C3 **Koukourou-Bamingui, Réserve de Faune du** *nature res.* C.A.R.
90 B5 **Koulamoutou** Gabon
84 D6 **Koulbo** Chad
Koulen Cambodia *see* **Kulen**
88 D3 **Koulikoro** Mali
88 D3 **Koulikoro** *admin. reg.* Mali
89 F3 **Koulou** Niger
84 B6 **Kouloudia** Chad
89 I4 **Koum** Cameroon
90 C3 **Kouma** *r.* C.A.R.
200 □5 **Koumac** New Caledonia
207 L6 **Koumala** *Qld* Austr.
90 A4 **Koumameyong** Gabon
90 D2 **Koumbala** C.A.R.
88 E4 **Koumbia** Burkina
88 B4 **Koumbia** Guinea
168 C5 **Koumenzi** *Xinjiang* China
167 H3 **Koumi** Japan
90 C2 **Koumra** Chad
88 B3 **Koundâra** Guinea
88 C3 **Koundian** Mali
88 D4 **Koundougou** Burkina
88 B3 **Koungheul** Senegal
99 □3b **Koungou** Mayotte
88 B3 **Kounkané** Senegal
79 H6 **Kounoupoi** *i.* Greece
183 P4 **Kounradskiy** *Karagandinskaya Oblast'* Kazakh.
Kounradskiy *Karagandinskaya Oblast'* Kazakh. *see* **Konyrat**
88 B4 **Kounsitél** Guinea
89 H3 **Kountchi** *well* Niger
121 H10 **Kountze** *TX* U.S.A.
96 F9 **Koup** S. Africa
88 E3 **Koupéla** Burkina
99 □3a **Kourani** *Njazidja* Comoros
90 B2 **Kourayadjé** Chad
89 I3 **Kouridinga** *well* Niger
164 □1 **Kouri-jima** *i.* *Okinawa* Japan
56 D2 **Kouřim** Czech Rep.
78 F7 **Kournas** *Kriti* Greece
137 H3 **Kourou** Fr. Guiana
78 G1 **Kourou** *r.* Greece
88 C2 **Koûroudjél** Maur.
88 C4 **Kouroussa** Guinea
88 B3 **Koussanar** Senegal
88 C3 **Koussané** Mali
89 I3 **Kousséri** Cameroon
89 F4 **Koussountou** Togo
88 D3 **Koutiala** Mali
53 N3 **Kout na Šumav** Czech Rep.
88 D4 **Kouto** Côte d'Ivoire
200 □5 **Koutouma** *i.* New Caledonia
78 D5 **Koutsopodi** Greece
202 M5 **Koutunui Head** *North I.* N.Z.
21 S6 **Kouvola** Fin.
90 C5 **Kouyou** *r.* Congo
76 I5 **Kovačica** *Vojvodina, Srbija* Serb. and Mont.
79 L5 **Kovada Gölü Milli Parkı** *nat. park* Turkey
57 H5 **Kővágószőlős** Hungary
16 J4 **Kovalivka** Ukr.
14 B2 **Kovallberget** Sweden
57 H3 **Kovarce** Slovakia
56 C1 **Kovářská** Czech Rep.
17 K2 **Kovchyn** Ukr.
20 U3 **Kovdor** Rus. Fed.
20 U3 **Kovdozero** Rus. Fed.
20 V3 **Kovdozero, Ozero** *l.* Rus. Fed.
16 D2 **Kovel'** Ukr.
14 H4 **Kovernino** Rus. Fed.
76 I5 **Kovilj** *Vojvodina, Srbija* Serb. and Mont.
176 E8 **Kovilpatti** *Tamil Nadu* India
76 I6 **Kovin** *Vojvodina, Srbija* Serb. and Mont.
Kovno Lith. *see* **Kaunas**
14 J2 **Kovriga, Gora** *hill* Rus. Fed.
19 Y5 **Kovrov** Rus. Fed.
17 S5 **Kovsuh** *r.* Ukr.
17 O4 **Kov''yahy** Ukr.
15 H5 **Kovylkino** Rus. Fed.
17 M8 **Kovyl'ne** Ukr.
19 U1 **Kovzha** *canal* Rus. Fed.
19 U1 **Kovzhskoye, Ozero** *l.* Rus. Fed.
55 H3 **Kowal** Pol.
54 G4 **Kowale** Pol.
55 K1 **Kowale Oleckie** Pol.
54 G4 **Kowale-Pańskie** Pol.
54 G2 **Kowalewo Pomorskie** Pol.
54 C3 **Kowalów** Pol.
157 M9 **Kowangge** *Sumbawa* Indon.
207 H3 **Kowanyama** *Qld* Austr.
207 H3 **Kowanyama Aboriginal Reserve** *Qld* Austr.
94 B3 **Kowares** *waterhole* Namibia
54 D5 **Kowary** Pol.
18 M8 **Kowbcha** Belarus
90 E5 **Kowe** Dem. Rep. Congo
203 F9 **Kowhitirangi** *South I.* N.Z.
55 I4 **Kowiesy** Pol.
184 E6 **Kowlī Kosh, Gardaneh-ye** *pass* Iran
171 □J7 **Kowloon** *H.K.* China
171 □ **Kowloon Peninsula** *H.K.* China
171 □J7 **Kowloon Peninsula** *pen.* *H.K.* China
171 □J7 **Kowloon Reservoirs** *H.K.* China
163 E9 **Kowŏn** N. Korea
168 C6 **Kox Kuduk** *well* *Xinjiang* China
173 E7 **Koxlax** *Xinjiang* China
173 D8 **Koxtag** *Xinjiang* China
166 C7 **Kōya** Japan
166 C7 **Kōyaguchi** Japan
88 C5 **Koyama** Guinea
165 I12 **Kōyama-misaki** *pt* Japan
166 C7 **Kōya-Ryūjin Quasi National Park** Japan
182 K1 **Koybagar, Ozero** *l.* Kazakh.
79 J6 **Köyceğiz** Turkey
79 J6 **Köyceğiz Gölü** *l.* Turkey
14 H2 **Koyda** Rus. Fed.
14 J3 **Koygorodok** Rus. Fed.
184 F1 **Koymatdag, Gory** *hills* Turkm.
77 M7 **Koynare** Bulg.
176 C4 **Koyna Reservoir** India
14 L3 **Koyp, Gora** *mt.* Rus. Fed.
104 C3 **Koyukuk** *r.* *AK* U.S.A.
188 H3 **Koyulhisar** Turkey
191 C5 **Koyunören** Turkey
89 I4 **Koza** Cameroon
14 G4 **Koza** Rus. Fed.
17 P3 **Kozacha Lopan'** Ukr.
17 N7 **Kozachi Laheri** Ukr.
166 F6 **Kozakai** Japan
167 L4 **Kōzaki** Japan
165 G12 **Kō-zaki** *pt* Japan
188 G5 **Kozan** Turkey
78 C2 **Kozani** Greece
186 E8 **Kozar, Ras** *pt* Eritrea
68 F3 **Kozara** *mts* Bos.-Herz.
68 F3 **Kozara** *nat. park* Bos.-Herz.
57 H5 **Kozármisleny** Hungary
17 K3 **Kozarn** Ukr.
57 H3 **Kozárovce** Slovakia
17 M7 **Kozats'ke** *Khersons'ka Oblast'* Ukr.
17 M2 **Kozats'ke** *Sums'ka Oblast'* Ukr.
17 K3 **Kozelets'** Ukr.
17 M4 **Kozel'shchyna** Ukr.
19 S7 **Kozel'sk** Rus. Fed.
84 C4 **Kozen** *well* Chad
57 J4 **Közép-tiszai** *park* Hungary
182 I5 **Kozhabakhy** Kazakh.
183 M2 **Kozhakol', Ozero** *l.* Kazakh.
16 I4 **Kozhanka** Ukr.
193 M2 **Kozhevnikovo** Rus. Fed.
14 L3 **Kozhim-Iz, Gora** *mt.* Rus. Fed.
16 G4 **Kozhukliv** Ukr.
14 L2 **Kozhva** Rus. Fed.
14 L2 **Kozhva** *r.* Rus. Fed.
14 L2 **Kozhym** *r.* Rus. Fed.
55 H5 **Koziegłowy** Pol.
54 C2 **Kozielice** Pol.
55 J4 **Kozienice** Pol.
16 A2 **Kozienicki Park Krajobrazowy** Pol.
68 D3 **Kozina** Slovenia
17 O3 **Koziyivka** Ukr.
56 C2 **Kožlany** Czech Rep.
77 L7 **Kozloduy** Bulg.
57 H2 **Kozlovice** Czech Rep.
14 J5 **Kozlovka** *Chuvashskaya Respublika* Rus. Fed.
15 I5 **Kozlovka** *Respublika Mordoviya* Rus. Fed.
15 H6 **Kozlovka** *Voronezhskaya Oblast'* Rus. Fed.
17 T3 **Kozlovka** *Voronezhskaya Oblast'* Rus. Fed.
19 T5 **Kozlovo** Rus. Fed.
55 I5 **Kozłów** Pol.
55 I3 **Kozłów Biskupi** Pol.
55 I2 **Kozłowo** Pol.
188 E3 **Kozlu** Turkey
79 L5 **Kozluca** Turkey
68 G3 **Kozluk** Bos.-Herz.
55 J3 **Kozły** Pol.
191 H2 **Koz'maaul** Rus. Fed.
54 G4 **Koźminek** Pol.
54 F4 **Koźmin Wielkopowski** Pol.
14 I4 **Koz'modem'yansk** Rus. Fed.
183 M6 **Kozmoldak** Kazakh.
77 L8 **Koznitsa** *mt.* Bulg.
16 E4 **Kozova** Ukr.
57 J1 **Kozubowski Park Krajobrazowy** Pol.
55 K4 **Kozubszczyzna** Pol.
54 D4 **Kożuchów** Pol.
77 K9 **Kožuf** *mts* Greece/Macedonia
167 J7 **Kōzu-shima** *i.* Japan
16 H4 **Kozyatyn** Ukr.
17 L2 **Kozylivka** Ukr.
16 J3 **Kozyn** *Kyivs'ka Oblast'* Ukr.
17 K4 **Kozyn** *Kyivs'ka Oblast'* Ukr.
79 H1 **Kozyörük** Turkey
17 K7 **Kozyrka** Ukr.
89 F5 **Kpalimé** Togo
89 E4 **Kpandae** Ghana
89 F5 **Kpandu** Ghana
89 F5 **Kpedze** Ghana
89 F4 **Kpèssi** Togo
158 C1 **Kpungan Pass** India/Myanmar
159 D9 **Kra, Isthmus of** Thai.
97 K6 **Kraai** *r.* S. Africa
96 I5 **Kraankuil** S. Africa
147 G5 **Krabbé** Arg.
45 F6 **Krabbendijke** Neth.
18 J4 **Krabi** Estonia
159 D10 **Krabi** Thai.
159 D9 **Kra Buri** Thai.
159 H8 **Krâchéh** Cambodia
21 M6 **Kräckelbäcken** Sweden
50 J4 **Krackow** Ger.
19 R4 **Kraftino, Ozero** *l.* Rus. Fed.
51 E9 **Kraftsdorf** Ger.
54 E1 **Krąg** Pol.
157 I8 **Kragan** *Jawa* Indon.
22 F3 **Kragerø** Norway
44 I3 **Kraggenburg** Neth.
54 E2 **Krągi** Pol.
76 I6 **Kragujevac** *Srbija* Serb. and Mont.
53 M5 **Kraiburg am Inn** Ger.
52 E3 **Kraichbach** *r.* Ger.
52 F3 **Kraichgau** *reg.* Ger.
53 K5 **Krailling** Ger.
54 F2 **Krajenka** Pol.
54 F2 **Krajeńskie, Pojezierze** *reg.* Pol.
54 C2 **Krajnik Dolny** Pol.
156 F8 **Krakatau** *i.* Indon.
156 F8 **Krakatau Volcano National Park** Indon.
Krakau Pol. *see* **Kraków**
20 K5 **Kråklivollen** Norway
159 G8 **Krâkôr** Cambodia
16 C4 **Krakovets'** Ukr.
55 H5 **Kraków** Pol.
110 F5 **Krakow** *WI* U.S.A.
50 F3 **Krakow am See** Ger.
50 F3 **Krakower See** *l.* Ger.
55 G4 **Krakowsko-Częstochowska, Wyżyna** *plat.* Pol.
159 F8 **Krâlănh** Cambodia
131 □8 **Kralendijk** *Bonaire* Neth. Antilles
159 D9 **Kra Lenya** *r.* Myanmar
56 F1 **Králíky** Czech Rep.
68 E3 **Kraljeviča** Croatia
76 I7 **Kraljevo** *Srbija* Serb. and Mont.
57 G3 **Kráľová, Vodná nádrž** *resr* Slovakia
57 J3 **Kráľova hoľa** *mt.* Slovakia
57 G3 **Kráľová nad Váhom** Slovakia
57 G3 **Kráľov Brod** Slovakia
56 E1 **Královéhradecký kraj** *admin. reg.* Czech Rep.
56 C2 **Kralovice** Czech Rep.
57 K3 **Kráľovský Chlmec** Slovakia
56 D1 **Kralupy nad Vltavou** Czech Rep.
56 D2 **Králův Dvůr** Czech Rep.
54 F1 **Kramarzyny** Pol.
17 Q5 **Kramators'k** Ukr.
20 N5 **Kramfors** Sweden
44 F5 **Krammer** *est.* Neth.
20 U1 **Krampenes** Norway
58 E5 **Kramsach** Austria
54 G3 **Kramsk** Pol.
78 C3 **Kranea** Greece
49 B7 **Kranenburg** Ger.
78 E5 **Kranidi** Greece
68 E2 **Kranj** Slovenia
156 □ **Kranji Reservoir** Sing.
59 I7 **Kranjska Gora** Slovenia
17 L7 **Kranoznam''yans'kyy Kanal** *canal* Ukr.
97 M4 **Kransfontein** S. Africa
97 O4 **Kranskop** S. Africa
97 N3 **Kranskop** *mt.* S. Africa
53 L5 **Kranzberg** Ger.
68 E4 **Krapanj** Croatia
54 D2 **Krąpiel** Pol.
68 E2 **Krapina** Croatia
68 E2 **Krapinske Toplice** Croatia
19 S8 **Krapivna** *Kaluzhskaya Oblast'* Rus. Fed.
19 Q7 **Krapivna** *Smolenskaya Oblast'* Rus. Fed.
54 F5 **Krapkowice** Pol.
59 I8 **Kras** *plat.* Slovenia
14 I3 **Krasavino** Rus. Fed.
17 L4 **Krasenivka** Ukr.
55 K6 **Krasiczyn** Pol.
Krasilov Ukr. *see* **Krasyliv**
Krasilovka *Chernihivs'ka Oblast'* Ukr. *see* **Krasylivka**
Krasilovka *Zhytomyrs'ka Oblast'* Ukr. *see* **Krasylivka**
192 G2 **Krasino** *Novaya Zemlya* Rus. Fed.
55 L6 **Krasiv** Ukr.
16 E4 **Krasiyiv** Ukr.
162 G7 **Kraskino** Rus. Fed.
18 K6 **Krāslava** Latvia
56 B1 **Kraslice** Czech Rep.
17 R4 **Krasna** *r.* Ukr.
51 K9 **Krásná Lípa** Czech Rep.
19 O8 **Krasnapollye** *Mahilyowskaya Voblasts'* Belarus
18 M6 **Krasnapollye** *Vitsyebskaya Voblasts'* Belarus
17 Q6 **Krasna Polyana** *Donets'ka Oblast'* Ukr.
17 L8 **Krasna Polyana** *Respublika Krym* Ukr.
16 J4 **Krasna Slobidka** Ukr.
18 H8 **Krasnasyel'ski** Belarus
19 O8 **Krasnaya Gora** Rus. Fed.
14 H5 **Krasnaya Gorbatka** Rus. Fed.
183 O3 **Krasnaya Polyana** Kazakh.
191 B2 **Krasnaya Polyana** Rus. Fed.
18 K9 **Krasnaya Slabada** Belarus
17 O3 **Krasnaya Yaruga** Rus. Fed.
19 U9 **Krasnaya Zarya** Rus. Fed.
55 I3 **Krasne** *Mazowieckie* Pol.
55 K5 **Krasne** *Podkarpackie* Pol.
17 K2 **Krasne** *Chernihivs'ka Oblast'* Ukr.
17 L2 **Krasne** *Chernihivs'ka Oblast'* Ukr.
16 D5 **Krasne** *Ivano-Frankivs'ka Oblast'* Ukr.
17 L7 **Krasne** *Khersons'ka Oblast'* Ukr.
16 D4 **Krasne** *L'vivs'ka Oblast'* Ukr.
16 F4 **Krasne** *Ternopils'ka Oblast'* Ukr.
16 H5 **Krasne** *Vinnyts'ka Oblast'* Ukr.
55 L5 **Kraśniczyn** Pol.
55 K5 **Kraśnik** Pol.
16 I6 **Krasni Okny** Ukr.
19 V5 **Krasnoarmeysk** *Moskovskaya Oblast'* Rus. Fed.
15 I6 **Krasnoarmeysk** *Saratovskaya Oblast'* Rus. Fed.
Krasnoarmeysk Ukr. *see* **Krasnoarmiys'k**
193 S3 **Krasnoarmeyskiy** *Chukotskiy Avtonomnyy Okrug* Rus. Fed.
15 H7 **Krasnoarmeyskiy** *Rostovskaya Oblast'* Rus. Fed.
17 Q5 **Krasnoarmiys'k** Ukr.
17 Q6 **Krasnoarmiys'ke** Ukr.
19 S2 **Krasnobarskiy** Rus. Fed.
14 I3 **Krasnoborsk** Rus. Fed.
55 L5 **Krasnobród** Pol.
57 M1 **Krasnobrodzki Park Krajobrazowy** Pol.
15 G7 **Krasnodar** Rus. Fed.
Krasnodar Kray *admin. div.* Rus. Fed. *see* **Krasnodarskiy Kray**
191 B1 **Krasnodarskiy Kray** *admin. div.* Rus. Fed.
17 S5 **Krasnodon** *Luhans'ka Oblast'* Ukr.
17 S5 **Krasnodon** *Luhans'ka Oblast'* Ukr.
19 O2 **Krasnofarfornyy** Rus. Fed.
17 N8 **Krasnoflots'ke** Ukr.
18 L5 **Krasnogorodskoye** Rus. Fed.
19 U6 **Krasnogorsk** *Moskovskaya Oblast'* Rus. Fed.
162 M4 **Krasnogorsk** *Sakhalin* Rus. Fed.
183 V1 **Krasnogorskoye** *Altayskiy Kray* Rus. Fed.
14 K4 **Krasnogorskoye** *Udmurtskaya Respublika* Rus. Fed.
Krasnograd Ukr. *see* **Krasnohrad**
19 X5 **Krasnogvardeyskiy** Rus. Fed.
17 R3 **Krasnogvardeyskoye** *Belgorodskaya Oblast'* Rus. Fed.
17 S8 **Krasnogvardeyskoye** *Respublika Adygeya* Rus. Fed.
15 H7 **Krasnogvardeyskoye** *Stavropol'skiy Kray* Rus. Fed.
17 O8 **Krasnohirka** Ukr.
17 Q5 **Krasnohorivka** Ukr.
17 O4 **Krasnohrad** Ukr.
17 N8 **Krasnohvardiys'ke** Ukr.
169 P2 **Krasnokamensk** Rus. Fed.
14 K4 **Krasnokamsk** Rus. Fed.
182 F2 **Krasnokholm** Rus. Fed.
17 O3 **Krasnokuts'k** Ukr.
15 G6 **Krasnolesnyy** Rus. Fed.
18 F7 **Krasnoles'ye** Rus. Fed.
17 R2 **Krasnolip'ye** Rus. Fed.
17 N9 **Krasnolissya** Ukr.
19 R4 **Krasnomayskiy** Rus. Fed.
57 H2 **Krásno nad Kysucou** Slovakia
18 L1 **Krasnoostrovskiy** Rus. Fed.
17 P4 **Krasnopavivs'ke Vodoskhovyshche** *l.* Ukr.
17 P4 **Krasnopavlivka** Ukr.
17 M8 **Krasnoperekops'k** Ukr.
16 H4 **Krasnopil'** Ukr.
16 J5 **Krasnopilka** Ukr.
17 O3 **Krasnopillya** Ukr.
55 L1 **Krasnopol** Pol.
162 M4 **Krasnopol'ye** *Sakhalin* Rus. Fed.
162 I6 **Krasnorechenskiy** Rus. Fed.
Krasnorechenskoye Ukr. *see* **Krasnorichens'ke**
17 R4 **Krasnorichens'ke** Ukr.
192 J3 **Krasnosel'kup** Rus. Fed.
18 M1 **Krasnosel'skoye** Rus. Fed.
183 T2 **Krasnoshchekovo** Rus. Fed.
14 G2 **Krasnoshchel'ye** Rus. Fed.
55 J2 **Krasnosielc** Pol.
16 I5 **Krasnosilka** *Vinnyts'ka Oblast'* Ukr.
16 G4 **Krasnosilka** *Zhytomyrs'ka Oblast'* Ukr.
17 L5 **Krasnosillya** Ukr.
15 H5 **Krasnoslobodsk** Rus. Fed.
17 U1 **Krasnosvobodnoye** Rus. Fed.
192 H4 **Krasnotur'insk** Rus. Fed.
14 L4 **Krasnoufimsk** Rus. Fed.
182 G1 **Krasnousol'skiy** Rus. Fed.
14 L3 **Krasnovishersk** Rus. Fed.
Krasnovodsk Turkm. *see* **Turkmenbashi**
184 E2 **Krasnovodsk, Mys** *pt* Turkm.
184 E2 **Krasnovodskiy Gosudarstvenny Zapovednik** *nature res.* Turkm.
184 E1 **Krasnovodskoye Plato** *plat.* Turkm.
162 F3 **Krasnoyarovo** Rus. Fed.
193 K4 **Krasnoyarsk** Rus. Fed.
182 H2 **Krasnoyarskiy** Rus. Fed.
160 F1 **Krasnoyarskiy Kray** *admin. div.* Rus. Fed.
Krasnoyarsk Kray *admin. div.* Rus. Fed. *see* **Krasnoyarskiy Kray**
15 G6 **Krasnoye** *Belgorodskaya Oblast'* Rus. Fed.
17 R3 **Krasnoye** *Belgorodskaya Oblast'* Rus. Fed.
19 Q8 **Krasnoye** *Bryanskaya Oblast'* Rus. Fed.
14 I4 **Krasnoye** *Kirovskaya Oblast'* Rus. Fed.
17 S7 **Krasnoye** *Krasnodarskiy Kray* Rus. Fed.
19 V9 **Krasnoye** *Lipetskaya Oblast'* Rus. Fed.
18 M5 **Krasnoye** *Pskovskaya Oblast'* Rus. Fed.
19 O7 **Krasnoye** *Smolenskaya Oblast'* Rus. Fed.
193 S3 **Krasnoye, Ozero** *l.* Rus. Fed.
19 X6 **Krasnoye Ekho** Rus. Fed.
19 Y4 **Krasnoye-na-Volge** Rus. Fed.
19 V5 **Krasnoye Plamya** Rus. Fed.
19 S4 **Krasnoye Znamya** Rus. Fed.
182 J9 **Krasnoye Znamya** Turkm.
16 E5 **Krasnoyil's'k** Ukr.
14 J3 **Krasnozatonskiy** Rus. Fed.
19 V5 **Krasnozavodsk** Rus. Fed.
18 F7 **Krasnoznamensk** Rus. Fed.
17 L7 **Krasnoznam''yanka** Ukr.
55 L5 **Krasnystaw** Pol.
19 O7 **Krasnyy** Rus. Fed.
169 K1 **Krasnyy Chikoy** Rus. Fed.
14 I4 **Krasnyye Baki** Rus. Fed.
15 I7 **Krasnyye Barrikady** Rus. Fed.
19 W4 **Krasnyye Tkachi** Rus. Fed.
19 Q4 **Krasnyy Gorodok** Rus. Fed.
Krasnyy Kamyshanik Rus. Fed. *see* **Komsomol'skiy**
19 U3 **Krasnyy Kholm** Rus. Fed.
182 B2 **Krasnyy Kut** Rus. Fed.
17 S2 **Krasnyy Liman** Rus. Fed.
19 N4 **Krasnyy Luch** Rus. Fed.
17 R5 **Krasnyy Luch** Ukr.
17 Q5 **Krasnyy Lyman** Ukr.
17 M9 **Krasnyy Mak** Ukr.
183 Q4 **Krasnyy Oktyabr'** Kazakh.
19 V5 **Krasnyy Oktyabr'** Rus. Fed.
19 X4 **Krasnyy Profintern** Rus. Fed.
19 Q8 **Krasnyy Rog** *Bryanskaya Oblast'* Rus. Fed.
19 Q9 **Krasnyy Rog** *Bryanskaya Oblast'* Rus. Fed.
17 T6 **Krasnyy Sulin** Rus. Fed.
15 I6 **Krasnyy Tekstil'shchik** Rus. Fed.
183 M1 **Krasnyy Yar** Kazakh.
182 C4 **Krasnyy Yar** *Astrakhanskaya Oblast'* Rus. Fed.
182 D1 **Krasnyy Yar** *Samarskaya Oblast'* Rus. Fed.
15 I6 **Krasnyy Yar** *Volgogradskaya Oblast'* Rus. Fed.
55 I5 **Krasocin** Pol.
16 I2 **Krasyatychi** Ukr.
16 F4 **Krasyliv** Ukr.
17 K2 **Krasylivka** *Chernihivs'ka Oblast'* Ukr.
16 H2 **Krasylivka** *Zhytomyrs'ka Oblast'* Ukr.
54 G4 **Kraszcwice** Pol.
55 I1 **Kraszewo** Pol.
57 L3 **Kraszna** *r.* Hungary
Kratie Cambodia *see* **Krâchéh**
77 K8 **Kratovo** Macedonia
52 G5 **Krauchenwies** Ger.
18 J6 **Krauja** Latvia
212 X2 **Kraul Mountains** Antarctica
Kraulshavn Greenland *see* **Nuussuaq**
51 K7 **Krauschwitz** Ger.
59 K4 **Kräuterin** *mts* Austria
52 H3 **Krautheim** Ger.
57 H2 **Kravaře** Czech Rep.
17 K1 **Krawtsowka** Belarus
191 I2 **Kraynovka** Rus. Fed.
51 K8 **Kreba-Neudorf** Ger.
49 J7 **Krebeck** Ger.
19 O3 **Krechevitsy** Rus. Fed.
49 C8 **Krefeld** Ger.
49 I7 **Kreiensen** Ger.
44 H3 **Kreileroord** Neth.
51 I9 **Kreischa** Ger.
18 H6 **Krekenava** Lith.
78 C4 **Kremaston, Techniti Limni** *resr* Greece
68 E3 **Kremen** *mt.* Croatia
Kremenchug Ukr. *see* **Kremenchuk**
17 M4 **Kremenchuk** Ukr.
17 L4 **Kremenchuts'ka Vodoskhovyshche** *resr* Ukr.
16 E3 **Kremenets'** Ukr.
19 U7 **Kremenki** Rus. Fed.
15 H6 **Kremenskaya** Rus. Fed.
19 S6 **Kremenskoye** Rus. Fed.
56 E2 **Křemešník** *hill* Czech Rep.
17 R4 **Kreminna** Ukr.
16 D5 **Kremintsi** Ukr.
50 H5 **Kremmen** Ger.
78 E6 **Kremmidi, Akra** *pt* Greece
122 K6 **Kremmling** *CO* U.S.A.
57 H3 **Kremnica** Slovakia
48 I3 **Krempe** Ger.
55 J6 **Krempna** Pol.
59 L3 **Krems** *r.* Austria
59 M3 **Krems an der Donau** Austria
59 I6 **Kremsbrücke** Austria
59 J3 **Kremsmünster** Austria
56 D3 **Křemže** Czech Rep.
104 B4 **Krenitzin Islands** *AK* U.S.A.
59 O2 **Křepice** Czech Rep.
17 S6 **Krepkaya** *r.* Rus. Fed./Ukr.
77 J6 **Krepoljin** *Srbija* Serb. and Mont.
118 E3 **Kresgeville** *PA* U.S.A.
51 J9 **Křešice** Czech Rep.
77 L9 **Kresna** Bulg.
59 K7 **Kresnice** Slovenia
52 H6 **Kressbronn am Bodensee** Ger.
193 T3 **Kresta, Zaliv** *g.* Rus. Fed.
78 C5 **Krestena** Greece
193 O3 **Krest-Khal'dzhayy** Rus. Fed.
14 K2 **Krestovka** Rus. Fed.
19 P3 **Kresttsy** Rus. Fed.
19 U6 **Kresty** *Moskovskaya Oblast'* Rus. Fed.
19 O6 **Kresty** *Pskovskaya Oblast'* Rus. Fed.
19 V8 **Kresty** *Tul'skaya Oblast'* Rus. Fed.
193 M3 **Krestyakh** Rus. Fed.
18 E6 **Kretinga** Lith.
51 F8 **Kretzschau** Ger.
53 L6 **Kreuth** Ger.
49 B9 **Kreuzau** Ger.
58 H6 **Kreuzeck** *mt.* Austria
58 G6 **Kreuzeck Gruppe** *mts* Austria
58 E5 **Kreuzjoch** *mt.* Austria
70 G1 **Kreuzlingen** Switz.
49 E9 **Kreuztal** Ger.
52 H2 **Kreuzwertheim** Ger.
18 J7 **Kreva** Belarus
89 H6 **Kribi** Cameroon
Krichev Belarus *see* **Krychaw**
77 M8 **Krichim** Bulg.
59 M4 **Krieglach** Austria
70 D1 **Kriegstetten** Switz.
97 N2 **Kriel** S. Africa
50 H3 **Krien** Ger.
70 E1 **Kriens** Switz.
18 E5 **Krievukalns** *hill* Latvia
78 F4 **Krieza** Greece
78 C4 **Krikellos** Greece
79 H6 **Krikelos, Akra** *pt* Greece
162 M6 **Kril'on, Mys** *c.* *Sakhalin* Rus. Fed.
59 J8 **Krim** *mt.* Slovenia
90 B2 **Krim-Krim** Chad
58 F5 **Krimmler Wasserfälle** *waterfall* Austria
44 G5 **Krimpen aan de IJssel** Neth.
56 E1 **Křinec** Czech Rep.
78 F1 **Krinides** Greece
78 E7 **Krios, Akra** *pt* *Kriti* Greece
Kripka *r.* Rus. Fed./Ukr. *see* **Krepkaya**
59 I4 **Krippenstein** *mt.* Austria
176 E4 **Krishna** *Andhra Prad.* India
176 G4 **Krishna** *r.* India
176 G5 **Krishna, Mouths of the** India
176 F6 **Krishnagiri** *Tamil Nadu* India
179 M6 **Krishnai** *r.* India
179 L8 **Krishnanagar** *W. Bengal* India
176 E6 **Krishnaraja Sagara** *l.* India
176 E6 **Krishnarajpet** *Karnataka* India
23 M4 **Kristdala** Sweden
Kristiania Norway *see* **Oslo**
22 D3 **Kristiansand** Norway
23 K5 **Kristianstad** Sweden
20 I5 **Kristiansund** Norway
Kristiinankaupunki Fin. *see* **Kristinestad**
23 K2 **Kristinehamn** Sweden
21 P5 **Kristinestad** Fin.
78 F8 **Kriti** *admin. reg.* Greece
78 F7 **Kriti** *i.* *Kriti* Greece
50 F2 **Kritzmow** Ger.
18 G6 **Kriūkai** Lith.
19 W7 **Kriusha** Rus. Fed.
76 I7 **Krivača** *mt.* Serb. and Mont.
68 G3 **Krivaja** *r.* Bos.-Herz.
57 I6 **Krivaja** *r.* Serb. and Mont.
19 W6 **Krivandino** Rus. Fed.
77 K8 **Kriva Palanka** Macedonia
77 J8 **Kriva Reka** *r.* Macedonia
17 S3 **Krivaya Polyana** Rus. Fed.
17 Q2 **Krivets** Rus. Fed.
71 R5 **Krivi Put** Croatia
76 J9 **Krivogaštani** Macedonia
56 C2 **Křivoklátská Vrchovina** *hills* Czech Rep.
19 P8 **Krivoles** Rus. Fed.
19 W8 **Krivopolyan'ye** Rus. Fed.
15 H6 **Krivorozh'ye** Rus. Fed.
14 F2 **Krivoy Porog** Rus. Fed.
Krivoy Rog Ukr. *see* **Kryvyy Rih**
71 P5 **Križ, Rt** *pt* Croatia
56 F2 **Křižanov** Czech Rep.
68 F2 **Križevci** Croatia
68 G3 **Krk** *mt.* Bos.-Herz.
68 E3 **Krk** Croatia
68 E3 **Krk** *i.* Croatia
68 E4 **Krka** *r.* Croatia
59 K8 **Krka** Slovenia
68 E3 **Krka** *r.* Slovenia
56 E1 **Krkonoše** *mts* Czech Rep.
54 D5 **Krkonošský narodní park** *nat. park* Czech Rep./Pol.
59 I7 **Krn** *mt.* Slovenia
71 Q6 **Krnica** Croatia
76 I6 **Krnjača** *Srbija* Serb. and Mont.
57 G1 **Krnov** Czech Rep.
54 E4 **Krobia** Pol.
55 H5 **Kroczyce** Pol.
22 F1 **Krøderen** Norway
22 F1 **Krøderen** *l.* Norway
51 H8 **Krögis** Ger.
88 D5 **Krohnwodoke** Liberia
Krokeaí Greece *see* **Krokees**
78 D6 **Krokees** Greece
23 M3 **Krokek** Sweden
20 U1 **Kroknes** Norway
20 M5 **Krokom** Sweden
159 J14 **Krokong** *Sarawak* Malaysia
23 O7 **Krokowa** Pol.
20 □C1 **Króksfjarðarnes** Iceland
20 J5 **Krokstadøra** Norway
20 M3 **Krokstranda** Norway
17 M2 **Krolevets'** Ukr.
55 L2 **Królowy Most** Pol.
51 E9 **Krölpa** Ger.
97 I10 **Krom** *r.* S. Africa
19 S9 **Kroma** *r.* Rus. Fed.
97 N1 **Kromdraai** S. Africa
56 G2 **Kroměříž** Czech Rep.
44 G3 **Krommenie** Neth.
57 J3 **Krompachy** Slovakia
51 D9 **Kromsdorf** Ger.
19 S9 **Kromy** Rus. Fed.
51 D10 **Kronach** Ger.
52 F3 **Kronau** Ger.
49 F10 **Kronberg im Taunus** Ger.
22 E2 **Kronfjell** *hill* Norway
159 F9 **Krŏng Kaôh Kŏng** Cambodia
179 O5 **Kronli** *Arun. Prad.* India
23 K5 **Kronoberg** *county* Sweden
20 Q5 **Kronoby** Fin.
193 R4 **Kronotskiy Poluostrov** *pen.* Rus. Fed.
193 R4 **Kronotskiy Zaliv** *b.* Rus. Fed.
193 R4 **Kronotskoye Ozero** *l.* Rus. Fed.
105 P1 **Kronprins Christian Land** *reg.* Greenland
105 O3 **Kronprins Frederik Bjerge** *nunataks* Greenland
48 G3 **Kronprinzenkoog** Ger.
48 J2 **Kronshagen** Ger.
18 M2 **Kronshtadt** Rus. Fed.
Kronstadt Rus. Fed. *see* **Kronshtadt**
59 J3 **Kronstorf** Austria
158 D7 **Kronwa** Myanmar
97 L3 **Kroonstad** S. Africa
59 J7 **Kropa** Slovenia
50 E2 **Kröpelin** Ger.
15 H7 **Kropotkin** Rus. Fed.
48 I2 **Kropp** Ger.
22 I3 **Kroppefjäll** *hills* Sweden
51 D7 **Kroppenstedt** Ger.
51 G7 **Kropstädt** Ger.
16 I3 **Kropyvnya** Ukr.
55 I6 **Krościenko nad Dunajcem** Pol.
50 I2 **Kröslin** Ger.
55 L1 **Krosna** Lith.
54 F4 **Krośnice** Pol.
55 H3 **Krośniewice** Pol.
55 J6 **Krosno** Pol.
54 D3 **Krosno Odrzańskie** Pol.
51 E9 **Krossen** Ger.
22 E2 **Krossen** Norway
51 F8 **Krostitz** Ger.
54 E4 **Krotoszyce** Pol.
54 F4 **Krotoszyn** Pol.
59 M5 **Krottendorf** Austria
121 J10 **Krotz Springs** *LA* U.S.A.
56 F2 **Krouna** Czech Rep.
78 F7 **Krousonas** *Kriti* Greece
52 C2 **Kröv** Ger.
157 H8 **Kroya** *Jawa* Indon.
71 Q5 **Kršan** Croatia
68 E3 **Krško** Slovenia
76 I8 **Krstača** *mt.* Serb. and Mont.
54 F3 **Kruchowo** Pol.
50 E5 **Krüden** Ger.
49 D10 **Kruft** Ger.
97 K4 **Krugerdrifdam** *resr* S. Africa
97 P1 **Kruger National Park** S. Africa
97 L2 **Krugersdorp** S. Africa
162 I4 **Kruglikovo** Rus. Fed.
191 D1 **Kruglolesskoye** Rus. Fed.
Kruglyakov Rus. Fed. *see* **Oktyabr'skiy**
18 M7 **Kruhlaye** Belarus
156 E7 **Krui** *Sumatera* Indon.
96 F8 **Kruidfontein** S. Africa
45 F6 **Kruiningen** Neth.
97 I10 **Kruisfontein** S. Africa
45 E7 **Kruishoutem** Belgium
76 H9 **Krujë** Albania
55 L6 **Krukenychi** Ukr.
55 J1 **Kruklanki** Pol.
55 J2 **Krukowo** Pol.
59 N4 **Krumbach** Austria
53 I5 **Krumbach (Schwaben)** Ger.
76 I8 **Krumë** Albania
48 K3 **Krummesse** Ger.
77 N9 **Krumovgrad** Bulg.
51 E8 **Krumpa (Geiseltal)** Ger.
59 J6 **Krumpendorf am Wörther See** Austria
53 K6 **Krün** Ger.
Krung Thep Thai. *see* **Bangkok**
18 G5 **Kruoja** *r.* Lith.
76 H6 **Krupanj** *Srbija* Serb. and Mont.
55 N2 **Krupava** Belarus
55 L4 **Krupe** Pol.
17 N2 **Krupets** Rus. Fed.
57 I3 **Krupina** Slovakia
57 H3 **Krupinica** *r.* Slovakia
57 I3 **Krupinská Planina** *plat.* Slovakia
56 C1 **Krupka** Czech Rep.
18 M7 **Krupki** Belarus
17 L4 **Krupodernytsi** Ukr.
17 L5 **Krups'ke** Ukr.
54 G5 **Krupski Młyn** Pol.
48 H1 **Kruså** Denmark
76 J7 **Kruševac** *Srbija* Serb. and Mont.
76 J9 **Kruševo** Macedonia
56 B1 **Krušné Hory** *mts* Czech Rep.
57 H3 **Krušovce** Slovakia
18 J5 **Krustkalnu rezervāts** *nature res.* Latvia
54 E3 **Kruszewo** Pol.
54 G3 **Kruszwica** Pol.
54 F1 **Kruszyna** *Pomorskie* Pol.
55 H5 **Kruszyna** *Śląskie* Pol.
54 F2 **Kruszyńskie, Jezioro** *l.* Pol.
17 S2 **Krutchenskaya Baygora** Rus. Fed.
17 K7 **Krutoyarka** Ukr.
19 U9 **Krutoye** *Orlovskaya Oblast'* Rus. Fed.
19 O6 **Krutoye** *Smolenskaya Oblast'* Rus. Fed.
17 L2 **Kruty** Ukr.
63 O2 **Krutzea** Spain
57 K2 **Kružlov** Slovakia
104 E4 **Kruzof Island** *AK* U.S.A.
18 M6 **Krybinka** *r.* Belarus
19 O8 **Krychaw** Belarus
76 I8 **Kryezi** Albania
16 F3 **Kryliv** Ukr.
214 H4 **Krylov Seamount** *sea feature* N. Atlantic Ocean
17 S7 **Krylovskaya** *Krasnodarskiy Kray* Rus. Fed.
17 S7 **Krylovskaya** *Krasnodarskiy Kray* Rus. Fed.
55 M5 **Kryłów** Pol.
Krym' *aut. rep.* Ukr. *see* **Krym, Respublika**
Krym' *pen.* Ukr. *see* **Kryms'kyy Pivostriv**
17 N8 **Krym, Respublika** *aut. rep.* Ukr.
191 D1 **Krymgireyevskoye** Rus. Fed.
55 M4 **Krymne** Ukr.
15 G7 **Krymsk** Rus. Fed.
Krymskaya Rus. Fed. *see* **Krymsk**
17 R5 **Kryms'ke** Ukr.
17 N9 **Kryms'ki Hori** *mts* Ukr.
17 N8 **Kryms'kyy Pivostriv** *pen.* Ukr.
17 N9 **Kryms'kyy Zapovidnyk** *nature res.* Ukr.
55 I6 **Krynica** Pol.
23 P7 **Krynica Morska** Pol.
54 F5 **Krynka** *r.* Pol.
17 R6 **Krynka** *r.* Ukr.
19 N6 **Krynki** Belarus
55 L2 **Krynki** Pol.
17 N5 **Krynychky** *Dnipropetrovs'ka Oblast'* Ukr.
17 K6 **Krynychky** *Mykolayivs'ka Oblast'* Ukr.
17 R5 **Krynychna** Ukr.
17 N6 **Krynychuvate** Ukr.
55 K2 **Krypno Kościelne** Pol.
183 P5 **Krypsalo** Kazakh.
51 H10 **Kryry** Czech Rep.
17 L2 **Krysky** Ukr.
78 G6 **Krytiko Pelagos** *sea* Greece
17 R9 **Kryukovskoye Vodokhranilishche** *resr* Rus. Fed.
17 R6 **Kryva Kosa** *spit* Ukr.
17 L4 **Kryva Ruda** Ukr.
16 I4 **Kryvchunka** Ukr.
16 J6 **Kryve Ozero** Ukr.
18 K7 **Kryvichy** Belarus
17 M6 **Kryvyy Rih** Ukr.
16 H5 **Kryzhopil'** Ukr.
54 G5 **Krzanowice** Pol.
55 K4 **Krzczonów-Wójtostwo** Pol.
54 D2 **Krzęcin** Pol.
54 E4 **Krzelów** Pol.
54 G5 **Krzepice** Pol.
54 E4 **Krzepielów** Pol.
55 K3 **Krzesk-Królowa Niwa** Pol.
55 K5 **Krzeszów** Pol.
55 H5 **Krzeszowice** Pol.
54 D3 **Krzeszyce** Pol.
55 H5 **Krzętów** Pol.
55 L3 **Krzna** *r.* Pol.
55 K4 **Krzna Południowa** *r.* Pol.
54 G3 **Krzymów** *Wielkopolskie* Pol.
50 J5 **Krzymów** *Zachodniopomorskie* Pol.
55 I2 **Krzynowłoga Mała** Pol.
54 D4 **Krzystkowice** Pol.
55 K6 **Krzywcza** Pol.
55 K4 **Krzywda** Pol.
54 E4 **Krzywiń** Pol.
50 J4 **Krzywin** Pol.
55 L4 **Krzywowierzba** Pol.
55 H3 **Krzyżanów** Pol.
54 G6 **Krzyżanowice** Pol.
54 E3 **Krzyż Wielkopolski** Pol.
87 E3 **Ksabi** Alg.
191 F4 **Ksani** *r.* Georgia
87 F2 **Ksar Chellala** Alg.
87 F2 **Ksar el Boukhari** Alg.
87 F2 **Ksar el Hirane** Alg.

Ksar el Kebir to Kyparissiakos Kolpos
288

86 D2 Ksar el Kebir Morocco
60 D5 Ksar Sghir Morocco
16 J3 Ksaverivka Ukr.
14 K3 Ksenofontova Rus. Fed.
19 U9 Kshen' r. Rus. Fed.
15 G6 Kshenskiy Rus. Fed.
56 F1 Książański Park Krajobrazowy Pol.
55 H2 Książki Pol.
55 I5 Książ Wielki Pol.
54 F3 Książ Wielkopolski Pol.
55 K5 Księżpol Pol.
184 E1 Kskyrbulak Yuzhnyy, Gora hill Turkm.
87 E2 Ksour, Monts des mts Alg.
87 H2 Ksour, Monts des mts Tunisia
87 H2 Ksour Essaf Tunisia
14 I4 Kstovo Rus. Fed.
19 S8 Ktsyn' Rus. Fed.
187 H2 Kū', Jabal al hill Saudi Arabia
84 E6 Ku, Wadi el watercourse Sudan
156 C1 Kuah Malaysia
157 K2 Kuala Belait Brunei
157 I6 Kualajelai Kalimantan Indon.
156 D2 Kuala Kangsar Malaysia
157 K6 Kualakapuas Kalimantan Indon.
156 E2 Kuala Kerai Malaysia
157 M2 Kuala Kinabatangan r. mouth Malaysia
157 J5 Kualakuayan Kalimantan Indon.
156 D3 Kuala Kubu Baharu Malaysia
157 J5 Kualakurun Kalimantan Indon.
156 B2 Kualalangsa Sumatera Indon.
156 D2 Kuala Lipis Malaysia
156 D3 Kuala Lumpur Malaysia
156 D1 Kuala Nerang Malaysia
157 J6 Kualapembuang Kalimantan Indon.
157 K2 Kuala Penyu Sabah Malaysia
156 E3 Kuala Pilah Malaysia
124 □D12 Kualapu'u HI U.S.A.
156 E3 Kuala Rompin Malaysia
157 J6 Kualasampit Indon.
156 D3 Kuala Selangor Malaysia
156 D2 Kuala Sepetang Malaysia
156 C2 Kualasimpang Sumatera Indon.
156 E2 Kuala Terengganu Malaysia
156 E5 Kualatungal Sumatera Indon.
157 L2 Kuamut Sabah Malaysia
157 L2 Kuamut r. Malaysia
169 P6 Kuancheng Hebei China
163 D8 Kuandian Liaoning China
171 M7 Kuanshan Taiwan
156 E3 Kuantan Malaysia
202 J3 Kuaotunu North I. N.Z.
191 E2 Kuba Rus. Fed.
191 I3 Kubachi Rus. Fed.
191 C2 Kuban' r. Rus. Fed.
191 A1 Kubanskaya Rus. Fed.
191 D1 Kubanskoye Vodokhranilishche resr Rus. Fed.
189 I6 Kubār Dayr az Zawr Syria
189 I6 Kubār Dayr az Zawr Syria
187 M4 Kubārah Oman
18 G3 Kübassaare poolsaar pen. Estonia
190 F3 Kubaybāt Syria
189 K7 Kubaysah Iraq
20 O5 Kubbe Sweden
90 D2 Kubbum Sudan
57 J5 Kübekháza Hungary
14 G4 Kubenskoye, Ozero l. Rus. Fed.
Kuberle Rus. Fed. see Krasnoarmeyskiy
167 H1 Kubiki Japan
19 T6 Kubinka Rus. Fed.
50 H2 Kubitzer Bodden b. Ger.
70 H2 Küblis Switz.
16 I5 Kublych r. Ukr.
14 J5 Kubnya r. Rus. Fed.
165 K13 Kubokawa Japan
77 O7 Kubrat Bulg.
19 V5 Kubrinsk Rus. Fed.
157 K9 Kubu Bali Indon.
157 H5 Kubu Kalimantan Indon.
157 K3 Kubuang Kalimantan Indon.
169 N1 Kubukhay Rus. Fed.
157 K4 Kubumesaäi Kalimantan Indon.
164 □22 Kubura Nansei-shotō Japan
77 J6 Kučevo Srbija Serb. and Mont.
178 E6 Kuchaman Rajasthan India
14 H2 Kuchema Rus. Fed.
52 H4 Kuchen Ger.
178 E6 Kuchera Rajasthan India
17 N2 Kucherivka Ukr.
157 I4 Kuching Sarawak Malaysia
164 □H16 Kuchino-Erabu-shima i. Japan
164 □G17 Kuchino-shima i. Nansei-shotō Japan
165 H14 Kuchinotsu Japan
58 H4 Kuchl Austria
183 R1 Kuchukskoye, Ozero salt l. Rus. Fed.
16 I7 Kuchurhan r. Ukr.
Kucing Sarawak Malaysia see Kuching
55 H4 Kuciny Pol.
55 L1 Kučiūnai Lith.
50 J3 Kückelsberg hill Ger.
78 A2 Kuçovë Albania
191 F6 Küçük Ağrı Dağı mt. Turkey
190 E2 Küçükdalyan Turkey
79 L5 Küçükköy Antalya Turkey
79 H3 Küçükköy Balıkesir Turkey
79 H3 Küçükkuyu Turkey
79 H2 Küçükmenderes r. Turkey
79 I5 Küçükmenderes r. Turkey
55 I2 Kuczbork-Osada Pol.
178 C8 Kuda Gujarat India
176 D4 Kudachi Karnataka India
175 □1 Kuda Finolhu i. S. Male Maldives
164 □1 Kudaka-jima i. Okinawa Japan
176 C5 Kudal Mahar. India
175 □1 Kudalhi i. N. Male Maldives
165 I13 Kudamatsu Japan
157 I5 Kudangan Kalimantan Indon.
156 E4 Kudap Sumatera Indon.
169 J1 Kudara-Somon Rus. Fed.
157 L1 Kudat Sabah Malaysia
186 E6 Kudayd Saudi Arabia
48 J3 Kuddewörde Ger.
18 L4 Kudev r. Rus. Fed.
18 M5 Kudever' Rus. Fed.
18 F7 Kudirkos Naumiestis Lith.
176 E5 Kudligi Karnataka India
54 E5 Kudowa-Zdrój Pol.
166 C7 Kudoyama Japan
176 D6 Kudremukh mt. Karnataka India
19 S7 Kudrinskaya Rus. Fed.
19 S8 Kudryavets Rus. Fed.
17 K6 Kudryavtsivka Ukr.
89 G4 Kudu Nigeria
157 I8 Kudus Jawa Indon.
14 K4 Kudymkar Rus. Fed.
171 N6 Kueishan Tao i. Taiwan
155 G5 Kufar Seram Indon.
58 F4 Kufstein Austria
105 J3 Kugaaruk Nunavut Can.
183 R5 Kugaly Kazakh.
14 I4 Kugesi Rus. Fed.
17 S7 Kugey Rus. Fed.
173 I11 Kugka Lhai Xizang China
104 G3 Kugluktuk Nunavut Can.
104 E3 Kugmallit Bay N.W.T. Can.
17 S7 Kugo-Eya r. Rus. Fed.
168 F9 Kugri Qinghai China
15 H7 Kugul'ta Rus. Fed.
166 F3 Kuguno Japan
184 G9 Kūh, Ra's-al- pt Iran
185 J8 Kūhak Iran
53 K5 Kühbach Ger.
50 F4 Kuhbier Ger.
184 G6 Kūhbonān Iran
184 B5 Kūhdasht Iran
184 G8 Kūhestak Iran
50 D5 Kuhfelde Ger.
184 C3 Kūhīn Iran
184 I8 Kūhīrī Iran
185 O3 Kŭhistoni Badakhshon aut. rep. Tajik.
50 E3 Kuhlen Ger.
50 E2 Kühlung park Ger.
20 T4 Kuhmo Fin.
21 R6 Kuhmoinen Fin.
49 J9 Kühndorf Ger.
184 E5 Kūhpāyeh Iran
184 G6 Kūhpāyeh mt. Iran
184 H8 Kūhrān, Kūh-e mt. Iran
184 D6 Kūhrang r. Iran
51 G8 Kühren Ger.
48 G3 Kührstedt Ger.
50 F3 Kuhs Ger.
48 G4 Kuhstedt Ger.
159 D8 Kui Buri Thai.
189 P5 Kuidzhuk Turkm.
169 S2 Kuile He r. China
18 I2 Kuimetsa Estonia
44 I3 Kuinre Neth.
94 C5 Kuis Namibia
94 B4 Kuiseb watercourse Namibia
171 J7 Kuitan Guangdong China
91 C8 Kuito Angola
Kuitun Xinjiang China see Kuytun
106 C3 Kuiu Island AK U.S.A.
20 R4 Kuivaniemi Fin.
18 G3 Kuivastu Estonia
18 J5 Kuja r. Latvia
54 G4 Kujakowice Dolne Pol.
179 K9 Kujang Orissa India
163 E9 Kujang N. Korea
54 G2 Kujawsko-Pomorskie prov. Pol.
164 S6 Kuji Japan
167 M3 Kuji-gawa r. Japan
167 L4 Kujikuri Japan
164 S6 Kuji-wan b. Japan
167 L5 Kujūkuri-hama coastal area Japan
165 I13 Kujū-san vol. Japan
184 D6 Kukālār, Kūh-e hill Iran
162 H4 Kukan Rus. Fed.
162 H4 Kukan r. Rus. Fed.
111 L1 Kukatush Ont. Can.
89 I3 Kukawa Nigeria
209 E12 Kukerin W.A. Austr.
76 I8 Kukës Albania
16 E2 Kukhits'ka Volya Ukr.
167 K3 Kuki Japan
167 L4 Kukizaki Japan
166 D7 Kuki-zaki pt Japan
20 R4 Kukkola Fin.
55 I2 Kuklin Pol.
54 F4 Kuklinów Pol.
59 N5 Kukmirn Austria
14 J4 Kukmor Rus. Fed.
14 G4 Kukoboy Rus. Fed.
18 K2 Kukruse Estonia
178 E8 Kukshi Madh. Prad. India
200 □6 Kukudu New Georgia Is Solomon Is
124 □F13 Kukuihaele HI U.S.A.
88 B4 Kukuna Sierra Leone
176 G4 Kukunuru Andhra Prad. India
156 E4 Kukup Malaysia
184 H2 Kukurtli Turkm.
157 K6 Kukusan, Gunung hill Indon.
14 L4 Kukushtan Rus. Fed.
184 F8 Kūl r. Iran
77 K7 Kula Bulg.
89 G5 Kula Nigeria
76 H5 Kula Vojvodina, Srbija Serb. and Mont.
76 H8 Kula mt. Serb. and Mont.
79 J4 Kula Turkey
156 C4 Kulabu, Gunung mt. Indon.
185 N6 Kulachi Pak.
19 P9 Kulagi Rus. Fed.
182 D3 Kulagino Kazakh.
179 M5 Kula Kangri mt. Bhutan
186 E5 Kulākh Saudi Arabia
92 C4 Kulal, Mount Kenya
182 D5 Kulaly, Ostrov i. Kazakh.
183 O6 Kulan Kazakh.
183 P7 Kulanak Kyrg.
182 H4 Kulandy Kazakh.
185 J9 Kulaneh reg. Pak.
183 M2 Kulanotpes watercourse Kazakh.
185 K7 Kulao r. Pak.
193 O2 Kular Rus. Fed.
154 C8 Kulassein i. Phil.
157 L4 Kulat, Gunung mt. Indon.
18 G7 Kulautuva Lith.
155 A4 Kulawi Sulawesi Indon.
85 F4 Kulb Sudan
17 N2 Kul'baki Rus. Fed.
18 E5 Kuldīga Latvia
162 G4 Kul'dur Rus. Fed.
94 D4 Kule Botswana
15 H5 Kulebaki Rus. Fed.
159 G8 Kulen Cambodia
79 L5 Kuleönü Turkey
19 U9 Kuleshi Rus. Fed.
17 S6 Kuleshovka Rus. Fed.
55 K2 Kulesze Pol.
55 K2 Kulesze Kościelne Pol.
182 I1 Kulevchinskoye Rus. Fed.
206 D8 Kulgera N.T. Austr.
182 G1 Kulgunino Rus. Fed.
191 I3 Kuli Rus. Fed.
18 E6 Kuliai Lith.
14 K4 Kuligi Rus. Fed.
183 R6 Kulikovka Kazakh.
14 I3 Kulikovo Arkhangel'skaya Oblast' Rus. Fed.
19 W9 Kulikovo Lipetskaya Oblast' Rus. Fed.
156 D2 Kulim Malaysia
209 E12 Kulin W.A. Austr.
176 F7 Kulittalai Tamil Nadu India
209 D11 Kulja W.A. Austr.
205 J4 Kulkyne watercourse N.S.W. Austr.
21 Q6 Kullaa Fin.
18 H3 Kullamaa Estonia
22 I5 Kullen pt Sweden
49 J8 Küllstedt Ger.
178 F4 Kullu Hima. Prad. India
53 L2 Kulmain Ger.
51 D10 Kulmbach Ger.
185 M3 Kŭlob Tajik.
19 Q3 Kulotino Rus. Fed.
14 H3 Kuloy Rus. Fed.
14 H2 Kuloy r. Rus. Fed.
189 J4 Kulp Turkey
204 F6 Kulpara S.A. Austr.
118 C3 Kulpmont PA U.S.A.
182 F4 Kul'sary Kazakh.
90 F2 Kulshabi Sudan
52 H2 Külsheim Ger.
57 G5 Kűlső-Somogy reg. Hungary
188 F4 Kulu Turkey
79 L5 Kulübe Tepe mt. Turkey
183 R1 Kulunda Rus. Fed.
183 R1 Kulunda r. Rus. Fed.
183 P1 Kulundinskaya Step' plain Kazakh./Rus. Fed.
183 R1 Kulundinskoye, Ozero salt l. Rus. Fed.
105 O3 Kulusuk Greenland
169 N1 Kulusutay Rus. Fed.
184 F6 Kūlvand Iran
205 I6 Kulwin Vic. Austr.
Kulyab Tajik. see Kŭlob
16 D4 Kulykiv Ukr.
17 K2 Kulykivka Ukr.
165 J13 Kuma Japan
191 H1 Kuma r. Rus. Fed.
20 U3 Kuma r. Rus. Fed.
55 I1 Kumachevo Rus. Fed.
17 R6 Kumachove Ukr.
167 J3 Kumagaya Japan
157 I6 Kumai Kalimantan Indon.
157 I6 Kumai, Teluk b. Indon.
164 Q4 Kumaishi Japan
182 I2 Kumak Rus. Fed.
182 H2 Kumak r. Rus. Fed.
137 G4 Kumaka Guyana
169 M1 Kumakhta Rus. Fed.
79 L4 Kumalar Dağı mts Turkey
165 H14 Kumamoto Japan
165 H14 Kumamoto pref. Japan
166 D8 Kumano Japan
166 C8 Kumanogawa Japan
77 J8 Kumanovo Macedonia
203 F9 Kumara South I. N.Z.
162 E3 Kumara Rus. Fed.
203 F9 Kumara Junction South I. N.Z.
179 L8 Kumarkhali Bangl.
88 E5 Kumasi Ghana
97 M7 Ku-Mayima S. Africa
89 H5 Kumba Cameroon
79 I2 Kumbağ Turkey
176 F7 Kumbakonam Tamil Nadu India
59 M5 Kumberg Austria
79 L3 Kümbet Turkey
176 C4 Kumbharli Ghat mt. Mahar. India
178 H5 Kumbher Nepal
176 D6 Kumbla Kerala India
89 H5 Kumbo Cameroon
18 F5 Kumbri Latvia
94 D4 Kumchuru Botswana
186 G5 Kumdah Saudi Arabia
79 L4 Kumdanlı Turkey
165 K11 Kume Japan
164 □D20 Kume-jima i. Nansei-shotō Japan
184 E4 Kumel well Iran
14 J4 Kumeny Rus. Fed.
182 F1 Kumertau Rus. Fed.
163 E11 Kŭm-gang r. S. Korea
163 F9 Kumgang-san mt. N. Korea
179 M6 Kumguri Assam India
173 C11 Kumharsain Hima. Prad. India
53 M4 Kumhausen Ger.
178 F6 Kumher Rajasthan India
163 F11 Kŭmho-gang r. S. Korea
163 F10 Kumi S. Korea
92 B4 Kumi Uganda
166 A4 Kumihama Japan
166 A4 Kumihama-wan l. Japan
84 B7 Kumishe Nigeria
166 C6 Kumiyama Japan
79 H3 Kumkale Turkey
172 J6 Kum Kuduk well Xinjiang China
23 L2 Kumla Sweden
21 P6 Kumlinge Åland Fin.
190 E2 Kumlu Turkey
79 L6 Kumluca Turkey
50 D4 Kummer Ger.
50 G3 Kummerow Ger.
50 G3 Kummerower See l. Ger.
53 L3 Kümmersbruck Ger.
51 H6 Kummersdorf-Alexanderdorf Ger.
51 H6 Kummersdorf Gut Ger.
89 H4 Kumo Nigeria
163 E11 Kŭmŏ-do i. S. Korea
183 L4 Kumola watercourse Kazakh.
158 C2 Kumon Range mts Myanmar
167 I4 Kumotori-yama mt. Japan
166 E6 Kumozu-gawa r. Japan
71 P6 Kumpare, Rt pt Croatia
158 F6 Kumphawapi Thai.
20 R3 Kumputunturi hill Fin.
59 M7 Kumrovec Croatia
96 D4 Kums Namibia
176 D5 Kumta Karnataka India
191 I2 Kumtorkala Rus. Fed.
90 E4 Kumu Dem. Rep. Congo
124 □G14 Kumukahi, Cape HI U.S.A.
191 I3 Kumukh Rus. Fed.
Kumul Xinjiang China see Hami
179 I9 Kumund Orissa India
191 E4 Kumurdo Georgia
172 I5 Kümüx Xinjiang China
Kumylzhenskaya Rus. Fed. see Kumylzhenskiy
15 H6 Kumylzhenskiy Rus. Fed.
183 N6 Kumyshtag, Pik mt. Kyrg.
158 C5 Kun r. Myanmar
57 I5 Kunadacs Hungary
57 K5 Kunágota Hungary
209 G7 Kunanaggi Well W.A. Austr.
185 N4 Kunar prov. Afgh.
185 N4 Kunar r. Afgh.
162 O6 Kunashir, Ostrov i. Kuril'skiye O-va Rus. Fed.
Kunashirskiy Proliv sea chan. Japan/Rus. Fed. see Nemuro-kaikyō
57 I5 Kunbaja Hungary
57 I5 Kunbaracs Hungary
191 G1 Kun'bator Rus. Fed.
158 C3 Kunchaung Myanmar
91 E5 Kunda Dem. Rep. Congo
18 J2 Kunda Estonia
18 J2 Kunda r. Estonia
178 H7 Kunda Uttar Prad. India
91 C7 Kunda-dia-Baze Angola
18 J2 Kunda laht b. Estonia
176 D6 Kundapura Karnataka India
185 M5 Kundar r. Afgh./Pak.
91 E7 Kundelungu, Parc National de nat. park Dem. Rep. Congo
91 E7 Kundelungu Ouest, Parc National de nat. park Dem. Rep. Congo
176 D5 Kundgol Karnataka India
185 N5 Kundian Pak.
58 E5 Kundl Austria
178 C9 Kundla Gujarat India
17 T6 Kundryuch'ya r. Rus. Fed./Ukr.
156 E4 Kundur i. Indon.
185 M3 Kunduz Afgh.
185 M3 Kunduz prov. Afgh.
91 B9 Kunene r. Angola/Namibia alt. Cunene
94 B3 Kunene admin. reg. Namibia
172 F5 Künes Chang Xinjiang China
172 E5 Künes He r. China
172 G5 Künes Linchang Xinjiang China
57 I5 Kunfehértó Hungary
22 H4 Kungälv Sweden
168 E1 Kungar-Tuk Rus. Fed.
183 Q6 Kungei Alatau mts Kazakh./Kyrg.
Kunggar Xizang China see Maizhokunggar
106 D4 Kunghit Island B.C. Can.
Küngöy Ala-Too mts Kazakh./Kyrg. see Kungei Alatau
23 N2 Kungsängen Sweden
22 I4 Kungsbacka Sweden
22 H3 Kungshamn Sweden
23 M2 Kungsör Sweden
90 C4 Kungu Dem. Rep. Congo
Kungur mt. Xinjiang China see Kongur Shan
14 L4 Kungur Rus. Fed.
158 B6 Kungyangon Myanmar
57 J4 Kunhegyes Hungary
37 O7 Kunheim France
170 B8 Kunhing Myanmar
176 F3 Kuni r. India
167 I2 Kuni Japan
54 E4 Kunice Pol.
184 H8 Kūnīch Iran
176 E6 Kunigai Karnataka India
166 D3 Kunimi-dake hill Japan
165 I14 Kunimi-dake mt. Japan
57 G2 Kunín Czech Rep.
18 K2 Kuningaküla Estonia
157 H8 Kuningan Jawa Indon.
54 G5 Kuniów Pol.
165 I13 Kunisaki Japan
179 J9 Kunjabar Orissa India
118 E3 Kunkletown PA U.S.A.
178 C9 Kunlavav Gujarat India
158 D3 Kunlong Myanmar
179 L7 Kunlui r. India/Nepal
168 C9 Kunlun Shan mts China
168 D9 Kunlun Shankou pass Qinghai China
57 J4 Kunmadaras Hungary
170 D6 Kunming Yunnan China
208 H3 Kunmunya Aboriginal Reserve W.A. Austr.
178 F6 Kuno r. India
56 G2 Kunovice Czech Rep.
55 J5 Kunów Pol.
51 K6 Kunowice Pol.
54 F4 Kunowo Pol.
24 D1 Kunoy i. Faroe Is
57 I4 Kunpeszér Hungary
50 D5 Kunrau Ger.
163 E11 Kunsan S. Korea
171 M3 Kunshan Jiangsu China
56 F2 Kunštát Czech Rep.
57 I5 Kunszállás Hungary
57 J5 Kunszentmárton Hungary
57 I4 Kunszentmiklós Hungary
91 D5 Kuntshankoie Dem. Rep. Congo
208 J3 Kununurra W.A. Austr.
107 L2 Kunwak r. Nunavut Can.
178 G6 Kunwari r. India
19 N5 Kun'ya Rus. Fed.
19 O4 Kun'ya r. Rus. Fed.
Kunyang Yunnan China see Jinning
Kunya-Urgench Turkm. see Keneurgench
17 Q4 Kun'ye Ukr.
169 Q8 Kunyu Shan mts China
56 E2 Kunžak Czech Rep.
49 I9 Künzell Ger.
52 H3 Künzelsau Ger.
51 D8 Künzels-Berg hill Ger.
53 O4 Künzing Ger.
91 C5 Kunzulu Dem. Rep. Congo
171 M4 Kuocang Shan mts China
20 T3 Kuolayarvi Rus. Fed.
21 S6 Kuolimo l. Fin.
20 S5 Kuopio Fin.
21 R6 Kuorevesi Fin.
20 T3 Kuosku Fin.
54 F5 Kup Pol.
68 F3 Kupa r. Croatia/Slovenia
155 C9 Kupang Timor Indon.
155 C9 Kupang, Teluk b. Timor Indon.
19 V5 Kupanskoye Rus. Fed.
179 K9 Kupari Orissa India
51 E10 Kupferberg Ger.
52 H3 Kupferzell Ger.
17 Q3 Kupino Rus. Fed.
18 H6 Kupiškis Lith.
71 R5 Kupjak Croatia
79 K2 Küplü Turkey
52 E4 Kuppenheim Ger.
18 K4 Kuprava Latvia
106 C3 Kupreanof AK U.S.A.
104 E4 Kupreanof Island AK U.S.A.
104 C4 Kupreanof Point AK U.S.A.
19 Y6 Kupreyevo Rus. Fed.
51 D10 Küps Ger.
19 N5 Kupuy Rus. Fed.
178 E2 Kupwara Jammu and Kashmir
17 Q4 Kup''yans'k Ukr.
17 Q4 Kup''yans'k-Vuzlovyy Ukr.
16 D3 Kupychiv Ukr.
172 F6 Kuqa Xinjiang China
191 H5 Kür Azer.
191 K6 Kür r. Azer.
189 L3 Kür r. Georgia
162 I4 Kur r. Rus. Fed.
191 G4 Kura r. Azer./Georgia
191 E2 Kura r. Rus. Fed.
191 E4 Kura r. Turkey
209 D8 Kurabuka r. W.A. Austr.
183 O6 Kuragaty Kazakh.
89 H4 Kuragwi Nigeria
165 J12 Kurahashi-jima i. Japan
166 F3 Kurai-yama mt. Japan
191 H5 Küräkçay r. Azer.
191 I4 Kurakh Rus. Fed.
17 Q6 Kurakhove Ukr.
Kurakhovo Ukr. see Kurakhove
Kurakhovstroy Ukr. see Kurakhove
Kura kurk sea chan. Estonia/Latvia see Irbe Strait
186 E3 Kuramā, Ḩarrat lava field Saudi Arabia
166 C5 Kurama-yama hill Japan
207 J4 Kuranda Qld Austr.
184 H8 Kūrān Dap Iran
182 G2 Kurashasayskiy Kazakh.
165 K12 Kurashiki Japan
178 I8 Kurasia Chhattisgarh India
208 I5 Kura Soak well W.A. Austr.
187 I2 Kurayn i. Saudi Arabia
165 K11 Kurayoshi Japan
168 A1 Kurayskiy Khrebet mts Rus. Fed.
19 W4 Kurba Rus. Fed.
79 K2 Kurban Dağı mt. Turkey
17 R2 Kurbatovo Rus. Fed.
162 F4 Kurbin He r. China
76 I4 Kurca r. Romania
191 H2 Kurchaloy Rus. Fed.
17 Q8 Kurchanskiy Liman salt l. Rus. Fed.
15 F6 Kurchatov Rus. Fed.
183 T3 Kurchum Kazakh.
183 T3 Kurchum r. Kazakh.
191 I5 Kürd Azer.
57 H5 Kurd Hungary
191 J5 Kürdämir Azer.
183 P6 Kurday Kazakh.
184 E7 Kūr Deh Iran
184 F8 Kūrdeh Iran
191 K7 Kür Dili pt Azer.
176 D3 Kurduvadi Mahar. India
77 N9 Kŭrdzhali Bulg.
191 B2 Kurdzhinovo Rus. Fed.
165 J12 Kure Japan
188 F3 Küre Turkey
197 G1 Kure Atoll HI U.S.A.
18 F3 Kuressaare Estonia
18 M3 Kureya r. Rus. Fed.
192 J3 Kureyskoye Vodokhranilishche resr Rus. Fed.
Kurgal'dzhino Kazakh. see Korgalzhyn
192 H4 Kurgan Rus. Fed.
15 H7 Kurganinsk Rus. Fed.
Kurgannaya Rus. Fed. see Kurganinsk
Kurgasyn Kazakh. see Korgasyn
178 G9 Kurhad Mahar. India
185 N3 Kuri Afgh.
178 C6 Kuri Rajasthan India
199 H1 Kuria is Gilbert Is Kiribati
Kuria Muria Bay Oman see Ḩalāniyāt, Khalīj al
Kuria Muria Islands Oman see Ḩalāniyāt, Juzur al
206 H6 Kuridala Qld Austr.
179 L7 Kurigram Bangl.
167 K5 Kurihama Japan
167 K3 Kurihashi Japan
20 Q5 Kurikka Fin.
164 R8 Kurikoma-yama vol. Japan
216 E2 Kuril Basin sea feature Sea of Okhotsk
76 H8 Kurile, Mal mt. Albania
Kuril Islands is Rus. Fed. see Kuril'skiye Ostrova
182 C2 Kurilovka Rus. Fed.
161 Q2 Kuril'sk Kuril'skiye O-va Rus. Fed.
161 Q2 Kuril'skiye Ostrova is Rus. Fed.
216 E3 Kuril Trench sea feature N. Pacific Ocean
56 F2 Kuřim Czech Rep.
57 K2 Kurima Slovakia
167 L4 Kurimoto Japan
165 H15 Kurino Japan
191 A1 Kurinskaya Rus. Fed.
164 S3 Kuriyama Hokkaidō Japan
167 K2 Kuriyama Tochigi Japan
19 V8 Kurkino Rus. Fed.
209 I7 Kurlkuta Aboriginal Reserve W.A. Austr.
19 X6 Kurlovskiy Rus. Fed.
182 D1 Kurmanayevka Rus. Fed.
Kurmashkino Kazakh. see Kurchum
18 H5 Kurmene Latvia
92 B2 Kurmuk Sudan
53 I2 Kürnach Ger.
52 F3 Kürnbach Ger.
16 H3 Kurne Ukr.
176 E5 Kurnool Andhra Prad. India
167 L2 Kurobane Japan
166 F2 Kurobe Japan
166 F2 Kurobe-gawa r. Japan
166 G2 Kurobe-ko resr Japan
166 B5 Kurodashō Japan
167 G2 Kurohime-yama mt. Japan
167 J3 Kurohone Japan
167 I1 Kurohume-yama hill Japan
164 R6 Kuroishi Japan
167 L2 Kuroiso Japan
164 R4 Kuromatsunai Japan
85 F4 Kuror, Jebel mt. Sudan
51 I9 Kurort Bad Gottleuba Ger.
51 I9 Kurort-Berggießhübel Ger.
49 J9 Kurort Brotterode Ger.
17 P8 Kurortne Ukr.
51 G10 Kurort Oberwiesenthal Ger.
49 J9 Kurort Schmalkalden Ger.
49 K9 Kurort Steinbach-Hallenberg Ger.
17 O6 Kuroshany r. Ukr.
164 □B22 Kuro-shima i. Nansei-shotō Japan
166 B7 Kuro-shima i. Japan
164 □G16 Kuro-shima i. Japan
166 D6 Kuroso-yama mt. Japan
162 E1 Kurovskiy Rus. Fed.
19 T7 Kurovskoy Rus. Fed.
19 V6 Kurovskoye Rus. Fed.
55 M6 Kurovychi Ukr.
203 E11 Kurow South I. N.Z.
55 K4 Kurów Pol.
55 H4 Kurowice Pol.
185 N5 Kurram r. Afgh./Pak.
185 N5 Kurram Pak.
205 M5 Kurri Kurri N.S.W. Austr.
191 D1 Kursavka Rus. Fed.
179 K7 Kursela Bihar India
18 F5 Kuršėnai Lith.
186 F4 Kursh, Jabal hill Saudi Arabia
Kürshim Kazakh. see Kurchum
18 J9 Kurshynavichy Belarus
18 F5 Kursīši Latvia
18 D6 Kuršių neringos nacionalinis parkas nat. park Lith.
15 G6 Kursk Rus. Fed.
191 F1 Kurskaya Rus. Fed.
15 G6 Kurskaya Oblast' admin. div. Rus. Fed.
Kursk Oblast admin. div. Rus. Fed. see Kurskaya Oblast'
17 O2 Kurskoye Vodokhranilishche resr Rus. Fed.
76 J7 Kuršumlija Srbija Serb. and Mont.
188 F3 Kurşunlu Turkey
189 J5 Kurtalan Turkey
79 H1 Kurtbey Turkey
Kürti r. Kazakh. see Kurtty
124 □F14 Kurtistown HI U.S.A.
191 F4 K'urt'lari Georgia
79 J6 Kurtoğlu Burnu pt Turkey
190 D2 Kurtpınar Turkey
190 D1 Kurttepe Turkey
183 Q5 Kurtty r. Kazakh.
Kurty r. Kazakh. see Kurtty
21 Q6 Kuru Fin.
Kurú r. Greece see Kourou
179 J8 Kuru Jharkhand India
90 E2 Kuru watercourse Sudan
88 C4 Kurubonla Sierra Leone
188 F3 Kurucaşile Turkey
191 B7 Kurucu Geçidi pass Turkey
178 H9 Kurud Chhattisgarh India
79 L2 Kurudere Turkey
178 F5 Kurukshetra Haryana India
172 H6 Kuruktag mts China
96 H3 Kuruman S. Africa
96 E2 Kuruman watercourse S. Africa
96 H3 Kuruman Hills S. Africa
165 H13 Kurume Japan
161 J1 Kurumkan Rus. Fed.
92 B3 Kurun r. Sudan
206 E6 Kurundi watercourse N.T. Austr.
176 D4 Kurundvad Mahar. India
176 G9 Kurunegala Sri Lanka
169 O1 Kurunzulay Rus. Fed.
177 H3 Kurupam Andhra Prad. India
137 G3 Kurupukari Guyana
85 F4 Kurush, Jebel hills Sudan
183 T2 Kur'ya Altayskiy Kray Rus. Fed.
14 L3 Kur'ya Respublika Komi Rus. Fed.
17 R4 Kuryachivka Ukr.
182 D6 Kuryk Kazakh.
55 M2 Kurylavichy Belarus
17 N5 Kurylivka Ukr.
55 K5 Kuryłówka Pol.
165 G11 Kuryongp'o S. Korea
55 H5 Kurzelów Pol.
55 I4 Kurzeszyn Pol.
55 H2 Kurzętnik Pol.
79 I5 Kuşadası Turkey
79 I5 Kuşadası Körfezi b. Turkey
Kusaie atoll Micronesia see Kosrae
190 E2 Kuşalanı Turkey
167 I2 Kusatsu Gunma Japan
166 C5 Kusatsu Shiga Japan
106 B2 Kusawa Lake Y.T. Can.
190 D2 Kuşcenneti nature res. Turkey
79 I2 Kuşcenneti Milli Parkı nat. park Turkey
165 K11 Kuse Japan
52 C2 Kusel Ger.
50 D5 Kusey Ger.
79 I2 Kuş Gölü l. Turkey
178 E8 Kushalgarh Rajasthan India
19 T4 Kushalino Rus. Fed.
184 G4 Kūshank Iran
15 G7 Kushchevskaya Rus. Fed.
89 G4 Kusheriki Nigeria
164 □1 Kushi Okinawa Japan
166 E6 Kushida-gawa r. Japan
167 H4 Kushigata Japan
166 F5 Kushihara Japan
165 H15 Kushikino Japan
165 I15 Kushima Japan
165 M13 Kushimoto Japan
164 V4 Kushiro Japan
164 V3 Kushiro-Shitsugen National Park Japan
184 B5 Kūshkī Iran
14 I3 Kushkopola Rus. Fed.
182 K1 Kushmurun Kazakh.
182 K1 Kushmurun, Ozero salt l. Kazakh.
14 K5 Kushnarenkovo Rus. Fed.
176 E5 Kushtagi Karnataka India
179 L8 Kushtia Bangl.
184 H7 Kushtih Iran
19 T1 Kushtozero, Ozero l. Rus. Fed.
17 O6 Kushuhum Ukr.
168 J7 Kushui He r. China
182 D2 Kushum Kazakh.
182 D3 Kushum r. Kazakh.
190 B2 Kuskan Turkey
104 B3 Kuskokwim r. AK U.S.A.
104 B4 Kuskokwim Bay AK U.S.A.
104 C3 Kuskokwim Mountains AK U.S.A.
19 S6 Kuskovo Rus. Fed.
70 F1 Küsnacht Switz.
163 D9 Kusŏng N. Korea
191 E2 Kusparty Rus. Fed.
164 V3 Kussharo-ko l. Japan
70 E1 Küssnacht Switz.
Kustanay Kazakh. see Kostanay
Kustanay Oblast admin. div. Kazakh. see Kostanayskaya Oblast'
21 P6 Kustavi Fin.
50 D5 Küsten Ger.
48 E4 Küstenkanal canal Ger.
52 G4 Kusterdingen Ger.
Kustia Bangl. see Kushtia
16 G4 Kustivtsi Ukr.
155 E3 Kusu Halmahera Indon.
166 E6 Kusu Japan
79 K4 Kuşu Turkey
191 H4 Kusur Rus. Fed.
184 C6 Kut Iran
159 F9 Kut, Ko i. Thai.
156 B2 Kutabagok Sumatera Indon.
184 C6 Kūt 'Abdollāh Iran
156 B3 Kutacane Sumatera Indon.
79 K3 Kütahya Turkey
79 K3 Kütahya prov. Turkey
157 L4 Kutai National Park Indon.
191 A1 Kutais Rus. Fed.
191 D3 K'ut'aisi Georgia
191 H1 Kutan Rus. Fed.
202 L5 Kutarere North I. N.Z.
57 K4 Kutas-főcsatorna canal Hungary
190 G7 Kutayfat Ţurayf vol. Saudi Arabia
Kutch, Gulf of Gujarat India see Kachchh, Gulf of
Kutch, Rann of marsh India see Rann of Kachchh
164 R4 Kutchan Japan
189 N7 Kūt-e Gapu tourist site Iran
48 H4 Kutenholz Ger.
17 R6 Kuteynykove Ukr.
68 F3 Kutina Croatia
68 F3 Kutjevo Croatia
158 C3 Kutkai Myanmar
97 K3 Kutloanong S. Africa
56 E2 Kutná Hora Czech Rep.
55 H3 Kutno Pol.
176 G3 Kutru Chhattisgarh India
166 C5 Kutsuki Japan
20 Q2 Kuttainen Sweden
90 C5 Kutu Dem. Rep. Congo
179 M9 Kutubdia Channel inlet Bangl.
179 M9 Kutubdia Island Bangl.
84 E6 Kutum Sudan
Kutuzov Moldova see Ialoveni
56 G3 Kúty Slovakia
16 F3 Kuty Ukr.
53 J5 Kutzenhausen Ger.
118 D3 Kutztown PA U.S.A.
104 G2 Kuujjua r. N.W.T. Can.
109 G1 Kuujjuaq Que. Can.
108 E2 Kuujjuarapik Que. Can.
184 E1 Kuuli-Mayak Turkm.
45 D7 Kuurne Belgium
20 R3 Kuusajoki Fin.
18 I2 Kuusalu Estonia
20 T4 Kuusamo Fin.
21 S6 Kuusankoski Fin.
18 G1 Kuusjoki Fin.
18 J3 Kuutse mägi hill Estonia
14 K4 Kuva Rus. Fed.
182 G2 Kuvandyk Rus. Fed.
91 C8 Kuvango Angola
19 R4 Kuvshinovo Rus. Fed.
Kuwait Kuwait see Al Kuwayt
189 M9 Kuwait country Asia
189 M9 Kuwait Jun b. Kuwait
Kuwajleen atoll Marshall Is see Kwajalein
166 E5 Kuwana Japan
14 H2 Kuya Rus. Fed.
184 E6 Kuyān Iran
Kūybyshev Kazakh. see Novoishimskiy
192 I4 Kuybyshev Novosibirskaya Oblast' Rus. Fed.
Kuybyshev Respublika Tatarstan Rus. Fed. see Bolgar
Kuybyshev Samarskaya Oblast' Rus. Fed. see Samara
17 Q6 Kuybysheve Donets'ka Oblast' Ukr.
17 P6 Kuybysheve Zaporiz'ka Oblast' Ukr.
17 R6 Kuybyshevo Rus. Fed.
15 J5 Kuybyshevskoye Vodokhranilishche resr Rus. Fed.
Kuybyshew Adyndaky Turkm. see imeni Kuybysheva
14 K4 Kuyeda Rus. Fed.
184 B2 Kūyeh Iran
169 L7 Kuye He r. China
183 P5 Kuygan Kazakh.
168 C5 Küysu Xinjiang China
172 G4 Kuytun Xinjiang China
172 F4 Kuytun He r. China
79 J5 Kuyucak Turkey
182 K2 Kuyukkol', Ozero salt l. Kazakh.
17 N7 Kuyuktuk, Ostriv i. Ukr.
190 C2 Kuyuluk Turkey
172 H1 Kuyus Rus. Fed.
126 □R10 Kuyu Tingni Nic.
137 G4 Kuyuwini r. Guyana
19 N1 Kuyvozi Rus. Fed.
166 E4 Kuze Japan
17 Q4 Kuzemivka Ukr.
17 N3 Kuzemyn Ukr.
14 J4 Kuzhener Rus. Fed.
19 Q4 Kuzhenkino Rus. Fed.
191 B1 Kuzhorskaya Rus. Fed.
18 G6 Kužiai Lith.
19 V2 Kuzino Rus. Fed.
57 K3 Kuzmice Slovakia
55 K6 Kuźmina Pol.
19 Q7 Kuz'minichi Rus. Fed.
19 W7 Kuz'minskoye Rus. Fed.
19 N1 Kuz'molovskiy Rus. Fed.
18 M1 Kuznechnoye Rus. Fed.
182 B1 Kuznetsk Rus. Fed.
162 K5 Kuznetsovo Rus. Fed.
16 E2 Kuznetsovs'k Ukr.
54 G5 Kuźnia Raciborska Pol.
55 L2 Kuźnica Pol.
54 E3 Kuźnica Czarnkowska Pol.
14 G2 Kuzomen' Rus. Fed.
15 I5 Kuzovatovo Rus. Fed.
19 V8 Kuzovka Rus. Fed.
164 S6 Kuzumaki Japan
166 D3 Kuzuryū-gawa r. Japan
166 E4 Kuzuryū-ko resr Japan
167 K3 Kuzuu Japan
20 P1 Kvænangen sea chan. Norway
22 G6 Kværndrup Denmark
48 H1 Kværs Denmark
20 O2 Kvaløya i. Norway
20 Q1 Kvaløya i. Norway
20 Q1 Kvalsund Norway
20 □ Kvalvågen b. Svalbard
182 H1 Kvarkeno Rus. Fed.
21 M6 Kvarnberg Sweden
68 E3 Kvarner g. Croatia
68 E3 Kvarnerić sea chan. Croatia
56 G2 Kvasice Czech Rep.
16 D5 Kvasy Ukr.
55 N3 Kvasyevichy Belarus
16 F3 Kvasyliv Ukr.
191 D2 K'veda Marghi Georgia
191 D4 K'veda Nasakirali Georgia
18 E6 Kvėdarna Lith.
22 F2 Kvelde Norway
191 G3 K'vemo Alvani Georgia
191 C2 K'vemo Azhara Georgia
191 G4 K'vemo Bodbe Georgia
191 F4 K'vemo Bolnisi Georgia
191 E4 K'vemo Boshuri Georgia
K'vemo-Marghi Georgia see K'veda Marghi
20 J5 Kvenvær Norway
104 C4 Kvichak Bay AK U.S.A.
22 D3 Kvifjorden l. Norway
20 N3 Kvikkjokk Sweden
23 L4 Kvillsfors Sweden
22 C3 Kvinesdal Norway
22 C3 Kvinlog Norway
21 N5 Kvissleby Sweden
21 I6 Kvitanosi mt. Norway
21 I5 Kvitegga mt. Norway
22 E2 Kviteseid Norway
20 □ Kvitøya i. Svalbard
22 B2 Kvitsøy Norway
91 C5 Kwa r. Dem. Rep. Congo
45 H6 Kwaadmechelen Belgium
Kwabhaca S. Africa see Mount Frere
97 O2 KwaChibukhulu S. Africa
106 E3 Kwadacha Wilderness Provincial Park B.C. Can.
97 N2 KwaDela S. Africa
Kwadelen atoll Marshall Is see Kwajalein
93 A6 Kwaga Tanz.
97 N1 KwaGuga S. Africa
171 □J7 Kwai Tau Leng hill H.K. China
200 □3a Kwajalein atoll Marshall Is
200 □3a Kwajalein i. Marshall Is
200 □3a Kwajalein Lagoon Kwajalein Marshall Is
137 H3 Kwakoegron Suriname
137 G3 Kwakwani Guyana
97 L3 Kwakwatse S. Africa
156 C3 Kwala Sumatera Indon.
93 C6 Kwale Kenya
89 G5 Kwale Nigeria
97 O5 KwaMashu S. Africa
97 Q4 Kwa-Mbonambi S. Africa
88 E5 Kwame Danso Ghana
97 M1 KwaMhlanga S. Africa
91 C5 Kwamouth Dem. Rep. Congo
93 B6 Kwa Mtoro Tanz.
155 C3 Kwandang Sulawesi Indon.
91 E6 Kwanga Dem. Rep. Congo
163 E11 Kwangju S. Korea
91 C5 Kwango r. Dem. Rep. Congo alt. Cuango (Angola)
Kwangtung prov. China see Guangdong
93 C6 Kwangwazi Tanz.
92 B4 Kwania, Lake Uganda
163 F8 Kwanmo-bong mt. N. Korea
97 J9 Kwanobuhle S. Africa
97 J8 KwaNojoli S. Africa
97 K9 Kwanonqubela S. Africa
97 I7 Kwanonzame S. Africa
97 L8 Kwa-Pita S. Africa
89 F4 Kwara state Nigeria
97 O2 KwaThandeka S. Africa
97 K8 Kwatinidubu S. Africa
97 N2 KwaZamokhule S. Africa
96 I8 Kwazamukucinga S. Africa
97 I7 Kwazamuxolo S. Africa
97 N2 KwaZanele S. Africa
97 O4 Kwazulu-Natal prov. S. Africa
95 F3 Kwekwe Zimbabwe
97 O1 Kwena Dam S. Africa
94 E4 Kweneng admin. dist. Botswana
91 C6 Kwenge r. Dem. Rep. Congo
108 D3 Kwetabohigan r. Ont. Can.
97 L6 Kwezi-Naledi S. Africa
89 G4 Kwiambana Nigeria
54 G2 Kwidzyn Pol.
104 B4 Kwigillingok AK U.S.A.
186 D9 Kwīhā Eth.
153 K8 Kwikila P.N.G.
54 E3 Kwilcz Pol.
91 C5 Kwilu r. Angola/Dem. Rep. Congo
209 C12 Kwinana W.A. Austr.
54 D4 Kwisa r. Pol.
137 G4 Kwitaro r. Guyana
171 □J7 Kwo Chau Kwan To is H.K. China
153 H7 Kwoka mt. Papua Indon.
90 E3 Kwoungo, Mont mt. C.A.R.
171 □J7 Kwun Tong H.K. China
90 C2 Kyabé Chad
158 B3 Kyabin Myanmar
207 I9 Kyabra Qld Austr.
207 I8 Kyabra watercourse Qld Austr.
205 J7 Kyabram Vic. Austr.
158 B4 Kyadet Myanmar
158 B6 Kyaiklat Myanmar
158 C6 Kyaikto Myanmar
158 D6 Kya-in Seikkyi Myanmar
168 J1 Kyakhta Rus. Fed.
205 I6 Kyalite N.S.W. Austr.
204 E5 Kyancutta S.A. Austr.
14 G2 Kyanda Rus. Fed.
158 B5 Kyangin Irrawaddy Myanmar
158 C5 Kyangin Mandalay Myanmar
173 L11 Kyangngoin Xizang China
158 C5 Kyaukhnyat Myanmar
158 C5 Kyaukkyi Myanmar
158 C3 Kyaukmaw Myanmar
158 C3 Kyaukme Myanmar
158 B3 Kyaukmyaung Myanmar
158 B4 Kyaukpadaung Myanmar
158 A5 Kyaukpyu Myanmar
158 C4 Kyaukse Myanmar
158 C6 Kyauktan Myanmar
158 A4 Kyauktaw Myanmar
158 B4 Kyaukyit Myanmar
158 B6 Kyaunggon Myanmar
18 F7 Kybartai Lith.
205 L7 Kybeyan Range mts N.S.W. Austr.
204 H7 Kybybolite S.A. Austr.
158 H3 Ky Cung, Sông r. Vietnam
203 E12 Kyeburn South I. N.Z.
158 D6 Kyeikdon Myanmar
158 B6 Kyeintali Myanmar
93 B7 Kyela Tanz.
178 F3 Kyelang Hima. Prad. India
92 A4 Kyenjojo Uganda
88 E5 Kyeraa Ghana
158 C5 Kyidaunggan Myanmar
168 G8 Kyikug Qinghai China
89 E4 Kyinderi Ghana
16 J3 Kyiv Ukr.
16 J3 Kyivs'ka Oblast' admin. div. Ukr.
56 G2 Kyjov Czech Rep.
78 G5 Kyklades dept Greece
188 B5 Kyklades is Greece
107 I5 Kyle Sask. Can.
29 O5 Kyle r. England U.K.
26 E8 Kyleakin Highland, Scotland U.K.
26 E8 Kyle of Lochalsh Highland, Scotland U.K.
26 H6 Kyle of Tongue inlet Scotland U.K.
26 E8 Kylerhea Highland, Scotland U.K.
26 F11 Kyles of Bute sea chan. Scotland U.K.
26 C7 Kyles Scalpay Western Isles, Scotland U.K.
26 F6 Kylestrome Highland, Scotland U.K.
49 C11 Kyll r. Ger.
49 C10 Kyllburg Ger.
78 C5 Kyllini Greece
78 D5 Kyllini mt. Greece
78 C5 Kyllinis, Akra pt Greece
21 Q6 Kylmäkoski Fin.
78 F4 Kymi Greece
18 J1 Kymijoki r. Fin.
78 F4 Kymis, Akra pt Greece
22 I2 Kymmen l. Sweden
205 J7 Kyneton Vic. Austr.
22 I1 Kynna r. Norway
56 B1 Kynšperk nad Ohří Czech Rep.
207 H6 Kynuna Qld Austr.
164 □1 Kyoda Okinawa Japan
92 B4 Kyoga, Lake Uganda
166 E3 Kyōga-dake mt. Japan
167 G4 Kyōga-dake mt. Japan
166 B4 Kyōga-misaki pt Japan
205 N3 Kyogle N.S.W. Austr.
90 F2 Kyom watercourse Sudan
167 K5 Kyonan Japan
158 D6 Kyondo Myanmar
207 J6 Kyong Qld Austr.
158 C4 Kyong Myanmar
163 D10 Kyŏnggi-man b. S. Korea
163 F11 Kyongjiu National Park S. Korea
163 F11 Kyŏngju S. Korea
158 B6 Kyonpyaw Myanmar
166 C6 Kyōtanabe Japan
166 C6 Kyōto Japan
166 B5 Kyōto pref. Japan
164 R7 Kyōwa Akita Japan
167 L3 Kyōwa Ibaraki Japan
78 C5 Kyparissia Greece
78 C5 Kyparissiakos Kolpos b. Greece

Kypshak, Ozero to Laï

289

33 M2 Kypshak, Ozero salt l. Kazakh.
59 M2 Kyra Rus. Fed.
78 F3 Kyra Panagia i. Greece
Kyrenia Cyprus see Keryneia
33 P7 Kyrgyzstan country Asia
16 I8 Kyrhyzh-Kytay r. Ukr.
78 F1 Kyria Greece
78 D4 Kyriaki Greece
50 F5 Kyritz Ger.
50 G4 Kyritz-Ruppiner Heide park Ger.
22 C2 Kyrkjenuten mt. Norway
32 D3 Kyrkopa Kazakh.
20 J5 Kyrksæterøra Norway
16 H5 Kyrnasivka Ukr.
16 I8 Kyrnychky Ukr.
14 L2 Kyrta Rus. Fed.
14 L4 Kyr'ya Rus. Fed.
17 O3 Kyrykivka Ukr.
17 O7 Kyrylivka Ukr.
17 P4 Kyseli Ukr.
16 E5 Kyseliv Ukr.
17 K2 Kyselivka Ukr.
16 G2 Kyshyy Ukr.
14 I2 Kyssa Rus. Fed.
57 I2 Kysuce park Slovakia
57 H2 Kysucké Nové Mesto Slovakia
93 O3 Kytalyktakh Rus. Fed.
16 I8 Kytay, Ozero l. Ukr.
17 N5 Kytayhorod Ukr.
78 D6 Kythira Kythira Greece
78 D6 Kythira i. Greece
78 F5 Kythnos i. Greece
78 F5 Kythnou, Steno sea chan. Greece
90 B3 Kythrea Cyprus
14 L4 Kytlym Rus. Fed.
Kyumyush-Tak, Pik mt. Kyrg. see Kumyshtag, Pik
73 E11 Kyunglung Xizang China
58 D7 Kyungyaung Myanmar
58 B3 Kyunhla Myanmar
59 C9 Kyun Pila i. Myanmar
06 E5 Kyuquot B.C. Can.
Kyurdamir Azer. see Kürdämir
32 G5 Kyushe Kazakh.
65 I15 Kyūshū i. Japan
16 E4 Kyushu-Palau Ridge sea feature N. Pacific Ocean
65 I14 Kyūshū-sanchi mts Japan
77 K8 Kyustendil Bulg.
58 C5 Kywebwe Myanmar
05 K6 Kywong N.S.W. Austr.
Kyyev Ukr. see Kyiv
Kyyiv Ukr. see Kyiv
16 J3 Kyyivs'ke Vodoskhovyshche resr Ukr.
20 R5 Kyyjärvi Fin.
21 S6 Kyyvesi l. Fin.
32 E5 Kyzan Kazakh.
91 E2 Kyzburun Tretiy Rus. Fed.
50 F1 Kyzyl Rus. Fed.
33 N6 Kyzyl-Adyr Kyrg.
33 R5 Kyzylagash Kazakh.
Kyzyl-Art, Pereval pass Kyrg./Tajik. see Kyzylart Pass
35 O2 Kyzylart Pass Kyrg./Tajik.
33 O5 Kyzylbelen, Gora hill Kazakh.
33 M3 Kyzyldyykan Kazakh.
33 T4 Kyzylkesek Kazakh.
Kyzylkesken Kazakh. see Kyzylkesek
68 A1 Kyzyl-Khaya Rus. Fed.
Kyzyl-Kiya Kyrg. see Kyzyl-Kyya
32 E3 Kyzylkoga Kazakh.
32 I3 Kyzylkol', Ozero l. Kazakh.
Kyzylkum, Peski des. Kazakh./Uzbek. see Kyzylkum Desert
32 K6 Kyzylkum Desert Kazakh./Uzbek.
33 O7 Kyzyl-Kyya Kyrg.
50 F1 Kyzyl-Mazhalyk Rus. Fed.
32 K5 Kyzylorda Kazakh.
Kyzyl-Orda Oblast admin. div. Kazakh. see Kyzylordinskaya Oblast'
32 J5 Kyzylordinskaya Oblast' admin. div. Kazakh.
32 K5 Kyzylordinskoye Vodokhranilishche resr Kazakh.
32 E6 Kyzylsay Kazakh.
33 Q6 Kyzyl-Suu Kyrg.
33 N8 Kyzyl-Suu r. Kyrg.
33 P2 Kyzyltas Kazakh.
33 O4 Kyzyltau Kazakh.
32 K3 Kyzyluy Kazakh.
32 D5 Kyzylysor Kazakh.
32 F2 Kyzylzhar Kazakh.
33 M3 Kyzylzhar Kazakh.
Kzyl-Dzhar Kazakh. see Kyzylzhar
Kzyl-Orda Kazakh. see Kyzylorda
Kzyltu Kazakh. see Kishkenekol'
91 L1 Kzyl-uzen Kazakh.

L

59 N2 Laa an der Thaya Austria
53 L3 Laaber Ger.
49 D10 Laacher See l. Ger.
47 E6 La Adela Arg.
50 F3 Laage Ger.
18 H2 Laagri Estonia
26 D6 La Aguja Mex.
62 H7 La Alberca Castilla y León Spain
67 C12 La Alberca Murcia Spain
63 P9 La Alberca de Záncara Spain
62 G8 La Alberguería de Argañán Spain
64 F3 La Albuera Spain
63 O7 La Alcarria reg. Spain
98 □3f La Aldea, Punta de pt Gran Canaria Canary Is
63 J8 La Aldehuela Spain
64 G6 La Algaba Spain
63 J8 La Aliseda de Tormes Spain
67 C12 La Aljorra Spain
63 P9 La Almarcha Spain
66 E4 La Almolda Spain
63 R6 La Almunia de Doña Godina Spain
46 E6 La Amarga, Laguna l. Arg.
26 □R13 La Amistad, Parque Internacional nat. park Costa Rica/Panama
98 □3b La Ampuyenta Fuerteventura Canary Is
27 M10 La Angostura, Presa de resr Mex.
14 D1 Laanila Fin.
18 K3 Lääniste Estonia
92 F2 Laanle well Somalia
46 D1 La Antigua, Salina salt pan Arg.
64 E6 La Antilla Spain
28 E3 La Ardilla, Cerro mt. Mex.
47 I5 La Argentina, Laguna l. Arg.
59 I4 Laarkirchen Austria
62 J6 La Armuña reg. Spain
45 E6 Laarne Belgium
92 F3 Laas Aano Somalia
92 E2 Laascaanood Somalia
27 P8 La Ascensión, Bahía de b. Mex.
92 F2 Laas Dawaco Somalia
92 F2 Laasgoray Somalia
50 E4 Laaslich Ger.
46 E5 La Asturiana Arg.
37 F2 La Asunción Venez.
62 F9 La Atalaya de Santiago hill Spain
49 I6 Laatzen Ger.
24 □D12 La'au Point HI U.S.A.
70 G2 Laax Switz.
86 B4 Laâyoune Western Sahara
67 C12 La Azohía Spain
76 J8 Lab r. Serb. and Mont.
191 B2 Laba r. Rus. Fed.
126 H3 La Babia Mex.
39 J5 La Baconnière France
66 I3 La Baells, Pantà de resr Spain
126 □P9 La Bahía, Islas de is Hond.
109 G3 La Baie Que. Can.
63 K7 Labajos Spain
155 C8 Labala Indon.
108 E2 La Baleine, Grande Rivière de r. Que. Can.
108 E2 La Baleine, Petite Rivière de r. Que. Can.
109 H1 La Baleine, Rivière à r. Que. Can.
98 □3b La Ballena, Punta de pt Fuerteventura Canary Is
40 I5 La Balme-de-Sillingy France
144 D2 La Banda Arg.
128 B1 La Bandera, Cerro mt. Mex.
62 I4 La Bañeza Spain
157 J3 Labang Sarawak Malaysia
18 I6 Labanoras Lith.
Labao Guangxi China see Liujiang
128 E5 La Barca Mex.
122 I5 La Barge WY U.S.A.
38 G8 La Barre-de-Monts France
39 M4 La Barre-en-Ouche France
43 E9 La Barthe-de-Neste France
43 F9 Labarthe-Rivière France
201 □1 Labasa Vanua Levu Fiji
36 E2 La Bassée France
43 B9 La Bastide-Clairence France
43 H9 Labastide-d'Anjou France
43 D8 Labastide-d'Armagnac France
43 H9 La Bastide-de Bousignac France
43 G9 La Bastide-de-Sérou France
41 H9 La Bastide-des-Jourdans France
43 I7 La Bastide-l'Évêque France
43 H6 Labastide-Murat France
41 D7 La Bastide-Puylaurent France
41 B10 Labastide-Rouairoux France
43 G8 Labastide-St-Pierre France
43 H10 La Bastide-sur-l'Hers France
40 I5 La Bâthie France
41 I7 La Bâtie-Neuve France
99 □3b Labattoir Mayotte
43 C8 Labatut France
43 E8 Labatut-Rivière France
38 G7 La Baule-Escoublac France
193 K2 Labaz, Ozero l. Rus. Fed.
14 K2 Labazhskoye Rus. Fed.
39 M5 La Bazoche-Gouet France
39 L5 La Bazoge France
70 A2 L'Abbaye Switz.
56 D1 Labe r. Czech Rep. alt. Elbe (Germany)
88 B4 Labé Guinea
41 F7 La Bégude-de-Mazenc France
43 E8 Labéjan France
108 F4 Labelle Que. Can.
115 G12 La Belle FL U.S.A.
155 C5 Labengke i. Indon.
43 B8 Labenne France
89 I4 La Bénoué, Parc National de nat. park Cameroon
41 I7 La Bérarde France
106 C2 Laberge, Lake Y.T. Can.
40 G2 Labergement-lès-Seurre France
147 F6 Laberinto, Punta pt Arg.
41 J9 La Bernarde, Sommet de mt. France
38 G7 La Bernerie-en-Retz France
70 C2 La Berra mt. Switz.
53 M4 Laberweinting Ger.
70 E5 La Bessa, Riserva Naturale nature res. Italy
157 K2 Labi Brunei
63 R3 Labia, Sierra de mts Spain
157 M2 Labian, Tanjung pt Malaysia
106 F3 La Biche r. N.W.T. Can.
107 H4 La Biche, Lac l. Alta Can.
68 E3 Labin Croatia
191 B1 Labinsk Rus. Fed.
40 H5 La Biolle France
156 E3 Labis Malaysia
66 G5 La Bisbal de Falset Spain
66 H5 La Bisbal del Penedès Spain
66 L4 La Bisbal d'Empordà Spain
54 F3 Łabiszyn Pol.
126 D3 La Biznaga Mex.
41 E8 Lablachère France
147 G2 La Blanca, Laguna l. Arg.
147 F6 La Blanca Grande Laguna l. Arg.
154 D4 Labo Luzon Phil.
62 G2 La Bobia, Sierra de mts Spain
155 C4 Labobo i. Indon.
191 E3 Laboda, Gora mt. Georgia/Rus. Fed.
63 O6 La Bodera mt. Spain
48 J2 Laboe Ger.
129 H2 La Bolsa Mex.
147 I2 La Bolsa Uru.
90 D3 La Bomu, Réserve de Faune de nature res. Dem. Rep. Congo
36 B6 La Bonneville-sur-Iton France
126 G4 La Boquilla Mex.
126 G4 La Boquilla, Presa de resr Mex.
94 C4 Labora Namibia
147 F3 Laborde Arg.
57 K3 Laborec r. Slovakia
131 □3 Laborie St Lucia
209 E8 Labouchere, Mount hill W.A. Austr.
88 C3 La Boucle du Baoulé, Parc National de nat. park Mali
190 E4 Laboué Lebanon
38 I5 La Bouëxière France
147 I2 Labougle Arg.
43 C7 Labouheyre France
41 H10 La Bouilladisse France
147 F4 Laboulaye Arg.
40 B5 La Bourboule France
43 A9 Labourd reg. France
38 H4 La Boussac France
43 I8 Laboutarie France
63 J6 La Bóveda de Toro Spain
55 I6 Łabowa Pol.
109 I2 Labrador reg. Nfld and Lab. Can.
109 H2 Labrador City Nfld and Lab. Can.
105 M3 Labrador Sea Can./Greenland
136 C3 Labranzagrande Col.
147 G2 La Brava Arg.
147 F3 La Brava, Laguna l. Arg.
138 D1 Lábrea Brazil
136 A6 La Brea Peru
131 □7 La Brea Trin. and Tob.
43 C6 La Brède France
65 J5 La Breña, Embalse de resr Spain
42 G2 La Brenne, Parc Naturel Régional de nature res. France
41 I8 La Bréole France
37 M7 La Bresse France
40 H5 La Bridoire France
43 C7 Labrit France
37 N7 La Broque France
38 I7 La Bruffière France
43 I8 Labruguière France
64 A2 Labrujeira Port.
39 J8 L'Absie France
157 K2 Labuan Malaysia
157 K2 Labuan i. Malaysia
157 K2 Labuan state Malaysia
155 B4 Labuanbajo Sulawesi Indon.
128 D7 La Bufa, Cerro mt. Mex.
156 F8 Labuhan Jawa Indon.
155 A8 Labuhanbajo Flores Indon.
156 D3 Labuhanbilik Sumatera Indon.
156 B3 Labuhanhaji Sumatera Indon.
156 F7 Labuhanmeringgai Sumatera Indon.
156 C3 Labuhanruku Sumatera Indon.
41 H6 La Buisse France
157 L2 Labuk r. Malaysia
157 L1 Labuk, Teluk b. Malaysia
155 E4 Labuna Maluku Indon.
55 L5 Łabunie Pol.
63 N3 La Bureba reg. Spain
36 E8 La Bussière France
158 B6 Labutta Myanmar
23 N1 Läby Sweden
204 E4 Labyrinth, Lake salt flat S.A. Austr.
107 J2 Labyrinth Lake N.W.T. Can.
192 H3 Labytnangi Rus. Fed.
76 H9 Laç Albania
84 B6 Lac pref. Chad
147 G2 La Cabral Arg.
63 M7 La Cabrera Spain
62 G4 La Cabrera, Sierra de mts Spain
126 G5 La Cadena Mex.
41 H10 La Cadière-d'Azur France
39 J8 La Caillère-St-Hilaire France
65 M6 Lacalahorra Spain
147 H2 La Calandria Arg.
65 L2 La Calderina mt. Spain
65 L2 La Calderina, Sierra de mts Spain
146 E2 La Calera Arg.
98 □3a La Calera La Gomera Canary Is
146 B3 La Calera Chile
98 □3c La Caleta Lanzarote Canary Is
72 D6 La Caletta Sardegna Italy
109 I3 Lac Allard Que. Can.
41 B7 Lacalm France
41 E9 La Calmette France
63 J9 La Calzada de Oropesa Spain
65 I5 La Campana Spain
146 B3 La Campana, Parque Nacional nat. park Chile
65 O7 La Cañada de San Urbano Spain
66 E6 La Cañada de Verich Spain
42 B6 Lacanau France
42 B6 Lacanau, Étang de l. France
42 B5 Lacanau-Océan France
40 F2 Lacanche France
127 N9 Lacandón, Parque Nacional nat. park Guat.
41 C8 La Canourgue France
127 N9 Lacantún r. Mex.
36 G4 La Capelle France
41 B7 Lacapelle-Barrès France
43 H6 Lacapelle-Marival France
43 I6 Lacapelle-Viescamp France
147 H2 La Capila Arg.
64 F3 Lácara r. Spain
76 H5 Laćarak Vojvodina, Srbija Serb. and Mont.
131 □3 La Caravelle, Presqu'île de pen. Martinique
62 G1 La Caridad Spain
147 F3 La Carlota Arg.
154 D6 La Carlota Negros Phil.
65 J5 La Carlota Spain
65 L4 La Carolina Spain
43 B9 Lacarre France
41 B9 Lacaune France
41 B9 Lacaune, Monts de mts France
63 M2 La Cavada Spain
41 C8 La Cavalerie France
43 H6 Lacave France
41 J8 La Cayolle, Col de pass France
43 J8 Lacaze France
117 □Q1 Lac-Baker N.B. Can.
Laccadive, Minicoy and Amindivi Islands union terr. India see Lakshadweep
176 C7 Laccadive Islands India
73 L6 Lacco Ameno Italy
107 L5 Lac du Bonnet Man. Can.
110 E4 Lac du Flambeau WI U.S.A.
29 Q6 Laceby North East Lincolnshire, England U.K.
73 O5 Lacedonia Italy
126 □P10 La Ceiba Hond.
66 K4 La Cellera de Ter Spain
39 M7 La Celle-St-Avant France
36 D6 La Celle-St-Cloud France
La Cenia Spain see La Sènia
204 G7 Lacepede Bay S.A. Austr.
208 G4 Lacepede Islands W.A. Austr.
63 N3 La Cerca Spain
66 E6 La Cerollera Spain
71 J2 Laces Italy
147 F3 La Cesira Arg.
109 G4 Lac-Etchemin Que. Can.
118 C1 Laceyville PA U.S.A.
117 □O2 Lac Frontière Que. Can.
14 G3 Lacha, Ozero l. Rus. Fed.
41 D6 La Chaise-Dieu France
38 I8 La Chaize-le-Vicomte France
41 I6 La Chambre France
40 B4 La Chapelaude France
37 J4 La Chapelle France
42 G5 La Chapelle-Aubareil France
37 L7 La Chapelle-aux-Bois France
42 H6 La Chapelle-aux-Saints France
40 J4 La Chapelle-d'Abondance France
39 K6 La Chapelle-d'Aligné France
39 K4 La Chapelle-d'Andaine France
39 P7 La Chapelle-d'Angillon France
38 H5 La Chapelle-des-Fougeretz France
38 G7 La-Chapelle-des-Marais France
41 I7 La Chapelle-en-Valgaudémar France
41 G7 La Chapelle-en-Vercors France
36 E7 La Chapelle-la-Reine France
41 C6 La Chapelle-Laurent France
40 C2 La Chapelle-St-André France
39 K8 La Chapelle-St-Laurent France
36 H7 La Chapelle-St-Luc France
36 C8 La Chapelle-St-Mesmin France
40 H2 La Chapelle-St-Quillain France
39 P7 La Chapelle-St-Ursin France
41 E7 Lachapelle-sous-Aubenas France
38 H7 La Chapelle-sur-Erdre France
40 C2 La Charité-sur-Loire France
39 M6 La Chartre-sur-le-Loir France
41 H6 La Chartreuse, Massif de mts France
42 C2 La Châtaigneraie France
42 H2 La Châtre France
42 G3 La Châtre-Langlin France
37 I8 La Chaume France
37 K5 Lachaussée, Étang de l. France
39 N6 La Chaussée-St-Victor France
36 I6 La Chaussée-sur-Marne France
70 B1 La Chaux-de-Fonds Switz.
40 H3 La Chaux-du-Dombief France
179 L6 Lachen Sikkim India
70 F1 Lachen Switz.
48 J5 Lachendorf Ger.
41 J9 Lachens, Montagne de mt. France
52 E3 Lachen-Speyerdorf Ger.
36 I5 La Cheppe France
38 B5 La Chèvre, Cap de c. France
38 H7 La Chevrolière France
38 F5 La Chèze France
111 K4 Lachine MI U.S.A.
17 Q2 Lachinovo Rus. Fed.
205 I6 Lachlan r. N.S.W. Austr.
136 C5 La Chorrera Col.
126 □T13 La Chorrera Panama
55 K2 Lachowo Pol.
48 J5 Lachte r. Ger.
65 I8 La Chullera, Punta de pt Spain
179 L6 Lachung Sikkim India
108 F4 Lachute Que. Can.
18 J6 Lāči Latvia
63 Q8 La Cierva Spain
191 H6 Laçın Azer.
41 H10 La Ciotat France
63 K5 La Cisterniga Spain
128 B2 La Ciudad Mex.
109 I2 Lac Joseph-Atikonak Wilderness Reserve Nfld and Lab. Can.
55 H3 Łąck Pol.
28 B4 Lack Northern Ireland U.K.
23 N3 Lacka naturreservat nature res. Sweden
116 G6 Lackawanna NY U.S.A.
118 D2 Lackawanna r. PA U.S.A.
118 D2 Lackawanna County county PA U.S.A.
118 F2 Lackawaxen r. PA U.S.A.
55 I6 Łącko Pol.
107 I4 Lac La Biche Alta Can.
Lac la Martre N.W.T. Can. see Wha Ti
107 J4 Lac La Ronge Provincial Park Sask. Can.
40 E4 La Clayette France
90 B4 Lac Lobeke, Réserve du res. Cameroon
40 I5 La Clusaz France
41 H7 La Cluse France
40 I3 La Cluse-et-Mijoux France
109 G4 Lac-Mégantic Que. Can.
144 D2 La Cocha Arg.
30 H5 Lacock Wiltshire, England U.K.
64 E2 La Codosera Spain
66 G5 La Cogulla mt. Spain
147 G5 La Colina Arg.
63 J3 La Collada pass Spain
117 L3 Lacolle Que. Can.
41 K9 La Colle-sur-Loup France
129 H3 La Colmena, Sierra mts Mex.
126 D3 La Colorada Sonora Mex.
128 E2 La Colorada Zacatecas Mex.
106 H4 Lacombe Alta Can.
88 E4 La Comoé, Parc National de nat. park Côte d'Ivoire
110 E8 Lacon IL U.S.A.
129 I2 La Concepción Mex.
126 □R13 La Concepción Panama
63 M2 La Concha Spain
127 M9 La Concordia Mex.
41 J8 La Condamine-Châtelard France
72 C8 Laconi Sardegna Italy
117 N5 Laconia NH U.S.A.
146 C3 La Consulta Arg.
147 G5 La Copeta Arg.
41 C9 La Coquillade hill France
42 F4 La Coquille France
107 I4 La Corey Alta Can.
111 Q1 La Corne Que. Can.
65 I4 La Coronada Andalucía Spain
64 H3 La Coronada Extremadura Spain
72 B2 La Corse, Parc Naturel Régional de nature res. Corse France
La Coruña Spain see A Coruña
108 F2 La Corvette, Lac de l. Que. Can.
41 G9 Lacoste France
41 G6 La Côte-St-André France
42 B3 La-Couarde-sur-Mer France
42 B4 La Coubre, Pointe de pt France
42 E4 La Couronne France
43 G10 Lacourt France
42 I4 La Courtine France
36 B6 La Couture-Boussey France
41 C9 La Couvertoirade France
130 □ Lacovia Jamaica
43 C9 Lacq France
41 I10 La Crau France
42 D3 La Crèche France
131 □8 Lacre Punt pt Bonaire Neth. Antilles
110 C6 La Crescent MN U.S.A.
106 G3 La Crete Alta Can.
66 G6 La Creu de Santos hill Spain
147 H2 La Criolla Entre Ríos Arg.
147 G2 La Criolla Santa Fé Arg.
110 C1 La Croix, Lac l. Can./U.S.A.
41 B7 Lacroix-Barrez France
70 A5 La Croix de Fer, Col de pass France
41 H7 La Croix-Haute, Col de pass France
39 I5 La Croixille France
36 E5 Lacroix-St-Ouen France
41 J10 La Croix-Valmer France
120 F6 La Crosse KS U.S.A.
116 G12 La Crosse VA U.S.A.
110 C6 La Crosse WI U.S.A.
43 I8 Lacrouzette France
146 E3 La Cruz Córdoba Arg.
144 F3 La Cruz Corrientes Arg.
136 B4 La Cruz Col.
126 □Q12 La Cruz Costa Rica
126 G4 La Cruz Chihuahua Mex.
126 F6 La Cruz Sinaloa Mex.
129 H1 La Cruz Tamaulipas Mex.
129 J2 La Cruz Tamaulipas Mex.
126 □Q11 La Cruz Nic.
147 I3 La Cruz Uru.
128 F8 La Cruz, Cerro mt. Mex.
128 B6 La Cruz de Loreto Mex.
63 M7 La Cuenca Alta del Manzanares, Parque Regional de park Spain
63 O5 La Cuerda del Pozo, Embalse de resr Spain
126 H3 La Cuesta Coahuila Mex.
128 C5 La Cuesta Jalisco Mex.
62 H5 La Culebra, Sierra de mts Spain
146 E2 La Cumbre Arg.
64 H2 La Cumbre Spain
Lacunza Spain see Lakuntza
123 K11 La Curva Mex.
120 H6 La Cygne KS U.S.A.
55 J4 Łączany Pol.
55 I5 Łączna Pol.
54 F5 Łącznik Pol.
55 K5 Łada r. Pol.
156 F8 Lada, Teluk b. Indon.
143 G2 Ladainha Brazil
178 F2 Ladakh reg. Jammu and Kashmir
178 F2 Ladakh Range mts India
17 L3 Ladan Ukr.
156 C1 Ladang, Ko i. Thai.
57 I4 Ladánybene Hungary
49 E6 Ladbergen Ger.
57 H2 Ladce Slovakia
110 E8 Ladd IL U.S.A.
54 F3 Lądek Pol.
54 E5 Lądek-Zdrój Pol.
48 H1 Ladelund Ger.
130 B3 La Demajagua Cuba
63 N4 La Demanda, Sierra de mts Spain
127 N10 La Democracia Guat.
52 F3 Ladenburg Ger.
38 G3 La Déroute, Passage de str. Channel Is/France
131 □2 La Désirade i. Guadeloupe
26 E8 Ladhar Bheinn mt. Scotland U.K.
42 G4 Ladignac-le-Long France
99 □2a La Digue i. Inner Islands Seychelles
188 G3 Ladik Turkey
59 K6 Ladinger Spitz mt. Austria
43 J6 Ladinhac France
96 F9 Ladismith S. Africa
72 I4 Ladispoli Italy
146 B3 La Disputada Chile
185 I7 Lādīz Iran
178 E6 Ladnun Rajasthan India
62 F9 Ladoeiro Port.
Ladoga, Lake Rus. Fed. see Ladozhskoye Ozero
70 A3 La Dôle mt. Switz.
36 E7 Ladon France
78 C5 Ladon r. Greece
170 G6 Ladong Guangxi China
146 D3 La Dormida Arg.
19 O1 Ladozhskoye Ozero l. Rus. Fed.
62 E2 Ladra r. Spain
145 A8 Ladrillero, Canal sea chan. Chile
Ladrones terr. N. Pacific Ocean see Northern Mariana Islands
126 □R14 Ladrones, Islas is Panama
179 N6 Ladu mt. Arun. Prad. India
106 A2 Ladue r. Can./U.S.A.
146 D6 La Dulce, Laguna l. Arg.
126 E3 La Dura Mex.
18 D7 Ladushkin Rus. Fed.
14 F3 Ladva Rus. Fed.
14 F3 Ladva-Vetka Rus. Fed.
178 F5 Ladwa Haryana India
105 J2 Lady Ann Strait Nunavut Can.
26 J10 Ladybank Fife, Scotland U.K.
205 L9 Lady Barron Tas. Austr.
29 N7 Ladybower Reservoir England U.K.
97 L5 Ladybrand S. Africa
111 N2 Lady Evelyn Lake Ont. Can.
97 L7 Lady Frere S. Africa
97 L6 Lady Grey S. Africa
16 G4 Ladyhy Ukr.
28 H2 Lady Isle i. Scotland U.K.
26 L11 Ladykirk Scottish Borders, Scotland U.K.
213 L2 Lady Newnes Bay Antarctica
26 L7 Ladysford Aberdeenshire, Scotland U.K.
106 F5 Ladysmith B.C. Can.
97 N4 Ladysmith S. Africa
110 C4 Ladysmith WI U.S.A.
183 M2 Ladyzhenka Kazakh.
16 I5 Ladyzhyn Ukr.
16 J5 Ladyzhynka Ukr.
Ladzhanurges Georgia see Lajanurpekhi
55 H4 Ładzice Pol.
50 K3 Ładzin Pol.
153 K8 Lae P.N.G.
147 G3 La Emilia Arg.
159 F8 Laem Ngop Thai.
23 L5 Läen l. Sweden
129 H5 La Encarnación Mex.
67 D10 La Encina Spain
136 E2 La Encrucijada Venez.
98 □3b La Entallada, Punta de pt Fuerteventura Canary Is
49 D6 Laer Ger.
63 J3 La Ercina Spain
21 I6 Lærdalsøyri Norway
72 B6 Laerru Sardegna Italy
La Escala Spain see L'Escala
128 E1 La Escalera Mex.
67 E10 La Escaleta, Punta de pt Spain
129 H1 La Escondida Mex.
147 H2 La Esmeralda Entre Ríos Arg.
144 D3 La Esmeralda Santiago del Estero Arg.
139 E5 La Esmeralda Bol.
137 E4 La Esmeralda Venez.
22 H4 Læsø i. Denmark
22 G4 Læsø Rende sea chan. Denmark
146 D5 La Esperanza Arg.
138 D3 La Esperanza Beni Bol.
139 E3 La Esperanza Santa Cruz Bol.
98 □3a La Esperanza Tenerife Canary Is
126 □O10 La Esperanza Hond.
126 □P10 La Esperanza, Sierra de mts Hond.
62 H2 La Espina Spain
146 E3 La Esquina Arg.
129 H5 La Estancia, Cerro mt. Mex.
146 D5 La Estrella Arg.
138 E4 La Estrella Bol.
146 B4 La Estrella Chile
63 J9 La Estrella Spain
18 J3 Laeva Estonia
41 C6 La Fageolle, Col de pass France
146 E2 La Falda Arg.
41 G9 La Fare-les-Oliviers France
110 D6 La Farge WI U.S.A.
117 J4 La Fargeville NY U.S.A.
41 I10 La Farlède France
92 E2 Lafaruug Somalia
66 F5 La Fatarrella Spain
40 I4 La Faucille, Col de pass France
41 H7 La Faurie France
42 B3 La Faute-sur-Mer France
115 E9 Lafayette AL U.S.A.
124 J4 Lafayette CA U.S.A.
122 L7 Lafayette CO U.S.A.
115 E8 La Fayette GA U.S.A.
114 D5 Lafayette IN U.S.A.
121 I10 Lafayette LA U.S.A.
118 F2 Lafayette NJ U.S.A.
116 B9 Lafayette OH U.S.A.
115 D7 Lafayette TN U.S.A.
99 □1b Lafayette, Pointe pt Mauritius
130 A2 Lafé Cuba
129 I1 La Fe del Golfo Mex.
65 P2 La Felipa Spain
36 F4 La Fère France
99 □1a La Ferme Rodrigues I. Mauritius
38 I8 La Ferrière France
39 J4 La Ferrière-aux-Etangs France
111 P1 Laferté Que. Can.
106 G2 Laferte r. N.W.T. Can.
36 D7 La Ferté-Alais France
39 M5 La Ferté-Bernard France
39 M4 La Ferté-Frênel France
36 F6 La Ferté-Gaucher France
39 O7 La Ferté-Imbault France
36 F8 La Ferté-Loupièrre France
39 K4 La Ferté-Macé France
36 F5 La-Ferté-Milon France
36 C8 La Ferté-St-Aubin France
36 C8 La Ferté-St-Cyr France
36 F6 La Ferté-sous-Jouarre France
37 K8 Laferté-sur-Amance France
37 I7 Laferté-sur-Aube France
39 M4 La Férte-Vidame France
36 B8 La Ferté-Villeneuil France
187 J3 Laffān, Ra's pt Qatar
89 H4 Lafia Nigeria
89 G4 Lafiagi Nigeria
43 E9 Lafitole France
108 E3 Laflamme r. Que. Can.
107 J5 Lafleche Sask. Can.
39 K6 La Flèche France
129 H4 La Florida Mex.
42 B3 La Flotte France
59 N5 Lafnitz Austria
59 N6 Lafnitz r. Austria
200 □5 La Foa New Caledonia
116 A12 La Follette TN U.S.A.
99 □1c La Fontaine Réunion
110 I9 La Fontaine IN U.S.A.
39 L6 La Fontaine-St-Martin France
67 D10 La Font de la Figuera Spain
41 J7 La Font Sancte, Pic de mt. France
111 P2 Laforce Que. Can.
43 E6 La Force France
70 C3 La Forclaz, Col de pass Switz.
111 M2 Laforest Ont. Can.
109 G2 La Forest, Lac l. Que. Can.
36 H7 La Forêt d'Orient, Parc Naturel Régional de nature res. France
38 D6 La Forêt-Fouesnant France
39 J8 La Forêt-sur-Sèvre France
109 F2 Laforge Que. Can.
109 F2 Laforge r. Que. Can.
37 M7 La Forge France
66 F2 Lafortunada Spain
La Fouce, Pointe pt Rodrigues I. Mauritius see La Fouche, Pointe
99 □1a La Fouche, Pointe pt Rodrigues I. Mauritius
43 I7 La Fouillade France
40 E5 La Fouillouse France
121 J11 Lafourche, Bayou r. LA U.S.A.
41 J8 La Foux-d'Allos France
43 G7 Lafrançaise France
36 I4 La Francheville France
147 F2 La Francia Arg.
108 F2 La Frégate, Lac de l. Que. Can.
62 G7 La Fregeneda Spain
39 L5 La Fresnaye-sur-Chédouat France
37 N6 Lafrimbolle France
63 P8 La Frontera Spain
184 F8 Lāft Iran
65 O4 La Fuensanta, Embalse de resr Spain
62 H7 La Fuente de San Esteban Spain
177 M9 Laful Andaman & Nicobar Is India
66 H4 La Fuliola Spain
38 G6 La Gacilly France
66 F6 La Galera Spain
87 H1 La Galite i. Tunisia
87 H1 La Galite, Canal de sea chan. Tunisia
144 E3 La Gallareta Arg.
126 G5 La Gallega Mex.
142 D3 Lagamar Brazil
182 B5 Lagan' Rus. Fed.
23 I5 Lagan r. Sweden
27 K3 Lagan r. Northern Ireland U.K.
78 B5 Lagana, Kolpos b. Zakynthos Greece
89 I3 Lagané well Niger
90 F3 La Garamba, Parc National de nat. park Dem. Rep. Congo
41 I10 La Garde France
41 F8 La Garde-Adhémar France
41 I10 La Garde-Freinet France
43 G9 Lagardelle-sur-Lèze France
62 F5 Lagarelhos Port.
62 E8 Lagares da Beira Port.
65 K4 La Garganta Spain
129 I4 La Garita Mex.
38 H8 La Garnache France
66 J4 La Garriga Spain
43 I8 Lagarrigue France
64 G3 La Garrovilla Spain
66 D6 La Garrucha, Sierra de mts Spain
63 J9 Lagartera Spain
140 F4 Lagarto Brazil
142 A5 Lagarto, Serra do hills Brazil
39 I8 La Gaubretière France
28 E3 Lagavara Northern Ireland U.K.
200 □5 La Gazelle, Récif de rf New Caledonia
88 B3 Lagbar Senegal
89 I4 Lagdo, Lac de l. Cameroon
49 C6 Lage Niedersachsen Ger.
49 G7 Lage Nordrhein-Westfalen Ger.
45 H6 Lage Mierde Neth.
22 E1 Lågen r. Norway
22 G2 Lågen r. Norway
48 I3 Lägerdorf Ger.
44 H4 Lage Vaart canal Neth.
26 F12 Lagg North Ayrshire, Scotland U.K.
26 G8 Laggan Highland, Scotland U.K.
26 H8 Laggan Highland, Scotland U.K.
26 G9 Laggan, Loch l. Scotland U.K.
28 E2 Laggan Bay Scotland U.K.
26 D10 Lagganulva Argyll and Bute, Scotland U.K.
92 D4 Lagh Bogal watercourse Kenya/Somalia
92 D4 Lagh Bor watercourse Kenya/Somalia
27 F3 Laghey Rep. of Ireland
92 D4 Lagh Kutulo watercourse Kenya/Somalia
185 N4 Laghmān prov. Afgh.
87 F2 Laghouat Alg.
27 E6 Laghtgeorge Rep. of Ireland
54 E5 Łagiewniki Pol.
146 E3 La Gilda Arg.
43 F9 La Gimonde, Barrage de dam France
65 P2 La Gineta Spain
72 C1 La Giraglia, Île de i. Corse France
78 E2 Lagkadas Greece
173 G10 Lagkor Co salt l. China
38 H2 La Glacerie France
136 C2 La Gloria Col.
129 M9 La Gloria Chiapas Mex.
121 F12 La Gloria Nuevo León Mex.
40 G5 Lagnieu France
36 E6 Lagny-sur-Marne France
73 Q9 Lago Italy
Lago prov. Moz. see Niassa
98 □1b Lagoa São Miguel Azores
62 G6 Lagoa Bragança Port.
64 C6 Lagoa Faro Port.
62 G6 Lagoaça Port.
143 E4 Lagoa da Prata Brazil
98 □1b Lagoa do Fogo nature res. São Miguel Azores
143 E4 Lagoa Dourada Brazil
142 D3 Lagoa Formosa Brazil
143 F3 Lagoa Santa Brazil
141 C9 Lagoa Vermelha Brazil
145 B7 Lago Belgrano Arg.
145 C8 Lago Cardiel Arg.
140 D3 Lago da Pedra Brazil
191 H4 Lagodekhi Georgia
191 H4 Lagodekhis Nakrdzali nature res. Georgia
62 G4 Lago del Sanabria, Parque Natural del nature res. Spain
72 I3 Lago di Vico, Riserva Naturale nature res. Italy
67 L8 Lago Menor Spain
98 □3a La Gomera i. Canary Is
127 N10 La Gomera Guat.
130 G4 La Gonâve, Île de i. Haiti
73 P7 Lagonegro Italy
157 H3 Lagong i. Indon.
154 D5 Lagonoy Gulf Luzon Phil.
206 G4 Lagoon Creek r. Qld Austr.
145 C7 Lago Posadas Arg.
43 C9 Lagor France
42 D5 Lagorce Aquitaine France
41 E8 Lagorce Rhône-Alpes France
212 O1 La Gorce Mountains Antarctica
42 B3 Lagord France
66 I5 La Gornal Spain
78 G1 Lagos Greece
128 E4 Lagos r. Mex.
89 F5 Lagos Nigeria
89 F5 Lagos state Nigeria
64 B6 Lagos Port.
93 A6 Lagosa Tanz.
71 M6 Lagosanto Italy
128 F4 Lagos de Moreno Mex.
139 E2 Lago Verde Brazil
145 B8 Lago Viedma Arg.
54 D3 Łagów Lubuskie Pol.
55 J5 Łagów Świętokrzyskie Pol.
51 L6 Łagowski Park Krajobrazowy Pol.
20 □ Lågøya i. Svalbard
63 O3 Lagran Spain
64 G5 La Granada de Riotinto Spain
66 G5 La Granadella Spain
40 F5 La Grand-Croix France
108 E2 La Grande r. Que. Can.
122 E4 La Grande OR U.S.A.
108 E2 La Grande 2, Réservoir resr Que. Can.
108 F2 La Grande 3, Réservoir resr Que. Can.
108 F2 La Grande 4, Réservoir resr Que. Can.
41 J6 La Grande Casse, Pointe de mt. France
41 E8 La Grande-Combe France
109 I3 La Grande Île i. Que. Can.
41 E9 La Grande-Motte France
131 □2 La Grande Vigie, Pointe de pt Guadeloupe
208 F5 Lagrange W.A. Austr.
124 L4 La Grange CA U.S.A.
115 E9 La Grange GA U.S.A.
114 E5 Lagrange IN U.S.A.
114 E6 La Grange KY U.S.A.
117 □Q3 La Grange ME U.S.A.
121 G11 La Grange TX U.S.A.
208 F5 Lagrange Bay W.A. Austr.
119 H1 Lagrangeville NY U.S.A.
66 F5 La Granja d'Escarp Spain
65 I4 La Granjuela Spain
137 F3 La Gran Sabana plat. Venez.
41 B10 Lagrasse France
41 I6 La Grave France
43 H7 La Grésigne, Forêt de reg. France
136 D2 La Grita Venez.
70 C2 La Gruyère, Lac de l. Switz.
109 G4 La Guadeloupe Que. Can.
136 E2 La Guaira Venez.
136 D2 La Guajira, Península de pen. Col.
98 □3a La Guancha Tenerife Canary Is
64 H3 La Guarda Spain
144 D3 La Guardia Arg.
144 C2 La Guardia Chile
63 N9 La Guardia Castilla-La Mancha Spain
63 O3 Laguardia Spain
65 L5 La Guardia de Jaén Spain
66 E3 Laguarta Spain
42 H5 Laguenne France
43 H7 Laguépie France
38 I6 La Guerche-de-Bretagne France
40 B3 La Guerche-sur-l'Aubois France
38 G8 La Guérinière France
40 E3 La Guiche France
41 B7 Laguiole France
128 B1 La Guitarra Mex.
131 □10 Lagún Curaçao Neth. Antilles
141 C9 Laguna Brazil
123 K9 Laguna NM U.S.A.
137 I5 Laguna, Ilha da i. Brazil
147 F5 Laguna Alsina Arg.
124 O8 Laguna Beach CA U.S.A.
146 B6 Laguna Blanca, Parque Nacional nat. park Arg.
62 I4 Laguna Dalga Spain
125 R9 Laguna Dam AZ/CA U.S.A.
63 K5 Laguna de Duero Spain
146 B5 Laguna de Laja, Parque Nacional nat. park Chile
62 I4 Laguna de Negrillos Spain
126 □R11 Laguna de Perlas Nic.
129 K7 Laguna de Temascal, Parque Natural nature res. Mex.
145 C8 Laguna Grande Arg.
127 N10 Laguna Lachua, Parque Nacional nat. park Guat.
125 P9 Laguna Mountains CA U.S.A.
147 G2 Laguna Paiva Arg.
138 C5 Lagunas Chile
136 C6 Lagunas Peru
145 B7 Laguna San Rafael, Parque Nacional nat. park Chile
129 L7 Lagunas de Catemaco, Parque Natural nature res. Mex.
129 J10 Lagunas de Chacahua, Parque Nacional nat. park Mex.
127 N9 Lagunas de Montebello, Parque Nacional nat. park Mex.
65 N2 Lagunas de Ruidera park Spain
129 H6 Lagunas de Zempoala, Parque Nacional nat. park Mex.
144 E2 Laguna Yema Arg.
71 K2 Lagundo Italy
129 H5 Lagunilla Mex.
62 I8 Lagunilla Spain
138 E4 Lagunillas Bol.
128 F8 Lagunillas Guerrero Mex.
129 H4 Lagunillas San Luis Potosí Mex.
136 D2 Lagunillas Venez.
169 S2 Laha Heilong. China
64 H3 La Haba Spain
130 B2 La Habana Cuba
124 O8 La Habra CA U.S.A.
157 M2 Lahad Datu Sabah Malaysia
157 M2 Lahad Datu, Teluk b. Malaysia
38 H2 La Hague, Cap de c. France
124 □E13 Lahaina HI U.S.A.
178 G6 Lahar Madh. Prad. India
27 D4 Lahardaun Rep. of Ireland
110 D9 La Harpe IL U.S.A.
178 H6 Laharpur Uttar Prad. India
118 E4 Lahaska PA U.S.A.
156 E6 Lahat Sumatera Indon.
36 C6 La Haute-Vallée-de-Chevreuse, Parc Naturel Régional de nature res. France
38 H3 La Haye-du-Puits France
38 I4 La Haye-Pesnel France
48 E5 Lähden Ger.
158 B1 Lahe Myanmar
18 I2 Lahemaa rahvuspark nat. park Estonia
18 H2 Lahepera laht b. Estonia
146 D4 La Herradura Arg.
146 B2 La Herradura Chile
129 J8 La Herradura Mex.
98 □3b La Herradura, Punta de pt Fuerteventura Canary Is
65 O3 La Herrera Spain
39 L2 La Hève, Cap de c. France
156 B4 Lahewa Indon.
37 J6 Laheycourt France
191 J5 Lahıc Azer.
147 H2 La Hierra Arg.
146 E2 La Higuera Arg.
67 C10 La Higuera Spain
186 G9 Laḩij Yemen
186 G9 Laḩij governorate Yemen
180 F2 Lāhījān Iran
124 □C12 Lahilahi Point HI U.S.A.
27 D7 Lahinch Rep. of Ireland
62 I5 La Hiniesta Spain
16 E1 Lahishyn Belarus
48 E5 Lahn Ger.
49 E10 Lahn r. Ger.
49 G9 Lahnau Ger.
59 L4 Lahnsattel pass Austria
49 E10 Lahnstein Ger.
49 G9 Lahntal-Goßfelden Ger.
22 J5 Laholm Sweden
22 I5 Laholmsbukten b. Sweden
59 N7 Lahonci Slovenia
128 D1 La Honda Mex.
124 M2 Lahontan Reservoir NV U.S.A.
63 J8 La Horcajada Spain
185 P6 Lahore Pak.
129 M8 La Horqueta Mex.
137 F3 La Horqueta Venez.
63 M5 La Horra Spain
36 I7 La Horre, Étang de l. France
130 F4 La Hotte, Massif de mts Haiti
99 □1c La Houssaye, Cap c. Réunion
18 K7 Lahoysk Belarus
52 D5 Lahr (Schwarzwald) Ger.
185 M7 Lahri Pak.
21 R6 Lahti Fin.
136 A6 La Huaca Peru
128 F7 La Huacana Mex.
128 C6 La Huerta Mex.
146 D2 La Huerta, Sierra de mts Arg.
90 C2 Laï Chad

171 L2 Lai'an Anhui China
Laibach Slovenia see Ljubljana
170 G7 Laibin Guangxi China
179 K9 Laichanpur Orissa India
53 H5 Laichingen Ger.
52 E7 Laide Highland, Scotland U.K.
207 N9 Laidley Qld Austr.
26 G9 Laidon, Loch l. Scotland U.K.
124 □D12 Lā'ie HI U.S.A.
124 □D12 Lā'ie Point HI U.S.A.
170 G4 Laifeng Hubei China
36 I4 Laifour France
39 N14 L'Aigle France
63 K8 La Iglesia Spain
66 E7 La Igleseula del Cid Spain
36 H8 Laignes France
70 E8 Laigueglia Italy
20 Q5 L'Aiguillon-sur-Mer France
20 Q5 Laihia Fin.
158 C4 Lai-hka Myanmar
158 C4 Lai-Hsak Myanmar
21 T6 Laikko Fin.
191 D3 Laila, Mt'a Georgia
36 C8 Lailly-en-Val France
207 J6 Laimbele, Mount hill Vanuatu
20 O4 Laimont France
70 G4 Lainate Italy
96 E9 Laingsburg S. Africa
111 J2 Laingsburg MI U.S.A.
20 Q3 Lainioälven r. Sweden
55 L2 Lainsitz r. Austria
119 A10 Lā'ī KY U.S.A.
89 H7 L'Aïr, Massif de mts Niger
118 B2 Lairdsville PA U.S.A.
26 H6 Lairg Highland, Scotland U.K.
65 N5 La Iruela Spain
156 E6 Lais Sumatera Indon.
158 E4 Lais Mindanao Phil.
130 C2 La Isabela Cuba
20 N4 Laislevenn r. Sweden
14 J5 Laishevo Rus. Fed.
169 O7 Laishui Hebei China
136 B3 La Isla Col.
144 C2 La Isla, Salar de salt flat Chile
98 □3b La Isleta pen. Gran Canaria Canary Is
41 B8 Laissac France
20 N3 Laisvall Sweden
21 P6 Laitila Fin.
191 C4 Lait'uri Georgia
93 C6 Laivera well Tanz.
71 K3 Laives Italy
169 O8 Laiwu Shandong China
155 E4 Laiwui Maluku Indon.
169 Q8 Laixi Shandong China
169 Q8 Laiyang Shandong China
169 N7 Laiyuan Hebei China
39 K3 Laize r. France
169 P8 Laizhou Shandong China
169 P8 Laizhou Wan b. China
39 K3 Laizon r. France
146 B5 Laja, Laguna de l. Chile
129 I5 La Jabonera Mex.
138 C2 La Jagua Col.
206 C5 Lajamanu N.T. Austr.
66 F6 La Jana Spain
191 D3 Lajanurpekhi Georgia
63 K9 La Jara reg. Spain
98 □3b Lajares Fuerteventura Canary Is
42 B3 La Jarrie France
71 J9 Lajatico Italy
41 I8 La Javie France
141 B9 Lajeado Brazil
140 F4 Lajeado Brazil
142 D6 Lajes dos Santos i. Brazil
62 E7 Lajeosa Guarda Port.
62 E7 Lajeosa Viseu Port.
62 F7 Lajeosa do Mondego Port.
98 □1a Lajes Terceira Azores
141 C8 Lajes Brazil
98 □1c Lajes do Pico Pico Azores
143 G4 Lajinha Brazil
76 I6 Lajkovac Srbija Serb. and Mont.
42 G3 La Jonchère-St-Maurice France
66 K3 La Jonquera Spain
57 H5 Lajoskomárom Hungary
57 I4 Lajosmizse Hungary
40 H3 La Joux, Forêt de for. France
129 N10 La Jova, Laguna l. Mex.
126 F4 La Joya Chihuahua Mex.
128 D2 La Joya Durango Mex.
138 C4 La Joya Peru
136 B5 La Joya de los Sachas Ecuador
56 G4 Lajta r. Austria/Hungary
39 J7 La Jumellière France
La Junquera Spain see La Jonquera
139 E3 La Junta Bol.
126 F3 La Junta Mex.
120 D7 La Junta CO U.S.A.
130 D3 La Juventud, Isla de i. Cuba
178 C8 Lakadiya Gujarat India
19 X7 Lakash Rus. Fed.
186 E6 Lakathah Saudi Arabia
91 □K3 Lakato Madag.
20 P3 Lakaträsk Sweden
116 B11 Lake KY U.S.A.
122 I4 Lake WY U.S.A.
202 J7 Lake Alice North I. N.Z.
120 F4 Lake Andes SD U.S.A.
120 F4 Lake Ariel PA U.S.A.
121 I10 Lake Arthur LA U.S.A.
205 I7 Lake Bolac Vic. Austr.
115 F10 Lake Butler FL U.S.A.
205 K5 Lake Cargelligo N.S.W. Austr.
119 H2 Lake Carmel NY U.S.A.
121 I10 Lake Charles LA U.S.A.
123 K8 Lake City AR U.S.A.
115 F10 Lake City CO U.S.A.
120 H4 Lake City IA U.S.A.
110 I5 Lake City MI U.S.A.
110 B5 Lake City MN U.S.A.
115 H9 Lake City SC U.S.A.
119 H4 Lake Clark National Park and Preserve AK U.S.A.
117 K4 Lake Clear NY U.S.A.
203 F10 Lake Coleridge South I. N.Z.
106 E5 Lake Cowichan B.C. Can.
17 R6 Lake Demonovka Rus. Fed.
29 K5 Lake District National Park England U.K.
205 J7 Lake Eildon State Park nature res. Vic. Austr.
111 M2 Lake Evelyn-Smoothwater Provincial Park Ont. Can.
204 F3 Lake Eyre National Park S.A. Austr.
203 J8 Lake Ferry North I. N.Z.
207 J3 Lakefield Qld Austr.
108 L4 Lakefield Ont. Can.
207 J3 Lakefield National Park Qld Austr.
125 W1 Lake Fork r. CO U.S.A.
204 G4 Lake Frome Regional Reserve nature res. S.A. Austr.
204 E4 Lake Gardner National Park S.A. Austr.
110 F7 Lake Geneva WI U.S.A.
117 L5 Lake George NY U.S.A.
204 F5 Lake Gilles Conservation Park nature res. S.A. Austr.
209 L12 Lake Grace W.A. Austr.
208 I6 Lake Gregory Aboriginal Reserve W.A. Austr.
Lake Harbour Nunavut Can. see Kimmirut
125 R7 Lake Havasu City AZ U.S.A.
119 G3 Lake Hiawatha NJ U.S.A.
118 F3 Lake Hopatcong NJ U.S.A.
119 G4 Lakehurst NJ U.S.A.
124 N6 Lake Isabella CA U.S.A.
121 H11 Lake Jackson TX U.S.A.
209 E12 Lake Katherine W.A. Austr.
209 E12 Lake King Nature Reserve W.A. Austr.
207 J3 Lakeland Qld Austr.
115 G12 Lakeland FL U.S.A.
115 F10 Lakeland GA U.S.A.
118 F3 Lake Lenape NJ U.S.A.

110 F2 Lake Linden MI U.S.A.
106 G5 Lake Louise Alta Can.
206 B6 Lake Mackay Aboriginal Land res. N.T. Austr.
209 E12 Lake Magenta Nature Reserve W.A. Austr.
93 B5 Lake Manyara National Park Tanz.
92 A5 Lake Mburo National Park Uganda
125 R5 Lake Mead National Recreation Area park U.S.A.
120 I4 Lake Mills IA U.S.A.
206 F6 Lake Nash N.T. Austr.
31 N3 Lakenheath Suffolk, England U.K.
122 C4 Lake Oswego OR U.S.A.
124 I4 Lakepa Niue
203 D10 Lake Paringa South I. N.Z.
115 G12 Lake Pine FL U.S.A.
115 G12 Lake Placid FL U.S.A.
117 L4 Lake Placid NY U.S.A.
117 K5 Lake Pleasant NY U.S.A.
122 J2 Lakeport CA U.S.A.
111 L6 Lakeport MI U.S.A.
121 J9 Lake Providence LA U.S.A.
89 F4 La Kéran, Parc National de nat. park Togo
124 M1 Lake Range mts NV U.S.A.
108 D2 Lake River Ont. Can.
115 P4 Lake St Peter Ont. Can.
205 L1 Lakes Entrance Vic. Austr.
124 M4 Lakeshore CA U.S.A.
118 C6 Lake Shore MD U.S.A.
125 W7 Lakeside AZ U.S.A.
119 I2 Lakeside CT U.S.A.
119 G2 Lakeside NJ U.S.A.
119 H3 Lake Success NY U.S.A.
203 G9 Lake Sumner Forest Park nature res. South I. N.Z.
110 J2 Lake Superior Provincial Park Ont. Can.
108 C4 Lake Superior Provincial Park park Ont. Can.
205 M6 Lake Tabourie N.S.W. Austr.
203 E11 Lake Tekapo South I. N.Z.
119 G3 Lake Telemark NJ U.S.A.
204 F4 Lake Torrens National Park S.A. Austr.
120 G3 Lake Traverse (Sisseton) Indian Reservation res. ND/SD U.S.A.
116 G6 Lake View NY U.S.A.
116 B8 Lakeview OH U.S.A.
120 D5 Lakeview OR U.S.A.
121 J9 Lake Village AR U.S.A.
110 A5 Lakeville MN U.S.A.
115 G12 Lake Wales FL U.S.A.
122 L7 Lakewood CO U.S.A.
119 G4 Lakewood NJ U.S.A.
116 F6 Lakewood NY U.S.A.
116 D7 Lakewood OH U.S.A.
178 C6 Lakha Rajasthan India
21 U6 Lakhdenpokh'ya Rus. Fed.
178 H6 Lakheri Rajasthan India
179 N7 Lakhimpur Uttar Prad. India
179 K7 Lakhisarai Bihar India
190 C7 Lakhish r. Israel
178 D8 Lakhnadon Madh. Prad. India
178 B8 Lakhpat Gujarat India
179 O6 Lakhuti Nagaland India
19 N8 Lakhva r. Belarus
191 I5 Lāki Azer.
54 F2 Łąkie Pol.
120 E7 Lakin KS U.S.A.
19 W5 Lakinsk Rus. Fed.
Lakinskiy Rus. Fed. see Meken-Yurt
57 I5 Lakitelek Hungary
108 D2 Lakitusaki r. Ont. Can.
191 G2 Lakki Pak.
185 N5 Lakki Pak.
65 J2 Lakkoma Samothraki Greece
155 B8 Lakomben Indon.
78 D6 Lakonikos Kolpos b. Greece
88 D5 Lakota Côte d'Ivoire
120 F1 Lakota ND U.S.A.
20 S1 Laksefjorden sea chan. Norway
20 R1 Lakselv Norway
20 L4 Laksfors Norway
Lakshadweep is India see Laccadive Islands
Lakshadweep union terr. India
176 C7 Laksham Bangl.
176 F3 Lakshettipet Andhra Prad. India
176 D5 Lakshmeshwar Karnataka India
179 L8 Lakshmikantapur W. Bengal India
18 J9 Laktyshy Vodaskhovishcha resr Belarus
63 P3 Lakuntza Spain
154 D6 Lala Mindanao Phil.
179 N7 Lalaghat Assam India
73 G9 Lalago Tanz.
147 F3 La Laguna Arg.
126 D6 La Laguna, Picacho de mt. Mex.
126 B4 La Laguna Ojo de Liebre, Parque Natural de nature res. Mex.
128 B3 La Lagunilla Mex.
146 A5 La Laja Chile
129 J4 La Laja Mex.
128 F5 La Laja r. Mex.
185 P5 Lala Musa Pak.
129 L8 Lalana r. Mex.
65 J5 La Lantejuela Spain
64 F4 La Lapa Spain
141 J3 Lalapansi Zimbabwe
90 A5 Lalara Gabon
143 H3 Lalaua Moz.
136 B5 La Libertad Ecuador
128 □O11 La Libertad El Salvador
127 H5 La Libertad Guat.
126 □Q11 La Libertad Nic.
138 B2 La Libertad Peru
119 G4 La Ligua Chile

65 I8 La Línea de la Concepción Spain
162 D6 Lalin He r. China
178 G7 Lalitpur Uttar Prad. India
178 G7 Lalitpur Nepal see Patan
41 B10 La Livinière France
147 H3 La Llave Arg.
41 H7 Lalley France
124 L2 La Loche Sask. Can.
107 I3 La Loche, Lac l. Sask. Can.
40 C3 La Loire et de l'Allier, Plaines de plain France
138 D5 La Loma Bol.
129 N4 La Loma Negra, Planicie de plain Arg.
29 N4 La Londe-les-Maures France
43 E9 La Lora reg. Spain
63 N3 La Losa reg. Spain
43 E9 Laloubère France
78 D4 La Louisa Arg.
36 B7 La Loupe France
41 F6 Lalouvesc France
59 L5 La Louvière Belgium
57 L3 Lalove Ukr.
40 H2 La Loye France
41 I6 L'Alpe-d'Huez France
41 I6 Lalpur Gujarat India
14 I3 Lal'sk Rus. Fed.
178 F6 Lalsot Rajasthan India
71 K11 L'Altissima mt. Austria/Italy
66 E4 Lalueza Spain
91 E7 La Lufira, Lac de retenue de resr Dem. Rep. Congo
155 E4 Laluin l. Maluku Indon.
65 I5 La Luisiana Spain
173 H12 Lalung La pass Xizang China
43 C8 Laluque France
128 E2 La Luz Mex.
53 O3 Lam Ger.
179 N9 Lama Bangl.
73 M3 Lama Italy
136 C4 La Macarena, Parque Nacional nat. park Col.
40 C3 La Machine France
72 C5 La Maddalena Sardegna Italy
72 C5 La Madeleine, Îles de is Que. Can.
40 D4 La Madeleine, Monts de mts France
169 S3 Lamadian Heilong. China
Lamadianzi Heilong. China see Lamadian
157 L2 Lamag Sabah Malaysia
62 I3 La Magdalena Mex.
67 C10 La Magdalena, Sierra de mts Spain
43 F7 Lamagistère France
90 E5 La Maiko, Parc National de nat. park Dem. Rep. Congo
71 L1 La Maira r. Italy
71 M6 La Malbaie Que. Can.
71 L7 La Malène France
129 I6 La Malinche, Parque Nacional nat. park Mex.
129 I6 La Malinche, Volcán vol. Mex.
40 C5 Lamalou-les-Bains France
158 H7 Lamam Laos
74 H9 Lama Mocogno Italy
126 H5 La Mancha Mex.
65 N2 La Mancha reg. Spain
La Manche str. France/U.K. see English Channel
70 C5 La Mandria, Parco Regionale park Italy
67 D12 La Manga del Mar Menor Spain
91 E7 La Manika, Plateau de plat. Dem. Rep. Congo
65 P5 La Manilla hill Spain
41 G9 Lamanon France
200 □5 Lamap Vanuatu
126 D6 La Máquina Mex.
121 D11 La Marca Coahuila Mex.
36 D5 Lamarche France
42 A2 La Marche France
43 G7 Lamarche-sur-Saône France
184 E8 Lamard Iran
40 F1 Lamargelle France
41 C6 La Margeride, Monts de mts France
72 C6 La Maroma mt. Spain
146 D4 La Maroma Arg.
146 B3 Lamarque Arg.
121 H11 La Marque TX U.S.A.
147 G5 La Martinetas Arg.
113 L8 La Martre, Lac l. N.W.T. Can.
146 C4 La Maruja Arg.
62 C7 Lamas r. Port.
190 D2 Lamas r. Turkey
126 □P10 Lamas de Olo Port.
66 I2 La Masica Hond.
154 D6 La Massana Andorra
44 F7 Lamastre France
63 I9 La Mata Spain
66 H4 La Mata de los Olmos Spain
98 □3a La Matanza de Acentejo Tenerife Canary Is
146 C5 La Matanzilla, Pampa de plain Arg.
146 C6 La Matilla Spain
109 H4 La Mauricie, Parc National nat. park Que. Can.
169 L6 Lamawan Nei Mongol China
130 T3 La Maya Cuba
63 M3 La Mazorra, Puerto de pass Spain
59 I3 Lambach Austria
38 F5 Lamballe France
90 A5 Lambaréné Gabon
143 E4 Lambari Brazil
89 E5 Lambasina i. Indon.
136 B6 Lambayeque Peru
136 B6 Lambayeque dept Peru
27 K6 Lambay Island Rep. of Ireland
157 K5 Lambeng Kalimantan Indon.
31 M5 Lamberhurst Kent, England U.K.
147 F3 Lambert France
146 B1 Lambert Chile
208 D6 Lambert, Cape Austr.
213 E2 Lambert Glacier Antarctica
118 F4 Lambertville NJ U.S.A.
141 G9 Lambesc France
65 M4 Lambesis France
178 E4 Lambi Punjab India
200 □5 Lambi Guadalcanal Solomon Is
204 E2 Lambina S.A. Austr.
63 L7 La Mira r. Spain
21 M6 Lamborn Sweden
31 I4 Lambourn West Berkshire, England U.K.
31 I4 Lambourn Downs hills England U.K.
52 E2 Lambrecht (Pfalz) Ger.
36 F3 Lambres-lez-Douai France
70 H5 Lambro r. Italy
45 I7 Lamb's Head Rep. of Ireland
159 F7 Lam Chi r. Thai.
156 B3 La Nao, Cabo de c. Spain
122 K4 Lame Deer MT U.S.A.
70 E5 Lame del Sesia, Parco Naturale nature res. Italy
26 I11 Lanark South Lanarkshire, Scotland U.K.

41 I6 La Meije mt. France
38 I6 La Meilleraye-de-Bretagne France
62 F7 Lameiras Peru
138 B3 La Mejorada Peru
59 L4 Lamen Bay Vanuatu
131 □2 Lamentin Guadeloupe
109 H4 Lameque, Île i. N.B. Can.
144 D3 La Merced Arg.
138 B2 La Merced Peru
53 J5 Lamerdingen Ger.
204 H6 Lameroo S.A. Austr.
73 L4 La Meta mt. Italy
73 L4 La Mesa Col.
129 H9 La Mesa Mex.
121 E9 La Mesa TX U.S.A.
29 N4 Lamesley Tyne and Wear, England U.K.
66 G6 L'Ametlla de Mar Spain
73 O10 Lamezia Italy
86 A5 Lamhar Touil, Sabkhet imp. l. Western Sahara
78 D4 Lamia Greece
154 C4 Lamigan Point Mindanao Phil.
39 L5 La Milesse France
59 L5 Laming r. Austria
205 N3 Lamington National Park Qld Austr.
64 G5 La Minilla, Embalse de resr Spain
184 C2 Lamir Iran
128 C7 La Mira Mex.
124 N8 La Mirada CA U.S.A.
126 D3 La Misa Mex.
124 P9 La Misión Mex.
154 D8 Lamitan Phil.
155 E4 Lamlam Papua Indon.
200 □1 Lamlam, Mount hill Guam
75 O3 Lamlash Scotland U.K.
26 F11 Lamlash North Ayrshire, Scotland U.K.
171 □J7 Lamma Island H.K. China
97 N1 Lammerkop S. Africa
53 N4 Landak r. Indon.
26 K11 Lammer Law hill Scotland U.K.
203 D12 Lammerlaw Range mts South I. N.Z.
203 D12 Lammerlaw Top mt. South I. N.Z.
26 K11 Lammermuir Hills Scotland U.K.
23 K4 Lammhult Sweden
21 R6 Lammi Fin.
206 C6 Lamm watercourse N.T. Austr.
122 J5 Lander WY U.S.A.
38 C5 Lamderneau France
37 N6 Landersheim France
38 H5 La Moille IL U.S.A.
45 J7 Lamouilly France
48 I5 Landesbergen Ger.
185 D6 Landi, Gunung mt. Indon.
185 D5 Landidre Gascogne, Parc Naturel Régional des nature res. France
49 I9 La Moine r. IL U.S.A.
22 G6 Landewiesen Ger.
169 O7 Landion r. France
21 L5 Landiras France
31 L3 Langford Bedfordshire, England U.K.
38 C5 Landivy France
156 D4 Lamgarf Norway
31 K2 Landquart Switz.

159 D9 Lanbi Kyun i. Myanmar
154 D7 Lamoon Point Mindanao Phil.
170 B7 Lancang Yunnan China
152 A1 Lancang Jiang r. Xizang China
170 C8 Lancang Jiang r. China conv. Mekong
29 L6 Lancashire admin. div. England U.K.
29 K7 Lancashire Plain England U.K.
117 K3 Lancaster Ont. Can.
114 C7 Lancaster Lancashire, England U.K.
124 N7 Lancaster CA U.S.A.
114 C7 Lancaster KY U.S.A.
120 I5 Lancaster MO U.S.A.
117 M4 Lancaster NH U.S.A.
116 E9 Lancaster OH U.S.A.
116 C5 Lancaster PA U.S.A.
115 G8 Lancaster SC U.S.A.
115 I11 Lancaster VA U.S.A.
120 J4 Lancaster WI U.S.A.
118 C4 Lancaster Canal England U.K.
118 C4 Lancaster County county PA U.S.A.
105 J2 Lancaster Sound str. Nunavut Can.
209 C11 Lancelin W.A. Austr.
209 C11 Lancelin Island W.A. Austr.
29 N4 Lanchester Durham, England U.K.
191 D3 Lanch'khut'i Georgia
73 M3 Lanciano Italy
63 P3 Lanciego Spain
145 B5 Lanco Chile
144 C3 Lancun Shandong China
55 K5 Łańcut Pol.
70 A3 Lancy Switz.
14 J2 Landa Rus. Fed.
129 H4 Landa de Matamoros Mex.
157 H5 Landak r. Indon.
53 N4 Landau an der Isar Ger.
53 K6 Landau in der Pfalz Ger.
55 N3 Landeck Austria
38 B4 Landéda France
38 B4 Landeleau France
192 I3 Langepas Rus. Fed.
20 Q5 Länsi-Suomi prov. Fin.
29 □c Langebak sea chan. Denmark
50 I5 Langer Berg hill Ger.
53 J5 Langerwisch Ger.
49 K9 Langewiesen Ger.
169 O7 Langfang Hebei China
21 L5 Långfjällets naturreservat nature res. Sweden
31 L3 Langford Bedfordshire, England U.K.
35 J4 Langfurth Ger.

43 E6 La Montagne hill Italy
145 B7 La Montagne Réunion
95 □K2 La Montagne d'Ambre, Parc National de nat. park Madag.
36 G5 La Montagne de Reims, Parc Naturel Régional de nature res. France
43 F7 Lamontjoie France
146 D4 La Mora Arg.
126 H4 La Mora Mex.
129 H4 La Morena Mex.
126 G3 La Morita Chihuahua Mex.
127 I4 La Morita Coahuila Mex.
36 D5 Lamorlaye France
74 H9 La Mostaza Chile
110 E3 Lamothe-Achard France
43 G6 Lamothe-Capdeville France
43 E6 Lamothe-Cassel France
43 D6 Lamothe-Landerron France
39 K8 La Mothe-St-Héray France
153 K5 Lamotrek atoll Micronesia
111 F1 La Motte r. Que. Can.
70 H2 La Motte France
36 C4 La Motte-Beuvron France
37 K5 La Motte-Chalancon France
41 J8 La Motte-d'Aveillans France
41 H7 La Motte-de-Caire France
41 H8 La Motte-Servolex France
90 A5 La Mougalaba, Réserve de nature res. Gabon
40 D5 La Moure France
115 F8 La Mudarra Spain
40 J3 La Muela Spain
66 D4 La Muela hill Spain
66 E3 La Muela Spain
66 H4 La Muga r. Spain
65 L4 La Mujer Muerta hill Spain
71 M6 La Mure France
40 H4 Lamure-sur-Azergues France
184 I4 Lana r. Albania
207 K2 Lana r. Qld Austr.
146 E4 La Nacional Arg.
124 □D13 Lāna'i i. HI U.S.A.
124 □D13 Lāna'i City HI U.S.A.
23 L5 Lānāsjö Sweden
66 E3 Lanaja Spain
45 I7 Lanaken Belgium
66 H2 La Nao, Cabo de c. Spain
154 D6 Lanao, Lake l. Mindanao Phil.
41 I9 Lanarce France
117 I4 Lanark Ont. Can.
41 I9 Lanark r. Scotland U.K.
57 E1 Lanark county Ont. Can.
157 L2 Lanas Sabah Malaysia
62 G3 La Nava Spain
63 K9 La Nava de Ricomalillo Spain
64 F3 La Nava de Santiago Spain
191 I5 Lānbāran Azer.

22 G6 Langeland i. Denmark
22 G7 Langelands Bælt str. Denmark
21 R6 Längelmäki r. Fin.
14 D3 Längelmävesi l. Fin.
49 K7 Langen Ger.
49 I7 Langen Ger.
48 C7 Langen Belgium
52 F2 Langen Hessen Ger.
48 D5 Langen Niedersachsen Ger.
48 G3 Langen Niedersachsen Ger.
53 H6 Langenargen Ger.
49 I6 Langenau Ger.
49 F9 Langenaubach Ger.
49 F9 Langenbach Ger.
58 A4 Langen bei Bregenz Austria
49 I7 Langenberg Ger.
49 F7 Langenberg Ger.
107 K5 Langenburg Sask. Can.
48 C8 Langenburg Ger.
51 E8 Langendorf Ger.
49 E9 Langeneichstädt Ger.
52 G5 Langenenslingen Ger.
53 K4 Langenfeld Ger.
53 J5 Langenfeld (Rheinland) Ger.
49 E8 Langenhagen Ger.
49 E9 Langenhahn Ger.
51 E8 Langenhessen Ger.
58 A4 Langenlois Austria
52 H6 Langenlonsheim Ger.
53 H4 Langenmosen Ger.
53 I5 Langennaudorf Ger.
53 J5 Langenneufnach Ger.
53 J5 Langenorla Ger.
53 L5 Langenpreising Ger.
49 H10 Langenselbold Ger.
53 K2 Langensendelbach Ger.
49 K7 Langenstein Ger.
50 F3 Langenthal Switz.
59 M4 Langenwang Austria
109 G3 L'Anse-St-Jean Que. Can.
51 F9 Langenweddingen Ger.
51 F9 Langenwetzendorf Ger.
53 J3 Langenzenn Ger.
59 N3 Langenzersdorf Austria
48 E3 Langeoog Ger.
48 E3 Langeoog i. Ger.
192 I3 Langepas Rus. Fed.
22 F2 Langesund Norway
22 G6 Langeskov Denmark
22 B2 Langevåg Norway
169 O7 Langfang Hebei China

145 C5 Lanín, Volcán vol. Arg./Chile
30 C7 Laniviet Cornwall, England U.K.
16 F4 Lanivtsi Ukr.
157 I4 Lanjak, Bukit mt. Malaysia
65 M7 Lanjarón Spain
179 □1 Lankā Madh. Prad. India
175 □1 Lankanfinolhu i. N. Male Maldives
Lankanfushifinolu i. N. Male Maldives see Lankanfinolhu
169 N9 Lankao Henan China
191 J7 Länkäran r. Azer.
171 □I7 Lan Kok Tsui pt H.K. China
138 C3 Lanlacuni Bajo Peru
38 D4 Lanloup France
38 C4 Lanmeur France
59 L6 Lannach Austria
43 E9 Lannemezan France
43 E9 Lannemezan, Plateau de France
43 E8 Lannepax France
38 C4 Lannilis France
38 D4 Lannion France
39 L8 Lannion, Baie de b. France
108 F4 L'Annonciation Que. Can.
36 F2 Lannoy France
40 D3 La Nocle-Maulaix France
66 I5 L'Anoia r. Spain
119 G5 Lanoka Harbor NJ U.S.A.
139 C5 La Noria Bol.
128 A2 La Noria Mex.
42 G5 Lanouaille France
170 B5 Lanping Yunnan China
58 D5 Lans Austria
41 H7 Lans, Montagne de mts France
43 H8 Lansargues France
43 C4 Lansdale PA U.S.A.
118 B6 Lansdowne MD U.S.A.
110 F3 L'Anse MI U.S.A.
50 G3 Lansen Ger.
109 G3 L'Anse-St-Jean Que. Can.
118 D3 Lansford PA U.S.A.
106 C2 Lansing r. Y.T. Can.
110 C6 Lansing IA U.S.A.
110 J7 Lansing MI U.S.A.
20 Q5 Lansing MN U.S.A.
110 J7 Lansing MI U.S.A.
22 J4 Länghem Sweden
70 I6 Langhirano Italy
96 H4 Langholm S. Africa
29 M4 Langholm Dumfries and Galloway, Scotland U.K.
22 H1 Langholsberget hill Norway
20 □1 Langjökull ice cap Iceland
54 G5 Lány Czech Rep.
146 E4 Lanya Sudan
169 L7 Lang He r. China
171 M7 Lan Yü i. Taiwan
50 L7 Lanz Ger.
21 I3 Lanzada Congo
63 □2 Lanzahita Spain
124 C8 Lanzarote i. Canary Is
77 I4 Lanzendorf Austria
41 E6 Lantriac France
40 D3 Lanty France
67 E10 La Nucía Spain
123 C8 Lanuéjols France
72 A6 Lanusei Sardegna Italy
147 H4 Lanús Arg.
72 D8 Lanusei Sardegna Italy
154 F7 Lanuza Mindanao Phil.
154 F7 Lanuza Bay Mindanao Phil.
38 B5 Lanvallay France
38 F4 Lanvollon France
42 E5 Lanxi Heilong. China
171 L4 Lanxi Zhejiang China
169 L4 Lanxian China
51 I10 Lány Czech Rep.
54 G5 Lány Czech Rep.
16 F4 Lanya Sudan
169 L7 Lang He r. China
171 M7 Lan Yü i. Taiwan
50 I4 Lanz Ger.
21 I3 Lanza Congo
63 □2 Lanzahita Spain
124 C8 Lanzarote i. Canary Is
170 E2 Lanzhou Gansu China
169 P4 Lanzijing Jilin China
170 C5 Lanzo Torinese Italy
73 P8 Lao r. Italy
36 H4 Laon France
98 □3a Laona i. Canary Is
41 I3 Laonnois reg. France
36 H4 Laon France
179 J5 Laoqitai Xinjiang China
158 H4 La Orotava Tenerife Canary Is
138 B2 La Oroya Peru
158 C1 Laos country Asia
170 G3 Laoshan Shandong China
179 J5 Laoshawan Xinjiang China
163 D8 Laotougou Jilin China
163 D8 Laotuding Shan hill Liaoning China
60 D5 Laou, Oued r. Morocco
90 D2 La Ouandja-Vakaga, Réserve de nat. park C.A.R.
88 E4 Laoudi-Ba Côte d'Ivoire
87 G5 Laou Oued watercourse Alg.
41 B9 Laouzas, Lac de l. France
168 G6 Laoximiao Nei Mongol China
168 H8 Laoyacheng Qinghai China
162 E3 Laoye Ling mts China
163 C8 Laoye Ling mts China
63 □2 Lapa Brazil
145 C4 Lapac i. Phil.
144 F2 Lapachito Arg.
89 F4 La Pacaudière France
62 F3 La Palma Panama
63 □2 La Palma Guat.
124 □D13 La Palma i. Canary Is
127 O9 La Palma Panama
63 □2 La Palma AZ U.S.A.
64 F6 La Palma del Condado Spain
127 □ La Palma del Condado Spain
41 E7 La Palme France
146 A3 La Paloma Uru.
144 F2 La Paloma Arg.
63 K9 La Palud-sur-Verdon France
55 I6 Łapanów Pol.
124 L6 La Panza Range mts CA U.S.A.

La Para to Laydennyy, Mys

291

147 F2 La Para Arg.
137 F3 La Paragua Venez.
63 K7 La Paramera, Puerto de pass Spain
63 J8 La Paramera, Sierra de mts Spain
154 B9 Laparan i. Phil.
72 B4 La Parata, Pointe de pt Corse France
128 F1 La Pardita Mex.
98 □3b La Pared Fuerteventura Canary Is
147 G3 La Parejas Arg.
128 C2 La Parilla Mex.
64 F3 La Parra Spain
63 P9 La Parra de Las Vegas Spain
64 G2 La Parrilla hill Spain
78 C4 Lapas Greece
62 C9 Lapas Port.
136 C4 La Paya, Parque Nacional nat. park Col.
146 E3 La Paz Córdoba Arg.
147 H2 La Paz Entre Ríos Arg.
146 D3 La Paz Mendoza Arg.
138 C4 La Paz Bol.
138 C3 La Paz dept Bol.
126 □P10 La Paz Hond.
126 D5 La Paz Mex.
126 □P11 La Paz Nic.
147 I4 La Paz Uru.
110 H8 Lapaz IN U.S.A.
136 C2 La Paz Venez.
126 D5 La Paz, Bahía b. Mex.
136 D5 La Pedrera Col.
67 D11 La Pedrera, Embalse de resr Spain
111 K6 Lapeer MI U.S.A.
64 □ Lapeiras Madeira
147 G2 La Pelada Arg.
39 I5 La Pellerine France
129 I2 La Peña Tamaulipas Mex.
129 L8 La Peña Veracruz Mex.
126 □S13 La Peña Panama
66 D3 La Peña, Embalse de resr Spain
62 H8 La Peña de Francia, Sierra de mts Spain
64 F2 La Peña del Águila, Embalse de resr Spain
89 F4 La Pendjari, Parc National de nat. park Benin
41 J9 La Penne France
41 H10 La Penne-sur-Huveaune France
63 O8 La Peraleja Spain
126 G3 La Perla Mex.
164 S1 La Pérouse Strait Japan/Rus. Fed.
146 D5 La Perra, Salitral de salt pan Arg.
129 J2 La Pesca Mex.
62 H8 La Pesga Spain
37 N6 La Petite-Pierre France
65 M6 La Peza Spain
30 E6 Lapford Devon, England U.K.
147 G2 La Picada Arg.
128 E5 La Piedad Mex.
67 C11 La Pila, Sierra de mts Spain
122 D5 La Pine OR U.S.A.
154 E5 Lapinig Samar Phil.
67 C12 La Pinilla Spain
21 S6 Lapinjärvi Fin.
20 S5 Lapinlahti Fin.
126 □S13 La Pintada Panama
190 B3 Lapithos Cyprus
74 E8 La Pizzuta mt. Sicilia Italy
121 J10 Laplace LA U.S.A.
158 E6 Lap Lae Thai.
40 J5 La Plagne France
99 □1c La Plaine-des-Cafres Réunion
99 □1c La Plaine-des-Palmistes Réunion
91 A5 La Plaine Ouanga, Réserve de nature res. Gabon
38 G7 La-Plaine-sur-Mer France
20 V3 Laplandskiy Zapovednik nature res. Rus. Fed.
120 E3 La Plant SD U.S.A.
147 I4 La Plata Arg.
116 I10 La Plata MD U.S.A.
120 I5 La Plata MO U.S.A.
147 I4 La Plata, Río de sea chan. Arg./Uru.
146 E2 La Playa Arg.
98 □3f La Playa de Mogán Gran Canaria Canary Is
147 F3 La Playosa Arg.
62 H2 La Plaza Spain
128 B1 La Plazuela Mex.
42 I5 Lapleau France
107 J4 La Plonge, Lac l. Sask. Can.
43 F7 Laplume France
18 G4 Lapmežciems Latvia
66 I3 La Pobla de Lillet Spain
66 G3 La Pobla de Segur Spain
65 P7 La Polacra, Punta de pt Spain
62 I3 La Pola de Gordón Spain
144 D2 La Poma Arg.
14 H2 Lapominka Rus. Fed.
39 J7 La Pommeraye France
72 C3 La Porta Corse France
114 D5 La Porte IN U.S.A.
111 R8 Laporte PA U.S.A.
106 E2 Laporte, Mount Y.T. Can.
66 F6 La Portellada Spain
67 C9 La Portera Spain
155 A6 Laposo, Bukit mt. Indon.
99 □1c La Possession Réunion
147 F2 La Posta Arg.
109 F1 La Potherie, Lac l. Que. Can.
39 J6 La Pouëze France
37 N7 Lapoutroie France
136 C3 La Poyata Col.
126 C5 La Poza Grande Mex.
20 Q5 Lappajärvi l. Fin.
23 L2 Lappe Sweden
21 T6 Lappeenranta Fin.
53 M3 Lappersdorf Ger.
21 P6 Lappi Fin.
20 S3 Lappi prov. Fin.
20 O3 Lappland reg. Europe
18 E1 Lappo Åland Fin.
18 G2 Lappohja Fin.
20 Q3 Lappträsk Sweden
117 L3 La Prairie Que. Can.
129 H2 La Presa Mex.
128 G1 La Presas Mex.
143 I11 La Preste France
147 G5 Laprida Arg.
147 G5 La Primavera Arg.
63 P4 La Proveda de Soria Spain
121 F11 La Pryor TX U.S.A.
79 H2 Lâpseki Turkey
41 E6 Lapte France
18 L5 Laptevo Pskovskaya Oblast' Rus. Fed.
Laptev Sea Rus. Fed. see Laptevykh, More
193 N2 Laptevykh, More sea Rus. Fed.
20 Q5 Lapua Fin.
20 Q5 Lapuanjoki r. Fin.
63 N9 La Puebla de Almoradiel Spain
63 O3 La Puebla de Arganzón Spain
65 I6 La Puebla de Cazalla Spain
66 E5 La Puebla de Híjar Spain
65 I5 La Puebla de los Infantes Spain
64 G6 La Puebla del Río Spain
63 L9 La Puebla de Montalbán Spain
63 K3 La Puebla de Valdavia Spain
67 D7 La Puebla de Valverde Spain
63 K9 La Pueblanueva Spain
144 D3 La Puerta Catamarca Arg.
147 F2 La Puerta Córdoba Arg.
136 D2 La Puerta Venez.
65 N4 La Puerta de Segura Spain
57 L6 Lăpugiu de Jos Romania
155 C6 Lapuko Sulawesi Indon.
154 D6 Lapu-Lapu Phil.
146 E3 La Punilla Arg.
144 C3 La Punilla, Cordillera de mts Chile
70 H2 La Punt Switz.
144 D3 La Punta Arg.
126 C4 La Purísima Mex.
77 M3 Lăpuș Romania
77 L3 Lăpuș r. Romania
77 J6 Lăpușnicu Mare Romania
76 I8 Lapušnik Kosovo, Srbija Serb. and Mont.
31 I3 Lapworth Warwickshire, England U.K.
55 K3 Łapy Pol.
84 F4 Laqiya Arbain well Sudan
84 F5 Laqiya 'Umran well Sudan
144 D1 La Quiaca Arg.
73 K3 L'Aquila Italy
73 L3 L'Aquila prov. Italy
125 P8 La Quinta CA U.S.A.
184 F8 Lār Iran
205 J8 Lara Vic. Austr.
136 D2 Lara state Venez.
62 C2 Laracha Spain
86 D2 Larache Morocco
60 C5 Larache prov. Morocco
28 D6 Laracor Rep. of Ireland
28 E7 Laragh Rep. of Ireland
41 H8 Laragne-Montéglin France
65 M6 La Ragua, Puerto de pass Spain
98 □3a La Rajita La Gomera Canary Is
184 G8 Lārak i. Iran
90 B2 Laramanay Chad
65 J5 La Rambla Spain
122 L6 Laramie WY U.S.A.
122 L5 Laramie r. WY U.S.A.
122 L5 Laramie Mountains WY U.S.A.
Laranda Turkey see Karaman
137 G6 Laranjal Brazil
142 D5 Laranjal Paulista Brazil
140 F4 Laranjeiras Brazil
142 C6 Laranjeiras, Baía das b. Brazil
142 A6 Laranjeiras do Sul Brazil
60 B3 Laranjeiro Port.
142 B5 Laranjinha r. Brazil
155 C8 Larantuka Flores Indon.
63 O7 Laranueva Spain
63 N5 La Rasa Spain
98 □3a La Rasca, Punta de pt Tenerife Canary Is
153 H8 Larat i. Indon.
41 B9 La Raviège, Lac de l. France
40 H5 La Ravoire France
41 G7 La Raye mt. France
86 B5 La Raygat reg. Western Sahara
26 I10 Larbert Falkirk, Scotland U.K.
66 I5 L'Arboç Spain
40 F5 L'Arbresle France
23 O4 Lärbro Gotland Sweden
43 B9 Larceveau-Arros-Cibits France
39 I5 Larchamp France
36 E7 Larchant France
42 G5 Larche Limousin France
41 J8 Larche Provence-Alpes-Côte d'Azur France
70 B7 Larche, Col de pass Italy
119 H3 Larchmont NY U.S.A.
111 M3 Larchwood Ont. Can.
71 J4 Lardaro Italy
71 J9 Larderello Italy
111 O1 Larder Lake Ont. Can.
111 O1 Larder Lake l. Ont. Can.
62 F9 Lardosa Port.
63 N2 Laredo Spain
121 F12 Laredo TX U.S.A.
41 B10 La Redorte France
146 D5 La Reforma Arg.
129 J9 La Reforma Oaxaca Mex.
123 I12 La Reforma Sonora Mex.
129 J5 La Reforma Veracruz Mex.
145 B9 La Reina Adelaida, Archipiélago de is Chile
111 O1 La Reine Que. Can.
44 J4 Laren Gelderland Neth.
44 H4 Laren Noord-Holland Neth.
43 D6 La Réole France
41 E6 La République, Col de pass France
131 □1 Lares Puerto Rico
184 F4 Lārestān Iran
98 □3e La Restinga El Hierro Canary Is
98 □3e La Restinga, Punta de pt El Hierro Canary Is
72 B2 La Revellata, Pointe de pt Corse France
27 E4 Largan Rep. of Ireland
41 E7 Largentière France
41 J7 L'Argentière-la-Bessée France
115 F12 Largo FL U.S.A.
130 C3 Largo, Cayo i. Cuba
26 K10 Largo Bay Scotland U.K.
26 K10 Largoward Fife, Scotland U.K.
26 G11 Largs North Ayrshire, Scotland U.K.
66 B1 La Rhune hill Spain
184 B2 Lārī Iran
71 J8 Lari Italy
87 H1 L'Ariana Tunisia
69 C7 L'Ariana admin. div. Tunisia
155 A4 Lariang Sulawesi Indon.
155 A4 Lariang r. Indon.
63 O6 La Riba de Escalote Spain
147 H4 La Rica Arg.
41 E6 La Ricamarie France
184 B2 Lārījān Iran
120 G1 Larimore ND U.S.A.
147 F2 La Rinconada Arg.
64 H6 La Rinconada Spain
65 J2 La Rinconada, Sierra de mts Spain
73 N4 Larino Italy
144 D3 La Rioja Arg.
146 D1 La Rioja prov. Arg.
63 P4 La Rioja aut. comm. Spain
19 N1 Larionovo Rus. Fed.
78 D3 Larisa Greece
Larissa Greece see Larisa
184 G8 Laristan reg. Iran
99 □1c La Rivière Réunion
185 M8 Larkana Pak.
26 I11 Larkhall South Lanarkshire, Scotland U.K.
109 J3 Lark Harbour Nfld and Lab. Can.
31 I5 Larkhill Wiltshire, England U.K.
185 J5 Lar Koh mt. Afgh.
207 J3 Lark Passage Qld Austr.
31 N3 Larling Norfolk, England U.K.
40 I3 Larmont mt. France/Switz.
38 E6 Larmor-Plage France
Larnaca Cyprus see Larnaka
190 B4 Larnaka Cyprus
27 K3 Larne Northern Ireland U.K.
120 F6 Larned KS U.S.A.
27 K3 Larne Lough inlet Northern Ireland U.K.
89 I4 Laro Cameroon
109 I3 La Robe Noire, Lac de l. Que. Can.
62 I3 La Robla Spain
64 F2 La Roca de la Sierra Spain
70 C2 La Roche Switz.
42 E5 La Rochebeaucourt-et-Argentine France
38 G6 La Roche-Bernard France
42 H5 La Roche-Canillac France
42 E5 La Roche-Chalais France
41 J7 La Roche-de-Rame France
38 E4 La Roche-Derrien France
41 H7 La Roche-des-Arnauds France
45 I8 La Roche-en-Ardenne Belgium
42 E4 La Rochefoucauld France
36 C5 La Roche-Guyon France
42 B3 La Rochelle France
40 E3 Larochemillay France
39 M8 La Roche-Posay France
40 F3 La Rochepot France
36 F8 Laroche-St-Cydroine France
40 I4 La Roche-sur-Foron France
38 I8 La Roche-sur-Yon France
41 I6 La Rochette France
45 J9 Larochette Lux.
65 O2 La Roda Spain
65 J6 La Roda de Andalucía Spain
39 I6 La Roë France
65 N6 Laroles Spain
131 I4 La Romana Dom. Rep.
67 D11 La Romana Spain
43 E8 La Romieu France
107 J4 La Ronge Sask. Can.
107 J4 La Ronge, Lac l. Sask. Can.
42 I6 Laroquebrou France
41 H10 La Roquebrussanne France
41 G9 La Roque-d'Anthéron France
43 H10 Laroque-d'Olmes France
41 C8 La Roque-Ste-Marguerite France
43 F7 Laroque-Timbaut France
127 I5 La Rosa Mex.
125 P9 La Rosa de Castilla Mex.
127 I3 La Rosita Mex.
62 E5 Larouco, Serra do mts Spain
43 H7 La Rouquette France
63 Q3 Larraga Spain
66 B2 Larrainzar Spain
63 Q3 Larrasoaina Spain
43 C9 Larrau France
43 G8 Larrazet France
43 E8 Larressingle France
43 B9 Larressore France
208 E5 Larrey Point W.A. Austr.
206 D3 Larrimah N.T. Austr.
206 D3 Larrimah Aboriginal Land res. N.T. Austr.
63 P3 Larrión Spain
147 H3 Larroque Arg.
213 E2 Lars Christensen Coast Antarctica
212 T2 Larsen Ice Shelf Antarctica
Larsmo Fin. see Luoto
20 H5 Larsnes Norway
75 □ L-Artal, Ras pt Malta
147 G2 La Rubia Arg.
43 D10 Laruns France
42 D5 Laruscade France
65 M5 Larva Spain
22 G2 Larvik Norway
192 J3 Lar'yak Rus. Fed.
17 Q6 Laryne Ukr.
41 C8 Larzac, Causse du plat. France
71 J2 Lasà Italy
144 F2 La Sabana Arg.
136 D4 La Sabana Col.
129 I2 Las Adjuntas, Presa de resr Mex.
63 M8 La Sagra reg. Spain
98 □3c Las Agujas hill Canary Is
155 C6 Lasahau Sulawesi Indon.
41 H10 La Ste-Baume, Chaîne de mts France
125 W3 La Sal UT U.S.A.
138 B2 La Sal, Cerros de mts Peru
147 I5 La Salada Grande, Laguna l. Arg.
128 G2 Las Albercas Mex.
146 C2 La Salina salt pan Arg.
99 □1c La Saline Réunion
125 W3 La Sal Junction UT U.S.A.
108 F4 La Salle Que. Can.
41 D8 Lasalle France
70 C4 La Salle Italy
110 E8 La Salle IL U.S.A.
41 J7 La Salle les Alpes France
90 D5 La Salonga Nord, Parc National de nat. park Dem. Rep. Congo
90 D5 La Salonga Sud, Parc National de nat. park Dem. Rep. Congo
43 I7 La Salvetat-Peyralès France
43 G8 La Salvetat-St-Gilles France
41 B9 La Salvetat-sur-Agout France
157 K4 Lasan Kalimantan Indon.
120 D6 Las Animas CO U.S.A.
126 C3 Las Ánimas, Punta pt Mex.
Las Anod Somalia see Laascaanood
98 □3c La Santa Lanzarote Canary Is
63 K2 Las Arenas Spain
70 C2 La Sarine r. Switz.
147 I5 Las Armas Arg.
108 E3 La Sarre Que. Can.
147 E3 Las Asequias Arg.
128 G4 La Sauceda Mex.
43 F8 La Sauvetat France
43 E6 La Sauvetat-du-Dropt France
41 I10 La Sauvette hill France
131 J8 Las Aves, Islas is West Indies
67 H10 La Savina Spain
147 G1 Las Avispas Arg.
126 D3 Las Avispas Mex.
109 F2 La Savonnière, Lac l. Que. Can.
147 G3 Las Bandurrias Arg.
59 K3 Lasberg Austria
63 K7 Las Berlanas Spain
137 E3 Las Bonitas Venez.
98 □3b Las Borriquillas, Punta de pt Fuerteventura Canary Is
144 E2 Las Breñas Arg.
22 F5 Låsby Denmark
64 H7 Las Cabezas de San Juan Spain
146 B4 Las Cabras Chile
128 B3 Las Cabras Mex.
65 O4 Las Cabras mt. Spain
64 H7 Las Cabras, Sierra de mts Spain
67 C11 Las Cabras, Sierra de mts Spain
98 □3d Las Caletas La Palma Canary Is
98 □3a Las Cañadas vol. crater Tenerife Canary Is
146 A4 Las Cañas Chile
147 H3 Las Cañas Uru.
74 F8 Lascari Sicilia Italy
67 E8 Las Casas Spain
146 C2 Las Casuarinas Arg.
146 C3 Las Catitas Arg.
128 B1 Las Cebollas Mex.
146 E3 Las Chacras Arg.
145 D6 Las Chapas Arg.
37 N7 La Schlucht, Col de pass France
129 M8 Las Choapas Mex.
109 K3 La Scie Nfld and Lab. Can.
139 F4 Las Conchas Bol.
126 F3 Las Cruces Mex.
124 L7 Las Cruces CA U.S.A.
123 K10 Las Cruces NM U.S.A.
65 O3 Las Crucetillas, Puerto de pass Spain
129 H2 Las Crucitas Mex.
66 G3 Lascuarre Spain
63 K6 La Seca Spain
39 J7 La Séguinière France
130 H4 La Selle, Pic mt. Haiti
66 H5 La Selva del Camp Spain
43 J7 La Selve France
66 F6 La Sènia Spain
41 D9 La Séranne, Montagne de ridge France
146 B1 La Serena Chile
64 H3 La Serena reg. Spain
65 I3 La Serena, Embalse de resr Spain
40 H2 La Serre, Massif de hills France
127 I4 Las Esperanças Mex.
65 O5 Las Estancias, Sierra de mts Spain
41 H10 La Seyne-sur-Mer France
147 H5 Las Flores Buenos Aires Arg.
144 E2 Las Flores Salta Arg.
146 C2 Las Flores San Juan Arg.
129 J3 Las Flores Mex.
146 B2 Las Galenas Chile
146 B4 Las Garzas Chile
147 H3 Las Golas Arg.
123 J11 Las Guacamatas, Cerro resr Mex.
128 E7 Las Guacamayas Mex.
185 I8 Lāshār r. Iran
107 I4 Lashburn Sask. Can.
146 C3 Las Heras Arg.
63 K9 Las Herencias Spain
136 C4 Las Hermosas, Parque Nacional nat. park Col.
126 G5 Las Herreras Mex.
147 E3 Las Higueras Arg.
158 C3 Lashio Myanmar
185 K6 Lashkar Gāh Afgh.
145 C8 Las Horquetas Arg.
146 A6 Las Hortensias Chile
128 F1 Las Huertas Mex.
67 E11 Las Huertas, Cabo de c. Spain
62 H8 Las Hurdes reg. Spain
75 L5 La Sila reg. Italy
55 H2 Łasin Pol.
98 □3d Las Indias La Palma Canary Is
129 K9 La Sirena, Cerro mt. Mex.
146 E3 Las Isletas Arg.
16 F2 Lasitsk Belarus
184 E4 Lāsjerd Iran
128 F5 Las Jicamas Mex.
146 C4 Las Juntas Arg.
144 C3 Las Juntas Chile
128 G6 Las Juntas Mex.
147 F2 Las Junturas Arg.
55 H4 Łask Pol.
189 O6 Laskarak Iran
55 J4 Łaskarzew Pol.
16 E4 Laskivtsi Ukr.
59 L7 Laško Slovenia
55 I6 Laskowa Pol.
54 G2 Laskowice Pol.
65 L2 Las Labores Spain
146 B6 Las Lajas Arg.
137 E3 Las Lajitas Venez.
129 I2 Las Lavaderos Mex.
146 B4 Las Leñas Arg.
136 A6 Las Lomas Peru
144 E2 Las Lomitas Arg.
63 P8 Las Majadas Spain
146 C4 Las Malvinas Arg.
64 F6 Las Marismas marsh Spain
145 D7 Las Martinetas Arg.
62 G4 Las Médulas tourist site Spain
65 O6 Las Menas Spain
136 E2 Las Mercedes Venez.
98 □3a Las Mercedes, Monte de hill Tenerife Canary Is
65 N2 Las Mesas Spain
126 G3 Las Mesteñas Mex.
55 K2 Łaśmiady, Jezioro l. Pol.
137 E2 Las Minas Venez.
127 O10 Las Minas, Cerro de mt. Hond.
127 O10 Las Minas, Sierra de mts Guat.
146 C4 Las Molles Arg.
129 H6 Las Navajas, Cerro mt. Mex.
65 I5 Las Navas de la Concepción Spain
63 L7 Las Navas del Marqués Spain
45 F7 Lasne Belgium
65 P7 Las Negras Spain
126 G4 Las Nieves Mex.
98 □3f Las Nieves, Pico de mt. Gran Canaria Canary Is
126 H5 Las Nopaleras, Cerro mt. Mex.
201 □3 La Société, Archipel de is Fr. Polynesia
65 M3 La Solana Spain
155 C5 Lasolo, Teluk b. Indon.
62 H3 Las Omañas reg. Spain
128 G8 La Sombra Mex.
36 C3 La Somme, Baie de b. France
136 B3 Las Orquideas, Parque Nacional nat. park Col.
42 G3 La Souterraine France
146 B5 Las Ovejas Arg.
54 G5 Lasowice Małe Pol.
144 F2 Las Palmas Arg.
128 E2 Las Palmas Mex.
125 O9 Las Palmas watercourse Mex.
126 □S13 Las Palmas Panama
98 □3f Las Palmas de Gran Canaria Gran Canaria Canary Is
146 C4 Las Paredes Arg.
128 G7 Las Parotas r. Mex.
65 N2 Las Pedroñeras Spain
147 F2 Las Peñas Arg.
128 B5 Las Peñitas, Punta pt Mex.
147 F3 Las Perdices Arg.
126 □T13 Las Perlas, Archipiélago de is Panama
139 F4 Las Petas Bol.
70 H7 La Spezia Italy
70 H7 La Spezia prov. Italy
147 I4 Las Piedras Uru.
138 C3 Las Piedras, Río de r. Peru
73 P7 La Spina, Monte mt. Italy
147 I4 Las Pipinas Arg.
126 □Q10 Las Planchas Hond.
72 B8 Las Plassas Sardegna Italy
145 D6 Las Plumas Arg.
66 F2 Laspuña Spain
185 O3 Laspur Pak.
147 G3 Las Rosas Arg.
67 F10 Las Rotas Spain
62 H3 Las Rozas, Embalse de resr Spain
63 M7 Las Rozas de Madrid Spain
48 K3 Lassahn Ger.
98 □3b Las Salinas Fuerteventura Canary Is
146 D2 Las Salinas, Pampa de salt pan Arg.
50 I3 Lassan Ger.
143 E2 Lassance Brazil
39 K5 Lassay-les-Châteaux France
124 K1 Lassen Peak vol. CA U.S.A.
124 K1 Lassen Volcanic National Park CA U.S.A.
43 D9 Lasseube France
36 E4 Lassigny France
59 K4 Lassing Niederösterreich Austria
59 J4 Lassing Steiermark Austria
59 M5 Laßnitzhöhe Austria
146 B3 Las Tablas Chile
129 H3 Las Tablas Mex.
126 □S14 Las Tablas Panama
65 L2 Las Tablas de Daimiel, Parque Nacional de nat. park Spain
145 B7 Lastarria, Parque Nacional de nat. park Chile
120 D6 Last Chance CO U.S.A.
71 K4 Lastebasse Italy
71 L3 Lastè delle Sute mt. Italy
144 D2 Las Termas Arg.
65 P5 Las Terreras Spain
107 J5 Last Mountain Lake Sask. Can.
66 C5 Las Torcas, Embalse de resr Spain
67 C11 Las Torres de Cotillas Spain
146 C1 Las Tórtolas, Cerro mt. Chile
43 I9 Lastours France
90 B5 Lastoursville Gabon
68 F4 Lastovo i. Croatia
68 F4 Lastovski Kanal sea chan. Croatia
147 G5 Lastra Arg.
66 D6 Lastra, Sierra de mts Spain
71 K8 Lastra a Signa Italy
63 L6 Lastras de Cuéllar Spain
63 J1 Lastres, Cabo c. Spain
126 C4 Las Tres Vírgenes, Volcán vol. Mex.
137 E3 Las Trincheras Venez.
48 E5 Lastrup Ger.
130 E3 Las Tunas Cuba
147 F4 Las Tunas Grandes, Laguna l. Arg.
45 I9 La Sûre, Vallée de val. Lux.
39 L6 La Suze-sur-Sarthe France
18 K4 Lasva Estonia
146 B2 Las Vacas Chile
136 D3 Las Varas Col.
126 F3 Las Varas Chihuahua Mex.
128 B4 Las Varas Nayarit Mex.
136 D3 Las Varas Venez.
147 F2 Las Varillas Arg.
128 B1 Las Vegas Mex.
123 L9 Las Vegas NM U.S.A.
125 Q5 Las Vegas NV U.S.A.
62 I7 Las Veguillas Spain
63 M6 Las Vencías, Embalse de resr Spain
63 L9 Las Ventas con Peña Aguilera Spain
63 J8 Las Ventas de San Julián Spain
146 E3 Las Vertientes Arg.
129 J6 Las Vigas de Ramirez Mex.
65 I2 Las Villuercas mt. Spain
65 H1 Las Villuercas, Sierra de mts Spain
138 C4 Las Yaras Peru
65 I6 Las Yeguas, Sierra de hills Spain
57 L1 Lasy Janowskie, Park Krajobrazowy Pol.
55 L5 Łaszczów Pol.
55 K5 Laszki Pol.
200 □6 Lata Santa Cruz Is Solomon Is
109 J3 La Tabatière Que. Can.
99 □1c La Table, Pointe de pt Réunion
136 B5 Latacunga Ecuador
212 S2 Latady Island Antarctica
40 E3 La Tagnière France
136 C5 La Tagua Col.
63 O7 La Tajera, Embalse de resr Spain
Latakia Syria see Al Lādhiqīyah
155 E4 Latalata i. Maluku Indon.
41 E6 La Talaudière France
39 J5 La Tannière France
128 G3 La Tapona Mex.
111 O2 Latchford Ont. Can.
31 N4 Latchingdon Essex, England U.K.
201 □2 Late i. Vava'u Gp Tonga
179 J8 Latehar Jharkhand India
38 E7 La Teignouse, Passage de str. France
71 L3 Latemar mt. Italy
75 L2 Laterza Italy
63 M3 La Tesla, Sierra de mts Spain
43 B6 La Teste-de-Buch France
128 C5 La Tetilla, Cerro mt. Mex.
18 K5 Latgales augstiene hills Latvia
209 D10 Latham W.A. Austr.
48 D5 Lathen Ger.
26 J6 Latheron Highland, Scotland U.K.
178 C9 Lathi Gujarat India
178 C6 Lathi Rajasthan India
178 F3 Latho Jammu and Kashmir
124 K4 Lathrop CA U.S.A.
70 B4 La Thuile Italy
42 F3 Lathus France
75 N2 Latiano Italy
184 F8 Lātīdān Iran
20 N4 Latikberg Sweden
155 B5 Latimojong Mountains Reserve nature res. Indon.
73 J5 Latina Italy
73 K5 Latina prov. Italy
129 K7 La Tinaja Mex.
71 O4 Latisana Italy
17 R2 Latnaya Rus. Fed.
75 L3 Lato r. Italy
146 E3 La Toma Arg.
57 K3 Latorica r. Slovakia
70 C3 La Tornette mt. Switz.
65 K2 La Torre de Abraham, Embalse de resr Spain
66 G3 La Torre de Cabdella Spain
130 G3 La Tortue, Île de i. Haiti
16 B5 Latorytsya r. Ukr.
208 F5 Latouche Treville, Cape W.A. Austr.
84 B4 Latouma well Niger
42 E5 La Tour-Blanche France
41 H9 La Tour-d'Aigues France
40 B5 La Tour-d'Auvergne France
43 H11 Latour-de-Carol France
43 J10 Latour-de-France France
43 H9 La Tour-du-Crieu France
40 G5 La Tour-du-Pin France
40 I5 La Tournette mt. France
41 C9 La Tour-sur-Orb France
41 I6 La Toussuire France
55 J3 Latowicz Pol.
146 D3 La Tranca Arg.
42 B3 La Tranche-sur-Mer France
63 Q6 La Tranquera, Embalse de resr Spain
43 G9 Latrape France
37 I8 Latrecey-Ormoy-sur-Aube France
42 B4 La Tremblade France
42 G3 La Trimouille France
126 □P11 La Trinidad Nic.
154 C3 La Trinidad Luzon Phil.
127 M9 La Trinitaria Mex.
41 K9 La Trinité France
131 □3 La Trinité Martinique
39 M4 La Trinité-de-Réville France
38 F5 La Trinité-Porhoët France
38 E6 La Trinité-sur-Mer France
42 I5 La Triouzoune, Lac de l. France
205 K9 Latrobe Tas. Austr.
116 F8 Latrobe PA U.S.A.
41 H6 La Tronche France
73 Q7 Latronico Italy
43 I6 Latronquière France
144 C3 La Troya r. Arg.
111 P2 La Truite, Lac à l. Que. Can.
190 C7 Latrun West Bank
19 V3 Latskoye Rus. Fed.
73 Q9 Lattarico Italy
Latte Island Vava'u Gp Tonga see Late
41 D9 Lattes France
44 K4 Lattrop Neth.
111 O2 Latulipe Que. Can.
109 F4 La Tuque Que. Can.
176 E3 Latur Mahar. India
38 G7 La Turballe France
18 G5 Latvia country Europe
Latvija country Europe see Latvia
Latviyskaya S.S.R. country Europe see Latvia
89 H4 Lau Nigeria
92 A3 Lau r. Sudan
179 J8 Laua r. Chhattisgarh India
49 G9 Laubach Hessen Ger.
49 D10 Laubach Rheinland-Pfalz Ger.
94 D3 Lauban waterhole Namibia
53 I5 Lauben Bayern Ger.
53 I6 Lauben Bayern Ger.
51 J8 Laubusch Ger.
138 C4 Lauca, Parque Nacional nat. park Chile
51 E8 Laucha (Unstrut) Ger.
52 G5 Lauchert r. Ger.
51 I8 Lauchhammer Ger.
53 I4 Lauchheim Ger.
52 E6 Lauchringen Ger.
52 H2 Lauda-Königshofen Ger.
52 F2 Laudenbach Ger.
26 K11 Lauder Scottish Borders, Scotland U.K.
118 F5 Lauderdale NJ U.S.A.
Laudio Spain see Llodio
41 F8 Laudun France
49 H6 Lauenau Ger.
48 I4 Lauenbrück Ger.
48 K4 Lauenburg (Elbe) Ger.
49 H7 Lauenförde Ger.
49 J10 Lauer r. Ger.
52 E4 Lauf Ger.
49 H10 Laufach Ger.
53 K2 Lauf an der Pegnitz Ger.
53 N6 Laufen Ger.
70 D1 Laufen Switz.
70 E1 Laufenberg Switz.
52 E6 Laufenburg (Baden) Ger.
20 □C1 Laugarbakki Iceland
105 L2 Lauge Koch Kyst reg. Greenland
30 D4 Laugharne Carmarthenshire, Wales U.K.
206 E7 Laughlen, Mount N.T. Austr.
123 L8 Laughlin Peak NM U.S.A.
43 F7 Laugnac France
21 Q5 Lauhanvuoren kansallispuisto nat. park Fin.
53 I4 Lauingen (Donau) Ger.
65 N7 Laujar de Andarax Spain
18 F3 Lauka Estonia
20 R5 Laukaa Fin.
18 F6 Laukuva Lith.
200 □2 Lauli'i Samoa
159 D9 Laun Thai.
43 G8 Launac France
111 P1 Launay Que. Can.
205 K9 Launceston Tas. Austr.
30 D6 Launceston Cornwall, England U.K.
27 C8 Laune r. Rep. of Ireland
158 D2 Launggyaung Myanmar
159 D8 Launglon Myanmar
159 C8 Launglon Bok Islands Myanmar
127 M10 La Unidad Mex.
139 E3 La Unión Bol.
145 B6 La Unión Chile
136 B4 La Unión Col.
126 □P11 La Unión El Salvador
126 □P10 La Unión Hond.
128 F8 La Unión Mex.
138 A2 La Unión Huánuco Peru
136 A6 La Unión Piura Peru
67 D12 La Unión Spain
36 I4 Launois-sur-Vence France
70 C2 Laupen Switz.
52 H5 Laupheim Ger.
154 C4 Laur Luzon Phil.
207 J3 Laura Qld Austr.
204 G5 Laura S.A. Austr.
43 H9 Lauragais reg. France
43 I9 Lauraguel France
136 E3 La Urbana Venez.
75 K7 Laureana di Borrello Italy
117 J10 Laurel DE U.S.A.
121 K10 Laurel MS U.S.A.
122 J4 Laurel MT U.S.A.
120 G4 Laurel NE U.S.A.
118 D4 Laureldale PA U.S.A.
139 F6 Laureles Para.
116 F9 Laurel Hill hills PA U.S.A.
118 E5 Laurel Springs NJ U.S.A.
118 A3 Laurelton PA U.S.A.
26 L9 Laurencekirk Aberdeenshire, Scotland U.K.
27 F6 Laurencetown Rep. of Ireland
41 C9 Laurens France
120 H4 Laurens IA U.S.A.
115 G8 Laurens SC U.S.A.
109 G4 Laurentides, Réserve Faunique des nature res. Que. Can.
73 P7 Laurenzana Italy
43 B9 Laurhibar r. France
178 H7 Lauri Madh. Prad. India
73 P7 Lauria Italy
212 V2 Laurie Island S. Orkney Is Antarctica
42 G3 Laurière France
26 H13 Laurieston Dumfries and Galloway, Scotland U.K.
205 N4 Laurieton N.S.W. Austr.
115 H8 Laurinburg NC U.S.A.
73 O7 Laurino Italy
41 G9 Lauris France
203 F10 Lauriston South I. N.Z.
110 F2 Laurium MI U.S.A.
74 H2 Lauro Italy
70 B2 Lausanne Switz.
51 D7 Lausehügel hill Ger.
51 K8 Lausitzer Gebirge hills Ger.
51 I7 Lausitzer Grenzwall park Ger.
51 G7 Laußig Ger.
51 I8 Laußnitz Ger.
41 E7 Laussonne France
43 F6 Laussou France
157 H2 Laut i. Indon.
157 H5 Laut i. Indon.
157 L6 Laut i. Indon.
157 K6 Laut, Selat sea chan. Indon.
51 J8 Lauta Ger.
41 I6 Lautaret, Col du pass France
146 A6 Lautaro Chile
145 B8 Lautaro, Volcán vol. Chile
155 E8 Lautem East Timor
52 E4 Lautenbach Ger.
37 P6 Lauter r. France/Ger.
51 G9 Lauter Ger.
58 A5 Lauterach Austria
53 L3 Lauterach r. Ger.
37 P6 Lauterbourg France
70 D2 Lauterbrunnen Switz.
52 D2 Lauterecken Ger.
53 L3 Lauterhofen Ger.
49 H9 Lautersbach (Hessen) Ger.
52 H4 Lauterstein Ger.
49 K10 Lautertal Ger.
157 K7 Laut Kecil, Kepulauan is Indon.
201 □1a Lautoka Viti Levu Fiji
43 I8 Lautrec France
155 B7 Laut Taka Bonerate National Park Indon.
156 B2 Lauttawar, Danau l. Indon.
20 K4 Lauvsnes Norway
20 T5 Lauvuskylä Fin.
44 J2 Lauwersmeer l. Neth.
43 G7 Lauzerte France
43 H6 Lauzès France
55 J1 Lava r. Rus. Fed.
118 E1 Lava NY U.S.A.
122 D6 Lava Beds National Monument nat. park CA U.S.A.
121 G11 Lavaca r. TX U.S.A.
72 A10 La Vacca, Isola i. Sardegna Italy
62 D1 Lavadoiro, Punta pt Spain
70 G7 Lavagna Italy
70 G7 Lavagne r. Italy
108 F4 Laval Que. Can.
39 J5 Laval France
43 I9 Lavalette France
116 C10 Lavalette WV U.S.A.
41 H10 La Valette-du-Var France
146 C3 Lavalle Arg.
71 L2 La Valle Italy
59 K6 Lavamünd Austria
184 E8 Lāvān Iran
200 □6 Lavanggu Rennell Solomon Is
41 J6 La Vanoise, Massif de mts France
41 J6 La Vanoise, Parc National de nat. park France
66 H3 Lavansa r. Spain
40 H4 Lavans-lès-St-Claude France
59 K6 Lavant r. Austria/Slovenia
59 K5 Lavanttal val. Austria
144 B5 Lavapié, Punta pt Chile
184 D7 Lāvar Iran
79 H1 Lavara Greece
95 □J4 Lavaraty Madag.
43 E7 Lavardac France
43 F8 Lavardens France
146 D4 La Varita, Pampa de plain Arg.
184 F6 Lāvar Meydān salt marsh Iran
90 C2 La Vassako-Bolo, Réserve National Intégral de nature res. C.A.R.
41 C6 Lavaudieu France
43 H8 Lavaur France
42 I3 Lavaveix-les-Mines France
124 K5 Laveaga Peak CA U.S.A.
63 J3 La Vecilla Spain
43 D10 Lavedan reg. France
130 H4 La Vega Dom. Rep.
128 D5 La Vega Mex.
62 I2 La Vega Spain
62 I2 La Vega Spain
63 K2 La Vega Cantabria Spain
136 D2 La Vela Venez.
136 C1 La Vela, Cabo de c. Col.
43 H10 Lavelanet France
62 I6 La Vellés Spain
73 P5 Lavello Italy
121 D11 La Venada r. Mex.
70 F4 Lavena Ponte Tresa Italy
31 N3 Lavenham Suffolk, England U.K.
70 F4 Laveno Italy
126 □P10 La Venta Hond.
129 N8 La Venta r. Mex.
147 F6 La Ventana, Sierra de hills Arg.
144 E5 La Ventana, Sierra de mts Arg.
36 E2 Laventie France
63 P8 La Ventosa Spain
136 D3 La Venturosa Col.
62 I9 La Vera reg. Spain
146 E4 La Verde Arg.
75 K7 La Verde r. Italy
41 H9 La Verdière France
108 E4 La Vérendrye, Réserve Faunique de nature res. Que. Can.
41 D8 La Vernarède France
121 F7 Laverne OK U.S.A.
30 F5 Lavernock Point Wales U.K.
40 G5 La Verpillière France
39 J8 La Verrie France
209 G10 Laverton W.A. Austr.
36 H5 La Veuve France
72 C5 Lavezzi, Îles i. Corse France
72 C5 Lavezzi, Réserve Naturelle des Îles nature res. Corse France
21 Q6 Lavia Fin.
73 O6 Laviano Italy
126 H4 La Víbora Mex.
128 G1 La Victoria Mex.
65 J5 La Victoria Spain
131 J8 La Victoria Venez.
61 □ La Victoria de Acentejo Tenerife Canary Is
63 N5 La Vid Spain
62 H9 La Vid, Río de r. Spain
111 P4 Lavieille, Lake Ont. Can.
111 N3 Lavigne Ont. Can.
72 E3 La Villa Italy
63 N9 La Villa de Don Fadrique Spain
36 B8 La Ville-aux-Clercs France
41 D7 La Villedieu France
41 E7 Lavilledieu France
42 E3 La Villedieu-du-Clain France
37 L8 La Villedieu-en-Fontenette France
129 I2 Lavin Mex.
144 D2 La Viña Arg.
136 B6 La Viña Peru
122 J3 Lavina MT U.S.A.
73 J5 Lavinio-Lido di Enea Italy
65 K7 La Viñuela, Embalse de resr Spain
66 D3 La Violada, Llanos de plain Spain
147 G3 La Violeta Arg.
65 O6 La Virgen, Puerto de pass Spain
63 Q5 La Virgen, Sierra de mts Spain
40 J2 Laviron France
71 K3 Lavis Italy
43 F8 Lavit France
147 F6 La Vitícola Arg.
37 L7 La Vôge reg. France
Lavongal i. P.N.G. see New Hanover
18 I7 Lavoriškės Lith.
62 C8 Lavos Port.
41 F7 La Voulte-sur-Rhône France
41 C6 Lavoûte-Chilhac France
41 D6 Lavoûte-sur-Loire France
143 E4 Lavras Brazil
141 B9 Lavras do Sul Brazil
64 C3 Lavre Port.
64 B3 Lavre r. Port.
182 K1 Lavrent'yevka Kazakh.
78 F5 Lavrio Greece
19 T9 Lavrovo Orlovskaya Oblast' Rus. Fed.
19 U2 Lavrovo Vologodskaya Oblast' Rus. Fed.
97 P3 Lavumisa Swaziland
93 A8 Lavushi-Manda National Park Zambia
88 C5 Lawa r. Liberia
158 C2 Lawa Myanmar
185 N5 Lawa Pak.
108 E3 Lawagamau r. Ont. Can.
178 I9 Lawan Chhattisgarh India
157 L9 Lawang i. Indon.
37 O6 La Wantzenau France
157 K2 Lawas Sarawak Malaysia
108 D2 Lawashi r. Ont. Can.
186 G9 Lawdar Yemen
213 H2 Law Dome ice feature Antarctica
155 C6 Lawele Sulawesi Indon.
26 H9 Lawers Perth and Kinross, Scotland U.K.
31 O4 Lawford Essex, England U.K.
155 F4 Lawin i. Maluku Indon.
157 J4 Lawit, Gunung mt. Indon./Malaysia
156 E2 Lawit, Gunung mt. Malaysia
158 C4 Lawksawk Myanmar
110 B6 Lawler IA U.S.A.
208 H3 Lawley r. W.A. Austr.
118 B4 Lawn PA U.S.A.
179 N8 Lawngtlai Mizoram India
206 G5 Lawn Hill Qld Austr.
206 G5 Lawn Hill Creek r. Qld Austr.
206 G5 Lawn Hill National Park Qld Austr.
37 K5 La Woëvre, Plaine de plain France
189 K9 Lawqah Saudi Arabia
88 E4 Lawra Ghana
203 D12 Lawrence South I. N.Z.
203 E10 Lawrence r. South I. N.Z.
120 H6 Lawrence KS U.S.A.
117 N6 Lawrence MA U.S.A.
115 D8 Lawrenceburg TN U.S.A.
117 □R3 Lawrence Station N.B. Can.
27 J4 Lawrencetown Northern Ireland U.K.
114 D6 Lawrenceville IL U.S.A.
118 F4 Lawrenceville NJ U.S.A.
116 H7 Lawrenceville PA U.S.A.
116 H12 Lawrenceville VA U.S.A.
209 F9 Lawrence Wells, Mount hill W.A. Austr.
55 K2 Ławsk Pol.
121 F8 Lawton OK U.S.A.
157 I8 Lawu, Gunung vol. Indon.
50 K5 Ławy Pol.
186 B1 Lawz, Jabal al mt. Saudi Arabia
23 K3 Laxå Sweden
62 C2 Laxe Spain
62 C2 Laxe, Cabo de c. Spain
28 I5 Laxey Isle of Man
96 H2 Laxey S. Africa
28 I5 Laxey Bay Isle of Man
26 F6 Laxford, Loch inlet Scotland U.K.
26 F6 Laxford Bridge Highland, Scotland U.K.
106 D4 Lax Kw'alaams B.C. Can.
26 □N2 Laxo Shetland, Scotland U.K.
173 G9 Laxong Co l. Xizang China
37 L6 Laxou France
20 M5 Laxsjö Sweden
23 K3 Laxsjön l. Sweden
42 B3 Lay r. France
14 L2 Laya r. Rus. Fed.
66 C3 Layana Spain
157 L7 Layar, Tanjung pt Indon.
138 C4 La Yarada Peru
90 D2 La Yata-Ngaya, Réserve de Faune de nature res. C.A.R.
14 I1 Laydennyy, Mys c. Rus. Fed.

Layeni to Les Cammazes

292

155 F7 **Layeni** *Maluku* Indon.
128 C4 **La Yesca** Mex.
186 H4 **Laylá** Saudi Arabia
190 G7 **Layla** *salt pan* Saudi Arabia
42 C1 **Layon** *r.* France
63 L9 **Layos** Spain
131 □3 **Layou** St Vincent
43 F7 **Layrac** France
197 H2 **Laysan Island** *HI* U.S.A.
172 F5 **Laysu** *Xinjiang* China
118 F2 **Layton** *NJ* U.S.A.
124 I2 **Laytonville** *CA* U.S.A.
Layturi Georgia *see* **Lait'uri**
59 N8 **Laz** Croatia
170 A5 **Laza** Myanmar
62 F4 **Laza** Spain
126 E6 **La Zacatosa, Picacho** *mt.* Mex.
63 P4 **Lazagurría** Spain
147 F5 **La Zanja** Arg.
99 □2b **Lazare, Pointe** *pt Mahé* Seychelles
57 L5 **Lăzăreni** Romania
162 L2 **Lazarev** Rus. Fed.
76 I6 **Lazarevac** *Srbija* Serb. and Mont.
19 U8 **Lazarevo** Rus. Fed.
191 A2 **Lazarevskoye** Rus. Fed.
126 E6 **Lázaro, Sierra de San** *mts* Mex.
126 B2 **Lázaro Cárdenas** *Baja California* Mex.
126 B2 **Lázaro Cárdenas** *Baja California* Mex.
129 N9 **Lázaro Cárdenas** *Chiapas* Mex.
128 E8 **Lázaro Cárdenas** *Michoacán* Mex.
57 J3 **Lazberci** *park* Hungary
144 G4 **Lazcano** Uru.
18 G7 **Lazdijai** Lith.
173 E9 **Lazhuglung** *Xizang* China
19 R7 **Lazinki** Rus. Fed.
73 J3 **Lazio** *admin. reg.* Italy
71 J5 **Lazise** Italy
55 J4 **Łaziska** Pol.
56 E1 **Lázně Bělohrad** Czech Rep.
56 E1 **Lázně Bohdaneč** Czech Rep.
56 B1 **Lázně Kynžvart** Czech Rep.
147 H3 **Lazo** Arg.
162 H7 **Lazo** *Primorskiy Kray* Rus. Fed.
193 O3 **Lazo** *Respublika Sakha (Yakutiya)* Rus. Fed.
29 L4 **Lazonby** *Cumbria, England* U.K.
121 E11 **La Zorra** *watercourse* Mex.
57 L4 **Lazuri** Romania
57 L5 **Lazuri de Beiuş** Romania
17 L7 **Lazurne** Ukr.
55 H5 **Łazy** Pol.
147 H5 **Lazzarino** Arg.
70 G6 **Lazzaro, Monte** *hill* Italy
28 E2 **Leacan, Rubha nan** *pt Scotland* U.K.
159 F8 **Leach** Cambodia
110 J2 **Leach Island** *Ont.* Can.
118 C4 **Leacock** *PA* U.S.A.
104 H5 **Lead** *SD* U.S.A.
26 J11 **Leadburn** *Midlothian, Scotland* U.K.
29 P7 **Leadenham** *Lincolnshire, England* U.K.
107 I5 **Leader** *Sask.* Can.
118 B5 **Leader Heights** *PA* U.S.A.
26 K11 **Leader Water** *r. Scotland* U.K.
29 N4 **Leadgate** *Durham, England* U.K.
26 I12 **Leadhills** *South Lanarkshire, Scotland* U.K.
205 L5 **Leadville** *N.S.W.* Austr.
123 K7 **Leadville** *CO* U.S.A.
121 K10 **Leaf** *r. MS* U.S.A.
107 K3 **Leaf Rapids** *Man.* Can.
212 Q2 **Leahy, Cape** Antarctica
208 I4 **Leake, Mount** *hill W.A.* Austr.
121 K10 **Leakesville** *MS* U.S.A.
121 F11 **Leakey** *TX* U.S.A.
208 D6 **Leal, Mount** *hill W.A.* Austr.
144 D2 **Leales** Arg.
108 D5 **Leamington** *Ont.* Can.
31 I3 **Leamington Spa, Royal** *Warwickshire, England* U.K.
171 J5 **Le'an** *Jiangxi* China
97 M2 **Leandra** S. Africa
147 G4 **Leandro N. Alem** *Buenos Aires* Arg.
144 G2 **Leandro N. Alem** *Misiones* Arg.
27 C8 **Leane, Lough** *l.* Rep. of Ireland
95 □J2 **Leanja** Madag.
57 I4 **Leányfalu** Hungary
27 D9 **Leap** Rep. of Ireland
208 C7 **Learmonth** *W.A.* Austr.
29 Q7 **Leasingham** *Lincolnshire, England* U.K.
31 L5 **Leatherhead** *Surrey, England* U.K.
45 F8 **L'Eau d'Heure** *l.* Belgium
45 F8 **L'Eau d'Heure** *r.* Belgium
29 P5 **Leavening** *North Yorkshire, England* U.K.
120 H6 **Leavenworth** *KS* U.S.A.
122 D3 **Leavenworth** *WA* U.S.A.
124 M3 **Leavitt Peak** *CA* U.S.A.
20 S2 **Leavvajohka** Norway
23 N7 **Łeba** Pol.
54 F1 **Łeba** *r.* Pol.
54 G1 **Łeba** *r.* Pol.
52 B3 **Lebach** Ger.
154 E8 **Lebak** *Mindanao* Phil.
97 J3 **Lebaleng** S. Africa
90 A5 **Lébamba** Gabon
77 J8 **Lebane** *Srbija* Serb. and Mont.
190 D5 **Lebanon** *country* Asia
114 D5 **Lebanon** *IN* U.S.A.
120 F6 **Lebanon** *KS* U.S.A.
114 E7 **Lebanon** *KY* U.S.A.
121 I7 **Lebanon** *MO* U.S.A.
117 M5 **Lebanon** *NH* U.S.A.
118 F3 **Lebanon** *NJ* U.S.A.
116 A9 **Lebanon** *OH* U.S.A.
122 C4 **Lebanon** *OR* U.S.A.
111 R9 **Lebanon** *PA* U.S.A.
115 D7 **Lebanon** *TN* U.S.A.
116 C12 **Lebanon** *VA* U.S.A.
118 C4 **Lebanon County** *county PA* U.S.A.
37 L5 **Le Ban-St-Martin** France
185 I1 **Lebap** Turkm.
Lebap Oblast *admin. div.* Turkm. *see* Lebapskaya Oblast'
185 J2 **Lebapskaya Oblast'** *admin. div.* Turkm.
43 K10 **Le Barcarès** France
43 C6 **Le Barp** France
45 F6 **Lebbeke** Belgium
Lebda *tourist site* Libya *see* **Leptis Magna**
41 E7 **Le Béage** France
41 H10 **Le Beausset** France
124 N7 **Lebec** *CA* U.S.A.
39 M3 **Le Bec-Hellouin** France
Lebedin Ukr. *see* **Lebedyn**
19 W8 **Lebedyan'** Rus. Fed.
17 N3 **Lebedyn** Ukr.
108 E3 **Lebel-sur-Quévillon** *Que.* Can.
51 E7 **Lebendorf** Ger.
39 J4 **Le Bény-Bocage** France
56 G4 **Lébényimiklós** Hungary
43 I8 **Le Bez** France
36 C3 **Lebiez** France
92 E3 **Lebiolali** *well* Eth.
40 J4 **Le Biot** France
42 G2 **Le Blanc** France
41 D8 **Le Bleymard** France
54 G1 **Łebno** Pol.
90 D3 **Lebo** Dem. Rep. Congo
155 C6 **Lebo** *Sulawesi* Indon.
40 F5 **Le Bois-d'Oingt** France
42 B3 **Le Bois-Plage-en-Ré** France
Lebomboberge *hills* Moz. *see* **Lebombo Mountains**
97 Q2 **Lebombo Mountains** *hills* Moz.
97 M2 **Lebonang** S. Africa
179 L6 **Lebong** *W. Bengal* India
41 K8 **Le Boréon** France
23 N7 **Lębork** Pol.
43 J10 **Le Boulou** France
39 J8 **Le Boupère** France
43 H6 **Le Bourg** France
41 I6 **Le Bourg-d'Oisans** France
40 H5 **Le Bourget-du-Lac** France
39 J5 **Le Bourgneuf-la-Forêt** France
43 C6 **Le Bouscat** France
41 C9 **Le Bousquet-d'Orb** France
95 F5 **Lebowakgomo** S. Africa
48 J2 **Lebrade** Ger.
40 E3 **Le Breuil** *Bourgogne* France
36 G6 **Le Breuil** *Champagne-Ardenne* France
40 J5 **Le Brévent** *mt.* France
64 G7 **Lebrija** Spain
59 M6 **Lebring-Sankt Margarethen** Austria
43 E8 **Le Brouilh-Monbert** France
99 □1c **Le Brûlé** Réunion
41 I8 **Le Brusquet** France
23 N7 **Łebsko, Jezioro** *lag.* Pol.
144 B5 **Lebu** Chile
62 F5 **Lebução** Port.
43 F6 **Le Bugue** France
41 C7 **Le Buisson** France
43 F6 **Le Buisson-de-Cadouin** France
51 K6 **Lebus** Ger.
51 H7 **Lebusa** Ger.
42 C2 **Le Busseau** France
17 O4 **Leb''yazhe** Ukr.
17 R8 **Lebyazhiy, Liman** *l.* Rus. Fed.
14 J4 **Lebyazh'ye** *Kirovskaya Oblast'* Rus. Fed.
18 M2 **Lebyazh'ye** *Leningradskaya Oblast'* Rus. Fed.
19 V9 **Lebyazh'ye** *Lipetskaya Oblast'* Rus. Fed.
62 C6 **Leça da Palmeira** Port.
62 C6 **Leça do Bailio** Port.
43 I10 **Lecamp, Plateau de** France
Le Caire Egypt *see* **Al Qāhirah**
41 K9 **Le Cannet** France
41 I10 **Le Cannet-des-Maures** France
38 B5 **Le Cap** *c.* France
131 □3 **Le Carbet** Martinique
27 F5 **Lecarrow** Rep. of Ireland
41 H10 **Le Castellet** France
36 G3 **Le Cateau-Cambrésis** France
36 F3 **Le Catelet** France
41 C9 **Le Caylar** France
41 B7 **Le Cayrol** France
75 O3 **Lecce** Italy
75 O3 **Lecce** *prov.* Italy
70 G4 **Lecco** Italy
70 G4 **Lecco** *prov.* Italy
70 G4 **Lecco, Lago di** *l.* Italy
120 I3 **Le Center** *MN* U.S.A.
66 D5 **Lécera** Spain
58 B5 **Lech** Austria
58 C4 **Lech** *r.* Austria/Ger.
78 C5 **Lechaina** Greece
41 E6 **Le Chambon-Feugerolles** France
41 E6 **Le Chambon-sur-Lignon** France
171 I6 **Lechang** *Guangdong* China
58 C5 **Lechaschau** Austria
70 B2 **Le Chasseron** *mt.* Switz.
42 B4 **Le Château-d'Oléron** France
40 I5 **Le Châtelard** France
39 P8 **Le Châtelet** France
36 E6 **Le Châtelet-en-Brie** France
53 J6 **Lechbruck** Ger.
36 H6 **Le Chêne** France
36 I4 **Le Chesne** France
40 J4 **Le Cheval Blanc** *mt.* France
41 I6 **Le Cheval Noir** *mt.* France
41 E7 **Le Cheylard** France
41 H6 **Le Cheylas** France
77 M3 **Lechința** Romania
77 M4 **Lechința** *r.* Romania
191 D3 **Lech'khumis K'edi** *hills* Georgia
31 I4 **Lechlade** *Gloucestershire, England* U.K.
58 B5 **Lechtal** *val.* Austria
58 B5 **Lechtaler Alpen** *mts* Austria
49 F6 **Lechtingen (Wallenhorst)** Ger.
66 D4 **Leciñena** Spain
48 G1 **Leck** Ger.
27 F4 **Leckaun** Rep. of Ireland
26 F7 **Leckmelm** *Highland, Scotland* U.K.
41 C9 **Le Clapier** France
41 D8 **Le Collet-de-Dèze** France
121 I10 **Lecompte** *LA* U.S.A.
38 B5 **Le Conquet** France
41 I6 **Le Corbier** France
40 E4 **Le Coteau** France
36 C5 **Le Coudray-St-Germer** France
38 I5 **Lécousse** France
41 D9 **Le Crès** France
40 E3 **Le Creusot** France
65 L7 **Lecrín** Spain
38 F7 **Le Croisic** France
36 C3 **Le Crotoy** France
43 F8 **Lectoure** France
55 K4 **Łęczna** Pol.
55 H3 **Łęczyca** Pol.
54 F1 **Łęczyce** Pol.
48 D4 **Leda** *r.* Ger.
26 F10 **Ledaig** *Argyll and Bute, Scotland* U.K.
65 P2 **Ledaña** Spain
63 O7 **Ledanca** Spain
156 E3 **Ledang, Gunung** *mt.* Malaysia
68 F2 **Ledava** *r.* Slovenia
31 K4 **Ledburn** *Buckinghamshire, England* U.K.
30 H3 **Ledbury** *Herefordshire, England* U.K.
45 E7 **Lede** Belgium
43 F7 **Lède** *r.* France
56 E2 **Ledeč nad Sázavou** Czech Rep.
45 D7 **Ledegem** Belgium
14 I4 **Ledengskoye** Rus. Fed.
56 D3 **Ledenice** Czech Rep.
43 I7 **Lédergues** France
62 I6 **Ledesma** Spain
43 C9 **Ledeuix** France
41 D7 **Le Devès** *mt.* France
131 □3 **Le Diamant** Martinique
91 C5 **Lediba** Dem. Rep. Congo
41 E9 **Lédignan** France
63 K4 **Ledigos** Spain
14 J2 **Ledkovo** Rus. Fed.
26 G6 **Ledmore** *Highland, Scotland* U.K.
14 F2 **Ledmozero** Rus. Fed.
57 H2 **Lednica** Slovakia
56 F3 **Lednice** Czech Rep.
157 H4 **Ledo** *Kalimantan* Indon.
170 G9 **Ledong** *Hainan* China
158 I5 **Ledong** *Hainan* China
40 D4 **Le Donjon** France
42 G3 **Le Dorat** France
Ledosus France *see* **Lezoux**
62 I8 **Ledrada** Spain
58 C8 **Ledro, Lago di** *l.* Italy
168 H8 **Ledu** *Qinghai* China
106 H4 **Leduc** *Alta* Can.
41 H8 **Le Duffre** *mt.* France
193 S3 **Ledyanaya, Gora** *mt.* Rus. Fed.
54 E2 **Lędyczek** Pol.
54 D1 **Lędzin** Pol.
55 H5 **Lędziny** Pol.
27 F9 **Lee** *r.* Rep. of Ireland
29 L6 **Lee** *Lancashire, England* U.K.
117 L6 **Lee** *MA* U.S.A.
117 □Q3 **Lee** *ME* U.S.A.
116 F8 **Leechburg** *PA* U.S.A.
120 H2 **Leech Lake** *MN* U.S.A.
120 H2 **Leech Lake Indian Reservation** *res. MN* U.S.A.
29 N6 **Leeds** *West Yorkshire, England* U.K.
29 N6 **Leeds Bradford International** *airport England* U.K.
30 B7 **Leedstown** *Cornwall, England* U.K.
44 J2 **Leek** Neth.
29 M7 **Leek** *Staffordshire, England* U.K.
209 C10 **Leeman** *W.A.* Austr.
29 N5 **Leeming** *North Yorkshire, England* U.K.
30 D7 **Lee Moor** *Devon, England* U.K.
27 C5 **Leenane** Rep. of Ireland
45 I6 **Leende** Neth.
44 J2 **Leens** Neth.
31 J6 **Lee-on-the-Solent** *Hampshire, England* U.K.
116 F7 **Leeper** *PA* U.S.A.
48 D4 **Leer (Ostfriesland)** Ger.
44 H5 **Leerdam** Neth.
44 H4 **Leersum** Neth.
43 C10 **Lées-Athas** France
115 G11 **Leesburg** *FL* U.S.A.
115 E10 **Leesburg** *GA* U.S.A.
116 A10 **Leesburg** *KY* U.S.A.
118 F6 **Leesburg** *NJ* U.S.A.
116 B9 **Leesburg** *OH* U.S.A.
116 H9 **Leesburg** *VA* U.S.A.
49 H5 **Leese** Ger.
118 D4 **Leesport** *PA* U.S.A.
120 H6 **Lees Summit** *MO* U.S.A.
209 F8 **Lee Steere Range** *hills W.A.* Austr.
203 G10 **Leeston** *South I.* N.Z.
121 I10 **Leesville** *LA* U.S.A.
116 F11 **Leesville Lake** *VA* U.S.A.
205 K6 **Leeton** *N.S.W.* Austr.
97 K3 **Leeudoringstad** S. Africa
96 F8 **Leeu-Gamka** S. Africa
97 J4 **Leeukop** *mt.* S. Africa
97 L5 **Leeurivierdam** *l.* S. Africa
96 F8 **Leeuw** *r.* S. Africa
44 I2 **Leeuwarden** Neth.
209 C13 **Leeuwin, Cape** *W.A.* Austr.
209 C12 **Leeuwin-Naturaliste National Park** *W.A.* Austr.
124 M4 **Lee Vining** *CA* U.S.A.
131 K4 **Leeward Islands** Caribbean Sea
50 D3 **Leezen** *Mecklenburg-Vorpommern* Ger.
48 J3 **Leezen** *Schleswig-Holstein* Ger.
38 C5 **Le Faou** France
38 E5 **Le Faouët** France
43 G9 **Le Fauga** France
77 N7 **Lefedzha** *r.* Bulg.
38 H8 **Le Fenouiller** France
36 D1 **Leffrinckoucke** France
190 A3 **Lefka** Cyprus
78 B4 **Lefkada** *Lefkada* Greece
78 B4 **Lefkada** *i.* Greece
78 E7 **Lefka Ori** *mts Kriti* Greece
Lefkás *Lefkada* Greece *see* Lefkada
Lefke Cyprus *see* **Lefka**
78 B3 **Lefkimmi** *Kerkyra* Greece
Lefkoniko Cyprus *see* Lefkonikon
190 B3 **Lefkonikon** Cyprus
78 E4 **Lefkonisia** *i.* Greece
Lefkoşa Cyprus *see* **Lefkosia**
190 B3 **Lefkosia** Cyprus
43 E6 **Le Fleix** France
38 C4 **Le Folgoët** France
36 F3 **Leforest** France
43 G9 **Le Fossat** France
43 G9 **Le Fousseret** France
131 □3 **Le François** Martinique
109 G1 **Lefroy** *r. Que.* Can.
209 G11 **Lefroy, Lake** *salt flat W.A.* Austr.
41 J8 **Le Fugeret** France
39 I7 **Le Fuilet** France
55 J5 **Łęg** *r.* Pol.
200 □3a **Legan** *i. Kwajalein* Marshall Is
63 M8 **Leganés** Spain
63 O8 **Leganiel** Spain
108 C3 **Legarde** *r. Ont.* Can.
154 D5 **Legaspi** *Luzon* Phil.
53 I6 **Legau** Ger.
36 B7 **Le Gault-St-Denis** France
36 G6 **Le Gault-Soigny** France
66 A1 **Legazpi** Spain
50 E5 **Legde** Ger.
49 D6 **Legden** Ger.
38 H8 **Legé** France
43 B6 **Lège-Cap-Ferret** France
208 D6 **Legendre Island** *W.A.* Austr.
39 J5 **Le Genest-St-Isle** France
205 K9 **Legges Tor** *mt. Tas.* Austr.
124 I2 **Leggett** *CA* U.S.A.
27 G3 **Leggs** *Northern Ireland* U.K.
Leghorn Italy *see* **Livorno**
55 I3 **Legionowo** Pol.
45 I9 **Léglise** Belgium
71 K5 **Legnago** Italy
70 F4 **Legnano** Italy
54 E4 **Legnica** Pol.
54 E4 **Legnickie Pole** Pol.
70 G3 **Legnone, Monte** *mt.* Italy
Legohli *N.W.T.* Can. *see* **Norman Wells**
42 E4 **Le Gond-Pontouvre** France
131 □2 **Le Gosier** Guadeloupe
54 G1 **Łęgowo** Pol.
59 O7 **Legrad** Croatia
124 L4 **Le Grand** *CA* U.S.A.
209 F13 **Le Grand, Cape** *W.A.* Austr.
99 □1c **Le Grand Bénare** *mt.* Réunion
40 I5 **Le Grand-Bornand** France
42 H3 **Le Grand-Bourg** France
41 J8 **Le Grand Coyer** *mt.* France
40 H4 **Le Grand Crêt d'Eau** *mt.* France
41 G6 **Le Grand-Lemps** France
39 L6 **Le Grand-Lucé** France
40 J5 **Le Grand Mont** *mt.* France
39 M8 **Le Grand-Pressigny** France
36 B5 **Le Grand-Quevilly** France
41 G6 **Le Grand-Serre** France
40 I3 **Le Grand Taureau** *mt.* France
41 H7 **Le Grand Veymont** *mt.* France
41 E9 **Le Grau-du-Roi** France
99 □1c **Le Gros Morne** *mt.* Réunion
39 M3 **Le Gros Theil** France
41 H6 **Le Gua** France
138 C5 **Leguena** Chile
38 E4 **Léguer** *r.* France
43 G8 **Léguevin** France
90 E4 **Leguga** Dem. Rep. Congo
147 H2 **Leguizamón** Arg.
206 B3 **Legune** *N.T.* Austr.
63 O3 **Legutiano** Spain
90 E4 **Legwe** *r.* Dem. Rep. Congo
158 C4 **Le-gya** Myanmar
178 F2 **Leh** Jammu and Kashmir
37 J8 **Le Haut du Sec** *hill* France
39 L2 **Le Havre** France
48 H2 **Lehe** Ger.
51 D10 **Lehesten** Ger.
125 U1 **Lehi** *UT* U.S.A.
118 E3 **Lehigh** *r. PA* U.S.A.
118 D3 **Lehigh County** *county PA* U.S.A.
118 D3 **Lehighton** *PA* U.S.A.
77 O6 **Lehliu-Gară** Romania
97 M6 **Lehlohonolo** S. Africa
147 G2 **Lehmann** Arg.
49 D10 **Lehmen** Ger.
48 J2 **Lehmkuhlen** Ger.
51 F9 **Lehndorf** Ger.
56 G3 **Lehnice** Slovakia
51 G6 **Lehnin** Ger.
50 H5 **Lehnitz** Ger.
37 N7 **Le Hohwald** France
38 G5 **Léhon** France
39 K5 **Le Horps** France
57 G3 **Lehota** Slovakia
43 D8 **Le Houga** France
53 J3 **Lehrberg** Ger.
49 K6 **Lehre** Ger.
49 I6 **Lehrte** Ger.
50 D4 **Lehsen** Ger.
20 Q5 **Lehtimäki** Fin.
124 □A11 **Lehua** *i. HI* U.S.A.
94 D4 **Lehututu** Botswana
72 B7 **Lei** *Sardegna* Italy
185 N6 **Leiah** Pak.
52 G5 **Leibertingen** Ger.
53 M4 **Leiblfing** Ger.
59 M6 **Leibnitz** Austria
170 D4 **Leibo** *Sichuan* China
51 I6 **Leibsch** Ger.
31 J2 **Leicester** *Leicester, England* U.K.
31 J2 **Leicester** *admin. div. England* U.K.
31 K2 **Leicestershire** *admin. div. England* U.K.
206 G4 **Leichhardt** *r. Qld* Austr.
206 G5 **Leichhardt Falls** *Qld* Austr.
207 K6 **Leichhardt Range** *mts Qld* Austr.
49 D8 **Leichlingen (Rheinland)** Ger.
44 G4 **Leiden** Neth.
44 G4 **Leiderdorp** Neth.
44 F4 **Leidschendam** Neth.
45 E6 **Leie** *r.* Belgium
18 J3 **Leie** Estonia
49 J6 **Leiferde** Ger.
204 G3 **Leigh** *watercourse S.A.* Austr.
202 I3 **Leigh** *North I.* N.Z.
29 L7 **Leigh** *Greater Manchester, England* U.K.
30 H3 **Leigh** *Worcestershire, England* U.K.
204 G4 **Leigh Creek** *S.A.* Austr.
27 I7 **Leighlinbridge** Rep. of Ireland
31 K4 **Leighton Buzzard** *Bedfordshire, England* U.K.
21 I6 **Leikanger** Norway
158 C5 **Leiktho** Myanmar
52 F3 **Leimen** Ger.
44 G4 **Leimuiden** Neth.
53 K3 **Leinburg** Ger.
49 I5 **Leine** *r.* Ger.
49 J8 **Leinefelde** Ger.
52 G4 **Leinfelden-Echterdingen** Ger.
70 D5 **Leinì** Italy
209 F10 **Leinster** *W.A.* Austr.
27 I6 **Leinster** *reg.* Rep. of Ireland
27 I7 **Leinster, Mount** *hill* Rep. of Ireland
52 H4 **Leinzell** Ger.
18 G7 **Leipalingis** Lith.
53 I5 **Leipheim** Ger.
20 P3 **Leipojärvi** Sweden
118 D6 **Leipsic** *DE* U.S.A.
116 B7 **Leipsic** *OH* U.S.A.
118 E6 **Leipsic** *r. DE* U.S.A.
79 H5 **Leipsoi** *i.* Greece
51 F8 **Leipzig** Ger.
51 G8 **Leipzig** *admin. reg.* Ger.
51 F8 **Leipzig-Halle** *airport* Ger.
20 J5 **Leira** *Møre og Romsdal* Norway
21 J6 **Leira** *Oppland* Norway
62 D4 **Leirado** Spain
20 M3 **Leiranger** Norway
40 C6 **Leiranoux** *mt.* France
20 Q1 **Leirbotn** Norway
62 C9 **Leiria** Port.
62 C9 **Leiria** *admin. dist.* Port.
62 D4 **Leiro** Spain
62 C8 **Leirosa** Port.
22 B2 **Leirvik** Norway
58 G6 **Leisach** Austria
59 N2 **Leiser Berge** *park* Austria
170 G5 **Leishan** *Guizhou* China
171 I5 **Lei Shui** *r.* China
18 F3 **Leisi** Estonia
206 B7 **Leisler, Mount** *hill N.T.* Austr.
204 C3 **Leisler Hills** *S.A.* Austr.
51 G8 **Leisnig** Ger.
31 P3 **Leiston** *Suffolk, England* U.K.
62 H3 **Leitariegos, Puerto de** *pass* Spain
114 D7 **Leitchfield** *KY* U.S.A.
29 K2 **Leith** *Edinburgh, Scotland* U.K.
59 O4 **Leithagebirge** *hills* Austria
203 G10 **Leithfield** *South I.* N.Z.
31 L5 **Leith Hill** *England* U.K.
27 F4 **Leitrim** *county* Rep. of Ireland
66 B1 **Leitza** Spain
53 L6 **Leitzach** *r.* Ger.
51 E6 **Leitzkau** Ger.
21 S6 **Leivonmäki** Fin.
52 B2 **Leiwen** Ger.
27 J6 **Leixlip** Rep. of Ireland
171 I5 **Leiyang** *Hunan* China
170 H8 **Leizhou** *Guangdong* China
170 G8 **Leizhou Bandao** *pen.* China
170 H8 **Leizhou Wan** *b.* China
23 K1 **Lejberget** *hill* Sweden
44 G5 **Lek** *r.* Neth.
20 K4 **Leka** Norway
20 K4 **Leka** *i.* Norway
90 B5 **Lékana** Congo
57 L3 **Lekárovce** Slovakia
90 D5 **Lekatero** Dem. Rep. Congo
55 H6 **Łękawica** Pol.
87 H1 **Le Kef** Tunisia
69 B8 **Le Kef** *admin. div.* Tunisia
63 P2 **Lekeitio** Spain
90 B5 **Lékéti** *r.* Congo
97 K9 **Lekfontein** S. Africa
Lekhainá Greece *see* Lechaina
88 C2 **Lekhcheb** Maur.
19 N6 **Lekhovo** Rus. Fed.
90 B5 **Lékila** Gabon
155 D4 **Lekitobi** *Maluku* Indon.
96 B5 **Lekkersing** S. Africa
54 C4 **Łęknica** Pol.
88 C3 **Léko** Mali
20 L2 **Lekoes** Norway
90 B5 **Lékoni** Gabon
91 B5 **Lékoumou** *admin. reg.* Congo
54 D2 **Lekowo** Pol.
23 L1 **Leksand** Sweden
Lek'suiri Georgia *see* Lentekhi
155 E5 **Leksula** *Buru* Indon.
Leksura Georgia *see* **Lentekhi**
20 K5 **Leksvik** Norway
66 B1 **Lekunberri** Spain
155 F3 **Lelai, Tanjung** *pt Halmahera* Indon.
131 □3 **Le Lamentin** Martinique
20 L3 **Leland** Norway
110 F8 **Leland** *IL* U.S.A.
110 I4 **Leland** *MI* U.S.A.
121 J9 **Leland** *MS* U.S.A.
22 I2 **Lelång** *l.* Sweden
42 C3 **Le Langon** France
42 G5 **Le Lardin-St-Lazare** France
41 I8 **Le Lauzet-Ubaye** France
41 I10 **Le Lavandou** France
145 C6 **Leleque** Arg.
57 L3 **Leles** Slovakia
57 L6 **Lelese** Romania
16 H2 **Leleta** Ukr.
43 C8 **Le Leuy** France
200 □6 **Leli** *i.* Solomon Is
55 H3 **Lelice** Pol.
68 G4 **Lelija** *mt.* Bos.-Herz.
169 O8 **Leling** *Shandong* China
155 G5 **Lelinta** *Papua* Indon.
39 J6 **Le Lion-d'Angers** France
55 J2 **Lelis** Pol.
55 I1 **Lelkowo** Pol.
70 B1 **Le Locle** Switz.
155 C8 **Lelogama** *Timor* Indon.
38 I7 **Le Loroux-Bottereau** France
131 □3 **Le Lorrain** Martinique
88 B4 **Lélouma** Guinea
39 J6 **Le Louroux-Béconnais** France
55 H5 **Lelów** Pol.
41 I10 **Le Luc** France
39 L6 **Le Lude** France
41 B6 **Le Luguet** *mt.* France
137 H3 **Lelydorp** Suriname
44 H3 **Lelystad** Neth.
145 D9 **Le Maire, Estrecho de** *sea chan.* Arg.
41 C7 **Le Malzieu-Ville** France
70 A3 **Léman, Lac** *l.* France/Switz.
39 L5 **Le Mans** France
131 □3 **Le Marin** Martinique
37 N8 **Le Markstein** France
120 G4 **Le Mars** *IA* U.S.A.
41 E8 **Le Martinet** France
43 E7 **Le Mas-d'Agenais** France
43 G9 **Le Mas-d'Azil** France
92 D3 **Lema Shilindi** Eth.
43 J8 **Le Masnau-Massuguiès** France
41 C8 **Le Massegros** France
40 D4 **Le Mayet-de-Montagne** France
212 T2 **LeMay Range** *mts* Antarctica
39 J7 **Le May-sur-Èvre** France
59 I2 **Lembach im Mühlkreis** Austria
93 C6 **Lembai** *well* Tanz.
157 L9 **Lembar** *Lombok* Indon.
155 D3 **Lembeh** *i.* Indon.
45 E6 **Lembeke** Belgium
37 N5 **Lemberg** France
52 D3 **Lemberg** Ger.
52 F5 **Lemberg** *mt.* Ger.
Lemberg Ukr. *see* **L'viv**
43 D9 **Lembeye** France
43 G7 **Lemboulas** *r.* France
43 F6 **Lembras** France
48 F5 **Lembruch** Ger.
157 L3 **Lembu** *Kalimantan* Indon.
156 B2 **Lembu, Gunung** *mt.* Indon.
157 L2 **Lembubut** *Kalimantan* Indon.
Lemdiyya Alg. *see* **Médéa**
142 D5 **Leme** Brazil
44 J4 **Lemele** Neth.
44 J4 **Lemelerveld** Neth.
39 L4 **Le Mêle-sur-Sarthe** France
92 E3 **Lemem Bar YeWha Gudgwad** *well* Eth.
39 L4 **Le Merlerault** France
41 G7 **Le Merlu Rocher** *mt.* France
57 K3 **Lemešany** Slovakia
19 O6 **Lemeshi** Rus. Fed.
17 K1 **Lemeshivka** Ukr.
36 H6 **Le Mesnil-sur-Oger** France
190 B4 **Lemesos** Cyprus
49 F6 **Lemförde** Ger.
49 G6 **Lemgo** Ger.
122 H4 **Lemhi** *r. ID* U.S.A.
122 H4 **Lemhi Range** *mts ID* U.S.A.
21 S6 **Lemi** Fin.
54 C3 **Lemierzyce** Pol.
105 L3 **Lemieux Islands** *Nunavut* Can.
21 P6 **Lemland** *Åland* Fin.
20 R2 **Lemmenjoen kansallispuisto** *nat. park* Fin.
44 I3 **Lemmer** Neth.
120 D3 **Lemmon** *SD* U.S.A.
125 V9 **Lemmon, Mount** *AZ* U.S.A.
Lemnos *i.* Greece *see* **Limnos**
96 E9 **Lemoenshoek** S. Africa
39 J3 **Le Molay-Littry** France
40 I4 **Le Môle** *mt.* France
70 C2 **Le Moleson** *mt.* Switz.
130 G4 **Le Môle St-Nicolas** Haiti
41 C7 **Le Monastier** France
41 D7 **Le Monastier-sur-Gazeille** France
124 M5 **Lemoncove** *CA* U.S.A.
41 J7 **Le Monêtier-les-Bains** France
124 O9 **Lemon Grove** *CA* U.S.A.
110 F8 **Lemont** *IL* U.S.A.
200 □5 **Le Mont-Dore** New Caledonia
40 C4 **Le Montet** France
38 H4 **Le Mont-St-Michel** *tourist site* France
124 M5 **Lemoore** *CA* U.S.A.
99 □1b **Le Morne Brabant** *pen.* Mauritius
131 □3 **Le Morne-Rouge** Martinique
200 □4a **Lemotol Bay** *Chuuk* Micronesia
131 □2 **Le Moule** Guadeloupe
41 D7 **Le Moure de la Gardille** *mt.* France
41 I7 **Le Mourre Froid** *mt.* France
109 G1 **Le Moyne, Lac** *l. Que.* Can.
21 Q6 **Lempäälä** Fin.
40 C5 **Lempdes** *Auvergne* France
41 C6 **Lempdes** *Auvergne* France
158 A4 **Lemro** *r.* Myanmar
14 L3 **Lemtybozh** Rus. Fed.
157 H4 **Lemukutan** *i.* Indon.
73 Q5 **Le Murge** *hills* Italy
41 J10 **Le Muy** France
14 M2 **Lemva** *r.* Rus. Fed.
22 E5 **Lemvig** Denmark
48 G4 **Lemwerder** Ger.
27 G8 **Lemybrien** Rep. of Ireland
158 B6 **Lemyethna** Myanmar
14 L3 **Lem'yu** *r.* Rus. Fed.
22 G1 **Lena** Norway
62 C9 **Lena** *r.* Port.
193 N3 **Lena** *r.* Rus. Fed.
110 E7 **Lena** *IL* U.S.A.
110 F5 **Lena** *WI* U.S.A.
27 D4 **Lenadoon Point** Rep. of Ireland
200 □5 **Lénakel** Vanuatu
157 L9 **Lenangguar** *Sumbawa* Indon.
59 M6 **Lenart** Slovenia
18 E5 **Lēnas** Latvia
57 J6 **Lenauheim** Romania
42 E2 **Lencloître** France
140 E2 **Lençóis Maranhenses, Parque Nacional dos** *nat. park* Brazil
142 C5 **Lençóis Paulista** Brazil
43 D7 **Lencouacq** France
58 H5 **Lend** Austria
90 F4 **Lenda** *r.* Dem. Rep. Congo
57 J2 **Lendak** Slovakia
68 F2 **Lendava** Slovenia
184 D6 **Lendeh** Iran
45 D7 **Lendelede** Belgium
14 E3 **Lendery** Rus. Fed.
71 L5 **Lendinara** Italy
59 H6 **Lendorf** Austria
28 C6 **Lene, Lough** *l.* Rep. of Ireland
56 C1 **Lenešice** Czech Rep.
39 M3 **Le Neubourg** France
58 H3 **Lengau** *Oberösterreich* Austria
58 G5 **Lengau** *Salzburg* Austria
184 H7 **Lengbarūt** Iran
53 M5 **Lengdorf** Ger.
49 J6 **Lengede** Ger.
51 H9 **Lengefeld** Ger.
51 F9 **Lengenfeld** Ger.
49 J8 **Lengenfeld unterm Stein** Ger.
53 J6 **Lengenwang** Ger.
183 M6 **Lenger** Kazakh.
48 E5 **Lengerich** *Niedersachsen* Ger.
49 E6 **Lengerich** *Nordrhein-Westfalen* Ger.
53 L6 **Lenggries** Ger.
172 K7 **Lenghuzhen** *Qinghai* China
168 G7 **Lenglong Ling** *mts* China
70 C1 **Lengnau** Switz.
90 C5 **Lengoué** *r.* Congo
171 H5 **Lengshuijiang** *Hunan* China
171 H5 **Lengshuitan** *Hunan* China
146 B2 **Lengua de Vaca, Punta** *pt* Chile
93 B8 **Lengwe National Park** Malawi
57 G5 **Lengyeltóti** Hungary
31 N5 **Lenham** *Kent, England* U.K.
118 D3 **Lenhartsville** *PA* U.S.A.
23 L5 **Lenhovda** Sweden
72 B9 **Leni** *r.* Italy
191 H5 **Lenin** Azer.
Lenīn Kazakh. *see* **Kazygurt**
185 M2 **Lenin** Tajik.
Lenin, Qullai *mt.* Kyrg./Tajik. *see* **Lenin Peak**
191 F2 **Lenina, Kanal** *canal* Rus. Fed.
Lenina, Pik *mt.* Kyrg./Tajik. *see* **Lenin Peak**
Leninabad Tajik. *see* **Khŭjand**
Lenin Atyndagy Choku *mt.* Kyrg./Tajik. *see* **Lenin Peak**
17 L6 **Lenine** *Mykolayivs'ka Oblast'* Ukr.
17 O8 **Lenine** *Respublika Krym* Ukr.
37 M6 **Léning** France
Leningrad Rus. Fed. *see* Sankt-Peterburg
185 N2 **Leningrad** Tajik.
Leningrad Oblast *admin. div.* Rus. Fed. *see* Leningradskaya **Oblast'**
15 G7 **Leningradskaya** Rus. Fed.
19 P2 **Leningradskaya Oblast'** *admin. div.* Rus. Fed.
193 S3 **Leningradskiy** Rus. Fed.
Leningradskiy Tajik. *see* Leningrad
17 K2 **Leninivka** Ukr.
191 I3 **Leninkent** Rus. Fed.
162 I6 **Lenino** Rus. Fed.
Lenino Ukr. *see* **Lenine**
Leninobod Tajik. *see* **Khŭjand**
Leninogor Kazakh. *see* Leninogorsk
183 T2 **Leninogorsk** Kazakh.
15 K5 **Leninogorsk** Rus. Fed.
183 O8 **Lenin Peak** Kyrg./Tajik.
183 N6 **Leninpol'** Kyrg.
15 I6 **Leninsk** Rus. Fed.
17 N6 **Lenins'ke** *Dnipropetrovs'ka Oblast'* Ukr.
17 N8 **Lenins'ke** *Respublika Krym* Ukr.
17 O8 **Lenins'ke** *Respublika Krym* Ukr.
182 G3 **Leninskiy** Kazakh.
19 U7 **Leninskiy** Rus. Fed.
192 J4 **Leninsk-Kuznetskiy** Rus. Fed.
Leninskoye *Yuzhnyy Kazakhstan* Kazakh. *see* **Kazygurt**
182 C3 **Leninskoye** *Zapadnyy Kazakhstan* Kazakh.
14 I4 **Leninskoye** *Kirovskaya Oblast'* Rus. Fed.
162 H5 **Leninskoye** *Yevreyskaya Avtonomnaya Oblast'* Rus. Fed.
43 D7 **Le Nizan** France
70 C3 **Lenk** Switz.
16 G4 **Lenkivtsi** Ukr.
Lenkoran' Azer. *see* **Länkäran**
208 H4 **Lennard** *r. W.A.* Austr.
49 I7 **Lenne** Ger.
49 D8 **Lenne** *r.* Ger.
49 F8 **Lennestadt** Ger.
52 G4 **Lenningen** Ger.
145 D9 **Lennox, Isla** *i.* Chile
213 L1 **Lennox-King Glacier** Antarctica
26 H11 **Lennoxtown** *East Dunbartonshire, Scotland* U.K.
70 I5 **Leno** Italy
115 G8 **Lenoir** *NC* U.S.A.
115 E8 **Lenoir City** *TN* U.S.A.
70 B1 **Le Noirmont** Switz.
73 K5 **Lenola** Italy
116 C11 **Lenore** *WV* U.S.A.
107 J4 **Lenore Lake** *Sask.* Can.
36 G3 **Le Nouvion-en-Thiérache** France
117 L6 **Lenox** *MA* U.S.A.
45 E7 **Lens** Belgium
36 E3 **Lens** France
48 K2 **Lensahn** Ger.
193 M3 **Lensk** Rus. Fed.
40 G4 **Lent** France
44 I5 **Lent** Neth.
191 D3 **Lentekhi** Georgia
48 I3 **Lentföhrden** Ger.
56 F5 **Lenti** Hungary
71 M3 **Lentiai** Italy
53 K4 **Lenting** Ger.
75 I9 **Lentini** *Sicilia* Italy
75 I9 **Lentini** *r. Sicilia* Italy
20 T4 **Lentua** *l.* Fin.
Lentvaravas Lith. *see* Lentvaris
18 I7 **Lentvaris** Lith.
19 T3 **Lent'yevo** Rus. Fed.
124 O7 **Lenwood** *CA* U.S.A.
159 D9 **Lenya** Myanmar
70 E1 **Lenzburg** Switz.
50 D4 **Lenzen** Ger.
59 I4 **Lenzing** Austria
52 E6 **Lenzkirch** Ger.
88 E4 **Léo** Burkina
71 J7 **Leo** *r.* Italy
59 I6 **Leoben** *Kärnten* Austria
59 L5 **Leoben** *Steiermark* Austria
59 N3 **Leobendorf** Austria
59 N4 **Leobersdorf** Austria
Leodhais, Eilean *i. Scotland* U.K. *see* **Lewis, Isle of**
130 G4 **Léogane** Haiti
58 G5 **Leogang** Austria
58 G5 **Leoganger Steinberge** *mts* Austria
43 C6 **Léognan** France
155 B3 **Leok** *Sulawesi* Indon.
120 F3 **Leola** *SD* U.S.A.
30 G3 **Leominster** *Herefordshire, England* U.K.
117 N6 **Leominster** *MA* U.S.A.
43 B8 **Léon** France
128 F4 **León** Mex.
126 □P11 **León** Nic.
62 I3 **León** Spain
62 I3 **León** *prov.* Spain
120 I5 **Leon** *IA* U.S.A.
121 G10 **Leon** *r. TX* U.S.A.
43 B8 **Léon, Étang de** *l.* France
64 G8 **León, Isla de** *i.* Spain
62 G4 **León, Montes de** *mts* Spain
121 G9 **Leonard** *TX* U.S.A.
73 I4 **Leonardo da Vinci** *airport* Italy
116 I10 **Leonardtown** *MD* U.S.A.
94 C4 **Leonardville** Namibia
Leonarisso Cyprus *see* Leonarisson
190 C3 **Leonarisson** Cyprus
127 P7 **Leona Vicario** Mex.
52 G4 **Leonberg** Ger.
41 G7 **Léoncel** France
Leondárion Greece *see* Leontari
59 J3 **Leonding** Austria
200 □2 **Leone** American Samoa
70 E3 **Leone, Monte** *mt.* Italy/Switz.
147 F3 **Leones** Arg.
73 J2 **Leonessa** Italy
74 G8 **Leonforte** *Sicilia* Italy
205 J8 **Leongatha** *Vic.* Austr.
72 G2 **Leoni, Monte** *hill* Italy
78 D5 **Leonidi** Greece
162 M4 **Leonidovo** *Sakhalin* Rus. Fed.
209 F10 **Leonora** *W.A.* Austr.
78 D3 **Leontari** Greece
179 M6 **Leopani** Bhutan
208 I5 **Leopold** *r. W.A.* Austr.
116 E9 **Leopold** *WV* U.S.A.
208 H5 **Leopold Downs** *W.A.* Austr.
208 H4 **Leopold Downs Aboriginal Reserve** *W.A.* Austr.
Léopold II, Lac *l.* Dem. Rep. Congo *see* **Mai-Ndombe, Lac**
143 F4 **Leopoldina** Brazil
142 C2 **Leopoldo de Bulhões** Brazil
45 H6 **Leopoldsburg** Belgium
59 O3 **Leopoldsdorf im Marchfelde** Austria
50 I3 **Leopoldshagen** Ger.
49 G6 **Leopoldshöhe** Ger.
52 D5 **Leopoldskanal** *canal* Ger.
Léopoldville Dem. Rep. Congo *see* **Kinshasa**
120 E6 **Leoti** *KS* U.S.A.
16 H7 **Leova** Moldova
107 J4 **Leoville** *Sask.* Can.
Leovo Moldova *see* **Leova**
38 E7 **Le Palais** France
42 G4 **Le Palais-sur-Vienne** France
38 I7 **Le Pallet** France
156 G6 **Lepar** *i.* Indon.
36 D3 **Le Parcq** France
43 F7 **Le Passage** France
36 G7 **Le Pavillon-Ste-Julie** France
146 B3 **Lepe** Chile
64 E6 **Lepe** Spain
41 F6 **Le Péage-de-Roussillon** France
42 H2 **Le Pêchereau** France
Lepel' Belarus *see* **Lyepyel'**
38 H7 **Le Pellerin** France
78 C4 **Lepenou** Greece
41 H7 **Le Périer** France
43 J11 **Le Perthus** France
39 I5 **Le Pertre** France
36 B5 **Le Petit-Quevilly** France
95 E4 **Lephalale** S. Africa
94 E4 **Lephepe** Botswana
97 J6 **Lephoi** S. Africa
42 C6 **Le Pian-Médoc** France
39 L4 **Le Pin-au-Haras** France
36 H6 **L'Épine** *Champagne-Ardenne* France
41 H8 **L'Épine** *Provence-Alpes-Côte d'Azur* France
171 K4 **Leping** *Jiangxi* China
39 M5 **Le Pin-la-Garenne** France
99 □1c **Le Piton** Réunion
42 E5 **Le Pizou** France
43 G9 **Le Plan** France
36 E5 **Le Plessis-Belleville** France
14 M3 **Lep'lya** *r.* Rus. Fed.
41 H8 **Le Poët** France
68 F2 **Lepoglava** Croatia
39 O8 **Le Poinçonnet** France
38 H8 **Le Poiré-sur-Vie** France
40 H5 **Le Pont-de-Beauvoisin** France
41 H6 **Le Pont-de-Claix** France
41 D8 **Le Pont-de-Monvert** France
41 F9 **Le Pontet** France
70 E3 **Lepontine, Alpi** *mts* Italy/Switz.
75 M3 **Leporano** Italy
43 B6 **Le Porge** France
43 B6 **Le Porge-Océan** France
99 □1c **Le Port** Réunion
36 C2 **Le Portel** France
76 I7 **Leposavić** *Kosovo, Srbija* Serb. and Mont.
99 □1b **Le Pouce** *hill* Mauritius
41 D9 **Le Pouget** France
38 D6 **Le Pouldu** France
38 G7 **Le Pouliguen** France
41 F7 **Le Pouzin** France
20 R5 **Leppävesi** Fin.
20 S5 **Leppävirta** Fin.
41 I10 **Le Pradet** France
109 H4 **Lepreau, Point** *N.B.* Can.
131 □3 **Le Prêcheur** Martinique
Lepsa Kazakh. *see* **Lepsy**
Lepsa *r.* Kazakh. *see* **Lepsy**
57 H4 **Lepsény** Hungary
Lepsi Kazakh. *see* **Lepsinsk**
183 S5 **Lepsinsk** Kazakh.
183 R4 **Lepsy** Kazakh.
183 R4 **Lepsy** *r.* Kazakh.
84 B1 **Leptis Magna** *tourist site* Libya
78 D2 **Leptokarya** Greece
36 C7 **Le Puiset** France
41 D6 **Le Puy-en-Velay** France
39 K7 **Le Puy-Notre-Dame** France
41 G9 **Le Puy-Ste-Réparade** France
88 B2 **Leqçeïba** Maur.
36 G3 **Le Quesnoy** France
88 D4 **Léraba** *r.* Burkina/Côte d'Ivoire
36 E6 **Le Raincy** France
95 E4 **Lerala** Botswana
43 H10 **Léran** France
97 L4 **Leratswana** S. Africa
74 F8 **Lercara Friddi** *Sicilia* Italy
205 J7 **Lerderderg State Park** *nature res. Vic.* Austr.
129 L7 **Lerdo** Mex.
90 B2 **Léré** Chad
40 B2 **Léré** France
88 D3 **Léré** Mali
89 H4 **Lere** Nigeria
155 A4 **Lereh, Tanjung** *pt* Indon.
38 C5 **Le Relecq-Kerhuon** France
62 C4 **Lérez** *r.* Spain
38 H5 **Le Rheu** France
70 H7 **Lerici** Italy
136 D5 **Lérida** Col.
Lérida Spain *see* **Lleida**
Lérida *prov. Cataluña* Spain *see* **Lleida**
191 J7 **Lerik** Azer.
63 Q4 **Lerín** Spain
41 K9 **Lérins, Îles de** *is* France
127 N8 **Lerma** Mex.
128 E5 **Lerma** *r.* Mex.
63 M4 **Lerma** Spain
129 H6 **Lerma de Vilada** Mex.
43 D7 **Lerm-et Musset** France
191 D1 **Lermontov** Rus. Fed.
162 I5 **Lermontovka** Rus. Fed.
Lermontovskiy Rus. Fed. *see* Lermontov
58 C5 **Lermoos** Austria
72 C6 **Lerno, Monte** *mt.* Italy
131 □3 **Le Robert** Martinique
40 J5 **Le Roignais** *mt.* France
79 H5 **Leros** *i.* Greece
43 I6 **Le Rouget** France
37 K6 **Lérouville** France
110 F9 **Le Roy** *IL* U.S.A.
110 B6 **Le Roy** *MN* U.S.A.
116 H6 **Le Roy** *NY* U.S.A.
118 B1 **Leroy** *PA* U.S.A.
108 F1 **Le Roy, Lac** *l. Que.* Can.
41 C8 **Le Rozier** France
37 L7 **Lerrain** France
70 E7 **Lerrone** *r.* Italy
22 I4 **Lerum** Sweden
40 J2 **Le Russey** France
26 □N2 **Lerwick** *Shetland, Scotland* U.K.
90 E2 **Ler Zerai** *well* Sudan
43 F10 **Lés** Spain
70 F4 **Lesa** Italy
40 H5 **Les Abrets** France
131 □2 **Les Abymes** Guadeloupe
58 G6 **Lesachtal** *val.* Austria
41 J9 **Les Adrets-de-l'Estérel** France
66 J4 **Les Agudes** *mt.* Spain
40 B2 **Les Aix-d'Angillon** France
66 B1 **Lesaka** Spain
43 J11 **Les Albères** *reg.* France
40 B5 **Les Ancizes-Comps** France
36 B5 **Les Andelys** France
41 F9 **Les Angles** *Languedoc-Roussillon* France
43 I10 **Les Angles** *Languedoc-Roussillon* France
131 □3 **Les Anses-d'Arlets** Martinique
39 L4 **Le Sap** France
41 I10 **Les Arcs** *Provence-Alpes-Côte d'Azur* France
40 J5 **Les Arcs** *Rhône-Alpes* France
39 J8 **Les Aubiers** France
41 J8 **Le Sauze-Super-Sauze** France
66 G4 **Les Avellanes** Spain
40 H5 **Les Avenières** France
99 □1c **Les Avirons** Réunion
41 D8 **Les Bondons** France
36 D8 **Les Bordes** France
43 G9 **Les Bordes-sur-Arize** France
66 G4 **Les Borges Blanques** Spain
66 H5 **Les Borges del Camp** Spain
Lesbos *i.* Greece *see* **Lesvos**
40 H4 **Les Bouchoux** France
70 B1 **Les Brenets** Switz.
29 N3 **Lesbury** *Northumberland, England* U.K.
43 H10 **Les Cabannes** France
66 L3 **L'Escala** Spain
41 I8 **L'Escale** France
99 □1b **L'Escalier** Mauritius
43 I9 **Les Cammazes** France

Lescar to Lingelihle 293

43 D9 Lescar France
41 K9 L'Escarène France
40 J4 Les Carroz-d'Arâches France
66 G6 Les Cases d'Alcanar Spain
130 G4 Les Cayes Haiti
59 J7 Lesce Slovenia
39 K5 Les Coëvrons hills France
38 C6 Lesconil France
40 J5 Les Contamines-Montjoie France
40 J4 Les Cornettes de Bise mts France/Switz.
43 I8 Lescure-d'Albigeois France
41 I6 Les Deux-Alpes France
70 C3 Les Diablerets Switz.
70 C3 Les Diablerets mts Switz.
90 D4 Lese r. Dem. Rep. Congo
75 L5 Lese r. Italy
41 H6 Les Échelles France
38 H3 Les Écréhou is Channel Is
42 D5 Les Églisottes-et-Chalaures France
41 J8 Le Seignus-d'Allos France
38 H6 Le Sel-de-Bretagne France
43 C7 Le Sen France
56 G5 Lesencetomaj Hungary
70 A2 Le Sentier Switz.
37 K5 Les Éparges France
39 J8 Les Epesses France
66 I2 Les Escaldes Andorra
109 G3 Les Escoumins Que. Can.
40 G3 Les Essards-Taignevaux France
38 I8 Les Essarts France
117 □Q1 Les Étroits Que. Can.
66 H3 Le Seu d'Urgell Spain
43 G6 Les Eyzies-de-Tayac-Sireuil France
40 J2 Les Fins France
37 L7 Les Forges France
40 I3 Les Fourgs France
40 J4 Les Gets France
170 D4 Leshan Sichuan China
37 I4 Les Hautes-Rivières France
17 P2 Leshchinka r. Rus. Fed.
42 B2 Les Herbiers France
40 J5 Les Houches France
14 I2 Leshukonskoye Rus. Fed.
191 D3 Lesichine Georgia
59 M7 Lesično Slovenia
36 E6 Lésigny France
70 G6 Lesima, Monte mt. Italy
73 O4 Lesina Italy
73 O4 Lesina, Lago di lag. Italy
41 J10 Les Issambres France
21 J5 Lesja Norway
23 K2 Lesjöfors Sweden
43 G6 Les Junies France
41 I6 Les Karellis France
191 E2 Lesken Rus. Fed.
55 K6 Lesko Pol.
77 J8 Leskovac Srbija Serb. and Mont.
78 B2 Leskovik Albania
213 F2 Leskov Island Antarctica
17 L4 Les'ky Ukr.
39 I8 Les Landes-Genusson France
42 E5 Les Lèches France
41 H10 Les Lecques France
26 J10 Leslie Fife, Scotland U.K.
110 J7 Leslie MI U.S.A.
38 I8 Les Lucs-sur-Boulogne France
26 I11 Lesmahagow South Lanarkshire, Scotland U.K.
40 G2 Les Maillys France
131 □2 Les Mangles Guadeloupe
40 I6 Les Marches France
40 C5 Les Martres-de-Veyre France
41 D9 Les Matelles France
39 J7 Les Mauges reg. France
36 I4 Les Mazures France
109 H3 Les Méchins Que. Can.
66 L3 Les Medes is Spain
41 H8 Les Mées France
41 J6 Les Menuires France
38 G4 Les Minquiers is Channel Is
41 I8 Les Monges mt. France
36 H7 Lesmont France
36 C6 Les Mureaux France
57 G2 Lešná Czech Rep.
54 D4 Leśna Pol.
55 L3 Leśna r. Pol.
38 C4 Lesneven France
54 G5 Leśnica Pol.
54 D4 Leśniów Wielki Pol.
36 H7 Les Noës-près-Troyes France
14 K4 Lesnoy Kirovskaya Oblast' Rus. Fed.
19 X7 Lesnoy Ryazanskaya Oblast' Rus. Fed.
19 O6 Lesnoy Smolenskaya Oblast' Rus. Fed.
18 L1 Lesnoy, Ostrov i. Rus. Fed.
19 S3 Lesnoye Rus. Fed.
14 K4 Lesnyye Polyany Rus. Fed.
162 M4 Lesogorsk Sakhalin Rus. Fed.
18 L1 Lesogorskiy Rus. Fed.
41 F7 Les Ollières-sur-Eyrieux France
162 I5 Lesopil'noye Rus. Fed.
41 J7 Les Orres France
193 K4 Lesosibirsk Rus. Fed.
97 M5 Lesotho country Africa
97 M5 Lesotho Highlands Water Project Lesotho
162 H6 Lesozavodsk Rus. Fed.
42 C5 Lesparre-Médoc France
42 D5 Les Peintures France
41 G10 Les Pennes-Mirabeau France
99 □2b L'Espérance Mahé Seychelles
199 I5 L'Espérance Rock i. N.Z.
43 B8 Lesperon France
36 H5 Les Petites-Loges France
77 L3 Lespezi hill Romania
38 H2 Les Pieux France
41 C10 Lespignan France
66 F6 L'Espina mt. Spain
43 J9 Lespinassière France
40 I3 Les Planches-en-Montagne France
66 H5 L'Espluga Calba Spain
66 H5 L'Espluga de Francolí Spain
42 C1 Les Ponts-de-Cé France
70 B1 Les Ponts-de-Martel Switz.
66 J3 Les Preses Spain
43 F9 Lespugue France
36 H8 Les Riceys France
39 K7 Les Rosiers-sur-Loire France
40 I4 Les Rousses France
42 A3 Les Sables-d'Olonne France
59 I5 Lessach Austria
41 E8 Les Salles-du-Gardon France
38 H3 Lessay France
45 G8 Lesse r. Belgium
45 H8 Lesse et Lomme, Parc Naturel de nature res. Belgium
38 E4 Les Sept-Îles is France
131 J7 Lesser Antilles is Caribbean Sea
191 D4 Lesser Caucasus mts Asia
178 F4 Lesser Himalaya mts India/Nepal
106 H4 Lesser Slave Lake Alta Can.
106 H4 Lesser Slave Lake Provincial Park Alta Can.
187 L2 Lesser Tunb i. The Gulf
36 G7 Les Sièges France
45 E7 Lessines Belgium
97 K5 Lessingskop mt. S. Africa
71 J4 Lessini, Monti mts Italy
99 □2a Les Sœurs is Inner Islands Seychelles
38 H7 Les Sorinières France
43 D9 Lestelle-Bétharram France
116 D11 Lester WV U.S.A.
41 C6 Les Ternes France
36 C5 Les Thilliers-en-Vexin France
41 J8 Les Thuiles France
20 R5 Lestijärvi Fin.
20 Q4 Lestijoki r. Fin.
41 B8 Lestrade France
38 D4 Les Triagoz is France
99 □1c Les Trois Bassins Réunion
131 □3 Les Trois-Îlets Martinique
39 L7 Les Trois-Moutiers France
90 E3 Les Trois Rivieres C.A.R.
41 B7 Les Trucs d'Aubrac mt. France
57 L5 Leșu, Lacul l. Romania
208 I2 Lesueur Island W.A. Austr.
36 D6 Les Ulis France
157 K4 Lesung, Bukit mt. Indon.
67 E7 Les Useres Spain
41 E8 Les Vans France
41 C8 Les Vignes France
79 G3 Lesvos i. Greece
54 D2 Leszczyn Pol.
55 K4 Leszkowice Pol.
55 I3 Leszno Mazowieckie Pol.
54 E4 Leszno Wielkopolskie Pol.
54 D4 Leszno Górne Pol.
41 H6 Le Taillefer mt. France
66 E2 Le Taillon mt. Spain
39 K8 Le Tallud France
23 K2 Letälven r. Sweden
99 □1c Le Tampon Réunion
41 E7 Le Tanargue mt. France
57 K4 Létavértes Hungary
31 L4 Letchworth Garden City Hertfordshire, England U.K.
43 B6 Le Teich France
41 F7 Le Teil France
39 J4 Le Teilleul France
40 E2 Le Télégraphe hill France
43 C6 Le Temple France
56 F5 Letenye Hungary
178 F7 Leteri Madh. Prad. India
97 L1 Lethabile S. Africa
158 A3 Letha Range mts Myanmar
106 H5 Lethbridge Alta Can.
109 K3 Lethbridge Nfld and Lab. Can.
48 F4 Lethe r. Ger.
39 M5 Le Theil France
38 I6 Le-Theil-de-Bretagne France
137 G4 Lethem Guyana
31 O2 Letheringsett Norfolk, England U.K.
37 M8 Le Thillot France
37 M7 Le Tholy France
41 I10 Le Thoronet France
155 E8 Leti i. Maluku Indon.
155 E8 Leti, Kepulauan is Maluku Indon.
136 D6 Leticia Col.
169 P7 Leting Hebei China
73 M5 Letino Italy
96 G8 Letjiesbos S. Africa
57 H4 Letkés Hungary
94 E4 Letlhakane Botswana
94 E5 Letlhakeng Botswana
14 F2 Letnerechenskiy Rus. Fed.
14 G2 Letniy Navolok Rus. Fed.
155 F8 Letoda Maluku Indon.
71 M2 Le Tofane mt. Italy
75 I8 Letoianni Sicilia Italy
59 O1 Letonice Czech Rep.
36 C2 Le Touquet-Paris-Plage France
41 C9 Le Tour d'Arre hill France
41 H6 Le Touvet France
56 F2 Letovice Czech Rep.
158 B6 Letpadan Myanmar
36 B3 Le Tréport France
41 B8 Le Truel France
21 M6 Letsbo Sweden
50 J5 Letschin Ger.
159 D9 Letsok-aw Kyun i. Myanmar
97 J2 Letsopa S. Africa
89 I5 Letta Cameroon
Lette Island Vava'u Gp Tonga see Late
22 I1 Letten l. Sweden
28 B5 Letterbreen Northern Ireland U.K.
27 C6 Lettercallow Rep. of Ireland
27 C9 Letterfinish Rep. of Ireland
27 C5 Letterfrack Rep. of Ireland
27 G3 Letterkenny Rep. of Ireland
30 C4 Letterston Pembrokeshire, Wales U.K.
156 F3 Letung Indon.
65 O4 Letur Spain
43 C7 Le Tuzan France
155 F7 Letwurung Maluku Indon.
15 H6 Letyazhevka Rus. Fed.
16 G4 Letychiv Ukr.
Lëtzebuerg country Europe see Luxembourg
51 D6 Letzlingen Ger.
77 M6 Leu Romania
91 D7 Léua Angola
51 H8 Leuben Ger.
51 D8 Leubingen Ger.
43 I9 Leuc France
Leucas Lefkada Greece see Lefkada
43 K10 Leucate France
43 K10 Leucate, Cap c. France
43 K10 Leucate, Étang de l. France
26 K10 Leuchars Fife, Scotland U.K.
53 M2 Leuchtenberg Ger.
50 I5 Leuenberg Ger.
37 I8 Leuglay France
70 D3 Leuk Switz.
Leukas Lefkada Greece see Lefkada
70 D3 Leukerbad Switz.
26 D6 Leumrabhagh Western Isles, Scotland U.K.
49 F9 Leun Ger.
171 □J7 Leung Shuen Wan Chau i. H.K. China
14 H2 Leunovo Rus. Fed.
125 V6 Leupp AZ U.S.A.
207 L7 Leura Qld Austr.
44 H4 Leusden Neth.
156 B3 Leuser, Gunung mt. Indon.
58 D5 Leutasch Austria
53 K7 Leutascher Dreitorspitze mt. Ger.
51 D9 Leutenberg Ger.
53 I3 Leutershausen Ger.
49 D10 Leutesdorf Ger.
53 I6 Leutkirch im Allgäu Ger.
59 L6 Leutschach Austria
45 G7 Leuven Belgium
45 E7 Leuze-en-Hainaut Belgium
78 D4 Levadeia Greece
41 I10 Le Val France
37 L8 Le Val-d'Ajol France
37 J8 Le Vallinot-Longeau-Percey France
38 I4 Le Val-St-Père France
78 A2 Levan Albania
125 U2 Levan UT U.S.A.
20 K5 Levanger Norway
41 I10 Levant, Île du i. France
70 F7 Levante, Riviera di coastal area Italy
70 H7 Levanto Italy
74 C8 Levanzo Sicilia Italy
74 C7 Levanzo, Isola di i. Sicilia Italy
191 I3 Levashi Rus. Fed.
131 □3 Le Vauclin Martinique
17 S2 Levaya Rossosh' Rus. Fed.
56 G4 Levél Hungary
121 D9 Levelland TX U.S.A.
203 F11 Levels South I. N.Z.
29 Q6 Leven East Riding of Yorkshire, England U.K.
26 K10 Leven Fife, Scotland U.K.
26 F9 Leven, Loch inlet Scotland U.K.
26 J10 Leven, Loch l. Scotland U.K.
41 K9 Levens France
29 L5 Levens Cumbria, England U.K.
70 F3 Leventina, Valle val. Switz.
26 □N3 Levenwick Shetland, Scotland U.K.
208 G4 Lévêque, Cape W.A. Austr.
202 □ L'Eveque, Cape Chatham Is S. Pacific Ocean
75 O3 Leverano Italy
26 B7 Leverburgh Western Isles, Scotland U.K.
42 B4 Le-Verdon-sur-Mer France
110 J4 Levering MI U.S.A.
49 C8 Leverkusen Ger.
106 G1 Lever Lake N.W.T. Can.
43 H9 Le Vernet France
Leverville Dem. Rep. Congo see Lusanga
36 B7 Lèves France
39 P8 Levet France
41 B8 Lévézou mts France
57 H3 Levice Slovakia
71 K3 Levico Terme Italy
78 D5 Levidi Greece
72 C4 Levie Corse France
40 I3 Levier France
41 D9 Le Vigan France
43 G8 Lévignac France
43 E6 Lévignac-de-Guyanne France
43 B7 Lévignacq France
71 M9 Le Ville Italy
202 J7 Levin North I. N.Z.
109 G4 Lévis Que. Can.
79 H6 Levitha i. Greece
119 H3 Levittown NY U.S.A.
118 F4 Levittown PA U.S.A.
38 H4 Le-Vivier-sur-Mer France
77 O9 Levka Bulg.
Levkás i. Greece see Lefkada
Levkímmi Kerkyra Greece see Lefkimmi
57 J2 Levoča Slovakia
57 J2 Levočské vrchy mts Slovakia
42 H2 Levroux France
77 N7 Levski Bulg.
Levskigrad Bulg. see Karlovo
19 W8 Lev Tolstoy Rus. Fed.
201 □1a Levuka Ovalau Fiji
18 H6 Lévuo r. Lith.
38 I2 Lévy, Cap c. France
155 A8 Lewa Sumba Indon.
158 C5 Lewe Myanmar
31 M6 Lewes East Sussex, England U.K.
117 J10 Lewes DE U.S.A.
54 F5 Lewin Brzeski Pol.
125 X4 Lewis CO U.S.A.
121 F7 Lewis KS U.S.A.
122 C4 Lewis r. WA U.S.A.
26 C6 Lewis, Isle of i. Scotland U.K.
206 D7 Lewis, Lake salt flat N.T. Austr.
118 B4 Lewisberry PA U.S.A.
116 A9 Lewisburg OH U.S.A.
111 R9 Lewisburg PA U.S.A.
115 D8 Lewisburg TN U.S.A.
116 E11 Lewisburg WV U.S.A.
106 D3 Lewis Cass, Mount Can./U.S.A.
109 J3 Lewis Hills Nfld and Lab. Can.
177 M6 Lewis Inlet Andaman & Nicobar Is India
203 G9 Lewis Pass South I. N.Z.
203 G9 Lewis Pass National Reserve nature res. South I. N.Z.
109 K3 Lewisporte Nfld and Lab. Can.
208 J6 Lewis Range hills W.A. Austr.
122 G2 Lewis Range mts MT U.S.A.
115 D8 Lewis Smith, Lake AL U.S.A.
122 F3 Lewiston ID U.S.A.
117 □O4 Lewiston ME U.S.A.
111 J5 Lewiston MI U.S.A.
110 C6 Lewiston MN U.S.A.
116 F5 Lewiston NY U.S.A.
110 D9 Lewistown IL U.S.A.
110 C9 Lewistown MO U.S.A.
122 J3 Lewistown MT U.S.A.
116 H8 Lewistown PA U.S.A.
121 I9 Lewisville AR U.S.A.
116 D9 Lewisville OH U.S.A.
121 G9 Lewisville, Lake TX U.S.A.
50 E4 Lewitz park Ger.
155 C8 Lewoleba Indon.
155 C8 Lewotobi, Gunung vol. Flores Indon.
115 F9 Lexington GA U.S.A.
110 F9 Lexington IL U.S.A.
114 E6 Lexington KY U.S.A.
111 L6 Lexington MI U.S.A.
120 I6 Lexington MO U.S.A.
121 J9 Lexington MS U.S.A.
115 G8 Lexington NC U.S.A.
120 F5 Lexington NE U.S.A.
116 C8 Lexington OH U.S.A.
115 G9 Lexington SC U.S.A.
121 K8 Lexington TN U.S.A.
116 F11 Lexington VA U.S.A.
116 I10 Lexington Park MD U.S.A.
29 N5 Leyburn North Yorkshire, England U.K.
Leyden Neth. see Leiden
170 F6 Leye Guangxi China
184 B3 Leyla Dāgh mt. Iran
29 L6 Leyland Lancashire, England U.K.
43 H6 Leyme France
31 N5 Leysdown-on-Sea Kent, England U.K.
70 C3 Leysin Switz.
154 E6 Leyte i. Phil.
154 E6 Leyte Gulf Phil.
70 C3 Leytron Switz.
43 G10 Lez r. France
63 P4 Leza r. Spain
55 K5 Leżajsk Pol.
136 E2 Lezama Venez.
41 E8 Lézan France
38 E4 Lézardrieux France
43 G9 Lézat-sur-Lèze France
42 D3 Lezay France
43 G9 Lèze r. France
76 H9 Lezhë Albania
170 E3 Lezhi Sichuan China
19 X5 Lezhnevo Rus. Fed.
41 B10 Lézignan-Corbières France
55 H2 Leźno Pol.
40 C5 Lezoux France
65 O3 Lezuza Spain
65 O2 Lezuza r. Spain
55 H4 Lgota Wielka Pol.
15 F6 L'gov Rus. Fed.
173 H12 Lhagoi Kangri mt. Xizang China
26 J7 Lhanbryde Moray, Scotland U.K.
173 K11 Lhari Xizang China
Lhari Xizang China see Sirdingka
209 B8 Lharidon Bight b. W.A. Austr.
173 J10 Lharigarbo Xizang China
173 J12 Lhasa Xizang China
173 J12 Lhasa He r. China
173 K12 Lhasoi Xizang China
170 A3 Lhatog Xizang China
36 D6 L'Hay-les-Roses France
173 H12 Lhazê Xizang China
173 L11 Lhazê Xizang China
59 J1 Lhenice Czech Rep.
43 G9 Lherm France
42 C2 L'Hermenault France
38 H5 L'Hermitage France
173 G10 Lhgu Xizang China
175 □1 Lhohifushi i. N. Male Maldives
156 A2 Lhokkruet Sumatera Indon.
156 B2 Lhokseumawe Sumatera Indon.
156 B2 Lhoksukon Sumatera Indon.
173 J11 Lhomar Xizang China
43 G7 L'Honor-de-Cos France
173 L11 Lhorong Xizang China
43 G7 L'Hospitalet France
66 G6 L'Hospitalet de l'Infant Spain
66 J5 L'Hospitalet de Llobregat Spain
41 C9 L'Hospitalet-du-Larzac France
43 H10 L'Hospitalet-près-l'Andorre France
66 G6 L'Hostal del Alls Spain
42 B3 L'Houmeau France
17 N8 L'hovs'ke Ukr.
173 J12 Lhozhag Xizang China
40 H5 Lhuis France
39 J5 L'Huisserie France
36 H6 Lhuître France
179 M6 Lhuntshi Bhutan
173 K12 Lhünzê Xizang China
158 D5 Li, Mae r. Thai.
191 F3 Liakhvis Nakrdzali nature res. Georgia
72 B3 Liamone r. Corse France
131 □2 Liamuiga, Mount vol. St Kitts and Nevis
171 K6 Liancheng Fujian China
36 D5 Liancourt France
163 G10 Liancourt Rocks i. N. Pacific Ocean
36 C2 Liane r. France
Lianfeng Fujian China see Liancheng
155 C4 Liang Sulawesi Indon.
154 F7 Lianga Mindanao Phil.
154 F7 Lianga Bay Mindanao Phil.
169 M6 Liangcheng Nei Mongol China
170 F2 Liangdang Gansu China
173 J11 Liangdaohe Xizang China
170 H6 Liangfeng Guangxi China
170 G4 Lianghe Chongqing China
170 B6 Lianghe Yunnan China
Lianghekou Chongqing China see Lianghe
170 E2 Lianghekou Gansu China
170 D3 Lianghekou Sichuan China
170 F3 Liangping Chongqing China
157 K4 Liangpran, Bukit mt. Indon.
Liangshan Chongqing China see Liangping
158 D2 Liang Shan mt. Myanmar
170 H8 Liangtian Guangxi China
156 D3 Liang Timur, Gunung mt. Malaysia
170 D6 Liangwang Shan mts Yunnan China
169 K8 Liangzhen Shaanxi China
171 J3 Liangzi Hu l. China
171 I5 Lianhua Jiangxi China
171 J7 Lianhua Shan mts China
171 L5 Lianjiang Fujian China
170 H8 Lianjiang Guangdong China
170 F6 Lian Jiang r. China
171 I6 Lianjiangkou Guangdong China
171 I6 Liannan Guangdong China
78 D4 Lianokladi Greece
171 J6 Lianping Guangdong China
171 I6 Lianshan Guangdong China
169 Q6 Lianshan Liaoning China
Liantang Jiangxi China see Nanchang
171 H3 Liantuo Hubei China
Lianxian Guangdong China see Lianzhou
162 C2 Lianyin Heilong. China
171 H5 Lianyuan Hunan China
169 P9 Lianyungang Jiangsu China
171 I6 Lianzhou Guangdong China
Lianzhou Guangxi China see Hepu
162 G6 Lianzhushan Heilong. China
169 N8 Liaocheng Shandong China
169 R6 Liaodong Bandao pen. China
169 Q6 Liaodong Wan b. China
168 C5 Liaodun Xinjiang China
168 C5 Liaodunzhan Xinjiang China
169 R6 Liao He r. China
169 R6 Liaoning prov. China
169 R6 Liaoyang Liaoning China
162 D7 Liaoyuan Jilin China
169 R6 Liaozhong Liaoning China
78 A3 Liapades Kerkyra Greece
185 N5 Liaqatabad Pak.
106 F2 Liard r. Can.
106 F2 Liard Highway N.W.T. Can.
106 E2 Liard Plateau Y.T. Can.
106 E3 Liard River B.C. Can.
185 L9 Liari Pak.
36 H4 Liart France
156 G6 Liat i. Indon.
26 F7 Liathach mt. Scotland U.K.
23 K5 Liatorp Sweden
Liban country Asia see Lebanon
56 E1 Libáň Czech Rep.
190 E4 Liban, Jebel mts Lebanon
147 G5 Líbano Arg.
136 C3 Libano Col.
65 I7 Líbar, Sierra de mts Spain
Libau Latvia see Liepāja
26 I11 Libberton South Lanarkshire, Scotland U.K.
122 G2 Libby MT U.S.A.
56 C1 Libčeves Czech Rep.
51 J10 Libčice nad Vltavou Czech Rep.
90 C4 Libenge Dem. Rep. Congo
55 I2 Liberadz Pol.
121 E7 Liberal KS U.S.A.
143 E5 Liberdade Brazil
140 B4 Liberdade r. Brazil
138 C1 Liberdade r. Brazil
56 E1 Liberec Czech Rep.
56 E1 Liberecký kraj admin. reg. Czech Rep.
88 C5 Liberia country Africa
126 □Q12 Liberia Costa Rica
131 □2 Liberta Antigua and Barbuda
147 I2 Libertad Arg.
147 I4 Libertad Uru.
136 D2 Libertad Venez.
144 D1 Libertador General San Martin Arg.
146 E3 Libertador General San Martín Arg.
97 L4 Libertase S. Africa
114 E6 Liberty IN U.S.A.
114 E7 Liberty KY U.S.A.
117 □P4 Liberty ME U.S.A.
120 H6 Liberty MO U.S.A.
117 K7 Liberty NY U.S.A.
118 A1 Liberty PA U.S.A.
121 H10 Liberty TX U.S.A.
116 A7 Liberty Center OH U.S.A.
118 B6 Liberty Lake MD U.S.A.
110 G7 Libertyville IL U.S.A.
51 J9 Liběšice Czech Rep.
55 H5 Libiąż Pol.
56 E1 Libice nad Cidlinou Czech Rep.
45 H9 Libin Belgium
56 D3 Libín mt. Czech Rep.
56 G2 Libina Czech Rep.
154 D5 Libmanan Luzon Phil.
190 B8 Libnī, Jabal hill Egypt
170 F6 Libo Guizhou China
155 F4 Libobo, Tanjung pt Halmahera Indon.
51 J10 Libochovice Czech Rep.
97 N7 Libode S. Africa
78 B2 Libohovë Albania
92 D4 Liboi Kenya
91 D8 Libonda Zambia
159 D11 Libong, Ko i. Thai.
97 M4 Libono Lesotho
146 E3 Liborio Luna Arg.
51 J9 Libouchec Czech Rep.
43 D6 Libourne France
208 H7 Libral Well W.A. Austr.
45 H9 Libramont Belgium
76 I9 Librazhd Albania
126 D3 Libre, Sierra mts Mex.
129 J6 Libres Mex.
90 A4 Libreville Gabon
67 C12 Librilla Spain
67 C7 Libros Spain
154 E8 Libuganon r. Mindanao Phil.
84 C3 Libya country Africa
84 E3 Libyan Desert Egypt/Libya
84 E2 Libyan Plateau Egypt
146 A4 Licantén Chile
74 F9 Licata Sicilia Italy
70 I7 Licciana Nardi Italy
189 J4 Lice Turkey
73 J3 Licenza Italy
63 N6 Liceras Spain
49 G9 Lich Ger.
78 D4 Lichas pen. Greece
Licheng Guangxi China see Lipu
169 O8 Licheng Shandong China
169 M8 Licheng Shanxi China
202 J5 Lichfield North I. N.Z.
31 I2 Lichfield Staffordshire, England U.K.
93 B8 Lichinga Moz.
57 G1 Lichnov Czech Rep.
54 G1 Lichnowy Pol.
51 D9 Lichte Ger.
52 E4 Lichtenau Baden-Württemberg Ger.
53 J3 Lichtenau Bayern Ger.
49 G7 Lichtenau Nordrhein-Westfalen Ger.
59 L2 Lichtenau im Waldviertel Austria
51 E10 Lichtenberg Bayern Ger.
51 H9 Lichtenberg Sachsen Ger.
97 K2 Lichtenburg S. Africa
51 D10 Lichtenfels Ger.
51 G9 Lichtenstein Ger.
44 K5 Lichtenvoorde Neth.
59 N4 Lichtenwörth Austria
50 I5 Lichterfelde Ger.
45 D6 Lichtervelde Belgium
170 G3 Lichuan Hubei China
171 K5 Lichuan Jiangxi China
95 H3 Liciro Moz.
116 A9 Licking r. KY U.S.A.
68 E3 Lički Osik Croatia
74 H9 Licodia Eubea Sicilia Italy
73 N7 Licosa, Isola i. Italy
43 C9 Licq-Athérey France
36 C2 Licques France
Licun Shandong China see Laoshan
19 S2 Lid' r. Rus. Fed.
18 I8 Lida Belarus
22 J3 Lidan r. Sweden
29 L3 Liddel Water r. England/Scotland U.K.
26 K12 Liddesdale val. Scotland U.K.
97 K8 Liddleton S. Africa
57 H2 Lidečko Czech Rep.
22 J5 Lidhult Sweden
23 O2 Lidingö Sweden
90 C4 Lidjombo C.A.R.
22 J3 Lidköping Sweden
71 M5 Lido Italy
71 M7 Lido Adriano Italy
71 M7 Lido di Classe Italy
73 J5 Lido di Foce Verde Italy
71 N4 Lido di Jesolo Italy
75 L3 Lido di Metaponto Italy
73 I4 Lido di Ostia Italy
73 P4 Lido di Siponto Italy
71 M6 Lido di Spina Italy
20 M4 Lidsjöberg Sweden
18 K5 Lidumnieki Latvia
55 H2 Lidzbark Pol.
23 Q7 Lidzbark Warmiński Pol.
59 K2 Liebenau Austria
49 H8 Liebenau Hessen Ger.
48 H5 Liebenau Niedersachsen Ger.
97 M3 Liebenbergs Vlei r. S. Africa
49 J6 Liebenburg Ger.
59 J6 Liebenfels Austria
50 H5 Liebenwalde Ger.
51 J7 Lieberose Ger.
51 F8 Liebertwolkwitz Ger.
206 C7 Liebig, Mount N.T. Austr.
76 J5 Liebling Romania
59 L6 Lieboch Austria
51 I9 Liebstadt Ger.
52 H7 Liechtenstein country Europe
63 R3 Liédena Spain
45 I7 Liège Belgium
45 I8 Liège prov. Belgium
Liegnitz Pol. see Legnica
20 U5 Lieksa Fin.
18 K5 Lielais Ludzas l. Latvia
18 H4 Lielupe r. Latvia
18 H5 Lielvārde Latvia
44 H5 Liempde Neth.
20 N5 Lien Sweden
44 I5 Lienden Neth.
49 E6 Lienen Ger.
159 I9 Liên Nghia Vietnam
159 I8 Liên Sơn Vietnam
58 G6 Lienz Austria
18 E5 Liepāja Latvia
Liepaya Latvia see Liepāja
50 I5 Liepe Ger.
50 H3 Liepen Ger.
50 J3 Liepgarten Ger.
18 K4 Liepna Latvia
55 M1 Lieponys Lith.
45 G6 Lier Belgium
40 E2 Liernais France
45 I8 Lierneux Belgium
Lierre Belgium see Lier
57 I2 Liesek Slovakia
52 C2 Lieser Ger.
44 I5 Lieshout Neth.
58 L5 Liesing r. Austria
18 G1 Liesjärven kansallispuisto nat. park Fin.
45 I6 Liessel Neth.
36 G4 Liesse-Notre-Dame France
70 D1 Liestal Switz.
57 H3 Lieštany Slovakia
18 F1 Lieto Fin.
65 P3 Liétor Spain
Lietuva country Europe see Lithuania
21 S6 Lietvesi l. Fin.
39 M3 Lieurey France
39 L3 Lieuvin reg. France
21 S5 Lievestuore Fin.
36 E3 Liévin France
108 F4 Lièvre r. Que. Can.
59 J4 Liezen Austria
155 E4 Lifamatola i. Indon.
90 D4 Lifanga Dem. Rep. Congo
28 E7 Liffey r. Rep. of Ireland
37 K7 Liffol-le-Grand France
27 H3 Lifford Rep. of Ireland
38 H5 Liffré France
145 C6 Lifi Mahuida mt. Arg.
200 □5 Lifou i. Îles Loyauté New Caledonia
30 D6 Lifton Devon, England U.K.
Lifu i. Îles Loyauté New Caledonia see Lifou
201 □2 Lifuka i. Tonga
154 D5 Ligao Luzon Phil.
43 E7 Ligardes France
90 D4 Ligasa Dem. Rep. Congo
18 I4 Līgatne Latvia
209 G10 Lightfoot Lake salt flat W.A. Austr.
127 P9 Lighthouse Reef Belize
205 K3 Lightning Ridge N.S.W. Austr.
118 C2 Lightstreet PA U.S.A.
59 L6 Ligist Austria
71 O4 Lignano Pineta Italy
71 O4 Lignano Sabbiadoro Italy
38 I7 Ligné France
38 H8 Ligneron r. France
45 J8 Ligneuville Belgium
39 P8 Lignières France
40 D5 Lignon r. France
41 E6 Lignon r. France
37 J6 Ligny-en-Barrois France
36 G8 Ligny-le-Châtel France
36 C8 Ligny-le-Ribault France
70 I7 Ligonchio Italy
95 H3 Ligonha r. Moz.
110 I8 Ligonier IN U.S.A.
116 F8 Ligonier PA U.S.A.
Ligoúrion Greece see Lygourio
55 H3 Ligowo Pol.
204 E6 Liguanea Island S.A. Austr.
39 M7 Ligueil France
42 E2 Ligugé France
126 D5 Ligui Mex.
Ligure, Mar sea France/Italy see Ligurian Sea
70 F7 Liguria admin. reg. Italy
68 B4 Ligurian Sea France/Italy
Ligurienne, Mer sea France/Italy see Ligurian Sea
125 R9 Ligurta AZ U.S.A.
203 □4 Liha Point Niue
153 L7 Lihir Group is P.N.G.
22 E5 Lihme Denmark
207 M4 Lihou Reef and Cays Coral Sea Is Terr. Austr.
124 □B11 Līhu'e HI U.S.A.
146 E5 Lihuel Calel, Parque Nacional nat. park Arg.
18 G3 Lihula Estonia
75 □ Lija Malta
65 O6 Lijar Spain
65 I7 Líjar, Sierra de mts Spain
170 C5 Lijiang Yunnan China
158 J2 Li Jiang r. China
171 J3 Lijiazhai Henan China
158 F5 Lik, Nam r. Laos
68 E3 Lika reg. Croatia
184 D6 Likak Iran
90 C4 Likala Dem. Rep. Congo
91 E7 Likasi Dem. Rep. Congo
90 D4 Likati Dem. Rep. Congo
90 E4 Likati r. Dem. Rep. Congo
106 F4 Likely B.C. Can.
Likhás pen. Greece see Lichas
19 S4 Likhoslavl' Rus. Fed.
17 T5 Likhovskoy Rus. Fed.
90 D4 Likimi Dem. Rep. Congo
19 V6 Likino-Dulevo Rus. Fed.
Likisia East Timor see Liquiçá
178 I9 Likma Chhattisgarh India
90 D5 Likolia Dem. Rep. Congo
90 C4 Likouala admin. reg. Congo
90 C5 Likouala r. Congo
90 C5 Likouala aux Herbes r. Congo
23 N3 Likstammen l. Sweden
157 H4 Liku Kalimantan Indon.
157 K2 Liku Sarawak Malaysia
203 □4 Liku Niue
155 D3 Likupang Sulawesi Indon.
14 H4 Likurga Rus. Fed.
201 □1a Likuri Harbour b. Viti Levu Fiji
39 L7 L'Île-Bouchard France
72 B2 L'Île-Rousse Corse France
59 M3 Lilienfeld Austria
48 G4 Lilienthal Ger.
171 I5 Liling Hunan China
18 J1 Liljendal Fin.
185 O5 Lilla Pak.
22 I3 Lilla Edet Sweden
20 P3 Lilla Luleälven r. Sweden
20 N4 Lillblaiken hill Sweden
45 G6 Lille Belgium
36 F2 Lille France
22 F6 Lille Bælt sea chan. Denmark
39 M2 Lillebonne France
21 K6 Lillehammer Norway
36 D2 Lillers France
22 E3 Lillesand Norway
30 H2 Lilleshall Telford and Wrekin, England U.K.
22 H2 Lillestrøm Norway
110 I6 Lilley MI U.S.A.
209 I9 Lillian, Point hill W.A. Austr.
213 L2 Lillie Glacier Antarctica
26 K11 Lilliesleaf Scottish Borders, Scotland U.K.
115 H8 Lillington NC U.S.A.
63 N9 Lillo Spain
106 F5 Lillooet B.C. Can.
106 F5 Lillooet r. B.C. Can.
106 F5 Lillooet Range mts B.C. Can.
90 E5 Lilo r. Dem. Rep. Congo
179 N7 Lilong Manipur India
93 B8 Lilongwe Malawi
144 E2 Lilo Viejo Arg.
154 D7 Liloy Mindanao Phil.
110 F4 Lily WI U.S.A.
204 G5 Lilydale S.A. Austr.
205 K9 Lilydale Tas. Austr.
76 H7 Lim r. Serb. and Mont.
147 H4 Lima Arg.
71 J7 Lima r. Italy
139 F5 Lima Para.
138 A3 Lima Peru
138 A2 Lima dept Peru
110 C9 Lima IL U.S.A.
122 H4 Lima MT U.S.A.
116 H6 Lima NY U.S.A.
116 A8 Lima OH U.S.A.
137 F4 Limaão Brazil
146 B3 Limache Chile
143 F4 Lima Duarte Brazil
40 C5 Limagne reg. France
187 M3 Līmah Oman
182 B5 Liman Rus. Fed.
58 F7 Limana Italy
55 I6 Limanowa Pol.
155 E7 Limar Maluku Indon.
146 B2 Limarí r. Chile
156 F4 Limas Indon.
154 E7 Limasawa i. Phil.
Limassol Cyprus see Lemesos
27 I2 Limavady Northern Ireland U.K.
146 D6 Limay r. Arg.
36 C5 Limay France
146 D5 Limay Mahuida Arg.
52 G3 Limbach Baden-Württemberg Ger.
52 B3 Limbach Saarland Ger.
51 F9 Limbach Sachsen Ger.
51 G9 Limbach-Oberfrohna Ger.
75 J6 Limbadi Italy
157 K2 Limbang Sarawak Malaysia
157 K2 Limbang r. Sarawak Malaysia
138 C3 Limbani Peru
72 C6 Limbara, Monte mts Sardegna Italy
18 H4 Limbaži Latvia
178 C8 Limbdi Gujarat India
89 H5 Limbe Cameroon
93 B8 Limbe Malawi
155 C3 Limboto Sulawesi Indon.
155 C3 Limboto, Danau l. Indon.
45 I7 Limbourg Belgium
95 H3 Limbuè Moz.
155 A6 Limbung Sulawesi Indon.
157 K6 Limbungan Kalimantan Indon.
206 B4 Limbunya N.T. Austr.
45 H6 Limburg prov. Belgium
45 I6 Limburg prov. Neth.
49 F10 Limburg an der Lahn Ger.
52 E3 Limburgerhof Ger.
156 □ Lim Chu Kang Sing.
156 □ Lim Chu Kang hill Sing.
96 H4 Lime Acres S. Africa
21 L6 Limedsforsen Sweden
203 C13 Limehills South I. N.Z.
142 D5 Limeira Brazil
29 K1 Limekilns Fife, Scotland U.K.
78 F2 Limenaria Thasos Greece
27 E7 Limerick Rep. of Ireland
27 E8 Limerick county Rep. of Ireland
110 B6 Lime Springs IA U.S.A.
117 □R2 Limestone ME U.S.A.
107 L4 Limestone Point Man. Can.
22 E5 Limfjorden sea chan. Denmark
62 D5 Limia r. Spain
79 G7 Limin Chersonisou Kriti Greece
20 L4 Limingen Norway
20 L4 Limingen l. Norway
117 □O5 Limington ME U.S.A.
20 R4 Liminka Fin.
22 J4 Limmared Sweden
44 G3 Limmen Neth.
206 F3 Limmen Bight b. N.T. Austr.
206 E3 Limmen Bight River r. N.T. Austr.
78 E4 Limni Greece
79 G3 Limnos i. Greece
140 G3 Limoeiro Brazil
117 J3 Limoges Ont. Can.
42 G4 Limoges France
43 H7 Limogne, Causse de hills France
43 H7 Limogne-en-Quercy France
126 □Q10 Limón Hond.
120 D6 Limon CO U.S.A.
99 □1a Limon, Mount hill Rodrigues I. Mauritius
70 D7 Limone Piemonte Italy
40 F5 Limonest France
71 J4 Limone sul Garda Italy
64 F3 Limonetes r. Spain
188 G5 Limonlu Turkey
138 D3 Limoquije Bol.
73 N4 Limosano Italy
42 H4 Limousin admin. reg. France
42 H4 Limousin, Monts du hills France
42 G4 Limousin, Plateaux du France
43 I9 Limoux France
95 F4 Limpopo prov. S. Africa
95 G5 Limpopo r. S. Africa/Zimbabwe
95 F4 Limpopo National Park S. Africa
170 H6 Limu Guangxi China
201 □2 Limu atoll Tonga
203 □4 Limufuafua Point Niue
91 D8 Limulunga Zambia
20 Q3 Linaälven r. Sweden
186 F1 Līnah Saudi Arabia
97 M5 Linakeng Lesotho
20 U2 Linakhamari Rus. Fed.
Lin'an Yunnan China see Jianshui
171 L3 Lin'an Zhejiang China
154 E8 Linao Bay Mindanao Phil.
154 B6 Linapacan i. Phil.
154 B6 Linapacan Strait Phil.
42 H4 Linards France
146 B4 Linares Chile
127 J5 Linares Mex.
65 L4 Linares Spain
63 M5 Linares, Embalse de resr Spain
67 D7 Linares de Mora Spain
62 I7 Linares de Riofrío Spain
72 B9 Linas, Monte mt. Sardegna Italy
70 G5 Linate airport Italy
157 K3 Linau Balui plat. Malaysia
170 C7 Lincang Yunnan China
45 H7 Lincent Belgium
Lincheng Hainan China see Lingao
Lincheng Hunan China see Huitong
212 R1 Linck Nunataks nunataks Antarctica
147 G4 Lincoln Arg.
203 G10 Lincoln South I. N.Z.
29 P7 Lincoln Lincolnshire, England U.K.
124 K3 Lincoln CA U.S.A.
118 E7 Lincoln DE U.S.A.
114 C5 Lincoln IL U.S.A.
120 F6 Lincoln KS U.S.A.
117 □Q3 Lincoln ME U.S.A.
111 K5 Lincoln MI U.S.A.
120 G5 Lincoln NE U.S.A.
117 N4 Lincoln NH U.S.A.
118 C4 Lincoln PA U.S.A.
122 B4 Lincoln City OR U.S.A.
152 D3 Lincoln Island Paracel Is
204 E6 Lincoln National Park S.A. Austr.
116 B6 Lincoln Park MI U.S.A.
105 N1 Lincoln Sea Can./Greenland
29 Q7 Lincolnshire admin. div. England U.K.
29 Q7 Lincolnshire Wolds hills England U.K.
115 F9 Lincolnton GA U.S.A.
118 D5 Lincoln University PA U.S.A.
119 G4 Lincroft NJ U.S.A.
140 E5 Linda, Serra hills Brazil
206 G7 Linda Creek watercourse Qld Austr.
24 J1 Lindas Norway
51 F6 Lindau Sachsen-Anhalt Ger.
48 I1 Lindau Schleswig-Holstein Ger.
52 H6 Lindau (Bodensee) Ger.
44 I3 Linde r. Neth.
48 K1 Lindelse Denmark
207 L6 Lindeman Group is Qld Austr.
106 H5 Linden Alta Can.
49 G9 Linden Hessen Ger.
48 H2 Linden Schleswig-Holstein Ger.
137 G3 Linden Guyana
115 D9 Linden AL U.S.A.
124 K3 Linden CA U.S.A.
116 B6 Linden MI U.S.A.
119 G3 Linden NJ U.S.A.
115 D8 Linden TN U.S.A.
121 H9 Linden TX U.S.A.
50 F4 Lindenberg Brandenburg Ger.
50 I5 Lindenberg Brandenburg Ger.
51 J6 Lindenberg Brandenburg Ger.
52 H6 Lindenberg im Allgäu Ger.
52 F2 Lindenfels Ger.
110 B2 Linden Grove MN U.S.A.
Lindenow Fjord inlet Greenland see Kangerlussuatsiaq
118 F5 Lindenwold NJ U.S.A.
48 E5 Lindern (Oldenburg) Ger.
23 L2 Lindesberg Sweden
22 D3 Lindesnes c. Norway
48 H1 Lindewitt Ger.
31 L5 Lindfield West Sussex, England U.K.
49 H6 Lindhorst Ger.
Líndhos Rodos Greece see Lindos
90 E4 Lindi r. Dem. Rep. Congo
93 C7 Lindi Tanz.
93 C7 Lindi admin. reg. Tanz.
169 S3 Lindian Heilong. China
Lindisfarne i. England U.K. see Holy Island
203 D11 Lindis Peak South I. N.Z.
49 D8 Lindlar Ger.
97 L3 Lindley S. Africa
142 D5 Lindóia Brazil
22 I4 Lindome Sweden
169 P5 Lindong Nei Mongol China
79 J6 Lindos Rodos Greece
79 J6 Lindos, Akra pt Rodos Greece
62 D5 Lindoso Port.
50 G5 Lindow Ger.
37 M6 Lindre, Étang de l. France
117 □R2 Lindsay N.B. Can.
108 E4 Lindsay Ont. Can.
124 M5 Lindsay CA U.S.A.
122 L3 Lindsay MT U.S.A.
209 F9 Lindsay Gordon Lagoon salt flat W.A. Austr.
120 G6 Lindsborg KS U.S.A.
23 M5 Lindsdal Sweden
116 E11 Lindside WV U.S.A.
50 E5 Lindstedt Ger.
Lindum Lincolnshire, England U.K. see Lincoln
48 I5 Lindwedel Ger.
56 C2 Líně Czech Rep.
118 B5 Lineboro MD U.S.A.
216 I5 Line Islands S. Pacific Ocean
118 E4 Line Lexington PA U.S.A.
17 O1 Linets Rus. Fed.
169 L8 Linfen Shanxi China
118 D4 Linfield PA U.S.A.
31 M5 Linford Thurrock, England U.K.
26 F8 Ling r. Scotland U.K.
176 H4 Lingamparti Andhra Prad. India
176 D6 Linganamakki Reservoir India
170 G9 Lingao Hainan China
41 D8 Lingas, Montagne du mt. France
154 C3 Lingayen Luzon Phil.
154 C3 Lingayen Gulf Luzon Phil.
169 L9 Lingbao Henan China
171 K2 Lingbi Anhui China
Lingcheng Anhui China see Lingbi
Lingcheng Guangxi China see Lingshan
Lingcheng Hainan China see Lingshui
Lingcheng Shandong China see Lingxian
170 H6 Lingchuan Guangxi China
169 M9 Lingchuan Shanxi China
97 K8 Lingelethu S. Africa
97 J8 Lingelihle S. Africa

48 D5 Lingen (Ems) Ger.
58 A5 Lingenau Austria
52 E3 Lingenfeld Ger.
31 L5 Lingfield Surrey, England U.K.
156 F5 Lingga i. Indon.
157 I4 Lingga Sarawak Malaysia
156 F5 Lingga, Kepulauan is Indon.
173 I10 Linggo Co l. Xizang China
169 Q6 Linghai Liaoning China
154 F8 Lingig Mindanao Phil.
157 L1 Lingkabau Sabah Malaysia
157 L3 Lingkas Kalimantan Indon.
122 L5 Lingle WY U.S.A.
118 B4 Linglestown PA U.S.A.
206 G4 Lingnoonganee Island Qld Austr.
37 O6 Lingolsheim France
90 D4 Lingomo Dem. Rep. Congo
169 N7 Lingqiu Shanxi China
170 G7 Lingshan Guangxi China
169 Q9 Lingshan Wan b. China
179 L6 Lingshi Bhutan
169 L8 Lingshi Shanxi China
170 G9 Lingshui Hainan China
170 G9 Lingshui Wan b. China
176 E4 Lingsugur Karnataka India
169 J9 Lingtai Gansu China
75 I8 Linguaglossa Sicilia Italy
88 B3 Linguère Senegal
170 H6 Lingui Guangxi China
72 C3 Linguizzetta Corse France
31 O2 Lingwood Norfolk, England U.K.
169 O8 Lingxian Shandong China
171 J3 Lingxiang Hubei China
169 P6 Lingyuan Liaoning China
170 F6 Lingyun Guangxi China
170 A4 Lingza Xizang China
Lingzhi Bhutan see Lingshi
173 D9 Lingzi Thang Plains reg. Aksai Chin
171 M4 Linhai Zhejiang China
143 G3 Linhares Brazil
62 F7 Linhares Port.
169 J6 Linhe Nei Mongol China
158 B2 Linhpa Myanmar
54 F1 Linia Pol.
203 D11 Linidis Valley South I. N.Z.
117 □O2 Linière Que. Can.
54 G1 Liniewo Pol.
170 E2 Linjiang Gansu China
163 E8 Linjiang Jilin China
52 E3 Linkenheim-Hochstetten Ger.
23 L3 Linköping Sweden
162 G6 Linkou Heilong. China
26 J5 Linksness Orkney, Scotland U.K.
18 G5 Linkuva Lith.
171 H4 Linli Hunan China
26 I11 Linlithgow West Lothian, Scotland U.K.
169 M8 Linlü Shan mt. Henan China
120 J6 Linn MO U.S.A.
121 F12 Linn TX U.S.A.
124 J1 Linn, Mount CA U.S.A.
21 T5 Linnansaaren kansallispuisto nat. park Fin.
22 H2 Linnekleppen hill Norway
117 □R2 Linneus ME U.S.A.
30 B4 Linney Head Wales U.K.
26 E9 Linnhe, Loch inlet Scotland U.K.
49 B9 Linnich Ger.
69 D8 Linosa, Isola di i. Sicilia Italy
18 H9 Linova Belarus
18 K4 Linovo Rus. Fed.
50 G4 Linow Ger.
158 C4 Linpo Myanmar
169 N8 Linqing Shandong China
169 M9 Linruzhen Henan China
142 C4 Lins Brazil
88 B4 Linsan Guinea
48 H5 Linsburg Ger.
170 F3 Linshui Sichuan China
130 □ Linstead Jamaica
95 □J5 Linta r. Madag.
155 A8 Lintah, Selat sea chan. Indon.
168 H9 Lintan Gansu China
168 H9 Lintao Gansu China
70 G1 Linth r. Switz.
70 G2 Linthal Switz.
51 G6 Linthe Ger.
118 B6 Linthicum Heights MD U.S.A.
48 G3 Lintig Ger.
202 J7 Linton North I. N.Z.
31 M3 Linton Cambridgeshire, England U.K.
120 E2 Linton ND U.S.A.
169 K9 Lintong Shaanxi China
66 C2 Lintzoain Spain
50 G5 Linum Ger.
118 F6 Linwood NJ U.S.A.
171 I6 Linwu Hunan China
43 B8 Linxe France
169 P5 Linxi Nei Mongol China
168 H9 Linxia Gansu China
168 H9 Linxia Gansu China
Linxian Henan China see Linzhou
169 L8 Linxian Shanxi China
171 I4 Linxiang Hunan China
94 E3 Linyanti r. Botswana/Namibia
94 D3 Linyanti Swamp Namibia
169 O8 Linyi Shandong China
169 P9 Linyi Shandong China
169 L9 Linyi Shanxi China
171 J2 Linying Henan China
66 G4 Linyola Spain
170 F1 Linyou Shaanxi China
59 J3 Linz Austria
49 D9 Linz am Rhein Ger.
168 G7 Linze Gansu China
52 G6 Linzgau reg. Ger.
169 M8 Linzhou Henan China
16 D2 Liobomlʹ Ukr.
95 H2 Lioma Moz.
157 K3 Lio Matoh Sarawak Malaysia
41 D11 Lion, Golfe du g. France
130 □ Lionel Town Jamaica
73 O6 Lioni Italy
Lions, Gulf of France see Lion, Golfe du
106 F5 Lions Bay B.C. Can.
95 F3 Lions Den Zimbabwe
111 M5 Lion's Head Ont. Can.
39 K3 Lion-sur-Mer France
155 E7 Lioppa Maluku Indon.
43 F6 Liorac-sur-Louyre France
84 B6 Lioua Chad
90 B4 Liouesso Congo
154 C5 Lipa Luzon Phil.
55 I2 Lipa Pol.
155 D2 Lipang i. Indon.
57 J2 Lipany Slovakia
74 H7 Lipari Isole Lipari Italy
74 H7 Lipari, Isola i. Isole Lipari Italy
74 H6 Lipari, Isole is Italy
156 D4 Lipatkain Sumatera Indon.
18 K6 Lipawki Belarus
16 F5 Lipcani Moldova
55 H4 Lipce Reymontowskie Pol.
20 T5 Liperi Fin.
19 W9 Lipetsk Rus. Fed.
19 V9 Lipetskaya Oblastʹ admin. div. Rus. Fed.
Lipetsk Oblast admin. div. Rus. Fed. see Lipetskaya Oblastʹ
138 D5 Lipez, Cordillera de mts Bol.
31 K5 Liphook Hampshire, England U.K.
54 C2 Lipiany Pol.
19 U1 Lipin Bor Rus. Fed.
170 G5 Liping Guizhou China
55 J6 Lipinki Pol.
54 D4 Lipinki Łużyckie Pol.
19 U8 Lipitsy Rus. Fed.
54 F2 Lipka Pol.
Lipkany Moldova see Lipcani
19 U8 Lipki Rus. Fed.
54 D3 Lipki Wielkie Pol.
76 J8 Lipljan Kosovo, Srbija Serb. and Mont.
19 Q2 Lipnaya Gorka Rus. Fed.
55 H2 Lipnica Kujawsko-Pomorskie Pol.
54 F2 Lipnica Pomorskie Pol.
55 I6 Lipnica Murowana Pol.
55 J5 Lipnik Pol.
55 H6 Lipnika Wielka Pol.
57 G2 Lipník nad Bečvou Czech Rep.
55 H3 Lipno Kujawsko-Pomorskie Pol.
54 E4 Lipno Wielkopolskie Pol.
56 D3 Lipno, Vodní nádrž resr Czech Rep.
43 C7 Liposthey France
77 J4 Lipova Romania
57 L6 Lipovei, Dealurile hills Romania
15 I6 Lipovka Volgogradskaya Oblastʹ Rus. Fed.
17 T3 Lipovka Voronezhskaya Oblastʹ Rus. Fed.
77 L6 Lipovu Romania
55 J2 Lipowiec Pol.
49 C7 Lippe r. Ger.
44 J2 Lippenhuizen Neth.
49 I7 Lippoldsberg (Wahlsburg) Ger.
49 F7 Lippstadt Ger.
121 E7 Lipscomb TX U.S.A.
55 L2 Lipsk Pol.
55 J4 Lipsko Pol.
Lipsoí i. Greece see Leipsoi
57 G2 Liptál Czech Rep.
178 H4 Lipti Lekh pass Nepal
89 F3 Liptougou Burkina
57 I2 Liptovská Kokava Slovakia
57 I2 Liptovská Mara, Vodná nádrž resr Slovakia
57 I3 Liptovská Osada Slovakia
57 J3 Liptovská Teplička Slovakia
57 I2 Liptovský Hrádok Slovakia
57 I2 Liptovský Mikuláš Slovakia
205 J8 Liptrap, Cape Vic. Austr.
19 R6 Liptsy Rus. Fed.
170 H6 Lipu Guangxi China
75 M5 Lipuda r. Italy
54 F1 Lipusz Pol.
155 D8 Liquiçá East Timor
Liquissa East Timor see Liquiçá
92 B4 Lira Uganda
155 D7 Liran i. Maluku Indon.
90 C5 Liranga Congo
39 I7 Liré France
62 B3 Lires, Ría de b. Spain
73 L5 Liri r. Italy
92 A2 Liri, Jebel el mt. Sudan
70 G3 Liro r. Italy
155 E2 Lirung Sulawesi Indon.
76 I9 Lis Albania
77 M5 Lisa Romania
27 E5 Lisacul Rep. of Ireland
182 J1 Lisakovsk Kazakh.
90 D4 Lisala Dem. Rep. Congo
131 □7 Lisas Bay Trin. and Tob.
28 F4 Lisbane Northern Ireland U.K.
27 G4 Lisbellaw Northern Ireland U.K.
64 A3 Lisboa Port.
64 A2 Lisboa admin. dist. Port.
Lisbon Port. see Lisboa
110 F8 Lisbon IL U.S.A.
118 A6 Lisbon MD U.S.A.
117 □O4 Lisbon ME U.S.A.
120 G2 Lisbon ND U.S.A.
117 N4 Lisbon NH U.S.A.
116 E8 Lisbon OH U.S.A.
117 □O5 Lisbon Falls ME U.S.A.
27 J3 Lisburn Northern Ireland U.K.
75 I6 Lisca Blanca, Isola i. Isole Lipari Italy
27 D7 Liscannor Rep. of Ireland
27 D7 Liscannor Bay Rep. of Ireland
27 C5 Liscarney Rep. of Ireland
27 E8 Liscarroll Rep. of Ireland
72 C5 Liscia r. Sardegna Italy
72 C5 Liscia, Lago di l. Sardegna Italy
72 C7 Liscoi r. Italy
109 I4 Liscomb Game Sanctuary nature res. N.S. Can.
27 D6 Lisdoonvarna Rep. of Ireland
27 H5 Lisduff Rep. of Ireland
77 K9 Lisec mt. Macedonia
22 H5 Liseleje Denmark
27 F7 Lisgarode Rep. of Ireland
27 F9 Lisgoold Rep. of Ireland
Lishan Shaanxi China see Lintong
171 M6 Lishan Taiwan
16 H3 Lishchyn Ukr.
170 C6 Lishe Jiang r. Yunnan China
169 L8 Lishi Shanxi China
184 D6 Līshtar-e Bālā Iran
162 D7 Lishu Jilin China
171 L3 Lishui Jiangsu China
171 L4 Lishui Zhejiang China
170 H4 Li Shui r. China
55 J5 Lisia Góra Pol.
197 H2 Lisianski Island HI U.S.A.
Lisichansk Ukr. see Lysychans'k
54 F5 Lisięcice Pol.
39 L3 Lisieux France
19 N1 Lisiy Nos Rus. Fed.
23 K1 Lisjön l. Sweden
30 D7 Liskeard Cornwall, England U.K.
15 G6 Liski Rus. Fed.
57 I2 Lisková Slovakia
42 F5 Lisle France
27 I3 Lislea Northern Ireland U.K.
36 D5 L'Isle-Adam France
40 G5 L'Isle-d'Abeau France
43 E8 L'Isle-de-Noé France
42 E4 L'Isle-d'Espagnac France
43 F9 L'Isle-en-Dodon France
43 G8 L'Isle-Jourdain Midi-Pyrénées France
42 F3 L'Isle-Jourdain Poitou-Charentes France
41 G9 L'Isle-sur-la-Sorgue France
40 J2 L'Isle-sur-le-Doubs France
40 E1 L'Isle-sur-Serein France
43 H8 Lisle-sur-Tarn France
205 N3 Lismore N.S.W. Austr.
203 F10 Lismore South I. N.Z.
27 G8 Lismore Rep. of Ireland
26 E10 Lismore i. Scotland U.K.
27 E7 Lisnagry Rep. of Ireland
27 H8 Lisnakill Rep. of Ireland
27 I3 Lisnamuck Northern Ireland U.K.
27 G4 Lisnarrick Northern Ireland U.K.
27 H4 Lisnaskea Northern Ireland U.K.
16 I7 Lisne Ukr.
72 G3 L'Isolotto i. Italy
40 H2 Lison r. France
56 D2 Lišov Czech Rep.
27 E9 Lispatrick Rep. of Ireland
27 B8 Lispole Rep. of Ireland
27 G8 Lisronagh Rep. of Ireland
28 C6 Lisryan Rep. of Ireland
190 G7 Liss mt. Saudi Arabia
31 K5 Liss Hampshire, England U.K.
Lissa Pol. see Leszno
43 H6 Lissac-et-Mouret France
28 D4 Lissan Northern Ireland U.K.
44 G4 Lisse Neth.
27 C8 Lisselton Rep. of Ireland
49 C10 Lissendorf Ger.
87 H2 Lisseri, Oued watercourse Tunisia
22 J1 Lisskogsbrändan Sweden
70 G4 Lissone Italy
27 D7 Lissycasey Rep. of Ireland
48 F1 List Ger.
22 C3 Lista pen. Norway
22 C3 Listafjorden b. Norway
23 L6 Listed Bornholm Denmark
213 K1 Lister, Mount Antarctica
27 H8 Listerlin Rep. of Ireland
28 F5 Listooder Northern Ireland U.K.
206 G8 Listore watercourse Qld Austr.
108 D5 Listowel Ont. Can.
27 D8 Listowel Rep. of Ireland
207 J8 Listowel Downs Qld Austr.
42 C5 Listrac-Médoc France
183 U3 Listvyaga, Khrebet mts Kazakh./Rus. Fed.
54 H4 Liswarta r. Pol.
30 G4 Liswerry Newport, Wales U.K.
55 H5 Liszki Pol.
54 F2 Liszkowo Pol.
20 M5 Lit Sweden
170 G7 Litang Guangxi China
170 C3 Litang Sichuan China
170 C4 Litang Qu r. Sichuan China
137 H4 Litani r. Fr. Guiana/Suriname
190 D5 Līţânî, Nahr el r. Lebanon
57 I3 Litava Slovakia
56 D2 Litavka r. Czech Rep.
124 L1 Litchfield CA U.S.A.
119 I1 Litchfield CT U.S.A.
120 K6 Litchfield IL U.S.A.
110 J7 Litchfield MI U.S.A.
120 H3 Litchfield MN U.S.A.
116 C7 Litchfield OH U.S.A.
118 I1 Litchfield County county CT U.S.A.
93 D7 Litembe Tanz.
18 K4 Litene Latvia
57 G4 Litér Hungary
43 B7 Lit-et-Mixe France
44 H5 Lith Neth.
186 E5 Līth, Wādī al watercourse Saudi Arabia
29 L7 Litherland Merseyside, England U.K.
205 M5 Lithgow N.S.W. Austr.
78 F8 Lithino, Akra pt Kriti Greece
18 G6 Lithuania country Europe
68 E2 Litija Slovenia
111 R9 Lititz PA U.S.A.
57 I3 Litke Hungary
193 T2 Litke, Mys c. Rus. Fed.
78 D2 Litochoro Greece
56 D1 Litoměřice Czech Rep.
56 F2 Litomyšl Czech Rep.
64 B1 Litoral reg. Port.
56 G2 Litovel Czech Rep.
162 I4 Litovko Rus. Fed.
Litovskaya S.S.R. country Europe see Lithuania
59 L2 Litschau Austria
70 E1 Littau Switz.
121 I10 Little r. LA U.S.A.
121 I9 Little r. OK U.S.A.
121 G10 Little r. TX U.S.A.
115 I12 Little Abaco i. Bahamas
108 D3 Little Abitibi r. Ont. Can.
108 D3 Little Abitibi Lake Ont. Can.
177 M7 Little Andaman i. Andaman & Nicobar Is India
Little Ararat mt. Turkey see Küçük Ağrı Dağı
120 G7 Little Arkansas r. KS U.S.A.
115 H12 Little Bahama Bank sea feature Bahamas
202 J3 Little Barrier i. North I. N.Z.
65 □ Little Bay Gibraltar
110 G4 Little Bay de Noc MI U.S.A.
Little Belt sea chan. Denmark see Lille Bælt
122 I3 Little Belt Mountains MT U.S.A.
122 K4 Little Bighorn r. MT U.S.A.
Little Bitter Lake Egypt see Murrah aş Şughrá, Al Buḩayrah al
120 G6 Little Blue r. KS U.S.A.
29 M6 Littleborough Greater Manchester, England U.K.
106 H5 Little Bow r. Alta Can.
106 H2 Little Buffalo r. N.W.T. Can.
130 C4 Little Cayman i. Cayman Is
107 M3 Little Churchill r. Man. Can.
31 O4 Little Clacton Essex, England U.K.
159 A8 Little Coco Island Cocos Is
26 D10 Little Colonsay i. Scotland U.K.
125 U5 Little Colorado r. AZ U.S.A.
31 M6 Little Common East Sussex, England U.K.
118 E6 Little Creek DE U.S.A.
125 T4 Little Creek Peak UT U.S.A.
28 H2 Little Cumbrae i. Scotland U.K.
108 D4 Little Current Ont. Can.
108 C3 Little Current r. Ont. Can.
30 E6 Little Dart r. England U.K.
30 H4 Littledean Gloucestershire, England U.K.
204 H7 Little Desert National Park Vic. Austr.
31 M3 Little Downham Cambridgeshire, England U.K.
119 G5 Little Egg Harbor inlet NJ U.S.A.
130 F2 Little Exuma i. Bahamas
120 H3 Little Falls MN U.S.A.
117 K5 Little Falls NY U.S.A.
26 H7 Littleferry Highland, Scotland U.K.
125 S5 Littlefield AZ U.S.A.
121 D9 Littlefield TX U.S.A.
97 K9 Little Fish r. S. Africa
110 A1 Little Fork MN U.S.A.
110 A1 Little Fork r. MN U.S.A.
106 F5 Little Fort B.C. Can.
118 D3 Little Gap PA U.S.A.
107 M4 Little Grand Rapids Man. Can.
124 K2 Little Grass Valley Reservoir CA U.S.A.
31 K6 Littlehampton West Sussex, England U.K.
130 G3 Little Inagua Island Bahamas
116 D9 Little Kanawha r. WV U.S.A.
96 C3 Little Karas Berg plat. Namibia
96 E9 Little Karoo plat. S. Africa
124 O6 Little Lake CA U.S.A.
26 F7 Little Loch Broom inlet Scotland U.K.
Little Mecatina r. Nfld and Lab./Que. Can. see Petit Mécatina
116 A9 Little Miami r. OH U.S.A.
26 I7 Littlemill Highland, Scotland U.K.
26 B7 Little Minch sea chan. Scotland U.K.
31 K4 Little Missenden Buckinghamshire, England U.K.
120 D2 Little Missouri r. ND U.S.A.
31 J4 Littlemore Oxfordshire, England U.K.
116 D9 Little Muskingum r. OH U.S.A.
177 M9 Little Nicobar i. Andaman & Nicobar Is India
31 O4 Little Oakley Essex, England U.K.
97 N1 Little Olifants r. S. Africa
31 M3 Little Ouse r. England U.K.
185 P3 Little Pamir mts Afgh.
119 K2 Little Peconic Bay NY U.S.A.
110 H1 Little Pic r. Ont. Can.
118 A2 Little Pine Creek r. PA U.S.A.
118 A5 Little Pipe Creek r. MD U.S.A.
31 M3 Littleport Cambridgeshire, England U.K.
122 L4 Little Powder r. MT U.S.A.
106 D2 Little Rancheria r. B.C. Can.
178 C8 Little Rann marsh Gujarat India
121 J8 Little Red r. AR U.S.A.
106 H3 Little Red River Alta Can.
203 G10 Little River South I. N.Z.
115 H9 Little River SC U.S.A.
121 I8 Little Rock AR U.S.A.
124 O7 Littlerock CA U.S.A.
110 H6 Little Sable Point MI U.S.A.
107 M4 Little Sachigo Lake Ont. Can.
106 C2 Little Salmon Lake Y.T. Can.
125 T4 Little Salt Lake UT U.S.A.
209 E7 Little Sandy Desert W.A. Austr.
130 F1 Little San Salvador i. Bahamas
120 G5 Little Sioux r. IA U.S.A.
104 A4 Little Sitkin Island AK U.S.A.
106 G4 Little Smoky Alta Can.
106 G4 Little Smoky r. Alta Can.
122 J6 Little Snake r. CO U.S.A.
115 □1 Little Sound b. Bermuda
31 N6 Littlestone-on-Sea Kent, England U.K.
118 A5 Littlestown PA U.S.A.
Little Tibet reg. Jammu and Kashmir see Ladakh
131 □5 Little Tobago i. Trin. and Tob.
28 B8 Littleton Rep. of Ireland
31 J5 Littleton Hampshire, England U.K.
110 D9 Littleton IL U.S.A.
117 N4 Littleton NH U.S.A.
116 E9 Littleton WV U.S.A.
110 I4 Little Traverse Bay MI U.S.A.
117 K4 Little Tupper Lake NY U.S.A.
110 B1 Little Turtle Lake Ont. Can.
116 G6 Little Valley NY U.S.A.
120 K7 Little Wabash r. IL U.S.A.
203 G8 Little Wanganui South I. N.Z.
120 E4 Little White r. SD U.S.A.
121 G9 Little Wichita r. TX U.S.A.
122 J5 Little Wind r. WY U.S.A.
122 G5 Little Wood r. ID U.S.A.
23 S1 Littoinen Fin.
89 H5 Littoral prov. Cameroon
146 B4 Litueche Chile
93 B8 Litunde Moz.
106 B3 Lituya Bay AK U.S.A.
56 C1 Litvínov Czech Rep.
16 H4 Lityn Ukr.
53 K2 Litzendorf Ger.
18 H3 Liu Estonia
Liu'an Anhui China see Lu'an
170 F2 Liuba Shaanxi China
55 L1 Liubavas Lith.
158 I2 Liucheng Guangxi China
171 L4 Liucheng Zhejiang China
171 M7 Liuchiu Yü i. Taiwan
170 F5 Liuchong He r. Guizhou China
Liuchow Guangxi China see Liuzhou
55 L1 Liudvinavas Lith.
169 R8 Liugong Dao i. China
169 Q6 Liugu He r. China
162 D7 Liuhe Jilin China
169 P6 Liu He r. China
169 R6 Liu He r. China
171 N4 Liuheng Dao i. China
171 H3 Liujiachang Hubei China
170 G6 Liujiang Guangxi China
168 H9 Liujiaxia Shuiku resr Gansu China
162 E5 Liukesong Heilong. China
170 B6 Liuku Yunnan China
Liulin Gansu China see Jonê
169 L8 Liulin Shanxi China
168 J9 Liupan Shan mts China
Liupanshui Guizhou China see Lupanshui
95 H2 Liupo Moz.
169 O9 Liuquan Jiangsu China
126 □P11 Liure Hond.
168 C5 Liushuquan Xinjiang China
91 D8 Liuwa Plain Zambia
91 D8 Liuwa Plain National Park Zambia
171 I4 Liuyang Hunan China
171 I4 Liuyang He r. China
172 L6 Liuyuan Gansu China
169 S1 Liuzhan Heilong. China
170 G6 Liuzhou Guangxi China
57 K5 Livada Arad Romania
77 L3 Livada Satu Mare Romania
79 G5 Livada, Akra pt Tinos Greece
78 D2 Livadi Greece
79 H6 Livadi i. Greece
78 E1 Livadia Greece
162 H7 Livadiya Rus. Fed.
78 E4 Livanates Greece
18 J5 Līvāni Latvia
68 F3 Livanjsko Polje plain Bos.-Herz.
39 L3 Livarot France
18 G5 Livbērze Latvia
17 R3 Livenka Rus. Fed.
71 M4 Livenza r. Italy
124 K2 Live Oak CA U.S.A.
115 F10 Live Oak FL U.S.A.
37 L6 Liverdun France
208 H5 Liveringa W.A. Austr.
124 K4 Livermore CA U.S.A.
123 L11 Livermore, Mount TX U.S.A.
117 □O4 Livermore Falls ME U.S.A.
43 H6 Livernon France
205 M5 Liverpool N.S.W. Austr.
206 E2 Liverpool r. N.T. Austr.
109 H4 Liverpool N.S. Can.
29 L7 Liverpool Merseyside, England U.K.
117 I5 Liverpool NY U.S.A.
118 B3 Liverpool PA U.S.A.
105 K2 Liverpool, Cape Nunavut Can.
104 E3 Liverpool Bay N.W.T. Can.
29 K7 Liverpool Bay England U.K.
205 M4 Liverpool Plains N.S.W. Austr.
205 L4 Liverpool Range mts N.S.W. Austr.
29 N6 Liversedge West Yorkshire, England U.K.
72 G3 Lividonia, Punta pt Italy
70 I2 Livigno Italy
127 O10 Livingston Guat.
26 I11 Livingston West Lothian, Scotland U.K.
121 K9 Livingston AL U.S.A.
124 L4 Livingston CA U.S.A.
116 A11 Livingston KY U.S.A.
121 J10 Livingston LA U.S.A.
122 I4 Livingston MT U.S.A.
119 G3 Livingston NJ U.S.A.
121 H10 Livingston TX U.S.A.
121 H10 Livingston, Lake TX U.S.A.
91 E9 Livingstone Zambia
93 B7 Livingstone Mountains Tanz.
93 B7 Livingstonia Malawi
212 T2 Livingston Island Antarctica
117 K7 Livingston Manor NY U.S.A.
203 C11 Livingston Mountains South I. N.Z.
68 F4 Livno Bos.-Herz.
19 U9 Livny Rus. Fed.
20 U4 Livo r. Rus. Fed.
71 R4 Livold Slovenia
111 K7 Livonia MI U.S.A.
116 H6 Livonia NY U.S.A.
70 I8 Livorno Italy
70 J9 Livorno prov. Italy
70 E5 Livorno Ferraris Italy
40 D6 Livradois, Monts du mts France
40 D5 Livradois Forez, Parc Naturel Régional du nature res. France
98 □1b Livramento São Miguel Azores
140 E5 Livramento do Brumado Brazil
41 F7 Livron-sur-Drôme France
55 J3 Liw Pol.
187 M3 Liwā Oman
190 E6 Liwāʹ, Wādī al watercourse Syria
93 C7 Liwale Tanz.
93 C7 Liwale Juu Tanz.
55 J3 Liwiec r. Pol.
93 B8 Liwonde Malawi
93 B8 Liwonde National Park Malawi
Liwu Hebei China see Lixian
168 I9 Lixian Gansu China
169 N7 Lixian Hebei China
171 H4 Lixian Hunan China
170 D3 Lixian Sichuan China
171 K2 Lixin Anhui China
37 M5 Lixing-lès-St-Avold France
78 B4 Lixouri Kefallonia Greece
Lixus Morocco see Larache
78 C2 Liyadero Greece
Liyang Anhui China see Hexian
Liyang Hunan China see Lixian
171 L3 Liyang Jiangsu China
62 C9 Liz r. Port.
30 B8 Lizard Cornwall, England U.K.
140 D4 Lizarda Brazil
207 J3 Lizard Island Qld Austr.
30 B8 Lizard Point England U.K.
63 P3 Lizarraga Spain
116 D10 Lizemores WV U.S.A.
17 S3 Lizinovka Rus. Fed.
170 D4 Liziping Sichuan China
42 E5 Lizonne r. France
36 F5 Lizy-sur-Ourcq France
75 O3 Lizzanello Italy
75 M3 Lizzano Italy
76 I6 Ljig Srbija Serb. and Mont.
22 D2 Ljomsnuten mt. Norway
68 F3 Ljubija Bos.-Herz.
76 H7 Ljubišnja mts Serb. and Mont.
68 E2 Ljubljana Slovenia
59 J7 Ljubljana airport Slovenia
59 K7 Ljubljanica r. Slovenia
76 H6 Ljubovija Srbija Serb. and Mont.
68 F4 Ljubuški Bos.-Herz.
23 O4 Ljugarn Gotland Sweden
20 N5 Ljungå Sweden
21 N5 Ljungan r. Sweden
21 N5 Ljungaverk Sweden
23 J5 Ljungby Sweden
23 M5 Ljungbyån r. Sweden
20 L5 Ljungdalen Sweden
23 L3 Ljungsbro Sweden
22 H3 Ljungskile Sweden
21 N6 Ljusdal Sweden
23 L3 Ljusfallshammar Sweden
22 J1 Ljusnan r. Sweden
21 N6 Ljusnan r. Sweden
21 N6 Ljusne Sweden
68 F2 Ljutomer Slovenia
66 K4 Llagostera Spain
146 B6 Llaima, Volcán vol. Chile
147 G2 Llambí Campbell Arg.
30 D2 Llanaelhaearn Gwynedd, Wales U.K.
30 F2 Llanarmon Dyffryn Ceiriog Wrexham, Wales U.K.
30 D3 Llanarth Ceredigion, Wales U.K.
30 D4 Llanarthney Carmarthenshire, Wales U.K.
30 F1 Llanasa Flintshire, Wales U.K.
30 D3 Llanbadarn Fawr Ceredigion, Wales U.K.
30 D1 Llanbadrig Isle of Anglesey, Wales U.K.
Llanbedr Ceredigion, Wales U.K. see Lampeter
30 D2 Llanbedr Gwynedd, Wales U.K.
30 D2 Llanbedrog Gwynedd, Wales U.K.
Llanbedr Pont Steffan Wales U.K. see Lampeter
30 D1 Llanberis Gwynedd, Wales U.K.
30 F3 Llanbister Powys, Wales U.K.
30 E2 Llanbryn-mair Powys, Wales U.K.
66 L3 Llançà Spain
146 C4 Llancanelo, Laguna l. Arg.
146 C4 Llancanelo, Salina salt flat Arg.
30 D2 Llandanwg Gwynedd, Wales U.K.
30 D4 Llanddarog Carmarthenshire, Wales U.K.
30 D1 Llanddeiniolen Gwynedd, Wales U.K.
30 E2 Llandderfel Gwynedd, Wales U.K.
30 C4 Llanddowror Carmarthenshire, Wales U.K.
30 E4 Llandeilo Carmarthenshire, Wales U.K.
30 G4 Llandinabo Herefordshire, England U.K.
30 F3 Llandinam Powys, Wales U.K.
30 C4 Llandissilio Pembrokeshire, Wales U.K.
30 E4 Llandovery Carmarthenshire, Wales U.K.
30 F2 Llandrillo Denbighshire, Wales U.K.
30 F3 Llandrindod Wells Powys, Wales U.K.
30 E1 Llandudno Conwy, Wales U.K.
30 D1 Llandwrog Gwynedd, Wales U.K.
30 D4 Llandybie Carmarthenshire, Wales U.K.
30 D3 Llandysul Ceredigion, Wales U.K.
30 D4 Llanegwad Carmarthenshire, Wales U.K.
30 D1 Llaneilian Isle of Anglesey, Wales U.K.
30 D4 Llanelli Carmarthenshire, Wales U.K.
30 E2 Llanelltyd Gwynedd, Wales U.K.
30 F4 Llanelly Monmouthshire, Wales U.K.
63 K2 Llanes Spain
30 D1 Llanfaelog Isle of Anglesey, Wales U.K.
30 F2 Llanfair Caereinion Powys, Wales U.K.
30 E1 Llanfairfechan Conwy, Wales U.K.
30 D1 Llanfairpwllgwyngyll Isle of Anglesey, Wales U.K.
30 E1 Llanfair Talhaiarn Conwy, Wales U.K.
30 C1 Llanfair-yn-Neubwll Isle of Anglesey, Wales U.K.
30 D3 Llanfarian Ceredigion, Wales U.K.
30 D3 Llanfihangel-ar-Arth Carmarthenshire, Wales U.K.
30 F2 Llanfyllin Powys, Wales U.K.
30 F1 Llanfynydd Flintshire, Wales U.K.
30 F2 Llangadfan Powys, Wales U.K.
30 E4 Llangadog Carmarthenshire, Wales U.K.
30 D1 Llangefni Isle of Anglesey, Wales U.K.
30 D3 Llangeler Carmarthenshire, Wales U.K.
30 D2 Llangelynin Gwynedd, Wales U.K.
30 D4 Llangendeirne Carmarthenshire, Wales U.K.
30 E1 Llangernyw Conwy, Wales U.K.
30 D1 Llangoed Isle of Anglesey, Wales U.K.
30 F2 Llangollen Denbighshire, Wales U.K.
30 D3 Llangrannog Ceredigion, Wales U.K.
30 D1 Llangristiolus Isle of Anglesey, Wales U.K.
30 D4 Llangunnor Carmarthenshire, Wales U.K.
30 E3 Llangurig Powys, Wales U.K.
30 C4 Llangwm Pembrokeshire, Wales U.K.
30 F4 Llangynidr Powys, Wales U.K.
30 F4 Llanharan Rhondda Cynon Taff, Wales U.K.
30 E3 Llanidloes Powys, Wales U.K.
30 D3 Llanilar Ceredigion, Wales U.K.
30 F4 Llanishen Cardiff, Wales U.K.
30 F2 Llanllwchaiarn Powys, Wales U.K.
30 D1 Llanllyfni Gwynedd, Wales U.K.
30 D1 Llannerch-y-medd Isle of Anglesey, Wales U.K.
30 D4 Llannon Carmarthenshire, Wales U.K.
30 D3 Llan-non Ceredigion, Wales U.K.
30 D2 Llannor Gwynedd, Wales U.K.
126 D2 Llano Mex.
121 F10 Llano TX U.S.A.
121 F10 Llano r. TX U.S.A.
121 D9 Llano Estacado plain NM/TX U.S.A.
128 B2 Llano Grande Durango Mex.
128 B3 Llano Grande Nayarit Mex.
136 D3 Llanos plain Col./Venez.
145 B6 Llanquihue, Lago l. Chile
30 F2 Llanrhaeadr-ym-Mochnant Powys, Wales U.K.
30 D4 Llanrhidian Swansea, Wales U.K.
30 D3 Llanrhystud Ceredigion, Wales U.K.
30 D1 Llanrug Gwynedd, Wales U.K.
30 F4 Llanrumney Cardiff, Wales U.K.
30 E1 Llanrwst Conwy, Wales U.K.
Llansá Spain see Llançà
30 E1 Llansanffraid Glan Conwy Conwy, Wales U.K.
30 E1 Llansannan Conwy, Wales U.K.
30 D3 Llansawel Carmarthenshire, Wales U.K.
30 D4 Llansteffan Carmarthenshire, Wales U.K.
Llanstephan Carmarthenshire, Wales U.K. see Llansteffan
30 F4 Llanthony Monmouthshire, Wales U.K.
30 F4 Llantilio Pertholey Monmouthshire, Wales U.K.
30 G4 Llantrisant Monmouthshire, Wales U.K.
30 F4 Llantrisant Rhondda Cynon Taff, Wales U.K.
30 F5 Llantwit Major Vale of Glamorgan, Wales U.K.
30 E2 Llanuwchllyn Gwynedd, Wales U.K.
30 F2 Llanwddyn Powys, Wales U.K.
30 D3 Llanwenog Ceredigion, Wales U.K.
30 D1 Llanwnda Gwynedd, Wales U.K.
30 F2 Llanwnog Powys, Wales U.K.
30 E4 Llanwrda Carmarthenshire, Wales U.K.
30 E3 Llanwrtyd Wells Powys, Wales U.K.
30 D3 Llanybydder Carmarthenshire, Wales U.K.
Llanymddyfri Carmarthenshire, Wales U.K. see Llandovery
Llanymddyfri Wales U.K. see Llandovery
30 C1 Llanynghenedl Isle of Anglesey, Wales U.K.
30 D2 Llanystumdwy Gwynedd, Wales U.K.
66 G5 Llardecans Spain
138 A2 Llata Peru
67 E9 Llaurí Spain
66 H2 Llavorsí Spain
30 F1 Llay Wrexham, Wales U.K.
146 B3 Llay-Llay Chile
67 K9 Llebeig, Cap de c. Spain
30 E3 Lledrod Ceredigion, Wales U.K.
66 G4 Lleida Spain
66 H3 Lleida prov. Cataluña Spain
67 H10 Llentrisca, Cap c. Spain
64 G4 Llera Spain
129 H2 Llera de Canales Mex.
64 G4 Llerena Spain
30 C2 Lleyn Peninsula Wales U.K.
138 C4 Llica Bol.
67 D8 Lliria Spain
66 I3 Llívia Spain
66 H4 Llobregós r. Spain
63 O2 Llodio Spain
146 B3 Llolleo Chile
66 I5 Llorenç del Penedès Spain
66 K4 Lloret de Mar Spain
78 A2 Llorgara nat. park Albania
67 D9 Llosa de Ranes Spain
67 K8 Lloseta Spain
207 I2 Lloyd Bay Qld Austr.
106 E3 Lloyd George, Mount B.C. Can.
119 I3 Lloyd Harbor NY U.S.A.
107 I3 Lloyd Lake Sask. Can.
107 I4 Lloydminster Alta Can.
67 L8 Llubí Spain
Lluchmayor Spain see Llucmajor
67 K9 Llucmajor Spain
130 □ Lluidas Vale Jamaica
138 C6 Llullaillaco, Parque Nacional nat. park Chile
138 C6 Llullaillaco, Volcán vol. Chile
Llyn Tegid Wales U.K. see Bala Lake
30 F3 Llyswen Powys, Wales U.K.
54 G2 Lniano Pol.
45 C7 Lo Belgium
Lo i. Vanuatu see Loh
158 G4 Lô, Sông r. China/Vietnam
138 C5 Loa r. Chile
125 U3 Loa UT U.S.A.
157 K3 Loagan Bunut National Park Malaysia
157 L5 Loakulu Kalimantan Indon.
142 A5 Loanda Brazil
26 J11 Loanhead Midlothian, Scotland U.K.
70 E7 Loano Italy
26 G11 Loans South Ayrshire, Scotland U.K.
66 D3 Loarre Spain
154 E7 Loay Bohol Phil.
19 S5 Lobʹ r. Rus. Fed.
55 M5 Lobachivka Ukr.
97 P2 Lobamba Swaziland
14 J4 Lobanʹ r. Rus. Fed.
19 V8 Lobanovo Rus. Fed.
155 C5 Lobata Sulawesi Indon.
65 K6 Lobatejo mt. Spain
94 E5 Lobatse Botswana
51 K8 Löbau Ger.
90 C3 Lobaye pref. C.A.R.
90 C4 Lobaye r. C.A.R.
41 K7 Lobbie, Cima delle mt. Italy
51 E7 Löbejün Ger.
51 G8 Löbenberg hill Ger.
66 C3 Lobera de Onsella Spain
147 H6 Loberia Arg.
54 D2 Łobez Pol.
154 E6 Lobi, Mount vol. Phil.
200 □3b Lobikaere i. Majuro Marshall Is
44 J5 Lobith Neth.
91 B8 Lobito Angola
136 A6 Lobitos Peru
50 G2 Löbnitz Mecklenburg-Vorpommern Ger.
51 F7 Löbnitz Sachsen Ger.
19 U5 Lobnya Rus. Fed.
90 C5 Loboko Congo
60 C3 Lobón Spain
147 H4 Lobos Arg.
98 □3b Lobos i. Canary Is
65 O5 Lobos mt. Spain
126 C3 Lobos, Cabo c. Mex.
126 D4 Lobos, Isla i. Mex.
129 J4 Lobos, Isla de i. Mex.
146 A4 Lobos, Punta de pt Chile
130 E2 Lobos Cay i. Cuba
136 A6 Lobos de Afuera, Islas is Peru
136 A6 Lobos de Tierra, Isla i. Peru
Lobositz Czech Rep. see Lovosice
17 N5 Loboykivka Ukr.
51 F8 Lobstädt Ger.
51 F6 Loburg Ger.
203 G10 Loburn South I. N.Z.
54 F2 Łobżenica Pol.
70 C5 Locana Italy
70 F3 Locarno Switz.
158 H4 Lôc Binh Vietnam
49 H6 Loccum (Rehburg-Loccum) Ger.
72 D8 Loceri Sardegna Italy
26 G9 Lochaber reg. Scotland U.K.
26 E9 Lochailort Highland, Scotland U.K.
26 E9 Lochaline Highland, Scotland U.K.
111 J1 Lochalsh Ont. Can.
26 F13 Lochans Dumfries and Galloway, Scotland U.K.
26 I12 Locharbriggs Dumfries and Galloway, Scotland U.K.
58 A4 Lochau Austria
171 □J7 Lo Chau i. H.K. China
26 F10 Lochawe Argyll and Bute, Scotland U.K.
26 H10 Lochay r. Scotland U.K.
Loch Baghasdail Western Isles, Scotland U.K. see Lochboisdale
26 B8 Lochboisdale Western Isles, Scotland U.K.
26 E10 Lochbuie Argyll and Bute, Scotland U.K.
26 E8 Lochcarron Highland, Scotland U.K.
26 E10 Lochdon Argyll and Bute, Scotland U.K.
26 H10 Lochearnhead Stirling, Scotland U.K.
44 J4 Lochem Neth.
58 H3 Lochen Austria
26 H8 Lochend Highland, Scotland U.K.
207 I8 Lochern National Park Qld Austr.
42 F1 Loches France
26 J10 Lochgelly Fife, Scotland U.K.
26 F10 Lochgilphead Argyll and Bute, Scotland U.K.
26 G10 Lochgoilhead Argyll and Bute, Scotland U.K.
203 C13 Lochiel South I. N.Z.
97 O2 Lochiel S. Africa
91 E8 Lochinvar National Park Zambia
26 F6 Lochinver Highland, Scotland U.K.
26 G10 Loch Lomond and the Trossachs National Park Scotland U.K.
26 J12 Lochmaben Dumfries and Galloway, Scotland U.K.
26 B7 Lochmaddy Western Isles, Scotland U.K.
203 C11 Lochnagar l. South I. N.Z.
26 J9 Lochnagar mt. Scotland U.K.
Loch na Madadh Western Isles, Scotland U.K. see Lochmaddy
56 C2 Lochovice Czech Rep.
55 J3 Łochów Pol.
26 F11 Lochranza North Ayrshire, Scotland U.K.
118 B6 Loch Raven Reservoir MD U.S.A.
45 E6 Lochristi Belgium
122 G3 Lochsa r. ID U.S.A.
26 B8 Loch Sgioport Western Isles, Scotland U.K.
26 G11 Lochwinnoch Renfrewshire, Scotland U.K.
26 G9 Lochy, Loch l. Scotland U.K.
204 E5 Lock S.A. Austr.
116 C9 Lockbourne OH U.S.A.
116 I6 Locke NY U.S.A.
124 K3 Lockeford CA U.S.A.
59 N5 Lockenhaus Austria
26 J12 Lockerbie Dumfries and Galloway, Scotland U.K.
208 C6 Locker Point W.A. Austr.
205 K6 Lockhart N.S.W. Austr.
121 G11 Lockhart TX U.S.A.
207 I2 Lockhart River Qld Austr.
207 I2 Lockhart River Aboriginal Reserve Qld Austr.
116 H7 Lock Haven PA U.S.A.
30 G5 Locking North Somerset, England U.K.
50 J4 Löcknitz Ger.
50 D4 Löcknitz r. Ger.
116 G5 Lockport NY U.S.A.
31 J6 Locks Heath Hampshire, England U.K.
29 P5 Lockton North Yorkshire, England U.K.
38 E7 Locmaria France
38 B5 Locmaria-Plouzané France
38 F6 Locmariaquer France
38 F6 Locminé France
38 E6 Locmiquélic France
159 H9 Lôc Ninh Vietnam
38 E6 Locoal-Mendon France
73 P5 Locone r. Italy
75 M2 Locorotondo Italy
38 D4 Locquirec France
75 K7 Locri Italy
38 C5 Locronan France
38 C6 Loctudy France
72 D7 Loculi Sardegna Italy
138 C4 Locumba r. Peru
119 G4 Locust NJ U.S.A.
119 H3 Locust Valley NY U.S.A.
190 C7 Lod Israel
51 E7 Lödderitz Ger.
50 J2 Loddin Ger.
30 E7 Loddiswell Devon, England U.K.
205 I6 Loddon r. Vic. Austr.
31 O2 Loddon Norfolk, England U.K.
72 D6 Lodè Sardegna Italy
18 I4 Lode Latvia
128 B5 Lo de Marcos Mex.
56 D1 Loděnice Czech Rep.
51 E8 Lodersleben Ger.
41 C9 Lodève France
19 Q1 Lodeynoye Pole Rus. Fed.
106 B3 Lodge, Mount Can./U.S.A.
107 I5 Lodge Creek r. Can./U.S.A.
122 K4 Lodge Grass MT U.S.A.
120 D5 Lodgepole Creek r. WY U.S.A.
178 G9 Lodhikheda Madh. Prad. India
185 N7 Lodhran Pak.
70 H5 Lodi Italy
70 H5 Lodi prov. Italy
124 K3 Lodi CA U.S.A.
119 G3 Lodi NJ U.S.A.
116 C7 Lodi OH U.S.A.
110 E6 Lodi WI U.S.A.
20 M3 Løding Norway
20 M2 Lødingen Norway
70 G5 Lodi Vecchio Italy
91 D5 Lodja Dem. Rep. Congo
201 □1a Lodoni Viti Levu Fiji
63 P4 Lodosa Spain
63 Q5 Lodosa, Canal de Spain
178 C8 Lodrani Gujarat India
92 B4 Lodwar Kenya
55 H6 Łodygowice Pol.
55 H4 Łódź Pol.
55 H4 Łódzkie prov. Pol.
63 N8 Loeches Spain
158 E6 Loei Thai.
44 J4 Loenen Gelderland Neth.
44 H4 Loenen Utrecht Neth.
97 J9 Loerie S. Africa
96 D6 Loeriesfontein S. Africa
49 D10 Löf Ger.
58 G4 Lofer Austria
52 E6 Löffingen Ger.
20 L2 Lofoten is Norway
21 L5 Lofsdalen Sweden
97 J6 Lofter S. Africa
29 P4 Loftus Redcar and Cleveland, England U.K.
209 E8 Lofty Range hills W.A. Austr.
92 B4 Lofusa Sudan
15 H6 Log Rus. Fed.
59 I7 Log Slovenia
89 F3 Loga Niger
96 I1 Logageng S. Africa

Column 1

26 H12 Logan East Ayrshire, Scotland U.K.
20 H5 Logan IA U.S.A.
21 D8 Logan NM U.S.A.
16 C9 Logan UT U.S.A.
22 I6 Logan UT U.S.A.
16 D11 Logan WV U.S.A.
06 A2 Logan, Mount Y.T. Can.
22 D2 Logan, Mount WA U.S.A.
07 K6 Logan Creek r. Qld Austr.
06 G5 Logan Creek r. NE U.S.A.
06 F5 Logandale NV U.S.A.
06 G5 Logan Lake B.C. Can.
06 F2 Logan Mountains N.W.T./Y.T. Can.
14 D5 Logansport IN U.S.A.
21 I10 Logansport LA U.S.A.
18 B5 Logatec Slovenia
68 E3 Lögda r. Sweden
20 O4 Lögdeälven r. Sweden
91 B6 Loge r. Angola
24 H2 Loggerheads Staffordshire, England U.K.
22 D3 Logna r. Norway
38 H7 Logne r. France
80 B1 Logone r. Africa
89 I4 Logone Birni Cameroon
90 B2 Logone Occidental pref. Chad
90 C2 Logone Oriental pref. Chad
68 D5 Logoualé Côte d'Ivoire
68 G9 Logouan Qinghai China
77 L6 Logreşti Romania
63 P4 Logroño Spain
65 I2 Logrosán Spain
79 N7 Logtak Lake India
72 B6 Logudoro reg. Sardegna Italy
22 E6 Løgumkloster Denmark
00 □5 Loh i. Vanuatu
22 C5 Lohals Denmark
91 D8 Lohardaga Jharkhand India
78 E5 Lohardaga Jharkhand India
86 H4 Loharu Haryana India
98 □¹⁰ Lohatha S. Africa
78 D6 Lohawat Rajasthan India
53 O3 Lohberg Ger.
38 H6 Lohéac France
48 H2 Lohe-Rickelshof Ger.
— Lohfelden Ger.
— Lohifushi i. N. Male Maldives see Lhohifushi
21 T6 Lohilahti Fin.
20 R3 Lohinina Fin.
21 R6 Lohja Fin.
18 G1 Lohjanjärvi l. Fin.
39 D9 Lohmar Ger.
51 J9 Lohme Ger.
50 F3 Lohmen Mecklenburg-Vorpommern Ger.
51 J9 Lohmen Sachsen Ger.
49 F9 Lohne Ger.
48 F5 Lohne Ger.
48 F5 Löhne Ger.
48 F5 Lohne (Oldenburg) Ger.
— Lohnsburg am Kobernaußerwald Austria
52 H2 Lohr r. Ger.
49 G9 Lohra Ger.
52 H7 Lohr am Main Ger.
48 J8 Lohsa Ger.
20 Q4 Lohtaja Fin.
58 H3 Lohusuu Estonia
58 E4 Loi, Nam r. Myanmar
71 K7 Loiano Italy
53 M4 Loiching Ger.
38 J6 Loigné-sur-Mayenne France
56 C7 Loigny-la-Bataille France
58 C5 Loikaw Myanmar
58 C5 Loi Lan mt. Myanmar/Thai.
90 C4 Loile r. Dem. Rep. Congo
58 C4 Loi-lem Myanmar
58 D3 Loi Lan Myanmar
41 Q6 Loimaa Fin.
18 F1 Loimaa kunta Fin.
18 F1 Loimijoki r. Fin.
38 E6 Loing r. France
58 C2 Loipyet Hills Myanmar
56 C7 Loir, r. France
56 C7 Loir, Les Vaux du val. France
39 J6 Loiré France
38 E7 Loire dept France
39 G7 Loire r. France
38 G7 Loire, Canal latéral à la France
40 E5 Loire, Gorges de la France
38 G7 Loire, Val de val. France
38 G7 Loire-Atlantique dept France
— Loire-Inférieure dept France see Loire-Atlantique
40 E5 Loire-sur-Rhône France
38 E6 Loiret dept France
56 C8 Loiret r. France
56 C8 Loir-et-Cher dept France
72 C6 Loiri-Porto San Paolo Sardegna Italy
39 J5 Loiron France
46 C5 Loisach r. Ger.
54 C4 Loi Sang mt. Myanmar
39 J6 Loise r. France
38 D7 Loison r. France
58 C2 Loi Song mt. Myanmar
38 H5 Loisy-sur-Marne France
96 I3 Loita Plains Kenya
52 F5 Loitz Ger.
92 F5 Loivos Port.
91 □¹ Loivos do Monte Port.
89 □¹ Loiza Aldea Puerto Rico
63 I3 Loja Ecuador
90 B6 Loja prov. Ecuador
95 H3 Loja Spain
66 E5 Lokachi Ukr.
67 L2 Lokan r. Malaysia
58 S2 Lokandu Dem. Rep. Congo
62 S3 Lokan tekojärvi l. Fin.
64 C4 Lokavec Slovenia
18 I5 Lokbatan Azer.
47 I2 Lokca Slovakia
42 H2 Lokchim r. Rus. Fed.
45 F6 Loken Norway
41 N5 Lokeren Belgium
93 U6 Loket Czech Rep.
44 D5 Lokgwabe Botswana
97 M3 Lokhvytsya Ukr.
92 B4 Lokichar Kenya
85 B4 Lokichokio Kenya
65 B4 Lokilalaki, Gunung mt. Indon.
60 S3 Lokitaung Kenya
60 S3 Loken r. Fin.
58 F4 Lakken Denmark
20 J5 Lakken Norway
19 N5 Loknya Rus. Fed.
90 D5 Loko Nigeria
90 C5 Lokofe Dem. Rep. Congo
96 G3 Lokoja Nigeria
90 C5 Lokolo r. Dem. Rep. Congo
90 C5 Lokolo i. Dem. Rep. Congo
90 I6 Lokomo Cameroon
90 C5 Lokona Dem. Rep. Congo
00 C4 Lokosafa C.A.R.
90 B5 Lökösháza Hungary
90 C5 Lokossa Benin
51 R9 Lokot' Rus. Fed.
18 I2 Loksa Estonia
08 I4 Loks Land i. Nunavut Can.
40 □ Lokuru New Georgia Is Solomon Is
91 ¹ R5 Lokve Croatia
91 J7 Lokve Slovenia
90 C4 Lol r. Sudan
90 C4 Lol watercourse Sudan
90 B5 Lola Guinea
13 C6 Lola, Mount CA U.S.A.
22 H7 Lolishniy Shepit Ukr.
22 D7 Lolland i. Denmark
90 D10 Lollar Ger.
92 B5 Lolle watercourse Sudan
95 H1 L'Olleria Spain
93 B5 Lollondo Tanz.

Column 2

90 D4 Lolo Dem. Rep. Congo
22 G3 Lolo MT U.S.A.
155 F3 Lolobata Halmahera Indon.
155 E3 Loloda Halmahera Indon.
155 E2 Loloda Utara, Kepulauan i. Maluku Indon.
89 H6 Lolodorf Cameroon
146 B4 Lolol Chile
122 G3 Lolo Pass MT U.S.A.
155 D8 Lolotoi East Timor
171 J6 Lolvavana, Passage Vanuatu
77 L1 Lom Bulg.
77 L7 Lom r. Bulg.
51 I9 Lom Czech Rep.
21 J6 Lom Norway
170 E4 Lom Rus. Fed.
125 X2 Loma CO U.S.A.
138 D2 Loma Alta Bol.
129 L7 Loma Bonita Mex.
65 M4 Loma de Chiclana reg. Spain
146 C5 Loma del Jaguel Moro Arg.
65 M5 Loma de Úbeda reg. Spain
43 F8 Lomagne reg. France
90 D4 Lomako r. Dem. Rep. Congo
124 O7 Loma Linda CA U.S.A.
199 I3 Lomaloma Fiji
91 E4 Lomami r. Dem. Rep. Congo
88 C4 Loma Mountains Sierra Leone
147 G5 Loma Negra Arg.
185 L5 Lomar Pass Afgh.
138 B3 Lomas Peru
212 T3 Lomas, Bahía de b. Chile
145 D6 Lomas Coloradas hills Arg.
147 N1 Lomas de Zamora Arg.
147 H4 Lomatí r. S. Africa see Mlumati
147 H4 Loma Verde Arg.
201 □¹ᵃ Lomawai Viti Levu Fiji
55 L4 Łomazy Pol.
91 D8 Lomba r. Angola
98 □¹ᵇ Lomba da Fazenda São Miguel Azores
42 B3 Lomba da Maia São Miguel Azores
27 G5 Lombarda, Serra hills Brazil
70 H5 Lombardia admin. reg. Italy
70 H5 Lombardina W.A. Austr.
43 I8 Lombers France
43 F9 Lombez France
155 C8 Lomblen i. Indon.
157 L9 Lombok Lombok Indon.
157 L9 Lombok i. Indon.
157 K9 Lombok, Selat sea chan. Indon.
39 L5 Lombron France
89 F5 Lomé Togo
90 D5 Lomela Dem. Rep. Congo
90 D5 Lomela r. Dem. Rep. Congo
70 F5 Lomello Italy
55 I3 Łomianki Pol.
89 I6 Lomié Cameroon
110 F6 Lomira WI U.S.A.
51 H8 Lommatzsch Ger.
36 E2 Lomme France
45 H6 Lommel Belgium
54 D3 Łomna r. Pol.
56 D2 Lomná r. Czech Rep.
56 D2 Lomnice r. Czech Rep.
59 K1 Lomnice nad Lužnicí Czech Rep.
57 L5 Lomnice nad Lužnicí Czech Rep.
212 U2 Lomnice nad Popelkou Czech Rep.
57 K5 Lomnice nad Popelkou Czech Rep.
207 L7 Lomo mt. Slovakia
109 J3 Lomond Nfld and Lab. Can.
26 G10 Lomond, Loch I. Scotland U.K.
109 H4 Lomond I. Scotland U.K.
108 E2 Lomond Nunavut Can.
218 M1 Lomonosov Rus. Fed.
177 M6 Lomonosov Ridge sea feature Arctic Ocean
40 J2 Lomont hills France
14 H2 Lomovoye Rus. Fed.
— Lomphat Cambodia see Lumphăt
155 A6 Lompobattang, Gunung mt. Indon.
124 L7 Lompoc CA U.S.A.
158 E6 Lom Sak Thai.
31 J3 Łomża Pol.
142 L6 Łomżyński Pol.
169 R3 Lonar r. India
169 Q6 Lonar India
169 Q8 Lonato Italy
176 C3 Lonavale Mahar. India
56 C6 Lončarica Croatia
117 □1 Loncem Chile
108 C3 Loncoche Chile
117 K5 Loncopangue Chile
146 B6 Loncoque r. Arg.
179 M8 Londa Bangl.
71 L8 Londa India
91 B6 Londela-Kayes Congo
45 F7 Londerzeel Belgium
36 B4 Londinières France
— Londinium Greater London, England U.K. see London
170 F5 London Kiribati
45 H9 London U.K.
170 E4 London Ont. Can.
117 M6 London Ont. Can.
31 N3 London area map U.K.
— London Bridge i. Grenada
31 □ London City airport England U.K.
— Londonderry Northern Ireland U.K.
170 F7 Londonderry county Northern Ireland U.K.
117 M5 Londonderry VT U.S.A.
208 I2 Londonderry, Cape W.A. Austr.
145 C9 Londonderry, Isla i. Chile
170 F7 Londoni Fiji see Lodoni
144 D2 Londres Arg.
142 B5 Londrina Brazil
91 B8 Londuimbali Angola
111 M4 Lonely Island Ont. Can.
95 F3 Lonely Mine Zimbabwe
119 I3 Lonelyville NY U.S.A.
124 N5 Lone Pine CA U.S.A.
15 D5 Long Thai.
26 G10 Long, Loch inlet Argyll and Bute, Scotland U.K.
159 H10 Long Phu Vietnam
91 C9 Longa Angola
91 C9 Longa r. Cuando Cubango Angola
91 B7 Longa r. Angola
78 C6 Longa Greece
193 S2 Longa, Proliv sea chan. Rus. Fed.
43 G9 Longages France
157 K3 Longageng Kalimantan Indon.
92 B3 Longagun Sudan
157 K3 Long Akah Sarawak Malaysia
91 D9 Longa-Mavinga, Coutada Pública do rio Angola
36 C3 Long'an Guangxi China
99 □³ᵇ Longani, Baie de b. Mayotte
162 C6 Longanqiao Heilong. China
29 M5 Longar India
12 E8 Longarni Italy
157 K3 Longares Spain
171 L4 Longarone Italy
171 M4 Longarsh W. Somerset, England U.K.
171 M4 Longavi Chile
109 J3 Longavi, Nevado de mt. Chile
42 D3 Longba Jamaica
130 □ Long Bay b. Jamaica
207 M7 Long Bay b. Jamaica
119 I9 Long Beach CA U.S.A.
119 I9 Long Beach WA U.S.A.
122 A3 Long Beach WA U.S.A.
119 G5 Long Beach coastal area NJ U.S.A.

Column 3

31 K2 Long Bennington Lincolnshire, England U.K.
29 N3 Longbenton Tyne and Wear, England U.K.
157 K3 Longberini Kalimantan Indon.
157 L3 Longbia Kalimantan Indon.
157 K4 Longbo Kalimantan Indon.
117 L8 Long Branch NJ U.S.A.
30 H5 Longbridge Deverill Wiltshire, England U.K.
171 J6 Longbu Jiangxi China
31 J3 Long Buckby Northamptonshire, England U.K.
202 J7 Longburn North I. N.Z.
130 F2 Long Cay i. Bahamas
170 E4 Longcha Sichuan China
40 H4 Longchamois France
— Longcheng Guangdong China see Longmen
171 J6 Longchuan Yunnan China see Chengxi
— Longchuan Yunnan China see Nanhua
170 A6 Longchuan Guangdong China
170 A7 Longchuan Jiang r. China
31 I4 Long Compton Warwickshire, England U.K.
204 E3 Long Creek watercourse Austr.
36 D4 Longeau France
42 D1 Longeau r. France
36 D2 Long Crendon Buckinghamshire, England U.K.
36 B4 Longde Ningxia China
36 B4 Longdon Staffordshire, England U.K.
124 I2 Longeau r. France
125 U7 Long Eaton Derbyshire, England U.K.
118 F3 Long Valley AZ U.S.A.
110 D4 Longetta WI U.S.A.
41 I9 Longues France
92 C4 Longue, Île i. Inner Islands Seychelles
36 D4 Longueau France
42 D1 Longué-Jumelles France
71 P9 Longuenesse France
109 H3 Longue-Pointe Que. Can.
117 L3 Longueuil Que. Can.
138 E3 Longueville France
137 G6 Longueville-sur-Scie France
154 E6 Longuyon France
124 I2 Longview TX U.S.A.
125 G3 Longview WA U.S.A.
157 I4 Longwa Kalimantan Indon.
162 H6 Longwangmiao Heilong. China
173 I10 Longwei Co i. Xizang China
28 D7 Longwood Rep. of Ireland
105 I3 Longwood St Helena
37 K4 Longwy France
122 K2 Longxi Gansu China
168 J3 Longxi Shaanxi China
171 K5 Longxi Shan mt. Fujian China
159 N8 Long Xuyên Vietnam
171 K6 Longyan Fujian China
169 N8 Longyao Hebei China
26 E10 Longyearbyen Svalbard
162 E4 Longzhen Heilong. China
170 F7 Longzhou Guangxi China
71 K5 Lonigo Italy
173 K12 Löningen Ger.
59 N8 Lonjica Croatia
68 F3 Lonjsko Polje plain Croatia
95 □K3 Lonkintsy Madag.
39 J4 Lonlay-l'Abbaye France
44 K4 Lonneker Neth.
36 I4 Lonny France
121 J8 Lonoke AR U.S.A.
147 I5 Lonquimay Arg.
146 B6 Lonquimay Chile
146 B6 Lonquimay, Volcán vol. Chile
43 D9 Lons France
— Lönsboda Sweden
39 J4 Lons-le-Saunier France
44 G5 Lonstrup Denmark
155 F5 Lontar i. Maluku Indon.
158 C2 Lonton Myanmar
137 I6 Lontra Brazil
71 K3 Lontra r. Brazil
45 I7 Lontué r. Chile
188 C4 Lontzen Belgium
57 L3 Lónya Hungary
18 H2 Loo Estonia
63 N3 Loo Rus. Fed.
62 H5 Looc Phil.
67 D8 Looe Cornwall, England U.K.
99 □³ᵃ Looking Glass r. MI U.S.A.
102 D2 Lookout, Cape Ont. Can.
115 I8 Lookout, Cape NC U.S.A.
124 N5 Lookout Mountain CA U.S.A.
123 K9 Lookout Point MT U.S.A.
67 D12 Lookout Ridge AK U.S.A.
127 J4 Loolmalasin vol. crater Tanz.
145 C6 Looma W.A. Austr.
208 H5 Loon W.A. Austr.
106 H3 Loon r. Alta Can.
209 I11 Loon Lake Sask. Can.
107 I4 Loon Lake ME U.S.A.
117 □P2 Loon op Zand Neth.
44 H5 Loop Head Rep. of Ireland
36 D2 Loon-Plage France
124 N6 Loonse en Drunense Duinen nature res. Neth.
145 C7 Loop Head Rep. of Ireland
130 C2 Loosdorf Austria
146 C3 Loose Kent, England U.K.
63 P3 Loosduinen S. Africa
173 E8 Lootsberg Pass S. Africa
17 P4 Lopan r. Xinjiang China
162 E4 Lopandino Rus. Fed.
95 H4 Lopar Croatia
19 U7 Lopasnya r. Rus. Fed.
191 I2 Lopatin Rus. Fed.
162 M3 Lopatina, Gora mt. Sakhalin Rus. Fed.
182 A1 Lopatinskiy Rus. Fed.
19 V6 Lopatino Rus. Fed.
193 Q3 Lopatka, Cape, Mys c. Rus. Fed.
193 Q4 Lopatka, Mys c. Rus. Fed.
16 G5 Lopatnic Moldova
18 L4 Lopatovo Ukr.
16 D3 Lopatyn Ukr.
16 D3 Lopatyn Ukr.
62 D4 Lopburi Thai.
90 C4 Lopburi r. Thai.
36 C3 Lop Buri Thai.
44 A5 Lope-Okanda, Réserve de nature res. Gabon
90 A5 Lopé-Okanda, Réserve de nature res. Gabon
91 R6 Lopeh Fiji
14 J3 Lopera Spain
55 I5 Lopez Phil.
63 P3 Lopez Luzon Phil.
118 C2 Lopez, Cap c. Gabon
90 A5 Lopez, Cap c. Gabon
19 N6 Lopik Neth.
172 J4 Lop Nur salt flat China
90 C4 Lopori r. Dem. Rep. Congo
44 C2 Loppersum Neth.
62 O2 Loppi Fin.
19 I5 Lopnur Rus. Fed.
55 I5 Lopuszno Pol.
63 B7 Lőr r. Spain
66 C5 Loscos Spain
63 P2 Lor r. Spain

Column 4

170 G4 Longshan Hunan China
— Longshan Hunan China see Longjiang
168 J3 Long Shan mts China
170 H6 Longsheng Guangxi China
30 □ Longsight England U.K.
168 G7 Longsong Shan mts China
203 A13 Long Sound inlet South I. N.Z.
122 L6 Longs Peak CO U.S.A.
31 O3 Long Stratton Norfolk, England U.K.
31 M2 Long Sutton Lincolnshire, England U.K.
30 G5 Long Sutton Somerset, England U.K.
157 K3 Long Teru Sarawak Malaysia
171 H4 Longtian Hunan China
106 G1 Longtom Lake N.W.T. Can.
97 O1 Long Tompas pass S. Africa
207 J6 Longton Qld Austr.
29 L6 Longton Lancashire, England U.K.
30 H2 Longton Stoke-on-Trent, England U.K.
169 R2 Longtou Nei Mongol China
29 L3 Longtown Cumbria, England U.K.
99 □²ᵇ Longue, Île i. Inner Islands Seychelles
36 D4 Longueau France
42 D1 Longué-Jumelles France
71 P9 Longuenesse France
109 H3 Longue-Pointe Que. Can.
117 L3 Longueuil Que. Can.
138 E3 Longueville France
137 G6 Longueville-sur-Scie France
154 E6 Longuyon France
124 I2 Longview TX U.S.A.
125 G3 Longview WA U.S.A.
157 I4 Longwa Kalimantan Indon.
162 H6 Longwangmiao Heilong. China
173 I10 Longwei Co i. Xizang China
28 D7 Longwood Rep. of Ireland
105 I3 Longwood St Helena
37 K4 Longwy France
122 K2 Longxi Gansu China
168 J3 Longxi Shaanxi China
171 K5 Longxi Shan mt. Fujian China
159 N8 Long Xuyên Vietnam
171 K6 Longyan Fujian China
169 N8 Longyao Hebei China
26 E10 Longyearbyen Svalbard
162 E4 Longzhen Heilong. China
170 F7 Longzhou Guangxi China
71 K5 Lonigo Italy
173 K12 Löningen Ger.
59 N8 Lonjica Croatia
68 F3 Lonjsko Polje plain Croatia
95 □K3 Lonkintsy Madag.
39 J4 Lonlay-l'Abbaye France
44 K4 Lonneker Neth.
36 I4 Lonny France
121 J8 Lonoke AR U.S.A.
147 I5 Lonquimay Arg.
146 B6 Lonquimay Chile
146 B6 Lonquimay, Volcán vol. Chile
43 D9 Lons France
— Lönsboda Sweden
39 J4 Lons-le-Saunier France
44 G5 Lonstrup Denmark
155 F5 Lontar i. Maluku Indon.
158 C2 Lonton Myanmar
137 I6 Lontra Brazil
71 K3 Lontra r. Brazil
45 I7 Lontué r. Chile
188 C4 Lontzen Belgium
57 L3 Lónya Hungary
18 H2 Loo Estonia
63 N3 Loo Rus. Fed.
62 H5 Looc Phil.
67 D8 Looe Cornwall, England U.K.
99 □³ᵃ Looking Glass r. MI U.S.A.

Column 5

52 H4 Lorch Baden-Württemberg Ger.
49 E10 Lorch Hessen Ger.
67 E10 Lorcha Spain
154 A6 Lord Auckland sea feature Phil.
62 D6 Lordelo Port.
— Lord Hood atoll Arch. des Tuamotu Fr. Polynesia see Marutea
204 □² Lord Howe Atoll Solomon Is see Ontong Java Atoll
216 F7 Lord Howe Island Austr.
— Lord Howe Rise sea feature S. Pacific Ocean
159 C9 Lord Loughborough Island Myanmar
62 E7 Lordosa Port.
123 J10 Lordsburg NM U.S.A.
155 E8 Lore East Timor
155 B4 Lore Lindu National Park Indon.
143 E5 Lorena Brazil
153 K7 Lorengau Admiralty Is P.N.G.
129 J3 Lorenzo Zacatecas Mex.
139 F5 Loreto Para.
154 E6 Loreto Prol.
73 L3 Loreto Aprutino Italy
110 D4 Loretta WI U.S.A.
41 I9 Lorgues France
92 C4 Loriac Kenya
136 C2 Lorica Col.
38 E6 Lorient Col.
42 C5 Loriga Port.
41 G8 Lorignac France
117 K3 L'Original Ont. Can.
162 H6 Loriguilla Spain
67 D8 Loriguilla, Embalse de resr Spain
185 J8 Lorikand Pak.
41 □ Lorino i. Nunavut Can.
105 I3 Lorinči Hungary
57 I4 Lórinci Hungary
122 K2 Loring MT U.S.A.
41 F7 Loriol-sur-Drôme France
40 D7 Lormes France
178 H8 Lormi Chhattisgarh India
43 C6 Lormont France
207 J8 Lorne Qld Austr.
205 I8 Lorne Vic. Austr.
206 F5 Lorne watercourse N.T. Austr.
173 K12 Lorn, Firth of est. Scotland U.K.
44 E5 Loro r. Spain
88 E4 Loropéni Burkina
73 K1 Loro Piceno Italy
43 G9 Lorp-Sentaraille France
37 M6 Lorquin France
52 D6 Lörrach Ger.
36 I4 Lorrain, Plateau France
145 D8 Lorraine Qld Austr.
37 L6 Lorraine admin. reg. France
37 K4 Lorraine reg. France
37 K7 Lorraine, Plaine plain France
37 E7 Lorrez-le-Bocage-Préaux France
36 E8 Lorris France
52 F7 Lorsch Ger.
209 T12 Lort r. W.A. Austr.
48 E5 Lörudden Sweden
87 H2 Lorzot Tunisia
88 B4 Los, Îles de i. Guinea
129 J4 Losa r. Spain
63 N3 Losa r. Spain
62 F5 Losacino Spain
67 D8 Los del Obispo Spain
65 O5 Losai National Reserve nature res. Kenya
178 E6 Losal Rajasthan India
126 H4 Los Alamitos, Sierra de mt. Mex.
124 L7 Los Alamos Chile
123 K9 Los Alamos NM U.S.A.
67 D12 Los Alcázares Spain
127 J4 Los Aldamas Mex.
145 C6 Los Alerces, Parque Nacional nat. park Arg.
65 C7 Los Algezares Spain
146 B3 Los Altos Mex.
128 G3 Los Amoles Mex.
144 F3 Los Amores Arg.
146 B3 Los Andes Chile
146 A5 Los Ángeles Chile
124 N6 Los Ángeles Aqueduct canal CA U.S.A.
145 C7 Los Antiguos Arg.
130 C2 Los Arabos Cuba
146 C3 Los Árboles Arg.
63 P3 Los Arcos Spain
19 E6 Los Arenales del Sol Spain
63 P8 Losares mt. Spain
64 H7 Los Argallanes, Sierra de hills Spain
146 A5 Los Arroyos Mex.
128 B4 Los Ayala Mex.
128 G6 Los Azufres, Parque Natural Mex.
126 F4 Los Baños Mex.
124 L4 Los Banos CA U.S.A.
65 O5 Los Barreros mt. Spain
64 I8 Los Barrios Spain
62 D3 Los Barrios de Luna Spain
67 D12 Los Belones Spain
65 K1 Los Bermejales, Embalse de resr Spain
146 A5 Los Blancos Arg.
126 E3 Los Caballos Mesteños, Llano de plain Mex.
130 D3 Los Canarreos, Archipiélago de is Cuba
64 F3 Los Canchales, Embalse de resr Spain
147 G5 Los Cardos Arg.
146 B5 Los Cardos Arg.
146 C2 Los Cerrillos Arg.
147 H2 Los Charrúas Arg.
129 K5 Los Chiles, Laguna i. Arg.
126 □C12 Los Chiles Costa Rica
145 B7 Los Chonos, Archipiélago de is Chile
19 E6 Los Choros, Islas de is Chile
146 C3 Los Cisnes, Lagunas de lakes Arg.
76 C5 Los Colorados Arg.
63 P8 Los Condores Arg.
146 C3 Los Conquistadores Arg.
63 L7 Los Corales del Rosario, Parque Nacional nat. park Col.

Column 6

129 I4 Los Gatos r. Mex.
124 K4 Los Gatos CA U.S.A.
98 □³ᵃ Los Gigantes Tenerife Canary Is
146 E2 Los Gigantes, Cerro mt. Arg.
145 B8 Los Glaciares, Parque Nacional nat. park Arg.
65 I2 Los Golondrinos, Sierra de mts Spain
131 I4 Los Haitíses nat. park Dom. Rep.
52 B2 Losheim Ger.
63 O9 Los Hinojosos Spain
126 E2 Los Hoyos Mex.
145 B7 Los Huemules, Parque Nacional nat. park Chile
128 C3 Los Huicholes, Sierra de mts Mex.
64 H7 Los Hurones, Embalse de resr Spain
55 K3 Łosice Pol.
127 M8 Los Idolos Mex.
55 L3 Łosiński i. Croatia
55 L3 Łosinka Pol.
130 D3 Los Jardines de la Reina, Archipiélago de is Cuba
144 E3 Los Juríes Arg.
136 B3 Los Katíos, Parque Nacional nat. park Col.
97 N4 Loskop S. Africa
97 N1 Loskop Dam Nature Reserve S. Africa
— Los Lagos Chile
— Los Lagos admin. reg. Chile
146 A5 Los Laureles Chile
126 G3 Los Leones Mex.
146 D2 Los Llanos, Sierra de mts Arg.
98 □³ᵈ Los Llanos de Aridane La Palma Canary Is
123 K9 Los Lunas NM U.S.A.
146 B3 Los Maitenes Santiago Chile
146 B3 Los Maitenes Valparaíso Chile
67 C12 Los Maldonados Spain
146 E5 Los Manatiales Arg.
129 H5 Los Mármoles, Parque Nacional nat. park Mex.
67 C12 Los Martínez Spain
145 C6 Los Menucos Arg.
126 F3 Los Mexicanos, Lago de Mex.
19 R6 Lo'smo Rus. Fed.
126 E5 Los Mochis Mex.
64 H6 Los Molares Spain
98 □³ᵇ Los Molinos Fuerteventura Canary Is
63 L7 Los Molinos Spain
124 I1 Los Molinos CA U.S.A.
64 G3 Los Molinos de Matachel, Embalse de resr Spain
66 D4 Los Molles r. Arg.
53 L3 Los Monegros reg. Spain
129 I1 Los Morales Mex.
67 C12 Los Mosquitos, Golfo de b. Panama
129 K7 Los Navalmorales Spain
63 K9 Los Navalucillos Spain
136 C3 Los Nevados, Parque Nacional nat. park Col.
145 D8 Los Nodales, Bahía de b. Arg.
129 I3 Los Olímpicos Mex.
70 F3 Losone Switz.
98 □³ᵃ Los Órganos, Punta de pt La Gomera Canary Is
55 I6 Łosośina Dolna Pol.
130 B2 Los Palacios Cuba
64 H6 Los Palacios y Villafranca Spain
63 M2 Los Pandos Spain
146 C3 Los Paramillos, Sierra de mts Arg.
155 E8 Los Patos East Timor
146 C2 Los Patos, Río de r. Arg.
63 I3 Los Pedroches plat. Spain
67 C9 Los Pedrones Spain
146 B2 Los Peladeros Chile
129 J2 Los Pericos Mex.
128 G7 Los Placeres del Oro Mex.
65 O5 Los Pocicos, Puerto de pass Spain
63 L6 Los Pozuelos de Calatrava Spain
19 R6 Los Rábanos Spain
144 D2 Los Rastros Arg.
98 □³ᵃ Los Realejos Tenerife Canary Is
129 I4 Los Remedios r. Mex.
128 A1 Los Reyes Mex.
128 E6 Los Reyes Mex.
98 □³ᵈ Los Reyes, Bahía de b. El Hierro Canary Is
41 G9 Los Riachos, Islas de is Arg.
136 B3 Los Ríos prov. Ecuador
146 C2 Los Rodríguez Mex.
63 L5 Los Roques, Islas is Venez.
64 G3 Los Royos Spain
146 B2 Los Santos Arg.
62 E7 Los Santos Spain
65 I4 Los Santos de Maimona Spain
98 □³ᵃ Los Sauces La Palma Canary Is
146 C3 Los Sauces Chile
52 E5 Loßburg Ger.
43 F8 Losse r. France
44 K3 Losser Neth.
26 J7 Lossiemouth Moray, Scotland U.K.
51 G7 Lößnitz Ger.
70 D2 Lostallo Switz.
67 E9 Los Taques Venez.
63 L2 Los Tepames Mex.
129 I5 Los Tepames Mex.
129 I2 Los Testigos i. Venez.
124 N6 Lost Hills CA U.S.A.
126 B3 Los Tigres Arg.
146 C3 Los Tigres Mex.
29 M7 Lostock Gralam Cheshire, England U.K.
63 M2 Los Tojos Spain
137 G5 Los Torneros, Sierra de mt. Spain
122 H4 Lost Trail Pass ID U.S.A.
30 C7 Lostwithiel Cornwall, England U.K.
19 N6 Losvida, Vozyera I. Belarus
125 S10 Los Vidrios Mex.
146 B3 Los Vientos Chile
146 B2 Los Vilares Chile
115 C6 Los Vilos Chile
146 A1 Los Yébenes Spain
43 F7 Lot dept France
43 C7 Lot r. France
21 K6 Løten Norway
57 I3 Lötgojad Swamp Kenya
21 K6 Løten Norway
31 O1 Lot-et-Garonne dept France
184 H3 Loţfābād Turkm.
26 I8 Lothian, Scotland U.K. hist. area
62 B3 Lothair S. Africa
14 F1 Lothmore Highland, Scotland U.K.
— Lotofaga Samoa
71 P5 Lothrair Rus. Fed.
— Lott r. Fr./Rus. Fed. alt. Lutto

Column 7

49 E6 Lotte Ger.
202 M4 Lottin Point North I. N.Z.
52 F6 Lottstetten Ger.
54 E2 Lotuke mt. Sudan
58 C2 Lotyń Pol.
72 D8 Lotzorai Sardegna Italy
39 K6 Louailles France
158 F3 Louangnamtha Laos
158 F5 Louangphabang Laos
36 E8 L'Ouanne r. France
38 E4 Louannec France
38 E4 Louargat France
91 B6 Loubomo Congo
51 C10 Loudéac France
56 C1 Loučná hill Czech Rep.
56 D3 Loučovice Czech Rep.
38 F5 Loudéac France
41 C6 Loudes France
171 H5 Loudi Hunan China
91 D7 Loudima Congo
115 E8 Loudon TN U.S.A.
116 C8 Loudonville OH U.S.A.
42 I1 Loudun France
39 K6 Loué France
40 G2 Loue r. France
91 B5 Louessé r. Congo
169 L7 Loufan Shanxi China
88 A3 Louga Senegal
147 G5 Louge r. Arg.
43 G9 Louge r. France
27 F2 Loughanure Rep. of Ireland
31 J2 Loughborough Leicestershire, England U.K.
27 J4 Loughbrickland Northern Ireland U.K.
105 H2 Lougheed Island Nunavut Can.
27 C8 Lougher Rep. of Ireland
27 I4 Loughgall Northern Ireland U.K.
27 G5 Lough Gowna Rep. of Ireland
27 K4 Loughinisland Northern Ireland U.K.
27 J6 Loughmoe Rep. of Ireland
30 D4 Loughor Swansea, Wales U.K.
30 C4 Loughor r. Wales U.K.
27 F6 Loughrea Rep. of Ireland
27 E3 Loughros More Bay Rep. of Ireland
31 M4 Loughton Essex, England U.K.
44 F6 Louhans France
40 G3 Louhuaro Fin.
116 C10 Louisa VA U.S.A.
116 H10 Louisa KY U.S.A.
208 I5 Louisa Downs Aboriginal Reserve W.A. Austr.
109 J4 Louisbourg N.S. Can.
— Louisbourg N.S. Can. see Louisburg
115 H7 Louisburg NC U.S.A.
106 G2 Louise Falls N.W.T. Can.
153 L9 Louisiade Archipelago is P.N.G.
120 J6 Louisiana MO U.S.A.
121 J10 Louisiana state U.S.A.
96 F4 Louisina S. Africa
115 F9 Louisville GA U.S.A.
120 K6 Louisville IL U.S.A.
114 C6 Louisville KY U.S.A.
121 K9 Louisville MS U.S.A.
116 D8 Louisville OH U.S.A.
216 H8 Louisville Ridge sea feature S. Pacific Ocean
108 E2 Louis-XIV, Pointe pt Que. Can.
14 F2 Loukhi Rus. Fed.
90 C5 Loukoléla Congo
91 C6 Loukouo Congo
40 I2 Loulans France
42 C3 Loulay France
64 C6 Loulé Port.
88 D4 Loulouni Mali
89 H6 Loum Cameroon
56 D1 Louny Czech Rep.
120 G5 Loup r. NE U.S.A.
120 F5 Loup City NE U.S.A.
109 F1 Loups Marins, Lacs des lakes Que. Can.
109 F1 Loups Marins, Petit lac des r. Que. Can.
109 J3 Lourdes Nfld and Lab. Can.
110 B6 Lourdes U.S.A.
42 H3 Lourdes France
137 I4 Lourdoueix-St-Pierre France
— Lourenço Brazil
— Lourenço Marques Moz. see Maputo
64 B5 Loures Port.
62 C7 Lourical Port.
62 C7 Lourinhã Port.
42 C5 Lourinha France
36 C3 Loury France
64 B3 Lousa Port.
62 D8 Lousã, Serra da mts Port.
62 B7 Lousã Port.
96 H9 Louterwater S. Africa
205 J4 Louth N.S.W. Austr.
27 I5 Louth county Rep. of Ireland
29 Q7 Louth Lincolnshire, England U.K.
78 C5 Loutra Greece
78 E4 Loutra Aidipsou Greece
78 D5 Loutraki Greece
78 D2 Loutros Greece
— Louvain Belgium see Leuven
45 I7 Louveigné Belgium
39 D9 Louvie-Juzon France
36 E5 Louviers France
39 K5 Louvigné-de-Bais France
39 I5 Louvigné-du-Désert France
36 E5 Louvres France
97 H3 Louwrois S. Africa
97 I3 Louwsburg S. Africa
36 I7 Louze France
57 H4 Lővänger Sweden
54 D3 Lovászi Hungary
57 M4 Lővászpatona Hungary
76 H5 Lovat' r. Rus. Fed.
77 M7 Lovech Bulg.
122 L6 Loveland CO U.S.A.
117 O4 Loveland OH U.S.A.
122 J4 Lovell WY U.S.A.
203 D13 Lovells Flat South I. N.Z.
131 □³ Lovell Village St Vincent
116 E12 Loves' Leap mt. VA U.S.A.
110 E6 Loves Park IL U.S.A.
21 S6 Loviisa Fin.
116 G11 Lovingston VA U.S.A.
121 D11 Loving NM U.S.A.
57 I3 Lovinobaňa Slovakia
18 J3 Lővnäsvallen Sweden
22 F1 Lovns Bredning b. Denmark
56 F1 Lovosice Czech Rep.
14 F1 Lovozero Rus. Fed.
68 E3 Lővran Croatia
71 P5 Lovran Croatia
76 I2 Lovrenc Slovenia
77 L5 Lovrin Romania
76 H5 Lovtsha r. Rus. Fed.
91 B8 Lóvua Angola
91 D7 Lóvua Angola
111 S4 Low Que. Can.
107 O2 Low, Cape Nunavut Can.

Lychkovo to Mahuva
297

19 P4 Lychkovo Rus. Fed.
20 O4 Lycksele Sweden
18 A2 Lycoming County county PA U.S.A.
18 A2 Lycoming Creek r. PA U.S.A.
31 N6 Lydd Kent, England U.K.
Lydda Israel see Lod
12 W2 Lyddan Island Antarctica
95 F5 Lydenburg S. Africa
30 D6 Lydford Devon, England U.K.
79 I4 Lydia reg. Turkey
30 G4 Lydney Gloucestershire, England U.K.
55 I3 Łydynia r. Pol.
18 I8 Lyebyada r. Belarus
16 H2 Lyel'chytsy Belarus
24 M4 Lyell, Mount CA U.S.A.
06 C7 Lyell Brown, Mount hill N.T. Austr.
06 D4 Lyell Island B.C. Can.
03 G8 Lyell Range mts South I. N.Z.
17 K1 Lyenina Belarus
55 M3 Lyeninski Belarus
18 L7 Lyepyel' Belarus
15 □2 Lyford Cay New Prov. Bahamas
22 I4 Lygnern l. Sweden
78 E5 Lygourio Greece
18 G5 Lygumai Lith.
17 P4 Lyhivka Ukr.
11 R9 Lykens PA U.S.A.
17 K2 Lykhachiv Ukr.
17 M5 Lykhivka Ukr.
19 Q3 Lykoshino Rus. Fed.
96 I3 Lykso S. Africa
10 B6 Lyle MN U.S.A.
16 I8 Lyman Ukr.
22 I6 Lyman WY U.S.A.
17 P4 Lyman, Ozero l. Ukr.
16 I7 Lymans'ke Ukr.
30 G6 Lyme Bay England U.K.
30 G6 Lyme Regis Dorset, England U.K.
31 O5 Lyminge Kent, England U.K.
31 I6 Lymington Hampshire, England U.K.
29 M7 Lymm Warrington, England U.K.
31 O5 Lympne Kent, England U.K.
30 F6 Lympstone Devon, England U.K.
23 R7 Łyna r. Pol.
16 C12 Lynch KY U.S.A.
15 D8 Lynchburg TN U.S.A.
16 F11 Lynchburg VA U.S.A.
15 H9 Lynches r. SC U.S.A.
16 F11 Lynch Station VA U.S.A.
17 □O4 Lynchville ME U.S.A.
07 I4 Lynd r. Qld Austr.
22 C2 Lynden WA U.S.A.
07 J5 Lyndhurst Qld Austr.
04 G4 Lyndhurst S.A. Austr.
31 I6 Lyndhurst Hampshire, England U.K.
09 C7 Lyndon W.A. Austr.
09 B7 Lyndon r. W.A. Austr.
20 H6 Lyndon KS U.S.A.
10 E6 Lyndon Station WI U.S.A.
16 G5 Lyndonville NY U.S.A.
17 M4 Lyndonville VT U.S.A.
29 K4 Lyne r. England U.K.
31 I4 Lyneham Wiltshire, England U.K.
29 N3 Lynemouth Northumberland, England U.K.
26 J5 Lyness Orkney, Scotland U.K.
22 E5 Lyngby nature res. Denmark
22 D3 Lyngdal Norway
20 P2 Lyngen sea chan. Norway
20 P2 Lyngseidet Norway
30 D7 Lynher r. England U.K.
08 F3 Lynher Reef W.A. Austr.
30 E5 Lynmouth Devon, England U.K.
Lynn Norfolk, England U.K. see King's Lynn
17 O6 Lynn MA U.S.A.
06 C3 Lynn Canal sea chan. AK U.S.A.
25 T2 Lynndyl UT U.S.A.
15 E10 Lynn Haven FL U.S.A.
07 K3 Lynn Lake Man. Can.
17 N2 Lynove Ukr.
17 L3 Lynovytsya Ukr.
09 C10 Lynton W.A. Austr.
30 E5 Lynton Devon, England U.K.
18 J6 Lyntupy Belarus
07 J2 Lynx Lake N.W.T. Can.
10 C6 Lynxville WI U.S.A.
40 F5 Lyon France
26 I9 Lyon r. Scotland U.K.
26 G9 Lyon, Loch l. Scotland U.K.
17 L4 Lyon Mountain NY U.S.A.
40 F5 Lyonnais, Monts du hills France
04 D4 Lyons S.A. Austr.
09 C8 Lyons r. W.A. Austr.
Lyons France see Lyon
15 F9 Lyons GA U.S.A.
20 F6 Lyons KS U.S.A.
16 I5 Lyons NY U.S.A.
17 J5 Lyons Falls NY U.S.A.
36 B5 Lyons-la-Forêt France
19 I2 Lyons Plain CT U.S.A.
18 D4 Lyon Station PA U.S.A.
19 N6 Lyozna Belarus
16 E3 Lypa r. Ukr.
16 H2 Lypnyky Ukr.
17 M3 Lypova Dolyna Ukr.
16 I4 Lypovets' Ukr.
17 P3 Lyptsi Ukr.
99 F2 Lyra Reef P.N.G.
36 F2 Lys r. France
70 D4 Lys r. Italy
48 J1 Lysabild Denmark
57 H2 Lysá Hora mt. Czech Rep.
17 K5 Lysa Hora Ukr.
51 K10 Lysá nad Labem Czech Rep.
57 H2 Lysá pod Makytou Slovakia
55 J2 Łyse Pol.
22 C2 Lysefjorden inlet Norway
22 C2 Lysekammen mt. Norway
22 H3 Lysekil Sweden
19 P9 Lyshchichi Rus. Fed.
55 L3 Lyshchytsy Belarus
90 B3 Lysi Cyprus
55 I5 Łysica hill Pol.
56 F2 Lysice Czech Rep.
78 C4 Lysimachia, Limni l. Greece
55 M3 Lyskava Belarus
19 N6 Lys'kava Belarus
54 G5 Łyski Pol.
14 I4 Lyskovo Rus. Fed.
17 S6 Lysogorka Rus. Fed.
54 G2 Łysomice Pol.
58 I7 Ly Sơn, Đao i. Vietnam
70 C1 Lyss Switz.
22 G5 Lystrup Denmark
14 L4 Lys'va Rus. Fed.
22 J1 Lysvik Sweden
16 J4 Lysyanka Ukr.
17 R5 Lysychans'k Ukr.
15 I6 Lysyye Gory Rus. Fed.
55 H4 Łyszkowice Pol.
30 H6 Lytchett Matravers Dorset, England U.K.
30 H6 Lytchett Minster Dorset, England U.K.
26 J5 Lyth Highland, Scotland U.K.
29 K6 Lytham St Anne's Lancashire, England U.K.
19 U6 Lytkarino Rus. Fed.
55 M5 Lytovezh Ukr.
03 G10 Lyttelton South I. N.Z.
03 G10 Lyttelton Harbour South I. N.Z.
06 F5 Lytton B.C. Can.
18 L9 Lyuban' Belarus
19 O2 Lyuban' Rus. Fed.
18 L9 Lyubanskaye Vodaskhovishcha resr Belarus
16 G4 Lyubar Ukr.
16 J6 Lyubashivka Ukr.
19 N7 Lyubavichi Rus. Fed.
17 O1 Lyubazh Rus. Fed.
18 J8 Lyubcha Belarus
16 J2 Lyubech Ukr.
19 U6 Lyubertsy Rus. Fed.
16 E2 Lyubeshiv Ukr.
14 H4 Lyubim Rus. Fed.
77 O9 Lyubimets Bulg.
17 O2 Lyubimovka Kurskaya Oblast' Rus. Fed.
19 V8 Lyubimovka Tul'skaya Oblast' Rus. Fed.
18 I9 Lyubishchytsy Belarus
19 R3 Lyubitovo Rus. Fed.
55 I1 Lyublino Rus. Fed.
55 M4 Lyublynets' Ukr.
19 R8 Lyubokhna Rus. Fed.
55 M4 Lyubokhyny Ukr.
17 L6 Lyubomyrivka Ukr.
17 O2 Lyubostan' Rus. Fed.
Lyubotin Ukr. see Lyubotyn
17 O4 Lyubotyn Ukr.
18 K8 Lyubyacha Belarus
17 P6 Lyubymivka Ukr.
55 L6 Lyubyntsi Ukr.
19 Q3 Lyubytino Rus. Fed.
19 R8 Lyudinovo Rus. Fed.
19 Q1 Lyugovichi Rus. Fed.
77 P8 Lyulyakovo Bulg.
14 I4 Lyunda r. Rus. Fed.
18 J9 Lyusina Belarus
17 O3 Lyutivka Ukr.
14 L2 Lyzha r. Rus. Fed.
17 R4 Lyzyne Ukr.
18 L4 Lzha r. Rus. Fed.

M

158 D3 Ma r. Myanmar
158 E4 Ma, Nam r. Laos
158 G5 Ma, Sông r. Vietnam
175 □1 Maabadi i. N. Male Maldives
Maafushi i. S. Male Maldives see Mafushi
124 □E13 Ma'alaea HI U.S.A.
176 C10 Maalhosmadulu Atoll Maldives
27 C5 Maam Rep. of Ireland
Maamakundhoo i. N. Male Maldives see Makunudhoo
91 E9 Maamba Zambia
27 C6 Maam Cross Rep. of Ireland
89 H6 Ma'an Cameroon
190 D8 Ma'ān Jordan
Maan Turkey see Nusratiye
20 S5 Maaninka Fin.
20 T3 Maaninkavaara Fin.
20 T5 Maanselkä Fin.
171 L3 Ma'anshan Anhui China
168 H2 Maanyt Bulgan Mongolia
169 J3 Maanyt Töv Mongolia
18 I2 Maardu Estonia
45 I6 Maarheeze Neth.
Maarianhamina Åland Fin. see Mariehamn
44 H4 Maarn Neth.
190 E2 Ma'arrat al Ikhwān Syria
190 E3 Ma'arrat an Nu'mān Syria
44 H4 Maarssen Neth.
44 H4 Maarssenbroek Neth.
44 H4 Maartensdijk Neth.
44 I6 Maas r. Neth.
alt. Meuse (Belgium/France)
27 F3 Maas Rep. of Ireland
45 I6 Maasbracht Neth.
45 J6 Maasbree Neth.
44 G5 Maasdam Neth.
45 I6 Maaseik Belgium
154 E6 Maasin Leyte Phil.
44 F5 Maasland Neth.
45 I7 Maasmechelen Belgium
49 A8 Maas-Schwalm-Nette nat. park Ger./Neth.
44 F5 Maassluis Neth.
45 I7 Maastricht Neth.
205 K10 Maatsuyker Group is Tas. Austr.
171 L2 Maba Jiangsu China
155 F3 Maba Halmahera Indon.
84 D6 Maba, Ouadi watercourse Chad
97 K1 Mabaalstad North West S. Africa
97 K1 Mabaalstad North West S. Africa
94 E3 Mababe Depression Botswana
154 C4 Mabalacat Luzon Phil.
95 G4 Mabalane Moz.
90 F4 Mabana Dem. Rep. Congo
90 A5 Mabanda Gabon
186 G8 Ma'bar Yemen
137 G2 Mabaruma Guyana
Mabating Yunnan China see Hongshan
158 C3 Mabein Myanmar
204 E3 Mabel Creek S.A. Austr.
208 I4 Mabel Downs W.A. Austr.
108 B3 Mabella Ont. Can.
106 G5 Mabel Lake B.C. Can.
111 R5 Maberly Ont. Can.
170 D4 Mabian Sichuan China
173 H12 Mabja Xizang China
29 R7 Mablethorpe Lincolnshire, England U.K.
40 E4 Mably France
97 M1 Mabopane S. Africa
95 G4 Mabote Moz.
109 I4 Mabou N.S. Can.
190 D8 Mabrak, Jabal mt. Jordan
88 E2 Mabroûk well Mali
84 B4 Mabrous well Niger
94 D5 Mabuasehube Game Reserve nature res. Botswana
154 C1 Mabudis i. Phil.
96 I1 Mabule Botswana
164 □1 Mabuni Okinawa Japan
84 D3 Ma'būs Yūsuf oasis Libya
94 D5 Mabutsane Botswana
145 B7 Macá, Monte mt. Chile
147 F5 Macachín Arg.
209 D8 Macadam Plains W.A. Austr.
206 B3 Macadam Range hills N.T. Austr.
143 G5 Macaé Brazil
65 O6 Macael Spain
191 C4 Maçahel Geçidi pass Turkey
140 G3 Macaíba Brazil
154 E7 Macajalar Bay Mindanao Phil.
140 E5 Macajuba Brazil
93 B8 Macaloge Moz.
105 H3 MacAlpine Lake Nunavut Can.
108 E3 Macamic Que. Can.
95 G4 Macandze Moz.
97 Q1 Macaneta, Ponta de pt Moz.
66 K3 Maçanet de Cabrenys Spain
Macao Macau China see Macau
62 E9 Mação Port.
137 I4 Macapá Amapá Brazil
138 D2 Macapá Amazonas Brazil
136 B6 Macará Ecuador
126 □S14 Macaracas Panama
141 E5 Macarani Brazil
136 C4 Macarena, Cordillera mts Col.
137 F2 Macareo, Caño r. Venez.
205 I8 Macarthur Vic. Austr.
136 B5 Macas Ecuador
62 G6 Maçãs r. Port./Spain
Macassar Sulawesi Indon. see Makassar
Macassar Strait Indon. see Makassar, Selat
67 D9 Macastre Spain
95 H3 Macatanja Moz.
140 F3 Macau Brazil
171 I7 Macau Macau China
42 C5 Macau France
138 C2 Macauã r. Brazil
140 C4 Macaúba Brazil
140 E5 Macaúbas Brazil
199 I5 Macauley Island N.Z.
136 C4 Macayari Col.
92 F2 Macbar, Raas pt Somalia
145 F8 Macbride Head Falkland Is
70 F3 Maccagno Italy
95 G5 Maccaretane Moz.
75 I8 Macchia r. Sicilia Italy
73 M4 Macchiagodena Italy
115 F10 Macclenny FL U.S.A.
29 M7 Macclesfield Cheshire, England U.K.
152 D3 Macclesfield Bank sea feature S. China Sea
108 B3 Macdiarmid Ont. Can.
208 J7 Macdonald, Lake salt flat W.A. Austr.
206 C7 Macdonnell Ranges mts N.T. Austr.
107 M4 MacDowell Lake Ont. Can.
26 L7 Macduff Aberdeenshire, Scotland U.K.
57 K5 Macea Romania
62 E4 Maceda Spain
147 I5 Macedo Arg.
62 G5 Macedo de Cavaleiros Port.
Macedon country Europe see Macedonia
77 J9 Macedonia country Europe
119 I1 Macedonia CT U.S.A.
140 G4 Maceió Brazil
140 F3 Maceio, Ponta da pt Brazil
62 F7 Maceira Guarda Port.
62 C9 Maceira Leiria Port.
59 M7 Macelj Croatia
88 C4 Macenta Guinea
71 O9 Macerata Italy
71 O9 Macerata prov. Italy
71 M8 Macerata Feltria Italy
204 F5 Macfarlane, Lake salt flat S.A. Austr.
27 C9 Macgillycuddy's Reeks mts Rep. of Ireland
28 E4 MacGregor's Corner Northern Ireland U.K.
185 L7 Mach Pak.
193 M3 Macha Rus. Fed.
143 G2 Machacalis Brazil
138 D4 Machacamarca Bol.
136 B5 Machachi Ecuador
139 E2 Machadinho r. Brazil
143 E4 Machado Brazil
97 O1 Machadodorp S. Africa
64 E4 Machados Port.
91 E8 Machai Zambia
95 G4 Machaila Moz.
93 C5 Machakos Kenya
136 B5 Machala Ecuador
146 B4 Machali Chile
Machali Qinghai China see Madoi
157 J4 Machan Sarawak Malaysia
200 □1 Machanao, Mount hill Guam
95 G4 Machanga Moz.
139 E5 Macharetí Bol.
92 B2 Machar Marshes Sudan
206 G8 Machattie, Lake salt flat Qld Austr.
97 Q1 Machatuine Moz.
36 I5 Machault France
38 H8 Machecoul France
45 F7 Machelen Belgium
30 F4 Machen Caerphilly, Wales U.K.
171 J3 Macheng Hubei China
37 M5 Macheren France
176 F4 Macherla Andhra Prad. India
51 G8 Machern Ger.
65 K2 Machero mt. Spain
110 E7 Machesney Park IL U.S.A.
179 K9 Machhagan Orissa India
178 F4 Machhiwara Punjab India
178 I7 Machhlishahr Uttar Prad. India
117 □R4 Machias ME U.S.A.
116 G6 Machias NY U.S.A.
117 □Q2 Machias r. ME U.S.A.
117 □R4 Machias Bay ME U.S.A.
64 □ Machico Madeira
167 J4 Machida Japan
176 G4 Machilipatnam Andhra Prad. India
93 B8 Machinga Malawi
136 C2 Machiques Venez.
26 D11 Machir Bay Scotland U.K.
Machiwara Punjab India see Machhiwara
185 I9 Māch Kowr Iran
123 L10 Macho, Arroyo del watercourse NM U.S.A.
129 N7 Machona, Laguna lag. Mex.
26 E12 Machrihanish Argyll and Bute, Scotland U.K.
17 N4 Machukhy Ukr.
138 B3 Machupicchu tourist site Peru
138 D3 Machupo r. Bol.
30 E2 Machynlleth Powys, Wales U.K.
95 G5 Macia Moz.
55 J4 Maciejowice Pol.
147 G3 Maciel Arg.
77 Q5 Măcin Romania
72 C2 Macinaggio Corse France
205 M3 Macintyre r. N.S.W. Austr.
205 M3 Macintyre Brook r. Qld Austr.
138 B3 Macizo de Tocate mts Peru
125 X2 Mack CO U.S.A.
191 A5 Maçka Turkey
207 L6 Mackay Qld Austr.
107 I3 MacKay r. Alta Can.
122 H4 Mackay ID U.S.A.
208 J7 Mackay, Lake salt flat W.A. Austr.
107 I2 MacKay Lake N.W.T. Can.
212 O1 Mackay Mountains Antarctica
52 D3 Mackenbach Ger.
49 K7 Mackenrode Ger.
207 L7 Mackenzie r. Qld Austr.
106 F4 Mackenzie B.C. Can.
110 F1 Mackenzie Ont. Can.
106 E1 Mackenzie r. N.W.T. Can.
Mackenzie Guyana see Linden
213 E2 Mackenzie Bay Antarctica
104 E3 Mackenzie Bay Y.T. Can.
106 G2 Mackenzie Bison Sanctuary nature res. N.W.T. Can.
106 G2 Mackenzie Highway N.W.T. Can.
105 G2 Mackenzie King Island N.W.T. Can.
106 C1 Mackenzie Mountains N.W.T./Y.T. Can.
110 I4 Mackinac, Straits of lake channel MI U.S.A.
110 J4 Mackinac Island MI U.S.A.
110 E9 Mackinaw r. IL U.S.A.
110 J4 Mackinaw City MI U.S.A.
107 I4 Macklin Sask. Can.
59 N6 Mačkovci Slovenia
205 N4 Macksville N.S.W. Austr.
207 H7 Mackunda Creek watercourse Qld Austr.
205 N3 Maclean N.S.W. Austr.
97 L8 Macleantown S. Africa
97 M7 Maclear S. Africa
205 N4 Macleay r. N.S.W. Austr.
209 B8 MacLeod, Lake imp. l. W.A. Austr.
Macleod's Table South hill Scotland U.K. see Healabhal Bheag
106 C2 Macmillan r. Y.T. Can.
106 D2 Macmillan Pass Y.T. Can.
27 G4 Macnean Lower, Lough l. Northern Ireland U.K.
27 G4 Macnean Upper, Lough l. Rep. of Ireland/U.K.
95 G4 Maçobere Moz.
91 C6 Macocola Angola
110 D9 Macomb IL U.S.A.
72 B7 Macomer Sardegna Italy
93 D8 Macomia Moz.
40 F4 Mâcon France
115 F9 Macon GA U.S.A.
120 I6 Macon MO U.S.A.
121 K9 Macon MS U.S.A.
116 B10 Macon OH U.S.A.
121 J10 Macon, Bayou r. LA U.S.A.
91 D8 Macondo Angola
40 F4 Mâconnais reg. France
119 G2 Macopin NJ U.S.A.
95 G3 Macossa Moz.
63 J7 Macotera Spain
107 K3 Macoun Lake Sask. Can.
95 G4 Macovane Moz.
Macpherson Robertson Land reg. Antarctica see Mac. Robertson Land
205 K4 Macquarie r. N.S.W. Austr.
205 K9 Macquarie r. Tas. Austr.
205 M5 Macquarie, Lake b. N.S.W. Austr.
205 J10 Macquarie Harbour Tas. Austr.
204 □3 Macquarie Island S. Pacific Ocean
205 K4 Macquarie Marshes N.S.W. Austr.
205 L5 Macquarie Mountain N.S.W. Austr.
216 F9 Macquarie Ridge sea feature S. Pacific Ocean
203 E12 Macraes Flat South I. N.Z.
156 □ MacRitchie Reservoir Sing.
213 E2 Mac. Robertson Land reg. Antarctica
27 E9 Macroom Rep. of Ireland
127 N9 Mactún Mex.
136 D4 Macú Brazil
70 D4 Macugnaga Italy
129 K8 Macuiltianguis Mex.
136 D1 Macuira, Parque Nacional nat. park Col.
136 C4 Macuje Col.
76 I9 Macukull Albania
204 E2 Macumba S.A. Austr.
204 F2 Macumba watercourse S.A. Austr.
118 D3 Macungie PA U.S.A.
140 F4 Macururé Brazil
138 C3 Macusani Peru
127 M9 Macuspana Mex.
126 E4 Macuzari, Presa resr Mex.
95 H3 Macuze Moz.
117 □Q3 Macwahoc ME U.S.A.
57 K3 Mád Hungary
190 D7 Mādabā Jordan
97 O3 Madadeni S. Africa
185 K7 Madagan Pak.
95 □ Madagascar i. Africa
215 H6 Madagascar Basin sea feature Indian Ocean
215 G7 Madagascar Ridge sea feature Indian Ocean
191 H5 Madagiz Azer.
89 I4 Madagli Nigeria
186 C2 Madā'in Şāliḩ Saudi Arabia
176 E6 Madakasira Andhra Prad. India
154 □ Madalai Palau
98 □1c Madalena Pico Azores
140 F3 Madalena Brazil
84 B4 Madama Niger
77 M9 Madan Bulg.
184 H3 Ma'dan Iran
90 C2 Madana Chad
84 C5 Madana well Chad
176 F6 Madanapalle Andhra Prad. India
153 K8 Madang P.N.G.
178 G7 Madaora Uttar Prad. India
89 G3 Madaoua Niger
77 P7 Madara Bulg.
57 I5 Madaras Hungary
77 J4 Mădăraş Romania
179 M8 Madaripur Bangl.
89 G3 Madarounfa Niger
184 F2 Madau Turkm.
Madaw Turkm. see Madau
111 Q4 Madawaska Ont. Can.
108 E4 Madawaska r. Ont. Can.
117 □Q1 Madawaska ME U.S.A.
158 C3 Madaya Myanmar
72 C5 Maddalena, Isola i. Sardegna Italy
75 I9 Maddalena, Penisola della pen. Sicilia Italy
72 C9 Maddalena Spiaggia Sardegna Italy
73 M5 Maddaloni Italy
176 G3 Madded Chhattisgarh India
176 E6 Maddur Karnataka India
44 G5 Made Neth.
90 F3 Madeir Sudan
137 G5 Madeira r. Brazil
64 □ Madeira terr. N. Atlantic Ocean
64 □ Madeira, Arquipélago da is N. Atlantic Ocean
Madeira, Arquipélago da terr. N. Atlantic Ocean see Madeira
64 □ Madeira, Ilha da i. Madeira
64 □ Madeira, Parque Natural de nature res. Madeira
Madeira Islands N. Atlantic Ocean see Madeira, Arquipélago da
139 E2 Madeirinha r. Brazil
30 H2 Madeley Staffordshire, England U.K.
30 H2 Madeley Telford and Wrekin, England U.K.
120 H3 Madelia MN U.S.A.
110 D3 Madeline Island WI U.S.A.
90 C2 Madel Ouèï Chad
188 I4 Maden Turkey
183 R4 Madeniyet Kazakh.
68 B2 Mäder Austria
126 E3 Madera Mex.
65 N4 Madera r. Spain
124 L5 Madera CA U.S.A.
63 K5 Maderano r. Spain
58 B5 Madererspitze mt. Austria
63 M6 Maderuelo Spain
20 S3 Madetkoski Fin.
176 C5 Madgaon Goa India
99 □2a Madge Rocks is Inner Islands Seychelles
92 D1 Madgoul Djibouti
178 C9 Madhavpur Gujarat India
179 K7 Madhepura Bihar India
173 E13 Madhoganj Uttar Prad. India
179 K6 Madhubani Bihar India
176 E6 Madhugiri Karnataka India
179 K7 Madhupur Jharkhand India
178 G8 Madhya Pradesh state India
157 J4 Madi, Dataran Tinggi plat. Indon.
93 B7 Madibira Tanz.
97 J2 Madibogo S. Africa
138 D3 Madidi r. Bol.
204 F3 Madigan Gulf salt flat S.A. Austr.
176 D6 Madikeri Karnataka India
121 G8 Madill OK U.S.A.
91 B6 Madimba Angola
91 B6 Madimba Dem. Rep. Congo
88 D4 Madinani Côte d'Ivoire
186 F8 Madīnat al 'Abīd Yemen
186 G9 Madīnat ash Sha'b Yemen
190 G3 Madīnat ath Thawrah Syria
37 K6 Madine, Lac de l. France
91 A6 Madingo-Kayes Congo
91 B6 Madingou Congo
89 I4 Madingrin Cameroon
43 D8 Madiran France
95 □J3 Madirovalo Madag.
115 D8 Madison AL U.S.A.
119 J2 Madison CT U.S.A.
115 F10 Madison FL U.S.A.
115 F9 Madison GA U.S.A.
114 E6 Madison IN U.S.A.
117 □P4 Madison ME U.S.A.
120 G3 Madison MN U.S.A.
120 G5 Madison NE U.S.A.
119 G3 Madison NJ U.S.A.
116 D7 Madison OH U.S.A.
120 G3 Madison SD U.S.A.
116 G10 Madison VA U.S.A.
110 E6 Madison WI U.S.A.
116 D10 Madison WV U.S.A.
122 I4 Madison r. MT U.S.A.
116 F11 Madison Heights VA U.S.A.
114 D7 Madisonville KY U.S.A.
115 E8 Madisonville TN U.S.A.
121 H10 Madisonville TX U.S.A.
155 B9 Madita Sumba Indon.
157 I8 Madiun Jawa Indon.
90 B4 Madjingo Gabon
87 I4 Madjūl Libya
30 G3 Madley Herefordshire, England U.K.
209 G8 Madley, Mount hill W.A. Austr.
18 I5 Madliena Latvia
90 F4 Mado Dem. Rep. Congo
108 E4 Madoc Ont. Can.
57 H5 Madocsa Hungary
92 C4 Mado Gashi Kenya
168 F9 Madoi Qinghai China
37 L6 Madon r. France
18 J5 Madona Latvia
94 D4 Madongo Pan salt pan Botswana
74 F8 Madonie mts Sicilia Italy
118 B5 Madonna MD U.S.A.
71 J3 Madonna di Campiglio Italy
178 C7 Madpura Rajasthan India
79 H3 Madra Dağı mts Turkey
186 D5 Madrakah Saudi Arabia
187 M6 Madrakah, Ra's c. Oman
Madras Tamil Nadu India see Chennai
Madras state India see Tamil Nadu
122 D4 Madras OR U.S.A.
191 J5 Mädräsä Azer.
129 J1 Madre, Laguna lag. Mex.
121 G12 Madre, Laguna lag. TX U.S.A.
154 C3 Madre, Sierra mt. Luzon Phil.
129 N9 Madre de Chiapas, Sierra mts Mex.
143 E4 Madre de Deus de Minas Brazil
138 C2 Madre de Dios dept Peru
145 B8 Madre de Dios, Isla i. Chile
128 F7 Madre del Sur, Sierra mts Mex.
90 F3 Madreggi Sudan
128 B1 Madre Occidental, Sierra mts Mex.
128 F1 Madre Oriental, Sierra mts Mex.
Madre, Sierra mts Mex. see Madre de Chiapas, Sierra
43 I10 Madrès, Pic de mt. France
154 E7 Madrid Mindanao Phil.
63 M8 Madrid Spain
63 M7 Madrid aut. comm. Spain
154 D6 Madridejos Phil.
65 L2 Madridejos Spain
63 K6 Madrigal de las Altas Torres Spain
63 J8 Madrigal de la Vera Spain
63 M4 Madrigal del Monte Spain
64 H2 Madrigalejo Spain
65 P2 Madrigueras Spain
58 A6 Madrisahorn mt. Austria/Switz.
23 L4 Madroken l. Sweden
30 □ Madron Cornwall, England U.K.
65 K4 Madrona, Sierra mts Spain
64 H2 Madroñera Spain
65 P3 Madroño mt. Spain
130 C2 Madruga Cuba
84 B3 Madrūsah Libya
155 B7 Madu i. Indon.
175 □1 Madu i. S. Male Maldives
91 B6 Maduda Dem. Rep. Congo
177 H4 Madugula Andhra Prad. India
209 I11 Madura W.A. Austr.
157 J8 Madura i. Indon.
157 J8 Madura, Selat sea chan. Indon.
176 F8 Madurai Tamil Nadu India
176 F6 Madurantakam Tamil Nadu India
184 F6 Madvār, Kūh-e mt. Iran
178 H7 Madwas Madh. Prad. India
185 O4 Madyan Pak.
93 B6 Madyo Tanz.
191 I3 Madzhalis Rus. Fed.
77 N9 Madzharovo Bulg.
95 F3 Madziwadzido Zimbabwe
95 F3 Madziwa Mine Zimbabwe
71 M3 Maè r. Italy
167 J3 Maebashi Japan
158 D5 Mae Chang Reservoir Thai.
158 C5 Mae Hong Son Thai.
164 □1 Mae-jima i. Okinawa Japan
155 C3 Maelang Sulawesi Indon.
38 E5 Maël-Carhaix France
22 E2 Mælefjell mt. Norway
66 F5 Maella Spain
63 K7 Maello Spain
30 C4 Maenclochog Pembrokeshire, Wales U.K.
158 D5 Mae Ngat Reservoir Thai.
30 E2 Maentwrog Gwynedd, Wales U.K.
73 K4 Maenza Italy
158 D6 Mae Ping National Park Thai.
158 D6 Mae Ramat Thai.
158 D5 Mae Rim Thai.
77 K3 Măerişte Romania
158 D4 Mae Sai Thai.
158 C5 Mae Sariang Thai.
158 D6 Mae Sot Thai.
30 E4 Maesteg Bridgend, Wales U.K.
130 E4 Maestra, Sierra mts Cuba
65 I6 Maestre hill Spain
154 C5 Maestre de Campo i. Phil.
71 L9 Maestro, Canale canal Italy
158 D5 Mae Suai Thai.
158 D6 Mae Tuen Wildlife Reserve nature res. Thai.
95 □J3 Maevatanana Madag.
200 □5 Maéwo i. Vanuatu
158 D7 Mae Wong National Park Thai.
158 E5 Mae Yom National Park Thai.
155 E3 Mafa Halmahera Indon.
99 □1c Mafaté, Cirque de vol. crater Réunion
107 K4 Mafeking Man. Can.
Mafeking S. Africa see Mafikeng
97 L5 Mafeteng Lesotho
205 K7 Maffra Vic. Austr.
93 C7 Mafia Channel Tanz.
93 C6 Mafia Island Tanz.
97 J1 Mafikeng S. Africa
93 B7 Mafinga Tanz.
141 C8 Mafra Brazil
64 A3 Mafra Port.
140 E4 Mafrense Brazil
95 F3 Mafungabusi Plateau Zimbabwe
175 □1 Mafushi i. S. Male Maldives
97 O6 Magabeni S. Africa
64 H3 Magacela hill Spain
193 Q4 Magadan Rus. Fed.
93 C5 Magadi Kenya
95 G4 Magaiza Moz.
41 C10 Magalas France
97 L1 Magaliesberg mts S. Africa
97 L1 Magaliesburg S. Africa
154 D5 Magallanes Luzon Phil.
145 C9 Magallanes, Estrecho de sea chan. Chile
130 E2 Magallanes Bank sea feature Bahamas
145 B9 Magallanes y Antártica Chilena admin. reg. Chile
63 R5 Magallón Spain
67 K8 Magalluf Spain
63 P5 Magaña Spain
27 I7 Maganey Rep. of Ireland
136 C2 Magangue Col.
188 F5 Mağara Turkey
191 E5 Mağara tourist site Turkey
190 A2 Mağara Dağı mt. Turkey
190 G2 Mağarali Turkey
191 J4 Magaramkent Rus. Fed.
89 H3 Magaria Niger
164 □1 Magari-zaki pt Okinawa Japan
191 F2 Magas Rus. Fed.
154 C3 Magat r. Luzon Phil.
63 L5 Magaz Spain
121 I8 Magazine Mountain hill AR U.S.A.
74 E9 Magazzolo r. Sicilia Italy
90 D4 Magbakele Dem. Rep. Congo
88 C4 Magburaka Sierra Leone
162 D2 Magdagachi Rus. Fed.
51 D9 Magdala Ger.
147 I4 Magdalena Arg.
138 D3 Magdalena Bol.
136 C2 Magdalena dept Col.
136 C2 Magdalena r. Col.
126 C4 Magdalena Baja California Sur Mex.
126 D2 Magdalena Sonora Mex.
126 D2 Magdalena r. Mex.
123 K9 Magdalena NM U.S.A.
136 B3 Magdalena, Bahía b. Col.
126 D5 Magdalena, Bahía b. Mex.
145 B7 Magdalena, Isla i. Chile
126 C5 Magdalena, Isla i. Mex.
129 J7 Magdalena Cuayucatepec Mex.
157 L2 Magdaline, Gunung mt. Malaysia
51 E6 Magdeburg Ger.
51 E6 Magdeburg admin. reg. Ger.
51 F6 Magdeburgerforth Ger.
207 M4 Magdelaine Cays atoll Coral Sea Is Terr. Austr.
121 K10 Magee MS U.S.A.
157 I8 Magelang Jawa Indon.
Magellan, Strait of Chile see Magallanes, Estrecho de
216 E4 Magellan Seamounts sea feature N. Pacific Ocean
70 F5 Magenta Italy
209 E12 Magenta, Lake salt flat W.A. Austr.
20 R1 Magerøya i. Norway
43 B8 Magescq France
164 □H16 Mage-shima i. Japan
57 L4 Măgeşti Romania
70 F3 Maggia Switz.
70 F3 Maggia r. Switz.
147 F3 Maggiolo Arg.
70 G6 Maggiorasca, Monte mt. Italy
72 I1 Maggiore, Isola i. Italy
70 F4 Maggiore, Lago l. Italy
Maggiore, Lake Italy see Maggiore, Lago
72 D6 Maggiore, Monte hill Sardegna Italy
73 M5 Maggiore, Monte mt. Italy
130 □ Maggotty Jamaica
85 F2 Maghāghah Egypt
190 C10 Maghā'ir Shu'ayb tourist site Saudi Arabia
88 B3 Maghama Maur.
27 C9 Maghanlawaun Rep. of Ireland
190 B8 Maghārah, Jabal hill Egypt
27 E3 Maghera Rep. of Ireland
27 I3 Maghera Northern Ireland U.K.
27 I3 Magherafelt Northern Ireland U.K.
28 E5 Magheralin Northern Ireland U.K.
27 H3 Magheramason Northern Ireland U.K.
27 I3 Maghery Northern Ireland U.K.
86 E2 Maghnia Alg.
185 J4 Maghor Afgh.
29 L6 Maghull Merseyside, England U.K.
28 D3 Magilligan Northern Ireland U.K.
27 I2 Magilligan Point Northern Ireland U.K.
65 M5 Mágina mt. Spain
65 L5 Mágina, Sierra mts Spain
93 B7 Magingo Tanz.
72 I1 Magione Italy
75 L5 Magisano Italy
129 I3 Magiscatzín Mex.
Magitang Qinghai China see Jainca
Magiyan Tajik. see Moghiyon
68 G3 Maglaj Bos.-Herz.
40 J4 Magland France
77 L6 Maglavit Romania
73 K3 Magliano de'Marsi Italy
72 G2 Magliano in Toscana Italy
73 I3 Magliano Sabina Italy
75 O3 Maglie Italy
57 I4 Maglód Hungary
125 U8 Magma AZ U.S.A.
42 G3 Magnac-Laval France
42 E4 Magnac-sur-Touvre France
74 C10 Magna Grande hill Italy
75 I8 Magna Grande mt. Sicilia Italy
42 C3 Magné France
213 D2 Magnet Bay Antarctica
207 K5 Magnetic Island Qld Austr.
207 K5 Magnetic Passage Qld Austr.
14 F1 Magnetity Rus. Fed.
37 M7 Magnières France
75 I9 Magnisi, Penisola pen. Sicilia Italy
19 S9 Magnitnyy Rus. Fed.
182 H1 Magnitogorsk Rus. Fed.
121 I9 Magnolia AR U.S.A.
118 E6 Magnolia DE U.S.A.
118 C6 Magnolia MD U.S.A.
121 J10 Magnolia MS U.S.A.
22 I2 Magnor Norway
55 J4 Magnuszew Pol.
40 C3 Magny-Cours France
36 C5 Magny-en-Vexin France
162 L2 Mago Rus. Fed.
57 H5 Mágocs Hungary
57 J5 Mágocs-ér r. Hungary
95 F2 Màgoé Moz.
109 F4 Magog Que. Can.
93 C6 Magole Tanz.
72 B7 Magomadas Sardegna Italy
92 C3 Mago National Park Eth.
91 E8 Magoye Zambia
129 J4 Magozal Mex.
109 H3 Magpie Que. Can.
108 C4 Magpie r. Ont. Can.
109 H3 Magpie r. Que. Can.
109 H3 Magpie, Lac l. Que. Can.
109 H3 Magpie-Ouest r. Que. Can.
70 H7 Magra r. Italy
106 H5 Magrath Alta Can.
67 E9 Magre r. Spain
124 O4 Magruder Mountain NV U.S.A.
85 F6 Magrur Sudan
84 E5 Magrur, Wadi watercourse Sudan
88 B2 Magţa' Laḩjar Maur.
93 B5 Magu Tanz.
162 J2 Magu, Khrebet mts Rus. Fed.
170 E7 Maguan Yunnan China
140 C2 Maguarinho, Cabo c. Brazil
95 G5 Magude Moz.
97 P3 Magudu S. Africa
62 E6 Magueija Port.
126 H4 Magueyal Mex.
98 □3c Máguez Lanzarote Canary Is
64 H4 Maguilla Spain
27 H4 Maguiresbridge Northern Ireland U.K.
89 I3 Magumeri Nigeria
117 □R3 Magundy N.B. Can.
95 F3 Magunge Zimbabwe
179 L8 Magura Bangl.
57 H3 Magura mt. Slovakia
16 G6 Măgura, Dealul hill Moldova
77 K3 Măgura Mare, Vârful hill Romania
77 K5 Măgurii, Vârful mt. Romania
107 M2 Maguse Lake Nunavut Can.
97 L8 Magwali S. Africa
Magway Myanmar see Magwe
Magway admin. div. Myanmar see Magwe
158 B4 Magwe Myanmar
158 B4 Magwe admin. div. Myanmar
92 B3 Magwe Sudan
94 D3 Magwegqana watercourse Botswana
57 K4 Magy Hungary
57 G5 Magyaratád Hungary
57 H6 Magyarbóly Hungary
Magyarkanizsa Vojvodina, Srbija Serb. and Mont. see Kanjiža
Magyar Köztársaság country Europe see Hungary
57 H5 Magyarszék Hungary
158 A4 Magyichaung Myanmar
184 A3 Mahābād Iran
176 C4 Mahabaleshwar Mahar. India
95 □J3 Mahabe Madag.
178 J6 Mahabharat Range mts Nepal
95 □J4 Mahabo Toliara Madag.
95 □J4 Mahabo Toliara Madag.
95 □J4 Mahaboboka Madag.
176 C3 Mahad Mahar. India
92 E4 Mahaddayweyne Somalia
178 F8 Mahadeo Hills Madh. Prad. India
176 G3 Mahadeopur Andhra Prad. India
201 □3a Mahaena Tahiti Fr. Polynesia
116 G8 Mahaffey PA U.S.A.
90 F4 Mahagi Dem. Rep. Congo
90 F4 Mahagi Port Dem. Rep. Congo
173 L7 Mahai Qinghai China
137 G3 Mahaicony Guyana
95 □J2 Mahajamba r. Madag.
178 D5 Mahajan Rajasthan India
95 □J2 Mahajanga Madag.
95 □J3 Mahajanga prov. Madag.
157 L5 Mahakam r. Indon.
95 E4 Mahalapye Botswana
93 A6 Mahale Mountains National Park Tanz.
95 □K2 Mahalevona Madag.
184 D5 Mahallāt Iran
178 F5 Maham Haryana India
184 G6 Māhān Iran
179 K9 Mahanadi r. India
95 □K3 Mahanoro Madag.
118 C3 Mahanoy City PA U.S.A.
118 B3 Mahanoy Creek r. PA U.S.A.
118 B3 Mahantango Creek r. PA U.S.A.
176 G9 Maha Oya Sri Lanka
179 J6 Maharajganj Bihar India
178 H6 Maharajganj Uttar Prad. India
179 I6 Maharajganj Uttar Prad. India
178 G7 Maharajpur Madh. Prad. India
176 D3 Maharashtra state India
186 B2 Mahārish, Ra's pt Saudi Arabia
184 E7 Mahārlū, Daryācheh-ye salt l. Iran
178 I9 Mahasamund Chhattisgarh India
158 F6 Maha Sarakham Thai.
95 □J5 Mahatalaky Madag.
190 E7 Maḩaţţat Ḑab'ah Jordan
131 □2 Mahaut Dominica
95 □J2 Mahavavy r. Madag.
95 □K3 Mahavelona Madag.
176 G8 Mahaweli Ganga r. Sri Lanka
95 □J3 Mahazoma Madag.
85 F6 Mahbub Sudan
176 G4 Mahbubabad Andhra Prad. India
176 E4 Mahbubnagar Andhra Prad. India
186 E4 Mahd adh Dhahab Saudi Arabia
187 L3 Maḩḑah Oman
17 N5 Mahdalynivka Dnipropetrovs'ka Oblast' Ukr.
17 M7 Mahdalynivka Khersons'ka Oblast' Ukr.
87 F2 Mahdia Alg.
137 G3 Mahdia Guyana
87 H2 Mahdia Tunisia
168 I9 Mahe Gansu China
176 D7 Mahe Pondicherry India
99 □2b Mahé i. Inner Islands Seychelles
99 □1b Mahébourg Mauritius
28 F5 Mahee Island Northern Ireland U.K.
179 L7 Mahendraganj Meghalaya India
178 F5 Mahendragarh Haryana India
177 I3 Mahendragiri mt. Orissa India
93 C7 Mahenge Tanz.
203 E12 Maheno South I. N.Z.
55 L5 Maheriv Ukr.
178 D8 Mahesana Gujarat India
178 E8 Maheshwar Madh. Prad. India
187 L9 Maḩfirhīn Suquţrā Yemen
178 G6 Mahgawan Madh. Prad. India
178 D8 Mahi r. Rajasthan India
184 H7 Māhī watercourse Iran
202 L6 Mahia North I. N.Z.
202 L6 Mahia Peninsula North I. N.Z.
62 H5 Mahíde Spain
200 □6 Mahige Island Solomon Is
19 N8 Mahilyow Belarus
Mahilyow Oblast admin. div. Belarus see Mahilyowskaya Voblasts'
19 N8 Mahilyowskaya Voblasts' admin. div. Belarus
176 C3 Mahim Mahar. India
89 G5 Mahin Nigeria
201 □3a Mahina Tahiti Fr. Polynesia
88 C3 Mahina Mali
203 E9 Mahinapua, Lake South I. N.Z.
203 D12 Mahinerangi, Lake South I. N.Z.
178 G3 Mahiya Jammu and Kashmir
176 G9 Mahiyangana Sri Lanka
184 E6 Mah Jān Iran
20 L4 Mahkene mt. Sweden
97 P4 Mahlabatini S. Africa
158 B4 Mahlaing Myanmar
97 P3 Mahlangasi S. Africa
97 L4 Mahlatswetsa S. Africa
52 D5 Mahlberg Ger.
51 H6 Mahlow Ger.
50 D5 Mahlsdorf Ger.
51 E6 Mahlwinkel Ger.
178 H6 Mahmudabad Uttar Prad. India
184 E3 Mahmudabad Iran
185 M4 Maḩmūd-e Rāqī Afgh.
77 R5 Mahmudia Romania
79 H3 Mahmudiye Çanakkale Turkey
79 L3 Mahmudiye Eskişehir Turkey
190 A2 Mahmutlar Turkey
79 K1 Mahmutşevketpaşa Turkey
184 C4 Mahniān Iran
120 G2 Mahnomen MN U.S.A.
176 G9 Maho Sri Lanka
178 G7 Mahoba Uttar Prad. India
202 I5 Mahoenui North I. N.Z.
178 H6 Maholi Uttar Prad. India
66 □ Mahón Spain
109 H4 Mahone Bay N.S. Can.
94 D3 Mahongo Game Park nature res. Namibia
106 E1 Mahony Lake N.W.T. Can.
119 H2 Mahopac NY U.S.A.
119 H2 Mahopac Lake NY U.S.A.
65 P2 Mahora Spain
88 D3 Mahou Mali
90 C2 Mahoua Chad
187 J7 Mahrāt, Jabal mt. Yemen
187 J7 Mahrāt, Wādī r. Yemen
178 G7 Mahrauni Uttar Prad. India
Mähren reg. Czech Rep. see Moravia
87 H2 Mahrès Tunisia
53 N2 Mähring Ger.
184 I5 Māhrūd Iran
Mahsana Gujarat India see Mahesana
173 L8 Mahuanggou Qinghai China
179 O8 Mahudaung mts Myanmar
124 □F13 Māhukona HI U.S.A.
179 N7 Mahur Assam India
176 E3 Mahur Mahar. India
89 G4 Mahuta Nigeria
93 C7 Mahuta Tanz.
178 C9 Mahuva Gujarat India

Mahwa to Mandhoúdhíon

298

178 F6 **Mahwa** *Rajasthan* India
77 P9 **Mahya Dağı** *mt.* Turkey
184 D5 **Mahyār** Iran
155 E6 **Mai** *i. Maluku* Indon.
200 □2 **Maia** American Samoa
98 □1b **Maia** *São Miguel* Azores
62 C6 **Maia** Port.
Maiaia Moz. *see* **Nacala**
66 G5 **Maials** Spain
199 H1 **Maiana** *atoll Gilbert Is* Kiribati
179 N7 **Maibang** *Assam* India
136 C2 **Maicao** Col.
108 E3 **Maicasagi** *r. Que.* Can.
108 E3 **Maicasagi, Lac** *l. Que.* Can.
40 J2 **Maîche** France
170 G8 **Maichen** *Guangdong* China
137 F6 **Maici** *r.* Brazil
137 H5 **Maicuru** *r.* Brazil
75 K6 **Maida** Italy
30 H5 **Maiden Bradley** *Wiltshire, England* U.K.
118 D4 **Maiden Creek** *r. PA* U.S.A.
31 K4 **Maidenhead** *Windsor and Maidenhead, England* U.K.
30 G6 **Maiden Newton** *Dorset, England* U.K.
110 B5 **Maiden Rock** *WI* U.S.A.
26 G12 **Maidens** *South Ayrshire, Scotland* U.K.
155 E3 **Maidi** *Halmahera* Indon.
107 I4 **Maidstone** *Sask.* Can.
31 N5 **Maidstone** *Kent, England* U.K.
89 I4 **Maiduguri** Nigeria
73 M3 **Maiella, Parco Nazionale della** *nat. park* Italy
70 H1 **Maienfeld** Switz.
75 K6 **Maierato** Italy
53 I6 **Maierhöfen** Ger.
77 M3 **Maieru** Romania
67 D10 **Maigmó** *mt.* Spain
36 E4 **Maignelay-Montigny** France
92 C3 **Mai Gudo** *mt.* Eth.
27 E7 **Maigue** *r.* Rep. of Ireland
178 H7 **Maihar** *Madh. Prad.* India
166 D5 **Maihara** Japan
202 J5 **Maihiihi** *North I.* N.Z.
179 M8 **Maijdi** Bangl.
170 F2 **Maiji Shan** *mt. Gansu* China
178 H8 **Maikala Range** *hills Madh. Prad.* India
52 E3 **Maikammer** Ger.
90 E4 **Maiko** *r.* Dem. Rep. Congo
179 I8 **Mailan Hill** *mt. Chhattisgarh* India
178 H5 **Mailani** *Uttar Prad.* India
90 B2 **Maïlao** Chad
156 C6 **Maileppe** Indon.
124 □C12 **Mā'ili** *HI* U.S.A.
43 D7 **Maillas** France
36 B6 **Maillebois** France
42 C3 **Maillezais** France
40 D1 **Mailly-la-Ville** France
36 H6 **Mailly-le-Camp** France
36 E3 **Mailly-Maillet** France
185 O7 **Mailsi** Pak.
170 D2 **Maima** *Gansu* China
49 F10 **Main** *r.* Ger.
186 G7 **Ma'īn** *tourist site* Yemen
179 L6 **Mainaguri** *W. Bengal* India
78 D5 **Mainalo** *mts* Greece
52 G2 **Mainaschaff** Ger.
53 I2 **Mainbernheim** Ger.
109 K3 **Main Brook** *Nfld and Lab.* Can.
53 L4 **Mainburg** Ger.
108 D4 **Main Channel** *lake channel Ont.* Can.
176 E4 **Maindargi** *Mahar.* India
90 C5 **Mai-Ndombe, Lac** *l.* Dem. Rep. Congo
53 J2 **Main-Donau-Kanal** *canal* Ger.
111 R6 **Main Duck Island** *Ont.* Can.
39 J7 **Maine** *r.* France
39 K5 **Maine** *reg.* France
117 □P3 **Maine** *state* U.S.A.
117 □P5 **Maine, Gulf of** U.S.A.
39 K7 **Maine-et-Loire** *dept* France
136 C5 **Mainé Hanari, Cerro** *hill* Col.
89 I3 **Maïné-Soroa** Niger
158 C1 **Maingkwan** Myanmar
159 D8 **Maingy Island** Myanmar
27 I6 **Mainham** Rep. of Ireland
52 H3 **Mainhardt** Ger.
154 E7 **Mainit** *Mindanao* Phil.
154 E7 **Mainit, Lake** *Mindanao* Phil.
170 B4 **Mainkung** *Xizang* China
26 J4 **Mainland** *i. Orkney, Scotland* U.K.
26 □N2 **Mainland** *i. Shetland, Scotland* U.K.
51 D10 **Mainleus** Ger.
173 L12 **Mainling** *Xizang* China
206 E3 **Mainoru** *N.T.* Austr.
206 E3 **Mainoru** *r. N.T.* Austr.
179 I8 **Mainpat** *reg. Chhattisgarh* India
178 G6 **Mainpuri** *Uttar Prad.* India
205 N3 **Main Range National Park** *Qld* Austr.
42 I3 **Mainsat** France
36 C6 **Maintenon** France
95 □J3 **Maintirano** Madag.
20 S4 **Mainua** Fin.
36 B7 **Mainvilliers** France
158 B3 **Mainyaung** Myanmar
49 F10 **Mainz** Ger.
88 □ **Maio** *i.* Cape Verde
71 O9 **Maiolati Spontini** Italy
64 B2 **Maior** *r.* Port.
62 C8 **Maiorca** Port.
62 C9 **Maiorga** Port.
74 H2 **Maiori** Italy
146 B3 **Maipó** *r.* Chile
146 C4 **Maipó, Volcán** *vol.* Chile
147 I5 **Maipú** *Buenos Aires* Arg.
146 C3 **Maipú** *Mendoza* Arg.
146 B3 **Maipú** Chile
136 E3 **Maipures** Col.
137 G3 **Maipuri Landing** Guyana
136 E2 **Maiquetía** Venez.
173 H12 **Maiqu Zangbo** *r. Xizang* China
70 D6 **Maira** *r.* Italy
64 H6 **Mairena del Alcor** Spain
140 E4 **Mairi** Brazil
142 D5 **Mairiporã** Brazil
142 C2 **Mairipotaba** Brazil
62 F5 **Mairos** *mt.* Spain
53 K5 **Maisach** Ger.
53 K5 **Maisach** *r.* Ger.
166 G6 **Maisaka** Japan
58 G5 **Maishofen** Austria
130 F3 **Maisí** Cuba
18 I7 **Maišiagala** Lith.
179 M9 **Maiskhal Channel** *inlet* Bangl.
179 M9 **Maiskhal Island** Bangl.
36 D6 **Maisons-Laffitte** France
59 M2 **Maissau** Austria
36 D7 **Maisse** France
45 H9 **Maissin** Belgium
Maitea *i. Arch. de la Société* Fr. Polynesia *see* **Mehetia**
53 M5 **Maitenbeth** Ger.
144 C3 **Maitencillo** Chile
95 E4 **Maitengwe** Botswana
179 K8 **Maithon** *W. Bengal* India
205 M5 **Maitland** *N.S.W.* Austr.
204 F6 **Maitland** *S.A.* Austr.
208 D6 **Maitland** *r. W.A.* Austr.
157 L2 **Maitland, Banjaran** *mts* Malaysia
209 F9 **Maitland, Lake** *salt flat W.A.* Austr.
213 A2 **Maitri** *research stn* Antarctica
Maiwo *i.* Vanuatu *see* **Maéwo**
206 E3 **Maiwok** *r. N.T.* Austr.
206 B4 **Maiyu, Mount** *hill N.T.* Austr.
126 □R11 **Maíz, Islas del** *is* Nic.
173 J12 **Maizhokunggar** *Xizang* China
36 G6 **Maizières-la-Grande-Paroisse** France
37 L5 **Maizières-lès-Metz** France
166 B5 **Maizuru** Japan
64 H7 **Majaceite** *r.* Spain
63 M8 **Majadahonda** Spain
62 I9 **Majadas de Tiétar** Spain
76 H8 **Maja Jezercë** *mt.* Albania
176 E3 **Majalgaon** *Mahar.* India
137 F4 **Majari** *r.* Brazil
187 I8 **Majdaḩah** Yemen
55 J5 **Majdan Królewski** Pol.
55 L5 **Majdan Niepryski** Pol.
77 J6 **Majdanpek** *Srbija* Serb. and Mont.
190 D5 **Majdel Aanjar** *tourist site* Lebanon
143 F5 **Majé** Brazil
155 A5 **Majene** *Sulawesi* Indon.
68 G3 **Majevica** *mts* Bos.-Herz.
178 H7 **Majhgawan** *Madh. Prad.* India
178 G8 **Majholi** *Madh. Prad.* India
187 J4 **Majhūd** *well* Saudi Arabia
169 O7 **Majia He** *r.* China
171 H7 **Majiang** *Guangxi* China
170 F5 **Majiang** *Guizhou* China
Majiawan *Ningxia* China *see* **Huinong**
162 D3 **Majiazi** *Nei Mongol* China
89 F3 **Majibo** *well* Mali
Majōl *country* N. Pacific Ocean *see* **Marshall Islands**
128 F2 **Majoma** Mex.
98 □3a **Majona, Punta** *pt La Gomera* Canary Is
Majorca *i.* Spain *see* **Mallorca**
204 □3 **Major Lake** S. Pacific Ocean
Majro *atoll* Marshall Is *see* **Majuro**
57 H6 **Majs** Hungary
59 M7 **Majšperk** Slovenia
179 N6 **Majuli Island** India
Majunga Madag. *see* **Mahajanga**
138 D1 **Majurá** Brazil
200 □3b **Majuro** *atoll* Marshall Is
200 □3b **Majuro Lagoon** *Majuro* Marshall Is
97 K4 **Majwemasweu** S. Africa
88 B3 **Maka** Senegal
200 □6 **Maka** *Malaita* Solomon Is
91 B5 **Makabana** Congo
167 L3 **Makabe** Japan
57 H4 **Makád** Hungary
191 H3 **Makadzhoy** Rus. Fed.
124 □C12 **Mākaha** *HI* U.S.A.
124 □B12 **Makahū'ena Point** *HI* U.S.A.
89 H6 **Makak** Cameroon
91 B5 **Makaka** Congo
90 E5 **Makalado** Dem. Rep. Congo
155 A5 **Makale** *Sulawesi* Indon.
155 D2 **Makalehi** *i.* Indon.
179 K6 **Makalu** *mt.* China/Nepal
179 K6 **Makalu Barun National Park** Nepal
93 A6 **Makamba** Burundi
183 T4 **Makanchi** Kazakh.
Makane Rus. Fed. *see* **Mekhen-Yurt**
93 B8 **Makanjila** Malawi
178 H6 **Makanpur** *Uttar Prad.* India
93 C6 **Makanya** Tanz.
90 C4 **Makanza** Dem. Rep. Congo
124 □D12 **Makapu'u Head** *HI* U.S.A.
95 □J3 **Makaraingo** Madag.
203 C13 **Makarewa** *South I.* N.Z.
89 I3 **Makari** Cameroon
14 J3 **Makar-Ib** Rus. Fed.
14 L2 **Makarikha** Rus. Fed.
Makari Mountain National Park Tanz. *see* **Mahale Mountains National Park**
16 I3 **Makariv** Ukr.
203 D11 **Makarora** *r. South I.* N.Z.
162 M4 **Makarov** *Sakhalin* Rus. Fed.
218 M1 **Makarov Basin** *sea feature* Arctic Ocean
16 B5 **Makarove** Ukr.
15 H5 **Makarovo** Rus. Fed.
68 F4 **Makarska** Croatia
185 N5 **Makarwal** Pak.
14 J4 **Makar'ye** Rus. Fed.
14 H4 **Makar'yev** Rus. Fed.
93 A7 **Makasa** Zambia
155 A6 **Makassar** *Sulawesi* Indon.
155 A3 **Makassar, Selat** *str.* Indon.
182 E4 **Makat** Kazakh.
97 Q3 **Makatini Flats** *lowland* S. Africa
158 C1 **Makaw** Myanmar
124 □E13 **Makawao** *HI* U.S.A.
95 □J4 **Makay, Massif du** *mts* Madag.
Makedonija *country* Europe *see* **Macedonia**
203 □4 **Makefu** Niue
97 K4 **Makeleketla** S. Africa
154 □ **Makelulu** *hill* Palau
201 □3 **Makemo** *atoll Arch. des Tuamotu* Fr. Polynesia
88 B4 **Makeni** Sierra Leone
93 B7 **Makete** Tanz.
Makeyevka Ukr. *see* **Makiyivka**
94 E4 **Makgadikgadi** *depr.* Botswana
94 E4 **Makgadikgadi Pans National Park** Botswana
191 I3 **Makhachkala** Rus. Fed.
185 N5 **Makhad** Pak.
95 F4 **Makhado** S. Africa
97 L6 **Makhaleng** *r.* Lesotho
182 D4 **Makhambet** Kazakh.
186 F3 **Makhāmīr, Jabal al** *hill* Saudi Arabia
Makharadze Georgia *see* **Ozurget'i**
190 A8 **Makhāzin, Kathīb al** *des.* Egypt
97 N5 **Makheka** *mt.* Lesotho
190 G3 **Makhfar al Ḩammām** Syria
184 I3 **Makhmal** Turkm.
191 G1 **Makhmud-Mekteb** Rus. Fed.
189 K6 **Makhmūr** Iraq
18 M4 **Makhnovka** Rus. Fed.
183 M1 **Makhorovka** Kazakh.
176 E4 **Makhtal** *Andhra Prad.* India
187 I7 **Makhyah, Wādī** *r.* Yemen
167 H1 **Maki** Japan
155 E3 **Makian** *vol. Maluku* Indon.
167 I2 **Makihata-yama** *mt.* Japan
203 F11 **Makikihi** *South I.* N.Z.
Makima *atoll Arch. des Tuamotu* Fr. Polynesia *see* **Makemo**
93 C5 **Makindu** Kenya
166 D5 **Makino** Japan
183 N1 **Makinsk** Kazakh.
105 J2 **Makinson Inlet** *Nunavut* Can.
167 I4 **Makioka** Japan
16 F5 **Makiv** Ukr.
17 K3 **Makiyivka** *Chernihivs'ka Oblast'* Ukr.
17 Q5 **Makiyivka** *Donets'ka Oblast'* Ukr.
186 D5 **Makkah** Saudi Arabia
186 E5 **Makkah** *prov.* Saudi Arabia
20 U1 **Makkaurhalvøya Naturreservat** *nature res.* Norway
109 J2 **Makkovik** *Nfld and Lab.* Can.
109 J2 **Makkovik, Cape** *Nfld and Lab.* Can.
44 H2 **Makkum** Neth.
19 R7 **Maklaki** Rus. Fed.
68 F4 **Makljen** *pass* Bos.-Herz.
57 J5 **Makó** Hungary
88 B3 **Mako** Senegal
137 G4 **Makoa, Serra** *hills* Brazil
201 □1 **Makogai** *i.* Fiji
90 B4 **Makokou** Gabon
97 K2 **Makokskraal** S. Africa
93 C7 **Makonde Plateau** Tanz.
Makongai *i.* Fiji *see* **Makogai**
93 B7 **Makongolosi** Tanz.
94 D5 **Makopong** Botswana
191 A2 **Makopse** Rus. Fed.
90 F4 **Makoro** Dem. Rep. Congo
95 G3 **Makosa** Zimbabwe
90 C5 **Makotipoko** Congo
202 K7 **Makotuku** *North I.* N.Z.
90 B5 **Makoua** Congo
91 B5 **Makoubi** Congo
57 H2 **Makov** Slovakia
68 E3 **Makovnik** *mt.* Croatia
55 I4 **Maków** Pol.
54 F2 **Makowarsko** Pol.
55 J3 **Maków Mazowiecki** Pol.
55 H6 **Maków Podhalański** Pol.
79 G6 **Makra** *i.* Greece
78 D4 **Makrakomi** Greece
184 I8 **Makran** *reg.* Iran/Pak.
178 E6 **Makrana** *Rajasthan* India
185 J9 **Makran Coast Range** *mts* Pak.
55 M4 **Makrany** Belarus
176 G3 **Makri** *Chhattisgarh* India
78 F5 **Makronisi** *i.* Greece
79 H5 **Makronisi** *i.* Greece
78 D2 **Makrygialos** *Kentriki Makedonia* Greece
79 G7 **Makrygialos** *Kriti* Greece
19 S4 **Maksatikha** Rus. Fed.
178 F8 **Maksi** *Madh. Prad.* India
162 J5 **Maksimovka** Rus. Fed.
185 J7 **Maksotag** Iran
178 F8 **Maksudangarh** *Madh. Prad.* India
191 H5 **Maksudlu** Azer.
54 G2 **Maksymilianowo** Pol.
184 A2 **Mākū** Iran
164 U4 **Makubetsu** Japan
179 O6 **Makum** *Assam* India
93 B7 **Makumbako** Tanz.
91 D6 **Makumbi** Dem. Rep. Congo
Makundu *i. N. Male* Maldives *see* **Makunudhoo**
93 C6 **Makunduchi** Tanz.
171 L7 **Makung** Taiwan
93 B7 **Makungu** Tanz.
93 C7 **Makunguwiro** Tanz.
175 □1 **Makunudhoo** *i. N. Male* Maldives
165 H15 **Makurazaki** Japan
89 H5 **Makurdi** Nigeria
202 J7 **Makuri** *North I.* N.Z.
92 D4 **Makuungo** Somalia
184 E7 **Makūyeh** Iran
93 C5 **Makuyuni** Tanz.
97 J3 **Makwassie** S. Africa
95 F3 **Makwiro** Zimbabwe
179 L6 **Mal** *W. Bengal* India
138 A3 **Mala** Peru
Mala Rep. of Ireland *see* **Mallow**
Mala *i.* Solomon Is *see* **Malaita**
65 L6 **Malá** Spain
20 O4 **Malå** Sweden
126 □S14 **Mala, Punta** *pt* Panama
65 I8 **Mala, Punta** *pt* Spain
206 C6 **Mala Aboriginal Land** *res. N.T.* Austr.
190 A9 **Mal'ab, Ra's** *pt* Egypt
154 E8 **Malabang** *Mindanao* Phil.
204 □2 **Malabar** *b. Lord Howe I.* Austr.
176 D6 **Malabar Coast** India
17 N6 **Mala Bilozerka** Ukr.
89 H6 **Malabo** Equat. Guinea
57 I5 **Mala Bosna** *Vojvodina, Srbija* Serb. and Mont.
147 I4 **Mal Abrigo** Uru.
154 A7 **Malabuñgan** *Palawan* Phil.
Malaca Spain *see* **Málaga**
143 F2 **Malacacheta** Brazil
Malacca Malaysia *see* **Melaka**
Malacca *state* Malaysia *see* **Melaka**
156 C2 **Malacca, Strait of** Indon./Malaysia
56 G3 **Malacky** Slovakia
122 H6 **Malad** *r. ID* U.S.A.
122 H5 **Malad City** *ID* U.S.A.
17 L3 **Mala Divytsya** Ukr.
18 J7 **Maladzyechna** Belarus
57 H2 **Malá Fatra** *mts* Slovakia
57 I2 **Malá Fatra** *nat. park* Slovakia
65 K7 **Málaga** Spain
65 J7 **Málaga** *prov.* Spain
118 E5 **Malaga** *NJ* U.S.A.
123 L10 **Malaga** *NM* U.S.A.
116 D9 **Malaga** *OH* U.S.A.
65 J7 **Málaga, Montes de** *mts* Spain
93 A6 **Malagarasi** *r.* Burundi/Tanz.
93 A6 **Malagarasi** Tanz.
65 L2 **Malagón** Spain
64 E5 **Malagon** *r.* Spain
63 L7 **Malagón, Sierra de** *mts* Spain
155 B8 **Malahar** *Sumba* Indon.
27 J6 **Malahide** Rep. of Ireland
95 □J4 **Malaimbandy** Madag.
54 D2 **Mała Ina** *r.* Pol.
200 □6 **Malaita** *i.* Solomon Is
157 M9 **Malaka** *mt. Sumbawa* Indon.
154 □ **Malakal** Palau
92 A2 **Malakal** Sudan
154 □ **Malakal Passage** Palau
68 E3 **Mala Kapela** *mts* Croatia
201 □1a **Malake** *i.* Fiji
178 H5 **Malakheti** Nepal
68 E3 **Mala Kladuša** Bos.-Herz.
206 C2 **Malak Malak Aboriginal Land** *res. N.T.* Austr.
200 □6 **Malakobi Island** Solomon Is
200 □5 **Malakula** *i.* Vanuatu
185 O5 **Malakwal** Pak.
71 L6 **Malalbergo** Italy
17 M6 **Mala Lepetykha** Ukr.
137 G3 **Malali** Guyana
155 B5 **Malamala** *Sulawesi* Indon.
154 C8 **Malamaui** *i.* Phil.
71 M5 **Malamocco** Italy
16 E3 **Mala Moshchanytsya** Ukr.
154 B6 **Malampaya Sound** *sea chan. Palawan* Phil.
185 K9 **Malan, Ras** *pt* Pak.
154 B7 **Malanao** *i.* Phil.
37 J5 **Malancourt** France
64 G7 **Malandar, Punta de** *pt* Spain
157 J8 **Malang** *Jawa* Indon.
95 H2 **Malanga** Moz.
93 B7 **Malangali** Tanz.
Malangana Nepal *see* **Malangwa**
Malange Angola *see* **Malanje**
20 O2 **Malangseidet** Norway
179 J6 **Malangwa** Nepal
154 D8 **Malanipa** *i.* Phil.
91 C7 **Malanje** Angola
91 C7 **Malanje** *prov.* Angola
54 G4 **Malanów** Pol.
38 G6 **Malansac** France
154 B7 **Malanut Bay** *Palawan* Phil.
89 F4 **Malanville** Benin
146 D2 **Malanzán** Arg.
146 D2 **Malanzán, Sierra de** *mts* Arg.
17 N4 **Mala Pereshchepyna** Ukr.
176 E7 **Malappuram** *Kerala* India
23 N2 **Mälaren** *l.* Sweden
146 C4 **Malargüe** Arg.
137 H4 **Malaripo** Brazil
108 E3 **Malartic** *Que.* Can.
111 P1 **Malartic, Lac** *l. Que.* Can.
16 D2 **Malaryta** Belarus
56 E1 **Malá Skála** Czech Rep.
155 A6 **Malasoro, Teluk** *b.* Indon.
145 D7 **Malaspina** Arg.
106 A3 **Malaspina Glacier** *AK* U.S.A.
106 E5 **Malaspina Strait** *B.C.* Can.
59 O7 **Mala Subotica** Croatia
157 J6 **Malatayur, Tanjung** *pt* Indon.
17 O5 **Mala Ternivka** *r.* Ukr.
188 I4 **Malatya** Turkey
41 G8 **Malaucène** France
36 B4 **Malaunay** France
43 D8 **Malaussanne** France
178 E4 **Malaut** *Punjab* India
176 E6 **Malavalli** *Karnataka* India
137 H4 **Malavate** Fr. Guiana
184 B5 **Malāvī** Iran
16 J4 **Mala Vil'shanka** Ukr.
17 K5 **Mala Vyska** Ukr.
89 H3 **Malawa** Niger
157 L1 **Malawali** *i.* Malaysia
54 F3 **Mała Wełna** *r.* Pol.
93 B7 **Malawi** *country* Africa
Malawi, Lake Africa *see* **Nyasa, Lake**
Malawi National Park Zambia *see* **Nyika National Park**
85 H6 **Malawiya** Sudan
20 P5 **Malax** Fin.
Malaya *pen.* Malaysia *see* **Malaysia, Semenanjung**
191 H1 **Malaya Areshevka** Rus. Fed.
18 G8 **Malaya Byerastavitsa** Belarus
14 K2 **Malaya Pera** Rus. Fed.
19 P3 **Malaya Vishera** Rus. Fed.
154 E7 **Malaybalay** *Mindanao* Phil.
184 C4 **Malāyer** Iran
36 F7 **Malay-le-Grand** France
207 L4 **Malay Reef** *Coral Sea Is Terr.* Austr.
183 Q5 **Malay Sary** Kazakh.
156 H3 **Malaysia** *country* Asia
156 E3 **Malaysia, Semenanjung** *pen.* Malaysia
189 K4 **Malazgirt** Turkey
109 G4 **Malbaie** *r. Que.* Can.
146 B5 **Malbarco, Laguna** *l.* Arg.
89 G3 **Malbaza** Niger
206 H6 **Malbon** *Qld* Austr.
55 H1 **Malbork** Pol.
52 B2 **Malborn** Ger.
41 C7 **Malbouzon** France
144 E3 **Malbrán** Arg.
40 I3 **Malbuisson** France
62 F8 **Malcata, Serra de** *mts* Port.
71 J4 **Malcesine** Italy
17 T4 **Mal'chevskaya** Rus. Fed.
50 G3 **Malchin** Ger.
50 G3 **Malchiner See** *l.* Ger.
50 F4 **Malchow** Ger.
57 K3 **Malčice** Slovakia
64 H4 **Malcocinado** Spain
209 F10 **Malcolm** *W.A.* Austr.
209 G12 **Malcolm, Point** *W.A.* Austr.
26 D10 **Malcolm's Point** *Scotland* U.K.
57 K2 **Malcov** Slovakia
54 E4 **Malczyce** Pol.
179 L7 **Maldah** *W. Bengal* India
45 D6 **Maldegem** Belgium
44 I5 **Malden** Neth.
121 K7 **Malden** *MO* U.S.A.
217 I6 **Malden Island** Kiribati
66 G2 **Malditos, Montes** *mts* Spain
72 A8 **Mal di Ventre, Isola di** *i. Sardegna* Italy
175 D10 **Maldives** *country* Indian Ocean
205 J7 **Maldon** *Vic.* Austr.
31 N4 **Maldon** *Essex, England* U.K.
144 G4 **Maldonado** Uru.
129 I9 **Maldonado, Punta** *pt* Mex.
55 H2 **Małdyty** Pol.
99 □3a **Male** *Njazidja* Comoros
71 J3 **Malè** Italy
175 □1 **Male** *N. Male* Maldives
158 C3 **Male** Myanmar
88 C4 **Maléa** Guinea
79 H3 **Maleas, Akra** *pt Lesvos* Greece
78 E6 **Maleas, Akra** *pt* Greece
175 □1 **Male Atoll** Maldives
97 J4 **Malebogo** S. Africa
54 E1 **Malechowo** Pol.
176 E3 **Malegaon** *Mahar.* India
178 E9 **Malegaon** *Mahar.* India
95 H3 **Malei** Moz.
63 Q5 **Maleján** Spain
92 A3 **Malek** Sudan
56 G3 **Malé Karpaty** *hills* Slovakia
56 G3 **Malé Karpaty** *park* Slovakia
97 M6 **Malekgonyane Wildlife Reserve** *nature res.* S. Africa
184 I7 **Malek Sīāh, Kūh-e** *mt.* Afgh.
90 E5 **Malela** *Maniema* Dem. Rep. Congo
91 E6 **Malela** *Maniema* Dem. Rep. Congo
91 B6 **Malélé** Congo
91 B6 **Malele** Dem. Rep. Congo
95 H2 **Malema** Moz.
91 E7 **Malemba Nkulu** Dem. Rep. Congo
41 G8 **Malemort-du-Comtat** France
42 H5 **Malemort-sur-Corrèze** France
89 G4 **Malendo** *watercourse* Nigeria
48 K2 **Malente** Ger.
97 N1 **Maleoskop** S. Africa
23 L5 **Målerås** Sweden
178 E4 **Maler Kotla** *Punjab* India
70 F3 **Malesco** Italy
77 K9 **Maleševske Planine** *mts* Bulg./Macedonia
36 D7 **Malesherbes** France
78 E4 **Malesina** Greece
Malesso' Guam *see* **Merizo**
185 L5 **Mālestān** Afgh.
38 G6 **Malestroit** France
169 K1 **Maleta** Rus. Fed.
74 H8 **Maletto** *Sicilia* Italy
200 □6 **Malevangga** *Choiseul* Solomon Is
19 V8 **Malevka** Rus. Fed.
74 H6 **Malfa** *Isole Lipari* Italy
96 E10 **Malgas** S. Africa
53 N4 **Malgersdorf** Ger.
191 F2 **Malgobek** Rus. Fed.
20 N4 **Malgomaj** *l.* Sweden
66 K4 **Malgrat de Mar** Spain
84 E6 **Malha** Sudan
140 E5 **Malhada** Brazil
62 H5 **Malhadas** Port.
186 H3 **Malham** Saudi Arabia
178 E7 **Malhargarh** *Madh. Prad.* India
122 F4 **Malheur** *r. OR* U.S.A.
99 □1b **Malheureux, Cape** Mauritius
122 E5 **Malheur Lake** *OR* U.S.A.
122 E5 **Malheur National Wildlife Refuge** *nature res. OR* U.S.A.
88 D3 **Mali** *country* Africa
90 E5 **Mali** Dem. Rep. Congo
88 B3 **Mali** Guinea
79 G7 **Malia** *Kriti* Greece
78 D4 **Maliakos Kolpos** *b.* Greece
162 G4 **Malian** *Heilong.* China
155 D8 **Maliana** East Timor
169 J9 **Malian He** *r.* China
168 D6 **Malianjing** *Gansu* China
168 G7 **Malianjing** *Gansu* China
97 M5 **Malibamatso** *r.* Lesotho
124 N7 **Malibu** *CA* U.S.A.
39 K6 **Malicorne-sur-Sarthe** France
154 D8 **Maligay Bay** *Mindanao* Phil.
36 G8 **Maligny** France
173 E13 **Malihabad** *Uttar Prad.* India
158 C2 **Mali Hka** *r.* Myanmar
57 I6 **Mali Iđoš** *Vojvodina, Srbija* Serb. and Mont.
41 I8 **Malijai** France
185 M5 **Malikdin** Afgh.
185 J7 **Malik Naro** *mt.* Pak.
155 C4 **Maliku** *Sulawesi* Indon.
159 D8 **Mali Kyun** *i.* Myanmar
155 B5 **Malili** *Sulawesi* Indon.
23 L4 **Målilla** Sweden
68 E3 **Mali Lošinj** Croatia
146 C1 **Malimán de Abajo** Arg.
91 F6 **Malimba, Monts** *mts* Dem. Rep. Congo
55 L6 **Mali Mokryany** Ukr.
156 G8 **Malimping** *Jawa* Indon.
27 H2 **Malin** Rep. of Ireland
Malin Ukr. *see* **Malyn**
16 E1 **Malinavka** Belarus
27 E3 **Malin Beg** Rep. of Ireland
93 D5 **Malindi** Kenya
95 E3 **Malindi** Zimbabwe
57 I3 **Málinec** Slovakia
Malines Belgium *see* **Mechelen**
169 J8 **Maling** *Gansu* China
90 B5 **Malinga** Gabon
27 H2 **Malin Head** Rep. of Ireland
77 O3 **Mălini** Romania
27 E3 **Malin More** Rep. of Ireland
155 A6 **Malino** *Sulawesi* Indon.
19 V6 **Malino** Rus. Fed.
155 B3 **Malino, Gunung** *mt.* Indon.
201 □2a **Malinoa** *i.* Tonga
183 N2 **Malinovka** Kazakh.
162 H6 **Malinovka** *r.* Rus. Fed.
183 R2 **Malinovoye Ozero** Rus. Fed.
71 R5 **Malinska** Croatia
93 C7 **Malinyi** Tanz.
79 G7 **Malion, Kolpos** *b. Kriti* Greece
170 E7 **Malipo** *Yunnan* China
78 B2 **Maliq** Albania
68 E3 **Mali Raginac** *mt.* Croatia
76 I8 **Malit, Qafa e** *pass* Albania
154 E8 **Malita** *Mindanao* Phil.
154 E6 **Malitbog** *Leyte* Phil.
159 D9 **Maliwun** Myanmar
178 C8 **Maliya** *Gujarat* India
17 L6 **Maliyivka** Ukr.
76 H6 **Mali Zvornik** *Srbija* Serb. and Mont.
191 E2 **Malka** Rus. Fed.
191 F2 **Malka** *r.* Rus. Fed.
184 B5 **Malkaili** Iran
92 D3 **Malka Mary** Kenya
176 G3 **Malkangiri** *Orissa* India
176 C4 **Malkapur** *Mahar.* India
178 F9 **Malkapur** *Mahar.* India
79 H2 **Malkara** Turkey
18 J9 **Mal'kavichy** Belarus
169 K1 **Malkhanskiy Khrebet** *mts* Rus. Fed.
55 K3 **Małkinia Górna** Pol.
77 P9 **Malko Tŭrnovo** Bulg.
205 L7 **Mallacoota** *Vic.* Austr.
205 L7 **Mallacoota Inlet** *b. Vic.* Austr.
26 E9 **Mallaig** *Highland, Scotland* U.K.
84 D5 **Mallanga** *well* Chad
178 C7 **Mallani** *reg.* India
85 F3 **Mallawī** Egypt
205 I6 **Mallee Cliffs National Park** *N.S.W.* Austr.
41 G9 **Mallemort** France
63 R5 **Mallén** Spain
50 D3 **Mallentin** Ger.
70 H3 **Mallero** *r.* Italy
53 M4 **Mallersdorf** Ger.
107 L1 **Mallery Lake** *Nunavut* Can.
71 J2 **Malles Venosta** Italy
141 C8 **Mallét** Brazil
Mallia *Kriti* Greece *see* **Malia**
50 D4 **Malliß** Ger.
58 H6 **Mallnitz** Austria
146 B4 **Malloa** Chile
67 K8 **Mallorca** *i.* Spain
27 E8 **Mallow** Rep. of Ireland
208 H7 **Mallowa Well** *W.A.* Austr.
30 D1 **Malltraeth Bay** *Wales* U.K.
30 E2 **Mallwyd** *Gwynedd, Wales* U.K.
20 K4 **Malm** Norway
185 J5 **Malman Rūd** *r.* Afgh.
20 P3 **Malmberget** Sweden
45 J8 **Malmédy** Belgium
96 C9 **Malmesbury** S. Africa
30 H4 **Malmesbury** *Wiltshire, England* U.K.
23 M2 **Malmköping** Sweden
22 J6 **Malmö** Sweden
131 □8 **Malmok** *hd Bonaire* Neth. Antilles
22 J6 **Malmö-Sturup** *airport* Sweden
23 L3 **Malmslätt** Sweden
14 J4 **Malmyzh** Rus. Fed.
70 F4 **Malnate** Italy
155 E1 **Malo** *i.* Indon.
71 K4 **Malo** Italy
200 □5 **Malo** *i.* Vanuatu
19 T9 **Maloarkhangel'sk** Rus. Fed.
137 F5 **Maloca** *Amazonas* Brazil
137 H4 **Maloca** *Pará* Brazil
139 E3 **Maloca Salamaim** Brazil
76 J6 **Malo Crniće** *Srbija* Serb. and Mont.
55 I5 **Małogoszcz** Pol.
201 □1a **Malolo** *i.* Fiji
201 □1a **Malolo Barrier Reef** Fiji
154 C4 **Malolos** *Luzon* Phil.
97 P2 **Malolotja Nature Reserve** Swaziland
97 P3 **Maloma** Swaziland
93 B8 **Malombe, Lake** Malawi
54 D4 **Małomice** Pol.
93 B8 **Malomo** Malawi
17 N5 **Malomykhaylivka** *Dnipropetrovs'ka Oblast'* Ukr.
17 P5 **Malomykhaylivka** *Dnipropetrovs'ka Oblast'* Ukr.
63 Q5 **Malón** Spain
70 D5 **Malone** *r.* Italy
117 K4 **Malone** *NY* U.S.A.
170 D6 **Malong** *Yunnan* China
91 D7 **Malonga** Dem. Rep. Congo
94 B2 **Malongo** Angola
70 I3 **Malonno** Italy
56 D3 **Malonty** Czech Rep.
55 I5 **Małopolska, Wyżyna** *hills* Pol.
55 I6 **Małopolskie** *prov.* Pol.
17 N9 **Malorichens'ke** Ukr.
Malorita Belarus *see* **Malaryta**
14 G3 **Maloshuyka** Rus. Fed.
68 F4 **Malovan** *pass* Bos.-Herz.
77 K6 **Malovăț** Romania
Malovata Moldova *see* **Molovata**
95 F2 **Malowera** Moz.
21 H6 **Måløy** Norway
19 T6 **Maloyaroslavets** Rus. Fed.
19 S9 **Maloye Bobrovo** Rus. Fed.
19 T2 **Maloye Borisovo** Rus. Fed.
55 I1 **Maloye-Lugovoye** Rus. Fed.
14 J2 **Malozemel'skaya Tundra** *lowland* Rus. Fed.
98 □3d **Malpaises** *La Palma* Canary Is
62 G7 **Malpartida** Port.
64 G2 **Malpartida de Cáceres** Spain
64 H3 **Malpartida de la Serena** Spain
62 H9 **Malpartida de Plasencia** Spain
29 L7 **Malpas** *Cheshire, England* U.K.
30 F4 **Malpas** *Newport, Wales* U.K.
98 □3e **Malpaso** *mt. El Hierro* Canary Is
128 E3 **Malpaso** Mex.
217 N5 **Malpelo, Isla de** *i.* N. Pacific Ocean
62 H1 **Mal Perro, Punta** *pt* Spain
62 C2 **Malpica** Spain
63 K9 **Malpica de Tajo** Spain
62 F9 **Malpica do Tejo** Port.
18 H4 **Mālpils** Latvia
176 E4 **Malprabha** *r.* India
178 E6 **Malpura** *Rajasthan* India
52 E4 **Malsch** Ger.
56 D3 **Malše** *r.* Czech Rep.
49 I8 **Malsfeld** Ger.
176 D4 **Malsiras** *Mahar.* India
59 I6 **Malta** Austria
69 E8 **Malta** *country* Europe
18 K5 **Malta** Latvia
18 K5 **Malta** *r.* Latvia
75 □ **Malta** *i.* Malta
62 F7 **Malta** Port.
122 H5 **Malta** *ID* U.S.A.
122 K2 **Malta** *MT* U.S.A.
94 C5 **Maltahöhe** Namibia
89 I3 **Maltam** Cameroon
29 O7 **Maltby** *South Yorkshire, England* U.K.
29 R7 **Maltby le Marsh** *Lincolnshire, England* U.K.
52 D5 **Malterdingen** Ger.
52 E7 **Malters** Switz.
20 T3 **Maltion luonnonpuisto** *nature res.* Fin.
29 P5 **Malton** *North Yorkshire, England* U.K.
200 □2 **Malua** Samoa
63 Q6 **Maluenda** Spain
Maluera Moz. *see* **Malowera**
Malukken *is* Indon. *see* **Maluku**
91 B6 **Maluku** Dem. Rep. Congo
155 E4 **Maluku** *is* Indon.
155 E3 **Maluku** *is* Indon.
155 F5 **Maluku** *prov.* Indon.
155 D4 **Maluku, Laut** *sea* Indon.
155 E4 **Maluku Utara** *prov.* Indon.
190 E5 **Ma'lūlā, Jabal** *mts* Syria
77 K4 **Malului, Vârful** *hill* Romania
89 G4 **Malumfashi** Nigeria
91 E9 **Malundano** Zambia
91 D8 **Malundo** Angola
23 J1 **Malung** Sweden
54 D3 **Małuszów** Pol.
55 H5 **Maluszyn** Pol.
97 M5 **Maluti Mountains** Lesotho
200 □6 **Malu'u** *Malaita* Solomon Is
88 E4 **Maluwe** Ghana
63 J5 **Malva** Spain
70 F3 **Malvaglia** Switz.
176 C4 **Malvan** *Mahar.* India
Malvasia Greece *see* **Monemvasia**
64 A3 **Malveira** Port.
130 □ **Malvern** Jamaica
130 □ **Malvern** *hill* Jamaica
121 I8 **Malvern** *AR* U.S.A.
116 D8 **Malvern** *OH* U.S.A.
30 H3 **Malvern Link** *Worcestershire, England* U.K.
178 F8 **Malwa** *reg. Madh. Prad.* India
92 A2 **Malwal** Sudan
51 J7 **Malxe** *r.* Ger.
57 H4 **Malý Dunaj** *r.* Slovakia
55 M3 **Malyech** Belarus
57 K3 **Malý Horeš** Slovakia
57 J3 **Mályi** Hungary
193 M3 **Malykay** Rus. Fed.
16 I3 **Malyn** Ukr.
17 P4 **Malynivka** Ukr.
16 F2 **Malyns'k** Ukr.
55 K2 **Mały Płock** Pol.
18 L1 **Malyy, Ostrov** *i.* Rus. Fed.
193 R3 **Malyy Anyuy** *r.* Rus. Fed.
184 F2 **Malyy Balkhan, Khrebet** *hill* Turkm.
57 L3 **Malyy Bereznyy** Ukr.
15 I7 **Malyye Derbety** Rus. Fed.
19 X4 **Malyye Soli** Rus. Fed.
15 J5 **Malyy Irgiz** *r.* Rus. Fed.
Malyy Kavkaz *mts* Asia *see* **Lesser Caucasus**
169 J1 **Malyy Kunaley** Rus. Fed.
193 P2 **Malyy Lyakhovskiy, Ostrov** *i. Novosibirskiye O-va* Rus. Fed.
16 F2 **Malyy Stydyn** Ukr.
193 L2 **Malyy Taymyr, Ostrov** *i.* Rus. Fed.
18 J2 **Malyy Tyuters, Ostrov** *i.* Estonia
182 C3 **Malyy Uzen'** *r.* Kazakh./Rus. Fed.
191 C1 **Malyy Zelenchuk** *r.* Rus. Fed.
193 P3 **Mama** *r.* Rus. Fed.
14 J5 **Mamadysh** Rus. Fed.
97 M3 **Mamafubedu** S. Africa
97 L4 **Mamahabane** S. Africa
201 □1 **Mamanuca-i-Cake Group** *is* Fiji
Mamanutha-i-Thake Group *is* Fiji *see* **Mamanuca-i-Cake Group**
202 H2 **Mamaranui** *North I.* N.Z.
119 H3 **Mamaroneck** *NY* U.S.A.
155 A5 **Mamasa** *Sulawesi* Indon.
185 K6 **Mamatān Nāvar** *l.* Afgh.
184 C6 **Māmātīn** Iran
173 K11 **Mamba** *Xizang* China
Mamba Japan *see* **Manba**
154 B8 **Mambahenauhan** *i.* Phil.
140 D5 **Mambai** Brazil
154 E7 **Mambajao** Phil.
89 I5 **Mambal** Cameroon
93 B6 **Mambali** Tanz.
90 F4 **Mambasa** Dem. Rep. Congo
90 C4 **Mambéré** *r.* C.A.R.
90 B3 **Mambéré-Kadéï** *pref.* C.A.R.
155 A5 **Mambi** *Sulawesi* Indon.
89 H5 **Mambila Mountains** Cameroon/Nigeria
90 C4 **Mambili** *r.* Congo
88 B4 **Mambolo** Sierra Leone
142 A6 **Mamborê** Brazil
63 M5 **Mambrilla de Castejón** Spain
93 D5 **Mambrui** Kenya
154 C5 **Mamburao** *Mindoro* Phil.
191 J3 **Mamedkala** Rus. Fed.
99 □2a **Mamelle** *i. Inner Islands* Seychelles
97 M1 **Mamelodi** S. Africa
39 L5 **Mamers** France
89 H5 **Mamfe** Cameroon
137 F6 **Mamiá** Brazil
137 F6 **Mamiá, Lago** *l.* Brazil
94 D3 **Mamili National Park** Namibia
138 C5 **Mamiña** Chile
136 E5 **Mamirauá, Reserve de Desenvolvimento Sustentável** *nature res.* Brazil
40 I2 **Mamirolle** France
191 E3 **Mamison Pass** Georgia/Rus. Fed.
179 N8 **Mamit** *Mizoram* India
183 M1 **Mamlyutka** Kazakh.
191 H6 **Mämmädbäyli** Azer.
53 K5 **Mammendorf** Ger.
53 N4 **Mamming** Ger.
75 K7 **Mammola** Italy
125 V9 **Mammoth** *AZ* U.S.A.
114 D7 **Mammoth Cave National Park** *KY* U.S.A.
124 N4 **Mammoth Lakes** *CA* U.S.A.
124 M4 **Mammoth Reservoir** *CA* U.S.A.
72 C7 **Mamoiada** *Sardegna* Italy
130 F8 **Mamonal** Col.
72 C6 **Mamone** *Sardegna* Italy
18 C7 **Mamonovo** *Kaliningradskaya Oblast'* Rus. Fed.
19 W8 **Mamonovo** *Ryazanskaya Oblast'* Rus. Fed.
183 S1 **Mamontovo** Rus. Fed.
118 F6 **Mamora** *NJ* U.S.A.
138 D2 **Mamoré** *r.* Bol./Brazil
136 E5 **Mamori** Brazil
137 F5 **Mamori, Lago** *l.* Brazil
138 D1 **Mamoriá** Brazil
88 B4 **Mamou** Guinea
99 □3b **Mamoudzou** Mayotte
Mamoutsou Mayotte *see* **Mamoudzou**
95 □J3 **Mampikony** Madag.
88 E5 **Mampong** Ghana
96 C9 **Mamre** S. Africa
55 J1 **Mamry, Jezioro** *l.* Pol.
155 A5 **Mamuju** *Sulawesi* Indon.
187 L6 **Ma'mūl** Oman
184 D4 **Māmūnīyeh** Iran
94 D4 **Mamuno** Botswana
76 H9 **Mamuras** Albania
164 R8 **Mamurogawa** Japan
Mamutzu Mayotte *see* **Mamoudzou**
182 H2 **Mamyt** Kazakh.
88 D5 **Man** Côte d'Ivoire
176 D4 **Man** *r.* India
178 G3 **Man** Jammu and Kashmir
116 D11 **Man** *WV* U.S.A.
201 □1a **Mana** *i.* Fiji
137 H3 **Mana** Fr. Guiana
57 H3 **Maňa** Slovakia
124 □B11 **Mānā** *HI* U.S.A.
136 C2 **Mana Bárbara** Venez.
136 B5 **Manabí** *prov.* Ecuador
136 C3 **Manacacias** *r.* Col.
137 F5 **Manacapuru** Brazil
67 L8 **Manacor** Spain
98 □1c **Manadas** *São Jorge* Azores
155 D3 **Manado** *Sulawesi* Indon.
155 D3 **Manadotua** *i.* Indon.
45 F8 **Manage** Belgium
126 □P11 **Managua** Nic.
126 □P11 **Managua, Lago de** *l.* Nic.
187 M4 **Manaḩ** Oman
119 G5 **Manahawkin Bay** *NJ* U.S.A.
202 I6 **Manaia** *North I.* N.Z.
95 □J4 **Manakara** Madag.
202 J7 **Manakau** *North I.* N.Z.
203 H9 **Manakau** *mt. South I.* N.Z.
186 F8 **Manākhah** Yemen
178 F3 **Manali** *Hima. Prad.* India
Manama Bahrain *see* **Al Manāmah**
176 F8 **Manamadurai** *Tamil Nadu* India
95 □J3 **Manambaho** *r.* Madag.
95 □J4 **Manambondro** Madag.
176 F7 **Manamelkudi** *Tamil Nadu* India
153 K7 **Manam Island** P.N.G.
137 F2 **Manamo, Caño** *r.* Venez.
154 C6 **Manamoc** *i.* Phil.
124 □D12 **Mānana** *i. HI* U.S.A.
95 □J4 **Mananantañana** *r.* Madag.
95 □J4 **Mananara** *r.* Madag.
95 □K3 **Mananara, Parc National de** *nat. park* Madag.
95 □K3 **Mananara Avaratra** Madag.
205 I6 **Manangatang** *Vic.* Austr.
206 F4 **Manangoora** *N.T.* Austr.
95 □K4 **Mananjary** Madag.
95 □J5 **Manankoliva** Madag.
88 D4 **Manankoro** Mali
88 C3 **Manantali, Lac de** *l.* Mali
176 E7 **Manantavadi** *Kerala* India
95 □J5 **Manantenina** Madag.
128 C6 **Manantlán, Sierra** *mts* Mex.
200 □6 **Manaoba Island** Solomon Is
173 D11 **Mana Pass** China/India
95 F3 **Mana Pools National Park** Zimbabwe
203 B12 **Manapouri** *South I.* N.Z.
203 B12 **Manapouri, Lake** *South I.* N.Z.
176 F7 **Manapparai** *Tamil Nadu* India
95 □J3 **Manarantsandry** Madag.
63 O2 **Mañaria** Spain
172 H4 **Manas** *Xinjiang* China
179 M6 **Manas** *r.* India
22 J1 **Månäs** Sweden
183 N6 **Manas, Gora** *mt.* Uzbek.
178 E7 **Manasa** *Madh. Prad.* India
191 I3 **Manasaul** Rus. Fed.
172 G4 **Manas He** *r.* China
172 H4 **Manas Hu** *l.* China
187 K4 **Manāṣīr** *reg.* U.A.E.
191 I3 **Manaskent** Rus. Fed.
179 J5 **Manaslu** *mt.* Nepal
179 J5 **Manaslu Conservation Area** *nature res.* Nepal
119 G4 **Manasquan** *NJ* U.S.A.
119 G4 **Manasquan** *r. NJ* U.S.A.
116 H10 **Manassas** *VA* U.S.A.
57 L6 **Mănăștiur** Romania
179 M6 **Manas Wildlife Sanctuary** *nature res.* Bhutan
155 D8 **Manatang** Indon.
131 □1 **Manatí** Puerto Rico
131 □1 **Manati, Río Grande de** *r.* Puerto Rico
98 □2b **Manati Bay** St Helena
167 J5 **Manatsuru** Japan
155 D8 **Manatuto** East Timor
158 A5 **Man-aung** Myanmar
158 A5 **Man-aung Kyun** *i.* Myanmar
137 F5 **Manaus** Brazil
188 E5 **Manavgat** Turkey
110 F5 **Manawa** *WI* U.S.A.
178 E8 **Manawar** *Madh. Prad.* India
202 J4 **Manawaru** *North I.* N.Z.
84 E6 **Manawashei** Sudan
202 J7 **Manawatu** *r. North I.* N.Z.
202 J6 **Manawatu-Wanganui** *admin. reg. North I.* N.Z.
154 F8 **Manay** *Mindanao* Phil.
19 T8 **Manayenki** Rus. Fed.
167 J5 **Manazuru-misaki** *pt* Japan
167 I3 **Manba** Japan
179 K8 **Manbazar** *W. Bengal* India
190 F2 **Manbij** Syria
29 R7 **Manby** *Lincolnshire, England* U.K.
39 K5 **Mancelles, Alpes** *hills* France
110 I5 **Mancelona** *MI* U.S.A.
63 J7 **Mancera de Abajo** Spain
176 C3 **Manchar** *Mahar.* India
65 L5 **Mancha Real** Spain
38 I4 **Manche** *dept* France
130 □ **Manchester** *parish* Jamaica
29 M7 **Manchester** *Greater Manchester, England* U.K.
117 M7 **Manchester** *CT* U.S.A.
120 J4 **Manchester** *IA* U.S.A.
116 B11 **Manchester** *KY* U.S.A.
118 B5 **Manchester** *MD* U.S.A.
111 J7 **Manchester** *MI* U.S.A.
117 N6 **Manchester** *NH* U.S.A.
116 B10 **Manchester** *OH* U.S.A.
118 B4 **Manchester** *PA* U.S.A.
115 D8 **Manchester** *TN* U.S.A.
117 L5 **Manchester** *VT* U.S.A.
185 L8 **Manchhar Lake** Pak.
53 K4 **Manching** Ger.
130 □ **Manchioneal** Jamaica
64 G3 **Manchita** Spain
Manchuria *reg. Heilong.* China *see* **Dongbei**
72 H2 **Manciano** Italy
43 E8 **Manciet** France
188 H4 **Mancılık** Turkey
79 I3 **Mancınık Dağı** *mts* Turkey
123 J8 **Mancos** *CO* U.S.A.
125 X5 **Mancos** *r. CO* U.S.A.
185 J8 **Mand** Pak.
184 D7 **Mand, Rūd-e** *r.* Iran
179 L7 **Manda** Bangl.
93 B7 **Manda** Malawi
93 B6 **Manda** Tanz.
90 E2 **Manda, Jebel** *mt.* Sudan
90 C2 **Manda, Parc National de** *nat. park* Chad
95 □J4 **Mandabe** Madag.
142 A5 **Mandaguaçu** Brazil
142 B5 **Mandaguari** Brazil
156 E5 **Mandah** *Sumatera* Indon.
156 □ **Mandai** Sing.
185 I5 **Mandal** Afgh.
178 C8 **Mandal** *Gujarat* India
178 E7 **Mandal** *Rajasthan* India
168 H2 **Mandal** *Bulgan* Mongolia
168 J2 **Mandal** *Töv* Mongolia
22 D3 **Mandal** Norway
153 J7 **Mandala, Puncak** *mt. Papua* Indon.
158 C4 **Mandalay** Myanmar
158 B4 **Mandalay** *admin. div.* Myanmar
Mandale Myanmar *see* **Mandalay**
Mandale *admin. div.* Myanmar *see* **Mandalay**
154 D6 **Mandalgan, Mount** *vol.* Phil.
178 E7 **Mandalgarh** *Rajasthan* India
168 J4 **Mandalgovĭ** Mongolia
189 L7 **Mandalī** Iraq
22 D3 **Mandalselva** *r.* Norway
169 M5 **Mandalt** *Nei Mongol* China
169 M4 **Mandalt Sum** *Nei Mongol* China
120 E2 **Mandan** *ND* U.S.A.
75 I7 **Mandanici** *Sicilia* Italy
154 D5 **Mandaon** *Masbate* Phil.
89 H3 **Mandaoua Soumounti** *well* Niger
176 F8 **Mandapam** *Tamil Nadu* India
155 A5 **Mandar, Teluk** *b.* Indon.
72 C8 **Mandas** *Sardegna* Italy
75 L5 **Mandatoriccio** Italy
178 C8 **Mandav Hills** *Gujarat* India
185 P7 **Mandawa** *Rajasthan* India
63 O7 **Mandayona** Spain
40 F4 **Mandé, Mont de** *hill* France
52 C3 **Mandelbachtal-Ormesheim** Ger.
41 J9 **Mandelieu-la-Napoule** France
70 G4 **Mandello del Lario** Italy
62 D2 **Mandeo** *r.* Spain
92 D4 **Mandera** Kenya
125 T3 **Manderfield** *UT* U.S.A.
49 C10 **Manderscheid** Ger.
40 J2 **Mandeure** France
130 □ **Mandeville** Jamaica
203 C12 **Mandeville** *South I.* N.Z.
178 C6 **Mandha** *Rajasthan* India
92 E2 **Mandheera** Somalia
Mandhoúdhíon Greece *see* **Mantoudi**

Marie Anne Island to Matawan

300

Marie Anne Island *Inner Islands* Seychelles *see* Marianne
212 P1 Marie Byrd Land *reg.* Antarctica
23 N2 Mariefred Sweden
131 □2 Marie-Galante *i.* Guadeloupe
21 O6 Mariehamn *Åland* Fin.
Mari El *aut. rep.* Rus. Fed. *see* Mariy El, Respublika
140 C5 Mariembero *r.* Brazil
45 G8 Mariembourg Belgium
Marienbad Czech Rep. *see* Mariánské Lázně
51 H9 Marienberg Ger.
Marienburg Pol. *see* Malbork
48 D3 Marienhafe Ger.
49 I6 Marienhagen Ger.
49 E8 Marienheide Ger.
49 K6 Mariental Ger.
94 C5 Mariental Namibia
116 F7 Marienville *PA* U.S.A.
Marienwerder Pol. *see* Kwidzyn
23 J3 Mariestad Sweden
108 E1 Mariet *r. Que.* Can.
115 E9 Marietta *GA* U.S.A.
116 D9 Marietta *OH* U.S.A.
121 G9 Marietta *OK* U.S.A.
118 B4 Marietta *PA* U.S.A.
117 L3 Marieville *Que.* Can.
89 G4 Mariga *r.* Nigeria
73 M6 Marigliano Italy
72 B3 Marignana *Corse* France
41 G10 Marignane France
39 L6 Marigné-Laillé France
40 J4 Marignier France
38 I3 Marigny France
36 G7 Marigny-le-Châtel France
40 D2 Marigny-l'Église France
131 □2 Marigot Dominica
131 L4 Marigot West Indies
162 M1 Marii, Mys *pt Sakhalin* Rus. Fed.
182 I1 Mariinskoye Rus. Fed.
18 G7 Marijampolė Lith.
97 L1 Marikana S. Africa
77 L9 Marikostinovo Bulg.
142 C5 Marília Brazil
208 E7 Marillana *W.A.* Austr.
142 A6 Mariluz Brazil
91 C7 Marimba Angola
157 K5 Marimun *Kalimantan* Indon.
127 I5 Marín Mex.
62 C4 Marín Spain
124 K5 Marina *CA* U.S.A.
72 G2 Marina di Alberese Italy
75 L4 Marina di Amendolara Italy
72 A8 Marina di Arbus *Sardegna* Italy
73 O7 Marina di Camerota Italy
72 E2 Marina di Campo Italy
72 F1 Marina di Castagneto Donoratico Italy
70 I9 Marina di Cecina Italy
73 O4 Marina di Chieuti Italy
75 L3 Marina di Ginosa Italy
75 K7 Marina di Gioiosa Ionica Italy
72 F2 Marina di Grosseto Italy
75 O4 Marina di Leuca Italy
70 I7 Marina di Massa Italy
74 F9 Marina di Palma *Sicilia* Italy
75 M3 Marina di Pulsano Italy
74 H10 Marina di Ragusa *Sicilia* Italy
71 M6 Marina di Ravenna Italy
Mar'ina Gorka Belarus *see* Mar''ina Horka
18 L8 Mar''ina Horka Belarus
65 J6 Marinaleda Spain
73 L1 Marina Palmense Italy
71 M6 Marina Romea Italy
75 L4 Marina Schiavonea Italy
154 C5 Marinduque *i.* Phil.
111 L7 Marine City *MI* U.S.A.
74 D8 Marinella *Sicilia* Italy
72 D5 Marinella, Golfo di *b. Sardegna* Italy
74 E8 Marineo *Sicilia* Italy
213 L2 Mariner Glacier Antarctica
36 C5 Marines France
67 D8 Marines Spain
110 G4 Marinette *WI* U.S.A.
142 B5 Maringá Brazil
90 C4 Maringa *r.* Dem. Rep. Congo
116 C8 Maringo *OH* U.S.A.
95 G3 Maringué Moz.
40 C5 Maringues France
62 C8 Marinha das Ondas Port.
62 C9 Marinha Grande Port.
64 B2 Marinhais Port.
62 C5 Marinhas Port.
71 Q5 Marinići Croatia
184 D4 Marinjab Iran
191 E1 Mar'in Kolodtsy Rus. Fed.
73 J4 Marino Italy
191 A2 Marino Rus. Fed.
18 L3 Mar'insko Rus. Fed.
115 D9 Marion *AL* U.S.A.
121 J8 Marion *AR* U.S.A.
119 J1 Marion *CT* U.S.A.
121 K7 Marion *IL* U.S.A.
114 E5 Marion *IN* U.S.A.
120 G6 Marion *KS* U.S.A.
121 K7 Marion *KY* U.S.A.
110 I5 Marion *MI* U.S.A.
115 F8 Marion *NC* U.S.A.
116 B8 Marion *OH* U.S.A.
115 H8 Marion *SC* U.S.A.
116 D12 Marion *VA* U.S.A.
110 F5 Marion *WI* U.S.A.
115 G9 Marion, Lake *SC* U.S.A.
204 F6 Marion Bay *S.A.* Austr.
206 G7 Marion Downs *Qld* Austr.
120 G6 Marion Lake *KS* U.S.A.
207 N5 Marion Reef *Coral Sea Is Terr.* Austr.
73 R5 Mariotto Italy
87 H5 Mariou, Adrar *mt.* Alg.
137 E3 Maripa Venez.
137 H4 Maripasoula Fr. Guiana
154 E6 Maripipi *i.* Phil.
124 M4 Mariposa *CA* U.S.A.
124 L4 Mariposa *r. CA* U.S.A.
136 C3 Mariquita Col.
155 B3 Marisa *Sulawesi* Indon.
129 I8 Mariscala Mex.
139 E5 Mariscal José Félix Estigarribia Para.
77 L4 Mărișel Romania
77 M3 Mărișelu Romania
41 J8 Maritime Alps *mts* France/Italy
77 O9 Maritsa *r.* Bulg. *alt.* Evros (Greece), *alt.* Meriç (Turkey)
14 J4 Mari-Turek Rus. Fed.
17 Q6 Mariupol' Ukr.
137 F2 Mariusa *nat. park* Venez.
137 F2 Mariusa, Isla *i.* Venez.
189 M6 Marīvān Iran
14 J4 Mariy El, Respublika *aut. rep.* Rus. Fed.
Mariyskaya A.S.S.R. *aut. rep.* Rus. Fed. *see* Mariy El, Respublika
40 E3 Marizy France
63 M9 Marjaliza Spain
18 H3 Märjamaa Estonia
184 E7 Marjān Iran
190 D5 Marjayoûn Lebanon
185 L2 Marjonbuloq Uzbek.
107 L1 Marjorie Lake *Nunavut* Can.
30 G5 Mark *Somerset, England* U.K.
190 E7 Mārkā Jordan
186 E6 Markā *i.* Saudi Arabia
92 E4 Marka Somalia
183 U3 Markakol', Ozero *l.* Kazakh.
88 D3 Markala Mali
14 L3 Markalasta Rus. Fed.
170 B4 Markam *Xizang* China
170 B4 Markam Shan *mts Xizang* China
191 G7 Mārkān Iran
176 F5 Markapur *Andhra Prad.* India
23 J5 Markaryd Sweden
92 E3 Markawene *well* Eth.
187 M6 Markaz, Ra's *c.* Oman
184 D4 Markazī *prov.* Iran
111 N5 Markdale *Ont.* Can.
52 G6 Markdorf Ger.
44 K4 Markelo Neth.
50 D1 Markelsdorfer Huk *pt* Ger.
44 H4 Marken *i.* Neth.
95 F4 Marken S. Africa
44 H3 Markermeer *l.* Neth.
51 G9 Markersdorf bei Burgstädt Ger.
31 J2 Market Bosworth *Leicestershire, England* U.K.
31 L2 Market Deeping *Lincolnshire, England* U.K.
30 H2 Market Drayton *Shropshire, England* U.K.
31 K3 Market Harborough *Leicestershire, England* U.K.
27 I4 Markethill *Northern Ireland* U.K.
31 I5 Market Lavington *Wiltshire, England* U.K.
29 Q7 Market Rasen *Lincolnshire, England* U.K.
29 O7 Market Warsop *Nottinghamshire, England* U.K.
29 P6 Market Weighton *East Riding of Yorkshire, England* U.K.
31 J2 Markfield *Leicestershire, England* U.K.
52 G4 Markgröningen Ger.
193 M3 Markha *r.* Rus. Fed.
108 E5 Markham *Ont.* Can.
213 K1 Markham, Mount Antarctica
107 K2 Markham Lake *N.W.T.* Can.
55 J3 Marki Pol.
17 S3 Marki Rus. Fed.
63 P2 Markina-Xemein Spain
26 J10 Markinch *Fife, Scotland* U.K.
51 I6 Märkisch Buchholz Ger.
172 C7 Markit *Xinjiang* China
20 P3 Markitta Sweden
17 S4 Markivka Ukr.
16 H5 Markivka *r.* Ukr.
51 F8 Markkleeberg Ger.
124 M3 Markleeville *CA* U.S.A.
116 F9 Markleysburg *PA* U.S.A.
53 N4 Marklkofen Ger.
48 H5 Marklohe Ger.
44 I3 Marknesse Neth.
51 F10 Markneukirchen Ger.
57 G4 Márkó Hungary
170 C2 Markog Qu *r. Sichuan* China
78 E5 Markopoulo Greece
90 C3 Markounda C.A.R.
59 O8 Markovac Trojstveni Croatia
193 S3 Markovo *Chukotskiy Avtonomnyy Okrug* Rus. Fed.
19 X4 Markovo *Ivanovskaya Oblast'* Rus. Fed.
17 N2 Markovo *Kurskaya Oblast'* Rus. Fed.
89 F3 Markoye Burkina
51 F8 Markranstädt Ger.
182 B2 Marks Rus. Fed.
121 J8 Marks *MS* U.S.A.
118 F3 Marksboro *NJ* U.S.A.
31 N4 Marks Tey *Essex, England* U.K.
49 J9 Marksuhl Ger.
121 I10 Marksville *LA* U.S.A.
59 N5 Markt Allhau Austria
53 I3 Marktbergel Ger.
53 J3 Markt Berolzheim Ger.
53 I2 Markt Bibart Ger.
53 I2 Marktbreit Ger.
53 J3 Markt Erlbach Ger.
59 M5 Markt Hartmannsdorf Austria
52 H2 Marktheidenfeld Ger.
53 K5 Markt Indersdorf Ger.
53 N5 Marktl Ger.
51 E10 Marktleugast Ger.
51 F10 Marktleuthen Ger.
53 J6 Marktoberdorf Ger.
53 I4 Marktoffingen Ger.
106 E5 Marktosis *B.C.* Can.
59 N4 Markt Piesting Austria
53 M1 Marktredwitz Ger.
53 I6 Markt Rettenbach Ger.
51 D10 Marktrodach Ger.
59 J3 Markt Sankt Florian Austria
59 N4 Markt Sankt Martin Austria
53 O6 Marktschellenberg Ger.
53 L5 Markt Schwaben Ger.
53 I2 Marktseft Ger.
53 J5 Markt Wald Ger.
59 N8 Markusevec Croatia
55 K4 Markuszów Pol.
31 L4 Markyate *Hertfordshire, England* U.K.
49 D7 Marl Ger.
204 D2 Marla *S.A.* Austr.
209 D10 Marlandy Hill *W.A.* Austr.
118 E6 Marlboro *NJ* U.S.A.
119 G4 Marlboro *NJ* U.S.A.
119 H1 Marlboro *NY* U.S.A.
207 L7 Marlborough *Qld* Austr.
203 H8 Marlborough *admin. reg. South I.* N.Z.
31 I5 Marlborough *Wiltshire, England* U.K.
119 K1 Marlborough *CT* U.S.A.
117 N6 Marlborough *MA* U.S.A.
117 M6 Marlborough *NH* U.S.A.
31 I5 Marlborough Downs *hills England* U.K.
30 E7 Marldon *Devon, England* U.K.
36 G4 Marle France
71 K2 Marlengo Italy
37 O6 Marlenheim France
71 P6 Marlera, Rt *pt* Croatia
111 K6 Marlette *MI* U.S.A.
41 E6 Marlhes France
40 G4 Marlieux France
121 G10 Marlin *TX* U.S.A.
116 E10 Marlinton *WV* U.S.A.
51 D9 Marlishausen Ger.
205 L7 Marlo *Vic.* Austr.
96 E10 Marloth Nature Reserve S. Africa
50 G2 Marlow Ger.
31 K4 Marlow *Buckinghamshire, England* U.K.
118 F5 Marlton *NJ* U.S.A.
37 L5 Marly *Lorraine* France
36 G3 Marly *Nord-Pas-de-Calais* France
70 C2 Marly Switz.
36 E5 Marly-la-Ville France
176 C5 Marmagao *Goa* India
40 E3 Marmagne *Bourgogne* France
39 P7 Marmagne *Centre* France
43 E6 Marmande France
79 I2 Marmara Turkey
Marmara, Sea of *g.* Turkey *see* Marmara Denizi
79 I2 Marmara Adası *i.* Turkey
79 J2 Marmara Denizi *g.* Turkey
79 I2 Marmaraereğlisi Turkey
79 J4 Marmara Gölü *l.* Turkey
84 E2 Marmarica *reg.* Libya
79 J6 Marmaris Turkey
79 H4 Marmaro *Chios* Greece
120 D2 Marmarth *ND* U.S.A.
173 F10 Marmê *Xizang* China
64 D4 Marmelar Port.
64 B2 Marmeleira Port.
64 B6 Marmelete Port.
137 F6 Marmelos *r.* Brazil
116 D10 Marmet *WV* U.S.A.
209 F10 Marmion, Lake *salt l. W.A.* Austr.
108 B3 Marmion Lake *Ont.* Can.
71 J5 Marmirolo Italy
128 A2 Mármol Mex.
71 L3 Marmolada *mt.* Italy
65 K4 Marmolejo Spain
70 D4 Marmore *r.* Italy
37 N6 Marmoutier France
40 H2 Marnay France
40 J4 Marnaz France
36 H5 Marne *dept* France
36 D6 Marne *r.* France
48 H3 Marne Ger.
37 J8 Marne, Source de la *r. source* France
37 J7 Marne à la Saône, Canal de la France
37 M6 Marne au Rhin, Canal de la France
36 E6 Marne-la-Vallée France
191 F4 Marneuli Georgia
52 E2 Marnheim Ger.
30 H6 Marnhull *Dorset, England* U.K.
50 E4 Marnitz Ger.
179 O6 Marniu *Arun. Prad.* India
205 I7 Marnoo *Vic.* Austr.
90 C2 Maro Chad
95 □K2 Maroambihy Madag.
95 □K2 Maroantsetra Madag.
143 H2 Maroba *r.* Brazil
95 □J4 Marofandilia Madag.
74 G9 Maroglio *r. Sicilia* Italy
201 □3 Marokau *atoll Arch. des Tuamotu* Fr. Polynesia
202 I5 Marokopa *North I.* N.Z.
178 F2 Marol Jammu and Kashmir
185 O7 Marol Pak.
95 □K4 Marolambo Madag.
49 K10 Maroldsweisach Ger.
39 L5 Marolles-les-Braults France
95 □K2 Maromandia Madag.
36 B5 Maromme France
95 □K2 Maromokotro *mt.* Madag.
95 F3 Marondera Zimbabwe
137 H3 Maroni *r.* Fr. Guiana
42 H5 Maronne *r.* France
207 N9 Maroochydore *Qld* Austr.
209 C7 Maroonah *W.A.* Austr.
123 K7 Maroon Peak *CO* U.S.A.
130 □ Maroon Town Jamaica
155 A6 Maros *Sulawesi* Indon.
155 A6 Maros *r.* Indon.
76 I4 Maros *r.* Romania
95 □K3 Maroseranana Madag.
57 J5 Maros-Körös Köze *plain* Hungary
57 J5 Maroslele Hungary
71 L4 Marostica Italy
95 □K3 Marotandrano Madag.
201 □3 Marotiri *is Îs Australes* Fr. Polynesia
202 I2 Marotiri Islands *North I.* N.Z.
95 □K2 Marotolana Madag.
89 I4 Maroua Cameroon
38 F5 Maroué France
137 F5 Marova Brazil
95 □K2 Marovato *Antsirañana* Madag.
95 □J5 Marovato *Toliara* Madag.
95 □J3 Marovoay *Mahajanga* Madag.
95 □K3 Marovoay *Toamasina* Madag.
95 □J3 Marovoay Atsimo Madag.
155 B4 Marowali *Sulawesi* Indon.
137 H3 Marowijne *r.* Suriname
55 I2 Maróz, Jezioro *l.* Pol.
52 C3 Marpingen Ger.
29 M7 Marple *Greater Manchester, England* U.K.
189 J6 Marqādah Syria
Marqaköl *l.* Kazakh. *see* Markakol', Ozero
97 L4 Marquard S. Africa
53 M6 Marquartstein Ger.
129 I9 Marquelia Mex.
36 C3 Marquenterre *reg.* France
63 O6 Marquesado de Berlanga *reg.* Spain
Marquesas Islands Fr. Polynesia *see* Marquises, Îles
115 F13 Marquesas Keys *is FL* U.S.A.
143 F5 Marquês de Valença Brazil
110 G3 Marquette *MI* U.S.A.
121 G10 Marquez *TX* U.S.A.
142 A6 Marquinho Brazil
36 F3 Marquion France
131 □3 Marquis, Cap *c.* St Lucia
36 C2 Marquise France
201 □3 Marquises, Îles *is* Fr. Polynesia
43 I10 Marquixanes France
205 I4 Marra *N.S.W.* Austr.
205 K4 Marra *r. N.S.W.* Austr.
84 E6 Marra, Jebel *mt.* Sudan
206 E3 Marra Aboriginal Land *res. N.T.* Austr.
95 H3 Marracua Moz.
95 G5 Marracuene Moz.
71 L7 Marradi Italy
186 E7 Marrāk *i.* Saudi Arabia
86 D3 Marrakech Morocco
Marrakesh Morocco *see* Marrakech
186 E6 Marrān Saudi Arabia
84 E6 Marra Plateau Sudan
20 R3 Marraskoski Fin.
205 J9 Marrawah *Tas.* Austr.
204 G3 Marree *S.A.* Austr.
121 J11 Marrero *LA* U.S.A.
95 G3 Marromeu Moz.
95 G3 Marromeu, Reserva de *nature res.* Moz.
129 H1 Marroquin Mex.
72 B8 Marrubiu *Sardegna* Italy
44 I2 Marrum Neth.
93 C8 Marrupa Moz.
204 D2 Marryat *S.A.* Austr.
41 A6 Mars *r.* France
116 E8 Mars *PA* U.S.A.
85 G3 Marsá al 'Alam Egypt
84 C2 Marsa al Burayqah Libya
61 E5 Marsa-Ben-Mehidi Alg.
92 C4 Marsabit Kenya
92 C4 Marsabit National Reserve *nature res.* Kenya
40 D6 Marsac-en-Livradois France
38 H6 Marsac-sur-Don France
85 H5 Marsa Darur Sudan
85 H4 Marsa Delwein Sudan
70 G6 Marsaglia Italy
186 B3 Marsá Ijlī Egypt
37 M6 Marsal France
74 C8 Marsala *Sicilia* Italy
75 □ Marsalforn *Gozo* Malta
186 C5 Marsa Mar'ob Sudan
84 E2 Marsá Maţrūḩ Egypt
40 F2 Marsannay-la-Côte France
41 F7 Marsanne France
85 H4 Marsa Oseif Sudan
186 C5 Marsa Salak Sudan
186 C5 Marsa Shin'ab Sudan
88 B3 Marsassoum Senegal
186 B3 Marsá Ţunḑubah Egypt
75 □ Marsaxlokk Malta
75 □ Marsaxlokk, Il-Bajja ta' *b.* Malta
130 E2 Mars Bay *Andros* Bahamas
98 □2a Mars Bay *Ascension* S. Atlantic Ocean
49 G8 Marsberg Ger.
48 J4 Marschacht Ger.
73 I2 Marsciano Italy
205 K5 Marsden *N.S.W.* Austr.
107 I4 Marsden *Sask.* Can.
29 N6 Marsden *West Yorkshire, England* U.K.
202 I2 Marsden Point N.Z.
44 G3 Marsdiep *sea chan.* Neth.
41 D10 Marseillan France
41 G10 Marseille France
41 F9 Marseille au Rhône, Canal de France
36 C4 Marseille-en-Beauvaisis France
Marseilles France *see* Marseille
110 F8 Marseilles *IL* U.S.A.
138 D3 Marsella Bol.
20 M4 Marsfjället *mt.* Sweden
190 C10 Marshah, Jabal *mt.* Saudi Arabia
206 F7 Marshall *watercourse N.T.* Austr.
107 I4 Marshall *Sask.* Can.
121 I8 Marshall *AR* U.S.A.
114 D6 Marshall *IL* U.S.A.
110 J7 Marshall *MI* U.S.A.
120 H3 Marshall *MN* U.S.A.
120 I6 Marshall *MO* U.S.A.
115 F8 Marshall *NC* U.S.A.
121 H9 Marshall *TX* U.S.A.
116 H10 Marshall *VA* U.S.A.
216 F5 Marshall Islands *country* N. Pacific Ocean
118 E2 Marshalls Creek *PA* U.S.A.
118 D5 Marshallton *DE* U.S.A.
120 I4 Marshalltown *IA* U.S.A.
118 D4 Marsh Creek Lake *PA* U.S.A.
30 H5 Marshfield *South Gloucestershire, England* U.K.
121 I7 Marshfield *MO* U.S.A.
110 D5 Marshfield *WI* U.S.A.
115 I12 Marsh Harbour Bahamas
117 □R2 Mars Hill *ME* U.S.A.
121 J11 Marsh Island *LA* U.S.A.
106 C2 Marsh Lake *Y.T.* Can.
106 C2 Marsh Lake *l. Y.T.* Can.
107 M3 Marsh Point *Man.* Can.
184 C3 Marshūn Iran
41 E9 Marsillargues France
122 F5 Marsing *ID* U.S.A.
29 O4 Marske-by-the-Sea *Redcar and Cleveland, England* U.K.
37 K5 Mars-la-Tour France
36 I6 Marson France
43 I8 Marssac-sur-Tarn France
23 N2 Märsta Sweden
22 G7 Marstal Denmark
48 K1 Marstal Bugt *b.* Denmark
70 G1 Märstetten Switz.
31 J4 Marston *Oxfordshire, England* U.K.
30 G6 Marston Magna *Somerset, England* U.K.
31 K3 Marston Moretaine *Bedfordshire, England* U.K.
200 □3a Marsugalt *i. Kwajalein* Marshall Is
179 J6 Marsyangdi *r.* Nepal
118 D7 Marsyhope *r. MD* U.S.A.
72 H2 Marta Italy
72 H3 Marta *r.* Italy
Martaban, Gulf of Myanmar *see* Mottama, Gulf of
72 H2 Martana, Isola *i.* Italy
157 L1 Martanai Besar *i.* Malaysia
75 O3 Martano Italy
73 J2 Martano, Monte *mt.* Italy
89 I5 Martap Cameroon
157 K6 Martapura *Kalimantan* Indon.
156 F7 Martapura *Sumatera* Indon.
89 I3 Marte Nigeria
42 H6 Martel France
116 C8 Martel *OH* U.S.A.
42 G6 Martel, Causse de *hills* France
45 I9 Martelange Belgium
71 M4 Martellago Italy
71 J2 Martello Italy
57 J5 Mártély Hungary
57 J5 Mártélyi *park* Hungary
108 E4 Marten River *Ont.* Can.
107 J4 Martensville *Sask.* Can.
127 J4 Marte R. Gómez, Presa *resr* Mex.
67 D9 Martés *mt.* Spain
67 C9 Martés, Serra *mts* Spain
48 H5 Martfeld Ger.
57 J4 Martfű Hungary
31 P2 Martham *Norfolk, England* U.K.
117 O7 Martha's Vineyard *i. MA* U.S.A.
42 E4 Marthon France
130 E3 Martí Cuba
62 H8 Martiago Spain
71 O3 Martignacco Italy
73 I3 Martignano, Lago di *l.* Italy
43 C6 Martignas-sur-Jalle France
39 K7 Martigné-Briand France
38 I6 Martigné-Ferchaud France
39 J5 Martigné-sur-Mayenne France
70 C3 Martigny Switz.
40 E3 Martigny-le-Comte France
37 K7 Martigny-les-Bains France
37 K7 Martigny-les-Gerbonvaux France
41 G10 Martigues France
63 K7 Martiherrero Spain
65 I9 Martil Morocco
43 C6 Martillac France
64 D6 Martim Longo Port.
Martim Vaz, Ilhas *is* S. Atlantic Ocean *see* Martin Vaz, Ilhas
106 F2 Martin *r. N.W.T.* Can.
57 H2 Martin Slovakia
66 E5 Martín *r.* Spain
120 E4 Martin *SD* U.S.A.
26 F7 Martin, Isle *i. Scotland* U.K.
115 E9 Martin, Lake *AL* U.S.A.
75 M2 Martina Franca Italy
203 J8 Martinborough *North I.* N.Z.
62 D9 Martinchel Port.
147 H4 Martín Chico Uru.
147 H5 Martín Colman Arg.
65 J6 Martín de la Jara Spain
146 D4 Martín de Loyola Arg.
62 H7 Martín de Yeltes Spain
70 H4 Martinengo Italy
66 I3 Martinet Spain
129 J5 Martínez Mex.
124 J3 Martinez *CA* U.S.A.
115 F9 Martinez *GA* U.S.A.
125 R9 Martinez Lake *AZ* U.S.A.
49 J8 Martinfeld Ger.
62 C9 Martingança Port.
147 H4 Martín García, Isla *i.* Arg.
65 K4 Martín Gonzalo, Embalse de *resr* Spain
143 E3 Martinho Campos Brazil
131 □3 Martinique *terr.* West Indies
131 □2 Martinique Passage Dominica/Martinique
63 K6 Martín Muñoz de las Posadas Spain
78 E4 Martino Greece
142 B5 Martinópolis Brazil
212 Q2 Martin Peninsula Antarctica
62 I2 Martinporra Spain
203 B11 Martins Bay *South I.* N.Z.
59 L3 Martinsberg Austria
116 C8 Martinsburg *OH* U.S.A.
116 G8 Martinsburg *PA* U.S.A.
116 H9 Martinsburg *WV* U.S.A.
71 Q6 Martinšćica Croatia
118 E3 Martins Creek *PA* U.S.A.
118 D1 Martins Creek *r. PA* U.S.A.
116 E8 Martins Ferry *OH* U.S.A.
73 L2 Martinsicuro Italy
27 F8 Martinstown Rep. of Ireland
114 D6 Martinsville *IN* U.S.A.
116 F12 Martinsville *VA* U.S.A.
214 H7 Martin Vaz, Ilhas *is* S. Atlantic Ocean
Martin Vaz Islands S. Atlantic Ocean *see* Martin Vaz, Ilhas
72 B6 Martis *Sardegna* Italy
39 N8 Martizay France
31 O3 Martlesham *Suffolk, England* U.K.
30 H3 Martley *Worcestershire, England* U.K.
30 G6 Martock *Somerset, England* U.K.
Martök Kazakh. *see* Martuk
173 E11 Martoli *Uttaranchal* India
202 J7 Marton *North I.* N.Z.
57 H4 Martonvásár Hungary
66 I5 Martorell Spain
65 L5 Martos Spain
43 G9 Martres-Tolosane France
20 T3 Martti Fin.
21 Q6 Marttila Fin.
182 G2 Martuk Kazakh.
191 G5 Martuni Armenia
191 D3 Martvili Georgia
17 L3 Martynivka Ukr.
16 I2 Martynovychi Ukr.
168 H9 Maru *Gansu* China
89 G3 Maru Nigeria
185 J4 Maruchak Afgh.
157 K2 Marudi *Sarawak* Malaysia
157 L1 Marudu, Teluk *b.* Malaysia
185 L6 Maruf Afgh.
165 K12 Marugame Japan
63 L7 Marugán Spain
75 N3 Maruggio Italy
203 G8 Maruia *r. South I.* N.Z.
140 F4 Maruim Brazil
191 C2 Marukhis Ugheltekhili *pass* Georgia/Rus. Fed.
167 H3 Maruko Japan
205 L6 Marulan *N.S.W.* Austr.
147 F2 Marull Arg.
44 J2 Marum Neth.
200 □5 Marum, Mount *vol.* Vanuatu
184 C6 Mārūn *r.* Iran
91 D9 Marunga Angola
166 D3 Maruoka Japan
183 U1 Marushka Rus. Fed.
178 C6 Marusthali *reg.* India
55 J4 Maruszów *Mazowieckie* Pol.
55 J5 Maruszów *Świętokrzyskie* Pol.
201 □3 Marutea *atoll Arch. des Tuamotu* Fr. Polynesia
201 □3 Marutea *atoll Arch. des Tuamotu* Fr. Polynesia
208 I7 Maruwa Aboriginal Reserve *W.A.* Austr.
92 B3 Maruwa Hills Sudan
167 K5 Maruyama Japan
166 A4 Maruyama-gawa *r.* Japan
64 E2 Marvão Port.
184 F6 Marvast Iran
184 E7 Marv Dasht Iran
41 C7 Marvejols France
209 E11 Marvel Loch *W.A.* Austr.
37 J5 Marville France
125 U3 Marvine, Mount *UT* U.S.A.
178 D7 Marwar Junction *Rajasthan* India
107 I4 Marwayne *Alta* Can.
53 J4 Marxheim Ger.
Marxwalde Ger. *see* Neuhardenberg
52 E4 Marxzell Ger.
206 C2 Mary *r. N.T.* Austr.
207 N8 Mary *r. Qld* Austr.
208 I5 Mary *r. W.A.* Austr.
185 I3 Mary Turkm.
90 E2 Maryal Bai Sudan
17 N8 Mar''yanivka *Respublika Krym* Ukr.
55 M5 Mar''yanivka *Volyns'ka Oblast'* Ukr.
17 P6 Mar''yanivka *Zaporiz'ka Oblast'* Ukr.
16 G3 Mar''yanivka *Zhytomyrs'ka Oblast'* Ukr.
17 R8 Mar'yanskaya Rus. Fed.
Mary A.S.S.R. *aut. rep.* Rus. Fed. *see* Mariy El, Respublika
26 G7 Marybank *Highland, Scotland* U.K.
207 N8 Maryborough *Qld* Austr.
205 I7 Maryborough *Vic.* Austr.
96 G5 Marydale S. Africa
118 D6 Marydel *MD* U.S.A.
182 C1 Mar'yevka Rus. Fed.
26 □N2 Maryfield *Shetland, Scotland* U.K.
107 J2 Mary Frances Lake *N.W.T.* Can.
17 Q6 Mar''yinka Ukr.
17 P8 Mar''yivka *Respublika Krym* Ukr.
17 N6 Mar''yivka *Zaporiz'ka Oblast'* Ukr.
26 K9 Marykirk *Aberdeenshire, Scotland* U.K.
107 K2 Mary Lake *N.W.T.* Can.
118 B7 Maryland *state* U.S.A.
118 B5 Maryland Line *MD* U.S.A.
16 E5 Marynychi Ukr.
Mary Oblast *admin. div.* Turkm. *see* Maryyskaya Oblast'
26 J8 Marypark *Moray, Scotland* U.K.
29 K4 Maryport *Cumbria, England* U.K.
109 K2 Mary's Harbour *Nfld and Lab.* Can.
109 K4 Marystown *Nfld and Lab.* Can.
125 T3 Marysvale *UT* U.S.A.
205 J7 Marysville *Vic.* Austr.
109 H4 Marysville *N.B.* Can.
124 K2 Marysville *CA* U.S.A.
120 G6 Marysville *KS* U.S.A.
111 L7 Marysville *MI* U.S.A.
116 B8 Marysville *OH* U.S.A.
118 B4 Marysville *PA* U.S.A.
122 C2 Marysville *WA* U.S.A.
206 E8 Maryvale *N.T.* Austr.
207 J5 Maryvale *Qld* Austr.
120 H5 Maryville *MO* U.S.A.
115 F8 Maryville *TN* U.S.A.
26 K8 Marywell *Aberdeenshire, Scotland* U.K.
184 J3 Maryyskaya Oblast' *admin. div.* Turkm.
71 K7 Marzabotto Italy
142 C2 Marzagão Brazil
51 G6 Marzahna Ger.
51 G5 Marzahne Ger.
75 I10 Marzamemi *Sicilia* Italy
38 G6 Marzan France
71 L7 Marzeno *r.* Italy
53 L5 Marzling Ger.
136 B3 Marzo, Cabo *c.* Col.
40 C3 Marzy France
63 M3 Masa Spain
126 □P12 Masachapa Nic.
190 D7 Masada *tourist site* Israel
92 E4 Masagaweyn Somalia
127 N10 Masagua Guat.
93 C7 Masaguro Tanz.
184 F6 Masāhūn, Kūh-e *mt.* Iran
93 B5 Masai Mara National Reserve *nature res.* Kenya
72 B9 Masainas *Sardegna* Italy
93 C6 Masai Steppe *plain* Tanz.
92 A5 Masaka Uganda
97 K7 Masakhane S. Africa
93 C6 Masaki Tanz.
94 D4 Masalanyane Pan *salt pan* Botswana
67 D9 Masalavés Spain
157 K7 Masalembu Besar *i.* Indon.
157 K7 Masalembu Kecil *i.* Indon.
191 J6 Masallı Azer.
155 B5 Masamba *Sulawesi* Indon.
155 B5 Masamba *mt.* Indon.
163 F11 Masan S. Korea
17 N9 Masandra Ukr.
155 E7 Masapun *Maluku* Indon.
186 F7 Masāqif *i.* Saudi Arabia
93 C7 Masasi Tanz.
126 □P12 Masatepe Nic.
139 E4 Masavi Bol.
126 □P12 Masaya Nic.
126 □P12 Masaya, Volcán *vol.* Nic.
154 D5 Masbate *Masbate* Phil.
154 D5 Masbate *i.* Phil.
43 I9 Mas-Cabardès France
75 I8 Mascali *Sicilia* Italy
75 I8 Mascalucia *Sicilia* Italy
87 F2 Mascara Alg.
63 M9 Mascaraque Spain
215 H6 Mascarene Basin *sea feature* Indian Ocean
215 H6 Mascarene Plain *sea feature* Indian Ocean
215 H5 Mascarene Ridge *sea feature* Indian Ocean
62 F5 Mascarenhas Port.
129 J4 Mascareños Mex.
146 D2 Mascasín Arg.
146 D2 Mascasín, Salinas de *salt pan* Arg.
73 P6 Maschito Italy
43 G6 Masclat France
128 C5 Mascota Mex.
128 B5 Mascota *r.* Mex.
114 K3 Mascouche *Que.* Can.
66 E3 Mascún *r.* Spain
66 F6 Mas de Barberans Spain
66 E6 Mas de las Matas Spain
63 P7 Masegosa Spain
65 O3 Masegoso Spain
63 O7 Masegoso de Tajuña Spain
158 B3 Masein Myanmar
157 L3 Ma Sekatok *b.* Indon.
155 F8 Masela *Maluku* Indon.
155 F8 Masela *i. Maluku* Indon.
52 H5 Maselheim Ger.
92 B4 Maseno Kenya
155 C5 Masepe *i.* Indon.
70 E3 Masera Italy
58 F8 Maserada sul Piave Italy
111 R1 Masères, Lac *l. Que.* Can.
97 L5 Maseru Lesotho
37 M8 Masevaux France
21 H6 Masfjorden Norway
43 G8 Mas-Grenier France
Mashaba Zimbabwe *see* Mashava
186 C3 Mashābih *i.* Saudi Arabia
97 M5 Mashai Lesotho
91 D6 Mashala Dem. Rep. Congo
29 N5 Masham *North Yorkshire, England* U.K.
170 G7 Mashan *Guangxi* China
95 F4 Mashava Zimbabwe
178 F2 Masherbrum *mt.* Jammu and Kashmir
17 L1 Masheve Ukr.
184 H3 Mashhad Iran
178 E6 Mashi *r.* India
164 S3 Mashike Japan
167 L3 Mashiko Japan
184 B2 Mashīrān Iran
17 N4 Mashivka Ukr.
185 J7 Mashkel, Hamun-i- *salt flat* Pak.
185 J8 Mashket *r.* Pak.
185 J7 Mashki Chah Pak.
185 J8 Māshkīd *r.* Iran
95 F3 Mashonaland Central *prov.* Zimbabwe
95 F3 Mashonaland East *prov.* Zimbabwe
95 F3 Mashonaland West *prov.* Zimbabwe
Mashtagi Azer. *see* Maştağa
20 Q2 Masi Norway
126 E4 Masiáca Mex.
91 C5 Masia-Mbia Dem. Rep. Congo
97 L7 Masibambane S. Africa
62 D4 Maside Spain
187 J8 Masīlah, Wādī al *watercourse* Yemen
97 K4 Masilo S. Africa
91 C6 Masi-Manimba Dem. Rep. Congo
155 A4 Masimbu *Sulawesi* Indon.
92 A4 Masindi Uganda
154 B4 Masinloc *Luzon* Phil.
70 H3 Masino *r.* Italy
96 H7 Masinyusane S. Africa
Masira, Gulf of Oman *see* Maşīrah, Khalīj
Masira Channel Oman *see* Maşīrah, Tur'at
187 N5 Maşīrah, Jazīrat *i.* Oman
187 N6 Maşīrah, Khalīj *b.* Oman
187 N5 Maşīrah, Tur'at *sea chan.* Oman
Masira Island Oman *see* Maşīrah, Jazīrat
191 F5 Masis Armenia
138 B2 Masisea Peru
90 F5 Masisi Dem. Rep. Congo
71 L6 Masi Torello Italy
155 G5 Masiwang *r. Seram* Indon.
97 M4 Masjaing S. Africa
184 C6 Masjed Soleymān Iran
27 D5 Mask, Lough *l.* Rep. of Ireland
187 I1 Maskān *i.* Kuwait
180 E7 Maskan, Raas *pt* Somalia
190 G2 Maskanah Syria
184 H8 Maskūtān Iran
43 C9 Maslacq France
57 K5 Maşloc Romania
17 P3 Maslova Pristan' Rus. Fed.
17 S2 Maslovka Rus. Fed.
55 H4 Masłowice Pol.
185 K7 Maslti Pak.
62 F1 Masma *r.* Spain
187 I8 Masna'ah Yemen
71 L3 Maso *r.* Italy
95 □K2 Masoala, Parc National de *nat. park* Madag.
95 □K2 Masoala, Tanjona *c.* Madag.
155 F5 Masohi *Seram* Indon.
110 J7 Mason *MI* U.S.A.
116 A9 Mason *OH* U.S.A.
121 F10 Mason *TX* U.S.A.
110 C3 Mason *WI* U.S.A.
116 C9 Mason *WV* U.S.A.
209 E9 Mason, Lake *salt flat W.A.* Austr.
203 B13 Mason Bay *Stewart I.* N.Z.
120 I4 Mason City *IA* U.S.A.
110 E9 Mason City *IL* U.S.A.
70 F6 Masone Italy
131 □5 Mason Hall Trin. and Tob.
155 D4 Masoni *i.* Indon.
203 G9 Masons Flat *South I.* N.Z.
116 F9 Masontown *PA* U.S.A.
116 F9 Masontown *WV* U.S.A.
98 □3f Maspalomas *Gran Canaria* Canary Is
98 □3f Maspalomas, Punta de *pt Gran Canaria* Canary Is
187 N4 Masqaţ Oman
187 N4 Masqaţ *governorate* Oman
187 M3 Masqaţ *reg.* Oman
91 B5 Massa Congo
70 I7 Massa Italy
117 M6 Massachusetts *state* U.S.A.
117 O6 Massachusetts Bay *MA* U.S.A.
70 I8 Massaciuccoli, Lago di *l.* Italy
125 X1 Massadona *CO* U.S.A.
70 H7 Massa e Carrara *prov.* Italy
71 M6 Massa Fiscaglia Italy
75 M2 Massafra Italy
84 B6 Massaguet Chad
41 C8 Mas-St-Chély France
84 B6 Massakory Chad
90 C2 Massalassef Chad
71 L7 Massa Lombarda Italy
73 M6 Massa Lubrense Italy
67 E8 Massamagrell Spain
72 F1 Massa Marittimo Italy
73 J2 Massa Martana Italy
95 G2 Massamba Moz.
141 B9 Massambará Brazil
90 A5 Massana Gabon
95 G4 Massangena Moz.
91 C7 Massango Angola
95 G2 Massangulo Moz.
119 I3 Massapequa *NY* U.S.A.
140 E4 Massaroca Brazil
70 I8 Massarosa Italy
43 G10 Massat France
91 C6 Massau Angola
85 H6 Massawa Eritrea
85 H5 Massawa Channel Eritrea
39 O7 Massay France
49 J10 Maßbach Ger.
51 I7 Massen Ger.
117 K4 Massena *NY* U.S.A.
90 C2 Massenya Chad
42 H4 Masseret France
75 M2 Masseria Risana *hill* Italy
106 C4 Masset *B.C.* Can.
106 C4 Masset Inlet *B.C.* Can.
43 F9 Masseube France
108 D4 Massey *Ont.* Can.
118 D6 Massey *MD* U.S.A.
41 C6 Massiac France
91 D7 Massibi Angola
73 L5 Massico, Monte *hill* Italy
116 C9 Massieville *OH* U.S.A.
41 C6 Massif Central *mts* France
88 D4 Massigui Mali
Massilia France *see* Marseille
116 D8 Massillon *OH* U.S.A.
70 E7 Massimino Italy
88 D3 Massina Mali
53 N5 Massing Ger.
95 G4 Massinga Moz.
95 G4 Massingir Moz.
111 S4 Masson *Que.* Can.
72 F2 Massoncello, Monte *hill* Italy
213 G2 Masson Island Antarctica
36 D6 Massy France
191 K5 Maştağa Azer.
70 E4 Mastallone, Parco Naturale *nature res.* Italy
185 M2 Mastchoh Tajik.
49 D10 Mastershausen Ger.
203 J7 Masterton *North I.* N.Z.
119 J3 Mastic *NY* U.S.A.
119 J3 Mastic Beach *NY* U.S.A.
79 H4 Masticho, Akra *pt Chios* Greece
130 E1 Mastic Point *Andros* Bahamas
108 F4 Mastigouche, Réserve Faunique de *nature res. Que.* Can.
72 D8 Mastixi, Punta su *pt Sardegna* Italy
24 J1 Mastrevik Norway
185 O3 Mastuj Pak.
185 L7 Mastung Pak.
186 D4 Mastūrah Saudi Arabia
18 H8 Masty Belarus
72 A9 Masua *Sardegna* Italy
165 I12 Masuda Japan
167 H4 Masuho Japan
91 D6 Masuika Dem. Rep. Congo
Masuku Gabon *see* Franceville
184 C3 Masuleh Iran
Masulipatam *Andhra Prad.* India *see* Machilipatnam
72 B8 Masullas *Sardegna* Italy
156 D6 Masurai, Bukit *mt.* Indon.
95 F4 Masvingo Zimbabwe
95 F4 Masvingo *prov.* Zimbabwe
93 B5 Maswa Tanz.
93 B5 Maswe Game Reserve *nature res.* Tanz.
190 E3 Maşyāf Syria
16 C2 Masyevichy Belarus
54 C3 Maszewo *Lubuskie* Pol.
54 F1 Maszewo *Pomorskie* Pol.
54 D2 Maszewo *Zachodniopomorskie* Pol.
76 H9 Mat *r.* Albania
158 G5 Mat, Nam *r.* Laos
99 □1c Mât, Rivière du *r.* Réunion
158 C1 Mata Myanmar
202 M4 Mata *r. North I.* N.Z.
137 E3 Mata, Serranía de *mts* Venez.
145 C8 Mata Amarilla Arg.
91 D8 Mataba Zambia
92 E3 Matabaan Somalia
95 E3 Matabeleland North *prov.* Zimbabwe
95 F4 Matabeleland South *prov.* Zimbabwe
179 L6 Matabhanga *W. Bengal* India
63 M6 Matabuena Spain
64 G3 Matachel *r.* Spain
108 D4 Matachewan *Ont.* Can.
126 F3 Matachic Mex.
91 B6 Matadi Dem. Rep. Congo
121 E8 Matador *TX* U.S.A.
66 J4 Matagalls *mt.* Spain
126 □Q11 Matagalpa Nic.
108 E3 Matagami *Que.* Can.
108 E3 Matagami, Lac *l. Que.* Can.
121 G11 Matagorda *TX* U.S.A.
121 G11 Matagorda Island *TX* U.S.A.
140 F4 Mata Grande Brazil
202 J6 Matahiwi *North I.* N.Z.
201 □3a Mataiea *Tahiti* Fr. Polynesia
156 G3 Matak *i.* Indon.
183 P3 Matak Kazakh.
202 K4 Matakana Island *North I.* N.Z.
202 M4 Matakaoa Point *North I.* N.Z.
203 G8 Matakitaki *South I.* N.Z.
91 B8 Matala Angola
64 F6 Matalascañas Spain
176 G9 Matale Sri Lanka
63 P5 Matalebreras Spain
96 I4 Mataleng S. Africa
186 E2 Maţāli', Jabal *hill* Saudi Arabia
63 J4 Matallana de Valmadrigal Spain
88 B3 Matam Senegal
63 O5 Matamala de Almazán Spain
202 J4 Matamata *North I.* N.Z.
96 E1 Mata-Mata S. Africa
202 K7 Matamau *North I.* N.Z.
89 H3 Matamey Niger
118 F2 Matamoras *PA* U.S.A.
127 N8 Matamoros *Campeche* Mex.
121 C12 Matamoros *Chihuahua* Mex.
126 H5 Matamoros *Coahuila* Mex.
129 L8 Matamoros *Oaxaca* Mex.
127 K5 Matamoros *Tamaulipas* Mex.
63 L3 Matamorosa Spain
88 B2 Ma'ta Moûlana *well* Maur.
62 C9 Mata Mourisca Port.
155 B5 Matana, Danau *l.* Indon.
154 D8 Matanal Point Phil.
84 D4 Ma'ţan as Sārah *well* Libya
84 D4 Ma'ţan Bishrah *well* Libya
146 B2 Matancilla Chile
93 C7 Matandu *r.* Tanz.
109 H3 Matane *Que.* Can.
109 H3 Matane, Réserve Faunique de *nature res. Que.* Can.
137 F2 Mata Negra Venez.
95 □J4 Matanga Madag.
202 J4 Matangi *North I.* N.Z.
89 G3 Matankari Niger
185 N5 Matanui Pak.
130 C2 Matanzas Cuba
142 C4 Matão Brazil
140 C4 Matão, Serra do *hills* Brazil
147 I2 Mataojo Uru.
126 □R13 Matapalo, Cabo *c.* Costa Rica
54 G5 Mata Panew *r.* Pol.
109 H3 Matapédia, Lac *l. Que.* Can.
203 □4 Mata Point Niue
63 L3 Mataporquera Spain
63 K6 Matapozuelos Spain
146 A4 Mataquito *r.* Chile
187 H2 Maţār *well* Saudi Arabia
144 E3 Matará Arg.
176 G10 Matara Sri Lanka
78 C4 Mataragka Greece
157 L9 Mataram *Lombok* Indon.
Mataránga Greece *see* Mataragka
138 B4 Matarani Peru
206 D3 Mataranka *N.T.* Austr.
155 C5 Matarape, Teluk *b.* Indon.
190 A9 Matārimah, Ra's *pt* Egypt
154 E6 Matarinao Bay *Samar* Phil.
86 E2 Matarka Morocco
66 J4 Mataró Spain
202 J6 Mataroa *North I.* N.Z.
155 C5 Matarombea *r.* Indon.
66 F5 Matarraña *r.* Spain
76 I7 Mataruška Banja *Srbija* Serb. and Mont.
98 □3b Matas Blancas *Fuerteventura* Canary Is
157 K7 Matasiri *i.* Indon.
85 F5 Matassi *well* Sudan
93 C6 Matassi Tanz.
97 M6 Matatiele S. Africa
178 G7 Matatila Dam India
200 □2 Matatula, Cape American Samoa
202 I6 Matau *North I.* N.Z.
203 C13 Mataura *South I.* N.Z.
203 C13 Mataura *r. South I.* N.Z.
200 □2 Matautu Samoa
199 I3 Matā'utu Wallis and Futuna Is
201 □3a Matavai, Baie de *b. Tahiti* Fr. Polynesia
200 □2 Matavanu Crater *vol. crater* Samoa
203 □3 Matavera *Rarotonga* Cook Is
202 L5 Matawai *North I.* N.Z.
202 H2 Matawaia *North I.* N.Z.
119 G4 Matawan *NJ* U.S.A.

Column 1

79 K6 **Megisti** i. Greece
19 R3 **Megletsy** Rus. Fed.
19 S3 **Meglino, Ozero** l. Rus. Fed.
19 S1 **Megra** r. Rus. Fed.
19 Q1 **Megrega** Rus. Fed.
19 Q1 **Megri** Armenia see **Meghri**
19 Q2 **Megrozero** Rus. Fed.
77 K5 **Mehadica** Romania
45 H7 **Mehaigne** r. Belgium
87 F2 **Mehaïguène, Oued** watercourse Alg.
20 S1 **Mehamn** Norway
17 O9 **Mehamon, Mys** pt Ukr.
185 L8 **Mehar** Pak.
209 E7 **Meharry, Mount** W.A. Austr.
184 B4 **Mehdia** Tunisia see **Mahdia**
184 B4 **Mehdikhān** Iran
184 E4 **Mehdishahr** Iran
48 H3 **Mehe** r. Ger.
23 N1 **Mehedeby** Sweden
178 F9 **Mehekar** Mahar. India
179 L8 **Meherpur** Bangl.
116 G11 **Meherrin** r. VA U.S.A.
116 I12 **Meherrin** r. VA U.S.A.
201 □3 **Mehetia** i. Arch. de la Société Fr. Polynesia
178 E8 **Mehidpur** Madh. Prad. India
47 J5 **Méhkérék** Hungary
51 F9 **Mehltheuer** Ger.
120 J6 **Mehlville** MO U.S.A.
179 D8 **Mehmadabad** Gujarat India
179 I6 **Mehndawal** Uttar Prad. India
118 C1 **Mehoopany** PA U.S.A.
184 B2 **Mehrābān** Iran
184 F8 **Mehrān** Iran
184 F8 **Mehrān** watercourse Iran
189 M7 **Mehrān** Iraq
49 C10 **Mehren** Ger.
52 B2 **Mehring** Ger.
51 E7 **Mehringen** Ger.
59 H3 **Mehrnbach** Austria
52 H5 **Mehrstetten** Ger.
185 N4 **Mehtar Lām** Afgh.
42 I1 **Mehun-sur-Yèvre** France
142 C3 **Meia Ponte** r. Brazil
Meicheng Fujian China see **Minqing**
171 H4 **Meichengzhen** Hunan China
170 E1 **Meichuan** Gansu China
89 I5 **Meidougou** Cameroon
30 D4 **Meidrim** Carmarthenshire, Wales U.K.
89 I5 **Meiganga** Cameroon
28 E5 **Meigh** Northern Ireland U.K.
105 I2 **Meighen Island** Nunavut Can.
26 J9 **Meigle** Perth and Kinross, Scotland U.K.
170 D4 **Meigu** Sichuan China
162 D7 **Meihekou** Jilin China
166 F4 **Meihō** Japan
45 I6 **Meijel** Neth.
44 F4 **Meijendel** nature res. Neth.
Meijiang Jiangxi China see **Ningdu**
171 J6 **Mei Jiang** r. China
171 J6 **Meikeng** Guangdong China
106 G3 **Meikle** r. Alta Can.
28 I1 **Meikle Bin** hill Scotland U.K.
28 G2 **Meikle Kilmory** Argyll and Bute, Scotland U.K.
26 J9 **Meiklecur** Perth and Kinross, Scotland U.K.
26 K11 **Meikle Says Law** hill Scotland U.K.
158 B4 **Meiktila** Myanmar
70 F1 **Meilen** Switz.
43 C8 **Meilhan** France
43 E6 **Meilhan-sur-Garonne** France
38 H5 **Meillac** France
40 A3 **Meillard** France
40 J4 **Meillerie** France
106 E2 **Meilleur** r. N.W.T. Can.
170 H8 **Meilu** Guangdong China
63 F8 **Meimoa** Port.
70 F4 **Meina** Italy
49 K6 **Meine** Ger.
49 J6 **Meinersen** Ger.
49 E8 **Meinerzhagen** Ger.
58 A5 **Meiningen** Austria
43 J9 **Meiningen** Ger.
62 F2 **Meira** Spain
62 F2 **Meira, Serra de** mts Spain
70 E2 **Meiringen** Switz.
96 G9 **Meiringspoort** pass S. Africa
26 D9 **Meirleach, Rubha nam** pt Scotland U.K.
51 D7 **Meisdorf** Ger.
52 D2 **Meissen** Ger.
Meishan Anhui China see **Jinzhai**
170 D3 **Meishan** Sichuan China
51 H8 **Meißen** Ger.
48 I5 **Meißendorf** Ger.
52 D5 **Meißenheim** Ger.
49 I8 **Meißner** hill Ger.
49 I8 **Meißner-Kaufunger Wald, Naturpark** nature res. Ger.
106 D2 **Meister** r. Y.T. Can.
170 F5 **Meitan** Guizhou China
53 J4 **Meitingen** Ger.
167 K3 **Meiwa** Gunma Japan
166 E8 **Meiwa** Mie Japan
45 H9 **Meix-devant-Virton** Belgium
162 F5 **Meixi** Heilong. China
Meixian Guangdong China see **Meizhou**
171 J6 **Meixian** Guangdong China
169 J9 **Meixian** Shaanxi China
171 K6 **Meizhou** Guangdong China
178 F7 **Mej** r. India
178 I7 **Meja** Uttar Prad. India
41 E7 **Mejan, Sommet de** mt. France
86 D5 **Mejaouda** well Maur.
200 □3a **Mejatto** i. Kwajalein Marshall Is
41 C8 **Méjean, Causse** plat. France
69 B7 **Mejez el Bab** Tunisia
144 D3 **Mejicana** mt. Arg.
138 C5 **Mejillones** Chile
138 C5 **Mejillones del Sur, Bahía de** b. Chile
63 K8 **Mejorada** Spain
63 N8 **Mejorada del Campo** Spain
85 G5 **Mekadio** well Sudan
90 B4 **Mékambo** Gabon
79 L2 **Mekece** Turkey
92 C1 **Mek'elē** Eth.
191 G2 **Meken-Yurt** Rus. Fed.
87 F4 **Mekerrhane, Sebkha** salt pan Alg.
19 Q1 **Mekhbaza** Rus. Fed.
45 H7 **Mékhé** Senegal
191 H3 **Mekhetʼta** Rus. Fed.
185 H6 **Mehtar** Pak.
92 C2 **Meki** Eth.
59 K7 **Mekinje** Slovenia
89 F5 **Mekkaw** Nigeria
86 D2 **Meknès** Morocco
170 C7 **Mekong** r. Asia
alt. **Lancang Jiang (China)**
Mekong r. Xizang/Yunnan China see **Lancang Jiang**
160 I8 **Mekong** r. Laos/Thai.
159 H10 **Mekong, Mouths of the Vietnam**
191 D3 **Mekʼvena** Georgia
71 M3 **Mel** Italy
90 D2 **Mela, Mont** hill C.A.R.
146 B4 **Melado** r. Chile
87 G3 **Melah, Oued el** watercourse Alg.
156 E3 **Melaka** Malaysia
156 E3 **Melaka** state Malaysia
157 K2 **Melalap** Sabah Malaysia
156 F5 **Melalo, Tanjung** pt Indon.
73 O6 **Melandro** r. Italy
216 F6 **Melanesia** is Oceania
216 F5 **Melanesian Basin** sea feature Pacific Ocean
20 □B1 **Melar** Iceland
71 K5 **Melara** Italy
157 I4 **Melawi** r. Indon.
40 E4 **Melay** Bourgogne France
37 K8 **Melay** Champagne-Ardenne France

Column 2

39 J7 **Melay** Pays de la Loire France
73 E6 **Melazzo** Italy
48 J4 **Melbeck** Ger.
31 M3 **Melbourn** Cambridgeshire, England U.K.
205 J7 **Melbourne** Vic. Austr.
31 J2 **Melbourne** Derbyshire, England U.K.
121 J7 **Melbourne** AR U.S.A.
115 G11 **Melbourne** FL U.S.A.
20 M2 **Melbu** Norway
26 □M2 **Melby** Shetland, Scotland U.K.
20 □ **Melchers, Kapp** c. Svalbard
146 B3 **Melchor, Isla** i. Chile
127 O9 **Melchor de Mencos** Guat.
127 I5 **Melchor Ocampo** Mex.
50 I5 **Melchow** Ger.
20 J5 **Meldal** Norway
71 M7 **Meldola** Italy
48 J2 **Meldorf** Ger.
116 B12 **Meldrum** KY U.S.A.
108 D4 **Meldrum Bay** Ont. Can.
66 **Mele** Italy
70 E8 **Mele, Capo** c. Italy
19 T4 **Melen** r. Rus. Fed.
70 E8 **Melenara** Gran Canaria Canary Is
76 I5 **Melenci** Vojvodina, Srbija Serb. and Mont.
188 G4 **Melendiz Daği** mt. Turkey
75 O3 **Melendugno** Italy
15 H5 **Melenki** Rus. Fed.
38 H5 **Melesse** France
Melet Turkey see **Mesudiye**
182 F1 **Meleuz** Rus. Fed.
109 G1 **Mélèzes, Rivière aux** r. Que. Can.
73 L4 **Melfa** Italy
115 J4 **Melfa** VA U.S.A.
90 C2 **Mélfi** Chad
73 J6 **Melfi** Italy
107 J4 **Melfort** Sask. Can.
137 I5 **Melgaço** Brazil
62 D4 **Melgaço** Port.
62 J5 **Melgar** r. Spain
63 J4 **Melgar de Arriba** Spain
63 L4 **Melgar de Fernamental** Spain
62 H5 **Melgar de Tera** Spain
38 D6 **Melgven** France
20 K5 **Melhus** Norway
107 M2 **Meliadine Lake** Nunavut Can.
157 I5 **Meliau** Kalimantan Indon.
45 J6 **Melick** Neth.
75 K7 **Melicucco** Italy
62 E3 **Melide** Spain
64 B4 **Melides** Port.
78 C5 **Meligalas** Greece
19 E5 **Melikköyü** Turkey
155 C4 **Melilli** r. Indon.
61 E5 **Melilla** N. Africa
75 I9 **Melilli** Sicilia Italy
145 B7 **Melimoyu, Monte** mt. Chile
203 □11 **Melina, Mount** S. I. N.Z.
137 G3 **Melincué** Arg.
147 G3 **Melincué, Laguna** l. Arg.
157 I5 **Melintang, Danau** l. Indon.
17 O5 **Melioratyvne** Ukr.
146 B6 **Melipeuco** Chile
146 B3 **Melipilla** Chile
37 M4 **Mélisey** France
44 E5 **Meliskerke** Neth.
75 M5 **Melissa** Italy
107 K5 **Melita** Man. Can.
78 C2 **Meliti** Greece
75 J8 **Melito** r. Italy
75 J8 **Melito di Porto Salvo** Italy
17 O7 **Melitopol'** Ukr.
59 L3 **Melk** Austria
59 L3 **Melk** r. Austria
97 I8 **Melk** r. S. Africa
92 C3 **Melka Guba** Eth.
96 B5 **Melkbospunt** pt S. Africa
96 B5 **Melkbosstrand** S. Africa
30 H5 **Melksham** Wiltshire, England U.K.
146 I. Italy
38 D6 **Mellac** France
20 R3 **Mellakoski** Fin.
79 I4 **Menderes** Turkey
183 L2 **Mendesh** Kazakh.
127 I3 **Méndez** Tamaulipas Mex.
127 J3 **Méndez** Veracruz Mex.
154 C4 **Mendez-Nuñez** Luzon Phil.
118 F3 **Mendham** NJ U.S.A.
92 B2 **Mendī** Eth.
153 J8 **Mendi** P.N.G.
63 Q3 **Mendigorria** Spain
30 G5 **Mendip Hills** England U.K.
124 I2 **Mendocino** CA U.S.A.
122 B6 **Mendocino, Cape** CA U.S.A.
124 I2 **Mendocino** r. CA U.S.A.
74 F8 **Mendola** r. Sicilia Italy
110 I7 **Mendon** MI U.S.A.
205 L4 **Mendooran** N.S.W. Austr.
124 L5 **Mendota** CA U.S.A.
110 E8 **Mendota** IL U.S.A.
110 E6 **Mendota, Lake** WI U.S.A.
146 C3 **Mendoza** Arg.
146 C3 **Mendoza** prov. Arg.
146 C3 **Mendoza** r. Arg.
138 D4 **Mendoza** Bol.
147 I4 **Mendoza** Peru
70 F4 **Mendrisio** Switz.
209 F12 **Mends, Lake** salt flat W.A. Austr.
38 G5 **Mené de Mauroa** Venez.
70 H6 **Menegosa, Monte** mt. Italy
130 H9 **Mene Grande** Venez.
79 I4 **Menemen** Turkey
45 D7 **Menen** Belgium
43 G9 **Ménerbes** France
40 E2 **Ménessaire** France
41 B6 **Menet** France
39 P7 **Menetou-Salon** France
38 E4 **Menez Bré** hill France
38 C6 **Menez Hom** hill France
73 D8 **Menfi** Sicilia Italy
63 D8 **Menga, Puerto de** pass Spain
72 B10 **Menga, Punta** pt Sardegna Italy
157 K1 **Mengalum** i. Malaysia
169 J9 **Mengba** Gansu China
170 C7 **Mengcun** Yunnan China
171 K2 **Mengcheng** Anhui China
52 G5 **Mengen** Ger.
188 D3 **Mengen** Turkey
49 F9 **Mengeringhausen** Ger.
59 K9 **Menges** Slovenia
118 B5 **Menges Mills** PA U.S.A.
157 I4 **Menggala** Sumatera Indon.
170 D8 **Menghai** Yunnan China
170 F4 **Mengjiawan** China
170 D7 **Menghe** China
170 C8 **Mengla** Yunnan China
170 C8 **Menglang** Yunnan China see **Lancang**
170 C8 **Menglian** Yunnan China
170 D7 **Menglie** Yunnan China see **Jiangcheng**
89 H5 **Mengong** Cameroon
170 H6 **Mengshan** Guangxi China
170 I5 **Mengyin** Shandong China
202 J3 **Mengzhou** Henan China see **Mengxian**
157 I4 **Mengzi** Sichuan China
169 O9 **Mengxian** Shandong China
169 M9 **Mengyin** Shandong China
170 D7 **Mengzi** Yunnan China
30 D7 **Menheniot** Cornwall, England U.K.

Column 3

26 I5 **Melvich** Highland, Scotland U.K.
107 K5 **Melville** Sask. Can.
207 J3 **Melville, Cape** Qld Austr.
154 A8 **Melville, Cape** Phil.
109 J2 **Melville, Lake** Nfld and Lab. Can.
206 F2 **Melville Bay** N.T. Austr.
206 C1 **Melville Island** N.T. Austr.
105 H2 **Melville Island** N.W.T./Nunavut Can.
105 J3 **Melville Peninsula** Nunavut Can.
204 G6 **Melvin** IL U.S.A.
184 C4 **Melvin, Lough** l. Rep. of Ireland/U.K.
193 N3 **Menkere** Rus. Fed.
27 D6 **Menlough** Rep. of Ireland
186 D9 **Menna** r. Eth.
36 D6 **Mennecy** France
139 F5 **Mennenom** sur-Cher France
40 C2 **Mennogue** Angola
86 E3 **Menor, Mar** lag. Spain
66 **Menorca** i. Spain
66 □ **Menorca, Cap** c. Spain
41 H7 **Mens** France
76 **Menoua** r. Cameroon
70 **Menouarar** Alg.
78 F5 **Menchas** Kythnos Greece
127 O7 **Méricourt** France
42 F5 **Mérida** Spain
64 G3 **Mérida** Venez.
136 D2 **Mérida** Venez.
136 D3 **Mérida, Cordillera de** mts Venez.
31 13 **Meriden** West Midlands, England U.K.
117 M7 **Meriden** CT U.S.A.
121 G10 **Meridian** MS U.S.A.
121 G10 **Meridian** MS U.S.A.
147 H4 **Meridiano** Arg.
43 C6 **Mérignac** France
20 R4 **Merijärvi** Fin.
21 P6 **Merikarvia** Fin.
205 L7 **Merimbula** N.S.W. Austr.
56 E2 **Mérin** Czech Rep.
209 C12 **Mentelle, Cape** W.A. Austr.
49 K8 **Menteroda** Ger.
79 L4 **Menteşe** Turkey
40 I5 **Menthon-St-Bernard** France
65 O4 **Mentiras** mt. Port.
125 X6 **Mentmore** NM U.S.A.
125 X6 **Mentok** Indon.
41 L9 **Menton** France
121 D10 **Mentone** TX U.S.A.
116 D7 **Mentor** OH U.S.A.
63 L8 **Mentrida** Spain
157 J6 **Menyapi, Gunung** mt. Indon.

Mfuwe to Miraflores
303

93 A8 Mfuwe Zambia
162 M3 Mgachi Sakhalin Rus. Fed.
75 □ Mġarr Gozo Malta
75 □ Mġarr Malta
89 G5 Mgbidi Nigeria
19 P8 Mglin Rus. Fed.
97 M7 Mgwali r. S. Africa
26 D11 Mhàil, Rubh' a' pt Scotland U.K.
95 F3 Mhangura Zimbabwe
64 H9 Mharhar, Oued r. Morocco
176 D4 Mhasvad Mahar. India
97 P2 Mhlambanyatsi Swaziland
97 P3 Mhlosheni Swaziland
97 P2 Mhlume Swaziland
97 N1 Mhluzi S. Africa
26 H8 Mhòr, Loch l. Scotland U.K.
178 E8 Mhow Madh. Prad. India
158 A4 Mi r. Myanmar
Miabhaig Scotland U.K. see Miavaig
129 H7 Miacatlan Mex.
55 L5 Miączyn Pol.
129 K9 Miahuatlán Mex.
129 K9 Miahuatlán, Sierra de mts Mex.
64 H2 Miajadas Spain
42 F4 Mialet France
54 E3 Miały Pol.
90 C2 Miaméré C.A.R.
125 V8 Miami AZ U.S.A.
115 G13 Miami FL U.S.A.
121 H7 Miami OK U.S.A.
121 E8 Miami TX U.S.A.
Miami Zimbabwe see Mwami
115 G13 Miami Beach FL U.S.A.
116 A9 Miamisburg OH U.S.A.
184 G3 Miānābād Iran
185 J8 Mianaz Pak.
168 F9 Miancaowan Qinghai China
185 O6 Mian Chanmun Pak.
169 L9 Mianchi Henan China
184 E4 Mīāndarreh Iran
184 G3 Mīāndasht Iran
184 H4 Mīāndehī Iran
184 B3 Miandowāb Iran
95 □J3 Miandrivazo Madag.
169 Q2 Mianduhe Nei Mongol China
184 B3 Mīāneh Iran
154 F9 Miangas i. Phil.
185 L9 Miani Hor b. Pak.
185 K5 Mianjoi Afgh.
185 N4 Mian Kalai Pak.
184 E3 Mian Kaleh Shebh-e Jazīreh-ye pen. Iran
170 C5 Mianmian Shan mts Sichuan/Yunnan China
170 D4 Mianning Sichuan China
185 N5 Mianwali Pak.
170 F2 Mianxian Shaanxi China
Mianyang Shaanxi China see Mianxian
170 E3 Mianyang Sichuan China
170 E3 Mianzhu Sichuan China
163 B10 Miao Dao i. China
169 Q8 Miaodao Liedao is China
172 F4 Miao'ergou Xinjiang China
171 M6 Miaoli Taiwan
95 □J3 Miarinarivo Madag.
167 G2 Miasa Japan
192 H4 Miass Rus. Fed.
54 F2 Miasteckzo Krajeńskie Pol.
54 E1 Miastko Pol.
55 J4 Miastków Kościelny Pol.
55 J2 Miastkowo Pol.
26 C6 Miavaig Western Isles, Scotland U.K.
166 E3 Miboro-ko l. Japan
167 K3 Mibu Japan
167 G4 Mibu-gawa r. Japan
138 C5 Mica, Cerro de mt. Chile
106 G4 Mica Creek B.C. Can.
147 G6 Micaela Cascallares Arg.
125 V9 Mica Mountain AZ U.S.A.
170 F2 Micang Shan mts China
95 H3 Micaune Moz.
14 J2 Michaichmon' Rus. Fed.
57 K3 Michaľany Slovakia
57 I3 Michalová Slovakia
57 K3 Michalovce Slovakia
55 I5 Michałów Pol.
55 J4 Michałów Górny Pol.
55 H5 Michałowice Małopolskie Pol.
54 F5 Michałowice Opolskie Pol.
55 L2 Michałowo Pol.
107 I4 Michel Sask. Can.
51 D10 Michelau in Oberfranken Ger.
52 H3 Michelbach an der Bilz Ger.
59 J6 Micheldorf Austria
59 J4 Micheldorf in Oberösterreich Austria
52 H3 Michelfeld Ger.
104 D5 Michelson, Mount AK U.S.A.
52 G2 Michelstadt Ger.
51 H6 Michendorf Ger.
Micheng Yunnan China see Midu
131 I4 Miches Dom. Rep.
110 F3 Michigamme Lake MI U.S.A.
110 F3 Michigamme Reservoir MI U.S.A.
120 K2 Michigan state U.S.A.
110 G6 Michigan, Lake MI/WI U.S.A.
114 D5 Michigan City IN U.S.A.
90 B2 Michika Nigeria
176 G3 Michinberi Chhattisgarh India
108 C4 Michipicoten Bay Ont. Can.
108 C4 Michipicoten Island Ont. Can.
108 C4 Michipicoten River Ont. Can.
128 E7 Michoacán state Mex.
55 K4 Michów Pol.
15 H5 Michurinsk Rus. Fed.
29 M4 Mickleton Durham, England U.K.
31 I3 Mickleton Gloucestershire, England U.K.
126 □Q11 Mico r. Nic.
129 H3 Micos Mex.
131 □3 Micoud St Lucia
216 E5 Micronesia is Pacific Ocean
153 L6 Micronesia, Federated States of country N. Pacific Ocean
77 K3 Micula Romania
157 G3 Midai i. Indon.
89 G2 Midal well Niger
107 K5 Midale Sask. Can.
214 F4 Mid-Atlantic Ridge sea feature Atlantic Ocean
26 K4 Midbea Orkney, Scotland U.K.
45 H6 Middelbeers Neth.
96 D8 Middelberg Pass S. Africa
44 E5 Middelburg Neth.
97 J7 Middelburg Eastern Cape S. Africa
97 N1 Middelburg Mpumalanga S. Africa
22 F6 Middelfart Denmark
44 F5 Middelharnis Neth.
45 C6 Middelkerke Belgium
96 E7 Middelpos S. Africa
44 K2 Middelstum Neth.
95 E5 Middelwit S. Africa
44 G3 Middenbeemster Neth.
44 H3 Middenmeer Neth.
122 D6 Middle Alkali Lake CA U.S.A.
217 M5 Middle America Trench sea feature N. Pacific Ocean
177 M6 Middle Andaman i. Andaman & Nicobar Is India
Middle Atlas mts Morocco see Moyen Atlas
31 J4 Middle Barton Oxfordshire, England U.K.
109 J3 Middle Bay Que. Can.
204 □2 Middle Beach b. Lord Howe I. Austr.
117 O7 Middleboro MA U.S.A.
114 G6 Middlebourne WV U.S.A.
111 Q9 Middleburg PA U.S.A.
116 H10 Middleburg VA U.S.A.
117 K6 Middleburgh NY U.S.A.
119 I1 Middlebury CT U.S.A.
110 I8 Middlebury IN U.S.A.
117 L4 Middlebury VT U.S.A.
130 H3 Middle Caicos i. Turks and Caicos Is
121 E10 Middle Concho r. TX U.S.A.
207 H4 Middle Creek r. Qld Austr.
118 E2 Middle Creek r. PA U.S.A.
119 J1 Middlefield CT U.S.A.
119 J1 Middle Haddam CT U.S.A.
29 N5 Middleham North Yorkshire, England U.K.
65 □ Middle Hill Gibraltar
119 G1 Middle Hope NY U.S.A.
98 □2c Middle Island Tristan da Cunha S. Atlantic Ocean
119 J3 Middle Island NY U.S.A.
120 G5 Middle Loup r. NE U.S.A.
30 H6 Middlemarsh Dorset, England U.K.
207 L7 Middlemount Qld Austr.
208 □1 Middle Point Christmas I.
116 C9 Middleport OH U.S.A.
118 C3 Middleport PA U.S.A.
120 I5 Middle Raccoon r. IA U.S.A.
29 Q7 Middle Rasen Lincolnshire, England U.K.
109 K3 Middle Ridge Wildlife Reserve nature res. Nfld and Lab. Can.
118 C6 Middle River MD U.S.A.
116 B12 Middlesboro KY U.S.A.
29 O4 Middlesbrough Middlesbrough, England U.K.
29 O4 Middlesbrough admin. div. England U.K.
127 O9 Middlesex Belize
130 □ Middlesex reg. Jamaica
116 H6 Middlesex NY U.S.A.
118 A4 Middlesex PA U.S.A.
119 J1 Middlesex County county CT U.S.A.
119 G4 Middlesex County county NJ U.S.A.
29 N5 Middlesmoor North Yorkshire, England U.K.
207 H7 Middleton Qld Austr.
109 H4 Middleton N.S. Can.
97 J8 Middleton S. Africa
29 M6 Middleton Greater Manchester, England U.K.
31 M2 Middleton Norfolk, England U.K.
116 A5 Middleton MI U.S.A.
110 E6 Middleton WI U.S.A.
31 J3 Middleton Cheney Northamptonshire, England U.K.
29 M4 Middleton in Teesdale Durham, England U.K.
31 K6 Middleton-on-Sea West Sussex, England U.K.
29 P6 Middleton-on-the-Wolds East Riding of Yorkshire, England U.K.
199 F4 Middleton Reef Austr.
31 J4 Middleton Stoney Oxfordshire, England U.K.
27 I4 Middletown Northern Ireland U.K.
124 J3 Middletown CA U.S.A.
119 J1 Middletown CT U.S.A.
118 D6 Middletown DE U.S.A.
116 H9 Middletown MD U.S.A.
119 G4 Middletown NJ U.S.A.
117 K7 Middletown NY U.S.A.
116 A9 Middletown OH U.S.A.
111 R9 Middletown PA U.S.A.
116 G9 Middletown VA U.S.A.
110 I7 Middleville MI U.S.A.
117 K5 Middleville NY U.S.A.
29 M7 Middlewich Cheshire, England U.K.
203 C12 Mid Dome mt. South I. N.Z.
86 D2 Midelt Morocco
202 I6 Midhirst North I. N.Z.
92 E2 Midhisho well Somalia
31 K6 Midhurst West Sussex, England U.K.
186 F7 Mīdī Yemen
43 I9 Midi, Canal du France
43 E10 Midi de Bigorre, Pic du mt. France
43 D10 Midi d'Ossau, Pic du mt. France
215 J5 Mid-Indian Basin sea feature Indian Ocean
215 I6 Mid-Indian Ridge sea feature Indian Ocean
41 A8 Midi-Pyrénées admin. reg. France
108 E4 Midland Ont. Can.
125 R8 Midland CA U.S.A.
111 J6 Midland MI U.S.A.
120 E3 Midland SD U.S.A.
121 E9 Midland TX U.S.A.
209 C11 Midland Junction W.A. Austr.
95 F3 Midlands prov. Zimbabwe
27 F9 Midleton Rep. of Ireland
26 J11 Midlothian admin. div. Scotland U.K.
121 G9 Midlothian TX U.S.A.
116 H11 Midlothian VA U.S.A.
48 G3 Midlum Ger.
97 O5 Midmar Nature Reserve S. Africa
111 M5 Midmay Ont. Can.
Midnapore W. Bengal India see Medinipur
95 □J4 Midongy Atsimo Madag.
167 K4 Midori Japan
165 H14 Midori-gawa r. Japan
43 C8 Midou r. France
43 C8 Midouze r. France
216 F4 Mid-Pacific Mountains sea feature N. Pacific Ocean
97 M1 Midrand S. Africa
154 E8 Midsayap Mindanao Phil.
30 H5 Midsomer Norton Bath and North East Somerset, England U.K.
20 I5 Midsund Norway
170 C6 Midu Yunnan China
175 □2 Midu i. Addu Atoll Maldives
122 F4 Midvale ID U.S.A.
125 U1 Midway UT U.S.A.
197 H2 Midway Islands N. Pacific Ocean
209 G7 Midway Well W.A. Austr.
122 K5 Midwest WY U.S.A.
121 G8 Midwest City OK U.S.A.
44 L2 Midwolda Neth.
186 B2 Midyan reg. Saudi Arabia
189 J5 Midyat Turkey
Midye Turkey see Kıyıköy
26 □N1 Mid Yell Shetland, Scotland U.K.
77 K7 Midzhur mt. Bulg./Yugo.
165 I14 Mie Japan
166 D7 Mie pref. Japan
55 I5 Miechów Pol.
57 L1 Mieczka r. Pol.
58 D5 Mieders Austria
63 R6 Miedes Spain
54 C2 Miedwie, Jezioro l. Pol.
55 I5 Miedziana Góra Pol.
54 D3 Miedzichowo Pol.
55 K3 Miedzna Pol.
55 H6 Miedźna Pol.
54 G5 Miedźno Pol.
54 F4 Międzybórz Pol.
54 D3 Międzychód Pol.
54 E5 Międzylesie Pol.
55 K4 Międzyrzec Podlaski Pol.
54 D3 Międzyrzecz Pol.
47 I3 Międzyrzecza Warty i Widawki, Park Krajobrazowy Pol.
54 C2 Międzyzdroje Pol.
21 S6 Miehikkälä Fin.
49 E10 Miehlen Ger.
55 J6 Miejsce Piastowe Pol.
54 E4 Miejska Górka Pol.
54 E4 Miękinia Pol.
43 E9 Miélan France
41 G8 Miélandre, Montagne de mt. France
55 J5 Mielec Pol.
50 K4 Mielęcin Pol.
54 F3 Mieleszyn Pol.
48 J2 Mielkendorf Ger.
55 L3 Mielnik Pol.
54 E1 Mielno Pol.
93 C7 Miembwe Tanz.
58 D5 Mieming Austria
58 C5 Mieminger Gebirge mts Austria
55 G3 Mień r. Pol.
23 K5 Mien l. Sweden
205 K9 Miena Tas. Austr.
91 C9 Mienga Angola
91 F8 Miengwe Zambia
171 N6 Mienhua Yü i. Taiwan
63 M2 Miera r. Spain
20 S2 Mieraslompolo Fin.
Mierašluoppal Fin. see Mieraslompolo
77 N4 Miercurea-Ciuc Romania
62 I2 Mieres Spain
Mieres del Camín Spain see Mieres
Mieres del Camino Spain see Mieres
45 I6 Mierlo Neth.
20 Q2 Mierojávri Norway
54 E5 Mieroszów Pol.
43 H6 Miers France
128 G2 Mier y Noriaga Mex.
55 I5 Mierzawa r. Pol.
23 O7 Mierzeja Helska spit Pol.
23 P7 Mierzeja Wiślana spit Pol.
50 J4 Mierzyn Pol.
52 C3 Miesau Ger.
53 L6 Miesbach Ger.
54 F3 Mieścisko Pol.
52 D3 Miesenbach Ger.
92 D2 Mī'ēso Eth.
51 D6 Mieste Ger.
51 D6 Miesterhorst Ger.
54 F3 Mieszków Pol.
54 C3 Mieszkowice Pol.
52 H5 Mietingen Ger.
21 P6 Mietoinen Fin.
40 J4 Mieussy France
62 G6 Mieza Spain
186 E6 Mīfah Saudi Arabia
116 C8 Mifflin OH U.S.A.
111 Q9 Mifflinburg PA U.S.A.
116 H8 Mifflintown PA U.S.A.
118 C2 Mifflinville PA U.S.A.
166 F1 Mifune-zaki pt Japan
168 J9 Migang Shan mt. Gansu/Ningxia China
97 J2 Migdol S. Africa
36 G8 Migennes France
184 H6 Mīghān Iran
179 O5 Miging Arun. Prad. India
71 L6 Migliarino Italy
70 I8 Migliarino-San Rossore-Massaciuccoli, Parco Naturale di nature res. Italy
71 L6 Migliaro Italy
75 K2 Miglionica Italy
42 E2 Mignaloux-Beauvoir France
73 L5 Mignano Monte Lungo Italy
72 H3 Mignone r. Italy
40 I3 Mignovillard France
173 J10 Migriggyangzham Co l. Qinghai China
109 H3 Miguasha, Parc de nature res. N.B. Can.
129 K7 Miguel Alemán Mex.
129 K7 Miguel Alemán, Presa resr Mex.
140 E3 Miguel Alves Brazil
128 D1 Miguel Auza Mex.
140 E4 Miguel Calmon Brazil
126 □S13 Miguel de la Borda Panama
129 K8 Miguel de la Madrid, Presa resr Mex.
63 N9 Miguel Esteban Spain
147 I4 Miguelete Uru.
129 H3 Miguel Hidalgo Mex.
126 E4 Miguel Hidalgo, Presa resr Mex.
143 F5 Miguel Pereira Brazil
147 F5 Miguel Riglos Arg.
65 L3 Miguelturra Spain
18 M6 Migushino Rus. Fed.
158 B5 Migyaunye Myanmar
77 N6 Mihăilești Romania
56 G5 Mihald Hungary
79 L2 Mihalgazi Turkey
188 E4 Mihalıççık Turkey
56 G4 Mihályi Hungary
166 E6 Mihama Aichi Japan
166 C4 Mihama Fukui Japan
166 D8 Mihama Mie Japan
166 B8 Mihama Wakayama Japan
165 K12 Mihara Hiroshima Japan
166 A7 Mihara Hyōgo Japan
167 J6 Mihara-yama vol. Japan
169 P8 Mi He r. China
179 K8 Mihijam Jharkhand India
176 G8 Mihintale Sri Lanka
49 J8 Mihla Ger.
167 L4 Mihō Japan
165 K11 Miho-wan b. Japan
93 C7 Mihumo Chini Tanz.
63 K8 Mijares Spain
67 D7 Mijares r. Spain
65 J7 Mijas Spain
65 J7 Mijas mt. Spain
44 G4 Mijdrecht Neth.
167 J1 Mijōga-take mt. Japan
40 I4 Mijoux France
164 S3 Mikasa Japan
16 G1 Mikashevichy Belarus
166 C4 Mikata Japan
166 C4 Mikata-ko l. Japan
166 D3 Mikawa Japan
166 F6 Mikawa-wan b. Japan
166 F6 Mikawa-wan Quasi National Park Japan
57 K4 Mikepércs Hungary
Mikhalevo Rus. Fed. see Paneyevo
19 W6 Mikhali Rus. Fed.
18 J7 Mikhalishki Belarus
18 K8 Mikhanavichy Belarus
19 W7 Mikhaylov Rus. Fed.
Mikhaylovgrad Bulg. see Montana
183 Q1 Mikhaylovka Pavlodarskaya Oblast' Kazakh.
162 F4 Mikhaylovka Amurskaya Oblast' Rus. Fed.
162 A3 Mikhaylovka Chitinskaya Oblast' Rus. Fed.
17 O1 Mikhaylovka Kurskaya Oblast' Rus. Fed.
162 H7 Mikhaylovka Primorskiy Kray Rus. Fed.
Mikhaylovka Tul'skaya Oblast' Rus. Fed. see Kimovsk
15 H6 Mikhaylovka Volgogradskaya Oblast' Rus. Fed.
77 L7 Mikhaylovo Bulg.
17 T4 Mikhaylovo-Aleksandrovskiy Rus. Fed.
Mikhaylovskiy Altayskiy Kray Rus. Fed. see Malinovoye Ozero
183 R2 Mikhaylovskiy Altayskiy Kray Rus. Fed.
213 F2 Mikhaytov Island Antarctica
19 U6 Mikhnevo Rus. Fed.
190 C9 Mikhrot Timna Israel
186 E6 Mikhwa Saudi Arabia
166 A6 Miki Japan
Mikínes tourist site Greece see Mykines
179 N6 Mikir Hills India
166 D8 Miki-zaki pt Japan
166 G6 Mikkabi Japan
21 S6 Mikkeli Fin.
21 S6 Mikkelin mlk Fin.
106 H3 Mikkwa r. Alta Can.
59 M6 Miklavž Slovenia
55 J2 Mikołajki Pol.
55 H2 Mikołajki Pomorskie Pol.
54 G5 Mikołów Pol.
Míkonos i. Greece see Mykonos
54 G1 Mikoszewo Pol.
Mikoyanovka Rus. Fed. see Oktyabr'skiy
78 E1 Mikropoli Greece
54 F4 Mikstat Pol.
51 J9 Mikulasovice Czech Rep.
56 G3 Mikulčice Czech Rep.
14 I2 Mikulkin, Mys c. Rus. Fed.
56 F3 Mikulov Czech Rep.
56 G1 Mikulovice Czech Rep.
93 C6 Mikumi Tanz.
93 C6 Mikumi National Park Tanz.
166 E6 Mikumo Japan
14 J3 Mikun' Rus. Fed.
166 D3 Mikuni Japan
167 I2 Mikuni-sanmyaku mts Japan
167 I4 Mikuni-yama mt. Japan
167 K8 Mikura-jima i. Japan
87 G1 Mila Alg.
120 I3 Milaca MN U.S.A.
176 C9 Miladhunmadulu Atoll Maldives
140 F3 Milagres Brazil
146 E2 Milagro Arg.
136 B5 Milagro Ecuador
63 Q4 Milagro Spain
63 M5 Milagros Spain
55 I1 Miłakowo Pol.
178 H4 Milam Uttaranchal India
Milan Italy see Milano
111 K7 Milan MI U.S.A.
120 I5 Milan MO U.S.A.
116 C7 Milan OH U.S.A.
91 C7 Milando Angola
91 C7 Milando, Reserva Especial do nature res. Angola
204 G6 Milang S.A. Austr.
95 G3 Milange Moz.
70 G5 Milano Italy
70 G5 Milano prov. Italy
70 F4 Milano (Malpensa) airport Italy
95 □K2 Milanoa Madag.
71 M7 Milano Marittima Italy
55 K4 Milanów Pol.
55 I3 Milanówek Pol.
118 E1 Milanville PA U.S.A.
77 M4 Milaș Romania
79 I5 Milas Turkey
16 G2 Milashavichy Belarus
19 P8 Milaslavichy Rus. Fed.
18 I9 Milavidy Belarus
75 I7 Milazzo Sicilia Italy
75 I7 Milazzo, Capo di c. Sicilia Italy
75 I7 Milazzo, Golfo di b. Sicilia Italy
120 G3 Milbank SD U.S.A.
30 H6 Milborne Port Somerset, England U.K.
30 H6 Milborne St Andrew Dorset, England U.K.
117 □R4 Milbridge ME U.S.A.
50 E5 Milde r. Ger.
31 N3 Mildenhall Suffolk, England U.K.
111 R8 Mildred PA U.S.A.
48 H2 Mildstedt Ger.
205 I6 Mildura Vic. Austr.
191 I5 Mil Düzü lowland Azer.
170 D6 Mile Yunnan China
92 D2 Mīlē Eth.
28 F4 Milebush Northern Ireland U.K.
31 N4 Mile End Essex, England U.K.
130 □ Mile Gully Jamaica
55 L3 Milejczyce Pol.
55 H1 Milejewo Pol.
55 K4 Milejów Pol.
74 F9 Milena Sicilia Italy
207 M9 Miles Qld Austr.
116 H8 Milesburg PA U.S.A.
122 L3 Miles City MT U.S.A.
92 D2 Mīlē Serdo Reserve nature res. Eth.
56 C1 Milešovka hill Czech Rep.
27 F7 Milestone Rep. of Ireland
77 P3 Miletin r. Romania
75 K6 Mileto Italy
73 M5 Miletto, Monte mt. Italy
209 D9 Mileura W.A. Austr.
56 D2 Mílevsko Czech Rep.
19 S8 Mileyevo Rus. Fed.
29 M2 Milfield Northumberland, England U.K.
64 B5 Milfontes Port.
27 E8 Milford Cork Rep. of Ireland
27 G2 Milford Donegal Rep. of Ireland
31 K5 Milford Surrey, England U.K.
119 I2 Milford CT U.S.A.
118 E7 Milford DE U.S.A.
110 G9 Milford IL U.S.A.
117 N6 Milford MA U.S.A.
118 B6 Milford MD U.S.A.
117 □Q4 Milford ME U.S.A.
116 B6 Milford MI U.S.A.
120 G5 Milford NE U.S.A.
117 N6 Milford NH U.S.A.
118 E3 Milford NJ U.S.A.
118 F2 Milford PA U.S.A.
125 S3 Milford UT U.S.A.
116 H10 Milford VA U.S.A.
30 B4 Milford Haven Pembrokeshire, Wales U.K.
120 G6 Milford Lake KS U.S.A.
31 I6 Milford on Sea Hampshire, England U.K.
203 B11 Milford Sound South I. N.Z.
203 B11 Milford Sound inlet South I. N.Z.
118 E4 Milford Square PA U.S.A.
207 H5 Milgarra Qld Austr.
209 E8 Milgun W.A. Austr.
62 G5 Milhão Port.
41 E9 Milhaud France
54 F4 Milicz Pol.
Milid Turkey see Malatya
206 C1 Milikapiti N.T. Austr.
209 D11 Miling W.A. Austr.
206 E2 Milingimbi N.T. Austr.
200 □5 Milip Vanuatu
72 B7 Milis Sardegna Italy
74 H9 Militello in Val di Catania Sicilia Italy
38 B5 Milizac France
59 M7 Miljana Croatia
122 K2 Milk r. MT U.S.A.
85 F5 Milk, Wadi el watercourse Sudan
51 J8 Milkel Ger.
55 J2 Miłki Pol.
193 Q4 Mil'kovo Rus. Fed.
54 E4 Miłkowice Pol.
107 H5 Milk River Alta Can.
44 I5 Mill Neth.
207 J4 Millaa Millaa Qld Austr.
110 B9 Millard MO U.S.A.
67 D9 Millares Spain
115 □2 Millars New Prov. Bahamas
41 C8 Millau France
40 E3 Millay France
116 F11 Millboro VA U.S.A.
111 P5 Millbrook Ont. Can.
30 D7 Millbrook Cornwall, England U.K.
115 D9 Millbrook AL U.S.A.
117 L7 Millbrook NY U.S.A.
26 I7 Mill Buie hill Scotland U.K.
122 C4 Mill City OR U.S.A.
116 F10 Mill Creek WV U.S.A.
124 J1 Mill Creek r. CA U.S.A.
118 C5 Mill Creek r. PA U.S.A.
119 J1 Milldale CT U.S.A.
115 F9 Milledgeville GA U.S.A.
110 E8 Milledgeville IL U.S.A.
120 I2 Mille Lacs lakes MN U.S.A.
108 B3 Mille Lacs, Lac des l. Ont. Can.
115 G9 Millen GA U.S.A.
Millennium Island atoll Kiribati see Caroline Island
204 E4 Miller watercourse S.A. Austr.
96 H9 Miller S. Africa
120 F3 Miller SD U.S.A.
110 D4 Miller Dam Flowage resr WI U.S.A.
111 M4 Miller Lake Ont. Can.
15 H6 Millerovo Rus. Fed.
125 V10 Miller Peak AZ U.S.A.
111 J4 Millersburg MI U.S.A.
116 D8 Millersburg OH U.S.A.
111 R9 Millersburg PA U.S.A.
204 F4 Millers Creek S.A. Austr.
116 B11 Millers Creek KY U.S.A.
117 M6 Millers Falls MA U.S.A.
203 D12 Millers Flat South I. N.Z.
116 C9 Millersport OH U.S.A.
118 A3 Millerstown PA U.S.A.
118 B6 Millersville MD U.S.A.
118 C5 Millersville PA U.S.A.
117 L7 Millerton NY U.S.A.
124 M4 Millerton Lake CA U.S.A.
26 F12 Milleur Point Scotland U.K.
42 I4 Millevaches France
42 H4 Millevaches, Plateau de France
27 I4 Millford Northern Ireland U.K.
213 L1 Mill Glacier Antarctica
116 H7 Mill Hall PA U.S.A.
119 G4 Millhurst NJ U.S.A.
204 H7 Millicent S.A. Austr.
37 J7 Millières France
208 H5 Millijiddie Aboriginal Reserve W.A. Austr.
44 J5 Millingen aan de Rijn Neth.
118 D6 Millington MD U.S.A.
111 K6 Millington MI U.S.A.
121 K8 Millington TN U.S.A.
212 T2 Mill Inlet Antarctica
117 □Q3 Millinocket ME U.S.A.
138 C5 Milliri, Cerro mt. Bol.
213 G2 Mill Island Antarctica
105 K3 Mill Island Nunavut Can.
27 K3 Millisle Northern Ireland U.K.
207 M9 Millmerran Qld Austr.
118 A3 Millmont PA U.S.A.
29 K5 Millom Cumbria, England U.K.
26 G11 Millport North Ayrshire, Scotland U.K.
118 F2 Millrift PA U.S.A.
117 J10 Millsboro DE U.S.A.
207 I7 Mills Creek watercourse Qld Austr.
106 G2 Mills Lake N.W.T. Can.
59 I6 Millstatt Austria
59 I6 Millstätter See l. Austria
110 D5 Millston WI U.S.A.
116 C11 Millstone KY U.S.A.
116 D10 Millstone WV U.S.A.
118 F3 Millstone r. NJ U.S.A.
208 D6 Millstream W.A. Austr.
208 D6 Millstream-Chichester National Park W.A. Austr.
27 D8 Millstreet Rep. of Ireland
109 H4 Milltown N.B. Can.
28 C5 Milltown Cavan Rep. of Ireland
27 E5 Milltown Galway Rep. of Ireland
27 C8 Milltown Kerry Rep. of Ireland
28 D7 Milltown Kildare Rep. of Ireland
28 E5 Milltown Northern Ireland U.K.
122 H3 Milltown MT U.S.A.
110 B4 Milltown WI U.S.A.
27 D7 Milltown Malbay Rep. of Ireland
26 K8 Milltown of Kildrummy Aberdeenshire, Scotland U.K.
26 K7 Milltown of Rothiemay Moray, Scotland U.K.
207 H5 Millungera Qld Austr.
97 K1 Millvale S. Africa
124 J4 Mill Valley CA U.S.A.
117 □R2 Millville N.B. Can.
118 E6 Millville NJ U.S.A.
118 B2 Millville PA U.S.A.
119 H2 Millwood NY U.S.A.
121 I9 Millwood Lake AR U.S.A.
36 D7 Milly-la-Forêt France
40 F4 Milly-Lamartine France
209 D9 Milly Milly W.A. Austr.
63 Q6 Milmarcos Spain
50 I4 Milmersdorf Ger.
45 I7 Milmort Belgium
26 J10 Milnathort Perth and Kinross, Scotland U.K.
Milne Land i. Greenland see Ilimananngip Nunaa
26 H11 Milngavie East Dunbartonshire, Scotland U.K.
29 M6 Milnrow Greater Manchester, England U.K.
29 L5 Milnthorpe Cumbria, England U.K.
88 C4 Milo r. Guinea
75 I8 Milo Sicilia Italy
117 □Q3 Milo ME U.S.A.
54 E2 Miłocice Pol.
162 I7 Milogradovo Rus. Fed.
71 Q5 Milohnić Croatia
124 □F14 Miloli'i HI U.S.A.
55 H2 Miłomłyn Pol.
54 G1 Miłoradz Pol.
78 F6 Milos i. Greece
19 W8 Miloslavskoye Rus. Fed.
54 F3 Miłosław Pol.
86 D4 Miloud well Alg.
26 C8 Milovaig Highland, Scotland U.K.
17 Q3 Milove Kharkivs'ka Oblast' Ukr.
17 T4 Milove Luhans'ka Oblast' Ukr.
51 K10 Milovice Czech Rep.
51 F5 Milow Brandenburg Ger.
50 E4 Milow Mecklenburg-Vorpommern Ger.
55 H6 Milówka Pol.
205 H3 Milparinka N.S.W. Austr.
124 K4 Milpitas CA U.S.A.
116 H8 Milroy PA U.S.A.
53 N3 Miltach Ger.
52 G2 Miltenberg Ger.
205 M6 Milton N.S.W. Austr.
111 O6 Milton Ont. Can.
203 D13 Milton South I. N.Z.
26 G8 Milton Highland, Scotland U.K.
26 I9 Milton Perth and Kinross, Scotland U.K.
117 J10 Milton DE U.S.A.
115 D10 Milton FL U.S.A.
117 □O5 Milton NH U.S.A.
119 H1 Milton NY U.S.A.
118 B2 Milton PA U.S.A.
117 L4 Milton VT U.S.A.
116 C10 Milton WV U.S.A.
30 D6 Milton Abbot Devon, England U.K.
122 E4 Milton-Freewater OR U.S.A.
31 K3 Milton Keynes Milton Keynes, England U.K.
31 K3 Milton Keynes admin. div. England U.K.
50 H2 Miltzow Ger.
171 I4 Miluo Hunan China
111 N6 Milverton Ont. Can.
30 F5 Milverton Somerset, England U.K.
110 G6 Milwaukee WI U.S.A.
214 E4 Milwaukee Deep sea feature Caribbean Sea
182 I3 Mily Kazakh.
183 P3 Milybulabk Kazakh.
15 H6 Milyutinskaya Rus. Fed.
49 K10 Milz Ger.
43 C8 Mimbaste France
90 C4 Mimbelly Congo
123 K10 Mimbres watercourse NM U.S.A.
63 N2 Mimetiz Spain
204 D2 Mimili S.A. Austr.
176 F8 Mimisal Tamil Nadu India
165 I14 Mimitsu Japan
43 B7 Mimizan France
43 B7 Mimizan-Plage France
56 D1 Mimoň Czech Rep.
90 A5 Mimongo Gabon
143 G4 Mimoso do Sul Brazil
165 L11 Mimuro-yama mt. Japan
127 I4 Mina Mex.
124 N3 Mina NV U.S.A.
138 C3 Mina, Nevado mt. Peru
187 I1 Mīnā' 'Abd Allāh Kuwait
184 G8 Mīnāb Iran
184 G8 Mīnāb r. Iran
185 M6 Mina Bazar Pak.
166 B8 Minabe Japan
166 B8 Minabegawa Japan
146 E2 Mina Clavero Arg.
140 C5 Minaçu Brazil
64 E5 Mina de São Domingos Port.
107 L4 Minago r. Man. Can.
155 B3 Minahasa, Semenanjung pen. Indon.
Minahassa Peninsula Indon. see Minahasa, Semenanjung
187 L3 Mina Jebel Ali U.A.E.
167 I2 Minakami Japan
190 F2 Mīnakh Syria
107 M5 Minaki Ont. Can.
166 D6 Minakuchi Japan
165 H14 Minamata Japan
166 E4 Minami Japan
206 E3 Minamia N.T. Austr.
167 H4 Minami Alps National Park Japan
167 J5 Minamiashigara Japan
167 K6 Minami-Bōsō Quasi National Park Japan
166 E6 Minamichita Japan
161 N6 Minami-Daitō-jima i. Japan
166 C4 Minami-gawa r. Japan
165 □2 Minami-Iō-jima vol. Kazan-rettō Japan
167 I6 Minamiizu Japan
167 J3 Minami-kawara Japan
167 H3 Minamimaki Japan
167 G4 Minamiminowa Japan
167 L2 Minaminasu Japan
167 G5 Minamishinano Japan
Min'an Hunan China see Longshan
167 J3 Minano Japan
26 F10 Minard Argyll and Bute, Scotland U.K.
203 D11 Minaret Peaks South I. N.Z.
130 E3 Minas Cuba
156 D4 Minas Sumatera Indon.
144 G4 Minas Uru.
189 N9 Mīnā' Sa'ūd Kuwait
109 H4 Minas Basin b. N.S. Can.
109 H4 Minas Channel N.S. Can.
144 G3 Minas de Corrales Uru.
130 B2 Minas de Matahambre Cuba
64 F5 Minas de Riotinto Spain
142 D3 Minas Gerais state Brazil
143 F2 Minas Novas Brazil
65 P4 Minateda Spain
128 C6 Minatitlán Colima Mex.
129 M7 Minatitlán Veracruz Mex.
65 O2 Minaya Spain
158 B4 Minbu Myanmar
158 A4 Minbya Myanmar
185 O6 Minchinabad Pak.
145 B6 Minchinmávida vol. Chile
26 J11 Minch Moor hill Scotland U.K.
71 J5 Mincio r. Italy
191 H6 Mincivan Azer.
154 E8 Mindanao i. Phil.
154 E8 Mindanao r. Mindanao Phil.
204 H6 Mindarie S.A. Austr.
158 A4 Mindat Sakan Myanmar
62 C9 Minde Port.
53 I4 Mindel r. Ger.
53 I5 Mindelheim Ger.
88 □ Mindelo Cape Verde
62 C6 Mindelo Port.
53 L4 Mindelstetten Ger.
108 E4 Minden Ont. Can.
49 G6 Minden Ger.
121 I9 Minden LA U.S.A.
120 F5 Minden NE U.S.A.
124 M3 Minden NV U.S.A.
111 L6 Minden City MI U.S.A.
45 G6 Minderhout Belgium
208 C6 Minderoo W.A. Austr.
158 B5 Mindon Myanmar
205 I5 Mindona Lake imp. l. N.S.W. Austr.
154 C5 Mindoro i. Phil.
154 B5 Mindoro Strait Phil.
91 B6 Mindouli Congo
57 J5 Mindszent Hungary
57 H5 Mindszentgodisa Hungary
143 E4 Minduri Brazil
182 H1 Mindyak Rus. Fed.
Mindzhivan Azer. see Mincivan
165 I12 Mine Japan
110 B1 Mine Centre Ont. Can.
27 G9 Mine Head Rep. of Ireland
25 D6 Mine Head hd Rep. of Ireland
30 F5 Minehead Somerset, England U.K.
142 A2 Mineiros Brazil
74 H9 Mineo Sicilia Italy
119 H3 Mineola NY U.S.A.
121 H9 Mineola TX U.S.A.
30 F1 Minera Wrexham, Wales U.K.
116 H10 Mineral VA U.S.A.
129 I5 Mineral del Monte Mex.
128 G4 Mineral del Refugio Mex.
146 E6 Minerales de la Pampa Arg.
191 E1 Mineral'nyye Vody Rus. Fed.
110 D7 Mineral Point WI U.S.A.
121 F9 Mineral Wells TX U.S.A.
116 D9 Mineralwells WV U.S.A.
71 K6 Minerbio Italy
118 C3 Minersville PA U.S.A.
125 T3 Minersville UT U.S.A.
116 D8 Minerva OH U.S.A.
199 I4 Minerva Reefs Fiji
73 Q5 Minervino Murge Italy
41 B10 Minervois reg. France
41 B10 Minervois, Monts du hills France
166 B4 Mineyama Japan
52 E3 Minfeld Ger.
173 F8 Minfeng Xinjiang China
91 E7 Minga Dem. Rep. Congo
93 A8 Minga Zambia
191 I5 Mingäçevir Azer.
191 H5 Mingäçevir Su Anbarı resr Azer.
90 D3 Mingala C.A.R.
109 H3 Mingan Que. Can.
109 I3 Mingan, Îles de is Que. Can.
73 O7 Mingardo r. Italy
204 H5 Mingary S.A. Austr.
182 J6 Mingbuloq Uzbek.
Mingechaur Azer. see Mingäçevir
Mingechaurskoye Vodokhranilishche resr Azer. see Mingäçevir Su Anbarı
207 K5 Mingela Qld Austr.
209 C10 Mingenew W.A. Austr.
206 F6 Mingera Creek watercourse Qld Austr.
171 J2 Minggang Henan China
171 L2 Mingguang Anhui China
158 B3 Mingin Myanmar
158 B3 Mingin Range mts Myanmar
183 P7 Ming-Kush Kyrg.
63 Q9 Minglanilla Spain
116 E8 Mingo Junction OH U.S.A.
63 K7 Mingorría Spain
93 C7 Mingoyo Tanz.
170 D3 Mingshan Sichuan China
168 E5 Mingshui Gansu China
162 D5 Mingshui Heilong. China
173 B8 Mingteke Xinjiang China
66 C6 Minguez, Puerto de pass Spain
26 A9 Mingulay i. Scotland U.K.
158 B3 Mingun Myanmar
95 I2 Mingùri Moz.
171 K5 Mingxi Fujian China
Minhe Jiangxi China see Jinxian
174 J4 Minhe Qinghai China
158 B5 Minhla Magwe Myanmar
158 B6 Minhla Pegu Myanmar
62 D5 Minho reg. Port.
171 L5 Minhou Fujian China
38 H4 Miniac-Morvan France
71 J5 Minico, Parco del park Italy
176 C8 Minicoy atoll India
122 G5 Minidoka Internment National Monument nat. park ID U.S.A.
209 G10 Minigwal, Lake salt flat W.A. Austr.
59 N6 Minihof-Liebau Austria
18 E6 Minija r. Lith.
209 C7 Minilya W.A. Austr.
209 B7 Minilya r. W.A. Austr.
138 C4 Miñimiñe Chile
146 A5 Mininco Chile
88 D4 Mininian Côte d'Ivoire
109 I2 Minipi Lake Nfld and Lab. Can.
108 B3 Miniss Lake Ont. Can.
63 P6 Ministra mt. Spain
63 O6 Ministra, Sierra mts Spain
107 K4 Minitonas Man. Can.
19 R1 Minitskaya Rus. Fed.
Minjian Sichuan China see Mabian
170 E4 Min Jiang r. Sichuan China
171 L5 Min Jiang r. China
206 D1 Minjilang N.T. Austr.
191 H6 Minkänd Azer.
Min-Kush Kyrg. see Ming-Kush
204 F6 Minlaton S.A. Austr.
168 G7 Minle Gansu China
89 G4 Minna Nigeria
213 L1 Minna Bluff pt Antarctica
164 □1 Minna-jima i. Okinawa Japan
164 □B22 Minna-shima i. Okinawa Japan
21 M5 Minne Sweden
120 G6 Minneapolis KS U.S.A.
110 A5 Minneapolis MN U.S.A.
107 L5 Minnedosa Man. Can.
116 F10 Minnehaha Springs WV U.S.A.
121 E7 Minneola KS U.S.A.
120 I3 Minnesota r. MN U.S.A.
120 I2 Minnesota state U.S.A.
110 C5 Minnesota City MN U.S.A.
120 F1 Minnewaukan ND U.S.A.
159 D8 Min-ngaw Myanmar
209 C7 Minnie Creek W.A. Austr.
26 H13 Minnigaff Dumfries and Galloway, Scotland U.K.
204 E5 Minnipa S.A. Austr.
108 B3 Minnitaki Lake Ont. Can.
166 E4 Mino Japan
62 C5 Miño r. Port./Spain
167 H5 Minobu Japan
167 H5 Minobu-san mt. Japan
167 H6 Minobu-sanchi mts Japan
166 F5 Minokamo Japan
166 F5 Mino-Mikawa-kōgen reg. Japan
147 H2 Miñones Arg.
110 C3 Minong WI U.S.A.
110 E9 Minonk IL U.S.A.
166 B6 Minoo Japan
Minorca i. Spain see Menorca
72 I1 Minore, Isola i. Italy
167 L3 Minori Japan
40 F1 Minot France
120 E1 Minot ND U.S.A.
167 G4 Minowa Japan
190 F6 Minqār, Ghadīr imp. l. Syria
168 H7 Minqin Gansu China
171 L5 Minqing Fujian China
118 D5 Minquadale DE U.S.A.
169 N9 Minquan Henan China
48 E3 Minsen Ger.
170 D2 Min Shan mts Sichuan China
158 B2 Minsin Myanmar
18 K8 Minsk Belarus
Minskaya Oblast' admin. div. Belarus see Minskaya Voblasts'
18 K8 Minskaya Voblasts' admin. div. Belarus
55 J3 Mińsk Mazowiecki Pol.
Minsk Oblast admin. div. Belarus see Minskaya Voblasts'
31 N5 Minster Kent, England U.K.
31 O5 Minster Kent, England U.K.
116 A8 Minster OH U.S.A.
30 G2 Minsterley Shropshire, England U.K.
89 I5 Minta Cameroon
183 P9 Mintaka Pass China/Jammu and Kashmir
170 C2 Mintang Qinghai China
26 M7 Mintlaw Aberdeenshire, Scotland U.K.
109 H4 Minto N.B. Can.
108 F1 Minto, Lac l. Que. Can.
213 L2 Minto, Mount Antarctica
104 G2 Minto Inlet N.W.T. Can.
89 I6 Mintom Cameroon
107 J5 Minton Sask. Can.
53 M4 Mintraching Ger.
123 K7 Minturn CO U.S.A.
Minturnae Italy see Minturno
73 L5 Minturno Italy
70 I7 Minucciano Italy
184 F3 Mīnudasht Iran
85 F2 Minūf Egypt
188 E8 Minūfīyah governorate Egypt
160 F1 Minusinsk Rus. Fed.
70 F3 Minusio Switz.
170 A4 Minutang Arun. Prad. India
64 C3 Minutos, Barragem dos resr Port.
90 B4 Minvoul Gabon
168 I9 Minxian Gansu China
14 L5 Minyar Rus. Fed.
205 I7 Minyip Vic. Austr.
158 B3 Minywa Myanmar
179 P6 Minzong Arun. Prad. India
89 H2 Mio well Niger
111 J5 Mio MI U.S.A.
76 I6 Mionica Srbija Serb. and Mont.
40 F5 Mionnay France
40 F5 Mions France
43 C6 Mios France
206 G8 Mipia, Lake salt flat Qld Austr.
172 H5 Miquan Xinjiang China
108 E3 Miquelon Que. Can.
109 J4 Miquelon i. St Pierre and Miquelon
129 H2 Miquihuana Mex.
18 J8 Mir Belarus
136 B4 Mira r. Col.
71 M5 Mira Italy
62 C8 Mira Port.
64 B5 Mira r. Port.
63 R9 Mira Spain
63 Q9 Mira r. Spain
67 C8 Mira, Sierra de mts Spain
41 H9 Mirabeau France
117 K3 Mirabel Que. Can.
43 G7 Mirabel France
62 H9 Mirabel Spain
143 E2 Mirabela Brazil
41 G8 Mirabel-aux-Baronnies France
74 G9 Mirabella Imbaccari Sicilia Italy
143 F4 Miracema Brazil
Miracema do Norte Brazil see Miracema do Tocantins
140 C4 Miracema do Tocantins Brazil
Mirada Hills CA U.S.A. see La Mirada
62 C9 Mira de Aire Port.
142 A5 Mirador Brazil
127 O9 Mirador-Dos Lagunos-Río Azul, Parque Nacional nat. park Guat.
143 F4 Miradouro Brazil
43 F8 Miradoux France
136 C3 Miraflores Boyaca Col.

Miraflores to Momence
304

136 C4 Miraflores Guaviare Col.
126 E6 Miraflores Mex.
63 M7 Miraflores de la Sierra Spain
189 J7 Mīrah, Wādī al watercourse Iraq/Saudi Arabia
143 F4 Miraí Brazil
176 D4 Miraj Mahar. India
143 F2 Miralta Brazil
147 I6 Miramar Buenos Aires Arg.
147 F2 Miramar Córdoba Arg.
145 B8 Miramar, Canal sea chan. Chile
127 N9 Miramar, Lago l. Mex.
71 N7 Miramare Italy
41 G9 Miramas France
42 C5 Mirambeau France
66 E6 Mirambel Spain
109 H4 Miramichi N.B. Can.
109 H4 Miramichi Bay N.B. Can.
43 E6 Miramont-de-Guyenne France
43 D8 Miramont-Sensacq France
185 N5 Miram Shah Pak.
172 I7 Miran Xinjiang China
136 D5 Miraña Col.
147 H5 Miranda Arg.
139 F5 Miranda Brazil
139 F4 Miranda r. Brazil
Miranda Moz. see Macaloge
124 I1 Miranda CA U.S.A.
136 E2 Miranda state Venez.
209 F9 Miranda, Lake salt flat W.A. Austr.
63 Q4 Miranda de Arga Spain
63 O3 Miranda de Ebro Spain
62 I8 Miranda del Castañar Spain
62 D8 Miranda do Corvo Port.
62 H5 Miranda do Douro Port.
43 E8 Mirande France
62 F6 Mirandela Port.
64 G2 Mirandilla Spain
128 E5 Mirandillas Mex.
71 K6 Mirandola Italy
43 I7 Mirandol-Bourgnounac France
142 B4 Mirandópolis Brazil
71 M5 Mirano Italy
142 B5 Mirante, Serra do hills Brazil
142 B5 Mirante do Paranapanema Brazil
147 F4 Mira Pampa Arg.
137 F5 Mirapinima Brazil
78 B2 Miras Albania
165 J12 Mirasaka Japan
142 C4 Mirassol Brazil
62 G3 Miravalles mt. Spain
62 I9 Miravete hill Spain
185 M4 Mir Bacheh Kowt Afgh.
187 L7 Mirbāṭ Oman
187 L7 Mirbāṭ, Ra's c. Oman
191 J6 Mircälal Azer.
55 L5 Mircze Pol.
Mirear Island Egypt see Murayr, Jazīrat
130 G4 Mirebalais Haiti
40 G2 Mirebeau Bourgogne France
42 E2 Mirebeau Poitou-Charentes France
37 L7 Mirecourt France
84 B6 Miréméné Chad
43 G9 Miremont France
59 I8 Miren Slovenia
43 H9 Mirepoix France
41 D9 Mireval France
179 J6 Mirganj Bihar India
Mirgorod Ukr. see Myrhorod
157 K2 Miri Sarawak Malaysia
185 J7 Miri mt. Pak.
89 H3 Miria Niger
176 F4 Mirialguda Andhra Prad. India
207 M8 Miriam Vale Qld Austr.
179 O6 Miri Hills India
144 G4 Mirim, Lagoa l. Brazil/Uru.
141 C9 Mirim, Lagoa do l. Brazil
136 D2 Mirimire Venez.
Mírina Limnos Greece see Myrina
205 I3 Mirintu watercourse Qld Austr.
176 D5 Mirjan Karnataka India
185 I7 Mīrjāveh Iran
77 M8 Mirkovo Bulg.
68 D3 Mirna r. Croatia
59 L8 Mirna Slovenia
59 L8 Mirna r. Slovenia
59 L8 Mirna Peč Slovenia
213 G2 Mirny research stn Antarctica
14 H3 Mirnyy Arkhangel'skaya Oblast' Rus. Fed.
19 O9 Mirnyy Bryanskaya Oblast' Rus. Fed.
193 M3 Mirnyy Respublika Sakha (Yakutiya) Rus. Fed.
191 F1 Mirnyy Stavropol'skiy Kray Rus. Fed.
77 K6 Miroč hills Serb. and Mont.
54 D4 Mirocin Górny Pol.
203 G9 Miromiro mt. South I. N.Z.
107 K4 Mirond Lake Sask. Can.
Mironovka Kharkivs'ka Oblast' Ukr. see Myronivka
Mironovka Kyivs'ka Oblast' Ukr. see Myronivka
59 N2 Miroslav Czech Rep.
54 E2 Mirosławiec Pol.
56 C2 Mirošov Czech Rep.
51 L7 Mirostowice Dolne Pol.
56 D2 Mirovice Czech Rep.
50 G4 Mirow Ger.
185 O5 Mirpur Pak.
185 M9 Mirpur Batoro Pak.
185 M9 Mirpur Khas Pak.
185 L9 Mirpur Sakro Pak.
106 H4 Mirror Alta Can.
92 E3 Mirsale Somalia
172 G6 Mirsali Xinjiang China
54 D5 Mirsk Pol.
207 K6 Mirtna Qld Austr.
Mirtoan Sea Greece see Mirtoö Pelagos
75 L4 Mirto Crosia Italy
78 E6 Mirtoö Pelagos sea Greece
63 J7 Mirueña de los Infanzones Spain
95 F2 Miruro Moz.
Miryalaguda Andhra Prad. India see Mirialguda
163 F11 Miryang S. Korea
Mirzachirla Turkm. see Murzechirla
179 I7 Mirzapur Uttar Prad. India
55 J4 Mirzec Pol.
71 M3 Mis, Lago del l. Italy
71 O8 Misa r. Italy
167 I4 Misaka Japan
167 L5 Misaki Chiba Japan
165 J13 Misaki Ehime Japan
166 B7 Misaki Ōsaka Japan
167 G5 Misakubo Japan
173 E7 Misalay Xinjiang China
71 N8 Misano Adriatico Italy
129 K6 Misantla Mex.
167 I3 Misato Gunma Japan
166 D6 Misato Mie Japan
167 G3 Misato Nagano Japan
164 □1 Misato Okinawa Japan
167 J3 Misato Saitama Japan
167 K4 Misato Saitama Japan
166 B7 Misato Wakayama Japan
89 H4 Misau Nigeria
164 S6 Misawa Japan
107 K3 Misaw Lake Sask. Can.
57 K5 Mişca Romania
73 N5 Miscano r. Italy
70 D3 Mischabel mt. Switz.
59 N5 Mischendorf Austria
109 H4 Miscou Island N.B. Can.
108 B3 Misehkow r. Ont. Can.
73 M6 Miseno, Capo c. Italy
40 H2 Miserey-Salines France
65 □ Misery, Mount hill Gibraltar
178 E1 Misgar Jammu and Kashmir
96 H9 Misgund S. Africa
184 G4 Mīsh, Kūh-e hill Iran
177 M9 Misha Andaman & Nicobar Is India
108 C2 Mishamattawa r. Ont. Can.
93 A6 Mishamo Tanz.
162 G6 Mishan Heilong. China
187 I3 Mishāsh al Ashāwī well Saudi Arabia
187 I2 Mishāsh al Hādī well Saudi Arabia
187 I3 Mishāsh az Zuayyinī well Saudi Arabia
187 I3 Mishāsh 'Uwayr well Saudi Arabia
110 H8 Mishawaka IN U.S.A.
19 W6 Misheronskiy Rus. Fed.
110 I1 Mishibishu Lake Ont. Can.
110 G5 Mishicot WI U.S.A.
167 I5 Mishima Japan
165 I12 Mi-shima i. Japan
14 L5 Mishkino Rus. Fed.
186 G5 Mishlah, Khashm hill Saudi Arabia
191 I4 Mishlesh Rus. Fed.
179 O5 Mishmi Hills India
19 N6 Mishutki Belarus
14 K2 Mishvan' Rus. Fed.
74 E7 Misilmeri Sicilia Italy
207 N1 Misima Island P.N.G.
144 G2 Misiones prov. Arg.
191 D4 Misırlı Turkey
190 D2 Misis Dağ hills Turkey
186 F3 Miskah Saudi Arabia
57 I5 Miske Hungary
187 M4 Miskin Oman
126 □R10 Miskitos, Cayos is Nic.
57 J3 Miskolc Hungary
59 L7 Mislinja Slovenia
68 E2 Mislinja r. Slovenia
186 E2 Mismā, Jibāl al mts Saudi Arabia
190 F6 Mismā, Tall al hill Jordan
138 C3 Mismi, Nevado mt. Peru
41 H8 Mison France
155 G4 Misoöl i. Papua Indon.
118 E7 Mispillion r. DE U.S.A.
110 C2 Misquah Hills MN U.S.A.
119 L2 Misquamicut RI U.S.A.
Misraç Turkey see Kurtalan
84 B1 Mişrātah Libya
178 H6 Misrikh Uttar Prad. India
111 J1 Missanabie Ont. Can.
73 Q7 Missanello Italy
38 G7 Missillac France
108 D3 Missinaibi r. Ont. Can.
111 K1 Missinaibi Lake Ont. Can.
107 J4 Missinipe Sask. Can.
207 H2 Mission r. Qld Austr.
120 E4 Mission SD U.S.A.
121 F12 Mission TX U.S.A.
207 K4 Mission Beach Qld Austr.
124 O8 Mission Viejo CA U.S.A.
88 B3 Missira Senegal
108 C2 Missisa r. Ont. Can.
108 C2 Missisa Lake Ont. Can.
108 E3 Missisicabi r. Que. Can.
108 D4 Mississagi r. Ont. Can.
108 E5 Mississauga Ont. Can.
110 I9 Mississinewa Lake IN U.S.A.
108 E4 Mississippi r. Ont. Can.
121 K11 Mississippi r. U.S.A.
121 K9 Mississippi state U.S.A.
121 K11 Mississippi Delta LA U.S.A.
111 R4 Mississippi Lake Ont. Can.
121 K10 Mississippi Sound sea chan. MS U.S.A.
Missolonghi Greece see Mesolongi
122 H3 Missoula MT U.S.A.
86 E2 Missour Morocco
120 J6 Missouri r. U.S.A.
120 I6 Missouri state U.S.A.
120 H5 Missouri Valley IA U.S.A.
206 B4 Mistake Creek N.T. Austr.
207 K6 Mistake Creek r. Qld Austr.
109 I3 Mistanipisipou r. Que. Can.
109 F3 Mistassibi r. Que. Can.
109 F3 Mistassini Que. Can.
109 F3 Mistassini r. Que. Can.
108 F3 Mistassini, Lac l. Que. Can.
109 I2 Mistastin Lake Nfld and Lab. Can.
59 O2 Mistelbach Austria
53 K2 Mistelgau Ger.
75 I8 Misterbianco Sicilia Italy
23 M4 Misterhults nature res. Sweden
130 B4 Misteriosa Bank sea feature Caribbean Sea
29 P7 Misterton Nottinghamshire, England U.K.
109 I1 Mistinibi, Lac l. Que. Can.
108 F3 Mistissini Que. Can.
17 R4 Mistky Ukr.
147 F2 Mistolar, Laguna del l. Arg.
78 D5 Mistras tourist site Greece
74 G8 Mistretta Sicilia Italy
104 E4 Misty Fiords National Monument Wilderness nat. park AK U.S.A.
107 K3 Misty Lake Man. Can.
166 D6 Misugi Japan
165 I12 Misumi Japan
Misuratah Libya see Mişrātah
71 M2 Misurina Italy
20 M3 Misvær Norway
128 B5 Mita, Punta de pt Mex.
167 K4 Mitaka Japan
166 F5 Mitake Gifu Japan
166 G4 Mitake Nagano Japan
95 G2 Mitande Moz.
137 H4 Mitaraca hill Suriname
136 D2 Mitare Venez.
85 H6 Mitatib Sudan
30 H4 Mitcheldean Gloucestershire, England U.K.
207 K9 Mitchell Qld Austr.
205 N3 Mitchell r. N.S.W. Austr.
207 H3 Mitchell r. Qld Austr.
205 K7 Mitchell r. Vic. Austr.
111 M6 Mitchell Ont. Can.
122 D4 Mitchell OR U.S.A.
120 F4 Mitchell SD U.S.A.
207 J4 Mitchell, Lake Qld Austr.
110 I5 Mitchell, Lake MI U.S.A.
115 F8 Mitchell, Mount NC U.S.A.
207 I3 Mitchell and Alice Rivers National Park Qld Austr.
Mitchell Island Cook Is see Nassau
Mitchell Island Tuvalu see Nukulaelae
206 C1 Mitchell Point N.T. Austr.
206 E2 Mitchell Range hills N.T. Austr.
205 K7 Mitchell River National Park Vic. Austr.
96 D9 Mitchells Pass S. Africa
116 F10 Mitchelltown VA U.S.A.
27 F8 Mitchelstown Rep. of Ireland
85 F2 Mīt Ghamr Egypt
178 B8 Mithapur Gujarat India
185 O5 Mitha Tiwano Pak.
185 M9 Mithi Pak.
Míthimna Greece see Mithymna
185 M9 Mithrani Can canal Pak.
185 M8 Mithrau Pak.
79 H3 Mithymna Greece
155 F3 Miti i. Maluku Indon.
203 □2 Mitiaro i. Cook Is
Mitiero i. Cook Is see Mitiaro
Mitilíni Lesvos Greece see Mytilini
19 Q7 Mitishkino Rus. Fed.
202 H3 Mititai North I. N.Z.
106 C3 Mitkof Island AK U.S.A.
129 K9 Mitla Mex.
166 F6 Mito Aichi Japan
167 L3 Mito Ibaraki Japan
165 I12 Mitō Japan
93 C7 Mitole Tanz.
167 I4 Mitomi Japan
93 B7 Mitomoni Tanz.
20 □ Mitra, Kapp c. Svalbard
202 J7 Mitre mt. North I. N.Z.
145 D9 Mitre, Península pen. Arg.
199 H3 Mitre Island Solomon Is
203 B11 Mitre Peak South I. N.Z.
15 G6 Mitrofanovka Rus. Fed.
Mitrovica Kosovo, Srbija Serb. and Mont. see Kosovska Mitrovica
36 E6 Mitry-Mory France
99 □3a Mitsamiouli Njazidja Comoros
78 B3 Mitsikeli mt. Greece
95 □J3 Mitsinjo Madag.
Mits'iwa Eritrea see Massawa
99 □3a Mitsoudjé Njazidja Comoros
166 D7 Mitsue Japan
164 T4 Mitsuishi Japan
167 K3 Mitsukaidō Japan
165 P9 Mitsuke Japan
166 G3 Mitsumatarenge-dake mt. Japan
165 G12 Mitsushima Japan
167 I4 Mitsutōge-yama mt. Japan
205 M6 Mittagong N.S.W. Austr.
205 K7 Mitta Mitta Vic. Austr.
58 C6 Mittelberg Tirol Austria
58 B5 Mittelberg Vorarlberg Austria
53 J3 Mittelberg hill Ger.
52 H5 Mittelbiberach Ger.
51 E7 Mittelelbe park Ger.
53 J3 Mittelfranken admin. reg. Ger.
51 D8 Mittelhausen Ger.
49 I10 Mittelkalbach Ger.
70 C2 Mittelland reg. Switz.
49 F6 Mittellandkanal canal Ger.
49 I10 Mittelsinn Ger.
53 N6 Mittelspitze mt. Ger.
53 K7 Mittenwald Ger.
50 I4 Mittenwalde Brandenburg Ger.
51 I6 Mittenwalde Brandenburg Ger.
59 L4 Mitterbach am Erlaufsee Austria
59 H3 Mitterding Austria
59 M4 Mitterdorf im Mürztal Austria
53 N4 Mitterfels Ger.
37 M6 Mittersheim France
58 F5 Mittersill Austria
53 N5 Mitterskirchen Ger.
53 M2 Mitterteich Ger.
20 I5 Mittet Norway
23 M5 Mittlands skogen reg. Öland Sweden
51 E9 Mittleres Saaletal park Ger.
51 G9 Mittweida Ger.
136 D4 Mitú Col.
136 D4 Mituas Col.
91 E7 Mitumba, Chaîne des mts Dem. Rep. Congo
90 F5 Mitumba, Monts mts Dem. Rep. Congo
91 E7 Mitwaba Dem. Rep. Congo
51 D10 Mitwitz Ger.
90 A4 Mitzic Gabon
Miughalaigh i. Scotland U.K. see Mingulay
167 K5 Miura Japan
167 K5 Miura-hantō pen. Japan
15 G7 Mius r. Rus. Fed.
17 R6 Miusskiy Liman est. Rus. Fed.
17 R5 Miusyns'k Ukr.
167 M1 Miwa Fukushima Japan
167 L2 Miwa Ibaraki Japan
166 B5 Miwa Kyōto Japan
129 I7 Mixteco r. Mex.
128 C5 Mixtlán Mex.
166 F3 Miya Japan
167 G4 Miyada Japan
167 J5 Miyagase-ko resr Japan
166 F3 Miyagawa Gifu Japan
166 D7 Miyagawa Mie Japan
166 E6 Miya-gawa r. Japan
166 F3 Miya-gawa r. Japan
164 □1 Miyagi Okinawa Japan
164 R8 Miyagi pref. Japan
164 □1 Miyagusuku-jima i. Okinawa Japan
186 F3 Miyah, Wādī al watercourse Saudi Arabia
188 I6 Miyāh, Wādī al watercourse Syria
165 J12 Miyajima Japan
167 K7 Miyake-jima i. Japan
164 S7 Miyako Japan
164 R9 Miyakoji Japan
164 □C22 Miyako-jima i. Nansei-shotō Japan
165 I15 Miyakonojō Japan
164 □B22 Miyako-rettō is Japan
164 S7 Miyako-wan b. Japan
182 E3 Miyaly Kazakh.
166 D3 Miyama Fukui Japan
166 E4 Miyama Gifu Japan
166 C5 Miyama Kyōto Japan
166 D7 Miyama Mie Japan
166 B8 Miyama Wakayama Japan
167 K4 Miyamae Japan
Miyang Yunnan China see Mile
178 B9 Miyani Gujarat India
165 H15 Miyanojō Japan
164 □H16 Miyanoura-dake mt. Japan
166 D4 Miyazaki Fukui Japan
165 I15 Miyazaki Miyazaki Japan
165 I14 Miyazaki pref. Japan
166 B4 Miyazu Japan
166 B4 Miyazu-wan b. Japan
170 D5 Miyi Sichuan China
166 F5 Miyoshi Aichi Japan
167 K5 Miyoshi Chiba Japan
165 J12 Miyoshi Hiroshima Japan
167 H3 Miyota Japan
169 O6 Miyun Beijing China
169 O6 Miyun Shuiku resr China
185 L5 Mīzāni Afgh.
92 B3 Mīzan Teferī Eth.
Mizar Turkey see Karakeçi
84 B2 Mizdah Libya
27 C10 Mizen Head Rep. of Ireland
27 J7 Mizen Head Rep. of Ireland
18 I9 Mizhevichy Belarus
16 C5 Mizhhir"ya Ukr.
169 L8 Mizhi Shaanxi China
77 O5 Mizil Romania
77 L7 Miziya Bulg.
16 F3 Mizoch Ukr.
75 L4 Mizofato r. Italy
Mizo Hills state India see Mizoram
179 N8 Mizoram state India
118 F6 Mizpah NJ U.S.A.
190 C8 Mizpe Ramon Israel
138 D4 Mizque Bol.
138 D4 Mizque r. Bol.
167 I4 Mizugaki-yama mt. Japan
166 F2 Mizuhashi Japan
166 B5 Mizuho Kyōto Japan
167 J4 Mizuho Tōkyō Japan
166 F5 Mizunami Japan
167 K3 Mizuno-gawa r. Japan
164 S7 Mizusawa Japan
20 M3 Mjelde Norway
23 L3 Mjölby Sweden
21 I6 Mjølfell Norway
22 G2 Mjøndalen Norway
22 I4 Mjörn l. Sweden
22 G1 Mjøsa l. Norway
97 N7 Mkambati S. Africa
97 O7 Mkambati Nature Reserve S. Africa
93 C6 Mkata Tanz.
93 C6 Mkata Plain Tanz.
97 P2 Mkhaya Game Reserve nature res. Swaziland
97 P2 Mkhondvo r. Swaziland
93 C6 Mkoani Tanz.
93 C6 Mkokotoni Tanz.
93 C6 Mkomazi Tanz.
93 C5 Mkomazi Game Reserve nature res. Tanz.
93 C6 Mkujani Tanz.
93 C6 Mkumbi, Ras pt Tanz.
Mkumvura Zimbabwe see Mukumbura
93 C7 Mkunja Tanz.
93 C6 Mkuranga Tanz.
93 B6 Mkurusi Tanz.
91 F8 Mkushi Zambia
97 Q3 Mkuze S. Africa
97 Q3 Mkuze r. S. Africa
97 Q3 Mkuzi Game Reserve nature res. S. Africa
56 D1 Mladá Boleslav Czech Rep.
56 D2 Mladá Vožice Czech Rep.
56 E1 Mladé Buky Czech Rep.
76 I6 Mladenovac Srbija Serb. and Mont.
77 J8 Mlado Nagoričane Macedonia
93 A6 Mlala Hills Tanz.
93 C6 Mlandizi Tanz.
93 B7 Mlangali Tanz.
97 Q2 Mlaula r. Swaziland
76 J6 Mlava r. Serb. and Mont.
55 I2 Mława Pol.
55 I3 Mławka r. Pol.
97 Q2 Mlawula Nature Reserve Swaziland
97 P2 Mlilwane Nature Reserve Swaziland
99 □3b Mlima Bénara hill Mayotte
99 □3b Mlima Choungui hill Mayotte
68 F4 Mljet i. Croatia
68 F4 Mljet nat. park Croatia
68 F4 Mljetski Kanal sea chan. Croatia
17 P2 Mlodat' r. Rus. Fed.
55 I3 Młodzieszyn Pol.
93 C7 Mlowoka Tanz.
97 P1 Mlumati r. S. Africa
97 K7 Mlungisi S. Africa
55 H1 Młynary Pol.
55 J3 Młynarze Pol.
16 E3 Mlyniv Ukr.
55 M6 Mlynys'ka Ukr.
97 J1 Mmabatho S. Africa
95 E4 Mmadinare Botswana
94 E4 Mmamabula Botswana
94 E4 Mmashoro Botswana
94 E5 Mmathethe Botswana
97 N8 Mncwasa Point S. Africa
56 D2 Mnichovice Czech Rep.
56 D1 Mnichovo Hradiště Czech Rep.
55 I5 Mnichów Pol.
55 I4 Mniów Pol.
57 J3 Mníšek nad Hnilcom Slovakia
55 J4 Mniszew Pol.
55 I4 Mniszków Pol.
97 P2 Mnjoli Dam Swaziland
162 K1 Mnogovershinnyy Rus. Fed.
21 H6 Mo Norway
138 B1 Moa r. Brazil
130 F3 Moa Cuba
155 F8 Moa i. Maluku Indon.
190 D7 Moab reg. Jordan
125 W3 Moab UT U.S.A.
90 A5 Moabi Gabon
138 C1 Moaco r. Brazil
153 J9 Moa Island Qld Austr.
201 □1 Moala i. Fiji
184 F4 Mo'allemān Iran
95 G5 Moamba Moz.
203 F9 Moana South I. N.Z.
62 C4 Moaña Spain
90 B5 Moanda Gabon
125 R5 Moapa NV U.S.A.
27 G6 Moate Rep. of Ireland
95 G3 Moatize Moz.
91 F6 Moba Dem. Rep. Congo
167 L5 Mobara Japan
184 E7 Mobārakābād Iran
184 D5 Mobārakeh Eşfahān Iran
184 F7 Mobārakeh Yazd Iran
90 D3 Mobaye C.A.R.
Mobayembongo Dem. Rep. Congo see Mobayi-Mbongo
90 D3 Mobayi-Mbongo Dem. Rep. Congo
29 M7 Mobberley Cheshire, England U.K.
90 C4 Mobeka Dem. Rep. Congo
120 I6 Moberly MO U.S.A.
106 F4 Moberly Lake B.C. Can.
110 I1 Mobert Ont. Can.
115 C10 Mobile AL U.S.A.
125 T8 Mobile AZ U.S.A.
121 K10 Mobile Bay AL U.S.A.
115 D10 Mobile Point AL U.S.A.
207 J9 Moble watercourse Qld Austr.
154 D5 Mobo Masbate Phil.
120 E3 Mobridge SD U.S.A.
130 H4 Moca Dom. Rep.
190 B2 Moca Geçidi pass Turkey
140 C2 Mocajuba Brazil
95 H2 Moçambicano, Planalto plat. Moz.
Moçambique country Africa see Mozambique
95 I2 Moçambique Moz.
95 I2 Mocambo, Porto b. Moz.
Moçâmedes Angola see Namibe
98 □3e Mocanal El Hierro Canary Is
118 C2 Mocanaqua PA U.S.A.
64 B2 Moçarria Port.
124 L4 Moccasin CA U.S.A.
116 C12 Moccasin Gap VA U.S.A.
158 G4 Môc Châu Vietnam
63 M9 Mocejón Spain
57 G3 Močenok Slovakia
19 U6 Mocha r. Rus. Fed.
Mocha Yemen see Al Mukhā
144 B5 Mocha, Isla i. Chile
63 Q6 Mochales Spain
200 □4a Mochenap sea chan. Chuuk Micronesia
126 E5 Mochicahui Mex.
19 V7 Mochily Rus. Fed.
137 E2 Mochirma, Parque Nacional nat. park Venez.
167 H3 Mochizuki Japan
130 □ Mocho Mountains Jamaica
200 □4a Mochonap sea chan. Chuuk Micronesia
55 H3 Mochowo Pol.
94 E5 Mochudi Botswana
54 E3 Mochy Pol.
93 D7 Mocimboa da Praia Moz.
93 C7 Mocimboa do Rovuma Moz.
77 M4 Mociu Romania
23 K2 Möckeln l. Sweden
23 K5 Möckeln l. Sweden
51 E6 Möckern Ger.
51 F6 Möckern-Magdeburger Forst park Ger.
52 G3 Möckmühl Ger.
51 G7 Mockrehna Ger.
115 G8 Mocksville NC U.S.A.
65 L6 Moclín Spain
65 K7 Moclinejo Spain
136 E5 Mocó r. Brazil
136 B4 Mocoa Col.
142 D4 Mococa Brazil
95 G4 Mocoduene Moz.
147 I2 Mocoretá r. Arg.
126 F5 Mocorito Mex.
126 F2 Moctezuma Chihuahua Mex.
128 F3 Moctezuma San Luis Potosí Mex.
126 E3 Moctezuma Sonora Mex.
129 I4 Moctezuma r. Mex.
123 J12 Moctezuma r. Mex.
95 H3 Mocuba Moz.
171 I7 Mocun Guangdong China
41 J6 Modane France
178 D8 Modasa Gujarat India
45 H8 Modave Belgium
30 E7 Modbury Devon, England U.K.
97 I5 Modder r. S. Africa
96 I5 Modderivier S. Africa
185 P6 Model Town Pak.
71 J6 Modena Italy
71 J7 Modena prov. Italy
119 G1 Modena NY U.S.A.
118 D5 Modena PA U.S.A.
125 S4 Modena UT U.S.A.
37 O6 Moder r. France
146 E4 Modestino Pizarro Arg.
124 L4 Modesto CA U.S.A.
74 H10 Modica Sicilia Italy
71 L7 Modigliana Italy
95 F5 Modimolle S. Africa
74 D8 Modione r. Sicilia Italy
55 K5 Modliborzyce Pol.
59 N3 Mödling Austria
55 I4 Modliszewice Pol.
72 B7 Modolo Sardegna Italy
169 K3 Modot Mongolia
56 G3 Modra Slovakia
59 L6 Modriach Austria
68 G3 Modriča Bos.-Herz.
56 F2 Modřice Czech Rep.
59 J6 Mödringberg mt. Austria
57 I3 Modrý Kameň Slovakia
75 L1 Modugno Italy
205 K8 Moe Vic. Austr.
95 H3 Moebase Moz.
202 J3 Moehau hill North I. N.Z.
38 D6 Moëlan-sur-Mer France
30 F1 Moel Famau hill Wales U.K.
30 D1 Moelfre Isle of Anglesey, Wales U.K.
30 F2 Moel Sych hill Wales U.K.
21 K6 Moelv Norway
97 L4 Moemaneng S. Africa
91 D6 Moembe Dem. Rep. Congo
20 O2 Moen Norway
71 L3 Moena Italy
137 H3 Moengo Suriname
125 U5 Moenkopi AZ U.S.A.
125 U6 Moenkopi Wash r. AZ U.S.A.
203 E12 Moeraki Point South I. N.Z.
45 E6 Moerbeke Belgium
202 I2 Moerewa North I. N.Z.
44 H5 Moergestel Neth.
45 D6 Moerkerke Belgium
Moero, Lake Dem. Rep. Congo/Zambia see Mweru, Lake
49 C8 Moers Ger.
70 G3 Moesa r. Switz.
96 G3 Moeswal S. Africa
200 □6 Moetambe, Mount Choiseul Solomon Is
26 J12 Moffat Dumfries and Galloway, Scotland U.K.
62 G5 Mofreita Port.
57 L4 Moftin Romania
178 E4 Moga Punjab India
Mogadishu Somalia see Muqdisho
62 G6 Mogadouro Port.
62 G6 Mogadouro, Serra de mts Port.
95 F4 Mogalakwena r. S. Africa
90 C4 Mogalo Dem. Rep. Congo
176 G4 Mogalturra Andhra Prad. India
164 Q8 Mogami-gawa r. Japan
98 □3f Mogán Gran Canaria Canary Is
90 E4 Mogandjo Dem. Rep. Congo
95 F5 Moganyaka S. Africa
172 L7 Mogao Ku Gansu China
186 C8 Mogareb watercourse Eritrea
158 C2 Mogaung Myanmar
162 H3 Mogdy Rus. Fed.
27 F9 Mogeely Rep. of Ireland
50 F5 Mögelin Ger.
48 G1 Møgeltønder Denmark
59 N6 Mogersdorf Austria
87 G2 Moggar Alg.
71 O3 Moggio Udinese Italy
52 H4 Mögglingen Ger.
185 L2 Moghiyon Tajik.
87 E2 Moghrar-Foukani Alg.
55 I4 Mogielnica Pol.
55 I6 Mogielnica mt. Pol.
142 D5 Mogi-Guaçu Brazil
76 J9 Mogila Macedonia
55 H6 Mogilany Pol.
Mogilev Belarus see Mahilyow
Mogilev Oblast admin. div. Belarus see Mahilyowskaya Voblasts'
Mogilev Podol'skiy Ukr. see Mohyliv Podil's'kyy
Mogilevskaya Oblast' admin. div. Belarus see Mahilyowskaya Voblasts'
54 E3 Mogilnica r. Pol.
54 F3 Mogilno Pol.
142 D5 Mogi-Mirim Brazil
95 I2 Mogincual Moz.
143 H2 Mogiquiçaba Brazil
71 J6 Moglia Italy
71 O9 Mogliano Italy
71 M4 Mogliano Veneto Italy
52 G4 Möglingen Ger.
146 C2 Mogna Arg.
162 A2 Mogocha Rus. Fed.
19 T4 Mogocha r. Rus. Fed.
87 H1 Mogod mts Tunisia
94 E5 Mogoditshane Botswana
62 D8 Mogofores Port.
92 A2 Mogogh Sudan
158 C3 Mogok Myanmar
125 U7 Mogollon Plateau AZ U.S.A.
65 M4 Mogón Spain
Mogontiacum Ger. see Mainz
92 D3 Mogor Eth.
72 B8 Mogorella Sardegna Italy
72 B8 Mogoro Sardegna Italy
72 B8 Mogoro r. Sardegna Italy
77 P3 Mogoşeşti Romania
147 I6 Mogotes, Punta pt Arg.
55 I3 Mogowo Pol.
169 N1 Mogoytuy Rus. Fed.
90 B2 Mogroum Chad
64 F6 Moguer Spain
169 R3 Moguqi Nei Mongol China
95 F4 Mogwadi S. Africa
97 L1 Mogwase S. Africa
57 I4 Mogyoród Hungary
57 H6 Mohács Hungary
202 L6 Mohaka r. North I. N.Z.
178 H9 Mohala Chhattisgarh India
97 M5 Mohale Dam Lesotho
97 L6 Mohale's Hoek Lesotho
120 E1 Mohall ND U.S.A.
184 H4 Mohammad Iran
87 F2 Mohammadia Alg.
178 H5 Mohan r. India/Nepal
178 F7 Mohana Madh. Prad. India
179 M7 Mohanganj Bangl.
178 G9 Mohari Mahar. India
65 P4 Moharque Spain
125 R6 Mohave, Lake NV U.S.A.
125 R7 Mohave Mountains AZ U.S.A.
110 F2 Mohawk MI U.S.A.
117 L6 Mohawk r. NY U.S.A.
125 S9 Mohawk Mountains AZ U.S.A.
178 H7 Mohdra Madh. Prad. India
162 C2 Mohe Heilong. China
21 N6 Mohed Sweden
23 K4 Moheda Sweden
62 H8 Mohedas de Granadilla Spain
119 K2 Mohegan CT U.S.A.
119 H2 Mohegan Lake NY U.S.A.
Mohéli i. Comoros see Mwali
56 F2 Mohelnice Czech Rep.
56 F2 Mohelno Czech Rep.
94 D3 Mohembo Botswana
185 M8 Mohenjo Daro tourist site Pak.
27 D7 Moher, Cliffs of Rep. of Ireland
63 N7 Mohernando Spain
27 H7 Mohil Rep. of Ireland
17 P6 Mohila Bel'mak, Hora hill Ukr.
27 G5 Mohill Rep. of Ireland
20 U5 Möhkö Fin.
97 L2 Mohlakeng S. Africa
51 F7 Möhlau Ger.
20 □ Mohn, Kapp c. Svalbard
49 E8 Möhne r. Ger.
49 F8 Möhnetalsperre resr Ger.
118 C4 Mohnton PA U.S.A.
158 C2 Mohnyin Myanmar
138 C3 Moho Peru
176 D4 Mohol Mahar. India
125 S7 Mohon Peak AZ U.S.A.
57 I4 Mohora Hungary
51 H9 Mohorn Ger.
99 □3a Mohoro Njazidja Comoros
93 C7 Mohoro Tanz.
178 G8 Mohpani Madh. Prad. India
53 J2 Möhrendorf Ger.
48 I1 Mohrkirch Ger.
118 D4 Mohrsville PA U.S.A.
16 G5 Mohyliv Podil's'kyy Ukr.
16 F3 Mohylyany Ukr.
22 C3 Moi Rogaland Norway
22 D3 Moi Vest-Agder Norway
66 J4 Moià Spain
74 H1 Moiano Italy
26 E9 Moidart reg. Scotland U.K.
94 E4 Moijabana Botswana
62 E7 Moimenta da Beira Port.
173 E11 Moincêr Xizang China
173 J12 Moinda Xizang China
179 M6 Moindawang Arun. Prad. India
200 □5 Moindou New Caledonia
39 I7 Moine r. France
95 G5 Moine Moz.
77 O4 Moineşti Romania
40 E5 Moingt France
Moinkum des. Kazakh. see Moyynkum, Peski
Mointy Kazakh. see Moyynty
27 J4 Moira Northern Ireland U.K.
137 I5 Moiraba Brazil
Moírai Kriti Greece see Moires
20 M3 Mo i Rana Norway
179 N7 Moirang Manipur India
40 H4 Moirans-en-Montagne France
43 F7 Moirax France
78 F7 Moires Kriti Greece
18 I3 Mõisaküla Estonia
48 I4 Moisburg Ger.
38 I6 Moisdon-la-Rivière France
77 M3 Moisei Romania
147 G2 Moisés Ville Arg.
109 H3 Moisie Que. Can.
109 H3 Moisie r. Que. Can.
36 E4 Moislains France
43 G7 Moissac France
41 I9 Moissac-Bellevue France
90 C2 Moïssala Chad
40 H2 Moissey France
72 C3 Moïta Corse France
62 D8 Moita Aveiro Port.
64 B3 Moita Setúbal Port.
137 E3 Moitaco Venez.
67 D10 Moixent-Mogente Spain
23 O2 Möja i. Sweden
65 P6 Mojácar Spain
63 K6 Mojados Spain
124 N6 Mojave CA U.S.A.
124 O7 Mojave r. CA U.S.A.
124 O6 Mojave Desert CA U.S.A.
170 C7 Mojiang Yunnan China
142 D5 Moji das Cruzes Brazil
142 C4 Moji-Guaçu r. Brazil
165 H13 Mojikō Japan
65 L3 Mojina mt. Spain
76 H8 Mojkovac Crna Gora Serb. and Mont.
138 D5 Mojo Bol.
92 C2 Mojo Eth.
157 J8 Mojokerto Jawa Indon.
65 M6 Mojón Alto mt. Spain
63 P9 Mojón Alto mt. Spain
144 D2 Mojones, Cerro mt. Arg.
138 D3 Mojos, Llanos de plain Bol.
92 D3 Mojo Shet' r. Eth.
138 D4 Mojotoro Bol.
59 I7 Mojstrana Slovenia
140 C2 Moju Brazil
167 L3 Mōka Japan
99 □1b Moka Mauritius
202 J5 Mokai North I. N.Z.
179 J7 Mokama Bihar India
91 F8 Mokambo Dem. Rep. Congo
124 □D12 Mōkapu Peninsula HI U.S.A.
90 D4 Mokaria Dem. Rep. Congo
202 I5 Mokau North I. N.Z.
202 I5 Mokau r. North I. N.Z.
90 B4 Mokéko Congo
124 K3 Mokelumne r. CA U.S.A.
124 K3 Mokelumne Aqueduct canal CA U.S.A.
97 M5 Mokhoabong Pass Lesotho
97 N5 Mokhotlong Lesotho
19 T9 Mokhovoye Rus. Fed.
193 N3 Mokhsogollokh Rus. Fed.
184 H5 Mokhtārān Iran
91 F6 Mokimbo Dem. Rep. Congo
203 B14 Mokinui Island Stewart I. N.Z.
16 G3 Mokiyivtsi Ukr.
87 H2 Moknine Tunisia
55 K3 Mokobody Pol.
Mokogai i. Fiji see Makogai
202 J2 Mokohinau Islands North I. N.Z.
179 O6 Mokokchung Nagaland India
89 I4 Mokolo Cameroon
95 E4 Mokolo r. S. Africa
95 F5 Mokopane S. Africa
203 D13 Mokoreta South I. N.Z.
203 D13 Mokoreta hill South I. N.Z.
203 C13 Mokotua South I. N.Z.
163 E11 Mokp'o S. Korea
76 I8 Mokra Gora mts Serb. and Mont.
17 K5 Mokra Kalyhirka Ukr.
57 K3 Mokrance Slovakia
55 J2 Mokre, Jezioro l. Pol.
76 I5 Mokrin Vojvodina, Srbija Serb. and Mont.
17 P6 Mokri Yaly r. Ukr.
59 L8 Mokronog Slovenia
182 B2 Mokrous Rus. Fed.
19 S6 Mokroye Moskovskaya Oblast' Rus. Fed.
19 T8 Mokroye Tul'skaya Oblast' Rus. Fed.
15 H5 Moksha r. Rus. Fed.
15 I5 Mokshan Rus. Fed.
Môktama Myanmar see Mottama
124 □D12 Moku 'Āuia i. HI U.S.A.
124 □C12 Mokulē'ia HI U.S.A.
124 □D12 Moku Lua is HI U.S.A.
Mokundurra Rajasthan India see Mukandwara
Mokvin Pershotravnevoye Ukr. see Mokvyn
16 F3 Mokvyn Ukr.
89 G4 Mokwa Nigeria
97 L3 Mokwallo S. Africa
45 H6 Mol Belgium
57 J6 Mol Vojvodina, Srbija Serb. and Mont.
75 M1 Mola di Bari Italy
Molaly Kazakh. see Mulaly
43 H9 Molandier France
129 I5 Molango Mex.
78 D6 Molaoi Greece
72 D6 Molara, Isola i. Sardegna Italy
70 F6 Molare Italy
71 R7 Molat Croatia
68 E3 Molat i. Croatia
67 C10 Molatón mt. Spain
48 E5 Molbergen Ger.
59 J6 Mölbling Austria
30 F1 Mold Flintshire, Wales U.K.
183 R2 Moldary Kazakh.
57 J3 Moldava nad Bodvou Slovakia
Moldavia country Europe see Moldova
Moldavskaya S.S.R. country Europe see Moldova
20 I5 Molde Norway
20 I5 Moldefjorden inlet Norway
20 M3 Moldjord Norway
16 H7 Moldova country Europe
77 O4 Moldova r. Romania
77 J6 Moldova Nouă Romania
77 M5 Moldoveanu, Vârful mt. Romania
77 M2 Moldovei, Podişul plat. Romania
16 G6 Moldovei Centrale, Podişul plat. Moldova
16 G6 Moldovei de Nord, Cîmpia lowland Moldova
16 G5 Moldovei de Nord, Podişul plat. Moldova
16 H7 Moldovei de Sud, Cîmpia plain Moldova
77 N3 Moldoviţa Romania
191 A2 Moldovka Rus. Fed.
93 B7 Mole Tanz.
30 E6 Mole r. England U.K.
170 A6 Mole Chaung r. Myanmar
62 C5 Moledo Viana do Castelo Port.
62 E7 Moledo Viseu Port.
109 H4 Molega Lake N.S. Can.
90 D3 Molegbe Dem. Rep. Congo
62 D7 Molelos Port.
97 M3 Molen r. S. Africa
88 E4 Mole National Park Ghana
45 F7 Molenbeek-St-Jean Belgium
38 B5 Molène, Île de i. France
94 E5 Molepolole Botswana
29 Q6 Molescroft East Riding of Yorkshire, England U.K.
36 H8 Molesmes France
18 I6 Molėtai Lith.
73 R5 Molfetta Italy
48 J2 Molfsee Ger.
20 O5 Moliden Sweden
43 G7 Molières Midi-Pyrénées France
43 H6 Molières Midi-Pyrénées France
41 E8 Molières-sur-Cèze France
43 B8 Moliets-et-Maa France
146 C3 Molina Arg.
146 B4 Molina Chile
73 L3 Molina Aterno Italy
63 Q7 Molina de Aragón Spain
67 C11 Molina de Segura Spain
71 J4 Molina di Ledro Italy
63 N2 Molinar Spain
73 N5 Molinara Italy
62 H3 Molinaseca Spain
120 J5 Moline IL U.S.A.
121 G7 Moline KS U.S.A.
71 L6 Molinella Italy
41 J7 Molines-en-Queyras France
40 D4 Molinet France
40 H4 Molinges France
65 O4 Molinicos Spain
71 L2 Molini di Tures Italy
115 D10 Molino FL U.S.A.
118 C3 Molino PA U.S.A.
66 E3 Molino de Villobas Spain
147 G3 Molino Doll Arg.
144 D2 Molinos Arg.
66 E6 Molinos Spain
66 J5 Molins de Rei Spain
91 F7 Moliro Dem. Rep. Congo
73 N4 Molise admin. reg. Italy
73 P7 Moliterno Italy
43 I10 Molitg-les-Bains France
57 L5 Moliviş mt. Romania
51 F8 Mölkau Ger.
23 J2 Molkom Sweden
58 H6 Möll r. Austria
72 A5 Molla, Capo c. Sardegna Italy
184 C4 Mollā Bodāgh Iran
Mollagara Turkm. see Mollakara
191 J5 Mollakänd Azer.
182 F8 Mollakara Turkm.
191 B6 Mollaömer Turkey
22 F6 Møllebjerg hill Denmark
63 L2 Molledo Spain
20 Q2 Mollejos hill Norway
179 O7 Mol Len mt. Nagaland India
50 H4 Möllenbeck Ger.
138 C4 Mollendo Peru
50 G3 Möllenhagen Ger.
209 D11 Mollerin, Lake salt flat W.A. Austr.
66 G4 Mollerussa Spain
40 D4 Molles France
66 J4 Mollet del Vallès Spain
36 D4 Molliens-Dreuil France
65 J6 Mollina Spain
70 G1 Mollis Switz.
59 J4 Molln Austria
50 H3 Mölln Mecklenburg-Vorpommern Ger.
48 K3 Mölln Schleswig-Holstein Ger.
66 J3 Molló Spain
58 G5 Mölltal val. Austria
23 K3 Mölltorp Sweden
22 I4 Mölnlycke Sweden
124 □B11 Moloa'a HI U.S.A.
17 O6 Molochans'k Ukr.
17 O7 Molochna r. Ukr.
17 M8 Molochne Ukr.
14 G4 Molochnoye Rus. Fed.
14 F1 Molochnyy Rus. Fed.
17 O7 Molochnyy Lyman inlet Ukr.
Molodechno Belarus see Maladzyechna
213 D2 Molodezhnaya research stn Antarctica
17 L5 Molodizhne Kirovohrads'ka Oblast' Ukr.
17 N9 Molodizhne Respublika Krym Ukr.
19 P8 Molod'kovo Rus. Fed.
88 D3 Molodo Mali
183 N1 Molodogvardeyskoye Kazakh.
19 Q5 Molodoy Tud Rus. Fed.
19 U3 Mologa r. Rus. Fed.
124 □D12 Moloka'i i. HI U.S.A.
19 T3 Molokovo Rus. Fed.
14 J4 Moloma r. Rus. Fed.
41 C6 Molompize France
205 L5 Molong N.S.W. Austr.
94 D6 Molopo watercourse Botswana/S. Africa
96 I1 Moloporivier Botswana
78 D4 Molos Greece
Molotovo Rus. Fed. see Oktyabr'skoye
Molotovsk Kyrg. see Kayyngdy
Molotovsk Kirovskaya Oblast' Rus. Fed. see Nolinsk
89 I6 Moloundou Cameroon
16 I6 Molovata Moldova
91 D6 Molowaie Dem. Rep. Congo
40 F1 Moloy France
49 K8 Molschleben Ger.
37 N6 Molsheim France
107 L5 Molson Man. Can.
107 L4 Molson Lake Man. Can.
97 K7 Molteno S. Africa
96 G8 Moltenopass pass S. Africa
72 C3 Moltifao Corse France
153 H8 Molu i. Indon.
Moluccas is Indon. see Maluku
Molucca Sea Indon. see Maluku, Laut
63 R10 Moluengo mt. Spain
95 H2 Molumbo Moz.
71 J3 Molveno Italy
71 J3 Molveno, Lago di l. Italy
19 P4 Molvotitsy Rus. Fed.
91 E7 Molwe Dem. Rep. Congo
90 D5 Moma Dem. Rep. Congo
95 H3 Moma Moz.
128 D4 Momax Mex.
205 I4 Momba N.S.W. Austr.
140 F3 Mombaça Brazil
70 E6 Mombaldone Italy
93 C5 Mombasa Kenya
64 C4 Mombeja Port.
63 J8 Mombeltrán Spain
90 C4 Mombenzélé Dem. Rep. Congo
70 E6 Mombercelli Italy
Mombetsu Hokkaidō Japan see Monbetsu
179 N7 Mombi New Manipur India
90 C5 Momboyo r. Dem. Rep. Congo
49 H10 Mömbris Ger.
142 A3 Mombuca, Serra da hills Brazil
62 H4 Mombuey Spain
77 N9 Momchilgrad Bulg.
186 E7 Momed i. Saudi Arabia
Momeik Myanmar see Mong Mit
110 G8 Momence IL U.S.A.

Momi, Ra's to **Moqor**

305

187 L9 **Momi, Ra's** *pt Suquṭrā* Yemen
64 H8 **Momia, Sierra** *mts* Spain
45 F8 **Momignies** Belgium
126 □P11 **Momotombo, Volcán** *vol.* Nic.
166 B7 **Momoyama** Japan
154 D5 **Mompog Passage** Phil.
90 D4 **Mompono** Dem. Rep. Congo
136 C2 **Mompós** Col.
193 P3 **Momskiy Khrebet** *mts* Rus. Fed.
43 C8 **Momuy** France
22 I6 **Møn** *i.* Denmark
179 O6 **Mon** *Nagaland* India
158 C6 **Mon** *state* Myanmar
125 U2 **Mona** *UT* U.S.A.
131 J4 **Mona, Isla** *i.* Puerto Rico
116 E8 **Monaca** *PA* U.S.A.
26 A7 **Monach, Sound of** *sea chan.* *Scotland* U.K.
65 L6 **Monachil** Spain
65 L6 **Monachil** *r.* Spain
26 A7 **Monach Islands** *Scotland* U.K.
72 C4 **Monacia-d'Aullène** *Corse* France
41 K9 **Monaco** *country* Europe
214 H4 **Monaco Basin** *sea feature* N. Atlantic Ocean
26 G8 **Monadhliath Mountains** *Scotland* U.K.
137 F2 **Monagas** *state* Venez.
27 I4 **Monaghan** Rep. of Ireland
27 I4 **Monaghan** *county* Rep. of Ireland
121 D10 **Monahans** *TX* U.S.A.
27 J7 **Monamolin** Rep. of Ireland
131 I4 **Mona Passage** Dom. Rep./Puerto Rico
95 I2 **Monapo** Moz.
91 C7 **Mona Quimbundo** Angola
26 F8 **Monar, Loch** *l.* *Scotland* U.K.
106 E5 **Monarch Mountain** *B.C.* Can.
123 K7 **Monarch Pass** *CO* U.S.A.
125 U2 **Mona Reservoir** *UT* U.S.A.
106 G5 **Monashee Mountains** *B.C.* Can.
75 L7 **Monasterace** Italy
27 H6 **Monasterevan** Rep. of Ireland
63 O4 **Monasterio de Suso** *tourist site* Spain
190 B10 **Monastery of St Catherine** *tourist site* Egypt
190 A10 **Monastery of St Anthony** *tourist site* Egypt
190 A10 **Monastery of St Paul** *tourist site* Egypt
72 C9 **Monastir** *Sardegna* Italy
87 H2 **Monastir** Tunisia
55 M6 **Monastyrets'** Ukr.
Monastyrishche Ukr. *see* Monastyryshche
19 O7 **Monastyrshchina** Rus. Fed.
16 I5 **Monastyryshche** Ukr.
16 E4 **Monastyrys'ka** Ukr.
89 H5 **Monatélé** Cameroon
203 E11 **Monavale** *South I.* N.Z.
201 □1a **Monavatu** *mt.* *Viti Levu* Fiji
27 G8 **Monavullagh Mountains** *hills* Rep. of Ireland
43 F6 **Monbahus** France
43 E6 **Monbazillac** France
43 G8 **Monbéqui** France
164 T4 **Monbetsu** *Hokkaidō* Japan
164 U2 **Monbetsu** *Hokkaidō* Japan
89 I4 **Monboré** Cameroon
43 G8 **Monbrun** France
67 E8 **Moncada** Spain
70 D5 **Moncalieri** Italy
70 E5 **Moncalvo** Italy
62 G4 **Moncalvo** *mt.* Spain
62 D4 **Monção** Port.
64 D6 **Moncarapacho** Port.
43 E7 **Moncaut** France
63 Q5 **Moncayo, Sierra del** *mts* Spain
39 L6 **Moncé-en-Belin** France
37 L6 **Moncel-sur-Seille** France
70 E2 **Mönch** *mt.* Switz.
20 V3 **Monchegorsk** Rus. Fed.
49 B8 **Mönchengladbach** Ger.
59 O4 **Mönchhof** Austria
70 I7 **Monchio delle Corti** Italy
64 B6 **Monchique** Port.
64 B6 **Monchique, Serra de** *mts* Port.
53 J4 **Mönchsdeggingen** Ger.
131 □3 **Monchy** St Lucia
115 G9 **Moncks Corner** *SC* U.S.A.
43 F7 **Monclar** France
43 H8 **Monclar-de-Quercy** France
127 I4 **Monclova** Mex.
67 E8 **Moncófar** Spain
38 F5 **Moncontour** *Bretagne* France
39 K8 **Moncontour** *Poitou-Charentes* France
109 G3 **Moncouche, Lac** *l.* *Que.* Can.
39 J8 **Moncoutant** France
43 E7 **Moncrabeau** France
109 H4 **Moncton** *N.B.* Can.
65 J7 **Monda** Spain
141 B8 **Mondai** Brazil
62 D4 **Mondariz** Spain
62 D4 **Mondariz-Balneario** Spain
43 G9 **Mondavezan** France
71 N8 **Mondavio** Italy
62 C8 **Mondego** *r.* Port.
62 C8 **Mondego, Cabo** *c.* Port.
63 N8 **Mondéjar** Spain
74 E7 **Mondello** *Sicilia* Italy
39 K3 **Mondeville** France
90 D4 **Mondimbi** Dem. Rep. Congo
62 E6 **Mondim de Basto** Port.
90 D4 **Mondjamboli** Dem. Rep. Congo
97 O3 **Mondlo** S. Africa
84 B6 **Mondo** Chad
71 O8 **Mondolfo** Italy
62 F2 **Mondoñedo** Spain
45 J9 **Mondorf-les-Bains** Lux.
39 M6 **Mondoubleau** France
70 D7 **Mondovì** Italy
110 C5 **Mondovi** *WI* U.S.A.
41 F8 **Mondragon** France
63 P2 **Mondragón-Arrasate** Spain
73 L5 **Mondragone** Italy
59 H4 **Mondsee** Austria
59 H4 **Mondsee** *l.* Austria
93 C5 **Monduli** Tanz.
67 E9 **Mondúver** *hill* Spain
130 □ **Moneague** Jamaica
57 L5 **Moneasa** Romania
42 H4 **Monédières, Massif des** *hills* France
110 G8 **Monee** *IL* U.S.A.
27 E6 **Moneen** Rep. of Ireland
70 G7 **Moneglia** Italy
66 E4 **Monegrillo** Spain
66 D4 **Monegros, Canal de** Spain
43 C9 **Monein** France
78 E6 **Monemvasia** Greece
162 L5 **Moneron, Ostrov** *i.* Rus. Fed.
116 F8 **Monessen** *PA* U.S.A.
64 G4 **Monesterio** Spain
41 H7 **Monestier-de-Clermont** France
43 I7 **Monestiés** France
111 S1 **Monet** *Que.* Can.
116 F11 **Moneta** *VA* U.S.A.
122 K5 **Moneta** *WY* U.S.A.
36 G8 **Monéteau** France
121 I7 **Monett** *MO* U.S.A.
66 D5 **Moneva, Embalse de** *resr* Spain
27 G7 **Moneygall** Rep. of Ireland
26 D13 **Moneyglass** *Northern Ireland* U.K.
27 I3 **Moneymore** *Northern Ireland* U.K.
28 D4 **Moneyneany** *Northern Ireland* U.K.
28 F4 **Moneyreagh** *Northern Ireland* U.K.
71 P4 **Monfalcone** Italy
73 N6 **Monfecorvino Rovella** Italy
43 F6 **Monflanquin** France
136 D4 **Monfort** Col.
43 F8 **Monfort** France
64 E2 **Monforte** Port.
62 E3 **Monforte** Spain
62 F9 **Monforte da Beira** Port.
70 D6 **Monforte d'Alba** Italy
67 D11 **Monforte del Cid** Spain
66 D5 **Monforte de Moyuela** Spain
62 G8 **Monfortinho** Port.
64 C3 **Monfurado** *hill* Port.
64 C3 **Monfurado, Serra de** *mts* Port.
91 E7 **Monga** *Katanga* Dem. Rep. Congo
90 D3 **Monga** *Orientale* Dem. Rep. Congo
142 D6 **Mongaguá** Brazil
90 C4 **Mongala** *r.* Dem. Rep. Congo
92 A3 **Mongalla** Sudan
179 M6 **Mongar** Bhutan
118 F2 **Mongaup** *r.* *NY* U.S.A.
118 F1 **Mongaup Valley** *NY* U.S.A.
90 F4 **Mongbwalu** Dem. Rep. Congo
158 H4 **Mông Cai** Vietnam
91 D5 **Mongemputu** Dem. Rep. Congo
209 D10 **Mongers Lake** *salt flat* *W.A.* Austr.
200 □6 **Mongga** *New Georgia Is* Solomon Is
169 P2 **Monggon Qulu** *Nei Mongol* China
158 D4 **Mong Hai** Myanmar
158 D4 **Mong Hang** Myanmar
71 K7 **Monghidoro** Italy
170 C8 **Mong Hkan** Myanmar
158 D4 **Mong Hkok** Myanmar
158 D4 **Mong Hpayak** Myanmar
158 D4 **Mong Hsat** Myanmar
158 C4 **Mong Hsawk** Myanmar
158 D4 **Mong Hsu** Myanmar
Monghyr *Bihar* India *see* Munger
158 C4 **Mong Kung** Myanmar
158 D5 **Mong Kyawt** Myanmar
179 L8 **Mongla** Bangl.
158 E4 **Mong La** Myanmar
158 C4 **Mong Lang** Myanmar
158 E4 **Mong Lin** Myanmar
158 E4 **Mong Loi** Myanmar
158 C3 **Mong Long** Myanmar
158 D4 **Mong Ma** Myanmar
158 C5 **Mong Mau** Myanmar
158 C3 **Mong Mit** Myanmar
158 C4 **Mong Nai** Myanmar
158 D4 **Mong Nawng** Myanmar
84 C6 **Mongo** Chad
Mongó *hill* Spain *see* **Montgó**
168 H3 **Mongolia** *country* Asia
Mongol Uls *country* Asia *see* Mongolia
89 H6 **Mongomo** Equat. Guinea
208 I3 **Mongona, Mount** *hill* *W.A.* Austr.
89 I3 **Mongonu** Nigeria
185 O4 **Mongora** Pak.
84 D6 **Mongororo** Chad
90 C4 **Mongoumba** C.A.R.
26 L9 **Mongour** *hill* *Scotland* U.K.
158 D4 **Mong Pan** Myanmar
158 D3 **Mong Pat** Myanmar
158 D3 **Mong Pawk** Myanmar
158 D4 **Mong Ping** Myanmar
158 D4 **Mong Pu** Myanmar
158 D4 **Mong Pu-awn** Myanmar
70 E4 **Mongrando** Italy
128 E8 **Mongrove, Punta** *pt* Mex.
158 D3 **Mong Si** Myanmar
170 B8 **Mong Ton** Myanmar
158 D4 **Mong Tum** Myanmar
170 A7 **Mong Tung** Myanmar
91 D8 **Mongu** Zambia
91 B9 **Mongua** Angola
88 B2 **Mônguel** Maur.
71 M2 **Monguelfo** Italy
158 E4 **Mong Un** Myanmar
158 D3 **Mong Yai** Myanmar
158 D4 **Mong Yang** Myanmar
158 D4 **Mong Yawn** Myanmar
158 E4 **Mong Yawng** Myanmar
158 C3 **Mong Yu** Myanmar
168 H3 **Mönhbulag** Mongolia
117 □P5 **Monhegan Island** *ME* U.S.A.
53 J4 **Monheim** Ger.
168 B3 **Mönh Hayrhan Uul** *mt.* Mongolia
26 I12 **Moniaive** *Dumfries and Galloway, Scotland* U.K.
110 E4 **Monico** *WI* U.S.A.
41 G8 **Monieux** France
26 K10 **Monifieth** *Angus, Scotland* U.K.
147 G2 **Monigotes** Arg.
28 C6 **Monilea** Rep. of Ireland
136 C3 **Moniquirá** Col.
41 D7 **Monistrol-d'Allier** France
66 I4 **Monistrol de Montserrat** Spain
41 E6 **Monistrol-sur-Loire** France
124 P3 **Monitor Mountain** *NV* U.S.A.
124 P3 **Monitor Range** *mts* *NV* U.S.A.
136 B2 **Moñitos** Col.
184 E6 **Monj** Iran
63 P9 **Monje, Sierra del** *mts* Spain
143 E3 **Monjolos** Brazil
48 J2 **Mönkeberg** Ger.
93 B8 **Monkey Bay** Malawi
209 B8 **Monkey Mia** *W.A.* Austr.
55 K2 **Mońki** Pol.
206 H8 **Monkira** *Qld* Austr.
106 F4 **Monkman Provincial Park** *park* *B.C.* Can.
30 D6 **Monkokehampton** *Devon, England* U.K.
90 D5 **Monkoto** Dem. Rep. Congo
31 N3 **Monks Eleigh** *Suffolk, England* U.K.
111 M6 **Monkton** *Ont.* Can.
118 B5 **Monkton** *MD* U.S.A.
67 E7 **Monleón** *r.* Spain
43 F9 **Monléon-Magnoac** France
30 G4 **Monmouth** *Monmouthshire, Wales* U.K.
124 M5 **Monmouth** *CA* U.S.A.
120 J5 **Monmouth** *IL* U.S.A.
119 G4 **Monmouth County** *county* *NJ* U.S.A.
118 F4 **Monmouth Junction** *NJ* U.S.A.
106 F5 **Monmouth Mountain** *B.C.* Can.
30 G4 **Monmouthshire** *admin. div.* *Wales* U.K.
39 M6 **Monnaie** France
116 B8 **Monnett** *OH* U.S.A.
44 H4 **Monnickendam** Neth.
30 G4 **Monnow** *r.* *England/Wales* U.K.
89 F5 **Mono** *r.* Togo
126 □R12 **Mono, Punta del** *pt* Nic.
200 □6 **Mono Island** Solomon Is
57 K3 **Monok** Hungary
124 N3 **Mono Lake** *CA* U.S.A.
79 I6 **Monolithos** *Rodos* Greece
117 P7 **Monomoy Island** *MA* U.S.A.
110 H9 **Monon** *IN* U.S.A.
110 C6 **Monona** *IA* U.S.A.
75 M2 **Monopoli** Italy
57 I4 **Monor** Hungary
116 F8 **Monorgahela** *r.* *PA* U.S.A.
131 □7 **Monos Island** Trin. and Tob.
57 K4 **Monostorpályi** Hungary
84 D5 **Monou** Chad
67 D11 **Monóvar** Spain
Monover Spain *see* **Monóvar**
203 B12 **Monowai, Lake** *South I.* N.Z.
43 F6 **Monpazier** France
63 R3 **Monreal** Spain
65 N2 **Monreal** *r.* Spain
66 C6 **Monreal del Campo** Spain
74 E7 **Monreale** *Sicilia* Italy
26 G13 **Monreith** *Dumfries and Galloway, Scotland* U.K.
115 F9 **Monroe** *GA* U.S.A.
120 I5 **Monroe** *IA* U.S.A.
121 I9 **Monroe** *LA* U.S.A.
111 K8 **Monroe** *MI* U.S.A.
115 G8 **Monroe** *NC* U.S.A.
118 F2 **Monroe** *NJ* U.S.A.
119 G2 **Monroe** *NY* U.S.A.
125 T3 **Monroe** *UT* U.S.A.
116 F11 **Monroe** *VA* U.S.A.
122 D3 **Monroe** *WA* U.S.A.
110 E7 **Monroe** *WI* U.S.A.
110 E5 **Monroe Center** *WI* U.S.A.
120 J6 **Monroe City** *MO* U.S.A.
118 E2 **Monroe County** *county* *PA* U.S.A.
114 D6 **Monroe Lake** *IN* U.S.A.
111 R8 **Monroeton** *PA* U.S.A.
115 D10 **Monroeville** *AL* U.S.A.
110 J9 **Monroeville** *IN* U.S.A.
118 E5 **Monroeville** *NJ* U.S.A.
116 C7 **Monroeville** *OH* U.S.A.
88 C5 **Monrovia** Liberia
62 H9 **Monroy** Spain
66 E6 **Monroyo** Spain
45 E8 **Mons** Belgium
41 B9 **Mons** *Languedoc-Roussillon* France
41 J9 **Mons** *Provence-Alpes-Côte d'Azur* France
147 I5 **Monsalvo** Arg.
73 L2 **Monsampolo del Tronto** Italy
62 F8 **Monsanto** Port.
143 H3 **Monsarás, Ponta de** *pt* Brazil
64 E4 **Monsaraz** Port.
49 B9 **Monschau** Ger.
42 F5 **Monsec** France
43 D9 **Monségur** *Aquitaine* France
43 E6 **Monségur** *Aquitaine* France
71 L5 **Monselice** Italy
43 F7 **Monsempron-Libos** France
36 F2 **Mons-en-Barœul** France
119 G2 **Monsey** *NY* U.S.A.
52 F4 **Mönsheim** Ger.
52 E2 **Monsheim** Ger.
22 I7 **Møns Klint** *cliff* Denmark
40 F4 **Monsols** France
117 □P3 **Monson** *ME* U.S.A.
44 F4 **Monster** Neth.
23 M4 **Mönsterås** Sweden
71 J8 **Monsummano Terme** Italy
70 D6 **Monta** Italy
49 E10 **Montabaur** Ger.
67 E10 **Montaberner** Spain
43 K9 **Montady** France
58 A5 **Montafon** *val.* Austria
41 C10 **Montagnac** France
71 K5 **Montagnana** Italy
42 D6 **Montagne** France
40 H2 **Montagney** France
41 C9 **Montagnol** France
40 E4 **Montagny** France
42 E5 **Montagrier** France
96 E9 **Montagu** S. Africa
109 I4 **Montague** *P.E.I.* Can.
118 F2 **Montague** *NJ* U.S.A.
121 G9 **Montague** *TX* U.S.A.
104 D3 **Montague Island** *AK* U.S.A.
209 E9 **Montague Range** *hills* *W.A.* Austr.
208 H3 **Montague Sound** *b.* *W.A.* Austr.
135 G7 **Montagu Island** S. Sandwich Is
Montagu Island Vanuatu *see* Nguna
38 I8 **Montaigu** France
43 G7 **Montaigu-de-Quercy** France
40 B4 **Montaigut** France
43 G8 **Montaigut-sur-Save** France
71 J8 **Montaione** Italy
157 K5 **Montalat** *r.* Indon.
66 D6 **Montalbán** Spain
65 J5 **Montalbán de Córdoba** Spain
75 I7 **Montalbano Elicona** *Sicilia* Italy
75 L3 **Montalbano Jonico** Italy
63 O9 **Montalbo** Spain
72 G1 **Montalcino** Italy
71 K8 **Montale** Italy
62 E5 **Montalegre** Port.
40 G5 **Montalieu-Vercieu** France
42 B5 **Montalivet-les-Bains** France
74 E9 **Montallegro** *Sicilia* Italy
75 J7 **Montalto** *mt.* Italy
73 L2 **Montalto delle Marche** Italy
72 H3 **Montalto di Castro** Italy
72 H3 **Montalto Marina** Italy
73 Q9 **Montalto Uffugo** Italy
62 E9 **Montalvão** Port.
136 B5 **Montalvo** Ecuador
124 M7 **Montalvo** *CA* U.S.A.
62 I5 **Montamarta** Spain
77 L7 **Montana** Bulg.
70 C3 **Montana** Switz.
122 J3 **Montana** *state* U.S.A.
98 □3c **Montaña Clara** *i.* Canary Is
126 □P10 **Montaña de Comayagua, Parque Nacional** *nat. park* Hond.
127 O10 **Montaña de Cusuco, Parque Nacional** *nat. park* Hond.
126 □P10 **Montaña de Yoro** *nat. park* Hond.
126 □Q10 **Montañas de Colón** *mts* Hond.
64 G2 **Montánchez** *hill* Spain
64 G2 **Montánchez, Sierra de** *mts* Spain
118 B3 **Montandon** *PA* U.S.A.
67 D7 **Montanejos** Spain
43 D9 **Montaner** France
143 G3 **Montanha** Brazil
137 H4 **Montanhas do Tumucumaque, Parque Nacional** *nat. park* Brazil
73 O7 **Montano Antilia** Italy
43 H8 **Montans** France
73 M4 **Montaquila** Italy
64 C2 **Montargil** Port.
64 C2 **Montargil, Barragem de** *resr* Port.
36 E8 **Montargis** France
43 H8 **Montastruc-la-Conseillère** France
36 D5 **Montataire** France
43 G7 **Montauban** France
38 G5 **Montauban-de-Bretagne** France
43 I9 **Montaud, Pic de** *mt.* France
39 J5 **Montaudin** France
117 N7 **Montauk** *NY* U.S.A.
119 L2 **Montauk, Lake** *b.* *NY* U.S.A.
117 N7 **Montauk Point** *NY* U.S.A.
43 F6 **Montauriol** France
41 J9 **Montauroux** France
43 C8 **Montaut** *Aquitaine* France
43 D9 **Montaut** *Aquitaine* France
43 H9 **Montaut** *Midi-Pyrénées* France
43 F8 **Montaut-les-Crénaux** France
97 M4 **Mont-aux-Sources** *mt.* Lesotho
43 F7 **Montayral** France
73 M4 **Montazzoli** Italy
40 E1 **Montbard** France
40 H2 **Montbarrey** France
43 G8 **Montbartier** France
43 I7 **Montbazens** France
41 D9 **Montbazin** France
39 M7 **Montbazon** France
40 J1 **Montbéliard** France
40 I3 **Montbenoît** France
43 F9 **Montbernard** France
43 G7 **Montbeton** France
41 C10 **Montblanc** France
40 J5 **Mont Blanc** *mt.* France/Italy
66 H5 **Montblanc** Spain
Montblanch Spain *see* Montblanc
99 □1b **Mont Blanche** Mauritius
40 J5 **Mont Blanc Tunnel** France/Italy
41 F7 **Montboucher-sur-Jabron** France
40 I2 **Montbozon** France
66 H5 **Montbrió del Camp** Spain
40 E5 **Montbrison** France
42 F4 **Montbron** France
43 H6 **Montbrun** France
41 G8 **Montbrun-les-Bains** France
116 D11 **Montcalm** *WV* U.S.A.
43 E6 **Montcaret** France
36 C2 **Montcavrel** France
40 E3 **Montceau-les-Mines** France
40 E3 **Montcenis** France
41 J6 **Mont Cenis, Lac du** *l.* France
40 E3 **Montchanin** France
119 G3 **Montclair** *NJ* U.S.A.
36 H4 **Montcornet** France
36 E8 **Montcresson** France
43 G7 **Montcuq** France
36 I4 **Montcy-Notre-Dame** France
41 D9 **Montdardier** France
41 J7 **Mont-Dauphin** France
43 D8 **Mont-de-Marsan** France
36 E4 **Montdidier** France
40 B5 **Mont-Dore** France
147 F5 **Monte, Laguna del** *l.* Arg.
73 P8 **Montea** *mt.* Italy
138 D4 **Monteagudo** Bol.
63 Q5 **Monteagudo** Spain
63 Q9 **Monteagudo de las Salinas** Spain
63 P6 **Monteagudo de las Vicarías** Spain
146 A5 **Monte Águila** Chile
129 K8 **Monte Alban** *tourist site* Mex.
137 H5 **Monte Alegre** Brazil
142 B2 **Monte Alegre** *r.* Brazil
140 D5 **Monte Alegre de Goiás** Brazil
67 C10 **Montealegre del Castillo** Spain
142 C3 **Monte Alegre de Minas** Brazil
142 C4 **Monte Alto** Brazil
142 C4 **Monte Aprazível** Brazil
141 E5 **Monte Azul** Brazil
142 C4 **Monte Azul Paulista** Brazil
108 F4 **Montebello** *Que.* Can.
136 C6 **Monte Bello** Peru
75 J8 **Montebello Ionico** Italy
208 C6 **Montebello Islands** *W.A.* Austr.
71 K5 **Montebello Vicentino** Italy
71 M4 **Montebelluna** Italy
38 I3 **Montebourg** France
70 G6 **Montebruno** Italy
147 F3 **Monte Buey** Arg.
71 N8 **Montecalvo in Foglia** Italy
144 G2 **Montecarlo** Arg.
41 K9 **Monte-Carlo** Monaco
142 D3 **Monte Carmelo** Brazil
147 I2 **Monte Caseros** Arg.
71 O9 **Montecassiano** Italy
73 I2 **Monte Castello di Vibio** Italy
73 I2 **Montecastrilli** Italy
71 J8 **Montecatini Terme** Italy
71 J9 **Montecatini Val di Cecina** Italy
71 N8 **Montecchio** Italy
70 I6 **Montecchio Emilia** Italy
71 K4 **Montecchio Maggiore** Italy
43 G8 **Montech** France
70 E5 **Montechiaro d'Asti** Italy
64 C6 **Montechoro** Port.
95 E4 **Monte Christo** S. Africa
73 N4 **Montecilfone** Italy
124 M7 **Montecito** *CA* U.S.A.
62 E9 **Monte Claro** Port.
146 D4 **Monte Comán** Arg.
62 D6 **Monte Córdova** Port.
73 N7 **Montecorice** Italy
71 K3 **Monte Corno, Parco Naturale** *nature res.* Italy
73 Q7 **Monte Cotugna, Lago di** *l.* Italy
71 N3 **Montecreale Valcellina** Italy
71 J7 **Montecreto** Italy
130 H4 **Monte Cristi** Dom. Rep.
130 H4 **Monte Cristi** *nat. park* Dom. Rep.
136 A5 **Montecristi** Ecuador
147 F2 **Monte Cristo** Arg.
139 E3 **Monte Cristo** Bol.
72 E3 **Montecristo, Isola di** *i.* Italy
71 N9 **Monte Cucco, Parco Naturale Regionale del** *park* Italy
64 D2 **Monte da Pedra** Port.
64 C5 **Monte da Rocha, Barragem do** *resr* Port.
62 F4 **Montederramo** Spain
145 C9 **Monte Dinero** Arg.
73 M6 **Monte di Procida** Italy
71 M8 **Montedoglio, Lago di** *l.* Italy
64 D4 **Monte do Trigo** Port.
137 H5 **Monte Dourado** Brazil
128 D3 **Monte Escobedo** Mex.
73 N6 **Montefalcione** Italy
73 J2 **Montefalco** Italy
73 N4 **Montefalcone** Italy
73 O5 **Montefalcone di Val Fortore** Italy
71 L8 **Monte Falterona, Campigna e delle Foreste Casentinesi, Parco Nazionale del** *nat. park* Italy
71 O9 **Montefano** Italy
71 N8 **Montefelcino** Italy
71 M8 **Montefeltro** *reg.* Italy
72 I2 **Montefiascone** Italy
64 C6 **Monte Figo, Serra de** *mts* Port.
73 L1 **Montefiore dell'Aso** Italy
71 J7 **Montefiorino** Italy
73 N6 **Monteforte Irpino** Italy
73 K2 **Montefortino** Italy
73 J2 **Montefranco** Italy
65 K6 **Montefrío** Spain
75 L3 **Montegiordano** Italy
73 L1 **Montegiorgio** Italy
130 □ **Montego Bay** Jamaica
130 □ **Montego Bay** *b.* Jamaica
64 E6 **Monte Gordo** Port.
71 P9 **Montegranaro** Italy
147 H4 **Monte Grande** Arg.
43 E9 **Montégut-Arros** France
147 G6 **Monte Hermoso** Arg.
62 H8 **Montehermoso** Spain
75 M3 **Monteiasi** Italy
43 H7 **Monteils** France
140 F3 **Monteiro** Brazil
98 □1c **Monteiros, Ponta dos** *pt* *São Jorge* Azores
65 I7 **Montejaque** Spain
65 M5 **Montejícar** Spain
206 C4 **Montejinnie** *N.T.* Austr.
63 M6 **Montejo de la Sierra** Spain
64 A2 **Montejunto, Serra de** *hill* Port.
71 N8 **Montelabbate** Italy
73 K4 **Montelanico** Italy
64 A3 **Montelavar** Port.
40 B5 **Montel-de-Gelat** France
145 C8 **Monte León** Arg.
73 O5 **Monteleone di Puglia** Italy
73 J2 **Monteleone di Spoleto** Italy
72 I2 **Monteleone d'Orvieto** Italy
72 B7 **Monteleone Rocca Doria** *Sardegna* Italy
73 J3 **Monteleone Sabino** Italy
74 E7 **Montelepre** *Sicilia* Italy
136 C2 **Monte Libano** Col.
73 J3 **Montelibretti** Italy
41 G7 **Montélier** France
41 F7 **Montélimar** France
139 F5 **Monte Lindo** *r.* Para.
73 O6 **Montella** Italy
64 H6 **Montellano** Spain
110 E6 **Montello** *WI* U.S.A.
43 G9 **Montels** France
71 K8 **Montelupo Fiorentino** Italy
71 P9 **Montelupone** Italy
74 F8 **Montemaggiore Belsito** *Sicilia* Italy
147 F3 **Monte Maíz** Arg.
73 O6 **Montemarano** Italy
71 O8 **Montemarciano** Italy
65 O3 **Montemayon** *r.* Spain
65 J5 **Montemayor** Spain
145 D7 **Montemayor, Meseta de** *plat.* Arg.
63 L5 **Montemayor de Pililla** Spain
42 F4 **Montemboeuf** France
75 M2 **Montemesola** Italy
73 P5 **Montemilone** Italy
64 G4 **Montemolín** Spain
73 K2 **Montemonaco** Italy
127 J5 **Montemorelos** Mex.
64 C3 **Montemor-o-Novo** Port.
62 C8 **Montemor-o-Velho** Port.
71 K8 **Montemurlo** Italy
62 D6 **Montemuro, Serra de** *mts* Port.
73 P7 **Montemurro** Italy
39 J5 **Montenay** France
42 D5 **Montendre** France
Montenegro *aut. rep.* Serb. and Mont. *see* **Crna Gora**
63 O4 **Montenegro de Cameros** Spain
73 N4 **Montenero di Bisaccia** Italy
73 M3 **Montenerodomo** Italy
75 M3 **Monteparano** Italy
143 H2 **Monte Pascoal, Parque Nacional** *nat. park* Brazil
146 B2 **Monte Patria** Chile
131 I4 **Monte Plata** Dom. Rep.
71 O8 **Monte Porzio** Italy
73 L2 **Monteprandone** Italy
93 C8 **Montepuez** Moz.
93 D8 **Montepuez** *r.* Moz.
72 H1 **Montepulciano** Italy
72 H1 **Montepulciano, Lago di** *l.* Italy
144 E2 **Monte Quemado** Arg.
38 F6 **Monterblanc** France
71 M9 **Monterchi** Italy
62 C9 **Monte Real** Port.
73 K2 **Montereale** Italy
36 E7 **Montereau-fault-Yonne** France
62 C9 **Monte Redondo** Port.
71 K7 **Monterenzio** Italy
Monterey Mex. *see* **Monterrey**
124 K5 **Monterey** *CA* U.S.A.
116 F10 **Monterey** *VA* U.S.A.
124 J5 **Monterey Bay** *CA* U.S.A.
124 J5 **Monterey Bay National Marine Sanctuary** *nature res.* *CA* U.S.A.
136 C2 **Montería** Col.
71 K9 **Monteriggioni** Italy
139 E4 **Montero** Bol.
73 M4 **Monteroduni** Italy
72 H3 **Monte Romano** Italy
71 K9 **Monteroni d'Arbia** Italy
75 O3 **Monteroni di Lecce** Italy
137 F3 **Monte Roraima, Parque Nacional do** *nat. park* Brazil
144 D2 **Monteros** Arg.
73 I3 **Monterosi** Italy
70 H7 **Monterosso al Mare** Italy
74 H9 **Monterosso Almo** *Sicilia* Italy
75 K6 **Monterosso Calabro** Italy
73 J3 **Monterotondo** Italy
72 F1 **Monterotondo Marittimo** Italy
62 F5 **Monterrei** Spain
125 Q9 **Monterrey** *Baja California* Mex.
127 I5 **Monterrey** *Nuevo León* Mex.
62 E3 **Monterroso** Spain
65 I3 **Monterrubio de la Serena** Spain
73 L1 **Monterubbiano** Italy
67 D10 **Montesa** Spain
140 D3 **Montes Altos** Brazil
73 K5 **Monte San Biagio** Italy
73 L4 **Monte San Giovanni Campano** Italy
122 C3 **Montesano** *WA* U.S.A.
75 O4 **Montesano Salentino** Italy
73 P7 **Montesano sulla Marcellana** Italy
71 L9 **Monte San Savino** Italy
71 M9 **Monte Santa Maria Tiberina** Italy
73 P4 **Monte Sant'Angelo** Italy
140 F4 **Monte Santo** Brazil
142 D4 **Monte Santo de Minas** Brazil
72 D7 **Monte Santu, Capo di** *c.* *Sardegna* Italy
73 N5 **Montesarchio** Italy
75 L2 **Montescaglioso** Italy
143 F2 **Montes Claros** Brazil
63 K8 **Montesclaros** Spain
71 J9 **Montescudaio** Italy
147 F6 **Montes de Oca** Arg.
71 J7 **Montese** Italy
73 M2 **Montesilvano** Italy
43 G7 **Montesquieu** France
43 G9 **Montesquieu-Volvestre** France
43 E8 **Montesquiou** France
43 F8 **Montestruc-sur-Gers** France
73 J1 **Monte Subasio, Parco Naturale Regionale del** *park* Italy
64 C5 **Montes Velhos** Port.
41 F8 **Monteux** France
74 D8 **Montevago** *Sicilia* Italy
71 L8 **Montevarchi** Italy
72 B8 **Montevecchia** *Sardegna* Italy
147 G2 **Monte Vera** Arg.
73 P5 **Monteverde** Italy
147 I4 **Montevideo** Uru.
147 I4 **Montevideo** *dept* Uru.
120 H3 **Montevideo** *MN* U.S.A.
64 B4 **Montevil** Port.
123 K8 **Monte Vista** *CO* U.S.A.
62 G5 **Montezinho, Parque Natural de** *nature res.* Port.
120 I5 **Montezuma** *IA* U.S.A.
121 E7 **Montezuma** *KS* U.S.A.
125 W4 **Montezuma Creek** *UT* U.S.A.
125 W4 **Montezuma Creek** *r.* *CO* U.S.A.
124 O4 **Montezuma Peak** *NV* U.S.A.
43 H6 **Montfaucon** *Midi-Pyrénées* France
39 I7 **Montfaucon** *Pays de la Loire* France
37 J5 **Montfaucon-d'Argonne** France
41 E6 **Montfaucon-en-Velay** France
43 F8 **Montferran-Savès** France
41 I9 **Montferrat** France
43 H10 **Montferrier** France
44 G4 **Montfoort** Neth.
43 C9 **Montfort** *Aquitaine* France
38 H5 **Montfort** *Bretagne* France
43 C8 **Montfort-en-Chalosse** France
36 C6 **Montfort-l'Amaury** France
39 L5 **Montfort-le-Gesnois** France
39 M3 **Montfort-sur-Risle** France
62 I9 **Montfragüe, Parque Natural de** *nature res.* Spain
66 G4 **Montgai** Spain
43 E9 **Montgaillard** *Midi-Pyrénées* France
43 F8 **Montgaillard** *Midi-Pyrénées* France
43 H10 **Montgaillard** *Midi-Pyrénées* France
41 J7 **Montgenèvre** France
41 J7 **Montgenèvre, Col de** *pass* France
36 D6 **Montgeron** France
43 H9 **Montgiscard** France
39 O8 **Montgivray** France
67 F10 **Montgó** *hill* Spain
66 L3 **Montgó, Cala** *b.* Spain
30 F2 **Montgomery** *Powys, Wales* U.K.
115 D9 **Montgomery** *AL* U.S.A.
119 G1 **Montgomery** *NY* U.S.A.
116 A9 **Montgomery** *OH* U.S.A.
111 R8 **Montgomery** *PA* U.S.A.
116 D10 **Montgomery** *WV* U.S.A.
120 J6 **Montgomery City** *MO* U.S.A.
118 A6 **Montgomery County** *county* *MD* U.S.A.
118 E4 **Montgomery County** *county* *PA* U.S.A.
208 G3 **Montgomery Islands** *W.A.* Austr.
42 D5 **Montguyon** France
36 I4 **Monthermé** France
70 B3 **Monthey** Switz.
36 I5 **Monthois** France
37 K7 **Monthureux-sur-Saône** France
72 C6 **Monti** *Sardegna* Italy
71 N4 **Monticano** *r.* Italy
70 H5 **Monticelli d'Ongina** Italy
72 B2 **Monticello** *Corse* France
121 J9 **Monticello** *AR* U.S.A.
115 F10 **Monticello** *FL* U.S.A.
115 F9 **Monticello** *GA* U.S.A.
120 K5 **Monticello** *IL* U.S.A.
114 D5 **Monticello** *IN* U.S.A.
114 E7 **Monticello** *KY* U.S.A.
117 □R2 **Monticello** *ME* U.S.A.
120 I3 **Monticello** *MN* U.S.A.
120 J5 **Monticello** *MO* U.S.A.
121 J10 **Monticello** *MS* U.S.A.
118 F1 **Monticello** *NY* U.S.A.
125 W4 **Monticello** *UT* U.S.A.
110 E7 **Monticello** *WI* U.S.A.
70 I5 **Montichiari** Italy
72 G1 **Monticiano** Italy
65 N3 **Montiel** Spain
147 H2 **Montiel, Cuchilla de** *hills* Arg.
39 O8 **Montierchaume** France
36 I7 **Montier-en-Der** France
72 G1 **Montieri** Italy
37 J6 **Montiers-sur-Saulx** France
42 G5 **Montignac** France
45 F8 **Montignies-le-Tilleul** Belgium
70 I7 **Montignoso** Italy
37 M6 **Montigny** France
111 Q1 **Montigny, Lac de** *l.* *Que.* Can.
36 G8 **Montigny-la-Resie** France
37 L5 **Montigny-lès-Metz** France
40 G1 **Montigny-Mornay-Villeneuve-sur-Vingeanne** France
37 I8 **Montigny-sur-Aube** France
64 B3 **Montijo** Port.
64 F3 **Montijo** Spain
65 J5 **Montilla** Spain
65 L5 **Montillana** Spain
91 B8 **Montipa** Angola
43 I7 **Montirat** France
73 K2 **Monti Sibillini, Parco Nazionale dei** *nat. park* Italy
73 K4 **Monti Simbruini, Parco Naturale Regionale dei** *nature res.* Italy
142 B2 **Montividiu** Brazil
39 L2 **Montivilliers** France
65 M4 **Montizón** Spain
65 M4 **Montizón** *r.* Spain
41 B8 **Montjaux** France
39 J5 **Montjean** France
39 J7 **Montjean-sur-Loire** France
109 G3 **Mont-Joli** *Que.* Can.
70 D4 **Montjovet** Italy
43 J9 **Montlaur** France
108 F4 **Mont-Laurier** *Que.* Can.
36 D6 **Montlhéry** France
42 D5 **Montlieu-la-Garde** France
109 H3 **Mont Louis** *Que.* Can.
43 I10 **Mont-Louis** France
39 M7 **Montlouis-sur-Loire** France
40 B4 **Montluçon** France
40 G5 **Montluel** France
105 K5 **Montmagny** *Que.* Can.
40 B4 **Montmarault** France
38 H4 **Montmartin-sur-Mer** France
37 J4 **Montmédy** France
40 I5 **Montmélian** France
40 F4 **Montmerle-sur-Saône** France
41 F7 **Montmeryran** France
41 I9 **Montmeyan** France
36 G6 **Montmirail** *Champagne-Ardenne* France
39 M5 **Montmirail** *Pays de la Loire* France
40 H2 **Montmirey-le-Château** France
42 E5 **Montmoreau-St-Cybard** France
110 G9 **Montmorenci** *IN* U.S.A.
114 L2 **Montmorency** *Que.* Can.
42 F3 **Montmorillon** France
41 H8 **Montmorin** France
40 H3 **Montmorot** France
36 G6 **Montmort-Lucy** France
66 K4 **Montnegre de Llevant** *hill* Spain
207 M8 **Monto** *Qld* Austr.
38 G7 **Montoir-de-Bretagne** France
39 M6 **Montoire-sur-le-Loir** France
36 F6 **Montois** *slope* France
41 F7 **Montoison** France
64 D3 **Montoito** Port.
43 I9 **Montolieu** France
63 R6 **Montón** Spain
71 M9 **Montone** Italy
71 M7 **Montone** *r.* Italy
73 J3 **Montopoli di Sabina** Italy
73 L2 **Montorio al Vomano** Italy
65 K4 **Montoro** Spain
65 L4 **Montoro** *r.* Spain
65 K3 **Montoro, Embalse de** *resr* Spain
43 C9 **Montory** France
118 B2 **Montour County** *county* *PA* U.S.A.
116 I6 **Montour Falls** *NY* U.S.A.
39 J8 **Montournais** France
111 R8 **Montoursville** *PA* U.S.A.
88 D5 **Mont Peko, Parc National du** *nat. park* Côte d'Ivoire
130 □ **Montpelier** Jamaica
122 I5 **Montpelier** *ID* U.S.A.
110 I9 **Montpelier** *IN* U.S.A.
116 A7 **Montpelier** *OH* U.S.A.
117 M4 **Montpelier** *VT* U.S.A.
41 D9 **Montpellier** France
41 B7 **Montpeyroux** France
43 F7 **Montpezat** France
43 F9 **Montpézat** France
43 G7 **Montpezat-de-Quercy** France
41 E7 **Montpezat-sous-Bauzon** France
42 E5 **Montpon-Ménestérol** France
40 G3 **Montpont-en-Bresse** France
39 N6 **Mont-près-Chambord** France
Montreal *Que.* Can. *see* Montréal
108 F4 **Montréal** *Que.* Can.
108 C4 **Montreal** *r.* *Ont.* Can.
108 E4 **Montreal** *r.* *Ont.* Can.
40 E1 **Montréal** *Bourgogne* France
43 I9 **Montréal** *Languedoc-Roussillon* France
43 E8 **Montréal** *Midi-Pyrénées* France
110 D3 **Montreal** *WI* U.S.A.
108 F4 **Montréal-Dorval** *airport* *Que.* Can.
110 J2 **Montreal Island** *Ont.* Can.
40 H4 **Montréal-la-Cluse** France
107 J4 **Montreal Lake** *Sask.* Can.
107 J4 **Montreal Lake** *l.* *Sask.* Can.
108 F4 **Montréal-Mirabel** *airport* *Que.* Can.
108 C4 **Montreal River** *Ont.* Can.
43 I8 **Montredon-Labessonnié** France
41 E6 **Montregard** France
43 F9 **Montréjeau** France
39 N7 **Montrésor** France
72 B7 **Montresta** *Sardegna* Italy
40 G3 **Montret** France
36 D6 **Montreuil** *Île-de-France* France
36 C3 **Montreuil** *Nord-Pas-de-Calais* France
39 K7 **Montreuil-Bellay** France
39 J6 **Montreuil-Juigné** France
70 B3 **Montreux** Switz.
39 I7 **Montrevault** France
40 G4 **Montrevel-en-Bresse** France
39 N7 **Montrichard** France
43 H7 **Montricoux** France
40 J4 **Montriond** France
41 C7 **Montrodat** France
41 B9 **Montrodre** *mt.* France
66 G5 **Mont-roig del Camp** Spain
40 H3 **Montrond** France
40 E5 **Montrond-les-Bains** France
96 E2 **Montrose** *well* S. Africa
26 L9 **Montrose** *Angus, Scotland* U.K.
123 K7 **Montrose** *CO* U.S.A.
111 K6 **Montrose** *MI* U.S.A.
119 H2 **Montrose** *NY* U.S.A.
117 J7 **Montrose** *PA* U.S.A.
116 F9 **Montrose** *WV* U.S.A.
116 I10 **Montross** *VA* U.S.A.
67 D9 **Montroy** Spain
41 B8 **Montrozier** France
42 F1 **Monts** France
36 B5 **Mont-St-Aignan** France
40 E2 **Mont-St-Jean** France
37 K4 **Mont-St-Martin** France
38 H4 **Mont-St-Michel, Baie du** *b.* France
36 G8 **Mont-St-Sulpice** France
40 E3 **Mont-St-Vincent** France
43 I6 **Montsalvy** France
88 D5 **Mont Sangbé, Parc National du** *nat. park* Côte d'Ivoire
66 G5 **Montsant** *r.* Spain
40 E2 **Montsauche-les-Settons** France
43 F9 **Montsaunès** France
66 G3 **Montsec, Serra del** *mts* Spain
43 H10 **Montségur** France
66 J4 **Montseny** Spain
66 J4 **Montseny, Parc Natural de** *nature res.* Spain
131 □2 **Montserrat** *terr.* West Indies
39 L7 **Montsoreau** France
43 C8 **Montsoué** France
40 H3 **Mont-sous-Vaudrey** France
39 L8 **Monts-sur-Guesnes** France
Mont St-Michel *tourist site* France *see* **Le Mont-St-Michel**
39 J5 **Montsûrs** France
36 H7 **Montsuzain** France
67 K8 **Montuïri** Spain
126 □R14 **Montuosa, Isla** *i.* Panama
65 J6 **Monturque** Spain
116 F11 **Montvale** *VA* U.S.A.
43 H6 **Montvalent** France
109 G2 **Montviel, Lac** *l.* *Que.* Can.
36 B4 **Montville** France
119 K2 **Montville** *CT* U.S.A.
45 I7 **Montzen** Belgium
37 J5 **Montzéville** France
121 D9 **Monument Draw** *watercourse* *NM/TX* U.S.A.
125 V5 **Monument Valley** *reg.* *AZ* U.S.A.
90 D4 **Monveda** Dem. Rep. Congo
97 K3 **Monyakeng** S. Africa
158 B3 **Monywa** Myanmar
70 G4 **Monza** Italy
91 E9 **Monze** Zambia
Monze, Cape *pt* Pak. *see* Muari, Ras
52 C2 **Monzelfeld** Ger.
166 E1 **Monzen** Japan
184 F2 **Monzhukly** Turkm.
52 D2 **Monzingen** Ger.
138 A2 **Monzón** Peru
66 F4 **Monzón** Spain
63 L4 **Monzón de Campos** Spain
119 K1 **Moodus** *CT* U.S.A.
119 K1 **Moodus Reservoir** *CT* U.S.A.
97 O4 **Mooi** *r.* *KwaZulu-Natal* S. Africa
97 K2 **Mooi** *r.* *North West* S. Africa
97 O5 **Mooirivier** S. Africa
44 I5 **Mook** Neth.
94 E4 **Mookane** Botswana
204 G3 **Moolawatana** *S.A.* Austr.
204 H3 **Moomba** *S.A.* Austr.
205 L3 **Moomin Creek** *r.* *N.S.W.* Austr.
206 G7 **Moonah Creek** *watercourse* *Qld* Austr.
204 E4 **Moonaree** *S.A.* Austr.
205 M4 **Moonbi Range** *mts* *N.S.W.* Austr.
27 H8 **Mooncoin** Rep. of Ireland
206 H8 **Moonda Lake** *salt flat* *Qld* Austr.
27 I7 **Moone** Rep. of Ireland
207 M9 **Moonie** *Qld* Austr.
205 L3 **Moonie** *r.* *N.S.W./Qld* Austr.
204 F6 **Moonta** *S.A.* Austr.
209 D11 **Moora** *W.A.* Austr.
207 H8 **Mooraberree** *Qld* Austr.
51 E10 **Moorbad Lobenstein** Ger.
122 L4 **Moorcroft** *WY* U.S.A.
97 M6 **Moordenaarsnek** *pass* S. Africa
48 D4 **Moordorf (Südbrookmerland)** Ger.
44 G5 **Moordrecht** Neth.
209 C11 **Moore** *r.* *W.A.* Austr.
122 J3 **Moore** *MT* U.S.A.
209 D10 **Moore, Lake** *salt flat* *W.A.* Austr.
201 □3a **Moorea** *i.* Fr. Polynesia
213 K1 **Moore Embayment** *b.* Antarctica
116 G9 **Moorefield** *WV* U.S.A.
115 G12 **Moore Haven** *FL* U.S.A.
29 P6 **Moorends** *South Yorkshire, England* U.K.
53 K5 **Moorenweis** Ger.
207 L4 **Moore Reef** *Coral Sea Is Terr.* Austr.
117 N4 **Moore Reservoir** *NH/VT* U.S.A.
209 C11 **Moore River National Park** *W.A.* Austr.
147 F4 **Moores** Arg.
118 B3 **Mooresburg** *PA* U.S.A.
130 E1 **Moores Island** Bahamas
117 □R3 **Moores Mills** *N.B.* Can.
118 F5 **Moorestown** *NJ* U.S.A.
130 □ **Moore Town** Jamaica
28 E4 **Moorfields** *Northern Ireland* U.K.
26 J11 **Moorfoot Hills** *Scotland* U.K.
120 G2 **Moorhead** *MN* U.S.A.
205 I5 **Moornanyah Lake** *imp. l.* *N.S.W.* Austr.
204 H6 **Moorook** *S.A.* Austr.
206 E1 **Mooroongga Island** *N.T.* Austr.
205 J7 **Mooroopna** *Vic.* Austr.
124 N7 **Moorpark** *CA* U.S.A.
96 C9 **Moorreesburg** S. Africa
207 J6 **Moorrinya National Park** *Qld* Austr.
45 D7 **Moorslede** Belgium
48 E3 **Moorweg** Ger.
52 F6 **Moos** *Baden-Württemberg* Ger.
53 N4 **Moos** *Bayern* Ger.
53 M2 **Moosbach** Ger.
59 J6 **Moosburg** Austria
53 L5 **Moosburg an der Isar** Ger.
108 D3 **Moose** *r.* *Ont.* Can.
108 D3 **Moose Factory** *Ont.* Can.
117 □P3 **Moosehead Lake** *ME* U.S.A.
107 J5 **Moose Jaw** *Sask.* Can.
107 J5 **Moose Jaw** *r.* *Sask.* Can.
110 B3 **Moose Lake** *MN* U.S.A.
117 □O4 **Mooselookmeguntic Lake** *ME* U.S.A.
107 K5 **Moose Mountain Creek** *r.* *Sask.* Can.
58 G5 **Mooserboden, Stausee** *resr* Austria
108 D3 **Moose River** *Ont.* Can.
117 N4 **Moosilauke, Mount** *NH* U.S.A.
53 L5 **Moosinning** Ger.
59 L6 **Mooskirchen** Austria
107 K5 **Moosomin** *Sask.* Can.
108 D3 **Moosonee** *Ont.* Can.
53 N4 **Moosthenning** Ger.
205 I4 **Mootwingee National Park** *N.S.W.* Austr.
95 F4 **Mopane** S. Africa
95 G3 **Mopeia** Moz.
Mopelia *atoll* *Arch. de la Société* Fr. Polynesia *see* Maupihaa
94 E4 **Mopipi** Botswana
88 D3 **Mopti** Mali
88 E3 **Mopti** *admin. reg.* Mali
92 B1 **Moqatta** Sudan
185 L5 **Moqor** Afgh.

Moquegua to Møysalen
306

138 C4 Moquegua Peru
138 C4 Moquegua dept Peru
147 H4 Moquehuá Arg.
57 H4 Mór Hungary
89 I4 Mora Cameroon
64 C3 Mora Port.
63 M9 Mora Spain
21 M6 Mora Sweden
110 A4 Mora MN U.S.A.
123 L9 Mora NM U.S.A.
123 L9 Mora r. NM U.S.A.
146 B4 Mora, Cerro mt. Arg./Chile
76 H8 Morača r. Serb. and Mont.
18 K9 Morach r. Belarus
185 L7 Morad r. Pak.
178 G5 Moradabad Uttar Prad. India
138 C1 Morada Nova Amazonas Brazil
140 F3 Morada Nova Ceará Brazil
143 E3 Morada Nova de Minas Brazil
66 G5 Móra d'Ebre Spain
67 D7 Mora de Rubielos Spain
63 M5 Moradillo de Roa Spain
191 J6 Morādlū Iran
95 □J3 Morafenobe Madag.
55 H2 Morąg Pol.
57 I5 Mórahalom Hungary
107 J1 Moraine Lake N.W.T. Can.
67 F10 Moraira, Punta de pt Spain
62 G5 Morais Port.
66 G5 Móra la Nova Spain
65 L3 Moral de Calatrava Spain
145 B7 Moraleda, Canal sea chan. Chile
65 L6 Moraleda de Zafayona Spain
62 G8 Moraleja Spain
62 I6 Moraleja del Vino Spain
62 I6 Moraleja de Sayago Spain
126 □O10 Morales Guat.
65 O7 Morales r. Spain
62 I6 Morales del Vino Spain
63 J5 Morales de Toro Spain
62 I5 Morales de Valverde Spain
62 H6 Moralina Spain
176 E4 Moram Mahar. India
95 □K3 Moramanga Madag.
110 J4 Moran MI U.S.A.
122 I5 Moran WY U.S.A.
207 L6 Moranbah Qld Austr.
178 G4 Morang Hima. Prad. India
142 A3 Morangas Brazil
179 O6 Moranhat Assam India
191 J6 Moranlı Azer.
73 Q8 Morano Calabro Italy
70 E5 Morano sul Po Italy
130 □ Morant Bay Jamaica
130 F5 Morant Cays is Jamaica
130 □ Morant Point Jamaica
176 F6 Morappur Tamil Nadu India
26 E9 Morar Highland, Scotland U.K.
26 E9 Morar hills Scotland U.K.
26 E9 Morar, Loch l. Scotland U.K.
178 G3 Morari, Tso l. Jammu and Kashmir
22 I5 Mörarp Sweden
62 F1 Morás, Punta de pt Spain
62 H7 Morasverdes Spain
63 R6 Morata de Jalón Spain
63 N8 Morata de Tajuña Spain
65 P4 Moratalla Spain
176 F9 Moratuwa Sri Lanka
Morava reg. Czech Rep. see Moravia
59 O3 Morava r. Europe alt. March (Austria)
71 R4 Morava Slovenia
59 O1 Moravany Czech Rep.
57 K3 Moravany Slovakia
95 □K2 Moravato Madag.
59 K8 Moravče Slovenia
184 F3 Moraveh Tappeh Iran
56 G2 Moravia reg. Czech Rep.
116 I6 Moravia NY U.S.A.
76 I7 Moravica r. Serb. and Mont.
77 J7 Moravica r. Serb. and Mont.
57 G2 Moravice r. Czech Rep.
57 H2 Morávka Czech Rep.
56 E3 Moravská Dyje r. Czech Rep.
59 P2 Moravská Nová Ves Czech Rep.
56 F2 Moravská Třebová Czech Rep.
56 E2 Moravské Budějovice Czech Rep.
57 H2 Moravskoslezské Beskydy mts Czech Rep.
57 H2 Moravskoslezský kraj admin. reg. Czech Rep.
56 G2 Moravský Beroun Czech Rep.
Moravský Ján Slovakia see Moravský Svätý Ján
56 F2 Moravský Kras park Czech Rep.
59 N1 Moravský Krumlov Czech Rep.
56 G3 Moravský Písek Czech Rep.
56 G3 Moravský Svätý Ján Slovakia
209 C10 Morawa W.A. Austr.
137 G2 Morawhanna Guyana
55 I5 Morawica Pol.
26 J7 Moray admin. div. Scotland U.K.
207 K6 Moray Downs Qld Austr.
26 H7 Moray Firth b. Scotland U.K.
206 C3 Moray Range hills N.T. Austr.
52 C2 Morbach Ger.
70 H3 Morbegno Italy
178 C8 Morbi Gujarat India
40 I3 Morbier France
38 F6 Morbihan dept France
59 O4 Mörbisch am See Austria
23 M5 Mörbylånga Öland Sweden
43 C7 Morcenx France
75 O4 Morciano di Leuca Italy
71 N8 Morciano di Romagna Italy
128 C1 Morcillo Mex.
73 N5 Morcone Italy
162 B3 Mordaga Nei Mongol China
189 L5 Mor Dağı mt. Turkey
38 H5 Mordelles France
107 L5 Morden Man. Can.
79 H4 Mordoğan Turkey
Mordovia aut. rep. Rus. Fed. see Mordoviya, Respublika
15 I5 Mordoviya, Respublika aut. rep. Rus. Fed.
15 H5 Mordoviya Zapovednik nature res. Rus. Fed.
15 H5 Mordovo Rus. Fed.
Mordovskaya A.S.S.R. aut. rep. Rus. Fed. see Mordoviya, Respublika
19 V7 Mordves Rus. Fed.
Mordvinia aut. rep. Rus. Fed. see Mordoviya, Respublika
17 O7 Mordvynivka Ukr.
55 K3 Mordy Pol.
26 G6 More, Loch l. Highland, Scotland U.K.
26 I6 More, Loch l. Highland, Scotland U.K.
38 F6 Moréac France
64 D5 Moreanes Port.
120 E3 Moreau r. SD U.S.A.
120 D3 Moreau, South Fork r. SD U.S.A.
26 L11 Morebattle Scottish Borders, Scotland U.K.
29 L5 Morecambe Lancashire, England U.K.
29 K5 Morecambe Bay England U.K.
62 I2 Moreda Spain
63 P3 Moreda de Álava Spain
205 L3 Moree N.S.W. Austr.
36 B8 Morée France
153 J8 Morehead P.N.G.
116 B10 Morehead KY U.S.A.
115 I8 Morehead City NC U.S.A.
137 F5 Moreira Brazil
62 D6 Moreira do Rei Port.
178 F6 Morel r. India
70 E3 Mörel Switz.
136 C4 Morelia Col.
128 F6 Morelia Mex.
207 I7 Morella Qld Austr.
66 E6 Morella Spain
74 G9 Morello r. Sicilia Italy
128 E3 Morelos Mex.
129 I7 Morelos state Mex.
129 J7 Morelos Cañada Mex.
94 D3 Moremi Wildlife Reserve nature res. Botswana
178 G6 Morena Madh. Prad. India
64 G5 Morena, Sierra mts Spain
125 W8 Morenci AZ U.S.A.
111 J8 Morenci MI U.S.A.
77 N6 Moreni Romania
147 H4 Moreno Arg.
126 D3 Moreno Mex.
124 O8 Moreno Valley CA U.S.A.
63 P3 Morentín Spain
20 I5 Møre og Romsdal county Norway
139 F2 Morerú r. Brazil
62 I5 Moreruela de Tábara Spain
72 B6 Mores Sardegna Italy
104 E4 Moresby, Mount B.C. Can.
106 C4 Moresby Island B.C. Can.
29 J4 Moresby Parks Cumbria, England U.K.
40 G5 Morestel France
207 N9 Moreton Bay Qld Austr.
30 E6 Moretonhampstead Devon, England U.K.
31 I4 Moreton-in-Marsh Gloucestershire, England U.K.
207 N9 Moreton Island Qld Austr.
30 G2 Moreton Say Shropshire, England U.K.
36 E7 Moret-sur-Loing France
70 D6 Moretta Italy
36 D4 Moreuil France
14 L1 Moreyu r. Rus. Fed.
40 I3 Morez France
30 C2 Morfa Nefyn Gwynedd, Wales U.K.
70 H6 Morfasso Italy
52 F2 Mörfelden Ger.
78 C2 Morfi Greece
190 A3 Morfou Cyprus
190 A3 Morfou Bay Cyprus
20 R2 Morgam-Viibus hill Fin.
204 G6 Morgan S.A. Austr.
115 E10 Morgan GA U.S.A.
116 A10 Morgan KY U.S.A.
124 N4 Morgan, Mount CA U.S.A.
121 J11 Morgan City LA U.S.A.
114 D7 Morganfield KY U.S.A.
124 K4 Morgan Hill CA U.S.A.
115 G8 Morganton NC U.S.A.
114 D7 Morgantown KY U.S.A.
118 D4 Morgantown PA U.S.A.
116 F9 Morgantown WV U.S.A.
119 G4 Morganville NJ U.S.A.
38 B5 Morgat France
64 B5 Morgavel, Barragem de resr Port.
97 N2 Morgenzon S. Africa
70 B2 Morges Switz.
70 C4 Morgex Italy
184 E6 Morghāb Iran
37 M6 Morhange France
179 J7 Morhar r. India
168 B5 Mori Xinjiang China
71 J4 Mori Italy
164 R4 Mori Hokkaidō Japan
167 G6 Mori Shizuoka Japan
131 □5 Moriah Trin. and Tob.
125 R2 Moriah, Mount NV U.S.A.
123 L9 Moriarty NM U.S.A.
205 J3 Moriarty's Range hills Qld Austr.
88 C4 Moribaya Guinea
29 K4 Moricambe b. England U.K.
106 E4 Morice Lake B.C. Can.
106 E4 Moricetown B.C. Can.
185 O3 Morich Pak.
136 D4 Morichal Col.
119 J3 Moriches Bay NY U.S.A.
73 J3 Moricone Italy
18 F4 Moricsalas rezervāts nature res. Latvia
36 E5 Morienval France
179 N6 Morigaon Assam India
166 C6 Moriguchi Japan
97 L5 Morija Lesotho
89 G3 Moriki Nigeria
65 J6 Moriles Spain
Morin Dawa Nei Mongol China see Nirji
68 G4 Morine pass Bos.-Herz.
49 I7 Moringen Ger.
73 K4 Morino Italy
19 N4 Morino Rus. Fed.
164 S7 Morioka Japan
95 G3 Morire Moz.
126 E3 Moris Mex.
77 O3 Morişca r. Romania
205 M5 Morisset N.S.W. Austr.
26 G8 Moriston r. Scotland U.K.
129 H3 Morita Mex.
51 I8 Moritzburg Ger.
167 K4 Moriya Japan
166 D5 Moriyama Japan
164 R6 Moriyoshi Japan
164 R7 Moriyoshi-zan vol. Japan
20 Q3 Morjärv Sweden
185 J7 Morjen r. Pak.
14 J4 Morki Rus. Fed.
19 T4 Morkiny Gory Rus. Fed.
43 D9 Morlaàs France
38 D4 Morlaix France
38 D4 Morlaix, Baie de b. France
43 C8 Morlanne France
45 F8 Morlanwelz Belgium
52 F2 Mörlenbach Ger.
106 H5 Morley Alta Can.
37 J6 Morley France
29 N6 Morley West Yorkshire, England U.K.
18 M9 Mormal' Belarus
73 Q8 Mormanno Italy
36 E6 Mormant France
41 G8 Mormoiron France
125 U7 Mormon Lake AZ U.S.A.
Mormugao Goa India see Marmagao
40 E5 Mornand France
40 F5 Mornant France
41 F8 Mornas France
131 □2 Morne-à-l'Eau Guadeloupe
131 □2 Morne Constant hill Guadeloupe
131 □ Morne Diablotin National Park Dominica
131 □2 Morne Diablotins vol. Dominica
131 □2 Morne Macaque vol. Dominica
70 F6 Mornese Italy
99 □2b Morne Seychellois hill Mahé Seychelles
131 □2 Morne Trois Pitons National Park Dominica
207 H8 Morney Qld Austr.
207 H8 Morney watercourse Qld Austr.
145 B8 Mornington, Isla i. Chile
214 D9 Mornington Abyssal Plain sea feature S. Atlantic Ocean
206 G4 Mornington Island Qld Austr.
205 J8 Mornington Peninsula National Park Vic. Austr.
78 C4 Mornos r. Greece
53 K4 Mörnsheim Ger.
185 L8 Moro Pak.
122 D4 Moro OR U.S.A.
63 P9 Moro, Cerro mts Spain
153 K8 Morobe P.N.G.
86 D3 Morocco country Africa
110 G9 Morocco IN U.S.A.
16 E2 Morochne Ukr.
121 I9 Moro Creek r. AR U.S.A.
93 C6 Morogoro Tanz.
93 C7 Morogoro admin. reg. Tanz.
154 D8 Moro Gulf Phil.
97 K5 Morojaneng S. Africa
96 H2 Morokweng S. Africa
128 F5 Moroleón Mex.
73 K4 Morolo Italy
155 D7 Moromaho i. Indon.
95 □I4 Morombe Madag.
138 D4 Moromoro Bol.
145 E6 Morón Arg.
130 D2 Morón Cuba
129 J3 Morón Mex.
168 G2 Mörön Mongolia
70 C1 Moron mt. Switz.
131 I8 Morón Venez.
136 B5 Morona Ecuador
136 B6 Morona r. Peru
136 B5 Morona-Santiago prov. Ecuador
95 □J4 Morondava Madag.
63 P6 Morón de Almazán Spain
65 I6 Morón de la Frontera Spain
88 D4 Morondo Côte d'Ivoire
128 D4 Morone, Sierra mts Mex.
124 P7 Morongo Valley CA U.S.A.
99 □3a Moroni Njazidja Comoros
125 U2 Moroni UT U.S.A.
63 Q6 Moros Spain
63 L6 Moros r. Spain
72 C3 Morosaglia Corse France
155 F2 Morotai i. Maluku Indon.
155 E2 Morotai, Selat sea chan. Maluku Indon.
92 B4 Moroto Uganda
92 B4 Moroto, Mount Uganda
165 I14 Morotsuka Japan
76 H5 Morović Vojvodina, Srbija Serb. and Mont.
131 □1 Morovis Puerto Rico
203 B12 Morowai South I. N.Z.
155 B4 Morowali Reserve nature res. Indon.
19 N2 Morozova Rus. Fed.
17 S3 Morozovka Rus. Fed.
19 X5 Morozovo Rus. Fed.
15 H6 Morozovsk Rus. Fed.
70 D7 Morozzo Italy
140 E4 Morpara Brazil
111 M7 Morpeth Ont. Can.
29 N3 Morpeth Northumberland, England U.K.
Morphou Cyprus see Morfou
52 G2 Morre r. Ger.
142 C6 Morretes Brazil
116 A11 Morrill KY U.S.A.
120 D4 Morrill NE U.S.A.
121 I8 Morrilton AR U.S.A.
106 H5 Morrin Alta Can.
142 C2 Morrinhos Brazil
202 J4 Morrinsville North I. N.Z.
107 L5 Morris Man. Can.
110 F8 Morris IL U.S.A.
120 H3 Morris MN U.S.A.
111 Q8 Morris PA U.S.A.
117 J4 Morrisburg Ont. Can.
118 F3 Morris County county NJ U.S.A.
105 O1 Morris Jesup, Kap c. Greenland
147 F3 Morrison Arg.
110 E8 Morrison IL U.S.A.
203 E12 Morrisons South I. N.Z.
119 G3 Morris Plains NJ U.S.A.
118 B1 Morris Run PA U.S.A.
30 E4 Morriston Swansea, Wales U.K.
125 T8 Morristown AZ U.S.A.
119 G3 Morristown NJ U.S.A.
117 J4 Morristown NY U.S.A.
115 F7 Morristown TN U.S.A.
117 J6 Morrisville NY U.S.A.
118 F4 Morrisville PA U.S.A.
117 M4 Morrisville VT U.S.A.
207 H4 Morr Morr Aboriginal Holding res. Qld Austr.
143 E2 Morro Brazil
72 D5 Morro, Monte hill Italy
144 C2 Morro, Punta pt Chile
142 C4 Morro Agudo Brazil
124 L6 Morro Bay CA U.S.A.
143 H3 Morro d'Anta Brazil
65 J3 Morro del Águila hill Spain
128 F8 Morro de Papanoa hd Mex.
128 F8 Morro de Petatlán hd Mex.
140 E4 Morro do Chapéu Brazil
143 G4 Morro do Coco Brazil
139 G2 Morro do Sinal hills Brazil
129 L9 Morro Mazatán Mex.
73 L3 Morrone, Monte mt. Italy
140 D2 Morros Brazil
136 C2 Morrosquillo, Golfo de b. Col.
71 P9 Morrovalle Italy
95 G3 Morrumbala Moz.
95 G4 Morrumbene Moz.
22 E5 Mors reg. Denmark
49 E9 Morsbach Ger.
52 F2 Morsberg hill Ger.
49 I8 Morschen Ger.
107 J5 Morse Sask. Can.
121 E7 Morse TX U.S.A.
110 D3 Morse WI U.S.A.
213 I2 Morse, Cape Antarctica
15 H5 Morshanka Rus. Fed.
Morshansk Rus. Fed. see Morshanka
16 C4 Morshyn Ukr.
178 G9 Morsi Mahar. India
191 I1 Morskaya Chapura, Ostrov i. Rus. Fed.
14 F3 Morskaya Masel'ga Rus. Fed.
17 N9 Mors'ke Ukr.
51 D6 Morsleben Ger.
48 H5 Morsum Ger.
20 M3 Mørsvikbotn Norway
206 H7 Mort watercourse Qld Austr.
107 I2 Mort, Lac du l. N.W.T. Can.
37 L6 Mortagne r. France
39 M4 Mortagne-au-Perche France
42 C5 Mortagne-sur-Gironde France
42 C1 Mortagne-sur-Sèvre France
62 D8 Mortágua Port.
39 J4 Mortain France
70 F5 Mortara Italy
40 H2 Morte r. France
40 J2 Morteau France
39 K4 Morteaux-Coulibœuf France
30 D5 Morte Bay England U.K.
36 E5 Mortefontaine France
71 O4 Mortegliano Italy
30 D5 Mortehoe Devon, England U.K.
75 J7 Mortelle Sicilia Italy
147 G2 Morteros Arg.
128 E1 Morteros Mex.
143 E4 Mortes, Rio das r. Brazil
140 C4 Mortes, Rio das r. Brazil
97 J8 Mortimer S. Africa
31 J5 Mortimer West Berkshire, England U.K.
130 F2 Mortimer's Long I. Bahamas
30 G3 Mortimer's Cross Herefordshire, England U.K.
107 J5 Mortlach Sask. Can.
205 I8 Mortlake Vic. Austr.
216 F5 Mortlock Islands Micronesia
31 L2 Morton Lincolnshire, England U.K.
29 P7 Morton Lincolnshire, England U.K.
110 E9 Morton IL U.S.A.
121 D9 Morton TX U.S.A.
122 C3 Morton WA U.S.A.
205 M6 Morton National Park N.S.W. Austr.
72 D5 Mortorio, Isola i. Sardegna Italy
39 L4 Mortrée France
58 G6 Mörtschach Austria
45 F6 Mortsel Belgium
131 □7 Moruga Trin. and Tob.
131 □7 Moruga Point Trin. and Tob.
205 K6 Morundah N.S.W. Austr.
92 B4 Morungole mt. Uganda
95 E4 Morupule Botswana
Moruroa atoll Arch. des Tuamotu Fr. Polynesia see Mururoa
205 M6 Moruya N.S.W. Austr.
40 D2 Morvan hills France
40 E2 Morvan, Parc Naturel Régional du nature res. France
207 K9 Morven Qld Austr.
203 F11 Morven South I. N.Z.
26 J8 Morven hill Aberdeenshire, Scotland U.K.
26 I6 Morven hill Highland, Scotland U.K.
26 E9 Morvern reg. Scotland U.K.
Morvi Gujarat India see Morbi
30 H2 Morville Shropshire, England U.K.
178 C7 Morwara Gujarat India
205 K8 Morwell Vic. Austr.
30 C6 Morwenstow Cornwall, England U.K.
19 O1 Mor'ye Rus. Fed.
54 C3 Moryń Pol.
54 G2 Morzeszczyn Pol.
14 H2 Morzhovets, Ostrov i. Rus. Fed.
40 J4 Morzine France
19 R7 Mosal'sk Rus. Fed.
16 G5 Moşana Moldova
52 G3 Mosbach Ger.
29 O7 Mosborough South Yorkshire, England U.K.
122 K3 Mosby MT U.S.A.
67 I9 Moscarter, Punta des pt Spain
64 A3 Moscavide Port.
71 Q5 Mošćenička Draga Croatia
71 L8 Moscia r. Italy
73 L2 Mosciano Sant'Angelo Italy
Moscow Rus. Fed. see Moskva
122 F3 Moscow ID U.S.A.
118 D2 Moscow PA U.S.A.
Moscow Oblast admin. div. Rus. Fed. see Moskovskaya Oblast'
213 I2 Moscow University Ice Shelf Antarctica
51 F9 Mosel Ger.
49 E10 Mosel r. Ger.
94 D5 Moselebe watercourse Botswana
116 H11 Moseley VA U.S.A.
37 M5 Moselle dept France
37 L5 Moselle r. France
51 E6 Möser Ger.
124 O1 Moses, Mount NV U.S.A.
122 E3 Moses Lake WA U.S.A.
94 E4 Mosetse Botswana
14 I2 Moseyevo Rus. Fed.
203 E12 Mosgiel South I. N.Z.
116 G7 Moshannon PA U.S.A.
96 G2 Moshaweng watercourse S. Africa
18 K2 Moshchnyy, Ostrov i. Rus. Fed.
19 R3 Moshenskoye Rus. Fed.
111 J1 Mosher Ont. Can.
184 F7 Moshgān Iran
89 G4 Moshi r. Nigeria
93 C5 Moshi Tanz.
17 K4 Moshny Ukr.
14 K2 Mosh'yuga Rus. Fed.
54 E3 Mosina Pol.
110 E5 Mosinee WI U.S.A.
97 I2 Mosita S. Africa
20 L4 Mosjøen Norway
162 M2 Moskal'vo Sakhalin Rus. Fed.
20 P2 Moskángáisi mt. Norway
20 L3 Moskenesøy i. Norway
20 L3 Moskenestraumen sea chan. Norway
55 H5 Moskorzew Pol.
20 O4 Moskosel Sweden
19 V6 Moskovskaya Oblast' admin. div. Rus. Fed.
17 S2 Moskovskoye Rus. Fed.
19 U6 Moskva Rus. Fed.
19 V6 Moskva r. Rus. Fed.
185 M3 Moskva Tajik.
19 U5 Moskvy, Kanal imeni canal Rus. Fed.
57 G6 Moslavna Podravska Croatia
146 D3 Mosmota Arg.
77 P4 Moşna Romania
57 K6 Moşniţa Nouă Romania
200 □5 Moso i. Vanuatu
71 K2 Moso in Passiria Italy
56 G4 Mosonmagyaróvár Hungary
68 F4 Mosor mts Croatia
57 H3 Mošovce Slovakia
17 P4 Mos'panove Ukr.
17 R6 Mospyne Ukr.
136 B4 Mosquera Col.
123 L9 Mosquero NM U.S.A.
67 E7 Mosqueruela Spain
126 □R10 Mosquitia reg. Hond.
131 □1 Mosquito Puerto Rico
116 E7 Mosquito Creek Lake OH U.S.A.
107 K2 Mosquito Lake N.W.T. Can.
22 G2 Moss Norway
90 C5 Mossaka Congo
Mossâmedes Angola see Namibe
142 B2 Mossâmedes Brazil
26 K8 Mossat Aberdeenshire, Scotland U.K.
203 C12 Mossburn South I. N.Z.
Mosselbaai S. Africa see Mossel Bay
96 G10 Mossel Bay S. Africa
96 G10 Mossel Bay b. S. Africa
91 B5 Mossendjo Congo
43 I10 Mosset France
205 J5 Mossgiel N.S.W. Austr.
97 N1 Mossiesdal S. Africa
52 G5 Mössingen Ger.
28 F4 Mossley Northern Ireland U.K.
207 J4 Mossman Qld Austr.
22 F5 Mossø l. Denmark
140 F3 Mossoró Brazil
27 J2 Moss-side Northern Ireland U.K.
26 J7 Mosstodloch Moray, Scotland U.K.
95 I2 Mossuril Moz.
205 M6 Moss Vale N.S.W. Austr.
107 K4 Mossy r. Sask. Can.
77 N9 Most Bulg.
56 C1 Most Czech Rep.
75 □ Mosta Malta
184 F5 Moştafaabad Iran
87 F2 Mostaganem Alg.
68 F4 Mostar Bos.-Herz.
141 C9 Mostardas Brazil
64 D5 Mosteiro Beja Port.
62 E9 Mosteiro Castelo Branco Port.
62 F2 Mosteiro Galicia Spain
98 □1b Mosteiros São Miguel Azores
77 N6 Moşteni Romania
77 O6 Mostiştea r. Romania
55 I2 Mostkowo Warmińsko-Mazurskie Pol.
54 D3 Mostkowo Zachodniopomorskie Pol.
59 I7 Most na Soči Slovenia
63 M8 Móstoles Spain
107 I4 Mostoos Hills Sask. Can.
16 J6 Mostove Ukr.
191 B1 Mostovskoy Rus. Fed.
55 J3 Mostówka Pol.
Mosty Belarus see Masty
55 L4 Mosty Pol.
157 M2 Mostyn Sabah Malaysia
16 C4 Mostys'ka Ukr.
55 L6 Mostys'ka Druha Ukr.
94 E4 Mosu Botswana
Mosul Iraq see Al Mawşil
172 H4 Mosuowan Xinjiang China
22 E2 Møsvatn Austfjell park Norway
22 E2 Møsvatnet l. Norway
20 K5 Mosvik Norway
55 M4 Mosyr Ukr.
55 H4 Moszczenica Pol.
92 C2 Mot'a Eth.
200 □5 Mota i. Vanuatu
90 C4 Motaba r. Congo
65 N2 Mota del Cuervo Spain
63 J5 Mota del Marqués Spain
127 O10 Motagua r. Guat.
170 B6 Motai Myanmar
16 E1 Motal' Belarus
23 L3 Motala Sweden
200 □5 Mota Lava i. Vanuatu
54 F1 Motarzyno Pol.
95 G5 Motaze Moz.
77 O3 Moţca Romania
167 L2 Motegi Japan
90 C4 Motenge-Boma Dem. Rep. Congo
97 M4 Moteng Pass Lesotho
95 F5 Motetema S. Africa
178 G7 Moth Uttar Prad. India
26 I11 Motherwell North Lanarkshire, Scotland U.K.
96 H3 Mothibistat S. Africa
78 E6 Mothonaio, Akra pt Kythira Greece
155 E3 Moti i. Maluku Indon.
163 C8 Motian Ling hill Liaoning China
70 B2 Môtiers Switz.
179 J6 Motihari Bihar India
65 I3 Motilla hill Spain
63 Q9 Motilla del Palancar Spain
202 K4 Motiti Island North I. N.Z.
23 J2 Motjärnshyttan Sweden
95 F4 Motloutse r. Botswana
164 □1 Motobu Okinawa Japan
164 □1 Motobu-hantō pen. Okinawa Japan
137 E3 Motocurunya Venez.
94 D5 Motokwe Botswana
167 L4 Motono Japan
63 Q7 Motos Spain
166 E5 Motosu Japan
167 I5 Motosu-ko l. Japan
20 V2 Motovskiy Zaliv sea chan. Rus. Fed.
71 P5 Motovun Croatia
165 □3 Moto-yama hill Iō-jima Japan
164 S8 Motoyoshi Japan
127 M10 Motozintla Mex.
65 L7 Motril Spain
77 K6 Motru Romania
77 L6 Motru r. Romania
97 L1 Motshikiri S. Africa
96 I5 Motswedimosa S. Africa
120 D2 Mott ND U.S.A.
158 C6 Mottama Myanmar
158 C6 Mottama, Gulf of Myanmar
73 O4 Motta Montecorvino Italy
75 J7 Motta San Giovanni Italy
70 F5 Motta Visconti Italy
49 I10 Motten Ger.
53 J4 Möttingen Ger.
138 D7 Motto Botello Arg.
75 M2 Mottola Italy
203 H8 Motueka South I. N.Z.
203 □1 Motu Fakataga i. Tokelau
Motuhora Island North I. N.Z. see Moutohora Island
Motuiti i. Fr. Polynesia see Motu Iti
201 □3 Motu Iti i. Fr. Polynesia
203 G10 Motukarara South I. N.Z.
127 O7 Motul Mex.
203 H10 Motunau Island South I. N.Z.
201 □3 Motu One atoll Arch. de la Société Fr. Polynesia
201 □3 Motu One i. Fr. Polynesia
203 G8 Motupiko South I. N.Z.
202 G7 Motupipi South I. N.Z.
201 □1a Moturiki i. Fiji
202 H1 Motutangi North I. N.Z.
203 □3 Motutapu i. Rarotonga Cook Is
201 □2a Motutapu i. Tonga
58 C5 Mötz Austria
22 G5 Mou Denmark
90 C4 Mouali Gbangba Congo
158 G5 Mouan, Nam r. Laos
89 H6 Mouanko Cameroon
41 J9 Mouans-Sartoux France
Mouaskar Alg. see Mascara
213 L2 Moubray Bay Antarctica
109 G3 Mouchalagane r. Que. Can.
39 I8 Mouchamps France
43 E8 Mouchan France
40 H3 Mouchard France
41 C7 Mouchet, Mont mt. France
130 H3 Mouchoir Bank sea feature Turks and Caicos Is
130 H3 Mouchoir Passage Turks and Caicos Is
62 E6 Mouçós Port.
170 C6 Mouding Yunnan China
88 B2 Moudjéria Maur.
70 B2 Moudon Switz.
78 G3 Moudros Limnos Greece
90 C2 Moufa Chad
41 K9 Mougins France
88 B2 Mougri well Maur.
21 Q6 Mouhijärvi Fin.
88 E4 Mouhoun r. Africa alt. Volta Noire, conv. Black Volta
90 A5 Mouila Gabon
87 E4 Mouilah well Alg.
39 J8 Mouilleron-en-Pareds France
90 D3 Mouka C.A.R.
89 I3 Moul well Niger
205 J6 Moulamein N.S.W. Austr.
205 I6 Moulamein Creek r. N.S.W. Austr.
43 I7 Moularès France
Moulavibazar Bangl. see Moulvibazar
39 J5 Moulay France
131 □3 Moule à Chique, Cape St Lucia
91 A5 Moulèngui Binza Gabon
88 D2 Moulentâr well Mali
43 F6 Mouleydier France
92 D1 Moulhoulé Djibouti
39 L7 Mouliherne France
43 H9 Moulin-Neuf France
40 C3 Moulins France
40 D3 Moulins-Engilbert France
39 L4 Moulins-la-Marche France
43 G10 Moulis France
42 C5 Moulis-en-Médoc France
42 F3 Moulismes France
43 D9 Moulle de Jaut, Pic du mt. France
Moulmein Myanmar see Mawlamyaing
86 E2 Moulouya, Oued r. Morocco
31 L6 Moulsecoomb Brighton and Hove, England U.K.
39 K3 Moult France
31 L2 Moulton Lincolnshire, England U.K.
31 K3 Moulton Northamptonshire, England U.K.
31 M3 Moulton Suffolk, England U.K.
115 D8 Moulton AL U.S.A.
212 P1 Moulton, Mount Antarctica
117 N5 Moultonborough NH U.S.A.
115 F10 Moultrie GA U.S.A.
115 H9 Moultrie, Lake SC U.S.A.
179 M7 Moulvibazar Bangl.
90 B5 Mounana Gabon
121 K7 Mound City IL U.S.A.
120 H6 Mound City KS U.S.A.
120 H5 Mound City MO U.S.A.
120 E3 Mound City SD U.S.A.
90 C2 Moundou Chad
116 E9 Moundsville WV U.S.A.
115 D9 Moundville AL U.S.A.
90 B5 Moungoundou-Sud Congo
41 J8 Mounier, Mont mt. France
78 B4 Mounta, Akra pt Kefallonia Greece
178 D7 Mount Abu Rajasthan India
118 C4 Mount Aetna PA U.S.A.
123 K9 Mountainair NM U.S.A.
30 F4 Mountain Ash Rhondda Cynon Taff, Wales U.K.
115 D9 Mountain Brook AL U.S.A.
116 D12 Mountain City TN U.S.A.
121 I7 Mountain Grove MO U.S.A.
121 I7 Mountain Home AR U.S.A.
122 G5 Mountain Home ID U.S.A.
118 E2 Mountainhome PA U.S.A.
125 V1 Mountain Home UT U.S.A.
110 B2 Mountain Iron MN U.S.A.
116 F9 Mountain Lake Park MD U.S.A.
119 G3 Mountain Lakes NJ U.S.A.
125 Q6 Mountain Pass CA U.S.A.
118 D2 Mountain Top PA U.S.A.
121 I8 Mountain View AR U.S.A.
124 J4 Mountain View CA U.S.A.
124 □F14 Mountain View HI U.S.A.
104 B3 Mountain Village AK U.S.A.
97 J8 Mountain Zebra National Park S. Africa
118 A6 Mount Airy MD U.S.A.
116 E12 Mount Airy NC U.S.A.
208 G4 Mount Anderson Aboriginal Reserve W.A. Austr.
204 H7 Mount Arapiles-Tooan State Park nature res. Vic. Austr.
118 F3 Mount Arlington NJ U.S.A.
203 C11 Mount Aspiring National Park South I. N.Z.
106 H5 Mount Assiniboine Provincial Park B.C. Can.
209 D8 Mount Augustus W.A. Austr.
97 N6 Mount Ayliff S. Africa
120 H5 Mount Ayr IA U.S.A.
124 O7 Mount Baldy CA U.S.A.
204 G6 Mount Barker S.A. Austr.
209 D13 Mount Barker W.A. Austr.
208 H4 Mount Barnett W.A. Austr.
208 I4 Mount Barnett Aboriginal Reserve W.A. Austr.
205 K7 Mount Beauty Vic. Austr.
27 F6 Mount Bellew Rep. of Ireland
26 J11 Mountbenger Scottish Borders, Scotland U.K.
202 J7 Mount Bruce North I. N.Z.
111 M7 Mount Brydges Ont. Can.
205 K7 Mount Buffalo National Park Vic. Austr.
207 J4 Mount Carbine Qld Austr.
117 □S1 Mount Carleton Provincial Park N.B. Can.
114 D6 Mount Carmel IL U.S.A.
118 C3 Mount Carmel PA U.S.A.
116 C12 Mount Carmel TN U.S.A.
125 T4 Mount Carmel Junction UT U.S.A.
110 E7 Mount Carroll IL U.S.A.
206 D8 Mount Cavenagh N.T. Austr.
27 F3 Mountcharles Rep. of Ireland
209 D8 Mount Clere W.A. Austr.
27 D8 Mountcollins Rep. of Ireland
Mount Cook South I. N.Z. see Aoraki
203 E10 Mount Cook National Park South I. N.Z.
207 K6 Mount Coolon Qld Austr.
97 N6 Mount Currie Nature Reserve S. Africa
95 F3 Mount Darwin Zimbabwe
206 D7 Mount Denison N.T. Austr.
117 □Q4 Mount Desert Island ME U.S.A.
204 E4 Mount Eba S.A. Austr.
206 D8 Mount Ebenezer N.T. Austr.
204 H8 Mount Eccles National Park Vic. Austr.
106 C3 Mount Edgecumbe AK U.S.A.
106 D3 Mount Edziza Provincial Park B.C. Can.
121 H10 Mount Enterprise TX U.S.A.
110 I9 Mount Etna IN U.S.A.
28 C4 Mountfield Northern Ireland U.K.
205 K10 Mount Field National Park Tas. Austr.
97 M6 Mount Fletcher S. Africa
108 D5 Mount Forest Ont. Can.
209 D13 Mount Frankland National Park W.A. Austr.
97 M6 Mount Frere S. Africa
204 H7 Mount Gambier S.A. Austr.
207 J4 Mount Garnet Qld Austr.
116 C11 Mount Gay WV U.S.A.
116 C8 Mount Gilead OH U.S.A.
153 J8 Mount Hagen P.N.G.
28 C4 Mount Hamilton Northern Ireland U.K.
118 F5 Mount Holly NJ U.S.A.
118 A4 Mount Holly Springs PA U.S.A.
205 J5 Mount Hope N.S.W. Austr.
204 E6 Mount Hope S.A. Austr.
116 D11 Mount Hope WV U.S.A.
110 E6 Mount Horeb WI U.S.A.
208 H4 Mount House W.A. Austr.
207 I9 Mount Howitt Qld Austr.
203 F10 Mount Hutt South I. N.Z.
121 I8 Mount Ida AR U.S.A.
206 G6 Mount Isa Qld Austr.
116 G10 Mount Jackson VA U.S.A.
209 D8 Mount James Aboriginal Reserve W.A. Austr.
116 G7 Mount Jewett PA U.S.A.
27 H3 Mountjoy Northern Ireland U.K.
27 I3 Mountjoy Northern Ireland U.K.
118 B4 Mount Joy PA U.S.A.
205 M4 Mount Kaputar National Park N.S.W. Austr.
209 F9 Mount Keith W.A. Austr.
92 C5 Mount Kenya National Park Kenya
119 H2 Mount Kisco NY U.S.A.
207 M7 Mount Larcom Qld Austr.
116 E8 Mount Lebanon PA U.S.A.
204 G6 Mount Lofty Range mts S.A. Austr.
157 M7 Mount Lompobatang Reserve nature res. Sulawesi Indon.
111 N2 Mount MacDonald Ont. Can.
209 D10 Mount Magnet W.A. Austr.
205 I5 Mount Manara N.S.W. Austr.
209 E10 Mount Manning Nature Reserve W.A. Austr.
202 K4 Mount Maunganui North I. N.Z.
124 L1 Mount Meadows Reservoir CA U.S.A.
27 H6 Mountmellick Rep. of Ireland
207 J4 Mount Molloy Qld Austr.
97 L6 Mount Moorosi Lesotho
207 M7 Mount Morgan Qld Austr.
110 E7 Mount Morris IL U.S.A.
111 K6 Mount Morris MI U.S.A.
116 H6 Mount Morris NY U.S.A.
205 I4 Mount Murchison N.S.W. Austr.
116 E10 Mount Nebo WV U.S.A.
209 E7 Mount Newman W.A. Austr.
27 J4 Mount Norris Northern Ireland U.K.
27 H5 Mount Nugent Rep. of Ireland
116 A10 Mount Olivet KY U.S.A.
116 B9 Mount Orab OH U.S.A.
109 K4 Mount Pearl Nfld and Lab. Can.
118 D4 Mount Penn PA U.S.A.
207 M8 Mount Perry Qld Austr.
208 I5 Mount Pierre Aboriginal Reserve W.A. Austr.
203 D11 Mount Pisa South I. N.Z.
204 G6 Mount Pleasant S.A. Austr.
115 □2 Mount Pleasant New Prov. Bahamas
109 H4 Mount Pleasant P.E.I. Can.
120 J5 Mount Pleasant IA U.S.A.
110 J6 Mount Pleasant MI U.S.A.
116 F8 Mount Pleasant PA U.S.A.
115 H9 Mount Pleasant SC U.S.A.
121 H9 Mount Pleasant TX U.S.A.
125 U2 Mount Pleasant UT U.S.A.
118 A3 Mount Pleasant Mills PA U.S.A.
118 E2 Mount Pocono PA U.S.A.
118 B7 Mount Rainier MD U.S.A.
122 D3 Mount Rainier National Park WA U.S.A.
27 H6 Mountrath Rep. of Ireland
204 G5 Mount Remarkable National Park S.A. Austr.
106 G5 Mount Revelstoke National Park B.C. Can.
203 H8 Mount Richmond Forest Park nature res. South I. N.Z.
106 G4 Mount Robson Provincial Park B.C. Can.
116 D12 Mount Rogers National Recreation Area park VA U.S.A.
96 I4 Mount Rupert S. Africa
122 C3 Mount St Helens National Volcanic Monument nat. park WA U.S.A.
118 F3 Mount Salem NJ U.S.A.
206 C4 Mount Sanford N.T. Austr.
30 B7 Mount's Bay England U.K.
27 F7 Mountshannon Rep. of Ireland
122 C6 Mount Shasta CA U.S.A.
203 F10 Mount Somers South I. N.Z.
31 J2 Mountsorrel Leicestershire, England U.K.
120 J6 Mount Sterling IL U.S.A.
116 B10 Mount Sterling KY U.S.A.
116 B9 Mount Sterling OH U.S.A.
96 I9 Mount Stewart S. Africa
116 F9 Mount Storm WV U.S.A.
207 J5 Mount Surprise Qld Austr.
206 E7 Mount Swan N.T. Austr.
27 F5 Mount Talbot Rep. of Ireland
116 H8 Mount Union PA U.S.A.
117 J6 Mount Upton NY U.S.A.
209 E8 Mount Vernon W.A. Austr.
121 K10 Mount Vernon AL U.S.A.
115 F9 Mount Vernon GA U.S.A.
120 K6 Mount Vernon IL U.S.A.
114 D7 Mount Vernon IN U.S.A.
116 A11 Mount Vernon KY U.S.A.
121 I7 Mount Vernon MO U.S.A.
119 H3 Mount Vernon NY U.S.A.
116 C8 Mount Vernon OH U.S.A.
121 H9 Mount Vernon TX U.S.A.
122 C2 Mount Vernon WA U.S.A.
118 C4 Mountville PA U.S.A.
206 D7 Mount Wedge N.T. Austr.
204 E5 Mount Wedge S.A. Austr.
208 D6 Mount Welcome Aboriginal Reserve W.A. Austr.
205 L9 Mount William National Park Tas. Austr.
204 E2 Mount Willoughby S.A. Austr.
118 B4 Mount Wolf PA U.S.A.
118 B7 Mount Zion MD U.S.A.
207 L8 Moura Qld Austr.
137 F5 Moura Brazil
138 B1 Moura r. Brazil
64 E4 Moura Port.
64 E4 Mourão Port.
90 D2 Mouraya Chad
84 D5 Mourdi, Dépression du depr. Chad
88 D3 Mourdiah Mali
62 D5 Moure Port.
43 C9 Mourenx France
41 F9 Mouriès France
62 D7 Mourisca do Vouga Port.
62 D9 Mouriscas Port.
36 H5 Mourmelon-le-Grand France
28 C4 Mourne r. Northern Ireland U.K.
27 J4 Mourne Mountains hills Northern Ireland U.K.
99 □1c Mourouvin, Forêt reg. Réunion
41 I9 Mourre de Chanier mt. France
41 G9 Mourre Nègre mt. France
78 G3 Mourtzeflos, Akra pt Limnos Greece
26 □N2 Mousa i. Scotland U.K.
45 D7 Mouscron Belgium
45 D7 Mouscron dept Belgium
90 C2 Mousgougou Chad
116 C11 Mousie KY U.S.A.
41 E9 Moussac France
90 C2 Moussafoyo Chad
41 B10 Moussan France
37 N7 Moussey France
84 C5 Mousso well Chad
84 C6 Moussoro Chad
43 I9 Moussoulens France
40 C2 Moussy France
38 E4 Moustéru France
43 C7 Moustey France
41 I9 Moustiers-Ste-Marie France
91 B5 Moutamba Congo
40 I3 Mouthe France
40 G3 Mouthier-en-Bresse France
40 I2 Mouthier-Haute-Pierre France
42 E4 Mouthiers-sur-Boëme France
116 D12 Mouth of Wilson VA U.S.A.
43 J10 Mouthoumet France
70 C1 Moutier Switz.
42 I3 Moutier-d'Ahun France
40 J6 Moûtiers France
42 B3 Moutiers-les-Mauxfaits France
59 O1 Moutnice Czech Rep.
202 K4 Moutohora Island North I. N.Z.
155 B3 Moutong Sulawesi Indon.
89 I4 Moutourwa Cameroon
41 B10 Moux France
40 E2 Moux-en-Morvan France
36 D5 Mouy France
87 F4 Mouydir, Monts du plat. Alg.
91 B5 Mouyondzi Congo
78 C3 Mouzaki Greece
84 B6 Mouzarak Chad
37 J5 Mouzay France
37 J4 Mouzon France
37 K7 Mouzon r. France
126 E3 Movas Mex.
184 C6 Moveyleh Iran
77 P5 Movila Miresii Romania
77 M6 Movileni Romania
27 H2 Moville Rep. of Ireland
208 G4 Mowanjum Aboriginal Reserve W.A. Austr.
207 M9 Mowbullan, Mount Qld Austr.
18 I8 Mowchadz' Belarus
26 L9 Mowtie Aberdeenshire, Scotland U.K.
116 C9 Moxahala OH U.S.A.
130 E1 Moxey Town Andros Bahamas
91 C8 Moxico prov. Angola
117 □P3 Moxie, Lake ME U.S.A.
27 D4 Moy r. Rep. of Ireland
26 H8 Moy Highland, Scotland U.K.
27 I4 Moy Northern Ireland U.K.
98 □3f Moya Gran Canaria Canary Is
99 □3 Moya Nzwani Comoros
67 C8 Moya Castilla-La Mancha Spain
Moya Cataluña Spain see Moià
128 D4 Moyahua Mex.
92 C4 Moyale Eth.
88 B4 Moyamba Sierra Leone
27 B5 Moyard Rep. of Ireland
27 D6 Moycullen Rep. of Ireland
36 F4 Moy-de-l'Aisne France
86 D2 Moyen Atlas mts Morocco
90 C2 Moyen-Chari pref. Chad
97 L6 Moyeni Lesotho
37 M7 Moyenmoutier France
99 □2b Moyenne, Île i. Inner Islands Seychelles
88 B4 Moyenne-Guinée admin. reg. Guinea
36 C3 Moyenneville France
90 A5 Moyen-Ogooué prov. Gabon
27 I5 Moyer hill Rep. of Ireland
37 L5 Moyeuvre-Grande France
27 I4 Moygashel Northern Ireland U.K.
27 D4 Moylaw Rep. of Ireland
28 C6 Moylett Rep. of Ireland
27 E6 Moylough Rep. of Ireland
19 S8 Moylovo Rus. Fed.
27 I5 Moynalty Rep. of Ireland
Moynaq Uzbek. see Mo'ynoq
27 G5 Moyne Rep. of Ireland
182 H6 Mo'ynoq Uzbek.
91 E5 Moyo Dem. Rep. Congo
157 L9 Moyo i. Indon.
92 A4 Moyo Uganda
136 B6 Moyobamba Peru
28 D4 Moyola r. Northern Ireland U.K.
93 A6 Moyowosi r. Tanz.
20 M2 Møysalen mt. Norway

Column 1

4 C6 Moyto Chad
3 D8 Moyu Xinjiang China
2 C4 Moyum waterhole Kenya
7 I6 Moyvalley Rep. of Ireland
8 B6 Moyvore Rep. of Ireland
8 B7 Moyvoughly Rep. of Ireland
3 O5 Moyynkum Kazakh.
3 O6 Moyynkum Kazakh.
3 L4 Moyynkum, Peski des. Kazakh.
3 M5 Moyynkum, Peski des. Kazakh.
0 A2 Moyynty Kazakh.
0 C5 Mozac France
5 G6 Mozambique country Africa
5 I4 Mozambique Channel Africa
5 G6 Mozambique Ridge sea feature Indian Ocean
2 I7 Mozárbez Spain
1 F2 Mozdok Rus. Fed.
4 I3 Mozdūrān Iran
8 B11 Mozelle KY U.S.A.
2 E7 Mozelos Port.
7 P4 Mozh r. Ukr.
8 M7 Mozha r. Belarus
7 S5 Mozhayevka Rus. Fed.
1 T6 Mozhaysk Rus. Fed.
4 K4 Mozhga Rus. Fed.
4 I4 Mozhnābād Iran
0 A2 Mozhong Qinghai China
9 K7 Mozirje Slovenia
9 K7 Mozirske Planine mts Slovenia
8 B3 Mozo Myanmar
3 L6 Mozolyivka Ukr.
7 G5 Mozoncillo Spain
7 G5 Mozsgó Hungary
8 M7 Mozyr' Belarus see Mazyr
92 A4 Mozyr' Rus. Fed.
5 J1 Mpal Senegal
3 A6 Mpanda Tanz.
3 E3 Mpandamatenga Botswana
3 A7 Mpande Zambia
0 B5 Mpen Congo
7 O3 Mpemvana S. Africa
7 O5 Mpessoba Mali
7 M8 Mpetu S. Africa
3 D3 Mpigi Uganda
8 B4 Mpika Zambia
7 K8 Mpofu Game Reserve nature res. S. Africa
0 C3 Mpoko r. C.A.R.
7 O5 Mpolweni S. Africa
1 F7 Mporokoso Zambia
0 C5 Mposa S. Africa
8 A7 Mpouya Congo
3 A7 Mpui Tanz.
139 E4 Mpulungu Zambia
7 O5 Mpumalanga S. Africa
7 N2 Mpumalanga prov. S. Africa
7 C6 Mpwapwa Tanz.
5 K8 Mqabba Malta
7 M7 Mqanduli S. Africa
Mqinvartsveri mt. Georgia/Rus. Fed. see Kazbek
5 J2 Mrągowo Pol.
3 N3 Mrákov Czech Rep.
5 I5 Mrakovo Rus. Fed.
8 A4 Mrauk-U Myanmar
206 D5 Mrewa Zimbabwe see Murehwa
8 E3 Mrežnica r. Croatia
8 E3 Mrkonjić-Grad Bos.-Herz.
8 F2 Mrkopalj Croatia
4 F2 Mrocza Pol.
26 ◻O1 Mroczeń Pol.
5 I4 Mroczków Pol.
5 I3 Mroczno Pol.
4 H3 Mroga r. Pol.
5 J3 Mrozy Pol.
7 K2 Mryn Ukr.
4 H2 M'Saken Tunisia
75 K5 Msambweni Kenya
3 C6 Msata Tanz.
4 E1 Mšćice Pol.
6 D1 Mšeno Czech Rep.
8 M2 Mshinskaya Rus. Fed.
9 R4 Msta r. Rus. Fed.
9 O3 Msta r. Rus. Fed.
9 P3 Mstinskiy Most Rus. Fed.
Mstislavl' Belarus see Mstsislaw
5 H5 Mstów Pol.
9 O7 Mstsislaw Belarus
5 H5 Msunduze r. S. Africa
5 I4 Mszana Dolna Pol.
5 I4 Mszczonów Pol.
3 C6 Mtama Tanz.
1 G3 Mt'at'usheti Nakrdzali nature res. Georgia
2 B4 Mtelo Kenya
3 B6 Mtera Reservoir Tanz.
Mtoko Zimbabwe see Mutoko
7 P4 Mtonjaneni S. Africa
176 D6 Mtorashanga Zimbabwe see Mutorashanga
9 ◻3b Mtsamboro Mayotte
9 T8 Mtsensk Rus. Fed.
Mts'khet'a Georgia
3 G5 Mtubatuba S. Africa
7 P4 Mtubatuba S. Africa
52 G2 Mtukula Tanz.
3 A7 Mtunzini S. Africa
3 P7 Mtwara Tanz.
8 A4 Mu r. Myanmar
4 C6 Mu hill Port.
1 ◻2a Mu'ab, Jibāl reg. Jordan see Moab
3 C8 Muaguide Moz.
5 G2 Mualadzi Moz.
5 H3 Mualama Moz.
3 C8 Muana Brazil
1 B6 Muanda Dem. Rep. Congo
8 G4 Muang Ham Laos
8 F4 Muang Hiam Laos
8 G6 Muang Hinboun Laos
8 F5 Muang Hôngsa Laos
*0 D8 Muang Hounxianghoung Laos
8 F5 Muang Kao Laos
8 E5 Muang Khi Laos
8 G7 Muang Khong Laos
8 F5 Muang Khôngxédôn Laos
8 E5 Muang Khoua Laos
8 G5 Muang Mok Laos
8 F4 Muang Ngoy Laos
8 H6 Muang Ou Nua Laos
8 E8 Muang Pakbeng Laos
8 E6 Muang Phalan Laos
8 E6 Muang Phiang Laos
8 H6 Muang Phin Laos
8 G7 Muang Phôn-Hông Laos
8 G7 Muang Sam Sip Thai.
8 G6 Muang Songkhon Laos
8 E5 Muang Soum Laos
8 E5 Muang Souy Laos
8 E5 Muang Thadua Laos
8 F4 Muang Va Laos
8 F4 Muang Vangviang Laos
8 G6 Muang Xon Laos
3 C6 Muanza Moz.
57 K2 Muar Malaysia
57 L2 Muar r. Malaysia
57 K2 Muara Brunei
Muaraancalong Kalimantan Indon.
57 L4 Muaraatap Kalimantan Indon.
57 L4 Muarabeliti Sumatera Indon.
57 K2 Muarabulian Sumatera Indon.
56 F7 Muaradua Sumatera Indon.
56 F7 Muaraenim Sumatera Indon.
57 K5 Muarainu Kalimantan Indon.
57 L4 Muarakaman Kalimantan Indon.

Column 2

157 L4 Muara Kaman Reserve nature res. Kalimantan Indon.
156 D5 Muaralabuh Sumatera Indon.
156 E6 Muaralakitan Sumatera Indon.
157 K5 Muaralaung Kalimantan Indon.
157 L4 Muaralesan Kalimantan Indon.
95 H3 Muaramayang Kalimantan Indon.
157 L4 Muaranawai Kalimantan Indon.
156 E6 Muararupit Sumatera Indon.
156 E5 Muarasabak Kalimantan Indon.
156 C5 Muarasiberut Indon.
156 C4 Muarasipongi Sumatera Indon.
156 C4 Muarasoma Sumatera Indon.
157 M4 Muaras Reef Indon.
156 E5 Muaratebo Sumatera Indon.
156 E5 Muaratembesi Sumatera Indon.
157 K5 Muarateweh Kalimantan Indon.
Muara Tuang Sarawak Malaysia see Kota Samarahan
157 L4 Muarawahau Kalimantan Indon.
155 E4 Muari r. Maluku Indon.
185 L9 Muari, Ras pt Pak.
187 I2 Mu'ayqil, Khashm al hill Saudi Arabia
178 E4 Muazzam Punjab India
178 H5 Mubārak, Jabal mt. Jordan/Saudi Arabia
179 I6 Mubarakpur Uttar Prad. India
173 L10 Mubarraz well Saudi Arabia
189 J9 Mubende Uganda
91 F6 Mubi Nigeria
182 K8 Mubrak Uzbek.
182 K8 Mubur i. Indon.
185 M8 Mucaba, Serra mts Angola
137 G5 Mucajá Brazil
137 F4 Mucajai r. Brazil
137 F4 Mucajaí, Serra do mts Brazil
109 I1 Mucalic r. Que. Can.
95 F2 Mucanha r. Moz.
76 I7 Muçanji mt. Serb. and Mont.
208 F6 Muccan W.A. Austr.
73 K1 Muccia Italy
49 D9 Much Ger.
190 H2 Muchas r. Spain
56 F4 Muchea W.A. Austr.
52 F4 Muchelhacker Ger.
51 G7 Mühlanger Ger.
52 G5 Mühlau Austria
59 J2 Mühlberg Brandenburg Ger.
51 H8 Mühlberg Thüringen Ger.
51 F7 Mühldorf Austria
51 N5 Mühldorf am Inn Ger.
59 K5 Mühlen Austria
50 G2 Mühlen hill Ger.
50 H5 Mühlenbeck Ger.
50 D3 Mühlen-Eichsen Ger.
52 F3 Mühlhausen Baden-Württemberg Ger.
53 K3 Mühlhausen Bayern Ger.
49 J8 Mühlhausen (Thüringen) Ger.
49 G10 Mühlheim am Main Ger.
52 F5 Mühlheim an der Donau Ger.
213 A2 Mühlig-Hofmann Mountains Antarctica
52 G6 Mühltal Ger.
51 E9 Mühltroff Ger.
59 J2 Mühlviertel reg. Austria
20 H4 Muhos Fin.
53 J3 Muhr am See Ger.
95 H2 Muhradah Syria
95 H2 Muhu r. Estonia
93 B7 Muhukuru Tanz.
95 H2 Muhula Tanz.
90 E5 Muhulu Dem. Rep. Congo
92 B3 Mui Eth.
Mui Bai Bung c. Vietnam see Mui Ca Mau
159 G10 Mui Ca Mau c. Vietnam
44 H4 Muiden Neth.
158 H6 Mui Đôc pt Vietnam
36 B5 Muids France
93 C7 Muidumbe Moz.
91 D8 Muié Angola
201 ◻3a Mui Hopohoponga pt Tongatapu Tonga
167 I1 Muika Japan
155 F4 Muiljk i. Maluku Indon.
26 J7 Muineachán Rep. of Ireland see Monaghan
209 C10 Muine Bheag Rep. of Ireland
62 E5 Muirancourt Brazil
110 J7 Muir MI U.S.A.
118 B3 Muir r. PA U.S.A.
26 K9 Muir Glacier Can./U.S.A.
106 B3 Muir hill Fuerteventura Canary Is
26 J10 Muirhead Angus, Scotland U.K.
26 H11 Muirkirk East Ayrshire, Scotland U.K.
26 D6 Muirneag hill Scotland U.K.
26 K8 Muir of Fowlis Aberdeenshire, Scotland U.K.
26 H7 Muir of Ord Highland, Scotland U.K.
158 H5 Mui Ron hd Vietnam
136 B4 Muisne Ecuador
95 H2 Muite Moz.
36 G5 Muizon France
153 F3 Mujeres, Isla i. Mex.
127 P7 Mujezi Xinjiang China
173 H3 Muji r. Tajik.
91 B8 Mujimbeji Angola
51 J6 Muju S. Korea
91 E6 Mujui dos Campos Brazil
27 C5 Mujumbar Iran
91 J6 Mukacheve Ukr.
Mukacheve Ukr. see Mukacheve
157 J3 Mukacheve Ukr.
155 N6 Mukah Sarawak Malaysia
185 N6 Mukah r. Malaysia
36 E5 Mukah r. Malaysia
178 F7 Mukandgarh Rajasthan India
178 E6 Mukandwara Rajasthan India
164 S4 Mukanga Dem. Rep. Congo
164 S4 Mukawa Hokkaidō Japan
164 O4 Mu-kawa r. Japan
91 E5 Mukawwar, Geziret i. Sudan
158 D6 Mukdahan Thai.
178 E4 Mukerian Punjab India
154 ◻1 Mukeru Palau
108 ◻2 Muketei r. Ont. Can.
92 C2 Muke T'uri Eth.
55 L3 Mukhavyets Belarus
55 M3 Mukhavyets r. Belarus
162 J4 Mukhen Rus. Fed.
162 E2 Mukhino Rus. Fed.
169 K1 Mukhorshibir' Rus. Fed.
Mukhtuya Rus. Fed. see Lensk
91 F6 Mükhür Iran
209 E11 Mukinbudin W.A. Austr.
70 D1 Mukkō Japan
89 J8 Mu Ko Chang Marine National Park Thai.
159 D11 Muko-jima i. Japan
165 ◻2 Mukomuko Sumatera Indon.
156 D6 Mukono Uganda
91 D7 Mukoshi Zambia
193 N3 Mukry Turkm.
185 N9 Muksu r. Tajik. see Mughsu
20 ◻C1 Muktinath Nepal
179 H3 Muktsar Punjab India
176 F4 Mukuku Zambia
165 H13 Mukumbura Zimbabwe
186 B4 Mukumbura Zambia
182 F4 Mukur Atyrauskaya Oblast' Kazakh.
184 C2 Mukur Vostochnyy Kazakhstan Kazakh.
107 L4 Mukur r. Man. Can.
110 F7 Mukwonago WI U.S.A.
178 G9 Mul Mahar. India

Column 3

191 J5 Muğan Azer.
185 L7 Muğan r. Pak.
67 C11 Mula Spain
65 Q4 Mula r. Spain
175 D11 Mulaku atoll Maldives see Mulaku Atoll
183 R5 Mulaku Atoll Maldives
162 F6 Mulan Heilong. China
154 C6 Mulanay Luzon Phil.
93 B8 Mulanje Malawi
95 G2 Mulanje, Mount Malawi
204 F3 Mulapula, Lake salt flat S.A. Austr.
72 C6 Mulargia, Lago l. Sardegna Italy
126 Z3 Mulatos Mex.
126 ◻U13 Mula-tupo Panama
186 G2 Mulayh Saudi Arabia
190 G9 Mulayh salt pan Saudi Arabia
187 I2 Mulayh Saudi Arabia
190 B8 Mulayz, Wādī al watercourse Egypt
70 H7 Mulazzo Italy
176 F6 Mulbagal Karnataka India
31 O2 Mulbarton Norfolk, England U.K.
178 F2 Mulbekh Jammu and Kashmir
26 J7 Mulben Moray, Scotland U.K.
121 H8 Mulberry AR U.S.A.
104 C3 Mulchatna r. AK U.S.A.
146 A5 Mulchén Chile
51 H9 Mulda Ger.
51 F7 Mulde r. Ger.
51 F7 Muldenstein Ger.
93 A5 Muleba Tanz.
122 L5 Mule Creek WY U.S.A.
126 C4 Mulegé Mex.
93 B7 Mulekatembo Zambia
140 E4 Mules i. Indon.
120 B8 Muleshoe TX U.S.A.
209 I11 Mulhacén mt. Spain
125 U7 Mulhacén mt. Spain
207 M8 Mülheim Dem. Rep. Congo
178 D6 Mulhacín r. W.A. Austr.
204 E4 Mülheim S.A. Austr.
65 M6 Mulhacén mt. Spain
50 C5 Mülheim an der Ruhr Ger.
49 D10 Mülheim-Kärlich Ger.
37 N8 Mulhouse France
170 C5 Muli Sichuan China
200 ◻2 Mulifanua Samoa
175 ◻2 Mulikatu i. Addu Atoll Maldives
90 F4 Mulila Gujarat India
93 B7 Mulilansolo Zambia
162 G6 Muling Heilong. China
162 G6 Muling Heilong. China
111 K6 Muling r. Heilong. China
162 H6 Muling He r. China
200 ◻3 Muitiapuili, Cape Samoa
59 K8 Muljava Slovenia
26 E10 Mull i. Scotland U.K.
26 D9 Mull, Sound of sea chan. Scotland U.K.
184 C5 Mulla Ali Iran
92 E2 Mulaaxe Boyle Somalia
28 D6 Mullagh Cavan Rep. of Ireland
27 D7 Mullagh Clare Rep. of Ireland
27 I6 Mullagh Mayo Rep. of Ireland
27 D8 Mullaghareirk hill Rep. of Ireland
27 D8 Mullaghareirk Mountains hills Rep. of Ireland
27 H3 Mullaghcarn hill Northern Ireland U.K.
27 J6 Mullaghcleevaun hill Rep. of Ireland
27 I4 Mullaghcloga hill Northern Ireland U.K.
27 F4 Mullaghmore Rep. of Ireland
176 G8 Mullaittivu Sri Lanka
205 L4 Mullaley N.S.W. Austr.
214 I4 Mullan Rep. of Ireland
27 G4 Mullan Northern Ireland U.K.
26 F8 Mullardoch, Loch l. Scotland U.K.
27 K4 Mullartown Northern Ireland U.K.
120 E4 Mullen NE U.S.A.
205 K4 Mullengudgery N.S.W. Austr.
119 D11 Mullens WV U.S.A.
206 E7 Muller, Pegunungan mts Indon.
45 J4 Mullett Lake MI U.S.A.
26 H7 Mullerup Denmark
49 J10 Mullewa W.A. Austr.
52 D6 Müllheim Ger.
95 H4 Mullica r. NJ U.S.A.
205 K3 Mulligan watercourse
207 H8 Mullinavat Rep. of Ireland
27 H5 Mullinawore Rep. of Ireland
115 H8 Mullins SC U.S.A.
30 B7 Mullion Cornwall, England U.K.
205 L5 Mullion Creek N.S.W. Austr.
25 E4 Mull of Galloway c. Scotland U.K.
26 D11 Mull of Kintyre hd Scotland U.K.
26 D11 Mull of Oa hd Scotland U.K.
15 J5 Mullovka Rus. Fed.
51 J6 Müllrose Ger.
23 E3 Mulltjärv l. Estonia
91 B8 Mulobezi Zambia
93 B8 Mulondo Angola
93 C6 Mulonga Plain Zambia
91 E6 Mulongo Dem. Rep. Congo
27 G5 Mulrany Rep. of Ireland
49 E6 Mulshi Bay Rep. of Ireland
209 E11 Multan W.A. Austr.
58 G5 Multan Austria
155 A3 Mulu, Gunung mt. Malaysia
77 L4 Multai Madh. Prad. India
44 K2 Multedam Neth.
77 75 Munteni Romania
70 D1 Muntendam Neth.
93 C6 Multaqan r. Turkey
92 E2 Mulugu Andhra Prad. India
91 E7 Mulukatu i. Addu Atoll Maldives
205 I5 Mulululu Lake N.S.W. Austr.
90 D4 Muma Dem. Rep. Congo
92 B4 Mumallah Sudan
184 D2 Mumān Iran
176 C3 Mumbai Mahar. India
93 D8 Mumbeji Zambia
205 L5 Mumbil N.S.W. Austr.
30 E4 Mumbles Head Wales U.K.
91 C8 Mumbondo Angola
91 C8 Mumbué Angola
93 C6 Mumbwa Zambia
169 K1 Mumbwi Tanz.
91 E7 Mumu Dem. Rep. Congo
Mume r. Ger.
94 B8 Mumra Rus. Fed.
85 F5 Mün, Mae Nam r. Thai.
92 A3 Muna r. Indon.
193 N3 Muna r. Rus. Fed.
185 N9 Munabao Pak.
20 ◻C1 Munaðarnes Iceland
92 A4 Munagala Andhra Prad. India
165 H13 Munakata Japan
167 K5 Munakata Japan
186 B4 Munayjah, Jabal mts Egypt/Sudan
182 F4 Munayly Kazakh.
182 E6 Munayshy Kazakh.
182 D4 Munayshy Kazakh.

Column 4

176 D3 Mula r. India
185 L7 Mula r. Pak.
67 C11 Mula Spain
65 Q4 Mula r. Spain
175 D11 Mulaku atoll Maldives
183 R5 Mulaku Atoll Maldives
162 F6 Mulan Heilong. China
154 C6 Mulanay Luzon Phil.
93 B8 Mulanje Malawi
95 G2 Mulanje, Mount Malawi
204 F3 Mulapula, Lake salt flat S.A. Austr.
72 C6 Mulargia, Lago l. Sardegna Italy
126 Z3 Mulatos Mex.
126 ◻U13 Mula-tupo Panama
186 G2 Mulayh Saudi Arabia
190 G9 Mulayh salt pan Saudi Arabia
187 I2 Mulayh Saudi Arabia
190 B8 Mulayz, Wādī al watercourse Egypt
70 H7 Mulazzo Italy
176 F6 Mulbagal Karnataka India
31 O2 Mulbarton Norfolk, England U.K.
178 F2 Mulbekh Jammu and Kashmir
26 J7 Mulben Moray, Scotland U.K.
121 H8 Mulberry AR U.S.A.
104 C3 Mulchatna r. AK U.S.A.
146 A5 Mulchén Chile
51 H9 Mulda Ger.
51 F7 Mulde r. Ger.
51 F7 Muldenstein Ger.
93 A5 Muleba Tanz.
122 L5 Mule Creek WY U.S.A.
126 C4 Mulegé Mex.
93 B7 Mulekatembo Zambia
140 E4 Mules i. Indon.
120 B8 Muleshoe TX U.S.A.
209 I11 Mulga Downs W.A. Austr.
207 M8 Mulga Park N.T. Austr.
204 E4 Mulga S.A. Austr.
65 M6 Mulhacén mt. Spain
50 C5 Mülheim an der Ruhr Ger.
49 D10 Mülheim-Kärlich Ger.
37 N8 Mulhouse France
170 C5 Muli Sichuan China
200 ◻2 Mulifanua Samoa
175 ◻2 Mulikatu i. Addu Atoll Maldives
90 F4 Mulila Gujarat India
93 B7 Mulilansolo Zambia
162 G6 Muling Heilong. China
162 G6 Muling Heilong. China
111 K6 Muling r. Heilong. China
162 H6 Muling He r. China
204 G3 Mungeranie S.A. Austr.
157 H4 Mungguresak, Tanjung pt Indon.
63 O2 Mungia Spain
209 H8 Mungi Aboriginal Reserve W.A. Austr.
205 L3 Mungindi N.S.W. Austr.
206 E6 Mungkarta Aboriginal Land res. N.T. Austr.
91 C7 Mungo Angola
205 I5 Mungo, Lake N.S.W. Austr.
205 I5 Mungo National Park N.S.W. Austr.
27 E7 Mungret Rep. of Ireland
Munguia Spain see Mungia
163 F10 Mun'gyŏng S. Korea
91 C8 Munhango Angola
91 B8 Munhino Angola
142 D5 Munhoz Brazil
63 J7 Munich Ger. see München
62 G2 Muñico Spain
62 D5 Muniellos, Reserva Natural Integral de nature res. Spain
66 D5 Muniesa Spain
93 A7 Munilla Spain
131 G9 Muniping MI U.S.A.
143 G4 Muniz Freire Brazil
178 C8 Munjpur Gujarat India
Munkács Ukr. see Mukacheve
14 E1 Munkbakken Norway
22 H3 Munkedal Sweden
22 H3 Munkflohögen Sweden
22 J2 Munkfors Sweden
168 G1 Munku-Sardyk, Gora mt. Mongolia/Rus. Fed.
45 I4 Munkzwalm Belgium
26 H7 Münnochy Highland, Scotland U.K.
49 J10 Münnerstadt Ger.
53 J4 Münningen Ger.
202 ◻ Munning Point Chatham Is S. Pacific Ocean
63 K7 Muñogalindo Spain
205 L3 Munro, Mount Tas. Austr.
107 L5 Munro Lake Man. Can.
53 M6 Münsing Ger.
53 K6 Münsingen Switz.
52 G5 Münsingen Ger.
59 T7 Münsingen Switz.
37 N7 Munster France
52 F2 Münster Hessen Ger.
49 E7 Münster Niedersachsen Ger.
45 J10 Münster Nordrhein-Westfalen Ger.
49 E6 Münster admin. reg. Ger.
56 D5 Münster admin. reg. Ger.
59 I1 Münster Switz.
209 E11 Muntadgin W.A. Austr.
77 M3 Muntenia reg. Romania
53 M6 Munster admin. reg. Ger.
143 F4 Munster r. Rep. of Ireland
49 E7 Münsterappel Ger.
70 E1 Münsterdorf Ger.
49 D6 Münsterland reg. Ger.
49 E6 Münstermaifeld Ger.
49 E6 Münster-Osnabrück airport Ger.
209 E11 Muntadgin W.A. Austr.
58 G5 Muntanjik r. Austria
155 A3 Muntele Mare, Vârful mt. Romania
77 L4 Muntok Indon.
44 K2 Munyal-Par sea feature India
77 75 Muonio Fin.
91 B8 Muonio r. Fin./Sweden
92 D2 Munyati r. Zimbabwe
169 K1 Muonioälven r. Fin./Sweden
18 I7 Muong Fin.
179 F4 Muong Ke Vietnam
158 F3 Muong Nhe Vietnam
155 F3 Muoni Fin.
19 X7 Muonio Fin.
53 K6 Muonionjoki r. Fin./Sweden
28 N9 Muor Iran
155 F3 Muor Austria
91 B9 Mupa, Parque Nacional da nat. park Angola
169 Q8 Muping Shandong China
95 F5 Mupini watercourse Sudan
92 E2 Muqaddam, watercourse
186 H9 Muqaynimah well Saudi Arabia
172 B4 Muqdisho Somalia
92 E4 Muqshin, Wādī r. Oman
143 H3 Muqui Brazil

Column 5

70 C1 Münchenbuchsee Switz.
München-Gladbach Ger. see Mönchengladbach
49 G9 Mönchhausen Ger.
136 B4 Munchique, Parque Nacional nat. park Col.
106 E3 Muncho Lake B.C. Can.
106 E3 Muncho Lake Provincial Park B.C. Can.
163 E9 Munch'ŏn N. Korea
53 L4 Münchsmünster Ger.
53 J2 Münchsteinach Ger.
145 B8 Münchweiler an der Rodalb Ger.
93 A5 Muncho r. Rus. Fed.
57 J3 Murah Slovakia
114 E5 Muncie IN U.S.A.
92 C5 Muncar a Kenya
206 G2 Muncoonie West, Lake salt flat Qld Austr.
111 R8 Muncy PA U.S.A.
118 B2 Muncy Creek r. PA U.S.A.
118 B2 Muncy Valley PA U.S.A.
91 B9 Munda Angola
90 D4 Munda Dem. Rep. Congo
185 N6 Munda Pak.
200 ◻6 Munda New Georgia Is Solomon Is
63 O2 Mundaka Spain
176 F9 Mundel Lake Sri Lanka
89 H5 Mundemba Cameroon
58 H3 Munderfing Austria
52 H5 Munderkingen Ger.
31 O2 Mundesley Norfolk, England U.K.
31 N2 Mundford Norfolk, England U.K.
209 F7 Mundiwindi W.A. Austr.
207 H5 Mundjura Creek r. Qld Austr.
65 P4 Mundo r. Spain
178 G7 Mundol Gujarat India
40 E4 Mundolsheim France
140 D6 Mundo Novo Brazil
178 B8 Mundra Gujarat India
207 H8 Munduberra Qld Austr.
184 D5 Murcheh Khvort Iran
50 I3 Munch r. Ger.
205 J7 Murchison Vic. Austr.
209 C9 Murchison watercourse W.A. Austr.
203 G8 Murchison South I. N.Z.
213 L2 Murchison, Mount Antarctica
209 C9 Murchison, Mount Hill W.A. Austr.
203 F10 Murchison, Mount South I. N.Z.
92 A4 Murchison Falls National Park Uganda
108 B3 Murchison Island Ont. Can.
203 B12 Murchison Mountains South I. N.Z.
206 E6 Murchison Range hills N.T. Austr.
67 C12 Murcia Spain
65 Q5 Murcia aut. comm. Spain
154 D7 Murcielagos Bay Mindanao Phil.
54 F3 Murczyn Pol.
41 B7 Mur-de-Barrez France
38 F5 Mur-de-Bretagne France
118 E6 Murderkill r. DE U.S.A.
39 O7 Mur-de-Sologne France
120 E4 Murdo SD U.S.A.
109 H3 Murdochville Que. Can.
167 H2 Mure Japan
59 M6 Mure Austria
79 I2 Mürefte Turkey
89 G4 Muregi Nigeria
76 J3 Mureș r. Romania
76 I4 Mures r. Romania
43 G9 Muret France
179 D5 Murewa Zimbabwe
186 G8 Murg r. Ger.
Murgab Tajik. see Murghob
Murgab Turkm. see Murgap
206 D1 Murgab r. Turkm.-see Murgap
185 J3 Murgap Turkm.
Murgap r. Turkm.
206 D1 Murgenella Creek r. N.T. Austr.
70 D1 Murgenthal Switz.
75 M2 Murgeni Romania
184 J2 Murgha Kibzai Pak.
185 I6 Murgha Mandau Pak.
185 N7 Murghob Tajik.
185 P4 Murghob r. Tajik.
191 C7 Murghub Tajik.
185 N7 Murgh Pass Afgh.
191 C5 Murghuz Lerr mt. Armenia
43 G9 Murgia Spain
73 M8 Murgia Sant'Elia Italy
207 M9 Murgon Qld Austr.
209 D9 Murgoo W.A. Austr.
191 C4 Murgul Turkey
168 F4 Murhash Afgh.
143 H2 Muriaé Brazil
137 F3 Muriá r. Brazil
81 G6 Muria, Gunung mt. Indon.
137 H5 Muriaú r. Brazil
137 H5 Muriel Brazil
38 H4 Murii-dake mt. Japan
110 E1 Murillo Port.
61 G6 Murillo el Fruto Spain
70 E5 Muri Bern Switz.
110 E1 Muriel Ont. Can.
57 H4 Muriaé Brazil

Column 6

59 O7 Mura r. Croatia/Slovenia
Mura r. Slovenia/Croatia see Mur (Austria)
53 M3 Murach r. Ger.
89 K3 Muradal, Serra do mts Port.
79 I4 Muradiye Manisa Turkey
189 K4 Muradiye Van Turkey
16 H5 Murafa r. Ukr.
156 ◻1 Murai, Tanjong pt Sing.
156 ◻1 Murai Reservoir Sing.
164 Q8 Murakami Japan
174 H3 Murakeresztúr Hungary
93 A5 Muramvya Burundi
57 J3 Murán Slovakia
92 C5 Muranga Kenya
71 M5 Murano Italy
57 I3 Mūránska planina park Slovakia
165 L13 Muraoka Japan
14 J4 Muras Spain
56 F5 Murashi Rus. Fed.
55 F5 Murassemenye Hungary
41 B6 Murat France
191 C7 Murat r. Turkey
54 F5 Murat, Tanjong pt Sing.
153 B8 Murau Austria
55 M3 Murava Belarus
166 A4 Muravera Sardegna Italy
164 R8 Murayama Japan
186 E3 Murayr, Jabal hill Saudi Arabia
85 G4 Murayr, Jazirat i. Egypt
84 E2 Muraysah, Ra's al pt Libya
70 E7 Murazzano Italy
63 G2 Murchante Spain
184 D5 Murcheh Khvort Iran
209 C9 Murchison watercourse W.A. Austr.
203 G8 Murchison South I. N.Z.
213 L2 Murchison, Mount Antarctica
209 C9 Murchison, Mount Hill W.A. Austr.
203 F10 Murchison, Mount South I. N.Z.
92 A4 Murchison Falls National Park Uganda
108 B3 Murchison Island Ont. Can.
203 B12 Murchison Mountains South I. N.Z.
206 E6 Murchison Range hills N.T. Austr.
67 C12 Murcia Spain
65 Q5 Murcia aut. comm. Spain
154 D7 Murcielagos Bay Mindanao Phil.
54 F3 Murczyn Pol.
41 B7 Mur-de-Barrez France
38 F5 Mur-de-Bretagne France
118 E6 Murderkill r. DE U.S.A.
39 O7 Mur-de-Sologne France
120 E4 Murdo SD U.S.A.
109 H3 Murdochville Que. Can.
167 H2 Mure Japan
59 M6 Mure Austria
79 I2 Mürefte Turkey
89 G4 Muregi Nigeria
76 J3 Mureș r. Romania
76 I4 Mures r. Romania
43 G9 Muret France
179 D5 Murewa Zimbabwe
186 G8 Murg r. Ger.
20 M4 Murfjället mt. Norway
115 F8 Murfreesboro AR U.S.A.
115 I7 Murfreesboro NC U.S.A.
115 D8 Murfreesboro TN U.S.A.
52 E6 Murg r. Ger.
52 E4 Murg r. Ger.
178 B8 Murgab Tajik. see Murghob
205 N3 Murgab r. Turkm. see Murgap
14 J4 Murygino Kirovskaya Oblast' Rus. Fed.
19 W7 Murygino Smolenskaya Oblast' Rus. Fed.
54 J1 Mürz r. Austria
184 L3 Mürzechirla Turkm.
59 M4 Mürzsteg Austria
59 M4 Mürzuq Libya
59 M4 Mürzzuschlag Austria
191 C7 Mus Turkey
90 E6 Musa Dem. Rep. Congo
90 F4 Musa r. Latvia/Lith.
184 C3 Mūsa r. Latvia/Lith.
191 C7 Müsa, Jabal mt. Egypt
176 F2 Müsa, Khowr-e b. Iran
179 K2 Musabeyli Turkey
191 D6 Musaköy Turkey
185 M6 Musakhel Pak.
185 I5 Müsá Qal'eh, Rūd-e r. Afgh.
167 K5 Musashino Japan
186 G9 Musaymir Yemen
84 E6 Musbat well Sudan
30 F6 Musbury Devon, England U.K.
Muscat Oman see Masqaţ
Muscat and Oman country Asia see Oman
120 J5 Muscatine IA U.S.A.
51 F8 Muschwitz Ger.
116 D3 Muscoda r. NJ U.S.A.
118 E3 Musconetcong r. NJ U.S.A.
117 ◻Q5 Muscongus Bay ME U.S.A.
18 H7 Muse r. Fin.
72 B9 Muse Sardegna Italy
207 I3 Musgrave Qld Austr.
203 ◻ Musgrave, Mount South I. N.Z.
109 K3 Musgrave Harbour Nfld and Lab. Can.
204 C2 Musgrave Ranges mts S.A. Austr.
185 M5 Müshaki Afgh.
190 H10 Mushāsh al Kabid well Jordan
190 H10 Mushāsh Dabl well Saudi Arabia
190 H9 Mushāsh Ḥaḍraj Jordan
190 H10 Mushāsh Muḍayyin well Saudi Arabia
186 G10 Mushayyish, Wādī al watercourse Jordan
91 C5 Mushie Dem. Rep. Congo
17 M9 Mushryn Rig Ukr.
156 E6 Musi r. Indon.
76 J9 Musica mt. Macedonia
Music Mountain AZ U.S.A.
179 I5 Musikot Nepal
71 M4 Musile di Piave Italy
109 J4 Musina S. Africa
106 D4 Musinia Peak UT U.S.A.
110 H5 Muskeg r. N.W.T. Can.
110 H5 Muskeget Channel MA U.S.A.
110 H6 Muskego WI U.S.A.
110 H6 Muskegon MI U.S.A.
110 H6 Muskegon r. MI U.S.A.
110 H6 Muskegon Heights MI U.S.A.
110 D8 Muskingum r. OH U.S.A.
121 H7 Muskogee OK U.S.A.

111 O5 Muskoka Ont. Can.
108 E4 Muskoka, Lake Ont. Can.
107 N4 Muskrat Dam Lake Ont. Can.
106 F3 Muskwa r. B.C. Can.
185 L6 Muslimbagh Pak.
190 F2 Muslimiyah Syria
14 K5 Muslyumovo Rus. Fed.
85 G5 Musmar Sudan
91 F8 Musofu Zambia
93 B5 Musoma Tanz.
93 B6 Musombe Tanz.
71 P9 Musone r. Italy
78 D1 Mušov Grob pass Macedonia
109 I3 Musquamousse, Lac l. Que. Can.
109 I3 Musquaro Que. Can.
109 I3 Musquaro, Lac l. Que. Can.
91 D8 Mussaca Angola
153 K7 Mussau Island P.N.G.
26 J11 Musselburgh East Lothian, Scotland U.K.
44 L3 Musselkanaal Neth.
122 K3 Musselshell r. M.T. U.S.A.
91 C7 Mussende Angola
191 B2 Mussera Georgia
91 B6 Mussera Angola
42 E5 Mussidan France
91 C7 Mussolo Angola
74 F8 Mussomeli Sicilia Italy
45 I9 Musson Belgium
178 G4 Mussoorie Uttaranchal India
91 D8 Mussuma Angola
91 D8 Mussuma r. Angola
36 I8 Mussy-sur-Seine France
178 G6 Mustafabad Uttar Prad. India
178 H7 Mustafabad Uttar Prad. India
79 J2 Mustafakemalpaşa Turkey
92 E3 Mustahīl Eth.
70 I2 Mustair Switz.
19 K1 Mustamaa r. Fin.
121 E10 Mustang Draw watercourse TX U.S.A.
172 G3 Mustau, Gora mt. Xinjiang China
182 E2 Mustayevo Rus. Fed.
145 C7 Musters, Lago l. Arg.
131 □3 Mustique l. St Vincent
18 F3 Mustjala Estonia
18 J4 Mustjõgi r. Estonia
18 I3 Mustla Estonia
20 T2 Mustola Fin.
18 F3 Mustvee Estonia
163 F8 Musu-dan pt N. Korea
191 I5 Müsüslü Azer.
205 M5 Muswellbrook N.S.W. Austr.
55 I2 Muszaki Pol.
55 I6 Muszyna Pol.
85 F3 Mût Egypt
44 F5 Mut Turkey
59 L6 Muta Slovenia
58 C6 Muta, Lago di l. Italy
140 F5 Mutá, Ponta do pt Brazil
203 □4 Mutalau Niue
93 C6 Mutanda Zambia
95 G3 Mutare Zimbabwe
186 G5 Mutarjim, Khashm hill Saudi Arabia
186 H2 Mutayr reg. Saudi Arabia
91 E6 Mutengwa Dem. Rep. Congo
59 P2 Mutěnice Czech Rep.
91 F7 Muteta Dem. Rep. Congo
26 I10 Muthill Perth and Kinross, Scotland U.K.
187 M4 Muti Oman
63 Q3 Mutiva Baja Spain
Mutina Italy see Modena
186 A2 Mu'tiq, Jabal mts Egypt
136 B3 Mutis Col.
155 D8 Mutis, Gunung mt. Timor Indon.
14 K2 Mutnyy Materik Rus. Fed.
95 G3 Mutoko Zimbabwe
91 D6 Mutombo Dem. Rep. Congo
204 H5 Mutooroo S.A. Austr.
95 F3 Mutorashanga Zimbabwe
91 D6 Mutoto Dem. Rep. Congo
73 N5 Mutria, Monte mt. Italy
99 □3 Mutsamudu Nzwani Comoros
91 E7 Mutshatsha Dem. Rep. Congo
164 S5 Mutsu Japan
164 S5 Mutsu-wan b. Japan
167 L5 Mutsuzawa Japan
207 J7 Muttaburra Qld Austr.
79 L3 Muttalip Turkey
58 C5 Muttekopf mt. Austria
70 D1 Muttenz Switz.
58 D5 Mutters Austria
52 E3 Mutterstadt Ger.
204 □2 Mutton Bird Island Lord Howe I. Austr.
203 C13 Muttonbird Islands Stewart I. N.Z.
27 C7 Mutton Island Rep. of Ireland
176 B3 Muttukuru Andhra Prad. India
176 F7 Muttupet Tamil Nadu India
95 H2 Mutuali Moz.
143 G3 Mutum Brazil
136 D6 Mutum r. Brazil
93 A5 Mutumba Burundi
89 H4 Mutum Biyu Nigeria
138 D2 Mutumparaná Brazil
91 C6 Mutungu-Tari Dem. Rep. Congo
140 C5 Mutunópolis Brazil
176 D8 Mutur Sri Lanka
67 E11 Mutxamel Spain
17 M2 Mutyn Ukr.
37 N6 Mutzig France
51 G8 Mutzschen Ger.
18 I2 Muuga Estonia
21 R5 Muurame Fin.
21 Q6 Muuruta Fin.
20 R3 Muurola Fin.
169 K7 Mu Us Shamo des. China
91 B7 Muxaluando Angola
191 H4 Muxax Azer.
Muxi Sichuan China see Muchuan
62 B2 Muxía Spain
91 B7 Muxima Angola
89 H4 Muya Nigeria
14 F3 Muyezerskiy Rus. Fed.
93 A5 Muyinga Burundi
Muyunkum sands see Mo'ynoq
93 B7 Muyombe Zambia
89 H5 Muyuka Cameroon
91 E6 Muyumba Dem. Rep. Congo
170 H3 Muyuping Hubei China
185 O4 Muzaffarabad Pak.
185 N6 Muzaffargarh Pak.
178 F5 Muzaffarnagar Uttar Prad. India
179 J6 Muzaffarpur Bihar India
95 G4 Muzamane Moz.
142 D4 Muzambinho Brazil
172 F6 Muzat He r. China
182 F6 Muzbel', Uval hills Kazakh.
95 F2 Muze Moz.
191 F2 Muzhi Rus. Fed.
38 G6 Muzillac France
185 I8 Muzo Col.
136 C3 Muzo Col.
165 Q15 Muzoi-sho l. Japan
165 R15 Muzoi-shō l. Japan
159 H9 My Phuoc Vietnam
173 E9 Muztag mt. Xinjiang China
173 H8 Muz Tag mt. Xinjiang China
172 B7 Muztagata mt. Xinjiang China
70 G5 Muzza, Canale canal Italy
71 O4 Muzzana del Turgnano Italy
90 B4 Mvadi Gabon
89 H6 Mvolo S. Sudan
90 F3 Mvomero Tanz.
90 B4 Mvoung r. Gabon
99 □3a Mvouni Njazidja Comoros
91 B6 Mvouti Congo
95 G3 Mvuma Zimbabwe
99 □3 Mwali l. Comoros
91 E9 Mwami Zimbabwe
91 B6 Mwandi Zambia
93 B6 Mwanga Tanz.
200 □6 Mwanihana San Cristobal Solomon Is

93 B8 Mwanjawira Zambia
93 B8 Mwanya Zambia
93 B8 Mwanza Malawi
93 B5 Mwanza admin. reg. Tanz.
93 B5 Mwanza Tanz.
93 A8 Mwapa Zambia
91 E6 Mwebe Dem. Rep. Congo
91 D6 Mweka Dem. Rep. Congo
93 C6 Mwele Tanz.
Mwene-Biji Dem. Rep. Congo
91 D6 Mwene-Ditu Dem. Rep. Congo
95 F4 Mwenezi Zimbabwe
95 F4 Mwenezi r. Zimbabwe
91 F5 Mwenga Dem. Rep. Congo
93 B8 Mwense Zambia
93 C6 Mwereni Kenya
91 F7 Mweru, Lake Dem. Rep. Congo/Zambia
93 C7 Mweru Wantipa, Lake Zambia
91 F7 Mweru Wantipa National Park Zambia
93 A7 Mwewa Zambia
93 C6 Mwimba Dem. Rep. Congo
93 C5 Mwingi Kenya
91 E7 Mwinilunga Zambia
87 G3 Mya, Oued watercourse Alg.
158 C3 Myadaung Myanmar
91 E7 Myadzyel Belarus
18 J7 Myadzyel, Vozyera l. Belarus
170 D3 Myaglo Sichuan China
158 A2 Myaing Myanmar
178 C6 Myajlar Rajasthan India
55 H1 Myakawo Pol.
55 J2 Myakshevo Rus. Fed.
193 Q3 Myakit Rus. Fed.
18 F3 M''yakoty Ukr.
205 N5 Myall Lakes National Park N.S.W. Austr.
158 B5 Myanaung Myanmar
158 B3 Myanmar country Asia
18 K6 Myaretskiya Belarus
19 S7 Myatlevo Rus. Fed.
193 P3 Myaundzha Rus. Fed.
158 B6 Myaungmya Myanmar
158 D6 Myawadi Thai.
26 J6 Mybster Highland, Scotland U.K.
23 L4 Myckelfärs l. Sweden
16 C2 Myebon Myanmar
159 D8 Myedna Belarus
159 C9 Myeik Myanmar
159 C9 Myeik Kyunzu is Myanmar
19 S7 Myerkulavichy Belarus
118 C4 Myers KY U.S.A.
118 B10 Myerstown PA U.S.A.
158 B4 Myingyan Myanmar
159 D8 Myinmoletkat mt. Myanmar
158 B4 Myitkyina Myanmar
158 C8 Myitson Myanmar
159 D7 Myitta Myanmar
158 C4 Myittha Myanmar
177 N1 Myittha r. Myanmar
57 J3 Myjava Slovakia
56 F3 Myjava r. Slovakia
17 L4 Mykhaylenky Ukr.
17 O5 Mykhaylivka Dnipropetrovs'ka Oblast' Ukr.
17 R6 Mykhaylivka Kharkivs'ka Oblast' Ukr.
17 N4 Mykhaylivka Poltavs'ka Oblast' Ukr.
17 O6 Mykhaylivka Zaporiz'ka Oblast' Ukr.
17 O6 Mykhaylivka Zaporiz'ka Oblast' Ukr.
17 K2 Mykhaylo-Kotsyubyns'ke Ukr.
16 G3 Mykhaylyuchka Ukr.
24 D1 Mykines i. Faroe Is
78 D5 Mykines tourist site Greece
20 M3 Myklebostad Norway
Mykolayiv L'viv's'ka
55 M5 Mykolayiv L'viv's'ka Ukr.
17 L7 Mykolayiv Mykolayiv's'ka Oblast' Ukr.
17 L1 Mykolayiv Chernihivs'ka Oblast' Ukr.
17 N6 Mykolayiv Dnipropetrovs'ka Oblast' Ukr.
16 J6 Mykolayiv Odes'ka Oblast' Ukr.
17 P5 Mykolayivka Dnipropetrovs'ka
17 Q5 Mykolayivka Donets'ka
17 P5 Mykolayivka Kharkivs'ka Oblast' Ukr.
17 N6 Mykolayivka Khersons'ka Oblast' Ukr.
16 J6 Mykolayivka Odes'ka Ukr.
17 P6 Mykolayivka Zaporiz'ka Oblast' Ukr.
16 I7 Mykolayivka-Novorosiys'ka Ukr.
Mykolayiv Oblast admin. div. Ukr. see Mykolayivs'ka Oblast'
17 L6 Mykolayivs'ka Oblast' admin. div. Ukr.
16 I6 Mykolo-Hulak Ukr.
78 E6 Mykonos Mykonos Greece
79 G5 Mykonos i. Greece
21 R5 Mykyntsi Ukr.
55 M5 Mykytychi Ukr.
14 N3 Myla Rus. Fed.
14 J2 Myla r. Rus. Fed.
Mylae Sicilia Italy see Milazzo
51 F9 Mylau Ger.
18 J1 Myllykoski Fin.
30 B7 Mylor Cornwall, England U.K.
Mymensing Bangl. see Mymensingh
179 M7 Mymensingh Bangl.
18 I1 Mynämäki r. Fin.
21 Q6 Mynämäki Fin.
96 H6 Mynfontein S. Africa
167 I3 Myōgi Japan
Myōgi-Arafune-Saku-kōgen Quasi National Park Japan
167 I3 Myōgi-san mt. Japan
166 A6 Myōken-yama hill Japan
167 H2 Myōkō Japan
167 H2 Myōkō Japan
40 H2 Myon France
167 I4 Myonji Japan

16 J4 Myronivka Kyivs'ka Oblast' Ukr.
16 G3 Myropil' Ukr.
17 O2 Myropillya Ukr.
17 N6 Myrove Ukr.
93 A5 Myrskylä Fin.
115 H9 Myrtle Beach SC U.S.A.
122 C5 Myrtle Creek OR U.S.A.
205 K7 Myrtleford Vic. Austr.
122 B5 Myrtle Point OR U.S.A.
183 M7 Myrzakent Kazakh.
22 H2 Mysen Norway
28 D8 Mysen Rep. of Ireland
18 I9 Myshanka r. Belarus
19 V4 Myshkin Rus. Fed.
Myshkino Rus. Fed. see Myshkin
17 Q9 Myshkin
54 C3 Myśla r. Pol.
Mys Lazareva Rus. Fed. see Lazarev
55 H6 Myślenice Pol.
54 C3 Myśliborskie, Jezioro l. Pol.
54 C3 Myślibórz Pol.
55 H5 Myślowice Pol.
Mysłowitz Pol. see Mysłowice
158 I7 My Son tourist site Vietnam
176 E6 Mysore Karnataka India
Mysore state India see Karnataka
17 N8 Mysove Ukr.
193 T3 Mys Shmidta Rus. Fed.
119 L2 Mystic CT U.S.A.
119 G5 Mystic Islands NJ U.S.A.
14 K3 Mysy Rus. Fed.
55 H1 Myszewo Pol.
55 J2 Myszków Pol.
55 J2 Myszyniec Pol.
14 N2 Myt Rus. Fed.
159 H9 My Tho Vietnam
Mytilene i. Greece see Lesvos
79 H3 Mytilini Lesvos Greece
79 H5 Mytilinioi Samos Greece
108 C4 Mytilini Strait Greece/Turkey
57 I3 Mytishchi Rus. Fed.
56 C2 Mýto Czech Rep.
125 V1 Myton UT U.S.A.
17 L5 Mytrofanivka Ukr.
191 I3 Myuregi Rus. Fed.
20 □E1 Mývatn i. Iceland
20 □E1 Mývatn-Laxá nature res. Iceland
20 □E1 Mývatnsöræfi lava field Iceland
14 K3 Myyeldino Rus. Fed.
Myylybulak Kazakh. see Milybulak
16 D2 Myzove Ukr.
87 F2 M'Zab Valley tourist site Alg.
97 K7 Mzamomhle S. Africa
56 B2 Mže r. Czech Rep.
93 C6 Mziha Tanz.
93 B7 Mzimba Malawi
95 F4 Mzingwani r. Zimbabwe
93 B7 Mzuzu Malawi
191 A2 Mzymta r. Rus. Fed.

N

158 F3 Na, Nam r. China/Vietnam
53 M3 Naab r. Ger.
44 F5 Naaldwijk Neth.
124 □F14 Nā'ālehu HI U.S.A.
90 F2 Naam Sudan
21 Q6 Naantali Fin.
59 K3 Naarn im Machlande Austria
27 I6 Naas Rep. of Ireland
20 T2 Näätämö Fin.
20 T5 Näätämöjoki r. Fin.
158 C2 Naba Myanmar
96 B5 Nababeep S. Africa
Nabadwip W. Bengal India see Navadwip
191 G3 Nabakevi Georgia
62 D9 Nabão r. Port.
177 H3 Nabarangapur Orissa India
166 D6 Nabari Japan
166 D6 Nabari-gawa r. Japan
154 D6 Nabas Panay Phil.
190 D5 Nabatîyé et Tahta Lebanon
209 F8 Nabberu, Lake salt flat W.A. Austr.
53 M3 Nabburg Ger.
88 E4 Nabéré, Réserve Partielle de nat. Burkina
93 C6 Nabera Tanz.
17 R2 Naberezhnoye Rus. Fed.
14 K5 Naberezhnyye Chelny Rus. Fed.
182 A2 Naberezhnyy Uvekh Rus. Fed.
87 G1 Nabeul Tunisia
69 □ Nabeul admin. div. Tunisia
178 F4 Nabha Punjab India
191 H5 Näbiağalı Azer.
72 □ Nabileque r. Brazil
179 J7 Nabinagar Bihar India
151 □ Nabire Papua Indon.
190 D5 Nabi Younés, Ras en pt Lebanon
190 D6 Nablus West Bank
88 E4 Nabolo Ghana
95 F5 Naboomspruit S. Africa
201 □1a Naboutini Viti Levu Fiji
201 □ Nabouwalu Vanua Levu Fiji
57 L3 Nábrád Hungary
159 D7 Nabule Myanmar
127 M8 Nacajuca Mex.
95 H2 Nacala Moz.
126 □P11 Nacaome Hond.
95 H2 Nacaroa Moz.
138 D2 Nacebe Bol.
56 D2 Náchod Czech Rep.
18 L7 Nacha r. Belarus
182 C4 Nachalovo Rus. Fed.
122 D3 Naches r. WA U.S.A.
109 H1 Nachicapau, Lac l. Que. Can.
93 C7 Nachingwea Tanz.
178 D6 Nachna Rajasthan India
56 F1 Náchod Czech Rep.
177 M7 Nachuge Andaman & Nicobar Is India
21 P6 Nacina Ves Pol.
131 □1a Nacilau Point Viti Levu Fiji
146 A5 Nacimiento Chile
65 N7 Nacimiento r. Spain
192 F1 Nacimiento Reservoir CA U.S.A.
50 G5 Nack Ger.
52 H4 Nackenheim Ger.
121 H10 Nacogdoches TX U.S.A.
126 C3 Nacozari de García Mex.
55 I3 Nacpolsk Pol.
18 L7 Nacuna r. Belarus
167 H2 Nadachi Japan
167 H1 Nadaillac-le-Lauze France
201 □1a Nadarivatu Viti Levu Fiji
54 E2 Nadarzyce Pol.
57 H4 Nádasdladány Hungary
178 F6 Nadbai Rajasthan India
31 I5 Nadder r. England U.K.
57 J4 Nádudvar Hungary
178 C8 Nadiad Gujarat India

57 J1 Nadnidziański Park Krajobrazowy Pol.
178 D7 Nadol Rajasthan India
86 E2 Nador Morocco
86 E2 Nador prov. Morocco
60 E5 Nadór Morocco
19 R1 Nadporozh'ye Rus. Fed.
77 K5 Nádrag Romania
201 □1a Nadrau Plateau Viti Levu Fiji
191 G2 Nadterechnaya Rus. Fed.
57 K4 Nádudvar Hungary
75 □ Nadur Gozo Malta
75 □ Nadur hill Malta
201 □1 Naduri Viti Levu Fiji
184 E5 Nadushan Iran
16 D5 Nadvirna Ukr.
Nadvornaya Ukr. see Nadvirna
192 I3 Nadym Rus. Fed.
178 E4 Naenwa Rajasthan India
54 G5 Næstved Denmark
56 G4 Naegyszénás Hungary
70 G1 Näfels Switz.
29 Q5 Nafferton East Riding of Yorkshire, England U.K.
78 C4 Nafpaktos Greece
78 D5 Nafplio Greece
191 H5 Naftalan Azer.
184 C5 Naftaln Iran
184 A4 Naft-e Safid Iran
186 G5 Naft-e Shah Iran
184 A4 Naft Shahr Iran
186 F3 Nafud ad Dahl des. Saudi Arabia
190 G2 Nafud al Ghuwaytah des. Saudi Arabia
184 F5 Nafud al Jur'ā des. Saudi Arabia
186 F3 Nafud as Sirr des. Saudi Arabia
186 F4 Nafud as Surrah des. Saudi Arabia
186 G3 Nafud Qunayfidhah des. Saudi Arabia
84 A2 Nafusah, Jabal hills Libya
186 F3 Nafy Saudi Arabia
173 J10 Nag, Co l. China
166 B7 Naga Japan
154 D5 Naga Luzon Phil.
108 C3 Nagagami r. Ont. Can.
166 D5 Nagahama Ehime Japan
166 B4 Nagahama Shiga Japan
179 O6 Naga Hills India
Naga Hills state India see Nagaland
164 R8 Nagai Japan
167 I5 Nagai Japan
179 O6 Nagaland state India
159 F10 Nagambie Vic. Austr.
164 □1 Nagannu-jima i. Okinawa
167 H2 Nagano Japan
167 H2 Nagano pref. Japan
167 I2 Naganohara Japan
167 L1 Naganuma Japan
166 C6 Nagaoka Japan
164 □1 Nagaokakyō Japan
179 N6 Nagaon Assam India
Nagapatam Tamil Nadu India see Nagapattinam
176 F4 Nagapattinam Tamil Nadu India
179 L7 Nagar r. Bangl./India
178 F3 Nagar Hima. Prad. India
176 D6 Nagar Karnataka India
178 F6 Nagar Rajasthan India
167 L5 Nagara Japan
167 L5 Nagara-gawa r. Japan
176 G3 Nagaram Andhra Prad. India
167 K4 Nagareyama Japan
179 I7 Nagarjuna Sagar Reservoir India
176 F4 Nagar Karnul Andhra Prad. India
178 D5 Nagar Parkar Pak.
173 J12 Nagarzê Xizang China
165 I3 Nagasaki Japan
165 G13 Nagasaki pref. Japan
165 G13 Nagashima Kagoshima Japan
166 C5 Nagashima Mie Japan
165 H14 Naga-shima i. Japan
165 I13 Naga-shima i. Japan
167 H3 Nagato Nagano Japan
165 I12 Nagato Yamaguchi Japan
178 D6 Nagaur Rajasthan India
176 D5 Nagavali r. India
52 □ Nagel Ger.
44 I3 Nagele Neth.
176 E8 Nagercoil Tamil Nadu India
185 K8 Nagha Kalat Pak.
173 L13 Nagina Uttar Prad. India
184 A4 Naginabad Iran
179 O6 Naginimara Nagaland India
165 K12 Nagiso Japan
169 R2 Naji Nei Mongol China
173 L13 Nagjog Xizang China
173 H11 Nag Qu r. Xizang China
55 I3 Nagłowice Pol.
89 H3 Nagode Nic.
185 N9 Nagor Nic.
191 G3 Nagore Xizang China
167 J2 Nagorge Japan
39 L8 Nagorje Slovenia
54 C2 Nagornyy Rus. Fed.
155 F5 Nagorye Rus. Fed.
Nagorno-Karabakh aut. reg. Azer. see Dağlıq Qarabağ
167 H1 Nagoya Japan
178 G8 Nagpur Mahar. India
184 H6 Nagqu Xizang China
173 K11 Nag Qu r. Xizang China
164 □1 Nag's Head pt St Kitts and Nevis
131 □ Nagua Puerto Rico
57 I3 Nagumbuaya Point Phil.
192 F1 Nagurskoye Zemlya Frantsa-Iosifa Rus. Fed.
191 D1 Nagutskoye Rus. Fed.
57 J5 Nagyatád Hungary
57 H4 Nagybajom Hungary
57 H4 Nagybánhegyes Hungary
57 H4 Nagybaracska Hungary
57 H5 Nagybereki Fehérvíz nature res. Hungary
57 H5 Nagyberény Hungary
57 H3 Nagybörzsöny Hungary
57 H5 Nagydorog Hungary
57 J4 Nagyecsed Hungary
57 J4 Nagyfüged Hungary
57 H5 Nagygyimót Hungary
57 H4 Nagyhalász Hungary
57 H4 Nagyharsány Hungary
57 G4 Nagyigmánd Hungary
57 K3 Nagykálló Hungary
56 F5 Nagykanizsa Hungary
57 H3 Nagykáta Hungary
57 I4 Nagykónyi Hungary

57 I4 Nagykőrös Hungary
57 H4 Nagykovácsi Hungary
57 J5 Nagykunság reg. Hungary
57 J5 Nagykunsági Öntöző Főcsatorna canal Hungary
57 J5 Nagylak Hungary
57 I3 Nagylóc Hungary
56 F4 Nagylózs Hungary
57 J5 Nagymágocs Hungary
57 H5 Nagymányok Hungary
57 H3 Nagymaros Hungary
57 K3 Nagy-Milic hill Hungary/Slovakia
57 H6 Nagynyárád Hungary
57 H4 Nagyoroszi Hungary
56 G5 Nagyrécse Hungary
57 J5 Nagy-sárrét reg. Hungary
57 I4 Nagyszénás Hungary
57 G4 Nagyszentjános Hungary
57 H5 Nagyszokoly Hungary
57 H4 Nagytarcsa Hungary
57 G4 Nagytőke Hungary
57 K4 Nagy-Vadas-tó l. Hungary
Nagyvárad Romania see Oradea
57 L3 Nagyvarsány Hungary
57 I5 Nagyvázsony Hungary
57 H3 Nagyvisnyó Hungary
18 K3 Naha Okinawa Japan
164 □1 Naha Okinawa Japan
178 F4 Nahan Hima. Prad. India
185 J8 Nahang r. Iran/Pak.
106 E2 Nahanni Butte N.W.T. Can.
106 E2 Nahanni National Park N.W.T. Can.
106 F2 Nahanni Range mts N.W.T. Can.
190 G2 Naharāyim Jordan
165 L13 Nahari Japan
190 D5 Nahariyya Israel
63 P8 Naharros Spain
184 C4 Nahāvand Iran
48 J3 Nahe r. Ger.
52 D2 Nahe r. Ger.
Na h-Eileanan an Iar admin. reg. Scotland U.K. see Western Isles
87 F4 N'Ahnet, Adrar mts Alg.
200 □5 Nahoi, Cap c. Vanuatu
39 O7 Nahon r. France
186 D2 Nahr, Jabal hill Saudi Arabia
48 K4 Nahrendorf Ger.
128 F6 Nahuatzen Mex.
146 D4 Nahuel Huapí Arg.
145 C6 Nahuel Huapi, Parque Nacional nat. park Arg.
146 D4 Nahuel Mapá Arg.
145 I5 Nahuel Niyeu Arg.
147 I5 Nahuel Rucá Arg.
185 J8 Nāhūg Iran
115 F10 Nahunta GA U.S.A.
185 L5 Naibabad Afgh.
154 C4 Naic Luzon Phil.
146 E5 Naicó Arg.
93 C6 Naicó well Tanz.
158 C1 Nai Ga Myanmar
201 □1a Naigani i. Fiji
169 J3 Naij Tal Qinghai China
155 C5 Nailiu Timor Indon.
106 C4 Naikoon Provincial Park park B.C. Can.
51 E10 Naila Ger.
43 E10 Nailloux France
30 G5 Nailsea North Somerset, England U.K.
30 H4 Nailsworth Gloucestershire, England U.K.
173 K12 Nailung Xizang China
178 B8 Naliya Gujarat India
178 F6 Nallhole Madh. Prad. India
42 B3 Nallbe r. Belarus
183 M2 Nallıhan Turkey
181 M8 Nalobino Kazakh.
178 D8 Nalolo Zambia
201 □ Nalón r. Spain
54 C2 Nałożovskè Hory Czech Rep.
155 F5 Namaa, Tanjung pt Seram Indon.
201 □ Namacha Moz.
95 H2 Namacala Moz.
166 E2 Namacunde Moz.
166 E2 Namacurra Moz.
205 L6 Namadgi National Park N.S.W. Austr.
93 B5 Namahadi S. Africa
154 □ Namai Bay Palau
184 G4 Namak, Daryācheh-ye salt flat Iran
184 F6 Namak, Kavīr-e salt flat Iran
184 F6 Namak-e Miqhān, Kavīr-e salt flat Iran
184 E2 Namakan Lake Can./U.S.A.
176 F7 Namakkal Tamil Nadu India
178 H6 Namakzar-e Shadad salt flat Iran
156 G6 Namang Indon.
92 C5 Namanga Kenya
201 □ Namangan Uzbek.
183 N7 Namangan Oblast admin. div. Uzbek. see Namangan
183 N7 Namangan Wiloyati admin. div. Uzbek. see Namangan
187 J2 Najmah Saudi Arabia
154 B3 Najran Saudi Arabia
186 E6 Najrān, Wādī watercourse Saudi Arabia
166 A5 Naka Hyōgo Japan
93 C6 Naka r. Japan
175 □3 Nakachaafushi i. N. Male Maldives
191 C5 Nakakanan Moz.
92 B4 Nakasale Uganda
95 H2 Nakashir Iran
95 B2 Nakasongola Uganda

94 B5 Namib Desert Namibia
91 B8 Namibe Angola
91 B8 Namibe prov. Angola
91 B8 Namibe, Reserva de nature res. Angola
94 A4 Namibia country Africa
214 J8 Namibia Abyssal Plain sea feature N. Atlantic Ocean
94 B5 Namib-Naukluft Game Park nature res. Namibia
95 C7 Namichiga Tanz.
95 H2 Namidobe Moz.
164 R9 Namie Japan
94 D5 Namies S. Africa
184 C2 Namin Iran
95 H2 Namina Moz.
173 L12 Namjagbarwa Feng mt. Xizang China
158 J12 Namka China
158 C3 Namlan Myanmar
158 C3 Namlea r. Myanmar
173 L13 Namlea Buru Indon.
158 E6 Nam Na National Park
158 F5 Nam Ngum Reservoir Laos
205 L4 Namoi r. N.S.W. Austr.
167 I3 Namoku Japan
152 □ Namonuito atoll Micronesia
95 H2 Nampa r. Nepal
122 F5 Nampa ID U.S.A.
88 B3 Nampala Mali
158 E6 Nam Pat Thai.
95 H3 Nampevo Moz.
158 F6 Nam Phong Thai.
163 D9 Nam Phung Reservoir Thai.
163 □ Nampo N. Korea
95 I2 Nampuecha Moz.
95 H2 Nampula prov. Moz.
95 H2 Nampula Moz.
158 C5 Namrole Buru Indon.
179 O6 Namrup Assam India
158 C4 Namsai Myanmar
158 C4 Namsang Myanmar
20 K4 Namsfjorden sea chan. Norway
158 H3 Nam Tha Tsim hill H.K. China
20 K4 Namsos Norway
20 L4 Namsskogan Norway
89 I4 Namtari Nigeria
159 D7 Namti Myanmar
158 C4 Namtok Myanmar
159 D7 Nam Tok Thai.
158 E6 Namtok Chattakan National Park Thai.
158 D5 Namtok Mae Surin National Park Thai.
158 C3 Namton Myanmar
193 N3 Namtsy Rus. Fed.
158 C4 Namtu Myanmar
106 C4 Namu B.C. Can.
203 □4 Namukulu Niue
Namuka i. Fiji see Nomuka
95 H2 Namuli, Monte mt. Moz.
95 H2 Namuno Moz.
45 H7 Namur Belgium
45 G8 Namur prov. Belgium
45 H7 Namutoni Namibia
91 E8 Namwala Zambia
91 E8 Namwera Malawi
83 B8 Namwŏn S. Korea
54 E4 Namysłów Pol.
158 E7 Nan Thai.
158 E6 Nan, Mae Nam r. Thai.
89 I4 Nan Cameroon
90 B3 Nana r. C.A.R.
158 A3 Nana Slovakia
90 C3 Nana-Bakassa C.A.R.
90 C3 Nana-Grébizi pref. C.A.R.
167 L3 Nanakai Japan
167 L3 Nānākuli HI U.S.A.
90 C3 Nana-Mambéré pref. C.A.R.
171 L6 Nan'an Fujian China
207 N9 Nanango Qld Austr.
94 C5 Nananib Plateau Namibia
201 □1a Nananu-i-Ra i. Fiji
166 E1 Nanao Japan
166 E1 Nanao-wan b. Japan
166 E2 Nanatsuka Japan
136 E1 Nanatsu-shima i. Japan
4 Nanay r. Peru
171 J4 Nanbaxian Qinghai China
170 H5 Nanbu Sichuan China
200 □3 Nanca Chile
39 P7 Nançay France
162 F5 Nancha Heilong. China
171 J4 Nanchang Jiangxi China
171 K5 Nanchang Jiangxi China
171 J4 Nanchital Mex.
170 D5 Nanchong Sichuan China
170 C5 Nanchuan Chongqing China
139 E5 Nancoroinza Bol.
177 M9 Nancowry i. Andaman & Nicobar Is India
106 E4 Nancut B.C. Can.
37 L6 Nancy France
203 B12 Nancy Sound inlet South I. N.Z.
178 H4 Nanda Devi mt. Uttaranchal India
178 H4 Nanda Kot mt. Uttaranchal India
170 H6 Nandan Guangxi China
89 I4 Nandan Cameroon
136 A7 Nandan r. Peru
176 E3 Nandarivatu Viti Levu Fiji
95 H4 Nanded Mahar. India
205 M4 Nandewar Range mts N.S.W. Austr.
178 E9 Nandgaon Mahar. India
95 H2 Nandi Fiji see Nadi
95 H3 Nandi Bay Viti Levu Fiji see Nadi Bay
176 G4 Nandigama Andhra Prad. India
176 D7 Nandikotkur Andhra Prad. India
178 D9 Nanding He r. Yunnan China
178 D9 Nandod Gujarat India
176 E5 Nandurbar Mahar. India
176 F5 Nandyal Andhra Prad. India
77 P5 Nănești Romania
173 K6 Namco Xizang China
173 K12 Nam Co salt l. China
184 D6 Namak watercourse Iran
173 K12 Nang Xizang China
171 J4 Nanfeng Guangdong China
171 K6 Nanfeng Jiangxi China
89 I3 Nanga Eboko Cameroon
157 J4 Nangahbaroh Kalimantan Indon.
157 J4 Nangah Dedai Kalimantan Indon.
157 J4 Nangahkantuk Kalimantan Indon.
157 J4 Nangahkemangai Kalimantan Indon.
157 J4 Nangah Merakai Kalimantan Indon.
157 I4 Nangahpinoh Kalimantan Indon.
157 J4 Nangahsuruk Kalimantan Indon.

Nelazskoye to Ngesebus
310

19 U2 Nelazskoye Rus. Fed.
207 I6 Nelia Qld Austr.
19 P5 Nelidovo Rus. Fed.
120 G4 Neligh NE U.S.A.
193 O4 Nel'kan Khabarovskiy Kray Rus. Fed.
193 P3 Nel'kan Respublika Sakha (Yakutiya) Rus. Fed.
200 □3a Nell i. Kwajalein Marshall Is
111 N1 Nellie Lake Ont. Can.
20 T2 Nellim Fin.
52 H4 Nellingen Ger.
176 F5 Nellore Andhra Prad. India
200 □3a Nell Passage Kwajalein Marshall Is
190 H2 Nelluz watercourse Turkey
162 K5 Nel'ma Rus. Fed.
97 O1 Nelshoogte pass S. Africa
147 G2 Nelson Arg.
106 G5 Nelson B.C. Can.
107 M3 Nelson r. Man. Can.
203 H8 Nelson South I. N.Z.
203 H8 Nelson admin. reg. South I. N.Z.
29 M6 Nelson Lancashire, England U.K.
125 S6 Nelson AZ U.S.A.
120 F5 Nelson NE U.S.A.
125 R6 Nelson NV U.S.A.
110 B5 Nelson WI U.S.A.
204 H8 Nelson, Cape Vic. Austr.
146 B8 Nelson, Estrecho str. Chile
205 N5 Nelson Bay N.S.W. Austr.
203 F9 Nelson Creek South I. N.Z.
106 F3 Nelson Forks B.C. Can.
107 L4 Nelson House Man. Can.
117 J11 Nelsonia VA U.S.A.
203 G9 Nelson Lakes National Park South I. N.Z.
119 H2 Nelsonville NY U.S.A.
96 H8 Nelspoort S. Africa
97 O1 Nelspruit S. Africa
14 K3 Nem r. Rus. Fed.
88 D2 Néma Maur.
14 J4 Nema Rus. Fed.
110 B3 Nemadji r. MN U.S.A.
Neman r. Belarus/Lith. see Nyoman
18 F6 Neman Rus. Fed.
18 F6 Neman r. Rus. Fed.
184 H7 Ne'matābād Iran
Nemausus France see Nîmes
200 □6 Nembao Santa Cruz Is Solomon Is
89 G5 Nembe Nigeria
70 D3 Nembro Italy
57 I3 Nemce Slovakia
14 H4 Nemda r. Rus. Fed.
78 D5 Nemea Greece
14 K3 Nemed Rus. Fed.
111 K2 Nemegos Ont. Can.
111 K1 Nemegosenda Lake Ont. Can.
18 I7 Nemenčinė Lith.
87 G2 Nementcha, Monts des mts Alg.
78 B2 Nëmerçkë, Mal ridge Albania
56 G4 Nemesszalók Hungary
56 G5 Nemesvid Hungary
57 H5 Németkér Hungary
20 U2 Nemetskiy, Mys c. Rus. Fed.
Nemirov Ukr. see Nemyriv
108 E3 Nemiscau r. Que. Can.
108 E3 Nemiscau, Lac l. Que. Can.
16 J3 Nemishayeve Ukr.
169 S2 Nemor He r. China
36 E7 Nemours France
189 K4 Nemrut Dağı mt. Turkey
51 E8 Nemsdorf-Göhrendorf Ger.
57 H3 Nemšová Slovakia
162 I4 Nemta r. Rus. Fed.
55 M1 Nemunaitis Lith.
18 E6 Nemunas r. Lith.
18 H5 Nemunėlio Radviliškis Lith.
18 I5 Nemunėlis r. Lith.
164 W3 Nemuro Japan
164 W3 Nemuro-hantō pen. Japan
164 W3 Nemuro-kaikyō sea chan. Japan/Rus. Fed.
164 W3 Nemuro-wan b. Japan
16 C3 Nemyriv L'vivs'ka Oblast' Ukr.
16 H5 Nemyriv Vinnyts'ka Oblast' Ukr.
16 G4 Nemyryntsi Ukr.
27 F7 Nenagh Rep. of Ireland
162 D4 Nenan Heilong. China
104 D3 Nenana AK U.S.A.
14 N7 Nenashevo Rus. Fed.
70 C3 Nendaz Switz.
31 M2 Nene r. England U.K.
Nenets Autonomous Okrug admin. div. Rus. Fed. see Nenetskiy Avtonomnyy Okrug
14 K2 Nenetskiy Avtonomnyy Okrug admin. div. Rus. Fed.
57 I3 Nenince Slovakia
169 S2 Nenjiang Heilong. China
169 S4 Nen Jiang r. China
48 D3 Nenndorf Ger.
50 G5 Nennhausen Ger.
53 K3 Nennslingen Ger.
14 G2 Nenoksa Rus. Fed.
49 I8 Nentershausen Hessen Ger.
49 E10 Nentershausen Rheinland-Pfalz Ger.
29 M4 Nenthead Cumbria, England U.K.
58 A5 Nenzing Austria
166 E4 Neo Japan
78 D2 Neo Agioneri Greece
200 □4a Neoch atoll Chuuk Micronesia
78 C3 Neochori Greece
78 F2 Neo Erasmio Greece
166 E5 Neo-gawa r. Japan
79 H5 Neo Karlovasi Samos Greece
Neokhórion Greece see Neochori
125 V1 Neola UT U.S.A.
26 J4 Neolithic Orkney tourist site Scotland U.K.
24 F2 Neolithic Orkney tourist site U.K.
78 D3 Neo Monastiri Greece
72 B7 Neoneli Sardegna Italy
Néon Karlovásion Samos Greece see Neo Karlovasi
110 F5 Neopit WI U.S.A.
121 H7 Neosho MO U.S.A.
121 H7 Neosho r. KS U.S.A.
78 E2 Neos Marmaras Greece
41 I10 Néoules France
66 F2 Néouvielle, Pic de mt. France
41 E6 Néouvielle, Réserve Naturelle de nature res. France
178 I5 Nepal country Asia
178 H5 Nepalganj Nepal
178 H6 Nepalganj Road Uttar Prad. India
178 F9 Nepanagar Madh. Prad. India
108 F4 Nepean Ont. Can.
204 □1 Nepean Island Norfolk I.
125 U2 Nephi UT U.S.A.
27 D4 Nephin hill Rep. of Ireland
27 C4 Nephin Beg Range hills Rep. of Ireland
73 I3 Nepi Italy
105 L5 Nepisiguit r. N.B. Can.
56 C2 Nepomuk Czech Rep.
19 V8 Nepryadva r. Rus. Fed.
119 G4 Neptune City NJ U.S.A.
204 F6 Neptune Islands S.A. Austr.
55 G3 Ner r. Pol.
73 I3 Nera r. Italy
43 E7 Nérac France
176 C3 Neral Mahar. India
207 N9 Nerang Qld Austr.
56 D1 Neratovice Czech Rep.
57 J6 Nerău Romania
18 H7 Neravai Lith.
51 G8 Nerchau Ger.
161 K1 Nerchinsk Rus. Fed.
162 A3 Nerchinskiy Zavod Rus. Fed.
42 D4 Nercillac France
72 D7 Nercone, Monte su mt. Italy
14 K4 Nerdva Rus. Fed.
42 D4 Néré France
77 O5 Nereju Romania
19 X4 Nerekhta Rus. Fed.
53 I4 Neresheim Ger.
109 G2 Néret, Lac l. Que. Can.
18 I5 Nereta Latvia
73 L2 Nereto Italy
68 F4 Neretva r. Bos.-Herz./Croatia
55 L4 Neretva r. Ukr.
68 F4 Neretvanski Kanal sea chan. Croatia
71 Q6 Nerezine Croatia
178 G9 Neri Mahar. India
173 J11 Nêri Pünco l. Xizang China
91 D8 Neriquinha Angola
18 G7 Neris r. Lith.
40 B4 Néris-les-Bains France
65 L7 Nerja Spain
104 C4 Nerka, Lake AK U.S.A.
19 X5 Nerl' Ivanovskaya Oblast' Rus. Fed.
19 V4 Nerl' Tverskaya Oblast' Rus. Fed.
19 U4 Nerl' r. Rus. Fed.
19 W4 Nero, Ozero l. Rus. Fed.
14 M3 Nerokhi Rus. Fed.
40 E5 Néronde France
40 B3 Nérondes France
142 C2 Nerópolis Brazil
49 C10 Neroth Ger.
17 S3 Nerovnovka Rus. Fed.
14 L2 Neroyka, Gora mt. Rus. Fed.
178 F9 Ner Pinglai Mahar. India
65 O4 Nerpio Spain
42 E4 Nersac France
53 I5 Nersingen Ger.
16 J7 Nerubays'ke Ukr.
19 T9 Neruch' r. Rus. Fed.
19 Q9 Nerussa r. Rus. Fed.
64 F5 Nerva Spain
71 M4 Nervesa della Battaglia Italy
40 E5 Nervieux France
63 O2 Nervión r. Spain
70 D4 Nery, Monte mt. Italy
193 N4 Neryungri Rus. Fed.
44 I2 Nes Neth.
22 F1 Nes Norway
14 I2 Nes' Rus. Fed.
14 I2 Nes' r. Rus. Fed.
184 G7 Nesā' Iran
184 D3 Nesa' Iran
22 F1 Nesbyen Norway
51 J8 Neschwitz Ger.
118 F5 Nesco NJ U.S.A.
118 C2 Nescopeck PA U.S.A.
118 C2 Nescopeck Creek r. PA U.S.A.
77 P8 Nesebŭr Bulg.
131 □4 Nesfield Barbados
22 C2 Nes Flaten Norway
118 F4 Neshaminy Creek r. PA U.S.A.
20 □G1 Neskaupstaður Iceland
36 E4 Nesle France
57 H2 Nesluša Slovakia
20 L3 Nesna Norway
16 G3 Nesolon' Ukr.
56 G2 Nesovice Czech Rep.
41 F8 Nesque r. France
118 D3 Nesquehoning PA U.S.A.
176 D4 Nesri Mahar. India
26 H8 Ness r. Scotland U.K.
26 G8 Ness, Loch l. Scotland U.K.
72 B2 Nessa Corse France
120 F6 Ness City KS U.S.A.
48 D3 Nesse Ger.
49 J9 Nesse r. Ger.
106 C3 Nesselrode, Mount Can./U.S.A.
53 J6 Nesselwang Ger.
70 G1 Nesslau Switz.
43 F9 Neste r. France
18 F7 Nesterov Rus. Fed.
19 Q7 Nestery Rus. Fed.
29 K7 Neston Cheshire, England U.K.
131 □7 Nestor Trin. and Tob.
73 I2 Nestore r. Italy
71 M9 Nestore r. Italy
107 M5 Nestor Falls Ont. Can.
110 F3 Nestoria MI U.S.A.
78 F2 Nestos r. Greece
22 E2 Nesvatn l. Norway
Nesvizh Belarus see Nyasvizh
190 C6 Netanya Israel
179 J8 Netarhat Jharkhand India
118 F3 Netcong NJ U.S.A.
49 H7 Nethe r. Ger.
44 I3 Netherlands country Europe
131 I7 Netherlands Antilles terr. West Indies
26 L8 Netherley Aberdeenshire, Scotland U.K.
30 F5 Nether Stowey Somerset, England U.K.
29 M3 Netherton Northumberland, England U.K.
26 I8 Nethy Bridge Highland, Scotland U.K.
95 H2 Netia Moz.
16 F3 Netishyn Ukr.
75 M5 Neto r. Italy
56 D2 Netolice Czech Rep.
49 F9 Netphen Ger.
49 J8 Netra (Ringgau) Ger.
179 M7 Netrakona Bangl.
178 D9 Netrang Gujarat India
70 G1 Netstal Switz.
37 I6 Nettancourt France
49 C10 Nettersheim Ger.
49 B8 Nettetal Ger.
105 K3 Nettilling Lake Nunavut Can.
110 A1 Nett Lake MN U.S.A.
29 Q7 Nettleham Lincolnshire, England U.K.
73 J5 Nettuno Italy
51 F9 Netzschkau Ger.
53 M2 Neualbenreuth Ger.
49 G10 Neu-Anspach Ger.
92 B3 Neubari r. Sudan
48 I1 Neuberend Ger.
59 M4 Neuberg an der Mürz Austria
53 M6 Neubeuern Ger.
53 L5 Neubiberg Ger.
48 D5 Neubörger Ger.
39 M3 Neubourg, Campagne du reg. France
50 H3 Neubrandenburg Ger.
48 G5 Neubruchhausen Ger.
52 H2 Neubrunn Ger.
50 E2 Neubukow Ger.
52 F4 Neubulach Ger.
53 O4 Neuburg am Inn Ger.
52 E4 Neuburg am Rhein Ger.
53 K4 Neuburg an der Donau Ger.
53 I5 Neuburg an der Kammel Ger.
50 E3 Neuburg-Steinhausen Ger.
51 H8 Neuburxdorf Ger.
70 B2 Neuchâtel Switz.
70 B1 Neuchâtel canton Switz.
70 B2 Neuchâtel, Lac de l. Switz.
48 K4 Neu Darchau Ger.
49 K9 Neudietendorf Ger.
59 N4 Neudorf Austria
51 G10 Neudorf Ger.
51 E10 Neudrossenfeld Ger.
52 F4 Neuenbürg Ger.
52 D6 Neuenburg am Rhein Ger.
53 J3 Neuendettelsau Ger.
51 I6 Neuendorfer See l. Ger.
50 J5 Neuenhagen Ger.
50 I5 Neuenhagen Berlin Ger.
49 C6 Neuenhaus Ger.
52 E7 Neuenhof Switz.
70 E1 Neuenkirch Switz.
50 H1 Neuenkirchen Mecklenburg-Vorpommern Ger.
50 H2 Neuenkirchen Mecklenburg-Vorpommern Ger.
48 G3 Neuenkirchen Niedersachsen Ger.
48 G4 Neuenkirchen Niedersachsen Ger.
48 G5 Neuenkirchen Niedersachsen Ger.
48 I4 Neuenkirchen Niedersachsen Ger.
49 E6 Neuenkirchen Niedersachsen Ger.
49 D6 Neuenkirchen Nordrhein-Westfalen Ger.
48 H2 Neuenkirchen Schleswig-Holstein Ger.
49 F5 Neuenkirchen (Oldenburg) Ger.
49 D9 Neuenkirchen-Seelscheid Ger.
49 E8 Neuenrade Ger.
52 G3 Neuenstadt am Kocher Ger.
52 H3 Neuenstein Ger.
48 G3 Neuenwalde Ger.
49 B10 Neuerburg Ger.
53 L5 Neufahrn bei Freising Ger.
53 M4 Neufahrn in Niederbayern Ger.
37 O7 Neuf-Brisach France
45 H9 Neufchâteau Belgium
37 K7 Neufchâteau France
36 B4 Neufchâtel-en-Bray France
39 L5 Neufchâtel-en-Saosnois France
36 C2 Neufchâtel-Hardelot France
36 H5 Neufchâtel-sur-Aisne France
48 H3 Neufeld Ger.
59 N4 Neufeld an der Leitha Austria
59 J3 Neufelden Austria
52 G4 Neuffen Ger.
37 I4 Neufmanil France
52 G5 Neufra Ger.
51 E7 Neugattersleben Ger.
51 K9 Neugersdorf Ger.
50 H4 Neuglobsow Ger.
50 J5 Neuhardenberg Ger.
48 E3 Neuharlingersiel Ger.
59 K6 Neuhaus Kärnten Austria
59 L4 Neuhaus Niederösterreich Austria
48 K4 Neuhaus (Elbe) Ger.
48 H3 Neuhaus (Oste) Ger.
53 O5 Neuhaus am Inn Ger.
59 N6 Neuhaus am Klausenbach Austria
51 D9 Neuhaus am Rennweg Ger.
53 L2 Neuhaus an der Pegnitz Ger.
52 F4 Neuhausen Baden-Württemberg Ger.
51 H9 Neuhausen Sachsen Ger.
70 F1 Neuhausen Switz.
52 F6 Neuhausen ob Eck Ger.
51 D10 Neuhaus-Schierschnitz Ger.
49 I10 Neuhof Ger.
53 J3 Neuhof an der Zenn Ger.
59 J3 Neuhofen an der Krems Austria
59 K3 Neuhofen an der Ybbs Austria
39 M6 Neuillé-Pont-Pierre France
40 D2 Neuilly France
36 D5 Neuilly-en-Thelle France
40 C4 Neuilly-le-Réal France
37 J8 Neuilly-l'Évêque France
36 F5 Neuilly-St-Front France
36 D6 Neuilly-sur-Seine France
49 G10 Neu-Isenburg Ger.
50 G3 Neukalen Ger.
50 D4 Neu Kaliß Ger.
48 E4 Neukamperfehn Ger.
51 F8 Neukieritzsch Ger.
52 H6 Neukirch Baden-Württemberg Ger.
51 J8 Neukirch Sachsen Ger.
49 H9 Neukirchen Hessen Ger.
51 F9 Neukirchen Sachsen Ger.
51 G9 Neukirchen Sachsen Ger.
50 D2 Neukirchen Schleswig-Holstein Ger.
48 G1 Neukirchen Schleswig-Holstein Ger.
58 F5 Neukirchen am Großvenediger Austria
58 H3 Neukirchen an der Enknach Austria
59 I3 Neukirchen an der Vöckla Austria
53 M3 Neukirchen-Balbini Ger.
53 L2 Neukirchen bei Sulzbach-Rosenberg Ger.
53 O4 Neukirchen vorm Wald Ger.
50 E3 Neukloster Ger.
48 D4 Neulehe Ger.
59 M3 Neulengbach Austria
53 I4 Neuler Ger.
50 J5 Neulewin Ger.
40 E5 Neulise France
66 K3 Neulós, Puig mt. Spain
51 I6 Neu Lübbenau Ger.
52 B2 Neumagen Ger.
51 F9 Neumark Sachsen Ger.
51 D8 Neumark Thüringen Ger.
58 H4 Neumarkt am Wallersee Austria
59 J3 Neumarkt im Mühlkreis Austria
53 K3 Neumarkt in der Oberpfalz Ger.
59 J5 Neumarkt in Steiermark Austria
53 N5 Neumarkt-Sankt Veit Ger.
212 X2 Neumayer research stn Antarctica
48 I2 Neumünster Ger.
158 G5 Neun, Nam r. Laos
53 M3 Neunburg vorm Wald Ger.
51 F9 Neundorf Ger.
39 O6 Neung-sur-Beuvron France
70 F1 Neunkirch Switz.
59 N4 Neunkirchen Austria
49 F9 Neunkirchen Nordrhein-Westfalen Ger.
52 C3 Neunkirchen Saarland Ger.
53 K2 Neunkirchen am Sand Ger.
53 N5 Neuötting Ger.
51 J7 Neupetershain Ger.
59 L2 Neupölla Austria
146 C6 Neuquén Arg.
146 C6 Neuquén prov. Arg.
146 D6 Neuquén r. Arg.
53 P4 Neureichenau Ger.
53 K5 Neuried Ger.
50 G5 Neuruppin Ger.
51 K8 Neusalza-Spremberg Ger.
Neu Sandez Pol. see Nowy Sącz
53 J5 Neusäß Ger.
53 O4 Neuschönau Ger.
115 I8 Neuse r. NC U.S.A.
51 G6 Neuseddin Ger.
59 O4 Neusiedl am See Austria
59 O4 Neusiedler See l. Austria/Hungary
59 O4 Neusiedler See Seewinkel, Nationalpark nat. park Austria
53 L2 Neusorg Ger.
49 C8 Neuss Ger.
41 B6 Neussargues-Moissac France
52 E6 Neustadt Baden-Württemberg Ger.
50 F5 Neustadt Brandenburg Ger.
51 E9 Neustadt Thüringen Ger.
49 K7 Neustadt (Harz) Ger.
49 H9 Neustadt (Hessen) Ger.
49 D9 Neustadt (Wied) Ger.
53 L2 Neustadt am Kulm Ger.
49 K9 Neustadt am Rennsteig Ger.
49 H5 Neustadt am Rübenberge Ger.
53 J2 Neustadt an der Aisch Ger.
53 L4 Neustadt an der Donau Ger.
Neustadt an der Hardt Ger. see Neustadt an der Weinstraße
53 M2 Neustadt an der Waldnaab Ger.
52 E3 Neustadt an der Weinstraße Ger.
51 D10 Neustadt bei Coburg Ger.
50 E4 Neustadt-Glewe Ger.
48 K2 Neustadt in Holstein Ger.
51 J8 Neustadt in Sachsen Ger.
58 D5 Neustift im Stubaital Austria
50 H4 Neustrelitz Ger.
53 M4 Neutraubling Ger.
50 J5 Neutrebbin Ger.
53 I5 Neu-Ulm Ger.
41 B7 Neuvéglise France
37 L6 Neuves-Maisons France
42 E5 Neuvic Aquitaine France
42 I5 Neuvic Limousin France
42 I5 Neuvic, Barrage de dam France
36 D7 Neuville-aux-Bois France
39 L8 Neuville-de-Poitou France
40 G4 Neuville-les-Dames France
36 B4 Neuville-lès-Dieppe France
40 F5 Neuville-sur-Saône France
39 L5 Neuville-sur-Sarthe France
37 J5 Neuvilly-en-Argonne France
40 D3 Neuvy-Grandchamp France
39 M6 Neuvy-le-Roi France
39 O8 Neuvy-Pailloux France
39 O8 Neuvy-St-Sépulchre France
36 G7 Neuvy-Sautour France
39 P7 Neuvy-sur-Barangeon France
51 D6 Neuwegersleben Ger.
52 F4 Neuweiler Ger.
48 G3 Neuwerk i. Ger.
21 J10 Neuwerker und Scharhoerner Watt nat. park Ger.
49 D10 Neuwied Ger.
48 J2 Neuwittenbek Ger.
48 I4 Neu Wulmstorf Ger.
51 G9 Neuwürschnitz Ger.
51 J7 Neu Zauche Ger.
51 K6 Neuzelle Ger.
51 I6 Neu Zittau Ger.
19 N2 Neva r. Rus. Fed.
41 J6 Névache France
120 I4 Nevada IA U.S.A.
121 H7 Nevada MO U.S.A.
124 O2 Nevada state U.S.A.
144 C2 Nevada, Sierra mt. Arg.
65 M6 Nevada, Sierra mts Spain
65 M6 Nevada, Sierra nature res. Spain
124 K1 Nevada, Sierra mts CA U.S.A.
124 K2 Nevada City CA U.S.A.
146 C4 Nevado, Cerro mt. Arg.
146 C5 Nevado, Sierra del mts Arg.
128 D6 Nevado de Colima, Parque Nacional nat. park Mex.
129 H6 Nevado de Tolúca, Parque Nacional nat. park Mex.
129 H6 Nevado de Toluca, Volcán vol. Mex.
65 I4 Névalo r. Spain
176 D3 Nevasa Mahar. India
190 C7 Nevatim Israel
17 N1 Nevdol'sk Rus. Fed.
Nevdubstroy Rus. Fed. see Kirovsk
91 B8 Neve, Serra da mts Angola
56 D2 Neveklov Czech Rep.
18 M5 Nevel' Rus. Fed.
19 M6 Nevel', Ozero l. Rus. Fed.
45 E6 Nevele Belgium
162 L5 Nevel'sk Sakhalin Rus. Fed.
63 Q7 Nevera mt. Spain
182 B1 Neverkino Rus. Fed.
30 C3 Nevern Pembrokeshire, Wales U.K.
18 H7 Neveronys Lith.
40 C2 Nevers France
118 F2 Neversink r. NY U.S.A.
205 K4 Nevertire N.S.W. Austr.
143 F5 Neves Brazil
71 L2 Neves, Lago di l. Italy
68 G4 Nevesinje Bos.-Herz.
38 D6 Névez France
18 G7 Nevėžis r. Lith.
41 B10 Névian France
75 O3 Neviano Italy
39 M2 Néville France
191 C1 Nevinnomyssk Rus. Fed.
131 □2 Nevis i. St Kitts and Nevis
26 E8 Nevis, Loch inlet Scotland U.K.
131 □2 Nevis Peak St Kitts and Nevis
188 G4 Nevşehir Turkey
162 H6 Nevskoye Rus. Fed.
125 Q8 New r. CA U.S.A.
116 D11 New r. WV U.S.A.
26 I13 New Abbey Dumfries and Galloway, Scotland U.K.
26 L7 New Aberdour Aberdeenshire, Scotland U.K.
31 L5 New Addington Greater London, England U.K.
106 D4 New Aiyansh B.C. Can.
93 C7 Newala Tanz.
114 E6 New Albany IN U.S.A.
121 K8 New Albany MS U.S.A.
118 C1 New Albany PA U.S.A.
110 F4 Newald WI U.S.A.
31 J5 New Alresford Hampshire, England U.K.
137 G3 New Amsterdam Guyana
205 K3 New Angledool N.S.W. Austr.
97 P5 Newark S. Africa
124 J4 Newark CA U.S.A.
118 D5 Newark DE U.S.A.
117 K8 Newark NJ U.S.A.
116 H5 Newark NY U.S.A.
116 C8 Newark OH U.S.A.
117 K8 Newark airport NJ U.S.A.
125 Q2 Newark Lake NV U.S.A.
29 P7 Newark-on-Trent Nottinghamshire, England U.K.
111 R7 Newark Valley NY U.S.A.
31 M5 New Ash Green Kent, England U.K.
121 K10 New Augusta MS U.S.A.
110 I6 Newaygo MI U.S.A.
117 O7 New Bedford MA U.S.A.
122 C4 Newberg OR U.S.A.
117 J6 New Berlin NY U.S.A.
118 B3 New Berlin PA U.S.A.
118 D4 New Berlinville PA U.S.A.
115 I8 New Bern NC U.S.A.
110 I3 Newberry MI U.S.A.
115 G8 Newberry SC U.S.A.
122 D5 Newberry National Volcanic Monument nat. park OR U.S.A.
124 P7 Newberry Springs CA U.S.A.
118 B4 Newberrytown PA U.S.A.
116 F7 New Bethlehem PA U.S.A.
29 N3 Newbiggin-by-the-Sea Northumberland, England U.K.
26 I11 Newbigging South Lanarkshire, Scotland U.K.
130 F1 New Bight Cat I. Bahamas
27 H4 Newbliss Rep. of Ireland
111 Q9 New Bloomfield PA U.S.A.
108 E4 Newboro Ont. Can.
116 C10 New Boston OH U.S.A.
121 H9 New Boston TX U.S.A.
121 F11 New Braunfels TX U.S.A.
27 F5 Newbridge Galway Rep. of Ireland
27 I6 Newbridge Kildare Rep. of Ireland
27 E7 Newbridge Limerick Rep. of Ireland
30 F4 Newbridge Caerphilly, Wales U.K.
30 F3 Newbridge on Wye Powys, Wales U.K.
116 E8 New Brighton PA U.S.A.
153 K8 New Britain i. P.N.G.
119 J1 New Britain CT U.S.A.
118 E4 New Britain PA U.S.A.
216 F6 New Britain Trench sea feature Pacific Ocean
130 □ New Broughton Jamaica
109 H4 New Brunswick prov. Can.
117 K8 New Brunswick NJ U.S.A.
110 H8 New Buffalo MI U.S.A.
118 B4 New Buffalo PA U.S.A.
27 H3 New Buildings Northern Ireland U.K.
116 H8 Newburg PA U.S.A.
111 R5 Newburgh Ont. Can.
26 L8 Newburgh Aberdeenshire, Scotland U.K.
26 J10 Newburgh Fife, Scotland U.K.
26 J12 Newburgh Scottish Borders, Scotland U.K.
117 K7 Newburgh NY U.S.A.
31 J5 Newbury West Berkshire, England U.K.
117 O6 Newburyport MA U.S.A.
89 G4 New Bussa Nigeria
29 L5 Newby Bridge Cumbria, England U.K.
26 L7 New Byth Aberdeenshire, Scotland U.K.
New Caledonia i. S. Pacific Ocean see Nouvelle Calédonie
200 □5 New Caledonia terr. S. Pacific Ocean
216 F7 New Caledonia Trough sea feature Tasman Sea
119 I2 New Canaan CT U.S.A.
109 H3 New Carlisle Que. Can.
116 A9 New Carlisle OH U.S.A.
118 B7 New Carrollton MD U.S.A.
205 M5 Newcastle N.S.W. Austr.
108 E5 Newcastle Ont. Can.
130 □ Newcastle Jamaica
27 J6 Newcastle Dublin Rep. of Ireland
27 E6 Newcastle Galway Rep. of Ireland
27 G8 Newcastle Tipperary Rep. of Ireland
27 J6 Newcastle Wicklow Rep. of Ireland
97 N3 Newcastle S. Africa
131 □2 Newcastle St Kitts and Nevis
27 K4 Newcastle Northern Ireland U.K.
30 F3 Newcastle Shropshire, England U.K.
124 K3 Newcastle CA U.S.A.
118 D5 New Castle DE U.S.A.
114 E6 New Castle IN U.S.A.
114 E6 New Castle KY U.S.A.
117 □P4 Newcastle ME U.S.A.
116 E7 New Castle PA U.S.A.
125 S4 Newcastle UT U.S.A.
116 E11 New Castle VA U.S.A.
122 L5 Newcastle WY U.S.A.
118 D5 New Castle County county DE U.S.A.
206 D4 Newcastle Creek r. N.T. Austr.
30 D3 Newcastle Emlyn Ceredigion, Wales U.K.
207 I5 Newcastle Range hills Qld Austr.
26 K12 Newcastleton Scottish Borders, Scotland U.K.
29 M7 Newcastle-under-Lyme Staffordshire, England U.K.
29 N4 Newcastle upon Tyne Tyne and Wear, England U.K.
206 D4 Newcastle Waters N.T. Austr.
27 D8 Newcastle West Rep. of Ireland
27 E9 Newcestown Rep. of Ireland
117 J11 New Church VA U.S.A.
119 H2 New City NY U.S.A.
118 B2 New Columbia PA U.S.A.
118 C2 New Columbus PA U.S.A.
125 X5 Newcomb NM U.S.A.
116 D8 Newcomerstown OH U.S.A.
116 D9 New Concord OH U.S.A.
119 H2 New Croton Reservoir NY U.S.A.
118 B4 New Cumberland PA U.S.A.
26 H12 New Cumnock East Ayrshire, Scotland U.K.
26 L7 New Deer Aberdeenshire, Scotland U.K.
209 E12 Newdegate W.A. Austr.
178 F5 New Delhi Delhi India
117 □R1 New Denmark N.B. Can.
124 L4 New Don Pedro Reservoir CA U.S.A.
29 O6 New Earswick York, England U.K.
118 F4 New Egypt NJ U.S.A.
52 B2 Newel Ger.
207 J4 Newell Qld Austr.
120 D3 Newell SD U.S.A.
116 E8 Newell WV U.S.A.
209 I8 Newell, Lake salt flat W.A. Austr.
107 I5 Newell, Lake Alta Can.
205 M4 New England Range mts N.S.W. Austr.
214 F3 New England Seamounts sea feature N. Atlantic Ocean
104 B4 Newenham, Cape AK U.S.A.
30 H4 Newent Gloucestershire, England U.K.
110 H6 New Era MI U.S.A.
116 G5 Newfane NY U.S.A.
117 M6 Newfane VT U.S.A.
118 E5 Newfield NJ U.S.A.
117 N5 Newfound Lake NH U.S.A.
109 J3 Newfoundland i. Nfld and Lab. Can.
119 G2 Newfoundland NJ U.S.A.
118 E2 Newfoundland PA U.S.A.
109 J2 Newfoundland and Labrador prov. Can.
122 H6 Newfoundland Evaporation Basin salt l. UT U.S.A.
118 B5 New Freedom PA U.S.A.
26 H12 New Galloway Dumfries and Galloway, Scotland U.K.
200 □6 New Georgia i. New Georgia Is Solomon Is
200 □6 New Georgia Islands Solomon Is
200 □6 New Georgia Sound sea chan. Solomon Is
110 E7 New Glarus WI U.S.A.
109 I4 New Glasgow N.S. Can.
27 J5 Newgrange Rep. of Ireland
25 D5 Newgrange Tomb tourist site Rep. of Ireland
131 □7 New Grant Trin. and Tob.
119 G5 New Gretna NJ U.S.A.
153 J8 New Guinea i. Indon./P.N.G.
85 G6 New Halfa Sudan
124 N7 Newhall CA U.S.A.
119 H1 New Hamburg NY U.S.A.
117 N4 New Hampshire state U.S.A.
110 B6 New Hampton IA U.S.A.
119 G2 New Hampton NY U.S.A.
153 L7 New Hanover i. P.N.G.
97 O5 New Hanover S. Africa
117 J5 New Hartford NY U.S.A.
31 M6 Newhaven East Sussex, England U.K.
117 M7 New Haven CT U.S.A.
110 B6 New Haven IA U.S.A.
110 I8 New Haven IN U.S.A.
111 L7 New Haven MI U.S.A.
116 D10 New Haven WV U.S.A.
119 J2 New Haven County county CT U.S.A.
106 E4 New Hazelton B.C. Can.
New Hebrides country S. Pacific Ocean see Vanuatu
216 G7 New Hebrides Trench sea feature Pacific Ocean
124 L3 New Hogan Reservoir CA U.S.A.
118 C4 New Holland PA U.S.A.
110 F6 New Holstein WI U.S.A.
118 F4 New Hope PA U.S.A.
121 J10 New Iberia LA U.S.A.
31 M6 Newick East Sussex, England U.K.
31 N5 Newington Kent, England U.K.
119 J1 Newington CT U.S.A.
28 C6 New Inn Cavan Rep. of Ireland
27 H6 New Inn Laois Rep. of Ireland
27 G8 Newinn Rep. of Ireland
153 L7 New Ireland i. P.N.G.
118 G5 New Jersey state U.S.A.
178 C8 New Kandla Gujarat India
116 F8 New Kensington PA U.S.A.
116 H11 New Kent VA U.S.A.
27 E7 New Kildimo Rep. of Ireland
123 L9 Newkirk NM U.S.A.
121 G7 Newkirk OK U.S.A.
26 I11 New Lanark Scotland U.K.
26 I11 New Lanark World Heritage Site tourist site Scotland U.K.
115 G7 Newland NC U.S.A.
209 G10 Newland Range hills W.A. Austr.
26 L7 New Leeds Aberdeenshire, Scotland U.K.
116 C9 New Lexington OH U.S.A.
110 D6 New Lisbon WI U.S.A.
108 E4 New Liskeard Ont. Can.
117 M7 New London CT U.S.A.
116 C7 New London OH U.S.A.
110 F5 New London WI U.S.A.
119 K1 New London County county CT U.S.A.
26 G13 New Luce Dumfries and Galloway, Scotland U.K.
30 □ Newlyn Cornwall, England U.K.
26 L8 Newmachar Aberdeenshire, Scotland U.K.
121 K7 New Madrid MO U.S.A.
209 E7 Newman W.A. Austr.
202 J7 Newman North I. N.Z.
124 K4 Newman CA U.S.A.
212 O1 Newman Island Antarctica
118 C4 Newmanstown PA U.S.A.
108 E4 Newmarket Ont. Can.
130 □ Newmarket Jamaica
27 D8 Newmarket Cork Rep. of Ireland
27 H8 Newmarket Kilkenny Rep. of Ireland
31 M3 Newmarket Suffolk, England U.K.
26 D6 Newmarket Western Isles, Scotland U.K.
117 □O5 Newmarket NH U.S.A.
116 G10 New Market VA U.S.A.
27 E7 Newmarket-on-Fergus Rep. of Ireland
116 E9 New Martinsville WV U.S.A.
122 F4 New Meadows ID U.S.A.
123 L9 New Mexico state U.S.A.
116 A9 New Miami OH U.S.A.
119 I1 New Milford CT U.S.A.
117 J7 New Milford PA U.S.A.
26 K7 Newmill Moray, Scotland U.K.
29 M7 New Mills Derbyshire, England U.K.
26 H11 Newmilns East Ayrshire, Scotland U.K.
31 I6 New Milton Hampshire, England U.K.
31 O4 New Mistley Essex, England U.K.
116 B9 New Moorefield OH U.S.A.
115 E9 Newnan GA U.S.A.
30 H4 Newnham Gloucestershire, England U.K.
209 D11 New Norcia W.A. Austr.
205 K10 New Norfolk Tas. Austr.
121 J11 New Orleans LA U.S.A.
118 A5 New Oxford PA U.S.A.
117 K7 New Paltz NY U.S.A.
110 I8 New Paris IN U.S.A.
116 A9 New Paris OH U.S.A.
116 D8 New Philadelphia OH U.S.A.
118 C3 New Philadelphia PA U.S.A.
26 L7 New Pitsligo Aberdeenshire, Scotland U.K.
202 I6 New Plymouth North I. N.Z.
30 C6 New Polzeath Cornwall, England U.K.
130 □ Newport Jamaica
27 C5 Newport Mayo Rep. of Ireland
27 F7 Newport Tipperary Rep. of Ireland
31 M4 Newport Essex, England U.K.
26 J6 Newport Highland, Scotland U.K.
31 J6 Newport Isle of Wight, England U.K.
30 F4 Newport Newport, Wales U.K.
30 C3 Newport Pembrokeshire, Wales U.K.
30 H2 Newport Telford and Wrekin, England U.K.
30 G4 Newport admin. div. Wales U.K.
121 J8 Newport AR U.S.A.
118 D5 Newport DE U.S.A.
114 D6 Newport IN U.S.A.
117 □P4 Newport ME U.S.A.
111 K8 Newport MI U.S.A.
117 M5 Newport NH U.S.A.
118 E6 Newport NJ U.S.A.
122 B4 Newport OR U.S.A.
118 A4 Newport PA U.S.A.
117 N7 Newport RI U.S.A.
115 F8 Newport TN U.S.A.
117 M4 Newport VT U.S.A.
122 F2 Newport WA U.S.A.
30 C3 Newport Bay Wales U.K.
124 O8 Newport Beach CA U.S.A.
116 I11 Newport News VA U.S.A.
26 K10 Newport-on-Tay Fife, Scotland U.K.
31 K3 Newport Pagnell Milton Keynes, England U.K.
115 F11 New Port Richey FL U.S.A.
27 I3 Newport Trench Northern Ireland U.K.
119 I1 New Preston CT U.S.A.
130 E1 New Providence i. Bahamas
119 G3 New Providence NJ U.S.A.
118 C5 New Providence PA U.S.A.
30 D3 New Quay Ceredigion, Wales U.K.
30 B7 Newquay Cornwall, England U.K.
30 F3 New Radnor Powys, Wales U.K.
109 H3 New Richmond Que. Can.
116 A10 New Richmond OH U.S.A.
110 B4 New Richmond WI U.S.A.
118 D3 New Ringgold PA U.S.A.
125 T8 New River AZ U.S.A.
203 C13 New River Estuary South I. N.Z.
121 J10 New Roads LA U.S.A.
119 H3 New Rochelle NY U.S.A.
120 F2 New Rockford ND U.S.A.
31 N6 New Romney Kent, England U.K.
109 H4 New Ross N.S. Can.
27 I8 New Ross Rep. of Ireland
206 B4 Newry N.T. Austr.
27 J4 Newry Northern Ireland U.K.
110 D6 Newry WI U.S.A.
27 J4 Newry Canal Northern Ireland U.K.
New Siberia Islands Rus. Fed. see Novosibirskiye Ostrova
115 G11 New Smyrna Beach FL U.S.A.
205 K5 New South Wales state Austr.
116 F8 New Stanton PA U.S.A.
119 K3 New Suffolk NY U.S.A.
116 B12 New Tazewell TN U.S.A.
147 H4 Newton Arg.
26 F10 Newton Argyll and Bute, Scotland U.K.
29 M6 Newton Lancashire, England U.K.
115 E10 Newton GA U.S.A.
120 I5 Newton IA U.S.A.
120 K6 Newton IL U.S.A.
120 G6 Newton KS U.S.A.
117 N6 Newton MA U.S.A.
121 K9 Newton MS U.S.A.
115 G8 Newton NC U.S.A.
118 F2 Newton NJ U.S.A.
121 I10 Newton TX U.S.A.
30 E6 Newton Abbot Devon, England U.K.
29 N4 Newton Aycliffe Durham, England U.K.
117 K4 Newton Falls NY U.S.A.
30 D7 Newton Ferrers Devon, England U.K.
26 L8 Newtonhill Aberdeenshire, Scotland U.K.
29 L7 Newton-le-Willows Merseyside, England U.K.
31 K4 Newton Longville Buckinghamshire, England U.K.
26 H11 Newton Mearns East Renfrewshire, Scotland U.K.
26 H8 Newtonmore Highland, Scotland U.K.
30 F6 Newton Poppleford Devon, England U.K.
30 E6 Newton St Cyres Devon, England U.K.
26 H13 Newton Stewart Dumfries and Galloway, Scotland U.K.
20 □ Newtontoppen mt. Svalbard
27 E8 Newtown Cork Rep. of Ireland
27 H7 Newtown Laois Rep. of Ireland
27 F6 Newtown Roscommon Rep. of Ireland
27 F8 Newtown Tipperary Rep. of Ireland
27 H8 Newtown Waterford Rep. of Ireland
30 G3 Newtown Herefordshire, England U.K.
30 F2 Newtown Powys, Wales U.K.
119 I2 Newtown CT U.S.A.
120 D1 New Town ND U.S.A.
118 C3 Newtown PA U.S.A.
118 F4 Newtown PA U.S.A.
27 K3 Newtownabbey Northern Ireland U.K.
27 K3 Newtownards Northern Ireland U.K.
27 H4 Newtownbutler Northern Ireland U.K.
28 E4 Newtown Crommelin Northern Ireland U.K.
27 G3 Newtowncunningham Rep. of Ireland
27 G5 Newtown Forbes Rep. of Ireland
27 G4 Newtown Gore Rep. of Ireland
27 I4 Newtownhamilton Northern Ireland U.K.
27 H6 Newtownlow Rep. of Ireland
27 J6 Newtownmountkennedy Rep. of Ireland
26 K11 Newtown St Boswells Scottish Borders, Scotland U.K.
27 D7 Newtown Sandes Rep. of Ireland
118 E5 Newtown Square PA U.S.A.
27 H3 Newtownstewart Northern Ireland U.K.
30 F4 New Tredegar Caerphilly, Wales U.K.
118 D3 New Tripoli PA U.S.A.
26 J9 Newtyle Angus, Scotland U.K.
120 H3 New Ulm MN U.S.A.
116 B9 New Vienna OH U.S.A.
116 H8 Newville PA U.S.A.
117 □O4 New Vineyard ME U.S.A.
29 Q6 New Waltham North East Lincolnshire, England U.K.
118 A5 New Windsor MD U.S.A.
119 G2 New Windsor NY U.S.A.
117 J6 New Woodstock NY U.S.A.
117 L8 New York NY U.S.A.
117 J6 New York state U.S.A.
119 H3 New York County county NY U.S.A.
125 Q6 New York Mountains CA U.S.A.
202 I9 New Zealand country Oceania
129 I7 Nexapa r. Mex.
42 G4 Nexon France
14 H4 Neya Rus. Fed.
14 H4 Neya r. Rus. Fed.
166 C6 Neyagawa Japan
184 I5 Neybasteh Afgh.
184 G7 Ney Bīd Iran
184 E5 Neyestānak Iran
30 C4 Neyland Pembrokeshire, Wales U.K.
184 F7 Neyrīz Iran
184 H3 Neyshābūr Iran
176 E8 Neyyattinkara Kerala India
129 H6 Nezahualcóyotl Mex.
129 N8 Nezahualcóyotl, Presa resr Mex.
56 G2 Nezamyslice Czech Rep.
56 D2 Nežárka r. Czech Rep.
99 □1c Nez de Bœuf mt. Réunion
17 P3 Nezhegol' r. Rus. Fed.
Nezhin Ukr. see Nizhyn
191 E1 Nezlobnaya Rus. Fed.
122 F3 Nezperce ID U.S.A.
122 F3 Nez Perce Indian Reservation res. ID U.S.A.
57 I4 Nézsa Hungary
56 C2 Nezvěstice Czech Rep.
16 E5 Nezvys'ko Ukr.
157 H4 Ngabang Kalimantan Indon.
91 C5 Ngabé Congo
159 D7 Nga Chong, Khao mt. Myanmar/Thai.
89 I3 Ngadda watercourse Nigeria
155 A8 Ngadubolu Sumba Indon.
158 C2 Ngagahtawng Myanmar
202 I2 Ngaiotonga North I. N.Z.
154 □ Ngajangel i. Palau
93 B6 Ngajira Tanz.
90 D4 Ngala Dem. Rep. Congo
89 I3 Ngala Nigeria
155 D2 Ngalipaëng Sulawesi Indon.
155 B9 Ngalu Sumba Indon.
90 C2 Ngam Chad
90 C2 Ngama Chad
94 D3 Ngamaseri watercourse Botswana
202 I6 Ngamatapouri North I. N.Z.
89 H5 Ngambé Cameroon
170 A3 Ngamda Xizang China
154 □ Ngamegei Passage Palau
94 D3 Ngamiland admin. dist. Botswana
173 H12 Ngamring Xizang China
92 A3 Ngangala Sudan
173 F11 Ngangla Ringco salt l. China
173 E10 Nganglong Kangri mt. Xizang China
173 E10 Nganglong Kangri mts Xizang China
91 B7 N'gangula Angola
173 H11 Ngangzê Co salt l. China
173 H11 Ngangzê Shan mts Xizang China
171 □J7 Ngan Hei Shui Tong resr H.K. China
157 I8 Nganjuk Jawa Indon.
170 E9 Ngan Sâu, Sông r. Vietnam
158 G3 Ngân Sơn Vietnam
158 D5 Ngao Thai.
89 I5 Ngaoundal Cameroon
89 I5 Ngaoundéré Cameroon
202 J5 Ngapuke North I. N.Z.
93 B7 Ngara Malawi
93 A5 Ngara Tanz.
156 F7 Ngaras Sumatera Indon.
154 □ Ngardmau Palau
154 □ Ngardmau Bay Palau
154 □ Ngaregur i. Palau
93 C7 Ngarimbi Tanz.
154 □ Ngariungs i. Palau
204 H6 Ngarkat Conservation Park nature res. S.A. Austr.
202 J4 Ngaruawahia North I. N.Z.
202 K6 Ngaruroro r. North I. N.Z.
202 H1 Ngataki North I. N.Z.
203 □3 Ngatangiia Rarotonga Cook Is
202 L5 Ngatapa North I. N.Z.
202 J4 Ngatea North I. N.Z.
154 □ Ngateguil, Point Palau
158 B6 Ngathainggyaung Myanmar
89 I6 Ngato Cameroon
171 □J7 Ngau Mei Hoi b. H.K. China
159 D8 Ngawan Chaung r. Myanmar
157 I8 Ngawi Jawa Indon.
158 B6 Ngayok Bay Myanmar
90 B4 Ngbala Congo
Ngcheangel atoll Palau see Kayangel Atoll
93 A6 Ngegera Tanz.
Ngemelachel Palau see Malakal
154 □ Ngemelis Islands Palau
154 □ Ngergoi i. Palau
153 H5 Ngeruangel i. Palau
154 □ Ngesebus i. Palau

Novoshakhtinsk to Ochakiv

313

15 G7 Novoshakhtinsk Rus. Fed.
62 H6 Novoshakhtinskiy Rus. Fed.
17 R7 Novoshcherbinovskaya Rus. Fed.
15 J5 Novosheshminsk Rus. Fed.
92 J4 Novosibirsk Rus. Fed.
93 P2 Novosibirskiye Ostrova is Rus. Fed.
19 U9 Novosil' Rus. Fed.
17 L8 Novosil's'ke Ukr.
17 R2 Novosil'skoye Rus. Fed.
17 L7 Novosofiyivka Ukr.
19 N5 Novosokol'niki Rus. Fed.
17 P7 Novospas'ke Ukr.
82 B1 Novospasskoye Rus. Fed.
55 J1 Novostroyevo Rus. Fed.
17 S5 Novosvitlivka Ukr.
57 I2 Novoť Slovakia
91 I1 Novoterechnoye Rus. Fed.
17 R8 Novotitarovskaya Rus. Fed.
62 G4 Novotroichkoye Rus. Fed.
82 H2 Novotroitsk Rus. Fed.
19 Q8 Novotroitskoye Rus. Fed.
17 Q5 Novotroyits'ke Donets'ka Oblast' Ukr.
17 Q6 Novotroyits'ke Donets'ka Oblast' Ukr.
17 N7 Novotroyits'ke Khersons'ka Oblast' Ukr.
17 O6 Novotroyits'ke Zaporiz'ka Oblast' Ukr.
Novoukrainka Kirovohrads'ka Oblast' Ukr. see Novoukrayinka
Novoukrainka Rivnens'ka Oblast' Ukr. see Novoukrayinka
17 K5 Novoukrayinka Kirovohrads'ka Oblast' Ukr.
16 E3 Novoukrayinka Rivnens'ka Oblast' Ukr.
82 G2 Novoural'sk Rus. Fed.
82 C2 Novouzensk Rus. Fed.
83 P1 Novovarshavka Rus. Fed.
17 O7 Novovasylivka Zaporiz'ka Oblast' Ukr.
17 P7 Novovasylivka Zaporiz'ka Oblast' Ukr.
68 F2 Novo Virje Croatia
16 D3 Novovolyns'k Ukr.
15 G6 Novovoronezh Rus. Fed.
Novovoronezhskiy Rus. Fed. see Novovoronezh
17 M6 Novovorontsovka Ukr.
62 E2 Novo-Voskresenovka Rus. Fed.
17 M6 Novovoskresens'ke Ukr.
83 R6 Novovoznesenovka Kyrg.
17 O5 Novov''yazivs'ke Ukr.
17 N1 Novoyamskoye Rus. Fed.
16 C4 Novoyavorivs'ke Ukr.
19 W9 Novoye Dubovoye Rus. Fed.
83 S2 Novoyegor'yevskoye Rus. Fed.
19 X5 Novoye Leushino Rus. Fed.
19 T5 Novozavidovskiy Rus. Fed.
14 J2 Novozhilovskaya Rus. Fed.
16 I4 Novozhyvotiv Ukr.
19 O9 Novozybkov Rus. Fed.
68 F3 Novska Croatia
16 J1 Novy Barsuk Belarus
19 N6 Novy Boletsk Belarus
56 D1 Nový Bor Czech Rep.
56 E1 Nový Bydžov Czech Rep.
19 N8 Novy Bykhaw Belarus
36 H4 Novy-Chevrières France
55 M2 Novy Dvor Hrodzyenskaya Voblasts' Belarus
18 H9 Novy Dvor Hrodzyenskaya Voblasts' Belarus
57 G2 Nový Jičín Czech Rep.
56 G2 Nový Malín Czech Rep.
18 K6 Novyya Kruki Belarus
18 L7 Novyya Valosavichy Belarus
19 N8 Novyya Zhuravichy Belarus
14 K2 Novyy Bor Rus. Fed.
Novyy Bug Ukr. see Novyy Buh
17 L6 Novyy Buh Ukr.
17 K3 Novyy Bykiv Ukr.
55 M5 Novyy Dvir Ukr.
Novyye Belokorovichi Ukr. see Novi Bilokorovychi
82 B1 Novyye Burasy Rus. Fed.
19 Q9 Novyye Ivaytenki Rus. Fed.
18 K4 Novyy Izborsk Rus. Fed.
17 O4 Novyy Merchyk Ukr.
19 V4 Novyy Nekouz Rus. Fed.
15 G6 Novyy Oskol Rus. Fed.
92 I3 Novyy Port Rus. Fed.
17 L1 Novyy Ropsk Rus. Fed.
16 D4 Novyy Rozdil Ukr.
19 T8 Novyy Sinets Rus. Fed.
17 M5 Novyystarodub Ukr.
17 R6 Novyy Svit Donets'ka Oblast' Ukr.
17 N9 Novyy Svit Respublika Krym Ukr.
91 I2 Novyy Terek r. Rus. Fed.
14 J4 Novyy Tor'yal Rus. Fed.
92 I3 Novyy Urengoy Rus. Fed.
62 H3 Novyy Urgal Rus. Fed.
55 M5 Novyy Vytkiv Ukr.
55 M6 Novyy Yarychiv Ukr.
14 K5 Novyy Zay Rus. Fed.
56 G3 Nový Šivot Slovakia
84 F6 Now Iran
55 H4 Nowa Brzeźnica Pol.
55 L2 Nowa Chodorówka Pol.
55 J5 Nowa Dęba Pol.
54 G1 Nowa Karczma Pol.
54 E5 Nowa Ruda Pol.
55 K5 Nowa Sarzyna Pol.
55 J5 Nowa Słupia Pol.
54 D4 Nowa Sól Pol.
21 H7 Nowata OK U.S.A.
51 L6 Nowa Wieś Pol.
55 K2 Nowa Wieś Ełcka Pol.
54 F1 Nowa Wieś Lęborskie Pol.
54 G3 Nowa Wieś Wielka Pol.
55 L2 Nowa Wola Pol.
55 J4 Nowa Wola Gołębiowska Pol.
84 C4 Nowbarān Iran
84 H5 Now Deh Iran
84 D4 Now Dezh Iran
84 C3 Nowdī Iran
54 G2 Nowe Pol.
55 I5 Nowe Brzesko Pol.
54 C2 Nowe Czarnowo Pol.
54 D4 Nowe Miasteczko Pol.
55 I3 Nowe Miasto Pol.
55 H2 Nowe Miasto Lubawskie Pol.
55 I4 Nowe Miasto nad Pilicą Pol.
27 D9 Nowen Hill Rep. of Ireland
55 H3 Nowe Ostrowy Pol.
55 K3 Nowe Piekuty Pol.
54 F4 Nowe Skalmierzyce Pol.
54 C2 Nowe Warpno Pol.
Nowfel low Shātow Iran see Kahak
84 E5 Now Gombad Iran
Nowgong Assam India see Nagaon
78 G7 Nowgong Madh. Prad. India
55 K2 Nowinka Pol.
89 N4 Nowjeh Deh Iran
84 F3 Now Kharegan Iran
07 K2 Nowleye Lake Nunavut Can.
55 K4 Nowodwór Pol.
54 D2 Nowogard Pol.
55 J2 Nowogród Pol.
54 D4 Nowogród Bobrzański Pol.
54 D3 Nowogródek Pomorski Pol.
54 D4 Nowogrodziec Pol.
22 K4 Nowood r. WY U.S.A.
55 L3 Nowosady Pol.
55 K6 Nowosielce Pol.
55 K5 Nowosielec Pol.
55 H4 Nowosolna Pol.
05 M6 Nowra N.S.W. Austr.
84 C2 Nowshahr Iran
84 D3 Now Shahr Iran
85 O4 Nowshera Pak.
84 B4 Nowsūd Iran
07 L2 Nowyak Lake Nunavut Can.
55 K3 Nowy Bartków Pol.
55 H3 Nowy Duninów Pol.
54 F2 Nowy Dwór Kujawsko-Pomorskie Pol.
55 L2 Nowy Dwór Podlaskie Pol.
23 P7 Nowy Dwór Gdański Pol.
55 I3 Nowy Dwór Mazowiecki Pol.
55 I5 Nowy Korczyn Pol.
55 L5 Nowy Lubliniec Pol.
55 I6 Nowy Sącz Pol.
23 P7 Nowy Staw Pol.
55 I6 Nowy Targ Pol.
54 E3 Nowy Tomyśl Pol.
55 J6 Nowy Żmigród Pol.
111 R8 Noxen PA U.S.A.
121 K9 Noxubee National Wildlife Refuge nature res. MS U.S.A.
158 G6 Noy, Xé r. Laos
Noya Galicia Spain see Noia
192 I3 Noyabr'sk Rus. Fed.
38 G6 Noyal-Muzillac France
38 F6 Noyalo France
38 F5 Noyal-Pontivy France
39 L6 Noyant France
39 K7 Noyant-la-Plaine France
41 H6 Noyarey France
189 Q5 Noyek Iran
191 G4 Noyemberyan Armenia
39 K6 Noyen-sur-Sarthe France
36 G8 Noyers France
39 N7 Noyers-sur-Cher France
41 H8 Noyers-sur-Jabron France
106 C4 Noyes Island AK U.S.A.
176 E7 Noyil r. India
36 E4 Noyon France
167 H2 Nozawaonsen-mura Japan
38 H6 Nozay France
55 K6 Nozdrzec Pol.
40 I3 Nozeroy France
191 H2 Nozhay-Yurt Rus. Fed.
97 J6 Nozizwe S. Africa
58 B8 Nozza r. Italy
92 B4 Npitamaiong mt. Kenya
97 O6 Nqabeni S. Africa
97 L8 Nqamakwe S. Africa
97 O4 Nqutu S. Africa
191 H7 Nrnadzor Armenia
90 B5 Nsa Congo
93 A8 Nsalamu Zambia
90 C5 Nsambi Dem. Rep. Congo
93 B8 Nsanje Malawi
88 E5 Nsawam Ghana
93 A7 Nseluka Zambia
89 H6 Nsoc Equat. Guinea
97 P3 Nsoko Swaziland
91 F7 Nsombo Zambia
90 C5 Nsondia Dem. Rep. Congo
89 G5 Nsukka Nigeria
86 B5 Ntalfa well Maur.
91 E8 Ntambu Zambia
90 C5 Ntandembele Dem. Rep. Congo
93 B8 Ntcheu Malawi
93 B8 Ntchisi Malawi
89 H6 Ntem r. Cameroon
97 L3 Ntha S. Africa
97 M2 Nthorwane S. Africa
97 M7 Ntibane S. Africa
84 B6 Ntiona Chad
92 A4 Ntoroko Uganda
90 A4 Ntoum Gabon
99 □3a Ntsamouéni Njazidja Comoros
97 N3 Ntshingwayo Dam S. Africa
99 □3a Ntsoudjini Njazidja Comoros
89 H5 Ntui Cameroon
93 A5 Ntungamo Uganda
94 E4 Ntwetwe Pan salt pan Botswana
97 M7 Ntywenka S. Africa
39 J7 Nuaillé France
42 C3 Nuaillé-d'Aunis France
Nuanetsi r. Zimbabwe see Mwenezi
155 D3 Nuangan Sulawesi Indon.
118 D2 Nuangola PA U.S.A.
179 I9 Nuapara Orissa India
187 L4 Nu'aym reg. Oman
85 F4 Nuba, Lake resr Sudan
92 A2 Nuba Mountains Sudan
48 I2 Nübbel Ger.
129 K9 Nube Flan, Cerro mt. Mex.
48 I1 Nübel Ger.
85 G4 Nubian Desert Sudan
20 Q2 Nubivarri hill Norway
146 A5 Ñuble r. Chile
62 I1 Nubledo Spain
178 F2 Nubra r. India
201 □1 Nubu Vanua Levu Fiji
77 K4 Nucet Romania
125 X3 Nucla CO U.S.A.
169 L5 Nüden Mongolia
51 G7 Nudersdorf Ger.
49 J10 Nüdlingen Ger.
19 T5 Nudol' Rus. Fed.
55 M4 Nudyzhe Ukr.
121 G12 Nueces r. TX U.S.A.
39 J8 Nueil-sur-Argent France
107 L2 Nueltin Lake Man./Nunavut Can.
45 I6 Nuenen Neth.
66 E3 Nueno Spain
67 I10 Nuestra Señora del Pilar Spain
63 K2 Nueva Spain
145 D9 Nueva, Isla i. Chile
136 C6 Nueva Alejandría Peru
126 □O10 Nueva Arcadia Hond.
146 C3 Nueva California Arg.
65 K5 Nueva-Carteya Spain
121 F12 Nueva Ciudad Guerrero Mex.
146 D4 Nueva Constitución Arg.
146 E3 Nueva Escocia Arg.
137 E2 Nueva Esparta state Venez.
136 D2 Nueva Florida Venez.
146 E4 Nueva Galia Arg.
139 F5 Nueva Germania Para.
130 B3 Nueva Gerona Cuba
145 D9 Nueva Harberton Arg.
147 I4 Nueva Helvecia Uru.
146 A6 Nueva Imperial Chile
128 E6 Nueva Italia de Ruiz Mex.
64 G7 Nueva Jarilla Spain
136 B4 Nueva Loja Ecuador
145 C7 Nueva Lubecka Arg.
126 □O10 Nueva Ocotepeque Hond.
147 H3 Nueva Palmira Uru.
144 E2 Nueva Población Arg.
129 I3 Nueva Polonia Mex.
127 I4 Nueva Rosita Mex.
127 O11 Nueva San Salvador El Salvador
129 I1 Nueva Villa de Padilla Mex.
130 E3 Nuevitas Cuba
127 N7 Nuevo, Cayo i. Mex.
145 D6 Nuevo, Golfo g. Arg.
147 I3 Nuevo Berlín Uru.
126 F2 Nuevo Casas Grandes Mex.
126 G5 Nuevo Ideal Mex.
127 J4 Nuevo Laredo Mex.
125 Q9 Nuevo León Mex.
128 G1 Nuevo León state Mex.
137 F2 Nuevo Mamo Venez.
129 H3 Nuevo-Morelos Mex.
128 C2 Nuevo Pilares Mex.
136 C5 Nuevo Rocatuerte Ecuador
128 F4 Nuevo Valle de Moreno Mex.
186 G4 Nufayyid Şabḩah des. Saudi Arabia
168 D2 Nuga Mongolia
92 F2 Nugaal admin. reg. Somalia
92 F3 Nugaal watercourse Somalia
207 L8 Nuga Nuga, Lake Qld Austr.
203 D13 Nugget Point South I. N.Z.
204 □3 Nuggetts Point S. Pacific Ocean
72 C6 Nughedu di San Nicolò Sardegna Italy
19 T8 Nugr' r. Rus. Fed.
176 E6 Nugu r. India
199 F2 Nuguria Islands P.N.G.
185 J9 Nuh, Ras pt Pak.
202 L6 Nuhaka North I. N.Z.
79 L4 Nuhköy Turkey
199 H2 Nui atoll Tuvalu
Nui Con Voi r. Vietnam see Hông, Sông
18 L1 Nuijamaa Fin.
39 J6 Nuillé-sur-Vicoin France
158 I7 Nui Thanh Vietnam
158 H7 Nui Ti On mt. Vietnam
36 H8 Nuits France
40 F2 Nuits-St-Georges France
170 B6 Nu Jiang r. China
166 F6 Nukata Japan
204 E5 Nukey Bluff hill S.A. Austr.
200 □6 Nukiki Choiseul Solomon Is
201 □2a Nuku i. Tonga
201 □2a Nuku'alofa Tongatapu Tonga
199 H2 Nukufetau atoll Tuvalu
201 □3 Nuku Hiva i. Fr. Polynesia
Nukuhiva i. Fr. Polynesia see Nuku Hiva
199 H2 Nukulaelae atoll Tuvalu
Nukulailai atoll Tuvalu see Nukulaelae
199 F2 Nukumanu Islands P.N.G.
Nukunau i. Gilbert Is Kiribati see Nikunau
Nukunono atoll Tokelau see Nukunonu
203 □1 Nukunonu Tokelau
203 □1 Nukunonu atoll Tokelau
182 H6 Nukus Uzbek.
44 H5 Nuland Neth.
104 C3 Nulato AK U.S.A.
72 C7 Nule Sardegna Italy
67 E8 Nules Spain
208 F6 Nullagine W.A. Austr.
208 F6 Nullagine r. W.A. Austr.
204 C4 Nullarbor S.A. Austr.
204 C4 Nullarbor National Park S.A. Austr.
204 B4 Nullarbor Plain S.A. Austr.
204 C4 Nullarbor Regional Reserve park S.A. Austr.
108 E1 Nuluarniavik, Lac l. Que. Can.
169 P6 Nulu'erhu Shan mts China
72 B6 Nulvi Sardegna Italy
153 I7 Num i. Papua Indon.
179 K6 Num Nepal
205 J3 Numalla, Lake salt flat Qld Austr.
89 I4 Numan Nigeria
186 B2 Nu'mān i. Saudi Arabia
71 P8 Numana Italy
154 E7 Numancia Phil.
44 F5 Numansdorp Neth.
167 J2 Numata Gunma Japan
164 S3 Numata Hokkaidō Japan
90 E3 Numatinna watercourse Sudan
167 I5 Numazu Japan
97 P1 Numbi Gate S. Africa
Numbu Vanua Levu Fiji see Nubu
206 E3 Numbulwar N.T. Austr.
22 F1 Numedal val. Norway
153 H7 Numfoor i. Papua Indon.
162 E5 Numin He r. China
94 C3 Numkaub Namibia
21 Q6 Nummi Fin.
205 J7 Numurkah Vic. Austr.
109 I2 Nunaksaluk Island Nfld and Lab. Can.
105 N3 Nunakuluut i. Greenland
105 N3 Nunap Isua c. Greenland
Nunarsuit i. Greenland see Nunakuluut
108 E1 Nunavik reg. Que. Can.
107 L2 Nunavut admin. div. Can.
136 C3 Nunchía Col.
51 H8 Nünchritz Ger.
91 F5 Nunda Dem. Rep. Congo
116 H6 Nunda NY U.S.A.
205 M4 Nundle N.S.W. Austr.
31 J2 Nuneaton Warwickshire, England U.K.
209 E11 Nungarin W.A. Austr.
179 N7 Nungba Manipur India
107 M5 Nungesser Lake Ont. Can.
169 P4 Nungnain Sum Nei Mongol China
95 H2 Nungo Moz.
93 C6 Nungwi, Ras pt Tanz.
104 B4 Nunivak Island AK U.S.A.
179 J9 Nunkapasi Orissa India
52 B3 Nunkirchen Ger.
178 F3 Nunkun mt. Jammu and Kashmir
193 T3 Nunligran Rus. Fed.
67 H9 Nunó, Cap c. Spain
138 C3 Nuñoa Peru
62 H8 Nuñomoral Spain
51 H6 Nunsdorf Ger.
44 I4 Nunspeet Neth.
157 L3 Nunukan i. Indon.
72 C7 Nuoro Sardegna Italy
72 C7 Nuoro prov. Sardegna Italy
200 □6 Nupani i. Santa Cruz Is Solomon Is
184 F6 Nūq Iran
84 C4 Nuqayy, Jabal mts Libya
186 E3 Nuqrah Saudi Arabia
85 G3 Nuqruş, Jabal mt. Egypt
136 B3 Nuquí Col.
173 E8 Nur Xinjiang China
184 E3 Nur r. Iran
55 K3 Nur Pol.
183 Q6 Nura Almatinskaya Oblast' Kazakh.
183 P3 Nura Kazakh.
183 M2 Nura r. Kazakh.
184 D6 Nūrābād Iran
184 C4 Nūrābād Iran
72 C8 Nuragus Sardegna Italy
Nurakita i. Tuvalu see Niulakita
72 C8 Nurallao Sardegna Italy
72 C9 Nuraminis Sardegna Italy
Nurata Uzbek. see Nurota
190 E1 Nurdağı Turkey
188 G5 Nur Dağları mts Turkey
70 H5 Nure r. Italy
72 B8 Nureci Sardegna Italy
Nurek Tajik. see Norak
Nurek Reservoir resr Tajik. see Obanbori Norak
Nurekskoye Vodokhranilishche resr Tajik. see Obanbori Norak
Nuremberg Ger. see Nürnberg
118 C3 Nuremberg PA U.S.A.
Nūrestān prov. Afgh. see Nuristan
185 N4 Nūr Gal Afgh.
185 L7 Nur Gama Pak.
126 E3 Nuri Mex.
85 G5 Nuri Sudan
157 H5 Nuri, Teluk b. Indon.
73 K3 Nuria, Monte mt. Italy
185 N4 Nuristan prov. Afgh.
185 N4 Nuristan reg. Afgh.
178 F2 Nurla Jammu and Kashmir
15 J5 Nurlat Rus. Fed.
14 J5 Nurlaty Rus. Fed.
20 T5 Nurmes Fin.
21 R6 Nurmijärvi Fin.
20 Q5 Nurmo Fin.
53 K3 Nürnberg Ger.
28 D8 Nurney Carlow Rep. of Ireland
28 D7 Nurney Kildare Rep. of Ireland
183 L8 Nurobad Uzbek.
182 K7 Nurota Uzbek.
183 L7 Nurota tizmasi mts Uzbek.
185 N6 Nurpur Pak.
204 C3 Nurrai Lakes salt flat S.A. Austr.
72 C8 Nurri Sardegna Italy
205 K4 Nurri, Mount hill N.S.W. Austr.
20 L4 Nursfjellet mt. Norway
Nursia Italy see Norcia
18 F3 Nurste Estonia
52 G4 Nürtingen Ger.
173 K8 Nur Turu Qinghai China
55 K3 Nurzec r. Pol.
55 L3 Nurzec-Stacja Pol.
70 C4 Nus Italy
157 H8 Nusa Kambangan Nature Reserve Jawa Indon.
155 F5 Nusa Laut i. Maluku Indon.
157 L9 Nusa Tenggara Barat prov. Indon.
155 B8 Nusa Tenggara Timur prov. Indon.
189 J5 Nusaybin Turkey
73 O6 Nusco Italy
155 G4 Nusela, Kepulauan is Papua Indon.
77 K3 Nuşfalău Romania
170 B5 Nu Shan mts China
166 A7 Nu-shima i. Japan
185 L7 Nushki Pak.
52 F5 Nusplingen Ger.
190 G2 Nusratiye Turkey
59 J4 Nußbach Austria
53 N6 Nußdorf Ger.
53 M6 Nußdorf am Inn Ger.
58 G6 Nußdorf-Debant Austria
48 K3 Nusse Ger.
109 I1 Nutak Nfld and Lab. Can.
107 L2 Nutarawit Lake Nunavut Can.
45 I7 Nuth Neth.
51 H6 Nuthe r. Ger.
31 L5 Nuthurst West Sussex, England U.K.
119 G3 Nutley NJ U.S.A.
125 W8 Nutrioso AZ U.S.A.
185 M7 Nuttal Pak.
27 J3 Nutt's Corner Northern Ireland U.K.
206 E3 Nutwood Downs N.T. Austr.
105 M2 Nuugaatsiaap Imaa inlet Greenland
105 M2 Nuugaatsiaq Greenland
105 M3 Nuuk Greenland
18 H1 Nuuksion kansallispuisto nat. park Fin.
20 S3 Nuupas Fin.
201 □3a Nuupere, Pointe pt Moorea Fr. Polynesia
105 M2 Nuussuaq Greenland
105 M2 Nuussuaq pen. Greenland
200 □2 Nu'uuli American Samoa
179 I5 Nuwakot Nepal
187 L3 Nuway Oman
85 G2 Nuwaybi' al Muzayyinah Egypt
96 H9 Nuwekloof pass S. Africa
96 C7 Nuwerus S. Africa
96 F8 Nuweveldberge mts S. Africa
128 G8 Nuxco Mex.
72 B9 Nuxis Sardegna Italy
55 M4 Nuyno Ukr.
209 D13 Nuyts, Point W.A. Austr.
204 D5 Nuyts Archipelago is S.A. Austr.
204 D5 Nuyts Archipelago Conservation Park nature res. S.A. Austr.
209 H12 Nuytsland Nature Reserve W.A. Austr.
190 H3 Nuzayzah reg. Syria
58 A5 Nüziders Austria
176 G4 Nuzvid Andhra Prad. India
89 H5 Nwa Cameroon
94 E3 Nxai Pan National Park Botswana
94 D3 Nxaunxau Botswana
157 K4 Nyaän, Bukit hill Indon.
89 H6 Nyabessan Cameroon
209 E12 Nyabing W.A. Austr.
117 L7 Nyack NY U.S.A.
192 H3 Nyagan' Rus. Fed.
93 B6 Nyahua Tanz.
92 C4 Nyahururu Kenya
205 I6 Nyah West Vic. Austr.
173 K12 Nyaimai Xizang China
173 J11 Nyainqêntanglha Feng mt. Xizang China
173 J12 Nyainqêntanglha Shan mts Xizang China
173 K10 Nyainrong Xizang China
93 A5 Nyakahanga Tanz.
93 A5 Nyakahura Kagera Tanz.
93 A6 Nyaka Kangaga Tanz.
93 B5 Nyakaliro Tanz.
97 K3 Nyakallong S. Africa
93 A5 Nyakanazi Tanz.
20 O5 Nyåker Sweden
Nyakh Rus. Fed. see Nyagan'
18 I9 Nyakhachava Belarus
88 E5 Nyakrom Ghana
14 M3 Nyaksimvol' Rus. Fed.
84 E6 Nyala Sudan
Nyalam Xizang China see Congdü
20 □ Ny-Ålesund Svalbard
91 F8 Nyama Zambia
95 F3 Nyamandhiovu Zimbabwe
95 G3 Nyamapanda Zimbabwe
93 B5 Nyambiti Tanz.
93 A5 Nyamirembe Kagera Tanz.
90 E2 Nyamlell Sudan
93 C7 Nyamtumbo Tanz.
55 N3 Nyamyerzha Belarus
Nyande Zimbabwe see Masvingo
14 H3 Nyandoma Rus. Fed.
14 G3 Nyandomskiy Vozvyshennost' hills Rus. Fed.
90 A5 Nyanga Congo
91 A5 Nyanga Gabon
91 A5 Nyanga prov. Gabon
95 G3 Nyanga Zimbabwe
95 G3 Nyanga National Park Zimbabwe
173 K11 Nyangbo Xizang China
173 I12 Nyang Qu r. China
173 L12 Nyang Qu r. China
88 E4 Nyankpala Ghana
93 A5 Nyanza Rwanda
93 A6 Nyanza-Lac Burundi
157 L4 Nyapa, Gunung mt. Indon.
92 B3 Nyapongeth Sudan
178 G4 Nyar r. India
56 G4 Nyárád Hungary
106 H2 Nyarling r. N.W.T. Can.
57 I5 Nyárlőrinc Hungary
57 I4 Nyársapát Hungary
93 A5 Nyarugumba Rwanda
93 B7 Nyasa, Lake Africa
Nyasaland country Africa see Malawi
14 K2 Nyashabozh Rus. Fed.
18 J8 Nyasvizh Belarus
95 F3 Nyathi Zimbabwe
158 C6 Nyaunglebin Myanmar
158 B4 Nyaungu Myanmar
14 M3 Nyays r. Rus. Fed.
95 G3 Nyazura Zimbabwe
48 I1 Nybøl Nor b. Denmark
22 G6 Nyborg Denmark
20 T1 Nyborg Norway
20 Q4 Nyborg Sweden
23 L5 Nybro Sweden
57 H2 Nýdek Czech Rep.
105 M1 Nyeboe Land reg. Greenland
18 K8 Nyeharelaye Belarus
173 J12 Nyêmo Xizang China
Nyenchen Tanglha Range mts Xizang China see Nyainqêntanglha Shan
92 C5 Nyeri Kenya
92 B2 Nyerol Sudan
18 M6 Nyeshcharda, Vozyera l. Belarus
20 □ Ny-Friesland reg. Svalbard
23 K1 Nyhammar Sweden
173 H9 Nyi, Co l. Xizang China
93 B7 Nyika National Park Zambia
93 B7 Nyika Plateau Malawi
173 H11 Nyima Xizang China
173 K11 Nyima Xizang China
93 A8 Nyimba Zambia
173 L12 Nyingchi Xizang China
173 J11 Nyingzhong Xizang China
Nyinma Gansu China see Maqu
57 L4 Nyírábrány Hungary
57 K4 Nyíracsád Hungary
56 G4 Nyirád Hungary
57 K4 Nyíradony Hungary
93 A5 Nyiragongo vol. Dem. Rep. Congo
57 L4 Nyírbátor Hungary
57 L4 Nyírbéltek Hungary
57 L4 Nyírbogát Hungary
57 K3 Nyírbogdány Hungary
57 L4 Nyírcsászári Hungary
57 K4 Nyíregyháza Hungary
57 K4 Nyírgelse Hungary
93 C5 Nyiri Desert Kenya
57 L4 Nyírlugos Hungary
57 K4 Nyírmártonfalva Hungary
57 K4 Nyírmihálydi Hungary
57 K3 Nyírtelek Hungary
57 K3 Nyírtét Hungary
57 K3 Nyírtura Hungary
92 C4 Nyiru, Mount Kenya
57 L4 Nyírvasvári Hungary
20 Q5 Nykarleby Fin.
22 H7 Nykøbing Denmark
22 E5 Nykøbing Mors Denmark
22 H6 Nykøbing Sjælland Denmark
23 N3 Nyköping Sweden
23 K2 Nykroppa Sweden
23 N2 Nykvarn Sweden
14 B3 Nyland Sweden
205 K5 Nymagee N.S.W. Austr.
205 N3 Nymboida N.S.W. Austr.
205 N3 Nymboida National Park N.S.W. Austr.
56 E1 Nymburk Czech Rep.
22 E6 Nymindegab Denmark
23 N3 Nynäshamn Sweden
205 K4 Nyngan N.S.W. Austr.
173 F11 Nyogzê Xizang China
167 K2 Nyohō-san mt. Japan
39 J6 Nyoiseau France
97 M8 Nyokana S. Africa
18 G8 Nyoman r. Belarus/Lith.
18 I8 Nyomanskaya Nizina lowland Belarus
70 A3 Nyon Switz.
89 H6 Nyong r. Cameroon
41 G8 Nyons France
50 F1 Nyord i. Denmark
50 E1 Nyråd Denmark
56 C2 Nýřany Czech Rep.
14 L3 Nyrob Rus. Fed.
56 C2 Nýrsko Czech Rep.
20 T2 Nyrud Norway
54 F5 Nysa Pol.
54 F5 Nysa Kłodzka r. Pol.
22 I2 Nysäter Sweden
20 L5 Nysätern Sweden
162 M3 Nysh Sakhalin Rus. Fed.
22 I2 Nysockensjön l. Sweden
122 F5 Nyssa OR U.S.A.
22 H7 Nysted Denmark
14 J3 Nyuchpas Rus. Fed.
164 Q7 Nyūdō-zaki pt Japan
167 H4 Nyūgasa-yama mt. Japan
57 K4 Nyugati-főcsatorna canal Hungary
166 F3 Nyūkawa Japan
14 I3 Nyukhcha Rus. Fed.
14 I3 Nyuksenitsa Rus. Fed.
57 G4 Nyúl Hungary
91 F6 Nyunzu Dem. Rep. Congo
193 M3 Nyurba Rus. Fed.
14 J3 Nyuvchim Rus. Fed.
193 M3 Nyuya Rus. Fed.
193 M3 Nyuya r. Rus. Fed.
166 G2 Nyūzen Japan
17 M8 Nyva Ukr.
162 M1 Nyvrovo Rus. Fed.
55 M5 Nyvytsi Ukr.
162 M2 Nyyskiy Zaliv lag. Sakhalin Rus. Fed.
16 B4 Nyzhankovychi Ukr.
17 N7 Nyzhni Sirohozy Ukr.
17 N7 Nyzhni Torhayi Ukr.
16 C5 Nyzhni Vorota Ukr.
16 C5 Nyzhniy Bystryy Ukr.
17 S5 Nyzhniy Nahol'chyk Ukr.
17 N8 Nyzhn'ohirs'kyy Ukr.
17 R4 Nyzhnya Dubanka Ukr.
17 N3 Nyzhnya Syrovatka Ukr.
17 O5 Nyzhnya Tersa r. Ukr.
57 M2 Nyzhnya Vysots'ke Ukr.
57 L2 Nyzhnya Yablun'ka Ukr.
17 N3 Nyzy Ukr.
90 D3 Nzako C.A.R.
91 A5 Nzambi Congo
90 F3 Nzara Sudan
88 C4 Nzébéla Guinea
93 B6 Nzega Tanz.
88 C5 Nzérékoré Guinea
91 B6 N'zeto Angola
88 D5 Nzi r. Côte d'Ivoire
91 E7 Nzilo, Lac l. Dem. Rep. Congo
91 E5 Nzingu Dem. Rep. Congo
88 D5 Nzo r. Côte d'Ivoire
88 D5 N'Zo, Réserve de Faune du nature res. Côte d'Ivoire
91 B6 Nzobe Dem. Rep. Congo
92 B4 Nzoia r. Kenya
90 F4 Nzoro r. Dem. Rep. Congo
99 □3 Nzwani i. Comoros

O

120 F4 Oacoma SD U.S.A.
31 J2 Oadby Leicestershire, England U.K.
120 E3 Oahe, Lake SD U.S.A.
124 □D12 O'ahu i. HI U.S.A.
204 H5 Oakbank S.A. Austr.
117 O7 Oak Bluffs MA U.S.A.
125 T2 Oak City UT U.S.A.
110 G7 Oak Creek WI U.S.A.
124 L4 Oakdale CA U.S.A.
119 K2 Oakdale CT U.S.A.
121 I10 Oakdale LA U.S.A.
119 I3 Oakdale NY U.S.A.
30 H2 Oakengates Telford and Wrekin, England U.K.
120 F2 Oakes ND U.S.A.
207 M9 Oakey Qld Austr.
116 G5 Oakfield NY U.S.A.
118 F4 Oakford PA U.S.A.
121 J9 Oak Grove LA U.S.A.
110 J5 Oak Grove MI U.S.A.
31 K2 Oakham Rutland, England U.K.
116 B7 Oak Harbor OH U.S.A.
122 C2 Oak Harbor WA U.S.A.
116 C10 Oak Hill OH U.S.A.
116 D11 Oak Hill WV U.S.A.
124 M4 Oakhurst CA U.S.A.
119 G4 Oakhurst NJ U.S.A.
110 D3 Oak Island WI U.S.A.
124 L7 Oak Knolls CA U.S.A.
107 K5 Oak Lake Man. Can.
124 J4 Oakland CA U.S.A.
116 F9 Oakland MD U.S.A.
117 □P4 Oakland ME U.S.A.
120 G5 Oakland NE U.S.A.
119 G2 Oakland NJ U.S.A.
122 C5 Oakland OR U.S.A.
124 J4 Oakland airport CA U.S.A.
114 D6 Oakland City IN U.S.A.
205 K6 Oaklands N.S.W. Austr.
110 G8 Oak Lawn IL U.S.A.
31 K3 Oakley Bedfordshire, England U.K.
31 J4 Oakley Buckinghamshire, England U.K.
26 I10 Oakley Fife, Scotland U.K.
31 J5 Oakley Hampshire, England U.K.
120 E6 Oakley KS U.S.A.
111 J6 Oakley MI U.S.A.
116 F8 Oakmont PA U.S.A.
208 F6 Oakover r. W.A. Austr.
110 G8 Oak Park IL U.S.A.
119 G2 Oak Ridge NJ U.S.A.
122 C5 Oakridge OR U.S.A.
115 E7 Oak Ridge TN U.S.A.
118 E4 Oaks PA U.S.A.
118 F5 Oak Shade NJ U.S.A.
202 H6 Oakura North I. N.Z.
204 H5 Oakvale S.A. Austr.
124 M7 Oak View CA U.S.A.
108 E5 Oakville Ont. Can.
119 I1 Oakville CT U.S.A.
116 A7 Oakwood OH U.S.A.
116 A9 Oakwood OH U.S.A.
118 D5 Oakwood Beach NJ U.S.A.
203 E12 Oamaru South I. N.Z.
167 L4 Ōamishirasato Japan
202 H6 Oaonui North I. N.Z.
167 M3 Ōarai Japan
203 H9 Oaro South I. N.Z.
62 C4 O Arrabal Spain
165 J12 Ōasa Japan
167 K3 Ōashi-gawa r. Japan
124 O4 Oasis CA U.S.A.
122 G6 Oasis NV U.S.A.
77 L2 Oaşului, Munţii mts Romania
Oates Coast reg. Antarctica see Oates Land
213 K2 Oates Land reg. Antarctica
205 K10 Oatlands Tas. Austr.
96 I8 Oatlands S. Africa
129 K8 Oaxaca Mex.
129 K8 Oaxaca state Mex.
183 M1 Ob' r. Rus. Fed.
Ob, Gulf of sea chan. Rus. Fed. see Obskaya Guba
108 C3 Oba Ont. Can.
166 C7 Obako-dake mt. Japan
190 A2 Obaköy Turkey
18 M6 Obal' Vitsyebskaya Voblasts' Belarus
18 M6 Obal' Vitsyebskaya Voblasts' Belarus
18 M6 Obal' canal Belarus
89 H5 Obala Cameroon
111 J1 Oba Lake Ont. Can.
166 C5 Obama Japan
166 C4 Obama-wan b. Japan
89 H5 Oban Nigeria
26 F10 Oban Argyll and Bute, Scotland U.K.
164 R8 Obanazawa Japan
185 M2 Obanbori Norak resr Tajik.
185 N1 Obanbori Qayroqqum resr Tajik.
89 H5 Oban Hills mt. Nigeria
166 F5 Obara Japan
62 G4 O Barco Spain
63 N3 Obarenes, Montes mts Spain
77 P4 Obârşeni, Dealul hill Romania
166 E6 Obata Japan
191 D5 Obayayla Turkey
Obbia Somalia see Hobyo
20 P5 Obbola Sweden
77 N3 Obcina Feredeului ridge Romania
77 N3 Obcina Mare ridge Romania
77 N3 Obcina Mestecănişului ridge Romania
59 K5 Obdach Austria
44 G3 Obdam Neth.
56 C2 Obecnice Czech Rep.
106 G4 Obed Alta Can.
65 J4 Obejo Spain
191 A5 Öbektaş Turkey
18 I6 Obeliai Lith.
55 L1 Obelija l. Lith.
203 D12 Obelisk mt. South I. N.Z.
144 G2 Oberá Arg.
59 L5 Oberaich Austria
58 H4 Oberalm Austria
70 F2 Oberalpstock mt. Switz.
53 K6 Oberammergau Ger.
53 J3 Oberasbach Ger.
53 K6 Oberau Ger.
53 M6 Oberaudorf Ger.
49 H9 Oberaula Ger.
53 L6 Oberbayern admin. reg. Ger.
52 F3 Oberderdingen Ger.
53 L5 Oberding Ger.
49 J8 Oberdorla Ger.
58 G6 Oberdrauburg Austria
52 F5 Obere Donau park Ger.
70 H1 Oberegg Switz.
49 J10 Oberelsbach Ger.
70 H2 Ober Engadin reg. Switz.
70 E1 Oberentfelden Switz.
53 N3 Oberer Bayerischer Wald park Ger.
51 E9 Obere Saale park Ger.
52 H6 Oberessendorf Ger.
51 G10 Oberes Westerzgebirge park Ger.
49 D10 Oberfell Ger.
51 D11 Oberfranken admin. reg. Ger.
49 J6 Oberg (Lahstedt) Ger.
70 D1 Obergösgen Switz.
59 M3 Ober-Grafendorf Austria
53 K5 Obergriesbach Ger.
53 I6 Obergünzburg Ger.
58 D6 Obergurgl Austria
51 J8 Obergurig Ger.
59 L6 Oberhaag Austria
53 L5 Oberhaching Ger.
53 J2 Oberhaid Ger.
52 E5 Oberharmersbach Ger.
53 K4 Oberhausen Bayern Ger.
49 C8 Oberhausen Nordrhein-Westfalen Ger.
49 K9 Oberhof Ger.
70 D2 Oberhofen Switz.
58 D5 Oberhofen im Inntal Austria
37 O6 Oberhoffen-sur-Moder France
58 B4 Oberjochpass pass Austria/Ger.
52 E4 Oberkirch Ger.
53 I4 Oberkochen Ger.
51 E10 Oberkotzau Ger.
48 D5 Oberlangen Ger.
51 J8 Oberlausitz reg. Ger.
51 J8 Oberlausitzer Bergland park Ger.
51 J8 Oberlichtenau Ger.
58 G6 Oberlienz Austria
120 E6 Oberlin KS U.S.A.
121 I10 Oberlin LA U.S.A.
116 C7 Oberlin OH U.S.A.
52 H5 Obermarchtal Ger.
49 J9 Obermaßfeld-Grimmenthal Ger.
52 D2 Obermoschel Ger.
37 N7 Obernai France
59 H3 Obernberg am Inn Austria
52 G2 Obernburg am Main Ger.
53 J4 Oberndorf am Lech Ger.
52 F5 Oberndorf am Neckar Ger.
59 L3 Oberndorf an der Melk Austria
58 G4 Oberndorf bei Salzburg Austria
59 J3 Oberneukirchen Austria
49 J7 Obernfeld Ger.
52 F5 Obernheim Ger.
52 D3 Obernheim-Kirchenarnbach Ger.
49 H6 Obernkirchen Ger.
53 P4 Obernzell Ger.
53 I3 Obernzenn Ger.
51 K9 Oberoderwitz Ger.
52 E2 Ober-Olm Ger.
205 L5 Oberon N.S.W. Austr.
53 J6 Oberostendorf Ger.
59 I3 Oberösterreich land Austria
53 L2 Oberpfalz admin. reg. Ger.
53 M2 Oberpfälzer Wald mts Ger.
56 B2 Oberpfälzer Wald park Ger.
53 L5 Oberpframmern Ger.
59 O4 Oberpullendorf Austria
52 F2 Ober-Ramstadt Ger.
52 H6 Oberreute Ger.
52 D6 Oberried Ger.
53 I5 Oberrieden Ger.
70 H1 Oberriet Switz.
51 D8 Oberröblingen Ger.
52 F2 Ober-Roden Ger.
51 D8 Oberroßla Ger.
52 H3 Oberrot Ger.
52 D5 Oberrotweil Ger.
53 L5 Oberschleißheim Ger.
53 N4 Oberschneiding Ger.
51 H9 Oberschöna Ger.
59 N5 Oberschützen Austria
59 O3 Obersiebenbrunn Austria
70 E1 Obersiggenthal Switz.
49 I10 Obersinn Ger.
52 H3 Obersontheim Ger.
49 K8 Oberspier Ger.
52 H5 Oberstadion Ger.
53 I6 Oberstaufen Ger.
53 I7 Oberstdorf Ger.
52 G3 Oberstenfeld Ger.
53 M5 Obertaufkirchen Ger.
52 G6 Oberteuringen Ger.
52 C2 Oberthal Ger.
49 I10 Oberthulba Ger.
58 G6 Obertilliach Austria
53 M4 Obertraubling Ger.
53 K2 Obertrubach Ger.
58 H4 Obertrum am See Austria
58 H4 Obertrumer See l. Austria
49 G10 Obertshausen Ger.
16 E5 Obertyn Ukr.
50 I4 Oberueckersee l. Ger.
49 G10 Oberursel (Taunus) Ger.
58 H6 Obervellach Austria
53 M3 Oberviechtach Ger.
70 E2 Oberwald Switz.
49 H7 Oberwälder Land reg. Ger.
59 N4 Oberwaltersdorf Austria
59 N5 Oberwart Austria
49 E10 Oberwesel Ger.
59 M3 Oberwölbling Austria
52 E5 Oberwolfach Ger.
59 J5 Oberwölz Austria
17 N2 Obesta r. Rus. Fed.
51 E8 Obhausen Ger.
155 E4 Obi i. Maluku Indon.
89 H4 Obi Nigeria
155 E4 Obi, Kepulauan is Maluku Indon.
155 E4 Obi, Selat sea chan. Maluku Indon.
137 H5 Óbidos Brazil
64 A2 Óbidos Port.
64 A2 Óbidos, Lagoa de lag. Port.
185 M2 Obigarm Tajik.
164 U4 Obihiro Japan
155 E4 Obilatu i. Maluku Indon.
76 J8 Obilić Kosovo, Srbija Serb. and Mont.
15 I7 Obil'noye Rus. Fed.
53 M5 Obing Ger.
121 K7 Obion r. TN U.S.A.
164 S2 Obira Japan
136 D2 Obispos Venez.
147 F2 Obispo Trejo Arg.
Obitochnaya Kosa spit Ukr. see Obytichna Kosa
167 K5 Obitsu-gawa r. Japan
42 G5 Objat France
54 F1 Objazda Pol.
55 M4 Oblapy Ukr.
59 I5 Öblarn Austria
15 H6 Oblivskaya Rus. Fed.
162 G4 Obluch'ye Rus. Fed.
19 T6 Obninsk Rus. Fed.
90 E3 Obo C.A.R.
168 G8 Obo Qinghai China
96 E3 Obobogorap S. Africa
92 D2 Obock Djibouti
16 I5 Obodivka Ukr.
163 F8 Ŏbŏk N. Korea
90 E5 Obokote Dem. Rep. Congo
172 K7 Obo Liang Qinghai China
89 G5 Obolo Nigeria
62 F4 O Bolo Spain
17 L4 Obolon' Ukr.
66 D6 Obón Spain
157 K2 Obong, Gunung mt. Malaysia
57 K3 Oborín Slovakia
54 E3 Oborniki Pol.
54 E4 Oborniki Śląskie Pol.
90 B5 Obouya Congo
15 G6 Oboyan' Rus. Fed.
14 H3 Obozerskiy Rus. Fed.
179 I7 Obra Uttar Prad. India
54 D3 Obra r. Pol.
144 F3 Obrage Arg.
126 E4 Obregón, Presa resr Mex.
107 K2 Obre Lake N.W.T. Can.
76 I6 Obrenovac Srbija Serb. and Mont.
122 C5 O'Brien OR U.S.A.
52 G3 Obrigheim Ger.
52 E2 Obrigheim (Pfalz) Ger.
56 C1 Obrnice Czech Rep.
77 Q7 Obrochishte Bulg.
71 Q4 Obrov Slovenia
54 G3 Obrowo Pol.
188 F4 Obruk Turkey
54 E4 Obry, Kanał canal Pol.
55 J3 Obryte Pol.
54 E3 Obrzycko Pol.
204 D3 Observatory Hill S.A. Austr.
106 D4 Observatory Inlet B.C. Can.
204 □2 Observatory Rock i. Lord Howe I. Austr.
19 P6 Obsha r. Rus. Fed.
182 D2 Obshchiy Syrt hills Rus. Fed.
192 I3 Obskaya Guba sea chan. Rus. Fed.
55 K5 Obsza Pol.
17 M2 Obtove Ukr.
166 E5 Ōbu Japan
88 E5 Obuasi Ghana
89 H5 Obubra Nigeria
68 G3 Obudovac Bos.-Herz.
89 H5 Obudu Nigeria
16 J3 Obukhiv Ukr.
Obukhov Ukr. see Obukhiv
19 V6 Obukhovo Rus. Fed.
167 H2 Obuse Japan
14 K4 Obva r. Rus. Fed.
70 E2 Obwalden canton Switz.
14 J3 Ob''yachevo Rus. Fed.
17 P7 Obytichna Kosa spit Ukr.
17 O7 Obytichna Zakota b. Ukr.
62 F2 O Cádabo Spain
115 F11 Ocala FL U.S.A.
62 C5 O Calvario Spain
126 E3 Ocampo Chihuahua Mex.
126 H4 Ocampo Coahuila Mex.
128 F4 Ocampo Guanajuato Mex.
129 H3 Ocampo Tamaulipas Mex.
62 D2 O Campo da Feira Spain
136 C2 Ocaña Col.
72 B4 Ocana Corse France
138 B3 Ocaña Peru
63 N9 Ocaña Spain
63 N9 Ocaña, Mesa de plat. Spain
62 D4 O Carballiño Spain
62 D4 O Castelo Spain
62 D3 O Castro Spain
71 L6 Occhiobello Italy
73 N4 Occhito, Lago di l. Italy
138 C4 Occidental, Cordillera mts Chile
136 B4 Occidental, Cordillera mts Col.
138 C4 Occidental, Cordillera mts Peru
70 F5 Occimiano Italy
116 H10 Occoquan VA U.S.A.
116 D11 Oceana WV U.S.A.
119 I3 Ocean Beach NY U.S.A.
106 B3 Ocean Cape AK U.S.A.
130 D1 Ocean Cay i. Bahamas
117 J10 Ocean City MD U.S.A.
118 F6 Ocean City NJ U.S.A.
119 G5 Ocean County county NJ U.S.A.
106 E4 Ocean Falls B.C. Can.
119 G5 Ocean Gate NJ U.S.A.
119 G4 Ocean Grove NJ U.S.A.
196 Oceania continent
Ocean Island Kiribati see Banaba
Ocean Island atoll HI U.S.A. see Kure Atoll
124 L6 Oceano CA U.S.A.
124 O8 Oceanside CA U.S.A.
121 K10 Ocean Springs MS U.S.A.
118 F6 Ocean View NJ U.S.A.
119 G6 Oceanville NJ U.S.A.
63 N6 Ocejón mt. Spain
200 □4a Ocha i. Chuuk Micronesia
200 □4a Ocha, Mochun sea chan. Chuuk Micronesia
66 C2 Ochagavía Spain
17 K7 Ochakiv Ukr.

Och'amch'ire to Ombrone
314

191 C3 Och'amch'ire Georgia
14 K4 Ocher Rus. Fed.
16 I4 Ocheretnya Ukr.
17 O6 Ocheretuvate Ukr.
37 K6 Ochey France
78 F4 Ochi mt. Greece
165 J11 Ōchi Japan
164 W3 Ochiishi-misaki pt Japan
26 I10 Ochil Hills Scotland U.K.
26 H12 Ochiltree East Ayrshire, Scotland U.K.
17 M1 Ochkyne Ukr.
115 E11 Ochlockonee r. GA U.S.A.
55 H3 Ochnia r. Pol.
48 E4 Ocholt Ger.
130 □ Ocho Rios Jamaica
Ochrida, Lake Albania/Macedonia see Ohrid, Lake
53 I2 Ochsenfurt Ger.
52 H5 Ochsenhausen Ger.
49 D10 Ochtendung Ger.
78 F4 Ochthonia Greece
78 F4 Ochthonia, Akra pt Greece
51 D6 Ochtmersleben Ger.
49 D6 Ochtrup Ger.
115 F10 Ocilla GA U.S.A.
21 N6 Ockelbo Sweden
48 G1 Ockholm Ger.
26 E9 Ockle Highland, Scotland U.K.
77 N4 Ocland Romania
115 F10 Ocmulgee r. GA U.S.A.
77 L4 Ocna Mureş Romania
77 M5 Ocna Sibiului Romania
16 G5 Ocniţa Moldova
77 N4 Ocolaşul Mare, Vârful mt. Romania
138 B4 Ocoña Peru
115 F9 Oconee, Lake resr GA U.S.A.
207 I6 O'Connell Creek r. Qld Austr.
110 F6 Oconomowoc WI U.S.A.
110 G5 Oconto WI U.S.A.
110 F5 Oconto Falls WI U.S.A.
62 C4 O Convento Spain
62 F3 O Corgo Spain
126 E5 Ocoroni Mex.
138 C3 Ocoruro Peru
127 M10 Ocos Guat.
127 M9 Ocosingo Mex.
126 □P11 Ocotal Nic.
129 K9 Ocotepec Mex.
128 E5 Ocotlán Jalisco Mex.
129 K9 Ocotlán Oaxaca Mex.
57 I3 Očová Slovakia
127 M9 Ocozocoautla Mex.
62 E9 Ocreza r. Port.
57 I4 Ócsa Hungary
57 I4 Ocsai park Hungary
57 H5 Őcsény Hungary
57 J5 Öcsöd Hungary
38 H2 Octeville France
39 L2 Octeville-sur-Mer France
October Revolution Island Severnaya Zemlya Rus. Fed. see Oktyabr'skoy Revolyutsii, Ostrov
118 C5 Octoraro Creek r. MD U.S.A.
118 C5 Octoraro Lake PA U.S.A.
126 □S14 Ocú Panama
95 H2 Ocua Moz.
129 H7 Ocuilan de Arteaga Mex.
131 J8 Ocumare del Tuy Venez.
138 D4 Ocurí Bol.
54 G2 Ocypel Pol.
88 E5 Oda Ghana
165 J11 Ōda Japan
85 H4 Oda, Jebel mt. Sudan
190 E2 Odabaşı Turkey
20 □E1 Ódáðahraun lava field Iceland
163 F8 Ŏdaejin N. Korea
163 F10 Odae-san National Park S. Korea
166 D7 Ōdai Japan
166 D7 Ōdaigahara-zan mt. Japan
166 G4 Odaira-tōge pass Japan
164 R9 Odaka Japan
110 D3 Odanah WI U.S.A.
164 R6 Ōdate Japan
167 J5 Odawara Japan
22 C1 Odda Norway
22 G6 Odder Denmark
26 □O1 Oddsta Shetland, Scotland U.K.
64 D4 Odearce r. Port.
64 B6 Odeceixe Port.
107 L3 Odei r. Man. Can.
64 E6 Odeleite Port.
64 E6 Odeleite r. Port.
110 F8 Odell IL U.S.A.
64 C6 Odelouca r. Port.
53 K5 Odelzhausen Ger.
121 G12 Odem TX U.S.A.
64 B5 Odemira Port.
79 I4 Ödemiş Turkey
65 H6 Odena Spain
97 K3 Odendaalsrus S. Africa
23 L2 Odensbacken Sweden
22 G6 Odense Denmark
22 G6 Odense Fjord b. Denmark
118 B6 Odenton MD U.S.A.
52 F2 Odenwald reg. Ger.
54 C3 Oder r. Ger. alt. Odra (Poland)
49 I7 Oder r. Ger./Pol.
50 J5 Oderberg Ger.
50 J5 Oderbruch reg. Ger.
50 J2 Oderbucht b. Ger.
50 J3 Oderhaff b. Ger.
50 H5 Oder-Havel-Kanal canal Ger.
51 I6 Oderin Ger.
52 D2 Odernheim am Glan Ger.
71 M4 Oderzo Italy
16 J7 Odesa Ukr.
14 K3 Odesdino Rus. Fed.
23 K3 Ödeshog Sweden
16 I6 Odes'ka Oblast' admin. div. Ukr.
Odessa Ukr. see Odesa
118 D6 Odessa DE U.S.A.
121 D10 Odessa TX U.S.A.
122 E3 Odessa WA U.S.A.
Odessa Oblast admin. div. Ukr. see Odes'ka Oblast'
Odesskaya Oblast' admin. div. Ukr. see Odes'ka Oblast'
183 O1 Odesskoye Rus. Fed.
38 C6 Odet r. France
85 H5 Odi watercourse Sudan
64 B6 Odiáxere Port.
64 F6 Odiel r. Spain
88 D4 Odienné Côte d'Ivoire
31 K5 Odiham Hampshire, England U.K.
44 H4 Odijk Neth.
90 A5 Odimba Gabon
19 U6 Odintsovo Rus. Fed.
64 C4 Odivelas Beja Port.
64 A3 Odivelas Lisboa Port.
64 C4 Odivelas r. Port.
64 C4 Odivelas, Barragem de resr Port.
77 P5 Odobeşti Romania
77 O5 Odobeştilor, Măgura hill Romania
54 F4 Odolanów Pol.
51 J10 Odolena Voda Czech Rep.
212 T2 Odom Inlet Antarctica
39 K3 Odon r. France
63 Q7 Odón Spain
159 G9 Ŏdŏngk Cambodia
44 K3 Odoorn Neth.
77 N4 Odorheiu Secuiesc Romania
19 T8 Odoyev Rus. Fed.
54 C3 Odra r. Pol. alt. Oder (Germany)
63 L4 Odra r. Spain
17 N7 Odradivka Ukr.
57 G2 Odry Czech Rep.
55 I4 Odrzywół Pol.
76 H5 Odžaci Vojvodina, Srbija Serb. and Mont.
90 B4 Odzala, Parc National d' nat. park Congo
95 G3 Odzi Zimbabwe
95 G3 Odzi r. Zimbabwe
166 B5 Ōe Japan
49 K6 Oebisfelde Ger.
49 I7 Oedelsheim (Oberweser) Ger.
51 H9 Oederan Ger.
48 H3 Oederquart Ger.
165 G11 Oedong S. Korea
44 I5 Oeffelt Neth.
44 G4 Oegstgeest Neth.
140 E3 Oeiras Brazil
64 A3 Oeiras Port.
64 D5 Oeiras r. Port.
49 F7 Oelde Ger.
48 I3 Oelixdorf Ger.
120 D4 Oelrichs SD U.S.A.
51 F10 Oelsnitz Sachsen Ger.
51 G9 Oelsnitz Sachsen Ger.
120 J4 Oelwein IA U.S.A.
44 J4 Oene Neth.
206 D2 Oenpelli N.T. Austr.
70 D1 Oensingen Switz.
48 H4 Oerel Ger.
48 J3 Oering Ger.
49 J10 Oerlenbach Ger.
49 G7 Oerlinghausen Ger.
Oesel i. Estonia see Hiiumaa
45 I9 Oesling hills Lux.
45 F6 Oesterdam barrage Neth.
144 E2 Oetling Arg.
51 E9 Oettersdorf Ger.
53 J4 Oettingen in Bayern Ger.
58 C5 Oetz Austria
48 K4 Oetzen Ger.
109 F2 Oeufs, Lac des l. Que. Can.
48 H1 Oeversee Ger.
166 B5 Ōe-yama hill Japan
43 B6 Œyreluy France
189 J3 Of Turkey
122 L3 O'Fallon r. MT U.S.A.
73 O5 Ofanto r. Italy
190 C7 Ofaqim Israel
73 L3 Ofena Italy
89 G4 Offa Nigeria
27 G6 Offaly county Rep. of Ireland
70 H5 Offanengo Italy
37 M8 Offemont France
49 G10 Offenbach am Main Ger.
52 E3 Offenbach an der Queich Ger.
53 N4 Offenberg Ger.
52 D5 Offenburg Ger.
59 I4 Offensee l. Austria
20 M5 Offerdal Sweden
73 L2 Offida Italy
53 I5 Offingen Ger.
36 B4 Offranville France
79 H6 Ofidoussa i. Greece
201 □2 Ofolanga atoll Tonga
62 D3 O Forte Spain
20 N2 Ofotfjorden sea chan. Norway
52 G5 Ofterdingen Ger.
200 □2 Ofu i. American Samoa
164 S7 Ōfunato Japan
157 K4 Oga r. Indon.
164 Q7 Oga Japan
164 R7 Ogachi Japan
167 K1 Oga-dake mt. Japan
92 E3 Ogadēn reg. Eth.
164 Q7 Oga-hantō pen. Japan
166 E5 Ōgaki Japan
120 E5 Ogallala NE U.S.A.
156 F6 Ogan r. Indon.
167 J3 Ogano Japan
167 H6 Ogasa Japan
165 □2 Ogasawara-shotō is N. Pacific Ocean
111 P2 Ogascanane, Lac l. Que. Can.
167 H1 Ōgata Japan
167 H3 Ōga-tō mt. Japan
167 M1 Ogawa Fukushima Japan
167 L3 Ogawa Ibaraki Japan
167 L2 Ogawa Ibaraki Japan
167 G2 Ogawa Nagano Japan
167 J3 Ogawa Saitama Japan
167 L2 Ōgawa Japan
164 R8 Ōgawara Japan
164 S6 Ogawara-ko l. Japan
89 G4 Ogbomosho Nigeria
Ogbomoso Nigeria see Ogbomosho
120 H4 Ogden IA U.S.A.
122 I6 Ogden UT U.S.A.
106 C3 Ogden, Mount B.C. Can.
118 F2 Ogdensburg NJ U.S.A.
117 J4 Ogdensburg NY U.S.A.
115 G10 Ogeechee r. GA U.S.A.
110 D4 Ogema WI U.S.A.
48 E3 Ogenbargen Ger.
36 H6 Oger France
43 C9 Ogeu-les-Bains France
37 M6 Ogéviller France
70 G4 Oggiono Italy
178 D7 Oghna Rajasthan India
200 □6 Ogho Choiseul Solomon Is
165 P9 Ogi Japan
108 C4 Ogidaki Ont. Can.
104 E3 Ogilvie r. Y.T. Can.
104 D3 Ogilvie Mountains Y.T. Can.
164 □1 Ogimi Okinawa Japan
191 D6 Oğlaksuyu Turkey
184 F2 Oglanly Turkm.
86 E5 'Oglât el Khnâchîch well Mali
86 D4 Oglat Sbot well Alg.
72 D8 Ogliastra reg. Sardegna Italy
72 D8 Ogliastra, Isola dell' i. Sardegna Italy
72 C2 Ogliastro Corse France
74 H9 Ogliastro, Lago di l. Sicilia Italy
70 J5 Oglio r. Italy
162 K2 Oglongi Rus. Fed.
207 L7 Ogmore Qld Austr.
30 E5 Ogmore Vale of Glamorgan, Wales U.K.
30 E4 Ogmore Vale Bridgend, Wales U.K.
40 G2 Ognon r. France
167 J3 Ōgo Japan
155 B3 Ogoamas, Gunung mt. Indon.
167 J4 Ogōchi Dam Japan
162 H2 Ogodzha Rus. Fed.
89 H5 Ogoja Nigeria
108 C3 Ogoki r. Ont. Can.
108 C3 Ogoki Lake Ont. Can.
108 B3 Ogoki Reservoir Ont. Can.
162 M5 Ogon'ki Rus. Fed.
63 O2 Ogoño, Cabo c. Spain
90 A5 Ogooué r. Gabon
90 B5 Ogooué-Ivindo prov. Gabon
90 B5 Ogooué-Lolo prov. Gabon
90 A5 Ogooué-Maritime prov. Gabon
165 I12 Ogōri Japan
162 F1 Ogoron Rus. Fed.
167 J4 Ogose Japan
77 L7 Ogosta r. Bulg.
89 F5 Ogou r. Togo
209 D11 O'Grady, Lake salt flat W.A. Austr.
77 K9 Ogražden mts Bulg./Macedonia
Ogradzhen mts Bulg./Macedonia see Ogražden
18 H5 Ogre Latvia
18 H5 Ogre r. Latvia
55 J3 Ogrodniki Pol.
55 H5 Ogrodzieniec Pol.
51 J7 Ogrosen Ger.
62 C4 O Grove Spain
166 E5 Ōguchi Japan
19 V5 Ogudnevo Rus. Fed.
86 E4 Oguilet Merzoug well Mali
68 E3 Ogulin Croatia
89 F5 Ogun state Nigeria
167 I1 Oguni Japan
117 □O5 Ogunquit ME U.S.A.
184 E2 Ogurchinskiy, Ostrov i. Turkm.
Ogurjaly Adasy i. Turkm. see Ogurchinskiy, Ostrov
191 I4 Oğuz Azer.
191 I1 Oguzer Rus. Fed.
57 K6 Ohaba Lungă Romania
89 G5 Ohafia Nigeria
203 B12 Ohai South I. N.Z.
202 J6 Ohakune North I. N.Z.
92 E3 Ohale well Somalia
65 N6 Ohanes Spain
87 H3 Ohanet Alg.
94 C3 Ohangwena admin. reg. Namibia
167 L5 Ōhara Japan
164 S5 Ōhata Japan
202 J7 Ohau North I. N.Z.
203 E11 Ohau r. South I. N.Z.
203 D11 Ohau, Lake South I. N.Z.
202 J4 Ohaupo North I. N.Z.
48 E4 Ohe r. Ger.
53 O4 Ohe r. Ger.
45 H8 Ohey Belgium
138 C5 O'Higgins Chile
146 B4 O'Higgins admin. reg. Chile
145 B8 O'Higgins, Lago l. Chile
202 J4 Ohinewai North I. N.Z.
110 E8 Ohio IL U.S.A.
120 K7 Ohio r. OH/WV U.S.A.
116 C8 Ohio state U.S.A.
116 A8 Ohio City OH U.S.A.
212 Q1 Ohio Range mts Antarctica
119 G1 Ohioville NY U.S.A.
167 K3 Ōhira Japan
167 I5 Ōhito Japan
202 L4 Ohiwa Harbour North I. N.Z.
17 O4 Ohiyivka Ukr.
52 D5 Ohlsbach Ger.
59 I4 Ohlsdorf Austria
53 K6 Ohlstadt Ger.
49 G9 Ohm r. Ger.
18 J3 Õhne r. Estonia
49 D6 Ohne Ger.
52 F6 Öhningen Ger.
201 □2 'Ohonua Tonga
202 L4 Ohope North I. N.Z.
57 G3 Ohrady Slovakia
49 K9 Ohrdruf Ger.
56 D1 Ohře r. Czech Rep.
51 E6 Ohre r. Ger.
76 I9 Ohrid Macedonia
76 I9 Ohrid, Lake Albania/Macedonia
Ohridsko Ezero l. Albania/Macedonia see Ohrid, Lake
95 F5 Ohrigstad S. Africa
52 G3 Öhringen Ger.
Ohrit, Liqeni i l. Albania/Macedonia see Ohrid, Lake
49 K6 Ohrum Ger.
202 I5 Ohura North I. N.Z.
166 C5 Ōi Fukui Japan
167 J5 Ōi Kanagawa Japan
62 C7 Oiã Port.
137 I4 Oiapoque Brazil
136 C3 Oiba Col.
26 G8 Oich r. Scotland U.K.
26 G8 Oich, Loch l. Scotland U.K.
175 □1 Oidhuni i. S. Male Maldives
173 K12 Oiga Xizang China
167 H6 Ōigawa Japan
166 C5 Ōi-gawa r. Japan
167 H6 Ōi-gawa r. Japan
26 C9 Oigh-sgeir is Scotland U.K.
36 E3 Oignies France
40 H4 Oignin r. France
62 D4 O Igrexario Spain
20 R4 Oijärvi Fin.
44 H5 Oijen Neth.
116 F7 Oil City PA U.S.A.
124 M6 Oildale CA U.S.A.
170 C4 Oilê Sichuan China
27 I8 Oilgate Rep. of Ireland
27 F3 Oily r. Rep. of Ireland
62 F5 Oímbra Spain
63 P3 Oion Spain
170 B4 Oi Qu r. Xizang China
164 S6 Oirase-gawa r. Japan
62 D3 O Irixo Spain
39 K8 Oiron France
44 H5 Oirschot Neth.
41 H6 Oisans reg. France
36 D5 Oise dept France
36 D6 Oise r. France
36 F5 Oise à l'Aisne, Canal de l' France
43 B6 Oiseaux, Île aux i. France
88 A2 Oiseaux du Djoudj, Parc National des nat. park Senegal
40 H2 Oiselay-et-Grachaux France
36 C4 Oisemont France
167 J5 Ōiso Japan
39 J5 Oisseau France
36 B5 Oissel France
44 H5 Oisterwijk Neth.
131 □4 Oistins Barbados
165 I13 Ōita Japan
165 I13 Ōita pref. Japan
62 C4 Oitavén r. Spain
78 D4 Oiti mt. Greece
78 D4 Oiti nat. park Greece
77 O4 Oituz r. Romania
78 D6 Oitylo Greece
84 C4 Oiuru well Libya
164 S4 Oiwake Japan
39 Q7 Oizon France
167 J3 Ōizumi Gunma Japan
167 H4 Ōizumi Yamanashi Japan
166 E3 Oizuruga-dake mt. Japan
23 N3 Öja i. Sweden
124 M7 Ojai CA U.S.A.
65 L3 Ojailén r. Spain
18 K2 Ojamaa r. Estonia
23 M1 Öjaren l. Sweden
55 H5 Ojcowski Park Narodowy nat. park Pol.
21 L6 Öje Sweden
147 E4 Ojeda Arg.
65 J7 Ojén Spain
166 C6 Ōji Japan
165 F13 Ojika-jima i. Japan
126 G3 Ojinaga Mex.
129 K7 Ojitlán Mex.
167 I1 Ojiya Japan
89 G5 Ojobo Nigeria
128 E3 Ojocaliente Mex.
123 K8 Ojo Caliente NM U.S.A.
146 E2 Ojo de Agua Arg.
128 G3 Ojo de Agua Mex.
126 F3 Ojo de Laguna Mex.
126 B4 Ojo de Liebre, Lago b. Mex.
65 L2 Ojos del Guadiana lakes Spain
144 C2 Ojos del Salado, Nevado mt. Arg./Chile
63 R7 Ojos Negros Spain
55 I3 Ojrzeń Pol.
89 H5 Oju Nigeria
128 F4 Ojuelos de Jalisco Mex.
21 M6 Öjung Sweden
89 G5 Oka Nigeria
19 W7 Oka r. Rus. Fed.
167 J3 Okabe Saitama Japan
167 H6 Okabe Shizuoka Japan
94 C4 Okahandja Namibia
Okahu b. South I. N.Z. see Jackson Bay
202 J5 Okahukura North I. N.Z.
202 I2 Okaihau North I. N.Z.
203 H10 Okains Bay South I. N.Z.
203 H10 Okains Bay b. South I. N.Z.
89 F4 Okaka Nigeria
94 C4 Okakarara Namibia
109 I1 Okak Islands Nfld and Lab. Can.
55 H2 Okalewo Pol.
106 G5 Okanagan Falls B.C. Can.
106 G5 Okanagan Lake B.C. Can.
176 G9 Okanda Sri Lanka
122 E2 Okanogan WA U.S.A.
122 E2 Okanogan r. WA U.S.A.
122 D2 Okanogan Range mts WA U.S.A.
57 K5 Okány Hungary
94 C4 Okaputa Namibia
185 O6 Okara Pak.
184 F2 Okarem Turkm.
203 E10 Okarito Lagoon South I. N.Z.
202 H6 Okato North I. N.Z.
94 B3 Okaukuejo Namibia
94 D3 Okavango r. Botswana/Namibia
94 C3 Okavango admin. reg. Namibia
94 D3 Okavango Delta swamp Botswana
165 H13 Ōkawa Japan
166 A5 Okawachi Japan
202 □ Okawa Point Chatham Is S. Pacific Ocean
167 H3 Okaya Japan
165 K12 Okayama Japan
165 K12 Okayama pref. Japan
166 F6 Okazaki Japan
191 B5 Okçular Dağı mt. Turkey
115 G12 Okeechobee FL U.S.A.
115 G12 Okeechobee, Lake FL U.S.A.
121 F7 Okeene OK U.S.A.
115 F10 Okefenokee National Wildlife Refuge and Wilderness nature res. GA U.S.A.
115 F10 Okefenokee Swamp GA U.S.A.
167 K3 Okegawa Japan
30 D6 Okehampton Devon, England U.K.
89 F4 Oke-Iho Nigeria
121 G8 Okemah OK U.S.A.
30 D6 Okement r. England U.K.
89 G5 Okene Nigeria
49 J5 Oker r. Ger.
164 U3 Oketo Japan
178 B8 Okha Gujarat India
162 M2 Okha Sakhalin Rus. Fed.
Okhadunga Nepal see Okhaldhunga
179 K6 Okhaldhunga Nepal
14 K4 Okhansk Rus. Fed.
178 G4 Okhimath Uttaranchal India
162 M1 Okhinskiy Peresheyek isth. Rus. Fed.
Ōkhi Óros mt. Greece see Ochi
17 P2 Okhochevka Rus. Fed.
19 V4 Okhotino Rus. Fed.
193 P4 Okhotka r. Rus. Fed.
17 M8 Okhotnykove Ukr.
193 P4 Okhotsk Rus. Fed.
164 V2 Okhotsk, Sea of Japan/Rus. Fed.
Okhotskoye More sea Japan/Rus. Fed. see Okhotsk, Sea of
17 O7 Okhrimivka Ukr.
Okhthonia Greece see Ochthonia
17 N3 Okhtyrka Ukr.
19 P5 Okhvat Rus. Fed.
96 B5 Okiep S. Africa
164 □1 Okinawa Okinawa Japan
164 □1 Okinawa i. Japan
164 □ Okinawa pref. Japan
Okinawa-guntō is Japan see Okinawa-shotō
164 □D20 Okinawa-shotō is Japan
161 N7 Okino-Daitō-jima i. Japan
164 □F19 Okinoerabu-jima i. Nansei-shotō Japan
166 B7 Okino-shima i. Japan
165 H12 Okino-shima i. Japan
165 J14 Okino-shima i. Japan
161 O7 Okino-Tori-shima i. Japan
165 J10 Oki-shotō is Japan
161 N4 Oki-shotō is Japan
89 G5 Okitipupa Nigeria
158 B6 Okkan Myanmar
121 G8 Oklahoma state U.S.A.
121 G8 Oklahoma City OK U.S.A.
115 G11 Oklawaha r. FL U.S.A.
121 G8 Okmulgee OK U.S.A.
57 L3 Okna r. Slovakia
Oknitsa Moldova see Ocniţa
85 H4 Oko, Wadi watercourse Sudan
57 G4 Okoč Slovakia
89 H5 Okola Cameroon
121 K8 Okolona MS U.S.A.
116 A7 Okolona OH U.S.A.
96 B3 Okombahe Namibia
90 B5 Okondja Gabon
54 E2 Okonek Pol.
55 L4 Okopy Pol.
57 G6 Okor r. Hungary
106 H5 Okotoks Alta Can.
94 A3 Okotusu well Namibia
19 P7 Okovskiy Les for. Rus. Fed.
90 B5 Okoyo Congo
183 S4 Okpety, Gora mt. Kazakh.
56 E2 Okříšky Czech Rep.
56 E2 Okrouhlice Czech Rep.
55 K4 Okrzeja Pol.
55 I5 Oksa Pol.
22 E6 Oksbøl Denmark
20 Q1 Øksfjord Norway
19 X7 Okskiy Zapovednik nature res. Rus. Fed.
14 G3 Oksovskiy Rus. Fed.
20 M3 Oksskolten mt. Norway
184 E1 Oktumkum, Peski des. Turkm.
158 C5 Oktwin Myanmar
Oktyabr' Aktyubinskaya Oblast' Kazakh. see Kandyagash
19 U4 Oktyabr' Rus. Fed.
Oktyabr'sk Kazakh. see Kandyagash
182 C1 Oktyabr'sk Rus. Fed.
184 H1 Oktyabr'sk Turkm.
17 S7 Oktyabr'skaya Rus. Fed.
182 J1 Oktyabr'skiy Kazakh.
162 F2 Oktyabr'skiy Amurskaya Oblast' Rus. Fed.
162 F2 Oktyabr'skiy Amurskaya Oblast' Rus. Fed.
14 H3 Oktyabr'skiy Arkhangel'skaya Oblast' Rus. Fed.
17 P3 Oktyabr'skiy Belgorodskaya Oblast' Rus. Fed.
19 X4 Oktyabr'skiy Ivanovskaya Oblast' Rus. Fed.
19 T7 Oktyabr'skiy Kaluzhskaya Oblast' Rus. Fed.
193 Q4 Oktyabr'skiy Kamchatskaya Oblast' Rus. Fed.
17 R8 Oktyabr'skiy Krasnodarskiy Kray Rus. Fed.
14 F2 Oktyabr'skiy Murmanskaya Oblast' Rus. Fed.
15 K5 Oktyabr'skiy Respublika Bashkortostan Rus. Fed.
17 S6 Oktyabr'skiy Rostovskaya Oblast' Rus. Fed.
19 V7 Oktyabr'skiy Ryazanskaya Oblast' Rus. Fed.
19 W8 Oktyabr'skiy Ryazanskaya Oblast' Rus. Fed.
14 L4 Oktyabr'skiy Sverdlovskaya Oblast' Rus. Fed.
15 H7 Oktyabr'skiy Volgogradskaya Oblast' Rus. Fed.
182 K1 Oktyabr'skoye Kazakh.
182 J1 Oktyabr'skoye Chelyabinskaya Oblast' Rus. Fed.
192 H3 Oktyabr'skoye Khanty-Mansiyskiy Avtonomnyy Okrug Rus. Fed.
19 W9 Oktyabr'skoye Lipetskaya Oblast' Rus. Fed.
182 F1 Oktyabr'skoye Orenburgskaya Oblast' Rus. Fed.
191 F2 Oktyabr'skoye Respublika Severnaya Osetiya-Alaniya Rus. Fed.
162 G5 Oktyabr'skoye Yevreyskaya Avtonomnaya Oblast' Rus. Fed.
193 K2 Oktyabr'skoy Revolyutsii, Ostrov i. Severnaya Zemlya Rus. Fed.
164 □1 Oku Okinawa Japan
68 F3 Okučani Croatia
166 E3 Okuchi Japan
165 H14 Ōkuchi Japan
19 Q3 Okulovka Rus. Fed.
191 C3 Ok'umi Georgia
Okureshi Georgia see Oqureshi
203 C10 Okuru South I. N.Z.
166 G4 Oku-sangai-dake mt. Japan
164 Q4 Okushiri-kaikyō sea chan. Japan
164 Q4 Okushiri-tō i. Japan
89 F4 Okuta Nigeria
167 J1 Okutadami-ko resr Japan
167 J4 Okutama Japan
167 J4 Okutama-ko l. Japan
166 B4 Okutango-hantō pen. Japan
167 J2 Okutone-ko resr Japan
166 G4 Okuwa Japan
94 E4 Okwa watercourse Botswana
193 Q4 Ola Rus. Fed.
121 I8 Ola AR U.S.A.
147 F3 Olaeta Arg.
20 □B1 Ólafsvík Iceland
62 D2 Olague Spain
175 □1 Olahali i. N. Male Maldives
18 G5 Olaine Latvia
176 F6 Olakkur Tamil Nadu India
62 D9 Olalhas Port.
41 I7 Olan, Pic d' mt. France
124 N5 Olancha CA U.S.A.
124 N5 Olancha Peak CA U.S.A.
126 □P10 Olanchito Hond.
23 N5 Öland i. Sweden
23 N4 Ölands norra udde pt Öland Sweden
23 M5 Ölands södra udde pt Öland Sweden
20 U3 Olanga Rus. Fed.
41 B9 Olargues France
57 K5 Olari Romania
204 H5 Olary S.A. Austr.
204 H5 Olary watercourse S.A. Austr.
147 G4 Olascoaga Arg.
57 K3 Olaszliszka Hungary
120 H6 Olathe KS U.S.A.
176 E7 Olavakod Kerala India
147 G5 Olavarría Arg.
63 Q3 Olave Spain
20 □ Olav V Land reg. Svalbard
54 F5 Oława Pol.
63 P3 Olazti Spain
67 D7 Olba Spain
59 N5 Olbendorf Austria
51 H9 Olbernhau Ger.
51 G9 Olbersdorf Ger.
51 D8 Olbersleben Ger.
72 C6 Olbia Sardegna Italy
72 D6 Olbia, Golfo di b. Sardegna Italy
55 K5 Olbięcin Pol.
56 D2 Olbramovice Czech Rep.
57 K5 Olcea Romania
191 D4 Olçek Turkey
191 C6 Ölçekli Turkey
193 P3 Ol'chan Rus. Fed.
53 K5 Olching Ger.
116 G5 Olcott NY U.S.A.
191 E5 Olçüllü Turkey
130 D2 Old Bahama Channel Bahamas/Cuba
31 J5 Old Basing Hampshire, England U.K.
176 G3 Old Bastar Chhattisgarh India
119 G4 Old Bridge NJ U.S.A.
30 H2 Oldbury West Midlands, England U.K.
27 H5 Oldcastle Rep. of Ireland
208 H5 Old Cherrabun W.A. Austr.
30 E1 Old Colwyn Conwy, Wales U.K.
207 H7 Old Cork Qld Austr.
104 E3 Old Crow Y.T. Can.
26 G12 Old Dailly South Ayrshire, Scotland U.K.
85 F5 Old Dongola Sudan
44 J3 Oldeberkoop Neth.
44 I4 Oldebroek Neth.
44 J2 Oldehove Neth.
21 H6 Oldeide Norway
44 I3 Oldemarkt Neth.
48 F4 Oldenbrok Ger.
48 F4 Oldenburg Ger.
48 K2 Oldenburg in Holstein Ger.
48 H3 Oldendorf Ger.
48 K4 Oldendorf (Luhe) Ger.
48 G2 Oldenswort Ger.
44 K4 Oldenzaal Neth.
20 P2 Olderdalen Norway
31 O4 Old Felixstowe Suffolk, England U.K.
209 F12 Oldfield r. W.A. Austr.
117 K5 Old Forge NY U.S.A.
118 E3 Old Forge PA U.S.A.
116 B7 Old Fort OH U.S.A.
115 □2 Old Fort Point New Prov. Bahamas
131 □2 Old Fort Point Montserrat
209 E9 Old Gidgee W.A. Austr.
29 M6 Oldham Greater Manchester, England U.K.
130 □ Old Harbour Jamaica
130 □ Old Harbour Bay Jamaica
27 E9 Old Head of Kinsale Rep. of Ireland
51 D8 Oldisleben Ger.
30 H5 Oldland South Gloucestershire, England U.K.
29 R7 Old Leake Lincolnshire, England U.K.
119 K2 Old Lyme CT U.S.A.
104 G5 Oldman r. Alta Can.
118 E5 Oldman's Creek r. NJ U.S.A.
26 L8 Oldmeldrum Aberdeenshire, Scotland U.K.
91 F8 Old Mkushi Zambia
97 N7 Old Morley S. Africa
119 L2 Old Mystic CT U.S.A.
117 □O5 Old Orchard Beach ME U.S.A.
109 K4 Old Perlican Nfld and Lab. Can.
124 M6 Old River CA U.S.A.
131 □2 Old Road Antigua and Barbuda
27 I8 Old Ross Rep. of Ireland
106 H5 Olds Alta Can.
119 K2 Old Saybrook CT U.S.A.
117 □O4 Old Speck Mountain ME U.S.A.
48 F1 Oldsum Ger.
27 J5 Old Town Rep. of Ireland
29 L5 Old Town Cumbria, England U.K.
116 C10 Oldtown KY U.S.A.
117 □Q4 Old Town ME U.S.A.
93 B5 Olduvai Gorge tourist site Tanz.
116 D8 Old Washington OH U.S.A.
118 F3 Oldwick NJ U.S.A.
105 J5 Old Wives Lake Sask. Can.
125 Q7 Old Woman Mountains CA U.S.A.
168 G2 Öldziyt Arhangay Mongolia
169 K4 Öldziyt Dornogovĭ Mongolia
116 G6 Olean NY U.S.A.
55 K1 Olecko Pol.
62 F9 Oledo Port.
70 F4 Oleggio Italy
62 E9 Oleiros Port.
193 N3 Olekma r. Rus. Fed.
193 N3 Olekminsk Rus. Fed.
17 L2 Oleksandrivka Chernihivs'ka Oblast' Ukr.
17 P6 Oleksandrivka Dnipropetrovs'ka Oblast' Ukr.
17 P5 Oleksandrivka Donets'ka Oblast' Ukr.
17 O3 Oleksandrivka Kharkivs'ka Oblast' Ukr.
17 K5 Oleksandrivka Kirovohrads'ka Oblast' Ukr.
17 L5 Oleksandrivka Kirovohrads'ka Oblast' Ukr.
17 K6 Oleksandrivka Mykolayivs'ka Oblast' Ukr.
17 L7 Oleksandrivka Mykolayivs'ka Oblast' Ukr.
17 N8 Oleksandrivka Respublika Krym Ukr.
17 O7 Oleksandrivka Zaporiz'ka Oblast' Ukr.
17 M5 Oleksandriya Kirovohrads'ka Oblast' Ukr.
16 F3 Oleksandriya Rivnens'ka Oblast' Ukr.
17 Q5 Oleksiyevo-Druzhkivka Ukr.
17 M7 Oleksiyivka Khersons'ka Oblast' Ukr.
17 R4 Oleksiyivka Luhans'ka Oblast' Ukr.
17 M8 Oleksiyivka Respublika Krym Ukr.
14 I2 Olema Rus. Fed.
45 G6 Olen Belgium
22 B2 Ølen Norway
14 F1 Olenegorsk Rus. Fed.
193 M3 Olenek Rus. Fed.
193 M2 Olenek r. Rus. Fed.
Olenek Bay Rus. Fed. see Olenekskiy Zaliv
193 N2 Olenekskiy Zaliv b. Rus. Fed.
Ölengti r. Kazakh. see Olenti
19 Q5 Olenino Rus. Fed.
14 F2 Olenitsa Rus. Fed.
17 Q6 Olenivka Ukr.
192 I2 Oleniy, Ostrov i. Rus. Fed.
182 E3 Olenti r. Kazakh.
183 P1 Olenti r. Kazakh.
169 N1 Olentuy Rus. Fed.
Olenya Rus. Fed. see Olenegorsk
42 B4 Oléron, Île d' i. France
66 I4 Olesa de Montserrat Spain
17 K2 Oleshnya Chernihivs'ka Oblast' Ukr.
17 N3 Oleshnya Sums'ka Oblast' Ukr.
16 D4 Oles'ko Ukr.
54 F5 Oleśnica Dolnośląskie Pol.
55 J5 Oleśnica Świętokrzyskie Pol.
55 I5 Olesno Małopolskie Pol.
54 G5 Olesno Opolskie Pol.
55 L5 Oleszyce Pol.
72 C2 Oletta Corse France
43 I10 Olette France
157 L9 Olet Tongo mt. Sumbawa Indon.
16 G2 Olevs'k Ukr.
118 D4 Oley PA U.S.A.
49 D7 Olfen Ger.
20 M3 Ølfjellet mt. Norway
162 I7 Ol'ga Rus. Fed.
108 E3 Olga, Lac l. Que. Can.
206 C8 Olga, Mount N.T. Austr.
20 □ Olgastretet str. Svalbard
70 G4 Olginate Italy
17 R9 Ol'ginka Rus. Fed.
162 H2 Ol'ginsk Rus. Fed.
17 R8 Ol'ginskaya Krasnodarskiy Kray Rus. Fed.
17 S6 Ol'ginskaya Rostovskaya Oblast' Rus. Fed.
Olginskoye Rus. Fed. see Kochubeyevskoye
168 A2 Ölgiy Mongolia
26 I6 Olgrinmore Highland, Scotland U.K.
64 A2 Olhalvo Port.
64 D6 Olhão Port.
20 R4 Olhava Fin.
64 A2 Olho Marinho Port.
143 F2 Olhos d'Agua Brazil
175 □1 Olhuveli i. S. Male Maldives
206 C8 Olia Chain mts N.T. Austr.
66 H3 Oliana Spain
66 H3 Oliana, Embassament d' resr Spain
63 M9 Olías del Rey Spain
71 R7 Olib Croatia
68 E3 Olib i. Croatia
72 C7 Oliena Sardegna Italy
72 C7 Oliena r. Sardegna Italy
66 D5 Oliete Spain
94 C5 Olifants watercourse Namibia
96 C7 Olifants r. Western Cape S. Africa
96 F9 Olifants r. Western Cape S. Africa
95 F4 Olifants r. S. Africa
96 G3 Olifantshoek S. Africa
96 C8 Olifantsrivierberge mts S. Africa
73 N7 Oligastro Marina Italy
153 K5 Olimarao atoll Micronesia
Olimbos hill Cyprus see Olympos
Olimbos mt. Greece see Olympos
142 C4 Olímpia Brazil
79 L6 Olimpos Beydağları Milli Parkı nat. park Turkey
129 I8 Olinalá Mex.
140 G3 Olinda Brazil
95 H3 Olinda, Ponta pt Moz.
207 J1 Olinda Entrance sea chan. Qld Austr.
95 H3 Olinga Moz.
21 M6 Olingsjövallen Sweden
207 I6 Olio Qld Austr.
66 H4 Oliola Spain
Olisipo Port. see Lisboa
63 Q4 Olite Spain
147 F3 Oliva Arg.
73 Q9 Oliva r. Italy
67 E10 Oliva Spain
64 G3 Oliva hill Spain
144 C3 Oliva, Cordillera de mts Arg./Chile
64 F4 Oliva de la Frontera Spain
64 G3 Oliva de Mérida Spain
62 C6 Olival Port.
146 C2 Olivares, Cerro de mt. Arg./Chile
63 P9 Olivares de Júcar Spain
116 B10 Olive Hill KY U.S.A.
124 K2 Olivehurst CA U.S.A.
143 E4 Oliveira Brazil
62 D7 Oliveira de Azeméis Port.
62 D7 Oliveira de Frades Port.
62 D7 Oliveira do Bairro Port.
62 E8 Oliveira do Conde Port.
62 C6 Oliveira do Douro Port.
62 E8 Oliveira do Hospital Port.
140 E5 Oliveira dos Brejinhos Brazil
Olivença Moz. see Lupilichi
73 P5 Olivento r. Italy
64 E3 Olivenza Spain
64 E3 Olivenza r. Port./Spain
64 E3 Olivenza, Llanos de plain Spain
106 G5 Oliver B.C. Can.
75 I7 Oliveri Sicilia Italy
107 K3 Oliver Lake Sask. Can.
147 G3 Oliveros Arg.
36 C8 Olivet France
110 J7 Olivet MI U.S.A.
120 G4 Olivet SD U.S.A.
73 O6 Oliveto Citra Italy
73 Q6 Oliveto Lucano Italy
120 H3 Olivia MN U.S.A.
203 C11 Olivine Range mts South I. N.Z.
70 F2 Olivone Switz.
16 E4 Oliyiv Ukr.
169 J7 Oljoq Nei Mongol China
93 C6 Oljoro Wells Tanz.
21 I6 Oljuvatnet l. Norway
57 K2 Ol'ka Slovakia
57 K3 Ol'ka r. Slovakia
92 C5 Ol Kalou Kenya
15 H5 Ol'khi Rus. Fed.
15 G6 Ol'khovatka Rus. Fed.
19 W8 Ol'khovets Rus. Fed.
15 I6 Ol'khovka Rus. Fed.
55 H5 Olkusz Pol.
26 □N1 Ollaberry Shetland, Scotland U.K.
138 C3 Ollachea Peru
138 C5 Ollagüe Chile
138 C5 Ollagüe, Volcán vol. Bol.
72 C9 Olla stu r. Italy
29 O7 Ollerton Nottinghamshire, England U.K.
40 D5 Olliergues France
41 H10 Ollioules France
146 B2 Ollita, Cordillera de mts Arg./Chile
146 B2 Ollitas mt. Arg.
63 Q3 Ollo Spain
20 U5 Öllölä Fin.
72 C7 Ollolai Sardegna Italy
90 B5 Ollombo Congo
70 B3 Ollon Switz.
183 M7 Olmaliq Uzbek.
63 M5 Olmedilla de Roa Spain
72 A6 Olmedo Sardegna Italy
63 K6 Olmedo Spain
72 C2 Olmeta-di-Tuda Corse France
72 B4 Olmeto Corse France
147 F3 Olmos Arg.
136 B6 Olmos Peru
63 L3 Olmos de Ojeda Spain
Olmütz Czech Rep. see Olomouc
31 K3 Olney Milton Keynes, England U.K.
120 K6 Olney IL U.S.A.
118 A6 Olney MD U.S.A.
121 F9 Olney TX U.S.A.
67 D8 Olocau Spain
66 E6 Olocau del Rey Spain
162 A3 Olochi Rus. Fed.
23 K5 Olofström Sweden
183 L1 Ol'oinka Kazakh.
109 I3 Olomane r. Que. Can.
200 □6 Olomburi Malaita Solomon Is
56 G2 Olomouc Czech Rep.
56 G2 Olomoucký kraj admin. reg. Czech Rep.
70 G5 Olona r. Italy
19 P1 Olonets Rus. Fed.
19 Q1 Olonetskaya Vozvyshennost' hills Rus. Fed.
154 C4 Olongapo Luzon Phil.
157 K5 Olongliko Kalimantan Indon.
19 P1 Olonka r. Rus. Fed.
42 A2 Olonne-sur-Mer France
41 B10 Olonzac France
43 C9 Oloron-Ste-Marie France
200 □2 Olosega i. American Samoa
66 J3 Olot Spain
182 J8 Olot Uzbek.
51 G10 Olovi Czech Rep.
68 G3 Olovo Bos.-Herz.
169 N1 Olovyannaya Rus. Fed.
124 □E13 Olowalu HI U.S.A.
178 D9 Olpad Gujarat India
146 D2 Olpas Arg.
49 E8 Olpe Ger.
58 E5 Olperer mt. Austria
18 M8 Ol'sa r. Belarus
56 F2 Olšany Czech Rep.
56 G2 Olšany u Prostějova Czech Rep.
22 J2 Olsätter Sweden
57 G2 Olšava r. Czech Rep.
57 K3 Olšava r. Slovakia
49 F8 Olsberg Ger.
57 H2 Olše r. Czech Rep.
19 O7 Ol'sha Rus. Fed.
17 Q2 Ol'shanka Rus. Fed.
17 K6 Ol'shans'ke Ukr.
44 J4 Olst Neth.
55 K3 Olszanka Mazowieckie Pol.
54 F5 Olszanka Opolskie Pol.
55 K6 Olszany Pol.
55 J2 Olszewka Pol.
55 J2 Olszewo-Borki Pol.
54 G3 Olszówka Pol.
55 H5 Olsztyn Śląskie Pol.
55 I2 Olsztyn Warmińsko-Mazurskie Pol.
55 I2 Olsztynek Pol.
55 L3 Olszyn Pol.
54 D4 Olszyna Pol.
77 M7 Olt r. Romania
146 D2 Olta Arg.
145 C6 Olte, Sierra de mts Arg.
22 C3 Oltedal Norway
70 D1 Olten Switz.
77 O6 Olteniţa Romania
77 M6 Olteţ r. Romania
77 P6 Oltina Romania
182 H6 Oltinko'l Uzbek.
Oltinkŭl Uzbek. see Oltinko'l
185 M1 Oltintopkan Tajik.
191 F3 Oltu Turkey
191 C5 Oltu r. Turkey
171 M8 Oluan Pi c. Taiwan
175 □1 Olugiri i. N. Male Maldives
191 D5 Oluklu Turkey
65 O6 Olula del Río Spain
191 D5 Olur Turkey
154 D8 Olutanga i. Phil.
63 Q5 Ólvega Spain
66 F3 Olvena Spain
65 I7 Olvera Spain
30 G4 Olveston South Gloucestershire, England U.K.
16 E3 Olyka Ukr.
19 V9 Olym r. Rus. Fed.
Olymbos hill Cyprus see Olympos
78 C5 Olympia tourist site Greece
122 C3 Olympia WA U.S.A.
78 E2 Olympiada Greece
122 C3 Olympic National Park WA U.S.A.
190 B3 Olympos hill Cyprus
78 D2 Olympos mt. Greece
78 D2 Olympos nat. park Greece
79 L6 Olympos tourist site Turkey
Olympus, Mount Greece see Olympos
122 C3 Olympus, Mount WA U.S.A.
17 R2 Olymskiy Rus. Fed.
118 D2 Olyphant PA U.S.A.
17 K2 Olyshivka Ukr.
193 R3 Olyutorskiy Rus. Fed.
193 S4 Olyutorskiy, Mys c. Rus. Fed.
193 R4 Olyutorskiy Zaliv b. Rus. Fed.
72 C7 Olzai Sardegna Italy
Olzheras Rus. Fed. see Mezhdurechensk
173 F10 Oma Xizang China
164 R5 Ōma Japan
14 I2 Oma r. Rus. Fed.
167 G3 Ōmachi Japan
167 H6 Omaezaki Japan
167 H6 Omae-zaki pt Japan
164 R7 Ōmagari Japan
27 H3 Omagh Northern Ireland U.K.
136 C6 Omaguas Peru
120 H5 Omaha NE U.S.A.
120 G4 Omaha Indian Reservation res. NE U.S.A.
94 C4 Omaheke admin. reg. Namibia
202 K7 Omakere North I. N.Z.
191 G3 Omalo Georgia
191 G3 Omalo Georgia
162 J2 Omal'skiy Khrebet mts Rus. Fed.
176 F7 Omalur Tamil Nadu India
167 J3 Ōmama Japan
187 K6 Oman country Asia
187 M3 Oman, Gulf of Asia
94 B4 Omangambo Namibia
202 H2 Omapere, Lake North I. N.Z.
203 D11 Omarama South I. N.Z.
77 O8 Omarchevo Bulg.
185 N7 Omarkot Pak.
68 F3 Omarska Bos.-Herz.
94 B4 Omaruru Namibia
138 A3 Omas Peru
94 D3 Omatako watercourse Namibia
138 C4 Omate Peru
94 B4 Omatjette Namibia
96 G1 Omaweneno Botswana
164 R5 Ōma-zaki c. Japan
155 D8 Ombai, Selat sea chan. Indon.
90 C3 Ombella-Mpoko pref. C.A.R.
30 H3 Ombersley Worcestershire, England U.K.
89 H5 Ombessa Cameroon
Ombetsu Japan see Onbetsu
94 B3 Ombika waterhole Namibia
156 B4 Ombolata Indon.
90 A5 Omboué Gabon
72 G2 Ombrone r. Italy

173 H11 Ombu Xizang China
147 I3 Ombúes de Lavalle Uru.
191 C6 Omcalı Turkey
96 H6 Omdraaisvlei S. Africa
85 G6 Omdurman Sudan
167 J4 Ōme Japan
129 K7 Omealca Mex.
27 J4 Omeath Rep. of Ireland
18 K3 Omedu Estonia
70 E4 Omegna Italy
17 M4 Omel'nyk Poltavs'ka Oblast' Ukr.
17 O6 Omel'nyk Zaporiz'ka Oblast' Ukr.
17 N8 Omelyanivka Ukr.
84 D5 Omena well Chad
205 K7 Omeo Vic. Austr.
116 B4 Omer MI U.S.A.
79 K3 Ömerler Turkey
62 D2 O Mesón do Vento Spain
72 C3 Omessa Corse France
126 □Q12 Ometepe, Isla de i. Nic.
129 I9 Ometepec Mex.
27 B5 Omey Island Rep. of Ireland
158 D6 Omgoy Wildlife Reserve nature res. Thai.
85 H6 Om Hajēr Eritrea
167 H3 Ōmi Japan
167 G1 Ōmi Niigata Japan
166 D5 Ōmi Shiga Japan
184 C6 Omīdīyeh Iran
167 M4 Omigawa Japan
166 D5 Ōmihachiman Japan
203 G10 Omihi South I. N.Z.
Omilo Georgia see Omalo
106 E3 Omineca Mountains B.C. Can.
106 E4 Omineca Provincial Park B.C. Can.
68 F4 Omiš Croatia
71 R5 Omišalj Croatia
165 I12 Ōmi-shima i. Japan
94 C4 Omitara Namibia
129 H8 Omitlán r. Mex.
167 L2 Ōmiya Ibaraki Japan
166 B4 Ōmiya Kyōto Japan
166 D7 Ōmiya Mie Japan
167 K4 Ōmiya Saitama Japan
106 C3 Ommaney, Cape AK U.S.A.
22 E6 Omme r. Denmark
48 J1 Ommel Denmark
44 J3 Ommen Neth.
168 I5 Ömnögovĭ prov. Mongolia
72 C7 Omodeo, Lago l. Sardegna Italy
167 K3 Omoi-gawa r. Japan
89 G5 Omoku Nigeria
78 D3 Omolio Greece
193 R3 Omolon Rus. Fed.
193 Q3 Omolon r. Rus. Fed.
92 B3 Omo National Park Eth.
164 R7 Omono-gawa r. Japan
36 I4 Omont France
164 R7 Ōmori Japan
62 C3 O Mosteiro Galicia Spain
167 L1 Omotegō Japan
92 C3 Omo Wenz r. Eth.
91 B9 Ompupa Angola
110 F5 Omro WI U.S.A.
192 I4 Omsk Rus. Fed.
193 Q3 Omsukchan Rus. Fed.
164 T2 Ōmu Japan
63 N5 O-mu Myanmar
77 N5 Omu, Vârful mt. Romania
89 G4 Omu-Aran Nigeria
55 J2 Omulew r. Pol.
55 I2 Omulew, Jezioro l. Pol.
89 G5 Omuo-Ekiti Nigeria
165 G14 Ōmura Japan
165 G14 Ōmura-wan b. Japan
167 J6 Ōmuro-yama hill Japan
167 I5 Ōmuro-yama mt. Japan
167 J4 Ōmuro-yama mt. Japan
77 O7 Omurtag Bulg.
94 B3 Omusati admin. reg. Namibia
165 H13 Ōmuta Japan
14 K4 Omutninsk Rus. Fed.
63 N3 Oña Spain
164 S8 Onagawa Japan
27 C6 Onaght Rep. of Ireland
202 K5 Onakuri, Lake North I. N.Z.
110 C6 Onalaska WI U.S.A.
108 C3 Onaman Lake Ont. Can.
120 I2 Onamia MN U.S.A.
200 □4a Onamue i. Chuuk Micronesia
117 J11 Onancock VA U.S.A.
155 A5 Onang Sulawesi Indon.
90 A5 Onangué, Lac l. Gabon
72 C7 Onani Sardegna Italy
72 H2 Onano Italy
108 D4 Onaping Lake Ont. Can.
110 F9 Onarga IL U.S.A.
109 G3 Onatchiway, Lac l. Que. Can.
63 P2 Oñati Spain
126 E3 Onavas Mex.
120 G4 Onawa IA U.S.A.
111 J4 Onaway MI U.S.A.
164 U4 Onbetsu Japan
159 C7 Onbingwin Myanmar
63 P5 Oncala Spain
63 P5 Oncala, Puerto de pass Spain
147 F2 Oncativo Arg.
28 I5 Onchan Isle of Man
91 B9 Oncócua Angola
190 H2 Öncül Turkey
67 E8 Onda Spain
94 B3 Ondangwa Namibia
67 F10 Ondara Spain
63 P2 Ondarroa Spain
57 K3 Ondava r. Slovakia
96 E6 Onderstedorings S. Africa
91 B9 Ondjiva Angola
89 G5 Ondo Nigeria
89 G5 Ondo state Nigeria
169 L3 Öndörhaan Mongolia
169 Q4 Ondor Had Nei Mongol China
169 M2 Öndörhushuu Mongolia
169 A3 Ondorkara Xinjiang China
168 I6 Ondor Mod Nei Mongol China
169 M5 Ondor Sum Nei Mongol China
14 F3 Ondozero Rus. Fed.
43 B8 Ondres France
94 D4 One Botswana
175 D11 One and a Half Degree Channel Maldives
207 J3 One and a Half Mile Opening sea chan. Qld Austr.
119 L1 Oneco CT U.S.A.
14 G3 Onega Rus. Fed.
14 G3 Onega r. Rus. Fed.
Onega Bay g. Rus. Fed. see Onezhskaya Guba
70 E8 Oneglia Italy
One Hundred and Fifty Mile House B.C. Can. see 150 Mile House
One Hundred Mile House B.C. Can. see 100 Mile House
117 J5 Oneida NY U.S.A.
118 C3 Oneida PA U.S.A.
117 J5 Oneida Lake NY U.S.A.
120 F4 O'Neill NE U.S.A.
202 G7 Onekaka South I. N.Z.
110 H5 Onekama MI U.S.A.
193 Q5 Onekotan, Ostrov i. Kuril'skiye O-va Rus. Fed.
200 □3a Onemak i. Kwajalein Marshall Is
115 D9 Oneonta AL U.S.A.
117 J6 Oneonta NY U.S.A.
200 □6 Onepusu Malaita Solomon Is
203 □3 Oneroa i. Rarotonga Cook Is
202 J3 Oneroa North I. N.Z.
43 B7 Onesse-et-Laharie France
77 O4 Onești Romania
41 B8 Onet-le-Château France
201 □2a Onevai i. Tonga
14 F2 Onezhskaya Guba g. Rus. Fed.
19 S1 Onezhskiy Kanal canal Rus. Fed.
192 E3 Onezhskoye Ozero l. Rus. Fed.
179 I9 Ong r. India
90 B5 Onga Gabon
94 B3 Ongandjera Namibia
202 K6 Ongaonga North I. N.Z.
159 G10 Ông Đốc, Sông r. Vietnam
91 E6 Ongeri Dem. Rep. Congo
96 H5 Ongers watercourse S. Africa
209 E12 Ongerup W.A. Austr.
168 H4 Ongi Dundgovĭ Mongolia
168 H3 Ongi Övörhangay Mongolia
168 H4 Ongiyn Gol r. Mongolia
163 D10 Ongjin N. Korea
176 G5 Ongole Andhra Prad. India
41 H8 Ongles France
168 H3 Ongon Mongolia
90 C5 Ongonyi Congo
172 H1 Onguday Rus. Fed.
191 E3 Oni Georgia
26 F9 Onich Highland, Scotland U.K.
120 E3 Onida SD U.S.A.
72 D7 Onifai Sardegna Italy
72 C7 Oniferi Sardegna Italy
167 J3 Oniishi Japan
67 D10 Onil Spain
95 □I4 Onilahy r. Madag.
109 G3 Onistagane, Lac l. Que. Can.
89 G5 Onitsha Nigeria
94 C4 Onjati Mountain Namibia
Onjiva Angola see Ondjiva
167 L5 Onjuku Japan
20 U5 Onkamo Fin.
20 S5 Onkivesi l. Fin.
164 □1 Onna Okinawa Japan
164 □1 Onna-dake hill Okinawa Japan
36 G3 Onnaing France
200 □4a Onnang i. Chuuk Micronesia
193 O3 Onnes Rus. Fed.
201 □1 Ono i. Fiji
166 D4 Ono Fukui Japan
167 M1 Ono Fukushima Japan
166 E5 Ōno Gifu Japan
164 R5 Ono Hokkaidō Japan
166 A6 Ono Hyōgo Japan
118 B4 Ono PA U.S.A.
165 I13 Ōnoda Japan
167 J7 Ōnohara-jima i. Japan
165 Q12 Ōnohara-jima i. Japan
199 I4 Ono-i-Lau i. Fiji
165 H13 Ōnojō Japan
165 K12 Onomichi Japan
Onon atoll Micronesia see Namonuito
169 L2 Onon Mongolia
169 N1 Onon r. Rus. Fed.
169 M2 Onon Gol r. Mongolia
162 M3 Onor Rus. Fed.
162 M3 Onor, Gora mt. Sakhalin Rus. Fed.
199 H2 Onotoa atoll Gilbert Is Kiribati
62 C4 Ons, Illa de i. Spain
165 G11 Onsan S. Korea
96 D4 Onseepkans S. Africa
66 C2 Onsella r. Spain
51 E1 Ønslev Denmark
208 C6 Onslow W.A. Austr.
203 D12 Onslow, Lake South I. N.Z.
115 I8 Onslow Bay NC U.S.A.
162 F7 Onsong N. Korea
52 F5 Onstmettingen Ger.
44 L2 Onstwedde Neth.
166 F4 Ontake-san vol. Japan
67 D9 Ontalafia, Laguna de l. Spain
107 N5 Ontario prov. Can.
124 O7 Ontario CA U.S.A.
122 F4 Ontario OR U.S.A.
110 D6 Ontario WI U.S.A.
111 Q6 Ontario, Lake Can./U.S.A.
118 D4 Ontelaunee, Lake PA U.S.A.
Onteniente Spain see Ontinyent
66 F4 Ontiñena Spain
67 D10 Ontinyent Spain
20 T4 Ontojärvi l. Fin.
110 E3 Ontonagon MI U.S.A.
200 □6 Ontong Java Atoll Solomon Is
67 C10 Ontur Spain
17 M5 Onufriyivka Ukr.
55 M1 Onuškis Lith.
Onutu atoll Gilbert Is Kiribati see Onotoa
137 H3 Onverwacht Suriname
124 N6 Onyx CA U.S.A.
39 N6 Onzain France
62 I3 Onzonilla Spain
43 E10 Oô, Lac d' l. France
204 E2 Oodnadatta S.A. Austr.
92 E2 Oodweyne Somalia
167 G2 Ōoka Japan
124 □F13 'Ō'ōkala HI U.S.A.
27 F7 Oola Rep. of Ireland
204 C4 Ooldea S.A. Austr.
204 C4 Ooldea Range hills S.A. Austr.
121 H7 Oologah Lake resr OK U.S.A.
44 F5 Ooltgensplaat Neth.
208 I3 Oombulg Aboriginal Reserve W.A. Austr.
208 I3 Oombulgurri W.A. Austr.
206 F6 Ooratippra r. N.T. Austr.
207 H6 Oorindi Qld Austr.
45 E6 Oostakker Belgium
115 E8 Oostanaula r. GA U.S.A.
45 D6 Oostburg Neth.
45 C6 Oostende Belgium
44 I4 Oostendorp Neth.
44 I5 Oosterbeek Neth.
44 G2 Oosterend Neth.
44 K3 Oosterhesselen Neth.
44 G5 Oosterhout Neth.
44 F5 Oosterland Neth.
44 E5 Oosterschelde est. Neth.
44 E5 Oosterscheldekering barrage Neth.
44 J3 Oosterwolde Neth.
45 E7 Oosterzele Belgium
37 J1 Oostham Belgium
44 G3 Oosthuizen Neth.
45 D6 Oostkamp Belgium
45 G6 Oostmalle Belgium
45 E6 Oost-Souburg Neth.
44 H4 Oostvaardersplassen nature res. Neth.
45 E7 Oost-Vlaanderen prov. Belgium
45 C7 Oostvleteren Belgium
44 H2 Oost-Vlieland Neth.
44 F5 Oostvoorne Neth.
44 G4 Oostzaan Neth.
Ootacamund Tamil Nadu India see Udagamandalam
44 K4 Ootmarsum Neth.
106 E4 Ootsa Lake B.C. Can.
106 E4 Ootsa Lake l. B.C. Can.
124 □C12 'Ōpae'ula r. HI U.S.A.
128 E1 Opal Mex.
90 E5 Opala Dem. Rep. Congo
54 E3 Opalenica Pol.
54 G2 Opalenie Pol.
57 L4 Ópályi Hungary
202 I5 Oparau North I. N.Z.
203 J7 Opari North I. N.Z.
92 B4 Opari Sudan
14 J4 Oparino Rus. Fed.
108 D3 Opasatika r. Ont. Can.
108 D3 Opasatika Lake Ont. Can.
107 M4 Opasquia Ont. Can.
107 M4 Opasquia Provincial Park Ont. Can.
108 F3 Opataca, Lac l. Que. Can.
68 E3 Opatija Croatia
56 F2 Opatov Czech Rep.
56 E1 Opatovice nad Labem Czech Rep.
54 G5 Opatów Śląskie Pol.
55 J5 Opatów Świętokrzyskie Pol.
54 G4 Opatów Wielkopolskie Pol.
54 G4 Opatówek Pol.
55 I5 Opatowiec Pol.
55 J5 Opatówka r. Pol.
57 G2 Opava Czech Rep.
57 G1 Opava r. Czech Rep.
62 D4 O Pazo Spain
62 D2 O Pazo de Irixoa Spain
19 R3 Opechenskiy Posad Rus. Fed.
62 D3 O Pedrouzo Spain
44 J2 Opeinde Neth.
52 D2 Opel hill Ger.
115 E9 Opelika AL U.S.A.
121 I10 Opelousas LA U.S.A.
44 J2 Opende Neth.
147 H4 Open Door Arg.
108 E4 Opeongo Lake Ont. Can.
52 H6 Opfenbach Ger.
52 F7 Opfikon Switz.
45 I6 Opglabbeek Belgium
122 K2 Opheim MT U.S.A.
44 I5 Opheusden Neth.
111 K3 Ophir Ont. Can.
203 D12 Ophir South I. N.Z.
156 D4 Ophir, Gunung vol. Indon.
73 L4 Opi Italy
90 E4 Opienge Dem. Rep. Congo
203 F11 Opihi r. South I. N.Z.
124 □G14 Opihikao HI U.S.A.
202 J7 Opiki North I. N.Z.
155 F5 Opin Seram Indon.
108 E2 Opinaca r. Que. Can.
108 E2 Opinaca, Réservoir resr Que. Can.
108 D2 Opinnagau r. Ont. Can.
41 J9 Opio France
189 L7 Opis tourist site Iraq
109 G2 Opiscotéo, Lac l. Que. Can.
17 N4 Opishnya Ukr.
44 I5 Oploo Neth.
59 L7 Oplotnica Slovenia
59 L7 Oplotnica r. Slovenia
158 D5 Op Luang National Park Thai.
44 G3 Opmeer Neth.
89 G5 Opobo Nigeria
18 L5 Opochka Rus. Fed.
56 F1 Opočno Czech Rep.
138 D4 Opoco Bol.
109 H2 Opocopa, Lac l. Que. Can.
55 I4 Opoczno Pol.
126 D3 Opodepe Mex.
45 I6 Opoeteren Belgium
54 F5 Opole Pol.
55 J4 Opole Lubelskie Pol.
54 F5 Opolskie prov. Pol.
202 H2 Opononi North I. N.Z.
16 G5 Oporets' Ukr.
62 C4 O Porriño Spain
Oporto Port. see Porto
202 L5 Opotiki North I. N.Z.
43 J10 Opoul-Périllos France
76 I5 Opovo Vojvodina, Srbija Serb. and Mont.
115 D10 Opp AL U.S.A.
51 K8 Oppach Ger.
164 S8 Oppa-wan b. Japan
20 J5 Oppdal Norway
71 K5 Oppeano Italy
21 H6 Oppedal Norway
Oppeln Pol. see Opole
52 E5 Oppenau Ger.
52 E2 Oppenheim Ger.
52 G4 Oppenweiler Ger.
73 P6 Oppido Lucano Italy
75 J7 Oppido Mamertina Italy
51 F7 Oppin Ger.
22 G1 Oppkuven hill Norway
21 J6 Oppland county Norway
59 K4 Opponitz Austria
122 F3 Opportunity WA U.S.A.
51 E9 Oppurg Ger.
77 L6 Oprișor Romania
71 P5 Oprtalj Croatia
77 M6 Optași-Măgura Romania
121 E7 Optima Lake OK U.S.A.
202 I2 Opua North I. N.Z.
202 I4 Opuatia North I. N.Z.
202 H6 Opunake North I. N.Z.
201 □3a Opunohu, Baie d' b. Moorea Fr. Polynesia
57 J5 Ópusztaszer Hungary
94 B3 Opuwo Namibia
45 F7 Opwijk Belgium
182 D4 Opytnoye Kazakh.
182 K6 Oqbaytal Uzbek.
182 H6 Oqqal'a Uzbek.
Oqqal'a Uzbek. see Oqqal'a
185 P2 Oqsu r. Tajik.
182 K8 Oqtosh Uzbek.
120 J5 Oquawka IL U.S.A.
126 D2 Oquitoa Mex.
117 □O4 Oquossoc ME U.S.A.
191 D3 Oqureshi Georgia
57 L4 Or Hungary
182 H2 Or' r. Rus. Fed.
40 I3 Or, Le Mont d' mt. France
71 K3 Ora Italy
167 J3 Ōra Japan
20 P1 Øra Norway
22 G2 Øra nature res. Norway
43 C9 Oraàs France
130 □ Oracabessa Jamaica
125 V9 Oracle AZ U.S.A.
64 E3 Orada Port.
77 J3 Oradea Romania
42 G4 Oradour-sur-Glane France
42 F4 Oradour-sur-Vayres France
76 I8 Orahovac Kosovo, Srbija Serb. and Mont.
68 F3 Orahovica Croatia
178 G7 Orai Uttar Prad. India
125 V6 Oraibi AZ U.S.A.
125 V6 Oraibi Wash watercourse AZ U.S.A.
40 G3 Orain r. France
41 H9 Oraison France
20 R3 Orajärvi Fin.
87 E2 Oran Alg.
144 D1 Orán Arg.
16 J2 Orane Ukr.
159 H8 O Rang Cambodia
179 N6 Orang Assam India
163 F8 Ŏrang N. Korea
205 L5 Orange N.S.W. Austr.
41 F8 Orange France
94 C6 Orange r. Namibia/S. Africa
124 O8 Orange CA U.S.A.
119 I2 Orange CT U.S.A.
121 I10 Orange TX U.S.A.
116 G10 Orange VA U.S.A.
137 I3 Orange, Cabo c. Brazil
119 H2 Orangeburg NY U.S.A.
115 G9 Orangeburg SC U.S.A.
130 D1 Orange Cay i. Bahamas
120 G4 Orange City IA U.S.A.
214 J8 Orange Cone sea feature S. Atlantic Ocean
119 G2 Orange County county NY U.S.A.
124 M5 Orange Cove CA U.S.A.
Orange Free State prov. S. Africa see Free State
119 G1 Orange Lake NY U.S.A.
115 G10 Orange Park FL U.S.A.
124 K3 Orangevale CA U.S.A.
108 D5 Orangeville Ont. Can.
118 C2 Orangeville PA U.S.A.
125 U2 Orangeville UT U.S.A.
127 O8 Orange Walk Belize
88 A4 Orango, Ilha de i. Guinea-Bissau
72 C7 Orani Sardegna Italy
154 C4 Orani Luzon Phil.
51 F7 Oranienbaum Ger.
50 H5 Oranienburg Ger.
Oranje r. Namibia/S. Africa see Orange
137 H4 Oranje Gebergte hills Suriname
44 K2 Oranjekanaal canal Neth.
94 C6 Oranjemund Namibia
96 I5 Oranjerivier S. Africa
131 □9 Oranjestad Aruba
131 □2 Oranjestad St Eustatius Neth. Antilles
97 M2 Oranjeville S. Africa
27 E6 Oranmore Rep. of Ireland
209 J7 Orantjugurr, Lake salt flat W.A. Austr.
15 I7 Oranzherei Rus. Fed.
94 E4 Orapa Botswana
64 F6 Oraque r. Spain
203 F11 Orari r. South I. N.Z.
154 E5 Oras Samar Phil.
68 F3 Orašac Bos.-Herz.
154 E5 Oras Bay Samar Phil.
77 L5 Orăștie Romania
77 L5 Orăștioara de Sus Romania
16 I4 Orativ Ukr.
200 □6 Orava P.N.G.
57 I2 Orava r. Slovakia
57 I2 Orava, Vodná nádrž resr Slovakia
20 Q5 Oravais Fin.
77 J5 Oravița Romania
57 I2 Oravská Lesná Slovakia
57 I2 Oravská Magura mts Slovakia
57 I2 Oravská Polhora Slovakia
203 B13 Orawia South I. N.Z.
41 B9 Orb r. France
70 F6 Orba r. Italy
67 E10 Orba Spain
62 C5 Orbacém Port.
173 E9 Orba Co l. China
22 G6 Ørbæk Denmark
36 G6 Orbais-l'Abbaye France
66 C2 Orbara Spain
70 D5 Orbassano Italy
70 B2 Orbe Switz.
70 B2 Orbe r. Switz.
77 N6 Orbeasca Romania
39 L3 Orbec France
72 G3 Orbetello Italy
72 G3 Orbetello, Laguna di lag. Italy
37 N7 Orbey France
43 J9 Orbieu r. France
62 I5 Orbigo r. Spain
116 H8 Orbisonia PA U.S.A.
205 L7 Orbost Vic. Austr.
23 N1 Örbyhus Sweden
62 F8 Orca Port.
212 V2 Orcadas research stn S. Orkney Is Antarctica
65 O5 Orce Spain
65 N4 Orcera Spain
40 J2 Orchamps-Vennes France
118 B6 Orchard Beach MD U.S.A.
125 X2 Orchard Mesa CO U.S.A.
178 G7 Orchha Madh. Prad. India
36 F3 Orchies France
137 E2 Orchila, Isla i. Venez.
98 □3e Orchila, Punta pt El Hierro Canary Is
78 D4 Orchomenos Greece
55 H4 Orchów Pol.
54 G3 Orchowo Pol.
26 F10 Orchy r. Scotland U.K.
72 G2 Orcia r. Italy
71 N8 Orciano di Pesaro Italy
41 I7 Orcières France
40 B5 Orcival France
70 D5 Orco r. Italy
191 I5 Orconikidze Azer.
191 I6 Orconikidze Azer.
138 B2 Orcotuna Peru
124 L7 Orcutt CA U.S.A.
208 J3 Ord r. W.A. Austr.
120 F5 Ord NE U.S.A.
208 H4 Ord, Mount hill W.A. Austr.
14 L4 Orda Rus. Fed.
43 E8 Ordan-Larroque France
Ordenes Spain see Ordes
125 T4 Orderville UT U.S.A.
62 D2 Ordes Spain
66 F2 Ordesa - Monte Perdido, Parque Nacional nat. park Spain
66 I2 Ordino Andorra
124 P7 Ord Mountain CA U.S.A.
73 P5 Ordona Italy
147 F3 Ordoñez Arg.
169 L7 Ordos Nei Mongol China
208 J4 Ord River Dam W.A. Austr.
208 J3 Ord River Nature Reserve W.A. Austr.
188 H3 Ordu Ordu Turkey
191 H7 Ordubad Azer.
63 O3 Orduña Spain
65 L6 Orduña mt. Spain
63 N2 Ordunte, Montes de mts Spain
120 D6 Ordway CO U.S.A.
Ordzhonikidze Georgia see Kharagauli
Ordzhonikidze Kazakh. see Denisovka
Ordzhonikidze Rus. Fed. see Vladikavkaz
17 M5 Ordzhonikidze Dnipropetrovs'ka Oblast' Ukr.
17 N6 Ordzhonikidze Dnipropetrovs'ka Oblast' Ukr.
Ordzhonikidzeabad Tajik. see Kofarnihon
191 C2 Ordzhonikidzevskiy Rus. Fed.
89 G5 Ore Nigeria
63 Q7 Orea Spain
62 D2 O Real Spain
137 G3 Orealla Guyana
21 M6 Oreälven r. Sweden
20 O5 Öreälven r. Sweden
124 N1 Oreana NV U.S.A.
200 □3a Oreba i. Kwajalein Marshall Is
21 L6 Örebäcken Sweden
23 L2 Örebro Sweden
23 K2 Örebro county Sweden
56 F2 Ořechov Czech Rep.
19 M3 Oredezh r. Rus. Fed.
118 D3 Orefield PA U.S.A.
57 H4 Öreg-Futóné hill Hungary
57 G5 Öreglak Hungary
110 E7 Oregon IL U.S.A.
120 H6 Oregon MO U.S.A.
116 B7 Oregon OH U.S.A.
110 E7 Oregon WI U.S.A.
122 D5 Oregon state U.S.A.
122 C4 Oregon City OR U.S.A.
23 O1 Öregrund Sweden
23 O1 Öregrundsgrepen b. Sweden
50 E1 Orehoved Denmark
Orekhov Ukr. see Orikhiv
19 V6 Orekhovo-Zuyevo Rus. Fed.
19 T9 Orel Orlovskaya Oblast' Rus. Fed.
14 L4 Orel Permskaya Oblast' Rus. Fed.
17 N5 Orel' r. Ukr.
162 K1 Orel', Gora mt. Rus. Fed.
162 K2 Orel', Ozero l. Rus. Fed.
77 L9 Orelek mt. Bulg.
136 B5 Orellana prov. Ecuador
136 C6 Orellana Peru
65 I2 Orellana, Embalse de resr Spain
64 H2 Orellana la Vieja Spain
Orel Oblast admin. div. Rus. Fed. see Orlovskaya Oblast'
125 U1 Orem UT U.S.A.
79 I5 Ören Muğla Turkey
79 K6 Ören Muğla Turkey
182 F2 Orenburg Rus. Fed.
Orenburg Oblast admin. div. Rus. Fed. see Orenburgskaya Oblast'
182 D2 Orenburgskaya Oblast' admin. div. Rus. Fed.
191 B5 Örence Turkey
79 K3 Örencik Turkey
52 B2 Orenhofen Ger.
147 H6 Orense Arg.
Orense Spain see Ourense
Orense prov. Galicia Spain see Ourense
Oreón, Dhíavlos sea chan. Greece see Oreon, Diavlos
78 D4 Oreon, Diavlos sea chan. Greece
Oreor Palau see Koror
Oreor i. Palau see Koror
203 B13 Orepuki South I. N.Z.
16 G3 Orepy Ukr.
66 C3 Orés Spain
77 N7 Oresh Bulg.
22 I4 Öresjön l. Sweden
22 H3 Öreskilsälven r. Sweden
79 H1 Orestiada Greece
Orestiás Greece see Orestiada
22 I6 Öresund str. Denmark/Sweden
203 C13 Oreti r. South I. N.Z.
202 I3 Orewa North I. N.Z.
45 H7 Oreye Belgium
89 G2 Orfane well Niger
78 E2 Orfanou, Kolpos b. Greece
205 K10 Orford Tas. Austr.
31 P3 Orford Suffolk, England U.K.
207 I1 Orford Bay Qld Austr.
31 P3 Orford Ness hd England U.K.
137 H3 Organabo Fr. Guiana
125 T9 Organ Pipe Cactus National Monument nat. park AZ U.S.A.
Organyà Spain see Organyà
66 H3 Organyà Spain
63 M9 Orgaz Spain
36 D6 Orge r. France
40 H3 Orgelet France
36 C7 Orgères-en-Beauce France
Orgeyev Moldova see Orhei
71 K5 Orgiano Italy
168 F2 Orgil Mongolia
65 M7 Orgiva Spain
41 G9 Orgon France
169 M5 Orgon Tal Nei Mongol China
72 C7 Orgosolo Sardegna Italy
57 I5 Orgovány Hungary
57 I5 Orgoványi park Hungary
19 X5 Orgtrud Rus. Fed.
185 M5 Orgūn Afgh.
57 I3 Orhalom Hungary
79 J3 Orhaneli Turkey
79 K2 Orhangazi Turkey
79 J6 Orhaniye Turkey
79 I3 Orhanlar Turkey
16 H6 Orhei Moldova
168 H2 Orhon Gol r. Mongolia
168 I2 Orhontuul Mongolia
66 C2 Orhy, Pic d' mt. France/Spain
75 N3 Oria Italy
65 O6 Oria Spain
66 A1 Oria r. Spain
62 C4 O Rial Spain
62 D4 O Ribeiro reg. Spain
97 O6 Oribi Gorge Nature Reserve S. Africa
14 J4 Orichi Rus. Fed.
117 □R3 Orient ME U.S.A.
119 K2 Orient NY U.S.A.
36 H7 Orient, Lac d' resr France
129 J6 Oriental Mex.
61 E5 Oriental prov. Morocco
138 D4 Oriental, Cordillera mts Bol.
136 C3 Oriental, Cordillera mts Col.
138 C3 Oriental, Cordillera mts Peru
90 E4 Orientale prov. Dem. Rep. Congo
147 G6 Oriente Arg.
138 D2 Oriente Rondônia Brazil
142 B5 Oriente São Paulo Brazil
119 K2 Orient Island NY U.S.A.
36 H4 Origny-en-Thiérache France
36 G7 Origny-le-Sec France
36 F4 Origny-Ste-Benoîte France
67 D11 Orihuela Spain
17 O6 Orikhiv Ukr.
78 A2 Orikum Albania
17 O4 Oril' r. Ukr.
17 P5 Oril'ka Ukr.
17 O5 Oril'ka r. Ukr.
108 E4 Orillia Ont. Can.
21 R6 Orimattila Fin.
122 L5 Orin WY U.S.A.
137 F3 Orinduik Falls Brazil/Guyana
137 F2 Orinoco r. Col./Venez.
137 F2 Orinoco Delta Venez.
66 A1 Orio Spain
64 D4 Oriola Port.
118 A2 Oriole PA U.S.A.
75 K3 Oriolo Italy
72 I3 Oriolo Romano Italy
21 Q6 Oripää Fin.
117 J5 Oriskany NY U.S.A.
179 J9 Orissa state India
18 G3 Orissaare Estonia
66 J4 Oristà Spain
72 B8 Oristano Sardegna Italy
72 B8 Oristano prov. Sardegna Italy
72 B8 Oristano, Golfo di b. Sardegna Italy
27 I5 Oristown Rep. of Ireland
56 F5 Őriszentpéter Hungary
55 L8 Oriv Ukr.
21 R6 Orivesi Fin.
20 T5 Orivesi l. Fin.
137 H5 Oriximiná Brazil
129 J7 Orizaba Mex.
129 J6 Orizaba, Pico de vol. Mex.
129 I4 Orizatlán Mex.
142 C2 Orizona Brazil
Orjonikidze Georgia see Kharagauli
Orjonikidzeobod Tajik. see Kofarnihon
22 J5 Örkelljunga Sweden
57 I4 Örkény Hungary
Orkhey Moldova see Orhei
Orkhomenós Greece see Orchomenos
97 K2 Orkney S. Africa
26 K5 Orkney admin. div. Scotland U.K.
26 K5 Orkney Islands Scotland U.K.
24 F2 Orla Pol.
55 L3 Orla Pol.
54 E4 Orla r. Pol.
54 F2 Orla r. Pol.
121 D10 Orla TX U.S.A.
51 E9 Orlamünde Ger.
124 J2 Orland CA U.S.A.
142 D4 Orlândia Brazil
115 G11 Orlando FL U.S.A.
55 L3 Orlanka r. Pol.
141 C9 Orleaes Brazil
36 C7 Orléanais reg. France
36 C8 Orléans France
117 P7 Orleans MA U.S.A.
117 M4 Orleans VT U.S.A.
36 E7 Orléans, Canal d' France
109 G4 Orléans, Île d' i. Que. Can.
36 D8 Orléans, Val d' val. France
43 E9 Orleix France
23 K3 Orlen l. Sweden
56 E1 Orlice r. Czech Rep.
57 I1 Orlich Gniazd, Park Krajobrazowy Pol.
56 E1 Orlické Hory mts Czech Rep.
56 F1 Orlické Hory park Czech Rep.
161 G1 Orlik Rus. Fed.
56 D2 Orlík, Vodní nádrž resr Czech Rep.
17 L2 Orlivka Chernihivs'ka Oblast' Ukr.
17 P7 Orlivka Zaporiz'ka Oblast' Ukr.
17 M8 Orlivs'ke Ukr.
68 F3 Orljava r. Croatia
14 J4 Orlov Rus. Fed.
57 H2 Orlová Czech Rep.
182 C2 Orlovka Rus. Fed.
15 G6 Orlovo Rus. Fed.
19 T9 Orlovskaya Oblast' admin. div. Rus. Fed.
15 H7 Orlovskiy Rus. Fed.
17 O6 Orlyans'ke Ukr.
17 N5 Orlyk Ukr.
17 M9 Orlyne Ukr.
21 P8 Ormankalns hill Latvia
57 I4 Ormánság reg. Hungary
185 K9 Ormara Pak.
185 K9 Ormara, Ras hd Pak.
70 D7 Ormea Italy
57 J5 Örménykút Hungary
31 P2 Ormesby St Margaret Norfolk, England U.K.
Ormília Greece see Ormylia
107 J5 Ormiston Sask. Can.
29 L2 Ormiston East Lothian, Scotland U.K.
154 E6 Ormoc Leyte Phil.
202 L5 Ormond North I. N.Z.
115 G11 Ormond Beach FL U.S.A.
59 N7 Ormož Slovenia
29 L6 Ormskirk Lancashire, England U.K.
117 L3 Ormstown Que. Can.
78 E2 Ormylia Greece
185 L8 Ornach Pak.
66 E3 Orna de Gállego Spain
37 I6 Ornain r. France
41 B10 Ornaisons France
40 I2 Ornans France
70 E4 Ornavasso Italy
53 J3 Ornbau Ger.
39 L4 Orne dept France
39 K3 Orne r. France
39 L5 Orne r. France
20 L3 Ørnes Norway
23 Q7 Orneta Pol.
23 O2 Ornö i. Sweden
43 H10 Ornolac-Ussat-les-Bains France
20 O5 Örnsköldsvik Sweden
18 F2 Örö i. Fin.
163 E8 Oro N. Korea
Oro r. Spain see Ouro
72 C3 Oro, Monte d' mt. Corse France
138 E3 Orobayaya Bol.
70 H3 Orobie, Alpi mts Italy
140 F4 Orocó Brazil
136 D3 Orocué Col.
88 D4 Orodara Burkina
Orodzholari Georgia see Orojolari
122 F3 Orofino ID U.S.A.
168 G4 Orog Nuur salt l. Mongolia
124 O7 Oro Grande CA U.S.A.
123 K10 Orogrande NM U.S.A.
201 □3a Orohena mt. Tahiti Fr. Polynesia
191 E4 Orojolari Georgia
71 L5 Orolo r. Italy
76 H5 Orom Vojvodina, Srbija Serb. and Mont.
92 C2 Oromīya admin. reg. Eth.
109 H4 Oromocto N.B. Can.
109 H4 Oromocto Lake N.B. Can.
190 D8 Oron Israel
89 H5 Oron Nigeria
199 I2 Orona atoll Phoenix Is Kiribati
70 B2 Oron-la-Ville Switz.
117 □Q4 Orono ME U.S.A.
137 G4 Oronoque Guyana
137 G4 Oronoque r. Guyana
66 B1 Oronoz Spain
26 D10 Oronsay i. Scotland U.K.
55 I4 Orońsko Pol.
Orontes r. Lebanon/Syria see 'Āṣī
190 E4 Orontes r. Asia
alt. Asi (Turkey),
alt. 'Āṣī, Nahr al
70 D4 Oropa Italy
136 C2 Oropa Venez.
128 F7 Oropeo Mex.
63 J9 Oropesa Castilla-La Mancha Spain
67 F7 Oropesa Valencia Spain
67 F7 Oropesa, Cabo de c. Spain
131 □7 Oropuche r. Trin. and Tob.
154 D7 Oroquieta Mindanao Phil.
63 Q3 Ororbia Spain
140 F3 Orós Brazil
140 F3 Orós, Açude resr Brazil
72 D7 Orosei Sardegna Italy
72 D7 Orosei, Golfo di b. Sardegna Italy
57 J5 Orosháza Hungary
76 F4 Oroslavje Croatia
57 H4 Oroszlány Hungary
72 C7 Orotelli Sardegna Italy
200 □1 Orote Peninsula Guam
193 Q3 Orotukan Rus. Fed.
125 V? Oro Valley AZ U.S.A.
124 K2 Oroville CA U.S.A.
122 E2 Oroville WA U.S.A.
124 K2 Oroville, Lake resr CA U.S.A.
41 H8 Orpierre France
169 Q2 Orqohan Nei Mongol China
110 B1 Orr MN U.S.A.
66 C1 Orreaga Navarra Spain
29 L6 Orrell Greater Manchester, England U.K.
72 B9 Orri, Monte hill Italy
66 H3 Orri, Tossal de l' mt. Spain
26 H7 Orrin r. Scotland U.K.
26 G7 Orrin Reservoir Scotland U.K.
66 D6 Orrios Spain
22 H1 Orrkjølen hill Norway
72 C8 Orroli Sardegna Italy
204 G5 Orroroo S.A. Austr.
116 D8 Orrville OH U.S.A.
21 M6 Orsa Sweden
73 O5 Orsara di Puglia Italy
36 D6 Orsay France
56 F5 Őrség reg. Hungary
56 F5 Őrségi Tájvédelmi Körzet nature res. Hungary
42 H3 Orsennes France
19 N7 Orsha Belarus
19 T5 Orsha Rus. Fed.
14 I4 Orshanka Rus. Fed.
70 C5 Orsiera-Rocciavrè, Parco Naturale nature res. Italy
70 C3 Orsières Switz.
21 N6 Orsjön l. Sweden
182 H2 Orsk Rus. Fed.
50 E1 Ørslev Denmark
73 M3 Orsogna Italy
73 P8 Orsomarso Italy
77 K6 Orșova Romania
20 I5 Ørsta Norway
23 N2 Örsundaån r. Sweden
23 N2 Örsundsbro Sweden
70 E4 Orta, Lago d' l. Italy
79 J6 Ortaca Turkey
191 B4 Ortaköy Turkey
73 P5 Orta Nova Italy
190 B2 Orta Toroslar plat. Turkey
191 G1 Orta-Tyube Rus. Fed.
73 I3 Orte Italy
62 E1 Ortegal, Cabo c. Spain
136 C4 Orteguaza r. Col.
52 D5 Ortenau reg. Ger.
52 D5 Ortenberg Baden-Württemberg Ger.
49 H10 Ortenberg Hessen Ger.
53 O4 Ortenburg Ger.
59 O3 Orth an der Donau Austria
43 C9 Orthez France
21 L5 Ortholmen Sweden
64 H3 Ortiga r. Spain
63 O4 Ortigosa Spain
142 B6 Ortigueira Brazil
62 E1 Ortigueira Spain
62 E1 Ortigueira, Ría de inlet Spain
71 L2 Ortisei Italy
76 J4 Ortișoara Romania
128 C2 Ortiz Mex.
136 E2 Ortiz Venez.
71 J2 Ortles mt. Italy
131 □7 Ortoire r. Trin. and Tob.
72 B4 Ortolo r. Corse France
29 L5 Orton Cumbria, England U.K.
73 M3 Ortona Italy
31 L2 Orton Longueville Peterborough, England U.K.
111 K7 Ortonville MI U.S.A.
120 G3 Ortonville MN U.S.A.
Ortospana Afgh. see Kābul
183 P6 Orto-Tokoy Kyrg.
70 E7 Ortovero Italy
51 I8 Ortrand Ger.
20 O4 Orträsk Sweden
73 L4 Ortucchio Italy
72 B7 Ortueri Sardegna Italy
48 I5 Örtze r. Ger.
18 I3 Oru Estonia
154 □ Orukuizu i. Palau
193 N3 Orulgan, Khrebet mts Rus. Fed.
94 C4 Orumbo Namibia
88 D5 Orumbo Boka hill Côte d'Ivoire
184 A3 Orūmīyeh Iran
184 A3 Orūmīyeh, Daryācheh-ye salt l. Iran
72 C7 Orune Sardegna Italy
138 D4 Oruro Bol.
138 D4 Oruro dept Bol.
63 N8 Orusco Spain
22 H3 Orust i. Sweden
185 L5 Orūzgān Afgh.
39 P8 Orval France
62 E8 Orvalho Port.
38 H7 Orvault France
72 I3 Orvieto Italy
212 T1 Orville Coast Antarctica
78 E1 Orvilos mts Greece
73 J3 Orvinio Italy
20 □ Orvin Land reg. Svalbard
31 O3 Orwell r. England U.K.
116 E7 Orwell OH U.S.A.
117 L5 Orwell VT U.S.A.
118 C3 Orwigsburg PA U.S.A.
169 O2 Orxon Gol r. China
77 L7 Oryakhovo Bulg.
16 F5 Orynyn Ukr.
Oryol Rus. Fed. see Orel
55 J3 Orz r. Pol.
54 F3 Orzechowo Pol.
54 G5 Orzesze Pol.
55 L3 Orzeszkowo Pol.
16 F3 Orzhiv Ukr.
17 L4 Orzhytsya Ukr.
17 L4 Orzhytsya r. Ukr.
70 H5 Orzinuovi Italy
98 □3c Orzola Lanzarote Canary Is
55 J3 Orzyc r. Pol.
55 J2 Orzyny Pol.
55 J2 Orzysz Pol.
55 K2 Orzysz, Jezioro l. Pol.
20 K5 Os Norway
18 J5 Oša r. Latvia
55 G2 Osa r. Pol.
14 K4 Osa Rus. Fed.
126 □R13 Osa, Península de pen. Costa Rica
63 Q9 Osa de Vega Spain
110 B6 Osage IA U.S.A.
116 E9 Osage WV U.S.A.
122 L4 Osage WY U.S.A.
120 I6 Osage r. MO U.S.A.
120 H6 Osage City KS U.S.A.
166 F4 Ōsaka Japan
166 B6 Ōsaka Japan
166 B6 Ōsaka pref. Japan
183 O2 Osakarovka Kazakh.
166 C7 Ōsakasayama Japan
166 B7 Ōsaka-wan b. Japan
70 H7 Osaro, Monte mt. Italy
142 D5 Osasco Brazil
166 F2 Ōsawano Japan
120 H6 Osawatomie KS U.S.A.
120 M1 Osawin r. Ont. Can.
29 O6 Osbaldwick York, England U.K.
62 E4 Os Blancos Spain
97 P4 Osborn S. Africa
120 F6 Osborne KS U.S.A.
52 B2 Osburg Ger.
52 B2 Osburger Hochwald mts Ger.
22 F6 Øsby Denmark
23 J5 Osby Sweden
57 H2 Oščadnica Slovakia
137 H4 Oscar Fr. Guiana
20 □ Oscar II Land reg. Svalbard
208 H4 Oscar Range hills W.A. Austr.
112 H5 Oscawana Lake NY U.S.A.
121 I8 Osceola AR U.S.A.
120 I5 Osceola IA U.S.A.
120 I6 Osceola MO U.S.A.
120 G5 Osceola NE U.S.A.
110 B4 Osceola WI U.S.A.
51 H8 Oschatz Ger.
51 D6 Oschersleben (Bode) Ger.
72 C6 Oschiri Sardegna Italy
111 K5 Oscoda MI U.S.A.
62 C3 Os Dices Spain
48 J2 Osdorf Ger.
76 H6 Osečina Srbija Serb. and Mont.
62 C5 O Seixo Spain
63 J2 Oseja de Sajambre Spain
53 P2 Osek Plzeňský kraj Czech Rep.
51 I9 Osek Ústecký kraj Czech Rep.
Osel i. Estonia see Hiiumaa
21 K6 Osensjøen l. Norway
66 D4 Osera Spain
17 T3 Osered' r. Rus. Fed.
54 E4 Osetno Pol.
165 G14 Ōseto Japan
19 V7 Osetr r. Rus. Fed.
165 F15 Ōse-zaki pt Japan
167 I5 Ōse-zaki pt Japan
108 F4 Osgoode Ont. Can.
122 F6 Osgood Mountains NV U.S.A.
183 O7 Osh Kyrg.
183 O7 Osh admin. div. Kyrg.
94 B3 Oshakati Namibia
Oshamambe Japan see Oshamanbe
164 R4 Oshamanbe Japan
94 B3 Oshana admin. reg. Namibia
108 E5 Oshawa Ont. Can.
164 S8 Oshika Japan
167 H4 Oshika Japan
164 S8 Oshika-hantō pen. Japan
94 B3 Oshikango Namibia
94 C3 Oshikoto admin. reg. Namibia
94 B3 Oshikuku Namibia
167 I1 Ōshima Niigata Japan
167 J6 Ōshima Tōkyō Japan
166 F2 Ōshima Toyama Japan
166 D3 Ō-shima i. Japan
164 Q5 Ō-shima i. Japan
167 J6 Ō-shima i. Japan
165 M13 Ō-shima i. Japan
164 Q4 Oshima-hantō pen. Japan
166 E2 Oshimizu Japan
89 G4 Oshin r. Nigeria
167 I5 Oshino Japan
94 C3 Oshivelo Namibia
120 D5 Oshkosh NE U.S.A.
110 F5 Oshkosh WI U.S.A.
14 L2 Oshkur'ya Rus. Fed.
184 A3 Oshnovīyeh Iran
Osh Oblast admin. div. Kyrg. see Osh
89 G5 Oshogbo Nigeria
14 M2 Oshper Rus. Fed.
Oshskaya Oblast' admin. div. Kyrg. see Osh
184 C5 Oshtorān Kūh mt. Iran
189 N7 Oshtorīnān Iran
89 G5 Oshun state Nigeria
14 M2 Oshvor Rus. Fed.
91 C5 Oshwe Dem. Rep. Congo
57 H4 Osi Hungary
77 M6 Osica de Sus Romania
72 C6 Osidda Sardegna Italy
54 G2 Osie Pol.
54 G3 Osięciny Pol.
54 G2 Osieczna Pomorskie Pol.
54 E4 Osieczna Wielkopolskie Pol.
54 D4 Osiecznica Pol.
55 H2 Osiek Kujawsko-Pomorskie Pol.
54 G2 Osiek Pomorskie Pol.
55 J5 Osiek Świętokrzyskie Pol.
55 J6 Osiek Jasielski Pol.
70 E7 Osiglia Italy
68 G3 Osijek Croatia
77 M8 Osikovitsa Bulg.
106 E3 Osilinka r. B.C. Can.
72 B6 Osilo Sardegna Italy
71 O9 Osimo Italy
54 D2 Osina Pol.
72 C8 Osini Sardegna Italy
169 K1 Osinovka Rus. Fed.
55 K4 Osiny Pol.
76 J6 Osipaonica Srbija Serb. and Mont.
94 C4 Osire Namibia
178 D6 Osiyan Rajasthan India
97 O3 Osizweni S. Africa
54 G4 Osjaków Pol.
68 F3 Osječenica mts Bos.-Herz.
14 A3 Ösjön l. Sweden
120 I5 Oskaloosa IA U.S.A.
120 H6 Oskaloosa KS U.S.A.
23 M4 Oskarshamn Sweden
22 I5 Oskarström Sweden
111 S1 Oskélanéo Que. Can.
17 R3 Oskil r. Ukr.
alt. Oskol (Rus. Fed.)
15 G6 Oskol r. Rus. Fed.
alt. Oskil (Ukraine)
51 L10 Oskořínek Czech Rep.
57 H4 Öskü Hungary
19 O2 Oskuya r. Rus. Fed.
57 H3 Osľany Slovakia
56 F2 Oslava r. Czech Rep.
56 F2 Oslavany Czech Rep.
55 K6 Osława r. Pol.
56 G4 Osli Hungary

97 K9	Padrone, Cape S. Africa
72 D6	Padria Sardegna Italy
30 C6	Padstow Cornwall, England U.K.
18 K6	Padsvillye Belarus
204 H7	Padthaway S. A. Austr.
177 H3	Padua Orissa India
	Padua Italy see Padova
121 K7	Paducah KY U.S.A.
121 E8	Paducah TX U.S.A.
73 P7	Padula Italy
73 N5	Paduli Italy
73 F8	Padum Jammu and Kashmir
77 K4	Pădurea Craiului, Munţii mts Romania
201 □3a	Paea Tahiti Fr. Polynesia
163 F8	Paegam N. Korea
203 I7	Paekakariki North I. N.Z.
163 D10	Paengnyŏng-do i. S. Korea
203 D12	Paerau South I. N.Z.
202 J4	Paeroa North I. N.Z.
203 I7	Paeroa North I. N.Z.
70 C6	Paesana Italy
71 M4	Paese Italy
75 H3	Paestum tourist site Italy
54 C4	Paete Luzon Phil.
80 A4	Pafos Cyprus
80 A4	Pafos airport Cyprus
95 F4	Pafúri Moz.
68 E3	Pag Croatia
68 E3	Pag i. Croatia
65 G5	Paga Flores Indon.
14 M2	Paga r. Rus. Fed.
137 H6	Paga Conta Brazil
157 G8	Pagadenbaru Jawa Indon.
54 D8	Pagadian Mindanao Phil.
156 D6	Pagai Selatan i. Indon.
156 D6	Pagai Utara i. Indon.
153 K3	Pagan i. N. Mariana Is
71 K3	Paganella mt. Italy
73 K3	Paganica Italy
72 G2	Paganico Italy
73 K3	Paganzo Arg.
146 D2	Pagaralam Sumatera Indon.
156 E6	Pagasitikos Kolpos b. Greece
157 K6	Pagatan Indon.
157 K6	Pagatan Kalimantan Indon.
125 U5	Page AZ U.S.A.
208 H4	Page, Mount hill W.A. Austr.
18 E6	Pagegiai Lith.
18 E6	Pagerdewa Sumatera Indon.
145 □	Paget, Mount S. Georgia
207 N5	Paget, Cape rf Coral Sea Is Terr. Austr.
53 K6	Pagham West Sussex, England U.K.
31 K6	Pagham mt. Afgh.
185 M4	Pagiriai Kaunas Lith.
18 H6	Pagiriai Vilnius Lith.
18 I7	Paglia r. Italy
72 I2	Paglieta Italy
73 M3	Pagny-sur-Moselle France
37 L6	Pago Bay Guam
200 □1	Pago Largo Arg.
147 L6	Pagon i. N. Mariana Is see Pagan
200 □2	Pago Pago American Samoa
123 K8	Pagosa Springs CO U.S.A.
89 F4	Pagouda Togo
173 I13	Pagri Xizang China
31 I3	Pagua Bay Dominica
108 C3	Pagwachuan r. Ont. Can.
108 C3	Pagwachuan r. Ont. Can.
108 C3	Pagwa River Ont. Can.
124 □F14	Pāhala HI U.S.A.
156 E3	Pahang r. Malaysia
156 E3	Pahang state Malaysia
78 F6	Paharı Rajasthan India
179 L7	Paharpur tourist site Bangl.
158 F5	Pahaua r. N.Z.
157 H4	Pahauman Kalimantan Indon.
203 B13	Pahia Point South I. N.Z.
202 J7	Pahiatua North I. N.Z.
53 K6	Pahl Ger.
48 H2	Pahlen Ger.
178 E2	Pahlgam Jammu and Kashmir
124 □G14	Pāhoa HI U.S.A.
115 G12	Pahokee FL U.S.A.
16 F1	Pahost Vodaskhovishcha resr Belarus
178 H7	Pahra Uttar Prad. India
185 I4	Pahra Kariz Afgh.
125 Q4	Pahranagat Range mts NV U.S.A.
18 G8	Pahranichny Belarus
125 Q5	Pahrump NV U.S.A.
178 G6	Pahuj r. India
124 □E14	Pāhute Mesa plat. NV U.S.A.
124 □E13	Pai HI U.S.A.
138 D5	Paí Brazil
124 □E13	Paia HI U.S.A.
139 F4	Paiaguás Brazil
62 C8	Paião Port.
124 K5	Paicines CA U.S.A.
18 I3	Paide Estonia
30 E7	Paignton Torbay, England U.K.
202 I7	Paihia North I. N.Z.
146 B2	Paihuano Chile
21 Q6	Paimio Fin.
18 F1	Paimionselkä b. Fin.
58 C4	Paimpol France
58 G5	Paimpont France
58 G6	Paimpont, Forêt de for. France
156 D5	Painan Sumatera Indon.
176 F4	Painavu Kerala India
146 B3	Paine Chile
148 B3	Paine Chile
146 C8	Paine, Cerro mt. Chile
141 C8	Painel Brazil
131 F5	Painesdale MI U.S.A.
116 D7	Painesville OH U.S.A.
53 E4	Painesville OH U.S.A.
30 H4	Painswick Gloucestershire, England U.K.
125 U5	Painted Desert AZ U.S.A.
125 T7	Painted Rock Dam AZ U.S.A.
107 L4	Paint Lake Man. Can.
107 L4	Paint Lake Provincial Recreation Park Man. Can.
121 F10	Paint Rock TX U.S.A.
116 C11	Paintsville KY U.S.A.
136 C1	Paipa Col.
178 H9	Paira r. India
111 M5	Paisley Ont. Can.
26 H11	Paisley Renfrewshire, Scotland U.K.
63 P2	País Vasco aut. comm. Spain
200 □1b	Paita New Caledonia
136 A6	Paita Peru
156 □	Paitan, Teluk b. Malaysia
176 D3	Paithan Mahar. India
172 I3	Paizhou Hubei China
62 D6	Paiva r. Port.
171 M4	Paiyun mt. Rus. Fed.
171 I3	Paizhai Hebei China
20 Q3	Pajala Sweden
129 I4	Pajapan Ecuador
129 H7	Pajapán Mex.
171 I3	Pajares, Puerto de pass Spain
136 C3	Pajarito Col.
63 Q9	Pajarón Spain
63 Q9	Pajaroncillo Spain
144 C3	Pájaros, Islotes Chile
54 F5	Pájaros Chile
54 F5	Pajecno Pol.
176 F6	Pajo Malaysia
176 F6	Pakala Andhra Prad. India
171 N2	Pakangyi Myanmar
18 G6	Pakapė Lith.

137 F4	Pakaraima Mountains S. America
108 B3	Pakashkan Lake Ont. Can.
179 K7	Pakaur Jharkhand India
202 G7	Pakawau South I. N.Z.
163 D9	Pakch'ŏn N. Korea
108 D4	Pakesley Ont. Can.
193 R3	Pakhachi Rus. Fed.
182 G3	Pakhar' Kazakh.
19 U7	Pakhi i. Greece see Pachia
185 K7	Pakhoi China see Beihai
19 U7	Pakhomovo Rus. Fed.
11 □J7	Pak Ka Shan hill H.K. China
156 C3	Pakkat Sumatera Indon.
68 E3	Paklenica nat. park Croatia
73 Q1	Pakleni Otoci is Croatia
	Paknampho Thai. see Nakhon Sawan
56 G5	Pakod Hungary
158 B4	Pakokku Myanmar
54 G3	Pakość Pol.
54 G3	Pakoskie, Jezioro l. Pol.
54 F4	Pakosław Pol.
58 C4	Pakoštane Croatia
202 H2	Pakotai North I. N.Z.
107 I5	Pakowki Lake imp. l. Alta Can.
57 K8	Pákozd Hungary
185 O6	Pakpattan Pak.
159 E10	Pak Phanang Thai.
159 E11	Pak Phayun Thai.
68 F3	Pakra r. Croatia
68 F3	Pakrac Croatia
18 G6	Pakruojis Lith.
57 H5	Paks Hungary
171 J4	Pakse Laos see Pakxé
171 □J7	Pak Tai To Yan mt. H.K. China
171 □J7	Pak Tam Chung H.K. China
159 F7	Pak Thong Chai Thai.
185 M5	Paktiä prov. Afgh.
185 M5	Paktika prov. Afgh.
157 J3	Paku r. Malaysia
155 B5	Paku, Tanjung pt Indon.
155 B5	Pakue Sulawesi Indon.
16 J2	Pakul' Ukr.
107 M5	Pakwash Lake Ont. Can.
158 F5	Pakxan Laos
158 G2	Pakxé Laos
158 F4	Pakxeng Laos
	Pal Senegal see Mpal
90 B2	Pala Chad
159 D8	Pala Myanmar
156 G3	Palabuhanratu Jawa Indon.
156 F8	Palabuhanratu, Teluk b. Indon.
147 G2	Palacios Arg.
138 D3	Palacios Arg.
63 K6	Palacios de Goda Spain
63 N5	Palacios de la Sierra Spain
62 H3	Palacios del Sil Spain
62 G4	Palacios de Sanabria Spain
58 E7	Pala di San Martino mt. Italy
41 H6	Paladru, Lac de l. France
	Palaestina reg. Asia see Palestine
66 L4	Palafrugell Spain
75 L2	Palagianello Italy
75 M2	Palagiano Italy
74 H9	Palagonia Sicilia Italy
71 J8	Palagruža i. Croatia
71 J8	Palaia Italy
78 E5	Palaia Fokaia Greece
190 B4	Palaichori Cyprus
79 H7	Palaikastro Kriti Greece
78 E7	Palaiochora Kriti Greece
	Palaiokastro Kriti Greece see Palaikastro
78 B4	Palaios Greece
36 D6	Palaiseau France
	Palakkad Kerala India see Palghat
179 J9	Pala Laharha Orissa India
177 M7	Palalankwe Andaman & Nicobar Is India
94 D4	Palamakoloi Botswana
78 D3	Palamas Greece
155 E4	Palamea Maluku Indon.
66 L4	Palamós Spain
178 F3	Palam Pur Hima. Prad. India
179 J8	Palamu Jharkhand India
178 D6	Palana Rajasthan India
193 Q4	Palana Rus. Fed.
154 D3	Palanan Luzon Phil.
154 D3	Palanan Point Luzon Phil.
72 E8	Palanca r. Corse France
191 B6	Palandöken Dağları mts Turkey
178 H9	Palandur Mahar. India
18 E6	Palanga Lith.
189 M6	Palangān Iran
184 I6	Palangān, Kūh-e mts Iran
41 I8	Palanges, Montagne des mts France
157 J6	Palangkaraya Kalimantan Indon.
176 F3	Palani Tamil Nadu India
178 D7	Palanpur Gujarat India
155 A6	Palanro Sulawesi Indon.
185 K6	Palantak Pak.
70 I7	Palanzano Italy
154 E5	Palapag Samar Phil.
95 F3	Palapye Botswana
176 G6	Palar r. India
155 D3	Palasa Sulawesi Indon.
179 M6	Palasbari Assam India
62 E3	Palas de Rei Spain
18 L6	Palata r. Belarus
73 N4	Palata Italy
193 Q3	Palatka Rus. Fed.
115 G11	Palatka FL U.S.A.
72 C5	Palau Sardegna Italy
154 □	Palau country N. Pacific Ocean
155 G6	Palau Hatta i. Maluku Indon.
154 A4	Palaui i. Phil.
154 A4	Palauig Luzon Phil.
153 H6	Palau Islands Palau
158 B5	Palaw Myanmar
200 □3	Palauli Bay Samoa
154 A5	Palausekong, Tanjung pt Indon.
216 D5	Palau Trench sea feature N. Pacific Ocean
41 K9	Pálava park Czech Rep.
159 D8	Palaw Myanmar
154 A7	Palawan i. Phil.
216 C5	Palawan Trough sea feature N. Pacific Ocean
154 C4	Palayan Luzon Phil.
176 F4	Palayankottai Tamil Nadu India
63 L7	Palazuelos de Eresma Spain
72 B3	Palazzo, Punta di pt Corse France
74 E8	Palazzo Adriano Sicilia Italy
70 H4	Palazzolo Acreide Sicilia Italy
71 M4	Palazzolo sull'Oglio Italy
72 C5	Palazzo San Gervasio Italy
176 G4	Palchal Lake India
59 M6	Palduno r. India
18 H2	Paldiski Estonia
158 B4	Pale Myanmar
14 H4	Palekh Rus. Fed.
	Palekhori Cyprus see Palaichori
155 E4	Palelen Sulawesi Indon.
156 F6	Palembang Sumatera Indon.
145 G6	Palemón Huérgo Arg.
148 C6	Palena Chile
73 M4	Palena Italy
63 K4	Palencia Spain
63 K4	Palencia prov. Spain
65 J6	Palenciana Spain
129 L9	Palenque Mex.
197 L3	Palenque Mex.
74 F7	Palermo Sicilia Italy
74 E7	Palermo prov. Sicilia Italy
74 E7	Palermo, Golfo di g. Sicilia Italy

190 D6	Palestine reg. Asia
121 H10	Palestine TX U.S.A.
73 J4	Palestrina Italy
158 A4	Paletwa Myanmar
162 M3	Palevo Rus. Fed.
185 M6	Palghar Mahar. India
57 H5	Pálfa Hungary
176 C3	Palghar Mahar. India
176 E7	Palghat Kerala India
209 C7	Palgrave, Mount hill W.A. Austr.
94 B4	Palgrave Point Namibia
62 C7	Palhaça Port.
57 K3	Pálháza Hungary
141 C8	Palhoca Brazil
178 H8	Pali Madh. Prad. India
176 C3	Pali Mahar. India
73 D7	Pali Rajasthan India
73 D7	Paliano Italy
157 K8	Paliat i. Indon.
57 L1	Palić Vojvodina, Srbija Serb. and Mont.
76 H4	Palić, Jezero l. Serb. and Mont.
18 L7	Paliceda Belarus
200 □4b	Palikir Pohnpei Micronesia
200 □4b	Palikir Passage Pohnpei Micronesia
154 E8	Palimbang Mindanao Phil.
40 E3	Palinges France
73 O7	Palinuro Italy
73 O7	Palinuro, Capo c. Italy
78 E3	Palioúri, Akra pt Greece
36 G7	Palis France
123 J7	Palisade CO U.S.A.
45 H9	Paliseul Belgium
178 C9	Palitana Gujarat India
18 G3	Palivere Estonia
75 K8	Palizzi Italy
20 O3	Pälja hill Sweden
20 T4	Pälkäne hill Fin.
21 R6	Pälkäne Fin.
176 F8	Palk Bay Sri Lanka
18 L4	Palkin Rus. Fed.
20 S2	Pälkisoja Fin.
177 H3	Palkonda Andhra Prad. India
176 F6	Palkonda Range mts India
179 J8	Palkot Jharkhand India
57 H2	Palkovice Czech Rep.
75 L5	Palladio Italy
138 B3	Pallapalla mt. Peru
64 G4	Pallarés Spain
66 H3	Pallaresa r. Spain
27 F7	Pallas Green Rep. of Ireland
20 □	Pallas ja Ounastunturin kansallispuisto nat. park Fin.
27 E7	Pallaskenry Rep. of Ireland
182 B2	Pallasovka Rus. Fed.
176 G6	Pallavaram Tamil Nadu India
209 E13	Pallinup r. W.A. Austr.
92 H4	Pallisa Uganda
203 J8	Palliser, Cape North I. N.Z.
201 □3	Palliser, Îles is Arch. des Tuamotu Fr. Polynesia
203 J8	Palliser Bay North I. N.Z.
72 A7	Pallosu, Cala su b. Sardegna Italy
178 E5	Palliu Rajasthan India
38 H8	Palluau France
39 N8	Palluau-sur-Indre France
140 D5	Palma r. Brazil
93 E6	Palma W. Bengal India
179 K8	Palma Moz.
64 B4	Palma Port.
67 K8	Palma, Badia de b. Spain
72 A8	Palma, Porto b. Sardegna Italy
73 N6	Palma, Campania Italy
63 O6	Palmaces, Embalse de resr Spain
65 I5	Palma del Rio Spain
67 K8	Palma de Mallorca Spain
74 F9	Palma di Montechiaro Sicilia Italy
72 A6	Palmadula Sardegna Italy
73 K3	Palmanova Italy
67 K8	Palma Nova Spain
128 F3	Palma Pegada Mex.
144 G4	Palmar, Punta del pt Uru.
128 G7	Palmar Chico Mex.
138 D2	Palmares Acre Brazil
140 G3	Palmares Pernambuco Brazil
141 C9	Palmares do Sul Brazil
70 H7	Palmaria, Isola i. Italy
136 D3	Palmarito Venez.
73 J6	Palmarola, Isola i. Italy
111 O1	Palmarolle Que. Can.
128 □R13	Palmar r. Sur Costa Rica
140 C4	Palmas Tocantins Brazil
88 B5	Palmas, Cape Liberia
72 B10	Palmas, Golfo di b. Sardegna Italy
129 K6	Palma Sola Mex.
131 I8	Palma Sola Venez.
157 J8	Palmasola Jawa Indon.
79 H3	Palmas Sola i. Venez.
59 O4	Palmas Sola i. Venez.
128 G7	Palmas, Punta de pt Mex.
73 B3	Palm Bay FL U.S.A.
115 G12	Palm Bay FL U.S.A.
115 G11	Palm Coast FL U.S.A.
124 N7	Palmdale CA U.S.A.
125 P8	Palm Desert CA U.S.A.
142 C6	Palmeira Brazil
62 D5	Palmeira Port.
141 B8	Palmeira das Missões Brazil
140 F4	Palmeira dos Índios Brazil
140 E3	Palmeirais Brazil
140 C5	Palmeiras de Goiás Brazil
91 B7	Palmeirinhas, Ponta das pt Angola
64 B3	Palmela Port.
212 T2	Palmer research stn Antarctica
207 I4	Palmer r. Qld Austr.
206 D8	Palmer watercourse N.T. Austr.
104 D3	Palmer AK U.S.A.
212 T2	Palmer Land reg. Antarctica
118 F7	Palmer MD U.S.A.
206 C2	Palmer Park N.T. Austr.
	Palmer N.T. Austr. see Darwin
111 N6	Palmerston Ont. Can.
203 □	Palmerston atoll Cook Is
203 E12	Palmerston South I. N.Z.
27 I4	Palmerston Rep. of Ireland
207 L6	Palmerston, Cape Qld Austr.
202 J7	Palmerston North North I. N.Z.
118 D3	Palmerton PA U.S.A.
25 D3	Palmerville Qld Austr.
115 F12	Palmetto FL U.S.A.
42 D5	Palmetto Point Antigua and Barbuda
31 M8	Palmetto Point Bahamas
79 K2	Palmi Italy
129 H2	Palmillas Mex.
136 B4	Palmira Col.
128 G3	Palmira Cuba
90 B5	Palmira Ecuador
120 M6	Palmira Ecuador
128 O7	Palmira r. Arg.
202 H2	Palmiro North I. N.Z.
156 C3	Palmitabun Bay Mindanao Phil.
25 R4	Palmas NV U.S.A.
78 C4	Panachaïkó mts Greece
78 C4	Panache, Lake Ont. Can.
77 N3	Panael Romania
207 N1	Panaeati Island P.N.G.
78 F2	Panagia Greece
77 M8	Panagyurishte Bulg.
54 C3	Panaitan i. Indon.
179 N9	Panaitolio Greece
185 K7	Panaji Goa India
130 C3	Panama country Central America

176 E7	Palni Hills India
14 K3	Pal'niki Rus. Fed.
154 E6	Palo Leyte Phil.
72 C4	Palo, Étang de lag. Corse France
62 G2	Palo, Puerto del pass Spain
128 E4	Palo Alto Aguascalientes Mex.
129 H1	Palo Alto Tamaulipas Mex.
124 J4	Palo Alto CA U.S.A.
144 D2	Palo Blanco Arg.
127 I4	Palo Blanco Mex.
136 C2	Palo de las Letras Col.
75 L1	Palo del Colle Italy
121 E8	Palo Duro watercourse TX U.S.A.
157 I3	Paloh Sarawak Malaysia
92 B2	Paloich Sudan
20 Q2	Palojärvi Fin.
20 Q2	Palojoensuu Fin.
20 S2	Palomaa Fin.
66 D6	Palomani mt. Peru
64 G6	Palomar de Arroyos Spain
129 L8	Palomares Mex.
64 G5	Palomares del Rio Spain
	Palomar Mountain CA U.S.A.
64 G3	Palomas Spain
64 H8	Palomas, Punta pt Spain
73 M3	Palombaro Italy
63 L2	Palombera, Embalse de mts Spain
63 L2	Palombera, Puerto de pass Spain
74 I10	Palombieri r. Sicilia Italy
63 P8	Palomera Spain
66 C6	Palomera, Sierra mts Spain
63 O9	Palomeras del Campo Spain
64 G3	Palomillas r. Spain
136 C2	Palomino Col.
144 D2	Palominos Arg.
73 D6	Palomonte Italy
71 K4	Palòn, Cima mt. Italy
176 G4	Palonchá Andhra Prad. India
121 F9	Palo Pinto TX U.S.A.
155 B5	Palopo Sulawesi Indon.
67 D12	Palos, Cabo de c. Spain
144 F2	Palo Santo Arg.
63 N3	Palos de la Frontera Spain
77 J4	Pâlosi Pak.
184 O4	Palos i. Peru
122 F3	Palouse r. WA U.S.A.
125 R8	Palouse r. WA U.S.A.
126 □Q12	Palo Verde, Parque Nacional nat. park Costa Rica
21 Q6	Palovesi l. Fin.
138 D3	Palpa Ica Peru
138 A2	Palpa Peru
207 H8	Palparara Qld Austr.
146 B3	Palpica Chile
178 D9	Palsana Gujarat India
20 S4	Palsmane r. Fin.
20 S4	Paltamo Fin.
155 D4	Paltaselkä i. Fin.
18 L1	Pal'tsevo Rus. Fed.
19 R8	Pal'tso Rus. Fed.
155 A4	Palu Sulawesi Indon.
155 B8	Palu i. Indon.
155 A4	Palu r. Indon.
191 H4	Palu Turkey
155 C5	Paluan Mindoro Phil.
75 L4	Paludi Italy
43 F8	Palue r. France
39 M2	Paluel France
71 O2	Paluzza Italy
185 K2	Pal'vart Turkm.
178 F5	Palwal Haryana India
	Palwancha Andhra Prad. India see Palonchá
192 I3	Pal'yanovo Rus. Fed.
182 S3	Palyatskishki Belarus
207 J1	Palyavaam r. Rus. Fed.
18 M9	Palyessye Homyel'skaya Voblasts' Belarus
19 O8	Palyessye Homyel'skaya Voblasts' Belarus
52 A2	Palzem Ger.
59 P3	Pama Burkina
90 C3	Pama r. C.A.R.
89 F4	Pama, Réserve Partielle de nature res. Burkina
205 I5	Pamamaroo Lake N.S.W. Austr.
155 C9	Pamana i. Indon.
155 C8	Pamana Besar i. Indon.
89 H6	Pamandzi Mayotte
157 G8	Pamanukan Jawa Indon.
99 □3b	Pamanzi, Récit rf Mayotte
78 B6	Pamarru Andhra Prad. India
95 H4	Pambarra Moz.
187 J3	Pambarra Moz.
59 L6	Pameče Slovenia
75 L7	Pamekasan Jawa Indon.
157 I8	Pamenang Sulawesi Indon.
79 I3	Pamfylla Lesvos Greece
59 O4	Pamhagen Austria
54 E3	Pamiątkowo Pol.
176 E5	Pamidi Andhra Prad. India
43 I9	Pamiers France
185 O3	Pamir r. Afgh./Tajik.
185 O3	Pamir mts Asia
115 I8	Pamlico r. NC U.S.A.
115 I8	Pamlico Sound sea chan. NC U.S.A.
109 □2	Pamouscachiou, Lac l. Que. Can.
128 C5	Pampa Chile
121 E8	Pampa TX U.S.A.
148 B3	Pampa Chica Arg.
138 B6	Pampachiri Peru
144 C2	Pampa de Infierno Arg.
146 D2	Pampa Grande Arg.
155 B6	Pampanua Sulawesi Indon.
60 I7	Pamparato Italy
147 I5	Pampas reg. Arg.
138 B3	Pampas r. Peru
74 B7	Pampas Peru
43 I7	Pamplonne France
	Pampeluna Spain see Pamplona
96 I3	Pamplemousses Mauritius
62 D6	Pamplhosa S. Africa
62 D6	Pamplhosa da Serra Port.
99 □1b	Pamplemousses Mauritius
136 C3	Pamplona Col.
63 Q3	Pamplona Negros Phil.
54 E8	Pamplona Spain
42 D1	Pamporovo Spain
77 M8	Pamporovo Bulg.
77 K7	Pamukova Turkey
191 N5	Pamukçu Turkey
191 N5	Pamukkale Turkey
116 I11	Pamunkey r. VA U.S.A.
178 E2	Pamzal Jammu and Kashmir
90 B5	Pana Gabon
120 K6	Pana IL U.S.A.
122 O7	Panabá Mex.
54 D8	Panabutan Bay Mindanao Phil.
204 C3	Panaca NV U.S.A.
78 C4	Panachaïkó mts Greece
110 D2	Panache, Lake Ont. Can.
77 N3	Panael Romania
207 N1	Panaeati Island P.N.G.
72 I5	Panagia Greece
77 M8	Panagyurishte Bulg.
54 C3	Panaitan i. Indon.
78 B6	Panaitolio Greece
185 K7	Panaji Goa India
130 C3	Panama country Central America

126 □T13	Panamá Panama
126 □T13	Panamá, Bahía de b. Panama
126 □T14	Panamá, Golfo de g. Panama
	Panamá, Gulf of Panama see Panamá, Golfo de
126 □T13	Panama Canal Panama
126 □T13	Panama City Panama
	Panamá City FL U.S.A.
115 C10	Panama City FL U.S.A.
178 F2	Panamik Jammu and Kashmir
124 O5	Panamint Range mts CA U.S.A.
124 O5	Panamint Valley CA U.S.A.
138 A2	Panao Peru
154 E7	Panaon i. Phil.
207 N1	Panapompom Island P.N.G.
179 L7	Panar r. India
75 I6	Panarea, Isola i. Isole Lipari Italy
157 H3	Panarik Indon.
71 K6	Panaro r. Italy
157 J8	Panarukan Jawa Indon.
43 F9	Panassac France
154 D6	Panay i. Phil.
154 D6	Panay Gulf Phil.
	Panayía i. Thasos Greece see Panagia
42 G4	Panazol France
97 O2	Panbult S. Africa
70 D6	Pancalieri Italy
143 G3	Pancas Brazil
76 I6	Pančevo Vojvodina, Srbija Serb. and Mont.
179 L6	Panchagarh Bangl.
178 G7	Panchanagar Madh. Prad. India
17 K5	Pancheve Ukr.
171 M6	Panch'iao Taiwan
178 F4	Panchkula Haryana India
157 K4	Pancingangan, Bukit mt. Indon.
77 P5	Panciu Romania
63 N3	Pancorbo Spain
77 J4	Pâncota Romania
66 C6	Pancrudo r. Spain
66 C6	Pancrudo r. Spain
	Pancsova Vojvodina, Srbija Serb. and Mont. see Pančevo
156 C3	Pancurbatu Sumatera Indon.
146 B4	Panda Moz.
176 I7	Pandan, Selat str. Sing.
154 D6	Pandan Panay Phil.
155 D4	Pandan Kalimantan Indon.
157 K5	Pandan Reservoir Sing.
156 □	Pandan Reservoir Sing.
178 D9	Pandaria Chhattisgarh India
178 H8	Pandatarai Chhattisgarh India
176 D4	Pandavapura Karnataka India
144 C2	Pan de Azúcar Chile
148 B2	Pan de Azúcar i. Chile
144 C2	Pan de Azúcar, Parque Nacional nat. park Chile
156 G8	Pandeglang Jawa Indon.
141 D5	Pandeiros r. Brazil
18 I5	Pandėlys Lith.
178 F9	Pandhana Madh. Prad. India
178 G9	Pandhurna Madh. Prad. India
204 G2	Pandie Pandie S.A. Austr.
70 H5	Pandino Italy
147 J4	Pando Uru.
	Pandokrátor hill Kerkyra Greece see Pantokratoras
126 □R13	Pandora Costa Rica
116 B6	Pandora OH U.S.A.
207 J1	Pandora Entrance sea chan. Qld Austr.
22 F4	Pandrup Denmark
30 G4	Pandy Monmouthshire, Wales U.K.
57 G4	Pándzsa r. Hungary
200 □1b	Pané, Mont mt. New Caledonia
208 J4	Panton r. W.A. Austr.
156 B2	Pantonlabu Sumatera Indon.
204 F2	Pantoowarinna, Lake salt flat S.A. Austr.
63 M8	Pantoja Spain
78 A3	Pantokratoras hill Kerkyra Greece
17 L3	Panʼtayivka Ukr.
14 H4	Pantelleria Sicilia Italy
74 B10	Pantelleria, Isola di i. Sicilia Italy
110 I3	Panther r. Ont. Can.
116 H2	Panther MI U.S.A.
124 □2	Paradise Island New Prov. Bahamas
74 B10	Pantelleria Sicilia Italy

40 E5	Panissières France
154 B7	Panitan Panay Phil.
128 J9	Panixtlahuaca Mex.
19 N7	Panizowye Belarus
185 J2	Panj r. Afgh./Tajik.
185 M3	Panj Tajik.
185 L4	Panjakent Tajik.
185 L2	Panjakent Tajik.
156 F7	Panjang Sumatera Indon.
157 H3	Panjang i. Indon.
157 M3	Panjang i. Indon.
156 □	Panjang, Bukit Sing.
156 E4	Panjang, Selat chan. Indon.
43 B8	Panjas France
184 B5	Panjbarār Iran
185 K8	Panjgur Pak.
178 E9	Panjhra r. India
185 M3	Panjikora r. Pak.
185 N7	Panjnad r. Pak.
185 N7	Panjnad Barrage Pak.
185 M4	Panjshir r. Afgh.
20 U5	Pankakoski Fin.
48 K2	Panker Ger.
54 G5	Panki Pol.
19 O3	Pankovka Rus. Fed.
89 H4	Pankshin Nigeria
	Panlian Sichuan China see Miyi
162 G7	Pan Ling mts China
160 D7	Panna Madh. Prad. India
208 D6	Pannawonica W.A. Austr.
36 E7	Pannes France
40 D2	Pannesière-Chaumard, Barrage de dam France
73 O5	Panni Italy
45 I6	Panningen Neth.
57 G4	Pannonhalma Hungary
185 M8	Pano Aqil Pak.
65 C5	Panóias Port.
190 B4	Pano Lefkara Cyprus
157 I5	Panopah Kalimantan Indon.
142 B4	Panorama Brazil
	Panormus Sicilia Italy see Palermo
176 F7	Panruti Tamil Nadu India
189 Q4	Panschwitz-Kuckau Ger.
169 R6	Panshan Liaoning China
162 E7	Panshi Jilin China
31 N4	Pant r. England U.K.
156 D5	Pantaicermin, Gunung mt. Indon.
139 F4	Pantanal reg. S. America
139 F4	Pantanal de São Lourenço marsh Brazil
139 F4	Pantanal do Taquari marsh Brazil
139 F4	Pantanal Matogrossense, Parque Nacional do nat. park Brazil
158 B6	Pantanaw Myanmar
125 V10	Pantano AZ U.S.A.
155 D8	Pantar i. Indon.
17 L5	Pantayivka Ukr.
178 E8	Panth Piploda Madh. Prad. India
66 E2	Pantic osa Spain
208 H4	Pantijan Aboriginal Reserve W.A. Austr.
66 E2	Panticosa Spain
63 M8	Pantoja Spain
78 A3	Pantokratoras hill Kerkyra Greece
17 L3	Pantayivka Ukr.
191 G3	Paraḡüyka Ukr.
140 G2	Paragominas Brazil
122 J7	Paragould AR U.S.A.
138 E4	Paraḡua r. Bol.
137 F3	Paraḡua r. Venez.
142 C5	Paraguaçu Brazil
140 E4	Paraguaçu Paulista Brazil
142 B2	Paraguaçu Paulista Brazil
136 C2	Paraguaipoa Venez.
136 D1	Paraguaná, Península de pen. Venez.

201 □3a	Papenoo r. Tahiti Fr. Polynesia
201 □3a	Papetoai Moorea Fr. Polynesia
	Papetoai, Baie de b. Moorea Fr. Polynesia see Opunohu, Baie d'
	Paphos Cyprus see Pafos
123 K12	Pápi Cyprus see Pafos
77 N9	Papikio mt. Bulg./Greece
18 F5	Papilė Lith.
120 G5	Papillion NE U.S.A.
57 L2	Papín Slovakia
108 F4	Papineau-Labelle, Réserve Faunique de nature res. Que. Can.
117 J3	Papineauville Que. Can.
77 P8	Papiu Ilvei Romania
57 H4	Papkeszi Hungary
125 Q4	Papoose Lake NV U.S.A.
54 G2	Papowo Biskupie Pol.
55 K3	Pappenheim Ger.
55 K3	Paprotnia Pol.
26 D11	Paps of Jura hills Scotland U.K.
155 F4	Papua prov. Indon.
153 J8	Papua, Gulf of P.N.G.
200 □6	Papua New Guinea country Oceania
146 B3	Papudo Chile
206 C7	Papunya N.T. Austr.
31 L3	Papworth Everard Cambridgeshire, England U.K.
30 C7	Par Cornwall, England U.K.
143 E3	Pará r. Brazil
137 I5	Pará state Brazil
155 D2	Pará i. Indon.
15 H5	Para r. Rus. Fed.
140 C2	Pará, Rio do r. Brazil
209 D7	Paraburdoo W.A. Austr.
57 I2	Paracal Slovakia
154 D4	Paracale Luzon Phil.
143 F5	Paracambi Brazil
138 A3	Paracas Peru
138 A3	Paracas, Peninsula pen. Peru
140 D2	Paracatu Brazil
142 D2	Paracatu r. Brazil
143 E2	Paracatu r. Brazil
152 D3	Paracel Islands S. China Sea
55 N2	Parachany Belarus
204 G4	Parachilna S.A. Austr.
185 N5	Parachinar Pak.
76 J6	Paraćin Srbija Serb. and Mont.
128 C5	Parácuaro Guanajuato Mex.
128 E6	Parácuaro Michoacán Mex.
63 Q9	Paracuellos Spain
140 F2	Paracuru Brazil
57 J4	Parád Hungary
62 F7	Parada Port.
141 E5	Parada, Punta pt Peru
62 D7	Parada de Ester Port.
62 D6	Parada de Pinhão Port.
63 J6	Parada de Rubiales Spain
62 G4	Parada de Sil Spain
68 I6	Paradas Spain
78 D5	Paradeisia Greece
62 E5	Paradela Viseu Port.
62 E6	Paradela Spain
62 E6	Paradela de Guiães Port.
143 E3	Pará de Minas Brazil
108 E3	Paradera Aruba
109 J2	Paradise r. Nfld and Lab. Can.
137 G3	Paradise Guyana
124 C2	Paradise CA U.S.A.
110 I3	Paradise MI U.S.A.
125 R4	Paradise NV U.S.A.
107 H4	Paradise Gardens N.W.T. Can.
107 J4	Paradise Hill Sask. Can.
124 □2	Paradise Island New Prov. Bahamas
118 C2	Paradise River Nfld and Lab. Can.
109 J2	Paradise River Nfld and Lab. Can.
122 C3	Paradise Valley NV U.S.A.
157 M9	Parado Sumbawa Indon.
179 K9	Paradwip Orissa India
55 I4	Parẑętniów Pol.
	Parae'tonium Egypt see Marsá Maţrūḩ
17 L3	Paraf'yivka Ukr.
191 G6	Parağlomas Brazil
122 J7	Paragould AR U.S.A.
138 E4	Paraguá r. Bol.
137 F3	Paraguá r. Venez.
142 C5	Paraguaçu Brazil
140 E4	Paraguaçu Brazil
142 B2	Paraguaçu Paulista Brazil
139 G3	Paraguaçu Paulista Brazil
130 C1	Paraguaipoa Venez.
138 D3	Paragua, Península de pen. Venez.
144 F2	Paraguaqu r. Brazil
139 G6	Paraguaná, Península de pen. Venez.
138 D4	Paraguari Para.
144 G1	Paraguari Para.
139 G1	Paraguay country S. America
138 E4	Paraíba do Sul r. Brazil
143 F5	Paraíba do Sul r. Brazil
143 G3	Paraíbuna Brazil
127 M8	Paraíso Campeche Mex.
129 L8	Paraíso Tabasco Mex.
129 N8	Paraíso Tabasco Mex.
140 C4	Paraíso Brazil
142 C2	Paraíso r. Brazil
143 F5	Paraíso do Norte Brazil
142 B1	Paraíso do Tocantins Brazil
143 A5	Paraisópolis Brazil
62 G5	Páramo Spain
140 C4	Páramo r. Brazil
62 E3	Páramo del Sil Spain
62 E3	Páramo hill Spain
63 M3	Páramo de Masa, Puerto del pass Spain
136 B4	Páramo Leonés reg. Spain
138 A2	Paramonga Peru
19 U8	Paramonovo Rus. Fed.
62 F3	Páramos Port.
193 Q4	Paramushir, Ostrov i. Kuril'skiye O-va Rus. Fed.
78 D8	Paramythia Greece
190 D8	Paran watercourse Israel
147 H2	Paraná Arg.
140 B5	Paraná Brazil
139 E5	Paraná r. Brazil
144 E2	Paraná state Brazil
144 F3	Paraná r. S. America
140 B4	Paraná, Delta del Arg.
141 C8	Paraná, Rio r. Brazil
144 C6	Paranaguá Brazil
142 D6	Paranaguá, Baía de b. Brazil
142 A2	Paranaíba Brazil
142 B2	Paranaíba r. Brazil
142 A4	Paranaíta Brazil
142 A4	Paraná Ibicuy r. Arg.
142 B3	Paranaíta r. Brazil
142 A3	Paranaíta r. Brazil
142 A5	Paranapanema r. Brazil
142 C5	Paranapiacaba, Serra mts Brazil
142 A5	Paranavaí Brazil
136 B6	Paranal Brazil
142 A4	Paranatinga r. Brazil
142 C5	Paranapanema Brazil
139 I3	Paranapuã Peru
142 A4	Paranatinga r. Brazil
54 F4	Parandak Iran
187 K2	Parandak Iran
18 C5	Parandówo Pol.
157 I4	Parang i. Phil.
185 L7	Parangi Aru r. Sri Lanka

Peixian Jiangsu China see Pizhou
42 D4 **Peixoto, Represa** resr Brazil
40 B4 **Peixoto de Azevedo** Brazil
39 G2 **Peixoto de Azevedo** r. Brazil
44 K2 **Peize** Neth.
56 G4 **Pejantan** i. Indon.
Peje Kosovo, Srbija Serb. and Mont. see **Peć**
77 J6 **Pek** r. Serb. and Mont.
97 L4 **Peka** Lesotho
55 A5 **Pekabata** Sulawesi Indon.
57 H8 **Pekalongan** Jawa Indon.
56 E3 **Pekan** Malaysia
56 D4 **Pekanbaru** Sumatera Indon.
09 H2 **Pékans, Rivière aux** r. Que. Can.
19 X8 **Pekhlets** Rus. Fed.
89 F5 **Peki** Ghana
10 E9 **Pekin** IL U.S.A.
Peking Beijing China see **Beijing**
19 Q8 **Peklino** Rus. Fed.
63 N6 **Pela, Sierra de** mts Spain
56 D3 **Pelabuhan Klang** Malaysia
57 M2 **Pelabuhan Sandakan** inlet Malaysia
45 C7 **Pelada, Pampa** hills Arg.
67 C8 **Pelado** mt. Spain
69 D8 **Pelagie, Isole** is Sicilia Italy
71 L8 **Pelago** Italy
76 J9 **Pelagonija** plain Macedonia
63 K8 **Pelahustán** Spain
57 K6 **Pelaihari** Kalimantan Indon.
56 E4 **Pelalawan** Sumatera Indon.
57 H5 **Pelapis** i. Indon.
46 B4 **Pelarco** Chile
62 C9 **Pelariga** Port.
62 H7 **Pelarrodríguez** Spain
78 D4 **Pelasgia** Greece
Pelasyía Greece see **Pelasgia**
41 J8 **Pelat, Mont** mt. France
97 M4 **Pelatsoeu** mt. Lesotho
00 □6 **Pelau** i. Solomon Is
57 L4 **Pelawanbesar** Kalimantan Indon.
54 D2 **Pełczyce** Pol.
77 K5 **Peleaga, Vârful** mt. Romania
63 J6 **Peleagonzalo** Spain
38 C3 **Pelechuco** Bol.
18 J5 **Pelēči** Latvia
31 □3 **Pelée, Montagne** vol. Martinique
08 D5 **Pelee Island** Ont. Can.
08 D5 **Pelee Point** Ont. Can.
73 Q1 **Pelegrin, Rt** pt Croatia
54 □ **Peleliu** i. Palau
55 C4 **Peleng** i. Indon.
55 C4 **Peleng, Selat** sea chan. Indon.
55 C4 **Peleng, Teluk** b. Indon.
14 J3 **Peles** Rus. Fed.
56 E2 **Pelhřimov** Czech Rep.
04 E4 **Pelican** AK U.S.A.
07 I4 **Pelican Creek** r. Qld Austr.
07 K4 **Pelican Lake** Man. Can.
10 E4 **Pelican Lake** WI U.S.A.
10 B1 **Pelican Lake** l. MN U.S.A.
07 K4 **Pelican Narrows** Sask. Can.
98 □3a **Peligro, Punta del** pt La Gomera Canary Is
65 L6 **Peligros** Spain
16 G6 **Pelinia** Moldova
41 G9 **Pélissanne** France
76 J10 **Pelister** mt. Macedonia
76 J10 **Pelister** nat. park Macedonia
68 F4 **Pelješac** pen. Croatia
20 S3 **Pelkosenniemi** Fin.
96 D5 **Pella** S. Africa
10 A1 **Pelland** MN U.S.A.
75 J7 **Pellaro** Italy
07 I1 **Pellatt Lake** N.W.T. Can.
15 D9 **Pell City** AL U.S.A.
47 F5 **Pellegrini** Arg.
46 D6 **Pellegrini, Lago** l. Arg.
70 H6 **Pellegrino Parmense** Italy
43 E6 **Pellegrue** France
53 J7 **Pelleluhu Islands** P.N.G.
57 H5 **Pellérd** Hungary
71 M5 **Pellestrina** Italy
39 N8 **Pellevoisin** France
70 D6 **Pellice** r. Italy
58 C7 **Pellizzano** Italy
20 Q3 **Pello** Fin.
10 J4 **Pellston** MI U.S.A.
46 A4 **Pelluhue** Chile
48 G1 **Pellworm** i. Ger.
06 B2 **Pelly** r. Y.T. Can.
Pelly Bay Nunavut Can. see **Kugaaruk**
06 B2 **Pelly Crossing** Y.T. Can.
06 C2 **Pelly Mountains** Y.T. Can.
49 C10 **Pelm** Ger.
58 F7 **Pelmo, Monte** mt. Italy
65 I2 **Peloche** Spain
57 M8 **Pelokang** is Indon.
Peloponnese admin. reg. Greece see **Peloponnisos**
Peloponnesus admin. reg. Greece see **Peloponnisos**
78 D5 **Peloponnisos** admin. reg. Greece
78 D5 **Peloponnisos** pen. Greece
75 H8 **Peloritani, Monti** mts Sicilia Italy
75 J7 **Peloro, Capo** c. Sicilia Italy
03 H8 **Pelorus Sound** sea chan. South I. N.Z.
44 G3 **Pelotas** Brazil
41 C8 **Pelotas, Rio das** r. Brazil
77 M7 **Pelovo** Bulg.
54 G2 **Pelplin** Pol.
31 I2 **Pelsall** West Midlands, England U.K.
09 B10 **Pelsart Group** is W.A. Austr.
50 I3 **Pelsin** Ger.
20 R2 **Peltovuoma** Fin.
90 A7 **Pelusium** tourist site Egypt
Pelusium, Bay of Egypt see **Ţīnah, Khalīj aţ**
41 F6 **Pélussin** France
41 I7 **Pelvoux** France
41 I7 **Pelvoux, Massif du** mts France
41 I7 **Pelvoux, Mont** mt. France
57 J4 **Pély** Hungary
30 C7 **Pelynt** Cornwall, England U.K.
11 K2 **Pemache** r. Ont. Can.
17 □Q3 **Pemadumcook Lake** ME U.S.A.
57 H8 **Pemalang** Jawa Indon.
57 H4 **Pemangkat** Kalimantan Indon.
57 L5 **Pemarung, Pulau** i. Indon.
56 C3 **Pematangsiantar** Sumatera Indon.
95 I2 **Pemba** Moz.
91 E9 **Pemba** Zambia
93 D8 **Pemba, Baía de** b. Moz.
93 C6 **Pemba Channel** Tanz.
93 C6 **Pemba Island** Tanz.
93 C6 **Pemba North** admin. reg. Tanz.
93 C6 **Pemba South** admin. reg. Tanz.
09 C13 **Pemberton** W.A. Austr.
06 F5 **Pemberton** B.C. Can.
18 F5 **Pemberton** NJ U.S.A.
06 H4 **Pembina** r. Alta Can.
20 G1 **Pembina** ND U.S.A.
20 G1 **Pembina** r. ND U.S.A.
10 G4 **Pembine** WI U.S.A.
30 D4 **Pembrey** Carmarthenshire, Wales U.K.
30 G3 **Pembridge** Herefordshire, England U.K.
08 E4 **Pembroke** Ont. Can.
30 C4 **Pembroke** Pembrokeshire, Wales U.K.
15 G9 **Pembroke** GA U.S.A.
17 □R4 **Pembroke** ME U.S.A.
45 F8 **Pembroke, Cape** Falkland Is
03 B11 **Pembroke, Mount** South I. N.Z.
30 C4 **Pembroke Dock** Pembrokeshire, Wales U.K.
15 G12 **Pembroke Pines** FL U.S.A.
30 C4 **Pembrokeshire** admin. div. Wales U.K.
30 B4 **Pembrokeshire Coast National Park** Wales U.K.
157 J6 **Pembuanghulu** Kalimantan Indon.
31 M5 **Pembury** Kent, England U.K.
146 B5 **Pemehue, Cordillera de** mts Chile
53 N3 **Pemfling** Ger.
157 I5 **Pemuar** Kalimantan Indon.
146 A5 **Pemuco** Chile
176 C3 **Pen** Mahar. India
158 A4 **Pen** r. Myanmar
17 O2 **Pena** r. Rus. Fed.
138 D5 **Pena Barrosa** Bol.
146 B2 **Peña Blanca** Chile
63 M6 **Peña Cabollera** mt. Spain
65 M5 **Peña Cambrón** mt. Spain
63 O3 **Peñacerrada** Spain
66 E2 **Peña Collarada** mt. Spain
63 J3 **Peña Corada** mt. Spain
62 D8 **Penacova** Port.
62 H7 **Peña de Francia** mt. Spain
63 R3 **Peña de Izaga** mt. Spain
63 N2 **Peña del Aro** mt. Spain
66 D2 **Peña de Oroel** mt. Spain
62 D6 **Penafiel** Port.
63 L5 **Peñafiel** Spain
65 I5 **Peñaflor** Spain
63 K5 **Peñaflor de Hornija** Spain
67 E7 **Peñagolosa** mt. Spain
63 M2 **Penagos** Spain
131 □7 **Penal** Trin. and Tob.
63 K2 **Peña Labra, Sierra de** mts Spain
63 M7 **Peñalara** mt. Spain
66 E5 **Peñalba** Spain
62 G4 **Peñalba de Santiago** tourist site Spain
63 P7 **Peñalén** Spain
30 C4 **Penally** Pembrokeshire, Wales U.K.
65 I3 **Peñalsordo** Spain
62 E7 **Penalva do Castelo** Port.
62 F8 **Penamacor** Port.
Penambo Range mts Malaysia see Tama Abu, Banjaran
129 H4 **Peñamiller** Mex.
62 H5 **Peña Mira** mt. Spain
157 L2 **Penampang** Sabah Malaysia
62 H4 **Peña Negra** mt. Spain
129 H2 **Peña Nevada, Cerro** mt. Mex.
Penang state Malaysia see Pinang
142 B4 **Penápolis** Brazil
63 K2 **Peña Prieta** mt. Spain
63 J7 **Peñaranda de Bracamonte** Spain
63 N5 **Peñaranda de Duero** Spain
118 E3 **Pen Argyl** PA U.S.A.
205 I6 **Penarie** N.S.W. Austr.
66 D7 **Peñarroya** mt. Spain
65 M2 **Peñarroya, Embalse de** resr Spain
65 I4 **Peñarroya-Pueblonuevo** Spain
65 O4 **Peñarrubia** Spain
30 F5 **Penarth** Vale of Glamorgan, Wales U.K.
62 I1 **Peñas, Cabo de** c. Spain
145 B7 **Penas, Golfo de** g. Chile
131 □7 **Peñas, Punta** pt Venez.
63 L2 **Peña Sagra, Sierra** mts Spain
63 K2 **Peña Santa de Enol** mt. Spain
146 D5 **Peñas Blancas** Arg.
126 □Q12 **Peñas Blancas** Nic.
123 L10 **Peñasco** watercourse NM U.S.A.
65 O3 **Peñascosa** Spain
63 M5 **Peñas de Cervera** hills Spain
65 P3 **Peñas de San Pedro** Spain
156 A2 **Penasi, Pulau** i. Indon.
62 H2 **Peña Treisa** mt. Spain
62 I2 **Peña Ubiña** mt. Spain
62 I6 **Peñausende** Spain
64 F4 **Peña Utrera** hill Spain
30 D3 **Penbryn** Ceredigion, Wales U.K.
57 I4 **Penc** Hungary
30 D3 **Pencader** Carmarthenshire, Wales U.K.
26 K11 **Pencaitland** East Lothian, Scotland U.K.
178 G9 **Pench** r. India
Pencheng Jiangxi China see Ruichang
213 F2 **Penck, Cape** Antarctica
30 F4 **Pencoed** Bridgend, Wales U.K.
90 C3 **Pendé** r. C.A.R.
30 □ **Pendeen** Cornwall, England U.K.
88 C4 **Pendembu** Eastern Sierra Leone
88 B4 **Pendembu** Northern Sierra Leone
120 G4 **Pender** NE U.S.A.
208 G4 **Pender Bay** W.A. Austr.
208 G4 **Pender Bay Aboriginal Reserve** W.A. Austr.
79 K2 **Pendik** Turkey
62 E7 **Pendilhe** Port.
30 C4 **Pendine** Carmarthenshire, Wales U.K.
29 M6 **Pendle Hill** England U.K.
122 E4 **Pendleton** OR U.S.A.
106 E4 **Pendleton Bay** B.C. Can.
156 E6 **Pendopo** Sumatera Indon.
122 F2 **Pend Oreille** r. WA U.S.A.
122 F2 **Pend Oreille Lake** ID U.S.A.
178 H8 **Pendra** Chhattisgarh India
178 H8 **Pendra Road** Chhattisgarh India
176 C4 **Penduv** Mahar. India
157 H5 **Penebangan** i. Indon.
62 D5 **Peneda, Serra da** mts Port.
62 D5 **Peneda Gerês, Parque Nacional da** nat. park Port.
64 D5 **Penedo Gordo** Port.
62 F7 **Penedono** Port.
62 D8 **Penela** Port.
91 F6 **Pene-Mende** Dem. Rep. Congo
89 F4 **Pénessoulou** Benin
38 G7 **Pénestin** France
57 L4 **Penészlek** Hungary
111 O5 **Penetanguishene** Ont. Can.
116 G7 **Penfield** PA U.S.A.
Penfro Pembrokeshire, Wales U.K. see **Pembroke**
170 F3 **Peng'an** Sichuan China
176 F3 **Penganga** r. India
171 □J7 **Peng Chau** i. H.K. China
171 N6 **P'engchia Yü** i. Taiwan
91 E6 **Penge** Dem. Rep. Congo
171 L7 **P'enghu Ch'üntao** is Taiwan
P'enghu Liehtao is Taiwan see **P'enghu Ch'üntao**
171 L7 **P'enghu Tao** i. Taiwan
157 H4 **Pengiki** i. Indon.
110 A2 **Pengilly** MN U.S.A.
156 D2 **Pengkalan Hulu** Malaysia
156 □ **Peng Kang** hill Sing.
169 Q8 **Penglai** Shandong China
170 D3 **Pengshan** Sichuan China
170 G4 **Pengshui** Chongqing China
156 □ **Peng Siang, Sungai** r. Sing.
158 A4 **Pengwa** Myanmar
170 E3 **Pengxi** Sichuan China
Pengxian Sichuan China see Pengzhou
171 K4 **Pengze** Jiangxi China
170 D3 **Pengzhou** Sichuan China
141 C8 **Penha** Brazil
62 F8 **Penha Garcia** Port.
95 G3 **Penhalonga** Zimbabwe
62 D9 **Penhascoso** Port.
38 B5 **Penhir, Pointe de** pt France
97 K7 **Penhoek Pass** S. Africa
116 F12 **Penhook** VA U.S.A.
64 A2 **Peniche** Port.
26 J11 **Penicuik** Midlothian, Scotland U.K.
157 K9 **Penida** i. Indon.
51 G9 **Penig** Ger.
14 F3 **Peninga** Rus. Fed.
26 E12 **Peninver** Argyll and Bute, Scotland U.K.
67 F7 **Peñíscola** Spain
29 N6 **Penistone** South Yorkshire, England U.K.
140 D4 **Penitente, Serra do** hills Brazil
89 H5 **Penja** Cameroon
128 F5 **Penjamo** Mex.
189 L6 **Pēnjwīn** Iraq
29 L7 **Penketh** Warrington, England U.K.
19 X5 **Penkino** Rus. Fed.
30 H2 **Penkridge** Staffordshire, England U.K.
50 J4 **Penkun** Ger.
30 G2 **Penley** Wrexham, Wales U.K.
36 B4 **Penly** France
38 C6 **Penmarch** France
38 C6 **Penmarch, Pointe de** pt France
Penn PA U.S.A. see **Penn Hills**
73 N3 **Penna, Punta della** pt Italy
73 I3 **Penna in Teverina** Italy
43 I9 **Pennautier** France
43 H7 **Penne** France
73 L3 **Penne** Italy
75 N2 **Penne, Punta** pt Italy
43 F7 **Penne-d'Agenais** France
213 L2 **Pennell Coast** Antarctica
176 G5 **Penner** r. India
204 F6 **Penneshaw** S.A. Austr.
117 □S3 **Pennfield** N.B. Can.
118 D3 **Penn Forest Reservoir** PA U.S.A.
116 F8 **Penn Hills** PA U.S.A.
40 K5 **Pennine, Alpi** mts Italy/Switz.
Pennine Alps mts Italy/Switz. see **Pennine, Alpi**
29 M5 **Pennines** hills England U.K.
97 O6 **Pennington** S. Africa
118 F4 **Pennington** NJ U.S.A.
116 B12 **Pennington Gap** VA U.S.A.
73 J1 **Pennino, Monte** mt. Italy
116 E9 **Pennsboro** WV U.S.A.
118 E4 **Pennsburg** PA U.S.A.
118 A3 **Penns Creek** PA U.S.A.
118 B3 **Penns Creek** r. PA U.S.A.
118 E5 **Penns Grove** NJ U.S.A.
118 D5 **Pennsville** NJ U.S.A.
111 P8 **Pennsylvania** state U.S.A.
131 □2 **Pennville** Dominica
116 H6 **Penn Yan** NY U.S.A.
26 D10 **Pennyghael** Argyll and Bute, Scotland U.K.
105 L3 **Penny Icecap** Nunavut Can.
213 K1 **Penny Point** Antarctica
118 F5 **Penny Pot** NJ U.S.A.
19 P5 **Peno** Rus. Fed.
117 □Q4 **Penobscot** r. ME U.S.A.
117 □Q4 **Penobscot Bay** ME U.S.A.
204 H7 **Penola** S.A. Austr.
126 G5 **Peñón Blanco** Mex.
67 F10 **Peñón de Ifach** pt Spain
204 D4 **Penong** S.A. Austr.
126 □S13 **Penonomé** Panama
30 D3 **Penrhiw-pâl** Ceredigion, Wales U.K.
203 □2 **Penrhyn** atoll Cook Is
217 I6 **Penrhyn Basin** sea feature Pacific Ocean
30 E1 **Penrhyn Bay** Conwy, Wales U.K.
30 D2 **Penrhyndeudraeth** Gwynedd, Wales U.K.
30 C2 **Penrhyn Mawr** pt Wales U.K.
205 M5 **Penrith** N.S.W. Austr.
29 L4 **Penrith** Cumbria, England U.K.
30 B7 **Penryn** Cornwall, England U.K.
115 D10 **Pensacola** FL U.S.A.
115 D10 **Pensacola Bay** b. FL U.S.A.
212 T1 **Pensacola Mountains** Antarctica
139 E3 **Pensamiento** Bol.
184 C2 **Pensär** Azer.
110 G5 **Pensaukee** WI U.S.A.
205 I7 **Penshurst** Vic. Austr.
157 L2 **Pensiangan** Sabah Malaysia
178 F3 **Pensi La** pass Jammu and Kashmir
30 D6 **Pensilva** Cornwall, England U.K.
190 B3 **Pentadaktylos Range** mts Cyprus
72 C3 **Penta-di-Casinca** Corse France
177 H4 **Pentakota** Andhra Prad. India
78 C2 **Pentalofos** Greece
208 I3 **Pentecost** r. W.A. Austr.
200 □5 **Pentecost Island** Vanuatu
109 H3 **Pentecôte** r. Que. Can.
Pentecôte, Île i. Vanuatu see **Pentecost Island**
77 O5 **Penteleu, Vârful** mt. Romania
38 F5 **Penthièvre** reg. France
106 G5 **Penticton** B.C. Can.
30 D1 **Pentir** Gwynedd, Wales U.K.
30 B6 **Pentire Point** England U.K.
207 J6 **Pentland** Qld Austr.
26 J5 **Pentland Firth** sea chan. Scotland U.K.
26 I11 **Pentland Hills** Scotland U.K.
53 M4 **Pentling** Ger.
30 D1 **Pentraeth** Isle of Anglesey, Wales U.K.
30 E1 **Pentrefoelas** Conwy, Wales U.K.
110 H6 **Pentwater** MI U.S.A.
156 F5 **Penuba** Indon.
156 F6 **Penuguan** Sumatera Indon.
176 E5 **Penukonda** Andhra Prad. India
156 E2 **Penunjuk, Tanjung** pt Malaysia
38 E4 **Penvénan** France
158 C5 **Penwegon** Myanmar
29 L6 **Penwortham** Lancashire, England U.K.
17 O2 **Peny** Rus. Fed.
30 F3 **Penybont** Powys, Wales U.K.
30 F2 **Penybontfawr** Powys, Wales U.K.
30 E4 **Pen-y-fai** Bridgend, Wales U.K.
30 E2 **Penygadair** hill Wales U.K.
29 M5 **Pen-y-Ghent** hill England U.K.
30 D1 **Penygroes** Gwynedd, Wales U.K.
107 J2 **Penylan Lake** N.W.T. Can.
155 E6 **Penyu, Kepulauan** is Maluku Indon.
30 F4 **Penywaun** Rhondda Cynon Taff, Wales U.K.
15 I5 **Penza** Rus. Fed.
30 □ **Penzance** Cornwall, England U.K.
Penza Oblast admin. div. Rus. Fed. see Penzenskaya Oblast'
53 K6 **Penzberg** Ger.
15 I5 **Penzenskaya Oblast'** admin. div. Rus. Fed.
193 R3 **Penzhinskaya Guba** b. Rus. Fed.
53 J5 **Penzing** Ger.
50 H4 **Penzlin** Ger.
41 J8 **Péone** France
122 J2 **Peoples Creek** r. MT U.S.A.
125 T8 **Peoria** AZ U.S.A.
110 E9 **Peoria** IL U.S.A.
110 E9 **Peoria Heights** IL U.S.A.
124 □F14 **Pepe'ekeo** HI U.S.A.
88 B4 **Pepel** Sierra Leone
50 E2 **Pepelow** Ger.
147 I2 **Pepe Nuñéz** Uru.
92 B3 **Peper** Sudan
41 B10 **Pépieux** France
45 F7 **Pepingen** Belgium
45 I7 **Pepinster** Belgium
54 F4 **Pępowo** Pol.
97 N4 **Pepworth** S. Africa
76 H9 **Pëqin** Albania
119 G3 **Pequannock** NJ U.S.A.
62 H4 **Peque** Spain
118 C5 **Pequea** PA U.S.A.
118 C5 **Pequea Creek** r. PA U.S.A.
126 C4 **Pequeña, Punta** pt Mex.
118 E3 **Pequest** r. NJ U.S.A.
143 E3 **Pequi** Brazil
57 G4 **Pér** Hungary
64 C6 **Pêra** Port.
78 D4 **Perachora** Greece
176 G9 **Peradeniya** Sri Lanka
207 H2 **Pera Head** Qld Austr.
159 E12 **Perai** Malaysia
62 E9 **Perais** Port.
137 F3 **Peraitepuy** Venez.
156 C2 **Perak** i. Malaysia
156 D2 **Perak** r. Malaysia
156 D2 **Perak** state Malaysia
66 L3 **Peralada** Spain
63 J9 **Peraleda de la Mata** Spain
64 H4 **Peraleda del Zaucejo** Spain
66 C7 **Peralejos** Spain
66 D6 **Perales del Alfambra** Spain
62 G8 **Perales del Puerto** Spain
147 G6 **Peralta** Arg.
63 Q4 **Peralta** Spain
66 E4 **Peralta de Alcofea** Spain
66 F4 **Peralta de la Sal** Spain
66 E3 **Peraltilla** Spain
64 D6 **Peralva** Port.
63 P7 **Peralveche** Spain
78 F7 **Perama** Kriti Greece
176 F7 **Perambalur** Tamil Nadu India
20 R4 **Perämeren kansallispuisto** nat. park Fin.
93 B7 **Peramiho** Tanz.
66 H3 **Peramola** Spain
64 E5 **Peramora** r. Spain
156 E5 **Peranap** Sumatera Indon.
20 S3 **Perä-Posio** Fin.
58 F7 **Perarolo di Cadore** Italy
109 H3 **Percé** Que. Can.
39 L4 **Perche, Collines du** hills France
59 N3 **Perchtoldsdorf** Austria
208 H6 **Percival Lakes** salt flat W.A. Austr.
38 I4 **Percy** France
117 N4 **Percy** NH U.S.A.
207 M6 **Percy Isles** Qld Austr.
111 Q5 **Percy Reach** l. Ont. Can.
72 C8 **Perdasdefogu** Sardegna Italy
72 B9 **Perdaxius** Sardegna Italy
97 N3 **Perdekop** S. Africa
96 H9 **Perdepoort** pass S. Africa
147 H3 **Perdices** Arg.
63 P5 **Perdices, Sierra de** mts Spain
140 D4 **Perdida** r. Brazil
147 H5 **Perdido** r. Arg.
139 F5 **Perdido** r. Brazil
66 F2 **Perdido, Monte** mt. Spain
73 O7 **Perdifumo** Italy
66 D4 **Perdiguera** Spain
66 G2 **Perdiguère, Pic** mt. France/Spain
78 B3 **Perdika** Greece
118 B4 **Perdix** PA U.S.A.
142 D3 **Perdizes** Brazil
143 E4 **Perdões** Brazil
109 G3 **Perdu, Lac** l. Que. Can.
65 O5 **Perea** mt. Spain
16 F2 **Perebrody** Ukr.
16 B5 **Perechyn** Ukr.
19 S6 **Peredel** Kaluzhskaya Oblast' Rus. Fed.
19 X6 **Peredel** Vladimirskaya Oblast' Rus. Fed.
62 G6 **Peredo** Port.
192 H3 **Peregrebnoye** Rus. Fed.
57 J5 **Peregu Mare** Romania
16 D5 **Perehins'ke** Ukr.
136 C3 **Pereira** Col.
142 B4 **Pereira Barreto** Brazil
64 C6 **Pereiras** Port.
140 F3 **Pereiro** Brazil
60 C4 **Pereiro** Port.
62 E1 **Pereiro** Spain
62 E4 **Pereiro de Aguiar** Spain
63 Q6 **Perejiles** r. Spain
19 O3 **Perekhoda** r. Rus. Fed.
17 M3 **Perekopivka** Ukr.
17 M8 **Perekops'ka Zatoka** b. Ukr.
15 H6 **Perelazovskiy** Rus. Fed.
19 O8 **Perelazy** Rus. Fed.
17 T2 **Pereleshinskiy** Rus. Fed.
182 D2 **Perelyub** Rus. Fed.
110 H6 **Pere Marquette** r. MI U.S.A.
182 D2 **Peremetnoye** Kazakh.
17 P4 **Peremoha** Kharkivs'ka Oblast' Ukr.
17 K3 **Peremoha** Kyivs'ka Oblast' Ukr.
176 C7 **Peremul Par** rf India
19 T7 **Peremyshl'** Rus. Fed.
16 D4 **Peremyshlyany** Ukr.
138 B2 **Perené** r. Peru
209 D10 **Perenjori** W.A. Austr.
62 I6 **Pereruela** Spain
16 H6 **Peresecina** Moldova
17 O4 **Pereshchepyne** Ukr.
19 V5 **Pereslavl'-Zalesskiy** Rus. Fed.
19 V5 **Pereslavskiy Natsional'nyy Park** nat. park Rus. Fed.
55 M5 **Perespa** Ukr.
59 O4 **Pereszteg** Hungary
71 K8 **Peretola** airport Italy
77 N6 **Peretu** Romania
17 R5 **Pereval's'k** Ukr.
17 L3 **Perevid** r. Ukr.
182 F2 **Perevolotskiy** Rus. Fed.
14 I5 **Perevoz** Rus. Fed.
162 I5 **Pereyaslavka** Rus. Fed.
Pereyaslav-Khmel'nitskiy Ukr. see **Pereyaslav-Khmel'nyts'kyy**
17 K3 **Pereyaslav-Khmel'nyts'kyy** Ukr.
147 G3 **Pérez** Arg.
144 C2 **Pérez** Chile
72 B6 **Perfugas** Sardegna Italy
59 K3 **Perg** Austria
147 G3 **Pergamino** Arg.
79 L6 **Perge** tourist site Turkey
71 L9 **Pergine Valdarno** Italy
71 K3 **Pergine Valsugana** Italy
71 N8 **Pergola** Italy
16 G2 **Perha** Ukr.
156 E2 **Perhentian Besar, Pulau** i. Malaysia
20 R5 **Perho** Fin.
76 I4 **Periam** Romania
65 K7 **Periana** Spain
128 E6 **Peribán de Ramos** Mex.
109 F3 **Péribonka** r. Que. Can.
109 G3 **Péribonka, Lac** l. Que. Can.
144 D2 **Perico** Arg.
128 B3 **Pericos** Nayarit Mex.
126 F5 **Pericos** Sinaloa Mex.
125 V8 **Peridot** AZ U.S.A.
77 P4 **Perieni** Romania
38 I3 **Périers** France
42 B3 **Périgny** France
42 F6 **Périgord** reg. France
42 F5 **Périgord Blanc** reg. France
43 F6 **Périgord Noir** reg. France
137 I5 **Perigoso, Canal** sea chan. Brazil
42 F5 **Périgueux** France
136 C2 **Perijá, Parque Nacional** nat. park Venez.
136 C2 **Perija, Sierra de** mts Venez.
62 I5 **Perilla de Castro** Spain
Perim Island Yemen see **Barīm**
57 K3 **Perín-Chym** Slovakia
156 E1 **Peringat** Malaysia
77 R5 **Periprava** Romania
77 P6 **Perişoru** Romania
78 E3 **Peristera** i. Greece
78 E4 **Peristerio** Greece
191 A7 **Peri Suyu** r. Turkey
77 R6 **Periteasca-Gura Portiţei** nature res. Romania
145 C7 **Perito Moreno** Arg.
145 B7 **Perito Moreno, Parque Nacional** nat. park Arg.
176 E7 **Perivar** r. India
78 B3 **Perivoli** Kerkyra Greece
78 F7 **Perivolia** Kriti Greece
57 J4 **Perje** r. Hungary
118 E4 **Perkasie** PA U.S.A.
156 F5 **Perkat, Tanjung** pt Indon.
57 H4 **Perkáta** Hungary
118 E4 **Perkiomen Creek** r. PA U.S.A.
52 A3 **Perl** Ger.
126 □R11 **Perlas, Laguna de** lag. Nic.
126 □R11 **Perlas, Punta de** pt Nic.
53 M3 **Perlbach** r. Ger.
50 E4 **Perleberg** Ger.
55 K3 **Perlejewo** Pol.
53 O4 **Perlesreut** Ger.
17 R2 **Perlevka** Rus. Fed.
156 D1 **Perlis** state Malaysia
55 M1 **Perloja** Lith.
55 J1 **Perły** Pol.
14 L4 **Perm'** Rus. Fed.
71 Q5 **Permani** Croatia
14 I4 **Permas** Rus. Fed.
78 B2 **Përmet** Albania
Perm Oblast admin. div. Rus. Fed. see Permskaya Oblast'
14 L4 **Permskaya Oblast'** admin. div. Rus. Fed.
71 R7 **Permuda** Croatia
68 E3 **Permuda** i. Croatia
18 J1 **Pernå** Fin.
Pernambuco Brazil see Recife
140 F4 **Pernambuco** state Brazil
214 H6 **Pernambuco Plain** sea feature S. Atlantic Ocean
40 F2 **Pernand-Vergelesses** France
56 C2 **Pernarec** Czech Rep.
64 C5 **Perna Seca, Barragem da** resr Port.
71 Q6 **Pernat, Rt** pt Croatia
204 F4 **Pernatty Lagoon** salt flat S.A. Austr.
59 L5 **Pernegg an der Mur** Austria
176 C5 **Pernem** Goa India
59 N2 **Pernersdorf** Austria
64 B2 **Pernes** Port.
41 G9 **Pernes-les-Fontaines** France
78 F1 **Perni** Greece
77 L8 **Pernik** Bulg.
21 Q6 **Perniö** Fin.
59 M4 **Pernitz** Austria
70 G4 **Pero** Italy
64 C4 **Peroguarda** Port.
142 A2 **Perolândia** Brazil
41 D9 **Pérols** France
40 H4 **Péron** France
209 B8 **Peron, Cape** W.A. Austr.
209 C12 **Peron, Point** W.A. Austr.
206 C2 **Peron Islands** N.T. Austr.
40 G4 **Péronnas** France
36 E4 **Péronne** France
209 B8 **Peron Peninsula** W.A. Austr.
70 C6 **Perosa Argentina** Italy
129 J6 **Perote** Mex.
40 G5 **Pérouges** France
62 F8 **Pero Viseu** Port.
205 M6 **Perpendicular, Point** N.S.W. Austr.
43 J10 **Perpignan** France
146 A6 **Perquenco** Chile
146 B4 **Perquilauquén** r. Chile
30 B7 **Perranporth** Cornwall, England U.K.
30 B7 **Perranzabuloe** Cornwall, England U.K.
40 E3 **Perrecy-les-Forges** France
40 E4 **Perreux** France
40 H3 **Perrigny** France
124 O8 **Perris** CA U.S.A.
64 G7 **Perro, Punta del** pt Spain
37 J8 **Perrogney-les-Fontaines** France
34 C2 **Perros-Guirec** France
117 L3 **Perrot, Île** i. Que. Can.
20 S2 **Perrum-Äbmir** Fin.
110 J2 **Perry** Ont. Can.
115 F10 **Perry** FL U.S.A.
115 F9 **Perry** GA U.S.A.
120 H5 **Perry** IA U.S.A.
117 □R4 **Perry** ME U.S.A.
111 J7 **Perry** MI U.S.A.
121 G7 **Perry** OK U.S.A.
118 A4 **Perry County** county PA U.S.A.
118 C6 **Perry Hall** MD U.S.A.
118 C6 **Perryman** MD U.S.A.
213 G2 **Perrymennyy, Cape** Antarctica
116 B7 **Perrysburg** OH U.S.A.
121 E7 **Perryton** TX U.S.A.
121 I8 **Perryville** AR U.S.A.
118 C5 **Perryville** MD U.S.A.
43 I6 **Pers** France
191 E4 **P'ersa** Georgia
36 D5 **Persan** France
191 D3 **P'ersat'i** Georgia
59 L3 **Persenbeug** Austria
184 E7 **Persepolis** tourist site Iran
139 E3 **Perseverancia** Bol.
23 N2 **Pershagen** Sweden
17 M5 **Pershe Travnya** Dnipropetrovs'ka Oblast' Ukr.
17 O5 **Pershe Travnya** Dnipropetrovs'ka Oblast' Ukr.
Pershnotravnevoye Ukr. see **Pershotravens'k**
30 H3 **Pershore** Worcestershire, England U.K.
17 P5 **Pershotravens'k** Ukr.
17 Q6 **Pershotravneve** Donets'ka Oblast' Ukr.
17 Q4 **Pershotravneve** Kharkivs'ka Oblast' Ukr.
17 L7 **Pershotravneve** Mykolayivs'ka Oblast' Ukr.
16 H2 **Pershotravneve** Zhytomyrs'ka Oblast' Ukr.
Persia country Asia see **Iran**
Persian Gulf Asia see **The Gulf**
23 M4 **Persnäs** Öland Sweden
23 N3 **Persö naturreservat** nature res. Sweden
22 J5 **Perstorp** Sweden
188 I4 **Pertek** Turkey
205 K9 **Perth** Tas. Austr.
209 C11 **Perth** W.A. Austr.
108 E4 **Perth** Ont. Can.
26 J10 **Perth** Perth and Kinross, Scotland U.K.
119 G3 **Perth Amboy** NJ U.S.A.
26 H9 **Perth and Kinross** admin. div. Scotland U.K.
109 H4 **Perth-Andover** N.B. Can.
215 L6 **Perth Basin** sea feature Indian Ocean
36 H5 **Perthes** Champagne-Ardenne France
36 E7 **Perthes** Île-de-France France
36 I6 **Perthois** reg. France
43 J11 **Perthus, Col du** pass France/Spain
14 G2 **Pertominsk** Rus. Fed.
21 Q6 **Pertteli** Fin.
41 H9 **Pertuis** France
42 A3 **Pertuis Breton** sea chan. France
42 A3 **Pertuis d'Antioche** sea chan. France
21 S6 **Pertunmaa** Fin.
66 E3 **Pertusa** Spain
72 C5 **Pertusato, Capo** c. Corse France
147 E5 **Perú** Arg.
138 D3 **Perú** Bol.
138 B2 **Peru** country S. America
110 E8 **Peru** IL U.S.A.
114 D5 **Peru** IN U.S.A.
117 L4 **Peru** NY U.S.A.
217 M7 **Peru Basin** sea feature S. Pacific Ocean
51 I10 **Peruc** Czech Rep.
217 N6 **Peru-Chile Trench** sea feature S. Pacific Ocean
68 F4 **Peručko Jezero** l. Croatia
73 I1 **Perugia** Italy
71 M9 **Perugia** prov. Italy
144 F3 **Perugorría** Arg.
155 B5 **Peruhumpenai Mountains Reserve** nature res. Indon.
142 D6 **Peruíbe** Brazil
176 E5 **Peruru** Andhra Prad. India
77 M8 **Perushtitsa** Bulg.
Perusia Italy see **Perugia**
45 E7 **Péruwelz** Belgium
191 C1 **Pervaya Sinyukha** Rus. Fed.
39 L5 **Pervenchères** France
45 C6 **Pervijze** Belgium
17 O1 **Pervoavgustovskiy** Rus. Fed.
16 I7 **Pervomaisc** Moldova
183 P6 **Pervomay** Kyrg.
183 N2 **Pervomayka** Kazakh.
15 H5 **Pervomaysk** Rus. Fed.
17 R5 **Pervomays'k** Luhans'ka Oblast' Ukr.
16 J5 **Pervomays'k** Mykolayivs'ka Oblast' Ukr.
18 L3 **Pervomayskaya** Rus. Fed.
17 L6 **Pervomays'ke** Mykolayivs'ka Oblast' Ukr.
17 M8 **Pervomays'ke** Respublika Krym Ukr.
183 T2 **Pervomayskiy** Kazakh.
Pervomayskiy Kyrg. see Pervomay
182 F2 **Pervomayskiy** Orenburgskaya Oblast' Rus. Fed.
19 P7 **Pervomayskiy** Smolenskaya Oblast' Rus. Fed.
19 X8 **Pervomayskiy** Tambovskaya Oblast' Rus. Fed.
19 U7 **Pervomayskiy** Tul'skaya Oblast' Rus. Fed.
Pervomayskoye Kyrg. see Pervomay
18 M1 **Pervomayskoye** Leningradskaya Oblast' Rus. Fed.
191 I3 **Pervomayskoye** Respublika Dagestan Rus. Fed.
162 M4 **Pervomayskoye** Sakhalinskaya Oblast' Rus. Fed.
17 P4 **Pervomays'kyy** Ukr.
193 R3 **Pervorechenskiy** Rus. Fed.
45 G7 **Perwez** Belgium
19 R3 **Pes'** Rus. Fed.
19 S2 **Pes'** r. Rus. Fed.
71 K8 **Pesa** r. Italy
63 M3 **Pesadas de Burgos** Spain
157 I5 **Pesaguan** Kalimantan Indon.
157 I6 **Pesaguan** r. Indon.
71 N8 **Pesaro** Italy
71 N8 **Pesaro e Urbino** prov. Italy
124 J4 **Pescadero** CA U.S.A.
Pescadores is Taiwan see **P'enghu Ch'üntao**
138 B4 **Pescadores, Punta** pt Peru
70 I8 **Pescaglia** Italy
71 J5 **Pescantina** Italy
73 M3 **Pescara** Italy
73 L3 **Pescara** prov. Italy
73 M3 **Pescara** r. Italy
77 J6 **Pescari** Romania
73 L4 **Pescasseroli** Italy
40 C5 **Peschadoires** France
15 H7 **Peschanokopskoye** Rus. Fed.
Peschanoye Rus. Fed. see **Yashkul'**
182 D6 **Peschanyy, Mys** pt Kazakh.
73 Q4 **Peschici** Italy
71 J8 **Pescia** Italy
73 L3 **Pescina** Italy
73 M4 **Pescocostanzo** Italy
73 M4 **Pescolanciano** Italy
73 O6 **Pescopagano** Italy
73 M4 **Pescopennataro** Italy
73 K3 **Pescorocchiano** Italy
73 N5 **Pesco Sannita** Italy
126 □S14 **Pesé** Panama
98 □3b **Pesebre, Punta** pt Fuerteventura Canary Is
156 □ **Pesek, Pulau** i. Sing.
156 □ **Pesek Kechil, Pulau** i. Sing.
70 B2 **Peseux** Switz.
14 I2 **Pesha** r. Rus. Fed.
185 I5 **Peshanjan** Afgh.
185 N4 **Peshawar** Pak.
76 I9 **Peshkopi** Albania
17 S7 **Peshkovo** Rus. Fed.
77 M8 **Peshtera** Bulg.
110 G4 **Peshtigo** WI U.S.A.
110 G5 **Peshtigo** r. WI U.S.A.
70 D7 **Pesio** r. Italy
183 L1 **Peski** Kazakh.
19 V6 **Peski** Moskovskaya Oblast' Rus. Fed.
15 H6 **Peski** Voronezhskaya Oblast' Rus. Fed.
185 J2 **Peski** Turkm.
14 K4 **Peskovka** Rus. Fed.
40 H2 **Pesmes** France
68 E2 **Pesnica** Slovenia
19 W3 **Pesochnoye** Rus. Fed.
19 Q8 **Pesochnya** Rus. Fed.
62 E6 **Peso da Régua** Port.
126 □P11 **Pespire** Hond.
140 F4 **Pesqueira** Brazil
126 D3 **Pesqueira** Mex.
63 L5 **Pesquera de Duero** Spain
43 C6 **Pessac** France
43 F8 **Pessan** France
44 J3 **Pesse** Neth.
50 G5 **Pessin** Ger.
57 I4 **Pest** county Hungary
19 S3 **Pestovo** Rus. Fed.
182 C1 **Pestravka** Rus. Fed.
14 H4 **Pestyaki** Rus. Fed.
63 L2 **Pesués** Spain
14 L1 **Pesyakov, Ostrov** i. Rus. Fed.
128 E8 **Petacalco, Bahía de** b. Mex.
73 N3 **Petacciato** Italy
190 C6 **Petah Tiqwa** Israel
21 R5 **Petäjävesi** Fin.
155 F3 **Petak, Tanjung** pt Halmahera Indon.
78 C6 **Petalidi** Greece
78 F4 **Petalioi** i. Greece
78 F4 **Petalion, Kolpos** sea chan. Greece
124 J3 **Petaluma** CA U.S.A.
45 I9 **Pétange** Lux.
157 K5 **Petangis** Kalimantan Indon.
136 E2 **Petare** Venez.
78 C3 **Petas** Greece
128 F8 **Petatlán** Mex.
93 A8 **Petauke** Zambia
111 S3 **Petawaga, Lac** l. Que. Can.
111 Q4 **Petawawa** Ont. Can.
127 O9 **Petén Itzá, Lago** l. Guat.
110 E5 **Petenwell Lake** WI U.S.A.
59 O7 **Peteranec** Croatia
108 D3 **Peterbell** Ont. Can.
204 G5 **Peterborough** S.A. Austr.
205 I8 **Peterborough** Vic. Austr.
108 E4 **Peterborough** Ont. Can.
31 L2 **Peterborough** Peterborough, England U.K.
31 L2 **Peterborough** admin. div. England U.K.
117 N6 **Peterborough** NH U.S.A.
26 L8 **Peterculter** Aberdeen, Scotland U.K.
26 M7 **Peterhead** Aberdeenshire, Scotland U.K.
57 I4 **Péteri** Hungary
212 R2 **Peter I Island** Antarctica
Peter I Øy i. Antarctica see **Peter I Island**
57 I5 **Péteri-tó** l. Hungary
107 M2 **Peter Lake** Nunavut Can.
29 O4 **Peterlee** Durham, England U.K.
106 H5 **Peter Lougheed Provincial Park** B.C. Can.
206 C8 **Petermann Aboriginal Land** res. N.T./W.A. Austr.
105 P2 **Petermann Bjerg** nunatak Greenland
206 B8 **Petermann Ranges** mts N.T. Austr.
146 B4 **Peteroa, Volcán** vol. Chile
107 I4 **Peter Pond Lake** Sask. Can.
109 G1 **Peters, Lac** l. Que. Can.
53 J3 **Petersaurach** Ger.
49 I9 **Petersberg** Ger.
97 I8 **Petersburg** S. Africa
104 E4 **Petersburg** AK U.S.A.
120 K6 **Petersburg** IL U.S.A.
114 D6 **Petersburg** IN U.S.A.
118 F6 **Petersburg** NJ U.S.A.
117 L6 **Petersburg** NY U.S.A.
116 E8 **Petersburg** OH U.S.A.
116 H11 **Petersburg** VA U.S.A.
116 F10 **Petersburg** WV U.S.A.
53 K4 **Petersdorf** Ger.
50 D2 **Petersdorf auf Fehmarn** Ger.
31 K5 **Petersfield** Hampshire, England U.K.
51 J6 **Petershagen** Brandenburg Ger.
49 G6 **Petershagen** Nordrhein-Westfalen Ger.
53 K5 **Petershausen** Ger.
137 G3 **Peters Mine** Guyana
116 E11 **Peterstown** WV U.S.A.
104 C3 **Petersville** AK U.S.A.
27 E6 **Peterswell** Rep. of Ireland
Peter the Great Bay Rus. Fed. see **Petra Velikogo, Zaliv**
Pétervárad Vojvodina, Srbija Serb. and Mont. see **Petrovaradin**
57 J3 **Pétervására** Hungary
Peterwardein Vojvodina, Srbija Serb. and Mont. see **Petrovaradin**
176 D4 **Peth** Mahar. India
75 L5 **Petilia Policastro** Italy
66 C3 **Petilla de Aragón** Spain
62 F4 **Petín** Spain
131 □2 **Petit-Bourg** Guadeloupe
131 □2 **Petit-Canal** Guadeloupe
109 H4 **Petitcodiac** N.B. Can.
39 N3 **Petit-Couronne** France
131 □2 **Petit Cul de Sac Marin** b. Guadeloupe
41 E10 **Petite Camargue** reg. France
42 H3 **Petite Creuse** r. France
99 □1c **Petite-Île** Réunion
43 C7 **Petite Leyre** r. France
131 □3 **Petite Martinique** i. Grenada
37 M5 **Petite-Rosselle** France
39 P7 **Petite Sauldre** r. France
45 J9 **Petite Suisse Luxembourgeoise** reg. Lux.
99 □3b **Petite Terre** i. Mayotte
130 G4 **Petit-Goâve** Haiti
Petitjean Morocco see **Sidi Kacem**
109 H2 **Petit Lac Manicouagan** l. Que. Can.
39 I8 **Petit Lay** r. France
90 A5 **Petit-Loango, Réserve de** nature res. Gabon
38 I7 **Petit Maine** r. France
117 □R4 **Petit Manan Point** ME U.S.A.
38 I7 **Petit-Mars** France
109 I3 **Petit Mécatina** r. Nfld and Lab./Que. Can.
105 M4 **Petit Mécatina** r. Que. Can.
109 J3 **Petit Mécatina, Île du** i. Que. Can.
37 M6 **Petitmont** France
36 F6 **Petit Morin** r. France
40 G3 **Petit-Noir** France
106 F2 **Petitot** r. Alta/B.C. Can.
41 E10 **Petit Rhône** r. France
40 J5 **Petit St-Bernard, Col du** pass France
19 W7 **Petkino** Rus. Fed.
20 S3 **Petkula** Fin.
51 H7 **Petkus** Ger.
178 D8 **Petlad** Gujarat India
129 J7 **Petlalcingo** Mex.
178 E8 **Petlawad** Madh. Prad. India
57 L3 **Petneháza** Hungary
127 O7 **Peto** Mex.
57 I4 **Petőfibánya** Hungary
57 I5 **Petőfiszállás** Hungary
146 B3 **Petorca** Chile
110 J4 **Petoskey** MI U.S.A.
190 D8 **Petra** tourist site Jordan
67 L8 **Petra** Spain
75 J7 **Petrace** r. Italy
74 G8 **Petralia-Soprana** Sicilia Italy
74 G8 **Petralia-Sottana** Sicilia Italy
212 P1 **Petras, Mount** Antarctica
162 G7 **Petra Velikogo, Zaliv** b. Rus. Fed.
111 Q6 **Petre, Point** Ont. Can.
202 □ **Petre Bay** Chatham Is S. Pacific Ocean
Petrel Valencia Spain see Petrer
73 L5 **Petrella, Monte** mt. Italy
73 K3 **Petrella Salto** Italy
73 N4 **Petrella Tifernina** Italy
67 D11 **Petrer** Spain
57 L4 **Petreşti** Romania
72 B4 **Petreto-Bicchisano** Corse France
71 N8 **Petriano** Italy
77 L9 **Petrich** Bulg.
200 □5 **Petrie, Récif** rf New Caledonia
125 W6 **Petrified Forest National Park** AZ U.S.A.
68 G3 **Petrijevci** Croatia
Petrikau Pol. see **Piotrków Trybunalski**
Petrikov Belarus see **Pyetrykaw**
77 L5 **Petrila** Romania
68 F3 **Petrinja** Croatia
57 L5 **Petriş** Romania
73 L1 **Petritoli** Italy
17 N7 **Petrivka** Khersons'ka Oblast' Ukr.
16 J7 **Petrivka** Odes'ka Oblast' Ukr.
17 Q6 **Petrivs'ke** Ukr.
17 M4 **Petrivtsi** Ukr.
144 C3 **Petro, Cerro de** mt. Chile
Petroaleksandrovsk Uzbek. see **To'rtko'l**
18 M2 **Petrodvorets** Rus. Fed.
Petrograd Rus. Fed. see **Sankt-Peterburg**
Petrokov Pol. see **Piotrków Trybunalski**
Petrokrepost' Rus. Fed. see **Shlissel'burg**
19 O1 **Petrokrepost', Bukhta** b. Rus. Fed.
65 P3 **Pétrola** Spain
140 F4 **Petrolândia** Brazil
136 C2 **Petrólea** Col.
111 L7 **Petrolia** Ont. Can.
124 H1 **Petrolia** CA U.S.A.
136 E5 **Petrolina** Amazonas Brazil
140 E4 **Petrolina** Pernambuco Brazil
142 C2 **Petrolina de Goiás** Brazil
Petromaryevka Ukr. see **Pervomays'k**
78 C2 **Petron, Limni** l. Greece
75 L5 **Petronà** Italy
Petropavl Kazakh. see **Petropavlovsk**
17 P5 **Petropavlivka** Ukr.
183 S5 **Petropavlovka** Kazakh.
162 E2 **Petropavlovka** Amurskaya Oblast' Rus. Fed.
168 I1 **Petropavlovka** Respublika Buryatiya Rus. Fed.
15 H6 **Petropavlovka** Voronezhskaya Oblast' Rus. Fed.
183 M1 **Petropavlovsk** Kazakh.
Petropavlovsk Rus. Fed. see **Petropavlovsk-Kamchatskiy**
193 Q4 **Petropavlovsk-Kamchatskiy** Rus. Fed.
183 U1 **Petropavlovskoye** Rus. Fed.
143 F5 **Petrópolis** Brazil
77 L5 **Petroşani** Romania
74 D8 **Petrosino** Sicilia Italy
56 G3 **Petrov** Czech Rep.

Petrovac to Pire Mahuida, Sierra

320

76 J6 Petrovac Srbija Serb. and Mont.
57 K3 Petrovany Slovakia
76 H5 Petrovaradin Vojvodina, Srbija Serb. and Mont.
17 M5 Petrove Ukr.
56 D2 Petrovice Czech Rep.
19 P8 Petrovichi Rus. Fed.
183 M1 Petrovka Kazakh.
182 A1 Petrovsk Rus. Fed.
15 G7 Petrovskaya Rus. Fed.
17 R5 Petrovs'ke Ukr.
19 X5 Petrovskiy Rus. Fed.
19 T5 Petrovskoye Moskovskaya Oblast' Rus. Fed.
182 G1 Petrovskoye Respublika Bashkortostan Rus. Fed.
Petrovskoye Stavropol'skiy Kray Rus. Fed. see Svetlograd
19 X9 Petrovskoye Tambovskaya Oblast' Rus. Fed.
19 W4 Petrovskoye Yaroslavskaya Oblast' Rus. Fed.
169 K1 Petrovsk-Zabaykal'skiy Rus. Fed.
15 I6 Petrov Val Rus. Fed.
14 F3 Petrozavodsk Rus. Fed.
77 M3 Petru Rareș Romania
97 J5 Petrusburg S. Africa
16 G6 Petrușeni Moldova
97 M3 Petrus Steyn S. Africa
96 I6 Petrusville S. Africa
57 H2 Petřvald Czech Rep.
17 N5 Petrykivka Ukr.
Petsamo Rus. Fed. see Pechenga
97 M3 Petsana S. Africa
Pettau Slovenia see Ptuj
44 G3 Petten Neth.
53 M3 Pettendorf Ger.
27 G3 Pettigo Northern Ireland U.K.
75 L5 Pettinascura, Monte mt. Italy
74 G8 Pettineo Sicilia Italy
53 N6 Petting Ger.
58 B5 Pettneu am Arlberg Austria
73 L4 Pettorano sul Gizio Italy
71 L3 Pettorina r. Italy
192 H4 Petukhovo Rus. Fed.
19 W6 Petushki Rus. Fed.
31 K6 Petworth West Sussex, England U.K.
58 G6 Petzeck mt. Austria
59 I3 Peuerbach Austria
156 B2 Peuetsagu, Gunung vol. Indon.
42 D5 Peujard France
146 B4 Peumo Chile
20 S3 Peurasuvanto Fin.
156 B2 Peureula Sumatera Indon.
193 S3 Pevek Rus. Fed.
31 M6 Pevensey East Sussex, England U.K.
31 M6 Pevensey Levels lowland England U.K.
70 D7 Peveragno Italy
31 I5 Pewsey Wiltshire, England U.K.
31 I5 Pewsey, Vale of val. England U.K.
48 D4 Pewsum (Krummhörn) Ger.
37 M7 Pexonne France
173 K10 Pêxung Xizang China
184 H9 Pey Beshk Iran
41 J9 Peymeinade France
41 C10 Peyne r. France
41 H10 Peynier France
184 G4 Pey Ostān Iran
41 H10 Peypin France
147 G3 Peyrano Arg.
42 H4 Peyrat-le-Château France
43 B8 Peyrehorade France
41 C8 Peyreleau France
42 I4 Peyrelevade France
43 E10 Peyresourde, Col de pass France
70 D8 Peyrevieille, Mont mt. Italy
41 B10 Peyriac-de-Mer France
43 J9 Peyriac-Minervois France
40 H5 Peyrieu France
41 G6 Peyrins France
41 H9 Peyrolles-en-Provence France
41 H8 Peyruis France
43 E8 Peyrusse-Grande France
43 I6 Peyrusse-le-Roc France
14 I2 Peza r. Rus. Fed.
41 C10 Pézenas France
54 D2 Pęzino Pol.
56 G3 Pezinok Slovakia
185 N5 Pezu Pak.
43 F6 Pezuls France
53 M4 Pfaffenberg Ger.
51 J6 Pfaffendorf Ger.
53 I5 Pfaffenhausen Ger.
53 L4 Pfaffenhofen an der Ilm Ger.
53 I5 Pfaffenhofen an der Roth Ger.
37 O6 Pfaffenhoffen France
59 M4 Pfaffensattel pass Austria
52 D6 Pfaffenweiler Ger.
70 F1 Pfäffikon Schwyz Switz.
70 F1 Pfäffikon Zürich Switz.
53 M5 Pfaffing Ger.
52 D3 Pfälzer Wald hills Ger.
52 D3 Pfälzer Wald park Ger.
49 E10 Pfalzfeld Ger.
52 F4 Pfalzgrafenweiler Ger.
53 N5 Pfarrkirchen Ger.
49 K10 Pfarrweisach Ger.
58 H5 Pfarrwerfen Austria
53 M4 Pfatter Ger.
52 G3 Pfedelbach Ger.
53 L4 Pfeffenhausen Ger.
58 C4 Pflach Austria
58 D5 Pfons Austria
53 L4 Pförring Ger.
53 J6 Pforzen Ger.
52 F4 Pforzheim Ger.
53 M5 Pfreimd Ger.
53 M2 Pfreimd r. Ger.
52 G5 Pfronstetten Ger.
53 J6 Pfronten Ger.
52 G6 Pfullendorf Ger.
52 G5 Pfullingen Ger.
58 C6 Pfunds Austria
52 F2 Pfungstadt Ger.
70 F1 Pfyn Switz.
178 E4 Phagwara Punjab India
97 K4 Phahameng Free State S. Africa
95 F5 Phahameng Limpopo S. Africa
95 F4 Phalaborwa S. Africa
185 O5 Phalia Pak.
178 D6 Phalodi Rajasthan India
37 N6 Phalsbourg France
178 C6 Phalsund Rajasthan India
178 D4 Phaltan Mahar. India
179 L6 Phalut Peak India/Nepal
159 E10 Phangan, Ko i. Thai.
158 E6 Phang Hoei, San Khao mts Thai.
159 D10 Phangnga Thai.
158 F3 Phăng Xi Păng mt. Vietnam
159 F7 Phanom Dong Rak, Thiu Khao mts Cambodia/Thai.
159 I9 Phan Rang - Thap Cham Vietnam
159 I9 Phan Ri Cưa Vietnam
159 I9 Phan Thiêt Vietnam
159 I9 Phan Thiêt, Vinh b. Vietnam
178 G6 Phaphund Uttar Prad. India
179 K6 Phaplu Nepal
28 E3 Pharis Northern Ireland U.K.
158 H4 Phat Diêm Vietnam
159 E11 Phatthalung Thai.
158 D5 Phayao Thai.
158 E7 Phayuhakhiri Thai.
179 O7 Phek Nagaland India
206 E3 Phelp r. N.T. Austr.
116 H6 Phelps NY U.S.A.
110 E3 Phelps WI U.S.A.
107 K3 Phelps Lake Sask. Can.
158 F6 Phen Thai.
116 G11 Phenix VA U.S.A.
115 E9 Phenix City AL U.S.A.
96 G1 Phephane watercourse S. Africa
159 D8 Phet Buri Thai.
158 E6 Phetchabun Thai.
159 G7 Phiafai Laos
158 E6 Phichai Thai.
158 E6 Phichit Thai.
96 C9 Philadelphia S. Africa
121 K9 Philadelphia MS U.S.A.
117 J4 Philadelphia NY U.S.A.
118 E5 Philadelphia PA U.S.A.
118 E5 Philadelphia County county PA U.S.A.
85 G4 Philae tourist site Egypt
120 E3 Philip SD U.S.A.
Philip Atoll Micronesia see Sorol
204 □1 Philip Island Norfolk I.
Philippeville Alg. see Skikda
45 G8 Philippeville Belgium
116 E9 Philippi WV U.S.A.
206 G8 Philippi, Lake salt flat Qld Austr.
45 E6 Philippine Neth.
216 D4 Philippine Basin sea feature N. Pacific Ocean
154 D4 Philippines country Asia
152 F3 Philippine Sea N. Pacific Ocean
216 D4 Philippine Trench sea feature N. Pacific Ocean
97 J6 Philippolis S. Africa
97 J6 Philippolis Road S. Africa
Philippopolis Bulg. see Plovdiv
52 E3 Philippsburg Ger.
53 P4 Philippsreut Ger.
49 J9 Philippsthal (Werra) Ger.
131 L4 Philipsburg St Maarten Neth. Antilles
122 H3 Philipsburg MT U.S.A.
116 G8 Philipsburg PA U.S.A.
44 F5 Philipsdam barrage Neth.
104 D3 Philip Smith Mountains AK U.S.A.
96 I6 Philipstown S. Africa
205 J8 Phillip Island Vic. Austr.
204 □2 Phillip Point Lord Howe I. Austr.
209 F12 Phillips r. W.A. Austr.
117 □O4 Phillips ME U.S.A.
110 D4 Phillips WI U.S.A.
106 E5 Phillips Arm B.C. Can.
120 F6 Phillipsburg KS U.S.A.
118 E3 Phillipsburg NJ U.S.A.
105 J1 Phillips Inlet Nunavut Can.
204 E3 Phillipson, Lake salt flat S.A. Austr.
208 H4 Phillips Range hills W.A. Austr.
116 F8 Phillipston PA U.S.A.
117 L6 Philmont NY U.S.A.
116 E12 Philpott Reservoir VA U.S.A.
158 G7 Phimun Mangsahan Thai.
97 L3 Phiritona S. Africa
158 E6 Phitsanulok Thai.
110 E4 Phlox WI U.S.A.
Phnom Penh Cambodia see Phnum Pénh
159 G9 Phnum Pénh Cambodia
159 E11 Pho, Laem pt Thai.
158 G5 Phô Châu Vietnam
117 K6 Phoenicia NY U.S.A.
99 □1b Phoenix Mauritius
125 T8 Phoenix AZ U.S.A.
117 I5 Phoenix NY U.S.A.
Phoenix Island Phoenix Is Kiribati see Rawaki
199 I2 Phoenix Islands Kiribati
118 D4 Phoenixville PA U.S.A.
97 N2 Phola S. Africa
158 G3 Phô Lu Vietnam
97 L3 Phomolong S. Africa
158 F7 Phon Thai.
158 H6 Phong Nha Vietnam
158 F4 Phôngsali Laos
Phong Saly Laos see Phôngsali
158 F3 Phong Thô Vietnam
158 F5 Phon Phisai Thai.
158 F6 Phon Thong Thai.
205 I8 Phoques Bay Tas. Austr.
206 H6 Phosphate Hill Qld Austr.
178 F2 Photaksur Jammu and Kashmir
158 F5 Phou San mt. Laos
158 E5 Phrae Thai.
158 D5 Phrao Thai.
159 D10 Phra Saeng Thai.
159 D10 Phra Thong, Ko i. Thai.
158 E6 Phrom Phiram Thai.
159 F9 Phsar Ream Cambodia
158 H6 Phu Bai Vietnam
159 G7 Phuchong-Nayoi National Park Thai.
Phu Cuong Vietnam see Thu Dâu Môt
158 G4 Phuc Yên Vietnam
94 E4 Phuduhudu Botswana
179 L6 Phuentsholing Bhutan
159 D11 Phuket Thai.
159 D11 Phuket, Ko i. Thai.
158 E6 Phu-khieo Wildlife Reserve nature res. Thai.
179 J9 Phulbani Orissa India
185 L8 Phulji Pak.
158 H6 Phu Lôc Vietnam
159 G10 Phu Lôc Vietnam
178 I7 Phulpur Uttar Prad. India
158 E6 Phu Luang National Park Thai.
158 G4 Phu Ly Vietnam
159 F8 Phumĭ Bânhchok Kon Cambodia
159 G8 Phumĭ Chhlong Cambodia
159 G9 Phumĭ Chhuk Cambodia
159 G7 Phumĭ Kâmpóng Srâlau Cambodia
159 G8 Phumĭ Kâmpóng Trâlach Cambodia
159 F9 Phumĭ Kaôh Kŏng Cambodia
159 F8 Phumĭ Kiliĕk Cambodia
159 F7 Phumĭ Kon Kriel Cambodia
159 F8 Phumĭ Koŭk Kduŏch Cambodia
159 G8 Phumĭ Mlu Prey Cambodia
159 F8 Phumĭ Prâmaôy Cambodia
159 G8 Phumĭ Prêk Kak Cambodia
159 F7 Phumĭ Sâmraông Cambodia
159 G8 Phumĭ Thalabârĭvăt Cambodia
159 G8 Phumĭ Toêng Cambodia
159 G9 Phumĭ Trâm Kak Cambodia
159 F7 Phumĭ Trom Cambodia
159 F9 Phumĭ Veal Renh Cambodia
159 I7 Phu My Vietnam
159 G10 Phung Hiêp Vietnam
Phuntsholing Bhutan see Phuentsholing
159 H9 Phước Bưu Vietnam
159 H9 Phước Hai Vietnam
159 G10 Phước Long Vietnam
158 F4 Phu Phac Mo mt. Vietnam
158 F6 Phu Phan National Park Thai.
159 F9 Phu Quôc, Đao i. Vietnam
159 I9 Phu Quy, Đao i. Vietnam
97 M4 Phuthaditjhaba S. Africa
158 G4 Phu Tho Vietnam
Phu Vinh Vietnam see Tra Vinh
158 F6 Phu Wiang Thai.
158 G4 Phu Yên Vietnam
158 C5 Phyu Myanmar
43 J10 Pia France
209 D9 Pia Aboriginal Reserve W.A. Austr.
157 J4 Piabung, Gunung mt. Indon.
140 D3 Piaca Brazil
142 B4 Piacatu Brazil
70 H5 Piacenza Italy
70 H6 Piacenza prov. Italy
109 G3 Piacouadie, Lac l. Que. Can.
70 I5 Piadena Italy
108 E2 Piagochioui r. Que. Can.
156 E4 Piai, Tanjung pt Malaysia
147 G3 Piamonte Arg.
205 L4 Pian r. N.S.W. Austr.
72 B3 Piana Corse France
72 A6 Piana, Isola i. Sardegna Italy
72 A9 Piana, Isola i. Sardegna Italy
70 E7 Piana Crixia Italy
74 E8 Piana degli Albanesi Sicilia Italy
73 K3 Piana del Fucino plain Italy
74 H9 Piana di Catania plain Sicilia Italy
72 H2 Piancastagnaio Italy
71 M8 Piandimeleto Italy
73 M3 Pianella Italy
70 G6 Pianello Val Tidone Italy
205 I6 Piangil Vic. Austr.
169 L7 Pianguan Shanxi China
158 D1 Pianma Yunnan China
71 K7 Piano del Voglio Italy
71 K7 Pianoro Italy
72 E2 Pianosa Italy
72 E2 Pianosa, Isola i. Italy
73 P3 Pianosa, Isole is Italy
72 C5 Pianotolli-Caldarello Corse France
72 H2 Piansano Italy
131 □7 Piarco airport Trin. and Tob.
64 E4 Pias Port.
62 G4 Pias, Embalse de resr Spain
55 J3 Piaseczno Mazowieckie Pol.
54 C2 Piaseczno Zachodniopomorskie Pol.
54 C3 Piasek Pol.
55 K4 Piaski Lubelskie Pol.
54 F4 Piaski Wielkopolskie Pol.
140 F4 Piassabussu Brazil
55 I3 Piastów Pol.
140 E5 Piatã Brazil
55 H3 Piątek Pol.
55 K2 Piątnica Poduchowna Pol.
77 N7 Piatra Romania
77 O4 Piatra Neamț Romania
77 M6 Piatra Olt Romania
77 O4 Piatra Șoimului Romania
43 E10 Piau-Engaly France
140 E3 Piauí r. Brazil
140 E3 Piauí state Brazil
140 E4 Piauí, Serra de hills Brazil
71 N4 Piave r. Italy
128 A2 Piaxtla r. Mex.
70 I7 Piazza al Serchio Italy
74 G9 Piazza Armerina Sicilia Italy
70 H4 Piazza Brembana Italy
70 H4 Piazzatorre Italy
70 I3 Piazzi, Cima de' mt. Italy
145 B8 Piazzi, Isla i. Chile
71 L4 Piazzola sul Brenta Italy
92 B2 Pibor r. Sudan
92 B3 Pibor Post Sudan
43 G8 Pibrac France
108 C3 Pic r. Ont. Can.
138 C5 Pica Chile
125 U9 Picacho AZ U.S.A.
128 B3 Picachos Mex.
126 B3 Picachos, Cerro dos mt. Mex.
71 Q5 Pićan Croatia
67 C8 Picaracho mt. Spain
36 E4 Picardie admin. reg. France
36 C4 Picardie reg. France
Picardy reg. France see Picardie
67 E9 Picassent Spain
38 I3 Picauville France
121 K10 Picayune MS U.S.A.
71 L2 Picco della Croce mt. Italy
41 K6 Piccolo, Lago l. Italy
127 N8 Pich Mex.
146 B5 Pichachén, Paso pass Arg./Chile
126 F3 Picháchic Mex.
144 D1 Pichanal Arg.
146 B2 Pichasca Chile
50 D4 Picher Ger.
146 C3 Pichi Ciego Arg.
146 B3 Pichidangui Chile
146 A4 Pichilemu Chile
126 D5 Pichilingue Mex.
146 E6 Pichi Mahuida Arg.
136 B5 Pichincha prov. Ecuador
59 I3 Pichl bei Wels Austria
178 G7 Pichor Madh. Prad. India
127 M9 Pichucalco Mex.
110 H1 Pic Island Ont. Can.
116 E10 Pickens WV U.S.A.
110 C1 Pickerel Lake Ont. Can.
111 O6 Pickering Ont. Can.
29 P5 Pickering North Yorkshire, England U.K.
29 P5 Pickering, Vale of val. England U.K.
137 G3 Pickersgill Guyana
111 J3 Pickford MI U.S.A.
130 C3 Pickle Bank sea feature Caribbean Sea
108 B3 Pickle Lake Ont. Can.
98 □1c Pico i. Azores
98 □1c Pico mt. Pico Azores
73 L5 Pico Italy
63 J8 Pico, Puerto del pass Spain
126 □P10 Pico Bonito, Parque Nacional nat. park Hond.
72 D9 Picocca r. Italy
137 E4 Pico da Neblina, Parque Nacional do nat. park Brazil
129 J6 Pico de Orizaba, Parque Nacional nat. park Mex.
128 E6 Pico de Tancítaro, Parque Nacional nat. park Mex.
98 □1c Pico Gorda vol. Faial Azores
65 K2 Picón Spain
140 E3 Picos Brazil
62 C5 Picos, Punta dos pt Spain
63 K2 Picos de Europa, Parque Nacional de los nat. park Spain
136 B6 Picota Peru
62 C6 Picoto Port.
145 D7 Pico Truncado Arg.
36 D4 Picquigny France
110 H1 Pic River Ont. Can.
205 M6 Picton N.S.W. Austr.
108 E5 Picton Ont. Can.
203 I8 Picton South I. N.Z.
205 K10 Picton, Mount Tas. Austr.
109 I4 Pictou N.S. Can.
106 H5 Picture Butte Alta Can.
110 H3 Pictured Rocks National Lakeshore nature res. MI U.S.A.
118 B2 Picture Rocks PA U.S.A.
131 □1 Picua, Punta pt Puerto Rico
140 F3 Picuí Brazil
146 C6 Picún Leufú Arg.
146 C6 Picún Leufú r. Arg.
185 J9 Pidarak Pak.
55 M5 Pidberezzya Ukr.
55 L6 Pidbuzh Ukr.
Piddle r. England U.K. see Trent
30 H6 Piddletrenthide Dorset, England U.K.
16 E4 Pidhaytsi Ukr.
16 J5 Pidhorodna Ukr.
17 O5 Pidhorodne Ukr.
55 L6 Pidhorodtsi Ukr.
53 N6 Piding Ger.
99 □3a Pidjani Njazidja Comoros
16 E4 Pidkamin' Ukr.
17 L5 Pidlisne Ukr.
19 R1 Pid'ma Rus. Fed.
176 G9 Pidurutalagala mt. Sri Lanka
16 F4 Pidvolochys'k Ukr.
16 J5 Pidvysoke Ukr.
54 G3 Piechcin Pol.
54 D5 Piechowice Pol.
55 J2 Piecki Pol.
54 E2 Piecnik Pol.
98 □1c Piedade Pico Azores
142 D5 Piedade Brazil
64 B6 Piedade, Ponta da pt Port.
146 C2 Pie de Palo, Sierra mts Arg.
72 C3 Piedicorte-di-Gaggio Corse France
72 C3 Piedicroce Corse France
73 J2 Piediluco, Lago di l. Italy
75 I8 Piedimonte Etneo Sicilia Italy
73 M5 Piedimonte Matese Italy
70 E3 Piedimulera Italy
Piedmont admin. reg. Italy see Piemonte
115 E9 Piedmont AL U.S.A.
121 J7 Piedmont MO U.S.A.
116 D8 Piedmont OH U.S.A.
116 D8 Piedmont Lake OH U.S.A.
63 Q6 Piedra r. Spain
64 F3 Piedra Aguda, Embalse de resr Spain
65 K2 Piedrabuena Spain
145 C6 Piedra de Águila Arg.
129 J8 Piedra de Olla, Cerro mt. Mex.
Piedrafita Spain see Pedrafita do Cebreiro
62 F3 Piedrafita, Porto de pass Spain
62 H3 Piedrafita de Babia Spain
63 J8 Piedrahita Spain
63 K8 Piedralaves Spain
64 E6 Piedras, Embalse de resr Spain
147 I4 Piedras, Punta pt Arg.
62 G9 Piedras Albas Spain
62 I1 Piedras Blancas Spain
124 K6 Piedras Blancas Point CA U.S.A.
63 L2 Piedrasluengas, Puerto de pass Spain
127 N9 Piedras Negras Guat.
127 I3 Piedras Negras Coahuila Mex.
129 K7 Piedras Negras Veracruz Mex.
147 I3 Piedra Sola Uru.
147 F4 Piedritas Arg.
72 I2 Piegaro Italy
42 F4 Piégut-Pluviers France
110 E1 Pie Island Ont. Can.
54 G5 Piekary Śląskie Pol.
50 I1 Piekberg hill Ger.
55 I5 Piekoszów Pol.
20 S5 Pieksämäki Fin.
89 E3 Piéla Burkina
59 L3 Pielach r. Austria
20 S5 Pielavesi Fin.
20 S5 Pielavesi l. Fin.
54 D4 Pielgrzymka Pol.
20 T5 Pielinen l. Fin.
20 N3 Pieljekaise nationalpark nat. park Sweden
41 F10 Piémanson, Plage de coastal area France
70 D6 Piemonte admin. reg. Italy
97 M1 Pienaarsrivier S. Africa
54 E2 Pieniężnica Pol.
23 Q7 Pieniężno Pol.
55 I6 Pieniński Park Narodowy nat. park Pol.
57 J2 Pieninský nat. park Slovakia
54 E1 Pieńkowo Pol.
37 K5 Piennes France
54 D4 Pieńsk Pol.
72 H1 Pienza Italy
66 I4 Piera Spain
120 G4 Pierce NE U.S.A.
107 M4 Pierce Lake Man./Ont. Can.
107 I4 Pierceland Sask. Can.
110 I8 Pierceton IN U.S.A.
147 H6 Pieres Arg.
78 D2 Pieria mts Greece
26 K4 Pierowall Orkney, Scotland U.K.
120 E3 Pierre SD U.S.A.
121 J10 Pierre, Bayou r. MS U.S.A.
121 I10 Pierre Bayou r. LA U.S.A.
42 G4 Pierre-Buffière France
41 H7 Pierre-Châtel France
40 G3 Pierre-de-Bresse France
41 I10 Pierrefeu-du-Var France
43 D10 Pierrefitte-Nestalas France
37 J6 Pierrefitte-sur-Aire France
40 D4 Pierrefitte-sur-Loire France
36 E5 Pierrefonds France
40 J2 Pierrefontaine-les-Varans France
41 B7 Pierrefort France
41 F8 Pierrelatte France
37 K5 Pierrepont France
36 C6 Pierres France
40 D5 Pierre-sur-Haute mt. France
41 H9 Pierrevert France
131 □7 Pierreville Trin. and Tob.
99 □1a Pierrot Island Rodrigues I. Mauritius
36 G5 Pierry France
44 F5 Piershil Neth.
55 I5 Pierzchnica Pol.
51 D9 Piesau Ger.
58 G5 Piesendorf Austria
20 N3 Pieskehaure l. Sweden
54 D3 Pieski Pol.
52 B2 Piesport Ger.
57 G3 Piešťany Slovakia
55 I1 Pieszkowo Pol.
54 E5 Pieszyce Pol.
99 □1b Pieter Both hill Mauritius
97 O5 Pietermaritzburg S. Africa
Pietersaari Fin. see Jakobstad
Pietersburg S. Africa see Polokwane
96 I2 Piet Plessis S. Africa
73 M4 Pietrabbondante Italy
73 N4 Pietracatella Italy
72 C2 Pietracorbara Corse France
72 C3 Pietra-di-Verde Corse France
73 P6 Pietragalla Italy
72 C2 Pietralba Corse France
70 E7 Pietra Ligure Italy
71 M9 Pietralunga Italy
73 M5 Pietramelara Italy
73 O4 Pietramontecorvino Italy
74 G9 Pietraperzia Sicilia Italy
70 C7 Pietraporzio Italy
70 I8 Pietrasanta Italy
75 K6 Pietra Spada, Passo di pass Italy
73 N6 Pietrastornina Italy
73 M5 Pietravairano Italy
73 N5 Pietrelcina Italy
97 O3 Piet Retief S. Africa
57 L5 Pietroasa Bihor Romania
57 L6 Pietroasa Timiș Romania
72 B4 Pietrosella Corse France
77 M3 Pietrosu, Vârful mt. Romania
77 N3 Pietrosu, Vârful mt. Romania
77 M3 Pietrosul Mare nature res. Romania
54 G5 Pietrowice Wielkie Pol.
71 M3 Pieve d'Alpago Italy
70 F5 Pieve del Cairo Italy
58 C8 Pieve di Bono Italy
71 M3 Pieve di Cadore Italy
71 M3 Pieve di Cadore, Lago di l. Italy
71 K6 Pieve di Cento Italy
71 M4 Pieve di Soligo Italy
70 D7 Pieve di Teco Italy
73 K1 Pievefavera, Lago di l. Italy
71 J7 Pievepelago Italy
71 M8 Pieve Santo Stefano Italy
73 K1 Pieve Torina Italy
70 E3 Pieve Vergonte Italy
36 F7 Piffonds France
108 B3 Pigeon r. Can./U.S.A.
111 K6 Pigeon MI U.S.A.
111 L8 Pigeon Bay Ont. Can.
203 G10 Pigeon Bay South I. N.Z.
130 □ Pigeon Island Jamaica
106 H4 Pigeon Lake Alta Can.
131 □3 Pigeon Point St Lucia
131 □5 Pigeon Point Trin. and Tob.
110 E1 Pigeon River MN U.S.A.
116 F11 Pigg r. VA U.S.A.
121 J7 Piggott AR U.S.A.
97 P1 Pigg's Peak Swaziland
73 K4 Piglio Italy
70 D8 Pigna Italy
41 D9 Pignan France
41 I10 Pignans France
73 L5 Pignataro Interamna Italy
74 G1 Pignataro Maggiore Italy
73 P6 Pignola Italy
78 C3 Pigon, Limni l. Greece
Pigs, Bay of Cuba see Cochinos, Bahía de
147 F5 Pigüé Arg.
129 H4 Piguicas mt. Mex.
202 I3 Piha North I. N.Z.
202 H6 Pihama North I. N.Z.
178 H6 Pihani Uttar Prad. India
201 □2a Piha Passage Tonga
171 K2 Pi He r. China
Pihkva järv l. Estonia/Rus. Fed. see Pskov, Lake
21 T6 Pihlajavesi l. Fin.
21 P6 Pihlava Fin.
20 R5 Pihtipudas Fin.
128 D6 Pihuamo Mex.
18 F1 Piikkiö Fin.
20 R4 Piippola Fin.
18 K3 Piirissaar i. Estonia
18 H2 Piirsalu Estonia
20 T4 Piispajärvi Fin.
200 □4a Piis-Panewu i. Chuuk Micronesia
Piji Sichuan China see Puge
127 M10 Pijijiapan Mex.
44 F4 Pijnacker Neth.
19 R2 Pikalevo Rus. Fed.
18 J3 Pikasilla Estonia
116 G6 Pike NY U.S.A.
116 D9 Pike WV U.S.A.
111 M5 Pike Bay Ont. Can.
118 E2 Pike County county PA U.S.A.
153 K5 Pikelot i. Micronesia
118 C2 Pikes Creek Reservoir PA U.S.A.
123 L7 Pikes Peak CO U.S.A.
118 B6 Pikesville MD U.S.A.
96 C8 Piketberg S. Africa
116 B9 Piketon OH U.S.A.
116 C11 Pikeville KY U.S.A.
115 E8 Pikeville TN U.S.A.
Pikihatiti b. Stewart I. N.Z. see Port Pegasus
44 I2 Pikmeer l. Neth.
169 R7 Pikou Liaoning China
90 C4 Pikounda Congo
147 H5 Pila Arg.
71 M6 Pila Italy
54 E2 Piła Pol.
67 C11 Pila mt. Spain
147 I5 Pila, Laguna de l. Arg.
144 F2 Pilagá r. Arg.
97 L1 Pilanesberg National Park S. Africa
178 E5 Pilani Rajasthan India
147 H4 Pilar Buenos Aires Arg.
147 F2 Pilar Córdoba Arg.
147 G2 Pilar Santa Fé Arg.
139 F6 Pilar Para.
154 F7 Pilar Phil.
145 B9 Pilar, Cabo c. Chile
140 C5 Pilar de Goiás Brazil
67 D12 Pilar de la Horadada Spain
142 D5 Pilar do Sul Brazil
154 C8 Pilas i. Phil.
64 G6 Pilas Spain
154 C8 Pilas Channel Phil.
41 F6 Pilat, Mont mt. France
41 F6 Pilat, Parc Naturel Régional du nature res. France
70 E2 Pilatus mt. Switz.
55 J4 Pilawa Pol.
54 E2 Piława r. Pol.
54 E5 Piława Górna Pol.
138 D5 Pilaya r. Bol.
145 C6 Pilcaniyeu Arg.
54 D5 Pilchowicie, Jezioro l. Pol.
50 J3 Pilchowo Pol.
139 F6 Pilcomayo r. Bol./Para.
54 E2 Pile, Jezioro l. Pol.
176 F6 Piler Andhra Prad. India
67 E10 Piles Spain
Píli Kos Greece see Pyli
154 D5 Pili Luzon Phil.
138 D5 Pili, Cerro mt. Chile
18 I6 Piliakalnis hill Lith.
178 E5 Pilibangan Rajasthan India
178 G5 Pilibhit Uttar Prad. India
55 H5 Pilica Pol.
55 J4 Pilica r. Pol.
Pilipinas country Asia see Philippines
57 I4 Pilis Hungary
57 H4 Pilis hill Hungary
57 H4 Piliscsév Hungary
57 H4 Pilisi park Hungary
57 H4 Pilisszentiván Hungary
57 H4 Pilisszentkereszt Hungary
57 H4 Pilisvörösvár Hungary
58 E5 Pill Austria
29 K5 Pillar hill England U.K.
98 □2a Pillar Bay Ascension S. Atlantic Ocean
138 C3 Pillcopata Peru
58 G4 Pillersee l. Austria
205 L4 Pilliga N.S.W. Austr.
29 L6 Pilling Lancashire, England U.K.
147 G3 Pillo, Isla del i. Arg.
118 B3 Pillow PA U.S.A.
124 J2 Pillsbury, Lake CA U.S.A.
14 I5 Pil'na Rus. Fed.
17 P3 Pil'na Ukr.
17 P3 Pil'na r. Ukr.
30 G4 Pilning South Gloucestershire, England U.K.
14 L1 Pil'nya, Ozero l. Rus. Fed.
142 D2 Pilões, Serra dos mts Brazil
130 E4 Pilón Cuba
63 J2 Piloña r. Spain
Pílos Greece see Pylos
107 I2 Pilot Lake N.W.T. Can.
128 B5 Piloto Mex.
147 H2 Piloto Ávila Arg.
124 O3 Pilot Peak NV U.S.A.
104 C4 Pilot Point AK U.S.A.
122 E4 Pilot Rock OR U.S.A.
104 B3 Pilot Station AK U.S.A.
121 K11 Pilottown LA U.S.A.
53 L3 Pilsach Ger.
Pilsen Czech Rep. see Plzeň
110 G5 Pilsen WI U.S.A.
55 H6 Pilsko mt. Pol.
53 N4 Pilsting Ger.
18 E4 Piltene Latvia
185 N9 Pilu Pak.
57 K5 Pilu Romania
158 C5 Pilu, Nam r. Myanmar
18 G7 Pilvė r. Lith.
18 G7 Pilviškiai Lith.
162 M3 Pil'vo Rus. Fed.
55 J6 Pilzno Pol.
125 W9 Pima AZ U.S.A.
139 E2 Pimenta Bueno Brazil
72 C9 Pimentel Sardegna Italy
178 E9 Pimpalner Mahar. India
30 H6 Pimperne Dorset, England U.K.
178 D9 Pimpri Gujarat India
90 D4 Pimu Dem. Rep. Congo
178 G3 Pin r. India
158 B4 Pin r. Myanmar
16 F1 Pina r. Belarus
66 D5 Pina Spain
67 D7 Pina mt. Spain
66 D4 Pina, Embalse de resr Spain
125 S10 Pinacate, Cerro del mt. Mex.
63 L5 Piña de Esgueva Spain
178 G6 Pinahat Uttar Prad. India
125 V9 Pinaleno Mountains AZ U.S.A.
154 C5 Pinamalayan Mindoro Phil.
147 I5 Pinamar Arg.
Pinang Malaysia see George Town
156 D2 Pinang i. Malaysia
156 D2 Pinang state Malaysia
157 L2 Pinangah Sabah Malaysia
65 I7 Pinar mt. Spain
67 L8 Pinar, Cap des c. Spain
65 O4 Pinar, Puerto del pass Spain
188 H4 Pınarbaşı Turkey
130 B2 Pinar del Río Cuba
188 C3 Pinarhisar Turkey
79 I5 Pınarköy Turkey
191 A7 Pınarlar Turkey
191 E6 Pınarlı Turkey
136 B5 Piñas Ecuador
70 C6 Pinasca Italy
152 F3 Pinatubo, Mount vol. Phil.
57 H5 Pincehely Hungary
31 L2 Pinchbeck Lincolnshire, England U.K.
106 H5 Pincher Creek Alta Can.
120 K6 Pinckneyville IL U.S.A.
39 J4 Pinçon, Mont hill France
111 K6 Pinconning MI U.S.A.
55 I5 Pińczów Pol.
140 B5 Pindaíba Brazil
143 E5 Pindamonhangaba Brazil
209 C10 Pindar W.A. Austr.
178 G4 Pindar r. India
140 D2 Pindaré r. Brazil
140 D2 Pindaré Mirim Brazil
185 O5 Pind Dadan Khay Pak.
Píndhos Óros mts Greece see Pindos
185 O6 Pindi Bhattian Pak.
185 O5 Pindi Gheb Pak.
140 C2 Pindobal Brazil
78 B3 Pindos mts Greece
78 C3 Pindos nat. park Greece
178 H8 Pindrei Madh. Prad. India
Pindus Mountains Greece see Pindos
178 D7 Pindwara Rajasthan India
204 H5 Pine watercourse N.S.W. Austr.
110 I5 Pine r. MI U.S.A.
110 J6 Pine r. MI U.S.A.
110 D6 Pine r. WI U.S.A.
110 F4 Pine r. WI U.S.A.
109 K4 Pine, Cape Nfld and Lab. Can.
121 I8 Pine Bluff AR U.S.A.
122 L6 Pine Bluffs WY U.S.A.
119 G1 Pine Bush NY U.S.A.
110 B4 Pine City MN U.S.A.
206 C2 Pine Creek N.T. Austr.
116 H7 Pine Creek r. PA U.S.A.
125 P1 Pine Creek watercourse NV U.S.A.
124 L3 Pinecrest CA U.S.A.
63 O8 Pineda de Cigüela Spain
63 N4 Pineda de la Sierra Spain
66 K4 Pineda de Mar Spain
122 J5 Pinedale WY U.S.A.
107 L5 Pine Dock Man. Can.
107 L5 Pine Falls Man. Can.
123 E8 Pine Flat Lake CA U.S.A.
14 H2 Pinega Rus. Fed.
14 H2 Pinega r. Rus. Fed.
209 C9 Pinegrove W.A. Austr.
116 A10 Pine Grove KY U.S.A.
111 R9 Pine Grove PA U.S.A.
116 E9 Pine Grove WV U.S.A.
206 D7 Pine Hill N.T. Austr.
118 F5 Pine Hill NJ U.S.A.
115 G11 Pine Hills FL U.S.A.
107 J4 Pinehouse Lake Sask. Can.
107 J4 Pinehouse Lake l. Sask. Can.
118 C6 Pinehurst MD U.S.A.
108 B2 Pineimuta r. Ont. Can.
78 D3 Pineios r. Greece
78 C5 Pineiou, Techniti Limni resr Greece
110 B5 Pine Island MN U.S.A.
119 G2 Pine Island NY U.S.A.
212 R2 Pine Island Bay Antarctica
212 R1 Pine Island Glacier Antarctica
115 F12 Pine Islands FL U.S.A.
115 G13 Pine Islands FL U.S.A.
62 G5 Pinela Port.
121 I10 Pineland TX U.S.A.
63 L5 Piñel de Abajo Spain
106 F4 Pine Le Moray Provincial Park park B.C. Can.
203 D12 Pinelheugh mt. South I. N.Z.
115 F12 Pinellas Park FL U.S.A.
124 K6 Pine Mountain CA U.S.A.
125 S7 Pine Peak AZ U.S.A.
106 H2 Pine Point N.W.T. Can.
106 H2 Pine Point pt N.W.T. Can.
147 I3 Piñera Uru.
124 M4 Pineridge CA U.S.A.
120 D4 Pine Ridge SD U.S.A.
120 D4 Pine Ridge Indian Reservation res. SD U.S.A.
70 C6 Pinerolo Italy
Pines, Isle of i. Cuba see La Juventud, Isla de
Pines, Isle of i. New Caledonia see Pins, Île des
121 H9 Pines, Lake o' the TX U.S.A.
70 F4 Pinet di Appiano Tradate, Parco del park Italy
73 M2 Pineto Italy
125 W7 Pinetop AZ U.S.A.
97 O5 Pinetown S. Africa
43 E6 Pineuilh France
111 R7 Pine Valley NY U.S.A.
116 B12 Pineville KY U.S.A.
121 I10 Pineville LA U.S.A.
118 E4 Pineville PA U.S.A.
116 D11 Pineville WV U.S.A.
36 H7 Piney France
158 E7 Ping, Mae Nam r. Thai.
178 D1 Pingal Jammu and Kashmir
168 H8 Ping'an Qinghai China
Ping'anyi Qinghai China see Ping'an
209 E12 Pingaring W.A. Austr.
170 F5 Pingba Guizhou China
170 D7 Pingbian Yunnan China
170 F3 Pingchang Sichuan China
170 C5 Pingchuan Sichuan China
169 P9 Ping Dao i. China
169 M8 Pingding Shanxi China
171 I2 Pingdingshan Henan China
Pingdong Taiwan see P'ingtung
169 P8 Pingdu Shandong China
209 D12 Pingelly W.A. Austr.
162 D7 Pinggang Liaoning China
59 N5 Pinggau Austria
169 O6 Pinggu Beijing China
170 F7 Pingguo Guangxi China
171 J7 Pinghai Guangdong China
171 K6 Pinghe Fujian China
Pinghu Guizhou China see Pingtang
171 M3 Pinghu Zhejiang China
171 I4 Pingjiang Hunan China
170 H6 Pingle Guangxi China
170 G2 Pingli Shaanxi China
168 J9 Pingliang Gansu China
169 L9 Pinglu Shanxi China
168 J7 Pingluo Ningxia China
168 J7 Pingluozhan Ningxia China
Pingma Guangxi China see Tiandong
171 L5 Pingnan Fujian China
170 H7 Pingnan Guangxi China
169 J9 Pingquan Gansu China
169 P6 Pingquan Hebei China
209 E12 Pingrup W.A. Austr.
169 N7 Pingshan Hebei China
170 E4 Pingshan Sichuan China
171 I6 Pingshi Guangdong China
171 L6 Pingtan Fujian China
170 F6 Pingtang Guizhou China
171 M7 P'ingtung Taiwan
20 □C1 Þingvallavatn l. Iceland
20 □C1 Þingvellir Iceland
170 E2 Pingwu Sichuan China
Pingxi Guizhou China see Yuping
Pingxiang Gansu China see Tongwei
170 F7 Pingxiang Guangxi China
171 I5 Pingxiang Jiangxi China
169 S2 Pingyang Heilong. China
171 M5 Pingyang Zhejiang China
169 M8 Pingyao Shanxi China
169 O9 Pingyi Shandong China
169 O8 Pingyin Shandong China
171 J2 Pingyu Henan China
171 J6 Pingyuan Guangdong China
169 O8 Pingyuan Shandong China
Pingyuan Yunnan China see Yingjiang
170 D7 Pingyuanjie Yunnan China
170 G6 Pingzhai Guizhou China
142 D5 Pinhal Brazil
64 B3 Pinhal Novo Port.
62 E6 Pinhão Port.
140 D2 Pinheiro Brazil
62 D6 Pinheiro Porto Port.
64 B4 Pinheiro Setúbal Port.
144 G3 Pinheiro Machado Brazil
143 G3 Pinheiros Brazil
62 F7 Pinhel Port.
30 F6 Pinhoe Devon, England U.K.
137 E6 Pinhuã r. Brazil
156 C4 Pini i. Indon.
65 N3 Pinilla r. Spain
63 M7 Pinilla, Embalse de resr Spain
63 Q7 Pinilla de Molina Spain
63 J5 Pinilla de Toro Spain
Piniós r. Greece see Pineios
209 C12 Pinjarra W.A. Austr.
209 G11 Pinjin W.A. Austr.
209 G11 Pinjin Aboriginal Reserve W.A. Austr.
59 N5 Pinkafeld Austria
204 E5 Pinkawilinie Conservation Park nature res. S.A. Austr.
206 B3 Pinkerton Range hills N.T. Austr.
106 F3 Pink Mountain B.C. Can.
158 C4 Pinlaung Myanmar
158 B2 Pinlebu Myanmar
203 H8 Pinnacle mt. South I. N.Z.
116 G9 Pinnacle hill VA/WV U.S.A.
124 K5 Pinnacles National Monument nat. park CA U.S.A.
204 H6 Pinnaroo S.A. Austr.
48 I3 Pinnau r. Ger.
48 I3 Pinneberg Ger.
78 F2 Pinnes, Akra pt Greece
51 K7 Pinnow Ger.
72 C2 Pino Corse France
62 H5 Pino Spain
63 K3 Pino del Río Spain
62 H8 Pinofranqueado Spain
157 I5 Pinoh r. Indon.
41 C6 Pinols France
124 O7 Pinon Hills CA U.S.A.
62 D3 Piñor Spain
128 F3 Pinos Mex.
66 I4 Pinós hill Spain
124 M7 Pinos, Mount CA U.S.A.
67 C11 Pinoso Spain
63 O7 Pinoso mt. Spain
65 L6 Pinos-Puente Spain
129 I9 Pinotepa Nacional Mex.
155 A5 Pinrang Sulawesi Indon.
155 B5 Pinrang Sulawesi Indon.
99 □2b Pins, Anse aux b. Mahé Seychelles
200 □5 Pins, Île des i. New Caledonia
111 M7 Pins, Pointe aux pt Ont. Can.
43 H6 Pinsac France
59 I4 Pinsdorf Austria
16 F1 Pinsk Belarus
63 R4 Pinsoro Spain
136 □ Pinta, Isla i. Islas Galápagos Ecuador
125 S9 Pinta, Sierra hill AZ U.S.A.
123 L9 Pintada Creek watercourse NM U.S.A.
147 I2 Pintado Grande Uru.
138 C5 Pintados Chile
66 C2 Pintano Spain
157 L2 Pintasan Sabah Malaysia
63 M8 Pinto Spain
125 S4 Pintura UT U.S.A.
72 C6 Pinu, Monte hill Italy
26 G12 Pinwherry South Ayrshire, Scotland U.K.
71 N3 Pinzano al Tagliamento Italy
58 F5 Pinzgau val. Austria
62 F7 Pinzio Port.
71 J3 Pinzolo Italy
71 N8 Piobbico Italy
125 R4 Pioche NV U.S.A.
91 E6 Piodi Dem. Rep. Congo
200 □6 Pio Island Solomon Is
140 E3 Pio IX Brazil
41 F8 Piolenc France
70 G5 Pioltello Italy
73 M2 Piomba r. Italy
72 F2 Piombino Italy
72 E2 Piombino, Canale di sea chan. Italy
71 L4 Piombino Dese Italy
116 A7 Pioneer OH U.S.A.
122 H4 Pioneer Mountains MT U.S.A.
193 K2 Pioner, Ostrov i. Severnaya Zemlya Rus. Fed.
18 D7 Pionerskiy Kaliningradskaya Oblast' Rus. Fed.
192 H3 Pionerskiy Khanty-Mansiyskiy Avtonomnyy Okrug Rus. Fed.
55 J4 Pionki Pol.
40 B4 Pionsat France
202 J5 Piopio North I. N.Z.
73 J1 Pioraco Italy
137 F5 Piorini r. Brazil
137 F5 Piorini, Lago l. Brazil
70 C6 Piossasco Italy
54 E4 Piotrkowice Pol.
54 G3 Piotrków Kujawski Pol.
55 H4 Piotrków Trybunalski Pol.
71 M5 Piove di Sacco Italy
71 K4 Piovene Rocchette Italy
70 G3 Pioverna r. Italy
184 I8 Pīp Iran
162 F7 Pipa Dingzi mt. China
144 D3 Pipanaco, Salar de salt flat Arg.
178 D6 Pipar Rajasthan India
178 D6 Pipar Road Rajasthan India
78 F3 Piperi i. Greece
124 O4 Piper Peak NV U.S.A.
118 E4 Pipersville PA U.S.A.
107 K5 Pipestone Man. Can.
108 B2 Pipestone r. Ont. Can.
120 G4 Pipestone MN U.S.A.
77 O3 Pipirig Romania
202 J6 Pipiriki North I. N.Z.
178 E5 Pipli Haryana India
109 G3 Pipmuacan, Réservoir resr Que. Can.
208 E6 Pippingarra Aboriginal Reserve W.A. Austr.
178 H9 Pipraud Chhattisgarh India
38 H6 Pipriac France
Piqan Xinjiang China see Shanshan
172 E6 Piqanlik Xinjiang China
116 A8 Piqua OH U.S.A.
43 F9 Pique r. France
63 O4 Piqueras, Puerto de pass Spain
140 F3 Piquet Carneiro Brazil
143 E5 Piquete Brazil
142 A6 Piquiri r. Brazil
139 G4 Piquiri r. Brazil
57 L4 Pir Romania
142 D5 Piracaia Brazil
142 C2 Piracanjuba Brazil
142 C3 Piracanjuba r. Brazil
142 D5 Piracicaba Brazil
142 C5 Piracicaba r. Brazil
143 F3 Piracicaba r. Brazil
142 D4 Piraçununga Brazil
140 E2 Piracuruca Brazil
201 □3a Pirae Tahiti Fr. Polynesia
Piraeus Greece see Peiraias
142 C6 Piraí do Sul Brazil
Piráievs Greece see Peiraias
74 H7 Piraino Sicilia Italy
142 C5 Piraju Brazil
142 C3 Pirajuba Brazil
142 C4 Pirajuí Brazil
191 L5 Pirallahı Adası Azer.
71 P4 Piran Slovenia
144 F2 Pirané Arg.
143 F4 Piranga Brazil
143 F4 Piranga r. Brazil
143 E5 Piranguinho Brazil
140 F4 Piranhas Alagoas Brazil
137 F6 Piranhas Amazonas Brazil
142 B2 Piranhas Goiás Brazil
142 B2 Piranhas r. Brazil
140 F3 Piranhas r. Brazil
140 D2 Pirapemas Brazil
139 E1 Pirapetinga Amazonas Brazil
143 F4 Pirapetinga Minas Gerais Brazil
142 A5 Pirapó r. Brazil
143 E2 Pirapora Brazil
142 B5 Pirapozinho Brazil
139 F4 Piraputangas Brazil
142 C6 Piraquara Brazil
137 G4 Pirara Guyana
144 G4 Pirarajá Uru.
179 J6 Pirari Nepal
144 G3 Piratini Brazil
142 C5 Piratininga Brazil
109 G3 Piraube, Lac l. Que. Can.
178 F7 Pirawa Rajasthan India
191 I5 Pirăză Azer.
31 K5 Pirbright Surrey, England U.K.
Pirchevan Azer. see Zängilan
55 M1 Pirčiupiai Lith.
145 C6 Pire Mahuida, Sierra mts Arg.

Pirenópolis Brazil
Pires do Rio Brazil
Pirganj Bangl.
Pirgos Greece see Pyrgos
Pirgovo Bulg.
Piriac-sur-Mer France
Piriaka North I. N.Z.
Piriápolis Uru.
Piricse Hungary
Pirin mts Bulg.
Pirin r. part Bulg.
Piripiri Brazil
Pirita r. Estonia
Piritu Falcón Venez.
Piritu Portuguesa Venez.
Pirizal Brazil
Pirka Austria
Pirkkala Fin.
Pir Kundil Afgh.
Pirlerkondu Turkey see Taşkent
Pirmasens Ger.
Pirmed Kerala India
Pir Morāl spring Iran
Pirna Ger.
Pirnmill North Ayrshire, Scotland U.K.
Pirojpur Bangl.
Piron r. Spain
Pirongia North I. N.Z.
Pirongia vol. North I. N.Z.
Pirongia Forest Park nature res. North I. N.Z.
Piros, Ozero i. Rus. Fed.
Pirot Srbija Serb. and Mont.
Pirovano Arg.
Pirpainti Bihar India
Pir Panjal Pass Jammu and Kashmir
Pir Panjal Range mts India/Pak.
Pirrasit Dağ hill Turkey
Pirsaat Azer.
Pirsaatçay r. Azer.
Pirto Hungary
Pirttivuopio Sweden
Piru Seram Indon.
Piru, Teluk b. Seram Indon.
Pir'yakh, Gora mt. Tajik. see Pir'yakh, Kühi
Pir'yakh, Kühi mt. Tajik.
Piryatin Ukr. see Pyryatyn
Piryetos Greece see Pyrgetos
Piryion Chios Greece see Pyrgi
Pirzada Afgh.
Pisa Italy
Pisa r. Pol.
Pisa r. Pol.
Pisae Italy see Pisa
Pisagua Chile
Pisamwe i. Chuuk Micronesia
Pisang i. Maluku Indon.
Pisany France
Pisar i. Chuuk Micronesia
Pisa Range mts South I. N.Z.
Pisau, Tanjung pt Malaysia
Pisaurum Italy see Pesaro
Pisba, Parque Nacional nat. park Col.
Piscataway U.S.A.
Pischelsdorf in der Steiermark Austria
Pişchia Romania
Pisciotta Italy
Pisco Peru
Pisco r. Peru
Pisco Elqui Chile
Pişcolt Romania
Pisek Czech Rep.
Piseco Lake N.Y. U.S.A.
Písek Czech Rep.
Pisgah, Mount South I. N.Z.
Pisgah, Mount South I. N.Z.
Pishan Xinjiang China
Pishcha Ukr.
Pishchane Ukr.
Pishchane Ukr.
Pishchanka Ukr.
Pishchanyy, Mys pt Ukr.
Pishin Iran
Pishin Pak.
Pishin Lora r. Pak.
Pishin, Ras pt Pak.
Pishpek Kyrg. see Bishkek
Pish Qal'eh Iran
Pisino i. Chuuk Micronesia
Pisidia reg. Turkey
Pising Sulawesi Indon.
Pisinimi AZ U.S.A.
Pisininin i. Chuuk Micronesia
Piskent Uzbek.
Piskivka Ukr.
Pisky Kharkiv'ska Oblast' Ukr.
Pisky Luhans'ka Oblast' Ukr.
Pismo Beach CA U.S.A.
Pismo Beach CA U.S.A.
Piso Firme Bol.
Pisogne Italy
Pissa r. Rus. Fed.
Pissis, Cerro mt. Arg.
Pisses France
Pistaos Rus. Fed.
Pistos r. Rus. Fed.
Pisticci Italy
Pistilfjörður b. Iceland
Pistoia Italy
Pistoia prov. Italy
Pistoriae Italy see Pistoia
Pistsovo Rus. Fed.
Pisuerga r. Spain
Piszczac Pol.
Pit r. CA U.S.A.
Pita Guinea
Pital Nfld and Lab. Can.
Pital Mex.
Pitalito Col.
Pitanga Brazil
Pitangueiras Brazil
Pitangui Brazil
Pitar Gujarat India
Pitarpunga Lake imp. l. N.S.W. Austr.
Pitarque Spain
Pitcairn Island S. Pacific Ocean
Pitche Guinea-Bissau
Pitch Lake Trin. and Tob.
Piteå Sweden
Piteälven r. Sweden
Piteglio Italy
Pitelino Rus. Fed.
Piterka Rus. Fed.
Piteşti Romania
Pithara W.A. Austr.
Pithiviers France
Pithoragarh Uttaranchal India
Piti Guam
Pitiquito Mex.
Pitigliano Italy
Pitihra Madh. Prad. India
Pitillas Spain
Pitillas, Laguna de l. Spain
Pituito Mex.
Pitlochry Perth and Kinross, Scotland U.K.
Pitman NJ U.S.A.
Pitmedden Aberdeenshire, Scotland U.K.
Pitminster Somerset, England U.K.
Pitoa Cameroon
Pitomača Croatia
Piton de la Fournaise vol. Réunion
Piton de la Petite Rivière Noire hill Mauritius
Piton des Neiges mt. Réunion
Pitong Sichuan China see Pixian
Pitres France
Pitrufquén Chile
Pitsane Siding Botswana
Pitschgau Austria
Pitseng Lesotho

Pitsford Reservoir England U.K.
Pitstone Buckinghamshire, England U.K.
Pitt Hampshire, England U.K.
Pittem Belgium
Pitten Austria
Pittentrail Highland, Scotland U.K.
Pittenweem Fife, Scotland U.K.
Pitti i. India
Pitti Sand Bank sea feature India
Pitt Island B.C. Can.
Pitt Island S. Pacific Ocean
Pitt Islands Santa Cruz Is Solomon Is see Vanikoro Islands
Pittsboro MS U.S.A.
Pittsboro NC U.S.A.
Pittsburg CA U.S.A.
Pittsburg KS U.S.A.
Pittsburg NH U.S.A.
Pittsburg TX U.S.A.
Pittsburgh PA U.S.A.
Pittsfield IL U.S.A.
Pittsfield MA U.S.A.
Pittsfield ME U.S.A.
Pittsfield NH U.S.A.
Pittsfield VT U.S.A.
Pittston PA U.S.A.
Pittston Farm ME U.S.A.
Pitt Strait Chatham Is S. Pacific Ocean
Pittsville WI U.S.A.
Pittsworth Qld Austr.
Pituri Creek watercourse Qld/S.A. Austr.
Pitvaros Hungary
Pitz Lake Nunavut Can.
Pitztal val. Austria
Pium Brazil
Piumhi Brazil
Piura Peru
Piura dept Peru
Piusa r. Estonia
Piute Mountains CA U.S.A.
Piute Peak CA U.S.A.
Piuthan Nepal
Pivabiska r. Ont. Can.
Pivashiani Lith.
Pivasinu r. Ont. Can.
Pivdennyy Buh r. Ukr.
Pivijay Col.
Pivka Slovenia
Pivka r. Slovenia
Pivnichno-Kryms'kyy Kanal canal Ukr.
Piwniczna-Zdrój Pol.
Pixa Xinjiang China
Pixariá mt. Greece see Pyxaria
Pixian China
Pixoyal Mex.
Pizacoma Peru
Pizarra Spain
Piz Bernina mt. Italy/Switz.
Piz Bom mt. Italy
Piz Buin mt. Austria/Switz.
Piz d'Anarosa mt. Switz.
Piz Duan mt. Switz.
Piz Ela mt. Switz.
Pizhma r. Rus. Fed.
Pizhma Rus. Fed.
Pizhma r. Rus. Fed.
Pizhma r. Rus. Fed.
Pizhou Jiangsu China
Piz Kesch mt. Switz.
Piz Medel mt. Switz.
Pizol mt. Switz.
Piz Pisoc mt. Switz.
Piz Platta mt. Switz.
Piz Varuna mt. Italy/Switz.
Pizzighettone Italy
Pizzo Italy
Pizzo Arera mt. Italy
Pizzo Cangialoso mt. Italy
Pizzo Carbonara mt. Italy
Pizzo della Presolana mt. Italy
Pizzo di Coca mt. Italy
Pizzoferrato Italy
Pizzoli Italy
Pizzo Rotondo mt. Switz.
Pizzo Telegrafo hill Italy
Pizzuto, Monte mt. Italy
Pjórsá r. Iceland
Pkulagalid Point Palau
Pkulagasemieg pt Palau
Pkulngril pt Palau
Pkurengel pt Palau
Plaaz Ger.
Plabennec France
Place Moulin, Lago di l. Italy
Placentia Nfld and Lab. Can.
Placentia Italy see Piacenza
Placentia Bay Nfld and Lab. Can.
Placer Masbate Phil.
Placer Mindanao Phil.
Placerville CA U.S.A.
Placerville CO U.S.A.
Placetas Cuba
Plácido de Castro Brazil
Placilla Chile
Plaffeien Switz.
Plaimpied-Givaudins France
Plain Dealing LA U.S.A.
Plaine France
Plainfield CT U.S.A.
Plainfield IN U.S.A.
Plainfield NJ U.S.A.
Plainfield VT U.S.A.
Plainfield WI U.S.A.
Plains KS U.S.A.
Plains TX U.S.A.
Plainsboro NJ U.S.A.
Plaintel France
Plainview MN U.S.A.
Plainview NE U.S.A.
Plainview NY U.S.A.
Plainview TX U.S.A.
Plainville CT U.S.A.
Plainville KS U.S.A.
Plaisance France
Plaisance Haiti
Plaisance-du-Touch France
Plaisir France
Plaistow NH U.S.A.
Plaju Sumatra Indon.
Plaka Greece
Plaka, Akra pt Kriti Greece
Plakoti, Cape Cyprus
Plampang Sumbawa Indon.
Planá Czech Rep.
Planada CA U.S.A.
Plana Cays is Bahamas
Planada Spain
Plana de Castelló plain Spain
Planaltina Brazil
Planay France
Plancher-Bas France
Plancher-les-Mines France
Planche France
Planchón, Paso del pass Arg.
Planchón, Portezuelo del pass Arg. see
Planchon, Paso del

Planegg Ger.
Planès France
Planèze reg. France
Plánice Czech Rep.
Planier, Île de i. France
Planik mt. Croatia
Planina Postojna Slovenia
Planina Žentjur pri Celju Slovenia
Plankenfels Ger.
Plankinton SD U.S.A.
Plano IL U.S.A.
Plano TX U.S.A.
Plano Alto Brazil
Plansee l. Austria
Plantagenet r. Jamaica
Plantain Garden r. Jamaica
Planta Los Quelthehues Chile
Plantation House St Helena
Plantaurel, Montagnes du hills France
Plant City FL U.S.A.
Plantsville CT U.S.A.
Plasencia Spain
Plashanovo Rus. Fed.
Plasencia Spain
Plasencia, Llano de plain Spain
Plasencia del Monte Spain
Plaska Pol.
Plaški Croatia
Plasnica Macedonia
Plast Rus. Fed.
Plaster City CA U.S.A.
Plaster Rock N.B. Can.
Plaston S. Africa
Plástovce Slovakia
Plastun Rus. Fed.
Plastunovskaya Rus. Fed.
Plasy Czech Rep.
Platamon, Rt pt Serb. and Mont.
Platamona Lido Sardegna Italy
Platamonas Greece
Platanal Peru
Platani r. Sicilia Italy
Platania Greece
Platania Italy
Platanillo Mex.
Platanistos Greece
Platbakkies S. Africa
Platberg mt. S. Africa
Plate Ger.
Plateau state Nigeria
Plateau des Tailles, Réserves Domaniales du nature res. Belgium
Plateaux admin. reg. Congo
Plateliai Lith.
Platen, Kapp c. Svalbard
Platenberg (Sassenburg) Ger.
Plateros Mex.
Plathus S. Africa
Plati Italy
Platičevo Vojvodina, Srbija Serb. and Mont.
Platykampos Greece see Platykampos
Platina CA U.S.A.
Platinum AK U.S.A.
Platja d'Aro Spain
Platnirovskaya Rus. Fed.
Plato Col.
Plato de Sopa Chile
Platón Sánchez Mex.
Platrand S. Africa
Platte r. MO U.S.A.
Platte r. NE U.S.A.
Platte City MO U.S.A.
Platte Island Seychelles
Plattekill NY U.S.A.
Plattenberg hill Austria
Platteville CO U.S.A.
Platteville WI U.S.A.
Plattling Ger.
Plattsburgh NY U.S.A.
Plattsmouth NE U.S.A.
Platy Greece
Plaue Ger.
Plauen Ger.
Plauer See l. Ger.
Plav Crna Gora Serb. and Mont.
Plav r. Ukr.
Plava r. Rus. Fed.
Plavecký Mikuláš Slovakia
Plavecký Štvrtok Slovakia
Plaviņas Latvia
Plavnik i. Croatia
Plavsk Rus. Fed.
Playa Azul Mex.
Playa Blanca Lanzarote Canary Is
Playa Blanca coastal area Fuerteventura Canary Is
Playa Chapadmalal Arg.
Playa Corrida de San Juan, Punta pt Mex.
Playa de Barlovento coastal area Fuerteventura Canary Is
Playa de Fajardo Puerto Rico
Playa de las Americas Tenerife Canary Is
Playa del Carmen Mex.
Playa del Inglés Gran Canaria Canary Is
Playa de Sotavento coastal area Fuerteventura Canary Is
Playa Hermosa Mex.
Playa Pascual Uru.
Playas Ecuador
Playas r. Mex.
Playas de Corralejo coastal area Fuerteventura Canary Is
Playa Vicente Mex.
Playford watercourse N.T. Austr.
Playgreen Lake Man. Can.
Play Ku Vietnam
Playón Mex.
Playones de Santa Ana l. Col.
Plazac France
Plaza de Judió mt. Spain
Plaza Huincul Arg.
Plazac France
Plazów Pol.
Pleasant, Lake AZ U.S.A.
Pleasant Bay MA U.S.A.
Pleasant Corners NY U.S.A.
Pleasant Grove NJ U.S.A.
Pleasant Grove UT U.S.A.
Pleasant Hill CA U.S.A.
Pleasant Hill OH U.S.A.
Pleasant Hill r. OR U.S.A.
Pleasant Hill r. TX U.S.A.
Pleasant Point N.Z.
Pleasant Valley NY U.S.A.
Pleasantville DE U.S.A.
Pleasantville NJ U.S.A.
Pleasantville PA U.S.A.
Pleasley Derbyshire, England U.K.
Pleasure Beach CT U.S.A.
Pleasureville KY U.S.A.
Plech Ger.
Plechý mt. Czech Rep.
Plecka Dąbrowa Pol.
Plédran France
Pléhédel France
Pléneuf-Val-André France
Pléchateau France
Plénée-Jugon France
Pléneuf-Val-André France

Plei Kần Vietnam
Pleine-Fougères France
Pleinfeld Ger.
Pleiskirchen Ger.
Pleißa Ger.
Pleiße r. Ger.
Plekhanovo Rus. Fed.
Plélan-le-Grand France
Plélan-le-Petit France
Plélo France
Plémet France
Plénée-Jugon France
Pléneuf-Val-André France
Plenty watercourse N.T. Austr.
Plenty, Bay of g. North I. N.Z.
Plentywood MT U.S.A.
Plérin France
Ples r. Ger.
Plescop France
Pleşcuţa Romania
Pleshanovo Rus. Fed.
Pleshchanitsy Belarus
Pleshcheyevo, Ozero l. Rus. Fed.
Plešivec Slovakia
Plešivec mt. Slovenia
Pleslin-Trigavou France
Plesná Czech Rep.
Pleso Rus. Fed.
Pleß hill Ger.
Pless Ger.
Plessé France
Plestin-les-Grèves France
Pleszew Pol.
Pletenyy Tashlyk Ukr.
Pletipi, Lac l. Que. Can.
Plettenberg Ger.
Plettenberg Bay S. Africa
Pletzen mt. Austria
Pleubian France
Pleucadeuc France
Pleudihen-sur-Rance France
Pleumartin France
Pleumeur-Bodou France
Pleurs France
Pleurtuit France
Pleuven France
Pleven Bulg.
Plevna Bulg. see Pleven
Plévenon France
Pleyben France
Pleystein Ger.
Pležuay r. France
Plieran r. Malaysia
Pliešovce Slovakia
Plieux France
Plima r. Italy
Plitviška Jezera l. Lith.
Plitra Greece
Plitvička Jezera nat. park Croatia
Plješevica mts Croatia
Pljevlja Crna Gora Serb. and Mont.
Ploaghe Sardegna Italy
Plobannalec France
Plobsheim France
Ploče Croatia
Plochingen Ger.
Płock Pol.
Płock r. Pol.
Plöckenpass pass Austria/Italy
Plockton Highland, Scotland U.K.
Plodovoye Rus. Fed.
Ploemeur France
Ploeren France
Ploërmel France
Ploeşti Romania see Ploiești
Plœuc-sur-Lié France
Plogastel-St-Germain France
Plogonnec France
Ploiești Romania
Plomari Lesvos Greece
Plomb du Cantal mt. France
Plombières-les-Bains France
Plomelin France
Plomeur France
Plomodiern France
Plomosas Mex.
Plön Ger.
Płoń, Jezioro l. Pol.
Plonéour-Lanvern France
Płonia r. Pol.
Płonia r. Pol.
Płońsk Pol.
Plopiş Romania
Ploskini Rus. Fed.
Ploskoye Rus. Fed.
Plošnica Pol.
Pöcking Ger.
Ploty Pol.
Plötzky Ger.
Plouagat France
Plouaret France
Plouarzel France
Plouay France
Ploubalay France
Ploubazlanec France
Ploudalmézeau France
Ploudaniel France
Plouescat France
Plouézec France
Ploufragan France
Plougasnou France
Plougastel-Daoulas France
Plougonvelin France
Plougonver France
Plougrescant France
Plouguenast France
Plouguerneau France
Plouguiel France
Plouha France
Plouharnel France
Plouhinec Bretagne France
Plouhinec Bretagne France
Plouider France
Plouigneau France
Plouisy France
Ploumanac'h France
Plounévez-Lochrist France
Plounévez-Moëdec France
Plounévez-Quintin France
Plouray France
Plourin-lès-Morlaix France
Plouvien France
Plouvorn France
Plouyé France
Plouzané France
Plovdiv Bulg.
Plover WI U.S.A.
Plover r. WI U.S.A.
Plover Cove Reservoir H.K. China
Plozévet France
Plŭk mt. Bulg.
Plŭckemin NJ U.S.A.
Plumbridge Northern Ireland U.K.
Plum Coulee Man. Can.

Plumelec France
Pluméliau France
Plumergat France
Plum Island NY U.S.A.
Plummer ID U.S.A.
Plumridge Lakes salt flat W.A. Austr.
Plumridge Lakes Nature Reserve W.A. Austr.
Plumsteadville PA U.S.A.
Plumtree Zimbabwe
Plunge Lith.
Plusko Pol.
Pluszkiejmy Pol.
Plutarco Elís Calles, Presa resr Mex.
Pluto, Lac l. Que. Can.
Plutos Rus. Fed.
Plužine Crna Gora Serb. and Mont.
Plužnica Pol.
Ply Huey Wati, Khao mt. Myanmar/Thai.
Plym r. England U.K.
Plymouth Montserrat
Plymouth Trin. and Tob.
Plymouth Plymouth, England U.K.
Plymouth admin. div. England U.K.
Plymouth CA U.S.A.
Plymouth CT U.S.A.
Plymouth IL U.S.A.
Plymouth IN U.S.A.
Plymouth MA U.S.A.
Plymouth NC U.S.A.
Plymouth NH U.S.A.
Plymouth PA U.S.A.
Plymouth WI U.S.A.
Plymouth Bay MA U.S.A.
Plympton Plymouth, England U.K.
Plymstock Plymouth, England U.K.
Plynlimon hill Wales U.K.
Plyskiv Ukr.
Plysky Ukr.
Plyussa Rus. Fed.
Plzeň Czech Rep.
Plzeňský kraj admin. reg. Czech Rep.
Pmere Nyente Aboriginal Land res. N.T. Austr.
Pniewo Pol.
Pniewy Mazowieckie Pol.
Pniewy Wielkopolskie Pol.
Pô Burkina
Po r. Italy
Pô, Parc National de nat. park Burkina
Pô Lak.r of Malaysia
Poás, Volcán vol. Costa Rica
Poat i. Indon.
Pobè Benin
Pobeda Mountain China/Kyrg. see Jengish Chokusu
Pobeda Ice Island Antarctica
Pobeda Peak China/Kyrg. see Jengish Chokusu
Pobedim Slovakia
Pobedino Sakhalin Rus. Fed. see Zarechnyy
Pobedy, Pik mt. China/Kyrg. see Jengish Chokusu
Poběžovice Czech Rep.
Pobiedziska Pol.
Pobierowo Pol.
Pobikry Pol.
Pohlibski Kanal sea chan. Croatia
Población Chile
Pobladura del Valle Spain
Poblet Arg.
Poblet tourist site Spain
Pobócie Spain
Poboleda Spain
Pobra do Caramiñal Spain
Pobre, Punta de pt Canary Is
Pobrzeże Koszalińskie Pol.
Pocahontas AR U.S.A.
Pocahontas IA U.S.A.
Pocatalico r. WV U.S.A.
Pocatello ID U.S.A.
Počátky Czech Rep.
Poceirão Port.
Pochala Sudan
Pochayiv Ukr.
Pochep Rus. Fed.
Pochinki Rus. Fed.
Pochinok Smolenskaya Oblast' Rus. Fed.
Pochinok Tverskaya Oblast' Rus. Fed.
Pochlarn Austria
Pocho, Sierra de mts Arg.
Pochutla Mex.
Pocillas Chile
Pock, Gunung hill Malaysia
Pockau Ger.
Pöcking Ger.
Pocklington East Riding of Yorkshire, England U.K.
Poços Brazil
Poço Fundo Brazil
Pocomoke City MD U.S.A.
Pocomoke Sound b. MD/VA U.S.A.
Pocona Bol.
Poconé Brazil
Pocono Mountains hills PA U.S.A.
Pocono Pines PA U.S.A.
Pocono Summit PA U.S.A.
Poço Ranakah vol. Flores Indon.
Poços de Caldas Brazil
Pocrane Brazil
Pocsaj Hungary
Poczesna Pol.
Poczesna r. Pol.
Podberez'ye Rus. Fed.
Podbořany Czech Rep.
Podbořany r. Czech Rep.
Podbrdo Slovenia
Podčetrtek Slovenia
Podcher'ye r. Rus. Fed.
Podcher'ye Rus. Fed.
Poddor'ye Rus. Fed.
Podebłocie Pol.
Poděbrady Czech Rep.
Podence Port.
Podensac France
Podgaytsy Ukr.
Podgorenskiy Rus. Fed.
Podgorica Crna Gora Serb. and Mont.
Podgornoye Rus. Fed.
Podgorny Rus. Fed.
Podgoryane Rus. Fed.
Podgorodnoye Rus. Fed.
Podhorod' Slovakia
Podil'sk Ukr.
Podişul Transilvaniei plat. Romania
Podium r. Indon.
Podkamennaya Tunguska Rus. Fed.
Podkamennaya Tunguska r. Rus. Fed.
Podkarpackie prov. Pol.
Podkova Bulg.
Podkumok r. Rus. Fed.

Podkumok r. Rus. Fed.
Podlaska, Nizina lowland Pol.
Podlaskie prov. Pol.
Podlesnoye Rus. Fed.
Podlib-Mihnik Slovenia
Podnart Slovenia
Pododarovo Rus. Fed.
Podofini S. Africa
Podoli Czech Rep.
Podol'sk Rus. Fed.
Podor Senegal
Podorozhnye Ukr.
Podosinki Rus. Fed.
Podove Ukr.
Podozerskiy Rus. Fed.
Podporozh'ye Rus. Fed.
Podravska Slatina Croatia
Podravske Sesvete Croatia
Podsreda Slovenia
Podtabor Slovenia
Podturen Croatia
Podujevo Kosovo, Srbija Serb. and Mont.
Podwilk Pol.
Podyji park Czech Rep.
Podyuga Rus. Fed.
Podvot've Rus. Fed.
Podz' Rus. Fed.
Poel i. Ger.
Poeldijk Neth.
Poeppel Corner salt flat N.T. Austr.
Poerio Slovenia see Ptuj
Pofadder S. Africa
Pofi Italy
Pogamasing Ont. Can.
Pogar r. Rus. Fed.
Poggendorf Ger.
Poggersdorf Austria
Poggiardo Italy
Poggibonsi Italy
Poggio Ballone hill Italy
Poggio Bustone Italy
Poggio del Leccio hill Italy
Poggio di Montieri mt. Italy
Poggiodomo Italy
Poggio Imperiale Italy
Poggio Lecci hill Italy
Poggio-Mezzana Corse France
Poggio Mirteto Italy
Poggio Moiano Italy
Poggio Peroni hill Italy
Poggio Picenze Italy
Poggioreale Sicilia Italy
Poggio Renatico Italy
Poggio Rusco Italy
Pöggstall Austria
Pogled mt. Serb. and Mont.
Poglina, Punta di pt Sardegna Italy
Pogny France
Pogoni Greece
Pogoreloye-Gorodishche Rus. Fed.
Pogorzela Pol.
Pogorzelice Pol.
Pogorzeheye Rus. Fed.
Pogradec Albania
Pogranichnyy Rus. Fed.
Pogrebishche Ukr.
Pogrodzie Pol.
Poguba r. Brazil
Poh Sulawesi Indon.
P'ohang S. Korea
Pohja Fin.
Pohja Fin.
Pöhl Ger.
Pohlibski Kanal sea chan. Croatia
Pohoralá Czech Rep.
Pohorje mts Slovenia
Pohrebyshche Ukr.
Pohrebyshche Ukr.
Pohri Madh. Prad. India
Pohronská pahorkatina mts Slovakia
Poi Manipur India
Poia r. Italy
Poiana Mare Romania
Poiana Ruscă, Munţii mts Romania
Poiana Stampei Romania
Poiana Vadului Romania
Poienaru Romania
Poienile de Sub Munte Romania
Poienia r. Pol.
Poieniţa, Vârful mt. Romania
Poigar Sulawesi Indon.
Poilly-lez-Gien France
Poim Rus. Fed.
Poinçon-lès-Larrey France
Poindexter KY U.S.A.
Poindimié r. New Caledonia
Poindimié r. New Caledonia
Point, Cape Antarctica
Point Arena CA U.S.A.
Point au Fer Island LA U.S.A.
Point Baker AK U.S.A.
Point-Comfort Que. Can.
Pointe à la Hache LA U.S.A.
Pointe-à-Pierre Trin. and Tob.
Pointe-à-Pitre Guadeloupe
Pointe au Baril Station Ont. Can.
Pointe Aux Pins MI U.S.A.
Pointe Michel Dominica
Pointe-Noire Guadeloupe
Point Fortin Trin. and Tob.
Point Hope AK U.S.A.
Pointis-Inard France
Point Kenny S.A. Austr.
Point Lay AK U.S.A.
Point Marion PA U.S.A.
Point of Rocks MD U.S.A.
Point of Rocks WY U.S.A.
Point Pelee National Park Ont. Can.
Point Pleasant NJ U.S.A.
Point Pleasant WV U.S.A.
Point Pleasant Beach NJ U.S.A.
Point Reyes National Seashore nature res. CA U.S.A.
Point Salvation Aboriginal Reserve W.A. Austr.
Point Samson W.A. Austr.
Point Somes Chatham Is S. Pacific Ocean
Poirino Italy
Poiseux France
Poisson Blanc, Lac du l. Que. Can.
Poissonnier Point W.A. Austr.
Poissons France
Poissy France
Poitiers France
Poitou reg. France
Poitou, Plaines et Seuil du plain France
Poitou-Charentes admin. reg. France
Poivre Atoll Seychelles
Poix-de-Picardie France
Poix-Terron France
Pojani r. Pol.
Pojarkovo Rus. Fed.
Pojezierze Iławskiego, Park Krajobrazowy Pol.
Pojezierze Łęczyńskie, Park Krajobrazowy Pol.
Pojo Bol.
Pojuca Brazil

Pôka'ī Bay HI U.S.A.
Pokal Fin.
Pokaran Rajasthan India
Pókaszepetk Hungary
Pokataroo N.S.W. Austr.
Pokats' r. Belarus
Pokcha Rus. Fed.
Pokeno North I. N.Z.
Pokhara Nepal
Pokhvistnevo Rus. Fed.
Pokigron Suriname
Pokka Fin.
Pokljuka reg. Slovenia
Poko Dem. Rep. Congo
Pokój Pol.
Pokoynoye Rus. Fed.
Pokran Pak.
Pokrov Smolenskaya Oblast' Rus. Fed.
Pokrov Vladimirskaya Oblast' Rus. Fed.
Pokrovka Azer.
Pokrovka Kazakh.
Pokrovka Talas Kyrg.
Pokrovka Chitinskaya Oblast' Rus. Fed.
Pokrovka Moskovskaya Oblast' Rus. Fed.
Pokrovka Orenburgskaya Oblast' Rus. Fed.
Pokrovka Primorskiy Kray Rus. Fed.
Pokrovka Yevreyskaya Avtonomnaya Oblast' Rus. Fed. see Priamurskiy
Pokrovka Mykolayiv's'ka Oblast' Ukr.
Pokrovka Mykolayiv's'ka Oblast' Ukr.
Pokrovka Sums'ka Oblast' Ukr.
Pokrovo-Marfino Rus. Fed.
Pokrovsk Respublika Sakha (Yakutiya) Rus. Fed.
Pokrovs'ke Dnipropetrovs'ka Oblast' Ukr.
Pokrovs'ke Luhans'ka Oblast' Ukr.
Pokrovskoye Lipetskaya Oblast' Rus. Fed.
Pokrovskoye Orlovskaya Oblast' Rus. Fed.
Pokrovskoye Rostovskaya Oblast' Rus. Fed.
Pokrovsk-Ural'skiy Rus. Fed.
Pokrówka Pol.
Poksha r. Rus. Fed.
Pokshen'ga r. Rus. Fed.
Pol Gujarat India
Pol' r. Rus. Fed.
Pola Croatia see Pula
Pola Mindoro Phil.
Pola r. Rus. Fed.
Pola r. Rus. Fed.
Polacca Wash watercourse AZ U.S.A.
Pola de Allande Spain
Pola de Laviana Spain
Pola de Siero Spain
Pola de Somiedo Spain
Polaincourt-et-Clairefontaine France
Polajewo Pol.
Polán Spain
Polán Iran
Poľana mt. Slovakia
Poľana mt. Slovakia
Poľana park Slovakia
Poland country Europe
Poland IN U.S.A.
Poland NY U.S.A.
Poland OH U.S.A.
Polanica-Zdrój Pol.
Polaniec Pol.
Polanów Pol.
Polar Bear Provincial Park Ont. Can.
Polar Plateau Antarctica
Polar Times Glacier Antarctica
Polatbey Turkey
Polatli Turkey
Polatsk Belarus
Polatskaya Nizina lowland Belarus
Polavaram Andhra Prad. India
Polcura Chile
Polczyn Zdrój Pol.
Poldarsa Rus. Fed.
Pol Dasht Iran
Pole 'Alam Afgh.
Poleax Rus. Fed.
Pole-e Fāsā Iran
Polegate East Sussex, England U.K.
Pole-e Khatum Iran
Pole-e Khomrī Afgh.
Polelino Spain
Polepy Czech Rep.
Pole-e Safīd Iran
Polesella Italy
Polesine, Isola di i. Italy
Poleski Park Narodowy nat. park Pol.
Polessk Rus. Fed.
Polesworth Warwickshire, England U.K.
Poles'ye marsh Belarus/Ukr. see Pripet Marshes
Poletayevo Rus. Fed.
Polevaya Rus. Fed.
Polewali Sulawesi Indon.
Polgahawela Sri Lanka
Polgár Hungary
Polhograjski Hribovje mts Slovenia
Polí Cameroon
Poli Shandong China
Poli Cyprus see Polis
Polia Italy
Poliaigos i. Greece see Polyaigos
Poliçan Albania
Polican Albania
Police Pol.
Police, Pointe pt Mahé Seychelles
Police nad Metují Czech Rep.
Polichni Lesvos Greece
Polička Czech Rep.
Policka r. Rus. Fed.
Polidhrosos Greece see Polydroso
Polidroso Greece
Polignano a Mare Italy
Poligny France
Polikastro Greece see Polykastro
Polikraishte Bulg.
Polillo i. Phil.
Polillo Islands Phil.
Polillo Strait Phil.
Polis Cyprus
Polis'ke Rivnens'ka Oblast' Ukr.
Polis'ke Zhytomyrs'ka Oblast' Ukr. see Poliss'ke
Polis'ke Zapovidnyk nature res. Ukr.
Polisot France
Poliss'ke Ukr.
Polistena Italy
Polistovo-Lovatskaya Rus. Fed.
Polithea Greece
Polittiko Cyprus
Polivanovo Rus. Fed.
Poliyiros Greece see Polygyros
Polizzi Generosa Sicilia Italy

Poljane to Posavina

322

59 J7 Poljane Slovenia
59 M7 Poljčane Slovenia
116 F7 Polk PA U.S.A.
18 J5 Polkorona Latvia
54 E4 Polkowice Pol.
73 O6 Polla Italy
176 E7 Pollachi Tamil Nadu India
59 M5 Pöllau Austria
59 M5 Pöllauberg Austria
59 M5 Pöllauer Tal nature res. Austria
49 H7 Polle Ger.
51 E7 Polleben Ger.
67 L8 Pollença Spain
67 L8 Pollença, Badia de b. Spain
53 K4 Pollenfeld Ger.
Pollensa Spain see Pollença
49 H6 Pollhagen Ger.
40 G4 Polliat France
73 O7 Pollica Italy
74 G8 Pollina Sicilia Italy
74 G7 Pollina r. Sicilia Italy
53 K6 Polling Bayern Ger.
53 N5 Polling Bayern Ger.
73 Q8 Pollino, Monte mt. Italy
73 Q8 Pollino, Parco Nazionale del nat. park Italy
50 E5 Pollitz Ger.
26 E9 Polloch Highland, Scotland U.K.
154 D8 Polloc Harbour b. Mindanao Phil.
124 L3 Pollock Pines CA U.S.A.
209 G13 Pollock Reef W.A. Austr.
202 I4 Pollok North I. N.Z.
63 J6 Pollos Spain
203 C11 Pollux mt. South I. N.Z.
20 S1 Polmak Norway
41 B7 Polminhac France
26 I11 Polmont Falkirk, Scotland U.K.
56 E2 Polná Czech Rep.
17 P2 Polnaya r. Rus. Fed.
54 F2 Polnica Pol.
192 H3 Polnovat Rus. Fed.
20 T4 Polo Fin.
110 E8 Polo IL U.S.A.
201 □2a Polo'a i. Tonga
Poloat atoll Micronesia see Puluwat
Pologi Ukr. see Polohy
17 P6 Polohy Ukr.
95 F4 Polokwane Limpopo S. Africa
14 J4 Polom Rus. Fed.
19 P4 Polomet' r. Rus. Fed.
154 E8 Polomoloc Mindanao Phil.
176 G9 Polonnaruwa Sri Lanka
16 G3 Polonne Ukr.
Polonnoye Ukr. see Polonne
65 M7 Polopos Spain
59 O6 Polöske Hungary
19 S7 Polotnyanyy Zavod Rus. Fed.
Polotsk Belarus see Polatsk
Polovinka Rus. Fed. see Ugleural'skiy
77 L5 Polovragi Romania
146 B3 Polpaico Chile
30 C7 Polperro Cornwall, England U.K.
59 K5 Pöls Austria
59 K5 Pöls r. Austria
44 G5 Polsbroek Neth.
53 J4 Polsingen Ger.
Polska country Europe see Poland
59 M7 Polskava r. Slovenia
77 N7 Polski Trŭmbesh Bulg.
122 G3 Polson MT U.S.A.
14 H2 Polta r. Rus. Fed.
57 I3 Poltár Slovakia
17 N4 Poltava Ukr.
Poltava Oblast admin. div. Ukr. see Poltavs'ka Oblast'
183 N1 Poltavka Omskaya Oblast' Rus. Fed.
162 G6 Poltavka Primorskiy Kray Rus. Fed.
17 Q5 Poltavka Donets'ka Oblast' Ukr.
17 L5 Poltavka Kirovohrads'ka Oblast' Ukr.
17 P6 Poltavka Zaporiz'ka Oblast' Ukr.
17 M4 Poltavs'ka Oblast' admin. div. Ukr.
15 G7 Poltavskaya Rus. Fed.
Poltavskaya Oblast' admin. div. Ukr. see Poltavs'ka Oblast'
18 I3 Põltsamaa Estonia
18 J3 Põltsamaa r. Estonia
183 M1 Poludino Kazakh.
16 C3 Południoworoztoczański Park Krajobrazowy Pol.
54 D3 Połupin Pol.
176 F6 Polur Tamil Nadu India
56 D3 Poluška hill Czech Rep.
18 K3 Põlva Estonia
123 K9 Polvadera NM U.S.A.
146 C3 Polvaredos Arg.
71 O8 Polverigi Italy
72 I1 Polvese, Isola i. Italy
20 T5 Polvijärvi Fin.
127 N8 Polvoxal Mex.
26 L11 Polwarth Scottish Borders, Scotland U.K.
19 W6 Polya r. Rus. Fed.
78 F6 Polyaigos i. Greece
16 B5 Polyana Ukr.
18 M1 Polyany Rus. Fed.
Polyarnoye Rus. Fed. see Russkoye Ust'ye
193 S3 Polyarnyy Chukotskiy Avtonomnyy Okrug Rus. Fed.
20 V2 Polyarnyy Murmanskaya Oblast' Rus. Fed.
20 V3 Polyarnyye Zori Rus. Fed.
14 M2 Polyarnyy Ural mts Rus. Fed.
78 D4 Polydroso Greece
78 E2 Polygyros Greece
78 F6 Polyiagou-Folegandrou, Steno sea chan. Greece
78 D2 Polykastro Greece
216 H6 Polynesia is Oceania
55 N4 Polytsi Ukr.
59 L7 Polzela Slovenia
51 F9 Pölzig Ger.
74 E8 Poma, Lago l. Sicilia Italy
138 A2 Pomabamba Peru
203 D13 Pomahaka r. South I. N.Z.
136 B6 Pomahuaca Peru
63 M2 Pomaluengo Spain
144 D3 Pomán Arg.
71 J9 Pomarance Italy
64 D5 Pomarão Port.
43 C8 Pomarez France
75 L2 Pomarico Italy
21 Q6 Pomarkku Fin.
57 I4 Pomáz Hungary
143 F4 Pomba r. Brazil
137 H5 Pombal Pará Brazil
140 F3 Pombal Paraíba Brazil
62 F6 Pombal Bragança Port.
62 C9 Pombal Leiria Port.
137 F6 Pombas r. Brazil
88 □ Pombas Cape Verde
142 A4 Pombo r. Brazil
41 G10 Pomègues, Île i. France
95 G4 Pomene Moz.
63 Q5 Pomer Spain
97 O4 Pomeroy S. Africa
27 I3 Pomeroy Northern Ireland U.K.
116 C9 Pomeroy OH U.S.A.
118 D5 Pomeroy PA U.S.A.
122 F3 Pomeroy WA U.S.A.
57 L5 Pomezeu Romania
56 F2 Pomezí Czech Rep.
73 J4 Pomezia Italy
96 H1 Pomfret S. Africa
17 K5 Pomichna Ukr.
55 I3 Pomiechówek Pol.
153 L8 Pomio New Britain P.N.G.
40 F2 Pommard France
38 E4 Pommerit-Jaudy France
53 J2 Pommersfelden Ger.
20 S3 Pomokaira reg. Fin.
207 N9 Pomona Qld Austr.
127 O9 Pomona Belize
94 B5 Pomona Namibia
124 O7 Pomona CA U.S.A.
118 F6 Pomona NJ U.S.A.
146 E6 Pomono Arg.
77 P8 Pomorie Bulg.
54 C1 Pomorska, Zatoka b. Pol.
54 F1 Pomorskie prov. Pol.
54 F2 Pomorskie, Pojezierze reg. Pol.
14 F2 Pomorskiy Bereg coastal area Rus. Fed.
14 J1 Pomorskiy Proliv sea chan. Rus. Fed.
54 D3 Pomorsko Pol.
71 L6 Po Morto di Primaro watercourse Italy
190 A3 Pomos Point Cyprus
Pomo Tso l. China see Puma Yumco
Pomou, Akra pt Cyprus see Pomos Point
14 K3 Pomozdino Rus. Fed.
173 K11 Pompain Xizang China
42 D2 Pompaire France
73 N6 Pompei Italy
142 B5 Pompéia Brazil
143 E3 Pompéu Brazil
37 L6 Pompey France
162 G4 Pompeyevka Rus. Fed.
122 K3 Pompeys Pillar National Monument nat. park MT U.S.A.
41 D9 Pompignan France
119 G2 Pompton Lakes NJ U.S.A.
54 F1 Pomysk Mały Pol.
Ponape atoll Micronesia see Pohnpei
107 M4 Ponask Lake Ont. Can.
14 I4 Ponazyrevo Rus. Fed.
120 G4 Ponca NE U.S.A.
121 G7 Ponca City OK U.S.A.
131 □1 Ponce Puerto Rico
115 G13 Ponce de Leon Bay FL U.S.A.
123 K7 Poncha Springs CO U.S.A.
108 E3 Poncheville, Lac l. Que. Can.
40 G4 Poncin France
128 E5 Poncitlán Mex.
208 H3 Pond, Cape W.A. Austr.
176 D5 Ponda Goa India
121 G7 Pond Creek OK U.S.A.
118 F2 Pond Eddy NY U.S.A.
31 L2 Pondersbridge Cambridgeshire, England U.K.
176 F7 Pondicherry Pondicherry India
176 F7 Pondicherry union terr. India
Pondichéry Pondicherry India see Pondicherry
105 K2 Pond Inlet Nunavut Can.
97 N7 Pondoland reg. S. Africa
59 H3 Pöndorf Austria
109 K2 Ponds, Island of Nfld and Lab. Can.
Ponds Bay Nunavut Can. see Pond Inlet
159 H7 Pơ Ne, Đak r. Vietnam
126 □P11 Poneloya Nic.
70 D8 Ponente, Riviera di coastal area Italy
200 □5 Ponérihouen New Caledonia
200 □4a Pones i. Chuuk Micronesia
17 S9 Ponezhukay Rus. Fed.
62 G3 Ponferrada Spain
202 K4 Pongakawa North I. N.Z.
90 A4 Pongara, Pointe pt Gabon
202 K7 Pongaroa North I. N.Z.
59 H5 Pongau val. Austria
179 O6 Pong-Chaa Arun. Prad. India
173 L11 Pongda Xizang China
90 E3 Pongo watercourse Sudan
136 B6 Pongo de Manseriche gorge Peru
97 P3 Pongola S. Africa
97 Q2 Pongola r. S. Africa
97 P3 Pongolapoort Dam l. S. Africa
97 P3 Pongolapoort Public Resort Nature Reserve S. Africa
88 E4 Pong Tamale Ghana
55 K4 Poniatowa Pol.
55 H2 Poniatowo Pol.
54 E4 Poniec Pol.
155 C3 Poniki, Gunung mt. Indon.
57 I3 Poniky Slovakia
155 B4 Ponindilisa, Tanjung pt Indon.
16 G3 Poninka Ukr.
57 H3 Ponitrie park Slovakia
51 F9 Ponitz Ger.
19 O6 Ponizov'ye Rus. Fed.
158 A4 Ponnagyun Myanmar
176 F7 Ponnaivar r. India
176 D6 Ponnampet Karnataka India
176 D7 Ponnani Kerala India
176 D7 Ponnani r. India
176 G6 Ponneri Tamil Nadu India
158 B3 Ponnyadaung Range mts Myanmar
106 H4 Ponoka Alta Can.
182 F1 Ponomarevka Rus. Fed.
17 L2 Ponornytsya Ukr.
157 I8 Ponorogo Jawa Indon.
14 H2 Ponoy Rus. Fed.
14 H2 Ponoy r. Rus. Fed.
109 G1 Pons r. Que. Can.
42 C4 Pons France
Pons Spain see Ponts
71 J8 Ponsacco Italy
154 E6 Ponson i. Phil.
62 F9 Ponsul r. Port.
40 E2 Pont, Lac de l. France
64 □ Ponta Madeira
45 F7 Pont-à-Celles Belgium
43 D9 Pontacq France
98 □1b Ponta Delgada São Miguel Azores
64 □ Ponta Delgada Madeira
140 C2 Ponta de Pedras Brazil
64 □ Ponta do Pargo Madeira
88 □ Ponta do Sol Cape Verde
64 □ Ponta do Sol Madeira
98 □1b Ponta Garça São Miguel Azores
142 B6 Ponta Grossa Brazil
40 G2 Pontailler-sur-Saône France
41 G7 Pontaix France
142 C4 Pontal Brazil
143 H3 Pontal do Ipiranga Brazil
142 C2 Pontalina Brazil
36 F2 Pont-à-Marcq France
37 L6 Pont-à-Mousson France
147 G5 Pontant Arg.
140 C3 Pontão Brazil
139 G5 Ponta Porã Brazil
30 E4 Pontardawe Neath Port Talbot, Wales U.K.
30 D4 Pontarddulais Swansea, Wales U.K.
Pontardulais Swansea, Wales U.K. see Pontarddulais
42 H4 Pontarion France
40 I3 Pontarlier France
71 K8 Pontassieve Italy
38 I4 Pontaubault France
39 M3 Pont-Audemer France
40 B5 Pontaumur France
38 D6 Pont-Aven France
108 E3 Pontax r. Que. Can.
70 D5 Pont-Canavese Italy
41 I6 Pontcharra France
121 J10 Pontchartrain, Lake LA U.S.A.
38 G7 Pontchâteau France
38 C5 Pont-Croix France
40 G4 Pont-d'Ain France
38 C5 Pont-de-Buis-lès-Quimerch France
40 G5 Pont-de-Chéruy France
43 I8 Pont-de-Larn France
41 F6 Pont-de-l'Isère France
45 G8 Pont-de-Loup Belgium
40 H3 Pont-de-Poitte France
40 J2 Pont-de-Roide France
41 B8 Pont-de-Salars France
66 G3 Pont de Suert Spain
40 F4 Pont-de-Vaux France
40 F4 Pont-de-Veyle France
41 D8 Pont-d'Hérault France
39 K4 Pont-d'Ouilly France
43 F7 Pont-du-Casse France
40 C5 Pont-du-Château France
41 F9 Pont du Gard tourist site France
40 H3 Pont-du-Navoy France
73 N5 Ponte Italy
62 D6 Ponte Port.
140 D4 Ponte Alta do Norte Brazil
62 E2 Ponte Aranga Spain
62 D4 Ponteareas Spain
71 O2 Pontebba Italy
142 A2 Ponte Branca Brazil
62 D4 Ponte Caldelas Spain
62 C2 Ponteceso Spain
70 C6 Pontechianale Italy
73 L5 Pontecorvo Italy
70 F6 Pontecurone Italy
62 D5 Ponte da Barca Port.
70 E8 Pontedassio Italy
62 C5 Ponte de Lima Port.
70 H6 Ponte dell'Olio Italy
139 F3 Ponte de Pedra Brazil
71 J8 Pontedera Italy
64 C2 Ponte de Sor Port.
62 D2 Pontedeume Spain
62 C8 Ponte de Vagos Port.
58 C7 Ponte di Legno Italy
71 M4 Ponte di Piave Italy
141 B6 Ponte do Rio Verde Brazil
64 A2 Ponte do Rol Port.
142 D3 Ponte Firme Brazil
29 O6 Pontefract West Yorkshire, England U.K.
71 L2 Ponte Gardena Italy
107 J5 Ponteix Sask. Can.
29 N3 Ponteland Northumberland, England U.K.
73 N5 Pontelandolfo Italy
72 C3 Ponte-Leccia Corse France
71 M5 Pontelongo Italy
71 M3 Ponte nelle Alpi Italy
70 H4 Ponte Nossa Italy
143 F4 Ponte Nova Brazil
71 K3 Ponte Nova Italy
41 G6 Pont-en-Royans France
70 H5 Pontenure Italy
43 B7 Pontenx-les-Forges France
30 E3 Ponterwyd Ceredigion, Wales U.K.
64 B3 Pontes Port.
71 L5 Ponte San Nicolò Italy
70 H4 Ponte San Pietro Italy
30 G2 Pontesbury Shropshire, England U.K.
58 F7 Pontesei, Lago di l. Italy
139 F3 Pontes-e-Lacerda Brazil
62 C3 Ponte Valga Spain
62 C4 Pontevedra Spain
62 D4 Pontevedra prov. Spain
62 C4 Pontevedra, Ría de est. Spain
64 B2 Pontével Port.
40 F5 Pont-Évêque France
70 I5 Pontevico Italy
39 I4 Pont-Farcy France
36 H5 Pontfaverger-Moronvilliers France
40 B5 Pontgibaud France
39 I3 Pont-Hébert France
Ponthierville Dem. Rep. Congo see Ubundu
36 C3 Ponthieu reg. France
110 F9 Pontiac IL U.S.A.
111 K7 Pontiac MI U.S.A.
Pontiae is Italy see Ponziane, Isole
157 H5 Pontianak Kalimantan Indon.
36 G8 Pontigny France
Pontine Islands is Italy see Ponziane, Isole
73 K5 Pontinia Italy
38 F5 Pontivy France
38 C6 Pont-l'Abbé France
42 C4 Pont-l'Abbé-d'Arnoult France
37 I7 Pont-la-Ville France
40 I2 Pont-les-Moulins France
39 L3 Pont-l'Évêque France
39 N7 Pontlevoy France
39 I5 Pontmain France
143 G3 Pontões Capixabas, Parque Nacional dos nat. park Brazil
137 H4 Pontoetoe Suriname
36 D5 Pontoise France
209 G10 Ponton watercourse W.A. Austr.
107 L4 Ponton Man. Can.
63 J2 Pontón, Puerto del pass Spain
65 N4 Pontones Spain
43 C8 Pontonx-sur-l'Adour France
27 D5 Pontoon Rep. of Ireland
38 H4 Pontorson France
191 D4 Pontos Mucha Nakrdzali nature res. Georgia
121 K8 Pontotoc MS U.S.A.
38 H5 Pont-Péan France
36 E5 Pontpoint France
70 H7 Pontremoli Italy
70 H3 Pontresina Switz.
30 E3 Pontrhydfendigaid Ceredigion, Wales U.K.
38 E4 Pontrieux France
30 G4 Pontrilas Herefordshire, England U.K.
66 H4 Ponts Spain
36 H7 Pont-Ste-Marie France
36 E5 Pont-Ste-Maxence France
41 F8 Pont-St-Esprit France
70 D4 Pont-St-Martin Italy
38 E6 Pont-Scorff France
30 F4 Pontsticill Reservoir Wales U.K.
36 G6 Pont-sur-Seine France
36 F7 Pont-sur-Yonne France
39 L6 Pontvallain France
30 D4 Pontyberem Carmarthenshire, Wales U.K.
111 P5 Pontypool Ont. Can.
30 F4 Pontypool Torfaen, Wales U.K.
30 F4 Pontypridd Rhondda Cynon Taff, Wales U.K.
202 J3 Ponui Island North I. N.Z.
17 R8 Ponura r. Rus. Fed.
17 L1 Ponurovka Rus. Fed.
19 P8 Ponyatovka Rus. Fed.
19 T9 Ponyri Rus. Fed.
73 J6 Ponza Italy
73 J6 Ponza, Isola di i. Italy
73 J6 Ponziane, Isole is Italy
70 E6 Ponzone Italy
70 E4 Ponzone r. Italy
204 E5 Poochera S.A. Austr.
91 B5 Pool admin. reg. Congo
29 N6 Pool West Yorkshire, England U.K.
203 D12 Poolburn Reservoir South I. N.Z.
131 □7 Poole Trin. and Tob.
31 I6 Poole Poole, England U.K.
31 I6 Poole admin. div. England U.K.
31 I6 Poole Bay England U.K.
26 E7 Poolewe Highland, Scotland U.K.
29 L4 Pooley Bridge Cumbria, England U.K.
204 F2 Poolowanna Lake salt flat S.A. Austr.
Poona Mahar. India see Pune
205 I5 Pooncarie N.S.W. Austr.
209 D9 Poondarrie, Mount hill W.A. Austr.
205 J4 Poopelloe Lake N.S.W. Austr.
138 D4 Poopó Bol.
138 D4 Poopó, Lago de l. Bol.
202 I2 Poor Knights Islands North I. N.Z.
183 N7 Pop Uzbek.
130 B9 Popa, Isla i. Panama
158 B4 Popa Mountain Myanmar
17 R5 Popasna Ukr.
Popasnaya Ukr. see Popasna
17 O5 Popasne Dnipropetrovs'ka Oblast' Ukr.
17 Q4 Popasne Kharkivs'ka Oblast' Ukr.
136 B4 Popayán Col.
18 E4 Pope Latvia
17 M5 Popel'naste Ukr.
45 C7 Poperinge Belgium
116 I10 Popes Creek MD U.S.A.
54 F5 Popielów Pol.
193 L2 Popigay r. Rus. Fed.
16 I4 Popil'nya Ukr.
205 H5 Popiltah Lake imp. l. N.S.W. Austr.
205 H5 Popio Lake N.S.W. Austr.
17 M3 Popivka Ukr.
107 L4 Poplar r. Man. Can.
106 G2 Poplar r. N.W.T. Can.
122 L2 Poplar MT U.S.A.
110 C3 Poplar WI U.S.A.
122 L2 Poplar r. MT U.S.A.
122 L2 Poplar, West Fork r. MT U.S.A.
121 J7 Poplar Bluff MO U.S.A.
116 E12 Poplar Camp VA U.S.A.
116 B10 Poplar Plains KY U.S.A.
121 K10 Poplarville MS U.S.A.
19 X8 Poplevino Rus. Fed.
19 W8 Poplevinskiy Rus. Fed.
129 I6 Popocatépetl, Volcán vol. Mex.
157 I9 Popoh Jawa Indon.
91 C6 Popokabaka Dem. Rep. Congo
73 L3 Popoli Italy
200 □6 Popomanaseu, Mount Guadalcanal Solomon Is
153 K8 Popondetta P.N.G.
68 F3 Popovača Croatia
19 U2 Popovka Rus. Fed.
77 O7 Popovo Bulg.
68 F4 Popovo Polje plain Bos.-Herz.
77 O8 Popovska Reka r. Bulg.
55 H3 Popów Łódzkie Pol.
54 G4 Popów Śląskie Pol.
53 L3 Poppberg hill Ger.
49 K7 Poppenberg hill Ger.
49 J10 Poppenhausen Ger.
49 I10 Poppenhausen (Wasserkuppe) Ger.
53 L3 Poppenricht Ger.
71 L8 Poppi Italy
55 I6 Poprad r. Pol.
57 J2 Poprad Slovakia
57 J2 Popradzki Park Krajobrazowy Pol.
57 J3 Poproč Slovakia
127 O9 Poptún Guat.
72 E2 Populonia Italy
191 C1 Poputnaya Rus. Fed.
119 K2 Poquetanuck CT U.S.A.
138 D5 Poquis, Nevado de mt. Chile
119 K2 Poquonock Bridge CT U.S.A.
117 I11 Poquoson VA U.S.A.
55 L5 Por r. Pol.
55 H6 Porąbka Pol.
55 H5 Poraj Pol.
185 L9 Porali r. Pak.
202 K7 Porangahau North I. N.Z.
140 C5 Porangatu Brazil
18 H9 Porazava Belarus
178 B9 Porbandar Gujarat India
71 J8 Porcari Italy
185 J5 Por Chaman Afgh.
106 D4 Porcher Island B.C. Can.
71 N4 Porcia Italy
36 H4 Porcien reg. France
143 F4 Porciúncula Brazil
138 D4 Porco Bol.
57 L4 Porcsalma Hungary
65 K5 Porcuna Spain
104 D3 Porcupine r. Can./U.S.A.
109 J2 Porcupine, Cape Nfld and Lab. Can.
214 H2 Porcupine Abyssal Plain sea feature N. Atlantic Ocean
207 J6 Porcupine Creek r. Qld Austr.
122 K2 Porcupine Creek r. MT U.S.A.
207 J6 Porcupine Gorge National Park Qld Austr.
107 K4 Porcupine Hills Man./Sask. Can.
110 E3 Porcupine Mountains MI U.S.A.
107 K4 Porcupine Plain Sask. Can.
107 K4 Porcupine Provincial Forest nature res. Sask. Can.
71 N4 Pordenone Italy
71 N3 Pordenone prov. Italy
38 F4 Pordic France
77 M7 Pordim Bulg.
136 D3 Pore Col.
68 D3 Poreč Croatia
142 B5 Porecatu Brazil
19 S6 Porech'ye Moskovskaya Oblast' Rus. Fed.
19 N5 Porech'ye Pskovskaya Oblast' Rus. Fed.
19 T3 Porech'ye Tverskaya Oblast' Rus. Fed.
19 W4 Porech'ye-Rybnoye Rus. Fed.
15 I5 Poretskoye Rus. Fed.
72 C2 Poretta airport Corse France
59 I7 Porezen mt. Slovenia
145 D6 Pórfido, Punta pt Arg.
89 F4 Porga Benin
173 F10 Porgyang Xizang China
21 P6 Pori Fin.
51 K10 Poříčany Czech Rep.
203 I8 Porirua North I. N.Z.
20 □D1 Þórisvatn l. Iceland
20 O3 Porjus Sweden
18 M4 Porkhov Rus. Fed.
18 H2 Porkkalafjärden b. Fin.
137 F2 Porlamar Venez.
70 G3 Porlezza Italy
30 E5 Porlock Somerset, England U.K.
63 J3 Porma r. Spain
63 J3 Porma, Embalse de resr Spain
207 H3 Pormpuraaw Qld Austr.
21 R6 Pornainen Fin.
70 D7 Pornassio Italy
53 K4 Pörnbach Ger.
38 G7 Pornic France
38 G7 Pornichet France
154 E6 Poro i. Phil.
200 □6 Poro Sta Isabel Solomon Is
75 J6 Poro, Monte hill Italy
14 L3 Porog Rus. Fed.
162 M4 Poronaysk Sakhalin Rus. Fed.
173 J11 Porong Xizang China
159 G8 Pôrông, Stœng r. Cambodia
146 D2 Porongo, Cerro mt. Arg.
78 E5 Poros Greece
78 E5 Poros i. Greece
16 B5 Poroshkove Ukr.
14 F3 Porosozero Rus. Fed.
57 J4 Poroszló Hungary
14 K3 Porozhsk Rus. Fed.
71 Q5 Porozina Croatia
213 I2 Porpoise Bay Antarctica
98 □2a Porpoise Point Ascension S. Atlantic Ocean
66 K3 Porqueres Spain
41 I11 Porquerolles, Île de i. France
111 N1 Porquis Junction Ont. Can.
73 M4 Porrara, Monte mt. Italy
70 C1 Porrentruy Switz.
67 L8 Porreres Spain
71 J7 Porretta Terme Italy
65 P4 Porrón hill Spain
20 R1 Porsangerfjorden sea chan. Norway
20 R1 Porsangerhalvøya pen. Norway
22 F2 Porsgrunn Norway
20 □F1 Þórshöfn Iceland
38 B4 Porspoder France
79 M3 Porsuk r. Turkey
27 E3 Port Rep. of Ireland
43 H10 Port, Pic du mt. France/Spain
43 H10 Porta France
27 C4 Portacloy Rep. of Ireland
146 B6 Portada Covunco Arg.
204 G6 Port Adelaide S.A. Austr.
27 J4 Portadown Northern Ireland U.K.
203 C14 Port Adventure b. Stewart I. N.Z.
27 K4 Portaferry Northern Ireland U.K.
110 G8 Portage IN U.S.A.
110 I7 Portage MI U.S.A.
116 G8 Portage PA U.S.A.
110 E6 Portage WI U.S.A.
116 D8 Portage Lakes OH U.S.A.
107 L5 Portage la Prairie Man. Can.
62 G9 Portaje Spain
120 D1 Portal ND U.S.A.
106 E5 Port Alberni B.C. Can.
205 K8 Port Albert Vic. Austr.
64 E2 Portalegre Port.
64 D2 Portalegre admin. dist. Port.
121 D8 Portales NM U.S.A.
104 E4 Port Alexander AK U.S.A.
97 K9 Port Alfred S. Africa
106 E5 Port Alice B.C. Can.
116 G7 Port Allegany PA U.S.A.
207 M7 Port Alma Qld Austr.
67 K9 Portals Vells Spain
122 C2 Port Angeles WA U.S.A.
130 □ Port Antonio Jamaica
130 F4 Port-à-Piment Haiti
26 F9 Port Appin Argyll and Bute, Scotland U.K.
78 E2 Portaria Greece
27 H6 Portarlington Rep. of Ireland
205 K10 Port Arthur Tas. Austr.
121 I11 Port Arthur TX U.S.A.
62 F4 Portas, Embalse das resr Spain
26 D11 Port Askaig Argyll and Bute, Scotland U.K.
204 F5 Port Augusta S.A. Austr.
109 J3 Port-au-Port Bay Nfld and Lab. Can.
130 G4 Port-au-Prince Haiti
111 L5 Port Austin MI U.S.A.
109 J3 Port aux Choix Nfld and Lab. Can.
28 G5 Portavogie Northern Ireland U.K.
38 H3 Portbail France
27 I2 Portballintrae Northern Ireland U.K.
26 F11 Port Bannatyne Argyll and Bute, Scotland U.K.
43 K10 Port-Barcarès France
154 B6 Port Barton b. Palawan Phil.
96 E10 Port Beaufort S. Africa
92 B4 Port Bell Uganda
177 M7 Port Blair Andaman & Nicobar Is India
111 O5 Port Bolster Ont. Can.
66 L3 Portbou Spain
206 F2 Port Bradshaw b. N.T. Austr.
39 J5 Port Brillet France
204 F5 Port Broughton S.A. Austr.
111 N7 Port Burwell Ont. Can.
205 I8 Port Campbell Vic. Austr.
205 I8 Port Campbell National Park Vic. Austr.
179 L8 Port Canning W. Bengal India
118 C3 Port Carbon PA U.S.A.
111 O4 Port Carling Ont. Can.
109 H3 Port-Cartier Que. Can.
203 E12 Port Chalmers South I. N.Z.
202 J3 Port Charles North I. N.Z.
115 F12 Port Charlotte FL U.S.A.
31 J6 Portchester Hampshire, England U.K.
119 H2 Port Chester NY U.S.A.
106 C4 Port Clements B.C. Can.
116 C7 Port Clinton OH U.S.A.
118 C3 Port Clinton PA U.S.A.
117 □P5 Port Clyde ME U.S.A.
108 E5 Port Colborne Ont. Can.
118 F3 Port Colden NJ U.S.A.
111 O6 Port Credit Ont. Can.
41 I10 Port-Cros, Île de i. France
41 I11 Port-Cros, Parc National de nat. park France
66 □ Port d'Addia Spain
67 J8 Port d'Andratx Spain
206 C2 Port Darwin b. N.T. Austr.
205 J10 Port Davey b. Tas. Austr.
41 F10 Port-de-Bouc France
66 G6 Port dels Alfacs b. Spain
42 C4 Port-d'Envaux France
43 I10 Port de Pailhères pass France
130 G4 Port-de-Paix Haiti
39 M7 Port-de-Piles France
67 L8 Port de Pollença Spain
118 C5 Port Deposit MD U.S.A.
42 B4 Port-des-Barques France
67 K8 Port de Sóller Spain
66 G2 Port de Venasque pass France/Spain
156 D3 Port Dickson Malaysia
207 J4 Port Douglas Qld Austr.
111 N7 Port Dover Ont. Can.
206 C1 Port Easington inlet N.T. Austr.
110 H4 Porte des Morts lake channel WI U.S.A.
106 D4 Port Edward B.C. Can.
97 O7 Port Edward S. Africa
110 E5 Port Edwards WI U.S.A.
137 G5 Porteira Brazil
143 F1 Porteirinha Brazil
137 I5 Portel Brazil
64 D4 Portel Port.
143 G4 Portela Brazil
142 A2 Portelândia Brazil
41 B10 Portel-des-Corbières France
109 H4 Port Elgin N.B. Can.
108 D4 Port Elgin Ont. Can.
97 J9 Port Elizabeth S. Africa
131 □3 Port Elizabeth St Vincent
66 E6 Portell de Morella Spain
26 D11 Port Ellen Argyll and Bute, Scotland U.K.
147 F2 Portena Arg.
39 J3 Port-en-Bessin-Huppain France
28 H5 Port Erin Isle of Man
107 J2 Porter Lake N.W.T. Can.
107 J3 Porter Lake Sask. Can.
106 D3 Porter Landing B.C. Can.
131 □3 Porter Point St Vincent
118 E2 Porters Lake PA U.S.A.
96 C9 Porterville S. Africa
124 M5 Porterville CA U.S.A.
30 G6 Portesham Dorset, England U.K.
41 F7 Portes-lès-Valence France
130 □ Port Esquivel Jamaica
43 F10 Portet d'Aspet, Col de pass France
30 D4 Port Eynon Swansea, Wales U.K.
205 I8 Port Fairy Vic. Austr.
202 J3 Port Fitzroy North I. N.Z.
90 A5 Port-Gentil Gabon
204 G5 Port Germein S.A. Austr.
121 J10 Port Gibson MS U.S.A.
26 G11 Port Glasgow Inverclyde, Scotland U.K.
27 J3 Portglenone Northern Ireland U.K.
203 I8 Port Gore b. South I. N.Z.
41 J10 Port Grimaud France
97 N7 Port Grosvenor S. Africa
30 F4 Porth Rhondda Cynon Taff, Wales U.K.
89 G5 Port Harcourt Nigeria
106 E5 Port Hardy B.C. Can.
Port Harrison Que. Can. see Inukjuak
109 I4 Port Hawkesbury N.S. Can.
30 E5 Porthcawl Bridgend, Wales U.K.
208 E6 Port Hedland W.A. Austr.
130 □ Port Henderson Jamaica
26 E7 Port Henderson Highland, Scotland U.K.
117 L4 Port Henry NY U.S.A.
30 B7 Porthleven Cornwall, England U.K.
30 D2 Porthmadog Gwynedd, Wales U.K.
78 B5 Porthmos Zakynthou sea chan. Greece
30 C2 Porth Neigwl b. Wales U.K.
111 P6 Port Hope Ont. Can.
111 L6 Port Hope MI U.S.A.
109 K2 Port Hope Simpson Nfld and Lab. Can.
124 M7 Port Hueneme CA U.S.A.
111 L7 Port Huron MI U.S.A.
72 B4 Porticcio Corse France
73 M6 Portici Italy
37 L7 Portieux France
191 J7 Port-İliç Azer.
63 P8 Portilla Spain
63 K2 Portilla de la Reina Spain
146 B3 Portillo Chile
130 E4 Portillo Cuba
63 K6 Portillo Spain
63 M2 Portillo de la Sía mt. Spain
63 L8 Portillo de Toledo Spain
43 F10 Portillon, Col du pass France
64 B6 Portimão Port.
20 S3 Portimo Fin.
67 I9 Portinatx Spain
30 C6 Port Isaac Bay England U.K.
30 G5 Portishead North Somerset, England U.K.
Port Jackson N.S.W. Austr. see Sydney
205 M5 Port Jackson inlet N.S.W. Austr.
119 I3 Port Jefferson NY U.S.A.
119 I3 Port Jefferson Station NY U.S.A.
118 F2 Port Jervis NY U.S.A.
38 G8 Port-Joinville France
130 □ Port Kaiser Jamaica
137 G3 Port Kaituma Guyana
Port Keats N.T. Austr. see Wadeye
205 M6 Port Kembla N.S.W. Austr.
117 L4 Port Kent NY U.S.A.
Port Klang Malaysia see Pelabuhan Klang
26 K7 Portknockie Moray, Scotland U.K.
Port Láirge Rep. of Ireland see Waterford
205 L5 Portland N.S.W. Austr.
204 H8 Portland Vic. Austr.
130 □ Portland parish Jamaica
202 I2 Portland North I. N.Z.
27 F6 Portland Rep. of Ireland
119 J1 Portland CT U.S.A.
114 E5 Portland IN U.S.A.
117 □O5 Portland ME U.S.A.
110 J7 Portland MI U.S.A.
122 C4 Portland OR U.S.A.
30 H6 Portland, Isle of pen. England U.K.
204 H8 Portland Bay Vic. Austr.
130 □ Portland Bight inlet Jamaica
106 D4 Portland Canal inlet B.C. Can.
109 J3 Portland Creek Pond l. Nfld and Lab. Can.
30 H6 Portland Harbour England U.K.
106 D4 Portland Inlet B.C. Can.
202 L6 Portland Island North I. N.Z.
130 □ Portland Point Jamaica
98 □2a Portland Point Ascension S. Atlantic Ocean
130 □ Portland Ridge hill Jamaica
207 I2 Portland Roads Qld Austr.
130 E5 Portland Rock i. Jamaica
41 C10 Port-la-Nouvelle France
27 H6 Portlaoise Rep. of Ireland
121 G11 Port Lavaca TX U.S.A.
27 H8 Portlaw Rep. of Ireland
26 L8 Portlethen Aberdeenshire, Scotland U.K.
43 K10 Port-Leucate France
204 E6 Port Lincoln S.A. Austr.
26 G13 Port Logan Dumfries and Galloway, Scotland U.K.
88 B4 Port Loko Sierra Leone
38 E6 Port-Louis France
131 □2 Port-Louis Guadeloupe
99 □1b Port Louis Mauritius
204 H8 Port MacDonnell S.A. Austr.
205 N4 Port Macquarie N.S.W. Austr.
Portmadoc Gwynedd, Wales U.K. see Porthmadog
27 B9 Portmagee Rep. of Ireland
26 I7 Portmahomack Highland, Scotland U.K.
118 E6 Port Mahon DE U.S.A.
67 D12 Portman Spain
38 D6 Port-Manec'h France
109 I1 Port Manvers inlet Nfld and Lab. Can.
130 □ Port Maria Jamaica
27 J6 Portmarnock Rep. of Ireland
99 □1a Port Mathurin Rodrigues I. Mauritius
206 F3 Port McArthur b. N.T. Austr.
106 E5 Port McNeill B.C. Can.
109 H3 Port-Menier Que. Can.
104 B4 Port Moller b. AK U.S.A.
130 □ Port Morant Jamaica
130 □ Portmore Jamaica
153 K8 Port Moresby P.N.G.
36 B5 Port-Mort France
27 K3 Portmuck Northern Ireland U.K.
207 H1 Port Musgrave b. Qld Austr.
26 F9 Portnacroish Argyll and Bute, Scotland U.K.
26 D6 Portnaguran Western Isles, Scotland U.K.
26 C11 Portnahaven Argyll and Bute, Scotland U.K.
26 D8 Portnalong Highland, Scotland U.K.
Port nan Giúran Scotland U.K. see Portnaguran
Port nan Giúran Western Isles, Scotland U.K. see Portnaguran
26 B7 Port nan Long Western Isles, Scotland U.K.
38 F6 Port-Navalo France
121 I11 Port Neches TX U.S.A.
204 F6 Port Neill S.A. Austr.
130 F2 Port Nelson Rum Cay Bahamas
26 D6 Port Ness Western Isles, Scotland U.K.
109 G3 Portneuf r. Que. Can.
122 H5 Portneuf r. ID U.S.A.
109 F4 Portneuf, Réserve Faunique de nature res. Que. Can.
Port Nis Scotland U.K. see Port Ness
204 G6 Port Noarlunga S.A. Austr.
96 A5 Port Nolloth S. Africa
27 F3 Portnoo Rep. of Ireland
118 E6 Port Norris NJ U.S.A.
Port-Nouveau-Québec Que. Can. see Kangiqsualujjuaq
140 E2 Porto Brazil
72 B3 Porto Corse France
62 C6 Porto Port.
62 D6 Porto admin. dist. Port.
62 G4 Porto Spain
72 B3 Porto, Golfe de b. Corse France
138 D2 Porto Acre Brazil
138 D2 Porto Alegre Amazonas Brazil
141 B7 Porto Alegre Mato Grosso do Sul Brazil
137 H6 Porto Alegre Pará Brazil
141 C9 Porto Alegre Rio Grande do Sul Brazil
142 B3 Porto Alencastro Brazil
Porto Alexandre Angola see Tombua
64 B3 Porto Alto Port.
139 E3 Porto Amarante Brazil
91 B7 Porto Amboim Angola
Porto Amélia Moz. see Pemba
139 G3 Porto Artur Brazil
72 E2 Porto Azzurro Italy
203 E12 Portobello South I. N.Z.
141 C8 Porto Belo Brazil
126 □T13 Portobelo Panama
126 □T13 Portobelo, Parque Nacional nat. park Panama
72 B9 Porto Botte Sardegna Italy
62 C3 Portobravo Spain
141 B7 Porto Camargo Brazil
140 G4 Porto Cavlo Brazil
72 D5 Porto Cervo Sardegna Italy
75 N3 Porto Cesareo Italy
67 L9 Porto Colom Spain
64 B5 Porto Covo da Bandeira Port.
67 L8 Porto Cristo Spain
64 □ Porto da Cruz Madeira
140 F4 Porto da Fôlha Brazil
137 H6 Porto da Lontra Brazil
140 B5 Porto de Meinacos Brazil
62 C9 Porto de Mós Port.
62 D3 Portodemouros, Encoro de resr Spain
137 H5 Porto de Moz Brazil
137 H6 Porto do Barka Brazil
62 E1 Porto do Barqueiro Spain
139 E3 Porto do Massacas Brazil
139 F2 Porto dos Gaúchos Óbidos Brazil
62 B3 Porto do Son Spain
74 F9 Porto Empedocle Sicilia Italy
72 G3 Porto Ercole Italy
139 F4 Porto Esperança Brazil
139 F3 Porto Esperidião Brazil
139 F3 Porto Estrêla Brazil
142 D5 Porto Feliz Brazil
72 E2 Portoferraio Italy
142 D4 Porto Ferreira Brazil
70 G7 Portofino Italy
143 F4 Porto Firme Brazil
26 H10 Port of Menteith Stirling, Scotland U.K.
140 D3 Porto Franco Brazil
131 □7 Port of Spain Trin. and Tob.
71 M6 Porto Garibaldi Italy
137 I4 Porto Grande Brazil
71 N4 Portogruaro Italy
141 B7 Porto Guareí Brazil
88 □ Porto Inglês Cape Verde
139 F4 Porto Jofre Brazil
98 □1a Porto Judeu Terceira Azores
124 L2 Portola CA U.S.A.
74 H7 Porto Levante Isole Lipari Italy
71 M5 Porto Levante Veneto Italy
141 B8 Porto Luceno Brazil
71 L6 Portomaggiore Italy
62 E3 Portomarín Spain
141 B8 Porto Mauá Brazil
64 □ Porto Moniz Madeira
139 F5 Porto Murtinho Brazil
140 C4 Porto Nacional Brazil
89 F5 Porto-Novo Benin
88 □ Porto Novo Cape Verde
74 D8 Porto Palo Sicilia Italy
69 E7 Portopalo di Capo Passero Sicilia Italy
67 L9 Porto Petra Spain
72 B10 Porto Pino Sardegna Italy
142 A5 Porto Primavera Brazil
142 A4 Porto Primavera, Represa resr Brazil
115 G11 Port Orange FL U.S.A.
122 C3 Port Orchard WA U.S.A.
71 P9 Porto Recanati Italy
122 B5 Port Orford OR U.S.A.
91 B6 Porto Rico Angola
88 □ Porto Rincão Santiago Cape Verde
72 D5 Porto Rotondo Sardegna Italy
71 P4 Portorož Slovenia
71 P9 Porto San Giorgio Italy
72 D6 Porto San Paolo Sardegna Italy
137 I5 Porto Santana Brazil
71 P9 Porto Sant'Elpidio Italy
64 □ Porto Santo, Ilha de i. Madeira
72 G3 Porto Santo Stefano Italy
142 A5 Porto São José Brazil
72 A9 Portoscuso Sardegna Italy
143 H2 Porto Seguro Brazil
71 M6 Porto Tolle Italy
72 A6 Porto Torres Sardegna Italy
139 E3 Porto Triunfo Brazil
141 C8 Porto União Brazil
72 C4 Porto-Vecchio Corse France
72 C4 Porto-Vecchio, Golfe de b. Corse France
138 E2 Porto Velho Brazil
70 H7 Portovenere Italy
136 A5 Portoviejo Ecuador
138 B2 Porto Wálter Brazil
26 F13 Portpatrick Dumfries and Galloway, Scotland U.K.
203 B14 Port Pegasus b. Stewart I. N.Z.
118 D5 Port Penn DE U.S.A.
111 P5 Port Perry Ont. Can.
205 J8 Port Phillip Bay Vic. Austr.
204 G5 Port Pirie S.A. Austr.
27 J6 Portrane Rep. of Ireland
30 B7 Portreath Cornwall, England U.K.
26 D8 Portree Highland, Scotland U.K.
106 E5 Port Renfrew B.C. Can.
109 K3 Port Rexton Nfld and Lab. Can.
27 F7 Portroe Rep. of Ireland
206 E3 Port Roper b. N.T. Austr.
111 N7 Port Rowan Ont. Can.
130 □ Port Royal Jamaica
116 H10 Port Royal VA U.S.A.
115 G9 Port Royal Sound inlet SC U.S.A.
27 I2 Portrush Northern Ireland U.K.
Port Said Egypt see Bûr Sa'îd
43 E6 Port-Ste-Foy-et-Ponchapt France
43 E7 Port-Ste-Marie France
115 E11 Port St Joe FL U.S.A.
97 N7 Port St Johns S. Africa
41 F10 Port-St-Louis-du-Rhône France
115 G12 Port St Lucie City FL U.S.A.
28 H5 Port St Mary Isle of Man
38 H7 Port-St-Père France
38 B4 Portsall France
27 G2 Portsalon Rep. of Ireland
145 F8 Port Salvador Falkland Is
111 L6 Port Sanilac MI U.S.A.
59 J6 Pörtschach am Wörther See Austria
66 F6 Ports de Beseit mts Spain
111 O5 Port Severn Ont. Can.
97 O6 Port Shepstone S. Africa
Port Simpson B.C. Can. see Lax Kw'alaams
131 □2 Portsmouth Dominica
31 J6 Portsmouth Portsmouth, England U.K.
31 J6 Portsmouth admin. div. England U.K.
117 □O5 Portsmouth NH U.S.A.
116 C10 Portsmouth OH U.S.A.
117 I12 Portsmouth VA U.S.A.
26 K7 Portsoy Aberdeenshire, Scotland U.K.
Port Stanley Falkland Is see Stanley
205 N5 Port Stephens b. N.S.W. Austr.
145 E9 Port Stephens Falkland Is
27 I2 Portstewart Northern Ireland U.K.
85 H5 Port Sudan Sudan
121 K11 Port Sulphur LA U.S.A.
37 L8 Port-sur-Saône France
Port Swettenham Malaysia see Pelabuhan Klang
30 E4 Port Talbot Neath Port Talbot, Wales U.K.
154 D5 Port Tambang b. Luzon Phil.
20 S2 Porttipahdan tekojärvi l. Fin.
122 C2 Port Townsend WA U.S.A.
118 B3 Port Trevorton PA U.S.A.
60 C3 Portugal country Europe
63 N2 Portugalete Spain
136 D2 Portuguesa state Venez.
27 F6 Portumna Rep. of Ireland
62 C5 Portuzelo Port.
43 K10 Port-Vendres France
204 F6 Port Victoria S.A. Austr.
200 □5 Port Vila Vanuatu
116 G6 Portville NY U.S.A.
204 F6 Port Vincent S.A. Austr.
20 V2 Port Vladimir Rus. Fed.
202 I4 Port Waikato North I. N.Z.
204 G6 Port Wakefield S.A. Austr.
208 H3 Port Warrender W.A. Austr.
119 H3 Port Washington NY U.S.A.
110 G6 Port Washington WI U.S.A.
Port Weld Malaysia see Kuala Sepetang
26 G13 Port William Dumfries and Galloway, Scotland U.K.
110 C3 Port Wing WI U.S.A.
176 F5 Porumamilla Andhra Prad. India
130 □ Porus Jamaica
19 O4 Porus'ya r. Rus. Fed.
20 □E1 Þorvaldsfell vol. Iceland
147 F4 Porvenir Arg.
138 C2 Porvenir Pando Bol.
139 E3 Porvenir Santa Cruz Bol.
145 C9 Porvenir Chile
147 I3 Porvenir Uru.
21 R6 Porvoo Fin.
18 I1 Porvoonjoki r. Fin.
163 E10 Poryŏng S. Korea
55 J3 Porządzie Pol.
65 K2 Porzuna Spain
19 R1 Posad Rus. Fed.
72 D6 Posada Sardegna Italy
72 D6 Posada r. Sardegna Italy
62 I2 Posada Spain
63 K2 Posada de Valdeón Spain
144 G2 Posadas Arg.
65 I5 Posadas Spain
213 G2 Posadowsky Bay Antarctica
17 L7 Posad-Pokrovs'ke Ukr.
68 F3 Posavina reg. Bos.-Herz./Croatia

Posavsko Hribovje to Ptsich

323

59 K7 Posavsko Hribovje reg. Slovenia
70 I3 Poschiavo Switz.
78 F5 Poseidonia Syros Greece
Posen Pol. see Poznań
11 K4 Posen MI U.S.A.
50 H2 Poseritz Ger.
66 F2 Posets mt. Spain
14 G4 Poshekhon'ye Rus. Fed.
Poshekon'ye-Volodarsk Rus. Fed. see Poshekhon'ye
84 H7 Posht watercourse Iran
84 G4 Posht-e Āsemān spring Iran
84 F5 Posht-e Badam Iran
84 H6 Poshteh-ye Chaqvīr hill Iran
84 B5 Posht-e Kūh mts Iran
84 C3 Posht Kūh hill Iran
17 M9 Poshtove Ukr.
58 D8 Posina r. Italy
53 N3 Pösing Ger.
20 T3 Posio Fin.
73 M6 Positano Italy
Poskam Xinjiang China see Zepu
19 J2 Posnet CT U.S.A.
55 B4 Poso Sulawesi Indon.
55 B4 Poso r. Indon.
55 B4 Poso, Danau l. Indon.
55 B4 Poso, Teluk b. Indon.
89 K3 Posof Turkey
91 D4 Posof r. Turkey
63 E11 Posŏng S. Korea
36 A5 Posorja Ecuador
83 S1 Pospelikha Rus. Fed.
58 E8 Possagno Italy
40 D5 Posse Brazil
90 C3 Possel C.A.R.
51 I9 Possendorf Ger.
37 I6 Possesse France
94 B5 Possession Island Namibia
13 L2 Possession Islands Antarctica
51 E9 Pößneck Ger.
27 J1 Possum Kingdom Lake TX U.S.A.
21 E9 Post TX U.S.A.
73 K2 Posta Italy
77 O5 Poşta Câlnău Romania
Poşta Cîlnău Romania see Poşta Câlnău
71 K2 Postal Italy
73 P5 Posta Piana Italy
53 M4 Postau Ger.
53 K3 Postbauer-Heng Ger.
97 J8 Post Chalmers S. Africa
99 □1b Poste de Flacq Mauritius
99 □1b Poste de Flacq, Rivière du r. Mauritius
Poste-de-la-Baleine Que. Can. see Kuujjuarapik
45 J6 Posterholt Neth.
96 H4 Postmasburg S. Africa
Post-Mawr Wales U.K. see Synod Inn
53 N5 Postmünster Ger.
68 E3 Postojna Slovenia
55 J3 Postoliska Pol.
56 C1 Postoloprty Czech Rep.
54 C3 Postomia r. Pol.
54 E1 Postomino Pol.
25 R7 Poston AZ U.S.A.
09 J2 Postville Nfld and Lab. Can.
10 C6 Postville IA U.S.A.
87 F4 Post Weygand Alg.
68 F4 Posušje Bos.-Herz.
55 I4 Poświętne Łódzkie Pol.
55 J3 Poświętne Pol.
55 K3 Poświętne Podlaskie Pol.
62 G7 Pos'yet Rus. Fed.
55 B8 Pota Flores Indon.
26 D4 Pótam Mex.
78 F2 Potamia Thasos Greece
78 D6 Potamos Kythira Greece
19 P1 Potanino Rus. Fed.
20 E4 Potato Creek SD U.S.A.
97 L2 Potchefstroom S. Africa
77 M6 Potcoava Romania
43 G2 Poté Brazil
21 H8 Poteau OK U.S.A.
76 G3 Potegaon Mahar. India
54 F1 Potęgowo Pol.
15 I6 Potemkino Rus. Fed.
Potentia Italy see Potenza
73 P6 Potenza Italy
73 P6 Potenza prov. Italy
71 P9 Potenza r. Italy
71 P9 Potenza Picena Italy
03 B13 Poteriteri, Lake South I. N.Z.
63 K2 Potes Spain
96 I6 Potfontein S. Africa
40 E3 Poti r. Brazil
91 C3 P'ot'i Georgia
39 K4 Potigny France
76 G3 Potikal Chhattisgarh India
41 F5 Potiraguá Brazil
89 H4 Potiskum Nigeria
16 H3 Potiyivka Ukr.
22 F3 Potlatch ID U.S.A.
00 □5 Potnarvin Vanuatu
38 C3 Poto Peru
71 □J7 Po Toi i. H.K. China
55 K5 Potok Górny Pol.
55 H5 Potok Złoty Pol.
16 H9 Potomac MD U.S.A.
16 I10 Potomac r. MD/VA U.S.A.
16 G9 Potomac, South Branch r. WV U.S.A.
16 F10 Potomac, South Fork South Branch r. WV U.S.A.
55 D8 Potomana, Gunung mt. Indon.
88 C5 Potoru Sierra Leone
38 D4 Potosí Bol.
38 D5 Potosí dept Bol.
14 B7 Potosi MO U.S.A.
25 Q6 Potosi Mountain NV U.S.A.
54 D6 Pototan Panay Phil.
44 C2 Potrerillos Chile
26 □P10 Potrerillos Hond.
46 C3 Potrerilos Arg.
26 G3 Potrero del Llano Chihuahua Mex.
29 J4 Potrero del Llano Veracruz Mex.
29 M8 Potrero Largo Mex.
36 B6 Potro r. Peru
51 H6 Potsdam Ger.
17 K4 Potsdam NY U.S.A.
51 G6 Potsdamer Havelseengebiet park Ger.
57 G2 Potštát Czech Rep.
00 □5 Pott, Île i. New Caledonia
77 H3 Pottangi Orissa India
59 N4 Pottendorf Austria
59 N4 Pottenstein Austria
53 K2 Pottenstein Ger.
20 D5 Potter NE U.S.A.
30 H5 Potterne Wiltshire, England U.K.
31 L4 Potters Bar Hertfordshire, England U.K.
24 I2 Potter Valley CA U.S.A.
16 A6 Potterville MI U.S.A.
53 K4 Pöttmes Ger.
31 L3 Potton Bedfordshire, England U.K.
59 N4 Pöttsching Austria
18 B2 Potts Grove PA U.S.A.
18 D4 Pottstown PA U.S.A.
18 C3 Pottsville PA U.S.A.
76 G9 Pottuvil Sri Lanka
17 S2 Potudan' r. Rus. Fed.
85 O5 Potwar reg. Pak.
55 I4 Potworów Pol.
52 C2 Potzberg hill Ger.
38 I6 Pouancé France
06 F4 Pouce Coupe B.C. Can.
09 K4 Pouch Cove Nfld and Lab. Can.
00 □5 Pouébo New Caledonia
00 □5 Pouembout New Caledonia
17 L7 Poughkeepsie NY U.S.A.
19 H1 Poughquag NY U.S.A.
40 C2 Pougny France
40 C2 Pougues-les-Eaux France
36 H7 Pougy France
40 H2 Pouilley-les-Vignes France
43 C8 Pouillon France
40 F2 Pouilly-en-Auxois France
40 E4 Pouilly-sous-Charlieu France
40 B2 Pouilly-sur-Loire France
40 G2 Pouilly-sur-Saône France
39 O7 Poulaines France
38 C6 Pouldreuzic France
38 D6 Pouldu, Anse de b. France
40 E4 Poule-les-Écharmeaux France
27 D9 Poulgorm Bridge Rep. of Ireland
39 N8 Pouligny-St-Pierre France
109 G3 Poulin de Courval, Lac l. Que. Can.
38 D5 Poullaouen France
27 G8 Poulnamucky Rep. of Ireland
117 L5 Poultney VT U.S.A.
29 L6 Poulton-le-Fylde Lancashire, England U.K.
200 □5 Poum New Caledonia
89 H6 Pouma Cameroon
116 C11 Pound VA U.S.A.
96 I6 Poupan S. Africa
43 F8 Poupas France
40 H3 Poupet, Mont hill France
41 H10 Pourcieux France
202 K7 Pourerere North I. N.Z.
36 F8 Pourrain France
40 J5 Pourri, Mont mt. France
41 H9 Pourrières France
147 G5 Pourtalé Arg.
43 D10 Pourtalet, Col du pass France
62 F7 Pousada Port.
143 E5 Pouso Alegre Brazil
142 A2 Pouso Alto Brazil
62 C9 Pousos Port.
41 D10 Poussan France
37 L7 Poussay France
20 T4 Poussu Fin.
200 □2 Poutasi Samoa
159 F8 Poŭthĭsăt Cambodia
202 I3 Pouto North I. N.Z.
37 M7 Pouxeux France
158 E5 Pouy, Nam r. Laos
43 E9 Pouyastruc France
43 D8 Pouydesseaux France
43 G9 Pouy-de-Touges France
42 C2 Pouzauges France
39 M7 Pouzay France
19 U5 Povarovo Rus. Fed.
57 H2 Považská Bystrica Slovakia
57 G3 Považský Inovec mts Slovakia
19 R4 Poved' r. Rus. Fed.
65 N3 Povedilla Spain
14 F3 Povenets Rus. Fed.
202 L5 Poverty Bay North I. N.Z.
71 J6 Poviglio Italy
76 H6 Povlen mt. Serb. and Mont.
64 D2 Póvoa, Barragem da resr Port.
98 □1b Povoação São Miguel Azores
143 H3 Povoação Brazil
62 D5 Póvoa de Lanhoso Port.
64 E4 Póvoa de São Miguel Port.
62 C6 Póvoa de Varzim Port.
62 F7 Póvoa do Concelho Port.
71 O3 Povoletto Italy
15 H6 Povorino Rus. Fed.
162 H7 Povorotnyy, Mys hd Rus. Fed.
16 E2 Povors'k Ukr.
51 J9 Povrly Czech Rep.
124 O9 Poway CA U.S.A.
29 N3 Powburn Northumberland, England U.K.
122 L3 Powder r. MT U.S.A.
122 F4 Powder r. OR U.S.A.
122 K5 Powder, South Fork r. WY U.S.A.
122 K5 Powder River WY U.S.A.
118 B1 Powell PA U.S.A.
122 J4 Powell WY U.S.A.
116 B12 Powell r. TN/VA U.S.A.
125 V4 Powell, Lake resr UT U.S.A.
207 I8 Powell Creek watercourse Qld Austr.
124 N3 Powell Mountain NV U.S.A.
130 E1 Powell Point Eleuthera Bahamas
106 E5 Powell River B.C. Can.
27 F9 Power Head Rep. of Ireland
110 G4 Powers MI U.S.A.
27 F6 Power's Cross Rep. of Ireland
121 J7 Powhatan AR U.S.A.
116 H11 Powhatan VA U.S.A.
116 E9 Powhatan Point OH U.S.A.
30 H3 Powick Worcestershire, England U.K.
54 F3 Powidz Pol.
54 F3 Powidzkie, Jezioro l. Pol.
26 I10 Powmill Perth and Kinross, Scotland U.K.
170 B2 Powo Sichuan China
30 F3 Powys admin. div. Wales U.K.
141 B5 Poxoréu Brazil
200 □5 Poya New Caledonia
63 J8 Poyales del Hoyo Spain
156 □ Poyan, Sungai r. Sing.
171 K4 Poyang Hu l. China
156 □ Poyan Reservoir Sing.
162 F4 Poyarkovo Rus. Fed.
63 P8 Poyatos Spain
110 F5 Poygan, Lake WI U.S.A.
191 H4 Poylu Azer.
110 E6 Poynette WI U.S.A.
29 M7 Poynton Cheshire, England U.K.
27 J4 Poyntz Pass Northern Ireland U.K.
65 O5 Poyo, Cerro mt. Spain
79 I3 Poyrazcık Turkey
59 O2 Poysdorf Austria
21 Q6 Pöytyä Fin.
63 N3 Poza de la Sal Spain
63 K6 Pozaldez Spain
188 G5 Pozantı Turkey
76 J6 Požarevac Srbija Serb. and Mont.
129 J5 Poza Rica Mex.
57 K3 Pozdišovce Slovakia
68 F3 Požega Croatia
76 I7 Požega Srbija Serb. and Mont.
55 J1 Pozezdrze Pol.
19 O5 Pozhnya Rus. Fed.
17 O3 Pozhnya Ukr.
14 L4 Pozhva Rus. Fed.
57 G2 Pozlovice Czech Rep.
54 E3 Poznań Pol.
65 N5 Pozo, Sierra del mts Spain
65 N5 Pozo Alcón Spain
63 J5 Pozoantiguo Spain
144 D2 Pozo Betbeder Arg.
65 J4 Pozoblanco Spain
65 P3 Pozo Cañada Spain
139 F5 Pozo Colorado Para.
63 N8 Pozo de Guadalajara Spain
147 F3 Pozo del Molle Arg.
144 E2 Pozo del Tigre Arg.
144 D2 Pozo Hondo Arg.
65 P3 Pozohondo Spain
65 Q2 Pozo-Lorente Spain
63 R7 Pozondón Spain
63 R7 Pozondón, Puerto de pass Spain
98 □3b Pozo Negro Fuerteventura Canary Is
126 D3 Pozo Nuevo Mex.
59 O1 Pozořice Czech Rep.
63 O9 Pozorrubio Spain
145 D7 Pozos, Punta pt Arg.
144 E2 Pozo San Martin Arg.
54 D2 Poźrzadło Wielkie Pol.
65 O3 Pozuelo Spain
63 M8 Pozuelo de Alarcón Spain
63 R5 Pozuelo de Aragón Spain
62 I4 Pozuelo del Páramo Spain
63 N8 Pozuelo del Rey Spain
62 H8 Pozuelo de Zarzón Spain
65 K3 Pozuelos de Calatrava Spain
138 B2 Pozuzo Peru
71 L3 Pozza di Fassa Italy
74 H10 Pozzallo Sicilia Italy
74 H8 Pozzillo, Lago di l. Sicilia Italy
70 F6 Pozzolo Formigaro Italy
72 B7 Pozzomaggiore Sardegna Italy
73 M6 Pozzuoli Italy
58 H8 Pozzuolo del Friuli Italy
88 E5 Pra r. Ghana
19 Y7 Pra r. Rus. Fed.
156 F6 Prabumulih Sumatera Indon.
55 H2 Prabuty Pol.
62 E9 Pracana, Barragem de resr Port.
56 D2 Prachatice Czech Rep.
177 J3 Prachi r. India
159 E7 Prachin Buri Thai.
49 E9 Pracht Ger.
159 D9 Prachuap Khiri Khan Thai.
53 N3 Prackenbach Ger.
62 G4 Prada, Embalse de resr Spain
62 F2 Pradairo mt. Spain
63 L3 Prádanos de Ojeda Spain
56 G1 Praděd mt. Czech Rep.
63 P4 Pradejón Spain
41 D7 Pradelles France
43 J9 Pradelles-en-Val France
63 M6 Prádena Spain
136 B4 Pradera Col.
43 I10 Prades Languedoc-Roussillon France
43 H10 Prades Midi-Pyrénées France
41 B7 Prades-d'Aubrac France
63 O4 Pradillo Spain
43 G7 Pradines France
143 H2 Prado Brazil
62 D5 Prado Port.
63 J3 Prado de la Guzpeña Spain
64 H7 Prado del Rey Spain
63 N4 Pradoluengo Spain
142 C4 Pradópolis Brazil
41 I8 Prads-Haute-Bléone France
22 I6 Præstø Denmark
70 B5 Pragelato Italy
59 M7 Pragersko Slovenia
58 F5 Prägraten Austria
Prague Czech Rep. see Praha
56 D1 Praha Czech Rep.
51 J10 Praha admin. reg. Czech Rep.
56 C2 Praha hill Czech Rep.
42 D3 Prahecq France
77 O6 Prahova r. Romania
Prai Malaysia see Perai
88 □ Praia Santiago Cape Verde
98 □1c Praia, Ilhéu da i. Azores
73 P8 Praia a Mare Italy
62 C7 Praia da Barra Port.
64 B6 Praia da Rocha Port.
62 C8 Praia da Tocha Port.
62 C7 Praia de Esmoriz Port.
62 C8 Praia de Mira Port.
98 □1c Praia do Almoxarife Faial Azores
95 G5 Praia do Bilene Moz.
98 □1c Praia do Norte Faial Azores
142 D6 Praia Grande Brazil
74 H2 Praiano Italy
139 G3 Praia Rica Brazil
64 B3 Praias do Sado Port.
98 □1c Prainha Pico Azores
139 E1 Prainha Amazonas Brazil
137 H5 Prainha Pará Brazil
207 J6 Prairie Qld Austr.
110 A2 Prairie r. MN U.S.A.
122 E4 Prairie City OR U.S.A.
121 E8 Prairie Dog Town Fork r. TX U.S.A.
110 C6 Prairie du Chien WI U.S.A.
107 K4 Prairie River Sask. Can.
157 J8 Prajekan Jawa Indon.
159 F7 Prakhon Chai Thai.
57 J3 Prakovce Slovakia
41 J6 Pralognan-la-Vanoise France
41 J8 Pra-Loup France
19 P8 Pralyetarskaye Belarus
59 H3 Pram r. Austria
78 C3 Pramanta Greece
59 I3 Prambachkirchen Austria
89 F5 Prampram Ghana
159 E8 Pran r. Thai.
159 D8 Pran Buri Thai.
88 E5 Prang Ghana
18 I2 Prangli i. Estonia
176 F3 Pranhita r. India
59 J5 Prankerhöhe mt. Austria
156 C3 Prapat Sumatera Indon.
57 H3 Prašice Slovakia
191 F1 Praskoveya Rus. Fed.
56 G2 Přáslavice Czech Rep.
37 J8 Praslay France
99 □2a Praslin i. Inner Islands Seychelles
131 □3 Praslin Bay St Lucia
79 I7 Prasonisi, Akra pt Rodos Greece
23 N2 Prästfjärden b. Sweden
54 G4 Praszka Pol.
145 B8 Prat i. Chile
142 C3 Prata Brazil
142 A3 Prata r. Brazil
142 C3 Prata r. Brazil
142 D2 Prata r. Brazil
71 N4 Prata di Pordenone Italy
178 E7 Pratapgarh Rajasthan India
51 G7 Pratau Ger.
66 F6 Prat de Comte Spain
66 G5 Pratdip Spain
73 M5 Pratella Italy
Prathes Thai country Asia see Thailand
142 D3 Pratinha Brazil
71 K8 Prato Italy
71 K8 Prato prov. Italy
71 J2 Prato allo Stelvio Italy
73 L3 Pratola Peligna Italy
74 H2 Pratola Serra Italy
71 L8 Pratovecchio Italy
66 J3 Prats de Lluçanès Spain
43 I11 Prats-de-Mollo-la-Preste France
121 F7 Pratt KS U.S.A.
70 D1 Pratteln Switz.
70 H2 Prättigau reg. Switz.
115 D9 Prattville AL U.S.A.
37 J8 Prauthoy France
176 D3 Pravara r. India
77 P7 Pravda Bulg.
18 E7 Pravdinsk Rus. Fed.
17 L7 Pravdyne Ukr.
62 H2 Pravia Spain
55 M2 Pravyya Masty Belarus
30 E7 Prawle Point England U.K.
157 L9 Praya Lombok Indon.
43 G6 Prayssac France
43 F7 Prayssas France
40 J5 Praz-sur-Arly France
159 H8 Preah, Prêk r. Cambodia
159 G8 Preăh Vihear Cambodia
59 I5 Prebersee l. Austria
117 I6 Preble NY U.S.A.
59 L7 Prebold Slovenia
43 D7 Préchac France
43 C8 Préchacq-les-Bains France
19 P6 Prechistoye Smolenskaya Oblast' Rus. Fed.
14 H4 Prechistoye Yaroslavskaya Oblast' Rus. Fed.
73 K2 Preci Italy
39 K6 Précigné France
57 H2 Prečín Slovakia
207 M8 Precipice National Park Qld Austr.
40 E2 Précy-sous-Thil France
71 L7 Predappio Italy
71 L3 Predazzo Italy
77 N5 Predeal Romania
59 L6 Preding Austria
59 I5 Predlitz Austria
59 I8 Predmeja Slovenia
70 F6 Predosa Italy
107 K5 Preeceville Sask. Can.
39 K5 Pré-en-Pail France
30 G2 Prees Shropshire, England U.K.
29 L6 Preesall Lancashire, England U.K.
48 J2 Preetz Ger.
38 G7 Préfailles France
71 M4 Preganziòl Italy
59 K3 Pregarten Austria
18 D7 Pregolya r. Rus. Fed.
66 □ Pregonda, Cala b. Spain
59 M7 Pregrada Croatia
191 C2 Pregradnaya Rus. Fed.
43 D6 Preignac France
43 F8 Preignan France
18 J5 Preiļi Latvia
111 P1 Preissac, Lac l. Que. Can.
59 K6 Preitenegg Austria
43 I9 Preixan France
77 N5 Prejmer Romania
76 H8 Prekornica mts Serb. and Mont.
107 I5 Prelate Sask. Can.
59 O3 Prellenkirchen Austria
59 O7 Prelog Croatia
56 E1 Přelouč Czech Rep.
71 Q4 Prem Slovenia
68 D3 Premantura Croatia
205 L4 Premer N.S.W. Austr.
40 C2 Prémery France
70 E3 Premia Italy
66 J5 Premià de Mar Spain
71 L8 Premilcuore Italy
40 B4 Prémilhat France
50 F5 Premnitz Ger.
36 F4 Prémontré France
70 E3 Premosello Chiovenda Italy
16 H6 Prenistrului, Dealurile hills Moldova
68 F4 Prenj mts Bos.-Herz.
110 D4 Prentice WI U.S.A.
121 K10 Prentiss MS U.S.A.
50 I4 Prenzlau Ger.
162 H7 Preobrazheniye Rus. Fed.
17 N6 Preobrazhenka Ukr.
191 E1 Preobrazhenskoye Rus. Fed.
159 A7 Preparis Island Cocos Is
158 A7 Preparis North Channel Cocos Is
159 A7 Preparis South Channel Cocos Is
40 D3 Préporché France
56 G2 Přerov Czech Rep.
62 D9 Presa Port.
128 G3 Presa de Guadalupe Mex.
127 I3 Presa de la Amistad, Parque Natural nature res. Mex.
41 E7 Présailles France
40 J5 Pre-St-Didier Italy
71 J3 Presanella, Cima mt. Italy
127 I5 Presa San Antonio Mex.
Prescelly Mts hills Wales U.K. see Preseli, Mynydd
29 L7 Prescot Merseyside, England U.K.
108 F4 Prescott Ont. Can.
121 I9 Prescott AR U.S.A.
125 T7 Prescott AZ U.S.A.
110 B5 Prescott WI U.S.A.
125 T7 Prescott Valley AZ U.S.A.
30 C4 Preseli, Mynydd hills Wales U.K.
203 A13 Preservation Inlet South I. N.Z.
77 J8 Preševo Srbija Serb. and Mont.
120 E4 Presho SD U.S.A.
75 O4 Presicce Italy
144 F2 Presidencia Roca Arg.
144 E2 Presidencia Roque Sáenz Peña Arg.
142 C5 Presidente Alves Brazil
142 B5 Presidente Bernardes Brazil
144 F2 Presidente de la Plaza Arg.
140 D3 Presidente Dutra Brazil
212 U2 Presidente Eduardo Frei research stn Antarctica
142 A4 Presidente Epitácio Brazil
139 E2 Presidente Hermes Brazil
143 E3 Presidente Juscelino Brazil
142 D3 Presidente Olegário Brazil
142 B5 Presidente Prudente Brazil
142 B4 Presidente Venceslau Brazil
128 A2 Presidio r. Mex.
123 L12 Presidio TX U.S.A.
Preslav Bulg. see Veliki Preslav
183 L1 Presnovka Kazakh.
57 K3 Prešov Slovakia
57 K2 Prešovský Kraj admin. reg. Slovakia
78 C2 Prespa, Lake Europe
Prespansko Ezero l. Europe see Prespa, Lake
78 C2 Prespes nat. park Greece
Prespës, Liqeni i l. Europe see Prespa, Lake
117 □Q2 Presque Isle ME U.S.A.
111 K4 Presque Isle MI U.S.A.
110 E3 Presque Isle WI U.S.A.
110 G3 Presque Isle Point MI U.S.A.
42 F3 Pressac France
53 L2 Pressath Ger.
59 N3 Pressbaum Austria
51 E10 Presseck Ger.
59 H6 Pressegger See l. Austria
51 G7 Pressel Ger.
51 D10 Pressig Ger.
30 F1 Prestatyn Denbighshire, Wales U.K.
29 M7 Prestbury Cheshire, England U.K.
30 H4 Prestbury Gloucestershire, England U.K.
88 E5 Prestea Ghana
22 H3 Prestebakke Norway
30 F3 Presteigne Powys, Wales U.K.
56 C2 Přeštice Czech Rep.
30 H6 Preston Dorset, England U.K.
29 Q6 Preston East Riding of Yorkshire, England U.K.
29 L6 Preston Lancashire, England U.K.
26 L11 Preston Scottish Borders, Scotland U.K.
115 E9 Preston GA U.S.A.
122 I5 Preston ID U.S.A.
117 J10 Preston MD U.S.A.
110 B6 Preston MN U.S.A.
121 I7 Preston MO U.S.A.
208 D6 Preston, Cape W.A. Austr.
29 L2 Prestonpans East Lothian, Scotland U.K.
116 C11 Prestonsburg KY U.S.A.
212 N1 Prestrud Inlet Antarctica
29 M6 Prestwich Greater Manchester, England U.K.
26 G12 Prestwick South Ayrshire, Scotland U.K.
142 B3 Preto r. Brazil
142 C4 Preto r. Brazil
142 D2 Preto r. Brazil
139 E2 Preto r. Brazil
140 E4 Preto r. Brazil
137 E5 Preto r. Brazil
137 F5 Preto r. Brazil
97 M1 Pretoria S. Africa
51 G7 Prettin Ger.
118 B5 Prettyboy Lake MD U.S.A.
53 K2 Pretzfeld Ger.
50 D5 Pretzier Ger.
51 G7 Pretzsch Ger.
51 I9 Pretzschendorf Ger.
39 M8 Preuilly-sur-Claise France
49 G6 Preußisch Oldendorf Ger.
Preußisch Stargard Pol. see Starogard Gdański
59 K6 Prevalje Slovenia
41 D7 Prévenchères France
42 I3 Préveranges France
78 B4 Preveza Greece
159 G9 Prey Vêng Cambodia
59 K7 Prežganje Slovenia
71 R4 Prezid Croatia
37 J7 Prez-sous-Lafauche France
58 D8 Priaforà, Monte mt. Italy
162 I4 Priamurskiy Rus. Fed.
182 J4 Priaral'skiye Karakumy, Peski des. Kazakh.
62 G3 Priaranza del Bierzo Spain
169 P1 Priargunsk Rus. Fed.
17 R8 Priazovskaya Rus. Fed.
57 H4 Pribeta Slovakia
56 F3 Přibice Czech Rep.
104 A4 Pribilof Islands AK U.S.A.
68 F3 Pribinić Bos.-Herz.
59 N7 Pribislavec Croatia
76 H7 Priboj Srbija Serb. and Mont.
57 H2 Příbor Czech Rep.
50 G4 Priborn Ger.
56 D2 Příbram Czech Rep.
55 I1 Pribrezhnoye Rus. Fed.
56 E2 Přibyslav Czech Rep.
206 C3 Price r. N.T. Austr.
109 G3 Price Que. Can.
116 F12 Price NC U.S.A.
125 V2 Price UT U.S.A.
125 V2 Price r. UT U.S.A.
106 D4 Price Island B.C. Can.
18 E6 Prichaly Rus. Fed.
121 K10 Prichard AL U.S.A.
116 C10 Prichard WV U.S.A.
53 I2 Prichsenstadt Ger.
131 □6 Prickly Point Grenada
63 P8 Priego Spain
65 K6 Priego de Córdoba Spain
18 E5 Priekule Latvia
18 E6 Priekulė Lith.
18 I4 Priekuļi Latvia
18 G7 Prienai Kaunas Lith.
18 I7 Prienai Vilnius Lith.
53 M6 Prien am Chiemsee Ger.
51 I6 Prieros Ger.
96 G5 Prieska S. Africa
96 G5 Prieskapoort pass S. Africa
51 G8 Prießnitz Sachsen Ger.
51 E8 Prießnitz Sachsen-Anhalt Ger.
51 I8 Priestewitz Ger.
Priestholm i. Wales U.K. see Puffin Island
122 F2 Priest Lake ID U.S.A.
130 □ Priestman's River Jamaica
65 J7 Prieta, Sierra mt. Spain
65 M3 Prieto hill Spain
56 G3 Prievaly Slovakia
57 H3 Prievidza Slovakia
50 F4 Prignitz reg. Ger.
19 Q8 Prigor'ye Rus. Fed.
68 F3 Prijedor Bos.-Herz.
76 H7 Prijepolje Srbija Serb. and Mont.
182 A5 Prikaspiyskaya Nizmennost' lowland Kazakh./Rus. Fed.
88 E5 Prikro Côte d'Ivoire
17 R8 Prikubanskaya Nizmennost' lowland Rus. Fed.
77 J9 Prilep Macedonia
Priluki Ukr. see Pryluky
67 H10 Prima, Punta pt Spain
138 D2 Primavera Bol.
140 B5 Primavera do Leste Brazil
56 B2 Přimda Czech Rep.
140 E2 Primeira Cruz Brazil
38 D4 Primel, Pointe de pt France
147 F2 Primero r. Arg.
130 D3 Primero de Enero Cuba
120 H4 Primghar IA U.S.A.
71 L4 Primolano Italy
55 I1 Primorsk Kaliningradskaya Oblast' Rus. Fed.
18 L1 Primorsk Leningradskaya Oblast' Rus. Fed.
15 I6 Primorsk Volgogradskaya Oblast' Rus. Fed.
Primorsk Ukr. see Prymors'k
162 G7 Primorskiy Rus. Fed.
162 I6 Primorskiy Kray admin. div. Rus. Fed.
15 G7 Primorsko-Akhtarsk Rus. Fed.
Primorskoye Ukr. see Prymors'ke
126 A1 Primo Tapia Mex.
106 B2 Primrose r. Y.T. Can.
107 I4 Primrose Lake Alta/Sask. Can.
52 B3 Prims r. Ger.
107 J4 Prince Albert Sask. Can.
96 G9 Prince Albert S. Africa
213 K1 Prince Albert Mountains Antarctica
107 J4 Prince Albert National Park Sask. Can.
104 G2 Prince Albert Peninsula N.W.T. Can.
96 F8 Prince Albert Road S. Africa
104 G2 Prince Albert Sound sea chan. N.W.T. Can.
104 F2 Prince Alfred, Cape N.W.T. Can.
96 D9 Prince Alfred Hamlet S. Africa
105 K3 Prince Charles Island Nunavut Can.
213 E2 Prince Charles Mountains Antarctica
109 I4 Prince Edward Island prov. Can.
215 G8 Prince Edward Islands Indian Ocean
111 R6 Prince Edward Point Ont. Can.
116 I10 Prince Frederick MD U.S.A.
208 H3 Prince Frederick Harbour W.A. Austr.
106 F4 Prince George B.C. Can.
118 B7 Prince George's County county MD U.S.A.
105 H2 Prince Gustaf Adolf Sea Nunavut Can.
213 C2 Prince Harald Coast Antarctica
104 B3 Prince of Wales, Cape AK U.S.A.
207 I1 Prince of Wales Island Qld Austr.
105 I2 Prince of Wales Island Nunavut Can.
104 E4 Prince of Wales Island AK U.S.A.
104 G2 Prince of Wales Strait N.W.T. Can.
104 G2 Prince Patrick Island N.W.T. Can.
208 H3 Prince Regent r. W.A. Austr.
105 I2 Prince Regent Inlet sea chan. Nunavut Can.
208 H3 Prince Regent Nature Reserve W.A. Austr.
106 D4 Prince Rupert B.C. Can.
131 □2 Prince Rupert Bay Dominica
31 K4 Princes Risborough Buckinghamshire, England U.K.
117 J10 Princess Anne MD U.S.A.
213 A2 Princess Astrid Coast Antarctica
207 I3 Princess Charlotte Bay Qld Austr.
213 F2 Princess Elizabeth Land reg. Antarctica
107 L1 Princess Mary Lake Nunavut Can.
208 H3 Princess May Range hills W.A. Austr.
203 B12 Princess Mountains South I. N.Z.
213 B2 Princess Ragnhild Coast Antarctica
209 F8 Princess Range hills W.A. Austr.
106 D4 Princess Royal Island B.C. Can.
131 □7 Prince's Town Trin. and Tob.
31 J3 Princethorpe Warwickshire, England U.K.
106 F5 Princeton B.C. Can.
124 J2 Princeton CA U.S.A.
110 E8 Princeton IL U.S.A.
114 D6 Princeton IN U.S.A.
114 D7 Princeton KY U.S.A.
117 □R3 Princeton ME U.S.A.
120 I5 Princeton MO U.S.A.
118 F4 Princeton NJ U.S.A.
110 E6 Princeton WI U.S.A.
116 D11 Princeton WV U.S.A.
118 F4 Princeton Junction NJ U.S.A.
30 E6 Princetown Devon, England U.K.
117 □R3 Prince William N.B. Can.
204 □2 Prince William Henry Bay Lord Howe I. Austr.
104 D3 Prince William Sound b. AK U.S.A.
89 G6 Príncipe i. São Tomé and Príncipe
122 D4 Prineville OR U.S.A.
78 F2 Prinos Thasos Greece
44 G5 Prinsenbeek Neth.
Prins Harald Kyst coastal area Antarctica see Prince Harald Coast
20 □ Prins Karls Forland i. Svalbard
17 Q3 Printsevka Rus. Fed.
126 □R11 Prinzapolca Nic.
48 G5 Prinzhöfte Ger.
75 I9 Priolo Gargallo Sicilia Italy
204 □3 Prion Lake S. Pacific Ocean
62 D1 Prior, Cabo c. Spain
62 D2 Prioriño Grande, Cabo c. Spain
63 K3 Prioro Spain
Priozernyy Kazakh. see Tugyl
19 N1 Priozersk Rus. Fed.
Priozyorsk Rus. Fed. see Priozersk
16 J2 Pripet r. Belarus/Ukr. alt. Pryp"yat' (Ukraine), alt. Prypyats' (Belarus)
16 D2 Pripet Marshes Belarus/Ukr.
173 K14 Priphema Nagaland India
14 L2 Pripolyarnyy Ural mts Rus. Fed.
77 P4 Priponeşti Romania
20 U2 Prirechnyy Rus. Fed.
77 P3 Prisăcani Romania
68 F3 Priseka hill Croatia
77 M3 Prislop, Pasul pass Romania
56 E1 Příšovice Czech Rep.
42 G2 Prissac France
40 F4 Prissé France
Pristan' Przheval'sk Kyrg. see Przheval'sk Pristany
17 P2 Pristen' Rus. Fed.
76 J8 Priština Kosovo, Srbija Serb. and Mont.
178 G7 Prithvipur Madh. Prad. India
53 J5 Prittriching Ger.
51 F6 Pritzerbe Ger.
50 D4 Pritzier Ger.
50 F4 Pritzwalk Ger.
41 F7 Privas France
73 K5 Priverno Italy
68 E3 Privlaka Croatia
19 S6 Privokzal'nyy Rus. Fed.
17 R7 Privol'naya Rus. Fed.
19 Y4 Privolzhsk Rus. Fed.
15 I6 Privolzhskaya Vozvyshennost' hills Rus. Fed.
15 I6 Privolzhskiy Rus. Fed.
182 A2 Privolzhskoye Rus. Fed.
182 C1 Privolzh'ye Rus. Fed.
15 H7 Priyutnoye Rus. Fed.
76 I8 Prizren Kosovo, Srbija Serb. and Mont.
74 E8 Prizzi Sicilia Italy
68 F3 Prnjavor Bos.-Herz.
62 H2 Proaza Spain
62 G3 Proba Spain
77 K8 Probištip Macedonia
157 J8 Probolinggo Jawa Indon.
48 J2 Probsteierhagen Ger.
51 D9 Probstzella Ger.
30 C7 Probus Cornwall, England U.K.
72 H2 Proceno Italy
54 E4 Prochowice Pol.
73 M6 Procida Italy
73 M6 Procida, Isola di i. Italy
110 B3 Proctor MN U.S.A.
117 L5 Proctor VT U.S.A.
116 C10 Proctorville OH U.S.A.
176 F5 Proddatur Andhra Prad. India
62 E9 Proença-a-Nova Port.
62 F8 Proença-a-Velha Port.
51 F8 Profen Ger.
137 H3 Professor van Blommestein Meer resr Suriname
45 G8 Profondeville Belgium
71 J5 Progno r. Italy
147 G2 Progreso Arg.
127 I4 Progreso Coahuila Mex.
129 H5 Progreso Hidalgo Mex.
129 K9 Progreso Oaxaca Mex.
127 O7 Progreso Yucatán Mex.
128 D2 Progreso Zacatecas Mex.
162 F4 Progress Rus. Fed.
138 C2 Progresso Brazil
50 H2 Prohn Ger.
122 C6 Project City CA U.S.A.
55 I1 Prokhladnaya r. Rus. Fed.
191 F2 Prokhladnyy Rus. Fed.
17 P2 Prokhorovka Rus. Fed.
17 L2 Prokhory Ukr.
76 H8 Prokletije mts Albania/Yugo.
78 E4 Prokopi Greece
192 J4 Prokop'yevsk Rus. Fed.
77 J7 Prokuplje Srbija Serb. and Mont.
19 O3 Proletariy Rus. Fed.
15 H7 Proletarsk Rus. Fed.
Proletarskaya Rus. Fed. see Proletarsk
17 O3 Proletarskiy Rus. Fed.
Prome Myanmar see Pyè
118 E2 Promised Land Lake PA U.S.A.
139 G4 Promissão Mato Grosso do Sul Brazil
142 C4 Promissão São Paulo Brazil
142 C4 Promissão, Represa resr Brazil
55 I4 Promna Pol.
73 P4 Promontorio del Gargano plat. Italy
118 E1 Prompton PA U.S.A.
118 E1 Prompton Lake PA U.S.A.
14 H4 Pronino Rus. Fed.
49 B10 Pronsfeld Ger.
19 W7 Pronsk Rus. Fed.
48 J3 Pronstorf Ger.
19 O8 Pronya r. Belarus
106 F3 Prophet r. B.C. Can.
106 F3 Prophet River B.C. Can.
110 E8 Prophetstown IL U.S.A.
140 F4 Propriá Brazil
72 B4 Propriano Corse France
50 I2 Prorer Wiek b. Ger.
191 H1 Prorva r. Rus. Fed.
182 K1 Proryvnoye Rus. Fed.
56 F2 Proseč Czech Rep.
51 I8 Prösen Ger.
59 N6 Prosenjakovci Slovenia
26 K9 Prosen Water r. Scotland U.K.
207 L6 Proserpine Qld Austr.
18 L6 Proshkava Belarus
79 G2 Proskynites Greece
54 F3 Prosna r. Pol.
78 E1 Prosotsani Greece
119 J1 Prospect CT U.S.A.
117 J5 Prospect NY U.S.A.
116 B8 Prospect OH U.S.A.
122 C5 Prospect OR U.S.A.
116 E8 Prospect PA U.S.A.
119 G4 Prospect Plains NJ U.S.A.
130 □ Prospect Point Jamaica
154 E7 Prosperidad Mindanao Phil.
28 D7 Prosperous Rep. of Ireland
98 □2b Prosperous Bay St Helena
122 E3 Prosser WA U.S.A.
56 G2 Prostějov Czech Rep.
55 K2 Prostki Pol.
207 M9 Proston Qld Austr.
17 N8 Prostorne Ukr.
183 O3 Prostornoye Kazakh.
14 K2 Prosunduy Rus. Fed.
17 O4 Prosyane Ukr.
54 F5 Prószków Pol.
55 I5 Proszowice Pol.
55 I5 Proszówki Pol.
96 E10 Protem S. Africa
78 C5 Proti i. Greece
56 F2 Protivanov Czech Rep.
56 D2 Protivín Czech Rep.
17 Q8 Protoka r. Rus. Fed.
17 P4 Protopopivka Ukr.
16 J3 Protsiv Ukr.
19 T6 Protva Rus. Fed.
19 U7 Protva r. Rus. Fed.
19 U7 Protvino Rus. Fed.
50 I5 Prötzel Ger.
77 P7 Provadiya Bulg.
64 B5 Provença Port.
41 G10 Provence airport France
41 I9 Provence-Alpes-Côte d'Azur admin. reg. France
37 N7 Provenchères-sur-Fave France
117 N7 Providence RI U.S.A.
203 A13 Providence, Cape South I. N.Z.
99 □2 Providence Atoll Seychelles
111 L4 Providence Bay Ont. Can.
136 B5 Providencia Ecuador
130 C7 Providencia, Isla de i. Caribbean Sea
139 E2 Providência, Serra de hills Brazil
130 G3 Providenciales Island Turks and Caicos Is
193 T3 Provideniya Rus. Fed.
207 I2 Providential Channel Qld Austr.
117 O6 Provincetown MA U.S.A.
136 C3 Provincia Col.
36 F6 Provins France
125 U1 Provo UT U.S.A.
107 I4 Provost Alta Can.
68 F4 Prozor Bos.-Herz.
19 U3 Prozorovo Rus. Fed.
76 I9 Prrenjas Albania
88 E4 Pru r. Ghana
14 K3 Prub r. Rus. Fed.
17 L8 Prubiynyy, Mys pt Ukr.
55 K6 Pruchnik Pol.
142 B6 Prudentópolis Brazil
29 N4 Prudhoe Northumberland, England U.K.
104 D2 Prudhoe Bay AK U.S.A.
207 L6 Prudhoe Island Qld Austr.
17 N8 Prudi Ukr.
19 P7 Prudki Rus. Fed.
54 F5 Prudnik Pol.
17 P3 Prudyanka Ukr.
18 L6 Prudzinki Belarus
57 K3 Prügy Hungary
51 K10 Průhonice Czech Rep.
49 B10 Prüm Ger.
49 B11 Prüm r. Ger.
65 I7 Pruna Spain
77 M6 Prundeni Romania
77 O6 Prundu Romania
77 M3 Prundu Bârgăului Romania
Prundu Bîrgăului Romania see Prundu Bârgăului
72 C3 Prunelli-di-Fiumorbo Corse France
43 I6 Prunet France
41 I7 Prunières France
39 O7 Pruniers-en-Sologne France
116 E9 Pruntytown WV U.S.A.
59 O2 Prušánky Czech Rep.
Prushkov Pol. see Pruszków
54 E4 Prusice Pol.
57 G2 Prusinovice Czech Rep.
54 G2 Pruszcz Pol.
23 O7 Pruszcz Gdański Pol.
55 I3 Pruszków Pol.
16 H8 Prut r. Europe
53 M6 Prutting Ger.
58 C5 Prutz Austria
18 H9 Pruzhany Belarus
19 W9 Pruzhinki Rus. Fed.
57 H2 Pružina Slovakia
59 I8 Prvačina Slovenia
68 E3 Prvić i. Croatia
17 O2 Pryamitsyno Rus. Fed.
17 O6 Pryazovs'ka Vysochyna hills Ukr.
17 O7 Pryazovs'ke Ukr.
17 L6 Prychornomors'ka Nyzovyna lowland Ukr.
213 F2 Prydz Bay Antarctica
191 D2 Pryelbrussky Natsional'nyy Park nat. park Rus. Fed.
17 Q3 Prykolotne Ukr.
17 L3 Pryluky Ukr.
17 P7 Prymors'k Ukr.
Prymors'ke Donets'ka Oblast' Ukr. see Sartana
17 M7 Prymors'ke Khersons'ka Oblast' Ukr.
16 I8 Prymors'ke Odes'ka Oblast' Ukr.
17 O6 Prymors'ke Zaporiz'ka Oblast' Ukr.
17 O8 Prymors'kyy Ukr.
121 H7 Pryor OK U.S.A.
16 J2 Pryp"yat' Ukr.
16 J2 Pryp"yat' r. Ukr. alt. Prypyats' (Belarus), conv. Pripet
16 H1 Prypyats' r. Belarus alt. Pryp"yat' (Ukraine), conv. Pripet
16 G2 Prypyatski Hidrlahichny Zapavyednik nature res. Belarus
18 K6 Prypyernaye Belarus
17 R4 Pryvillya Ukr.
17 L6 Pryvil'ne Ukr.
17 O8 Pryvitne Respublika Krym Ukr.
16 D3 Pryvitne Volyns'ka Oblast' Ukr.
17 M5 Pryyutivka Ukr.
55 I2 Przasnysz Pol.
54 F2 Przechlewo Pol.
55 H5 Przeciszów Pol.
55 J5 Przecław Pol.
57 I1 Przedborski Park Krajobrazowy Pol.
55 H4 Przedbórz Pol.
54 G3 Przedecz Pol.
54 D2 Przelewice Pol.
47 H3 Przemęcki Park Krajobrazowy Pol.
54 D4 Przemków Pol.
57 I1 Przemsza r. Pol.
55 K6 Przemyśl Pol.
55 K1 Przerośl Pol.
55 K3 Przesmyki Pol.
55 L5 Przewale Pol.
55 L4 Przewłoka Pol.
54 F5 Przeworno Pol.
55 K5 Przeworsk Pol.
54 C4 Przewóz Pol.
55 K3 Przeździatka Pol.
55 I2 Przezdzięk Wielki Pol.
55 H2 Przezmark Pol.
162 H7 Przheval'skogo, Gory mts Rus. Fed.
19 O6 Przheval'skoye Rus. Fed.
183 R6 Przheval'sk Pristany Kyrg.
54 G1 Przodkowo Pol.
54 C2 Przybiernów Pol.
55 I3 Przyborowice Pol.
54 G3 Przybranowo Pol.
54 F4 Przygodzice Pol.
54 G4 Przykona Pol.
55 H5 Przyrów Pol.
55 J5 Przyrwa r. Pol.
54 G5 Przystajń Pol.
55 I4 Przysucha Pol.
54 D3 Przytoczna Pol.
55 K4 Przytoczno Pol.
55 K2 Przytuły Pol.
55 I4 Przytyk Pol.
54 G1 Przywidz Pol.
78 E4 Psachna Greece
Psakhná Greece see Psachna
78 F6 Psalidis, Akra pt Milos Greece
79 G4 Psara Greece
79 G4 Psara i. Greece
78 F3 Psathoura i. Greece
191 B1 Psebay Rus. Fed.
191 F2 Psedakh Rus. Fed.
191 A1 Psekups r. Rus. Fed.
Psel r. Rus. Fed./Ukr. see Ps'ol
17 P2 Pselets Rus. Fed.
79 I6 Pserimos i. Greece
17 R9 Pshada Rus. Fed.
191 A1 Pshekha r. Rus. Fed.
Pskent Uzbek. see Piskent
17 N8 Pshenychne Ukr.
191 A1 Pshish r. Rus. Fed.
191 B2 P'skhu Georgia
191 C2 P'skhus Nakrdzali nature res. Georgia
18 L4 Pskov Rus. Fed.
18 K3 Pskov, Lake Estonia/Rus. Fed.
18 L4 Pskova r. Rus. Fed.
Pskov Oblast admin. div. Rus. Fed. see Pskovskaya Oblast'
18 M4 Pskovskaya Oblast' admin. div. Rus. Fed.
Pskovskoye Ozero l. Estonia/Rus. Fed. see Pskov, Lake
17 O2 Ps'ol r. Rus. Fed./Ukr.
68 F3 Psunj mts Croatia
191 E2 Psynodakh Rus. Fed.
54 D3 Pszczew Pol.
47 G2 Pszczewski Park Krajobrazowy Pol.
54 G1 Pszczółki Pol.
55 H4 Pszczonów Pol.
54 G6 Pszczyna Pol.
19 V8 Ptan' r. Rus. Fed.
78 D3 Pteleos Greece
Ptich' Belarus see Ptsich
78 C2 Ptolemaïda Greece
16 H1 Ptsich Belarus
18 L9 Ptsich r. Belarus

68 E2 Ptuj Slovenia
59 M7 Ptujsko jezero l. Slovenia
16 E3 Ptycha Ukr.
156 E6 Pu r. Indon.
146 A6 Púa Chile
158 E5 Pua Thai.
156 □ Puaka hill Sing.
124 □F14 Puakō HI U.S.A.
147 F5 Puán Arg.
170 E6 Pu'an Guizhou China
170 E3 Pu'an Sichuan China
200 □2 Pu'apu'a Samoa
200 □2 Puava, Cape Samoa
158 I3 Pubei Guangxi China
40 J4 Publier France
136 B6 Pucacaca Peru
136 C5 Pucacuro Peru
136 C5 Pucacuro r. Peru
136 B6 Pucalá Peru
138 B2 Pucallpa Peru
138 D4 Pucará Bol.
138 C3 Pucara Peru
138 C4 Pucarani Bol.
136 D5 Puca Urco Peru
58 H4 Puch bei Hallein Austria
59 M4 Puchberg am Schneeberg Austria
171 L5 Pucheng Fujian China
169 K9 Pucheng Shaanxi China
14 H4 Puchezh Rus. Fed.
53 K5 Puchheim Ger.
163 E10 Puch'ŏn S. Korea
57 H2 Púchov Slovakia
146 C2 Puchuzúh Arg.
77 N5 Pucioasa Romania
154 C6 Pucio Point Panay Phil.
23 O7 Puck Pol.
23 O7 Pucka, Zatoka b. Pol.
27 F7 Puckaun Rep. of Ireland
209 D8 Puckford, Mount hill W.A. Austr.
67 E8 Puçol Spain
146 B6 Pucón Chile
184 F5 Pūdanū Iran
20 S4 Pudasjärvi Fin.
30 H6 Puddletown Dorset, England U.K.
49 E9 Puderbach Ger.
157 L6 Pudi Kalimantan Indon.
97 I3 Pudimoe S. Africa
170 E5 Puding Guizhou China
171 M3 Pudong Shanghai China
161 L5 Pudong airport Shanghai China
171 M3 Pudong airport China
14 G3 Pudozh Rus. Fed.
29 N6 Pudsey West Yorkshire, England U.K.
Pudu Hubei China see Suizhou
Puduchcheri Pondicherry India see Pondicherry
176 F7 Pudukkottai Tamil Nadu India
129 J5 Puebillo Mex.
125 Q9 Puebla Baja California Mex.
129 I6 Puebla Puebla Mex.
129 I7 Puebla state Mex.
147 G2 Puebla Brugo Arg.
66 D5 Puebla de Albortón Spain
65 I3 Puebla de Alcocer Spain
66 D4 Puebla de Alfindén Spain
63 O9 Puebla de Almenara Spain
63 N7 Puebla de Beleña Spain
66 F6 Puebla de Benifasar Spain
62 F3 Puebla de Brollón Spain
65 O5 Puebla de Don Fadrique Spain
65 J2 Puebla de Don Rodrigo Spain
64 E5 Puebla de Guzmán Spain
64 F3 Puebla de la Calzada Spain
64 G3 Puebla de la Reina Spain
63 J2 Puebla de Lillo Spain
64 G4 Puebla del Maestre Spain
65 N3 Puebla del Príncipe Spain
64 G3 Puebla del Prior Spain
64 F2 Puebla de Obando Spain
62 G4 Puebla de Sanabria Spain
64 G4 Puebla de Sancho Pérez Spain
Puebla de San Julián Spain see Puebla de San Xulián
67 C7 Puebla de San Miguel Spain
62 F3 Puebla de San Xulián Spain
62 H7 Puebla de Yeltes Spain
Puebla de Zaragoza Mex. see Puebla
130 F8 Pueblito Col.
123 L7 Pueblo CO U.S.A.
147 H2 Pueblo Arrúa Arg.
144 C2 Pueblo Hundido Chile
147 F3 Pueblo Italiano Arg.
147 H2 Pueblo Libertador Arg.
147 G2 Pueblo Marini Arg.
128 B2 Pueblo Nuevo Mex.
126 □P11 Pueblo Nuevo Nic.
136 E4 Pueblo Viejo Col.
129 J3 Pueblo Viejo, Laguna de lag. Mex.
126 D4 Pueblo Yaqui Mex.
41 B8 Puech del Pal mt. France
43 I7 Puech de Rouet hill France
146 E6 Puelches Arg.
146 D5 Puelén Arg.
146 B3 Puente Alto Chile
Puenteareas Spain see Ponteareas
Puente Caldelas Spain see Ponte Caldelas
128 D4 Puente de Camotlán Mex.
62 G4 Puente de Domingo Flórez Spain
65 N4 Puente de Génave Spain
129 H7 Puente de Ixtla Mex.
62 I8 Puente del Congosto Spain
146 C3 Puente del Inca Arg.
66 G3 Puente de Montañana Spain
63 L2 Puente de San Miguel Spain
65 J6 Puente-Genil Spain
63 Q3 Puente la Reina Spain
63 L2 Puentenansa Spain
65 J4 Puente Nuevo, Embalse de resr Spain
65 P5 Puentes, Embalse de resr Spain
63 M6 Puentes Viejas, Embalse de resr Spain
136 D2 Puente Torres Venez.
63 M2 Puente Viesgo Spain
170 C7 Pu'er Yunnan China
131 □1 Puerca, Punta pt Puerto Rico
125 V7 Puerco watercourse AZ U.S.A.
123 K9 Puerco watercourse NM U.S.A.
138 C3 Puerto Acosta Bol.
145 B7 Puerto Aisén Chile
139 E3 Puerto Alegre Bol.
138 D3 Puerto Alejandría Bol.
136 D5 Puerto Alfonso Col.
136 B6 Puerto America Peru
127 K10 Puerto Ángel Mex.
129 K10 Puerto Angel Mex.
139 F6 Puerto Antequera Para.
129 N10 Puerto Arista Mex.
126 □R13 Puerto Armuelles Panama
136 B4 Puerto Asís Col.
136 E3 Puerto Ayacucho Venez.
136 □ Puerto Ayora Islas Galápagos Ecuador
145 B7 Puerto Bajo Pisagua Chile
136 □ Puerto Baquerizo Moreno Islas Galápagos Ecuador
126 □O10 Puerto Barrios Guat.
147 F6 Puerto Belgrano Arg.
144 F2 Puerto Bermejo Arg.
136 C3 Puerto Berrío Col.
136 C3 Puerto Boyaca Col.
136 D2 Puerto Cabello Venez.
126 □R10 Puerto Cabezas Nic.
126 □R10 Puerto Cabo Gracias á Dios Nic.
136 E3 Puerto Carreño Col.
139 F5 Puerto Casado Para.
138 D3 Puerto Cavinas Bol.
136 C5 Puerto Cerpera Peru
138 C2 Puerto Ceticayo Peru
145 B7 Puerto Chacabuco Chile
136 B6 Puerto Chicama Peru
145 B7 Puerto Cisnes Chile
145 C8 Puerto Coig Arg.
130 F8 Puerto Colombia Col.
147 H3 Puerto Constanza Arg.
136 D5 Puerto Córdoba Col.
126 □R13 Puerto Cortés Costa Rica
126 □P10 Puerto Cortés Hond.
126 D5 Puerto Cortés Mex.
136 C4 Puerto Cuemaní Col.
136 D2 Puerto Cumarebo Venez.
62 I8 Puerto de Béjar Spain
Puerto de Cabras Fuerteventura Canary Is see Puerto del Rosario
136 A5 Puerto de Cayo Ecuador
138 C3 Puerto Definitivo Peru
131 L8 Puerto de Hierro Venez.
98 □3b Puerto de la Cruz Fuerteventura Canary Is
98 □3a Puerto de la Cruz Tenerife Canary Is
98 □3e Puerto de la Estaca El Hierro Canary Is
128 G2 Puerto del Aire Mex.
98 □3b Puerto de la Peña Fuerteventura Canary Is
98 □3c Puerto del Carmen Lanzarote Canary Is
128 G8 Puerto del Gallo Mex.
129 H3 Puerto del Higuerón Mex.
126 C2 Puerto de Lobos Mex.
128 B2 Puerto de Los Ángeles, Parque Natural nature res. Mex.
129 I1 Puerto de los Ébanos Mex.
98 □3b Puerto del Rosario Fuerteventura Canary Is
Puerto del Son Galicia Spain see Porto do Son
67 C12 Puerto de Mazarrón Spain
127 P7 Puerto de Morelos Mex.
136 D2 Puerto de Nutrias Venez.
128 G4 Puerto de Palmas Mex.
128 G1 Puerto de Pastores Mex.
Puerto de Pollensa Spain see Port de Pollença
65 I1 Puerto de San Vicente Spain
Puerto de Sóller Spain see Port de Sóller
129 J10 Puerto Escondido Mex.
136 D1 Puerto Estrella Col.
136 B6 Puerto Eten Peru
144 C2 Puerto Flamenco Chile
139 E3 Puerto Frey Bol.
147 F6 Puerto Galván Arg.
138 D3 Puerto Génova Bol.
138 D4 Puerto Grether Bol.
139 F5 Puerto Guarani Para.
145 D9 Puerto Harberton Arg.
138 C3 Puerto Heath Bol.
136 C4 Puerto Huitoto Col.
147 H3 Puerto Ibicuy Arg.
138 B2 Puerto Inca Peru
145 B7 Puerto Ingeniero Ibáñez Chile
147 F6 Puerto Ingeniero White Arg.
136 E4 Puerto Inírida Col.
144 E1 Puerto Irigoyen Arg.
139 F4 Puerto Isabel Bol.
126 □Q12 Puerto Jesus Costa Rica
127 P7 Puerto Juáres Mex.
131 K8 Puerto La Cruz Venez.
144 E1 Puerto La Paz Arg.
65 M2 Puerto Lápice Spain
66 F2 Puértolas Spain
136 C5 Puerto Leguizamo Col.
126 □R10 Puerto Lempira Hond.
126 C3 Puerto Libertad Mex.
126 □R12 Puerto Limón Costa Rica
65 K3 Puertollano Spain
145 D6 Puerto Lobos Arg.
136 D2 Puerto Lopez Col.
136 C3 Puerto Lopéz Col.
136 A5 Puerto López Ecuador
65 P5 Puerto Lumbreras Spain
127 M10 Puerto Madero Mex.
145 D6 Puerto Madryn Arg.
126 C5 Puerto Magdalena Mex.
138 C3 Puerto Maldonado Peru
138 D4 Puerto Mamoré Bol.
130 E3 Puerto Manatí Cuba
136 A6 Puerto Máncora Peru
139 F5 Puerto María Auxiliadora Para.
Puertomarín Spain see Portomarín
138 D3 Puerto Marquez Bol.
145 B6 Puerto Melinka Chile
136 C4 Puerto Mercedes Col.
139 F5 Puerto Mihanovich Para.
67 E7 Puertomingalvo Spain
136 E3 Puerto Miranda Venez.
145 B6 Puerto Montt Chile
126 □P11 Puerto Morazán Nic.
136 B7 Puerto Morín Peru
98 □3d Puerto Naos La Palma Canary Is
145 B8 Puerto Natales Chile
136 D3 Puerto Nuevo Col.
136 C3 Puerto Olaya Col.
137 F2 Puerto Ordaz Venez.
136 C4 Puerto Ospina Col.
130 E3 Puerto Padre Cuba
136 E3 Puerto Páez Venez.
138 D3 Puerto Pando Bol.
136 B5 Puerto Pardo Peru
138 C3 Puerto Pariamanu Peru
126 C2 Puerto Peñasco Mex.
139 F5 Puerto Pinasco Para.
145 D6 Puerto Pirámides Arg.
137 E2 Puerto Píritu Venez.
136 C5 Puerto Pizarro Col.
130 H4 Puerto Plata Dom. Rep.
138 B2 Puerto Portillo Peru
138 B2 Puerto Prado Peru
154 B7 Puerto Princesa Palawan Phil.
126 □Q13 Puerto Quepos Costa Rica
126 N11 Puerto Quetzal Guat.
127 N8 Puerto Real Mex.
64 G7 Puerto Real Spain
144 G2 Puerto Rico Arg.
138 D2 Puerto Rico Bol.
98 □3f Puerto Rico Gran Canaria Canary Is
136 C4 Puerto Rico Col.
131 □1 Puerto Rico terr. West Indies
214 E4 Puerto Rico Trench sea feature Caribbean Sea
147 H3 Puerto Ruiz Arg.
145 B5 Puerto Saavedra Chile
136 C3 Puerto Salgar Col.
Puerto Sama Cuba see Samá
136 D5 Puerto San Agustin Peru
145 B7 Puerto San Carlos Chile
126 □P11 Puerto Sandino Nic.
127 N11 Puerto San José Guat.
145 C8 Puerto Santa Cruz Arg.
139 F5 Puerto Sastre Para.
139 E3 Puerto Saucedo Bol.
Puertos de Beceite mts Spain see Ports de Beseit
62 G7 Puerto Seguro Spain
64 H7 Puerto Serrano Spain
138 D3 Puerto Siles Bol.
136 D5 Puerto Socorro Peru
Puerto Somoza Nic. see Puerto Sandino
139 F4 Puerto Suárez Bol.
138 A2 Puerto Supe Peru
138 C3 Puerto Tahuantisuyo Peru
136 B4 Puerto Tejado Col.
136 B5 Puerto Tunigrama Peru
136 B4 Puerto Umbría Col.
145 E6 Puerto Valdés Arg.
128 B5 Puerto Vallarta Mex.
145 B6 Puerto Varas Chile
136 □ Puerto Velasco Ibarra Islas Galápagos Ecuador
138 B2 Puerto Victoria Peru
136 □ Puerto Villamil Islas Galápagos Ecuador
139 E3 Puerto Villazon Bol.
145 D7 Puerto Visser Arg.
136 C3 Puerto Wilches Col.
145 C9 Puerto Yartou Chile
147 H2 Puerto Yerua Arg.
136 C5 Puesto Arturo Peru
146 D6 Puesto Sánchez Arg.
201 □3a Pueu Tahiti Fr. Polynesia
63 Q3 Pueyo Spain
71 L2 Puez-Odle, Parco Naturale nature res. Italy
30 D1 Puffin Island Wales U.K.
139 F4 Puga Brazil
182 C1 Pugachev Rus. Fed.
14 K4 Pugachevo Rus. Fed.
178 D5 Pugal Rajasthan India
93 C8 Puga Puga, Ilha i. Moz.
170 D5 Puge Sichuan China
157 J9 Puger Jawa Indon.
41 J10 Puget-sur-Argens France
41 J9 Puget-Théniers France
41 I10 Puget-Ville France
118 D4 Pughtown PA U.S.A.
73 P5 Puglia admin. reg. Italy
73 I2 Puglia r. Italy
42 C5 Pugnac France
73 Q4 Pugnochiuso Italy
109 I4 Pugwash N.S. Can.
202 L5 Puha North I. N.Z.
184 F8 Pūhāl-e Khamīr, Kūh-e mts Iran
169 J9 Pu He r. China
Puhiwaero c. Stewart I. N.Z. see South West Cape
18 J3 Puhja Estonia
77 L5 Pui Romania
41 B10 Puichéric France
77 P5 Puiești Romania
67 E8 Puig Spain
66 I3 Puigcerdà Spain
61 H1 Puig de Comanegra mt. Spain
66 I3 Puig de les Morreres mt. Spain
67 L9 Puig de Sant Salvador hill Spain
67 K8 Puig des Galatzó mt. Spain
67 K8 Puig Major mt. Spain
66 J3 Puigmal mt. France/Spain
66 I3 Puig Pedrós mt. Spain
66 I4 Puig-reig Spain
66 G4 Puigverd de Lleida Spain
41 I9 Puimoisson France
171 □I7 Pui O Wan b. H.K. China
40 B2 Puisaye reg. France
36 D7 Puiseaux France
36 E3 Puisieux France
43 D6 Puisseguin France
41 C10 Puisserguier France
36 H6 Puits r. France
84 C6 Puits 29 well Chad
84 C6 Puits 30 well Chad
43 I10 Puivert France
154 F8 Pujada Bay Mindanao Phil.
41 F8 Pujaut France
88 C5 Pujehun Sierra Leone
Puji Shaanxi China see Wugong
171 L4 Pujiang Zhejiang China
43 E9 Pujo France
43 D6 Pujols Aquitaine France
43 F7 Pujols Aquitaine France
203 E11 Pukaki, Lake South I. N.Z.
57 H3 Pukanec Slovakia
163 E10 Puk'an-san National Park S. Korea
203 □2 Pukapuka atoll Cook Is
201 □3 Pukapuka atoll Arch. des Tuamotu Fr. Polynesia
201 □3 Pukarua atoll Arch. des Tuamotu Fr. Polynesia
110 I1 Pukaskwa r. Ont. Can.
108 C3 Pukaskwa National Park Ont. Can.
107 K4 Pukatawagan Man. Can.
163 D8 Pukchin N. Korea
163 F8 Pukch'ŏng N. Korea
76 H8 Pukë Albania
202 M4 Pukeamaru hill North I. N.Z.
202 I5 Pukearuhe North I. N.Z.
202 K6 Pukehoi North I. N.Z.
202 I4 Pukekohe North I. N.Z.
202 H1 Pukenui North I. N.Z.
202 J6 Pukeokahu North I. N.Z.
203 E12 Pukerangi South I. N.Z.
203 D13 Pukerau South I. N.Z.
202 J6 Pukeroa North I. N.Z.
203 I8 Pukerua Bay North I. N.Z.
203 G10 Puketeraki Range mts South I. N.Z.
202 K6 Puketitiri North I. N.Z.
202 L4 Puketoetoe mt. North I. N.Z.
202 K7 Puketoi Range hills North I. N.Z.
202 J5 Puketutu North I. N.Z.
203 F12 Pukeuri Junction South I. N.Z.
19 O6 Pukhnovo Rus. Fed.
17 S3 Pukhovo Rus. Fed.
21 R6 Pukkila Fin.
14 K4 Puksib Rus. Fed.
14 H3 Puksoozero Rus. Fed.
163 E8 Puksubaek-san mt. N. Korea
68 D3 Pula Croatia
71 P6 Pula airport Croatia
72 C9 Pula Sardegna Italy
72 C10 Pula, Capo di c. Sardegna Italy
138 D5 Pulacayo Bol.
169 R7 Pulandian Liaoning China
169 Q7 Pulandian Wan b. China
154 E8 Pulangi r. Mindanao Phil.
157 K6 Pulangpisau Kalimantan Indon.
153 K5 Pulap atoll Micronesia
138 C6 Pular, Cerro mt. Chile
155 B7 Pulasi i. Indon.
117 I5 Pulaski NY U.S.A.
115 D8 Pulaski TN U.S.A.
116 E11 Pulaski VA U.S.A.
110 F5 Pulaski WI U.S.A.
153 I8 Pulau r. Papua Indon.
156 E5 Pulaukijang Sumatera Indon.
157 J4 Pulaumajang Kalimantan Indon.
Pulau Pinang state Malaysia see Pinang
55 J4 Puławy Pol.
31 K6 Pulborough West Sussex, England U.K.
71 O3 Pulfero Italy
178 G9 Pulgaon Mahar. India
63 L9 Pulgar Spain
49 C8 Pulheim Ger.
176 G6 Pulicat Tamil Nadu India
176 G6 Pulicat Lake inlet India
40 F3 Puligny-Montrachet France
176 F5 Pulivendla Andhra Prad. India
20 R2 Pulju Fin.
59 M2 Pulkau Austria
59 N2 Pulkau r. Austria
20 R4 Pulkkila Fin.
53 L5 Pullach in Isartal Ger.
122 F3 Pullman WA U.S.A.
138 B3 Pullo Peru
153 H6 Pulo Anna i. Palau
154 C3 Pulog, Mount Luzon Phil.
20 V2 Pulozero Rus. Fed.
65 P6 Pulpí Spain
126 D4 Púlpito, Punta pt Mex.
75 M3 Pulsano Italy
51 H8 Pulsen Ger.
51 J8 Pulsnitz Ger.
51 I8 Pulsnitz r. Ger.
55 J3 Pułtusk Pol.
173 E8 Pulu Xinjiang China
208 □2 Pulu Capelok i. Cocos Is
189 I4 Pülümür Turkey
208 □2 Pulu Pandang i. Cocos Is
153 K5 Pulusuk atoll Micronesia
155 E1 Pulutan Sulawesi Indon.
153 K5 Puluwat atoll Micronesia
37 N8 Pulversheim France
178 E3 Pulwama Jammu and Kashmir
93 B6 Puma Tanz.
145 B6 Pumalin, Parque nat. park Chile
146 B4 Pumanque Chile
173 J12 Puma Yumco l. China
Pumiao Guangxi China see Yongning
122 L3 Pumpkin Creek r. MT U.S.A.
30 E3 Pumsaint Carmarthenshire, Wales U.K.
144 E2 Puna Arg.
136 A5 Puná, Isla i. Ecuador
201 □3a Punaauia Tahiti Fr. Polynesia
201 □3a Punaauia, Pointe pt Tahiti Fr. Polynesia
144 D2 Puna de Atacama plat. Arg.
203 F9 Punakaiki South I. N.Z.
179 L6 Punakha Bhutan
124 □F14 Punalu'u HI U.S.A.
201 □3a Punaruu r. Tahiti Fr. Polynesia
71 R5 Punat Croatia
138 D4 Punata Bol.
185 P5 Punch Pak.
106 F4 Punchaw B.C. Can.
95 F4 Punda Maria S. Africa
178 F5 Pundri Haryana India
176 C3 Pune Mahar. India
176 F6 Punganuru Andhra Prad. India
156 □ Punggol Sing.
156 □ Punggol, Sungai r. Sing.
91 B7 Pungo Andango Angola
163 F8 P'ungsan N. Korea
95 G3 Púnguè r. Moz.
71 J2 Puni r. Italy
90 E5 Punia Dem. Rep. Congo
55 M1 Punia Lith.
171 K7 Puning Guangdong China
146 B2 Punitaqui Chile
178 E4 Punjab state India
185 N6 Punjab prov. Pak.
21 T6 Punkaharju Fin.
178 F2 Punmah Glacier China/Jammu and Kashmir
138 C3 Puno Peru
138 C3 Puno dept Peru
179 J7 Punpun r. India
55 L1 Puńsk Pol.
131 □1 Punta, Cerro de mt. Puerto Rico
72 F2 Punta Ala Italy
147 F6 Punta Alta Arg.
145 C9 Punta Arenas Chile
72 C6 Punta Balestrieri mt. Italy
136 D2 Punta Cardón Venez.
138 C4 Punta de Bombón Peru
144 C3 Punta de Diaz Chile
146 C4 Punta del Agua Arg.
137 E2 La Tortuga, Isla i. Venez.
144 G4 Punta del Este Uru.
145 E6 Punta Delgada Arg.
146 D2 Punta de los Llanos Arg.
128 B5 Punta de Mita Mex.
146 C3 Punta de Vacas Arg.
126 □O9 Punta Gorda Belize
98 □3d Puntagorda La Palma Canary Is
126 □R12 Punta Gorda Nic.
115 F12 Punta Gorda FL U.S.A.
147 I4 Punta Indio Arg.
71 Q6 Punta Križa Croatia
98 □3d Puntallana La Palma Canary Is
72 A9 Punta Mumullonis hill Italy
146 D4 Puntana, Travesía des. Arg.
138 C6 Punta Negra, Salar salt flat Chile
145 E6 Punta Norte Arg.
126 B3 Punta Prieta Mex.
126 □Q12 Puntarenas Costa Rica
71 M5 Punta Sabbioni Italy
131 □1 Punta Santiago Puerto Rico
138 D5 Puntas Negras, Cerro mt. Chile
64 F6 Punta Umbría Spain
129 K5 Puntilla Aldama Mex.
136 D2 Punto Fijo Venez.
66 E3 Puntón de Guara mt. Spain
116 G8 Punxsutawney PA U.S.A.
20 S4 Puokio Fin.
20 S4 Puolanka Fin.
20 P3 Puoltikasvaara Sweden
138 B3 Puquio Peru
138 C4 Puquios Chile
192 I3 Pur r. Rus. Fed.
136 B4 Puracé, Parque Nacional nat. park Col.
176 D3 Purandhar Mahar. India
178 H5 Puranpur Uttar Prad. India
153 J8 Purari r. P.N.G.
59 O4 Purbach am Neusiedler See Austria
157 H8 Purbalingga Jawa Indon.
30 H6 Purbeck, Isle of pen. England U.K.
121 G8 Purcell OK U.S.A.
106 G5 Purcell Mountains B.C. Can.
116 H9 Purcellville VA U.S.A.
65 O6 Purchena Spain
65 L6 Purchil Spain
173 E9 Pur Co l. China
204 E4 Pureba Conservation Park nature res. S.A. Austr.
18 I2 Purekkari neem pt Estonia
144 B5 Purén Chile
202 J5 Pureora Forest Park nature res. North I. N.Z.
128 E6 Purépero Mex.
31 M5 Purfleet Thurrock, England U.K.
173 G10 Purgadala Xizang China
121 D6 Purgatoire r. CO U.S.A.
53 J5 Pürgen Ger.
59 L3 Purgstall an der Erlauf Austria
91 B6 Puri Angola
177 I3 Puri Orissa India
128 C6 Purificación Mex.
129 I2 Purificación r. Mex.
30 G5 Puriton Somerset, England U.K.
59 N3 Purkersdorf Austria
31 L5 Purley Greater London, England U.K.
31 J5 Purley on Thames West Berkshire, England U.K.
44 G3 Purmerend Neth.
176 E3 Purna Mahar. India
176 E3 Purna r. Mahar. India
178 F9 Purna r. Mahar. India
179 L7 Purnabhaba r. India
176 C4 Purnagad Mahar. India
204 C2 Purndu Saltpan salt flat S.A. Austr.
Purnea Bihar India see Purnia
179 K7 Purnia Bihar India
208 J4 Purnululu National Park W.A. Austr.
145 B6 Purranque Chile
Pursat Cambodia see Poŭthĭsăt
31 I4 Purton Wiltshire, England U.K.
105 K3 Purtuniq Que. Can.
128 F5 Puruandíro Mex.
128 F6 Puruarán Mex.
136 D5 Puruê r. Brazil
63 Q5 Purujosa Spain
157 K5 Purukcahu Kalimantan Indon.
179 K8 Puruliya W. Bengal India
65 M6 Purullena Spain
137 F5 Purus r. Peru
21 T6 Puruvesi l. Fin.
121 K10 Purvis MS U.S.A.
77 N8 Pŭrvomay Bulg.
178 H6 Purwa Uttar Prad. India
156 G8 Purwakarta Jawa Indon.
157 I8 Purwareja Jawa Indon.
157 I8 Purwodadi Jawa Indon.
157 H8 Purwokerto Jawa Indon.
163 F7 Puryŏng N. Korea
176 E3 Pus r. India
179 J7 Pusa Bihar India
18 K5 Puša Latvia
157 I4 Pusa Sarawak Malaysia
63 K9 Pusa r. Spain
176 E3 Pusad Mahar. India
163 F11 Pusan S. Korea
154 F8 Pusan Point Mindanao Phil.
157 I4 Pusatdamai Kalimantan Indon.
53 J2 Puschendorf Ger.
51 J8 Puschwitz Ger.
117 □Q4 Pushaw Lake ME U.S.A.
16 J3 Pushcha-Vodytsya Ukr.
19 U7 Pushchino Rus. Fed.
14 I3 Pushemskiy Rus. Fed.
178 E6 Pushkar Rajasthan India
19 N2 Pushkin Rus. Fed.
182 B2 Pushkino Rus. Fed.
162 M5 Pushkinskaya, Gora mt. Sakhalin Rus. Fed.
18 L4 Pushkinskiye Gory Rus. Fed.
66 D3 Pusilibro mt. Spain
57 K4 Püspökladány Hungary
18 K2 Püssi Estonia
57 H2 Pustá Polom Czech Rep.
71 L2 Pusteria, Val val. Italy
58 F6 Pustertal val. Austria
59 J5 Pusterwald Austria
57 G3 Pusté Úľany Slovakia
76 G8 Pusti Lisac mt. Serb. and Mont.
56 G2 Pustiměř Czech Rep.
16 C4 Pustomyty Ukr.
18 M5 Pustoshka Rus. Fed.
16 J4 Pustovity Ukr.
18 G1 Pusula Fin.
179 L9 Pusur r. Bangl.
55 L2 Puszcza Augustowska for. Pol.
55 I4 Puszcza Mariańska Pol.
54 D3 Puszcza Natecka for. Pol.
47 K2 Puszczy Knyszyńskiej, Park Krajobrazowy Pol.
54 E3 Puszczykowo Pol.
57 M1 Puszczy Solskiej, Park Krajobrazowy Pol.
57 J4 Pusztakocsi mocsarak nature res. Hungary
57 G5 Pusztakovácsi Hungary
57 I5 Pusztamérges Hungary
57 I4 Pusztamonostor Hungary
57 H4 Pusztaszabolcs Hungary
57 I5 Pusztaszer Hungary
57 J5 Pusztaszeri park Hungary
57 I4 Pusztavacs Hungary
57 H4 Pusztavám Hungary
146 B3 Putaendo Chile
107 K3 Putahow Lake Man. Can.
155 D8 Putain Timor Indon.
39 K4 Putanges-Pont-Écrepin France
158 C1 Putao Myanmar
202 J5 Putaruru North I. N.Z.
50 H2 Putbus Ger.
Puteoli Italy see Pozzuoli
157 K8 Puteran i. Indon.
202 L5 Putere North I. N.Z.
14 L2 Puteyets Rus. Fed.
184 I8 Puthak Iran
171 L6 Putian Fujian China
72 A6 Putifigari Sardegna Italy
75 M2 Putignano Italy
14 I4 Putilovo Rus. Fed.
19 T9 Putimets Rus. Fed.
138 C3 Putina Peru
157 I6 Puting, Tanjung pt Indon.
183 U3 Putintsevo Kazakh.
129 J8 Putla Mex.
185 L6 Putla Khan Afgh.
50 F4 Putlitz Ger.
77 O5 Putna r. Romania
117 N7 Putnam CT U.S.A.
119 H2 Putnam County county NY U.S.A.
119 H2 Putnam Valley NY U.S.A.
117 M6 Putney VT U.S.A.
57 J3 Putnok Hungary
170 B4 Putog Xizang China
Putoi i. H.K. China see Po Toi
193 K3 Putorana, Gory mts Rus. Fed.
156 D3 Putrajaya Malaysia
138 C4 Putre Chile
96 F5 Putsonderwater S. Africa
176 F8 Puttalam Sri Lanka
176 F8 Puttalam Lagoon Sri Lanka
45 G6 Putte Belgium
45 F6 Putte Neth.
37 M5 Puttelange-aux-Lacs France
44 I4 Putten Neth.
50 D1 Puttgarden Ger.
52 B3 Püttlingen Ger.
176 D6 Puttur Karnataka India
146 A4 Putú Chile
91 C6 Putubumba Dem. Rep. Congo
136 C4 Putumayo dept Col.
136 D5 Putumayo r. Col.
188 I4 Pütürge Turkey
157 J4 Putusibau Kalimantan Indon.
15 H5 Putyatino Rus. Fed.
16 E6 Putyla Ukr.
16 H2 Putylovychi Ukr.
17 M2 Putyvl' Ukr.
50 I3 Putzar Ger.
51 J8 Putzkau Ger.
124 □F14 Pu'uanahulu HI U.S.A.
124 □E13 Pu'ukoli'i HI U.S.A.
21 S6 Puula l. Fin.
21 T6 Puumala Fin.
45 F6 Puurs Belgium
124 □A12 Pu'uwai HI U.S.A.
105 K3 Puvirnituq Que. Can.
169 L8 Puxian Shanxi China
122 C3 Puyallup WA U.S.A.
169 N9 Puyang Henan China
Puyang Zhejiang China see Pujiang
43 H6 Puybrun France
43 F8 Puycasquier France
39 J8 Puy Crapaud hill France
40 C5 Puy-de-Dôme dept France
40 B5 Puy de Dôme mt. France
43 H9 Puy de Faucher hill France
41 G7 Puy de la Gagère mt. France
40 D5 Puy de Montoncel mt. France
40 B5 Puy de Sancy mt. France
42 H3 Puy des Trois-Cornes hill France
145 C6 Puyehue, Parque Nacional nat. park Chile
145 C6 Puyel Arg.
43 I8 Puygouzon France
41 B6 Puy Griou mt. France
41 I6 Puy Gris mt. France
40 C5 Puy-Guillaume France
43 H7 Puylaroque France
43 I8 Puylaurens France
43 G6 Puy-l'Évêque France
41 B6 Puy Mary mt. France
43 F9 Puymaurin France
43 F7 Puymirol France
43 H10 Puymorens, Col de pass France
42 E4 Puymoyen France
136 B5 Puyo Ecuador
43 C8 Puyôo France
41 I7 Puy-St-Vincent France
203 A13 Puysegur Point South I. N.Z.
14 K3 Puzla Rus. Fed.
Puzol Valencia Spain see Puçol
93 C6 Pwani admin. reg. Tanz.
200 □4b Pwel Weite Pohnpei Micronesia
91 F7 Pweto Dem. Rep. Congo
30 D2 Pwllheli Gwynedd, Wales U.K.
200 □4b Pwok Pohnpei Micronesia
14 G2 Pyalitsa Rus. Fed.
14 F3 Pyal'ma Rus. Fed.
158 B5 Pyalo Myanmar
158 B7 Pyamalaw r. Myanmar
Pyanskiy Perevoz Rus. Fed. see Perevoz
14 L3 Pyanteg Rus. Fed.
20 U3 Pyaozero, Ozero l. Rus. Fed.
20 U4 Pyaozerskiy Rus. Fed.
158 B6 Pyapon Myanmar
192 J2 Pyasina r. Rus. Fed.
192 J3 Pyasino, Ozero l. Rus. Fed.
192 J2 Pyasinskiy Zaliv b. Rus. Fed.
77 M8 Pyasŭchnik r. Bulg.
55 I1 Pyatidorozhnoye Rus. Fed.
191 E1 Pyatigorsk Rus. Fed.
Pyatikhatka Ukr. see P''yatykhatka
Pyatikhatki Ukr. see P''yatykhatky
Pyatimar Kazakh. see Pyatimarskoye
182 D3 Pyatimarskoye Kazakh.
19 N1 Pyatirech'ye Rus. Fed.
16 H3 P''yatka Ukr.
17 Q3 Pyatnitskoye Rus. Fed.
19 T7 Pyatovskiy Rus. Fed.
17 N8 P''yatykhatka Ukr.
17 M5 P''yatykhatky Ukr.
158 C5 Pyaunglaung r. Myanmar
158 C4 Pyawbwe Myanmar
19 S1 Pyazhelka Rus. Fed.
19 S1 Pyazhozero, Ozero l. Rus. Fed.
14 K4 Pychas Rus. Fed.
158 B5 Pyè Myanmar
203 D13 Pye, Mount hill South I. N.Z.
55 L3 Pyelishcha Belarus
18 I8 Pyershamayski Belarus
18 H8 Pyeski Belarus
202 K4 Pyes Pa North I. N.Z.
16 H1 Pyetrykaw Belarus
177 M9 Pygmalion Point Andaman & Nicobar Is India
18 G1 Pyhäjärvi l. Fin.
21 Q6 Pyhäjärvi l. Fin.
20 R5 Pyhäjärvi l. Fin.
20 R5 Pyhäjärvi l. Fin.
21 S6 Pyhäjärvi l. Fin.
21 U6 Pyhäjärvi l. Fin.
20 R4 Pyhäjoki Fin.
20 R4 Pyhäjoki r. Fin.
18 K1 Pyhältö Fin.
20 S4 Pyhäntä Fin.
21 P6 Pyhäranta Fin.
20 R5 Pyhäsalmi Fin.
20 T5 Pyhäselkä Fin.
20 T5 Pyhäselkä l. Fin.
20 S3 Pyhätunturin kansallispuisto nat. park Fin.
59 M3 Pyhra Austria
21 S6 Pyhtää Fin.
Pyin Myanmar see Pyè
158 B3 Pyingaing Myanmar
158 C5 Pyinmana Myanmar
158 C3 Pyin-U-Lwin Myanmar
43 B6 Pyla-sur-Mer France
30 E4 Pyle Bridgend, Wales U.K.
79 I6 Pyli Kos Greece
78 C3 Pyli Thessalia Greece
192 J3 Pyl'karamo Rus. Fed.
20 R5 Pylkönmäki Fin.
78 C6 Pylos Greece
16 G3 Pylypovychi Ukr.
116 E7 Pymatuning Reservoir PA U.S.A.
163 D9 Pyŏksŏng N. Korea
163 D8 Pyŏktong N. Korea
163 E9 P'yŏnggang N. Korea
163 E9 P'yŏngsan N. Korea
163 D9 P'yŏngsong N. Korea
163 E10 P'yŏngt'aek S. Korea
163 D9 P'yŏngyang N. Korea
163 E11 Pyŏnsan Bando National Park S. Korea
58 F4 Pyramidenspitze mt. Austria
205 J7 Pyramid Hill Vic. Austr.
202 □ Pyramid Island Chatham Is S. Pacific Ocean
209 F12 Pyramid Lake salt flat W.A. Austr.
124 M1 Pyramid Lake NV U.S.A.
124 M1 Pyramid Lake Indian Reservation res. NV U.S.A.
98 □2a Pyramid Point Ascension S. Atlantic Ocean
110 I5 Pyramid Point MI U.S.A.
124 M2 Pyramid Range mts NV U.S.A.
188 E9 Pyramids of Giza tourist site Egypt
53 K3 Pyrbaum Ger.
66 J3 Pyrenees mts Europe
43 D9 Pyrénées airport France
43 C9 Pyrénées-Atlantiques dept France
66 D2 Pyrénées Occidentales, Parc National des nat. park France/Spain
43 J10 Pyrénées-Orientales dept France
78 D3 Pyrgetos Greece
79 G4 Pyrgi Chios Greece
78 C5 Pyrgos Greece
16 I3 Pyrizhky Ukr.
17 M4 Pyrohy Ukr.
78 B2 Pyrsogianni Greece
208 D6 Pyrton, Mount hill W.A. Austr.
17 L3 Pyryatyn Ukr.
54 C2 Pyrzyce Pol.
14 I4 Pyshchug Rus. Fed.
17 N8 Pyshkine Ukr.
18 L7 Pyshna Belarus
54 G5 Pyskowice Pol.
17 O5 Pys'menne Ukr.
54 G4 Pyszna r. Pol.
55 K5 Pysznica Pol.
18 K4 Pytalovo Rus. Fed.
111 R3 Pythonga, Lac l. Que. Can.
78 E4 Pyxaria mt. Greece

Q

186 D2 Qā', Wādī al watercourse Saudi Arabia
188 H6 Qaa Lebanon
105 L2 Qaanaaq Greenland
191 I5 Qäbälä Azer.
190 D6 Qabātiya West Bank
187 L4 Qābil Oman
191 H4 Qabırrı r. Azer.
173 L12 Qabnag Xizang China
187 I7 Qabr Hūd Oman
191 F4 Qach'aghani Georgia
97 M6 Qacha's Nek Lesotho
191 J4 Qäçräş Azer.
184 H3 Qadamgāli Iran
186 F6 Qaḍḍā Saudi Arabia
185 J4 Qādes Afgh.
186 D4 Qaḍīmah Saudi Arabia
189 L6 Qādir Karam Iraq
189 K6 Qādisīyah, Sadd dam Iraq
Qadisiyah Dam Iraq see Qādisīyah, Sadd
187 K9 Qādub Suquṭrā Yemen
184 I6 Qa'emabad Iran
184 D7 Qā'emiyeh Iran
78 B2 Qafzez Albania
169 P2 Qagan Nei Mongol China
168 J6 Qagan Ders Nei Mongol China
169 K7 Qagan Nur Nei Mongol China
169 M5 Qagan Nur Nei Mongol China
169 N5 Qagan Nur Nei Mongol China
168 F8 Qagan Nur Qinghai China
172 H5 Qagan Nur Xinjiang China
169 S4 Qagan Nur l. China
169 N5 Qagan Nur resr China
169 L4 Qagan Obo Nei Mongol China
169 P3 Qagan Qulut Nei Mongol China
169 M5 Qagan Teg Nei Mongol China
168 D9 Qagan Tohoi Qinghai China
168 E8 Qagan Us He r. China
170 B2 Qagca Sichuan China
Qagchêng Sichuan China see Xiangcheng
Qahar Youyi Qianqi Nei Mongol China see Togrog Ul
188 I8 Qā' Ḥazawzā' salt pan Saudi Arabia
186 F3 Qahd, Wādī watercourse Saudi Arabia
186 G6 Qahr, Jibāl al hills Saudi Arabia
191 I6 Qährämanlı Azer.
186 F5 Qaḥṭān reg. Saudi Arabia
168 D8 Qaidam He r. China
173 K8 Qaidam Pendi basin China
168 D8 Qaidam Shan mts Qinghai China
173 I10 Qainaqangma Xizang China
185 K4 Qaisar Afgh.
185 K3 Qaisar r. Afgh.
173 E8 Qakar Xinjiang China
75 □ Qala Gozo Malta
87 G2 Qal'a Beni Hammad tourist site Alg.
97 M3 Qalabotjha S. Africa
189 L5 Qalā Diza Iraq
85 G6 Qala'en Nahl Sudan
185 M4 Qalagai Afgh.
185 N2 Qal'aikhum Tajik.
185 J5 Qala Jamal Afgh.
187 K5 Qalamat Abū Shafrah Saudi Arabia
187 J5 Qalamat Al Juḥaysh oasis Saudi Arabia
187 K5 Qalamat ar Rakabah oasis Saudi Arabia
187 J6 Qalamat Fāris oasis Saudi Arabia
187 J4 Qalamat Nadqān well Saudi Arabia
187 K4 Qalamat Shutfah well Saudi Arabia
187 K9 Qalansīyah Suquṭrā Yemen
185 L4 Qala Shinia Takht Afgh.
189 P9 Qalāt Iran
186 B2 Qal'at al Azlam Saudi Arabia
190 E4 Qal'at al Ḥiṣn Syria
190 E4 Qal'at al Ḥiṣn tourist site Syria
190 D3 Qal'at al Marqab tourist site Syria
186 C2 Qal'at al Mu'aẓẓam Saudi Arabia
186 F5 Qal'at Bīshah Saudi Arabia
190 G3 Qal'at Muqaybirah, Jabal mt. Syria
189 M8 Qal'at Ṣāliḥ Iraq
189 M8 Qal'at Sukkar Iraq
185 J4 Qala Vali Afgh.
184 F3 Qal'eh Iran
184 A2 Qal'eh Dāgh mt. Iran
185 I4 Qal'eh Tirpul Afgh.
185 K6 Qal'eh-ye Bost Afgh.
185 I6 Qal'eh-ye Fatḥ Afgh.
184 G8 Qal'eh-ye Ganj Iran
185 J4 Qal'eh-ye Now Afgh.
189 N7 Qal'eh-ye Now Iran
184 H5 Qal'eh-ye Shūrak well Iran
168 I8 Qalgar Nei Mongol China
187 N4 Qalhāt Oman
189 L9 Qalīb Bāqūr well Iraq
108 F1 Qalluviartuuq, Lac l. Que. Can.
190 C6 Qalqīlya West Bank
84 E5 Qalti el Adusa well Sudan
85 F2 Qalyūb Egypt
188 E8 Qalyūbīyah governorate Egypt
168 F9 Qamalung Qinghai China
107 M2 Qamanirjuaq Lake Nunavut Can.
187 K7 Qamar, Ghubbat al b. Yemen
187 K7 Qamar, Jabal al mts Oman
191 I4 Qämärvan Azer.
183 L8 Qamashi Uzbek.
185 M8 Qambar Pak.
184 B4 Qāmchīān Iran
170 A3 Qamdo Xizang China
201 □1 Qamea i. Fiji
186 E6 Qam Hadīl Saudi Arabia
84 C2 Qamīnis Libya
75 □ Qammieħ, Il-Ponta tal- pt Malta
185 M6 Qamruddin Karez Pak.
184 D5 Qamṣar Iran
190 E6 Qanawāt Syria
187 L7 Qanawt Oman
92 F2 Qandala Somalia
184 B2 Qandarānbāshī, Kūh-e mt. Iran
184 B2 Qandarān-Hūrand Iran
169 N5 Qangdin Sum Nei Mongol China
173 E10 Qangdoi Xizang China
173 D11 Qangzê Xizang China
182 H6 Qanliko'l Uzbek.
184 F3 Qapan Iran
172 E5 Qapqal Xinjiang China
105 N3 Qaqortoq Greenland
187 K7 Qarā', Jabal al mts Oman
190 D5 Qaraaoun Lebanon
185 I4 Qarabagh Afgh.
191 H5 Qarabağ Silsiläsi hills Azer.
191 G6 Qarabağ Yaylası plat. Armenia/Azer.
191 J6 Qaraçala Azer.
189 K6 Qarachōq, Jabal mts Iraq
191 J6 Qaradonlu Azer.
188 C9 Qārah Egypt
189 J9 Qārah Saudi Arabia
186 G6 Qārah, Jabal al hill Saudi Arabia
185 M5 Qarah Bāgh Ghaznī Afgh.
185 M4 Qarah Bāgh Kābul Afgh.
Qarah Tappah Iraq see Qara Tepe
172 C7 Qarak Xinjiang China
191 G5 Qaralar Azer.
191 J5 Qaramäryam Azer.
184 B3 Qaranqu r. Iran
Qara Özek Uzbek. see Qorao'zak
Qaraqalpaqstan Respublikasi aut. rep. Uzbek. see Qoraqalpog'iston Respublikasi
184 F3 Qara Quzi Iran
191 J5 Qarasu Azer.
191 I5 Qarasu r. Azer.
191 I6 Qarasu r. Azer.
191 K6 Qarasu Adası i. Azer.
185 K4 Qara Tarai mt. Afgh.
189 L6 Qara Tepe Iraq
189 N5 Qara Tikan Iran
191 H5 Qarayeri Azer.
92 F2 Qardho Somalia
90 F2 Qardud Sudan
191 I6 Qareh Āghāj Iran
184 B3 Qar'eh Aqāj Iran
184 D4 Qareh Chāy r. Iran
184 A2 Qareh Dāgh mt. Iran
184 B2 Qareh Dāgh mts Iran
184 B3 Qareh Dāsh, Kūh-e mt. Iran
191 F6 Qareh Khāj Iran
184 E4 Qareh Qāch, Kūh-e mts Iran
184 B2 Qareh Sū r. Iran
184 I3 Qareh Tekān Turkm.
191 G7 Qareh Ẕīā' od Dīn Iran
168 D8 Qarhan Qinghai China
Qarkilik Xinjiang China see Ruoqiang
85 G2 Qarn al Kabsh, Jabal mt. Egypt
187 K3 Qarnayn i. U.A.E.
186 E5 Qarnayṭ, Jabal hill Saudi Arabia
182 K8 Qarnobcho'l cho'li plain Uzbek.
185 O2 Qarokŭl l. Tajik.
Qarqan Xinjiang China see Qiemo
172 H7 Qarqan He r. China
191 I6 Qarqarçay r. Azer.
172 E6 Qarqi Xinjiang China
172 G6 Qarqi Xinjiang China
182 F9 Qārqi Iran
185 L3 Qarqīn Afgh.
78 B2 Qarrit, Qafa e pass Albania
182 K8 Qarshi Qashqadaryo Uzbek.
182 K8 Qarshi cho'li plain Uzbek.
Qarshi Chŭli plain Uzbek. see Qarshi cho'li
190 D4 Qartaba Lebanon
189 N9 Qārūh, Jazīrat i. Kuwait
85 F2 Qārūn, Birkat l. Egypt
186 G6 Qaryat al Faw tourist site Saudi Arabia
187 H2 Qaryat al Ulyā Saudi Arabia
187 H2 Qaryat as Sufla Saudi Arabia
184 F3 Qāsam, Kūh-e mt. Iran
184 G5 Qasamī Iran
185 J4 Qasa Murg mts Afgh.
179 K7 Qasba Bihar India
187 M4 Qaṣbīyat al Burayk Oman
184 G4 Qāsemābād Khorāsān Iran
184 H3 Qāsemābād Khorāsān Iran
183 L8 Qashqadaryo admin. div. Uzbek.
185 K2 Qashqadaryo r. Uzbek.
Qashqadaryo Wiloyati admin. div. Uzbek. see Qashqadaryo
184 D6 Qash Qai reg. Iran
105 M3 Qasigiannguit Greenland
186 F2 Qasīm reg. Saudi Arabia
169 L6 Qasq Nei Mongol China
190 D8 Qaṣr ad Dayr, Jabal mt. Jordan
190 E7 Qaṣr al Azraq Jordan
84 E3 Qaṣr al Farāfirah Egypt
190 F4 Qasr al Ḥayr tourist site Syria
190 E7 Qaṣr al Kharānah Jordan
189 K7 Qasr al Khubbāz Iraq
190 E7 Qaṣr 'Amrah tourist site Jordan
189 N9 Qaṣr aṣ Ṣabīyah Kuwait
84 C2 Qaṣr Bū Hādī Libya
190 F6 Qaṣr Burqu' tourist site Jordan
184 I8 Qaṣr-e Qand Iran
189 L6 Qaṣr-e Shīrīn Iran
186 G5 Qaṣr Ḥimām Saudi Arabia
84 B3 Qaṣr Larocu Libya
105 N3 Qassimiut Greenland
186 G9 Qa'tabah Yemen
190 E5 Qaṭanā Syria
187 J3 Qatar country Asia

Qatār, Jabal to Raini
325

181 H5 Qatār, Jabal hill Oman
184 G3 Qatlish Iran
190 E2 Qaṭmah Syria
85 F2 Qaṭrānī, Jabal esc. Egypt
184 F7 Qaṭrūyeh Iran
190 F7 Qaṭṭāfī, Wādī al watercourse Jordan
Qâttara Depression Egypt see Qaṭṭārah, Munkhafaḍ al
84 E2 Qaṭṭārah, Munkhafaḍ al depr. Egypt
84 E2 Qaṭṭārah, Ra's esc. Egypt
190 E4 Qaṭṭīnah, Buḥayrat resr Syria
Qausuittuq Nunavut Can. see Resolute
184 G6 Qavāmābād Iran
191 H4 Qax Azer.
172 F5 Qaxi Xinjiang China
184 H5 Qāyen Iran
185 M1 Qayroqqum Tajik.
191 H4 Qaysa Georgia
190 E7 Qaysīyah, Qa' al imp. l. Jordan
186 A2 Qaysūm, Juzur is Egypt
173 K12 Qayü Xizang China
189 K6 Qayyārah Iraq
191 H6 Qazangödağ mt. Armenia/Azer.
191 H6 Qazanzämi Azer.
191 G4 Qazax Azer.
191 F3 Qazbegi Georgia
185 M8 Qazi Ahmad Pak.
191 J5 Qazımämmäd Azer.
184 C3 Qazvīn Iran
184 C3 Qazvīn prov. Iran
172 G6 Qedir Xinjiang China
168 G5 Qeh Nei Mongol China
Qeisûm Islands Egypt see Qaysūm, Juzur
78 B2 Qelqëzës, Mali i mt. Albania
191 E3 Qemult'a Georgia
Qena Egypt see Qinā
105 M3 Qeqertarsuaq Greenland
105 M3 Qeqertarsuaq i. Greenland
105 M3 Qeqertarsuatsiaat Greenland
105 M2 Qeqertarsuatsiaq i. Greenland
105 M3 Qeqertarsuup Tunua b. Greenland
184 B4 Qeshlāq Iran
184 D4 Qeshlāq-e Ḩoseyn Iran
184 G8 Qeshm Iran
184 G8 Qeshm i. Iran
184 C3 Qeydār Iran
184 F8 Qeys i. Iran
185 K5 Qeyṣār, Kūh-e mt. Afgh.
184 C3 Qezel Owzan, Rūdkhāneh-ye r. Iran
191 G6 Qezel Qeshlāq Iran
190 C8 Qeẕi'ot Israel
169 P7 Qian'an Hebei China
169 S4 Qian'an Jilin China
172 F6 Qianfodong Xinjiang China
162 D6 Qianguozhen Jilin China
169 P9 Qiangwei He r. China
169 J9 Qian He r. China
170 G4 Qianjiang Chongqing China
171 I3 Qianjiang Hubei China
162 H5 Qianjin Heilong. China
162 F6 Qianjin Jilin China
170 C3 Qianning Sichuan China
169 R4 Qianqihao Jilin China
171 K3 Qianshan Anhui China
169 R6 Qian Shan mts China
172 G4 Qianshanlaoba Xinjiang China
214 R4 Qiansuo Zhejiang China
170 D4 Qianwei Sichuan China
170 F5 Qianxi Guizhou China
169 P6 Qianxi Hebei China
169 K9 Qianxian Shaanxi China
170 H5 Qianyang Hunan China
169 J9 Qianyang Shaanxi China
Qianyou Shaanxi China see Zhashui
169 M7 Qiaocun Shanxi China
170 D5 Qiaojia Yunnan China
168 E6 Qiaowan Gansu China
Qiaozhuang Sichuan China see Qingchuan
184 A2 Qīās Iran
186 G2 Qibā' Saudi Arabia
97 L5 Qibing S. Africa
183 M7 Qibray Uzbek.
171 J3 Qichun Hubei China
171 I5 Qidong Hunan China
171 M3 Qidong Jiangsu China
173 G7 Qiemo Xinjiang China
169 O8 Qihe Shandong China
169 N9 Qi He r. China
170 F4 Qijiang Chongqing China
168 B5 Qijiaojing Xinjiang China
105 L3 Qikiqtarjuaq Nunavut Can.
168 B5 Qiktim Xinjiang China
185 L6 Qila Abdullah Pak.
185 J8 Qila Ladgasht Pak.
169 O6 Qilaotu Shan mts China
185 I7 Qila Safed Pak.
185 M6 Qila Saifullah Pak.
Qili Anhui China see Shitai
168 G7 Qilian Qinghai China
168 F7 Qilian Shan mt. China
168 E7 Qilian Shan mts China
172 L6 Qilizhen Gansu China
105 O3 Qillak i. Greenland
172 F6 Qiman Xinjiang China
173 J8 Qiman Tag mts China
171 K4 Qimen Anhui China
105 L2 Qimusseriarsuaq b. Greenland
85 G3 Qinā Qinā Egypt
186 A3 Qinā governorate Egypt
85 G3 Qinā, Wādī watercourse Egypt
187 I7 Qināb, Wādī r. Yemen
168 I9 Qin'an Gansu China
168 D5 Qincheng Xinjiang China
162 E5 Qing'an Heilong. China
Qingcheng Gansu China see Qingyang
163 C8 Qingchengzi Liaoning China
170 E2 Qingchuan Sichuan China
169 Q8 Qingdao Shandong China
162 E5 Qinggang Heilong. China
Qinggil Xinjiang China see Qinghe
173 G8 Qinggilik Xinjiang China
170 H4 Qingguandu Hunan China
168 E8 Qinghai prov. China
168 G8 Qinghai Hu salt l. Qinghai China
168 F8 Qinghai Nanshan mts China
169 N8 Qinghe Hebei China
162 F5 Qinghe Heilong. China
168 B3 Qinghe Xinjiang China
162 C7 Qing He r. China
163 D8 Qinghecheng Liaoning China
169 L8 Qingjian Shaanxi China
Qingjiang Jiangxi China see Zhangshu
170 H3 Qing Jiang r. China
170 H9 Qinglan Hainan China
171 K5 Qingliu Fujian China
170 E6 Qinglong Guizhou China
169 P6 Qinglong Hebei China
169 P7 Qinglong He r. China
173 J11 Qinglung Xizang China
158 I4 Qingping Guangdong China
171 M3 Qingpu Shanghai China
Qingquan Hubei China see Xishui
Qingshan Heilong. China see Wudalianchi
170 D4 Qingshen Sichuan China
168 G8 Qingshizui Qinghai China
Qingshui Gansu China see Qingshuipu
168 J9 Qingshui Gansu China
169 L7 Qingshuihe Nei Mongol China
170 A2 Qingshuihe Qinghai China
172 E4 Qingshuihezi Xinjiang China
172 H5 Qingshuihezi Xinjiang China
170 B5 Qingshuilang Shan mts Yunnan China
168 F7 Qingshuipu Gansu China
171 M4 Qingtian Zhejiang China
168 J7 Qingtongxia Ningxia China
169 O7 Qingxian Hebei China
171 I7 Qingxin Guangdong China
169 M8 Qingxu Shanxi China
171 K3 Qingyang Anhui China
169 J8 Qingyang Gansu China
Qingyang Jiangsu China see Sihong
Qingyuan Gansu China see Weiyuan
171 I7 Qingyuan Guangdong China
Qingyuan Guangxi China see Yizhou
162 D7 Qingyuan Liaoning China
Qingyuan Shanxi China see Qingxu
171 L5 Qingyuan Zhejiang China
169 O8 Qingyun Shandong China
173 G10 Qingzang Gaoyuan plat. Xizang China
170 F5 Qingzhen Guizhou China
Qingzhou Hebei China see Qingxian
171 H3 Qingzhou Hubei China
169 P8 Qingzhou Shandong China
169 M9 Qin He r. China
169 P7 Qinhuangdao Hebei China
Qinjiang Jiangxi China see Shicheng
170 F2 Qin Ling mts China
Qinshan Heilong. China see Wudalianchi
169 M9 Qinshui Shanxi China
169 M8 Qinxian Shanxi China
169 M9 Qinyang Henan China
169 M8 Qinyuan Shanxi China
170 G8 Qinzhou Guangxi China
170 G8 Qinzhou Wan b. China
170 H9 Qionghai Hainan China
Qiongjiexue Xizang China see Qonggyai
170 D3 Qionglai Sichuan China
170 D3 Qionglai Shan mts Sichuan China
170 H9 Qiongshan Hainan China
170 G9 Qiongzhong Hainan China
170 G9 Qiongzhou Haixia str. China
191 H4 Qıpçaq Azer.
168 E7 Qiping Gansu China
169 R3 Qiqihar Heilong. China
172 I5 Qiquanhu Xinjiang China
184 E7 Qīr Fārs Iran
184 C5 Qīr Lorestān Iran
173 E8 Qira Xinjiang China
191 H6 Qırmızı Bazar Azer.
191 H5 Qırmızı Samux Azer.
191 J6 Qırmızıkänd Azer.
190 C7 Qiryat Gat Israel
190 D5 Qiryat Shemona Israel
170 G8 Qisha Guangxi China
Qishan Anhui China see Qimen
169 J9 Qishan Shaanxi China
187 J8 Qishn Yemen
190 D6 Qishon r. Israel
186 E5 Qishrān Island Saudi Arabia
188 H8 Qitab ash Shāmah vol. crater Saudi Arabia
172 I5 Qitai Xinjiang China
162 G6 Qitaihe Heilong. China
187 L7 Qitbīt, Wādī r. Oman
170 E6 Qiubei Yunnan China
171 J4 Qiujin Jiangxi China
169 Q8 Qixia Shandong China
169 N9 Qixian Henan China
169 N9 Qixian Henan China
169 M8 Qixian Shanxi China
162 H5 Qixing He r. China
162 D4 Qixingpao Heilong. China
171 H5 Qiyang Hunan China
168 J8 Qiying Ningxia China
170 B4 Qizhong Xizang China
171 H9 Qizhou Liedao i. China
191 K6 Qızılağac Körfäzi b. Azer.
191 K6 Qızılağaç Qoruğu nature res. Azer.
185 I4 Qizil Bulak Afgh.
191 K5 Qızıldaş Azer.
185 P3 Qizilrabot Tajik.
182 J7 Qizilravot Uzbek.
182 H6 Qizketkan Uzbek.
Qizqetkan Uzbek. see Qizketkan
97 M8 Qoboqobo S. Africa
191 K5 Qobustan Azer.
191 K5 Qobustan qoruğu nature res. Azer.
169 O4 Qog Ul Nei Mongol China
168 G9 Qoigargoinba Qinghai China
168 F8 Qoijê Qinghai China
184 B3 Qojūr Iran
97 M8 Qolora Mouth S. Africa
172 I5 Qoltag mts China
184 D4 Qom Iran
184 D4 Qom prov. Iran
Qomdo Xizang China see Qumdo
Qomishēh Iran see Shahrezā
Qomolangma Feng mt. China/Nepal see Everest, Mount
191 J4 Qonaqkänd Azer.
173 J12 Qonggyai Xizang China
182 H6 Qo'ng'irot Uzbek.
169 K6 Qongj Nei Mongol China
172 H6 Qongkol Xinjiang China
173 F9 Qong Muztag mt. Xinjiang/Xizang China
Qongrat Uzbek. see Qo'ng'irot
168 F8 Qonj Qinghai China
92 F3 Qooriga Neegro b. Somalia
105 M3 Qoornoq Greenland
Qoqek Xinjiang China see Tacheng
97 K7 Qoqodala S. Africa
183 N7 Qo'qon Farg'ona Uzbek.
182 H6 Qorajar Uzbek.
182 J8 Qorako'l Buxoro Uzbek.
182 J8 Qorako'l Buxoro Uzbek.
182 H6 Qorao'zak Uzbek.
Qoraqalpoghiston Uzbek. see Qoraqalpog'iston
Qoraqalpoghiston Respublikasi aut. rep. Uzbek. see Qoraqalpog'iston Respublikasi
182 G5 Qoraqalpog'iston Uzbek.
182 H6 Qoraqalpog'iston Respublikasi aut. rep. Uzbek.
182 K7 Qoraqata botig'i depr. Uzbek.
Qoraŭzak Uzbek. see Qorao'zak
75 □ Qormi Malta
190 E4 Qornet es Saouda mt. Lebanon
191 E3 Qornisi Georgia
182 K8 Qorovulbozor Uzbek.
Qorowulbozor Uzbek. see Qorovulbozor
184 D3 Qoroy, Gardaneh-ye pass Iran
184 B4 Qorveh Iran
191 I5 Qoşaqovaq Azer.
182 I7 Qo'shko'pir Uzbek.
183 L7 Qo'shrabot Uzbek.
189 K5 Qosh Tepe Iraq
191 H5 Qoşqarçay r. Azer.
184 G8 Qoṭbābād Iran
184 A2 Qoṭūr Iran
190 E4 Qoubaiyat Lebanon
191 G5 Qovlar Azer.
185 N3 Qozideh Kŭhistoni Badakhshon Tajik.
182 H6 Qozonketkan Uzbek.
182 H6 Qozoqdaryo Uzbek.
75 □ Qrejten, Il-Ponta tal- pt Malta
75 □ Qrendi Malta
117 M6 Quabbin Reservoir MA U.S.A.
106 E5 Quadra Island B.C. Can.
62 G8 Quadrazais Port.
73 M4 Quadri Italy
141 C9 Quadros, Lago dos l. Brazil
96 E7 Quaggasfontein Poort pass S. Africa
26 I9 Quaich r. Scotland U.K.
185 N5 Quaidabad Pak.
124 O6 Quail Mountains CA U.S.A.
209 D12 Quairading W.A. Austr.
48 E5 Quakenbrück Ger.
119 K2 Quaker Hill CT U.S.A.
118 F3 Quakertown NJ U.S.A.
118 E4 Quakertown PA U.S.A.
118 C3 Qualake PA U.S.A.
187 I2 Qualay'ah, Ra's al pt Saudi Arabia
73 M6 Qualiano Italy
205 I6 Quambatook Vic. Austr.
205 K4 Quambone N.S.W. Austr.
206 H6 Quamby Qld Austr.
121 F8 Quanah TX U.S.A.
169 L9 Quanbao Shan mt. Henan China
158 H4 Quân Đao Cô Tô is Vietnam
159 G10 Quân Đao Nam Du i. Vietnam
Quan Dao Truong Sa is S. China Sea see Spratly Islands
158 H4 Quang Ha Vietnam
158 I7 Quang Ngai Vietnam
158 H6 Quang Tri Vietnam
158 H4 Quang Yên Vietnam
171 J2 Quan He r. China
158 G4 Quan Hoa Vietnam
Quanjiang Jiangxi China see Suichuan
171 J6 Quannan Jiangxi China
Quan Phu Quoc i. Vietnam see Phu Quôc, Đao
171 K5 Quanshang Fujian China
178 G2 Quanshuigou Aksai Chin
30 F5 Quantock Hills England U.K.
Quanwan H.K. China see Tsuen Wan
171 L6 Quanzhou Fujian China
171 H6 Quanzhou Guangxi China
107 K5 Qu'Appelle Sask. Can.
107 K5 Qu'Appelle r. Man./Sask. Can.
105 L3 Quaqtaq Que. Can.
141 A9 Quaraí Brazil
147 I2 Quaraí r. Brazil
45 E8 Quaregnon Belgium
91 C7 Quarenta Angola
26 □N2 Quarff Shetland, Scotland U.K.
70 F6 Quargnento Italy
22 F7 Quarnbek Ger.
70 E4 Quarona Italy
71 J8 Quarrata Italy
40 D2 Quarré-les-Tombes France
171 □J7 Quarry Bay H.K. China
203 D13 Quarry Hills South I. N.Z.
118 C5 Quarryville PA U.S.A.
64 C6 Quarteira Port.
67 E8 Quartell Spain
70 G1 Quarten Switz.
99 □1c Quartier-Français Réunion
99 □1b Quartier Militaire Mauritius
71 M8 Quarto, Lago di l. Italy
72 C9 Quartu Sant'Elena Sardegna Italy
125 P4 Quartzite Mountain NV U.S.A.
125 R8 Quartzsite AZ U.S.A.
142 B5 Quatá Brazil
131 □3 Quatre, Isle á i. St Vincent
99 □1b Quatre Bornes Mauritius
36 I5 Quatre-Champs France
99 □1b Quatre Cocos, Pointe pt Mauritius
67 E10 Quatretonda Spain
98 □1a Quatro Ribeiras Terceira Azores
191 J4 Quba Azer.
191 H6 Qubadlı Azer.
191 K5 Qubalıbalaoğlan Azer.
184 H3 Quchan Iran
190 G3 Qudaym Syria
187 M6 Qudaysah well Oman
97 O4 Qudeni S. Africa
191 J4 Qudıyalçay r. Azer.
94 B2 Qué Angola
205 L6 Queanbeyan A.C.T. Austr.
109 G4 Québec Que. Can.
109 F2 Québec prov. Can.
142 D3 Quebra Anzol r. Brazil
147 I3 Quebracho Uru.
144 E3 Quebrachos Arg.
146 E2 Quebrada del Condorito, Parque Nacional nat. park Arg.
131 □1 Quebradillas Puerto Rico
129 H8 Quechultenango Mex.
145 B6 Quedal, Cabo c. Chile
95 G3 Quedas Moz.
30 H4 Quedgeley Gloucestershire, England U.K.
51 D7 Quedlinburg Ger.
190 D7 Queen Alia airport Jordan
118 D7 Queen Anne MD U.S.A.
118 C6 Queen Anne's County county MD U.S.A.
106 E5 Queen Bess, Mount B.C. Can.
31 N5 Queenborough Kent, England U.K.
106 C4 Queen Charlotte B.C. Can.
145 E8 Queen Charlotte Bay Falkland Is
106 C4 Queen Charlotte Islands B.C. Can.
106 D5 Queen Charlotte Sound sea chan. B.C. Can.
203 H8 Queen Charlotte Sound sea chan. South I. N.Z.
106 E5 Queen Charlotte Strait B.C. Can.
110 B9 Queen City MO U.S.A.
125 U8 Queen Creek AZ U.S.A.
105 H2 Queen Elizabeth Islands N.W.T./Nunavut Can.
92 A5 Queen Elizabeth National Park Uganda
213 K1 Queen Elizabeth Range mts Antarctica
213 C2 Queen Fabiola Mountains Antarctica
106 B2 Queen Mary, Mount Y.T. Can.
213 G2 Queen Mary Land reg. Antarctica
98 □2c Queen Mary's Peak Tristan da Cunha S. Atlantic Ocean
105 H3 Queen Maud Gulf Nunavut Can.
213 A2 Queen Maud Land reg. Antarctica
212 O1 Queen Maud Mountains Antarctica
97 O5 Queensburgh S. Africa
29 N6 Queensbury West Yorkshire, England U.K.
206 B3 Queens Channel N.T. Austr.
105 I2 Queens Channel Nunavut Can.
205 J8 Queenscliff Vic. Austr.
119 H3 Queens County county NY U.S.A.
207 J7 Queensland state Austr.
205 J10 Queenstown Tas. Austr.
203 C12 Queenstown South I. N.Z.
97 K7 Queenstown S. Africa
156 □ Queenstown Sing.
118 C7 Queenstown MD U.S.A.
209 G11 Queen Victoria Spring Nature Reserve W.A. Austr.
122 B3 Queets WA U.S.A.
147 H3 Queguay Grande r. Uru.
138 D4 Quehua Bol.
146 E5 Quehué Arg.
84 D5 Queiba well Chad
40 I5 Queige France
63 M1 Queijo, Cabo c. Spain
139 E2 Queimada Brazil
137 I5 Queimada, Ilha i. Brazil
98 □1c Queimada, Ponta da pt Pico Azores
140 F4 Queimadas Brazil
98 □1a Queimado, Ponta do pt Terceira Azores
62 E7 Queiriga Port.
142 B4 Queiroz Brazil
63 P4 Quel Spain
91 C7 Quela Angola
39 J6 Quelaines-St-Gault France
95 H3 Quelimane Moz.
128 A2 Quelite Mex.
146 A5 Quella Chile
51 F7 Quellendorf Ger.
145 B6 Quellón Chile
91 B6 Quelo Angola
143 E5 Queluz Brazil
64 A3 Queluz Port.
63 M5 Quemada Spain
142 D6 Quemada Grande, Ilha i. Brazil
123 J9 Quemado NM U.S.A.
91 D8 Quembo r. Angola
145 B6 Quemchi Chile
Quemoy i. Taiwan see Chinmen Tao
147 F5 Quemú-Quemú Arg.
36 C3 Quend France
49 D6 Quendorf Ger.
51 D7 Quenstedt Ger.
65 M6 Quéntar Spain
118 C4 Quentin PA U.S.A.
176 D5 Quepem Goa India
147 H6 Quequén Arg.
147 H6 Quequén Grande r. Arg.
66 J3 Queralbs Spain
70 I9 Quercianella Italy
43 G7 Quercy reg. France
64 D6 Querença Port.
140 B5 Querência Brazil
142 A5 Querência do Norte Brazil
128 G6 Queréndaro Mex.
49 K6 Querenhorst Ger.
128 G5 Querétaro Mex.
129 H5 Querétaro state Mex.
51 E8 Querfurt Ger.
43 I10 Quérigut France
48 I1 Quern Ger.
49 F6 Quernheim Ger.
29 L5 Quernmore Lancashire, England U.K.
71 L4 Quero Italy
63 N9 Quero Spain
126 D2 Querobabi Mex.
66 H5 Querol Spain
136 B6 Querpon Peru
38 H2 Querqueville France
36 D4 Querrieu France
37 L8 Quers France
67 D9 Quesa Spain
65 M5 Quesada Spain
65 M5 Quesada r. Spain
86 C4 Quesat watercourse Western Sahara
171 J2 Queshan Henan China
106 F4 Quesnel B.C. Can.
106 F4 Quesnel r. B.C. Can.
106 F4 Quesnel Lake B.C. Can.
36 F2 Quesnoy-sur-Deûle France
38 F5 Quessoy France
36 F4 Quessy France
38 G6 Questembert France
138 D5 Quetena de Lipez r. Bol.
108 B3 Quetico Provincial Park Ont. Can.
40 G2 Quetigny France
185 L6 Quetta Pak.
38 I2 Quettehou France
38 I4 Quettreville-sur-Sienne France
129 I9 Quetzala r. Mex.
129 H7 Quetzalapa Guerrero Mex.
129 H5 Quetzalapa Hidalgo Mex.
127 N10 Quetzaltenango Guat.
146 B5 Queuco Chile
145 B7 Queulat, Parque Nacional nat. park Chile
145 B5 Queule Chile
145 D6 Queupán Arg.
36 D4 Quevauvillers France
38 E6 Quéven France
38 G5 Quévert France
42 C5 Queyrac France
41 J7 Queyras, Parc Naturel Régional du nature res. France
43 I6 Quézac France
127 O11 Quezaltepeque El Salvador
154 D6 Quezon Negros Phil.
154 B7 Quezon Palawan Phil.
154 C4 Quezon City Luzon Phil.
186 E2 Qufār Saudi Arabia
169 O9 Qufu Shandong China
62 C8 Quiaios Port.
91 B7 Quibala Angola
91 B7 Quibaxe Angola
136 B3 Quibdó Col.
38 E7 Quiberon France
38 E6 Quiberon, Baie de b. France
38 E6 Quiberon, Presqu'île de pen. France
136 D2 Quíbor Venez.
91 B7 Quicabo Angola
91 B7 Quiçama, Parque Nacional do nat. park Angola
158 G5 Qui Châu Vietnam
48 I3 Quickborn Ger.
91 B7 Quiculungo Angola
37 N5 Quierschied Ger.
36 F4 Quierzy France
106 C2 Quiet Lake Y.T. Can.
36 G3 Quiévrechain France
91 B8 Quihita Angola
91 C6 Quihuhu Angola
139 F6 Quiindy Para.
126 F5 Quilá Mex.
146 A5 Quilaco Chile
126 □P11 Quilalí Nic.
145 B6 Quilán, Cabo c. Chile
176 D7 Quilandi Kerala India
138 B4 Quilca Peru
147 G5 Quilco Arg.
91 B7 Quilenda Angola
91 B8 Quilengues Angola
70 E7 Quiliano Italy
146 B3 Quilimarí Chile
146 E2 Quilino Arg.
138 D4 Quillacollo Bol.
146 B2 Quillaicillo Chile
43 I10 Quillan France
107 J5 Quill Lakes Sask. Can.
146 A5 Quillón Chile
146 B3 Quillota Chile
147 H4 Quilmes Arg.
91 B7 Quilombo dos Dembos Angola
176 E8 Quilon Kerala India
207 J9 Quilpie Qld Austr.
146 B3 Quilpué Chile
95 H3 Quilua Moz.
91 C7 Quimbango Angola
91 C6 Quimbele Angola
91 C7 Quimbonge Angola
138 D4 Quime Bol.
128 B3 Quimichis Mex.
144 E2 Quimilí Arg.
139 E4 Quimome Bol.
38 C6 Quimper France
38 D6 Quimperlé France
27 E7 Quin Rep. of Ireland
26 F6 Quinag hill Scotland U.K.
154 D5 Quinalasag i. Phil.
122 B3 Quinault r. WA U.S.A.
122 B3 Quinault Indian Reservation res. WA U.S.A.
138 C3 Quince Mil Peru
70 D4 Quincinetto Italy
124 L2 Quincy CA U.S.A.
115 E10 Quincy FL U.S.A.
114 B6 Quincy IL U.S.A.
117 N6 Quincy MA U.S.A.
110 J8 Quincy MI U.S.A.
116 B8 Quincy OH U.S.A.
36 E6 Quincy-Voisins France
136 C3 Quindío dept Col.
146 E3 Quines Arg.
38 I2 Quinéville France
95 I2 Quinga Moz.
40 H2 Quingey France
172 I6 Quinggir Xinjiang China
104 B4 Quinhagak AK U.S.A.
88 B4 Quinhámel Guinea-Bissau
137 E3 Quinigua, Cerro mts Venez.
147 G5 Quiñihual Arg.
154 C6 Quiniluban i. Phil.
136 B4 Quinindé Ecuador
207 J3 Quinkan Aboriginal Holding res. Qld Austr.
122 E6 Quinn r. NV U.S.A.
125 Q4 Quinn Canyon Range mts NV U.S.A.
116 D11 Quinnimont WV U.S.A.
138 D2 Quiñones Bol.
41 I9 Quinson France
40 B4 Quinssaines France
64 D6 Quintã hill Port.
64 B3 Quinta do Anjo Port.
142 B5 Quintana Brazil
64 H3 Quintana de la Serena Spain
62 H3 Quintana del Castillo Spain
63 M3 Quintana del Pino Spain
63 L4 Quintana del Puente Spain
63 J3 Quintana de Rueda Spain
63 M4 Quintanapalla Spain
63 N9 Quintanar de la Orden Spain
63 N5 Quintanar de la Sierra Spain
65 P2 Quintanar del Rey Spain
63 O5 Quintana Redonda Spain
127 O8 Quintana Roo state Mex.
62 G5 Quintanilha Port.
Quintanilla de Abajo Spain see Quintanilla de Onésimo
63 L5 Quintanilla de Onésimo Spain
62 C7 Quintãs Port.
146 B3 Quintay Chile
41 F6 Quintenas France
120 E6 Quinter KS U.S.A.
146 B3 Quintero Chile
38 F5 Quintin France
146 E4 Quinto r. Arg.
66 E5 Quinto Spain
70 F2 Quinto Switz.
118 E5 Quinton NJ U.S.A.
62 D5 Quinxo, Monte do mts Port.
91 B6 Quinzau Angola
111 O2 Quinze, Lac des l. Que. Can.
93 D7 Quionga Moz.
129 K8 Quiotepec Mex.
140 G4 Quipapá Brazil
65 P4 Quipar r. Spain
91 B8 Quipungo Angola
138 D3 Quiquive r. Bol.
126 □O10 Quiriguá tourist site Guat.
146 A5 Quirihue Chile
91 C7 Quirima Angola
93 D8 Quirimbas, Parque Nacional das nat. park Moz.
205 M4 Quirindi N.S.W. Austr.
142 B3 Quirinópolis Brazil
131 L9 Quiriquire Venez.
111 L3 Quirke Lake Ont. Can.
147 G4 Quiroga Arg.
138 D4 Quiroga Bol.
128 F6 Quiroga Mex.
62 F4 Quiroga Spain
72 D8 Quirra, Isola di i. Sardegna Italy
62 I4 Quiruelas de Vidriales Spain
136 D2 Quisiro Venez.
63 L8 Quismondo Spain
41 E9 Quissac France
143 G5 Quissamã Brazil
93 D8 Quissanga Moz.
95 G5 Quissico Moz.
91 C7 Quitapa Angola
130 C6 Quita Sueño Bank sea feature Caribbean Sea
93 D7 Quiterajo Moz.
142 B4 Quitéria r. Brazil
91 B9 Quiteve Angola
144 E2 Quitilipi Arg.
115 F10 Quitman GA U.S.A.
121 K9 Quitman MS U.S.A.
121 H9 Quitman TX U.S.A.
136 B5 Quito Ecuador
126 C2 Quitovac Mex.
145 B7 Quitralco, Parque Nacional nat. park Chile
36 A5 Quittebeuf France
140 F3 Quixadá Brazil
95 I2 Quixaxe Moz.
140 F3 Quixeramobim Brazil
91 B7 Quixinge Angola
171 I6 Qujiang Guangdong China
Qujiang Sichuan China see Quxian
170 F3 Qu Jiang r. China
170 H8 Qujie Guangdong China
170 D6 Qujing Yunnan China
97 M8 Quko S. Africa
85 G3 Qul'ān, Jazā'ir i. Egypt
189 M9 Qulbān Layyah well Iraq
191 C3 Qulevi Georgia
173 G11 Qulho Xizang China
169 R3 Qulin Gol r. China
182 J7 Quljuqtov tog'lari hills Uzbek.
Quljuqtow Toghi hills Uzbek. see Quljuqtov tog'lari
188 E9 Qulūṣanā Egypt
190 A9 Qulzum, Baḩr al b. Egypt
168 D9 Qumar He r. China
168 C9 Qumarheyan Qinghai China
173 L10 Qumarlêb Qinghai China
97 M7 Qumbu S. Africa
173 L11 Qumdo Xizang China
173 H11 Qumigxung Xizang China
97 L8 Qumrha S. Africa
191 G4 Qünäşli Azer.
186 G4 Qunayy well Saudi Arabia
84 D2 Qunayyin, Sabkhat al salt marsh Libya
187 I7 Qunfudh Yemen
Qŭnghirot Uzbek. see Qo'ng'irot
168 G9 Qu'ngoin r. Qinghai China
173 J10 Quntamari Xizang China
170 A3 Qu'nyido Xizang China
107 M1 Quoich r. Nunavut Can.
26 F8 Quoich, Loch l. Scotland U.K.
27 K4 Quoile r. Northern Ireland U.K.
99 □1b Quoin Channel Mauritius
206 B3 Quoin Island N.T. Austr.
96 D10 Quoin Point S. Africa
204 G5 Quorn S.A. Austr.
94 E4 Quoxo r. Botswana
184 E5 Qūptān Iran
Qŭqon Uzbek. see Qo'qon
180 C7 Quraid Sudan
187 N4 Qurayat Oman
190 E10 Qurayyah tourist site Saudi Arabia
190 C8 Qurayyah, Wādī watercourse Egypt
190 F7 Qurayyat al Milḩ l. Jordan
185 M3 Qŭrghonteppa Tajik.
191 H4 Qurmuxçay r. Azer.
191 F7 Qūrū Gol pass Iran
85 G3 Qūş Egypt
191 J4 Qusar Azer.
191 J4 Qusarçay r. Azer.
187 J8 Quşay'ir Saudi Arabia
184 A3 Qūshchī Iran
184 B2 Qūsheh Dāgh mts Iran
Qŭshkŭpir Uzbek. see Qo'shko'pir
Qŭshrabot Uzbek. see Qo'shrabot
173 D10 Qusum Xizang China
173 K12 Qusum Xizang China
97 L6 Quthing r. Lesotho
184 C4 Qūṭīābād Iran
186 F2 Quṭn, Jabal hill Saudi Arabia
105 K1 Quttinirpaaq National Park Nunavut Can.
186 E6 Qutū' Island Saudi Arabia
190 F3 Quwayq, Nahr r. Syria/Turkey
187 L6 Qū' Wishām reg. Oman
169 L9 Quwo Shanxi China
168 I8 Quwu Shan mts China
170 F3 Quxian Sichuan China
Quxian Zhejiang China see Quzhou
173 J12 Qūxü Xizang China
158 F4 Quynh Nhai Vietnam
159 I8 Quy Nhơn Vietnam
111 R4 Quyon Que. Can.
184 A3 Qūyūn Eshek i. Iran
186 E6 Qūz Saudi Arabia
191 I5 Quzanlı Azer.
169 N8 Quzhou Hebei China
171 L4 Quzhou Zhejiang China
169 J8 Quzi Gansu China
191 G4 Qvareli Georgia
191 E3 Qvirila r. Georgia

R

59 I3 Raab Austria
59 N6 Raab r. Austria
59 L2 Raabs an der Thaya Austria
20 R4 Raahe Fin.
20 T5 Rääkkylä Fin.
44 J4 Raalte Neth.
44 G5 Raamsdonksveer Neth.
186 F2 Ra'an, Khashm ar hill Saudi Arabia
20 R3 Raanujärvi Fin.
157 K8 Raas i. Indon.
26 D8 Raasay i. Scotland U.K.
26 D8 Raasay, Sound of sea chan. Scotland U.K.
18 I2 Raasiku Estonia
20 T4 Raate Fin.
71 R6 Rab Croatia
68 E3 Rab i. Croatia
56 G4 Rába r. Hungary
157 M9 Raba Sumbawa Indon.
55 I5 Raba r. Pol.
92 F2 Rabaale Somalia
71 Q5 Rabac Croatia
62 D8 Rabaçal Coimbra Port.
62 F7 Rabaçal Guarda Port.
62 F5 Rabaçal r. Port./Spain
62 E2 Rábade Spain
57 L5 Răbăgani Romania
56 F4 Rábahidvég Hungary
85 G6 Rabak Sudan
56 G4 Rábakecöl Hungary
62 H5 Rabanales Spain
173 E10 Rabang Xizang China
56 F4 Rábapaty Hungary
56 G4 Rábapordány Hungary
43 H8 Rabastens France
43 E9 Rabastens-de-Bigorre France
Rabat Gozo Malta see Victoria
75 □ Rabat Malta
86 D2 Rabat Morocco
Rabatakbaytal Tajik. see Rabotoqbaytal
184 H4 Rabāt-e Kamah Iran
153 L7 Rabaul New Britain P.N.G.
55 H6 Raba Wyżna Pol.
71 M7 Rabbi r. Italy
71 J3 Rabbies r. Italy
106 E3 Rabbit r. B.C. Can.
206 C6 Rabbit Flat N.T. Austr.
106 F2 Rabbitskin r. N.W.T. Can.
57 G4 Rábca r. Hungary
57 I2 Rabča Slovakia
57 I2 Rabčice Slovakia
57 J5 Rabe Vojvodina, Srbija Serb. and Mont.
51 I9 Rabenau Ger.
59 L3 Rabenstein an der Pielach Austria
50 E3 Raben Steinfeld Ger.
19 Q4 Rabezha Rus. Fed.
201 □1 Rabi i. Fiji
155 G4 Rabia Papua Indon.
89 G3 Rabidine well Niger
186 D4 Rābigh Saudi Arabia
127 N10 Rabinal Guat.
54 D2 Rąbino Pol.
98 □3d Rabisca, Punta de pt La Palma Canary Is
70 G2 Rabiusa r. Switz.
22 G4 Rabjerg nature res. Denmark
55 H6 Rabka Pol.
49 K6 Räbke Ger.
179 M9 Rabnabad Islands Bangl.
Râbniţa Moldova see Rîbniţa
98 □1b Rabo de Peixe São Miguel Azores
184 G7 Rābor Iran
71 M4 Raboso r. Italy
185 O2 Rabotoqbaytal Kŭhistoni Badakhshon Tajik.
19 R1 Rabovichi Rus. Fed.
86 B5 Rabt Sbayta des. Western Sahara
84 D3 Rabyānah oasis Libya
84 D3 Rabyānah, Ramlat des. Libya
76 I6 Rača Srbija Serb. and Mont.
174 I5 Racaka Xizang China
75 O4 Racale Italy
57 H4 Rácalmás Hungary
74 F9 Racalmuto Sicilia Italy
73 Q7 Racanello r. Italy
71 O3 Raccolana r. Italy
70 D6 Racconigi Italy
130 F2 Raccoon Cay i. Bahamas
118 E5 Raccoon Creek r. NJ U.S.A.
116 C10 Raccoon Creek r. OH U.S.A.
74 H7 Raccuia Sicilia Italy
59 M7 Rače Slovenia
109 K4 Race, Cape Nfld and Lab. Can.
121 J11 Raceland LA U.S.A.
117 O6 Race Point MA U.S.A.
190 D5 Rachaïya Lebanon
121 F12 Rachal TX U.S.A.
55 L5 Rachanie Pol.
156 C1 Racha Noi, Ko i. Thai.
156 C1 Racha Yai, Ko i. Thai.
37 J6 Rachecourt-sur-Marne France
125 Q4 Rachel NV U.S.A.
19 U3 Rachevo Rus. Fed.
159 G10 Rach Gia Vietnam
159 G10 Rach Gia, Vinh b. Vietnam
191 E3 Rachis K'edi hills Georgia
54 F2 Raciąż Kujawsko-Pomorskie Pol.
55 I3 Raciąż Mazowieckie Pol.
55 I3 Raciążnica r. Pol.
54 G5 Racibórz Pol.
55 I6 Raciechowice Pol.
54 C2 Racimierz Pol.
110 G7 Racine WI U.S.A.
116 D10 Racine WV U.S.A.
111 K1 Racine Lake Ont. Can.
77 M4 Râciu Romania
57 H4 Ráckeve Hungary
26 J5 Rackwick Orkney, Scotland U.K.
51 F8 Rackwitz Ger.
55 I5 Racławice Pol.
77 N4 Racoș Romania
77 P5 Racoviţa Brăila Romania
57 K6 Racoviţa Timiş Romania
55 K2 Raczki Pol.
55 I2 Rączki Pol.
186 G8 Radā' Yemen
146 A6 Radal Chile
18 K7 Radashkovichy Belarus
77 N3 Rădăuţi Romania
56 C2 Radbuza r. Czech Rep.
19 T5 Radchenko Rus. Fed.
17 T4 Radchenskoye Rus. Fed.
114 E7 Radcliff KY U.S.A.
29 M6 Radcliffe Greater Manchester, England U.K.
31 J2 Radcliffe on Trent Nottinghamshire, England U.K.
162 G4 Radde Rus. Fed.
74 H9 Raddusa Sicilia Italy
22 G2 Rade Norway
51 I8 Radeberg Ger.
51 I8 Radebeul Ger.
51 I8 Radeburg Ger.
59 L7 Radeče Slovenia
51 F8 Radefeld Ger.
51 F7 Radegast Ger.
16 D3 Radekhiv Ukr.
59 N6 Radenci Slovenia
17 L7 Radens'k Ukr.
50 G5 Radensleben Ger.
59 I6 Radenthein Austria
49 D8 Radevormwald Ger.
54 D1 Radew r. Pol.
58 E5 Radfeld Austria
116 E11 Radford VA U.S.A.
206 C1 Radford Point N.T. Austr.
31 J3 Radford Semele Warwickshire, England U.K.
178 C8 Radhanpur Gujarat India
51 J8 Radibor Ger.
72 H2 Radicofani Italy
71 K9 Radicondoli Italy
73 O4 Radicosa r. Italy
51 G7 Radis Ger.
182 B1 Radishchevo Rus. Fed.
108 E2 Radisson Que. Can.
107 J4 Radisson Sask. Can.
110 C4 Radisson WI U.S.A.
19 R8 Raditsa-Krylovka Rus. Fed.
106 G5 Radium Hot Springs B.C. Can.
59 M7 Radizelj Slovenia
17 P2 Rad'kovka Rus. Fed.
54 E5 Radków Dolnośląskie Pol.
55 H5 Radków Świętokrzyskie Pol.
31 L4 Radlett Hertfordshire, England U.K.
212 R1 Radlinski, Mount Antarctica
59 L6 Radlje ob Dravi Slovenia
55 I5 Radłów Małopolskie Pol.
54 G5 Radłów Opolskie Pol.
77 N8 Radnevo Bulg.
56 C2 Radnice Czech Rep.
136 B4 Rado de Tumaco inlet Col.
19 R2 Radogoshcha Rus. Fed.
57 J6 Radojevo Vojvodina, Srbija Serb. and Mont.
52 F6 Radolfzell am Bodensee Ger.
55 J4 Radom Pol.
90 E2 Radom Sudan
55 H2 Radomin Pol.
77 K8 Radomir Bulg.
77 L9 Radomir mt. Bulg./Greece
55 J4 Radomka r. Pol.
57 K2 Radomka r. Slovakia
17 L2 Radomka Ukr.
90 D2 Radom National Park Sudan
55 J4 Radomska, Równina plain Pol.
55 H4 Radomsko Pol.
16 I3 Radomyshl' Ukr.
55 J5 Radomyśl nad Sanem Pol.
55 J5 Radomyśl Wielki Pol.
56 C1 Radonice Czech Rep.
Radoshkovichi Belarus see Radashkovichy
57 G3 Radošina Slovakia
56 G3 Radošovce Slovakia
55 I4 Radoszyce Pol.
54 D3 Radoszyn Pol.
77 O9 Radovets Bulg.
77 K9 Radoviš Macedonia
19 W6 Radovitskiy Rus. Fed.
68 E2 Radovljica Slovenia
54 D2 Radowo Małe Pol.
24 J1 Radøy i. Norway
59 H5 Radstadt Austria
59 H5 Radstädter Tauern mts Austria
59 I5 Radstädter Tauern pass Austria
30 H5 Radstock Bath and North East Somerset, England U.K.
204 E5 Radstock, Cape S.A. Austr.
77 P4 Răducăneni Romania
16 J2 Radul' Ukr.
18 H7 Radun' Belarus
23 O7 Radunia r. Pol.
17 M6 Radushne Ukr.
57 K2 Radvaň nad Laborcom Slovakia
18 G6 Radviliškis Lith.
186 D3 Raḑwá, Jabal mt. Saudi Arabia
54 D4 Radwanice Pol.
55 K6 Radymno Pol.
17 M4 Radyvonivka Ukr.
16 E3 Radyvyliv Ukr.
55 I3 Radzanów Pol.
55 I4 Radzice Duże Pol.
54 F2 Radzicz Pol.
55 J1 Radzieje Pol.
54 G3 Radziejów Pol.
55 I6 Radziejowa mt. Pol.
55 I3 Radziejowice Pol.
55 I5 Radziemice Pol.
54 C3 Radzików Pol.
55 K2 Radziłów Pol.
57 I3 Radzovce Slovakia
55 J3 Radzymin Pol.
54 G2 Radzyń Chełminski Pol.
55 K4 Radzyń Podlaski Pol.
178 H6 Rae Bareli Uttar Prad. India
106 G2 Rae-Edzo N.W.T. Can.
115 H8 Raeford NC U.S.A.
106 G1 Rae Lakes N.W.T. Can.
45 J7 Raeren Belgium
49 C7 Raesfeld Ger.
209 F10 Raeside, Lake salt flat W.A. Austr.
202 H2 Raetea hill North I. N.Z.
202 J6 Raetihi North I. N.Z.
189 I9 Rāf hill Saudi Arabia
146 A5 Rafael Chile
147 G2 Rafaela Arg.
130 F3 Rafael Freyre Cuba
129 J6 Rafael J. Garcia Mex.
147 G4 Rafael Obligado Arg.
Rafaḩ Gaza see Rafiaḩ
90 D3 Rafaï C.A.R.
16 F2 Rafalivka Ukr.
67 E8 Rafelbunyol Spain
74 F9 Raffadali Sicilia Italy
106 K5 Rafferty Reservoir Can.
26 I7 Rafford Moray, Scotland U.K.
27 K4 Raffrey Northern Ireland U.K.
189 K9 Rafḩā' Saudi Arabia
190 C7 Rafiaḩ Gaza
90 E3 Rafili Sudan
78 F4 Rafina Greece
27 E6 Raford r. Rep. of Ireland
184 F6 Rafsanjān Iran
122 H5 Raft r. ID/NV U.S.A.
90 E2 Raga Sudan
90 E2 Ragag Sudan
63 J7 Rágama Spain
18 H4 Ragana Latvia
75 K4 Raganello r. Italy
154 E8 Ragang, Mount vol. Mindanao Phil.
154 D5 Ragay Gulf Luzon Phil.
50 G4 Rägelin Ger.
209 G12 Ragged, Mount hill W.A. Austr.
130 F2 Ragged Island Bahamas
117 □Q5 Ragged Island ME U.S.A.
131 □4 Ragged Point Barbados
185 N3 Rāgh Afgh.
178 F7 Raghogarh Madh. Prad. India
186 G1 Raghwah Saudi Arabia
186 G8 Raghwān, Wādī watercourse Yemen
202 I4 Raglan North I. N.Z.
30 G4 Raglan Monmouthshire, Wales U.K.
202 I4 Raglan Harbour North I. N.Z.
59 M6 Ragnitz Austria
20 N3 Rago Nasjonalpark nat. park Norway
51 G6 Ragösen Ger.
109 G3 Ragueneau Que. Can.
51 F7 Raguhn Ger.
74 H10 Ragusa Sicilia Italy
74 H10 Ragusa prov. Sicilia Italy
173 K11 Ragxi Xizang China
168 G9 Ra'gyagoinba Qinghai China
158 A1 Raha Assam India
155 C6 Raha Sulawesi Indon.
19 N8 Rahachow Belarus
85 G6 Rahad r. Sudan
85 G6 Rahad Canal Sudan
90 D2 Rahad el Berdi Sudan
84 E6 Rahad Wahal well Sudan
Rahaeng Thai. see Tak
186 E4 Rahaţ, Ḩarrat lava field Saudi Arabia
178 F8 Rahatgaon Madh. Prad. India
49 G6 Rahden Ger.
176 D4 Rahimatpur Mahar. India
185 N7 Rahimyar Khan Pak.
37 L8 Rahin r. France
184 D4 Rāhjerd Iran
202 H6 Rahotu North I. N.Z.
146 B6 Rahué Arg.
146 B6 Rahue mt. Chile
18 K3 Rahumäe Estonia
176 D3 Rahuri Mahar. India
185 I4 Rahzanak Afgh.
73 L3 Raiano Italy
201 □3 Raiatea i. Arch. de la Société Fr. Polynesia
147 H2 Raices Arg.
176 E4 Raichur Karnataka India
179 L7 Raiganj W. Bengal India
179 I9 Raigarh Chhattisgarh India
176 H3 Raigarh Orissa India
155 B9 Raijua i. Indon.
178 E4 Raikot Punjab India
125 Q3 Railroad Valley NV U.S.A.
179 L9 Raimangal r. Bangl.
109 G2 Raimbault, Lac l. Que. Can.
53 J4 Rain Bayern Ger.
53 M4 Rain Bayern Ger.
59 J2 Rainbach im Mühlkreis Austria
205 I6 Rainbow Vic. Austr.
207 N8 Rainbow Beach Qld Austr.
106 G3 Rainbow Lake Alta Can.
207 J1 Raine Entrance sea chan. Qld Austr.
207 J1 Raine Island Qld Austr.
116 E11 Rainelle WV U.S.A.
29 L6 Rainford Merseyside, England U.K.
185 M7 Raini r. Pak.

122 D3 **Rainier, Mount** vol. WA U.S.A.
155 E1 **Rainis** Sulawesi Indon.
29 M7 **Rainow** Cheshire, England U.K.
29 O7 **Rainworth** Nottinghamshire, England U.K.
120 H1 **Rainy** r. MN U.S.A.
107 M5 **Rainy Lake** Ont. Can.
107 M5 **Rainy River** Ont. Can.
20 P5 **Raippaluoto** i. Fin.
179 M8 **Raipur** Bangl.
178 H9 **Raipur** Chhattisgarh India
178 E6 **Raipur** Rajasthan India
179 K8 **Raipur** W. Bengal India
179 K8 **Rairangpur** Orissa India
200 ☐1b **Rairik** i. Majuro Marshall Is
62 E4 **Rairiz de Veiga** Spain
Rairoa atoll Arch. des Tuamotu Fr. Polynesia see Rangiroa
48 J2 **Raisdorf** Ger.
178 F8 **Raisen** Madh. Prad. India
74 E7 **Raisi, Punta** di Sicilia Italy
178 D5 **Raisinghnagar** Rajasthan India
21 Q6 **Raisio** Fin.
36 F3 **Raismes** France
20 T3 **Raistakka** Fin.
178 F9 **Raitalai** Madh. Prad. India
53 K3 **Raitenbuch** Ger.
110 E1 **Raith** Ont. Can.
203 H8 **Rai Valley** South I. N.Z.
201 ☐3 **Raivavae** i. Is Australes Fr. Polynesia
185 P6 **Raiwind** Pak.
18 J3 **Raja** Estonia
157 J8 **Raja** i. Indon.
156 B3 **Raja, Ujung** pt Indon.
155 F4 **Rajaampat, Kepulauan** is Papua Indon.
156 F7 **Rajabasa, Gunung** vol. Indon.
179 J8 **Rajaganga** Orissa India
176 G4 **Rajahmundry** Andhra Prad. India
20 T2 **Raja-Jooseppi** Fin.
178 E5 **Rajaldesar** Rajasthan India
18 H1 **Rajaniki** Fin.
176 F5 **Rajampet** Andhra Prad. India
157 I3 **Rajang** Sarawak Malaysia
157 I3 **Rajang** r. Malaysia
185 N7 **Rajanpur** Pak.
176 E8 **Rajapalaiyam** Tamil Nadu India
178 D6 **Rajapur** Mahar. India
178 D5 **Rajasthan** state India
179 J7 **Rajauli** Bihar India
179 L8 **Rajbari** Bangl.
56 F2 **Rajec** Slovakia
57 H2 **Rajec** Slovakia
57 H2 **Rajecká Lesná** Slovakia
178 F7 **Rajgarh** Madh. Prad. India
176 C3 **Rajgarh** Mahar. India
178 E5 **Rajgarh** Rajasthan India
178 F6 **Rajgarh** Rajasthan India
179 J7 **Rajgir** Bihar India
55 K2 **Rajgród** Pol.
55 K2 **Rajgrodzkie, Jezioro** l. Pol.
179 J7 **Rajhara** Jharkhand India
59 O1 **Rajhrad** Czech Rep.
59 O1 **Rajhradice** Czech Rep.
Rájijovsset Fin. see Raja-Jooseppi
156 F6 **Rajik** Indon.
179 H8 **Rajim** Chhattisgarh India
77 J8 **Rajince** Srbija Serb. and Mont.
56 G3 **Rajka** Hungary
178 C8 **Rajkot** Gujarat India
179 K7 **Rajmahal** Jharkhand India
178 E7 **Raj Mahal** Rajasthan India
179 J7 **Rajmahal Hills** India
178 H3 **Rajnagar** W. Bengal India
178 H9 **Raj Nandgaon** Chhattisgarh India
178 E3 **Rajouri** Jammu and Kashmir
178 D9 **Rajpipla** Gujarat India
178 D9 **Rajpur** Madh. Prad. India
178 F4 **Rajpura** Punjab India
Rajputana Agency state India see Rajasthan
178 D7 **Rajsamand** Rajasthan India
179 L7 **Rajshahi** Bangl.
179 L7 **Rajshahi** admin. div. Bangl.
190 E2 **Rajula** Syria
178 C9 **Rajula** Gujarat India
178 G9 **Rajur** Mahar. India
176 F3 **Rajura** Mahar. India
173 G12 **Raka** Xizang China
59 L8 **Raka** Slovenia
57 J3 **Rakaca** r. Hungary
203 ☐2 **Rakahanga** atoll Cook Is
92 A5 **Rakai** Uganda
203 G10 **Rakaia** South I. N.Z.
203 G10 **Rakaia** r. South I. N.Z.
57 K3 **Rakamaz** Hungary
187 J2 **Rakan, Ra's** pt Qatar
178 E1 **Rakaposhi** mt. Jammu and Kashmir
203 B13 **Rakeahua, Mount** hill Stewart I. N.Z.
59 J8 **Rakek** Slovenia
Rakhine state Myanmar see Arakan
16 D5 **Rakhiv** Ukr.
17 M6 **Rakhmanivka** Ukr.
185 M6 **Rakhni** Pak.
185 J8 **Rakhshan** r. Pak.
201 ☐1a **Rakiraki** Viti Levu Fiji
157 H7 **Rakit** i. Indon.
59 J8 **Rakitna** Slovenia
77 N8 **Rakitnitsa** r. Bulg.
15 F6 **Rakitnoye** Belgorodskaya Oblast' Rus. Fed.
162 I6 **Rakitnoye** Primorskiy Kray Rus. Fed.
71 P5 **Rakitovec** Slovenia
202 J3 **Rakiura Island** North I. N.Z.
Rakiura i. N.Z. see Stewart Island
18 J3 **Rakke** Estonia
22 H2 **Rakkestad** Norway
172 H2 **Rakmanovskie Klyuchi** Kazakh.
185 N6 **Rakni** r. Pak.
57 J4 **Rákóczifalva** Hungary
57 J4 **Rákócziújfalu** Hungary
54 E3 **Rakoniewice** Pol.
94 E4 **Rakops** Botswana
57 J3 **Rakovica** Ukr.
57 H2 **Raková** Slovakia
77 K7 **Rakovitsa** Bulg.
56 C1 **Rakovnická Pahorkatina** hills Czech Rep.
56 C1 **Rakovník** Czech Rep.
77 M8 **Rakovski** Bulg.
50 H2 **Rakow** Ger.
55 K5 **Raków** Pol.
55 K5 **Rakszawa** Pol.
15 K7 **Rakulka** Rus. Fed.
182 D6 **Rakushechnyy, Mys** pt Kazakh.
18 J2 **Rakvere** Estonia
56 F3 **Rakvice** Czech Rep.
93 M6 **Rakwere** Lesotho
121 K9 **Raleigh** MS U.S.A.
115 H8 **Raleigh** NC U.S.A.
137 G3 **Raleighvallen Voltsberg, Natuurreservaat** nature res. Suriname
52 B2 **Ralingen** Ger.
155 A6 **Ralla** Sulawesi Indon.
121 H8 **Ralph** MI U.S.A.
107 I5 **Ralston** Alta Can.
111 R8 **Ralston** PA U.S.A.
175 ☐1 **Raluana Giri** i. N. Male Maldives
106 F2 **Ram** r. N.W.T. Can.
190 D6 **Rama** Israel
126 ☐Q11 **Rama** Nic.
16 D3 **Rama** r. Ukr.
74 H4 **Ramacca** Sicilia Italy
146 B3 **Ramada, Cerro de la** mt. Arg.
138 C5 **Ramaditas** Chile
177 I3 **Ramagiri** Orissa India
109 I1 **Ramah** Nfld and Lab. Can.
64 A2 **Ramales de la Victoria** Spain
140 D6 **Ramalho, Serra do** hills Brazil
190 D7 **Ramallah** West Bank
147 G3 **Ramallo** Arg.
176 E6 **Ramanagaram** Karnataka India

176 F8 **Ramanathapuram** Tamil Nadu India
179 I8 **Ramanuj Ganj** Chhattisgarh India
119 G3 **Ramapo** r. NJ U.S.A.
216 E3 **Ramapo Deep** sea feature N. Pacific Ocean
179 I9 **Ramapur** Orissa India
97 J1 **Ramaphaleng** S. Africa
Ramas, Cape India see Ramasukha
14 G9 **Ramasukha** Rus. Fed.
97 J1 **Ramatlabama** watercourse Botswana/S. Africa
97 J1 **Ramatlabama** S. Africa
41 J10 **Ramatuelle** France
176 F3 **Ramayampet** Andhra Prad. India
20 L2 **Ramberg** Norway
37 M7 **Rambervillers** France
178 E8 **Rambha** Madh. Prad. India
201 ☐3b **Rambi** i. Fiji see Rabi
50 H2 **Rambin** Ger.
67 C11 **Rambla de Judío** r. Spain
59 K3 **Rambla del Moro** r. Spain
36 C6 **Rambouillet** France
36 C6 **Rambouillet, Forêt de** for. France
45 I9 **Rambrouch** Lux.
37 K6 **Rambucourt** France
153 K7 **Rambutyo Island** Admiralty Is P.N.G.
176 D5 **Ramdurg** Karnataka India
30 D7 **Rame** Cornwall, England U.K.
179 K6 **Ramechhap** Nepal
97 N7 **Rame Head** S. Africa
30 D7 **Rame Head** England U.K.
22 G1 **Ramelton** Rep. of Ireland
23 L1 **Rämen** l. Sweden
95 ☐K2 **Ramena** Madag.
21 J6 **Ramendik** Norway
97 M2 **Ramenskoye** Rus. Fed.
36 H6 **Ramerupt** France
203 F19 **Rameses, Mount** South I. N.Z.
19 T4 **Rameshki** Rus. Fed.
176 F8 **Rameswaram** Tamil Nadu India
184 I9 **Ramezān Kalak** Iran
13 D13 **Ramganga** r. India
179 M8 **Ramgarh** Bangl.
178 C6 **Ramgarh** Jharkhand India
178 E6 **Ramgarh** Rajasthan India
178 F6 **Ramgarh** Rajasthan India
185 N4 **Ramgul** reg. Afgh.
184 C6 **Rāmhormoz** Iran
45 G7 **Ramillies** Belgium
206 E2 **Ramingining** N.T. Austr.
59 I5 **Ramingstein** Austria
98 ☐1a **Raminho** Terceira Azores
62 E4 **Ramirás** Spain
Ramit Tajik. see Romit
179 I8 **Ramkola** Uttar Prad. India
190 C7 **Ramla** Israel
187 N5 **Ramlat al Wahībah** des. Oman
187 K6 **Ramlat Amilhayt** des. Oman
186 G8 **Ramlat as Sab'atayn** des. Yemen
186 E2 **Ramlat Dahm** des. Saudi Arabia/Yemen
190 D9 **Ramm, Jabal** mts Jordan
51 J2 **Rammelsbach** Ger.
53 I4 **Rammenau** Ger.
97 K3 **Rammulotsi** S. Africa
Ramnad Tamil Nadu India see Ramanathapuram
178 H7 **Ramnagar** Madh. Prad. India
178 H8 **Ramnagar** Madh. Prad. India
178 G5 **Ramnagar** Uttaranchal India
23 M2 **Ramnäs** Sweden
19 N6 **Ramni** Belarus
77 P5 **Râmnicu Sărat** r. Romania
77 P5 **Râmnicu Sărat** Romania
77 M5 **Râmnicu Vâlcea** Romania
92 D3 **Ramo** Eth.
95 E4 **Ramokgwebane** Botswana
17 S2 **Ramon'** Rus. Fed.
124 P8 **Ramona** CA U.S.A.
37 M8 **Ramonchamp** France
128 D1 **Ramón Corona** Mex.
62 E7 **Ramonde** Port.
146 C6 **Ramón M. Castro** Arg.
147 H6 **Ramón Santamarina** Arg.
43 G8 **Ramonville-St-Agne** France
27 H5 **Ramor, Lough** l. Rep. of Ireland
111 N1 **Ramore** Ont. Can.
144 D1 **Ramos** Mex.
128 G5 **Ramos** Mex.
121 C13 **Ramos** r. Mex.
127 I5 **Ramos Arizpe** Mex.
70 I2 **Ramosch** Switz.
94 E2 **Ramotswa** Botswana
169 M2 **Rampart of Genghis Khan** tourist site Asia
29 K5 **Rampside** Cumbria, England U.K.
121 E10 **Rankin** TX U.S.A.
107 M2 **Rankin Inlet** inlet Nunavut Can.
107 M2 **Rankin Inlet** Nunavut Can.
205 K5 **Rankin's Springs** N.S.W. Austr.
58 A5 **Rankweil** Austria
18 K3 **Ranna** Estonia
207 M8 **Ranna** S. Africa
182 E2 **Ranneye** Rus. Fed.
179 K7 **Rannoch, Loch** l. Scotland U.K.
26 G9 **Rannoch Moor** moorland Scotland U.K.
26 G9 **Rannoch Station** Perth and Kinross, Scotland U.K.
173 B5 **Rann of Kachchh** marsh India
18 J3 **Rannu** Estonia
89 H4 **Rano** Nigeria
23 O3 **Rånö** i. Sweden
155 I3 **Rano, Mount** New Georgia Is Solomon Is
95 ☐J3 **Ranobe** r. Madag.
95 ☐J4 **Ranohira** Madag.
95 ☐J3 **Ranomafana** Madag.
95 ☐J4 **Ranomena** Madag.
159 T0 **Ranong** Thai.
200 ☐5 **Ranongga** i. New Georgia Is Solomon Is
159 E11 **Ranot** Thai.
95 ☐J4 **Ranotsara Avaratra** Madag.
19 X7 **Ranova** r. Rus. Fed.
178 C8 **Ranpur** Gujarat India
179 I7 **Ranrikke** Sweden
146 C5 **Ranquilco, Salitral** salt pan Arg.
146 B6 **Ranquil del Norte** Arg.
185 M6 **Ranrkan** Pak.
187 J8 **Ra's Sharwayn** c. Yemen
99 ☐3b **Rasi Douamoungo** c. Mayotte
187 M6 **Ra's Şīrāb** Oman
54 J5 **Ras Jebel** Tunisia
207 J8 **Rasskazovo** Rus. Fed.
77 T1 **Rast** Romania
15 H5 **Rasta** r. Belarus
187 K1 **Ras Tannūrah** Saudi Arabia
58 J5 **Rastatt** Ger.
50 S2 **Rastde** Denmark
48 F5 **Rastede** Ger.
55 D7 **Rastede** Ger.
59 L2 **Rastenberg** Austria
18 H7 **Rastorf** Ger.
77 M7 **Rastorguyevo** Rus. Fed. see Vidnoye
63 D6 **Rasueros** Spain
68 F3 **Rasun Anterselva/Rasen-Antholz** Italy
92 I2 **Rasvag** Norway
23 L2 **Rasvåg** i. Sweden
63 O3 **Rasyny** Belarus
155 B6 **Rata** r. Indon.
155 K6 **Rataj** Slovenia
156 I6 **Ratak Chain** is Marshall Is
59 L3 **Ratan** Austria
65 K6 **Rataje nad Sázavou** Czech Rep.
155 I3 **Rataje** Slovenia

Red Wing to **Rinkenæs**
327

10 B5 **Red Wing** MN U.S.A.
51 D10 **Redwitz an der Rodach** Ger.
24 J4 **Redwood City** CA U.S.A.
20 H3 **Redwood Falls** MN U.S.A.
22 B6 **Redwood National Park** CA U.S.A.
24 I2 **Redwood Valley** CA U.S.A.
55 H5 **Rędziny** Pol.
27 G5 **Ree, Lough** l. Rep. of Ireland
10 I6 **Reed City** MI U.S.A.
07 K4 **Reed Lake** Man. Can.
24 M5 **Reedley** CA U.S.A.
19 G6 **Reeds Bay** NJ U.S.A.
10 E6 **Reedsburg** WI U.S.A.
22 B5 **Reedsport** OR U.S.A.
16 D9 **Reedsville** OH U.S.A.
16 H8 **Reedsville** PA U.S.A.
17 I11 **Reedville** VA U.S.A.
16 D10 **Reedy** WV U.S.A.
07 J7 **Reedy Creek** watercourse Qld Austr.
12 P1 **Reedy Glacier** Antarctica
Reef Islands Vanuatu see Rowa
03 F9 **Reefton** South I. N.Z.
27 E7 **Reens** Rep. of Ireland
31 O2 **Reepham** Norfolk, England U.K.
49 B7 **Rees** Ger.
11 K6 **Reese** MI U.S.A.
24 P1 **Reese** r. NV U.S.A.
48 H4 **Reeßum** Ger.
50 E4 **Reetz** Brandenburg Ger.
51 F6 **Reetz** Brandenburg Ger.
44 G4 **Reeuwijksebrug** Neth.
88 I4 **Refahiye** Turkey
62 C5 **Refóios do Lima** Port.
21 K9 **Reform** AL U.S.A.
27 M9 **Reforma** Chiapas Mex.
29 M9 **Reforma** Oaxaca Mex.
18 C5 **Refton** PA U.S.A.
21 G11 **Refugio** TX U.S.A.
54 D1 **Rega** r. Pol.
62 D6 **Regadas** Port.
28 F8 **Regaditos** Mex.
67 E8 **Regajo, Embalse del** resr Spain
74 H8 **Regalbuto** Sicilia Italy
66 E5 **Regallo** r. Spain
59 I4 **Regau** Austria
53 O4 **Regen** Ger.
53 M3 **Regen** r. Ger.
43 H3 **Regência** Brazil
53 M3 **Regensburg** Ger.
70 E1 **Regensdorf** Switz.
53 M3 **Regenstauf** Ger.
42 B5 **Regente Feijó** Brazil
87 F4 **Reggane** Alg.
44 J3 **Regge** r. Neth.
71 L8 **Reggello** Italy
Reggio Calabria Italy see **Reggio di Calabria**
Reggio Emilia-Romagna Italy see **Reggio nell'Emilia**
75 J7 **Reggio di Calabria** Italy
75 K7 **Reggio di Calabria** prov. Italy
Reggio Emilia Italy see **Reggio nell'Emilia**
71 J6 **Reggio nell'Emilia** Italy
71 J6 **Reggio nell'Emilia** prov. Italy
77 M4 **Reghin** Romania
85 K5 **Regi** Afgh.
73 L6 **Regi Lagni** canal Italy
55 I3 **Regimin** Pol.
07 J5 **Regina** Sask. Can.
37 H3 **Régina** Fr. Guiana
85 K6 **Registān** reg. Afgh.
42 D6 **Registro** Brazil
42 B1 **Registro do Araguaia** Brazil
Regium Lepidum Italy see **Reggio nell'Emilia**
51 F10 **Regnitzlosau** Ger.
40 E5 **Régny** France
79 O5 **Regong** Arun. Prad. India
20 U4 **Regozero** Rus. Fed.
62 C4 **Reguengo** Spain
64 D4 **Reguengos de Monsaraz** Port.
38 F6 **Réguiny** France
51 F10 **Rehau** Ger.
49 H6 **Rehburg (Rehburg-Loccum)** Ger.
48 F5 **Rehden** Ger.
78 G8 **Rehli** Madh. Prad. India
53 J5 **Rehling** Ger.
52 B3 **Rehlingen-Siersburg** Ger.
51 I9 **Řehlovice** Czech Rep.
50 D3 **Rehna** Ger.
94 C4 **Rehoboth** Namibia
17 J10 **Rehoboth Bay** DE U.S.A.
17 J10 **Rehoboth Beach** DE U.S.A.
37 K4 **Réhon** France
90 C7 **Rehovot** Israel
51 F7 **Reibitz** Ger.
53 J2 **Reiche Ebrach** r. Ger.
52 F2 **Reichelsheim (Odenwald)** Ger.
49 G10 **Reichelsheim (Wetterau)** Ger.
52 G6 **Reichenau** Ger.
59 M4 **Reichenau an der Rax** Austria
52 F2 **Reichenbach** Hessen Ger.
51 F9 **Reichenbach** Sachsen Ger.
70 D2 **Reichenbach** Switz.
51 K8 **Reichenbach (Oberlausitz)** Ger.
52 H2 **Reichenberg** Ger.
59 K5 **Reichenfels** Austria
49 J8 **Reichensachsen (Wehretal)** Ger.
53 K2 **Reichenschwand** Ger.
58 F5 **Reichenspitze** mt. Austria
59 J2 **Reichenthal** Austria
53 L5 **Reichertshausen** Ger.
53 M5 **Reichertsheim** Ger.
53 K4 **Reichertshofen** Ger.
53 J6 **Reichling** Ger.
51 D9 **Reichmannsdorf** Ger.
52 H2 **Reicholzheim** Ger.
59 J4 **Reichraming** Austria
37 O6 **Reichshoffen** France
37 O6 **Reichstett** France
09 J11 **Reid** W.A. Austr.
70 D1 **Reiden** Switz.
26 E7 **Reidh, Rubha** pt Scotland U.K.
15 F9 **Reidsville** GA U.S.A.
15 H7 **Reidsville** NC U.S.A.
62 G7 **Reigada** Port.
31 L5 **Reigate** Surrey, England U.K.
42 C5 **Reignac** France
40 I4 **Reignier** France
49 D10 **Reil** Ger.
25 V9 **Reiley Peak** AZ U.S.A.
43 G6 **Reilhaguet** France
52 F3 **Reilingen** Ger.
41 H9 **Reillanne** France
63 Q9 **Reillo** Spain
36 H5 **Reims** France
64 H4 **Reina** Spain
70 E1 **Reinach** Aargau Switz.
70 D1 **Reinach** Basellandschaft Switz.
22 C2 **Reinaknuten** hill Norway
48 J3 **Reinbek** Ger.
50 H2 **Reinberg** Ger.
07 K4 **Reindeer** r. Sask. Can.
07 L4 **Reindeer Island** Man. Can.
07 K3 **Reindeer Lake** Man./Sask. Can.
20 L3 **Reine** Norway
16 D9 **Reinersville** OH U.S.A.
21 J6 **Reineskarvet** mt. Norway
48 J3 **Reinfeld (Holstein)** Ger.
02 G1 **Reinga, Cape** North I. N.Z.
49 H7 **Reinhardswald** mts Ger.
52 F2 **Reinheim** Ger.
18 C4 **Reinholds** PA U.S.A.
63 L3 **Reinosa** Spain
40 E4 **Reins** r. France
51 G7 **Reinsdorf** Sachsen-Anhalt Ger.
51 D8 **Reinsdorf** Thüringen Ger.
52 B2 **Reinsfeld** Ger.
22 C2 **Reinsnosi** mt. Norway
20 □B1 **Reipholsfjöll** hill Iceland
Reirson Island atoll Cook Is see **Rakahanga**
20 Q2 **Reisa Nasjonalpark** nat. park Norway
53 N4 **Reisbach** Ger.
53 N5 **Reischach** Ger.
20 R5 **Reisjärvi** Fin.
49 G9 **Reiskirchen** Ger.
118 B6 **Reisterstown** MD U.S.A.
74 G8 **Reitano** Sicilia Italy
44 J2 **Reitdiep** r. Neth.
53 M6 **Reit im Winkl** Ger.
97 M3 **Reitz** S. Africa
97 L3 **Reitzburg** S. Africa
18 H3 **Reiu** r. Estonia
96 I3 **Reivilo** S. Africa
92 A3 **Rejaf** Sudan
23 L3 **Rejmyre** Sweden
55 L4 **Rejowiec** Pol.
55 L4 **Rejowiec Fabryczny** Pol.
59 O7 **Reka** Croatia
71 Q5 **Reka** r. Slovenia
176 G4 **Rekapalle** Andhra Prad. India
49 D7 **Reken** Ger.
185 L7 **Rekgwash** Pak.
44 K4 **Rekken** Neth.
55 M5 **Reklynets'** Ukr.
76 J7 **Rekovac** Srbija Serb. and Mont.
55 M6 **Rekshyn** Ukr.
22 E1 **Reksjåeggi** mt. Norway
18 G6 **Rėkyvos ežeras** l. Lith.
107 I2 **Reliance** N.W.T. Can.
74 H10 **Religione, Punta** pt Sicilia Italy
64 C5 **Relíquias** Port.
87 F2 **Relizane** Alg.
126 G4 **Rellano** Mex.
67 E10 **Relleu** Spain
177 H4 **Relli** Andhra Prad. India
48 I3 **Rellingen** Ger.
98 □1b **Relva** São Miguel Azores
57 I5 **Rém** Hungary
87 H2 **Remada** Tunisia
49 D9 **Remagen** Ger.
39 M5 **Rémalard** France
204 G5 **Remarkable, Mount** hill S.A. Austr.
157 I8 **Rembang** Jawa Indon.
37 J6 **Rembercourt-Sommaisne** France
51 D9 **Remda** Ger.
147 F5 **Remecó** Arg.
98 □1b **Remédios** São Miguel Azores
136 C3 **Remedios** Col.
130 D2 **Remedios** Cuba
128 A1 **Remedios** Mex.
127 O11 **Remedios, Punta** pt El Salvador
62 B3 **Remedios, Punta dos** pt Spain
87 H3 **Remel el Abiod** des. Tunisia
48 E4 **Remels (Uplengen)** Ger.
18 L5 **Remennikovo** Rus. Fed.
120 I2 **Remer** MN U.S.A.
184 H8 **Remeshk** Iran
20 S5 **Remeskylä** Fin.
57 L5 **Remetea** Romania
57 K6 **Remetea Mare** Romania
77 L3 **Remeți** Romania
59 N7 **Remetinec** Croatia
Remi France see **Reims**
45 J9 **Remich** Lux.
45 H7 **Remicourt** Belgium
37 I4 **Remilly-Aillicourt** France
116 H10 **Remington** VA U.S.A.
137 H3 **Rémire** Fr. Guiana
99 □2 **Rémire** i. Seychelles
37 M7 **Remiremont** France
49 K6 **Remlingen** Ger.
122 D2 **Remmel Mountain** WA U.S.A.
66 C4 **Remolinos** Spain
37 L7 **Remoncourt** France
15 H7 **Remontnoye** Rus. Fed.
45 I8 **Remouchamps** Belgium
41 F9 **Remoulins** France
156 F4 **Rempang** i. Indon.
99 □1c **Remparts, Rivière des** r. Réunion
50 G3 **Remplin** Ger.
51 E9 **Remptendorf** Ger.
52 G4 **Rems** r. Ger.
49 D8 **Remscheid** Ger.
58 B7 **Remulo** r. Italy
38 F6 **Remungol** France
110 I6 **Remus** MI U.S.A.
41 G8 **Rémuzat** France
21 K6 **Rena** Norway
21 K6 **Rena** r. Norway
64 H2 **Rena** Spain
111 K1 **Renabie** Ont. Can.
41 G6 **Renage** France
146 A5 **Renaico** Chile
40 D4 **Renaison** France
Renaix Belgium see **Ronse**
158 D1 **Renam** Myanmar
176 E3 **Renapur** Mahar. India
39 I6 **Renazé** France
146 E3 **Renca** Arg.
52 E4 **Renchen** Ger.
95 F4 **Renco** Zimbabwe
Rende Yunnan China see **Xundian**
73 Q9 **Rende** Italy
120 K6 **Rend Lake** IL U.S.A.
200 □6 **Rendova** i. New Georgia Is Solomon Is
48 I2 **Rendsburg** Ger.
63 M2 **Renedo** Cantabria Spain
63 K5 **Renedo** Castilla y León Spain
63 K4 **Renedo de la Vega** Spain
109 G3 **René-Levasseur, Île** i. Que. Can.
70 B2 **Renens** Switz.
44 E5 **Renesse** Neth.
109 K4 **Renews** Nfld and Lab. Can.
108 E4 **Renfrew** Ont. Can.
26 H11 **Renfrew** Renfrewshire, Scotland U.K.
26 G11 **Renfrewshire** admin. div. Scotland U.K.
179 J9 **Rengali Reservoir** Orissa India
156 E5 **Rengat** Sumatera Indon.
146 B4 **Rengo** Chile
49 D9 **Rengsdorf** Ger.
49 I8 **Rengshausen (Knüllwald)** Ger.
170 G2 **Ren He** r. China
171 J3 **Renheji** Henan China
Renhou Hebei China see **Tangxian**
171 I6 **Renhua** Guangdong China
170 F5 **Renhuai** Guizhou China
16 H8 **Reni** Ukr.
116 E11 **Renick** WV U.S.A.
176 F6 **Renigunta** Andhra Prad. India
26 C7 **Renish Point** Scotland U.K.
48 D5 **Renkenberge** Ger.
18 H1 **Renko** Fin.
44 I5 **Renkum** Neth.
Renland reg. Greenland see **Tuttut Nunaat**
204 H6 **Renmark** S.A. Austr.
74 H10 **Renna** r. Sicilia Italy
49 K6 **Rennau** Ger.
200 □6 **Rennell** i. Solomon Is
145 B8 **Rennell, Islas** is Chile
49 F9 **Rennerod** Ger.
206 D5 **Renner Springs** N.T. Austr.
53 K4 **Rennertshofen** Ger.
38 H5 **Rennes** France
38 H5 **Rennes, Bassin de** basin France
43 I10 **Rennes-les-Bains** France
22 B2 **Rennesøy** i. Norway
213 K2 **Rennick Glacier** Antarctica
107 M5 **Rennie** Man. Can.
107 J2 **Rennie Lake** N.W.T. Can.
52 F4 **Renningen** Ger.
29 N3 **Rennington** Northumberland, England U.K.
59 I5 **Rennweg** Austria
71 M6 **Reno** r. Italy
110 C6 **Reno** MN U.S.A.
124 M2 **Reno** NV U.S.A.
71 K2 **Renòn** Italy
72 C3 **Rénoso, Monte** mt. Corse France
97 K2 **Renoster** r. S. Africa
96 E7 **Renoster** watercourse S. Africa
96 G8 **Renosterkop** S. Africa
97 K2 **Renosterspruit** S. Africa
116 H7 **Renovo** PA U.S.A.
169 O7 **Renqiu** Hebei China
48 H1 **Rens** Denmark
170 E4 **Renshou** Sichuan China
54 F5 **Reńska Wieś** Opolskie Pol.
54 G5 **Reńska Wieś** Opolskie Pol.
114 D5 **Rensselaer** IN U.S.A.
117 L6 **Rensselaer** NY U.S.A.
44 I4 **Renswoude** Neth.
66 B1 **Rentería** Spain
78 C3 **Rentina** Greece
20 O4 **Rentjärn** Sweden
122 C3 **Renton** WA U.S.A.
49 K10 **Rentweinsdorf** Ger.
179 I7 **Renukut** Uttar Prad. India
36 I4 **Renwez** France
203 H8 **Renwick** South I. N.Z.
19 U3 **Renya** r. Rus. Fed.
50 D3 **Renzow** Ger.
88 E3 **Réo** Burkina
155 B8 **Reo** Flores Indon.
137 G5 **Repartimento** Brazil
56 F4 **Répce** r. Hungary
56 G4 **Répcelak** Hungary
95 G4 **Repembe** r. Moz.
185 J2 **Repetek** Turkm.
185 J2 **Repetekskiy Zapovednik** nature res. Turkm.
19 P6 **Repino** Rus. Fed.
55 K3 **Repki** Pol.
40 F4 **Replonges** France
20 R2 **Repokaira** reg. Fin.
18 M2 **Repolka** Rus. Fed.
202 K5 **Reporoa** North I. N.Z.
21 P6 **Reposaari** Fin.
50 F2 **Reppelin** Ger.
48 J4 **Reppenstedt** Ger.
116 B7 **Republic** OH U.S.A.
122 E2 **Republic** WA U.S.A.
120 G6 **Republican** r. NE U.S.A.
120 E5 **Republican, South Fork** r. NE U.S.A.
68 F3 **Republika Srpska** aut. div. Bos.-Herz.
207 L6 **Repulse Bay** Qld Austr.
105 J3 **Repulse Bay** Nunavut Can.
20 R1 **Repvåg** Norway
15 G6 **Rep'yevka** Rus. Fed.
75 □ **Reqqa, Il-Ponta ta'** pt Gozo Malta
63 L3 **Requejada, Embalse de** resr Spain
62 G4 **Requejo** Spain
136 C6 **Requena** Peru
67 C9 **Requena** Spain
146 B4 **Requinoa** Chile
43 J7 **Réquista** France
200 □6 **Rere** Guadalcanal Solomon Is
140 E3 **Reriutaba** Brazil
189 K4 **Reşadiye** Turkey
Reşadiye Bolu Turkey see **Yeniçağa**
188 H3 **Reşadiye** Tokat Turkey
79 I6 **Reşadiye Yarımadası** pen. Turkey
156 F7 **Resag, Gunung** mt. Indon.
71 L4 **Resana** Italy
77 J6 **Resava** r. Serb. and Mont.
77 J6 **Resavica** Srbija Serb. and Mont.
26 K9 **Rescobie** Angus, Scotland U.K.
76 J9 **Resen** Macedonia
143 E5 **Resende** Brazil
62 E6 **Resende** Port.
142 B6 **Reserva** Brazil
123 J10 **Reserve** NM U.S.A.
19 T5 **Reshetnikovo** Rus. Fed.
17 N4 **Reshetylivka** Ukr.
171 H4 **Reshi** Hunan China
168 G8 **Reshui** Qinghai China
71 J2 **Resia, Lago di** l. Italy
58 C6 **Resia, Passo di** pass Austria/Italy
118 E2 **Resica Falls** PA U.S.A.
144 F2 **Resistencia** Arg.
77 J5 **Reșița** Romania
54 D2 **Resko** Pol.
54 D1 **Resko Przymorskie, Jezioro** lag. Pol.
105 I2 **Resolute** Nunavut Can.
105 L3 **Resolution Island** Nunavut Can.
203 A12 **Resolution Island** South I. N.Z.
30 E4 **Resolven** Neath Port Talbot, Wales U.K.
26 B6 **Resort, Loch** inlet Scotland U.K.
63 K3 **Respenda de la Peña** Spain
143 G3 **Resplendor** Brazil
19 S7 **Ressa** r. Rus. Fed.
137 G5 **Ressaca** Brazil
97 P1 **Ressango Garcia** S. Africa
19 S8 **Resseta** r. Rus. Fed.
36 E4 **Ressons-sur-Matz** France
138 B2 **Restauração** Brazil
41 J8 **Restefond, Col de** pass France
76 I9 **Restelica** Kosovo, Srbija Serb. and Mont.
117 □S1 **Restigouche** r. N.B. Can.
60 D5 **Restinga** Morocco
143 E5 **Restinga de Marambaia** coastal area Brazil
141 B9 **Restinga Seca** Brazil
136 C3 **Restrepo** Col.
74 G8 **Resuttano** Sicilia Italy
17 M2 **Ret'** r. Ukr.
127 N10 **Retalhuleu** Guat.
64 H3 **Retamal** Spain
146 C3 **Retamito** Arg.
156 □ **Retan Laut, Pulau** i. Sing.
62 E9 **Retaxo** Port.
87 G2 **Retem, Oued er** watercourse Alg.
146 B3 **Retén Atalaya** Chile
146 A4 **Retén Llico** Chile
77 K5 **Retezat, Parcul Național** nat. park Romania
29 P7 **Retford** Nottinghamshire, England U.K.
36 H4 **Rethel** France
48 H5 **Rethem (Aller)** Ger.
Réthimnon Kriti Greece see **Rethymno**
36 E5 **Rethondes** France
78 F7 **Rethymno** Kriti Greece
45 H6 **Retie** Belgium
63 N7 **Retiendas** Spain
38 I6 **Retiers** France
64 G3 **Retín** r. Spain
146 B5 **Retiro** Chile
71 R4 **Retje** Slovenia
57 K3 **Rétköz** reg. Hungary
62 H7 **Retortillo** Spain
63 L3 **Retortillo** tourist site Spain
65 I5 **Retortillo, Embalse de** resr Spain
63 O6 **Retortillo de Soria** Spain
41 E6 **Retournac** France
207 I8 **Retreat** Qld Austr.
57 I4 **Rétság** Hungary
53 I6 **Rettenberg** Ger.
66 C6 **Retuerta** mt. Spain
65 K2 **Retuerta del Bullaque** Spain
59 M2 **Retz** Austria
51 F6 **Reuden** Sachsen-Anhalt Ger.
51 F8 **Reuden** Sachsen-Anhalt Ger.
39 P7 **Reuilly** France
146 A5 **Reunión** Chile
99 □1c **Réunion** terr. Indian Ocean
49 K10 **Reurieth** Ger.
66 H5 **Reus** Spain
156 B3 **Reusam, Pulau** i. Indon.
45 H6 **Reusel** Neth.
45 H5 **Reusel** r. Neth.
70 E1 **Reuss** r. Switz.
53 N5 **Reut** Ger.
Reut r. Moldova see **Răut**
17 O2 **Reut** r. Rus. Fed.
52 D5 **Reute** Ger.
16 G6 **Reuțel** Moldova
50 G3 **Reuterstadt Stavenhagen** Ger.
53 M2 **Reuth bei Erbendorf** Ger.
52 G5 **Reutlingen** Ger.
19 U6 **Reutov** Rus. Fed.
58 C5 **Reutte** Austria
45 J6 **Reuver** Neth.
185 N3 **Revak** Afgh.
Reval Estonia see **Tallinn**
14 F2 **Revda** Rus. Fed.
125 P4 **Reveille Peak** NV U.S.A.
Revel Estonia see **Tallinn**
43 I9 **Revel** France
179 J7 **Revelganj** Bihar India
70 C6 **Revello** Italy
106 G5 **Revelstoke** B.C. Can.
129 I3 **Reventadero** Mex.
136 A6 **Reventazón** Peru
118 E3 **Revere** PA U.S.A.
40 G5 **Revermont** reg. France
41 H8 **Revest-du-Bion** France
57 G5 **Révfülöp** Hungary
95 H2 **Rèvia** Moz.
77 P6 **Reviga** Romania
77 P6 **Reviga** r. Romania
37 I6 **Revigny-sur-Ornain** France
63 L3 **Revilla de Collazos** Spain
63 M4 **Revilla del Campo** Spain
112 D7 **Revillagigedo, Islas** is Mex.
104 E4 **Revillagigedo Island** AK U.S.A.
36 I4 **Revin** France
71 M4 **Revine-Lago** Italy
190 C7 **Revivim** Israel
19 R9 **Revna** r. Rus. Fed.
56 D2 **Řevnice** Czech Rep.
56 C1 **Řevničov** Czech Rep.
71 K3 **Revò** Italy
65 O4 **Revolcadores** mt. Spain
Revolyutsii, Pik mt. Tajik. see **Revolyutsiya, Qullai**
185 O2 **Revolyutsiya, Qullai** mt. Tajik.
20 N2 **Revsnes** Norway
57 J3 **Revúca** Slovakia
95 G3 **Revuè** r. Moz.
19 U7 **Revyakino** Rus. Fed.
201 □1a **Rewa** r. Viti Levu Fiji
178 H7 **Rewa** Madh. Prad. India
203 J8 **Rewa** hill North I. N.Z.
54 D1 **Rewal** Pol.
178 F5 **Rewari** Haryana India
212 S2 **Rex, Mount** Antarctica
122 I5 **Rexburg** ID U.S.A.
109 H4 **Rexton** N.B. Can.
126 □T13 **Rey, Isla del** i. Panama
16 H3 **Reya** Ukr.
89 I4 **Rey Bouba** Cameroon
31 P3 **Reydon** Suffolk, England U.K.
138 D3 **Reyes** Bol.
124 I3 **Reyes, Point** CA U.S.A.
136 B4 **Reyes, Punta** pt Col.
190 E2 **Reyhanlı** Turkey
20 □C1 **Reykir** Iceland
20 □B2 **Reykjanes** constituency Iceland
214 G2 **Reykjanes Ridge** sea feature N. Atlantic Ocean
20 □B2 **Reykjanestá** pt Iceland
20 □C1 **Reykjavík** Iceland
206 C2 **Reynolds** r. N.T. Austr.
116 C9 **Reynoldsburg** OH U.S.A.
206 D7 **Reynolds Range** mts N.T. Austr.
127 J4 **Reynosa** Mex.
40 F5 **Reyrieux** France
40 F4 **Reyssouze** r. France
184 E5 **Rezā** Iran
184 D5 **Rezā, Kūh-e** hill Iran
184 E6 **Rezāābād** Iran
38 H7 **Rezé** France
18 K5 **Rēzekne** Latvia
18 K5 **Rēzekne** r. Latvia
56 G5 **Rezi** Hungary
16 H6 **Rezina** Moldova
68 E3 **Rezinjski vrh** mt. Slovenia
77 Q9 **Rezovska Reka** r. Bulg./Turkey
185 I7 **Rezvān** Iran
Rezvāndeh Iran see **Rezvānshahr**
184 C3 **Rezvānshahr** Iran
70 I4 **Rezzato** Italy
70 D7 **Rezzo** Italy
70 G6 **Rezzoaglio** Italy
R. F. Magón Mex. see **Ricardo Flores Magón**
77 K6 **Rgotina** Srbija Serb. and Mont.
48 H4 **Rhade** Ger.
Rhaeadr Gwy Wales U.K. see **Rhayader**
87 F3 **Rharbi, Oued el** watercourse Alg.
70 H1 **Rhätikon** mts Switz.
52 C2 **Rhaunen** Ger.
30 E3 **Rhayader** Powys, Wales U.K.
49 F7 **Rheda-Wiedenbrück** Ger.
49 C7 **Rhede** Ger.
48 D4 **Rhede (Ems)** Ger.
49 I6 **Rheden** Ger.
118 B4 **Rheems** PA U.S.A.
Rhegium Italy see **Reggio di Calabria**
30 D3 **Rheidol** r. Wales U.K.
Rheims France see **Reims**
52 E4 **Rhein** r. Ger. alt. **Rhin (France)**, conv. **Rhine**
52 D4 **Rheinau** Ger.
49 C9 **Rheinbach** Ger.
49 C7 **Rheinberg** Ger.
52 D2 **Rheinböllen** Ger.
49 D9 **Rheinbreitbach** Ger.
49 D10 **Rheinbrohl** Ger.
49 D6 **Rheine** Ger.
70 H1 **Rheineck** Switz.
70 D1 **Rheinfelden** Switz.
52 D6 **Rheinfelden (Baden)** Ger.
49 E10 **Rheingaugebirge** hills Ger.
52 D3 **Rheinhessen-Pfalz** admin. reg. Ger.
49 B10 **Rheinisches Schiefergebirge** hills Ger.
49 D11 **Rheinland-Pfalz** land Ger.
49 C8 **Rhein-Ruhr** airport Ger.
50 G4 **Rheinsberg** Ger.
52 E4 **Rheinstetten** Ger.
49 F10 **Rhein-Taunus, Naturpark** nature res. Ger.
70 G2 **Rheinwaldhorn** mt. Switz.
49 D9 **Rhein-Westerwald, Naturpark** nature res. Ger.
52 E3 **Rheinzabern** Ger.
70 C4 **Rhêmes-Notre-Dame** Italy
70 C4 **Rhêmes-St-Georges** Italy
86 D3 **Rhemilès** well Alg.
44 I5 **Rhenen** Neth.
49 E10 **Rhens** Ger.
86 D3 **Rheris, Oued** watercourse Morocco
26 G6 **Rhiconich** Highland, Scotland U.K.
40 L1 **Rhin** r. France alt. **Rhein (Germany)**, conv. **Rhine**
50 G4 **Rhin** r. Ger.
37 O7 **Rhinau** France
37 P6 **Rhine** r. Europe alt. **Rhein (Germany)**, alt. **Rhin (France)**
117 L7 **Rhinebeck** NY U.S.A.
110 E4 **Rhinelander** WI U.S.A.
Rhineland-Palatinate land Ger. see **Rheinland-Pfalz**
50 G5 **Rhinkanal** canal Ger.
50 G5 **Rhinluch** marsh Ger.
26 H12 **Rhinns of Kells** hills Scotland U.K.
92 A4 **Rhino Camp** Uganda
50 F5 **Rhinow** Ger.
50 F5 **Rhinowes Berge** hills Ger.
86 C3 **Rhir, Cap** c. Morocco
45 G7 **Rhisnes** Belgium
Rhiwabon Wales U.K. see **Ruabon**
70 G4 **Rho** Italy
130 □ **Rhoades, Point** Jamaica
27 H6 **Rhode** Rep. of Ireland
117 N7 **Rhode Island** state U.S.A.
49 H8 **Rhoden (Diemelstadt)** Ger.
Rhodes Rodos Greece see **Rodos**
Rhodes i. Greece see **Rodos**
Rhodesia country Africa see **Zimbabwe**
122 G3 **Rhodes Peak** ID U.S.A.
77 L9 **Rhodope Mountains** Bulg./Greece
Rhodus i. Greece see **Rodos**
49 I10 **Rhön** mts Ger.
30 F4 **Rhondda** reg. Wales U.K.
30 F4 **Rhondda Cynon Taff** admin. div. Wales U.K.
40 F5 **Rhône** dept France
41 F9 **Rhône** r. France/Switz.
41 G6 **Rhône-Alpes** admin. reg. France
41 E9 **Rhône à Sète, Canal du** France
37 N8 **Rhône au Rhin, Canal du** France
30 F5 **Rhoose** Vale of Glamorgan, Wales U.K.
53 M6 **Rhordorf** Ger.
30 E4 **Rhos** Neath Port Talbot, Wales U.K.
30 F1 **Rhosllanerchrugog** Wrexham, Wales U.K.
30 E1 **Rhôs-on-Sea** Conwy, Wales U.K.
30 D4 **Rhossili** Swansea, Wales U.K.
87 G2 **Rhoufi** Alg.
28 H1 **Rhu** Argyll and Bute, Scotland U.K.
Rhube, Oasis of Syria see **Ruḥbah**
30 F1 **Rhuddlan** Denbighshire, Wales U.K.
41 A6 **Rhue** r. France
Rhum i. Scotland U.K. see **Rum**
49 J7 **Rhumspringe** Ger.
Rhuthun Denbighshire, Wales U.K. see **Ruthin**
38 F6 **Rhuys, Presqu'île de** pen. France
30 F1 **Rhyl** Denbighshire, Wales U.K.
30 F4 **Rhymney** Caerphilly, Wales U.K.
26 K8 **Rhynie** Aberdeenshire, Scotland U.K.
89 H6 **Riaba** Equat. Guinea
75 K7 **Riace** Italy
140 D3 **Riachão** Brazil
140 D4 **Riachão das Neves** Brazil
143 G3 **Riacho** Brazil
140 E5 **Riacho de Santana** Brazil
143 F1 **Riacho dos Machados** Brazil
64 D6 **Ria Formosa, Parque Natural da** nature res. Port.
63 N6 **Riaguas** r. Spain
38 I6 **Riaillé** France
Rialb de Noguera Spain see **Rialp**
141 C5 **Rialma** Brazil
66 H3 **Rialp** Spain
66 H4 **Rialp, Pantà de** resr Spain
124 O7 **Rialto** CA U.S.A.
157 I5 **Riam** Kalimantan Indon.
179 N6 **Riang** Arun. Prad. India
90 F2 **Riangnom** Sudan
Rianjo Galicia Spain see **Rianxo**
73 J3 **Riano** Italy
63 K3 **Riaño** Spain
63 J3 **Riaño, Embalse de** resr Spain
139 H3 **Rianópolis** Brazil
41 H9 **Rians** France
63 N9 **Riansáres** r. Spain
38 E6 **Riantec** France
62 C3 **Rianxo** Spain
178 E3 **Riasi** Jammu and Kashmir
156 E4 **Riau** prov. Indon.
156 F4 **Riau, Kepulauan** is Indon.
70 C2 **Riaz** Switz.
63 N6 **Riaza** Spain
63 M5 **Riaza** r. Spain
63 M2 **Riba** Spain
62 D4 **Ribadavia** Spain
62 G4 **Ribadelago** Spain
62 F1 **Ribadeo** Spain
63 P7 **Riba de Saelices** Spain
63 J2 **Ribadesella** Spain
63 Q4 **Ribaforada** Spain
63 P4 **Ribafrecha** Spain
66 F5 **Riba-roja, Pantà de** resr Spain
66 F5 **Riba-roja d'Ebre** Spain
Ribas de Fresser Spain see **Ribes de Freser**
141 B7 **Ribas do Rio Pardo** Brazil
185 M3 **Ribat** Afgh.
64 C2 **Ribatejo** reg. Port.
95 H2 **Ribáuè** Moz.
49 K6 **Ribbesbüttel** Ger.
29 L6 **Ribble** r. England U.K.
29 M5 **Ribblesdale** val. England U.K.
22 E6 **Ribe** Denmark
22 E6 **Ribe** county Denmark
37 N7 **Ribeauvillé** France
36 E4 **Ribécourt-Dreslincourt** France
142 C6 **Ribeira** Brazil
142 D6 **Ribeira** r. Brazil
62 E2 **Ribeira, Encoro da** resr Spain
64 □ **Ribeira Brava** Madeira
64 □ **Ribeira da Janela** Madeira
62 E5 **Ribeira de Pena** Port.
98 □1b **Ribeira Grande** São Miguel Azores
138 D2 **Ribeirão** Brazil
62 C6 **Ribeirão** Port.
142 C6 **Ribeirão Branco** Brazil
143 E3 **Ribeirão das Neves** Brazil
142 B5 **Ribeirão do Pinhal** Brazil
142 D4 **Ribeirão Preto** Brazil
98 □1c **Ribeiras** Pico Azores
98 □1c **Ribeira Seca** São Jorge Azores
98 □1b **Ribeira Seca** São Miguel Azores
98 □1c **Ribeirinha** Faial Azores
98 □1c **Ribeirinha** Pico Azores
98 □1a **Ribeirinha** Terceira Azores
36 F4 **Ribemont** France
74 E8 **Ribera** Sicilia Italy
42 E5 **Ribérac** France
64 G3 **Ribera del Fresno** Spain
138 D2 **Riberalta** Bol.
63 Q4 **Ribera Navarra** reg. Spain
67 E7 **Ribesalbes** Spain
66 J3 **Ribes de Freser** Spain
41 H8 **Ribiers** France
57 L5 **Ribița** Romania
59 L6 **Ribnica** Radlje Ob Dravi Slovenia
68 E3 **Ribnica** Ribnica Slovenia
16 I6 **Rîbnița** Moldova
50 F2 **Ribnitz-Damgarten** Ger.
77 L9 **Ribnovo** Bulg.
162 L2 **Ribnovsk** Rus. Fed.
63 N6 **Ribota** Spain
138 C5 **Rica Aventura** Chile
75 J6 **Ricadi** Italy
59 N1 **Říčany** Jihomoravský kraj Czech Rep.
56 D2 **Říčany** Středočeský kraj Czech Rep.
126 F3 **Ricardo Flores Magón** Mex.
29 P5 **Riccal** r. England U.K.
73 N5 **Riccia** Italy
71 M9 **Riccio** Italy
71 N7 **Riccione** Italy
70 H7 **Riccò del Golfo di Spezia** Italy
125 R7 **Rice** CA U.S.A.
116 G11 **Rice** VA U.S.A.
111 L2 **Rice Lake** Ont. Can.
108 E4 **Rice Lake** Ont. Can.
110 C4 **Rice Lake** WI U.S.A.
110 A3 **Rice Lake** l. MN U.S.A.
110 B6 **Riceville** IA U.S.A.
116 C11 **Riceville** KY U.S.A.
37 L6 **Richardménil** France
97 Q4 **Richards Bay** S. Africa
213 L1 **Richards Inlet** Antarctica
104 E3 **Richards Island** N.W.T. Can.
107 I3 **Richardson** r. Alta Can.
106 G1 **Richardson Island** N.W.T. Can.
117 □O4 **Richardson Lakes** ME U.S.A.
104 E3 **Richardson Mountains** N.W.T. Can.
203 C11 **Richardson Mountains** South I. N.Z.
88 B2 **Richard Toll** Senegal
118 E4 **Richboro** PA U.S.A.
99 □1b **Riche en Eau** Mauritius
44 H2 **Richel** i. Neth.
117 L3 **Richelieu** Que. Can.
42 E1 **Richelieu** France
118 A3 **Richfield** PA U.S.A.
125 T3 **Richfield** UT U.S.A.
117 K6 **Richfield Springs** NY U.S.A.
117 I6 **Richford** NY U.S.A.
117 M4 **Richford** VT U.S.A.
124 M6 **Richgrove** CA U.S.A.
27 I4 **Richhill** Northern Ireland U.K.
109 H4 **Richibucto** N.B. Can.
107 I4 **Rich Lake** Alta Can.
118 F6 **Richland** NJ U.S.A.
118 C4 **Richland** PA U.S.A.
122 E3 **Richland** WA U.S.A.
110 D6 **Richland Center** WI U.S.A.
116 D11 **Richlands** VA U.S.A.
118 E4 **Richlandtown** PA U.S.A.
205 M5 **Richmond** N.S.W. Austr.
207 I6 **Richmond** Qld Austr.
111 S4 **Richmond** Ont. Can.
109 F4 **Richmond** Que. Can.
130 □ **Richmond** Jamaica
203 H8 **Richmond** South I. N.Z.
97 O5 **Richmond** KwaZulu-Natal S. Africa
96 H7 **Richmond** Northern Cape S. Africa
29 N5 **Richmond** North Yorkshire, England U.K.
124 J4 **Richmond** CA U.S.A.
110 F7 **Richmond** IL U.S.A.
114 E6 **Richmond** IN U.S.A.
116 A11 **Richmond** KY U.S.A.
117 □P4 **Richmond** ME U.S.A.
111 L7 **Richmond** MI U.S.A.
121 H11 **Richmond** TX U.S.A.
116 H11 **Richmond** VA U.S.A.
117 M4 **Richmond** VT U.S.A.
203 H8 **Richmond, Mount** South I. N.Z.
119 G3 **Richmond County** county NY U.S.A.
116 C9 **Richmond Dale** OH U.S.A.
108 E5 **Richmond Hill** Ont. Can.
115 G10 **Richmond Hill** GA U.S.A.
131 □3 **Richmond Peak** St Vincent
205 N3 **Richmond Range** hills N.S.W. Austr.
203 H8 **Richmond Range** mts South I. N.Z.
117 K6 **Richmondville** NY U.S.A.
173 H11 **Richoi** Xizang China
50 G2 **Richtenberg** Ger.
96 B4 **Richtersveld National Park** S. Africa
52 F7 **Richterswil** Switz.
121 K10 **Richton** MS U.S.A.
57 K2 **Richvald** Slovakia
124 K2 **Richvale** CA U.S.A.
116 B8 **Richwood** OH U.S.A.
116 E10 **Richwood** WV U.S.A.
73 O6 **Ricigliano** Italy
52 D6 **Rickenbach** Ger.
31 N3 **Rickinghall** Suffolk, England U.K.
20 P4 **Rickleån** r. Sweden
48 J2 **Rickling** Ger.
31 L4 **Rickmansworth** Hertfordshire, England U.K.
63 R5 **Ricla** Spain
62 I5 **Ricobayo, Embalse de** resr Spain
Ricomagus France see **Riom**
57 K3 **Ricse** Hungary
213 E2 **Riddell Nunataks** nunataks Antarctica
44 G5 **Ridderkerk** Neth.
70 C3 **Riddes** Switz.
116 G8 **Riddlesburg** PA U.S.A.
111 S4 **Rideau** r. Ont. Can.
108 E4 **Rideau Lakes** Ont. Can.
118 B6 **Riderwood** MD U.S.A.
108 C3 **Ridge** r. Ont. Can.
119 J3 **Ridge** NY U.S.A.
124 O6 **Ridgecrest** CA U.S.A.
119 I2 **Ridgefield** CT U.S.A.
119 G3 **Ridgefield** NJ U.S.A.
121 J9 **Ridgeland** MS U.S.A.
115 G9 **Ridgeland** SC U.S.A.
110 C4 **Ridgeland** WI U.S.A.
118 D7 **Ridgely** MD U.S.A.
111 M7 **Ridgetown** Ont. Can.
110 C6 **Ridgeway** IA U.S.A.
119 G4 **Ridgeway** NJ U.S.A.
116 F12 **Ridgeway** VA U.S.A.
119 G3 **Ridgewood** NJ U.S.A.
116 G7 **Ridgway** PA U.S.A.
57 I6 **Riđica** Vojvodina, Srbija Serb. and Mont.
26 M13 **Riding Mill** Northumberland, England U.K.
107 K5 **Riding Mountain National Park** Man. Can.
208 E6 **Ridley** r. W.A. Austr.
97 K3 **Riebeeckstad** S. Africa
96 C9 **Riebeek-Kasteel** S. Africa
97 K9 **Riebeek-Oos** S. Africa
96 C9 **Riebeek Wes** S. Africa
20 N3 **Riebnes** l. Sweden
136 D2 **Riecito** Venez.
38 D6 **Riec-sur-Belon** France
53 K5 **Ried** Ger.
70 E3 **Ried** Switz.
53 I7 **Riedbergerhorn** mt. Ger.
48 G5 **Riede** Ger.
53 L3 **Rieden** Ger.
53 L4 **Riedenburg** Ger.
53 M6 **Riedering** Ger.
59 H3 **Ried im Innkreis** Austria
58 C5 **Ried im Oberinntal** Austria
58 E5 **Ried im Zillertal** Austria
59 K3 **Ried in der Riedmark** Austria
37 N8 **Riedisheim** France
52 G5 **Riedlingen** Ger.
52 B3 **Riegelsberg** Ger.
59 M5 **Riegersburg** Austria
118 E3 **Rieglelsville** PA U.S.A.
64 H7 **Riego, Canal de** Spain
62 I4 **Riego de la Vega** Spain
70 D1 **Riehen** Switz.
97 K1 **Riekertsdam** S. Africa
52 F6 **Rielasingen-Worblingen** Ger.
62 I3 **Riello** Spain
63 L9 **Rielves** Spain
45 I7 **Riemst** Belgium
49 I10 **Rieneck** Ger.
57 L5 **Rieni** Romania
71 L2 **Rienza** r. Italy
20 P2 **Rieppesgai'sa** mt. Norway
48 K2 **Riepsdorf** Ger.
66 I4 **Riera de Rajadell** r. Spain
51 H8 **Riesa** Ger.
145 B9 **Riesco, Isla** i. Chile
48 I1 **Rieseby** Ger.
74 G9 **Riesi** Sicilia Italy
49 F6 **Rieste** Ger.
51 D8 **Riestedt** Ger.
96 H5 **Riet** r. S. Africa
96 E7 **Riet** watercourse S. Africa
18 E6 **Rietavas** Lith.
49 F7 **Rietberg** Ger.
96 H8 **Rietbron** S. Africa
96 E2 **Rietfontein** S. Africa
50 J3 **Rieth** Ger.
45 H6 **Riethoven** Neth.
96 F10 **Riethuiskraal** S. Africa
73 J3 **Rieti** Italy
73 J3 **Rieti** prov. Italy
97 N3 **Rietkuil** S. Africa
96 C6 **Rietpoort** S. Africa
51 K8 **Rietschen** Ger.
96 E6 **Riet se Vloer** salt pan S. Africa
97 O5 **Rietvlei** S. Africa
97 M1 **Rietvlei Nature Reserve** S. Africa
58 D5 **Rietz** Austria
43 G9 **Rieumes** France
43 I7 **Rieupeyroux** France
41 C7 **Rieutort-de-Randon** France
38 G6 **Rieux** Bretagne France
43 G9 **Rieux** Midi-Pyrénées France
43 J9 **Rieux-Minervois** France
41 I9 **Riez** France
190 E6 **Rifā'ī, Tall** mt. Jordan/Syria
142 D4 **Rifaina** Brazil
58 H4 **Rifflkopf** mt. Austria
71 K2 **Rifiano** Italy
123 K7 **Rifle** CO U.S.A.
92 B4 **Rift Valley** prov. Kenya
173 L12 **Riga** Arun. Prad. India
18 H5 **Rīga** Latvia
18 G4 **Riga, Gulf of** Estonia/Latvia
89 G4 **Rigacikun** Nigeria
173 H10 **Rigain Pünco** l. Xizang China
78 D3 **Rigaio** Greece
184 H7 **Rīgān** Iran
Rīgas jūras līcis b. Estonia/Latvia see **Riga, Gulf of**
117 K3 **Rigaud** Que. Can.
41 J9 **Rigaud** France
122 I5 **Rigby** ID U.S.A.
122 F4 **Riggins** ID U.S.A.
40 K3 **Riggisberg** Switz.
26 E11 **Righ Mòr, Loch** l. Scotland U.K.
70 F1 **Rigi** mts Switz.
70 H5 **Riglio** r. Italy
184 H8 **Rīg Matī** Iran
43 I7 **Rignac** France
73 I3 **Rignano Flaminio** Italy
73 P4 **Rignano Garganico** Italy
71 K8 **Rignano sull'Arno** Italy
36 G7 **Rigny-le-Ferron** France
40 E3 **Rigny-sur-Arroux** France
39 L7 **Rigny-Ussé** France
109 J2 **Rigolet** Nfld and Lab. Can.
84 B6 **Rig-Rig** Chad
26 I11 **Rigside** South Lanarkshire, Scotland U.K.
63 R4 **Riguel** r. Spain
186 D6 **Rīḩ, Gezirat er** i. Sudan
186 D6 **Rīḩ, Gezirat er** i. Sudan
175 □1 **Rihiveli** i. S. Male Maldives
Riia laht b. Estonia/Latvia see **Riga, Gulf of**
21 R6 **Riihimäki** Fin.
20 S3 **Riipi** Fin.
212 W2 **Riiser-Larsen Ice Shelf** Antarctica
18 H2 **Riisipere** Estonia
20 T3 **Riisitunturin kansallispuisto** nat. park Fin.
126 B1 **Riito** Mex.
89 G4 **Rijau** Nigeria
68 E3 **Riječki Zaliv** b. Croatia
68 E3 **Rijeka** Croatia
71 R5 **Rijeka** airport Croatia
44 G5 **Rijen** Neth.
45 G6 **Rijkevorsel** Belgium
44 G4 **Rijnsaterwoude** Neth.
44 F4 **Rijnsburg** Neth.
20 □ **Rijpfjorden** inlet Svalbard
44 G5 **Rijsbergen** Neth.
44 K4 **Rijssen** Neth.
44 F4 **Rijswijk** Neth.
16 C5 **Rika** r. Ukr.
186 G4 **Rikā, Wādī ar** watercourse Saudi Arabia
156 B2 **Rikitgaib** Sumatera Indon.
179 O5 **Rikor** Arun. Prad. India
20 O2 **Riksgränsen** Sweden
164 U3 **Rikubetsu** Japan
164 T7 **Rikuchū-kaigan National Park** Japan
164 S7 **Rikuzen-takata** Japan
77 L8 **Rila** Bulg.
77 L8 **Rila** mts Bulg.
173 G12 **Rila** Xizang China
122 E5 **Riley** OR U.S.A.
116 G10 **Rileyville** VA U.S.A.
42 G4 **Rilhac-Rancon** France
45 F6 **Rilland** Neth.
39 L7 **Rillé** France
40 F5 **Rillieux-la-Pape** France
125 U9 **Rillito** AZ U.S.A.
66 D6 **Rillo** Spain
63 Q7 **Rillo de Gallo** Spain
36 H5 **Rilly-la-Montagne** France
89 G3 **Rima** watercourse Niger/Nigeria
186 F2 **Rimah, Wādī al** watercourse Saudi Arabia
201 □3 **Rimatara** i. Îs Australes Fr. Polynesia
Rimatera i. Îs Australes Fr. Polynesia see **Rimatara**
156 F6 **Rimau, Pulau** i. Indon.
37 J7 **Rimaucourt** France
57 J3 **Rimava** r. Slovakia
57 I3 **Rimavská Baňa** Slovakia
57 J3 **Rimavská Seč** Slovakia
57 J3 **Rimavská Sobota** Slovakia
53 N3 **Rimbach** Bayern Ger.
52 F2 **Rimbach** Hessen Ger.
106 H4 **Rimbey** Alta Can.
23 O2 **Rimbo** Sweden
116 F7 **Rimersburg** PA U.S.A.
77 L4 **Rimetea** Romania
23 L3 **Rimforsa** Sweden
71 N7 **Rimini** Italy
71 M7 **Rimini** prov. Italy
Rîmnicu Sărat Romania see **Râmnicu Sărat**
Rîmnicu Vîlcea Romania see **Râmnicu Vâlcea**
178 F2 **Rimo Glacier** Jammu and Kashmir
36 I4 **Rimogne** France
43 G10 **Rimont** France
109 G3 **Rimouski** Que. Can.
109 G3 **Rimouski, Réserve Faunique de** nature res. Que. Can.
52 H2 **Rimpar** Ger.
59 L7 **Rimske Toplice** Slovenia
53 M6 **Rimsting** Ger.
203 J8 **Rimutaka Forest Park** nature res. North I. N.Z.
173 I12 **Rinbung** Xizang China
155 A8 **Rinca** i. Indon.
142 C4 **Rincão** Brazil
53 O4 **Rinchnach** Ger.
144 D2 **Rincón** Arg.
131 □8 **Rincón** Bonaire Neth. Antilles
131 □1 **Rincón** Puerto Rico
131 □1 **Rincón, Bahía de** b. Puerto Rico
138 D6 **Rincón, Cerro del** mt. Chile
144 D1 **Rinconada** Arg.
129 K6 **Rinconada** Mex.
67 C7 **Rincón de Ademuz** reg. Spain
147 I3 **Rincón de Cololó** Uru.
146 C4 **Rincón del Atuel** Arg.
65 K7 **Rincón de la Victoria** Spain
147 I3 **Rincón del Bonete, Lago Artificial de** resr Uru.
146 C5 **Rincón de los Sauces** Arg.
147 I4 **Rincón del Pino** Uru.
147 I3 **Rincón de Palacio** Uru.
128 E3 **Rincón de Romos** Mex.
63 Q4 **Rincón de Soto** Spain
178 H7 **Rind** r. India
18 E4 **Rinda** r. Latvia
20 J5 **Rindal** Norway
179 L5 **Rindü** Xizang China
78 G5 **Rineia** i. Greece
74 H6 **Rinella** Isole Lipari Italy
116 E11 **Riner** VA U.S.A.
205 K9 **Ringarooma Bay** Tas. Austr.
23 M3 **Ringarum** Sweden
178 E6 **Ringas** Rajasthan India
27 F9 **Ringaskiddy** Rep. of Ireland
22 G6 **Ringe** Denmark
48 C5 **Ringe** Ger.
21 K6 **Ringebu** Norway
70 G2 **Ringelspitz** mt. Switz.
50 I4 **Ringenwalde** Ger.
115 E8 **Ringgold** GA U.S.A.
158 D1 **Ringhkung** Myanmar
89 H3 **Ringim** Nigeria
22 E5 **Ringkøbing** Denmark
22 E5 **Ringkøbing** county Denmark
22 E6 **Ringkøbing Fjord** lag. Denmark
31 O2 **Ringland** Norfolk, England U.K.
51 D8 **Ringleben** Ger.
31 M6 **Ringmer** East Sussex, England U.K.
118 F4 **Ringoes** NJ U.S.A.
28 D3 **Ringsend** Northern Ireland U.K.
22 H6 **Ringsted** Denmark
173 F11 **Ringtor** Xizang China
20 O2 **Ringvassøya** i. Norway
27 G8 **Ringville** Rep. of Ireland
31 I6 **Ringwood** Hampshire, England U.K.
117 K7 **Ringwood** NJ U.S.A.
Rinía i. Greece see **Rineia**
48 I1 **Rinkenæs** Denmark

Roosevelt Island to Russkaya-Polyana

329

212 N1 Roosevelt Island Antarctica
27 G5 Roosky *Leitrim* Rep. of Ireland
27 E5 Roosky *Mayo* Rep. of Ireland
18 I2 Roosna-Alliku Estonia
97 N1 Roossenekal S. Africa
106 F2 Root *r. N.W.T.* Can.
110 C6 Root *r. MN* U.S.A.
55 J6 Ropa Pol.
55 J6 Ropa *r.* Pol.
18 H5 Ropaži Latvia
55 J5 Ropczyce Pol.
206 E3 Roper *r. N.T.* Austr.
206 E3 Roper Bar *N.T.* Austr.
206 E3 Roper Bar Aboriginal Land *res. N.T.* Austr.
207 L7 Roper Creek *r. Qld* Austr.
62 I4 Roperuelos del Páramo Spain
206 E3 Roper Valley *N.T.* Austr.
55 K6 Ropienka Pol.
20 P2 Ropinsalmi Fin.
58 C5 Roppen Austria
41 K8 Roquebillière France
41 C9 Roquebrun France
41 K9 Roquebrune-Cap-Martin France
41 J10 Roquebrune-sur-Argens France
43 F7 Roquecor France
43 I8 Roquecourbe France
98 □3c Roque del Este *i.* Canary Is
98 □3d Roque de los Muchachos *vol. La Palma* Canary Is
43 D7 Roquefort France
41 B9 Roquefort-sur-Soulzon France
41 F8 Roquemaure France
147 H4 Roque Pérez Arg.
41 K9 Roquesteron France
66 G6 Roquetas Spain
65 N7 Roquetas de Mar Spain
41 H10 Roquevaire France
137 F4 Roraima *state* Brazil
137 F3 Roraima, Mount Guyana
22 E3 Rore *l.* Norway
178 E5 Rori *Punjab* India
20 K5 Røros Norway
70 H1 Rorschach Switz.
22 H6 Rørvig Denmark
20 K4 Rørvik Norway
55 M2 Ros' Belarus
18 H8 Ros' *r.* Belarus
16 K4 Ros' *r.* Ukr.
55 J2 Roś, Jezioro *l.* Pol.
71 L4 Rosà Italy
130 G3 Rosa, Lake *Gt Inagua* Bahamas
70 D4 Rosa, Monte *mt.* Italy/Switz.
126 E4 Rosa, Punta *pt* Mex.
70 C3 Rosablanche *mt.* Switz.
98 □1c Rosais *São Jorge* Azores
98 □1c Rosais, Ponta dos *pt São Jorge* Azores
62 C5 Rosal, Val do *reg.* Spain
64 E5 Rosal de la Frontera Spain
126 G3 Rosales Mex.
122 F3 Rosalia *WA* U.S.A.
131 □2 Rosalie Bay Dominica
130 C5 Rosalind Bank *sea feature* Caribbean Sea
124 N7 Rosamond *CA* U.S.A.
124 N7 Rosamond Lake *CA* U.S.A.
128 B3 Rosamorada Mex.
142 A5 Rosana Brazil
58 B5 Rosanna *r.* Austria
41 G8 Rosans France
27 G2 Rosapenna Rep. of Ireland
144 D1 Rosario *Jujuy* Arg.
147 G3 Rosario *Santa Fé* Arg.
140 D2 Rosário Brazil
138 C6 Rosario Chile
126 B2 Rosario *Baja California* Mex.
126 F2 Rosario *Coahuila* Mex.
126 B3 Rosario *Sinaloa* Mex.
126 E4 Rosario *Sonora* Mex.
128 F1 Rosario *Zacatecas* Mex.
139 F6 Rosario Para.
154 C3 Rosario *Luzon* Phil.
154 C5 Rosario *Luzon* Phil.
64 C5 Rosário Port.
147 I4 Rosario Uru.
136 C2 Rosario Venez.
130 C3 Rosario, Cayo del *i.* Cuba
130 A4 Rosario Bank *sea feature* Caribbean Sea
144 D2 Rosario de la Frontera Arg.
144 D2 Rosario de Lerma Arg.
147 H3 Rosario del Tala Arg.
142 D2 Rosario del Tama Arg.
141 B9 Rosário do Sul Brazil
139 F3 Rosário Oeste Brazil
126 A1 Rosarito *Baja California* Mex.
126 B3 Rosarito *Baja California* Mex.
126 D4 Rosarito *Baja California Sur* Mex.
63 J8 Rosarito, Embalse de *resr* Spain
75 J7 Rosarno Italy
Rosas Spain *see* Roses
Rosas, Golfo de *b.* Spain *see* Roses, Golf de
17 K4 Rosava *r.* Ukr.
49 G10 Rosbach vor der Höhe Ger.
27 E3 Rosbeg Rep. of Ireland
27 I8 Rosbercon Rep. of Ireland
41 B5 Roscanvel France
48 K5 Rosche Ger.
59 M2 Röschitz Austria
55 H3 Rościszewo Pol.
110 E7 Roscoe *SD* U.S.A.
38 D4 Roscoff France
27 F5 Roscommon Rep. of Ireland
27 F5 Roscommon *county* Rep. of Ireland
110 J5 Roscommon *MI* U.S.A.
27 G7 Roscrea Rep. of Ireland
49 I8 Rosdorf Ger.
206 E3 Rose *r. N.T.* Austr.
73 Q9 Rose Italy
124 M2 Rose, Mount *NV* U.S.A.
131 □2 Roseau Dominica
120 H1 Roseau *MN* U.S.A.
120 G1 Roseau *r. MN* U.S.A.
99 □1b Rose Belle Mauritius
29 O4 Roseberry Topping *hill England* U.K.
206 G8 Roseberth *Qld* Austr.
205 J9 Rosebery *Tas.* Austr.
109 J4 Rose Blanche *Nfld and Lab.* Can.
106 H5 Rosebud *r. Alta* Can.
122 K3 Rosebud *MT* U.S.A.
122 K3 Rosebud Creek *r. MT* U.S.A.
120 E4 Rosebud Indian Reservation *res. SD* U.S.A.
122 C5 Roseburg *OR* U.S.A.
111 J5 Rose City *MI* U.S.A.
110 B6 Rose Creek *MN* U.S.A.
207 M8 Rosedale *Qld* Austr.
205 K8 Rosedale *Vic.* Austr.
118 B6 Rosedale *MD* U.S.A.
121 J9 Rosedale *MS* U.S.A.
29 P5 Rosedale Abbey *North Yorkshire, England* U.K.
96 G8 Rosedene S. Africa
45 G8 Rosée Belgium
59 J6 Rosegg Austria
137 G3 Rosehall Guyana
130 □ Rose Hall Jamaica
26 L7 Rosehearty *Aberdeenshire, Scotland* U.K.
99 □1b Rose Hill Mauritius
92 B2 Roseires Reservoir Sudan
197 H4 Rose Island American Samoa
115 □2 Rose Island Bahamas
40 J5 Roselend, Barrage de *dam* France
66 F6 Rosell Spain
119 G3 Roselle *NJ* U.S.A.
26 H7 Rosemarkie *Highland, Scotland* U.K.
208 D6 Rosemary Island *W.A.* Austr.
27 H6 Rosenallis Rep. of Ireland
121 H11 Rosenberg *TX* U.S.A.
22 C2 Rosendal Norway
97 L4 Rosendal S. Africa
110 F6 Rosendale *WI* U.S.A.
26 K5 Rose Ness *hd Scotland* U.K.
52 F5 Rosenfeld Ger.
48 I4 Rosengarten Ger.
118 E6 Rosenhayn *NJ* U.S.A.
53 M6 Rosenheim Ger.
59 I6 Rosennock *mt.* Austria
50 H3 Rosenow Ger.
59 J6 Rosental *val.* Austria
49 G9 Rosenthal Ger.
125 W8 Rose Peak *AZ* U.S.A.
106 D4 Rose Point *B.C.* Can.
23 N2 Roserberg Sweden
66 L3 Roses Spain
66 L3 Roses, Golf de *b.* Spain
118 E3 Roseto *PA* U.S.A.
75 L4 Roseto Capo Spulico Italy
73 M2 Roseto degli Abruzzi Italy
73 O5 Roseto Valfortore Italy
107 J5 Rosetown *Sask.* Can.
Rosetta Egypt *see* Rashīd
207 K6 Rosetta Creek *r. Qld* Austr.
107 K4 Rose Valley *Sask.* Can.
124 K3 Roseville *CA* U.S.A.
120 J5 Roseville *IL* U.S.A.
111 L7 Roseville *MI* U.S.A.
116 C9 Roseville *OH* U.S.A.
26 J11 Rosewell *Midlothian, Scotland* U.K.
207 N9 Rosewood *Qld* Austr.
116 B8 Rosewood *OH* U.S.A.
19 W6 Roshal' Rus. Fed.
18 M1 Roshchino *Leningradskaya Oblast'* Rus. Fed.
191 G1 Roshchino *Stavropol'skiy Kray* Rus. Fed.
17 N8 Roshchyne Ukr.
37 N6 Rosheim France
184 H4 Roshkhvār Iran
191 G2 Roshni-Chu Rus. Fed.
110 E5 Rosholt *WI* U.S.A.
94 C5 Rosh Pinah Namibia
Roshtkala Tajik. *see* Roshtqal'a
185 N3 Roshtqal'a Tajik.
26 E9 Roshven *Highland, Scotland* U.K.
65 □ Rosia Gibraltar
57 L5 Roșia Romania
65 □ Rosia Bay Gibraltar
56 F2 Rosice Czech Rep.
41 D6 Rosières France
36 E4 Rosières-en-Santerre France
36 H7 Rosières-près-Troyes France
70 I9 Rosignano Marittimo Italy
208 C6 Rosily Island *W.A.* Austr.
57 H2 Rosina Slovakia
77 P6 Roșiori Romania
77 N6 Roșiori de Vede Romania
18 K6 Rositsa Belarus
77 P7 Rositsa Bulg.
77 N7 Rositsa *r.* Bulg.
51 F8 Rositz Ger.
27 E4 Roskeeragh Point Rep. of Ireland
26 C8 Roskhill *Highland, Scotland* U.K.
22 I6 Roskilde Denmark
22 I6 Roskilde *county* Denmark
54 E3 Rosko Pol.
78 A2 Roskovec Albania
51 G6 Roskow Ger.
125 U9 Roskruge Mountains *AZ* U.S.A.
51 E10 Röslau Ger.
51 F10 Röslau *r.* Ger.
19 P8 Roslavl' Rus. Fed.
26 J11 Roslin *Midlothian, Scotland* U.K.
20 V2 Roslyakovo Rus. Fed.
14 I4 Roslyatino Rus. Fed.
44 H5 Rosmalen Neth.
62 F9 Rosmaninhal Port.
97 J7 Rosmead S. Africa
27 C6 Rosmuck Rep. of Ireland
54 E1 Rosnowo Pol.
71 M5 Rosolina Italy
71 M5 Rosolina Mare Italy
74 H10 Rosolini *Sicilia* Italy
77 J9 Rosoman Macedonia
36 F7 Rosoy France
58 F5 Röspitze *mt.* Austria/Italy
38 D6 Rosporden France
49 D9 Rösrath Ger.
205 K10 Ross *Tas.* Austr.
106 C2 Ross *r. Y.T.* Can.
203 E9 Ross *South I.* N.Z.
203 J8 Ross, Mount *hill North I.* N.Z.
75 L4 Rossano Italy
71 L4 Rossano Veneto Italy
27 E3 Rossan Point Rep. of Ireland
62 D5 Rossas Port.
27 C6 Rossaveel Rep. of Ireland
53 N4 Roßbach *Bayern* Ger.
51 E8 Roßbach *Sachsen-Anhalt* Ger.
121 K9 Ross Barnett Reservoir *MS* U.S.A.
109 H2 Ross Bay Junction *Nfld and Lab.* Can.
27 D9 Rossbrin Rep. of Ireland
27 D6 Rosscahill Rep. of Ireland
27 D9 Ross Carbery Rep. of Ireland
27 F4 Rosscor *Northern Ireland* U.K.
212 N2 Ross Dependency Antarctica
52 F2 Roßdorf Ger.
111 O4 Rosseau, Lake *Ont.* Can.
153 L9 Rossel Island P.N.G.
66 G4 Rosselló Spain
71 J7 Rossenno *r.* Italy
27 F2 Rosses Bay Rep. of Ireland
27 E4 Rosses Point Rep. of Ireland
30 G1 Rossett *Wrexham, Wales* U.K.
53 J6 Roßhaupten Ger.
208 □1 Ross Hill Christmas I.
213 M1 Ross Ice Shelf Antarctica
70 F6 Rossiglione Italy
45 H9 Rossignol Belgium
108 F2 Rossignol, Lac *l. Que.* Can.
109 H4 Rossignol, Lake *N.S.* Can.
94 B4 Rössing Namibia
49 I6 Rössing (Nordstemmen) Ger.
29 O7 Rossington *South Yorkshire, England* U.K.
27 F4 Rossinver Rep. of Ireland
64 C2 Rossio ao Sul do Tejo Port.
213 L1 Ross Island Antarctica
209 G12 Rossiter Bay *W.A.* Austr.
Rossiyskaya Sovetskaya Federativnaya Sotsialisticheskaya Respublika *country* Asia/Europe *see* Russian Federation
22 D2 Rosskreppfjorden *l.* Norway
51 D8 Roßla Ger.
106 G5 Rossland *B.C.* Can.
27 J8 Rosslare Rep. of Ireland
27 J8 Rosslare Harbour Rep. of Ireland
27 J8 Rosslare Point Rep. of Ireland
51 F7 Roßlau Ger.
27 H4 Rosslea *Northern Ireland* U.K.
51 D8 Roßleben Ger.
59 J4 Roßleithen Austria
111 Q5 Rossmore *Ont.* Can.
27 F3 Rossnowlagh Rep. of Ireland
88 B2 Rosso Maur.
72 B3 Rosso, Capo *c. Corse* France
20 N5 Rossön Sweden
30 G4 Ross-on-Wye *Herefordshire, England* U.K.
Rossony Belarus *see* Rasony
15 G6 Rossosh' Rus. Fed.
55 L4 Rossosz Pol.
54 G4 Rossoszyca Pol.
97 L7 Rossouw S. Africa
50 G4 Rossow Ger.
110 G1 Rossport *Ont.* Can.
206 E7 Ross River *N.T.* Austr.
106 C2 Ross River *Y.T.* Can.
213 L1 Ross Sea Antarctica
53 J3 Roßtal Ger.
44 H5 Rossum Neth.
20 M4 Rossvatnet *l.* Norway
110 C6 Rossville *IA* U.S.A.
110 G9 Rossville *IL* U.S.A.
110 H9 Rossville *IN* U.S.A.
118 B4 Rossville *PA* U.S.A.
51 H8 Roßwein Ger.
106 D4 Rosswood *B.C.* Can.
189 L5 Rōst Iraq
20 L3 Røst Norway
16 J4 Rostabytsya *r.* Ukr.
185 M3 Rostāq Afgh.
184 F7 Rostāq *Fārs* Iran
184 E8 Rostāq *Hormozgan* Iran
54 E3 Rostarzewo Pol.
20 L3 Røsthavet *sea chan.* Norway
107 J4 Rosthern *Sask.* Can.
50 F2 Rostock Ger.
20 P2 Rostonsölkä *ridge* Sweden
17 T2 Rostoshi Rus. Fed.
19 W4 Rostov Rus. Fed.
15 G7 Rostov-na-Donu Rus. Fed.
Rostov Oblast *admin. div.* Rus. Fed. *see* Rostovskaya Oblast'
Rostov-on-Don Rus. Fed. *see* Rostov-na-Donu
15 H7 Rostovskaya Oblast' *admin. div.* Rus. Fed.
97 J2 Rostrataville S. Africa
38 E5 Rostrenen France
27 J4 Rostrevor *Northern Ireland* U.K.
20 R2 Rostujávri *l.* Sweden
27 C5 Rosturk Rep. of Ireland
20 M3 Røsvik Norway
20 P4 Rosvik Sweden
119 E9 Roswell *GA* U.S.A.
123 L10 Roswell *NM* U.S.A.
29 K1 Rosyth *Fife, Scotland* U.K.
57 J5 Röszke Hungary
52 H5 Rot *r.* Ger.
153 K4 Rota *i.* N. Mariana Is
64 G7 Rota Spain
52 H6 Rotach *r.* Ger.
73 Q9 Rota Greca Italy
53 I3 Rot am See Ger.
53 I5 Rot an der Rot Ger.
51 G10 Rotava Czech Rep.
Rotch Island *Gilbert Is* Kiribati *see* Tamana
155 C9 Rote *i.* Indon.
73 N4 Rotello Italy
48 H4 Rotenburg (Wümme) Ger.
49 I8 Rotenburg an der Fulda Ger.
51 D10 Roter Main *r.* Ger.
53 K3 Rote Wand *mt.* Austria
59 H5 Rotgülden Austria
53 K3 Roth Ger.
53 I5 Roth *r.* Ger.
53 K3 Roth *r.* Ger.
51 F8 Rötha Ger.
49 F9 Rothaargebirge *hills* Ger.
29 N3 Rothbury *Northumberland, England* U.K.
29 N3 Rothbury Forest *England* U.K.
53 K3 Röthenbach an der Pegnitz Ger.
52 F2 Rothenberg Ger.
52 G2 Rothenbuch Ger.
51 E7 Rothenburg Ger.
51 K8 Rothenburg (Oberlausitz) Ger.
53 I3 Rothenburg ob der Tauber Ger.
38 H4 Rothéneuf France
52 H2 Rothenfels Ger.
51 E9 Rothenstein Ger.
31 K6 Rother *r. England* U.K.
212 T2 Rothera *research stn* Antarctica
31 M5 Rotherfield *East Sussex, England* U.K.
203 G9 Rotherham *South I.* N.Z.
29 O7 Rotherham *South Yorkshire, England* U.K.
26 J7 Rothes *Moray, Scotland* U.K.
26 F11 Rothesay *Argyll and Bute, Scotland* U.K.
45 H7 Rotheux-Rimière Belgium
26 K4 Rothiesholm *Orkney, Scotland* U.K.
53 I2 Röthlein Ger.
52 D7 Rothrist Switz.
110 E5 Rothschild *WI* U.S.A.
212 T2 Rothschild Island Antarctica
118 C4 Rothsville *PA* U.S.A.
31 K3 Rothwell *Northamptonshire, England* U.K.
29 O6 Rothwell *West Yorkshire, England* U.K.
49 I8 Rothwesten (Fuldatal) Ger.
155 C9 Roti Indon.
Roti *i.* Indon. *see* Rote
155 C9 Roti, Selat *sea chan.* Indon.
Rotja, Punta *pt* Spain *see* Roja, Punta
205 J5 Roto *N.S.W.* Austr.
202 J6 Rotoaira, Lake *North I.* N.Z.
202 K5 Rotoehu, Lake *North I.* N.Z.
202 K5 Rotoiti, Lake *North I.* N.Z.
203 G8 Rotoiti, Lake *South I.* N.Z.
202 K5 Rotoma, Lake *North I.* N.Z.
Rotomagus France *see* Rouen
202 K5 Rotomahana, Lake *North I.* N.Z.
203 F9 Rotomanu *South I.* N.Z.
73 O8 Rotonda Italy
75 L3 Rotondella Italy
72 C3 Rotondo, Monte *mt. Corse* France
203 G8 Rotoroa, Lake *South I.* N.Z.
202 K5 Rotorua *North I.* N.Z.
202 K5 Rotorua, Lake *North I.* N.Z.
45 G7 Rotselaar Belgium
58 G6 Rotsteinberg *mt.* Austria
53 J6 Rott Ger.
53 O5 Rott *r.* Ger.
51 G7 Rotta Ger.
53 L6 Rottach-Egern Ger.
53 M6 Rott am Inn Ger.
37 L6 Rotte *r.* France
52 H5 Rottenacker Ger.
53 J2 Röttenbach *Bayern* Ger.
53 K3 Röttenbach *Bayern* Ger.
51 D9 Rottenbach Ger.
53 J6 Rottenbuch Ger.
52 F5 Rottenburg am Neckar Ger.
53 M4 Rottenburg an der Laaber Ger.
53 I2 Rottendorf Ger.
59 J4 Rottenmann Austria
59 J5 Rottenmanner Tauern *mts* Austria
44 G5 Rotterdam Neth.
117 L6 Rotterdam *NY* U.S.A.
44 J2 Rottevalle Neth.
53 O5 Rotthalmünster Ger.
31 L6 Rottingdean *Brighton and Hove, England* U.K.
52 H2 Röttingham Ger.
49 K7 Rottleberode Ger.
22 I2 Rottnan *r.* Sweden
23 L5 Rottnen *l.* Sweden
209 C12 Rottnest Island *W.A.* Austr.
70 H5 Rottofreno Italy
44 K1 Rottumeroog *i.* Neth.
44 J1 Rottumerplaat *i.* Neth.
52 F5 Rottweil Ger.
199 H3 Rotuma *i.* Fiji
77 M7 Rotunda Romania
20 M5 Rötviken Sweden
53 L6 Rotwand *mt.* Ger.
53 N3 Rötz Ger.
38 H7 Rouans France
36 F2 Roubaix France
41 F7 Roubion *r.* France
66 H2 Rouch, Mont *mt.* France/Spain
40 D4 Rouchain, Barrage du *dam* France
56 F2 Rouchovany Czech Rep.
56 D1 Roudnice nad Labem Czech Rep.
36 B5 Rouen France
43 I7 Rouergue *reg.* France
37 N8 Rouffach France
42 I5 Rouffiac France
42 F5 Rouffignac France
18 J4 Rõuge Estonia
38 I6 Rougé France
131 □7 Rouge, Point Trin. and Tob.
108 F4 Rouge-Matawin, Réserve Faunique *nature res. Que.* Can.
40 I2 Rougemont France
37 M8 Rougemont-le-Château France
203 D12 Rough Ridge *South I.* N.Z.
31 O2 Roughton *Norfolk, England* U.K.
27 C9 Roughty *r.* Rep. of Ireland
42 E4 Rougnac France
84 A4 Roui, Oued er *watercourse* Niger
42 D4 Rouillac France
42 E3 Rouillé France
41 C9 Roujan France
40 I2 Roulans France
Roulers Belgium *see* Roeselare
116 G7 Roulette *PA* U.S.A.
206 D7 Roulpmaulpma Aboriginal Land *res. N.T.* Austr.
Roumania *country* Europe *see* Romania
42 F4 Roumazières-Loubert France
39 M3 Roumois *reg.* France
41 I9 Roumoules France
109 G2 Roundeyed Lake *Que.* Can.
116 B8 Round Head *OH* U.S.A.
29 O5 Round Hill *England* U.K.
205 K5 Round Hill Nature Reserve *N.S.W.* Austr.
99 □1b Round Island Mauritius
108 E4 Round Lake *Ont.* Can.
205 N4 Round Mountain *N.S.W.* Austr.
124 O3 Round Mountain *NV* U.S.A.
125 W5 Round Rock *AZ* U.S.A.
121 G10 Round Rock *TX* U.S.A.
27 C6 Roundstone Rep. of Ireland
118 B3 Round Top *hill PA* U.S.A.
122 J3 Roundup *MT* U.S.A.
118 F3 Round Valley Reservoir *NJ* U.S.A.
31 I5 Roundway *Wiltshire, England* U.K.
28 E7 Roundwood Rep. of Ireland
137 H3 Roura Fr. Guiana
70 C5 Roure Italy
26 J4 Rousay *i. Scotland* U.K.
117 L4 Rouses Point *NY* U.S.A.
56 F2 Rousinov Czech Rep.
28 C4 Rousky *Northern Ireland* U.K.
41 H10 Rousset France
41 G7 Rousset, Col de *pass* France
41 G9 Roussillon *Provence-Alpes-Côte d'Azur* France
35 G4 Roussillon *Rhône-Alpes* France
43 J10 Roussillon *reg.* France
41 E8 Rousson France
Routh Bank *sea feature* Phil. *see* Seahorse Bank
39 M3 Routot France
44 J3 Rouveen Neth.
39 K4 Rouvre *r.* France
36 E3 Rouvroy France
36 I4 Rouvroy-sur-Audry France
41 J10 Roux, Cap *c.* France
97 K6 Rouxville S. Africa
40 D2 Rouy France
108 E3 Rouyn-Noranda *Que.* Can.
20 R3 Rovaniemi Fin.
70 E5 Rovasenda *r.* Italy
70 I4 Rovato Italy
70 G6 Rovegno Italy
15 G6 Roven'ki Rus. Fed.
Rovenki Ukr. *see* Roven'ky
17 S5 Roven'ky Ukr.
Rovenskaya Oblast' *admin. div.* Ukr. *see* Rivnens'ka Oblast'
71 J5 Roverbella Italy
70 G3 Roveredo Switz.
71 K4 Rovereto Italy
50 F2 Rövershagen Ger.
144 E2 Roversi Arg.
73 J3 Roviano Italy
159 G8 Rôviĕng Tbong Cambodia
71 L5 Rovigo Italy
71 L5 Rovigo *prov.* Italy
77 L6 Rovinari Romania
68 D3 Rovinj Croatia
56 G3 Rovinka Slovakia
59 O8 Rovišće Croatia
Rovno Ukr. *see* Rivne
Rovno Oblast *admin. div.* Ukr. *see* Rivnens'ka Oblast'
18 L3 Rovnoye *Pskovskaya Oblast'* Rus. Fed.
182 B2 Rovnoye *Saratovskaya Oblast'* Rus. Fed.
54 C3 Rów Pol.
200 □5 Rowa Vanuatu
30 H5 Rowde *Wiltshire, England* U.K.
205 L3 Rowena *N.S.W.* Austr.
118 F2 Rowland *PA* U.S.A.
116 F9 Rowlesburg *WV* U.S.A.
105 K3 Rowley Island *Nunavut* Can.
208 E4 Rowley Shoals *sea feature W.A.* Austr.
18 M6 Rownaye Belarus
Równe Ukr. *see* Rivne
54 E4 Rów Polski *r.* Pol.
116 C8 Rowsburg *OH* U.S.A.
154 C3 Roxas *Luzon* Phil.
154 D7 Roxas *Mindanao* Phil.
154 C5 Roxas *Mindoro* Phil.
154 B6 Roxas *Palawan* Phil.
154 D6 Roxas *Panay* Phil.
115 H7 Roxboro *NC* U.S.A.
131 □5 Roxborough Trin. and Tob.
206 G7 Roxborough Downs *Qld* Austr.
203 D12 Roxburgh *South I.* N.Z.
Roxburgh Island Cook Is *see* Rarotonga
119 I1 Roxbury *CT* U.S.A.
119 I1 Roxbury Falls *CT* U.S.A.
204 F4 Roxby Downs *S.A.* Austr.
23 L3 Roxen *l.* Sweden
64 C5 Roxo *r.* Port.
64 C5 Roxo, Barragem do *resr* Port.
31 L3 Roxton *Bedfordshire, England* U.K.
26 G9 Roy *r. Scotland* U.K.
122 J3 Roy *MT* U.S.A.
123 L8 Roy *NM* U.S.A.
41 L9 Roya *r.* France/Italy
27 H6 Royal Canal Rep. of Ireland
110 H9 Royal Center *IN* U.S.A.
179 J6 Royal Chitwan National Park Nepal
110 F1 Royale, Isle *i. MI* U.S.A.
97 M4 Royal Natal National Park S. Africa
111 K7 Royal Oak *MI* U.S.A.
213 K1 Royal Society Range *mts* Antarctica
178 H5 Royal Sukla Phanta Wildlife Reserve *nature res.* Nepal
118 B4 Royalton *PA* U.S.A.
110 F5 Royalton *WI* U.S.A.
42 B4 Royan France
40 C5 Royat France
41 G6 Roybon France
31 N2 Roydon *Norfolk, England* U.K.
31 O3 Roydon *Norfolk, England* U.K.
36 E4 Roye France
42 H4 Royère-de-Vassivière France
118 D4 Royersford *PA* U.S.A.
208 E7 Roy Hill *W.A.* Austr.
17 K2 Royishche Ukr.
31 L3 Royston *Hertfordshire, England* U.K.
29 O6 Royston *South Yorkshire, England* U.K.
29 M6 Royton *Greater Manchester, England* U.K.
20 R4 Röyttä Fin.
63 R8 Royuela Spain
76 I8 Rožaje *Crna Gora* Serb. and Mont.
63 O9 Rozalén del Monte Spain
55 J3 Różan Pol.
76 H6 Rožanj *hill* Serb. and Mont.
54 D3 Różanki Pol.
36 E6 Rozay-en-Brie France
56 E1 Rožďalovice Czech Rep.
55 M6 Rozdil Ukr.
16 J7 Rozdil'na Ukr.
17 R6 Rozdol'ne *Donets'ka Oblast'* Ukr.
17 M8 Rozdol'ne *Respublika Krym* Ukr.
17 O5 Rozdory Ukr.
54 F4 Rozdrażew Pol.
44 F5 Rozenburg Neth.
44 I4 Rozendaal Neth.
183 N2 Rozhdestvenka Kazakh.
19 T5 Rozhdestveno *Tverskaya Oblast'* Rus. Fed.
19 U4 Rozhdestveno *Yaroslavskaya Oblast'* Rus. Fed.
14 I4 Rozhdestvenskoye Rus. Fed.
19 Q4 Rozhdestvo Rus. Fed.
191 B2 Rozhkao Rus. Fed.
17 N1 Rozhkovychi Rus. Fed.
17 L3 Rozhnivka Ukr.
16 J3 Rozhny Ukr.
16 D5 Rozhnyativ Ukr.
16 E3 Rozhyshche Ukr.
77 M8 Rozino Bulg.
17 Q6 Rozivka Ukr.
56 C2 Rožmitál pod Třemšínem Czech Rep.
57 J3 Rožňava Slovakia
54 G3 Rożniatów Pol.
57 H2 Rožnov pod Radhoštěm Czech Rep.
55 I6 Rożnów Pol.
54 E3 Roznowo Pol.
55 J2 Rozoga *r.* Pol.
55 J2 Rozogi Pol.
36 H4 Rozoy-sur-Serre France
55 H4 Rozprza Pol.
17 R4 Rozsypne Ukr.
55 L5 Roztoczański Park Narodowy *nat. park* Pol.
55 I6 Roztoka Wielka Pol.
51 I10 Roztoky *Středočeský kraj* Czech Rep.
51 J10 Roztoky *Středočeský kraj* Czech Rep.
184 D5 Rozveh Iran
70 G5 Rozzano Italy
76 H9 Rrëshen Albania
76 H9 Rrogozhinë Albania
15 H5 Rtishchevo Rus. Fed.
62 D2 Ru Spain
62 E7 Rua Port.
155 A8 Rua, Tanjung *pt Sumba* Indon.
30 F2 Ruabon *Wrexham, Wales* U.K.
94 B3 Ruacana Namibia
93 B6 Ruaha National Park Tanz.
202 K6 Ruahine Forest Park *nature res. North I.* N.Z.
202 K7 Ruahine Range *mts North I.* N.Z.
202 I2 Ruakaka *North I.* N.Z.
27 E7 Ruan Rep. of Ireland
Ruanda *country* Africa *see* Rwanda
155 D2 Ruang *i.* Indon.
202 J6 Ruapehu, Mount *vol. North I.* N.Z.
203 C13 Ruapuke Island *South I.* N.Z.
30 G4 Ruardean *Gloucestershire, England* U.K.
93 B7 Ruarwe Malawi
202 I2 Ruatangata *North I.* N.Z.
203 E9 Ruatapu *South I.* N.Z.
202 M4 Ruatoria *North I.* N.Z.
39 L6 Ruaudin France
200 □6 Ruavatu *Guadalcanal* Solomon Is
19 N6 Ruba Belarus
186 H6 Rub' al Khālī *des.* Saudi Arabia
57 H4 Rúbaň Slovakia
28 G5 Rubane *Northern Ireland* U.K.
17 N7 Rubanivka Ukr.
71 L5 Rubano Italy
18 K6 Rubashki Belarus
187 I3 Rubaydā *reg.* Saudi Arabia
63 M2 Rubayo Spain
93 C6 Rubeho Mountains Tanz.
49 K7 Rübeland Ger.
143 F2 Rubelita Brazil
63 M4 Rubena Spain
51 H9 Rübenau Ger.
128 G8 Rubén Figueroa Mex.
164 U3 Rubeshibe Japan
Rubezhnoye Ukr. *see* Rubizhne
Rubha an t-Siumpain *hd* Scotland U.K. *see* Tiumpan Head
90 E4 Rubi *r.* Dem. Rep. Congo
66 J5 Rubí Spain
62 G4 Rubiá Spain
142 B4 Rubiácea Brazil
67 C8 Rubial, Serra de *mts* Spain
124 K3 Rubicon *r. CA* U.S.A.
71 N7 Rubicone *r.* Italy
63 K6 Rubí de Bracamonte Spain
66 C6 Rubielos de la Cérida Spain
67 D7 Rubielos de Mora Spain
71 J6 Rubiera Italy
143 G2 Rubim Brazil
142 B4 Rubinéia Brazil
63 M6 Rubio *mt.* Spain
17 R4 Rubizhne Ukr.
50 I3 Rubkow Ger.
63 N3 Rublacedo de Abajo Spain
93 A5 Rubondo National Park Tanz.
17 Q4 Rubtsi Ukr.
183 S2 Rubtsovsk Rus. Fed.
93 B6 Rubuga Tanz.
186 F6 Rubūţ, Jabal ar *hill* Saudi Arabia
104 C3 Ruby *AK* U.S.A.
203 H8 Ruby Bay *South I.* N.Z.
122 G6 Ruby Dome *mt. NV* U.S.A.
16 G2 Rubyel' Belarus
19 N6 Rubyezhnitsa Belarus
125 Q1 Ruby Lake *NV* U.S.A.
125 Q1 Ruby Lake National Wildlife Refuge *nature res. NV* U.S.A.
125 Q1 Ruby Mountains *NV* U.S.A.
106 E4 Rubyrock Lake Provincial Park *nat. park B.C.* Can.
125 T4 Rubys Inn *UT* U.S.A.
207 K7 Rubyvale *Qld* Austr.
125 Q1 Ruby Valley *NV* U.S.A.
146 E5 Rucanelo Arg.
77 N5 Rucăr Romania
18 K6 Ruchay Belarus
Rucheng *Guangdong* China *see* Ruyuan
171 I6 Rucheng *Hunan* China
17 M3 Ruchky Ukr.
17 M8 Ruch"yi Ukr.
55 J2 Ruciane-Nida Pol.
51 I7 Rückersdorf Ger.
116 G10 Ruckersville *VA* U.S.A.
44 G5 Rucphen Neth.
54 G4 Ruda Pol.
57 J3 Rudabánya Hungary
55 L4 Ruda-Huta Pol.
208 G7 Rudall *watercourse W.A.* Austr.
208 G7 Rudall River National Park *W.A.* Austr.
209 L7 Rudalls *watercourse N.T.* Austr.
55 I4 Ruda Maleniecka Pol.
55 L1 Rudamina Lith.
55 L5 Ruda Różaniecka Pol.
179 I6 Rudarpur *Uttar Prad.* India
54 G5 Ruda Śląska Pol.
178 H6 Rudauli *Uttar Prad.* India
56 E1 Rudawski Park Krajobrazowy Pol.
185 J6 Rudbar Afgh.
189 P9 Rūdbār *Fārs* Iran
184 C3 Rūdbār *Gīlān* Iran
45 D6 Ruddervoorde Belgium
31 J2 Ruddington *Nottinghamshire, England* U.K.
184 E7 Rūd-e Kor *watercourse* Iran
53 L4 Rudelzhausen Ger.
59 K6 Ruden Austria
50 I2 Ruden *i.* Ger.
52 H4 Rudersberg Ger.
59 N5 Rudersdorf Austria
51 I6 Rüdersdorf Berlin Ger.
49 J7 Rüdershausen Ger.
53 O4 Ruderting Ger.
16 I4 Rude Selo Ukr.
52 D2 Rüdesheim Ger.
52 D2 Rüdesheim am Rhein Ger.
31 L5 Rudgwick *West Sussex, England* U.K.
76 H7 Rudina *pass* Serb. and Mont.
18 H7 Rūdiškės Lith.
49 K9 Rudisleben Ger.
17 L3 Rudivka *Chernihivs'ka Oblast'* Ukr.
17 R4 Rudivka *Luhans'ka Oblast'* Ukr.
55 K3 Rudka Pol.
55 L3 Rudka *r.* Pol.
22 G7 Rudkøbing Denmark
55 L6 Rudky Ukr.
51 J10 Rudná Czech Rep.
54 E4 Rudna Pol.
77 K6 Rudna Glava *Srbija* Serb. and Mont.
54 E4 Rudna Wielka Pol.
162 I6 Rudnaya Pristan' *Primorskiy Kray* Rus. Fed.
162 I7 Rudnaya Pristan' *Primorskiy Kray* Rus. Fed.
16 C4 Rudne Ukr.
57 I1 Rudniański, Park Krajobrazowy Pol.
50 L5 Rudnica Pol.
14 K4 Rudnichnyy Rus. Fed.
54 G5 Rudnik *Śląskie* Pol.
54 G4 Rudniki Pol.
55 K5 Rudnik nad Sadem *Podkarpackie* Pol.
50 I5 Rüdnitz Ger.
55 M3 Rudnya Belarus
19 O7 Rudnya *Smolenskaya Oblast'* Rus. Fed.
19 O5 Rudnya *Tverskaya Oblast'* Rus. Fed.
15 I6 Rudnya *Volgogradskaya Oblast'* Rus. Fed.
16 G3 Rudnya-Ivanivs'ka Ukr.
55 L6 Rudnyky Ukr.
16 H5 Rudnytsya Ukr.
182 J1 Rudnyy Kazakh.
162 I6 Rudnyy Rus. Fed.
Rudolf, Lake *salt l.* Eth./Kenya *see* Turkana, Lake
192 G1 Rudol'fa, Ostrov *i. Zemlya Frantsa-Iosifa* Rus. Fed.
146 C4 Rudolfo Iselin Arg.
59 K2 Rudolfov Czech Rep.
Rudolph Island *Zemlya Frantsa-Iosifa* Rus. Fed. *see* Rudol'fa, Ostrov
51 D9 Rudolstadt Ger.
171 M2 Rudong *Jiangsu* China
77 M9 Rudozem Bulg.
63 M3 Rudrón *resr* Spain
184 D3 Rūdsar Iran
22 E2 Rudsgrendi Norway
29 Q5 Rudston *East Riding of Yorkshire, England* U.K.
110 J3 Rudyard *MI* U.S.A.
54 F5 Rudziczka Pol.
18 K8 Rudzyensk Belarus
36 C3 Rue France
64 H2 Ruecas *r.* Spain
63 K6 Rueda Spain
36 D6 Rueil-Malmaison France
111 M2 Ruel *Ont.* Can.
Ruen *mt.* Macedonia *see* Rujen
63 L2 Ruente Spain
95 G3 Ruenya *r.* Zimbabwe
58 D5 Ruetz *r.* Austria
85 G6 Rufa'a Sudan
75 O4 Ruffano Italy
39 N8 Ruffec *Centre* France
42 E3 Ruffec *Poitou-Charentes* France
40 G2 Ruffey-lès-Echirey France
40 G3 Ruffey-sur-Seille France
38 G6 Ruffiac France
40 H4 Ruffieu France
40 H5 Ruffieux France
29 L6 Rufford *Lancashire, England* U.K.
93 C7 Rufiji *r.* Tanz.
71 K8 Rufina Italy
147 F4 Rufino Arg.
88 A3 Rufisque Senegal
91 F8 Rufunsa Zambia
18 K4 Rugāji Latvia
171 M2 Rugao *Jiangsu* China
50 E3 Rugberg *hill* Ger.
31 J3 Rugby *Warwickshire, England* U.K.
120 E1 Rugby *ND* U.S.A.
31 I2 Rugeley *Staffordshire, England* U.K.
50 H2 Rügen *i.* Ger.
50 H1 Rügen, Naturpark *nature res.* Ger.
106 E5 Rugged Mountain *B.C.* Can.
85 F5 Rugheiwa *well* Sudan
53 J3 Rügland Ger.
39 M4 Rugles France
59 N8 Rugvica Croatia
93 C7 Ruhangino Tanz.
187 H3 Ruḩayyat al Ḩamr'ā' *waterhole* Saudi Arabia
188 H7 Ruḩbah *oasis* Syria
49 K6 Rühen Ger.
93 A5 Ruhengeri Rwanda
49 J9 Ruhla Ger.
51 I8 Ruhland Ger.
53 N4 Ruhmannsfelden Ger.
50 E3 Rühn Ger.
18 G4 Ruhnu *i.* Estonia
53 N6 Ruhpolding Ger.
49 C8 Ruhr *r.* Ger.
53 O5 Ruhstorf an der Rott Ger.
93 B7 Ruhudji *r.* Tanz.
176 G9 Ruhuna National Park Sri Lanka
171 M5 Rui'an *Zhejiang* China
171 J4 Ruichang *Jiangxi* China
65 N3 Ruidera Spain
123 L12 Ruidosa *TX* U.S.A.
123 L10 Ruidoso *NM* U.S.A.
171 J6 Ruijin *Jiangxi* China
170 A6 Ruili *Yunnan* China
72 B8 Ruinas *Sardegna* Italy
44 J3 Ruinen Neth.
44 J3 Ruinerwold Neth.
93 C7 Ruipa Tanz.
45 D6 Ruiselede Belgium
62 D5 Ruivães Port.
64 □ Ruivo, Pico *mt.* Madeira
128 B4 Ruiz Mex.
129 I3 Ruiz Cortines Mex.
77 K8 Ruj *mt.* Bulg.
18 I4 Rūja *r.* Latvia
54 E4 Ruja Pol.
190 F6 Rujaylah, Ḩarrat ar *lava field* Jordan
77 K8 Rujen *mt.* Macedonia
18 I4 Rūjiena Latvia
191 J4 Rük Azer.
185 M8 Ruk Pak.
185 O7 Rukanpur Pak.
187 I2 Rukbah *well* Saudi Arabia
191 J3 Rukel' Rus. Fed.
191 C3 Rukhi Georgia
90 C4 Ruki *r.* Dem. Rep. Congo
179 I5 Rukumkot Nepal
92 A5 Rukungiri Uganda
155 D6 Rukuwa *Sulawesi* Indon.
93 A6 Rukwa *admin. reg.* Tanz.
93 B7 Rukwa, Lake Tanz.
21 M6 Rulbo Sweden
187 M3 Rūl Ḑadnah U.A.E.
121 J9 Ruleville *MS* U.S.A.
208 I2 Rulhieres, Cape *W.A.* Austr.
49 F6 Rulle (Wallenhorst) Ger.
48 K4 Rullstorf Ger.
40 F3 Rully France
Rulong *Sichuan* China *see* Xinlong
52 E3 Rülzheim Ger.
58 D5 Rum Austria
56 F4 Rum Hungary
184 H5 Rūm Iran
Rum Jordan *see* Ramm
26 D9 Rum *i. Scotland* U.K.
120 I3 Rum *r. MN* U.S.A.
Rum, Jebel *mts* Jordan *see* Ramm, Jabal
26 D9 Rum, Sound of *sea chan. Scotland* U.K.
89 G3 Ruma Nigeria
76 H5 Ruma *Vojvodina, Srbija* Serb. and Mont.
186 F9 Rumādah Yemen
187 H3 Rumāh Saudi Arabia
92 B5 Ruma National Park Kenya
Rumania *country* Europe *see* Romania
186 F7 Rumayn *i.* Saudi Arabia
155 D3 Rumbai *Sulawesi* Indon.
90 F3 Rumbek Sudan
65 L4 Rumblar *r.* Spain
65 L4 Rumblar, Embalse del *resr* Spain
56 D1 Rumburk Czech Rep.
130 F2 Rum Cay *i.* Bahamas
45 J10 Rumelange Lux.
45 D7 Rumes Belgium
117 □O4 Rumford *ME* U.S.A.
23 O7 Rumia Pol.
36 H4 Rumigny France
40 H5 Rumilly France
206 C2 Rum Jungle *N.T.* Austr.
186 E2 Rummān, Jabal ar *mts* Saudi Arabia
190 G5 Rummānā *hill* Syria
30 F4 Rumney *Cardiff, Wales* U.K.
164 S3 Rumoi Japan
93 A5 Rumonge Burundi
37 J6 Rumont France
93 B7 Rumphi Malawi
119 H4 Rumson *NJ* U.S.A.
45 F6 Rumst Belgium
207 J4 Rumula *Qld* Austr.
92 C4 Rumuruti Kenya
155 F6 Run *i. Maluku* Indon.
64 A2 Runa Port.
27 J2 Runabay Head *Northern Ireland* U.K.
171 J2 Runan *Henan* China
203 F9 Runanga *South I.* N.Z.
202 L4 Runaway, Cape *North I.* N.Z.
130 □ Runaway Bay Jamaica
29 L7 Runcorn *Halton, England* U.K.
77 L5 Runcu Romania
57 L6 Runcu *r.* Romania
95 G4 Runde *r.* Zimbabwe
94 C3 Rundu Namibia
155 D6 Runduma *i.* Indon.
20 O5 Rundvik Sweden
159 F9 Rŭng, Kaôh *i.* Cambodia
157 J6 Rungan *r.* Indon.
90 E4 Rungu Dem. Rep. Congo
93 A6 Rungwa *Rukwa* Tanz.
93 B6 Rungwa *Singida* Tanz.
93 A6 Rungwa *r.* Tanz.
93 B6 Rungwa Game Reserve *nature res.* Tanz.
171 K2 Runheji *Anhui* China
Runing *Henan* China *see* Runan
184 E7 Rūnīz-e Bālā Iran
49 F10 Runkel Ger.
23 O2 Runmarö *i.* Sweden
23 L1 Runn *l.* Sweden
124 O7 Running Springs *CA* U.S.A.
121 E9 Running Water *watercourse NM/TX* U.S.A.
23 M4 Runnö *i.* Sweden
209 G7 Runton Range *hills W.A.* Austr.
31 N4 Runwell *Essex, England* U.K.
200 □4a Ruo *i. Chuuk* Micronesia
21 T6 Ruokolahti Fin.
41 E8 Ruoms France
172 I7 Ruoqiang *Xinjiang* China
172 I7 Ruoqiang He *r.* China
168 G6 Ruo Shui *watercourse* China
73 P6 Ruoti Italy
21 S6 Ruotsinpyhtää Fin.
21 R6 Ruovesi Fin.
71 Q5 Rupa Croatia
179 N6 Rupa *Arun. Prad.* India
156 D4 Rupat *i.* Indon.
77 N4 Rupea Romania
108 E3 Rupert *r. Que.* Can.
122 H5 Rupert *ID* U.S.A.
116 E11 Rupert *WV* U.S.A.
108 E3 Rupert Bay *Que.* Can.
212 O1 Rupert Coast Antarctica
207 I6 Rupert Creek *r. Qld* Austr.
178 F4 Rupnagar *Punjab* India
178 E6 Rupnagar *Rajasthan* India
93 C7 Ruponda Tanz.
50 G5 Ruppiner See *l.* Ger.
59 L3 Ruprechtshofen Austria
178 F3 Rupshu *reg.* Jammu and Kashmir
37 M8 Rupt-sur-Moselle France
186 F5 Ruqayţah Saudi Arabia
190 D6 Ruqqād, Wādī ar *watercourse* Israel
116 D12 Rural Retreat *VA* U.S.A.
138 D3 Rurrenabaque Bol.
49 B9 Rurstausee *resr* Ger.
201 □3 Rurutu *i. Îs Australes* Fr. Polynesia
77 L3 Rus Romania
65 M4 Rus Spain
65 N2 Rus *r.* Spain
17 N8 Rusakivka Ukr.
17 M3 Rusanivka Ukr.
95 G3 Rusape Zimbabwe
77 K5 Rusca Montană Romania
Ruschuk Bulg. *see* Ruse
77 M3 Ruscova Romania
77 N7 Ruse Bulg.
59 M6 Ruše Slovenia
77 O7 Rusenski Lom *nat. park* Bulg.
179 K7 Rusera *Bihar* India
77 P6 Rușețu Romania
27 J5 Rush Rep. of Ireland
31 I2 Rushall *West Midlands, England* U.K.
169 Q8 Rushan *Shandong* China
Rushan Tajik. *see* Rushon
Rushanskiy Khrebet *mts* Tajik. *see* Rushon, Qatorkŭhi
120 D6 Rush Creek *r. CO* U.S.A.
31 K3 Rushden *Northamptonshire, England* U.K.
110 C6 Rushford *MN* U.S.A.
95 G3 Rushinga Zimbabwe
110 F6 Rush Lake *WI* U.S.A.
116 I11 Rushmere *VA* U.S.A.
31 O3 Rushmere St Andrew *Suffolk, England* U.K.
179 O5 Rushon *Arun. Prad.* India
185 N2 Rushon Tajik.
185 N3 Rushon, Qatorkŭhi *mts* Tajik.
168 J9 Rushui He *r.* China
120 J5 Rushville *IL* U.S.A.
114 E6 Rushville *IN* U.S.A.
120 D4 Rushville *NE* U.S.A.
116 C9 Rushville *OH* U.S.A.
205 J7 Rushworth *Vic.* Austr.
54 G4 Rusiec Pol.
55 I4 Rusinów Pol.
54 E2 Rusinowo Pol.
121 H10 Rusk *TX* U.S.A.
20 O4 Ruskele Sweden
23 K4 Rusken *l.* Sweden
76 H5 Ruski Krstur *Vojvodina, Srbija* Serb. and Mont.
115 F12 Ruskin *FL* U.S.A.
29 Q7 Ruskington *Lincolnshire, England* U.K.
17 P3 Rus'ki Tyshky Ukr.
57 J6 Rusko Selo *Vojvodina, Srbija* Serb. and Mont.
57 K3 Ruskov Slovakia
18 E6 Rusnė Lith.
77 P8 Rusokastro Bulg.
18 J5 Rušona Latvia
18 J5 Rušonu ezers *l.* Latvia
16 H5 Rusova *r.* Ukr.
30 G4 Ruspidge *Gloucestershire, England* U.K.
18 F2 Russarö *i.* Fin.
140 F3 Russas Brazil
107 K5 Russell *Man.* Can.
117 J3 Russell *Ont.* Can.
202 I2 Russell *North I.* N.Z.
120 F6 Russell *KS* U.S.A.
116 F7 Russell *PA* U.S.A.
212 P2 Russell Bay Antarctica
105 I2 Russell Island *Nunavut* Can.
200 □6 Russell Islands Solomon Is
107 K3 Russell Lake *Man.* Can.
106 H2 Russell Lake *N.W.T.* Can.
107 J3 Russell Lake *Sask.* Can.
115 D8 Russellville *AL* U.S.A.
121 I8 Russellville *AR* U.S.A.
114 D7 Russellville *KY* U.S.A.
116 B10 Russellville *OH* U.S.A.
118 D5 Russellville *PA* U.S.A.
52 E1 Rüsselsheim Ger.
71 M7 Russi Italy
Russia *country* Asia/Europe *see* Russian Federation
192 F4 Russian Federation *country* Asia/Europe
Russian Soviet Federal Socialist Republic *country* Asia/Europe *see* Russian Federation
183 O1 Russkaya-Polyana Rus. Fed.

Column 1

- 15 H6 Russkaya Zhuravka Rus. Fed.
- 19 I9 Russkiy Brod Rus. Fed.
- 182 B1 Russkiy Kameshkir Rus. Fed.
- 14 K1 Russkiy Zavorot, Poluostrov pen. Rus. Fed.
- 19 P8 Russkoye Smolenskaya Oblast' Rus. Fed.
- 191 F2 Russkoye Stavropol'skiy Kray Rus. Fed.
- 193 P2 Russkoye Ust'ye Rus. Fed.
- 59 O4 Rust Austria
- 191 G5 Rüstäm Äliyev Azer.
- 191 G4 Rust'avi Georgia
- 116 F11 Rustburg VA U.S.A.
- 97 M1 Rust de Winter S. Africa
- 97 M1 Rust de Winter Nature Reserve S. Africa
- 191 D6 Rüstemgedik Turkey
- 97 L1 Rustenburg S. Africa
- 97 L1 Rustenburg Nature Reserve S. Africa
- 22 D3 Rustfjellheii mt. Norway
- 97 K5 Rustfontein Dam l. S. Africa
- 97 L3 Rustig S. Africa
- 31 K6 Rustington West Sussex, England U.K.
- 121 I9 Ruston Azer.
- 191 J4 Ruston Azer.
- 41 G9 Rustrel France
- 70 E1 Rusviel Rus. Fed.
- 54 D4 Ruszów Pol.
- 19 T6 Rut' r. Rus. Fed.
- 155 E4 Ruta Maluku Indon.
- 203 □³ Rutaki Passage Rarotonga Cook Is
- 72 G2 Rutali Corse France
- 93 A5 Rutana Burundi
- Rutanzige, Lake Dem. Rep. Congo/Uganda see Edward, Lake
- 65 K6 Rute Spain
- 155 B8 Ruteng Flores Indon.
- 95 F4 Rutenga Zimbabwe
- 52 F4 Rüthesheim Ger.
- 125 Q2 Ruth NV U.S.A.
- 49 F8 Rüthen Ger.
- Ruthenia admin. div. Ukr. see Zakarpats'ka Oblast'
- 119 G3 Rutherford NJ U.S.A.
- 115 G8 Rutherfordton NC U.S.A.
- 205 K7 Rutherglen Vic. Austr.
- 111 O3 Rutherglen Ont. Can.
- 26 H11 Rutherglen South Lanarkshire, Scotland U.K.
- 116 H11 Ruther Glen VA U.S.A.
- 30 F1 Ruthin Denbighshire, Wales U.K.
- 178 F7 Ruthiyai Madh. Prad. India
- 70 F1 Rüti Switz.
- 75 M1 Rutigliano Italy
- 73 O7 Rutino Italy
- 14 I4 Rutka r. Pol.
- 55 K1 Rutka-Tartak Pol.
- 55 K2 Rutki-Kossaki Pol.
- 31 K2 Rutland admin. div. England U.K.
- 117 M5 Rutland VT U.S.A.
- 177 M7 Rutland Island Andaman & Nicobar Is India
- 207 H3 Rutland Plains Qld Austr.
- 31 K2 Rutland Water resr England U.K.
- 116 B12 Rutledge TN U.S.A.
- 107 I2 Rutledge Lake N.W.T. Can.
- 173 H12 Rutog Xizang China
- 173 K12 Rutog Xizang China
- 173 D10 Rutog Xizang China
- 90 F5 Rutshuru Dem. Rep. Congo
- 44 I3 Rutten Neth.
- 111 N3 Rutter Ont. Can.
- 191 I4 Rutul Rus. Fed.
- 20 R4 Ruukki Fin.
- 44 J4 Ruurlo Neth.
- 34 K3 Ruusa Estonia
- 20 T5 Ruvaslahti Fin.
- 73 P6 Ruvo del Monte Italy
- 73 Q5 Ruvo di Puglia Italy
- 20 U3 Ruvozero Rus. Fed.
- 20 U3 Ruvozero, Ozero l. Rus. Fed.
- 93 D7 Ruvuma r. Moz./Tanz.
- 93 C7 Ruvuma admin. reg. Tanz.
- 186 G3 Ruwaydah Saudi Arabia
- 187 N5 Ruways, Ra's ar c. Oman
- 190 F6 Ruwayshid, Wādī watercourse Jordan
- 190 E9 Ruwaytah, Wādī watercourse Jordan
- 190 C9 Ruweijil pt Saudi Arabia
- 187 K3 Ruweis U.A.E.
- Ruwenzori National Park Uganda see Queen Elizabeth National Park
- 40 G5 Ruy France
- 95 G3 Ruya r. Zimbabwe
- 189 Q5 Ruyan Iran
- 93 A5 Ruyigi Burundi
- 64 O5 Ruynes-en-Margeride France
- 30 G2 Ruyton-XI-Towns Shropshire, England U.K.
- 171 I6 Ruyuan Guangdong China
- 19 T6 Ruza Rus. Fed.
- 183 L1 Ruzayevka Kazakh.
- 15 I5 Ruzayevka Rus. Fed.
- 18 H9 Ruzhany Belarus
- 19 R9 Ruzhnoye Rus. Fed.
- 169 M9 Ruzhou Henan China
- 16 I4 Ruzhyn Ukr.
- 57 I2 Ružomberok Slovakia
- 57 I5 Ruzsa Hungary
- 93 A5 Rwanda country Africa
- 90 F5 Rwenzori mts Dem. Rep. Congo/Uganda
- 92 A4 Rwenzori Mountains National Park Uganda
- 22 F5 Ry Denmark
- 22 F4 Ryā r. Denmark
- 184 F3 Ryābād Iran
- 18 L1 Ryabovo Rus. Fed.
- 17 O3 Ryabyna Ukr.
- 203 C13 Ryal Bush South I. N.Z.
- 203 F9 Ryall, Mount South I. N.Z.
- 26 F12 Ryan, Loch in Scotland U.K.
- 17 N4 Ryasne Ukr.
- 17 O3 Ryasne Ukr.
- 17 K6 Ryasnopil' Ukr.
- 19 W7 Ryazan' Rus. Fed.
- Ryazan Oblast admin. div. Rus. Fed. see Ryazanskaya Oblast'
- 19 W6 Ryazanovskiy Rus. Fed.
- 17 S9 Ryazanskaya Rus. Fed.
- 19 X7 Ryazanskaya Oblast' admin. div. Rus. Fed.
- 19 W5 Ryazantsevo Rus. Fed.
- 19 X8 Ryazhsk Rus. Fed.
- 20 V2 Rybachiy, Poluostrov pen. Rus. Fed.
- Rybach'ye Kazakh. see Balykchy
- 19 W7 Rybnoye Rus. Fed.
- 55 L3 Ryboly Pol.
- 19 T3 Ryboreka Rus. Fed.
- 56 F1 Rychliki Pol.
- 56 F1 Rychnov nad Kněžnou Czech Rep.
- 51 L9 Rychnov u Jablonce nad Nisou Czech Rep.
- 55 I2 Rychtal Pol.
- 54 F4 Rychwał Pol.
- 50 H2 Ryck r. Ger.
- 106 G4 Rycroft Alta Can.
- 55 J4 Ryczywół Mazowieckie Pol.
- 54 G2 Ryczywół Wielkopolskie Pol.
- 23 K5 Ryd Sweden
- 212 S2 Rydberg Peninsula Antarctica
- 31 J6 Ryde Isle of Wight, England U.K.

Column 2

- 16 E4 Rydomyl' Ukr.
- 54 G5 Rydułtowy Pol.
- 54 E4 Rydzyna Pol.
- 31 N6 Rye East Sussex, England U.K.
- 31 N6 Rye r. England U.K.
- 119 H3 Rye NY U.S.A.
- 31 N6 Rye Bay England U.K.
- 117 O6 Rye Beach NH U.S.A.
- 122 J3 Ryegate MT U.S.A.
- 124 N1 Rye Patch Dam NV U.S.A.
- 124 N1 Rye Patch Reservoir NV U.S.A.
- 39 J3 Ryes France
- 55 J6 Ryglice Pol.
- 31 L2 Ryhall Rutland, England U.K.
- 16 G3 Ryhiv Ukr.
- 55 J4 Ryki Pol.
- Rykovo Ukr. see Yenakiyeve
- 55 M1 Rykoyshchi Ukr.
- 55 M1 Ryliškiai Lith.
- 205 L5 Rylstone N.S.W. Austr.
- 55 J6 Rymanów Pol.
- 56 E2 Rýmařov Czech Rep.
- 21 P6 Rymättylä Fin.
- 23 R8 Ryn Pol.
- 54 F2 Rynarzewo Pol.
- 14 G1 Ryńsk Pol.
- 182 C4 Ryn-Peski des. Kazakh.
- 54 G2 Ryńsk Pol.
- 55 J2 Ryńskie, Jezioro l. Pol.
- 167 I3 Ryōgami-san mt. Japan
- 166 E4 Ryōhaku-sanchi mts Japan
- 167 I3 Ryōkami Japan
- 164 S7 Ryōri-zaki pt Japan
- 164 P8 Ryōtsu Japan
- 166 D5 Ryōzen-zan mt. Japan
- 55 H2 Ryńkany Moldova see Rişcani
- 17 O1 Ryn'kovka Rus. Fed.
- 21 H6 Rysjedal Norway
- 48 D4 Rysum (Krummhörn) Ger.
- 57 J2 Rysy mt. Pol.
- 55 I4 Rytel Pol.
- 23 K6 Rytterknaegten hill Bornholm Denmark
- 18 H1 Ryttylä Fin.
- 55 H4 Rytwiany Pol.
- 166 D5 Ryūga-dake mt. Japan
- 167 L4 Ryūgasaki Japan
- 166 B8 Ryūjin Japan
- 19 P9 Ryukhovo Rus. Fed.
- Ryukyu Islands Japan see Nansei-shotō
- 216 D4 Ryukyu Trench sea feature N. Pacific Ocean
- 166 D3 Ryūō Shiga Japan
- 167 I4 Ryūō Yamanashi Japan
- 167 H5 Ryūōdō Japan
- 167 Q6 Ryūyō Japan
- 19 O7 Ryzhikovo Rus. Fed.
- 19 N8 Ryzhkavka Belarus
- 16 J4 Ryzyne Ukr.
- 55 J3 Rząca r. Pol.
- 55 H4 Rząśnia Pol.
- 68 G4 Rzav r. Bos.-Herz.
- 54 F2 Rzeczenica Pol.
- 54 G4 Rzeczyca Łódzkie Pol.
- 55 I4 Rzeczyca Łódzkie Pol.
- 55 H4 Rzegnowo Pol.
- 54 E3 Rzepin Pol.
- 55 J6 Rzepiennik Strzyżewski Pol.
- 54 C3 Rzepin Pol.
- 55 K5 Rzeszników Pol.
- 55 K6 Rzeszów Pol.
- 54 G3 Rzgów Pierwszy Pol.
- 15 H5 Rzhaksa Rus. Fed.
- 19 Q8 Rzhanitsa Rus. Fed.
- 18 N9 Rzhavka r. Belarus
- 19 R5 Rzhev Rus. Fed.
- 17 K4 Rzhyshchiv Ukr.
- 55 I4 Rzucow Pol.

S

Column 3

- 131 I4 Sabana de la Mar Dom. Rep.
- 126 □P11 Sabanagrande Hond.
- 131 □¹ Sabana Grande Puerto Rico
- 130 □ Sabanalarga Col.
- Sabana Seca Aruba see Savaneta
- 130 H4 Sabaneta Dom. Rep.
- 130 I8 Sabaneta Venez.
- 156 A2 Sabang Aceh Indon.
- 155 A3 Sabang Sulawesi Indon.
- 155 B5 Sabang Sulawesi Indon.
- 155 C8 Sabang Sulawesi Indon.
- 77 O3 Săbăoani Romania
- 143 F3 Sabará Brazil
- 43 G9 Sabarat France
- 178 C8 Sabari r. India
- 178 D8 Sabarmati r. Gujarat India
- 55 A7 Sabari r. Indon.
- 190 D6 Sabastiya West Bank
- 73 N5 Sabato r. Italy
- 73 K5 Sabaudia Italy
- 73 K5 Sabaudia, Lago di lag. Italy
- 138 C4 Sabaya Bol.
- 186 E6 Şabbah Saudi Arabia
- 191 C3 Sabazho Georgia
- 70 I6 Sabbioneta Italy
- 84 B3 Sabha S. Africa
- 92 C4 Sabena Desert Kenya
- 63 J3 Sabero Spain
- 190 E6 Şabḥā Jordan
- 84 B3 Şabḥā Libya
- 186 G4 Şabḥāʾ Saudi Arabia
- 178 B8 Sabhrai Gujarat India
- 178 F5 Sabi r. India
- Sabi r. Moz./Zimbabwe see Save
- 95 G5 Sabie Moz.
- 97 Q1 Sabie r. Moz./S. Africa
- 95 F5 Sabie S. Africa
- 188 D3 Sabiha Gökçen airport Turkey
- 18 I4 Sabile Latvia
- 116 B9 Sabina OH U.S.A.
- 126 F2 Sabinal Mex.
- 130 E3 Sabinal, Cayo i. Cuba
- 65 N7 Sabinánigo Spain
- 66 E3 Sabinar, Punta del mt. Spain
- 127 I4 Sabinas Mex.
- 121 I12 Sabinas r. Mex.
- 121 F12 Sabinas r. Mex.
- 121 I11 Sabinas Hidalgo Mex.
- 121 I11 Sabine r. LA/TX U.S.A.
- 20 □ Sabine r. Svalbard
- 121 I11 Sabine Lake LA/TX U.S.A.
- 121 I11 Sabine National Wildlife Refuge nature res. LA U.S.A.
- 121 I11 Sabine Pass TX U.S.A.
- 73 J3 Sabini, Monti mts Italy
- 143 F3 Sabinópolis Brazil
- 98 □³ᵉ Sabinosa El Hierro Canary Is
- 57 K2 Sabinov Slovakia
- 191 J5 Sabiote Spain
- 154 C5 Sablan Mindoro Phil.
- 109 H5 Sable, Cape N.S. Can.
- 115 G13 Sable, Cape FL U.S.A.
- 200 □⁵ Sable, Île de i. New Caledonia
- 109 H2 Sable, Lac du l. Que. Can.
- 109 G2 Sable, Rivière du r. Que. Can.
- 99 □³ᵇ Sable Blanc, Récif du rf Mayotte
- 99 □¹ᵃ Sable Island N.S. Can.
- 99 □¹ᵃ Sables, River aux r. Ont. Can.
- Sables, îles aux i. Rodrigues I. Mauritius
- 111 L3 Sables, River aux r. Ont. Can.
- 38 G4 Sables-d'Or-les-Pins France
- 39 K6 Sablé-sur-Sarthe France
- 41 G8 Sablet France
- 41 E7 Sablières France
- 191 I1 Sablinskoye Rus. Fed.
- 41 F10 Sablon, Pointe du pt France
- 41 F6 Sablons France
- 184 G6 Sablū'īyeh Iran
- 140 F3 Saboeiro Brazil
- 64 C5 Sabóia Port.
- 89 H3 Sabon Kafi Niger
- 62 F6 Sabor r. Port.
- 88 E3 Sabou Burkina
- 90 B3 Sabourin, Lac l. Que. Can.
- 84 B1 Sabrātah Libya
- 43 C7 Sabres France
- 213 H2 Sabrina Coast Antarctica
- 62 E6 Sabrosa Port.
- 154 C1 Sabtang i. Phil.
- 62 E3 Sabugal Port.
- 62 F8 Sabugal Port.
- 64 C3 Sabugueiro Évora Port.
- 62 E8 Sabugueiro Guarda Port.
- 155 B4 Sabulu Sulawesi Indon.
- 191 K5 Sabunçu Turkey
- 79 L3 Sabuncu Turkey
- 157 K8 Sabunten i. Indon.
- 167 I2 Saburō-yama mt. Japan
- 186 F7 Sabyā Saudi Arabia
- 184 G3 Sabzawar Afgh. see Shindand
- 184 F2 Sabzevār Fārs Iran
- 184 F1 Sabzvārān Hormozgan Iran
- 50 F7 Saal r. Ger.
- 53 O6 Saalach r. Ger.
- 53 L4 Saal an der Donau Ger.
- 49 J10 Saal an der Saale Ger.
- 53 L4 Saalbach r. Ger.
- 58 S5 Saalbach-Hinterglemm Austria
- 51 E10 Saalburg Ger.
- 53 N6 Saaldorf Ger.
- 51 E8 Saale park Ger.
- 51 E7 Saale r. Ger.
- 50 F2 Saaler Bodden inlet Ger.
- 37 N7 Saales France
- 51 D9 Saalfeld Ger.
- 58 S5 Saalfelden am Steinernen Meer Austria
- 36 A4 Saâne r. France
- 70 C2 Saane r. Switz.
- 70 C3 Saanen Switz.
- 106 F5 Saanich B.C. Can.
- Saar land Ger. see Saarland
- 52 B2 Saar r. Ger.
- 52 B2 Saarbrücken Ger.
- 52 B2 Saarburg Ger.
- 18 J3 Saare Estonia
- 18 J3 Saaremaa i. Estonia
- 52 A3 Saaren Estonia
- 52 B2 Saar-Hunsrück, Naturpark Ger.
- 21 T6 Saari Fin.
- 20 R5 Saarijärvi Fin.
- 20 S3 Saari-Kämä Fin.
- 20 P2 Saarikoski Fin.
- 20 S2 Saaristomeren Kansallispuisto nat. park Fin. see Skärgårdshavets nationalpark
- 52 B3 Saarland land Ger.
- 52 B3 Saarlouis Ger.
- 52 B3 Saarwellingen Ger.
- 70 H2 Saas Fee Switz.
- 70 D3 Saas Grund Switz.
- 70 D3 Saastal val. Switz.
- 85 F6 Saatâ Sudan
- 191 H6 Saatlı Azer.
- 18 K4 Saatse Estonia
- 147 F5 Saavedra Buenos Aires Arg.
- 131 L5 Saba i. Neth. Antilles
- 84 □ Sab' Âbâr Syria
- 49 I7 Sababurg Ger.
- 70 H6 Sabuie i. (Serbia Serb. and Mont.)
- 66 D4 Sabadell Spain
- 89 D4 Sabadou Baranama Guinea
- 166 D4 Sae-gawa r. Japan
- 93 A6 Sabagusi Tanz.
- 158 B3 Sabah state Malaysia
- 156 D3 Sabak Malaysia
- 155 A7 Sabalana i. Indon.
- 155 A7 Sabalana, Kepulauan is Indon.
- 124 J7 Sacramento Mountains NM U.S.A.
- 130 □ Sabana, Archipiélago de is Cuba

Column 4

- 73 I3 Sacrofano Italy
- 57 L5 Săcueni Romania
- 139 F3 Sacuriuiná r. Brazil
- 127 O8 Sacxán Mex.
- 93 □ Sada Mayotte
- 62 D2 Sada Spain
- 43 B10 Sádaba Spain
- 63 R4 Sádaba Spain
- 178 G6 Sadabad Uttar Prad. India
- 184 D7 Sa'dābād Iran
- 190 E4 Şadad Syria
- 186 F7 Şa'dah Yemen
- 186 F7 Şa'dah governorate Yemen
- 72 C8 Sadali Sardegna Italy
- 165 J13 Sada-misaki pt Japan
- 155 A5 Sadang r. Indon.
- 93 C6 Sadani Tanz.
- 159 E11 Sadao Thai.
- 176 E4 Sadārak Azer.
- 176 E4 Sadasivpet Andhra Prad. India
- 185 N5 Sadda Pak.
- 190 E7 Saddat as Sultānī Jordan
- 189 L7 Saddat al Hindīyah Iraq
- 26 E11 Saddell Argyll and Bute, Scotland U.K.
- 97 P1 Saddleback pass S. Africa
- 121 D8 Saddleback Mesa mt. NM U.S.A.
- 207 J3 Saddle Hill Qld Austr.
- 203 C8 Saddle Hill mt. South I. N.Z.
- 177 M6 Saddle Peak hill Andaman & Nicobar Is India
- 159 G9 Sa Đéc Vietnam
- 187 L7 Sadh Oman
- 178 E4 Sadhaura Haryana India
- 181 □ Sadhoowa Trin. and Tob.
- 92 B2 Sadi Eth.
- 184 H9 Sadij watercourse Iran
- 185 M7 Sadiqabad Pak.
- 191 H5 Sädiqli Azer.
- 179 O6 Sadiya Assam India
- 189 M7 Sa'dīyah, Hawr as imp. l. Iraq
- 187 L3 Sa'dīyat i. U.A.E.
- 95 □K2 Sadjoavato Madag.
- 184 G3 Sadkī Iran
- 55 I4 Sadki Pol.
- 54 G2 Sadlinki Pol.
- 54 G2 Sadłno Pol.
- 19 R6 Sadnoye Rus. Fed.
- 31 N2 Sadham Toney Norfolk, England U.K.
- 17 T2 Sadove Voronezhskaya Oblast' Rus. Fed.
- 55 S5 Sadowie Pol.
- 67 J8 Sa Dragonera i. Spain
- 55 J5 Sadowne Pol.
- 92 C7 Sadūt Egypt
- 22 G4 Sæby Denmark
- 48 I1 Sæd Denmark
- 116 E7 Saegertown PA U.S.A.
- 63 O9 Saelices Spain
- 63 J7 Saelices de la Sal Spain
- 63 J3 Saelices del Rio Spain
- 63 J3 Saelices de Mayorga Spain
- 49 E6 Saerbeck Ger.
- 45 I9 Saeul Lux.
- Safad Israel see Zefat
- 84 F2 Safājah Libya
- 43 C7 Safáfah, Jazīrat i. Egypt
- 88 E3 Safané Burkina
- Safárikovo Slovakia see Tornaľa
- 191 I6 Safārī Iran
- 200 □³ᵇ Safata Bay Samoa
- 189 M8 Safayal Maqūf well Iraq
- 185 N2 Safed Khirs mts Afgh.
- 185 N4 Safed Koh mts Afgh./Pak.
- 188 I1 Saffārīnīyah, Ra's as pt Saudi Arabia
- 22 I2 Säffle Sweden
- 125 W9 Safford AZ U.S.A.
- 31 M4 Saffron Walden Essex, England U.K.
- 86 C2 Safi Morocco
- 184 G3 Safiabad Iran
- 185 H3 Safīd, Darya-ye r. Afgh.
- 184 E4 Safīd Dasht Iran
- 184 I6 Safīdabeh Iran
- 184 I4 Safīd Kūh mts Iran
- 184 H8 Safīd, Kūh-e mt. Iran
- 187 M7 Safīd Yemen
- 143 G3 Safiras, Serra das mts Brazil
- 190 D5 Şāfītā Syria
- 185 J8 Safī, Jaz esc. Iran
- 187 M4 Sa'īd Bin Şahrān Oman
- 185 J8 Sa'īd Iran
- 86 □ Safidiye Morocco
- 88 B2 Saïnsoubou Senegal
- 40 E4 Sains-Richaumont France
- 29 J4 St Bees Scotland U.K.
- 41 I7 St Abb's Head Scotland U.K.
- 65 □ St Abb's Head Gibraltar
- 41 I7 St Abbs Scottish Borders, Scotland U.K.
- 36 E3 St-Acheul France
- 41 B8 St-Affrique, Causse de plat. France
- 90 A5 St Abb's Head
- 29 N4 Sacriston Durham, England U.K.

Column 5

- 122 I6 Sage WY U.S.A.
- 122 I2 Sage Creek r. MT U.S.A.
- 23 K1 Sågen Sweden
- 27 J6 Saggart Rep. of Ireland
- 20 N3 Saggat l. Sweden
- 190 C8 Sagi, Har mt. Israel
- 184 F5 Saghand Iran
- 185 J5 Saghar Afgh.
- 119 K3 Sag Harbor NY U.S.A.
- Saghyz Kazakh. see Sagiz
- 111 K6 Saginaw MI U.S.A.
- 110 B3 Saginaw MN U.S.A.
- 111 K6 Saginaw Bay MI U.S.A.
- 79 J3 Sağırlar Turkey
- 73 L3 Sagittario r. Italy
- 182 E4 Sagiz Atyrauskaya Oblast' Kazakh.
- 182 F3 Sagiz r. Kazakh. see Sagyz
- 79 I2 Sağlamtaş Turkey
- 191 J7 Sağlasär Azer.
- 88 C5 Saglei peie Liberia
- 109 I1 Saglek Bay Nfld and Lab. Can.
- Saglouc Que. Can. see Salluit
- 65 N5 Sagra r. Spain
- 146 B4 Sagrada Familia Chile
- 64 B6 Sagres Port.
- 65 K6 Sagres, Ponta de pt Port.
- 168 E4 Sagsay watercourse Mongolia
- 168 E4 Sagsay Rajasthan India
- 155 C8 Sagu Indon.
- 158 B4 Sagu Myanmar
- 77 J2 Sagu Romania
- 123 K7 Saguache CO U.S.A.
- 123 L8 Saguache Creek r. CO U.S.A.
- 130 F3 Sagua de Tánamo Cuba
- 130 C2 Sagua la Grande Cuba
- Sagunt Spain see Sagunto
- Saguntum Spain see Sagunto
- 67 E8 Sagunto Spain
- 182 F3 Sagyndyk, Mys pt Kazakh.
- 190 E7 Şaḥāb Jordan
- 178 G5 Sahabab Uttar Prad. India
- 120 I6 Sahagún Col.
- 63 J3 Sahagún Spain
- 21 R6 Sahalahti Fin.
- 31 N2 Saham Toney Norfolk, England U.K.
- 184 B3 Sahand, Kūh-e mt. Iran
- 191 D5 Sahandöken Turkey
- 86 G6 Sahara des. Africa
- 178 F5 Saharanpur Uttar Prad. India
- 208 G6 Sahara Well W.A. Austr.
- 179 K7 Sadras Tamil Nadu India
- 179 L5 Saharsa Bihar India
- 184 F4 Sahat, Kūh-e hill Iran
- 95 □K4 Sahavato Madag.
- 187 I4 Sahbā', Wādī as watercourse Saudi Arabia
- 191 G5 Şahbuz Silsiläsi hills Armenia/Azer.
- 92 B3 Sahel reg. Africa
- 186 D7 Sahel prov. Eritrea
- 88 D3 Sahel, Réserve Partielle du nature res. Burkina
- 179 N7 Sahibganj Jharkhand India
- 185 O6 Sahiwal Punjab Pak.
- 185 O5 Sahiwal Punjab Pak.
- 186 D2 Sahl al Maţran Saudi Arabia
- 186 E5 Sahl Rakbah plain Saudi Arabia
- 187 M3 Saḩm Oman
- 184 B4 Saḩneh Iran
- 189 L8 Şaḩrāʾ al Ḩijārah reg. Iraq
- Sahra Qinghai China see Zadoi
- 155 B3 Sahu Halmahera Indon.
- 126 F3 Sahuaripa Mex.
- 125 V10 Sahuarita AZ U.S.A.
- 128 E5 Sahuayo Mex.
- 66 F2 Sahún Spain
- 17 L4 Sahun'ya Ukr.
- 159 I7 Sa Huynh Vietnam
- 191 I7 Sahveletverenik Dağları mts Turkey
- 57 H3 Sahy Slovakia
- 178 E9 Sahyadriparvat Range hills India
- 190 D3 Şaḩyūn tourist site Syria
- 178 I7 Sai r. India
- 153 J8 Saibai Island Qld Austr.
- 159 E11 Sai Buri Thai.
- 159 E11 Sai Buri, Mae Nam r. Thai.
- 87 F2 Saïda Alg.
- 190 D5 Saïda Lebanon
- 84 □ Saïda Morocco
- 189 L4 Sa'īdīyeh Iran see Solţānīyeh
- 179 L7 Saidpur Uttar Prad. India
- 185 O4 Saidu Pak.
- 88 B2 Sai-gawa r. Japan
- 166 E4 Sa-gawa r. Japan
- 188 F3 Şafranbolu Turkey
- 41 I9 Saignelégier Switz.
- 40 C5 Saignes France
- 165 K10 Saigō Japan
- Saigon Vietnam see Hồ Chí Minh
- 179 N8 Saiha Mizoram India
- 169 M5 Saihan Tal Nei Mongol China
- 168 G6 Saihan Toroi Nei Mongol China
- 20 T3 Saija Fin.
- 165 K13 Saijō Japan
- 165 G13 Saikai National Park Japan
- 95 □K4 Saikanosy Masoala pen.
- 165 I14 Saiki Japan
- 158 B8 Sagaing Myanmar
- 171 □J7 Sai Kung H.K. China
- 171 □J7 Sai Kung H.K. China
- 178 E8 Sailana Madh. Prad. India
- 43 E2 Saillans France

Column 6

- 40 E2 St-Agnan Bourgogne France
- 40 D3 St-Agnan Bourgogne France
- 41 G7 St-Agnan-en-Vercors France
- 42 C4 St-Agnant France
- 42 H3 St-Agnant-de-Versillat France
- 30 B7 St Agnes Cornwall, England U.K.
- 30 □ St Agnes i. England U.K.
- 41 E6 St-Agrève France
- 42 G1 St-Aignan France
- 39 I6 St-Aignan-sur-Roë France
- 42 D5 St-Aigulin France
- 40 F4 St-Alban France
- 38 F4 St-Alban France
- 41 H6 St-Alban-d'Ay France
- 40 H5 St-Alban-Leysse France
- 109 K4 St Alban's Nfld and Lab. Can.
- 31 L4 St Albans Hertfordshire, England U.K.
- 117 L4 St Albans VT U.S.A.
- 116 D10 St Albans WV U.S.A.
- St Alban's Head England U.K. see St Aldhelm's Head
- 41 C7 St-Alban-sur-Limagnole France
- 106 H4 St Albert Alta Can.
- 39 J3 St-Amand France
- 40 C1 St-Amand-en-Puisaye France
- 36 F3 St-Amand-les-Eaux France
- 39 N6 St-Amand-Longpré France
- 40 B3 St-Amand-Montrond France
- 38 I6 St-Amand-sur-Fion France
- 41 B7 St-Amans France
- 41 B7 St-Amans-des-Cots France
- 42 I5 St-Amans-Soult France
- 42 E4 St-Amant-de-Boixe France
- 41 D8 St-Amant-Roche-Savine France
- 40 C5 St-Amant-Tallende France
- 37 N8 St-Amarin France
- 109 G3 St-Ambroise Que. Can.
- 41 E8 St-Ambroix France
- 40 G4 St-Amour France
- 41 F9 St-Andiol France
- 43 J10 St-André Languedoc-Roussillon France
- 41 K9 St-André Provence-Alpes-Côte d'Azur France
- 99 □¹ᵇ St-André Mauritius
- 99 □¹ᶜ St-André Réunion
- St-André, Cap pt Madag. see Vilanandro, Tanjona
- 36 B6 St-André, Plaine de plain France
- 42 D6 St-André-de-Cubzac France
- 36 B6 St-André-de-l'Eure France
- 41 J7 St-André-d'Embrun France
- 43 B8 St-André-de-Seignanx France
- 41 D8 St-André-de-Valborgne France
- 40 D2 St-André-en-Morvan France
- 40 H5 St-André-le-Gaz France
- 41 J7 St-André-les-Alpes France
- 36 H7 St-André-les-Vergers France
- 130 □ St Andrew county Jamaica
- 117 □R3 St Andrews N.B. Can.
- 203 F11 St Andrews South I. N.Z.
- 26 L9 St Andrews Fife, Scotland U.K.
- 115 G10 St Andrew Sound inlet GA U.S.A.
- 42 I4 St-Angel France
- 130 □ St Ann parish Jamaica
- 41 C8 St-Anthème France
- 109 K3 St Anthony Nfld and Lab. Can.
- 122 H5 St Anthony ID U.S.A.
- 130 □ St Ann's Bay Jamaica
- 110 B6 St Ansgar IA U.S.A.
- 40 D5 St-Anthème France
- 40 G8 St-Antonin-Noble-Val France
- 42 D5 St-Apollinaire France
- 41 D6 St-Arcons-d'Allier France
- 205 L7 St Arnaud Vic. Austr.
- 203 G8 St Arnaud South I. N.Z.
- 203 G8 St Arnaud Range mts South I. N.Z.
- 36 C6 St-Arnoult-en-Yvelines France
- 30 F1 St Asaph Denbighshire, Wales U.K.
- 206 C1 St Asaph Bay N.T. Austr.
- 42 F5 St-Astier Aquitaine France
- 42 E5 St-Astier Aquitaine France
- 30 F5 St Athan Vale of Glamorgan, Wales U.K.
- 42 I5 St-Auban France
- 41 J9 St-Auban-sur-l'Ouvèze France
- 40 G2 St-Aubin France
- 38 H5 St-Aubin-d'Aubigné France
- 38 I5 St-Aubin-du-Cormier France
- 36 B5 St-Aubin-lès-Elbeuf France
- 39 M3 St-Aubin-sur-Mer France
- 42 I4 St-Augustin France
- 109 J3 St Augustin Que. Can.
- 115 G11 St Augustine FL U.S.A.
- 42 C5 St-Aulaye France
- 31 □ St Austell Cornwall, England U.K.
- 30 □ St Austell Bay England U.K.
- 30 C7 St-Avertin France
- 37 M5 St-Avold France
- 37 N6 St-Ay France
- 41 J10 St-Aygulf France
- 40 H5 St-Baldoph France
- 109 H3 St Barbe Nfld and Lab. Can.
- 131 L5 St-Barthélemy i. West Indies
- 43 H10 St-Barthélemy, Pic de mt. France
- 43 E8 St-Barthélemy-d'Agenais France
- 38 K7 St-Barthélemy-d'Anjou France
- 42 E5 St-Barthélemy-de-Bellegarde France
- 41 E6 St-Barthélemy-de-Vals France
- 203 D11 St Bathans South I. N.Z.
- 203 D11 St Bathans, Mount South I. N.Z.
- 41 D9 St-Bauzille-de-Putois France
- 41 B9 St-Béat France
- 41 D9 St-Beauzély France
- 29 J5 St Bees Cumbria, England U.K.
- 29 J4 St Bees Head England U.K.
- 40 C2 St-Benin-d'Azy France
- 43 E8 St-Benoît Languedoc-Roussillon France
- 42 E2 St-Benoît Poitou-Charentes France
- 99 □¹ᶜ St-Benoît Réunion
- 39 P7 St-Benoît-du-Sault France
- 42 C6 St-Benoît-sur-Loire France
- 42 E5 St-Bernard France
- 41 B8 St-Bertrand-de-Comminges France
- 43 F9 St-Biez-en-Belin France
- 70 B1 St-Blaise Switz.
- 37 N7 St-Blin-Semilly France
- 40 F3 St-Bonnet-de-Bellac France
- 40 F4 St-Bonnet-de-Joux France
- 41 I7 St-Bonnet-en-Champsaur France
- 40 C5 St-Bonnet-le-Château France
- 42 C6 St-Bonnet-sur-Gironde France
- 38 H7 St-Branchs France
- 38 F5 St Brelade Channel Is
- 40 D3 St-Brevin-les-Pins France

Column 7

- 38 G4 St-Briac-sur-Mer France
- 41 G7 St Briavels Gloucestershire, England U.K.
- 36 H5 St-Brice-Courcelles France
- 38 I5 St-Brice-en-Coglès France
- 30 B4 St Brides Pembrokeshire, Wales U.K.
- 30 B4 St Bride's Bay Wales U.K.
- 30 E5 St Brides Major Vale of Glamorgan, Wales U.K.
- 38 F4 St-Brieuc France
- 38 G4 St-Brieuc, Baie de b. France
- 36 G8 St-Bris-le-Vineux France
- 40 E2 St-Brisson France
- 37 I8 St-Broing-les-Moines France
- 30 □ St Buryan Cornwall, England U.K.

Column 8

- 39 M6 St-Calais France
- 41 G9 St-Cannat France
- 38 G4 St-Cast-le-Guildo France
- 108 E5 St Catharines Ont. Can.
- 130 □ St Catherine parish Jamaica
- 131 □¹ St Catherine, Mount hill Grenada
- 109 K4 St Catherine's Nfld and Lab. Can.
- 115 G10 St Catherines Island GA U.S.A.
- 115 □¹ St Catherine's Point Bermuda
- 31 J6 St Catherine's Point England U.K.
- 41 C7 St-Céré France
- 70 A3 St-Cergue Switz.
- 40 I4 St-Cergues France
- 42 I5 St-Cernin France
- 117 L3 St-Césaire Que. Can.
- 41 J7 St-Chaffrey France
- 41 E6 St-Chamas France
- 41 E6 St-Chamond France
- 41 E9 St-Chaptes France
- 111 N3 St Charles Ont. Can.
- 122 I5 St Charles ID U.S.A.
- 116 I10 St Charles MD U.S.A.
- 111 J6 St Charles MI U.S.A.
- 120 J6 St Charles MO U.S.A.
- 40 C5 St-Chef France
- 42 C5 St-Chély-d'Apcher France
- 41 B7 St-Chély-d'Aubrac France
- 41 I10 St-Chinian France
- 41 G8 St-Christol France
- 42 C5 St-Christol-lès-Alès France
- 42 C5 St-Christoly-de-Blaye France
- 42 C5 St-Christoly-Médoc France
- 40 C5 St-Christophe Italy
- 39 O7 St-Christophe-en-Bazelle France
- 40 E4 St-Christophe-en-Brionnais France
- 43 C5 St-Ciers-sur-Gironde France
- 43 C8 St-Cirgues-en-Montagne France
- 43 H7 St-Cirq-Lapopie France
- 108 D5 St Clair r. Can./U.S.A.
- 111 L7 St Clair MI U.S.A.
- 118 C3 St Clair PA U.S.A.
- 111 L7 St Clair, Lake Can./U.S.A.
- 36 C5 St-Clair-sur-Epte France
- 39 I3 St-Clair-sur-l'Elle France
- 117 □R3 St Clairsville OH U.S.A.
- 43 F8 St-Clar France
- 42 F8 St-Claud France
- 40 H4 St-Claude France
- 131 □ St-Claude Guadeloupe
- 30 D4 St Clears Carmarthenshire, Wales U.K.
- 38 G5 St Clement Channel Is
- 39 F7 St-Clément Bourgogne France
- 41 D8 St-Clément Lorraine France
- 37 M6 St-Clément Lorraine France
- 41 D9 St-Clément-de-Rivière France
- 115 G11 St Cloud FL U.S.A.
- 120 G2 St Cloud MN U.S.A.
- 30 C7 St Columb Major Cornwall, England U.K.
- 26 M7 St Combs Aberdeenshire, Scotland U.K.
- 39 I6 St-Constant France
- 36 C5 St-Cosme-en-Vairais France
- 42 F5 St-Crépin-de-Richemont France
- 105 L3 St Croix r. Can./U.S.A.
- 110 A4 St Croix r. WI U.S.A.
- 131 K5 St Croix i. Virgin Is (U.S.A.)
- 110 A4 St Croix Falls WI U.S.A.
- 42 E5 St-Cyprien Aquitaine France
- 43 K10 St-Cyprien Languedoc-Roussillon France
- 43 G7 St-Cyprien Midi-Pyrénées France
- 36 D6 St-Cyr-l'École France
- 41 H10 St-Cyr-sur-Mer France
- 41 J8 St-Cyr-sur-Morin France
- 131 □¹ St David county Trin. and Tob.
- 125 V10 St David AZ U.S.A.
- 110 D9 St David IL U.S.A.
- 30 B4 St David's Pembrokeshire, Wales U.K.
- 30 B4 St David's Head Wales U.K.
- 115 □¹ St David's Island Bermuda
- 30 B7 St Day Cornwall, England U.K.
- 43 □ St-Denis France
- 99 □¹ᶜ St-Denis Réunion
- 39 □ St-Denis-d'Anjou France
- 42 D6 St-Denis-de-Gastines France
- 38 K6 St-Denis-de-Jouhet France
- 40 D3 St-Denis-d'Oléron France
- 39 K5 St-Denis-d'Orques France
- St-Denis-du-Sig Alg. see Sig
- 40 G4 St-Denis-en-Bugey France
- 40 G4 St-Denis-lès-Bourg France
- 30 C7 St Dennis Cornwall, England U.K.
- 41 E6 St-Désert France
- 41 E6 St-Didier-en-Velay France
- 40 G4 St-Didier-sur-Chalaronne France
- 40 D5 St-Didier-sur-Rochefort France
- 37 M7 St-Dié France
- 40 I5 St-Dier-d'Auvergne France
- 37 I6 St-Dizier France
- 41 D7 St-Dizier-Leyrenne France
- 38 G5 St Dogmaels Pembrokeshire, Wales U.K.
- 38 G5 St-Dolay France
- 38 F5 St-Dominec France
- 42 E2 St-Donan France
- 41 F8 St-Donat-sur-l'Herbasse France
- 39 P7 St-Doulchard France
- 42 L6 St-Adresse France
- 41 F8 Ste-Alvère France
- 107 L5 Sainte Anne Alta Can.
- 99 □¹ᶜ Ste-Anne Guadeloupe
- 99 □¹ᵇ Ste-Anne Réunion
- 99 □¹ Ste-Anne i. Seychelles
- 107 L4 Sainte Anne, Lac l. Alta Can.
- 99 □²ᵇ Ste-Anne Réunion
- 109 H4 Ste-Anne-de-Beaupré Que. Can.
- 109 G4 Ste-Anne-de-Madawaska N.B. Can.
- 117 Q1 Ste-Anne-de-Portneuf Que. Can.
- 109 H3 Ste-Anne-des-Monts Que. Can.
- 117 □ Ste-Anne-du-Lac Que. Can.
- 117 □O2 Ste-Camille-de-Lellis Que. Can.
- 90 A5 Ste-Catherine, Pointe pt Gabon
- 41 F8 Ste-Cécile-les-Vignes France

Ste-Croix to St-Zacharie 331

40 G3 Ste-Croix *Bourgogne* France
41 G7 Ste-Croix *Rhône-Alpes* France
70 B2 Ste-Croix Switz.
41 I9 Ste-Croix, Barrage de *dam* France
41 I9 Ste-Croix, Lac de *l.* France
43 G9 Ste-Croix-Volvestre France
08 F4 Ste-Émélie-de-l'Énergie *Que.* Can.
43 C9 Ste-Engrâce France
41 C8 Ste-Énimie France
41 B8 Ste-Eulalie d'Olt France
43 B7 Ste-Eulalie-en-Born France
42 H3 Ste-Feyre France
41 C6 Ste-Florine France
42 H5 Ste-Fortunade France
43 G9 Ste-Foy-de-Peyrolières France
43 E6 Ste-Foy-la-Grande France
40 E5 Ste-Foy-l'Argentière France
40 F5 Ste-Foy-lès-Lyon France
40 J5 Ste-Foy-Tarentaise France
39 L4 Ste-Gauburge-Ste-Colombe France
42 B3 Ste-Gemme-la-Plaine France
36 D5 Ste-Geneviève France
20 J7 Sainte Genevieve *MO* U.S.A.
41 B7 Ste-Geneviève-sur-Argence France
41 H6 St-Égrève France
42 C6 Ste-Hélène France
42 B2 Ste-Hermine France
17 □O2 Ste-Justine *Que.* Can.
17 □P1 St-Éleuthère *Que.* Can.
04 D4 St Elias, Cape *AK* U.S.A.
06 A2 St Elias, Mount *AK* U.S.A.
06 A2 St Elias Mountains *Y.T.* Can.
37 H3 St-Élie Fr. Guiana
43 F7 Ste-Livrade-sur-Lot France
43 G9 St-Élix-le-Château France
43 E9 St-Élix-Theux France
30 □ St Elizabeth *parish* Jamaica
39 P7 Ste-Lizaigne France
40 B4 St-Éloy-les-Mines France
31 □3 Ste-Luce Martinique
72 C4 Ste-Lucie-de-Tallano *Corse* France
09 H3 Ste-Marguerite *r. Que.* Can.
09 H3 Sainte-Marguerite 3 *resr Que.* Can.
37 M7 Ste-Marguerite France
09 G4 Ste-Marie *Que.* Can.
41 B7 Ste-Marie *Auvergne* France
43 K10 Ste-Marie *Languedoc-Roussillon* France
31 □3 Ste-Marie Martinique
99 □1c Ste-Marie Réunion
Ste-Marie, Cap *c.* Madag. *see* Vohimena, Tanjona
37 N7 Ste-Marie-aux-Mines France
39 M7 Ste-Maure, Plateau de France
43 E7 Ste-Maure-de-Peyriac France
42 F1 Ste-Maure-de-Touraine France
41 J10 Ste-Maxime France
37 I5 Ste-Menehould France
38 I3 Ste-Mère-Église France
40 E3 St-Émiland France
43 D6 St-Émilion France
30 C6 St Endellion *Cornwall, England* U.K.
30 C7 St Enoder *Cornwall, England* U.K.
42 G5 Ste-Orse France
38 H7 Ste-Pazanne France
39 K8 Ste-Radegonde France
36 G4 St-Erme-Outre-et-Ramecourt France
31 □2 Ste-Rose Guadeloupe
99 □1c Ste-Rose Réunion
07 L5 Sainte Rose du Lac *Man.* Can.
30 B7 St Erth *Cornwall, England* U.K.
42 C4 Saintes France
31 □2 Saintes, Îles des *is* Guadeloupe
40 F2 Ste-Sabine France
36 H7 Ste-Savine France
42 I3 Ste-Sévère-sur-Indre France
41 E6 Ste-Sigolène France
31 □3 St-Esprit Martinique
43 B9 St-Esteben France
42 C5 St-Estèphe France
43 J10 St-Estève France
39 K5 Ste-Suzanne France
99 □1c Ste-Suzanne Réunion
17 L3 Ste-Thérèse *Que.* Can.
06 F1 Sainte Thérèse, Lac *l. N.W.T.* Can.
41 E6 St-Étienne France
42 I6 St-Étienne-Cantalès France
43 B9 St-Étienne-de-Baïgorry France
41 H6 St-Étienne-de-Crossey France
41 E7 St-Étienne-de-Fontbellon France
42 H3 St-Étienne-de-Fursac France
41 D7 St-Étienne-de-Lugdarès France
38 H7 St-Étienne-de-Montluc France
41 G6 St-Étienne-de-St-Geoirs France
41 J8 St-Étienne-de-Tinée France
43 G7 St-Étienne-de-Tulmont France
40 G4 St-Étienne-du-Bois France
36 B5 St-Étienne-du-Rouvray France
41 H7 St-Étienne-en-Dévoluy France
41 H8 St-Étienne-les-Orgues France
37 M7 St-Étienne-lès-Remiremont France
41 D8 St-Étienne-Vallée-Française France
41 H9 Ste-Tulle France
17 K3 St Eugene *Ont.* Can.
17 □Q1 St-Eusèbe *Que.* Can.
17 L3 St-Eustache *Que.* Can.
38 C6 St-Évarzec France
36 G8 Ste-Vertu France
41 H9 Ste-Victoire, Montagne *mt.* France
09 G3 St-Fabien *Que.* Can.
97 O6 St Faith's S. Africa
40 C1 St-Fargeau France
09 F3 St-Félicien *Que.* Can.
41 F6 St-Félicien France
11 P1 St-Félix-de-Dalquier *Que.* Can.
43 H9 St-Félix-Lauragais France
26 M7 St Fergus *Aberdeenshire, Scotland* U.K.
43 E6 St-Ferme France
27 K4 Saintfield *Northern Ireland* U.K.
26 H10 St Fillans *Perth and Kinross, Scotland* U.K.
37 L7 St-Firmin *Lorraine* France
41 I7 St-Firmin *Provence-Alpes-Côte d'Azur* France
36 G7 St-Flavy France
72 C2 St-Florent *Corse* France
72 C2 St-Florent, Golfe de *b. Corse* France
42 B2 St-Florent-des-Bois France
36 G7 St-Florentin France
39 I7 St-Florent-le-Vieil France
42 I2 St-Florent-sur-Cher France
90 D2 St Floris, Parc National *nat. park* C.A.R.
41 C6 St-Flour France
39 N8 St-Flovier France
40 F5 St-Fons France
42 C5 St-Fort-sur-Gironde France
43 F9 St-Frajou France
121 J10 St Francesville *LA* U.S.A.
117 □Q1 St Francis *r.* Can./U.S.A.
120 E6 St Francis *KS* U.S.A.
117 □Q1 St Francis *ME* U.S.A.
121 J8 St Francis *r. AR/MO* U.S.A.
97 I10 St Francis, Cape S. Africa
97 J10 St Francis Bay S. Africa
204 D5 St Francis Isles *S.A.* Austr.
109 F4 St-François *r. Que.* Can.
131 □2 St-François Guadeloupe
99 □2 St François *i.* Seychelles
109 G4 St-François, Lac *l. Que.* Can.
41 I6 St-François-Longchamp France
117 □Q2 St Froid Lake *ME* U.S.A.
41 E7 St-Front France
42 E5 St-Front-de-Pradoux France
39 I8 St-Fulgent France
40 E5 St-Galmier France
39 L3 St-Gatien-des-Bois France
43 F9 St-Gaudens France
42 G2 St-Gaultier France
117 □O3 St-Gédéon *Que.* Can.
43 D8 St-Gein France
41 D9 St-Gély-du-Fesc France
41 E6 St-Genest-Malifaux France
40 F3 St-Gengoux-le-National France
41 E9 St-Geniès-de-Malgoirès France
41 I8 St-Geniez France
41 B8 St-Geniez-d'Olt France
42 C5 St-Genis-de-Saintonge France
43 J10 St-Génis-des-Fontaines France
40 F5 St-Genis-Laval France
40 I4 St-Genis-Pouilly France
40 H5 St-Genix-sur-Guiers France
30 C6 St Gennys *Cornwall, England* U.K.
39 N8 St-Genou France
41 H6 St-Geoire-en-Valdaine France
205 L3 St George *Qld* Austr.
207 J4 St George *r. Qld* Austr.
115 □1 St George Bermuda
109 H4 St George *N.B.* Can.
131 □7 St George *county* Trin. and Tob.
104 B4 St George *AK* U.S.A.
115 G9 St George *SC* U.S.A.
125 S4 St George *UT* U.S.A.
153 L7 St George, Cape *New Ireland* P.N.G.
122 B6 St George, Point *CA* U.S.A.
205 M6 St George Head *A.C.T.* Austr.
104 B4 St George Island *AK* U.S.A.
115 E11 St George Island *FL* U.S.A.
208 H5 St George Range *hills W.A.* Austr.
109 J3 St George's *Nfld and Lab.* Can.
109 G4 St-Georges *Que.* Can.
137 I4 St-Georges Fr. Guiana
131 □6 St George's Grenada
118 D5 St Georges *DE* U.S.A.
109 J3 St George's Bay *Nfld and Lab.* Can.
109 I4 St George's Bay *N.S.* Can.
39 J5 St-Georges-Buttavent France
127 P9 St George's Cay *i.* Belize
177 M9 St George's Channel *Andaman & Nicobar Is* India
153 L7 St George's Channel P.N.G.
27 J9 St George's Channel Rep. of Ireland/U.K.
41 D6 St-Georges-d'Aurac France
41 H6 St-Georges-de-Commiers France
42 C4 St-Georges-de-Didonne France
41 B8 St-Georges-de-Luzençon France
40 B5 St-Georges-de-Mons France
38 I8 St-Georges-de-Montaigu France
40 F4 St-Georges-de-Reneins France
39 J4 St-Georges-des-Groseillers France
40 G5 St-Georges-d'Espéranche France
42 B4 St-Georges-d'Oléron France
39 M3 St-Georges-du-Vièvre France
40 D5 St-Georges-en-Couzan France
115 □1 St George's Harbour *b.* Bermuda
115 □1 St George's Island Bermuda
39 L8 St-Georges-lès-Baillargeaux France
36 G8 St-Georges-sur-Baulche France
39 N7 St-Georges-sur-Cher France
36 B7 St-Georges-sur-Eure France
39 J7 St-Georges-sur-Loire France
43 B8 St-Geours-de-Maremne France
40 D4 St-Gérand-le-Puy France
110 E4 St Germain *WI* U.S.A.
40 C3 St-Germain-Chassenay France
41 D8 St-Germain-de-Calberte France
39 M5 St-Germain-de-la-Coudre France
40 C4 St-Germain-des-Fossés France
42 C5 St-Germain-d'Esteuil France
43 G6 St-Germain-du-Bel-Air France
40 G3 St-Germain-du-Bois France
39 L5 St-Germain-du-Corbéis France
40 F3 St-Germain-du-Plain France
42 I1 St-Germain-du-Puy France
41 C8 St-Germain-du-Teil France
36 D6 St-Germain-en-Laye France
40 E5 St-Germain-Laval France
41 C6 St-Germain-Lembron France
42 G4 St-Germain-les-Belles France
40 D4 St-Germain-Lespinasse France
42 H5 St-Germain-les-Vergnes France
41 D6 St-Germain-l'Herm France
30 D7 St Germans *Cornwall, England* U.K.
43 D8 St-Germé France
36 C5 St-Germer-de-Fly France
38 G8 St-Gervais *Pays de la Loire* France
41 G6 St-Gervais *Rhône-Alpes* France
40 B4 St-Gervais-d'Auvergne France
39 N6 St-Gervais-la-Forêt France
40 J5 St-Gervais-les-Bains France
39 L8 St-Gervais-les-Trois-Clochers France
41 C9 St-Gervais-sur-Mare France
43 H7 St-Géry France
45 E8 St-Ghislain Belgium
38 G7 St-Gildas, Pointe de *pt* France
38 F6 St-Gildas-de-Rhuys France
38 G6 St-Gildas-des-Bois France
131 □5 St Giles Islands Trin. and Tob.
41 E9 St-Gilles France
38 H8 St-Gilles-Croix-de-Vie France
99 □1c St-Gilles-les-Bains Réunion
40 J4 St-Gingolph France
43 G10 St-Girons France
43 B8 St-Girons-Plage France
36 F4 St-Gobain France
St Gotthard Pass *pass* Switz. *see* San Gottardo, Passo del
30 C4 St Govan's Head *Wales* U.K.
38 H5 St-Grégoire France
38 C6 St-Guénolé France
41 D9 St-Guilhem-le-Désert France
40 D4 St-Haon-le-Châtel France
40 E5 St-Héand France
110 J5 St Helen *MI* U.S.A.
98 □2b St Helena *terr.* S. Atlantic Ocean
124 J3 St Helena *CA* U.S.A.
96 C8 St Helena Bay S. Africa
96 C8 St Helena Bay *b.* S. Africa
115 G9 St Helena Sound *inlet SC* U.S.A.
205 L9 St Helens *Tas.* Austr.
29 L7 St Helens *Merseyside, England* U.K.
122 C4 St Helens *OR* U.S.A.
122 C3 St Helens, Mount *vol. WA* U.S.A.
205 L9 St Helens Point *Tas.* Austr.
38 G3 St Helier Channel Is
38 H7 St-Herblain France
43 I9 St-Hilaire France
36 H5 St-Hilaire-au-Temple France
41 E8 St-Hilaire-de-Brethmas France
38 I7 St-Hilaire-de-Loulay France
43 F7 St-Hilaire-de-Lusignan France
38 H8 St-Hilaire-de-Riez France
42 C3 St-Hilaire-des-Loges France
42 C4 St-Hilaire-de-Villefranche France
39 I4 St-Hilaire-du-Harcouët France
41 G6 St-Hilaire-du-Rosier France
40 D3 St-Hilaire-Fontaine France
36 H5 St-Hilaire-le-Grand France
39 K7 St-Hilaire-St-Florent France
37 N7 St-Hippolyte *Alsace* France
40 J2 St-Hippolyte *Franche-Comté* France
41 D9 St-Hippolyte-du-Fort France
179 K8 Sainthiya *W. Bengal* India
41 J8 St-Honorat, Mont *mt.* France
40 D3 St-Honoré-les-Bains France
41 E6 St-Hostien France
45 H8 St-Hubert Belgium
109 F4 St-Hyacinthe *Que.* Can.
110 J4 St Ignace *MI* U.S.A.
108 C3 St Ignace Island *Ont.* Can.
137 G4 St Ignatius Guyana
70 B1 St-Imier Switz.
70 B1 St-Imier, Vallon de *val.* Switz.
30 D4 St Ishmael *Carmarthenshire, Wales* U.K.
41 H6 St-Ismier France
30 D7 St Ive *Cornwall, England* U.K.
31 L3 St Ives *Cambridgeshire, England* U.K.
30 □ St Ives *Cornwall, England* U.K.
30 B7 St Ives Bay *England* U.K.
41 B9 St-Izaire France
117 □Q1 St-Jacques *N.B.* Can.
St Jacques, Cap Vietnam *see* Vung Tau
108 E3 St-Jacques-de-Dupuy *Que.* Can.
38 H5 St-Jacques-de-la-Lande France
38 G4 St-Jacut-de-la-Mer France
38 I4 St-James France
130 □ St James *parish* Jamaica
110 I4 St James *MI* U.S.A.
120 H4 St James *MN* U.S.A.
120 J6 St James *MO* U.S.A.
119 I3 St James *NY* U.S.A.
106 D5 St James, Cape *B.C.* Can.
109 H3 St-Jean *r. Que.* Can.
109 H3 St-Jean *r. Que.* Can.
43 G8 St-Jean France
137 H3 St-Jean Fr. Guiana
109 F3 St-Jean, Lac *l. Que.* Can.
38 F6 St-Jean-Brévelay France
41 K9 St-Jean-Cap-Ferrat France
42 C4 St-Jean-d'Angély France
39 L5 St-Jean-d'Assé France
40 G5 St-Jean-de-Bournay France
36 C8 St-Jean-de-Braye France
39 I3 St-Jean-de-Daye France
36 C8 St-Jean-de-la-Ruelle France
40 G2 St-Jean-de-Losne France
43 A9 St-Jean-de-Luz France
41 E8 St-Jean-de-Maurejols-et-Avéjan France
41 I6 St-Jean-de-Maurienne France
38 G8 St-Jean-de-Monts France
41 F6 St-Jean-de-Muzols France
109 G4 St-Jean-de-Port-Joli *Que.* Can.
39 L8 St-Jean-de-Sauves France
40 I5 St-Jean-de-Sixt France
41 D9 St-Jean-de-Védas France
43 C6 St-Jean-d'Illac France
41 C8 St-Jean-du-Bruel France
43 H9 St-Jean-du-Falga France
41 D8 St-Jean-du-Gard France
41 G6 St-Jean-en-Royans France
43 B9 St-Jean-Pied-de-Port France
43 E8 St-Jean-Poutge France
40 E6 St-Jean-Soleymieux France
39 K5 St-Jean-sur-Erve France
40 G4 St-Jean-sur-Reyssouze France
109 F4 St-Jean-sur-Richelieu *Que.* Can.
40 I4 St-Jeoire France
108 F4 St-Jérôme *Que.* Can.
41 F6 St-Jeure-d'Ay France
41 E6 St-Jeures France
38 G7 St-Joachim France
122 F3 St Joe *r. ID* U.S.A.
109 H4 Saint John *N.B.* Can.
38 G3 St John Channel Is
88 C5 St John *r.* Liberia
120 F6 St John *KS* U.S.A.
117 □S3 St John *r. ME* U.S.A.
131 K4 St John *i.* Virgin Is (U.S.A.)
109 K3 St John, Cape *Nfld and Lab.* Can.
109 J3 St John Bay *Nfld and Lab.* Can.
109 J3 St John Island *Nfld and Lab.* Can.
131 □2 St John's Antigua and Barbuda
109 K4 St John's *Nfld and Lab.* Can.
125 W7 St Johns *AZ* U.S.A.
110 J6 St Johns *MI* U.S.A.
116 A8 St Johns *OH* U.S.A.
115 G10 St Johns *r. FL* U.S.A.
117 M4 St Johnsbury *VT* U.S.A.
27 K4 St John's Point *Northern Ireland* U.K.
28 C4 St Johnstown Rep. of Ireland
26 H12 St John's Town of Dalry *Dumfries and Galloway, Scotland* U.K.
117 K6 St Johnsville *NY* U.S.A.
38 I3 St-Jores France
40 I5 St-Jorioz France
43 G8 St-Jory France
42 F4 St-Jory-de-Chalais France
131 □2 St Joseph Dominica
131 □3 St-Joseph Martinique
99 □1c St-Joseph Réunion
121 J10 St Joseph *LA* U.S.A.
110 H7 St Joseph *MI* U.S.A.
120 H6 St Joseph *MO* U.S.A.
110 H7 St Joseph *r. MI* U.S.A.
110 I8 St Joseph *r. MI* U.S.A.
108 B3 St Joseph, Lake *Ont.* Can.
108 D4 St Joseph Island *Ont.* Can.
121 G12 St Joseph Island *TX* U.S.A.
38 H4 St-Jouan-des-Guérets France
39 L2 St-Jouin-Bruneval France
39 K8 St-Jouin-de-Marnes France
108 F4 St-Jovité *Que.* Can.
43 I8 St-Juéry France
St Julian's Malta *see* San Ġiljan
St Julian's Bay Malta *see* Spinola, Ix-Xatt ta'
40 G4 St-Julien *Franche-Comté* France
43 G9 St-Julien *Midi-Pyrénées* France
42 C5 St-Julien-Beychevelle France
41 E7 St-Julien-Boutières France
40 E4 St-Julien-de-Civry France
34 D3 St-Julien-de-Concelles France
38 I6 St-Julien-de-Vouvantes France
36 F7 St-Julien-du-Sault France
41 J9 St-Julien-du-Verdon France
41 H7 St-Julien-en-Beauchêne France
43 B7 St-Julien-en-Born France
40 I4 St-Julien-en-Genevois France
41 G7 St-Julien-en-Quint France
42 F2 St-Julien-l'Ars France
41 E8 St-Julien-les-Rosiers France
36 H7 St-Julien-les-Villas France
40 G4 St-Julien-sur-Reyssouze France
42 F4 St-Junien France
41 F8 St-Just France
30 □ St Just *Cornwall, England* U.K.
36 D4 St-Just-en-Chaussée France
40 D5 St-Just-en-Chevalet France
43 B9 St-Just-Ibarre France
43 D8 St-Justin France
30 B7 St Just in Roseland *Cornwall, England* U.K.
40 E5 St-Just-la-Pendue France
42 B4 St-Just-Luzac France
36 G6 St-Just-Sauvage France
40 E6 St-Just-St-Rambert France
30 B7 St Keverne *Cornwall, England* U.K.
26 □1 St Kilda *i. Western Isles, Scotland* U.K.
26 □1 St Kilda *is Scotland* U.K.
131 □2 St Kitts *i.* St Kitts and Nevis
131 □2 St Kitts and Nevis *country* West Indies
39 K7 St-Lambert-des-Levées France
39 J7 St-Lambert-du-Lattay France
43 E8 St-Lary France
43 E10 St-Lary-Soulan France
St-Laurent, Golfe du *g. Que.* Can. *see* St Lawrence, Gulf of
36 E3 St-Laurent-Blangy France
43 D9 St-Laurent-Bretagne France
41 E9 St-Laurent-d'Aigouze France
41 F8 St-Laurent-de-Carnols France
66 K3 St-Laurent-de-Cerdans France
40 E5 St-Laurent-de-Chamousset France
41 B10 St-Laurent-de-la-Cabrerisse France
43 J10 St-Laurent-de-la-Salanque France
43 E9 St-Laurent-de-Neste France
137 H3 St-Laurent-du-Maroni Fr. Guiana
41 H6 St-Laurent-du-Pont France
41 K9 St-Laurent-du-Var France
41 J8 St-Laurent-du-Verdon France
39 M2 St-Laurent-en-Caux France
40 H3 St-Laurent-en-Grandvaux France
41 D7 St-Laurent-les-Bains France
42 C5 St-Laurent-Médoc France
36 C8 St-Laurent-Nouan France
42 F4 St-Laurent-sur-Gorre France
37 K5 St-Laurent-sur-Othain France
39 J8 St-Laurent-sur-Sèvre France
207 L7 St Lawrence *Qld* Austr.
109 K4 St Lawrence *Nfld and Lab.* Can.
109 G3 St Lawrence *inlet Que.* Can.
118 D4 St Lawrence *PA* U.S.A.
109 I4 St Lawrence, Cape *N.S.* Can.
109 I3 St Lawrence, Gulf of *Que.* Can.
104 B3 St Lawrence Island *AK* U.S.A.
111 S5 St Lawrence Islands National Park *Ont.* Can.
108 F4 St Lawrence Seaway *sea chan.* Can./U.S.A.
107 K5 St Lazare *Man.* Can.
45 I9 St-Léger Belgium
40 D2 St-Léger-de-Fougeret France
40 C3 St-Léger-des-Vignes France
36 C6 St-Léger-en-Yvelines France
40 E3 St-Léger-sous-Beuvray France
40 F3 St-Léger-sur-Dheune France
109 H4 St-Léonard *N.B.* Can.
109 F4 St-Léonard *Que.* Can.
37 M7 St-Léonard France
116 I10 St Leonard *MD* U.S.A.
42 G4 St-Léonard-de-Noblat France
31 I6 St Leonards *Dorset, England* U.K.
42 F5 St-Léon-sur-l'Isle France
99 □1c St-Leu Réunion
36 D5 St-Leu-d'Esserent France
109 K2 St Lewis *Nfld and Lab.* Can.
109 J2 St Lewis *r. Nfld and Lab.* Can.
43 G9 St-Lizier France
39 I3 St-Lô France
43 B8 St-Lon-les-Mines France
40 H3 St-Lothian France
43 D6 St-Loubès France
40 L1 St-Louis France
131 □2 St-Louis Guadeloupe
99 □1c St-Louis Réunion
88 A2 St-Louis Senegal
110 J6 St Louis *MI* U.S.A.
120 J6 St Louis *MO* U.S.A.
110 B3 St Louis *r. MN* U.S.A.
117 L3 St-Louis, Lac *l. Que.* Can.
130 G4 St-Louis du Nord Haiti
37 N6 St-Louis-lès-Bitche France
41 D9 St-Loup, Pic *hill* France
40 F3 St-Loup-de-la-Salle France
36 F6 St-Loup-de-Naud France
39 K8 St-Loup-Lamairé France
37 L8 St-Loup-sur-Semouse France
36 B6 St-Lubin-des-Joncherets France
38 I7 St-Luce-sur-Loire France
131 □3 St Lucia *country* West Indies
97 Q4 St Lucia, Lake S. Africa
131 □3 St Lucia Channel Martinique/St Lucia
97 Q4 St Lucia Estuary S. Africa
97 Q4 St Lucia Game Reserve *nature res.* S. Africa
97 Q4 St Lucia Park *nature res.* S. Africa
St Luke's Island Myanmar *see* Zadetkale Kyun
38 G4 St-Lunaire France
40 H4 St-Lupicin France
36 H7 St-Lyé France
43 G8 St-Lys France
43 D6 St-Macaire France
42 C1 St-Macaire-en-Mauges France
43 C6 St-Magne France
43 D6 St-Magne-de-Castillon France
26 □M2 St Magnus Bay *Scotland* U.K.
41 H9 St-Maime France
42 D3 St-Maixent-l'École France
38 G4 St-Malo France
38 G4 St-Malo, Golfe de *g.* France
38 H3 St-Malo-de-la-Lande France
41 E9 St-Mamert-du-Gard France
43 I6 St-Mamet-la-Salvetat France
41 H10 St-Mandrier-sur-Mer France
130 G4 St-Marc Haiti
130 G4 St-Marc, Canal de *sea chan.* Haiti
40 F3 St-Marcel *Bourgogne* France
42 H2 St-Marcel *Centre* France
36 B5 St-Marcel *Haute-Normandie* France
41 F8 St-Marcel-d'Ardèche France
41 F6 St-Marcel-lès-Annonay France
41 F7 St-Marcel-lès-Sauzet France
41 F7 St-Marcel-lès-Valence France
41 G6 St-Marcellin France
43 F9 St-Marcet France
39 I3 St-Marcouf, Îles *is* France
36 I8 St-Marc-sur-Seine France
36 G7 St-Mards-en-Othe France
31 O5 St Margaret's at Cliffe *Kent, England* U.K.
130 □ St Margaret's Bay Jamaica
26 K5 St Margaret's Hope *Orkney, Scotland* U.K.
122 F3 St Maries *ID* U.S.A.
97 L8 St Marks S. Africa
115 E10 St Marks National Wildlife Refuge *nature res. FL* U.S.A.
43 J10 St-Marsal France
39 L6 St-Mars-d'Outillé France
38 I7 St-Mars-du-Désert France
39 L5 St-Mars-la-Brière France
38 I6 St-Mars-la-Jaille France
41 D8 St-Martial France
43 G6 St-Martial-de-Nabirat France
42 F4 St-Martial-de-Valette France
38 F3 St Martin *Guernsey* Channel Is
38 G3 St Martin *Jersey* Channel Is
41 H9 St-Martin France
131 L4 St-Martin *i.* West Indies
131 □3 St Martin, Cap *c.* Martinique
96 B8 St Martin, Cape S. Africa
107 L5 St Martin, Lake *Man.* Can.
36 C2 St-Martin-Boulogne France
36 G5 St-Martin-d'Ablois France
43 B9 St-Martin-d'Arrossa France
39 P7 St-Martin-d'Auxigny France
41 J6 St-Martin-de-Belleville France
41 H9 St-Martin-de-Castillon France
41 F9 St-Martin-de-Crau France
41 D7 St-Martin-de-Fugères France
38 I4 St-Martin-de-Landelles France
41 D9 St-Martin-de-Londres France
41 J8 St-Martin-d'Entraunes France
42 B3 St-Martin-de-Ré France
39 J3 St-Martin-des-Besaces France
38 I4 St-Martin-des-Champs *Basse-Normandie* France
38 D4 St-Martin-des-Champs *Bretagne* France
43 B8 St-Martin-de-Seignanx France
41 E7 St-Martin-de-Valamas France
41 E8 St-Martin-de-Valgalgues France
41 H6 St-Martin-d'Hères France
43 C8 St-Martin-d'Oney France
40 H4 St-Martin-du-Frêne France
40 G4 St-Martin-du-Mont France
41 K9 St-Martin-du-Var France
40 G3 St-Martin-en-Bresse France
40 F5 St-Martin-en-Haut France
110 H4 St Martin Island *MI* U.S.A.
40 F5 St-Martin-la-Plaine France
39 M7 St-Martin-le-Beau France
30 F2 St Martin's *Shropshire, England* U.K.
30 □ St Martin's *i. England* U.K.
179 N9 St Martin's Island Bangl.
36 F8 St-Martin-sur-Ouanne France
42 I5 St-Martin-Valmeroux France
41 K8 St-Martin-Vésubie France
43 F9 St-Martory France
106 H5 St Mary *r. B.C.* Can.
130 □ St Mary *parish* Jamaica
203 D11 St Mary, Mount *South I.* N.Z.
31 J5 St Mary Bourne *Hampshire, England* U.K.
31 N5 St Mary in the Marsh *Kent, England* U.K.
204 G4 St Mary Peak *S.A.* Austr.
205 L9 St Marys *Tas.* Austr.
111 M6 St Mary's *Ont.* Can.
131 □7 St Mary's Trin. and Tob.
26 K5 St Mary's *Orkney, Scotland* U.K.
30 □ St Mary's *i. England* U.K.
120 G6 St Marys *KS* U.S.A.
116 A8 St Marys *OH* U.S.A.
116 G7 St Marys *PA* U.S.A.
116 D9 St Marys *WV* U.S.A.
120 M5 St Marys *r. OH* U.S.A.
109 K4 St Mary's, Cape *Nfld and Lab.* Can.
109 K4 St Mary's Bay *Nfld and Lab.* Can.
31 N5 St Mary's Bay *Kent, England* U.K.
116 I10 St Marys City *MD* U.S.A.
26 J12 St Mary's Loch *l. Scotland* U.K.
111 P1 St-Mathieu *Que.* Can.
42 F4 St-Mathieu France
38 B5 St-Mathieu, Pointe de *pt* France
42 A2 St-Mathurin France
104 A3 St Matthew Island *AK* U.S.A.
115 G9 St Matthews *SC* U.S.A.
St Matthew's Island Myanmar *see* Zadetkyi Kyun
153 K7 St Matthias Group *is* P.N.G.
39 O8 St-Maur France
36 E6 St-Maur-des-Fossés France
108 F4 St-Maurice *r. Que.* Can.
70 B3 St-Maurice Switz.
108 F4 St-Maurice, Réserve Faunique du *nature res. Que.* Can.
40 F5 St-Maurice-de-Beynost France
41 E6 St-Maurice-de-Lignon France
42 F4 St-Maurice-des-Lions France
42 G3 St-Maurice-la-Souterraine France
41 F6 St-Maurice-l'Exil France
41 D9 St-Maurice-Navacelles France
43 F7 St-Maurin France
30 B7 St Mawes *Cornwall, England* U.K.
37 L6 St-Max France
36 C3 St-Maxent France
36 D5 St-Maximin France
41 H10 St-Maximin-la-Ste-Baume France
42 E5 St-Méard-de-Drône France
42 D5 St-Médard-de-Guizières France
43 C6 St-Médard-en-Jalles France
38 G5 St-Méen-le-Grand France
38 H4 St-Méloir-des-Ondes France
42 D4 St-Même-les-Carrières France
36 H6 St-Memmie France
37 I4 St-Menges France
40 C3 St-Menoux France
30 C6 St Merryn *Cornwall, England* U.K.
42 G5 St-Mesmin *Aquitaine* France
36 G7 St-Mesmin *Champagne-Ardenne* France
39 J8 St-Mesmin *Pays de la Loire* France
43 F7 St-Mézard France
117 I10 St Michaels *MD* U.S.A.
109 K2 St Michael's Bay *Nfld and Lab.* Can.
30 □ St Michael's Mount *tourist site England* U.K.
43 E9 St-Michel *Midi-Pyrénées* France
36 H4 St-Michel *Picardie* France
42 E4 St-Michel *Poitou-Charentes* France
38 D5 St-Michel, Montagne *hill* France
38 D5 St-Michel, Réservoir de *resr* France
38 G7 St-Michel-Chef-Chef France
43 D7 St-Michel-de-Castelnau France
41 I6 St-Michel-de-Maurienne France
108 F4 St-Michel-des-Saints *Que.* Can.
38 D4 St-Michel-en-Grève France
42 B3 St-Michel-en-l'Herm France
39 J8 St-Michel-Mont-Mercure France
37 M7 St-Michel-sur-Meurthe France
37 K6 St-Mihiel France
26 K10 St Monans *Fife, Scotland* U.K.
43 D8 St-Mont France
41 F8 St-Montant France
37 M7 St-Nabord France
43 G8 St-Nauphary France
38 G7 St-Nazaire France
41 G6 St-Nazaire-en-Royans France
41 G7 St-Nazaire-le-Désert France
40 B5 St-Nectaire France
31 L3 St Neots *Cambridgeshire, England* U.K.
St Nicolas Belgium *see* Sint-Niklaas
36 E3 St-Nicolas France
45 J9 St-Nicolas, Mont *hill* Lux.
36 B4 St-Nicolas-d'Aliermont France
43 G7 St-Nicolas-de-la-Grave France
37 L6 St-Nicolas-de-Port France
38 G6 St-Nicolas-de-Redon France
38 E5 St-Nicolas-du-Pélem France
26 □N3 St Ninian's Isle *i. Scotland* U.K.
38 F6 St-Nolff France
44 H5 St-Oedenrode Neth.
36 D2 St-Omer France
42 C4 Saintonge *reg.* France
43 H8 St-Orens-de-Gameville France
43 E9 St-Ost France
31 O4 St Osyth *Essex, England* U.K.
38 G3 St Ouen Channel Is
36 B8 St-Ouen *Centre* France
36 D3 St-Ouen *Picardie* France
39 J5 St-Ouen-des-Toits France
36 H6 St-Ouen-Domprot France
30 G4 St Owen's Cross *Herefordshire, England* U.K.
109 G4 St-Pacôme *Que.* Can.
38 H4 St-Pair-sur-Mer France
43 B9 St-Palais France
42 B4 St-Palais-sur-Mer France
41 D6 St-Pal-de-Chalancon France
41 E6 St-Pal-de-Mons France
117 □P2 St-Pamphile *Que.* Can.
40 E3 St-Pantaléon *Bourgogne* France
43 G7 St-Pantaléon *Midi-Pyrénées* France
42 G5 St-Pantaléon-de-Larche France
43 I9 St-Papoul France
42 G3 St-Pardoux, Lac de *l.* France
43 E6 St-Pardoux-Isaac France
42 F5 St-Pardoux-la-Rivière France
116 B8 St Paris *OH* U.S.A.
40 C3 St-Parize-le-Châtel France
36 H7 St-Parres-lès-Vaudes France
109 G4 St-Pascal *Que.* Can.
39 L5 St-Paterne France
39 L6 St-Paterne-Racan France
111 Q3 St-Patrice, Lac *l. Que.* Can.
131 □7 St Patrick *county* Trin. and Tob.
107 I4 St Paul *Alta* Can.
109 J3 St Paul *r. Nfld and Lab./Que.* Can.
41 J7 St-Paul France
88 C5 St Paul *r.* Liberia
99 □1c St-Paul Réunion
110 A5 St Paul *MN* U.S.A.
120 F5 St Paul *NE* U.S.A.
116 C12 St Paul *VA* U.S.A.
99 □1c St Paul, Baie de *b.* Réunion
89 F5 St Paul, Cape Ghana
215 J7 St-Paul, Île *i.* Indian Ocean
43 H8 St-Paul-Cap-de-Joux France
43 J10 St-Paul-de-Fenouillet France
43 H10 St-Paul-de-Jarrat France
42 I6 St-Paul-des-Landes France
43 F7 St-Paul-d'Espis France
43 B7 St-Paul-en-Born France
41 J9 St-Paul-en-Forêt France
41 D9 St-Paul-et-Valmalle France
41 D6 St-Paulien France
109 I4 St Paul Island *N.S.* Can.
104 A4 St Paul Island *AK* U.S.A.
41 E8 St-Paul-le-Jeune France
43 B8 St-Paul-lès-Dax France
41 H9 St-Paul-lès-Durance France
41 G6 St-Paul-lès-Romans France
131 □2 St Paul's St Kitts and Nevis
St Paul's Bay Malta *see* San Pawl il-Baħar
St Paul's Bay *b.* Malta *see* San Pawl-il-Baħar, Il-Bajja ta'
St Paul's Islands Malta *see* San Pawl, Gżejjer ta'
154 B6 St Paul Subterranean River National Park Phil.
41 F8 St-Paul-Trois-Châteaux France
43 D9 St-Pé-de-Bigorre France
43 A9 St-Pée-sur-Nivelle France
41 F7 St-Péray France
40 D2 St-Père France
38 G7 St-Père-en-Retz France
120 I3 St Peter *MN* U.S.A.
St Peter and St Paul Rocks *is* N. Atlantic Ocean *see* São Pedro e São Paulo
38 F3 St Peter in the Wood Channel Is
38 F3 St Peter Port Channel Is
109 I4 St Peter's *N.S.* Can.
109 I4 St Peters *P.E.I.* Can.
31 O5 St Peter's *Kent, England* U.K.
St Petersburg Rus. Fed. *see* Sankt-Peterburg
115 F12 St Petersburg *FL* U.S.A.
36 G7 St-Phal France
38 H8 St-Philbert-de-Bouaine France
38 H7 St-Philbert-de-Grand-Lieu France
99 □1c St-Philippe Réunion
41 G9 St-Pierre *mt.* France
40 K5 St-Pierre Italy
131 □3 St-Pierre Martinique
99 □1b St-Pierre Mauritius
99 □1c St-Pierre Réunion
99 □2 St Pierre *i.* Seychelles
109 K4 St-Pierre St Pierre and Miquelon
109 F4 St-Pierre, Lac *l. Que.* Can.
109 J4 St Pierre and Miquelon *terr.* N. America
40 I5 St-Pierre-d'Albigny France
41 I6 St-Pierre-d'Allevard France
43 D6 St-Pierre-d'Aurillac France
41 H6 St-Pierre-de-Chartreuse France
42 F5 St-Pierre-de-Chignac France
42 F5 St-Pierre-de-Côle France
41 C9 St-Pierre-de-la-Fage France
39 M8 St-Pierre-de-Maillé France
38 H5 St-Pierre-de-Plesguen France
42 F1 St-Pierre-des-Corps France
39 J7 St-Pierre-des-Échaubrognes France
39 I5 St-Pierre-des-Landes France
39 K5 St-Pierre-des-Nids France
43 I8 St-Pierre-de-Trivisy France
43 B9 St-Pierre-d'Irube France
42 B4 St-Pierre-d'Oléron France
39 J8 St-Pierre-du-Chemin France
43 C8 St-Pierre-du-Mont France
38 I2 St-Pierre-Église France
40 I4 St-Pierre-en-Faucigny France
39 L2 St-Pierre-en-Port France
39 I5 St-Pierre-la-Cour France
40 C3 St-Pierre-le-Moûtier France
36 B5 St-Pierre-lès-Elbeuf France
36 E7 St-Pierre-lès-Nemours France
38 E6 St-Pierre-Quiberon France
39 K3 St-Pierre-sur-Dives France
41 E7 St-Pierreville France
43 F9 St-Plancard France
40 I3 St-Point, Lac de *l.* France
39 I4 St-Pois France
39 I6 St-Poix France
38 D4 St-Pol-de-Léon France
36 D1 St-Pol-sur-Mer France
36 D3 St-Pol-sur-Ternoise France
43 G6 St-Pompont France
41 J8 St-Pons France
41 B10 St-Pons-de-Thomières France
42 C4 St-Porchaire France
43 G7 St-Porquier France
40 C4 St-Pourçain-sur-Sioule France
70 A3 St-Prex Switz.
40 F5 St-Priest France
40 B5 St-Priest-de-Champs France
40 D5 St-Priest-Laprugne France
42 G4 St-Priest-Taurion France
42 I5 St-Privat France
41 D7 St-Privat-d'Allier France
41 E8 St-Privat-des-Vieux France
40 D4 St-Prix *Auvergne* France
41 F7 St-Prix *Rhône-Alpes* France
43 H7 St-Projet France
117 □O2 St-Prosper *Que.* Can.
43 E8 St-Puy France
109 H4 St Quentin *N.B.* Can.
36 F4 St-Quentin France
36 F4 St-Quentin, Canal de France
41 E8 St-Quentin-la-Poterie France
41 H6 St-Quentin-sur-Isère France
37 N6 St-Quirin France
41 F6 St-Rambert-d'Albon France
40 G5 St-Rambert-en-Bugey France
41 J10 St-Raphaël France
122 G3 St Regis *MT* U.S.A.
117 K4 St Regis *r. NY* U.S.A.
117 K4 St Regis Falls *NY* U.S.A.
41 E8 St-Remèze France
117 L3 St-Rémi *Que.* Can.
40 F3 St-Rémy France
41 F9 St-Rémy-de-Provence France
36 I6 St-Remy-en-Bouzemont-St-Genest-et-Isson France
36 B6 St-Rémy-sur-Avre France
40 D5 St-Rémy-sur-Durolle France
38 B5 St-Renan France
40 D2 St-Révérien France
70 C4 St-Rhemy Italy
40 E4 St-Rigaud, Mont *mt.* France
36 C3 St-Riquier France
39 L2 St-Romain-de-Colbosc France
40 G5 St-Romain-de-Jalionas France
40 F5 St-Romain-en-Gal France
40 E5 St-Romain-le-Puy France
40 E3 St-Romain-sous-Versigny France
39 N7 St-Romain-sur-Cher France
41 G6 St-Romans France
41 B8 St-Rome-de-Cernon France
41 B8 St-Rome-de-Tarn France
36 B4 St-Saëns France
38 F3 St Sampson Channel Is
43 I6 St-Santin France
42 I2 St-Saturnin France
41 G9 St-Saturnin-lès-Apt France
42 F4 St-Saud-Lacoussière France
40 D2 St-Saulge France
40 B5 St-Sauves-d'Auvergne France
38 C5 St-Sauveur *Bretagne* France
37 L8 St-Sauveur *Franche-Comté* France
41 F7 St-Sauveur-de-Montagut France
108 F4 St-Sauveur-des-Monts *Que.* Can.
40 C1 St-Sauveur-en-Puisaye France
41 G8 St-Sauveur-Gouvernet France
38 I3 St-Sauveur-Lendelin France
38 H3 St-Sauveur-le-Vicomte France
41 K8 St-Sauveur-sur-Tinée France
43 F8 St-Sauvy France
42 D5 St-Savin *Aquitaine* France
42 F2 St-Savin *Poitou-Charentes* France
42 C4 St-Savinien France
38 G3 St Saviour Channel Is
96 E10 St Sebastian Bay S. Africa
117 □O3 St-Sébastien *Que.* Can.
36 B5 St-Sébastien-de-Morsent France
38 H7 St-Sébastien-sur-Loire France
40 F2 St-Seine-l'Abbaye France
43 D6 St-Selve France
41 E7 St-Semin France
41 B9 St-Sernin-sur-Rance France
36 F7 St-Sérotin France
43 C8 St-Sever France
39 I4 St-Sever-Calvados France
109 G4 St-Siméon *Que.* Can.
41 G6 St-Siméon-de-Bressieux France
42 J6 St-Simon *Auvergne* France
36 F4 St-Simon *Picardie* France
115 G10 St Simons Island *GA* U.S.A.
40 I3 St-Sorlin, Mont de *mt.* France
41 I6 St-Sorlin-d'Arves France
36 E5 St-Soupplets France
117 □R3 St Stephen *N.B.* Can.
30 C7 St Stephen *Cornwall, England* U.K.
115 H9 St Stephen *SC* U.S.A.
43 H8 St-Sulpice France
42 B4 St-Sulpice-de-Royan France
38 H6 St-Sulpice-des-Landes France
42 G3 St-Sulpice-Laurière France
42 H3 St-Sulpice-le-Guérétois France
42 I4 St-Sulpice-les-Champs France
42 G3 St-Sulpice-les-Feuilles France
43 G9 St-Sulpice-sur-Lèze France
39 M4 St-Sulpice-sur-Risle France
39 K3 St-Sylvain France
39 K6 St-Sylvain-d'Anjou France
43 F7 St-Sylvestre-sur-Lot France
43 D7 St-Symphorien France
40 E5 St-Symphorien-de-Lay France
40 F5 St-Symphorien-d'Ozon France
40 E5 St-Symphorien-sur-Coise France
30 C6 St Teath *Cornwall, England* U.K.
106 C3 St Terese *AK* U.S.A.
38 D4 St-Thégonnec France
117 □O3 St-Théophile *Que.* Can.
107 M4 St Theresa Point *Man.* Can.
41 C10 St-Thibéry France
37 K7 St-Thiébault France
108 D5 St Thomas *Ont.* Can.
130 □ St Thomas *parish* Jamaica
131 K4 St Thomas *i.* Virgin Is (U.S.A.)
St Thomas Bay Malta *see* San Tumas, Il-Bajja ta'
38 D6 St-Thurien France
109 G4 St-Tite-des-Caps *Que.* Can.
40 G4 St-Trivier-de-Courtes France
40 F4 St-Trivier-sur-Moignans France
42 B4 St-Trojan-les-Bains France
St Trond Belgium *see* Sint-Truiden
41 J10 St-Tropez France
41 J10 St-Tropez, Cap de *c.* France
41 J10 St-Tropez, Golfe de *b.* France
30 D2 St Tudwal's Road *b. Wales* U.K.
43 H8 St-Urcisse France
41 C7 St-Urcize France
41 F6 St-Uze France
38 I2 St-Vaast-la-Hougue France
36 F7 St-Valérien France
39 M2 St-Valery-en-Caux France
36 C3 St-Valery-sur-Somme France
40 E3 St-Vallier *Bourgogne* France
41 F6 St-Vallier *Rhône-Alpes* France
41 J9 St-Vallier-de-Thiey France
39 K8 St-Varent France
42 H3 St-Vaury France
41 J7 St-Véran France
41 F6 St-Victor France
41 G10 St-Victoret France
41 F8 St-Victor-la-Coste France
39 J3 St-Vigor-le-Grand France
70 D4 St-Vincent Italy
120 G1 St Vincent *MN* U.S.A.
131 □3 St Vincent *i.* West Indies
205 J10 St Vincent, Cape *Tas.* Austr.
St Vincent, Cape Port. *see* São Vicente, Cabo de
204 F6 St Vincent, Gulf *S.A.* Austr.
131 □3 St Vincent and the Grenadines *country* West Indies
42 E5 St-Vincent-de-Connezac France
43 C8 St-Vincent-de-Paul France
43 B8 St-Vincent-de-Tyrosse France
115 E11 St Vincent Island *FL* U.S.A.
41 I8 St-Vincent-les-Forts France
131 □3 St Vincent Passage St Lucia/St Vincent
40 H2 St-Vit France
43 F7 St-Vite France
45 J8 St-Vith Belgium
42 B5 St-Vivien-de-Médoc France
107 I4 St Walburg *Sask.* Can.
111 N7 St Williams *Ont.* Can.
42 B3 St-Xandre France
40 E4 St-Yan France
43 G9 St-Ybars France
40 C4 St-Yorre France
42 G4 St-Yrieix-la-Perche France
42 E4 St-Yrieix-sur-Charente France
38 D6 St-Yvy France
41 H10 St-Zacharie France

San Cristóbal to Sannicandro di Bari

333

128 F4 **San Cristóbal** *Jalisco* Mex.
200 □6 **San Cristobal** *i.* Solomon Is
136 C3 **San Cristóbal** Venez.
136 □ **San Cristóbal, Isla** *i.* *Islas Galápagos* Ecuador
126 □P11 **San Cristóbal, Volcán** *vol.* Nic.
62 I4 **San Cristóbal de Entreviñas** Spain
128 D4 **San Cristóbal de la Barranca** Mex.
98 □3a **San Cristóbal de la Laguna** *Tenerife* Canary Is
127 M9 **San Cristóbal de las Casas** Mex.
63 K6 **San Cristóbal de la Vega** Spain
125 S9 **San Cristobal Wash** *watercourse AZ* U.S.A.
73 P6 **San Croce, Monte** *mt.* Italy
64 G8 **Sancti Petri, Isla** *i.* Spain
147 F3 **Sancti Spíritu** Arg.
130 D3 **Sancti Spíritus** Cuba
130 D3 **Sancti Spíritus** *prov.* Cuba
62 H7 **Sancti-Spíritus** Spain
65 I3 **Sancti-Spíritus** Spain
37 K5 **Sancy** France
22 C2 **Sand** Norway
97 K4 **Sand** *r. Free State* S. Africa
95 F4 **Sand** *r. Limpopo* S. Africa
166 B6 **Sanda** Japan
162 I7 **Sandagou** Rus. Fed.
157 I5 **Sandai** *Kalimantan* Indon.
26 E12 **Sanda Island** *Scotland* U.K.
157 M2 **Sandakan** *Sabah* Malaysia
179 L6 **Sandakphu Peak** *Sikkim* India
70 E6 **San Damiano d'Asti** Italy
70 C7 **San Damiano Macra** Italy
49 K11 **Sand am Main** Ger.
159 H8 **Sândăn** Cambodia
21 I6 **Sandane** Norway
58 H7 **San Daniele del Friuli** Italy
70 I5 **San Daniele Po** Italy
77 L9 **Sandanski** Bulg.
Sandaohezi *Xinjiang* China *see* Shawan
88 C3 **Sandaré** Mali
50 F5 **Sandau** Ger.
26 L4 **Sanday** *i. Scotland* U.K.
26 K4 **Sanday Sound** *sea chan. Scotland* U.K.
29 M7 **Sandbach** *Cheshire, England* U.K.
49 J10 **Sandberg** Ger.
96 C8 **Sandberg** S. Africa
48 L1 **Sandby** Denmark
176 C7 **Sand Cay** *rf* India
20 L4 **Sanddøla** *r.* Norway
48 F4 **Sande** Ger.
21 H6 **Sande** *Sogn og Fjordane* Norway
22 G2 **Sande** *Vestfold* Norway
62 D6 **Sande** Port.
22 G2 **Sandefjord** Norway
22 G2 **Sandefjord (Torp)** *airport* Norway
22 B2 **Sandeid** Norway
204 □3 **Sandell Bay** S. Pacific Ocean
20 P2 **Sandelva** Norway
75 K4 **San Demetrio Corone** Italy
73 L3 **San Demetrio ne Vestini** Italy
213 D2 **Sandercock Nunataks** *nunataks* Antarctica
125 W6 **Sanders** *AZ* U.S.A.
51 F7 **Sandersdorf** Ger.
49 I8 **Sandershausen (Niestetal)** Ger.
51 E7 **Sandersleben** Ger.
121 D10 **Sanderson** *TX* U.S.A.
115 F9 **Sandersville** *GA* U.S.A.
48 J3 **Sandesneben** Ger.
208 F5 **Sandfire Roadhouse** *W.A.* Austr.
22 D2 **Sandfloeggi** *mt.* Norway
116 E10 **Sand Fork** *WV* U.S.A.
26 K4 **Sandgarth** *Orkney, Scotland* U.K.
52 F3 **Sandhausen** Ger.
26 G13 **Sandhead** *Dumfries and Galloway, Scotland* U.K.
120 G2 **Sand Hill** *r. MN* U.S.A.
120 D5 **Sand Hills** *NE* U.S.A.
20 M3 **Sandhornøy** *i.* Norway
31 K5 **Sandhurst** *Bracknell Forest, England* U.K.
178 H6 **Sandi** *Uttar Prad.* India
138 C3 **Sandia** Peru
62 E4 **Sandiás** Spain
126 G3 **San Diego** *Chihuahua* Mex.
123 J11 **San Diego** *Chihuahua* Mex.
128 G4 **San Diego** *Guanajuato* Mex.
124 O9 **San Diego** *CA* U.S.A.
121 F12 **San Diego** *TX* U.S.A.
145 D9 **San Diego, Cabo** *c.* Arg.
126 E2 **San Diego, Sierra** *mts* Mex.
129 H6 **San Diego Alcalá** Mex.
137 E2 **San Diego de Cabrutica** Venez.
129 H3 **San Dieguito** Mex.
79 L4 **Sandıklı** Turkey
178 H6 **Sandila** *Uttar Prad.* India
115 □2 **Sandilands Village** *New Prov.* Bahamas
36 D8 **Sandillon** France
209 C8 **Sandiman, Mount** *hill W.A.* Austr.
75 □ **San Dimitri, Il-Ponta ta'** *pt Gozo* Malta
156 D6 **Sanding** *i.* Indon.
129 M9 **San Dionisio del Mar** Mex.
110 D3 **Sand Island** *WI* U.S.A.
14 L2 **Sandivey** *r.* Rus. Fed.
50 I5 **Sandkrug** Ger.
59 K2 **Sandl** Austria
108 C4 **Sand Lake** *Ont.* Can.
107 M5 **Sand Lake** *l. Ont.* Can.
22 B3 **Sandnes** Norway
26 □M2 **Sandness** *Shetland, Scotland* U.K.
20 L3 **Sandnessjøen** Norway
Sandø *i.* Faroe Is *see* **Sandoy**
62 H7 **Sando** Spain
91 D7 **Sandoa** Dem. Rep. Congo
55 J5 **Sandomierz** Pol.
77 N4 **Sândominic** Romania
73 O3 **San Domino, Isola** *i.* Italy
136 B4 **Sandoná** Col.
75 N3 **San Donaci** Italy
71 N4 **San Donà di Piave** Italy
75 O3 **San Donato di Lecce** Italy
73 Q8 **San Donato di Ninea** Italy
70 G5 **San Donato Milanese** Italy
73 L4 **San Donato Val di Comino** Italy
57 J5 **Sándorfalva** Hungary
206 F6 **Sandover** *watercourse N.T.* Austr.
19 T3 **Sandovo** Rus. Fed.
213 G2 **Sandow, Mount** Antarctica
Sandoway Myanmar *see* **Thandwè**
31 J6 **Sandown** *Isle of Wight, England* U.K.
96 C10 **Sandown Bay** S. Africa
24 D1 **Sandoy** *i.* Faroe Is
20 I5 **Sandøy** Norway
30 D7 **Sandplace** *Cornwall, England* U.K.
122 F2 **Sandpoint** *ID* U.S.A.
26 B9 **Sandray** *i. Scotland* U.K.
31 L4 **Sandridge** *Hertfordshire, England* U.K.
206 G8 **Sandringham** *Qld* Austr.
97 P2 **Sand River Reservoir** Swaziland
56 G6 **Šandrovac** Croatia
20 N4 **Sandsele** Sweden
29 P4 **Sandsend** *North Yorkshire, England* U.K.
106 D4 **Sandspit** *B.C.* Can.
121 G7 **Sand Springs** *OK* U.S.A.
124 N2 **Sand Springs Salt Flat** *NV* U.S.A.
97 K3 **Sandspruit** *r.* S. Africa
48 G4 **Sandstedt** Ger.
116 H11 **Sandston** *VA* U.S.A.
209 E9 **Sandstone** *W.A.* Austr.
110 B3 **Sandstone** *MN* U.S.A.
124 N7 **Sandstone Peak** *hill CA* U.S.A.
125 T9 **Sand Tank Mountains** *AZ* U.S.A.
97 M2 **Sandton** S. Africa
118 E3 **Sandts Eddy** *PA* U.S.A.
170 F6 **Sandu** *Guizhou* China
171 I6 **Sandu** *Hunan* China
176 E5 **Sandur** *Karnataka* India
111 L6 **Sandusky** *MI* U.S.A.
116 C7 **Sandusky** *OH* U.S.A.
116 C7 **Sandusky Bay** *OH* U.S.A.
96 C7 **Sandveld** *mts* S. Africa
97 J3 **Sandveld Nature Reserve** S. Africa
96 B2 **Sandverhaar** Namibia
22 G2 **Sandvika** *Akershus* Norway
20 L5 **Sandvika** *Nord-Trøndelag* Norway
23 M1 **Sandviken** Sweden
96 I9 **Sandvlakte** S. Africa
31 O5 **Sandwich** *Kent, England* U.K.
117 O7 **Sandwich** *MA* U.S.A.
109 J2 **Sandwich Bay** *Nfld and Lab.* Can.
94 B4 **Sandwich Bay** Namibia
179 M8 **Sandwip** Bangl.
179 M8 **Sandwip Channel** Bangl.
31 L3 **Sandy** *Bedfordshire, England* U.K.
122 I6 **Sandy** *UT* U.S.A.
117 □P4 **Sandy** *r. ME* U.S.A.
107 K4 **Sandy Bay** *Sask.* Can.
65 □ **Sandy Bay** Gibraltar
130 □ **Sandy Bay** Jamaica
202 I2 **Sandy Bay** *North I.* N.Z.
204 □3 **Sandy Bay** S. Pacific Ocean
98 □2b **Sandy Bay** St Helena
209 G12 **Sandy Bight** *b. W.A.* Austr.
207 N8 **Sandy Cape** *Qld* Austr.
205 J9 **Sandy Cape** *Tas.* Austr.
206 G5 **Sandy Creek** *r. Qld* Austr.
28 H5 **Sandygate** Isle of Man
119 I2 **Sandy Hook** *CT* U.S.A.
116 B10 **Sandy Hook** *KY* U.S.A.
119 G4 **Sandy Hook** *pt NJ* U.S.A.
208 F3 **Sandy Island** *W.A.* Austr.
Sandy Island *Rodrigues I.* Mauritius *see* **Sables, Île aux**
185 J3 **Sandykachi** Turkm.
Sandykly Gumy *des.* Turkm. *see* **Sundukli, Peski**
106 H4 **Sandy Lake** *Alta* Can.
107 M4 **Sandy Lake** *Ont.* Can.
107 M4 **Sandy Lake** *l. Ont.* Can.
98 □2c **Sandy Point** *Tristan da Cunha* S. Atlantic Ocean
131 □2 **Sandy Point Town** St Kitts and Nevis
115 E9 **Sandy Springs** *GA* U.S.A.
116 D10 **Sandyville** *WV* U.S.A.
40 G3 **Sâne** *r.* France
45 I9 **Sanem** Lux.
62 I3 **San Emiliano** Spain
147 G4 **San Enrique** Arg.
139 F6 **San Estanislao** Para.
126 □Q10 **San Esteban** Hond.
129 J3 **San Esteban** Mex.
126 C3 **San Esteban, Isla** *i.* Mex.
129 J6 **San Esteban Cuautempan** Mex.
63 N5 **San Esteban de Gormaz** Spain
62 I7 **San Esteban de la Sierra** Spain
146 B5 **San Fabián de Alico** Chile
73 P6 **San Fele** Italy
73 M5 **San Felice a Cancello** Italy
73 K5 **San Felice Circeo** Italy
62 G7 **San Felices de los Gallegos** Spain
71 K6 **San Felice sul Panaro** Italy
146 B3 **San Felipe** Chile
126 B2 **San Felipe** *Baja California* Mex.
126 F4 **San Felipe** *Chihuahua* Mex.
128 F4 **San Felipe** *Guanajuato* Mex.
63 Q8 **San Felipe** *mt.* Spain
136 D2 **San Felipe** Venez.
130 B3 **San Felipe, Cayos de** *is* Cuba
125 Q8 **San Felipe Creek** *watercourse CA* U.S.A.
128 E1 **San Felipe de Teyra** Mex.
128 E1 **San Felipe Nuevo Mercurio** Mex.
129 K8 **San Felipe Usila** Mex.
San Feliú de Guíxols Spain *see* **Sant Feliu de Guíxols**
San Feliú de Pallarols Spain *see* **Sant Feliu de Pallerols**
San Feliú Sasssera Spain *see* **Sant Feliu Sasserra**
138 A6 **San Félix, Isla** *i. Islas de los Desventurados* S. Pacific Ocean
75 J7 **San Ferdinando** Italy
73 Q5 **San Ferdinando di Puglia** Italy
147 H4 **San Fernando** Arg.
146 B4 **San Fernando** Chile
126 B3 **San Fernando** *Baja California* Mex.
127 J5 **San Fernando** *Tamaulipas* Mex.
154 C3 **San Fernando** *Luzon* Phil.
154 C4 **San Fernando** *Luzon* Phil.
64 G8 **San Fernando** Spain
131 □7 **San Fernando** Trin. and Tob.
124 N7 **San Fernando** *CA* U.S.A.
136 E3 **San Fernando de Apure** Venez.
136 E3 **San Fernando de Atabapo** Venez.
63 M8 **San Fernando de Henares** Spain
73 Q9 **San Fili** Italy
75 I7 **San Filippo del Mela** *Sicilia* Italy
62 F6 **Sanfins do Douro** Port.
21 L5 **Sånfjället nationalpark** *nat. park* Sweden
209 C9 **Sanford** *r. W.A.* Austr.
115 G11 **Sanford** *FL* U.S.A.
117 □O5 **Sanford** *ME* U.S.A.
110 J6 **Sanford** *MI* U.S.A.
115 H8 **Sanford** *NC* U.S.A.
131 □7 **San Francique** Trin. and Tob.
147 F2 **San Francisco** Arg.
138 D3 **San Francisco** Bol.
128 F2 **San Francisco** *San Luis Potosí* Mex.
129 H3 **San Francisco** *San Luis Potosí* Mex.
126 C2 **San Francisco** *Sonora* Mex.
124 J4 **San Francisco** *CA* U.S.A.
123 J10 **San Francisco** *r. NM* U.S.A.
130 H8 **San Francisco** Venez.
136 A4 **San Francisco, Cabo de** *c.* Ecuador
144 C2 **San Francisco, Paso de** *pass* Arg.
126 C4 **San Francisco, Sierra** *mts* Mex.
124 J4 **San Francisco Bay** *inlet CA* U.S.A.
129 K10 **San Francisco Cozoaltepec** Mex.
147 G6 **San Francisco de Bellocq** Arg.
126 G4 **San Francisco de Conchos** Mex.
144 E3 **San Francisco del Chañar** Arg.
146 D3 **San Francisco del Monte de Oro** Arg.
126 G4 **San Francisco del Oro** Mex.
139 E5 **San Francisco del Parapetí** Bol.
128 F4 **San Francisco del Rincón** Mex.
130 H4 **San Francisco de Macorís** Dom. Rep.
146 B3 **San Francisco de Mostazal** Chile
145 D8 **San Francisco de Paula, Cabo** *c.* Arg.
129 I2 **San Francisco el Alto** Mex.
126 □O11 **San Francisco Gotera** El Salvador
67 H10 **San Francisco Javier** Spain
74 H7 **San Fratello** *Sicilia* Italy
70 C6 **Sanfront** Italy
91 B7 **Sanga** Angola
91 F6 **Sanga** Dem. Rep. Congo
146 B3 **San Gabriel** Chile
136 B4 **San Gabriel** Ecuador
126 C3 **San Gabriel, Punta** *pt* Mex.
129 J7 **San Gabriel Chilac** Mex.
124 N7 **San Gabriel Mountains** *CA* U.S.A.
191 K5 **Sängäçal Burnu** *pt* Azer.
Sangachaly Azer. *see* Sanqaçal
156 F6 **Sangaigerong** *Sumatera* Indon.
170 B3 **Sa'ngain** *Xizang* China
62 D8 **Sangalhos** Port.
138 A3 **San Gallan, Isla** *i.* Peru
176 F5 **Sangam** *Andhra Prad.* India
176 C4 **Sangameshwar** *Mahar.* India
176 D3 **Sangamner** *Mahar.* India
120 J5 **Sangamon** *r. IL* U.S.A.
185 K5 **Sangan** Afgh.
184 H4 **Sangān** *Khorāsān* Iran
184 I4 **Sangan** Iran
185 I7 **Sangān** *Sīstān va Balūchestān* Iran
185 L7 **Sangan** Pak.
185 K5 **Sangān, Kūh-e** *mt.* Afgh.
185 N6 **Sangar** *r.* Pak.
193 N3 **Sangar** Rus. Fed.
63 L7 **Sangarcía** Spain
88 B4 **Sangaréa** Guinea
176 F4 **Sangareddi** *Andhra Prad.* India
88 B4 **Sangarédi** Guinea
178 E5 **Sangaria** *Rajasthan* India
157 L5 **Sangasanga** *Kalimantan* Indon.
154 B9 **Sanga Sanga** *i.* Phil.
Sangasso Mali *see* **Zangasso**
18 J4 **Sangaste** Estonia
90 A5 **Sangatanga** Gabon
36 C2 **Sangatte** France
72 B8 **San Gavino Monreale** *Sardegna* Italy
136 B5 **Sangay, Parque Nacional** *nat. park* Ecuador
136 B5 **Sangay, Volcán** *vol.* Ecuador
173 K11 **Sangba** *Xizang* China
21 M5 **Sångbäcken** Sweden
184 H4 **Sang Bast** Iran
89 I5 **Sangbé** Cameroon
154 C8 **Sangboy Islands** Phil.
185 I5 **Sangbur** Afgh.
155 A8 **Sangeang** *i.* Indon.
168 I6 **Sangejing** *Nei Mongol* China
73 J2 **San Gemini** Italy
147 G3 **San Genaro** Arg.
Sangenjo *Galicia* Spain *see* Sanxenxo
75 O2 **San Gennaro, Capo** *c.* Italy
77 M4 **Sângeorgiu de Pădure** Romania
77 M3 **Sângeorz-Băi** Romania
168 B5 **Sangequanzi** *Xinjiang* China
77 M4 **Sânger** Romania
124 M5 **Sanger** *CA* U.S.A.
Sângera Moldova *see* Sîngera
Sângerei Moldova *see* Sîngerei
117 J6 **Sangerfield** *NY* U.S.A.
51 D8 **Sangerhausen** Ger.
147 F6 **San German** Arg.
131 □1 **San Germán** Puerto Rico
41 K7 **San Germano Chisone** Italy
146 D3 **San Gerónimo** Arg.
169 N6 **Sanggan He** *r.* China
157 M9 **Sanggar, Teluk** *b. Sumbawa* Indon.
157 I4 **Sanggau** *Kalimantan* Indon.
157 H4 **Sanggauledo** *Kalimantan* Indon.
155 D2 **Sanggeluhang** *i.* Indon.
169 R8 **Sanggou Wan** *b.* China
89 F4 **Sangha** Burkina
90 B4 **Sangha** *admin. reg.* Congo
90 C5 **Sangha** *r.* Congo
90 C4 **Sangha-Mbaéré** *pref.* C.A.R.
185 M8 **Sanghar** Pak.
71 K2 **San Giacomo, Cima** *mt.* Italy
70 I2 **San Giacomo, Lago di** *l.* Italy
136 C3 **San Gil** Col.
168 D1 **Sangilen, Nagor'ye** *mts* Rus. Fed.
75 □ **San Ġiljan** Malta
71 K9 **San Gimignano** Italy
185 K5 **Sangīn** Afgh.
63 R7 **San Ginés** *mt.* Spain
73 K1 **San Ginesio** Italy
73 L5 **San Giorgio a Liri** Italy
71 N3 **San Giorgio della Richinvelda** Italy
71 O4 **San Giorgio di Nogaro** Italy
71 K6 **San Giorgio di Piano** Italy
75 M3 **San Giorgio Ionico** Italy
73 N5 **San Giorgio la Molara** Italy
75 K3 **San Giorgio Lucano** Italy
73 O7 **San Giovanni a Piro** Italy
70 H4 **San Giovanni Bianco** Italy
72 H1 **San Giovanni d'Asso** Italy
74 F8 **San Giovanni Gemini** *Sicilia* Italy
73 K4 **San Giovanni Incarico** Italy
70 I5 **San Giovanni in Croce** Italy
75 L5 **San Giovanni in Fiore** Italy
71 K6 **San Giovanni in Persiceto** Italy
71 K5 **San Giovanni Lupatoto** Italy
73 P4 **San Giovanni Rotondo** Italy
72 B9 **San Giovanni Suegiu** *Sardegna* Italy
73 M3 **San Giovanni Teatino** Italy
71 L8 **San Giovanni Valdarno** Italy
178 E9 **Sangir** *Mahar.* India
155 D2 **Sangir** *i.* Indon.
155 D2 **Sangir, Kepulauan** *is* Indon.
75 K2 **San Giuliano, Lago di** *l.* Italy
70 I8 **San Giuliano Terme** Italy
74 E8 **San Giuseppe Jato** *Sicilia* Italy
74 H2 **San Giuseppe Vesuviano** Italy
71 M8 **San Giustino** Italy
168 I3 **Sangiyn Dalay** Mongolia
168 F2 **Sangiyn Dalay Nuur** *salt l.* Mongolia
163 F10 **Sangju** S. Korea
157 J7 **Sangkapura** *Jawa* Indon.
155 A6 **Sangkarang, Kepulauan** *is* Indon.
159 F8 **Sângke, Stœ̆ng** *r.* Cambodia
159 D7 **Sangkhla Buri** Thai.
157 M4 **Sangkulirang** *Kalimantan* Indon.
157 M4 **Sangkulirang, Teluk** *b.* Indon.
185 O6 **Sangla** Pak.
176 D4 **Sangli** *Mahar.* India
185 N3 **Sanglich** Afgh.
63 K2 **San Glorio, Puerto de** *pass* Spain
89 H6 **Sangmélima** Cameroon
178 G4 **Sangnam** *Hima. Prad.* India
173 K12 **Sangngagqoiling** *Xizang* China
95 F4 **Sango** Zimbabwe
178 F7 **Sangod** *Rajasthan* India
71 L8 **San Godenzo** Italy
176 D4 **Sangole** *Mahar.* India
67 C12 **Sangonera** *r.* Spain
124 P7 **San Gorgonio Mountain** *CA* U.S.A.
70 F2 **San Gottardo, Passo del** *pass* Switz.
155 F2 **Sangowo** *Maluku* Indon.
Sangpi *Sichuan* China *see* **Xiangcheng**
170 A4 **Sang Qu** *r. Xizang* China
123 K7 **Sangre de Cristo Range** *mts CO* U.S.A.
147 F4 **San Gregorio** Arg.
146 B5 **San Gregorio** Chile
147 I3 **San Gregorio** Uru.
144 G4 **San Gregorio de Polanca** Uru.
73 O6 **San Gregorio Magno** Italy
73 M5 **San Gregorio Matese** Italy
131 □7 **Sangre Grande** Trin. and Tob.
63 K9 **Sangrera** *r.* Spain
173 K12 **Sangri** *Xizang* China
73 N3 **Sangro** *r.* Italy
55 L1 **Sangrūda** Lith.
170 B2 **Sangruma** *Qinghai* China
178 E4 **Sangrur** *Punjab* India
173 H12 **Sangsang** *Xizang* China
179 M8 **Sangu** *r.* Bangl.
106 H4 **Sangudo** *Alta* Can.
139 F2 **Sangue** *r.* Brazil
63 R3 **Sangüesa** Spain
70 G5 **San Guiliano Milanese** Italy
147 G2 **San Guillermo** Arg.
144 C3 **San Guillermo, Parque Nacional** *nat. park* Arg.
66 H4 **San Guim de Freixenet** Spain
72 B4 **Sanguinaires, Îles** *i. Corse* France
43 B7 **Sanguinet** France
71 K5 **Sanguinetto** Italy
184 G7 **Sangū'īyeh** Iran
147 H2 **San Gustavo** Arg.
185 N2 **Sangvor** Tajik.
Sangyuan *Hebei* China *see* **Wuqiao**
170 H4 **Sangzhi** *Hunan* China
88 D4 **Sanhala** Côte d'Ivoire
Sanhe *Guizhou* China *see* Sandu
169 Q1 **Sanhe** *Nei Mongol* China
171 K3 **Sanhezhen** *Anhui* China
126 D5 **San Hilario** Mex.
San Hilario Sacalm Spain *see* Sant Hilari Sacalm
126 B4 **San Hipólito, Punta** *pt* Mex.
85 F2 **Sanhūr** Egypt
115 F12 **Sanibel Island** *FL* U.S.A.
147 H5 **San Ignacio** Arg.
127 O9 **San Ignacio** Belize
138 D3 **San Ignacio** *Beni* Bol.
138 E4 **San Ignacio** *Santa Cruz* Bol.
139 E4 **San Ignacio** *Santa Cruz* Bol.
126 C3 **San Ignacio** *Baja California* Mex.
126 C4 **San Ignacio** *Baja California Sur* Mex.
128 A2 **San Ignacio** *Sinaloa* Mex.
126 D2 **San Ignacio** *Sonora* Mex.
139 F6 **San Ignacio** Para.
136 B6 **San Ignacio** Peru
126 C4 **San Ignacio, Laguna** *l.* Mex.
108 E1 **Sanikiluaq** *Nunavut* Can.
63 M7 **San Ildefonso** Spain
154 D3 **San Ildefonso Peninsula** *Luzon* Phil.
166 A4 **Sanin-kaigan National Park** Japan
97 N5 **Sanipas** *pass* S. Africa
146 D3 **San Isidro** Arg.
129 K10 **San Isidro** *Oaxaca* Mex.
129 I1 **San Isidro** *Tamaulipas* Mex.
128 E1 **San Isidro** *Zacatecas* Mex.
63 J2 **San Isidro, Puerto de** *pass* Spain
129 L10 **San Isidro Chacalapa** Mex.
129 K10 **San Isidro del Palmar** Mex.
77 K3 **Sanislău** Romania
50 F2 **Sanitz** Ger.
84 C3 **Sāniyat al Fawākhir** *well* Libya
136 C2 **San Jacinto** Col.
154 D5 **San Jacinto** *Masbate* Phil.
124 P8 **San Jacinto** *CA* U.S.A.
124 P8 **San Jacinto Peak** *CA* U.S.A.
179 K8 **Sanjai** *r. Jharkhand* India
147 H2 **San Jaime** Arg.
147 H2 **San Javier** Arg.
138 D3 **San Javier** *Beni* Bol.
139 E4 **San Javier** *Santa Cruz* Bol.
129 H5 **San Javier** Mex.
67 D12 **San Javier** Spain
147 H3 **San Javier** Uru.
146 B4 **San Javier de Loncomilla** Chile
185 M6 **Sanjawi** Pak.
184 C3 **Sanjbod** Iran
128 G8 **San Jerónimo** *Guerrero* Mex.
128 D2 **San Jerónimo** *Zacatecas* Mex.
138 B1 **San Jerónimo** Peru
129 K9 **San Jerónimo Taviche** Mex.
170 G6 **Sanjiang** *Guangxi* China
169 R5 **Sanjiangkou** *Liaoning* China
170 H4 **Sanjiaoping** *Hunan* China
171 M4 **Sanjie** *Zhejiang* China
165 P9 **Sanjō** Japan
138 D3 **San Joaquín** Bol.
129 H5 **San Joaquin** Mex.
139 F6 **San Joaquin** Para.
124 L5 **San Joaquin** *CA* U.S.A.
124 K3 **San Joaquin** *r. CA* U.S.A.
124 L4 **San Joaquin Valley** *CA* U.S.A.
121 D8 **San Jon** *NM* U.S.A.
146 D3 **San Jorge** *San Luis* Arg.
147 G2 **San Jorge** *Santa Fé* Arg.
200 □6 **San Jorge** *i.* Solomon Is
66 F6 **San Jorge** Spain
145 D7 **San Jorge, Golfo de** *g.* Arg.
San Jorge, Golfo de *g.* Spain *see* **Sant Jordi, Golf de**
64 E3 **San Jorge de Alor** Spain
146 C3 **San José** Arg.
136 D4 **San José** Col.
126 □Q13 **San José** Costa Rica
128 G1 **San Jose** Mex.
154 C4 **San Jose** *Luzon* Phil.
154 C5 **San Jose** *Mindoro* Phil.
154 C5 **San Jose** *Mindoro* Phil.
65 O7 **San José** *Andalucía* Spain
67 H10 **San José** *Illes Balears* Spain
147 I4 **San José** *dept* Uru.
147 I4 **San José** *r.* Uru.
124 K4 **San Jose** *CA* U.S.A.
123 L9 **San Jose** *NM* U.S.A.
123 K9 **San Jose** *watercourse NM* U.S.A.
136 E2 **San José** Venez.
145 D7 **San José, Cabo** *c.* Arg.
147 I2 **San José, Cuchilla de** *hills* Uru.
145 D6 **San José, Golfo** *g.* Arg.
126 D5 **San José, Isla** *i.* Mex.
146 C3 **San José, Volcán** *vol.* Chile
128 G6 **San Jose Allende** Mex.
127 N8 **San José Carpizo** Mex.
128 G4 **San José de Alburquerque** Mex.
137 F2 **San José de Amacuro** Venez.
126 F3 **San José de Bavicora** Mex.
154 C6 **San Jose de Buenavista** *Panay* Phil.
139 E4 **San José de Chiquitos** Bol.
126 D4 **San José de Comondú** Mex.
147 H2 **San José de Feliciano** Arg.
128 G3 **San José de Gallinas** Mex.
128 E3 **San Jose de Gracia** Mex.
126 C4 **San José de Gracia** *Baja California Sur* Mex.
128 D6 **San José de Gracia** *Michoacán* Mex.
126 F4 **San José de Gracia** *Sinaloa* Mex.
126 D3 **San José de Gracia** *Sonora* Mex.
131 K9 **San José de Guaribe** Venez.
146 C2 **San Jose de Jáchal** Arg.
126 E5 **San Joséde la Brecha** Mex.
147 F2 **San José de la Dormida** Arg.
147 G3 **San José de la Esquina** Arg.
145 B5 **San José de la Mariquina** Chile
128 D7 **San José de la Montaña** Mex.
146 E2 **San José de las Salinas** Arg.
144 E2 **San José del Boquerón** Arg.
126 E6 **San José del Cabo** Mex.
136 C4 **San José del Guaviare** Col.
146 E3 **San José del Morro** Arg.
129 J9 **San José del Progreso** Mex.
64 H7 **San José del Valle** Spain
146 B3 **San José de Maipó** Chile
147 I4 **San José de Mayo** Uru.
130 H4 **San José de Ocoa** Dom. Rep.
136 D3 **San José de Ocuné** Col.
123 I12 **San José de Primas** Mex.
128 G1 **San José de Raíces** Mex.
128 D1 **San José de Reyes** Mex.
128 G4 **San José Iturbide** Mex.
173 D8 **Sanju** *Xinjiang* China
146 C2 **San Juan** Arg.
146 C2 **San Juan** *prov.* Arg.
139 E4 **San Juan** Bol.
98 □3a **San Juan** *Tenerife* Canary Is
136 B2 **San Juan** Col.
136 B3 **San Juan** *r.* Col.
126 □R12 **San Juan** *r.* Costa Rica/Nic.
130 C3 **San Juan** *mt.* Cuba
130 H4 **San Juan** Dom. Rep.
126 F4 **San Juan** *Chihuahua* Mex.
127 I4 **San Juan** *Coahuila* Mex.
128 E2 **San Juan** *Zacatecas* Mex.
128 E4 **San Juan** *r.* Mex.
129 L7 **San Juan** *r.* Mex.
138 B3 **San Juan** Peru
154 E6 **San Juan** *Leyte* Phil.
154 F7 **San Juan** *Mindanao* Phil.
131 □1 **San Juan** Puerto Rico
64 G3 **San Juan** *r.* Spain
131 □7 **San Juan** Trin. and Tob.
124 L6 **San Juan** *r. CA* U.S.A.
125 V4 **San Juan** *r. UT* U.S.A.
137 E3 **San Juan** Venez.
131 □1 **San Juan, Bahía de** *b.* Puerto Rico
145 E9 **San Juan, Cabo** *c.* Arg.
89 H6 **San Juan, Cabo** *c.* Equat. Guinea
63 L8 **San Juan, Embalse de** *resr* Spain
126 □O11 **San Juan, Punta** *pt* El Salvador
65 I7 **San Juan, Sierra de** *hills* Spain
129 J8 **San Juan Achiutla** Mex.
139 F6 **San Juan Bautista** Para.
138 □ **San Juan Bautista** S. Pacific Ocean
67 I9 **San Juan Bautista** Spain
124 K5 **San Juan Bautista** *CA* U.S.A.
129 I9 **San Juan Bautista lo de Soto** Mex.
129 J8 **San Juan Bautista Suchitepec** Mex.
129 K7 **San Juan Bautista Tuxtepec** Mex.
124 O8 **San Juan Capistrano** *CA* U.S.A.
126 □P10 **San Juancito** Hond.
128 B5 **San Juan de Abajo** Mex.
67 E11 **San Juan de Alicante** Spain
64 G6 **San Juan de Aznalfarache** Spain
136 C2 **San Juan de César** Col.
128 E1 **San Juan de Guadalupe** Mex.
130 F8 **San Juan de Guía, Cabo de** *c.* Col.
145 B6 **San Juan dela Costa** Chile
66 D3 **San Juan de la Peña, Sierra de** *mts* Spain
129 H6 **San Juan de las Huertas** Mex.
126 □R12 **San Juan del Norte** Nic.
126 □R12 **San Juan del Norte, Bahía de** *b.* Nic.
136 D2 **San Juan de los Cayos** Venez.
128 E4 **San Juan de los Lagos** Mex.
136 E2 **San Juan de los Morros** Venez.
128 D4 **San Juan de los Potreros** Mex.
64 F6 **San Juan del Puerto** Spain
126 G5 **San Juan del Río** *Durango* Mex.
129 L8 **San Juan del Río** *Oaxaca* Mex.
129 H5 **San Juan del Río** *Querétaro* Mex.
126 □Q12 **San Juan del Sur** Nic.
145 E9 **San Juan de Salvamento** Arg.
129 L8 **San Juan Evangelista** Mex.
126 C4 **San Juanico, Punta** *pt* Mex.
122 C2 **San Juan Islands** *WA* U.S.A.
126 F4 **San Juanito** Mex.
128 A4 **San Juanito, Isla** *i.* Mex.
129 J7 **San Juan Ixcaquixtla** Mex.
127 N10 **San Juan Ixcoy** Guat.
129 L9 **San Juan Lachixila** Mex.
129 L8 **San Juan Mazatlán** Mex.
129 K9 **San Juan Mixtepec** Mex.
123 K8 **San Juan Mountains** *CO* U.S.A.
129 K8 **San Juan Tepeuxila** Mex.
130 B2 **San Juan y Martínez** Cuba
173 D8 **Sanju He** *watercourse* China
145 D8 **San Julián** Arg.
128 E4 **San Julian** Mex.
66 D6 **San Just** *mt.* Spain
147 G2 **San Justo** Arg.
62 H4 **San Justo de la Vega** Spain
158 C4 **Sanka** Myanmar
88 C4 **Sankanbiaiwa** *mt.* Sierra Leone
88 C4 **Sankarani** *r.* Côte d'Ivoire/Guinea
176 E8 **Sankarankovil** *Tamil Nadu* India
176 D4 **Sankeshwar** *Karnataka* India
179 J8 **Sankh** *r. Jharkhand* India
184 G3 **Sankhāş** Iran
178 E5 **Sankhu** *Rajasthan* India
Sankosh *r.* Bhutan *see* Sunkosh Chhu
178 I9 **Sankra** *Chhattisgarh* India
178 C6 **Sankra** *Rajasthan* India
59 M4 **Sankt Aegyd am Neuwalde** Austria
59 K6 **Sankt Andrä** Austria
59 O4 **Sankt Andrä am Zicksee** Austria
49 K7 **Sankt Andreasberg** Ger.
59 M6 **Sankt Anna am Aigen** Austria
58 B5 **Sankt Anton am Arlberg** Austria
59 L4 **Sankt Anton an der Jeßnitz** Austria
49 D9 **Sankt Augustin** Ger.
52 E6 **Sankt Blasien** Ger.
51 G9 **Sankt Egidien** Ger.
59 K4 **Sankt Gallen** Austria
70 G1 **Sankt Gallen** Switz.
70 G1 **Sankt Gallen** *canton* Switz.
58 A5 **Sankt Gallenkirch** Austria
51 E9 **Sankt Gangloff** Ger.
59 J6 **Sankt Georgen am Längsee** Austria
59 K3 **Sankt Georgen am Walde** Austria
59 J3 **Sankt Georgen an der Gusen** Austria
59 H4 **Sankt Georgen im Attergau** Austria
59 K6 **Sankt Georgen im Lavanttal** Austria
52 E5 **Sankt Georgen im Schwarzwald** Ger.
59 H4 **Sankt Gilgen** Austria
49 E10 **Sankt Goar** Ger.
49 E10 **Sankt Goarshausen** Ger.
Sankt Gotthard Hungary *see* Szentgotthárd
52 C3 **Sankt Ingbert** Ger.
59 J6 **Sankt Jakob im Rosental** Austria
59 M5 **Sankt Jakob im Walde** Austria
58 F6 **Sankt Jakob in Defereggen** Austria
59 J5 **Sankt Johann am Tauern** Austria
58 H5 **Sankt Johann im Pongau** Austria
59 L6 **Sankt Johann im Saggautal** Austria
58 G6 **Sankt Johann im Walde** Austria
58 F4 **Sankt Johann in Tirol** Austria
52 D2 **Sankt Julian** Ger.
59 K6 **Sankt Kanzian am Klopeiner See** Austria
59 J5 **Sankt Lambrecht** Austria
59 L3 **Sankt Leonhard am Forst** Austria
59 M2 **Sankt Leonhard am Hornerwald** Austria
58 C5 **Sankt Leonhard im Pitztal** Austria
59 H4 **Sankt Lorenz** Austria
58 H6 **Sankt Lorenzen im Gitschtal** Austria
58 G6 **Sankt Lorenzen im Lesachtal** Austria
59 L5 **Sankt Lorenzen im Mürztal** Austria
59 J5 **Sankt Lorenzen ob Murau** Austria
59 L5 **Sankt Marein im Mürztal** Austria
59 J6 **Sankt Margareten im Rosental** Austria
48 H3 **Sankt Margarethen** Ger.
59 M5 **Sankt Margarethen an der Raab** Austria
59 K5 **Sankt Margarethen bei Knittelfeld** Austria
59 O4 **Sankt Margarethen im Burgenland** Austria
52 E5 **Sankt Märgen** Ger.
59 J3 **Sankt Marien** Austria
59 I3 **Sankt Marienkirchen an der Polsenz** Austria
59 K2 **Sankt Martin** *Niederösterreich* Austria
59 H5 **Sankt Martin** *Salzburg* Austria
59 N6 **Sankt Martin an der Raab** Austria
59 J3 **Sankt Martin im Mühlkreis** Austria
59 L6 **Sankt Martin im Sulmtal** Austria
59 N5 **Sankt Michael im Burgenland** Austria
59 I5 **Sankt Michael im Lungau** Austria
59 L5 **Sankt Michael in Obersteiermark** Austria
48 H3 **Sankt Michaelisdonn** Ger.
70 H2 **Sankt Moritz** Switz.
70 D3 **Sankt Niklaus** Switz.
59 L6 **Sankt Nikolai im Saustal** Austria
59 J5 **Sankt Nikolai im Sölktal** Austria
59 K2 **Sankt Oswald bei Freistadt** Austria
59 L6 **Sankt Oswald ob Eibiswald** Austria
53 O4 **Sankt Oswald-Riedlhütte** Ger.
59 J4 **Sankt Pankraz** Austria
58 G3 **Sankt Pantaleon** Austria
59 K6 **Sankt Paul im Lavanttal** Austria
52 E5 **Sankt Peter** Ger.
58 H3 **Sankt Peter am Hart** Austria
59 J5 **Sankt Peter am Kammersberg** Austria
59 M6 **Sankt Peter am Ottersbach** Austria
19 N2 **Sankt-Peterburg** Rus. Fed.
59 L5 **Sankt Peter-Freienstein** Austria
59 L6 **Sankt Peter im Sulmtal** Austria
59 K3 **Sankt Peter in der Au** Austria
48 G2 **Sankt Peter-Ording** Ger.
Sankt Petersburg Rus. Fed. *see* **Sankt-Peterburg**
59 M3 **Sankt Pölten** Austria
58 G3 **Sankt Radegund** Austria
59 M5 **Sankt Ruprecht an der Raab** Austria
59 K6 **Sankt Stefan** Austria
59 I6 **Sankt Stefan im Gailtal** Austria
59 M6 **Sankt Stefan im Rosental** Austria
59 K5 **Sankt Stefan ob Leoben** Austria
59 L6 **Sankt Stefan ob Stainz** Austria
58 G4 **Sankt Ulrich am Pillersee** Austria
59 J3 **Sankt Ulrich bei Steyr** Austria
59 J6 **Sankt Urban** Austria
59 K3 **Sankt Valentin** Austria
59 M6 **Sankt Veit am Vogau** Austria
59 J6 **Sankt Veit an der Glan** Austria
59 M3 **Sankt Veit an der Gölsen** Austria
58 H5 **Sankt Veit im Pongau** Austria
58 F6 **Sankt Veit in Defereggen** Austria
52 C3 **Sankt Wendel** Ger.
53 M5 **Sankt Wolfgang** Ger.
59 H4 **Sankt Wolfgang im Salzkammergut** Austria
178 F2 **Sanku** Jammu and Kashmir
91 D6 **Sankuru** *r.* Dem. Rep. Congo
75 □ **San Lawrenz** *Gozo* Malta
139 F5 **San Lázaro** Para.
126 C5 **San Lázaro, Cabo** *c.* Mex.
71 K7 **San Lazzaro di Savena** Italy
124 J4 **San Leandro** *CA* U.S.A.
71 M8 **San Leo** Italy
74 F8 **San Leonardo** *r. Sicilia* Italy
63 N5 **San Leonardo de Yagüe** Spain
71 K2 **San Leonardo in Passiria** Italy
188 I5 **Şanlıurfa** Turkey
190 H1 **Şanlıurfa** *prov.* Turkey
144 F3 **San Lorenzo** *Corrientes* Arg.
147 G3 **San Lorenzo** *Santa Fé* Arg.
138 D3 **San Lorenzo** *Beni* Bol.
138 D2 **San Lorenzo** *Pando* Bol.
138 D5 **San Lorenzo** *Tarija* Bol.
136 B4 **San Lorenzo** Ecuador
126 □P11 **San Lorenzo** Hond.
75 J8 **San Lorenzo** Italy
126 F3 **San Lorenzo** Mex.
138 C2 **San Lorenzo** Peru
63 O4 **San Lorenzo** *mt.* Spain
136 A5 **San Lorenzo, Cabo** *c.* Ecuador
72 D9 **San Lorenzo, Capo** *c. Sardegna* Italy
145 B7 **San Lorenzo, Cerro** *mt.* Arg./Chile
126 C3 **San Lorenzo, Isla** *i.* Mex.
138 A3 **San Lorenzo, Isla** *i.* Peru
70 D8 **San Lorenzo al Mare** Italy
73 Q8 **San Lorenzo Bellizzi** Italy
129 K8 **San Lorenzo Cacaotepec** Mex.
65 L4 **San Lorenzo de Calatrava** Spain
63 L7 **San Lorenzo de El Escorial** Spain
63 P9 **San Lorenzo de la Parrilla** Spain
San Lorenzo de Morunys Spain *see* Sant Llorenç de Morunys
71 L2 **San Lorenzo di Sebato** Italy
71 N8 **San Lorenzo in Campo** Italy
72 H2 **San Lorenzo Nuovo** Italy
75 K7 **San Luca** Italy
64 G7 **Sanlúcar de Barrameda** Spain
64 E6 **Sanlúcar de Guadiana** Spain
64 G6 **Sanlúcar la Mayor** Spain
138 D5 **San Lucas** Bol.
126 C4 **San Lucas** *Baja California Sur* Mex.
126 E6 **San Lucas** *Baja California Sur* Mex.
128 G7 **San Lucas** *Michoacán* Mex.
126 E6 **San Lucas, Cabo** *c.* Mex.
136 C3 **San Lucas, Serranía de** *mts* Col.
73 Q9 **San Lucido** Italy
146 D3 **San Luis** Arg.
146 D3 **San Luis** *prov.* Arg.
138 D2 **San Luís** Brazil
130 F3 **San Luis** Cuba
127 O9 **San Luis** Guat.
128 G8 **San Luis** *Guerrero* Mex.
129 M8 **San Luis** *Veracruz* Mex.
136 C5 **San Luis** Peru
66 □ **San Luis** Spain
125 R9 **San Luis** *AZ* U.S.A.
125 U9 **San Luis** *AZ* U.S.A.
123 L8 **San Luis** *CO* U.S.A.
136 D2 **San Luis** Venez.
126 B3 **San Luís, Isla** *i.* Mex.
125 R9 **San Luis, Mesa de** *plat.* Mex.
146 D3 **San Luis, Sierra de** *mts* Arg.
129 I9 **San Luis Acatlán** Mex.
129 K9 **San Luis Amatlán** Mex.
128 G4 **San Luis de la Paz** Mex.
144 F2 **San Luis del Palmar** Arg.
126 D5 **San Luis Gonzaga** Mex.
126 C2 **San Luisito** Mex.
124 L6 **San Luis Obispo** *CA* U.S.A.
124 L6 **San Luis Obispo Bay** *CA* U.S.A.
126 □O10 **San Luis Pajón** Hond.
128 G3 **San Luis Potosí** Mex.
128 G3 **San Luis Potosí** *state* Mex.
124 K4 **San Luis Reservoir** *CA* U.S.A.
126 B1 **San Luis Río Colorado** Mex.
72 B8 **Sanluri** *Sardegna* Italy
71 M2 **San Maddalena Vallalta** Italy
62 E4 **San Mamede, Serra do** *mts* Spain
63 K4 **San Mamés de Campos** Spain
73 Q9 **San Mango d'Aquino** Italy
147 H5 **San Manuel** Arg.
146 B3 **San Manuel** Chile
125 V9 **San Manuel** *AZ* U.S.A.
71 O8 **San Marcello** Italy
71 J7 **San Marcello Pistoiese** Italy
126 D5 **San Marcial, Punta** *pt* Mex.
72 A8 **San Marco, Capo** *c. Sardegna* Italy
74 E9 **San Marco, Capo** *c. Sicilia* Italy
73 Q8 **San Marco Argentano** Italy
74 H7 **San Marco d'Alunzio** *Sicilia* Italy
73 N5 **San Marco dei Cavoti** Italy
73 P4 **San Marco in Lamis** Italy
146 B2 **San Marcos** Chile
136 C2 **San Marcos** Col.
127 N10 **San Marcos** Guat.
126 □P11 **San Marcos** Hond.
129 H9 **San Marcos** *Guerrero* Mex.
128 C5 **San Marcos** *Jalisco* Mex.
138 A1 **San Marcos** Peru
62 D2 **San Marcos** Spain
124 O8 **San Marcos** *CA* U.S.A.
121 G11 **San Marcos** *TX* U.S.A.
121 G11 **San Marcos** *r. TX* U.S.A.
126 C4 **San Marcos, Isla** *i.* Mex.
71 M8 **San Marino** *country* Europe
71 M8 **San Marino** San Marino
212 T2 **San Martín** *research stn* Antarctica
144 D3 **San Martín** *Catamarca* Arg.
146 C3 **San Martín** *Mendoza* Arg.
139 E3 **San Martín** *r.* Bol.
129 I6 **San Martín** Mex.
138 A1 **San Martín** *dept* Peru
57 K4 **Sânmartin** Romania
66 A1 **San Martín** Spain
67 F10 **San Martín, Cabo de** *c.* Spain
145 B8 **San Martín, Lago** *l.* Arg./Chile
129 L7 **San Martín, Volcán** *vol.* Mex.
129 I4 **San Martín Chalchicuautla** Mex.
128 D4 **San Martin de Bolaños** Mex.
63 M8 **San Martín de la Vega** Spain
63 J8 **San Martín de la Vega del Alberche** Spain
145 C6 **San Martín de los Andes** Arg.
63 J8 **San Martin del Pimpollar** Spain
63 L9 **San Martín de Montalbán** Spain
63 K9 **San Martín de Pusa** Spain
63 Q3 **San Martin de Unx** Spain
63 L8 **San Martín de Valdeiglesias** Spain
128 D5 **San Martín Hidalgo** Mex.
71 K5 **San Martino Buon Albergo** Italy
71 L3 **San Martino di Castrozza** Italy
72 C2 **San-Martino-di-Lota** *Corse* France
71 L4 **San Martino di Lupari** Italy
71 L5 **San Martino di Venezze** Italy
71 L2 **San Martino in Badia** Italy
71 K2 **San Martino in Passiria** Italy
73 O4 **San Martino in Pensilis** Italy
136 D5 **San Mateo** Peru
San Mateo Spain *see* Sant Mateu
124 J4 **San Mateo** *CA* U.S.A.
137 E2 **San Mateo** Venez.
66 D4 **San Mateo de Gállego** Spain
127 N10 **San Mateo Ixtatán** Guat.
139 F4 **San Matías** Bol.
145 D6 **San Matías, Golfo** *g.* Arg.
136 E2 **San Mauricio** Venez.
74 G8 **San Mauro Castelverde** *Sicilia* Italy
73 Q7 **San Mauro Forte** Italy
71 M7 **San Mauro Pascoli** Italy
70 D5 **San Mauro Torinese** Italy
171 M4 **Sanmen** *Zhejiang* China
73 P4 **San Menaio** Italy
171 M4 **Sanmen Wan** *b.* China
169 L9 **Sanmenxia** *Henan* China
71 N4 **San Michele al Tagliamento** Italy
70 D7 **San Michele Mondovì** Italy
75 N2 **San Michele Salentino** Italy
144 F3 **San Miguel** *Corrientes* Arg.
146 D3 **San Miguel** *San Juan* Arg.
139 E4 **San Miguel** Bol.
138 E3 **San Miguel** *r.* Bol.
136 C4 **San Miguel** *r.* Col.
126 □O11 **San Miguel** El Salvador
128 B3 **San Miguel** Mex.
126 □T13 **San Miguel** Panama
138 B3 **San Miguel** Peru
154 C5 **San Miguel** *Luzon* Phil.
San Miguel Spain *see* Sant Miquel
67 F7 **San Miguel** *r.* Spain
124 L6 **San Miguel** *CA* U.S.A.
123 J7 **San Miguel** *r. CO* U.S.A.
137 E2 **San Miguel** Venez.
154 D5 **San Miguel Bay** *Luzon* Phil.
129 K9 **San Miguel Coatlán** Mex.
98 □3a **San Miguel de Abona** *Tenerife* Canary Is
128 G5 **San Miguel de Allende** Mex.
63 L6 **San Miguel de Arroyo** Spain
63 M6 **San Miguel de Bernuy** Spain
128 B1 **San Miguel de Cruces** Mex.
128 G5 **San Miguel Deheti** Mex.
126 D3 **San Miguel de Horcasitas** *r.* Mex.
138 D3 **San Miguel de Huachi** Bol.
128 C5 **San Miguel de la Sierra** Mex.
147 H4 **San Miguel del Monte** Arg.
129 K10 **San Miguel del Puerto** Mex.
67 D12 **San Miguel de Salinas** Spain
144 D2 **San Miguel de Tucumán** Arg.
140 C5 **San Miguel do Araguaia** Brazil
128 E4 **San Miguel el Alto** Mex.
124 L7 **San Miguel Island** *CA* U.S.A.
154 B8 **San Miguel Islands** Phil.
128 G2 **San Miguelito** Mex.
126 □T13 **San Miguelito** Panama
128 G5 **San Miguel Octopan** Mex.
129 K9 **San Miguel Sola de Vega** Mex.
129 H8 **San Miguel Tecuixiapan** Mex.
63 N4 **San Millán** *mt.* Spain
63 O4 **San Millán de la Cogolla** Spain
171 K5 **Sanming** *Fujian* China
71 J8 **San Miniato** Italy
55 J5 **Sanna** *r.* Pol.
166 B5 **Sannan** Japan
154 C4 **San Narciso** *Luzon* Phil.
97 K5 **Sannaspos** S. Africa
75 □ **Sannat** *Gozo* Malta
70 F5 **Sannazzaro de'Burgondi** Italy
176 D5 **Sanndatti** *Karnataka* India
Sanndraigh *i. Scotland* U.K. *see* **Sandray**
185 L7 **Sanni** Pak.
75 L2 **Sannicandro di Bari** Italy

73 P4 Sannicandro Garganico Italy
75 O3 Sannicola Italy
73 P3 San Nicola, Isole is Italy
75 L5 San Nicola dell'Alto Italy
72 C3 San-Nicolao Corse France
146 A5 San Nicolás Chile
129 I9 San Nicolás Guerrero Mex.
129 I1 San Nicolás Tamaulipas Mex.
128 B6 San Nicolás r. Mex.
136 D5 San Nicolás Peru
154 C3 San Nicolas Luzon Phil.
138 B3 San Nicolás, Bahía b. Peru
128 G5 San Nicolás de los Agustinos Mex.
147 G3 San Nicolás de los Arroyos Arg.
126 G5 San Nicolás del Presidio Mex.
64 H4 San Nicolás del Puerto Spain
98 □3f San Nicolás de Tolentino Gran Canaria Canary Is
123 E10 San Nicolas Island CA U.S.A.
128 G3 San Nicolás Tolentino Mex.
76 I4 Sânnicolau Mare Romania
71 L6 San Nicolò Italy
72 B8 San Nicolò d'Arcidano Sardegna Italy
72 C9 San Nicolò Gerrei Sardegna Italy
97 J2 Sannieshof S. Africa
55 H3 Sanniki Pol.
73 N4 Sannio, Monti del mts Italy
88 C5 Sanniquellie Liberia
164 S6 Sannohe Japan
167 K3 Sano Japan
140 D3 Sañogasta, Sierra de mts Arg.
55 K6 Sanok Pol.
136 C2 San Onofre Col.
145 D9 San Pablo Arg.
138 D5 San Pablo Potosí Bol.
139 E3 San Pablo Santa Cruz Bol.
139 E3 San Pablo r. Bol.
136 D3 San Pablo Col.
129 H5 San Pablo Mex.
154 C4 San Pablo Luzon Phil.
124 J4 San Pablo CA U.S.A.
63 L9 San Pablo de los Montes Spain
71 K2 San Pancrazio Italy
75 N3 San Pancrazio Salentino Italy
58 B8 San Paolo, Isola i. Italy
73 O4 San Paolo di Civitate Italy
75 □ San Pawl, Gżejjer ta' is Malta
75 □ San Pawl il-Baħar Malta
75 □ San Pawl-il-Baħar, Il-Bajja ta' b. Malta
147 H3 San Pedro Buenos Aires Arg.
144 D2 San Pedro Catamarca Arg.
146 E2 San Pedro Córdoba Arg.
144 D2 San Pedro Jujuy Arg.
144 G2 San Pedro Misiones Arg.
127 P9 San Pedro Belize
138 D3 San Pedro Beni Bol.
139 E4 San Pedro Santa Cruz Bol.
138 D4 San Pedro r. Bol.
146 B3 San Pedro Santiago Chile
146 B3 San Pedro Valparaíso Chile
88 D5 San-Pédro Côte d'Ivoire
130 D3 San Pedro r. Cuba
126 D6 San Pedro Baja California Sur Mex.
126 F3 San Pedro Chihuahua Mex.
128 B4 San Pedro r. Mex.
123 L12 San Pedro r. Mex.
138 C2 San Pedro Peru
154 C5 San Pedro Mindoro Phil.
65 O3 San Pedro Spain
147 I4 San Pedro Uru.
125 V9 San Pedro watercourse AZ U.S.A.
126 □R13 San Pedro, Punta pt Costa Rica
64 E1 San Pedro, Sierra de mts Spain
128 F4 San Pedro Almoloyan Mex.
128 C4 San Pedro Analco Mex.
129 K9 San Pedro Apóstol Mex.
127 N10 San Pedro Carchá Guat.
124 N8 San Pedro Channel CA U.S.A.
65 J8 San Pedro de Alcántara Spain
136 D3 San Pedro de Arimena Col.
138 C5 San Pedro de Atacama Chile
62 H4 San Pedro de Ceque Spain
123 J12 San Pedro de la Cueva Mex.
63 K7 San Pedro del Arroyo Spain
126 H5 San Pedro de las Colonias Mex.
63 J5 San Pedro de Latarce Spain
136 B6 San Pedro de Lloc Peru
139 F6 San Pedro del Paraná Para.
67 D12 San Pedro del Pinatar Spain
63 M2 San Pedro del Romeral Spain
131 I4 San Pedro de Macorís Dom. Rep.
62 I7 San Pedro de Rozados Spain
139 F6 San Pedro de Ycuamandyyú Para.
129 K9 San Pedro el Alto Mex.
126 D3 San Pedro el Saucito Mex.
63 P4 San Pedro Manrique Spain
126 B2 San Pedro Mártir, Parque Nacional nat. park Mex.
129 J10 San Pedro Mixtepec Mex.
126 □O10 San Pedro Sula Hond.
57 J5 Sânpetru Mare Romania
71 K8 San Piero a Sieve Italy
75 H7 San Piero Patti Sicilia Italy
75 H7 San Pietro Isole Lipari Italy
72 A9 San Pietro, Isola di i. Sardegna Italy
58 G6 San Pietro di Cadore Italy
71 J4 San Pietro in Cariano Italy
71 K6 San Pietro in Casale Italy
75 K8 San Pietro Vernotico Italy
125 U2 San Pitch r. UT U.S.A.
70 I6 San Polo d'Enza Italy
71 K6 San Prospero Italy
168 G7 Sanpu Gansu China
191 K5 Sanqaçal Azer.
26 I12 Sanquhar Dumfries and Galloway, Scotland U.K.
136 B4 Sanquianga, Parque Nacional nat. park Col.
66 F4 San Quilez mt. Spain
126 A2 San Quintín, Cabo c. Mex.
72 H1 San Quirico d'Orcia Italy
146 C4 San Rafael Arg.
139 E4 San Rafael Bol.
146 B4 San Rafael Chile
136 D3 San Rafael Col.
128 F2 San Rafael San Luis Potosí Mex.
129 K5 San Rafael Veracruz Mex.
124 J4 San Rafael CA U.S.A.
125 V3 San Rafael r. UT U.S.A.
136 D2 San Rafael Venez.
San Rafael del Moján Venez. see San Rafael
126 □P11 San Rafael del Norte Nic.
66 F6 San Rafael del Río Spain
131 I4 San Rafael del Yuma Dom. Rep.
125 V3 San Rafael Knob mt. UT U.S.A.
124 L7 San Rafael Mountains CA U.S.A.
65 J5 San Rafael Navallana, Embalse de resr Spain
146 D2 San Ramón Arg.
139 D3 San Ramón Beni Bol.
139 E4 San Ramón Santa Cruz Bol.
129 I2 San Ramón Mex.
147 J4 San Ramón Uru.
171 K6 Sanrao Guangdong China
70 D8 San Remo Italy
119 I3 San Remo NY U.S.A.
164 S7 Sanriku Japan
121 E11 San Rodrigo watercourse Mex.
147 G6 San Román Arg.
62 F3 San Román Spain
136 D1 San Román, Cabo c. Venez.
63 K4 San Román de la Cuba Spain
63 K8 San Román de los Montes Spain
65 I8 San Roque Andalucía Spain
62 C2 San Roque Galicia Spain
62 D4 San Roque Galicia Spain
126 B4 San Roque, Punta pt Mex.
73 O7 San Rufo Italy
121 F10 San Saba TX U.S.A.
121 F10 San Saba r. TX U.S.A.
43 I6 Sansac-de-Marmiesse France
146 E2 San Salano Arg.
129 J6 San Salvador el Seco Mex.
88 B4 Sansalé Guinea
147 H2 San Salvador Arg.
130 F1 San Salvador i. Bahamas
127 O11 San Salvador El Salvador
129 H1 San Salvador Mex.
136 D5 San Salvador Peru
147 H3 San Salvador r. Uru.
136 □ San Salvador, Isla i. Islas Galápagos Ecuador
63 L3 San Salvador de Cantamunda Spain
144 D2 San Salvador de Jujuy Arg.
72 A8 San Salvatore Sardegna Italy
70 F6 San Salvatore Monferrato Italy
73 M5 San Salvatore Telesino Italy
73 N3 San Salvo Italy
89 F3 Sansané Haoussa Niger
89 F4 Sansanné-Mango Togo
145 C9 San Sebastián Arg.
128 C5 San Sebastián Mex.
131 □1 San Sebastián Puerto Rico
62 D3 San Sebastián hill Spain
145 C9 San Sebastián, Bahía de b. Arg.
62 G4 San Sebastián, Embalse de resr Spain
98 □3a San Sebastián de la Gomera La Gomera Canary Is
63 M7 San Sebastián de los Reyes Spain
129 K9 San Sebastián Río Hondo Mex.
129 J7 San Sebastián Zinacatepec Mex.
70 I6 San Secondo Parmense Italy
71 M8 Sansepolcro Italy
72 H3 San Severa Italy
73 Q7 San Severino Lucano Italy
71 O9 San Severino Marche Italy
73 O4 San Severo Italy
171 M5 Sansha Fujian China
138 C2 San Silvestre Bol.
136 D2 San Silvestre Venez.
125 W9 San Simon AZ U.S.A.
68 F3 Sanski Most Bos.-Herz.
63 P3 Sansol Spain
202 J7 Sanson North I. N.Z.
Sansoral Islands Palau see Sonsorol Islands
73 Q8 San Sosti Italy
72 C9 San Sperate Sardegna Italy
75 L1 San Spirito Italy
131 □2 Sans Toucher mt. Guadeloupe
170 G5 Sansui Guizhou China
138 A2 Santa Peru
138 A2 Santa r. Peru
142 C4 Santa Adélia Brazil
64 G2 Santa Amalia Spain
127 O9 Santa Amelia Guat.
147 I2 Santa Ana Entre Ríos Arg.
144 D2 Santa Ana Tucumán Arg.
138 D3 Santa Ana La Paz Bol.
139 E4 Santa Ana Santa Cruz Bol.
139 F4 Santa Ana Santa Cruz Bol.
127 O10 Santa Ana El Salvador
200 □1 Santa Ana Guam
129 H6 Santa Ana México Mex.
128 G1 Santa Ana Nuevo León Mex.
126 D2 Santa Ana Sonora Mex.
200 □6 Santa Ana i. Solomon Is
65 P3 Santa Ana Spain
63 L8 Santa Ana hill Spain
124 O8 Santa Ana CA U.S.A.
66 G4 Santa Ana, Embassament de resr Spain
63 K9 Santa Ana de Pusa Spain
138 D3 Santa Ana de Yacuma Bol.
147 H3 Santa Anita Arg.
126 E6 Santa Anita Baja California Sur Mex.
128 D5 Santa Anita Jalisco Mex.
121 F10 Santa Anna TX U.S.A.
98 □1a Santa Bárbara Terceira Azores
139 F3 Santa Bárbara Mato Grosso Brazil
143 F3 Santa Bárbara Minas Gerais Brazil
146 A5 Santa Bárbara Chile
126 □O10 Santa Bárbara Hond.
126 G4 Santa Bárbara Chihuahua Mex.
128 E4 Santa Bárbara Jalisco Mex.
66 G6 Santa Bárbara Spain
67 C10 Santa Bárbara mt. Spain
65 N6 Santa Bárbara mt. Spain
124 M7 Santa Barbara CA U.S.A.
136 E4 Santa Bárbara Amazonas Venez.
136 D3 Santa Bárbara Barinas Venez.
143 H2 Santa Bárbara, Ilha i. Brazil
141 B7 Santa Bárbara, Serra de hills Brazil
124 L7 Santa Barbara Channel CA U.S.A.
64 F5 Santa Bárbara de Casa Spain
64 D5 Santa Bárbara de Padrões Port.
142 D5 Santa Bárbara d'Oeste Brazil
141 B9 Santa Bárbara do Sul Brazil
124 M8 Santa Barbara Island CA U.S.A.
147 I3 Santa Bernardina Uru.
98 □3f Santa Brígida Gran Canaria Canary Is
63 Q4 Santacara Spain
146 E3 Santa Catalina Arg.
144 C2 Santa Catalina Chile
126 □S13 Santa Catalina Panama
200 □6 Santa Catalina i. Solomon Is
137 F2 Santa Catalina Venez.
124 O8 Santa Catalina, Gulf of CA U.S.A.
126 D5 Santa Catalina, Isla i. Mex.
62 C2 Santa Catalina de Armada Spain
124 N8 Santa Catalina Island CA U.S.A.
141 C8 Santa Catarina state Brazil
126 B3 Santa Catarina Baja California Mex.
127 I5 Santa Catarina Nuevo León Mex.
129 H4 Santa Catarina San Luis Potosí Mex.
129 I9 Santa Catarina r. Mex.
131 □10 Santa Catarina Curaçao Neth. Antilles
64 C4 Santa Catarina Port.
141 C8 Santa Catarina, Ilha de i. Brazil
75 L6 Santa Caterina dello Ionio Italy
72 B7 Santa Caterina di Pittinuri Sardegna Italy
129 J9 Santa Catarina Juquila Mex.
74 G8 Santa Caterina Villarmosa Sicilia Italy
75 O3 Santa Cesarea Terme Italy
66 D2 Santa Cilia de Jaca Spain
146 A5 Santa Clara Chile
136 D5 Santa Clara Col.
130 D2 Santa Clara Cuba
126 F3 Santa Clara Chihuahua Mex.
128 D1 Santa Clara Durango Mex.
125 P10 Santa Clara r. Mex.
123 K12 Santa Clara r. Mex.
124 K4 Santa Clara CA U.S.A.
125 S4 Santa Clara UT U.S.A.
124 M7 Santa Clara r. CA U.S.A.
64 C5 Santa Clara, Barragem de resr Port.
138 □ Santa Clara, Isla i. S. Pacific Ocean
64 C6 Santa Clara-a-Nova Port.
64 C5 Santa Clara-a-Velha Port.
147 G2 Santa Clara de Buena Vista Arg.
64 D5 Santa Clara de Louredo Port.
147 G2 Santa Clara de Saguier Arg.
124 N7 Santa Clarita CA U.S.A.
136 C5 Santa Clotilde Peru
66 K4 Santa Coloma de Farners Spain
66 J5 Santa Coloma de Gramanet Spain
66 H4 Santa Coloma de Queralt Spain
62 H4 Santa Colomba de Somoza Spain
63 J3 Santa Columba de Curueño Spain
Santa Comba Angola see Waku-Kungo
62 D8 Santa Comba Dão Port.
62 G5 Santa Comba de Rossas Port.
66 K4 Santa Cristina d'Aro Spain
62 I4 Santa Cristina de la Polvorosa Spain
75 I9 Santa Croce, Capo c. Sicilia Italy
74 H10 Santa Croce Camerina Sicilia Italy
73 N5 Santa Croce del Sannio Italy
73 O4 Santa Croce di Magliano Italy
71 J8 Santa Croce sull'Arno Italy
147 E2 Santa Cruz Arg.
145 C8 Santa Cruz prov. Arg.
145 C8 Santa Cruz r. Arg.
131 □9 Santa Cruz Aruba
139 E4 Santa Cruz Bol.
139 E4 Santa Cruz dept Bol.
136 D5 Santa Cruz Amazonas Brazil
143 G2 Santa Cruz Espírito Santo Brazil
137 H5 Santa Cruz Pará Brazil
137 I5 Santa Cruz Pará Brazil
140 G3 Santa Cruz Rio Grande do Norte Brazil
146 B4 Santa Cruz Chile
126 □Q12 Santa Cruz Costa Rica
130 □ Santa Cruz Jamaica
64 □ Santa Cruz Madeira
128 B4 Santa Cruz Nayarit Mex.
128 B4 Santa Cruz Nayarit Mex.
126 D2 Santa Cruz Sonora Mex.
136 C6 Santa Cruz Peru
154 B4 Santa Cruz Luzon Phil.
154 C3 Santa Cruz Luzon Phil.
154 C4 Santa Cruz Luzon Phil.
64 A2 Santa Cruz Port.
63 Q6 Santa Cruz mt. Spain
124 J5 Santa Cruz CA U.S.A.
125 T8 Santa Cruz watercourse AZ U.S.A.
136 D2 Santa Cruz Venez.
136 □ Santa Cruz, Isla i. Islas Galápagos Ecuador
126 D5 Santa Cruz, Isla i. Mex.
145 C8 Santa Cruz, Puerto inlet Arg.
63 Q6 Santa Cruz, Sierra de mts Spain
127 N10 Santa Cruz Barillas Guat.
143 H2 Santa Cruz Cabrália Brazil
142 D4 Santa Cruz das Palmeiras Brazil
62 D7 Santa Cruz da Tapa Port.
63 M2 Santa Cruz de Bezana Spain
142 C2 Santa Cruz de Goiás Brazil
98 □3d Santa Cruz de la Palma La Palma Canary Is
43 C10 Santa Cruz de la Serós Spain
128 D5 Santa Cruz de las Flores Mex.
64 H2 Santa Cruz de la Sierra Spain
63 N9 Santa Cruz de la Zarza Spain
127 N10 Santa Cruz del Quiché Guat.
63 L8 Santa Cruz del Retamar Spain
130 E3 Santa Cruz del Sur Cuba
67 C8 Santa Cruz de Moya Spain
65 M3 Santa Cruz de Mudela Spain
98 □3e Santa Cruz de Tenerife Tenerife Canary Is
126 □P10 Santa Cruz de Yojoa Hond.
142 C5 Santa Cruz do Rio Pardo Brazil
141 B9 Santa Cruz do Sul Brazil
129 K10 Santa Cruz Huatulco Mex.
124 M7 Santa Cruz Island CA U.S.A.
200 □6 Santa Cruz Islands Solomon Is
130 □ Santa Cruz Mountains hills Jamaica
72 B9 Santadi Sardegna Italy
73 P8 Santa Domenica Talao Italy
74 H8 Santa Domenica Vittoria Sicilia Italy
143 F3 Santa Efigênia de Minas Brazil
147 G5 Santa Elena Buenos Aires Arg.
147 F2 Santa Elena Córdoba Arg.
147 H2 Santa Elena Entre Ríos Arg.
138 D5 Santa Elena Bol.
136 C6 Santa Elena Peru
65 L4 Santa Elena Spain
137 F3 Santa Elena Venez.
126 □Q12 Santa Elena, Cabo c. Costa Rica
136 A5 Santa Elena, Punta pt Ecuador
62 I4 Santa Elena de Jamuz Spain
147 F4 Santa Eleonora Arg.
74 F9 Santa Elisabetta Sicilia Italy
65 J5 Santaella Spain
63 P4 Santa Engracia Spain
142 D4 Santa Eudóxia Brazil
147 F3 Santa Eufemia Arg.
65 J3 Santa Eufemia Spain
73 Q10 Santa Eufemia, Golfo di g. Italy
Santa Eugenia Galicia Spain see Santa Uxía de Ribeira
127 I3 Santa Eulalia Mex.
64 E2 Santa Eulália Port.
66 C6 Santa Eulalia Aragón Spain
62 I2 Santa Eulalia Asturias Spain
63 J2 Santa Eulalia Asturias Spain
67 I10 Santa Eulalia del Río Spain
62 F2 Santa Eulalia de Oscos Spain
66 J4 Santa Eulàlia de Riuprimer Spain
147 G2 Santa Fé Arg.
147 G2 Santa Fé prov. Arg.
130 B3 Santa Fé Cuba
126 □S13 Santa Fé Panama
154 C5 Santa Fe Phil.
65 L6 Santa Fé Spain
123 L9 Santa Fe NM U.S.A.
136 □ Santa Fé, Isla i. Islas Galápagos Ecuador
143 E2 Santa Fé de Minas Brazil
142 B4 Santa Fé do Sul Brazil
140 D4 Santa Filomena Brazil
72 H2 Santa Fiora Italy
73 N5 Sant'Agata de'Goti Italy
75 K7 Sant'Agata del Bianco Italy
73 P8 Sant'Agata di Esaro Italy
74 H7 Sant'Agata di Militello Sicilia Italy
73 O5 Sant'Agata di Puglia Italy
71 M8 Sant'Agata Feltria Italy
126 G4 Santa Gertrudis Mex.
72 B8 Santa Giusta Sardegna Italy
72 B9 Santa Giusta, Stagno di l. Sardegna Italy
71 M3 Santa Giustina Italy
71 K6 Sant'Agostino Italy
140 D2 Santa Helena Brazil
142 B2 Santa Helena de Goiás Brazil
170 E3 Santai Sichuan China
172 E4 Santai Xinjiang China
172 I4 Santai Xinjiang China
170 C5 Santai Yunnan China
140 F5 Santa Inês Bahia Brazil
140 D2 Santa Inês Maranhão Brazil
129 K9 Santa Inés Mex.
145 B9 Santa Inés, Isla i. Chile
64 D5 Santa Iria Port.
146 D5 Santa Isabel La Pampa Arg.
147 G3 Santa Isabel Santa Fé Arg.
138 D5 Santa Isabel Bol.
139 E3 Santa Isabel Brazil
136 B5 Santa Isabel Ecuador
129 N9 Santa Isabel Mex.
136 C6 Santa Isabel Peru
131 □1 Santa Isabel Puerto Rico
200 □6 Santa Isabel i. Solomon Is
140 E2 Santa Isabel, Ilha Grande de i. Brazil
126 B2 Santa Isabel, Sierra mts Mex.
138 B4 Santa Isabel de Sihuas Peru
142 A5 Santa Isabel do Ivaí Brazil
146 A5 Santa Juana Chile
142 D3 Santa Juliana Brazil
64 C2 Santa Justa Port.
131 □10 Santa Krus Curaçao Neth. Antilles
63 P3 Santa Kurutze Kanpezu Spain
71 M6 Sant'Alberto Italy
62 F5 Santalha Port.
66 F3 Santa Liestra y San Quílez Spain
178 C8 Santalpur Gujarat India
71 J9 Santa Luce Italy
147 G3 Santa Lucia Arg.
138 C5 Santa Lucia Chile
Santa Lucía Cuba see Rafael Freyre
136 B5 Santa Lucía Ecuador
127 N10 Santa Lucia Guat.
72 D6 Santa Lucia Sardegna Italy
147 I4 Santa Lucía Uru.
147 I4 Santa Lucía r. Uru.
65 K6 Santa Lucía, Cerro de mt. Spain
147 F3 Santa Lucia, Lago l. Arg.
128 C3 Santa Lucía de la Sierra Mex.
75 I7 Santa Lucia del Mela Sicilia Italy
62 C3 Santa Lucía de Moraña Spain
98 □3f Santa Lucía de Tirajana Gran Canaria Canary Is
124 K5 Santa Lucia Range mts CA U.S.A.
147 G5 Santa Luisa Arg.
98 □1c Santa Luzia Pico Azores
140 D3 Santa Luzia Maranhão Brazil
140 F3 Santa Luzia Paraíba Brazil
88 □ Santa Luzia i. Cape Verde
64 C5 Santa Luzia Beja Port.
64 D6 Santa Luzia Faro Port.
147 F4 Santa Magdalena Arg.
67 F7 Santa Magdalena de Pulpís Spain
72 C5 Santa-Manza, Golfe de b. Corse France
77 P3 Santa Mare Romania
66 I4 Santa Margarida de Montbui Spain
64 C4 Santa Margarida do Sádão Port.
144 E3 Santa Margarita Arg.
67 L8 Santa Margarita Spain
124 L6 Santa Margarita CA U.S.A.
126 D5 Santa Margarita, Isla i. Mex.
74 E8 Santa Margherita di Belice Sicilia Italy
70 G7 Santa Margherita Ligure Italy
144 D2 Santa María Arg.
98 □1b Santa Maria i. Azores
138 E3 Santa María Bol.
137 F5 Santa Maria Amazonas Brazil
137 G5 Santa Maria Amazonas Brazil
137 H5 Santa Maria Pará Brazil
141 B9 Santa Maria Rio Grande do Sul Brazil
144 G3 Santa Maria r. Brazil
88 □ Santa Maria Cape Verde
127 N8 Santa María Mex.
126 F2 Santa María r. Mex.
128 H4 Santa María r. Mex.
66 D3 Santa María Spain
67 D8 Santa María mt. Spain
64 G6 Santa María r. Spain
70 I2 Santa Maria Switz.
124 L7 Santa Maria CA U.S.A.
125 S7 Santa Maria r. AZ U.S.A.
136 E4 Santa María Venez.
144 G4 Santa María, Cabo c. Uru.
95 G5 Santa Maria, Cabo de c. Moz.
64 D7 Santa Maria, Cabo de c. Port.
115 J14 Santa Maria, Cape Bahamas
130 D2 Santa María, Cayo i. Cuba
141 D5 Santa Maria, Chapadão de hills Brazil
144 B5 Santa María, Isla i. Chile
136 □ Santa María, Isla i. Islas Galápagos Ecuador
72 C5 Santa Maria, Isola i. Sardegna Italy
138 B3 Santa María, Punta pt Peru
140 D5 Santa Maria, Serra de hills Brazil
146 C5 Santa María, Volcán vol. Arg.
129 H6 Santa María Ajoloapan Mex.
73 M5 Santa Maria Capua Vetere Italy
140 F4 Santa Maria da Boa Vista Brazil
62 C7 Santa Maria da Feira Port.
140 C4 Santa Maria das Barreiras Brazil
142 C5 Santa Maria da Serra Brazil
140 D5 Santa Maria da Vitória Brazil
63 M2 Santa María de Cayón Spain
126 F4 Santa María de Cuevas Mex.
129 H3 Santa María de Guadalupe Mex.
98 □3f Santa María de Guía Gran Canaria Canary Is
128 C3 Santa Maria de Huazamota Mex.
63 P6 Santa María de Huertas Spain
137 E2 Santa María de Ipire Venez.
63 J7 Santa Maria del Berrocal Spain
63 M4 Santa María del Campo Spain
63 P9 Santa María del Campo Rus Spain
73 P8 Santa Maria del Cedro Italy
70 G6 Santa Maria della Versa Italy
129 J7 Santa María del Monte Mex.
126 G5 Santa María del Oro Mex.
128 C4 Santa María del Oro Mex.
62 I4 Santa María del Páramo Spain
128 F2 Santa María del Refugio Mex.
128 G4 Santa María del Río Mex.
63 P7 Santa María del Val Spain
65 P6 Santa María de Nieva Spain
65 O5 Santa María de Nieva, Puerto de pass Spain
73 N7 Santa Maria di Castellabate Italy
75 O4 Santa Maria di Leuca, Capo c. Italy
74 H8 Santa Maria di Licodia Sicilia Italy
72 C2 Santa-Maria-di-Lota Corse France
71 M4 Santa Maria di Sala Italy
143 G2 Santa Maria do Salto Brazil
143 F3 Santa Maria do Suaçuí Brazil
129 L9 Santa María Ecatepec Mex.
129 K10 Santa María Huatulco Mex.
200 □5 Santa Maria Island Vanuatu
129 J8 Santa María Ixcatlán Mex.
63 L6 Santa María la Real de Nieva Spain
143 F4 Santa Maria Madalena Brazil
70 E3 Santa Maria Maggiore Italy
125 T7 Santa Maria Mountains AZ U.S.A.
72 D8 Santa Maria Navarrese Sardegna Italy
70 G3 Santa Maria Rezzonico Italy
72 B4 Santa-Maria-Siché Corse France
129 K8 Santa María Tlalixtac Mex.
129 J9 Santa María Zaniza Mex.
129 K9 Santa María Zoquitlán Mex.
73 P7 Santa Marina Italy
62 I3 Santa Marina del Rey Spain
74 H6 Santa Marina Salina Isole Lipari Italy
72 H3 Santa Marinella Italy
136 C2 Santa Marta Col.
65 O2 Santa Marta Castilla-La Mancha Spain
64 F3 Santa Marta Extremadura Spain
91 B8 Santa Marta, Cabo de c. Angola
62 I7 Santa Marta de Tormes Spain
141 C9 Santa Marta Grande, Cabo de c. Brazil
129 M7 Santa Martha, Cerro mt. Mex.
72 B2 Sant'Ambroggio Corse France
124 N7 Santa Monica CA U.S.A.
123 H13 Santa Monica, Pico mt. Mex.
124 N8 Santa Monica Bay CA U.S.A.
124 N7 Santa Monica Mountains National Recreation Area park CA U.S.A.
157 L5 Santan Kalimantan Indon.
136 E4 Santana Amazonas Brazil
140 E5 Santana Bahia Brazil
142 B3 Santana r. Brazil
64 □ Santana Madeira
62 C8 Santana Coimbra Port.
64 D4 Santana Évora Port.
64 A4 Santana Setúbal Port.
77 J4 Sântana Romania
141 B9 Santana da Boa Vista Brazil
64 C5 Santana da Serra Port.
64 D5 Santana de Cambas Port.
140 E2 Santana do Acarau Brazil
140 C4 Santana do Araguaia Brazil
64 C3 Santana do Campo Port.
140 F3 Santana do Cariri Brazil
141 B9 Santana do Livramento Brazil
64 C3 Santana do Mato Port.
143 F3 Santana do Paraíso Brazil
74 G2 Sant'Anastasia Italy
73 J2 Sant'Anatolia di Narco Italy
136 B4 Santander Col.
136 C3 Santander dept Col.
63 M2 Santander Spain
63 L2 Santander prov. Spain
63 M2 Santander, Bahía de b. Spain
75 N3 Sant'Andrea, Isola i. Italy
75 L6 Sant'Andrea Apostolo dello Ionio Italy
72 C9 Sant'Andrea Frius Sardegna Italy
57 K4 Sântandrei Romania
124 K4 Santa Nella CA U.S.A.
75 K6 Sant'Angelo Italy
73 N5 Sant'Angelo a Cupolo Italy
73 O7 Sant'Angelo a Fasanella Italy
73 O6 Sant'Angelo dei Lombardi Italy
71 N8 Sant'Angelo in Lizzola Italy
71 M8 Sant'Angelo in Vado Italy
70 G5 Sant'Angelo Lodigiano Italy
168 C4 Santanghu Xinjiang China
Santanilla, Islas is Caribbean Sea see Swan Islands
74 D8 Santa Ninfa Sicilia Italy
125 U8 Santan Mountain hill AZ U.S.A.
143 G5 Sant'Anna, Ilha de i. Brazil
72 B9 Sant'Anna Arresi Sardegna Italy
72 A9 Sant'Antioco Sardegna Italy
72 A9 Sant'Antioco, Isola di i. Sardegna Italy
72 C6 Sant'Antonio di Gallura Sardegna Italy
72 A8 Sant'Antonio di Santadi Sardegna Italy
Santañy Spain see Santanyí
67 L9 Santanyí Spain
63 L8 Santa Olalla Spain
62 G8 Santa Olalla hill Spain
66 I5 Santa Oliva Spain
64 G5 Santa Ollala del Cala Spain
75 I9 Santa Panagia, Capo c. Sicilia Italy
66 K3 Santa Pau Spain
124 M7 Santa Paula CA U.S.A.
177 H3 Santapilly Andhra Prad. India
67 D11 Santa Pola Spain
67 E11 Santa Pola, Cabo de c. Spain
125 U2 Santaquin UT U.S.A.
140 E3 Santa Quitéria Brazil
62 E7 Santar Port.
73 Q7 Sant'Arcangelo Italy
71 M7 Santarcangelo di Romagna Italy
147 F4 Santa Regina Arg.
137 H5 Santarém Brazil
64 B2 Santarém Port.
64 B2 Santarém admin. dist. Port.
130 D2 Santaren Channel Bahamas
139 F1 Santa Rita Mato Grosso Brazil
140 G3 Santa Rita Paraíba Brazil
136 C4 Santa Rita Col.
200 □1 Santa Rita Guam
127 I4 Santa Rita Coahuila Mex.
128 G1 Santa Rita Nuevo León Mex.
136 E2 Santa Rita Guárico Venez.
130 H8 Santa Rita Zulia Venez.
140 D4 Santa Rita de Cassia Brazil
142 A2 Santa Rita do Araguaia Brazil
142 A4 Santa Rita do Pardo Brazil
143 E5 Santa Rita do Sapucaí Brazil
136 D5 Santa Rita do Weil Brazil
144 F3 Santa Rosa Corrientes Arg.
147 E5 Santa Rosa La Pampa Arg.
146 C3 Santa Rosa Mendoza Arg.
145 D6 Santa Rosa Río Negro Arg.
144 D2 Santa Rosa Salta Arg.
138 D3 Santa Rosa Bol.
138 C2 Santa Rosa Acre Brazil
141 B8 Santa Rosa Rio Grande do Sul Brazil
136 D4 Santa Rosa Col.
136 B5 Santa Rosa Ecuador
128 G6 Santa Rosa Michoacán Mex.
128 G1 Santa Rosa Nuevo León Mex.
127 O8 Santa Rosa Quintana Roo Mex.
129 I4 Santa Rosa San Luis Potosí Mex.
129 J1 Santa Rosa Tamaulipas Mex.
139 F6 Santa Rosa Para.
136 C5 Santa Rosa Loreto Peru
138 C3 Santa Rosa Puno Peru
147 I4 Santa Rosa Uru.
124 J3 Santa Rosa CA U.S.A.
123 L9 Santa Rosa NM U.S.A.
136 E4 Santa Rosa Amazonas Venez.
137 E2 Santa Rosa Anzoátegui Venez.
136 E3 Santa Rosa Apure Venez.
200 □1 Santa Rosa, Mount Guam
125 P8 Santa Rosa and San Jacinto Mountains National Monument nat. park CA U.S.A.
126 □O10 Santa Rosa de Copán Hond.
139 E4 Santa Rosa de la Roca Bol.
146 E3 Santa Rosa del Conlara Arg.
139 E4 Santa Rosa del Palmar Bol.
147 F2 Santa Rosa del Río Primero Arg.
136 C3 Santa Rosa de Osos Col.
136 B4 Santa Rosa de Sucumbio Ecuador
138 D3 Santa Rosa de Vigo Bol.
142 D4 Santa Rosa de Viterbo Brazil
124 L8 Santa Rosa Island CA U.S.A.
128 G5 Santa Rosa Jauregui Mex.
126 C4 Santa Rosalía Mex.
125 P8 Santa Rosa Mountains CA U.S.A.
122 F6 Santa Rosa Range mts NV U.S.A.
125 T8 Santa Rosa Wash watercourse AZ U.S.A.
73 O7 Sant'Arsenio Italy
75 L5 Santa Severina Italy
63 J4 Santas Martas Spain
71 L8 Santa Sofia Italy
64 C3 Santa Sofia Port.
64 D3 Santa Susana Évora Port.
64 C4 Santa Susana Setúbal Port.
144 E2 Santa Sylvina Arg.
147 G3 Santa Teresa Arg.
206 E8 Santa Teresa N.T. Austr.
143 G3 Santa Teresa Brazil
140 C4 Santa Teresa r. Brazil
128 C1 Santa Teresa Durango Mex.
128 C3 Santa Teresa Nayarit Mex.
127 K5 Santa Teresa Tamaulipas Mex.
131 J8 Santa Teresa Venez.
62 I7 Santa Teresa, Embalse de resr Spain
72 C5 Santa Teresa di Gallura Sardegna Italy
75 I8 Santa Teresa di Riva Sicilia Italy
147 I5 Santa Teresita Arg.
140 C4 Santa Terezinha Brazil
57 L4 Santău Romania
98 □3a Santa Úrsula Tenerife Canary Is
62 C3 Santa Uxía de Ribeira Galicia Spain
75 I8 Santa Venerina Sicilia Italy
142 B3 Santa Vitória Brazil
64 C5 Santa Vitória Port.
64 D3 Santa Vitória do Ameixial Port.
144 G4 Santa Vitória do Palmar Brazil
72 C8 Santa Vittoria, Monte mt. Sardegna Italy
124 L7 Santa Ynez r. CA U.S.A.
Santa Ysabel i. Solomon Is see Santa Isabel
66 K4 Sant Benet mt. Spain
66 J5 Sant Boi de Llobregat Spain
66 G6 Sant Carles de la Ràpita Spain
66 J4 Sant Celoni Spain
66 J5 Sant Cugat del Vallès Spain
38 C4 Santec France
124 P9 Santee CA U.S.A.
115 H9 Santee r. SC U.S.A.
73 L2 Sant'Egidio alla Vibrata Italy
72 C9 Sant'Elia, Capo c. Sardegna Italy
73 N4 Sant'Elia a Pianisi Italy
73 L4 Sant Elia Fiumerapido Italy
126 A2 San Telmo Mex.
64 F5 San Telmo Spain
71 P9 Sant'Elpidio a Mare Italy
72 D6 San Teodoro Sardegna Italy
69 F5 Santeramo in Colle Italy
71 L6 Santerno r. Italy
36 D4 Santerre reg. France
63 K3 Santervás de la Vega Spain
66 H5 Santes Creus Spain
75 J7 Sant'Eufemia d'Aspromonte Italy
66 L4 Sant Feliu de Guíxols Spain
66 K3 Sant Feliu de Pallerols Spain
66 J4 Sant Feliu Sasserra Spain
70 E5 Santhià Italy
66 K4 Sant Hilari Sacalm Spain
66 J3 Sant Hipòlit de Voltregà Spain
141 B9 Santiago Brazil
88 □ Santiago i. Cape Verde
146 B3 Santiago Chile
146 B3 Santiago admin. reg. Chile
130 H4 Santiago Dom. Rep.
126 E6 Santiago Baja California Sur Mex.
128 C6 Santiago Colima Mex.
127 I5 Santiago Nuevo León Mex.
128 B1 Santiago r. Mex.
126 □S13 Santiago Panama
139 F6 Santiago Para.
138 B3 Santiago Peru
136 B6 Santiago r. Peru
154 C3 Santiago Luzon Phil.
145 B8 Santiago, Cabo c. Chile
126 □S13 Santiago, Cerro mt. Panama
128 B4 Santiago, Río Grande de r. Mex.
139 F4 Santiago, Sierra de hills Bol.
129 L9 Santiago Astata Mex.
62 F9 Santiago de Alcántara Spain
65 K5 Santiago de Calatrava Spain
136 B6 Santiago de Cao Peru
Santiago de Carbajo Spain see Santiago de Alcántara
62 C3 Santiago de Compostela Spain
62 D4 Santiago de Covelo Spain
130 F3 Santiago de Cuba Cuba
65 N4 Santiago de la Espada Spain
129 J5 Santiago de la Peña Mex.
67 D12 Santiago de la Ribera Spain
62 H9 Santiago del Campo Spain
144 D2 Santiago del Estero Arg.
147 F1 Santiago del Estero prov. Arg.
Santiago de los Caballeros Dom. Rep. see Santiago
98 □3a Santiago del Teide Tenerife Canary Is
136 B5 Santiago de Méndez Ecuador
138 C3 Santiago de Pacaguaras Bol.
64 B4 Santiago do Cacém Port.
64 C3 Santiago do Escoural Port.
128 B4 Santiago Ixcuintla Mex.
129 J9 Santiago Ixtayutla Mex.
129 I8 Santiago Juxtlahuaca Mex.
129 J9 Santiago Minas Mex.
129 J8 Santiago Mitlatengo Mex.
124 O8 Santiago Peak CA U.S.A.
147 F2 Santiago Temple Arg.
129 L8 Santiago Tutla Mex.
129 L7 Santiago Tuxtla Mex.
147 I4 Santiago Vazquez Uru.
128 C1 Santiaguillo, Laguna de l. Mex.
62 I8 Santibáñez de Béjar Spain
63 K3 Santibáñez de la Peña Spain
62 I7 Santibáñez de la Sierra Spain
62 H4 Santibáñez de Vidriales Spain
62 H8 Santibáñez el Bajo Spain
63 M4 Santibáñez Zarzaguda Spain
128 F1 San Tiburcio Mex.
155 B3 Santigi Sulawesi Indon.
155 B3 Santiki, Tanjung pt Indon.
70 I6 Sant'Ilario d'Enza Italy
63 L2 Santillana Spain
63 M7 Santillana, Embalse de resr Spain
136 D2 San Timoteo Venez.
64 G6 Santiponce Spain
Santipur W. Bengal India see Shantipur
70 G1 Säntis mt. Switz.
65 M4 Santisteban del Puerto Spain
63 K6 Santiuste de San Juan Bautista Spain
62 I6 Santiz Spain
66 □ Sant Jaume del Mediterrani Spain
66 G6 Sant Jaume d'Enveja Spain
66 J3 Sant Joan de les Abadesses Spain
66 I4 Sant Joan de Vilatorrada Spain
66 □ Sant Joan Gran Spain
66 G6 Sant Jordi, Golf de g. Spain
66 I3 Sant Julià de Lòria Andorra
66 I3 Sant Llorenç de Morunys Spain
66 I4 Sant Llorenç de Munt, Parc Natural del nature res. Spain
67 L8 Sant Llorenç des Cardassar Spain
Sant Lluís Spain see San Luis
66 I4 Sant Martí de Tous Spain
66 I5 Sant Martí Sarroca Spain
66 F7 Sant Mateu Spain
67 H9 Sant Miquel Spain
166 A5 Santō Hyōgo Japan
166 D5 Santō Shiga Japan
64 E3 Santo Aleixo Port.
64 E4 Santo Aleixo da Restauração Port.
98 □1c Santo Amaro Pico Azores
98 □1c Santo Amaro São Jorge Azores
140 F5 Santo Amaro Brazil
143 G4 Santo Amaro de Campos Brazil
142 B4 Santo Anastácio Brazil
142 A4 Santo Anastácio r. Brazil
142 D5 Santo André Brazil
64 B4 Santo André Port.
64 B4 Santo André, Lagoa de lag. Port.
141 B9 Santo Angelo Brazil
98 □1c Santo Antão São Jorge Azores
88 □ Santo Antão i. Cape Verde
62 C3 Santo Antoniño Spain
98 □1c Santo António Pico Azores
98 □1b Santo António São Miguel Azores
137 F5 Santo Antônio Amazonas Brazil
140 D3 Santo Antônio Maranhão Brazil
140 G3 Santo Antônio Rio Grande do Norte Brazil
143 F3 Santo Antônio r. Brazil
89 G6 Santo António São Tomé and Príncipe
143 H2 Santo Antônio, Ponta pt Brazil
142 B2 Santo Antônio da Barra Brazil
137 H5 Santo Antônio da Cachoeira Brazil
142 B5 Santo Antônio da Platina Brazil
140 F5 Santo Antônio de Jesus Brazil
139 F3 Santo Antônio de Leverger Brazil
143 F4 Santo Antônio de Pádua Brazil
143 E4 Santo Antônio do Amparo Brazil
136 E5 Santo Antônio do Içá Brazil
143 G2 Santo Antônio do Jacinto Brazil
143 E4 Santo Antônio do Monte Brazil
142 D2 Santo Antônio do Rio Verde Brazil
64 A3 Santo António dos Cavaleiros Port.
Santo António do Zaire Angola see Soyo
139 F4 Santo Corazón Bol.
71 M3 Santo Croce, Lago di l. Italy
147 I5 Santo Domingo Arg.
146 B3 Santo Domingo Chile
130 C2 Santo Domingo Cuba
130 I4 Santo Domingo Dom. Rep.
127 O10 Santo Domingo Guat.
126 B3 Santo Domingo Baja California Mex.
126 D5 Santo Domingo Baja California Sur Mex.
129 M9 Santo Domingo Oaxaca Mex.
128 F2 Santo Domingo San Luis Potosí Mex.
129 K7 Santo Domingo r. Mex.
126 □Q11 Santo Domingo Nic.
138 C3 Santo Domingo Peru
66 D3 Santo Domingo mt. Spain
63 O4 Santo Domingo de la Calzada Spain
129 K10 Santo Domingo de Morelos Mex.
63 N5 Santo Domingo de Silos Spain
129 K9 Santo Domingo Ozolotepec Mex.
129 L9 Santo Domingo Petapa Mex.
123 K9 Santo Domingo Pueblo NM U.S.A.
129 L9 Santo Domingo Tehuantepec Mex.
143 G4 Santo Eduardo Brazil
64 D6 Santo Estêvão Faro Port.
64 B3 Santo Estêvão Santarém Port.
62 F4 Santo Estevo, Embalse de resr Spain
202 J7 Santoft North I. N.Z.
143 E3 Santo Hipólito Brazil
140 E4 Santo Inácio Bahia Brazil
142 B5 Santo Inácio Paraná Brazil
64 B3 Santo Isidro de Pegões Port.
137 E2 San Tomé Venez.
67 C11 Santomera Spain
67 C11 Santomera, Embalse de resr Spain
73 L2 Sant Omero Italy
63 N2 Santoña Spain
162 E7 Santong He r. China
154 E6 Santo Niño i. Phil.
75 K6 Sant'Onofrio Italy
74 H9 Santo Pietro Sicilia Italy
72 C2 Santo-Pietro-di-Tenda Corse France
72 C3 Santo-Pietro-di-Venaco Corse France
Santorini i. Greece see Thira
142 D5 Santos Brazil
143 F4 Santos Dumont Brazil
138 D2 Santos Mercado Bol.
214 F7 Santos Plateau sea feature S. Atlantic Ocean
70 E6 Santo Stefano Belbo Italy
71 N2 Santo Stefano di Cadore Italy
74 G7 Santo Stefano di Camastra Sicilia Italy
70 H7 Santo Stefano di Magra Italy
74 E8 Santo Stefano Quisquina Sicilia Italy
71 N4 Santo Stino di Livenza Italy
62 D6 Santo Tirso Port.
123 K12 Santo Tomás Chihuahua Mex.
123 H11 Santo Tomás Sonora Mex.
126 □P11 Santo Tomás Nic.
138 B3 Santo Tomás Peru
144 F3 Santo Tomé Corrientes Arg.
147 G2 Santo Tomé Santa Fé Arg.
65 M4 Santo Tomé Spain
62 I5 Santovenia Spain
66 I5 Sant Pere de Ribes Spain
66 J3 Sant Pere de Torelló Spain
66 L3 Sant Pere Pescador Spain
44 G4 Santpoort Neth.
66 J3 Sant Privat d'en Bas Spain
66 I5 Sant Quintí de Mediona Spain
178 D8 Santrampur Gujarat India
66 I5 Sant Sadurní d'Anoia Spain
67 J8 Sant Telm Spain
62 I2 Santullano Spain
72 B7 Santu Lussurgiu Sardegna Italy
75 □ San Tumas, Il-Bajja ta' b. Malta
Santurce País Vasco Spain see Santurtzi
63 O4 Santurde Spain
63 N2 Santurtzi Spain
66 I4 Sant Vincenç de Castellet Spain
125 S5 Sanup Plateau AZ U.S.A.
145 B7 San Valentín, Cerro mt. Chile
58 F8 San Vendemiano Italy
72 B7 San Vero Milis Sardegna Italy
147 G2 San Vicente Arg.
138 D5 San Vicente Bol.
146 B4 San Vicente Chile
126 □O11 San Vicente El Salvador
126 A2 San Vicente Baja California Mex.
128 G1 San Vicente San Luis Potosí Mex.
154 D2 San Vicente Luzon Phil.
63 K8 San Vicente, Sierra de mts Spain
64 E2 San Vicente de Alcántara Spain
138 A3 San Vicente de Cañete Peru

San Vicente de Castellet to Sayam
335
San Vicente de Castellet Spain see Sant Vicenç de Castellet
63 L2 San Vicente de la Barquera Spain
63 O3 San Vicente de la Sonsierra Spain
36 C4 San Vicente del Caguán Col.
67 D11 San Vicente del Raspeig Spain
63 K6 San Vicente de Palacio Spain
63 M2 San Vicente de Toranzo Spain
29 I4 San Vicente Tancuayalab Mex.
62 C3 San Vicenzo Spain
71 O9 San Vicino, Monte mt. Italy
47 H2 San Victor Arg.
40 E3 Sanvignes-les-Mines France
28 G8 San Vincente de Benitez Mex.
75 I6 San Vincenzo Isole Lipari Italy
72 F1 San Vincenzo Toscana Italy
62 H5 San Vitero Spain
72 D9 San Vito Sardegna Italy
74 D7 San Vito, Capo c. Sicilia Italy
75 M3 San Vito, Capo c. Italy
71 N4 San Vito al Tagliamento Italy
73 M3 San Vito Chietino Italy
75 N2 San Vito dei Normanni Italy
71 M3 San Vito di Cadore Italy
74 D7 San Vito lo Capo Sicilia Italy
73 J4 San Vito Romano Italy
75 K6 San Vito sullo Ionio Italy
67 K3 Sanwa Ibaraki Japan
67 H1 Sanwa Niigata Japan
78 E8 Sanwer Madh. Prad. India
62 C4 Sanxenxo Spain
79 G5 Sanya Hainan China
36 D4 San Yanaro Col.
95 F3 Sanyati r. Zimbabwe
69 K9 Sanyuan Shaanxi China
73 P7 Sanza Italy
91 C6 Sanza Pombo Angola
62 I6 Sanzoles Spain
58 F5 Sao, Phou mt. Laos
64 C6 São Barnabé Port.
98 □1a São Bartolomeu Terceira Azores
42 D2 São Bartolomeu r. Brazil
64 D2 São Bartolomeu Port.
64 B4 São Bartolomeu da Serra Port.
64 C6 São Bartolomeu de Messines Port.
40 E3 São Benedito Brazil
98 □1a São Bento Terceira Azores
38 D1 São Bento Amazonas Brazil
40 D2 São Bento Maranhão Brazil
37 F4 São Bento Roraima Brazil
42 B6 São Bento do Amparo Brazil
40 G3 São Bento do Norte Brazil
40 E2 São Bernardo Brazil
42 D5 São Bernardo do Campo Brazil
39 F7 São Borja Brazil
64 D5 São Brás Port.
64 D6 São Brás de Alportel Port.
64 C4 São Brás do Regedouro Port.
98 □1c São Caetano Pico Azores
38 D2 São Carlos Rondônia Brazil
39 E2 São Carlos Rondônia Brazil
41 B8 São Carlos Santa Catarina Brazil
42 D5 São Carlos São Paulo Brazil
62 E6 São Cosmado Port.
64 C4 São Cristóvão Port.
64 B4 São Cristóvão r. Port.
40 D5 São Desidério Brazil
40 D5 São Domingos Brazil
42 A4 São Domingos r. Brazil
42 B3 São Domingos r. Brazil
64 B5 São Domingos Port.
43 G3 São Domingos do Norte Brazil
64 C2 São Facundo Port.
43 E1 São Felipe, Serra de hills Brazil
40 F5 São Félix Bahia Brazil
40 C4 São Félix Mato Grosso Brazil
37 I6 São Félix Pará Brazil
62 C6 São Félix da Marinha Port.
43 G4 São Fidélis Brazil
88 □ São Filipe Cape Verde
38 C2 São Francisco Acre Brazil
37 F6 São Francisco Amazonas Brazil
43 E1 São Francisco Minas Gerais Brazil
43 E1 São Francisco r. Brazil
38 D2 São Francisco r. Brazil
41 C8 São Francisco, Ilha de i. Brazil
64 B4 São Francisco da Serra Port.
41 B9 São Francisco de Assis Brazil
42 C1 São Francisco de Goiás Brazil
41 C9 São Francisco de Paula Brazil
42 C3 São Francisco de Sales Brazil
40 E3 São Francisco do Maranhão Brazil
41 C8 São Francisco do Sul Brazil
41 B9 São Gabriel Brazil
43 G3 São Gabriel da Palha Brazil
64 C3 São Geraldo Port.
43 F5 São Gonçalo Brazil
43 E3 São Gonçalo do Abaeté Brazil
43 E3 São Gonçalo do Pará Brazil
43 E4 São Gonçalo do Sapucaí Brazil
43 E3 São Gotardo Brazil
64 D3 São Gregório Port.
93 B7 Sao Hill Tanz.
62 C7 São Jacinto Port.
42 B5 São Jerônimo da Serra Brazil
98 □1c São João Pico Azores
36 E5 São João Brazil
40 D2 São João, Ilhas de is Brazil
39 E2 São João, Serra de hills Brazil
40 D5 São João da Aliança Brazil
43 G4 São João da Barra Brazil
42 D4 São João da Boa Vista Brazil
62 D7 São João da Madeira Port.
62 F6 São João da Pesqueira Port.
43 E1 São João da Ponte Brazil
42 B4 São João das Duas Pontas Brazil
43 E4 São João del Rei Brazil
43 F5 São João de Meriti Brazil
62 E7 São João de Tarouca Port.
40 C3 São João do Araguaia Brazil
42 A5 São João do Caiuá Brazil
62 D8 São João do Campo Port.
40 F3 São João do Cariri Brazil
41 E5 São João do Paraíso Brazil
40 E4 São João do Piauí Brazil
64 D5 São João dos Caldeireiros Port.
40 E3 São João dos Patos Brazil
91 B8 São João do Sul Angola
43 F3 São João Evangelista Brazil
43 F4 São João Nepomuceno Brazil
36 E4 São Joaquim Amazonas Brazil
41 C9 São Joaquim Santa Catarina Brazil
42 D4 São Joaquim da Barra Brazil
98 □1c São Jorge i. Azores
64 □ São Jorge Madeira
98 □1c São Jorge, Canal de sea chan. Azores
42 A5 São Jorge do Ivaí Brazil
36 E5 São José Amazonas Brazil
41 C8 São José Santa Catarina Brazil
42 D4 São José da Boa Vista Brazil
64 C2 São José da Lamarosa Port.
37 F4 São José do Anauá Brazil
43 E5 São José do Barreiro Brazil
40 F3 São José do Belmonte Brazil
43 G4 São José do Calçado Brazil
43 G3 São José do Divino Brazil
40 F3 São José do Egito Brazil
43 F3 São José do Jacurí Brazil
44 G4 São José do Norte Brazil
140 E3 São José do Peixe Brazil
142 D4 São José do Rio Pardo Brazil
142 C4 São José do Rio Preto Brazil
143 E5 São José dos Campos Brazil
142 B4 São José dos Dourados r. Brazil
141 C8 São José dos Pinhais Brazil
62 F5 São Julião de Montenegro Port.
139 G4 São Lourenço Mato Grosso Brazil
143 E5 São Lourenço Minas Gerais Brazil
139 F4 São Lourenço r. Brazil
64 □ São Lourenço, Ponta de pt Madeira
64 D3 São Lourenço de Mamporcão Port.
144 H3 São Lourenço do Sul Brazil
91 C7 São Lucas Angola
140 D2 São Luís Brazil
137 G6 São Luís Brazil
64 B5 São Luís Port.
138 D1 São Luís de Cassianã Brazil
142 B2 São Luís de Montes Belos Brazil
143 E5 São Luís do Paraitinga Brazil
140 G4 São Luís do Quitunde Brazil
141 B9 São Luís Gonzaga Brazil
64 E2 São Mamede, Serra de mts Port.
64 C4 São Mamede do Sádão Port.
64 D4 São Manços Port.
142 C5 São Manuel Brazil
136 E4 São Marceline Brazil
142 D3 São Marcos r. Brazil
140 D2 São Marcos, Baía de b. Brazil
64 D5 São Marcos da Ataboeira Port.
64 C6 São Marcos da Serra Port.
64 D4 São Marcos do Campo Port.
137 G6 São Martinho Brazil
62 D8 São Martinho da Cortiça Port.
64 C5 São Martinho das Amoreiras Port.
62 H5 São Martinho de Angueira Port.
62 B9 São Martinho do Porto Port.
98 □1c São Mateus Pico Azores
98 □1a São Mateus Terceira Azores
143 H3 São Mateus Brazil
143 H3 São Mateus r. Brazil
141 C8 São Mateus do Sul Brazil
64 D4 São Matias Port.
98 □1b São Miguel i. Azores
142 D2 São Miguel r. Brazil
62 E9 São Miguel hill Port.
142 D5 São Miguel Arcanjo Brazil
62 F8 São Miguel de Acha Port.
64 D3 São Miguel de Machede Port.
64 C2 São Miguel de Rio Torto Port.
64 D5 São Miguel do Pinheiro Port.
140 E3 São Miguel do Tapuio Brazil
141 B9 São Miguel Jesuit Missions tourist site Brazil
131 I4 Saona, Isla i. Dom. Rep.
71 N9 Saonda r. Italy
99 □3a Saondzou mt. Njazidja Comoros
40 I2 Saône France
37 L7 Saône r. France
40 F3 Saône-et-Loire dept France
178 G9 Saoner Mahar. India
139 G7 São Nicolau Brazil
88 □ São Nicolau i. Cape Verde
142 D5 São Paulo Brazil
142 C5 São Paulo state Brazil
136 D5 São Paulo de Olivença Brazil
137 G6 São Pedro Amazonas Brazil
142 B3 São Pedro Mato Grosso do Sul Brazil
139 E2 São Pedro Rondônia Brazil
142 D5 São Pedro São Paulo Brazil
143 F5 São Pedro da Aldeia Brazil
64 A2 São Pedro da Cadeira Port.
62 F5 São Pedro de Agostem Port.
62 B9 São Pedro de Muel Port.
64 D6 São Pedro de Solis Port.
64 E4 São Pedro do Corval Port.
138 D2 São Pedro do Desterro Brazil
142 B5 São Pedro do Ivaí Brazil
141 B9 São Pedro do Sul Brazil
62 D7 São Pedro do Sul Port.
214 H5 São Pedro e São Paulo is N. Atlantic Ocean
São Pires r. Brazil see Teles Pires
140 D3 São Raimundo das Mangabeiras Brazil
140 E4 São Raimundo Nonato Brazil
41 L9 Saorge France
166 E5 Saori Japan
136 E6 São Romão Amazonas Brazil
143 E2 São Romão Minas Gerais Brazil
64 E3 São Romão Évora Port.
62 E8 São Romão Guarda Port.
64 C4 São Romão do Sado Port.
98 □1c São Roque Pico Azores
142 D5 São Roque Brazil
142 D4 São Roque de Minas Brazil
98 □1a São Sebastião Terceira Azores
138 C1 São Sebastião Amazonas Brazil
137 H6 São Sebastião Pará Brazil
139 E2 São Sebastião Rondônia Brazil
139 I5 São Sebastião São Paulo Brazil
143 E5 São Sebastião, Ilha do i. Brazil
142 B5 São Sebastião da Amoreira Brazil
137 I5 São Sebastião da Boa Vista Brazil
137 F6 São Sebastião de Tapuru Brazil
142 D4 São Sebastião do Paraíso Brazil
141 B9 São Sepé Brazil
62 C8 São Silvestre Port.
139 F5 São Simão Mato Grosso do Sul Brazil
142 B3 São Simão Minas Gerais Brazil
142 D4 São Simão São Paulo Brazil
142 B3 São Simão, Barragem de resr Brazil
142 C3 São Simão, Represa de resr Brazil
155 E3 Sao-Siu Maluku Indon.
64 B5 São Teotónio Port.
143 E4 São Tiago Brazil
São Tiago i. Cape Verde see Santiago
89 G6 São Tomé São Tomé and Príncipe
89 G6 São Tomé i. São Tomé and Príncipe
143 G5 São Tomé, Cabo de c. Brazil
89 G6 São Tomé, Pico de mt. São Tomé and Príncipe
89 G6 São Tomé and Príncipe country Africa
64 B3 São Torcato hill Port.
41 G7 Saou France
86 E3 Saoura, Oued watercourse Alg.
142 D5 São Vicente Brazil
88 □ São Vicente i. Cape Verde
64 □ São Vicente Madeira
64 E3 São Vicente Portalegre Port.
62 F5 São Vicente Vila Real Port.
64 B6 São Vicente, Cabo de c. Port.
62 E8 São Vicente da Beira Port.
140 D2 São Vicente Ferrer Brazil
57 K4 Sáp Hungary
Sápai Greece see Sapes
156 C5 Sapako Indon.
64 E6 Sapal de Castro Marim e Vila Real de Santo António, Reserva Natural do nature res. Spain
138 B3 Sapallanga Peru
79 L2 Sapanca Turkey
79 L2 Sapanca Gölü l. Turkey
140 D4 Sapão r. Brazil
155 F5 Saparua Maluku Indon.
155 F5 Saparua i. Maluku Indon.
31 J2 Sapcote Leicestershire, England U.K.
155 A8 Sape, Selat sea chan. Indon.
157 M9 Sape, Teluk b. Sumbawa Indon.
89 G5 Sapele Nigeria
79 G1 Sapes Greece
79 K3 Şaphane Turkey
72 C6 Sa Pianedda, Monte hill Italy
78 C6 Sapientza i. Greece
126 □T14 Sapo, Serranía del mts Panama
67 L8 Sa Pobla Spain
75 I7 Saponara Sicilia Italy
88 C5 Sapo National Park Liberia
142 B5 Sapopema Brazil
18 G8 Sapotskin Belarus
88 E4 Sapouy Burkina
19 X8 Sapozhok Rus. Fed.
120 F5 Sappa Creek r. NE U.S.A.
71 N2 Sappada Italy
115 □1 Sapphire Bay Bermuda
164 S3 Sapporo Japan
179 L9 Saptamukhi r. India
142 C4 Sapucai r. Brazil
143 E4 Sapucai r. Brazil
137 G5 Sapucaia Brazil
157 K8 Sapudi i. Indon.
121 G7 Sapulpa OK U.S.A.
157 J8 Sapulu Jawa Indon.
157 L2 Sapulut Sabah Malaysia
186 F2 Sāq, Jabal hill Saudi Arabia
184 H5 Sāqī Iran
105 M2 Saqqaq Greenland
184 B3 Saqqez Iran
186 F7 Saqr Saudi Arabia
191 D3 Saqulia Georgia
179 L7 Sara Bangl.
184 B3 Sarā Iran
184 B3 Sarāb Āžarbāyjān-e Sharqī Iran
184 H5 Sarāb Khorāsān Iran
189 M7 Sarābe Meymeh Iran
190 B9 Sarābīţ al Khādim tourist site Egypt
159 E7 Sara Buri Thai.
20 Q1 Saraby Norway
137 G5 Saracá, Lago l. Brazil
75 L4 Saraceno r. Italy
74 D7 Saraceno, Punta del pt Sicilia Italy
59 N7 Saračinec Croatia
178 C9 Saradiya Gujarat India
84 C6 Saraf Doungous Chad
Saragossa Spain see Zaragoza
136 B5 Saraguro Ecuador
185 L5 Sarai Afgh.
15 H5 Sarai Rus. Fed.
179 J8 Saraikela Jharkhand India
185 O6 Sarai Sidhu Pak.
20 S4 Säräisniemi Fin.
68 G4 Sarajevo Bos.-Herz.
207 L7 Saraji Qld Austr.
185 I3 Sarakhs Iran
185 I3 Sarakhs Turkm.
78 E4 Sarakiniko, Akra pt Greece
78 F4 Sarakino i. Greece
182 G2 Saraktash Rus. Fed.
121 K10 Saraland AL U.S.A.
182 F3 Saralzhin Kazakh.
179 O7 Saramati mt. India/Myanmar
136 B6 Sarameriza Peru
43 F8 Saramon France
36 C8 Saran France
183 O3 Saran' Kazakh.
157 I5 Saran, Gunung mt. Indon.
117 L4 Saranac r. NY U.S.A.
117 K4 Saranac Lake NY U.S.A.
57 K4 Sáránd Hungary
78 B3 Sarandë Albania
142 B5 Sarandi Paraná Brazil
141 B8 Sarandi Rio Grande do Sul Brazil
Sarandib country Asia see Sri Lanka
144 G4 Sarandí del Yí Uru.
147 I3 Sarandí de Navarro Uru.
147 I3 Sarandí Grande Uru.
154 E9 Sarangani i. Phil.
154 E9 Sarangani Bay Mindanao Phil.
154 E9 Sarangani Islands Phil.
154 E9 Sarangani Strait Phil.
179 I9 Sarangarh Chhattisgarh India
178 F8 Sarangpur Madh. Prad. India
15 I5 Saransk Rus. Fed.
89 H4 Sara Peak Nigeria
158 D5 Saraphi Thai.
14 K4 Sarapul Rus. Fed.
190 E3 Sarāqib Syria
115 F12 Sarasota FL U.S.A.
178 C8 Saraswati r. Gujarat India
16 H7 Sărata r. Moldova
77 O6 Sărata r. Romania
16 I7 Sarata Ukr.
16 I8 Sarata r. Ukr.
16 H6 Sărătenii Vechi Moldova
124 J4 Saratoga CA U.S.A.
122 K6 Saratoga WY U.S.A.
117 L5 Saratoga Lake NY U.S.A.
117 L5 Saratoga Springs NY U.S.A.
157 I4 Saratok Sarawak Malaysia
182 A2 Saratov Rus. Fed.
Saratov Oblast admin. div. Rus. Fed. see Saratovskaya Oblast'
191 A1 Saratovskaya Rus. Fed.
182 B2 Saratovskaya Oblast' admin. div. Rus. Fed.
182 B1 Saratovskoye Vodokhranilishche resr Rus. Fed.
185 J8 Saravan Iran
154 D6 Saravia Negros Phil.
159 D8 Sarawa r. Myanmar
157 I4 Sarawak state Malaysia
191 K5 Saray Azer.
188 C3 Saray Turkey
88 C4 Saraya Guinea
88 C3 Saraya Senegal
190 D3 Şarāyā Syria
79 K4 Saraycık Turkey
79 J5 Sarayköy Turkey
79 I2 Saraylar Turkey
188 F4 Sarayönü Turkey
185 I8 Sarbāz Iran
185 I9 Sarbāz r. Iran
185 I8 Sarbāz reg. Iran
77 N6 Sârbeni Romania
179 M6 Sarbhang Bhutan
57 L4 Sârbi Romania
184 H5 Sarbīsheh Iran
57 H5 Sárbogárd Hungary
54 F1 Sarbsko, Jezioro lag. Pol.
168 A3 Sarbulak Xinjiang China
71 J4 Sarca r. Italy
58 C7 Sarca di Genova r. Italy
36 D6 Sarcelles France
184 C3 Sarcham Iran
191 F4 Sarch'apet Armenia
72 B8 Sarcidano reg. Sardegna Italy
144 C3 Sarco Chile
173 E12 Sarda r. India/Nepal
178 H5 Sarda r. Nepal
185 I8 Sardāb Iran
185 N3 Sardab Pass Afgh.
64 B5 Sardão, Cabo c. Port.
72 B8 Sardara Sardegna Italy
178 E8 Sardarpur Madh. Prad. India
178 E5 Sardarshahr Rajasthan India
184 A3 Sar Dasht Iran
184 C5 Sardasht Khūzestān Iran
184 D6 Sardasht Khūzestān Iran
72 C7 Sardegna admin. reg. Italy
72 A7 Sardegna i. Sardegna Italy
Sardica Bulg. see Sofiya
56 G3 Šardice Czech Rep.
98 □3f Sardina Gran Canaria Canary Is
98 □3f Sardina, Punta de pt Gran Canaria Canary Is
136 C2 Sardinata Col.
126 □Q12 Sardinia Costa Rica
Sardinia i. Sardegna Italy see Sardegna
65 L4 Sardinilla r. Spain
121 K8 Sardis MS U.S.A.
116 E9 Sardis WV U.S.A.
121 K8 Sardis Lake resr MS U.S.A.
62 D9 Sardoal Port.
189 M5 Sardrūd Iran
43 A9 Sare France
187 J3 Sareb, Rās as pt U.A.E.
185 L4 Sar-e Būm Afgh.
20 N3 Sareks nationalpark nat. park Sweden
20 N3 Sarektjåkkå mt. Sweden
157 K5 Sarempaka, Gunung mt. Indon.
67 K8 S'Arenal Spain
71 K2 Sarentino Italy
185 K3 Sar-e Pol Afgh.
185 L4 Sar-e Pol Afgh.
185 L3 Sar-e Pol prov. Afgh.
189 L6 Sar-e Pol-e Žahāb Iran
70 C4 Sareva r. Italy
184 F6 Sare Yazd Iran
185 O2 Sarez, Kŭli l. Tajik.
Sarezskoye Ozero l. Tajik. see Sarez, Kŭli
70 G1 Sargans Switz.
214 E4 Sargasso Sea Atlantic Ocean
136 C5 Sargentu Loros Peru
185 O5 Sargodha Pak.
90 C2 Sarh Chad
184 I7 Sarhad reg. Iran
88 D4 Sarhala Côte d'Ivoire
86 D3 Sarhro, Jbel mt. Morocco
184 E3 Sārī Iran
79 I7 Saria i. Karpathos Greece
126 D2 Sáric Mex.
79 L2 Sarıcakaya Turkey
191 B7 Sarıcan Turkey
77 Q6 Sarichioi Romania
191 E6 Sarıçiçek Dağı mt. Turkey
72 B3 Sari-d'Orcino Corse France
62 I3 Sariegos Spain
153 K3 Sarigan i. N. Mariana Is
191 C5 Sarıgöl Artvin Turkey
79 J4 Sarıgöl Manisa Turkey
79 M5 Sarıidris Turkey
189 K3 Sarıkamış Turkey
190 B2 Sarıkavak Turkey
157 I3 Sarikei Sarawak Malaysia
79 I5 Sarıkemer Turkey
79 I2 Sarıköy Turkey
Sarikŭl, Qatorkŭhi mts China/Tajik. see Sarykol Range
178 G7 Sarila Uttar Prad. India
156 □ Sarimbun Reservoir Sing.
207 L6 Sarina Qld Austr.
66 E4 Sariñena Spain
92 D4 Sarinleev Somalia
191 D6 Sarıpınar Turkey
184 F3 Sāri Qamīsh Iran
Sariqamish Kuli salt l. Turkm./Uzbek. see Sarykamyshskoye Ozero
84 C4 Sarīr Tibesti des. Libya
84 D3 Sarir Water Wells Field Libya
179 L7 Sarishabari Bangl.
191 B4 Sarısu Turkey
191 J5 Sarısu Gölü l. Azer.
121 G12 Sarita TX U.S.A.
190 A2 Sarıveliler Turkey
163 D9 Sariwŏn N. Korea
191 I6 Sarıxanlı Azer.
79 M2 Sarıyar Turkey
79 K1 Sarıyer Turkey
188 H4 Sarız Turkey
38 G3 Sark i. Channel Is
57 K5 Sarkad Hungary
57 K5 Sarkadkeresztúr Hungary
183 R5 Sarkand Kazakh.
178 C6 Sarkari Tala Rajasthan India
57 H4 Sárkeresztes Hungary
57 H4 Sárkeresztúr Hungary
188 E4 Şarkikaraağaç Turkey
21 Q6 Särkisalo Fin.
188 H4 Şarkışla Turkey
79 I2 Şarköy Turkey
185 L7 Sarlath Range mts Afgh./Pak.
43 G6 Sarlat-la-Canéda France
59 I2 Sarleinsbach Austria
42 F5 Sarliac-sur-l'Isle France
191 E2 Sarmakovo Rus. Fed.
185 K5 Sarmalan Afgh.
14 K5 Sarmanovo Rus. Fed.
77 K3 Şărmăşag Romania
77 M4 Sărmaşu Romania
75 K3 Sarmento r. Italy
153 I7 Sarmi Papua Indon.
145 C7 Sarmiento Arg.
21 L6 Särna Sweden
62 E9 Sarnadas do Ródão Port.
55 K3 Sarnaki Pol.
73 K1 Sarnano Italy
18 E4 Sārnate Latvia
179 I7 Sarnath Uttar Prad. India
184 B5 Sarneh Iran
70 E2 Sarnen Switz.
70 E2 Sarner See l. Switz.
108 D5 Sarnia Ont. Can.
70 H4 Sarnico Italy
73 N6 Sarno Italy
54 E4 Sarnowa Pol.
16 F2 Sarny Ukr.
155 B5 Saroako Sulawesi Indon.
19 S3 Sarogozha r. Rus. Fed.
156 E6 Sarolangun Sumatera Indon.
164 U2 Saroma-ko l. Japan
110 C4 Sarona WI U.S.A.
78 E5 Saronikos Kolpos g. Greece
70 G4 Saronno Italy
57 H4 Sárosd Hungary
79 H2 Saros Körfezi b. Turkey
57 K3 Sárospatak Hungary
178 D7 Sarotra Gujarat India
15 H5 Sarova Rus. Fed.
57 H3 Šarovce Slovakia
50 H3 Sarow Ger.
185 M4 Sarowbī Afgh.
15 I6 Sarpa, Ozero l. Rus. Fed.
15 I7 Sarpa, Ozero l. Rus. Fed.
Sarpan i. N. Mariana Is see Rota
154 □ Sar Passage Palau
76 I9 Šar Planina mts Macedonia/Yugo.
22 H2 Sarpsborg Norway
Sarqant Kazakh. see Sarkand
72 C9 Sarrabus reg. Sardegna Italy
63 M4 Sarracín Spain
66 H5 Sarral Spain
37 N6 Sarralbe France
43 C9 Sarrance France
43 E10 Sarrancolin France
41 B7 Sarrans, Barrage de dam France
62 E5 Sarraquinhos Port.
41 F6 Sarras France
37 N5 Sarre r. France
70 C4 Sarre Italy
31 O5 Sarre Kent, England U.K.
Sarreal Spain see Sarral
62 E4 Sarreaus Spain
37 N6 Sarre Blanche r. France
37 N6 Sarrebourg France
37 N5 Sarreguemines France
57 H4 Sarreti park Hungary
57 K4 Sárrétudvari Hungary
37 N6 Sarre-Union France
62 F3 Sarria Spain
66 K3 Sarrià de Ter Spain
41 F8 Sarrians France
67 D7 Sarrión Spain
88 D3 Sarro Mali
66 G5 Sarroca de Lleida Spain
72 C9 Sarròch Sardegna Italy
59 O4 Sarród Hungary
72 B3 Sarrola-Carcopino Corse France
43 D8 Sarron France
36 H6 Sarry France
14 L4 Sars Rus. Fed.
71 M8 Sarsina Italy
42 I4 Sarssonne r. France
49 I6 Sarstedt Ger.
57 H5 Sárszentágota Hungary
57 H4 Sárszentmihály Hungary
45 I7 Sart Belgium
63 P4 Sartaguda Spain
17 Q6 Sartana Ukr.
185 N8 Sartanahu Pak.
72 H2 Sarteano Italy
72 B4 Sartène Corse France
39 L6 Sarthe dept France
39 J6 Sarthe r. France
78 E2 Sarti Greece
191 G4 Sart'ichala Georgia
38 I4 Sartilly France
18 E6 Sartininkai Lith.
168 A3 Sartokay Xinjiang China
57 J4 Sarud Hungary
184 D4 Sarud, Rūdkhāneh-ye r. Iran
164 T4 Saru-gawa r. Japan
79 I4 Saruhanlı Turkey
72 C7 Sarule Sardegna Italy
185 L8 Saruna Pak.
185 L8 Saruna r. Pak.
178 D5 Sarupsar Rajasthan India
184 C4 Saruq Iran
191 F6 Şarur Azer.
185 J6 Saru Tara tourist site Afgh.
187 O2 Sarvāb Iran
184 B4 Sarvābād Iran
56 F4 Sárvár Hungary
184 E7 Sarvestān Iran
66 E2 Sarvisé Spain
76 G4 Sárvíz r. Romania
57 H5 Sárvíz-malomcsatorna canal Hungary
178 E6 Sarwar Rajasthan India
176 C3 Sarya r. India
183 M7 Saryagash Kazakh.
18 K6 Sar"yanka r. Belarus/Latvia
182 I4 Sarybasat Kazakh.
183 O7 Sary-Bulak Kyrg.
Sarydhaz r. Kyrg. see Sary-Jaz
Sarydzhas Kazakh. see Saryzhaz
Sarygamysh Köli salt l. Turkm./Uzbek. see Sarykamyshskoye Ozero
Sary-Ishikotrau, Peski des. Kazakh. see Saryyesik-Atyrau, Peski
183 R6 Sary-Jaz r. Kyrg.
182 E5 Sarykamys Atyrauskaya Oblast' Kazakh.
183 L3 Sarykamys Karagandinskaya Oblast' Kazakh.
184 G1 Sarykamyshskoye Ozero salt l. Turkm./Uzbek.
183 N6 Sarykemer Kazakh.
183 P2 Sarykiyak Kazakh.
182 K1 Sarykol' Kazakh.
185 P2 Sarykol Range mts China/Tajik.
183 P5 Sarykomey Kazakh.
182 K2 Sarymoyyn, Ozero salt l. Kazakh.
183 R5 Saryozek Kazakh.
Saryqamys Kazakh. see Sarykamys
183 O4 Saryshagan Kazakh.
183 L5 Sarysu watercourse Kazakh.
191 H2 Sarysu Rus. Fed.
182 D5 Sarytash Kazakh.
183 O8 Sary-Tash Kyrg.
183 Q7 Saryter, Gora mt. Kyrg.
182 D2 Saryumir Kazakh.
185 J3 Sary Yazikskoye Vodokhranilishche resr Turkm.
183 P5 Saryyesik-Atyrau, Peski des. Kazakh.
Saryzhal Kazakh. see Sarzhal
183 R6 Saryzhaz Kazakh.
70 H7 Sarzana Italy
38 F6 Sarzeau France
62 E9 Sarzedas Port.
182 D6 Sarzha Kazakh.
183 R3 Sarzhal Kazakh.
125 U10 Sasabe AZ U.S.A.
92 D2 Sasabeneh Eth.
156 C4 Sasak Sumatera Indon.
63 L4 Sasamón Spain
200 □6 Sasamungga Choiseul Solomon Is
155 A8 Sasar, Tanjung pt Sumba Indon.
179 J7 Sasaram Bihar India
200 □6 Sasari, Mount Sta Isabel Solomon Is
166 B5 Sasayama Japan
52 D5 Sasbach Baden-Württemberg Ger.
52 E4 Sasbach Baden-Württemberg Ger.
52 E4 Sasbachwalden Ger.
17 L3 Saschnivka Ukr.
57 H5 Sásd Hungary
165 G13 Sasebo Japan
55 I2 Sasek Wielki, Jezioro l. Pol.
167 K3 Sashima Japan
17 L5 Sasivka Ukr.
107 J4 Saskatchewan prov. Can.
107 K4 Saskatchewan r. Man./Sask. Can.
106 J5 Saskatchewan Landing Provincial Park Sask. Can.
107 J4 Saskatoon Sask. Can.
193 M2 Saskylakh Rus. Fed.
126 □Q11 Saslaya mt. Nic.
126 □Q11 Saslaya, Parque Nacional nat. park Nic.
16 I1 Sasnovy Bor Belarus
97 L2 Sasolburg S. Africa
15 H5 Sasovo Rus. Fed.
106 H2 Sass r. N.W.T. Can.
118 D6 Sassafras MD U.S.A.
88 D5 Sassandra Côte d'Ivoire
88 D5 Sassandra r. Côte d'Ivoire
73 P7 Sassano Italy
72 B6 Sassari Sardegna Italy
72 B6 Sassari prov. Sardegna Italy
70 E7 Sassello Italy
50 H2 Sassen Ger.
41 H6 Sassenage France
49 F7 Sassenberg Ger.
44 G4 Sassenheim Neth.
72 F1 Sassetta Italy
50 I1 Sassnitz Ger.
71 M8 Sassocorvaro Italy
70 G3 Sasso della Paglia mt. Switz.
71 K7 Sasso di Castro mt. Italy
71 N9 Sassoferrato Italy
71 L2 Sasso Lungo mt. Italy
71 K7 Sasso Marconi Italy
71 L2 Sass Rigais mt. Italy
88 C5 Sass Town Liberia
71 J6 Sassuolo Italy
66 E5 Sástago Spain
56 G3 Šaštín-Stráže Slovakia
183 N6 Sastobe Kazakh.
147 G2 Sastre Arg.
176 D3 Sasvad Mahar. India
45 E6 Sas Van Gent Neth.
17 K7 Sasyk r. Ukr.
17 M8 Sasyk, Ozero l. Ukr.
183 S4 Sasykkol', Ozero l. Kazakh.
15 I7 Sasykoli Rus. Fed.
Sasyqköl l. Kazakh. see Sasykkol', Ozero
88 C3 Satadougou Mali
Satahual i. Micronesia see Satawal
88 D5 Satama-Sokoura Côte d'Ivoire
165 H16 Sata-misaki c. Japan
178 E9 Satana Mahar. India
16 F4 Sataniv Ukr.
62 E7 Satão Port.
200 □2 Satapuala Samoa
176 D4 Satara Mahar. India
95 F5 Satara S. Africa
200 □2 Sataua Samoa
153 K5 Satawal i. Micronesia
Sätbaev Kazakh. see Satpayev
76 J5 Satchinez Romania
90 D3 Satéma C.A.R.
157 L8 Satengar i. Indon.
23 L1 Säter Sweden
126 F4 Satevó Mex.
123 K13 Satevo r. Mex.
124 M7 Saticoy CA U.S.A.
20 O3 Satihaure l. Sweden
115 G10 Satilla r. GA U.S.A.
41 F6 Satillieu France
15 H5 Satinka Rus. Fed.
138 B2 Satipo Peru
88 D4 Satiri Burkina
Satırlar Turkey see Yeşilova
192 G4 Satka Rus. Fed.
179 N9 Satkania Bangl.
191 E4 Sat'khe Georgia
179 L8 Satkhira Bangl.
Satluj r. India/Pak. see Sutlej
176 F3 Satmala Range hills India
178 H7 Satna Madh. Prad. India
40 G5 Satolas airport France
167 L2 Satomi Japan
157 L9 Satonda i. Indon.
57 K3 Sátoraljaújhely Hungary
68 E3 Satorina mt. Croatia
50 E3 Satow Ger.
183 L3 Satpayev Karagandinskaya Oblast' Kazakh.
183 L4 Satpayev Karagandinskaya Oblast' Kazakh.
178 E9 Satpura Range mts India
73 P6 Satriano di Lucania Italy
18 F6 Šatrijos kalnis hill Lith.
48 I1 Satrup Ger.
165 H15 Satsuma-hantō pen. Japan
164 U4 Satsunai-gawa r. Japan
159 E8 Sattahip Thai.
20 S3 Sattanen Fin.
167 K3 Satte Japan
58 A5 Satteins Austria
53 I3 Satteldorf Ger.
176 G4 Sattenapalle Andhra Prad. India
158 B5 Satthwa Myanmar
178 F2 Satti Jammu and Kashmir
59 J3 Sattledt Austria
59 J6 Sattnitz reg. Austria
157 K6 Satui Kalimantan Indon.
77 K3 Satu Mare Romania
57 L4 Satu Mare county Romania
159 E11 Satun Thai.
164 □F18 Satunan-shotō is Japan
200 □2 Satupa'itea Samoa
147 F2 Saturnino M. Laspiur Arg.
178 F8 Satwas Madh. Prad. India
66 J4 Sau, Pantà de resr Spain
59 K6 Saualpe mts Austria
22 C2 Sauanuten mt. Norway
157 K8 Saubi i. Indon.
43 B8 Saubusse France
57 L4 Săuca Romania
63 O6 Saúca Spain
43 C6 Saucats France
147 H2 Sauce Arg.
147 G6 Sauce r. Arg.
121 E13 Sauceda Mex.
125 T9 Sauceda Mountains AZ U.S.A.
147 H2 Sauce de Luna Arg.
147 I2 Saucedo Uru.
62 G6 Saucelle, Embalse de resr Port./Spain
126 G3 Saucillo Mex.
41 C9 Sauclières France
22 C2 Sauda Norway
183 M6 Saudakent Kazakh.
20 □D1 Sauðárkrókur Iceland
180 E5 Saudi Arabia country Asia
18 H2 Saue Estonia
48 I4 Sauensiek Ger.
37 P6 Sauer r. France
53 L6 Sauerlach Ger.
49 E8 Sauerland reg. Ger.
139 F3 Sauêruiná r. Brazil
154 E8 Saug r. Mindanao Phil.
18 H3 Sauga r. Estonia
110 H7 Saugatuck MI U.S.A.
119 I2 Saugatuck Reservoir CT U.S.A.
108 D4 Saugeen r. Ont. Can.
117 L6 Saugerties NY U.S.A.
29 L7 Saughall Cheshire, England U.K.
43 C7 Saugnacq-et-Muret France
41 D7 Saugues France
144 D2 Saujil Arg.
42 C4 Saujon France
18 I5 Saukas ezers l. Latvia
120 H3 Sauk Center MN U.S.A.
110 E6 Sauk City WI U.S.A.
137 H4 Saül Fr. Guiana
27 K4 Saul Northern Ireland U.K.
43 G10 Saula, Port de pass Spain
22 E2 Sauland Norway
41 F7 Saulce-sur-Rhône France
37 M7 Saulcy-sur-Meurthe France
52 G6 Sauldorf Ger.
42 G1 Sauldre r. France
52 H5 Saulgau Ger.
42 F3 Saulgé France
53 K6 Saulgrub Ger.
52 E2 Saulheim Ger.
40 E2 Saulieu France
18 H4 Saulkrasti Latvia
37 L6 Saulnois reg. France
41 G8 Sault France
43 C8 Sault-de-Navailles France
36 H5 Sault-lès-Rethel France
108 C4 Sault Sainte Marie Ont. Can.
111 J3 Sault Sainte Marie MI U.S.A.
37 L8 Saulx France
37 I6 Saulx r. France
37 M8 Saulxures-sur-Moselotte France
40 B3 Saulzais-le-Potier France
183 M1 Saumalkol' Kazakh.
207 N6 Saumarez Reef Coral Sea Is Terr. Austr.
153 H8 Saumlakki Maluku Indon.
43 B6 Saumos France
42 D1 Saumur France
39 K7 Saumurois reg. France
20 S3 Saunavaara Fin.
206 C2 Saunders, Mount hill N.T. Austr.
212 O1 Saunders Coast Antarctica
30 C4 Saundersfoot Pembrokeshire, Wales U.K.
145 E8 Saunders Island Falkland Is
135 G7 Saunders Island S. Sandwich Is
110 F9 Saunemin IL U.S.A.
159 D10 Saung Thai.
158 C2 Saungka Myanmar
117 J5 Sauquoit NY U.S.A.
183 U4 Saur, Khrebet mts China/Kazakh.
182 D5 Saura Kazakh.
43 H10 Saurat France
18 H5 Saurieši Latvia
91 D7 Saurimo Angola
71 N3 Sauris Italy
71 N3 Sauris, Lago di l. Italy
73 Q7 Sauro r. Italy
59 L6 Sausal hills Austria
124 J4 Sausalito CA U.S.A.
178 G9 Sausar Madh. Prad. India
41 G10 Sausset-les-Pins France
40 F2 Saussy France
155 B4 Sausu Sulawesi Indon.
91 C7 Sautar Angola
58 C5 Sautens Austria
43 D6 Sauternes France
131 □6 Sauteurs Grenada
38 H7 Sautron France
43 D9 Sauvagnon France
41 D9 Sauve France
41 C8 Sauveterre, Causse de plat. France
43 C9 Sauveterre-de-Béarn France
43 D6 Sauveterre-de-Guyenne France
43 I7 Sauveterre-de Rouergue France
43 G6 Sauveterre-la-Lémance France
42 H4 Sauviat-sur-Vige France
40 C3 Sauvigny-les-Bois France
21 Q6 Sauvo Fin.
44 K2 Sauwerd Neth.
40 C5 Sauxillanges France
146 A4 Sauzal Maule Chile
146 B4 Sauzal O'Higgins Chile
128 C1 Sauz de Arriba Mex.
43 G7 Sauzet France
42 E3 Sauzé-Vaussais France
38 E7 Sauzon France
47 J6 Sava r. Europe
126 □P10 Savá Hond.
75 N3 Sava Italy
59 K7 Sava Slovenia
118 B6 Savage MD U.S.A.
205 J9 Savage River Tas. Austr.
200 □2 Savai'i i. Samoa
15 H6 Savala r. Rus. Fed.
89 F5 Savalou Benin
109 G3 Savane r. Que. Can.
95 G3 Savane Moz.
131 □9 Savaneta Aruba
120 J4 Savanna IL U.S.A.
115 G9 Savannah GA U.S.A.
120 H6 Savannah MO U.S.A.
116 C8 Savannah OH U.S.A.
121 K8 Savannah TN U.S.A.
115 G9 Savannah r. GA/SC U.S.A.
130 E1 Savannah Sound Eleuthera Bahamas
158 G6 Savannakhét Laos
130 □ Savanna-la-Mar Jamaica
110 D1 Savanne Ont. Can.
108 B3 Savant Lake Ont. Can.
108 B3 Savant Lake l. Ont. Can.
Savantvadi Mahar. India see Vadi
176 D5 Savanur Karnataka India
20 P5 Sävar Sweden
77 K4 Săvârşin Romania
20 P4 Sävast Sweden
79 I3 Savaştepe Turkey
59 N7 Savci Slovenia
89 F4 Savè Benin
43 G8 Save r. France
95 G4 Save Moz.
95 G4 Save r. Moz./Zimbabwe
184 D4 Sāveh Iran
75 L5 Savelli Italy
88 E4 Savelugu Ghana
71 K7 Savena r. Italy
38 H7 Savenay France
77 O3 Săveni Romania
43 H9 Saverdun France
137 G3 Saveretik Guyana
37 N6 Saverne France
20 T5 Saviaho Fin.
36 G7 Savières France
70 D6 Savigliano Italy
42 F5 Savignac-les-Églises France
73 O5 Savignano Irpino Italy
71 M7 Savignano sul Rubicone Italy
39 L5 Savigné-l'Évêque France
40 E5 Savigneux France
40 B2 Savigny-en-Sancerre France
40 F2 Savigny-lès-Beaune France
39 M6 Savigny-sur-Braye France
36 D6 Savigny-sur-Orge France
41 I7 Savines-le-Lac France
77 O4 Săvineşti Romania
19 O8 Savinichy Belarus
68 E2 Savinja r. Slovenia
182 B2 Savinka Rus. Fed.
19 Y5 Savino Rus. Fed.
14 L3 Savinobor Rus. Fed.
14 H3 Savinskiy Rus. Fed.
19 W6 Savinskoye Rus. Fed.
71 M7 Savio r. Italy
21 S6 Savitaipale Fin.
176 C3 Savitri r. India
23 N2 Sävja Sweden
79 L5 Savköy Turkey
76 H8 Šavnik Crna Gora Serb. and Mont.
200 □6 Savo i. Solomon Is
70 H2 Savognin Switz.
73 P6 Savoia di Lucania Italy
40 J6 Savoie dept France
40 I4 Savoie reg. France
36 H8 Savoisy France
70 E7 Savona Italy
70 E7 Savona prov. Italy
73 L5 Savone r. Italy
21 T6 Savonlinna Fin.
20 T5 Savonranta Fin.
104 A3 Savoonga AK U.S.A.
Savoy reg. France see Savoie
19 Q1 Savozero, Ozero l. Rus. Fed.
16 J5 Savran' Ukr.
16 J5 Savranka r. Ukr.
189 K3 Şavşat Turkey
23 K4 Sävsjö Sweden
155 B9 Savu i. Indon.
71 O5 Savudrija Croatia
68 D3 Savudrija, Rt pt Croatia
20 T3 Savukoski Fin.
189 J5 Savur Turkey
201 □1 Savusavu Vanua Levu Fiji
201 □1 Savusavu Bay Vanua Levu Fiji
Savu Sea Indon. see Sawu, Laut
94 E3 Savute r. Botswana
94 E3 Savuti Botswana
73 Q9 Savuto r. Italy
169 P1 Savvo-Borzya Rus. Fed.
17 L2 Savynky Ukr.
17 Q4 Savyntsi Ukr.
158 B4 Saw Myanmar
156 D5 Sawahlunto Sumatera Indon.
155 F5 Sawai, Teluk b. Seram Indon.
178 F7 Sawai Madhopur Rajasthan India
201 □1 Sawaleke Fiji
157 K5 Sawan Kalimantan Indon.
158 C1 Sawan Myanmar
158 D6 Sawankhalok Thai.
178 E7 Sawar Rajasthan India
167 M4 Sawara Japan
165 P9 Sawasaki-bana pt Japan
164 P9 Sawata Japan
123 K7 Sawatch Range mts CO U.S.A.
31 M4 Sawbridgeworth Hertfordshire, England U.K.
84 B2 Sawdā', Jabal as hills Libya
27 H3 Sawel Mountain hill Northern Ireland U.K.
85 F3 Sawhāj Sawhāj Egypt
159 D9 Sawi, Ao b. Thai.
55 L4 Sawin Pol.
88 E4 Sawla Ghana
95 F3 Sawmills Zimbabwe
158 C3 Sawn Yunnan China
187 M6 Şawqirah, Dawḩat b. Oman
187 M6 Şawqirah, Ra's c. Oman
Şawqirah Bay Oman see Şawqirah, Dawḩat
31 M3 Sawston Cambridgeshire, England U.K.
205 N4 Sawtell N.S.W. Austr.
110 C2 Sawtooth Mountains hills MN U.S.A.
122 G4 Sawtooth Range mts ID U.S.A.
122 D2 Sawtooth Range mts WA U.S.A.
31 L3 Sawtry Cambridgeshire, England U.K.
155 B9 Sawu Indon.
Sawu i. Indon. see Savu
155 B8 Sawu, Laut sea Indon.
67 D10 Sax Spain
26 □O1 Saxa Vord hill Scotland U.K.
207 H5 Saxby r. Qld Austr.
59 K3 Saxen Austria
29 P7 Saxilby Lincolnshire, England U.K.
106 D4 Saxman AK U.S.A.
31 O3 Saxmundham Suffolk, England U.K.
20 M4 Saxnäs Sweden
70 C3 Saxon Switz.
Saxony land Ger. see Sachsen
Saxony-Anhalt land Ger. see Sachsen-Anhalt
31 O2 Saxthorpe Norfolk, England U.K.
116 A12 Saxton KY U.S.A.
116 G8 Saxton PA U.S.A.
88 D3 Say Mali
89 F3 Say Niger
170 C2 Saya Sichuan China
166 E5 Saya Japan
190 D3 Şāyā Syria
Sayabouri Laos see Xaignabouli
155 F3 Sayafi i. Maluku Indon.
62 H6 Sayago reg. Spain
183 Q4 Sayak Kazakh.
176 F8 Sayalkudi Tamil Nadu India
89 I3 Sayam well Niger

Sayama to Selenge Mörön

336

167 J4 Sayama Japan
138 A2 Sayán Peru
155 F3 Sayang i. Papua Indon.
160 F1 Sayano-Shushenskoye Vodokhranilishche resr Rus. Fed.
Sayaq Kazakh. see Sayak
185 J2 Sayat Turkm.
63 O8 Sayatón Spain
127 N9 Sayaxché Guat.
51 H9 Sayda Ger.
Sayda Lebanon see Saïda
42 D6 Saye r. France
184 F6 Sāyen Iran
190 D1 Saygeçit Turkey
185 L4 Sayghān Afgh.
186 G7 Şayḩ well Yemen
187 M5 Şayḩ al Aḩmar reg. Oman
187 J8 Sayḩūt Yemen
191 H6 Şayıflı Azer.
170 D5 Sayingpan Yunnan China
182 B3 Saykhin Kazakh.
92 D2 Saylac Somalia
Saylan country Asia see Sri Lanka
118 E3 Saylorsburg PA U.S.A.
169 L4 Saynshand Mongolia
168 D3 Sayn-Ust Mongolia
Sayot Turkm. see Sayat
Say-Ötesh Kazakh. see Say-Utes
190 F5 Şayqal, Baḩr imp. l. Syria
Sayqyn Kazakh. see Saykhin
172 E4 Sayram Hu salt l. China
183 N6 Sayramskiy, Pik mt. Uzbek.
121 F8 Sayre OK U.S.A.
111 R8 Sayre PA U.S.A.
119 G4 Sayreville NJ U.S.A.
185 L3 Sayrob Uzbek.
168 D5 Saysu Xinjiang China
128 D6 Sayula Jalisco Mex.
129 M8 Sayula Veracruz Mex.
128 D6 Sayula, Laguna de imp. l. Mex.
187 I7 Say'ūn Yemen
182 E5 Say-Utes Kazakh.
119 I3 Sayville NY U.S.A.
106 E5 Sayward B.C. Can.
187 M6 Sayy well Oman
Sayyod Turkm. see Sayat
78 A2 Sazan i. Albania
56 D2 Sázava r. Czech Rep.
182 C4 Sazdy Kazakh.
14 L4 Sazhino Rus. Fed.
17 P3 Sazhnoye Rus. Fed.
99 □3b Sazile, Pointe pt Mayotte
185 O4 Sazin Pak.
19 S2 Sazonovo Rus. Fed.
Saztöbe Kazakh. see Sastobe
87 E3 Sbaa Alg.
87 H2 Sbeitla Tunisia
209 F12 Scaddan W.A. Austr.
38 D5 Scaër France
73 M3 Scafa Italy
29 K5 Scafell Pike hill England U.K.
118 B6 Scaggsville MD U.S.A.
74 G9 Scala, Monte della hill Italy
26 D10 Scalasaig Argyll and Bute, Scotland U.K.
29 Q5 Scalby North Yorkshire, England U.K.
29 K2 Scald Law hill Scotland U.K.
73 P8 Scalea Italy
73 P8 Scalea, Capo c. Italy
75 I7 Scaletta Zanclea Sicilia Italy
26 □N2 Scalloway Shetland, Scotland U.K.
Scalpaigh, Eilean i. Western Isles, Scotland U.K. see Scalpay
26 E8 Scalpay i. Highland, Scotland U.K.
26 C7 Scalpay i. Western Isles, Scotland U.K.
27 H2 Scalp Mountain hill Rep. of Ireland
205 L9 Scamander Tas. Austr.
41 E9 Scamandre, Étang de lag. France
104 B3 Scammon Bay AK U.S.A.
29 P7 Scampton Lincolnshire, England U.K.
75 L5 Scandale Italy
73 K2 Scandarello, Lago di l. Italy
71 J6 Scandiano Italy
71 K8 Scandicci Italy
73 J3 Scandriglia Italy
Scania reg. Sweden see Skåne
73 L4 Scanno Italy
73 L4 Scanno, Lago di l. Italy
72 B7 Scano di Montiferro Sardegna Italy
72 G2 Scansano Italy
77 P6 Scânteia Romania
75 L3 Scanzano Jonico Italy
26 K5 Scapa Orkney, Scotland U.K.
26 J5 Scapa Flow inlet Scotland U.K.
26 I6 Scaraben hill Scotland U.K.
26 E10 Scarba i. Scotland U.K.
108 E5 Scarborough Ont. Can.
131 □5 Scarborough Trin. and Tob.
29 Q5 Scarborough North Yorkshire, England U.K.
152 E3 Scarborough Shoal sea feature S. China Sea
116 D11 Scarbro WV U.S.A.
71 M6 Scardovari Italy
203 G9 Scargill South I. N.Z.
27 B9 Scariff Island Rep. of Ireland
26 C9 Scarinish Argyll and Bute, Scotland U.K.
29 L6 Scarisbrick Lancashire, England U.K.
118 D4 Scarlets Mill PA U.S.A.
72 F2 Scarlino Italy
26 B6 Scarp i. Scotland U.K.
36 F2 Scarpe r. France
71 K8 Scarperia Italy
27 E7 Scarriff Rep. of Ireland
119 H2 Scarsdale NY U.S.A.
27 J4 Scarva Northern Ireland U.K.
109 J4 Scaterie Island N.S. Can.
74 B10 Scauri Sicilia Italy
26 D8 Scavaig, Loch b. Scotland U.K.
59 N6 Ščavnica r. Slovenia
156 G1 Scawfell Shoal sea feature S. China Sea
204 E5 Sceale Bay S.A. Austr.
68 F4 Šćedro i. Croatia
73 N3 Scerni Italy
37 K8 Scey-sur-Saône-et-St-Albin France
52 G2 Schaafheim Ger.
48 I1 Schaalby Ger.
48 K4 Schaale r. Ger.
48 K3 Schaalsee l. Ger.
48 K3 Schaalsee park Ger.
52 H7 Schaan Liechtenstein
44 I4 Schaarsbergen Neth.
48 I2 Schacht-Audorf Ger.
118 C4 Schaefferstown PA U.S.A.
45 F7 Schaerbeek Belgium
45 J7 Schaesberg Neth.
70 F1 Schaffhausen Switz.
70 F1 Schaffhausen canton Switz.
48 H1 Schafflund Ger.
48 H2 Schafstedt Ger.
53 K6 Schäftlarn Ger.
44 G3 Schagen Neth.
44 G3 Schagerbrug Neth.
44 I5 Schaijk Neth.
94 C5 Schakalskuppe Namibia
58 H3 Schalchen Austria
51 D10 Schalkau Ger.
44 J4 Schalkhaar Neth.
49 E8 Schalksmühle Ger.
52 D6 Schallstadt Ger.
70 G1 Schänis Switz.
184 I6 Schao watercourse Afgh./Iran
49 E6 Schapen Ger.
50 H1 Schaprode Ger.
48 K2 Scharbeutz Ger.
59 H2 Schardenberg Austria
59 H3 Schärding Austria
58 H5 Schareck mt. Austria
44 E5 Scharendijke Neth.
58 E4 Scharfreiter mt. Austria/Ger.
48 F3 Scharhörn sea feature Ger.
51 J6 Scharmützelsee l. Ger.
48 K4 Scharnebeck Ger.
44 I2 Scharnegoutum Neth.
58 D5 Scharnitz Austria
59 I4 Scharnstein Austria
48 E4 Scharrel (Oldenburg) Ger.
49 C10 Scharteberg hill Ger.
44 H3 Scharwoude Neth.
48 K2 Schashagen Ger.
59 O4 Schattendorf Austria
110 F7 Schaumburg IL U.S.A.
53 I2 Schebheim Ger.
53 M6 Schechen Ger.
49 I8 Scheden Ger.
44 K2 Scheemda Neth.
52 G5 Scheer Ger.
48 H4 Scheeßel Ger.
58 H4 Scheffau am Tennengebirge Austria
58 F4 Scheffau am Wilden Kaiser Austria
109 H2 Schefferville Nfld and Lab. Can.
52 G3 Schefflenz Ger.
71 N9 Scheggia e Pascelupo Italy
73 J2 Scheggino Italy
59 L3 Scheibbs Austria
59 N4 Scheiblingkirchen Austria
52 H6 Scheidegg Ger.
59 J5 Scheifling Austria
53 I2 Scheinfeld Ger.
52 H5 Schelklingen Ger.
125 R3 Schell Creek Range mts NV U.S.A.
45 F6 Schelle Belgium
49 J6 Schellerten Ger.
48 J2 Schellhorn Ger.
116 G8 Schellsburg PA U.S.A.
124 J3 Schellville CA U.S.A.
52 H5 Schemmerhofen Ger.
117 L6 Schenectady NY U.S.A.
48 H2 Schenefeld Schleswig-Holstein Ger.
48 I3 Schenefeld Schleswig-Holstein Ger.
59 J2 Schenkenfelden Austria
52 E5 Schenkenzell Ger.
49 I9 Schenklengsfeld Ger.
49 C7 Schermbeck Ger.
51 E6 Schermen Ger.
44 G3 Schermerhorn Neth.
49 K8 Schernberg Ger.
53 K4 Schernfeld Ger.
45 G7 Scherpenheuvel Belgium
44 H4 Scherpenzeel Neth.
121 F11 Schertz TX U.S.A.
37 N7 Scherwiller France
70 G1 Scherzingen Switz.
58 A5 Schesaplana mt. Austria/Switz.
53 K2 Scheßlitz Ger.
53 K5 Scheyern Ger.
71 M3 Schiara, Monte mt. Italy
73 M4 Schiavi di Abruzzo Italy
44 F5 Schiedam Neth.
49 H7 Schieder-Schwalenberg Ger.
59 J6 Schiefling am See Austria
26 H9 Schiehallion mt. Scotland U.K.
45 J9 Schieren Lux.
49 K7 Schierke Ger.
53 M4 Schierling Ger.
44 J2 Schiermonnikoog Neth.
44 J1 Schiermonnikoog i. Neth.
44 J1 Schiermonnikoog Nationaal Park nat. park Neth.
70 H2 Schiers Switz.
48 G3 Schiffdorf Ger.
52 E3 Schifferstadt Ger.
45 J9 Schifflange Lux.
52 C3 Schiffweiler Ger.
44 H5 Schijndel Neth.
45 G6 Schilde Belgium
48 K4 Schilde r. Ger.
44 K2 Schildmeer l. Neth.
50 H5 Schildow Ger.
44 K2 Schildwolde-Hellum Neth.
52 B2 Schillingen Ger.
53 I3 Schillingsfürst Ger.
70 I3 Schilpario Italy
52 E5 Schiltach Ger.
53 K5 Schiltberg Ger.
37 O6 Schiltigheim France
78 E4 Schimatari Greece
45 I7 Schinnen Neth.
45 I7 Schinveld Neth.
71 K4 Schio Italy
44 J4 Schipbeek r. Neth.
44 G4 Schiphol airport Neth.
51 I7 Schipkau Ger.
37 N7 Schirmeck France
53 M2 Schirmitz Ger.
51 F10 Schirnding Ger.
77 P3 Schitu Duca Romania
78 C6 Schiza i. Greece
51 F8 Schkeuditz Ger.
51 E8 Schkölen Ger.
51 G7 Schköna Ger.
51 E8 Schkopau Ger.
51 I7 Schlabendorf Ger.
49 K6 Schladen Ger.
59 I5 Schladming Austria
59 I5 Schladminger Tauern mts Austria
48 K3 Schlagsdorf Ger.
49 G7 Schlangen Ger.
49 F10 Schlangenbad Ger.
51 D6 Schlanstedt Ger.
53 M6 Schleching Ger.
58 E5 Schlegeisspeicher l. Austria
48 J1 Schlei r. Ger.
49 B9 Schleiden Ger.
51 K7 Schleife Ger.
59 N3 Schleinbach Austria
70 E1 Schleitheim Switz.
51 E9 Schleiz Ger.
51 G9 Schlema Ger.
51 I6 Schlepzig Ger.
Schlesien reg. Europe see Silesia
48 I1 Schleswig Ger.
48 I2 Schleswig-Holstein land Ger.
48 G2 Schleswig-Holsteinisches Wattenmeer, Nationalpark nat. park Ger.
51 G9 Schlettau Ger.
49 K9 Schleusingen Ger.
51 H7 Schlieben Ger.
52 D6 Schliengen Ger.
52 H6 Schlier Ger.
59 J4 Schlierbach Austria
70 E1 Schlieren Switz.
53 L6 Schliersee Ger.
53 L6 Schliersee l. Ger.
58 A5 Schlins Austria
58 E5 Schlitters Austria
49 I9 Schlitz Ger.
49 G7 Schloss Holte-Stukenbrock Ger.
70 D2 Schlosswil Switz.
49 K8 Schlotheim Ger.
52 E6 Schluchsee Ger.
52 E6 Schluchsee l. Ger.
49 I10 Schlüchtern Ger.
Schlüsselburg Rus. Fed. see Shlissel'burg
53 J2 Schlüsselfeld Ger.
48 I3 Schmalfeld Ger.
49 F8 Schmallenberg Ger.
52 B3 Schmelz Ger.
53 M3 Schmidgaden Ger.
53 L3 Schmidmühlen Ger.
Schmidt Island Rus. Fed. see Shmidta, Ostrov
96 I4 Schmidtsdrif S. Africa
51 I9 Schmiedeberg Ger.
58 E5 Schmirn Austria
58 G5 Schmittenhöhe mt. Austria
50 J4 Schmölln Brandenburg Ger.
51 F9 Schmölln Thüringen Ger.
53 L2 Schnabelwaid Ger.
50 E4 Schnackenburg Ger.
53 M5 Schnaitsee Ger.
53 K2 Schnaittach Ger.
53 M2 Schnaittenbach Ger.
70 F1 Schnebelhorn mt. Switz.
118 D3 Schnecksville PA U.S.A.
51 G9 Schneeberg Ger.
48 K5 Schnega Ger.
Schneidemühl Pol. see Piła
51 D7 Schneidlingen Ger.
49 B10 Schneifel hills Ger.
53 N6 Schneizlreuth Ger.
53 I3 Schnelldorf Ger.
48 I4 Schneverdingen Ger.
52 H5 Schnürpflingen Ger.
48 H1 Schobüll Ger.
131 □3 Schœlcher Martinique
97 O1 Schoemanskloof pass S. Africa
45 J8 Schoenberg Belgium
110 E5 Schofield WI U.S.A.
124 □C12 Schofield Barracks military base HI U.S.A.
117 K6 Schoharie NY U.S.A.
44 I3 Schokland tourist site Neth.
48 G5 Scholen Ger.
29 O6 Scholes West Yorkshire, England U.K.
50 F5 Schollene Ger.
49 H10 Schöllkrippen Ger.
53 O4 Schöllnach Ger.
97 J7 Schombee S. Africa
52 F4 Schömberg Baden-Württemberg Ger.
52 F5 Schömberg Baden-Württemberg Ger.
52 G4 Schönaich Ger.
52 F3 Schönau Baden-Württemberg Ger.
53 N5 Schönau Bayern Ger.
53 N6 Schönau am Königssee Ger.
52 D6 Schönau im Schwarzwald Ger.
59 L3 Schönbach Austria
53 O4 Schönberg Bayern Ger.
50 G5 Schönberg Brandenburg Ger.
48 K3 Schönberg Mecklenburg-Vorpommern Ger.
48 J3 Schönberg Schleswig-Holstein Ger.
48 J2 Schönberg (Holstein) Ger.
59 M2 Schönberg am Kamp Austria
48 J2 Schönbergerstrand Ger.
58 D5 Schönberg im Stubaital Austria
51 I7 Schönborn Ger.
49 K9 Schönbrunn Ger.
52 F4 Schönbuch reg. Ger.
52 G4 Schönbuch, Naturpark nature res. Ger.
51 E8 Schönburg Ger.
49 I10 Schondra Ger.
50 F4 Schönebeck Ger.
51 E6 Schönebeck (Elbe) Ger.
51 F10 Schöneck Ger.
49 B10 Schönecken Ger.
51 H6 Schönefeld Ger.
51 I6 Schönefeld airport Ger.
51 I6 Schöneiche Berlin Ger.
52 C3 Schönenberg-Kübelberg Ger.
50 I4 Schönermark Brandenburg Ger.
50 J4 Schönermark Brandenburg Ger.
51 H7 Schönewalde Ger.
48 K5 Schönewörde Ger.
51 I8 Schönfeld Ger.
53 J6 Schongau Ger.
50 F5 Schönhausen Ger.
51 G9 Schönheide Ger.
49 K6 Schöningen Ger.
48 J2 Schönkirchen Ger.
53 N2 Schönsee Ger.
49 K8 Schönstedt Ger.
52 H3 Schöntal Ger.
53 N3 Schönthal Ger.
49 J10 Schonungen Ger.
51 F10 Schönwald Ger.
50 H5 Schönwalde Brandenburg Ger.
50 H5 Schönwalde Brandenburg Ger.
51 I7 Schönwalde Brandenburg Ger.
48 K2 Schönwalde am Bungsberg Ger.
58 C5 Schönwies Austria
117 □Q3 Schoodic Lake ME U.S.A.
117 □R4 Schoodic Point ME U.S.A.
110 I7 Schoolcraft MI U.S.A.
45 E6 Schoondijke Neth.
44 K3 Schoonebeek Neth.
44 G5 Schoonhoven Neth.
44 K3 Schoonoord Neth.
44 G3 Schoorl Neth.
52 D6 Schopfheim Ger.
59 M3 Schöpfl hill Austria
53 I3 Schopfloch Ger.
49 K6 Schöppenstedt Ger.
58 B5 Schoppernau Austria
49 D6 Schöppingen Ger.
50 I5 Schorfheide reg. Ger.
59 I4 Schörfling am Attersee Austria
52 H4 Schorndorf Baden-Württemberg Ger.
53 N3 Schorndorf Bayern Ger.
48 E3 Schortens Ger.
45 F6 Schoten Belgium
49 H10 Schotten Ger.
205 L10 Schouten Island Tas. Austr.
153 J7 Schouten Islands P.N.G.
118 C1 Schrader r. PA U.S.A.
52 E5 Schramberg Ger.
58 D5 Schrankogel mt. Austria
51 E8 Schraplau Ger.
49 H9 Schrecksbach Ger.
108 C3 Schreiber Ont. Can.
59 L2 Schrems Austria
50 F5 Schrepkow Ger.
52 F3 Schriesheim Ger.
53 K4 Schrobenhausen Ger.
59 J5 Schröder Austria
117 L5 Schroon Lake NY U.S.A.
117 L5 Schroon Lake l. NY U.S.A.
Schröttersburg Pol. see Płock
52 H3 Schrozberg Ger.
58 A5 Schruns Austria
70 F1 Schübelbach Switz.
48 H1 Schuby Ger.
49 J7 Schulenberg im Oberharz Ger.
121 G11 Schulenburg TX U.S.A.
107 I5 Schuler Alta Can.
27 C9 Schull Rep. of Ireland
107 L1 Schultz Lake Nunavut Can.
50 J5 Schulzendorf Ger.
51 I6 Schulzendorf bei Eichwalde Ger.
70 E2 Schüpfheim Switz.
52 G4 Schurwald for. Ger.
124 N3 Schurz NV U.S.A.
52 H6 Schussen r. Ger.
52 D4 Schutter r. Ger.
53 K4 Schutter r. Ger.
52 D5 Schuttertal Ger.
52 D5 Schutterwald Ger.
49 D6 Schüttorf Ger.
120 G5 Schuyler NE U.S.A.
117 J6 Schuyler Lake NY U.S.A.
117 L5 Schuylerville NY U.S.A.
118 E5 Schuylkill r. PA U.S.A.
118 C3 Schuylkill County county PA U.S.A.
111 R9 Schuylkill Haven PA U.S.A.
50 F3 Schwaan Ger.
53 K3 Schwabach Ger.
53 I5 Schwaben admin. reg. Ger.
52 F6 Schwäbische Alb mts Ger.
52 H4 Schwäbisch-Fränkischer Wald, Naturpark nature res. Ger.
52 H4 Schwäbisch Gmünd Ger.
52 H3 Schwäbisch Hall Ger.
53 J5 Schwabmünchen Ger.
48 H2 Schwabstedt Ger.
48 G5 Schwaförden Ger.
53 K3 Schwaig bei Nürnberg Ger.
52 G3 Schwaigern Ger.
52 B3 Schwalbach Ger.
49 J9 Schwallungen Ger.
49 H8 Schwalm r. Ger.
49 H9 Schwalmstadt-Treysa Ger.
49 H9 Schwalmstadt-Ziegenhain Ger.
59 L6 Schwanberg Austria
70 G1 Schwanden Switz.
53 M3 Schwandorf Ger.
50 I5 Schwanebeck Brandenburg Ger.
51 D7 Schwanebeck Sachsen-Anhalt Ger.
59 I3 Schwanenstadt Austria
157 J5 Schwaner, Pegunungan mts Indon.
48 G4 Schwanewede Ger.
53 J6 Schwangau Ger.
48 K4 Schwanheide Ger.
48 I1 Schwansen reg. Ger.
53 K3 Schwanstetten Ger.
48 H5 Schwarme Ger.
48 I5 Schwarmstedt Ger.
213 D2 Schwartz Range mts Antarctica
50 G4 Schwarz Ger.
49 K9 Schwarza Ger.
52 E6 Schwarza r. Ger.
51 D9 Schwarza r. Ger.
58 A5 Schwarzach Austria
53 N4 Schwarzach Ger.
53 K4 Schwarzach r. Ger.
53 M3 Schwarzach r. Ger.
58 H5 Schwarzach im Pongau Austria
59 M4 Schwarzau im Gebirge Austria
51 G7 Schwarze Elster r. Ger.
53 M4 Schwarze Laber r. Ger.
59 L2 Schwarzenau Austria
59 N4 Schwarzenbach Austria
51 E10 Schwarzenbach am Wald Ger.
51 E10 Schwarzenbach an der Saale Ger.
48 J3 Schwarzenbek Ger.
51 G9 Schwarzenberg Ger.
49 H9 Schwarzenborn Ger.
53 K3 Schwarzenbruck Ger.
70 C2 Schwarzenburg Switz.
53 M3 Schwarzenfeld Ger.
58 E5 Schwarzenstein mt. Austria/Italy
51 J7 Schwarze Pumpe Ger.
53 M3 Schwarzer Bach r. Ger.
49 B10 Schwarzer Mann hill Ger.
53 N3 Schwarzer Regen r. Ger.
51 K8 Schwarzer Schöps r. Ger.
71 P1 Schwarzersee l. Austria
51 I8 Schwarzheide Ger.
53 M3 Schwarzhofen Ger.
58 D5 Schwarzhorn mt. Austria
70 E2 Schwarzhorn mt. Switz.
94 C5 Schwarzrand mts Namibia
53 N3 Schwarzriegel mt. Ger.
52 E6 Schwarzwald mts Ger.
58 E5 Schwaz Austria
59 N3 Schwechat Austria
48 J2 Schwedeneck Ger.
50 J4 Schwedt an der Oder Ger.
52 E3 Schwegenheim Ger.
48 F4 Schwei (Stadland) Ger.
48 F4 Schweiburg Ger.
52 B2 Schweich Ger.
52 D3 Schweigen-Rechtenbach Ger.
37 O6 Schweighouse-sur-Moder France
49 J9 Schweina Ger.
49 J10 Schweinfurt Ger.
51 H7 Schweinitz Ger.
50 G4 Schweinrich Ger.
53 L4 Schweitenkirchen Ger.
Schweiz country Europe see Switzerland
97 J3 Schweizer-Reneke S. Africa
49 D8 Schwelm Ger.
58 E5 Schwendau Austria
52 H5 Schwendi Ger.
52 F5 Schwenningen Baden-Württemberg Ger.
52 F5 Schwenningen Baden-Württemberg Ger.
51 I8 Schwepnitz Ger.
50 D3 Schwerin Ger.
50 D3 Schweriner See l. Ger.
50 D3 Schweriner Seenlandschaft park Ger.
48 H5 Schweringen Ger.
59 K3 Schwertberg Austria
49 E8 Schwerte Ger.
52 F3 Schwetzingen Ger.
50 I3 Schwichtenberg Ger.
52 G4 Schwieberdingen Ger.
51 J6 Schwielochsee l. Ger.
50 D5 Schwiesau Ger.
53 M5 Schwindegg Ger.
48 H3 Schwinge r. Ger.
50 G3 Schwinkendorf Ger.
58 F4 Schwoich Austria
52 D6 Schwörstadt Ger.
70 F1 Schwyz Switz.
70 F1 Schwyz canton Switz.
74 E8 Sciacca Sicilia Italy
74 H10 Scicli Sicilia Italy
36 B4 Scie r. France
40 I4 Sciez France
75 K5 Scigliano Italy
71 L3 Sciliar, Parco Naturale dello nature res. Italy
75 J7 Scilla Italy
30 □ Scilly, Isles of England U.K.
54 E4 Ścinawa Pol.
54 E5 Ścinawka r. Pol.
116 D8 Scio OH U.S.A.
40 J4 Scionzier France
118 E3 Sciota PA U.S.A.
116 C10 Scioto r. OH U.S.A.
125 T2 Scipio UT U.S.A.
30 C4 Scleddau Pembrokeshire, Wales U.K.
122 L2 Scobey MT U.S.A.
Scodra Albania see Shkodër
125 U2 Scofield Reservoir UT U.S.A.
72 F2 Scoglia dello Sparviero i. Italy
74 G10 Scoglitti Sicilia Italy
75 H7 Scolaticci Isole Lipari Italy
31 O3 Scole Norfolk, England U.K.
71 J7 Scoltenna r. Italy
205 M5 Scone N.S.W. Austr.
26 J10 Scone Perth and Kinross, Scotland U.K.
26 D8 Sconser Highland, Scotland U.K.
70 E4 Scopello Italy
73 K3 Scoppito Italy
39 L8 Scorbé-Clairvaux France
74 H9 Scordia Sicilia Italy
105 P2 Scoresby Land reg. Greenland
Scoresbysund Greenland see Ittoqqortoormiit
38 E6 Scorff r. France
77 M6 Scornicești Romania
209 I12 Scorpion Bight b. W.A. Austr.
75 O3 Scorrano Italy
29 N5 Scorton North Yorkshire, England U.K.
71 M4 Scorzè Italy
28 D5 Scotch Corner Rep. of Ireland
29 N5 Scotch Corner North Yorkshire, England U.K.
119 G3 Scotch Plains NJ U.S.A.
214 F9 Scotia Ridge sea feature S. Atlantic Ocean
215 B9 Scotia Ridge sea feature S. Atlantic Ocean
214 G9 Scotia Sea S. Atlantic Ocean
111 N6 Scotland Ont. Can.
26 I8 Scotland admin. div. U.K.
117 I10 Scotland MD U.S.A.
118 E2 Scotrun PA U.S.A.
27 H4 Scotshouse Rep. of Ireland
109 G4 Scotstown Que. Can.
206 B2 Scott, Cape N.T. Austr.
106 D5 Scott, Cape B.C. Can.
121 G9 Scott, Mount hill OK U.S.A.
213 L1 Scott Base research stn Antarctica
97 O6 Scottburgh S. Africa
120 E6 Scott City KS U.S.A.
213 K1 Scott Coast Antarctica
29 P7 Scotter Lincolnshire, England U.K.
212 N1 Scott Glacier Antarctica
213 G2 Scott Glacier Antarctica
105 K2 Scott Inlet Nunavut Can.
26 K11 Scottish Borders admin. div. Scotland U.K.
213 L2 Scott Island Antarctica
106 D5 Scott Islands B.C. Can.
107 J3 Scott Lake Sask. Can.
213 D2 Scott Mountains Antarctica
29 N5 Scotton North Yorkshire, England U.K.
31 O2 Scottow Norfolk, England U.K.
202 G1 Scott Point North I. N.Z.
208 G3 Scott Reef W.A. Austr.
120 D5 Scottsbluff NE U.S.A.
115 D8 Scottsboro AL U.S.A.
114 E6 Scottsburg IN U.S.A.
205 K9 Scottsdale Tas. Austr.
125 U8 Scottsdale AZ U.S.A.
131 □2 Scotts Head Dominica
114 D7 Scottsville KY U.S.A.
116 G11 Scottsville VA U.S.A.
110 H6 Scottville MI U.S.A.
26 F6 Scourie Highland, Scotland U.K.
26 □N3 Scousburgh Shetland, Scotland U.K.
26 I5 Scrabster Highland, Scotland U.K.
118 D2 Scranton PA U.S.A.
27 C6 Screeb Rep. of Ireland
27 G6 Screggan Rep. of Ireland
27 F4 Scribbagh Northern Ireland U.K.
26 D10 Scridain, Loch inlet Scotland U.K.
70 F5 Scrivia r. Italy
108 E4 Scugog, Lake Ont. Can.
29 P6 Scunthorpe North Lincolnshire, England U.K.
70 I2 Scuol Switz.
Scupi Macedonia see Skopje
73 K3 Scurcola Marsicana Italy
26 B8 Scurrival Point Scotland U.K.
Scutari Albania see Shkodër
76 H8 Scutari, Lake Albania/Yugo.
116 H12 Seaboard NC U.S.A.
118 E5 Seabrook NJ U.S.A.
209 E11 Seabrook, Lake salt flat W.A. Austr.
77 M6 Seaca Romania
31 M6 Seaford East Sussex, England U.K.
117 J10 Seaford DE U.S.A.
111 M6 Seaforth Ont. Can.
130 □ Seaforth Jamaica
26 C7 Seaforth, Loch inlet Scotland U.K.
29 O4 Seaham Durham, England U.K.
154 A6 Seahorse Bank sea feature Phil.
29 N2 Seahouses Northumberland, England U.K.
118 F6 Sea Isle City NJ U.S.A.
107 M3 Seal r. Man. Can.
96 H10 Seal, Cape S. Africa
205 I6 Sea Lake Vic. Austr.
212 X2 Seal Bay Antarctica
98 □2c Seal Bay Tristan da Cunha S. Atlantic Ocean
130 H3 Seal Cays is Turks and Caicos Is
117 □S4 Seal Cove N.B. Can.
109 J3 Seal Cove Nfld and Lab. Can.
26 F7 Sealga, Loch na l. Scotland U.K.
117 □Q5 Seal Island ME U.S.A.
109 I2 Seal Lake Nfld and Lab. Can.
107 I1 Seal Lake N.W.T. Can.
97 I10 Seal Point S. Africa
121 G11 Sealy TX U.S.A.
116 B10 Seaman OH U.S.A.
125 Q4 Seaman Range mts NV U.S.A.
29 Q5 Seamer North Yorkshire, England U.K.
28 H2 Seamill North Ayrshire, Scotland U.K.
62 C5 Seara Port.
125 R6 Searchlight NV U.S.A.
121 J8 Searcy AR U.S.A.
124 O6 Searles Lake CA U.S.A.
117 □Q4 Searsport ME U.S.A.
29 K5 Seascale Cumbria, England U.K.
124 K5 Seaside CA U.S.A.
122 C4 Seaside OR U.S.A.
119 G5 Seaside Park NJ U.S.A.
29 J4 Seaton Cumbria, England U.K.
30 F6 Seaton Devon, England U.K.
29 N3 Seaton Delaval Northumberland, England U.K.
213 D2 Seaton Glacier Antarctica
29 O3 Seaton Sluice Northumberland, England U.K.
122 C3 Seattle WA U.S.A.
106 B2 Seattle, Mount Can./U.S.A.
97 J10 Sea View S. Africa
31 J6 Seaview Isle of Wight, England U.K.
207 J5 Seaview Range mts Qld Austr.
118 F6 Seaville NJ U.S.A.
203 H9 Seaward Kaikoura Range mts South I. N.Z.
155 B9 Seba Indon.
126 □P11 Sebaco Nic.
117 □O5 Sebago Lake ME U.S.A.
157 L5 Sebakung Kalimantan Indon.
62 C8 Sebal Port.
157 J6 Sebangan, Teluk b. Indon.
156 F4 Sebangka i. Indon.
Sebastea Turkey see Sivas
115 G12 Sebastian FL U.S.A.
147 F2 Sebastián Elcano Arg.
126 B3 Sebastián Vizcaíno, Bahía b. Mex.
117 □P4 Sebasticook r. ME U.S.A.
117 □P4 Sebasticook Lake ME U.S.A.
Sebastopol Ukr. see Sevastopol'
124 J3 Sebastopol CA U.S.A.
157 L2 Sebatik i. Indon.
157 J3 Sebauh Sarawak Malaysia
157 I5 Sebayan, Bukit mt. Indon.
41 B8 Sébazac-Concourès France
89 F3 Sebba Burkina
22 F5 Sebbersund Denmark
85 H6 Sebderat Eritrea
87 E2 Sebdou Alg.
88 C3 Sébékoro Mali
188 E3 Seben Turkey
Sebenico Croatia see Šibenik
Sebennytos Egypt see Samannūd
77 L5 Sebeș Romania
77 L4 Sebeș r. Romania
156 F7 Sebesi i. Indon.
57 J5 Sebes-Körös r. Hungary
111 K6 Sebewaing MI U.S.A.
18 L5 Sebezh Rus. Fed.
188 I3 Şebinkarahisar Turkey
77 K4 Sebiș Romania
19 U3 Sebla r. Rus. Fed.
156 E6 Seblat, Gunung mt. Indon.
51 J9 Sebnitz Ger.
117 □Q3 Seboeis ME U.S.A.
117 □Q3 Seboeis Lake ME U.S.A.
117 □P3 Seboomook Lake ME U.S.A.
116 H12 Sebrell VA U.S.A.
115 G12 Sebring FL U.S.A.
15 H6 Sebrovo Rus. Fed.
157 L6 Sebuku i. Indon.
157 L2 Sebuku r. Indon.
157 L3 Sebuku, Teluk b. Indon.
157 L2 Sebuku-Sembakung National Park Kalimantan Indon.
157 I4 Sebuyau Sarawak Malaysia
146 D5 Seca, Pampa plain Arg.
76 I5 Sečanj Vojvodina, Srbija Serb. and Mont.
62 D8 Secarias Port.
57 K6 Secaș Romania
77 L4 Secaș r. Romania
126 □S14 Secas, Islas is Panama
71 K5 Secchia r. Italy
92 C3 Seccia mts Eth.
55 H5 Secemin Pol.
106 F5 Sechelt B.C. Can.
15 I5 Sechenovo Rus. Fed.
136 A6 Sechura Peru
136 A6 Sechura, Bahía de b. Peru
52 G3 Seckach Ger.
59 K5 Seckau Austria
59 K5 Seckauer Alpen mts Austria
36 F2 Seclin France
66 F7 Seco r. Spain
42 D2 Secondigny France
117 □N3 Second Lake NH U.S.A.
125 V6 Second Mesa AZ U.S.A.
118 B4 Second Mountain ridge PA U.S.A.
88 □ Secos, Ilhéus is Cape Verde
57 K3 Sečovce Slovakia
203 A12 Secretary Island South I. N.Z.
97 N2 Secunda S. Africa
176 F4 Secunderabad Andhra Prad. India
138 D3 Sécure r. Bol.
57 J5 Secusigiu Romania
18 I4 Seda Latvia
18 I4 Seda r. Latvia
18 F5 Seda Lith.
64 D2 Seda Port.
64 C3 Seda r. Port.
120 I6 Sedalia MO U.S.A.
176 E4 Sedam Karnataka India
204 G6 Sedan S.A. Austr.
37 I4 Sedan France
121 G7 Sedan KS U.S.A.
207 H5 Sedan Dip Qld Austr.
63 M3 Sedano Spain
29 L5 Sedbergh Cumbria, England U.K.
203 I8 Seddon South I. N.Z.
203 F8 Seddonville South I. N.Z.
79 H2 Seddülbahir Turkey
190 C8 Sedé Boqer Israel
184 E6 Sedeh Fārs Iran
184 H5 Sedeh Khorāsān Iran
41 H8 Séderon France
190 C7 Sederot Israel
29 O4 Sedgefield Durham, England U.K.
107 I4 Sedgewick Alta Can.
30 H2 Sedgley West Midlands, England U.K.
117 □Q4 Sedgwick ME U.S.A.
88 B3 Sédhiou Senegal
71 M3 Sedico Italy
72 B7 Sedilo Sardegna Italy
72 B6 Sedini Sardegna Italy
56 G6 Sedlarica Croatia
56 D2 Sedlčany Czech Rep.
56 D2 Sedlec Prčice Czech Rep.
Sedlets Pol. see Siedlce
57 K3 Sedlice Slovakia
51 J7 Sedlitz Ger.
51 J9 Sedlo hill Czech Rep.
16 E2 Sedlyshche Ukr.
190 D7 Sedom Israel
125 U7 Sedona AZ U.S.A.
Sedovo Ukr. see Syedove
87 G1 Sédrata Alg.
70 H4 Sedrina Italy
157 L4 Sedulang Kalimantan Indon.
18 G6 Šeduva Lith.
55 H4 Sędziejowice Pol.
54 G3 Sędzin Pol.
55 I5 Sędziszów Pol.
55 J5 Sędziszów Małopolski Pol.
58 H5 See Salzburg Austria
58 B5 See Tirol Austria
39 I4 Sée r. France
52 E4 Seebach Baden-Württemberg Ger.
49 J9 Seebach Thüringen Ger.
50 J3 Seebad Ahlbeck Ger.
50 J3 Seebad Bansin Ger.
50 J3 Seebad Heringsdorf Ger.
59 K7 Seeberg pass Austria/Slovenia
49 K9 Seebergen Ger.
59 I6 Seeboden Austria
53 M6 Seebruck Ger.
49 J7 Seeburg Ger.
48 J2 Seedorf Schleswig-Holstein Ger.
48 K3 Seedorf Schleswig-Holstein Ger.
53 K5 Seefeld Bayern Ger.
50 I5 Seefeld Brandenburg Ger.
48 F4 Seefeld (Stadland) Ger.
58 D5 Seefeld in Tirol Austria
27 G8 Seefin hill Rep. of Ireland
53 J6 Seeg Ger.
51 G7 Seegrehna Ger.
50 I4 Seehausen Brandenburg Ger.
51 D6 Seehausen Sachsen-Anhalt Ger.
50 E5 Seehausen (Altmark) Ger.
53 K6 Seehausen am Staffelsee Ger.
94 C5 Seeheim Namibia
52 F2 Seeheim-Jugenheim Ger.
58 H4 Seekirchen am Wallersee Austria
96 G9 Seekoegat S. Africa
97 I6 Seekoei r. S. Africa
97 N3 Seekoevlei Nature Reserve S. Africa
52 D5 Seelbach Ger.
125 Q9 Seeley CA U.S.A.
212 R1 Seelig, Mount Antarctica
51 F9 Seelingstädt Ger.
50 J5 Seelow Ger.
49 I6 Seelze Ger.
53 M6 Seeon Ger.
70 F1 Seerücken val. Switz.
39 L4 Sées France
49 J7 Seesen Ger.
53 K6 Seeshaupt Ger.
59 J5 Seetaler Alpen mts Austria
59 I5 Seethal Austria
48 J4 Seevetal Ger.
59 I4 Seewalchen am Attersee Austria
59 L4 Seewiesen Austria
59 P4 Seewinkel reg. Austria
40 J5 Séez France
88 C4 Sefadu Sierra Leone
79 H4 Seferihisar Turkey
88 C3 Séféto Mali
184 C5 Sefīd, Kūh-e mt. Iran
184 D6 Sefīd, Kūh-e mts Iran
184 D5 Sefīd Dasht Iran
95 E4 Sefophe Botswana
86 D2 Sefrou Morocco
203 E10 Sefton, Mount South I. N.Z.
43 I7 Ségala reg. France
88 C3 Ségala Mali
21 K6 Segalstad Norway
157 M2 Segama r. Malaysia
156 E3 Segamat Malaysia
60 E5 Segangane Morocco
77 L6 Șegarcea Romania
66 H4 Segarra reg. Spain
89 F4 Ségbana Benin
92 C3 Segen Wenz watercourse Eth.
93 C6 Segera Tanz.
155 A6 Segeri Sulawesi Indon.
56 G5 Segesd Hungary
14 F3 Segezha Rus. Fed.
87 F2 Seggeur, Oued watercourse Alg.
72 H2 Seggiano Italy
200 □6 Seghe New Georgia Is Solomon Is
185 N3 Seghnān Afgh.
183 L5 Segiz, Ozera lakes Kazakh.
70 H3 Segl, Lago da l. Switz.
38 E5 Séglien France
73 K4 Segni Italy
42 D4 Segonzac France
67 E8 Segorbe Spain
88 D3 Ségou Mali
88 D3 Ségou admin. reg. Mali
136 C3 Segovia Col.
63 L7 Segovia Spain
63 L6 Segovia prov. Spain
14 F3 Segozerskoye, Ozero resr Rus. Fed.
39 J6 Segré France
66 F5 Segre r. Spain
39 J6 Segréen reg. France
66 G4 Segrià reg. Spain
39 L5 Ségrie France
104 A4 Seguam Island AK U.S.A.
89 I1 Séguédine Niger
88 D5 Séguéla Côte d'Ivoire
88 D3 Séguéla Mali
88 D4 Séguélon Côte d'Ivoire
88 E3 Séguénéga Burkina
147 G3 Seguí Arg.
121 G11 Seguin TX U.S.A.
147 F2 Segundo r. Arg.
41 B8 Ségur France
62 G9 Segura Port.
65 N4 Segura r. Spain
65 N5 Segura, Sierra de mts Spain
65 N4 Segura de la Sierra Spain
64 F4 Segura de León Spain
66 D6 Segura de los Baños Spain
63 K8 Segurilla Spain
94 D4 Sehithwa Botswana
97 N5 Sehlabathebe Lesotho
97 N5 Sehlabathebe National Park Lesotho
49 J6 Sehlde Ger.
49 I6 Sehnde Ger.
155 D4 Seho i. Indon.
178 F8 Sehore Madh. Prad. India
185 L8 Sehwan Pak.
62 E8 Seia Port.
120 D6 Seibert CO U.S.A.
38 H6 Seiche r. France
39 K6 Seiches-sur-le-Loir France
166 A7 Seidan Japan
59 L5 Seiersberg Austria
20 K4 Seierstad Norway
51 K9 Seifhennersdorf Ger.
30 H2 Seighford Staffordshire, England U.K.
41 B8 Seigne, Mont mt. France
109 G3 Seignelay r. Que. Can.
36 G8 Seignelay France
70 B1 Seignelégier Switz.
43 B8 Seignosse France
166 C6 Seika Japan
158 B4 Seikphyu Myanmar
26 E10 Seil i. Scotland U.K.
20 Q1 Seiland i. Norway
42 H5 Seilhac France
121 F7 Seiling OK U.S.A.
41 J9 Seillans France
40 F3 Seille r. France
37 L5 Seille r. France
45 H8 Seilles Belgium
18 F7 Šeimena r. Lith.
38 B5 Sein, Île de i. France
166 G5 Seinaiji Japan
20 Q5 Seinäjoki Fin.
108 B3 Seine r. Ont. Can.
36 B5 Seine r. France
39 J3 Seine, Baie de b. France
40 F2 Seine, Sources de la r. source France
36 F7 Seine, Val de val. France
36 F6 Seine-et-Marne dept France
Seine-Inférieure dept France see Seine-Maritime
36 A4 Seine-Maritime dept France
39 P4 Seine-St-Denis dept France
77 L3 Seini Romania
53 I2 Seinsheim Ger.
157 K5 Seipinang Kalimantan Indon.
55 L1 Seira l. Lith.
66 F3 Seira Spain
55 L1 Seirijai Lith.
55 L1 Seirijis l. Lith.
43 F9 Seissan France
Seistan reg. Iran see Sīstān
59 K3 Seitenstetten Austria
57 J5 Șeitin Romania
21 Q6 Seitsemisen kansallispuisto nat. park Fin.
144 G3 Seival Brazil
166 D7 Seiwa Japan
43 G10 Seix France
64 □ Seixal Madeira
64 A3 Seixal Port.
62 C5 Seixas Port.
64 B6 Seixe r. Port.
62 E8 Seixo da Beira Port.
157 L6 Sejaka Kalimantan Indon.
157 H4 Sejangkung Kalimantan Indon.
22 H6 Sejerby Denmark
22 H6 Sejerø i. Denmark
22 H6 Sejerø Bugt b. Denmark
55 L1 Sejny Pol.
157 I4 Sekadau Kalimantan Indon.
156 F5 Sekanak, Teluk b. Indon.
157 L3 Sekatak Bengara Kalimantan Indon.
156 E6 Sekayu Sumatera Indon.
57 K3 Sekčov r. Slovakia
Seke Sichuan China see Sêrtar
93 B5 Seke Tanz.
91 B6 Seke-Banza Dem. Rep. Congo
93 B6 Sekenke Tanz.
200 □4b Sekeren Iap Pohnpei Micronesia
166 E5 Seki Gifu Japan
166 D6 Seki Mie Japan
79 K6 Seki Turkey
79 K6 Seki r. Turkey
164 □B21 Sekibi-sho i. Nansei-shotō Japan
156 F7 Sekicau, Gunung vol. Indon.
166 E2 Sekidō-san hill Japan
166 D5 Sekigahara Japan
167 K3 Sekijō Japan
167 K3 Sekiyado Japan
94 D5 Sekoma Botswana
88 E5 Sekondi Ghana
92 C1 Sek'ot'a Eth.
55 J6 Sękowa Pol.
Sekseūil Kazakh. see Saksaul'skiy
185 I6 Sekūheh Iran
157 H4 Sekura Kalimantan Indon.
99 □2b Sel, Pointe au pt Mahé Seychelles
Şela Rus. Fed. see Shali
92 C2 Šela Dingay Eth.
156 D6 Selagan r. Indon.
122 D3 Selah WA U.S.A.
157 H4 Selakau Kalimantan Indon.
157 I3 Selalang Sarawak Malaysia
156 D3 Selangor state Malaysia
72 C9 Selargius Sardegna Italy
155 G8 Selaru i. Maluku Indon.
157 K7 Selatan, Tanjung pt Indon.
156 E4 Selatpanjang Sumatera Indon.
30 F2 Selattyn Shropshire, England U.K.
104 B3 Selawik AK U.S.A.
63 M2 Selaya Spain
51 F10 Selb Ger.
58 G5 Selbhorn mt. Austria
51 E10 Selbitz Ger.
22 A2 Selbjørnsfjorden sea chan. Norway
20 K5 Selbu Norway
29 O6 Selby North Yorkshire, England U.K.
120 E3 Selby SD U.S.A.
117 J10 Selbyville DE U.S.A.
71 R5 Selce Croatia
79 I5 Selçuk Turkey
120 E6 Selden KS U.S.A.
104 C4 Seldovia AK U.S.A.
155 G4 Sele Papua Indon.
73 N7 Sele r. Italy
155 G4 Sele, Selat sea chan. Papua Indon.
95 E4 Selebi-Phikwe Botswana
Selebi-Pikwe Botswana see Selebi-Phikwe
77 J9 Selečka Planina mts Macedonia
72 C8 Selegas Sardegna Italy
72 C6 S'Elema r. Sardegna Italy
162 F2 Selemdzha r. Rus. Fed.
162 G2 Selemdzhinsk Rus. Fed.
162 H2 Selemdzhinskiy Khrebet mts Rus. Fed.
79 J4 Selendi Turkey
168 J1 Selenduma Rus. Fed.
168 J1 Selenga r. Rus. Fed. alt. Selenge Mörön (Mongolia)
90 C5 Selenge Dem. Rep. Congo
168 G2 Selenge Mongolia
168 J2 Selenge prov. Mongolia
168 J1 Selenge Mörön r. Mongolia
168 J1 Selenge Mörön r. Mongolia alt. Selenga (Rus. Fed.)

78 A2 Selenicë Albania
48 J2 Selent Ger.
48 J2 Selenter See l. Ger.
173 F11 Sêlêpug Xizang China
37 N7 Sélestat France
156 □ Seletar Sing.
156 □ Seletar, Pulau i. Sing.
156 □ Seletar Reservoir Sing.
183 O1 Seletinkoye Kazakh.
Selety r. Kazakh. see Sileti
Seletyteniz, Oz. salt l. Kazakh. see Siletiteniz, Ozero
Seleucia Turkey see Silifke
Seleucia Pieria Turkey see Samandağı
57 K5 Seleuş Romania
53 L1 Selezneve Rus. Fed.
19 O6 Selezni Rus. Fed.
20 □C2 Selfoss Iceland
120 E2 Selfridge ND U.S.A.
162 I4 Sel'gon Stantsiya Rus. Fed.
14 J3 Sélibabi Maur.
88 B3 Sélibabi Maur.
19 R9 Seligdar Rus. Fed.
49 G10 Seligenstadt Ger.
19 U4 Seliger, Ozero l. Rus. Fed.
125 T6 Seligman AZ U.S.A.
162 I3 Selikhino Rus. Fed.
90 D3 Sélim C.A.R.
191 D5 Selim Turkey
85 F4 Selima Oasis Sudan
157 J4 Selimbau Kalimantan Indon.
79 I5 Selimiye Turkey
88 C4 Sélingué, Lac de l. Mali
88 D3 Selinkegni Mali
78 D4 Selinous r. Greece
118 B3 Selinsgrove PA U.S.A.
19 O5 Selishche Rus. Fed.
15 H5 Selishchi Rus. Fed.
182 B4 Selitrennoye Rus. Fed.
157 G6 Seliu i. Indon.
19 Q5 Selizharovo Rus. Fed.
21 H5 Selje Norway
22 E2 Seljord Norway
51 D7 Selke r. Ger.
107 L5 Selkirk Man. Can.
26 K11 Selkirk Scottish Borders, Scotland U.K.
106 G4 Selkirk Mountains B.C. Can.
20 R1 Selkopp Norway
Şelkovski Rus. Fed. see Shelkovskaya
97 M5 Semonkong Lesotho
37 J7 Semouliers-Montsaon France
67 E10 Sella Spain
63 J2 Sella r. Spain
73 N5 Sella Canala pass Italy
73 P7 Sella Cessuta pass Italy
73 M5 Sella del Perrone pass Italy
29 K5 Sellafield Cumbria, England U.K.
26 □N1 Sellafirth Shetland, Scotland U.K.
73 J2 Sellano Italy
118 E4 Sellersville PA U.S.A.
42 H1 Selles-St-Denis France
39 O7 Selles-sur-Cher France
107 K6 Sellheim r. Qld Austr.
78 F7 Sellia Kriti Greece
73 K6 Sellia Marina Italy
40 H3 Sellières France
31 N5 Sellindge Kent, England U.K.
44 L3 Sellingen Neth.
Sellore Island Myanmar see Saganthit Kyun
58 D5 Sellrain Austria
25 U10 Sells AZ U.S.A.
57 G6 Sellye Hungary
49 D7 Selm Ger.
13 A3 Selma AL U.S.A.
124 M5 Selma CA U.S.A.
21 K8 Selmer TN U.S.A.
64 K4 Selmes Port.
191 E5 Selmet Wielki, Jezioro l. Pol.
62 G3 Selmir r. Spain
48 K3 Selmsdorf Ger.
Selmunett, Gżejjer is Malta see San Pawl, Gżejjer ta'
36 B8 Selommes France
57 L9 Selong Lombok Indon.
40 G1 Selongey France
41 I8 Selonnet France
97 N1 Selonsrivier S. Africa
88 C4 Selouma Guinea
06 C2 Selous, Mount Y.T. Can.
93 C7 Selous Game Reserve nature res. Tanz.
50 E5 Selow Ger.
84 I7 Selseleh-ye Pir Shūrān mts Iran
29 M4 Selset Reservoir England U.K.
31 K6 Selsey West Sussex, England U.K.
31 K6 Selsey Bill hd England U.K.
48 H4 Selsingen Ger.
49 E9 Selters (Westerwald) Ger.
19 R8 Sel'tso Bryanskaya Oblast' Rus. Fed.
19 R8 Sel'tso Bryanskaya Oblast' Rus. Fed.
14 K4 Selty Rus. Fed.
37 P6 Seltz France
20 J2 Selukwe Zimbabwe see Shurugwi
39 I4 Selune r. France
44 E3 Selva Arg.
75 M2 Selva Italy
67 K8 Selva r. Spain
66 C3 Selva mt. Spain
71 L2 Selva dei Molini Italy
58 E6 Selva di Progno Italy
58 E6 Selva di Val Gardena Italy
86 B3 Selvagens, Ilhas is Madeira
46 A6 Selva Obscura Chile
76 B3 Selvas reg. Brazil
71 L1 Selvazzano Dentro Italy
70 H4 Selvino Italy
54 B4 Selviria Brazil
22 G3 Selway r. ID U.S.A.
07 J2 Selwyn Lake l. N.W.T./Sask. Can.
06 D1 Selwyn Mountains N.W.T./Y.T. Can.
06 G6 Selwyn Range hills Qld Austr.
16 E6 Selyatyn Ukr.
20 J2 Selydove Ukr.
52 G2 Selz r. Ger.
59 J4 Selzthal Austria
45 I4 Sémalens France
78 A2 Semama France
67 F7 Semani r. Albania
57 I8 Semarang Java Indon.
57 H4 Sematan Sarawak Malaysia
56 □ Semau i. Indon.
41 D6 Semayang, Danau l. Indon.
41 D6 Sembabor France
56 □ Sembawang Sing.
56 □ Sembawang, Sungai r. Sing.
90 B4 Sembé Congo
39 M6 Semblançay France
70 C3 Sembrancher Switz.
69 L5 Semdinli Turkey
40 D3 Sémelay France
Semendire Srbija see Smederevo
91 C5 Semendua Dem. Rep. Congo
19 V4 Semendyayevo Rus. Fed.
91 C5 Semenic, Vârful mt. Romania
17 L1 Semenivka Chernihivs'ka Oblast' Ukr.
17 P5 Semenivka Kharkivs'ka Oblast' Ukr.
17 K3 Semenivka Kyivs'ka Oblast' Ukr.
47 M4 Semenivka Poltavs'ka Oblast' Ukr.
82 F1 Semenkino Rus. Fed.
17 T2 Semeno-Aleksandrovka Rus. Fed.
14 I4 Semenov Rus. Fed.
19 S6 Semenovskoye Rus. Fed.

156 J9 Semeru, Gunung vol. Indon.
96 H1 Semey Kazakh. see Semipalatinsk
186 D8 Semien prov. Eritrea
17 S6 Semibalki Rus. Fed.
19 W4 Semibratovo Rus. Fed.
62 D8 Semide Port.
17 R2 Semidesyatnoye Rus. Fed.
104 C4 Semidi Islands AK U.S.A.
14 H4 Semigorodnyaya Rus. Fed.
15 H7 Semiddarskorsk Rus. Fed.
184 D5 Semiluki Rus. Fed.
56 E1 Semily Czech Rep.
75 J7 Seminara Italy
40 H4 Semine r. France
122 K5 Seminoe Reservoir WY U.S.A.
121 D9 Seminole TX U.S.A.
115 E10 Seminole, Lake FL/GA U.S.A.
183 U2 Seminskiy Khrebet mts Rus. Fed.
19 X7 Semion Rus. Fed.
162 B2 Semiozernyy Rus. Fed.
183 S2 Semipalatinsk Kazakh.
183 L1 Semipolka Kazakh.
154 C5 Semirara i. Phil.
154 C6 Semirara Islands Phil.
184 D6 Semirom Iran
404 A4 Semisopochnoi Island AK U.S.A.
157 I4 Semitau Kalimantan Indon.
183 R2 Semiyarka Kazakh.
183 P2 Semizbughy Kazakh. see Semizbuga
19 V5 Semizbuga
76 I4 Semlac Romania
19 Q6 Semlevo Smolenskaya Oblast' Rus. Fed.
19 Q6 Semlevo Smolenskaya Oblast' Rus. Fed.
90 F4 Semliki r. Dem. Rep. Congo/Uganda
50 G2 Semlow Ger.
49 K6 Semmenstedt Ger.
184 E4 Semnān Iran
184 D4 Semnān prov. Iran
168 G8 Shēmnyi Qinghai China
45 G9 Semois r. Belgium
45 G9 Semois, Vallée de la val. Belgium/France
97 M5 Semonkong Lesotho

Semuliki r. Dem. Rep. Congo/Uganda see Semliki
97 M5 Semonkong Lesotho
137 H6 Sem Tripa Brazil
19 Q9 Semtsy Rus. Fed.
40 E2 Semur-en-Auxois France
40 F2 Semur-en-Brionnais France
42 C4 Semussac France
14 I2 Semzha Rus. Fed.
159 G8 Sên, Stœng r. Cambodia
138 D2 Sena Bol.
184 D7 Sená Iran
44 J3 Sena Slovakia
66 E4 Sena Spain
142 C2 Senador Canedo Brazil
140 F3 Senador Pompeu Brazil
85 H6 Senafe Eritrea
71 L3 Senaiga r. Italy
157 L1 Senaja Sabah Malaysia
191 D3 Senak Georgia
71 J2 Senales Italy
72 C6 Senales, Val di val. Italy
138 C2 Sena Madureira Brazil
176 G9 Senanayake Samudra l. Sri Lanka
91 D9 Senanga Zambia
157 I4 Senaning Kalimantan Indon.
36 C4 Senarpont France
41 I9 Sénas France
121 K8 Senatobia MS U.S.A.
179 N6 Sendai Kagoshima Japan
164 H8 Sendai Miyagi Japan
165 H15 Sendai-gawa r. Japan
165 H15 Sendai-wan b. Japan
97 K2 Sendelingsfontein S. Africa
53 I5 Senden Bayern Ger.
38 E4 Senden Nordrhein-Westfalen Ger.
49 E7 Senenhorst Ger.
62 H6 Sendim Bragança Port.
62 H6 Sendim Porto Port.
173 L11 Sêndo Xizang China
77 P5 Şendreni Romania
157 I5 Şenduruhan Kalimantan Indon.
38 F6 Séné France
88 E5 Sene r. Ghana
37 L7 Senebier France
56 G3 Senec Slovakia
110 F8 Seneca IL U.S.A.
120 G6 Seneca KS U.S.A.
122 K4 Seneca OR U.S.A.
116 F7 Seneca SC U.S.A.
116 H10 Seneca r. NY U.S.A.
116 D9 Seneca Falls NY U.S.A.
45 F7 Seneffe Belgium
88 D3 Senegal country Africa
88 B3 Sénégal r. Maur./Senegal
72 B7 Senerchia Italy
162 J1 Seneka, Mys hd Rus. Fed.
97 L4 Senekal S. Africa
65 G6 Senes Spain
72 D7 Senes, Monte hill Italy
72 B4 Senetosa, Capu di c. Corse France
110 J3 Seney MI U.S.A.
110 J3 Seney National Wildlife Refuge nature res. MI U.S.A.
52 M2 Senez France
53 I3 Senftenberg Austria
51 J7 Senftenberg Ger.
93 B8 Senga Malawi
93 A7 Senga Hill Zambia
178 G6 Sengar r. India
187 G3 Sengata Kalimantan Indon.
173 K11 Sêngdoi Xizang China
93 B5 Sengerema Tanz.
76 I6 Senggi prov. Indon.
14 J1 Sengiley Rus. Fed.
15 J5 Sengiri Rus. Fed.
182 E6 Sengiri, Mys pt Kazakh.
Sengirli, Mys pt Kazakh. see Syngyrli, Mys
173 G11 Sêngli Co l. Xizang China
43 F10 Sengouagnet France
175 C3 Sengqu r. Qinghai China see
92 G2 Sengurovo Rus. Fed.
15 I5 Senhit prov. Eritrea
64 C2 Senhora do Rosário Port.
140 E4 Senhor do Bonfim Brazil
62 A5 Senica Slovakia
56 G2 Senica Slovakia
71 O8 Senigallia Italy
146 C6 Senillosa Arg.
71 M6 Senio r. Italy
79 L4 Senirkent Turkey
72 B8 Senis Sardegna Italy
73 Q7 Senise Italy
68 E3 Senj Croatia
20 L2 Senja i. Norway
20 N2 Senjehopen Norway
166 C2 Senjō-ga-dake mt. Japan
167 H4 Senjō-ga-dake mt. Japan
48 I3 Senkaki-shotō is Japan
189 K3 Şenkaya Turkey
14 J2 Sen'kina Rus. Fed.
88 C4 Senko Guinea
91 E9 Senkobo Zambia
19 N6 Sen'kovo Rus. Fed.

190 E2 Şenköy Turkey
96 H1 Semey Kazakh. see
162 G7 Senlin Shan mt. Jilin China
36 E5 Senlis France
159 H8 Senmonorom Cambodia
166 B7 Sennan Japan
85 G6 Sennar Sudan
85 G6 Sennar state Sudan
72 B7 Sennariolo Sardegna Italy
17 Q8 Sennaya Rus. Fed.
49 G7 Senne reg. Ger.
40 F3 Sennecey-le-Grand France
40 G2 Sennecey-lès-Dijon France
30 □ Sennen Cornwall, England U.K.
108 E3 Senneterre Que. Can.
51 E7 Sennewitz Ger.
Senno Belarus see Syanno
167 I2 Sennokura-yama mt. Japan
72 B6 Sennori Sardegna Italy
70 G1 Sennwald Switz.
30 E4 Sennybridge Powys, Wales U.K.
57 I3 Senohrad Slovakia
36 F7 Sénonhais reg. France
36 B6 Senonches France
37 M7 Senones France
72 C8 Senorbì Sardegna Italy
43 H8 Senouillac France
41 C6 Senoure r. France
59 L7 Senovo Slovenia
59 J8 Senovože Slovenia
97 L6 Senqu r. Lesotho
36 F7 Sens France
38 H5 Sens-de-Bretagne France
36 F3 Sensée, Canal de la r. France
126 □O11 Sensuntepeque El Salvador
76 I5 Senta Vojvodina, Srbija Serb. and Mont.
57 I3 Sentaš Kazakh.
43 F10 Sentein France
66 G3 Sentenac-d'Oust France
59 N6 Sentijl Slovenia
125 S9 Sentinel AZ U.S.A.
73 N4 Sentinelle, Colle della hill Italy
106 F4 Sentinel Peak B.C. Can.
212 S1 Sentinel Range mts Antarctica
Sentinum Italy see Sassoferrato
128 B4 Sentispac Mex.
59 L8 Šentjernej Slovenia
59 L7 Šentjur pri Celju Slovenia
156 □ Sentosa i. Sing.
37 I5 Senuc France
157 L4 Senyiur Kalimantan Indon.
57 K4 Şenyô Hungary
191 C5 Şenyurt Turkey
189 K5 Şenyurt Turkey
165 N14 Senzaki Japan
165 J14 Sen-zaki pt Japan
92 E1 Senzig Ger.
70 E1 Seon Switz.
178 I9 Seonath r. India
178 D6 Seondha Madh. Prad. India
178 G8 Seoni Madh. Prad. India
178 Q3 Seoni Chhapara Madh. Prad. India
178 F8 Seoni-Malwa Madh. Prad. India
178 I9 Seorinarayan Chhattisgarh India
Seoul S. Korea see Sŏul
43 F7 Sepanjang i. Indon.
157 K8 Separation Point South l. N.Z.
202 G7 Separation Well W.A. Austr.
208 Q7 Sepang Sabah Malaysia
157 L1 Sepasu Kalimantan Indon.
191 D3 Sepatini r. Brazil
138 D1 Sepauk Kalimantan Indon.
157 I4 Sepetiba, Baía de b. Brazil
143 E5 Sepik r. P.N.G.
153 J7 Sepinang Kalimantan Indon.
157 K3 Seping r. Malaysia
73 N5 Sepino Italy
163 E9 Sep'o N. Korea
54 F2 Sępólno Krajeńskie Pol.
54 E2 Sępólno Wielkie Pol.
73 K4 Sępopol r. Pol.
40 F3 Seppa Arun. Prad. India
18 I4 Seppois-le-Bas France
62 F7 Serne r. Ukr.
55 K4 Serniki Pol.
15 I5 Sernovodsk Rus. Fed.
14 J4 Sernur Rus. Fed.
16 F2 Sernyky Ukr.
54 D4 Serock Kujawsko-Pomorskie Pol.
55 J3 Serock Mazowieckie Pol.
127 □5 Sero Colorado Aruba see Seroe Colorado
147 G3 Serodino Arg.
131 □9 Seroe Colorado Aruba
15 I7 Seroglazka Rus. Fed.
95 D6 Serón Spain
63 P6 Serón de Nájima Spain
63 L7 Serones, Embalse de resr Spain
94 D3 Seronga Botswana
65 F6 Seroskerke Neth.
66 F5 Serós Spain
87 G4 Seroue well Alg.
192 H4 Serov Rus. Fed.
94 E4 Serowe Botswana
94 E4 Serpa Port.
65 D3 Serpent r. Que. Can.
88 C3 Serpent, Vallée du watercourse Mali
72 D9 Serpentara, Isola i. Sardegna Italy
209 C12 Serpentine r. W.A. Austr.
204 B3 Serpentine Lakes salt flat S.A. Austr.
131 M9 Serpent's Mouth sea chan. Trin. and Tob./Venez.
19 V7 Serpukhov Rus. Fed.
62 G7 Serpins Port.
67 E10 Serpis r. Spain
59 M3 Serpneve Ukr.
19 U7 Serpukhov Rus. Fed.
37 M3 Serqueux France
39 M3 Serquigny France
143 G4 Serra Italy
72 B9 Serra Spain
73 O4 Serracapriola Italy
63 K6 Serrada Spain
143 E5 Serra da Bocaina, Parque Nacional da nat. park Brazil
142 D4 Serra da Canastra, Parque Nacional da nat. park Brazil
140 C4 Serra da Capivara, Parque Nacional da nat. park Brazil
138 D2 Serra da Cutia, Parque Nacional da nat. park Brazil
140 E4 Serra da Estrela, Parque Natural da nature res. Port.
72 B7 Serra da Mesa, Represa resr Brazil
143 F5 Serra da Mociade, Parque Nacional da nat. park Brazil
140 C4 Serra das Confusões, Parque Nacional da nat. park Brazil
71 O4 Serra de'Conti Italy
73 Q6 Serra del Corvo, Lago di l.
86 D2 Serra de Santa Barbara vol.
90 A5 Serra do Divisor, Parque Nacional da nat. park Brazil
98 □1a Serra de São Mamede, Parque Natural da nature res. Port.
98 □1a Serra de São Mamede, Parque Natural da n. Terceira Azores
60 C3 Serra-di-Ferro Corse France
79 F8 Serra-di-Ferro Corse France
72 B4 Serra-di-Scopamène Corse France
142 D4 Serra-di-Ferro Corse France
143 F3 Serradilla del Arroyo Spain
63 J8 Serradilla Spain
137 G4 Serra do Divisor, Parque Nacional da nat. park Brazil
137 H4 Serra do Navio Brazil
142 D2 Serra Dourada Brazil
142 D3 Serra Grande Brazil
98 □2 Serra Greca see Serres
54 H1 Serra Almorós Brazil
70 B2 Serra Azul Brazil
142 D3 Serra Branca Brazil
71 J7 Serra San Bruno Italy

130 C6 Serrana Bank sea feature Caribbean Sea
137 E4 Serrania de la Neblina, Parque Nacional nat. park Venez.
130 D6 Serrana Bank sea feature Caribbean Sea
63 K8 Serranillos Spain
147 F4 Serrano i. Chile
145 B8 Serrano i. Chile
142 A3 Serrano r. Chile
70 F6 Serra Riccò Italy
75 K6 Serra San Bruno Italy
72 C9 Serra San Quirico Italy
62 C9 Serra San Quirico Italy
17 N1 Sev r. Rus. Fed.
66 J4 Sevan Armenia
191 F5 Sevan Armenia
140 F3 Serra Talhada Brazil
71 M8 Serravalle di Chienti Italy
73 J1 Serravalle Scrivia Italy
76 F4 Serre r. France
73 O6 Serre Italy
41 J7 Serre-Chevalier France
62 I9 Serrejón Spain
72 B9 Serrenti Sardegna Italy
41 I8 Serre-Ponçon, Lac de l. France
Serrera, Pic de la mt. Andorra see Serrère, Pic de
66 I2 Serres France
41 H8 Serres France
78 E1 Serres Greece
43 D9 Serres-Castet France
98 □1a Serreta Terceira Azores
146 E2 Serrezuela Arg.
207 M8 Serrinha Brazil
45 J6 Serrig Ger.
140 F4 Serrinha Brazil
140 F3 Sèrro Brazil
143 F3 Sèrro Brazil
63 J8 Serrota mt. Spain
42 E4 Sers France
69 B7 Sers Tunisia
75 L5 Sersale Italy
62 D9 Sertã Port.
140 F4 Sertânia Brazil
142 B5 Sertanópolis Brazil
142 A3 Sertão de Camapuã reg. Brazil
142 D2 Sertãozinho Brazil
118 B6 Severna Park MD U.S.A.
116 H12 Severn NC U.S.A.
118 C7 Severn r. Md U.S.A.
114 L3 Severnaya Mylva r. Rus. Fed.
192 H3 Severnaya Sos'va r. Rus. Fed.
193 L1 Severnaya Zemlya is Rus. Fed.
108 B2 Severn Lake Ont. Can.
15 K5 Severnoye Rus. Fed.
108 B2 Severn River Provincial Park park Ont. Can.
17 P3 Severnyy Belgorodskaya Oblast' Rus. Fed.
19 U5 Severnyy Nenetskiy Avtonomnyy Okrug Rus. Fed.
14 N2 Severnyy Respublika Komi Rus. Fed.
55 H1 Severnyy, Mys pt Rus. Fed.
162 L1 Severnyy, Ostrov i. Rus. Fed.
193 S3 Severnyy Anyuyskiy Khrebet mts Rus. Fed.
184 E2 Severnyy Berezovyy, Ostrov i. Rus. Fed.
18 L1 Severnyy Chink Ustyurta esc. Kazakh.
183 M1 Severnyy Kazakhstan admin. div. Kazakh.
14 K4 Severnyy Kommunar Rus. Fed.
191 C2 Severnyy Priyut Rus. Fed.
14 L3 Severnyy Suchan Rus. Fed.
15 I5 Severnyy Ural mts Rus. Fed.
161 I1 Severo-Baykal'sk Rus. Fed.
193 M4 Severo-Baykal'skoye Nagor'ye mts Rus. Fed.
172 H1 Severo-Chuyskiy Khrebet mts Rus. Fed.
Severodonetsk Ukr. see Syeverodonets'k
Severodvinsk Rus. Fed. see Severnaya Dvina
193 Q4 Severo-Kuril'sk Kuril'skiye O-va Rus. Fed.
20 V2 Severomorsk Rus. Fed.
14 G3 Severoonezhsk Rus. Fed.
14 K3 Severo-Osetinskaya A.S.S.R. aut. rep. Rus. Fed. see Severnaya Osetiya - Alaniya, Respublika
191 F3 Severo-Osetinskiy Zapovednik nature res. Rus. Fed.
162 M2 Severo-Sakhalinskaya Ravnina plain Rus. Fed.
193 □ Severo-Sibirskaya Nizmennost' lowland Rus. Fed.
14 L3 Severoural'sk Rus. Fed.
193 K3 Severo-Yeniseyskiy Rus. Fed.
19 V7 Severo-Zadonsk Rus. Fed.
15 H7 Seversk Rus. Fed.
17 N9 Seversk Ukr. see Sivers'k
17 N9 Sivers'kyy Donets' r. Rus. Fed./Ukr. see Seversky Donets
70 G2 Sevi, Col de pass France
72 B3 Sévi, Col de pass France
125 G4 Sevier r. UT U.S.A.
125 H2 Sevier r. UT U.S.A.
125 F2 Sevier Bridge Reservoir UT U.S.A.
123 D10 Sevier Desert UT U.S.A.
125 H2 Sevier Lake UT U.S.A.
115 F8 Sevierville TN U.S.A.
43 H7 Sévignac France
43 D9 Sévignac France
137 □ Sévigné-Wappe France
48 J3 Setit r. Africa
178 H5 Seti r. Nepal
178 H3 Seti r. Nepal
63 K8 Setenil de las Bodegas Spain
93 C8 Setete Sezze Italy
87 G1 Sétif Alg.
85 G6 Setit r. Eth.
66 J4 Setit r. Africa

130 C6 Serrana Bank sea feature
143 F2 Setubinha Brazil
53 L3 Seubersdorf in der Oberpfalz Ger.
42 C4 Seudre r. France
42 C4 Seudre r. France
72 C8 Seugne r. France
37 J6 Seuil-d'Argonne France
107 M5 Seul, Lac l. Ont. Can.
110 I4 Seul Choix Point MI U.S.A.
156 A2 Seulimeum Sumatera Indon.
49 J7 Seulingen Ger.
39 K3 Seulles r. France
72 C8 Seulo Sardegna Italy
40 G2 Seurre France
17 N1 Sev r. Rus. Fed.
66 J4 Sevan Armenia
191 F5 Sevan Armenia
Sevan, Lake Armenia see Sevana Lich
Sevan Lich l. Armenia see Sevana Lich
Sevan, Ozero l. Armenia see Sevana Lich
191 G5 Sevana Lich l. Armenia
53 L3 Sevana Bol.
46 D9 Sevard r. France
19 M8 Sevastopol' Ukr.
29 P5 Seven r. England U.K.
27 E9 Seven Heads Rep. of Ireland
Seven Islands Que. Can. see Sept-Îles
109 I1 Seven Islands Bay Nfld and Lab. Can.
209 D7 Seven Mile Creek r. W.A. Austr.
97 O5 Sevenoaks S. Africa
31 M5 Sevenoaks Kent, England U.K.
30 E4 Seven Sisters Neath Port Talbot, Wales U.K.
98 □1a Seven Stones is England U.K.
146 E2 Seventeen Seventy Qld Austr.
45 M8 Sevenum Neth.
70 C4 Seveno, Col di mt. Italy
118 B5 Seven Valleys PA U.S.A.
72 C6 Severac-le-Château France
62 D7 Sever do Vouga Port.
56 F6 Severin Croatia
141 B9 Severino Ribeiro Brazil
19 V6 Severka r. Rus. Fed.
205 M3 Severn r. N.S.W. Austr.
108 C2 Severn r. Ont. Can.
203 H9 Severn mt. South l. N.Z.
96 G2 Severn S. Africa
30 H4 Severn r. England/Wales U.K.
118 B6 Severn MD U.S.A.

185 J5 Seyah Band Koh mts Afgh.
192 I2 Seyakha Rus. Fed.
127 N8 Seybaplaya Mex.
99 □2 Seychelles country Indian Ocean
43 G6 Seyches France
51 G7 Seyda Ger.
79 M3 Seydi r. Turkey
185 J2 Seydi Turkey
188 F5 Seydişehir Turkey
20 □F1 Seyðisfjörður Iceland
38 H3 Seyer r. France
188 G4 Seyhan r. Turkey
Seyhan Turkey see Adana
188 G4 Seyhan r. Turkey
190 D1 Seyhan r. Turkey
191 H5 Seyhan r. Turkey
79 L3 Seyitgazi Turkey
79 K3 Seyitömer Turkey
17 Q2 Seym r. Rus. Fed.
17 N2 Seym r. Rus. Fed./Ukr.
193 Q3 Seymchan Rus. Fed.
205 J2 Seymour Vic. Austr.
97 K8 Seymour S. Africa
112 I12 Seymour CT U.S.A.
114 E6 Seymour IN U.S.A.
121 F9 Seymour TX U.S.A.
106 E5 Seymour Inlet B.C. Can.
206 D8 Seymour Range mts N.T. Austr.
41 I8 Seyne France
40 I5 Seynod France
88 D4 Seypan i. N. Mariana Is see Saipan
40 H5 Seyssel France
40 F5 Seysses France
40 F5 Seysseuel France
43 F9 Seyssins France
41 P7 Seyssuel France
21 N2 Seytan r. Turkey
185 H4 Seyyedābād Afgh.
68 D3 Seyyedeşan Slovenia
36 G6 Sézanne France
97 O6 Sezela S. Africa
19 R6 Sezha r. Rus. Fed.
56 D2 Sezimovo Ústí Czech Rep.
73 K5 Sezze Italy
79 G7 Sfaka Kriti Greece
78 F7 Sfakia Kriti Greece
77 N5 Sfântu Gheorghe Covasna Romania
77 M8 Sfântu Gheorghe Tulcea Romania
77 R6 Sfântu Gheorghe, Brațul watercourse Romania
77 R6 Sfântu Gheorghe-Palade-Perişor nature res. Romania
87 H2 Sfax Tunisia
72 D8 Sferracavallo, Capo c. Sardegna Italy
78 D2 Sfikia, Limni resr Greece
97 O6 Sfântu Gheorghe Romania
49 Sfântu Gheorghe
26 D6 Sgiersch Pol. see Zgierz
26 E7 Sgiogarstaigh Western Isles, Scotland U.K.
26 E7 Sgorr Ruadh hill Scotland U.K.
44 G5 's-Gravendeel Neth.
44 F4 's-Gravenhage Neth.
45 I6 's-Gravenpolder Neth.
45 I7 's-Gravenvoeren Belgium
44 F5 's-Gravenzande Neth.
73 K4 Sgurdola Italy
26 D8 Sgurr a' Chaorachain mt. Scotland U.K.
26 D8 Sgurr a' Choire Ghlais mt. Scotland U.K.
26 D8 Sgurr Alasdair hill Scotland U.K.
26 E7 Sgurr a' Mhuilinn hill Scotland U.K.
26 E9 Sgurr Dhomhnuill hill Scotland U.K.
26 E7 Sgurr Fhuaran mt. Scotland U.K.
26 E7 Sgurr Mhòr mt. Scotland U.K.
26 E8 Sgurr na Ciche mt. Scotland U.K.
191 G2 Shaami-Yurt Rus. Fed.
169 K9 Shaanxi prov. China
Shaartuz Tajik. see Shahrtuz
187 I3 Sha'b, Jabal ash hills Saudi Arabia
Shaba prov. Dem. Rep. Congo see Katanga
185 L7 Shaaban Pak.
94 E3 Shabani Zimbabwe see Zvishavane
17 N9 Shabanovskoye Rus. Fed.
92 D4 Shabeelle, Webi r. Somalia
93 E2 Shabeellaha Dhexe admin. reg. Somalia
92 D4 Shabeellaha Hoose admin. reg. Somalia
15 G2 Shabel'sk Rus. Fed.
76 A2 Shabestar Iran
77 Q7 Shabla Bulg.
77 Q7 Shabla, Nos pt Bulg.
93 B6 Shablykino Rus. Fed.
109 H2 Shabogamo Lake l. Nfld and Lab. Can.
90 E5 Shabunda Dem. Rep. Congo
186 H8 Shabwah Yemen
172 C7 Shache Xinjiang China
213 L1 Shackleton Coast Antarctica
213 M1 Shackleton Glacier Antarctica
213 G2 Shackleton Ice Shelf Antarctica
159 Shackleton Range mts Antarctica
185 H4 Shadād Saudi Arabia
185 J5 Shadadkot Pak.
170 D4 Shadi Hubei China
170 E4 Shade Myanmar
116 C9 Shade OH U.S.A.
116 H1 Shades Glen PA U.S.A.
185 I5 Shadihar Pak.
185 L8 Shadian watercourse Iran
116 D4 Shadow Lake l. Can.
192 H4 Shadrinsk Rus. Fed.
184 M4 Shadwan Island Egypt see Shākir, Gezirat
116 G10 Shady Grove OR U.S.A.
122 C6 Shady Grove OR U.S.A.
118 E7 Shady Side MD U.S.A.
110 H2 Shady Spring WV U.S.A.
213 K2 Shafer Peak Antarctica
184 G4 Shafi'ābad Iran
176 G6 Shafranovo Rus. Fed.
178 H4 Shahabad Rajasthan India
176 C3 Shahabad Karnataka India
178 H5 Shahābād Iran
146 K6 Shāh Alam Malaysia
156 □ Shah Alam Malaysia
182 F1 Shafranovo Rus. Fed.
184 B2 Shāghān r. Iran
184 C3 Shaghyray Üstirti plat.
185 H2 Shaghrāy, Plato plat.
183 M5 Shaglik Kazakh.
169 N8 Shaglteng, Ozero l. Kazakh.
203 I2 Shag Point South l. N.Z.
135 G2 Shag Rocks is S. Georgia
185 H3 Shagray, Plato plat.
178 F4 Shahabad India
178 F4 Shahabad Haryana India
176 D3 Shahabad Karnataka India
178 H4 Shahabad Uttar Prad. India
178 E5 Shahābād Rajasthan India
184 K2 Shahbandar Pak.
178 E4 Shahbāz Kalat Pak.
178 E4 Shahbazpur India
182 G3 Shahdad Iran
184 F4 Shahdad, Namakzar-e marsh Iran
185 H5 Shahdadkot Pak.
184 M2 Shahdara Afgh.
178 H8 Shahdol Madh. Prad. India
154 B2 Shaheed Pak.
185 J3 Shaharak Afgh.
178 F4 Shahbad India
177 M3 Shahapur Mahar. India
176 C3 Shahapur Karnataka India
176 C3 Shahapur Mahar. India

Shahbā' to Shoemakersville
338

190 E6 Shahbā' Syria
185 L9 Shahbandar Pak.
184 C3 Shahbanu Farah Dam Iran
185 K8 Shahbaz Kalat Pak.
179 M8 Shahbazpur sea chan. Bangl.
185 L9 Shahbeg Pak.
185 L9 Shah Bilawal Pak.
184 G6 Shahdād Iran
185 M9 Shahdadpur Pak.
178 H8 Shahdol Madh. Prad. India
185 P6 Shahdura Pak.
170 G3 Shahe Chongqing China
169 P8 Shahe Shandong China
169 N8 Sha He r. China
185 L4 Shah Fuladi mt. Afgh.
179 I6 Shahganj Uttar Prad. India
178 G7 Shahgarh Madh. Prad. India
178 B6 Shahgarh Rajasthan India
84 D1 Shaḥḥāt Libya
185 O6 Shah Hussain Pak.
185 J9 Shahid, Ras pt Pak.
Shāhīn Dezh Iran see Sa'īndezh
185 K7 Shah Ismail Afgh.
178 F6 Shahjahanpur Rajasthan India
178 G6 Shahjahanpur Uttar Prad. India
184 H3 Shāh Jehān, Kūh-e mts Iran
185 L5 Shāh Jūy Afgh.
184 H6 Shāh Kūh mt. Iran
189 P6 Shahmīrzād Iran
169 Q6 Shahousuo Liaoning China
176 E4 Shahpur Karnataka India
178 F8 Shahpur Madh. Prad. India
178 F9 Shahpur Madh. Prad. India
178 G8 Shahpur Madh. Prad. India
178 H8 Shahpur Madh. Prad. India
Shāhpūr Iran see Salmās
185 M7 Shahpur Balochistan Pak.
185 O5 Shahpur Punjab Pak.
185 M8 Shahpur Sindh Pak.
178 G8 Shahpura Madh. Prad. India
178 H8 Shahpura Madh. Prad. India
178 E7 Shahpura Rajasthan India
187 J6 Shahr oasis Saudi Arabia
185 K4 Shahrak Afgh.
184 I5 Shāhrakht Iran
186 F6 Shahrān reg. Saudi Arabia
184 F6 Shahr-e Bābak Iran
184 D5 Shahr-e Kord Iran
184 I4 Shahr-e Now Iran
185 L6 Shahr-e Şafā Afgh.
184 D5 Shahrezā Iran
185 L6 Shahrig Pak.
183 O7 Shahrihon Uzbek.
183 L8 Shahrisabz Uzbek.
185 M2 Shahriston Tajik.
184 D4 Shahr Rey Iran
185 N7 Shahr Sultan Pak.
185 M3 Shahrtuz Tajik.
184 C3 Shāhrūd, Rūdkhāneh-ye r. Iran
184 F4 Shahrud Bustam reg. Iran
184 H7 Shāh Savārān, Kūh-e mts Iran
185 K7 Shah Umar Pak.
185 M6 Shaighalu Pak.
185 K7 Shaikh Husain mt. Pak.
190 F4 Shā'īr, Jabal mts Syria
190 C9 Sha'īrah, Jabal mt. Egypt
179 M7 Shaistaganj Bangl.
187 I3 Shaj'ah, Jabal hill Saudi Arabia
178 F8 Shajapur Madh. Prad. India
163 D8 Shajianzi Liaoning China
166 C7 Shakaga-dake mt. Japan
184 B3 Shakar Bolāghī Iran
97 P5 Shakaskraal S. Africa
97 P5 Shakaville S. Africa
94 D3 Shakawe Botswana
108 B3 Shakespeare Island Ont. Can.
Shakh Khatlon Tajik. see Shoh
Shakhagach Azer. see Şahağac
Shakhbuz Azer. see Şahbuz
184 H5 Shākhen Iran
17 P3 Shakhovo Rus. Fed.
19 S5 Shakhovskaya Rus. Fed.
Shakhrisabz Uzbek. see Shahrisabz
Shakhristan Tajik. see Shahriston
186 E8 Shakhs, Ras pt Eritrea
17 R5 Shakhtars'k Ukr.
Shakhtersk Ukr. see Shakhtars'k
Shakhterskoye Ukr. see Pershotravens'k
183 O3 Shakhtinsk Kazakh.
182 H3 Shakhty Kazakh.
15 H7 Shakhty Rostovskaya Oblast' Rus. Fed.
Shakhtyorsk Ukr. see Shakhtars'k
Shakhtyorskoye Ukr. see Pershotravens'k
14 I4 Shakhun'ya Rus. Fed.
89 F4 Shaki Nigeria
85 G3 Shâkir, Gezîret i. Egypt
120 I3 Shakopee MN U.S.A.
164 R3 Shakotan-hantō pen. Japan
164 R3 Shakotan-misaki c. Japan
171 I6 Shakou Guangdong China
84 A1 Shakshūk Libya
92 C3 Shala Hāyk' l. Eth.
14 H3 Shalakusha Rus. Fed.
184 D5 Shālamzār Iran
171 H8 Shalang Guangdong China
191 I4 Shalbuzdag, Gora mt. Rus. Fed.
183 R2 Shalday Kazakh.
31 J6 Shalfleet Isle of Wight, England U.K.
31 K5 Shalford Surrey, England U.K.
183 N4 Shalginskiy Kazakh.
Shalgiya Kazakh. see Shalginskiy
191 G2 Shali Rus. Fed.
168 C8 Shaliangzi Qinghai China
187 L6 Shalim Oman
178 G4 Shalkar Hima. Prad. India
182 H4 Shalkar Aktyubinskaya Oblast' Kazakh.
182 D2 Shalkar, Ozero salt l. Kazakh.
182 I2 Shalkar Karashatau salt l. Kazakh.
182 I2 Shalkar-Yega-Kara, Ozero l. Rus. Fed.
Shalqar Aktyubinskaya Oblast' Kazakh. see Shalkar
Shalqar Köli salt l. Kazakh. see Shalkar, Ozero
Shalqīya Kazakh. see Shalginskiy
184 D3 Shaltrak Iran
170 B3 Shaluli Shan mts Sichuan China
179 P5 Shaluni mt. Arun. Prad. India
14 L4 Shalya Rus. Fed.
17 N2 Shalyhyne Ukr.
181 H5 Shām, Jabal mt. Oman
93 B6 Shama r. Tanz.
190 A8 Shamāl Sīnā' governorate Egypt
185 L6 Shamalzā'ī Afgh.
14 L4 Shamary Rus. Fed.
186 F1 Shāmat al Akbād des. Saudi Arabia
107 M3 Shamattawa Man. Can.
108 C2 Shamattawa r. Ont. Can.
19 O7 Shamava Belarus
184 C5 Shambār Iran
92 A3 Shambe Sudan
92 C2 Shambu Eth.
91 D6 Shambuanda Dem. Rep. Congo
171 □ Sham Chun r. Guangdong/H.K. China
178 E7 Shamgarh Madh. Prad. India
Shamgong Bhutan see Shemgang
184 G8 Shamīl Iran
191 H3 Shamil'kala Rus. Fed.
187 K4 Shamis U.A.E.
191 I2 Shamkhal Rus. Fed.
Shamkhor Azer. see Şämkir
186 F2 Shammar, Jabal reg. Saudi Arabia
118 B3 Shamokin PA U.S.A.
118 B3 Shamokin Dam PA U.S.A.
19 Q1 Shamoksha Rus. Fed.
16 I4 Shamrayivka Ukr.
121 E8 Shamrock TX U.S.A.
95 F3 Shamva Zimbabwe
97 K9 Shamwari Game Reserve nature res. S. Africa
158 D4 Shan state Myanmar
Shancheng Shandong China see Shanxian
185 I6 Shand Afgh.
184 I7 Shāndak Iran
168 G7 Shandan Gansu China
168 G7 Shandan He r. Gansu China
169 O6 Shandian He r. China
184 H3 Shandiz Iran
169 O8 Shandong prov. China
169 Q8 Shandong Bandao pen. China
17 K4 Shandra Ukr.
189 L7 Shandrūkh Iraq
185 O3 Shandur Pass Pak.
118 D4 Shanesville PA U.S.A.
95 F3 Shangani Zimbabwe
95 E3 Shangani r. Zimbabwe
170 B2 Shang Boingor Qinghai China
171 J2 Shangcai Henan China
170 G6 Shangchao Guangxi China
171 J3 Shangcheng Henan China
173 I12 Shang Chu r. China
171 I8 Shangchuan Dao i. Guangdong China
169 M6 Shangdu Nei Mongol China
162 F5 Shangganling Heilong. China
171 J4 Shanggao Jiangxi China
171 M3 Shanghai Shanghai China
171 M3 Shanghai mun. China
171 K6 Shanghang Fujian China
169 O8 Shanghe Shandong China
163 D8 Shanghekou Liaoning China
Shangji Henan China see Xichuan
Shangjie Yunnan China see Yangbi
170 H2 Shangjin Hubei China
170 B2 Shang Kongma Qinghai China
169 Q1 Shangkuli Nei Mongol China
170 G2 Shangluo Shaanxi China
Shangmei Hunan China see Xinhua
170 H2 Shangnan Shaanxi China
91 D9 Shangombo Zambia
169 N9 Shangqiu Henan China
171 K4 Shangrao Jiangxi China
172 F3 Shangsanshilipu Xinjiang China
171 J2 Shangshui Henan China
170 G7 Shangsi Guangxi China
Shangtang Zhejiang China see Yongjia
171 J6 Shangyou Jiangxi China
172 E6 Shangyou Shuiku resr China
171 M3 Shangyu Zhejiang China
170 A4 Shang Zayü Xizang China
162 E6 Shangzhi Heilong. China
Shangzhou Shaanxi China see Shangluo
169 P6 Shanhaiguan Hebei China
Shanhe Gansu China see Zhengning
162 E6 Shanhetun Heilong. China
55 M3 Shani Belarus
89 I4 Shani Nigeria
191 F3 Shani, Mt'a Georgia/Rus. Fed.
31 J6 Shanklin Isle of Wight, England U.K.
170 G8 Shankou Guangxi China
171 H4 Shankou Hunan China
168 D5 Shankou Xinjiang China
202 J7 Shannon North I. N.Z.
27 E7 Shannon airport Rep. of Ireland
27 E7 Shannon est. Rep. of Ireland
27 E7 Shannon r. Rep. of Ireland
97 K5 Shannon S. Africa
110 E7 Shannon IL U.S.A.
27 C7 Shannon, Mouth of the Rep. of Ireland
209 D13 Shannon National Park W.A. Austr.
105 Q2 Shannon Ø i. Greenland
158 C4 Shan Plateau Myanmar
168 B5 Shanshan Xinjiang China
168 B5 Shanshanzhan Xinjiang China
Shansi prov. China see Shanxi
193 O4 Shantarskiye Ostrova is Rus. Fed.
171 □J7 Shan Tei Tong hill H.K. China
Shan Teng hill H.K. China see Victoria Peak
179 L8 Shantipur W. Bengal India
28 D5 Shantonagh Rep. of Ireland
171 K7 Shantou Guangdong China
Shantung prov. China see Shandong
27 F4 Shanvus Rep. of Ireland
171 J7 Shanwei Guangdong China
169 L7 Shanxi prov. China
169 O9 Shanxian Shandong China
19 S7 Shanya r. Rus. Fed.
170 G2 Shanyang Shaanxi China
169 M7 Shanyin Shanxi China
171 H5 Shaodong Hunan China
171 I6 Shaoguan Guangdong China
171 I5 Shaoshan Hunan China
171 K5 Shaowu Fujian China
171 M3 Shaoxing Zhejiang China
171 H5 Shaoyang Hunan China
171 H5 Shaoyang Hunan China
29 L4 Shap Cumbria, England U.K.
171 H8 Shapa Guangdong China
91 D6 Shapembe Dem. Rep. Congo
26 K4 Shapinsay i. Scotland U.K.
26 K4 Shapinsay Sound sea chan. Scotland U.K.
19 O2 Shapki Rus. Fed.
14 K2 Shapkina r. Rus. Fed.
17 L2 Shapovalivka Ukr.
19 R1 Shapsha Rus. Fed.
172 I1 Shapshal'skiy Khrebet mts Rus. Fed.
17 R9 Shapsugskaya Rus. Fed.
17 R9 Shapsugskoye Vodokhranilishche resr Rus. Fed.
18 M7 Shapyalyevichy Belarus
172 I4 Shaqiuhe Xinjiang China
84 E6 Shaqq el Giefer, Wadi watercourse Sudan
84 E6 Shaqq el Khadir Sudan
186 G3 Shaqrā' Saudi Arabia
172 F4 Shaquanzi Xinjiang China
183 S3 Shar Kazakh.
186 B2 Shār, Jabal mt. Saudi Arabia
189 K8 Sharaf well Iraq
84 E6 Sharafa Sudan
189 L4 Sharaf-Khāneh Iran
190 D8 Sharāh, Jibāl ash mts Jordan
169 J1 Sharalday Rus. Fed.
185 M5 Sharan Afgh.
14 K5 Sharan Rus. Fed.
14 I4 Sharanga Rus. Fed.
185 M6 Sharan Jogizai Pak.
19 U6 Sharapovo Rus. Fed.
190 G2 Sharaqraq Syria
18 H9 Sharashova Belarus
190 B10 Sharātīb, Ra's pt Egypt
27 G6 Sharavogue Rep. of Ireland
190 E10 Sharawrā, Jabal hills Saudi Arabia
190 E10 Sharawrā', Qa' salt pan Saudi Arabia
Sharbaqty Kazakh. see Shcherbakty
187 M7 Sharbithāt, Ra's c. Oman
168 C2 Sharbulag Mongolia
183 S1 Sharchino Rus. Fed.
183 L7 Shardara Kazakh.
185 P4 Shardi Pak.
168 D3 Sharga Govĭ-Altay Mongolia
168 F2 Sharga Hövsgöl Mongolia
Shargorod Ukr. see Sharhorod
183 L8 Shargʻun Uzbek.
16 H5 Sharhorod Ukr.
168 I4 Sharhulsan Mongolia
Shari r. Cameroon/Chad see Chari
164 V3 Shari Japan
189 L6 Shārī, Buḥayrat imp. l. Iraq
164 V3 Shari-dake vol. Japan
190 F4 Sharīfah Syria
190 C10 Sharīrah Pass Egypt
17 O3 Sharivka Kharkivs'ka Oblast' Ukr.
17 R4 Sharivka Luhans'ka Oblast' Ukr.
191 E3 Sharivtsek, Pereval pass Georgia/Rus. Fed.
Sharjah U.A.E. see Ash Shāriqah
173 J12 Sharka-leb La pass Xizang China
14 K4 Sharkan Rus. Fed.
18 K6 Sharkawshchyna Belarus
209 B8 Shark Bay W.A. Austr.
154 B6 Shark Fin Bay Palawan Phil.
187 J8 Sharkhāt Yemen
207 K3 Shark Reef Coral Sea Is Terr. Austr.
119 G4 Shark River Hills NJ U.S.A.
Sharlawuk Turkm. see Sharlouk
184 F2 Sharlouk Turkm.
182 F1 Sharlyk Rus. Fed.
186 B1 Sharmah Saudi Arabia
85 G3 Sharm ash Shaykh Egypt
191 G2 Sharo-Argun r. Rus. Fed.
116 E7 Sharon PA U.S.A.
110 F7 Sharon WI U.S.A.
120 E6 Sharon Springs KS U.S.A.
116 A9 Sharonville OH U.S.A.
191 G3 Sharoy Rus. Fed.
209 F12 Sharpe, Lake salt flat W.A. Austr.
107 M4 Sharpe Lake Man. Can.
30 H4 Sharpness Gloucestershire, England U.K.
116 H9 Sharpsburg MD U.S.A.
116 D9 Sharpsburg OH U.S.A.
190 D5 Sharqī, Jabal ash mts Lebanon/Syria
182 H6 Sharqiy Ustyurt Chink esc. Uzbek.
185 P6 Sharqpur Pak.
118 C3 Shartlesville PA U.S.A.
Sharur Azer. see Şärur
168 E3 Shar Us Gol r. Mongolia
186 F2 Shary well Saudi Arabia
14 I4 Shar'ya Rus. Fed.
19 P2 Shar'ya r. Rus. Fed.
89 G5 Shasha Nigeria
95 E4 Shashe Botswana
95 F4 Shashe r. Botswana/Zimbabwe
95 E4 Shashe Dam resr Botswana
92 C3 Shashemenē Eth.
183 P4 Shashubay Kazakh.
122 C6 Shasta, Mount vol. CA U.S.A.
122 C6 Shasta Lake CA U.S.A.
17 R2 Shatalovka Rus. Fed.
19 P7 Shatalovo Rus. Fed.
171 □J7 Sha Tau Kok Hoi inlet H.K. China
84 B3 Shāṭi', Wādī ash watercourse Libya
191 G3 Shatili Georgia
Shatilki Belarus see Svyetlahorsk
171 □J7 Sha Tin H.K. China
171 □J7 Sha Tin Hoi b. H.K. China
15 I5 Shatki Rus. Fed.
190 G3 Shaţnat as Salmās, Wādī watercourse Syria
171 □J7 Sha Tong Hau Shan i. H.K. China
189 L2 Shatoy Rus. Fed.
15 H5 Shatsk Rus. Fed.
16 C2 Shats'k Ukr.
16 C2 Shats'k nat. park Ukr.
184 D7 Shaṭṭ, Ra's osh pt Iran
184 C7 Shaṭṭ al 'Arab r. Iran/Iraq
189 M8 Shaṭṭ al Gharrāf r. Iraq
121 F7 Shattuck OK U.S.A.
19 W6 Shatura Rus. Fed.
19 W6 Shaturtorf Rus. Fed.
Shäüildir Kazakh. see Shaul'der
183 M6 Shaul'der Kazakh.
107 I5 Shaunavon Sask. Can.
20 U5 Shaverki Rus. Fed.
124 M4 Shaver Lake CA U.S.A.
116 F10 Shavers Fork r. WV U.S.A.
191 G3 Shavi Klde, Mt'a Georgia/Rus. Fed.
29 M7 Shavington Cheshire, England U.K.
147 H5 Shaw Arg.
208 E6 Shaw r. W.A. Austr.
29 M6 Shaw Greater Manchester, England U.K.
172 G4 Shawan Xinjiang China
118 B6 Shawan MD U.S.A.
119 G1 Shawangunk Kill r. NY U.S.A.
119 F2 Shawangunk Mountains hills NY U.S.A.
110 F5 Shawano WI U.S.A.
110 F5 Shawano Lake WI U.S.A.
186 C2 Shawāq well Saudi Arabia
26 C6 Shawbost Western Isles, Scotland U.K.
116 A10 Shawhan KY U.S.A.
121 G8 Shawnee OK U.S.A.
122 L5 Shawnee WY U.S.A.
116 E11 Shawsville VA U.S.A.
171 L5 Sha Xi r. China
171 K5 Shaxian Fujian China
183 M6 Shayan Kazakh.
171 I3 Shayang Hubei China
186 C3 Shaybārā i. Saudi Arabia
193 R3 Shayboveyem r. Rus. Fed.
208 F6 Shay Gap W.A. Austr.
190 B10 Shaykh, Wādī ash watercourse Egypt
189 M7 Shaykh Jūwī Iraq
190 E6 Shaykh Miskīn Syria
189 M7 Shaykh Sa'd Iraq
19 R7 Shaykovka Rus. Fed.
17 P6 Shaytanka r. Ukr.
184 F6 Shayṭūr Iran
190 E3 Shayzar Syria
184 C5 Shāzand Iran
172 L7 Shazaoyuan Gansu China
186 E2 Shaẓāẓ, Jabal mt. Saudi Arabia
185 O3 Shazud Tajik.
18 H8 Shchara r. Belarus
55 M3 Shcharchova Belarus
17 S5 Shchastya Ukr.
17 O9 Shchebetovka Ukr.
19 R9 Shcheglovka Rus. Fed.
19 U7 Shchekino Rus. Fed.
16 F3 Shchekychyn Ukr.
19 S7 Shchelkanovo Rus. Fed.
19 V6 Shchelkovo Rus. Fed.
14 K2 Shchel'yayur Rus. Fed.
Shcherbakov Rus. Fed. see Rybinsk
183 R1 Shcherbakty Kazakh.
17 K6 Shcherbani Ukr.
14 G4 Shchetinskoye Rus. Fed.
15 G6 Shchigry Rus. Fed.
17 O8 Shcholkine Ukr.
18 K8 Shchomyslitsa Belarus
17 K2 Shchors Ukr.
17 N5 Shchors'k Ukr.
Shchuchin Belarus see Shchuchyn
183 N1 Shchuchinsk Kazakh.
17 T2 Shchuch'ye Rus. Fed.
18 H8 Shchuchyn Belarus
14 L2 Shchuger r. Rus. Fed.
16 C4 Shchyrets' Ukr.
18 L8 Shchytkavichy Belarus
137 G4 Shea Guyana
183 U2 Shebalino Rus. Fed.
110 D1 Shebandowan Lakes Ont. Can.
15 G6 Shebekino Rus. Fed.
185 K3 Sheberghān Afgh.
110 G6 Sheboygan WI U.S.A.
17 R9 Shebsh r. Rus. Fed.
89 H4 Shebshi Mountains Nigeria
162 L5 Shebunino Sakhalin Rus. Fed.
Shecheng Hebei China see Shexian
109 H4 Shediac N.B. Can.
106 E4 Shedin Peak B.C. Can.
191 B1 Shedok Rus. Fed.
27 H5 Sheelin, Lough l. Rep. of Ireland
27 G2 Sheep Haven b. Rep. of Ireland
97 O2 Sheepmoor S. Africa
125 Q5 Sheep Peak NV U.S.A.
44 J5 's-Heerenberg Neth.
31 M4 Sheering Essex, England U.K.
31 N5 Sheerness Kent, England U.K.
109 I4 Sheet Harbour N.S. Can.
190 D6 Shefar'am Israel
203 G10 Sheffield South I. N.Z.
29 O7 Sheffield South Yorkshire, England U.K.
115 D8 Sheffield AL U.S.A.
110 E8 Sheffield IL U.S.A.
116 F7 Sheffield PA U.S.A.
121 E10 Sheffield TX U.S.A.
109 J3 Sheffield Lake Nfld and Lab. Can.
31 L3 Shefford Bedfordshire, England U.K.
185 K6 Shegah Afgh.
178 F9 Shegaon Mahar. India
14 J2 Shegmas Rus. Fed.
111 M4 Sheguiandah Ont. Can.
92 D3 Shēh Husēn Eth.
170 E3 Shehong Sichuan China
27 D9 Shehy Mountains hills Rep. of Ireland
108 C3 Shekak r. Ont. Can.
184 F5 Shekār Āb Iran
178 E6 Shekhawati reg. India
17 T1 Shekhman' Rus. Fed.
185 P6 Shekhupura Pak.
Sheki Azer. see Şäki
171 □I7 Shekka Ch'ün-Tao is H.K. China
171 □I7 Shek Kwu Chau i. H.K. China
171 □I7 Shek Pik resr H.K. China
Shek Pik Reservoir H.K. China see Shek Pik
14 G4 Sheksna Rus. Fed.
14 G4 Sheksninskoye Vodokhranilishche resr Rus. Fed.
171 □J7 Shek Uk Shan mt. H.K. China
173 K11 Shela Xizang China
183 T1 Shelabolikha Rus. Fed.
185 I7 Shelag watercourse Afgh./Iran
193 S2 Shelagskiy, Mys pt Rus. Fed.
116 C11 Shelbiana KY U.S.A.
120 I6 Shelbina MO U.S.A.
114 D6 Shelburn IN U.S.A.
109 H5 Shelburne N.S. Can.
111 N5 Shelburne Ont. Can.
207 I1 Shelburne Bay Qld Austr.
117 M6 Shelburne Falls MA U.S.A.
110 H6 Shelby MI U.S.A.
121 J9 Shelby MS U.S.A.
122 I2 Shelby MT U.S.A.
115 G8 Shelby NC U.S.A.
116 C8 Shelby OH U.S.A.
120 K6 Shelbyville IL U.S.A.
114 E6 Shelbyville IN U.S.A.
120 I6 Shelbyville MO U.S.A.
115 D8 Shelbyville TN U.S.A.
120 K6 Shelbyville, Lake IL U.S.A.
97 J9 Sheldon S. Africa
120 H4 Sheldon IA U.S.A.
110 G9 Sheldon IL U.S.A.
110 D4 Sheldon WI U.S.A.
122 E6 Sheldon National Wildlife Refuge nature res. NV U.S.A.
117 M4 Sheldon Springs VT U.S.A.
109 H3 Sheldrake Que. Can.
16 J6 Shelekhove Ukr.
193 Q3 Shelikhova, Zaliv g. Rus. Fed.
104 C4 Shelikof Strait AK U.S.A.
191 H2 Shelkovskaya Rus. Fed.
122 K4 Shell WY U.S.A.
26 C6 Shell, Loch inlet Scotland U.K.
107 J4 Shellbrook Sask. Can.
122 H5 Shelley ID U.S.A.
205 M6 Shellharbour N.S.W. Austr.
107 J4 Shell Lake Sask. Can.
110 C4 Shell Lake WI U.S.A.
209 I10 Shell Lakes salt flat W.A. Austr.
124 I1 Shell Mountain CA U.S.A.
18 N3 Shelon' r. Rus. Fed.
Shelter Bay Que. Can. see Port-Cartier
119 K2 Shelter Island NY U.S.A.
119 K2 Shelter Island i. NY U.S.A.
119 K2 Shelter Island Heights NY U.S.A.
119 K2 Shelter Island Sound str. NY U.S.A.
203 C14 Shelter Point Stewart I. N.Z.
119 I2 Shelton CT U.S.A.
122 C3 Shelton WA U.S.A.
14 F3 Sheltozero Rus. Fed.
Shelyakino Rus. Fed. see Sovetskoye
184 D3 Shem Iran
Shemakha Azer. see Şamaxı
89 H4 Shemankar r. Nigeria
19 R1 Shemenichi Rus. Fed.
179 M6 Shemgang Bhutan
191 D4 Shemok'medi Georgia
183 S2 Shemonaikha Kazakh.
14 J4 Shemordan Rus. Fed.
15 I5 Shemursha Rus. Fed.
15 I5 Shemysheyka Rus. Fed.
120 H5 Shenandoah IA U.S.A.
111 R9 Shenandoah PA U.S.A.
116 G10 Shenandoah VA U.S.A.
116 H9 Shenandoah r. VA U.S.A.
116 F10 Shenandoah Mountains VA/WV U.S.A.
116 G10 Shenandoah National Park VA U.S.A.
171 K7 Shen'ao Guangdong China
182 I3 Shenbertal Kazakh.
169 M7 Shenchi Shanxi China
89 H4 Shendam Nigeria
85 G5 Shendi Sudan
162 H5 Shending Shan hill Heilong. China
88 B5 Shenge Sierra Leone
183 Q5 Shengel'dy Almatinskaya Oblast' Kazakh.
182 I5 Shengel'dy Kyzylordinskaya Oblast' Kazakh.
Shenggeldy Kazakh. see Shengel'dy
76 H9 Shëngjin Albania
171 J3 Shengli Hubei China
172 H5 Shengli Daban pass Xinjiang China
172 D6 Shengli Qichang Xinjiang China
172 E6 Shengli Shibachang Xinjiang China
Shengrenjian Shanxi China see Pinglu
171 N3 Shengsi Zhejiang China
171 N3 Shengsi Liedao is China
Shengxian Zhejiang China see Shengzhou
171 M4 Shengzhou Zhejiang China
163 C14 Shenjiamen Zhejiang China
76 H9 Shënkoll Albania
14 H3 Shenkursk Rus. Fed.
169 L7 Shenmu Shaanxi China
170 H3 Shennongjia Hubei China
171 J2 Shenqiu Henan China
162 F5 Shenshu Heilong. China
Shensi prov. China see Shaanxi
31 I2 Shenstone Staffordshire, England U.K.
15 J5 Shentala Rus. Fed.
209 G10 Shenton, Mount hill W.A. Austr.
Shenxian Hebei China see Shenzhou
169 N8 Shenxian Shandong China
169 R6 Shenyang Liaoning China
171 J7 Shenzhen Guangdong China
171 □I7 Shenzhen Wan b. H.K. China
169 N8 Shenzhou Hebei China
178 D7 Sheoganj Rajasthan India
178 F7 Sheopur Madh. Prad. India
212 P2 Shepard Island Antarctica
16 G3 Shepetivka Ukr.
Shepetovka Ukr. see Shepetivka
116 A5 Shepherd MI U.S.A.
200 □5 Shepherd Islands Vanuatu
205 J7 Shepparton Vic. Austr.
31 L5 Shepperton Surrey, England U.K.
31 N5 Sheppey, Isle of i. England U.K.
118 C3 Sheppton PA U.S.A.
31 J2 Shepshed Leicestershire, England U.K.
17 M1 Sheptaky Ukr.
30 G5 Shepton Mallet Somerset, England U.K.
17 O2 Sheptukhovka Rus. Fed.
171 I2 Sheqi Henan China
90 E2 Sherab Sudan
Sherabad Uzbek. see Sherobod
105 J2 Sherard, Cape Nunavut Can.
185 I5 Sher Bakhsh Afgh.
97 I7 Sherborne S. Africa
30 G6 Sherborne Dorset, England U.K.
31 J5 Sherborne St John Hampshire, England U.K.
88 B5 Sherbro Island Sierra Leone
109 I4 Sherbrooke N.S. Can.
109 G4 Sherbrooke Que. Can.
29 N4 Sherburn Durham, England U.K.
117 J6 Sherburne NY U.S.A.
29 O6 Sherburn in Elmet North Yorkshire, England U.K.
27 I5 Shercock Rep. of Ireland
84 C4 Sherda well Chad
31 L5 Shere Surrey, England U.K.
85 G5 Shereiq Sudan
178 D6 Shergarh Rajasthan India
179 J7 Sherghati Bihar India
121 I8 Sheridan AR U.S.A.
122 K4 Sheridan WY U.S.A.
105 L1 Sheridan, Cape Nunavut Can.
29 O5 Sheriff Hutton North Yorkshire, England U.K.
204 E5 Sheringa S.A. Austr.
31 O2 Sheringham Norfolk, England U.K.
192 H3 Sherkaly Rus. Fed.
185 L7 Sher Khan Qala Afgh.
27 D10 Sherkin Island Rep. of Ireland
208 D6 Sherlock r. W.A. Austr.
169 O1 Sherlovaya Gora Rus. Fed.
116 F6 Sherman NY U.S.A.
121 G9 Sherman TX U.S.A.
117 □Q3 Sherman Mills ME U.S.A.
125 Q1 Sherman Mountain NV U.S.A.
183 L9 Sherobod Uzbek.
19 O7 Sherovichi Rus. Fed.
179 M7 Sherpur Dhaka Bangl.
179 L7 Sherpur Rajshahi Bangl.
178 E1 Sher Qila Jammu and Kashmir
107 K4 Sherridon Man. Can.
30 H4 Sherston Wiltshire, England U.K.
176 E8 Shertally Kerala India
44 H5 's-Hertogenbosch Neth.
116 A7 Sherwood OH U.S.A.
203 E10 Sherwood Downs South I. N.Z.
29 O7 Sherwood Forest reg. England U.K.
107 K2 Sherwood Lake N.W.T. Can.
162 F3 Sheryshevo Rus. Fed.
111 L4 Sheshegwaning Ont. Can.
184 G3 Sheshtamad Iran
106 D3 Sheslay B.C. Can.
106 C3 Sheslay r. B.C. Can.
14 J4 Shestakovo Kirovskaya Oblast' Rus. Fed.
17 T3 Shestakovo Voronezhskaya Oblast' Rus. Fed.
19 V4 Shestikhino Rus. Fed.
17 M6 Shestirnya Ukr.
120 H3 Shetek, Lake MN U.S.A.
107 L3 Shethanei Lake Man. Can.
26 □O2 Shetland admin. div. Scotland U.K.
24 G1 Shetland Islands Scotland U.K.
182 E5 Shetpe Kazakh.
119 K1 Shetucket r. CT U.S.A.
171 □J7 Sheung Shui H.K. China
171 □J7 Sheung Sze Mun sea chan. H.K. China
171 □J7 Sheung Yue Ho r. H.K. China
176 F7 Shevaroy Hills India
17 N5 Shevchenkivka Ukr.
182 I4 Shevchenko, Zaliv l. Kazakh.
17 K4 Shevchenkove Cherkas'ka Oblast' Ukr.
17 Q4 Shevchenkove Kharkivs'ka Oblast' Ukr.
17 M2 Shevchen Kove Ukr.
176 D3 Shevgaon Mahar. India
162 H1 Shevli r. Rus. Fed.
92 B3 Shewa Gīmīra Eth.
171 L4 Shexian Anhui China
169 M8 Shexian Hebei China
193 M3 Sheya Rus. Fed.
171 M2 Sheyang Jiangsu China
14 H4 Sheybukhta Rus. Fed.
120 F2 Sheyenne ND U.S.A.
120 G2 Sheyenne r. ND U.S.A.
184 E8 Sheykh Sho'eyb i. Iran
19 O5 Sheykino Rus. Fed.
189 O8 Sheykkī Iran
179 I5 Shey Phoksundo National Park Nepal
26 D7 Shiant, Sound of str. Scotland U.K.
26 D7 Shiant Islands Scotland U.K.
193 Q5 Shiashkotan, Ostrov i. Kuril'skiye O-va Rus. Fed.
111 K6 Shiawassee r. MI U.S.A.
167 I5 Shibakawa Japan
187 I8 Shibām Yemen
168 D6 Shibandong Jing well China
168 F6 Shiban Jing well China
168 E7 Shibaocheng Gansu China
185 M4 Shibar Pass Afgh.
164 Q9 Shibata Japan
167 L4 Shibayama Japan
166 D3 Shibayama-gata l. Japan
162 D2 Shibazhan Heilong. China
164 T2 Shibetsu Hokkaidō Japan
164 W3 Shibetsu Hokkaidō Japan
85 F2 Shibīn al Kawm Egypt
170 G5 Shibing Guizhou China
108 B2 Shibogama Lake Ont. Can.
Shibotsu-jima i. Kuril'skiye O-va Rus. Fed. see Zelenyy, Ostrov
167 J3 Shibukawa Japan
165 I15 Shibushi Japan
165 I15 Shibushi-wan b. Japan
167 I2 Shibu-tōge pass Japan
167 J2 Shibutsu-san mt. Japan
Shicheng Fujian China see Zhouning
171 K5 Shicheng Jiangxi China
169 R7 Shicheng Dao i. China
167 H5 Shichimen-zan mt. Japan
164 S6 Shichinohe Japan
111 R8 Shickshinny PA U.S.A.
Shicun Shanxi China see Xiangfen
190 G7 Shidād al Mismā' hill Saudi Arabia
169 R8 Shidao Shandong China
169 R8 Shidao Wan b. China
183 P1 Shiderti r. Kazakh.
170 B6 Shidian Yunnan China
165 L12 Shido Japan
185 N3 Shidud Afgh.
26 E9 Shiel, Loch l. Scotland U.K.
26 F8 Shiel Bridge Highland, Scotland U.K.
206 F2 Shield, Cape N.T. Austr.
26 E7 Shieldaig Highland, Scotland U.K.
29 J2 Shieldhill Falkirk, Scotland U.K.
186 B1 Shifa, Jabal ash mts Saudi Arabia
170 E3 Shifang Sichuan China
30 H2 Shifnal Shropshire, England U.K.
167 G3 Shiga Nagano Japan
166 C5 Shiga Shiga Japan
166 C5 Shiga pref. Japan
178 E2 Shigar Jammu and Kashmir
166 D6 Shigaraki Japan
Shigatse Xizang China see Xigazê
176 D5 Shiggaon Karnataka India
172 L6 Shigong Gansu China
182 C1 Shigony Rus. Fed.
169 L6 Shiguai Nei Mongol China
Shiguaigou Nei Mongol China see Shiguai
187 K7 Shiḥan Yemen
187 K7 Shiḥan, Wādī r. Oman
172 H4 Shihezi Xinjiang China
Shihkiachwang Hebei China see Shijiazhuang
92 E2 Shiikh Somalia
76 H9 Shijak Albania
169 N7 Shijiazhuang Hebei China
171 L3 Shijiu Hu l. China
Shijiusuo Shandong China see Rizhao
166 E1 Shika Japan
164 R4 Shikabe Japan
108 B3 Shikag Lake Ont. Can.
170 G8 Shikang Guangxi China
185 J7 Shikar r. Pak.
176 D5 Shikarpur Karnataka India
185 M8 Shikarpur Pak.
171 I6 Shikengkong mt. Guangdong China
182 B1 Shikhany Rus. Fed.
167 K4 Shiki Japan
167 J7 Shikine-jima i. Japan
167 I4 Shikishima Japan
178 G6 Shikohabad Uttar Prad. India
165 K13 Shikoku i. Japan
165 J13 Shikoku-sanchi mts Japan
161 Q3 Shikotan, Ostrov i. Kuril'skiye O-va Rus. Fed.
Shikotan-tō i. Kuril'skiye O-va Rus. Fed. see Shikotan, Ostrov
164 S4 Shikotsu vol. Japan
164 R4 Shikotsu-Tōya National Park Japan
29 N3 Shilbottle Northumberland, England U.K.
182 H2 Shil'da Rus. Fed.
29 N4 Shildon Durham, England U.K.
14 I2 Shilega Rus. Fed.
169 P9 Shilianghe Shuiku resr China
179 L6 Shiliguri W. Bengal India
170 D6 Shilin Yunnan China
171 I3 Shilipu Hubei China
178 G3 Shilla mt. Jammu and Kashmir
26 B7 Shillay i. Scotland U.K.
27 I7 Shillelagh Rep. of Ireland
111 N1 Shillington Ont. Can.
118 D4 Shillington PA U.S.A.
190 C6 Shillo r. Israel
179 M7 Shillong Meghalaya India
182 C2 Shil'naya Balka Kazakh.
118 E6 Shiloh NJ U.S.A.
116 C8 Shiloh OH U.S.A.
169 L8 Shilou Shanxi China
15 H5 Shilovo Ryazanskaya Oblast' Rus. Fed.
19 V8 Shilovo Tul'skaya Oblast' Rus. Fed.
166 E7 Shima Japan
167 I2 Shima spring Japan
165 H14 Shimabara Japan
165 H14 Shimabara-wan b. Japan
167 H6 Shimada Japan
166 D6 Shimagahara Japan
166 D7 Shima-hantō pen. Japan
164 R4 Shimamaki Japan
166 C6 Shimamoto Japan
165 J12 Shimane pref. Japan
165 J11 Shimane-hantō pen. Japan
162 E2 Shimanovsk Rus. Fed.
92 E2 Shimbiris mt. Somalia
92 D4 Shimbirre waterhole Kenya
171 H4 Shimen Hunan China
Shimen Yunnan China see Yunlong
170 D4 Shimian Sichuan China
166 D3 Shimizu Fukui Japan
164 T3 Shimizu Hokkaidō Japan
167 H5 Shimizu Shizuoka Japan
167 I5 Shimizu Shizuoka Japan
166 B7 Shimizu Wakayama Japan
178 F4 Shimla Hima. Prad. India
Shimminato Japan see Shinminato
166 F2 Shimo Japan
167 H5 Shimobe Japan
167 I6 Shimoda Japan
167 K3 Shimodate Japan
167 L4 Shimofusa Japan
176 D6 Shimoga Karnataka India
167 K1 Shimogō Japan
166 C7 Shimoichi Japan
167 G5 Shimojō Japan
164 T2 Shimokawa Japan
164 R5 Shimokita-hantō pen. Japan
166 C7 Shimokitayama Japan
165 G15 Shimo-Koshiki-jima i. Japan
93 C6 Shimoni Kenya
167 I3 Shimonita Japan
165 H13 Shimonoseki Japan
167 H3 Shimosuwa Japan
166 B7 Shimotsu Japan
167 K3 Shimotsuma Japan
166 F5 Shimoyama Japan
176 E6 Shimsha r. India
178 E1 Shimshal Jammu and Kashmir
19 N3 Shimsk Rus. Fed.
167 J3 Shin Japan
26 G6 Shin, Loch l. Scotland U.K.
Shinan Guangxi China see Xingye
167 H2 Shinano Japan
166 D5 Shin-asahi Japan
164 □H16 Shin-dake vol. Japan
185 J5 Shīndand Afgh.
31 K5 Shinfield Wokingham, England U.K.
91 F8 Shingana Dem. Rep. Congo
158 C1 Shingbwiyang Myanmar
158 C1 Shing-gai Myanmar
185 P3 Shinghshal Pass Pak.
116 G7 Shinglehouse PA U.S.A.
110 H3 Shingleton MI U.S.A.
183 S4 Shingozha Kazakh.
165 N13 Shingū Japan
95 F4 Shingwedzi S. Africa
29 M7 Shining Tor hill England U.K.
111 M2 Shining Tree Ont. Can.
164 R8 Shinjō Japan
185 M5 Shinkai Hills Afgh.
185 L6 Shīnkāy Afgh.
166 F2 Shinminato Japan
165 I12 Shinnan-yō Japan
185 L6 Shin Narai Thana Afgh.
119 K3 Shinnecock Bay NY U.S.A.
26 H6 Shinness Lodge Highland, Scotland U.K.
116 E9 Shinnston WV U.S.A.
166 E6 Shino-jima i. Japan
167 H2 Shinonoi Japan
185 N4 Shinpokh Pak.
27 G7 Shinrone Rep. of Ireland
166 E5 Shinsei Japan
190 E4 Shinshār Syria
166 F6 Shinshiro Japan
167 H2 Shinshūshin Japan
167 I3 Shintō Japan
164 T3 Shintoku Japan
167 L4 Shintone Japan
191 H6 Shinuhayr Armenia
93 B5 Shinyanga Tanz.
93 B5 Shinyanga admin. reg. Tanz.
166 E2 Shio Japan
167 K2 Shiobara Japan
164 S8 Shiogama Japan
167 G3 Shiojiri Japan
164 □B22 Shiokawa Nansei-shotō Japan
167 H4 Shiomi-dake mt. Japan
165 M13 Shiono-misaki c. Japan
167 K2 Shioya Japan
167 M1 Shioya-zaki pt Japan
167 I1 Shiozawa Japan
171 K3 Shipai Anhui China
117 K9 Ship Bottom NJ U.S.A.
130 E1 Ship Chan Cay i. Bahamas
77 N8 Shipchenski Prokhod pass Bulg.
19 V4 Shipilovo Rus. Fed.
170 D7 Shiping Yunnan China
173 D11 Shipki Pass China/India
31 K5 Shiplake Oxfordshire, England U.K.
29 N6 Shipley West Yorkshire, England U.K.
116 G11 Shipman VA U.S.A.
109 H4 Shippegan N.B. Can.
109 H4 Shippegan Island N.B. Can.
116 H8 Shippensburg PA U.S.A.
116 F7 Shippenville PA U.S.A.
166 E5 Shippō Japan
125 X5 Shiprock NM U.S.A.
125 X5 Shiprock Peak NM U.S.A.
31 I3 Shipston on Stour Warwickshire, England U.K.
29 O5 Shipton North Yorkshire, England U.K.
30 G2 Shipton Shropshire, England U.K.
31 I4 Shipton-under-Wychwood Oxfordshire, England U.K.
171 M4 Shipu Zhejiang China
193 R4 Shipunskiy, Mys hd Rus. Fed.
170 G5 Shiqian Guizhou China
Shiqizhen Guangdong China see Zhongshan
186 H7 Shiqqat al Kharītah des. Saudi Arabia
170 G2 Shiquan Shaanxi China
178 A8 Shiquan He r. China conv. Indus
170 G2 Shiquan Shuiku resr China
186 F3 Shi'r, Jabal hill Saudi Arabia
26 F10 Shira r. Scotland U.K.
187 K3 Shirā'awh i. Qatar
184 C2 Shīrābād Iran
167 K6 Shirahama Chiba Japan
165 M13 Shirahama Wakayama Japan
166 D6 Shirai-san hill Japan
164 R5 Shirakami-misaki pt Japan
167 L1 Shirakawa Fukushima Japan
166 E3 Shirakawa Gifu Japan
166 F4 Shirakawa Gifu Japan
166 F3 Shirake-mine mt. Japan
167 L5 Shirako Japan
166 G5 Shirakura-yama mt. Japan
166 B7 Shirama-yama hill Japan
166 E3 Shiramine Japan
167 H4 Shirane Japan
167 H4 Shirane-san mt. Japan
167 I2 Shirane-san mt. Japan
167 J2 Shirane-san vol. Japan
164 V4 Shiranuka Japan
164 S4 Shiraoi Japan
167 J2 Shirasawa Japan
212 O1 Shirase Coast Antarctica
213 C2 Shirase Glacier Antarctica
164 U3 Shirataki Japan
93 B5 Shirati Tanz.
184 E7 Shīrāz Iran
188 E8 Shirbīn Egypt
93 B8 Shire r. Malawi
29 O7 Shirebrook Derbyshire, England U.K.
169 M4 Shireet Mongolia
184 B3 Shīreh Jīn Iran
30 G4 Shirenewton Monmouthshire, Wales U.K.
164 V3 Shiretoko-hantō pen. Japan
164 W2 Shiretoko-misaki c. Japan
164 W2 Shiretoko National Park Japan
185 K8 Shireza Pak.
183 M7 Shirin Uzbek.
185 L6 Shirinab r. Pak.
185 K3 Shīrīn Tagāb Afgh.
164 R5 Shiriuchi Japan
164 S5 Shiriya-zaki c. Japan
182 G4 Shirkala reg. Kazakh.
184 F6 Shīr Kūh mt. Iran
29 O7 Shirland Derbyshire, England U.K.
119 J3 Shirley NY U.S.A.
65 □ Shirley Cove b. Gibraltar
167 L4 Shiroi Japan
164 R9 Shiroishi Japan
167 G5 Shirokura-yama mt. Japan
164 Q9 Shirone Japan
89 G4 Shiroro Reservoir Nigeria
166 E4 Shirotori Japan
166 G2 Shirouma-dake mt. Japan
167 J4 Shiroyama Japan
178 E9 Shirpur Mahar. India
168 E5 Shirten Holoy Gobi des. China
184 G3 Shīrvān Iran
168 B5 Shisanjianfang Xinjiang China
162 D3 Shisanzhan Heilong. China
97 P3 Shiselweni admin. dist. Swaziland
104 B4 Shishaldin Volcano AK U.S.A.
Shisha Pangma mt. Xizang China see Xixabangma Feng
165 L13 Shishikui Japan
171 I4 Shishou Hubei China
167 L4 Shisui Japan
171 K3 Shitai Anhui China
171 I6 Shitan Guangdong China
171 M4 Shitang Zhejiang China
168 J7 Shitanjing Ningxia China
166 G5 Shitara Japan
85 I1 Shithāthah Iraq
162 D7 Shitoukoumen Shuiku resr Jilin China
178 C6 Shiv Rajasthan India
193 R4 Shiveluch, Sopka vol. Rus. Fed.
178 F7 Shivpuri Madh. Prad. India
190 C8 Shivta tourist site Israel
125 S4 Shivwits UT U.S.A.
125 S5 Shivwits Plateau AZ U.S.A.
185 N3 Shiwal l. Afgh.
169 K8 Shiwan Shaanxi China
170 F8 Shiwan Dashan mts China
158 H3 Shiwan Dashan mts China
93 A7 Shiwa Ngandu Zambia
171 J6 Shixing Guangdong China
170 H2 Shiyan Hubei China
170 G4 Shizhu Chongqing China
169 J9 Shizi Gansu China
171 L3 Shizipu Anhui China
170 D6 Shizong Yunnan China
164 S8 Shizugawa Japan
168 J7 Shizuishan Ningxia China
168 J7 Shizuishanzhan Ningxia China
164 R7 Shizukuishi Japan
164 T4 Shizunai Japan
167 H6 Shizuoka Japan
167 H6 Shizuoka pref. Japan
76 I8 Shkëlzenit, Maja e mt. Albania
191 E3 Shkhara mt. Georgia/Rus. Fed.
16 C4 Shklo Ukr.
Shklov Belarus see Shklow
19 N7 Shklow Belarus
16 E3 Shklyn' Ukr.
191 E3 Shk'meri Georgia
76 H8 Shkodër Albania
Shkodrës, Liqeni i l. Albania/Yugo. see Scutari, Lake
76 H9 Shkumbin r. Albania
17 S7 Shkurinskaya Rus. Fed.
16 E2 Shlapan' Ukr.
19 R4 Shlina r. Rus. Fed.
19 Q4 Shlino, Ozero l. Rus. Fed.
19 O2 Shlissel'burg Rus. Fed.
193 K1 Shmidta, Ostrov i. Rus. Fed.
162 M1 Shmidta, Poluostrov pen. Sakhalin Rus. Fed.
18 L4 Shmoylovo Rus. Fed.
18 L6 Sho, Vozyera l. Belarus
205 L6 Shoalhaven r. N.S.W. Austr.
107 K5 Shoal Lake Man. Can.
107 K4 Shoal Lake Sask. Can.
114 D6 Shoals IN U.S.A.
207 M7 Shoalwater Bay Qld Austr.
165 K12 Shōbara Japan
165 L12 Shōdo-shima i. Japan
31 N4 Shoeburyness Southend, England U.K.
118 D3 Shoemakersville PA U.S.A.

Column 1

82 K7 Shofirkon Uzbek.
66 F2 Shōgawa Japan
66 F2 Shō-gawa r. Japan
84 H3 Shoghlābād Iran
85 M3 Shoh Khatlon Tajik.
Shoh Pass Pak. see Tal Pass
18 F2 Shohola PA U.S.A.
64 S3 Shokanbetsu-dake mt. Japan
19 U1 Shola r. Rus. Fed.
83 M6 Sholaqkorgan Kazakh.
82 K2 Sholaksay Kazakh.
Sholapur Mahar. India see Solapur
82 K2 Sholaqorghan Kazakh. see Sholakkorgan
Sholaqsay Kazakh. see Sholaksay
08 C6 Sholl Island W.A. Austr.
14 F2 Shomba r. Rus. Fed.
82 H4 Shomishkol' Kazakh.
14 F2 Shomvuva Rus. Fed.
18 M2 Shōmaru-ko l. Japan
76 E9 Shona, Eilean i. Scotland U.K.
14 J9 Shona Ridge sea feature S. Atlantic Ocean
79 M6 Shongar Bhutan
19 W4 Shongzha Rus. Fed.
28 E4 Shoptown Northern Ireland U.K.
82 G4 Shoptykol' Aktyubinskaya Oblast' Kazakh.
33 P2 Shoptykol' Pavlodarskaya Oblast' Kazakh.
85 F3 Shor Hima. Prad. India
85 L7 Shoran Pak.
76 E7 Shorapur Kerala India
85 K9 Shorap Pak.
76 E4 Shorapur Karnataka India
85 K6 Shorawak reg. Afgh.
83 L9 Sho'rchi Uzbek.
19 N6 Shore Acres NJ U.S.A.
31 M5 Shoreham Kent, England U.K.
31 L6 Shoreham-by-Sea West Sussex, England U.K.
Shorgun Uzbek. see Shargʻun
85 O6 Shorkot Pak.
84 G1 Shorkozakhly, Solonchak salt flat Turkm.
85 P2 Shorkūl i. Tajik.
36 D3 Shorobe Botswana
33 N2 Shortandy Kazakh.
35 L3 Shor Tepe Afgh.
00 □6 Shortland Island Solomon Is
00 □6 Shortland Islands Solomon Is
16 H6 Shortsville NY U.S.A.
84 D4 Shosambetsu Japan see Shosanbetsu
64 S2 Shosanbetsu Japan
19 T5 Shosha r. Rus. Fed.
25 P6 Shoshone CA U.S.A.
22 G5 Shoshone ID U.S.A.
22 I4 Shoshone r. WY U.S.A.
22 I4 Shoshone Lake WY U.S.A.
24 O2 Shoshone Mountains NV U.S.A.
25 P5 Shoshone Peak NV U.S.A.
39 E4 Shoshong Botswana
22 J5 Shoshoni WY U.S.A.
17 M2 Shostka Ukr.
17 M2 Shostka r. Ukr.
31 O4 Shotley Gate Suffolk, England U.K.
30 F1 Shotton Flintshire, Wales U.K.
26 I11 Shotts North Lanarkshire, Scotland U.K.
Shouchun Anhui China see Shouxian
79 P8 Shouguang Shandong China
71 K2 Shouxian Anhui China
59 M8 Shouyang Shanxi China
70 G2 Shouyang Shan mt. Shaanxi China
67 J2 Shōwa Japan
35 G6 Showak Sudan
25 V7 Show Low AZ U.S.A.
91 H6 Showt Iran
14 I2 Shoyna Rus. Fed.
15 H7 Shpakovskoye Rus. Fed.
17 K4 Shpola Ukr.
16 H5 Shpykiv Ukr.
16 H5 Shpyli Ukr.
17 L3 Shramkivka Ukr.
15 J9 Shreve OH U.S.A.
21 I9 Shreveport LA U.S.A.
30 G2 Shrewsbury Shropshire, England U.K.
19 L4 Shrewsbury NJ U.S.A.
18 B3 Shrewsbury PA U.S.A.
31 I5 Shrewton Wiltshire, England U.K.
28 F5 Shrigley Northern Ireland U.K.
76 D3 Shriqonda Mahar. India
Shri Lanka country Asia see Sri Lanka
78 C6 Shri Mohangarh Rajasthan India
78 E6 Shrirampur W. Bengal India
76 E6 Shrirangapattana Karnataka India
30 I2 Shrivenham Oxfordshire, England U.K.
30 G2 Shropshire admin. div. England U.K.
19 H7 Shrub Oak NY U.S.A.
Shtefan-Vode Moldova see Ştefan Vodă
76 I10 Shtërmen Albania
76 I4 Shtigjën Albania
17 M8 Shtormove Ukr.
30 C6 Shu Kazakh.
85 N7 Shu'ab, Ghubbat b. Suquţrā Yemen
87 K9 Shu'ab, Ra's pt Suquţrā Yemen
89 M8 Shu'aiba Iraq
70 D2 Shuajingsi Sichuan China
15 H7 Shuakhevi Georgia
70 C6 Shuangbai Yunnan China
Shuangcheng Fujian China see Zherong
62 E6 Shuangcheng Heilong. China
71 I3 Shuangfeng Hubei China
70 F3 Shuangchang Sichuan China
73 G2 Shuangchiang Yunnan China see Zhenyuan
73 H10 Shuangliu Sichuan China
73 J10 Shuangjingkuang Qinghai China
71 J7 Shuangjiang Hunan China
71 H5 Shuangjiang Yunnan China
70 F7 Shuangshipu Shaanxi China
71 I5 Shuikoushan Hunan China

Column 2

Shuiluocheng Gansu China see Zhuangliang
213 L2 Shuiquan Gansu China
49 I6 Shuiquanzi Gansu China
21 R6 Shuituo He r. Sichuan China
ShuiXi Guangdong China see Wuhua
185 N7 Shujaabad Pak.
162 H3 Shulan Jilin China
172 C7 Shule Xinjiang China
172 M6 Shule Gansu China
168 C6 Shule He r. China
168 E7 Shule Nanshan mts China
17 R4 Shul'hynka Ukr.
169 L6 Shulinzhao Nei Mongol China
Shulu Hebei China see Xinji
19 O2 Shum Rus. Fed.
104 B4 Shumagin Islands AK U.S.A.
17 P2 Shumakovo Rus. Fed.
182 H6 Shumanay Uzbek.
164 T2 Shumerinai-ko l. Japan
18 M6 Shumba Zimbabwe
77 O7 Shumen Bulg.
77 O7 Shumensko Plato nat. park Bulg.
14 I5 Shumerlya Rus. Fed.
192 H4 Shumikha Rus. Fed.
16 C4 Shumilina Belarus
193 Q4 Shumshu, Ostrov i. Kuril'skiye O-va Rus. Fed.
97 P2 Shumshu's Ukr.
179 O6 Shutagar Assam India
29 R7 Shumyachi Rus. Fed.
157 I3 Sibu Sarawak Malaysia
154 D8 Sibuco Mindanao Phil.
154 D8 Sibuco Bay Mindanao Phil.
154 D8 Sibuguey r. Mindanao Phil.
154 D8 Sibuguey Bay Mindanao Phil.
90 C3 Siburi P.C.A.R.T.
157 J2 Sibuti Sarawak Malaysia
154 B9 Sibutu i. Phil.
154 B9 Sibutu Passage Phil.
154 D5 Sibuyan i. Phil.
154 D5 Sibuyan Sea Phil.
77 L4 Sic Romania
106 G5 Sicamous B.C. Can.
154 C2 Sicapoo mt. Luzon Phil.
138 D4 Sicasica Bol.
154 D7 Sicayac Mindanao Phil.
204 G4 Siccus watercourse S.A. Austr.
184 E5 Si Chah Iran
159 D10 Sichon Thai.
170 D3 Sichuan prov. China
170 E4 Sichuan Pendi basin Sichuan China
41 H10 Sicié, Cap c. France
74 G8 Sicilia admin. reg. Italy
74 G7 Sicilia i. Italy
74 C9 Sicilian Channel Italy/Tunisia
Sicily i. Italy see Sicilia
54 E4 Siciny Pol.
118 F5 Sicklerville NJ U.S.A.
49 K6 Sickte Ger.
138 C3 Sicuani Peru
57 K5 Sicula Romania
74 E9 Šiculiana Sicilia Italy
76 H5 Šid Vojvodina, Srbija Serb. and Mont.
57 I3 Šid Slovakia
155 E3 Sidangoli Halmahera Indon.
30 F6 Sidbury Devon, England U.K.
44 K2 Siddeburen Neth.
178 D8 Siddhapur Gujarat India
176 F3 Siddipet Andhra Prad. India
21 P5 Sideby Fin.
155 A5 Sidenreng, Danau l. Indon.
30 B4 Sidensjö Sweden
74 G3 Sideradougou Burkina
75 K7 Siderno Italy
79 H7 Sideros, Akra pt Kriti Greece
76 I3 Sidesaviwa S. Africa
30 F6 Sidford Devon, England U.K.
185 O6 Sidhai Pak.
178 H6 Sidhauli Uttar Prad. India
178 H7 Sidhi Madh. Prad. India
Sidhirokastron Greece see Sidirokastro
92 D1 Sidi N'Srit Morocco
88 D5 Sïfié Côte d'Ivoire
78 F5 Sifnos i. Greece
78 F5 Sifnou, Steno sea chan. Greece
87 E2 Sig Alg.
19 U4 Sig, Ozero l. Rus. Fed.
187 K6 Sigani well Saudi Arabia
201 □1a Sigave Viti Levu Fiji
199 I3 Sigave Wallis and Futuna Is
41 B10 Sigean France
54 E4 Sigep, Tanjung pt Indon.
50 E4 Sigg Switz.
79 I4 Siggiewi Malta
29 Q6 Sigglesthorne East Riding of Yorkshire, England U.K.
105 M2 Sigguup Nunaa pen. Greenland
77 L3 Sighetu Marmaţiei Romania
77 M4 Sighişoara Romania
71 N9 Sigillo Italy
176 D9 Sigiriya Sri Lanka
191 J5 Sigʻnri Azer.
12 G4 Sigli Sumatera Indon.
20 □D1 Siglufjörður Iceland
154 D6 Sigma Panay Phil.
48 E4 Sigmaringen Ger.
48 E4 Sigmaringendorf Ger.
84 R8 Signa Italy
53 N3 Signalberg hill Ger.
38 E4 Signal de Botrange hill Belgium
41 I10 Signal de la Ste-Baume mt. France
41 I7 Signal de Mailhebiau mt. France
41 D7 Signal de Randon mt. France
40 F5 Signal de St-André hill France
42 G3 Signal de Sauvagnac hill France
42 H4 Signal du Pic hill France
39 K5 Signal du Viviers hill France
65 □ Signal Hill Gibraltar
125 F8 Signal Peak AZ U.S.A.
20 L3 Sigmatkylä Fin.
84 B5 Sillod Mahar. India
71 K8 Signa Italy
53 N3 Signalberg hill Ger.

Column 3

182 H1 Sibay Rus. Fed.
97 Q3 Sibayi, Lake S. Africa
213 L2 Sibbald, Cape Antarctica
49 I6 Sibbesse Ger.
21 R6 Sibbo Fin.
21 R6 Sibböjärden b. Fin.
184 H5 Sib Chāh Iran
68 E4 Šibenik Croatia
71 K9 Siena Italy
Siberia reg. Rus. Fed. see Sibir'
71 K9 Siena prov. Italy
K5 Sienawa Indon.
55 K3 Sienno Pol.
183 N7 Sijjak Uzbek. see Sijjaq
Siberut i. Indon.
55 J4 Sienno Pol.
Siberut, Selat sea chan. Indon.
20 O3 Sieppijärvi Fin.
55 H6 Siepraw Pol.
47 J3 Sieradowicki Park Krajobrazowy Pol.
54 G4 Sieradz Pol.
54 G5 Sieraków Śląskie Pol.
54 E3 Sieraków Wielkopolskie Pol.
55 H3 Sierakówek Pol.
54 F1 Sierakowice Pol.
47 H2 Sierakowski Park Krajobrazowy Pol.
37 L5 Sierck-les-Bains France
37 N8 Sierentz France
48 K2 Sierksdorf Ger.
52 E2 Sierrczyno Pol.
59 N3 Sierndorf Austria
59 J3 Sierning Austria
59 M4 Sierningtal nature res. Austria
54 F4 Sieroszewice Pol.
55 H3 Sierpc Pol.
55 H3 Sierpienica r. Pol.
145 D6 Sierra, Punta de la pt Arg.
63 J2 Sierra, Punta de la pt Spain
130 H4 Sierra Blanca TX U.S.A.
123 L11 Sierra Boyer, Embalse de resr Spain
65 J4 Sierra Chica r. Arg.
147 G5 Sierra Colorada Arg.
145 D6 Sierra de Cazorla Segura y las Villas park Spain
65 N4 Sierra de Fuentes Spain
64 G2 Sierra de la Culata nat. park Venez.
136 D2 Sierra de las Quijadas, Parque Nacional nat. park Arg.
144 D4 Sierra del Gistral mts Spain
66 D3 Sierra de Luna Spain
65 J6 Sierra de Yeguas Spain
67 F7 Sierra Engarcerán Spain
145 D6 Sierra Grande Arg.
88 C4 Sierra Leone country Africa
214 H5 Sierra Leone Basin sea feature N. Atlantic Ocean
214 H5 Sierra Leone Rise sea feature N. Atlantic Ocean
124 L6 Sierra Madre Mountains CA U.S.A.
126 H4 Sierra Mojada Mex.
129 N9 Sierra Morena Mex.
136 D2 Sierra Nevada, Parque Nacional nat. park Venez.
136 C2 Sierra Nevada de Santa Marta, Parque Nacional nat. park Col.
147 G5 Sierras Bayas Arg.
124 L2 Sierraville CA U.S.A.
125 V10 Sierra Vista AZ U.S.A.
70 D3 Sierre Switz.
183 O1 Sierro r. Spain
88 D5 Sïfié Côte d'Ivoire
78 F5 Sifnos i. Greece

Column 4

55 K3 Siemiatycze Pol.
55 K4 Siemień Pol.
54 G4 Siemkowice Pol.
159 H7 Siĕmpang Cambodia
159 F8 Siĕmréab Cambodia
Siem Reap Cambodia see Siĕmréab
54 D1 Siemyśl Pol.
71 K9 Siena Italy
71 K9 Siena prov. Italy
55 K5 Sienawa Indon.
58 I3 Sienne r. France
55 J4 Sienno Pol.
71 J6 Sienno Pol.
20 O3 Sieppijärvi Fin.
55 H6 Siepraw Pol.
47 J3 Sieradowicki Park Krajobrazowy Pol.
54 G4 Sieradz Pol.
54 G5 Sieraków Śląskie Pol.
54 E3 Sieraków Wielkopolskie Pol.
55 H3 Sierakówek Pol.
54 F1 Sierakowice Pol.
47 H2 Sierakowski Park Krajobrazowy Pol.
37 L5 Sierck-les-Bains France
37 N8 Sierentz France
48 K2 Sierksdorf Ger.
52 E2 Sierrczyno Pol.
59 N3 Sierndorf Austria
59 J3 Sierning Austria
59 M4 Sierningtal nature res. Austria
54 F4 Sieroszewice Pol.
55 H3 Sierpc Pol.
55 H3 Sierpienica r. Pol.
145 D6 Sierra, Punta de la pt Arg.
63 J2 Sierra, Punta de la pt Spain
130 H4 Sierra Blanca TX U.S.A.
59 M4 Sierra, Parque Nacional nat. park Arg.
156 A2 Silawah Agam vol. Indon.
154 D6 Silay Negros Phil.
68 G3 Silba i. Croatia
71 R7 Silbanski Kanal sea chan. Croatia
48 I5 Silberberg hill Ger.
55 M3 Silberstedt Ger.
184 H3 Silchar Assam India
79 K1 Sile r. Italy
31 J2 Şile Turkey
29 K6 Sileby Leicestershire, England U.K.
29 K5 Silecroft Cumbria, England U.K.
18 J6 Silene Latvia
70 F2 Silenen Switz.
45 F8 Silenrieux Belgium
115 H8 Siler City NC U.S.A.
65 N4 Siles Spain
54 F4 Silesia reg. Pol.
87 G5 Silet Alg.
Sileti r. Kazakh. see Seletinskoye
183 O1 Sileti Kazakh.
183 O1 Siletiteniz, Ozero salt l. Kazakh.
38 E5 Silfiac France
178 H5 Silgadi Nepal see Silgarhi
178 H5 Silgarhi Nepal
179 N6 Silghat Assam India
99 □2a Silhouette i. Inner Islands Seychelles
50 G4 Siliana Tunisia
69 B8 Siliana admin. div. Tunisia
31 J8 Silifke Turkey
72 B6 Siligo Sardegna Italy
179 J7 Siliguri W. Bengal India see Shiliguri
91 E9 Sililo Zambia
57 L3 Silindia Romania
73 L1 Sifeni Eth.
128 O3 Silip Mach. Prad. India
72 B9 Siliqua Sardegna Italy
72 B6 Silis r. Italy
200 □1a Silisili, Mount Samoa
77 N6 Silişteni Romania
77 M6 Siliştea Nouă Romania
77 O5 Silistra Bulg. see Silistra
77 O5 Silistra Bulg.
79 I1 Silivri Turkey
22 F2 Siljan l. Sweden
21 M6 Siljan Norway
23 K1 Siljansnäs Sweden
22 F5 Silkeborg Denmark
207 K4 Silkwood Qld Austr.
118 C2 Silkworth PA U.S.A.
58 D7 Sill r. Austria
18 K2 Sill r. Austria
20 S3 Silláa Estonia
72 D7 Sillano Italy
41 J9 Sillans-la-Cascade France
71 L6 Sillaro r. Italy
188 F5 Sille Turkey
122 D1 Silleda Spain
40 D2 Sillé-le-Guillaume France
36 H5 Sillery France
49 K7 Silstedt Ger.
20 L3 Silsbee TX U.S.A.
20 J1 Sitakylä Fin.
84 C5 Siitou well Chad
185 I9 Siluas Kalimantan Indon.
185 I9 Sïlûp r. Iran
18 E6 Silutė Lith.

Column 5

183 N7 Sijjak Uzbek. see Sijjaq
183 N7 Sijjaq Uzbek.
45 D6 Sijsele Belgium
156 D5 Sikanang Sumatera Indon.
178 B8 Sika Gujarat India
Sikakah Saudi Arabia see Sakākah
156 D6 Sikakap Indon.
178 F6 Sikandra Uttar Prad. India
178 H3 Sikandra Rao Uttar Prad. India
106 F3 Sikanni Chief B.C. Can.
106 F3 Sikanni Chief r. B.C. Can.
178 E6 Sikar Rajasthan India
185 M4 Sikaram mt. Afgh.
88 D3 Sikasso Mali
88 D4 Sikasso admin. reg. Mali
158 C3 Sikaw Myanmar
78 E2 Sikea Greece
Sikéa Greece see Sykea
155 B6 Sikeli Sulawesi Indon.
57 H4 Sikenica r. Slovakia
121 K7 Sikeston MO U.S.A.
57 I5 Sik-hegy hill Hungary
162 H7 Sikhote-Alin' mts Rus. Fed.
162 J6 Sikhote-Alinskiy Zapovednik nature res. Rus. Fed.
78 G6 Sikinos Greece
78 G6 Sikinos i. Greece
191 J5 Sikirevci Croatia
179 L6 Sikkim state India
14 L5 Siklós Hungary
57 K5 Siko i. Maluku Indon.
91 D8 Sikongo Zambia
55 H3 Sikórz Pol.
162 H2 Siksjö Sweden
154 C8 Sikta Dihar India
169 R7 Sikuaishi Liaoning China
157 L1 Sikuati Sabah Malaysia
62 E4 Sil r. Spain
186 B2 Şilaʼ i. Saudi Arabia
63 L6 Silaçayopan Mex.
154 E6 Silago Leyte Phil.
18 F6 Silalė Lith.
71 J2 Silando Italy
72 B7 Si Lanna National Park Thai.
72 B7 Silanus Sardegna Italy
154 E5 Sila Pat Samar Phil.
121 K10 Silas AL U.S.A.
156 A2 Silavatturai Sri Lanka

Column 6

27 F7 Silvermine Mountains hills Rep. of Ireland
27 F7 Silvermines Rep. of Ireland
124 O4 Silver Peak Range mts NV U.S.A.
118 B7 Silver Spring MD U.S.A.
124 M2 Silver Springs NV U.S.A.
31 J3 Silverstone Northamptonshire, England U.K.
96 H4 Silver Streams S. Africa
106 E5 Silverthrone Mountain B.C. Can.
122 D2 Silvertip Mountain B.C. Can.
204 H4 Silverton N.S.W. Austr.
106 G5 Silverton B.C. Can.
119 G4 Silverton NJ U.S.A.
121 E8 Silverton TX U.S.A.
111 L4 Silver Water Ont. Can.
137 G5 Silves Brazil
64 C6 Silves Port.
21 T1 Silvi Italy
62 C4 Silvia Col.
115 F9 Silvies r. OR U.S.A.
127 N8 Silvituc Mex.
70 I2 Silvretta Gruppe mts Switz.
58 B6 Silvrettahorn mt. Austria
191 J5 Silyan Azer.
14 L5 Sim Rus. Fed.
14 L5 Sim r. Rus. Fed.
173 J11 Sima Nzwani Comoros
99 □3 Sima i. Comoros
158 C2 Simao Yunnan China
19 V5 Sima Rus. Fed.
72 B8 Simala Sardegna Italy
63 K5 Simancas Spain
57 K5 Şimand Romania
40 F3 Simandre France
178 C7 Simari Rajasthan India
156 B4 Simeleue, Pulau i. Indon.
78 E2 Simao Yunnan China
185 M9 Simara i. Phil.
137 F3 Simaraña Venez.
108 E4 Simard, Lac l. Que. Can.
189 M7 Simareh, Rūdkhāneh-ye r. Iran
179 J7 Simaria Jharkhand India
178 H7 Simaria Madh. Prad. India
179 K7 Simaria Ghat Bihar India
55 B3 Simatang i. Indon.
50 J3 Simat de la Valldigna Spain
79 J3 Simav Turkey
79 J3 Simav Dağları mts Turkey
173 E8 Simawat Xinjiang China
145 S3 Simaxis Sardegna Italy
186 E7 Simaya i. Saudi Arabia
90 D4 Simba Dem. Rep. Congo
53 N4 Simbach Ger.
53 O5 Simbach am Inn Ger.
75 K6 Simbario Italy
31 P3 Simbirsk Rus. Fed. see Ul'yanovsk
200 □1a Simbo i. New Georgia Is Solomon Is
73 K4 Simbruini, Monti mts Italy
79 N3 Simbukhovo Rus. Fed.
108 D5 Simcoe Ont. Can.
108 E4 Simcoe, Lake Ont. Can.
179 J8 Simdega Jharkhand India
31 N6 Simi'nel'nikovo Ukr.
89 F4 Simdou Burkina
64 D5 Simdou Burkina
88 D4 Siméandou Burkina
176 I3 Simdhara r. India
179 J8 Simdhara r. India
185 N6 Sind Sagar Doab lowland Pak.
14 J4 Sinegor'ye Rus. Fed.
79 I2 Sinekçi Turkey
73 N3 Sinello r. Italy
35 □ Sinet'nikovo Ukr. see Synel'nykove
79 P2 Sinende Benin
89 F4 Sinendé Benin
64 B5 Sines Port.
64 B5 Sines, Cabo de c. Port.
23 N7 Sinettä Fin.
67 I8 Sineu Spain
89 I8 Sineu Spain
88 D5 Sinfra Côte d'Ivoire
158 D4 Sing Sudan
85 G6 Singa Sudan

Column 7

128 A2 Silvermine Mountains hills Mex.
71 L9 Silverton NV U.S.A.
136 D2 Sinaloa state Mex.
128 A2 Sinalunga Italy
71 N4 Sinamaica Venez.
163 D9 Sinan N. Korea
78 A3 Sinarades Kerkyra Greece
67 C8 Sinarcas Spain
84 A2 Sinawin Libya
84 H2 Sinazongwe Zambia
158 B5 Sinbaungwe Myanmar
158 C2 Sinbo Myanmar
158 B3 Sinbyugyun Myanmar
191 I5 Sincan Azer.
188 G3 Sincan Turkey
79 I4 Sincanli Turkey
136 C2 Sincé Col.
136 C2 Sincelejo Col.
36 F4 Sinceny France
115 C10 Sinclair, Lake U.S.A.
203 I8 Sinclair Head hill N.Z.
106 F4 Sinclair Mills B.C. Can.
26 J5 Sinclair's Bay Scotland U.K.
140 E5 Sincora, Serra do hills Brazil
178 G6 Sind r. India
179 P4 Sinda Xizang China
162 J4 Sinda Rus. Fed.
93 A8 Sinda Zambia
22 G4 Sindal Denmark
92 C5 Sindangan Mindanao Phil.
154 D7 Sindangan Bay Mindanao Phil.
156 G8 Sindangbarang Jawa Indon.
90 A5 Sindara Gabon
178 C7 Sindari Rajasthan India
158 B5 Sindeh, Teluk b. Flores Indon.
52 F4 Sindelfingen Ger.
176 E4 Sindgi Karnataka India
185 M9 Sindh prov. Pak.
Sindhnur Karnataka India
179 J6 Sindhnur Karnataka India
Sindhos Greece see Sindos
179 J6 Sindhnurari Nepal
Sindhuli Garhi
18 I3 Sindi Estonia
178 G9 Sindi India
72 B7 Sindia Sardegna Italy
129 J3 Sindihui Mex.
Sındırġı Turkey
178 F8 Sindkheda Mahar. India
178 F9 Sindkheda Mahar. India
Sindominic Romania see Sândominic
14 J3 Sindor Rus. Fed.
78 D2 Sindos Greece
88 D4 Sindou Burkina
179 K4 Sindphana r. India
179 J8 Sindhara r. India
179 J8 Sindhara r. India
185 N6 Sind Sagar Doab lowland Pak.
14 J4 Sinegor'ye Rus. Fed.
79 I2 Sinekçi Turkey
73 N3 Sinello r. Italy
89 F4 Sinende Benin
64 B5 Sines Port.
64 B5 Sines, Cabo de c. Port.
23 N7 Sinettä Fin.
67 I8 Sineu Spain
88 D5 Sinfra Côte d'Ivoire
85 G6 Singa Sudan

Column 8

159 D7 Si Nakarin Reservoir Thai.
200 □6 Sinalagu Malaita Solomon Is
128 A2 Sinaloa state Mex.
128 A2 Sinalunga Italy
71 N4 Sinamaica Venez.
163 D9 Sinan N. Korea
78 A3 Sinarades Kerkyra Greece
67 C8 Sinarcas Spain
84 A2 Sinawin Libya
84 H2 Sinazongwe Zambia
158 B5 Sinbaungwe Myanmar
158 C2 Sinbo Myanmar
158 B3 Sinbyugyun Myanmar
191 I5 Sincan Azer.
188 G3 Sincan Turkey
79 I4 Sincanli Turkey
136 C2 Sincé Col.
136 C2 Sincelejo Col.
36 F4 Sinceny France
115 C10 Sinclair, Lake U.S.A.
203 I8 Sinclair Head hill N.Z.
106 F4 Sinclair Mills B.C. Can.
26 J5 Sinclair's Bay Scotland U.K.
140 E5 Sincora, Serra do hills Brazil
178 G6 Sind r. India
179 P4 Sinda Xizang China
162 J4 Sinda Rus. Fed.
93 A8 Sinda Zambia
22 G4 Sindal Denmark
92 C5 Sindangan Mindanao Phil.
154 D7 Sindangan Bay Mindanao Phil.
156 G8 Sindangbarang Jawa Indon.
90 A5 Sindara Gabon
178 C7 Sindari Rajasthan India
158 B5 Sindeh, Teluk b. Flores Indon.
52 F4 Sindelfingen Ger.
176 E4 Sindgi Karnataka India
185 M9 Sindh prov. Pak.
179 J6 Sindhnur Karnataka India
179 J6 Sindhnurari Nepal Sindhuli Garhi
18 I3 Sindi Estonia
178 G9 Sindi India
72 B7 Sindia Sardegna Italy
129 J3 Sindihui Mex.
178 F8 Sindkheda Mahar. India
14 J3 Sindor Rus. Fed.
78 D2 Sindos Greece
88 D4 Sindou Burkina
179 K4 Sindphana r. India
185 N6 Sind Sagar Doab lowland Pak.
14 J4 Sinegor'ye Rus. Fed.
79 I2 Sinekçi Turkey
73 N3 Sinello r. Italy
89 F4 Sinende Benin
64 B5 Sines Port.
64 B5 Sines, Cabo de c. Port.
23 N7 Sinettä Fin.
67 I8 Sineu Spain
88 D5 Sinfra Côte d'Ivoire
85 G6 Singa Sudan
177 H3 Singa Valley CA U.S.A.
176 I2 Singapuru Orissa India
176 Ia Singareni Andhra Prad. India
201 □1a Singatoka Viti Levu Fiji see Sigatoka
199 I3 Singave Wallis and Futuna Is
159 D7 Sing Buri Thai.
52 F6 Singen (Hohentwiel) Ger.
156 □ Singapore Sing.
156 □ Singapore country Asia
156 □ Singapore, Strait of Indon./Sing.
156 □ Singapura Sing.
156 □ Singapura country Asia
176 Ia Singareni Andhra Prad. India
176 Ia Singatoka Viti Levu Fiji see Sigatoka
16 H7 Singen (Hohentwiel) Ger.
16 H6 Singera Moldova
172 I5 Singgimtay Xinjiang China
111 N5 Singhampton Ont. Can.
59 J6 Singhofen Ger.
158 C3 Singida admin. reg. Tanz.
93 B6 Singida Tanz.
155 B6 Singimale Myanmar
158 G4 Singkaling Hkamti Myanmar
155 B6 Singkang Sulawesi Indon.
156 A4 Singkawak Sumatera Indon.
157 H4 Singkawang Kalimantan Indon.
156 □ Singkep i. Indon.
156 D5 Singkil Sumatera Indon.
205 M5 Singleton N.S.W. Austr.
31 L6 Singleton W. Sussex, England U.K.
206 D7 Singleton, Mount hill N.T. Austr.
209 D10 Singleton, Mount hill W.A. Austr.
23 O1 Singö i. Sweden
178 I5 Singoli Madh. Prad. India
158 B3 Singu Myanmar
Sing, Gunung mt. Indon. see Songkhla
179 N7 Singra Assam India
129 I6 Singuilucan Mex.
178 H8 Singrauli Madh. Prad. India
163 E8 Sin'gwang-ri N. Korea
186 G6 Sinḥ, Jabal hill Saudi Arabia
176 □ Sinhala country Asia see Sri Lanka
176 □ Sinharaja Forest Reserve nature res. Sri Lanka
163 E8 Sinhŭng N. Korea
163 D9 Sini Sardegna Italy
72 C9 Sinigo r. Italy
154 C4 Siniloan Luzon Phil.
168 E5 Sining Qinghai China see Xining

Column 9

155 A4 Sini, Gunung mt. Indon.
72 B6 Sinis pen. Italy
91 N9 Siní Vrūkh mt. Bulg.
79 R2 Sinyaya Lipyagi Rus. Fed.
20 R5 Siniscola Sardegna Italy
138 H3 Sinj Croatia
72 C6 Sinjai Sulawesi Indon.
189 M9 Sinjār, Jabal mt. Iraq
190 N5 Sinkat Sudan
85 H5 Sinkiang aut. reg. China see Xinjiang Uygur Zizhiqu
Sinkiang Uighur Autonomous Region aut. reg. China see Xinjiang Uygur Zizhiqu
27 E7 Sinking Spring OH U.S.A.
116 D10 Sinking Spring PA U.S.A.
36 H5 Sinkyevichy Belarus
185 I8 Sin-le-Noble France
163 D9 Sinmartin Romania see Sânmartin
163 D9 Sinmi-do i. N. Korea

49 F9 Sinn Ger.
49 I10 Sinn r. Ger.
72 C9 Sinnai Sardegna Italy
137 H3 Sinnamary Fr. Guiana
176 D3 Sinnar Mahar. India
190 A9 Sinn Bishr, Jabal hill Egypt
17 O3 Sinne Ukr.
Sinneh Iran see Sanandaj
116 G7 Sinnemahoning PA U.S.A.
73 R7 Sinni r. Italy
Sînnicolau Mare Romania see Sânnicolau Mare
77 Q6 Sinoie, Lacul lag. Romania
18 J4 Sinole Latvia
139 G2 Sinop Brazil
188 G2 Sinop Turkey
Sinope Turkey see Sinop
75 J7 Sinopoli Italy
126 D2 Sinoquipe Mex.
163 E8 Sinp'a N. Korea
Sînpetru Mare Romania see Sânpetru Mare
163 F8 Sinp'o N. Korea
163 E9 Sinp'yŏng N. Korea
52 E7 Sins Switz.
163 E9 Sinsang N. Korea
52 F3 Sinsheim Ger.
157 I4 Sintang Kalimantan Indon.
131 □10 Sint Annabaai b. Curaçao Neth. Antilles
44 F5 Sint Annaland Neth.
44 I2 Sint Annaparochie Neth.
44 I5 Sint Anthonis Neth.
131 □10 Sint Christoffelberg hill Curaçao Neth. Antilles
57 K5 Sintea Mare Romania
57 L4 Şinteu Romania
131 □2 Sint Eustatius i. Neth. Antilles
45 F7 Sint-Genesius-Rode Belgium
45 F6 Sint-Gillis-Waas Belgium
45 H6 Sint-Huibrechts-Lille Belgium
44 I2 Sint Jacobiparochie Neth.
45 F6 Sint Jansteen Neth.
45 D6 Sint-Joris Belgium
45 G6 Sint-Katelijne-Waver Belgium
Sint Kruis Curaçao Neth. Antilles see Santa Krus
45 E6 Sint-Laureins Belgium
45 G6 Sint-Lenaarts Belgium
131 L4 Sint Maarten i. Neth. Antilles
44 F5 Sint Maartensdijk Neth.
45 E6 Sint-Margriete Belgium
45 E7 Sint-Maria-Lierde Belgium
45 E6 Sint-Martens-Latem Belgium
131 □10 Sint Michiel Curaçao Neth. Antilles
131 □9 Sint Nicolaas Aruba
44 I3 Sint Nicolaasga Neth.
45 F6 Sint-Niklaas Belgium
121 G11 Sinton TX U.S.A.
44 G3 Sint Pancras Neth.
44 F5 Sint Philipsland Neth.
45 F7 Sint-Pieters-Leeuw Belgium
64 A3 Sintra Port.
60 B3 Sintra-Cascais, Parque Natural de nature res. Port.
71 L7 Sintria r. Italy
19 T5 Sintsovo Rus. Fed.
45 H7 Sint-Truiden Belgium
131 □10 Sint Willebrordus Curaçao Neth. Antilles
136 C2 Sinú r. Col.
163 D8 Sinŭiju N. Korea
92 F2 Sinujiif Somalia
18 L4 Sinyaya r. Rus. Fed.
52 E4 Sinzheim Ger.
49 D9 Sinzig Ger.
53 M4 Sinzing Ger.
57 H5 Sió r. Romania
66 G4 Sió r. Spain
57 H5 Sióagárd Hungary
154 D8 Siocon Mindanao Phil.
57 H5 Siófok Hungary
91 D9 Sioma Zambia
91 D9 Sioma Ngwezi National Park Zambia
70 C3 Sion Switz.
26 F6 Sionascaig, Loch l. Scotland U.K.
191 G4 Sioni Georgia
27 H3 Sion Mills Northern Ireland U.K.
Sionmsheni Georgia see Sioni
105 K2 Siorapaluk Greenland
200 □6 Siota Solomon Is
40 C4 Sioule r. France
120 G4 Sioux Center IA U.S.A.
120 G4 Sioux City IA U.S.A.
120 G4 Sioux Falls SD U.S.A.
108 B3 Sioux Lookout Ont. Can.
127 N11 Sipacate Guat.
157 M2 Sipadan, Pulau i. Sabah Malaysia
154 D7 Sipalay Negros Phil.
68 F4 Šipan i. Croatia
157 I4 Sipang, Tanjung pt Malaysia
131 □7 Siparia Trin. and Tob.
158 C3 Sipein Myanmar
162 D7 Siping Jilin China
157 K2 Sipitang Sabah Malaysia
107 L4 Sipiwesk Man. Can.
107 L4 Sipiwesk Lake Man. Can.
212 P2 Siple, Mount Antarctica
212 N1 Siple Coast Antarctica
212 P2 Siple Island Antarctica
77 P3 Şipote Romania
68 F3 Šipovo Bos.-Herz.
52 G6 Sipplingen Ger.
121 K9 Sipsey r. AL U.S.A.
156 C6 Sipura i. Indon.
156 C6 Sipura, Selat sea chan. Indon.
190 A9 Sīq, Wādī as watercourse Egypt
187 L9 Siqirah Suquṭrā Yemen
142 C5 Siqueira Campos Brazil
128 A2 Siqueiros Mex.
126 □Q11 Siquia r. Nic.
154 D7 Siquijor Phil.
154 D7 Siquijor i. Phil.
136 D2 Siquisique Venez.
185 M10 Sir r. Pak.
176 E6 Sira Karnataka India
22 C3 Sira Norway
22 C3 Sira r. Norway
187 L3 Şīr Abū Nu'āyr i. U.A.E.
41 I7 Sirac mt. France
159 E8 Si Racha Thai.
75 I9 Siracusa Sicilia Italy
75 I9 Siracusa prov. Sicilia Italy
Siraha Nepal see Sirha
179 L7 Sirajganj Bangl.
106 F4 Sir Alexander, Mount B.C. Can.
42 I6 Siran France
188 I3 Şiran Turkey
185 L9 Siranda Lake Pak.
178 H7 Sirathu Uttar Prad. India
89 F3 Sirba r. Burkina/Niger
190 B10 Sirbāl, Jabal mt. Egypt
187 K3 Şīr Banī Yās i. U.A.E.
Sircilla Andhra Prad. India see Sirsilla
189 N5 Sīrdān Iran
Sirdaryo r. Asia see Syrdar'ya
183 M7 Sirdaryo Uzbek.
183 M7 Sirdaryo admin. div. Uzbek.
Sirdaryo Wiloyati admin. div. Uzbek. see Sirdaryo
173 K11 Sirdingka Xizang China
92 C2 Sīrē Oromīya Eth.
92 C2 Sīrē Oromīya Eth.
93 A6 Sire Tanz.
206 F3 Sir Edward Pellew Group is N.T. Austr.
110 B4 Siren WI U.S.A.
73 L3 Sirente, Monte mt. Italy
77 O3 Siret Romania
77 Q5 Siret r. Romania
Siret r. Ukr. see Seret
208 I2 Sir Graham Moore Islands W.A. Austr.
179 K6 Sirha Nepal
190 F7 Sirḥān, Wādī as watercourse Jordan/Saudi Arabia
77 J4 Şiria Romania
184 G8 Šīrīk Iran
157 I3 Sirik, Tanjung pt Malaysia
158 E6 Siri Kit Dam Thai.
22 F2 Sirikjerka hill Norway
Sirína i. Greece see Syrna
159 D10 Sirinat National Park Thai.
185 M6 Siritoi r. Pak.
184 F6 Sīrīz Iran
185 I9 Sīrjā Iran
106 E2 Sir James MacBrien, Mount N.W.T. Can.
184 F7 Sīrjān Iran
184 F7 Sīrjān salt flat Iran
204 F6 Sir Joseph Banks Group Conservation Park nature res. S.A. Austr.
20 R3 Sirkka Fin.
178 F4 Sirmaur Hima. Prad. India
105 K2 Sirmilik National Park Nunavut Can.
71 J5 Sirmione Italy
Sirmium Vojvodina, Srbija Serb. and Mont. see Sremska Mitrovica
178 H7 Sirmour Madh. Prad. India
Sirmur Hima. Prad. India see Sirmaur
70 G1 Sirnach Switz.
189 K5 Şırnak Turkey
20 T4 Sirniö Fin.
59 J6 Sirnitz Austria
40 I3 Sirod France
178 D7 Sirohi Rajasthan India
57 J4 Sirok Hungary
57 J2 Široké Slovakia
92 B4 Siroko Uganda
71 P8 Sirolo Italy
156 B4 Sirombu Indon.
176 G3 Sironcha Mahar. India
155 C4 Sirong Sulawesi Indon.
178 F7 Sironj Madh. Prad. India
71 L3 Siròr Italy
Síros i. Greece see Syros
18 M6 Sirotsina Belarus
86 D3 Siroua, Jbel mt. Morocco
176 F3 Sirpur Andhra Prad. India
186 E6 Sirrayn Island Saudi Arabia
92 D3 Sirrei Eth.
124 N6 Sirretta Peak CA U.S.A.
184 F9 Sirrī, Jazīreh-ye i. Iran
178 E5 Sirsa Haryana India
106 G5 Sir Sandford, Mount B.C. Can.
176 D5 Sirsi Karnataka India
178 F7 Sirsi Madh. Prad. India
178 G5 Sirsi Uttar Prad. India
176 F3 Sirsilla Andhra Prad. India
Sirte Libya see Surt
Sirte, Gulf of Libya see Surt, Khalīj
204 B2 Sir Thomas, Mount hill S.A. Austr.
65 I3 Siruela Spain
176 E5 Siruguppa Karnataka India
123 J12 Sirupa r. Mex.
176 D4 Sirur Karnataka India
176 D3 Sirur Mahar. India
18 G6 Sirutiškis Lith.
189 K4 Şirvan Turkey
191 I5 Şirvan Düzü lowland Azer.
184 B1 Şirvan Düzü plain Azer.
191 J4 Şirvanovka Azer.
191 K6 Şirvan Qoruğu nature res. Azer.
176 F5 Sirvel Andhra Prad. India
55 K1 Širvinta r. Lith.
18 H6 Širvintos Lith.
186 G8 Şirwāḩ Yemen
189 L6 Sīrwān r. Iraq
106 G4 Sir Wilfrid Laurier, Mount B.C. Can.
207 I2 Sir William Thompson Range hills Qld Austr.
184 H5 Siryan Iran
185 L9 Sisa Creek inlet Pak.
68 F3 Sisak Croatia
158 G7 Sisaket Thai.
127 N7 Sisal Mex.
65 O2 Sisante Spain
62 C2 Sisargas, Illas is Spain
Siscia Croatia see Sisak
72 C2 Sisco Corse France
96 H3 Sishen S. Africa
168 J9 Sishilipu Gansu China
171 M5 Sishuang Liedao is China
191 H6 Sisian Armenia
191 G6 Sisiani Lerrnants'k pass Armenia/Azer.
88 E4 Sisili r. Burkina/Ghana
105 M3 Sisimiut Greenland
107 K4 Sisipuk Lake Man./Sask. Can.
110 F2 Siskiwit Bay MI U.S.A.
126 F4 Sisogúichic Mex.
159 F8 Sisŏphŏn Cambodia
124 L7 Sisquoc r. CA U.S.A.
70 D1 Sissach Switz.
120 G3 Sisseton SD U.S.A.
88 E4 Sissili r. Burkina
117 □R1 Sisson Branch Reservoir N.B. Can.
36 G4 Sissonne France
116 D10 Sissonville WV U.S.A.
185 I6 Sīstān reg. Iran
185 I6 Sīstan, Daryācheh-ye marsh Afgh.
184 I8 Sīstān va Balūchestān prov. Iran
57 K5 Şiştarovăț Romania
110 G4 Sister Bay WI U.S.A.
41 H8 Sisteron France
177 M7 Sisters is Andaman & Nicobar Is India
122 D4 Sisters OR U.S.A.
98 □2a Sisters Peak hill Ascension S. Atlantic Ocean
116 E9 Sistersville WV U.S.A.
73 K5 Sisto r. Italy
58 D5 Sistrans Austria
184 H8 Sīt Iran
19 U3 Sit' r. Rus. Fed.
93 A6 Sitalike Tanz.
179 J6 Sitamarhi Bihar India
178 E8 Sitamau Madh. Prad. India
95 □J3 Sitampiky Madag.
154 B9 Sitangkai Phil.
55 L5 Sitaniec Pol.
178 H6 Sitapur Uttar Prad. India
56 F2 Šitbořice Czech Rep.
79 H7 Siteia Kriti Greece
97 P2 Siteki Swaziland
66 I5 Sitges Spain
78 E2 Sithonia pen. Greece
Sitía Kriti Greece see Siteia
168 D5 Sitian Xinjiang China
95 G4 Sitila Moz.
158 H2 Siting Guizhou China
140 D5 Sítio da Abadia Brazil
140 E5 Sítio do Mato Brazil
67 E7 Sitjar, Embalse de resr Spain
104 E4 Sitka AK U.S.A.
55 I5 Sitkówka-Nowiny Pol.
178 H7 Sitlaha Madh. Prad. India
76 I8 Sitnica r. Serb. and Mont.
57 H3 Sitno mt. Slovakia
18 M4 Sitnya r. Rus. Fed.
84 E2 Sitrah oasis Egypt
18 M6 Sitsyenyets Belarus
Sittang r. Myanmar see Sittaung
45 I7 Sittard Neth.
158 B2 Sittaung Myanmar
158 C6 Sittaung r. Myanmar
48 I4 Sittensen Ger.
52 G6 Sitter r. Ger.
59 K6 Sittersdorf Austria
97 L9 Sittingbourne S. Africa
31 N5 Sittingbourne Kent, England U.K.
Sittoung r. Myanmar see Sittaung
158 A4 Sittwe Myanmar
157 K8 Situbondo Jawa Indon.
51 D9 Sitzendorf Ger.
59 M2 Sitzendorf an der Schmida Austria
51 G8 Sitzenroda Ger.
171 □I7 Siu A Chau i. H.K. China
155 C6 Siumpu i. Indon.
200 □2 Si'umu Samoa
126 □Q11 Siuna Nic.
21 R6 Siuntio Fin.
72 C8 Siurgus Donigala Sardegna Italy
179 K8 Siuri W. Bengal India
14 K4 Siva Rus. Fed.
57 I6 Sivac Vojvodina, Srbija Serb. and Mont.
176 F8 Sivaganga Tamil Nadu India
176 E8 Sivakasi Tamil Nadu India
162 E2 Sivaki Rus. Fed.
184 E6 Sivand Iran
188 H4 Sivas Turkey
79 K4 Sivaslı Turkey
88 B3 Sivé Maur.
188 I5 Siverek Turkey
18 K5 Sīvers l. Latvia
17 R5 Sivers'k Ukr.
19 N2 Siverskiy Rus. Fed.
Sivers'kyy Donets' r. Rus. Fed. see Severskiy Donets
17 S5 Sivers'kyy Donets' r. Ukr.
55 M6 Sivka-Voynylivs'ka Ukr.
14 M2 Sivomaskinskiy Rus. Fed.
188 I4 Sivrice Turkey
188 E4 Sivrihisar Turkey
45 F8 Sivry Belgium
37 J5 Sivry-sur-Meuse France
97 N2 Sivukile S. Africa
155 B5 Siwa Sulawesi Indon.
84 E2 Sīwah Egypt
84 E2 Sīwah, Wāḩāt oasis Egypt
178 F4 Siwalik Range mts India/Nepal
179 J6 Siwan Bihar India
178 D7 Siwana Rajasthan India
Siwa Oasis Egypt see Sīwah, Wāḩāt
191 H5 Şıxarx Azer.
131 □4 Six Cross Roads Barbados
41 H10 Six-Fours-les-Plages France
171 K2 Sixian Anhui China
110 I6 Six Lakes MI U.S.A.
27 E7 Sixmilebridge Rep. of Ireland
27 H3 Sixmilecross Northern Ireland U.K.
40 J5 Sixt, Réserve Naturelle de nature res. France
40 J4 Sixt-Fer-à-Cheval France
97 N1 Siyabuswa S. Africa
191 H7 Siyah Rud Iran
Siyang Guangxi China see Shangsi
171 L2 Siyang Jiangsu China
97 M2 Siyathemba S. Africa
97 O1 Siyathuthuka S. Africa
191 K4 Siyäzän Azer.
169 K6 Siyitang Nei Mongol China
184 E5 Sīyunī Iran
64 A2 Sizandro r. Port.
31 P3 Sizewell Suffolk, England U.K.
Siziwang Qi Nei Mongol China see Ulan Hua
38 C5 Sizun France
14 K2 Sizyabsk Rus. Fed.
22 H6 Sjælland i. Denmark
20 O3 Sjaunja naturreservat nature res. Sweden
76 I7 Sjenica Srbija Serb. and Mont.
21 J6 Sjoa Norway
23 J6 Sjöbo Sweden
20 I5 Sjøholt Norway
20 L3 Sjona sea chan. Norway
20 M4 Sjoutnäset Sweden
20 N2 Sjøvegan Norway
20 P4 Sjulsmark Sweden
20 □ Sjuøyane is Svalbard
20 L5 Skäckerfjällen mts Sweden
76 H8 Skadarsko Jezero nat. park Serb. and Mont.
17 L7 Skadovs'k Ukr.
22 H6 Skælsør Denmark
22 E6 Skærbæk Denmark
105 Q2 Skærfjorden inlet Greenland
105 Q3 Skaftafell nat. park Iceland
20 □E1 Skaftafell nat. park Iceland
20 □E2 Skaftárós r. mouth Iceland
20 □D1 Skagafjörður inlet Iceland
20 □C1 Skagaheiði reg. Iceland
22 G4 Skagen Denmark
22 G4 Skagen nature res. Denmark
23 K3 Skagern l. Sweden
22 E4 Skagerrak str. Denmark/Norway
122 C2 Skagit r. WA U.S.A.
106 F5 Skagit Mountain B.C. Can.
104 E4 Skagway AK U.S.A.
20 R1 Skaidi Norway
18 I7 Skaidiškės Lith.
26 J4 Skaill Orkney, Scotland U.K.
26 K5 Skaill Orkney, Scotland U.K.
79 H5 Skala Notio Aigaio Greece
78 D6 Skala Peloponnisos Greece
55 H5 Skała Pol.
79 H3 Skala Kallonis Lesvos Greece
20 N2 Skaland Norway
16 F5 Skala-Podil's'ka Ukr.
22 I5 Skälderviken b. Sweden
51 K9 Skalice Czech Rep.
191 B1 Skalistyy Khrebet reg. Rus. Fed.
57 H2 Skalité Slovakia
20 U1 Skallelv Norway
20 M4 Skalmodal Sweden
56 B1 Skalná Czech Rep.
22 F5 Skals r. Denmark
17 M9 Skalyste Ukr.
22 F5 Skanderborg Denmark
22 J6 Skåne county Sweden
23 J6 Skåne reg. Sweden
116 I6 Skaneateles NY U.S.A.
117 I6 Skaneateles Lake NY U.S.A.
22 B2 Skånevik Norway
22 B2 Skånevikfjorden sea chan. Norway
20 N4 Skansholm Sweden
78 F3 Skantzoura i. Greece
54 D3 Skąpe Pol.
22 J3 Skara Sweden
26 J4 Skara Brae tourist site Scotland U.K.
20 N2 Skarberget Norway
71 R7 Škarda i. Croatia
Skardarsko Jezero l. Albania/Yugo. see Scutari, Lake
207 I1 Skardon r. Qld Austr.
178 E2 Skardu Jammu and Kashmir
22 C2 Skare Norway
22 C3 Skåreheia mt. Norway
21 P7 Skärgårdshavets nationalpark nat. park Fin.
22 H4 Skärhamn Sweden
22 H1 Skarnes Norway
48 J1 Skarø i. Denmark
16 H2 Skarodnaye Belarus
23 N1 Skärplinge Sweden
21 L5 Skärsjövålen Sweden
21 J5 Skarstind mt. Norway
54 G1 Skarszewy Pol.
21 J5 Skarvedalseggen mt. Norway
20 N4 Skarvsjöby Sweden
55 J4 Skaryszew Pol.
16 F4 Skarzhyntsi Ukr.
55 I4 Skarżysko-Kamienna Pol.
22 I1 Skasberget hill Norway
22 I1 Skasen l. Norway
18 F6 Skaudvilė Lith.
20 P3 Skaulo Sweden
22 D1 Skaupsjøen-Hardangerjøkulen park Norway
22 E5 Skave Denmark
26 □O2 Skaw Shetland, Scotland U.K.
55 H5 Skawa r. Pol.
55 H6 Skawina Pol.
86 B4 Skaymat Western Sahara
23 O2 Skebobruk Sweden
23 L3 Skeda udde Sweden
23 O2 Skedviken l. Sweden
23 L2 Skedvisjön l. Sweden
106 D4 Skeena r. B.C. Can.
106 D3 Skeena Mountains B.C. Can.
29 R7 Skegness Lincolnshire, England U.K.
20 □E2 Skeiðarársandur sand area Iceland
26 □N2 Skeld Shetland, Scotland U.K.
26 □N2 Skelda Ness hd Scotland U.K.
48 I1 Skelde Denmark
94 B3 Skeleton Coast Game Park nature res. Namibia
20 P4 Skellefteå Sweden
20 P4 Skellefteälven r. Sweden
20 P4 Skelleftebukten b. Sweden
20 P4 Skelleftehamn Sweden
27 A9 Skellig Rocks is Rep. of Ireland
29 L6 Skelmersdale Lancashire, England U.K.
26 G11 Skelmorlie North Ayrshire, Scotland U.K.
29 P4 Skelton Redcar and Cleveland, England U.K.
Skelton-in-Cleveland England U.K. see Skelton
30 G4 Skenfrith Monmouthshire, Wales U.K.
55 H3 Skępe Pol.
21 N5 Skeppshamn Sweden
96 G4 Skerpioenpunt S. Africa
26 H5 Skerray Highland, Scotland U.K.
27 J5 Skerries Rep. of Ireland
30 E4 Sketty Swansea, Wales U.K.
16 B4 Skhidni Beskydy mts Pol./Ukr.
16 B4 Skhidni Karpaty mts Ukr.
55 L6 Skhidnytsya Ukr.
Skhimatárion Greece see Schimatari
87 H2 Skhira Tunisia
Skhíza i. Greece see Schiza
22 G2 Ski Norway
78 E3 Skiathos Greece
78 E3 Skiathos i. Greece
27 D9 Skibbereen Rep. of Ireland
20 P2 Skibotn Norway
18 H8 Skidal' Belarus
29 K4 Skiddaw hill England U.K.
106 D4 Skidegate Mission B.C. Can.
Skidel' Belarus see Skidal'
118 C6 Skidmore MD U.S.A.
18 I6 Skiemonys Lith.
22 F2 Skien Norway
55 L5 Skierbieszów Pol.
55 I4 Skierniewice Pol.
87 G1 Skikda Alg.
18 K4 Šķilbēni Latvia
78 B5 Skinari, Akra pt Zakynthos Greece
23 L2 Skinnskatteberg Sweden
178 F3 Skio Jammu and Kashmir
26 F11 Skipness Argyll and Bute, Scotland U.K.
118 E4 Skippack PA U.S.A.
29 Q6 Skipsea East Riding of Yorkshire, England U.K.
96 E10 Skipskop S. Africa
205 I7 Skipton Vic. Austr.
29 M6 Skipton North Yorkshire, England U.K.
118 C7 Skipton MD U.S.A.
29 Q6 Skirlaugh East Riding of Yorkshire, England U.K.
Skiropoúla i. Greece see Skyropoula
Skíros i. Greece see Skyros
22 F5 Skive Denmark
55 K3 Skiwy Duże Pol.
20 □E1 Skjálfandafljót r. Iceland
20 □E1 Skjálfandi b. Iceland
20 M3 Skjelatinden mt. Norway
20 L4 Skjellbreid Norway
22 G1 Skjellinhovde hill Norway
22 C1 Skjemmene mt. Norway
22 D3 Skjerkeknuten hill Norway
22 E6 Skjern Denmark
22 E6 Skjern r. Denmark
20 K4 Skjern Norway
20 M3 Skjerstadejorden inlet Norway
20 P1 Skjervøy Norway
21 I6 Skjolden Norway
48 J1 Skjoldnæs pen. Denmark
78 D3 Sklithro Greece
19 U4 Sknyatino Rus. Fed.
183 O8 Skobeleva, Pik mt. Kyrg.
59 L8 Škocjan Slovenia
59 I8 Skocjanske Jame tourist site Slovenia
54 G6 Skoczów Pol.
97 J10 Skoenmakerskop S. Africa
68 E2 Škofja Loka Slovenia
59 K8 Skofljica Slovenia
21 N6 Skog Sweden
20 R2 Skoganvarri Norway
20 T2 Skogfoss Norway
23 L5 Skoghult Sweden
30 B4 Skokholm Island Wales U.K.
54 F3 Skoki Pol.
110 G7 Skokie IL U.S.A.
182 I3 Skol' Kazakh.
16 C4 Skole Ukr.
23 L2 Sköllersta Sweden
55 J6 Skołyszyn Pol.
30 B4 Skomer Island Wales U.K.
54 G4 Skomlin Pol.
20 K3 Skomvær is Norway
97 K3 Skoonspruit r. S. Africa
78 E3 Skopelos Greece
78 E3 Skopelos i. Greece
78 G4 Skopelos i. Greece
78 G3 Skopia hill Limnos Greece
19 W8 Skopin Rus. Fed.
76 J9 Skopje Macedonia
Skoplje Macedonia see Skopje
24 D1 Skopunarfjørður sea chan. Faroe Is
54 G2 Skórcz Pol.
15 G6 Skorodnoye Rus. Fed.
54 F5 Skorogoszcz Pol.
54 F5 Skoroszyce Pol.
20 L4 Skorovatn Norway
24 J1 Skorpa i. Norway
22 F5 Skørping Denmark
55 K3 Skórzec Pol.
54 F3 Skorzęcińskie, Jezioro l. Pol.
78 E1 Skotoussa Greece
22 I2 Skotterud Norway
78 E1 Skoutari Greece
79 H3 Skoutaros Lesvos Greece
23 J3 Skövde Sweden
162 C2 Skovorodino Rus. Fed.
117 □P4 Skowhegan ME U.S.A.
22 F2 Skrimfjell hill Norway
18 I5 Skrīveri Latvia
68 D2 Škrlatica mt. Slovenia
55 J2 Skroda r. Pol.
20 P3 Skröven Sweden
18 F5 Skrunda Latvia
55 H3 Skrwa r. Pol.
55 H2 Skrwilno Pol.
19 N6 Skrydlyeva Belarus
54 E2 Skrzatusz Pol.
55 G6 Skrzyczne mt. Pol.
55 I4 Skrzyńsko Pol.
55 J6 Skrzyszów Pol.
22 B2 Skudeneshavn Norway
97 K1 Skuinsdrif S. Africa
106 C2 Skukum, Mount Y.T. Can.
95 F5 Skukuza S. Africa
20 O5 Skuleskogens nationalpark nat. park Sweden
125 P5 Skull Peak NV U.S.A.
125 T7 Skull Valley AZ U.S.A.
96 B6 Skulpfonteinpunt pt S. Africa
54 G3 Skulsk Pol.
23 M2 Skultuna Sweden
120 J5 Skunk r. IA U.S.A.
18 E5 Skuodas Lith.
19 U7 Skuratovskiy Rus. Fed.
22 J6 Skurup Sweden
77 L7 Skŭt r. Bulg.
23 N1 Skutskär Sweden
20 M2 Skutvik Norway
24 D1 Skúvoy i. Faroe Is
55 M6 Skvaryava Ukr.
16 I4 Skvyra Ukr.
54 D3 Skwierzyna Pol.
57 H3 Skýcov Slovakia
78 D2 Skydra Greece
26 D8 Skye i. Scotland U.K.
22 C3 Skykula hill Norway
145 B9 Skyring, Seno b. Chile
78 F4 Skyropoula i. Greece
78 F4 Skyros Skyros Greece
78 F4 Skyros i. Greece
118 E2 Skytop PA U.S.A.
212 S1 Skytrain Ice Rise Antarctica
18 K6 Slabodka Belarus
55 I5 Słaboszów Pol.
118 C3 Slabtown PA U.S.A.
118 F4 Slack Woods NJ U.S.A.
17 R7 Sladkiy, Liman salt l. Rus. Fed.
24 D1 Slættaratindur hill Faroe Is
22 H6 Slagelse Denmark
44 K3 Slagharen Neth.
20 O4 Slagnäs Sweden
29 M6 Slaidburn Lancashire, England U.K.
26 I11 Slamannan Falkirk, Scotland U.K.
157 H8 Slamet, Gunung vol. Indon.
57 J3 Slaná r. Slovakia
27 I5 Slane Rep. of Ireland
57 K3 Slanec Slovakia
27 I8 Slaney r. Rep. of Ireland
77 N5 Slănic Romania
77 O5 Slănic r. Romania
77 O4 Slănic Moldova Romania
57 K3 Slanské Vrchy mts Slovakia
18 L2 Slantsy Rus. Fed.
56 D1 Slaný Czech Rep.
59 I7 Slap Slovenia
18 G6 Slapaberžė Lith.
56 F2 Šlapanice Czech Rep.
68 E4 Slapovi Krke nat. park Croatia
15 H6 Slashchevskaya Rus. Fed.
207 K5 Slashers Reefs Qld Austr.
Śląsk reg. Europe see Silesia
54 F4 Śląska, Nizina lowland Pol.
55 G5 Śląska, Wyżyna hills Pol.
54 G5 Śląskie prov. Pol.
118 E3 Slateford PA U.S.A.
119 G2 Slate Hill NY U.S.A.
108 C3 Slate Islands Ont. Can.
208 J5 Slatey watercourse W.A. Austr.
68 F3 Slatina Croatia
77 M6 Slatina Romania
57 I3 Slatina r. Slovakia
77 K5 Slatina-Timiş Romania
118 D3 Slatington PA U.S.A.
56 G2 Slatinice Czech Rep.
116 E10 Slaty Fork WV U.S.A.
17 P3 Slatyne Ukr.
193 R3 Slautnoye Rus. Fed.
162 F2 Slava Rus. Fed.
106 H2 Slave r. Alta/N.W.T. Can.
89 F5 Slave Coast Africa
106 H4 Slave Lake Alta Can.
106 H2 Slave Point N.W.T. Can.
Slavgorod Belarus see Slawharad
183 R1 Slavgorod Rus. Fed.
Slavgorod Ukr. see Slavhorod
17 O5 Slavhorod Dnipropetrovs'ka Oblast' Ukr.
17 O3 Slavhorod Sums'ka Oblast' Ukr.
57 G2 Slavičín Czech Rep.
77 K7 Slavinja Srbija Serb. and Mont.
18 M4 Slavkovichi Rus. Fed.
56 B1 Slavkovský Les for. Czech Rep.
56 F2 Slavkov u Brna Czech Rep.
71 P4 Slavnik mt. Slovenia
19 T5 Slavnoye Rus. Fed.
Slavonia reg. Croatia see Slavonija
56 E3 Slavonice Czech Rep.
68 F3 Slavonija reg. Croatia
Slavonska Požega Croatia see Požega
68 G3 Slavonski Brod Croatia
57 J3 Slavošovce Slovakia
18 E6 Slavsk Rus. Fed.
16 F3 Slavuta Ukr.
16 J2 Slavutych Ukr.
162 G7 Slavyanka Rus. Fed.
77 M7 Slavyanovo Bulg.
Slavyansk Ukr. see Slov''yans'k
Slavyanskaya Rus. Fed. see Slavyansk-na-Kubani
15 G7 Slavyansk-na-Kubani Rus. Fed.
54 E4 Sława Pol.
55 L4 Sławatycze Pol.
54 F2 Sławęcin Pol.
19 O8 Slawharad Belarus
54 F2 Sławianowskie Wielkie, Jezioro l. Pol.
23 M7 Sławno Pol.
54 D2 Sławoborze Pol.
54 E4 Sławskie, Jezioro l. Pol.
54 E1 Sławsko Pol.
120 H4 Slayton MN U.S.A.
29 Q7 Slea r. England U.K.
29 Q7 Sleaford Lincolnshire, England U.K.
204 E6 Sleaford Bay S.A. Austr.
27 B8 Slea Head Rep. of Ireland
26 E8 Sleat pen. Scotland U.K.
26 D8 Sleat, Point of Scotland U.K.
26 E8 Sleat, Sound of sea chan. Scotland U.K.
107 J4 Sled Lake Sask. Can.
29 P5 Sledmere East Riding of Yorkshire, England U.K.
178 H8 Sleemanabad Madh. Prad. India
44 K3 Sleen Neth.
108 E1 Sleeper Islands Nunavut Can.
110 H5 Sleeping Bear Dunes National Lakeshore nature res. MI U.S.A.
110 H5 Sleeping Bear Point MI U.S.A.
171 □J7 Sleep Island H.K. China
44 G5 Sleeuwijk Neth.
29 P5 Sleights North Yorkshire, England U.K.
157 I8 Sleman Indon.
55 H6 Ślemień Pol.
191 G2 Sleptsovskaya Rus. Fed.
54 G3 Ślesin Pol.
212 W1 Slessor Glacier Antarctica
54 E5 Ślęża hill Pol.
54 E4 Ślęża r. Pol.
56 F1 Ślężański Park Krajobrazowy Pol.
Slezsko reg. Europe see Silesia
57 I3 Sliač Slovakia
125 X3 Slick Rock CO U.S.A.
121 K10 Slidell LA U.S.A.
117 K7 Slide Mountain NY U.S.A.
21 J6 Slidre Norway
44 G5 Sliedrecht Neth.
75 □ Sliema Malta
27 B8 Slievanea hill Rep. of Ireland
27 G4 Slieve Anierin hill Rep. of Ireland
27 G7 Slieveardagh Hills Rep. of Ireland
27 E6 Slieve Aughty Mountains hills Rep. of Ireland
27 H4 Slieve Beagh hill Rep. of Ireland/U.K.
27 E7 Slieve Bernagh hills Rep. of Ireland
27 G7 Slieve Bloom Mountains hills Rep. of Ireland
27 D7 Slievecallan hill Rep. of Ireland
27 C4 Slieve Car hill Rep. of Ireland
27 K4 Slieve Donard hill Northern Ireland U.K.
27 F7 Slievefelim Mountains hills Rep. of Ireland
28 D4 Slieve Gallion hill Northern Ireland U.K.
27 D5 Slieve Gamph hills Rep. of Ireland
27 F7 Slievekimalta hill Rep. of Ireland
27 H3 Slievekirk hill Northern Ireland U.K.
27 B8 Slieve Mish Mountains hills Rep. of Ireland
27 B9 Slieve Miskish Mountains hills Rep. of Ireland
27 G4 Slievenakilla hill Rep. of Ireland
27 G8 Slievenamon hill Rep. of Ireland
28 B5 Slieve Rushen hill Northern Ireland U.K.
27 F3 Slieve Snaght hill Rep. of Ireland
27 H2 Slieve Snaght hill Rep. of Ireland
26 D8 Sligachan Highland, Scotland U.K.
Sligeach Rep. of Ireland see Sligo
27 F4 Sligo Rep. of Ireland
27 E4 Sligo county Rep. of Ireland
116 F7 Sligo PA U.S.A.
27 E4 Sligo Bay Rep. of Ireland
55 K2 Ślina r. Pol.
31 L5 Slinfold West Sussex, England U.K.
44 J4 Slinge r. Neth.
26 F7 Slioch hill Scotland U.K.
17 L4 Sliporid r. Ukr.
202 J4 Slipper Island North I. N.Z.
116 E7 Slippery Rock PA U.S.A.
23 O4 Slite Gotland Sweden
18 F4 Slīteres rezervāts nature res. Latvia
77 O8 Sliven Bulg.
77 L8 Slivnitsa Bulg.
77 O7 Slivo Pole Bulg.
54 G2 Śliwice Pol.
68 E3 Sljeme mt. Croatia
57 G3 Sĺňava l. Slovakia
125 Q6 Sloan NV U.S.A.
124 L2 Sloat CA U.S.A.
119 G2 Sloatsburg NY U.S.A.
16 I6 Slobidka Ukr.
14 I3 Sloboda Arkhangel'skaya Oblast' Rus. Fed.
Sloboda Smolenskaya Oblast' Rus. Fed. see Przheval'skoye
15 H6 Sloboda Voronezhskaya Oblast' Rus. Fed.
17 M2 Sloboda Ukr.
14 J3 Slobodchikovo Rus. Fed.
19 R7 Slobodka Rus. Fed.
14 J4 Slobodskoy Rus. Fed.
Slobodzeya Moldova see Slobozia
16 I7 Slobozia Moldova
77 P6 Slobozia Romania
77 P5 Slobozia Bradului Romania
106 G5 Slocan B.C. Can.
44 K2 Slochteren Neth.
55 I5 Słomniki Pol.
18 I8 Slonim Belarus
17 Q3 Slonovka Rus. Fed.
54 D2 Słonowice Pol.
54 C3 Słońsk Pol.
44 G3 Slootdorp Neth.
44 I3 Sloten Neth.
44 I3 Slotermeer l. Neth.
31 K4 Slough Slough, England U.K.
31 K4 Slough admin. div. England U.K.
56 F2 Sloupnice Czech Rep.
17 M2 Slout Ukr.
57 I3 Slovakia country Europe
16 H2 Slovechna r. Ukr.
16 H2 Slovechne Ukr.
68 E2 Slovenia country Europe
Slovenija country Europe see Slovenia
68 E2 Slovenj Gradec Slovenia
68 E2 Slovenska Bistrica Slovenia
57 J2 Slovenská Ves Slovakia
68 E2 Slovenske Gorice hills Slovenia
59 L7 Slovenske Konjice Slovenia
57 K3 Slovenské Nové Mesto Slovakia
57 I3 Slovenské Rudohorie mts Slovakia
Slovensko country Europe see Slovakia
57 J3 Slovenský kras mts Slovakia
57 J3 Slovenský kras park Slovakia
57 J3 Slovenský raj nat. park Slovakia
57 J3 Slovinky Slovakia
55 M6 Slovita Ukr.
17 P5 Slov''yanka Ukr.
17 Q4 Slov''yanohirs'k Ukr.
17 R5 Slov''yanoserbs'k Ukr.
17 Q5 Slov''yans'k Ukr.
17 M8 Slov''yans'ke Ukr.
16 I2 Slovyechna r. Belarus
55 H4 Słowik Pol.
23 N7 Słowiński Park Narodowy nat. park Pol.
54 C3 Słubice Lubuskie Pol.
55 H3 Słubice Mazowieckie Pol.
18 K9 Sluch r. Belarus
16 F2 Sluch r. Ukr.
71 J2 Sluderno Italy
14 L4 Sludka Permskaya Oblast' Rus. Fed.
14 J4 Sludka Respublika Komi Rus. Fed.
45 D6 Sluis Neth.
45 E6 Sluiskil Neth.
56 D1 Šluknov Czech Rep.
56 G2 Slunečná hill Czech Rep.
159 H9 S'Lung, B'Nom mt. Vietnam
68 E3 Slunj Croatia
54 F3 Słupca Pol.
55 J5 Słupcza Pol.
55 H4 Słupia Łódzkie Pol.
55 H5 Słupia Świętokrzyskie Pol.
55 I4 Słupia Świętokrzyskie Pol.
23 M7 Słupia r. Pol.
55 H3 Słupno Pol.
23 N7 Słupsk Pol.
20 N4 Slussfors Sweden
54 G4 Słuszków Pol.
18 K8 Slutsk Belarus
18 F6 Šlyna r. Lith.
27 B6 Slyne Head Rep. of Ireland
160 H1 Slyudyanka Rus. Fed.
121 I9 Smackover AR U.S.A.
42 B2 Smagne r. France
26 K11 Smailholm Scottish Borders, Scotland U.K.
23 K4 Småland reg. Sweden
22 H6 Smålandsfarvandet sea chan. Denmark
22 J4 Smålandsstenar Sweden
31 J2 Smalley Derbyshire, England U.K.
117 □P5 Small Point ME U.S.A.
109 H2 Smallwood Reservoir Nfld and Lab. Can.
19 N6 Smalowka Belarus
55 M3 Smalyanitsa Belarus
18 L7 Smalyavichy Belarus
55 I4 Smardzewice Pol.
54 D3 Smardzewo Pol.
54 D2 Smardzko Pol.
18 J7 Smarhon' Belarus
59 M7 Šmarje pri Jelšah Slovenia
59 L8 Šmarjeta Slovenia
59 L7 Šmartinsko jezero l. Slovenia
107 J2 Smart Lake N.W.T. Can.
59 K7 Šmartno Mozirje Slovenia
59 L7 Šmartno Slovenj Gradec Slovenia
96 H6 Smartt Syndicate Dam resr S. Africa
42 E2 Smarves France
107 J4 Smeaton Sask. Can.
51 J10 Smečno Czech Rep.
56 D1 Smědá r. Czech Rep.
23 M5 Smedby Sweden
76 I6 Smederevo Srbija Serb. and Mont.
76 I6 Smederevska Palanka Srbija Serb. and Mont.
77 O5 Smeeni Romania
31 N5 Smeeth Kent, England U.K.
Smela Ukr. see Smila
20 U1 Smelror Norway
116 G7 Smethport PA U.S.A.
31 I3 Smethwick West Midlands, England U.K.
54 G2 Smętowo Graniczne Pol.
56 E1 Smidary Czech Rep.
55 M4 Smidyn Ukr.
54 E3 Śmigiel Pol.
17 K4 Smila Ukr.
18 L8 Smilavichy Belarus
44 J3 Smilde Neth.
17 M3 Smile Ukr.
16 G3 Smilka r. Ukr.
54 E2 Śmiłowo Pol.
18 I4 Smiltene Latvia
18 F5 Smiltiņu kalns hill Latvia
20 M2 Smines Norway
56 E1 Smiřice Czech Rep.
183 M1 Smirnovo Kazakh.
Smirnovskiy Kazakh. see Smirnovo
162 M4 Smirnykh Sakhalin Rus. Fed.
106 H4 Smith Alta Can.
122 I3 Smith r. MT U.S.A.
116 F12 Smith r. VA U.S.A.
104 F3 Smith Arm b. N.W.T. Can.
104 C2 Smith Bay AK U.S.A.
27 H4 Smithborough Rep. of Ireland
120 F6 Smith Center KS U.S.A.
106 E4 Smithers B.C. Can.
106 E4 Smithers Landing B.C. Can.
97 K6 Smithfield S. Africa
115 H8 Smithfield NC U.S.A.
122 I6 Smithfield UT U.S.A.
116 I12 Smithfield VA U.S.A.
212 Q1 Smith Glacier Antarctica
212 T2 Smith Island Antarctica
105 K3 Smith Island Nunavut Can.
177 M6 Smith Island Andaman & Nicobar Is India
117 I10 Smith Island MD U.S.A.
117 J11 Smith Island VA U.S.A.
121 K7 Smithland KY U.S.A.
116 F11 Smith Mountain Lake VA U.S.A.
206 C1 Smith Point N.T. Austr.
106 E3 Smith River B.C. Can.
116 H9 Smithsburg MD U.S.A.
108 E4 Smiths Falls Ont. Can.
208 □1 Smithson Bight b. Christmas I.
105 K2 Smith Sound sea chan. Can./Greenland
205 J9 Smithton Tas. Austr.
205 N4 Smithtown N.S.W. Austr.
119 I3 Smithtown NY U.S.A.
119 G6 Smithville NJ U.S.A.
121 H8 Smithville OK U.S.A.
115 E8 Smithville TN U.S.A.
116 D9 Smithville WV U.S.A.
96 I9 Smitskraal S. Africa
57 J3 Smižany Slovakia
20 □F1 Smjörfjöll mts Iceland
124 M1 Smoke Creek Desert NV U.S.A.
106 G3 Smoky r. Alta Can.
204 D5 Smoky Bay S.A. Austr.
204 D5 Smoky Bay b. S.A. Austr.
205 N4 Smoky Cape N.S.W. Austr.
206 G7 Smoky Creek watercourse Qld Austr.
108 D3 Smoky Falls Ont. Can.
120 E6 Smoky Hill r. KS U.S.A.
120 E6 Smoky Hill, North Fork r. KS U.S.A.
112 G3 Smoky Hills KS U.S.A.
120 F6 Smoky Hills KS U.S.A.
107 H4 Smoky Lake Alta Can.
122 G5 Smoky Mountains ID U.S.A.
20 I5 Smøla i. Norway
54 F1 Smołdzino Pol.
182 C2 Smolenka Rus. Fed.
19 P7 Smolensk Rus. Fed.
19 Q7 Smolenskaya Oblast' admin. div. Rus. Fed.
Smolensk Oblast admin. div. Rus. Fed. see Smolenskaya Oblast'
19 P7 Smolensko-Moskovskaya Vozvyshennost' hills Rus. Fed.
183 U1 Smolenskoye Rus. Fed.
Smolevichi Belarus see Smalyavichy
54 F4 Smolice Pol.
78 B2 Smolikas mt. Greece
17 K5 Smoline Ukr.
22 I2 Smolmark Sweden
50 K5 Smolnica Pol.
57 J3 Smolník Slovakia
77 M9 Smolyan Bulg.
162 H7 Smolyoninovo Rus. Fed.
108 D3 Smooth Rock Falls Ont. Can.
108 B3 Smoothrock Lake Ont. Can.
107 J4 Smoothstone Lake Sask. Can.
20 R1 Smørfjord Norway
Smorgon' Belarus see Smarhon'
19 P9 Smotrova Buda Rus. Fed.
16 F5 Smotrych Ukr.
17 L3 Smotryky Ukr.
56 G1 Smrk mt. Czech Rep.
51 L9 Smrk mt. Czech Rep.
17 K2 Smyach Ukr.
77 P7 Smyadovo Bulg.
22 J6 Smygehamn Sweden
16 E3 Smyha Ukr.
55 I4 Smyków Pol.
212 S2 Smyley Island Antarctica
Smyrna Turkey see İzmir
118 D6 Smyrna DE U.S.A.
115 E9 Smyrna GA U.S.A.
115 D8 Smyrna TN U.S.A.
118 D6 Smyrna r. DE U.S.A.
117 □Q2 Smyrna Mills ME U.S.A.
145 B8 Smyth, Canal sea chan. Chile
20 □F1 Snæfell mt. Iceland
28 I5 Snaefell hill Isle of Man
20 □B1 Snæfellsjökull ice cap Iceland
20 □B1 Snæfellsnes pen. Iceland
106 A2 Snag Y.T. Can.
29 P5 Snainton North Yorkshire, England U.K.
29 O6 Snaith East Riding of Yorkshire, England U.K.
120 E4 Snake r. NE U.S.A.
122 E3 Snake r. U.S.A.
206 B3 Snake Creek r. N.T. Austr.
125 R2 Snake Range mts NV U.S.A.
106 F3 Snake River B.C. Can.
122 G5 Snake River Plain ID U.S.A.
106 G2 Snare r. N.W.T. Can.
106 H1 Snare Lake N.W.T. Can.
107 J3 Snare Lake Sask. Can.
Snare Lakes N.W.T. Can. see Wekweti
199 G6 Snares Islands N.Z.
20 L4 Snåsa Norway
20 L4 Snåsvatn l. Norway
116 B12 Sneedville TN U.S.A.
44 I2 Sneek Neth.
44 I2 Sneekermeer l. Neth.
27 C9 Sneem Rep. of Ireland
96 D8 Sneeuberg mt. S. Africa
96 I7 Sneeuberge mts S. Africa
109 I2 Snegamook Lake Nfld and Lab. Can.
Snegurovka Ukr. see Tetiyiv
124 L4 Snelling CA U.S.A.
18 E5 Snēpele Latvia
31 N2 Snettisham Norfolk, England U.K.
19 T8 Snezhed' r. Rus. Fed.
192 J3 Snezhnogorsk Rus. Fed.
162 E1 Snezhnogorskiy Rus. Fed.
Snezhnoye Ukr. see Snizhne
56 E1 Sněžka mt. Czech Rep.
68 E3 Snežnik mt. Slovenia
55 J2 Śniadowo Pol.
55 J2 Śniardwy, Jezioro l. Pol.
Sniečkus Lith. see Visaginas
Snieżka mt. Czech Rep. see Sněžka
56 F1 Śnieżnicki Park Krajobrazowy Pol.
54 E5 Śnieżnik mt. Pol.
17 L6 Snihurivka Ukr.
57 L3 Snina Slovakia
31 I3 Snitterfield Warwickshire, England U.K.
17 M3 Snityn Ukr.
17 R5 Snizhne Ukr.
26 D7 Snizort, Loch b. Scotland U.K.
21 J5 Snøhetta mt. Norway
122 C3 Snohomish WA U.S.A.
22 C2 Snønuten mt. Norway
19 Q8 Snopot' r. Rus. Fed.
Snoul Cambodia see Snuŏl
17 K2 Snov r. Ukr.

South Brook to **Staroye Melkovo**

342

109 J3 **South Brook** *Nfld and Lab.* Can.
97 O6 **Southbroom** S. Africa
117 L4 **South Burlington** *VT* U.S.A.
203 F11 **Southburn** *South I.* N.Z.
119 I2 **Southbury** *CT* U.S.A.
118 E1 **South Canaan** *PA* U.S.A.
115 G8 **South Carolina** *state* U.S.A.
29 P6 **South Cave** *East Riding of Yorkshire, England* U.K.
31 I4 **South Cerney** *Gloucestershire, England* U.K.
30 G6 **South Chard** *Somerset, England* U.K.
116 B9 **South Charleston** *OH* U.S.A.
116 D10 **South Charleston** *WV* U.S.A.
152 E4 **South China Sea** N. Pacific Ocean
120 E3 **South Dakota** *state* U.S.A.
26 K12 **Southdean** *Scottish Borders, Scotland* U.K.
117 M6 **South Deerfield** *MA* U.S.A.
118 F6 **South Dennis** *NJ* U.S.A.
30 G6 **South Dorset Downs** *hills England* U.K.
31 L6 **South Downs** *hills England* U.K.
98 □2a **South East Bay** *Ascension* S. Atlantic Ocean
205 K10 **South East Cape** *Tas.* Austr.
205 L7 **South East Forests National Park** *N.S.W.* Austr.
215 J7 **Southeast Indian Ridge** *sea feature* Indian Ocean
South-East Island *Inner Islands* Seychelles *see* **Suète, Île du**
209 G13 **South East Isles** *W.A.* Austr.
217 L10 **Southeast Pacific Basin** *sea feature* S. Pacific Ocean
130 G3 **Southeast Point** *Gt Inagua* Bahamas
204 □3 **South East Reef** S. Pacific Ocean
204 □2 **South East Rock** *i. Lord Howe I.* Austr.
118 F5 **South Egg Harbor** *NJ* U.S.A.
107 K3 **Southend** *Sask.* Can.
26 E12 **Southend** *Argyll and Bute, Scotland* U.K.
31 N4 **Southend** *admin. div. England* U.K.
31 N4 **Southend-on-Sea** *Southend, England* U.K.
99 □1b **South Entrance** *sea chan.* Mauritius
93 B8 **Southern** *admin. reg.* Malawi
88 B5 **Southern** *prov.* Sierra Leone
91 E9 **Southern** *prov.* Zambia
203 E10 **Southern Alps** *mts South I.* N.Z.
209 H9 **Southern Central Aboriginal Reserve** *W.A.* Austr.
203 □2 **Southern Cook Islands** Cook Is
209 E11 **Southern Cross** *W.A.* Austr.
90 E2 **Southern Darfur** *state* Sudan
107 L3 **Southern Indian Lake** *Man.* Can.
90 F2 **Southern Kordofan** *state* Sudan
199 I3 **Southern Lau Group** *is* Fiji
91 D9 **Southern Lueti** *watercourse* Angola/Zambia
90 F3 **Southern National Park** Sudan
212 R3 **Southern Ocean**
115 H8 **Southern Pines** *NC* U.S.A.
Southern Rhodesia *country* Africa *see* **Zimbabwe**
135 G7 **Southern Thule** *is* S. Sandwich Is
26 G12 **Southern Uplands** *hills Scotland* U.K.
Southern Urals *mts* Rus. Fed. *see* **Yuzhnyy Ural**
123 K8 **Southern Ute Indian Reservation** *res. CO* U.S.A.
31 M2 **Southery** *Norfolk, England* U.K.
26 K9 **South Esk** *r. Angus, Scotland* U.K.
208 I5 **South Esk Tableland** *reg. W.A.* Austr.
107 J5 **Southey** *Sask.* Can.
97 L7 **Southeyville** S. Africa
120 J6 **South Fabius** *r. MO* U.S.A.
121 K6 **Southfield** *MI* U.S.A.
119 J2 **Southfields** *NY* U.S.A.
216 G7 **South Fiji Basin** *sea feature* S. Pacific Ocean
31 O5 **South Foreland** *pt England* U.K.
124 I1 **South Fork** *CA* U.S.A.
123 K8 **South Fork** *CO* U.S.A.
116 G8 **South Fork** *PA* U.S.A.
110 I4 **South Fox Island** *MI* U.S.A.
131 □2 **South Friar's Bay** St Kitts and Nevis
106 E5 **Southgate** *r. B.C.* Can.
31 L4 **Southgate** *Greater London, England* U.K.
213 H1 **South Geomagnetic Pole** Antarctica
135 G7 **South Georgia and South Sandwich Islands** *terr.* S. Atlantic Ocean
118 D1 **South Gibson** *PA* U.S.A.
110 E1 **South Gillies** *Ont.* Can.
119 J1 **South Glastonbury** *CT* U.S.A.
30 H4 **South Gloucestershire** *admin. div. England* U.K.
120 H6 **South Grand** *r. MO* U.S.A.
31 K6 **South Harting** *West Sussex, England* U.K.
179 M8 **South Hatia Island** Bangl.
110 H7 **South Haven** *MI* U.S.A.
31 K6 **South Hayling** *Hampshire, England* U.K.
202 I3 **South Head** *North I.* N.Z.
202 I3 **South Head** *hd North I.* N.Z.
107 L2 **South Henik Lake** *Nunavut* Can.
117 L4 **South Hero** *VT* U.S.A.
29 O4 **South Hetton** *Durham, England* U.K.
98 □2c **South Hill** *Tristan da Cunha* S. Atlantic Ocean
116 G12 **South Hill** *VA* U.S.A.
216 E3 **South Honshu Ridge** *sea feature* N. Pacific Ocean
92 C4 **South Horr** Kenya
107 L3 **South Indian Lake** *Man.* Can.
119 J1 **Southington** *CT* U.S.A.
208 □2 **South Island** Cocos Is
176 C7 **South Island** India
203 G11 **South Island** N.Z.
92 C4 **South Island National Park** Kenya
154 B7 **South Islet** *rf* Phil.
107 M5 **South Junction** *Man.* Can.
South Kazakhstan Oblast *admin. div.* Kazakh. *see* **Yuzhnyy Kazakhstan**
29 Q7 **South Kelsey** *Lincolnshire, England* U.K.
29 O6 **South Kirkby** *West Yorkshire, England* U.K.
93 C5 **South Kitui National Reserve** *nature res.* Kenya
179 J8 **South Koel** *r. Jharkhand* India
124 L3 **South Lake Tahoe** *CA* U.S.A.
26 I11 **South Lanarkshire** *admin. div. Scotland* U.K.
203 B12 **Southland** *admin. reg. South I.* N.Z.
31 N3 **South Lopham** *Norfolk, England* U.K.
120 F5 **South Loup** *r. NE* U.S.A.
93 A8 **South Luangwa National Park** Zambia
119 K2 **South Lyme** *CT* U.S.A.
106 C2 **South Macmillan** *r. Y.T.* Can.
213 J2 **South Magnetic Pole** Antarctica
175 □1 **South Male Atoll** Maldives
31 N4 **Southminster** *Essex, England* U.K.
65 □ **South Mole** Gibraltar
30 E5 **South Molton** *Devon, England* U.K.
107 K4 **South Moose Lake** *Man.* Can.
118 A5 **South Mountains** *hills PA* U.S.A.
208 C6 **South Muiron Island** *W.A.* Austr.
106 D1 **South Nahanni** *r. N.W.T.* Can.
130 □ **South Negril Point** Jamaica
26 □N2 **South Nesting Bay** *Scotland* U.K.
117 J6 **South New Berlin** *NY* U.S.A.
31 M4 **South Ockendon** *Thurrock, England* U.K.
119 K2 **Southold** *NY* U.S.A.
214 G10 **South Orkney Islands** S. Atlantic Ocean
South Ossetia *aut. reg.* Georgia *see* **Samkhret' Oset'i**
31 L4 **South Oxhey** *Hertfordshire, England* U.K.
119 I3 **South Oyster Bay** *NY* U.S.A.
117 □O4 **South Paris** *ME* U.S.A.
209 B9 **South Passage** *W.A.* Austr.
200 □3a **South Passage** *Kwajalein* Marshall Is
115 G11 **South Patrick Shores** *FL* U.S.A.
30 G6 **South Petherton** *Somerset, England* U.K.
119 G3 **South Plainfield** *NJ* U.S.A.
120 E5 **South Platte** *r. CO* U.S.A.
130 F2 **South Point** *Long I.* Bahamas
131 □ **South Point** Barbados
208 □1 **South Point** Christmas I.
98 □2a **South Point** *Ascension* S. Atlantic Ocean
212 T1 **South Pole** Antarctica
108 D3 **South Porcupine** *Ont.* Can.
207 N9 **Southport** *Qld* Austr.
205 K10 **Southport** *Tas.* Austr.
29 K6 **Southport** *Merseyside, England* U.K.
119 I2 **Southport** *CT* U.S.A.
115 H9 **Southport** *NC* U.S.A.
117 I6 **Southport** *NY* U.S.A.
117 □O5 **South Portland** *ME* U.S.A.
26 J11 **South Queensferry** *Edinburgh, Scotland* U.K.
204 □3 **South Reef** S. Pacific Ocean
111 O4 **South River** *Ont.* Can.
26 □ **South Rona** *i. Highland, Scotland* U.K. *see* **Rona**
26 K5 **South Ronaldsay** *i. Scotland* U.K.
117 M5 **South Royalton** *VT* U.S.A.
110 A5 **South St Paul** *MN* U.S.A.
214 H9 **South Sandwich Islands** S. Atlantic Ocean
214 H9 **South Sandwich Trench** *sea feature* S. Atlantic Ocean
124 J4 **South San Francisco** *CA* U.S.A.
107 J4 **South Saskatchewan** *r. Alta/Sask.* Can.
107 L3 **South Seal** *r. Man.* Can.
212 U2 **South Shetland Islands** Antarctica
214 E10 **South Shetland Trough** *sea feature* S. Atlantic Ocean
29 O3 **South Shields** *Tyne and Wear, England* U.K.
120 I5 **South Skunk** *r. IA* U.S.A.
216 F6 **South Solomon Trench** *sea feature* Pacific Ocean
27 D6 **South Sound** *sea chan.* Rep. of Ireland
105 K3 **South Spicer Island** *Nunavut* Can.
118 E2 **South Sterling** *PA* U.S.A.
118 D3 **South Tamaqua** *PA* U.S.A.
202 I6 **South Taranaki Bight** *b. North I.* N.Z.
215 N8 **South Tasman Rise** *sea feature* Southern Ocean
122 J5 **South Tent** *mt. UT* U.S.A.
119 G5 **South Toms River** *NJ* U.S.A.
178 I7 **South Tons** *r.* India
125 V9 **South Tucson** *AZ* U.S.A.
92 B4 **South Turkana Nature Reserve** Kenya
108 E2 **South Twin Island** *Nunavut* Can.
109 K3 **South Twin Lake** *Nfld and Lab.* Can.
29 M4 **South Tyne** *r. England* U.K.
26 B8 **South Uist** *i. Scotland* U.K.
122 C5 **South Umpqua** *r. OR* U.S.A.
26 J5 **South Walls** *pen. Scotland* U.K.
31 L5 **Southwater** *West Sussex, England* U.K.
29 P7 **Southwell** *Nottinghamshire, England* U.K.
206 G4 **South Wellesley Islands** *Qld* Austr.
South-West Africa *country* Africa *see* **Namibia**
115 □2 **South West Bay** *New Prov.* Bahamas
98 □2a **South West Bay** *Ascension* S. Atlantic Ocean
205 K10 **South West Cape** *Tas.* Austr.
203 B14 **South West Cape** *Stewart I.* N.Z.
207 N6 **South West Cay** *rf Coral Sea Is Terr.* Austr.
205 J9 **Southwest Conservation Area** *nature res. Tas.* Austr.
207 M1 **South West Entrance** *sea chan.* P.N.G.
117 □Q4 **Southwest Harbor** *ME* U.S.A.
215 G7 **Southwest Indian Ridge** *sea feature* Indian Ocean
207 L4 **South West Island** *Coral Sea Is Terr.* Austr.
205 K10 **South West National Park** *Tas.* Austr.
217 I8 **Southwest Pacific Basin** *sea feature* S. Pacific Ocean
130 □ **South West Point** Jamaica
98 □2b **South West Point** *St Helena*
130 □ **Southwest Rock** *i.* Jamaica
205 N4 **South West Rocks** *N.S.W.* Austr.
110 I8 **South Whitley** *IN* U.S.A.
121 F9 **South Wichita** *r. TX* U.S.A.
30 H5 **Southwick** *Wiltshire, England* U.K.
116 C11 **South Williamson** *KY* U.S.A.
111 R8 **South Williamsport** *PA* U.S.A.
117 □O5 **South Windham** *ME* U.S.A.
31 P3 **Southwold** *Suffolk, England* U.K.
31 N4 **South Woodham Ferrers** *Essex, England* U.K.
207 M9 **Southwood National Park** *Qld* Austr.
30 G2 **South Wootton** *Norfolk, England* U.K.
29 O7 **South Yorkshire** *admin. div. England* U.K.
116 C9 **South Zanesville** *OH* U.S.A.
62 G8 **Souto** *Guarda* Port.
62 D9 **Souto** *Santarém* Port.
62 E3 **Souto** Spain
62 B8 **Souto da Casa** Port.
97 K4 **Soutpan** S. Africa
95 F4 **Soutpansberg** *mts* S. Africa
86 B5 **Souttouf, Adrar** *mts* Western Sahara
40 C3 **Souvigny** France
22 C1 **Sovarnuten** *mt.* Norway
77 N4 **Sovata** Romania
77 O4 **Soveja** Romania
146 E4 **Soven** Arg.
75 L6 **Soverato** Italy
72 C3 **Soveria** *Corse* France
75 K5 **Soveria Mannelli** Italy
183 N7 **Sovet** Kyrg.
185 M2 **Sovet** Tajik.
Sovetabad Uzbek. *see* **Xonobod**
Sovetashen Armenia *see* **Zangakatun**
18 E6 **Sovetsk** *Kaliningradskaya Oblast'* Rus. Fed.
14 J4 **Sovetsk** *Kirovskaya Oblast'* Rus. Fed.
19 U8 **Sovetsk** *Tul'skaya Oblast'* Rus. Fed.
191 C1 **Sovetskaya** *Krasnodarskiy Kray* Rus. Fed.
191 F1 **Sovetskaya** *Stavropol'skiy Kray* Rus. Fed.
162 L4 **Sovetskaya Gavan'** Rus. Fed.
Sovetskiy Kyrg. *see* **Sovet**
192 H3 **Sovetskiy** *Khanty-Mansiyskiy Avtonomnyy Okrug* Rus. Fed.
18 L1 **Sovetskiy** *Leningradskaya Oblast'* Rus. Fed.
14 N2 **Sovetskiy** *Respublika Komi* Rus. Fed.
14 J4 **Sovetskiy** *Respublika Mariy El* Rus. Fed.
Sovetskiy Tajik. *see* **Sovet**
17 S3 **Sovetskoye** *Belgorodskaya Oblast'* Rus. Fed.
Sovetskoye *Chechenskaya Respublika* Rus. Fed. *see* **Shatoy**
182 B2 **Sovetskoye** *Saratovskaya Oblast'* Rus. Fed.
Sovetskoye *Stavropol'skiy Kray* Rus. Fed. *see* **Zelenokumsk**
68 F4 **Sovići** Bos.-Herz.
71 K9 **Sovicille** Italy
14 H2 **Sovpol'ye** Rus. Fed.
17 N8 **Sovyets'kyy** Ukr.
94 E4 **Sowa** Botswana
170 B4 **Sowa** *Sichuan* China
167 K3 **Sōwa** Japan
94 E4 **Sowa Pan** *salt pan* Botswana
29 O5 **Sowerby** *North Yorkshire, England* U.K.
29 N6 **Sowerby Bridge** *West Yorkshire, England* U.K.
97 L2 **Soweto** S. Africa
54 C2 **Sowno** *Zachodniopomorskie* Pol.
54 E1 **Sowno** *Zachodniopomorskie* Pol.
127 M9 **Soyaló** Mex.
164 S1 **Sōya-misaki** *c.* Japan
14 H2 **Soyana** *r.* Rus. Fed.
163 E9 **Soyang-ho** *l.* S. Korea
42 E4 **Soyaux** France
164 S1 **Sōya-wan** *b.* Japan
40 I2 **Soye** France
53 M5 **Soyen** Ger.
Soylan Armenia *see* **Vayk'**
14 J2 **Soyma** *r.* Rus. Fed.
91 B6 **Soyo** Angola
41 F7 **Soyons** France
126 E3 **Soyopa** Mex.
191 G5 **Soyuqbulaq** Azer.
Sozaq Kazakh. *see* **Suzak**
19 N9 **Sozh** *r.* Europe
14 K4 **Sozimskiy** Rus. Fed.
77 P8 **Sozopol** Bulg.
45 I8 **Spa** Belgium
212 T2 **Spaatz Island** Antarctica
52 D2 **Spabrücken** Ger.
75 I7 **Spadafora** *Sicilia* Italy
48 E5 **Spahnharrenstätte** Ger.
52 F5 **Spaichingen** Ger.
60 E2 **Spain** *country* Europe
Spalato Croatia *see* **Split**
Spalatum Croatia *see* **Split**
204 G5 **Spalding** *S.A.* Austr.
31 L2 **Spalding** *Lincolnshire, England* U.K.
56 C2 **Spálené Poříčí** Czech Rep.
53 J3 **Spalt** Ger.
49 I8 **Spangenberg** Ger.
30 E5 **Span Head** *hill England* U.K.
109 K4 **Spaniard's Bay** *Nfld and Lab.* Can.
108 D4 **Spanish** *Ont.* Can.
108 D4 **Spanish** *r. Ont.* Can.
125 U1 **Spanish Fork** *UT* U.S.A.
131 □2 **Spanish Point** Antigua and Barbuda
115 □1 **Spanish Point** Bermuda
25 C5 **Spanish Point** Rep. of Ireland
Spanish Sahara *terr.* Africa *see* **Western Sahara**
130 □ **Spanish Town** Jamaica
130 E1 **Spanish Wells** *Eleuthera* Bahamas
50 I3 **Spantekow** Ger.
74 D7 **Sparagio, Monte** *mt.* Italy
73 M5 **Sparanise** Italy
72 C5 **Spargi, Isola** *i. Sardegna* Italy
124 M2 **Sparks** *NV* U.S.A.
110 G5 **Sparlingville** *MI* U.S.A.
118 F2 **Sparrow Bush** *NY* U.S.A.
Sparta Greece *see* **Sparti**
75 J7 **Spartà** *Sicilia* Italy
115 F9 **Sparta** *GA* U.S.A.
110 I6 **Sparta** *MI* U.S.A.
116 D12 **Sparta** *NC* U.S.A.
118 F2 **Sparta** *NJ* U.S.A.
115 E8 **Sparta** *TN* U.S.A.
110 D6 **Sparta** *WI* U.S.A.
115 G8 **Spartanburg** *SC* U.S.A.
116 F7 **Spartansburg** *PA* U.S.A.
60 D5 **Spartel, Cap** *c.* Morocco
79 I5 **Sparti** Greece
72 B10 **Spartivento, Capo** *c. Sardegna* Italy
75 K8 **Spartivento, Capo** *c.* Italy
106 H5 **Sparwood** *B.C.* Can.
19 R7 **Spas-Demensk** Rus. Fed.
17 O5 **Spas'ke** Ukr.
19 X6 **Spas-Klepiki** Rus. Fed.
17 P5 **Spas'ko-Mykhaylivka** Ukr.
17 M5 **Spasove** Ukr.
19 S6 **Spass** Rus. Fed.
14 F3 **Spasskaya Guba** Rus. Fed.
19 O3 **Spasskaya Polist'** Rus. Fed.
162 H6 **Spassk-Dal'niy** Rus. Fed.
183 M1 **Spasskoye** Kazakh.
19 T8 **Spasskoye-Lutovinovo** Rus. Fed.
19 X7 **Spassk-Ryazanskiy** Rus. Fed.
19 U5 **Spas-Ugol** Rus. Fed.
78 F7 **Spatha, Akra** *pt Kriti* Greece
78 D6 **Spathi, Akra** *pt Kythira* Greece
106 D3 **Spatsizi Plateau Wilderness Provincial Park** *B.C.* Can.
49 E10 **Spay** Ger.
26 G9 **Spean Bridge** *Highland, Scotland* U.K.
120 D3 **Spearfish** *SD* U.S.A.
121 E7 **Spearman** *TX* U.S.A.
75 O4 **Specchia** Italy
117 K5 **Speculator** *NY* U.S.A.
31 J5 **Speen** *West Berkshire, England* U.K.
70 G1 **Speer** *mt.* Switz.
107 J4 **Speers** *Sask.* Can.
98 □2b **Speery Island** St Helena
52 G2 **Speicher** Ger.
59 H5 **Speicher Sameralm** *l.* Austria
53 L2 **Speichersdorf** Ger.
131 □4 **Speightstown** Barbados
59 K6 **Speikkogel** *mt.* Austria
93 B5 **Speke Gulf** Tanz.
49 D6 **Spelle** Ger.
73 J2 **Spello** Italy
26 E10 **Spelve, Loch** *inlet Scotland* U.K.
Spence Bay *Nunavut* Can. *see* **Taloyoak**
120 H4 **Spencer** *IA* U.S.A.
122 H4 **Spencer** *ID* U.S.A.
114 D6 **Spencer** *IN* U.S.A.
117 N6 **Spencer** *MA* U.S.A.
120 G4 **Spencer** *NE* U.S.A.
111 R7 **Spencer** *NY* U.S.A.
116 E12 **Spencer** *VA* U.S.A.
116 D10 **Spencer** *WV* U.S.A.
204 F6 **Spencer, Cape** *S.A.* Austr.
106 B3 **Spencer, Cape** *AK* U.S.A.
104 B5 **Spencer, Point** *AK* U.S.A.
94 B5 **Spencer Bay** Namibia
204 F6 **Spencer Gulf** *est. S.A.* Austr.
117 □O3 **Spencer Lake** *ME* U.S.A.
206 B3 **Spencer Range** *hills N.T.* Austr.
206 D2 **Spencer Range** *hills N.T.* Austr.
106 F5 **Spences Bridge** *B.C.* Can.
49 F6 **Spenge** Ger.
29 N4 **Spennymoor** *Durham, England* U.K.
203 G9 **Spenser Mountains** *South I.* N.Z.
78 D4 **Sperchelos** *r.* Greece
51 H6 **Sperenberg** Ger.
22 G1 **Sperillen** *l.* Norway
Sperkhiós *r.* Greece *see* **Spercheios**
74 G8 **Sperlinga** *Sicilia* Italy
73 K5 **Sperlonga** Italy
77 M3 **Spermezeu** Romania
72 A10 **Sperone, Capo** *c. Sardegna* Italy
27 H3 **Sperrin Mountains** *hills Northern Ireland* U.K.
116 G10 **Sperryville** *VA* U.S.A.
49 H11 **Spessart** *reg.* Ger.
118 C6 **Spesutie Island** *MD* U.S.A.
Spétsai *i.* Greece *see* **Spetses**
78 E5 **Spetses** Greece
78 E5 **Spetses** *i.* Greece
26 J7 **Spey** *r. Scotland* U.K.
26 J7 **Spey Bay** *Moray, Scotland* U.K.
52 E3 **Speyer** Ger.
131 □5 **Speyside** Trin. and Tob.
185 L7 **Spezand** Pak.
38 D5 **Spézet** France
73 Q8 **Spezzano Albanese** Italy
55 K4 **Spiczyn** Pol.
27 D6 **Spiddal** Rep. of Ireland
53 O4 **Spiegelau** Ger.
48 E3 **Spiekeroog** Ger.
48 E3 **Spiekeroog** *i.* Ger.
59 K5 **Spielberg bei Knittelfeld** Austria
59 M6 **Spielfeld** Austria
52 C3 **Spiesen-Elversberg** Ger.
70 D2 **Spiez** Switz.
70 E6 **Spigno Monferrato** Italy
73 L5 **Spigno Saturnia** Italy
44 K2 **Spijk** Neth.
44 F5 **Spijkenisse** Neth.
191 A6 **Spikör Geçidi** *pass* Turkey
71 K6 **Spilamberto** Italy
79 I4 **Spil Dağı Milli Parkı** *nat. park* Turkey
78 F7 **Spili** *Kriti* Greece
71 N3 **Spilimbergo** Italy
75 J6 **Spilinga** Italy
29 R7 **Spilsby** *Lincolnshire, England* U.K.
73 Q6 **Spinazzola** Italy
185 L6 **Spin Búldak** Afgh.
37 K5 **Spincourt** France
71 M5 **Spinea** Italy
73 L2 **Spinetoli** Italy
118 E4 **Spinnerstown** *PA* U.S.A.
75 □ **Spinola, Ix-Xatt ta'** *b.* Malta
73 P8 **Spinoso** Italy
185 M7 **Spintangi** Pak.
57 L4 **Spinuş** Romania
185 N5 **Spinwam** Pak.
97 N4 **Spioenkop Dam Nature Reserve** S. Africa
120 H4 **Spirit Lake** *IA* U.S.A.
122 F2 **Spirit Lake** *ID* U.S.A.
107 J4 **Spiritwood** *Sask.* Can.
19 R4 **Spirovo** Rus. Fed.
56 G6 **Spišić-Bukovica** Croatia
58 G6 **Spiss** Austria
56 G3 **Spišská Belá** Slovakia
57 J2 **Spišská Nová Ves** Slovakia
57 J2 **Spišská Stará Ves** Slovakia
57 J3 **Spišské Podhradie** Slovakia
57 J3 **Spišské Vlachy** Slovakia
57 J2 **Spišský Hrad** Slovakia
57 J2 **Spišský Štvrtok** Slovakia
191 F5 **Spitak** Armenia
59 J4 **Spital am Pyhrn** Austria
59 M4 **Spital am Semmering** Austria
178 G4 **Spiti** *r.* India
208 E6 **Spit Point** *W.A.* Austr.
20 □ **Spitsbergen** *i.* Svalbard
96 G9 **Spitskop** *mt.* S. Africa
97 J7 **Spitskopvlei** S. Africa
18 K3 **Spitsyno** Rus. Fed.
59 H6 **Spittal an der Drau** Austria
26 J9 **Spittal of Glenshee** *Perth and Kinross, Scotland* U.K.
115 □1 **Spittal Pond** Bermuda
59 L3 **Spitz** Austria
Spitzbergen *i.* Svalbard *see* **Spitsbergen**
58 G6 **Spitzkofel** *mt.* Austria
70 G1 **Spitzmeilen** *mt.* Switz.
17 R4 **Spivakivka** Ukr.
31 O2 **Spixworth** *Norfolk, England* U.K.
22 E5 **Spjald** Denmark
68 F4 **Split** Croatia
107 L3 **Split Lake** *Man.* Can.
107 L3 **Split Lake** *l. Man.* Can.
70 G2 **Spluga, Passo dello** *pass* Italy/Switz.
70 G2 **Splügen** Switz.
16 H4 **Spodakhy** Ukr.
59 J7 **Spodnja Idrija** Slovenia
59 M6 **Spodnje Hoče** Slovenia
48 K1 **Spodsbjerg** Denmark
29 O6 **Spofforth** *North Yorkshire, England* U.K.
122 F3 **Spokane** *WA* U.S.A.
122 E3 **Spokane** *r. WA* U.S.A.
122 E3 **Spokane Indian Reservation** *res. WA* U.S.A.
191 C1 **Spokoynaya** Rus. Fed.
70 I2 **Spöl** *r.* Italy
Spoletium Italy *see* **Spoleto**
73 J3 **Spoleto** Italy
73 M3 **Spoltore** Italy
71 J2 **Spondigna** Italy
44 H8 **Spontin** Belgium
110 D9 **Spoon** *r. IL* U.S.A.
110 C4 **Spooner** *WI* U.S.A.
51 F8 **Spora** Ger.
50 E4 **Spornitz** Ger.
118 C3 **Sporting Hill** *PA* U.S.A.
130 D7 **Spot Bay** Cayman Is
70 E7 **Spotorno** Italy
119 G4 **Spotswood** *NJ* U.S.A.
116 H10 **Spotsylvania** *VA* U.S.A.
122 D4 **Spotted Horse** *WY* U.S.A.
122 D5 **Sprague** *OR* U.S.A.
122 D5 **Sprague** *r. OR* U.S.A.
52 H4 **Spraitbach** Ger.
48 K5 **Sprakensehl** Ger.
106 F4 **Spranger, Mount** *B.C.* Can.
152 D5 **Spratly Island** S. China Sea
152 D5 **Spratly Islands** S. China Sea
122 E4 **Spray** *OR* U.S.A.
110 F4 **Spread Eagle** *WI* U.S.A.
68 G3 **Spreča** *r.* Bos.-Herz.
51 H5 **Spree** *r.* Ger.
51 I6 **Spreenhagen** Ger.
51 J6 **Spreewald** *park* Ger.
51 J6 **Spreewald** *reg.* Ger.
52 E7 **Spreitenbach** Switz.
51 J7 **Spremberg** Ger.
52 D2 **Sprendlingen** Ger.
71 M4 **Spresiano** Italy
44 J8 **Sprimont** Belgium
45 I7 **Sprimont** Belgium
121 H7 **Spring** *r. MO* U.S.A.
111 P4 **Spring Bay** *Ont.* Can.
96 B5 **Springbok** S. Africa
118 D4 **Spring City** *PA* U.S.A.
125 U2 **Spring City** *UT* U.S.A.
206 F5 **Spring Creek** *r. N.T.* Austr.
207 H8 **Spring Creek** *watercourse Qld* Austr.
120 E5 **Spring Creek** *r. NE* U.S.A.
109 K3 **Springdale** *Nfld and Lab.* Can.
121 H7 **Springdale** *AR* U.S.A.
49 I6 **Springe** Ger.
123 L8 **Springer** *NM* U.S.A.
125 W7 **Springerville** *AZ* U.S.A.
203 F10 **Springfield** *South I.* N.Z.
27 G4 **Springfield** *Northern Ireland* U.K.
121 D7 **Springfield** *CO* U.S.A.
115 G9 **Springfield** *GA* U.S.A.
122 H5 **Springfield** *ID* U.S.A.
110 D9 **Springfield** *IL* U.S.A.
114 E7 **Springfield** *KY* U.S.A.
117 M6 **Springfield** *MA* U.S.A.
117 □Q3 **Springfield** *ME* U.S.A.
120 H3 **Springfield** *MN* U.S.A.
121 I7 **Springfield** *MO* U.S.A.
116 B9 **Springfield** *OH* U.S.A.
122 C4 **Springfield** *OR* U.S.A.
118 E5 **Springfield** *PA* U.S.A.
115 D7 **Springfield** *TN* U.S.A.
117 M5 **Springfield** *VT* U.S.A.
116 G9 **Springfield** *WV* U.S.A.
97 J9 **Springfontein** S. Africa
119 G3 **Spring Garden** Guyana
119 G1 **Spring Glen** *NY* U.S.A.
118 B3 **Spring Glen** *PA* U.S.A.
125 V2 **Spring Glen** *UT* U.S.A.
110 D6 **Spring Green** *WI* U.S.A.
110 C6 **Spring Grove** *MN* U.S.A.
118 B5 **Spring Grove** *PA* U.S.A.
116 I11 **Spring Grove** *VA* U.S.A.
109 H4 **Springhill** *N.S.* Can.
115 F11 **Spring Hill** *FL* U.S.A.
26 I12 **Springholm** *Dumfries and Galloway, Scotland* U.K.
106 F5 **Springhouse** *B.C.* Can.
110 H6 **Spring Lake** *MI* U.S.A.
119 G4 **Spring Lake Heights** *NJ* U.S.A.
125 Q5 **Spring Mountains** *NV* U.S.A.
110 J7 **Springport** *MI* U.S.A.
97 M2 **Springs** S. Africa
119 K2 **Springs** *NY* U.S.A.
203 G9 **Springs Junction** *South I.* N.Z.
207 L8 **Springsure** *Qld* Austr.
118 E5 **Springton Reservoir** *PA* U.S.A.
207 H7 **Springvale** *Qld* Austr.
97 K8 **Spring Valley** S. Africa
124 P9 **Spring Valley** *CA* U.S.A.
110 B6 **Spring Valley** *MN* U.S.A.
119 G2 **Spring Valley** *NY* U.S.A.
110 B5 **Spring Valley** *WI* U.S.A.
120 F4 **Springview** *NE* U.S.A.
124 M5 **Springville** *CA* U.S.A.
116 G6 **Springville** *NY* U.S.A.
118 D1 **Springville** *PA* U.S.A.
125 U1 **Springville** *UT* U.S.A.
118 C1 **Springwater** *NY* U.S.A.
29 Q6 **Sproatley** *East Riding of Yorkshire, England* U.K.
49 D8 **Sprockhövel** Ger.
31 O2 **Sprowston** *Norfolk, England* U.K.
106 H4 **Spruce Grove** *Alta* Can.
116 F10 **Spruce Knob** *mt. WV* U.S.A.
125 X3 **Spruce Mountain** *CO* U.S.A.
125 R1 **Spruce Mountain** *NV* U.S.A.
118 F3 **Spruce Run Reservoir** *NJ* U.S.A.
44 G5 **Sprundel** Neth.
118 B5 **Spry** *PA* U.S.A.
75 L4 **Spulico, Capo** *c.* Italy
29 R6 **Spurn Head** *England* U.K.
104 C3 **Spurr, Mount** *vol. AK* U.S.A.
106 F5 **Spuzzum** *B.C.* Can.
55 J2 **Spychowo** Pol.
106 F5 **Squamish** *B.C.* Can.
106 F5 **Squamish** *r. B.C.* Can.
117 N5 **Squam Lake** *NH* U.S.A.
117 □Q2 **Squapan Lake** *ME* U.S.A.
71 K5 **Squaranto** *r.* Italy
117 □Q1 **Square Lake** *ME* U.S.A.
75 L6 **Squillace** Italy
75 L6 **Squillace, Golfo di** *g.* Italy
75 O3 **Squinzano** Italy
116 D11 **Squire** *WV* U.S.A.
209 I9 **Squires, Mount** *hill W.A.* Austr.
157 I8 **Sragen** *Jawa* Indon.
76 I8 **Srbica** *Kosovo, Srbija* Serb. and Mont.
76 I7 **Srbija** *aut. rep.* Serb. and Mont.
76 H5 **Srbobran** *Vojvodina, Srbija* Serb. and Mont.
159 F9 **Srê Âmbĕl** Cambodia
77 P6 **Srebărna** *tourist site* Bulg.
68 G3 **Srebrenica** Bos.-Herz.
77 P8 **Sredets** *Burgas* Bulg.
Sredets *Sofiya-Grad* Bulg. *see* **Sofiya**
77 P8 **Sredetska Reka** *r.* Bulg.
193 Q4 **Sredinnyy Khrebet** *mts* Rus. Fed.
59 N7 **Središće** Slovenia
77 P7 **Sredishte** Bulg.
77 J8 **Sredna Gora** *mts* Bulg.
162 E3 **Srednebelaya** Rus. Fed.
193 Q3 **Srednekolymsk** Rus. Fed.
19 T7 **Sredne-Russkaya Vozvyshennost'** *hills* Rus. Fed.
193 M3 **Sredne-Sibirskoye Ploskogor'ye** *plat.* Rus. Fed.
20 U4 **Sredneye Kuyto, Ozero** *l.* Rus. Fed.
17 S2 **Sredniy Ikorets** Rus. Fed.
162 H3 **Sredniy Urgal** Rus. Fed.
71 Q5 **Srednja Vrata, Kanal** *sea chan.* Croatia
77 M8 **Srednogorie** Bulg.
19 W4 **Srednyaya Akhtuba** Rus. Fed.
15 I6 **Srednyaya Akhtuba** Rus. Fed.
159 H8 **Srê Khtum** Cambodia
54 F3 **Śrem** Pol.
76 H5 **Srem** *reg.* Serb. and Mont.
76 H6 **Sremska Mitrovica** *Vojvodina, Srbija* Serb. and Mont.
159 G8 **Srê Noy** Cambodia
159 H8 **Srêpok, Tônlé** *r.* Cambodia
161 K1 **Sretensk** Rus. Fed.
157 I4 **Sri Aman** *Sarawak* Malaysia
17 L3 **Sribne** Ukr.
176 G6 **Sriharikota Island** India
176 F9 **Sri Jayewardenepura Kotte** Sri Lanka
177 I3 **Srikakulam** *Andhra Prad.* India
176 F6 **Sri Kalahasti** *Andhra Prad.* India
176 G9 **Sri Lanka** *country* Asia
178 E6 **Sri Madhopur** *Rajasthan* India
179 M7 **Srimangal** Bangl.
178 D2 **Srinagar** *Uttaranchal* India
178 E2 **Srinagar** *Jammu and Kashmir* India
176 D6 **Sringeri** *Karnataka* India
176 G9 **Sri Pada** *mt.* Sri Lanka
176 F7 **Srirangam** *Tamil Nadu* India
176 F4 **Srisailam** *Andhra Prad.* India
176 F8 **Srivaikuntam** *Tamil Nadu* India
176 C3 **Srivardhan** *Mahar.* India
176 E8 **Srivilliputtur** *Tamil Nadu* India
68 F3 **Srnetica** *mts* Bos.-Herz.
68 G3 **Srnice** Bos.-Herz.
55 J1 **Srockowo** Pol.
54 E4 **Środa Śląska** Pol.
54 F3 **Środa Wielkopolska** Pol.
54 E3 **Środkowy Kanał Obry** *canal* Pol.
26 G8 **Srón a' Choire Ghairbh** *hill Scotland* U.K.
183 U1 **Srostki** Rus. Fed.
76 I5 **Srpska Crnja** *Vojvodina, Srbija* Serb. and Mont.
76 I5 **Srpski Itebej** *Vojvodina, Srbija* Serb. and Mont.
177 H3 **Srungavarapukota** *Andhra Prad.* India
19 W9 **Sselki** Rus. Fed.
96 E3 **Staansaam** S. Africa
207 H4 **Staaten** *r. Qld* Austr.
207 I4 **Staaten River National Park** *Qld* Austr.
59 N2 **Staatz** Austria
20 R1 **Stabbursdalen Nasjonalpark** *nat. park* Norway
50 D2 **Staberhuk** *c.* Ger.
45 F6 **Stabroek** Belgium
56 C2 **Stachy** Czech Rep.
26 F6 **Stac Pollaidh** *hill Scotland* U.K.
Stac Polly *hill Scotland* U.K. *see* **Stac Pollaidh**
110 B4 **Stacy** *MN* U.S.A.
110 B6 **Stacyville** *IA* U.S.A.
48 H3 **Stade** Ger.
53 N6 **Stadelhorn** *mt.* Ger.
45 D7 **Staden** Belgium
48 K5 **Stadensen** Ger.
31 J4 **Stadhampton** *Oxfordshire, England* U.K.
Stadhlaigearraidh *Scotland* U.K. *see* **Stilligarry**
21 L6 **Städjan-Nipfjällets naturreservat** *nature res.* Sweden
59 I3 **Stadl-Paura** Austria
44 K3 **Stadskanaal** Neth.
44 K2 **Stadskanaal** *canal* Neth.
49 H9 **Stadtallendorf** Ger.
53 J5 **Stadtbergen** Ger.
49 H6 **Stadthagen** Ger.
51 D9 **Stadtilm** Ger.
49 C10 **Stadtkyll** Ger.
49 J10 **Stadtlauringen** Ger.
49 J9 **Stadtlengsfeld** Ger.
49 C7 **Stadtlohn** Ger.
49 I7 **Stadtoldendorf** Ger.
52 G2 **Stadtprozelten** Ger.
51 E9 **Stadtroda** Ger.
59 N5 **Stadtschlaining** Austria
51 E10 **Stadtsteinach** Ger.
48 H1 **Stadum** Ger.
70 F1 **Stäfa** Switz.
26 D10 **Staffa** *i. Scotland* U.K.
51 D10 **Staffelberg** *hill* Ger.
37 N8 **Staffelfelden** France
53 K6 **Staffelsee** *l.* Ger.
49 K10 **Staffelstein** Ger.
48 G5 **Stafforst** Ger.
26 D7 **Staffin** *Highland, Scotland* U.K.
26 D7 **Staffin Bay** *Scotland* U.K.
71 O9 **Staffolo** Italy
70 G5 **Staffora** *r.* Italy
30 H2 **Stafford** *Staffordshire, England* U.K.
116 H10 **Stafford** *VA* U.S.A.
130 E1 **Stafford Creek** *Andros* Bahamas
30 H2 **Staffordshire** *admin. div. England* U.K.
97 N6 **Stafford's Post** S. Africa
117 M7 **Stafford Springs** *CT* U.S.A.
157 L6 **Stagen** *Kalimantan* Indon.
106 H2 **Stagg Lake** *N.W.T.* Can.
27 C4 **Stags of Broad Haven** *is* Rep. of Ireland
53 P2 **Stáhlavy** Czech Rep.
116 F8 **Stahlstown** *PA* U.S.A.
51 H6 **Stahnsdorf** Ger.
59 K7 **Stahovica** Slovenia
18 H4 **Staicele** Latvia
52 H5 **Staig** Ger.
73 O4 **Staimi** *r.* Italy
59 J4 **Stainach** Austria
29 N4 **Staindrop** *Durham, England* U.K.
31 K5 **Staines** *Surrey, England* U.K.
29 M5 **Stainforth** *North Yorkshire, England* U.K.
29 O6 **Stainforth** *South Yorkshire, England* U.K.
29 Q5 **Staintondale** *North Yorkshire, England* U.K.
37 J6 **Stainville** France
59 L6 **Stainz** Austria
75 K8 **Staiti** Italy
57 L3 **Stakčín** Slovakia
26 G11 **Stake, Hill of** *Scotland* U.K.
17 R5 **Stakhanov** Ukr.
17 M8 **Stakhanovka** Ukr.
Stakhanovo Rus. Fed. *see* **Zhukovskiy**
30 H6 **Stalbridge** *Dorset, England* U.K.
70 D3 **Stalden** Switz.
48 L1 **Stalدby** *sea chan.* Denmark
31 P2 **Stalham** *Norfolk, England* U.K.
Stalin Bulg. *see* **Varna**
106 E3 **Stalin, Mount** *B.C.* Can.
Stalingrad Rus. Fed. *see* **Volgograd**
Stalingradskaya Oblast' *admin. div.* Rus. Fed. *see* **Volgogradskaya Oblast'**
Staliniri Georgia *see* **Ts'khinvali**
Stalino Uzbek. *see* **Shahrihon**
58 H6 **Stall** Austria
23 N2 **Stallarholmen** Sweden
59 L5 **Stallhofen** Austria
29 M5 **Stalling Busk** *North Yorkshire, England* U.K.
53 N3 **Stallwang** Ger.
55 K5 **Stalowa Wola** Pol.
77 O5 **Stâlpu** Romania
97 L9 **Stalwart Point** S. Africa
29 M7 **Stalybridge** *Greater Manchester, England* U.K.
77 M8 **Stamboliyski** Bulg.
207 I6 **Stamford** *Qld* Austr.
31 L2 **Stamford** *Lincolnshire, England* U.K.
117 L7 **Stamford** *CT* U.S.A.
117 K6 **Stamford** *NY* U.S.A.
121 F9 **Stamford** *TX* U.S.A.
29 P6 **Stamford Bridge** *East Riding of Yorkshire, England* U.K.
29 N3 **Stamfordham** *Northumberland, England* U.K.
51 E10 **Stammbach** Ger.
53 K4 **Stammham** Ger.
94 C5 **Stampriet** Namibia
58 C5 **Stams** Austria
53 N3 **Stamsried** Ger.
20 L2 **Stamsund** Norway
27 J5 **Stamullen** Rep. of Ireland
116 G10 **Stanardsville** *VA* U.S.A.
120 I6 **Stanberry** *MO* U.S.A.
212 W1 **Stancomb-Wills Glacier** Antarctica
106 H5 **Standard** *Alta* Can.
44 G5 **Standdaarbuiten** Neth.
95 E4 **Standerton** S. Africa
120 E2 **Standing Rock Indian Reservation** *res. ND/SD* U.S.A.
29 L6 **Standish** *Greater Manchester, England* U.K.
111 K6 **Standish** *MI* U.S.A.
31 M4 **Standon** *Hertfordshire, England* U.K.
28 J2 **Stane** *North Lanarkshire, Scotland* U.K.
77 M6 **Stănești** Romania
125 U9 **Stanfield** *AZ* U.S.A.
96 D10 **Stanford** S. Africa
114 E7 **Stanford** *KY* U.S.A.
122 I3 **Stanford** *MT* U.S.A.
31 M4 **Stanford-le-Hope** *Thurrock, England* U.K.
23 O4 **Stånga** *Gotland* Sweden
23 M4 **Stångån** *r.* Sweden
20 T1 **Stáŋganasčohkka** *hill* Norway
97 P5 **Stanger** S. Africa
20 J5 **Stangvikfjorden** *inlet* Norway
31 M2 **Stanhoe** *Norfolk, England* U.K.
29 M4 **Stanhope** *Durham, England* U.K.
118 F3 **Stanhope** *NJ* U.S.A.
77 Q4 **Stănilești** Romania
55 K4 **Stanin** Pol.
76 H5 **Stanišić** *Vojvodina, Srbija* Serb. and Mont.
17 L7 **Stanislav** *Khersons'ka Oblast'* Ukr.
55 M5 **Stanislavchyk** Ukr.
55 J3 **Stanisławów** Pol.
77 N3 **Stănișoarei, Munții** *mts* Romania
59 I8 **Štanjel** Slovenia
56 C2 **Staňkov** Czech Rep.
205 J9 **Stanley** *Tas.* Austr.
109 H4 **Stanley** *N.B.* Can.
171 □J7 **Stanley** *H.K.* China
145 F8 **Stanley** Falkland Is
29 N4 **Stanley** *Durham, England* U.K.
26 J10 **Stanley** *Perth and Kinross, Scotland* U.K.
122 G4 **Stanley** *ID* U.S.A.
120 D1 **Stanley** *ND* U.S.A.
116 G10 **Stanley** *VA* U.S.A.
110 D5 **Stanley** *WI* U.S.A.
Stanley, Chutes *waterfall* Dem. Rep. Congo *see* **Boyoma, Chutes**
206 C7 **Stanley, Mount** *hill N.T.* Austr.
205 J9 **Stanley, Mount** *hill Tas.* Austr.
Stanley, Mount Dem. Rep. Congo/Uganda *see* **Margherita Peak**
Stanley Falls Dem. Rep. Congo *see* **Boyoma, Chutes**
176 E7 **Stanley Reservoir** India
Stanleyville Dem. Rep. Congo *see* **Kisangani**
95 F4 **Stanmore** Zimbabwe
29 N3 **Stannington** *Northumberland, England* U.K.
54 D2 **Stanomino** Pol.
78 C4 **Stanos** Greece
19 V9 **Stanovaya** Rus. Fed.
19 W8 **Stanovaya Ryasa** *r.* Rus. Fed.
51 G10 **Stanovice, Vodní nádrž** *resr* Czech Rep.
19 V9 **Stanovoye** Rus. Fed.
193 M4 **Stanovoye Nagor'ye** *mts* Rus. Fed.
193 N4 **Stanovoy Khrebet** *mts* Rus. Fed.
19 T9 **Stanovoy Kolodez'** Rus. Fed.
58 E5 **Stans** Austria
70 E2 **Stans** Switz.
204 F6 **Stansbury** *S.A.* Austr.
208 J6 **Stansmore Range** *hills W.A.* Austr.
31 M4 **Stansted** *airport England* U.K.
31 M4 **Stansted Mountfitchet** *Essex, England* U.K.
205 M3 **Stanthorpe** *Qld* Austr.
31 N3 **Stanton** *Suffolk, England* U.K.
118 D5 **Stanton** *DE* U.S.A.
116 B11 **Stanton** *KY* U.S.A.
110 I6 **Stanton** *MI* U.S.A.
120 E2 **Stanton** *ND* U.S.A.
120 G5 **Stanton** *NE* U.S.A.
121 E9 **Stanton** *TX* U.S.A.
19 V9 **Stantsiya Babarykino** Rus. Fed.
19 U8 **Stantsiya Skuratovo** Rus. Fed.
Stantsiya-Yakkabag Uzbek. *see* **Yakkabog'**
31 N4 **Stanway** *Essex, England* U.K.
17 S5 **Stanychno-Luhans'ke** Ukr.
58 C5 **Stanzach** Austria
59 M5 **Stanz im Mürztal** Austria
48 K4 **Stapel** Ger.
49 K7 **Stapelburg** Ger.
48 J3 **Stapelfeld** Ger.
44 J3 **Staphorst** Neth.
31 J2 **Stapleford** *Nottinghamshire, England* U.K.
31 N5 **Staplehurst** *Kent, England* U.K.
120 H2 **Staples** *MN* U.S.A.
120 E5 **Stapleton** *NE* U.S.A.
55 I4 **Stąporków** Pol.
207 J5 **Star** *r. Qld* Austr.
19 R8 **Star'** Rus. Fed.
17 K3 **Stara Basan'** Ukr.
57 H2 **Stará Bystrica** Slovakia
16 G3 **Stara Chortoryya** Ukr.
55 J4 **Starachowice** Pol.
56 D2 **Stará Huť** Czech Rep.
17 M1 **Stara Huta** Ukr.
54 G2 **Stara Kiszewa** Pol.
55 K3 **Stara Kornica** Pol.
16 H3 **Stara Kotel'nya** Ukr.
54 E2 **Stara Łubianka** Pol.
57 J2 **Stará Ľubovňa** Slovakia
57 I6 **Stara Moravica** *Vojvodina, Srbija* Serb. and Mont.
71 R6 **Stara Novalja** Croatia
56 E1 **Stará Paka** Czech Rep.
76 I6 **Stara Pazova** *Vojvodina, Srbija* Serb. and Mont.
77 K7 **Stara Planina** *mts* Bulg./Yugo.
58 F9 **Stara Ploščica** Croatia
50 J5 **Stara Rudnica** Pol.
55 K6 **Stara Sil'** Ukr.
57 G3 **Stará Turá** Slovakia
16 G5 **Stara Ushytsya** Ukr.
59 M8 **Stara vas-Bizeljsko** Slovenia
16 D2 **Stara Vyzhivka** Ukr.
55 K5 **Stara Wieś** Pol.
17 T2 **Staraya Chigla** Rus. Fed.
17 S3 **Staraya Kalitva** Rus. Fed.
182 B1 **Staraya Kulatka** Rus. Fed.
182 B2 **Staraya Poltavka** Rus. Fed.
19 O4 **Staraya Russa** Rus. Fed.
19 O5 **Staraya Toropa** Rus. Fed.
15 J5 **Staraya Tumba** Rus. Fed.
77 N8 **Stara Zagora** Bulg.
16 E5 **Stara Zhadova** Ukr.
217 I6 **Starbuck Island** Kiribati
17 P6 **Starchenkove** Ukr.
77 O5 **Starchiojd** Romania
121 I9 **Star City** *AR* U.S.A.
110 H9 **Star City** *IN* U.S.A.
207 J3 **Starcke National Park** *Qld* Austr.
30 F6 **Starcross** *Devon, England* U.K.
17 M8 **Stare, Ozero** *l.* Ukr.
54 F3 **Stare Budkowice** Pol.
59 M1 **Stareč** Czech Rep.
54 C2 **Stare Czarnowo** Pol.
54 G2 **Stare Dąbrowa** Pol.
55 K2 **Stare Dolistowo** Pol.
55 K3 **Stare Hołowczyce** Pol.
51 J9 **Staré Křečany** Czech Rep.
54 D3 **Stare Kurowo** Pol.
56 F1 **Staré Město** Czech Rep.
54 E3 **Stare Miasto** Pol.
55 H1 **Stare Pole** Pol.
16 D4 **Stare Selo** Ukr.
54 E4 **Stare Strącze** Pol.
Stargard in Pommern Pol. *see* **Stargard Szczeciński**
54 D2 **Stargard Szczeciński** Pol.
57 I3 **Star Huta** Slovakia
71 R6 **Starigrad** Croatia
55 M4 **Stari Koshary** Ukr.
71 R4 **Stari Log** Slovenia
57 I2 **Starina, Vodná nádrž** *resr* Slovakia
16 J3 **Stari Petrivtsi** Ukr.
76 I7 **Stari Ras and Sopoćani** *tourist site* Serb. and Mont.
71 Q4 **Stari Trg** Slovenia
19 R5 **Staritsa** Rus. Fed.
182 H3 **Star Karabutak** Kazakh.
115 F11 **Starke** *FL* U.S.A.
51 F9 **Starkenberg** Ger.
116 F11 **Starkey** *VA* U.S.A.
202 □ **Star Keys** *is Chatham Is* S. Pacific Ocean
19 X6 **Starkovo** Rus. Fed.
121 K9 **Starkville** *MS* U.S.A.
117 J4 **Star Lake** *NY* U.S.A.
Starling Inlet *H.K.* China *see* **Sha Tau Kok Hoi**
53 K6 **Starnberg** Ger.
53 K6 **Starnberger See** *l.* Ger.
172 F1 **Staroaleyskoye** Rus. Fed.
Starobel'sk Ukr. *see* **Starobil's'k**
17 R6 **Starobesheve** Ukr.
17 R6 **Starobesheve** Ukr.
Starobeshivs'ke Vodoskhovyshche *resr* Ukr.
17 R4 **Starobil's'k** Ukr.
18 K9 **Starobin** Belarus
17 O6 **Starobohdanivka** Ukr.
17 R7 **Starodereveyankovskaya** Rus. Fed.
19 P9 **Starodub** Rus. Fed.
54 D2 **Starogard** Pol.
54 G2 **Starogard Gdański** Pol.
191 H2 **Starogladkovskaya** Rus. Fed.
Starokonstantinov Ukr. *see* **Starokostyantyniv**
16 G4 **Starokostyantyniv** Ukr.
16 I7 **Starokozache** Ukr.
19 W7 **Staroletovo** Rus. Fed.
17 S8 **Staroleushkovskaya** Rus. Fed.
15 G7 **Staromanskaya** Rus. Fed.
17 P6 **Staromlynivka** Ukr.
17 R8 **Staronizhesteblievskaya** Rus. Fed.
77 P8 **Staro Oryakhovo** Bulg.
17 Q2 **Starooskol'skoye Vodokhranilishche** *resr* Rus. Fed.
77 M8 **Starosel** Bulg.
77 O7 **Staro Selo** Bulg.
19 X8 **Staroseslavino** Rus. Fed.
15 G7 **Starosherbinovskaya** Rus. Fed.
54 C4 **Starosiedle** Pol.
182 G1 **Starosubkhangulovo** Rus. Fed.
17 Q8 **Starotitarovskaya** Rus. Fed.
17 O4 **Starovirivka** Ukr.
55 H4 **Starowa Góra** Pol.
14 H4 **Staroye** Rus. Fed.
15 I5 **Staroye Drozhzhanoye** Rus. Fed.
19 Q6 **Staroye Istomino** Rus. Fed.
19 T5 **Staroye Melkovo** Rus. Fed.

Staroye Sandovo to Stubno

343

19 T3 **Staroye Sandovo** Rus. Fed.
55 M3 **Staroye Syalo** *Brestskaya Voblasts'* Belarus
18 M6 **Staroye Syalo** *Vitsyebskaya Voblasts'* Belarus
15 H5 **Staroyur'yevo** Rus. Fed.
19 W7 **Starozhilovo** Rus. Fed.
55 H3 **Staroźreby** Pol.
124 N1 **Star Peak** *NV* U.S.A.
30 E7 **Start Bay** *England* U.K.
29 N4 **Startforth** *Durham, England* U.K.
30 E7 **Start Point** *England* U.K.
Starve Island Kiribati *see* **Starbuck Island**
55 H2 **Stary Dzierzgoń** Pol.
57 L1 **Stary Dzików** Pol.
57 G2 **Starý Jičín** Czech Rep.
54 D4 **Stary Kisielin** Pol.
55 H3 **Stary Kobrzyniec** Pol.
55 K5 **Stary Majdan** Pol.
18 K7 **Starynki** Belarus
18 M6 **Starynovichy** Belarus
56 C2 **Starý Plzenec** Czech Rep.
55 I6 **Stary Sącz** Pol.
57 J2 **Starý Smokovec** Slovakia
55 J3 **Stary Szelków** Pol.
55 H2 **Stary Targ** Pol.
57 H3 **Starý Tekov** Slovakia
17 P3 **Starytsya** Ukr.
55 K4 **Stary Uścimów** Pol.
18 L8 **Staryya Darohi** Belarus
16 E2 **Staryy Chortoryys'k** Ukr.
19 X5 **Staryy Dvor** Rus. Fed.
Staryye Dorogi Belarus *see* Staryya Darohi
17 K1 **Staryye Yurkovichi** Rus. Fed.
193 L2 **Staryy Kayak** Rus. Fed.
17 Q6 **Staryy Krym** *Donets'ka Oblast'* Ukr.
17 O8 **Staryy Krym** *Respublika Krym* Ukr.
191 E2 **Staryy Lesken** Rus. Fed.
192 I3 **Staryy Nadym** Rus. Fed.
16 E4 **Staryy Oleksynets'** Ukr.
15 G6 **Staryy Oskol** Rus. Fed.
16 G4 **Staryy Ostropil'** Ukr.
17 P3 **Staryy Saltiv** Ukr.
16 B4 **Staryy Sambir** Ukr.
Staryy Sambor Ukr. *see* Staryy Sambir
191 I2 **Staryy Terek** *r.* Rus. Fed.
191 F2 **Staryy Urukh** Rus. Fed.
54 G1 **Starzyno** Pol.
17 N4 **Stasi** Ukr.
51 E7 **Staßfurt** Ger.
55 J5 **Staszów** Pol.
116 H8 **State College** *PA* U.S.A.
121 K10 **State Line** *MS* U.S.A.
119 G3 **Staten Island** *NY* U.S.A.
115 F10 **Statenville** *GA* U.S.A.
115 G9 **Statesboro** *GA* U.S.A.
115 G8 **Statesville** *NC* U.S.A.
22 F2 **Stathelle** Norway
85 G4 **Station No. 6** Sudan
85 G5 **Station No. 10** Sudan
105 Q1 **Station Nord** Greenland
119 G3 **Statue of Liberty** *tourist site NJ* U.S.A.
59 L3 **Statzberg** *hill* Austria
59 M3 **Statzendorf** Austria
16 H6 **Stăuceni** Moldova
51 H8 **Stauchitz** Ger.
52 D6 **Staufen im Breisgau** Ger.
53 J5 **Staufersberg** *hill* Ger.
30 H4 **Staunton** *Gloucestershire, England* U.K.
116 F10 **Staunton** *VA* U.S.A.
51 I7 **Staupitz** Ger.
22 B3 **Stavanger** Norway
203 F10 **Staveley** *South I.* N.Z.
29 O7 **Staveley** *Derbyshire, England* U.K.
45 I8 **Stavelot** Belgium
44 F5 **Stavenisse** Neth.
22 G3 **Stavern** Norway
77 M7 **Stavertsi** Bulg.
16 J6 **Stavkove** Ukr.
55 M4 **Stavky** Ukr.
57 L3 **Stavne** Ukr.
44 H3 **Stavoren** Neth.
78 C5 **Stavrodromi** Greece
15 H7 **Stavropol'** Rus. Fed.
183 L1 **Stavropolka** Kazakh.
Stavropol Kray *admin. div.* Rus. Fed. *see* **Stavropol'skiy Kray**
Stavropol'-na-Volge Rus. Fed. *see* **Tol'yatti**
15 H7 **Stavropol'skaya Vozvyshennost'** *hills* Rus. Fed.
191 E1 **Stavropol'skiy Kray** *admin. div.* Rus. Fed.
78 D2 **Stavros** *Kentriki Makedonia* Greece
78 E2 **Stavros** *Kentriki Makedonia* Greece
78 F7 **Stavros, Akra** *pt Kriti* Greece
79 G5 **Stavros, Akra** *pt Naxos* Greece
78 F1 **Stavroupoli** Greece
50 K5 **Staw** Pol.
19 O9 **Stawbun** Belarus
205 I7 **Stawell** *Vic.* Austr.
207 I6 **Stawell** *r. Qld* Austr.
55 I2 **Stawiguda** Pol.
55 K2 **Stawiski** Pol.
54 G4 **Stawiszyn** Pol.
47 I3 **Stawki, Park Krajobrazowy** Pol.
29 Q5 **Staxton** *North Yorkshire, England* U.K.
19 S8 **Stayki** Rus. Fed.
16 J3 **Stayky** Ukr.
111 N5 **Stayner** *Ont.* Can.
122 C4 **Stayton** *OR* U.S.A.
97 N4 **Steadville** S. Africa
124 M2 **Steamboat** *NV* U.S.A.
122 K6 **Steamboat Springs** *CO* U.S.A.
55 I2 **Stębark** Pol.
104 B3 **Stebbins** *AK* U.S.A.
17 K4 **Stebliv** Ukr.
55 L6 **Stebnyk** Ukr.
75 L6 **Steccato** Italy
56 D2 **Štěchovice** Czech Rep.
50 F5 **Stechow** Ger.
70 F1 **Steckborn** Switz.
48 E3 **Stedesdorf** Ger.
51 E8 **Stedten** Ger.
44 K2 **Stedum** Neth.
58 B5 **Steeg** Austria
96 I3 **Steekdorings** S. Africa
108 C3 **Steel** *r. Ont.* Can.
120 F2 **Steele** *ND* U.S.A.
212 T2 **Steele Island** Antarctica
204 □1 **Steel's Point** Norfolk I.
118 B4 **Steelton** *PA* U.S.A.
120 J7 **Steelville** *MO* U.S.A.
106 G3 **Steen** *r. Alta* Can.
44 F5 **Steenbergen** Neth.
44 J4 **Steenderen** Neth.
97 O1 **Steenkampsberge** *mts* S. Africa
106 G3 **Steen River** *Alta* Can.
122 E5 **Steens Mountain** *OR* U.S.A.
Steenstrup Gletscher *glacier* Greenland *see* **Sermersuaq**
36 E2 **Steenvoorde** France
44 J3 **Steenwijk** Neth.
30 F5 **Steep Holm** *i. England* U.K.
29 R7 **Steeping** *r. England* U.K.
31 K4 **Steeple Claydon** *Buckinghamshire, England* U.K.
209 B9 **Steep Point** *W.A.* Austr.
29 N6 **Steeton** *West Yorkshire, England* U.K.
59 O8 **Štefanje** Croatia
56 G3 **Štefanov** Slovakia
78 D3 **Stefanoviki** Greece
213 D2 **Stefansson Bay** Antarctica
105 H2 **Stefansson Island** *Nunavut* Can.
116 I7 **Ştefan Vodă** Moldova
77 P6 **Ştefan Vodă** Romania
70 D2 **Steffisburg** Switz.
19 V9 **Stegalovka** Rus. Fed.
53 J2 **Stegaurath** Ger.
22 I7 **Stege** Denmark
50 F1 **Stege Bugt** *b.* Denmark
51 E6 **Stegelitz** Ger.
50 F1 **Stege Nor** *lag.* Denmark
59 N5 **Stegersbach** Austria
44 J3 **Steggerda** Neth.
Stegi Swaziland *see* **Siteki**
55 H1 **Stegny** Pol.
19 O7 **Stegrimovo** Rus. Fed.
77 K4 **Ştei** Romania
59 L5 **Steiermark** *land* Austria
53 I2 **Steigerwald** *mts* Ger.
53 J2 **Steigerwald** *park* Ger.
97 P3 **Steilrand** S. Africa
48 H5 **Steimbke** Ger.
53 K3 **Stein** Ger.
45 I7 **Stein** Neth.
52 D6 **Stein** Switz.
52 E6 **Steina** *r.* Ger.
52 E5 **Steinach** *Baden-Württemberg* Ger.
53 N4 **Steinach** *Bayern* Ger.
51 D10 **Steinach** *Thüringen* Ger.
58 D5 **Steinach am Brenner** Austria
59 L3 **Steinakirchen am Forst** Austria
70 F1 **Stein am Rhein** Switz.
20 □D2 **Steinar** Iceland
48 G3 **Steinau** Ger.
49 H10 **Steinau an der Straße** Ger.
107 L5 **Steinbach** *Man.* Can.
51 H9 **Steinbach** Ger.
49 G10 **Steinbach (Taunus)** Ger.
59 I4 **Steinbach am Attersee** Austria
51 D10 **Steinbach am Wald** Ger.
59 J4 **Steinbach an der Steyr** Austria
53 M3 **Steinberg** *Bayern* Ger.
48 I1 **Steinberg** *Schleswig-Holstein* Ger.
48 I1 **Steinbergkirche** Ger.
48 J3 **Steinburg** Ger.
59 J6 **Steindorf am Ossiacher See** Austria
52 D6 **Steinen** Ger.
58 G4 **Steinernes Meer** *mts* Austria
58 H6 **Steinfeld** Austria
52 H2 **Steinfeld** *Bayern* Ger.
52 E3 **Steinfeld** *Rheinland-Pfalz* Ger.
48 F5 **Steinfeld (Oldenburg)** Ger.
45 I9 **Steinfort** Lux.
49 D6 **Steinfurt** Ger.
53 J6 **Steingaden** Ger.
50 G2 **Steinhagen** *Mecklenburg-Vorpommern* Ger.
49 F6 **Steinhagen** *Nordrhein-Westfalen* Ger.
94 C4 **Steinhausen** Namibia
51 D10 **Steinheid** Ger.
49 H7 **Steinheim** Ger.
53 I4 **Steinheim am Albuch** Ger.
52 G4 **Steinheim an der Murr** Ger.
51 J6 **Steinhöfel** Ger.
53 M5 **Steinhöring** Ger.
48 J5 **Steinhorst** *Niedersachsen* Ger.
48 J3 **Steinhorst** *Schleswig-Holstein* Ger.
49 H6 **Steinhuder Meer** *l.* Ger.
48 H5 **Steinhuder Meer, Naturpark** *nature res.* Ger.
51 J8 **Steinigtwolmsdorf** Ger.
48 I3 **Steinkirchen** Ger.
20 K4 **Steinkjer** Norway
49 G10 **Steinkopf** *hill* Ger.
96 B5 **Steinkopf** S. Africa
51 K6 **Steinsdorf** Ger.
53 I3 **Steinsfeld** Ger.
22 B1 **Steinsland** Norway
52 D3 **Steinwenden** Ger.
51 D10 **Steinwiesen** Ger.
52 F6 **Steißlingen** Ger.
96 H7 **Stekaar** S. Africa
45 F6 **Stekene** Belgium
71 K8 **Stella** *r.* Italy
71 O4 **Stella** *r.* Italy
97 I2 **Stella** S. Africa
130 F2 **Stella Maris** *Long I.* Bahamas
99 □1c **Stella Matutina** Réunion
48 J4 **Stelle** Ger.
96 C9 **Stellenbosch** S. Africa
44 F5 **Stellendam** Neth.
72 C2 **Stello, Monte** *mt. Corse* France
70 I3 **Stelvio, Parco Nazionale dello** *nat. park* Italy
70 I2 **Stelvio, Passo dello** *pass* Italy
48 I4 **Stemmen** Ger.
49 F6 **Stemshorn** Ger.
54 E5 **Stěnava** *r.* Pol.
37 J5 **Stenay** France
23 M4 **Stenbo** Sweden
50 E5 **Stendal** Ger.
18 F4 **Stende** Latvia
23 J4 **Stengårdshultasjön** *l.* Sweden
23 N2 **Stenhamra** Sweden
Stenhouse, Mount *hill H.K.* China *see* **Shan Tei Tong**
26 I10 **Stenhousemuir** *Falkirk, Scotland* U.K.
71 J3 **Stenico** Italy
22 I6 **Stenløse** Denmark
26 □M2 **Stenness** *Shetland, Scotland* U.K.
26 J4 **Stenness, Loch of** *l. Scotland* U.K.
78 D5 **Steno** Greece
53 O2 **Štěnovice** Czech Rep.
23 K6 **Stenshuvuds nationalpark** *nat. park* Sweden
22 I7 **Stensved** Denmark
26 K11 **Stenton** *East Lothian, Scotland* U.K.
20 N3 **Stenudden** Sweden
22 H3 **Stenungsund** Sweden
55 M5 **Stenyatyn** Ukr.
16 D3 **Stenzharychi** Ukr.
Steornabhagh *Western Isles, Scotland* U.K. *see* **Stornoway**
16 F2 **Stepan'** Ukr.
Stepanakert Azer. *see* **Xankändi**
191 F4 **Step'anavan** Armenia
17 L2 **Stepanivka** *Chernihivs'ka Oblast'* Ukr.
17 R6 **Stepanivka** *Donets'ka Oblast'* Ukr.
16 F3 **Stepanivka** *Khmel'nyts'ka Oblast'* Ukr.
17 N3 **Stepanivka** *Sums'ka Oblast'* Ukr.
17 O7 **Stepanivka Persha** Ukr.
182 G2 **Stepanovka** Kazakh.
19 V6 **Stepanshchino** Rus. Fed.
19 T5 **Stepantsevo** Rus. Fed.
27 J6 **Stepaside** Rep. of Ireland
48 K3 **Stepenitz** *r.* Ger.
53 M6 **Stephanskirchen** Ger.
53 N4 **Stephansposching** Ger.
120 G1 **Stephen** *MN* U.S.A.
205 I5 **Stephens** *watercourse N.S.W.* Austr.
202 H7 **Stephens, Cape** *South I.* N.Z.
118 F3 **Stephensburg** *NJ* U.S.A.
116 G9 **Stephens City** *VA* U.S.A.
205 H4 **Stephens Creek** *N.S.W.* Austr.
106 D4 **Stephens Island** *B.C.* Can.
107 M3 **Stephens Lake** *Man.* Can.
110 G4 **Stephenson** *MI* U.S.A.
212 T2 **Stephenson, Mount** Antarctica
109 J3 **Stephenville** *Nfld and Lab.* Can.
121 F9 **Stephenville** *TX* U.S.A.
17 R8 **Stepnaya** Rus. Fed.
17 M1 **Stepne** Ukr.
119 I2 **Stepney** *CT* U.S.A.
54 C2 **Stepnica** Pol.
183 O1 **Stepnogorsk** Kazakh.
17 O6 **Stepnohirs'k** Ukr.
183 O6 **Stepnoy** Kyrg.
182 I1 **Stepnoye** *Chelyabinskaya Oblast'* Rus. Fed.
182 B2 **Stepnoye** *Saratovskaya Oblast'* Rus. Fed.
191 F1 **Stepnoye** *Stavropol'skiy Kray* Rus. Fed.
183 N1 **Stepnyak** Kazakh.
76 I6 **Stepojevac** *Srbija* Serb. and Mont.
200 □2 **Steps Point** American Samoa
19 S5 **Stepurino** Rus. Fed.
55 K3 **Sterdyń-Osada** Pol.
78 E4 **Sterea Ellas** *admin. reg.* Greece
97 N4 **Sterkfontein Dam** *resr* S. Africa
97 L6 **Sterkspruit** S. Africa
97 K7 **Sterkstroom** S. Africa
55 J1 **Sterławki-Wielkie** Pol.
107 I1 **Sterlet Lake** *N.W.T.* Can.
182 F1 **Sterlibashevo** Rus. Fed.
96 F7 **Sterling** S. Africa
120 D5 **Sterling** *CO* U.S.A.
119 L1 **Sterling** *CT* U.S.A.
110 E8 **Sterling** *IL* U.S.A.
120 F6 **Sterling** *KS* U.S.A.
111 J5 **Sterling** *MI* U.S.A.
120 E2 **Sterling** *ND* U.S.A.
125 U2 **Sterling** *UT* U.S.A.
121 E10 **Sterling City** *TX* U.S.A.
111 K7 **Sterling Heights** *MI* U.S.A.
182 F1 **Sterlitamak** Rus. Fed.
71 P5 **Sterna** Croatia
78 D5 **Sterna** Greece
50 E3 **Sternberg** Ger.
56 G2 **Šternberk** Czech Rep.
48 I1 **Sterup** Ger.
41 F10 **Stes Maries, Golfe des** *b.* France
41 E10 **Stes-Maries-de-la-Mer** France
54 E3 **Stęszew** Pol.
56 D1 **Štětí** Czech Rep.
17 L4 **Stetsivka** Ukr.
17 N2 **Stets'kivka** Ukr.
52 G5 **Stetten am kalten Markt** Ger.
Stettin Pol. *see* **Szczecin**
122 H1 **Stettler** *Alta* Can.
116 E8 **Steubenville** *OH* U.S.A.
59 J6 **Steuerberg** Austria
51 F7 **Steutz** Ger.
31 L4 **Stevenage** *Hertfordshire, England* U.K.
202 G7 **Stevens, Mount** *South I.* N.Z.
122 D4 **Stevenson** *WA* U.S.A.
204 E2 **Stevenson Creek** *watercourse S.A.* Austr.
107 L4 **Stevenson Lake** *Man.* Can.
110 E5 **Stevens Point** *WI* U.S.A.
26 G11 **Stevenston** *North Ayrshire, Scotland* U.K.
104 D3 **Stevens Village** *AK* U.S.A.
118 C7 **Stevensville** *MD* U.S.A.
110 H7 **Stevensville** *MI* U.S.A.
111 R8 **Stevensville** *PA* U.S.A.
212 O1 **Steventon Island** Antarctica
22 I6 **Stevns Klint** *cliff* Denmark
207 I3 **Stewart** *r. Qld* Austr.
106 D4 **Stewart** *B.C.* Can.
106 B2 **Stewart** *r. Y.T.* Can.
124 U8 **Stewart** *NV* U.S.A.
206 E1 **Stewart, Cape** *N.T.* Austr.
145 C9 **Stewart, Isla** *i.* Chile
106 B2 **Stewart Crossing** *Y.T.* Can.
203 B14 **Stewart Island** N.Z.
203 B14 **Stewart Island** *nature res. Stewart I.* N.Z.
200 □6 **Stewart Islands** Solomon Is
105 J3 **Stewart Lake** *Nunavut* Can.
26 G11 **Stewarton** *East Ayrshire, Scotland* U.K.
124 I3 **Stewarts Point** *CA* U.S.A.
27 I3 **Stewartstown** *Northern Ireland* U.K.
118 B5 **Stewartstown** *PA* U.S.A.
130 □ **Stewart Town** Jamaica
107 J5 **Stewart Valley** *Sask.* Can.
110 B6 **Stewartville** *MN* U.S.A.
109 I4 **Stewiacke** *N.S.* Can.
48 H5 **Steyerberg** Ger.
31 L6 **Steyning** *West Sussex, England* U.K.
97 L3 **Steynrus** S. Africa
97 J7 **Steynsburg** S. Africa
59 J3 **Steyr** Austria
59 J4 **Steyr** *r.* Austria
59 J3 **Steyregg** Austria
96 I9 **Steytlerville** S. Africa
55 J4 **Stężyca** *Lubelskie* Pol.
54 F1 **Stężyca** *Pomorskie* Pol.
71 L8 **Stia** Italy
57 H3 **Štiavnické Vrchy** *mts* Slovakia
57 H3 **Štiavnické Vrchy** *park* Slovakia
57 H2 **Štiavnik** Slovakia
30 D6 **Stibb Cross** *Devon, England* U.K.
29 M2 **Stichill** *Scottish Borders, Scotland* U.K.
29 R7 **Stickney** *Lincolnshire, England* U.K.
49 K7 **Stiege** Ger.
44 I2 **Stiens** Neth.
71 L6 **Stienta** Italy
Stif Alg. *see* **Sétif**
121 H8 **Stigler** *OK* U.S.A.
73 Q7 **Stigliano** Italy
75 K7 **Stignano** Italy
23 M3 **Stigtomta** Sweden
106 C3 **Stikine** *r. B.C.* Can.
106 D3 **Stikine Plateau** *B.C.* Can.
106 C3 **Stikine Ranges** *mts B.C.* Can.
22 G2 **Stikkvasskollen** *hill* Norway
96 F10 **Stilbaai** S. Africa
96 F10 **Stilbaai** *b.* S. Africa
110 F5 **Stiles** *WI* U.S.A.
97 K2 **Stilfontein** S. Africa
Stilís Greece *see* **Stylida**
26 B8 **Stilligarry** *Western Isles, Scotland* U.K.
29 O5 **Stillington** *North Yorkshire, England* U.K.
118 C6 **Still Pond** *MD* U.S.A.
110 B4 **Stillwater** *MN* U.S.A.
121 G7 **Stillwater** *OK* U.S.A.
122 J4 **Stillwater** *r. MT* U.S.A.
124 N2 **Stillwater National Wildlife Refuge** *nature res. NV* U.S.A.
124 N2 **Stillwater Range** *mts NV* U.S.A.
75 K7 **Stilo** Italy
75 L7 **Stilo, Punta** *pt* Italy
68 F4 **Štilt** *mt.* Bos.-Herz.
31 L3 **Stilton** *Cambridgeshire, England* U.K.
121 H8 **Stilwell** *OK* U.S.A.
76 J8 **Štimlje** *Kosovo, Srbija* Serb. and Mont.
53 I3 **Stimpfach** Ger.
213 E2 **Stinear, Mount** Antarctica
77 Q3 **Stînga Nistrului** *reg.* Moldova
121 E8 **Stinnett** *TX* U.S.A.
72 A6 **Stintino** *Sardegna* Italy
73 O7 **Stio** Italy
77 K9 **Štip** Macedonia
68 E3 **Stipanov Grič** *mt.* Croatia
37 M5 **Stiring-Wendel** France
206 D6 **Stirling** *N.T.* Austr.
111 Q5 **Stirling** *Ont.* Can.
26 I10 **Stirling** *Stirling, Scotland* U.K.
26 H10 **Stirling** *admin. div. Scotland* U.K.
119 G3 **Stirling** *NJ* U.S.A.
209 D11 **Stirling, Mount** *hill W.A.* Austr.
206 B4 **Stirling Creek** *r. N.T.* Austr.
204 F5 **Stirling North** *S.A.* Austr.
209 D13 **Stirling Range** *mts W.A.* Austr.
209 D13 **Stirling Range National Park** *W.A.* Austr.
70 I6 **Stirone** *r.* Italy
116 C11 **Stirrat** *WV* U.S.A.
30 B7 **Stithians** *Cornwall, England* U.K.
57 J3 **Štítnik** Slovakia
111 S4 **Stittsville** *Ont.* Can.
56 F2 **Štíty** Czech Rep.
71 Q6 **Štivan** Croatia
71 L4 **Stizzon** *r.* Italy
20 Q1 **Stjernøya** *i.* Norway
20 K5 **Stjørdalshalsen** Norway
26 G9 **Stob Choire Claurigh** *mt. Scotland* U.K.
26 G9 **Stob Ghabhar** *mt. Scotland* U.K.
55 J6 **Stobnica** *r.* Pol.
54 F5 **Stobrawa** *r.* Pol.
56 C1 **Stochov** Czech Rep.
31 M4 **Stock** *Essex, England* U.K.
37 M6 **Stock, Étang du** *l.* France
52 G6 **Stockach** Ger.
31 J5 **Stockbridge** *Hampshire, England* U.K.
111 J7 **Stockbridge** *MI* U.S.A.
48 K3 **Stockelsdorf** Ger.
59 I6 **Stockenboi** Austria
59 N3 **Stockerau** Austria
118 E3 **Stockertown** *PA* U.S.A.
51 D10 **Stockheim** Ger.
23 O2 **Stockholm** Sweden
23 N2 **Stockholm** *county* Sweden
117 □Q1 **Stockholm** *ME* U.S.A.
119 F2 **Stockholm** *NJ* U.S.A.
70 D2 **Stockhorn** *mt.* Switz.
205 K6 **Stockinbingal** *N.S.W.* Austr.
59 M6 **Stocking** Austria
29 M7 **Stockport** *Greater Manchester, England* U.K.
29 N7 **Stocksbridge** *South Yorkshire, England* U.K.
48 H5 **Stöckse** Ger.
29 N4 **Stocksfield** *Northumberland, England* U.K.
29 M5 **Stocks Reservoir** *England* U.K.
214 G6 **Stocks Seamount** *sea feature* S. Atlantic Ocean
52 G2 **Stockstadt am Main** Ger.
52 E2 **Stockstadt am Rhein** Ger.
124 K4 **Stockton** *CA* U.S.A.
110 D7 **Stockton** *IL* U.S.A.
120 F6 **Stockton** *KS* U.S.A.
121 I7 **Stockton** *MO* U.S.A.
118 F4 **Stockton** *NJ* U.S.A.
125 T1 **Stockton** *UT* U.S.A.
29 L7 **Stockton Heath** *Warrington, England* U.K.
110 D3 **Stockton Island** *WI* U.S.A.
121 I7 **Stockton Lake** *MO* U.S.A.
29 O4 **Stockton-on-Tees** *Stockton-on-Tees, England* U.K.
29 O4 **Stockton-on-Tees** *admin. div. England* U.K.
121 D10 **Stockton Plateau** *TX* U.S.A.
117 □Q4 **Stockton Springs** *ME* U.S.A.
120 E5 **Stockville** *NE* U.S.A.
55 J3 **Stoczek** Pol.
55 J4 **Stoczek Łukowski** Pol.
56 C2 **Stod** Czech Rep.
21 N5 **Stöde** Sweden
19 P7 **Stodolishche** Rus. Fed.
159 G8 **Stœng Trêng** Cambodia
26 F6 **Stoer** *Highland, Scotland* U.K.
26 F6 **Stoer, Point of** *Scotland* U.K.
97 N1 **Stoffberg** S. Africa
76 I9 **Stogovo Planina** *mts* Macedonia
30 F5 **Stogursey** *Somerset, England* U.K.
59 M8 **Stojdraga** Croatia
59 M7 **Stojnci** Slovenia
31 K3 **Stoke Albany** *Northamptonshire, England* U.K.
31 O3 **Stoke Ash** *Suffolk, England* U.K.
31 N4 **Stoke-by-Nayland** *Suffolk, England* U.K.
31 O2 **Stoke Holy Cross** *Norfolk, England* U.K.
31 K4 **Stoke Mandeville** *Buckinghamshire, England* U.K.
31 K4 **Stokenchurch** *Buckinghamshire, England* U.K.
30 E7 **Stokenham** *Devon, England* U.K.
29 M7 **Stoke-on-Trent** *Stoke-on-Trent, England* U.K.
29 M7 **Stoke-on-Trent** *admin. div. England* U.K.
31 K4 **Stoke Poges** *Buckinghamshire, England* U.K.
30 H3 **Stoke Prior** *Worcestershire, England* U.K.
203 I8 **Stokes, Mount** *South I.* N.Z.
30 G3 **Stokesay** *Shropshire, England* U.K.
209 F12 **Stokes Inlet** *W.A.* Austr.
29 O5 **Stokesley** *North Yorkshire, England* U.K.
205 I9 **Stokes Point** *Tas.* Austr.
206 C4 **Stokes Range** *hills N.T.* Austr.
30 F6 **Stoke St Mary** *Somerset, England* U.K.
30 G6 **Stoke sub Hamdon** *Somerset, England* U.K.
203 I8 **Stokes Valley** *North I.* N.Z.
16 E2 **Stokhid** *r.* Ukr.
48 L1 **Stokkemarke** Denmark
20 □C2 **Stokkseyri** Iceland
20 L3 **Stokkvågen** Norway
20 M2 **Stokmarknes** Norway
56 E2 **Štoky** Czech Rep.
77 K6 **Stol** *mt.* Serb. and Mont.
59 H7 **Stol** *mt.* Slovenia
68 F4 **Stolac** Bos.-Herz.
49 K7 **Stolberg (Harz) Kurort** Ger.
49 B9 **Stolberg (Rheinland)** Ger.
183 U2 **Stolboukha** *Vostochnyy Kazakhstan* Kazakh.
183 U3 **Stolboukha** *Vostochnyy Kazakhstan* Kazakh.
192 G2 **Stolbovoy** *Novaya Zemlya* Rus. Fed.
193 O2 **Stolbovoy, Ostrov** *i. Novosibirskiye O-va* Rus. Fed.
Stolbtsy Belarus *see* **Stowbtsy**
54 F2 **Stołczno** Pol.
57 J3 **Stolica** *mt.* Slovakia
68 G3 **Stolice** *hill* Bos.-Herz.
16 F2 **Stolin** Belarus
51 G9 **Stollberg** Ger.
48 F3 **Stollhamm (Butjadingen)** Ger.
54 G2 **Stolno** Pol.
Stolp Pol. *see* **Słupsk**
50 J5 **Stolpe** *Brandenburg* Ger.
48 J2 **Stolpe** *Schleswig-Holstein* Ger.
51 J8 **Stolpen** Ger.
21 I6 **Stolsheimen** *park* Norway
21 J6 **Stolsvatnet** *l.* Norway
98 □2c **Stoltenhoff Island** *Tristan da Cunha* S. Atlantic Ocean
44 G5 **Stolwijk** Neth.
49 H5 **Stolzenau** Ger.
96 B8 **Stompneusbaai** S. Africa
73 Q1 **Stončica, Rt** *pt* Croatia
30 H4 **Stone** *Gloucestershire, England* U.K.
31 M5 **Stone** *Kent, England* U.K.
30 H2 **Stone** *Staffordshire, England* U.K.
116 E7 **Stoneboro** *PA* U.S.A.
20 □ **Stonebreen** *glacier* Svalbard
108 E4 **Stonecliffe** *Ont.* Can.
120 D5 **Stoneham** *CO* U.S.A.
118 F6 **Stone Harbor** *NJ* U.S.A.
26 L9 **Stonehaven** *Aberdeenshire, Scotland* U.K.
207 I8 **Stonehenge** *Qld* Austr.
31 I5 **Stonehenge** *tourist site England* U.K.
30 H4 **Stonehouse** *Gloucestershire, England* U.K.
26 I11 **Stonehouse** *South Lanarkshire, Scotland* U.K.
110 C4 **Stone Lake** *WI* U.S.A.
106 E3 **Stone Mountain Provincial Park** *B.C.* Can.
117 K7 **Stone Ridge** *NY* U.S.A.
116 F12 **Stoneville** *NC* U.S.A.
107 L5 **Stonewall** *Man.* Can.
121 G8 **Stonewall** *OK* U.S.A.
111 O6 **Stoney Creek** *Ont.* Can.
118 D4 **Stoney Creek Mills** *PA* U.S.A.
27 H7 **Stoneyford** Rep. of Ireland
26 G13 **Stoneykirk** *Dumfries and Galloway, Scotland* U.K.
111 L7 **Stoney Point** *Ont.* Can.
97 M7 **Stoneyride** S. Africa
22 B2 **Stong** Norway
24 J1 **Stongfjorden** Norway
119 L2 **Stonington** *CT* U.S.A.
117 □Q4 **Stonington** *ME* U.S.A.
93 C5 **Stony Athi** Kenya
26 □M3 **Stonybreck** *Shetland, Scotland* U.K.
119 I3 **Stony Brook** *NY* U.S.A.
118 B5 **Stony Brook** *PA* U.S.A.
119 J2 **Stony Creek** *CT* U.S.A.
116 H12 **Stony Creek** *VA* U.S.A.
124 J2 **Stony Gorge Reservoir** *CA* U.S.A.
130 □ **Stony Hill** Jamaica
98 □2c **Stonyhill Point** *Tristan da Cunha* S. Atlantic Ocean
107 L3 **Stony Lake** *Man.* Can.
106 H4 **Stony Plain** *Alta* Can.
117 I5 **Stony Point** *NY* U.S.A.
107 J3 **Stony Rapids** *Sask.* Can.
31 K3 **Stony Stratford** *Milton Keynes, England* U.K.
59 O4 **Stoob** Austria
108 D2 **Stooping** *r. Ont.* Can.
59 L8 **Stopiče** Slovenia
55 J1 **Stopki** Pol.
55 I5 **Stopnica** Pol.
48 H3 **Stör** *r.* Ger.
22 E5 **Stora** *r.* Denmark
23 L2 **Storå** Sweden
23 M5 **Stora Alvaret** *pen.* Sweden
23 M4 **Stora Askö** *i.* Sweden
22 I2 **Stora Bör** *l.* Sweden
22 I2 **Stora Gla** *l.* Sweden
22 I4 **Stora Horredssjön** *l.* Sweden
22 H3 **Stora Le** *l.* Sweden
20 O3 **Stora Lulevatten** *l.* Sweden
23 P2 **Stora Nassa naturreservat** *nature res.* Sweden
20 N3 **Stora Sjöfallets nationalpark** *nat. park* Sweden
20 O4 **Storavan** *l.* Sweden
21 L6 **Storbäcken** Sweden
21 K6 **Storbekkfjellet** *mt.* Norway
21 L6 **Storbo** Sweden
22 B2 **Stord** *i.* Norway
20 I5 **Stordal** Norway
21 K6 **Store** *mt.* Norway
59 L7 **Štore** Slovenia
22 G6 **Store Bælt** *sea chan.* Denmark
22 B1 **Storebø** Norway
50 F1 **Store Damme** Denmark
22 I6 **Store Heddinge** Denmark
21 J6 **Store Jukleeggi** *mt.* Norway
105 Q2 **Store Koldewey** *i.* Greenland
20 P2 **Store Lenangstind** *mt.* Norway
20 Q1 **Storelv** Norway
20 T1 **Store Molvik** Norway
23 J4 **Store Moss nationalpark** *nat. park* Sweden
20 K5 **Støren** Norway
22 D2 **Store Nup** *mt.* Norway
48 J1 **Store Rise** Denmark
22 B1 **Store Sotra** *i.* Norway
22 D2 **Store Urevatnet** *l.* Norway
23 N1 **Storfjärden** *l.* Sweden
20 S1 **Storfjordbotn** Norway
20 □ **Storfjorden** *sea chan.* Svalbard
23 K2 **Storfors** Sweden
20 M3 **Storforshei** Norway
59 I8 **Štorje** Slovenia
20 M4 **Storjola** Sweden
20 M3 **Storjord** Norway
20 N4 **Storjuktan** *l.* Sweden
22 D3 **Storkarshei** *hill* Norway
105 H2 **Storkerson Peninsula** *Nunavut* Can.
51 I6 **Storkow** Ger.
48 J3 **Stormarn** *reg.* Ger.
205 K10 **Storm Bay** *Tas.* Austr.
97 K7 **Stormberg** S. Africa
97 K6 **Stormberg** *mt.* S. Africa
97 K6 **Stormberg** *r.* S. Africa
97 K7 **Stormberge** *mts* S. Africa
120 H4 **Storm Lake** *IA* U.S.A.
96 H9 **Stormsrivier** S. Africa
73 P5 **Stornara** Italy
73 P5 **Stornarella** Italy
26 D6 **Stornoway** *Western Isles, Scotland* U.K.
71 J4 **Storo** Italy
23 O2 **Storö-Bockö-Lökaöns naturreservat** *nature res.* Sweden
20 □ **Storøya** *i.* Svalbard
19 P1 **Storozhenskiy, Mys** *pt* Rus. Fed.
14 K3 **Storozhevsk** Rus. Fed.
19 P1 **Storozhno** Rus. Fed.
16 E5 **Storozhynets'** Ukr.
31 L6 **Storrington** *West Sussex, England* U.K.
22 E2 **Stor-Roan** *mt.* Norway
117 M7 **Storrs** *CT* U.S.A.
20 N4 **Storseleby** Sweden
22 H1 **Storsjøen** *l.* Norway
23 M1 **Storsjön** *l.* Sweden
20 M5 **Storsjön** *l.* Sweden
23 N2 **Storsjön** *l.* Sweden
20 J5 **Storskarhø** *mt.* Norway
20 M4 **Storskog** Sweden
20 P2 **Storslett** Norway
22 G7 **Storstrøm** *county* Denmark
22 H7 **Storstrømmen** *sea chan.* Denmark
20 P4 **Storsund** Sweden
31 M4 **Stort** *r. England* U.K.
44 H2 **Stortemelk** *sea chan.* Neth.
20 N4 **Storuman** Sweden
20 N4 **Storuman** *l.* Sweden
20 L5 **Storvigelen** *mt.* Norway
23 M1 **Storvik** Sweden
20 N4 **Storvindeln** *l.* Sweden
22 G4 **Storvorde** Denmark
23 N2 **Storvreta** Sweden
122 K4 **Story** *WY* U.S.A.
76 I2 **Štós** Slovakia
145 B8 **Stosch, Isla** *i.* Chile
51 E8 **Stößen** Ger.
59 M3 **Stössing** Austria
31 L3 **Stotfold** *Bedfordshire, England* U.K.
53 J6 **Stötten am Auerberg** Ger.
51 D8 **Stotternheim** Ger.
118 C4 **Stouchsburg** *PA* U.S.A.
107 K5 **Stoughton** *Sask.* Can.
45 I8 **Stoumont** Belgium
159 G8 **Stoŭng, Stœng** *r.* Cambodia
30 I6 **Stour** *r. Dorset, England* U.K.
31 O4 **Stour** *r. Essex/Suffolk, England* U.K.
31 O5 **Stour** *r. Kent, England* U.K.
31 I3 **Stour** *r. Oxfordshire/Warwickshire, England* U.K.
30 H3 **Stourbridge** *West Midlands, England* U.K.
30 H3 **Stourport-on-Severn** *Worcestershire, England* U.K.
107 M4 **Stout Lake** *Ont.* Can.
26 K11 **Stow** *Scottish Borders, Scotland* U.K.
18 J8 **Stowbtsy** Belarus
118 D4 **Stowe** *PA* U.S.A.
54 F1 **Stowięcino** Pol.
31 N3 **Stowmarket** *Suffolk, England* U.K.
31 I4 **Stow-on-the-Wold** *Gloucestershire, England* U.K.
16 D3 **Stoyaniv** Ukr.
162 G2 **Stoyba** Rus. Fed.
55 K1 **Stożne** Pol.
71 M5 **Stra** Italy
51 G7 **Straach** Ger.
97 K1 **Straatsdrif** S. Africa
27 H3 **Strabane** *Northern Ireland* U.K.
55 L3 **Strabla** Pol.
26 K8 **Strachan** *Aberdeenshire, Scotland* U.K.
26 F10 **Strachur** *Argyll and Bute, Scotland* U.K.
55 M1 **Stračiūnai** Lith.
48 E4 **Strackholt (Großefehn)** Ger.
54 E2 **Strączno** Pol.
27 H6 **Stradbally** Rep. of Ireland
31 O3 **Stradbroke** *Suffolk, England* U.K.
70 G5 **Stradella** Italy
59 M6 **Straden** Austria
31 N3 **Stradishall** *Suffolk, England* U.K.
27 H5 **Stradone** Rep. of Ireland
31 M2 **Stradsett** *Norfolk, England* U.K.
49 B8 **Straelen** Ger.
205 J10 **Strahan** *Tas.* Austr.
125 U4 **Straight Cliffs** *ridge UT* U.S.A.
45 H9 **Straimont** Belgium
56 C2 **Strakonice** Czech Rep.
77 O8 **Straldzha** Bulg.
59 M5 **Strallegg** Austria
26 I9 **Straloch** *Perth and Kinross, Scotland* U.K.
50 H2 **Stralsund** Ger.
70 D5 **Strambino** Italy
45 I6 **Stramproy** Neth.
96 C10 **Strand** S. Africa
20 I5 **Stranda** Norway
22 D1 **Strandavatnet** *l.* Norway
48 J2 **Strande** Ger.
27 E4 **Strandhill** Rep. of Ireland
115 H12 **Strangers Cay** *i.* Bahamas
27 K4 **Strangford** *Northern Ireland* U.K.
27 K4 **Strangford Lough** *inlet Northern Ireland* U.K.
23 N2 **Strängnäs** Sweden
73 K4 **Strangolagalli** Italy
206 D3 **Strangways** *r. N.T.* Austr.
206 E7 **Strangways Range** *mts N.T.* Austr.
57 G3 **Strání** Czech Rep.
27 J2 **Stranocum** *Northern Ireland* U.K.
27 G3 **Stranorlar** Rep. of Ireland
26 F13 **Stranraer** *Dumfries and Galloway, Scotland* U.K.
74 D8 **Strasatti** *Sicilia* Italy
37 O6 **Strasbourg** France
50 I4 **Strasburg** Ger.
116 D8 **Strasburg** *OH* U.S.A.
118 C5 **Strasburg** *PA* U.S.A.
116 G10 **Strasburg** *VA* U.S.A.
16 H6 **Străşeni** Moldova
Strasheny Moldova *see* **Străşeni**
53 P2 **Strašice** Czech Rep.
52 G5 **Straßberg** *Baden-Württemberg* Ger.
51 D7 **Straßberg** *Sachsen-Anhalt* Ger.
59 J6 **Straßburg** Austria
Strassburg France *see* **Strasbourg**
45 J9 **Strassen** Lux.
59 L5 **Straßengel** Austria
49 E9 **Straßenhaus** Ger.
59 O3 **Strasshof an der Norbahn** Austria
53 N4 **Straßkirchen** Ger.
58 H4 **Straßwalchen** Austria
31 J5 **Stratfield Mortimer** *West Berkshire, England* U.K.
108 D5 **Stratford** *Ont.* Can.
202 I6 **Stratford** *North I.* N.Z.
27 I7 **Stratford** Rep. of Ireland
124 M5 **Stratford** *CA* U.S.A.
119 I2 **Stratford** *CT* U.S.A.
121 D7 **Stratford** *TX* U.S.A.
110 D5 **Stratford** *WI* U.S.A.
31 I3 **Stratford-upon-Avon** *Warwickshire, England* U.K.
204 G6 **Strathalbyn** *S.A.* Austr.
26 H11 **Strathaven** *South Lanarkshire, Scotland* U.K.
28 I2 **Strathblane** *Stirling, Scotland* U.K.
26 K8 **Strathbogie** *reg. Scotland* U.K.
26 G7 **Strathcarron** *val. Scotland* U.K.
213 G2 **Strathcona, Mount** Antarctica
106 E5 **Strathcona Provincial Park** *B.C.* Can.
26 G7 **Strathconon** *val. Scotland* U.K.
26 H8 **Strath Dearn** *val. Scotland* U.K.
26 J8 **Strathdon** *Aberdeenshire, Scotland* U.K.
26 H10 **Strath Earn** *val. Scotland* U.K.
26 H6 **Strath Fleet** *val. Scotland* U.K.
26 G8 **Strathglass** *val. Scotland* U.K.
205 K10 **Strathgordon** *Tas.* Austr.
26 I6 **Strath Halladale** *val. Scotland* U.K.
106 H5 **Strathmore** *Alta* Can.
26 G5 **Strathmore** *r. Scotland* U.K.
124 M5 **Strathmore** *CA* U.S.A.
106 F4 **Strathnaver** *B.C.* Can.
26 H6 **Strathnaver** *val. Scotland* U.K.
26 I6 **Strath of Kildonan** *val. Scotland* U.K.
26 G7 **Strathpeffer** *Highland, Scotland* U.K.
111 M7 **Strathroy** *Ont.* Can.
26 I8 **Strathspey** *val. Scotland* U.K.
26 I9 **Strath Tay** *val. Scotland* U.K.
26 I5 **Strathy** *Highland, Scotland* U.K.
26 H5 **Strathy Point** *Scotland* U.K.
26 H10 **Strathyre** *Stirling, Scotland* U.K.
78 E2 **Stratoni** Greece
79 J5 **Stratonıkeıa** *tourist site* Turkey
78 C4 **Stratos** Greece
30 C6 **Stratton** *Cornwall, England* U.K.
117 □O3 **Stratton** *ME* U.S.A.
117 M5 **Stratton Mountain** *VT* U.S.A.
31 I4 **Stratton St Margaret** *Swindon, England* U.K.
53 N4 **Straubing** Ger.
20 M2 **Straume** Norway
20 M3 **Straumen** *Nordland* Norway
20 M3 **Straumen** *Nordland* Norway
20 □B1 **Straumnes** *pt* Iceland
51 J7 **Straupitz** Ger.
50 I5 **Strausberg** Ger.
49 K8 **Straußfurt** Ger.
118 C3 **Strausstown** *PA* U.S.A.
125 U7 **Strawberry** *AZ* U.S.A.
122 E4 **Strawberry Mountain** *OR* U.S.A.
125 U1 **Strawberry Reservoir** *UT* U.S.A.
55 I5 **Strawczyn** Pol.
110 F9 **Strawn** *IL* U.S.A.
77 K8 **Straža** *mt.* Macedonia
77 N7 **Strazhitsa** Bulg.
56 D2 **Stráž nad Nežárkou** Czech Rep.
51 L9 **Stráž nad Nisou** Czech Rep.
59 I2 **Strážný** Czech Rep.
56 C2 **Strážov** Czech Rep.
57 H3 **Strážov** *mt.* Slovakia
51 K9 **Stráž pod Ralskem** Czech Rep.
57 K3 **Strážske** Slovakia
204 E5 **Streaky Bay** *S.A.* Austr.
204 E5 **Streaky Bay** *b. S.A.* Austr.
27 G6 **Streamstown** Rep. of Ireland
31 J4 **Streatley** *West Berkshire, England* U.K.
110 F8 **Streator** *IL* U.S.A.
56 D2 **Středočeský Kraj** *admin. reg.* Czech Rep.
48 F4 **Streek** Ger.
30 G5 **Street** *Somerset, England* U.K.
77 L6 **Strehaia** Romania
51 H8 **Strehla** Ger.
77 L5 **Strei** *r.* Romania
209 G11 **Streich Mound** *hill W.A.* Austr.
57 H4 **Strekov** Slovakia
56 C2 **Střela** *r.* Czech Rep.
77 M8 **Strelcha** Bulg.
17 R1 **Strelets** Rus. Fed.
17 P3 **Streletskoye** Rus. Fed.
56 F2 **Střelice** Czech Rep.
17 R2 **Strelitsa** Rus. Fed.
193 Q3 **Strelka** Rus. Fed.
19 R1 **Strelkovo** Rus. Fed.
208 E6 **Strelley** *W.A.* Austr.
208 E6 **Strelley** *r. W.A.* Austr.
208 E6 **Strelley Aboriginal Reserve** *W.A.* Austr.
14 G2 **Strel'na** *r.* Rus. Fed.
59 N5 **Strem** Austria
71 J3 **Strembo** Italy
51 F5 **Stremme** *r.* Ger.
16 H3 **Stremyhorod** Ukr.
18 I4 **Strenči** Latvia
59 K3 **Strengberg** Austria
58 B5 **Strengen** Austria
29 O5 **Strensall** *York, England* U.K.
55 M5 **Streptiv** Ukr.
70 F4 **Stresa** Italy
29 M7 **Stretford** *Greater Manchester, England* U.K.
31 M3 **Stretham** *Cambridgeshire, England* U.K.
31 I2 **Stretton** *Staffordshire, England* U.K.
49 J10 **Streu** *r.* Ger.
49 K10 **Streufdorf** Ger.
24 D1 **Streymoy** *i.* Faroe Is
192 I3 **Strezhevoy** Rus. Fed.
56 B2 **Stříbro** Czech Rep.
26 L7 **Strichen** *Aberdeenshire, Scotland* U.K.
153 J8 **Strickland** *r.* P.N.G.
71 L3 **Strigno** Italy
59 N6 **Štrigova** Croatia
44 G5 **Strijen** Neth.
17 P3 **Strilechna** Ukr.
56 E2 **Strimilov** Czech Rep.
78 E2 **Strimonas** *r.* Greece
Strimonikón Greece *see* **Strymoniko**
28 G2 **Striven, Loch** *inlet Scotland* U.K.
68 G3 **Strizivojna** Croatia
59 M8 **Strmec** Croatia
49 K7 **Ströbeck** Ger.
59 H4 **Strobl** Austria
145 E6 **Stroeder** Arg.
78 C5 **Strofades** *i.* Greece
53 L5 **Strogen** *r.* Ger.
17 M7 **Strohanivka** Ukr.
48 G5 **Ströhen** Ger.
16 H6 **Stroieşti** Moldova
17 P3 **Stroitel'** Rus. Fed.
27 F5 **Strokestown** Rep. of Ireland
50 I4 **Strom** *r.* Ger.
26 J5 **Stroma, Island of** *Scotland* U.K.
23 N1 **Strömaren** *l.* Sweden
21 N6 **Strömbacka** Sweden
52 D2 **Stromberg** Ger.
52 F3 **Stromberg-Heuchelberg, Naturpark** *nature res.* Ger.
75 I6 **Stromboli, Isola** *i. Isole Lipari* Italy
75 I6 **Strombolicchio, Isola** *i. Isole Lipari* Italy
26 E8 **Stromeferry** *Highland, Scotland* U.K.
145 □ **Stromness** S. Georgia
26 J5 **Stromness** *Orkney, Scotland* U.K.
21 N6 **Strömsbruk** Sweden
120 G5 **Stromsburg** *NE* U.S.A.
20 O2 **Strømsmoen** Norway
22 H3 **Strömstad** Sweden
20 M5 **Strömsund** Sweden
73 J3 **Stroncone** Italy
70 I5 **Strone** *r.* Italy
26 G11 **Strone** *Argyll and Bute, Scotland* U.K.
121 I9 **Strong** *AR* U.S.A.
75 M5 **Strongoli** Italy
116 D7 **Strongsville** *OH* U.S.A.
54 E5 **Stronie Śląskie** Pol.
26 K4 **Stronsay** *i. Scotland* U.K.
26 K4 **Stronsay Firth** *sea chan. Scotland* U.K.
59 N2 **Stronsdorf** Austria
26 E9 **Strontian** *Highland, Scotland* U.K.
57 K2 **Stropkov** Slovakia
56 D3 **Stropnice** *r.* Czech Rep.
70 E5 **Stroppiana** Italy
70 C6 **Stroppo** Italy
30 H4 **Stroud** *Gloucestershire, England* U.K.
205 M5 **Stroud Road** *N.S.W.* Austr.
118 E3 **Stroudsburg** *PA* U.S.A.
Stroyentsy Moldova *see* **Stroieşti**
55 H6 **Stróża** Pol.
48 E4 **Strücklingen (Saterland)** Ger.
22 E5 **Struer** Denmark
76 I9 **Struga** Macedonia
54 F3 **Struga** *r.* Pol.
18 M3 **Strugi-Krasnyye** Rus. Fed.
19 P8 **Strugovskaya Buda** Rus. Fed.
96 E10 **Struis Bay** S. Africa
96 E10 **Struis Bay** *b.* S. Africa
27 H3 **Strule** *r. Northern Ireland* U.K.
53 J2 **Strullendorf** Ger.
77 L9 **Struma** *r.* Bulg.
30 B3 **Strumble Head** *Wales* U.K.
78 E1 **Strumeshnitsa** *r.* Bulg.
77 K9 **Strumica** Macedonia
77 K9 **Strumica** *r.* Macedonia
54 G6 **Strumień** Pol.
57 L3 **Strumkivka** Ukr.
19 V5 **Strunino** Rus. Fed.
59 J1 **Strunkovice nad Blanicí** Czech Rep.
49 J8 **Struth** Ger.
116 E7 **Struthers** *OH* U.S.A.
77 M8 **Stryama** *r.* Bulg.
96 H5 **Strydenburg** S. Africa
97 J2 **Strydpoort** S. Africa
55 H4 **Stryków** Pol.
78 E1 **Strymoniko** Greece
21 I6 **Stryn** Norway
48 K1 **Strynø** *i.* Denmark
16 E5 **Strypa** *r.* Ukr.
16 J6 **Stryukove** Ukr.
16 C4 **Stryy** Ukr.
16 D4 **Stryy** *r.* Ukr.
16 H4 **Stryzhavka** Ukr.
54 F3 **Strzałkowo** Pol.
54 G5 **Strzebień** Pol.
55 I3 **Strzegocin** Pol.
54 E5 **Strzegom** Pol.
54 E4 **Strzegomka** *r.* Pol.
55 I3 **Strzegowo** Pol.
55 H3 **Strzelce** Pol.
54 D3 **Strzelce Krajeńskie** Pol.
54 G5 **Strzelce Opolskie** Pol.
55 H4 **Strzelce Wielkie** Pol.
206 D6 **Strzelecki, Mount** *hill N.T.* Austr.
204 G3 **Strzelecki Creek** *watercourse S.A.* Austr.
204 G3 **Strzelecki Regional Reserve** *nature res. S.A.* Austr.
54 F5 **Strzeleczki** Pol.
54 F5 **Strzelin** Pol.
54 G3 **Strzelno** Pol.
54 G1 **Strzepcz** Pol.
55 J6 **Strzyżów** Pol.
37 J8 **Sts-Geosmes** France
16 G1 **Stsvina** *r.* Belarus
207 M9 **Stuart** *r. Qld* Austr.
115 G12 **Stuart** *FL* U.S.A.
120 H5 **Stuart** *IA* U.S.A.
120 F4 **Stuart** *NE* U.S.A.
116 E12 **Stuart** *VA* U.S.A.
206 D7 **Stuart Bluff Range** *mts N.T.* Austr.
26 L7 **Stuartfield** *Aberdeenshire, Scotland* U.K.
106 E4 **Stuart Lake** *B.C.* Can.
203 B12 **Stuart Mountains** *South I.* N.Z.
204 E3 **Stuart Range** *hills S.A.* Austr.
116 F10 **Stuarts Draft** *VA* U.S.A.
58 D5 **Stubaier Alpen** *mts* Austria
58 D5 **Stubaital** *val.* Austria
59 K5 **Stubalpe** *mt.* Austria
48 H1 **Stubbæk** Denmark
50 F1 **Stubbekøbing** Denmark
48 G4 **Stubben** Ger.
50 I1 **Stubbenkammer** *hd* Ger.
208 □1 **Stubbings Point** Christmas I.
31 J6 **Stubbington** *Hampshire, England* U.K.
131 □3 **Stubbs** St Vincent
59 M5 **Stubenberg** Austria
76 J7 **Stubica** *Srbija* Serb. and Mont.
76 I6 **Stubline** *Srbija* Serb. and Mont.
55 K6 **Stubno** Pol.

Stuchowo to **Svartevatn**

344

54 D2 **Stuchowo** Pol.
56 E2 **Studená** Czech Rep.
16 H5 **Studena** Ukr.
59 I2 **Studená Vltava** *r.* Czech Rep.
76 I7 **Studenica** *tourist site* Serb. and Mont.
50 F5 **Stüdenitz** Ger.
57 H2 **Studénka** Czech Rep.
77 N9 **Studen Kladenets, Yazovir** *resr* Bulg.
17 Q1 **Studenoye** Rus. Fed.
16 G2 **Studenytsya** *r.* Ukr.
31 K4 **Studham** *Bedfordshire, England* U.K.
203 F11 **Studholme Junction** *South I.* N.Z.
56 G3 **Studienka** Slovakia
96 I9 **Studis** S. Africa
31 I6 **Studland** *Dorset, England* U.K.
31 I3 **Studley** *Warwickshire, England* U.K.
23 N3 **Studsvik** Sweden
14 B3 **Studsviken** Sweden
121 D11 **Study Butte** *TX* U.S.A.
54 F1 **Studzienice** Pol.
20 M5 **Stugun** Sweden
58 G5 **Stuhlfelden** Austria
52 E6 **Stühlingen** Ger.
16 J3 **Stuhna** *r.* Ukr.
48 G4 **Stuhr** Ger.
107 M4 **Stull Lake** *Man./Ont.* Can.
51 H6 **Stülpe** Ger.
77 N3 **Stulpicani** Romania
58 E5 **Stumm** Austria
107 L6 **Stump Lake** *ND* U.S.A.
Stung Treng Cambodia *see* **Stœ̆ng Trêng**
107 M4 **Stupart** *r. Man.* Can.
56 G3 **Stupava** Slovakia
19 V7 **Stupino** Rus. Fed.
73 Q1 **Stupišće, Rt** *pt* Croatia
55 I2 **Stupsk** Pol.
70 E5 **Stura** *r.* Italy
70 C5 **Stura di Ala** *r.* Italy
70 D6 **Stura di Demonte** *r.* Italy
41 K6 **Stura di Val Grande** *r.* Italy
70 C5 **Stura di Viù** *r.* Italy
213 K2 **Sturge Island** Antarctica
108 E4 **Sturgeon** *r. Ont.* Can.
107 J4 **Sturgeon** *r. Sask.* Can.
110 H4 **Sturgeon** *r. MI* U.S.A.
110 C1 **Sturgeon, Lake** *Ont.* Can.
107 L4 **Sturgeon Bay** *Man.* Can.
110 G5 **Sturgeon Bay** *WI* U.S.A.
110 J4 **Sturgeon Bay** *b. MI* U.S.A.
110 G5 **Sturgeon Bay Canal** *lake channel WI* U.S.A.
108 E4 **Sturgeon Falls** *Ont.* Can.
111 P5 **Sturgeon Lake** *Ont.* Can.
108 B3 **Sturgeon Lake** *Ont.* Can.
114 D7 **Sturgis** *KY* U.S.A.
110 I8 **Sturgis** *MI* U.S.A.
120 D3 **Sturgis** *SD* U.S.A.
70 G7 **Sturla** *r.* Italy
68 E3 **Šturlić** Bos.-Herz.
30 H6 **Sturminster Newton** *Dorset, England* U.K.
57 H4 **Štúrovo** Slovakia
31 O5 **Sturry** *Kent, England* U.K.
205 H3 **Sturt, Mount** *hill N.S.W.* Austr.
204 F6 **Sturt Bay** *S.A.* Austr.
208 J5 **Sturt Creek** *W.A.* Austr.
208 I5 **Sturt Creek** *watercourse W.A.* Austr.
110 G7 **Sturtevant** *WI* U.S.A.
205 H3 **Sturt National Park** *N.S.W.* Austr.
206 D4 **Sturt Plain** *N.T.* Austr.
204 H3 **Sturt Stony Desert** *Qld* Austr.
37 O5 **Sturzelbronn** France
97 L8 **Stutterheim** S. Africa
52 G4 **Stuttgart** Ger.
52 H3 **Stuttgart** *admin. reg.* Ger.
121 J8 **Stuttgart** *AR* U.S.A.
Stutthof Pol. *see* **Sztutowo**
49 K9 **Stützerbach** Ger.
16 G2 **Stvyha** *r.* Ukr.
20 □B1 **Stykkishólmur** Iceland
17 Q6 **Styla** Ukr.
78 D4 **Stylida** Greece
16 F1 **Styr** *r.* Belarus/Ukr.
Styria *land* Austria *see* **Steiermark**
143 G3 **Suaçuí Grande** *r.* Brazil
155 D8 **Suai** East Timor
157 J3 **Suai** *Sarawak* Malaysia
136 C3 **Suaita** Col.
85 H5 **Suakin** Sudan
186 D6 **Suakin Archipelago** *is* Sudan
85 H5 **Suakin Archipelago** *is* Sudan
91 D6 **Suana** Dem. Rep. Congo
63 L2 **Suances** Spain
171 M6 **Suao** Taiwan
126 E3 **Suaqui Grande** Mex.
85 H5 **Suara, Mount** Eritrea
147 G2 **Suardi** Arg.
136 B4 **Suárez** Col.
191 L1 **Suat** Kazakh.
137 E2 **Suata** Venez.
200 □6 **Suavanao** *Sta Isabel* Solomon Is
18 H6 **Subačius** Lith.
157 G8 **Subang** *Jawa* Indon.
179 M6 **Subankhata** *Assam* India
173 L13 **Subansiri** *r.* India
179 K9 **Subarnarekha** *r. W. Bengal* India
184 C4 **Sūbāshī** Iran
79 J1 **Subaşı** *İstanbul* Turkey
79 I4 **Subaşı** *İzmir* Turkey
73 J1 **Subasio, Monte** *mt.* Italy
18 I5 **Subate** Latvia
187 H2 **Subay** *reg.* Saudi Arabia
188 I8 **Şubayḩah** Saudi Arabia
186 G9 **Şubayḩī** *reg.* Yemen
71 L8 **Subbiano** Italy
77 N4 **Subcetate** Romania
172 L7 **Subei** *Gansu* China
Subeita *tourist site* Israel *see* **Shivta**
59 H3 **Suben** Austria
73 K4 **Subiaco** Italy
157 H3 **Subi Besar** *i.* Indon.
157 H3 **Subi Kecil** *i.* Indon.
54 G1 **Subkowy** Pol.
121 E7 **Sublette** *KS* U.S.A.
76 H4 **Subotica** *Vojvodina, Srbija* Serb. and Mont.
85 I6 **Subucle** *mt.* Eritrea
93 B5 **Subugo** *mt.* Kenya
57 H2 **Sučany** Slovakia
42 H5 **Suc-au-May** *hill* France
118 F3 **Succasunna** *NJ* U.S.A.
124 N5 **Success, Lake** *CA* U.S.A.
70 I7 **Succiso, Alpi di** *mts* Italy
77 O3 **Suceava** Romania
77 N3 **Suceava** *r.* Romania
38 H7 **Sucé-sur-Erdre** France
55 H6 **Sucha Beskidzka** Pol.
55 H1 **Suchacz** Pol.
57 G3 **Suchá Loz** Czech Rep.
54 D2 **Suchań** Pol.
162 H7 **Suchan** *r.* Rus. Fed.
56 E2 **Suchdol** Czech Rep.
56 D3 **Suchdol nad Lužnicí** Czech Rep.
55 I4 **Suchedniów** Pol.
47 J3 **Suchedniowsko-Oblęgorski Park Krajobrazowy** Pol.
70 A2 **Suchet, Mont** *mt.* Switz.
128 D2 **Suchil** Mex.
55 L2 **Suchowola** Pol.
55 K3 **Suchożebry** Pol.
131 □1 **Sucia, Bahía** *b.* Puerto Rico
67 D12 **Sucina** Spain
136 B3 **Sucio** *r.* Col.
77 M3 **Suciu de Sus** Romania
27 F6 **Suck** *r.* Rep. of Ireland
111 N3 **Sucker Creek Landing** *Ont.* Can.
50 E4 **Suckow** Ger.
138 D4 **Sucre** Bol.
136 C2 **Sucre** *dept* Col.
137 F2 **Sucre** *state* Venez.
136 D3 **Sucuaro** Col.
136 B5 **Sucumbíos** *prov.* Ecuador
137 G6 **Sucunduri** *r.* Brazil
142 B4 **Sucuriú** *r.* Brazil
Suczawa Romania *see* **Suceava**
89 H6 **Sud** *prov.* Cameroon
99 □3a **Sud, Pointe** *pt Njazidja* Comoros
99 □2b **Sud, Pointe du** *c. Mahé* Seychelles
99 □3b **Sud, Récif du** *rf* Mayotte
117 L3 **Sud, Rivière du** *r. Que.* Can.
19 U2 **Suda** Rus. Fed.
19 U2 **Suda** *r.* Rus. Fed.
17 N9 **Sudak** Ukr.
167 H4 **Sudama** Japan
85 F6 **Sudan** *country* Africa
14 H4 **Suday** Rus. Fed.
186 G3 **Sudayr** *reg.* Saudi Arabia
189 L8 **Sudayr, Sha'īb** *watercourse* Iraq
19 U9 **Sudbishchi** Rus. Fed.
182 E1 **Sud'bodarovka** Rus. Fed.
108 D4 **Sudbury** *Ont.* Can.
31 I2 **Sudbury** *Derbyshire, England* U.K.
31 N3 **Sudbury** *Suffolk, England* U.K.
92 A3 **Sudd** *swamp* Sudan
49 D6 **Suddendorf** Ger.
137 G3 **Suddie** Guyana
48 K4 **Sude** *r.* Ger.
48 G2 **Süden** Ger.
48 I1 **Süderbrarup** Ger.
48 J5 **Suderburg** Ger.
48 J4 **Südergellersen** Ger.
48 H2 **Süderhastedt** Ger.
48 G1 **Süderlügum** Ger.
48 G2 **Süderoog** *i.* Ger.
48 F2 **Süderoogsand** *i.* Ger.
48 H2 **Süderstapel** Ger.
Sudest Island P.N.G. *see* **Tagula Island**
Sudetenland *mts* Czech Rep./Pol. *see* **Sudety**
54 D5 **Sudety** *mts* Czech Rep./Pol.
48 G2 **Südfall** *i.* Ger.
19 R8 **Sudimir** Rus. Fed.
19 Y4 **Sudislavl'** Rus. Fed.
91 F5 **Sud-Kivu** *prov.* Dem. Rep. Congo
118 D6 **Sudlersville** *MD* U.S.A.
49 C7 **Südlohn** Ger.
48 D5 **Süd-Nord-Kanal** *canal* Ger.
64 B6 **Sudoeste Alentejano e Costa Vicentina, Parque Natural do** *nature res.* Port.
19 X6 **Sudogda** Rus. Fed.
19 X5 **Sudogda** *r.* Rus. Fed.
56 G3 **Sudoměřice** Czech Rep.
18 M4 **Sudomskiye Vysoty** *hills* Rus. Fed.
19 Q9 **Sudost'** *r.* Rus. Fed.
89 H5 **Sud-Ouest** *prov.* Cameroon
99 □1b **Sud Ouest, Pointe** *pt* Mauritius
16 C4 **Sudova Vyshnya** Ukr.
59 N7 **Sudovec** Croatia
85 G2 **Sudr** Egypt
191 I4 **Sudur** Azer.
191 B6 **Sudurağı** Turkey
20 □B1 **Suðurland** *constituency* Iceland
192 A3 **Suðuroy** *i.* Faroe Is
24 D1 **Suðuroy** *i.* Faroe Is
24 D1 **Suðuroyarfjørður** *sea chan.* Faroe Is
48 G5 **Sudwalde** Ger.
17 O2 **Sudzha** Rus. Fed.
17 O2 **Sudzha** *r.* Rus. Fed.
90 F3 **Sue** *watercourse* Sudan
67 E9 **Sueca** Spain
77 M8 **Sŭedinenie** Bulg.
72 C8 **Suelli** *Sardegna* Italy
99 □2b **Suète, Île du** *i. Inner Islands* Seychelles
63 J2 **Sueva, Reserva Nacional de** *nature res.* Spain
36 B8 **Suèvres** France
115 □1 **Sue Wood Bay** Bermuda
Suez Egypt *see* **As Suways**
Suez, Gulf of Egypt *see* **Suways, Khalīj as**
Suez Bay Egypt *see* **Qulzum, Baḩr al**
Suez Canal *canal* Egypt *see* **Suways,Qanāt as**
186 E4 **Şufaynah** Saudi Arabia
119 G2 **Suffern** *NY* U.S.A.
31 N3 **Suffolk** *admin. div. England* U.K.
116 I12 **Suffolk** *VA* U.S.A.
119 J3 **Suffolk County** *county NY* U.S.A.
184 A2 **Sūfiān** Iran
Sufi-Kurgan Kyrg. *see* **Sopu-Korgon**
191 E3 **Sugan, Gora** *mt.* Rus. Fed.
110 E7 **Sugar** *r. WI* U.S.A.
110 F4 **Sugarbush Hill** *WI* U.S.A.
116 C9 **Sugar Grove** *OH* U.S.A.
119 G2 **Sugar Loaf** *NY* U.S.A.
27 C9 **Sugarloaf Mountain** *hill* Rep. of Ireland
117 □O3 **Sugarloaf Mountain** *ME* U.S.A.
205 N5 **Sugarloaf Point** *N.S.W.* Austr.
98 □2b **Sugar Loaf Point** St Helena
118 D2 **Sugar Notch** *PA* U.S.A.
118 C1 **Sugar Run** *PA* U.S.A.
166 E7 **Suga-shima** *i.* Japan
154 F6 **Sugbuhan Point** Phil.
53 I2 **Sugenheim** Ger.
Süget *Xinjiang* China *see* **Sogat**
185 M2 **Sughd** *admin. div.* Tajik.
156 E4 **Sugi** *i.* Indon.
172 C7 **Sugun** *Xinjiang* China
157 L1 **Sugut** *r.* Malaysia
157 L1 **Sugut, Tanjung** *pt* Malaysia
77 N7 **Suhaia** Romania
172 K7 **Suhai Hu** *l. Qinghai* China
168 J6 **Suhai Obo** *Nei Mongol* China
168 I7 **Suhait** *Nei Mongol* China
Sūhāj Egypt *see* **Sawhāj**
59 K8 **Suha Krajina** *reg.* Slovenia
187 M3 **Şuḩār** Oman
77 O2 **Suharău** Romania
190 B8 **Suhaymī, Wādī as** *watercourse* Egypt
168 J1 **Sühbaatar** Mongolia
169 M3 **Sühbaatar** *prov.* Mongolia
176 C7 **Suheli Par** *i.* India
59 J8 **Suhi vrh** *mt.* Slovenia
49 K9 **Suhl** Ger.
48 K5 **Suhlendorf** Ger.
68 F3 **Suhopolje** Croatia
52 E7 **Suhr** Switz.
186 G4 **Suhul** *reg.* Saudi Arabia
187 K4 **Suhūl al Kidan** *plain* Saudi Arabia
88 E5 **Suhum** Ghana
79 L4 **Şuhut** Turkey
185 M7 **Sui** Pak.
159 D10 **Sui, Laem** *pt* Thai.
140 B4 **Suiá Missur** *r.* Brazil
Sui'an *Fujian* China *see* **Zhangpu**
162 G5 **Suibin** *Heilong.* China
171 L4 **Suichang** *Zhejiang* China
Suicheng *Guangdong* China *see* **Suixi**
171 J5 **Suichuan** *Jiangxi* China
Suid-Afrika *country* Africa *see* **South Africa, Republic of**
169 L8 **Suide** *Shaanxi* China
62 D3 **Suído, Serra do** *mts* Spain
162 G6 **Suifenhe** *Heilong.* China
162 G7 **Suifen He** *r.* China
167 L2 **Suifu** Japan
178 C7 **Suigam** *Gujarat* India
166 C4 **Suigetsu-ko** *l.* Japan
167 L3 **Suigō-Tsukuba Quasi National Park** Japan
162 E5 **Suihua** *Heilong.* China
170 D4 **Suijiang** *Yunnan* China
162 E5 **Suileng** *Heilong.* China
40 C2 **Suilly-la-Tour** France
26 F6 **Suilven** *hill Scotland* U.K.
170 H5 **Suining** *Hunan* China
171 K2 **Suining** *Jiangsu* China
170 E3 **Suining** *Sichuan* China
147 H4 **Suipacha** Arg.
138 D5 **Suipacha** Bol.
171 J2 **Suiping** *Henan* China
36 G5 **Suippe** *r.* France
36 I5 **Suippes** France
27 H8 **Suir** *r.* Rep. of Ireland
Suisse *country* Europe *see* **Switzerland**
39 K4 **Suisse Normande** *reg.* France
166 C6 **Suita** Japan
191 L5 **Suiti Burunu** *pt* Azer.
118 B7 **Suitland** *MD* U.S.A.
171 K2 **Suixi** *Anhui* China
170 H8 **Suixi** *Guangdong* China
169 N9 **Suixian** *Henan* China
Suixian *Hubei* China *see* **Suizhou**
170 F5 **Suiyang** *Guizhou* China
169 N9 **Suiyang** *Henan* China
Suizhai *Henan* China *see* **Xiangcheng**
169 Q6 **Suizhong** *Liaoning* China
171 I3 **Suizhou** *Hubei* China
169 J5 **Suj** *Nei Mongol* China
178 E6 **Sujangarh** *Rajasthan* India
185 M9 **Sujawal** Pak.
Suk *atoll* Micronesia *see* **Pulusuk**
156 G8 **Sukabumi** *Jawa* Indon.
157 H5 **Sukadana** *Kalimantan* Indon.
156 F7 **Sukadana** *Sumatera* Indon.
157 H5 **Sukadana, Teluk** *b.* Indon.
167 L1 **Sukagawa** Japan
156 G8 **Sukanegara** *Jawa* Indon.
157 I6 **Sukaraja** *Kalimantan* Indon.
157 I6 **Sukaramai** *Kalimantan* Indon.
157 M2 **Sukau** *Sabah* Malaysia
178 F7 **Suket** *Rajasthan* India
20 S5 **Sukeva** Fin.
162 H5 **Sukhanovka** Rus. Fed.
19 N8 **Sukhary** Belarus
19 S7 **Sukhinichi** Rus. Fed.
17 Q6 **Sukhi Yaly** *r.* Ukr.
55 M6 **Sukhodil** Ukr.
19 V8 **Sukhodol'skiy** Rus. Fed.
19 N1 **Sukhodol'skoye, Ozero** *l.* Rus. Fed.
19 S7 **Sukhodrev** *r.* Rus. Fed.
Sukhoivanovka Ukr. *see* **Stepnohirs'k**
191 G1 **Sukhokumskiy Kanal** *canal* Rus. Fed.
14 I3 **Sukhona** *r.* Rus. Fed.
158 D6 **Sukhothai** Thai.
162 E3 **Sukhotino** Rus. Fed.
19 S5 **Sukhoverkovo** Rus. Fed.
Sukhumi Georgia *see* **Sokhumi**
Sukhum-Kale Georgia *see* **Sokhumi**
17 Q5 **Sukhyy Torets'** *r.* Ukr.
17 K6 **Sukhyy Yelanets'** Ukr.
14 F3 **Sukkozero** Rus. Fed.
185 M8 **Sukkur** Pak.
185 M8 **Sukkur Barrage** Pak.
176 G3 **Sukma** *Chhattisgarh* India
84 B2 **Sūknah** Libya
157 I8 **Sukolilo** *Jawa* Indon.
57 H5 **Sükösd** Hungary
50 E3 **Sukow** Ger.
162 J5 **Sukpay** Rus. Fed.
162 J5 **Sukpay** *r.* Rus. Fed.
178 D7 **Sukri** *r.* India
178 D7 **Sukri** *r.* India
19 R5 **Sukromlya** Rus. Fed.
19 T4 **Sukromny** Rus. Fed.
94 C4 **Sukses** Namibia
14 L4 **Suksun** Rus. Fed.
179 I9 **Suktel** *r.* India
165 J14 **Sukumo** Japan
165 J14 **Sukumo-wan** *b.* Japan
155 C8 **Sukun** *i.* Indon.
191 I6 **Şükürbäyli** Azer.
137 I5 **Sul, Canal do** *sea chan.* Brazil
143 F4 **Sul, Pico do** *mt.* Brazil
24 J1 **Sula** *i.* Norway
14 J2 **Sula** *r.* Rus. Fed.
17 L4 **Sula** *r.* Ukr.
155 D4 **Sula, Kepulauan** *is* Indon.
155 D5 **Sulabesi** *i.* Indon.
185 M6 **Sulaiman Range** *mts* Pak.
191 I2 **Sulak** Rus. Fed.
191 I2 **Sulak** *r.* Rus. Fed.
184 D6 **Sūlār** Iran
26 D4 **Sula Sgeir** *i. Scotland* U.K.
156 D5 **Sulasih, Gunung** *vol.* Indon.
157 L9 **Sulat** *i.* Indon.
154 E6 **Sulat** *Samar* Phil.
155 B5 **Sulawesi** *i.* Indon.
155 A5 **Sulawesi Selatan** *prov.* Indon.
155 B4 **Sulawesi Tengah** *prov.* Indon.
155 C6 **Sulawesi Tenggara** *prov.* Indon.
155 D3 **Sulawesi Utara** *prov.* Indon.
189 L6 **Sulaymān Beg** Iraq
186 G5 **Sulayyimah** Saudi Arabia
Sulci *Sardegna* Italy *see* **Sant'Antioco**
Sulcis *Sardegna* Italy *see* **Sant'Antioco**
72 B9 **Sulcis** *reg. Sardegna* Italy
22 C2 **Suldalsvatnet** *l.* Norway
54 D3 **Sulechów** Pol.
54 D3 **Sulęcin** Pol.
54 F3 **Sulęcinek** Pol.
54 F1 **Sulęczyno** Pol.
184 D3 **Suledeh** Iran
89 G4 **Suleja** Nigeria
55 H4 **Sulejów** Pol.
55 J3 **Sulejówek** Pol.
55 H4 **Sulejowskie, Jezioro** *l.* Pol.
157 M4 **Suleman, Teluk** *b.* Indon.
72 D6 **Su Lernu** *r.* Italy
26 H4 **Sule Skerry** *i. Scotland* U.K.
26 G4 **Sule Stack** *i. Scotland* U.K.
188 H5 **Süleymanlı** *Kahramanmaraş* Turkey
79 I4 **Süleymanlı** *Manisa* Turkey
156 D5 **Suliki** *Sumatera* Indon.
54 D4 **Sulików** Pol.
88 C5 **Sulima** Sierra Leone
77 R5 **Sulina** Romania
77 R5 **Sulina, Braţul** *watercourse* Romania
48 G5 **Sulingen** Ger.
168 D8 **Sulin Gol** *r. Qinghai* China
20 N3 **Suliskongen** *mt.* Norway
54 D2 **Suliszewo** Pol.
20 N3 **Sulitjelma** Norway
21 T6 **Sulkava** Fin.
55 H6 **Sułkowice** Pol.
191 H2 **Sulla-Chubutla** *r.* Rus. Fed.
136 A6 **Sullana** Peru
27 E9 **Sullane** *r.* Rep. of Ireland
79 K4 **Süller** Turkey
31 L6 **Sullington** *West Sussex, England* U.K.
120 K6 **Sullivan** *IL* U.S.A.
114 D6 **Sullivan** *IN* U.S.A.
120 J6 **Sullivan** *MO* U.S.A.
106 E5 **Sullivan Bay** *B.C.* Can.
118 F1 **Sullivan County** *county NY* U.S.A.
118 B2 **Sullivan County** *county PA* U.S.A.
107 I5 **Sullivan Lake** *Alta* Can.
26 □N2 **Sullom Voe** *inlet Scotland* U.K.
117 □P1 **Sully** *Que.* Can.
40 E2 **Sully** France
30 F5 **Sully** *Vale of Glamorgan, Wales* U.K.
36 D8 **Sully-sur-Loire** France
59 M6 **Sulm** *r.* Austria
55 H4 **Sulmierzyce** *Łódzkie* Pol.
54 F4 **Sulmierzyce** *Wielkopolskie* Pol.
Sulmo Italy *see* **Sulmona**
73 L3 **Sulmona** Italy
38 F6 **Sulniac** France
200 □6 **Sulofoloa** *Malaita* Solomon Is
77 O9 **Süloğlu** Turkey
55 H5 **Sułoszowa** Pol.
54 F4 **Sułów** *Dolnośląskie* Pol.
55 K5 **Sułów** *Lubelskie* Pol.
121 I10 **Sulphur** *LA* U.S.A.
121 G8 **Sulphur** *OK* U.S.A.
121 H9 **Sulphur** *r. TX* U.S.A.
121 D9 **Sulphur Draw** *watercourse TX* U.S.A.
121 H9 **Sulphur Springs** *TX* U.S.A.
121 E9 **Sulphur Springs Draw** *watercourse NM/TX* U.S.A.
108 D4 **Sultan** *Ont.* Can.
84 D2 **Sultan** Libya
185 J7 **Sultan, Koh-i-** *mts* Pak.
79 K2 **Sultanbeyli** Turkey
79 M4 **Sultandağı** Turkey
188 F4 **Sultanhanı** Turkey
79 J5 **Sultanhisar** Turkey
79 H2 **Sultaniça** Turkey
178 I6 **Sultanpur** *Uttar Prad.* India
185 I1 **Sultansandzharskoye Vodokhranilishche** *resr* Turkm.
191 D1 **Sultanskoye** Rus. Fed.
91 E6 **Sulu** Dem. Rep. Congo
154 E6 **Suluan** *i.* Phil.
154 D8 **Sulu Archipelago** *is* Phil.
188 F4 **Sülüklü** Turkey
183 M8 **Sülüktü** Kyrg.
179 N6 **Sulung** *Arun. Prad.* India
84 D1 **Suluntah** Libya
84 D2 **Sulūq** Libya
176 G6 **Suluru** *Andhra Prad.* India
216 C5 **Sulu Sea** N. Pacific Ocean
191 J5 **Sulut** Azer.
109 F1 **Suluvvaulik, Lac** *l. Que.* Can.
17 K3 **Sulymivka** Ukr.
Sulyukta Kyrg. *see* **Sülüktü**
58 A5 **Sulz** Austria
53 K3 **Sulz** *r.* Ger.
53 I3 **Sulzach** *r.* Ger.
52 F5 **Sulz am Neckar** Ger.
53 O4 **Sulzbach** *r.* Ger.
52 G2 **Sulzbach am Main** Ger.
52 G3 **Sulzbach an der Murr** Ger.
52 H4 **Sulzbach-Laufen** Ger.
53 L2 **Sulzbach-Rosenberg** Ger.
52 C3 **Sulzbach/Saar** Ger.
58 A4 **Sulzberg** Austria
53 I6 **Sulzberg** Ger.
212 N1 **Sulzberger Bay** Antarctica
52 D6 **Sulzburg** Ger.
49 K10 **Sulzdorf an der Lederhecke** Ger.
53 K5 **Sulzemoos** Ger.
52 F3 **Sulzfeld** *Baden-Württemberg* Ger.
49 J10 **Sulzfeld** *Bayern* Ger.
53 I2 **Sulzheim** Ger.
49 J10 **Sulzthal** Ger.
166 B6 **Suma** Japan
136 B5 **Sumaco, Volcán** *vol.* Ecuador
76 I6 **Šumadija** *reg.* Serb. and Mont.
187 N4 **Sumāil** Oman
155 C3 **Sumalata** *Sulawesi* Indon.
92 D3 **Sumalē** *admin. reg.* Eth.
144 E3 **Sumampa** Arg.
157 L1 **Sumangat, Tanjung** *pt* Malaysia
136 C4 **Sumapaz, Parque Nacional** *nat. park* Col.
184 A5 **Sūmār** Iran
44 J2 **Sumar** Neth.
156 C3 **Sumatera** *i.* Indon.
156 D5 **Sumatera Barat** *prov.* Indon.
156 E6 **Sumatera Selatan** *prov.* Indon.
156 C3 **Sumatera Utara** *prov.* Indon.
Sumatra *i.* Indon. *see* **Sumatera**
139 E1 **Sumaúma** Brazil
56 C2 **Šumava** *mts* Czech Rep.
56 C2 **Šumava** *nat. park* Czech Rep.
200 □1 **Sumay** Guam
155 B8 **Sumba** *i.* Indon.
90 C4 **Sumba, Île** *i.* Dem. Rep. Congo
155 A8 **Sumba, Selat** *sea chan.* Indon.
184 F3 **Sumbar** *r.* Turkm.
155 A8 **Sumbawa** *i.* Indon.
157 L9 **Sumbawabesar** *Sumbawa* Indon.
93 A6 **Sumbawanga** Tanz.
138 C3 **Sumbay** Peru
91 B7 **Sumbe** Angola
156 D6 **Sumbing, Gunung** *vol.* Indon.
91 F7 **Sumbu** Zambia
91 F7 **Sumbu National Park** Zambia
26 □N3 **Sumburgh** *Shetland, Scotland* U.K.
26 □N3 **Sumburgh Head** *Scotland* U.K.
88 C5 **Sumbuya** Sierra Leone
14 J4 **Sumchino** Rus. Fed.
173 D9 **Sumdo** Aksai Chin
170 C4 **Sumdo** *Sichuan* China
106 C3 **Sumdum** *AK* U.S.A.
106 C3 **Sumdum, Mount** *AK* U.S.A.
140 F3 **Sumé** Brazil
59 N8 **Šumećani** Croatia
157 G8 **Sumedang** *Jawa* Indon.
184 C3 **Sume'eh Sarā** Iran
56 G5 **Sümeg** Hungary
90 E2 **Sumeih** Sudan
41 D9 **Sumène** France
157 J8 **Sumenep** *Jawa* Indon.
178 D7 **Sumerpur** *Rajasthan* India
Sumgait Azer. *see* **Sumqayıt**
57 J3 **Šumiac** Slovakia
165 R15 **Sumisu-jima** *i.* Japan
70 D1 **Sumiswald** Switz.
169 N2 **Sümiyn Bulag** Mongolia
164 □G18 **Sumiyō** *Nansei-shotō* Japan
189 K5 **Summēl** Iraq
108 B2 **Summer Beaver** *Ont.* Can.
29 N5 **Summer Bridge** *North Yorkshire, England* U.K.
94 C4 **Summerdown** Namibia
109 K3 **Summerford** *Nfld and Lab.* Can.
27 I6 **Summerhill** Rep. of Ireland
110 H4 **Summer Island** *MI* U.S.A.
26 E6 **Summer Isles** *Scotland* U.K.
106 G5 **Summerland** *B.C.* Can.
109 I4 **Summerside** *P.E.I.* Can.
116 E10 **Summersville** *WV* U.S.A.
116 E10 **Summersville Lake** *WV* U.S.A.
115 E8 **Summerville** *GA* U.S.A.
115 G9 **Summerville** *SC* U.S.A.
202 K7 **Summit** *hill North I.* N.Z.
119 G3 **Summit** *NJ* U.S.A.
120 G3 **Summit** *SD* U.S.A.
118 D3 **Summit Hill** *PA* U.S.A.
106 E3 **Summit Lake** *B.C.* Can.
106 F4 **Summit Lake** *B.C.* Can.
125 P2 **Summit Mountain** *NV* U.S.A.
123 K8 **Summit Peak** *CO* U.S.A.
118 C3 **Summit Station** *PA* U.S.A.
59 M2 **Šumná** Czech Rep.
173 D9 **Sumnal** Aksai Chin
203 G10 **Sumner** *South I.* N.Z.
121 J9 **Sumner** *MS* U.S.A.
203 G9 **Sumner, Lake** *South I.* N.Z.
106 C3 **Sumner Strait** *AK* U.S.A.
167 J1 **Sumon** Japan
165 Q9 **Sumon-dake** *mt.* Japan
166 A7 **Sumoto** Japan
155 A6 **Sumpangbinangae** *Sulawesi* Indon.
56 F2 **Šumperk** Czech Rep.
158 C1 **Sumprabum** Myanmar
Sumpu Japan *see* **Shizuoka**
191 K5 **Sumqayıt** Azer.
191 K5 **Sumqayıt** *r.* Azer.
185 N8 **Sumrahu** Pak.
183 N7 **Sumsar** Kyrg.
17 M2 **Sums'ka Oblast'** *admin. div.* Ukr.
Sumskaya Oblast' *admin. div.* Ukr. *see* **Sums'ka Oblast'**
14 F2 **Sumskiy Posad** Rus. Fed.
48 K4 **Sumte** Ger.
115 G9 **Sumter** *SC* U.S.A.
178 F2 **Sumur** Jammu and Kashmir
56 G2 **Šumvald** Czech Rep.
70 F2 **Sumvitg** Switz.
173 E9 **Sumxi** *Xizang* China
17 N3 **Sumy** Ukr.
Sumy Oblast *admin. div.* Ukr. *see* **Sums'ka Oblast'**
170 A4 **Sumzom** *Xizang* China
122 I3 **Sun** *r. MT* U.S.A.
14 J4 **Suna** Rus. Fed.
164 S3 **Sunagawa** Japan
178 F7 **Sunaj** *Madh. Prad.* India
178 E4 **Sunam** *Punjab* India
179 M7 **Sunamganj** Bangl.
166 E5 **Sunami** Japan
168 F7 **Sunan** *Gansu* China
163 D9 **Sunan** N. Korea
26 E9 **Sunart, Loch** *inlet Scotland* U.K.
57 J2 **Šuňava** Slovakia
187 L4 **Şunaynah** Oman
66 B1 **Sunbilla** Spain
184 A4 **Sunbula Kuh** *mts* Iran
122 I2 **Sunburst** *MT* U.S.A.
205 J7 **Sunbury** *Vic.* Austr.
31 L5 **Sunbury** *Surrey, England* U.K.
116 C8 **Sunbury** *OH* U.S.A.
111 R9 **Sunbury** *PA* U.S.A.
147 G2 **Sunchales** Arg.
53 M4 **Sünching** Ger.
139 E6 **Suncho Corral** Arg.
163 D9 **Sunch'ŏn** N. Korea
163 E11 **Sunch'ŏn** S. Korea
97 L1 **Sun City** S. Africa
125 T8 **Sun City** *AZ* U.S.A.
124 O8 **Sun City** *CA* U.S.A.
117 N5 **Suncook** *NH* U.S.A.
57 L5 **Şuncuiuş** Romania
18 D1 **Sund** *Åland* Fin.
156 F8 **Sunda, Selat** *str.* Indon.
122 L4 **Sundance** *WY* U.S.A.
179 L9 **Sundarbans** *coastal area* Bangl./India
179 L9 **Sundarbans National Park** Bangl./India
179 J8 **Sundargarh** *Orissa* India
178 F4 **Sundarnagar** *Hima. Prad.* India
215 L4 **Sunda Shelf** *sea feature* Indian Ocean
Sunda Strait Indon. *see* **Sunda, Selat**
Sunda Trench *sea feature* Indian Ocean *see* **Java Trench**
96 J9 **Sundays** *r. Eastern Cape* S. Africa
97 O4 **Sundays** *r. KwaZulu-Natal* S. Africa
208 G4 **Sunday Strait** *W.A.* Austr.
147 F4 **Sundblad** Arg.
22 B2 **Sunde** *Hordaland* Norway
20 J5 **Sunde** *Sør-Trøndelag* Norway
29 O4 **Sunderland** *Tyne and Wear, England* U.K.
49 F8 **Sundern (Sauerland)** Ger.
40 K1 **Sundgau** *reg.* France
49 K8 **Sundhausen** Ger.
79 L3 **Sündiken Dağları** *mts* Turkey
91 B6 **Sundi-Mamba** Dem. Rep. Congo
106 H5 **Sundre** *Alta* Can.
108 E4 **Sundridge** *Ont.* Can.
22 F5 **Sunds** Denmark
22 E2 **Sundsli** Norway
21 N5 **Sundsvall** Sweden
191 J5 **Sündü** Azer.
185 J2 **Sundukli, Peski** *des.* Turkm.
97 P5 **Sundumbili** S. Africa
169 L2 **Sunduyka** Rus. Fed.
178 F7 **Sunel** *Rajasthan* India
93 C6 **Sunga** Tanz.
156 E4 **Sungaiapit** *Sumatera* Indon.
157 I4 **Sungai Ayak** *Kalimantan* Indon.
156 E4 **Sungaiguntung** *Sumatera* Indon.
156 E4 **Sungaikabung** *Sumatera* Indon.
157 H5 **Sungaikakap** *Kalimantan* Indon.
156 G5 **Sungailiat** *Sumatera* Indon.
156 D6 **Sungaipenuh** *Sumatera* Indon.
156 D2 **Sungai Petani** Malaysia
157 H4 **Sungaipinyuh** *Kalimantan* Indon.
156 G6 **Sungaiselan** Indon.
156 □ **Sungai Tuas Basin** *dock* Sing.
Sungari *r.* China *see* **Songhua Jiang**
156 □ **Sungei Seletar Reservoir** Sing.
155 A6 **Sungguminasa** *Sulawesi* Indon.
85 F6 **Sungikai** Sudan
Sungkiang *Shanghai* China *see* **Songjiang**
171 □J7 **Sung Kong** *i. H.K.* China
95 G3 **Sungo** Moz.
Sungqu *Sichuan* China *see* **Songpan**
156 F6 **Sungsang** *Sumatera* Indon.
191 D4 **Süngülü** Turkey
77 O8 **Sungurlare** Bulg.
188 G3 **Sungurlu** Turkey
72 B7 **Suni** *Sardegna* Italy
68 F3 **Sunja** Croatia
183 O5 **Sunkar, Gora** *mt.* Kazakh.
179 L7 **Sunkosh Chhu** *r.* Bhutan
179 K6 **Sun Kosi** *r.* Nepal
17 L4 **Sunky** Ukr.
49 J9 **Sünna** Ger.
22 C1 **Sunndal** Norway
20 J5 **Sunndalsøra** Norway
22 J2 **Sunne** Sweden
21 H6 **Sunnfjord** *reg.* Norway
31 K5 **Sunninghill** *Windsor and Maidenhead, England* U.K.
125 V2 **Sunnyside** *UT* U.S.A.
122 E3 **Sunnyside** *WA* U.S.A.
124 J4 **Sunnyvale** *CA* U.S.A.
167 K6 **Suno-saki** *pt* Japan
110 E6 **Sun Prairie** *WI* U.S.A.
139 F4 **Sunsas, Sierra de** *hills* Bol.
124 □C12 **Sunset Beach** *HI* U.S.A.
106 G4 **Sunset House** *Alta* Can.
Sunset Peak *hill H.K.* China *see* **Tai Tung Shan**
193 M3 **Suntar** Rus. Fed.
185 J9 **Suntsar** Pak.
92 C2 **Suntu** Eth.
122 G5 **Sun Valley** *ID* U.S.A.
163 D10 **Sunwi-do** *i.* N. Korea
162 E4 **Sunwu** *Heilong.* China
88 E5 **Sunyani** Ghana
191 H2 **Sunzha** *r.* Rus. Fed.
20 T2 **Suojanperä** Fin.
20 R5 **Suolahti** Fin.
14 E2 **Suolijärvet** *l.* Fin.
Suoločielgi Fin. *see* **Saariselkä**
20 Q2 **Suoluvuobmi** Norway
21 S6 **Suomenniemi** Fin.
110 E1 **Suomi** *Ont.* Can.
18 G1 **Suomusjärvi** Fin.
20 T4 **Suomussalmi** Fin.
165 I13 **Suō-nada** *b.* Japan
20 S5 **Suonenjoki** Fin.
159 G9 **Suŏng** Cambodia
158 F5 **Suong** *r.* Laos
20 S5 **Suontee** Fin.
20 S5 **Suontienselkä** *l.* Fin.
14 F3 **Suoyarvi** Rus. Fed.
176 D5 **Supa** *Karnataka* India
125 T5 **Supai** *AZ* U.S.A.
179 K6 **Supaul** *Bihar* India
43 F10 **Superbagnères** France
36 G6 **Superbe** *r.* France
40 B5 **Superbesse** France
41 H7 **Superdévoluy** France
125 U8 **Superior** *AZ* U.S.A.
122 G3 **Superior** *MT* U.S.A.
120 F5 **Superior** *NE* U.S.A.
110 B3 **Superior** *WI* U.S.A.
129 M9 **Superior, Laguna** *lag.* Mex.
110 G2 **Superior, Lake** Can./U.S.A.
71 J5 **Superiore, Lago** *l.* Italy
41 B6 **Superlioran** France
71 R6 **Supertarska Draga** Croatia
68 F4 **Supetar** Croatia
159 E7 **Suphan Buri** Thai.
189 K4 **Süphan Dağı** *mt.* Turkey
73 K4 **Supino** Italy
153 I7 **Supiori** *i. Papua* Indon.
17 K4 **Supiy** *r.* Ukr.
57 L4 **Suplacu de Barcău** Romania
19 R8 **Suponevo** Rus. Fed.
49 K6 **Süpplingen** Ger.
212 V1 **Support Force Glacier** Antarctica
55 L2 **Supraśl** Pol.
55 K2 **Supraśl** *r.* Pol.
191 C3 **Sup'sa** *r.* Georgia
163 D8 **Supung** N. Korea
57 L4 **Supur** Romania
186 G7 **Sūq al Inān** Yemen
186 E5 **Sūq ar Rubū'** Saudi Arabia
189 M8 **Sūq ash Shuyūkh** Iraq
171 L2 **Suqian** *Jiangsu* China
186 D3 **Sūq Suwayq** Saudi Arabia
187 L9 **Suquṭrá** *i.* Yemen
53 N6 **Sur** *r.* Ger.
88 E4 **Sur** *r.* Ghana
57 H4 **Súr** Hungary
187 N4 **Şūr** Oman
124 K5 **Sur, Point** *CA* U.S.A.
147 I5 **Sur, Punta** *pt* Arg.
15 I5 **Sura** Rus. Fed.
182 B1 **Sura** *r.* Rus. Fed.
191 K5 **Şuraabad** Azer.
185 L7 **Surab** Pak.
157 J8 **Surabaya** *Jawa* Indon.
185 K7 **Surai** Pak.
179 I8 **Surajpur** *Chhattisgarh* India
184 H9 **Sūrak** Iran
157 I8 **Surakarta** *Jawa* Indon.
155 A4 **Suramana** *Sulawesi* Indon.
77 M5 **Şura Mare** Romania
40 G4 **Suran** *r.* France
185 I8 **Sūran** Iran
190 E3 **Şūrān** Syria
57 H3 **Šurany** Slovakia
92 D3 **Surar** Eth.
137 F6 **Surára** Brazil
207 L9 **Surat** *Qld* Austr.
178 D9 **Surat** *Gujarat* India
178 D5 **Suratgarh** *Rajasthan* India
159 D10 **Surat Thani** Thai.
55 K3 **Suraż** Pol.
19 N6 **Surazh** Belarus
19 P8 **Surazh** Rus. Fed.
53 N6 **Surberg** Ger.
207 K7 **Surbiton** *Qld* Austr.
75 O3 **Surbo** Italy
189 L6 **Sūrdāsh** Iraq
77 P5 **Surdila-Greci** Romania
77 L3 **Surduc** Romania
77 K8 **Surdulica** *Srbija* Serb. and Mont.
52 B2 **Sûre** *r.* Ger./Lux.
178 C8 **Surendranagar** *Gujarat* India
126 □R13 **Suretka** Costa Rica
124 L7 **Surf** *CA* U.S.A.
119 G5 **Surf City** *NJ* U.S.A.
31 L2 **Surfleet** *Lincolnshire, England* U.K.
178 D9 **Surgana** *Mahar.* India
42 C3 **Surgères** France
130 B2 **Surgidero de Batabanó** Cuba
192 I3 **Surgut** Rus. Fed.
44 J2 **Surhuizum** Neth.
Suri *W. Bengal* India *see* **Siuri**
66 I4 **Súria** Spain
176 F4 **Suriapet** *Andhra Prad.* India
165 □3 **Suribachi-yama** *hill Iō-jima* Japan
70 C4 **Surier** Italy
154 E7 **Surigao** *Mindanao* Phil.
154 E6 **Surigao Strait** Phil.
136 C4 **Surimena** Col.
159 F7 **Surin** Thai.
99 □1b **Surinam** Mauritius
Surinam *country* S. America *see* **Suriname**
137 G3 **Suriname** *country* S. America
137 H3 **Suriname** *r.* Suriname
159 C10 **Surin Nua, Ko** *i.* Thai.
136 D3 **Suripá** Venez.
184 E6 **Suriyān** Iran
189 P6 **Surkhābād** Iran
183 L9 **Surkhandar'ya** *r.* Uzbek.
Surkhandarya Oblast *admin. div.* Uzbek. *see* **Surxondaryo**
185 K6 **Surkhduz** Afgh.
178 H5 **Surkhet** Nepal
185 M2 **Surkhob** *r.* Tajik.
Surkhondaryo *r.* Uzbek. *see* **Surkhandar'ya**
Surkhondaryo Wiloyati *admin. div.* Uzbek. *see* **Surxondaryo**
184 E6 **Surmāq** Iran
36 G5 **Surmelin** *r.* France
189 J3 **Sürmene** Turkey
20 J5 **Surnadalsøra** Norway
77 N8 **Sŭrnevo** Bulg.
15 H6 **Surovikino** Rus. Fed.
106 C3 **Surprise** *B.C.* Can.
200 □5 **Surprise, Île** *i.* New Caledonia
106 C3 **Surprise Lake** *B.C.* Can.
64 D2 **Surrazala** *r.* Port.
106 F5 **Surrey** *B.C.* Can.
130 □ **Surrey** *reg.* Jamaica
31 L5 **Surrey** *admin. div. England* U.K.
70 E1 **Sursee** Switz.
70 F2 **Surselva** *reg.* Switz.
17 N5 **Surs'ko-Mykhaylivka** Ukr.
15 I5 **Surskoye** Rus. Fed.
84 C2 **Surt** Libya
84 C2 **Surt, Khalīj** *g.* Libya
20 □C2 **Surtsey** *i.* Iceland
184 G8 **Sūrū** *Hormozgan* Iran
184 H9 **Sūrū** *Sīstān va Balūchestān* Iran
77 M5 **Suru, Vârful** *mt.* Romania
140 C2 **Surubiú** *r.* Brazil
188 I5 **Suruç** Turkey
92 E2 **Surud, Raas** *pt* Somalia
Surud Ad *mt.* Somalia *see* **Shimbiris**
167 H6 **Suruga-wan** *b.* Japan
156 E6 **Surulangun** *Sumatera* Indon.
137 F4 **Surumú** *r.* Brazil
154 F8 **Surup** *Mindanao* Phil.
36 E5 **Survilliers** France
48 E5 **Surwold** Ger.
183 L9 **Surxondaryo** *admin. div.* Uzbek.
Suryapet *Andhra Prad.* India *see* **Suriapet**
40 E5 **Sury-le-Comtal** France
38 F6 **Surzur** France
191 H6 **Şuşa** Azer.
22 H6 **Suså** *r.* Denmark
70 C5 **Susa** Italy
165 I12 **Susa** Japan
70 B5 **Susa, Valle di** *val.* Italy
68 F4 **Sušac** *i.* Croatia
Susah Tunisia *see* **Sousse**
71 Q6 **Susak** Croatia
68 E3 **Susak** *i.* Croatia
165 K13 **Susaki** Japan
165 M13 **Susami** Japan
Susamyr Kyrg. *see* **Suusamyr**
117 I11 **Susan** *VA* U.S.A.
184 C6 **Sūsangerd** Iran
162 L2 **Susanino** *Khabarovskiy Kray* Rus. Fed.
14 H4 **Susanino** *Kostromskaya Oblast'* Rus. Fed.
124 L1 **Susanville** *CA* U.S.A.
70 I2 **Susch** Switz.
16 G2 **Suschany** Ukr.
71 M4 **Susegana** Italy
188 I3 **Suşehri** Turkey
48 K2 **Süsel** Ger.
77 N7 **Sushitsa** Bulg.
169 L9 **Sushui He** *r.* China
56 C2 **Sušice** Czech Rep.
55 L5 **Susiec** Pol.
18 L5 **Šuškova** Latvia
178 F8 **Susner** *Madh. Prad.* India
159 D11 **Suso** Thai.
167 H2 **Susobana-gawa** *r.* Japan
171 K3 **Susong** *Anhui* China
167 I5 **Susono** Japan
66 K4 **Susqueda, Pantà de** *resr* Spain
117 J7 **Susquehanna** *PA* U.S.A.
111 R9 **Susquehanna** *r. PA* U.S.A.
116 I8 **Susquehanna, West Branch** *r. PA* U.S.A.
144 D1 **Susques** Arg.
52 H4 **Süßen** Ger.
109 H4 **Sussex** *N.B.* Can.
118 F2 **Sussex** *NJ* U.S.A.
116 H12 **Sussex** *VA* U.S.A.
118 F2 **Sussex County** *county NJ* U.S.A.
48 G5 **Süstedt** Ger.
45 I6 **Susteren** Neth.
128 D3 **Susticacán** Mex.
71 K5 **Sustinente** Italy
48 D5 **Sustrum** Ger.
106 E3 **Sustut Provincial Park** *B.C.* Can.
155 B5 **Susua** *Sulawesi* Indon.
200 □6 **Susubona** *Sta Isabel* Solomon Is
200 □6 **Susuka** *Choiseul* Solomon Is
157 L2 **Susul** *Sabah* Malaysia
193 P3 **Susuman** Rus. Fed.
155 E2 **Susupu** *Halmahera* Indon.
79 J3 **Susurluk** Turkey
191 E5 **Susuz** Turkey
18 G6 **Šušvė** *r.* Lith.
55 H2 **Susz** Pol.
178 F3 **Sutak** Jammu and Kashmir
168 C3 **Sutay Uul** *mt.* Mongolia
79 L5 **Sütçüler** Turkey
74 F8 **Sutera** *Sicilia* Italy
205 M6 **Sutherland** *N.S.W.* Austr.
96 E8 **Sutherland** S. Africa
26 H6 **Sutherland** *reg. Scotland* U.K.
120 E5 **Sutherland** *NE* U.S.A.
116 H11 **Sutherland** *VA* U.S.A.
209 H9 **Sutherland Range** *hills W.A.* Austr.
68 G4 **Sutjeska** *nat. park* Bos.-Herz.
178 C5 **Sutlej** *r.* India/Pak.
18 G2 **Sutlepa meri** *l.* Estonia
190 B2 **Sütlüce** *İçel* Turkey
77 P9 **Sütlüce** *Kırklareli* Turkey
72 I3 **Sutri** Italy
124 K2 **Sutter** *CA* U.S.A.
124 L3 **Sutter Creek** *CA* U.S.A.
31 L2 **Sutterton** *Lincolnshire, England* U.K.
117 M3 **Sutton** *Que.* Can.
108 D2 **Sutton** *r. Ont.* Can.
203 E12 **Sutton** *South I.* N.Z.
31 M3 **Sutton** *Cambridgeshire, England* U.K.
120 G5 **Sutton** *NE* U.S.A.
116 E10 **Sutton** *WV* U.S.A.
31 M2 **Sutton Bridge** *Lincolnshire, England* U.K.
31 I2 **Sutton Coldfield** *West Midlands, England* U.K.
31 J4 **Sutton Courtenay** *Oxfordshire, England* U.K.
29 O7 **Sutton in Ashfield** *Nottinghamshire, England* U.K.
108 C2 **Sutton Lake** *Ont.* Can.
116 E10 **Sutton Lake** *WV* U.S.A.
29 O5 **Sutton-on-the-Forest** *North Yorkshire, England* U.K.
29 P7 **Sutton on Trent** *Nottinghamshire, England* U.K.
31 N5 **Sutton Valence** *Kent, England* U.K.
207 K6 **Suttor** *r. Qld* Austr.
164 R4 **Suttsu** Japan
104 C4 **Sutwik Island** *AK* U.S.A.
162 H3 **Sutyr'** *r.* Rus. Fed.
16 H4 **Sutysky** Ukr.
200 □6 **Su'u** *Malaita* Solomon Is
169 J4 **Suugant** Mongolia
200 □6 **Su'uholo** Solomon Is
97 J7 **Suurberg** *mt.* S. Africa
97 J9 **Suurberg** *mts* S. Africa
96 E10 **Suurbraak** S. Africa
18 I3 **Suure-Jaani** Estonia
18 F3 **Suuremõisa** Estonia
18 F3 **Suur katel** *b.* Estonia
18 G2 **Suur-Pakri** *i.* Estonia
18 I2 **Suurpea** Estonia
18 G3 **Suur väin** *sea chan.* Estonia
183 O6 **Suusamyr** Kyrg.
201 □1a **Suva** *Viti Levu* Fiji
Suvalki Pol. *see* **Suwałki**
76 I8 **Suva Reka** *Kosovo, Srbija* Serb. and Mont.
191 F6 **Suveren** Turkey
72 F1 **Suvereto** Italy
73 Q10 **Suvero, Capo** *c.* Italy
71 K7 **Suviano, Lago di** *l.* Italy
Suvorov *atoll* Cook Is *see* **Suwarrow**
16 H8 **Suvorov** Moldova
19 T7 **Suvorov** Rus. Fed.
17 M6 **Suvorove** *Dnipropetrovs'ka Oblast'* Ukr.
16 H8 **Suvorove** *Odes'ka Oblast'* Ukr.
77 P7 **Suvorovo** Bulg.
Suvorovo Moldova *see* **Ştefan Vodă**
191 D1 **Suvorovskaya** Rus. Fed.
17 M8 **Suvorovs'ke** Ukr.
167 H3 **Suwa** Japan
167 H3 **Suwa-ko** *l.* Japan
157 K5 **Suwakong** *Kalimantan* Indon.
55 K1 **Suwałki** Pol.
158 F7 **Suwannaphum** Thai.
115 F11 **Suwannee** *r. FL* U.S.A.
164 □G17 **Suwanose-jima** *i. Nansei-shotō* Japan
157 L4 **Suwaran, Gunung** *mt.* Indon.
203 □2 **Suwarrow** *atoll* Cook Is
190 D6 **Suwaylih** Jordan
189 L7 **Suwayqīyah, Hawr as** *imp. l.* Iraq
189 J8 **Suwayr** *well* Saudi Arabia
85 G2 **Suways, Khalīj as** *g.* Egypt
85 G2 **Suways, Qanāt as** *canal* Egypt
190 C10 **Suweihil** *pt* Saudi Arabia
Suweilih Jordan *see* **Suwaylih**
Suweis, Khalîg el *g.* Egypt *see* **Suways, Khalīj as**
163 E10 **Suwŏn** S. Korea
168 D7 **Suxik** *Qinghai* China
170 G7 **Suxu** *Guangxi* China
183 S3 **Suykbulak** Kazakh.
136 A6 **Suyo** Peru
Sūyqbulaq Kazakh. *see* **Suykbulak**
186 F9 **Suyūl Ḩanīsh** *i.* Yemen
191 I1 **Suyutkina Kosa** Rus. Fed.
191 I1 **Suyutkina Kosa, Mys** *pt* Rus. Fed.
182 E7 **Suz, Mys** *pt* Kazakh.
184 G8 **Sūzā** Iran
183 M5 **Suzak** Kazakh.
167 H2 **Suzaka** Japan
19 X5 **Suzdal'** Rus. Fed.
41 F8 **Suze-la-Rousse** France
17 N1 **Suzemka** Rus. Fed.
171 K2 **Suzhou** *Anhui* China
171 M3 **Suzhou** *Jiangsu* China
163 D8 **Suzi He** *r.* China
165 O9 **Suzu** Japan
166 E6 **Suzuka** Japan
166 E6 **Suzuka-gawa** *r.* Japan
166 D5 **Suzuka Quasi National Park** Japan
166 D6 **Suzuka-sanmyaku** *mts* Japan
165 O9 **Suzu-misaki** *pt* Japan
71 J6 **Suzzara** Italy
21 M6 **Svabensverk** Sweden
20 S1 **Sværholthalvøya** *pen.* Norway
20 □ **Svalbard** *terr.* Arctic Ocean
77 O7 **Svalenik** Bulg.
22 H6 **Svallerup** Denmark
16 B5 **Svalyava** Ukr.
23 O2 **Svanberga** Sweden
191 D3 **Svanet'is K'edi** *hills* Georgia
23 K5 **Svängsta** Sweden
20 Q3 **Svanstein** Sweden
17 N2 **Svapa** *r.* Rus. Fed.
20 P3 **Svappavaara** Sweden
19 P4 **Svapushcha** Rus. Fed.
56 C3 **Švarcenberský kanál** *canal* Czech Rep.
23 L1 **Svärdsjö** Sweden
22 F2 **Svarstad** Norway
18 I1 **Svarta** *r.* Fin.
23 K2 **Svartå** Sweden
23 K2 **Svartälven** *r.* Sweden
23 J1 **Svartån** *r.* Sweden
23 M2 **Svartån** *r.* Sweden
20 Q3 **Svartbyn** Sweden
Svartenhuk Halvø *pen.* Greenland *see* **Sigguup Nunaa**
22 C2 **Svartevatn** *l.* Norway

Svartlä to Täklä
345

20 P3 Svartlä Sweden
23 P2 Svartlögafjärden b. Sweden
16 F2 Svarytsevychi Ukr.
51 G10 Svatava Czech Rep.
24 J1 Svatjell hill Norway
59 P2 Svatobořice-Mistřín Czech Rep.
17 R4 Svatove Ukr.
57 K3 Svätuše Slovakia
56 G3 Svätý Jur Slovakia
57 H4 Svätý Peter Slovakia
59 G9 Svay Riĕng Cambodia
20 □ Sveagruva Svalbard
14 I4 Svecha Rus. Fed.
18 I6 Svėdasai Lith.
21 M5 Sveg Sweden
21 M5 Svegsjön l. Sweden
22 B2 Sveio Norway
18 J4 Sveķi Latvia
18 E6 Švėkšna Lith.
21 H6 Svelgen Norway
20 J5 Svellingen Norway
17 N1 Sven' Rus. Fed.
18 I6 Švenčionėliai Lith.
18 J6 Švenčionys Lith.
22 G6 Svendborg Denmark
22 J4 Svenljunga Sweden
20 □ Svenskøya i. Svalbard
20 M5 Svenstavik Sweden
55 L1 Šventežeris Lith.
18 H6 Šventoji r. Lith.
62 C2 Sverbeyevo Rus. Fed.
19 S6 Sverchkovo Rus. Fed.
15 I6 Sverdlovo Rus. Fed.
Sverdlovsk Rus. Fed. see Yekaterinburg
17 S5 Sverdlovs'k Ukr.
14 M4 Sverdlovskaya Oblast' admin. div. Rus. Fed.
Sverdlovsk Oblast admin. div. Rus. Fed. see Sverdlovskaya Oblast'
05 I2 Sverdrup Channel Nunavut Can.
05 I2 Sverdrup Islands Nunavut Can.
Sverige country Europe see Sweden
Švermovo Slovakia see Telgárt
17 M2 Svesa Ukr.
77 O7 Sveshtari, Tomb of tourist site Bulg.
68 E4 Sveta Andrija i. Croatia
59 O7 Sveta Marija Croatia
18 G5 Švėtė r. Lith.
71 R6 Sveti Damjan, Rt pt Croatia
71 R6 Sveti Grgur i. Croatia
Sveti Ivan Zelina Croatia see Zelina
68 F4 Sveti Jure mt. Croatia
77 J9 Sveti Nikole Macedonia
56 G1 Světlá Hora Czech Rep.
56 E2 Světlá nad Sázavou Czech Rep.
62 K5 Svetlaya Rus. Fed.
62 M4 Svetlodarskoye Sakhalin Rus. Fed.
Svetlogorsk Belarus see Svyetlahorsk
18 D7 Svetlogorsk Kaliningradskaya Oblast' Rus. Fed.
92 J3 Svetlogorsk Krasnoyarskiy Kray Rus. Fed.
15 H7 Svetlograd Rus. Fed.
14 K4 Svetlopolyansk Rus. Fed.
Svetlovodsk Ukr. see Svitlovods'k
18 D7 Svetlyy Kaliningradskaya Oblast' Rus. Fed.
82 I2 Svetlyy Orenburgskaya Oblast' Rus. Fed.
15 I6 Svetlyy Yar Rus. Fed.
18 L1 Svetogorsk Leningradskaya Oblast' Rus. Fed.
Svetogorsk Respublika Dagestan Rus. Fed. see Shamil'kala
76 H5 Svetozar Miletić Vojvodina, Srbija Serb. and Mont.
18 H4 Svētupe r. Latvia
71 P5 Svetvinčenat Croatia
20 □E1 Svíahnúkar vol. Iceland
16 D4 Svicha r. Ukr.
57 K2 Svidník Slovakia
56 C2 Švihov Czech Rep.
18 G3 Sviibi Estonia
68 F4 Svilaja mts Croatia
76 J6 Svilajnac Srbija Serb. and Mont.
77 O9 Svilengrad Bulg.
77 K6 Svinecea Mare, Vârful mt. Romania
57 K2 Svinia Slovakia
57 H3 Svinná Slovakia
22 H6 Svinninge Denmark
Svinø i. Faroe Is see Svínoy
24 D1 Svínoy i. Faroe Is
85 L3 Svintsovyy Rudnik Turkm.
18 J7 Svir Belarus
19 S1 Svir' r. Rus. Fed.
18 J7 Svir, Vozyera l. Belarus
19 P1 Sviritsa Rus. Fed.
19 P1 Svirskaya Guba b. Rus. Fed.
19 Q1 Svir'stroy Rus. Fed.
55 M6 Svirzh r. Ukr.
77 N7 Svishtov Bulg.
18 H8 Svislach Hrodzyenskaya Voblasts' Belarus
18 K8 Svislach Minskaya Voblasts' Belarus
55 M2 Svislach r. Belarus
18 L8 Svislach r. Belarus
18 L8 Svislach r. Belarus
Svisloch r. Belarus see Svislach
57 J2 Svit Slovakia
56 F3 Svitava r. Czech Rep.
56 F2 Svitavy Czech Rep.
17 R5 Svitlodars'k Ukr.
17 N5 Svitlohirs'ke Ukr.
17 M4 Svitlovods'k Ukr.
55 L4 Svityaz' Ukr.
Svizzera country Europe see Switzerland
18 E7 Svoboda Kaliningradskaya Oblast' Rus. Fed.
17 P2 Svoboda Kurskaya Oblast' Rus. Fed.
56 E1 Svoboda nad Úpou Czech Rep.
62 F3 Svobodnyy Rus. Fed.
91 E1 Svobody Rus. Fed.
77 L8 Svoge Bulg.
18 L6 Svol'nya r. Belarus
20 M2 Svolvær Norway
56 F2 Svratka Czech Rep.
56 F2 Svratka r. Czech Rep.
57 H2 Svrčinovec Slovakia
77 K7 Svrljig Srbija Serb. and Mont.
77 K7 Svrljiške Planine mts Serb. and Mont.
18 J7 Svyantsyanskiya Hrady hills Belarus
19 X6 Svyatoye, Ozero l. Rus. Fed.
14 J2 Svyatoy Nos, Mys c. Rus. Fed.
19 O9 Svyatsk Rus. Fed.
18 M9 Svyetlahorsk Belarus
17 M1 Svyha r. Ukr.
16 D3 Svynya r. Ukr.
16 F3 Svyten'ka r. Ukr.
85 O4 Swabi Pak.
31 I2 Swadlincote Derbyshire, England U.K.
97 J8 Swaershoek S. Africa
97 J8 Swaershoekpas pass S. Africa
31 N2 Swaffham Norfolk, England U.K.
07 N6 Swain Reefs Qld Austr.
15 F9 Swainsboro GA U.S.A.
99 I3 Swains Island American Samoa
94 B4 Swakop watercourse Namibia
94 B4 Swakopmund Namibia
29 O5 Swale r. England U.K.
00 □6 Swallow Islands Santa Cruz Is Solomon Is
45 J6 Swalmen Neth.
176 E5 Swamihalli Karnataka India
109 G1 Swampy r. Que. Can.
209 C11 Swan r. W.A. Austr.
107 K4 Swan r. Man./Sask. Can.
108 D2 Swan r. Ont. Can.
28 C8 Swan Rep. of Ireland
31 I6 Swanage Dorset, England U.K.
91 E7 Swana-Mume Dem. Rep. Congo
116 E10 Swandale WV U.S.A.
96 H9 Swanepoelspoort mt. S. Africa
205 I6 Swan Hill Vic. Austr.
106 H4 Swan Hills Alta Can.
130 B5 Swan Islands is Caribbean Sea
106 D4 Swan Lake B.C. Can.
107 K4 Swan Lake Man. Can.
118 F1 Swan Lake NY U.S.A.
120 H3 Swan Lake l. MN U.S.A.
31 M5 Swanley Kent, England U.K.
27 G4 Swanlinbar Rep. of Ireland
203 G10 Swannanoa South I. N.Z.
115 I8 Swanquarter NC U.S.A.
115 I8 Swanquarter National Wildlife Refuge nature res. NC U.S.A.
204 G6 Swan Reach S.A. Austr.
107 K4 Swan River Man. Can.
110 A2 Swan River MN U.S.A.
28 D5 Swan's Cross Roads Rep. of Ireland
205 L10 Swansea Tas. Austr.
30 E4 Swansea Swansea, Wales U.K.
30 E4 Swansea admin. div. Wales U.K.
30 E4 Swansea Bay Wales U.K.
117 □Q4 Swans Island ME U.S.A.
124 J4 Swanton CA U.S.A.
117 L4 Swanton VT U.S.A.
31 N2 Swanton Morley Norfolk, England U.K.
54 G1 Swarożyn Pol.
97 N6 Swartberg S. Africa
96 D10 Swartberg mt. S. Africa
96 F9 Swartbergpas pass S. Africa
96 B6 Swartdoorn r. S. Africa
118 E5 Swarthmore PA U.S.A.
97 L8 Swart Kei r. S. Africa
96 E6 Swartkolkvloer salt pan S. Africa
97 J9 Swartkops S. Africa
97 J9 Swartkops r. S. Africa
97 K2 Swartplaas S. Africa
96 H4 Swartputs S. Africa
96 D2 Swartput se Pan salt pan Namibia
97 K1 Swartruggens S. Africa
97 K1 Swartruggens mts S. Africa
118 F2 Swartswood NJ U.S.A.
118 F2 Swartswood Lake NJ U.S.A.
97 P3 Swart Umfolozi S. Africa
111 K7 Swartz Creek MI U.S.A.
54 F3 Swarzędz Pol.
125 S2 Swasey Peak UT U.S.A.
111 N1 Swastika Ont. Can.
185 N4 Swat r. Pak.
118 B4 Swatara Creek r. PA U.S.A.
185 O4 Swat Kohistan reg. Pak.
Swatow Guangdong China see Shantou
28 D4 Swatragh Northern Ireland U.K.
31 I6 Sway Hampshire, England U.K.
97 P2 Swaziland country Africa
21 M6 Sweden country Europe
118 E5 Swedesboro NJ U.S.A.
206 G4 Sweers Island Qld Austr.
116 F11 Sweet Briar VA U.S.A.
122 C4 Sweet Home OR U.S.A.
116 E11 Sweet Springs WV U.S.A.
118 C2 Sweet Valley PA U.S.A.
121 E9 Sweetwater TX U.S.A.
122 K5 Sweetwater r. WY U.S.A.
122 J5 Sweetwater Station WY U.S.A.
96 E10 Swellendam S. Africa
97 L7 Swempoort S. Africa
55 I2 Świątki Pol.
54 G1 Świbno Pol.
55 J3 Świder r. Pol.
54 E5 Świdnica Dolnośląskie Pol.
54 D4 Świdnica Lubuskie Pol.
55 K4 Świdnik Pol.
54 D2 Świdwin Pol.
54 E5 Świebodzice Pol.
54 D3 Świebodzin Pol.
54 G2 Świecie Pol.
54 E4 Święciechowa Pol.
55 H2 Świecie nad Osą Pol.
51 K6 Świecko Pol.
55 H2 Świedziebnia Pol.
54 G2 Świekatowo Pol.
54 D5 Świeradów-Zdrój Pol.
55 I3 Świercze Pol.
54 F5 Świerczów Pol.
54 G5 Świerklaniec Pol.
54 D4 Świerzawa Pol.
54 E1 Świerzenko Pol.
54 C2 Świerzno Pol.
54 E1 Świeszyno Pol.
55 J2 Świętajno Warmińsko-Mazurskie Pol.
55 K1 Świętajno Warmińsko-Mazurskie Pol.
55 I5 Świętokrzyskie prov. Pol.
55 I5 Świętokrzyskie, Góry hills Pol.
55 I5 Świętokrzyski Park Narodowy nat. park Pol.
117 □O4 Swift r. ME U.S.A.
107 J5 Swift Current Sask. Can.
107 J5 Swiftcurrent Creek r. Sask. Can.
44 I3 Swifterbant Neth.
118 E2 Swiftwater PA U.S.A.
28 B4 Swilly r. Rep. of Ireland
27 G2 Swilly, Lough inlet Rep. of Ireland
31 I4 Swindon Swindon, England U.K.
31 I4 Swindon admin. div. England U.K.
29 P6 Swinefleet East Riding of Yorkshire, England U.K.
31 L2 Swineshead Lincolnshire, England U.K.
27 E5 Swinford Rep. of Ireland
118 F1 Swinging Bridge Reservoir NY U.S.A.
54 G3 Świnice Warckie Pol.
97 J4 Swinkpan imp. l. S. Africa
55 H6 Świnna Pol.
54 C2 Świnoujście Pol.
26 L11 Swinton Scottish Borders, Scotland U.K.
29 O7 Swinton South Yorkshire, England U.K.
Swiss Confederation country Europe see Switzerland
70 I2 Swiss National Park Switz.
Świstocz r. Belarus see Svislach
70 E2 Switzerland country Europe
54 C2 Swobnica Pol.
27 J6 Swords Rep. of Ireland
207 H6 Swords Range hills Qld Austr.
54 F2 Swornegacie Pol.
118 D2 Swoyerville PA U.S.A.
18 M7 Syalyava, Vozyera l. Belarus
55 M3 Syalyets Brestskaya Voblasts' Belarus
19 N8 Syalyets Mahilyowskaya Voblasts' Belarus
18 H9 Syalyets Vodaskhovishcha resr Belarus
14 F3 Syamozero, Ozero l. Rus. Fed.
14 H3 Syamzha Rus. Fed.
179 I5 Syang Nepal
18 M7 Syanno Belarus
18 H8 Syarednenemanskaya Nizina lowland Belarus/Lith.
18 K8 Syarhyeyevichy Belarus
19 P1 Syas' r. Rus. Fed.
19 P1 Syas'troy Rus. Fed.
14 I4 Syava Rus. Fed.
27 B8 Sybil Point Rep. of Ireland
97 M1 Sybrandskraal S. Africa
110 F8 Sycamore IL U.S.A.
54 E1 Sycewice Pol.
19 R6 Sychevka Rus. Fed.
19 T6 Sychevo Rus. Fed.
18 M8 Sychkava Belarus
54 F4 Syców Pol.
205 M5 Sydney N.S.W. Austr.
109 I4 Sydney N.S. Can.
204 □1 Sydney Bay Norfolk I.
206 G4 Sydney Island Qld Austr.
107 M5 Sydney Lake Ont. Can.
109 I4 Sydney Mines N.S. Can.
Sydzhak Uzbek. see Sijjaq
17 R6 Syedove Ukr.
190 A2 Syedra tourist site Turkey
17 R5 Syeverne Ukr.
17 R5 Syeverodonets'k Ukr.
48 G5 Syke Ger.
78 D6 Sykea Greece
118 B6 Sykesville MD U.S.A.
116 G7 Sykesville PA U.S.A.
20 I5 Sykkylven Norway
14 J3 Syktyvkar Rus. Fed.
115 D9 Sylacauga AL U.S.A.
179 M7 Sylhet Bangl.
179 M7 Sylhet admin. div. Bangl.
14 H3 Syloga Rus. Fed.
48 F1 Sylt i. Ger.
48 F1 Sylt-Ost Ger.
14 L4 Sylva r. Rus. Fed.
115 F8 Sylva NC U.S.A.
209 E7 Sylvania W.A. Austr.
115 G9 Sylvania GA U.S.A.
116 B7 Sylvania OH U.S.A.
106 H4 Sylvan Lake Alta Can.
53 L6 Sylvensteinsee l. Ger.
115 F10 Sylvester GA U.S.A.
206 E5 Sylvester, Lake salt flat N.T. Austr.
106 E3 Sylvia, Mount B.C. Can.
79 I6 Symi Greece
79 I6 Symi i. Greece
26 I11 Symington South Lanarkshire, Scotland U.K.
17 N9 Synape Ukr.
154 D5 Syndicate Masbate Phil.
17 O5 Synel'nykove Ukr.
Syngyrli, Mys pt Kazakh. see Sengirli, Mys
189 P2 Syngyrli, Mys pt Kazakh.
17 N3 Synivka Ukr.
193 N4 Synnagyn, Khrebet mts Rus. Fed.
21 J6 Synnfjell mt. Norway
208 H4 Synnot, Mount hill W.A. Austr.
208 H4 Synnott Range hills W.A. Austr.
30 D3 Synod Inn Ceredigion, Wales U.K.
14 L2 Synya Rus. Fed.
14 N2 Synya r. Rus. Fed.
16 J5 Synytsya r. Ukr.
16 J5 Synyukha r. Ukr.
Synzhera Moldova see Sîngerei
Synzheray Moldova see Sîngerei
119 H3 Syosset NY U.S.A.
213 C2 Syowa research stn Antarctica
55 J2 Sypniewo Mazowieckie Pol.
54 E2 Sypniewo Wielkopolskie Pol.
Syracusae Sicilia Italy see Siracusa
Syracuse Sicilia Italy see Siracusa
120 E6 Syracuse KS U.S.A.
117 I5 Syracuse NY U.S.A.
51 F9 Syrau Ger.
183 I4 Syrdar'ya r. Asia
Syrdar'ya Uzbek. see Sirdaryo
Syrdarya Oblast admin. div. Uzbek. see Sirdaryo
Syrdaryinskiy Uzbek. see Sirdaryo
53 I4 Syrgenstein Ger.
188 I6 Syria country Asia
Syrian Desert Asia see Bādiyat ash Shām
79 H6 Syrna i. Greece
19 N5 Syrokvashino Rus. Fed.
78 F5 Syros i. Greece
19 W9 Syrskiy Rus. Fed.
21 R6 Sysmä Fin.
14 J3 Sysola r. Rus. Fed.
19 T2 Sysoyevo Rus. Fed.
31 J2 Syston Leicestershire, England U.K.
16 I5 Sytkivtsi Ukr.
14 J4 Syumsi Rus. Fed.
14 K5 Syun r. Rus. Fed.
162 L3 Syurkum Rus. Fed.
162 L3 Syurkum, Mys pt Rus. Fed.
17 O8 Syvash, Zatoka lag. Ukr.
17 N7 Syvas'ke Ukr.
21 T6 Syyspohja Fin.
17 M8 Syzivka Ukr.
182 C1 Syzran' Rus. Fed.
57 H4 Szabadbattyán Hungary
57 H4 Szabadegyháza Hungary
Szabadka Vojvodina, Srbija Serb. and Mont. see Subotica
57 K5 Szabadkígyós Hungary
57 K5 Szabadkígyósi park Hungary
57 I5 Szabadszállás Hungary
57 L3 Szabolcs-Szatmár-Bereg county Hungary
54 G4 Szadek Pol.
55 I6 Szaflary Pol.
57 J4 Szajol Hungary
57 H5 Szakcs Hungary
57 I5 Szakmár Hungary
57 H4 Szákszend Hungary
57 K3 Szalaszend Hungary
57 I5 Szalkszentmárton Hungary
57 J3 Szalonna Hungary
54 F2 Szamocin Pol.
57 L3 Szamos r. Hungary
57 L3 Szamosszeg Hungary
54 E3 Szamotuły Pol.
57 J1 Szaniecki Park Krajobrazowy Pol.
57 I5 Szank Hungary
56 G4 Szany Hungary
57 H4 Szár Hungary
57 J5 Szárazér-Porgányi-főcsatorna canal Hungary
57 J5 Szarvas Hungary
57 J4 Szászberek Hungary
57 H5 Szászvár Hungary
57 L3 Szatmár-Beregi park Hungary
57 L3 Szatmárcseke Hungary
57 J5 Szatymaz Hungary
57 H4 Százhalombatta Hungary
54 D3 Szczaniec Pol.
55 K6 Szczawne Pol.
55 I6 Szczawnica Pol.
54 E5 Szczawno-Zdrój Pol.
55 K5 Szczebrzeszyn Pol.
54 C2 Szczecin Pol.
54 E2 Szczecinek Pol.
54 D2 Szczecińskie reg. Pol.
50 K4 Szczeciński Park Krajobrazowy Pol.
55 H5 Szczekociny Pol.
55 J2 Szczepankowo Pol.
55 H4 Szczerców Pol.
55 J5 Szczucin Pol.
55 K2 Szczuczyn Pol.
55 I1 Szczurkowo Pol.
55 I5 Szczurowa Pol.
55 H6 Szczyrk Pol.
54 E5 Szczytna Pol.
54 G4 Szczytniki Pol.
55 I2 Szczytno Pol.
54 F2 Szczytno, Jezioro l. Pol.
Szechwan prov. China see Sichuan
57 I3 Szécsény Hungary
57 H5 Szederkény Hungary
57 H5 Szedres Hungary
57 J5 Szeged Hungary
57 K4 Szeghalom Hungary
57 J5 Szegvár Hungary
57 H4 Székesfehérvár Hungary
57 J5 Székkutas Hungary
57 H5 Szekszárd Hungary
55 I2 Szeląg Wielki, Jezioro l. Pol.
54 G1 Szemud Pol.
57 I4 Szendehely Hungary
57 J3 Szendrő Hungary
57 J3 Szendrőlád Hungary
57 I4 Szentendre Hungary
57 J5 Szentes Hungary
56 F5 Szentgotthárd Hungary
56 F5 Szentgyörgyvölgyi park Hungary
57 J4 Szentistván Hungary
57 I5 Szentkirály Hungary
57 G5 Szentlászló Hungary
57 I4 Szentlőrinckáta Hungary
57 I4 Szentmártonkáta Hungary
57 G5 Szentőrinc Hungary
56 F4 Szentpéterfa Hungary
57 K4 Szentpéterszeg Hungary
56 F5 Szepetnek Hungary
55 K3 Szepietowo Pol.
57 H5 Szeremle Hungary
57 K3 Szerencs Hungary
57 K4 Szerep Hungary
55 J6 Szerzyny Pol.
55 K1 Szeska Góra hill Pol.
55 J2 Szestno Pol.
57 H4 Szigetbecse Hungary
57 H4 Szigethalom Hungary
57 I4 Szigetszentmiklós Hungary
57 H4 Szigetújfalu Hungary
57 G5 Szigetvár Hungary
56 G5 Szigliget Hungary
57 J4 Szihalom Hungary
57 J3 Szikszó Hungary
56 G4 Szil Hungary
57 J3 Szilvásvárad Hungary
54 F4 Szkaradowo Pol.
54 D5 Szklarska Poręba Pol.
54 E4 Szklary Górne Pol.
55 K6 Szkło r. Pol.
55 J2 Szkwa r. Pol.
54 E4 Szlichtyngowa Pol.
57 H4 Szob Hungary
57 J3 Szögliget Hungary
57 J4 Szolnok Hungary
57 G5 Szőlősgyörök Hungary
56 F4 Szombathely Hungary
57 J4 Szomolya Hungary
55 K5 Szówsko Pol.
54 D4 Szprotawa Pol.
54 D4 Szprotawa r. Pol.
55 I5 Szreniawa r. Pol.
56 E1 Szrenica mt. Czech Rep.
55 I2 Szreńsk Pol.
55 H2 Szropy Pol.
55 L2 Sztabin Pol.
55 H2 Sztum Pol.
55 H1 Sztutowo Pol.
54 F2 Szubin Pol.
57 I4 Szűcsi Hungary
55 L2 Szudziałowo Pol.
57 I3 Szügy Hungary
57 J3 Szuhogy Hungary
55 K3 Szulborze Wielkie Pol.
55 K3 Szumowo Pol.
57 I4 Szurdokpüspöki Hungary
55 I4 Szydłowiec Pol.
55 I2 Szydłowo Mazowieckie Pol.
54 E2 Szydłowo Wielkopolskie Pol.
55 J2 Szymonka Pol.
54 F4 Szymonków Pol.
54 G4 Szynkielów Pol.
55 L1 Szypliszki Pol.

T

88 D5 Taabo, Lac de l. Côte d'Ivoire
92 D2 Taagga Duudka reg. Somalia
203 □3 Taakoka i. Rarotonga Cook Is
154 C4 Taal, Lake Luzon Phil.
190 D5 Taalabaya Lebanon
201 □3a Taapuna Tahiti Fr. Polynesia
22 I6 Taastrup Denmark
57 H5 Tab Hungary
17 M9 Tabachne Ukr.
154 D5 Tabaco Luzon Phil.
184 H3 Tabādkān Iran
186 F2 Tābah Saudi Arabia
139 E2 Tabajara Brazil
57 H4 Tabajd Hungary
87 E5 Tabakat well Mali
157 K9 Tabanan Bali Indon.
63 L4 Tabanera de Cerrato Spain
157 L4 Tabang Kalimantan Indon.
157 K4 Tabang r. Indon.
97 N6 Tabankulu S. Africa
188 I6 Ţabaqah Ar Raqqah Syria
131 □7 Tabaquite Trin. and Tob.
62 I5 Tábara Spain
153 L7 Tabar Islands P.N.G.
69 B7 Tabarka Tunisia
49 K9 Tabarz Ger.
184 G5 Ţabas Khorāsān Iran
184 I5 Ţabas Khorāsān Iran
18 H2 Tabasalu Estonia
128 E4 Tabasco Mex.
129 N8 Tabasco state Mex.
184 G6 Tabāsin Iran
184 D7 Tābask, Kūh-e mt. Iran
136 D6 Tabatinga Amazonas Brazil
142 C4 Tabatinga São Paulo Brazil
140 D4 Tabatinga, Serra da hills Brazil
167 I4 Tabayama Japan
158 B3 Tabayin Myanmar
154 C3 Tabayoo, Mount Luzon Phil.
57 I5 Tabdi Hungary
84 B6 Tabédé well Chad
86 E3 Tabelbala Alg.
107 H5 Taber Alta Can.
87 G2 Taberdga Alg.
23 K4 Taberg hill Sweden
65 O6 Tabernas Spain
Tabernes de Valldigna Spain see Tavernes de la Valldigna
65 O6 Taberno Spain
158 C2 Tabet, Nam r. Myanmar
91 B7 Tabi Angola
173 G11 Tabia Tsaka salt l. China
200 □3a Tabik i. Kwajalein Marshall Is
200 □3a Tabik Channel Kwajalein Marshall Is
90 F4 Tabili Dem. Rep. Congo
157 M2 Tabin Wildlife Reserve nature res. Malaysia
156 E5 Tabir r. Indon.
199 H2 Tabiteuea atoll Gilbert Is Kiribati
18 J3 Tabivere Estonia
154 D5 Tablas i. Phil.
146 B2 Tablas, Cabo c. Chile
154 C5 Tablas Strait Phil.
96 C9 Table Bay S. Africa
202 L6 Table Cape North I. N.Z.
177 M6 Table Islands Andaman & Nicobar Is India
96 C9 Table Mountain hill S. Africa
154 B6 Table Point Palawan Phil.
121 I7 Table Rock Reservoir MO U.S.A.
89 F5 Tabligbo Togo
65 K3 Tablillas r. Spain
62 E3 Taboada Spain
137 F5 Taboca Brazil
137 G5 Tabocal Brazil
137 F6 Tabocal r. Brazil
139 G4 Tabocó r. Brazil
158 C1 Tabong Myanmar
56 D2 Tábor Czech Rep.
93 B6 Tabora Tanz.
93 B6 Tabora admin. reg. Tanz.
57 I4 Táborfalva Hungary
185 M1 Taboshar Tajik.
147 H2 Tabossi Arg.
88 D5 Tabou Côte d'Ivoire
89 F2 Tabrichat well Mali
184 B2 Tabrīz Iran
62 D8 Tábua Port.
62 E6 Tabuaço Port.
217 I5 Tabuaeran atoll Kiribati
63 Q5 Tabuenca Spain
186 C1 Tabūk Saudi Arabia
186 C1 Tabūk prov. Saudi Arabia
205 N3 Tabulam N.S.W. Austr.
155 C4 Tabulan Sulawesi Indon.
183 R1 Tabuny Rus. Fed.
73 N5 Taburno, Monte mt. Italy
156 C4 Tabuyung Sumatera Indon.
200 □5 Tabwémasana hill Vanuatu
200 □5 Tabwémasana, Mount Vanuatu
23 O2 Täby Sweden
57 H4 Tác Hungary
137 H5 Tacaipu, Serra hills Brazil
137 H4 Tacalé Brazil
128 F6 Tacámbaro Mex.
127 M10 Tacaná, Volcán de vol. Mex.
126 □U13 Tacarcuna, Cerro mt. Panama
59 J7 Tacen Slovenia
172 G4 Tachakou Xinjiang China
89 F2 Tachdaït well Mali
172 F3 Tacheng Xinjiang China
53 N5 Tacherting Ger.
165 G14 Tachibana-wan b. Japan
106 E4 Tachie B.C. Can.
167 J4 Tachikawa Tōkyō Japan
164 Q8 Tachikawa Yamagata Japan
53 N6 Tachinger See l. Ger.
136 C2 Táchira state Venez.
84 A3 Tachiumet well Libya
56 B2 Tachov Czech Rep.
75 L6 Tacina r. Italy
155 B6 Tacipi Sulawesi Indon.
137 F6 Taciuã, Lago l. Brazil
154 E6 Tacloban Leyte Phil.
136 D5 Tacna Col.
138 C4 Tacna Peru
138 C4 Tacna dept Peru
125 S9 Tacna AZ U.S.A.
122 C3 Tacoma WA U.S.A.
110 D2 Taconite Harbor MN U.S.A.
144 E2 Taco Pozo Arg.
98 □3a Tacoronte Tenerife Canary Is
144 G3 Tacuarembó Uru.
147 J3 Tacuarembó dept Uru.
147 G4 Tacuari Arg.
126 E3 Tacupeto Mex.
54 F4 Taczanów Drugi Pol.
165 Q9 Tadami Japan
165 Q9 Tadami-gawa r. Japan
72 B7 Tadasuni Sardegna Italy
29 O6 Tadcaster North Yorkshire, England U.K.
87 G5 Tadeinte, Oued watercourse Alg.
89 G3 Tadélaka well Niger
87 F3 Tademaït, Plateau du Alg.
200 □5 Tadin Îles Loyauté New Caledonia
87 H4 Tadjentourt hill Alg.
87 F5 Tadjeraout, Oued watercourse Alg.
Tadjikistan country Asia see Tajikistan
87 F4 Tadjmout Alg.
92 D2 Tadjoura Djibouti
92 D2 Tadjoura, Golfe de g. Djibouti
87 F2 Tadjrouna Alg.
31 J5 Tadley Hampshire, England U.K.
190 G4 Tadmur Syria
136 B3 Tadó Col.
166 E5 Tado Japan
163 E11 Tadohae Haesang National Park S. Korea
107 L3 Tadoule Lake Man. Can.
109 G3 Tadoussac Que. Can.
176 E5 Tadpatri Andhra Prad. India
87 H4 Tadrart hills Alg.
84 A3 Tadrart Acacus tourist site Libya
176 E3 Tadwale Mahar. India
31 L5 Tadworth Surrey, England U.K.
Tadzhikabad Tajik. see Tojikobod
Tadzhikskaya S.S.R. country Asia see Tajikistan
163 E10 T'aean Haean National Park S. Korea
163 E9 T'aebaek-sanmaek mts N. Korea/S. Korea
18 G3 Taebla Estonia
Taech'ŏn S. Korea see Poryŏng
163 D10 Taech'ŏng-do i. S. Korea
163 D9 Taedong-gang r. N. Korea
163 D10 Taedong-man b. N. Korea
163 F11 Taegu S. Korea
163 D11 Taehŭksan-kundo is S. Korea
163 E10 Taejŏn S. Korea
163 E12 Taejŏng S. Korea
163 F10 T'aepaek S. Korea
169 Q3 Ta'erqi Nei Mongol China
18 K3 Taevaskoja Estonia
30 D4 Taf r. Wales U.K.
199 I3 Tafahi i. Tonga
63 Q3 Tafalla Spain
87 H5 Tafassasset, Oued watercourse Alg./Niger
131 □10 Tafelberg hill Curaçao Neth. Antilles
97 J7 Tafelberg S. Africa
96 F8 Tafelberg mt. S. Africa
137 G4 Tafelberg mt. Suriname
137 G4 Tafelberg, Natuurreservaat nature res. Suriname
70 C2 Tafers Switz.
30 F4 Taff's Well Cardiff, Wales U.K.
98 □3f Tafira Gran Canaria Canary Is
88 D4 Tafiré Côte d'Ivoire
144 D2 Tafi Viejo Arg.
21 I5 Tafjord Norway
86 C3 Tafraoute Morocco
184 C4 Tafresh Iran
184 F6 Taft Iran
124 M6 Taft CA U.S.A.
185 I7 Taftān, Kūh-e mt. Iran
190 E3 Taftanāz Syria
118 E2 Tafton PA U.S.A.
177 M9 Tafwap Andaman & Nicobar Is India
166 D5 Taga Japan
200 □2 Taga Samoa
66 J3 Taga mt. Spain
185 L5 Tagāb Afgh.
85 F5 Tagab Sudan
164 R8 Tagajō Japan
88 E2 Tagânet Keyna well Mali
15 G7 Taganrog Rus. Fed.
17 R7 Taganrog, Gulf of Rus. Fed./Ukr.
Taganrogskiy Zaliv b. Rus. Fed./Ukr. see Taganrog, Gulf of
88 C2 Tagant admin. reg. Maur.
184 G2 Tagarev, Gora mt. Iran/Turkm.
158 C3 Tagaung Myanmar
165 H13 Tagawa Japan
15 I5 Tagay Rus. Fed.
89 G2 Tagaza well Niger
154 D7 Tagbilaran Bohol Phil.
173 F10 Tagchagpu Ri mt. Xizang China
Tagdempt Alg. see Tiaret
70 D8 Taggia Italy
88 E3 Taghin-Dassouri Burkina
Tâghira Moldova see Ţighira
86 D4 Taghmanant well Mali
106 C2 Tagish Y.T. Can.
106 C3 Tagish Lake B.C. Can.
73 K3 Tagliacozzo Italy
71 O4 Tagliamento r. Italy
72 C3 Taglio-Isolaccio Corse France
36 H5 Tagnon France
87 E5 Tagnout Chagguerret well Mali
167 J1 Tagokura-ko resr Japan
154 E7 Tagoloan r. Mindanao Phil.
67 I9 Tagomago i. Spain
88 D2 Tagourâret well Maur.
184 H1 Tagta Turkm.
185 J4 Tagtabazar Turkm.
142 C1 Taguatinga Minas Gerais Brazil
140 D5 Taguatinga Tocantins Brazil
166 B7 Taguchi-zaki pt Japan
154 C3 Tagudin Luzon Phil.
89 H2 Taguedoufat well Niger
Taguenout Haggueret well Mali see Tagnout Chagguerret
199 F3 Tagula Island P.N.G.
154 E8 Tagum Mindanao Phil.
64 D2 Tagus r. Port./Spain alt. Tajo (Spain), alt. Tejo (Portugal)
86 B4 Tah, Sabkhat salt pan Morocco
169 S3 Taha Heilong. China
106 G5 Tahaetkun Mountain B.C. Can.
65 O6 Tahal Spain
156 E2 Tahan, Gunung mt. Malaysia
86 D3 Tahanaoute Morocco
201 □3 Tahanea atoll Arch. des Tuamotu Fr. Polynesia
Tahanroz'ka Zatoka b. Rus. Fed./Ukr. see Taganrog, Gulf of
166 F6 Tahara Japan
202 H2 Taharoa, Lake North I. N.Z.
201 □3a Taharuu r. Tahiti Fr. Polynesia
87 G5 Tahat, Mont mt. Alg.
127 O7 Tahdzibichén Mex.
162 D2 Tahe Heilong. China
202 H2 Taheke North I. N.Z.
18 K3 Tähemaa Estonia
184 G8 Tāherū'ī Iran
87 G5 Tahifet Alg.
27 C9 Tahilla Rep. of Ireland
168 E4 Tahilt Mongolia
201 □3a Tahiti i. Fr. Polynesia
57 I4 Tahitótfalu Hungary
18 F2 Tahkuna nina pt Estonia
185 J7 Tahlab r. Iran/Pak.
185 J7 Tahlab, Dasht-i- plain Pak.
121 H8 Tahlequah OK U.S.A.
106 D3 Tahltan B.C. Can.
124 L2 Tahoe, Lake CA U.S.A.
124 L2 Tahoe City CA U.S.A.
104 H3 Tahoe Lake Nunavut Can.
124 L2 Tahoe Vista CA U.S.A.
121 E9 Tahoka TX U.S.A.
202 I6 Tahora North I. N.Z.
202 K5 Tahorakuri North I. N.Z.
89 G3 Tahoua Niger
89 G3 Tahoua dept Niger
184 G7 Tahrūd Iran
184 H7 Tahrūd r. Iran
158 D4 Ta Hsai Myanmar
106 E5 Tahsis B.C. Can.
85 F3 Ţahţā Egypt
79 K3 Tahtaköprü Turkey
79 L6 Tahtali Dağ mt. Turkey
106 E4 Tahtsa Peak B.C. Can.
138 D4 Tahua Bol.
138 D2 Tahuamanú r. Bol.
138 C2 Tahuamanú Peru
201 □3 Tahuata i. Fr. Polynesia
155 D2 Tahulandang i. Indon.
155 D2 Tahuna Sulawesi Indon.
88 D5 Taï Côte d'Ivoire
88 D5 Taï, Parc National de nat. park Côte d'Ivoire
179 L6 Taiabpur Bihar India
171 □I7 Tai A Chau i. H.K. China
169 R6 Tai'an Liaoning China
169 O8 Tai'an Shandong China
201 □3a Taiarapu, Presqu'île de pen. Tahiti Fr. Polynesia
203 E12 Taiaroa Head South I. N.Z.
169 K8 Taibai Gansu China
169 J9 Taibai Shaanxi China
170 F2 Taibai Shan mt. Shaanxi China
Taibei Taiwan see T'aipei
87 G2 Taïbet Alg.
65 O4 Taibilla r. Spain
67 C12 Taibilla, Canal del Spain
67 A11 Taibilla, Embalse de resr Spain
65 O4 Taibilla, Sierra de mts Spain
98 □3e Taibique El Hierro Canary Is
71 M3 Taibòn Agordino Italy
171 M6 T'aichung Taiwan
Taidong Taiwan see T'aitung
167 L4 Taiei Japan
203 E13 Taieri r. South I. N.Z.
203 E12 Taieri Ridge South I. N.Z.
Taigong Guizhou China see Taijiang
169 M8 Taigu Shanxi China
169 M8 Taihang Shan mts China
169 N7 Taihang Shan mts China
202 J6 Taihape North I. N.Z.
171 J2 Taihe Anhui China
Taihe Guangdong China see Qingxin
171 J5 Taihe Jiangxi China
Taihe Sichuan China see Shehong
Taihezhen Sichuan China see Shehong
164 □1 Taiho Okinawa Japan
171 □J7 Tai Ho Wan H.K. China
171 K3 Taihu Anhui China
171 M3 Tai Hu l. China
169 M7 Taihuai Shanxi China
165 M13 Taiji Japan
170 G5 Taijiang Guizhou China
169 S3 Taikang Heilong. China
169 N9 Taikang Henan China
164 U4 Taiki Japan
158 B6 Taikkyi Myanmar
166 B4 Taiko-yama hill Japan
155 D8 Tailaco East Timor
169 R3 Tailai Heilong. China
171 □J7 Tai Lam Chung Shui Tong resr H.K. China
156 C5 Taileleo Indon.
204 G6 Tailem Bend S.A. Austr.
171 □J7 Tai Long Wan b. H.K. China
Tailuge Taiwan see T'ailuko
171 M6 T'ailuko Taiwan
144 G4 Taim Brazil
185 J5 Taimani reg. Afgh.
171 □J7 Tai Mo Shan hill H.K. China
88 E4 Tain r. Ghana
26 H7 Tain Highland, Scotland U.K.
171 M7 T'ainan Taiwan
78 D6 Tainaro, Akra pt Greece
40 C1 Taingy France
41 F6 Tain-l'Hermitage France
37 M7 Taintrux France
171 □I7 Tai O H.K. China
71 K3 Taio Italy
143 F1 Taiobeiras Brazil
155 B4 Taipa Sulawesi Indon.
202 H2 Taipa North I. N.Z.
171 □J7 Tai Pak Wan b. H.K. China
21 T6 Taipalsaari Fin.
171 M6 T'aipei Taiwan
171 I7 Taiping Guangdong China
Taiping Guangdong China see Shixing
170 H7 Taiping Guangxi China
156 D2 Taiping Malaysia
169 R4 Taipingchuan Jilin China
169 Q3 Taiping Ling mt. Nei Mongol China
171 □J7 Tai Po H.K. China
171 □J7 Tai Po Hoi b. H.K. China
Tai Poutini National Park South I. N.Z. see Westland National Park
140 G3 Taipu Brazil
179 O6 Taipudia Arun. Prad. India
169 N9 Taiqian Henan China
164 □1 Taira Okinawa Japan
166 E3 Taira Toyama Japan
164 R5 Tairadate-kaikyō sea chan. Japan
164 □G17 Taira-jima i. Nansei-shotō Japan
Tairbeart Western Isles, Scotland U.K. see Tarbert
159 D10 Tai Rom Yen National Park Thai.
202 J4 Tairua North I. N.Z.
184 A4 Tairuq Iran
156 E7 Tais Sumatera Indon.
164 Q4 Taisei Japan
164 T3 Taisetsu-zan mts Japan
167 J2 Taishaku-san mt. Japan
171 I7 Taishan Guangdong China
171 □J7 Tai Shek Mo hill H.K. China
167 L1 Taishin Japan
171 L5 Taishun Zhejiang China
171 □I7 Tai Siu Mo To is H.K. China
59 I3 Taiskirchen im Innkreis Austria
36 H5 Taissy France
93 C5 Taita Hills Kenya
156 D6 Taitaitanopo i. Indon.
171 □J7 Tai Tan Hoi Hap inlet H.K. China
203 G10 Taitanu South I. N.Z.
145 B7 Taitao, Península de pen. Chile
145 B7 Taitao, Punta pt Chile
92 B4 Taiti mt. Kenya
171 □J7 Tai To Yan mt. H.K. China
167 L5 Taitō-zaki pt Japan
171 M7 T'aitung Taiwan
171 □I7 Tai Tung Shan hill H.K. China
171 M7 T'aitung Shan mts Taiwan
20 T4 Taivalkoski Fin.
20 R2 Taivaskero hill Fin.
21 P6 Taivassalo Fin.
171 M7 Taiwan country Asia
Taiwan Haixia str. China/Taiwan see Taiwan Strait
171 L7 Taiwan Strait China/Taiwan
171 M2 Taixing Jiangsu China
Taïyetos Óros mts Greece see Tavgetos
169 M8 Taiyuan Shanxi China
169 L8 Taiyue Shan mts China
40 F3 Taizé France
173 K11 Taizhao Xizang China
Taizhong Taiwan see T'aichung
171 L2 Taizhou Jiangsu China
171 M4 Taizhou Zhejiang China
171 M4 Taizhou Liedao i. China
171 M4 Taizhou Wan b. China
163 D8 Taizi He r. China
186 F9 Ta'izz Yemen
186 F9 Ta'izz governorate Yemen
185 M8 Tajal Pak.
156 □ Tajam, Tanjong pt Sing.
127 N10 Tajamulco, Volcán de vol. Guat.
84 B3 Tajarḩī Libya
157 G6 Tajem, Gunung hill Indon.
184 D7 Tāj-e Malekī Iran
87 H2 Tajerouine Tunisia
185 N2 Tajikistan country Asia
167 K1 Tajima Japan
166 F5 Tajimi Japan
166 B7 Tajiri Japan
126 C2 Tajitos Mex.
178 G6 Taj Mahal tourist site Uttar Prad. India
60 C3 Tajo r. Spain alt. Tejo (Portugal), conv. Tagus
179 P5 Tajobum Arun. Prad. India
179 J7 Tajpur Bihar India
189 O6 Tajrīsh Iran
138 D5 Tajsara, Cordillera de mts Bol.
63 M8 Tajuña r. Spain
84 B1 Tājūra Libya
158 D6 Tak Thai.
184 B3 Takāb Iran
92 D4 Takabba Kenya
155 B7 Taka'Bonerate, Kepulauan atolls Indon.
56 G4 Takácsi Hungary
90 D2 Takadja C.A.R.
167 G4 Takagi Japan
167 M2 Takahagi Japan
166 E6 Takahama Aichi Japan
166 C5 Takahama Fukui Japan
166 F3 Takahara-gawa r. Japan
165 K12 Takahashi Japan
212 Q1 Takahe, Mount Antarctica
166 B6 Takaishi Japan
166 E1 Takaiwa-misaki pt Japan
203 G7 Takaka South I. N.Z.
178 F9 Takal Madh. Prad. India
90 C2 Takalaou Chad
93 C6 Takaloi well Tanz.
87 G5 Takalous, Oued watercourse Alg.
137 G3 Takama Guyana
99 □2b Takamaka Mahé Seychelles
166 E2 Takamatsu Ishikawa Japan
165 L12 Takamatsu Kagawa Japan
166 D7 Takami-yama mt. Japan
165 I14 Takamori Kumamoto Japan
167 G4 Takamori Nagano Japan
165 I14 Takanabe Japan
166 F3 Takane Gifu Japan
167 H4 Takane Yamanashi Japan
167 K2 Takanezawa Japan
164 R6 Takanosu Japan
166 F2 Takaoka Japan
202 K7 Takapau North I. N.Z.
202 M5 Takapau North I. N.Z.
202 I3 Takapuna North I. N.Z.
164 □G17 Takara-jima i. Nansei-shotō Japan
166 B6 Takarazuka Japan
166 A6 Takasago Japan
167 J3 Takasaki Japan
166 D5 Takashima Japan
166 E3 Takashōzu-yama mt. Japan
166 E4 Takasu Japan
167 H2 Takasuma-yama mt. Japan
167 M2 Takasuzu-san hill Japan
167 H4 Takatō Japan
94 E5 Takatokwane Botswana
166 E4 Takatomi Japan
166 C7 Takatori Japan
94 D4 Takatshwaane Botswana
166 C6 Takatsuki Ōsaka Japan
166 D5 Takatsuki Shiga Japan
165 J13 Takatsuki-yama mt. Japan
137 G4 Takatu r. Brazil/Guyana
93 C5 Takaungu Kenya
158 D4 Ta-Kaw Myanmar
166 F3 Takayama Gifu Japan
167 I2 Takayama Gunma Japan
167 I1 Takayanagi Japan
159 E11 Tak Bai Thai.
166 D4 Takefu Japan
165 J12 Takehara Japan
31 M4 Takeley Essex, England U.K.
156 B2 Takengon Sumatera Indon.
166 A4 Takeno Japan
Takeo Cambodia see Takêv
165 H13 Takeo Japan
23 K3 Tåkern l. Sweden
23 K3 Tåkern naturreservat nature res. Sweden
167 H3 Takeshi Japan
164 □H16 Take-shima i. Japan
Take-shima i. N. Pacific Ocean see Liancourt Rocks
184 C3 Takestān Iran
91 C5 Taketa Dem. Rep. Congo
165 I14 Taketa Japan
166 E6 Taketoyo Japan
159 G9 Takêv Cambodia
185 M2 Takfon Tajik.
189 L9 Takhādīd well Iraq
185 M3 Takhār prov. Afgh.
178 H8 Takhatpur Chhattisgarh India
61 G5 Takhemaret Alg.
Takhiatash Uzbek. see Taxiatosh
106 C2 Takhini r. Y.T. Can.
106 C2 Takhini Hotspring Y.T. Can.
158 E7 Ta Khli Thai.
159 G9 Ta Khmau Cambodia
15 H7 Takhta Rus. Fed.
Takhta Turkm. see Tagta
Takhta-Bazar Turkm. see Tagtabazar
183 L1 Takhtabrod Kazakh.
17 R9 Takhtamukay Rus. Fed.
Takhtamukayskiy Rus. Fed. see Takhtamukay
184 C5 Takht Apān, Kūh-e mt. Iran
185 K6 Takhta Pul Post Afgh.
184 E7 Takhteh Iran
189 P9 Takht-e Jamshīd tourist site Iran
184 D3 Takht-e Soleymān mt. Iran
185 N6 Takht-i-Sulaiman mt. Pak.
166 E7 Taki Mie Japan
165 J11 Taki Shimane Japan
89 H3 Takiéta Niger
164 S3 Takikawa Japan
166 A6 Takino Japan
164 U2 Takinoue Japan
87 H4 Takisset, Oued watercourse Alg./Libya
157 K6 Takisung Kalimantan Indon.
203 B12 Takitimu Mountains South I. N.Z.
191 J6 Täklä Azer.

Täklä to Tarrabool Lake

346

191 J6 Täklä Azer.
106 E4 Takla Lake B.C. Can.
106 E4 Takla Landing B.C. Can.
Takla Makan des. China see Taklimakan Shamo
Taklimakan Desert China see Taklimakan Shamo
172 E7 Taklimakan Shamo des. China
167 L4 Tako Japan
185 M2 Takob Tajik.
88 E5 Takoradi Ghana
202 H2 Takou Bay North I. N.Z.
173 K12 Takpa Shiri mt. Xizang China
57 I4 Taksony Hungary
57 K4 Takta r. Hungary
57 K3 Taktaharkány Hungary
57 K3 Taktakenéz Hungary
106 C3 Taku B.C. Can.
104 E4 Taku r. Can./U.S.A.
165 H13 Taku Japan
200 □6 Takuan, Mount P.N.G.
159 D10 Takua Pa Thai.
159 D10 Takua Thung Thai.
89 H5 Takum Nigeria
91 C6 Takundi Dem. Rep. Congo
203 □2 Takutea i. Cook Is
199 F2 Takuu Islands P.N.G.
200 □6 Takwa Malaita Solomon Is
17 P8 Takyl, Mys pt Ukr.
178 E8 Tal Madh. Prad. India
185 O4 Tal Pak.
128 D5 Tala Mex.
144 G4 Tala Uru.
146 C2 Talacasto Arg.
18 M7 Talachyn Belarus
185 O5 Talagang Pak.
146 B3 Talagante Chile
67 H10 Talaiassa, Serra hill Spain
176 F8 Talaimannar Sri Lanka
41 B10 Talairan France
42 B5 Talais France
178 D9 Talaja Gujarat India
162 G3 Talakan Amurskaya Oblast' Rus. Fed.
162 H4 Talakan Khabarovskiy Kray Rus. Fed.
178 C9 Talala Gujarat India
17 M3 Talalayivka Ukr.
126 □R13 Talamanca, Cordillera de mts Costa Rica
63 Q5 Talamantes Spain
70 H3 Talamona Italy
72 G2 Talamone Italy
146 D1 Talampaya, Parque Nacional nat. park Arg.
72 C7 Talana Sardegna Italy
162 G4 Talandzha Rus. Fed.
156 D6 Talang, Gunung vol. Indon.
156 F6 Talangbatu Sumatera Indon.
156 F6 Talangbetutu Sumatera Indon.
147 F2 Tala Norte Arg.
40 G2 Talant France
179 O6 Talap Assam India
136 A6 Talara Peru
Talar-i-Band mts Pak. see Makran Coast Range
66 G3 Talarn, Embassament de resr Spain
65 I2 Talarrubias Spain
183 M5 Talas r. Kazakh./Kyrg.
183 O6 Talas Kyrg.
183 N6 Talas admin. div. Kyrg.
183 N6 Talas Ala-Too mts Kyrg.
153 L8 Talasea New Britain P.N.G.
19 P7 Talashkino Rus. Fed.
Talas Oblast admin. div. Kyrg. see Talas
Talas Range mts Kyrg. see Talas Ala-Too
Talasskaya Oblast' admin. div. Kyrg. see Talas
Talasskiy Alatau, Khrebet mts Kyrg. see Talas Ala-Too
155 B4 Talatakoh i. Indon.
190 D8 Tal'at al Jamā'ah, Rujm mt. Jordan
89 G3 Talata-Mafara Nigeria
190 E4 Ţal'at Mūsá mt. Lebanon/Syria
155 E1 Talaud, Kepulauan is Indon.
62 H9 Talaván Spain
65 P3 Talave, Embalse de resr Spain
63 K9 Talavera de la Reina Spain
64 F3 Talavera la Real Spain
206 H5 Talawanta Qld Austr.
158 C2 Talawgyi Myanmar
193 Q3 Talaya Rus. Fed.
154 E8 Talayan Mindanao Phil.
67 B12 Talayón hill Spain
62 I9 Talayuela Spain
67 C8 Talayuelas Spain
63 P9 Talayuelo mt. Spain
178 G7 Talbehat Uttar Prad. India
190 E4 Talbīsah Syria
209 I9 Talbot, Mount hill W.A. Austr.
118 C7 Talbot County county MD U.S.A.
105 K2 Talbot Inlet Nunavut Can.
107 L4 Talbot Lake Man. Can.
115 E9 Talbotton GA U.S.A.
205 L5 Talbragar r. N.S.W. Austr.
146 B4 Talca Chile
146 B3 Talca, Punta pt Chile
144 B5 Talcahuano Chile
146 A5 Talcamávida Chile
179 J9 Talcher Orissa India
162 D2 Taldan Rus. Fed.
19 U5 Taldom Rus. Fed.
183 O8 Taldyk, Pereval pass Kyrg.
183 R5 Taldykorgan Kazakh.
Taldy-Kurgan Kazakh. see Taldykorgan
Taldyqorghan Kazakh. see Taldykorgan
183 M3 Taldysay Kazakh.
Taldysu Kyrg. see Taldy-Suu
183 R6 Taldy-Suu Kyrg.
129 K8 Talea de Castro Mex.
176 D3 Talegaon Mahar. India
176 F2 Talegaon Mahar. India
184 C5 Taleh Zang Iran
178 F8 Talen Madh. Prad. India
43 C6 Talence France
97 M8 Taleni S. Africa
38 H5 Talensac France
67 E8 Tales Spain
184 C3 Tālesh Gīlān Iran
19 T2 Talets, Ozero l. Rus. Fed.
208 E6 Talga r. W.A. Austr.
183 Q6 Talgar Kazakh.
183 Q6 Talgar, Pik mt. Kazakh.
30 D3 Talgarreg Ceredigion, Wales U.K.
30 F4 Talgarth Powys, Wales U.K.
85 G5 Talguharai Sudan
62 D7 Talhadas Port.
186 F7 Ţalḩah Saudi Arabia
204 E5 Talia S.A. Austr.
155 D4 Taliabu i. Indon.
41 I8 Taliard France
154 E6 Talibon Bohol Phil.
30 E3 Taliesin Ceredigion, Wales U.K.
64 E3 Táliga Spain
176 E4 Talikota Karnataka India
154 E8 Talikud i. Phil.
Talimardzhan Uzbek. see Tollimarjon
191 E5 T'alin Armenia
169 S3 Talin Hiag Heilong. China
86 D3 Taliouine Morocco
176 D6 Taliparamba Kerala India
92 A3 Tali Post Sudan
154 D6 Talisay Cebu Phil.
157 M4 Talisayan Kalimantan Indon.
154 E7 Talisayan Mindanao Phil.
191 J7 Taliş Dağları mts Azer./Iran
155 D3 Talisei i. Indon.
26 D8 Talisker Highland, Scotland U.K.
146 E3 Talita Arg.
14 I4 Talitsa Kostromskaya Oblast' Rus. Fed.
19 V9 Talitsa Lipetskaya Oblast' Rus. Fed.
17 T1 Talitskiy Chamlyk Rus. Fed.
157 L9 Taliwang Sumbawa Indon.
18 L8 Tal'ka Belarus
48 K3 Talkau Ger.
71 L8 Talla Italy
204 D4 Tallacootra, Lake salt flat S.A. Austr.
26 F7 Talladale Highland, Scotland U.K.
115 D9 Talladega AL U.S.A.
189 K5 Tall 'Afar Iraq
27 J6 Tallaght Rep. of Ireland
115 E10 Tallahassee FL U.S.A.
190 G2 Tall al Aḩmar Syria
205 K7 Tallangatta Vic. Austr.
27 I5 Tallanstown Rep. of Ireland
115 D9 Tallapoosa r. AL U.S.A.
204 D3 Tallaringa Conservation Park nature res. S.A. Austr.
115 E9 Tallassee AL U.S.A.
85 H5 Talla Talla Seghir Island Sudan
189 J5 Tall Baydar Syria
43 B8 Taller France
209 C10 Tallering Peak hill W.A. Austr.
118 D5 Talleyville DE U.S.A.
18 H2 Tallinn Estonia
18 H2 Tallinna laht b. Estonia
190 E4 Tall Kalakh Syria
189 K5 Tall Kayf Iraq
189 K5 Tall Kūjik Syria
116 D7 Tallmadge OH U.S.A.
40 I5 Talloires France
72 D3 Tallone Corse France
62 C3 Tallós Spain
27 F8 Tallow Rep. of Ireland
121 J9 Tallulah LA U.S.A.
189 K5 Tall 'Uwaynāt Iraq
Tallymerjen Uzbek. see Tollimarjon
77 M5 Tălmaciu Romania
118 C4 Talmage PA U.S.A.
40 G2 Talmay France
86 C3 Talmest Morocco
137 H4 Talmiã Brazil
26 H5 Talmine Highland, Scotland U.K.
42 C4 Talmont France
42 A3 Talmont-St-Hilaire France
16 J5 Tal'ne Ukr.
Tal'noye Ukr. see Tal'ne
178 D8 Talod Gujarat India
178 E9 Taloda Mahar. India
90 F2 Talodi Sudan
200 □1 Talofofo Guam
200 □1 Talofofo Bay Guam
121 F7 Taloga OK U.S.A.
185 K9 Taloi Range mts Pak.
109 H2 Talon, Lac l. Que. Can.
158 D4 Ta-long Myanmar
185 M3 Tāloqān Afgh.
72 C7 Talora r. Sardegna Italy
213 K2 Talos Dome ice feature Antarctica
158 F4 Ta Loung San mt. Laos
17 M5 Talova Balka Ukr.
182 D2 Talovaya Kazakh.
15 H6 Talovaya Rus. Fed.
191 H1 Talovka Rus. Fed.
105 I3 Taloyoak Nunavut Can.
128 C5 Talpa Mex.
185 O4 Tal Pass Pak.
89 H3 Talras well Niger
75 M3 Talsano Italy
168 E4 Talshand Mongolia
18 F4 Talsi Latvia
184 I7 Tal Sīyāh Iran
51 K8 Talsperre Quitzdorf Kollmer Höhen park Ger.
144 C2 Taltal Chile
107 H2 Taltson r. N.W.T. Can.
55 J2 Tałty, Jezioro l. Pol.
173 L11 Talu Xizang China
156 C4 Talu Sumatera Indon.
155 C3 Taludaa Sulawesi Indon.
155 F5 Taluti, Teluk b. Seram Indon.
71 K3 Talvera r. Italy
20 Q1 Talvik Norway
205 L3 Talwood Qld Austr.
15 H6 Taly Rus. Fed.
16 J5 Tal'yanky Ukr.
205 I5 Talyawalka r. N.S.W. Austr.
Talyshskiye Gory mts Azer./Iran see Taliş Dağları
14 K2 Talyy Rus. Fed.
167 J4 Tama Japan
63 K2 Tama Spain
157 K3 Tama Abu, Banjaran mts Malaysia
Tamabo Range mts Malaysia see Tama Abu, Banjaran
158 B3 Tamadaw Myanmar
167 K4 Tama-gawa r. Japan
164 □1 Tamagusuku Okinawa Japan
158 D1 Tamai, Nam r. Myanmar
63 N6 Tamajón Spain
203 □4 Tamakautoga Niue
167 L1 Tamakawa Japan
166 E7 Tamaki Japan
202 I3 Tamaki Strait North I. N.Z.
209 B9 Tamala W.A. Austr.
15 H5 Tamala Rus. Fed.
136 C2 Tamalameque Col.
88 E4 Tamale Ghana
89 F3 Tamalelt well Mali
157 J5 Tamalung Kalimantan Indon.
62 H7 Tamames Spain
167 J3 Tamamura Japan
165 H14 Tamana Japan
199 H2 Tamana i. Gilbert Is Kiribati
86 C3 Tamanar Morocco
147 H6 Tamangueyú Arg.
84 B3 Tamanhint Libya
88 D3 Tamani Mali
156 E2 Taman Negara National Park Malaysia
165 K12 Tamano Japan
87 G5 Tamanrasset Alg.
87 F5 Tamanrasset, Oued watercourse Alg.
158 B2 Tamanthi Myanmar
129 H4 Tamapatz Mex.
118 D3 Tamaqua PA U.S.A.
179 J8 Tamar Jharkhand India
Tamar Syria see Tadmur
30 D7 Tamar r. England U.K.
89 F2 Tamaradant well Mali
165 I14 Tamarai Japan
167 L3 Tamari Japan
99 □1b Tamarin Mauritius
131 L9 Tamarindo Venez.
66 F4 Tamarite de Litera Spain
138 C4 Tamarugal, Pampa de plain Chile
95 E4 Tamasane Botswana
89 G2 Tamasgoï well Niger
55 L4 Tamashowka Belarus
57 H5 Tamási Hungary
77 P4 Tamaşi Romania
129 H4 Tamasopo Mex.
Tamatave Madag. see Toamasina
167 L3 Tamatsukuri Japan
129 H3 Tamaulipas state Mex.
129 I2 Tamaulipas, Sierra de mts Mex.
92 C3 Tama Wildlife Reserve nature res. Eth.
164 S7 Tamayama Japan
126 F5 Tamazula Durango Mex.
128 D6 Tamazula Jalisco Mex.
129 J8 Tamazulápam Mex.
129 I4 Tamazunchale Mex.
Tamba Japan see Tanba
92 B4 Tambach Kenya
49 K9 Tambach-Dietharz Ger.
88 B3 Tambacounda Senegal
Tamba-kōchi plat. Japan see Tanba-kōchi
155 B7 Tambalongang i. Indon.
157 I5 Tambangmunjul Kalimantan Indon.
156 E6 Tambangsawah Sumatera Indon.
97 P2 Tambankulu Swaziland
89 F3 Tambao Burkina
88 C3 Tambaoura, Falaise de esc. Mali
137 F6 Tambaqui Brazil
95 G3 Tambara Moz.
205 L4 Tambar Springs N.S.W. Austr.
142 D4 Tambau Brazil
89 G3 Tambawel Nigeria
155 B6 Tambea Sulawesi Indon.
156 G4 Tambelan, Kepulauan is Indon.
157 G4 Tambelan Besar i. Indon.
209 D13 Tambellup W.A. Austr.
146 C2 Tamberías Arg.
157 J8 Tamberu Jawa Indon.
146 C3 Tambillo, Cerro mt. Arg.
157 M2 Tambisan Sabah Malaysia
207 K8 Tambo Qld Austr.
205 K7 Tambo r. Vic. Austr.
138 C4 Tambo r. Peru
138 B3 Tambobamba Peru
138 A3 Tambo de Mora Peru
136 A6 Tambo Grande Peru
95 □I3 Tambohorano Madag.
155 B5 Tamboli Sulawesi Indon.
138 C3 Tambopata r. Peru
91 B9 Tambor Angola
126 G5 Tambor Mex.
157 L9 Tambora, Gunung vol. Sumbawa Indon.
147 I2 Tambores Uru.
140 E3 Tamboril Brazil
136 C5 Tamboryacu r. Peru
90 E3 Tamboura C.A.R.
15 H5 Tambov Rus. Fed.
191 E4 Tambovka Georgia
162 F3 Tambovka Rus. Fed.
Tambov Oblast admin. div. Rus. Fed. see Tambovskaya Oblast'
15 H5 Tambovskaya Oblast' admin. div. Rus. Fed.
62 C3 Tambre r. Spain
155 A3 Tambu, Teluk b. Indon.
157 M5 Tambulan Sulawesi Indon.
157 L2 Tambulanan, Bukit hill Malaysia
157 L2 Tambunan Sabah Malaysia
90 E3 Tambura Sudan
157 L1 Tambuyukon, Gunung mt. Malaysia
88 C2 Tâmchekkeţ Maur.
182 G3 Tamdy Kazakh.
Tamdybulak Uzbek. see Tomdibuloq
136 D3 Tame Col.
62 D6 Tâmega r. Port.
145 C8 Tamel Aike Arg.
78 F5 Tamelos, Akra pt Kea Greece
Tamenghest Alg. see Tamanrasset
179 N7 Tamenglong Manipur India
Tamerlanovka Kazakh. see Temirlanovka
89 G2 Tamesna reg. Niger
89 H2 Tamgak, Adrar mt. Niger
88 B3 Tamgué, Massif du mt. Guinea
178 G8 Tamia Madh. Prad. India
129 J4 Tamiahua Mex.
129 J4 Tamiahua, Laguna de lag. Mex.
115 G13 Tamiami Canal FL U.S.A.
156 C2 Tamiang r. Indon.
156 C2 Tamiang, Ujung pt Indon.
176 F7 Tamil Nadu state India
118 E2 Tamiment PA U.S.A.
157 K6 Taminglayang Kalimantan Indon.
70 G2 Tamins Switz.
168 H3 Tamirin Gol r. Mongolia
76 I6 Tamiš r. Serb. and Mont.
140 B5 Tamitatoala r. Brazil
14 G2 Tamitsa Rus. Fed.
85 F2 Ţāmīyah Egypt
186 F3 Tamīyah, Jabal hill Saudi Arabia
89 H1 Tamjit well Niger
182 J3 Tamkamys Kazakh.
179 J6 Tamkuhi Uttar Prad. India
158 I7 Tam Ky Vietnam
86 E2 Tamlelt, Plaine de plain Morocco
179 K8 Tamluk W. Bengal India
52 G4 Tamm Ger.
73 N5 Tammaro r. Italy
107 K1 Tammarvi r. Nunavut Can.
18 G1 Tammela Etelä-Suomi Fin.
20 U4 Tammela Oulu Fin.
48 G1 Tammensiel Ger.
Tammerfors Fin. see Tampere
18 K1 Tammio i. Fin.
18 K3 Tammispää Estonia
23 N1 Tämnaren l. Sweden
76 I6 Tamnava r. Serb. and Mont.
40 D2 Tamnay-en-Bazois France
62 E2 Támoga r. Spain
89 F3 Tamou Niger
89 F3 Tamou, Réserve Totale de Faune de nature res. Niger
115 F12 Tampa FL U.S.A.
115 F12 Tampa Bay FL U.S.A.
129 I4 Tampacán Mex.
129 I4 Tampamolón Mex.
156 F7 Tampang Sumatera Indon.
21 Q6 Tampere Fin.
129 J3 Tampico Mex.
129 J3 Tampico el Alto Mex.
156 E3 Tampin Malaysia
156 □ Tampines Sing.
156 □ Tampines, Sungai r. Sing.
155 C6 Tampo Sulawesi Indon.
159 I7 Tam Quan Vietnam
186 G5 Tamrah Saudi Arabia
169 O3 Tamsagbulag Mongolia
168 H6 Tamsag Muchang Nei Mongol China
18 J2 Tamsalu Estonia
136 C6 Tamshiyacu Peru
59 I5 Tamsweg Austria
158 B2 Tamu Myanmar
129 I4 Tamuín Mex.
200 □1 Tamuning Guam
179 K6 Tamur r. Nepal
65 J3 Tamurejo Spain
200 □4b Tamworohi Pohnpei Micronesia
205 M4 Tamworth N.S.W. Austr.
29 N8 Tamworth Staffordshire, England U.K.
183 Q3 Tan Kazakh.
Tana r. Fin./Norway see Tenojoki
92 D5 Tana r. Kenya
Tana i. Vanuatu see Tanna
Tana, Lake Eth. see T'ana Hāyk'
165 M13 Tanabe Japan
142 C4 Tanabi Brazil
20 T1 Tana Bru Norway
20 T1 Tanafjorden inlet Norway
104 A4 Tanaga vol. AK U.S.A.
104 A4 Tanaga Island AK U.S.A.
73 O6 Tanagro r. Italy
167 L1 Tanagura Japan
157 H8 Tanah, Tanjung pt Indon.
92 C2 T'ana Hāyk' l. Eth.
156 C5 Tanahbala i. Indon.
157 L5 Tanahgrogot Kalimantan Indon.
155 B7 Tanahjampea i. Indon.
156 C5 Tanahmasa i. Indon.
157 L3 Tanahmerah Kalimantan Indon.
156 E2 Tanah Merah Malaysia
156 D4 Tanahputih Sumatera Indon.
156 D2 Tanah Rata Malaysia
155 A6 Tanakeke i. Indon.
178 H5 Tanakpur Uttaranchal India
155 A5 Tanambung Sulawesi Indon.
206 B5 Tanami N.T. Austr.
206 C5 Tanami Desert N.T. Austr.
206 B6 Tanami Downs Aboriginal Land res. N.T. Austr.
159 H9 Tân An Vietnam
104 C3 Tanana AK U.S.A.
Tananarive Madag. see Antananarivo
95 □I4 Tanandava Madag.
187 I2 Tanāqīb, Ra's pt Saudi Arabia
70 F5 Tanaro r. Italy
30 F2 Tanat r. Wales U.K.
154 E6 Tanauan Leyte Phil.
72 D6 Tanaunella Sardegna Italy
201 □1a Tanavuso Point Viti Levu Fiji
166 B5 Tanba Japan
166 B5 Tanba-kōchi plat. Japan
207 H8 Tanbar Qld Austr.
169 P9 Tanbu Shandong China
39 L3 Tancarville France
Tancheng Fujian China see Pingtan
169 P9 Tancheng Shandong China
163 F8 Tanch'ŏn N. Korea
128 E6 Tancítaro Mex.
128 E6 Tancítaro, Cerro de mt. Mex.
129 N8 Tancochapa r. Mex.
88 E5 Tanda Côte d'Ivoire
178 E4 Tanda Punjab India
178 G5 Tanda Uttar Prad. India
179 I6 Tanda Uttar Prad. India
21 L6 Tandådalen Sweden
154 F7 Tandag Mindanao Phil.
77 P6 Ţăndărei Romania
91 C9 Tandaué Angola
157 L1 Tandek Sabah Malaysia
53 K5 Tandern Ger.
178 F3 Tandi Hima. Prad. India
147 H5 Tandil Arg.
147 H5 Tandil, Sierra del hills Arg.
90 C2 Tandjilé pref. Chad
185 M9 Tando Adam Pak.
185 M9 Tando Alahyar Pak.
185 M9 Tando Bago Pak.
185 M9 Tando Muhammmad Khan Pak.
205 I5 Tandou Lake imp. l. N.S.W. Austr.
27 J4 Tandragee Northern Ireland U.K.
21 M6 Tandsjöborg Sweden
154 C9 Tandubatu i. Phil.
178 H9 Tandula r. India
176 E4 Tandur Andhra Prad. India
176 F3 Tandur Andhra Prad. India
185 L7 Tanduri Pak.
202 K5 Taneatua North I. N.Z.
164 □H16 Tanega-shima i. Japan
164 S6 Taneichi Japan
158 D5 Tanen Taunggyi mts Thai.
155 E4 Taneti i. Maluku Indon.
55 K5 Tanew r. Pol.
118 A5 Taneytown MD U.S.A.
87 E5 Tanezrouft reg. Alg./Mali
87 E5 Tanezrouft Tan-Ahenet reg. Alg.
190 G5 Ţanf, Jabal aţ hill Syria
184 H9 Tang Iran
28 B6 Tang Rep. of Ireland
184 H9 Tang, Ra's-e pt Iran
169 L1 Tanga Rus. Fed.
93 C6 Tanga Tanz.
93 C6 Tanga admin. reg. Tanz.
202 I3 Tangaehe North I. N.Z.
179 L7 Tangail Bangl.
95 □J4 Tangainony Madag.
153 L7 Tanga Islands P.N.G.
176 G9 Tangalla Sri Lanka
128 E6 Tangamandapio Mex.
128 E6 Tangancícuaro de Arista Mex.
Tanganyika country Africa see Tanzania
93 A6 Tanganyika, Lake Africa
184 F3 Tangar Iran
141 C8 Tangará Brazil
200 □6 Tangarare Guadalcanal Solomon Is
90 C2 Tangaray Chad
176 E8 Tangasseri Kerala India
170 D5 Tangdan Yunnan China
173 K11 Tangdê Xizang China
Tangdukou Hunan China see Shaoyang
189 P9 Tang-e Kalleh Iran
184 F3 Tangeli Iran
22 H1 Tangen Norway
213 D2 Tange Promontory hd Antarctica
86 D2 Tanger Morocco
60 D5 Tanger prov. Morocco
156 G8 Tangerang Jawa Indon.
51 E6 Tangerhütte Ger.
50 E5 Tangermünde Ger.
60 D5 Tanger-Tétouan prov. Morocco
184 H8 Tang-e Sarkheh Iran
168 F8 Tanggarma Qinghai China
173 J11 Tanggo Xizang China
170 D2 Tanggor Sichuan China
169 O7 Tanggu Tianjin China
168 C9 Tanggulashan Qinghai China
173 J10 Tanggula Shan mt. Qinghai/Xizang China
173 I10 Tanggula Shan mts Xizang China
173 J10 Tanggula Shankou pass Xizang China
173 G12 Tangguo Xizang China
169 O7 Tanghai Hebei China
171 I2 Tanghe Henan China
171 I2 Tang He r. China
185 N4 Tangi Pak.
Tangier Morocco see Tanger
117 I11 Tangier Island VA U.S.A.
202 J7 Tangimoana North I. N.Z.
155 B5 Tangkelemboko, Gunung mt. Indon.
156 F7 Tangkittebak, Gunung mt. Indon.
173 I13 Tang La pass Xizang China
158 A1 Tangla Assam India
170 B2 Tanglag Qinghai China
156 □ Tanglin Sing.
173 L11 Tangmai Xizang China
168 G9 Tangnag Qinghai China
166 B4 Tango Japan
207 J6 Tangorin Qld Austr.
173 H11 Tangra Yumco salt l. China
156 A2 Tangse Sumatera Indon.
Tangshan Guizhou China see Shiqian
169 P7 Tangshan Hebei China
48 J3 Tangstedt Ger.
Tangsyq Kazakh. see Tansyk
158 C3 Tangte mt. Myanmar
154 D7 Tangub Mindanao Phil.
154 D6 Tangub Negros Phil.
89 F4 Tanguieta Benin
170 H5 Tangwan Hunan China
162 F4 Tangwanghe Heilong. China
162 F5 Tangwang He r. China
169 N7 Tangxian Hebei China
171 I3 Tangxianzhen Hubei China
158 D3 Tang-yan Myanmar
170 G4 Tangyan He r. China
169 N9 Tangyin Henan China
162 F5 Tangyuan Heilong. China
140 E5 Tanhaçu Brazil
20 S3 Tanhua Fin.
129 J4 Tanhuijo, Arrecife rf Mex.
159 G9 Tani Cambodia
170 A3 Taniantaweng Shan mts Xizang China
167 I2 Tanigawa-dake mt. Japan
166 E4 Tanigumi Japan
153 H8 Tanimbar, Kepulauan is Indon.
40 J4 Taninges France
Taninthari Myanmar see Tenasserim
Tanintharyi Myanmar see Tenasserim
Tanintharyi admin. div. Myanmar see Tenasserim
Taninthayi Myanmar see Tenasserim
155 F5 Taniwel Seram Indon.
165 H15 Taniyama Japan
Tanjah Morocco see Tanger
154 D7 Tanjay Negros Phil.
168 H8 Tanjiajing Gansu China
Tanjore Tamil Nadu India see Thanjavur
157 K6 Tanjung Kalimantan Indon.
156 F5 Tanjung Sumatera Indon.
156 C3 Tanjungbalai Sumatera Indon.
156 E4 Tanjungbalai Sumatera Indon.
155 E5 Tanjungbaliha Maluku Indon.
157 M3 Tanjungbatu Kalimantan Indon.
156 E4 Tanjungbatu Sumatera Indon.
157 M4 Tanjungbuayabuaya, Pulau i. Indon.
156 E6 Tanjungenim Sumatera Indon.
157 L6 Tanjunggaru Kalimantan Indon.
Tanjungkarang-Telukbetung Sumatera Indon. see Bandar Lampung
157 G6 Tanjungpandan Indon.
156 F4 Tanjungpinang Indon.
156 C3 Tanjungpura Sumatera Indon.
157 J6 Tanjung Puting National Park Indon.
156 F6 Tanjungraja Sumatera Indon.
157 L3 Tanjungredeb Kalimantan Indon.
157 H5 Tanjungsaleh i. Indon.
157 H5 Tanjungsatai Kalimantan Indon.
157 L3 Tanjungselor Kalimantan Indon.
185 N5 Tank Pak.
178 C8 Tankara Gujarat India
20 S2 Tankavaara Fin.
178 D9 Tankhala Gujarat India
168 I1 Tankhoy Rus. Fed.
178 G2 Tanktse Jammu and Kashmir
96 D8 Tankwa r. S. Africa
96 D8 Tankwa-Karoo National Park S. Africa
129 H4 Tanlacut Mex.
129 I4 Tanlajas Mex.
36 H8 Tanlay France
158 B5 Tanlwe r. Myanmar
53 N5 Tann Ger.
49 J9 Tann (Rhon) Ger.
51 E10 Tanna Ger.
200 □5 Tanna i. Vanuatu
26 K9 Tannadice Angus, Scotland U.K.
166 B5 Tannan Japan
21 L5 Tännäs Sweden
40 D2 Tannay Bourgogne France
37 I4 Tannay Champagne-Ardenne France
49 K7 Tanne Ger.
Tannenberg Pol. see Stębark
106 G5 Tanner, Mount B.C. Can.
41 J9 Tanneron France
118 E2 Tannersville PA U.S.A.
53 M2 Tännesberg Ger.
53 I4 Tannhausen Ger.
58 C5 Tannheim Austria
53 I6 Tannheim Ger.
58 B4 Tannheimer Gebirge mts Austria/Ger.
20 R4 Tannila Fin.
22 G4 Tannis Bugt b. Denmark
Tannoa i. Vanuatu see Tongoa
51 D9 Tannroda Ger.
207 M7 Tannum Sands Qld Austr.
168 B1 Tannu-Ola, Khrebet mts Rus. Fed.
Tannu Tuva aut. rep. Rus. Fed. see Tyva, Respublika
165 I15 Tano Japan
154 D7 Tañon Strait Phil.
178 C6 Tanot Rajasthan India
89 H3 Tanout Niger
54 C2 Tanowo Pol.
129 I4 Tanquian Mex.
179 I6 Tansen Nepal
171 M6 Tanshui Taiwan
88 D3 Tansilla Burkina
29 N7 Tansley Derbyshire, England U.K.
183 R4 Tansyk Kazakh.
85 F2 Ţanţā Egypt
158 C5 Tantabin Pegu Myanmar
158 B3 Tantabin Sagaing Myanmar
158 B6 Tantabin Yangôn Myanmar
86 C3 Tan-Tan Morocco
204 H7 Tantanoola S.A. Austr.
166 A5 Tantō Japan
37 L7 Tantonville France
50 J4 Tantow Ger.
129 I4 Tantoyuca Mex.
178 F6 Tantpur Uttar Prad. India
169 R3 Tantu Jilin China
190 C6 Tantura Israel
176 G4 Tanuku Andhra Prad. India
167 K3 Tanuma Japan
206 E4 Tanumbirini N.T. Austr.
22 H3 Tanumshede Sweden
56 E1 Tanvald Czech Rep.
86 B5 Tanwakka, Sabkhat well Western Sahara
158 I3 Tanxu Guangxi China
17 R4 Tanyushivka Ukr.
93 B6 Tanzania country Africa
167 J5 Tanzawa-Ōyama Quasi National Park Japan
106 D3 Tanzilla r. B.C. Can.
98 □3c Tao Lanzarote Canary Is
159 D9 Tao, Ko i. Thai.
Tao'an Jilin China see Taonan
Taocheng Fujian China see Yongchun
171 H6 Taochuan Hunan China
169 Q8 Taocun Shandong China
Taodeni Mali see Taoudenni
169 R4 Tao'er He r. China
168 H9 Tao He r. China
Taohuajiang Hunan China see Taojiang
171 I4 Taojiang Hunan China
Taolanaro Madag. see Tôlañaro
168 J7 Taole Ningxia China
169 R4 Taonan Jilin China
75 I8 Taormina Sicilia Italy
123 L8 Taos NM U.S.A.
89 F2 Taouârdeï well Mali
86 E5 Taoudenni Mali
86 D2 Taounate Morocco
87 E5 Taounnant well Mali
86 E2 Taourirt Morocco
86 D3 Taouz Morocco
171 K6 Taoxi Fujian China
171 H4 Taoyuan Hunan China
171 M6 T'aoyüan Taiwan
18 I2 Tapa Estonia
154 C9 Tapaan Passage Phil.
127 M10 Tapachula Mex.
200 □2 Tapaga Point Samoa
156 D2 Tapah Malaysia
137 H5 Tapajós r. Brazil
156 B3 Tapaktuan Sumatera Indon.
128 D6 Tapalpa Mex.
147 G5 Tapalqué Arg.
156 D6 Tapan Sumatera Indon.
137 H3 Tapanahoni r. Suriname
129 M9 Tapanatepec Mex.
156 C4 Tapanuli, Teluk b. Indon.
137 H5 Tapará, Ilha Grande do i. Brazil
137 H5 Tapara, Serra do hills Brazil
155 E4 Tapat i. Maluku Indon.
137 E6 Tapauá Brazil
137 E6 Tapauá r. Brazil
203 G8 Tapawera South I. N.Z.
141 B9 Tapera Rio Grande do Sul Brazil
137 F5 Tapera Roraima Brazil
145 C7 Tapera Chile
139 E3 Tapera Pesoe Brazil
140 F5 Taperoá Brazil
141 C9 Tapes Brazil
88 C5 Tapeta Liberia
53 J4 Tapfheim Ger.
178 D9 Tapi r. India
159 D10 Ta Pi, Mae Nam r. Thai.
139 F4 Tapia, Sierra de hills Bol.
62 G1 Tapia de Casariego Spain
145 C8 Tapi Aike Arg.
154 D8 Tapiantana i. Phil.
136 C6 Tapiche r. Peru
127 M9 Tapijulapa Mex.
157 I5 Tapinbini Kalimantan Indon.
57 J4 Tápió r. Hungary
57 I4 Tápióbicske Hungary
142 D2 Tapiocanga, Chapada do hills Brazil
57 I4 Tápiógyörgye Hungary
57 I4 Tápióság Hungary
57 I4 Tápiószecső Hungary
57 I4 Tápiószele Hungary
57 I4 Tápiószőlős Hungary
142 D3 Tapira Minas Gerais Brazil
142 A5 Tapira Paraná Brazil
140 D5 Tapiracanga Brazil
142 D5 Tapiraí Brazil
139 H2 Tapirapé r. Brazil
137 E4 Tapirapecó, Sierra mts Brazil/Venez.
139 F3 Tapirapuã Brazil
156 E2 Tapis, Gunung mt. Malaysia
126 E4 Tapisuelas Mex.
56 F4 Táplánszentkereszt Hungary
179 K6 Taplejung Nepal
171 □J7 Tap Mun Chau i. H.K. China
89 F3 Tapoa watercourse Burkina
90 B2 Tapol Chad
56 G5 Tapolca Hungary
158 D4 Ta-pom Myanmar
26 K8 Tap o' Noth hill Scotland U.K.
116 I11 Tappahannock VA U.S.A.
178 F5 Tappal Uttar Prad. India
157 M6 Tappalang Sulawesi Indon.
119 H2 Tappan NY U.S.A.
116 D8 Tappan Lake OH U.S.A.
184 D4 Tappeh, Kūh-e hill Iran
164 R5 Tappi-zaki pt Japan
191 H5 Tap Qaraqoyunlu Azer.
Taprobane country Asia see Sri Lanka
56 G5 Tapsony Hungary
162 B2 Taptugary Rus. Fed.
203 H8 Tapuaenuku mt. South I. N.Z.
154 C9 Tapul Phil.
154 C9 Tapul Group is Phil.
156 C4 Tapulonanjing mt. Indon.
156 D4 Tapung r. Indon.
137 F6 Tapurú Brazil
137 E5 Tapurucuara Brazil
200 □2 Taputapu, Cape American Samoa
Taputeouea atoll Gilbert Is Kiribati see Tabiteuea
186 G9 Taqar mt. Yemen
189 L6 Ţaqţaq Iraq
141 C9 Taquara Brazil
142 A1 Taquaral, Serra do hills Brazil
139 F4 Taquarí r. Brazil
142 C4 Taquaritinga Brazil
142 C5 Taquarituba Brazil
142 A4 Taquaruçu r. Brazil
146 B5 Taquimilán Arg.
57 I4 Tar Hungary
27 G8 Tar r. Rep. of Ireland
207 M9 Tara Qld Austr.
76 G7 Tara r. Bos.-Herz./Yugo.
76 H7 Tara nat. park Serb. and Mont.
27 I5 Tara, Hill of Rep. of Ireland
89 H4 Taraba r. Nigeria
89 H4 Taraba state Nigeria
142 B5 Tarabaí Brazil
138 D4 Tarabuco Bol.
84 B1 Ţarābulus Libya
63 N7 Taracena Spain
16 H8 Taraclia Moldova
138 C3 Taraco Peru
136 D4 Taracua Brazil
202 K6 Taradale North I. N.Z.
41 I10 Taradeau France
84 B3 Tarāghin Libya
185 N9 Tar Ahmad Rind Pak.
179 L6 Tarai reg. India
Taraíra r. Brazil see Traíra
138 E5 Tarairí Bol.
98 □3b Tarajalejo Fuerteventura Canary Is
157 L3 Tarakan Kalimantan Indon.
157 L3 Tarakan i. Indon.
185 L5 Tarakki reg. Afgh.
79 L2 Taraklı Turkey
Tarakliya Moldova see Taraclia
199 I3 Tarakua Fiji
164 X3 Taraku-shima i. Kuril'skiye O-va Rus. Fed.
205 L6 Taralga N.S.W. Austr.
164 □B22 Tarama-jima i. Nansei-shotō Japan
62 F2 Taramundi Spain
18 C7 Taran, Mys pt Rus. Fed.
178 F8 Tarana Madh. Prad. India
178 E5 Taranagar Rajasthan India
202 H6 Taranaki admin. reg. North I. N.Z.
202 I6 Taranaki, Mount vol. North I. N.Z.
63 N8 Tarancón Spain
17 L3 Tarandyntsi Ukr.
202 I2 Taranga Island North I. N.Z.
176 F7 Tarangambadi Tamil Nadu India
90 C2 Tarangara Chad
93 C6 Tarangire National Park Tanz.
Tarangul l. Kazakh. see Tarankol', Ozero
183 M1 Tarankol', Ozero l. Kazakh.
182 J1 Taranovskoye Kazakh.
26 B7 Taransay i. Scotland U.K.
75 M3 Taranto Italy
75 M2 Taranto prov. Italy
75 M3 Taranto, Golfo di g. Italy
56 G5 Tarany Hungary
138 C4 Tarapacá admin. reg. Chile
136 D5 Tarapacá Col.
200 □6 Tarapaina Malaita Solomon Is
136 B6 Tarapoto Peru
40 E5 Tarare France
147 I4 Tarariras Uru.
202 J7 Tararua Forest Park nature res. North I. N.Z.
203 J7 Tararua Range mts North I. N.Z.
Tarasaigh i. Scotland U.K. see Taransay
41 F9 Tarascon France
43 H10 Tarascon-sur-Ariège France
16 F5 Tarashany Ukr.
16 J4 Tarashcha Ukr.
184 G5 Tarasht Iran
17 M7 Tarasivka Khersons'ka Oblast' Ukr.
17 M7 Tarasivka Khersons'ka Oblast' Ukr.
17 L5 Tarasivka Kirovohrads'ka Oblast' Ukr.
17 R4 Tarasivka Luhans'ka Oblast' Ukr.
14 I2 Tarasovo Rus. Fed.
15 H6 Tarasovskiy Rus. Fed.
87 H4 Tarat Alg.
138 C4 Tarata Peru
138 C2 Tarauacá Brazil
136 D6 Tarauacá r. Brazil
201 □3a Taravao Tahiti Fr. Polynesia
201 □3a Taravao, Baie de b. Tahiti Fr. Polynesia
201 □3a Taravao, Isthme de isth. Tahiti Fr. Polynesia
71 P3 Taravisio, Foresta di Italy
72 B4 Taravo r. Corse France
199 H1 Tarawa atoll Kiribati
202 K6 Tarawera North I. N.Z.
202 K5 Tarawera, Lake North I. N.Z.
202 K5 Tarawera, Mount North I. N.Z.
183 N6 Taraz Kazakh.
63 Q5 Tarazona Spain
65 P2 Tarazona de la Mancha Spain
183 S4 Tarbagatay Kazakh.
169 J1 Tarbagatay Rus. Fed.
183 S4 Tarbagatay, Khrebet mts Kazakh.
26 I7 Tarbat Ness pt Scotland U.K.
67 E10 Tárbena Spain
27 D7 Tarbert Rep. of Ireland
26 E11 Tarbert Argyll and Bute, Scotland U.K.
26 F11 Tarbert Argyll and Bute, Scotland U.K.
26 C7 Tarbert Western Isles, Scotland U.K.
26 D11 Tarbert, Loch inlet Scotland U.K.
43 E9 Tarbes France
26 G10 Tarbet Argyll and Bute, Scotland U.K.
26 H11 Tarbolton South Ayrshire, Scotland U.K.
115 I8 Tarboro NC U.S.A.
57 L5 Tărcaia Romania
57 K3 Tarcal Hungary
57 L4 Tarcea Romania
71 O3 Tarcento Italy
204 E4 Tarcoola S.A. Austr.
205 K4 Tarcoon N.S.W. Austr.
204 D2 Tarcoonyinna watercourse S.A. Austr.
77 K5 Ţarcului, Munţii mts Romania
205 K6 Tarcutta N.S.W. Austr.
55 I4 Tarczyn Pol.
38 H4 Tard r. France
63 M4 Tardajos Spain
63 O5 Tardelcuende Spain
36 F5 Tardenois reg. France
42 J3 Tardes r. France
43 C9 Tardets-Sorholus France
66 D4 Tardienta Spain
42 E4 Tardoire r. France
162 K4 Tardoki-Yani, Gora mt. Rus. Fed.
205 N4 Taree N.S.W. Austr.
92 B2 Tareifing Sudan
205 I4 Tarella N.S.W. Austr.
20 Q3 Tärendö Sweden
128 F5 Tarengo Mex.
89 F2 Tarenkat well Mali
Tarentum Italy see Taranto
128 F6 Taretán Mex.
193 K2 Tareya Rus. Fed.
186 F7 Ţarfā, Ra's aţ pt Saudi Arabia
86 B4 Tarfaya Morocco
26 K9 Tarfside Angus, Scotland U.K.
89 G2 Targa well Niger
Targan Heilong. China see Talin Hiag
Targan Kazakh. see Targyn
122 I4 Targhee Pass ID U.S.A.
43 D6 Targon France
77 N6 Târgovişte Romania
54 F3 Targowa Górka Pol.
77 P5 Târgu Bujor Romania
77 L6 Târgu Cărbuneşti Romania
77 O3 Târgu Frumos Romania
86 D2 Targuist Morocco
77 L5 Târgu Jiu Romania
77 L3 Târgu Lăpuş Romania
77 M4 Târgu Mureş Romania
77 O3 Târgu Neamţ Romania
77 O4 Târgu Ocna Romania
77 O4 Târgu Secuiesc Romania
173 G12 Targyailing Xizang China
183 T3 Targyn Kazakh.
184 B5 Tarhān Iran
86 D3 Tarhbalt Morocco
Tarhmanant well Mali see Taghmanant
57 K5 Tarhos Hungary
84 B1 Tarhūnah Libya
153 J8 Tari P.N.G.
169 K7 Tarian Gol Nei Mongol China
186 F6 Tarib, Wādī watercourse Saudi Arabia
187 K3 Tarif U.A.E.
64 H8 Tarifa Spain
64 H8 Tarifa, Punta de pt Spain
154 D3 Tarigtig Point Luzon Phil.
138 D5 Tarija Bol.
138 D5 Tarija dept Bol.
176 D6 Tarikere Karnataka India
153 I7 Tariku r. Papua Indon.
172 F6 Tarim Xinjiang China
187 I7 Tarīm Yemen
Tarim Basin China see Tarim Pendi
93 B5 Tarime Tanz.
172 H6 Tarim He r. China
172 H6 Tarim Liuchang Xinjiang China
128 G5 Tarimoro Mex.
172 E7 Tarim Pendi basin China
172 H6 Tarim Qichang Xinjiang China
139 E5 Taringuiti Bol.
185 K5 Tarīn Kowt Afgh.
153 I7 Taritatu r. Papua Indon.
Taritipan Sabah Malaysia see Tandek
57 H4 Tarján Hungary
97 J8 Tarka r. S. Africa
89 G3 Tarka, Vallée de watercourse Niger
57 G4 Tárkány Hungary
97 K8 Tarkastad S. Africa
17 P8 Tarkhan, Mys pt Ukr.
17 L8 Tarkhankut, Mys pt Ukr.
191 I3 Tarki Rus. Fed.
120 H5 Tarkio MO U.S.A.
192 I3 Tarko-Sale Rus. Fed.
88 E5 Tarkwa Ghana
154 C4 Tarlac Luzon Phil.
154 C3 Tarlac r. Luzon Phil.
183 R4 Tarlauly Kazakh.
29 L6 Tarleton Lancashire, England U.K.
205 L6 Tarlo River National Park N.S.W. Austr.
116 C9 Tarlton OH U.S.A.
22 E6 Tarm Denmark
138 B2 Tarma Junín Peru
136 D5 Tarma Loreto Peru
179 L5 Tarmar Xizang China
48 H4 Tarmstedt Ger.
43 I8 Tarn dept France
41 B8 Tarn r. France
41 C8 Tarn, Gorges du France
57 I4 Tarna r. Hungary
63 J2 Tarna, Puerto de pass Spain
20 M4 Tärnaby Sweden
185 K6 Tarnak r. Afgh.
57 J3 Tarnalelesz Hungary
57 J4 Tarnaméra Hungary
57 J4 Tarnaőrs Hungary
57 J4 Tarnaszentmiklós Hungary
77 L4 Târnava Mare r. Romania
77 L4 Târnava Mică r. Romania
77 M4 Târnăveni Romania
55 K5 Tarnawa Duża Pol.
55 L5 Tarnawatka Pol.
43 G7 Tarn-et-Garonne dept France
55 K6 Tarnica mt. Pol.
55 J5 Tarnobrzeg Pol.
55 K5 Tarnogród Pol.
14 H3 Tarnogskiy Gorodok Rus. Fed.
57 H4 Tárnok Hungary
Tarnopol Ukr. see Ternopil'
43 B8 Tarnos France
55 L5 Tarnoszyn Pol.
57 K5 Târnova Arad Romania
77 K5 Târnova Caraş-Severin Romania
50 F3 Tarnow Ger.
54 C3 Tarnów Lubuskie Pol.
55 I5 Tarnów Małopolskie Pol.
55 J6 Tarnowiec Pol.
Tarnowitz Pol. see Tarnowskie Góry
54 E2 Tarnówka Pol.
54 E3 Tarnowo Podgórne Pol.
54 G5 Tarnów Opolski Pol.
54 G5 Tarnowskie Góry Pol.
20 M3 Tårnvik Norway
70 I6 Taro r. Italy
164 S7 Tarō Japan
173 F11 Taro Co salt l. China
184 F7 Ţārom Iran
17 N5 Taroms'ke Ukr.
43 D8 Taron-Sadirac-Viellenave France
207 L8 Taroom Qld Austr.
167 J2 Tarō-san mt. Japan
62 E6 Tarouca Port.
86 C3 Taroudannt Morocco
62 D6 Tarouquela Port.
48 H1 Tarp Ger.
57 L3 Tarpa Hungary
179 M8 Tarpasa Bangl.
206 F5 Tarpaulin Swamp N.T. Austr.
204 H7 Tarpeena S.A. Austr.
115 F11 Tarpon Springs FL U.S.A.
29 L7 Tarporley Cheshire, England U.K.
55 L1 Tarprubežiai Lith.
130 E1 Tarpum Bay Eleuthera Bahamas
184 D5 Tarq Iran
184 D6 Tarqān Iran
72 H3 Tarquinia Italy
72 H3 Tarquinia Lido Italy
Tarquinii Italy see Tarquinia
206 E5 Tarrabool Lake salt flat N.T. Austr.

Column 1

Tarracina Italy see Terracina
Tarraco Spain see Tarragona
88 □ Tarrafal Santiago Cape Verde
66 H5 Tarragona Spain
66 G5 Tarragona prov. Spain
205 K10 Tarraleah Tas. Austr.
205 K5 Tarran Hills N.S.W. Austr.
206 G4 Tarrant Point Qld Austr.
203 D11 Tarras South I. N.Z.
66 H4 Tárrega Spain
26 I7 Tarrel Highland, Scotland U.K.
58 C5 Tarrenz Austria
157 J3 Tarrena Austria
184 A3 Tatavi r. Iran
191 I2 Tatayurt Rus. Fed.
207 I4 Tate r. Qld Austr.
19 H2 Társ Denmark
166 D4 Tatebayashi Japan
167 K1 Tateishi-misaki pt Japan
167 H3 Tateiwa Japan
167 H3 Tateshina Japan
167 H3 Tateshina-yama mt. Japan
167 K6 Tateyama Chiba Japan
166 G2 Tateyama Toyama Japan
166 G2 Tate-yama vol. Japan
106 G2 Tathlina Lake N.W.T. Can.
186 F6 Tathlith Saudi Arabia
186 G5 Tathlīth, Wādī watercourse Saudi Arabia
205 L7 Tathra N.S.W. Austr.
95 E4 Tati Botswana
88 B2 Tatitlek Alaska U.S.A.
48 G2 Tating Ger.
107 L2 Tatinnai Lake Nunavut Can.
182 A2 Tatishchevo Rus. Fed.
121 H9 Tatkon Myanmar
206 E3 Tatlawiksuk r. Alaska U.S.A.
71 N7 Tatnam, Cape Man. Can.
167 I4 Tatomi Japan

Column 2

Tatarskaya A.S.S.R. aut. rep. Rus. Fed. see
Tatarstan, Respublika
162 L3 Tatarskiy Proliv str. Rus. Fed.
14 J5 Tatarstan, Respublika aut. rep. Rus. Fed.
Tatar Strait Rus. Fed. see Tatarskiy Proliv
57 I4 Tatárszentgyörgy Hungary
77 O3 Tătăruşi Romania
201 □3a Tatatua, Pointe pt Tahiti Fr. Polynesia
184 A3 Tatau Sarawak Malaysia
111 N6 Tatvan Turkey
30 D6 Tavan Myanmar
73 M3 Tavo r. Italy
72 D6 Tavoy r. Qld Austr.

Tatra Mountains Pol./Slovakia see Tatry
173 Q7 Tatrang Xinjiang China
57 J2 Tátra-vidék Slovakia
57 J2 Tatranská Javorina Slovakia
57 J2 Tatranský nat. park Slovakia
55 H6 Tatry mts Pol./Slovakia
55 H6 Tatrzański Park Narodowy nat. park Pol.
106 B3 Tatshenshini r. B.C. Can.
106 B3 Tatshenshini-Alsek Provincial Wilderness Park B.C. Can.
186 A2 Tatsinskiy Rus. Fed.
165 L12 Tatsuno Hyōgo Japan
166 E3 Tatsuno Nagano Japan
166 E3 Tatsunokuchi Japan
166 E1 Tatsuruhama Japan
167 G2 Tatsuyama Japan
185 L9 Tatta Pak.
29 Q7 Tattershall Lincolnshire, England U.K.
183 O6 Tatti Kazakh.
202 I5 Tatu well North I. N.Z.
142 D5 Tatuí Brazil
106 E4 Tatuk Mountain B.C. Can.
181 H5 Tatula r. Lith.
121 D9 Tatum NM U.S.A.
91 H4 Tatvan Turkey
189 K4 Tau i. American Samoa
138 A2 Tayabamba Peru
154 C5 Tayabas Bay Luzon Phil.
157 I4 Tayan Kalimantan Indon.
14 F1 Taybola Rus. Fed.
92 I3 Tayeeglow Somalia
79 N2 Tayfur Turkey
192 J4 Tayga Rus. Fed.
184 D4 Täygän Iran
168 E3 Taygan Mongolia
129 I7 Tayinloan Argyll and Bute, Scotland U.K.
125 D6 Tayirove Ukr.
162 I1 Taykanskiy Khrebet mts Rus. Fed.

Column 3

89 G2 Tchidoutene watercourse Niger
84 C5 Tchie well Chad
84 B4 Tchigaï, Plateau du Niger
91 B8 Tchihepepe Angola
91 C8 Tchikala-Tcholohanga Angola
90 C5 Tshikala Congo
91 B8 Tchindjenje Angola
73 Chin Garaguene well Niger
89 G3 Tchin-Tabaradene Niger
89 I4 Tchollire Cameroon
77 L4 Tchou-m-Adegdeg well Niger
23 O7 Tczew Pol.
159 H8 Te, Prêk r. Cambodia
136 E5 Tea r. Spain
62 D4 Tea r. Spain
128 B3 Teacapán Mex.
209 F8 Teague, Lake salt flat W.A. Austr.
201 □3a Teahupoo Tahiti Fr. Polynesia
203 □3 Te Aiti Point Rarotonga Cook Is
26 K9 Tealing Angus, Scotland U.K.
203 B12 Te Anau South I. N.Z.
203 B12 Te Anau, Lake South I. N.Z.
119 G3 Teaneck NJ U.S.A.
202 I5 Te Anga North I. N.Z.
73 M5 Teano Italy
209 D8 Teano Range mts W.A. Austr.
127 M9 Teapa Mex.
202 M4 Te Araroa North I. N.Z.
76 J8 Tearce Macedonia
202 J4 Te Aroha North I. N.Z.
202 J4 Te Aroha, Mount hill North I. N.Z.
201 □3a Teavaro Moorea Fr. Polynesia
202 J5 Te Awamutu North I. N.Z.
65 J7 Teba Spain
89 G3 Tebar Niger
89 G3 Tébarat Niger
157 H4 Tebas Kalimantan Indon.
29 L5 Tebay Cumbria, England U.K.
157 H4 Tebedu Sarawak Malaysia
191 C2 Teberda Rus. Fed.
191 C2 Teberda r. Rus. Fed.
191 C2 Teberdinskiy Zapovednik nature res. Rus. Fed.
107 L2 Tebesjuak Lake Nunavut Can.
87 H2 Tébessa Alg.
87 H2 Tébessa, Monts de mts Alg.
139 F6 Tebicuary r. Para.
139 F6 Tebicuary r. Para.
156 C3 Tebingtinggi Sumatera Indon.
156 E6 Tebingtinggi Sumatera Indon.
156 C5 Tebo r. Indon.
69 B7 Téboursouk Tunisia
87 H1 Téboursouk Tunisia

Column 4

164 □1 Teima Okinawa Japan
53 N6 Teisendorf Ger.
89 F2 Teïskot well Mali
53 O3 Teisnach Ger.
41 I7 Teissières-lès-Bouliès France
49 J8 Teistungen Ger.
129 K9 Teitipac Mex.
70 N6 Teiu Romania
77 L4 Teiuş Romania
143 F3 Teixeira Brazil
142 B5 Teixeira de Freitas Brazil
143 F4 Teixeiras Brazil
142 B6 Teixeira Soares Brazil
62 D2 Teixeiro Spain
62 F8 Teixoso Port.
62 F6 Teja r. Port.
62 D3 Teixido Spain
89 F5 Tejakula Bali Indon.
128 E4 Tejamen Mex.
129 K6 Tejas Mex.
98 □3a Tejeda Gran Canaria Canary Is
65 L7 Tejeda de Tiétar Spain
Tejeda y Almijara, Sierra de nature res. Spain
Tejen Turkm. see Tedzhen
179 M8 Tejgaon Bangl.
89 I3 Tejira well Niger
64 D1 Tejo r. Port.
alt. Tago (Spain), conv. Tagus
64 E1 Tejo Internacional, Parque Natural do nature res. Port.
128 D7 Tejupan, Punta pt Mex.
128 G7 Tejupilco Mex.
202 L4 Te Kaha North I. N.Z.
202 L4 Te Kaha Point North I. N.Z.
202 L4 Te Kao North I. N.Z.
203 E11 Tekapo r. South I. N.Z.
203 E10 Tekapo, Lake South I. N.Z.
167 J7 Tekari Bihar India
84 G2 Te Kauwhata North I. N.Z.
203 I8 Te Kuaha Point North I. N.Z.
202 J4 Te Kauwhata North I. N.Z.
127 O7 Tekax Mex.
77 O9 Teke r. Turkey
183 O1 Teke, Ozero salt l. Kazakh.
63 N9 Tekebaşı Turkey
91 C6 Tekeköy Turkey
79 K2 Tekeli Aktyubinskaya Oblast' Kazakh.
183 R7 Tekeli Almatinskaya Oblast' Kazakh.
172 E5 Tekes Xinjiang China
183 S6 Tekes Kazakh.
172 E5 Tekes He r. China
85 H6 Tekezê Wenz r. Eritrea/Eth.
173 E8 Tekiliktag mt. Xinjiang China
162 H4 Tekin Rus. Fed.
79 I2 Tekirdağ Turkey
79 I1 Tekirdağ prov. Turkey

Column 5

157 H5 Telukbajur Sumatera Indon. see Telukbayur
156 D5 Telukbatang Kalimantan Indon.
Telukbetung Indon. see Bandar Lampung
156 B4 Telukdalam Indon.
156 D2 Teluk Intan Malaysia
156 D5 Telukkuantan Sumatera Indon.
157 H5 Telukmelano Kalimantan Indon.
156 G8 Telukuga Jawa Indon.
157 H5 Telukpakedai Kalimantan Indon.
176 G9 Telulla Sri Lanka
19 U9 Telyazh'ye Rus. Fed.
89 F5 Tema Ghana
128 E4 Temacapulín Mex.
129 K6 Tema Mex.
111 O2 Temagami Ont. Can.
111 O2 Temagami, Lake Ont. Can.
157 H4 Temaju i. Indon.
203 □3 Te Manga hill Rarotonga Cook Is
202 I6 Temapache Mex.
64 E1 Te Mata hill North I. N.Z.
201 □3 Tematangi atoll Arch. des Tuamotu Fr. Polynesia
127 O7 Temax Mex.
97 M1 Temba S. Africa
153 I7 Tembagapura Papua Indon.
97 Q2 Tembe r. Moz.
157 L5 Tembe Elephant Park nature res. S. Africa
156 E5 Tembesi r. Indon.
156 C5 Tembilahan Sumatera Indon.
97 M2 Tembisa S. Africa
63 K9 Temblador Venezuela
91 C6 Temblor Range mts U.S.A.
91 C6 Tembo Aluma Angola
190 Tembo Falls Angola/Dem. Rep. Congo
97 M7 Tembuland reg. S. Africa
93 B7 Tembwe Zambia
30 H3 Teme r. England U.K.
124 D8 Temecula CA U.S.A.
188 F4 Temelli Turkey
168 E1 Temenchula, Gora mt. Rus. Fed.
156 D2 Temengor, Tasik resr Malaysia
76 H5 Temenica r. Slovenia
76 H5 Temerin Vojvodina, Srbija Serb. and Mont.
156 E3 Temerluh Malaysia
156 F3 Temiang, Bukit mt. Malaysia
97 M2 Temba S. Africa
189 M4 Temirtau Rus. Fed.
179 N9 Teknaf Bangl.
191 B5 Tekneciler Turkey
202 J5 Tekoa, Mount South I. N.Z.
156 □ Tekong Kechil, Pulau i. Sing.
110 J7 Tekonsha MI U.S.A.

Column 6

70 D7 Tende, Col de pass France/Italy
177 M8 Ten Degree Channel Andaman & Nicobar Is India
85 F6 Tendelti Sudan
88 B2 Te-n-Dghàmcha, Sebkhet salt marsh Maur.
63 O7 Tendilla Spain
164 R8 Tendō Japan
86 E2 Tendrara Morocco
70 A2 Tenero, Mont mt. Switz.
17 K7 Tendriv'ka Kosa, Ostriv i. Ukr.
17 K7 Tendriv'ka Zatoka b. Ukr.
39 O8 Tendu France
178 G8 Tendükheda Madh. Prad. India
191 E6 Tendürek Dağı mt. Turkey
88 D3 Tenekou Mali
18 E6 Tenenys r. Lith.
89 H1 Ténéré du Tafassâsset des. Niger
98 □3a Tenerife i. Canary Is
87 F1 Ténès Alg.
77 O8 Tenevo Bulg.
158 C5 Teng, Nam r. Myanmar
157 L8 Tengah, Kepulauan is Indon.
156 □ Tengah, Sungai r. Sing.
155 C8 Tengchong Yunnan China
Tengchow Guangxi China see Tengxian
170 B6 Tengchong Yunnan China
182 E6 Tenge Kazakh.
156 □ Tengeh Reservoir Sing.
157 I5 Tengelic Hungary
52 F6 Tenggara Indon.
200 □6 Te Nggano lag. Rennell Solomon Is
157 L5 Tenggarong Kalimantan Indon.
168 I8 Tengger Els Nei Mongol China
168 I7 Tengger Shamo des. Nei Mongol China
156 E2 Tenggul i. Malaysia
183 M2 Tengiz, Ozero salt l. Kazakh.
170 G9 Tengqiao Hainan China
88 D4 Tengréla Côte d'Ivoire
15 H5 Tengushevo Rus. Fed.
170 F2 Tengxian Guangxi China
Tengxian Shandong China see Tengzhou
169 O9 Tengzhou Shandong China
41 J8 Ténibre, Mont mt. France/Italy
139 E5 Teniente Enciso, Parque Nacional nat. park Para.
147 F6 Tenille FL U.S.A.
115 F11 Tenille GA U.S.A.
52 D5 Teningen Ger.
88 A2 Te-n-Isoubrar, Sebkhet salt marsh Maur.
129 J5 Tenixtepec Mex.
182 K1 Teniz, Ozero l. Kazakh.
57 J4 Tenk Hungary
177 J4 Tenkasi Tamil Nadu India
90 C4 Tenke Dem. Rep. Congo
193 P2 Tenkeli Rus. Fed.
14 J5 Ten'ki Rus. Fed.
88 E4 Tenkodogo Burkina
109 J3 Ten Mile Lake Nfld and Lab. Can.
71 P9 Tenna r. Italy
206 E5 Tennant Creek N.T. Austr.
52 E5 Tennenbronn Ger.
58 I5 Tennengau val. Austria
58 H5 Tennengebirge mts Austria
119 G4 Tennent NJ U.S.A.
121 K7 Tennessee r. U.S.A.
116 B12 Tennessee state U.S.A.
123 K7 Tennessee Pass CO U.S.A.
119 K6 Tennille Belgium
20 N2 Tennevoll Norway
20 L3 Tennholmfjorden sea chan. Norway
19 I5 Tenniöjoki r. Fin./Rus. Fed.
63 O7 Tennsift r. Morocco
146 B4 Teno r. Chile
98 □3a Teno, Punta de pt Tenerife Canary Is
129 K6 Tenochtitlán Mex.
71 I8 Tenojoki r. Fin./Norway
157 K2 Tenom Sabah Malaysia
127 N9 Tenosique Mex.
166 E5 Tenpaku Japan
166 C6 Tenri Japan
167 G3 Tenryū Nagano Japan
167 G4 Tenryū-Shizuoka Japan
167 G3 Tenryū-gawa r. Japan
167 G5 Tenryū-Ōkumikawa Quasi National Park Japan
122 G6 Ten Sleep WY U.S.A.
111 O3 Tennoz Sulawesi Indon.
88 E4 Tenterden Kent, England U.K.
205 N2 Tenterfield N.S.W. Austr.
115 G13 Ten Thousand Islands FL U.S.A.
107 L4 Tent Lake N.W.T. Can.
155 B2 Tentolomatinan, Gunung mt. Indon.
64 G4 Tentudia mt. Spain
57 I3 Tentügai Port.
38 H7 Tenu r. France
71 C8 Ténya Hungary
128 C5 Teocaltiche Mex.
130 C6 Teocelo Mex.
128 G7 Teococuilco de Corona Mex.
127 G4 Teodelina Arg.
72 D6 Teodoro, Stagno di l. Sardegna Italy
141 B7 Teodoro Beltrán Mex.
142 A5 Teodoro Sampaio Brazil
146 A6 Teodoro Schmidt Chile
143 G2 Teófilo Otôni Brazil
154 C8 Teófilo' Ukr.
172 B7 Teomabal i. Phil.
128 D7 Teonthar Madh. Prad. India
73 O6 Teora Italy
66 E3 Teotihuacán tourist site Mex.
127 H5 Teotitlán del Valle Mex.
129 K8 Teotitlán Mex.
128 G7 Tepa Ghana
155 F4 Tepa Maluku Indon.
88 C3 Te Paki North I. N.Z.
56 C1 Tepalcatepec Mex.
128 C7 Tepalcatepec r. Mex.
129 I7 Tepalcingo Mex.
200 □6a Tepa Point Niue
20 R3 Tepasto Fin.
73 O6 Tepatitlán Mex.
88 C7 Tepatitlán Mex.
157 L4 Tepianlangsat Kalimantan Indon.
128 B5 Tepic Mex.
56 C1 Teplá Czech Rep.
56 B1 Teplá r. Czech Rep.
56 B1 Teplá Vltava r. Czech Rep.
23 P7 Teplice Pol.
15 G5 Teplaya Gora Rus. Fed.
17 S5 Teplice Ukr.
54 C1 Teplice Czech Rep.
191 E3 Tepli, Gora mt. Rus. Fed.
56 C1 Teplice Czech Rep.

Column 1

26 I6 Trantlemore Highland, Scotland U.K.
159 G10 Tra Ôn Vietnam
74 D7 Trapani Sicilia Italy
74 D8 Trapani prov. Sicilia Italy
Trapezus Turkey see Trabzon
146 D3 Trapiche Arg.
118 E4 Trappe PA U.S.A.
48 J2 Trappenkamp Ger.
122 G4 Trapper Peak MT U.S.A.
36 D6 Trappes France
1 B9 Trapiá r. Brazil
205 K8 Traralgon Vic. Austr.
52 C2 Trarbach Ger.
23 J5 Traryd Sweden
88 B2 Trarza admin. reg. Maur.
73 L4 Trasacco Italy
88 B2 Trascău, Munții mts Romania
Trashigang Bhutan see Tashigang
72 I1 Trasimeno, Lago l. Italy
62 E4 Trasmiras Spain
62 F5 Tras-os-Montes reg. Port.
72 G2 Trasubbie r. Italy
63 P9 Trasvase, Canal de Spain
65 O2 Trasvase Tajo-Segura, Canal de Spain
159 F8 Trat Thai.
72 B9 Tratalias Sardegna Italy
59 M3 Trate Slovenia
59 J6 Traun Austria
53 N5 Traun r. Ger.
53 N5 Traun r. Austria
59 N6 Traunreut Ger.
59 I4 Traunsee l. Austria
59 L3 Traunstein Austria
59 N6 Traunstein Ger.
18 H6 Traupis Lith.
59 O3 Trautmannsdorf an der Leitha Austria
71 R4 Trava Slovenia
71 O4 Travagliato Italy
62 D8 Travanca do Mondego Port.
62 E7 Travancas Port.
62 E7 Travassós de Cima Port.
48 K3 Traver r. Ger.
205 I5 Travellers Lake imp. l. N.S.W. Austr.
48 K3 Travemünde Ger.
48 J3 Travenbrück Ger.
70 B2 Travers Switz.
203 G9 Travers, Mount South I. N.Z.
71 L3 Travignolo r. Italy
159 H10 Tra Vinh Vietnam
121 F10 Travis, Lake TX U.S.A.
53 F13 Travnik Bos.-Herz.
72 C4 Travo r. Corse France
72 H6 Travo r. Italy
68 E4 Trawmore Bay Rep. of Ireland
30 E2 Trawsfynydd Gwynedd, Wales U.K.
30 E2 Trawsfynydd, Llyn resr Wales U.K.
209 D11 Trayning W.A. Austr.
68 E2 Trbovlje Slovenia
27 D5 Trean Rep. of Ireland
30 □ Treasure Beach Jamaica
57 G3 Treasury Islands Solomon Is
200 □6 Trebatice Slovakia
57 G3 Trebatsch Ger.
70 H5 Trebbia r. Italy
51 H6 Trebbin Ger.
53 F13 Trebević nat. park Bos.-Herz.
48 D5 Trebel Ger.
50 D5 Trebel r. Ger.
50 H1 Trebenow Ger.
56 C11 Trebenice Czech Rep.
43 I9 Trèbes France
59 I6 Trebesing Austria
41 B8 Trébeurden France
56 E2 Trebíč Czech Rep.
68 H3 Trebinje Bos.-Herz.
75 L4 Trebisacce Italy
57 K3 Trebišnjica r. Bos.-Herz.
57 K3 Trebišov Slovakia
68 F7 Trebizat r. Bos.-Herz.
Trebizond Turkey see Trabzon
68 E3 Trebnje Slovenia
147 F6 Treboiares Arg.
62 E3 Treboille Spain
56 D2 Treboň Czech Rep.
57 K5 Trebonne Qld Austr.
38 C5 Tréboul France
51 G8 Trebsen Ger.
64 G7 Trebujena Spain
52 F5 Trebur Ger.
30 F4 Trecastle Powys, Wales U.K.
70 F5 Trecate Italy
77 T7 Trecchina Italy
71 K5 Trecenta Italy
30 F4 Tredegar Blaenau Gwent, Wales U.K.
31 I3 Tredington Warwickshire, England U.K.
71 L7 Tredozio Italy
28 C5 Treehoo Rep. of Ireland
116 □ Tree Island India
48 H2 Treene r. Ger.
19 P4 Trefeglwys Powys, Wales U.K.
59 I6 Treffen Austria
36 D8 Treffiagat France
40 G4 Treffort-Cuisiat France
49 J8 Treffurt Ger.
30 E1 Trefriw Conwy, Wales U.K.
30 E3 Tregaron Ceredigion, Wales U.K.
38 C5 Trégastel France
71 K4 Tregnago Italy
10 C4 Tregony Cornwall, England U.K.
38 C4 Trégorrois reg. France
207 M4 Tregrosse Islets and Reefs Coral Sea Is Terr. Austr.
146 A5 Treguaco Chile
38 E5 Trégueux France
38 C5 Tréguier France
38 C5 Trégunc France
30 F2 Tregynon Powys, Wales U.K.
22 F5 Trehörningsjö Sweden
20 O5 Treia Ger.
72 G6 Treia Italy
69 I4 Treig, Loch l. Scotland U.K.
42 H4 Treignac France
41 O7 Treigny France
144 G4 Treinta y Tres Uru.
38 E3 Trélazé France
30 D7 Trelech Carmarthenshire, Wales U.K.
38 C4 Trélévern France
42 F5 Trélissac France
38 G5 Trélivan France
22 J6 Trelleborg Sweden
38 E3 Trélon France
67 K7 Trem mt. Serb. and Mont.
30 D2 Tremadog Bay Wales U.K.
30 D2 Tremblant, Mont hill Que. Can.
99 □1b Tremblay Réunion
36 B6 Tremblay-les-Villages France
38 E3 Trembleur, Lake B.C. Can.
63 Q7 Tremedal, Sierra del mts Spain
62 H6 Tremedal de Tormes Spain
45 □ Tremelo Belgium
39 J7 Tréméntines France
38 B2 Tréméoc France
38 D6 Tréméven France
70 □ Tremezzo Italy
48 M9 Treml, Isole i. Italy
71 R9 Tremonte r. Italy
17 T7 Tremonton UT U.S.A.

Column 2

56 C2 Třemošná Czech Rep.
56 E2 Třemošnice Czech Rep.
41 B8 Trémouilles France
66 G3 Tremp Spain
110 C5 Trempealeau r. WI U.S.A.
48 J3 Tremsbüttel Ger.
30 B7 Trenance Cornwall, England U.K.
110 H3 Trenary MI U.S.A.
109 F4 Trenche r. Que. Can.
57 H3 Trenčianska Turná Slovakia
57 G3 Trenčianske Stankovce Slovakia
57 H3 Trenčianske Teplice Slovakia
57 H3 Trenčiansky Kraj admin. reg. Slovakia
57 H3 Trenčín Slovakia
49 H7 Trendelburg Ger.
147 E4 Trenel Arg.
159 F8 Trêng Cambodia
157 I9 Trengganu state Malaysia see Terengganu
147 F4 Trenque Lauquén Arg.
43 C7 Trensacq France
50 H1 Trent Ger.
29 F6 Trent r. Dorset, England U.K.
30 H6 Trent r. England U.K.
Trent Italy see Trento
71 K3 Trentino - Alto Adige admin. reg. Italy
71 K3 Trento Italy
71 K3 Trento prov. Italy
110 C1 Trenton Ont. Can.
115 F11 Trenton FL U.S.A.
115 E8 Trenton GA U.S.A.
120 I5 Trenton MO U.S.A.
115 I8 Trenton NC U.S.A.
120 E5 Trenton NE U.S.A.
118 F4 Trenton NJ U.S.A.
121 K8 Trenton TN U.S.A.
36 B6 Tréon France
30 E4 Treorchy Rhondda Cynon Taff, Wales U.K.
206 C1 Trepassey Nfld and Lab. Can.
109 K4 Trepassey Bay N.T. Austr.
17 L5 Treppeln Ger.
51 K6 Treppeln Ger.
40 G5 Trept France
72 O11 Trepuzzi Italy
70 F3 Tresa r. Italy
147 F4 Tres Algarrobas Arg.
70 H7 Tresana Italy
147 I3 Tres Arboles Uru.
147 G3 Tres Arroyos Arg.
142 B6 Três Bicos Brazil
147 H3 Tres Bocas Arg.
147 H3 Tres Bocas Uru.
137 F6 Três Casas Brazil
145 D8 Tres Cerros Arg.
118 D3 Tresco PA U.S.A.
41 H8 Tresco i. France
30 □ Tresco i. England U.K.
143 E4 Três Corações Brazil
70 H4 Trescore Balneario Italy
144 D1 Tres Cruces Arg.
144 C3 Tres Cruces Chile
70 I3 Tresenda Italy
136 C4 Tres Esquinas Col.
147 I4 Tres Esquinas Uru.
31 O4 Tres Forcas, Cabo c. Morocco
29 O4 Tres Picachos, Sierra mts Mex.
72 B6 Trinità d'Agultu Sardegna Italy
70 H2 Tresnuraghes Sardegna Italy
63 N3 Trespaderne Spain
129 H9 Tres Palos Guerrero Mex.
129 H5 Tres Palos Tamaulipas Mex.
129 H9 Tres Palos, Laguna lag. Mex.
123 K12 Tres Picachos, Sierra mts Mex.
147 F6 Tres Picos Arg.
145 C6 Tres Picos Arg.
127 M10 Tres Picos mt. Arg.
147 G6 Tres Picos, Cerro mt. Arg.
129 N9 Tres Picos, Cerro mt. Mex.
123 L8 Tres Piedras NM U.S.A.
124 K5 Tres Pinos CA U.S.A.
143 E4 Tres Pontas Brazil
142 C6 Tres Pontões, Pico mt. Brazil
146 C3 Tres Porteñas Arg.
144 C2 Tres Puentes Chile
145 D7 Tres Puntas, Cabo c. Arg.
142 D3 Três Ranchos Brazil
143 F5 Três Rios Brazil
26 I9 Tressait Perth and Kinross, Scotland U.K.
147 H4 Tres Sargentos Arg.
40 H5 Tresserve France
56 E2 Třešť Czech Rep.
73 N4 Treste r. Italy
19 Q4 Trestna Rus. Fed.
19 S4 Trestna Rus. Fed.
136 D6 Três Unidos Brazil
129 K7 Tres Valles Mex.
30 F4 Treswell Notts, England U.K.
41 H10 Trets France
21 K6 Tretten Norway
53 J4 Treuchtlingen Ger.
51 F9 Treuen Ger.
51 G6 Treuenbrietzen Ger.
21 I6 Treungen Norway
38 F5 Trévé France
65 M7 Trevélez Spain
65 M7 Trevélez r. Spain
145 C6 Trevelin Arg.
42 J6 Tréveray France
41 C8 Trèves France
Trèves Ger. see Trier
72 I5 Treviglio Italy
143 D3 Trevignano Romano Italy
63 □ Treviño Spain
71 M4 Treviso Italy
71 M4 Treviso prov. Italy
71 M4 Treviso airport Italy
178 G4 Trevor i. Uttaranchal India
78 D5 Trévoux France
30 B6 Trewose Head England U.K.
40 F5 Trévoux France

Column 3

185 N5 Tribal Areas admin. div. Pak.
71 K3 Tribalj Croatia
57 H3 Tribeč mts Slovakia
38 I3 Tribehou France
52 I5 Triberg im Schwarzwald Ger.
162 M1 Tri Brata, Gora hill Sakhalin Rus. Fed.
50 G2 Tribsees Ger.
207 J4 Tribulation, Cape Qld Austr.
120 E6 Tribune KS U.S.A.
73 Q6 Tricarico Italy
75 O4 Tricase Italy
71 O3 Triceesimo Italy
71 M3 Trichiana Italy
Trichinopoly Tamil Nadu India see Tiruchchirappalli
78 C4 Trichonida, Limni l. Greece
176 C4 Trichur Kerala India
36 E4 Tricot France
205 J5 Trida N.S.W. Austr.
Tridentum Italy see Trento
51 F10 Triebel Ger.
59 J4 Trieben Austria
51 F9 Triebes Ger.
36 C5 Trie-Château France
72 D7 Triei Sardegna Italy
52 E7 Triengen Switz.
52 B2 Trier Ger.
49 C10 Trier admin. reg. Ger.
52 B7 Trierweiler Ger.
71 P4 Trieste Italy
71 P4 Trieste prov. Italy
71 P4 Trieste, Golfo di g. Europe see Trieste, Gulf of
68 D3 Trieste, Gulf of Europe
71 O4 Trieste - Ronchi dei Legionari airport Italy
43 E9 Trie-sur-Baïse France
37 K5 Trieux France
38 E4 Trieux r. France
53 O5 Triftern Ger.
64 D4 Trigaches Port.
41 I9 Trigance France
75 L1 Triggiano Italy
59 I7 Triglav mt. Slovenia
68 D2 Triglavski Narodni Park nat. park Slovenia
50 F4 Triglitz Ger.
38 G7 Trignac France
73 N3 Trigno r. Italy
98 □1c Trigo, Monte hill São Jorge Azores
36 E8 Triguères France
64 F6 Trigueros Spain
63 K5 Trigueros del Valle Spain
78 C3 Trikala Greece
78 D3 Trikeri, Diavlos sea chan. Greece
Trikkala Greece see Trikala
Trikomo Cyprus see Trikomon
190 B3 Trikomon Cyprus
153 I7 Trikora, Puncak mt. Papua Indon.
78 D4 Triklino mt. Greece
68 F4 Trilj Croatia
147 F4 Trill Arg.
27 H4 Trillick Northern Ireland U.K.
63 O7 Trillo Spain
78 D5 Trilofo Greece
178 F3 Triloknath Hima. Prad. India
36 E6 Trilport France
27 I5 Trim Rep. of Ireland
29 O4 Trimdon Durham, England U.K.
31 O4 Trimley St Mary Suffolk, England U.K.
70 H2 Trimmis Switz.
208 C6 Trimouille Island W.A. Austr.
30 D4 Trimsaran Carmarthenshire, Wales U.K.
126 D2 Trincheras Mex.
176 G2 Trincomalee Sri Lanka
64 D5 Trindade Beja Port.
62 F6 Trindade Bragança Port.
214 H7 Trindade, Ilha da i. S. Atlantic Ocean
57 H2 Třinec Czech Rep.
31 K4 Tring Hertfordshire, England U.K.
78 C3 Tringia mt. Greece
138 D3 Trinidad Bol.
130 D3 Trinidad Cuba
129 L8 Trinidad i. Mex.
131 □7 Trinidad i. Trin. and Tob.
147 I3 Trinidad Uru.
123 L8 Trinidad CO U.S.A.
145 B8 Trinidad, Golfo b. Chile
147 G6 Trinidad, Isla i. Arg.
131 M8 Trinidad and Tobago country West Indies
74 D8 Trinità, Lago della l. Sicilia Italy
72 B6 Trinità d'Agultu Sardegna Italy
73 G5 Trinitápoli Italy
121 H10 Trinity TX U.S.A.
122 C6 Trinity r. CA U.S.A.
121 H11 Trinity r. TX U.S.A.
121 G9 Trinity, West Fork r. OK U.S.A.
207 J4 Trinity Bay Qld Austr.
109 K4 Trinity Bay Nfld and Lab. Can.
131 □7 Trinity Hills Trin. and Tob.
104 C4 Trinity Islands AK U.S.A.
124 M1 Trinity Range mts NV U.S.A.
177 M8 Trinkat Island Andaman & Nicobar Is India
186 C6 Trinkitat Sudan
70 E5 Trino Italy
58 B5 Trins Austria
73 O7 Trinta Port.
116 C8 Trinwillershagen Ger.
99 □1b Triolet Mauritius
63 K3 Triollo Spain
59 N7 Triolo r. Italy
73 L1 Trionto, Capo c. Italy
75 L4 Triora Italy
156 B3 Tripa r. Indon.
50 D4 Tripkau Ger.
78 D5 Tripi Sicilia Italy
79 P9 Tripoli Greece
Tripoli Lebanon see Trâblous
Tripoli Libya see Ṭarābulus
78 D5 Tripolis Greece see Tripoli
Tripolis Lebanon see Trâblous
84 B2 Tripolitania reg. Libya
205 J9 Tripotama Greece
39 P9 Trippstadt Ger.
176 F2 Triprayar Kerala India
179 M8 Tripura state India
48 G2 Trischen i. Ger.
58 G6 Trisanna r. Austria
98 □2c Tristan da Cunha i. S. Atlantic Ocean
88 B4 Tristão, Îles is Guinea
64 □ Tristão, Ponta do pt Madeira
58 H6 Tristenspitze mt. Austria
178 C4 Trisul mt. Uttaranchal India
50 D4 Trittau Ger.
78 D5 Trittenheim Ger.
140 D3 Triunfo Pernambuco Brazil
139 D2 Triunfo Rondônia Brazil
126 □P1 Triunfo Mex.
176 F2 Trivandrum Kerala India
70 H6 Trivento Italy
73 N3 Trivero Italy
75 H3 Trizac France
19 J6 Trizina Greece

Column 4

62 C6 Trofa Port.
59 L5 Trofaiach Austria
20 L4 Trofors Norway
71 K3 Trogir Croatia
58 H6 Trogkofel mt. Austria/Italy
68 F4 Troglav mt. Croatia
73 O5 Tregstad Norway
64 B4 Tróia Port.
74 H8 Troina Sicilia Italy
74 H8 Troina r. Sicilia Italy
49 D9 Troisdorf Ger.
37 N6 Troisfontaines France see Yusta
86 E2 Trois Fourches, Cap des c. Morocco
109 G3 Trois-Pistoles Que. Can.
45 I8 Trois-Ponts Belgium
109 F4 Trois-Rivières Que. Can.
131 □2 Trois-Rivières Guadeloupe
43 G10 Trois Seigneurs, Pic des mt. France
36 D5 Troissereux France
40 C3 Trois-Vèvres France
45 J8 Troisvierges Lux.
192 H3 Troitsa Khanty-Mansiyskiy Avtonomnyy Okrug Rus. Fed.
19 X7 Troitsa Ryazanskaya Oblast' Rus. Fed.
182 I1 Troitsk Chelyabinskaya Oblast' Rus. Fed.
19 U6 Troitsk Moskovskaya Oblast' Rus. Fed.
17 Q2 Troitskiy Belgorodskaya Oblast' Rus. Fed.
Troitskiy Moskovskaya Oblast' Rus. Fed. see Troitsk
14 L3 Troitsko-Pechorsk Rus. Fed.
183 U1 Troitskoye Altayskiy Kray Rus. Fed.
162 J4 Troitskoye Khabarovskiy Kray Rus. Fed.
182 E1 Troitskoye Orenburgskaya Oblast' Rus. Fed.
182 G1 Troitskoye Respublika Bashkortostan Rus. Fed.
15 I7 Troitskoye Respublika Kalmykiya-Khalm'g-Tangch Rus. Fed.
130 □ Troja Jamaica
54 G5 Troja r. Pol.
59 K7 Trojane Slovenia
23 O7 Trójmiejski Park Krajobrazowy Pol.
84 B6 Trolla well Chad
22 I3 Trollhättan Sweden
20 J5 Trollheimen park Norway
137 G5 Trombetas r. Brazil
99 □1 Tromelin, Île i. Indian Ocean
145 B5 Tromen, Volcán vol. Arg.
26 H8 Tromie r. Scotland U.K.
50 H1 Tromper Wiek b. Ger.
97 J6 Trompsburg S. Africa
20 O2 Troms county Norway
124 O6 Troms CA U.S.A.
145 C6 Tronador, Monte mt. Arg.
40 B3 Tronçais, Forêt de for. France
55 K5 Trončica Pol.
128 E3 Troncoso Mex.
20 K5 Trondheim Norway
20 J5 Trondheimsfjorden sea chan. Norway
20 J5 Trondheimsleia sea chan. Norway
Trongsa Bhutan see Tongsa
73 L2 Trons Chhu r. Bhutan
37 J6 Tronto r. Italy
70 E5 Tronville-en-Barrois France
70 E5 Tronville Vercellese Italy
39 M6 Troo France
80 C5 Troödos Cyprus
190 A4 Troödos, Mount Cyprus
190 A4 Troödos Mountains Cyprus
26 G11 Troon South Ayrshire, Scotland U.K.
78 C5 Tropaia Greece
19 S6 Troparevo Rus. Fed.
137 G6 Tropas r. Brazil
75 J6 Tropea Italy
140 D5 Tropeiros, Serra dos hills Brazil
125 T4 Tropic UT U.S.A.
27 G4 Tropi Northern Ireland U.K.
14 K2 Trosh Rus. Fed.
19 S9 Trosna Rus. Fed.
51 G7 Trossin Ger.
19 P9 Trostan r. Ukr.
27 J2 Trostan hill Northern Ireland U.K.
53 N5 Trostberg Ger.
17 N3 Trostyanets' Sums'ka Oblast' Ukr.
16 I5 Trostyanets' Vinnyts'ka Oblast' Ukr.
16 E3 Trostyanets' Volyns'ka Oblast' Ukr.
26 D7 Trotternish hills Scotland U.K.
77 O4 Trotuș r. Romania
43 E10 Trounoue, Cirque de corrie France/Spain
26 E7 Troup Head Scotland U.K.
117 □S1 Trousers Lake N.B. Can.
106 E3 Trout r. B.C. Can.
107 H1 Trout r. N.W.T. Can.
29 L5 Trout Cumbria, England U.K.
111 A4 Trout Creek Ont. Can.
110 E3 Trout Creek MI U.S.A.
116 D12 Trout Dale VA U.S.A.
106 H3 Trout Lake Alta Can.
106 C2 Trout Lake N.W.T. Can.
107 M5 Trout Lake N.W.T. Can.
110 I3 Trout Lake MI U.S.A.
110 E3 Trout Lake l. Ont. Can.
109 J3 Trout River Nfld and Lab. Can.
111 Q8 Trout Run PA U.S.A.
116 F11 Troutville VA U.S.A.
39 I3 Trouville-sur-Mer France
77 P7 Troviscal Port.
62 D9 Troviscal Port.
30 H5 Trowbridge Wiltshire, England U.K.
205 J9 Trowutta Tas. Austr.
130 □ Troy tourist site Turkey see Truva
115 E10 Troy AL U.S.A.
120 H6 Troy KS U.S.A.
111 K7 Troy KY U.S.A.
120 J6 Troy MO U.S.A.
122 G2 Troy MT U.S.A.
115 I8 Troy NC U.S.A.
117 M6 Troy NH U.S.A.
117 L6 Troy NY U.S.A.
116 D9 Troy OH U.S.A.
116 F8 Troy PA U.S.A.
77 M8 Troyan Bulg.
16 J5 Troyanivka Ukr.
16 J5 Troyanka Ukr.
19 W8 Troyekurovo Lipetskaya Oblast' Rus. Fed.
J4 Troyekurovo Tul'skaya Oblast' Rus. Fed.
36 H7 Troyes France
17 R4 Troyits'ke Luhans'ka Oblast' Ukr.
16 J6 Troyits'ke Odes'ka Oblast' Ukr.
17 R4 Troyits'ko-Safonovo Ukr.

Column 5

62 I2 Trubia r. Spain
17 K3 Trubizh r. Ukr.
41 C7 Truc de la Garde mt. France
62 H4 Truchas Spain
37 O6 Truchtersheim France
Trucial Coast country Asia see United Arab Emirates
Trucial States country Asia see United Arab Emirates
124 L2 Truckee CA U.S.A.
19 Q4 Trud Rus. Fed.
182 B5 Trudfront Rus. Fed.
162 H7 Trudovoye Rus. Fed.
19 U9 Trudovoye Rus. Fed.
206 C7 Truer Range hills N.T. Austr.
14 I2 Trufanovo Rus. Fed.
64 G3 Trujillo Spain
126 □Q10 Trujillo Hond.
138 A2 Trujillo Peru
64 H2 Trujillo Spain
136 D2 Trujillo Venez.
131 □1 Trujillo Alto Puerto Rico
136 D2 Trujillo state Venez.
30 F6 Trull Somerset, England U.K.
121 J8 Trumann AR U.S.A.
119 I2 Trumansburg NY U.S.A.
119 I2 Trumbull CT U.S.A.
125 T7 Trumbull, Mount AZ U.S.A.
156 B3 Trumon Sumatera Indon.
31 M3 Trumpington Cambridgeshire, England U.K.
77 K8 Trün Bulg.
59 L4 Trun France
70 F2 Trun Switz.
77 L8 Trüna mt. Bulg.
205 K5 Trundle N.S.W. Austr.
158 H3 Trung Khanh Vietnam
Truong Sa is S. China Sea see Spratly Islands
56 I1 Trutnov Czech Rep.
79 H3 Truro N.S. Can.
33 B10 Truro Cornwall, England U.K.
48 K7 Truro Cornwall, England U.K.
77 P3 Trușești Romania
49 J9 Trusetal Ger.
76 H9 Trush Albania
19 S3 Truskavets' Ukr.
16 C4 Truskavets' Ukr.
27 F4 Truskmore hill Rep. of Ireland
157 L2 Trus Madi, Gunung mt. Malaysia
56 E1 Trutnov Czech Rep.
79 H3 Truva tourist site Turkey
55 J3 Trzciana Mazowieckie Pol.
54 E2 Trzcianka Wielkopolskie Pol.
54 C4 Trzcianne Pol.
54 F1 Trzcielino Pol.
54 D4 Trzcinica Pol.
55 K5 Trzciniec Pol.
54 E4 Trzebiatów Pol.
55 I4 Trzebiechów Pol.
55 H5 Trzebiel Pol.
55 I4 Trzebielino Pol.
54 C2 Trzebież Pol.
55 H5 Trzebnica Pol.
54 E4 Trzebownisko Pol.
55 L5 Trzemeszno Pol.
55 L5 Trzemeszno Lubuskie Pol.
55 L3 Trześcianka Pol.
55 L5 Trzeszczany Pierwsze Pol.
68 E3 Tržič Slovenia
59 K7 Tržin Slovenia
19 P9 Trzcińsko-Zdrój Pol.
168 A2 Trzydnik Duży Pol.
169 P3 Tsagaannuur Bayan-Ölgiy Mongolia
169 J3 Tsagaannuur Dornod Mongolia
168 D3 Tsagaan Nuur salt l. Mongolia
168 I3 Tsagaan-Olom Mongolia
169 M2 Tsagaan-Ovoo Mongolia
168 I3 Tsagaan-Ovoo Mongolia see Sharga
26 D7 Tsagaan-Uul Mongolia
182 B3 Tsagan Aman Rus. Fed.
15 I7 Tsagan-Nur Rus. Fed.
191 B3 Ts'ageri Georgia
Tsaidam Basin China see Qaidam Pendi
191 A4 Tsakhur Rus. Fed.
94 D3 Tsamkong Guangdong China see Zhanjiang
95 □K2 Tsaratanana Madag.
95 □K2 Tsaratanana, Massif du mts Madag.
77 P8 Tsarevo Bulg.
19 R6 Tsarevo-Zaymishche Rus. Fed.
77 M8 Tsarimir Bulg.
17 O5 Tsaritsyn Rus. Fed. see Volgograd
17 O5 Tsarychanka Ukr.
15 I6 Tsatsane S. Africa
97 M6 Tsatsu Botswana
165 G12 Tsashima s. Japan
165 I11 Tsashima Japan
77 L9 Tsvetkove Bulg.
17 L5 Tsvitne Ukr.

Column 6

91 B6 Tshela Dem. Rep. Congo
91 C6 Tshene Dem. Rep. Congo
95 E4 Tsheseebe Botswana
91 D6 Tshibala Dem. Rep. Congo
91 D6 Tshibuka Dem. Rep. Congo
96 I1 Tshidilamolomo Botswana
91 D6 Tshikapa Dem. Rep. Congo
91 D6 Tshikapa r. Dem. Rep. Congo
91 D6 Tshilenge Dem. Rep. Congo
91 D6 Tshimbo Dem. Rep. Congo
91 D6 Tshimbulu Dem. Rep. Congo
95 F2 Tshipise S. Africa
91 D7 Tshintanzu Dem. Rep. Congo
91 D6 Tshitupa Dem. Rep. Congo
91 D6 Tshiumbe r. Angola/Dem. Rep. Congo
91 E6 Tshofa Dem. Rep. Congo
64 H2 Tshopo r. Dem. Rep. Congo
95 E3 Tsholotsho Zimbabwe
91 D6 Tshongwe Dem. Rep. Congo
94 D4 Tshootsha Botswana
91 C6 Tshuapa r. Dem. Rep. Congo
90 C5 Tshumbiri Dem. Rep. Congo
94 D3 Tshwane Botswana
Tshwane S. Africa see Pretoria
95 □J3 Tsiazonano mt. Madag.
77 L7 Tsibritsa r. Bulg.
104 E3 Tsiigehtchic N.W.T. Can.
18 J8 Tsimkavichy Belarus
15 H7 Tsimlyansk Rus. Fed.
15 H7 Tsimlyanskoye Vodokhranilishche resr Rus. Fed.
162 K3 Tsimmermanovka Rus. Fed.
96 H3 Tsineng S. Africa
Tsinan Shandong China see Jinan
Tsinghai prov. China see Qinghai
171 □I7 Tsing Shan hill H.K. China
171 □I7 Tsing Shan Wan b. H.K. China
171 □J7 Tsing Shui Wan b. H.K. China
Tsingtao Shandong China see Qingdao
95 □J3 Tsingy de Bemaraha, Réserve nature res. Madag.
99 □3a Tsingy Y. i. H.K. China
99 □3a Tsininouapanga Njazidja Comoros
95 □J3 Tsinjomay mt. Madag.
94 C3 Tsintsabis Namibia
95 □J5 Tsiombe Madag.
95 □J3 Tsiroanomandidy Madag.
191 C4 Tsiskara Nakrdzali nature res. Georgia
95 □J3 Tsitondroina Madag.
Tsitsihar Heilong. China see Qiqihar
96 H10 Tsitsikamma Forest and Coastal National Park S. Africa
106 E4 Tsitsutl Peak B.C. Can.
191 C3 Ts'iv'i Georgia
191 G4 Ts'nori Georgia
120 E5 Tryon NE U.S.A.
202 J3 Tryphena Harbour North I. N.Z.
Tsitsikamma Georgia see Senaki
Tskhakaia Georgia see Senaki
Tskhaltubo Georgia see Sqaltubo
191 E3 Ts'khinvali Georgia
191 F4 Ts'khneti Georgia
18 K9 Tsna r. Belarus
19 R4 Tsna r. Rus. Fed.
191 F4 Tsodilo Hills Botswana
178 B3 Tsokar Chumo l. Jammu and Kashmir
97 M7 Tsolo S. Africa
97 L8 Tsomo S. Africa
97 L8 Tsomo r. S. Africa
78 C2 Tsotili Greece
191 D3 Tsovinar Armenia
191 C3 Tsqaltubo Georgia
166 E6 Tsu Japan
165 P9 Tsubame Japan
164 V3 Tsubetsu Japan
167 H3 Tsuchiura Japan
167 I3 Tsuchiyama Japan
165 J13 Tsudakhar Rus. Fed.
171 □J7 Tsuen Wan H.K. China
167 I3 Tsugaru-kaikyō str. Japan
164 R5 Tsugaru Strait Japan
166 C6 Tsuge Japan
166 C5 Tsukechi Japan
164 □1 Tsuken-jima i. Okinawa Japan
167 I3 Tsukigase Japan
167 I2 Tsukigata Japan
167 I2 Tsukiyono Japan
167 H2 Tsukuba Japan
165 J14 Tsukude Japan
166 S5 Tsukumi Japan
168 I13 Tsul-Ulaan Mongolia
165 D13 Tsumagoi Japan
16 E3 Tsuman' Ukr.
94 B3 Tsumeb Namibia
94 C5 Tsumkwe Namibia
167 H1 Tsuna Japan
166 A7 Tsuna Japan
166 C6 Tsuno Japan
166 H12 Tsunega-misaki pt Japan
167 I4 Tsuno Japan
166 C6 Tsuruga Japan
166 D5 Tsuruga-wan b. Japan
167 I4 Tsurugi-dake mt. Japan
165 J13 Tsurugi-san mt. Japan
Tsuruhaytuy Rus. Fed. see Priargunsk
165 J14 Tsurumi-zaki pt Japan
165 I14 Tsuruoka Japan
165 E5 Tsuruta Japan
165 G12 Tsushima Japan
165 I11 Tsushima is Japan
167 I3 Tsushima Japan
77 L9 Tsvetnitsa Bulg.
14 L5 Tsvitkove Ukr.
17 L5 Tsvitne Ukr.
77 M7 Tsyelyakhany Belarus
20 V2 Tsyp-Navolok Rus. Fed.
55 N4 Tsyr r. Ukr.
18 G5 Tsyurupyns'k Ukr.

Columns 7–8 (Tu)

99 P5 Tua r. Port.
97 M4 Tua, Tanjung pt Indon.
200 □2 Tua North I. N.Z.
72 B8 Tua Sardegna Italy
95 C5 Tua r. Port.
173 K11 Tuglung Xizang China
154 E6 Tuguancun China
170 C5 Tuguegarao Luzon Phil.
129 F4 Tuguan Point Mindanao Phil.
129 H4 Tuguegarao Luzon Phil.
162 J2 Tugur Rus. Fed.
162 J2 Tugurskiy Zaliv b. Rus. Fed.
183 U4 Tugyl Kazakh.
169 F4 Tuhai r. China
96 E5 Tsael Israel see Zefat
15 H1 Tselina Rus. Fed.
183 U1 Tselinnoye Rus. Fed.
182 I2 Tsel'ye Rus. Fed.
191 F4 Tsentral'nyy Kirovskaya Oblast' Rus. Fed.
J4 Tsentral'nyy Kirovskaya Oblast' Rus. Fed.
36 H7 Tsentral'nyy Moskovskaya Oblast' Rus. Fed.
17 R4 Tsentral'nyy Ryazanskaya Oblast' Rus. Fed.
19 W8 Tsentral'nyy Ryazanskaya Oblast' Rus. Fed.
96 E5 Tsentralnyi Balkan nat. park Bulg.
Tschechoe N.W.T. Can. see Wrigley
62 C5 Tua r. Port.
201 □3 Tua, Tanjung pt Indon.
202 L1 Tua North I. N.Z.
184 B8 Tual Maluku Indon.
191 H6 Tü 'Alï-ye Iran
27 D5 Tuam Rep. of Ireland
203 E7 Tuamarina South I. N.Z.
201 □3 Tuamotu, Archipel des is Fr. Polynesia
Tuamotu Islands Fr. Polynesia see Tuamotu, Archipel des
28 C5 Tuamgraney Rep. of Ireland
154 F4 Tsolo... Maputi i. Indon.
173 K11 Tuân Giao Vietnam
171 □J7 Tuanji Japan
161 □J7 Tuangku Sabah Malaysia
17 O3 Tuapeka Mouth South I. N.Z.
15 G7 Tuapse Rus. Fed.
191 A1 Tuapse Rus. Fed.
157 L1 Tuaran Sabah Malaysia
185 J5 Tuariq...
200 □1 Tuasivi Samoa
203 B13 Tuatapere South I. N.Z.

26 D9 Tuath, Loch sea chan. Scotland U.K.
26 D6 Tuath, Loch a' b. Scotland U.K.
125 U5 Tuba City AZ U.S.A.
155 F4 Tubalai i. Maluku Indon.
157 J8 Tubalai i. Jawa Indon.
141 C9 Tubarão Brazil
188 I8 Tubarjal Saudi Arabia
190 D6 Tûbâs West Bank
157 J3 Tubau Sarawak Malaysia
154 B7 Tubbataha Reefs Phil.
44 K4 Tubbergen Neth.
28 B8 Tubbrid Rep. of Ireland
154 C8 Tubigan i. Phil.
63 M3 Tubilla del Agua Spain
52 G4 Tübingen Ger.
52 H5 Tübingen admin. reg. Ger.
45 F7 Tubize Belgium
88 C4 Tubmanburg Liberia
89 G4 Tubo r. Nigeria
154 D7 Tubod Mindanao Phil.
70 I2 Tubou Fiji
208 C6 Tubridgi Point W.A. Austr.
84 D1 Tubruq Libya
157 L3 Tubu r. Indon.
201 □3 Tubuai i. Is Australes Fr. Polynesia
Tubuai Islands Fr. Polynesia see Australes, Îles
126 D2 Tucacas Venez.
131 I8 Tucandera Brazil
122 E3 Tucannon r. WA U.S.A.
140 F4 Tucano Brazil
146 B5 Tucapel Chile
139 F4 Tucavaca Bol.
139 F4 Tucavaca r. Bol.
43 F10 Tuc de les Carants mt. Spain
43 J10 Tuchan France
50 F4 Tüchen Ger.
51 F6 Tuchheim Ger.
19 T6 Tuchkovo Rus. Fed.
54 F2 Tuchola Pol.
47 H2 Tucholski Park Krajobrazowy Pol.
54 F1 Tuchomie Pol.
55 J6 Tuchów Pol.
16 I3 Tuchyn Ukr.
118 F6 Tuckahoe NJ U.S.A.
119 K3 Tuckahoe NY U.S.A.
118 F6 Tuckahoe r. NJ U.S.A.
118 D7 Tuckahoe Creek r. MD U.S.A.
209 F9 Tuckanarra W.A. Austr.
213 L2 Tucker Glacier Antarctica
115 □1 Tucker's Town Bermuda
119 G5 Tuckerton NJ U.S.A.
118 D4 Tuckerton PA U.S.A.
Tucopia i. Solomon Is see Tikopia
125 V9 Tucson AZ U.S.A.
125 V9 Tucson Mountains AZ U.S.A.
109 H1 Tuctac r. Que. Can.
144 D2 Tucumán prov. Arg.
121 D8 Tucumcari NM U.S.A.
146 C2 Tucunuco Arg.
137 H6 Tucuparé Brazil
137 F2 Tucupita Venez.
136 C2 Tucuracas Col.
137 I5 Tucuruí Brazil
137 I6 Tucuruí, Represa resr Brazil
55 L4 Tuczna Pol.
54 E2 Tuczno Pol.
63 Q3 Tudela Spain
63 K5 Tudela de Duero Spain
Tuder Italy see Todi
77 O3 Tudora Romania
77 P5 Tudor Vladimirescu Romania
19 Q5 Tudovka r. Rus. Fed.
18 J2 Tudu Estonia
30 C2 Tudweiliog Gwynedd, Wales U.K.
62 F5 Tuela r. Port.
171 □I7 Tuen Mun H.K. China
71 K3 Tuenno Italy
187 I3 Tuensang Nagaland India
62 I4 Tuerto r. Spain
187 L2 Tufayh Saudi Arabia
153 K6 Tufi P.N.G.
217 J2 Tufts Abyssal Plain sea feature N. Pacific Ocean
97 P5 Tugela r. S. Africa
97 P4 Tugela Falls S. Africa
97 O4 Tugela Ferry S. Africa
158 D1 Tuhtong Myanmar
158 D1 Tui r. Bol.
138 D4 Tuichi r. Bol.
72 B8 Tuili Sardegna Italy
179 N8 Tuipang Mizoram India
98 □3b Tuineje Fuerteventura Canary Is
96 E4 Tuins watercourse S. Africa
184 A3 Tūja Latvia
Tujiabu Jiangxi China see Yongxiu
156 E3 Tujuh, Kepulauan is Indon.
157 L3 Tujung Kalimantan Indon.
182 C4 Tukan Rus. Fed.
155 C6 Tukangbesi, Kepulauan is Indon.
108 L1 Tukarak Island Nunavut Can.
92 E2 Tukayel Eth.
18 I9 Tukhavichy Belarus
58 F4 Tükhtamish Tajik.
202 K6 Tukituki r. N.Z.
104 F3 Tuktoyaktuk N.W.T. Can.
104 E3 Tuktut Nogait National Park N.W.T. Can.
18 G5 Tukums Latvia
162 E1 Tukuringra, Khrebet mts Rus. Fed.
191 E1 Tukuy-Mekteb Rus. Fed.
200 □2 Tula American Samoa
72 B6 Tula Sardegna Italy
92 C5 Tula watercourse Kenya
129 F4 Tula Hidalgo Mex.
129 I4 Tula Tamaulipas Mex.
128 E4 Tula r. Mex.
19 U8 Tula Rus. Fed.
126 E4 Tula Mex.
213 D2 Tula Mountains Antarctica
129 I5 Tulancingo Mex.
156 F7 Tulangbawang r. Indon.

Tula Oblast admin. div.
Rus. Fed. see
Tul'skaya Oblast'
124 K5 Tulare CA U.S.A.
124 M6 Tulare Lake Bed CA U.S.A.
123 L10 Tularosa NM U.S.A.
176 H3 Tulasi mt. Madh. Prad./Orissa India
48 K5 Tülau Ger.
55 I2 Tulawki Pol.
96 D9 Tulbagh S. Africa
59 N3 Tulbing Austria
57 K5 Tulca Romania
136 B4 Tulcán Ecuador
54 F3 Tulcea Rom.
77 Q5 Tul'chyn Ukr.
Tul'chin Ukr. see Tul'chyn
16 H5 Tulear Iran
129 I7 Tulcingo Mex.
124 M5 Tule CA U.S.A.
130 G8 Tule Venez.
Tuléar Madag. see Toliara
184 K4 Tuleh Iran
155 F5 Tulehu Maluku Indon.
122 D6 Tulelake CA U.S.A.
107 L2 Tulemalu Lake Nunavut Can.
169 Q4 Tule Mod Nei Mongol China
41 F8 Tulette France
56 F5 Tulfás r. Hungary
58 E5 Tulghes Romania
77 N4 Tulghes Romania
121 E8 Tulia TX U.S.A.
169 Q1 Tulihe Nei Mongol China
54 G3 Tuliszków Pol.
106 E1 Tulita N.W.T. Can.
176 E3 Tuljapur Mahar. India
190 D6 Tülkarm West Bank
27 F7 Tulla Rep. of Ireland
27 F4 Tullaghan Rep. of Ireland
115 D8 Tullahoma TN U.S.A.
205 K5 Tullamore N.S.W. Austr.
27 H6 Tullamore Rep. of Ireland
28 C8 Tullamarine Rep. of Ireland
42 H5 Tulle France
48 K1 Tullebelle Denmark
205 K1 Tullibigeal N.S.W. Austr.
41 G6 Tullins France
59 N3 Tulln Austria
59 M3 Tulner Feld plain Austria
124 L4 Tullock CA U.S.A.
121 I10 Tullos LA U.S.A.
27 I7 Tullow Rep. of Ireland
207 K4 Tully Qld Austr.
27 G4 Tully Northern Ireland U.K.
27 H4 Tully Northern Ireland U.K.
27 J5 Tullyallen Rep. of Ireland
27 G4 Tullybrack hill Northern Ireland U.K.
27 I8 Tullycanna Rep. of Ireland
207 J4 Tully Falls Qld Austr.
27 I3 Tullyhogue Northern Ireland U.K.
118 F4 Tullytown PA U.S.A.
27 H4 Tullyvin Rep. of Ireland
27 F3 Tullyvoos Rep. of Ireland
77 O5 Tulnici Romania
20 V2 Tuloma r. Rus. Fed.
20 U5 Tulos Rus. Fed.
55 I3 Tułowice Mazowieckie Pol.
54 F5 Tułowice Opolskie Pol.
14 L3 Tulpan Rus. Fed.
73 J1 Tulppio Fin.
121 H7 Tulsa OK U.S.A.
106 C3 Tulsequah B.C. Can.
178 I5 Tulsipur Nepal
27 F5 Tulsk Rep. of Ireland
19 U8 Tul'skaya Oblast' admin. div. Rus. Fed.
191 B1 Tul'skiy Rus. Fed.
183 P1 Tul'skoye Kazakh.
136 B3 Tulu Eth.
92 C2 Tulu Bolo Eth.
77 Q5 Tulucesti Romania
57 J5 Tulu Dimtu mt. Eth.
104 B3 Tuluksak AK U.S.A.
190 F6 Tülül al Ashaqif hills Jordan
127 P7 Tulum tourist site Mex.
146 C2 Tulum, Valle de val. Mex.
160 H1 Tulun Rus. Fed.
157 I9 Tulungagung Jawa Indon.
Tulusdu i. N. Male Maldives see Thulusdhu
137 F4 Tulu-Tuloi, Serra hills Brazil
92 B2 Tulu Welel mt. Eth.
14 K4 Tulun r. Rus. Fed.
55 M4 Tulychiv Ukr.
17 M2 Tulyholove Ukr.
126 □Q11 Tuma r. Nic.
19 X6 Tuma Rus. Fed.
136 B4 Tumaco Col.
57 J3 Tumahole S. Africa
173 J10 Tumain Xizang China
182 C4 Tumak Rus. Fed.
184 I4 Tümän Äqä Iran
Tuman-gang r. Asia see Tumen Jiang
Tumannaya r. Asia see Tumen Jiang
14 F1 Tumannyy Rus. Fed.
19 R6 Tumanovo Rus. Fed.
193 S3 Tumanskiy Rus. Fed.
Tumasik Sing. see Singapore
137 G3 Tumatumari Guyana
19 R1 Tumaz Rus. Fed.
168 Q8 Tumba Qinghai China
91 D5 Tumba Dem. Rep. Congo
23 N2 Tumba Sweden
90 C5 Tumba, Lac l. Dem. Rep. Congo
90 C5 Tumba, Lac l. Dem. Rep. Congo
157 J5 Tumbangmiri Kalimantan Indon.
157 J5 Tumbangsamba Kalimantan Indon.
157 J5 Tumbangsenamang Kalimantan Indon.
157 I5 Tumbangtiti Kalimantan Indon.
154 E8 Tumbao Mindanao Phil.
72 A5 Tumbarumba, Punta c pt Sardegna Italy
205 L6 Tumbarumba N.S.W. Austr.
136 A5 Tumbes Peru
136 A5 Tumbes dept Peru
128 E7 Tumbiscatio Mex.
106 F4 Tumbler Ridge B.C. Can.
Tumbu Fin. see Tubou
204 F6 Tumby Bay S.A. Austr.
20 U3 Tumcha r. Fin./Rus. Fed.
Tumd Youqi Nei Mongol China see Salaqi
Tumd Zuoqi Nei Mongol China see Qasq
162 F7 Tumen Jilin China
170 H2 Tumen Shaanxi China
162 G7 Tumen Jiang r. Asia
137 F3 Tumeremo Venez.
137 F3 Tumereng Guyana
154 B9 Tumindao i. Phil.
143 G3 Tumiritinga Brazil
176 E6 Tumkur Karnataka India
179 K6 Tumlingtar Nepal
26 I9 Tummel, Loch l. Scotland U.K.
26 H9 Tummel Bridge Perth and Kinross, Scotland U.K.
84 B4 Tummo, Mountains of Libya/Niger
162 L4 Tump Pak.
200 □1 Tumon Bay Guam
185 J8 Tumpah Kalimantan Indon.
157 K5 Tumpat Malaysia
159 F8 Tumpok, Phnum mt. Cambodia
155 C4 Tumpu, Gunung mt. Indon.
155 C4 Tumputiga, Gunung mt. Indon.
178 G9 Tumsar Mahar. India
88 E4 Tumu Ghana
137 G4 Tumucumaque, Serra hills Brazil
177 H3 Tumudibandh Orissa India
62 H9 Tumuli r. Spain
138 D3 Tumupasa Bol.
138 D5 Tumupasa Bol.
205 L6 Tumut N.S.W. Austr.
14 K5 Tumutuk Rus. Fed.
72 E6 Tumxuk Xinjiang China

88 E4 Tuna Ghana
131 □1 Tuna, Punta pt Puerto Rico
154 E8 Tuna Bay Mindanao Phil.
23 I1 Tuna-Hästberg Sweden
131 □7 Tunapuna Trin. and Tob.
130 D3 Tunas de Zaza Cuba
Tunb al Kubrá i. The Gulf see Greater Tunb
Tunb as Sughrá i. The Gulf see Lesser Tunb
31 M5 Tunbridge Wells, Royal Kent, England U.K.
79 K3 Tunçbilek Turkey
188 I4 Tunceli Turkey
191 A6 Tunceli prov. Turkey
170 H9 Tunchang Hainan China
191 D4 Tunçoluk Turkey
205 N5 Tuncurry N.S.W. Austr.
173 D13 Tundla Uttar Prad. India
85 F6 Tundubai well Sudan
93 D7 Tunduru Tanz.
89 H4 Tundun-Wada Nigeria
93 C7 Tunduru Tanz.
77 O9 Tundzha r. Bulg.
26 D6 Tunga Western Isles, Scotland U.K.
176 F5 Tungabhadra r. India
178 E5 Tungabhadra Reservoir India
92 A2 Tungaru Sudan
154 D8 Tungawan Mindanao Phil.
171 □I7 Tung Chung H.K. China
171 □I7 Tung Chung Wan b. H.K. China
179 M8 Tungi Bangl.
157 M2 Tungku Sabah Malaysia
126 □Q11 Tungla Nic.
171 □J7 Tung Lung Chau i. H.K. China
Tung Lung Island H.K. China see Tung Lung Chau
20 □D1 Tungnaá i. Iceland
162 M2 Tungor r. Sakhalin Rus. Fed.
20 L4 Tungozero Rus. Fed.
171 □J7 Tung Pok Liu Hoi Hap sea chan. H.K. China
106 D2 Tungsten N.W.T. Can.
209 E8 Tunnel Creek watercourse W.A. Austr.
116 F9 Tunnelton WV U.S.A.
22 E1 Tunnhovd Norway
22 E1 Tunnhovdfjorden l. Norway
20 L4 Tunnsjøen l. Norway
19 X4 Tunoshna Rus. Fed.
31 O3 Tunstall Suffolk, England U.K.
53 M6 Tunstein Ger.
20 T3 Tuntsa Fin.
109 H1 Tunulic r. Que. Can.
104 B3 Tununak AK U.S.A.
109 I1 Tunungayualok Island Nfld and Lab. Can.
146 C3 Tunuyán Arg.
146 D4 Tunuyán r. Arg.
146 C3 Tunuyán, Sierra de mts Arg.
146 D3 Tunuyán, Travesia des. Arg.
57 L4 Tunyogmatolcs Hungary
Tuodian Yunnan China see Shuangbai
171 K2 Tuo Jiang r. Sichuan China
159 E4 Tuôl Khpos Cambodia
124 L4 Tuolumne CA U.S.A.
124 L4 Tuolumne r. CA U.S.A.
186 F2 Tuómmale Meadows CA U.S.A.
72 H1 Tuoma r. Italy
Tuoniang Jiang r. Guangxi China
71 M9 Tuoro sul Trasimeno Italy
Tuotuoheyan Qinghai China see Tanggulashan
183 R6 Tüp Kyrg.
142 B4 Tupã Brazil
142 C3 Tupaciguara Brazil
184 B3 Tüp Äghaj Iran
137 F5 Tupanaóca Brazil
141 B9 Tupanciretã Brazil
121 K8 Tupelo MS U.S.A.
56 G2 Tupesy Czech Rep.
143 G3 Tupinambarama, Ilha i. Brazil
31 L1 Tupinambá Brazil
142 B4 Tupã Paulista Brazil
139 H2 Tupiratins Brazil
138 D5 Tupiza Bol.
54 C4 Tupia Pol.
106 F4 Tupper B.C. Can.
119 L2 Tupper Lake NY U.S.A.
117 K4 Tupper Lake l. NY U.S.A.
146 C3 Tupungato Arg.
146 C3 Tupungato, Cerro mt. Arg./Chile
189 L9 Tuqayyid well Iraq
169 Q4 Tuqqu Nei Mongol China
136 B4 Túquerres Col.
77 K2 Tura r. Rus. Fed.
173 H8 Tura Xinjiang China
57 I4 Tura Hungary
179 M7 Tura Meghalaya India
193 L3 Tura Rus. Fed.
186 F1 Turabah Hā'il Saudi Arabia
186 E5 Turabah Makkah Saudi Arabia
186 E5 Turabah, Wādī watercourse Saudi Arabia
137 E3 Turagua, Serranía mt. Venez.
176 F7 Turaiyur Tamil Nadu India
202 J7 Turakina North I. N.Z.
202 J7 Turakina r. North I. N.Z.
203 I8 Turakirae Head North I. N.Z.
184 G4 Turan Iran
162 G3 Turana, Khrebet mts Rus. Fed.
202 J5 Turangi North I. N.Z.
182 G8 Turan Lowland Asia
73 J3 Turano r. Italy
Turanskaya Nizmennost' lowland Asia see Turan Lowland
190 D5 Turāq al 'Ilab hills Syria
183 N6 Turar Ryskulov Kazakh.
16 G1 Turaw Belarus
54 G3 Turawa Pol.
188 I8 Turayf Saudi Arabia
182 H2 Turayf well Saudi Arabia
18 H2 Turba Estonia
136 C2 Turbaco Col.
55 I6 Turbacz mt. Pol.
185 J4 Turbat Pak.
58 F1 Turbenthal Switz.
185 I3 Turbio r. Mex.
16 H4 Turbiv Ukr.
136 B2 Turbo Col.
118 B2 Turbotville PA U.S.A.
58 H1 Türchlwand mt. Austria
58 C4 Turckheim France
174 L1 Turco Bol.
19 U8 Turdei Rus. Fed.
58 F2 Turdine r. France
77 J4 Turda Romania
54 G3 Turek Pol.
54 E1 Turee Creek r. W.A. Austr.
63 D7 Turégano Spain
184 I4 Türek Iran
54 G3 Turenki Fin.
54 E3 Turew Pol.
Turfan Xinjiang China see Turpan
Turfan Depression China see Turpan Pendi
183 O2 Turgay Akmolinskaya Oblast' Kazakh.
182 J3 Turgay Kostanayskaya Oblast' Kazakh.

182 J4 Turgay r. Kazakh.
182 J3 Turgayskaya Dolina val. Kazakh.
182 I2 Turgayskaya Stolovaya Strana reg. Kazakh.
168 B2 Türgen Uul mt. Mongolia
168 B2 Türgen Uul mts Mongolia
77 O7 Turgeon r. Ont./Que. Can.
188 I4 Turgoin Konya Turkey
79 I3 Turgut Turkey
79 I4 Turgutalp Turkey
79 I4 Turgutlu Turkey
79 J4 Turgutreis Turkey
188 H3 Turhal Turkey
17 M9 Turhenyevka Ukr.
18 I3 Türi Estonia
75 M2 Turi Italy
67 E9 Turia r. Spain
139 L2 Turiaçu Brazil
140 D2 Turiaçu r. Brazil
140 D2 Turiaçu, Baia de b. Brazil
131 □8 Turiamo Venez.
93 C6 Turiani Tanz.
57 H2 Turie Slovakia
77 I3 Turi r. Slovakia
107 H5 Turin Alta Can.
Turin Italy see Torino
192 H4 Turinsk Rus. Fed.
67 D9 Turís Spain
79 L1 Turi r. Ukr.
162 E2 Turiy Rog Rus. Fed.
16 D2 Turiys'k Ukr.
55 G5 Türje Hungary
161 I1 Turka Rus. Fed.
16 C4 Turka Ukr.
Turkana, Lake salt l. Eth./Kenya
79 I2 Türkeli Turkey
79 I2 Türkeli Adasi i. Turkey
53 K5 Türkenfeld Ger.
185 M6 Turkestan Kazakh.
185 L2 Turkestan Range mts Asia
57 J4 Turkeve Hungary
188 G4 Turkey country Asia/Europe
115 D11 Turkey KY U.S.A.
120 J4 Turkey r. IA U.S.A.
208 J4 Turkey Creek W.A. Austr.
15 H6 Turki Rus. Fed.
Türkistan Kazakh. see Turkestan
185 J2 Turkmenabat Lebapskaya Oblast' Turkm.
Türkmen Aylagy b. Turkm. see Türkmenskiy Zaliv
184 E2 Turkmenbashi Turkm.
184 E2 Turkmenbashi, Zaliv b. Turkm.
79 L3 Türkmen Dağı mt. Turkey
185 J3 Türkmengala Turkm.
184 H1 Turkmenistan country Asia
Turkmeniya country Asia see Turkmenistan
Turkmen-Kala Turkm. see Türkmenkarakul
185 J4 Türkmenkarakul' Turkm.
Türkmenostan country Asia see Turkmenistan
Turkmenskaya S.S.R. country Asia see Turkmenistan
184 E2 Türkmenskiy Zaliv b. Turkm.
79 L3 Türkoğlu Turkey
188 H5 Türkoğlu Turkey
18 I6 Turkova Belarus
130 H3 Turks and Caicos Islands terr. West Indies
130 H3 Turks Island Passage Turks and Caicos Is
130 H3 Turks Islands Turks and Caicos Is
21 Q6 Turku Fin.
92 C4 Turkwel watercourse Kenya
124 L4 Turlock CA U.S.A.
124 L4 Turlock Lake CA U.S.A.
27 D6 Turlough Clare Rep. of Ireland
27 D5 Turlough Mayo Rep. of Ireland
143 F2 Turmalina Brazil
186 F2 Turmus, Wādī at watercourse Saudi Arabia
146 B3 Turnagain r. B.C. Can.
202 K7 Turnagain, Cape North I. N.Z.
191 A5 Turnalı Turkey
57 J3 Turña nad Bodvou Slovakia
26 G12 Turnberry South Ayrshire, Scotland U.K.
203 C12 Turnbull, Mount South I. N.Z.
125 V8 Turnbull, Mount AZ U.S.A.
127 P9 Turneffe Islands Belize
208 E6 Turner r. W.A. Austr.
209 E8 Turner watercourse W.A. Austr.
111 K5 Turner MI U.S.A.
128 D4 Turner River W.A. Austr.
31 L5 Turners Hill West Sussex, England U.K.
88 B5 Turner's Peninsula Sierra Leone
106 H5 Turner Valley Alta Can.
45 G6 Turnhout Belgium
59 N4 Turnitz Austria
107 I3 Turnor Lake Sask. Can.
107 I3 Turnor Lake l. Sask. Can.
56 E1 Turnov Czech Rep.
Târnovo Bulg. see Veliko Tŭrnovo
77 M7 Turnu Măgurele Romania
55 K5 Turobin Pol.
205 L5 Turon r. N.S.W. Austr.
77 K2 Turon r. N.S.W. Austr.
Turones France see Tours
68 E3 Turoni plain Croatia
55 J2 Turośl Podlaskie Pol.
55 J2 Turośl Warmińsko-Mazurskie Pol.
14 H4 Turovets Rus. Fed.
19 U7 Turovo Rus. Fed.
55 K4 Turów Pol.
172 E2 Turpan Xinjiang China
172 E2 Turpan Xinjiang China
64 B2 Turquel Port.
59 I6 Turre Spain
22 I4 Turri Sardegna Italy
56 F2 Turriaco Italy
57 L3 Turracher Höhe pass Austria
84 F4 Turreh Sudan
126 □R13 Turrialba Costa Rica
26 L7 Turriff Aberdeenshire, Scotland U.K.
Turris Libisonis Sardegna Italy see Porto Torres
189 L6 Tursāq Iraq
75 K3 Tursi Italy
16 G2 Turskyy Kanal canal Ukr.
77 I3 Turt Romania
110 D3 Turtle Flambeau Flowage resr WI U.S.A.
107 I4 Turtleford Sask. Can.
Turtle I. Fiji see Vatoa
154 E8 Turtle Islands Fiji
88 B5 Turtle Islands Sierra Leone
107 I4 Turtle Lake Sask. Can.
110 B3 Turtle Lake WI U.S.A.
120 F2 Turtle Lake ND U.S.A.
111 G5 Turtle Pt

182 H4 Turgay r. Kazakh.
57 L3 Tur'ya-Polyana Ukr.
16 C4 Tur''ye Ukr.
57 L3 Tur''yi Remety Ukr.
16 D3 Turynka Ukr.
57 H2 Turzovka Slovakia
184 H3 Tüs Iran
65 O4 Tús r. Spain
74 G8 Tusa Sicilia Italy
74 G7 Tusa r. Sicilia Italy
125 T6 Tusayan AZ U.S.A.
115 D9 Tuscaloosa AL U.S.A.
Tuscania Italy
Tuscany reg. Italy see Toscana
116 D8 Tuscarawas r. OH U.S.A.
118 C3 Tuscarora PA U.S.A.
118 C3 Tuscarora Mountains hills PA U.S.A.
120 K6 Tuscola IL U.S.A.
121 F9 Tuscola TX U.S.A.
115 D8 Tuscumbia AL U.S.A.
120 I6 Tuscumbia MO U.S.A.
184 G4 Tusharik Iran
17 P2 Tuskar r. Rep. of Ireland
115 D8 Tuskegee AL U.S.A.
77 N4 Tuşnad Romania
53 J5 Tussenhausen Ger.
116 B8 Tussey Mountains hills PA U.S.A.
53 N5 Tüßling Ger.
55 I5 Tuszów Narodowy Pol.
55 H4 Tuszyma Pol.
55 H4 Tuszyn Pol.
184 F5 Tüt Iran
189 K4 Tutak Turkey
184 H8 Tutak Turkey
19 W4 Tutayev Rus. Fed.
31 I2 Tutbury Staffordshire, England U.K.
26 H13 Tutbury ...
176 F7 Tuticorin Tamil Nadu India
157 K3 Tutoh r. Malaysia
77 O4 Tutona r. Romania
50 H3 Tutow Ger.
77 O6 Tutrakan Bulg.
30 G4 Tutshill Gloucestershire, England U.K.
120 G6 Tuttle Creek Reservoir KS U.S.A.
118 F2 Tuttles Corner NJ U.S.A.
52 F6 Tüttlingen Ger.
105 P2 Tuttut Nunaat reg. Greenland
155 E8 Tutuala East Timor
53 B6 Tütük Yemen
200 □3 Tutuila i. American Samoa
212 S2 Tutukaka N. I. N.Z.
95 E4 Tutume Botswana
154 B9 Tutupaca, Volcán vol. Peru
79 H1 Tuttytere Greece
17 L2 Tutkovnovychi Ukr.
26 G10 Tuva country
199 H J. Pacific Ocean
199 I4 Tuvalu country S. Pacific Ocean
199 H4 Tuvana-i-Colo i. Fiji
199 I4 Tuvana-i-Tholo i. Fiji see Tuvana-i-Colo
212 S2 Tuve, Mount Antarctica
Tuvinskaya A.S.S.R. aut. rep. Rus. Fed. see Tyva, Respublika
201 □1a Tuvuca i. Viti Levu Fiji
186 G2 Tuwayq, Jabal hills Saudi Arabia
186 G2 Tuwayq, Jabal mts Saudi Arabia
186 D3 Tuwayrah Saudi Arabia
190 D7 Tuwayyil al Ḥajj mt. Jordan
190 E8 Tuwayyil ash Shihāq mt. Jordan
186 D6 Tuwwal Saudi Arabia
128 D5 Tuxcacuesco Mex.
29 O3 Tuxedo Park NY U.S.A.
59 I1 Tuxer Gebirge mts Austria
29 P7 Tuxford Nottinghamshire, England U.K.
128 B4 Tuxpan Jalisco Mex.
128 B4 Tuxpan Nayarit Mex.
129 L5 Tuxpan Veracruz Mex.
129 J4 Tuxpan, Arrecife rf Mex.
127 M9 Tuxtla Gutiérrez Mex.
131 K8 Tuy r. Venez.
106 D3 Tuy Duc Vietnam
159 H8 Tuy Duc Vietnam
158 G4 Tuyên Quang Vietnam
191 D5 Tuyguon Turkey
159 I8 Tuy Hoa Vietnam
15 K5 Tuymazy Rus. Fed.
184 C4 Tüysarkan Iran
77 M7 Tuz, Lake salt l. Turkey see Tuz Gölü
183 R6 Tuz Gölü salt l. Turkey
188 F4 Tüzha Bulg.
14 I4 Tuzi Crna Gora Serb. and Mont.
76 H8 Tuzla Bos.-Herz.
189 L6 Tuzla r. Romania
116 G10 Tuzla Turkey
205 I6 Tuzla Turkey
205 I6 Tuzluca Turkey
107 J2 Tuzly Ukr.
27 H6 Tvååker Sweden
69 C5 Tværåna r. Norway
16 A5 Tvarozná Czech Rep.
22 H2 Tveateigen Norway
22 B1 Tveit Norway
19 S5 Tver' Rus. Fed.
Tver Oblast admin. div. Rus. Fed. see Tverskaya Oblast'
19 S4 Tverskaya Oblast' admin. div. Rus. Fed.
30 E5 Tvertsa r. Rus. Fed.
31 M6 Tverøyri Faroe Is
18 I6 Tverskoye Rus. Fed.
191 L1 Tvyrdivka Ukr.
192 I4 Tyub i. Rus. Fed.
205 N3 Tvøroyri Faroe Is
108 B3 Tvrdošín Slovakia
18 G6 Tvŭrditsa Bulg.
191 I2 Tytyvenai Lith.
193 P3 Tyube Rus. Fed.
191 D1 Tyubelyakh Rus. Fed.
191 N1 Tyukyan r. Rus. Fed.

44 J4 Twentekanaal canal Neth.
125 P7 Twentynine Palms CA U.S.A.
90 C5 Tweya Dem. Rep. Congo
109 K3 Twillingate Nfld and Lab. Can.
124 L3 Twin Bridges CA U.S.A.
122 H2 Twin Bridges MT U.S.A.
121 E10 Twin Buttes Reservoir TX U.S.A.
109 H2 Twin Falls Nfld and Lab. Can.
122 G5 Twin Falls ID U.S.A.
91 F7 Twingi Zambia
208 I6 Twin Heads hill W.A. Austr.
114 L3 Twin Lakes PA U.S.A.
117 N4 Twin Mountain NH U.S.A.
124 L2 Twin Peak CA U.S.A.
209 D13 Twin Peaks hill W.A. Austr.
116 D7 Twinsburg OH U.S.A.
118 D7 Twins Creek watercourse
122 D2 Twisp WA U.S.A.
48 D5 Twist Ger.
49 G8 Twiste (Twistetal) Ger.
48 G5 Twistringen Ger.
124 L6 Twitchen Reservoir CA U.S.A.
106 D1 Twitya r. N.W.T. Can.
203 E11 Twizel South I. N.Z.
98 □2a Two Boats Village Ascension S. Atlantic Ocean
121 D6 Two Butte Creek r. CO U.S.A.
110 C2 Two Harbors MN U.S.A.
107 I4 Two Hills Alta Can.
28 B8 Twomileborris Rep. of Ireland
27 H6 Two Mile Bridge Rep. of Ireland
110 G5 Two Rivers WI U.S.A.
54 G5 Tworóg Pol.
31 J5 Tworth England U.K.
26 H13 Twynholm Dumfries and Galloway, Scotland U.K.
Tyachev Ukr. see Tyachiv
16 C5 Tyachiv Ukr.
17 M7 Tyahynka Ukr.
Tyan' Shan' mts China/Kyrg. see Tien Shan
158 A3 Tyao r. India/Myanmar
77 I4 Tyasmyn r. Ukr.
164 X2 Tyatya, Vulkan vol. Rus. Fed.
54 E2 Tychowo Pol.
54 G5 Tychowo Pol.
55 J6 Tyczyn Pol.
20 K5 Tydal Norway
28 C5 Tydd St Mary's England U.K.
116 F10 Tygart Valley WV U.S.A.
162 E2 Tygda Rus. Fed.
162 E2 Tygda r. Rus. Fed.
27 I4 Tyholland Rep. of Ireland
55 L2 Tykocin Pol.
55 J6 Tylawa Pol.
121 H9 Tyler TX U.S.A.
121 J10 Tylertown MS U.S.A.
55 J4 Tylicz Pol.
162 I2 Tyl'skiy Khrebet mts Rus. Fed.
162 M3 Tym' r. Sakhalin Rus. Fed.
55 I6 Tymbark Pol.
17 L4 Tymchenky Ukr.
78 T2 Tymfi mts Greece
54 D1 Tymień Pol.
77 R4 Tymná r. Ukr.
17 L1 Tymonovychi Ukr.
79 O6 Tymoshivka Ukr.
162 M3 Tymovskoye Sakhalin Rus. Fed.
54 F7 Týn nad Vltavou Czech Rep.
16 F2 Tynne Ukr.
21 K5 Tynset Norway
Tyr Lebanon see Sūr
55 K6 Tyrawa Wołoska Pol.
Tyre Lebanon see Soûr
212 S1 Tyree, Mount Antarctica
28 F5 Tyrella Northern Ireland U.K.
23 O2 Tyresö Sweden
48 F8 Tyrifjorden l. Norway
57 M1 Tyrlaching Ger.
23 N5 Tyrma r. Rus. Fed.
162 H7 Tyrma Rus. Fed.
22 F3 Tyrnavos Greece
20 R4 Tyrnyauz Rus. Fed.
Tyrol land Austria see Tirol
27 H3 Tyrone Northern Ireland U.K.
123 L10 Tyrone NM U.S.A.
116 G10 Tyrone PA U.S.A.
205 I6 Tyrrell, Lake dry lake Vic. Austr.
107 J2 Tyrrell, Lake N.W.T. Can.
27 H6 Tyrrellspass Rep. of Ireland
69 C5 Tyrrhenian Sea France/Italy
16 A5 Tyrus Lebanon see Soûr

168 E1 Tyva, Respublika aut. rep. Rus. Fed.
16 H4 Tyvriv Ukr.
54 C7 Tywardreath Cornwall, England U.K.
30 D7 Tywi r. Wales U.K.
30 C7 Tywyn Gwynedd, Wales U.K.
97 F4 Tzaneen S. Africa
127 O4 Tzucacab Mex.
44 I2 Tzummarum Neth.

U

137 F3 Uacauyén Venez.
Uaco Congo Angola see Waku-Kungo
200 □3 Uafato Samoa
201 □3 Uainambi Brazil
136 D4 Ualikhanov Kazakh. see Valikhanovo
91 D7 Uamanda Angola
95 H3 Uape Moz.
Ua Pou i. Fr. Polynesia see
201 □3 Ua Pou i. Fr. Polynesia

137 F5 Uara Brazil
137 G5 Uarc, Ras c. Morocco see Trois Fourches, Cap des
209 C7 Uaroo W.A. Austr.
136 D4 Uaruma Brazil
137 E3 Uatatás r. Brazil
140 F4 Uatumã r. Brazil
136 E4 Uaupés r. Brazil
127 O9 Uaxactún Guat.
186 G3 U'ayfirah well Saudi Arabia
186 G1 U'ayli, Wādī al watercourse Saudi Arabia
189 K9 U'aywij well Saudi Arabia
186 G1 U'aywij, Wādī al watercourse Saudi Arabia
76 I6 Ub Srbija Serb. and Mont.
143 F4 Uba Brazil
183 S2 Uba r. Kazakh.
49 B9 Übach-Palenberg Ger.
182 K1 Ubagan r. Kazakh.
143 G3 Ubaí Brazil
84 E6 Ubaid well Sudan
143 F4 Ubaitaba Brazil
90 C4 Ubangi r. C.A.R./Dem. Rep. Congo
143 F3 Ubaporanga Brazil
16 D5 Ubarts r. Belarus
136 C3 Ubate Col.
143 E5 Ubatuba Brazil
185 M5 Ubauro Pak.
41 I8 Ubaye r. France
189 K7 Ubayyiḍ, Wādī al watercourse Iraq/Saudi Arabia
49 C6 Ubbergen Neth.
68 I4 Ube Japan
65 M4 Úbeda Spain
93 D6 Ubenazomozi Tanz.
142 C4 Uberaba Brazil
142 C3 Uberaba r. Brazil
142 C3 Überlandia Brazil
49 G9 Überherrn Ger.
52 G6 Überlingen Ger.
52 G6 Überlinger See l. Ger.
53 I5 Übersee Ger.
63 O2 Ubidea Spain
185 J8 Ubin, Pulau i. Sing.
53 K6 Ubinskaya Rus. Fed.
192 I4 Ubinskoye, Ozero l. Rus. Fed.
142 A6 Ubiratã Brazil
49 K7 Ubly MI U.S.A.
14 I3 Ubolratna Reservoir Thai.
98 F3 Ubombo S. Africa
97 O3 Ubon Ratchathani Thai.
158 F6 Ubori Sudan
90 F3 Ubrique Spain
63 O1 Ubstadt-Weiher Ger.
52 I7 Ucacha Arg.
48 H1 Ucar Azer.
75 O4 Uçarı Turkey
190 A2 Ucayali dept Peru
138 B2 Ucayali r. Peru
136 C6 Ucciani Corse France
72 B3 Uccle Belgium
63 N5 Ucel France
41 E7 Ucero Spain
63 N5 Ucero r. Spain
21 K5 Uch Port.
62 C5 Uch-Adzhi Turkm.
205 L6 Uchajdyn, Khrebet mts Rus. Fed.
184 D7 Üchān Iran
131 K8 Ucharal Kazakh.
16 J4 Uchaux France
68 C6 Uchiko Japan
165 I13 Uchinada Japan
166 E2 Uchinada Japan
165 I3 Uchinomaki Japan
165 O9 Uchiura Japan
167 I3 Uchiura-wan b. Japan
167 H3 Uchiyama-tōge pass Japan
167 J3 Uchiza Peru
40 F7 Uchiza France
162 J5 Uchkeken Rus. Fed.
185 L2 Uchkuduk Uzbek.
182 J6 Uchkuduq Uzbek.
182 J6 Uchkuduk Uzbek.
27 H3 Uchkyr Uzbek.
191 C1 Uchquduq Uzbek.
191 D1 Uchsoy Uzbek.
182 H6 Uchtagan, Peski des. Turkm.
48 H5 Uchte Ger.
49 J10 Üchtelhausen Ger.
50 G5 Uchtspringe Ger.
63 O4 Ucieza r. Spain
48 C5 Uckange France
31 L6 Uckermark reg. Ger.
31 M6 Uckfield East Sussex, England U.K.
63 O9 Uckro Ger.
101 □ Uclulet B.C. Can.
62 C5 Uçmakdere Turkey

177 I3 Udayagiri Orissa India
187 I4 'Udayn well Saudi Arabia
23 J7 Uddeholm Sweden
44 I4 Uddel Neth.
22 H3 Uddevalla Sweden
28 I2 Uddingston South Lanarkshire, Scotland U.K.
26 I11 Uddington South Lanarkshire, Scotland U.K.
20 N4 Uddjaure l. Sweden
191 D4 Ude Georgia
187 J3 'Udeid, Khōr al inlet Qatar
14 H5 Udelnaya Rus. Fed.
49 J8 Uden Neth.
48 J6 Uder Ger.
49 C10 Üdersdorf Ger.
176 E3 Udgir Mahar. India
178 D3 Udhagamandalam Tamil Nadu India see Udagamandalam
178 D3 Udhampur Jammu and Kashmir
57 H2 Udiča Slovakia
14 I3 Udimskiy Rus. Fed.
71 N3 Udine Italy
71 N3 Udine prov. Italy
178 D6 Udit Rajasthan India
109 I2 Udjuktok Bay Nfld and Lab. Can.
Udmalaippettai Tamil Nadu India see Udumalaippettai
Udmurtia aut. rep. Rus. Fed. see Udmurtskaya Respublika
14 K4 Udmurtskaya Respublika aut. rep. Rus. Fed.
19 S4 Udomlya Rus. Fed.
167 J7 Udone-jima i. Japan
158 F6 Udon Thani Thai.
54 F1 Udorpie Pol.
200 □4a Udot i. Chuuk Micronesia
55 L5 Údrzyce Pol.
162 I1 Udskoye Rus. Fed.
176 D6 Udumalaippettai Tamil Nadu India
17 P3 Udy Ukr.
162 K2 Udyl', Ozero l. Rus. Fed.
Udzharma Georgia see Ujarma
93 C6 Udzungwa mts Tanz.
191 C1 Udzungwa Azer. see Ucar
193 M3 Uedineniya, Ostrov i. Rus. Fed.
49 C7 Uedem Ger.
89 H6 Uell Cameroon
193 U3 Uelen Rus. Fed.
193 T3 Uel'kal' Rus. Fed.
48 J5 Uelsen Ger.
48 K6 Uelzen Ger.
167 I3 Ueno Gunma Japan
166 D6 Ueno Mie Japan
167 J4 Ueno Japan
90 E4 Uere r. Dem. Rep. Congo
70 D2 Uetendorf Switz.
48 I3 Uetersen Ger.
52 I2 Uettingen Ger.
49 J6 Uetze Ger.
14 L5 Ufa Rus. Fed.
14 L5 Ufa r. Rus. Fed.
30 D7 Uffculme Devon, England U.K.
53 K6 Uffenheim Ger.
53 J6 Uffing am Staffelsee Ger.
73 O5 Uffita r. Italy
49 K7 Uftrungen Ger.
14 I3 Uftyuga r. Rus. Fed.
94 B4 Ugab watercourse Namibia
18 E4 Ugāle Latvia
93 A6 Ugalla r. Tanz.
93 A6 Ugalla River Game Reserve nature res. Tanz.
92 B4 Uganda country Africa
76 H3 Ugao-Miraballes Spain
63 O2 Ugarana Spain
146 C3 Ugarche Arg.
30 F6 Ugborough Devon, England U.K.
48 H1 Uge Denmark
75 O4 Ugento Italy
52 B1 Uggerby r. Denmark
75 O3 Uggerby Denmark
72 C3 Uggiano la Chiesa Italy
91 J6 Ughelli Nigeria
97 M7 Ugie S. Africa
18 J4 Uglich Solomon Is see Uki Island
65 M7 Ugíjar Spain
184 I5 Uğinak Iran
40 I5 Ugine France
18 I4 Uglegorsk Sakhalin Rus. Fed.
162 M7 Uglegorsk Sakhalin Rus. Fed.
14 V4 Uglekamensk Rus. Fed.
19 V4 Uglerodny Rus. Fed.
68 E3 Uglian i. Croatia
30 C7 Uglian i. Croatia
19 W4 Uglich Rus. Fed.
19 W4 Uglovka Rus. Fed.
183 O2 Uglovoye Amurskaya Oblast' Rus. Fed.
162 H7 Uglovoye Primorskiy Kray Rus. Fed.
57 G4 Ugod Hungary
Ugodskiy Zavod Rus. Fed. see Zhukovo
193 M3 Ugol'noye Rus. Fed.
193 E2 Ugol'nyye Kopi Rus. Fed.
19 T7 Ugra r. Rus. Fed.
14 I3 Ugūrchin Bulg.
189 G2 Uğurlu Gökeada Turkey
191 B4 Uğurludağ Turkey
91 B6 Ugut Rus. Fed.
63 E10 Uharte-Arakil Spain
169 L6 Uher Hudag Nei Mongol China
56 G2 Uherka r. Pol.
56 G2 Uherské Hradiště Czech Rep.
56 G2 Uherský Brod Czech Rep.
52 H2 Uhingen Ger.
56 F2 Uhldingen Ger.
56 E2 Uhlířská Janovica Czech Rep.
58 H1 Uhldingen-Mühlhofen Ger.
50 F5 Uhrsleben Ger.
57 H3 Uhrovec Slovakia
17 H6 Uhryniv Ukr.
140 E4 Uíbh Fhailí county Rep. of Ireland see Offaly
51 D9 Uhlstädt Ger.
53 L4 Uhyst Ger.
57 H3 Uhlava r. Czech Rep.
91 B6 Uige Angola
91 B6 Uíge prov. Angola
13 I10 Uiju N. Korea
182 K1 Uil Kazakh.
182 K1 Uil r. Kazakh.
163 E10 Ŭijŏngbu S. Korea
182 D8 Uinta r. UT U.S.A.
182 J2 Uintah and Ouray Indian Reservation res. UT U.S.A.
125 W1 Uinta Mountains UT U.S.A.
94 B3 Uis Mine Namibia
94 B3 Uitenhage S. Africa
44 K2 Uitgeest Neth.
44 K2 Uithoorn Neth.
44 L1 Uithuizen Neth.
44 L1 Uithuizermeeden Neth.
96 E3 Uitkyk S. Africa
176 F5 Uitsakpan salt pan S. Africa

96 D8 Uitspankraal S. Africa
109 I1 Uivak, Cape
 Nfld and Lab. Can.
57 J6 Uivar Romania
191 G4 Ujarma Georgia
55 H4 Ujazd Łódzkie Pol.
54 G5 Ujazd Opolskie Pol.
57 G2 Ujezd Czech Rep.
56 F2 Ujezd u Brna Czech Rep.
57 K6 Újfehértó Hungary
178 G4 Ujhani Uttar Prad. India
57 I4 Újhartyán Hungary
166 C6 Uji Japan
166 C6 Uji-gawa r. Japan
165 G15 Uji-guntō is Japan
167 K2 Ujiie Japan
166 C6 Ujitawara Japan
178 E8 Ujjain Madh. Prad. India
57 L3 Újkenéz Hungary
56 F4 Újker Hungary
57 K5 Újkígyós Hungary
157 K4 Újléta Hungary
157 K4 Újohbilang Kalimantan Indon.
208 □? Ujong Tanjong pt Cocos Is
54 F2 Újsoly Pol.
57 H6 Újsoly Pol.
55 H6 Újszalonta Hungary
57 J5 Újszász Hungary
57 J5 Újszentiván Hungary
57 K5 Újszentmargita Hungary
57 I4 Újszilvás Hungary
57 K4 Újtikos Hungary
57 J5 Újudvar Hungary
156 F8 Ujung Kulon National Park Indon.
 Ujung Pandang Sulawesi Indon. see Makassar
164 □1 Uka Okinawa Japan
178 D9 Ukal Sagar l. India
83 G4 Ukata Nigeria
166 F1 Ukawa Japan
164 □G19 Uke-jima i. Nansei-shotō Japan
93 B5 Ukerewe Island Tanz.
189 K7 Ukhaydir tourist site Iraq
189 K7 Ukhdūd tourist site Saudi Arabia
15 H5 Ukholovo Rus. Fed.
55 M4 Ukhovets'k Ukr.
179 O7 Ukhrul Manipur India
14 K3 Ukhta Respublika Komi Rus. Fed.
14 K3 Ukhta r. Rus. Fed.
18 M7 Ukhvala Belarus
205 N3 Uki N.S.W. Austr.
124 I2 Ukiah CA U.S.A.
126 B3 Ukiah OR U.S.A.
200 □6 Uki Island Solomon Is
105 M2 Ukkusissat Greenland
54 D2 Ukleja r. Pol.
18 H6 Ukmergė Lith.
19 S8 Ukolitsa Rus. Fed.
58 K4 Ukraine country Europe
 Ukraina Kyiv's'ka Oblast' Ukr. see Ukrayinka
 Ukrainas Respublika Krym Ukr. see Ukrayinka
 Ukrainskaya S.S.R. country Europe see Ukraine
 Ukrainskoye Ukr. see Ukrayins'ke
 Ukrayina country Europe see Ukraine
16 I3 Ukrayinka Kyiv's'ka Oblast' Ukr.
17 N9 Ukrayinka Respublika Krym Ukr.
17 L3 Ukrayins'ke Ukr.
68 F3 Ukrina r. Bos.-Herz.
91 B7 Uku Angola
165 G13 Uku-jima i. Japan
91 B8 Ukuma Angola
94 D4 Uku Botswana
73 C11 Ul r. India
18 M6 Ula r. Belarus
18 M6 Ula r. Belarus
55 M1 Ula r. Lith.
68 J3 Ulaanbaatar Mongolia
68 J3 Ulaanbaatar mun. Mongolia
69 K3 Ulaan-Ereg Mongolia
68 C2 Ulaangom Mongolia
68 I3 Ulaanhudag Mongolia
68 H4 Ulaan Nuur salt l. Mongolia
68 D4 Ulaan-Uul Bayanhongor Mongolia
68 G3 Ulaan-Uul Dornogovĭ Mongolia
69 L4 Ulaanbaatar
05 L5 Ulan N.S.W. Austr.
69 K7 Ulan Nei Mongol China
68 F8 Ulan Qinghai China
 Ulan Bator Mongolia see Ulaanbaatar
83 N5 Ulanbel' Kazakh.
15 I7 Ulan Buh Shamo des. China
69 K3 Ulanhot Nei Mongol China
69 L6 Ulan Hua Nei Mongol China
16 H4 Ulaniv Ukr.
15 I7 Ulan-Khol Rus. Fed.
72 H5 Ulanlingzi Xinjiang China
55 K4 Ulan-Majorat Pol.
68 I7 Ulan Mod Nei Mongol China
17 N2 Ulanove Ukr.
55 L5 Ulanów Pol.
68 I5 Ulan Suhai Nei Mongol China
19 M6 Ulanukhai Nur l. China
68 G6 Ulan Tohoi Nei Mongol China
60 I1 Ulan-Ude Rus. Fed.
73 J9 Ulan Ul Hu l. China
46 D2 Ulapes, Sierra mts Arg.
46 D2 Ulapes, Sierra mts Arg.
68 H4 Ulas Sivas Turkey
79 I1 Ulas Tekirdağ Turkey
72 D8 Ulastai Sardegna Italy
72 H5 Ulastai Xinjiang China
00 □5 Ulawa Island Solomon Is
93 C6 Ulaya Tanz.
93 H6 Ulayyah reg. Saudi Arabia
63 T2 Ul'ba Kazakh.
62 J2 Ul'banskiy Zaliv b. Rus. Fed.
22 K3 UL Bend National Wildlife Refuge nature res. MT U.S.A.
18 H5 Ulbroka Latvia
29 □6 Ulbster Highland, Scotland U.K.
 Ulceby North Lincolnshire, England U.K.
63 F10 Ulcinj S. Korea
76 H9 Ulcinj Crna Gora Serb. and Mont.
96 I4 Ulco S. Africa
22 E4 Uldum Denmark
69 L2 Uldz Mongolia
69 N2 Uldz r. Mongolia
 Uleåborg Fin. see Oulu
72 F5 Ülenurme Estonia
00 □5 Uléi Vanuatu
65 O6 Uleila del Campo Spain
68 I1 Ulekchin Rus. Fed.
18 F4 Ulenurme Estonia
21 M1 Uley England U.K.
25 K4 Ulețu Pol.
22 E5 Ulfborg Denmark
22 E5 Ulfborg Vind nature res. Denmark
 Ulflingen Lux. see Troisvierges
44 J5 Ulft Neth.
59 H4 Ulgain Gol r. China
63 F10 Ulgham Northumberland, England U.K.
33 L2 Ulhasnagar Mahar. India
76 C3 Ulhowek Pol.
91 G4 Ulianovka Georgia
53 G4 Uliastai Nei Mongol China
 Uliastay Mongolia
 Uliatea i. Arch. de la Société Fr. Polynesia see Raiatea
33 J3 Ulić Slovakia
45 G6 Ulicoten Neth.

14 F1 Ulita r. Rus. Fed.
153 I4 Ulithi atoll Micronesia
 Uljanovsk Rus. Fed. see
182 J3 Ul'yanovsk
183 N1 Ul'ken-Karoy, Ozero salt l.
 Kazakh.
183 P6 Ul'ken Sulutor Kazakh.
62 C3 Ulla r. Spain
205 M6 Ulladulla N.S.W. Austr.
26 F7 Ullapool Highland, Scotland U.K.
22 I4 Ullared Sweden
20 P3 Ullatti Sweden
138 C3 Ulla Ulla, Parque Nacional nat. park Bol.
209 D7 Ullawarra Aboriginal Reserve W.A. Austr.
66 F6 Ulldecona Spain
66 G5 Ulldemolins Spain
32 G6 Ullerslev Denmark
57 I5 Ülles Hungary
29 O6 Ulleskelf North Yorkshire, England U.K.
63 O3 Ullibarri, Embalse de resr Spain
212 S1 Ullmer, Mount Antarctica
138 C4 Ulloma Bol.
20 O2 Ullsfjorden sea chan. Norway
29 L4 Ullswater l. England U.K.
191 J3 Ulluchay r. Rus. Fed.
163 C10 Ullŭng-do i. S. Korea
52 H5 Ulm Ger.
162 F3 Ul'ma r. Rus. Fed.
49 H10 Ulmbach Ger.
64 B2 Ulmen r. Port.
57 O6 Ulmen Ger.
77 O6 Ulmeni Călăraşi Romania
77 L3 Ulmeni Maramureş Romania
68 G4 Ulog Bos.-Herz.
204 G2 Uloowaranie, Lake salt flat S.A. Austr.
29 K5 Ulpha Cumbria, England U.K.
22 J4 Ulricehamn Sweden
59 I2 Ulrichsberg Austria
49 H9 Ulrichstein Ger.
44 J2 Ulrum Neth.
163 F11 Ulsan S. Korea
20 J5 Ulsberg Norway
26 □N1 Ulsta Shetland, Scotland U.K.
22 G4 Ulsted Denmark
20 H5 Ulsteinvik Norway
27 H3 Ulster reg. Rep. of Ireland/U.K.
111 R8 Ulster PA U.S.A.
27 H4 Ulster Canal Rep. of Ireland/U.K.
119 G1 Ulster County county NY U.S.A.
130 □ Ulster Spring Jamaica
205 I6 Ultima Vic. Austr.
138 B1 Ultraoriental, Cordillera mts Peru
63 Q3 Ultzama r. Spain
65 M2 Ultzama, Valle de val. Spain
155 D2 Ulu Sulawesi Indon.
92 B2 Ulu Sudan
126 □P10 Ulúa r. Hond.
191 C5 Uluabat Turkey
79 J2 Ulubat Gölü l. Turkey
79 K4 Uluborlu Turkey
79 I4 Uluborlu Turkey
79 K2 Uludağ mt. Turkey
79 K2 Uludağ Milli Parkı nat. park Turkey
 Uluqqat Xinjiang China see
156 D3 Ulu Kali, Gunung mt. Malaysia
191 C7 Ulukaya Turkey
188 G5 Ulukışla Turkey
91 B8 Ulukŏy Turkey
97 N4 Ulundi S. Africa
172 H3 Ulungur He r. China
172 N3 Ulungur Hu l. China
124 □E13 Ulupalakua HI U.S.A.
156 □ Ulu Pandan Sing.
206 C8 Uluru hill N.T. Austr.
206 C8 Uluru - Kata Tjuṯa National Park N.T. Austr.
79 J3 Ulus Dağı mt. Turkey
 Ulutau Kazakh. see Ulytau
95 H2 Ulutay Moz.
122 B5 Ulupqua r. OR U.S.A.
91 B3 Ulpuqua r. OR U.S.A.
157 K2 Ulu Temburong National Park Brunei
26 D10 Ulva i. Scotland U.K.
20 □ Ulvebreen glacier Svalbard
22 B2 Ulvenåso mt. Norway
44 G5 Ulvenhout Neth.
29 K5 Ulverston Cumbria, England U.K.
205 □ Ulverstone Tas. Austr.
22 C1 Ulvik Norway
21 N5 Ulvsjön Sweden
19 U3 Ul'yanikha Rus. Fed.
13 V6 Ul'yanino Rus. Fed.
17 K6 Ulyanivka Mykolayivs'ka Oblast' Ukr.
79 I2 Ulyanivka Sums'ka Oblast' Ukr.
202 J7 Ul'yanov Turkey
97 P5 Ul'yanovi r. S. Africa
97 N7 Ulyanivka r. S. Africa
97 N6 Ulyanivka Kirovohrads'ka Oblast' Ukr.
97 O6 Umzimkulu r. S. Africa
19 N2 Ulyanivka Kaliningradskaya Oblast' Rus. Fed.
16 J5 Ulyanivka Kirovohrads'ka Oblast' Ukr.
17 L3 Ulyanivka Poltavs'ka Oblast' Ukr.
18 F7 Ulyanivka Kaliningradskaya Oblast' Rus. Fed.
19 S8 Ulyanovo Kaluzhskaya Oblast' Rus. Fed.
13 J5 Ul'yanovsk Rus. Fed.
15 I5 Ul'yanovskaya Oblast' admin. div. Rus. Fed.
183 O2 Ul'yanovskiy Kazakh.
 Ul'yanovsk Oblast admin. div. Rus. Fed. see Ul'yanovskaya Oblast'
68 F3 Ulyatuy r. Rus. Fed.
62 H4 Ulyshylo Kazakh.
42 H5 Ulytau Kazakh.
185 M4 Ulytau, Gory mts Kazakh.
183 I4 Ulytau, Gory mts Kazakh.
183 L4 Ulytau, Gory mts Kazakh.
55 I3 Ulz-Zhylamshyk r. Kazakh.
82 B2 Uma Rus. Fed.
63 D3 Uma Rus. Fed.
138 D4 Uma Bol.
162 H3 Umaltinskiy Rus. Fed.
127 O7 Uman Mex.
200 □14? Uman i. Chuuk Micronesia
31 □ Uman' Ukr.
144 C3 Umanao, Cerro mt. Arg.
185 K7 Umarao Bah.
190 E7 Umari, Qa' al salt pan Jordan
178 H6 Umaria Madh. Prad. India
188 F3 Umaria Madh. Prad. India
176 H3 Umarkot Mahar. India
185 M9 Umarkot Pak.
204 G2 Umaroona, Lake salt flat S.A. Austr.
178 D9 Umarpada Gujarat India
200 □11 Umatac Guam
178 G2 Umatilla r. India
154 E2 Umatilla r. Indon.
97 N5 Umbagog Lake l. NH U.S.A.
25 H1 Umberumberka watercourse
97 N6 Umerkot Sindh Pak.
48 J5 Umatilla watercourse Sudan
155 B3 Umatilla watercourse Indon.
18 E3 Umbrete Spain
66 E2 Umbria r. Ger.
71 M9 Umbrete Spain
153 K8 Umboi i. P.N.G.
203 □12 Umbrella Mountains South I. N.Z.
130 □ Umbrella Point Jamaica
71 M9 Umbria admin. reg. Italy
204 E6 Umbratico Italy
69 P5 Umbriático Italy
95 K3 Umbro Italy
20 R4 Umeå Sweden
20 P5 Umeälven r. Sweden

155 F4 Umera Maluku Indon.
15 H5 Umet Rus. Fed.
97 Q4 Umfolozi r. S. Africa
97 P4 Umfolozi Game Reserve nature res. S. Africa
20 M4 Umfors Sweden
107 M5 Umfreville Lake Man./Ont. Can.
97 O6 Umgababa S. Africa
97 P5 Umgeni r. S. Africa
187 H1 Umgharah Kuwait
97 P5 Umhali S. Africa
58 C5 Umhausen Austria
97 P5 Umhlanga Rocks S. Africa
97 Q4 Umhlatuzi Lagoon S. Africa
62 C3 Umia r. Spain
167 G1 Umi-gawa r. Japan
105 N3 Umiiviip Kangertiva inlet Greenland
 Umiikon S. Africa
124 □F14 'Umikoa HI U.S.A.
104 H3 Umingmaktok Nunavut Can.
182 D6 Umist Rus. Fed.
108 E1 Umiujaq Que. Can.
52 D5 Umkirch Ger.
97 O6 Umkomaas S. Africa
97 O6 Umkomaas r. S. Africa
97 O5 Umlazi S. Africa
189 L8 Umm tourist site Iraq
190 D6 Umm ad Daraj, Jabal mt. Jordan
190 F4 Umm al 'Amad Syria
186 D4 Umm al Birak Saudi Arabia
190 D9 Umm al Hashim, Jabal mt. Jordan
186 G2 Umm al Jamājim well Saudi Arabia
187 L3 Umm al Qaiwain U.A.E. see
50 H2 Ummanz i. Ger.
190 F9 Umm ar Raqabah, Khabrat imp. l. Saudi Arabia
187 L5 Umm as Samim salt flat
186 E2 Umm at Qalbān Saudi Arabia
187 L4 Umm az Zumūl well Oman
187 J3 Umm Bāb Qatar
84 E6 Umm Badr Sudan
190 B10 Umm Bujmah Egypt
85 F6 Umm Dam Sudan
52 H5 Ummendorf Ger.
84 C2 Umm Farud Libya
85 G4 Umm Gerifat waterhole Sudan
186 C2 Umm Harb Saudi Arabia
90 F2 Umm Heitan Sudan
84 E6 Umm Keddada Sudan
186 C3 Umm Lajj Saudi Arabia
190 C9 Umm Mafrūd, Jabal mt. Egypt
186 D4 Umm Mukhbār, Jabal hill Saudi Arabia
190 D9 Umm Nukhaylah hill Saudi Arabia
190 D10 Umm Nukhaylah well Saudi Arabia
189 M8 Umm Qaşr Iraq
85 F5 Umm Qurein well Sudan
186 B2 Umm Quşur i. Saudi Arabia
85 G5 Umm Rumeila well Sudan
85 F6 Umm Ruwaba Sudan
84 E2 Umm Sa'ad Libya
187 J3 Umm Sa'id Qatar
187 J3 Umm Şalāl 'Alī Qatar
184 D4 Umm Samā Saudi Arabia
190 D9 Umm Saysabān, Jabal mt. Jordan
190 E9 Umm Shaitiya well Jordan
190 B10 Umm Shawmar, Jabal mt. Egypt
85 F6 Umm Shugeira Sudan
190 A10 Umm Tināşşib, Jabal mt. Egypt
186 C3 Umm Urūmah i. Saudi Arabia
190 G7 Umm Wa'āl hill Saudi Arabia
186 G4 Umm Wazir well Saudi Arabia
190 A10 Umm Zanātīr mt. Egypt
104 B4 Umnak Island AK U.S.A.
158 D7 Um Phang Wildlife Reserve nature res. Thai.
95 H2 Umpilua Moz.
122 B5 Umpqua r. OR U.S.A.
91 B3 Umpulo Angola
179 M3 Umrangso Assam India
178 G9 Umred Mahar. India
176 C1 Umreth Gujarat India
97 O7 Umtamvuna r. S. Africa
97 M7 Umtata S. Africa
97 M7 Umtata Dam resr S. Africa
97 M7 Umtentweni S. Africa
89 G5 Umuahia Nigeria
142 A5 Umuarama Brazil
178 D8 Umudu r. India
191 C5 Umudum Turkey
79 H2 Umurbey Turkey
79 J3 Umurlar Turkey
202 J7 Umutoi North I. N.Z.
97 P5 Umvoti r. S. Africa
97 N7 Umzimhlava r. S. Africa
97 O6 Umzimkulu S. Africa
97 O6 Umzimkulu r. S. Africa
97 N7 Umzimvubu r. S. Africa
97 O6 Umzinto S. Africa
97 P5 Umzumbe S. Africa
20 R3 Una r. Brazil
155 B4 Una r. Brazil
16 J3 Una r. Ukr.
141 B8 Una Brazil
140 G4 Una r. Brazil
178 F4 Una Hima. Prad. India
63 G8 Uña Spain
12 N3 Una, Mount South I. N.Z.
51 E8 Unabäb, Jabal al hill Jordan
51 E8 'Unāb, Wādī al watercourse Jordan
179 I7 Unac r. Bos.-Herz.
164 □1 Unten Okinawa Japan
77 O3 Unţeni Romania
70 F1 Unterägeri Switz.
53 K6 Unterammergau Ger.
49 I8 Unterbreizbach Ger.
53 J6 Unterdietfurt Ger.
50 F5 Untere Havel park Ger.
70 I2 Unter Engadin reg. Switz.
50 J5 Unteres Odertal, Nationalpark nat. park Ger.
49 I10 Unterfranken admin. reg. Ger.
14 L2 Untergriesbach Ger.
53 L5 Unterhaching Ger.
58 D5 Unter Inn Thal val. Austria
70 E1 Unterkulm Switz.
14 L1 Untermaßfeld Ger.
53 L6 Untermeitingen Ger.
49 J10 Untermünkheim Ger.
49 K10 Unternkirchen Ger.
53 M4 Unterpleichfeld Ger.
53 L5 Unterreit Ger.
53 K4 Unterschleißheim Ger.
53 I4 Unterschneidheim Ger.
58 B5 Untersee l. Ger./Switz.
53 K5 Untersiemau Ger.
51 E10 Untersteinach Ger.
50 I4 Unterthingau Ger.
51 I6 Unterwalden reg. Switz.
59 K4 Unterweißenbach Austria
51 I6 Unterwellenborn Ger.
59 M5 Unterwössen Ger.
188 F3 Unţur Romania
137 E4 Untuca, Sierra de mts Venez.
186 G2 Unūk r. Saudi Arabia
168 B9 Unur Hoog Qinghai China
36 B7 Unun r. Rus. Fed.
14 J4 Unuwera Nigeria
12 N5 Unye Turkey
49 J6 Unzen-Amakusa National Park Japan
14 I4 Unzha Rus. Fed.
14 I4 Unzha r. Rus. Fed.
120 F5 Upa r. Rus. Fed.
15 G5 Upa r. Czech Rep.
28 S6 Upa r. Czech Rep.
125 V1 Upalco UT U.S.A.

53 I5 Ungava, Péninsule d'
162 G7 Ungava Peninsula Que. Can.
16 G6 Ungeni Moldova
77 M4 Ungheni Romania
95 G4 Unguana Moz.
 Ungüja i. Tanz. see Zanzibar Island
 Unguja North admin. reg. Tanz. see Zanzibar North
48 D3 Ungujja South admin. reg. Tanz. see Zanzibar South
154 E8 Unguja West admin. reg. Tanz. see Zanzibar West
56 F1 Unguraşi Romania
77 M3 Unguri Moldova
184 H2 Unguz, Solonchakovyye Vpadiny salt flat Turkm.
 Üngüz Angyrsyndaky Garagum des. Turkm. see Zaunguzskiy Karakumy
93 D5 Ungvár Ukr. see Uzhhorod
62 D5 Ungwana Bay Kenya
62 E8 Unhais da Serra Port.
51 J10 Unhais-o-Velho Port.
14 J4 Unhošt' Czech Rep.
138 C2 Uni Rus. Fed.
142 B3 União Acre Brazil
140 E3 União Minas Gerais Brazil
141 C8 União Piauí Brazil
137 F5 União da Vitória Brazil
140 G4 União do Maranã Brazil
178 F7 União dos Palmares Brazil
30 F3 Uniara Rajasthan India
 Unicorn Point Ascension S. Atlantic Ocean
56 G2 Uničov Czech Rep.
54 G4 Unieów Poland
41 E6 Unije i. Croatia
68 E3 Unije i. Croatia
104 B4 Unimak Island AK U.S.A.
56 G3 Unín Slovakia
137 F5 Uníní r. Brazil
142 D1 Uníni Peru
146 E4 Unión Arg.
139 F6 Unión Para.
117 □P4 Union ME U.S.A.
119 J3 Union MO U.S.A.
116 G3 Union NJ U.S.A.
122 F4 Union OR U.S.A.
115 G3 Union SC U.S.A.
116 E11 Union WV U.S.A.
145 E5 Unión, Bahía b. Arg.
125 T7 Unión, Mount AZ U.S.A.
119 G4 Union Beach NJ U.S.A.
118 A5 Union Bridge MD U.S.A.
116 A8 Union City OH U.S.A.
116 F7 Union City PA U.S.A.
121 K7 Union City TN U.S.A.
119 G3 Union County county NJ U.S.A.
118 B7 Union County county PA U.S.A.
96 H9 Uniondale S. Africa
119 J2 Union Dale PA U.S.A.
130 C2 Unión de Reyes Cuba
128 C6 Unión de Tula Mex.
27 D9 Unionhall Rep. of Ireland
129 M9 Unión Hidalgo Mex.
131 □3 Union Island St Vincent
116 I6 Union Lake NJ U.S.A.
116 I6 Union Springs NY U.S.A.
99 □1b Union Vale Mauritius
124 L3 Union Valley Reservoir CA U.S.A.
119 J1 Unionville CT U.S.A.
111 K6 Unionville MO U.S.A.
120 I5 Unionville MO U.S.A.
124 N1 Unionville NV U.S.A.
118 F2 Unionville NY U.S.A.
118 D5 Unionville NY U.S.A.
116 H10 Unionville VA U.S.A.
54 G2 Uniscaw Pol.
187 K4 United Arab Emirates country Asia
 United Kingdom country Europe
 United Provinces state India see Uttar Pradesh
112 G3 United States of America country N. America
105 L1 United States Range mts Nunavut Can.
71 M7 Uniti r. Italy
107 I4 Unity Sask. Can.
122 E4 Unity OR U.S.A.
118 F2 Unity Reservoir OR U.S.A.
63 G8 Universales, Montes reg. Spain
94 B4 Unjab watercourse Namibia
178 D8 Unjha Gujarat India
49 I8 Unkel Ger.
58 C4 Unken Austria
52 H5 Unlingen Ger.
49 E7 Unna Ger.
178 H6 Unnao Uttar Prad. India
49 E9 Unnau Ger.
162 D2 Unnuk r. Rus. Fed.
163 B10 Unp'a N. Korea
163 B10 Unsan N. Korea
163 E9 Unsan N. Korea
191 F7 Únşeli Turkey
26 □O1 Unst i. Scotland U.K.
29 O7 Unstone Derbyshire, England U.K.
51 E8 Unstrut r. Ger.
51 E8 Unstrut-Trias-Land park Ger.
179 I7 Unţāb Jharkhand India
164 □1 Unten Okinawa Japan
77 O3 Unţeni Romania
70 F1 Unterägeri Switz.

63 M4 Urbel r. Spain
205 N3 Urbenville N.S.W. Austr.
52 F2 Urberach Ger.
191 N8 Urbino Italy
72 C3 Urbino, Étang d' lag. Corse France
 Urbinum Italy see Urbino
63 O4 Urbión mt. Spain
63 O4 Urbión, Picos de mts Spain
71 O9 Urbisaglia Italy
40 D4 Urbise France
56 G2 Urbísc r. Czech Rep.
138 C3 Urcos Peru
43 B9 Urçay France
182 B3 Urda Kazakh.
65 I5 Urda Spain
203 K8 Uruti Point North I. N.Z.
93 A6 Uruwira Tanz.
185 L5 Urüzgán prov. Afgh.
191 E2 Urvan' Rus. Fed.
38 H2 Urville Nacqueville France
183 V3 Uryl' Kazakh.
166 B2 Uryū Japan
162 B2 Uryupino Rus. Fed.
64 C5 Urza hill Port.
 Urzedów Pol.
98 □1c Urzela r. São Jorge Azores
 Urzhar Kazakh. see Urdzhar
14 J4 Urzhum Rus. Fed.
77 O6 Urziceni Ialomiţa Romania
57 L4 Urziceni Satu Mare Romania
17 Q7 Urzuf Ukr.
72 D7 Urzulei Sardegna Italy
40 C2 Urzy France
18 L8 Usa r. Belarus
165 I13 Usa Japan
182 C1 Usa r. Rus. Fed.
14 L2 Usa r. Rus. Fed.
154 C9 Usacá i. Phil.
64 G4 Usagre Spain
79 K4 Uşak Turkey
79 K4 Uşak prov. Turkey
94 B4 Usakos Namibia
93 C6 Usambara Mountains Tanz.
93 B7 Usangu Flats plain Tanz.
213 K2 Usarp Mountains Antarctica
145 F8 Usborne, Mount hill Falkland Is
14 J4 Ushako Srbija Serb. and Mont.
77 O6 Usellus Sardegna Italy
181 L8 Usha r. Belarus
 Usha r. Belarus
48 L3 Úshachy Belarus
66 B1 Urdax-Urdazubi Spain
 Ur'devarri hill Fin./Norway see Urtivaara
147 H3 Urdinarrain Arg.
143 J4 Urdoma Rus. Fed.
13 E7 Urdorf Switz.
43 C10 Urdos France
168 G3 Urd Tamir Gol r. Mongolia
191 L1 Urdyuk, Mys pt Kazakh.
14 J2 Urdyuzhskoye, Ozero l. Rus. Fed.
29 S4 Ure r. England U.K.
77 P4 Urecheşti Romania
14 J4 Urengoy Rus. Fed.
21 J4 Urenui North I. N.Z.
22 D2 Urenui r. Norway
202 I5 Ureparapara i. Vanuatu
43 B9 Urepel France
203 K8 Urewera National Park North I. N.Z.
31 J5 Urfa Turkey see Şanlıurfa
14 J3 Urft r. Ger.
49 D9 Urga Mongolia see Ulaanbaatar
162 H3 Urgal r. Rus. Fed.
79 I4 Urganlı Turkey
64 H4 Urgell, Canal d' Spain
29 O5 Urgench Uzbek. see Urganch
27 I3 Urgnach Switz.
106 D2 Upper Liard Y.T. Can.
27 G4 Upper Lough Erne l. Northern Ireland U.K.
108 A3 Upper Manitou Lake Ont. Can.
131 □7 Upper Manzanilla Trin. and Tob.
118 B7 Upper Marlboro MD U.S.A.
111 Q5 Upper Mazinaw Lake Ont. Can.
26 L8 Upper Missouri Breaks National Monument nat. park MT U.S.A.
92 B2 Upper Nile state Sudan
119 H2 Upper Nyack NY U.S.A.
156 □ Upper Peirce Reservoir Sing.
110 E9 Upper Preoria Lake IL U.S.A.
120 H1 Upper Red Lake MN U.S.A.
116 B8 Upper Sandusky OH U.S.A.
117 K4 Upper Saranac Lake NY U.S.A.
203 G8 Upper Takaka South I. N.Z.
31 I2 Upper Tean Staffordshire, England U.K.
176 D6 Uppinangadi Karnataka India
31 K2 Uppingham Rutland, England U.K.
23 N2 Uppland reg. Sweden
23 N1 Upplands Sweden
23 N2 Upplands-Väsby Sweden
23 N1 Uppsala Sweden
23 N1 Uppsala county Sweden
178 F3 Uprara Chhattisgarh India
110 D3 Upsala Ont. Can.
179 H11 Upshi Jammu and Kashmir India
207 K5 Upstart, Cape Qld Austr.
207 K5 Upstart Bay Qld Austr.
30 H6 Upton Dorset, England U.K.
117 N6 Upton MA U.S.A.
30 H4 Upton St Leonards Gloucestershire, England U.K.
30 D3 Upton upon Severn Worcestershire, England U.K.
171 □I7 Urmston Road sea chan. H.K. China
18 K8 Urnäsch Switz.
66 A1 Uroa r. Spain
79 I1 Uröševac Kosovo, Srbija Serb. and Mont.
76 J8 Uröševac Kosovo, Srbija Serb. and Mont.
14 F3 Urozero Rus. Fed.
182 M5 Urotepa Tajik.
173 H11 Urqinza r. Brazil
191 F2 Ur,Urrmari Rus. Fed.
64 C2 Urra Port.
66 G5 Urrea de Gaén Spain
66 C6 Urrea de Jalón Spain
147 G1 Urrao Col.
174 J7 Urrao Col.
63 O3 Urriés Spain

185 Q1 Uru Pass China/Kyrg.
142 C4 Urupês Brazil
 Urupskaya Rus. Fed. see Sovetskaya
186 H6 'Urüq al Awärik des. Saudi Arabia
187 L4 'Urüq ash Shaybah des. Saudi Arabia
73 O4 Ururi Italy
162 C1 Urusha Rus. Fed.
162 C2 Urusha Rus. Fed.
191 G2 Urus-Martan Rus. Fed.
15 K5 Urussu Rus. Fed.
142 C2 Uruul Brazil
202 I5 Uruti North I. N.Z.
203 K8 Uruti Point North I. N.Z.
93 A6 Uruwira Tanz.
185 L5 Urüzgán prov. Afgh.
191 E2 Urvan' Rus. Fed.
38 H2 Urville Nacqueville France
183 V3 Uryl' Kazakh.
166 B2 Uryū Japan
162 B2 Uryupino Rus. Fed.
64 C5 Urza hill Port.
98 □1c Urzela r. São Jorge Azores
14 J4 Urzhum Rus. Fed.
77 O6 Urziceni Ialomiţa Romania
57 L4 Urziceni Satu Mare Romania
17 Q7 Urzuf Ukr.
72 D7 Urzulei Sardegna Italy
40 C2 Urzy France
18 L8 Usa r. Belarus
165 I13 Usa Japan
182 C1 Usa r. Rus. Fed.
14 L2 Usa r. Rus. Fed.
154 C9 Usacá i. Phil.
64 G4 Usagre Spain
79 K4 Uşak Turkey
79 K4 Uşak prov. Turkey
94 B4 Usakos Namibia
93 C6 Usambara Mountains Tanz.
93 B7 Usangu Flats plain Tanz.
213 K2 Usarp Mountains Antarctica
145 F8 Usborne, Mount hill Falkland Is
14 J4 Ushachi Belarus see Ushachy
192 I1 Ushakova, Ostrov i. Rus. Fed.
183 T3 Ushanovo Kazakh.
1 □ Ushant i. France see Ouessant, Île d'
 Ushant i. France see Ouessant, Île d'
183 N6 Usharal Kazakh.
29 N4 Ushaw Moor Durham, England U.K.
186 G3 'Ushayrah Saudi Arabia
186 E5 'Ushayrah Saudi Arabia
191 D2 Ushba, Mt'a Georgia
18 M6 Ushcha r. Rus. Fed.
19 O9 Ushcherp'ye Rus. Fed.
167 M4 Ushibori Japan
165 H14 Ushibuka Japan
167 L3 Ushioda Japan
166 C8 Ushimawashi-yama mt. Japan
93 A5 Ushirombo Tanz.
14 M3 Ushkalka Ukr.
29 M7 Ush-Kuduk Kazakh.
171 N1 Ushtagan Kazakh.
183 Q5 Ushtobe Kazakh.
 Ush-Tyube Kazakh. see Ushtobe
145 C8 Ushuaia Arg.
16 G5 Ushytsya r. Ukr.
18 F4 Usi Latvia
140 B3 Usina Brazil
49 G10 Usingen Ger.
72 B6 Usini Sardegna Italy
14 L2 Usinsk Rus. Fed.
30 D4 Usk Monmouthshire, Wales U.K.
30 C4 Usk r. Wales U.K.
179 I6 Uska Uttar Prad. India
18 K8 Uskhodni Belarus
79 N1 Üsküdar Turkey
77 P9 Üsküp Turkey
52 H6 Uslar Ger.
54 L2 Úslava r. Czech Rep.
74 G6 Ustica Sicilia Italy
74 G6 Ustica, Isola di i. Sicilia Italy
193 L4 Ust'-Ilimsk Rus. Fed.
 Vodokhranilishche resr Rus. Fed.
169 M1 Ust'-Ilya Rus. Fed.
54 D1 Ustí nad Labem Czech Rep.
56 F2 Ústí nad Orlicí Czech Rep.
56 F2 Ustirt plat. Kazakh./Uzbek.
 Ustyurt Plateau
23 M7 Ustka Pol.

183 T1	Ust'-Kalmanka Rus. Fed.

Ust'-Kalmanka Rus. Fed.
183 T1
193 R4 Ust'-Kamchatsk Rus. Fed.
183 T3 Ust'-Kamenogorsk Kazakh.
172 G1 Ust'-Kan Rus. Fed.
162 A2 Ust'-Karsk Rus. Fed.
172 G1 Ust'-Koksa Rus. Fed.
14 K3 Ust'-Kulom Rus. Fed.
193 L4 Ust'-Kut Rus. Fed.
193 O2 Ust'-Kuyga Rus. Fed.
15 G7 Ust'-Labinsk Rus. Fed.
162 B2 Ust'-Labinskaya Rus. Fed. see Ust'-Labinsk
18 L2 Ust'-Lubiya Rus. Fed.
14 L2 Ust'-Luga Rus. Fed.
14 M3 Ust'-Lyzha Rus. Fed.
193 O3 Ust'-Man'ya Rus. Fed.
Ust'-Maya Rus. Fed.
Ust'-Mongunay Rus. Fed. see Primorskiy
192 J3 Ust'-Munduyka Rus. Fed.
14 K3 Ust'-Nem Rus. Fed.
193 P3 Ust'-Nera Rus. Fed.
14 J3 Ust'-Ocheya Rus. Fed.
193 M2 Ust'-Olenek Rus. Fed.
193 P3 Ust'-Omchug Rus. Fed.
160 H1 Ust'-Ordynskiy Rus. Fed.
160 H1 Ust'-Ordynskiy Buryatskiy Avtonomnyy Okrug admin. div. Rus. Fed.
43 G10 Ustou France
192 J3 Ust'-Port Rus. Fed.
77 O8 Ustrem Bulg.
54 G6 Ustroń Pol.
54 D1 Ustronie Morskie Pol.
55 K6 Ustrzyki Dolne Pol.
19 Q1 Ust'-Sara Rus. Fed.
14 H3 Ust'-Shonosha Rus. Fed.
14 K2 Ust'-Tsil'ma Rus. Fed.
172 H1 Ust'-Ulagan Rus. Fed.
14 L3 Ust'-Uls Rus. Fed.
162 H3 Ust'-Umalta Rus. Fed.
14 L3 Ust'-Unya Rus. Fed.
14 I3 Ust'-Ura Rus. Fed.
162 H3 Ust'-Urgal Rus. Fed.
162 B2 Ust'-Urov Rus. Fed.
14 L2 Ust'-Usa Rus. Fed.
182 J1 Ust'-Uyskoye Kazakh.
14 H3 Ust'wer'ga Rus. Fed.
14 L2 Ust'-Voya Rus. Fed.
14 I3 Ust'-Vyyskaya Rus. Fed.
14 H3 Ust'ya r. Rus. Fed.
193 O2 Ust'-Yansk Rus. Fed.
19 O5 Ust'ye r. Tverskaya Oblast' Rus. Fed.
14 G4 Ust'ye Vologodskaya Oblast' Rus. Fed.
14 H4 Ust'ye Vologodskaya Oblast' Rus. Fed.
19 W4 Ust'ye Yaroslavskaya Oblast' Rus. Fed.
19 W4 Ust'ye r. Rus. Fed.
19 S8 Ust'ye-Kirovskoye Rus. Fed.
16 D3 Ustylüh Ukr.
17 L6 Ustynivka Ukr.
Ustyurt, Plato plat. Kazakh./Uzbek. see
182 G6 Ustyurt Plateau
182 O2 Ustyurt Plateau
Ustyurt Platosi plat. Kazakh./Uzbek. see
Ustyurt Plateau
19 S3 Ustyutskoye Rus. Fed.
19 T3 Ustyutskoye
172 G4 Usu Xinjiang China
155 C9 Usu i. Indon.
167 H3 Usuda Japan
191 I4 Usukhchay Rus. Fed.
165 I13 Usuki Japan
126 ☐O11 Usulután El Salvador
127 M8 Usumacinta r. Guat./Mex.
157 K3 Usun Apau, Dataran Tinggi plat. Malaysia
66 A1 Usurbil Spain
55 H6 Ušust mt. Pol.
97 Q2 Usutu r. Africa
14 L4 Us'va Rus. Fed.
19 N6 Usvyaty Rus. Fed.
18 M7 Usvyeyka r. Belarus
55 I6 Uszew Pol.
57 H5 Uszód Hungary
55 J5 Uszwica r. Pol.
153 I7 Uta i. Papua Indon.
155 F3 Uta i. Maluku Indon.
72 B9 Uta Sardegna Italy
125 U2 Utah state U.S.A.
125 U11 Utah Lake UT U.S.A.
20 S4 Utajärvi Fin.
157 L9 Utan Sumbawa Indon.
166 C7 Utano Japan
48 D3 Utarp Ger.
Utashinai Kuril'skiye O-va Rus. Fed. see Yuzhno-Kuril'sk
168 H1 Utashud I. Rus. Fed.
201 I12 'Uta Vava'u Vava'u Gp Tonga
186 E4 'Utaybah reg. Saudi Arabia
190 E5 'Utaybah, Buhayrat al imp. l. Syria
190 B10 Utayrtir ad Dahami, Jabal mt. Egypt
187 I2 Utayyiq Saudi Arabia
22 B2 Utbjoa Norway
66 D4 Utebo Spain
121 D8 Ute Creek r. NM U.S.A.
41 K9 Utelle France
91 D9 Utembo r. Angola
125 X4 Ute Mountain Indian Reservation res. CO/NM U.S.A.
18 I6 Utena Lith.
162 B1 Uteni Rus. Fed.
178 C7 Uterlai Rajasthan India
48 F1 Utgart Ger.
93 C7 Utete Tanz.
178 F6 Utetei Rajasthan India
188 L9 Uthal Pak.
185 L9 Uthlede Ger.
48 G4 Uthlede Ger.
190 F4 'Uthmaniyah Syria
159 D7 U Thong Thai.
158 G7 Uthumphon Phisai Thai.
139 F3 Utiariti Brazil
111 K7 Utica MI U.S.A.
121 J9 Utica MS U.S.A.
117 J5 Utica NY U.S.A.
116 C8 Utica OH U.S.A.
67 C8 Utiel Spain
106 H4 Utikuma Lake Alta Can.
126 ☐P9 Utila Hond.
140 E2 Utinga r. Brazil
21 I6 Utladalen park Norway
23 L5 Utlängan i. Sweden
97 J3 Utlwanang S. Africa
97 I3 Utlyuks'kyy Lyman b. Ukr.
165 H14 Uto Japan
23 O3 Utö i. Sweden
206 E7 Utopia N.T. Austr.
146 E5 Utracán Arg.
53 I3 Utrata r. Pol.
178 I6 Utraula Uttar Prad. India
44 H4 Utrecht Neth.
97 O3 Utrecht prov. Neth.
64 H6 Utrera Spain
66 Utrillas Spain
57 I6 Utrine Vojvodina, Srbija Serb. and Mont.
18 L4 Utroya r. Rus. Fed.
22 A2 Utsira Norway
20 S2 Utsjoki Fin.
20 M2 Utskor Norway
167 I6 Utsugi-dake mt. Japan
167 K2 Utsunomiya Japan
15 I7 Utta Rus. Fed.
176 F6 Uttangarai Tamil Nadu India
158 E6 Uttaradit Thai.
Uttarakhand state India see Uttaranchal
178 G4 Uttaranchal state India
178 G4 Uttarkashi Uttaranchal India
178 D3 Uttar Pradesh state India
58 H3 Uttendorf Oberösterreich Austria
Uttendorf Salzburg Austria
53 K2 Uttenreuth Ger.
52 H5 Uttenweiler Ger.
48 L1 Uttersleb Denmark

53 K5 Utting am Ammersee Ger.
31 I2 Uttoxeter Staffordshire, England U.K.
131 ☐1 Utuado Puerto Rico
172 H3 Utubulak Xinjiang China
201 ☐3a Utuofai Tahiti Fr. Polynesia
200 ☐6 Utupua i. Santa Cruz Is Solomon Is
182 E2 Utva r. Kazakh.
50 H3 Utzedel Ger.
18 H3 Uulu Estonia
105 L2 Uummannaq Avanersuaq Greenland
105 M2 Uummannaq Kitaa Greenland
105 M2 Uummannaq Fjord inlet Greenland
20 R5 Uurainen Fin.
168 B1 Üüreg Nuur salt l. Mongolia
168 G1 Üür Gol r. Mongolia
21 P6 Uusikaupunki Fin.
94 B3 Uutapi Namibia
136 D4 Uva r. Col.
14 K4 Uva Rus. Fed.
76 H7 Uvac r. Bos.-Herz./Yugo.
121 F11 Uvalde TX U.S.A.
56 D1 Uvaly Czech Rep.
19 N9 Uvarovichi Belarus
19 S6 Uvarovo Rus. Fed.
15 H6 Uvarovo Rus. Fed.
182 I1 Uver'k r. Rus. Fed.
19 R3 Uver' r. Rus. Fed.
41 J8 Uvernet-Fours France
93 A6 Uvinza Tanz.
91 F5 Uvira Dem. Rep. Congo
19 Y5 Uvod' r. Rus. Fed.
91 B7 Uvongo S. Africa
168 C2 Uvs prov. Mongolia
168 C1 Uvs Nuur salt l. Mongolia
165 J13 Uwa Japan
165 J13 Uwa-kai b. Japan
187 M4 'Uwayfi Oman
188 E3 'Uwayja well Saudi Arabia
84 B2 'Uwaynat Wannin Libya
186 C2 'Uwayriq, Harrat al lava field Saudi Arabia
190 G8 Uwaysit well Saudi Arabia
84 E4 Uweinat, Jebel mt. Sudan
93 B7 Uwimberi r. Tanz.
156 G4 Uwi i. Indon.
111 O5 Uxbridge Ont. Can.
31 Uxbridge Greater London, England U.K.
40 E3 Uxeau France
49 C10 Uxheim Ger.
169 K7 Uxin Ju Nei Mongol China
137 H6 Uxituba Brazil
127 O7 Uxmal tourist site Mex.
91 A6 Uxpanapa r. Mex.
172 G4 Uxxaktal Xinjiang China
182 J1 Uy r. Rus. Fed.
182 I5 Uyaly Kazakh.
191 A7 Uyandik Turkey
193 K4 Uya r. Rus. Fed.
168 I2 Üydzin Mongolia
26 ☐O1 Uyea i. Scotland U.K.
26 ☐O1 Uyeasound Shetland, Scotland U.K.
89 G5 Üyo Nigeria
168 G3 Üyönch Mongolia
168 B4 Üyönch Gol r. China
93 A6 Uyowa Tanz.
182 I1 Uyskoye Rus. Fed.
158 B2 Uyu Chaung r. Myanmar
183 N6 Uyuk Kazakh.
187 I3 Uyuni Bol.
138 D5 Uyuni Bol.
138 D5 Uyuni, Salar de salt flat Bol.
43 B7 Uza France
182 A1 Uza r. Rus. Fed.
189 L6 'Uzaym, Nahr al r. Iraq
182 I6 Uzbekistan country Asia
Uzbekskaya S.S.R. country Asia see Uzbekistan
Uzbek S.S.R. country Asia see Uzbekistan
18 K8 Uzda Belarus
38 F5 Uzel France
41 E7 Uzer France
42 H5 Uzerche France
38 E5 Uzès France
16 B5 Uzh r. Ukr.
19 Q7 Uzha r. Rus. Fed.
16 B5 Uzhgorod Ukr. see Uzhhorod
16 B5 Uzhhorod Ukr.
Uzhorod Ukr. see Uzhhorod
76 H7 Užice Srbija Serb. and Mont.
19 V8 Uzlovaya Rus. Fed.
14 H4 Uzmorye Belarus
183 R7 Üzöngü Toosu mt. China/Kyrg.
191 A6 Üzümlü Erzincan Turkey
79 K6 Üzümlü Muğla Turkey
79 H4 Uzun Ada i. Turkey
183 Q6 Uzunagach Almatinskaya Oblast' Kazakh.
183 Q6 Uzunagach Almatinskaya Oblast' Kazakh.
191 C4 Uzunark Turkey
172 G4 Uzunbulak Xinjiang China
172 I6 Uzun Bulak spring Xinjiang China
190 B2 Uzuncaburç Turkey
191 C5 Uzundere Turkey
191 B5 Uzunisa Turkey
79 H1 Uzunköprü Turkey
17 P8 Uzunlar, Ozero l. Ukr.
191 J1 Uzunoba Azer.
176 O9 Uzunsavat Turkey
191 J6 Uzuntäğä Azer.
18 I5 Üzventis Lith.
19 O6 Uzvoz Rus. Fed.
16 J4 Uzyn Ukr.
Uzynagash Kazakh. see Uzunagach
182 I5 Uzynkair Kazakh.
182 K1 Uzynkol' Kostanayskaya Oblast' Kazakh.

V

175 ☐1 Vaadhu i. S. Male Maldives
175 ☐1 Vaadhu Channel Maldives
175 ☐1 Vaadhu i. S. Male Maldives
14 D3 Vaajakoski Fin.
97 H5 Vaal r. S. Africa
20 S4 Vaala Fin.
97 M3 Vaal Dam S. Africa
97 M2 Vaal Dam Nature Reserve S. Africa
63 L5 Vaalbos National Park S. Africa
48 H3 Vaale Ger.
97 M1 Vaalpaaza S. Africa
97 N5 Vaalwater S. Africa
48 J4 Vaalserberg hill Neth.
45 I7 Vaals Neth.
20 P5 Vaasa Fin.
44 I4 Vaassen Neth.
175 ☐1 Vaattaru i. N. Male Maldives
18 H6 Vabalninkas Lith.
18 M8 Vabich r. Belarus
71 M2 Vablya r. Rus. Fed.
63 M3 Vabres r. Rus. Fed.
43 H9 Vabres-l'Abbaye France
57 I4 Vác Hungary
75 K7 Vacale r. Italy
143 E4 Vacaré r. Brazil
141 C9 Vacaria Brazil
143 F2 Vacaria r. Brazil
141 B7 Vacaria r. Brazil
141 C9 Vacaria, Campo da plain Brazil
141 B7 Vacaria, Serra hills Brazil
124 K3 Vacaville CA U.S.A.
96 F10 Vacca, Cape S. Africa
41 F9 Vaccarès, Étang de lag. France
75 K4 Vaccarizzo Albanese Italy
70 H5 Vacchelli, Canale canal Italy
49 J9 Vacha Ger.
14 H5 Vacha Rus. Fed.
57 I4 Váchartyán Hungary
40 J4 Vacheresse France
99 ☐2b Vaches, Île aux i. Inner Islands Seychelles
191 I3 Vachi Rus. Fed.
23 K5 Väckelsång Sweden
99 ☐1b Vacoas Mauritius
53 P3 Vacov Czech Rep.
43 H7 Vacqueyras France
77 O3 Vacvil Romania
14 I5 Vad Rus. Fed.
15 H5 Vad r. Rus. Fed.
176 C3 Vada Mahar. India
18 I4 Vadakaste r. Latvia/Lith.
23 M3 Vademarpils Latvia
77 M7 Vădăstriţa Romania
22 E6 Vadehavet nature res. Denmark
22 E6 Vadehavet sea chan. Denmark
77 P5 Vădeni Romania
77 O2 Vădeni, Dealul hill Moldova
22 H3 Väderön i. Sweden
24 J1 Vadheim Norway
176 C5 Vadi Mahar. India
15 H5 Vadinsk Rus. Fed.
22 C2 Vada Norway
70 E7 Vado, Capo di c. Italy
63 M6 Vado, Embalse del resr Spain
63 N5 Vadocondes Spain
178 D8 Vadodara Gujarat India
70 E7 Vado Ligure Italy
20 T1 Vadsø Norway
23 K3 Vadstena Sweden
57 K4 Vadu Crişului Romania
52 H7 Vaduz Liechtenstein
50 L1 Væggerløse Denmark
20 L3 Værøy i. Norway
14 H3 Vaga r. Rus. Fed.
21 J6 Vågåmo Norway
68 E3 Vaganski Vrh mt. Croatia
24 D1 Vágar i. Faroe Is
176 D4 Vagavaram Andhra Prad. India
21 J6 Vågen Norway
23 K4 Väggeryd Sweden
74 E4 Vaglia Italy
73 P6 Vaglio Basilicata Italy
70 I7 Vagli Sotto Italy
37 M7 Vagney France
23 N3 Vagnhärad Sweden
62 C7 Vagos Port.
20 O4 Vågsele Sweden
20 N2 Vågsfjorden sea chan. Norway
57 I4 Váh r. Slovakia
20 Q5 Vähäkyrö Fin.
184 G7 Vahhabi Iran
49 H7 Vahlbruch Ger.
145 Vahsel, Cape S. Georgia
21 Q6 Vahto Fin.
201 ☐3a Vahitu, Lac i. Tahiti Fr. Polynesia
176 D3 Vai Kerala India
176 E8 Vaikam Kerala India
18 J3 Väike Emajõgi r. Estonia
18 G2 Väike-Maarja Estonia
18 G2 Väike-Pakri i. Estonia
18 G3 Vaikijaur Sweden
120 B6 Vail CO U.S.A.
26 ☐M2 Vaila i. Scotland U.K.
36 G5 Vailly-sur-Aisne France
40 B2 Vailly-sur-Sauldre France
200 ☐2 Vailoa Samoa
119 G2 Vails Gate NY U.S.A.
18 G3 Vaimõisa Estonia
201 ☐3a Vainsia Estonia
200 ☐2 Vaini Tonga
176 F8 Vainode Latvia
176 F8 Vaippar r. India
37 K7 Vaire r. France
73 M5 Vairano Patenora Italy
201 ☐3a Vairao Tahiti Fr. Polynesia
41 J9 Vaire r. France
62 C8 Vairowal Punjab India
155 Vais Port.
30 C4 Vaison-la-Romaine France
43 H7 Vaison France
200 ☐2 Vaisigano r. American Samoa
199 H2 Vaitupu i. Tuvalu
200 ☐2 Vaitupu i. Tuvalu
71 J5 Vaiusu Samoa
106 C4 Vakaga pref. C.A.R.
62 C4 Vakarai Sri Lanka
140 F3 Vakaré r. France
42 H1 Vakfıkebir Turkey
41 I7 Vajasnó r. France
43 I7 Vajza Albania
17 P5 Vakhrusheve Ukr.
185 M3 Vakhsh Tajik.
185 M3 Vakhsh r. Tajik.
Vakhstroy Tajik. see Vakhsh
67 D9 Vakia Greece
67 D9 Vakia prov. Greece
18 F3 Väki Estonia
14 I4 Vaksala Rus. Fed.
184 H7 Vakilabad Iran
22 B1 Vakstad Norway
77 J4 Vakneala Macedonia
57 H4 Val Hungary
162 M2 Val Rus. Fed.
21 U6 Vaala Fin.
176 G8 Valaam r. Rus. Fed.
62 D4 Valadares Port.
84 F1 Valais Spain
70 D3 Valais canton Switz.
97 K3 Valaika Slovakia
77 K9 Valamaz Rus. Fed.
77 K9 Valandovo Macedonia
39 J1 Valanjou France
57 I3 Valaská Slovakia
57 G2 Valašská Polanka Czech Rep.
57 H2 Valašské Klobouky Czech Rep.
57 G2 Valašské Meziříčí Czech Rep.
53 P4 Valbo Sweden
111 S3 Val-Barrette Que. Can.
23 N1 Valberg France
72 B3 Valbo Sweden
70 I3 Valbona Italy
70 I3 Valbonnais France
63 O4 Valbornedo, Embalse de resr Spain
63 L5 Valbuena de Duero Spain
73 H2 Valča Slovakia
63 P9 Valca de Arriba Spain
41 H8 Valcabrère France
77 N5 Vălcănești, Munţii mts Romania
57 L4 Vălcău de Jos Romania
145 D6 Valcheta Arg.
77 K4 Valcani Romania
73 O1 Valcimarra Italy
18 K4 Valcoava Romania
18 I6 Valdai Hills Rus. Fed.
19 P5 Valday Rus. Fed.
19 P5 Valday Rus. Fed.
19 Q3 Valdayskaya Vozvyshennost' hills Rus. Fed.

66 E5 Valdealgorfa Spain
65 J3 Valdeazogues r. Spain
41 K8 Valdeblore France
65 I2 Valdecaballeros Spain
62 J9 Valdecañas, Embalse de resr Spain
62 I9 Valdecarros Spain
63 L3 Valdecebollas mt. Spain
63 M2 Valdecilla Spain
63 R8 Valdecuenca Spain
65 P2 Valdeganga Spain
63 J9 Valdeginate r. Spain
63 Q8 Valdeinfierno, Embalse de resr Spain
65 P5 Valdelacasa Spain
62 I7 Valdelacasa Spain
63 J9 Valdelacasa de Tajo Spain
64 F5 Valdelamusa Spain
66 D7 Valdelinares Spain
63 R7 Valdellosa mt. Spain
70 F5 Valle del Ticino, Parco della park Italy
63 Q10 Valde de Tajo Spain
63 L7 Valdemanco Spain
63 M3 Valdemarillo Spain
63 N8 Valdemoro Spain
63 N7 Valdemoro-Sierra Spain
147 I4 Valdenoches Spain
Valdes Uru.
62 H8 Valdeobispo Spain
62 H8 Valdeobispo, Embalse de resr Spain
65 M3 Valdepeñas Spain
65 L5 Valdepeñas de Jaén Spain
63 J3 Valdepiélago Spain
63 I5 Valderaduey r. Spain
63 J4 Valderas Spain
36 E5 Val-de-Reuil France
74 D7 Valderice Sicilia Italy
43 I7 Valderies France
66 F6 Valderrobres Spain
63 K3 Valderrueda Spain
110 G5 Valders WI U.S.A.
147 G4 Valdés Arg.
145 E6 Valdés, Península pen. Arg.
63 L8 Val de Santo Domingo Spain
111 S4 Val-des-Bois Que. Can.
63 K6 Valdesalor Spain
63 R8 Valdestillas Spain
65 J4 Valdetorres Spain
36 E5 Val-de-Saâne France
63 J9 Valdeverdeja Spain
62 I4 Valdevimbre Spain
136 D3 Valdez Ecuador
64 C4 Valdez AK U.S.A.
74 G8 Val di Demone reg. Sicilia Italy
70 I3 Valdidentro Italy
63 L7 Valdihuelo mt. Spain
70 I3 Valdilecha Spain
74 G9 Val di Noto reg. Sicilia Italy
41 J6 Val-d'Isère France
70 I3 Valdisotto Italy
145 B5 Valdivia Chile
136 C3 Valdivia Col.
42 F2 Valdivienne France
38 I5 Val-d'Izé France
71 L4 Valdobbiadene Italy
37 M8 Val-d'Oise dept France
36 D5 Val-d'Oise dept France
108 E3 Val-d'Or Que. Can.
63 N5 Valdosa r. Spain
115 F10 Valdosta GA U.S.A.
21 J6 Valdres val. Norway
63 J4 Valdres r. Norway
38 F7 Vale Channel Is
191 D4 Vale Georgia
122 F4 Vale OR U.S.A.
77 K3 Valea lui Mihai Romania
77 M7 Valea Lungă Alba Romania
77 N5 Valea Lungă Dâmbovita Romania
64 D6 Vale da Rosa Port.
26 ☐M2 Vale i. Scotland U.K.
64 C6 Vale das Mós Port.
64 D5 Vale do Açor Beja Port.
64 D2 Vale do Açor Portalegre Port.
62 D7 Vale de Cambra Port.
64 C4 Vale de Cavalos Port.
62 E7 Vale de Espinho Port.
129 K8 Vale Nacional Brazil
62 F7 Vale de Estrela Port.
64 C4 Vale de Figueira Port.
62 D8 Vale do Gaio, Barragem de resr Port.
62 E8 Vale de Guiso Port.
64 F8 Vale de Prazeres Port.
64 C4 Vale de Reis Port.
64 C5 Vale de Salgueiro Port.
64 B2 Vale de Santarém Port.
64 C4 Vale de Vargo Port.
64 D5 Vale do Guadiana, Parque Natural do nature res. Port.
64 D3 Vale de Pereiro Port.
64 D6 Vale do Peso Port.
62 E7 Valega Port.
106 C4 Valemount B.C. Can.
124 O8 Valencia CA U.S.A.
120 F2 Valencia City ND U.S.A.
122 D5 Valença do Piauí Brazil
42 H1 Valençay France
41 F7 Valence Midi-Pyrénées France
41 G7 Valence Rhône-Alpes France
43 H7 Valence-sur-Baïse France
67 E9 Valencia Spain
67 D9 Valencia prov. Spain
67 D9 Valencia aut. comm. Spain
67 D9 Valencia, Trin. and Tob.
136 E2 Valencia Venez.
67 D9 Valencia, Golfo de g. Spain
62 I4 Valencia de Don Juan Spain
64 F3 Valencia de las Torres Spain
64 G4 Valencia de Alcántara Spain
64 I4 Valencia del Mombuey Spain
27 B6 Valencia del Ventoso Spain
Valencia Island Rep. of Ireland
Valenciana, Comunidad aut. comm. Spain see Valencia
36 G1 Valenciennes France
77 O5 Vălenii de Munte Romania
40 I4 Valensole France
40 I4 Valensole, Plateau de France
72 H2 Valentano Italy
129 K6 Valente Brazil
67 F9 Valentigney France
162 I7 Valentin Rus. Fed.
120 E4 Valentine NE U.S.A.
123 L11 Valentine TX U.S.A.
120 E4 Valentine National Wildlife Refuge nature res. NE U.S.A.
18 I4 Valmiera Latvia
41 I8 Valmojado Spain
73 J4 Valmontone France
41 I6 Valmorel France
41 I9 Valmy France
36 I5 Valois reg. France
36 E5 Valois Albania see Vlorë

74 G9 Valguarnera Caropepe Sicilia Italy
119 H2 Valhalla NY U.S.A.
106 G5 Valhalla Provincial Park B.C. Can.
62 F8 Valhelhas Port.
93 G7 Valhermoso Spain
43 G10 Valier, Mont mt. France
183 N1 Valikhanovo Kazakh.
72 B4 Valinco, Golfe de b. Corse France
142 D5 Valinhos Brazil
66 H3 Valira r. Andorra/Spain
76 H6 Valjevo Srbija Serb. and Mont.
66 F6 Valjunquera Spain
18 J4 Valka Latvia
21 R6 Valkeakoski Fin.
45 I7 Valkenburg Limburg Neth.
44 F4 Valkenburg Zuid-Holland Neth.
45 H6 Valkenswaard Neth.
18 L2 Valkininkai Lith.
18 I2 Valko Estonia
18 J1 Valko Fin.
57 I4 Valkó Hungary
Valkoni Fin. see Valko
17 O4 Val'kumey Rus. Fed.
213 C1 Valkyrie Dome ice feature Antarctica
178 C9 Vallabhipur Gujarat India
41 F9 Vallabrègues France
67 D10 Vallada Spain
127 O7 Valladolid Mex.
63 K5 Valladolid Spain
63 K5 Valladolid prov. Spain
67 C12 Valladolises Spain
37 J7 Vallage reg. France
57 L4 Vállaj Hungary
Vall'Alta, Cala b. Sardegna Italy
109 G2 Vallard, Lac l. Que. Can.
41 K9 Vallauris France
26 B7 Vallay i. Scotland U.K.
20 I5 Valldal Norway
67 E7 Vall d'Alba Spain
67 K8 Valldemossa Spain
67 E8 Vall de Uxó Spain
22 D2 Valle Norway
63 L2 Valle Spain
67 J7 Valle Castellana Italy
127 J4 Vallecillos Mex.
146 D2 Vallecito Arg.
131 I9 Vallecitos Mex.
128 G1 Vallecitos Spain
73 K5 Vallecorsa Italy
70 C4 Valle d'Aosta admin. reg. Italy
146 E5 Valle Daza Arg.
65 J7 Valle de Abdalajís Spain
128 B5 Valle de Banderas Mex.
128 E4 Valle de Bravo Mex.
128 E4 Valle de Guadalupe Mex.
137 E2 Valle de la Pascua Venez.
64 H3 Valle de la Serena Spain
128 D3 Valle de Matamoros Spain
126 F4 Valle de Olivos Mex.
128 D3 Valle de Rosario Mex.
64 F4 Valle de Santa Ana Spain
128 F5 Valle de Santiago Mex.
128 G4 Valle de Zaragoza Mex.
71 M3 Valle di Cadore Italy
74 F8 Valledolmo Sicilia Italy
136 C2 Valledupar Col.
36 F7 Vallée de la Scarpe et de l'Escaut park France
99 ☐2a Vallée de Mai tourist site Seychelles
70 A2 Vallée du Doubs nature res. Switz.
109 G4 Vallée-Jonction Que. Can.
146 C2 Vallée Fértil, Sierra de mts Arg.
138 D4 Valle Grande Bol.
98 ☐3a Vallehermoso La Gomera Canary Is
127 K5 Valle Hermoso Mex.
40 H4 Valleiry France
128 G2 Vallejo Mex.
124 J3 Vallejo CA U.S.A.
22 J1 Vallen Sweden
111 J7 Valley, Parco della park Italy
74 F8 Vallelunga Pratameno Sicilia Italy
70 E4 Valle Mosso Italy
58 N5 Vallen Sweden
129 K8 Valle Nacional Mex.
144 C3 Vallenar Chile
49 E10 Vallendar Ger.
36 I7 Vallentigny France
23 O2 Vallentuna Sweden
72 B9 Vallermosa Sardegna Italy
73 L4 Vallerotonda Italy
99 ☐3f Valleseco Gran Canaria Canary Is
38 I7 Valletta Malta
75 L5 Valletta Malta
107 L5 Valley r. Man. Can.
30 C1 Valley Isle of Anglesey, Wales U.K.
124 O8 Valley Center CA U.S.A.
120 F2 Valley City ND U.S.A.
122 D5 Valley Falls OR U.S.A.
118 E4 Valley Forge PA U.S.A.
154 D3 Valley Head Luzon Phil.
27 I6 Valley Mouth Rep. of Ireland
85 G3 Valley of the Kings tourist site Egypt
124 L3 Valley Springs CA U.S.A.
131 E9 Valley Station KY U.S.A.
119 H3 Valley Stream NY U.S.A.
118 D4 Valley View PA U.S.A.
63 H4 Vallfogona de Riucorb Spain
42 I4 Vallgrund i. Fin.
Vallibona Spain
66 H5 Vallières France
41 E8 Vallnord Andorra
41 F9 Vallon-Pont-d'Arc France
40 A4 Vallorbe Switz.
41 I7 Vallorcine France
40 I8 Vallouise France
23 K4 Valls Spain
63 I3 Valls Sweden
Vallsjön l. Sweden
54 D1 Vallstena Sweden
70 G4 Valmadrera Italy
107 J5 Val Marie Sask. Can.
71 K2 Valmayor r. Spain
93 D6 Vanga Kenya

68 G3 Valpovo Croatia
119 H2 Valras-Plage France
106 G5 Valréas France
65 K2 Valronquillo hill Spain
41 C10 Valros France
97 K3 Vals r. S. Africa
70 G2 Vals Switz.
181 Vals, Tanjung c. Papua Indon.
178 D9 Vasad Gujarat India
70 C4 Valsavarenche Italy
50 E1 Valse Denmark
63 L6 Valseca Spain
65 I4 Valsequillo Spain
40 H4 Valserine r. France
125 T10 Valshui Wash watercourse AZ U.S.A.
75 K3 Valsinni Italy
190 M4 Valsjöbyn Sweden
41 E7 Vals-les-Bains France
97 I3 Valspan S. Africa
97 M4 Valsrivier S. Africa
71 L4 Valstagna Italy
71 K2 Valtellina val. Italy
40 I2 Val'tevo Rus. Fed.
56 Valtice Czech Rep.
46 M5 Valtiendas Spain
63 Q4 Valtierra Spain
20 T5 Valtimo Fin.
99 ☐1b Valton Mauritius
73 J1 Valtopina Italy
78 C3 Valtos Greece
70 D4 Valtournenche Italy
70 B6 Valtos
71 P6 Valtura Croatia
81 B6 Valujôls France
71 Q6 Valun Croatia
17 R3 Valuy r. Rus. Fed.
19 Q9 Valuyets Rus. Fed.
15 H7 Valuyevka Rus. Fed.
15 G6 Valuyki Rus. Fed.
191 K4 Välväläçay r. Azer.
98 ☐3e Valverde El Hierro Canary Is
63 I9 Valverde Spain
64 F5 Valverde de Burguillos Spain
63 F9 Valverde de Júcar Spain
64 F5 Valverde del Camino Spain
96 G2 Valverde del Fresno Spain
62 G8 Valverde de Leganés Spain
64 G4 Valverde de Llerena Spain
63 N6 Valverde de los Arroyos Spain
Valverde de Mérida Spain
18 L5 Valvestino, Lago di l. Italy
20 M3 Valvik Norway
18 I5 Valyasy Belarus
77 N3 Vama Suceava Romania
77 M4 Vama Mureş Romania
65 L4 Vamberk Czech Rep.
159 H9 Vam Co Đông r. Vietnam
159 H9 Vam Co Tây r. Vietnam
22 G5 Vamdrup Denmark
22 I3 Vamlingbo Sweden
167 I4 Vammala Fin.
57 I4 Vámosgyörk Hungary
57 I4 Vámospércs Hungary
57 K4 Vámosmikola Hungary
21 Q6 Vampula Fin.
177 I3 Vamsadhara r. India
79 H4 Vamvakas, Akra pt Chios Greece
79 Van Turkey
191 E7 Van, Lake salt l. Turkey see Van Gölü
191 F5 Vanadzor Armenia
21 R6 Vanajavesi l. Fin.
18 K4 Vana-Koiola Estonia
22 G6 Vanavara Rus. Fed.
99 ☐3a Vanault-les-Dames France
193 L3 Vanavara Rus. Fed.
128 G2 Vancejo Mex.
124 J3 Van Buren AR U.S.A.
110 I9 Van Buren IN U.S.A.
117 □11 Van Buren ME U.S.A.
121 J7 Van Buren MO U.S.A.
159 I8 Văn Canh Vietnam
159 H9 Vanceburg KY U.S.A.
116 B10 Vanceburg KY U.S.A.
Vances-Allières-et-Risset France
185 C1 Varchen Iran
115 L5 Vancleave MS U.S.A.
78 C4 Varda Greece
119 H2 Van Cortlandtville NY U.S.A.
106 Vancouver B.C. Can.
209 L13 Vancouver, Cape W.A. Austr.
106 B2 Vancouver, Mount Can./U.S.A.
106 C4 Vancouver Island B.C. Can.
57 K4 Vancsod Hungary
Vanda Fin. see Vantaa
120 K6 Vandalia IL U.S.A.
116 A11 Vandalia OH U.S.A.
58 Vandans Austria
176 Vandavasi Tamil Nadu India
107 K3 Vanderhoof B.C. Can.
40 G5 Vandenesse France
40 G5 Vandenesse-en-Auxois France
97 L2 Vanderbijlpark S. Africa
110 I4 Vanderbilt MI U.S.A.
118 Vandergrift PA U.S.A.
106 E4 Vanderkloof Dam resr S. Africa
208 D1 Vansittart Bay W.A. Austr.
105 J3 Vansittart Island Nunavut Can.
21 J1 Vansjø l. Norway
97 L5 Vanstadensrus S. Africa
44 J2 Van Starkenborgh Kanaal canal Neth.
21 R6 Vantaa Fin.
18 H1 Vantaa r. Fin.
209 G9 Van Truer Tableland reg. Austr.

20 ☐ Van Mijenfjorden inlet Svalbard
20 O5 Vännäs Sweden
36 F7 Vanne r. France
38 F6 Vennes France
109 H2 Vannes France
Vannes, Lac l. Que. Can. see Turar Ryskulov
20 O1 Vannoya r. Norway
20 O1 Vanntinden mt. Norway
71 L4 Vanoi r. Italy
97 N4 Van Reenen S. Africa
153 I7 Van Rees, Pegunungan mts Indon.
96 C7 Vanrhynsdorp S. Africa
207 H4 Vanrook Qld Austr.
207 H4 Vanrook Creek r. Qld Austr.
178 D9 Vansada Gujarat India
116 C11 Vansant VA U.S.A.
22 C3 Vanse Norway
208 H2 Vansittart Bay W.A. Austr.
22 G2 Vansjö l. Norway
97 L5 Vanstadensrus S. Africa
44 J2 Van Starkenborgh Kanaal canal Neth.
21 R6 Vanse Norway
18 H1 Vantaa Fin.
209 G9 Van Truer Tableland reg. Austr.
97 O4 Vant's Drift S. Africa
199 I3 Vanua Balavu i. Fiji
200 ☐5 Vanua Balavu i. Vanuatu
201 ☐1a Vanua Levu Barrier Reef Fiji
Vanua Mbalavu i. Fiji see Vanua Balavu
200 ☐5 Vanuatu country S. Pacific Ocean
Vanua Valavo i. Fiji see Vanua Balavu
191 K4 Vanvey France
120 M5 Van Wert OH U.S.A.
96 F9 Vanwyksdorp S. Africa
96 F6 Vanwyksvlei S. Africa
96 F6 Vanwyksvlei i. S. Africa
191 J2 Vanzare Hungary
97 O4 Vanzone Italy
96 G2 Vao New Caledonia
200 ☐5 Vao New Caledonia
203 ☐1 Vao Tokelau
62 F4 Vao, Embalse de resr Spain
43 H7 Vaour France
56 G1 Vápenná Czech Rep.
76 H5 Vapnyarka Ukr.
41 K9 Var dept France
41 K9 Var r. France
18 J3 Vara Estonia
20 H7 Vara r. Italy
22 I3 Vara Sweden
176 E5 Vara r. India
65 O2 Vara da Rei Spain
130 C2 Vara del
39 I7 Varades France
191 D6 Varades de Mureş Romania
41 H9 Varages France
178 C8 Varahi Gujarat India
43 H7 Vairaire France
16 G2 Vărăjäni Latvia
85 L4 Varakläni Latvia
... Varalé Côte d'Ivoire
70 H5 Varaita r. Italy
88 E4 Varalé Côte d'Ivoire
70 H5 Varallo Italy
190 I1 Varämïn Iran
119 I7 Varanasi Uttar Prad. India
14 L1 Varandey Rus. Fed.
20 T1 Varangerfjorden sea chan. Norway
20 T1 Varangerhalvøya pen. Norway
73 P4 Varano, Lago di lag. Italy
91 D8 Varão de Melegari Italy
77 O5 Varapayeva Belarus
185 L4 Varas Afgh.
184 E8 Väravi Iran
68 E3 Varaždin Croatia
69 ... Varaždinske Toplice Croatia
70 F7 Varazze Italy
22 I4 Varberg Sweden
18 G3 Varbla Estonia
184 C5 Varchen Iran
57 L5 Vârciorog Romania
78 C4 Varda Greece
Vardannapet Andhra Prad.
190 H5 Vardar r. Macedonia
22 E6 Varde Denmark
22 E6 Varde r. Denmark
191 G5 Vardenis Armenia
191 ... Vardenisi Lerr mt. Armenia
191 F6 Vardenisi Lerrnashght'a mts Armenia
191 F5 Vardubani Georgia
21 P6 Várdö Åland Fin.
20 U1 Vardø Norway
57 H5 Várdomb Hungary
19 V5 Vardousia mts Greece
18 E5 Vardva r. Lith.
146 D4 Varela Arg.
143 H7 Varela Guinea-Bissau
18 H7 Varèna Lith.
36 E5 Varengeville-sur-Mer France
71 Q8 Varengeville France
40 F5 Varennes-Changy France
37 J5 Varennes-en-Argonne France
40 I7 Varennes-sur-Allier France
37 S8 Varennes-Vauzelles France
85 J6 Varennes Rus. Fed.
70 F4 Varese Italy
70 F4 Varese, Lago di l. Italy
70 F4 Varese Ligure Italy
73 N2 Varès France
73 H1 Vardia r. Fin.
97 N2 Varfullyekyt S. Africa
162 H6 Vargashi Rus. Fed.
57 L5 Vârfuraşu, Vârful mt. Romania
57 L5 Vârfurile Romania
57 J3 Varin Slovakia
77 J5 Varkaus Fin.
57 J3 Variaş Romania
18 M6 Varkhi Belarus
49 I8 Varlosen (Niemetal) Ger.
20 ☐1 Varmahlíð Iceland
22 H2 Varmeln l. Sweden
22 H1 Värmland county Sweden
22 H1 Värmland reg. Sweden
22 H2 Värmland naturreservat nature res. Sweden
23 J2 Värmlandsskärgårdens nature res. Sweden
176 D4 Varna Bulg.
182 I1 Varna r. India
22 I3 Varna Italy
77 O4 Varna Rus. Fed.
18 I1 Varnja Estonia

Várnjárg to Vetsikko
355

Várnjárg pen. Norway see Varangerhalvøya
56 D1 Varnsdorf Czech Rep.
115 G9 Varnville SC U.S.A.
18 J7 Varnyany Belarus
18 K6 Varonka Belarus
57 I5 Városföld Hungary
Varosha Cyprus see Varosia
190 B3 Varosia Cyprus
68 F3 Varoška Rijeka Bos.-Herz.
57 G4 Városlőd Hungary
20 S5 Varpaisjärvi Fin.
57 H4 Várpalota Hungary
48 G5 Varrel Ger.
20 T3 Värriön luonnonpuisto nature res. Fin.
42 E4 Vars Poitou-Charentes France
41 J7 Vars Provence-Alpes-Côte d'Azur France
41 J7 Vars, Col de pass France
77 N4 Vărșag Romania
185 N3 Varsaj Afgh.
79 L6 Varsak Turkey
76 J4 Vărșand Romania
57 I3 Varsány Hungary
14 I2 Varsh, Ozero l. Rus. Fed.
70 H6 Varsi Italy
21 Q6 Varsinais-Suomi reg. Fin.
18 K4 Värska Estonia
44 J5 Varsseveld Neth.
23 N2 Vårsta Sweden
20 I5 Vartdalsfjorden inlet Norway
22 H2 Varteig Norway
78 C5 Vartholomio Greece
189 J4 Varto Turkey
77 L6 Vârtop Romania
77 K4 Vârtop, Pasul pass Romania
28 E7 Vartry Reservoir Rep. of Ireland
191 D3 Varts'ikhe Georgia
20 U5 Värtsilä Fin.
17 L3 Varva Ukr.
146 B5 Varvarco Campos, Lago l. Arg.
17 O5 Varvarivka Dnipropetrovs'ka Oblast' Ukr.
17 Q3 Varvarivka Kharkivs'ka Oblast' Ukr.
16 F3 Varvarivka Khmel'nyts'ka Oblast' Ukr.
17 R3 Varvarovka Rus. Fed.
57 L3 Vary Ukr.
16 D3 Varyazh Ukr.
192 I3 Var'yegan Rus. Fed.
184 E5 Varzaneh Iran
184 B2 Varzaqān Iran
140 F3 Várzea Alegre Brazil
143 E2 Várzea da Palma Brazil
140 E3 Várzea Grande Brazil
70 G6 Varzi Italy
14 G1 Varzino Rus. Fed.
70 E3 Varzo Italy
185 M2 Varzob Tajik.
14 G2 Varzuga Rus. Fed.
40 C2 Varzy France
56 F4 Vas county Hungary
Vasa Fin. see Vaasa
140 F4 Vasa Barris r. Brazil
57 I4 Vasad Hungary
176 C3 Vasai Mahar. India
18 H2 Vasalemma Estonia
18 H2 Vasalemma r. Estonia
73 I3 Vasanello Italy
57 H5 Vásárosdombó Hungary
57 L3 Vásárosnamény Hungary
64 D5 Vascão r. Port.
77 K4 Vașcău Romania
14 I2 Vashka r. Rus. Fed.
16 E5 Vashkivtsi Ukr.
191 H4 Vashlovanis Nakrdzali nature res. Georgia
14 I3 Vasilevo Rus. Fed.
78 E2 Vasilika Greece
78 B4 Vasiliki Lefkada Greece
55 M2 Vasilishki Belarus
Vasilkov Ukr. see Vasyl'kiv
Vasilkovka Ukr. see Vasyl'kivka
14 I4 Vasil'sursk Rus. Fed.
16 I1 Vasilyevichy Belarus
15 H6 Vasil'yevka Rus. Fed.
18 K4 Vasil'yevo Rus. Fed.
19 S4 Vasil'yevskiy Mokh Rus. Fed.
19 N8 Vas'kavichy Belarus
18 F1 Vaskijärven luonnonpuisto nature res. Fin.
21 Q5 Vaskivesi Fin.
18 K2 Vasknarva Estonia
16 H2 Vas'kovychi Ukr.
57 H5 Vaskút Hungary
42 D2 Vasles France
77 P4 Vaslui Romania
23 K1 Väsman l. Sweden
57 K3 Vasmegyer Hungary
111 K6 Vassar MI U.S.A.
21 L6 Vassbo Sweden
21 I6 Vassenden Norway
22 F1 Vassfaret og Vidalen park Norway
41 G7 Vassieux-en-Vercors France
42 H4 Vassivière, Lac de l. France
56 F4 Vas-Soproni-síkság hills Hungary
143 F5 Vassouras Brazil
39 J4 Vassy France
56 F4 Vasszécseny Hungary
20 N5 Västana Sweden
18 F1 Västanfjärd Fin.
20 N4 Västansjö Sweden
18 I3 Vastemõisa Estonia
20 N3 Vastenjaure l. Sweden
23 M2 Västerås Sweden
20 M4 Västerbotten county Sweden
21 M6 Västerdalälven r. Sweden
20 N3 Västerfjäll Sweden
22 J4 Västergötland reg. Sweden
23 O2 Västerhaninge Sweden
20 N5 Västernorrland county Sweden
23 M4 Västervik Sweden
23 L2 Västlandasjön l. Sweden
23 L2 Västmanland county Sweden
73 N3 Vasto Italy
48 K4 Vastorf Ger.
22 J2 Västra Åmtervik Sweden
22 J4 Västra Fegen l. Sweden
22 I3 Västra Götaland county Sweden
20 P5 Västra Kvarken sea chan. Sweden
20 N4 Västra Ormsjö Sweden
22 I2 Västra Silen l. Sweden
18 J3 Vastse-Kuuste Estonia
56 F4 Vasvár Hungary
17 L5 Vasylivka Kirovohrads'ka Oblast' Ukr.
17 N3 Vasylivka Sums'ka Oblast' Ukr.
17 O6 Vasylivka Zaporiz'ka Oblast' Ukr.
16 J3 Vasyl'kiv Ukr.
17 P5 Vasyl'kivka Ukr.
55 M6 Vasyuchyn Ukr.
17 L4 Vasyutyntsi Ukr.
57 G4 Vaszar Hungary
57 L5 Vața de Jos Romania
42 H1 Vatan France
23 O4 Väte Gotland Sweden
26 C7 Vaternish Point Scotland U.K.
26 A9 Vatersay Western Isles, Scotland U.K.
26 A9 Vatersay i. Scotland U.K.
53 L5 Vaterstetten Ger.
Vathí Greece see Vathy
78 D6 Vathia Greece
79 H6 Vathy Notio Aigaio Greece
79 H5 Vathy Voreio Aigaio Greece
201 □1a Vatia Point Viti Levu Fiji
73 I4 Vatican City Europe
75 J6 Vaticano, Capo c. Italy
Vaticano, Città del Europe see Vatican City
200 □6 Vatilau i. Solomon Is
79 I6 Vatio Rodos Greece
20 □E1 Vatnajökull ice cap Iceland
20 I5 Vatne Norway
99 I3 Vatoa i. Fiji
95 □K3 Vatomandry Madag.
79 H3 Vatoussa Lesvos Greece
77 N3 Vatra Dornei Romania
57 J4 Vatta Hungary
Vätter, Lake Sweden see Vättern
23 K3 Vättern l. Sweden
23 N1 Vattholma Sweden
21 N6 Vattrång Sweden
201 □1a Vatu-i-Cake i. Fiji
201 □1a Vatu-i-Ra Channel Fiji
Vatu-i-Thake i. Fiji see Vatu-i-Cake
201 □1a Vatukoula Viti Levu Fiji
201 □1 Vatulele i. Fiji
39 J3 Vaubadon France
37 J6 Vaubecourt France
36 G7 Vauchassis France
40 D2 Vauclaix France
41 G8 Vaucluse dept France
41 G9 Vaucluse, Monts de mts France
40 H1 Vauconcourt-Nervezain France
37 K6 Vaucouleurs France
70 B2 Vaud canton Switz.
37 L7 Vaudémont France
36 G7 Vaudeurs France
206 C7 Vaughan Springs N.T. Austr.
123 L9 Vaughn NM U.S.A.
40 F5 Vaugneray France
40 D1 Vault-de-Lugny France
40 F5 Vaulx-en-Velin France
40 G5 Vaulx-Milieu France
136 D4 Vaupés dept Col.
136 D4 Vaupés r. Col.
108 E2 Vauquelin r. Que. Can.
41 H9 Vauvenargues France
41 E9 Vauvert France
37 L8 Vauvillers France
40 D2 Vaux, Étang de l. France
37 J5 Vaux-devant-Damloup France
107 H5 Vauxhall Alta Can.
36 E6 Vaux-le-Pénil France
42 B4 Vaux-sur-Mer France
45 I9 Vaux-sur-Sûre Belgium
178 C7 Vav Gujarat India
95 □K3 Vavatenina Madag.
199 I3 Vava'u i. Tonga
201 □2 Vava'u Group is Tonga
37 J6 Vavincourt France
Vavitao i. Îs Australes Fr. Polynesia see Raivavae
88 D5 Vavoua Côte d'Ivoire
14 J4 Vavozh Rus. Fed.
176 G8 Vavuniya Sri Lanka
18 K7 Vawkalata Belarus
19 N8 Vawkavichy Belarus
18 H8 Vawkavysk Belarus
18 H8 Vawkavyskaye Wzvyshsha hills Belarus
23 O2 Vaxholm Sweden
23 K5 Växjö Sweden
159 F10 Vay, Đao i. Vietnam
176 F6 Vayalpad Andhra Prad. India
Vayenga Rus. Fed. see Severomorsk
192 G2 Vaygach, Ostrov i. Rus. Fed.
176 E7 Vayittiri Kerala India
191 G6 Vayk' Armenia
20 S2 Väylä Fin.
42 H6 Vayrac France
42 F4 Vayres France
142 D2 Vazante Brazil
Vazáš Sweden see Vittangi
191 G5 Vazashen Armenia
57 I2 Važec Slovakia
19 R1 Vazhinka r. Rus. Fed.
191 G4 Vaziani Georgia
95 □J3 Vazobe mt. Madag.
147 G6 Vázquez Arg.
19 R6 Vazuza r. Rus. Fed.
19 R6 Vazuzskoye Vodokhranilishche resr Rus. Fed.
56 D3 Včelná Czech Rep.
Veaikevárri Sweden see Svappavaara
159 F8 Veal Vêng Cambodia
40 E5 Veauche France
22 J6 Veberöd Sweden
20 P4 Vebomark Sweden
41 D8 Vebron France
70 I8 Vecchiano Italy
57 K3 Vechec Slovakia
49 J6 Vechelde Ger.
44 J3 Vecht r. Neth. alt. Vechte (Germany)
48 F5 Vechta Ger.
49 C5 Vechte r. Ger. alt. Vecht (Neth.)
98 □3f Vecindario Gran Canaria Canary Is
62 I7 Vecinos Spain
49 K7 Veckenstedt Ger.
49 I8 Veckerhagen (Reinhardshagen) Ger.
18 G5 Vecmikeļi Latvia
57 I4 Vecsés Hungary
56 E2 Vectec hill Czech Rep.
18 H5 Vecumnieki Latvia
Vedana Rus. Fed. see Vedeno
176 F7 Vedaranniyam Tamil Nadu India
176 E7 Vedasandur Tamil Nadu India
22 I4 Veddige Sweden
77 M6 Vedea Argeș Romania
77 N7 Vedea Giurgiu Romania
77 N7 Vedea r. Romania
71 M4 Vedelago Italy
41 F9 Vedène France
191 H3 Vedeno Rus. Fed.
23 L2 Vedevåg Sweden
191 F6 Vedi Armenia
147 G4 Vedia Arg.
14 F3 Vedlozero Rus. Fed.
17 S5 Vedmezha r. Ukr.
62 D3 Vedra Spain
41 C6 Védrines-St-Loup France
16 J1 Vedrych r. Belarus
17 S2 Veduga r. Rus. Fed.
44 K2 Veendam Neth.
44 I4 Veenendaal Neth.
44 J2 Veenhuizen Neth.
48 D4 Veenhusen Ger.
44 K3 Veenoord Neth.
26 □N2 Veensgarth Shetland, Scotland U.K.
44 I2 Veenwouden Neth.
44 E5 Veere Neth.
48 H4 Veerse r. Ger.
44 E5 Veerse Meer resr Neth.
20 L4 Vefsnfjord sea chan. Norway
20 K4 Vega i. Norway
121 D8 Vega TX U.S.A.
131 □1 Vega Alta Puerto Rico
131 □1 Vega Baja Puerto Rico
62 I3 Vegacervera Spain
129 K5 Vega de Alatorre Mex.
62 G3 Vega de Espinareda Spain
62 F2 Vegadeo Spain
63 M2 Vega de Pas Spain
98 □3f Vega de San Mateo Gran Canaria Canary Is
62 I6 Vega de Tirados Spain
62 G3 Vega de Valcarce Spain
63 J5 Vega de Valdetronco Spain
63 M6 Veganzones Spain
22 E3 Vegar l. Norway
62 H3 Vegarienza Spain
22 E3 Vegarshei Norway
63 J3 Vegas del Condado Spain
63 L7 Vegas de Matute Spain
44 I5 Veghel Neth.
75 N3 Veglie Italy
78 C2 Vegoritis, Limni l. Greece
39 K6 Vègre r. France
107 H4 Vegreville Alta Can.
138 A2 Végueta Peru
18 K1 Vehkalahti Fin.
50 F4 Vehlow Ger.
21 P6 Vehmaa Fin.
185 N6 Vehoa Pak.
185 N6 Vehoa r. Pak.
20 S1 Veidneset Norway
39 M7 Veigné France
40 I4 Veigy-Foncenex France
49 K10 Veilsdorf Ger.
137 H5 Veiros Brazil
64 D3 Veiros Port.
185 M9 Veirwaro Pak.
55 L1 Veisiejai l. Lith.
18 G7 Veisiejis Lith.
53 J2 Veitsbronn Ger.
59 M4 Veitsch Austria
59 L4 Veitsch mt. Austria
52 H2 Veitshöchheim Ger.
20 R4 Veitsiluoto Fin.
18 E6 Veiviržas r. Lith.
72 I3 Vejano Italy
22 F6 Vejen Denmark
64 H8 Vejer de la Frontera Spain
22 F6 Vejle Denmark
22 F6 Vejle county Denmark
53 O2 Vejprnice Czech Rep.
56 C1 Vejprty Czech Rep.
48 J1 Vejsnæs Nakke pt Denmark
182 I9 Vekil'bazar Turkm.
178 D9 Velachha Gujarat India
63 K9 Velada Spain
68 F4 Vela Luka Croatia
63 O6 Velamazán Spain
126 H5 Velardena Mex.
98 □1c Velas São Jorge Azores
126 □Q12 Velas, Cabo c. Costa Rica
129 I3 Velasco Mex.
144 D3 Velasco, Sierra de mts Arg.
175 □1 Velassary i. S. Male Maldives
57 K3 Veľaty Slovakia
41 G9 Velaux France
68 E3 Vela Vrata, Kanal sea chan. Croatia
41 D6 Velay reg. France
144 G4 Velázquez Uru.
49 D8 Velbert Ger.
53 L3 Velburg Ger.
77 K8 Velbŭzhdki Prokhod pass Macedonia
96 C8 Velddrif S. Africa
45 D6 Veldegem Belgium
53 L2 Velden Bayern Ger.
53 M5 Velden Bayern Ger.
45 J6 Velden Neth.
59 J6 Velden am Wörther See Austria
45 H6 Veldhoven Neth.
176 E5 Veldurti Andhra Prad. India
68 E3 Velebit mts Croatia
68 E3 Velebitski Kanal sea chan. Croatia
65 O6 Velefique Spain
77 P8 Veleka r. Bulg.
49 C7 Velen Ger.
57 H4 Velence Hungary
57 H4 Velencei-tó l. Hungary
68 E2 Velenje Slovenia
77 J9 Veles Macedonia
76 H9 Velës, Mali i mt. Albania
56 D3 Velešín Czech Rep.
71 Q6 Vele Srakane i. Croatia
65 M6 Veleta, Pico mt. Spain
68 F4 Velež mts Bos.-Herz.
136 C3 Vélez Col.
65 O5 Vélez-Blanco Spain
65 M7 Vélez de Benaudalla Spain
65 K7 Vélez-Málaga Spain
65 O5 Vélez-Rubio Spain
20 L4 Velfjorden inlet Norway
50 G2 Velgast Ger.
142 D3 Velhas r. Brazil
143 E2 Velhas r. Brazil
15 I7 Velichayevskoye Rus. Fed.
16 E4 Velika Berezovytsya Ukr.
76 J7 Velika Drenova Srbija Serb. and Mont.
68 F3 Velika Gorica Croatia
16 E2 Velika Hlusha Ukr.
68 E3 Velika Kapela mts Croatia
68 E3 Velika Kladuša Bos.-Herz.
68 F3 Velika Mlaka Croatia
76 J6 Velika Morava canal Serb. and Mont.
16 F2 Velika Ozera Ukr.
56 G6 Velika Pisanica Croatia
76 J6 Velika Plana Srbija Serb. and Mont.
59 K8 Velika Račna Slovenia
59 K7 Velika Rogatec mt. Slovenia
14 J4 Velikaya Rus. Fed.
14 J4 Velikaya r. Rus. Fed.
193 S3 Velikaya r. Rus. Fed.
18 L4 Velikaya r. Rus. Fed.
14 F3 Velikaya Guba Rus. Fed.
162 J6 Velikaya Kema Rus. Fed.
Velikaya Novoselka Ukr. see Velyka Novosilka
17 L1 Velikaya Topal' Rus. Fed.
59 K8 Velike Lašče Slovenia
68 F4 Veliki Drvenik i. Croatia
56 G6 Veliki Grđevac Croatia
76 J7 Veliki Jastrebac mts Serb. and Mont.
16 E4 Veliki Kunynets' Ukr.
77 O7 Veliki Preslav Bulg.
68 E3 Veliki Risnjak mt. Croatia
77 J7 Veliki Šiljegovac Srbija Serb. and Mont.
77 K8 Veliki Strešer mt. Serb. and Mont.
76 I6 Veliki Šturac mt. Serb. and Mont.
19 N5 Velikiye Luki Rus. Fed.
17 K2 Velikiy Lystven Ukr.
16 C4 Velikiy Lyubin' Ukr.
19 O3 Velikiy Novgorod Rus. Fed.
14 I3 Velikiy Ustyug Rus. Fed.
17 T3 Velikoarkhangel'skoye Rus. Fed.
19 X6 Velikodvorskiy Rus. Fed.
17 Q3 Velikomikhaylovka Rus. Fed.
176 F5 Velikonda Range hills India
19 Q4 Velikooktyabr'skiy Rus. Fed.
56 F6 Veliko Trojstvo Croatia
77 N7 Veliko Tŭrnovo Bulg.
191 D4 Veliköy Turkey
19 T2 Velikoye Vologodskaya Oblast' Rus. Fed.
19 W4 Velikoye Yaroslavskaya Oblast' Rus. Fed.
19 X6 Velikoye, Ozero l. Ryazanskaya Oblast' Rus. Fed.
19 T4 Velikoye, Ozero l. Tverskaya Oblast' Rus. Fed.
66 F4 Velilla de Cinca Spain
66 E5 Velilla de Ebro Spain
Velilla de Guardo Spain see Velilla del Río Carrión
63 K3 Velilla del Río Carrión Spain
65 L6 Velillas r. Spain
68 E3 Veli Lošinj Croatia
76 G8 Velimlje Crna Gora Serb. and Mont.
43 E6 Vélines France
88 B3 Vélingara Kolda Senegal
88 B3 Vélingara Louga Senegal
77 M8 Velingrad Bulg.
73 J2 Velino r. Italy
73 K3 Velino, Monte mt. Italy
18 G6 Veliuona Lith.
19 O6 Velizh Rus. Fed.
56 F2 Velká Bíteš Czech Rep.
56 D1 Velká Dobrá Czech Rep.
57 K2 Veľká Domaša, Vodná nádrž resr Slovakia
57 H3 Veľká Fatra mts Slovakia
57 I3 Veľká Fatra park Slovakia
56 G2 Velká Haná r. Czech Rep.
53 N2 Velká Hleďsebe Czech Rep.
57 G3 Velká Javořina hill Czech Rep./Slovakia
57 K2 Veľká Javorina mt. Slovakia
57 H3 Veľká Lehota Slovakia
57 H2 Veľká Lúka mt. Slovakia
57 I3 Veľká nad Ipľom Slovakia
57 H2 Velká Polom Czech Rep.
Veľká Rača mt. Pol./Slovakia see Wielka Racza
56 F3 Velké Bílovice Czech Rep.
51 J9 Velké Březno Czech Rep.
57 L3 Veľké Kapušany Slovakia
57 H2 Velké Karlovice Czech Rep.
59 P2 Veľké Leváre Slovakia
56 G1 Velké Losiny Czech Rep.
57 H3 Veľké Lovce Slovakia
57 H4 Veľké Ludince Slovakia
56 F2 Velké Meziříčí Czech Rep.
56 F3 Velké Němčice Czech Rep.
56 F3 Velké Pavlovice Czech Rep.
57 G3 Veľké Rípňany Slovakia
57 L3 Veľké Trakany Slovakia
57 H3 Veľké Uherce Slovakia
18 E1 Velkua Fin.
57 J3 Veľký Blh Slovakia
57 H3 Veľký Ďur Slovakia
57 H2 Veľký Javorník mt. Slovakia
57 I2 Veľký Kriváň mt. Slovakia
57 I3 Veľký Krtíš Slovakia
57 H3 Veľký Kýr Slovakia
57 G3 Velký Lopeník hill Czech Rep.
57 G4 Veľký Meder Slovakia
57 K2 Veľký Šariš Slovakia
57 H3 Veľký Tribeč hill Slovakia
56 G2 Velký Týnec Czech Rep.
56 B2 Velký Zvon hill Czech Rep.
59 J6 Vellach r. Austria
200 □6 Vella Gulf sea chan. New Georgia Is Solomon Is
48 K4 Vellahn Ger.
200 □6 Vella Lavella i. New Georgia Is Solomon Is
176 F7 Vellar r. India
52 H3 Vellberg Ger.
62 E4 Velle, Embalse de resr Spain
73 J4 Velletri Italy
40 J2 Vellevans France
40 H1 Vellexon-Queutrey-et-Vaudey France
22 J6 Vellinge Sweden
63 O8 Vellisca Spain
49 I8 Vellmar Ger.
176 F6 Vellore Tamil Nadu India
66 F2 Vellos r. Spain
193 K3 Vel'mo r. Rus. Fed.
78 D5 Velo Greece
78 E6 Velopoula i. Greece
37 J4 Velosnes France
45 H7 Velp r. Belgium
44 I5 Velp Neth.
49 K6 Velpke Ger.
14 H3 Vel'sk Rus. Fed.
14 J1 Vel't Rus. Fed.
50 H5 Velten Ger.
49 K6 Veltheim (Ohe) Ger.
56 D1 Veltrusy Czech Rep.
71 L2 Velturno Italy
44 H4 Veluwe reg. Neth.
44 I4 Veluwemeer l. Neth.
44 I4 Veluwezoom, Nationaal Park nat. park Neth.
120 E1 Velva ND U.S.A.
56 D1 Velvary Czech Rep.
78 D2 Velvendos Greece
19 P4 Vel'ye, Ozero l. Rus. Fed.
17 L4 Velyka Andrusivka Ukr.
17 P4 Velyka Babka Ukr.
17 M4 Velyka Bahachka Ukr.
17 N6 Velyka Bilozerka Ukr.
17 N6 Velyka Bilozerka r. Ukr.
17 L4 Velyka Burimka Ukr.
16 J3 Velyka Dymerka Ukr.
55 L6 Velyka Horozhanna Ukr.
16 H5 Velyka Kisnytsya Ukr.
17 P4 Velyka Komyshuvakha Ukr.
57 M3 Velyka Kopanya Ukr.
17 K7 Velyka Korenykha Ukr.
17 M6 Velyka Kostromka Ukr.
17 M6 Velyka Lepetykha Ukr.
16 I6 Velyka Mykhaylivka Ukr.
17 P6 Velyka Novosilka Ukr.
17 M6 Velyka Oleksandrivka Ukr.
17 O3 Velyka Pysarivka Ukr.
17 N4 Velyka Rublivka Ukr.
17 L5 Velyka Severynka Ukr.
16 G3 Velyka Tsvilya Ukr.
17 J5 Velyka Vys' r. Ukr.
17 K5 Velyka Vyska Ukr.
17 N6 Velyka Znam''yanka Ukr.
57 L3 Velyki Kom''yaty Ukr.
17 L7 Velyki Kopani Ukr.
16 H4 Velyki Korovyntsi Ukr.
17 M4 Velyki Krynky Ukr.
57 L3 Velyki Luchky Ukr.
16 D3 Velyki Mosty Ukr.
17 M3 Velyki Sorochyntsi Ukr.
17 L4 Velykiy Khutir Ukr.
16 J7 Velykiy Kuyal'nyk r. Ukr.
17 M2 Velykiy Sambir Ukr.
16 J7 Velykodolyns'ke Ukr.
17 O5 Velykomykhaylivka Dnipropetrovs'ka Oblast' Ukr.
17 P6 Velykomykhaylivka Dnipropetrovs'ka Oblast' Ukr.
17 O5 Velykooleksandrivka Ukr.
17 K6 Velykoserbulivka Ukr.
16 B5 Velykyy Bereznyy Ukr.
17 Q3 Velykyy Burluk Ukr.
16 D6 Velykyy Bychkiv Ukr.
Velykyy Tokmak Ukr. see Tokmak
14 K3 Vel'yu r. Rus. Fed.
176 F3 Vemalwada Andhra Prad. India
214 J8 Vema Seamount sea feature S. Atlantic Ocean
215 I5 Vema Trench sea feature Indian Ocean
176 E8 Vembanad Lake India
57 H5 Véménd Hungary
162 M5 Vemor'ye Sakhalin Rus. Fed.
176 F5 Vempalle Andhra Prad. India
22 I6 Ven i. Sweden
72 C3 Venaco Corse France
128 F3 Venado Mex.
126 □R12 Venado, Isla del i. Nic.
129 I5 Venados r. Mex.
147 G3 Venado Tuerto Arg.
73 M5 Venafro Italy
137 F3 Venamo r. Venez. alt. Wenamu (Guyana)
137 F3 Venamo, Cerro mt. Venez.
38 H8 Venansault France
40 E1 Venarey-les-Laumes France
70 D5 Venaria Italy
73 K2 Venarotta Italy
41 K7 Venasca Italy
41 K9 Vence France
137 F6 Vencedor Brazil
142 C5 Venceslau Bráz Brazil
18 H7 Venciūnai Lith.
71 L5 Venda, Monte hill Italy
64 A3 Venda do Pinheiro Port.
143 G4 Venda Nova Brazil
62 E5 Venda Nova, Barragem de resr Port.
41 D9 Vendargues France
64 B3 Vendas de Azeitão Port.
64 C3 Vendas Novas Port.
40 C4 Vendat France
42 B5 Vendays-Montalivet France
38 I8 Vendée dept France
42 C3 Vendée r. France
37 O6 Vendenheim France
39 L8 Vendeuvre-du-Poitou France
36 H7 Vendeuvre-sur-Barse France
75 I10 Vendicari, Isola i. Sicilia Italy
14 I3 Vendinga Rus. Fed.
64 D4 Vendinha Port.
39 N8 Vendœuvres France
36 B8 Vendôme France
64 G4 Vendoval r. Spain
16 G5 Vendychany Ukr.
136 C4 Venecia Col.
128 G2 Venegas Mex.
41 G9 Venelles France
43 I8 Vénès France
71 M5 Veneta, Laguna lag. Italy
Venetia Italy see Venezia
71 L5 Veneto admin. reg. Italy
19 V7 Venev Rus. Fed.
71 M5 Venezia Italy
71 N4 Venezia prov. Italy
Venezia, Golfo di g. Europe see Venice, Gulf of
137 E3 Venezuela country S. America
136 D2 Venezuela, Golfo de g. Venez.
214 E4 Venezuelan Basin sea feature S. Atlantic Ocean
176 C5 Vengurla Mahar. India
44 H3 Venhuizen Neth.
62 I6 Venialbo Spain
104 C4 Veniaminof Volcano AK U.S.A.
Venice Italy see Venezia
115 F12 Venice FL U.S.A.
121 K11 Venice LA U.S.A.
68 D3 Venice, Gulf of Europe
70 H3 Venina r. Italy
40 F5 Vénissieux France
36 F5 Venizel France
21 L6 Venjan Sweden
176 F6 Venkatagiri Andhra Prad. India
176 G3 Venkatapalem Orissa India
176 G3 Venkatapuram Andhra Prad. India
45 J6 Venlo Neth.
22 D3 Vennesla Norway
22 E5 Venø Bugt b. Denmark
73 P6 Venosa Italy
73 P5 Venosa r. Italy
71 I2 Venosta, Val val. Italy
36 G8 Venoy France
44 I5 Venray Neth.
58 C6 Vent Austria
201 □3 Vent, Îles du is Arch. de la Société Fr. Polynesia
18 F5 Venta r. Latvia/Lith.
18 F5 Venta Lith.
41 G9 Ventabren France
41 K9 Ventabren, Mont mt. France
63 L5 Venta de Baños Spain
65 K4 Venta del Charco Spain
67 C9 Venta del Moro Spain
65 M4 Venta de los Santos Spain
62 I1 Venta las Ranas Spain
142 B6 Ventania Brazil
62 G2 Venta Nueva Spain
65 L6 Ventas de Huelma Spain
65 K7 Ventas de Zafarraya Spain
41 H8 Ventavon France
97 L4 Ventersburg S. Africa
97 K2 Ventersdorp S. Africa
97 L2 Venterskroon S. Africa
97 J6 Venterstad S. Africa
41 D7 Venteuges France
72 C5 Ventilegne, Golfe de b. Corse France
70 D8 Ventimiglia Italy
72 C4 Ventiseri Corse France
145 C6 Ventisquero mt. Arg.
31 J6 Ventnor Isle of Wight, England U.K.
119 G6 Ventnor City NJ U.S.A.
73 K6 Ventotene, Isola i. Italy
41 G8 Ventoux, Mont mt. France
50 E3 Ventschow Ger.
18 E4 Ventspils Latvia
137 E3 Ventuari r. Venez.
124 M7 Ventura CA U.S.A.
201 □3a Vénus, Pointe pt Tahiti Fr. Polynesia
205 J8 Venus Bay Vic. Austr.
Venusia Italy see Venosa
128 D6 Venustiano Mex.
129 N9 Venustiano Carranza Chiapas Mex.
129 J5 Venustiano Carranza Puebla Mex.
127 I4 Venustiano Carranza, Presa resr Mex.
72 C3 Venzolasca Corse France
71 O3 Venzone Italy
56 F4 Vép Hungary
17 N3 Vepryk Ukr.
19 R1 Vepsovskaya Vozvyshennost' hills Rus. Fed.
144 E3 Vera Arg.
65 P6 Vera Spain
139 F6 Verá, Lago l. Para.
138 D2 Vera Cruz Amazonas Brazil
142 C5 Vera Cruz São Paulo Brazil
129 K6 Veracruz Mex.
Vera Cruz Mex. see Veracruz
129 J5 Veracruz state Mex.
64 D4 Vera Cruz Port.
118 E3 Vera Cruz PA U.S.A.
66 D2 Veral r. Spain
141 C9 Veranópolis Brazil
178 C9 Veraval Gujarat India
147 G2 Vera y Pintado Arg.
16 E3 Verba Rivnens'ka Oblast' Ukr.
16 D3 Verba Volyns'ka Oblast' Ukr.
70 F4 Verbania Italy
119 H1 Verbank NY U.S.A.
70 E3 Verbano-Cusio-Ossola prov. Italy
36 E5 Verberie France
73 P8 Verbicaro Italy
70 C3 Verbier Switz.
19 U5 Verbilki Rus. Fed.
17 L5 Verblyuzhka Ukr.
17 O6 Verbove Ukr.
16 E4 Verbovets' Ukr.
15 H5 Verbovskiy Rus. Fed.
17 N7 Verby Ukr.
70 G3 Verceia Italy
70 E5 Vercelli Italy
70 E5 Vercelli prov. Italy
40 I2 Vercel-Villedieu-le-Camp France
50 G3 Verchen Ger.
41 G7 Vercors reg. France
41 G7 Vercors, Parc Naturel Régional du nature res. France
59 J8 Verd Slovenia
19 X8 Verda r. Rus. Fed.
41 I8 Verdaches France
20 K5 Verdalsøra Norway
145 D6 Verde r. Arg.
142 B3 Verde r. Brazil
142 B3 Verde r. Brazil
142 B4 Verde r. Brazil
142 C3 Verde r. Brazil
142 D3 Verde r. Brazil
143 E4 Verde r. Brazil
140 E4 Verde r. Brazil
139 F3 Verde r. Brazil
139 G2 Verde r. Brazil
128 D5 Verde r. Aguascalientes/Jalisco Mex.
126 F4 Verde r. Chihuahua/Durango Mex.
129 I9 Verde r. Guerrero/Oaxaca Mex.
129 H4 Verde r. Mex.
129 J10 Verde r. Mex.
139 F5 Verde r. Para.
65 L7 Verde r. Spain
65 M6 Verde r. Spain
125 U8 Verde r. AZ U.S.A.
Verde, Cabo c. Senegal see Vert, Cap
147 F6 Verde, Península pen. Arg.
143 F1 Verde Grande r. Brazil
154 C5 Verde Island Passage Phil.
48 H5 Verden (Aller) Ger.
140 E5 Verde Pequeno r. Brazil
124 M2 Verdi NV U.S.A.
121 H8 Verdigris r. KS U.S.A.
78 C3 Verdikoussa Greece
142 B2 Verdinho r. Brazil
142 B3 Verdinho, Serra do mts Brazil
129 H2 Verdolaga Mex.
41 H9 Verdon r. France
41 I9 Verdon, Grand Canyon du gorge France
62 C4 Verdugo r. Spain
37 J5 Verdun France
43 G8 Verdun-sur-Garonne France
40 G3 Verdun-sur-le-Doubs France
74 E9 Verdura r. Sicilia Italy
55 L1 Verebiejai Lith.
97 L2 Vereeniging S. Africa
17 L4 Veremiyivka Ukr.
97 N1 Verena S. Africa
57 I4 Veresegyház Hungary
14 K4 Vereshchagino Rus. Fed.
17 K2 Veresoch Ukr.
19 T4 Verestovo, Ozero l. Rus. Fed.
19 T6 Vereya Rus. Fed.
43 H7 Verfeil Midi-Pyrénées France
43 H8 Verfeil Midi-Pyrénées France
88 B4 Verga, Cap c. Guinea
147 I4 Vergara Arg.
144 G4 Vergara Uru.
71 K7 Vergato Italy
37 M6 Vergaville France
96 I1 Vergeleë S. Africa
207 I8 Vergemont Creek watercourse Qld Austr.
117 L4 Vergennes VT U.S.A.
66 L3 Verges Spain
41 E9 Vergèze France
71 M8 Verghereto Italy
36 G8 Vergigny France
78 D2 Vergina Greece
72 B3 Vergio, Col de pass France
41 C6 Vergongheon France
42 F5 Vergt France
17 L4 Verhuny Cherkas'ka Oblast' Ukr.
17 M4 Verhuny Poltavs'ka Oblast' Ukr.
Véria Greece see Veroia
19 V5 Verigino Rus. Fed.
62 F5 Verín Spain
52 G5 Veringenstadt Ger.
Verin T'alin Armenia see T'alin
18 K3 Veriora Estonia
142 C3 Veríssimo Brazil
97 K4 Verkeerdevlei S. Africa
17 N5 Verkhivtseve Ukr.
182 G1 Verkhne-Avzyan Rus. Fed.
17 Q9 Verkhnebakanskiy Rus. Fed.
183 T2 Verkhne-berezovskiy Kazakh.
Verkhnedneprovsk Ukr. see Verkhn'odniprovs'k
19 Q7 Verkhnedneprovskiy Rus. Fed.
192 J3 Verkhneimbatsk Rus. Fed.
14 L2 Verkhnekolvinsk Rus. Fed.
19 S6 Verkhneruzskoye Vodokhranilishche resr Rus. Fed.
14 I4 Verkhnespasskoye Rus. Fed.
20 U2 Verkhnetulomskiy Rus. Fed.
20 U2 Verkhnetulomskoye Vodokhranilishche resr Rus. Fed.
17 R2 Verkhneturovo Rus. Fed.
182 H1 Verkhneural'sk Rus. Fed.
193 N3 Verkhnevilyuysk Rus. Fed.
19 P4 Verkhnevolzhskoye Vodokhranilishche resr Rus. Fed.
14 K5 Verkhneyarkeyevo Rus. Fed.
20 U4 Verkhneye Kuyto, Ozero l. Rus. Fed.
162 F1 Verkhnezeysk Rus. Fed.
193 Q3 Verkhniy At-Uryakh Rus. Fed.
191 D2 Verkhniy Baksan Rus. Fed.
15 I6 Verkhniy Baskunchak Rus. Fed.
17 P4 Verkhniy Byshkyn Ukr.
191 E2 Verkhniy Chegem Rus. Fed.
191 F2 Verkhniye Achaluki Rus. Fed.
19 O6 Verkhniye Koshevichi Rus. Fed.
19 O6 Verkhniye Mokhovichi Rus. Fed.
191 F3 Verkhniy Fiagdon Rus. Fed.
Verkhniy Karabulag Georgia see Zemo Qarabulakhi
19 V9 Verkhniy Lomovets Rus. Fed.
15 H6 Verkhniy Mamon Rus. Fed.
17 N6 Verkhniy Rohachyk Ukr.
14 J1 Verkhniy Shar Rus. Fed.
169 K1 Verkhniy Shergol'dzhin Rus. Fed.
14 K4 Verkhniy Tatyshly Rus. Fed.
17 P6 Verkhniytokmak Ukr.
169 M2 Verkhniy Ul'khun Rus. Fed.
14 F2 Verkhniy Vyalozerskiy Rus. Fed.
17 N5 Verkhn'odniprovs'k Ukr.
16 J5 Verkhnyachka Ukr.
55 M6 Verkhnya Lypytsya Ukr.
17 N3 Verkhnya Syrovatka Ukr.
17 O5 Verkhnya Tersa r. Ukr.
16 C5 Verkhnya Vysots'ke Ukr.
57 L3 Verkhnya Vyznytsya Ukr.
191 E2 Verkhnyaya Balkariya Rus. Fed.
57 L2 Verkhnya Yablun'ka Ukr.
17 Q2 Verkhnyaya Grayvoronka Rus. Fed.
14 M2 Verkhnyaya Inta Rus. Fed.
15 G6 Verkhnyaya Khava Rus. Fed.
191 D2 Verkhnyaya Mara Rus. Fed.
193 R3 Verkhnyaya Pakhachi Rus. Fed.
17 T2 Verkhnyaya Plavitsa Rus. Fed.
193 K2 Verkhnyaya Taymyra r. Rus. Fed.
191 C2 Verkhnyaya Teberda Rus. Fed.
17 T2 Verkhnyaya Tishanka Rus. Fed.
17 T2 Verkhnyaya Toyda Rus. Fed.
14 I3 Verkhnyaya Toyma Rus. Fed.
19 U4 Verkhnyaya Troitsa Rus. Fed.
16 C4 Verkhnye Syn'ovydne Ukr.
14 J4 Verkhoramen'ye Rus. Fed.
17 M9 Verkhorichchya Ukr.
14 J4 Verkhoshizhem'ye Rus. Fed.
17 N3 Verkhosulka Ukr.
19 Z1 Verkhovazh'ye Rus. Fed.
Verkhovina Ukr. see Verkhovyna
19 U9 Verkhov'ye Rus. Fed.
16 D5 Verkhovyna Ukr.
193 N2 Verkhoyanskiy Khrebet mts Rus. Fed.
183 T2 Verkhuba Kazakh.
55 N4 Verkhy Ukr.
18 H7 Verknė r. Lith.
14 I3 Verkola Rus. Fed.
97 N3 Verkykerskop S. Africa
49 G7 Verl Ger.
45 H7 Verlaine Belgium
96 E8 Verlatekloof pass S. Africa
20 □ Verlegenhuken pt Svalbard
20 J5 Verma Norway
96 F10 Vermaaklikheid S. Africa
36 F4 Vermand France
36 F4 Vermandois reg. France
142 B5 Vermelha, Serra hills Brazil
140 C3 Vermelho r. Brazil
140 D3 Vermelho r. Brazil
139 H3 Vermelho r. Brazil
36 G8 Vermenton France
77 J5 Vermeș Romania
71 J3 Vermiglio Italy
107 I4 Vermilion Alta Can.
116 C7 Vermilion OH U.S.A.
110 E8 Vermilion r. IL U.S.A.
121 J11 Vermilion Bay LA U.S.A.
125 T5 Vermilion Cliffs esc. AZ U.S.A.
125 T4 Vermilion Cliffs esc. UT U.S.A.
110 B2 Vermilion Lake MN U.S.A.
110 B2 Vermilion Range hills MN U.S.A.
120 G4 Vermillion SD U.S.A.
120 G4 Vermillion r. SD U.S.A.
120 G4 Vermillion, East Fork r. SD U.S.A.
107 M5 Vermillion Bay Ont. Can.
114 K2 Vermillon r. Que. Can.
78 C2 Vermio mt. Greece
62 G7 Vermiosa Port.
62 C9 Vermoil Port.
131 □3 Vermont St Vincent
117 M4 Vermont state U.S.A.
212 T2 Vernadsky research stn Antarctica
71 J2 Vernago, Lago di l. Italy
43 H10 Vernajoul France
122 J6 Vernal UT U.S.A.
70 D7 Vernante Italy
39 L7 Vernantes France
70 C3 Vernayaz Switz.
39 J6 Vern-d'Anjou France
108 D4 Verner Ont. Can.
56 D1 Verneřice Czech Rep.
43 G9 Vernet France
43 I10 Vernet-les-Bains France
39 M4 Verneuil-sur-Avre France
42 G4 Verneuil-sur-Vienne France
96 F5 Verneuk Pan salt pan S. Africa
70 A3 Vernier Switz.
71 K7 Vernio Italy
43 H9 Verniolle France
78 C2 Verno mt. Greece
75 O3 Vernole Italy
106 G5 Vernon B.C. Can.
36 B5 Vernon France
121 K9 Vernon AL U.S.A.
114 E6 Vernon IN U.S.A.
119 G2 Vernon NJ U.S.A.
121 F8 Vernon TX U.S.A.
125 T1 Vernon UT U.S.A.
209 E8 Vernon, Mount hill W.A. Austr.
206 C2 Vernon Islands N.T. Austr.
36 B6 Vernouillet France
41 F7 Vernoux-en-Vivarais France
118 F3 Vernoy NJ U.S.A.
162 F3 Vernoye Rus. Fed.
38 H5 Vern-sur-Seiche France
37 L5 Verny France
72 B3 Vero Corse France
66 F4 Vero r. Spain
115 G12 Vero Beach FL U.S.A.
57 I4 Verőcemaros Hungary
78 D2 Veroia Greece
70 I5 Verolanuova Italy
73 K4 Veroli Italy
36 F7 Véron France
71 J5 Verona Italy
71 K5 Verona prov. Italy
116 F10 Verona VA U.S.A.
110 E7 Verona WI U.S.A.
147 I4 Verónica Arg.
40 E4 Verosvres France
57 J4 Verpelét Hungary
119 H2 Verplanck NY U.S.A.
204 F5 Verran S.A. Austr.
70 D4 Verres Italy
42 F3 Verrières France
73 M4 Verrino r. Italy
70 E6 Versa r. Italy
70 G5 Versa r. Italy
71 O4 Versa r. Italy
36 D6 Versailles France
114 E6 Versailles IN U.S.A.
114 E6 Versailles KY U.S.A.
120 I6 Versailles MO U.S.A.
116 A8 Versailles OH U.S.A.
138 E3 Versalles Bol.
Versec Vojvodina, Srbija Serb. and Mont. see Vršac
18 H7 Verseka r. Lith.
40 H3 Vers-en-Montage France
17 L4 Vershatsi Ukr.
49 F6 Versmold Ger.
70 A3 Versoix Switz.
41 B9 Versols-et-Lapeyre France
39 K3 Verson France
41 F9 Vers-Pont-du-Gard France
43 C7 Vert France
43 G6 Vert r. France
88 A3 Vert, Cap c. Senegal
109 G3 Vert, Île i. Que. Can.
40 C5 Vertaizon France
42 E5 Verteillac France
140 C4 Vertentes r. Brazil
57 H4 Vértesacsa Hungary
57 H4 Vértesboglár Hungary
57 H4 Vertesi park Hungary
43 E7 Verteuil-d'Agenais France
42 E4 Verteuil-sur-Charente France
42 C5 Vertheuil France
130 D3 Vertientes Cuba
17 K2 Vertiyivka Ukr.
147 F4 Vertiz Arg.
36 C3 Verton France
71 J2 Vertona, Cima mt. Italy
38 I7 Vertou France
36 H6 Vertus France
71 M8 Verucchio Italy
97 P5 Verulam S. Africa
Verulamium Hertfordshire, England U.K. see St Albans
45 I7 Verviers Belgium
36 G4 Vervins France
58 A5 Verwallgruppe mts Austria
107 J5 Verwood Sask. Can.
31 I6 Verwood Dorset, England U.K.
Veryína Greece see Vergina
39 J6 Verzée r. France
36 H5 Verzenay France
75 L5 Verzino Italy
70 C6 Verzuolo Italy
36 H5 Verzy France
20 S5 Vesanto Fin.
72 C3 Vescovato Corse France
70 I5 Vescovato Italy
45 I7 Vesdre r. Belgium
56 G5 Vése Hungary
192 G4 Veselaya, Gora mt. Rus. Fed.
17 N6 Vesele Ukr.
19 T6 Veselevo Rus. Fed.
77 N7 Veselina r. Bulg.
56 D2 Veselí nad Lužnicí Czech Rep.
56 G3 Veselí nad Moravou Czech Rep.
17 L6 Veselivka Kirovohrads'ka Oblast' Ukr.
16 H3 Veselivka Zhytomyrs'ka Oblast' Ukr.
17 R6 Veselo-Voznesenka Rus. Fed.
15 H7 Veselovskoye Vodokhranilishche resr Rus. Fed.
183 S2 Veseloyarsk Rus. Fed.
17 R3 Veseloye Rus. Fed.
17 K3 Veselynivka Ukr.
17 K6 Veselynove Ukr.
15 H7 Veselyy Rus. Fed.
182 K1 Veselyy Podol Kazakh.
36 B6 Vesgre r. France
15 H6 Veshenskaya Rus. Fed.
14 H2 Veshkoma Rus. Fed.
21 R6 Vesijärvi l. Fin.
70 E6 Vesime Italy
36 F5 Vesle r. France
14 K3 Veslyana r. Rus. Fed.
40 I1 Vesoul France
70 F5 Vespolate Italy
162 I7 Vesselyy Yar Rus. Fed.
45 H6 Vessem Neth.
22 D3 Vest-Agder county Norway
20 L2 Vesterålen is Norway
20 L2 Vesterålsfjorden sea chan. Norway
48 L1 Vesterby Denmark
50 E1 Vestermark Denmark
48 I1 Vester Sottrup Denmark
20 S1 Vestertana Norway
20 □B1 Vestfirðir constituency Iceland
22 E2 Vestfjorddalen val. Norway
20 L3 Vestfjorden sea chan. Norway
22 G2 Vestfold county Norway
213 F2 Vestfold Hills Antarctica
20 □ Vestfonna ice cap Svalbard
142 B4 Véstia Brazil
24 D1 Vestmanna Faroe Is
20 □C2 Vestmannaeyjar is Iceland
20 I5 Vestnes Norway
70 I4 Vestone Italy
20 T1 Vestre Jakobselv Norway
22 H6 Vestsjælland county Denmark
212 X2 Veststraumen Glacier Antarctica
20 □B1 Vesturland constituency Iceland
20 L2 Vestvågøy i. Norway
41 K9 Vésubie r. France
73 M6 Vesuvio vol. Italy
73 M6 Vesuvio, Parco Nazionale del nat. park Italy
Vesuvius vol. Italy see Vesuvio
19 U3 Ves'yegonsk Rus. Fed.
56 G4 Veszkény Hungary
57 G4 Veszprém Hungary
56 G4 Veszprém county Hungary
57 G4 Veszprémvarsány Hungary
57 K5 Vésztő Hungary
97 J3 Vet r. S. Africa
201 □1 Vetauua i. Fiji
20 Q5 Veteli Fin.
107 I4 Veteran Alta Can.
76 H5 Veternik Vojvodina, Srbija Serb. and Mont.
36 C5 Vétheuil France
57 L4 Vetiș Romania
23 L4 Vetlanda Sweden
21 I6 Vetlefjorden Norway
14 I4 Vetluga Rus. Fed.
14 I4 Vetluga r. Rus. Fed.
192 F4 Vetluzhskiy Kostromskaya Oblast' Rus. Fed.
14 I4 Vetluzhskiy Nizhegorodskaya Oblast' Rus. Fed.
16 E2 Vetly Ukr.
19 Q8 Vet'ma r. Rus. Fed.
77 O7 Vetovo Bulg.
72 I3 Vetralla Italy
77 P8 Vetren Bulg.
77 Q4 Vetrișoaia Romania
56 D3 Větřní Czech Rep.
51 J7 Vetschau Ger.
20 S2 Vetsikko Fin.

Vettasjärvi to Villetta Barrea

356

20 P3 **Vettasjärvi** Sweden
49 D9 **Vettelschoss** Ger.
70 I7 **Vetto** Italy
73 K2 **Vettore, Monte** mt. Italy
39 L7 **Veude** r. France
39 M2 **Veules-les-Roses** France
39 M2 **Veulettes-sur-Mer** France
45 C6 **Veurne** Belgium
114 E6 **Vevay** IN U.S.A.
92 B3 **Veveno** r. Sudan
70 B3 **Vevey** Switz.
70 C3 **Vex** Switz.
36 C5 **Vexin Français** reg. France
36 B5 **Vexin Normand** reg. France
15 G6 **Veydelevka** Rus. Fed.
40 F4 **Veyle** r. France
41 H7 **Veynes** France
40 D3 **Veynon** r. France
125 S4 **Veyo** UT U.S.A.
40 C5 **Veyre-Monton** France
40 I5 **Veyrier-du-Lac** France
184 C6 **Veys** Iran
18 E6 **Vėžaičiai** Lith.
40 D2 **Vézelay** France
37 L7 **Vézelise** France
41 E8 **Vézénobres** France
42 F6 **Vézère** r. France
14 K3 **Vezhayu** Rus. Fed.
77 M8 **Vezhen** mt. Bulg.
39 J7 **Vezins** France
41 B8 **Vézins-de-Lévézou** France
79 K2 **Vezirhan** Turkey
188 G3 **Vezirköprü** Turkey
37 L6 **Vezouze** r. France
70 I3 **Vezza d'Oglio** Italy
58 E7 **Vezzana, Cima della** mt. Italy
72 C3 **Vezzani** Corse France
71 K3 **Vezzano** Italy
95 F4 **Vhembe Dongola National Park** S. Africa
88 C5 **Via** r. Liberia
138 C4 **Viacha** Bol.
71 J6 **Viadana** Italy
62 E5 **Viade de Baixo** Port.
41 K9 **Vial, Mont** mt. France
41 B8 **Viala du Tarn** France
Vialar Alg. see **Tissemsilt**
41 D8 **Vialas** France
147 G2 **Viale** Arg.
141 C9 **Viamao** Brazil
147 F3 **Viamonte** Córdoba Arg.
145 D9 **Viamonte** Tierra del Fuego Arg.
91 B7 **Viana** Angola
143 G4 **Viana** Espírito Santo Brazil
140 D2 **Viana** Maranhão Brazil
63 P3 **Viana** Spain
63 K5 **Viana de Cega** Spain
Viana del Bollo Spain see **Viana do Bolo**
64 D4 **Viana do Alentejo** Port.
62 F4 **Viana do Bolo** Spain
62 C5 **Viana do Castelo** Port.
62 D5 **Viana do Castelo** admin. dist. Port.
45 J9 **Vianden** Lux.
41 B9 **Viane** France
44 H5 **Vianen** Neth.
158 F6 **Viangchan** Laos
158 E4 **Viangphoukha** Laos
43 E7 **Vianne** France
62 D2 **Viaño Pequeno** Spain
142 C2 **Vianópolis** Brazil
65 O3 **Vianos** Spain
64 H5 **Viar** r. Spain
70 I8 **Viareggio** Italy
36 D5 **Viarmes** France
41 C10 **Vias** France
62 C6 **Viatodos** Port.
65 O7 **Viator** Spain
43 H7 **Viaur** r. France
43 I6 **Viazac** France
73 P7 **Vibonati** Italy
65 K5 **Víboras** r. Spain
22 F5 **Viborg** Denmark
22 F5 **Viborg** county Denmark
Viborg Rus. Fed. see **Vyborg**
75 K6 **Vibo Valentia** Italy
75 K6 **Vibo Valentia** prov. Italy
39 M5 **Vibraye** France
66 J4 **Vic** Spain
126 D4 **Vicam** Mex.
65 N7 **Vícar** Spain
74 F8 **Vicari** Sicilia Italy
28 C7 **Vicarstown** Rep. of Ireland
71 K8 **Vicchio** Italy
43 H10 **Vicdessos** France
43 H10 **Vicdessos** r. France
62 E1 **Vicedo** Spain
43 E9 **Vic-en-Bigorre** France
124 N8 **Vicente, Point** CA U.S.A.
147 H4 **Vicente Casares** Arg.
146 D4 **Vicente Dupuy** Arg.
126 A2 **Vicente Guerrero** Baja California Mex.
128 D2 **Vicente Guerrero** Durango Mex.
129 N7 **Vicente Guerrero** Tabasco Mex.
129 I6 **Vicente Guerrero** Tlaxcala Mex.
129 K7 **Vicente y Camalote** Mex.
71 L4 **Vicenza** Italy
71 K4 **Vicenza** prov. Italy
43 E8 **Vic-Fezensac** France
Vich Spain see **Vic**
136 D3 **Vichada** dept Col.
136 E3 **Vichada** r. Col.
144 G3 **Vichadero** Uru.
129 I3 **Vichinchijol Nuevo** Mex.
14 H4 **Vichuga** Rus. Fed.
146 A4 **Vichuquén** Chile
40 C4 **Vichy** France
121 F7 **Vici** OK U.S.A.
66 E3 **Vicién** Spain
29 K5 **Vickerstown** Cumbria, England U.K.
125 S8 **Vicksburg** AZ U.S.A.
110 I7 **Vicksburg** MI U.S.A.
121 J9 **Vicksburg** MS U.S.A.
118 B3 **Vicksburg** PA U.S.A.
40 C5 **Vic-le-Comte** France
72 B3 **Vico** Corse France
72 I3 **Vico, Lago di** l. Italy
73 P4 **Vico del Gargano** Italy
73 M6 **Vico Equense** Italy
70 D7 **Vicoforte** Italy
73 K4 **Vico nel Lazio** Italy
63 Q6 **Vicort, Sierra de** mts Spain
140 F4 **Viçosa** Alagoas Brazil
143 F4 **Viçosa** Minas Gerais Brazil
73 J3 **Vicovaro** Italy
77 N3 **Vicovu de Sus** Romania
39 P8 **Vicq-Exemplet** France
42 G4 **Vicq-sur-Breuilh** France
36 F5 **Vic-sur-Aisne** France
41 B7 **Vic-sur-Cère** France
37 M6 **Vic-sur-Seille** France
213 C2 **Victor, Mount** Antarctica
48 D4 **Victorbur (Südbrookmerland)** Ger.
204 G6 **Victor Harbor** S.A. Austr.
147 G3 **Victoria** Arg.
147 H3 **Victoria** r. Arg.
206 C3 **Victoria** r. N.T. Austr.
205 J7 **Victoria** state Austr.
106 F5 **Victoria** B.C. Can.
146 A6 **Victoria** Araucanía Chile
145 C9 **Victoria** Magallanes y Antártica Chilena Chile
131 □6 **Victoria** Grenada
126 □P10 **Victoria** Hond.
75 □ **Victoria** Gozo Malta
128 G4 **Victoria** Mex.
154 C4 **Victoria** Luzon Phil.
77 P6 **Victoria** Brăila Romania
77 M5 **Victoria** Brașov Romania
99 □2b **Victoria** Mahé Seychelles
131 □7 **Victoria** county Trin. and Tob.
121 G11 **Victoria** TX U.S.A.
116 G12 **Victoria** VA U.S.A.
145 B7 **Victoria, Isla** i. Chile
92 B4 **Victoria, Lake** Africa
204 H5 **Victoria, Lake** N.S.W. Austr.
Victoria, Mount Viti Levu Fiji see **Tomanivi**
158 A4 **Victoria, Mount** Myanmar
203 G9 **Victoria, Mount** South I. N.Z.
153 K8 **Victoria, Mount** P.N.G.
105 K2 **Victoria and Albert Mountains** Nunavut Can.
91 E9 **Victoria Falls** Zambia/Zimbabwe
94 E3 **Victoria Falls** Zimbabwe
94 E3 **Victoria Falls National Park** Zimbabwe
105 N1 **Victoria Fjord** inlet Greenland
203 G8 **Victoria Forest Park** nature res. South I. N.Z.
99 □2b **Victoria Harbour** b. Mahé Seychelles
104 H2 **Victoria Island** N.W.T./Nunavut Can.
109 J3 **Victoria Lake** Nfld and Lab. Can.
213 K2 **Victoria Land** coastal area Antarctica
171 □J7 **Victoria Peak** hill H.K. China
204 □3 **Victoria Point** S. Pacific Ocean
203 G9 **Victoria Range** mts South I. N.Z.
206 C3 **Victoria River** N.T. Austr.
206 C4 **Victoria River Downs** N.T. Austr.
202 H2 **Victoria Valley** North I. N.Z.
109 G4 **Victoriaville** Que. Can.
96 H7 **Victoria West** S. Africa
146 E5 **Victorica** Arg.
136 E4 **Victorino** Venez.
128 E3 **Víctor Rosales** Mex.
124 O7 **Victorville** CA U.S.A.
57 K6 **Victor Vlad Delamarina** Romania
116 I5 **Victory** NY U.S.A.
206 D8 **Victory Downs** N.T. Austr.
146 B2 **Vicuña** Chile
146 E3 **Vicuña Mackenna** Arg.
62 E5 **Vidago** Port.
64 A2 **Vidais** Port.
145 B8 **Vidal, Isla** i. Chile
121 J10 **Vidalia** LA U.S.A.
125 R7 **Vidal Junction** CA U.S.A.
18 G9 **Vidamlya** Belarus
66 C2 **Vidángoz** Spain
41 I10 **Vidauban** France
72 B6 **Viddalba** Sardegna Italy
22 E5 **Videbæk** Denmark
141 C8 **Videira** Brazil
147 G2 **Videla** Arg.
77 N6 **Videle** Romania
59 N6 **Videm** Gornja Radgona Slovenia
59 K8 **Videm** Grosuplje Slovenia
62 F7 **Videmonte** Port.
77 K8 **Viden** mt. Bulg.
Viderø i. Faroe Is see **Viðoy**
55 K1 **Vidgiriu kalnas** hill Lith.
64 D4 **Vidigueira** Port.
77 N8 **Vidima** r. Bulg.
77 K7 **Vidin** Bulg.
57 I3 **Vidiná** Slovakia
62 H1 **Vidio, Cabo** c. Spain
178 F8 **Vidisha** Madh. Prad. India
26 □N2 **Vidlin** Shetland, Scotland U.K.
19 P1 **Vidlitsa** Rus. Fed.
22 D2 **Vidmyr** nature res. Norway
56 G1 **Vidnava** Czech Rep.
19 U6 **Vidnoye** Rus. Fed.
23 J4 **Vidöstern** l. Sweden
41 E9 **Vidourle** r. France
68 F4 **Vidova Gora** hill Croatia
59 N7 **Vidovec** Croatia
24 D1 **Viðoy** i. Faroe Is
57 L5 **Vidra** Romania
Vidreras Spain see **Vidrieres**
66 K4 **Vidrieres** Spain
20 P4 **Vidsel** Sweden
18 F6 **Viduklė** Lith.
68 G4 **Viduša** mts Bos.-Herz.
18 I5 **Vidzemes centrālā augstiene** hills Latvia
18 J6 **Vidzy** Belarus
38 H8 **Vie** r. France
39 K3 **Vie** r. France
53 N3 **Viechtach** Ger.
55 M1 **Viečiūnai** Lith.
97 M7 **Viedgesville** S. Africa
145 E6 **Viedma** Arg.
145 B8 **Viedma, Lago** l. Arg.
59 K2 **Viehberg** mt. Austria
38 I8 **Vieillevigne** France
62 C9 **Vieira de Leiria** Port.
62 D5 **Vieira do Minho** Port.
128 C2 **Viejo** r. Mex.
126 C2 **Viejo, Cerro** mt. Mex.
18 F5 **Viekšniai** Lith.
50 D4 **Vielank** Ger.
66 G2 **Vielha** Spain
43 D8 **Viella** France
Viella Spain see **Vielha**
43 E10 **Vielle-Aure** France
41 C6 **Vielle-Brioude** France
43 B8 **Vielle-St-Girons** France
43 I8 **Vielmur-sur-Agout** France
45 I8 **Vielsalm** Belgium
40 G2 **Vielverge** France
49 K7 **Vienenburg** Ger.
Vienna Austria see **Wien**
115 F9 **Vienna** GA U.S.A.
121 K7 **Vienna** IL U.S.A.
117 J10 **Vienna** MD U.S.A.
120 J6 **Vienna** MO U.S.A.
118 F3 **Vienna** NJ U.S.A.
116 D9 **Vienna** WV U.S.A.
40 F5 **Vienne** France
39 L8 **Vienne** dept France
42 E1 **Vienne** r. France
37 I5 **Vienne-le-Château** France
Vientiane Laos see **Viangchan**
146 B5 **Viento, Cordillera del** mts Arg.
65 I7 **Viento, Puerto del** pass Spain
131 □1 **Vieques** i. Puerto Rico
37 I6 **Vière** r. France
50 J3 **Viereck** Ger.
20 S5 **Vieremä** Fin.
53 J2 **Viereth-Trunstadt** Ger.
53 K5 **Vierkirchen** Ger.
44 I5 **Vierlingsbeek** Neth.
49 K9 **Viernau** Ger.
52 F2 **Viernheim** Ger.
50 J4 **Vierraden** Ger.
49 B8 **Viersen** Ger.
39 J3 **Vierville-sur-Mer** France
70 E1 **Vierwaldstätter See** l. Switz.
42 I1 **Vierzon** France
126 H5 **Viesca** Mex.
50 F4 **Viesecke** Ger.
51 D9 **Vieselbach** Ger.
18 I5 **Viesīte** Latvia
73 Q4 **Vieste** Italy
18 F6 **Viešvilės rezervatas** nature res. Lith.
20 O3 **Vietas** Sweden
Viet Nam country Asia see **Vietnam**
158 G5 **Vietnam** country Asia
158 G3 **Viêt Quang** Vietnam
73 P6 **Vietri di Potenza** Italy
73 N6 **Vietri sul Mare** Italy
158 G4 **Viêt Tri** Vietnam
43 B8 **Vieux-Boucau-les-Bains** France
131 □2 **Vieux-Bourg** Guadeloupe
41 I7 **Vieux Chaillol** mt. France
40 J1 **Vieux-Charmont** France
108 E2 **Vieux Comptoir, Lac du** l. Que. Can.
36 G3 **Vieux-Condé** France
109 J3 **Vieux-Fort** Que. Can.
131 □2 **Vieux-Fort** Guadeloupe
131 □3 **Vieux Fort** St Lucia
131 □2 **Vieux-Fort, Pointe de** pt Guadeloupe
131 □2 **Vieux-Habitants** Guadeloupe
109 I3 **Vieux Poste, Pointe du** pt Que. Can.
18 H7 **Vievis** Lith.
28 I2 **Viewpark** North Lanarkshire, Scotland U.K.
147 I4 **Vieytes** Arg.
41 H6 **Vif** France
18 H3 **Vigala** r. Estonia
154 C3 **Vigan** Luzon Phil.
71 K6 **Vigarano Mainarda** Italy
71 J5 **Vigasio** Italy
58 H4 **Vigaun** Austria
42 H5 **Vigeois** France
70 F5 **Vigevano** Italy
72 B4 **Viggianello** Corse France
73 Q8 **Viggianello** Italy
73 P7 **Viggiano** Italy
70 F4 **Viggiù** Italy
140 C2 **Vigia** Brazil
64 C5 **Vigia** hill Port.
64 D3 **Vigia, Barragem da** resr Port.
145 D8 **Vigía, Cabo** c. Arg.
127 P8 **Vigía Chico** Mex.
57 I3 **Vígľaš** Slovakia
73 K4 **Viglio, Monte** mt. Italy
36 D3 **Vignacourt** France
70 E5 **Vignale Monferrato** Italy
73 I3 **Vignanello** Italy
43 D10 **Vignemale** mt. France
37 K6 **Vigneulles-lès-Hattonchâtel** France
40 H3 **Vignoble** reg. France
71 K7 **Vignola** Italy
72 C5 **Vignola** r. Italy
72 C5 **Vignola Mare l'Agnata** Sardegna Italy
37 J7 **Vignory** France
36 C5 **Vigny** France
62 C4 **Vigo** Spain
62 C4 **Vigo, Ría de** est. Spain
71 M3 **Vigo di Cadore** Italy
58 E7 **Vigo di Fassa** Italy
70 C6 **Vigone** Italy
71 L5 **Vigonza** Italy
71 J3 **Vigo Rendena** Italy
208 E7 **Vigors, Mount** W.A. Austr.
22 E4 **Vigsø Bugt** b. Denmark
70 F6 **Viguzzolo** Italy
37 L5 **Vigy** France
20 R4 **Vihanti** Fin.
185 O6 **Vihari** Pak.
42 C1 **Vihiers** France
57 L3 **Vihorlat** mt. Slovakia
57 L3 **Vihorlat** park Slovakia
57 K3 **Vihorlatské vrchy** mts Slovakia
18 G2 **Vihterpalu** r. Estonia
21 R6 **Vihti** Fin.
21 Q6 **Viiala** Fin.
57 L4 **Viile Satu Mare** Romania
Viipuri Rus. Fed. see **Vyborg**
20 S3 **Viirinkylä** Fin.
57 L4 **Viișoara** Romania
20 R5 **Viitasaari** Fin.
18 K4 **Viitka** Estonia
178 D5 **Vijainagar** Rajasthan India
178 D8 **Vijapur** Gujarat India
176 C4 **Vijayadurg** Mahar. India
176 E8 **Vijayapati** Tamil Nadu India
176 G4 **Vijayawada** Andhra Prad. India
20 □D2 **Vík** Iceland
20 L4 **Vik** Norway
20 S3 **Vikajärvi** Fin.
176 E4 **Vikarabad** Andhra Prad. India
23 M3 **Vikbolandet** pen. Sweden
22 B2 **Vikedal** Norway
Vikeke East Timor see **Viqueque**
23 K3 **Viken** l. Sweden
22 F2 **Vikersund** Norway
22 B2 **Vikevåg** Norway
19 O7 **Vikhra** r. Rus. Fed.
77 L9 **Vikhren** mt. Bulg.
107 I4 **Viking** Alta Can.
20 K4 **Vikna** i. Norway
57 I2 **Vikolínec** Slovakia
78 B3 **Vikos-Aoos** nat. park Greece
21 I6 **Vikøyri** Norway
20 O2 **Vikran** Norway
55 L1 **Viktarinas** Lith.
16 J6 **Viktorivka** Ukr.
Viktorovka Kazakh. see **Taranovskoye**
51 D7 **Viktorshöhe** hill Ger.
62 D5 **Vila** Spain
Vila Vanuatu see **Port Vila**
64 D4 **Vila Alva** Port.
64 □ **Vila Baleira** Madeira
136 D5 **Vila Bittencourt** Brazil
62 G8 **Vila Boa** Port.
64 E3 **Vila Boim** Port.
137 G6 **Vila Braga** Brazil
62 D6 **Vila Caiz** Port.
138 D4 **Vilacaya** Bol.
62 C6 **Vila Chã** Port.
62 E7 **Vila Chã de Sá** Port.
62 D6 **Vila Chão do Marão** Port.
Vila Coutinho Moz. see **Ulongue**
62 E7 **Vila Cova à Coelheira** Port.
62 D6 **Vila Cova da Lixa** Port.
66 I3 **Vilada** Spain
66 L3 **Viladamat** Spain
62 E5 **Vila da Ponte** Port.
98 □1a **Vila da Praia da Vitória** Terceira Azores
88 □ **Vila da Ribeira Brava** Cape Verde
66 J5 **Viladecans** Spain
62 D3 **Vila de Cruces** Spain
Vila de João Belo Moz. see **Xai-Xai**
147 F1 **Vila de María** Arg.
Vilademat Spain see **Viladamat**
62 D9 **Vila de Rei** Port.
95 G3 **Vila de Sena** Moz.
64 B6 **Vila do Bispo** Port.
62 C6 **Vila do Conde** Port.
66 J4 **Viladrau** Spain
66 K3 **Vilafant** Spain
64 E3 **Vila Fernando** Port.
98 □3a **Vilaflor** Tenerife Canary Is
62 F6 **Vila Flor** Port.
98 □1b **Vila Franca, Ilhéu de** i. Azores
62 F7 **Vila Franca das Naves** Port.
66 I5 **Vilafranca del Penedès** Spain
64 B3 **Vila Franca de Xira** Port.
98 □1b **Vila Franca do Campo** São Miguel Azores
62 C3 **Vilagarcía de Arousa** Spain
95 G5 **Vila Gomes da Costa** Moz.
62 D2 **Vilagudín, Encoro de** resr Spain
38 G6 **Vilaine** r. France
66 L3 **Vilajuiga** Spain
18 K4 **Viļaka** Latvia
62 E2 **Vilalba** Spain
66 J3 **Vilallonga** Spain
Vila Marechal Carmona Angola see **Uíge**
62 F4 **Vilamartín de Valdeorras** Spain
67 D8 **Vilamarxant** Spain
146 A5 **Vila Mercedes** Chile
64 B2 **Vila Moreira** Port.
64 C6 **Vilamoura** Port.
138 D2 **Vila Murtinho** Brazil
62 B2 **Vilán, Cabo** c. Spain
95 □J3 **Vilanandro, Tanjona** pt Madag.
95 G4 **Vilanculos** Moz.
18 J5 **Viļāni** Latvia
64 A3 **Vila Nogueira de Azeitão** Port.
Vila Nova Angola see **Tchikala-Tcholohanga**
98 □1a **Vila Nova** Terceira Azores
64 C4 **Vila Nova da Baronia** Port.
95 G3 **Vila Nova da Fronteira** Moz.
67 F7 **Vilanova d'Alcolea** Spain
62 C8 **Vila Nova de Anços** Port.
62 C3 **Vilanova de Arousa** Spain
Vilanova de Castelló Spain see **Villanueva de Castellón**
62 C5 **Vila Nova de Cerveira** Port.
62 C6 **Vila Nova de Famalicão** Port.
62 F6 **Vila Nova de Foz Coa** Port.
62 C6 **Vila Nova de Gaia** Port.
66 H4 **Vilanova de l'Aguda** Spain
62 F2 **Vilanova de Lourenzá** Spain
66 H4 **Vilanova de Meià** Spain
62 C9 **Vila Nova de Ourém** Port.
62 E7 **Vila Nova de Paiva** Port.
62 D8 **Vila Nova de Poiares** Port.
64 E5 **Vila Nova de São Bento** Port.
Vila Nova do Seles Angola see **Uku**
66 I5 **Vilanova i la Geltrú** Spain
88 □ **Vila Nova Sintra** Cape Verde
62 E8 **Vila Pouca da Beira** Port.
62 E5 **Vila Pouca de Aguiar** Port.
62 C5 **Vila Praia de Âncora** Port.
62 F7 **Vilar, Barragem de** resr Port.
62 F5 **Vilarandelo** Port.
62 E4 **Vilarchao** Spain
62 D5 **Vilar da Veiga** Port.
62 C6 **Vilar de Andorinho** Port.
62 E4 **Vilar de Barrio** Spain
62 E4 **Vilar de Santos** Spain
62 F5 **Vilardevós** Spain
62 E6 **Vila Real** Port.
62 E5 **Vila Real** admin. dist. Port.
67 E8 **Vila-real de los Infantes** Spain
64 E6 **Vila Real de Santo António** Port.
62 F5 **Vilarelho da Raia** Port.
62 G7 **Vilar Formoso** Port.
62 F6 **Vilarinho da Castanheira** Port.
62 C8 **Vilarinho do Bairro** Port.
62 F4 **Vilariño de Conso** Spain
66 H5 **Vila-rodona** Spain
64 D4 **Vila Ruiva** Port.
Vilas i. S. Male Maldives see **Velassary**
Vila Salazar Zimbabwe see **Sango**
191 J6 **Viläşçay** r. Azer.
62 C5 **Vila Seca** Port.
66 H5 **Vilaseca de Solcina** Spain
147 G2 **Vila Trinidad** Arg.
176 E8 **Vilavankod** Tamil Nadu India
137 I4 **Vila Velha** Amapá Brazil
143 G4 **Vila Velha** Espírito Santo Brazil
62 E9 **Vila Velha de Ródão** Port.
62 D5 **Vila Verde** Braga Port.
62 C8 **Vila Verde** Coimbra Port.
62 E6 **Vila Verde** Vila Real Port.
62 F5 **Vila Verde da Raia** Port.
64 E5 **Vila Verde de Ficalho** Port.
64 E3 **Vila Viçosa** Port.
138 B3 **Vilcabamba, Cordillera** mts Peru
138 C3 **Vilcanota, Cordillera de** mts Peru
16 I2 **Vil'cha** Ukr.
65 M4 **Vilches** Spain
146 A6 **Vilcun** Chile
14 I3 **Viled'** r. Rus. Fed.
147 H4 **Vilela** Arg.
Vileyka Belarus see **Vilyeyka**
14 L3 **Vil'gort** Permskaya Oblast' Rus. Fed.
14 J3 **Vil'gort** Respublika Komi Rus. Fed.
20 N4 **Vilhelmina** Sweden
139 E3 **Vilhena** Brazil
Viligili i. N. Male Maldives see **Vilingli**
17 M9 **Viline** Ukr.
175 □1 **Vilingli** i. N. Male Maldives
175 □1 **Vilingli** i. N. Male Maldives
18 I7 **Viliya** r. Belarus/Lith.
16 F3 **Viliya** r. Ukr.
18 I3 **Viljandi** Estonia
96 D10 **Viljoenshof** S. Africa
97 K3 **Viljoenskroon** S. Africa
18 G7 **Vilkaviškis** Lith.
17 S5 **Vil'khova** r. Ukr.
18 G6 **Vilkija** Lith.
192 I2 **Vil'kitskogo, Ostrov** i. Rus. Fed.
193 K2 **Vil'kitskogo, Proliv** str. Rus. Fed.
138 D5 **Villa Abecia** Bol.
146 C2 **Villa Aberastain** Arg.
73 J4 **Villa Adriana** tourist site Italy
126 F2 **Villa Ahumada** Mex.
147 F6 **Villa Alba** Arg.
146 B4 **Villa Alegre** Chile
146 B3 **Villa Alemana** Chile
129 K8 **Villa Alta** Mex.
130 H4 **Villa Altagracia** Dom. Rep.
144 F3 **Villa Ana** Arg.
147 G3 **Villa Ángela** Arg.
144 E2 **Villa Ángela** Arg.
128 G5 **Villa Apaseo El Alto** Mex.
147 F6 **Villa Atlántica** Arg.
146 D4 **Villa Atuel** Arg.
129 J5 **Villa Ávila Camacho** Mex.
129 L7 **Villa Azueta** Mex.
71 K5 **Villa Bartolomea** Italy
74 E7 **Villabate** Sicilia Italy
138 D2 **Villa Bella** Bol.
Villa Bens Morocco see **Tarfaya**
144 E2 **Villa Berthet** Arg.
64 E6 **Villablanca** Spain
62 H3 **Villablino** Spain
66 A1 **Villabona** Spain
63 J5 **Villabrágima** Spain
63 J6 **Villabuena del Puente** Spain
42 G5 **Villac** France
147 G4 **Villa Cañás** Arg.
63 N9 **Villacañas** Spain
70 I4 **Villa Carcina** Italy
66 □ **Villacarlos** Spain
146 E2 **Villa Carlos Paz** Arg.
65 M4 **Villacarrillo** Spain
147 F5 **Villa Castelar** Arg.
75 M2 **Villa Castelli** Italy
63 L7 **Villacastín** Spain
59 I6 **Villach** Austria
72 B9 **Villacidro** Sardegna Italy
63 O5 **Villaciervos** Spain
Villa Cisneros, Ría de b. Western Sahara see **Río de Oro, Bahía de**
127 M10 **Villa Comaltitlán** Mex.
147 F2 **Villa Concepción del Tío** Arg.
63 N8 **Villaconejos** Spain
63 P8 **Villaconejos de Trabaque** Spain
147 G3 **Villa Constitución** Arg.
128 D5 **Villa Corona** Mex.
126 G4 **Villa Coronado** Mex.
127 M9 **Villa Corzo** Mex.
146 E2 **Villa Cura Brochero** Arg.
147 G3 **Villada** Arg.
63 K4 **Villada** Spain
70 H4 **Villa d'Almè** Italy
128 D6 **Villa de Álvarez** Mex.
128 E2 **Villa de Cos** Mex.
136 E2 **Villa de Cura** Venez.
127 N8 **Villa de Guadalupe** Campeche Mex.
128 G2 **Villa de Guadalupe** San Luis Potosí Mex.
146 E3 **Villa del Carmen** Arg.
63 L8 **Villa del Prado** Spain
128 G5 **Villa del Pueblito** Mex.
65 K5 **Villa del Río** Spain
147 F2 **Villa del Rosario** Arg.
146 C2 **Villa del Salvador** Arg.
147 E2 **Villa del Totoral** Arg.
62 H5 **Villadepera** Spain
67 C9 **Villa de Ves** Spain
147 G3 **Villa Diego** Arg.
63 L3 **Villadiego** Spain
146 E2 **Villa Dolores** Arg.
147 H3 **Villa Domínguez** Arg.
71 L5 **Villadose** Italy
70 E3 **Villadossola** Italy
66 C5 **Villadoz** Spain
146 C6 **Villa El Chocón** Arg.
63 K3 **Villaeles de Valdavia** Spain
147 H3 **Villa Elisa** Arg.
147 G3 **Villa Eloisa** Arg.
128 F6 **Villa Escalante** Mex.
63 O9 **Villaescusa de Haro** Spain
63 N4 **Villaescusa la Sombría** Spain
62 I5 **Villafáfila** Spain
67 E7 **Villafamés** Spain
63 R6 **Villafeliche** Spain
127 M9 **Villa Flores** Mex.
63 J6 **Villaflores** Spain
139 F6 **Villa Florida** Para.
63 Q4 **Villafranca** Spain
70 E6 **Villafranca d'Asti** Italy
67 L8 **Villafranca de Bonany** Spain
65 J5 **Villafranca de Córdoba** Spain
66 D4 **Villafranca de Ebro** Spain
62 G3 **Villafranca del Bierzo** Spain
66 C6 **Villafranca del Campo** Spain
66 E7 **Villafranca del Cid** Spain
64 G3 **Villafranca de los Barros** Spain
65 M2 **Villafranca de los Caballeros** Spain
Villafranca del Penedès Spain see **Vilafranca del Penedès**
71 J5 **Villafranca di Verona** Italy
70 H7 **Villafranca in Lunigiana** Italy
63 N4 **Villafranca-Montes de Oca** Spain
75 I7 **Villafranca Tirrena** Sicilia Italy
71 J5 **Villafranca Veronese** airport Italy
64 G6 **Villafranco del Guadalquivir** Spain
74 E8 **Villafrati** Sicilia Italy
63 J5 **Villafrechos** Spain
63 M5 **Villafruela** Spain
63 L5 **Villafuerte** Spain
Villagarcía de Arosa Spain see **Vilagarcía de Arousa**
63 J5 **Villagarcía de Campos** Spain
64 G4 **Villagarcía de la Torre** Spain
65 P2 **Villagarcía del Llano** Spain
146 D3 **Villa General Roca** Arg.
147 I5 **Villa Gesell** Arg.
75 L5 **Villagio Mancuso** Italy
64 G3 **Villagonzalo** Spain
147 G3 **Villa Governador Gálvez** Arg.
129 H1 **Villagrán** Mex.
72 D8 **Villagrande Strisaili** Sardegna Italy
147 H2 **Villaguay** Arg.
128 D4 **Villa Guerrero** Mex.
144 F3 **Villa Guillermina** Arg.
65 J4 **Villaharta** Spain
139 F6 **Villa Hayes** Para.
127 M8 **Villahermosa** Mex.
65 N3 **Villahermosa** Spain
67 E7 **Villahermosa del Río** Spain
147 H2 **Villa Hernandarias** Arg.
63 L4 **Villaherreros** Spain
128 E4 **Villa Hidalgo** Jalisco Mex.
128 B4 **Villa Hidalgo** Nayarit Mex.
128 G3 **Villa Hidalgo** San Luis Potosí Mex.
123 J11 **Villa Hidalgo** Sonora Mex.
63 M4 **Villahizán** Spain
63 M4 **Villahoz** Spain
146 E4 **Villa Huidobro** Arg.
36 I8 **Villaines-en-Duesmois** France
39 K5 **Villaines-la-Juhel** France
39 K6 **Villaines-sous-Malicorne** France
126 D5 **Villa Insurgentes** Mex.
147 F6 **Villa Iris** Arg.
67 E10 **Villajoyosa - La Vila Joíosa** Spain
128 B4 **Villa Juárez** Nayarit Mex.
128 G3 **Villa Juárez** San Luis Potosí Mex.
71 K4 **Villa Lagarina** Italy
73 L4 **Villalago** Italy
63 J5 **Villalar de los Comuneros** Spain
73 L4 **Villa Latina** Italy
129 M7 **Villa La Venta** Mex.
129 J5 **Villa Lázaro Cárdenas** Mex.
74 F8 **Villalba** Sicilia Italy
131 □1 **Villalba** Puerto Rico
63 M5 **Villalba de Duero** Spain
63 K3 **Villalba de Guardo** Spain
64 G6 **Villalba del Alcor** Spain
63 P8 **Villalba de la Sierra** Spain
63 K5 **Villalba de los Alcores** Spain
64 F3 **Villalba de los Barros** Spain
63 O8 **Villalba del Rey** Spain
66 F5 **Villalba dels Arcs** Spain
63 O3 **Villalba de Rioja** Spain
62 H5 **Villalcampo** Spain
62 H6 **Villalcampo, Embalse de** resr Spain
63 K4 **Villalcázar de Sirga** Spain
127 I4 **Villaldama** Mex.
63 Q6 **Villalengua** Spain
65 O2 **Villalgordo del Júcar** Spain
63 P9 **Villalgordo del Marquesado** Spain
147 H4 **Villa Lía** Arg.
147 H3 **Villa Lila** Arg.
73 M5 **Villa Literno** Italy
63 J5 **Villalobos** Spain
63 J4 **Villalón de Campos** Spain
145 E5 **Villalonga** Arg.
67 E10 **Villalonga** Spain
63 J5 **Villalpando** Spain
65 P2 **Villalpardo** Spain
63 M8 **Villaluenga de la Sagra** Spain
63 K4 **Villalumbroso** Spain
128 F6 **Villa Madero** Mex.
129 H1 **Villa Mainero** Mex.
65 P2 **Villamalea** Spain
62 I4 **Villamañán** Spain
62 I4 **Villamandos** Spain
65 N3 **Villamanrique** Spain
64 G6 **Villamanrique de la Condesa** Spain
63 L8 **Villamanta** Spain
72 B8 **Villamar** Sardegna Italy
Villamarchante Spain see **Vilamarxant**
147 G4 **Villa Maria** Arg.
147 F3 **Villa María** Córdoba Arg.
147 G2 **Villa María** Entre Ríos Arg.
147 H2 **Villa María Grande** Arg.
138 D5 **Villa Martín** Bol.
64 H7 **Villamartín** Spain
63 K4 **Villamartín de Campos** Spain
72 B9 **Villamassargia** Sardegna Italy
144 E2 **Villa Matoque** Arg.
62 I7 **Villamayor** Spain
65 K3 **Villamayor de Calatrava** Spain
63 J5 **Villamayor de Campos** Spain
63 O9 **Villamayor de Santiago** Spain
63 L4 **Villamayor de Treviño** Spain
42 F5 **Villamblard** France
63 L4 **Villamediana** Spain
63 P4 **Villamediana de Iregua** Spain
62 H3 **Villamejil** Spain
146 C2 **Villa Mercedes** Arg.
146 E3 **Villa Mercedes** San Luis Arg.
64 H2 **Villamesías** Spain
62 G8 **Villamiel** Spain
70 I7 **Villa Minozzo** Italy
138 E5 **Villa Montes** Bol.
62 I6 **Villamor de los Escuderos** Spain
128 F5 **Villa Morelos** Mex.
63 M9 **Villamuelas** Spain
63 L5 **Villamuriel de Cerrato** Spain
43 D7 **Villandraut** France
63 O2 **Villano, Cabo** c. Spain
75 N2 **Villanova** Italy
70 E7 **Villanova d'Albenga** Italy
70 D6 **Villanova d'Asti** Italy
73 O5 **Villanova del Battista** Italy
72 C8 **Villanovafranca** Sardegna Italy
72 A6 **Villanova Monteleone** Sardegna Italy
72 B8 **Villanova Truschedu** Sardegna Italy
72 C8 **Villanova Tulo** Sardegna Italy
70 G5 **Villanterio** Italy
66 D2 **Villanúa** Spain
63 K5 **Villanubla** Spain
147 F3 **Villa Nueva** Córdoba Arg.
146 C3 **Villa Nueva** Mendoza Arg.
136 C2 **Villanueva** Col.
128 E3 **Villanueva** Mex.
Villanueva Spain see **Vilanova de Lourenzá**
63 O9 **Villanueva de Alcardete** Spain
Villanueva de Alcolea Spain see **Vilanova d'Alcolea**
63 P7 **Villanueva de Alcorón** Spain
65 K6 **Villanueva de Algaidas** Spain
63 M4 **Villanueva de Argaño** Spain
Villanueva de Arosa Spain see **Vilanova de Arousa**
63 M9 **Villanueva de Bogas** Spain
63 O4 **Villanueva de Cameros** Spain
67 E9 **Villanueva de Castellón** Spain
65 J4 **Villanueva de Córdoba** Spain
66 D4 **Villanueva de Gállego** Spain
63 K7 **Villanueva de Gómez** Spain
63 M8 **Villanueva de la Cañada** Spain
65 J7 **Villanueva de la Concepción** Spain
65 N3 **Villanueva de la Fuente** Spain
65 P2 **Villanueva de la Jara** Spain
65 L4 **Villanueva de la Reina** Spain
65 M4 **Villanueva del Arzobispo** Spain
64 E5 **Villanueva de las Cruces** Spain
64 H3 **Villanueva de la Serena** Spain
62 H8 **Villanueva de la Sierra** Spain
65 M5 **Villanueva de las Torres** Spain
63 J8 **Villanueva de la Vera** Spain
63 J5 **Villanueva del Campo** Spain
65 J4 **Villanueva del Duque** Spain
64 E4 **Villanueva del Fresno** Spain
64 E5 **Villanueva de los Castillejos** Spain
65 N3 **Villanueva de los Infantes** Spain
65 I4 **Villanueva del Rey** Spain
67 C11 **Villanueva del Río Segura** Spain
64 H5 **Villanueva del Río y Minas** Spain
65 K7 **Villanueva del Rosario** Spain
65 K6 **Villanueva del Trabuco** Spain
65 L3 **Villanueva de San Carlos** Spain
65 I6 **Villanueva de San Juan** Spain
65 K6 **Villanueva de Tapia** Spain
63 N3 **Villanueva de Valdegovia** Spain
Villanueva-y-Geltrú Spain see **Vilanova i la Geltrú**
63 K3 **Villanuño de Valdavia** Spain
57 H6 **Villány** Hungary
57 H6 **Villányi-hegység** ridge Hungary
144 F3 **Villa Ocampo** Arg.
126 G4 **Villa Ocampo** Mex.
145 B8 **Villa O'Higgins** Chile
144 E3 **Villa Ojo de Agua** Arg.
139 F6 **Villa Oliva** Para.
Villa O. Pereyra Mex. see **Villa Orestes Pereyra**
71 P4 **Villa Opicina** Italy
126 G4 **Villa Orestes Pereyra** Mex.
138 D4 **Villa Oropeza** Bol.
65 N3 **Villapalacios** Spain
72 B9 **Villaperuccio** Sardegna Italy
123 J12 **Villa Pesqueira** Mex.
75 K4 **Villapiana** Italy
75 K4 **Villapiana Lido** Italy
71 K6 **Villa Poma** Italy
40 D3 **Villapourçon** France
146 B4 **Villa Prat** Chile
72 D9 **Villaputzu** Sardegna Italy
62 I4 **Villaquejida** Spain
62 I3 **Villaquilambre** Spain
138 D4 **Villar** Bol.
62 I6 **Villaralbo** Spain
65 J4 **Villaralto** Spain
147 G3 **Villa Ramírez** Arg.
63 M3 **Villarcayo** Spain
41 I6 **Villar-d'Arêne** France
41 H6 **Villard-Bonnot** France
41 H6 **Villard-de-Lans** France
65 P3 **Villar de Chinchilla** Spain
62 G7 **Villar de Ciervo** Spain
62 H5 **Villardeciervos** Spain
63 J5 **Villardefrades** Spain
67 D8 **Villar del Arzobispo** Spain
62 G7 **Villar de la Yegua** Spain
62 H6 **Villar del Buey** Spain
63 Q8 **Villar del Cobo** Spain
63 Q9 **Villar del Humo** Spain
62 G3 **Villar de los Barrios** Spain
66 C5 **Villar de los Navarros** Spain
63 J9 **Villar del Pedroso** Spain
64 F2 **Villar del Rey** Spain
63 R7 **Villar del Salz** Spain
63 P8 **Villar de Olalla** Spain
62 H6 **Villar de Peralonso** Spain
64 H2 **Villar de Rena** Spain
63 O4 **Villar de Torre** Spain
65 K5 **Villardompardo** Spain
Villareal Spain see **Vila-real de los Infantes**
Villareal de los Infantes Spain see **Vila-real de los Infantes**
147 F3 **Villa Reducción** Arg.
146 D6 **Villa Regina** Arg.
63 O9 **Villarejo de Fuentes** Spain
63 K9 **Villarejo de Montalbán** Spain
62 I4 **Villarejo de Orbigo** Spain
63 N8 **Villarejo de Salvanés** Spain
71 J3 **Villa Rendena** Italy
63 J3 **Villarente** Spain
62 I6 **Villares de la Reina** Spain
139 F6 **Villa Rey** Para.
146 E3 **Villa Reynolds** Arg.
65 L5 **Villargordo** Spain
62 H6 **Villarino de los Aires** Spain
66 D6 **Villarluengo** Spain
74 G9 **Villa Romana del casale** tourist site Italy
74 G8 **Villarosa** Sicilia Italy
66 C6 **Villarquemado** Spain
63 K4 **Villarramiel** Spain
66 C5 **Villarreal de Huerva** Spain
146 A6 **Villarrica** Chile
139 F6 **Villarrica** Para.
146 A6 **Villarrica, Lago** l. Chile
146 B6 **Villarrica, Parque Nacional** nat. park Chile
62 I5 **Villarrín de Campos** Spain
65 N2 **Villarrobledo** Spain
65 N4 **Villarrodrigo** Spain
63 P4 **Villarroya** Spain
66 D6 **Villarroya de los Pinares** Spain
65 L2 **Villarrubia de los Ojos** Spain
63 N9 **Villarrubia de Santiago** Spain
63 O9 **Villarrubio** Spain
147 H4 **Villars** Arg.
42 F5 **Villars** Aquitaine France
41 E6 **Villars** Rhône-Alpes France
41 J7 **Villar-St-Pancrace** France
63 P9 **Villars del Saz** Spain
40 J2 **Villars-lès-Blamont** France
40 G5 **Villars-les-Dombes** France
41 K9 **Villars-sur-Var** France
65 P2 **Villarta** Spain
65 J2 **Villarta de los Montes** Spain
65 M2 **Villarta de San Juan** Spain
118 F6 **Villas** NJ U.S.A.
Villasalazar Zimbabwe see **Sango**
72 C9 **Villasalto** Sardegna Italy
60 E1 **Villasana de Mena** Spain
63 L4 **Villasandino** Spain
75 J7 **Villa San Giovanni** Italy
147 H3 **Villa San José** Arg.
147 H3 **Villa San Marcial** Arg.
144 D3 **Villa San Martin** Arg.
73 M4 **Villa Santa Maria** Italy
146 D2 **Villa Santa Rita de Catuna** Arg.
146 C2 **Villa Santa Rosa** Arg.
63 N2 **Villasante de Montija** Spain
71 N3 **Villa Santina** Italy
146 E4 **Villa Sarmiento** Arg.
63 L4 **Villasarracino** Spain
147 F4 **Villa Sauze** Arg.
43 I9 **Villasavary** France
63 O6 **Villasayas** Spain
147 I3 **Villasboas** Uru.
62 G6 **Villasbuenas** Spain
62 H6 **Villasdardo** Spain
62 H3 **Villaseca de Laciana** Spain
63 M9 **Villaseca de la Sagra** Spain
62 H6 **Villaseco de los Gamitos** Spain
62 H6 **Villaseco de los Reyes** Spain
62 I6 **Villaseco del Pan** Spain
63 M9 **Villasequilla de Yepes** Spain
138 D4 **Villa Serrano** Bol.
72 D9 **Villasimius** Sardegna Italy
75 I9 **Villasmundo** Sicilia Italy
72 B9 **Villasor** Sardegna Italy
72 B9 **Villaspeciosa** Sardegna Italy
62 G8 **Villasrubias** Spain
67 C7 **Villastar** Spain
63 N4 **Villasur de Herreros** Spain
63 N9 **Villatobas** Spain
63 J7 **Villatoro** Spain
67 C9 **Villatoya** Spain
147 E2 **Villa Tulumba** Arg.
63 J3 **Villaturiel** Spain
63 K4 **Villaumbrales** Spain
144 C3 **Villa Unión** Arg.
127 I3 **Villa Unión** Coahuila Mex.
128 C2 **Villa Unión** Durango Mex.
128 A2 **Villa Unión** Sinaloa Mex.
72 B8 **Villaurbana** Sardegna Italy
147 G2 **Villa Urquiza** Arg.
146 E4 **Villa Valeria** Arg.
73 L4 **Villavallelonga** Italy
130 H4 **Villa Vasquez** Dom. Rep.
63 O4 **Villavelayo** Spain
98 □3b **Villaverde** Fuerteventura Canary Is
72 B8 **Villa Verde** Sardegna Italy
65 N4 **Villaverde de Guadalimar** Spain
64 H5 **Villaverde del Río** Spain
67 A8 **Villaverde y Pasaconsol** Spain
70 F6 **Villavernia** Italy
136 C3 **Villavicencio** Col.
63 J2 **Villaviciosa** Spain
63 J1 **Villaviciosa, Ría de** inlet Spain
65 I4 **Villaviciosa de Córdoba** Spain
63 M8 **Villaviciosa de Odón** Spain
128 D7 **Villa Victoria** Mex.
67 E8 **Villavieja** Spain
63 M6 **Villavieja del Lozoya** Spain
62 H7 **Villavieja de Yeltes** Spain
138 D4 **Villa Viscarra** Bol.
63 L5 **Villaviudas** Spain
62 G2 **Villayón** Spain
63 K3 **Villazanzo de Valderaduey** Spain
138 D5 **Villazon** Bol.
37 N7 **Villé** France
40 G5 **Villebois** France
42 E5 **Villebois-Lavalette** France
43 G8 **Villebrumier** France
43 E9 **Villecomtal-sur-Arros** France
40 G1 **Villecomte** France
41 I9 **Villecroze** France
41 B10 **Villedaigne** France
128 F3 **Ville de Ramos** Mex.
128 G4 **Ville de Reyes** Mex.
39 I7 **Villedieu-la-Blouère** France
38 I4 **Villedieu-les-Poêles** France
39 O8 **Villedieu-sur-Indre** France
72 C2 **Ville-di-Pietrabugno** Corse France
39 M6 **Villedômer** France
36 G5 **Ville-en-Tardenois** France
42 E3 **Villefagnan** France
40 G5 **Villefontaine** France
41 D8 **Villefort** France
36 F8 **Villefranche** Bourgogne France
43 F9 **Villefranche** Midi-Pyrénées France
43 I8 **Villefranche-d'Albigeois** France
40 B4 **Villefranche-d'Allier** France
43 I10 **Villefranche-de-Conflent** France
43 H9 **Villefranche-de-Lauragais** France
42 E6 **Villefranche-de-Lonchat** France
41 B8 **Villefranche-de-Panat** France
43 I7 **Villefranche-de-Rouergue** France
43 G6 **Villefranche-du-Périgord** France
39 O7 **Villefranche-sur-Cher** France
41 K9 **Villefranche-sur-Mer** France
40 F5 **Villefranche-sur-Saône** France
43 B9 **Villefranque** France
63 L4 **Villegas** Spain
128 E3 **Ville Juarez** Mex.
67 C7 **Villel** Spain
128 G4 **Villela** Mex.
41 G9 **Villelaure** France
36 E8 **Villemandeur** France
111 O2 **Ville-Marie** Que. Can.
36 G7 **Villemaur-sur-Vanne** France
111 P1 **Villemontel** Que. Can.
36 H7 **Villemorien** France
43 I9 **Villemoustaussou** France
43 H8 **Villemur-sur-Tarn** France
67 D10 **Villena** Spain
36 G6 **Villenauxe-la-Grande** France
43 C6 **Villenave-d'Ornon** France
43 I7 **Villeneuve** Midi-Pyrénées France
41 H9 **Villeneuve** Provence-Alpes-Côte d'Azur France
40 F4 **Villeneuve** Rhône-Alpes France
70 B3 **Villeneuve** Switz.
36 G7 **Villeneuve-au-Chemin** France
41 C6 **Villeneuve-d'Allier** France
36 F2 **Villeneuve-d'Ascq** France
41 F7 **Villeneuve-de-Berg** France
43 D8 **Villeneuve-de-Marsan** France
43 F9 **Villeneuve-de-Rivière** France
43 H10 **Villeneuve-d'Olmes** France
43 H9 **Villeneuve-du-Paréage** France
36 F7 **Villeneuve-la-Guyard** France
36 G7 **Villeneuve-l'Archevêque** France
41 F9 **Villeneuve-lès-Avignon** France
41 C10 **Villeneuve-lès-Béziers** France
41 D9 **Villeneuve-lès-Maguelone** France
41 K9 **Villeneuve-Loubet** France
36 F5 **Villeneuve-St-Germain** France
40 C3 **Villeneuve-sur-Allier** France
43 F7 **Villeneuve-sur-Lot** France
36 F7 **Villeneuve-sur-Yonne** France
43 G8 **Villeneuve-Tolosane** France
43 H9 **Villenouvelle** France
43 I9 **Villepinte** France
121 I10 **Ville Platte** LA U.S.A.
39 M2 **Villequier** France
41 B7 **Villercomtal** France
43 F6 **Villeréal** France
40 E5 **Villerest** France
40 E5 **Villerest, Barrage de** dam France
63 K5 **Villerías** Spain
41 B10 **Villerouge-Termenès** France
39 J3 **Villers-Bocage** Basse-Normandie France
36 D4 **Villers-Bocage** Picardie France
36 E4 **Villers-Bretonneux** France
36 E4 **Villers-Carbonnel** France
36 F5 **Villers-Cotterêts** France
36 A4 **Villers-Écalles** France
37 I5 **Villers-en-Argonne** France
40 I1 **Villersexel** France
40 H2 **Villers-Farlay** France
45 H7 **Villers-le-Bouillet** Belgium
40 J2 **Villers-le-lac** France
37 L6 **Villers-lès-Nancy** France
36 F3 **Villers-Outréaux** France
45 B10 **Villers-St-Paul** France
36 I4 **Villers-Semeuse** France
70 C2 **Villers-sur-Glâne** Switz.
39 K3 **Villers-sur-Mer** France
37 J5 **Villers-sur-Meuse** France
37 K5 **Villerupt** France
39 L3 **Villerville** France
36 H7 **Villery** France
36 H6 **Villeseneux** France
41 G8 **Villes-sur-Auzon** France
37 I5 **Ville-sur-Tourbe** France
139 F6 **Villeta** Para.
73 L4 **Villetta Barrea** Italy

40 G5 Villette-d'Anthon France
40 F5 Villeurbanne France
41 D9 Villeveyrac France
40 G5 Villevocance France
128 G3 Vilia Zaragoza Mex.
146 C2 Villicun, Sierra mt. Arg.
40 F4 Villié-Morgon France
97 M3 Villiers S. Africa
39 J6 Villiers-Charlemagne France
96 D9 Villiersdorp S. Africa
37 I6 Villiers-en-l'Isle France
40 F2 Villiers-en-Plaine France
36 D5 Villiers-le-Bel France
36 F6 Villiers-St-Benoît France
27 Q8 Villierstown Rep. of Ireland
40 G5 Villieu-Loyes-Mollon France
52 F5 Villingen Ger.
52 F5 Villingendorf Ger.
49 F10 Villmar Ger.
63 K4 Villoldo Spain
63 Q9 Villora Spain
63 J6 Villora Spain
71 M4 Villorba Italy
70 G4 Villores, Canale canal Italy
63 J2 Viloria Spain
63 J6 Viloria Spain
176 F7 Villupuram Tamil Nadu India
50 I2 Vilm i. Ger.
57 K3 Vilmány Hungary
107 I4 Vilna Alta Can.
24 J1 Vilna Lith. see Vilnius
18 I7 Vilnjusfjorden inlet Norway
17 N5 Vil'nohirs'k Ukr.
17 O6 Vil'nyans'k Ukr.
66 K4 Vilovi d'Onyar Spain
21 F5 Vilppula Fin.
58 C4 Vils Austria
53 L3 Vils r. Ger.
53 O4 Vils r. Ger.
18 E3 Vilsandi i. Estonia
18 E3 Vilsandi nature res. Estonia
53 M5 Vilsbiburg Ger.
53 L2 Vilseck Ger.
17 K4 Vil'shana Cherkas'ka Oblast' Ukr.
17 L3 Vil'shana Chernihivs'ka Oblast' Ukr.
17 Q4 Vil'shana Kharkivs'ka Oblast' Ukr.
16 J5 Vil'shana Kirovohrads'ka Oblast' Ukr.
16 H5 Vil'shana Vinnyts'ka Oblast' Ukr.
16 H3 Vil'shana Zhytomyrs'ka Oblast' Ukr.
53 O4 Vilshofen Ger.
22 E5 Vilsund Vest Denmark
176 C4 Viluppuram Tamil Nadu India see Villupuram
18 K4 Viluste Estonia
62 G6 Vilvestre Spain
45 F7 Vilvoorde Belgium
18 J7 Vilyeyka Belarus
18 K7 Vilyeyskaye, Vozyera l. Belarus
193 N3 Vilyuy r. Rus. Fed.
193 M3 Vilyuyskoye Vodokhranilishche resr Rus. Fed.
91 F8 Vimbe mt. Zambia
66 H5 Vimbodi Spain
64 A2 Vimeiro Port.
70 G4 Vimercate Italy
36 C3 Vimeu r. France
62 B2 Vimianzo Spain
64 D3 Vimieiro Port.
62 G5 Vimioso Port.
23 L4 Vimmerby Sweden
36 E8 Vimory France
39 J6 Vimoutiers France
20 Q5 Vimpeli Fin.
56 C2 Vimperk Czech Rep.
124 J2 Vina r. Cameroon
124 J2 Vina CA U.S.A.
66 F7 Vinaceite Spain
146 B3 Viña del Mar Chile
70 C7 Vinadio Italy
66 G5 Vinaixa Spain
130 B2 Viñales Cuba
130 E4 Viñales Valley tourist site Cuba
117 □Q4 Vinalhaven ME U.S.A.
117 Q4 Vinalhaven Island ME U.S.A.
67 D11 Vinalopó r. Spain
95 □K2 Vinanivao Madag.
91 J10 Vinarice Czech Rep.
200 □⁶ Vinarori, Mount New Georgia Is Solomon Is
66 F7 Vinaròs Spain
Vinarós Spain see Vinaròs
41 C10 Vinassan France
40 I4 Vinay France
129 J5 Vinazco r. Mex.
43 J10 Vinça France
109 F2 Vincelotte, Lac l. Que. Can.
191 □¹c Vincendo Réunion
114 D6 Vincennes IN U.S.A.
213 H2 Vincennes Bay Antarctica
204 □¹ Vincent, Point Norfolk I.
118 F5 Vincentown NJ U.S.A.
118 E5 Vincentown NJ U.S.A.
37 L7 Vincey France
73 N5 Vinchiaturo Italy
43 J8 Vinchina Arg.
138 B3 Vinchos Peru
22 J1 Vindeby Denmark
48 J1 Vindelälven r. Sweden
20 O5 Vindeln Sweden
20 M3 Vindelfjällens naturreservat nature res. Sweden
20 O4 Vindeln Denmark
22 E5 Vinderup Denmark
178 E8 Vindhya Range hills Madh. Prad. India
Vindobona Austria see Wien
59 S9 Vinebre Spain
118 E6 Vineland NJ U.S.A.
41 I7 Vineuil Centre France
39 N6 Vineuil Centre France
39 O8 Vineuil Centre France
97 K6 Vineyard S. Africa
19 Q3 Vingaa Romania
76 J4 Vingái, Câmpia plain Romania
23 L2 Vingåker Sweden
40 G2 Vingeanne r. France
43 J10 Vingrau France
158 G5 Vinh Vietnam
158 G5 Vinh Port.
158 G3 Vinhais Port.
159 Loc Vinh Loc Vietnam
159 G9 Vinh Long Vietnam
158 H4 Vinh Thuc, Dao i. Vietnam
158 G4 Vinh Yên Vietnam
59 N7 Vinica Croatia
19 P9 Vinica Macedonia
77 K9 Vinica Slovakia
59 O1 Viniegra de Arriba Spain
59 O3 Vininé Šumice Czech Rep.
121 H7 Vinita OK U.S.A.
178 B8 Vinjhan Gujarat India
Vinju Mare Romania see Vânju Mare

23 L2 Vinon i. Sweden
41 H9 Vinon-sur-Verdon France
41 G8 Vinsobres France
212 S1 Vinson Massif mt. Antarctica
21 J6 Vinstra Norway
120 I4 Vinton LA U.S.A.
120 I4 Vinton i. Luzon Phil.
63 N7 Viñuelas Spain
91 B5 Vinuesa Spain
155 E8 Vinukunda Andhra Prad. India
176 F4 Vinukonda Andhra Prad. India
50 E5 Vinzelberg Ger.
48 H1 Viöl Ger.
40 E5 Violay France
41 F8 Violès France
18 F7 Violeta Cuba see Primero de Enero
55 K1 Violet Valley Aboriginal Reserve W.A. Austr.
17 L6 Viols-le-Fort France
179 O7 Vioolsdrif S. Africa
57 J4 Viosne r. France
77 M7 Vipava Slovenia
136 E3 Vipava r. Slovenia
73 A8 Viphya Mountains Malawi
185 M7 Vipiteno Italy
76 G7 Vipperow Ger.
57 J3 Viqueque East Timor
72 I3 Vir i. Croatia
57 G2 Vir Slovenia
59 O4 Virac Phil.
200 □6 Virac Point Phil.
79 J9 Viradouro Brazil
76 I8 Viramgam Gujarat India
138 C4 Viranşehir Turkey
138 B4 Virarajendrapet Karnataka India
72 I3 Virawah Pak.
143 G4 Virawluy Belarus
137 H5 Virazeil France
Vircava r. Latvia/Lith.
63 O3 Virchow, Mount hill W.A. Austr.
Virdáánjarga Fin. see Virtaniemi
131 K4 Virden Man. Can.
27 H5 Virden Rep. of Ireland
97 K4 Virginia S. Africa
116 G11 Virginia state U.S.A.
117 J12 Virginia Beach VA U.S.A.
77 L8 Virginia City MT U.S.A.
75 M5 Virginia City NV U.S.A.
38 I5 Virginia Falls N.W.T. Can.
37 K8 Virginia Water Surrey, England U.K.
36 I3 Virgin Islands (U.K.) terr. West Indies
131 K4 Virgin Islands (U.S.A.) terr. West Indies
125 R5 Virgin Mountains AZ U.S.A.
143 F3 Virginópolis Brazil
40 G4 Viriat France
40 H5 Vireux-Molhain France
40 E5 Vireux-Wallerand France
41 G6 Virey-sous-Bar France
12 I6 Virgem da Lapa Brazil
19 N6 Virgen Austria
18 L6 Virgines, Cabo c. Arg.
20 P3 Virgental val. Austria
40 F2 Virginia VA U.S.A.
37 K7 Virgin r. U.S.A. (U.K.)
74 H10 Virginia S. Africa
71 M4 Virginia Rep. of Ireland
48 S5 Virginia S. Africa
21 S6 Virginia airport Spain
17 Q8 Virginia da Conquista Brazil
77 L8 Virginia Seamount sea feature S. Atlantic Ocean
36 D6 Vitry-la-Ville France
40 G3 Vitry-le-François France
41 E9 Vitry-sur-Loire France
12 I6 Vitry-sur-Seine France
19 N6 Vits' r. Belarus
18 L6 Vitsyebsk Belarus
20 P3 Vitsyebskaya Voblasts' admin. div. Belarus
40 F2 Vittangi r. Sweden
37 K7 Vittaresjaure l. Sweden
74 H10 Vittel France
71 M4 Vittoria Sicilia Italy
71 M4 Vittorio Veneto Italy
45 G8 Vityaz-vos Rus. Fed.
21 S6 Vityazevo Rus. Fed.
17 Q8 Vityazevskiy Liman lag. Rus. Fed.

137 F6 Vista Alegre Amazonas Brazil
139 F4 Vista Alegre Mato Grosso do Sul Brazil
137 F4 Vista Alegre Roraima Brazil
67 E7 Vistabella del Maestrazgo Spain
146 C3 Vista Flores Arg.
128 J3 Vista Hermosa Mex.
124 M6 Vista Lake CA U.S.A.
132 I5 Visten l. Sweden
78 G1 Vistonida, Limni lag. Greece
Vistula r. Pol. see Wisła
18 F7 Vištytis Lith.
55 K1 Vištytis r. Lith./Rus. Fed.
17 L6 Visun' r. Ukr.
179 O7 Viswema Nagaland India
57 J4 Viszneek Hungary
77 M7 Vit r. Bulg.
136 E3 Vita r. Col.
73 A8 Vita Sicilia Italy
185 M7 Vitakri Pak.
76 G7 Vita mt. Serb. and Mont.
57 J3 Vitaz Slovakia
138 C4 Vitavo r. Italy
138 B4 Vitré France
72 I3 Vitiaz Strait P.N.G.
143 G4 Vitichi Bol.
137 H5 Vitigudino Spain
201 □¹⁰ Vitileva i. Fiji
161 K1 Vitim r. Rus. Fed.
161 J1 Vitimskoye Ploskogor'ye plat. Rus. Fed.
76 J3 Vitina Kosovo, Srbija Serb. and Mont.
59 L1 Vitis Austria
57 G2 Vitkov Czech Rep.
59 O4 Vito r. Italy
200 □6 Vito P.N.G.
77 J9 Vitolište Macedonia
76 I8 Vitomirica Kosovo, Srbija Serb. and Mont.
138 C4 Vitor r. Peru
138 B4 Vitor r. Peru
72 I3 Vitória Espírito Santo Brazil
143 G4 Vitória Pará Brazil
137 H5 Vitória Spain see Vitoria-Gasteiz
63 O3 Vitória airport Spain
63 O3 Vitória, Montes de mts Spain
141 E5 Vitória da Conquista Brazil
63 O3 Vitória-Gasteiz Spain
214 G7 Vitória Seamount sea feature S. Atlantic Ocean
77 L8 Vitré nat. park Bulg.
75 M5 Vitravo r. Italy
38 I5 Vitré France
37 K8 Vitrey-sur-Mance France
41 G10 Vitrolles France
36 I5 Vitry-en-Artois France
36 H6 Vitry-en-Perthois France
40 D3 Vitry-la-Ville France
36 D6 Vitry-le-François France
12 I6 Vitry-sur-Loire France
19 N6 Vitry-sur-Seine France
18 L6 Vits' r. Belarus
37 K7 Vitsyebsk Belarus
37 K7 Vitsyebskaya Voblasts' admin. div. Belarus
74 H10 Vittangi Sweden
71 M4 Vittaresjaure l. Sweden
71 M4 Vittel France
17 Q8 Vittoria Sicilia Italy
71 M4 Vittorio Veneto Italy
17 Q8 Vityaz-vos Rus. Fed.
17 Q8 Vityazevo Rus. Fed.
51 E8 Vitzenburg Ger.
51 E8 Viuz-la-Chiésaz Ger.
40 I4 Viuz-en-Sallaz France
88 G4 Vivaro, Monts du mts France
59 K7 Vivario Corse France
72 C3 Vivaro Italy
72 E1 Vivcharove Ukr.
62 E1 Vivero Spain see Viveiro
62 C1 Viveiro Spain
85 F5 Vivel del Río Martín Spain
57 K3 Vivero Spain
22 E6 Viverols France
20 N4 Viverone, Lago di l. Italy
55 L6 Vivers Spain
76 I5 Vivi r. Rus. Fed.
18 K2 Voka Estonia
57 H6 Vivian LA U.S.A.
14 I4 Vivier-au-Court France
41 I8 Viviers France
41 E9 Viviez France
59 K7 Vivo di. Africa
18 G3 Vivod nik mt. Slovenia
56 C3 Vivonne France
Visé Guadalcanal Solomon Is
147 I5 Vivoratá Arg.
126 □R10 Vivorillo, Cayos is Hond.
36 I8 Vix Bourgogne France
42 C3 Vix Pays de la Loire France
55 M5 Viysk'ove Ukr.
16 F4 Viys'kove Ukr.

19 Q6 Vladimirskiy Tupik Rus. Fed.
Vladimir-Volyns'kyy Ukr. see Volodymyr-Volyns'kyy
56 E2 Vladislav Czech Rep.
162 G7 Vladivostok Rus. Fed.
51 E7 Vladychnoye Rus. Fed.
77 N4 Vlăhiţa Romania
77 J8 Vlajna mt. Serb. and Mont.
Vlakhokerassia Greece see
68 G3 Vlasenica Bos.-Herz.
78 H6 Vlašić Planina mts Serb. and Mont.
56 E2 Vlašim Czech Rep.
71 M4 Vlasiva Ukr.
77 K8 Vlasotince Srbija Serb. and Mont.
19 W6 Vlasovo Rus. Fed.
162 L2 Vlas'yevo Rus. Fed.
19 P8 Vlazovichi Rus. Fed.
57 G3 Vlčany Slovakia
185 M7 Vlieland S. Africa
57 J3 Vlkaş mt. Serb. and Mont.
96 F9 Vlieland S. Africa
44 H4 Vleuten Neth.
44 G2 Vlieland i. Neth.
44 H2 Vliimen Neth.
45 E5 Vlissingen Neth.
78 A2 Vlorë Albania
78 A2 Vlorës, Gjiri i b. Albania
49 G6 Vlotho Ger.
56 D1 Vltava r. Czech Rep.
59 J7 Vnáña r. Rus. Fed.
19 T2 Vodice Istra Croatia
182 K7 Vobkent Uzbek.
59 I3 Vöcklabruck Austria
59 H3 Vöcklamarkt Austria
71 Q5 Voderady Slovakia
68 E4 Vodice Šibenik Croatia
56 D2 Vodňany Czech Rep.
14 J2 Vodnjan Croatia
71 Q5 Vodice Istra Croatia
19 S5 Vodokolamsk Rus. Fed.
16 I4 Vodlozero, Ozero l. Rus. Fed.
14 I4 Vodlovozero Rus. Fed.
183 S5 Vodokovaya Rus. Fed.
17 N2 Voerde (Niederrhein) Ger.
22 G4 Voersaa Denmark
89 F5 Vogan Togo
17 Q4 Vogelenzang Neth.
17 P4 Vogelgram France
18 M2 Vogel Peak Nigeria
57 L3 Voghera Italy
19 N4 Voghera Italy
17 R3 Votovo Rus. Fed.
16 G5 Vogelheim France
15 G5 Vogelwehr Ger.
15 G5 Vokov Lipetskaya Oblast' Rus. Fed.
70 G6 Voghera Italy
21 L6 Voghiera Italy
191 H5 Voghji r. Armenia
20 J5 Voghill Norway
19 R7 Vogoča Bos.-Herz.
52 H6 Vogt Ger.
59 S8 Vogtareuth Ger.
70 F6 Volpago del Mòntello Italy
57 J3 Vogtland reg. Ger.
73 L5 Vogtsburg im Kaiserstuhl Ger.
86 D2 Vohburg an der Donau Ger.
53 M2 Vohenstrauß Ger.
95 □J4 Vohemar Madag. see Vohimarina
95 □J4 Vohilava Fianarantsoa Madag.
95 □J4 Vohilava Fianarantsoa Madag.
95 □J4 Vohimena, Tanjona c. Madag.
95 □J4 Vohipeno Madag.
95 □J4 Vohitrandriana Madag.
49 G8 Vöhl Ger.
19 W4 Vöhma Estonia
143 E5 Vöhrenbach Ger.
52 F5 Vöhringen Baden-Württemberg Ger.
53 J5 Vöhringen Bayern Ger.
71 J9 Voi Kenya
49 E6 Void-Vacon France
63 K6 Voigtstedt Ger.
21 S6 Voikoski Fin.
73 P7 Voillecomte France
77 L5 Voineasa Romania
18 L3 Voineşti Romania
86 D2 Voinjama Liberia
40 H3 Voiron France
36 C6 Voise r. France
109 I1 Voisey Bay Nfld and Lab. Can.
40 C5 Voisines France
49 H3 Voise France
55 L3 Vojtište Austria
56 C2 Vojčice Slovakia
22 E6 Vojens Denmark
21 S6 Vojmsjön l. Sweden
55 L7 Vojnić Slovenia
76 I5 Vojvodina prov. Serb. and Mont.
18 K2 Voka Estonia
57 H6 Vokány Hungary
14 I4 Voknavolok Rus. Fed.
89 U4 Voko Cameroon
14 K3 Vol'r. Rus. Fed.
56 C3 Volary Czech Rep.
122 L4 Volborg MT U.S.A.
138 D5 Volcán Arg.
182 D1 Volcán, Cerro del vol. Chile
146 B2 Volcán, Cerro del hills Arg.
126 □R13 Volcán Barú, Parque Nacional nat. park Panama

18 G2 Vormsi i. Estonia
22 H1 Vormsund Norway
19 W9 Vorob'yevka Lipetskaya Oblast' Rus. Fed.
15 H6 Vorob'yevka Voronezhskaya Oblast' Rus. Fed.
17 M1 Vorob'yivka Ukr.
17 M8 Vorob'yivka Ukr.
19 V4 Vorobyova Ukr.
192 J3 Vorogovo Rus. Fed.
16 D5 Vorokhta Ukr.
77 O3 Vorona Romania
15 H6 Vorona r. Rus. Fed.
15 G6 Voronezh Rus. Fed.
19 W9 Voronezh r. Rus. Fed.
162 G7 Vol'no-Nadezhdinskoye Rus. Fed.
17 L8 Vol'noye Ukr.
183 N1 Vol'nyansk Ukr. see Vil'nyans'k
19 V5 Voronezh Oblast admin. div. Rus. Fed.
193 K2 Vyazov'yevskiy Zapovednik nature res. Rus. Fed.
162 I4 Voronezhskaya Oblast' admin. div. Rus. Fed.
17 S2 Voronezhskoye Rus. Fed.
17 M2 Voronizh Ukr.
17 M3 Voron'ky Ukr.
16 F2 Voronok Rus. Fed.
17 L1 Voronok Rus. Fed.
19 U6 Voronov, Mys pt Rus. Fed.
19 P1 Voronovo Rus. Fed.
19 U6 Voronovo Rus. Fed.
17 N2 Voronovo Rus. Fed.
16 H4 Voronovytsya Ukr.
18 L4 Vorontsova Rus. Fed.
16 D4 Vorontsovka Ukr.
183 S5 Vorota val. Kazakh.
191 H6 Vorotan r. Armenia
17 K6 Vorotynets Rus. Fed.
14 I4 Vorotynets Rus. Fed.
17 T7 Vorotynsk Rus. Fed.
191 D1 Voroykoleskaya Rus. Fed.
17 N2 Vorozhba Sums'ka Oblast' Ukr.
17 N3 Vorozhba Sums'ka Oblast' Ukr.
50 G2 Vorpommersche Boddenlandschaft, Nationalpark nat. park Ger.
213 B2 Vorposten Peak Antarctica
59 M5 Vorra Ger.
59 M5 Vörsar Austria
15 F6 Vorskla r. Ukr.
59 M1 Vorsklitsa r. Rus. Fed.
45 H6 Vorst Belgium
96 F1 Vorsterhoop S. Africa
19 R7 Vorta Romania
213 B2 Vorterkaka Nunatak mt. Antarctica
18 I3 Vörtsjärv l. Estonia
18 L4 Võru Estonia
185 N2 Vorukh Tajik.
58 H4 Vorwerk Ger.
14 J3 Vorya r. Rus. Fed.
16 J3 Vorzel' Ukr.
70 F6 Vosa Belarus
96 G6 Vosburg S. Africa
37 M8 Vose Tajik.
59 N3 Vösendorf Austria
37 L7 Vosges dept France
37 M8 Vosges mts France
37 O6 Vosges du Nord, Parc Naturel Régional des nat. park France
19 W4 Voshchazhnikovo Rus. Fed.
191 G4 Voskevan Armenia
17 N8 Voskhod Ukr.
19 V6 Voskresensk Rus. Fed.
17 L6 Voskresens'ke Ukr.
14 M3 Vol'ya r. Rus. Fed.
55 L6 Volya Belarus
71 R5 Volya r. Ukr.
40 C5 Volya Arlamivs'ka Ukr.
21 I6 Volyně Czech Rep.
56 C2 Volyňka r. Czech Rep.
19 N1 Vojvodina r. Serb. and Mont.
182 G1 Voskresenskoye Respublika Bashkortostan Rus. Fed.
19 U7 Voskresenskoye Tul'skaya Oblast' Rus. Fed.
19 U4 Voskresenskoye Vologodskaya Oblast' Rus. Fed.
16 D2 Voskresenskoye Yaroslavskaya Oblast' Rus. Fed.
162 M3 Vostochno-Sakhalinskiy Gory mts Sakhalin Rus. Fed.
193 P2 Vostochno-Sibirskoye More sea Rus. Fed.
14 F2 Vostochnoye Munozero Rus. Fed.
14 K4 Vostochnyy Kirovskaya Oblast' Rus. Fed.
17 Q8 Vostochnyy Sakhalin Rus. Fed.
17 Q8 Vostochnyy, Liman l. Rus. Fed.
1 □ Vostochnyy Kazakhstan admin. div. Kazakh.
36 A4 Vron France
77 M9 Vrosina Greece
15 K6 Vroutek Czech Rep.
54 E4 Vrouwenpolder Neth.
74 H9 Vrsi Albania
46 H5 Vršac Vojvodina, Srbija Serb. and Mont.

18 G2 Vormsi i. Estonia

14 J4 Voya r. Rus. Fed.
120 I1 Voyageurs National Park MN U.S.A.
17 K5 Voyevods'ke Ukr.
20 U4 Voynitsa Rus. Fed.
55 M6 Voynyliv Ukr.
14 K2 Vöyri Fin. see Vörå
192 J3 Voyvozh Respublika Komi Rus. Fed.
14 K3 Voyvozh Respublika Komi Rus. Fed.
200 □6 Voza Choiseul Solomon Is
Vozdvizhenskoye Moskovskaya Oblast' Rus. Fed.
14 H3 Vozha r. Rus. Fed.
14 G3 Vozhe, Ozero l. Rus. Fed.
14 H3 Vozhega Rus. Fed.
14 G3 Vozhgora Rus. Fed.
63 Q5 Vozmediano Spain
183 N1 Voznesenka Rus. Fed.
17 K6 Voznesens'ke Ukr.
191 C1 Voznesenskaya Krasnodarskiy Kray Rus. Fed.
191 E2 Voznesenskaya Respublika Ingushetiya Rus. Fed.
19 Y5 Voznesenskoye Ivanovskaya Oblast' Rus. Fed.
182 H5 Voznesens'ke Ukr.
182 H5 Voznesens'ke Ukr.
17 L6 Voznesens'k Ukr.
183 N1 Vozrozhdenya Island Uzbek.
17 Q8 Vozsiyats'ke Ukr.
183 N1 Vozvyshenka Kazakh.
Vozvyshenskiy Kazakh. see
162 F3 Vozzhayevka Rus. Fed.
22 F4 Vrå Denmark
77 M8 Vrabevo Bulg.
57 H3 Vráble Slovakia
78 B5 Vrachionas hill Zakynthos Greece
78 C4 Vrachnaíka Greece
22 E2 Vrådal Norway
16 J6 Vradiyivka Ukr.
Vrakhiónas Óros hill Zakynthos Greece see Vrachionas
Vrakhnaíika Greece see Vrachnaíka
77 O7 Vran mt. Bos.-Herz.
77 O7 Vrana r. Bulg.
72 F4 Vrangel' Rus. Fed.
162 K1 Vrangelya, Mys pt Rus. Fed.
193 T2 Vrangelya, Ostrov i. Rus. Fed.
22 H4 Vrångö naturreservat nature res. Sweden
68 G3 Vranja Croatia
77 J8 Vranje Srbija Serb. and Mont.
55 M3 Vranjska Banja Srbija Serb. and Mont.
56 E3 Vranov, Vodní nádrž resr Czech Rep.
59 O2 Vranovice Czech Rep.
57 K3 Vranov nad Topľou Slovakia
59 K7 Vransko Slovenia
17 O6 Vransko Jezero l. Croatia
57 K3 Vransko Jezero l. Croatia
76 I9 Vrapčište Macedonia
77 K7 Vrasidas, Akra pt Greece
Srbija
77 O8 Vratnik pass Bulg.
77 L7 Vratsa Bulg.
68 F3 Vrbanja r. Bos.-Herz.
68 F3 Vrbas r. Bos.-Herz.
19 S9 Vrbas Vojvodina, Srbija Serb. and Mont.
57 J5 Vrbica Vojvodina, Srbija Serb. and Mont.
71 R5 Vrbnik Croatia
56 G1 Vrbno pod Pradědem Czech Rep.
57 G3 Vrbov Slovakia
56 G3 Vrbovce Slovakia
68 E3 Vrbovec Croatia
57 G3 Vrbové Slovakia
68 E3 Vrbovsko Croatia
37 N7 Vrécourt France
59 I8 Vrede S. Africa
49 C6 Vredefort S. Africa
96 B8 Vredenburg S. Africa
96 C7 Vredendal S. Africa
137 G3 Vredeshoop Namibia
44 H4 Vreeland Neth.
62 E6 Vrees Ger.
64 E6 Vreia de Jales Port.
59 I8 Vrelo S. Africa
Serb. and Mont.
71 P5 Vresse Belgium
45 G9 Vresse Belgium
59 I2 Vrhnika Slovenia
73 O4 Vrbyberd Czech Rep.
53 O2 Vrchlabí Czech Rep.
57 G2 Vsetín Czech Rep.
104 B4 Vsevolozhsk Rus. Fed.
19 N1 Vshyva r. Ukr.
15 H5 Vskhody Rus. Fed.
17 R7 Vtáčnik mts Slovakia
57 H3 Vtáčnik mt. Slovakia
44 H5 Vught Neth.
76 J9 Vučje Srbija Serb. and Mont.

358 **Vuntut National Park** to **Washburn**

104 E3 **Vuntut National Park** *Y.T.* Can.
18 J1 **Vuohijärvi** Fin.
21 S6 **Vuohijärvi** *l.* Fin.
20 T4 **Vuokatti** Fin.
18 N1 **Vuoksa** *r.* Rus. Fed.
18 M1 **Vuoksa, Ozero** *l.* Rus. Fed.
18 L1 **Vuoksi** *r.* Fin.
20 S4 **Vuolijoki** Fin.
20 P3 **Vuollerim** Sweden
20 O3 **Vuolvojaure** *l.* Sweden
20 S3 **Vuostimo** Fin.
20 S2 **Vuotso** Fin.
200 □6 **Vuranimala** Solomon Is
77 O8 **Vŭrbitsa** Bulg.
77 M5 **Vurpær** Romania
77 L7 **Vŭrshets** Bulg.
18 K6 **Vustsye** Belarus
77 P4 **Vutcani** Romania
176 G4 **Vuyyuru** *Andhra Prad.* India
59 L6 **Vuzenica** Slovenia
16 D3 **Vuzlove** *L'vivs'ka Oblast'* Ukr.
16 B5 **Vuzlove** *Zakarpats'ka Oblast'* Ukr.
18 J7 **Vuzlyanka** *r.* Belarus
182 J1 **Vvedenka** Kazakh.
19 Y5 **Vveden'ye** Rus. Fed.
93 B7 **Vwawa** Tanz.
93 B7 **Vwaza Game Reserve** *nature res.* Malawi
17 P7 **Vyacheslavka** Ukr.
55 M2 **Vyalikaya Byerastavitsa** Belarus
18 H8 **Vyalikaya Mazheykava** Belarus
18 M8 **Vyalikiya Bortniki** Belarus
18 J8 **Vyalikiya Zhukhavichy** Belarus
19 N2 **Vyal'ye, Ozero** *l.* Rus. Fed.
178 D9 **Vyara** *Gujarat* India
19 N6 **Vyarechcha** Belarus
18 G9 **Vyarkhovichy** Belarus
Vyarkhowye Belarus *see* **Ruba**
18 L9 **Vyatchyn** Belarus
14 J5 **Vyatka** *r.* Rus. Fed.
14 J4 **Vyatskiye Polyany** Rus. Fed.
19 X4 **Vyatskoye** Rus. Fed.
18 M5 **Vyaz** Rus. Fed.
162 I5 **Vyazemskiy** Rus. Fed.
19 R6 **Vyaz'ma** Rus. Fed.
19 Q6 **Vyaz'ma** *r.* Rus. Fed.
14 H4 **Vyazniki** Rus. Fed.
15 I6 **Vyazovka** *Astrakhanskaya Oblast'* Rus. Fed.
182 A2 **Vyazovka** *Saratovskaya Oblast'* Rus. Fed.
182 B1 **Vyazovka** *Saratovskaya Oblast'* Rus. Fed.
15 H6 **Vyazovka** *Volgogradskaya Oblast'* Rus. Fed.
19 W8 **Vyazovo** Rus. Fed.
17 P2 **Vyazovoye** Rus. Fed.
18 L1 **Vyborg** Rus. Fed.
18 L1 **Vyborgskiy Zaliv** *b.* Rus. Fed.
14 I3 **Vychegda** *r.* Rus. Fed.
14 I3 **Vychegodskiy** Rus. Fed.
57 I2 **Východná** Slovakia
57 L2 **Východné Karpaty** *park* Slovakia
55 M1 **Vydeniai** Lith.
55 N4 **Vyderta** Ukr.
55 M4 **Vydranytsya** Ukr.
168 I1 **Vydrino** Rus. Fed.
55 M4 **Vydrychi** Ukr.
19 O8 **Vyeramyeyki** Belarus
18 K6 **Vyerkhnyadzvinsk** Belarus
19 O9 **Vyetka** Belarus
18 L6 **Vyetryna** Belarus
19 R8 **Vygonichi** Rus. Fed.
14 F3 **Vygozero, Ozero** *l.* Rus. Fed.
16 E1 **Vyhanashchy** Belarus
57 H3 **Vyhne** Slovakia
15 H5 **Vyksa** Rus. Fed.
40 I1 **Vy-lès-Lure** France
16 I8 **Vylkove** Ukr.
16 B5 **Vylok** Ukr.
14 J3 **Vym'** *r.* Rus. Fed.
16 D4 **Vynnyky** Ukr.
16 C5 **Vynohradiv** Ukr.
17 M5 **Vynohradivka** Ukr.
17 K6 **Vynohradne** Ukr.
17 L7 **Vynohradove** *Khersons'ka Oblast'* Ukr.
17 M8 **Vynohradove** *Respublika Krym* Ukr.
176 E7 **Vypin Island** India
19 Q4 **Vypolzovo** Rus. Fed.
17 M3 **Vyrishal'ne** Ukr.
19 N2 **Vyritsa** Rus. Fed.
30 F2 **Vyrnwy, Lake** *Wales* U.K.
17 N2 **Vyry** Ukr.
15 G7 **Vyselki** Rus. Fed.
16 J3 **Vyshcha Dubechnya** Ukr.
17 Q4 **Vyshche Solone** Ukr.
17 N6 **Vyshchetarasivka** Ukr.
19 X7 **Vyshgorod** Rus. Fed.
18 K4 **Vyshgorodok** Rus. Fed.
16 J3 **Vyshhorod** Ukr.
16 B5 **Vyshka** Ukr.
19 O9 **Vyshkov** Rus. Fed.
16 C5 **Vyshkove** Ukr.
19 S4 **Vyshkovo** Rus. Fed.
17 M5 **Vyshneve** *Dnipropetrovs'ka Oblast'* Ukr.
16 J3 **Vyshneve** *Kyivs'ka Oblast'* Ukr.
19 R5 **Vyshnevolotskaya Gryada** *ridge* Rus. Fed.
19 R4 **Vyshnevolotskoye Vodokhranilishche** *resr* Rus. Fed.
17 Q1 **Vyshneye-Ol'shanoye** Rus. Fed.
55 M4 **Vyshniv** Ukr.
16 E4 **Vyshnivets'** Ukr.
19 R4 **Vyshniy-Volochek** Rus. Fed.
16 C4 **Vyshnya** *r.* Ukr.
17 M4 **Vyshnyaky** Ukr.
19 N4 **Vyskod'** Rus. Fed.
56 G2 **Vyškov** Czech Rep.
57 K2 **Vyšný Mirošov** Slovakia
57 K2 **Vyšný Orlík** Slovakia
56 E2 **Vysočina** *admin. reg.* Czech Rep.
56 D3 **Vysoká** *mt.* Czech Rep.
56 G3 **Vysoká** *hill* Slovakia
16 H3 **Vysoka Pich** Ukr.
56 F3 **Vysoká pri Morave** Slovakia
18 G9 **Vysokaye** *Brestskaya Voblasts'* Belarus
19 N7 **Vysokaye** *Vitsyebskaya Voblasts'* Belarus
17 M7 **Vysoke** Ukr.
56 F2 **Vysoké Mýto** Czech Rep.
19 T7 **Vysokinichi** Rus. Fed.
162 K3 **Vysokogorniy** Rus. Fed.
17 Q5 **Vysokopillya** *Donets'ka Oblast'* Ukr.
17 O4 **Vysokopillya** *Kharkivs'ka Oblast'* Ukr.
17 M6 **Vysokopillya** *Khersons'ka Oblast'* Ukr.
19 V4 **Vysokovo** Rus. Fed.
19 T5 **Vysokovsk** Rus. Fed.
Vysokoye Belarus *see* Vysokaye
19 R5 **Vysokoye** Rus. Fed.
18 L1 **Vysotsk** Rus. Fed.
16 F2 **Vysots'k** Ukr.
59 J2 **Vyšší Brod** Czech Rep.
16 I2 **Vystupovychi** Ukr.
19 T1 **Vytegra** Rus. Fed.
193 R3 **Vyvenka** Rus. Fed.
14 I3 **Vyya** *r.* Rus. Fed.
16 D2 **Vyzhivka** *r.* Ukr.
16 E5 **Vyzhnytsya** Ukr.
18 I6 **Vyžuona** *r.* Lith.
55 I1 **Vzmor'ye** Rus. Fed.

W

88 E4 **Wa** Ghana
48 I1 **Waabs** Ger.
92 D4 **Waajid** Somalia
49 J7 **Waake** Ger.
53 L6 **Waakirchen** Ger.
53 J6 **Waal** Ger.
44 G5 **Waal** *r.* Neth.
45 H6 **Waalre** Neth.
44 H5 **Waalwijk** Neth.
206 F5 **Waanyi/Garawa Aboriginal Land** *res. N.T.* Austr.
44 G3 **Waarland** Neth.
45 E6 **Waarschoot** Belgium
45 F6 **Waasmunster** Belgium
92 B2 **Waat** Sudan
153 J8 **Wabag** P.N.G.
108 B3 **Wabakimi Lake** *Ont.* Can.
108 B3 **Wabakimi Provincial Park** *park Ont.* Can.
187 M4 **Wabal** *well* Oman
106 H4 **Wabamun** *Alta* Can.
106 H4 **Wabamun Lake** *Alta* Can.
106 H3 **Wabasca** *r. Alta* Can.
106 H4 **Wabasca-Desmarais** *Alta* Can.
114 E5 **Wabash** *IN* U.S.A.
116 A8 **Wabash** *OH* U.S.A.
120 K7 **Wabash** *r. IN* U.S.A.
110 B5 **Wabasha** *MN* U.S.A.
108 C3 **Wabassi** *r. Ont.* Can.
111 J1 **Wabatongushi Lake** *Ont.* Can.
92 D3 **Wabē Gestro** *r.* Eth.
92 D3 **Wabē Mena** *r.* Eth.
110 F4 **Wabeno** *WI* U.S.A.
49 H8 **Wabern** Ger.
92 E3 **Wabē Shebelē Wenz** *r.* Eth.
108 A3 **Wabigoon Lake** *Ont.* Can.
107 L4 **Wabowden** *Man.* Can.
187 H2 **Wabrah** *well* Saudi Arabia
54 G2 **Wąbrzeźno** Pol.
171 K2 **Wabu** *Anhui* China
108 C2 **Wabuk Point** *Ont.* Can.
109 H2 **Wabush** *Nfld and Lab.* Can.
109 H2 **Wabush Lake** *Nfld and Lab.* Can.
115 H9 **Waccamaw** *r. SC* U.S.A.
115 H8 **Waccamaw, Lake** *NC* U.S.A.
115 F11 **Waccasassa Bay** *FL* U.S.A.
117 J11 **Wachapreague** *VA* U.S.A.
59 L3 **Wachau** *reg.* Austria
52 E3 **Wachenheim an der Weinstraße** Ger.
166 B5 **Wachi** Japan
92 C3 **Wach'īlē** Eth.
50 G5 **Wachow** Ger.
45 E6 **Wachtebeke** Belgium
49 H10 **Wächtersbach** Ger.
117 N6 **Wachusett Reservoir** *MA* U.S.A.
48 H2 **Wacken** Ger.
53 M3 **Wackersdorf** Ger.
109 H3 **Waco** *Que.* Can.
121 G10 **Waco** *TX* U.S.A.
120 F6 **Waconda Lake** *KS* U.S.A.
110 B5 **Wacouta** *MN* U.S.A.
185 L8 **Wad** Pak.
167 L5 **Wada** Japan
84 E6 **Wada'a** Sudan
166 B6 **Wada-misaki** *pt* Japan
167 H3 **Wada-tōge** *pass* Japan
206 F3 **Wada Wadalla Aboriginal Land** *res. N.T.* Austr.
166 A5 **Wadayama** Japan
84 E6 **Wad Banda** Sudan
205 L7 **Wadbilliga National Park** *N.S.W.* Austr.
84 C2 **Waddān** Libya
84 B2 **Waddān, Jabal** *hills* Libya
125 T8 **Waddell Dam** *AZ* U.S.A.
44 G2 **Waddeneilanden** *is* Neth.
Wadden Islands Neth. *see* Waddeneilanden
44 G3 **Waddenzee** *sea chan.* Neth.
31 K4 **Waddesdon** *Buckinghamshire, England* U.K.
48 K4 **Waddeweitz** Ger.
204 F5 **Waddikee** *S.A.* Austr.
29 P7 **Waddington** *Lincolnshire, England* U.K.
106 E5 **Waddington, Mount** *B.C.* Can.
27 I8 **Waddingtown** Rep. of Ireland
44 G4 **Waddinxveen** Neth.
207 N8 **Waddy Point** *Qld* Austr.
30 C6 **Wadebridge** *Cornwall, England* U.K.
92 B2 **Wadega** Sudan
107 K5 **Wadena** *Sask.* Can.
120 H2 **Wadena** *MN* U.S.A.
180 C7 **Wad en Nail** Sudan
70 F1 **Wädenswil** Switz.
52 B2 **Wadern** Ger.
49 F7 **Wadersloh** Ger.
115 G8 **Wadesboro** *NC* U.S.A.
206 B3 **Wadeye** *N.T.* Austr.
176 C3 **Wadgaon** *Mahar.* India
178 F9 **Wadgaon** *Mahar.* India
52 B3 **Wadgassen** Ger.
85 G5 **Wad Hamid** Sudan
90 E2 **Wad Hassib** Sudan
31 M5 **Wadhurst** *East Sussex, England* U.K.
178 C8 **Wadhwan** *Gujarat* India
Wadhwan *Gujarat* India *see* Surendranagar
176 E4 **Wadi** *Karnataka* India
171 I2 **Wadian** *Henan* China
190 D7 **Wādī as Sīr** Jordan
190 B10 **Wādī Fayrān** Egypt
Wâdi Gimâl Island Egypt *see* Wādī Jimāl, Jazīrat
85 F4 **Wadi Halfa** Sudan
186 E4 **Wādī Ḥammah** Saudi Arabia
186 B3 **Wādī Jimāl, Jazīrat** *i.* Egypt
190 D8 **Wādī Mūsá** Jordan
118 G5 **Wading** *r. NJ* U.S.A.
119 J3 **Wading River** *NY* U.S.A.
55 H4 **Wadlew** Pol.
85 G6 **Wad Medani** Sudan
164 □F19 **Wadomari** *Nansei-shotō* Japan
55 H6 **Wadowice** Pol.
55 J5 **Wadowice Górne** Pol.
124 M2 **Wadsworth** *NV* U.S.A.
116 D7 **Wadsworth** *OH* U.S.A.
Wadu *i. S. Male* Maldives *see* Vaadhu
Wadu Channel Maldives *see* Vaadhu Channel
96 E10 **Waenhuiskrans** S. Africa
212 P1 **Waesche, Mount** Antarctica
169 R7 **Wafangdian** *Liaoning* China
90 D5 **Wafania** Dem. Rep. Congo
164 S7 **Waga-gawa** *r.* Japan
178 E4 **Wagah** *Punjab* India
206 C2 **Wagait Aboriginal Land** *res. N.T.* Austr.
54 G3 **Waganiec** Pol.
48 G5 **Wagenfeld** Ger.
48 K5 **Wagenhoff** Ger.
44 I5 **Wageningen** Neth.
137 G3 **Wageningen** Suriname
105 J3 **Wager Bay** *Nunavut* Can.
205 K6 **Wagga Wagga** *N.S.W.* Austr.
178 D9 **Waghai** *Gujarat* India
52 F3 **Waghäusel** Ger.
206 C3 **Wagiman Aboriginal Land** *res. N.T.* Austr.
209 D12 **Wagin** *W.A.* Austr.
53 N6 **Waging am See** Ger.
53 N6 **Waginger See** *l.* Ger.
70 F1 **Wägitaler See** *l.* Switz.
106 D4 **Waglisla** *B.C.* Can.
140 E5 **Wagner** Brazil
120 F4 **Wagner** *SD* U.S.A.
121 H7 **Wagoner** *OK* U.S.A.
123 L8 **Wagon Mound** *NM* U.S.A.
58 H5 **Wagrain** Austria
48 J2 **Wagrien** *reg.* Ger.
54 F3 **Wągrowiec** Pol.
185 O5 **Wah** Pak.
155 F5 **Wahai** *Seram* Indon.
89 F5 **Wahala** Togo
84 D2 **Wāḥāt Jālū** Libya
90 F2 **Wahda** *state* Sudan
109 G2 **Wahemen, Lac** *l. Que.* Can.
124 □C12 **Wahiawā** *HI* U.S.A.
20 □ **Wahlenbergfjorden** *inlet* Svalbard
49 I8 **Wahlhausen** Ger.
51 H7 **Wahlsdorf** Ger.
48 J3 **Wahlstedt** Ger.
120 G5 **Wahoo** *NE* U.S.A.
120 G2 **Wahpeton** *ND* U.S.A.
48 K5 **Wahrenholz** Ger.
125 S3 **Wah Wah Mountains** *UT* U.S.A.
176 C4 **Wai** *Mahar.* India
124 □D12 **Waiāhole** *HI* U.S.A.
124 □E13 **Waiakoa** *HI* U.S.A.
124 □B11 **Wai'ale'ale** *mt. HI* U.S.A.
124 □C12 **Wai'ale'e** *HI* U.S.A.
124 □C12 **Waialua** *HI* U.S.A.
124 □C12 **Waialua Bay** *HI* U.S.A.
124 □C12 **Wai'anae** *HI* U.S.A.
124 □C12 **Wai'anae Range** *mts HI* U.S.A.
202 M4 **Waiapu** *r. North I.* N.Z.
202 K7 **Waiaruhe** *North I.* N.Z.
203 H9 **Waiau** *South I.* N.Z.
202 L5 **Waiau** *r. North I.* N.Z.
203 B13 **Waiau** *r. South I.* N.Z.
203 H9 **Waiau** *r. South I.* N.Z.
52 G4 **Waiblingen** Ger.
52 F3 **Waibstadt** Ger.
53 N2 **Waidhaus** Ger.
53 K4 **Waidhofen** Ger.
59 L2 **Waidhofen an der Thaya** Austria
59 K4 **Waidhofen an der Ybbs** Austria
155 F4 **Waigama** *Papua* Indon.
155 G4 **Waigeo** *i. Papua* Indon.
53 I2 **Waigolshausen** Ger.
203 E11 **Waihao Downs** *South I.* N.Z.
202 H1 **Waiharara** *North I.* N.Z.
202 J4 **Waiharoa** *North I.* N.Z.
202 J3 **Waiheke Island** *North I.* N.Z.
202 J4 **Waihi** *North I.* N.Z.
202 J4 **Waihi Beach** *North I.* N.Z.
202 K4 **Waihi Estuary** *North I.* N.Z.
203 E13 **Waihola, Lake** *South I.* N.Z.
202 J4 **Waihou** *r. North I.* N.Z.
202 L6 **Waihua** *North I.* N.Z.
90 E5 **Waika** Dem. Rep. Congo
155 A8 **Waikabubak** *Sumba* Indon.
203 C12 **Waikaia** *South I.* N.Z.
203 C12 **Waikaia** *r. South I.* N.Z.
203 D12 **Waikaka** *South I.* N.Z.
203 J7 **Waikanae** *North I.* N.Z.
124 □D12 **Waikāne** *HI* U.S.A.
124 □E13 **Waikapu** *HI* U.S.A.
202 J4 **Waikare, Lake** *North I.* N.Z.
202 L5 **Waikareiti, Lake** *North I.* N.Z.
202 K5 **Waikaremoana, Lake** *North I.* N.Z.
202 I4 **Waikaretu** *North I.* N.Z.
203 G9 **Waikari** *South I.* N.Z.
202 I4 **Waikato** *admin. reg. North I.* N.Z.
202 I4 **Waikato** *r. North I.* N.Z.
203 D13 **Waikawa** *South I.* N.Z.
202 L4 **Waikawa Point** *North I.* N.Z.
202 J5 **Waikeria** *North I.* N.Z.
204 G6 **Waikerie** *S.A.* Austr.
124 □F14 **Waiki'i** *HI* U.S.A.
124 □D12 **Waikīkī Beach** *HI* U.S.A.
202 K5 **Waikirikiri** *North I.* N.Z.
155 C8 **Waiklibang** *Flores* Indon.
203 D13 **Waikoikoi** *South I.* N.Z.
202 L6 **Waikokopa** *North I.* N.Z.
203 E12 **Waikouaiti** *South I.* N.Z.
201 □1a **Wailotua** *Viti Levu* Fiji
124 □B11 **Wailua** *HI* U.S.A.
124 □E13 **Wailua** *HI* U.S.A.
124 □E13 **Wailuku** *HI* U.S.A.
203 C13 **Waimahake** *South I.* N.Z.
203 G10 **Waimakariri** *r. South I.* N.Z.
202 L5 **Waimana** *North I.* N.Z.
124 □D12 **Waimānalo** *HI* U.S.A.
124 □D12 **Waimānalo Beach** *HI* U.S.A.
203 F8 **Waimangaroa** *South I.* N.Z.
202 K6 **Waimarama** *North I.* N.Z.
203 F8 **Waimarie** *South I.* N.Z.
203 F11 **Waimate** *South I.* N.Z.
202 H2 **Waimatenui** *North I.* N.Z.
202 I3 **Waimauku** *North I.* N.Z.
124 □B12 **Waimea** *HI* U.S.A.
124 □C12 **Waimea** *HI* U.S.A.
124 □F13 **Waimea** *HI* U.S.A.
124 □C12 **Waimea Bay** *HI* U.S.A.
155 B5 **Waimenda** *Sulawesi* Indon.
45 J8 **Waimes** Belgium
53 I5 **Wain** Ger.
116 F6 **Wainfleet** *Ont.* Can.
29 R7 **Wainfleet All Saints** *Lincolnshire, England* U.K.
176 F3 **Wainganga** *r.* India
155 B8 **Waingapu** *Sumba* Indon.
203 J7 **Waingawa** *North I.* N.Z.
30 C6 **Wainhouse Corner** *Cornwall, England* U.K.
137 G2 **Waini Point** Guyana
203 F11 **Wainono Lagoon** *South I.* N.Z.
107 I4 **Wainwright** *Alta* Can.
104 C2 **Wainwright** *AK* U.S.A.
202 L5 **Waioeka** *r. North I.* N.Z.
202 I2 **Waiotira** *North I.* N.Z.
202 J6 **Waiouru** *North I.* N.Z.
202 J4 **Waipa** *r. North I.* N.Z.
203 D13 **Waipahi** *South I.* N.Z.
124 □C12 **Waipahu** *HI* U.S.A.
202 L5 **Waipaoa** *r. North I.* N.Z.
203 C13 **Waipapa Point** *South I.* N.Z.
203 G10 **Waipara** *South I.* N.Z.
202 K6 **Waipawa** *North I.* N.Z.
202 I4 **Waipipi** *North I.* N.Z.
202 I2 **Waipu** *North I.* N.Z.
202 K6 **Waipukurau** *North I.* N.Z.
202 K5 **Wairakei** *North I.* N.Z.
203 J8 **Wairarapa, Lake** *North I.* N.Z.
203 I8 **Wairau** *r. South I.* N.Z.
203 H8 **Wairau Valley** *South I.* N.Z.
202 L6 **Wairoa** *North I.* N.Z.
202 I3 **Wairoa** *r. North I.* N.Z.
202 L6 **Wairoa** *r. North I.* N.Z.
155 C8 **Wairunu** *Flores* Indon.
155 G4 **Waisai** *Papua* Indon.
53 K2 **Waischenfeld** Ger.
171 L4 **Waishe** *Zhejiang* China
202 K5 **Waitahanui** *North I.* N.Z.
203 D12 **Waitahuna** *South I.* N.Z.
202 J4 **Waitakaruru** *North I.* N.Z.
203 F11 **Waitaki** *South I.* N.Z.
203 F11 **Waitaki** *r. South I.* N.Z.
202 □ **Waitangi** *Chatham Is* S. Pacific Ocean
203 E10 **Waitangitaona** *r. South I.* N.Z.
202 I5 **Waitara** *North I.* N.Z.
203 E12 **Waitati** *South I.* N.Z.
204 □3 **Waite, Mount** *hill* S. Pacific Ocean
206 E7 **Waite River** *N.T.* Austr.
202 J4 **Waitoa** *North I.* N.Z.
202 J5 **Waitomo Caves** *North I.* N.Z.
202 I6 **Waitotara** *North I.* N.Z.
202 I6 **Waitotari** *r. North I.* N.Z.
122 E3 **Waitsburg** *WA* U.S.A.
202 I4 **Waiuku** *North I.* N.Z.
203 D13 **Waiwera South** *South I.* N.Z.
155 F5 **Waiya** *Seram* Indon.
171 L5 **Waiyang** *Fujian* China
201 □1 **Waiyevu** *Taveuni* Fiji
59 I3 **Waizenkirchen** Austria
186 G6 **Wajīd, Jabal al** *hills* Saudi Arabia
165 L13 **Wajiki** Japan
165 N9 **Wajima** Japan
92 D4 **Wajir** Kenya
90 D4 **Waka** *Équateur* Dem. Rep. Congo
90 D5 **Waka** *Équateur* Dem. Rep. Congo
155 B8 **Waka** *Flores* Indon.
155 E5 **Waka, Tanjung** *pt* Indon.
111 L2 **Wakami Lake** *Ont.* Can.
203 H8 **Wakapuaka** *South I.* N.Z.
165 L11 **Wakasa** Japan
166 C4 **Wakasa-wan** *b.* Japan
166 C4 **Wakasa-wan Quasi National Park** Japan
203 C12 **Wakatipu, Lake** *South I.* N.Z.
155 C6 **Wakatobi Marine National Park** *nat. park* Indon.
111 K3 **Wakatoma Lake** *Ont.* Can.
107 J4 **Wakaw** *Sask.* Can.
201 □1 **Wakaya** *i.* Fiji
206 F5 **Wakaya Aboriginal Land** *res. N.T.* Austr.
166 B7 **Wakayama** Japan
166 B8 **Wakayama** *pref.* Japan
164 S8 **Wakayanagi** Japan
Wake Atoll N. Pacific Ocean *see* **Wake Island**
120 F6 **WaKeeney** *KS* U.S.A.
111 S4 **Wakefield** *Que.* Can.
130 □ **Wakefield** Jamaica
203 H8 **Wakefield** *South I.* N.Z.
29 N6 **Wakefield** *West Yorkshire, England* U.K.
110 E3 **Wakefield** *MI* U.S.A.
116 B10 **Wakefield** *OH* U.S.A.
118 C5 **Wakefield** *PA* U.S.A.
117 N7 **Wakefield** *RI* U.S.A.
116 I12 **Wakefield** *VA* U.S.A.
197 F2 **Wake Island** N. Pacific Ocean
158 B6 **Wakema** Myanmar
185 O3 **Wakhan** *reg.* Afgh.
165 L12 **Waki** Japan
164 R5 **Wakinosawa** Japan
186 D8 **Wakiro** *watercourse* Eritrea
92 B4 **Wakiso** Uganda
164 S1 **Wakkanai** Japan
97 O3 **Wakkerstroom** S. Africa
205 J6 **Wakool** *N.S.W.* Austr.
205 I6 **Wakool** *r. N.S.W.* Austr.
109 H2 **Wakuach, Lac** *l. Que.* Can.
91 B7 **Waku-Kungo** Angola
164 S8 **Wakuya** Japan
108 D3 **Wakwayowkastic** *r. Ont.* Can.
200 □6 **Walade** Solomon Is
208 F7 **Walagunya Aboriginal Reserve** *W.A.* Austr.
176 F6 **Walajapet** *Tamil Nadu* India
51 D6 **Walbeck** Ger.
31 P3 **Walberswick** *Suffolk, England* U.K.
54 E5 **Wałbrzych** Pol.
49 I8 **Walburg** Ger.
205 M4 **Walcha** *N.S.W.* Austr.
53 K6 **Walchensee** *l.* Ger.
58 F4 **Walchsee** Austria
58 F4 **Walchsee** *l.* Austria
48 D5 **Walchum** Ger.
122 K6 **Walcott** *WY* U.S.A.
208 H4 **Walcott Inlet** *W.A.* Austr.
45 F8 **Walcourt** Belgium
54 E2 **Wałcz** Pol.
52 G6 **Wald** *Baden-Württemberg* Ger.
53 M3 **Wald** *Bayern* Ger.
52 F7 **Wald** Switz.
52 F5 **Waldachtal** Ger.
59 K3 **Waldaist** *r.* Austria
52 D2 **Waldböckelheim** Ger.
49 D9 **Waldbreitbach** Ger.
49 E9 **Waldbröl** Ger.
52 H2 **Waldbrunn** Ger.
49 F9 **Waldbrunn-Lahr** Ger.
52 H6 **Waldburg** Ger.
209 D8 **Waldburg Range** *mts W.A.* Austr.
51 I7 **Walddrehna** Ger.
49 H8 **Waldeck** Ger.
59 N4 **Waldegg** Austria
119 G1 **Walden** *NY* U.S.A.
52 G4 **Waldenbuch** Ger.
52 H3 **Waldenburg** *Baden-Württemberg* Ger.
51 G9 **Waldenburg** *Sachsen* Ger.
Waldenburg Pol. *see* Wałbrzych
70 D1 **Waldenburg** Switz.
53 M3 **Walderbach** Ger.
53 M2 **Waldershof** Ger.
31 N5 **Walderslade** *Medway, England* U.K.
52 D3 **Waldfischbach-Burgalben** Ger.
59 L2 **Waldhausen** Austria
59 K3 **Waldhausen im Strudengau** Austria
51 H8 **Waldheim** Ger.
59 J3 **Walding** Austria
49 I8 **Waldkappel** Ger.
52 D5 **Waldkirch** Ger.
53 P4 **Waldkirchen** Ger.
53 M5 **Waldkraiburg** Ger.
52 F2 **Wald-Michelbach** Ger.
52 C3 **Waldmohr** Ger.
53 N3 **Waldmünchen** Ger.
115 F11 **Waldo** *FL* U.S.A.
110 G6 **Waldo** *WI* U.S.A.
117 □P4 **Waldoboro** *ME* U.S.A.
30 D6 **Waldon** *r. England* U.K.
116 I10 **Waldorf** *MD* U.S.A.
54 G2 **Waldowo-Szlacheckie** Pol.
122 B4 **Waldport** *OR* U.S.A.
52 B2 **Waldrach** Ger.
121 H8 **Waldron** *AR* U.S.A.
110 J8 **Waldron** *MI* U.S.A.
213 H2 **Waldron, Cape** Antarctica
51 F10 **Waldsassen** Ger.
52 E6 **Waldshut** Ger.
70 G1 **Waldstatt** Switz.
52 H4 **Waldstetten** *Baden-Württemberg* Ger.
53 I5 **Waldstetten** *Bayern* Ger.
53 M2 **Waldthurn** Ger.
59 L3 **Waldviertel** *reg.* Austria
155 C4 **Walea, Selat** *sea chan.* Indon.
155 C4 **Waleabahi** *i.* Indon.
155 C4 **Waleakodi** *i.* Indon.
209 D11 **Walebing** *W.A.* Austr.
170 C4 **Walêg** *Sichuan* China
70 G1 **Walenstadt** Switz.
30 E3 **Wales** *admin. div.* U.K.
88 E4 **Walewale** Ghana
45 J9 **Walferdange** Lux.
205 L4 **Walgett** *N.S.W.* Austr.
212 Q1 **Walgreen Coast** Antarctica
110 H6 **Walhalla** *MI* U.S.A.
120 G1 **Walhalla** *ND* U.S.A.
115 F8 **Walhalla** *SC* U.S.A.
185 M7 **Walhar** Pak.
90 F5 **Walikale** Dem. Rep. Congo
209 C10 **Walkaway** *W.A.* Austr.
50 G3 **Walkendorf** Ger.
49 K7 **Walkenried** Ger.
206 E2 **Walker** *r. N.T.* Austr.
206 D8 **Walker** *watercourse N.T.* Austr.
110 I6 **Walker** *MI* U.S.A.
120 H2 **Walker** *MN* U.S.A.
124 N3 **Walker** *r. NV* U.S.A.
96 D10 **Walker Bay** S. Africa
115 H12 **Walker Cay** *i.* Bahamas
207 H4 **Walker Creek** *r. Qld* Austr.
107 L4 **Walker Lake** *Man.* Can.
124 N3 **Walker Lake** *NV* U.S.A.
124 N3 **Walker Lake** *l. NV* U.S.A.
212 R2 **Walker Mountains** Antarctica
124 N3 **Walker River Indian Reservation** *res. NV* U.S.A.
116 H9 **Walkersville** *MD* U.S.A.
116 E10 **Walkersville** *WV* U.S.A.
111 M5 **Walkerton** *Ont.* Can.
110 H8 **Walkerton** *IN* U.S.A.
119 G1 **Walker Valley** *NY* U.S.A.
120 D3 **Wall** *SD* U.S.A.
209 D7 **Wall, Mount** *hill W.A.* Austr.
209 B10 **Wallabi Group** *is W.A.* Austr.
207 H3 **Wallaby Island** *Qld* Austr.
122 F3 **Wallace** *ID* U.S.A.
115 I8 **Wallace** *NC* U.S.A.
120 E5 **Wallace** *NE* U.S.A.
116 C12 **Wallace** *VA* U.S.A.
108 D5 **Wallaceburg** *Ont.* Can.
203 C13 **Wallacetown** *South I.* N.Z.
208 F5 **Wallal Downs** *W.A.* Austr.
209 D11 **Wallambin, Lake** *salt flat W.A.* Austr.
205 M3 **Wallangarra** *Qld* Austr.
204 F5 **Wallaroo** *S.A.* Austr.
29 K7 **Wallasey** *Merseyside, England* U.K.
207 M8 **Wallaville** *Qld* Austr.
122 E3 **Walla Walla** *WA* U.S.A.
52 F3 **Walldorf** *Baden-Württemberg* Ger.
52 F1 **Walldorf** *Hessen* Ger.
49 J9 **Walldorf** *Thüringen* Ger.
52 G2 **Walldürn** Ger.
96 B6 **Wallekraal** S. Africa
205 L6 **Wallendbeen** *N.S.W.* Austr.
51 D10 **Wallenfels** Ger.
118 E2 **Wallenpaupack, Lake** *PA* U.S.A.
70 G1 **Wallensee** *l.* Switz.
53 N4 **Wallerfing** Ger.
59 O4 **Wallern im Burgenland** Austria
53 N4 **Wallersdorf** Ger.
58 H4 **Wallersee** *l.* Austria
53 I4 **Wallerstein** Ger.
53 K6 **Wallgau** Ger.
53 I3 **Wallhausen** *Baden-Württemberg* Ger.
52 D2 **Wallhausen** *Rheinland-Pfalz* Ger.
202 K7 **Wallingford** *North I.* N.Z.
31 J4 **Wallingford** *Oxfordshire, England* U.K.
119 J2 **Wallingford** *CT* U.S.A.
117 M5 **Wallingford** *VT* U.S.A.
Wallis *canton* Switz. *see* **Valais**
199 I3 **Wallis, Îles** *is* Wallis and Futuna Is
199 I3 **Wallis and Futuna Islands** *terr.* S. Pacific Ocean
52 F7 **Wallisellen** Switz.
Wallis et Futuna, Îles *terr.* S. Pacific Ocean *see* Wallis and Futuna Islands
Wallis Islands Wallis and Futuna Is *see* Wallis, Îles
119 G1 **Wallkill** *NY* U.S.A.
119 H1 **Wallkill** *r. NY* U.S.A.
117 J11 **Wallops Island** *VA* U.S.A.
122 F4 **Wallowa** *OR* U.S.A.
122 F4 **Wallowa Mountains** *OR* U.S.A.
26 □M2 **Walls** *Shetland, Scotland* U.K.
48 H1 **Wallsbüll** Ger.
29 N4 **Wallsend** *Tyne and Wear, England* U.K.
205 K9 **Walls of Jerusalem National Park** *Tas.* Austr.
50 D5 **Wallstawe** Ger.
49 F10 **Walluf** Ger.
122 E3 **Wallula** *WA* U.S.A.
207 L9 **Wallumbilla** *Qld* Austr.
185 J5 **Walma** Afgh.
31 O5 **Walmer** *Kent, England* U.K.
107 I2 **Walmsley Lake** *N.W.T.* Can.
29 K5 **Walney, Isle of** *i. England* U.K.
110 E8 **Walnut** *IL* U.S.A.
116 H8 **Walnut Bottom** *PA* U.S.A.
124 J4 **Walnut Creek** *CA* U.S.A.
120 F6 **Walnut Creek** *r. KS* U.S.A.
124 K3 **Walnut Grove** *CA* U.S.A.
118 D3 **Walnutport** *PA* U.S.A.
121 J7 **Walnut Ridge** *AR* U.S.A.
179 P5 **Walong** *Arun. Prad.* India
51 K7 **Wałowice** Pol.
53 L5 **Walpertskirchen** Ger.
209 D13 **Walpole** *W.A.* Austr.
117 M5 **Walpole** *NH* U.S.A.
200 □5 **Walpole, Île** *i.* New Caledonia
55 J2 **Wałpusza** *r.* Pol.
58 G4 **Wals** Austria
31 I2 **Walsall** *West Midlands, England* U.K.
53 J2 **Walsdorf** Ger.
123 L8 **Walsenburg** *CO* U.S.A.
207 I4 **Walsh** *r. Qld* Austr.
121 D7 **Walsh** *CO* U.S.A.
50 G5 **Walsleben** Ger.
31 M2 **Walsoken** *Cambridgeshire, England* U.K.
48 I5 **Walsrode** Ger.
55 H1 **Wałsza** *r.* Pol.
177 H4 **Waltair** *Andhra Prad.* India
53 I6 **Waltenhofen** Ger.
115 G9 **Walterboro** *SC* U.S.A.
115 E10 **Walter F. George Reservoir** *AL/GA* U.S.A.
121 F8 **Walters** *OK* U.S.A.
49 K9 **Waltershausen** Ger.
205 J3 **Walter's Range** *hills Qld* Austr.
121 K9 **Walthall** *MS* U.S.A.
111 R4 **Waltham** *Que.* Can.
29 Q6 **Waltham** *North East Lincolnshire, England* U.K.
117 N6 **Waltham** *MA* U.S.A.
117 □Q4 **Waltham** *ME* U.S.A.
31 M4 **Waltham Abbey** *Essex, England* U.K.
31 K2 **Waltham on the Wolds** *Leicestershire, England* U.K.
53 K4 **Walting** Ger.
110 H9 **Walton** *IN* U.S.A.
117 J6 **Walton** *NY* U.S.A.
116 D10 **Walton** *WV* U.S.A.
130 D5 **Walton Bank** *sea feature* Jamaica
31 L5 **Walton-on-Thames** *Surrey, England* U.K.
31 O4 **Walton on the Naze** *Essex, England* U.K.
Walvisbaai Namibia *see* Walvis Bay
94 B4 **Walvis Bay** Namibia
94 B4 **Walvis Bay** *b.* Namibia
214 I8 **Walvis Ridge** *sea feature* S. Atlantic Ocean
209 E11 **Walyahmoing** *hill W.A.* Austr.
185 N4 **Wama** Afgh.
92 A4 **Wamala, Lake** Uganda
91 E6 **Wamaza** Dem. Rep. Congo
90 D5 **Wamba** *Équateur* Dem. Rep. Congo
90 E4 **Wamba** *Orientale* Dem. Rep. Congo
91 C5 **Wamba** *r.* Dem. Rep. Congo
89 H4 **Wamba** Nigeria
63 K5 **Wamba** Spain
206 C3 **Wambardi Aboriginal Land** *res. N.T.* Austr.
120 G6 **Wamego** *KS* U.S.A.
153 I7 **Wamena** *Papua* Indon.
93 C6 **Wami** *r.* Tanz.
155 E5 **Wamlana** *Buru* Indon.
206 E4 **Wampaya Aboriginal Land** *res. Qld* Austr.
126 □Q10 **Wampusirpi** Hond.
122 K6 **Wamsutter** *WY* U.S.A.
155 E5 **Wamulan** *Buru* Indon.
185 M5 **Wana** Pak.
205 J3 **Wanaaring** *N.S.W.* Austr.
203 D11 **Wanaka** *South I.* N.Z.
203 D11 **Wanaka, Lake** *South I.* N.Z.
119 G4 **Wanamassa** *NJ* U.S.A.
118 C2 **Wanamie** *PA* U.S.A.
171 J5 **Wan'an** *Jiangxi* China
108 D4 **Wanapitei Lake** *Ont.* Can.
119 G2 **Wanaque** *NJ* U.S.A.
119 G2 **Wanaque Reservoir** *NJ* U.S.A.
155 C6 **Wanasabari** *Sulawesi* Indon.
204 H6 **Wanbi** *S.A.* Austr.
170 C5 **Wanbi** *Yunnan* China
203 E12 **Wanbrow, Cape** *South I.* N.Z.
115 J8 **Wanchese** *NC* U.S.A.
155 C6 **Wanci** *Sulawesi* Indon.
144 G2 **Wanda** Arg.
209 C10 **Wandana Nature Reserve** *W.A.* Austr.
162 H6 **Wanda Shan** *mts* China
107 H4 **Wandering River** *Alta* Can.
49 K9 **Wandersleben** Ger.
48 H1 **Wanderup** Ger.
170 B6 **Wanding** *Yunnan* China
Wandingzhen *Yunnan* China *see* **Wanding**
Wandiwash *Tamil Nadu* India *see* **Vandavasi**
203 H9 **Wandle Downs** *South I.* N.Z.
50 H5 **Wandlitz** Ger.
163 E11 **Wando** S. Korea
207 L9 **Wandoan** *Qld* Austr.
31 L5 **Wandsworth** *Greater London, England* U.K.
59 L3 **Wang** Austria
158 D6 **Wang, Mae Nam** *r.* Thai.
90 F4 **Wanga** Dem. Rep. Congo
202 J6 **Wanganui** *North I.* N.Z.
202 I6 **Wanganui** *r. North I.* N.Z.
203 E10 **Wanganui** *r. South I.* N.Z.
205 K7 **Wangaratta** *Vic.* Austr.
204 E6 **Wangary** *S.A.* Austr.
170 F2 **Wangcang** *Sichuan* China
171 I4 **Wangcheng** *Hunan* China
169 Q8 **Wangcun** *Shandong* China
Wangda *Xizang* China *see* Zogang
173 I12 **Wangdain** *Xizang* China
179 L6 **Wangdi Phodrang** Bhutan
169 N7 **Wangdu** *Hebei* China
49 I7 **Wangelnstedt** Ger.
48 K2 **Wangels** Ger.
70 D1 **Wangen** Switz.
52 H6 **Wangen im Allgäu** Ger.
48 E3 **Wangerooge** Ger.
48 E3 **Wangerooge** *i.* Ger.
155 B9 **Wanggamet, Gunung** *mt. Sumba* Indon.
168 E8 **Wang Gaxun** *Qinghai* China
70 F1 **Wängi** Switz.
155 C6 **Wangiwangi** *i.* Indon.
171 K3 **Wangjiang** *Anhui* China
169 K8 **Wangjiawan** *Shaanxi* China
126 □Q10 **Wangkibila** Hond.
162 E5 **Wangkui** *Heilong.* China
58 C5 **Wängle** Austria
Wang Mai Khon Thai. *see* Sawankhalok
170 G7 **Wangmao** *Guangxi* China
170 F6 **Wangmo** *Guizhou* China
162 F7 **Wangqing** *Jilin* China
170 E2 **Wangziguan** *Gansu* China
106 G4 **Wanham** *Alta* Can.
137 H3 **Wanhatti** Suriname
158 D4 **Wan Hsa-la** Myanmar
90 E4 **Wanie-Rukula** Dem. Rep. Congo
206 C3 **Wanimiyn Aboriginal Land** *res. N.T.* Austr.
209 F9 **Wanjarri Nature Reserve** *W.A.* Austr.
178 C8 **Wankaner** *Gujarat* India
48 J2 **Wankendorf** Ger.
Wankie Zimbabwe *see* **Hwange**
92 E4 **Wanlaweyn** Somalia
48 G3 **Wanna** Ger.
209 J10 **Wanna Lakes** *salt flat W.A.* Austr.
209 C11 **Wanneroo** *W.A.* Austr.
171 K4 **Wannian** *Jiangxi* China
170 H9 **Wanning** *Hainan* China
166 E5 **Wanouchi** Japan
44 I5 **Wanroij** Neth.
169 L9 **Wanrong** *Shanxi* China
170 G5 **Wanshan** *Guizhou* China
171 I8 **Wanshan Qundao** *is Guangdong* China
51 E8 **Wansleben am See** Ger.
202 K7 **Wanstead** *North I.* N.Z.
31 J4 **Wantage** *Oxfordshire, England* U.K.
119 H3 **Wantagh** *NY* U.S.A.
111 N3 **Wanup** *Ont.* Can.
170 G3 **Wanxian** *Chongqing* China
170 G2 **Wanyuan** *Sichuan* China
171 J4 **Wanzai** *Jiangxi* China
45 H7 **Wanze** Belgium
Wanzhi *Anhui* China *see* **Wuhu**
116 A8 **Wapakoneta** *OH* U.S.A.
107 J4 **Wapawekka Lake** *Sask.* Can.
44 J4 **Wapenveld** Neth.
55 H2 **Wąpiersk** Pol.
108 B3 **Wapikaimaski Lake** *Ont.* Can.
108 B2 **Wapikopa Lake** *Ont.* Can.
106 G4 **Wapiti** *r. Alta* Can.
55 I2 **Waplewo** Pol.
54 D2 **Wapnica** Pol.
54 F3 **Wapno** Pol.
155 E5 **Wapotih** *Buru* Indon.
121 J7 **Wappapello Lake** *resr MO* U.S.A.
119 H1 **Wappinger Creek** *r. NY* U.S.A.
119 H1 **Wappingers Falls** *NY* U.S.A.
120 J5 **Wapsipinicon** *r. IA* U.S.A.
105 I4 **Wapusk National Park** *Man.* Can.
170 D2 **Waqên** *Sichuan* China
190 E7 **Waqf aş Şawwān, Jibāl** *hills* Jordan
189 K8 **Wāqişah** *well* Iraq
187 I4 **Waqr** *well* Saudi Arabia
186 G7 **Waqr Maryamah** *well* Yemen
116 D11 **War** *WV* U.S.A.
166 F4 **Wara** Japan
90 F2 **Warab** Sudan
90 F2 **Warab** *state* Sudan
167 K4 **Warabi** Japan
92 D4 **Waradi** *waterhole* Kenya
185 L8 **Warah** Pak.
209 J9 **Warakurna-Wingellina-Irrunytju Aboriginal Reserve** *W.A.* Austr.
92 E3 **Warandab** Eth.
176 F4 **Warangal** *Andhra Prad.* India
178 H9 **Waraseoni** *Madh. Prad.* India
205 J9 **Waratah** *Tas.* Austr.
187 I1 **Warbah Island** Iraq
49 K6 **Warberg** Ger.
31 L3 **Warboys** *Cambridgeshire, England* U.K.
207 I8 **Warbreccan** *Qld* Austr.
106 H4 **Warburg** *Alta* Can.
49 H8 **Warburg** Ger.
49 H8 **Warburger Börde** *reg.* Ger.
205 J7 **Warburton** *Vic.* Austr.
209 I9 **Warburton** *W.A.* Austr.
204 F2 **Warburton** *watercourse S.A.* Austr.
97 O2 **Warburton** S. Africa
209 I9 **Warburton Aboriginal Reserve** *W.A.* Austr.
107 I2 **Warburton Bay** *N.W.T.* Can.
209 I8 **Warburton Range** *hills W.A.* Austr.
185 O5 **Warcha** Pak.
45 I8 **Warche** *r.* Belgium
29 M4 **Warcop** *Cumbria, England* U.K.
37 K5 **Warcq** France
207 K9 **Ward** *watercourse Qld* Austr.
203 I8 **Ward** *South I.* N.Z.
212 T2 **Ward, Mount** Antarctica
203 B12 **Ward, Mount** *South I.* N.Z.
203 D10 **Ward, Mount** *South I.* N.Z.
185 M4 **Wardag** *prov.* Afgh.
204 F6 **Wardang Island** *S.A.* Austr.
92 D4 **Wardeglo** *waterhole* Kenya
97 M3 **Warden** S. Africa
48 F4 **Wardenburg** Ger.
178 G9 **Wardha** *Mahar.* India
176 F3 **Wardha** *r.* India
26 J5 **Ward Hill** *Scotland* U.K.
75 □ **Wardija, Il-Ponta tal-** *pt Gozo* Malta
75 □ **Wardija Ridge** Malta
31 J3 **Wardington** *Oxfordshire, England* U.K.
26 □N2 **Ward of Bressay** *hill Scotland* U.K.
50 F3 **Wardow** Ger.
29 L5 **Ward's Stone** *hill England* U.K.
106 E3 **Ware** *B.C.* Can.
31 L4 **Ware** *Hertfordshire, England* U.K.
117 M6 **Ware** *MA* U.S.A.
45 D7 **Waregem** Belgium
30 H6 **Wareham** *Dorset, England* U.K.
117 O7 **Wareham** *MA* U.S.A.
45 H7 **Waremme** Belgium
50 G3 **Waren** Ger.
49 E7 **Warendorf** Ger.
44 K2 **Warffum** Neth.
Wargili *i. S. Male* Maldives *see* Vaagali
207 M7 **Warginburra Peninsula** *Qld* Austr.
31 K5 **Wargrave** *Wokingham, England* U.K.
92 E2 **War Gunbi** *waterhole* Somalia
205 M3 **Warialda** *N.S.W.* Austr.
185 L10 **Wari Creek** *inlet* Pak.
207 M1 **Wari Island** P.N.G.
50 E3 **Warin** Ger.
158 G7 **Warin Chamrap** Thai.
27 J4 **Waringstown** *Northern Ireland* U.K.
29 M3 **Wark** *Northumberland, England* U.K.
55 J4 **Warka** Pol.
202 I3 **Warkworth** *North I.* N.Z.
29 N3 **Warkworth** *Northumberland, England* U.K.
92 E2 **War Idaad** Somalia
Warli *Sichuan* China *see* **Walêg**
31 L5 **Warlingham** *Surrey, England* U.K.
36 E3 **Warloy-Baillon** France
54 G2 **Warlubie** Pol.
107 J4 **Warman** *Sask.* Can.
94 C6 **Warmbad** Namibia
53 L2 **Warmensteinach** Ger.
36 H5 **Warmeriville** France
96 D3 **Warmfontein** Namibia
23 Q7 **Warmia** *reg.* Pol.
31 J3 **Warmington** *Warwickshire, England* U.K.
55 I2 **Warmińsko-Mazurskie** *prov.* Pol.
30 H5 **Warminster** *Wiltshire, England* U.K.
118 E4 **Warminster** *PA* U.S.A.
44 G4 **Warmond** Neth.
49 G6 **Warmsen** Ger.
125 P3 **Warm Springs** *NV* U.S.A.
116 F10 **Warm Springs** *VA* U.S.A.
122 D4 **Warm Springs Indian Reservation** *res. OR* U.S.A.
96 E9 **Warmwaterberg** S. Africa
96 E9 **Warmwaterberg** *mts* S. Africa
50 F2 **Warnemünde** Ger.
107 H5 **Warner** *Alta* Can.
117 N5 **Warner** *NH* U.S.A.
122 E5 **Warner Lakes** *OR* U.S.A.
122 D6 **Warner Mountains** *CA* U.S.A.
115 F9 **Warner Robins** *GA* U.S.A.
124 P8 **Warner Springs** *CA* U.S.A.
139 E4 **Warnes** Bol.
45 C7 **Warneton** Belgium
53 L6 **Warngau** Ger.
31 L5 **Warnham** *West Sussex, England* U.K.
54 C2 **Warnice** *Zachodniopomorskie* Pol.
50 K5 **Warnice** *Zachodniopomorskie* Pol.
54 E2 **Warnino** Pol.
50 E3 **Warnow** Ger.
50 F2 **Warnow** *r.* Ger.
44 J4 **Warnsveld** Neth.
176 E3 **Waronda** *Mahar.* India
209 C12 **Waroona** *W.A.* Austr.
178 G9 **Warora** *Mahar.* India
48 H5 **Warpe** Ger.
207 M9 **Warra** *Qld* Austr.
206 E6 **Warrabri Aboriginal Land** *res. N.T.* Austr.
205 I7 **Warracknabeal** *Vic.* Austr.
205 M6 **Warragamba Reservoir** *N.S.W.* Austr.
205 J8 **Warragul** *Vic.* Austr.
204 G3 **Warrakalanna, Lake** *salt flat S.A.* Austr.
119 I1 **Warramaug, Lake** *CT* U.S.A.
204 E5 **Warramboo** *S.A.* Austr.
209 D10 **Warramboo** *hill W.A.* Austr.
205 K4 **Warrambool** *r. N.S.W.* Austr.
204 F2 **Warrandirinna, Lake** *salt flat S.A.* Austr.
205 J7 **Warrandyte** *Vic.* Austr.
208 F6 **Warrawagine** *W.A.* Austr.
205 J4 **Warrego** *r. N.S.W./Qld* Austr.
207 J8 **Warrego Range** *hills Qld* Austr.
205 K4 **Warren** *N.S.W.* Austr.
209 C13 **Warren** *r. W.A.* Austr.
111 N3 **Warren** *Ont.* Can.
121 I9 **Warren** *AR* U.S.A.
110 E7 **Warren** *IL* U.S.A.
110 I9 **Warren** *IN* U.S.A.
111 K7 **Warren** *MI* U.S.A.
120 G1 **Warren** *MN* U.S.A.
116 E7 **Warren** *OH* U.S.A.
116 F7 **Warren** *PA* U.S.A.
118 F3 **Warren County** *county NJ* U.S.A.
119 G5 **Warren Grove** *NJ* U.S.A.
106 C4 **Warren Island** *AK* U.S.A.
27 J4 **Warrenpoint** *Northern Ireland* U.K.
110 D5 **Warrens** *WI* U.S.A.
120 I6 **Warrensburg** *MO* U.S.A.
117 L5 **Warrensburg** *NY* U.S.A.
118 B2 **Warrensville** *PA* U.S.A.
97 I4 **Warrenton** S. Africa
115 F9 **Warrenton** *GA* U.S.A.
120 J6 **Warrenton** *MO* U.S.A.
115 H7 **Warrenton** *NC* U.S.A.
116 H10 **Warrenton** *VA* U.S.A.
89 G5 **Warri** Nigeria
209 D10 **Warriedar** *hill W.A.* Austr.
204 F3 **Warriners Creek** *watercourse S.A.* Austr.
203 E12 **Warrington** *South I.* N.Z.
29 L7 **Warrington** *Warrington, England* U.K.
29 L7 **Warrington** *admin. div. England* U.K.
115 D10 **Warrington** *FL* U.S.A.
204 G4 **Warriota** *watercourse S.A.* Austr.
205 I8 **Warrnambool** *Vic.* Austr.
120 H1 **Warroad** *MN* U.S.A.
204 E6 **Warrow** *S.A.* Austr.
205 L4 **Warrumbungle National Park** *N.S.W.* Austr.
206 D1 **Warruwi** *N.T.* Austr.
205 H3 **Warry Warry** *watercourse Qld* Austr.
Warsaw Pol. *see* **Warszawa**
110 C9 **Warsaw** *IL* U.S.A.
114 E5 **Warsaw** *IN* U.S.A.
114 E6 **Warsaw** *KY* U.S.A.
120 I6 **Warsaw** *MO* U.S.A.
116 G6 **Warsaw** *NY* U.S.A.
116 I11 **Warsaw** *VA* U.S.A.
59 J4 **Warscheneck** *mt.* Austria
92 E4 **Warshiikh** Somalia
48 D4 **Warsingsfehn** Ger.
29 N7 **Warslow** *Staffordshire, England* U.K.
49 F8 **Warstein** Ger.
55 J3 **Warszawa** Pol.
54 E1 **Warszkowo** Pol.
54 G4 **Warta** Pol.
54 C3 **Warta** *r.* Pol.
54 D4 **Warta Bolesławiecka** Pol.
54 G3 **Warta-Gopło, Kanał** *canal* Pol.
59 J4 **Wartberg an der Krems** Austria
115 E7 **Wartburg** *TN* U.S.A.
51 B9 **Wartburg, Schloss** *tourist site* Ger.
51 B9 **Wartburg Schloß** *tourist site* Ger.
53 L5 **Wartenberg** Ger.
49 H9 **Wartenberg-Angersbach** Ger.
58 B5 **Warth** Austria
52 H5 **Warthausen** Ger.
50 J4 **Wartin** Ger.
55 H4 **Wartkowice** Pol.
49 I10 **Wartmannsroth** Ger.
29 L5 **Warton** *Lancashire, England* U.K.
157 L5 **Waru** *Kalimantan* Indon.
178 G9 **Warud** *Mahar.* India
206 E5 **Warumungu Aboriginal Land** *res. N.T.* Austr.
205 N3 **Warwick** *Qld* Austr.
31 I3 **Warwick** *Warwickshire, England* U.K.
118 D6 **Warwick** *MD* U.S.A.
119 G2 **Warwick** *NY* U.S.A.
117 N7 **Warwick** *RI* U.S.A.
29 L4 **Warwick Bridge** *Cumbria, England* U.K.
206 F3 **Warwick Channel** *N.T.* Austr.
31 I3 **Warwickshire** *admin. div. England* U.K.
170 C4 **Warzhong** *Sichuan* China
106 H5 **Wasa** *B.C.* Can.
111 N5 **Wasaga Beach** *Ont.* Can.
89 G4 **Wasagu** Nigeria
125 U2 **Wasatch Range** *mts UT* U.S.A.
97 O4 **Wasbank** S. Africa
48 I2 **Wasbek** Ger.
26 J4 **Wasbister** *Orkney, Scotland* U.K.
49 K6 **Wasbüttel** Ger.
107 J5 **Wascana Creek** *r. Sask.* Can.
52 H4 **Wäschenbeuren** Ger.
124 M6 **Wasco** *CA* U.S.A.
110 C3 **Wascott** *WI* U.S.A.
120 I3 **Waseca** *MN* U.S.A.
107 I3 **Wasekamio Lake** *Sask.* Can.
55 J3 **Wąsewo** Pol.
137 G3 **Washado** Suriname
185 J8 **Washap** Pak.
110 E9 **Washburn** *IL* U.S.A.
117 □Q2 **Washburn** *ME* U.S.A.
120 E2 **Washburn** *ND* U.S.A.
116 B12 **Washburn** *TN* U.S.A.

Washburn to Westport

359

110 D3 **Washburn** *WI* U.S.A.
166 E4 **Washiga-take** *mt.* Japan
178 F9 **Washim** *Mahar.* India
109 F3 **Washimeska** *r. Que.* Can.
146 E3 **Washington** Arg.
29 N4 **Washington** *Tyne and Wear, England* U.K.
119 I1 **Washington** *CT* U.S.A.
118 A7 **Washington** *DC* U.S.A.
115 F9 **Washington** *GA* U.S.A.
120 J5 **Washington** *IA* U.S.A.
110 E9 **Washington** *IL* U.S.A.
114 D6 **Washington** *IN* U.S.A.
120 G6 **Washington** *KS* U.S.A.
116 B10 **Washington** *KY* U.S.A.
115 I8 **Washington** *NC* U.S.A.
117 M5 **Washington** *NH* U.S.A.
118 F3 **Washington** *NJ* U.S.A.
116 E8 **Washington** *PA* U.S.A.
125 S4 **Washington** *UT* U.S.A.
116 G10 **Washington** *VA* U.S.A.
122 D3 **Washington** *state* U.S.A.
213 L2 **Washington, Cape** Antarctica
117 N4 **Washington, Mount** *NH* U.S.A.
116 B9 **Washington Court House** *OH* U.S.A.
118 F4 **Washington Crossing** *NJ* U.S.A.
119 I1 **Washington Depot** *CT* U.S.A.
118 A6 **Washington Grove** *MD* U.S.A.
110 H4 **Washington Island** *WI* U.S.A.
110 H4 **Washington Island** *i. WI* U.S.A.
105 L2 **Washington Land** *reg.* Greenland
119 G2 **Washingtonville** *NY* U.S.A.
118 B3 **Washingtonville** *PA* U.S.A.
185 J5 **Washir** Afgh.
121 G8 **Washita** *r. OK* U.S.A.
205 N3 **Washpool National Park** *N.S.W.* Austr.
122 E3 **Washtucna** *WA* U.S.A.
185 K8 **Washuk** Pak.
176 D3 **Wasi** *Mahar.* India
187 H3 **Wasiʿ** Saudi Arabia
187 J4 **Wasiʿ** *well* Saudi Arabia
36 H4 **Wasigny** France
55 L2 **Wasilków** Pol.
104 D3 **Wasilla** *AK* U.S.A.
89 F4 **Wasinmi** Nigeria
155 E7 **Wasiri** *Maluku* Indon.
155 E5 **Wasisi** *Buru* Indon.
190 C9 **Wāsiṭ** Egypt
189 L7 **Wāsiṭ** *governorate* Iraq
189 M7 **Wāsiṭ** *tourist site* Iraq
187 M4 **Wāsiṭ** Oman
186 D4 **Wāsiṭah** Saudi Arabia
108 E3 **Waskaganish** *Que.* Can.
107 L3 **Waskaiowaka Lake** *Man.* Can.
106 H4 **Waskatenau** *Alta* Can.
54 E4 **Wąsosz** *Dolnośląskie* Pol.
55 K2 **Wąsosz** *Podlaskie* Pol.
54 E3 **Wąsowo** Pol.
126 □Q10 **Waspán** Nic.
44 G5 **Waspik** Neth.
29 O5 **Wass** *North Yorkshire, England* U.K.
88 B3 **Wassadou** Senegal
164 T2 **Wassamu** Japan
45 H7 **Wasseiges** Belgium
37 N6 **Wasselonne** France
70 F2 **Wassen** Switz.
44 F4 **Wassenaar** Neth.
49 B8 **Wassenberg** Ger.
95 C5 **Wasser** Namibia
53 I4 **Wasseralfingen** Ger.
53 M5 **Wasserburg am Inn** Ger.
49 I10 **Wasserkuppe** *hill* Ger.
49 K7 **Wasserleben** Ger.
52 B2 **Wasserliesch** Ger.
49 J10 **Wasserlosen** Ger.
53 J3 **Wassertrüdingen** Ger.
36 G3 **Wassigny** France
88 B4 **Wassou** Guinea
124 N3 **Wassuk Range** *mts NV* U.S.A.
37 I6 **Wassy** France
186 D4 **Wasta** Saudi Arabia
29 K5 **Wast Water** *l. England* U.K.
49 J9 **Wasungen** Ger.
108 E3 **Waswanipi, Lac** *l. Que.* Can.
111 N1 **Watabeag Lake** *Ont.* Can.
155 B4 **Watambayoli** *Sulawesi* Indon.
155 B6 **Watampone** *Sulawesi* Indon.
155 A6 **Watansoppeng** *Sulawesi* Indon.
107 I4 **Watapi Lake** *Sask.* Can.
166 E7 **Watarai** Japan
167 K3 **Watarase-gawa** *r.* Japan
206 C8 **Watarrka National Park** *N.T.* Austr.
167 H2 **Watauchi** Japan
116 C12 **Watauga** *r. TN* U.S.A.
158 D5 **Wat Chan** Thai.
30 F5 **Watchet** *Somerset, England* U.K.
29 L5 **Watchgate** *Cumbria, England* U.K.
119 L2 **Watch Hill Point** *RI* U.S.A.
48 K5 **Watenstedt-Salzgitter** Ger. *see* Salzgitter
31 M3 **Waterbeach** *Cambridgeshire, England* U.K.
94 C4 **Waterberg** Namibia
94 C4 **Waterberg Plateau Game Park** *nature res.* Namibia
117 L7 **Waterbury** *CT* U.S.A.
117 M4 **Waterbury** *VT* U.S.A.
107 J3 **Waterbury Lake** *Sask.* Can.
130 E2 **Water Cays** *i.* Bahamas
111 O6 **Waterdown** *Ont.* Can.
115 G9 **Wateree** *r. SC* U.S.A.
106 C4 **Waterfall** *AK* U.S.A.
204 □3 **Waterfall Lake** S. Pacific Ocean
27 H8 **Waterford** Rep. of Ireland
27 G8 **Waterford** *county* Rep. of Ireland
97 G9 **Waterford** S. Africa
124 L4 **Waterford** *CA* U.S.A.
119 K2 **Waterford** *CT* U.S.A.
116 F7 **Waterford** *PA* U.S.A.
27 I8 **Waterford Harbour** Rep. of Ireland
118 F5 **Waterford Works** *NJ* U.S.A.
30 B7 **Watergate Bay** *England* U.K.
107 J4 **Waterhen** *r. Sask.* Can.
107 L4 **Waterhen Lake** *Man.* Can.
206 D3 **Waterhouse** *r. N.T.* Austr.
206 D8 **Waterhouse Range** *mts N.T.* Austr.
44 F4 **Wateringen** Neth.
45 E6 **Waterland-Oudeman** Belgium
206 B4 **Waterloo** *N.T.* Austr.
45 F7 **Waterloo** Belgium
108 D5 **Waterloo** *Ont.* Can.
88 B4 **Waterloo** Sierra Leone
31 □7 **Waterloo** Trin. and Tob.
120 I4 **Waterloo** *IA* U.S.A.
120 J6 **Waterloo** *IL* U.S.A.
118 B6 **Waterloo** *MD* U.S.A.
116 I6 **Waterloo** *NY* U.S.A.
110 F6 **Waterloo** *WI* U.S.A.
31 J6 **Waterlooville** *Hampshire, England* U.K.
110 F8 **Waterman** *IL* U.S.A.
119 K3 **Watermill** *NY* U.S.A.
26 K2 **Water of Leith** *r. Scotland* U.K.
26 G9 **Water of Tulla** *r. Scotland* U.K.
31 I2 **Water Orton** *Warwickshire, England* U.K.
95 F4 **Waterpoort** S. Africa
27 H3 **Waterside** *Northern Ireland* U.K.
110 E3 **Watersmeet** *MI* U.S.A.
106 H5 **Waterton Lakes National Park** *B.C.* Can.
106 H5 **Waterton Park** *Alta* Can.
119 I1 **Watertown** *CT* U.S.A.
117 J5 **Watertown** *NY* U.S.A.
120 G3 **Watertown** *SD* U.S.A.
110 F6 **Watertown** *WI* U.S.A.
97 M2 **Waterval** *r.* S. Africa
97 O1 **Waterval-Boven** S. Africa
104 G5 **Watervale** *S.A.* Austr.
121 K8 **Water Valley** *MS* U.S.A.
28 H3 **Waterville** Rep. of Ireland
117 □P4 **Waterville** *ME* U.S.A.
116 B7 **Waterville** *OH* U.S.A.
122 D3 **Waterville** *WA* U.S.A.
117 L6 **Watervliet** *NY* U.S.A.
157 I8 **Wates** Indon.
111 M7 **Watford** *Ont.* Can.
31 L4 **Watford** *Hertfordshire, England* U.K.
120 D2 **Watford City** *ND* U.S.A.
107 K3 **Wathaman** *r. Sask.* Can.
107 K3 **Wathaman Lake** *Sask.* Can.
209 D11 **Watheroo** *W.A.* Austr.
209 C11 **Watheroo National Park** *W.A.* Austr.
106 G4 **Watino** *Alta* Can.
190 C9 **Watīr, Wādī** *watercourse* Egypt
116 I6 **Watkins Glen** *NY* U.S.A.
115 F9 **Watkinsville** *GA* U.S.A.
Watling Island Bahamas *see* San Salvador
31 J4 **Watlington** *Oxfordshire, England* U.K.
121 F8 **Watonga** *OK* U.S.A.
155 F3 **Watowato, Bukit** *mt. Halmahera* Indon.
107 J5 **Watrous** *Sask.* Can.
123 L9 **Watrous** *NM* U.S.A.
90 F4 **Watsa** Dem. Rep. Congo
110 G9 **Watseka** *IL* U.S.A.
90 D5 **Watsi Kengo** Dem. Rep. Congo
207 H2 **Watson** *r. Qld* Austr.
107 J4 **Watson** *Sask.* Can.
212 P1 **Watson Escarpment** Antarctica
106 D2 **Watson Lake** *Y.T.* Can.
118 D2 **Watsontown** *PA* U.S.A.
124 K5 **Watsonville** *CA* U.S.A.
209 I9 **Watt, Mount** *hill W.A.* Austr.
36 D2 **Watten** France
26 J6 **Watten** *Highland, Scotland* U.K.
26 J6 **Watten, Loch** *l. Scotland* U.K.
48 J2 **Wattenbek** Ger.
58 E5 **Wattens** Austria
70 D2 **Wattenwil** Switz.
107 L2 **Watterson Lake** *Nunavut* Can.
36 H3 **Wattignies-la-Victoire** France
204 F3 **Wattiwarriganna** *watercourse S.A.* Austr.
27 H4 **Wattlebridge** *Northern Ireland* U.K.
50 F3 **Wattmannshagen** Ger.
31 N2 **Watton** *Norfolk, England* U.K.
31 L4 **Watton at Stone** *Hertfordshire, England* U.K.
36 F2 **Wattrelos** France
115 E8 **Watts Bar Lake** *resr TN* U.S.A.
116 F6 **Wattsburg** *PA* U.S.A.
70 G1 **Wattwil** Switz.
153 H7 **Watubela, Kepulauan** *is* Indon.
155 B5 **Watuwila, Bukit** *mt.* Indon.
49 G9 **Watzenborn-Steinberg** Ger.
153 K8 **Wau** P.N.G.
90 E3 **Wau** Sudan
90 E3 **Wau** *watercourse* Sudan
120 G3 **Waubay Lake** *SD* U.S.A.
205 N4 **Wauchope** *N.S.W.* Austr.
206 E6 **Wauchope** *N.T.* Austr.
115 G12 **Wauchula** *FL* U.S.A.
155 A4 **Waukara, Gunung** *mt.* Indon.
208 F6 **Waukarlycarly, Lake** *salt flat W.A.* Austr.
110 F6 **Waukau** *WI* U.S.A.
110 G7 **Waukegan** *IL* U.S.A.
110 F6 **Waukesha** *WI* U.S.A.
110 C6 **Waukon** *IA* U.S.A.
110 E6 **Waunakee** *WI* U.S.A.
120 E5 **Wauneta** *NE* U.S.A.
110 E5 **Waupaca** *WI* U.S.A.
110 F6 **Waupun** *WI* U.S.A.
119 L1 **Wauregan** *CT* U.S.A.
121 G8 **Waurika** *OK* U.S.A.
110 E5 **Wausau** *WI* U.S.A.
110 G4 **Wausaukee** *WI* U.S.A.
116 A7 **Wauseon** *OH* U.S.A.
110 E5 **Wautoma** *WI* U.S.A.
206 C4 **Wave Hill** *N.T.* Austr.
31 P3 **Waveney** *r. England* U.K.
202 I6 **Waverley** *North I.* N.Z.
120 I4 **Waverly** *IA* U.S.A.
116 I6 **Waverly** *NY* U.S.A.
116 C9 **Waverly** *OH* U.S.A.
115 D7 **Waverly** *TN* U.S.A.
116 H11 **Waverly** *VA* U.S.A.
45 G7 **Wavre** Belgium
36 E2 **Wavrin** France
158 C6 **Waw** Myanmar
108 C4 **Wawa** *Ont.* Can.
89 G4 **Wawa** Nigeria
108 E3 **Wawagosic** *r. Que.* Can.
155 C5 **Wawalalindu** *Sulawesi* Indon.
84 C3 **Wāw al Kabīr** Libya
84 C3 **Wāw an Nāmūs** *waterhole* Libya
119 G1 **Wawarsing** *NY* U.S.A.
110 I8 **Wawasee, Lake** *IN* U.S.A.
54 F5 **Wawelno** Pol.
155 B5 **Wawo** *Sulawesi* Indon.
153 J8 **Wawoi** *r.* P.N.G.
55 K4 **Wawolnica** Pol.
155 C5 **Wawotebi** *Sulawesi* Indon.
54 D3 **Wawrów** Pol.
55 I5 **Wawrzeńczyce** Pol.
121 G9 **Waxahachie** *TX* U.S.A.
168 H9 **Waxü** *Gansu* China
49 B10 **Waxweiler** Ger.
172 H7 **Waxxari** *Xinjiang* China
209 F9 **Way, Lake** *salt flat W.A.* Austr.
201 □1a **Waya** *i.* Fiji
155 F2 **Wayabula** *Maluku* Indon.
155 G3 **Wayag** *i. Papua* Indon.
Wayaq Lailai *i.* Fiji *see* Wayasewa
155 F3 **Wayamli** *Halmahera* Indon.
Wayaobu *Shaanxi* China *see* Zichang
201 □1a **Wayasewa** *i.* Fiji
115 F10 **Waycross** *GA* U.S.A.
155 D4 **Wayhaya** *Maluku* Indon.
156 F7 **Way Kambas National Park** Indon.
155 D4 **Waykilo** *Maluku* Indon.
116 C11 **Wayland** *KY* U.S.A.
110 I7 **Wayland** *MI* U.S.A.
110 C9 **Wayland** *MO* U.S.A.
116 H6 **Wayland** *NY* U.S.A.
111 K7 **Wayne** *MI* U.S.A.
120 G4 **Wayne** *NE* U.S.A.
119 G3 **Wayne** *NJ* U.S.A.
118 E4 **Wayne** *PA* U.S.A.
116 C10 **Wayne** *WV* U.S.A.
118 E1 **Wayne County** *county PA* U.S.A.
115 F9 **Waynesboro** *GA* U.S.A.
121 K10 **Waynesboro** *MS* U.S.A.
116 H9 **Waynesboro** *PA* U.S.A.
115 D8 **Waynesboro** *TN* U.S.A.
116 G10 **Waynesboro** *VA* U.S.A.
116 E9 **Waynesburg** *PA* U.S.A.
121 I7 **Waynesville** *MO* U.S.A.
115 F8 **Waynesville** *NC* U.S.A.
121 F7 **Waynoka** *OK* U.S.A.
89 I4 **Waza** Cameroon
158 C2 **Waza** Myanmar
89 I4 **Waza, Parc National de** *nat. park* Cameroon
36 F3 **Waziers** France
185 M3 **Wazi Khwa** Afgh.
185 P5 **Wazirabad** Pak.
166 C6 **Wazuka** Japan
54 G2 **Wda** *r.* Pol.
52 I2 **Wdecki Park Krajobrazowy** Pol.
89 F4 **W du Niger, Parcs Nationaux du** *nat. park* Niger
54 F2 **Wdzydze, Jezioro** *l.* Pol.
47 H1 **Wdzydzki Park Krajobrazowy** Pol.
200 □5 **We** *Îles Loyauté* New Caledonia
156 A2 **We, Pulau** *i.* Indon.
108 B2 **Weagamow Lake** *Ont.* Can.
29 O4 **Wear** *r. England* U.K.
117 N5 **Weare** *NH* U.S.A.
206 F4 **Wearyan** *r. N.T.* Austr.
207 J3 **Weary Bay** *Qld* Austr.
121 F8 **Weatherford** *OK* U.S.A.
121 G9 **Weatherford** *TX* U.S.A.
118 D3 **Weatherly** *PA* U.S.A.
29 L7 **Weaverham** *Cheshire, England* U.K.
107 L4 **Weaver Lake** *Man.* Can.
122 C6 **Weaverville** *CA* U.S.A.
208 J7 **Webb, Mount** *hill W.A.* Austr.
108 D4 **Webbwood** *Ont.* Can.
108 C2 **Webequie** *Ont.* Can.
202 K7 **Weber** *North I.* N.Z.
122 H6 **Weber** *r. UT* U.S.A.
106 D4 **Weber, Mount** *B.C.* Can.
215 M5 **Weber Basin** *sea feature* Indon.
212 T2 **Weber Inlet** Antarctica
92 D4 **Webi Shabeelle** *r.* Somalia
117 N6 **Webster** *MA* U.S.A.
118 A7 **Webster** *MD* U.S.A.
120 G3 **Webster** *SD* U.S.A.
110 B4 **Webster** *WI* U.S.A.
120 I4 **Webster City** *IA* U.S.A.
116 E10 **Webster Springs** *WV* U.S.A.
92 B4 **Webuye** Kenya
45 G6 **Wechelderzande** Belgium
49 K9 **Wechmar** Ger.
106 H2 **Wecho** *r. N.W.T.* Can.
106 H2 **Wecho Lake** *N.W.T.* Can.
51 G8 **Wechselburg** Ger.
155 E3 **Weda** *Halmahera* Indon.
155 F3 **Weda, Teluk** *b. Halmahera* Indon.
44 L2 **Wedde** Neth.
212 V2 **Weddell Abyssal Plain** *sea feature* Southern Ocean
145 E8 **Weddell Island** Falkland Is
212 V2 **Weddell Sea** Antarctica
205 I7 **Wedderburn** *Vic.* Austr.
203 E12 **Wedderburn** *South I.* N.Z.
48 H2 **Weddingstedt** Ger.
48 I3 **Wedel (Holstein)** Ger.
20 □ **Wedel Jarlsberg Land** *reg.* Svalbard
106 F5 **Wedge Mountain** *B.C.* Can.
30 G5 **Wedmore** *Somerset, England* U.K.
30 H2 **Wednesbury** *West Midlands, England* U.K.
115 E9 **Wedowee** *AL* U.S.A.
122 C6 **Weed** *CA* U.S.A.
48 J3 **Weede** Ger.
31 J3 **Weedon Bec** *Northamptonshire, England* U.K.
116 G7 **Weedville** *PA* U.S.A.
155 G4 **Weeim** *i. Papua* Indon.
118 F5 **Weekstown** *NJ* U.S.A.
45 G6 **Weelde** Belgium
205 L3 **Weemelah** *N.S.W.* Austr.
97 O4 **Weenen** S. Africa
97 O4 **Weenen Nature Reserve** S. Africa
48 D4 **Weener** Ger.
58 E5 **Weerberg** Austria
44 K4 **Weerselo** Neth.
45 I6 **Weert** Neth.
48 I1 **Wees** Ger.
70 G1 **Weesen** Switz.
44 H4 **Weesp** Neth.
205 K5 **Weethalle** *N.S.W.* Austr.
205 L4 **Wee Waa** *N.S.W.* Austr.
49 B7 **Weeze** Ger.
51 D6 **Weferlingen** Ger.
49 B8 **Wegberg** Ger.
96 F4 **Wegdraai** S. Africa
51 D7 **Wegeleben** Ger.
51 D6 **Wegenstedt** Ger.
52 E7 **Weggis** Switz.
54 D4 **Węgliniec** Pol.
55 J1 **Węgorzewo** Pol.
54 D2 **Węgorzyno** Pol.
55 K4 **Węgrów** Pol.
54 D3 **Węgrzynice** Pol.
55 I3 **Węgrzynowo** Pol.
59 L4 **Wegscheid** Austria
53 P4 **Wegscheid** Ger.
48 G3 **Wehdel** Ger.
44 J2 **Wehe-den Hoorn** Neth.
45 J5 **Wehl** Neth.
Wehlau Rus. Fed. *see* Znamensk
92 C1 **Wehni** Eth.
52 D6 **Wehr** Ger.
49 G9 **Wehrheim** Ger.
53 I5 **Wehringen** Ger.
49 D10 **Wehrheim** Ger.
52 G2 **Weibersbrunn** Ger.
169 O6 **Weichang** *Hebei* China
53 K4 **Weichering** Ger.
53 K5 **Weichs** Ger.
51 F9 **Weida** Ger.
51 F9 **Weida** *r.* Ger.
53 J3 **Weidenbach** Ger.
53 L2 **Weidenberg** Ger.
53 M2 **Weiden in der Oberpfalz** Ger.
52 H4 **Weidenstetten** Ger.
52 D3 **Weidenthal** Ger.
53 N3 **Weiding** Ger.
Weidongmen *Heilong.* China *see* Qianjin
52 C2 **Weiersbach** Ger.
169 P8 **Weifang** *Shandong* China
51 K8 **Weigersdorf** Ger.
118 B5 **Weiglestown** *PA* U.S.A.
169 P8 **Weihai** *Shandong* China
169 R8 **Weihai** *Shandong* China
169 N8 **Wei He** *r. Henan* China
169 L9 **Wei He** *r. Shaanxi* China
169 P8 **Wei He** *r. Shandong* China
53 J3 **Weihenzell** Ger.
53 M2 **Weiherhammer** Ger.
53 K5 **Weihmichl** Ger.
169 N9 **Weihui** *Henan* China
162 E7 **Weihu Ling** *mts* China
59 O3 **Weikendorf** Austria
52 H3 **Weikersheim** Ger.
53 J5 **Weil** Ger.
52 D6 **Weil am Rhein** Ger.
52 D6 **Weilbach** Ger.
49 F10 **Weilburg** Ger.
52 F4 **Weil der Stadt** Ger.
58 A5 **Weiler** Austria
52 H6 **Weiler** Ger.
52 D3 **Weilerbach** Ger.
52 E6 **Weilersbach** Ger.
52 E6 **Weilheim** Ger.
52 H4 **Weilheim an der Teck** Ger.
53 K6 **Weilheim in Oberbayern** Ger.
205 K3 **Weilmoringle** *N.S.W.* Austr.
49 F10 **Weilmünster** Ger.
51 D9 **Weimar** Ger.
49 H8 **Weimar (Ahnatal)** Ger.
169 K9 **Weinan** *Shaanxi* China
49 F10 **Weinbach** Ger.
51 I8 **Weinböhla** Ger.
70 G1 **Weinfelden** Switz.
52 H5 **Weingarten** Ger.
52 F3 **Weingarten (Baden)** Ger.
52 F3 **Weinheim** Ger.
170 E5 **Weining** *Guizhou* China
52 G3 **Weinsberg** Ger.
59 K2 **Weinsberger Wald** *for.* Austria
52 D2 **Weinsheim** *Rheinland-Pfalz* Ger.
49 B10 **Weinsheim** *Rheinland-Pfalz* Ger.
52 G4 **Weinstadt** Ger.
59 N3 **Weinviertel** *reg.* Austria
207 H2 **Weipa** *Qld* Austr.
207 H2 **Weipa Aboriginal Reserve** *Qld* Austr.
207 I2 **Weipa South Aboriginal Reserve** *Qld* Austr.
205 L3 **Weir** *r. Qld* Austr.
209 D9 **Weiragoo Range** *hills W.A.* Austr.
168 I9 **Weirong** *Gansu* China
107 M3 **Weir River** *Man.* Can.
116 E8 **Weirton** *WV* U.S.A.
51 F10 **Weischlitz** Ger.
26 □N2 **Weisdale** *Shetland, Scotland* U.K.
50 E4 **Weisen** Ger.
53 J2 **Weisendorf** Ger.
122 F4 **Weiser** *ID* U.S.A.
122 F4 **Weiser** *r. ID* U.S.A.
169 O9 **Weishan** *Shandong* China
170 C6 **Weishan** *Yunnan* China
169 O9 **Weishan Hu** *l.* China
169 N9 **Weishi** *Henan* China
52 B2 **Weiskirchen** Ger.
51 D10 **Weismain** Ger.
53 L6 **Weißach** *r.* Ger.
58 H6 **Weißbriach** Austria
51 E8 **Weiße Elster** *r.* Ger.
53 L3 **Weiße Laber** *r.* Ger.
58 C5 **Weißenbach am Lech** Austria
53 K6 **Weißenberg** Ger.
49 J8 **Weißenborn** *Hessen* Ger.
51 H9 **Weißenborn** *Sachsen* Ger.
49 J7 **Weißenborn-Lüderode** Ger.
51 D10 **Weißenbrunn** Ger.
53 J3 **Weißenburg in Bayern** Ger.
51 E8 **Weißenfels** Ger.
53 I5 **Weißenhorn** Ger.
52 H6 **Weißensberg** Ger.
59 H6 **Weißensee** *l.* Austria
51 D8 **Weißensee** Ger.
51 E10 **Weißenstadt** Ger.
59 I6 **Weißenstein** Austria
49 D10 **Weißenthurm** Ger.
51 D10 **Weißer Main** *r.* Ger.
53 N3 **Weißer Regen** *r.* Ger.
51 K8 **Weißer Schöps** *r.* Ger.
70 D3 **Weisshorn** *mt.* Switz.
51 I8 **Weißig** Ger.
51 K8 **Weißkeißel** Ger.
59 J3 **Weißkirchen an der Traun** Austria
59 K5 **Weißkirchen in Steiermark** Austria
51 J8 **Weißkollm** Ger.
58 C6 **Weißkugel** *mt.* Austria/Italy
115 E8 **Weiss Lake** *AL* U.S.A.
70 E3 **Weissmies** *mt.* Switz.
94 C5 **Weissrand Mountains** Namibia
51 K7 **Weißwasser** Ger.
59 K3 **Weistrach** Austria
45 J8 **Weiswampach** Lux.
52 D5 **Weisweil** Ger.
37 O6 **Weitbruch** France
49 E9 **Weitefeld** Ger.
59 L3 **Weiten** Austria
59 L6 **Weitendorf** Austria
50 H2 **Weitenhagen** Ger.
59 J6 **Weitensfeld** Austria
59 M2 **Weitersfeld** Austria
52 F2 **Weiterstadt** Ger.
44 L3 **Weiteveen** Neth.
53 I6 **Weitnau** Ger.
59 K2 **Weitra** Austria
49 K10 **Weitramsdorf** Ger.
107 J3 **Weitzel Lake** *Sask.* Can.
51 I8 **Weixdorf** Ger.
170 B5 **Weixi** *Yunnan* China
169 N8 **Weixian** *Hebei* China
170 E5 **Weixin** *Yunnan* China
168 D6 **Weiya** *Xinjiang* China
168 I9 **Weiyuan** *Gansu* China
170 C7 **Weiyuan Jiang** *r. Yunnan* China
59 L5 **Weiz** Austria
168 J8 **Weizhou** *Ningxia* China
Weizhou *Sichuan* China *see* Wenchuan
170 G8 **Weizhou Dao** *i.* China
169 R6 **Weizi** *Liaoning* China
23 O7 **Wejherowo** Pol.
107 L4 **Wekusko** *Man.* Can.
107 L4 **Wekusko Lake** *Man.* Can.
106 H1 **Wekweti** *N.W.T.* Can.
116 F2 **Wel** *r.* Pol.
158 D1 **Welatam** Myanmar
97 K5 **Welbedacht Dam** S. Africa
204 B2 **Welbourn Hill** *S.A.* Austr.
116 D11 **Welch** *WV* U.S.A.
117 □O4 **Weld** *ME* U.S.A.
209 G10 **Weld, Mount** *hill W.A.* Austr.
53 J5 **Welden** Ger.
92 C2 **Weldiya** Eth.
31 K3 **Weldon** *Northamptonshire, England* U.K.
209 D9 **Weld Range** *hills W.A.* Austr.
207 I8 **Welford National Park** *Qld* Austr.
45 I7 **Welkenraedt** Belgium
51 F6 **Welkiek** Eth.
92 C2 **Welkīt'ē** Eth.
97 K3 **Welkom** S. Africa
44 J5 **Well** Neth.
111 O7 **Welland** *Ont.* Can.
31 L2 **Welland** *r. England* U.K.
111 O6 **Welland Canal** *Ont.* Can.
51 G7 **Wellaune** Ger.
176 G9 **Wellawaya** Sri Lanka
48 I4 **Welle** Ger.
45 H7 **Wellen** Belgium
52 F5 **Wellendingen** Ger.
31 I3 **Wellesbourne** *Warwickshire, England* U.K.
111 N6 **Wellesley** *Ont.* Can.
206 G4 **Wellesley Islands** *Qld* Austr.
206 G4 **Wellesley Islands Aboriginal Reserve** *Qld* Austr.
106 B2 **Wellesley Lake** *Y.T.* Can.
117 O7 **Wellfleet** *MA* U.S.A.
53 K4 **Wellheim** Ger.
45 H8 **Wellin** Belgium
49 D10 **Welling** Ger.
31 K3 **Wellingborough** *Northamptonshire, England* U.K.
205 L5 **Wellington** *N.S.W.* Austr.
204 G6 **Wellington** *S.A.* Austr.
111 Q6 **Wellington** *Ont.* Can.
203 I8 **Wellington** *North I.* N.Z.
203 J8 **Wellington** *admin. reg. North I.* N.Z.
96 C9 **Wellington** S. Africa
30 F6 **Wellington** *Somerset, England* U.K.
30 G2 **Wellington** *Telford and Wrekin, England* U.K.
122 L6 **Wellington** *CO* U.S.A.
121 G7 **Wellington** *KS* U.S.A.
124 M3 **Wellington** *NV* U.S.A.
116 C7 **Wellington** *OH* U.S.A.
121 E8 **Wellington** *TX* U.S.A.
125 V2 **Wellington** *UT* U.S.A.
145 B8 **Wellington, Isla** *i.* Chile
27 I8 **Wellington Bridge** Rep. of Ireland
206 D2 **Wellington Range** *hills N.T.* Austr.
209 F9 **Wellington Range** *hills W.A.* Austr.
106 F4 **Wells** *B.C.* Can.
30 G5 **Wells** *Somerset, England* U.K.
122 G6 **Wells** *NV* U.S.A.
209 G9 **Wells, Lake** *salt flat W.A.* Austr.
116 H7 **Wellsboro** *PA* U.S.A.
116 E8 **Wellsburg** *WV* U.S.A.
202 I3 **Wellsford** *North I.* N.Z.
106 F4 **Wells Gray Provincial Park** *B.C.* Can.
31 N2 **Wells-next-the-Sea** *Norfolk, England* U.K.
110 I5 **Wellston** *MI* U.S.A.
116 H6 **Wellsville** *NY* U.S.A.
116 E8 **Wellsville** *OH* U.S.A.
118 B4 **Wellsville** *PA* U.S.A.
125 R9 **Wellton** *AZ* U.S.A.
54 E3 **Wełna** *r.* Pol.
31 M2 **Welney** *Norfolk, England* U.K.
55 L4 **Wełnianka** *r.* Pol.
124 □1 **Weloka** *HI* U.S.A.
59 J3 **Wels** Austria
52 B2 **Welschbillig** Ger.
59 J4 **Welse** *r.* Ger.
30 L4 **Welsh Newton** *Herefordshire, England* U.K.
30 F2 **Welshpool** *Powys, Wales* U.K.
51 H7 **Welsickendorf** Ger.
51 E7 **Welsleben** Ger.
29 Q7 **Welton** *Lincolnshire, England* U.K.
49 E7 **Welver** Ger.
92 E3 **Welwel** Eth.
31 L4 **Welwyn** *Hertfordshire, England* U.K.
31 L4 **Welwyn Garden City** *Hertfordshire, England* U.K.
48 H2 **Welzheim** Ger.
52 H4 **Welzheimer Wald** *hills* Ger.
31 J7 **Welzow** Ger.
30 G2 **Wem** *Shropshire, England* U.K.
90 D5 **Wema** Dem. Rep. Congo
30 F5 **Wembdon** *Somerset, England* U.K.
93 B6 **Wembere** *r.* Tanz.
97 N5 **Wembesi** S. Africa
106 G4 **Wembley** *Alta* Can.
53 J4 **Wemding** Ger.
44 F5 **Wemeldinge** Neth.
92 D3 **Wemel Shet'** *r.* Eth.
108 E2 **Wemindji** *Que.* Can.
26 G11 **Wemyss Bay** *Inverclyde, Scotland* U.K.
130 E1 **Wemyss Bight** *Eleuthera* Bahamas
137 F3 **Wenamu** *r.* Guyana *alt.* Venamo (Venezuela)
122 D3 **Wenatchee** *WA* U.S.A.
122 D3 **Wenatchee Mountains** *WA* U.S.A.
170 H9 **Wenchang** *Hainan* China
Wenchang *Sichuan* China *see* Zitong
171 M5 **Wencheng** *Zhejiang* China
88 E5 **Wenchi** Ghana
92 C2 **Wench'it Shet'** *r.* Eth.
Wenchow *Zhejiang* China *see* Wenzhou
170 D3 **Wenchuan** *Sichuan* China
49 J6 **Wendeburg** Ger.
52 E2 **Wendelsheim** Ger.
53 K3 **Wendelstein** Ger.
53 M6 **Wendelstein** *mt.* Ger.
49 E9 **Wenden** Ger.
125 S8 **Wenden** *AZ* U.S.A.
169 R8 **Wendeng** *Shandong* China
31 M3 **Wendens Ambo** *Essex, England* U.K.
48 J4 **Wendisch Evern** Ger.
50 F4 **Wendisch Priborn** Ger.
51 J6 **Wendisch Rietz** Ger.
50 D4 **Wendland** *reg.* Ger.
52 G4 **Wendlingen am Neckar** Ger.
92 C3 **Wendo** Eth.
88 B4 **Wendou Mbôrou** Guinea
31 K4 **Wendover** *Buckinghamshire, England* U.K.
122 G6 **Wendover** *UT* U.S.A.
30 B7 **Wendron** *Cornwall, England* U.K.
45 D6 **Wenduine** Belgium
111 K2 **Wenebegon Lake** *Ont.* Can.
170 E1 **Wenfengzhen** *Gansu* China
90 D4 **Wenge** Dem. Rep. Congo
70 D2 **Wengen** Switz.
49 D6 **Wengsel (Isterberg)** Ger.
170 B4 **Wengshui** *Yunnan* China
171 J6 **Wengyuan** *Guangdong* China
169 P9 **Wen He** *r.* China
Wenhua *Yunnan* China *see* Weishan
170 E4 **Wenjiang** *Sichuan* China
171 I5 **Wenjiashi** *Hunan* China
162 C4 **Wenkutu** *Nei Mongol* China
Wenlin *Sichuan* China *see* Renshou
171 M4 **Wenling** *Zhejiang* China
207 H2 **Wenlock** *r. Qld* Austr.
30 G3 **Wenlock Edge** *ridge England* U.K.
136 □ **Wenman, Isla** *i. Islas Galápagos* Ecuador
49 F8 **Wenne** *r.* Ger.
49 I6 **Wennigsen (Deister)** Ger.
29 L5 **Wenning** *r. England* U.K.
48 F1 **Wenningstedt** Ger.
58 C5 **Wenns** Austria
200 □4a **Weno** *Chuuk* Micronesia
200 □4a **Weno** *i. Chuuk* Micronesia
110 E8 **Wenona** *IL* U.S.A.
117 J10 **Wenona** *MD* U.S.A.
170 F3 **Wenquan** *Chongqing* China
Wenquan *Guizhou* China
Wenquan *Hubei* China *see* Yingshan
168 F9 **Wenquan** *Qinghai* China
173 J10 **Wenquan** *Qinghai* China
172 E4 **Wenquan** *Xinjiang* China
Wenquanzhen *Hubei* China
170 E7 **Wenshan** *Yunnan* China
170 F4 **Wenshui** *Guizhou* China
29 N5 **Wensley** *North Yorkshire, England* U.K.
29 M5 **Wensleydale** *val. England* U.K.
172 E6 **Wensu** *Xinjiang* China
31 O2 **Wensum** *r. England* U.K.
29 P6 **Went** *r. England* U.K.
51 F9 **Wenthorf** Ger.
48 J3 **Wentorf bei Hamburg** Ger.
205 H6 **Wentworth** *N.S.W.* Austr.
115 H7 **Wentworth** *NC* U.S.A.
117 N5 **Wentworth** *NH* U.S.A.
110 C3 **Wentworth** *WI* U.S.A.
169 L9 **Wenxi** *Shanxi* China
170 E2 **Wenxian** *Gansu* China
Wenxing *Hunan* China *see* Xiangyin
169 L8 **Wenyu He** *r.* China
53 M3 **Wenzenbach** Ger.
171 M5 **Wenzhou** *Zhejiang* China
51 F6 **Wenzlow** Ger.
30 G3 **Weobley** *Herefordshire, England* U.K.
97 L5 **Wepener** S. Africa
45 G8 **Wépion** Belgium
178 F6 **Wer** *Rajasthan* India
52 H2 **Werbach** Ger.
50 I5 **Werbellin** Ger.
50 I5 **Werbellinsee** *l.* Ger.
51 J7 **Werben** Ger.
50 E5 **Werben (Elbe)** Ger.
51 H7 **Werbig** Ger.
55 L5 **Werbkowice** Pol.
45 I8 **Werbomont** Belgium
94 D5 **Werda** Botswana
51 F9 **Werda** Ger.
92 E3 **Werdër** Eth.
51 G6 **Werder** *Brandenburg* Ger.
50 H3 **Werder** *Mecklenburg-Vorpommern* Ger.
49 E8 **Werdohl** Ger.
48 E3 **Werdum** Ger.
31 M2 **Wereham** *Norfolk, England* U.K.
58 H5 **Werfen** Austria
44 I2 **Wergea** Neth.
155 G5 **Werinama** *Seram* Indon.
49 E7 **Werl** Ger.
48 E5 **Werlte** Ger.
49 D8 **Wermelskirchen** Ger.
51 G8 **Wermsdorf** Ger.
51 G8 **Wermsdorfer Forst** *park* Ger.
49 I10 **Wern** *r.* Ger.
53 K4 **Wernau** Ger.
59 I6 **Wernberg** Austria
53 L2 **Wernberg-Köblitz** Ger.
53 M2 **Werndorf** Austria
59 M6 **Werndorf** Austria
49 E7 **Werne** Ger.
51 B11 **Werneck** Ger.
50 I5 **Werneuchen** Ger.
49 K7 **Wernigerode** Ger.
53 J3 **Wernshausen** Ger.
92 C2 **Werota** Eth.
48 E5 **Werpeloh** Ger.
49 I8 **Werra** *r.* Ger.
49 G6 **Werre** *r.* Ger.
204 H6 **Werrimull** *Vic.* Austr.
205 M4 **Werris Creek** *N.S.W.* Austr.
53 I6 **Wertach** Ger.
53 J5 **Wertach** *r.* Ger.
52 H2 **Wertheim** Ger.
52 F7 **Werthenstein** Switz.
49 K8 **Wether** Ger.
49 F6 **Werther (Westfalen)** Ger.
53 I4 **Wertingen** Ger.
44 H3 **Wervershoof** Neth.
45 D7 **Wervik** Belgium
155 F8 **Werwaru** *Maluku* Indon.
49 C7 **Wesel** Ger.
49 C7 **Wesel-Datteln-Kanal** *canal* Ger.
50 G4 **Wesenberg** Ger.
48 K5 **Wesendorf** Ger.
44 J4 **Wesepe** Neth.
49 F7 **Weser** *r.* Ger.
48 F3 **Weser** *sea chan.* Ger.
49 G5 **Weser-Ems** *admin. reg.* Ger.
49 G6 **Wesergebirge** *hills* Ger.
120 E6 **Weskan** *KS* U.S.A.
92 B3 **Weska Weka** Eth.
121 G12 **Weslaco** *TX* U.S.A.
111 Q4 **Weslemkoon Lake** *Ont.* Can.
97 L9 **Wesley** S. Africa
117 □R4 **Wesley** *ME* U.S.A.
109 K3 **Wesleyville** *Nfld and Lab.* Can.
116 E6 **Wesleyville** *PA* U.S.A.
55 J3 **Wesoła** Pol.
206 F1 **Wessel, Cape** *N.T.* Austr.
48 G2 **Wesselburen** Ger.
49 C9 **Wesseling** Ger.
206 F1 **Wessel Islands** *N.T.* Austr.
48 H2 **Wesseln** Ger.
97 K3 **Wesselsbron** S. Africa
96 H3 **Wesselsvlei** S. Africa
97 N2 **Wesselton** S. Africa
45 I6 **Wessem** Neth.
120 F3 **Wessington Springs** *SD* U.S.A.
53 K5 **Weßling** Ger.
53 K6 **Wessobrunn** Ger.
118 C7 **West** *r. MD* U.S.A.
204 E5 **Westall, Point** *S.A.* Austr.
206 D2 **West Alligator** *r. N.T.* Austr.
110 F6 **West Allis** *WI* U.S.A.
212 P1 **West Antarctica** *reg.* Antarctica
119 G6 **West Atlantic City** *NJ* U.S.A.
29 N4 **West Auckland** *Durham, England* U.K.
215 K6 **West Australian Basin** *sea feature* Indian Ocean
119 I3 **West Babylon** *NY* U.S.A.
206 C3 **West Baines** *r. N.T.* Austr.
178 C8 **West Banas** *r.* India
190 D7 **West Bank** *terr.* Asia
118 F6 **West Bay** *Nfld and Lab.* Can.
130 C4 **West Bay** Cayman Is
121 K11 **West Bay** *LA* U.S.A.
115 E10 **West Bay** *FL* U.S.A.
110 F6 **West Bend** *WI* U.S.A.
179 K8 **West Bengal** *state* India
31 N4 **West Bergholt** *Essex, England* U.K.
31 J5 **West Berkshire** *admin. div. England* U.K.
118 F5 **West Berlin** *NJ* U.S.A.
116 B9 **Westboro** *OH* U.S.A.
111 J5 **West Branch** *MI* U.S.A.
31 J2 **West Bridgford** *Nottinghamshire, England* U.K.
31 I2 **West Bromwich** *West Midlands, England* U.K.
119 K2 **Westbrook** *CT* U.S.A.
117 □O5 **Westbrook** *ME* U.S.A.
118 F1 **Westbrookville** *NY* U.S.A.
117 N4 **West Burke** *VT* U.S.A.
205 K9 **Westbury** *Tas.* Austr.
30 H5 **Westbury** *Wiltshire, England* U.K.
110 D6 **Westby** *WI* U.S.A.
130 G3 **West Caicos** *i.* Turks and Caicos Is
26 I11 **West Calder** *West Lothian, Scotland* U.K.
118 B3 **West Cameron** *PA* U.S.A.
203 A12 **West Cape** *South I.* N.Z.
209 D13 **West Cape Howe** *W.A.* Austr.
118 F7 **West Cape May** *NJ* U.S.A.
216 E5 **West Caroline Basin** *sea feature* N. Pacific Ocean
118 D5 **West Chester** *PA* U.S.A.
119 H2 **Westchester County** *county NY* U.S.A.
123 L7 **Westcliffe** *CO* U.S.A.
203 E9 **West Coast** *admin. reg. South I.* N.Z.
96 C9 **West Coast National Park** S. Africa
30 G6 **West Coker** *Somerset, England* U.K.
110 B5 **West Concord** *MN* U.S.A.
31 L5 **Westcott** *Surrey, England* U.K.
119 G5 **West Creek** *NJ* U.S.A.
203 C12 **West Dome** *mt. South I.* N.Z.
45 E6 **Westdorpe** Neth.
111 K4 **West Duck Island** *Ont.* Can.
26 G11 **West Dunbartonshire** *admin. div. Scotland* U.K.
115 H12 **West End** *Gd Bahama* Bahamas
117 J6 **West End** *NY* U.S.A.
45 C6 **Westende** Belgium
58 F5 **Westendorf** Austria
115 H12 **West End Point** *Gd Bahama* Bahamas
44 J3 **Westenholte** Neth.
48 I2 **Westensee** Ger.
48 I2 **Westensee** *l.* Ger.
48 K5 **Westerbeck (Sassenburg)** Ger.
96 G5 **Westerberg** S. Africa
44 K3 **Westerbork** Neth.
49 E9 **Westerburg** Ger.
26 I6 **Westerdale** *Highland, Scotland* U.K.
51 D7 **Westeregeln** Ger.
48 D4 **Westerende-Kirchloog (Ihlow)** Ger.
203 F10 **Westerfield** *South I.* N.Z.
31 K6 **Westergate** *West Sussex, England* U.K.
48 J4 **Westergellersen** Ger.
44 K4 **Westerhaar** Neth.
Westerhall Grenada *see* Westerhall Point
131 □6 **Westerhall Point** Grenada
31 M5 **Westerham** *Kent, England* U.K.
51 D7 **Westerhausen** Ger.
52 H4 **Westerheim** *Baden-Württemberg* Ger.
53 I5 **Westerheim** *Bayern* Ger.
48 D3 **Westerholt** Ger.
48 I3 **Westerhorn** Ger.
45 H6 **Westerhoven** Neth.
48 F1 **Westerland** Ger.
45 G6 **Westerlo** Belgium
119 L2 **Westerly** *RI* U.S.A.
207 I7 **Western** *watercourse Qld* Austr.
88 E5 **Western** *admin. reg.* Ghana
91 D8 **Western** *prov.* Zambia
88 B4 **Western Area** *admin. div.* Sierra Leone
209 F8 **Western Australia** *state* Austr.
90 E3 **Western Bahr el Ghazal** *state* Sudan
96 E9 **Western Cape** *prov.* S. Africa
84 D6 **Western Darfur** *state* Sudan
Western Desert Egypt *see* Aş Şaḩrāʾ al Gharbīyah
206 B5 **Western Desert Aboriginal Land** *res. N.T.* Austr.
Western Dvina *r.* Europe *see* Zapadnaya Dvina
90 F3 **Western Equatoria** *state* Sudan
176 D5 **Western Ghats** *mts* India
26 C6 **Western Isles** *admin. div. Scotland* U.K.
90 F2 **Western Kordofan** *state* Sudan
205 J8 **Western Port** *b. Vic.* Austr.
202 □ **Western Reef** *is Chatham Is* S. Pacific Ocean
30 □ **Western Rocks** *is England* U.K.
86 D3 **Western Sahara** *terr.* Africa
Western Samoa *country* S. Pacific Ocean *see* Samoa
Western Sayan Mountains *reg.* Rus. Fed. *see* Zapadnyy Sayan
48 H1 **Wester-Ohrstedt** Ger.
26 I12 **Wester Parkgate** *Dumfries and Galloway, Scotland* U.K.
26 F7 **Wester Ross** *reg. Scotland* U.K.
45 D6 **Westerschelde** *est.* Neth.
48 E4 **Westerstede** Ger.
48 H4 **Westerstetten** Ger.
116 C8 **Westerville** *OH* U.S.A.
44 I5 **Westervoort** Neth.
49 E10 **Westerwald** *hills* Ger.
51 H8 **Westewitz** Ger.
145 E8 **West Falkland** *i.* Falkland Is
120 G2 **West Fargo** *ND* U.S.A.
153 K5 **West Fayu** *atoll* Micronesia
29 Q7 **West Fen** *reg. Lincolnshire, England* U.K.
31 N6 **Westfield** *East Sussex, England* U.K.
117 M6 **Westfield** *MA* U.S.A.
117 □R2 **Westfield** *ME* U.S.A.
119 G3 **Westfield** *NJ* U.S.A.
116 F6 **Westfield** *NY* U.S.A.
116 H7 **Westfield** *PA* U.S.A.
110 E6 **Westfield** *WI* U.S.A.
West Flanders *prov.* Belgium *see* West-Vlaanderen
117 □P3 **West Forks** *ME* U.S.A.
119 G4 **West Freehold** *NJ* U.S.A.
44 H3 **West Friesland** *reg.* Neth.
West Frisian Islands Neth. *see* Waddeneilanden
44 J1 **Westgat** *sea chan.* Neth.
207 K9 **Westgate** *Qld* Austr.
29 M4 **Westgate** *Durham, England* U.K.
122 H2 **West Glacier** *MT* U.S.A.
117 □R3 **West Grand Lake** *ME* U.S.A.
31 L6 **West Grinstead** *West Sussex, England* U.K.
118 D5 **West Grove** *PA* U.S.A.
31 J3 **West Haddon** *Northamptonshire, England* U.K.
116 C10 **West Hamlin** *WV* U.S.A.
119 J3 **Westhampton** *NY* U.S.A.
30 G5 **West Harptree** *Bath and North East Somerset, England* U.K.
119 J1 **West Hartford** *CT* U.S.A.
53 I4 **Westhausen** Ger.
119 J2 **West Haven** *CT* U.S.A.
119 H2 **West Haverstraw** *NY* U.S.A.
118 D3 **West Hazleton** *PA* U.S.A.
26 L8 **Westhill** *Aberdeenshire, Scotland* U.K.
52 E2 **Westhofen** Ger.
37 N6 **Westhoffen** France
120 E1 **Westhope** *ND* U.S.A.
213 F2 **West Ice Shelf** Antarctica
131 L4 **West Indies** *N. America*
26 □O1 **Westing** *Shetland, Scotland* U.K.
West Irian *prov.* Indon. *see* Papua
206 F3 **West Island** *N.T.* Austr.
208 □2 **West Island** Cocos Is
177 M6 **West Island** *Andaman & Nicobar Is* India
119 I3 **West Islip** *NY* U.S.A.
116 B9 **West Jefferson** *OH* U.S.A.
44 D5 **Westkapelle** Neth.
West Kazakhstan Oblast *admin. div.* Kazakh. *see* Zapadnyy Kazakhstan
26 G11 **West Kilbride** *North Ayrshire, Scotland* U.K.
117 N7 **West Kingston** *RI* U.S.A.
29 K7 **West Kirby** *Merseyside, England* U.K.
29 P5 **West Knapton** *North Yorkshire, England* U.K.
114 D5 **West Lafayette** *IN* U.S.A.
West Lamma Channel *H.K.* China *see* Sai Pok Liu Hoi Hap
207 I7 **Westland** *Qld* Austr.
116 B6 **Westland** *MI* U.S.A.
200 □3b **West Landing** *i. Majuro* Marshall Is
203 E10 **Westland National Park** *South I.* N.Z.
31 I5 **West Lavington** *Wiltshire, England* U.K.
118 E4 **West Lawn** *PA* U.S.A.
97 L3 **Westleigh** S. Africa
31 P3 **Westleton** *Suffolk, England* U.K.
116 B11 **West Liberty** *KY* U.S.A.
116 B8 **West Liberty** *OH* U.S.A.
26 J11 **West Linton** *Scottish Borders, Scotland* U.K.
26 C6 **West Loch Roag** *b. Scotland* U.K.
26 E11 **West Loch Tarbert** *inlet Scotland* U.K.
106 H4 **Westlock** *Alta* Can.
30 D7 **West Looe** *Cornwall, England* U.K.
108 D5 **West Lorne** *Ont.* Can.
26 I11 **West Lothian** *admin. div. Scotland* U.K.
30 H6 **West Lulworth** *Dorset, England* U.K.
91 E8 **West Lunga** *r.* Zambia
91 E8 **West Lunga National Park** Zambia
206 D7 **West MacDonnell National Park** *N.T.* Austr.
45 G6 **Westmalle** Belgium
31 M5 **West Malling** *Kent, England* U.K.
Westman Islands Iceland *see* Vestmannaeyjar
207 L9 **Westmar** *Qld* Austr.
216 E4 **West Mariana Basin** *sea feature* N. Pacific Ocean
27 H5 **Westmeath** *county* Rep. of Ireland
121 J8 **West Memphis** *AR* U.S.A.
31 J5 **West Meon Hut** *Hampshire, England* U.K.
202 I6 **Westmere** *North I.* N.Z.
31 N4 **West Mersea** *Essex, England* U.K.
31 I3 **West Midlands** *admin. div. England* U.K.
119 G2 **West Milford** *NJ* U.S.A.
111 K8 **West Millgrove** *OH* U.S.A.
116 A9 **West Milton** *OH* U.S.A.
118 B2 **West Milton** *PA* U.S.A.
118 B5 **Westminster** *MD* U.S.A.
30 F5 **West Monkton** *Somerset, England* U.K.
121 I9 **West Monroe** *LA* U.S.A.
31 I6 **West Moors** *Dorset, England* U.K.
206 G4 **Westmoreland** *Qld* Austr.
130 □ **Westmoreland** Jamaica
120 G6 **Westmoreland** *KS* U.S.A.
125 Q8 **Westmorland** *CA* U.S.A.
118 C2 **West Nanticoke** *PA* U.S.A.
29 J4 **Westness** *Orkney, Scotland* U.K.
Westnewton *Cumbria, England* U.K.
95 F4 **West Nicholson** Zimbabwe
121 F11 **West Nueces** *r. TX* U.S.A.
119 H2 **West Nyack** *NY* U.S.A.
97 O2 **Weston** S. Africa
157 K2 **Weston** *Sabah* Malaysia
203 E12 **Weston** *South I.* N.Z.
30 H6 **Weston** *Dorset, England* U.K.
30 H2 **Weston** *Staffordshire, England* U.K.
119 I2 **Weston** *CT* U.S.A.
116 B7 **Weston** *OH* U.S.A.
116 E9 **Weston** *WV* U.S.A.
97 L2 **Westonaria** S. Africa
30 G5 **Weston-super-Mare** *North Somerset, England* U.K.
30 G5 **Westonzoyland** *Somerset, England* U.K.
117 J10 **Westover** *MD* U.S.A.
115 G12 **West Palm Beach** *FL* U.S.A.
West Papua *prov.* Indon. *see* Papua
West Passage Palau *see* Toagel Mlungui
121 J7 **West Plains** *MO* U.S.A.
205 J9 **West Point** *Tas.* Austr.
98 □2c **West Point** *Tristan da Cunha* S. Atlantic Ocean
124 L3 **West Point** *CA* U.S.A.
110 G9 **Westpoint** *IN* U.S.A.
121 K9 **West Point** *MS* U.S.A.
120 G5 **West Point** *NE* U.S.A.
117 L7 **West Point** *NY* U.S.A.
116 E8 **West Point** *OH* U.S.A.
116 I11 **West Point** *VA* U.S.A.
115 E9 **West Point Lake** *resr AL/GA* U.S.A.
111 R5 **Westport** *Ont.* Can.
203 F8 **Westport** *South I.* N.Z.
27 C5 **Westport** Rep. of Ireland
124 I2 **Westport** *CA* U.S.A.

Column 1

119 I2 Westport CT U.S.A.
117 L4 Westport NY U.S.A.
27 C5 Westport Quay Rep. of Ireland
131 □10 Westpunt Curaçao Neth. Antilles
29 N4 West Rainton Durham, England U.K.
107 K4 Westray Man. Can.
26 J4 Westray i. Scotland U.K.
26 J4 Westray Firth sea chan. Scotland U.K.
119 I2 West Redding CT U.S.A.
108 D4 Westree Ont. Can.
52 C3 Westrich reg. Ger.
106 F4 West Road r. B.C. Can.
26 K11 Westruther Scottish Borders, Scotland U.K.
117 L5 West Rutland VT U.S.A.
124 K3 West Sacramento CA U.S.A.
116 C8 West Salem OH U.S.A.
111 P7 West Seneca NY U.S.A.
West Siberian Plain Rus. Fed. see Zapadno-Sibirskaya Ravnina
205 K8 West Sister Island Tas. Austr.
31 P2 West Somerton Norfolk, England U.K.
117 N4 West Stewartstown NH U.S.A.
31 L5 West Sussex admin. div. England U.K.
44 H7 West-Terschelling Neth.
117 M4 West Topsham VT U.S.A.
31 K6 West Town Hampshire, England U.K.
118 F2 Westtown NY U.S.A.
110 J5 West Twin Lake MI U.S.A.
110 C7 West Union IA U.S.A.
116 B10 West Union OH U.S.A.
116 E9 West Union WV U.S.A.
122 I6 West Valley City UT U.S.A.
110 H8 Westville IN U.S.A.
121 H8 Westville OK U.S.A.
116 E10 West Virginia state U.S.A.
45 C7 West-Vlaanderen prov. Belgium
124 M3 West Walker r. NV U.S.A.
30 D5 Westward Ho! Devon, England U.K.
31 I6 West Wellow Hampshire, England U.K.
26 J10 West Wemyss Fife, Scotland U.K.
29 R8 West Winch Norfolk, England U.K.
207 M7 Westwood Qld Austr.
124 L1 Westwood CA U.S.A.
119 G3 Westwood NJ U.S.A.
205 K5 West Wyalong N.S.W. Austr.
31 K4 West Wycombe Buckinghamshire, England U.K.
26 □N1 West Yell Shetland, Scotland U.K.
122 I4 West Yellowstone MT U.S.A.
118 B5 West York PA U.S.A.
29 M6 West Yorkshire admin. div. England U.K.
44 G4 Wetaskiwin Neth.
155 F7 Wetan i. Maluku Indon.
155 F7 Wetar i. Maluku Indon.
155 L8 Wetar, Selat sea chan. Indon.
106 H4 Wetaskiwin Alta Can.
91 E6 Wete Dem. Rep. Congo
93 C6 Wete Tanz.
51 E8 Wethau Ger.
29 L4 Wetheral Cumbria, England U.K.
29 O6 Wetherby West Yorkshire, England U.K.
119 J1 Wethersfield CT U.S.A.
203 A12 Wet Jacket Arm inlet South I. N.Z.
55 K6 Wetlina Pol.
110 H3 Wetmore MI U.S.A.
212 T2 Wetmore Glacier Antarctica
48 F5 Wetschen Ger.
49 G9 Wetter r. Ger.
49 G10 Wetter (Hessen) Ger.
49 D8 Wetter (Ruhr) Ger.
49 G10 Wetterau reg. Ger.
45 E6 Wetteren Belgium
51 E7 Wettin Ger.
70 E1 Wettingen Switz.
49 D6 Wettringen Ger.
48 E5 Wettrup Ger.
53 K4 Wettstetten Ger.
115 D9 Wetumka OK U.S.A.
153 C3 Wetwun Myanmar
70 F1 Wetzikon Switz.
49 G9 Wetzlar Ger.
45 D7 Wevelgem Belgium
115 E10 Wewahitchka FL U.S.A.
153 J7 Wewak P.N.G.
48 H3 Wewelsfleth Ger.
121 G8 Wewoka OK U.S.A.
27 J8 Wexford Rep. of Ireland
27 I7 Wexford county Rep. of Ireland
27 J8 Wexford Bay Rep. of Ireland
27 J8 Wexford Harbour b. Rep. of Ireland
107 J4 Weyakwin Sask. Can.
53 L6 Weyarn Ger.
110 F5 Weyauwega WI U.S.A.
31 L5 Weybridge Surrey, England U.K.
107 K5 Weyburn Sask. Can.
49 E9 Weyerbusch Ger.
59 K4 Weyer Markt Austria
49 F6 Weyersheim France
49 K6 Weyhausen Ger.
48 G5 Weyhe Ger.
109 H4 Weymouth N.S. Can.
30 H6 Weymouth Dorset, England U.K.
117 O6 Weymouth MA U.S.A.
118 F5 Weymouth NJ U.S.A.
207 I2 Weymouth, Cape Qld Austr.
44 J4 Wezep Neth.
202 L4 Whakaari i. North I. N.Z.
202 L6 Whakaki North I. N.Z.
202 J5 Whakamaru North I. N.Z.
202 L5 Whakapunake hill North I. N.Z.
202 K4 Whakarewarewa Forest Park nature res. North I. N.Z.
202 K4 Whakatane North I. N.Z.
205 L3 Whalan Creek r. N.S.W. Austr.
106 C3 Whale Bay AK U.S.A.
130 E1 Whale Cay i. Bahamas
107 M2 Whale Cove Nunavut Can.
Whale Island North I. N.Z. see Moutohora Island
106 C3 Whale Pass AK U.S.A.
97 N7 Whale Rock i. S. Africa
29 N7 Whaley Bridge Derbyshire, England U.K.
116 I12 Whaleyville VA U.S.A.
26 □O2 Whalsay i. Scotland U.K.
29 N3 Whalton Northumberland, England U.K.
156 □ Whampoa, Sungai i. Sing.
202 J4 Whangaehu r. North I. N.Z.
202 J4 Whangamata North I. N.Z.
203 H8 Whangamoa North I. N.Z.
202 I6 Whangamomona North I. N.Z.
202 I6 Whanganui Inlet b. South I. N.Z.
202 I6 Whanganui National Park North I. N.Z.
202 I3 Whangaparaoa North I. N.Z.
202 L4 Whangaparaoa Bay North I. N.Z.
202 I3 Whangaparaoa Head North I. N.Z.
202 H2 Whangape Harbour North I. N.Z.
202 M5 Whangarei North I. N.Z.
202 M5 Whangarei North I. N.Z.
202 I2 Whangaroa Bay North I. N.Z.
202 I2 Whangaruru Harbour b. North I. N.Z.
31 L2 Whaplode Lincolnshire, England U.K.
108 E2 Whapmagoostui Que. Can.
203 I8 Wharanui South I. N.Z.
203 K7 Whareama South I. N.Z.

Column 2

29 O6 Wharfe r. England U.K.
29 N5 Wharfedale val. England U.K.
111 K3 Wharncliffe Ont. Can.
116 D11 Wharncliffe WV U.S.A.
118 F3 Wharton NJ U.S.A.
121 G11 Wharton TX U.S.A.
107 L1 Wharton Lake Nunavut Can.
203 E10 Whataroa South I. N.Z.
106 G2 Wha Ti N.W.T. Can.
26 H13 Whauphill Dumfries and Galloway, Scotland U.K.
124 K2 Wheatland CA U.S.A.
122 L5 Wheatland WY U.S.A.
111 L7 Wheatley Ont. Can.
110 F8 Wheaton IL U.S.A.
120 G3 Wheaton MN U.S.A.
30 H2 Wheaton Aston Staffordshire, England U.K.
118 A6 Wheaton-Glenmont MD U.S.A.
204 □ Wheatsheaf Island Lord Howe I. Austr.
30 E5 Wheddon Cross Somerset, England U.K.
121 E8 Wheeler TX U.S.A.
125 W8 Wheeler WI U.S.A.
124 M2 Wheeler Lake N.W.T. Can.
115 D8 Wheeler Lake resr AL U.S.A.
123 L8 Wheeler Peak NM U.S.A.
125 R3 Wheeler Peak NV U.S.A.
124 M7 Wheelersburg OH U.S.A.
116 E8 Wheeling WV U.S.A.
147 G3 Wheelwright Arg.
29 M5 Whernside hill England U.K.
31 J5 Wherwell Hampshire, England U.K.
29 N4 Whickham Tyne and Wear, England U.K.
30 E6 Whiddon Down Devon, England U.K.
27 D9 Whiddy Island Rep. of Ireland
208 D6 Whim Creek W.A. Austr.
30 F6 Whimple Devon, England U.K.
204 C2 Whinham, Mount S.A. Austr.
119 G3 Whippany NJ U.S.A.
202 K5 Whirinaki Forest Park nature res. North I. N.Z.
107 K3 Whiskey Jack Lake Man. Can.
124 J3 Whispering Pines CA U.S.A.
206 E6 Whistleduck Creek watercourse N.T. Austr.
106 F5 Whistler B.C. Can.
109 K4 Whitburn Tyne and Wear, England U.K.
26 I11 Whitburn West Lothian, Scotland U.K.
111 P6 Whitby Ont. Can.
29 P5 Whitby North Yorkshire, England U.K.
31 K4 Whitchurch Buckinghamshire, England U.K.
30 F4 Whitchurch Cardiff, Wales U.K.
31 J5 Whitchurch Hampshire, England U.K.
30 G2 Whitchurch Shropshire, England U.K.
111 O6 Whitchurch-Stouffville Ont. Can.
203 E10 Whitcombe, Mount South I. N.Z.
108 C3 White r. Ont. Can.
106 B2 White r. Can./U.S.A.
130 □ White r. Jamaica
113 H4 White r. AR U.S.A.
121 J9 White r. AR U.S.A.
125 W1 White r. CO U.S.A.
114 C6 White r. IN U.S.A.
110 H6 White r. MI U.S.A.
125 R5 White r. NV U.S.A.
124 M2 White r. SD U.S.A.
117 M5 White r. VT U.S.A.
110 D3 White r. WI U.S.A.
125 V8 White watercourse AZ U.S.A.
121 E9 White watercourse TX U.S.A.
114 D6 White, East Fork r. IN U.S.A.
206 B6 White, Lake salt flat N.T. Austr.
121 I7 White, North Fork r. MO U.S.A.
29 M2 Whiteadder Water r. Scotland U.K.
109 J3 White Bay Nfld and Lab. Can.
120 D2 White Butte mt. ND U.S.A.
125 V4 White Canyon UT U.S.A.
27 E9 Whitechurch Cork Rep. of Ireland
27 G8 Whitechurch Waterford Rep. of Ireland
205 I4 White Cliffs N.S.W. Austr.
110 I6 White Cloud MI U.S.A.
203 D12 Whitecoomb mt. South I. N.Z.
26 J12 White Coomb hill Scotland U.K.
106 H4 Whitecourt Alta Can.
26 J11 Whitecraig East Lothian, Scotland U.K.
27 J4 Whitecross Northern Ireland U.K.
118 B2 White Deer PA U.S.A.
120 H2 White Earth Indian Reservation res. MN U.S.A.
110 B2 Whiteface r. MN U.S.A.
117 L4 Whiteface Mountain NY U.S.A.
117 N4 Whitefield NH U.S.A.
111 M3 Whitefish Ont. Can.
106 E1 Whitefish r. N.W.T. Can.
122 G1 Whitefish MT U.S.A.
110 H4 Whitefish r. MI U.S.A.
110 G5 Whitefish Bay WI U.S.A.
107 J2 Whitefish Lake N.W.T. Can.
110 I1 Whitefish Lake Ont. Can.
110 I3 Whitefish Point MI U.S.A.
118 C5 Whiteford MD U.S.A.
27 F7 Whitegate Clare Rep. of Ireland
27 F9 Whitegate Cork Rep. of Ireland
27 D9 White Hall Rep. of Ireland
27 H7 Whitehall Rep. of Ireland
26 K4 Whitehall Orkney, Scotland U.K.
120 J6 White Hall IL U.S.A.
118 D3 White Hall MD U.S.A.
110 H4 White Hall MI U.S.A.
117 L5 Whitehall NY U.S.A.
110 G9 Whitehall OH U.S.A.
118 B2 White Hall PA U.S.A.
110 D5 Whitehall WI U.S.A.
205 K6 White Horse NJ U.S.A.
207 H8 Whitula watercourse Qld Austr.
29 M6 Whitworth Lancashire, England U.K.
118 D2 White Haven PA U.S.A.
27 K3 Whitehead Northern Ireland U.K.
109 I4 White Hill N.S. Can.
31 K5 Whitehill Hampshire, England U.K.
26 K7 Whitehills Aberdeenshire, Scotland U.K.
106 C2 Whitehorse Y.T. Can.
31 I4 White Horse, Vale of val. England U.K.
130 □ White Horses Jamaica
118 F3 Whitehouse NJ U.S.A.
118 F3 White House Station NJ U.S.A.
213 D2 White Island Antarctica
202 L3 White Island North I. N.Z. see Whakaari
97 L8 White Kei r. S. Africa
209 F8 White Lake N.S.W. Austr.
108 C3 White Lake Ont. Can.
108 E4 White Lake Ont. Can.
118 F1 White Lake NY U.S.A.
121 H11 White Lake r. LA U.S.A.
110 H6 White Lake MI U.S.A.
205 L9 White Lake Tas. Austr.
118 E1 White Mills PA U.S.A.
124 N4 White Mountain Peak CA U.S.A.
117 N4 White Mountains NH U.S.A.
207 J6 White Mountains National Park Qld Austr.

Column 3

112 G1 Whitemouth r. Man. Can.
107 M5 Whitemouth Lake Man. Can.
106 G3 Whitemud r. Alta Can.
85 G6 Whiten Head Sudan
85 G6 White Nile state Sudan
85 G6 White Nile r. Sudan/Uganda alt. Abiad, Bahr el, alt. Jebel, Bahr el
85 G6 White Nile Dam Sudan
94 C4 White Nossob watercourse Namibia
116 B11 White Oak KY U.S.A.
111 J6 White Otter Lake Ont. Can.
106 C3 White Pass Can./U.S.A.
110 I8 White Pigeon MI U.S.A.
110 J3 White Pine MI U.S.A.
125 U3 White Pine Range mts NV U.S.A.
119 H2 White Plains NY U.S.A.
26 L8 Whiterashes Aberdeenshire, Scotland U.K.
108 C3 White River Ont. Can.
125 W8 Whiteriver AZ U.S.A.
120 C4 White River SD U.S.A.
117 M5 White River Junction VT U.S.A.
121 J8 White River National Wildlife Refuge nature res. AR U.S.A.
125 Q3 White River Valley NV U.S.A.
106 E4 Whitesail Lake B.C. Can.
122 D4 White Salmon WA U.S.A.
106 H2 Whitesand r. Alta/N.W.T. Can.
107 K5 Whitesand r. Sask. Can.
123 K10 White Sands National Monument nat. park NM U.S.A.
118 F6 Whitesboro NJ U.S.A.
117 J5 Whitesboro NY U.S.A.
116 C11 Whitesburg KY U.S.A.
White Sea Rus. Fed. see Beloye More
107 M5 Whiteshell Provincial Park park Man. Can.
111 I11 White Stone VA U.S.A.
122 I3 White Sulphur Springs MT U.S.A.
116 E11 White Sulphur Springs WV U.S.A.
118 E1 Whites Valley PA U.S.A.
116 D11 Whitesville WV U.S.A.
97 M4 White Umfolozi r. S. Africa
115 H8 Whiteville NC U.S.A.
88 E4 White Volta watercourse Burkina/Ghana alt. Nakambé, alt. Nakambe, alt. Volta Blanche
88 E4 White Volta r. Ghana
124 P8 White Water CA U.S.A.
125 X3 Whitewater CO U.S.A.
110 F7 Whitewater WI U.S.A.
123 J10 Whitewater Baldy mt. NM U.S.A.
108 B3 Whitewater Lake Ont. Can.
204 C4 White Well S.A. Austr.
120 E6 White Woman Creek r. KS U.S.A.
207 I6 Whitewood Qld Austr.
107 K5 Whitewood Sask. Can.
205 K7 Whitfield Vic. Austr.
31 O5 Whitfield Kent, England U.K.
30 F1 Whitford Flintshire, Wales U.K.
26 H13 Whithorn Dumfries and Galloway, Scotland U.K.
202 J3 Whitianga North I. N.Z.
117 □R4 Whiting ME U.S.A.
119 G5 Whiting NJ U.S.A.
110 E5 Whiting WI U.S.A.
26 F12 Whiting Bay North Ayrshire, Scotland U.K.
30 C4 Whitland Carmarthenshire, Wales U.K.
29 O3 Whitley Bay Tyne and Wear, England U.K.
115 E7 Whitley City KY U.S.A.
118 E5 Whitman Square NJ U.S.A.
97 M7 Whitmore S. Africa
212 Q1 Whitmore Mountains Antarctica
31 I3 Whitnash Warwickshire, England U.K.
111 P4 Whitney Ont. Can.
121 G10 Whitney, Lake TX U.S.A.
124 N5 Whitney, Mount CA U.S.A.
117 J6 Whitney Point NY U.S.A.
30 D7 Whitsand Bay England U.K.
118 D5 Whittingham Kent, England U.K.
207 L6 Whitsunday Group is Qld Austr.
207 L6 Whitsunday Island Qld Austr.
207 L6 Whitsunday Island National Park Qld Austr.
207 L6 Whitsunday Passage Qld Austr.
Whitsun Island Vanuatu see Pentecost Island
111 N5 Whittemore MI U.S.A.
124 N8 Whittier CA U.S.A.
29 N3 Whittingham Northumberland, England U.K.
30 F2 Whittington Shropshire, England U.K.
206 D5 Whittington Range hills N.T. Austr.
205 J3 Whittlesea Vic. Austr.
97 K8 Whittlesea S. Africa
31 L2 Whittlesey Cambridgeshire, England U.K.
110 D4 Whittlesey WI U.S.A.
110 D3 Whittlesey, Mount hill WI U.S.A.
205 K6 Whitton N.S.W. Austr.

Column 4

27 J6 Wicklow county Rep. of Ireland
27 K7 Wicklow Head Rep. of Ireland
27 J7 Wicklow Mountains Rep. of Ireland
27 J6 Wicklow Mountains National Park Rep. of Ireland
54 F1 Wicko Pol.
23 M7 Wicko, Jezioro lag. Pol.
30 H4 Wickwar South Gloucestershire, England U.K.
118 D3 Wiconisco PA U.S.A.
118 B3 Wiconisco Creek r. PA U.S.A.
54 G4 Widawa r. Pol.
54 E4 Widawa r. Pol.
54 G4 Widawka r. Pol.
207 N8 Wide Bay Qld Austr.
30 E6 Widecombe in the Moor Devon, England U.K.
26 J4 Wide Firth sea chan. Scotland U.K.
209 K8 Wide Gum watercourse
213 B2 Wideroe, Mount Antarctica
31 M4 Widford Hertfordshire, England U.K.
207 J9 Widgeegoara watercourse Qld Austr.
209 F11 Widgiemooltha W.A. Austr.
155 F4 Widi, Kepulauan is Maluku Indon.
70 H1 Widnau Switz.
29 M6 Widnes Halton, England U.K.
163 E11 Wi-do i. S. Korea
54 C2 Widuchowa Pol.
54 F2 Wiecbork Pol.
50 G2 Wieck am Darß Ger.
55 I2 Wieczno, Jezioro l. Pol.
49 D10 Wied r. Ger.
51 I8 Wieda Ger.
48 F4 Wiefelstede Ger.
51 D8 Wiehe Ger.
50 H1 Wiek Ger.
54 G5 Wiehengebirge hills Ger.
49 E9 Wiehl Ger.
52 F4 Większyce Pol.
55 I2 Wielbark Pol.
54 F5 Wieleń Pol.
53 H6 Wielenbach Ger.
54 D5 Wielichowo Pol.
55 I6 Wieliczka Pol.
55 K2 Wieliczki Pol.
57 H2 Wielka Racza mt. Pol./Slovakia
55 K6 Wielka Rawka mt. Pol.
54 E5 Wielka Sowa mt. Pol.
55 L5 Wielkie Oczy Pol.
54 G1 Wielkie Partęczyny, Jezioro l. Pol.
54 G1 Wielki Klincz Pol.
54 F4 Wielkopolska, Nizina lowland Pol.
54 F3 Wielkopolskie prov. Pol.
54 F3 Wielkopolskie, Pojezierze reg. Pol.
54 H6 Wielkopolski Park Narodowy nat. park Pol.
55 J6 Wielopole Skrzyńskie Pol.
55 G5 Wielowieś Pol.
45 D7 Wielsbeke Belgium
54 G4 Wieluń Pol.
59 N3 Wien Austria
59 L4 Wiener Neudorf Austria
59 L4 Wiener Neustadt Austria
59 N3 Wiener Wald mts Austria
48 J5 Wienhausen Ger.
59 N3 Wieniawa Pol.
54 G3 Wieniec Pol.
59 L3 Wiensberg mt. Austria
50 D5 Wienrode Ger.
55 J4 Wieprz r. Pol.
23 M7 Wieprza r. Pol.
49 F10 Wiera-Krzna, Kanał canal Pol.
55 K3 Wiercień Duży Pol.
55 K4 Wiercany Pol.
54 F4 Wierciszów Pol.
48 G3 Wieringermeer Polder Neth.
44 H3 Wieringerwerf Neth.
52 F4 Wiernsheim Ger.
59 N3 Wierzawice Pol.
54 F3 Wierzbica Lubelskie Pol.
55 J4 Wierzbica Mazowieckie Pol.
54 F2 Wierzbica Górna Pol.
54 O2 Wierzbięcin Pol.
54 F5 Wierzbinek Pol.
54 F5 Wierzbnik Pol.
55 L2 Wierzchlesie Pol.
54 F3 Wierchosławice Kujawsko-Pomorskie Pol.
55 I5 Wierzchosławice Małopolskie Pol.
54 E2 Wierzchowo Zachodniopomorskie Pol.
54 F2 Wierzchowo Zachodniopomorskie Pol.
54 E2 Wierzchowo, Jezioro l. Pol.
54 G1 Wierzyca r. Pol.
55 I6 Wies Austria
53 J6 Wies Ger.
53 M2 Wiesau Ger.
49 F10 Wiesbaden Ger.
52 D6 Wiese r. Ger.
51 J4 Wieselburg Austria
59 N4 Wiesen Austria
70 H2 Wiesen Switz.
51 F6 Wiesenburg Ger.
51 F6 Wiesenburg Ger.
52 H4 Wiesensteig Ger.
53 M3 Wiesent r. Ger.
53 K2 Wiesent Ger.
53 L2 Wiesenthau Ger.
58 E5 Wiesenttal Ger.
48 H4 Wiesloch Ger.
54 H3 Wiesmoor Ger.
59 M5 Wiespach SA U.S.A.
48 E4 Wiesmoor Ger.
48 E4 Wietze Ger.
48 I5 Wietzendorf Ger.
29 L6 Wieżyca hill Pol.
29 L6 Wigan Greater Manchester, England U.K.
53 I6 Wiggen Switz.
121 K10 Wiggins MS U.S.A.
20 □ Wiggins, Isle i. England U.K.
55 L1 Wigierski Park Narodowy nat. park Pol.
30 D3 Wigmore Herefordshire, England U.K.
107 M2 Wiggins Lake N.W.T. Can.
55 L1 Wigry, Jezioro l. Pol.
153 I8 Wigram Leicestershire, England U.K.
29 K4 Wigton Cumbria, England U.K.
26 H13 Wigtown Dumfries and Galloway, Scotland U.K.
26 H13 Wigtown Bay Scotland U.K.

Column 5

125 S7 Wikieup AZ U.S.A.
49 K9 Wik'ro Eth.
111 M4 Wikwemikong Ont. Can.
70 G1 Wil Switz.
55 H6 Wilamowice Pol.
120 G5 Wilber NE U.S.A.
205 D10 Wilberforce r. South I. N.Z.
206 F1 Wilberforce, Cape N.T. Austr.
122 E3 Wilbur WA U.S.A.
121 H8 Wilburton OK U.S.A.
205 I4 Wilcannia N.S.W. Austr.
54 G4 Wilcza Pol.
116 G7 Wilcox PA U.S.A.
54 G3 Wilczogóra Pol.
Wilczek Land i. Zemlya Frantsa-Iosifa Rus. Fed. see Zemlya Vil'cheka
55 H1 Wilczęta Pol.
52 F4 Wilczkowo Pol.
59 N4 Wild Austria
54 G3 Wildalpener Salzatal nature res. Austria
51 I6 Wildau Ger.
52 F4 Wildbad im Schwarzwald Ger.
52 F4 Wildberg Baden-Württemberg Ger.
50 G5 Wildberg Brandenburg Ger.
50 I3 Wildberg Mecklenburg-Vorpommern Ger.
107 K4 Wildcat Hill Provincial Wilderness Park nature res. Sask. Can.
124 P3 Wildcat Peak NV U.S.A.
97 N7 Wildcliff S. Africa
49 J9 Wildeck-Obersuhl Ger.
49 J9 Wildeck-Richelsdorf Ger.
49 J7 Wildemann Ger.
59 N2 Wildendürnbach Austria
51 G9 Wildenfels Ger.
49 J9 Wildenhain Ger.
53 I6 Wildenstein Ger.
48 F5 Wildeshausen Ger.
49 I10 Wildflecken Ger.
54 G5 Wildhaus Switz.
50 E4 Wildpoldsried Ger.
120 G2 Wild Rice r. MN U.S.A.
120 G2 Wild Rice r. ND U.S.A.
110 B3 Wild Rice Lake MN U.S.A.
58 C5 Wildseeloder mt. Austria
58 C6 Wildspitz mt. Austria
106 F4 Wildwood Alta Can.
115 F11 Wildwood FL U.S.A.
118 F7 Wildwood NJ U.S.A.
118 F7 Wildwood Crest NJ U.S.A.
116 F9 Wiley CO U.S.A.
116 F9 Wiley Ford WV U.S.A.
55 J4 Wilga r. Pol.
54 G3 Wilga r. Pol.
97 M3 Wilge r. Free State S. Africa
97 N1 Wilge r. S. Africa
204 E4 Wilgena S.A. Austr.
153 J8 Wilhelm, Mount P.N.G.
137 G4 Wilhelm Gebergte mts Suriname
44 H6 Wilhelmina Kanaal canal Neth.
20 □ Wilhelmøya i. Svalbard
59 M3 Wilhelmsburg Austria
50 I3 Wilhelmsburg Ger.
52 G6 Wilhelmsdorf Ger.
48 F3 Wilhelmshaven Ger.
94 C4 Wilhelmstal Namibia
51 D10 Wilhelmsthal Ger.
59 J3 Wilhering Austria
53 J3 Wilhermsdorf Ger.
175 □2 Wilingili i. Addu Atoll Maldives
51 G9 Wilkau-Haßlau Ger.
118 D2 Wilkes-Barre PA U.S.A.
115 G7 Wilkesboro NC U.S.A.
213 I2 Wilkes Coast Antarctica
213 I2 Wilkes Land reg. Antarctica
213 T2 Wilkins Ice Shelf Antarctica
204 D3 Wilkinson Lakes salt flat S.A. Austr.
27 I5 Wilkinstown Rep. of Ireland
54 F4 Wilkołaz Pierwszy Pol.
55 K4 Wilków Lubelskie Pol.
54 F4 Wilków Opolskie Pol.
55 J4 Wilków Pol.
106 D3 Will, Mount B.C. Can.
122 C4 Willamette r. OR U.S.A.
30 F6 Willand Devon, England U.K.
205 J3 Willandra Billabong watercourse N.S.W. Austr.
205 J5 Willandra National Park N.S.W. Austr.
122 B3 Willapa Bay WA U.S.A.
123 K9 Willard Mex.
116 C7 Willard OH U.S.A.
122 H6 Willard UT U.S.A.
29 J10 Willaston Cheshire, England U.K.
125 U9 Willcox AZ U.S.A.
125 W9 Willcox Playa salt flat AZ U.S.A.
49 I7 Willebadessen Ger.
45 F6 Willebroek Belgium
97 L4 Willem Pretorius Game Reserve nature res. S. Africa
44 F5 Willemstad Neth.
131 □10 Willemstad Curaçao Neth. Antilles
206 E3 Willeroo N.T. Austr.
107 I3 William r. Sask. Can.
209 C7 William, Mount Vic. Austr.
209 D7 Willaumez W.A. Austr.
204 F3 William Creek S.A. Austr.
107 L4 William Lake Man. Can.
209 D12 Williams W.A. Austr.
207 I4 Williams r. W.A. Austr.
125 T6 Williams AZ U.S.A.
124 J2 Williams CA U.S.A.
116 A12 Williamsburg KY U.S.A.
110 I5 Williamsburg MI U.S.A.
118 A4 Williamsburg PA U.S.A.
116 H11 Williamsburg VA U.S.A.
106 F4 Williams Lake B.C. Can.
130 □ Williams Island Bahamas
107 I4 Williams Lake Can.
116 C11 Williamson WV U.S.A.
116 H7 Williamson NY U.S.A.
114 D5 Williamsport IN U.S.A.
118 B3 Williamsport PA U.S.A.
115 I7 Williamston NC U.S.A.
117 L6 Williamstown MA U.S.A.
118 E3 Williamstown NJ U.S.A.
117 I7 Williamstown NY U.S.A.
27 I8 Williamstown Rep. of Ireland
111 L7 Williamsville NY U.S.A.
49 H7 Willich Ger.
88 E3 Willikies Antigua and Barbuda
131 □10 Willimantic CT U.S.A.
119 K1 Willimantic CT U.S.A.
118 F6 Willingboro NJ U.S.A.
49 I7 Willingen (Upland) Ger.
31 M3 Willingham Cambridgeshire, England U.K.
49 J8 Willingshausen Ger.
70 H2 Willisau Switz.
145 □ Willis Group atolls
96 E7 Willis Islands S. Georgia

Column 6

115 F11 Williston FL U.S.A.
120 D1 Williston ND U.S.A.
115 G9 Williston SC U.S.A.
106 F4 Williston Lake B.C. Can.
30 F5 Williton Somerset, England U.K.
124 I1 Willits CA U.S.A.
120 H3 Willmar MN U.S.A.
106 G4 Willmore Wilderness Provincial Park Alta Can.
204 F4 Willochra watercourse S.A. Austr.
29 R7 Willoughby Lincolnshire, England U.K.
116 D7 Willoughby OH U.S.A.
117 M4 Willoughby, Lake VT U.S.A.
106 F4 Willow r. B.C. Can.
125 R6 Willow Beach AZ U.S.A.
107 J5 Willow Bunch Sask. Can.
106 H5 Willow Creek r. Alta Can.
124 D4 Willow Creek r. CA U.S.A.
122 G4 Willow Creek r. ID U.S.A.
125 W1 Willow Creek r. UT U.S.A.
118 D6 Willow Grove DE U.S.A.
118 E4 Willow Grove PA U.S.A.
116 H8 Willow Hill PA U.S.A.
106 F2 Willow Lake N.W.T. Can.
106 F2 Willowlake r. N.W.T. Can.
97 J5 Willowmore S. Africa
206 D6 Willowra N.T. Austr.
110 E4 Willow Reservoir WI U.S.A.
124 J2 Willows CA U.S.A.
121 J7 Willow Springs MO U.S.A.
118 C5 Willow Street PA U.S.A.
97 M8 Willowvale S. Africa
208 J6 Wills, Lake salt flat W.A. Austr.
206 H7 Wills Creek watercourse Qld Austr.
52 D4 Willstätt Ger.
204 G6 Willunga S.A. Austr.
31 □3 Wilmcote England U.K.
118 D5 Wilmington DE U.S.A.
115 I8 Wilmington NC U.S.A.
116 B10 Wilmington OH U.S.A.
117 M6 Wilmington VT U.S.A.
115 I9 Wilmington Island GA U.S.A.
29 M7 Wilmslow Cheshire, England U.K.
44 G4 Wilnis Neth.
Wilno Lith. see Vilnius
49 F9 Wilnsdorf Ger.
44 J4 Wilp Neth.
176 G8 Wilpattu National Park Sri Lanka
204 G4 Wilpena watercourse S.A. Austr.
51 I8 Wilsdruff Ger.
48 I4 Wilseder Berg hill Ger.
50 I4 Wilsickow Ger.
208 J4 Wilson r. W.A. Austr.
207 I9 Wilson watercourse Qld Austr.
120 G5 Wilson KS U.S.A.
110 C6 Wilson MN U.S.A.
115 I8 Wilson NC U.S.A.
116 G5 Wilson NY U.S.A.
118 C3 Wilson PA U.S.A.
105 J3 Wilson, Cape Nunavut Can.
123 K8 Wilson, Mount CO U.S.A.
125 R3 Wilson, Mount NV U.S.A.
122 D4 Wilson, Mount OR U.S.A.
206 C5 Wilson Creek watercourse N.T. Austr.
213 K2 Wilson Hills Antarctica
124 N5 Wilsonia CA U.S.A.
115 D8 Wilson Lake resr AL U.S.A.
116 H11 Wilson's Mills VA U.S.A.
205 K8 Wilson's Promontory pen. Vic. Austr.
205 K8 Wilson's Promontory National Park Vic. Austr.
48 H5 Wilstedt Ger.
48 I3 Wilster Ger.
48 C5 Wilsum Ger.
59 O2 Wilten Austria
51 J8 Wilthen Ger.
52 B2 Wiltingen Ger.
206 E3 Wilton r. N.T. Austr.
31 I5 Wilton Wiltshire, England U.K.
117 □O4 Wilton ME U.S.A.
120 E2 Wilton ND U.S.A.
117 N6 Wilton NH U.S.A.
31 I5 Wiltshire admin. div. England U.K.
45 I9 Wiltz Lux.
209 F9 Wiluna W.A. Austr.

Column 7

205 K11 Wimbleball Lake England U.K.
202 K7 Wimbledon North I. N.Z.
31 M2 Wimblington Cambridgeshire, England U.K.
31 I6 Wimborne Minster Dorset, England U.K.
36 C2 Wimereux France
51 E7 Wimmelburg Ger.
205 H7 Wimmera r. Vic. Austr.
Wina r. Cameroon see Vina
114 D5 Winamac IN U.S.A.
92 B5 Winam Gulf Kenya
207 J9 Winbin watercourse Qld Austr.
97 L4 Winburg S. Africa
30 H5 Wincanton Somerset, England U.K.
31 N6 Winchcombe Gloucestershire, England U.K.
31 N6 Winchelsea East Sussex, England U.K.
117 M6 Winchendon MA U.S.A.
110 H3 Winchester Ont. Can.
203 F11 Winchester South I. N.Z.
31 J6 Winchester Hampshire, England U.K.
121 K9 Winchester U.S.A.
114 C4 Winchester IL U.S.A.
116 A11 Winchester KY U.S.A.
115 D8 Winchester TN U.S.A.
116 G9 Winchester VA U.S.A.
48 I3 Windbergen Ger.
104 E3 Wind r. Y.T. Can.
122 K4 Wind r. WY U.S.A.
125 V6 Windach Ger.
Windau Latvia see Ventspils
118 B3 Windber PA U.S.A.
116 G8 Wind Cave National Park SD U.S.A.
48 I2 Windeby Ger.
49 E8 Windeck Ger.
29 L5 Windermere Cumbria, England U.K.
29 L5 Windermere l. England U.K.
49 D7 Windeshausen Ger.
49 E8 Windhagen Ger.
49 K7 Windhausen Ger.
94 C3 Windhoek Namibia
209 G9 Windidda Aboriginal Reserve W.A. Austr.
105 I4 Windigo Lake Ont. Can.
108 B2 Windigo Lake Ont. Can.
70 E1 Windisch Switz.
53 L3 Windischeschenbach Ger.
59 J4 Windischgarsten Austria
30 □ Windmill Hill Flats Gibraltar
120 H4 Windom MN U.S.A.
207 I8 Windorah Qld Austr.

Column 8

53 O4 Windorf Ger.
125 W6 Window Rock AZ U.S.A.
110 O7 Wind Point WI U.S.A.
116 E9 Wind Ridge PA U.S.A.
122 J5 Wind River Indian Reservation res. WY U.S.A.
31 J4 Windrush r. England U.K.
213 G2 Winds, Bay of Antarctica
53 J3 Windsbach Ger.
205 M5 Windsor N.S.W. Austr.
109 K3 Windsor Nfld and Lab. Can.
109 H4 Windsor N.S. Can.
108 D5 Windsor Ont. Can.
109 F4 Windsor Que. Can.
31 K5 Windsor Windsor and Maidenhead, England U.K.
117 M7 Windsor CT U.S.A.
115 I7 Windsor NC U.S.A.
118 F4 Windsor NJ U.S.A.
116 I12 Windsor VA U.S.A.
117 M5 Windsor VT U.S.A.
31 K5 Windsor and Maidenhead admin. div. England U.K.
117 M6 Windsor Locks CT U.S.A.
96 I4 Windsorton S. Africa
207 H9 Windula watercourse Qld Austr.
131 I3 Windward Grenada
131 M6 Windward Islands Caribbean Sea
Windward Islands Arch. de la Société Fr. Polynesia see Vent, Îles du
130 F4 Windward Passage Cuba/Haiti
209 C13 Windy Harbour W.A. Austr.
107 I4 Winefred Lake Alta Can.
115 D9 Winfield AL U.S.A.
121 G7 Winfield KS U.S.A.
116 D10 Winfield WV U.S.A.
30 G5 Winford North Somerset, England U.K.
31 K4 Wing Buckinghamshire, England U.K.
29 O4 Wingate Durham, England U.K.
206 C3 Wingate Mountains hills N.T. Austr.
119 H1 Wingdale NY U.S.A.
205 M4 Wingen N.S.W. Austr.
45 I6 Wingene Belgium
37 N6 Wingen-sur-Moder France
205 N4 Wingham N.S.W. Austr.
108 D5 Wingham Ont. Can.
31 O5 Wingham Kent, England U.K.
36 E3 Wingles France
48 H3 Wingst Ger.
53 N5 Winhöring Ger.
155 D8 Wini East Timor
208 G7 Winifred, Lake salt flat W.A. Austr.
147 E5 Winifreda Arg.
200 □4a Winion, Mochun sea chan. Chuuk Micronesia
108 C2 Winisk Ont. Can.
108 C2 Winisk r. Ont. Can.
108 C2 Winisk Lake Ont. Can.
108 C2 Winisk River Provincial Park Ont. Can.
158 C7 Winkana Myanmar
96 I4 Winkelhaaks r. S. Africa
53 K3 Winkelhaid Ger.
125 V9 Winkelman AZ U.S.A.
97 K3 Winkelspruit S. Africa
48 G5 Winkelsett Ger.
31 K5 Winkfield Bracknell Forest, England U.K.
53 M3 Winklarn Ger.
30 E6 Winkleigh Devon, England U.K.
107 L5 Winkler Man. Can.
59 G6 Winklern Austria
59 J5 Winklern bei Oberwölz Austria
122 C2 Winlock WA U.S.A.
206 C8 Winnall's Ridge N.T. Austr.
88 E5 Winneba Ghana
120 H4 Winnebago MN U.S.A.
110 F5 Winnebago, Lake WI U.S.A.
120 G4 Winnebago Indian Reservation res. NE U.S.A.
206 C5 Winnecke Creek watercourse N.T. Austr.
110 E5 Winneconne WI U.S.A.
124 M1 Winnemucca NV U.S.A.
124 M1 Winnemucca Lake NV U.S.A.
52 D2 Winnenden Ger.
58 F3 Winner SD U.S.A.
31 K5 Winnersh Wokingham, England U.K.
122 F2 Winnett MT U.S.A.
121 I10 Winnfield LA U.S.A.
120 H2 Winnibigoshish, Lake MN U.S.A.
55 I3 Winnica Pol.
121 H11 Winnie TX U.S.A.
209 C7 Winning W.A. Austr.
49 E10 Winningen Rheinland-Pfalz Ger.
51 D7 Winningen Sachsen-Anhalt Ger.
107 L5 Winnipeg Man. Can.
107 L5 Winnipeg r. Man./Ont. Can.
107 L5 Winnipeg, Lake Man. Can.
107 K4 Winnipegosis Man. Can.
107 K4 Winnipegosis, Lake Man. Can.
117 N5 Winnipesaukee, Lake NH U.S.A.
121 J9 Winnsboro LA U.S.A.
115 G8 Winnsboro SC U.S.A.
121 H9 Winnsboro TX U.S.A.
52 D3 Winnweiler Ger.
120 I4 Winona MN U.S.A.
110 I8 Winona MI U.S.A.
120 I3 Winona MN U.S.A.
121 K9 Winona MS U.S.A.
117 L4 Winooski VT U.S.A.
117 L4 Winooski r. VT U.S.A.
30 G5 Winscombe North Somerset, England U.K.
48 J4 Winsen (Aller) Ger.
29 L7 Winsen (Luhe) Ger.
29 L7 Winsford Cheshire, England U.K.
54 E4 Wińsko Pol.
31 K4 Winslow Buckinghamshire, England U.K.
125 V6 Winslow AZ U.S.A.
117 □P4 Winslow ME U.S.A.
118 E5 Winslow NJ U.S.A.
31 L3 Winston Durham, England U.K.
115 G7 Winston-Salem NC U.S.A.
48 D5 Winsum Friesland Neth.
44 K2 Winsum Groningen Neth.
49 □ Winter Switz.
30 □ Winterberg Ger.
97 K8 Winterberg mts S. Africa
49 H8 Winterberg Ger.
Winterbourne South Gloucestershire, England U.K.
131 M6 Winterbourne Abbas Dorset, England U.K.
50 D5 Winterfeld Ger.
117 L6 Winter Harbor ME U.S.A.
115 G11 Winter Haven FL U.S.A.
115 G11 Winterlingen Ger.
115 F11 Winter Park FL U.S.A.
124 J5 Winterport ME U.S.A.
124 F10 Winters CA U.S.A.
121 F10 Winters TX U.S.A.
52 F2 Winterset IA U.S.A.
118 B5 Winterstown PA U.S.A.
44 K5 Winterswijk Neth.
70 F1 Winterthur Switz.
29 P6 Winterton North Lincolnshire, England U.K.
109 K3 Winterton Nfld and Lab. Can.
97 N4 Winterton S. Africa
29 P6 Winterton North Lincolnshire, England U.K.

Winterveld to Xincheng 361

97 M1 **Winterveld** S. Africa
117 □Q2 **Winterville** ME U.S.A.
119 K2 **Winthrop** CT U.S.A.
117 □P4 **Winthrop** ME U.S.A.
207 I7 **Winton** Qld Austr.
115 □2 **Winton** New Prov. Bahamas
203 C13 **Winton** South I. N.Z.
29 M5 **Winton** Cumbria, England U.K.
115 I7 **Winton** NC U.S.A.
52 B2 **Wintrich** Ger.
37 N7 **Wintzenheim** France
31 L3 **Winwick** Cambridgeshire, England U.K.
49 I7 **Winzenburg** Ger.
59 N4 **Winzendorf** Austria
53 O4 **Winzer** Ger.
51 D8 **Wipper** r. Ger.
49 K8 **Wipperdorf** Ger.
49 D8 **Wipperfürth** Ger.
48 D5 **Wippingen** Ger.
51 D7 **Wippra Kurort** Ger.
58 D5 **Wipptal** val. Austria
156 F6 **Wiralaga** Sumatera Indon.
48 D4 **Wirdumer (Wirdum)** Ger.
49 E10 **Wirges** Ger.
29 N7 **Wirksworth** Derbyshire, England U.K.
206 D6 **Wirliyajarrayi Aboriginal Land Trust** res. N.T. Austr.
204 G5 **Wirrabara** S.A. Austr.
29 K7 **Wirral** pen. England U.K.
204 F4 **Wirraminna** S.A. Austr.
204 H7 **Wirrega** S.A. Austr.
204 E3 **Wirrida, Lake** salt flat S.A. Austr.
205 N4 **Wirrikimbe National Park** N.S.W. Austr.
204 E5 **Wirrulla** S.A. Austr.
51 E10 **Wirsberg** Ger.
200 □4a **Wisas** i. Chuuk Micronesia
31 M2 **Wisbech** Cambridgeshire, England U.K.
117 □P4 **Wiscasset** ME U.S.A.
48 H3 **Wischhafen** Ger.
110 C6 **Wisconsin** r. WI U.S.A.
120 K3 **Wisconsin** state U.S.A.
110 E6 **Wisconsin, Lake** WI U.S.A.
110 E6 **Wisconsin Dells** WI U.S.A.
110 E5 **Wisconsin Rapids** WI U.S.A.
116 C12 **Wise** VA U.S.A.
26 I11 **Wishaw** North Lanarkshire, Scotland U.K.
120 F2 **Wisher** ND U.S.A.
92 F3 **Wisil Dabarow** Somalia
29 O5 **Wiske** r. England U.K.
55 I3 **Wiskitki** Pol.
54 G6 **Wisła** Pol.
23 O7 **Wisła** r. Pol.
55 I5 **Wiślica** Pol.
55 K5 **Wisłok** r. Pol.
55 J5 **Wisłoka** r. Pol.
50 D3 **Wismar** Ger.
50 D2 **Wismarbucht** b. Ger.
121 J10 **Wisner** LA U.S.A.
55 K3 **Wiśniew** Pol.
55 I2 **Wiśniewo** Pol.
55 I6 **Wiśniowa** Pol.
36 C2 **Wissant** France
37 O5 **Wissembourg** France
49 E9 **Wissen** Ger.
110 C5 **Wissota Lake** WI U.S.A.
30 G3 **Wistanstow** Shropshire, England U.K.
106 E4 **Wistaria** B.C. Can.
29 M7 **Wistaston** Cheshire, England U.K.
48 I4 **Wistedt** Ger.
55 K6 **Wisznia** r. Pol.
54 F4 **Wisznia Mała** Pol.
55 L4 **Wisznice** Pol.
97 N1 **Witbank** S. Africa
94 C5 **Witbooisvlei** Namibia
96 E2 **Witdraai** S. Africa
31 N4 **Witham** Essex, England U.K.
31 M2 **Witham** r. England U.K.
117 L4 **Witherbee** NY U.S.A.
30 E6 **Witheridge** Devon, England U.K.
29 R6 **Withernsea** East Riding of Yorkshire, England U.K.
115 F10 **Withlacoochee** r. FL U.S.A.
115 F11 **Withlacoochee** r. FL U.S.A.
204 E2 **Witjira National Park** S.A. Austr.
97 N3 **Witkoppies** mt. S. Africa
54 F3 **Witkowo** Wielkopolskie Pol.
54 D2 **Witkowo** Zachodniopomorskie Pol.
97 J7 **Witkransnek** pass S. Africa
31 K5 **Witley** Surrey, England U.K.
44 H2 **Witmarsum** Neth.
97 J8 **Witmos** S. Africa
97 M1 **Witnek** S. Africa
31 J4 **Witney** Oxfordshire, England U.K.
54 C3 **Witnica** Lubuskie Pol.
54 C3 **Witnica** Zachodniopomorskie Pol.
55 H3 **Witonia** Pol.
54 F2 **Witosław** Pol.
96 I5 **Witput** S. Africa
97 P1 **Witrivier** S. Africa
36 H5 **Witry-lès-Reims** France
96 G4 **Witsand Nature Reserve** S. Africa
48 F1 **Wittdün** Ger.
96 G9 **Witteberg** mt. Eastern Cape S. Africa
97 M4 **Witteberg** mt. Free State S. Africa
97 L6 **Witteberg** mts S. Africa
96 E9 **Witteberge** mts S. Africa
37 N8 **Wittelsheim** France
49 D8 **Witten** Ger.
52 G7 **Wittenbach** Switz.
Wittenberg Ger. see **Lutherstadt Wittenberg**
110 E5 **Wittenberg** WI U.S.A.
50 E5 **Wittenberge** Ger.
50 D3 **Wittenburg** Ger.
50 D3 **Wittenförden** Ger.
50 H2 **Wittenhagen** Ger.
37 N8 **Wittenheim** France
208 E7 **Wittenoom** W.A. Austr.
Wittenoom Gorge W.A. Austr. see **Wittenoom**
48 I2 **Wittensee** l. Ger.
31 □8 **Witte Pan** salt l. Bonaire Neth. Antilles
31 L2 **Wittering** Peterborough, England U.K.
51 G9 **Wittgensdorf** Ger.
57 L2 **Witti, Banjaran** mts Malaysia
53 N5 **Wittibreut** Ger.
51 J8 **Wittichenau** Ger.
52 H2 **Wittighausen** Ger.
48 K5 **Wittingen** Ger.
53 I4 **Wittislingen** Ger.
52 B2 **Wittlich** Ger.
18 C7 **Wittman** MD U.S.A.
49 K6 **Wittmar** Ger.
48 E3 **Wittmund** Ger.
29 N4 **Witton Gilbert** Durham, England U.K.
50 H1 **Wittow** pen. Ger.
50 F4 **Wittstock** Ger.
93 D5 **Witu** Kenya
53 K7 **Witu Islands** P.N.G.
94 C4 **Witvlei** Namibia
97 L2 **Witwatersberg** mts S. Africa
97 K2 **Witwatersrand** mts S. Africa
49 I8 **Witzenhausen** Ger.
48 J3 **Witzhave** Ger.
50 E3 **Witzin** Ger.
48 G2 **Witzwort** Ger.
30 F5 **Wiveliscombe** Somerset, England U.K.
31 N4 **Wivenhoe** Essex, England U.K.
207 N9 **Wivenhoe, Lake** Qld Austr.
55 K1 **Wiżajny** Pol.
36 D2 **Wizernes** France
55 K2 **Wizna** Pol.
55 I3 **Wkra** r. Pol.
54 G3 **Władysławów** Pol.
23 O7 **Władysławowo** Pol.
54 D4 **Wleń** Pol.
55 H3 **Włocławek** Pol.
55 L4 **Włodawa** Pol.
55 L4 **Włodawka** r. Pol.
55 H5 **Włodowice** Pol.
54 F5 **Włodzienin** Pol.
55 H4 **Włodzimierzów** Pol.
54 E4 **Włoszakowice** Pol.
55 H5 **Włoszczowa** Pol.
50 E4 **Wöbbelin** Ger.
Wobkent Uzbek. see **Vobkent**
117 □O3 **Woburn** Que. Can.
31 K4 **Woburn** Bedfordshire, England U.K.
31 K3 **Woburn Sands** Milton Keynes, England U.K.
205 K7 **Wodonga** Vic. Austr.
55 J3 **Wodynie** Pol.
55 H4 **Wodzierady** Pol.
55 I5 **Wodzisław** Pol.
54 G5 **Wodzisław Śląski** Pol.
44 G4 **Woerden** Neth.
37 O6 **Wœrth** France
37 J5 **Wœvre, Forêt de** for. France
44 H3 **Wognum** Neth.
90 F3 **Wohko** watercourse Sudan
70 E1 **Wohlen** Aargau Switz.
70 C2 **Wohlen** Bern Switz.
51 D8 **Wohlmirstedt** Ger.
213 A2 **Wohlthat Mountains** Antarctica
48 J3 **Wohltorf** Ger.
49 G9 **Wohra** r. Ger.
48 H2 **Wöhrden** Ger.
55 K4 **Wohyń** Pol.
170 B2 **Woinbo** Sichuan China
37 L5 **Woippy** France
55 J6 **Wojaszówka** Pol.
55 J5 **Wojciechowice** Pol.
55 K4 **Wojcieszków** Pol.
54 D5 **Wojcieszów** Pol.
54 G3 **Wójcin** Pol.
200 □3b **Woje Majuro** i. Majuro Marshall Is
Wōjjā atoll Marshall Is see **Wotje**
55 H5 **Wojkowice** Pol.
55 I6 **Wojnicz** Pol.
54 F2 **Wojnowo** Pol.
55 L5 **Wojsławice** Pol.
55 L5 **Wojsławka** r. Pol.
153 H8 **Wokam** i. Indon.
162 F5 **Woken He** r. China
179 O6 **Wokha** Nagaland India
31 K5 **Woking** Surrey, England U.K.
207 I7 **Wokingham** watercourse Qld Austr.
31 K5 **Wokingham** Wokingham, England U.K.
31 K5 **Wokingham** admin. div. England U.K.
205 M4 **Woko National Park** N.S.W. Austr.
50 H4 **Wokuhl** Ger.
55 H3 **Wola** Pol.
55 J4 **Wola Mysłowska** Pol.
55 I4 **Wolanów** Pol.
55 L4 **Wola Uhruska** Pol.
55 I3 **Wola Wierzbowska** Pol.
59 I6 **Wolayersee und Umgobung** nature res. Austria
55 H4 **Wolbórz** Pol.
55 H5 **Wolbrom** Pol.
119 J1 **Wolcott** CT U.S.A.
110 G9 **Wolcott** IN U.S.A.
116 I5 **Wolcott** NY U.S.A.
117 M4 **Wolcott** VT U.S.A.
110 I8 **Wolcottville** IN U.S.A.
54 G4 **Wołczyn** Pol.
50 I4 **Woldegk** Ger.
44 L2 **Woldendorp** Neth.
29 Q5 **Wold Newton** East Riding of Yorkshire, England U.K.
Wolea atoll Micronesia see **Woleai**
153 J5 **Woleai** atoll Micronesia
90 A4 **Woleu-Ntem** prov. Gabon
106 C2 **Wolf** r. Y.T. Can.
121 J8 **Wolf** r. TN U.S.A.
110 F5 **Wolf** r. WI U.S.A.
136 □ **Wolf, Volcán** vol. Islas Galápagos Ecuador
52 E5 **Wolfach** Ger.
122 H3 **Wolf Creek** MT U.S.A.
122 C5 **Wolf Creek** OR U.S.A.
121 F7 **Wolf Creek** r. OK U.S.A.
123 K8 **Wolf Creek Pass** CO U.S.A.
117 □N5 **Wolfeboro** NH U.S.A.
52 H6 **Wolfegg** Ger.
111 R5 **Wolfe Island** Ont. Can.
51 F7 **Wolfen** Ger.
49 K6 **Wolfenbüttel** Ger.
49 G10 **Wölfersheim** Ger.
59 H4 **Wolfgangsee** l. Austria
49 H8 **Wolfhagen** Ger.
49 K9 **Wölfis** Ger.
Wolf Island Islas Galápagos Ecuador see **Wenman, Isla**
106 D2 **Wolf Lake** Y.T. Can.
110 H6 **Wolf Lake** MI U.S.A.
59 L3 **Wolfpassing** Austria
122 L2 **Wolf Point** MT U.S.A.
53 J3 **Wolframs-Eschenbach** Ger.
53 K6 **Wolfratshausen** Ger.
59 K6 **Wolfsberg** Austria
49 K6 **Wolfsburg** Ger.
52 D2 **Wolfstein** Ger.
109 H4 **Wolfville** N.S. Can.
50 I2 **Wolgast** Ger.
70 E1 **Wolhusen** Switz.
55 L5 **Wolica** r. Pol.
54 C2 **Wolin** Pol.
54 C2 **Wolin** i. Pol.
54 C2 **Woliński Park Narodowy** nat. park Pol.
55 H3 **Wólka** Kujawsko-Pomorskie Pol.
55 K4 **Wólka** Lubelskie Pol.
55 L3 **Wólka Dobryńska** Pol.
51 H9 **Wolkenstein** Ger.
59 O3 **Wolkersdorf** Austria
49 K8 **Wolkramshausen** Ger.
31 K3 **Wollaston** Northamptonshire, England U.K.
145 D9 **Wollaston, Islas** is Chile
107 K3 **Wollaston Lake** Sask. Can.
107 K3 **Wollaston Lake** l. Sask. Can.
104 G3 **Wollaston Peninsula** N.W.T./Nunavut Can.
205 M5 **Wollemi National Park** N.S.W. Austr.
70 F1 **Wollerau** Switz.
50 I4 **Wolletzsee** l. Ger.
205 M6 **Wollongong** N.S.W. Austr.
97 J3 **Wolmaransstad** S. Africa
51 D7 **Wolmirsleben** Ger.
51 E6 **Wolmirstedt** Ger.
53 L4 **Wolnzach** Ger.
55 J3 **Wołomin** Pol.
170 D3 **Wolong Reserve** nature res. China
54 E4 **Wołów** Pol.
155 B8 **Wolowaru** Flores Indon.
52 H3 **Wolpertshausen** Ger.
52 H6 **Wolpertswende** Ger.
49 H6 **Wölpinghausen** Ger.
49 K6 **Wolsdorf** Ger.
204 H7 **Wolseley** S.A. Austr.
96 D9 **Wolseley** S. Africa
120 F3 **Wolsey** SD U.S.A.
29 N4 **Wolsingham** Durham, England U.K.
105 K3 **Wolstenholme, Cap** c. Que. Can.
31 J3 **Wolston** Warwickshire, England U.K.
54 E3 **Wolsztyn** Pol.
51 H6 **Woltersdorf** Brandenburg Ger.
51 I6 **Woltersdorf** Brandenburg Ger.
50 D5 **Woltersdorf** Niedersachsen Ger.
49 I7 **Woltershausen** Ger.
44 J3 **Wolvega** Neth.
30 H2 **Wolverhampton** West Midlands, England U.K.
110 J4 **Wolverine** MI U.S.A.
97 I9 **Wolwefontein** S. Africa
97 J4 **Wolwespruit** S. Africa
156 A2 **Wolya** r. Indon.
59 J5 **Wölzer Tauern** mts Austria
30 H2 **Wombourne** Staffordshire, England U.K.
29 O6 **Wombwell** South Yorkshire, England U.K.
118 C4 **Womelsdorf** PA U.S.A.
44 I2 **Wommels** Neth.
52 C2 **Womrather Höhe** hill Ger.
206 F5 **Wonarah** N.T. Austr.
207 M9 **Wondai** Qld Austr.
45 E6 **Wondelgem** Belgium
97 N1 **Wonderfontein** S. Africa
97 L3 **Wonderkop** S. Africa
97 L4 **Wonderkop** mt. S. Africa
97 K1 **Wondermere** S. Africa
53 M1 **Wondreb** r. Ger.
205 J4 **Wongalarroo Lake** salt l. N.S.W. Austr.
209 D11 **Wongan Hills** W.A. Austr.
90 A5 **Wonga Wongué, Réserve de** nature res. Gabon
179 L6 **Wong Chhu** r. Bhutan
171 □J7 **Wong Chuk Hang** H.K. China
171 □J7 **Wong Leng** hill H.K. China
171 □J7 **Wong Wan Chau** i. H.K. China
163 E10 **Wŏnju** S. Korea
157 I8 **Wonogiri** Jawa Indon.
157 I8 **Wonosari** Indon.
157 H8 **Wonosobo** Jawa Indon.
106 F3 **Wonowon** B.C. Can.
155 E8 **Wonreli** Maluku Indon.
163 E9 **Wŏnsan** N. Korea
53 K2 **Wonsees** Ger.
31 J5 **Wonston** Hampshire, England U.K.
205 J8 **Wonthaggi** Vic. Austr.
209 E8 **Wonyulgunna, Mount** hill W.A. Austr.
31 K4 **Wooburn** Buckinghamshire, England U.K.
204 F4 **Woocalla** S.A. Austr.
147 F6 **Wood, Isla** i. Arg.
106 A2 **Wood, Mount** Y.T. Can.
206 F2 **Woodah, Isle** i. N.T. Austr.
115 G10 **Woodbine** GA U.S.A.
118 A6 **Woodbine** MD U.S.A.
118 F6 **Woodbine** NJ U.S.A.
110 E4 **Woodboro** WI U.S.A.
203 H8 **Woodbourne** South I. N.Z.
118 F1 **Woodbourne** NY U.S.A.
31 O3 **Woodbridge** Suffolk, England U.K.
119 I2 **Woodbridge** CT U.S.A.
119 G3 **Woodbridge** NJ U.S.A.
116 H10 **Woodbridge** VA U.S.A.
106 H3 **Wood Buffalo National Park** Alta Can.
205 N3 **Woodburn** N.S.W. Austr.
110 J8 **Woodburn** IN U.S.A.
122 C4 **Woodburn** OR U.S.A.
119 I1 **Woodbury** CT U.S.A.
110 I7 **Woodbury** MI U.S.A.
118 E5 **Woodbury** NJ U.S.A.
118 E5 **Woodbury Heights** NJ U.S.A.
206 E5 **Woodcock, Mount** hill N.T. Austr.
31 J4 **Woodcote** Oxfordshire, England U.K.
205 N3 **Wooded Bluff** hd N.S.W./Qld Austr.
205 N3 **Woodenbong** N.S.W. Austr.
27 J7 **Woodenbridge** Rep. of Ireland
205 J7 **Woodend** Vic. Austr.
203 C13 **Woodend** South I. N.Z.
203 G10 **Woodend** South I. N.Z.
20 □ **Woodfjorden** inlet Svalbard
131 □6 **Woodford** Grenada
27 F6 **Woodford** Rep. of Ireland
124 M3 **Woodfords** CA U.S.A.
29 Q7 **Woodhall Spa** Lincolnshire, England U.K.
31 L6 **Woodingdean** Brighton and Hove, England U.K.
107 K4 **Wood Lake** Sask. Can.
124 M5 **Woodlake** CA U.S.A.
124 K3 **Woodland** CA U.S.A.
117 □R3 **Woodland** ME U.S.A.
122 C4 **Woodland** WA U.S.A.
118 B7 **Woodland Beach** MD U.S.A.
107 M5 **Woodland Caribou Provincial Park** park Ont. Can.
123 L7 **Woodland Park** CO U.S.A.
156 □ **Woodlands** Sing.
153 L8 **Woodlark Island** P.N.G.
118 B6 **Woodlawn** MD U.S.A.
31 K5 **Woodley** Wokingham, England U.K.
118 E5 **Woodlyn** PA U.S.A.
29 Q6 **Woodmansey** East Riding of Yorkshire, England U.K.
204 F2 **Woodmurra Creek** watercourse S.A. Austr.
29 L6 **Woodplumpton** Lancashire, England U.K.
107 L5 **Woodridge** Man. Can.
118 F1 **Woodridge** NY U.S.A.
206 G6 **Woodroffe** watercourse N.T. Austr.
204 C2 **Woodroffe, Mount** S.A. Austr.
122 I6 **Woodruff** UT U.S.A.
110 E4 **Woodruff** WI U.S.A.
206 D4 **Woods, Lake** salt flat N.T. Austr.
112 H1 **Woods, Lake of the** Can./U.S.A.
116 D9 **Woodsfield** OH U.S.A.
117 O7 **Woods Hole** MA U.S.A.
205 K8 **Woodside** Vic. Austr.
118 D6 **Woodside** DE U.S.A.
205 L5 **Woodstock** N.S.W. Austr.
207 K5 **Woodstock** Qld Austr.
109 H4 **Woodstock** N.B. Can.
108 D5 **Woodstock** Ont. Can.
31 J4 **Woodstock** Oxfordshire, England U.K.
110 F7 **Woodstock** IL U.S.A.
116 G10 **Woodstock** VA U.S.A.
117 M5 **Woodstock** VT U.S.A.
97 N4 **Woodstock Dam** resr S. Africa
27 H8 **Woodstown** Rep. of Ireland
118 E5 **Woodstown** NJ U.S.A.
117 M4 **Woodsville** NH U.S.A.
31 O3 **Woodton** Norfolk, England U.K.
27 I5 **Woodtown** Rep. of Ireland
111 P5 **Woodville** Ont. Can.
202 J7 **Woodville** North I. N.Z.
121 J10 **Woodville** MS U.S.A.
116 B7 **Woodville** OH U.S.A.
121 H10 **Woodville** TX U.S.A.
121 F7 **Woodward** OK U.S.A.
124 L4 **Woodward Reservoir** CA U.S.A.
124 N6 **Woody** CA U.S.A.
97 K9 **Woody Cape Nature Reserve** S. Africa
30 G3 **Woofferton** Shropshire, England U.K.
153 I7 **Woöi** Papua Indon.
30 H6 **Wool** Dorset, England U.K.
30 D5 **Woolacombe** Devon, England U.K.
206 E2 **Woolen** r. N.T. Austr.
29 M2 **Wooler** Northumberland, England U.K.
207 I6 **Woolgar** r. Qld Austr.
205 N4 **Woolgoolga** N.S.W. Austr.
205 N3 **Wooli** N.S.W. Austr.
206 D7 **Woolla Downs** N.T. Austr.
212 W1 **Woollard, Mount** Antarctica
204 G4 **Wooltana** S.A. Austr.
116 E12 **Woolwine** VA U.S.A.
209 F12 **Woolyeenyer Hill** W.A. Austr.
204 F4 **Woomera** S.A. Austr.
204 D3 **Woomera Prohibited Area** S.A. Austr.
117 N6 **Woonsocket** RI U.S.A.
120 F3 **Woonsocket** SD U.S.A.
207 L8 **Woorabinda** Qld Austr.
209 C8 **Wooramel** r. W.A. Austr.
116 D8 **Wooster** OH U.S.A.
31 K3 **Wootton** Bedfordshire, England U.K.
31 I4 **Wootton Bassett** Wiltshire, England U.K.
92 D2 **Woqooyi Galbeed** admin. reg. Somalia
163 F10 **Worak-san National Park** S. Korea
70 D2 **Worb** Switz.
207 H2 **Worbody Point** Qld Austr.
96 D9 **Worcester** S. Africa
30 H3 **Worcester** Worcestershire, England U.K.
117 N6 **Worcester** MA U.S.A.
117 K6 **Worcester** NY U.S.A.
30 H3 **Worcestershire** admin. div. England U.K.
59 N3 **Wördern** Austria
30 H2 **Worfield** Shropshire, England U.K.
58 F5 **Wörgl** Austria
53 I6 **Woringen** Ger.
153 H8 **Workai** i. Indon.
29 J4 **Workington** Cumbria, England U.K.
29 O7 **Worksop** Nottinghamshire, England U.K.
44 H3 **Workum** Neth.
122 K4 **Worland** WY U.S.A.
51 F7 **Wörlitz** Ger.
45 J9 **Wormeldange** Lux.
44 G4 **Wormer** Neth.
36 D2 **Wormhout** France
26 K10 **Wormit** Fife, Scotland U.K.
52 E2 **Worms** Ger.
30 D4 **Worms Head** Wales U.K.
53 J4 **Wörnitz** r. Ger.
88 D4 **Worofla** Côte d'Ivoire
31 K5 **Worplesdon** Surrey, England U.K.
48 G4 **Worpswede** Ger.
52 E2 **Wörrstadt** Ger.
59 J4 **Wörschach** Austria
45 G6 **Wortel** Belgium
58 G5 **Wörth** Austria
53 L5 **Wörth** Ger.
31 L5 **Worth** West Sussex, England U.K.
52 G2 **Wörth am Main** Ger.
52 E3 **Wörth am Rhein** Ger.
53 M3 **Wörth an der Donau** Ger.
53 M4 **Wörth an der Isar** Ger.
59 J6 **Wörther See** l. Austria
31 L6 **Worthing** West Sussex, England U.K.
120 H4 **Worthington** MN U.S.A.
116 B8 **Worthington** OH U.S.A.
118 C6 **Worton** MD U.S.A.
155 E4 **Wosi** Halmahera Indon.
155 B5 **Wosu** Sulawesi Indon.
54 D2 **Woświn, Jezioro** l. Pol.
208 G4 **Wotjalum Aboriginal Reserve** W.A. Austr.
216 G6 **Wotje** atoll Marshall Is
30 H4 **Wotton-under-Edge** Gloucestershire, England U.K.
155 B5 **Wotu** Sulawesi Indon.
44 H4 **Woudenberg** Neth.
44 G5 **Woudrichem** Neth.
44 I3 **Woudsend** Neth.
31 K3 **Woughton on the Green** Milton Keynes, England U.K.
120 D4 **Wounded Knee** SD U.S.A.
84 B4 **Wour** Chad
89 H5 **Wouri** r. Cameroon
37 N5 **Woustviller** France
44 F5 **Wouw** Neth.
207 M7 **Wowan** Qld Austr.
155 C6 **Wowoni** i. Indon.
155 C5 **Wowoni, Selat** sea chan. Indon.
55 H5 **Woźniki** Pol.
Wozrojdeniye Oroli pen. Uzbek. see **Vozrozhdenya Island**
29 Q7 **Wragby** Lincolnshire, England U.K.
Wrangel Island Rus. Fed. see **Vrangelya, Ostrov**
104 E4 **Wrangell** AK U.S.A.
106 C3 **Wrangell Island** AK U.S.A.
104 C4 **Wrangell Mountains** AK U.S.A.
104 D3 **Wrangell-St Elias National Park and Preserve** AK U.S.A.
29 R7 **Wrangle** Lincolnshire, England U.K.
26 F5 **Wrath, Cape** Scotland U.K.
120 D5 **Wray** CO U.S.A.
31 J2 **Wreake** r. England U.K.
208 □2 **Wreck Point** Cocos Is
130 □ **Wreck Point** Jamaica
96 A4 **Wreck Point** S. Africa
Wrecsam Wrexham, Wales U.K. see **Wrexham**
54 G5 **Wręczyca Wielka** Pol.
50 G4 **Wredenhagen** Ger.
29 P5 **Wrelton** North Yorkshire, England U.K.
48 G3 **Wremen** Ger.
115 F9 **Wrens** GA U.S.A.
48 K5 **Wrestedt** Ger.
49 G7 **Wrexen (Diemelstadt)** Ger.
30 G1 **Wrexham** Wrexham, Wales U.K.
30 G1 **Wrexham** admin. div. Wales U.K.
203 C13 **Wreys Bush** South I. N.Z.
48 J4 **Wriedel** Ger.
50 J5 **Wriezen** Ger.
154 E6 **Wright** Samar Phil.
122 L5 **Wright** WY U.S.A.
177 M7 **Wrightmyo** Andaman & Nicobar Is India
121 H9 **Wright Patman Lake** TX U.S.A.
125 V10 **Wrightson, Mount** AZ U.S.A.
118 F4 **Wrightstown** PA U.S.A.
110 F5 **Wrightstown** WI U.S.A.
115 F9 **Wrightsville** GA U.S.A.
118 B4 **Wrightsville** PA U.S.A.
124 O7 **Wrightwood** CA U.S.A.
106 F2 **Wrigley** N.W.T. Can.
116 B10 **Wrigley** KY U.S.A.
212 P2 **Wrigley Gulf** Antarctica
30 G5 **Wrington** North Somerset, England U.K.
48 I3 **Wrist** Ger.
31 M4 **Writtle** Essex, England U.K.
54 G4 **Wróblew** Pol.
54 F4 **Wrocław** Pol.
48 H2 **Wrohm** Ger.
55 K1 **Wronki** Warmińsko-Mazurskie Pol.
54 E3 **Wronki** Wielkopolskie Pol.
55 K3 **Wrotnów** Pol.
31 I4 **Wroughton** Swindon, England U.K.
54 G3 **Wrząielka** Pol.
55 J4 **Wrzelowiec** Pol.
54 F1 **Wrzeście** Pol.
54 F3 **Września** Pol.
54 F3 **Wrześnica** r. Pol.
54 D1 **Wrzosowo** Pol.
55 J5 **Wschodnía** r. Pol.
54 E4 **Wschowa** Pol.
169 N8 **Wu'an** Hebei China
209 D11 **Wubin** W.A. Austr.
169 L8 **Wubu** Shaanxi China
169 Q3 **Wuchagou** Nei Mongol China
162 E6 **Wuchang** Heilong. China
Wuchang Hubei China see **Jiangxia**
171 L4 **Wucheng** Anhui China
Wucheng Anhui China see **Wuwei**
Wuchow Guangxi China see **Wuzhou**
170 F4 **Wuchuan** Guizhou China
169 L6 **Wuchuan** Nei Mongol China
168 J7 **Wuda** Nei Mongol China
162 E4 **Wudalianchi** Heilong. China
187 M4 **Wuḑām 'Alwā** Oman
169 P5 **Wudan** Nei Mongol China
170 G2 **Wudang Shan** mts China
169 Q7 **Wudao** Liaoning China
162 E3 **Wudaogou** Heilong. China
168 C9 **Wudaoliang** Qinghai China
187 H7 **Wuday'ah** well Saudi Arabia
169 O8 **Wudi** Shandong China
89 H4 **Wudil** Nigeria
170 D6 **Wuding** Yunnan China
169 L8 **Wuding He** r. China
204 E5 **Wudinna** S.A. Austr.
170 E2 **Wudu** Gansu China
170 H3 **Wufeng** Hubei China
Wufeng Yunnan China see **Zhenxiong**
168 I8 **Wufoshan** Gansu China
170 H5 **Wugang** Hunan China
169 K9 **Wugong** Shaanxi China
168 J7 **Wuhai** Nei Mongol China
171 J3 **Wuhan** Hubei China
171 K2 **Wuhe** Anhui China
171 L3 **Wuhu** Anhui China
171 L3 **Wuhu** Anhui China
171 J7 **Wuhua** Guangdong China
173 D10 **Wūjang** Xizang China
170 G8 **Wujia** Guangxi China
171 M3 **Wujiang** Jiangsu China
170 F4 **Wu Jiang** r. China
Wujin Sichuan China see **Xinjin**
89 H5 **Wukari** Nigeria
169 Q8 **Wuleidao Wan** b. China
51 E7 **Wulfen** Ger.
50 F4 **Wulfersdorf** Ger.
49 J10 **Wülfershausen an der Saale** Ger.
48 J4 **Wulfsen** Ger.
49 J7 **Wulften** Ger.
168 C9 **Wuli** Qinghai China
170 D4 **Wulian Feng** mts Yunnan China
170 C6 **Wuliang Shan** mts Yunnan China
153 H8 **Wuliaru** i. Indon.
170 G8 **Wuli Jiang** r. China
170 G4 **Wuling Shan** mts China
50 F5 **Wulkau** Ger.
59 N2 **Wullersdorf** Austria
170 F4 **Wulong** Chongqing China
169 Q8 **Wulong He** r. China
55 I2 **Wulpińskie, Jezioro** l. Pol.
48 G4 **Wulsbüttel** Ger.
155 F7 **Wulur** Maluku Indon.
89 H5 **Wum** Cameroon
173 J11 **Wumatang** Xizang China
170 D5 **Wumeng Shan** mts Guizhou/Yunnan China
170 G7 **Wuming** Guangxi China
48 G4 **Wümme** r. Ger.
177 O2 **Wundwin** Myanmar
170 C3 **Wungda** Sichuan China
171 J4 **Wuning** Jiangxi China
49 G7 **Wünnenberg** Ger.
108 B2 **Wunnummin Lake** Ont. Can.
90 F2 **Wun Rog** Sudan
51 F9 **Wünschendorf** Ger.
51 H6 **Wünsdorf** Ger.
90 F2 **Wun Shwai** Sudan
51 F10 **Wunsiedel** Ger.
49 H6 **Wunstorf** Ger.
92 B2 **Wuntau** Sudan
158 B3 **Wuntho** Myanmar
125 U6 **Wupatki National Monument** nat. park AZ U.S.A.
171 K6 **Wuping** Fujian China
49 D8 **Wuppertal** Ger.
96 D8 **Wuppertal** S. Africa
169 K8 **Wuqi** Shaanxi China
172 B7 **Wuqia** Xinjiang China
172 B7 **Wuqia** Xinjiang China
169 N7 **Wuqiang** Hebei China
169 O8 **Wuqiao** Hebei China
169 O7 **Wuqing** Tianjin China
Wuquan Henan China see **Wuyang**
209 D10 **Wuranga** W.A. Austr.
53 K5 **Würm** r. Ger.
53 N5 **Wurmannsquick** Ger.
52 F5 **Wurmlingen** Ger.
89 G3 **Wurno** Nigeria
206 F3 **Wurralibi Aboriginal Land** res. N.T. Austr.
49 B9 **Würselen** Ger.
119 G1 **Wurtsboro** NY U.S.A.
51 E10 **Wurzbach** Ger.
52 H2 **Würzburg** Ger.
51 G8 **Wurzen** Ger.
170 G3 **Wushan** Chongqing China
168 I9 **Wushan** Gansu China
170 H3 **Wu Shan** mts China
170 F3 **Wusheng** Sichuan China
170 G8 **Wushi** Guangdong China
172 D6 **Wushi** Xinjiang China
50 F5 **Wust** Ger.
49 H8 **Wüstegarten** hill Ger.
52 G3 **Wüstenrot** Ger.
50 F5 **Wusterhausen** Ger.
50 I2 **Wusterhusen** Ger.
50 G5 **Wustermark** Ger.
51 F6 **Wusterwitz** Ger.
49 J8 **Wüstheuterode** Ger.
50 G5 **Wustrau-Altfriesack** Ger.
50 G4 **Wustrow** Mecklenburg-Vorpommern Ger.
50 D5 **Wustrow** Niedersachsen Ger.
50 E2 **Wustrow, Halbinsel** spit Ger.
Wusuli Jiang r. Rus. Fed. see **Ussuri**
52 E6 **Wutach** r. Ger.
169 M7 **Wutai** Shanxi China
172 F4 **Wutai** Xinjiang China
169 M7 **Wutaishan** Shanxi China
171 H4 **Wutan** Hunan China
49 J9 **Wutha** Ger.
168 F6 **Wutonggou** Nei Mongol China
172 I6 **Wutonggou** Xinjiang China
162 G5 **Wutong He** r. China
168 D5 **Wutongwozi Quan** well Xinjiang China
45 G6 **Wuustwezel** Belgium
153 J7 **Wuvulu Island** P.N.G.
171 K3 **Wuwei** Anhui China
168 H8 **Wuwei** Gansu China
170 G3 **Wuxi** Chongqing China
170 H4 **Wuxi** Hunan China
Wuxi Hunan China see **Qiyang**
171 M3 **Wuxi** Jiangsu China
Wuxia Chongqing China see **Wushan**
169 M8 **Wuxiang** Shanxi China
170 G7 **Wuxu** Guangxi China
170 G7 **Wuxuan** Guangxi China
171 J4 **Wuxue** Hubei China
Wuyang Guizhou China see **Zhenyuan**
171 I2 **Wuyang** Henan China
169 M8 **Wuyang** Shanxi China
Wuyang Zhejiang China see **Wuyi**
171 L4 **Wuyi** Zhejiang China
162 F4 **Wuyiling** Heilong. China
171 L5 **Wuyishan** Fujian China
171 K6 **Wuyi Shan** mts China
171 L5 **Wuyi Shan** tourist site Fujian China
171 K4 **Wuyuan** Jiangxi China
169 K6 **Wuyuan** Nei Mongol China
169 L7 **Wuzhai** Shanxi China
171 H3 **Wuzhen** Hubei China
169 M9 **Wuzhi** Henan China
170 G9 **Wuzhishan** Hainan China
170 G9 **Wuzhi Shan** mts China
168 J8 **Wuzhong** Ningxia China
171 H7 **Wuzhou** Guangxi China
207 H4 **Wyaaba Creek** r. Qld Austr.
110 C9 **Wyaconda** r. MO U.S.A.
209 D11 **Wyalkatchem** W.A. Austr.
111 R8 **Wyalusing** PA U.S.A.
111 K7 **Wyandotte** MI U.S.A.
207 J9 **Wyandra** Qld Austr.
110 E8 **Wyanet** IL U.S.A.
205 L5 **Wyangala Reservoir** N.S.W. Austr.
205 J3 **Wyara, Lake** salt flat Qld Austr.
31 L2 **Wyberton** Lincolnshire, England U.K.
205 I7 **Wycheproof** Vic. Austr.
119 G2 **Wyckoff** NJ U.S.A.
54 F2 **Wyczechy** Pol.
55 K2 **Wydminy** Pol.
31 N5 **Wye** Kent, England U.K.
29 N7 **Wye** r. Derbyshire, England U.K.
30 G4 **Wye** r. England/Wales U.K.
209 E10 **Wyemandoo** hill W.A. Austr.
118 C7 **Wye Mills** MD U.S.A.
110 D5 **Wyeville** WI U.S.A.
57 I1 **Wygoda** Pol.
54 D2 **Wygon** Pol.
52 D5 **Wyhl** Ger.
51 F8 **Wyhra** r. Ger.
48 G1 **Wyk auf Föhr** Ger.
54 F3 **Wylatowo** Pol.
116 G12 **Wylliesburg** VA U.S.A.
209 D7 **Wyloo** W.A. Austr.
31 I5 **Wylye** Wiltshire, England U.K.
31 I5 **Wylye** r. England U.K.
48 D4 **Wymeer** Ger.
51 L7 **Wymiarki** Pol.
31 O2 **Wymondham** Norfolk, England U.K.
120 G5 **Wymore** NE U.S.A.
204 D4 **Wynbring** S.A. Austr.
208 J3 **Wyndham** W.A. Austr.
203 C13 **Wyndham** South I. N.Z.
205 J7 **Wyndham-Werribee** Vic. Austr.
121 J8 **Wynne** AR U.S.A.
104 G2 **Wynniatt Bay** N.W.T. Can.
205 J9 **Wynyard** Tas. Austr.
107 J5 **Wynyard** Sask. Can.
110 E6 **Wyocena** WI U.S.A.
204 C3 **Wyola Lake** salt flat S.A. Austr.
118 D6 **Wyoming** DE U.S.A.
110 E8 **Wyoming** IL U.S.A.
110 I7 **Wyoming** MI U.S.A.
122 K5 **Wyoming** state U.S.A.
118 C1 **Wyoming County** county PA U.S.A.
122 I5 **Wyoming Peak** WY U.S.A.
122 I5 **Wyoming Range** mts WY U.S.A.
118 D4 **Wyomissing** PA U.S.A.
205 M5 **Wyong** N.S.W. Austr.
206 F2 **Wyonga** r. N.T. Austr.
204 I6 **Wyperfeld National Park** Vic. Austr.
26 K4 **Wyre** i. Scotland U.K.
29 L6 **Wyre** r. England U.K.
55 L4 **Wyryki-Połód** Pol.
54 F2 **Wyrzysk** Pol.
55 I4 **Wyśmierzyce** Pol.
54 D3 **Wysoka** Lubuskie Pol.
55 J6 **Wysoka** Podkarpackie Pol.
54 F2 **Wysoka** Wielkopolskie Pol.
54 C2 **Wysoka Kamieńska** Pol.
54 D5 **Wysoka Kopa** mt. Pol.
55 K5 **Wysokie** Lubelskie Pol.
55 K2 **Wysokie** Warmińsko-Mazurskie Pol.
55 K3 **Wysokie Mazowieckie** Pol.
55 J6 **Wysowa** Pol.
111 R8 **Wysox** PA U.S.A.
55 K3 **Wyszki** Pol.
55 J3 **Wyszków** Pol.
55 I3 **Wyszogród** Pol.
31 I3 **Wythall** Worcestershire, England U.K.
116 D12 **Wytheville** VA U.S.A.
55 L4 **Wytyczno** Pol.
55 J4 **Wyżnica** r. Pol.
23 P7 **Wzniesienie Elbląskie, Park Krajobrazowy** Pol.

X

92 F2 **Xaafuun** Somalia
92 F2 **Xaafuun, Raas** pt Somalia
92 F2 **Xabo** Somalia
173 M11 **Xabyai** Xizang China
191 I5 **Xaçınçay** r. Azer.
191 J4 **Xaçmaz** Azer.
94 D4 **Xade** Botswana
75 □ **Xagħra** Gozo Malta
173 K12 **Xagjang** Xizang China
173 E10 **Xagnag** Xizang China
173 I11 **Xago** Xizang China
173 K11 **Xagquka** Xizang China
173 D8 **Xaidulla** Xinjiang China
158 E5 **Xaignabouli** Laos
37 L7 **Xaintois** reg. France
173 I11 **Xainza** Xizang China
173 I12 **Xaitongmoin** Xizang China
95 G5 **Xai-Xai** Moz.
172 D7 **Xakur** Xinjiang China
127 O7 **Xal, Cerro de** hill Mex.
191 I5 **Xaldan** Azer.
92 F2 **Xalin** Somalia
62 B3 **Xallas** r. Spain
182 H6 **Xalqobod** Uzbek.
191 J5 **Xaltan** Azer.
129 H8 **Xaltianguis** Mex.
91 D9 **Xamavera** Angola
169 J6 **Xamba** Nei Mongol China
140 C3 **Xambioa** Brazil
142 A5 **Xambrê** Brazil
158 G4 **Xam Nua** Laos
91 C7 **Xá-Muteba** Angola
158 F5 **Xan** r. Laos
62 D2 **Xanceda** Spain
168 H6 **Xangd** Nei Mongol China
169 L5 **Xangdin Hural** Nei Mongol China
173 E10 **Xangdoring** Xizang China
91 B9 **Xangongo** Angola
158 G6 **Xangxoy, Xé** r. Laos
173 L11 **Xangzha** Xizang China
129 K9 **Xanica** Mex.
191 H6 **Xankändi** Azer.
191 H5 **Xanlar** Azer.
191 H6 **Xanlıq** Azer.
49 B7 **Xanten** Ger.
78 F1 **Xanthi** Greece
188 D5 **Xanthos** tourist site Turkey
141 B8 **Xanxerê** Brazil
138 C2 **Xapuri** Brazil
138 C2 **Xapuri** r. Brazil
184 C2 **Xaraba Şähär Sayı** i. Azer.
168 F8 **Xarag** Qinghai China
92 E3 **Xarardheere** Somalia
191 K6 **Xärä Zirä Adası** is Azer.
173 G12 **Xarba La** pass Xizang China
173 G11 **Xardong** Xizang China
62 F4 **Xares** r. Spain
169 N4 **Xar Hudag** Nei Mongol China
169 L5 **Xar Moron** r. China
169 Q5 **Xar Moron** r. China
64 C4 **Xarrama** r. Port.
78 B3 **Xarrë** Albania
179 K5 **Xarru** Xizang China
Xarsingma Xizang China see **Yadong**
91 C7 **Xassengue** Angola
191 G4 **Xatınlı** Azer.
67 D10 **Xátiva** Spain
94 E4 **Xau, Lake** Botswana
94 D3 **Xaudum** watercourse Botswana/Namibia
142 C5 **Xavantes, Represa de** resr Brazil
140 C5 **Xavantes, Serra dos** hills Brazil
173 F10 **Xaxa** Xizang China
158 F4 **Xay** Laos
172 F6 **Xayar** Xinjiang China
172 H3 **Xazgat** Xinjiang China
127 P8 **Xcalak** Mex.
127 P7 **X-Can** Mex.
172 D6 **Xegil** Xinjiang China
172 C7 **Xekar** Xinjiang China
116 B9 **Xenia** OH U.S.A.
173 I11 **Xênkyêr** Xizang China
91 C9 **Xequessa** Angola
67 E9 **Xeraco** Spain
67 E9 **Xeresa** Spain
137 F5 **Xeriuini** r. Brazil
62 E2 **Xermade** Spain
Xero Potamos r. Cyprus see **Xeros**
190 A4 **Xeros** r. Cyprus
66 G6 **Xerta** Spain
37 L7 **Xertigny** France
75 □ **Xewkija** Gozo Malta
94 E4 **Xhorodomo Pan** salt pan Botswana
94 E4 **Xhumo** Botswana
172 C7 **Xia Awat** Xinjiang China
172 C7 **Xia Bazar** Xinjiang China
162 D3 **Xiabole Shan** mt. China
162 G6 **Xiachengzi** Heilong. China
171 I8 **Xiachuan Dao** i. Guangdong China
Xiacun Shandong China see **Rushan**
168 F9 **Xia Dawo** Qinghai China
168 D6 **Xiadong** Gansu China
168 I9 **Xiaguanying** Gansu China
168 H9 **Xiahe** Gansu China
Xiajiang Xizang China see **Xagjang**
169 O8 **Xiajin** Shandong China
170 A2 **Xialaxiu** Qinghai China
170 A4 **Xia Lingka** Xizang China
168 D5 **Xiamaya** Xinjiang China
171 L6 **Xiamen** Fujian China
169 K9 **Xi'an** Shaanxi China
170 G4 **Xianfeng** Hubei China
171 I2 **Xiangcheng** Henan China
171 J2 **Xiangcheng** Henan China
170 B4 **Xiangcheng** Sichuan China
Xiangcheng Yunnan China see **Xiangyun**
171 I2 **Xiangfan** Hubei China
169 L9 **Xiangfen** Shanxi China
170 B5 **Xianggelila** Yunnan China
Xianghuang Qi Nei Mongol China see **Xin Bulag**
171 I4 **Xiang Jiang** r. China
158 F5 **Xiangkhoang** Laos
158 F5 **Xiangkhoang Plateau** Laos
Xiangkou Chongqing China see **Wulong**
169 L9 **Xiangning** Shanxi China
168 E9 **Xiangride** Qinghai China
171 M4 **Xiangshan** Zhejiang China
171 M4 **Xiangshan Gang** b. Zhejiang China
169 P9 **Xiangshui** Jiangsu China
170 G5 **Xiangshuiba** Hunan China
171 I5 **Xiangtan** Hunan China
171 I5 **Xiangxiang** Hunan China
Xiangyang Hubei China see **Xiangfan**
171 I2 **Xiangyang** Hubei China
173 I9 **Xiangyang Hu** l. Xizang China
171 I4 **Xiangyin** Hunan China
170 C6 **Xiangyun** Yunnan China
170 G7 **Xiangzhou** Guangxi China
171 M4 **Xianju** Zhejiang China
171 J4 **Xianning** Hubei China
170 C3 **Xianshui He** r. Sichuan China
171 I3 **Xiantao** Hubei China
171 K5 **Xianxia Ling** mts China
169 O7 **Xianxian** Hebei China
169 K9 **Xianyang** Shaanxi China
171 L6 **Xianyou** Fujian China
168 I8 **Xi'anzhou** Ningxia China
Xiaoba Ningxia China see **Qingtongxia**
169 N6 **Xiaochang** Hebei China
171 I3 **Xiaochang** Hubei China
170 E2 **Xiaochuan** Gansu China
170 G7 **Xiaodong** Guangxi China
169 R2 **Xiao'ergou** Nei Mongol China
Xiaofan Hebei China see **Wuqiang**
171 I3 **Xiaogan** Hubei China
172 G4 **Xiaoguai** Xinjiang China
169 J8 **Xiaoguan** Gansu China
172 D7 **Xiaohaizi Shuiku** resr Xinjiang China
162 E3 **Xiao Hinggan Ling** mts China
Xiaojiang Guangxi China see **Pubei**
169 J9 **Xiaojin** Gansu China
170 D3 **Xiaojin** Sichuan China
169 M9 **Xiaolangdi Shuiku** resr Henan/Shanxi China
171 L5 **Xiaomei** Zhejiang China
Xiaonan Gansu China see **Dongxiangzu**
168 D9 **Xiaonanchuan** Qinghai China
173 L8 **Xiao Qaidam** Qinghai China
169 P8 **Xiaoqing He** r. China
171 I6 **Xiaosanjiang** Guangdong China
171 M3 **Xiaoshan** Zhejiang China
169 L9 **Xiao Shan** mts China
170 E4 **Xiaoshi** Sichuan China
170 A2 **Xiao Surmang** Qinghai China
171 K6 **Xiaotao** Fujian China
169 N7 **Xiaowutai Shan** mt. Hebei China
Xiaoxi Fujian China see **Pinghe**
169 O9 **Xiaoxian** Anhui China
170 D4 **Xiaoxiang Ling** mts Sichuan China
169 L8 **Xiaoyi** Shanxi China
172 E4 **Xiaoyingpan** Xinjiang China
171 M5 **Xiapu** Fujian China
170 C5 **Xiaqiaotou** Yunnan China
Xiashan Guangdong China see **Zhanjiang**
168 H7 **Xiasifen** Gansu China
127 O8 **Xiatil** Mex.
169 L9 **Xiaxian** Shanxi China
Xiayang Hunan China see **Yanling**
Xiayanjing Xizang China see **Yanjing**
170 C2 **Xia Zanggor** Qinghai China
170 C3 **Xiazhai** Sichuan China
Xiazhen Shandong China see **Weishan**
170 B4 **Xibdê** Sichuan China
172 I3 **Xibet** Xinjiang China
171 L5 **Xibing** Fujian China
170 G8 **Xichang** Guangxi China
170 D5 **Xichang** Sichuan China
Xicheng Hebei China see **Yangyuan**
170 E7 **Xichou** Yunnan China
171 H2 **Xichuan** Henan China
129 J6 **Xico** Mex.
129 I2 **Xicohténcatl** Mex.
129 J5 **Xicotepec de Juárez** Mex.
170 D4 **Xide** Sichuan China
136 E4 **Xié** r. Brazil
Xiejiaji Shandong China see **Qingyun**
171 H3 **Xiemahe'** Hubei China
Xieng Khouang Laos see **Xiangkhoang**
158 G5 **Xiêng Lam** Vietnam
170 G8 **Xieyang Dao** i. China
171 K2 **Xifei He** r. China
169 J9 **Xifeng** Gansu China
170 F5 **Xifeng** Guizhou China
162 D7 **Xifeng** Liaoning China
Xifengzhen Gansu China see **Xifeng**
173 I12 **Xigazê** Xizang China
170 F2 **Xihan Shui** r. Gansu China
170 E2 **Xihe** Gansu China
169 Q6 **Xi He** r. Liaoning China
170 F3 **Xi He** r. Sichuan China
168 G5 **Xi He** watercourse China
172 L6 **Xihu** Gansu China
171 J2 **Xihua** Henan China
92 E2 **Xiis** Somalia
168 I9 **Xiji** Ningxia China
171 I7 **Xi Jiang** r. Guangdong China
168 E6 **Xijian Quan** well Gansu China
170 G7 **Xijin** Guangxi China
168 B9 **Xijir** Qinghai China
173 J9 **Xijir Ulan Hu** salt l. China
168 H8 **Xijishui** Gansu China
162 F4 **Xikelin** Heilong. China
162 B2 **Xikouzi** Nei Mongol China
169 M5 **Xil** Nei Mongol China
Xilaganí Greece see **Xylagani**
169 Q4 **Xilaotou Shan** mt. Nei Mongol China
172 K7 **Xiliangzi** Qinghai China
169 R5 **Xiliao He** r. China
Xiligou Qinghai China see **Ulan**
170 E6 **Xilin** Guangxi China
169 O5 **Xilinhot** Nei Mongol China
Xilin Qagan Obo Nei Mongol China see **Qagan Obo**
129 I4 **Xilitla** Mex.
191 K6 **Xıllı** Azer.
191 J5 **Xılmilli** Azer.
Xilókastron Greece see **Xylokastro**
Xilópolis Greece see **Xylopoli**
170 B7 **Ximeng** Yunnan China
168 G6 **Ximiao** Nei Mongol China
169 K7 **Xin** Nei Mongol China
191 J4 **Xınalıq** Azer.
169 M9 **Xin'an** Henan China
171 L4 **Xin'anjiang Shuiku** resr China
163 D8 **Xinbin** Liaoning China
193 M5 **Xin Bulag** Nei Mongol China
169 P2 **Xin Bulag Dong** Nei Mongol China
171 J2 **Xincai** Henan China
Xinchang Jiangxi China see **Yifeng**
171 M4 **Xinchang** Zhejiang China
168 G7 **Xincheng** Gansu China
Xincheng Guangdong China see **Xinxing**
170 G6 **Xincheng** Guangxi China
168 J7 **Xincheng** Ningxia China

Xincheng to **Yeniseyskiy Kryazh**

362

Xincheng *Shanxi* China *see* **Yuanqu**
Xincheng *Sichuan* China *see* **Zhaojue**
169 K8 **Xinchengbu** *Shaanxi* China
172 G4 **Xinchepaizi** *Xinjiang* China
171 H7 **Xindi** *Guangxi* China
169 S3 **Xindian** *Heilong.* China
171 H7 **Xindu** *Guangxi* China
170 E3 **Xindu** *Sichuan* China
170 C3 **Xinduqiao** *Sichuan* China
171 J6 **Xinfeng** *Guangdong* China
171 J6 **Xinfeng** *Jiangxi* China
171 J7 **Xinfengjiang Shuiku** *resr* China
170 H6 **Xing'an** *Guangxi* China
171 J5 **Xingan** *Jiangxi* China
169 Q7 **Xingangzhen** *Liaoning* China
173 K12 **Xingba** *Xizang* China
Xingcheng *Hebei* China *see* **Qianxi**
169 Q6 **Xingcheng** *Liaoning* China
172 H6 **Xingdi** *Xinjiang* China
91 C7 **Xinge** Angola
Xingguo *Gansu* China *see* **Qin'an**
171 J5 **Xingguo** *Jiangxi* China
168 F9 **Xinghai** *Qinghai* China
162 D2 **Xinghua** *Heilong.* China
171 L2 **Xinghua** *Jiangsu* China
171 L6 **Xinghua Wan** *b.* China
162 H6 **Xingkai** *Heilong.* China
169 O6 **Xinglong** *Hebei* China
162 D3 **Xinglong** *Heilong.* China
162 E5 **Xinglongzhen** *Heilong.* China
171 J6 **Xingning** *Guangdong* China
171 I6 **Xingning** *Hunan* China
171 I3 **Xingou** *Hubei* China
169 K9 **Xingping** *Shaanxi* China
170 E6 **Xingren** *Guizhou* China
168 I8 **Xingrenbu** *Ningxia* China
168 G9 **Xingsagoinba** *Qinghai* China
170 H3 **Xingshan** *Hubei* China
169 N8 **Xingtai** *Hebei* China
169 N7 **Xingtang** *Hebei* China
137 H5 **Xingu** *r.* Brazil
140 B4 **Xingu, Parque Indígena do** *res.* Brazil
169 M7 **Xinguangwu** *Shanxi* China
140 C3 **Xinguara** Brazil
170 E4 **Xingwen** *Sichuan* China
169 L7 **Xingxian** *Shanxi* China
168 D6 **Xingxingxia** *Xinjiang* China
169 M9 **Xingyang** *Henan* China
170 G7 **Xingye** *Guangxi* China
170 E6 **Xingyi** *Guizhou* China
171 K4 **Xingzi** *Jiangxi* China
169 N8 **Xinhe** *Hebei* China
172 F6 **Xinhe** *Xinjiang* China
169 N5 **Xin Hot** *Nei Mongol* China
171 H5 **Xinhua** *Hunan* China
Xinhua *Yunnan* China *see* **Qiaojia**
170 G5 **Xinhuang** *Hunan* China
169 P5 **Xinhui** *Nei Mongol* China
168 G8 **Xining** *Qinghai* China
169 N8 **Xinji** *Hebei* China
Xinji *Henan* China *see* **Xinxian**
171 J4 **Xinjian** *Jiangxi* China
169 L9 **Xinjiang** *Shanxi* China
Xinjiang *aut. reg.* China *see* **Xinjiang Uygur Zizhiqu**
171 K4 **Xin Jiang** *r.* China
Xinjiangkou *Hubei* China *see* **Songzi**
168 B5 **Xinjiang Uygur Zizhiqu** *aut. reg.* China
169 K7 **Xinjie** *Nei Mongol* China
170 B6 **Xinjie** *Yunnan* China
170 D7 **Xinjie** *Yunnan* China
Xinjin *Liaoning* China *see* **Pulandian**
170 D3 **Xinjin** *Sichuan* China
169 R5 **Xinkai He** *r.* China
162 D7 **Xinlicheng Shuiku** *resr Jilin* China
162 E3 **Xinlitun** *Heilong.* China
170 C3 **Xinlong** *Sichuan* China
169 M9 **Xinmi** *Henan* China
Xinmian *Sichuan* China *see* **Shimian**
162 E4 **Xinmin** *Heilong.* China
169 R6 **Xinmin** *Liaoning* China
169 L7 **Xinminzhen** *Shaanxi* China
170 H5 **Xinning** *Hunan* China
Xinning *Jiangxi* China *see* **Wuning**
170 C6 **Xinping** *Yunnan* China
162 F4 **Xinqing** *Heilong.* China
171 K6 **Xinquan** *Fujian* China
171 H5 **Xinshao** *Hunan* China
169 O9 **Xintai** *Shandong* China
162 D3 **Xintain** *Nei Mongol* China
171 J4 **Xintanpu** *Hubei* China
171 I6 **Xintian** *Hunan* China
171 J3 **Xinxian** *Henan* China
Xinxian *Shanxi* China *see* **Xinzhou**
169 M9 **Xinxiang** *Henan* China
171 I7 **Xinxing** *Guangdong* China
171 J2 **Xinyang** *Henan* China
171 M2 **Xinyang Gang** *r.* China
171 I2 **Xinye** *Henan* China
171 H7 **Xinyi** *Guangdong* China
169 P9 **Xinyi** *Jiangsu* China
169 P9 **Xinyi He** *r.* China
170 G9 **Xinying** *Hainan* China
171 J5 **Xinyu** *Jiangxi* China
Xinyuan *Qinghai* China *see* **Tianjun**
172 F5 **Xinyuan** *Xinjiang* China
169 Q1 **Xinzhangfang** *Nei Mongol* China
169 M9 **Xinzheng** *Henan* China
171 J3 **Xinzhou** *Hubei* China
169 M7 **Xinzhou** *Shanxi* China
62 E4 **Xinzo de Limia** Spain
Xiongshan *Fujian* China *see* **Zhenghe**
138 D2 **Xipamanu** *r.* Bol./Brazil
171 H2 **Xiping** *Henan* China
171 J2 **Xiping** *Henan* China
168 G9 **Xiqing Shan** *mts* China
168 H7 **Xiqu** *Gansu* China
140 E4 **Xique Xique** Brazil
191 K5 **Xırdalan** Azer.
67 E9 **Xirivella** Spain
78 E4 **Xiro** *hill* Greece
79 H5 **Xirokampo** Greece
136 E6 **Xiruá** *r.* Brazil
Xisa *Yunnan* China *see* **Xichou**
169 K6 **Xishanzui** *Nei Mongol* China
170 C7 **Xishuangbanna** *reg. Yunnan* China
170 F4 **Xishui** *Guizhou* China
171 J3 **Xishui** *Hubei* China
62 E2 **Xistral, Serra do** *mts* Spain
173 K8 **Xi Taijnar Hu** *l. Qinghai* China
168 D8 **Xitieshan** *Qinghai* China
129 K9 **Xitla** Mex.
88 B4 **Xitole** Guinea-Bissau
171 L4 **Xiuning** *Anhui* China
170 G4 **Xiushan** *Chongqing* China
Xiushan *Yunnan* China *see* **Tonghai**
171 J4 **Xiushui** *Jiangxi* China
171 J4 **Xiu Shui** *r.* China
170 F5 **Xiuwen** *Guizhou* China
169 M9 **Xiuwu** *Henan* China
169 R6 **Xiuyan** *Liaoning* China
Xiuyan *Shaanxi* China *see* **Qingjian**
170 H8 **Xiuying** *Hainan* China
182 I7 **Xiva** Uzbek.
170 A2 **Xiwu** *Qinghai* China
173 G12 **Xixabangma Feng** *mt. Xizang* China
171 H2 **Xixia** *Henan* China
171 J2 **Xixian** *Henan* China
169 L8 **Xixian** *Shanxi* China
170 F2 **Xixiang** *Shaanxi* China
169 M8 **Xiyang** *Shanxi* China
171 M5 **Xiyang Dao** *i.* China
170 E6 **Xiyang Jiang** *r. Yunnan* China
168 H8 **Xiying** *Gansu* China
Xizang *aut. reg.* China *see* **Xizang Zizhiqu**
Xizang Gaoyuan *plat. Xizang* China *see* **Qingzang Gaoyuan**
170 A3 **Xizang Zizhiqu** *aut. reg.* China
169 Q7 **Xizhong Dao** *i.* China
191 K5 **Xızı** Azer.
173 L11 **Xobando** *Xizang* China
191 H6 **Xocalı** Azer.
191 I6 **Xocavänd** Azer.
129 L8 **Xochiapa** Mex.
129 I5 **Xochiatipan** Mex.
129 H7 **Xochicalco** *tourist site* Mex.
129 H6 **Xochimilco** Mex.
129 I9 **Xochistlahuaca** Mex.
79 H6 **Xodoto, Akra** *pt* Greece
Xoi *Xizang* China *see* **Qüxü**
182 J8 **Xo'jadavlat** Uzbek.
181 J2 **Xo'japiryox tog'i** *mt.* Uzbek.
182 H6 **Xo'jayli** *Qoraqalpog'iston Respublikasi* Uzbek.
173 K12 **Xoka** *Xizang* China
97 L8 **Xolobe** S. Africa
191 J6 **Xol Qarabucaq** Azer.
129 H6 **Xonacatlán** Mex.
183 O7 **Xonobod** Uzbek.
182 I7 **Xonqa** Uzbek.
Xonrupt France *see* **Xonrupt-Longemer**
37 M7 **Xonrupt-Longemer** France
97 L7 **Xonxa Dam** S. Africa
170 B4 **Xo Qu** *r. Sichuan* China
182 I7 **Xorazm** *admin. div.* Uzbek.
172 J7 **Xorkol** *Xinjiang* China
173 G8 **Xortang** *Xinjiang* China
191 I5 **Xosrov** Azer.
62 E1 **Xove** Spain
183 M7 **Xovos** Uzbek.
171 L3 **Xuancheng** *Anhui* China
170 G3 **Xuan'en** *Hubei* China
170 F3 **Xuanhan** *Sichuan* China
169 N6 **Xuanhua** *Hebei* China
159 H9 **Xuân Lôc** Vietnam
170 E5 **Xuanwei** *Yunnan* China
Xuanzhou *Anhui* China *see* **Xuancheng**
62 D4 **Xubín** Spain
171 I2 **Xuchang** *Henan* China
161 J5 **Xuchang** *Henan* China
Xucheng *Guangdong* China *see* **Xuwen**
191 J4 **Xudat** Azer.
92 D3 **Xuddur** Somalia
92 E2 **Xudun** Somalia
173 K12 **Xueba** *Xizang* China
170 G5 **Xuefeng Shan** *mts* China
169 L9 **Xuehua Shan** *hill Shanxi* China
169 L7 **Xuejiawan** *Nei Mongol* China
170 B5 **Xue Shan** *mts Yunnan* China
168 D9 **Xugin Gol** *r. Qinghai* China
169 P9 **Xugou** *Jiangsu* China
168 H6 **Xugui** *Nei Mongol* China
168 D9 **Xugui** *Qinghai* China
Xuguit Qi *Nei Mongol* China *see* **Yakeshi**
Xulun Hobot Qagan Qi *Nei Mongol* China *see* **Qagan Nur**
170 D6 **Xundian** *Yunnan* China
Xungba *Xizang* China *see* **Xangdoring**
173 I11 **Xungmai** *Xizang* China
173 K11 **Xung Qu** *r. Xizang* China
173 G12 **Xungru** *Xizang* China
162 E4 **Xunhe** *Heilong.* China
162 F4 **Xun He** *r.* China
170 G2 **Xun He** *r.* China
168 H9 **Xunhua** *Qinghai* China
170 H7 **Xun Jiang** *r.* China
162 F4 **Xunke** *Heilong.* China
62 E4 **Xunqueira de Ambía** Spain
171 J6 **Xunwu** *Jiangxi* China
169 N9 **Xunxian** *Henan* China
170 G2 **Xunyang** *Shaanxi* China
169 K9 **Xunyi** *Shaanxi* China
170 H5 **Xupu** *Hunan* China
168 D9 **Xurgan** *Qinghai* China
173 H11 **Xuru Co** *salt l.* China
169 N7 **Xushui** *Hebei* China
170 H8 **Xuwen** *Guangdong* China
Xuyang *Sichuan* China *see* **Rongxian**
171 L2 **Xuyi** *Jiangsu* China
170 E4 **Xuyong** *Sichuan* China
Xuzhou *Jiangsu* China *see* **Tongshan**
79 G2 **Xylagani** Greece
78 D4 **Xylokastro** Greece
78 E2 **Xylopoli** Greece

Y

207 M7 **Yaamba** *Qld* Austr.
170 D3 **Ya'an** *Sichuan* China
205 I6 **Yaapeet** *Vic.* Austr.
155 E4 **Yaba** *Maluku* Indon.
89 H5 **Yabassi** Cameroon
200 □3a **Yabbenohr** *i. Kwajalein* Marshall Is
92 C3 **Yabēlo** Eth.
92 C3 **Yabēlo Wildlife Sanctuary** *nature res.* Eth.
90 D4 **Yabia** Dem. Rep. Congo
77 M7 **Yablanitsa** Bulg.
77 O8 **Yablanovo** Bulg.
17 S2 **Yablochnoye** Rus. Fed.
17 T1 **Yablonovets** Rus. Fed.
17 R9 **Yablonovskiy** Rus. Fed.
169 K1 **Yablonovyy Khrebet** *mts* Rus. Fed.
16 D5 **Yabluniv** Ukr.
17 K4 **Yablunivka** Ukr.
89 G3 **Yabo** Nigeria
168 H7 **Yabrai Shan** *mts* China
168 H7 **Yabrai Yanchang** *Nei Mongol* China
187 I4 **Yabrīn** *reg.* Saudi Arabia
190 E5 **Yabrūd** Syria
166 A5 **Yabu** Japan
131 □1 **Yabucoa** Puerto Rico
131 □1 **Yabucoa, Puerto** *b.* Puerto Rico
167 L1 **Yabuki** Japan
162 F6 **Yabuli** *Heilong.* China
16 H3 **Yabunets'** Ukr.
136 C5 **Yabuyanos** Peru
167 J3 **Yabuzukahon** Japan
170 G9 **Yacheng** *Hainan* China
170 F5 **Yachi He** *r.* China
167 L4 **Yachimata** Japan
167 L4 **Yachiyo** *Chiba* Japan
167 K3 **Yachiyo** *Ibaraki* Japan
141 A8 **Yaciretá, Isla** *i.* Para.
205 K7 **Yackandandah** *Vic.* Austr.
138 E5 **Yacuiba** Bol.
136 E3 **Yacurai** Venez.
144 F2 **Yacyretá Apipé, Embalse** *resr* Arg./Para.
90 B3 **Yadé, Massif du** *mts* C.A.R.
176 E4 **Yadgir** *Karnataka* India
176 E5 **Yadiki** *Andhra Prad.* India
115 G8 **Yadkin** *r. NC* U.S.A.
115 G7 **Yadkinville** *NC* U.S.A.
173 I13 **Yadong** *Xizang* China
14 I5 **Yadrin** Rus. Fed.
201 □1 **Yadua** *i.* Fiji
164 □A22 **Yaeyama-rettō** *is* Japan
Yafa Israel *see* **Tel Aviv-Yafo**
84 B1 **Yafran** Libya
88 E4 **Yagaba** Ghana
164 □1 **Yagaji-jima** *i. Okinawa* Japan
165 G14 **Yagami** Japan
168 H6 **Yagan** *Nei Mongol* China
79 I3 **Yağcılı** Turkey
214 E9 **Yaghan Basin** *sea feature* S. Atlantic Ocean
166 C5 **Yagi** Japan
164 S2 **Yagishiri-tō** *i.* Japan
190 D1 **Yağızlar** Turkey
168 F8 **Yagkêng** *Qinghai* China
191 E5 **Yağlıca Dağı** *mt.* Turkey
14 E3 **Yaglyayarvi** Rus. Fed.
184 F2 **Yagman** Turkm.
191 E6 **Yağmurlu** *r.* Turkey
19 U3 **Yagnitsa** Rus. Fed.
128 B4 **Yago** Mex.
77 N8 **Yagoda** Bulg.
182 A2 **Yagodnaya Polyana** Rus. Fed.
19 S8 **Yagodnoye** *Kaluzhskaya Oblast'* Rus. Fed.
193 P3 **Yagodnoye** *Magadanskaya Oblast'* Rus. Fed.
162 K3 **Yagodnyy** Rus. Fed.
Yagotin Ukr. *see* **Yahotyn**
89 I4 **Yagoua** Cameroon
173 F11 **Yagra** *Xizang* China
168 D9 **Yagradagzê Shan** *mt. Qinghai* China
130 D2 **Yaguajay** Cuba
136 D5 **Yaguas** *r.* Peru
159 E11 **Yaha** Thai.
166 E6 **Yahagi-gawa** *r.* Japan
90 D4 **Yahila** Dem. Rep. Congo
106 G5 **Yahk** *B.C.* Can.
16 I6 **Yahorlyk** *r.* Ukr.
17 K3 **Yahotyn** Ukr.
128 E4 **Yahualica** Mex.
90 D4 **Yahuma** Dem. Rep. Congo
180 D2 **Yahyalı** Turkey
185 M6 **Yahya Wana** Afgh.
159 D8 **Yai, Khao** *mt.* Thai.
167 K2 **Yaita** Japan
98 □3c **Yaiza** *Lanzarote* Canary Is
167 H6 **Yaizu** Japan
170 C3 **Yajiang** *Sichuan* China
90 C3 **Yaka** C.A.R.
190 E2 **Yakacık** Turkey
190 D2 **Yakapınar** Turkey
172 H7 **Yakatograk** *Xinjiang* China
185 K5 **Yak Dar** Afgh.
166 G3 **Yake-dake** *vol.* Japan
169 Q2 **Yakeshi** *Nei Mongol* China
184 G4 **Yakhab** *waterhole* Iran
185 K6 **Yakhehal** Afgh.
16 F4 **Yakhivtsi** Ukr.
17 M3 **Yakhnyky** Ukr.
19 U5 **Yakhroma** Rus. Fed.
122 D3 **Yakima** *WA* U.S.A.
122 E3 **Yakima** *r. WA* U.S.A.
122 D3 **Yakima Indian Reservation** *res. WA* U.S.A.
184 E5 **Yakinish** Iran
183 L8 **Yakkabog'** Uzbek.
185 J7 **Yakmach** Pak.
88 E3 **Yako** Burkina
106 B3 **Yakobi Island** *AK* U.S.A.
90 D3 **Yakoma** Dem. Rep. Congo
77 L8 **Yakoruda** Bulg.
17 P4 **Yakovenkove** Ukr.
162 H6 **Yakovlevka** Rus. Fed.
17 P3 **Yakovlevo** Rus. Fed.
14 K4 **Yakskur-Bod'ya** Rus. Fed.
164 R4 **Yakumo** Japan
166 A5 **Yakuno** Japan
164 □H16 **Yaku-shima** *i.* Japan
104 E4 **Yakutat** *AK* U.S.A.
104 D4 **Yakutat Bay** *AK* U.S.A.
193 N3 **Yakutsk** Rus. Fed.
17 O7 **Yakymivka** Ukr.
88 E4 **Yala** Ghana
92 B4 **Yala** Kenya
176 G9 **Yala** Sri Lanka
159 E11 **Yala** Thai.
173 H12 **Yalai** *Xizang* China
170 C3 **Yalakan** *Sichuan* China
79 K2 **Yalakdere** Turkey
191 J4 **Yalama** Azer.
190 A2 **Yalan Dünya Mağarası** *tourist site* Turkey
204 C4 **Yalata Aboriginal Lands** *res. S.A.* Austr.
203 G10 **Yaldhurst** *South I.* N.Z.
106 F5 **Yale** *B.C.* Can.
111 L6 **Yale** *MI* U.S.A.
90 E4 **Yaleko** Dem. Rep. Congo
88 E3 **Yalgo** Burkina
209 D10 **Yalgoo** *W.A.* Austr.
79 I5 **Yalıkavak** Turkey
77 Q9 **Yalıköy** Turkey
191 C6 **Yalınca** Turkey
90 D3 **Yalinga** C.A.R.
18 M8 **Yalizava** Belarus
127 O7 **Yalkubul, Punta** *pt* Mex.
130 □ **Yallahs** Jamaica
207 J8 **Yalleroi** *Qld* Austr.
209 C12 **Yallingup** *W.A.* Austr.
88 E3 **Yallo** Burkina
205 K8 **Yallourn** *Vic.* Austr.
191 D5 **Yalnızçam Dağları** *mts* Turkey
121 J9 **Yalobusha** *r. MS* U.S.A.
Yalogo Burkina *see* **Yalgo**
90 C3 **Yaloké** C.A.R.
170 C5 **Yalong Jiang** *r. Sichuan* China
79 K2 **Yalova** Turkey
77 R10 **Yalova** *prov.* Turkey
206 D7 **Yalpirakinu Aboriginal Land** *res. N.T.* Austr.
16 H8 **Yalpuh, Ozero** *l.* Ukr.
17 Q7 **Yalta** *Donets'ka Oblast'* Ukr.
17 N9 **Yalta** *Respublika Krym* Ukr.
17 N9 **Yaltins'kyy Zapovidnyk** *nature res.* Ukr.
16 G5 **Yaltushkiv** Ukr.
169 R3 **Yalu He** *r.* China
163 D8 **Yalu Jiang** *r.* China/N. Korea
90 D5 **Yalusaka** Dem. Rep. Congo
192 H4 **Yalutorovsk** Rus. Fed.
79 M4 **Yalvaç** Turkey
186 G7 **Yām** *reg.* Saudi Arabia
Yama Ukr. *see* **Sivers'k**
167 M4 **Yamada** *Chiba* Japan
164 S7 **Yamada** *Iwate* Japan
166 F2 **Yamada** *Toyama* Japan
165 H13 **Yamaga** Japan
167 L2 **Yamagata** *Ibaraki* Japan
164 S6 **Yamagata** *Iwate* Japan
167 G3 **Yamagata** *Nagano* Japan
164 R8 **Yamagata** *Yamagata* Japan
164 Q8 **Yamagata** *pref.* Japan
166 G4 **Yamaguchi** *Nagano* Japan
165 I12 **Yamaguchi** *Yamaguchi* Japan
165 I12 **Yamaguchi** *pref.* Japan
167 J5 **Yamakita** Japan
192 H2 **Yamal, Poluostrov** *pen.* Rus. Fed.
162 I2 **Yam Alin', Khrebet** *mts* Rus. Fed.
Yamal Peninsula Rus. Fed. *see* **Yamal, Poluostrov**
166 D3 **Yamanaka** Japan
167 I5 **Yamanaka-ko** *l.* Japan
167 I4 **Yamanashi** Japan
167 H4 **Yamanashi** *pref.* Japan
207 J5 **Yamanie Falls National Park** *Qld* Austr.
167 I5 **Yamanokako** Japan
167 H2 **Yamanouchi** Japan
168 C6 **Yamansu** *Xinjiang* China
166 F5 **Yamaoka** Japan
169 L1 **Yamarovka** Rus. Fed.
165 L11 **Yamasaki** Japan
166 C6 **Yamashiro** Japan
166 E4 **Yamato** *Gifu* Japan
167 L3 **Yamato** *Ibaraki* Japan
167 J5 **Yamato** *Kanagawa* Japan
164 □G18 **Yamato** *Nansei-shotō* Japan
167 I1 **Yamato** *Niigata* Japan
166 C6 **Yamato-Aogaki Quasi National Park** Japan
166 C6 **Yamato-kōriyama** Japan
166 C6 **Yamatotakada** Japan
167 L2 **Yamatsuri** Japan
166 D6 **Yamazoe** Japan
205 N3 **Yamba** *N.S.W.* Austr.
205 I8 **Yambacoona** *Tas.* Austr.
107 I1 **Yamba Lake** *N.W.T.* Can.
206 C3 **Yambarran Range** *hills N.T.* Austr.
90 B2 **Yamba Tchangsou** Chad
88 B4 **Yambéring** Guinea
136 D4 **Yambi, Mesa de** *hills* Col.
90 F3 **Yambio** Sudan
77 O8 **Yambol** Bulg.
136 B6 **Yambrasbamba** Peru
153 H8 **Yamdena** *i.* Indon.
165 H13 **Yame** Japan
158 C4 **Yamethin** Myanmar
154 C1 **Y'ami** *i.* Phil.
167 L2 **Yamizo-san** *mt.* Japan
176 D4 **Yamkanmardi** *Karnataka* India
18 M4 **Yamkino** Rus. Fed.
18 L3 **Yamm** Rus. Fed.
207 H9 **Yamma Yamma, Lake** *salt flat Qld* Austr.
17 O3 **Yamne** Ukr.
88 D5 **Yamoussoukro** Côte d'Ivoire
17 K5 **Yampil'** *Cherkas'ka Oblast'* Ukr.
16 F4 **Yampil'** *Khmel'nyts'ka Oblast'* Ukr.
17 M2 **Yampil'** *Sums'ka Oblast'* Ukr.
16 H5 **Yampil'** *Vinnyts'ka Oblast'* Ukr.
Yampol' *Cherkas'ka Oblast'* Ukr. *see* **Yampil'**
Yampol' *Khmel'nyts'ka Oblast'* Ukr. *see* **Yampil'**
Yampol' *Sums'ka Oblast'* Ukr. *see* **Yampil'**
Yampol' *Vinnyts'ka Oblast'* Ukr. *see* **Yampil'**
178 H7 **Yamuna** *r.* India
178 F4 **Yamunanagar** *Haryana* India
173 J12 **Yamzho Yumco** *l.* China
89 H4 **Yana** Nigeria
193 O2 **Yana** *r.* Rus. Fed.
204 H7 **Yanac** *Vic.* Austr.
138 B2 **Yanachaga-Chemillen, Parque Nacional** *nat. park* Peru
165 K13 **Yanadani** Japan
164 R9 **Yanagawa** Japan
164 □1 **Yanaha-jima** *i. Okinawa* Japan
165 J13 **Yanai** Japan
176 H4 **Yanam** *Pondicherry* India
169 K8 **Yan'an** *Shaanxi* China
138 C3 **Yanaoca** Peru
Yanaon *Pondicherry* India *see* **Yanam**
14 K4 **Yanaul** Rus. Fed.
19 N6 **Yanavichy** Belarus
136 C5 **Yanayacu** Peru
170 C5 **Yanbian** *Yunnan* China
186 C3 **Yanbu, Sharm** *b.* Saudi Arabia
186 D3 **Yanbu' al Baḥr** Saudi Arabia
186 D3 **Yanbu' an Nakhl** *reg.* Saudi Arabia
115 H7 **Yanceyville** *NC* U.S.A.
169 L8 **Yanchang** *Shaanxi* China
171 M2 **Yancheng** *Jiangsu* China
Yancheng *Shandong* China *see* **Qihe**
209 C11 **Yanchep** *W.A.* Austr.
169 J8 **Yanchi** *Ningxia* China
168 D5 **Yanchi** *Xinjiang* China
172 H3 **Yanchi** *Xinjiang* China
172 L7 **Yanchiwan** *Gansu* China
169 L8 **Yanchuan** *Shaanxi* China
17 P6 **Yanchur** *r.* Ukr.
205 K6 **Yanco** *N.S.W.* Austr.
205 J6 **Yanco Creek** *r. N.S.W.* Austr.
205 H4 **Yanco Glen** *N.S.W.* Austr.
205 J4 **Yanda** *watercourse N.S.W.* Austr.
204 H4 **Yandama Creek** *watercourse S.A.* Austr.
171 M5 **Yandang Shan** *mts* China
Yandao *Sichuan* China *see* **Yingjing**
208 E6 **Yandeyarra Aboriginal Reserve** *W.A.* Austr.
208 E7 **Yandicoogina Mine** *W.A.* Austr.
209 E9 **Yandil** *W.A.* Austr.
207 N9 **Yandina** *Qld* Austr.
200 □6 **Yandina** Solomon Is
90 C5 **Yandja** Dem. Rep. Congo
158 B6 **Yandoon** Myanmar
Yandua *i.* Fiji *see* **Yadua**
168 D5 **Yandun** *Xinjiang* China
19 Q1 **Yanega** Rus. Fed.
88 C4 **Yanfolila** Mali
90 D3 **Yangalia** C.A.R.
90 E4 **Yangambi** Dem. Rep. Congo
173 L11 **Ya'ngamdo** *Xizang* China
173 L11 **Ya'ngamdo** *Xizang* China
88 D3 **Yangasso** Mali
173 J11 **Yangbajain** *Xizang* China
170 B6 **Yangbi** *Yunnan* China
Yangcheng *Guangdong* China *see* **Yangshan**
169 M9 **Yangcheng** *Shanxi* China
Yangchuan *Guizhou* China *see* **Suiyang**
171 H7 **Yangchun** *Guangdong* China
171 J7 **Yangcun** *Guangdong* China
Yangcun *Tianjin* China *see* **Wuqing**
172 I7 **Yangdaxkak** *Xinjiang* China
163 E9 **Yangdok** N. Korea
171 H8 **Yangdong** *Guangdong* China
169 M6 **Yanggao** *Shanxi* China
169 N8 **Yanggu** *Shandong* China
Yanghe *Ningxia* China *see* **Yongning**
169 N6 **Yang He** *r.* China
173 G9 **Yang Hu** *l. Xizang* China
182 I7 **Yangiariq** Uzbek.
173 D9 **Yangi Davan** *pass* Aksai Chin/China
182 K8 **Yangi Nishon** Uzbek.
185 M3 **Yangi Qal'eh** Afgh.
183 L7 **Yangiqishloq** Uzbek.
182 K7 **Yangirabot** Uzbek.
183 M7 **Yangiyo'l** Uzbek.
169 K8 **Yangjialing** *Shaanxi* China
171 H8 **Yangjiang** *Guangdong* China
169 P8 **Yangjiaogou** *Shandong* China
158 C6 **Yangôn** Myanmar
177 O4 **Yangôn** *admin. div.* Myanmar
171 H3 **Yangping** *Hubei* China
169 M8 **Yangquan** *Shanxi* China
169 L8 **Yangquangu** *Shanxi* China
171 I6 **Yangshan** *Guangdong* China
170 H6 **Yangshuo** *Guangxi* China
158 F6 **Yang Talat** Thai.
170 C6 **Yangtouyan** *Yunnan* China
Yangtze *r. Qinghai* China *see* **Tongtian He**
171 K3 **Yangtze** *r.* China
alt. **Chang Jiang,**
alt. **Jinsha Jiang,**
alt. **Tongtian He,**
long **Yangtze Kiang**
170 E1 **Yanguan** *Gansu* China
63 P4 **Yanguas** Spain
92 D2 **Yangudi Rassa National Park** Eth.
169 P9 **Yangweigang** *Jiangsu* China
171 H8 **Yangxi** *Guangdong* China
170 F2 **Yangxian** *Shaanxi* China
163 F9 **Yangyang** S. Korea
169 N6 **Yangyuan** *Hebei* China
171 L2 **Yangzhou** *Jiangsu* China
Yangzhou *Shaanxi* China *see* **Yangxian**
170 G4 **Yanhe** *Guizhou* China
169 L8 **Yan He** *r.* China
172 I5 **Yanhu** *Xinjiang* China
173 F10 **Yanhu** *Xizang* China
204 E5 **Yaninee, Lake** *salt flat S.A.* Austr.
14 F3 **Yanishpole** Rus. Fed.
20 U5 **Yanis''yarvi, Ozero** *l.* Rus. Fed.
162 F7 **Yanji** *Jilin* China
169 N9 **Yanjin** *Henan* China
170 E4 **Yanjin** *Yunnan* China
Yanjing *Sichuan* China *see* **Yanyuan**
170 B4 **Yanjing** *Xizang* China
Yanjing *Yunnan* China *see* **Yanjin**
89 H4 **Yankara National Park** Nigeria
18 L6 **Yankavichy** Belarus
Yankou *Sichuan* China *see* **Wusheng**
120 G4 **Yankton** *SD* U.S.A.
120 F4 **Yankton Indian Reservation** *res. SD* U.S.A.
191 D1 **Yankul'** Rus. Fed.
191 D1 **Yankul'** *r.* Rus. Fed.
169 N9 **Yanling** *Henan* China
171 I5 **Yanling** *Hunan* China
193 P2 **Yano-Indigirskaya Nizmennost'** *lowland* Rus. Fed.
19 P7 **Yanovo** Rus. Fed.
192 J3 **Yanov-Stan** Rus. Fed.
176 G8 **Yan Oya** *r.* Sri Lanka
172 H5 **Yanqi** *Xinjiang* China
169 N6 **Yanqing** *Beijing* China
187 M4 **Yanqul** Oman
209 C7 **Yanrey** *r. W.A.* Austr.
169 O7 **Yanshan** *Hebei* China
171 K4 **Yanshan** *Jiangxi* China
170 E7 **Yanshan** *Yunnan* China
169 O6 **Yan Shan** *mts* China
169 M9 **Yanshi** *Henan* China
173 K10 **Yanshiping** *Qinghai* China
162 F6 **Yanshou** *Heilong.* China
193 O2 **Yanskiy Zaliv** *g.* Rus. Fed.
205 J3 **Yantabulla** *N.S.W.* Austr.
184 C2 **Yantagh** Iran
169 Q8 **Yantai** *Shandong* China
145 B6 **Yántales, Cerro** *mt.* Chile
17 N8 **Yantarne** Ukr.
18 C7 **Yantarnyy** Rus. Fed.
119 K1 **Yantic** *r. CT* U.S.A.
170 E3 **Yanting** *Sichuan* China
162 E7 **Yantongshan** *Jilin* China
171 M4 **Yantou** *Zhejiang* China
77 N7 **Yantra** *r.* Bulg.
201 □1a **Yanuca** *i.* Fiji
186 F4 **Yanūfī, Jabal al** *hill* Saudi Arabia
Yanutha *i.* Fiji *see* **Yanuca**
170 B5 **Yanwa** *Yunnan* China
170 H4 **Yanxi** *Hunan* China
Yany-Kurgan Kazakh. *see* **Zhanakorgan**
170 C5 **Yanyuan** *Sichuan* China
169 O9 **Yanzhou** *Shandong* China
166 C6 **Yao** Japan
170 C6 **Yao'an** *Yunnan* China
169 K8 **Yaodian** *Shaanxi* China
171 K4 **Yaoli** *Jiangxi* China
168 E7 **Yaoquanzi** *Gansu* China
166 F5 **Yaotsu** Japan
89 H6 **Yaoundé** Cameroon
169 K9 **Yaoxian** *Shaanxi* China
159 D10 **Yao Yai, Ko** *i.* Thai.
169 L7 **Yaozhen** *Shaanxi* China
153 I5 **Yap** *i.* Micronesia
136 E4 **Yapacana, Parque Nacional** *nat. park* Venez.
138 D3 **Yapacani** *r.* Bol.
88 E4 **Yapei** Ghana
153 I7 **Yapen** *i. Papua* Indon.
153 I7 **Yapen, Selat** *sea chan. Papua* Indon.
144 F3 **Yapeyú** Arg.
119 J3 **Yaphank** *NY* U.S.A.
207 H5 **Yappar** *r. Qld* Austr.
31 K6 **Yapton** *West Sussex, England* U.K.
216 E5 **Yap Trench** *sea feature* N. Pacific Ocean
137 G4 **Yapukarri** Guyana
209 I9 **Yapuparra Aboriginal Reserve** *W.A.* Austr.
126 D4 **Yaqui** *r.* Mex.
14 K4 **Yar** Rus. Fed.
130 E3 **Yara** Cuba
136 D2 **Yaracal** Venez.
136 D2 **Yaracuy** *state* Venez.
Yaradzha Turkm. *see* **Yaradzhi**
184 G2 **Yaradzhi** Turkm.
207 J8 **Yaraka** *Qld* Austr.
Yarangüme Turkey *see* **Tavas**
14 I4 **Yaransk** Rus. Fed.
Yardan Uzbek. *see* **Yordon**
204 E5 **Yardea** *S.A.* Austr.
79 L6 **Yardımcı Burnu** *pt* Turkey
191 J7 **Yardımlı** Azer.
118 F4 **Yardley** *PA* U.S.A.
173 J12 **Yardoi** *Xizang* China
118 F4 **Yardville** *NJ* U.S.A.
Yardymly Azer. *see* **Yardımlı**
31 P3 **Yare** *r. England* U.K.
14 K3 **Yarega** Rus. Fed.
16 D5 **Yaremcha** Ukr.
199 G2 **Yaren** Nauru
14 J3 **Yarenga** *r.* Rus. Fed.
129 K8 **Yareni** Mex.
14 J3 **Yarensk** Rus. Fed.
17 M4 **Yares'ky** Ukr.
136 C5 **Yari** *r.* Col.
166 G3 **Yariga-take** *mt.* Japan
186 G8 **Yarīm** Yemen
206 G6 **Yaringa** *watercourse Qld* Austr.
137 H4 **Yaripo** Brazil
89 G3 **Yaris** *well* Niger
131 I8 **Yaritagua** Venez.
Yarkand *Xinjiang* China *see* **Shache**
Yarkant *Xinjiang* China *see* **Shache**
173 D7 **Yarkant He** *r.* China
111 R5 **Yarker** *Ont.* Can.
185 O3 **Yarkhun** *r.* Pak.
209 K11 **Yarle Lakes** *salt flat S.A.* Austr.
77 L8 **Yarlovo** Bulg.
173 L12 **Yarlung Zangbo** *r.* China
alt. **Dihang (China),**
alt. **Jamuna (Bangladesh),**
alt. **Yarlung Zangbo (China),**
conv. **Brahmaputra**
29 O4 **Yarm** *Stockton-on-Tees, England* U.K.
16 F4 **Yarmolyntsi** Ukr.
109 H5 **Yarmouth** *N.S.* Can.
31 J6 **Yarmouth** *Isle of Wight, England* U.K.
117 □O5 **Yarmouth** *ME* U.S.A.
190 D6 **Yarmuk** *r.* Asia
125 T7 **Yarnell** *AZ* U.S.A.
31 J4 **Yarnton** *Oxfordshire, England* U.K.
19 X9 **Yarok** Rus. Fed.
19 N6 **Yaromina** Belarus
17 M3 **Yaroshivka** Ukr.
17 M2 **Yaroslavets'** Ukr.
19 R1 **Yaroslavichi** Rus. Fed.
19 W4 **Yaroslavl'** Rus. Fed.
Yaroslavl Oblast *admin. div.* Rus. Fed. *see* **Yaroslavskaya Oblast'**
191 B1 **Yaroslavskaya** Rus. Fed.
19 W4 **Yaroslavskaya Oblast'** *admin. div.* Rus. Fed.
162 H6 **Yaroslavskiy** Rus. Fed.
207 J4 **Yarrabah Aboriginal Reserve** *Qld* Austr.
207 I3 **Yarraden** *Qld* Austr.
205 J7 **Yarra Junction** *Vic.* Austr.
206 C4 **Yarralin Aboriginal Land** *res. N.T.* Austr.
208 C6 **Yarraloola** *W.A.* Austr.
205 K8 **Yarram** *Vic.* Austr.
207 M9 **Yarraman** *Qld* Austr.
205 J7 **Yarrawonga** *Vic.* Austr.
209 C10 **Yarra Yarra Lakes** *salt flat W.A.* Austr.
208 F6 **Yarrie** *W.A.* Austr.
207 J9 **Yarronvale** *Qld* Austr.
207 J6 **Yarrowmere** *Qld* Austr.
179 N5 **Yartö Tra La** *pass Xizang* China
192 J3 **Yartsevo** *Krasnoyarskiy Kray* Rus. Fed.
19 P6 **Yartsevo** *Smolenskaya Oblast'* Rus. Fed.
173 H12 **Yaru** *r.* China
136 C3 **Yarumal** Col.
170 B3 **Yarwa** *Sichuan* China
191 H2 **Yaryk-Aul** Rus. Fed.
170 A4 **Yarzhong** *Xizang* China
91 D5 **Yasa** Dem. Rep. Congo
177 J1 **Yasai** *r. W. Bengal* India
166 B4 **Yasaka** *Kyōto* Japan
167 G3 **Yasaka** *Nagano* Japan
167 L3 **Yasato** Japan
201 □1 **Yasawa** *i.* Fiji
201 □1 **Yasawa Group** *is* Fiji
16 D5 **Yasen'** Ukr.
17 R7 **Yaseni** *r.* Rus. Fed.
77 O7 **Yasenkovo** Bulg.
15 G7 **Yasenskaya** Rus. Fed.
15 H7 **Yashalta** Rus. Fed.
89 G3 **Yashi** Nigeria
89 F4 **Yashikera** Nigeria
185 O3 **Yashilkŭl** *l.* Tajik.
164 R7 **Yashima** Japan
165 J13 **Ya-shima** *i.* Japan
167 H2 **Yashira** Japan
166 A6 **Yashiro** Japan
165 J13 **Yashiro-jima** *i.* Japan
15 K5 **Yashkino** Rus. Fed.
15 I7 **Yashkul'** Rus. Fed.
178 D1 **Yasin** Jammu and Kashmir
Yasinovataya Ukr. *see* **Yasynuvata**
16 D5 **Yasinya** Ukr.
18 K9 **Yaskavichy** Belarus
191 K5 **Yaşma** Azer.
191 K5 **Yaşma Adası** *i.* Azer.
77 P8 **Yasna Polyana** Bulg.
19 U7 **Yasnogorsk** Rus. Fed.
17 Q5 **Yasnohirka** Ukr.
16 J3 **Yasnohorodka** Ukr.
162 F2 **Yasnyy** *Amurskaya Oblast'* Rus. Fed.
182 H2 **Yasnyy** *Orenburgskaya Oblast'* Rus. Fed.
158 G7 **Yasothon** Thai.
205 L6 **Yass** *N.S.W.* Austr.
205 L6 **Yass** *r. N.S.W.* Austr.
Yassı Burnu *c.* Cyprus *see* **Plakoti, Cape**
79 K5 **Yassıhüyük** Turkey
19 N4 **Yasski** Rus. Fed.
191 C6 **Yastıktepe** Turkey
17 Q2 **Yastrebovka** Rus. Fed.
17 N2 **Yastrubyne** Ukr.
166 D5 **Yasu** Japan
165 K13 **Yasuda** Japan
165 K11 **Yasugi** Japan
184 D6 **Yāsūj** Iran
136 C5 **Yasuní, Parque Nacional** *nat. park* Ecuador
167 G5 **Yasuoka** Japan
199 G3 **Yasur** *vol.* Vanuatu
167 H1 **Yasuzuka** Japan
16 F1 **Yasyel'da** *r.* Belarus
17 Q5 **Yasynuvata** Ukr.
89 I1 **Yat** *well* Niger
138 D2 **Yata** *r.* Bol.
90 D2 **Yata** *r.* C.A.R.
79 J5 **Yatağan** Turkey
89 F3 **Yatakala** Niger
93 C5 **Yata Plateau** Kenya
200 □5 **Yaté** New Caledonia
30 H4 **Yate** *South Gloucestershire, England* U.K.
31 K5 **Yateley** *Hampshire, England* U.K.
106 H2 **Yates** *r. Alta/N.W.T.* Can.
121 H7 **Yates Center** *KS* U.S.A.
107 L2 **Yathkyed Lake** *Nunavut* Can.
205 J5 **Yathong Nature Reserve** *N.S.W.* Austr.
129 I5 **Yatipan** Mex.
90 E4 **Yatolema** Dem. Rep. Congo
166 E5 **Yatomi** Japan
Yatou *Shandong* China *see* **Rongcheng**
67 D9 **Yatova** Spain
16 J5 **Yatran'** *r.* Ukr.
167 H4 **Yatsuga-take** *vol.* Japan
167 H3 **Yatsuga-take-Chūshin-kōgen Quasi National Park** Japan
166 F2 **Yatsuo** Japan
165 H14 **Yatsushiro** Japan
165 H14 **Yatsushiro-kai** *b.* Japan
190 D7 **Yaṭṭa** West Bank
30 G5 **Yatton** *North Somerset, England* U.K.
138 B3 **Yauca** Peru
138 B3 **Yauca** *r.* Peru
131 □1 **Yauco** Puerto Rico
138 A2 **Yauli** Peru
136 D5 **Yauna Maloca** Col.
138 C3 **Yauri** Peru
138 B3 **Yauricocha** Peru
129 H7 **Yautepec** *Morelos* Mex.
129 K9 **Yautepec** *Oaxaca* Mex.
171 □J7 **Yau Tong** *b. H.K.* China
138 B3 **Yauyos** Peru
126 □P11 **Yauyupe** Hond.
Yavan Tajik. *see* **Yovon**
136 D6 **Yavari** *r.* Brazil/Peru *alt.* **Javari**
126 E4 **Yávaros** Mex.
178 G9 **Yavatmal** *Mahar.* India
138 B3 **Yavero** *r.* Peru
137 E3 **Yaví, Cerro** *mt.* Venez.
17 L6 **Yavkyne** Ukr.
183 M1 **Yavlenka** Kazakh.
55 L6 **Yavora** Ukr.
16 D5 **Yavoriv** *Ivano-Frankivs'ka Oblast'* Ukr.
16 C4 **Yavoriv** *L'vivs'ka Oblast'* Ukr.
20 U2 **Yavr** *r.* Fin./Rus. Fed.
190 F2 **Yavuzlu** Turkey
166 C6 **Yawata** Japan
165 J13 **Yawatahama** Japan
173 F8 **Yawatongguz He** *r.* China
173 F8 **Yawatongguzlangar** *Xinjiang* China
158 B4 **Yaw Chaung** *r.* Myanmar
158 C4 **Yawng-hwe** Myanmar
127 N9 **Yaxchilan** *tourist site* Guat.
Yaxian *Hainan* China *see* **Sanya**
31 L2 **Yaxley** *Cambridgeshire, England* U.K.
191 C7 **Yaygın** Turkey
191 A6 **Yaylabaşı** Turkey
190 E3 **Yayladağı** Turkey
191 B6 **Yayladere** Turkey
191 D6 **Yayladüzü** Turkey
14 L4 **Yayva** Rus. Fed.
158 B3 **Yazagyo** Myanmar
184 F6 **Yazd** Iran
184 F6 **Yazd** *prov.* Iran
184 I5 **Yazdān** Iran
184 E6 **Yazd-e Khvāst** Iran
Yazgulemskiy Khrebet *mts* Tajik. *see* **Yazgulom, Qatorkŭhi**
185 N2 **Yazgulom, Qatorkŭhi** *mts* Tajik.
19 P3 **Yazhelbitsy** Rus. Fed.
188 I4 **Yazıhan** Turkey
79 J5 **Yazıkent** Turkey
79 I6 **Yazıköy** Turkey
79 L5 **Yazır** Turkey
121 J9 **Yazoo** *r. MS* U.S.A.
121 J9 **Yazoo City** *MS* U.S.A.
167 L2 **Yazukami** Japan
14 L3 **Yaz'va** *r.* Rus. Fed.
84 B4 **Ybakoura** *well* Chad
59 L3 **Ybbs** *r.* Austria
59 L3 **Ybbs an der Donau** Austria
59 K4 **Ybbsitz** Austria
139 F6 **Ybycui** Para.
43 C7 **Ychoux** France
42 I5 **Ydes** France
22 F6 **Yding Skovhøj** *hill* Denmark
78 E5 **Ydra** Greece
78 E5 **Ydra** *i.* Greece
78 E5 **Ydras, Kolpos** *sea chan.* Greece
158 C7 **Ye** Myanmar
158 C7 **Ye** *r.* Myanmar
29 N6 **Yeadon** *West Yorkshire, England* U.K.
30 E7 **Yealmpton** *Devon, England* U.K.
158 B2 **Yebawmi** Myanmar
84 C4 **Yebbi-Bou** Chad
84 C4 **Yebbi-Souma** Chad
63 L9 **Yébenes, Sierra de** *mts* Spain
63 O8 **Yebra** Spain
66 E3 **Yebra de Basa** Spain
173 C8 **Yecheng** *Xinjiang* China
67 C10 **Yecla** Spain
62 H7 **Yecla de Yeltes** Spain
126 E3 **Yécora** Mex.
129 K6 **Yecuautla** Mex.
158 C5 **Yedashe** Myanmar
176 E6 **Yedatore** *Karnataka* India
92 C3 **YeDebub Bihēroch Bihēreseboch na Hizboch** *admin. reg.* Eth.
79 K6 **Yedi Burun Başı** *pt* Turkey
191 B6 **Yedisu** Turkey
190 D3 **Yeditepe** Turkey
14 I3 **Yedoma** Rus. Fed.
84 C4 **Yedri** *well* Chad
19 Q4 **Yedrovo** Rus. Fed.
18 K6 **Yedy** Belarus
92 D3 **Yeed** Eth.
208 G4 **Yeeda River** *W.A.* Austr.
115 G12 **Yeehaw Junction** *FL* U.S.A.
204 E6 **Yeelanna** *S.A.* Austr.
19 R2 **Yefimovskiy** Rus. Fed.
19 V8 **Yefremov** Rus. Fed.
89 I2 **Yeggueba** *well* Niger
191 G6 **Yeghegis** *r.* Armenia
191 G6 **Yeghegnadzor** Armenia
191 F5 **Yeghvard** Armenia
183 Q3 **Yegindybulak** Kazakh.
183 M2 **Yegindykol'** Kazakh.
15 H7 **Yegorlyk** *r.* Rus. Fed.
15 H7 **Yegorlykskaya** Rus. Fed.
162 J6 **Yegorova, Mys** *pt* Rus. Fed.
19 Q6 **Yegor'ye** Rus. Fed.
19 W6 **Yegor'yevsk** Rus. Fed.
65 K4 **Yeguas** *r.* Spain
65 K4 **Yeguas, Embalse del** *resr* Spain
146 B4 **Yeguas, Volcán** *vol.* Chile
89 F4 **Yégué** Togo
92 A3 **Yei** Sudan
92 A3 **Yei** *r.* Sudan
171 J3 **Yeji** *Anhui* China
88 E4 **Yeji** Ghana
Yejiaji *Anhui* China *see* **Yeji**
192 H4 **Yekaterinburg** Rus. Fed.
Yekaterinodar Rus. Fed. *see* **Krasnodar**
162 F3 **Yekaterinoslavka** Rus. Fed.
19 V9 **Yekaterinovka** *Lipetskaya Oblast'* Rus. Fed.
17 R6 **Yekaterinovka** *Rostovskaya Oblast'* Rus. Fed.
15 I5 **Yekaterinovka** *Saratovskaya Oblast'* Rus. Fed.
191 F2 **Yekatorinogradskaya** Rus. Fed.
Yekhegnadzor Armenia *see* **Yeghegnadzor**
19 Q7 **Yekimovichi** Rus. Fed.
90 D4 **Yekokora** *r.* Dem. Rep. Congo
162 I4 **Yelabuga** *Khabarovskiy Kray* Rus. Fed.
14 J5 **Yelabuga** *Respublika Tatarstan* Rus. Fed.
15 H6 **Yelan'** Rus. Fed.
15 H6 **Yelan'** *r.* Rus. Fed.
15 H6 **Yelan'** *r.* Rus. Fed.
17 K6 **Yelanets'** Ukr.
205 M3 **Yelarbon** *Qld* Austr.
15 H5 **Yelat'ma** Rus. Fed.
184 I2 **Yelbarsli** Turkm.
79 J4 **Yeleğen** Turkey
Yelenovka Ukr. *see* **Zoryns'k**
19 S8 **Yelenskiy** Rus. Fed.
19 V9 **Yelets** Rus. Fed.
14 N2 **Yeletskiy** Rus. Fed.
19 Q3 **Yeligovo** Rus. Fed.
168 H9 **Yeliguan** *Gansu* China
88 C3 **Yélimané** Mali
19 W7 **Yelino** Rus. Fed.
17 N5 **Yelizarove** Ukr.
17 R7 **Yelizavetovka** *Rostovskaya Oblast'* Rus. Fed.
17 T3 **Yelizavetovka** *Voronezhskaya Oblast'* Rus. Fed.
193 P4 **Yelizavety, Mys** *c. Sakhalin* Rus. Fed.
193 Q4 **Yelizovo** Rus. Fed.
15 J5 **Yelkhovka** Rus. Fed.
26 □N1 **Yell** *i. Scotland* U.K.
204 D4 **Yellabina Regional Reserve** *nature res. S.A.* Austr.
176 G4 **Yellandu** *Andhra Prad.* India
176 D5 **Yellapur** *Karnataka* India
176 E3 **Yellareddi** *Andhra Prad.* India
110 D6 **Yellow** *r. WI* U.S.A.
209 E11 **Yellowdine** *W.A.* Austr.
118 F3 **Yellow Frame** *NJ* U.S.A.
106 G4 **Yellowhead Pass** *Alta/B.C.* Can.
118 D4 **Yellow House** *PA* U.S.A.
106 H2 **Yellowknife** *N.W.T.* Can.
106 H2 **Yellowknife** *r. N.W.T.* Can.
205 K5 **Yellow Mountain** *hill N.S.W.* Austr.
Yellow River *r.* China *see* **Huang He**
216 D3 **Yellow Sea** N. Pacific Ocean
116 B9 **Yellow Springs** *OH* U.S.A.
120 D2 **Yellowstone** *r. MT* U.S.A.
122 I4 **Yellowstone Lake** *WY* U.S.A.
122 I4 **Yellowstone National Park** U.S.A.
26 □N1 **Yell Sound** *str. Scotland* U.K.
121 I7 **Yellville** *AR* U.S.A.
122 C3 **Yelm** *WA* U.S.A.
65 N4 **Yelmo** *mt.* Spain
15 H5 **Yel'niki** Rus. Fed.
19 Q7 **Yel'nya** Rus. Fed.
185 J3 **Yeloten** Turkm.
14 K4 **Yelovo** Rus. Fed.
191 G6 **Yelp'in** Armenia
16 I2 **Yel'sk** Belarus
183 S4 **Yel'tay** Kazakh.
62 H7 **Yeltes** *r.* Spain
19 Q5 **Yel'tsy** Rus. Fed.
126 □Q10 **Yelucá** *mt.* Nic.
14 J3 **Yelva** *r.* Rus. Fed.
105 J1 **Yelverton Bay** *Nunavut* Can.
89 G4 **Yelwa** *Kebbi* Nigeria
89 H4 **Yelwa** *Plateau* Nigeria
17 P6 **Yelyseyivka** Ukr.
17 L5 **Yelyzavethradka** Ukr.
168 D7 **Yema Nanshan** *mts* China
172 L7 **Yema Shan** *mts* China
168 E9 **Yematan** *Qinghai* China
168 F8 **Yematan** *Qinghai* China
92 C2 **Yembo** Eth.
63 Q9 **Yémeda** Spain
186 G8 **Yemen** *country* Asia
14 H3 **Yemetsk** Rus. Fed.
16 G3 **Yemil'chyne** Ukr.
Yemişenbükü Turkey *see* **Taşova**
14 H3 **Yemtsa** Rus. Fed.
14 J3 **Yemva** Rus. Fed.
89 I6 **Yen** Cameroon
20 U3 **Yena** Rus. Fed.
89 G5 **Yenagoa** Nigeria
17 R5 **Yenakiyeve** Ukr.
Yenakiyevo Ukr. *see* **Yenakiyeve**
158 B4 **Yenangyat** Myanmar
158 B4 **Yenangyaung** Myanmar
158 B5 **Yenanma** Myanmar
158 G4 **Yên Bai** Vietnam
183 M7 **Yenbekshi** Kazakh.
158 G4 **Yên Châu** Vietnam
205 K6 **Yenda** *N.S.W.* Austr.
89 E4 **Yendi** Ghana
Yêndum *Xizang* China *see* **Zhag'yab**
91 B5 **Yénéganou** Congo
91 C6 **Yenga-Lusundji** Dem. Rep. Congo
158 C4 **Yengan** Myanmar
90 D5 **Yenge** *r.* Dem. Rep. Congo
184 B3 **Yengejeh** Iran
88 C4 **Yengema** Sierra Leone
172 C7 **Yengisar** *Xinjiang* China
172 G6 **Yengisar** *Xinjiang* China
172 H6 **Yengisu** *Xinjiang* China
90 B4 **Yengo** Congo
205 M5 **Yengo National Park** *N.S.W.* Austr.
191 B6 **Yenibaşlar** Turkey
15 F8 **Yeniçağa** Turkey
79 I3 **Yenice** *Çanakkale* Turkey
190 D2 **Yenice** *İçel* Turkey
79 K2 **Yeniceköy** Turkey
188 F4 **Yeniceoba** Turkey
79 I2 **Yeniçiftlik** *Çanakkale* Turkey
79 I1 **Yeniçiftlik** *Tekirdağ* Turkey
191 B7 **Yenidal** Turkey
79 J5 **Yenidere** *r.* Turkey
79 H4 **Yenifoça** Turkey
191 G5 **Yeni Göyçä** Azer.
Yenihan Turkey *see* **Yıldızeli**
79 I5 **Yenihisar** Turkey
191 H5 **Yenikänd** Azer.
191 J5 **Yenikänd** Azer.
190 E2 **Yeniköy** *Hatay* Turkey
79 I4 **Yeniköy** *İzmir* Turkey
79 J3 **Yeniköy** *Kütahya* Turkey
79 K4 **Yeniköy** *Kütahya* Turkey
79 H2 **Yenimuhacirköy** Turkey
79 J5 **Yenipazar** *Aydın* Turkey
79 L2 **Yenipazar** *Bilecik* Turkey
79 I4 **Yenişakran** Turkey
79 K2 **Yenişehir** Turkey
193 J2 **Yenisey** *r.* Rus. Fed.
193 K4 **Yeniseysk** Rus. Fed.
193 K4 **Yeniseyskiy Kryazh** *ridge* Rus. Fed.

Yeniseyskiy Zaliv to Zambue
363

192 I2 Yeniseyskiy Zaliv inlet Rus. Fed.
168 E9 Yeniugou Qinghai China
168 F7 Yeniugou Qinghai China
158 G3 Yên Minh Vietnam
40 H5 Yenne France
15 I7 Yenotayevka Rus. Fed.
30 E6 Yeo r. England U.K.
178 E9 Yeola Mahar. India
209 H9 Yeo Lake salt flat W.A. Austr.
209 H10 Yeo Lake Nature Reserve W.A. Austr.
Yeotmal Mahar. India see Yavatmal
205 L5 Yeoval N.S.W. Austr.
30 G6 Yeovil Somerset, England U.K.
30 G5 Yeovilton Somerset, England U.K.
126 E3 Yepachi Mex.
63 M9 Yepes Spain
19 V8 Yepifan' Rus. Fed.
207 M7 Yeppoon Qld Austr.
15 H5 Yerakhtur Rus. Fed.
128 F2 Yerbabuena Mex.
184 H2 Yerbent Turkm.
193 L3 Yerbogachen Rus. Fed.
176 F7 Yercaud Tamil Nadu India
183 O2 Yerementau, Gory hills Kazakh.
191 F5 Yerevan Armenia
183 O2 Yereymentau Kazakh.
191 J4 Yerfi Azer.
176 E4 Yergara Karnataka India
15 I7 Yergeni hills Rus. Fed.
209 F10 Yerilla W.A. Austr.
124 M3 Yerington NV U.S.A.
79 J5 Yerkesik Turkey
190 A1 Yerköprü Mağarası tourist site Turkey
188 G4 Yerköy Turkey
176 D4 Yerla r. India
162 E2 Yermakovo Rus. Fed.
218 A1 Yermak Plateau sea feature Arctic Ocean
Yermentau Kazakh. see Yereymentau
15 H5 Yermish' Rus. Fed.
14 K2 Yermitsa Rus. Fed.
126 G4 Yermo Mex.
124 P7 Yermo CA U.S.A.
19 Y4 Yermolino Rus. Fed.
162 B2 Yerofey Pavlovich Rus. Fed.
190 C8 Yeroham Israel
36 B7 Yerre r. France
36 D6 Yerres r. France
14 K2 Yersa r. Rus. Fed.
44 F6 Yerseke Neth.
191 F3 Yersh Rus. Fed.
19 R7 Yershi Rus. Fed.
19 P8 Yershichi Rus. Fed.
182 C2 Yershov Rus. Fed.
18 L4 Yershovo Rus. Fed.
19 X1 Yertsevo Rus. Fed.
138 A2 Yerupaja mt. Peru
Yerushalayim Israel/West Bank see Jerusalem
182 B2 Yeruslan r. Rus. Fed.
39 M2 Yerville France
17 T3 Yeryshevka Rus. Fed.
66 C2 Yesa Spain
66 C2 Yesa, Embalse de resr Spain
19 R4 Yesenovichi Rus. Fed.
183 Q6 Yesik Kazakh.
183 L2 Yesil' Kazakh.
190 E2 Yeşil Turkey
79 K5 Yeşildere Burdur Turkey
190 F2 Yeşildere Gaziantep Turkey
190 B1 Yeşildere Karaman Turkey
188 G4 Yeşilhisar Turkey
188 H3 Yeşilırmak r. Turkey
190 F1 Yeşilkent Turkey
79 K3 Yeşilköy Turkey
79 K5 Yeşilova Burdur Turkey
Yeşilova Yozgat Turkey see Sorgun
79 L5 Yeşilyayla Turkey
79 J4 Yeşilyurt Turkey
79 K5 Yeşilyuva Turkey
19 W5 Yesiplevo Rus. Fed.
19 O6 Yes'kovo Rus. Fed.
26 J4 Yesnaby Orkney, Scotland U.K.
147 H2 Yeso Arg.
146 B4 Yeso, Cerro mt. Chile
191 D1 Yessentuki Rus. Fed.
191 D1 Yessentukskaya Rus. Fed.
193 L3 Yessey Rus. Fed.
65 O4 Yeste Spain
30 D6 Yes Tor hill England U.K.
190 D5 Yesud HaMa'ala Israel
65 O4 Yetas de Abajo Spain
205 M3 Yetman N.S.W. Austr.
158 B3 Ye-U Myanmar
38 G8 Yeu, Île d' i. France
17 S3 Yevdakovo Rus. Fed.
Yevlakh Azer. see Yevlax
17 Q1 Yevlanovo Rus. Fed.
191 I5 Yevlax Azer.
17 M8 Yevpatoriya Ukr.
17 M8 Yevpatoriys'kyy, Mys pt Ukr.
40 A2 Yèvre r. France
162 H4 Yevreyskaya Avtonomnaya Oblast' admin. div. Rus. Fed.
19 O6 Yevseyevka Rus. Fed.
17 S3 Yevstratovka Rus. Fed.
17 S5 Yevsuh r. Ukr.
171 I2 Yexian Henan China
183 Q6 Yeygen'yevka Kazakh.
173 F8 Yeyik Xinjiang China
15 G7 Yeysk Rus. Fed.
17 R7 Yeyskiy Liman inlet Rus. Fed.
17 R7 Yeyskoye Ukreplenie Rus. Fed.
172 G6 Yeyungou Xinjiang China
18 N6 Yezerishche, Ozero l. Belarus/Rus. Fed.
14 I2 Yezhuga r. Rus. Fed.
18 M6 Yezyaryshcha Belarus
Y Fali Wales U.K. see Valley
38 F5 Yffiniac France
139 G6 Ygatimí Para.
43 C8 Ygos-St-Saturnin France
40 B3 Ygrande France
139 G6 Yhú Para.
147 I3 Yí r. Uru.
162 D5 Yi'an Heilong. China
186 E6 Yibā, Wādī watercourse Saudi Arabia
170 E4 Yibin Sichuan China
170 E4 Yibin Sichuan China
173 H10 Yibug Caka salt l. China
171 H3 Yichang Hubei China
Yicheng Henan China see Zhumadian
171 I3 Yicheng Hubei China
169 L9 Yicheng Shanxi China
169 M9 Yichuan Henan China
169 L9 Yichuan Shaanxi China
162 F5 Yichun Heilong. China
171 J5 Yichun Jiangxi China
Yidu Shandong China see Qingzhou
170 B3 Yidun Sichuan China
171 J4 Yifeng Jiangxi China
Yiggêtang Qinghai China see Sêrwolungwa
170 A2 Yiggêtang Qinghai China
79 M2 Yığılca Turkey
191 A6 Yiğitler Turkey
190 E2 Yiğityolu Turkey
200 □1 Yigo Guam
Yigu Guam see Yigo
168 E5 Yihatuoli Gansu China
169 M9 Yi He r. Henan China
169 P9 Yi He r. Shandong China
171 K5 Yihuang Jiangxi China
Yijiang Jiangxi China see Yiyang
169 K9 Yijun Shaanxi China
169 S2 Yilaha Heilong. China
162 F5 Yilan Heilong. China
191 B5 Yıldırım Turkey
188 C3 Yıldız Dağları mts Turkey
188 H4 Yıldızeli Turkey
162 C3 Yilehuli Shan mts China
170 D6 Yiliang Yunnan China
170 E5 Yiliang Yunnan China
173 K8 Yiliping Qinghai China
209 D12 Yilliminning W.A. Austr.
162 D5 Yilong Heilong. China
170 F3 Yilong Sichuan China
Yilong Yunnan China see Shiping
170 D7 Yilong Hu l. China
169 O6 Yimatu He r. China
158 F2 Yimen Yunnan China
162 F6 Yimianpo Heilong. China
169 P2 Yimin He r. China
162 B2 Yimuhe Nei Mongol China
169 P9 Yinan Shandong China
158 C6 Yinbaing Myanmar
168 J7 Yinchuan Ningxia China
209 G11 Yindarlgooda, Lake salt flat W.A. Austr.
206 C4 Yingawunarri Aboriginal Land res. N.T. Austr.
171 I3 Yingcheng Hubei China
162 D7 Yingchengzi Jilin China
171 I6 Yingde Guangdong China
170 G9 Yinggehai Hainan China
Yinggen Hainan China see Qiongzhong
171 K2 Ying He r. China
170 A6 Yingjiang Yunnan China
170 D4 Yingjing Sichuan China
169 R6 Yingkou Liaoning China
168 I8 Yingpanshui Ningxia China
171 J3 Yingshan Hubei China
170 F3 Yingshan Sichuan China
171 K2 Yingshang Anhui China
171 K4 Yingtan Jiangxi China
89 H5 Yingui Cameroon
169 M7 Yingxian Shanxi China
Yining Jiangxi China see Xiushui
172 E5 Yining Xinjiang China
172 E5 Yining Xinjiang China
206 B6 Yiningarra Aboriginal Land res. N.T. Austr.
170 G5 Yinjiang Guizhou China
171 J5 Yinkengxu Jiangxi China
158 B3 Yinmabin Myanmar
162 D6 Yinma He r. China
158 C6 Yinnyein Myanmar
169 K6 Yin Shan mts China
173 L11 Yi'ong Nongchang Xizang China
173 L11 Yi'ong Zangbo r. Xizang China
170 C6 Yipinglang Yunnan China
79 L4 Yıprak Turkey
143 E5 Yira Chapéu, Monte mt. Brazil
173 K10 Yiran Co l. Qinghai China
92 C3 Yirga Alem Eth.
92 C3 Yirga Ch'efē Eth.
92 A3 Yirol Sudan
206 F2 Yirrkala N.T. Austr.
169 P3 Yirshi Nei Mongol China
172 I6 Yirtkuq Bulak spring Xinjiang China
Yirxie Nei Mongol China see Yirshi
Yishan Guangxi China see Yizhou
169 P8 Yi Shan mt. Shandong China
169 P8 Yi Shan mts China
169 P9 Yishui Shandong China
156 □ Yishun Sing.
89 I1 Yi Tchouma well Niger
162 D7 Yitong Jilin China
162 D6 Yitong He r. China
158 C3 Yi Tu, Nam r. Myanmar
169 Q1 Yitulihe Nei Mongol China
168 C5 Yiwanquan Xinjiang China
168 D5 Yiwu Xinjiang China
170 C8 Yiwu Yunnan China
169 Q6 Yiwulü Shan mts China
171 K4 Yixian Anhui China
169 N7 Yixian Hebei China
169 Q6 Yixian Liaoning China
162 D2 Yixiken Heilong. China
171 L3 Yixing Jiangsu China
169 O6 Yixun He r. China
171 I4 Yiyang Hunan China
171 K4 Yiyang Jiangxi China
169 P8 Yiyuan Shandong China
171 I6 Yizhang Hunan China
171 L2 Yizheng Jiangsu China
170 G6 Yizhou Guangxi China
Yizhou Hebei China see Yixian
Yizhou Liaoning China see Yixian
20 R5 Ylä-Keitele l. Fin.
21 T6 Ylämaa Fin.
21 Q6 Yläne Fin.
200 □1 Ylig Bay Guam
20 Q5 Ylihärmä Fin.
20 R4 Yli-Ii Fin.
20 R4 Yli-Kärppä Fin.
20 S4 Ylikiiminki Fin.
20 T3 Yli-Kitka l. Fin.
20 Q5 Ylistaro Fin.
20 Q3 Ylitornio Fin.
20 R4 Ylivieska Fin.
20 R3 Ylläs hill Fin.
30 E2 Y Llethr hill Wales U.K.
21 Q6 Ylöjärvi Fin.
105 P2 Ymer Nunatak Greenland
105 P2 Ymer Ø i. Greenland
36 C7 Ymonville France
23 J3 Ymsen l. Sweden
14 K3 Yndin Rus. Fed.
23 M3 Yngaren l. Sweden
23 K2 Yngen l. Sweden
23 N2 Yngern l. Sweden
183 N3 Yntaly Kazakh.
193 O3 Ynykchanskiy Rus. Fed.
Ynys Môn i. Wales U.K. see Anglesey
121 G11 Yoakum TX U.S.A.
89 H4 Yobe state Nigeria
164 R3 Yobetsu-dake vol. Japan
92 D2 Yoboki Djibouti
165 G13 Yobuko Japan
85 H5 Yob Wildlife Reserve nature res. Eritrea
166 B6 Yodo-gawa r. Japan
118 B5 Yoe PA U.S.A.
145 C9 Yogan, Cerro mt. Chile
129 K9 Yogana Mex.
166 D4 Yogo Japan
84 C5 Yogoum well Chad
157 I8 Yogyakarta Indon.
157 I9 Yogyakarta admin. dist. Indon.
106 G5 Yoho National Park B.C. Can.
164 R3 Yoichi Japan
164 S3 Yoichi-dake mt. Japan
173 M9 Yoigilanglêb r. Qinghai China
126 □P10 Yojoa, Lago de l. Hond.
163 E10 Yŏju S. Korea
166 A5 Yōka Japan
89 I6 Yokadouma Cameroon
165 J13 Yokagawara Japan
166 D5 Yōkaichi Japan
167 M4 Yōkaichiba Japan
164 □F18 Yokate-jima i. Nansei-shotō Japan
166 B6 Yokawa Japan
166 E6 Yokkaichi Japan
89 I5 Yoko Cameroon
164 S5 Yokohama Aomori Japan
167 K5 Yokohama Kanagawa Japan
167 I3 Yokokawa Japan
167 L4 Yokoshiba Japan
167 K5 Yokosuka Japan
165 K11 Yokota Japan
164 R7 Yokote Japan
164 R5 Yokotsu-dake mt. Japan
167 J4 Yokoze Japan
178 F3 Yol Hima. Prad. India
89 I4 Yola Nigeria
126 □Q12 Yolaina, Cordillera de mts Nic.
124 J1 Yolla Bolly Middle Eel Wilderness CA U.S.A.
124 K3 Yolo CA U.S.A.
90 D5 Yolombo Dem. Rep. Congo
Yolöten Turkm. see Yeloten
129 J9 Yolotepec Mex.
129 K8 Yolox Mex.
129 I9 Yoloxóchitl Mex.
127 P7 Yoluk Mex.
158 E7 Yom, Mae Nam r. Thai.
165 □2 Yome-jima i. Japan
167 M1 Yomogida-dake hill Japan
88 C5 Yomou Guinea
191 A5 Yomra Turkey
179 N6 Yomtam Arun. Prad. India
42 B2 Yon r. France
200 □1 Yona Guam
164 □1 Yona Okinawa Japan
164 □1 Yonabaru Okinawa Japan
165 K11 Yonago Japan
164 □A22 Yonaguni-jima i. Nansei-shotō Japan
164 □1 Yonaha-dake hill Okinawa Japan
163 E10 Yŏnan N. Korea
164 R6 Yoneshiro-gawa r. Japan
167 I1 Yone-yama hill Japan
164 R9 Yonezawa Japan
204 G5 Yongala S.A. Austr.
163 E11 Yŏng-am S. Korea
171 K6 Yong'an Fujian China
Yongbei Yunnan China see Yongsheng
168 G7 Yongchang Gansu China
171 K2 Yongcheng Henan China
163 F11 Yŏngch'ŏn S. Korea
170 E4 Yongchuan Chongqing China
171 L6 Yongchun Fujian China
170 B6 Yongde Yunnan China
168 H8 Yongdeng Gansu China
171 K6 Yongding Fujian China
Yongding Yunnan China see Yongren
169 O7 Yongding He r. China
163 F10 Yŏngdŏk S. Korea
171 J5 Yongfeng Jiangxi China
172 H5 Yongfengqu Xinjiang China
170 G6 Yongfu Guangxi China
163 E11 Yŏnggwang S. Korea
169 L8 Yonghe Shanxi China
163 E9 Yŏnghŭng N. Korea
163 E9 Yŏnghŭng-man b. N. Korea
165 G11 Yŏngil-man b. S. Korea
162 E7 Yongji Jilin China
171 M4 Yongjia Zhejiang China
168 H9 Yongjing Gansu China
Yongjing Guizhou China see Xifeng
Yongjing Liaoning China see Xifeng
169 M8 Yongjin Qu r. China
163 F10 Yŏngju S. Korea
170 B6 Yongkang Yunnan China
171 M4 Yongkang Zhejiang China
170 C3 Yonglaxi Sichuan China
Yongle Shaanxi China see Zhen'an
163 D8 Yongling Liaoning China
169 N8 Yongnian Hebei China
170 G7 Yongning Guangxi China
Yongning Jiangxi China see Tonggu
168 J7 Yongning Ningxia China
Yongning Sichuan China see Xuyong
170 B6 Yongping Yunnan China
Yongqing Gansu China see Qingshui
170 C5 Yongren Yunnan China
163 E11 Yŏngsan-gang r. S. Korea
170 D4 Yongshan Yunnan China
170 C5 Yongsheng Yunnan China
169 K9 Yongshou Shaanxi China
170 G4 Yongshun Hunan China
171 L6 Yongtai Fujian China
163 F10 Yŏngwol S. Korea
171 I5 Yongxing Hunan China
171 J5 Yongxing Jiangxi China
169 L7 Yongxing Shaanxi China
171 J4 Yongxiu Jiangxi China
171 H5 Yongzhou Hunan China
117 L8 Yonkers NY U.S.A.
36 G8 Yonne dept France
36 E7 Yonne r. France
88 B3 Yonoféré Senegal
89 I2 Yoo Baba well Niger
136 C3 Yopal Col.
172 C7 Yopurga Xinjiang China
126 F4 Yoquivo Mex.
183 N7 Yordon Uzbek.
178 E3 Yordu Jammu and Kashmir
128 F6 Yoricostío Mex.
167 J3 Yorii Japan
209 D11 York W.A. Austr.
111 O6 York Ont. Can.
107 M4 York r. Man. Can.
29 O6 York York, England U.K.
29 O6 York admin. div. England U.K.
121 K9 York AL U.S.A.
120 G5 York NE U.S.A.
118 B5 York PA U.S.A.
115 G8 York SC U.S.A.
207 I1 York, Cape Qld Austr.
29 N5 York, Vale of val. England U.K.
118 B5 York County county PA U.S.A.
207 I2 York Downs Qld Austr.
204 F6 Yorke Peninsula S.A. Austr.
204 F6 Yorketown S.A. Austr.
118 B4 York Haven PA U.S.A.
29 M5 Yorkshire Dales National Park England U.K.
29 P6 Yorkshire Wolds hills England U.K.
118 A4 York Springs PA U.S.A.
107 K5 Yorkton Sask. Can.
116 I11 Yorktown VA U.S.A.
119 H2 Yorktown Heights NY U.S.A.
108 B5 Yorkville IL U.S.A.
126 □P10 Yoro Hond.
166 E5 Yōrō Japan
166 E7 Yoroi-zaki pt Japan
164 □G18 Yoro-jima i. Nansei-shotō Japan
155 F4 Yoronga i. Maluku Indon.
164 □F19 Yoron-tō i. Nansei-shotō Japan
168 J2 Yöröö Gol r. Mongolia
88 D3 Yorosso Mali
124 M4 Yosemite National Park CA U.S.A.
124 M4 Yosemite Village CA U.S.A.
165 J13 Yoshida Ehime Japan
165 J12 Yoshida Hiroshima Japan
167 J3 Yoshida Saitama Japan
167 H6 Yoshida Shizuoka Japan
165 H13 Yoshii Fukuoka Japan
167 I3 Yoshii Gunma Japan
165 L12 Yoshii-gawa r. Japan
167 H1 Yoshikawa Japan
167 M1 Yoshima Japan
166 C7 Yoshino Japan
166 E3 Yoshinodani Japan
166 C7 Yoshino-gawa r. Japan
165 L12 Yoshino-gawa r. Japan
166 D8 Yoshino-Kumano National Park Japan
14 I4 Yoshkar-Ola Rus. Fed.
163 E11 Yŏsu S. Korea
139 E4 Yotau Bol.
164 R4 Yōtei-zan mt. Japan
167 L4 Yotsukaidō Japan
167 M1 Yotsukura Japan
190 D9 Yotvata Israel
92 E3 Yoube well Eth.
106 E5 Youbou B.C. Can.
173 J7 Youdunzi Qinghai China
27 G9 Youghal Rep. of Ireland
27 F9 Youghal Bay Rep. of Ireland
170 G7 You Jiang r. China
29 N7 Youlgreave Derbyshire, England U.K.
169 P8 Youlin Shandong China
90 C5 Youmba Congo
205 L6 Young N.S.W. Austr.
209 F12 Young r. W.A. Austr.
147 I3 Young Uru.
125 V7 Young AZ U.S.A.
202 □ Young, Cape Chatham Is S. Pacific Ocean
204 F4 Younghusband, Lake salt flat S.A. Austr.
204 G6 Younghusband Peninsula S.A. Austr.
213 K2 Young Island Antarctica
202 L5 Young Nicks Head North I. N.Z.
203 D11 Young Range mts South I. N.Z.
107 I5 Youngstown Alta Can.
116 E7 Youngstown OH U.S.A.
116 F7 Youngsville PA U.S.A.
124 J3 Yountville CA U.S.A.
173 J7 Youshashan Qinghai China
170 H4 You Shui r. China
86 C2 Youssoufia Morocco
88 D3 Youvarou Mali
171 L5 Youxi Fujian China
171 I5 Youxian Hunan China
170 G4 Youyang Chongqing China
162 G5 Youyi Heilong. China
172 H2 Youyi Feng mt. China/Rus. Fed.
169 M7 Youyu Shanxi China
185 M2 Yovon Tajik.
205 J3 Yowah watercourse Qld Austr.
209 E8 Yowereena Hill W.A. Austr.
31 I2 Yoxall Staffordshire, England U.K.
31 P3 Yoxford Suffolk, England U.K.
188 G4 Yozgat Turkey
139 G5 Ypé-Jhú Para.
39 L2 Yport France
20 R4 Yppäri Fin.
Ypres West-Vlaanderen Belgium see Ieper
111 K7 Ypsilanti MI U.S.A.
122 C6 Yreka CA U.S.A.
Yr Wyddfa mt. Wales U.K. see Snowdon
30 E3 Ysbyty Ystwyth Ceredigion, Wales U.K.
36 E2 Yser r. France alt. IJzer (Belgium)
44 I6 Ysselsteyn Neth.
41 E6 Yssingeaux France
23 J6 Ystad Sweden
30 E4 Ystalyfera Neath Port Talbot, Wales U.K.
30 F1 Ystrad r. Wales U.K.
30 E4 Ystradgynlais Powys, Wales U.K.
30 D3 Ystwyth r. Wales U.K.
183 P6 Ysyk-Ata Kyrg.
Ysyk-Köl Kyrg. see Balykchy
183 R7 Ysyk-Köl admin. div. Kyrg.
183 Q6 Ysyk-Köl salt l. Kyrg.
26 L8 Ythan r. Scotland U.K.
Y Trallwng Powys, Wales U.K. see Welshpool
22 C1 Ytre Samlen b. Norway
193 O3 Ytyk-Kyuyel' Rus. Fed.
155 F4 Yu i. Maluku Indon.
190 B8 Yu'alliq, Jabal mt. Egypt
171 H3 Yuan'an Hubei China
169 P5 Yuanbaoshan Nei Mongol China
170 G6 Yuanbao Shan mt. Guangxi China
171 I4 Yuanjiang Hunan China
170 C7 Yuanjiang Yunnan China
170 H4 Yuan Jiang r. Hunan China
170 D7 Yuan Jiang r. Yunnan China
171 M6 Yüanli Taiwan
169 Q2 Yuanlin Nei Mongol China
170 H4 Yuanling Hunan China
Yuanma Yunnan China see Yuanmou
170 C6 Yuanmou Yunnan China
169 M7 Yuanping Shanxi China
169 L9 Yuanqu Shanxi China
168 F7 Yuanshanzi Gansu China
170 D7 Yuanyang Yunnan China
Yuanyang Yunnan China see Xinjie
166 B7 Yuasa Japan
186 B2 Yub'ā i. Saudi Arabia
124 K2 Yuba City CA U.S.A.
164 S3 Yūbari Japan
164 T3 Yūbari-dake mt. Japan
164 T3 Yūbari-sanchi mts Japan
170 F4 Yubei Chongqing China
164 U2 Yūbetsu Japan
164 U2 Yūbetsu-gawa r. Japan
90 E3 Yubu Sudan
124 O7 Yucaipa CA U.S.A.
127 N8 Yucatán pen. Mex.
127 O7 Yucatán state Mex.
127 P6 Yucatan Channel Cuba/Mex.
125 R7 Yucca AZ U.S.A.
125 P5 Yucca Lake NV U.S.A.
125 P7 Yucca Valley CA U.S.A.
191 C7 Yücetepe Turkey
169 N9 Yucheng Henan China
169 O8 Yucheng Shandong China
Yucheng Sichuan China see Ya'an
138 D3 Yucumo Bol.
19 U5 Yudino Moskovskaya Oblast' Rus. Fed.
14 J5 Yudino Respublika Tatarstan Rus. Fed.
14 G4 Yudino Yaroslavskaya Oblast' Rus. Fed.
162 B2 Yudi Shan mt. China
193 O4 Yudoma r. Rus. Fed.
171 J6 Yudu Jiangxi China
Yuecheng Sichuan China see Yuexi
170 F3 Yuechi Sichuan China
169 R4 Yueliang Pao l. China
206 C7 Yuendumu N.T. Austr.
206 C7 Yuendumu Aboriginal Land res. N.T. Austr.
171 □J7 Yuen Long H.K. China
171 M4 Yueqing Zhejiang China
171 K3 Yuexi Anhui China
170 D4 Yuexi Sichuan China
171 I4 Yueyang Hunan China
171 I4 Yueyang Hunan China
14 L4 Yug Rus. Fed.
14 I3 Yug r. Rus. Fed.
171 K4 Yugan Jiangxi China
167 J5 Yugawara Japan
173 L9 Yuge Qinghai China
190 B1 Yuğluk Dağı mts Turkey
14 K4 Yugo-Kamskiy Rus. Fed.
Yugo-Osetinskaya Avtonomnaya Oblast' aut. reg. Georgia see Samkhret' Oset'i
192 H3 Yugorsk Rus. Fed.
14 M1 Yugorskiy Poluostrov pen. Rus. Fed.
14 M2 Yugud-Vayskiy Natsional'nyy Park nat. park Rus. Fed.
171 M3 Yuhang Zhejiang China
169 M7 Yu He r. China
171 M4 Yuhuan Zhejiang China
169 O8 Yuhuang Ding mt. Shandong China
167 I5 Yui Japan
209 D9 Yuin W.A. Austr.
171 K4 Yujiang Jiangxi China
170 H7 Yu Jiang r. China
Yujin Sichuan China see Qianwei
193 Q3 Yukagirskoye Ploskogor'ye plat. Rus. Fed.
14 K4 Yukamenskoye Rus. Fed.
191 F7 Yukarıbalçıklı Turkey
79 I3 Yukarıbey Turkey
191 B5 Yukarıcanören Turkey
191 D4 Yukarıgündeş Turkey
191 E5 Yukarıkaragüney Turkey
79 M3 Yukarı Sakarya Ovaları plain Turkey
191 D5 Yukarısarıkamış Turkey
188 G4 Yukarısarıkaya Turkey
18 L5 Yukhavichy Belarus
15 J5 Yukhmachi Rus. Fed.
19 S7 Yukhnov Rus. Fed.
19 N5 Yukhovo Rus. Fed.
91 C5 Yuki Dem. Rep. Congo
165 K12 Yuki Japan
167 K3 Yūki Japan
104 B3 Yukon r. Can./U.S.A.
104 D3 Yukon-Charley Rivers National Preserve nature res. AK U.S.A.
106 B2 Yukon Crossing Y.T. Can.
106 C2 Yukon Territory admin. div. Can.
189 L5 Yüksekova Turkey
165 H13 Yukuhashi Japan
206 C8 Yulara N.T. Austr.
182 G1 Yuldybayevo Rus. Fed.
208 E6 Yule r. W.A. Austr.
207 L9 Yuleba Qld Austr.
115 G10 Yulee FL U.S.A.
172 H6 Yuli Xinjiang China
171 M7 Yüli Taiwan
170 H7 Yulin Guangxi China
170 G9 Yulin Hainan China
169 K7 Yulin Shaanxi China
170 C5 Yulong Xueshan mt. Yunnan China
125 R9 Yuma AZ U.S.A.
120 D5 Yuma CO U.S.A.
125 R9 Yuma Desert AZ U.S.A.
182 G1 Yumaguzino Rus. Fed.
204 D4 Yumbarra Conservation Park nature res. S.A. Austr.
92 A4 Yumbe Uganda
146 A5 Yumbel Chile
90 C5 Yumbi Bandundu Dem. Rep. Congo
90 E5 Yumbi Maniema Dem. Rep. Congo
136 B4 Yumbo Col.
173 G11 Yumco Xizang China
168 E7 Yumen Gansu China
168 E7 Yumendongzhan Gansu China
172 K6 Yumenguan Gansu China
168 E6 Yumenzhen Gansu China
172 F3 Yumin Xinjiang China
168 E4 Yumt Uul mt. Mongolia
190 D2 Yumurtalık Turkey
209 C10 Yuna W.A. Austr.
130 I4 Yuna r. Dom. Rep.
188 E4 Yunak Turkey
17 O2 Yunakivka Ukr.
171 H7 Yunan Guangdong China
171 I7 Yun'an Guangdong China
104 A4 Yunaska Island AK U.S.A.
138 D5 Yunchara Bol.
169 N9 Yuncheng Shandong China
169 L9 Yuncheng Shanxi China
191 C5 Yüncüler Turkey
209 G10 Yundamindera W.A. Austr.
171 I7 Yunfu Guangdong China
138 D4 Yungas reg. Bol.
138 C6 Yungay Antofagasta Chile
146 A5 Yungay Bíobío Chile
138 C4 Yungayo Peru
170 D6 Yungui Gaoyuan plat. Guizhou/Yunnan China
Yunhe Jiangsu China see Pizhou
171 L4 Yunhe Zhejiang China
170 H7 Yunkai Dashan mts China
206 C7 Yunkanjini Aboriginal Land res. N.T. Austr.
Yunling Fujian China see Yunxiao
170 B5 Yun Ling mts Yunnan China
170 B6 Yunlong Yunnan China
171 I3 Yunmeng Hubei China
170 C6 Yunnan prov. China
17 R5 Yunokomunarivs'k Ukr.
167 J1 Yunotani Japan
165 J11 Yunotsu Japan
65 J7 Yunquera Spain
63 N7 Yunquera de Henares Spain
171 I3 Yun Shui r. China
204 G5 Yunta S.A. Austr.
190 A2 Yunt Dağı mt. Turkey
79 K3 Yunuslar Turkey
171 H7 Yunwu Shan mts China
170 H2 Yunxi Hubei China
Yunxi Sichuan China see Yanting
170 H2 Yunxian Hubei China
170 C6 Yunxian Yunnan China
171 K7 Yunxiao Fujian China
14 M2 Yun'yakha r. Rus. Fed.
170 G3 Yunyang Chongqing China
171 I2 Yunyang Henan China
Yupin Yunnan China see Pingbian
170 G5 Yuping Guizhou China
171 L3 Yuqian Zhejiang China
170 F5 Yuqing Guizhou China
138 D5 Yura Bol.
138 D5 Yura r. Bol.
166 B8 Yura Japan
138 C4 Yura Peru
136 B6 Yuracyacu Peru
166 B5 Yura-gawa r. Japan
164 R4 Yūrappu-dake mt. Japan
17 S3 Yurasovka Rus. Fed.
18 I7 Yuratsishki Belarus
16 I2 Yuravichy Belarus
205 N3 Yuraygir National Park N.S.W. Austr.
173 H9 Yurba Co l. Xizang China
17 Q4 Yurchenkove Ukr.
128 E5 Yurécuaro Mex.
190 D2 Yürekli Turkey
192 J4 Yurga Rus. Fed.
136 B6 Yurimaguas Peru
14 I4 Yurino Rus. Fed.
128 F5 Yuriria Mex.
128 F5 Yuriria, Laguna l. Mex.
191 H1 Yurkovka Rus. Fed.
14 K4 Yurla Rus. Fed.
17 T1 Yurlovka Rus. Fed.
14 I2 Yuroma Rus. Fed.
17 Q8 Yurovka Rus. Fed.
79 I2 Yürük Turkey
173 E7 Yurungkax He r. China
164 W3 Yururi-jima i. Japan
14 J4 Yur'ya Rus. Fed.
14 K2 Yur'yakha r. Rus. Fed.
Yuryev Estonia see Tartu
14 H4 Yur'yevets Ivanovskaya Oblast' Rus. Fed.
19 X5 Yur'yevets Vladimirskaya Oblast' Rus. Fed.
19 W5 Yur'yev-Pol'skiy Rus. Fed.
17 P5 Yur''yivka Dnipropetrovs'ka Oblast' Ukr.
17 P7 Yur''yivka Zaporiz'ka Oblast' Ukr.
126 □P11 Yuscarán Hond.
171 L5 Yushan Fujian China
171 L4 Yushan Jiangxi China
171 M7 Yü Shan mt. Taiwan
171 M4 Yushan Liedao is China
169 M8 Yushe Shanxi China
14 K1 Yushino Rus. Fed.
14 F2 Yushkozero Rus. Fed.
162 E6 Yushu Jilin China
170 A2 Yushu Qinghai China
172 H5 Yushugou Xinjiang China
14 J4 Yushut r. Rus. Fed.
15 I7 Yusta Rus. Fed.
189 J3 Yusufeli Turkey
165 K13 Yusuhara Japan
14 K4 Yus'va Rus. Fed.
169 O9 Yutai Shandong China
15 K5 Yutaza Rus. Fed.
169 O7 Yutian Hebei China
173 E8 Yutian Xinjiang China
169 P5 Yutiangao Nei Mongol China
166 G6 Yūtō Japan
Yutpundji Djindiniwirritj res. N.T. Austr. see Roper Bar Aboriginal Land
147 F5 Yutuyaco Arg.
139 F6 Yuty Para.
37 L5 Yutz France
79 K6 Yuva Turkey
191 A5 Yuvacık Turkey
164 □G18 Yuwan-dake hill Nansei-shotō Japan
168 J8 Yuwang Ningxia China
191 I5 Yuxarı Garabağ Kanalı canal Azer.
191 G4 Yuxarı Salahlı Azer.
191 H4 Yuxarı Tala Azer.
171 H3 Yuxi Hubei China
170 D6 Yuxi Yunnan China
170 H3 Yuxiakou Hubei China
169 N7 Yuxian Hebei China
169 M7 Yuxian Shanxi China
171 L3 Yuxikou Anhui China
171 H3 Yuyangguan Hubei China
171 M3 Yuyao Zhejiang China
164 Q7 Yuza Japan
164 R7 Yuzawa Japan
191 F5 Yüzbaşılar Turkey
14 H4 Yuzha Rus. Fed.
17 K7 Yuzhne Ukr.
162 M5 Yuzhno-Kamyshovyy Khrebet ridge Sakhalin Rus. Fed.
Yuzhno-Kazakhstanskaya Oblast' admin. div. Kazakh. see Yuzhnyy Kazakhstan
161 Q3 Yuzhno-Kuril'sk Kuril'skiye O-va Rus. Fed.
193 M4 Yuzhno-Muyskiy Khrebet mts Rus. Fed.
162 M5 Yuzhno-Sakhalinsk Sakhalin Rus. Fed.
191 G1 Yuzhno-Sukhokumsk Rus. Fed.
15 E7 Yuzhnoukrayinsk Ukr.
182 I1 Yuzhnoural'sk Rus. Fed.
183 T1 Yuzhnyy Altayskiy Kray Rus. Fed.
55 I1 Yuzhnyy Kaliningradskaya Oblast' Rus. Fed.
15 H7 Yuzhnyy Rostovskaya Oblast' Rus. Fed.
193 Q4 Yuzhnyy, Mys hd Rus. Fed.
183 V3 Yuzhnyy Altay, Khrebet mts Kazakh.
Yuzhnyy Bug r. Ukr. see Pivdennyy Buh
183 M6 Yuzhnyy Kazakhstan admin. div. Kazakh.
182 G1 Yuzhnyy Ural mts Rus. Fed.
168 I9 Yuzhong Gansu China
Yuzhou Hebei China see Yuxian
169 M9 Yuzhou Henan China
Yuzkuduk Uzbek. see Yuzquduq
182 J6 Yuzquduq Uzbek.
166 A7 Yuzuruha-yama hill Japan
38 G5 Yvel r. France
36 C6 Yvelines dept France
70 B2 Yverdon Switz.
39 M2 Yvetot France
38 G5 Yvignac France
45 G8 Yvoir Belgium
40 I4 Yvoire France
70 B2 Yvonand Switz.
158 B4 Ywamun Myanmar
158 C5 Ywathit Myanmar
23 M4 Yxern l. Sweden
23 M3 Yxningen l. Sweden
23 M3 Yxnö i. Sweden
184 H1 Ylanly Turkm.
96 C9 Yzerfontein S. Africa
96 C9 Yzerfonteinpunt pt S. Africa
40 C3 Yzeure France
39 M8 Yzeures-sur-Creuse France

Z

Zaamin Uzbek. see Zomin
86 E2 Za, Oued r. Morocco
129 K9 Zaachila Mex.
96 H9 Zaaimansdal S. Africa
45 E6 Zaamslag Neth.
44 G4 Zaandam Neth.
44 G4 Zaandijk Neth.
77 O5 Zăbala r. Romania
76 I5 Žabalj Vojvodina, Srbija Serb. and Mont.
189 K5 Zāb al Kabīr, Nahr az r. Iraq
18 K4 Zabalova Latvia
184 G4 Zabānābād Iran
186 C4 Zabarjad, Jazīrat i. Egypt
189 K6 Zāb aş Şaghīr, Nahr az r. Iraq
169 O2 Zabaykal'sk Rus. Fed.
75 □ Żabbar Malta
56 F2 Žabčice Czech Rep.
184 A4 Zab-e Kuchek r. Iran
51 I8 Zabeltitz-Treugeböhla Ger.
90 E4 Zabia Dem. Rep. Congo
55 I3 Żabia Wola Pol.
71 Q4 Zabiče Slovenia
186 F8 Zabīd Yemen
186 F8 Zabīd, Wādī watercourse Yemen
55 J2 Zabiele Pol.
55 J3 Ząbki Pol.
54 E5 Ząbkowice Śląskie Pol.
55 L4 Zabłocie Pol.
55 L2 Zabłudów Pol.
59 O8 Žabno Croatia
55 I5 Żabno Pol.
68 E2 Zabok Croatia
57 H2 Žabokreky Slovakia
185 I6 Zābol Iran
185 I8 Zābolī Iran
16 E5 Zabolotiv Ukr.
16 D2 Zabolottya Ukr.
47 H2 Zaborski Park Krajobrazowy Pol.
19 S2 Zabor'ye Rus. Fed.
50 K4 Żabów Pol.
54 D2 Żabowo Pol.
173 H11 Zabqung Xizang China
77 J4 Zăbrani Romania
191 K5 Zabrat Azer.
88 E4 Zabré Burkina
56 F2 Zábřeh Czech Rep.
54 G5 Zabrze Pol.
185 L5 Zābul prov. Afgh.
182 D4 Zaburun'ye Kazakh.
16 I3 Zabuyannya Ukr.
16 C2 Zabuzhzhya Ukr.
89 F4 Zabzugu Ghana
127 O10 Zacapa Guat.
129 J6 Zacapoaxtla Mex.
128 F6 Zacapu Mex.
128 G7 Zacapuato Mex.
140 C4 Zacarias r. Brazil
127 N8 Zacatal Mex.
128 E3 Zacatecas Mex.
128 E2 Zacatecas state Mex.
126 □O11 Zacatecoluca El Salvador
129 I6 Zacatelco Mex.
129 H7 Zacatepec Morelos Mex.
129 J9 Zacatepec Oaxaca Mex.
129 L8 Zacatepec Oaxaca Mex.
129 J6 Zacatlán Mex.
182 D2 Zachagansk Kazakh.
78 C5 Zacharo Greece
54 F2 Zacharzyn Pol.
53 O4 Zachenberg Ger.
17 O4 Zachepylivka Ukr.
54 D2 Zachodniopomorskie prov. Pol.
128 D5 Zacoalco Mex.
129 H7 Zacualpán Mex.
128 B4 Zacualpan Nayarit Mex.
129 I5 Zacualpan Veracruz Mex.
129 I5 Zacualtipán Mex.
Zacynthus i. Greece see Zakynthos
55 L3 Zaczopki Pol.
86 D2 Zad, Col du pass Morocco
68 E3 Zadar Croatia
68 E3 Zadarski Kanal sea chan. Croatia
16 J2 Zaderiyivka Ukr.
159 D9 Zadetkale Kyun i. Myanmar
159 D10 Zadetkyi Kyun i. Myanmar
159 C7 Zadi Myanmar
173 L10 Zadoi Qinghai China
19 V9 Zadonsk Rus. Fed.
63 O3 Zadorra r. Spain
185 M5 Zadran reg. Afgh.
19 N6 Zadubrowye Belarus
57 G2 Zádveřice Czech Rep.
19 N6 Zadzyetuni Belarus
85 G2 Za'farānah Egypt
190 A9 Za'farānah, Ra's pt Egypt
65 K7 Zafarraya Spain
185 P5 Zafarwal Pak.
75 I8 Zafferana Etnea Sicilia Italy
74 F7 Zafferano, Capo c. Sicilia Italy
79 H6 Zafora i. Greece
64 G4 Zafra Spain
63 O9 Zafra de Záncara Spain
63 Q8 Zafrilla Spain
63 Q8 Zafrilla, Sierra de mts Spain
86 C3 Zag Morocco
59 H7 Žaga Slovenia
54 D4 Żagań Pol.
18 G5 Žagarė Lith.
73 J4 Zagarolo Italy
Zagazig Egypt see Az Zaqāzīq
191 F4 Zages Georgia
184 G4 Zaghdeh well Iran
184 D4 Zāgheh Iran
184 B4 Zāgheh-ye Bālā Iran
87 H1 Zaghouan Tunisia
69 C7 Zaghouan admin. div. Tunisia
55 I5 Zagnańsk Pol.
77 O5 Zagon Romania
78 E3 Zagora Greece
86 D3 Zagora Morocco
59 M7 Zagorje reg. Croatia
71 Q4 Zagorje Slovenia
68 E2 Zagorje ob Savi Slovenia
54 F3 Zagórów Pol.
Zagorsk Rus. Fed. see Sergiyev Posad
55 K6 Zagórz Pol.
65 K6 Zagra Spain
77 M9 Zagrazhden Bulg.
68 E3 Zagreb Croatia
54 D4 Zagrodno Pol.
184 B4 Zagros, Kūhhā-ye mts Iran
Zagros Mountains Iran see Zagros, Kūhhā-ye
77 J6 Žagubica Srbija Serb. and Mont.
173 I11 Za'gya Zangbo r. Xizang China
57 J4 Zagyva r. Hungary
57 J4 Zagyvarékas Hungary
16 I3 Zahal'tsi Ukr.
95 □K3 Zahamena, Réserve de nature res. Madag.
65 I7 Zahara Spain
64 H8 Zahara de los Atunes Spain
65 I7 Zahara - El Gastor, Embalse de resr Spain
55 M3 Zaharoddzye reg. Belarus
187 J7 Zaḩawn, Wādī r. Yemen
184 E7 Zāhedān Fārs Iran
184 I7 Zāhedān Sīstān va Balūchestān Iran
64 F4 Zahinos Spain
190 D5 Zahlé Lebanon
191 G5 Zähmätkänd Azer.
Zähmet Turkm. see Zakhmet
51 G7 Zahna Ger.
57 L3 Záhony Hungary
57 G2 Záhorovice Czech Rep.
56 F3 Záhorská Ves Slovakia
186 F7 Zaḩrān Saudi Arabia
18 K4 Zaiceva Latvia
63 Q6 Zaida, Laguna de resr Spain
66 F4 Zaidín Spain
18 G6 Žaiginys Lith.
186 G5 Zā'in, Jabal hill Saudi Arabia
184 E5 Zaindeh r. Iran
Zainlha Sichuan China see Xiaojin
Zair Uzbek. see Zoir
Zaire country Africa see Congo, Democratic Republic of
91 B6 Zaire prov. Angola
Zaïre r. Congo/Dem. Rep. Congo see Congo
76 I9 Zajas Macedonia
77 K7 Zaječar Srbija Serb. and Mont.
53 P2 Zaječov Czech Rep.
54 D2 Zajezierze Pol.
95 F4 Zaka Zimbabwe
168 H1 Zakamensk Rus. Fed.
56 F5 Zákány Hungary
57 I5 Zákányszek Hungary
16 C5 Zakarpats'ka Oblast' admin. div. Ukr.
Zakarpatskaya Oblast' admin. div. Ukr. see Zakarpats'ka Oblast'
Zakataly Azer. see Zaqatala
Zakháro Greece see Zacharo
19 W7 Zakharovo Rus. Fed.
16 D3 Zakhidnyy Buh r. Ukr.
185 J3 Zakhmet Turkm.
189 K5 Zākhō Iraq
Zakhodnyaya Dzvina r. Europe see Zapadnaya Dvina
14 G1 Zakhrebetnoye Rus. Fed.
184 A2 Zakī, Kūh-e mt. Iran
Zákinthos i. Greece see Zakynthos
55 I6 Zakliczyn Pol.
55 K5 Zaklików Pol.
55 H6 Zakopane Pol.
90 C2 Zakouma Chad
90 C2 Zakouma, Parc National de nat. park Chad
79 H7 Zakros Kriti Greece
55 K5 Zakrzew Lubelskie Pol.
55 J4 Zakrzew Mazowieckie Pol.
54 G3 Zakrzewo Kujawsko-Pomorskie Pol.
54 F2 Zakrzewo Wielkopolskie Pol.
55 K5 Zakrzówek-Wieś Pol.
56 D1 Zákupy Czech Rep.
106 F5 Zakwaski, Mount B.C. Can.
78 B5 Zakynthos Zakynthos Greece
78 B5 Zakynthos i. Greece
91 B6 Zala Angola
173 L11 Zala Xizang China
56 F5 Zala county Hungary
76 F4 Zala r. Romania
56 G5 Zalaapáti Hungary
56 F5 Zalaegerszeg Hungary
56 F5 Zalai-domsag hills Hungary
56 G5 Zalakaros Hungary
56 G5 Zalakomár Hungary
56 F5 Zalalövő Hungary
64 H3 Zalamea de la Serena Spain
64 F5 Zalamea la Real Spain
89 H4 Zalanga Nigeria
169 R3 Zalantun Nei Mongol China
56 G5 Zalaszántó Hungary
56 F5 Zalaszentbalázs Hungary
56 G5 Zalaszentgrót Hungary
56 F5 Zalaszentiván Hungary
56 F5 Zalaszentmihály Hungary
77 L3 Zalău Romania
57 L4 Zalău r. Romania
56 G5 Zalavár Hungary
18 J7 Zalavas Lith.
55 J4 Załazy Pol.
68 E2 Žalec Slovenia
47 I3 Załęczański Park Krajobrazowy Pol.
19 T9 Zalegoshch' Rus. Fed.
54 F3 Zalesie Kujawsko-Pomorskie Pol.
55 L3 Zalesie Lubelskie Pol.
116 C9 Zaleski OH U.S.A.
19 T3 Zales'ye Rus. Fed.
55 H2 Zalewo Pol.
54 C2 Zalew Szczeciński b. Pol.
23 P7 Zalew Wiślany b. Pol.
186 F4 Zalim Saudi Arabia
84 D6 Zalingei Sudan
16 E5 Zalishchyky Ukr.
16 E5 Zalissya Ukr.
17 P6 Zaliznychne Ukr.
17 L7 Zaliznyy Port Ukr.
16 E4 Zaliztsi Ukr.
186 D2 Zalmā, Jabal az mt. Saudi Arabia
54 F2 Żalno Pol.
84 A1 Zalţan Libya
84 C2 Zaltan, Jabal hills Libya
44 H5 Zaltbommel Neth.
55 L1 Žaltytis l. Lith.
19 O4 Zaluch'ye Rus. Fed.
16 D2 Zalukhiv Ukr.
191 E2 Zalukokoazhe Rus. Fed.
177 N4 Zalun Myanmar
18 L8 Zaluzhzha Belarus
55 M2 Zal'vyanka r. Belarus
57 L5 Zam Romania
167 J5 Zama Japan
89 F3 Zama Niger
106 G3 Zama City Alta Can.
187 H7 Zamakh Saudi Arabia
97 N3 Zamani S. Africa
188 G4 Zamanti r. Turkey
57 G5 Zamárdi Hungary
54 F2 Zamarte Pol.
154 C4 Zambales Mountains Luzon Phil.
56 F1 Žamberk Czech Rep.
91 D8 Zambeze r. Africa alt. Zambezi
91 D7 Zambezi r. Africa alt. Zambeze
91 D8 Zambezi Zambia
95 H3 Zambézia prov. Moz.
91 E9 Zambezi Escarpment Zambia/Zimbabwe
94 E3 Zambezi National Park Zimbabwe
91 E8 Zambia country Africa
154 D8 Zamboanga Mindanao Phil.
154 D8 Zamboanga Peninsula Mindanao Phil.
154 D7 Zamboanguita Negros Phil.
63 O3 Zambrana Spain
130 F9 Zambrano Col.
55 K3 Zambrów Pol.
95 F2 Zambue Moz.

Zambujal de Cima to Žilinai

364

64 A4 **Zambujal de Cima** Port.
64 B5 **Zambujeira do Mar** Port.
54 D2 **Zamęcin** Pol.
89 G3 **Zamfara** *state* Nigeria
89 G3 **Zamfara** *watercourse* Nigeria
185 J6 **Zamīndāvar** *reg.* Afgh.
Zamkog *Sichuan* China *see* Zamtang
86 B4 **Zamlat Amagraj** *hills* Western Sahara
18 K3 **Zamogil'ye** Rus. Fed.
57 H4 **Zámoly** Hungary
136 B6 **Zamora** Ecuador
136 B5 **Zamora** *r.* Ecuador
62 I5 **Zamora** Spain
62 I5 **Zamora** *prov.* Spain
128 E6 **Zamora de Hidalgo** Mex.
55 L5 **Zamość** *Lubelskie* Pol.
55 J2 **Zamość** *Mazowieckie* Pol.
Zamost'ye Pol. *see* **Zamość**
17 Q6 **Zamozhne** Ukr.
Zampa-misaki *hd* *Okinawa* Japan *see* **Zanpa-misaki**
191 D5 **Zamp Dağı** *mt.* Turkey
58 C5 **Zams** Austria
170 C2 **Zamtang** *Sichuan* China
136 D2 **Zamuro, Punta** *pt* Venez.
137 F3 **Zamuro, Sierra del** *mts* Venez.
84 B2 **Zamzam, Wādī** *watercourse* Libya
136 B6 **Zaña** Peru
90 B5 **Zanaga** Congo
129 M9 **Zanatepec** Mex.
191 K5 **Zänbil Adası** *i.* Azer.
63 N10 **Záncara** *r.* Spain
173 D11 **Zanda** *Xizang* China
95 G5 **Zandamela** Moz.
137 H3 **Zanderij** Suriname
45 G6 **Zandhoven** Belgium
51 J9 **Žandov** Czech Rep.
45 F6 **Zandvliet** Belgium
44 G4 **Zandvoort** Neth.
116 C9 **Zanesville** *OH* U.S.A.
191 G6 **Zangakatun** Armenia
88 D3 **Zangasso** Mali
Zangelan Azer. *see* **Zängilan**
191 G6 **Zangezuri Lerrnashght'a** *mts* Armenia/Azer.
173 D8 **Zangguy** *Xinjiang* China
191 H6 **Zängilan** Azer.
178 F3 **Zangla** Jammu and Kashmir
173 G9 **Zangsêr Kangri** *mt.* *Xizang* China
169 N8 **Zanhuang** *Hebei* China
90 F4 **Zani** Dem. Rep. Congo
185 M7 **Zani** Pak.
54 F3 **Zaniemyśl** Pol.
184 C3 **Zanjān** Iran
184 C3 **Zanjān** *prov.* Iran
189 M5 **Zanjān Rūd** *r.* Iran
146 D3 **Zanjitas** Arg.
187 K3 **Zannah, Jabal az** *hill* U.A.E.
73 K6 **Zannone, Isola** *i.* Italy
164 □1 **Zanpa-misaki** *hd* *Okinawa* Japan
178 F2 **Zanskar** *r.* India
178 F3 **Zanskar** *reg.* Jammu and Kashmir
178 F2 **Zanskar Mountains** India
Zante *i.* *Ionioi Nisoi* Greece *see* Zakynthos
209 G11 **Zanthus** *W.A.* Austr.
88 D4 **Zantiébougou** Mali
93 C6 **Zanzibar** Tanz.
93 C6 **Zanzibar Channel** Tanz.
93 C6 **Zanzibar Island** Tanz.
93 C6 **Zanzibar North** *admin. reg.* Tanz.
93 C6 **Zanzibar South** *admin. reg.* Tanz.
93 C6 **Zanzibar West** *admin. reg.* Tanz.
213 H1 **Zaohe** *Jiangsu* China
19 U7 **Zaokskiy** Rus. Fed.
69 C7 **Zaonia Mornag** Tunisia
63 P7 **Zaorejas** Spain
90 C3 **Zaoro-Songou** C.A.R.
169 K9 **Zaosheng** *Gansu* China
171 I3 **Zaoshi** *Hubei* China
171 I5 **Zaoshi** *Hunan* China
19 Q1 **Zaostrov'ye** Rus. Fed.
87 H4 **Zaouatallaz** Alg.
87 E4 **Zaouiet Kounta** Alg.
171 I2 **Zaoyang** *Hubei* China
171 I2 **Zaoyangzhan** *Hubei* China
172 H4 **Zaoyuan** *Xinjiang* China
164 R8 **Zaō-zan** *vol.* Japan
17 M8 **Zaozerne** Ukr.
183 N1 **Zaozernyy** Kazakh.
193 K4 **Zaozernyy** Rus. Fed.
19 V4 **Zaozer'ye** Rus. Fed.
169 O9 **Zaozhuang** *Shandong* China
189 K5 **Zap** *r.* Turkey
76 J7 **Zapadna Morava** *r.* Serb. and Mont.
19 P5 **Zapadnaya Dvina** *r.* Europe *alt.* **Daugava (Latvia),** *alt.* **Zakhodnyaya Dzvina,** *conv.* **Western Dvina**
19 P5 **Zapadnaya Dvina** Rus. Fed.
77 L9 **Zapadni Rodopi** *mts* Bulg.
Zapadno-Kazakhstanskaya Oblast' *admin. div.* Kazakh. *see* **Zapadnyy Kazakhstan**
162 M3 **Zapadno-Sakhalinskiy Khrebet** *mts* Rus. Fed.
Zapadno-Sibirskaya Nizmennost' *plain* Rus. Fed. *see* **Zapadno-Sibirskaya Ravnina**
192 J3 **Zapadno-Sibirskaya Ravnina** *plain* Rus. Fed.
183 P6 **Zapadnyy Alamedin, Pik** *mt.* Kyrg.
18 L1 **Zapadnyy Berezovyy, Ostrov** *i.* Rus. Fed.
182 F7 **Zapadnyy Chink Ustyurta** *esc.* Kazakh.
189 Q3 **Zapadnyy Chink Ustyurta** *esc.* Kazakh.
182 D3 **Zapadnyy Kazakhstan** *admin. div.* Kazakh.
14 F1 **Zapadnyy Kil'din** Rus. Fed.
160 E1 **Zapadnyy Sayan** *reg.* Rus. Fed.
16 G4 **Zapadyntsi** Ukr.
146 B6 **Zapala** Arg.
146 B3 **Zapallar** Chile
55 K5 **Zapałów** Pol.
63 J6 **Zapardiel** *r.* Spain
146 C3 **Zapata** Arg.
121 F12 **Zapata** *TX* U.S.A.
130 C2 **Zapata, Península de** *pen.* Cuba
136 C3 **Zapatoca** Col.
64 F3 **Zapatón** *r.* Spain
136 C2 **Zapatoza, Ciénaga de** *l.* Col.
49 K10 **Zapfendorf** Ger.
138 C4 **Zapiga** Chile
Zápio Greece *see* **Zappeio**
18 M3 **Zaplyus'ye** Rus. Fed.
77 P4 **Zăpodeni** Romania
54 G4 **Zapolice** Pol.
20 U2 **Zapolyarnyy** *Murmanskaya Oblast'* Rus. Fed.
14 M2 **Zapolyarnyy** *Respublika Komi* Rus. Fed.
18 M3 **Zapol'ye** *Pskovskaya Oblast'* Rus. Fed.
19 T2 **Zapol'ye** *Vologodskaya Oblast'* Rus. Fed.
128 D5 **Zapopan** Mex.
17 O6 **Zaporizhzhya** Ukr.
Zaporizhzhya Oblast *admin. div.* Ukr. *see* Zaporiz'ka Oblast'
17 O6 **Zaporiz'ka Oblast'** *admin. div.* Ukr.
Zaporozhskaya Oblast' *admin. div.* Ukr. *see* Zaporiz'ka Oblast'
19 N1 **Zaporozhskoye** Rus. Fed.
Zaporozh'ye Ukr. *see* **Zaporizhzhya**
Zaporozhye Oblast *admin. div.* Ukr. *see* Zaporiz'ka Oblast'
128 D6 **Zapotiltic** Mex.
128 D6 **Zapotitlán** *Jalisco* Mex.
129 J6 **Zapotitlán** *Puebla* Mex.
129 J7 **Zapotitlán Salinas** Mex.
128 D5 **Zapotlanejo** Mex.
162 H7 **Zapovednyy** Rus. Fed.
78 D3 **Zappeio** Greece
51 E7 **Zappendorf** Ger.
73 P5 **Zapponeta** Italy
68 E3 **Zaprešić** Croatia
19 U5 **Zaprudnya** Rus. Fed.
18 H9 **Zaprudy** Belarus
173 E10 **Zapug** *Xizang* China
55 M6 **Zapytiv** Ukr.
191 H4 **Zaqatala** Azer.
191 H4 **Zaqatala qoruğu** *nature res.* Azer.
173 L10 **Zaqên** *Qinghai* China
84 C2 **Zaqqui** Libya
170 A3 **Za Qu** *r.* *Qinghai* China
173 I10 **Zaqungngomar** *mt.* *Xizang* China
Zara Croatia *see* **Zadar**
188 H4 **Zara** Turkey
Zarafshan Uzbek. *see* Zarafshon
185 M2 **Zarafshon** Tajik.
185 M2 **Zarafshon** *r.* Tajik.
182 K7 **Zarafshon** Uzbek.
183 J8 **Zarafshon** *r.* Uzbek.
185 L2 **Zarafshon, Qatorkŭhi** *mts* Tajik.
136 C3 **Zaragoza** Col.
127 I3 **Zaragoza** *Coahuila* Mex.
129 H2 **Zaragoza** *Nuevo León* Mex.
129 J6 **Zaragoza** *Puebla* Mex.
66 D4 **Zaragoza** Spain
63 R5 **Zaragoza** *prov.* Spain
66 D7 **Zaragozana** *mt.* Spain
184 G6 **Zarand** *Kermān* Iran
184 D4 **Zarand** *Markazī* Iran
57 K5 **Zărand** Romania
77 K4 **Zarandului, Munții** *hills* Romania
173 D11 **Zarang** *Xizang* China
185 I6 **Zaranj** Afgh.
54 D2 **Zarańsko** Pol.
18 J6 **Zarasai** Lith.
191 K5 **Zarat** Azer.
63 O2 **Zaratamo** Spain
63 K5 **Zaratán** Spain
147 H4 **Zárate** Arg.
66 A1 **Zarautz** Spain
19 V7 **Zaraysk** Rus. Fed.
137 E2 **Zaraza** Venez.
183 M7 **Zarbdor** Uzbek.
65 P5 **Zarcilla de Ramos** Spain
185 K7 **Zard** Pak.
191 I5 **Zärdab** Azer.
184 H4 **Zardak** Iran
184 C5 **Zard Kuh** *mts* Iran
55 J2 **Zaręby** Pol.
55 K3 **Zaręby-Kościelne** Pol.
14 E2 **Zarechensk** Rus. Fed.
16 E1 **Zarechka** Belarus
14 L3 **Zarechka** Rus. Fed.
19 W8 **Zarechnyy** Rus. Fed.
19 X7 **Zarech'ye** Rus. Fed.
184 C4 **Zāreh** Iran
106 C3 **Zarembo Island** *AK* U.S.A.
18 F6 **Žarėnai** Lith.
186 E2 **Zarghat** Saudi Arabia
185 M5 **Zarghūn Shahr** Afgh.
185 L6 **Zargun** *mt.* Pak.
185 L4 **Zari** Afgh.
89 G4 **Zaria** Nigeria
57 L3 **Zaricheve** Ukr.
17 N8 **Zarichne** *Respublika Krym* Ukr.
16 F2 **Zarichne** *Rivnens'ka Oblast'* Ukr.
184 F6 **Zarīgān** Iran
184 A3 **Zarīneh Rūd** *r.* Iran
55 H5 **Żarki** Pol.
54 C4 **Żarki Wielkie** Pol.
185 J5 **Zarmardan** Afgh.
191 J5 **Zarnava** Azer.
184 B5 **Zarneh** Iran
77 N5 **Zărnești** Romania
57 H3 **Žarnovica** Slovakia
55 I4 **Żarnów** Pol.
55 H5 **Żarnowiec** Pol.
23 O7 **Żarnowieckie, Jezioro** *l.* Pol.
54 E5 **Żarów** Pol.
48 K3 **Zarpen** Ger.
190 D6 **Zarqā', Nahr az** *r.* Jordan
184 E7 **Zarqān** Iran
191 J4 **Zärqava** Azer.
45 C6 **Zarren** Belgium
48 K3 **Zarrentin** Ger.
184 F5 **Zarrīn** Iran
55 K6 **Zarszyn** Pol.
184 E6 **Zarū** Iran
19 Q3 **Zarubino** *Novgorodskaya Oblast'* Rus. Fed.
162 G7 **Zarubino** *Primorskiy Kray* Rus. Fed.
167 H5 **Zaruga-dake** *mt.* Japan
54 D4 **Żary** Pol.
182 G3 **Zarya Oktyabrya** Kazakh.
65 I3 **Zarza Capilla** Spain
64 G3 **Zarza de Alange** Spain
62 H8 **Zarza de Granadilla** Spain
63 N8 **Zarza de Tajo** Spain
65 P5 **Zarzadilla de Totana** Spain
87 H3 **Zarzaïtine** Alg.
136 B3 **Zarzal** Col.
62 G9 **Zarza la Mayor** Spain
55 K6 **Zarzecze** Pol.
87 H2 **Zarzis** Tunisia
63 L7 **Zarzuela del Monte** Spain
63 L6 **Zarzuela del Pinar** Spain
62 C2 **Zas** Spain
18 I5 **Zasa** Latvia
183 T3 **Zashchita** Kazakh.
20 U3 **Zasheyek** Rus. Fed.
Zaskar *reg.* Jammu and Kashmir *see* **Zanskar**
18 L6 **Zaskarki** Belarus
57 I2 **Žaškov** Slovakia
18 K8 **Zaslawkaye Vodaskhovishcha** *resr* Belarus
18 K7 **Zaslawye** Belarus
56 E2 **Zásmuky** Czech Rep.
17 R3 **Zasosna** Rus. Fed.
55 J5 **Zasów** Pol.
191 B1 **Zassovskaya** Rus. Fed.
16 E5 **Zastavna** Ukr.
97 L6 **Zastron** S. Africa
55 K3 **Zaszków** Pol.
190 E6 **Za'tarī, Wādī az** *watercourse* Jordan
56 C1 **Žatec** Czech Rep.
191 G1 **Zaterechnyy** Rus. Fed.
182 J1 **Zatobol'sk** Kazakh.
16 J7 **Zatoka** Ukr.
57 G1 **Zátor** Czech Rep.
55 H6 **Zator** Pol.
55 J3 **Zatory** Pol.
16 D3 **Zaturtsi** Ukr.
16 I6 **Zatyshshya** Ukr.
51 G6 **Zauche** *reg.* Ger.
184 H1 **Zaunguzskiye Karakumy** *des.* Turkm.
129 J6 **Zautla** Mex.
57 M2 **Zavadka** Ukr.
57 I3 **Závadka nad Hronom** Slovakia
213 F2 **Zavadovskiy Island** Antarctica
147 G4 **Zavalía** Arg.
147 G3 **Zavalla** Arg.
121 H10 **Zavalla** *TX* U.S.A.
16 J5 **Zavallya** Ukr.
184 E5 **Zavareh** Iran
70 G6 **Zavattarello** Italy
45 F7 **Zaventem** Belgium
15 H7 **Zavetnoye** Rus. Fed.
162 L4 **Zavety Il'icha** Rus. Fed.
68 G3 **Zavidoviči** Bos.-Herz.
19 T5 **Zavidovskiy Zapovednik** *nature res.* Rus. Fed.
Zavitaya Rus. Fed. *see* Zavitinsk
162 F3 **Zavitinsk** Rus. Fed.
17 N8 **Zavit-Lenins'ky** Ukr.
56 G3 **Závod** Slovakia
55 M5 **Zavods'ke** *L'vivs'ka Oblast'* Ukr.
16 E4 **Zavods'ke** *Ternopils'ka Oblast'* Ukr.
183 U1 **Zavodskoy** *Altayskiy Kray* Rus. Fed.
191 F3 **Zavodskoy** *Respublika Severnaya Osetiya-Alaniya* Rus. Fed.
77 K7 **Zavojsko Jezero** *resr* Serb. and Mont.
14 H4 **Zavolzhsk** Rus. Fed.
Zavolzh'ye Rus. Fed. *see* Zavolzhsk
95 G5 **Závora, Ponta** *pt* Moz.
17 K3 **Zavorychi** Ukr.
18 L6 **Zavutstsye** Belarus
18 L6 **Zavyachellye** Belarus
193 Q4 **Zav'yalova, Ostrov** *i.* Rus. Fed.
183 S1 **Zav'yalovo** Rus. Fed.
55 L6 **Zavydovychi** Ukr.
168 G8 **Zawa** *Qinghai* China
173 D8 **Zawa** *Xinjiang* China
55 H4 **Zawada** *Łódzkie* Pol.
55 L5 **Zawada** *Lubelskie* Pol.
54 D4 **Zawada** *Lubuskie* Pol.
54 F5 **Zawada** *Opolskie* Pol.
55 H5 **Zawada** *Śląskie* Pol.
55 K2 **Zawady** Pol.
54 G5 **Zawadzkie** Pol.
158 C4 **Zawgyi** *r.* Myanmar
55 J5 **Zawichost** Pol.
54 D4 **Zawidów** Pol.
55 H3 **Zawidz Kościelny** Pol.
55 H5 **Zawiercie** Pol.
84 B3 **Zawīlah** Libya
190 E3 **Zāwīyah, Jabal az** *hills* Syria
84 D2 **Zāwiyat Masūs** Libya
188 C8 **Zāwiyat Shammās** *pt* Egypt
187 L5 **Zawlīyah, Jiddat az** *plain* Oman
55 H6 **Zawoja** Pol.
54 F4 **Zawonia** Pol.
187 I2 **Zawr, Ra's az** *pt* Saudi Arabia
173 J11 **Zaxoi** *Xizang* China
14 J5 **Zay** *r.* Rus. Fed.
59 O2 **Zaya** *r.* Austria
191 G5 **Zäyäm** Azer.
191 G4 **Zäyämçay** *r.* Azer.
190 E6 **Zaydī, Wādī az** *watercourse* Syria
19 N6 **Zaykava** Belarus
183 U4 **Zaysan** Kazakh.
Zaysan, Lake Kazakh. *see* Zaysan, Ozero
183 T3 **Zaysan, Ozero** *l.* Kazakh.
17 R5 **Zaytseve** Ukr.
18 L4 **Zaytsevo** Rus. Fed.
170 A4 **Zayü** *Xizang* China
170 A4 **Zayü** *Xizang* China
Zayü *Xizang* China *see* Gyigang
191 E2 **Zayukovo** Rus. Fed.
170 A4 **Zayü Qu** *r.* China/India
Zayyr Uzbek. *see* **Zoir**
95 □J4 **Zazafotsy** Madag.
89 G3 **Zazagawa** Nigeria
87 G6 **Zazir, Oued** *watercourse* Alg.
57 I2 **Zázrivá** Slovakia
16 E4 **Zbarazh** Ukr.
54 D3 **Zbąszyn** Pol.
54 D3 **Zbąszynek** Pol.
54 D3 **Zbąszyńskie, Jezioro** *l.* Pol.
55 H2 **Zbiczno** Pol.
54 G4 **Zbiersk** Pol.
53 P2 **Zbiroh** Czech Rep.
54 G2 **Zblewo** Pol.
55 I5 **Zbludowice** Pol.
55 J2 **Zbójna** Pol.
55 H2 **Zbójno** Pol.
76 H7 **Zborište** *mt.* Serb. and Mont.
16 E4 **Zboriv** Ukr.
57 K2 **Zborov** Slovakia
54 F6 **Zborovice** Czech Rep.
59 N1 **Zbraslav** Czech Rep.
56 E2 **Zbraslavice** Czech Rep.
16 F5 **Zbruch** *r.* Ukr.
56 C2 **Zbůch** Czech Rep.
55 K3 **Zbuczyn Poduchowny** Pol.
17 L7 **Zbur''yivka** Ukr.
59 N1 **Zbýšov** Czech Rep.
56 G5 **Ždala** Croatia
59 P1 **Ždánice** Czech Rep.
56 F2 **Ždánický Les** *for.* Czech Rep.
51 L9 **Žďár** Czech Rep.
56 E2 **Žďár nad Sázavou** Czech Rep.
56 E2 **Žďárské Vrchy** *hills* Czech Rep.
56 E2 **Zdárské vrchy** *park* Czech Rep.
57 J2 **Ždiar** Slovakia
56 C2 **Zdíkov** Czech Rep.
56 E2 **Ždírec nad Doubravou** Czech Rep.
16 F3 **Zdolbuniv** Ukr.
Zdolbunov Ukr. *see* **Zdolbuniv**
56 G2 **Zdounky** Czech Rep.
54 G4 **Zduńska Wola** Pol.
55 H3 **Zduny** *Łódzkie* Pol.
54 F4 **Zduny** *Wielkopolskie* Pol.
16 J2 **Zdvyzh** *r.* Ukr.
55 J6 **Zdynia** Pol.
54 G4 **Zdziechowice** *Opolskie* Pol.
55 K5 **Zdziechowice** *Podkarpackie* Pol.
54 G5 **Zdzieszowice** Pol.
55 K5 **Zdziłowice** Pol.
55 N3 **Zdzitava** Belarus
Zealand *i.* Denmark *see* Sjælland
185 N3 **Zēbāk** Afgh.
145 C7 **Zeballos** *mt.* Arg.
106 E5 **Zeballos** *B.C.* Can.
189 L5 **Zēbār** Iraq
75 □ **Żebbiegħ** Malta
75 □ **Żebbuġ** *Gozo* Malta
75 □ **Żebbuġ** Malta
Zebirget Island Egypt *see* Zabarjad, Jazīrat
54 G5 **Zębowice** Pol.
53 P2 **Žebrák** Czech Rep.
62 F9 **Zebreira** Port.
54 D4 **Zebrzydowa** Pol.
54 G6 **Zebrzydowice Dolne** Pol.
115 E9 **Zebulon** *GA* U.S.A.
116 C11 **Zebulon** *KY* U.S.A.
115 H8 **Zebulon** *NC* U.S.A.
71 Q6 **Zeča** *i.* Croatia
50 G4 **Zechlin Dorf** Ger.
50 G4 **Zechlinerhütte** Ger.
44 J5 **Zeddam** Neth.
72 B8 **Zeddiani** *Sardegna* Italy
45 D6 **Zedelgem** Belgium
59 I5 **Zederhaus** Austria
57 I6 **Žednik** *Vojvodina, Srbija* Serb. and Mont.
45 D6 **Zeebrugge** Belgium
205 J9 **Zeehan** *Tas.* Austr.
44 I5 **Zeeland** Neth.
44 E5 **Zeeland** *prov.* Neth.
110 H7 **Zeeland** *MI* U.S.A.
190 C7 **Ze'elim** Israel
97 K1 **Zeerust** S. Africa
51 I6 **Zeesen** Ger.
45 D6 **Zeeuwsch-Vlaanderen** *reg.* Neth.
44 I4 **Zeewolde** Neth.
190 D6 **Zefat** Israel
184 E5 **Zefreh** Iran
66 A2 **Zegama** Spain
55 I6 **Żegiestów** Pol.
55 I6 **Żegocina** Pol.
55 J3 **Zegrzyńskie, Jezioro** *l.* Pol.
50 H5 **Zehdenick** Ger.
50 F3 **Zehna** Ger.
51 H8 **Zehren** Ger.
206 D7 **Zeil, Mount** *N.T.* Austr.
49 K10 **Zeil am Main** Ger.
53 N5 **Zeilarn** Ger.
18 H5 **Žeimelis** Lith.
59 N3 **Zeiselmauer** Austria
44 H4 **Zeist** Neth.
51 H8 **Zeithain** Ger.
53 M3 **Zeitlarn** Ger.
49 I10 **Zeitlofs** Ger.
51 F8 **Zeitz** Ger.
75 □ **Żejtun** Malta
168 G9 **Zêkog** *Qinghai* China
172 F5 **Zekti** *Xinjiang* China
Zela Turkey *see* **Zile**
54 G4 **Żelazków** Pol.
45 F6 **Zele** Belgium
55 I4 **Żelechlinek** Pol.
55 J4 **Żelechów** Pol.
16 F5 **Zelena** *Chernivets'ka Oblast'* Ukr.
16 D5 **Zelena** *Ivano-Frankivs'ka Oblast'* Ukr.
16 D5 **Zelena** *Ivano-Frankivs'ka Oblast'* Ukr.
68 F4 **Zelena Gora** *mt.* Bos.-Herz.
56 G2 **Zelená Hora** *tourist site* Czech Rep.
183 P1 **Zelenaya Roshcha** Kazakh.
191 C2 **Zelenchukskaya** Rus. Fed.
51 K10 **Zeleneč** Czech Rep.
57 G3 **Zeleneč** Slovakia
17 P6 **Zelene Pole** Ukr.
68 G4 **Zelengora** *mts* Bos.-Herz.
17 L7 **Zelenivka** Ukr.
17 N4 **Zelenkivka** Ukr.
14 I3 **Zelennik** Rus. Fed.
20 V3 **Zelenoborskiy** Rus. Fed.
14 J5 **Zelenodol'sk** Rus. Fed.
17 M6 **Zelenodol's'k** Ukr.
18 M1 **Zelenogorsk** Rus. Fed.
19 U5 **Zelenograd** Rus. Fed.
18 D7 **Zelenogradsk** Rus. Fed.
16 J6 **Zelenohirs'ke** Ukr.
191 E1 **Zelenokumsk** Rus. Fed.
14 I4 **Zelentsovo** Rus. Fed.
161 Q3 **Zelenyy, Ostrov** *i.* *Kuril'skiye O-va* Rus. Fed.
183 N2 **Zelenyy Gay** Kazakh.
59 O1 **Želešice** Czech Rep.
56 E2 **Želetava** Czech Rep.
56 C2 **Železná Ruda** Czech Rep.
57 I3 **Železné** Slovakia
56 E2 **Železné Hory** *hills* Czech Rep.
59 J7 **Železniki** Slovenia
56 E1 **Železný Brod** Czech Rep.
44 J4 **Zelhem** Neth.
116 E8 **Zelienople** *PA* U.S.A.
57 H3 **Želiezovce** Slovakia
68 F3 **Zelina** Croatia
168 E8 **Zelinggou** *Qinghai* China
76 J9 **Želino** Macedonia
56 E2 **Želivka** *r.* Czech Rep.
56 E2 **Želivka, Vodní nádrž** *resr* Czech Rep.
76 I7 **Željin** *mt.* Serb. and Mont.
55 K3 **Żelków-Kolonia** Pol.
51 E10 **Zell** Ger.
49 D10 **Zell (Mosel)** Ger.
49 K9 **Zella-Mehlis** Ger.
52 E5 **Zell am Harmersbach** Ger.
58 G5 **Zell am See** Austria
58 E5 **Zell am Ziller** Austria
59 I3 **Zell an der Pram** Austria
59 M2 **Zellerndorf** Austria
59 L4 **Zellerrain** *pass* Austria
58 G5 **Zeller See** *l.* Austria
59 H4 **Zellersee** *l.* Austria
52 G6 **Zellersee** *l.* Ger.
52 D6 **Zell im Wiesental** Ger.
52 H2 **Zellingen** Ger.
59 J7 **Zell-Pfarre** Austria
57 I3 **Želovce** Slovakia
55 H4 **Zelów** Pol.
52 C2 **Zeltingen-Rachtig** Ger.
18 J4 **Zeltiņi** Latvia
59 K5 **Zeltweg** Austria
18 H8 **Zel'va** Belarus
55 M2 **Zel'vyenskaye Vodaskhovishcha** *resr* Belarus
45 E6 **Zelzate** Belgium
18 E6 **Žemaičių Naumiestis** Lith.
18 E5 **Žemaitijos nacionalinis parkas** *nat. park* Lith.
57 H3 **Žemberovce** Slovakia
78 B2 **Zemblak** Albania
55 K3 **Zembrów** Pol.
55 H6 **Zembrzyce** Pol.
77 K8 **Zemen** Bulg.
77 O4 **Zemeș** Romania
15 H5 **Zemetchino** Rus. Fed.
57 G4 **Zemianska Olča** Slovakia
90 E3 **Zémio** C.A.R.
50 I3 **Zemitz** Ger.
192 F1 **Zemlya Aleksandry** *i.* *Zemlya Frantsa-Iosifa* Rus. Fed.
192 G2 **Zemlya Frantsa-Iosifa** *is* Rus. Fed.
192 F1 **Zemlya Georga** *i.* *Zemlya Frantsa-Iosifa* Rus. Fed.
17 R2 **Zemlyansk** Rus. Fed.
192 H1 **Zemlya Vil'cheka** *i.* *Zemlya Frantsa-Iosifa* Rus. Fed.
52 B2 **Zemmer** Ger.
191 C3 **Zemo Barghebi** Georgia
191 E4 **Zemo Khveduret'i** Georgia
90 E3 **Zémongo, Réserve de Faune de** *nature res.* C.A.R.
191 F4 **Zemo Qarabulakhi** Georgia
57 L3 **Zemplénagárd** Hungary
57 K3 **Zempleni** *park* Hungary
57 K3 **Zempléni-hegység** *hills* Hungary
57 L3 **Zemplínska šírava** *l.* Slovakia
57 K3 **Zemplínska Teplica** Slovakia
57 L3 **Zemplínske Hámre** Slovakia
129 I6 **Zempoala** *Hidalgo* Mex.
129 K6 **Zempoala** *Veracruz* Mex.
129 L8 **Zempoaltépetl, Nudo de** *mt.* Mex.
45 F7 **Zemst** Belgium
19 P5 **Zemtsy** Rus. Fed.
76 I6 **Zemun** *Srbija* Serb. and Mont.
170 A2 **Zênda** *Sichuan* China
171 I7 **Zengcheng** *Guangdong* China
162 F7 **Zengfeng Shan** *mt.* China
57 H5 **Zengő** *hill* Hungary
68 F3 **Zenica** Bos.-Herz.
190 C8 **Zenifim** *watercourse* Israel
53 J2 **Zenn** *r.* Ger.
30 □ **Zennor** *Cornwall, England* U.K.
Zenta *Vojvodina, Srbija* Serb. and Mont. *see* **Senta**
165 K12 **Zentsūji** Japan
185 M4 **Zenyeh** Afgh.
87 F2 **Zenzach** Alg.
129 J9 **Zenzontepec** Mex.
68 G3 **Žepče** Bos.-Herz.
50 I5 **Zepernick** Ger.
124 M2 **Zephyr Cove** *NV* U.S.A.
115 F11 **Zephyrhills** *FL* U.S.A.
173 C7 **Zepu** *Xinjiang* China
90 C2 **Zérab, Ouadi** *watercourse* Chad
92 A2 **Zeraf, Bahr el** *r.* Sudan
Zeravshan Tajik. *see* Zarafshon
Zeravshan *r.* Tajik. *see* Zarafshon
Zeravshan *r.* Uzbek. *see* Zarafshon
Zeravshanskiy Khrebet *mts* Tajik. *see* Zarafshon, Qatorkŭhi
51 F7 **Zerbst** Ger.
185 I6 **Zereh, Gowd-e** *depr.* Afgh.
185 J7 **Zereh, Gowd-e** *depr.* Afgh.
183 M1 **Zerenda** Kazakh.
52 B2 **Zerf** Ger.
87 G2 **Zeribet el Oued** Alg.
57 K5 **Zerind** Romania
54 F3 **Żerków** Pol.
70 D3 **Zermatt** Switz.
70 I2 **Zernez** Switz.
48 K4 **Zernien** Ger.
50 F5 **Zernitz** Ger.
15 H7 **Zernograd** Rus. Fed.
Zernovoy Rus. Fed. *see* Zernograd
71 M4 **Zero** *r.* Italy
50 I5 **Zerpenschleuse** Ger.
50 J4 **Zerrenthin** Ger.
47 I2 **Zespół Nadwiślanskich Parków Krajobrazowych** Pol.
47 I2 **Zespół Nadwiślanskich Parków Krajobrazowych** Pol.
Zestafoni Georgia *see* Zestap'oni
191 E3 **Zestap'oni** Georgia
66 A1 **Zestoa** Spain
179 L5 **Zêsum** *Xizang* China
76 H8 **Zeta** *r.* Serb. and Mont.
59 M7 **Žetale** Slovenia
173 J12 **Zêtang** *Xizang* China
77 N4 **Zetea** Romania
48 E4 **Zetel** Ger.
51 E9 **Zeulenroda** Ger.
51 I6 **Zeuthen** Ger.
48 H4 **Zeven** Ger.
44 J5 **Zevenaar** Neth.
44 G5 **Zevenbergen** Neth.
44 J2 **Zevenhuizen** Neth.
190 A4 **Zevgari, Cape** Cyprus
78 D5 **Zevgolatio** Greece
71 K5 **Zevio** Italy
162 E2 **Zeya** Rus. Fed.
162 E3 **Zeya** *r.* Rus. Fed.
184 F7 **Zeydābād** Iran
184 G3 **Zeydar** Iran
185 J8 **Zeydī** Iran
184 G7 **Zeynalābād** Iran
162 E1 **Zeyskiy Zapovednik** *nature res.* Rus. Fed.
162 G3 **Zeysko-Bureinskaya Vpadina** *depr.* Rus. Fed.
162 E1 **Zeyskoye Vodokhranilishche** *resr* Rus. Fed.
79 I4 **Zeytindağ** Turkey
78 B2 **Zezë, Maja e** *mt.* Albania
62 D10 **Zêzere** *r.* Port.
169 M9 **Zezhou** *Shanxi* China
190 D4 **Zgharta** Lebanon
55 H4 **Zgierz** Pol.
55 I6 **Zgłobice** Pol.
59 J7 **Zgornje Bitnje** Slovenia
59 J7 **Zgornje Jezersko** Slovenia
59 M6 **Zgornji Duplek** Slovenia
54 D4 **Zgorzelec** Pol.
16 G5 **Zgurița** Moldova
16 D1 **Zhabinka** Belarus
16 H5 **Zhabokrychka** Ukr.
Zhabye Ukr. *see* **Verkhovyna**
16 H3 **Zhad'ky** Ukr.
17 L1 **Zhadove** Ukr.
170 B2 **Zhaglag** *Sichuan* China
170 A3 **Zhag'yab** *Xizang* China
182 I2 **Zhailma** Kazakh.
183 L2 **Zhaksy** Kazakh.
183 M3 **Zhaksy-Kon** *watercourse* Kazakh.
182 I4 **Zhaksykylysh** Kazakh.
182 I4 **Zhaksykylysh, Ozero** *salt l.* Kazakh.
Zhaksy Sarysu *watercourse* Kazakh. *see* **Sarysu**
183 R6 **Zhalanash** *Almatinskaya Oblast'* Kazakh.
Zhalgyztöbe Kazakh. *see* Zhangiztobe
182 C3 **Zhalpaktal** Kazakh.
Zhalpaqtal Kazakh. *see* Zhalpaktal
183 M2 **Zhaltyr** *Akmolinskaya Oblast'* Kazakh.
183 Q2 **Zhaltyr** *Pavlodarskaya Oblast'* Kazakh.
182 D4 **Zhaltyr, Ozero** *l.* Kazakh.
18 H8 **Zhaludok** Belarus
182 J3 **Zhamanakkol', Ozero** *salt l.* Kazakh.
182 E4 **Zhamansor** Kazakh.
183 N4 **Zhambyl** *Karagandinskaya Oblast'* Kazakh.
Zhambyl *Zhambylskaya Oblast'* Kazakh. *see* **Taraz**
Zhambyl Oblast *admin. div.* Kazakh. *see* Zhambylskaya **Oblast'**
183 O5 **Zhambylskaya Oblast'** *admin. div.* Kazakh.
183 S4 **Zhameuka** Kazakh.
183 M4 **Zhanabas** Kazakh.
183 L6 **Zhanakorgan** Kazakh.
182 I5 **Zhanakurylys** Kazakh.
173 J12 **Zhanang** *Xizang* China
183 P4 **Zhanaortalyk** Kazakh.
182 E6 **Zhanaozen** Kazakh.
183 R6 **Zhanatalan** Kazakh.
183 M6 **Zhanatas** Kazakh.
182 I5 **Zhanay** Kazakh.
182 D4 **Zhanbay** Kazakh.
162 E4 **Zhanbei** *Heilong.* China
Zhangaözen Kazakh. *see* Zhanaozen
Zhangaqorghan Kazakh. *see* Zhanakorgan
Zhangatas Kazakh. *see* Zhanatas
169 N6 **Zhangbei** *Hebei* China
Zhangcheng *Fujian* China *see* Yongtai
171 K2 **Zhangcunpu** *Anhui* China
Zhangdian *Shandong* China *see* **Zibo**
162 F5 **Zhangguangcai Ling** *mts* China
169 R5 **Zhanggutai** *Liaoning* China
169 N8 **Zhang He** *r.* China
170 G8 **Zhanghuang** *Guangxi* China
183 S3 **Zhangiztobe** Kazakh.
170 F1 **Zhangjiachuan** *Gansu* China
170 H4 **Zhangjiajie** *Hunan* China
169 N6 **Zhangjiakou** *Hebei* China
171 K4 **Zhangjialing** *Jiangxi* China
Zhangjiang *Hunan* China *see* Taoyuan
162 C2 **Zhangling** *Heilong.* China
171 K2 **Zhanglou** *Anhui* China
171 K6 **Zhangping** *Fujian* China
171 K6 **Zhangpu** *Fujian* China
169 R5 **Zhangqiangzhen** *Liaoning* China
169 O8 **Zhangqiu** *Shandong* China
171 J4 **Zhangshu** *Jiangxi* China
Zhangwan *Hubei* China *see* Xiangyang
169 O7 **Zhangwei Xinhe** *r.* China
169 R5 **Zhangwu** *Liaoning* China
168 I9 **Zhangxian** *Gansu* China
168 G7 **Zhangye** *Gansu* China
171 K6 **Zhangzhou** *Fujian* China
169 M8 **Zhangzi** *Shanxi* China
Zhanhe *Heilong.* China *see* Zhanbei
162 F4 **Zhan He** *r.* China
169 P8 **Zhanhua** *Shandong* China
182 B3 **Zhanibek** Kazakh.
Zhänibek Kazakh. *see* Zhanibek
170 H8 **Zhanjiang** *Guangdong* China
182 F4 **Zhanterek** Kazakh.
170 D6 **Zhanyi** *Yunnan* China
171 K7 **Zhao'an** *Fujian* China
162 D5 **Zhaodong** *Heilong.* China
Zhaoge *Henan* China *see* Qixian
170 D4 **Zhaojue** *Sichuan* China
171 I4 **Zhaoliqiao** *Hubei* China
170 H6 **Zhaoping** *Guangxi* China
171 I7 **Zhaoqing** *Guangdong* China
172 E5 **Zhaosu** *Xinjiang* China
169 R5 **Zhaosutai He** *r.* China
170 D5 **Zhaotong** *Yunnan* China
169 N8 **Zhaoxian** *Hebei* China
169 O9 **Zhaoyang Hu** *l.* China
162 D6 **Zhaoyuan** *Heilong.* China
169 Q8 **Zhaoyuan** *Shandong* China
Zhaozhou *Hebei* China *see* Zhaoxian
162 D6 **Zhaozhou** *Heilong.* China
171 H8 **Zhapo** *Guangdong* China
Zhaqsy Kazakh. *see* **Zhaksy**
16 H4 **Zhar** *r.* Ukr.
183 T4 **Zharbulak** Kazakh.
18 K7 **Zhardzyazhzha** Belarus
173 G11 **Zhari Namco** *salt l.* China
182 G4 **Zharkamys** Kazakh.
183 S5 **Zharkent** Kazakh.
19 P6 **Zharkovskiy** Rus. Fed.
182 E6 **Zharma** *Mangistauskaya Oblast'* Kazakh.
183 S3 **Zharma** *Vostochnyy Kazakhstan* Kazakh.
182 E5 **Zharmysh-Ondy** Kazakh.
183 S4 **Zharsuat** Kazakh.
Zharyk Kazakh. *see* Saken Seyfullin
183 S3 **Zharyk** Kazakh.
16 J4 **Zhashkiv** Ukr.
Zhashkov Ukr. *see* **Zhashkiv**
170 G2 **Zhashui** *Shaanxi* China
Zhaslyk Uzbek. *see* **Jasliq**
19 P8 **Zhastkovo** Rus. Fed.
Zhaxi *Yunnan* China *see* **Weixin**
173 G10 **Zhaxi Co** *salt l.* China
173 D10 **Zhaxigang** *Xizang* China
173 I12 **Zhaxigang** *Xizang* China
170 A3 **Zhaxizê** *Xizang* China
173 H12 **Zhaxizong** *Xizang* China
183 N3 **Zhayrem** Kazakh.
170 B4 **Zhayü** *Xizang* China
Zhayylma Kazakh. *see* **Zhailma**
Zhayyq *r.* Kazakh./Rus. Fed. *see* **Ural**
17 O5 **Zhdanivka** Ukr.
183 N6 **Zhdanovo** Kazakh.
19 Q4 **Zhdanovo** Rus. Fed.
17 M3 **Zhdany** Ukr.
Zhdenevo Ukr. *see* Zhdeniyevo
16 C5 **Zhdeniyevo** Ukr.
169 N9 **Zhecheng** *Henan* China
170 C3 **Zhêhor** *Sichuan* China
171 M4 **Zhejiang** *prov.* China
183 P3 **Zhekezhal** Kazakh.
171 J7 **Zhelang** *Guangdong* China
192 H2 **Zhelaniya, Mys** *c.* *Novaya Zemlya* Rus. Fed.
18 K3 **Zhelcha** *r.* Rus. Fed.
183 P1 **Zhelezinka** Kazakh.
18 E7 **Zheleznodorozhnyy** *Kaliningradskaya Oblast'* Rus. Fed.
Zheleznodorozhnyy *Respublika Komi* Rus. Fed. *see* Yemva
Zheleznodorozhnyy Uzbek. *see* **Qo'ng'irot**
19 S9 **Zheleznogorsk** Rus. Fed.
191 E1 **Zheleznovodsk** Rus. Fed.
19 U7 **Zheleznya** Rus. Fed.
183 P5 **Zheltorangy** Kazakh.
Zheltyye Vody Ukr. *see* Zhovti Vody
17 N8 **Zhelyabovka** Ukr.
77 O8 **Zhelyu Voyvoda** Bulg.
170 G2 **Zhen'an** *Shaanxi* China
170 F2 **Zhenba** *Shaanxi* China
170 E6 **Zhenfeng** *Guizhou* China
170 F4 **Zheng'an** *Guizhou* China
169 N7 **Zhengding** *Hebei* China
171 L5 **Zhenghe** *Fujian* China
Zhengjiatun *Jilin* China *see* Shuangliao
168 H8 **Zhenglubu** *Gansu* China
169 K9 **Zhengning** *Gansu* China
Zhengxiangbai Qi *Nei Mongol* China *see* **Qagan Nur**
171 J2 **Zhengyang** *Henan* China
169 M9 **Zhengzhou** *Henan* China
171 M4 **Zhenhai** *Zhejiang* China
170 D2 **Zhenjiangguan** *Sichuan* China
Zhenkang *Yunnan* China *see* Fengwei
170 B7 **Zhenkang** *Yunnan* China
169 R4 **Zhenlai** *Jilin* China
170 E5 **Zhenning** *Guizhou* China
170 G3 **Zhenping** *Shaanxi* China
169 R4 **Zhenxi** *Jilin* China
170 E5 **Zhenxiong** *Yunnan* China
Zhenyang *Henan* China *see* Zhengyang
169 J9 **Zhenyuan** *Gansu* China
170 G5 **Zhenyuan** *Guizhou* China
170 C7 **Zhenyuan** *Yunnan* China
170 H3 **Zhenziling** *Hubei* China
15 H6 **Zherdevka** Rus. Fed.
19 T8 **Zherdevo** Rus. Fed.
16 F5 **Zherdya** Ukr.
17 R5 **Zherebets'** *r.* Ukr.
16 I2 **Zheriv** *r.* Ukr.
16 I3 **Zheriv** *r.* Ukr.
171 L5 **Zherong** *Fujian* China
14 J3 **Zheshart** Rus. Fed.
19 U5 **Zhestylevo** Rus. Fed.
Zhetibay Kazakh. *see* Zhetybay
Zhetikara Kazakh. *see* Zhitikara
Zhetisay Kazakh. *see* Zhetysay
182 E6 **Zhetybay** Kazakh.
182 I2 **Zhety-Kol', Ozero** *l.* Rus. Fed.
183 M7 **Zhetysay** Kazakh.
173 H11 **Zhêxam** *Xizang* China
171 H4 **Zhexi Shuiku** *resr* China
183 L3 **Zhezdy** Kazakh.
183 L4 **Zhezkazgan** *Karagandinskaya Oblast'* Kazakh.
183 L4 **Zhezkazgan** *Karagandinskaya Oblast'* Kazakh.
Zhezqazghan Kazakh. *see* Zhezkazgan
Zhicheng *Shandong* China *see* Qingzhou
19 O6 **Zhichitsy** Rus. Fed.
169 K8 **Zhidan** *Shaanxi* China
173 L10 **Zhidoi** *Qinghai* China
193 N3 **Zhigansk** Rus. Fed.
169 P9 **Zhigou** *Shandong* China
182 C1 **Zhigulevsk** Rus. Fed.
173 J11 **Zhigung** *Xizang* China
170 G5 **Zhijiang** *Hunan* China
170 E5 **Zhijin** *Guizhou* China
19 V7 **Zhilevo** Rus. Fed.
19 T8 **Zhilino** *Orlovskaya Oblast'* Rus. Fed.
17 S4 **Zhilino** *Voronezhskaya Oblast'* Rus. Fed.
Zhilong *Guangdong* China *see* Yangxi
169 K9 **Zhiluozhen** *Shaanxi* China
15 I6 **Zhirnovsk** Rus. Fed.
Zhirnovskiy Rus. Fed. *see* Zhirnovsk
Zhirnoye Rus. Fed. *see* Zhirnovsk
19 Q8 **Zhiryatino** Rus. Fed.
Zhitarovo Bulg. *see* **Vetren**
182 I1 **Zhitikara** Kazakh.
Zhitkovichi Belarus *see* Zhytkavichy
18 M1 **Zhitkovo** Rus. Fed.
15 I6 **Zhitkur** Rus. Fed.
78 A2 **Zhitom** Albania
Zhitomir Ukr. *see* **Zhytomyr**
Zhitomir Oblast *admin. div.* Ukr. *see* **Zhytomyrs'ka Oblast'**
Zhitomirskaya Oblast' *admin. div.* Ukr. *see* Zhytomyrs'ka Oblast'
189 M6 **Zhīvār** Iran
19 R8 **Zhizdra** Rus. Fed.
19 T7 **Zhizdra** *r.* Rus. Fed.
19 O5 **Zhizhitsa** Rus. Fed.
19 O5 **Zhizhitskoye, Ozero** *l.* Rus. Fed.
170 B5 **Zhiziluo** *Yunnan* China
19 N9 **Zhlobin** Belarus
Zhmerinka Ukr. *see* Zhmerynka
16 H4 **Zhmerynka** Ukr.
185 M6 **Zhob** Pak.
185 M5 **Zhob** *r.* Pak.
18 L7 **Zhodzina** Belarus
193 Q2 **Zhokhova, Ostrov** *i.* *Novosibirskiye O-va* Rus. Fed.
Zholkva Ukr. *see* **Zhovkva**
183 T3 **Zholnuskay** Kazakh.
183 N2 **Zholymbet** Kazakh.
171 J7 **Zhongba** *Guangdong* China
173 G12 **Zhongba** *Xizang* China
Zhongcheng *Sichuan* China *see* **Xingwen**
Zhongcheng *Yunnan* China *see* **Suijiang**
Zhongduo *Chongqing* China *see* **Youyang**
Zhonghe *Chongqing* China *see* Xiushan
169 N9 **Zhongmou** *Henan* China
168 I8 **Zhongning** *Ningxia* China
168 H8 **Zhongpu** *Gansu* China
213 F2 **Zhongshan** *research stn* Antarctica
171 I7 **Zhongshan** *Guangdong* China
171 H6 **Zhongshan** *Guangxi* China
169 L9 **Zhongtiao Shan** *mts* China
168 I8 **Zhongwei** *Ningxia* China
170 G3 **Zhongxian** *Chongqing* China
171 J6 **Zhongxin** *Guangdong* China
Zhongxing *Jiangsu* China *see* Siyang
171 K3 **Zhongxingji** *Anhui* China
170 B1 **Zhongxinzhan** *Qinghai* China
169 L8 **Zhongyang** *Shanxi* China
162 D3 **Zhongyaozhan** *Heilong.* China
170 D6 **Zhongyicun** *Yunnan* China
170 H9 **Zhongyuan** *Hainan* China
170 E2 **Zhongzhai** *Gansu* China
171 N4 **Zhongzhai** *Zhejiang* China
Zhongzhou *Chongqing* China *see* **Zhongxian**
55 L4 **Zhorany** Ukr.
17 M5 **Zhorte** Ukr.
17 L2 **Zhortneve** Ukr.
183 Q2 **Zhosaly** *Pavlodarskaya Oblast'* Kazakh.
169 O9 **Zhoucheng** *Shandong* China
170 F3 **Zhou He** *r.* China
168 H7 **Zhoujiajing** *Gansu* China
170 F2 **Zhoujiaping** *Shaanxi* China
171 J2 **Zhoukou** *Henan* China
Zhoukou *Sichuan* China *see* Peng'an
169 N7 **Zhoukoudian** *tourist site* China
171 L5 **Zhouning** *Fujian* China
171 N3 **Zhoushan** *Zhejiang* China
171 N3 **Zhoushan Dao** *i.* China
171 N3 **Zhoushan Qundao** *is* China
169 K9 **Zhouzhi** *Shaanxi* China
16 C3 **Zhovkva** Ukr.
17 M6 **Zhovta** *r.* Ukr.
16 J6 **Zhovten'** Ukr.
17 M5 **Zhovti Vody** Ukr.
17 Q4 **Zhovtneve** *Kharkivs'ka Oblast'* Ukr.
17 N4 **Zhovtneve** *Poltavs'ka Oblast'* Ukr.
17 N3 **Zhovtneve** *Sums'ka Oblast'* Ukr.
55 M5 **Zhovtneve** *Volyns'ka Oblast'* Ukr.
182 I2 **Zhualy** Kazakh.
169 R7 **Zhuanghe** *Liaoning* China
168 I9 **Zhuanglang** *Gansu* China
183 M5 **Zhuantobe** Kazakh.
170 A2 **Zhubgyügoin** *Qinghai* China
16 G2 **Zhubrovychi** Ukr.
169 P9 **Zhucheng** *Shandong* China
168 F8 **Zhugkyung** *Qinghai* China
173 K11 **Zhugla** *Xizang* China
170 E2 **Zhugqu** *Gansu* China
171 I7 **Zhuhai** *Guangdong* China
171 M4 **Zhuji** *Zhejiang* China
169 L7 **Zhujia Chuan** *r.* China
171 I7 **Zhu Jiang** *r.* *Guangdong* China
171 M3 **Zhujing** *Shanghai* China
171 I7 **Zhukeng** *Guangdong* China
19 P5 **Zhukopa** *r.* Rus. Fed.
19 Q8 **Zhukovka** Rus. Fed.
19 T6 **Zhukovo** Rus. Fed.
19 V6 **Zhukovskiy** Rus. Fed.
16 J3 **Zhukyn** Ukr.
169 N7 **Zhulong He** *r.* China
171 J2 **Zhumadian** *Henan* China
182 D4 **Zhumysker** Kazakh.
169 N6 **Zhuolu** *Hebei* China
Zhuoyang *Henan* China *see* Suiping
169 O7 **Zhuozhou** *Hebei* China
169 M6 **Zhuozi** *Nei Mongol* China
Zhuozishan *Nei Mongol* China *see* **Zhuozi**
17 T3 **Zhuravka** Rus. Fed.
17 O8 **Zhuravky** Ukr.
183 M2 **Zhuravlevka** Kazakh.
16 D4 **Zhuravno** Ukr.
17 S8 **Zhuravskaya** Rus. Fed.
17 L1 **Zhurbin** Rus. Fed.
17 K3 **Zhurivka** Ukr.
18 K6 **Zhurki** Belarus
182 G3 **Zhuryn** Kazakh.
183 O5 **Zhusandala, Step'** *plain* Kazakh.
Zhushan *Hubei* China *see* Xuan'en
170 H2 **Zhushan** *Hubei* China
170 G2 **Zhuxi** *Hubei* China
171 I5 **Zhuzhou** *Hunan* China
171 I5 **Zhuzhou** *Hunan* China
55 M5 **Zhvyrka** Ukr.
16 D4 **Zhydachiv** Ukr.
182 E2 **Zhympity** Kazakh.
182 D5 **Zhyngyldy** Kazakh.
55 N1 **Zhyrmuny** Belarus
55 N2 **Zhyrovichy** Belarus
55 M4 **Zhyrychi** Ukr.
16 G1 **Zhytkavichy** Belarus
16 H3 **Zhytomyr** Ukr.
Zhytomyr Oblast *admin. div.* Ukr. *see* **Zhytomyrs'ka Oblast'**
16 G3 **Zhytomyrs'ka Oblast'** *admin. div.* Ukr.
16 I4 **Zhyvka** *r.* Ukr.
18 I8 **Zhyzhma** *r.* Belarus
88 C4 **Ziama** *mt.* Guinea
184 D3 **Ziārān** Iran
184 G3 **Ziarat** Iran
185 L6 **Ziarat** Pak.
57 H3 **Žiar nad Hronom** Slovakia
190 G8 **Zibā** *salt pan* Saudi Arabia
189 K5 **Zībār** Iraq
70 I5 **Zibello** Italy
169 P8 **Zibo** *Shandong* China
64 B2 **Zibreira** Port.
72 C4 **Zicavo** *Corse* France
169 K8 **Zichang** *Shaanxi* China
Zicheng *Guangdong* China *see* Zijin
53 P3 **Žichovice** Czech Rep.
50 D5 **Zichtauer Berge und Klötzer Forst** *park* Ger.
50 D3 **Zickhusen** Ger.
128 F7 **Zicuirán** Mex.
59 L7 **Zidani Most** Slovenia
185 M2 **Ziddí** Tajik.
185 L8 **Zidi** Pak.
17 P4 **Zid'ky** Ukr.
54 F5 **Ziębice** Pol.
50 E4 **Ziegendorf** Ger.
51 E9 **Ziegenrück** Ger.
51 H8 **Ziegra** Ger.
Ziel, Mount *N.T.* Austr. *see* Zeil, Mount
55 L4 **Zielawa** *r.* Pol.
54 D1 **Zieleniewo** *Zachodniopomorskie* Pol.
54 D2 **Zieleniewo** *Zachodniopomorskie* Pol.
51 E6 **Zielitz** Ger.
55 I3 **Zielkowice** Pol.
55 H2 **Zielona** Pol.
54 F2 **Zielona Chocina** Pol.
54 D4 **Zielona Góra** *Lubuskie* Pol.
54 E3 **Zielona Góra** *Wielkopolskie* Pol.
55 J3 **Zielonka** Pol.
55 H2 **Zieluń** Pol.
18 F4 **Ziemelkursas augstiene** *hills* Latvia
18 K4 **Ziemeris** Latvia
53 J5 **Ziemetshausen** Ger.
18 E5 **Ziemupe** Latvia
49 H8 **Zierenberg** Ger.
44 E5 **Zierikzee** Neth.
59 M2 **Ziersdorf** Austria
50 E4 **Zierzow** Ger.
51 F6 **Ziesar** Ger.
85 F2 **Ziftá** Egypt
158 A4 **Zigaing** Myanmar
191 A5 **Zigana Geçidi** *pass* Turkey
173 J10 **Zigê Tangco** *l.* China
84 D3 **Zīghan** Libya
71 N4 **Zignago, Valle** *lag.* Italy
158 B5 **Zigon** Myanmar
170 E4 **Zigong** *Sichuan* China
84 B6 **Ziguey** Chad
170 H3 **Zigui** *Hubei* China
88 A3 **Ziguinchor** Senegal
18 K4 **Žīguri** Latvia
169 P8 **Zi He** *r.* China
56 C1 **Žihle** Czech Rep.
128 F7 **Zihuaquio** Mex.
128 F8 **Zihuatanejo** Mex.
171 J7 **Zijin** *Guangdong* China
44 J4 **Zijpenberg** *hill* Neth.
Ziketan *Qinghai* China *see* Xinghai
19 R8 **Zikeyevo** Rus. Fed.
190 C6 **Zikhron Ya'aqov** Israel
182 G1 **Zilair** Rus. Fed.
18 I4 **Zilaiskalns** Latvia
188 G3 **Zile** Turkey
15 L5 **Zilim** *r.* Rus. Fed.
57 H2 **Žilina** Slovakia
55 M1 **Žilinai** Lith.

57 I2 Žilinský Kraj admin. reg. Slovakia
84 C2 Zillah Libya
58 E5 Ziller r. Austria
58 E5 Zillertal val. Austria
58 E5 Zillertaler Alpen mts Austria
70 G2 Zillis Switz.
49 K7 Zilly Ger.
51 K6 Ziltendorf Ger.
18 L5 Zilupe Latvia
160 H1 Zima Rus. Fed.
57 K5 Zimandu Nou Romania
129 H5 Zimapán Mex.
129 K9 Zimatlán Mex.
91 E9 Zimba Zambia
95 F4 Zimbabwe country Africa
　　Zimbabwe tourist site
　　Zimbabwe see Great Zimbabwe National Monument
184 A4 Zimkān, Rūdkhāneh-ye r. Iran
　　Zimmerbude Rus. Fed. see Svetlyy
52 F5 Zimmern ob Rottweil Ger.
49 H8 Zimmersrode (Neuental) Ger.
88 C5 Zimmi Sierra Leone
77 N7 Zimnicea Romania
14 G2 Zimniy Bereg coastal area Rus. Fed.
15 H7 Zimovniki Rus. Fed.
188 G6 Zimrin Syria
190 D7 Zin watercourse Israel
129 M8 Zinapa r. Mex.
128 F5 Zináparo Mex.
128 G6 Zinapécuaro Mex.
79 L4 Zinave, Parque Nacional de nat. park Moz.
185 N6 Zindawar Pak.
89 H3 Zinder Niger
89 H3 Zinder dept Niger
170 C3 Zindo Sichuan China
89 H4 Zinga Nigeria
93 C7 Zinga Mulike Tanz.
50 G2 Zingst reg. Ger.
88 E3 Ziniaré Burkina
186 G9 Zinjibār Yemen
17 N3 Zin'kiv Ukr.
53 O3 Zinkovy Czech Rep.
97 P5 Zinkwazi Beach S. Africa
19 X5 Zinnowitz Ger.
170 B3 Zinov o r. Sichuan China
88 D3 Zinzana Mali
81 C2 Zion II. U.S.A.
110 C2 Zion IL U.S.A.
118 D5 Zion MD U.S.A.
118 C3 Zion Grove PA U.S.A.
125 S4 Zion National Park UT U.S.A.
108 B3 Zionz Lake Ont. Can.
173 H3 Zi Qu r. Qinghai China
170 A2 Ziqudukou Qinghai China
28 I3 Zirab Iran
28 C7 Zirándaro Mex.
59 K5 Ziritzkogel mt. Austria
27 K6 Zirc Hungary
50 J3 Zirchow Ger.
187 J7 Zirekli Turkey
59 J7 Žiri Slovenia
22 K6 Zirkel i. Croatia
68 E4 Zirkel, Mount CO U.S.A.
187 A3 Zīrkūh i. U.A.E.
59 J7 Zirl Austria
53 J3 Zirndorf Ger.
79 N6 Ziro Arun. Prad. India
59 L1 Žirovnice Czech Rep.
85 I7 Zīrreh Afgh.
84 D7 Zīr Rūd Iran

171 I4 Zi Shui r. China
59 O2 Zistersdorf Austria
128 G6 Zitácuaro Mex.
57 H4 Zitava r. Slovakia
76 I5 Žitište Vojvodina, Srbija Serb. and Mont.
140 D2 Zitiua r. Brazil
170 E3 Zitong Sichuan China
77 J7 Žitorsđa Srbija Serb. and Mont.
51 K9 Zittau Ger.
51 K9 Zittauer Gebirge park Ger.
58 A5 Zitterklapfen mt. Austria
51 F6 Zitz Ger.
189 L5 Ziveh Iran
68 G3 Živinice Bos.-Herz.
92 C2 Ziway Hāyk' l. Eth.
171 K5 Zixi Jiangxi China
171 I6 Zixing Hunan China
169 O7 Ziya He r. China
182 G2 Ziyang Jiangxi China see Wuyuan
170 G2 Ziyang Shaanxi China
170 E3 Ziyang Sichuan China
184 G8 Ziyārat Iran
190 C2 Ziyaret Dağı hill Turkey
191 A5 Ziyaret Dağı mt. Turkey
170 H5 Ziyuan Guangxi China
170 F6 Ziyun Guizhou China
86 D3 Ziz, Oued watercourse Morocco
70 H2 Zizers Switz.
170 E4 Zizhong Sichuan China
169 L8 Zizhou Shaanxi China
22 K6 Zizurkil Spain
59 N7 Zlatar Croatia
59 N7 Zlatar mts Serb. and Mont.
57 H3 Zlatar-Bistrica Croatia
56 G1 Zlatá Studňa mt. Slovakia
57 H3 Zlaté Hory Czech Rep.
77 K6 Zlaté Moravce Slovakia
76 H7 Zlatibor mts Serb. and Mont.
76 I5 Zlatica r. Serb. and Mont.
77 L4 Zlatna Romania
77 Q7 Zlatni Pyasŭtsi nat. park Bulg.
77 N9 Zlatograd Bulg.
192 G4 Zlatoust Rus. Fed.
17 M6 Zlatoustivka Dnipropetrovs'ka Oblast' Ukr.
17 Q6 Zlatoustivka Donets'ka Oblast' Ukr.
162 H2 Zlatoustovsk Rus. Fed.
57 J3 Zlatý Stôl mt. Slovakia
54 G2 Zławieś Wielka Pol.
16 F3 Zlazne Ukr.
59 K8 Žlebič Slovenia
57 G2 Zlín Czech Rep.
57 G2 Zlínský kraj admin. reg. Czech Rep.
84 B1 Zlītan Libya
56 D2 Zliv Czech Rep.
54 E2 Złocieniec Pol.
54 G4 Złoczew Pol.
51 J10 Zlonice Czech Rep.
55 I4 Złoów Pol.
54 G3 Złotniki Kujawskie Pol.
54 D4 Złotoryja Pol.
54 F2 Złotów Pol.
54 E5 Złoty Stok Pol.
56 C1 Žlutice Czech Rep.
17 K5 Zlynka Rus. Fed.
183 T2 Zmeinogorsk Rus. Fed.
54 E4 Żmigród Pol.
71 P5 Žminj Croatia
19 T9 Zmiyev Ukr. see Zmiyiv
77 S5 Zmiyinyy, Ostriv i. Ukr.

17 P4 Zmiyiv Ukr.
17 M7 Zmiyivka Ukr.
55 L4 Žmudź Pol.
183 R2 Znamenka Kazakh.
183 R1 Znamenka Altayskiy Kray Rus. Fed.
19 S9 Znamenka Orlovskaya Oblast' Rus. Fed.
19 R7 Znamenka Smolenskaya Oblast' Rus. Fed.
　　Znamenka Ukr. see
55 J1 Znam''yanka
19 W8 Znamenskoye Lipetskaya Oblast' Rus. Fed.
19 S8 Znamenskoye Orlovskaya Oblast' Rus. Fed.
17 L5 Znam''yanka Ukr.
17 L5 Znam''yanka Druha Ukr.
54 F3 Żnin Pol.
17 M1 Znobivka r. Ukr.
17 M1 Znob Novhorods'ke Ukr.
56 F3 Znojmo Czech Rep.
70 G7 Zoagli Italy
96 F9 Zoar S. Africa
184 B4 Zōbuē Moz.
95 G2 Zóbuè Moz.
58 C6 Zoccola, Lago di l. Italy
173 E10 Zoco Xizang China
191 E3 Zodi Georgia
　　Zodi-Qornisi Georgia see Zodi
44 H5 Zoelen Neth.
45 G6 Zoersel Belgium
89 H6 Zoetelé Cameroon
44 F4 Zoetermeer Neth.
44 F4 Zoeterwoude Neth.
70 D1 Zofingen Switz.
170 A4 Zogang Xizang China
70 H4 Zogno Italy
170 B2 Zogqên Sichuan China
78 E5 Zografos Greece
184 A4 Zoháb Iran
53 L5 Zohor Slovakia
184 C6 Zohreh r. Iran
173 I10 Zoidê Lhai Xizang China
170 D2 Zoigê Sichuan China
182 H6 Zoir Uzbek.
53 G9 Zoissa Tanz.
178 E2 Zoji La pass Jammu & Kashmir
97 K8 Zola S. Africa
71 K6 Zola Predosa Italy
45 H6 Zolder Belgium
71 M3 Zoldo Alto Italy
55 K5 Zółkiewka-Osada Pol.
50 E3 Zölkow Ger.
70 C1 Zollikofen Switz.
70 F1 Zollikon Switz.
53 L5 Zolling Ger.
17 O3 Zolochev Kharkivs'ka Oblast' Ukr. see Zolochiv
16 D4 Zolochiv L'vivs'ka Oblast' Ukr.
16 E5 Zolota Lypa r. Ukr.
162 E1 Zolotaya Gora Rus. Fed.
17 R5 Zolote Ukr.
17 O8 Zolote Pole Ukr.
55 K6 Zolotkovychi Ukr.
16 E4 Zolotnyky Ukr.
17 K5 Zolotonosha Ukr.
182 A2 Zolotoye Rus. Fed.
　　Zolotoye Ukr. see Zolote
15 G5 Zolotukhino Rus. Fed.
16 E5 Zolotyy Potik Ukr.
54 E2 Zółtnica Pol.
55 K5 Żołynia Pol.

95 □J4 Zomandao r. Madag.
57 H5 Zomba Hungary
93 B8 Zomba Malawi
　　Zombor Vojvodina, Srbija Serb. and Mont. see Sombor
45 E6 Zomergem Belgium
146 C2 Zomin Uzbek.
168 E8 Zongjiafangzi Qinghai China
90 C3 Zongo Dem. Rep. Congo
129 K7 Zongolica Mex.
188 E3 Zonguldak Turkey
79 M1 Zonguldak prov. Turkey
171 K3 Zongyang Anhui China
170 B4 Zongza Sichuan China
168 F7 Zongzhai Gansu China
45 H7 Zonhoven Belgium
45 C7 Zonnebeke Belgium
75 □ Żonqor, Il-Ponta taż- pt Malta
184 A2 Zonūz Iran
72 C4 Zonza Corse France
89 I7 Zoo Baba well Niger
129 K8 Zoogocho Mex.
74 H8 Zoppo, Portella dello pass Italy
129 I6 Zoquiapán y Anexas, Parque Nacional nat. park Mex.
129 J7 Zoquitlán Mex.
54 F5 Zórawina Pol.
54 D3 Żórawino Pol.
19 R5 Zörbig Ger.
191 E6 Zor Dağ mt. Turkey
88 E3 Zorgho Burkina
　　Zorgo Burkina see Zorgho
　　Zorinsk Ukr. see Zoryns'k
64 H2 Zorita Spain
63 L7 Zorita r. Spain
66 E6 Zorita del Maestrazgo Spain
17 N8 Zorkine Ukr.
185 O3 Zorkūl l. Afgh./Tajik.
77 P4 Zorleni Romania
77 J5 Zorlenţu Mare Romania
37 P6 Zorn r. France
57 G5 Zorneding Ger.
53 L2 Zornheim Ger.
52 E2 Zornotza País Vasco Spain
77 O8 Zornitsa Bulg.
63 O2 Zornotza País Vasco Spain
136 A5 Zorritos Peru
54 G5 Zory Pol.
17 R5 Zoryns'k Ukr.
88 C5 Zorzor Liberia
51 H6 Zossen Ger.
45 E7 Zottegem Belgium
88 C5 Zouan-Hounien Côte d'Ivoire
84 C4 Zouar Chad
169 O9 Zoucheng Shandong China
78 E5 Zourva, Akra pt Greece
171 H4 Zoushi Hunan China
44 J2 Zoutkamp Neth.
45 H7 Zoutleeuw Belgium
45 D6 Zouxian Shandong China see Zoucheng
　　Zoushui Shaanxi China see Taibai
184 E5 Zovar Iran
18 L3 Zoviy Spain

57 I4 Zsámbok Hungary
57 I5 Zsana Hungary
51 H8 Zschaitz Ger.
51 H9 Zschopau r. Ger.
51 F8 Zschortau Ger.
57 G5 Zselic hills Hungary
57 G5 Zselicsegi park Hungary
185 N3 Zu Afgh.
137 E3 Zuata r. Venez.
63 O3 Zuazo de Cuartango Spain
71 P5 Zub, Rt pt Croatia
186 F8 Zubayr, Jazā'ir az i. Yemen
57 I2 Zuberec Slovakia
60 E4 Zubia Spain
63 O2 Zubiaur Spain
70 E5 Zubiena Italy
63 O1 Zubieta Spain
66 B1 Zubieta Spain
66 A1 Zubieta Spain
147 F5 Zubillaga Arg.
63 Q3 Zubiri Spain
19 T8 Zubkovo Rus. Fed.
19 T8 Zubova Polyana Rus. Fed.
15 J5 Zubovka Rus. Fed.
19 S7 Zubtsov Rus. Fed.
16 C4 Zubra r. Ukr.
54 D3 Żubrów Pol.
67 E7 Zucaina Spain
89 I2 Zucchero, Monte mt. Switz.
52 D7 Zuchwil Switz.
58 D6 Zuckerhütl mt. Austria
107 J2 Zucker Lake N.W.T. Can.
63 P3 Zudaire Spain
50 H2 Zudar Ger.
88 D5 Zuénoula Côte d'Ivoire
66 D4 Zuera Spain
187 L7 Zufār admin. reg. Oman
64 G5 Zufre Spain
64 G5 Zufre, Embalse de resr Spain
70 F1 Zug Switz.
66 B1 Zugarramurdi Spain
191 C3 Zugdidi Georgia
70 E1 Zuger See l. Switz.
58 C5 Zugspitze mt. Austria/Ger.
89 G4 Zugu Nigeria
65 K5 Zuheros Spain
167 K5 Zuhres Ukr.
44 F5 Zuid-Beijerland Neth.
44 F3 Zuider Zee l. Neth. see IJsselmeer
44 F3 Zuid-Holland prov. Neth.
44 J4 Zuidhorn Neth.
44 G4 Zuid-Kennemerland Nationaal Park nat. park Neth.
44 K2 Zuidlaardermeer l. Neth.
44 F5 Zuidland Neth.
44 I6 Zuid-Willemsvaart canal Neth.
45 D6 Zuienkerke Belgium
65 N5 Zújar Spain
65 N5 Zújar r. Spain
65 H2 Zújar, Embalse del resr Spain
55 L4 Żuków Lubelskie Pol.
55 I3 Żuków Mazowieckie Pol.
54 D4 Żukowice Pol.
54 G2 Żukowo Pol.
23 O7 Žukovka Rus. Fed.
136 D2 Zulia state Venez.
168 I8 Zuli He r. Gansu China
23 O7 Zulová Czech Rep.
57 K5 Zsadány Hungary
57 K4 Zsáka Hungary
57 H4 Zsámbék Hungary

66 A1 Zumarraga Spain
136 B6 Zumba Ecuador
59 L8 Žumberačka Gora mts Croatia
95 F2 Zumbo Moz.
110 B5 Zumbro r. MN U.S.A.
110 B5 Zumbrota MN U.S.A.
65 O4 Zumeta r. Spain
129 H7 Zumpahuacán Mex.
129 H6 Zumpango Mex.
129 H8 Zumpango del Río Mex.
45 G6 Zundert Neth.
89 G4 Zungeru Nigeria
75 J6 Zungri Italy
169 P6 Zunhua Hebei China
125 X6 Zuni NM U.S.A.
125 W7 Zuni watercourse AZ/NM U.S.A.
123 J9 Zuni Mountains NM U.S.A.
169 N1 Zun-Torey, Ozero l. Rus. Fed.
170 F5 Zunyi Guizhou China
170 F5 Zunyi Guizhou China
63 R3 Zunzarren Spain
158 I3 Zuoquan Shanxi China
169 M8 Zuoyun Shanxi China
169 M7 Zuoyun Shanxi China
70 H2 Zuoz Switz.
68 G3 Županja Croatia
186 E6 Zuqāq i. Saudi Arabia
76 I8 Zur Kosovo, Srbija Serb. and Mont.
14 K4 Zura Rus. Fed.
189 L4 Zūrābād Āzarbāyjān-e Gharbī Iran
182 G9 Zurabad Iran
185 I4 Zūrābād Khorāsān Iran
184 B5 Zurbāţīyah Iraq
65 O6 Zürgena Spain
173 J9 Zurhen Ul Shan mts China
70 F1 Zürich Switz.
70 F1 Zürich canton Switz.
70 F1 Zürichsee l. Switz.
185 M5 Zürmat reg. Afgh.
14 H4 Zürnabad Azer.
59 P4 Zürndorf Austria
77 P7 Žurnevo Bulg.
50 E3 Žuromin Pol.
75 □ Żurrieq Malta
89 G4 Zuru Nigeria
70 E1 Zurzach Switz.
53 J4 Zusam r. Ger.
19 T8 Zusmarshausen Ger.
50 E3 Züssow Ger.
50 I3 Züssow Ger.
45 I7 Zutendaal Belgium
44 J4 Zutphen Neth.
97 J3 Zuurberg National Park S. Africa
18 G7 Žuvintas l. Lith.
18 G7 Žuvinto rezervatas nature res. Lith.
84 B1 Zuwārah Libya
17 N8 Zuya r. Ukr.
36 D1 Zuydcoote France
209 C9 Zuytdorp Nature Reserve W.A. Austr.
184 H4 Zūzan Iran
59 J8 Žuženberk Slovenia
16 J4 Zvenigorod Rus. Fed.
17 T5 Zverevo Rus. Fed.
77 L7 Zverino Bulg.

182 K1 Zverinogolovskoye Rus. Fed.
78 B2 Zvezdë Albania
95 F4 Zvishavane Zimbabwe
57 I3 Zvolen Slovakia
77 K8 Zvonce Srbija Serb. and Mont.
68 G3 Zvornik Bos.-Herz.
55 M5 Zvyniyache Ukr.
44 J2 Zwaagwesteinde Neth.
59 L6 Zwaring Austria
96 F6 Zwarkop S. Africa
44 J3 Zwartewater r. Neth.
44 J3 Zwartsluis Neth.
88 C5 Zwedru Liberia
44 K3 Zweeloo Neth.
52 C3 Zweibrücken Ger.
70 C2 Zweisimmen Switz.
53 N6 Zwenkau Ger.
97 L8 Zwelitsha S. Africa
59 M3 Zwentendorf an der Donau Austria
51 H7 Zwethau Ger.
59 L2 Zwettl Austria
59 L2 Zwettl r. Austria
45 D7 Zwevegem Belgium
45 D6 Zwevezele Belgium
51 G8 Zwickau Ger.
51 G8 Zwickauer Mulde r. Ger.
52 G5 Zwiefalten Ger.
54 D3 Zwierzyn Pol.
55 K5 Zwierzyniec Pol.
53 O3 Zwiesel Ger.
53 N6 Zwiesel mt. Ger.
45 F6 Zwijndrecht Belgium
44 G5 Zwijndrecht Neth.
70 D1 Zwingen Switz.
52 F2 Zwingenberg Ger.
48 F4 Zwischenahner Meer l. Ger.
51 F8 Zwochau Ger.
55 J4 Zwolen Pol.
51 G9 Zwönitz Ger.
51 F10 Zwota Pol.
14 K4 Zyablovo Rus. Fed.
18 L6 Zyal'ki Belarus
17 N8 Zybyny Ukr.
55 H3 Zychlin Pol.
54 F3 Żydowo Wielkopolskie Pol.
54 E1 Żydowo Zachodniopomorskie Pol.
55 M3 Zyelyanyevichy Belarus
18 L7 Zyembin Belarus
190 B4 Zygi Cyprus
54 G4 Zygry Pol.
55 M5 Zymne Ukr.
17 N5 Zymohor'ye Ukr. see Zymohir''ya
17 M8 Zymohir''ya Ukr.
55 I3 Zyrardów Pol.
193 Q3 Zyryan Kazakh. see Zyryanovsk
192 J3 Zyryanka Rus. Fed.
183 U3 Zyryanovsk Kazakh.
55 K4 Zyrzyn Pol.
55 H5 Żytkiejny Pol.
55 H6 Żytno Pol.
57 I2 Żywiecki Park Krajobrazowy Pol.
54 F5 Żywocice Pol.
　　Zyyi Cyprus see Zygi

ACKNOWLEDGEMENTS

MAPS AND DATA

Maps designed and created by
HarperCollins*Reference*, Glasgow

Pages 212–213: Antarctic Digital Database (versions 1 and 2),
© Scientific Committee on Antarctic Research (SCAR), Cambridge (1993, 1998)

Bathymetric data: The GEBCO Digital Atlas published by
the British Oceanographic Data Centre on behalf of IOC and IHO, 1994

All mapping in this atlas is generated from Collins Bartholomew digital databases.
Collins Bartholomew, the UK's leading independent geographical information supplier,
can provide a digital, custom, and premium mapping service to a variety of markets.
For further information:
Tel: +44 (0) 141 306 3752
e-mail: collinsbartholomew@harpercollins.co.uk
www.collinsbartholomew.com

IMAGE CREDITS

Pages 10–11 (Atlas), 80–81, 100–101, 132–133, 148–149,194–195
Remote Sensing Applications Consultants Ltd
2 Prospect Place, Mill Lane, Alton, Hants
GU34 2SX

Pages 210–211
NRSC Ltd/Science Photo Library

Pages 10–11
The Sun: Jisas/Lockheed/Science Photo Library
Mercury: NASA/Science Photo Library
Venus: NASA/Science Photo Library
Earth: Photo Library International/Science Photo Library
Mars: US Geological Survey/Science Photo Library
Jupiter: NASA/Science Photo Library
Saturn: Space Telescope Science Institute/NASA/
Science Photo Library
Uranus: NASA/Science Photo Library
Neptune: NASA/Science Photo Library
Pluto and Charon: Space Telescope Science Institute/NASA/Science Photo Library

Page 15
Hurricane Ivan: Image courtesy of Space Science and Engineering Center,
University of Wisconsin-Madison/NASA

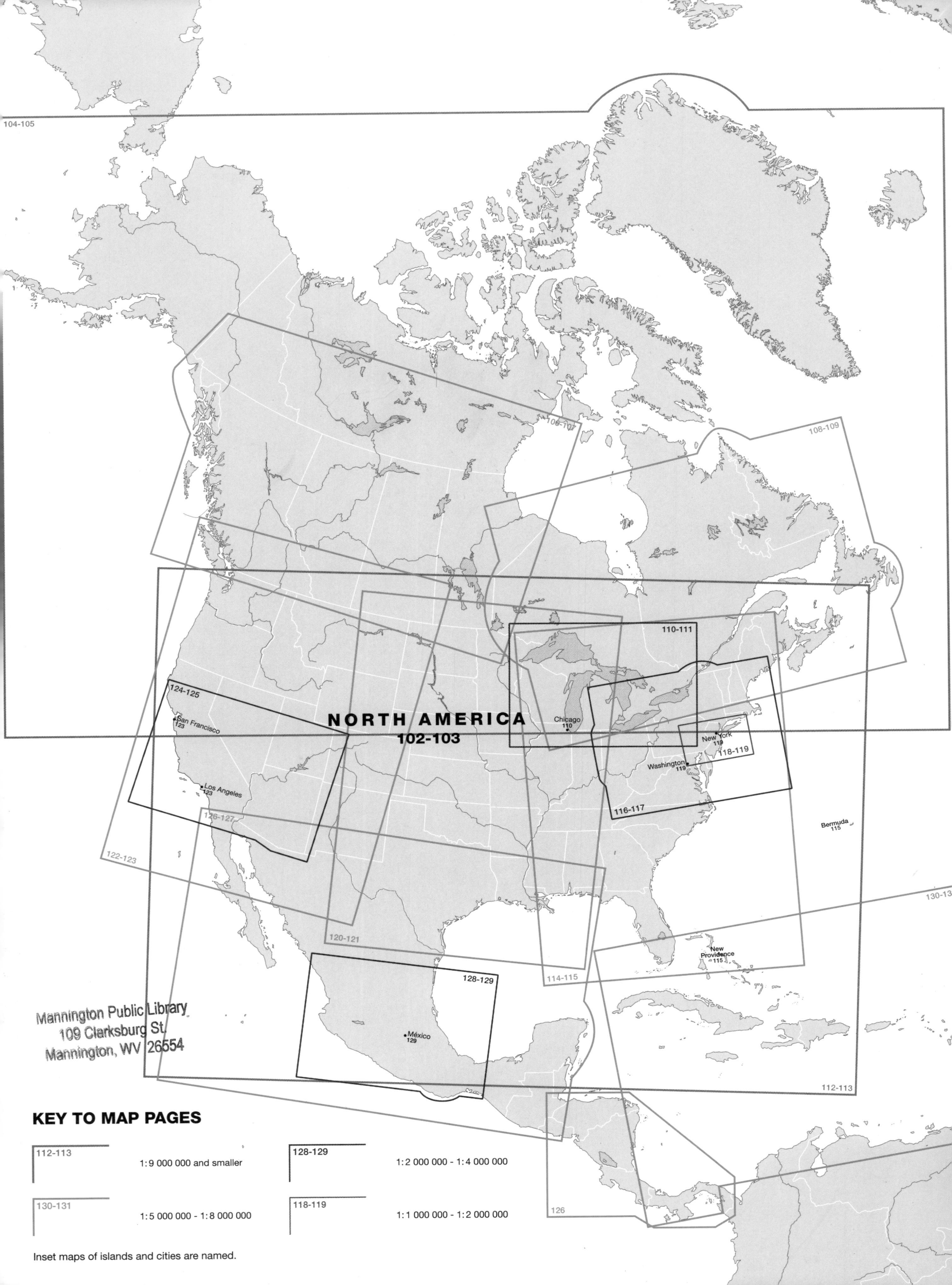

104-105

106-107

108-109

110-111

124-125

NORTH AMERICA
102-103

San Francisco
123

Chicago
110

New York
119

118-119

Washington
119

126-127

116-117

122-123

Bermuda
115

130-13

120-121

New
Providence
115

128-129

114-115

Mannington Public Library
109 Clarksburg St.
Mannington, WV 26554

México
129

112-113

KEY TO MAP PAGES

| 112-113 | 1:9 000 000 and smaller | 128-129 | 1:2 000 000 - 1:4 000 000 |

| 130-131 | 1:5 000 000 - 1:8 000 000 | 118-119 | 1:1 000 000 - 1:2 000 000 |

126

Inset maps of islands and cities are named.